DICTIONARY OF CANADIAN BIOGRAPHY

DICTIONARY OF CANADIAN BIOGRAPHY
DICTIONNAIRE BIOGRAPHIQUE DU CANADA

FRANCESS G. HALPENNY GENERAL EDITOR

JEAN HAMELIN DIRECTEUR GÉNÉRAL ADJOINT

VOLUME VIII

TORONTO

HENRI PILON executive officer CHARLES DOUGALL supervisory editor

MARGARET FILSHIE, JEAN HOFF, DAVID ROBERTS
CATHERINE A. WAITE, ROBERT G. WUETHERICK
manuscript editors

PHYLLIS CREIGHTON translations editor
SUSAN E. BÉLANGER bibliographies editor
DEBORAH MARSHALL editorial assistant

QUEBEC

HUGUETTE FILTEAU, MICHEL PAQUIN codirecteurs de la rédaction
THÉRÈSE P. LEMAY rédactrice-historienne principale

PAULETTE M. CHIASSON, CHRISTIANE DEMERS, FRANCE GALARNEAU
JOHN KEYES, MICHEL DE LORIMIER, JACQUELINE ROY
rédacteurs-historiens

JEAN-PIERRE ASSELIN réviseur-historien
SUZANNE ALLAIRE-POIRIER éditrice

TRANSLATOR J. S. WOOD

UNIVERSITY OF TORONTO PRESS
LES PRESSES DE L'UNIVERSITÉ LAVAL

DICTIONARY

OF CANADIAN

BIOGRAPHY

VOLUME VIII

1851 TO 1860

UNIVERSITY OF TORONTO PRESS

Toronto Buffalo London

©University of Toronto Press and
Les Presses de l'université Laval, 1985
Printed in Canada

ISBN 0-8020-3422-5 (regular edition)

Canadian Cataloguing in Publication Data
Main entry under title:

Dictionary of Canadian biography.

Added t.p. in English and French.
Issued also in French.
Contents: v.1. 1000–1700. – v.2. 1701–1740. – v.3. 1741–1770. –
v.4. 1771–1800. – v.5. 1801–1820. – v.8. 1851–1860. – v.9. 1861–1870. –
v.10. 1871–1880. – v.11. 1881–1890.
Includes bibliographies and indexes.
ISBN 0-8020-3142-0 (v.1)   ISBN 0-8020-3240-0 (v.2)
ISBN 0-8020-3314-8 (v.3)   ISBN 0-8020-3351-2 (v.4)
ISBN 0-8020-3398-9 (v.5)   ISBN 0-8020-3422-5 (v.8)
ISBN 0-8020-3319-9 (v.9)   ISBN 0-8020-3287-7 (v.10)
ISBN 0-8020-3367-9 (v.11)
1. Canada – Biography
FC25.D52 1966   920′.071   C66-3974-5 rev.5
F1005.D49 1966

Contents

Introduction

VOLUME VIII is the ninth volume of the *Dictionary of Canadian biography/Dictionnaire biographique du Canada* to be published. Volume I, presenting persons who died or flourished between the years 1000 and 1700, appeared in 1966; volume II (1701–40) in 1969; volume III (1741–70) in 1974; volume IV (1771–1800) in 1979. A separate *Index, volumes I to IV* was issued in 1981. The publication of volumes for the 19th century began in 1972 with volume X (1871–80) and has continued with volume IX (1861–70) in 1976, volume XI (1881–90) in 1982, and volume V (1801–20) in 1983. At present the DCB/DBC is concentrating its efforts on completing its program for the 19th century and is at work on volumes VI, VII, and XII; volume VI (1821–35) will be the next volume to appear.

The Introduction to volume I contains an account of the founding of the DCB by means of the generous bequest of James Nicholson (1861–1952), and of the establishment of the DBC with the support of the Université Laval. The DCB/DBC, while continuing to develop the collaboration on which its immense bicultural and bilingual project depends, has maintained the principles and standards of operation and selection set out in the preliminary pages of its first volumes. Acknowledgements of volume VIII record the gratitude of the DCB/DBC for the assistance of the Social Sciences and Humanities Research Council of Canada, which has supported our work generously and sympathetically. This support has enabled us to carry the project forward in the spirit and manner of its founders.

The 351 contributors to volume VIII, writing in either English or French, have provided 521 biographies ranging in length from fewer than 600 words to more than 10,000 words. They were invited to contribute because of their special knowledge of the period and of the persons who figured in it, and have been asked to write in accordance with the DCB/DBC's *Directives to contributors*. It sets out a general aim for authors of articles:

> Biographers should endeavour to provide a readable and stimulating treatment of their subject. Factual information should come from primary sources if possible. Biographies should not be mere catalogues of events nor should they be compilations of previous studies of the subject. The achievements of the subjects should be seen against the background of the period in which they lived and the events in which they participated. Relevant anecdote and/or quotation of the subject's own words should be used discreetly to illuminate character or personality.

As always, our contributors bring to the volume the benefit of new knowledge on both major and minor figures.

Volume VIII also contains an introductory essay, "The Colonial Office and British North America, 1801–50," in which Phillip Buckner chronicles the birth and early growth of the department in the expanding British bureaucracy which "played a decisive part in determining the destiny of the North American Colonies" for more than a century. The essay will be of interest to readers of volumes V through XII. In this volume we again offer finding aids for the biographies in the form of cross-references, the list of subjects of the biographies, the nominal index, and special indexes of identifications and geographical location. The General Bibliography, and individual bibliographies, identify the sources our contributors and DCB staff have consulted.

The lives presented in volume VIII reflect the development of British North America through the disruptions of the Napoleonic Wars, the War of 1812, the rebellions of 1837–38, and the union of Upper and Lower Canada in 1841. Attempts to reach the goal of responsible government create another of the leading themes. In February 1848, in Nova Scotia, climaxing years of dispute and struggle, the first formally responsible ministry in an overseas British colony took office under James Boyle Uniacke; shortly thereafter, a similarly responsible ministry led by Robert Baldwin and Louis-Hippolyte La Fontaine* was inaugurated in the Canadas. Yet another link within the volume is the search in all colonies for the security provided by property, business, and office, a search which was characteristic not only of their established inhabitants but especially of the thousands of newcomers – loyalists and later arrivals from the United States and overseas. The effect of this movement of peoples was in itself dramatic; in Upper Canada, for example, the population between 1806 and 1817 rose from 46,000 to 83,000 and such growth led to careers that created many of the towns along the shores of the upper St Lawrence and Lake Ontario.

In this period of conflict and growth, the War of 1812 appears in the biographies of commanders such as Sir Gordon Drummond, Dominique Ducharme, and Sir Roger Hale Sheaffe. The chances of rebellion are experienced by Patriote teacher Siméon Marchesseault or Upper Canadian farmer Martin Switzer. To the people of this volume, the challenges of creating the social institutions of religion and education, the press, medicine and the law, charity and emigrant relief loomed equally large. From time to time the leaders of communities had to face the calamities of cholera and typhus epidemics and fires that almost destroyed cities such as Saint John, St John's, and Quebec. A corps of architects, builders, and artisans, including Thomas Baillairgé, Henry Bowyer Joseph Lane, James Purcell, Thomas Rogers, William Thomas, and Frank Wills, created a physical face for towns and cities and were responsible for many structures admired today as lasting achievements. Joseph Légaré catches the attention as a painter and also as a creator of taste through his art galleries. Among compilers of directories and guidebooks, travel writers and versifiers, several figures stand out – Robert Christie, for his history of Lower Canada and his crusade for archives; Jacques Viger, for his collection of materials that would prove invaluable to future historians; Anna Jameson, for her perceptive and pungent comments on the people and landscape of Upper Canada; and John Richardson, for the power of his melding of fact and fiction in order to render his imaginative reaction to life in British North America. Through their written accounts, we are also able to follow the important Arctic voyages of Elisha Kent Kane, Sir William Edward Parry, and Sir John Ross.

In the west, and reaching far into the north, the bitter struggle of the Hudson's Bay Company and the North West Company for control of the fur trade engages the attention. The HBC's push into the Athabasca country is represented by John Clarke and the well-entrenched NWC interests by John McGillivray (Dalcrombie). Competition for furs on the

Pacific coast encouraged David Thompson's explorations across the Rocky Mountains and motivated the activities of Ross Cox and Alexander Ross at Fort Astoria. This volume demonstrates how the rivalries of the fur trade companies seriously compromised the existence of the fledgling Red River settlement. The involvement there of the Métis in this rivalry appears in the story of Cuthbert Grant. Conflict between the NWC and the HBC ended in the amalgamation of 1821, implemented by Nicholas Garry. The subsequent consolidation of the fur trade across the continent under the efficient management of Sir George Simpson is illustrated in the careers of John McLoughlin on the Pacific coast and Peter Skene Ogden in the arduous Snake River country, and in John Rowand's 30 years at Fort Edmonton. Life at the isolated trading posts is illuminated by the correspondence of Letitia Hargrave, and the changing status of mixed-blood women in Red River society is recounted in the unhappy stories of Sarah Ballenden and Nancy McTavish.

Of the few subject areas that can be referred to more specifically here, one is business and industry, which contributes many figures to a volume so concerned with the growth of early communities. The importance of banking appears early in its pages with William Allan of the Bank of Upper Canada, and continues through Henry Hezekiah Cogswell and William Pryor of the Halifax Banking Company, Jacob De Witt and Louis-Michel Viger of the Banque du Peuple, and Samuel Gerrard of the Bank of Montreal. With them may be associated Receiver General John Henry Dunn, who struggled with the financing of Upper Canada. The forwarding trade – the lifeline of the colonies that brought finished goods from overseas and sent out local staples such as fish, flour, and timber – makes many appearances from places large and small: in Newfoundland, Robert Pack of Carbonear; in Nova Scotia, James Foreman and Richard Tremain of Halifax; in New Brunswick, William Crane of Sackville and James Taylor of Fredericton; in Lower Canada, William Cuthbert of Baie des Chaleurs, James Gibb of Quebec, Moses Hart of Trois-Rivières, David Le Boutillier of the Gaspé, and Peter McGill and William Ritchie of Montreal; in Upper Canada, Samuel Crane of Prescott, James Crooks of West Flamborough, Colin Campbell Ferrie of Hamilton, George Rykert of St Catharines, and David Barker Stevenson of Picton. Timber, a great resource industry on the Miramichi, the Saguenay, and the Ottawa, fills the holds of ships heading across the Atlantic, ships indeed often built in British North America for the trade. Entrepreneurs include John Saxton Campbell and Peter Patterson of Quebec, John Egan (the "Napoleon of the Ottawa") of Aylmer, Alexis Tremblay, dit Picoté, of La Malbaie; Noah Disbrow of Saint John and timber baron Alexander Rankin and Joseph Russell of the Miramichi; Alexander Campbell of Tatamagouche, N.S. Opposite the shipbuilding activities of John Munn of Quebec can be set the steamboat interests of Henry Gildersleeve of Kingston. Mills, and ancillary activities, were another need of settlers and the site of local development and outward exports, as witnessed in the careers of John DeCow of Thorold, James Bell Ewart of Dundas, John McDonald of Gananoque, Thomas McKay of Ottawa, Siméon Gautron, dit Larochelle, of the Beauce, and Peter McLeod of Chicoutimi. In a small workshop on the family farm Daniel Massey begins what will be a long story of family enterprise. John Molson of Montreal was active in almost all the important business and economic undertakings of his day. John Macaulay of Kingston used his experience of business, a newspaper, and public office to further in several ways the development of Upper Canada.

Entrepreneurship with land and settlement is represented in many places and at many levels, from Thomas Blinkhorn of Vancouver Island, through Zacheus Burnham of Cobourg, Alexander Fraser in Glengarry County, Hamnett Kirkes Pinhey and Nathaniel Hazard Tredwell on the Ottawa, Joseph-Édouard Faribault in L'Assomption, and William Hall of the Beauce, to horticulturalist Charles Ramage Prescott in the Annapolis valley of Nova Scotia and John O'Brien in Freshwater, Newfoundland. Two colourful and dominating figures, in their very different ways, are Archibald McNab, 17th Chief of Clan Macnab, of the Ottawa valley and Thomas Talbot of the London district. Waterways, as territorial boundaries or avenues of commerce, were the concern of surveyors and engineers such as William Fitz William Owen in Upper Canada and in the Bay of Fundy, James Bucknall Bucknall Estcourt on the St Croix boundary, Peter Fleming with the St Lawrence and Richelieu canals, and George Keefer with the Welland Canal.

The customary procession of governors through the British American colonies brings a varied set to volume VIII. The group of officers who served the crown in the Napoleonic Wars and who continued to serve it in its outposts, includes here Charles Murray Cathcart, 2nd Earl Cathcart, governor-in-chief of the Province of Canada, and also Sir James Kempt and Sir George Arthur. Kempt served first in Nova Scotia before moving in 1828, as governor-in-chief, to Lower Canada, where he found himself in the midst of disputes with the assembly on such matters as the civil list. Francis Gore and Sir Peregrine Maitland faced a similar climate in Upper Canada, hampered by conflicts over land policy, the treatment of aliens, and the use of the clergy reserves. Sir George Arthur, who took control of Upper Canada shortly after the abortive rebellion in 1837, proved to be its last lieutenant governor. Charles Douglass Smith might have been the "worst Governor" ever of Prince Edward Island. On the other hand, Sir John Harvey, beginning his series of governorships there, went on to make a distinguished and conciliatory career of his service in New Brunswick, Newfoundland, and Nova Scotia.

Politicians, whether conservatives or reformers, who attempted to represent the interests of their growing communities in development and who supported or opposed the series of governors and executive councils, make a strong appearance in the volume, working through the shifting alignments of the 1820s–40s towards the parties that were to carry responsible government forward. Although these achievements are familiarly connected with the major figures such as Baldwin, there is in this volume a vigorous company of other campaigners with a range of opinions: Charles Simonds and Thomas Harding of Saint John, Herbert Huntington of Yarmouth and George Renny Young of Halifax, Patrick Doyle of St John's, George Dalrymple and Duncan Maclean of Prince Edward Island, Jean Chabot of Quebec and François-Xavier Larue of Pointe-aux-Trembles, and Henry Sherwood of Brockville and the changeable Robert Baldwin Sullivan of Toronto. The concerns of the Patriotes through opposition, rebellion, and aftermath can be followed with Patriote party members Marcus Child and Joseph Roy and also with Pierre-Paul Démaray, Édouard-Raymond Fabre, Toussaint Peltier, or William Henry Scott. Some of this large group of campaigners had a base in business or property; some came, as might be expected, from the law. This profession contributes to the volume a chief justice of New Brunswick, Ward Chipman, another of Nova Scotia, Sir Brenton Halliburton, one of Prince Edward Island, Edward James Jarvis, and also Sir James Stuart of Lower Canada. Other men of the law who put themselves variously in the public eye are represented here by Alexander Buchanan, notaries Nicolas-Benjamin Doucet and André Jobin, Sir James Buchanan Macaulay, and Thomas Ritchie.

Old and new inhabitants of British North America were intent upon providing educational opportunities at all levels. Alexander Davidson produced *The Canada spelling book* in 1840, significantly the first book copyrighted in Upper Canada. Samuel Codner helped to establish the Newfoundland School Society. Antoine Parant, as head of the Petit Séminaire, encouraged two exceptional colleagues, Jérôme Demers and John Holmes, who were responsible for much needed texts and the introduction of new courses of study; Holmes was posthumously named a founder of Université Laval. Charles Frederick Allison, the founder of Mount Allison University, appears, as does John Mowat, active in the development of Queen's University, and Charlottetown's bishop Bernard Donald MacDonald of St Dunstan's College. Ann Cuthbert Rae set up private schools in Montreal and developed textbooks using Canadian material; Olympe Tanner contributed to Protestant evangelizing in Lower Canada through schools for boys and girls.

The importance of the press for debate of public issues is shown in the number of journalists in the volume. The Atlantic provinces read the papers of Henry David Winton of St John's, Henry Chubb of Saint John and Thomas Hill of Fredericton, Duncan Maclean of Prince Edward Island, and Richard Nugent of Halifax. Conservative or reform opinion in the Canadas was supported in Robert Reid Smiley's *Hamilton Spectator*, Charles Donlevy's *Mirror* or Hugh Scobie's *British Colonist* of Toronto, and Ludger Duvernay's *La Minerve* of Montreal.

The conditions of life in the colonies demanded much of the doctors who carried on professional careers, many of them prepared by study abroad in centres such as Edinburgh, London, or Paris. The needs of seamen and immigrants were faced by Alexander Boyle in Saint John and Matthias Francis Hoffmann in Halifax; development of hospitals and the medical profession was assisted by William Grigor in Halifax, Jean Blanchet and Joseph Parant in Quebec, Andrew Fernando Holmes in Montreal, and Walter Telfer in Toronto; Thomas David Morrison mixed the politics of reform with his medicine and Christopher Widmer exhibited great skill both as practitioner and as administrator. In the northwest William Todd attended fur traders and their families, and also concerned himself with the European diseases affecting Indians.

The years covered by this volume provide a wealth of figures who demonstrate the concern with religion in the colonies of British North America. All the denominations are represented and each attempts to extend the faith by missionary endeavour among white settlers and Indian tribes and by establishing churches and organizational structures, schools, and charitable aids. These efforts were frequently complicated by disputes between denominations over such matters as recognition to perform marriages or support from public funds and within denominations by clashes of personality or doctrinal disputes. Only a few figures of the many can be mentioned here for the leads into the volume they provide. For Roman Catholics, Bishop William Fraser, a Scot in Antigonish, is set against William Walsh, an Irishman in Halifax and the first Catholic archbishop to be created in British North America outside Quebec; working among immigrants was William Dollard in New Brunswick and Patrick McMahon at Quebec, among the Indians was Nicolas-Marie-

Joseph Frémiot of Manitoulin Island and Joseph Marcoux of Caughnawaga; the strength of building is in Jean-Baptiste Kelly and Thomas Maguire, Patrick Phelan and Jean-Charles Prince, and especially in Joseph-Norbert Provencher. Anglicans range from William Arnold in the Gaspé and Jacob George Mountain in the Newfoundland outports, both in rigorous pastoral service, to George Coster, high churchman, of Fredericton. The momentous disruption in the Church of Scotland dramatically affected Presbyterians, such as John MacLennan among the Gaels of Cape Breton, Murdoch Sutherland in Nova Scotia, John Keir on Prince Edward Island, and, in Upper Canada, Andrew Bell of Streetsville, William Bell of Perth, William Proudfoot of London, and William Rintoul of Toronto. The character of Methodism, influenced from both Britain and the United States, is shown in the biographies of William Case, William Martin Harvard, James Jackson, and Ojibwa convert Peter Jones in the Canadas, and Richard Knight and Albert Des Brisay in the Maritimes. The efforts of the Baptists, particularly in the Maritimes, in itinerancy, churches, and education are represented by Joseph Crandall, Edward Manning, and Richard McLearn.

Devoted and arduous itinerancy was provided by Bible Christians Elizabeth Dart and Ann Vickery. These two women of strong religious convictions have a number of companions in this volume, of several faiths, such as, in the Maritimes, Eliza Ann Chipman of the Baptists or Mary Bradley of the Methodists, who left revealing spiritual narratives. Women who entered religious orders, including Sister Mary Bernard in Newfoundland, Émilie Gamelin in Montreal, and Sister Delphine in Toronto, took on roles of leadership in social service. So too did Marie-Amable Viger in Montreal with the Association des Dames de la Charité.

Volume VIII, like other volumes, does not lack variety in its people, who include midwife "Granny Ross," Inuit guide Kallihirua, spy John Henry, fur-trade messenger Jean-Baptiste Lagimonière, filibuster Thomas Jefferson Sutherland, sorcerer Louis Gamache of Anticosti, and poet John Smyth ("a genius above commas"). There is variety always in the lives, which show Donald McKenzie, fur trader and governor of Assiniboia, settling "the most knotty points with a joke and a laugh, seated on a mortar opposite the gate of his fort," or farmer and politician Thomas Marchildon of Batiscan attacking the railways as "a punishment imposed by God" and surely "the ruin of dairying," or James Foreman of Halifax enjoying a daily sea-bath, even if that meant breaking through the ice in the harbour. One might wish to have been present in the House of Assembly with reformer Peter Perry to witness the enthusiastic waving of hats after each legislative success and to have seen the launching from the yard of John Munn in Quebec of his splendid new ships, including the *United Kingdom*, described in a Liverpool paper as looking "most beautiful upon the water."

As volume VIII goes on its way to readers, the general editors are conscious once again of the services rendered to it and to its companions by the staff of the DCB/DBC. These services have been constant through all the complexities of assembly from choice of entries to final text, and we are grateful.

FRANCESS G. HALPENNY

JEAN HAMELIN

Acknowledgements

THE *Dictionary of Canadian biography/Dictionnaire biographique du Canada* receives assistance, advice, and encouragement from many institutions and individuals. They cannot all be named nor can their kindness and support be adequately acknowledged.

The DCB/DBC, which owes its founding to the generosity of the late James Nicholson, has been sustained over the years by its parent institutions, the University of Toronto and the University of Toronto Press and the Université Laval and Les Presses de l'université Laval. Beginning in 1973 the Canada Council provided grants to the two university presses which made possible the continuation and acceleration of the DCB/DBC's publication program, and this assistance has been maintained and amplified by the Social Sciences and Humanities Research Council of Canada, created in 1978. We should like to give special thanks to the SSHRCC not only for its financial support but also for the encouragement it has given us as we strive to complete our volumes for the 19th century. We are grateful also for the financial assistance accorded us by the Université Laval.

Of the numerous individuals who assisted in the preparation of volume VIII, we owe particular thanks to our contributors. In addition, we have had the benefit of special consultation with a number of persons, some of them also contributors. We should like to thank: Peter Baskerville, Phyllis R. Blakeley, Denise Bousquet, Phillip Buckner, Gaston Deschênes, R. B. Donovan, C.S.B., Raymond Dumais, Micheline Fortin, Armand Gagné, Frances Gundry, David M. Hayne, Gilles Héon, H. T. Holman, Susan Johnston, Orlo Jones, Patricia Kennedy, Marion MacRae, Monique Mailloux, André Martineau, Marianne Morrow, Patrick O'Flaherty, G. D. O'Gorman, C.S.B., J. E. Rea, Dennis Reid, D. S. Richardson, Paul Romney, Shirlee Anne Smith, David A. Sutherland, M. Brook Taylor, and Sylvia M. Van Kirk.

Throughout the preparation of volume VIII we have enjoyed willing cooperation from libraries and archives in Canada and elsewhere. We are particularly grateful to the administrators and staffs of those institutions to which we have most frequently appealed. In addition to the Public Archives of Canada in Ottawa and the provincial archives in all the provinces, they are: in Manitoba, the Hudson's Bay Company Archives (Winnipeg); in New Brunswick, the New Brunswick Museum (Saint John); in Ontario, the Art Gallery of Ontario (Toronto), the Kingston Public Library, the Metropolitan Toronto Library, the Queen's University Library (Kingston), the United Church Archives (Toronto), and the University of Toronto Library; in Prince Edward Island, the Prince Edward Island Museum and Heritage Foundation (Charlottetown); in Quebec, the *archives civiles* and *judiciaires*, the Archives de l'archidiocèse de Québec, the Bibliothèque de l'Assemblée nationale, the Bibliothèque and Archives du Séminaire de Québec, the Bibliothèque générale de l'université Laval, and the Montreal Business History Project. We should like to thank as well the staffs of the *archives départementales* and *municipales* in France and of the various record offices in the United Kingdom and Republic of Ireland who answered our numerous requests for information so kindly.

The editors of volume VIII were helped in the preparation of the volume by colleagues in both offices. In Toronto, editorial and research assistance has been given by Wendy Cameron, Robert Fraser, Jane Graham, and Bruce Ward. Special thanks must be extended to Mary Bentley, Curtis Fahey, and Stuart Sutherland. We should like to make mention of the devoted services of a former bibliographies editor, Joan Mitchell. Deborah Marshall provided invaluable editorial assistance and was in charge of the secretariat in Toronto, where secretarial and administrative services were provided by Heddi Keil, Kent Lebsock, Eileen McAuley, Lina Peres, and Maggie Reeves. In Quebec, Michèle Brassard, Céline Cyr, Marcelle Duquet, Gérard Goyer, James H. Lambert, Marie-Hélène Lévesque, Jean Provencher, and Robert Tremblay aided the editors at one stage or another of volume VIII. Pierrette Desrosiers was in charge of secretarial services, assisted by Hélène Packenham and Suzanne East. We have also benefited from the advice of Jacques Chouinard of the Service des éditions des Presses de l'université Laval and also of the staff of the Office de la langue française as well as that of the Translation Bureau of the Department of the Secretary of State.

We should like to recognize the guidance and encouragement we have received from the two presses with which the DCB/DBC is associated, and in particular from Harald Bohne, H. C. Van Ierssel, Peter Scaggs, and Stephen Phillips at the University of Toronto Press and Marc Boucher and Jacques Beaulieu at Les Presses de l'université Laval.

DICTIONNAIRE BIOGRAPHIQUE DU CANADA   DICTIONARY OF CANADIAN BIOGRAPHY

Subjects of Biographies

A-CA-OO-MAH-CA-YE (Feathers, Old Swan) (d. 1859 or 1860)
Allan, William (d. 1853)
Allanson, John (d. 1853)
Allison, Charles Frederick (1795–1858)
Angers, François-Réal (1812–60)
Antrobus, Edmund William Romer (1795–1852)
Archambault, Paul-Loup (1787–1858)
Armour, Robert (1781–1857)
Arms, William (1794–1853)
Armstrong, Sir Richard (d. 1854)
Arnold, William (1804–57)
Arthur, Sir George (1784–1854)
Ayre, William (d. 1855)

BABEY, Peter Paul Toney (fl. 1849–55)
Baby, François (1768–1852)
Bagnall, James (d. 1855)
Baillairgé, Thomas (1791–1859)
Baird, Edmond (1802–59)
Baird, John (1795–1858)
Baker, Hugh Cossart (1818–59)
Baldwin, Robert (1804–58)
Ballenden, John (d. 1856)
Barbier, Louis-Marie-Raphaël (1792–1852)
Barclay, George (d. 1857)
Barnston, James (1831–58)
Barss, John (1778–1851)
Bartlett, William Henry (1809–54)
Basquet, Pierre (fl. 1841–52)
Baudrand, Fleury (1811–53)
Bayne, John (1806–59)
Beardsley, Bartholomew Crannell (1775–1855)
Beechey, Frederick William (1796–1856)
Bell, Andrew (1803–56)
Bell, Hugh (1780–1860)
Bell, John (1788–1855)
Bell, William (1780–1857)
Bellenger, Joseph-Marie (1788–1856)
Bellot, Joseph-René (1826–53)
Benedict, Roswell Gardinier (1815–59)
Bennett, William (d. 1857)
Berczy, Charles Albert (1794–1858)
Bethune, Angus (1783–1858)
Betzner, Samuel D. (1771–1856)
Bibaud, Michel (1782–1857)
Bibb, Henry Walton (1815–54)

Bird, James (d. 1856)
Birdsall, Richard (1799–1852)
Black, George (d. 1854)
Blackman, Charles (d. 1853)
Blake, Dominick Edward (1806–59)
Blanchet, Jean (1795–1857)
Blinkhorn, Thomas (1806–56)
Bond, George (d. 1852)
Booker, Alfred (1800–57)
Boucher de Boucherville, Thomas-René-Verchères (1784–1857)
Boxer, Edward (1784–1855)
Boyle, Alexander (1771–1854)
Bridge, Thomas Finch Hobday (1807–56)
Brouse, George (1790–1860)
Brown, Paola (fl. 1828–52)
Browne, Timothy (d. 1855)
Bruneau, François-Pierre (1799–1851)
Buchanan, Alexander (1798–1851)
Buchanan, Peter (1805–60)
Bulger, Andrew H. (1789–1858)
Burn, William Scott (1797–1851)
Burnet, David (d. 1853)
Burnham, Zacheus (1777–1857)
Burpee, Richard E. (1810–53)

CALDWELL, Francis Xavier (1792–1851)
Cameron, John Dugald (d. 1857)
Campbell, Alexander (d. 1854)
Campbell, John Saxton (d. 1855)
Carey, John (1780–1851)
Carmichael, James (1788–1860)
Caron, Charles (1768–1853)
Carrier, Michel (1805–59)
Cartier, Claude (d. 1855)
Cary, George Marcus (1795–1858)
Case, William (1780–1855)
Cathcart, Charles Murray, 2nd Earl Cathcart (1783–1859)
Cazeneuve, Louis-Joseph-Charles (1795–1856)
Chabot, Jean (1806–60)
Chandler, William (1804–56)
Chaperon, John (1825–51)
Chartier, Étienne (1798–1853)
Child, Marcus (1792–1859)
Chipman, Eliza Ann (Chipman) (1807–53)
Chipman, Ward (1787–1851)

Christie, Robert (1787–1856)
Chubb, Henry (1787–1855)
Clarke, John (1781–1852)
Clarke, Septimus D. (1787–1859)
Clemo, Ebenezer (d. c. 1860)
Clench, Joseph Brant (d. 1857)
Clitherow, John (1782–1852)
Codner, Samuel (d. 1858)
Cogswell, Henry Hezekiah (1776–1854)
Corrigan, Robert (d. 1855)
Coster, George (1794–1859)
Couillard-Després, Emmanuel (1792–1853)
Cox, Ross (1793–1853)
Coy, Mary (Morris; Bradley) (1771–1859)
Craig, John (1804–54)
Crandall, Joseph (d. 1858)
Crandall, Reuben (1767–1853)
Crane, Samuel (1794–1858)
Crane, William (1785–1853)
Creedon, Marianne, named Mother Mary Francis (1811–55)
Crooks, James (1778–1860)
Crooks, Ramsay (1787–1859)
Crookshank, George (1773–1859)
Crosskill, John Henry (1817–57)
Crysler, John (1770–1852)
Cuthbert, William (1795–1854)

Dalrymple, George R. (d. 1851)
Dalton, Charles (1786–1859)
Dart, Elizabeth (Eynon) (1792–1857)
Daulé, Jean-Denis (1766–1852)
Davidson, Alexander (1794–1856)
de Blaquière, Peter Boyle (1783–1860)
Deblois, Joseph-François (1797–1860)
DeCow, John (1766–1855)
Démaray, Pierre-Paul (1798–1854)
Demers, Jérôme (1774–1853)
Des Brisay, Albert (1795–1857)
Désilets, Aimé (1826–60)
Desrochers, Urbain (1781–1860)
De Witt, Jacob (1785–1859)
Dickerson, Silas Horton (1799–1857)
Dickson, Thomas (1791–1855)
Dionne, Amable (1781–1852)
Disbrow, Noah (1772–1853)
Doak, Robert (1785–1857)
Dodd, Charles (d. 1860)
Dollard, William (d. 1851)
Donlevy, Charles (d. 1858)
Doucet, Nicolas-Benjamin (1781–1858)
Douglas, James (1789–1854)
Doyle, Patrick (1777–1857)
Drouin, Pierre (1810–60)
Drummond, Sir Gordon (1772–1854)
Duchaîne, Amable-Daniel (1774–1853)
Ducharme, Charles-Joseph (1786–1853)

Ducharme, Dominique (1765–1853)
Duffy, James W. (d. 1860)
Dumoulin, Jean-Gaspard (1832–60)
Dumoulin, Pierre-Benjamin (d. 1856)
Dumoulin, Sévère (1793–1853)
Dunn, John Henry (d. 1854)
Du Val, Peter (1767–1851)
Duvernay, Ludger (1799–1852)

Eaststaff, Thomas George William (d. 1854)
Eby, Benjamin (1785–1853)
Edmundson, William Graham (d. 1852)
Egan, John (1811–57)
Ellis, William (1774–1855)
Enslin, Christian (1800–56)
Esson, Henry (d. 1853)
Estcourt, James Bucknall Bucknall (1802–55)
Evans, Francis (1801–58)
Evans, William (1786–1857)
Ewart, James Bell (d. 1853)
Ewart, John (1788–1856)

Fabre, Édouard-Raymond (1799–1854)
Faribault, Jean-Baptiste (1775–1860)
Faribault, Joseph-Édouard (1773–1859)
Fassio, Gerome (d. 1851)
Fenouillet, Émile de (1807–59)
Ferguson, Robert (1768–1851)
Ferrie, Colin Campbell (d. 1856)
FitzRoy, Sir Charles Augustus (1796–1858)
Fleming, Peter (fl. 1815–52)
Fontbonne, Marie-Antoinette, named Sister Delphine (1813–56)
Foreman, James (1763–1854)
Foretier, Marie-Amable (Viger) (1778–1854)
Fortier, Narcisse-Charles (1800–59)
Fraser, Alexander (1786–1853)
Fraser, Richard Duncan (d. 1857)
Fraser, William (d. 1851)
Frémiot, Nicolas-Marie-Joseph (1818–54)

Gage, James (1774–1854)
Gale, Alexander (d. 1854)
Gamache, Louis (fl. 1808–52)
Gamelin, Pierre (1789–1856)
Garry, Nicholas (d. 1856)
Gaukel, Friedrich (1785–1853)
Gaulin, Rémi (1787–1857)
Gautron, dit Larochelle, Siméon (1808–59)
Gerrard, Samuel (1767–1857)
Gibb, James (1799–1858)
Gilchrist, John (1792–1859)
Gildersleeve, Henry (1785–1851)
Gilkison, David (d. 1851)
Gingras, Édouard (1806–57)
Gingras, Léon (1808–60)
Girouard, Jean-Joseph (1794–1855)

Editorial Notes

PROPER NAMES

Persons have been entered under family name rather than title, pseudonym, popular name, nickname, or name in religion. Where possible the form of the surname is based on the signature, although contemporary usage is taken into account. Common variant spellings are included in parenthesis.

In the case of French names, "La," "Le," "Du," "Des," and sometimes "De" are considered part of the name and are capitalized; when both parts of the name are capitalized in the signature, French style treats the family name as two words. Compound names often appear, such as Emmanuel COUILLARD-DESPRÉS and Jean-Baptiste-René HERTEL de Rouville; cross-references are made in the text from the compounds to the main entry under the family name: from Després to Couillard-Després and from Rouville to Hertel.

Where a signature was not available for a subject whose name began with Mc or Mac, the form Mac, followed by a capital letter, has been used. Scottish-born immigrants who were entitled under Scottish law to a territorial designation as part of their names appear with that designation included, such as John MacDonald* of Glenaladale in volume V. Scots for whom the designation was used merely as a convenient way of distinguishing one individual from another have the designation in parenthesis: John McGILLIVRAY (Dalcrombie). Subjects are entered under their Gaelic names only when it is clear that they spoke Gaelic and moved in a Gaelic environment: Iain MacDHÒMHNAILL' Ic IAIN (John Mac-Donald). In all cases, appropriate cross-references are provided.

Married women and *religieuses* have been entered under their maiden names, with cross-references to the entries from their married names or their names in religion: Letitia MACTAVISH (Hargrave) and Marie-Antoinette FONTBONNE, named Sister Delphine.

Indian names have presented a particular problem, since an Indian might be known by his own name (written in a variety of ways by people unfamiliar with Indian languages) and by a nickname or baptismal name. Moreover, by the late 18th century some Indian families, such as the Joneses, were beginning to use family surnames in the European style and in these cases this is the form used in the main entry, especially where signatures are available, such as for Peter JONES. Otherwise, Indian names have been used when they could be found, and, because it is often impossible to establish an original spelling for an Indian name, the form generally chosen is the one found in standard sources or the one linguists now regard as correct, with variants following in parenthesis: HWISTESMETXĒ'qEn (Shiwelean, Nicola, N'Kuala). Appropriate cross-references are included.

For reference works used in establishing the names of persons not receiving biographies in the DCB/DBC, the reader is referred to section III of the General Bibliography.

CROSS-REFERENCES WITHIN VOLUME VIII

The first time the name of a person who has a biography in volume VIII appears in another biography his or her family name is printed in capitals and level small capitals: Robert BALDWIN and Joseph LÉGARÉ.

CROSS-REFERENCES TO OTHER VOLUMES

An asterisk following a name indicates either that the person has a biography in a volume already published – Sir Isaac Brock* and Louis-Joseph Papineau* – or that he or she will receive a biography in a volume to be published – Joseph-Octave Plessis* and Christopher Alexander Hagerman*. Birth and death (or floruit) dates for such persons are given in the index as an indication of the volume in which the biography will be found.

PLACE-NAMES

Place-names are generally given in the form used at the time of reference; where necessary, the modern name and/or the present name of the province, territory, state, or country in which the place is located have been included in parenthesis: York (Toronto), Norway House (Man.), Great Bear Lake (N.W.T.), Great Salt Lake (Utah), and Mainz (Federal Republic of Germany). The English edition cites well-known place-names in their present-day English form: St Lawrence River, Montreal, Quebec, Marseilles, and Florence. The *Encyclopædia Britannica* has been followed in determining whether place-names outside Canada have accepted English forms. Cities considered to be easily recognizable (such as London, Paris, Rome, Boston, and Rio de Janeiro) are not identified by country; within Canada, provincial capitals and several well-known cities (such as Montreal and Vancouver) are not identified by province.

Many sources have been used as guides to establish 18th- and 19th-century place-names: G. P. V. Akrigg and H. B. Akrigg, *1001 British Columbia place names* (3rd ed., Vancouver, 1973); Joseph Bouchette, *A topographical description of the province of Lower Canada . . .* (London, 1815; repr. [Saint-Lambert, Que., 1973]); *Encyclopædia Britannica*; *Encyclopedia Canadiana*; *HBRS* (several volumes of this series have been used); "Historic forts and trading posts of the French regime and of the English fur trading companies," comp. Ernest Voorhis (mimeograph, Ottawa, 1930); *Lovell's gazetteer of British North America . . .*, ed. P. A. Crossby (Montreal, 1881); Hormisdas Magnan, *Dictionnaire historique et géographique des paroisses, missions et municipalités de la province de Québec* (Arthabaska, Qué., 1925); *Place-names of N.S.*; *Places in Ont.* (Mika); Rayburn, *Geographical names of N.B.* and *Geographical names of P.E.I.*; P.-G. Roy, *Inv. concessions*; W. H. Smith, *Canada: past, present and future*; Walbran, *B.C. coast names.* For complete information about titles given in shortened form the reader is referred to the General Bibliography.

Modern Canadian names are based whenever possible on the Gazetteer of Canada series issued by the Canadian Permanent Committee on Geographical Names, Ottawa, on the *Canada gazetteer atlas* (n.p., 1980), and on the *Répertoire toponymique du Québec* (Québec, 1979) and the supplements published in the *Gazette officielle du Québec*. For places outside Canada the following have been major sources of reference: *Bartholomew gazetteer of Britain*, comp. Oliver Mason ([Edinburgh, 1977]); Albert Dauzat et Charles Rostaing, *Dictionnaire étymologique des noms de lieux en France* (Paris, [1963]); *Dictionnaire universel des noms propres . . . le Petit Robert 2*, Paul Robert *et al.*, édit. (3ᵉ éd., Paris, 1977); *Grand Larousse encyclopédique*; *National Geographic atlas of the world*, ed. W. E. Garrett *et al.* (5th ed., Washington, 1981).

For the period 1841–67 Upper and Lower Canada are used rather than Canada West and East.

CONTEMPORARY USAGE

Useful reference works for contemporary usage are *A dictionary of Canadianisms on historical principles*, ed. W. S. Avis *et al.* (Toronto, 1967) and *Dictionary of Newfoundland English*, ed. G. M. Story *et al.* (Toronto, [1982]). For the use of cognate terms or names in French and English, particularly in the administrative and business worlds, the statutes of Lower Canada and the Province of Canada were a helpful source, as was the *Quebec Gazette/La Gazette de Québec*. A microfilm copy of the index to the commissions register (PAC, RG 8, General index, 1651–1841 and 1841–67) was used frequently in establishing the English form for official appointments.

QUOTATIONS

Quotations have been translated when the language of the original passage is different from that of the text of the biography. Readers of the DCB may consult the DBC for the original French of quotations that have been translated into English. When a passage in French is quoted from a work that has appeared in both languages, the published English version is generally used. The wording, spelling, punctuation, and capitalization of original quotations are not altered unless it is necessary to do so for meaning, in which case the changes are made within square brackets. A name appearing within square brackets has been substituted for the original in order to identify the person more precisely or to indicate that he/she has a biography within the volume or in another volume.

DATES

If, in spite of assiduous inquiry, it is impossible to uncover a subject's birth and death dates, only the dates of his/her active career are documented. In the introductory paragraphs and in the various indexes the outside dates of activity are presented as floruit (fl.) dates.

BIBLIOGRAPHIES

Each biography is followed by a bibliography. Published works that are cited in the text appear in complete form unless they are included in the bibliography, in which case the citation is usually shortened. Sources frequently used by authors and editors are cited in shortened form in individual bibliographies; the General Bibliography (pp.973–1012) gives these sources in full. Many abbreviations are used in the individual bibliographies, especially for archival sources; a list of these can be found on p.2 and p.972.

The individual bibliographies are generally arranged alphabetically according to the five sections of the General Bibliography: manuscript sources, printed primary sources (including a section on contemporary newspapers), reference works, studies and theses, and journals. Wherever possible, manuscript material is cited under the location of the original documents; the location of copies used by contributors is included in the citation. In general, the items in individual bibliographies are the sources listed by the contributors, but these items have often been supplemented by bibliographic investigation in the DCB/DBC offices. Any special bibliographical comments by contributors appear within square brackets.

The Colonial Office and British North America, 1801–50

PHILLIP BUCKNER

DURING THE 18th century both the territorial limits of the British empire, in North America and elsewhere, and the institutions of the imperial government in London were in an almost constant state of flux. The Seven Years' War and the American revolution clarified the boundaries of the empire and in 1801 responsibility for the colonies was given to the secretary of state for war and the colonies. With the end of the Napoleonic Wars the department was preoccupied with colonial business and became generally known as the Colonial Office. During the Crimean War another secretary of state was created to take over the war department, and from 1854 until 1925, when a separate Dominions Office was established, the Colonial Office had the primary responsibility for managing the overseas possessions of the crown (excluding India).

For a century and a quarter the Colonial Office played a decisive part in determining the destiny of the North American colonies. Particularly before responsible government was introduced into those colonies in the 1840s and 1850s, its views were a critical factor in the calculations of the governors and the governed in British North America. The files of the department literally bulge with letters of advice, of warning, of complaint, and of special pleading from priests and politicians, businessmen and landowners, immigrants and sojourners who had interests to pursue or to protect in the colonies. Frequently the colonists had only a hazy idea of how the Colonial Office was organized and how it functioned but they knew it was an institution that in innumerable ways affected them in their daily lives.

For most of the 19th century the Colonial Office was housed in two dilapidated buildings in London which were condemned in 1839 by the select committee on public offices as unsafe and unworthy of repair. Within these crowded and inadequate quarters at 13 and 14 Downing Street a handful of public servants laboured to run the British empire. They received limited praise from their contemporaries. During the first half of the century the Colonial Office was the object of continuous abuse by a wide range of interest groups both in London and in the colonies. Its principal critics in Britain were the so-called colonial reformers, particularly Edward Gibbon Wakefield*

and Charles Buller*; they fabricated the stereotype of "Mr Mother Country," the faceless and ignorant bureaucrat who was presumed to exercise a baneful influence over the colonial policy of the British government and to be responsible for the maladministration of the colonies. The myth that imperial policy was formulated in this way crossed the Atlantic and was eagerly espoused by all those discontented with that policy. From very different perspectives both the reformers and the conservatives in British North America – William Lyon Mackenzie* and John Beverley Robinson* alike – blamed the Canadian rebellions of 1837–38 on the weaknesses and ignorance of the Colonial Office. Even those officials who visited London and were received at the Colonial Office frequently returned disillusioned after their experience with what Chief Justice Jonathan Sewell* of Lower Canada cynically described as "the Patience Chamber of Downing St."

This view of the Colonial Office as an ignorant and unresponsive bureaucracy answerable for all of the disasters in imperial policy has become so deeply entrenched in Canadian historiography that it is unlikely ever to be entirely eradicated. Yet it is based upon a distorted image of the Colonial Office. During the first half of the 19th century the Colonial Office evolved from a department organized around the personality of the secretary of state into the prototype of a modern bureaucracy. In 1801 the office possessed neither the administrative competence nor the bureaucratic machinery to play a major role in the formulation of policy. Lacking the assistance of an efficient and knowledgeable body of subordinates, the secretary of state had to rely for advice upon reports from officials in the colonies or from self-interested pressure groups in London. Inevitably information about the colonies collected in this haphazard fashion was defective. Year by year after 1801, however, the quantity and quality of information received by the Colonial Office improved. The institution of the blue books in the 1820s, prepared in the colonies according to general guide-lines laid down in London, provided one source of valuable knowledge and in the 1830s colonial authorities were required to send home reports on an ever wider variety of subjects. A representative sample of newspapers and a comprehensive collection of books and pamphlets about

British North America were diligently examined by the expanding bureaucracy of the Colonial Office. In fact, by the 1830s the office had evolved what was by contemporary standards a relatively efficient system of collecting, storing, and retrieving information. Egerton Ryerson* was exaggerating in 1836 when he reported that, "in respect to *Upper Canada,* nearly as much is known in the Colonial Office of our affairs and our public men as we know ourselves," but he was a good deal closer to the truth than he would have been a decade earlier.

As the internal organization of the Colonial Office improved, British ministers were able to supervise more effectively the activities of their subordinates in British North America. Prior to the mid 1820s the department exercised only a perfunctory control over British officials in the colonies. Indeed, many lesser officials were appointed and dismissed by other government departments in Britain, and the Colonial Office had little knowledge of how adequately or inadequately such officials performed their duties. Until the 1820s it did not even realize how grossly overpaid many of these functionaries were, since they were frequently rewarded by fees rather than paid salaries. Even the governors, whom it appointed and whose salaries it monitored, received few positive instructions from the Colonial Office, and as a result they had nearly unlimited freedom of action. Of course, governors did not always get their own way. On questions of patronage they were frequently disappointed when positions in the colony were distributed according to the exigencies of British and not colonial politics. Thomas Carleton*, for example, was deeply affronted when Edward Winslow* was appointed to the Supreme Court of New Brunswick in 1807 rather than his own candidate, Ward Chipman*. Similarly, when a governor appealed to his superiors to introduce changes in a colonial constitution, as Sir James Henry Craig* did in 1810 for Lower Canada, he was usually disillusioned by the refusal of the government in London to act, even when, as in Craig's case, it shared his desire to restructure the constitution. The perspective of most secretaries of state was that of Lord Bathurst, who is alleged to have said to a governor departing for his post, "Joy be with you, and let us hear as little of you as possible." Governors were seldom exhorted to do anything positive. More likely, they would be rebuked for trying to do too much or for using heated or extravagant language that threatened to destroy the tranquillity of the colonial political scene. But rarely would they be recalled unless guilty of the grossest stupidity or misconduct, and sometimes not even then. Dismissals were even rarer. As late as the early 1820s a complete incompetent like Charles Douglass SMITH was permitted to retain office until he had nearly precipitated a minor uprising in Prince Edward Island. Several governors – most notably Thomas Carleton and Robert Prescott* – continued to hold office for years after leaving a colony to which they had no intention of ever going back.

Somewhat greater attention was paid to the affairs of the larger North American colonies because of their strategic location on the border of the United States, particularly during and immediately following the War of 1812. Indeed, in 1815 Sir George Prevost* suffered the indignity of dismissal because of his military failures during the war. Thereafter the British government reverted to its normal inactivity. Until 1828 the Colonial Office had no conception of the degree of popular discontent aroused by Lord Dalhousie [Ramsay*] in Lower Canada or by Sir Peregrine MAITLAND in Upper Canada. After 1828, the British government embarked upon a policy of conciliating the British North American assemblies which required giving more detailed instructions to the governors and exercising closer supervision over them. Sir John Colborne* was removed from Upper Canada in 1835, Sir Archibald Campbell* from New Brunswick in 1837, and Sir Colin Campbell* from Nova Scotia in 1839 for resisting, albeit passively, this program of conciliation. Sir Francis Bond Head*, the most colourful and least obedient governor of the 1830s, was only saved from dismissal by submitting his resignation as lieutenant governor of Upper Canada in 1837. Even Sir John HARVEY, who won high praise for conciliating New Brunswick, was demoted to the less prestigious and less remunerative government of Newfoundland in 1841 for disobeying instructions.

During and immediately following the Napoleonic Wars all of the governors of the British North American colonies were, like Sir John Coape Sherbrooke*, military men; they were usually given their positions in the colonies as a reward for distinguished military service. Although many of the governors of the 1830s and 1840s also had a military background, they began to be chosen, as was Sir William MacBean George Colebrooke*, more for their political and diplomatic skills. As they crossed and recrossed the empire and worked their way up the ladder of colonial governorships, they came to form the nucleus of a quasi-professional colonial service. On the peripheries of the empire they might be given a great deal of latitude and might frequently be able to disobey with impunity the instructions they received from London, but not in the North American colonies, where the Colonial Office could regulate their activities with increasing effectiveness. Because of the political crisis in the Canadas in the 1830s, the British government did devolve considerable authority upon Lord Gosford [Acheson*], who became governor-in-chief of British North America in 1835, and even more extensive powers upon his successors,

Lord Durham [Lambton*] and Charles Edward Poulett Thomson*, later Lord Sydenham. Moreover, because of the sheer size and the political complexity of the Province of Canada (formed by the union of Upper and Lower Canada in 1841), the post of governor there was held by a series of imperial proconsuls – Sydenham, Sir Charles Bagot*, Sir Charles Theophilus Metcalfe*, and Lord Elgin [Bruce*] – who were given an unusual degree of discretionary authority and played a positive role in shaping imperial policy. But they were the exceptions. As a general rule the governors of the British North American colonies had become, in practice as well as in theory, the agents of the Colonial Office.

During the first half of the 19th century the ability of colonial visitors to influence imperial policy-making also declined. As late as the 1820s representatives of the colonial élite who travelled to London – men like John Beverley Robinson and Jonathan Sewell – were co-opted into assisting the staff of the Colonial Office in formulating policy. By the 1830s the permanent officials in the department no longer required this assistance and the access of colonial visitors to the secretary of state was restricted and their influence greatly reduced. Simultaneously, the role of interest groups in Britain was drastically curtailed. In the 18th century British merchants and colonial agents, such as Joshua Mauger*, Brook Watson*, and Francis Maseres*, had played an important role in determining policy. The factionalized and undisciplined nature of the British political system had given interest groups considerable leverage as had the inadequacy of the administrative machinery for governing the empire, with no clear demarcation of authority between departments in London, little centralized control, and few permanent officials to provide continuity. Although some of these conditions persisted into the early 19th century, the emergence of the modern cabinet and of a rudimentary party system made it easier for ministers to resist self-interested pressure groups. Moreover, communications with the colonies were rapidly improving, and the Colonial Office had begun to coordinate the work of the various government departments with responsibilities overseas.

There remained, of course, a vast complex of interest groups directly or indirectly concerned with specific colonial subjects. The religious lobbies were particularly active both in parliament and outside it. The strongest lobby was inevitably the Church of England and an assiduous lobbyist such as Bishop John Inglis* or Archdeacon John Strachan* could bring considerable pressure to bear on the Colonial Office. The Church of Scotland and the Methodists also had active organizations on both sides of the Atlantic [see William MORRIS; George Ryerson*]. The other dissenting sects had less influence in government circles but could count on radical support in parliament and moral support from dissenting congregations. Many Irish and Canadian Roman Catholics looked to Daniel O'Connell and his Irish followers for assistance on religious issues. The Catholic hierarchy in Lower Canada worked mainly through the apostolic vicars in London, and Scottish Catholics, Bishop Alexander McDonell* of Kingston among them, made use of their political influence on such Scottish MPs as Charles Grant, later Lord Glenelg. Particularly after the Whigs came to power in 1830 the Catholic lobby had considerable clout. None the less, the interest of the religious lobbies in colonial affairs remained specific, not general, and was usually limited to advancing or protecting the position of their own churches.

Although other pressure groups inevitably paled before the great religious lobbies of the period, a web of vested interests stretched across the Atlantic. The single most important strand in it was the timber trade. In the colonies the trade provided the foundation of the personal fortunes and political influence of such prominent merchants as Alexander RANKIN and Peter PATTERSON. In Britain it gave rise to a lobby of formidable proportions, which had to maintain an active presence in parliament because the market for British North America timber had been artificially created by the preference against Baltic timber adopted during the Napoleonic Wars, and this preference came increasingly under attack from free traders after 1815. Even at the peak of the trade, however, the number of merchants in Britain engaged in importing timber was not big and their influence was local in nature, confined largely to Glasgow, Liverpool, and London, where the only important concentrations of merchants were found. What gave the timber merchants considerable influence was their alliance with the Society of Shipowners, perhaps the best organized commercial association in early 19th-century Britain. But when many shipowners came to the conclusion in the 1840s that they would benefit from a general reduction in tariffs, they abandoned their former friends.

Without the backing of the shipowners the timber merchants were too weak to protect the preference on colonial timber. Other groups in Britain with a financial or commercial stake in British North America, such as the Hudson's Bay Company and the North American fisheries interest, were not without political influence, and to some extent their concerns were intertwined with those of the timber lobby since they also had a vested interest in the protective system. None the less, by the 1840s they were fighting a rearguard action to defend their own privileges and could provide only limited support for the timber merchants. Of course, there were numerous merchants who like Peter BUCHANAN were engaged in the wholesaling or retailing of British goods in the colonies, but in the main they ran small-scale operations and could bring little pressure to bear on the Colonial Office. Far more important was the much smaller number of merchant bankers with investments in the colonies, the firms – Baring Brothers among them – to which such colonial officials as Receiver General John Henry DUNN of Upper Canada had recourse when they went to London to borrow money. Yet as a proportion of the total of their overseas investments, the stake of British financial institutions in the North American colonies remained small until the building of the railways. Except for a handful of land speculators, who purchased estates or bought shares in one of the land companies founded during the 1820s and 1830s, there were few investors whose fortunes depended upon the commercial health of the North American colonies, and with rare exceptions these men had little access to the councils of the great in Britain.

One of the exceptions was Edward Ellice*. Heir to a substantial fortune, Ellice had sizeable investments in the West Indies, in the United States, and in British North America. He visited North America on occasion, played a critical part in the negotiations which led to the North West Company's amalgamation with the Hudson's Bay Company, and was involved in several speculative ventures, including John Galt*'s Canada Company, the North American Colonial Association of Ireland, and William Hamilton Merritt*'s Welland Canal Company. In 1809 he married the younger daughter of the 1st Earl Grey and thus joined one of the most powerful political dynasties in Great Britain. Entering politics, he served during the 1820s as one of the Whig's principal spokesmen on economic questions, in 1830 became a secretary to the Treasury and chief whip, and in 1833 entered the cabinet as secretary at war. This combination of interest and influence has led historians to exaggerate the extent to which Ellice could and did affect the course of British colonial policy. For all his connections, Ellice remained something of a lone wolf. Despite extensive investments in the Caribbean he seldom acted in concert with the West Indies interest in parliament, and during the latter part of the 1830s his influence waned rapidly. Although Ellice freely offered advice about the course of events in British North America, he was legitimately suspected of interpreting those events in the light of his own self-interest. He did have some impact upon the policy of successive governments, but his counsel was seldom decisive.

Indeed, the merchants concerned with North America never rivalled in influence the far stronger West Indies interest. One glaring weakness of their organizations, such as the Canada Club (formed by Isaac Todd* and others) and the North American Colonial Association, was that these bodies could not claim to reflect the views of the colonial legislatures. The only colonial agent associated with the merchants was Henry Bliss*, who from 1824 acted for the New Brunswick assembly. The reform parties in the Canadas had their own agents in the House of Commons during the 1830s. John Arthur Roebuck* served as the agent for Lower Canada and Joseph Hume unofficially represented the views of the radical reformers in Upper Canada. By the mid 1830s the interests of British merchants with investments to protect in the Canadas and the concerns of the Canadian reformers diverged widely. The merchants were represented in the Commons by such men as George Richard Robinson and Patrick Maxwell Stewart, but Hume and Roebuck were more than a match for them and the debates on Canadian policy during this period reflected a growing polarization. If all the groups claiming to speak for the North American colonies in London had been able to agree on what they wanted, they might well have exercised greater influence. But since they could not agree, the Colonial Office could to a considerable degree act, as it claimed to act, as an arbiter between the different pressure groups.

By the 1830s and 1840s the Colonial Office had developed the administrative competence to play a much more positive role in the government of the colonies. In fact, it rarely did so. The government in London seldom anticipated events; it simply responded to external pressures. The Colonial Office was essentially a regulatory agency, primarily concerned with the security of the empire, not with the growth or development of the colonies. Its major functions were to protect imperial interests by supervising the activities of the colonial governors and by scrutinizing colonial legislation and to coordinate the activities of all those metropolitan bodies with a role to play in colonial government.

In the 18th century there had been no real equivalent of the 19th-century Colonial Office. The ministers and departments of state in Britain simply assumed for the colonies responsibilities similar to those they undertook at home. A limited degree of coordination was provided by the Board of Trade and after 1768 by the short-lived American Department, but in 1782 both bodies were abolished and their supervisory role was transferred to the two secretaries of state. Later that year one secretary of state became responsible for foreign affairs and one for home affairs; the colonies were placed under the jurisdiction of the Home Department, which had little experience in colonial matters, and was unable to give much coherence or direction to the conduct of colonial policy. In 1801, largely for reasons of political convenience, the colonies were transferred to the secretary of state for war, a position created in 1794. For the duration of the Napoleonic Wars the secretary of state for war and the colonies concentrated on military affairs, but after 1815 he was relieved of a whole range of administrative duties and became, virtually by accident, primarily concerned with the colonies.

In one sense the Colonial Office as it developed in the early 1800s was a new department, providing a service that had been performed inadequately and fitfully in the previous century. Certainly the scale of its responsibilities was new. The second British empire was both larger and more diverse than the first. In theory, secretaries of state were expected to "be minutely acquainted with all the details of the business of their offices, and the only way of being constantly armed with such information is to conduct and direct those details themselves." In practice, no secretary of state could be well informed about all the details of the affairs of a vast and heterogeneous empire. In 1846 the 3rd Earl Grey, probably the most conscientious colonial minister in the 19th century, admitted to a subordinate that he did not know whether the Auckland Islands were part of the British empire: "I see that they are coloured red in Arrowsmith's map of the world which I suppose implies some sort of claim on our part." Yet, although the secretary of state might know little about the distant and less important parts of the empire, he usually had some general knowledge about the British North American colonies and an idea of the principles upon which he wished those colonies to be governed. In British North American affairs he always paid comparatively close attention to the activities of his subordinates and performed much of the work himself.

Inevitably the personal ability of successive secretaries of state and the degree of interest they showed in the colonies fluctuated greatly. The six men who held the seals of the office between 1801 and 1812 – Henry Dundas, Lord Hobart, Lord Camden, Lord Castlereagh, William Windham, and Lord Liverpool – concentrated on military affairs and showed a minimum of concern with the colonies. Their successors had very limited responsibilities for military affairs after 1815, however, and were compelled to devote their primary attention to the colonies. The Colonial Office continued to suffer occasionally from poor appointments, but since the post of secretary of state carried considerable prestige and a position in the cabinet, it was usually held by a senior and distinguished politician. Collectively the 12 men who served as secretary of state between 1812 and 1850 had impressive credentials. Five – Lord Goderich, Lord Stanley, Lord Aberdeen, Lord John Russell, and William Ewart Gladstone – had been or were to become prime minister. With the exception of Sir George Murray*, who was parachuted into the office by the Duke of Wellington in 1828, all 12 were

in the first rank of politicians and had considerable administrative experience.

Under the direction of Lord Bathurst, the secretary of state from 1812 to 1827, the Colonial Office was reorganized in the 1820s. Revisionism has been kind to Lord Bathurst. Recent studies have painted a picture of a reasonably intelligent and capable man, deeply conservative in his political philosophy but prepared to deal with specific issues pragmatically. Unfortunately Bathurst was past his prime by the 1820s and he allowed his under-secretary, Robert John Wilmot-Horton, to persuade him to adopt, during Dalhousie's administration of Lower Canada, a policy of confrontation with the assembly over the civil list question. During the rapid change of ministries in Britain in 1827–28, neither Lord Goderich nor William Huskisson found time to make much of an impact at the Colonial Office, although Huskisson was responsible for the appointment of the House of Commons select committee on Canada in 1828 [see Sir James KEMPT]. Between 1828 and 1830 Sir George Murray proved incapable of formulating a coherent response to the report of that committee, which had recognized the claims of the Lower Canadian assembly as represented by Denis-Benjamin Viger*, Augustin Cuvillier*, and John Neilson* and whose consideration of both Lower and Upper Canadian affairs had thoroughly antagonized such conservatives as John Strachan. Lord Goderich returned to the Colonial Office in 1830 but increasingly was overshadowed by his parliamentary under-secretary, Lord Howick, the eldest son of the prime minister, the 2nd Earl Grey. Until his resignation in 1833 Howick was the real architect of the Whig government's North American policy, which was based on a sincere effort to implement the recommendations of the Canada committee and to conciliate reform parties throughout British North America. Stanley, who had served as under-secretary in 1827–28 and had played a key role as a member of the Canada committee in formulating its report, returned to the Colonial Office as secretary of state in 1833 and alienated reformers in both Canadas, Mackenzie and Viger alike. In 1834 and 1835 Thomas Spring-Rice and Lord Aberdeen struggled without success to reach an accommodation with the Canadian assemblies.

Between 1835 and 1839 poor Lord Glenelg, the most maligned of the secretaries of state of this period, presided over the failure of the imperial government to find a peaceful resolution to the crisis in the Canadas. His successor, Lord Normanby, was even less capable and was quickly transferred to the Home Office. Lord John Russell, secretary of state from 1839 to 1841, and Lord Stanley, from 1841 to 1845, dominated the decision-making process within the Colonial Office in the years when the introduction of responsible government was an overriding issue. Contemporary historiography tends to assign the decision to introduce responsible government to the 3rd Earl Grey (as Lord Howick became) in the period 1846–52; in practice, however, as Adam Shortt* argued many years ago, that decision was taken in the Province of Canada by Sydenham in 1841 and Russell approved it. In 1842 Stanley and Sir Robert Peel were forced to accept, albeit reluctantly, that Sir Charles Bagot had no choice but to reorganize his government in order to ensure that it had the confidence of the Canadian legislature. After 1842 no one within the Colonial Office doubted that the essential principle of responsible government had been conceded, but Stanley and his successor, William Ewart Gladstone, tried to delay the extension of that principle to the other North American colonies and to exercise a degree of influence in Canadian politics that could not be sustained indefinitely. Gladstone was secretary of state for only six months before the Whigs returned to power in 1846 and the 3rd Earl Grey returned to the Colonial Office. Almost immediately Grey had to deal with the implications of the decision to introduce responsible government in Nova Scotia [see Sir John Harvey], and before his departure from office in 1852 he presided over the transition to responsible government in most of the British North American colonies. In the process he was compelled to accept that he must avoid even the appearance of interfering in the partisan struggles within the colonies, a necessity that would severely circumscribe the ability of any future colonial minister to influence developments in North America.

Even before responsible government was conceded, the authority of the secretary of state was constrained by a variety of factors. The military departments – the Admiralty, the War Office, the Ordnance, and the Horse Guards – had their own representatives overseas and were a law unto themselves. The Treasury, the Post Office, and the Board of Customs also stationed their own officials in the colonies and only gradually relinquished control over them to the local executive. The Colonial Office had running battles with the Treasury, which wished to pare imperial expenditures in the colonies to levels the Colonial Office considered unacceptable, and with the Privy Council committee for trade, established in 1784 and commonly called the Board of Trade, which sought to exercise greater control over colonial legislation than the Colonial Office believed was practicable. During the 1830s and 1840s the Colonial Office was able to exert considerable influence over other departments with lingering responsibilities in the colonies, but it could not impose its will. Frequently inter-departmental rivalries could be resolved only at the cabinet level, and sometimes not even there.

With the decline of royal authority in the 19th century the cabinet became the focus of the executive government. Yet it was, as Lord John Russell noted in 1854, "a cumbrous and unwieldy instrument" for formulating policy unless given clear guide-lines by a strong minister. In fact, the degree of interest shown by the cabinet in colonial affairs normally reflected the degree of interest shown by parliament, where the affairs of British North America were of concern only to a small minority of members. "I almost despair," Henry Bliss, the colonial agent for New Brunswick, lamented in 1826. "The Empire is so vast and we are so distant, our affairs are but a bore." It is true that, during the 1830s and 1840s, a significant proportion of the time of the House of Commons was devoted to British North American, and particularly Canadian, affairs. None the less, it would be wrong to conclude that those colonies had assumed an unusual importance in the collective mind of the house. The rebellions of 1837–38 in the Canadas coincided with a domestic political crisis during which the parties in the Commons were almost equal in strength, and partisan considerations gave to colonial issues a transitory importance. After 1841, with the Conservatives again possessing a clear majority, the interest in debating British North American issues dissolved, to be reconstituted only when this period of political stability came to an end in 1846.

Longevity in office, the pressures and demands of domestic politics, and the complexity of the difficulties confronted were all critical factors limiting the freedom of action of the secretary of state. Equally important in determining whether he succeeded or failed in his objectives was the quality of information and advice he received from his subordinates in the Colonial Office. By far the most influential of these subordinates were the under-secretaries of state. In 1801 there was one under-secretary; after 1806 there were two; in 1816, as a measure of post-war retrenchment, the number was reduced to one. The duties of an under-secretary fluctuated with the needs and whims of his superior. Lord Bathurst left much of the daily routine of the office in the hands of his subordinates and so placed an almost unbearable work-load on their shoulders. At the end of his first day as under-secretary in 1821, Wilmot-Horton, a man of immense if not always well-directed energy, confided to his wife that he was "daunted by the *enormous* Mass of Papers and correspondence, which I must conquer and carry on." To deal with this mass Henry Goulburn and Wilmot-Horton, under-secretaries in 1812–21 and 1821–28, devoted considerable attention to internal improvements within the department. At the end of 1823 the establishment of the Colonial Office was composed of one under-secretary, a private secretary, a librarian, ten clerks, and a part-time legal counsel. By the end of August 1825 the staff had been expanded to two under-secretaries, three private secretaries, two librarians, fifteen clerks, two registrars, a précis writer, and a full-time legal counsel shared with the Board of Trade. Thereafter only slight additions were made to the establishment until the 1870s. Prior to the expansion of the 1820s individual clerks had been responsible for specific colonies, but after 1822 the business of the empire was divided into geographical areas and a senior clerk, assisted by two to four junior clerks, was placed in charge of each. After 1824 there were four geographic departments, one of which dealt with North American affairs.

Perhaps the most important innovation was the decision to reappoint a second under-secretary in 1825, because in time he became a permanent under-secretary with control over the establishment of the Colonial Office. Initially, there was no clear functional division of labour between the two under-secretaries. Wilmot-Horton simply shared the business with his new colleague on a geographical basis, retaining for himself the colonies, including the British North American colonies, in which he was most interested or which attracted the most attention in the House of Commons. After Wilmot-Horton was forced to retire from office in 1828, he was replaced by a series of parliamentary under-secretaries. Some of them played an important role in evolving Colonial Office policy in British North America. Particularly active were Stanley, who had been appointed additional parliamentary under-secretary in 1827 and who succeeded Wilmot-Horton the following year, and Lord Howick, who served as parliamentary under-secretary between 1830 and 1833. It was Stanley, for example, who shaped the more conciliatory policy adopted by the British government toward the Canadas in 1827–28, and Howick drafted virtually all of the important dispatches dealing with those colonies in the early 1830s. Other parliamentary under-secretaries were nonentities who left the running of the North American department in the hands of the second under-secretary, Robert William Hay. Appointed in 1825, Hay was theoretically responsible for overseeing the work of the North American department for most of the period between 1828 and 1836.

Although Hay became the first permanent under-secretary, he was no innovator. He continued to conduct the business in the old manner, he seldom took the initiative, and he avoided controversial subjects. To a considerable degree his views were shaped by the reports he received from the numerous colonial officials with whom he carried on an extensive private correspondence. There was nothing unusual or sinister in this practice. Goulburn and Wilmot-Horton had conducted their work in the same way and many of the clerks regularly corresponded with friends or acquaintances who were serving in the colonies. Even James Stephen, who as under-secretary was to end the practice, admitted "a sort of propensity to make acquaintance with the crowd of Colonial Officers who are constantly passing and repassing through Downing St." But while these informal channels frequently provided useful information about the colonies, they were not an adequate foundation upon which to base decisions and they left the Colonial Office open to the charge of taking sides in the struggles within the colonies. Indeed, as political changes in Britain in the later 1820s and the 1830s brought shifts in the policies of the imperial government, correspondence with officials in the colonies whose activities were no longer condoned by the government at home could be dangerous. Part of Hay's dilemma in the 1830s was that he found himself more sympathetic to the views of his acquaintances overseas than to those of the Whig governments he served. His passive role was easily interpreted by some of the Whigs as hostile to their interests. Moreover, it created a vacuum at the top in the Colonial Office which annoyed those clerks within the department who did sympathize with Whig policies.

To some extent, this vacuum was filled by James Stephen, who, as legal adviser to the Colonial Office, was already performing in the 1820s duties that would later be assigned to the permanent under-secretary. Although the outlines of Stephen's character are well known and he has been the subject of a useful biography by Paul Knaplund, the definitive study has yet to be written of the man who more than any other individual influenced the development of the Colonial Office in the 19th century and who played a very important role in shaping the North American policy of the British government.

Sir James Stephen was a child of the evangelical revival. His father was prominent in the movement; his father's second wife was a sister of William Wilberforce. Stephen was brought up within the confines of the "Clapham sect," the name he gave to that group of prominent evangelical families who congregated in the fashionable London suburb of Clapham, and his close friends were drawn almost entirely from the inner circle of the evangelical movement. Naturally shy, "sensitive beyond what was reasonable," "a man without a skin," in later life he became something of a recluse. His aloofness was reinforced by asceticism. He never went to the theatre or dances, was uninterested in food, seldom drank, and once smoked a cigar but never repeated the experience because he enjoyed it so much. Involvement in the affairs of the world was implicit in the evangelical creed and Stephen entered the Colonial Office to perform God's work, to assist in the movement to abolish slavery. He was, in Henry Walter Parris's felicitous phrase, "a zealot." His dedication to his work was almost total. Stephen's superiors, his colleagues, and his subordinates might break down under the pressure of a constant influx of dispatches and retreat from London, but Stephen remained at his post "to give an example." He rose early and worked late. Almost his sole diversion in later years was to devote part of the morning or evening to the preparation of articles for the *Edinburgh Review*.

Evangelicals drew a distinction, which was not merely casuistical, between temporal evils, intrinsic in a society of sinners, and moral wrongs, which fly in the face of God's laws. With the latter there could be no compromise. This moral absolutism had both a positive and a negative side. Evangelicals led the crusade against slavery; they also led the crusade to destroy non-Christian systems of belief among native peoples in British North America and throughout the empire. The energy of the movement was focused on the Church Missionary Society (of which Stephen was a member for many years) and the British and Foreign Bible Society, organizations represented in British North America by such men as William Cockran* and John West*, and on a host of other religious or quasi-religious bodies that were concerned with the spiritual and only incidentally the material well-being of their fellow men. Stephen, for example, played a negative role in dealing with efforts to regulate the transatlantic emigrant trade and not infrequently "contented himself with a melancholy contemplation of the folly and hopeless misery of mortals." Other examples could be given of Stephen's insensitivity, but they should not be blown out of proportion. By the standards of his age Stephen was humane. But with his pessimistic views on the nature of man and the inevitable misery in human society, he could not be a great social reformer.

Stephen's disdain for partisan politics, as well as his intense dedication and his acute intelligence, made him far more suitable than Hay for the position of permanent under-secretary. His legal training was another advantage. The vast expansion of the empire during the Napoleonic Wars had created complex constitutional and legal problems for the Colonial Office and in 1813 Stephen was retained on a commission basis to examine colonial laws. He gradually came to occupy a position of unique importance in the Colonial Office as "the single student and Professor in England of my art – the art of understanding everything connected with the Constitutions, Charters and Written Laws, of some 40 Colonies." In 1824 Wilmot-Horton wrote to assure the West Indian lobby that Stephen's duty was to report whether colonial laws were compatible with the laws of England, not whether they were "expedient" or "inexpedient." Wilmot-Horton was not quite honest. Since the law itself is crystallized policy, legal advice

inevitably involves some statement concerning that policy and from there it is no distance to discussing the merits of a policy. Stephen did not adopt a narrow interpretation of his responsibilities and it soon became "something of a fiction to regard as mere legal opinions Reports which embrace or advert to every topic which seems to me to demand the notice of the Secretary of State." His work grew rapidly in scope and complexity and he was consulted whenever a legal or constitutional question was involved. Yet even after becoming a permanent employee in 1825, he held only "an obscure and secondary Place" in the official hierarchy and he began to work, perhaps subconsciously at first, to replace Hay as permanent under-secretary.

When Hay entered the Colonial Office in 1825, he did not think of himself as a civil servant in any modern sense. As Henry Parris has pointed out, the "permanent civil service" in the early 19th century was neither permanent nor civil nor a service. Entry was by patronage, did not require any particular expertise or even a high level of administrative competence, and conferred financial rewards but limited intrinsic social status. Since the duties of government were few and simple and the business in most departments was conducted by the ministers themselves, a large number of highly qualified, well-motivated public servants was hardly necessary and the civil service could be staffed by men appointed because of their influence. Hay had emerged from precisely the right background. The grandson of an archbishop of York and the nephew of the 10th Earl of Kinnoull, he had attended Christ Church College, Oxford, had been appointed in 1812 private secretary to Lord Melville, first lord of the Admiralty, and had subsequently become a commissioner of the Victualling Board. His transfer to a higher position at the Colonial Office he owed primarily to his close personal friendship with Wilmot-Horton. There is little doubt that he found his duties at the Colonial Office tedious. Stephen was cut from a different cloth and it was considerably less purple. Although he owed his initial appointment at the Colonial Office to his father's influence, thereafter he advanced through his own merits. Firmly entrenched in the Victorian upper middle class and sharing the evangelical disdain for idle aristocrats, he found subordination to a dilettante like Hay increasingly irritating.

After the Whigs came to power in 1830, Stephen had an important ally in the new parliamentary under-secretary, Lord Howick. Early in 1832, having persuaded the secretary of state, Lord Goderich, to agree, Howick took charge of the North American department, and he began to work for Hay's dismissal and Stephen's promotion. When Howick resigned from the Colonial Office in March 1833, however, Hay resumed control over North American affairs. In

April 1835, with the Whigs back in power, Howick entered the cabinet as secretary at war, and in February 1836 he coerced the colonial minister, Lord Glenelg, into dismissing Hay and appointing Stephen permanent under-secretary.

Under Stephen's direction, the reorganization of the Colonial Office, begun in the 1820s, was completed. No fundamental changes were introduced until the 1870s and the significance of the later innovations is easily exaggerated. Immediately upon becoming permanent under-secretary, Stephen introduced a comprehensive system of minuting and brought to an end the division of business on a geographical basis between the two under-secretaries. Henceforth, every letter, every dispatch, with the relevant enclosures, was sent from the senior clerk of the geographical department concerned, or his assistant, to the permanent under-secretary, then to the parliamentary under-secretary, and finally to the secretary of state. In the vast majority of cases Stephen indicated in a minute the answer that should be given or the course of action to be adopted. Usually the parliamentary under-secretary and the secretary of state needed to do little more than to note whether they agreed with Stephen's recommendation. The papers were then returned to Stephen, who prepared the draft of any letters that were necessary to implement the decision taken or indicated to a clerk the form which should be followed in preparing these documents. All drafts were circulated to both under-secretaries and to the secretary of state for revision and approval.

In theory, little distinction was drawn between the duties of the two under-secretaries. In practice, a dichotomy was established. The parliamentary under-secretary became a political adviser to the secretary of state with a special responsibility for dealing with questions that were likely to arouse comment in parliament, while the permanent under-secretary became increasingly anonymous and apolitical with the primary responsibility of supervising the work of the clerical establishment and all routine business. In the past, parliamentary under-secretaries such as Wilmot-Horton and Howick had overshadowed the permanent under-secretary and occasionally even the secretary of state. But after 1836 the parliamentary under-secretary no longer kept the detailed business of half the empire, frequently the more important half, in his own hands. His work had increased immensely, since he was expected to read all the dispatches and letters that came into the Colonial Office. His ability to influence the decisions of the secretary of state had declined, his advice having to compete with that of the permanent under-secretary whose knowledge was inevitably greater.

Yet in the formulation of North American policy even Stephen's role was extremely limited after 1836. Between 1828 and 1830 he had been one of the principal architects of government policy. Following Stanley's resignation as under-secretary in January 1828, William Huskisson turned to him for assistance in formulating a policy to meet the crisis in Lower Canada and that year Stephen appeared as a witness before the select committee on Canada, where he defended the legal claim of the Canadian legislatures to the revenues in dispute. His views carried weight with the committee and were embodied in its report. Moreover, Sir George Murray assigned Stephen the duty of preparing the Colonial Office's response to that report, although he followed Stephen's advice only on minor issues. After 1830 Stephen exercised considerable indirect influence over policy because of his direct influence over Lord Howick, who derived many of his views from Stephen. When Stanley became secretary of state in 1833, he deliberately relegated Stephen to a minor role in policy-making, but during the rapid turnover of ministers in 1834 and 1835 Thomas Spring-Rice, Lord Aberdeen, and Lord Glenelg all looked to Stephen for guidance. Over his fellow evangelical and boyhood friend, Glenelg, Stephen had a particularly strong influence and from 1835 to 1837 a number of Stephen's memoranda were circulated to the cabinet and formed the basis of its discussions. None the less, as the situation in the Canadas deteriorated and Canadian issues moved to the centre of British politics, the real focus of decision-making shifted from the Colonial Office to the cabinet, where Stephen's voice was only one among many. Moreover, after Glenelg was forced out of office in 1839, he was replaced by a series of strong secretaries of state who required little instruction from their permanent under-secretary on the major questions of Canadian policy. Stephen, under increasing attack from his critics in Britain and in the colonies, was pleased to play a less prominent role in formulating policy. On routine matters his advice still carried great weight. When the issue was whether to approve an appointment or any administrative or financial decision taken by a governor, or if it involved essentially a legal or technical question, Stephen's minute on the incoming dispatch normally formed the basis of the secretary of state's decision. If the dispatch raised a more general issue of policy, his minute usually outlined the alternatives available and subtly pushed the secretary of state in the direction he preferred. Occasionally but rarely was Stephen's advice on such matters challenged by the parliamentary under-secretary and even more rarely would the latter's opinion be favoured by the secretary of state. Because of his own reorganization of the Colonial Office, Stephen had neither the time nor the inclination to prepare those lengthy and comprehensive memoranda on general issues which had accounted for much of his influence before he had become permanent under-secretary. But next to the secretary of state, whose voice remained decisive, Stephen exercised the greatest control over the decision-making process within the Colonial Office.

Another shift of power within the Colonial Office is discernible after 1836. In the 1820s and during the first half of the 1830s a number of the more able clerks had been doing the work of statesmen. After 1836 Stephen absorbed many of their duties. He decided what functions the clerks should perform and what information should be given to the secretary of state. With his extensive knowledge, long experience, and truly remarkable memory, he seldom had to call upon his subordinates for assistance. Even when Stephen was in error, the clerks were reluctant to point this fact out to him.

The significance of this change is clearly observable in the North American department. When Wilmot-Horton arrived at the Colonial Office in 1821, North American business was handled by Adam Gordon, the son of an American loyalist, who had been appointed to the Home Department in 1795 and then transferred along with responsibility for the colonies to the secretary of state for war in 1801. For several years the agent for Lower Canada, Gordon had been a friend of Sir George Prevost, knew many of the officials in British North America personally, and was related to Jonathan Sewell, the chief justice of Lower Canada. Gordon regularly corresponded with his friends across the Atlantic and looked after their interests in London. In 1824 he became chief clerk and George Baillie became senior clerk in charge of the North American department. Appointed to the Colonial Office in 1810, Baillie was one of Lord Bathurst's favourites and secured a position in the office for his brother Thomas*, who subsequently became commissioner of crown lands in New Brunswick. George Baillie had been involved in duties relating to British North America long before his appointment as senior clerk and he had many contacts in the colonies. He also corresponded privately with the officials and local governors, gave them confidential papers and advice, and approached Lord Bathurst on their behalf when they sought a favour. Occasionally he probably went beyond the ill-defined limits of official propriety. In one instance he even wrote to advise Sir Howard Douglas*, the lieutenant governor of New Brunswick, on the best way to deal with a disagreeable decision made by Lord Bathurst.

Although Gordon and Baillie undoubtedly had some influence upon the decisions taken on questions relating to British North America, much of the correspondence in the North American department, which remained small in volume, was too important to be delegated to a clerk. In any event, Gordon and Baillie were clerks of the old style. They were useful in dealing with procedural questions, in remembering precedents, and in supplying a certain amount of background material when decisions had to be taken. But they seldom wrote lengthy memoranda and they showed little desire to take the initiative in the formulation of policy. As the political crisis in the Canadas grew more serious during the 1830s and parliament began to take a greater interest in the affairs of British North America, there was an obvious need for more energetic and able clerks. For this reason Lord Howick persuaded Lord Goderich to appoint Baillie one of the agents general for the colonies in 1833 and to place Thomas Frederick Elliot in charge of the North American department.

The son of a colonial governor, a cousin of the 2nd Earl of Minto, and a future second cousin by marriage of Lord John Russell, Elliot had entered the Colonial Office in 1825, became précis writer in 1827, and served as secretary to the emigration commission of 1831–32. In 1833 he succeeded to the first vacant senior clerkship, much to the chagrin of some of his more senior, but less able, colleagues. Under his direction the North American department was run with a new sense of purpose. In 1835 he was appointed secretary to the commission headed by Lord Gosford that was to inquire into the political impasse in Lower Canada, and he went with it to Quebec. In effect, he became a fourth commissioner. His letters to Henry Taylor, another senior clerk in the Colonial Office, were circulated to the cabinet and on his return he published a pamphlet defending the government's policy in British North America. In April 1837 he became agent general for emigration, in 1840 one of the colonial land and emigration commissioners, and in 1847 an assistant under-secretary.

Elliot's place at the North American department was filled in 1837 by Thomas William Clinton Murdoch, another exceptionally able public servant. The son of a fellow of the Royal Society, Murdoch was first employed by the Colonial Office in 1826 as a copying clerk. Promoted to the establishment in 1828, he served his apprenticeship in the West Indian department before transferring to the North American section to assist Elliot. Although still very junior he was allowed to perform the duties of a senior clerk during Elliot's absence in Lower Canada and on 20 Jan. 1836 was promoted from the fourth class in the clerical hierarchy to the second. Those clerks in the office who had been passed over vigorously complained about Murdoch's rapid advancement and in 1839 he was demoted to the third class, although given the salary of a higher rank. Since he could no longer serve as senior clerk of the North American department, he agreed to become civil secretary to Charles Edward Poulett Thomson, when the latter was appointed governor-in-chief of British North America; he served with distinction under Thomson in 1839–41 and then in 1841–42 under Sir Charles

Bagot, who praised him as "nearly the best man of business I ever knew." Bagot tried to persuade Murdoch to settle in Canada but could not promise him secure employment so Murdoch returned to the Colonial Office. His return was not a happy one. Because of his lowly status in the official hierarchy he could not be given a position commensurate with his abilities. Eventually he became senior clerk in 1846 and had a new department created for him. He held this position, and performed in addition the work of a précis writer, until 1847 when he was promoted to the colonial land and emigration commission to succeed Elliot. In 1850 he was offered but declined the position of lieutenant governor of Prince Edward Island.

From 1833 to 1835 Elliot had virtually performed the duties of an under-secretary, and Murdoch continued to undertake important and responsible work from 1835 to 1839, although his influence declined after Stephen became under-secretary. Their successors played no such active role in the formulation of policy. In 1839 Edmund Thomas Harrison took charge of the North American department. Already twice passed over by men who were his junior in the official hierarchy, he was conscientious – so conscientious that he apparently died of overwork in 1840 – but without intellectual distinction. His successor was Arthur Johnstone Blackwood, the son of an admiral and a graduate of Harrow, who, like Harrison, had entered the Colonial Office in 1824. His promotion was also overdue. He was to hold his position until 1867 and to perform his duties diligently. Occasionally he took the initiative, and longevity in office inevitably gave him a grasp of the details of his department that few men could rival. Yet he too was to have an extremely limited impact upon the larger issues of colonial policy. Elliot and Murdoch had done work equal to that of an under-secretary; Harrison and Blackwood remained useful clerks.

The waning importance of the senior clerks in the North American department can in part be attributed to the personal qualities of the individuals who held the post. But even Henry Taylor, the senior clerk in the West Indian department, whose ability cannot be doubted, found that the atmosphere of the office changed after Stephen became under-secretary. The formal system of written minutes and the channelling of all papers through the permanent under-secretary tended to isolate the clerical staff from the secretary of state. Stephen had complained in 1832 that "the senior Clerks have virtually become under-secretaries, and are often drawn into personal and direct communication with the secretary of state." After 1836 he discouraged the clerks from having private interviews with the head of the Colonial Office and, when Murdoch returned from Canada in 1842, he found that

he had restricted access to Lord Stanley, the secretary of state.

One has the feeling that during Stephen's years as permanent under-secretary the Colonial Office became a less happy place in which to work. Because of the extensive hiring of new clerks in the 1820s, promotion was extremely slow and many of the junior clerks were confined to the drudgery of menial work, such as copying. Moreover, Stephen inspired little devotion, since he brought to his work a degree of moral earnestness that left little room for light-heartedness and he was critical of his subordinates. There was good reason for Stephen's attitude. The Colonial Office appealed to a "better class" of candidate than departments such as the Board of Customs which engaged in work that was considered less suitable for a gentleman. Not all of the clerks were as highly connected as Elliot but all of them came from the respectable ranks in society. The atmosphere within the Colonial Office resembled that of a gentlemen's club. The duties of most of the clerks were seldom onerous: each clerk had an office to himself or shared one, his hours were short, and he worked under inadequate supervision. There were a handful of able and an even larger number of conscientious clerks, and the senior clerks in particular had heavy responsibilities. However, since clerks were appointed because they were well connected and rose through the ranks by seniority, there was no guarantee that they would be conscientious or capable of taking on ever more responsible duties.

As a group, the clerks at the Colonial Office were probably no less capable than their counterparts in other departments. But the "appropriate functions" of a clerk were changing. Those who entered government service in the 1820s expected to perform relatively simple tasks. Increasingly they were criticized for not undertaking duties for which they were equipped neither by experience nor by training. Not surprisingly they resented this criticism and opposed the changes that were taking place within the office. Since the clerks were a highly cohesive body who considered themselves gentlemen and the social equals of Stephen, they resisted his efforts to enforce more stringent regulations governing their hours of attendance, the work they performed, and their holidays. They were not afraid to protest decisions that hindered their chances of promotion, adversely affected their emoluments, or infringed upon the freedom to which they believed they were entitled. Stephen could issue orders. He could not necessarily enforce them and many of the reforms introduced into the procedure of the department in the mid 1830s were ultimately abandoned.

To some extent Stephen was obliged by the strong

resistance to change within the Colonial Office and by his inability to promote more able men to positions of responsibility to concentrate the work in his own hands. Under his direction the Colonial Office became more centralized than it had been in the past or would ever be again in the future. The parliamentary under-secretary had been largely excluded from effective control over the routine business of the office. Stephen remained legal adviser, a position he had made second in importance to that of the permanent under-secretary. The senior clerks seldom had contact with the secretary of state and the junior clerks were largely confined to purely clerical tasks. Stephen could hardly conduct all the detailed work of the department himself and he frequently had to call on his colleague or on the clerks for assistance. But if ever there was a "Mr Mother Country" (a title Stephen loathed), it was during this period.

Yet Stephen accepted that there must be limits to the undoubtedly considerable influence he possessed in the formulation of policies. He was not a member of that "heroic generation" of civil servants, so vividly described by George Kitson Clark, who were prepared to work through sympathetic members of parliament, the press, and public opinion to achieve their goals, even if it meant ignoring or opposing the wishes of their superiors. Stephen never sought to influence public opinion by releasing confidential documents or by writing articles on colonial affairs. Many civil servants eagerly sought to appear before select committees of parliament in order to promote their views but, when Stephen was interviewed by the select committee on Canada in 1828 and defended the financial claims of the Canadian legislatures, his evidence aroused so much antagonism among colonial conservatives such as John Strachan and Lord Dalhousie's supporters that he wished to avoid a repetition of the experience.

Partly because he was the subject of virulent abuse by a number of pressure groups in Britain and partly because of his own personality, Stephen was one of the first senior civil servants of his generation to accept that to hold a permanent position a civil servant must be prepared to remain anonymous. As early as 1829 he wrote to friends in the colonies to ask them not to correspond with him unofficially and to burn any of his confidential letters they possessed. When he became under-secretary, he not only tried to end the habit of officials in the department of corresponding privately with officials overseas, but enthusiastically endorsed the rule, apparently laid down by Stanley in 1833–34, that no under-secretary should write a dispatch to a governor on any private business. He ensured that all the relevant documents on any matter, important or trivial, were laid before the secretary of state. For the execution of a decision made by his superior Stephen was prepared to accept responsibili-

ty, but only for the details, never for the "substance." In this way he hoped to "obviate the reproach of undue interference" in the formulation of policy.

In fact, Stephen's appointment as under-secretary made it even more difficult to maintain the impression of bureaucratic neutrality. Prior to 1836 there were several officials against whom disgruntled pressure groups could vent their dissatisfaction. After 1836 the only visible and logical subject for these attacks was Stephen – "Mr Mother Country," "Mr Oversecretary Stephen," "King Stephen" – even though Stephen's influence on policy was not at its highest in these years. Sir John Colborne and Sir Francis Bond Head condemned Stephen for the failure to end popular agitation in Upper Canada. The Conservative opposition in parliament laid much of the blame for the government's policy at Stephen's feet. In 1838 Sir William Molesworth attacked Lord Glenelg for allowing his subordinates to make policy. The following year Bond Head published in London an account of his administration in Upper Canada which included disparaging comments about Stephen. Ironically, the appearance of Bond Head's *A narrative* may have saved Stephen from removal to another department. After the rebellions in the Canadas, the government of Lord Melbourne was eager to find a scapegoat for the ostensible failure of its policy. Glenelg, the colonial minister, was sacrificed early in 1839 and Stephen had become a distinct political liability. But to remove Stephen immediately after the publication of Head's book would have created the impression that not only were his attacks on Stephen legitimate, but also his criticisms of the government's policy. Fortunately for Stephen, Lord John Russell, who took charge of the Colonial Office in 1839, came to appreciate his worth. So Stephen remained at his post, although the volume of criticism did not abate.

In 1847 Stephen fell seriously ill. He was forced to accept a six months' leave of absence and then to resign in 1848. No one person could replace him and his duties were apportioned between Frederic Rogers, who gave legal advice to the colonial department, Elliot, who was promoted assistant under-secretary, and Herman Merivale, who became permanent under-secretary. After a relatively undistinguished career at the bar, Merivale had become professor of political economy at Oxford, published a series of lectures on colonies and colonization, and frequently contributed articles to the *Edinburgh Review*. These publications brought him to Stephen's attention and Stephen put Merivale's name forward, although he knew him only by reputation. At first Merivale made little impression upon the policies of the department. The secretary of state from 1846 to 1852, the 3rd Earl Grey, had a much greater knowledge of colonial affairs than his new under-secretary and when he needed help he still turned to Stephen. During the political instability of the 1850s, when Grey was replaced by a series of less able and less knowledgeable politicians, Merivale's influence undoubtedly grew. But Merivale was no Stephen. He was conscientious but without Stephen's masochistic devotion to duty.

In his formative study of the Colonial Office, Ralph Bernard Pugh has argued that by his emphasis upon regular, written minutes "Stephen decelerated the machine and brought some discredit upon his Department." Both Pugh and John Semple Galbraith have criticized Stephen for failing to develop an adequate system of inter-departmental liaison. Yet these criticisms simply do not bear up under careful scrutiny. By contemporary standards the Colonial Office had evolved by the end of Stephen's career into a relatively efficient government department. With only slight additions to the strength of the establishment, it dealt with a rapidly increasing volume of business in an age when technological advances were narrowing the distance between London and the colonies and leaving less time for leisurely deliberation. The staff of the Colonial Office dispatched their business as quickly as their political superiors would allow, and the overall impression one takes away from a detailed study of the records during this period is of an accelerating, not a decelerating, administrative machine. One can still find evidence of the occasional delay, the misplaced document or memorandum, but by the 1840s examples of administrative confusion are progressively more difficult to uncover.

In the area of inter-departmental relations Stephen's work has been particularly maligned. Following his retirement there does seem to have been considerable improvement in the degree of coordination between those departments in London with responsibilities in the colonies, but Merivale did not change the administrative structure he inherited and his approach to the question of inter-departmental liaison was not fundamentally different from Stephen's. If improvements took place, they were due to external factors which neither Stephen nor Merivale controlled. The abolition of the protective system and the navigation laws made it impossible for the Board of Trade and the Treasury to justify retaining their own officials in the colonies or to interfere on the same scale with colonial legislation. The grant of responsible government to the more mature colonies gradually reduced the potential areas of friction. Increasingly, departments could not pursue their own policies without any concern for the impact those policies had upon the affairs of other departments. If Merivale had more successful informal contacts with officials in other departments, it was because devolution had begun to place greater authority in the hands of subordinate officials. Moreover, the gradual growth of a sense of corporatism among civil servants in all departments, as the higher civil service became a more homogeneous group with close social and cultural affinities, created an environment in which cooperation was more easily achieved.

A more sophisticated critique of the mid-19th-century Colonial Office, advanced by John Whitson Cell and David John Murray among others, is that it was not well equipped for the formulation of long-term policies. This criticism is not wholly without foundation. As structured by Stephen, the Colonial Office did become the slave of a routine, but the routine itself prevented every decision from being taken on a purely *ad hoc* basis. The primary function of any bureaucracy must be to narrow the range of questions upon which an individual decision must be taken and to establish precedents which remove the need to consider each case in isolation as it occurs. No one who has examined in depth the records of the Colonial Office during this period can fail to be impressed with how efficiently the department performed this function under Stephen's direction. The secretary of state might consider every dispatch and letter, but usually he had only to initial the document to indicate his concurrence with the routine course of action recommended by his subordinates. This is why the Colonial Office minutes can be so misleading. It is the extraordinary, the unusual, or the unique problem which consumes the bureaucrat's time, once a body of precedents and clearly understood procedures have been established. Those who criticize Stephen as an administrator do not recognize how successful he had been in establishing a routine which minimized the labours of the decision-making process.

In one sense the critics of the 19th-century Colonial Office are undeniably right: the office was best suited for handling current and routine business. Yet those modern critics who condemn the Colonial Office for not becoming a more dynamic administrative agency have missed the point. The Colonial Office was organized, and functioned, on the principle that power ought to be centralized in the hands of the politicians placed by parliament in charge of the office. It was also organized on the assumption that the initiative in colonial government would and ought to come from the colonies.

When Sir George Murray declared in 1830 his belief "that to abstain from any extraordinary activity in the measures to be carried into effect with respect to the Colonies was a merit rather than a defect," he was stating what had long been an axiom of British colonial policy. Regardless of appearances to the contrary, it remained an axiom of British policy. What creates the opposite impression is the fact that while the Colonial Office assumed few new responsibilities after 1830, it was able to perform its traditional duties with increased efficiency. The land and emigration policies of the Colonial Office, for example, are usually seen as the ingredients of a new imperialism that led the British government to adopt "an interfering spirit" after 1830. But interference with colonial land-granting procedures was not new, although in the past such interference had been neither coordinated nor consistent. Nor was there anything new in laying down regulations in London concerning emigration. Before 1815 there had been legislative restrictions to hinder emigration; after 1815 various efforts were made to encourage and assist emigrants. In the cases of both emigration and land policies there was a shift in the purpose of British regulations, but what was unusual was the systematic way in which a vastly improved administrative machine sought to bring order out of chaos and to lay down policies in London that could be applied with a degree of consistency impossible in the past.

Although these tasks involved the Colonial Office in a more detailed and careful supervision of colonial activity in certain areas, they are not indicative of any fundamental change in the prevailing attitude of the British authorities in regard to their proper role in the conduct of colonial government. Essentially a regulatory rather than an executive agency, the Colonial Office was neither well designed nor well equipped to handle land and emigration policy, and because of the complexity and sheer volume of the business the work was devolved upon a separate division in the department in the 1830s and upon the colonial land and emigration commission in 1840. By 1850 the staff of the commission – 3 commissioners, 11 established clerks, and around 30 temporary clerks – was approximately as large as the Colonial Office had been two decades earlier. Much of its work, such as the preparation of emigration returns and the supervision of the passenger acts, had little to do *per se* with the colonies and, when the commission was abolished in 1878, this business was transferred to the Board of Trade, where it more properly belonged. Moreover, the staff of the Colonial Office did not enthusiastically assume these responsibilities. The supervision of land-granting policies in the colonies, in particular, was viewed as a transitory duty to be transferred to the colonies when they were mature enough to deal with such problems themselves. By the 1840s the North American colonies controlled their own waste lands and disposed of the funds arising from their sale.

The other area where historians have seen "an interfering spirit" at work within the Colonial Office after 1830 was in its efforts to protect the welfare of non-Europeans overseas. Although negotiations with native peoples had always been considered an imperial rather than a colonial problem, the pressure of the humanitarian lobbies and a growing concern for the well-being of native peoples among the rulers of the empire did lead to greater activity in the Colonial Office and the broadening of the imperial government's responsibilities. But the commitment of the department to what has been glorified as the doctrine of imperial trusteeship was not consistent. Only Lord Glenelg of the secretaries of state of the period took more than a passing interest in such questions unless they had immediate political implications. Although Stephen and some of the clerks within the office were more deeply concerned about the plight of native peoples, they accepted that there were severe limitations upon what they could do in colonies with representative institutions. Attempts were made to ensure that colonial legislation did not discriminate against non-Europeans and occasionally overtly discriminatory acts were disallowed. Exhortations were frequently sent to governors and to local legislatures to encourage them to improve the condition of the non-Europeans. Yet direct interference in the internal affairs of the colonies was undertaken only with great reluctance.

In fact, the whole trend of Colonial Office policy in the decades following 1815 was in the direction of a clearer definition and therefore a limitation of imperial responsibilities. Long before Lord Durham recommended in 1839 a division between matters of imperial and colonial responsibility, the Colonial Office was already acting upon a similar, although more flexible, division. It was this flexibility that enabled the Colonial Office to endorse, with mounting enthusiasm, the introduction of the principle of responsible government into the British North American colonies and the gradual extinction of its responsibilities in those colonies. Too much of the literature dealing with British policy in British North America during the first half of the 19th century implies that it was a disastrous failure. If so, the failure seems curious, since the policy laid the foundation for a continuing connection between Britain and Canada which persists – even if only in unimportant ways – to the present. The British ministers and the departmental officials upon whom they relied for advice frequently made errors in judgement but in the end they did succeed in reconciling the desire for greater colonial self-government with the imperial need to exercise some measure of control over the colonial legislatures. When viewed from this perspective, the Colonial Office does not merit the bad press it was accorded by contemporaries and has received from most historians.

[Every student of 19th-century British North America will be aware of the value of the Colonial Office files housed in the Public Record Office in London and duplicated on microfilm in the Public Archives of Canada. Particularly valuable are the letters between the secretaries of state and the governors contained in CO 42 and CO 43 (Canada), CO 188 and CO 189 (New Brunswick), CO 194 and CO 195 (Newfoundland), CO 217 and CO 218 (Nova Scotia and Cape Breton), and CO 226 and CO 227 (Prince Edward Island). Less well known are the various files of miscellanea relating to British North America, especially CO 47 and CO 325 which consist largely of précis and memoranda written by the staff of the Colonial Office, CO 380 which contains copies of the commissions and instructions sent to the governors, CO 537 which holds several volumes of supplementary correspondence, and CO 880 where one finds the confidential prints circulated to the British cabinet. Particularly important for the period before 1836 are the private letters between the under-secretaries and officials in the colonies found in CO 323 and CO 324. These series also contain the reports of the legal adviser to the Colonial Office, many of which deal with British North America, and considerable information about the internal organization of the department. More details on the latter subject can be found in CO 325, CO 537, CO 854, and CO 885. The best overview of the archival resources of the Colonial Office and their organization is R. B. Pugh's *The records of the Colonial and Dominions offices* (London, 1964). For materials in the PAC readers should consult its *General inventory, manuscripts, volume 2, MG 11–MG 16* (Ottawa, 1976).

The indispensable source for understanding how the Colonial Office operated is D. M. Young's *The Colonial Office in the early nineteenth century* ([London], 1961). Paul Knaplund's *James Stephen and the British colonial system, 1813–1847* (Madison, Wis., 1953), Helen Taft Manning's *British colonial government after the American revolution, 1782–1820* (New Haven, Conn., 1953), and R. B. Pugh's "The Colonial Office," *The Cambridge history of the British empire*, ed. J. H. Rose *et al.* (8v., Cambridge, Eng., 1929–59), 3: 711–68, are still useful, although dated. The best recent overview is contained in R. C. Snelling and T. J. Barron, "The Colonial Office and its permanent officials, 1801–1914," *Studies in the growth of nineteenth-century government*, ed. Gillian Sutherland (London, 1972), which should be supplemented by D. J. Murray, *The West Indies and the development of colonial government, 1801–1834* (Oxford, 1965), J. S. Galbraith, *Reluctant empire: British policy on the South African frontier, 1834–1854* (Berkeley and Los Angeles, 1963), and J. W. Cell, *British colonial administration in the mid-nineteenth century: the policy-making process* (New Haven and London, 1970). H. [W.] Parris, *Constitutional bureaucracy: the development of*

British central administration since the eighteenth century (London, 1969), and George Kitson Clark, "'Statesmen in disguise': reflexions on the history of the neutrality of the civil service," *Hist. Journal* (Cambridge), 2 (1959): 19–39, are useful on the emergence of the modern civil service in the 19th century.

The vast secondary literature dealing with British imperial policy and the North American colonies is assessed at considerable length in Phillip Buckner, "Britain and British North America before confederation," *A reader's guide to Canadian history, 1: Beginnings to confederation*, ed. D. A. Muise (Toronto, 1982). Of the earlier works C. B. Martin's *Empire & commonwealth: studies in governance and self-government in Canada* (Oxford, 1929), Aileen Dunham's *Political unrest in Upper Canada, 1815–1836* (London, 1927; repr. Toronto, 1963), and Adam Shortt's *Lord Sydenham* (Toronto, 1908) are the most useful but must be supplemented by Taft Manning's "The colonial policy of the Whig ministers, 1830–37," *CHR*, 33 (1952): 203–36, 341–68, and *Revolt of French Canada*. Ged Martin's *The Durham report and British policy: a critical essay* (Cambridge, 1972) and the chapters he wrote for Ronald Hyam and Ged Martin, *Reappraisals in British imperial history* (London, 1975) contain a stimulating but controversial interpretation which is supported by J. M. Ward in *Colonial self-government: the British experience, 1759–1856* (Toronto, 1976) and rejected by Phillip Buckner in *The transition to responsible government: British policy in British North America, 1815–1850* (Westport, Conn., 1985). Of the many recent articles on British policy the most useful are Peter Burroughs, "The determinants of colonial self-government," *Journal of Imperial and Commonwealth Hist.* (London), 6 (1977–78): 314–29; Philip Goldring, "Province and nation: problems of imperial rule in Lower Canada, 1820 to 1841," *ibid.*, 9 (1980–81): 38–56; Peter Burroughs, "The Canadian rebellions in British politics," *Perspectives of empire: essays presented to Gerald S. Graham*, ed. J. E. Flint and Glyndwr Williams (London, 1973), 54–92; and Ged Martin, "Confederation rejected: the British debate on Canada, 1837–1840," *Journal of Imperial and Commonwealth Hist.*, 11 (1982–83): 33–57, and "Launching Canadian confederation: means to ends, 1836–1864," *Hist. Journal* (Cambridge), 27 (1984): 575–602. P.B.]

BIOGRAPHIES

List of Abbreviations

AAH	Archives of the Archdiocese of Halifax	GS	Genealogical Society of the Church of Jesus Christ of Latter-Day Saints
AAQ	Archives de l'archidiocèse de Québec		
AASJ	Archives of the Archdiocese of Saint John's	HBC	Hudson's Bay Company
		HBCA	Hudson's Bay Company Archives
AAT	Archives of the Archdiocese of Toronto	*HBRS*	Hudson's Bay Record Society, *Publications*
ABHC	Atlantic Baptist Historical Collection		
AC	Archives civiles	HPL	Hamilton Public Library
ACAM	Archives de la chancellerie de l'archevêché de Montréal	MAC-CD	Ministère des Affaires culturelles, Centre de documentation
ACC	Anglican Church of Canada	MCA	Maritime Conference Archives
AD	Archives départementales	MHGA	Maritime History Group Archives
ADB	*Australian dictionary of biography*	MTL	Metropolitan Toronto Library
ANQ	Archives nationales du Québec	NLS	National Library of Scotland
AO	Archives of Ontario	NWC	North West Company
AP	Archives paroissiales	*OH*	*Ontario History*
ASN	Archives du séminaire de Nicolet	PABC	Provincial Archives of British Columbia
ASQ	Archives du séminaire de Québec		
ASSH	Archives du séminaire de Saint-Hyacinthe	PAC	Public Archives of Canada
		PAM	Provincial Archives of Manitoba
ASSM	Archives du séminaire de Saint-Sulpice, Montréal	PANB	Provincial Archives of New Brunswick
ASTR	Archives du séminaire de Trois-Rivières	PANL	Provincial Archives of Newfoundland and Labrador
AUM	Archives de l'université de Montréal	PANS	Public Archives of Nova Scotia
AVQ	Archives de la ville de Québec	PAPEI	Public Archives of Prince Edward Island
BCHQ	*British Columbia Historical Quarterly*		
BE	Bureau d'enregistrement	PCA	Presbyterian Church in Canada Archives
BLHU	Baker Library, Harvard University		
BNQ	Bibliothèque nationale du Québec	PRO	Public Record Office
BRH	*Le Bulletin des recherches historiques*	QUA	Queen's University Archives
BVM-G	Bibliothèque de la ville de Montréal, Salle Gagnon	*RHAF*	*Revue d'histoire de l'Amérique française*
CCHA	Canadian Catholic Historical Association	RSC	Royal Society of Canada
		SCHÉC	Société canadienne d'histoire de l'Église catholique
CCHS	Canadian Church Historical Society		
CHA	Canadian Historical Association	SGCF	Société généalogique canadienne-française
CHR	*Canadian Historical Review*		
CLA	Canadian Library Association	SOAS	School of Oriental and African Studies
CTA	City of Toronto Archives	SPG	Society for the Propagation of the Gospel
DAB	*Dictionary of American biography*		
DCB	*Dictionary of Canadian biography*	SRO	Scottish Record Office
DHB	*Dictionary of Hamilton biography*	UCA	United Church Archives
DNB	*Dictionary of national biography*	UNBL	University of New Brunswick Library
DOLQ	*Dictionnaire des œuvres littéraires du Québec*	USPG	United Society for the Propagation of the Gospel
GRO	General Register Office	UWOL	University of Western Ontario Library

Biographies

A

A-CA-OO-MAH-CA-YE (Ac ko mok ki, Ak ko mock ki, A'kow-muk-ai, known as **Feathers** and **Old Swan**), Blackfoot chief; d. 1859 or 1860.

During the later years of the 18th and the first half of the 19th centuries there were at least three leaders of the Blackfoot tribe who bore the name of Old Swan. With the Blood and Peigan Indians, the Blackfeet were loosely united in the Blackfoot confederacy which occupied the western Prairies south from the North Saskatchewan River to the Missouri River. In 1795 Duncan McGillivray*, North West Company clerk at Fort George (near Lindbergh, Alta), noted that Old Swan, the earliest known leader with that name, had once been the greatest chief of the Blackfeet and "was respected and esteemed by all the neighbouring tribes; his intentions towards the white people have been always honest and upright, and while he retained any authority his band never attempted anything to our predjudice." Because of his advanced age Old Swan had relinquished the chieftainship to Gros Blanc, "a man of unbounded ambition and ferocity" according to McGillivray. Old Swan died in January 1795 and by the turn of the century his son, the Feathers, had become chief. He adopted his father's name.

In temperament, the second Old Swan was much like his father and was well regarded by his people as an effective leader and peacemaker. In 1801 and 1802 he drew maps for Peter Fidler*, Hudson's Bay Company surveyor at Chesterfield House on the South Saskatchewan River, where he was a regular visitor. These maps, which bear his name, indicated the geographical areas known to the Blackfeet, and information from the first of them was instrumental in the drafting of Aaron Arrowsmith's 1802 map of North America, used by Meriwether Lewis and William Clark in their exploration up the Missouri in 1804. Old Swan was respected by the traders as a friend of white men and recognized as a peacemaker in the relations of his tribe with the Gros Ventres, Northern Arapaho, Cree, and Assiniboin Indians. In 1814 he was shot and killed by a Blood Indian, and a feud broke out between the Blackfeet and the Bloods, two normally friendly tribes.

The leadership of what continued to be identified for some time after the tragedy as "Old Feathers' band" was probably assumed by a son or nephew, the subject of this biography. Known also as the Feathers, he was described in the HBC's Chesterfield House journal in 1822 as "a Blackfoot Chief (much attached to the whites)," and like both of his predecessors he earned a reputation as a peacemaker. When he visited Edmonton House (Edmonton) in the spring of 1828, for instance, he stated that his people had become troublesome while he had been ill, but that he was there to negotiate a peace treaty with the Crees. Some time after 1828 the Feathers took the name of Old Swan and was thenceforth known by that name. In 1854 he prevented the shedding of blood during a drunken altercation between Blackfoot and Blood Indians at Rocky Mountain House (Alta) by coolly ordering both factions back to their camps; he then forced the traders to destroy the supply of liquor on hand. Henry John Moberly, HBC apprentice clerk in charge of Rocky Mountain House at that time, described him as "a Blackfoot of great authority, aged but still active," and in gratitude for the intervention of the chief gave him one of his best horses. "Not that it meant much to Old Swan," he observed, "he had three hundred of his own."

By the early 1850s the leadership of the Blackfoot tribe was shared by three chiefs. The most influential of these was the third Old Swan, whose personal following, known as the Bad Guns band, consisted of about 400 persons. The other two chiefs were Nato'sapi (Old Sun), leader of the All Medicine Men band, and No-okskatos (Three Suns), leader of the Biters band. In 1858 Old Swan was listed as one of the principal chiefs of the Blackfoot tribe by Dr James Hector* of the British North American exploration party under John Palliser*. Palliser was apparently highly regarded by Old Swan, who called him his grandson, and in July 1859 he accepted the chief's invitation to visit his camp on the Red Deer River (Alta). "This very large camp was in many ways a novel sight," said Palliser, "even to us who had seen so many Indian camps. We now found the Blackfeet here numbering about 400 tents." When Palliser's party left the camp the following day, Old Swan and a number of his soldiers accompanied them back to the safety of their expedition.

Shortly after Palliser's visit Old Swan died, either late in 1859 or early in 1860, and his chieftainship was

Allan

taken by a man named Omukaiee (Big Swan). Whereas Old Swan had been a friend of the traders, his successor despised them. William Francis Butler* described him as "a man of colossal size and savage disposition, crafty and treacherous." Big Swan died of tuberculosis in 1872 and the leadership of the tribe passed to two chiefs from other bands, Nato'sapi* (son of Chief Nato'sapi) and Crowfoot [Isapo-muxika*].

HUGH A. DEMPSEY

PAM, HBCA, B.34/a/4: f.18; B.60/a/13: f.3d; B.60/a/25: f.55. W. F. Butler, *The great lone land: a narrative of travel and adventure in the north-west of America* (7th ed., London, 1875). *HBRS*, 26 (Johnson). Duncan McGillivray, *The journal of Duncan M'Gillivray of the North West Company at Fort George on the Saskatchewan, 1794–5*, ed. and intro. A. S. Morton (Toronto, 1929). H. J. Moberly and W. B. Cameron, *When fur was king* (Toronto, 1929). *The papers of the Palliser expedition, 1857–1860*, ed. I. M. Spry (Toronto, 1968). H. A. Dempsey, *Crowfoot, chief of the Blackfeet* (Edmonton, 1972).

ALLAN, WILLIAM, businessman, militia officer, justice of the peace, office holder, judge, and politician; b. *c.* 1770 at the Moss, near Huntly, Scotland, son of Alexander Allan and Margaret Mowatt; m. 24 July 1809 Leah Tyrer Gamble in Kingston, Upper Canada; d. 11 July 1853 in Toronto.

William Allan's family background and early training remain obscure. His lack of formal education and bad penmanship were sufficiently marked to cause him some concern in later life. He came to Canada about 1787, probably as a clerk for Robert Ellice and Company of Montreal, which was reorganized in 1790 as Forsyth, Richardson and Company. Since the Forsyth family was from Huntly, and John Forsyth* was a partner in the Ellice firm, it may have been through this family that Allan obtained his post in Canada.

In 1788 or 1789 he came to Niagara (Niagara-on-the-Lake, Ont.), probably as a clerk under George Forsyth, head of the firm's branch there. An important trans-shipment centre on the route to the upper Great Lakes, Niagara provided Allan with an excellent opportunity to learn all the details of the general merchant's operations, the Indian trade, and garrison supply. In 1795 he applied for and received a town lot and an additional grant of 200 acres at Upper Canada's new capital, York (Toronto). He moved there, becoming the local agent for Forsyth, Richardson and Company. Because of the firm's Montreal location, excellent financial rating, and transatlantic trade connections, the agency gave Allan a lead over many rival merchants at the backwoods capital.

The move to York may have been something of a gamble: virtually only Lieutenant Governor John Graves Simcoe* liked the site. But Allan's relocation paid off. He almost immediately exchanged his town lot for a harbourside property and in 1798 he was granted the adjoining water-lot for a wharf. About 1797 he had formed a partnership with Alexander Wood* in a general store. Wood, another Scottish emigrant, had worked for the Forsyth firm in Kingston before coming to York. The partnership lasted until 1801, when it was dissolved with some recrimination. Apparently the buildings were on Allan's lot, for he ended up with the store and stock. As well, Allan purchased the debts due to the partnership, at what Wood claimed was far too low a price. Whatever the case, each went back into business for himself and both prospered. Most important, Allan was able to retain the agency for Forsyth, Richardson and Company.

As was usual at the time, he soon developed his own agencies in York's growing hinterland centres. Although Laurent Quetton* de Saint-Georges was probably the leading merchant in York prior to the War of 1812, Allan quickly gained an excellent reputation. As the *Church* stated in his obituary, he "acquired the entire confidence of all classes of the community by his excellent habits of business, his punctuality in all transactions, and his perfect integrity." Further, in May 1811, he entered into partnership with William Jarvie, forming William Allan and Company, which was dissolved in April of the following year.

The field of local government had quickly occupied Allan's attention, particularly during slack seasons of trade when he had time on his hands. York formed part of the Home District, which was administered by local justices of the peace sitting in a court of quarter sessions. On 1 Jan. 1800 Allan joined their ranks and began to play a major role in district government. His work involved issuing various licences, including those for marriages and for shops and taverns. He was appointed to the onerous post of district treasurer on 9 April 1800 and his name appears on commissions for various public works. On 6 August he became collector of customs at York and district inspector of flour, potash, and pearl ash. (He was particularly familiar with potash for he had erected a potashery in 1800.) As well, in 1801 he succeeded William Willcocks* as postmaster at York and, commencing that year, Allan served as a returning officer in a number of provincial elections. In 1807 he presided over the election of Robert Thorpe*, whose traitorous remarks he reported to Lieutenant Governor Francis GORE.

Allan was also active within York's small social élite. During the first decade of the 1800s he gained influential friends in official quarters, including two other Scots: Inspector General of Public Accounts John McGill* and Alexander Grant*, the provincial

4

administrator (1805–6), who for a time lived with Allan. He was an early supporter of the Church of England. He and Duncan Cameron were the treasurers for the building fund of St James' Church in 1803 and Allan was chief custodian for the expansion of the church in 1818. At the end of his term as people's warden, an office he held from 1807 to 1812, he welcomed a new rector, the Reverend John Strachan*, another Aberdeenshire man who was to become a close friend. Allan had also married, in 1809. His wife, Leah Tyrer Gamble, a daughter of a surgeon with Simcoe's Queen's Rangers, had wide family connections which can have done Allan's career no harm; Samuel Smith*, for example, who later became provincial administrator (1817–18, 1820), was Leah's uncle. Thus, though the War of 1812 would, in some ways, be a watershed in Allan's career, he had laid the foundations of his future activities and influence well before the war, obtaining the respect and patronage of the local and provincial governing groups and building up a prosperous business.

Allan had been commissioned in the Lincoln militia in 1795 and three years later his lieutenancy was transferred to the York militia. In April 1812, on the eve of the war, he was promoted major of the 3rd York Militia, whose territory encompassed the town and its environs. With the beginning of hostilities in June the regiment's flank companies, 120 strong, entered the garrison. Allan spent the winter of 1812–13 on garrison duty and escorting prisoners to Kingston. During the first capitulation of York, in April 1813, Major-General Sir Roger Hale SHEAFFE and the British regulars retreated to Kingston, leaving Allan and Lieutenant-Colonel William Chewett*, as the senior militia officers, to negotiate the terms of surrender, which provided that private property was not to be touched. Allan then became a prisoner on parole. He saw his store looted, but, with John Strachan, was successful in the keeping of order in the town. Justifiably, he went down as one of the heroes of the capitulation.

As a prisoner on parole Allan could not bear arms, but he was active as a government agent in curbing disloyalty and searching out enemy agents in the Home District. His zeal made a good impression on Judge William Dummer Powell*, an executive councillor and probably the leading figure in the government. Allan also impressed the Americans, who regarded him as "obnoxious," and when the town was about to be captured for the second time, in July, he quickly fled. His store was looted again. The public declarations of sympathy for the enemy which had resulted from the occupations of York prompted such authorities as Allan and Powell to urge suppressive measures. In August, Allan, Strachan, and four others formed a committee of investigation, the findings of which led to the sentencing of such spokesmen as

Elijah Bentley*. In May 1814 Allan was back on active duty after a prisoner-on-parole exchange. He saw no more action, however, although he was commander of the militia at the garrison until the fall of 1815.

During the war Allan was kept busy with the very profitable pursuit of supplying the garrison through the office of the commissary general. In all, the commissariat paid out more than £50,000 to York merchants, most of it to Laurent Quetton de Saint-Georges and Allan. The latter received at least £12,724, which represented a mark-up of about 100 per cent. Of course he also had claims for compensation for the damage to his store during the occupations and after the war he received 1,000 acres of land under the Prince Regent's bounty. In 1815 he took his brother-in-law John William Gamble* as a partner in the store and they were later joined by another brother-in-law, William Gamble*.

The post-war years saw Allan's gradual development from a leading merchant and holder of multiple local offices into the province's principal financial figure. Politically his offices, in keeping with his growing reputation, were increasingly of provincial rather than local importance. But, in this sphere, Allan seemed to hold back, perhaps to ensure his flexibility in the economic enterprises that engaged his main attention. He always refused to run for elected office. When, in the election of 1800, the *Upper Canada Gazette*, the official government newspaper, stated that he would become a candidate for the York riding, he was furious. He complained to the government that if the assertion reached his commercial connections in Lower Canada uncontradicted, it would "very materially affect his Interests." He therefore demanded that the editors, William Waters and Titus Geer Simons, be fired as government printers.

Though he was averse to seeking elective office, Allan continued and increased his early involvement in official administration. Probably because of his experience as a justice of the peace, in 1818 he was an associate judge along with the three justices of the Court of King's Bench, William Dummer Powell, William Campbell*, and D'Arcy Boulton*, at the trial in York of two of the North West Company supporters involved with Cuthbert GRANT in the murder of Governor Robert Semple* at Seven Oaks (Winnipeg). Later, in 1826, Allan was one of the justices sitting in the trial of the rioters who had destroyed William Lyon Mackenzie*'s printing-press. Allan was also in charge of the finances of such important public works as the rebuilding of the parliament houses in 1819–20. When they had to be rebuilt again after a fire, he assisted in 1826–29 in having the plans and estimates prepared. These can hardly have been profitable posts; however, when he was paymaster of the militia from 1818 to 1825, more than £28,000 passed through his hands, doubtless resulting in a fine commission. Also, he was gazetted in 1822 one of the commissioners for investigating claims for war losses and thus, with Alexander Wood and others, authorized the compensation for himself and his friends.

The fact that some of the offices he held enabled him to watch over his own interests may have made these services almost mandatory, but Allan's public contributions merited recognition. His services were well appreciated within the "family compact" and in 1825 he was appointed to the Legislative Council. The following year, evidently with regard to the appointment of a new deputy postmaster general, Attorney General John Beverley Robinson* remarked to John MACAULAY of Kingston, "He is really so very good a man & so upright & valuable a public officer, that everyone would be reluctant as well as yourself to interfere with any expectation he might reasonably indulge."

In the years after his appointment to council, Allan gradually retired from the local offices that he had held for so many years: he ceased serving as postmaster and collector of customs in 1828 and as treasurer of the Home District the next year. Although deputies had done much of the work in these offices, the responsibilities must have consumed much time and conflicted with his banking interests, which were then at full tide. Also, the barbs of such radical reformers as William Lyon Mackenzie, who saw him as a political figure and accused him of monopolizing offices, must have been galling.

Allan's business career underwent a complete redirection in the 1820s, but again this adjustment built upon earlier foundations. Like all pioneer merchants, he had acted as a banker, handling a considerable portion of the local exchange business for Forsyth, Richardson and Company. In 1818, the year after the Bank of Montreal was founded, he became its agent in York, a position he held for three years. The success of the Bank of Montreal and the need for banking services were quickly reflected in Upper Canada, where, as early as 1817, rival groups in York and Kingston [see Thomas Markland*] had begun to contend for the first bank charter. The York group was led initially by John Strachan and Alexander Wood rather than by Allan, with his Montreal connections, but by about 1819 he had taken over the leadership. Through various complex manœuvres in the House of Assembly and the Legislative Council, combined with the vital support of Lieutenant Governor Sir Peregrine MAITLAND, the York group appropriated the charter originally granted to Kingston, and in 1821 the Bank of Upper Canada was incorporated. Allan headed the subscription committee. By November of that year the necessary 4,000 shares, including a government purchase of 2,000 shares, had been subscribed. To start operations

£20,000 in gold or silver had to be paid up, but the money was not forthcoming. The York group consequently had the bank's charter amended to allow business to begin upon the payment of £10,000, Maitland gave royal assent to this legislation on 17 Jan. 1822, and by June enough capital had been paid up. Business commenced the following month. The bank did not, however, obtain the account of the province's receiver general, John Henry DUNN, who continued to deal with Forsyth, Richardson and Company and the Bank of Montreal in matters of colonial finance and exchange, and used the Bank of Upper Canada only for transactions within the province. As a result of Allan's increasing activity within the bank, which operated out of his store building until 1825, he sold his store interests in July 1822 to his partners, the Gambles, and "gave up all his concern in trade."

The bank's first directors in 1822 included George CROOKSHANK, Provincial Secretary Duncan Cameron, Surveyor General Thomas Ridout*, Solicitor General Henry John Boulton*, and John Henry Dunn in addition to Allan and John Strachan. At the election for president, there was apparently some support for both Dunn and Crookshank (who was out of the province), but because of Allan's mercantile success, experience with the Bank of Montreal, and hard work on behalf of the new bank, the directors elected him to the office. Except for 1825–26, when he did not stand because of a trip abroad and Crookshank held the presidency, Allan was re-elected annually until his resignation in 1835. Thomas Ridout's son, Thomas Gibbs Ridout*, became the bank's first cashier (general manager), a position he would hold for nearly 40 years.

The directorate, as William Lyon Mackenzie was constantly to remind it, comprised a "family compact" group. The reformers had early had representatives within the bank – Francis Jackson and William Warren Baldwin* – but as members of the founding group in 1821, these representatives were hardly in a position at the outset to quarrel with bank policy. The image of the bank as a government body was reinforced in January 1823 by legislation which authorized the lieutenant governor to appoint 4 of the bank's 15 directors, of whom a large number were already executive or legislative councillors. Banking had not yet become a major political issue, however, and Allan received the cooperation of the House of Assembly on banking matters. In 1823, in an attempt to align capitalization with the exigencies of the province's economy, the capital of the bank was reduced from £200,000 to £100,000. The following year it achieved a monopoly on note issuing in the province through an act which required, for five years, all banks operating there to redeem their notes in Upper Canada. The bank, however, did not operate without internal friction. In 1825 a group headed by William Warren Baldwin and Thomas Gibbs Ridout made a determined effort to dominate the board of directors, evidently during Allan's absence. Although the group canvassed extensively for votes, especially in Niagara and Kingston, it was soundly defeated.

Allan's caution and sound judgement made him a very successful banker and contributed to the Bank of Upper Canada's prosperous situation at the end of the 1820s. From 1824 it had paid annual dividends of eight per cent on paid-up capital, plus some bonuses. Following the expiry in 1829 of the note redemption act, the bank became engaged in a specie war with the Bank of Montreal, which had sent its agents back into York and Kingston, in part to take advantage of imperial spending on the Rideau Canal. Each bank purchased the other's notes with the intention of demanding payment in specie upon presenting the notes. Allan played his cards boldly, sending Thomas Gibbs Ridout to Montreal to arrange weekly shipments of specie. In the end, Allan later informed Lieutenant Governor Sir John Colborne*, he and his bank "met the exigency triumphantly & were above all difficulty." The banks reached an agreement whereby the Montreal bank withdrew all its Upper Canadian agents except Henry Dupuy at Kingston and acted as agent in Montreal for the Upper Canadian bank; Allan subsequently used his personal friendship with Peter McGill, an influential director of the Bank of Montreal, to maintain smooth relations. The Bank of Upper Canada benefited too from the increasing number of public works in the province, which were financed by government debentures. These were bought by the bank at six per cent and negotiated in Montreal, London, or New York. Early in 1833 Allan secured for the bank the business of the British Treasury in Upper Canada, including the lucrative commissarial business at Kingston.

By the opening of the 1830s the bank, despite its success, was confronted with continuing internal dissent, political opposition, and new competition. In a colony that was undergoing a rapid increase in population as a result of immigration and that was heading into boom times, Allan's strict policies on the function and expansion of the bank were becoming increasingly unpopular. As a merchant running a bank, Allan regarded it as a centre for financial transactions such as the making of loans on, or the discounting of, promissory notes and bills of exchange; the handling of coin and bullion; and the purchase and resale of government debentures. The bank's circulation of capital in the form of loans to merchants [see James CROOKS] constituted its main source of profit. In 1837 Thomas Gibbs Ridout reported that about one-third of the bank's business had been enabling "the Merchant to transact through its medium and assistance his remittances to other

Countries," for which service a premium was charged on the normal rate of exchange. According to Allan in 1831, the negotiation of bills on Montreal and New York "in aid" of the wheat, flour, and general export trade averaged £500,000 annually. The bank maintained deposits of capital in those places and in London in order to sell bills on the markets there at any time of the year; in New York it dealt regularly with Prime, Ward, and King, and in London with Thomas Wilson and Company.

The bank had opened agencies at Kingston (1823), Niagara (1824), Montreal (1829), and Cobourg (1830). In 1830, however, Allan advised John Macaulay, a close friend and the bank's Kingston agent, of his preference for "keeping *within bounds* on the *secure side*," thus avoiding too rapid growth that might later necessitate the contraction or withdrawal of agencies. Accustomed to running his own business, Allan was ready in the interest of prompt action to do what he conceived was "right & safe" without referring every decision to the directors. He could not, however, carry them on all points. He preached restraint to a board which supported his management but which, as early as 1823, contained a majority out of sympathy with his policies. Allan decried his associates' involvement with speculative ventures. His pessimism was on occasion borne out, as in the reckless entrepreneurial practices and financial collapse in 1833 of James Gray Bethune*, the bank's cashier at Cobourg. Losses resulting from such failures were absorbed without harm to the bank's reputation. But even the success of the bank became controversial, and serious discontent developed among businessmen who wanted to break the banking monopoly of the York élite and to use the bank more as a source of investment capital.

In 1830 Allan faced concentrated, politically motivated opposition. William Warren Baldwin and his son ROBERT, supported by William Lyon Mackenzie, sought disclosure of shareholdings and a full reporting of the bank's affairs. Allan resisted the demands of a House of Assembly committee headed by Mackenzie, but failed to counter effectively Robert Baldwin's charges there in February that the bank acted as a "dangerous engine of political oppression" and that notes had been blackballed and discounted "from political motives." This challenge was followed in June by an unsuccessful bid, originating within the same committee and led by the Baldwins, to obtain disclosure by securing the election of a sympathetic director. Allan, who was observed on such occasions to express himself heatedly in a "rich Aberdeen brogue," believed that George Ridout* and possibly his brother Thomas Gibbs Ridout had also been involved, apparently in the hope of getting George on the board.

Balked in this area, political opponents of the Bank

Allan

of Upper Canada regrouped around John Solomon Cartwright* and other Kingston businessmen seeking a bank charter. This attempt attracted wide support, since it appealed to those who favoured the American system of numerous banks as well as to those who believed that the York bank deliberately retarded development in order to preserve a profitable monopoly. Allan's response was dictated by his policy on expansion and by political necessity. He believed that safe banking required hard money – paper currency "of a proper value with Gold and Silver." In his opinion this monetary objective could best be achieved by a single bank, with adequate capital, establishing branches throughout the province. To achieve expansion on these terms, the Bank of Upper Canada now needed additional capital, but Allan was in a stalemate with the assembly, whose authorization was needed. So long as Allan and other members of the Legislative Council blocked a charter for the Kingston bank, the assembly would refuse to restore the Bank of Upper Canada's capital to £200,000. In late 1830 Allan appears to have initiated a bid to secure government support for capitalization when he encouraged John Macaulay to discuss the matter with Peter PERRY, a member of the assembly, and to "pursuade" Cartwright to write to Solicitor General Christopher Alexander Hagerman*, presumably to find a resolution to the political impasse. Two years later bills of incorporation, for the Commercial Bank of the Midland District, and capitalization, for the Bank of Upper Canada, were passed. In contrast to Allan, John Strachan, who no longer sat on the board but reflected the thinking of many directors, did not fully recognize a need to relate paper to metallic currency; he argued for the careful expansion of the Bank of Upper Canada but believed that Allan's inhibitions had hurt it.

While Allan settled in to do business with the Commercial Bank on the basis of "amiable" rivalry, William Lyon Mackenzie carried to the Colonial Office his opposition to the privileged position of all chartered banks. He convinced British officials that the bank acts passed in 1832 did not contain adequate safeguards and brought home rumours in 1833 of their impending disallowance. This threat brought Allan into community of purpose with other businessmen in Upper Canada: he lent his weight to calming alarm and to a successful campaign to persuade the British authorities to withdraw their opposition. Yet this victory over "scandulous misrepresentation" and deception did not bring lasting peace.

Once the Kingston bank was chartered, Allan had informed William Hamilton Merritt* in December 1831, "common Justice" must open the door to others and he promised to support Merritt's proposal for a bank at St Catharines and "all future applications that appear *reasonable*." By 1834 the Bank of Upper

Canada itself had established new branches, at Hamilton and Brockville, as well as agencies at Amherstburg, Penetanguishene, Prescott, and Bytown (Ottawa). Private partnership banks were also making their appearance, one of which, George TRUSCOTT's Agricultural Bank, opened in Toronto in 1834 and paid interest on deposits, thus setting a controversial precedent which other institutions followed of necessity. Allan deeply distrusted Truscott and his methods of banking, and the two soon became locked in a specie war. Truscott, who had heard rumours that Allan's board did not support his campaign wholeheartedly, characterized the Bank of Upper Canada in 1835 as a "discreet old lady" and attacked the integrity of its president with biting sarcasm.

Meanwhile, Allan was becoming progressively more dissatisfied in the bank. In 1832 death in his family and his own serious illness had left him "very much depressed." He pondered about building a small cottage and taking a trip abroad, and suggested that "if spared" he would in a year's time have "left all this," including the bank, "for others." He rallied, but felt increasingly isolated within a bank board which, he confided to John Macaulay, no longer supported him fully and undervalued his service.

During the winter of 1834–35 Allan was equally frustrated in his dealings with the government. He believed the connection had outlived its usefulness to the bank, but Lieutenant Governor Colborne and the government directors had blocked his attempt to have the government's shares sold, thus forcing him to face continued criticism from the bank's political opponents. His objections to John Henry Dunn's plan to circumvent the bank by selling debentures directly on the British market were also set aside. Allan had argued that if the interest on the debentures was paid in Upper Canada, capital and capitalists would be attracted to the colony. As well, he knew that the position of the Bank of Upper Canada as the intermediary for such internal financing would be altered if, along the lines of Dunn's plan, interest was paid in England. Weary of the struggle, he resigned as president in 1835.

Allan saw Dunn as the leading presidential candidate and the one favoured by Colborne and the government directors. He nevertheless disliked, thoroughly, Dunn's policies on public borrowing and his attempts to curry political and popular favour. He thought better of John Spread Baldwin, a former director, but Baldwin was not a member of the board and thus received few votes. The directors subsequently elected the pliable William Proudfoot*. Allan had no intention of accepting a secondary role as a director of an institution which, he believed, soon deviated "very much" from his "system" and "management." After he had resigned, the bank

experienced increasing subordination to political interests, which contributed much to its ultimate decline [*see* Robert Cassels*; Thomas Gibbs Ridout]. Allan nevertheless established a working relationship with it in the interest of such ventures as the Welland Canal Company, the Canada Company, and the British America Fire and Life Assurance Company, his other major corporate concerns.

The Welland Canal Company had been chartered in 1824 under the aegis of William Hamilton Merritt. The next year Allan invested the £250 necessary to become a director of the company, and he was duly elected along with such leading provincial figures as John Henry Dunn and John Beverley Robinson. In time Allan became vice-president. Convinced of the value to the Canadas of the inland water-way, he was one of those to whom Merritt turned for support when he approached the Bank of Upper Canada, which by statute in 1824 became treasurer for the canal company, for loans for the canal. The bank refused to lend the company any money directly, but did lend sums to its directors on their personal security. Although the bank purchased debentures from the government, with the money going to the company, these were resold. In 1830 Allan warned Merritt that a canal project undertaken in the public interest offered insufficient inducement to private financing. And, while the sums he sought from the bank might be of the "utmost consequence" in the short term, Allan added, "It is not a little [money] that does for your wants – it is large sums that will only do for you." After he withdrew from the boards of both the bank and the canal company, Allan continued his interest, at least until 1837, in Merritt's efforts to raise money.

In 1829 Allan agreed to become "for a limited period" one of the two Upper Canadian commissioners appointed by the Canada Company to replace John Galt*. Set up to sell a large tract of land along Lake Huron, as well as lots elsewhere in the province, the company had been badly managed by Galt, and the directors in London wanted a complete reorganization. Allan initiated the transfer of the company's Upper Canadian headquarters from Guelph to York, where he assumed responsibility for managing the scattered former crown reserves that had been transferred to the company in 1825. The other commissioner, Thomas Mercer Jones*, took charge of sales in the Huron Tract. As part of the reorganization, Allan moved quickly to deal with outstanding claims, re-establish public trust, and institute a complete review of the company's books. He warned the company that giving his full time to its affairs would be "rather too much to be expected constantly," but he did so as long as the review was in progress. He was confident of his managerial skills, although less so when the London directors asked him to produce a full report of Canadian operations.

Allan feared that his analysis of possible courses of action in the Huron Tract was "too tedious and lengthy" for the directors. His report of September 1829 nevertheless demonstrated the considerable thought that he, a major landowner on his own account, had given to the problems of immigration and settlement and to the work of such successful promoters as Colonel Thomas TALBOT and Peter Robinson*. Allan's advice to the directors was clear. The development of crown reserves offered immediate profit, the Huron Tract the best future prospects. The Canada Company's stock was depressed for two reasons: shareholders misunderstood the kind of investment involved and they were hesitant "in advancing the capital necessary." If the shareholders were to realize the excellent, long-term financial potential offered by the venture, Allan argued, they should put up the full amount of their instalment payments as well as assume a large proportion of the expenses of the early years. To encourage investment, he recommended the payment of a dividend tied to land sales by the company.

In February 1830 Allan was shocked to find that the directors were considering dissolution of the company at a time when he had committed his reputation to its renewal. It survived, but Allan does not seem to have given the company his full attention. He had obtained a portion of its Upper Canadian business for the Bank of Upper Canada and continued to interest himself, on the company's behalf, in financial matters and in questions of monetary exchange. As well, from about 1834 and possibly earlier, the Canada Company's offices in York were housed in premises owned by Allan. In 1835 the directors signified their appreciation of his services by increasing his salary by £200 sterling. By 1839, however, they were once more wishing for new direction in their affairs in Upper Canada. Frederick Widder* was sent out that year to replace Allan, who retired from the company in 1841.

Allan's last major directorship was with the British America Fire and Life Assurance Company. Founded in 1833 to fulfil the need of obtaining fire and navigation insurance at reasonable rates in York, the company had William Proudfoot as its first governor and Allan headed its subscription committee. Allan's brother-in-law Thomas William Birchall became general manager in 1834, and two years later, after Proudfoot had gone to the Bank of Upper Canada, Allan was elected governor. The business, of which he remained governor until his death, was soundly underwritten and proved highly successful.

In addition to these business and financial institutions, Allan was for some time interested in the development of transportation systems. In 1827 he served, as a legislative councillor, on a government committee dealing with navigation on the St Lawrence River. By 1835 he believed that too much public

Allan

funding was going to the St Lawrence canals and that some should be appropriated to inland water-ways. During the 1830s he also became interested in railways, but in that new field his achievements as a promoter fell far short of his successes elsewhere as a financier.

When the City of Toronto and Lake Huron Rail Road Company was organized in 1837 he was elected to its board of directors with the greatest number of votes, thus becoming president. Before adequate funds could be raised, however, the depression of 1837 set in and plans to build the railway had to wait for the return of prosperity in the mid 1840s. Allan and his associates revived the project in December 1844. Almost immediately their scheme was confronted with energetic opposition from the principal promoters of the Great Western Rail-Road, Sir Allan Napier MacNab* in Hamilton and Peter BUCHANAN in London, England. As well, Allan's entrepreneurial role within the Toronto company was to be successfully challenged by John Wellington Gwynne* and Frederick Chase Capreol*, whose aggressive promotional tactics contrasted sharply with Allan's cautious, methodical management. In 1847 his ill-timed prosecution of George Crookshank for defaulting on stock payments was publicly criticized and allowed Gwynne and Capreol to come to the fore. Under the latter's direction the project eventually led to the construction of the Toronto, Simcoe and Huron Union Rail-Road (later renamed the Northern Railway), which became a profitable enterprise for both its shareholders and the developers of the city of Toronto.

Allan was unanimously elected first president of the Toronto Board of Trade when it was initially founded in 1834. By that time, despite the decline of the "family compact" in politics, he had become the unquestioned doyen of Upper Canadian business. Allan's withdrawal from mercantile business in 1822 and his corporate involvement for more than 20 years did not mean that he gave up all his private interests or terminated the excellent network of connections that he had developed over the years. Thus he was still engaged in various personal investments and when the British-based Bank of British North America was founded in 1836, he became a shareholder. A number of his activities were of the type that would now be carried on by a lawyer or trust company, for he was an agent, trustee, financial adviser, realtor, and estate administrator or executor. The management of estates in Upper Canada was one of his most time-consuming tasks, and could frequently be complicated by the existence of landholdings and heirs in England and Scotland. The tangled affairs of the estate of William Berczy*, who died in 1813, took until 1841 to settle, the major creditor being Forsyth, Richardson and Company. Settlement of the estate of Chief Justice Thomas Scott*, for which Allan and John Strachan

were co-executors, dragged on for a decade after Scott died in 1824. Thus, while Allan may be best known as a financier, his work as a trustee also occupied a great deal of his time and energy.

In carrying out these duties he had working with and advising him a wide network of friends and associates. Some of these, such as John Macaulay, were personal friends as well as close business associates. For another valuable Upper Canadian connection, Colonel Thomas Talbot of the London District, Allan handled investments and Talbot, in return, advised him on western land purchases. Beyond Upper Canada, Allan's correspondents included Peter McGill, in Montreal, and a variety of persons in England. Allan helped the family of John Graves Simcoe with its Upper Canadian investments: between 1832 and 1853 he bought or handled the sale of much of its landed property in the province. As well, he took care of various business matters for retired officials and officers, such as former Surveyor General Sir David William Smith* and Robert Pilkington*. His most influential British correspondent, however, was Edward Ellice*, whom he had known since his early days in the mercantile business. Ellice probably secured for Allan his commissionership with the Canada Company. As Ellice's attorney in Upper Canada, Allan attended to land speculation and financial matters; in 1845 Ellice advised him, "I am perfectly satisfied that you do for me, as you do for yourself, in these matters, & thank you sincerely for your kindness & attention to them" – the sort of expression that Allan received from many. Thus, even beyond Upper Canada, he came to be regarded as a financial expert on the colony.

Allan's own land speculations occupied a good deal of his time. The amount of land that he held at different times is impossible to estimate, but for some 60 years he was continuously involved in the land market, dealing in both wild land and areas which he hoped to develop. By 1829 he had held land in townships in almost every district of the province. An idea of the size of his holdings may be judged from the request he made to John George Howard* in 1841, noted in Howard's diary, "to get the List of 20 thousand acres of Land to sell for him." Not all his speculations were immediately successful. In 1832 he attempted to found a recreation and cottage community at Niagara Falls in association with some of the most astute investors in Upper Canadian lands, including Thomas Clark* and Samuel Street*. Sales for the "City of the Falls" failed to come up to expectations and by 1837 the property was being divided among the proprietors. Allan was still winding up his part in 1850 through the agency of Thomas Clark Street*.

His most valuable land was his own park lot in York, which he had purchased in 1819. Subdivided after Allan's death by his son, George William*, the land stretched roughly a mile and a half from present-day Richmond Street to Bloor Street in Toronto, running west from Sherbourne Street to about Jarvis Street. On this wooded lot, in about 1828, Allan built a large house, Moss Park. His family life there, unfortunately, was tragic. The death in 1832 of his eldest daughter, "lovely" Elizabeth, was, in the opinion of Mrs Anne Powell [Murray*], "lamentable proof of the insufficiency of wealth to promote or rather confer happiness; Allan from a state of indigence is one of the richest men in the community; his house as you know is a Palace; its splendour has become desolation." Nine of Allan's eleven children died before the age of 20, many of them of the consumption that carried off his wife in 1848 and probably his last daughter in 1850. Only one son, George William, survived him.

During the mid 1830s Allan appears to have played a diminishing role in politics, the result, perhaps, of family circumstances, his withdrawal from the Bank of Upper Canada, and the waning political power of such veteran associates as John Strachan. In March 1836, however, Lieutenant Governor Sir Francis Bond Head* got into a quarrel with his Executive Council over the constitutional question of whether or not he had to consult that body, and the entire council resigned. Allan, with three other legislative councillors, Augustus Warren Baldwin*, John Elmsley*, and Robert Baldwin SULLIVAN, was called by Head to sit on his new council, and he accepted as his duty. Special arrangements were made so that he would act as administrator of the province if the governor were absent or incapacitated. Again, the honour showed Allan's position in the community. Head described him privately as "an excellent honest honorable man of high character and sound principles" but without "much talent or education" and "led a little by the Scotch." Sir George ARTHUR, Head's successor in 1838, would look to more politically oriented survivors of the old tory group such as John Beverley Robinson and John Macaulay for advice, so that Allan's executive posting did not keep him at centre stage. His authority also declined within the Legislative Council, to which he gave a stern warning in 1839 of the likely results of uncontrolled public spending and borrowing. He pointed out that the public debt, which exceeded £1,200,000, was absorbing all revenue and that there was no provision to repay capital. Knowing that he was in a minority on this issue, he acted not to influence policy but to record his "sentiments" in anticipation of the "consequence of a fictitious credit." His analysis echoed arguments on monetary policy and financial management that he had used six years earlier in banking.

As a major landholder and Canada Company commissioner, Allan also maintained a clearly defined position on land policy. In council debate in 1840 over free grants to immigrants, he and Richard Alexander Tucker*, the provincial secretary, spoke out for the large landholders bent on preserving their market by preventing areas of crown land from being opened up to settlement at either low prices or by free grants. Governor Charles Edward Poulett Thomson* (later Lord Sydenham), however, believed that Allan was out of touch with the needs of a developing province and suspected him "of having the Canada Company a little too much in his mind to give an unbiased opinion."

Allan served with greater effectiveness on a number of special commissions, such as those formed to examine persons arrested for high treason after the rebellion of 1837–38, to investigate in 1838 the sexual conduct of George Herchmer Markland*, the province's inspector general of public accounts, and to inspect in 1839–40 the administration of public departments. As a committee chairman on the last commission, Allan was responsible for the examination of eight departments, notably those of Crown Lands Commissioner Robert Baldwin Sullivan and Receiver General John Henry Dunn. Allan's committee focused on the totally inadequate method of accounting in Sullivan's office and recommended, in its place, the double-entry system with which Allan was familiar as a businessman. As for the Receiver General's Department, Allan, who was already deeply suspicious of Dunn's unprecedented powers in raising public loans, pressed for a careful distinction between his public and private transactions. Although Dunn intervened personally to limit Allan's investigation, Allan had had adequate time to show that he still possessed a flair for incisive analysis in matters of finance. Dunn's department and others were later reorganized under Lord Sydenham.

Allan remained on the Executive and Legislative councils until the union of the Canadas in February 1841 and then retired from politics. He was, however, still to be found chairing meetings of the tory British Constitutional Society during the 1840s, and in 1849 was a vice-president of the British American League [see George Moffatt*]. Two years later he supported John Strachan in the founding of Trinity College and was a member of its board when he died. As well, he sat on the board of the Church Society, which handled funds for the Anglican diocese of Toronto. Outside the church, however, his charitable activities appear to have been limited; in 1836 he had been instrumental in organizing a local St Andrew's society, of which he became first president.

Allan was fortunate in enjoying "a long life of almost uninterrupted health"; after being in a weak state for some time he died "at last from sheer exhaustion" on 11 July 1853. He was probably the oldest inhabitant of the city, the only person who

Allan

could speak of its earliest history from personal knowledge. How much wealth he left is unknown. In his very business-like will he left everything to his son, George William, after making minor bequests to relatives, the church, and local charities.

At the end of his life Allan became somewhat crotchety. Charles Morrison Durand, a Hamilton lawyer, later recalled his demeanour as "proud and austere, at least to strangers." At the same time he had outlived many of the antagonisms of the 1820s and 1830s. When he died, the *Toronto Mirror*, the reform journal published by Charles DONLEVY, assessed his political career: "His politics we judge with leniency. Connected with the early history of the Province and the compact that ruled its destinies, he belonged to a school that has become obsolete and incapable of renovation. The liberal policy of a more enlightened and progressive period was unknown in his day, and it would be unjust to subject his conduct to the rules of modern improvement. We believe, however, that neither by natural nor acquired abilities he was adapted for political life, and his errors he only shared in common with his more gifted associates."

Allan, though always identified with the "family compact," was never a member of the inner circle of government. But for the crisis precipitated by Sir Francis Bond Head, he might never have sat on the Executive Council. Before his rise to prominence as president of the Bank of Upper Canada, contemporaries as far apart politically as John Beverley Robinson and William Lyon Mackenzie agreed in portraying Allan as an administrator rather than an initiator of government policy.

His reputation rested on his success in business. As his obituary in the *Church* correctly noted, "Whatever success he had in life was due chiefly to his persevering industry, for he hazarded little in doubtful enterprises and had no fondness for speculation." He did a great deal for the successful development of Ontario's first corporations and set standards of management which few contemporaries could equal. At the height of his career, businessmen were willing to invest in the Bank of Upper Canada on the strength of his reputation and, in his old age, he was remembered for his wealth. Some of his associates, such as William Hamilton Merritt, also gave Allan credit for more than an eye for profit. Within the context of his admittedly rigid views on business and development in Upper Canada, he appears to have had a genuine concern for his adopted country. Possibly he saw the province in much the same light as he had the Bank of Upper Canada. For each he argued for expansion tempered by enough fiscal restraint to ensure independence from outside control.

IN COLLABORATION

The largest collection of Allan papers is at the MTL. Because he was prominently involved in public life and business for more than 50 years, material on Allan can be found in most collections pertaining to early Toronto. For this reason only the most important sources consulted are listed.

AO, MS 74, packages 11–15, 30, 34; MS 78; RG 22, ser.155, will of William Allan. MTL, J. G. Howard papers, sect.II, diaries, 1834, 1841; misc. accounts, "Memorandum of papers burnt," 88; S. P. Jarvis papers; W. D. Powell papers, A99 (M. B. Powell [Jarvis] corr.): 138–39. PAC, MG 24, E1: 620–1797; RG 1, L3, 2: A3/39; 3: A4/40, A5/18; 4: A8/1; RG 5, A1: 5291–92, 19002–5, 22083–85, 27080, 29004–9, 29022–23, 29116–18, 30700–4, 31823–24, 32175–78, 37790–92, 38244–45, 38792–95, 71640, 82370–72, 82614, 82674–84, 83514–16, 83831, 117145–48; RG 68, General index, 1651–1841: 181, 245, 407, 525, 670–71, 678. PRO, CO 42/393: 273 *et seq.*; 42/415: 2, 4, 6, 20, 22, 24, 28–29. Toronto Land Registry Office (Toronto), Abstract index to deeds, 581, park lots 4–5. Can., Prov. of, Legislative Assembly, *App. to the journals*, 1841, app.F; 1843, app.I. *The correspondence of the Honourable Peter Russell, with allied documents relating to his administration of the government of Upper Canada . . .* , ed. E. A. Cruikshank and A. F. Hunter (3v., Toronto, 1932–36), 3: 15–16. *Doc. hist. of campaign upon Niagara frontier* (Cruikshank), vols.2–9. "Grants of crown lands in U.C.," AO *Report*, 1929: 121, 157, 162. "Journals of Legislative Assembly of U.C.," AO *Report*, 1911: 92, 127–28, 216; 1912: 419; 1913: 230–31; 1914: 60–63, 543, 732–33, 752, 755. "Minutes of the Court of General Quarter Sessions of the Peace for the Home District, 13th March, 1800, to 28th December, 1811," AO *Report*, 1932: 3. *The parish register of Kingston, Upper Canada, 1785–1811*, ed. A. H. Young (Kingston, Ont., 1921), 108, 135, 149. *Select British docs. of War of 1812* (Wood), 1: 400; 2: 84, 189–90, 192, 194. *The Talbot papers*, ed. J. H. Coyne (2v., Ottawa, 1908–9). *Town of York, 1793–1815* (Firth); *Town of York, 1815–34* (Firth). U.C., House of Assembly, *App. to the journal*, 1835, 1, no.3; 1836, 3, no.106; 1837–38, 1: 212–34; 1839–40, 1, pt.I: 308–19; 2: vi–vii; *Journal*, app., 1829: 43–44 (2nd group); 1830: 21–48; 1831–32: 96–99; 1832–33: 75; 1833–34: 162–74, 213–14; Legislative Council, *Journal*, 1828–40, especially 1831–32: 51; 1839: 204–5. "Upper Canada land book B, 19th August, 1796, to 7th April, 1797," AO *Report*, 1930: 102. "Upper Canada land book C, 11th April, 1797, to 30th June, 1797," AO *Report*, 1930: 151. "Upper Canada land book D, 22nd December, 1797, to 13th July, 1798," AO *Report*, 1931: 145.

Church, 14, 21 July 1853. *Colonial Advocate*, 19 Aug. 1814; 7 April, 23 May 1825; 25 Feb. 1830–21 Dec. 1833, especially 10 June 1830, 6–27 May, 3, 10 June 1833. *Daily Leader* (Toronto), 12 July 1853. *Toronto Mirror*, 15 July 1853. *Upper Canada Gazette*, 30 April, 4 June 1821; 11 July 1822. *York Gazette*, 11 May 1811, 28 July 1812. Chadwick, *Ontario families*, 1: 79–80. *Toronto directory*, 1833–51.

Lucy Booth Martyn, *The face of early Toronto: an archival record, 1797–1936* (Sutton West, Ont., and Santa Barbara, Calif., 1982). *The defended border: Upper Canada and the War of 1812 . . .* , ed. Morris Zaslow and W. B. Turner (Toronto, 1964). Denison, *Canada's first bank*, vol.1. Charles Durand, *Reminiscences of Charles Durand of*

Toronto, barrister (Toronto, 1897), 130–31. B. D. Dyster, "Toronto, 1840–1860: making it in a British Protestant town" (1v. in 2, PHD thesis, Univ. of Toronto, 1970). "Historical sketch of the British America Assurance Company," *Canadian annual review of public affairs*, ed. J. C. Hopkins (Toronto), 1911, *Special supplement . . .* : 96–104. M. L. Magill, "William Allan: a pioneer business executive," *Aspects of nineteenth-century Ontario . . .* , ed. F. H. Armstrong et al. (Toronto and Buffalo, N.Y., 1974), 101–13. Middleton, *Municipality of Toronto. Robertson's landmarks of Toronto*, 1: 251–53, 366, 561; 6: 275, 300. V. Ross and Trigge, *Hist. of Canadian Bank of Commerce*, vol.2. Scadding, *Toronto of old* (1873; ed. Armstrong, 1966). T. W. Acheson, "The nature and structure of York commerce in the 1820s," *CHR*, 50 (1969): 406–28. H. G. J. Aitken, "The Family Compact and the Welland Canal Company," *Canadian Journal of Economics and Political Science* (Toronto), 18 (1952): 63–76. P. A. Baskerville, "Entrepreneurship and the Family Compact: York–Toronto, 1822–55," *Urban Hist. Rev.* (Ottawa), 9 (1980–81), no.3: 15–34. R. M. Breckenridge, "The Canadian banking system, 1817–1890," Canadian Bankers' Assoc., *Journal* (Toronto), 2 (1894–95): 105–96. L. F. [Cowdell] Gates, "The decided policy of William Lyon Mackenzie," *CHR*, 40 (1959): 185–208. E. C. Guillet, "Pioneer banking in Ontario: the Bank of Upper Canada, 1822–1866," *Canadian Banker* (Toronto), 55 (1948), no.1: 115–32. L. B. Jackes, "Toronto's first bank," *Toronto Sunday World*, 26 March 1922; repub. in *Canadian Paper Money Journal* (Toronto), 17 (1981): 71–74. M. L. Magill, "William Allan and the War of 1812," *OH*, 64 (1972): 132–41. R. C. B. Risk, "The nineteenth-century foundations of the business corporation in Ontario," *Univ. of Toronto Law Journal* (Toronto), 23 (1973): 270–306. Adam Shortt, "The early history of Canadian banking," "The history of Canadian currency, banking and exchange . . . ," and "Founders of Canadian banking: the Hon. William Allan, merchant and banker," Canadian Bankers' Assoc., *Journal*, 5 (1897–98): 1–21; 8 (1900–1): 4–6, 227–43, 305–26; 30 (1922–3): 154–66. C. L. Vaughan, "The Bank of Upper Canada in politics, 1817–1840," *OH*, 60 (1968): 185–204.

ALLANSON, JOHN, wood-engraver; b. *c.* 1813 in England; his wife, Elizabeth ——, and a child predeceased him; d. 11 Feb. 1853 in Toronto.

Where or under whom John Allanson trained as a wood-engraver is not known. Many reference books repeat the assertion of a later associate in Leipzig (German Democratic Republic) that he had been a pupil of the renowned Newcastle engraver Thomas Bewick, but Allanson was only about 15 when Bewick died in 1828 after years of illness and semi-retirement. Allanson was perhaps finishing his apprenticeship when an illustrated weekly, the *Penny Magazine*, was launched in London in 1832. Its immediate popularity produced a flock of imitators in England and abroad, and a demand for engravers who had been trained by Bewick or a pupil of his. One such imitator, the *Musée des Familles*, launched in Paris in 1833, carried during its first year 20 engravings signed

by Allanson. They reveal that, while still a youth, he had already mastered a variety of styles and had the skill to retain the spontaneity of sketches by Paul Gavarni and Henry Monnier, to render finely detailed vignettes in Bewick's miniature style, and to reproduce the subtle gradations of tone found in Salon paintings. However, after about two or three years, growing nationalist sentiment increasingly favoured the rising generation of French engravers and illustrators, and Allanson departed for the United States.

Once settled in New York, Allanson found little difficulty at first in finding commissions. In May 1836 he attracted critical approval in the *New York Mirror* for a frame of vignettes shown at the spring exhibition of the city's National Academy of Design. Three topographical views by Allanson had already appeared in the *American Magazine of Useful and Entertaining Knowledge* (Boston), and were followed by ten illustrations in the French narrative style to accompany a serialized short story published in the *Mirror* at the end of 1837. His residence in New York, however, lasted at most four years. He returned to England, probably because he could not find continuing work in New York, where the art of wood-engraving was not yet highly developed.

Allanson's name next appears in Leipzig in 1843 when a magazine called the *Illustrirte Zeitung*, launched that year, began carrying regular contributions by him of portraits, reproductions of old master paintings, architectural views, and glimpses of current events. He and other engravers had been lured from London by the Leipzig publisher Georg Wigand, and Allanson later became the principal engraver of the romantic illustrations by the artist Adrian Ludwig Richter which appeared in Wigand's collections of German myths and folk tales. But history was to repeat itself for John Allanson. National pride in the group of accomplished native engravers coupled with uneasiness over the English engravers' seeming obsession with technique at the expense of feeling brought an end to his career in Germany by 1848.

One can only speculate why Allanson, now about 35, decided that Upper Canada would be an appropriate residence for one of his skill and experience. As a wood-engraver, he had been trained to reproduce the form and spirit of an artist's sketch, and when, as in Germany, the necessary equipment, materials, and technical assistance were put at his disposal, wood-engraving in his hands became indeed "this beautiful art," as a contemporary editorial had described it. In Upper Canada the conditions would be far from ideal. Allanson may have chosen the province to avoid the relative anonymity and lack of independence that would have been his lot in a large London firm. Although local publishers had for some

Allanson

years made scattered attempts to appease their readers' growing appetite for illustrations by inserting the occasional cut, these were usually copied from imported publications. In 1848, when he arrived in Toronto, the tiny audience for Upper Canadian publications translated into less than full-time employment for one wood-engraver, Frederick C. Lowe. However, to an immigrant British wood-engraver who was prepared to establish roots, and if necessary work at a variety of jobs in the publishing and printing trades, Toronto, already an active publishing community, offered security for Allanson and his family.

Information about the four to five years Allanson spent in Toronto before his death is scanty, but it suggests that he did indeed draw upon his past experience in publishing to establish a solid future for himself. In March 1849, giving a commercial address on King Street, he placed an advertisement in the city's *British Colonist* offering for sale a set of steel engravings by William Hogarth, and another of Paris and its environs. By late spring he had set up his own lithographic press. In November he was elected a member of the Toronto Mechanics' Institute, which maintained a reading-room; it may not have been a coincidence that at this time he also began business as a subscription agent for periodicals.

From the first, Allanson undoubtedly developed working relationships with established figures in the Toronto publishing world. His name is not mentioned on the topographical plan of Toronto prepared by Sandford Fleming* and published by Hugh Scobie, but Fleming recorded in 1849 that he traced the plan on a lithographic stone at Allanson's premises. It included a border in the form of a series of public buildings engraved by Allanson after drawings by architect Thomas Young, and was completed in time for the Great Exhibition in London in 1851. A reviewer in Toronto, praising its execution, remarked that "this new plan of the city is, in every respect, Canadian." In a land of recent immigrants, Allanson, three years after his arrival, finally was as much at home as other citizens.

It was customary in Upper Canada at that time for amateur and professional artists alike to have their work viewed by the public, and judged for prizes, at the annual Upper Canada Provincial Exhibition. The first prize in wood-engraving in the fine arts department was taken by Allanson on three occasions between 1849 and 1852. By 1850 Allanson was renting domestic and business premises on Yonge Street, beside Holy Trinity Church, from which address he advertised in Scobie's *Canadian almanac* for 1851 a wide range of services as an "engraver on wood": "Historical Subjects, Public Buildings, Hotels, Official and Municipal Seals, Arms, &c., &c." He evidently attracted commissions, and illustrations with "Allanson" signed in the block

began to be seen with some frequency. In the same almanac, Young's drawings of a painting and decorating shop and a combined livery stable and bowling saloon are precisely documented in a pair of full-page advertisements engraved by Allanson. The *Canadian Agriculturist*, of Toronto, employed him in 1852 to do small cuts copied from the American press, and for a view of the provincial exhibition grounds. The unaccustomed "Allanson del & sc" on an engraving of the newly erected Trinity College, Toronto, by architect Kivas Tully*, acknowledges his responsibility for both the original design and the wood-block.

Allanson returned to working on magazines when Thomas Maclear* made illustrations a feature of his *Anglo-American Magazine*, launched in July 1852 in Toronto. A monthly view of a provincial town printed on a separate page, a fashion plate, and one other engraving, usually of a literary subject, were Allanson's responsibility. Proof impressions of these engravings, including views of Kingston, Hamilton, and Brockville, were "very much admired" at the provincial exhibition that year, and were republished posthumously as separate plates in some later impressions of William Henry Smith*'s *Canada: past, present and future*. The last of Allanson's contributions to the *Anglo-American* appeared in the October 1852 issue, and in November he was succeeded by Frederick C. Lowe. John Allanson may already have encountered the ill health that would lead to his death the following February.

Having to substitute softer local woods for the more desirable European boxwood, and probably having to make do with unsuitable printing-presses and paper and with pressmen unaccustomed to printing from wood-blocks, Allanson could not have been satisfied that the impressions made from his Canadian wood-blocks did justice to his training, skill, and reputation. To earn a living he must have routinely undertaken commercial assignments such as seals, small advertising cuts, and letterheads, and in much of this work he was a typical engraver of his time. But his peripatetic career was characteristic of only a small number of English engravers who carried the secrets of Thomas Bewick's techniques to receptive audiences in other countries.

Mary F. Williamson

AO, MU 1050, diary, 26 June 1849 (transcript). MTL, Toronto, Mechanics Institute papers, G4 (General accounts, 1849–58): 29. Toronto Necropolis and Crematorium, Reg. of burials (Elizabeth Allanson, d. 23 Dec. 1851; (child) Allanson, d. 12 July 1852; John Allanson, d. 11 Feb. 1853). *Canadian Agriculturist* (Toronto), 1 (1849): 281; 2 (1850): 235; 4 (1852): 292, 311, 365. *British Colonist* (Toronto), 27 March 1849, 29 Aug. 1851, 15 Feb. 1853. *Globe*, "Pictorial Suppl.," December 1856: 3. *Canadian almanac*, 1851:

78–79, 83. J. F. Hoff, *Adrian Ludwig Richter, maler und radierer*. . . (2nd ed., Freiburg, [German Federal Republic], 1922), 405. M. F. Williamson, "'Description fails . . .'; periodical illustration in 19th century Ontario," *The art and pictorial press in Canada; two centuries of art magazines*, ed. Karen McKenzie and M. F. Williamson (Toronto, 1979), 11–19. Patricia Stone, "The publishing history of W. H. Smith's *Canada: past, present and future*: a preliminary investigation," Biblio. Soc. of Canada, *Papers* (Toronto), 19 (1980): 38–68.

ALLISON, CHARLES FREDERICK, merchant, philanthropist, and college administrator; b. 25 Jan. 1795 in Cornwallis, N.S., son of James Allison, farmer and merchant, and Margaret Hutchinson; m. 23 June 1840 Milcah Trueman, and they had at least one daughter; d. 20 Nov. 1858 in Sackville, N.B.

Of Ulster Scottish descent, Charles Frederick Allison grew up in Cornwallis, N.S., where he received his education. After moving to Parrsboro, he spent several years working as a clerk in a store owned by James Ratchford, a relative by marriage. At the age of 21 he joined the expanding mercantile firm run by his cousin William CRANE and Bardin Turner in Sackville, N.B., and within a few years became a partner. The Crane and Allison concern operated both in the Sackville area, as a distributor of local agricultural produce and imported goods, and on the Miramichi River, exporting timber to Liverpool and selling provisions and imported commodities. The firm's widespread trading links in both Great Britain and the New England states enabled it also to play a significant role in stimulating the development of shipbuilding in Sackville parish, since it bought several vessels from local yards during the 1820s. Allison's cautious approach to business transactions – a contemporary remarked that he was "inclined to pursue safe rather than rapid modes of acquiring wealth" – made him an effective counterpart to the ebullient Crane. As Crane was active in provincial politics from 1824, the daily conduct of the firm's affairs fell largely to Allison, until he retired from active business in early 1840 to devote himself to the establishment of Mount Allison Wesleyan Academy in Sackville.

The roots of Allison's interest in education lay in a spiritual crisis during the mid 1830s which resulted in his conversion from the Church of England to the Methodist denomination. Through the influence of the Reverend William Smithson, he began to attend Methodist services in 1833, and in 1836 he was among those converted at a series of revival meetings held in Sackville by the Reverend John Bass Strong. Allison thus joined a denomination which had aspired for some years to open an educational institution in the Maritime provinces but had been unable to raise the necessary funds. In 1839 he resolved this difficulty by offering to buy land in Sackville for a school and to

construct a suitable building at his own expense, and to donate £100 annually for its first ten years of operation. He wanted a preparatory school for boys where "not only the Elementary, but higher branches of Education may be taught."

First broached at a meeting of New Brunswick Methodist ministers in Saint John, Allison's offer was then put to a joint meeting of the New Brunswick and Nova Scotia districts in Halifax on 12 July 1839. An observer, the Reverend Enoch Wood*, later recalled Allison's characteristically unassuming demeanour at the meeting. "One sentence of his address," Wood wrote, "I have never forgotten. . . . 'The Lord hath put it into my heart to give this sum towards building a Wesleyan Academy,' – and then he made a short pause, as though he was afraid he had spoken too strongly, resuming – ' I know the impression is from the Lord, for I am naturally fond of money.'"

Allison's "munificent offer" was accepted by the meeting. Winding up his business affairs by the following January, he laid the foundation-stone for the Mount Allison Wesleyan Academy on 9 July 1840, supervised the construction personally, and saw it opened to students on 19 Jan. 1843. In the years that followed, he took an active interest in its operation: he was a frequent visitor to the school and served as treasurer until his death. Shy by nature and quiet in manner, Allison shunned public attention. In 1849 he declined an appointment to the Legislative Council of New Brunswick offered by the government leader, Edward Barron Chandler*, even though he had been assured that he would not be called upon to identify himself with any political party. Most of his energy continued to be expended on the academy, and during the late 1840s and early 1850s he played a leading role in promoting the idea of adding a school for girls. He again supervised the construction of a building and, in the summer of 1854, after donating £1,000, had the satisfaction of seeing the female academy, with Mary Electa Adams* as lady preceptress, begin to receive students. Allison did not live to see the inauguration of yet a further institution bearing his name – the Mount Allison Wesleyan College, opened in 1862 – but it benefited from a sum left in his will to be put towards a degree-granting college.

Yet when Allison died, it was not his money that was chiefly remembered at Mount Allison, important though his donations had been. In fact, his retirement from business in 1840 had limited his wealth and his fortune was described as "a small one"; his estate was estimated at only £10,000. Humphrey Pickard*, the academy's principal, declared that Allison's gift had also included his time and energy, and his passing was mourned as the loss of an able counsellor and a loyal and constant friend of the institution. As a merchant, Allison had participated successfully in the commercial economy of the Maritime provinces; as the

Angers

founder of Mount Allison, he turned both his wealth and his personal abilities to the service of his religious denomination and to the cause of education in the region.

JOHN G. REID

A large, full-length oil portrait of Charles Frederick Allison, begun by the English artist William Gush shortly before Allison's death in 1858 and completed subsequently, hangs in the Owens Art Gallery of Mount Allison Univ. (Sackville, N.B.). A smaller portrait by the same artist is in the university's Alumni and Continuing Education Centre. Details regarding these portraits are available in Mount Allison Univ. Arch., F. W. W. DesBarres, "Correspondence from Alice Borden and L. M. Fortier concerning William Gush (artist), his career, and his painting of the Allison portraits" (MS, 1929).

BLHU, R. G. Dun & Co. credit ledger, Canada, 7: 203. Mount Allison Univ. Arch., C. F. Allison papers. N.B. Museum, N.B. Hist. Soc. papers, Crane & Allison corr., 1834–52. PANB, MC 218, MS3/17; "New Brunswick political biography," comp. J. C. and H. B. Graves (11v., typescript), IV; RG 7, RS74A, 1858, C. F. Allison. PANS, MG 3, 300. SOAS, Methodist Missionary Soc. Arch., Wesleyan Methodist Missionary Soc., corr., N. Am., C. F. Allison to William Temple, 4 June 1839 (mfm. at UCA and United Church of Canada, Maritime Conference Arch. (Halifax)). United Church of Canada, Maritime Conference Arch., Wesleyan Methodist Church, New Brunswick District, minutes, 12 July 1839 (mfm. at UCA). *British North American Wesleyan Methodist Magazine* (Saint John, N.B.), 1 (1840–41): 79–80; 2 (1842): 274; 3 (1843): 198–99 [a series of short, uncredited articles on the foundation of the Wesleyan Academy, the first of which reprints Allison's endowment proposal]. *A catalogue of the officers and students of the Wesleyan Academy, Mount Allison, Sackville, New Brunswick* (Saint John; Sackville), 1843–52 (copies in Mount Allison Univ. Arch.). Richard Knight and William Temple, "Address of the Wesleyan missionaries in the Nova Scotia and New-Brunswick districts to the members of society, and congregations attending their ministry, and friends of religious education generally," *British North American Wesleyan Methodist Magazine*, 1: 558. *Mount Allison Academic Gazette* (Sackville), nos.1 (December 1853)–6 (1857), especially no.3 (December 1854): 2–4; no.8 (1859): 13–14 (copies in Mount Allison Univ. Arch.). Humphrey Pickard, "A discourse commemoratory of the late Chas. F. Allison, esq., founder of the Mount Allison Wesleyan Academy, delivered in Lingley Hall, Sabbath evening, May 29th, 1859, at the request of the students," *Mount Allison Academic Gazette*, no.8: 5–9. *Provincial Wesleyan* (Halifax), 14 Feb. 1852, 18 March 1853. *Royal Gazette* (Fredericton), 21 Feb. 1849.

L. A. Morrison, *The history of the Alison, or Allison family in Europe and America, A.D. 1135 to 1893; giving an account of the family in Scotland, England, Ireland, Australia, Canada, and the United States* (Boston, 1893). D. E. Alward, "Down Sackville ways: shipbuilding in a nineteenth century New Brunswick outport" (BA thesis, Mount Allison Univ., 1978), 136–37. W. C. Milner, *History of Sackville, New Brunswick* (Sackville, 1934). J. G. Reid, *Mount Allison University: a history, to 1963* (2v.,

Toronto, 1984). Smith, *Hist. of Methodist Church*. Wynn, *Timber colony*. [M. C. Maxwell] Mrs A. E. Vesey, "Founder's Day address," *Mount Allison Record* (Sackville), 17 (1933–34): 14–22 (copy in Mount Allison Univ. Arch.). "The old Sackville Academy," *Argosy* (Sackville), 39 (1912–13): 262–64 (copy in Mount Allison Univ. Arch.). Enoch Wood, "Wesleyan Academy, Mount Allison, Sackville, N.B.," *Wesleyan* (Halifax), 19 May 1882: [6].

ANGERS, FRANÇOIS-RÉAL, author, lawyer, office holder, and journalist; b. 20 Nov. 1812 at Pointe-aux-Trembles (Neuville), Lower Canada, son of François Angers, a farmer, and Marie-Desanges Larue; m. 4 April 1842 Louise-Adèle Taschereau at Sainte-Marie-de-la-Nouvelle-Beauce (Sainte-Marie), Lower Canada; m. secondly 23 Nov. 1853 Louise Panet at Quebec; d. there 27 March 1860, and was buried four days later at Pointe-aux-Trembles.

François-Réal Angers received his classical education at the Petit Séminaire de Québec. He was in the fifth-year class (Belles-Lettres) when on 9 Dec. 1830 he and some fellow students founded the Société littéraire, the first of its kind to be set up there, as Honorius Provost confirms in his volume on the Séminaire de Québec. With two other students he was chosen as a member of a committee charged with "drawing up a constitution for the Société littéraire and proposing regulations." The constitution for the society, which lasted only four months, was presented and approved with some amendments at a meeting on 14 December.

In 1836, when he was a law student, Angers published a pamphlet entitled *Système de sténographie, applicable au français et à l'anglais*. Called to the bar on 6 Oct. 1837, he was immediately appointed official reporter of the debates in the House of Assembly of Lower Canada, and his publication was no doubt extremely useful to him in carrying out his duties. While practising law he was co-editor, from 1845 to 1848, of the *Revue de législation et de jurisprudence* which, according to historians André Beaulieu and Jean Hamelin, constitutes "one of [the] oldest collections of the rulings of the courts of Lower Canada." In 1850 and 1851 he was president of the Institut Canadien in Quebec; however, his name does not appear on the list of founding members published by Alphonse Désilets in 1948. From 1851 until his death Angers was one of the principal contributors to the *Décisions des tribunaux du Bas-Canada*.

Before entering upon his legal career, Angers had made himself known as a writer. Five of his poems, many in the form of songs, appeared in *Le répertoire national* compiled by James HUSTON in the years 1848–50. In his poem "L'avenir" Angers extols liberty, condemns slavery, and devoutly hopes that French Canadians and the sons of Albion will form one nation. In "Réconciliation" he opposes armed conflict, which usually leads to division, to separation, indeed to death. In "La voix d'une ombre" he disapproves of the insurrection by the Patriotes and deplores the fate held in store for his "most unhappy brothers / Led astray by their hearts" and forced into exile. In the poem "À Saint Jean-Baptiste" he pays homage to the noble patron saint of French Canadians, from whom he seeks protection.

But Angers's greatest success was unquestionably *Les révélations du crime ou Cambray et ses complices*, published at Quebec in 1837, in which he reconstructs the climate of terror created at Quebec between 1832 and 1834 by a group of brigands who were hiding out at nearby Cap-Rouge under the leadership of Charles Cambray (actually Charles Chambers*), a timber merchant of Quebec and the brother of Robert Chambers, a future mayor of the city. This fictional account about the crimes of the "Chambers gang," a work some wrongly consider to be the first French Canadian novel, remains according to Professor David M. Hayne "one of the most readable and widely circulated books of the first half of the 19th century in Canada." Republished in 1867, 1880, and again in 1969, it was serialized in at least three newspapers and was translated into English in 1867 as *The Canadian brigands; an intensely exciting story of crime in Quebec, thirty years ago!*

Angers soon gave up literature to devote himself entirely to practising law. It was he who with Thomas-Jean-Jacques Loranger* defended the *censitaires* in the years 1854–56 before the Seigneurial Court, presided over by the chief justice, Louis-Hippolyte La Fontaine*, which had the responsibility of adjudging the claims made following the passing of the bill abolishing the seigneurial régime. During the long debates that marked the hearing of the numerous cases, he showed himself to be an outstanding jurist and a speaker as talented as he was convincing.

Although he had a brilliant career in law, François-Réal Angers is little known. The brief, scattered obituaries contain errors concerning his writings and the date of his death. When he died on 27 March 1860, an anonymous reporter for *Le Canadien* wrote that "the bar was losing . . . its foremost lawyer [and] its most distinguished speaker; Canadian literature, one of its finest ornaments; the country, an ardent and devoted patriot." One of the sons born of his first marriage, Auguste-Réal*, had a distinguished political career, and in 1887 became lieutenant governor of Quebec.

AURÉLIEN BOIVIN

François-Réal Angers published poems in newspapers between 1836 and 1843, which were reproduced, with one exception, in *Le répertoire national* (Huston, 1848–50; 1893). He also wrote *Système de sténographie, applicable au français et à l'anglais* (Québec, 1836), and *Les révélations du crime ou Cambray et ses complices; chroniques canadiennes de 1834* (Québec, 1837). Further editions of the latter work were published at Quebec in 1867 and 1880, and in Montréal in 1969; it was also translated into English under the title *The Canadian brigands; an intensely exciting story of crime in Quebec, thirty years ago!* (Montreal, 1867).

ANQ-Q, CE1-1, 23 nov. 1853, 31 mars 1860; ZQ6, 4 avril 1842. *Le Séminaire de Québec: documents et biographies*, Honorius Provost, édit. (Québec, 1964). *Le Canadien*, 28, 30 mars 1860. *DOLQ*, 1: 578–79, 655–56. Réginald Hamel *et al.*, *Dictionnaire pratique des auteurs québécois* (Montréal, 1976). Morgan, *Bibliotheca Canadensis*, 10. P.-G. Roy, *Les avocats de la région de Québec*. Wallace, *Macmillan dict.* Alphonse Désilets, "Les fondateurs de l'Institut canadien," *Rev. de l'univ. Laval* (Québec), 2 (1947–48): 708–12. P.-G. Roy, "La bande de chambers," *Cahiers des Dix*, 3 (1938): 89–113.

ANTROBUS, EDMUND WILLIAM ROMER, army officer, office holder, and justice of the peace; b. 16 Jan. 1795 in Berthier-en-Haut (Berthierville, Que.), son of John Antrobus*, a merchant, and Catherine Betsey Isabella Cuthbert, daughter of the seigneur of Berthier, James Cuthbert*; m. 1 June 1830 Catharine Esther Brehaut, daughter of merchant Pierre Brehaut*, at Quebec, and they had 13 children, 12 of whom survived infancy; d. 31 Oct. 1852 at Quebec.

Descended from eminent families on both sides, Edmund William Romer Antrobus was brought up in a strict, religious atmosphere and remained a faithful member of the Church of England throughout his life. At age 17 he was studying law in the office of the acting attorney general, Edward Bowen*, but he decided instead to follow in the footsteps of his brother and uncle by choosing a military career. Colonel George Robertson, married to his mother's sister, was commanding officer of the Canadian Fencibles, and on 4 April 1812, shortly before the War of 1812 broke out, Antrobus signed on with the unit as a volunteer. He was promoted ensign on 2 Sept. 1812 and lieutenant on 14 Nov. 1813.

Antrobus is said to have distinguished himself in various engagements in Upper Canada, for which he received a war medal, before being involved in his most memorable battle. On 30 March 1814, 4,000 American troops made a serious attempt to reach Montreal. Two hundred men from a small British post on the Rivière Lacolle commanded by Major Richard Butler Handcock of the 13th Foot, together with another 300 men seven miles away, put an end to the attempted invasion. Antrobus had been in the thick of the battle and his joy at the victory was immeasurably increased by the invitation to exchange into the 13th Foot. He did so on 24 Aug. 1815 and served overseas in Spain and Portugal, presumably in mopping up operations after the Peninsular War. He was on half pay from 1817 to 1829. In England he obtained a

Antrobus

miniature portrait of himself, thought to have been painted by the artist Sir Thomas Lawrence.

Antrobus probably returned to Quebec in 1818 and on 6 July 1819 he was appointed deputy to his father, overseer of highways for the district of Three Rivers. The following year, on 28 January, he succeeded his father. In 1821 he was appointed justice of the peace. Three years later he ran for a seat in the House of Assembly for the riding of Saint-Maurice but was badly defeated by Charles CARON and Pierre Bureau*. When Thomas-Pierre-Joseph Taschereau* died, Antrobus was asked to assume his duties as overseer of highways for the district of Quebec. He was commissioned on 11 Nov. 1826.

When the governor-in-chief, Lord Dalhousie [Ramsay*], founded the Literary and Historical Society of Quebec in 1824, Antrobus was among the charter members. The following year he was in a deputation with Mathew Bell* and Pierre-Joseph Godefroy* de Tonnancour to deliver an address welcoming Dalhousie to Trois-Rivières. In 1827 Dalhousie set up a joint monument to James Wolfe* and Louis-Joseph de Montcalm*; Antrobus's name was listed among the donors. Presumably then, the governor-in-chief knew him when he asked Antrobus to become his extra provincial aide-de-camp in 1828. Antrobus succeeded the chief provincial aide-de-camp, Jean-Baptiste Juchereau* Duchesnay, after the latter's sudden death on 12 Jan. 1833, and thus attended Governor Lord Aylmer [Whitworth-Aylmer*].

A few years later, in protest against the plurality of government posts, the House of Assembly resolved on 26 Feb. 1836 "that the cumulation of the Offices of Grand Voyer [overseer of highways] of the District of *Quebec*, and of Provincial Aide-de-Camp, in the same person, is contrary to the public good, and incompatible with the due and efficient performance of the duties of the said Offices." Antrobus continued, however, to occupy the post of overseer of highways until it was abolished in 1841 and that of aide-de-camp until his death in 1852. On the suggestion of Colonel Charles Stephen Gore*, Governor Lord Gosford [Acheson*] also made him deputy adjutant general of militia for Lower Canada on 14 Dec. 1837.

Antrobus was very much a military man. During the second half of his life, at a time when the British military were looked up to by the inhabitants, he was a proud member of the 71st Foot. He always enjoyed the camaraderie of his fellow officers and made them feel welcome in his home.

As aide-de-camp, Antrobus often became attached to the governor he was serving. His diary indicates that the parting at the end of a term of office could be quite emotional, especially in the case of Sir Charles Theophilus Metcalfe*, who was critically ill. Proba-

bly the only time Antrobus was called upon to defend a governor was on 25 April 1849, when Lord Elgin [Bruce*] signed the Rebellion Losses Bill at the parliament buildings in Montreal and was subsequently pelted with rotten eggs and stones by infuriated tories as he drove away in his open landau. Despite his aide-de-camp's efforts, Elgin was hit as was Antrobus himself.

Throughout his years of involvement with the governors and their entourages, Antrobus frequently dined with small groups at Government House or planned gala receptions for 500 guests, each of whom he presented to their excellencies. Consequently he became acquainted with a large number of the social élite, vividly catalogued in his diaries, at the successive seats of government: Quebec, Kingston, Montreal, Toronto, and again Quebec. Often he preferred to dine at home with his family and friends. His concern for his children is apparent in a passage from his diary dated 7 Dec. 1845: "To bed at 12, kept watching the children who coughed dreadfully [eight of them had whooping cough], until 6 this morning when I took an hour's nap." The last entry in his diary tells of having spent the evening playing whist with Lord Elgin and ends with, "I feel very ill." He died five hours later of cholera. Lord Elgin recommended to the Legislative Assembly that the widow of his faithful aide-de-camp, left with 12 children, be awarded a pension for life of not more than £200 a year. After some lively debate, the motion was amended to provide for an annual grant and was passed.

Antrobus was remembered by author Charlotte Holt Macpherson as figuring among the prominent characters of Quebec and as "just the right man in the right place, handsome, dignified, overflowing with *bonhomie*, a favourite with all."

VIRGINIA RYERSON WHITELAW

ANQ-Q, CE1-61, 1er juin 1830, 1er nov. 1852. PAC, MG 24, F50; MG 30, D1, 2: 345; RG 68, General index, 1651–1841: 352, 361, 364, 367, 373, 518. Private arch., W. G. Antrobus (Downsview [Toronto]), Geneal. information; Doris Hart and Valerie Maxwell (New Milford, N.J.), E. W. R. Antrobus, journal, 1832–34; Lucienne Minguy (Québec), Geneal. information. PRO, WO 17/1519: 163, 178, 193, 211, 217. Bas-Canada, Chambre d'Assemblée, *Journaux*, 1836: 525. *Debates of the Legislative Assembly of United Canada* (Abbott Gibbs *et al.*), 11: 1420–23. *Quebec Gazette*, 8 July 1819, 27 Oct. 1825, 27 Dec. 1837, 3 Nov. 1852. G.B., WO, *Army list*, 1813, 1815–16, 1818, 1830. *Officers of British forces in Canada* (Irving). P.-G. Roy, *Fils de Québec*, 3: 73–75. [C. H. Gethings] Mrs Daniel Macpherson, *Reminiscences of old Quebec* (Montreal, 1890). "Edmund-William-Romer Antrobus," *BRH*, 12 (1906): 78–80. "La famille Antrobus," *BRH*, 41 (1935): 506–8. P.-G. Roy, "Les grands voyers de la Nouvelle-

France et leurs successeurs," *Cahiers des Dix*, 8 (1943): 181–233. "Valuable miniature donated to Chateau," *Gazette* (Montreal), 19 Jan. 1938: 13.

ARCHAMBAULT, PAUL-LOUP (baptized **Paul**), Roman Catholic priest, vicar general, and seminary administrator; b. 29 Sept. 1787 in Rivière-des-Prairies (Montreal), son of Jean-Baptiste Archambault and Marie-Angélique Hachin, *dit* Baron; d. 20 Feb. 1858 in Vaudreuil, Lower Canada.

The son of an illiterate habitant, Paul-Loup Archambault received his secondary education from 1800 to 1809 at the Collège Saint-Raphaël (which in 1806 became the Petit Séminaire de Montréal). Throughout his studies he showed unusual discretion and piety. Having donned the soutane, by the autumn of 1809 he held the post of regent at the Séminaire de Nicolet. He taught in succession the second and third year classes (respectively, Syntaxe and Méthode), while learning theology through textbooks and the commentaries of the principal. He was probably engaged in similar tasks in the year he spent at the Séminaire de Québec prior to his ordination on 18 Oct. 1812. In November he was appointed curate at Les Cèdres. The people in this large parish had experienced a poor harvest and its priest, Laurent Aubry, was infirm. During his short stay, the young curate was universally esteemed, even by the least devout.

The dearth of priests at the time was so serious that Bishop Joseph-Octave Plessis* summoned Archambault to become the principal of the Séminaire de Nicolet on 1 Oct. 1813. There he was under the immediate authority of the curé of Nicolet, Jean Raimbault*, who made the decisions on admissions and important undertakings. In return, the principal was assigned the task of being pastoral assistant to the priests of the five surrounding parishes. It is easy, then, to understand why during his three years as principal Archambault constantly felt torn and overwhelmed by his duties, and caught in a position of uneasy authority, last in line after the bishop and the parish priest. Yet he was immediately responsible for the studies of the 79 pupils, divided into five classes, and for the regents, all of whom were young clergymen in training; he was responsible also for lay employees and for the state of the supplies and finances. Conditions were far from satisfactory in the seminary at the outset of the war with the United States in 1812.

As the principal objective of the seminary was to train priests, Archambault busied himself recreating a more élite fraternity, and reinstating for the clerics prayers said in common at least weekly, although he despaired of the theological training being acquired by regents who were left to their own devices with textbooks as their sole resource. He watched carefully over moral conduct, whether it was a question of close relationships between adolescents or of dangerous theatrical performances encouraged by Raimbault. His efforts did not, however, produce many recruits for the priesthood, since at the end of his term of office Archambault only had two candidates to present. He left his post as principal in September 1816 without regret, to become priest in the parish of Vaudreuil, which had been left vacant by Jean-Baptiste Deguire's death.

Archambault found himself once more in a parish hard hit by a series of poor harvests; it was also split over a plan to rebuild the presbytery, which had become uninhabitable. Various influential people had for several months been challenging the report by Joseph-Norbert PROVENCHER, the priest of Pointe-Claire, which had rendered a decision on the matter in the bishop's name. They elaborated legal arguments, and explored the question of the autonomy of laymen who they thought should no longer let themselves be overruled by the church hierarchy. Archambault acted cautiously; he communicated to Plessis the seven arguments of the opposing party (six valid, in his view) and awaited orders. The bishop instructed him to proceed immediately with apportioning the cost of the reconstruction among the parishioners and to be ready to leave the parish without a priest if the opposition went to court. This piece of blackmail was likely to be effective, for the parishioners had soon taken a liking to their new priest, who had not been party to the dispute. The legal resolution of the conflict did not come for years, and the rebuilding took longer still. It was ten years before Archambault could write that the agitation had subsided. Some aspects of religious practice did, however, improve and in 1817 and 1818 the number of Easter confessions increased by about 20 per cent. More than half the parishioners gave him good reasons for cheer, but Archambault must have been somewhat disillusioned when he discovered that people were seeking absolution from their faults rather than improvement in their conduct, the goal behind the whole pastoral strategy of meting out penance. He attempted to encourage the fervour of at least a minority by bringing in the Confrérie du Saint-Scapulaire, but the bishop of Quebec's consent took five years to come, and even then the associates were refused the privilege of being able to have the special service of Benediction. This delay could be taken as evidence of the episcopal apathy that formed part of the context of a troubled period. During these years Archambault regularly dispatched to his bishop the records of irregular conjugal circumstances, both public scandals and secret ones divulged at confession. He usually recommended a lenient solution after satisfying himself as to the good intentions of those involved.

Archambault

The difficult economic conditions experienced by many of the habitants in the parish and the extra burden of debt resulting from the construction of a presbytery gave rise to an incident that would weigh heavily on Archambault for many years. Between 10 and 11 o'clock on the evening of 20 Dec. 1822, two people in disguise broke into his room, held a knife to his throat, and forced him to hand over about £6,000 belonging to the *fabrique* that had been left on his desk. A few days later sizeable payments were made by some of the *fabrique*'s debtors. Archambault was put in a difficult position by the loss of the £6,000, which he wanted to conceal because it was partly caused by his negligence. He had to postpone the annual rendering of accounts, and as he could not replace the missing sum the only solution appeared to be to sue his personal debtors, and in so doing render himself odious, hurt the clergy, and then be forced to leave his parish. Things did not, however, come to this pass.

In February 1830 the parish of Saint-Michel at Vaudreuil was canonically erected with boundaries extended at the behest of the seigneur Robert Unwin Harwood*, who did not want to see his domain split. Since losing the hearing in his right ear in 1827, Archambault had been convinced that he could not meet the needs of his parish and he now felt overwhelmed. However, he held out for many years against the appointment of a curate, and attended on his own to the requirements of the parishioners, even those living farthest away. The neighbouring parish priests reproached him on several occasions for extending his services to their parishioners by hearing their confessions, sometimes conducting burials, or giving opinions contrary to theirs. Perhaps all this should be attributed to his seniority in the region or to his great knowledge of people. In any case it is certain that Archambault maintained excellent relations with his neighbours, and sometimes enjoyed ties of the deepest affection, for instance with Augustin Blanchet, the parish priest of Les Cèdres from 1832 to 1833, and then of Coteau-du-Lac from 1833 to 1835. As archpriest of five adjoining parishes, Archambault chaired meetings of the priests in the county and ecclesiastical conferences without imposing his authority.

His notion of the obedience owed to bishops was no mere consent to blind submission, and Archambault made it clearly known. It may have been this liberty of mind that a colleague, who doubtless was jealous, denounced in an anonymous letter sent in August 1835 to Bishop Joseph Signay* of Quebec when there was a possibility that Archambault would be appointed vicar general. The letter made him out to be an enemy of the bishops and of Jean-Jacques Lartigue* in particular, an embarrassment for the neighbouring parish priests, a friend of the Sulpicians and the English party, and an ignoramus. But it is known that Archambault, in the name of the public interest, supported Lartigue at the height of his struggle with the Séminaire de Montréal [*see* Joseph-Vincent QUIBLIER]. As for his ties with the English party, the safest conjecture is that he did everything possible to stay out of their conflict with the Patriotes, although he came close to attacking Ludger DUVERNAY when Duvernay refused to tell him the name of the anonymous author making disparaging remarks about him in the final December issue of *La Minerve* in 1832. He watched with some misgiving the consideration shown in his parish in January 1840 to local heroes of the rebellion. But when the principal agitators of his region became reconciled with the church by taking their Easter communion in April 1841, he regarded the opposition as ended.

The systematic process of consultation with the clergy set up by Ignace Bourget* in the first years of his episcopate reveals Archambault's opinion on many subjects related to the reappraisal of church discipline. In March 1841 he spoke out against dancing outside the family setting: it was a sin that must be confessed. In his view the bishop of Montreal should continue to forbid mixed marriages, which always produced bad results. Every religious denomination should be allowed to build schools in accordance with its convictions, and the priest or minister should by right be a compulsory visitor. It would be very dangerous to carry out the proposal made by the bishops of Quebec and Montreal to put the New Testament in the vernacular into each school, even if the text had accompanying notes. Admitting landowners to the meetings of the *fabrique* would be advisable, but only for the election of churchwardens and the rendering of accounts. When in 1847 Bourget raised the question of reducing the number of cases of absolution reserved for the bishop, Archambault proved a bit more of a rigorist than his younger colleagues. These views provide an interesting illustration of the thinking of a parish priest in the mid 19th century.

Archambault's association with Esther Sureau*, *dit* Blondin, to found the Sisters of St Anne constitutes unquestionably the outstanding achievement of the final part of his life. For 15 years he had followed the slow development of the project conceived by this teacher from Vaudreuil: to bring together a number of women who had not found a place in any community of female religious to teach at Vaudreuil and in the neighbouring parishes in both the girls' schools and the mixed schools set up by law. Archambault was convinced of the timeliness of the project, which Bourget was also encouraging, and from 1848 he supported Esther Sureau's initial experiments. He gave the community its first rule and its first name (Filles de Notre-Dame de Bonsecours et de Sainte-Anne), and decided that the sisters would not wear special clothing except for a black dress when they went out on Sundays and feast-days. The first recruitment surprised him: 35 candidates applied, of whom 15 became postulants after a retreat and 16 a little later. The level of their ability and the financial support available to them appeared to be excellent. This situation reflected the marked resurgence of a religious fervour that was in direct touch with the educational needs of the people. The priest's hopes were, however, to be dashed by the long-standing lay resistance so often encountered in meetings of the *fabrique*. In April 1853 the influential members of the parish exerted pressure to secure a veto on the building on the *fabrique*'s land of a convent that had become absolutely essential. Only three nuns then remained at Vaudreuil, and for Archambault this was a shock from which it was hard to recover. Although he retained a keen interest in the community that he had encouraged, after the sisters left for Saint-Jacques-de-l'Achigan (Saint-Jacques) in August 1853 virtually the only direct action he took was to support them in a conflict with their chaplain, Louis-Adolphe Maréchal*. On this occasion Bourget did not follow his advice, however, and excluded the founder from the management of the community.

When Paul-Loup Archambault died he left a parish equipped with schools, confréries, and a temperance movement, all structures characterizing the revival of Catholicism after 1840. Fervour and unanimity were, however, less evident among the parishioners than would have been expected.

LOUIS ROUSSEAU

AAQ, 12 A, H: f.53v; 1 CB, VIII: 2; 515 CD, I: 179–80, 184–85, 194, 208–9, 217, 231, 235; II: 18a, 22, 24, 26. ACAM, 401.130. AP, Saint-Joseph (Rivière-des-Prairies), Reg. des baptêmes, mariages et sépultures, 22 févr. 1858; Saint-Michel (Vaudreuil), Reg. des baptêmes, mariages et sépultures, 22 févr. 1858. Arch. de la chancellerie de l'évêché de Valleyfield (Valleyfield, Qué.), Île-Perrot, corr., 3 nov., 5 déc. 1835; Saint-Michel, corr., 9 mars 1813; 11 nov. 1815; 25 janv., 22 avril, 30 juill., 24 sept., 8 nov., 9 déc. 1816; 18 mars 1817; 2 mai, 3 déc. 1818; 3 juin 1819; 27 août 1821; 6 août, 29 déc. 1822; 26 avril 1823; 13 déc. 1824; 30 juill. 1826; 22 févr. 1827; 16, 23 nov. 1829; 2 mai 1830; 17 avril 1831; 25 nov. 1832; 4 mars 1833; 11 févr., 14 avril, 29 août 1834; 7 août 1835; 6 déc. 1836; 30 avril, 4 nov. 1838; 1er, 12 janv. 1840; 7 mars, 7 avril, 6 août 1841; 11 juin, 25 juill., 25 nov. 1848; 25 avril, 12 août 1853; 21 févr. 1854; 21 févr. 1858; 18 janv. 1859; Soulanges, corr., 30 juill., 14 août, 24 sept. 1813. ASN, AO, Séminaire, I: 9. *La Minerve*, 4 mars 1858. Allaire, *Dictionnaire*. É.-J.[-A.] Auclair, *Histoire des Sœurs de Sainte-Anne; les premiers cinquante ans, 1850–1900* (Montréal, 1922). Douville, *Hist. du collège-séminaire de Nicolet*, 2: 5. Frédéric Langevin, *Mère Marie-Anne, fondatrice de l'Institut des Sœurs de Sainte-Anne, 1809–1890; esquisse biographique* (2e éd., Montréal, 1937). Sœur Marie-Jean de Pathmos [Laura Jean], *Les Sœurs de Sainte-Anne; un siècle d'histoire* (1v. paru, Lachine, Qué., 1950–). Louis Martin, "Jean Raimbault, curé à Nicolet de 1806 à 1841" (thèse de MA, univ. de Montréal, 1977), 102–20. Eugène Nadeau, *Martyre du silence; mère Marie-Anne, fondatrice des Sœurs de Sainte-Anne (1809–1890)* (Montréal et Lachine, [1956]). Pouliot, *Mgr Bourget et son temps*, 3: 75–97. F.-J. Audet, "Les députés de la vallée de l'Ottawa, John Simpson (1788–1873)," CHA *Report*, 1936: 34.

ARMOUR, ROBERT, businessman, militia officer, and office holder; b. 13 June 1781 in Kilmarnock, Scotland, son of Robert Armour, a shoemaker, and Jean Shaw; m. 1806 Elizabeth Harvie of Kilmarnock, and they had five children; d. 16 April 1857 in Montreal.

Arriving in Montreal in 1798, probably with his brothers Hugh and Shaw, Robert Armour became an auctioneer, and then, at least until 1816, was a partner in the firm Henderson, Armour and Company, general merchants. In 1815 he was appointed a warden of Trinity House, Montreal, an organization which regulated shipping on the St Lawrence. The following year he was named a commissioner for improving inland navigation and also became a partner in the Quebec Steamboat Company which built the *Lauzon*, the first steamboat to ply between Quebec and Pointe-Lévy (Lauzon and Lévis). By 1820 he owned shares in another vessel, the steamboat *Car of Commerce*, travelling between Quebec and Montreal.

In May 1816 Armour had formed a partnership with George Davis (Davies). In June of the following year, together with eight others including George Moffatt*, James Leslie*, and Augustin Cuvillier*, he was a founder of the Bank of Montreal. The bank opened the following December on premises originally owned by Armour and his partner, but then in receivership. Their merchandising business was in serious financial difficulty; Armour had misused £5,024 in public funds with which he had been entrusted and the government had begun to take legal action. Although the outcome of his financial problem is not known, Armour seems to have recovered. Two years later he was cashier (general manager) of the short-lived Bank of Canada. By the late 1820s he was selling dry goods and insurance in Montreal.

Armour became involved in numerous activities outside of his business interests. He was a lieutenant in Montreal's 1st Militia Battalion from at least 1815 to 1821. He served as treasurer of the Scotch Presbyterian Church, later known as the St Gabriel Street Church, from 1815 to 1817 and was ordained elder in 1819. When the congregation split in 1832 between the conservative Reverend Henry ESSON and the evangelical Reverend Edward Black*, the Armours went with Black to form St Paul's Church, but Robert, Esson's friend, helped to calm the dispute.

In April 1827 Armour obtained the office of king's

Armour

printer for the district of Montreal, a post he held until his dismissal on 1 Dec. 1832. Using money from the estate of his late wife which was to have been held in trust for their children, he purchased the languishing *Montreal Gazette* from his friend Thomas Andrew Turner* in May 1827 for £750 and invested another £1,150 in the printing and publishing company. Late in the next year, he transferred ownership to his children as security for the gradual repayment of the £1,900. He would continue to operate the business in trust, paying an annual rent of £100, and was to assume complete control upon the full repayment of the sum due the estate. Under his direction, the refurbished *Montreal Gazette* had a handsome format, was enlarged from four to five columns per page, and by the mid 1830s appeared three times a week. It also fostered local literary and cultural activities. In the growing political unrest after 1828, the *Gazette*, as the leading tory newspaper in Lower Canada, espoused the merchants' complaints about the restrictions of the Constitutional Act of 1791 and even sanctioned the annexation of Montreal to Upper Canada. The newspaper pressed for increased immigration from Britain to the Canadas and urged a larger role for the St Lawrence as a route for American and Canadian produce to Britain, accusing the assembly, which was dominated by French-speaking members, of being anti-trade for refusing to go into debt to improve the waterways. Critical of Louis-Joseph Papineau*, the *Gazette* opposed French Canadian nationalism for its "republicanism," "feudalism," and "corruption." It openly supported the tory constitutionalists and gave its blessing to paramilitary organizations formed by the British population. In March 1836 the paper even predicted "civil warfare" and in June, angry over the attempts of Governor Gosford [Acheson*] to court members of the Patriote party in order to achieve political reconciliation, insisted that he leave the country.

During the 1830s there were numerous changes at the *Gazette*. In May 1831 Armour formed a partnership with his son Andrew Harvie (1809–59) and the printing and publishing firm became known as Andrew H. Armour and Company. Robert Armour may then have taken a less direct role in the business, although he continued to operate his dry goods firm and acted as a real estate and fire insurance agent. From 1828 to 1831 his eldest son, Robert Jr (1806–45), edited *The Montreal almanack, or Lower Canada register . . .*, founded and published by the father. Robert Jr was also "principal Editor" of the *Gazette* "for several years" until 1836. He had attended the University of Edinburgh and read law under Samuel Gale*, receiving his commission as a lawyer in 1829. Robert Jr was appointed registrar and clerk of Trinity House in 1832. In September 1837 he purchased the *Farmer's Advocate and Townships Gazette* (Sherbrooke) and, changing its name to the *Sherbrooke Gazette and Townships Advertiser*, turned the newspaper into a tory organ. The paper ceased publication in 1839. He then served as school visitor for 1839–40 and as law clerk and translator to the Legislative Council from 1841 until his death in 1845.

Meanwhile, in May 1835 Andrew Harvie terminated the partnership with his father and formed another with his brother-in-law, bookseller and publisher Hew Ramsay. The firm Armour and Ramsay acquired Robert Armour's interest in the *Montreal Gazette* in May 1836, publishing it until 1 Aug. 1843. With editors such as David Chisholme* and David Kinnear*, both anti-French and possessing extensive knowledge of constitutional law, the *Gazette* continued to represent British and tory interests in Montreal. The paper was opposed to the establishment of responsible government, which it perceived as a loosening of imperial control over Canadian affairs and an invitation to party corruption and rule by demagogues. It attacked Robert BALDWIN and the entry of the French Canadians, led by Louis-Hippolyte La Fontaine*, into the Executive Council in 1842. For the *Gazette*, this was the loss of everything the tories had gained after 1837, since it signalled the end of attempts to assimilate French Canadians.

Armour and Ramsay were queen's printers to the Special Council from 1838 to 1840. When they sold the *Montreal Gazette* to Robert Abraham in 1843, it was appearing as a daily in the summer months. During the 1840s Armour and Ramsay were the leading booksellers in the Province of Canada, with branches in Kingston and Hamilton, and their business extended into the United States. They countered the growing flood of pirated books and periodicals from the United States by importing cheap "colonial editions" of standard British works, and published reprint editions of the Irish National Series of school-books to meet the increasing demand for textbooks. To publicize these activities they issued *Armour and Ramsay's literary news-letter, and general record of British literature* (1845). In addition, they manufactured ledgers, journals, and cash-books and published the *Presbyterian*, established in 1848 as the organ of the Presbyterian Church of Canada in connection with the Church of Scotland. Earlier, their 1840 publication of John RICHARDSON's historical romance, *The Canadian brothers; or, the prophecy fulfilled*, spurred hopes for a native literature. After their partnership dissolved in 1850, Ramsay conducted the Montreal business until his death in 1857. Andrew Harvie conducted a Toronto bookstore until his death in 1859.

Robert Armour Sr continued his career in the dry goods business. By 1843, apart from his firm Robert Armour and Company, he seems to have formed a partnership with William Whiteford in another wholesale dry goods firm, Armour, Whiteford and Company. During the 1840s Armour also served as director of various businesses including the Montreal Gas Light Company, the Montreal Fire Assurance Company, the City Bank, and the Montreal Provident and Savings Bank. He had withdrawn from the dry goods business by 1850 and probably retired shortly afterwards. He nevertheless continued to hold the position of master of Trinity House, to which he had been appointed in 1834, until his death in 1857.

Robert Armour and his sons Robert Jr and Andrew Harvie were among that group of Scottish businessmen in Montreal whose commercial and political activities clashed with the nationalistic aspirations of the French Canadians. The Armours came to prominence in the final decades of the old British mercantile system. Their successes in business, journalism, and bookselling were undoubtedly due to their own astuteness, but they also gave eloquent voice to the tory views which sustained the British merchant class in the Canadas. Unfortunately for this group, by 1850 their vision of a colonial community was shattered by a combination of local and international changes in politics and trade.

GEORGE L. PARKER

ANQ-M, CN1-7, 13 nov., 30 déc. 1828; CN1-87, 5 juin 1822. GRO (Edinburgh), Kilmarnock, reg. of births and baptisms, 13 June 1781. PAC, MG 24, B2: 858–59, 1612; D8: 8898; L3: 9143 (copies); RG 4, A1, 144: 88; 256: 13, 58; 264: 133; 574: 244–45; RG 7, G20, 2, no.101; 4, no.403; RG 8, I (C ser.), 168: 91–92; 688D: 92. *Chronicle & Gazette*, 9 Dec. 1843. *Montreal Gazette*, 12 Oct. 1813, 3 May 1827–1 Aug. 1843, 6 Oct. 1845, 24 Feb. 1857. *Montreal Herald*, 11 May 1816. *Montreal Transcript*, 17 April 1857. Beaulieu et Hamelin, *La presse québécoise*, 1: 4–7, 71. Borthwick, *Hist. and biog. gazetteer. Montreal directory*, 1843–58. Morgan, *Bibliotheca Canadensis*, 12. Campbell, *Hist. of Scotch Presbyterian Church*, 265–67. D. [G.] Creighton, *The empire of the St. Lawrence* (Toronto, 1956). Denison, *Canada's first bank*. Labarrère-Paulé, *Les instituteurs laïques*. André Lefebvre, *La "Montreal Gazette" et le nationalisme canadien (1835–1842)* (Montréal, 1970). J.-E. Roy, *Hist. de Lauzon*, 4: 59. G. L. Parker, "The British North American book trade in the 1840s: the first crisis," Biblio. Soc. of Canada, *Papers* (Toronto), 12 (1973): 82–99.

ARMS, WILLIAM, blacksmith, businessman, and office holder; b. 28 May 1794 in Deerfield, Mass., son of William Arms and Mercy ——; m. 29 Oct. 1818 Miranda Haven, daughter of a minister at Croydon, N.H., and they had numerous children, of whom four girls and one boy reached adulthood; d. 4 Feb. 1853 in Sherbrooke, Lower Canada.

William Arms immigrated to Lower Canada at an unknown date and settled at Stanstead, an important point of contact between Lower Canada and the United States. There is evidence that he was there by 1816, when the Congregational church was being organized. In addition to working as a blacksmith,

Arms made axes, ploughs, and other equipment. This business expanded as the region developed and in 1832 he formed a partnership with Alba Brown. The firm Arms and Brown concentrated on forging ploughs from American models. In May of that year Arms was a member of a company financing construction of an aqueduct at Stanstead-Plain; the contract included a stipulation that water was to be brought to the Arms and Brown factory.

Arms was a prominent figure in his village. He became an elder of the Congregational church in 1822, and four years later was elected secretary of the Bible Society's local branch. Like several influential people in his circle, he belonged to the famous Golden Rule Lodge; founded in 1814, it was one of the oldest non-military masonic lodges in Lower Canada. In 1821 he had been made an officer of the regional Royal Arch Chapter.

Arms moved his business in 1836 to the village of Sherbrooke, which had been humming with activity since the arrival of the British American Land Company [*see* Sir Alexander Tilloch Galt*]. This company, which planned to develop its vast holdings in the region, owned almost all the commercial and industrial sites in Sherbrooke, so Arms and Brown entered into an agreement with it. In 1839 the firm, which had changed its name to the Sherbrooke Foundry, announced a new model for a kitchen stove invented by Arms, and in 1851 the manufacture of sugar kettles and "any tools needed for Rail road contracts."

Well thought of by his fellow-citizens, Arms often stood surety when contracts were signed, and he was appointed a magistrate in 1841. Aware that means of communication were of vital importance, that year he joined the promoters organizing the Company of Proprietors of the Eastern Townships Rail-road, to link Sherbrooke and Saint-Jean (Saint-Jean-sur-Richelieu). He remained engaged in business until 1851, when he announced his retirement for reasons of health, and sold some of the industrial plant. However, the Sherbrooke Foundry continued to prosper under the management of his son-in-law Samuel Tuck, and profited from the boom in railway construction.

William Arms illustrates well how such pioneers of American origin helped transform their adopted country. Enterprising and resourceful people, they sought to improve their personal circumstances while manifesting civic and community spirit.

MARIE-PAULE R. LABRÈQUE

ANQ-E, CM1, 11 févr. 1853. N.H., Secretary of State Office (Concord), Division of Records Management and Arch., Records of Croydon, selectmen's records (1796–1821). PAC, MG 24, I54, 1: 137; RG 1, L3L: 33952. *Docs. relating to constitutional hist., 1819–28* (Doughty and Story). L.C., Special Council, *Ordinances*, 1840–41, c.10.

Armstrong

British Colonist and St. Francis Gazette (Stanstead, Que.), 1 Dec. 1823, 4 Nov. 1825, 9 Feb. 1826. *Farmer's Advocate and Townships Gazette* (Sherbrooke, Que.), 6 Oct. 1834. *Sherbrooke Gazette and Eastern Townships Advertiser*, 6 Oct. 1834, 31 Aug. 1839, 8 March 1851. Joseph Bouchette, *A topographical description of the province of Lower Canada with remarks upon Upper Canada, and on the relative connexion of both provinces with the United States of America* (London, 1815; repr. [Saint-Lambert, Que., 1973]). C. P. De Volpi and P. H. Scowen, *The Eastern Townships: a pictorial record; historical prints and illustrations of the Eastern Townships of the province of Quebec, Canada* (Montreal, 1962). *Vital records of Deerfield, Massachusetts, to the year 1850*, comp. T. W. Baldwin (Boston, 1920), 20. H. I. Cowan, *British emigration to British North America; the first hundred years* (rev. ed., Toronto, 1961). L.-P. Demers, *Sherbrooke, découvertes, légendes, documents, nos rues et leurs symboles* ([Sherbrooke, 1969]), 88–89, 141–42. B. F. Hubbard, *Forest and clearings; the history of Stanstead County, province of Quebec, with sketches of more than five hundred families*, ed. John Lawrence (Montreal, 1874; repr. 1963).

ARMSTRONG, Sir RICHARD, army officer; b. *c.* 1782 in Lincoln, England, only son of Lieutenant-Colonel Richard Armstrong; m. 3 Nov. 1803 Elizabeth Champion in Edgbaston (Birmingham), England, and they had at least two daughters; d. 3 March 1854 at sea en route from India to England.

Richard Armstrong entered the British army as an ensign on 23 June 1796 and was made captain in the 9th Battalion of Reserve on 9 July 1803. On 31 Jan. 1805 he was appointed to the 8th Veteran Battalion and on 7 July 1808 he joined the 97th Foot. He served on the Iberian Peninsula from August 1808 to the end of the campaign in 1814, during which period he attained the brevet rank of major (30 May 1811) and then the rank of lieutenant-colonel (26 Aug. 1813). He saw service in many battle areas, and while commanding Portuguese regiments in the Pyrenees in 1813 was severely wounded in the arm. He continued in the service of Portugal for six years after the conclusion of the Napoleonic Wars and was remembered with affection by many friends in that country. Armstrong served as a brigadier in the first Burmese War, in the campaigns of 1825–26. He stormed and carried the stockades near Prome (Pye) on 1–5 Dec. 1825. He was promoted colonel on 22 July 1830 and knighted a year later for his military services.

Armstrong was appointed to the army's general staff in Canada in 1841 with the rank of major-general. In July 1842 he succeeded Lieutenant-General John CLITHEROW as commander of the forces in Canada West, with headquarters in Kingston, then the provincial capital. The forces stationed there under Armstrong included royal engineers, companies of artillery, infantry regiments, officials of the commissariat, and detachments of the medical department,

ranging in total strength from about 900 to 1,000. As commander, Armstrong was also responsible for a host of routine administrative matters: transmitting reports on accidental deaths, arguing with Ordnance officers about moth-eaten greatcoats, negotiating deals with deserters, making good the debts of officers, issuing promotions, and responding to officers' requests for ensigncies for their sons.

During his six years in Kingston, Armstrong made a very favourable impression on the populace through his involvement in the community. On 27 Feb. 1844, for instance, he took personal command of the fire-fighting efforts when the Globe Hotel burned, and on 21 November of that year he sat beside Mayor Thomas Weeks Robison at the opening of the new town hall and market building [*see* George Browne*]. Between 300 and 400 people were present at the ceremonies, with music provided by the 14th Foot. In 1846 the Philharmonic Society was founded under the presidency of Armstrong and it flourished until 1849, the year following his departure.

In late September 1848 he left Kingston for New York, where he boarded the *Europa* and sailed back to England. On 16 September Edward John Barker*, the editor of the *British Whig*, had written: "His unostentatious manners, his urbanity and kindness of disposition, the willingness with which he lent his name in aid of all kinds of public undertakings and amusements, his charity and good feeling, have all conspired to render him most extremely popular, and to cause his departure from Kingston to be regretted as a severe loss, a feeling assuaged only by the recollection that the illness from which the gallant soldier has suffered recently, will be entirely removed by the change in air and clime." He was followed as commander at Kingston by Major-General William Rowan*.

In 1849 Armstrong was gazetted colonel of the 95th Foot and a year later he became colonel of the 32nd Foot. He was appointed commander-in-chief of the Madras presidency in 1851 and that November was promoted lieutenant-general. A knight commander of the Portuguese orders of St Benedict of Avís and of the Tower and Sword, he was made a KCB in 1852. His continued ill health forced him to resign his command in Madras in early 1854. He died on his homeward voyage on board the *Barham* on 3 March at the age of 72. Under the terms of his will he left sums of money to various relatives as well as a number of leasehold houses in London to his daughter Emma Champion Roberts.

OTTE A. ROSENKRANTZ

Birmingham Reference Library (Birmingham, Eng.), Reg. of marriages for the parish of St Bartholomew, Edgbaston [Birmingham], 3 Nov. 1803. PAC, RG 8, I (C ser.). PRO, PROB 11/2189/27. *Annual Reg.* (London), 1854: 273–74.

Gentleman's Magazine, 1803: 1085; July–December 1833: 380; July–December 1854: 191. *British Whig*, 30 Jan. 1844; 9, 16 Sept. 1848. *Chronicle & Gazette*, 23 Nov. 1844. *Times* (London), 13 April 1854. G.B., WO, *Army list*, 1805–6. *Hart's army list*, 1853. Peter Kemp, *The British sailor: a social history of the lower deck* (London, 1970). A. M. Machar, *The story of old Kingston* (Toronto, 1908). J. A. Roy, *Kingston: the king's town* (Toronto, 1952). J. [W.] Spurr, "The Kingston Garrison, 1815–1870," *Historic Kingston*, no.20 (1972): 14–34.

ARNOLD, WILLIAM, Church of England clergyman; b. 25 Dec. 1804 in Blackrock (Republic of Ireland); m. first probably in 1828 Maria Charlotte O'Hara, granddaughter of Felix O'Hara*, and they had four daughters; m. secondly *c.* 1842 Ellen Boyle of Gaspé, Canada East, and they had one daughter; d. 25 May 1857 in Gaspé.

William Arnold immigrated to Upper Canada with his parents, who settled near Hamilton. He studied for some time under the direction of two missionaries of the Society for the Propagation of the Gospel, the reverends Robert Blakey and John Wilson. On the recommendation of Bishop Jacob Mountain* in 1824, Arnold, the son "of parents very respectable, but much straitened in their means," received an SPG studentship. Two years later he was summoned to Quebec, ordained deacon, and appointed to the mission of New Carlisle and Paspébiac, with a salary of £100 paid by the SPG. Ordained priest at Quebec on 28 Oct. 1827, Arnold was unable to return immediately to his Baie des Chaleurs mission because of ice conditions and thus ministered to isolated settlements in the Quebec region throughout the winter and early spring.

Not long after his return to Baie des Chaleurs, Arnold married Maria Charlotte O'Hara, a member of a prominent Gaspé family. Some time before November 1828 he wrote to the bishop of Quebec and the SPG requesting that the cure of Gaspé be annexed to his charge so that he could be near his wife who had returned to live with her family because of illness. The SPG replied in January 1829 by transferring him to Gaspé. Arnold's new mission included the settlements from Grande-Grève to Percé on the northeastern tip of the peninsula and he seems to have endured the difficulties of travelling between the scattered and isolated villages of his charge with patience and fortitude. He was active in promoting education and was a frequent visitor to many small community schools. Although he probably had no formal medical training, he had acquired a reputation as a doctor by bandaging wounds and setting broken bones. By 1835, however, Bishop Charles James Stewart* wrote to the SPG that Arnold had "a permanent rheumatic affection of the thigh and cannot stand the boats and snowshoes" and recommended that "as he believed he could do good work in another place . . . he should be removed before the winter." No action was taken. Two years later Bishop George Jehoshaphat Mountain* visited him and reported that "poor Mr Arnold contracted at Gaspé a habit of too free indulgence in the use of liquor." Arnold appears to have left Gaspé under a cloud.

During 1837–38 Arnold served the missions of Lachute and Gore Township. In October of the latter year he began work in the area around Bury and Dudswell in the Eastern Townships, where he took a special interest in Sunday schools and, according to Bishop Mountain, "gained the respect and affection of everybody." None the less, Mountain also wrote that "poor Mr Arnold . . . became ensnared again at Montreal, on a visit to that City, & so lost himself that he cannot be again employed in the Church." Mountain seems to have relented, for Arnold was appointed assistant to the Reverend William Devereux Baldwyn at Saint-Jean (Saint-Jean-sur-Richelieu) in late 1839. Arnold was active in this ministry: he served Lachine and La Prairie, established congregations at Sabrevois and L'Acadie, and was military chaplain. However, on 4 March 1840 his wife died and, faced with the prospect of bringing up four young daughters, he requested that he be stationed at the Gaspé mission so that his children could live with their maternal grandmother. Permission was granted and Arnold was at Gaspé by spring 1842.

Shortly after his return, Arnold married Ellen Boyle and settled his family in the home he had built some years previously. In 1844 he applied to the SPG for a post in Van Diemen's Land (Tasmania, Australia) but did not go. Instead he ministered to the people of Gaspé for another 13 years. In his reports to the SPG he explained some of the difficulties faced by his parishioners, mainly poor fishermen and their families, who were "charged 150 to 200 per cent above the regular market price for food, clothing & fishing tackle." They "commence the fishing season overwhelmed with a debt previously contracted, for articles consumed before hand, which the most successful result of their endeavour can scarcely meet." According to Arnold, as long as the bartering system continued, "the few capitalists" would continue to hold the fishermen "in complete thraldom."

By the early 1850s the Gaspé mission had increased in size so as to require two ministers. Despite the setbacks of his early career, Arnold continued his ministry until his death, establishing churches and chapels and promoting education. A devoted husband and father, he had also shown concern for both the spiritual and the temporal welfare of his parishioners.

MALCOLM A. HUGHES

AC, Gaspé (Percé), État civil, Anglicans, Protestant Episcopal Congregation (Gaspé), 26 May 1857. ACC-Q, 52;

Arthur

105: 26, 36. USPG, C/CAN/Que./folders 368, 370, 420; Journal of SPG, 35: 201–2; 37: 32–33; 38: 351; 40: 318–23. *Morning Chronicle* (Quebec), 10 June 1857. Millman, *Life of Charles James Stewart*. E. B. Mills, *Remembrance* (n.p., [1932]). C.-E. Roy et Lucien Brault, *Gaspé depuis Cartier* (Québec, 1934).

ARTHUR, Sir GEORGE, army officer and colonial administrator; b. 21 June 1784 in Plymouth, England, youngest son of John Arthur and Catherine Cornish; m. 13 June 1814 Elizabeth Orde Usher Smith in Half Way Tree (Kingston), Jamaica, and they had seven sons and five daughters; d. 19 Sept. 1854 in London.

George Arthur passed his youth in "comfortable circumstances" in Plymouth, where his father, a wealthy brewer, had been elected mayor the year prior to his birth. On 25 Aug. 1804 George became an ensign in the 91st Foot and the following June he was promoted to lieutenant in the 35th Foot. His military career was not unusually distinguished, since it was confined to participation in a series of relatively unimportant and mainly ill-fated campaigns against Napoleon. In 1806 he was incapacitated by fever while serving in Sir James Henry Craig*'s abortive expedition in Italy. The following year he was wounded during the unsuccessful siege of Rosetta (Rashīd) in Egypt. On 5 May 1808 while on leave in England he purchased his captaincy.

During the disastrous expedition to Walcheren, Netherlands, in 1809, he served as deputy assistant adjutant-general and received praise for his part in the attack on Flushing (Vlissingen), in which he was wounded once again. From 1810 to 1812 he acted as aide-de-camp and military secretary to Lieutenant-General George Don, the lieutenant governor of Jersey, and on 5 Nov. 1812 he was gazetted major in the 7th West India Regiment, which he joined in Jamaica. There he acted as assistant quartermaster general and for a few months as paymaster general, and he met and married Elizabeth, the second daughter of Colonel John Frederick Sigismund Smith, the officer commanding the artillery in the colony. Shortly after the marriage, Arthur was appointed superintendent and commandant of the British settlement on the coast of Honduras (Belize) and assumed office in July 1814. He was given the local rank of colonel and on 1 June 1815 became a lieutenant-colonel in the army.

Although Honduras was technically in Spanish territory, its rich timber resources had attracted British settlers who established a community that by 1816 numbered 3,800, of whom 2,740 were slaves. Initially, as he embarked upon a program of civic improvement, Arthur was popular with the small white élite. Gradually, however, his authoritarian manner and the rigid way in which he enforced the imperial customs regulations caused his popularity to

wane. In 1820 an expedition which he led to suppress a slave revolt aroused his hitherto dormant humanitarianism and he sought to introduce the Jamaican slave code into Honduras in order to provide legal protection for the local slaves. In 1822 he decided to free the descendants of the Miskito Indians who he believed had been illegally enslaved. These actions alienated the slave owners and led to growing opposition. Arthur responded by dismissing his opponents from office and by attempting to render the system of government in the settlement less democratic. When he went back to England on sick leave in 1822, the settlers sent an agent to London to lobby against his return. Arthur was also embarrassed by a court action brought by Lieutenant-Colonel Thomas Bradley whom he had dismissed for disobedience and thrown into prison in 1820. Bradley was awarded compensation for his ten-month confinement and a confidential report from Sir Herbert Taylor, secretary to the commander-in-chief, the Duke of York, criticized Arthur for his "most tyrannical, arbitrary and capricious conduct." None the less Arthur was appointed lieutenant governor of Van Diemen's Land (Tasmania, Australia) in 1823 and took control of the government in May the following year.

In 1824 half of the population of Van Diemen's Land were convicts and their number would increase from 6,000 to 18,000 by 1836. Faced with this rapidly growing convict population and persistent complaints in Britain that transportation was not a sufficiently severe deterrent to crime, Arthur created a carefully graded system of reward and punishment for convicts sent to the colony. At one extreme were the penal settlements, particularly Port Arthur which he founded in 1830, where conditions were harsh and the labour unremitting. At the other extreme was the assignment of prisoners to work for settlers. In between were the work gangs where conditions varied with the behaviour of the convicts. Arthur personally supervised every part of the system and believed in its efficiency as a means of discouraging criminal behaviour. Although his primary concern was to control the convict population, he also sought to prevent unnecessary brutality and to encourage reformation, particularly of younger offenders for whom he established a separate institution. In two pamphlets published in 1833 and 1835 and in the evidence he gave to a select committee of the House of Commons in 1837, he defended transportation as "the most effective, as well as the most humane punishment that the wit of man ever devised." Viewing Van Diemen's Land as "an extensive Gaol," he opposed the introduction of trial by jury and representative institutions and thus antagonized the free settlers and the emancipated convicts. As in Honduras, he reacted violently to any sign of opposition and sought to muzzle the local press and to dismiss his opponents from office. Amid a growing volume of criticism he was recalled in 1836 but again succeeded in vindicating his conduct on his return to England in 1837. That spring he received a KCH from William IV and on 19 July was among the first to be knighted by the young Queen Victoria. In November he was appointed lieutenant governor of Upper Canada and, when word of rebellion there reached England, he was given the local rank of major-general.

Arthur took control of the government of Upper Canada from Sir Francis Bond Head* on 23 March 1838. His immediate problem was to dispose of the prisoners arrested during the abortive rebellion. The reformers appealed to him to adopt a "lenient Course" while the conservatives demanded "energetic measures." Since Arthur believed that "a few" of the leading rebels ought to be punished "with comparative severity," he allowed Samuel Lount* and Peter Matthews* to be put to death on 12 April, even though he received numerous petitions on their behalf. Arthur was also prepared to execute the Irish-American Patriot Edward Alexander THELLER, but, in view of the legal objections raised by Chief Justice John Beverley Robinson*, granted a respite and referred the case to London for instructions. The execution of Lount and Matthews was a harsh act but both Head and the members of the Executive Council had wanted more Draconian measures and most moderates, including many reformers, approved of Arthur's decision. Moreover, Arthur sought to "temper justice with mercy" by releasing those against whom the evidence was weak, by keeping to a minimum the number sentenced to transportation, and by pardoning as many as possible. The Executive Council wished to banish anyone implicated in the rebellion, but Arthur refused, even though he distrusted the loyalty of the reformers and was aware that his policy was not popular with the conservatives.

During 1838, the activities of American Patriots and Canadian refugees kept the Upper Canadian border in a state of almost constant turmoil. Though subordinate to and occasionally at odds with Sir John Colborne*, the commander-in-chief of the forces in the Canadas, Arthur personally supervised the defence of Upper Canada. For 12 months, he noted at the end of 1839, he had had nearly 18,000 men under his command and he greatly improved the efficiency of the militia. Although Arthur shared the anti-American sentiments of his predecessor and at times exaggerated the extent of rebel activity, he believed that Head's incautious language was partly responsible for the crisis along the border and he sought to establish cordial relations with officials in New York State. When the American government failed to restrain the Patriots, Arthur gloomily predicted that a war with the United States was inevitable, but he adhered to a policy of cooperating with American

officials and of preventing the militia from engaging in actions that would give the Americans grounds for retaliation. By his moderation he thus contributed to a peaceful solution to the crisis in American-Canadian relations.

None the less, in order to crush "this most unparalleled, wicked conspiracy," Arthur concluded that it was necessary to deal more severely with those captured in the border raids than with those involved in the original rebellion. His reaction in June 1838 to the Short Hills raid on the Niagara frontier was to call for the execution of "no less than four prisoners," one in ten of those arrested. In fact, only James Morreau was put to death before the new governor-in-chief, Lord Durham [Lambton*], decided to issue a general amnesty. Arthur had learned "with equal surprise and disappointment" that Durham was to be given extensive powers over the lieutenant governors. Although Arthur, with the full support of his Executive Council, continued to deny that Durham had the constitutional authority to interfere with "the ordinary course of justice" in Upper Canada when not actually in residence there, he followed Durham's orders and in late August commuted the sentences of Jacob R. Beamer*, Samuel Chandler*, and Benjamin Wait*. Relations between the two men remained strained. When Durham had visited Upper Canada in July, he found Arthur "full of littlenesses about etiquette, precedence, official dignity, etc." Arthur was convinced that Durham's initial constitutional proposals for a union of the Canadas were unsound and that Durham's policy of granting clemency to captured Patriots had failed to act as a deterrent to further raids, although on 1 October he claimed to "deeply lament" Durham's decision to resign.

Following two major clashes, at Prescott in November 1838 and at Windsor in December, 17 of those taken prisoner were executed. Arthur examined each case with "the utmost deliberation" and ensured that only the most prominent of those captured, such as Nils Gustaf von Schoultz* and Joshua Gwillen Doan*, were put to death. Over the objections of Henry Stephen Fox, the British minister in Washington, he released all those recommended for mercy and all those under 21 years of age. After tempers had cooled in Upper Canada, he also released a number of those condemned to transportation to Australia and induced his Executive Council to approve a more lenient policy than they wished. Even Francis Hincks*'s *Examiner*, a Toronto reform newspaper usually critical of Arthur, admitted in 1840 that he deserved "credit for a greater degree of tact than we had previously thought him possessed of." Yet Arthur's position was a difficult one since he was concerned not to antagonize the loyalist militia of the colony. For this reason he did not publicly criticize Colonel John Prince* for ordering the summary

Arthur

execution of five prisoners at Windsor, although he was enraged by Prince's "injudicious and improper" behaviour.

In allying himself with the province's conservatives on most issues Arthur was following the instructions he had been given in London. But these instructions had been prepared before the Colonial Office realized that Head had deliberately underestimated the extent of the discontent in the colony, and after the rebellion the Colonial Office stressed the need to reconcile the moderate reformers who had been alienated by Head's partisanship. Arthur, too, soon came to believe that disaffection was more widespread than Head had indicated, but feared that the number of reformers "decidedly attached to British Connexion" was "limited." En route to Upper Canada in March 1838 he had visited the home of Governor William Learned Marcy of New York where he met Marshall Spring Bidwell*, a meeting which convinced him that the "real object of the leaders" of the reform party was "the subversion of the Government." Although he was prepared to allow the majority of Canadian refugees in the United States to return to Upper Canada, he would not encourage Bidwell to return from the exile into which he had unfairly been forced by Head. Arthur also supported Head's refusal to reinstate George Ridout*, a known reformer, as a district judge and he declined to restore James Scott Howard* to the office of postmaster of Toronto, even though there was no evidence that Howard was linked to the rebellion. Arthur justified his policy by arguing that it was important not to annoy the "loyal population" since upon them "I must mainly depend for the protection of this Province." He surrounded himself with advisers associated with the old "family compact," such as John Beverley Robinson, Christopher Alexander Hagerman*, and John MACAULAY. He even reappointed Head's secretary, John JOSEPH, as his own, though he soon replaced him with Macaulay. Although claiming that he sought "Recruits" from among the moderate reformers, Arthur, in fact, made no serious effort to do so, thus confirming the suspicion of moderates such as Egerton Ryerson* that he was not to be trusted.

Arthur also antagonized many colonists by his cool and aloof manner. A devout evangelical, he preferred to abstain "from all public amusements" and refused to patronize activities, such as horse-racing, of which he disapproved. He normally dressed in dark clothes and entertained reluctantly. Like many evangelicals, he was extremely conservative in his political and social views. But he also embraced the evangelical commitment to the doctrine of "imperial trusteeship." In Honduras he had espoused the cause of the slaves and the native peoples. In Van Diemen's Land he issued a proclamation warning the settlers that he would prosecute those who committed acts of aggression against the rapidly declining aboriginal population but, because of pressure from the colonists, he decided to remove the natives from the settled areas of the colony and thus inadvertently contributed to the extinction of the very people he sought to help. In Upper Canada he also revealed a genuine concern for the welfare of the "much ill used" native peoples. In September 1838 he visited the Six Nations Indians, who had loyally responded to his request for military assistance during the Short Hills affair, and he promised to prevent any further alienation of their land without their consent. That December he instructed the provincial secretary, Richard Alexander Tucker*, to examine how intruders upon Indian lands could be summarily removed and two years later he argued that the Ojibwas of the Saugeen (Bruce) Peninsula should be given additional compensation for the land that Head had persuaded them to surrender to the government in 1836. Yet Arthur's ultimate concern, like that of most evangelicals and indeed of most men of the time, was not to preserve the Indians' culture but to ease their total assimilation into white society.

As a devout evangelical, Arthur was also determined to assist the activities of the Church of England, including its missionary efforts. He corresponded with the archbishop of Canterbury and with the bishop of London and, according to George Ryerson*, travelled in Upper Canada "with two and sometimes three Episcopal ministers." His relations with Archdeacon John Strachan* of Toronto were less cordial. In 1838 he supported Strachan's imminent appointment as the first bishop of Upper Canada solely because Strachan was willing to serve without an additional salary. During 1839 and 1840 the two men quarrelled violently over educational policy as Arthur proposed diverting funds from King's College (University of Toronto) to Upper Canada College, and in 1840 Arthur privately rebuked Strachan for publicly opposing government policy. Arthur also disagreed with Strachan's efforts to secure all the funds arising from the sale of the clergy reserves for the Church of England, but he himself favoured the Anglican church and seriously underestimated the degree of resentment which had developed in Upper Canada against its privileged position. He approved of former lieutenant governor Sir John Colborne's unpopular decision to endow 44 rectories for the Church of England, the legality of which had been affirmed in January 1838 while Arthur was en route to Canada. His own efforts to resolve the clergy reserves issue were well intentioned but naïve. In 1839 he persuaded the Upper Canadian legislature to pass a bill reinvesting the reserves in the crown, but his critics legitimately viewed the proposed division of the reserves by an Anglican-dominated British parliament as unfairly benefiting the established church. Arthur's Clergy

Reserves Bill was disallowed in London on technical grounds and his intervention simply added to the distrust in which he was held by the reformers. So did his support for Wesleyan Methodists connected with the conservative British Wesleyan Conference instead of for the more numerous members of the Canada Conference led by Egerton Ryerson and his brothers William* and John*.

Arthur repeatedly claimed he was not a "party man" and in a literal sense this was so. His relationship with the conservative majority in the House of Assembly was extremely tenuous and during the 1839 session he was unable to persuade them to adopt most of the measures he had recommended in his speech from the throne. Sensitive to complaints that the "Canadian Party . . . monopolized all Political influence and Patronage," he did broaden the base of his administration by distributing appointments to recent immigrants to the colony, such as Richard Alexander Tucker, the former chief justice of Newfoundland, who had become his provincial secretary in 1838, and Samuel Bealey Harrison*, whom he recruited as his civil secretary in 1839. None the less, he did bestow his patronage almost exclusively on conservatives. In 1838 he had submitted to Lord Glenelg, the colonial secretary, a list of 27 names he recommended as possible appointees to the Legislative Council; 20 were members of the Church of England and the nominees included such prominent conservatives as Robert Sympson JAMESON, John Simcoe MACAULAY, and Peter Boyle DE BLAQUIÈRE. According to the *British Colonist* in March 1839, Arthur's opinions were largely "derived from the *clique* by whom he is surrounded." When Lord Durham delivered a stinging attack on that clique in his famous *Report on the affairs of British North America* (1839), Arthur claimed that he was "much misinformed." He rejected Durham's proposals for reform and vainly sought to contain the rapidly growing popular movement in favour of responsible government. At the same time he did not deny that many of Durham's specific criticisms of the administrative structure of the colony were valid.

Arthur had already taken some measures to improve the efficiency of the government. In 1838 he had pushed for, and eventually was allowed to make, changes in the commissariat but failed to get "a good Militia Act" through the assembly the following year. Early in 1839 he had commissioned John Macaulay to investigate and redefine the secretarial offices and to suggest which functions of the civil secretary might be transferred to the provincial secretary. That February he asked Justice James Buchanan MACAULAY to report on the workings of the Indian Department. In April he ordered an investigation into the management of the endowments of Upper Canada College and King's College and subsequently dismissed the

bursar, Colonel Joseph WELLS, for misusing the funds placed under his control. The publication of the Durham report in February added to the pressure for administrative reform and in May the assembly asked Arthur to appoint a commission of inquiry into the operation of most public offices. Although the commission and the eight subcommittees appointed by Arthur were staffed mainly by office holders, including William ALLAN, Augustus Warren Baldwin*, and Henry SHERWOOD, sweeping changes were recommended in 1840 for a number of departments. Particularly damning were the revelations of financial incompetence and mismanagement in the offices of Robert Baldwin SULLIVAN (commissioner of crown lands and surveyor general), John Henry DUNN (receiver general), and John Macaulay (inspector general of public accounts). Arthur began introducing reforms in various departments but the union of the Canadas delayed the further implementation of the commission's reports and it was Charles Edward Poulett Thomson* who would reap the benefits of Arthur's labours.

To Arthur's dismay, Thomson was commissioned governor-in-chief in September 1839 with the same extensive powers over the lieutenant governors as Durham had possessed. On 21 November Thomson arrived in Toronto and assumed control of the administration in order to persuade the legislature to vote for union with Lower Canada. Arthur believed that union would give power to the reformers whose loyalty was suspect and would ultimately lead to separation from Great Britain. Although he tried to dissuade Thomson from implementing union, he obediently followed his instructions. He acted as Thomson's intermediary with William Henry Draper* and other Upper Canadian conservatives and helped to persuade several of them to vote for union. In private, he remained sympathetic to the views of those ultra conservatives, such as John Beverley Robinson, who continued to oppose union. As well, he caballed with a former lieutenant governor, Lord Seaton [Colborne], to undermine those parts of Thomson's measure, particularly the creation of powerful district councils, which were most objectionable to the conservatives. Ironically, in playing this double game Arthur alienated Robinson and many other former friends among the ultra conservatives.

On 19 Feb. 1840 Thomson, who would become Baron Sydenham that summer, returned to Lower Canada and, though Arthur resumed only nominal control of the government of Upper Canada, he became actively involved in the political prelude to union. He repeatedly warned Thomson against placing too much faith in Robert BALDWIN and correctly assessed the danger which Baldwin posed to the governor's system of non-party government under union, as Thomson later admitted. After the conservatives won the municipal election in Toronto in late 1840, Baldwin withdrew as a candidate for the city in the subsequent provincial election but Arthur claimed some responsibility for persuading his running mate, the influential pro-union reformer John Henry Dunn, to stay in the race. Yet Arthur antagonized the reformers by showing favouritism to the conservatives in the distribution of patronage in Upper Canada. Baldwin warned Sydenham in January 1841 that Arthur's actions were causing "jealousies & dissentions." Sydenham therefore increasingly distributed patronage himself, but was sufficiently pleased with Arthur's behaviour to ask him to remain in Upper Canada after union was proclaimed. He reluctantly agreed and on 10 February assumed office as deputy governor of the united province.

Despite his conservative sympathies, when the first general election under the union was held in March 1841 Arthur assisted Samuel Bealey Harrison, the provincial secretary and a moderate reformer, in ensuring that a majority of the candidates elected were sympathetic to Sydenham's views. But Arthur's health was not good and he found the role of deputy governor "unpleasant"; in late March he left for England. His departure was little mourned. Many conservatives considered him a turncoat and they boycotted a public dinner held in his honour. He was only marginally more popular with the reformers, who justly remained suspicious of his commitment to the new order.

Upon his return to England Arthur was created a baronet as a reward for what Sydenham described as the "very generous and disinterested assistance" he had given him. For nearly a year Arthur sought more tangible proof of the government's gratitude and in March 1842 was appointed governor and commander-in-chief of the presidency of Bombay. He arrived in India in June and was plunged into the war against Afghanistan. He also assisted in the campaign in Sind (Pakistan) and in 1844–45 suppressed a rebellion in his presidency. Although subordinate to the central government in Calcutta, he was able to introduce some useful reforms in Bombay and supported a revision of the land assessment system. In 1846 he was nominated to succeed Lord Hardinge as governor general of India in the event of an emergency but fell seriously ill and was forced to resign. That September he arrived back in England and two months later was promoted to major-general. He was also made a member of the Privy Council and was awarded the honorary degree of DCL by the University of Oxford. But he did not forget Canada and maintained a private correspondence on affairs there. He regarded Robert Baldwin's appointment as attorney general for Upper Canada in 1848 as an "extraordinary" step and predicted trouble from the association in the "Responsible Govt. party" of "some Ultra Republicans of

Upper Canada" and the "most violent men of the French Party in Lower Canada." In May 1849 he joined with his predecessor as lieutenant governor, Sir Francis Bond Head, in blaming Durham's policy of responsible government for the rebellion losses crisis in Montreal in late April [see James Bruce*]. Arthur devoted most of his time, however, to family and personal business. He rose to the rank of lieutenant-general in June 1854, and died in retirement in London that September.

Over the next half-century Arthur's reputation was blackened by hostile and exaggerated accounts of his activities in Van Diemen's Land and Canada circulated in North America by Patriots who had been exiled to Australia [see Daniel D. Heustis*]. These stories hardened into a tradition perpetuated by later apologists of the Patriots such as Charles Lindsey* and Edwin Clarence Guillet*. Despite the efforts of Charles Rupert Sanderson* and Alan George Lewers Shaw to redeem Arthur's reputation, he is still best remembered in Canada for allowing the execution of Lount and Matthews and for opposing responsible government. This emphasis is undoubtedly unfair. Arthur was not primarily responsible for the blood shed in 1838 and 1839. Indeed he played a moderating role under difficult circumstances and may well have prevented greater violence. He did oppose responsible government but he also introduced a number of useful administrative reforms into the existing system of government in Upper Canada, and the claim of his opponents that he was not fit for the government of a free colony was patently unfair. None the less, while he was neither bloodthirsty nor completely reactionary, he remains a rather unattractive figure. He was frequently petty and vindictive and he could be self-serving and hypocritical. By his dutiful support of Sydenham's policies, he did betray those conservatives who had trusted him. He condemned land speculation and nepotism in Upper Canada but had been guilty of both in Van Diemen's Land. In the midst of a severe financial crisis in Upper Canada he spent more than £2,000 on improvements to Government House and asked for another £1,000 for furniture.

George Arthur was the last lieutenant governor of Upper Canada. He was also one of the last of a dying breed of soldier-administrators who served their apprenticeship in the Napoleonic Wars and rose by ability rather than through interest. The Upper Canadian House of Assembly praised his "ability, uprightness and impartiality," yet Charles Poulett Thomson was also justified in describing him as "well intentioned" but "with the narrowest mind I ever met." While Arthur was a competent administrator he was also immune to most of the currents of reform of the period. He believed that his duty was simply "to serve faithfully the *Government*" in London, even if it meant abandoning his own principles, and since the British government of the day was more liberal than he was, his term of office in Canada was productive of more good than evil.

PHILLIP BUCKNER

[A handsome oil portrait of Sir George Arthur, now in the possession of Lady Raynor Arthur, is reproduced on the frontispiece of A. G. L. Shaw's biography, cited below.

The major sources for this study were the Colonial Office files in the PRO, especially CO 42/446–77, and Arthur's Canadian papers in the MTL. Most of these have been published in the *Arthur papers* (Sanderson), but an additional volume of Canadian material remains in manuscript, as does the MTL's collection of Arthur's India papers, which deal with his later Indian career and the last few years of his life in England. Other useful primary sources include the Upper Canada state books (PAC, RG 1, E1), vols.55–57, and the *Journal* of its House of Assembly for 1839; [Charles] Grey, *Crisis in the Canadas: 1838–1839, the Grey journals and letters*, ed. W. G. Ormsby (Toronto, 1964); [C. E. P. Thomson, 1st Baron] Sydenham, *Letters from Lord Sydenham, governor-general of Canada, 1839–1841, to Lord John Russell*, ed. Paul Knaplund (London, 1931); and Benjamin Wait, *The Wait letters*, ed. Mary Brown (Erin, Ont., 1976). Numerous references to Arthur occur in Toronto newspapers of the period 1838–41, especially in the *British Colonist*, *Christian Guardian*, and *Examiner*. There is a useful "Military obituary" in the *United Service Gazette, and Naval and Military Chronicle* (London), 30 Sept. 1854, also published as a separate pamphlet under the title *Lieutenant General the Right Hon. Sir George Arthur, bart., K.C.H., D.C.L.* (n.p., n.d.); a copy of the latter is available at MTL.

The definitive biography is A. G. L. Shaw, *Sir George Arthur, bart., 1784–1854: superintendent of British Honduras, lieutenant-governor of Van Diemen's Land and of Upper Canada, governor of the Bombay presidency* (Melbourne, Australia, 1980). Also useful are W. D. Forsyth, *Governor Arthur's convict system, Van Diemen's Land, 1824–36: a study in colonization* (London, 1935); S. W. Jackman, *A slave to duty: a portrait sketch of Sir George Arthur, bart., PC, KCH* (Melbourne, 1979); M. C. I. Levy, *Governor George Arthur, a colonial benevolent despot* (Melbourne, 1953); Walter Sage, "Sir George Arthur and his administration of Upper Canada," Queen's Univ., Depts. of Hist. and of Political and Economic Science, *Bull.* (Kingston, Ont.), no.28 (July 1918); C. R. Sanderson, "Sir George Arthur, last lieutenant governor of Upper Canada, 1838–1841: a vindication" (MA thesis, Univ. of Toronto, 1940); and the entries in D. B. Read, *The lieutenant-governors of Upper Canada and Ontario, 1792–1899* (Toronto, 1900), ADB, and DNB. Particularly valuable for Arthur's Canadian career is B. C. Murison, "'Enlightened government': Sir George Arthur and the Upper Canadian administration," *Journal of Imperial and Commonwealth Hist.* (London), 8 (1979–80): 161–80, which is based upon her MA thesis, "Sir George Arthur in Upper Canada: politics and administration, 1838–41" (Univ. of Western Ont., London, 1977).

Arthur's role in dealing with the unrest along the border is variously assessed in Guillet, *Lives and times of Patriots*;

Fred Landon, *An exile from Canada to Van Diemen's Land; being the story of Elijah Woodman, transported overseas for participation in the Upper Canada troubles of 1837–38* (Toronto, 1960); J. P. Martyn, "Upper Canada and border incidents, 1837–38: a study of the troubles on the American frontier following the rebellion of 1837" (MA thesis, Univ. of Toronto, 1962); two works by Colin Read, *The rising in western Upper Canada, 1837–8: the Duncombe revolt and after* (Toronto, 1982) and "The Short Hills raid of June, 1838, and its aftermath," *OH*, 68 (1976): 93–109; and R. C. Watt, "The political prisoners in Upper Canada," *English Hist. Rev.* (London and New York), 41 (1926): 526–55. Other aspects of Arthur's career are discussed in I. M. Abella, "The 'Sydenham election' of 1841," *CHR*, 47 (1966): 326–43; C. M. H. Clark, *A history of Australia* (5v., [Melbourne], 1962–81); G. [S.] French, *Parsons & politics: the rôle of the Wesleyan Methodists in Upper Canada and the Maritimes from 1780 to 1855* (Toronto, 1962); J. E. Hodgetts, *Pioneer public service: an administrative history of the united Canadas, 1841–1867* (Toronto, 1955); A. G. L. Shaw, *Convicts and the colonies: a study of penal transportation from Great Britain and Ireland to Australia and other parts of the British Empire* (London, 1966); Clive Turnbull, *Black war: the extermination of the Tasmanian aborigines* (Melbourne and London, 1948); and [G.] A. Wilson, *The clergy reserves of Upper Canada, a Canadian mortmain* (Toronto, 1968).   P.B.]

AYRE, WILLIAM, teacher; b. 1782 or 1783 in Ireland; d. 14 April 1855 in Halifax.

Little is known of William Ayre's early life. By his own account, he taught school in Nova Scotia for some time before 1832 when he was teaching in the vicinity of Antigonish. In 1835 he left the mainland for Port Hood, Cape Breton, where after a short stay his licence was withdrawn. Despite reputedly excellent qualifications, his career was marred by one serious flaw – he found it difficult to remain sober for any length of time! His career thereafter was remarkable for great bouts of spending, innumerable debts, and an almost constant flow of petitions to government officials to have his licence restored.

In 1836 Ayre left Port Hood but remained in Cape Breton, teaching without a licence and without government assistance in Hillsboro and Mabou during the following year. In June 1837 he began building a seminary for general education at Mabou, but lack of money soon caused his school to become known as "Ayre's Folly." In 1839 he sent a petition to Lieutenant Governor Sir Colin Campbell* asking that his licence be restored, which would make his school eligible for government aid. He tried yet again in the following year, but his application was opposed by the authorities at his former school in Port Hood. Defending himself against their allegations, Ayre argued that the "petitioner's school regulations provide that after each examination, he shall have a few days vacation, when if he visits his friends and takes a Gala day to himself, it is not understood that he was accountable for the same. . . . It is notorious that the Port Hood schoolhouse was the place where the guardians of youth and education met to fight their family battles. . . . Petitioner quit Port Hood schoolhouse. The school did not quit him." Despite his best efforts both petitions were refused. Undaunted, he appealed again, and on 22 April 1841, by order in council "in consideration of his age and great usefulness as a teacher," the amount owing him was paid, and it is presumed his licence was reissued at this time as he continued to teach in the province.

In 1844, while teaching in North East Margaree, Ayre advertised his school in the *Novascotian*, noting that "the School Department is furnished by the Teacher with a Library consisting of: approved School Books, Nautical and Scientific works, Drawing Paper, Stationery, . . . Spelling Books, Chambers' Educational course, Grammars, Dictionaries, Jones's writing system, Morrison's and other Arithmetics, . . . all of which he vends to his students on accommodating terms." He also appears to have had an interest in adult education for he added, "to which Library, as well as to the perusal of two weekly newspapers, adult scholars have access on favourable conditions."

Ayre's well-written complaints to various school boards and government officials suggest that he himself had probably had a superior education. His bills were always detailed. In 1849, when his annual salary was about £128, he sent in another petition claiming £121, including five shillings for the "treats" of rum and shrub, a beverage made from fruit, sometimes containing spirits. Writing to the *Nova-scotian* in April 1851 from a school at the Ross settlement (Rossville), Margaree, where he had constructed a sundial for the use of his students and had purchased a globe recommended by the superintendent of education, John William Dawson*, Ayre described the general indifference of the community toward his efforts to improve education: "I cannot offend truth when I assert that the majority of this community have not acquired a desire of reading, either as regards mental improvement, or amusement; that to read or understand what we read, are indubitably the first requisites; [with] which to establish a sound system of Education."

William Ayre was still teaching in Cape Breton and writing letters to government officials in 1852. By this time he had taught in Nova Scotia for more than 35 years and was anxious to "secure a resting place for the remainder of my days." Teaching in Inverness County until 1854, he eventually retired to Halifax where he died on 14 April 1855, aged 72 years.

HOPE H. JOHNSTON

PANS, MG 5, Halifax County, Camp Hill Cemetery, Halifax, reg. of burials, 1855 (mfm.); RG 14, 3, 1832; 39, nos.64–65; 70, 1852. St Paul's Anglican Church (Halifax), Reg. of burials, 1855 (mfm. at PANS). "A documentary study of early educational policy," ed. D. C. Harvey, PANS *Bull.* (Halifax), 1 (1937–39), no.1. *Novascotian*, 18 Nov. 1844, 28 April 1851, 21 April 1853. *Place-names of N.S.*, 399, 409. H. H. Johnston, "The contributions of the Scottish teachers to early Cape Breton education, 1802–1865" (MA thesis, Dalhousie Univ., Halifax, 1973), 99–105.

B

BABEY, PETER PAUL TONEY (also known as **Peter Bobbeie**), Micmac chief and doctor; fl. 1849–55 in Nova Scotia.

Peter Paul Toney Babey was born some time around the turn of the 19th century and by 1849 he was chief of the Micmac band living at Bear River in Kings County, N.S. At that point he was married and had a 13-year-old child. In an 1855 petition he is described as "Governor of the Aborigines of the Counties of Queen's, Shelburne, Anapolis and King's."

On 26 Jan. 1842 Ebenezer Fitch Harding, justice of the peace for Kings, had reported to the House of Assembly that there were approximately 280 Micmacs living in the county and that their principal means of support came from hunting, fishing, coopering, basket making, and fancy quill work. He went on to say that they lived "in comparative comfort and contentment where they are temperate and sickness or old age do not prevent." However, he lamented that they lacked "provident forethought" and were thus barred from the "accumulation of means for meeting future exigences." He suggested that they be "relieved by a reasonable supply" of blankets, clothing, food, and medical help.

When famine hit the Micmacs in the mid 1840s the Nova Scotia House of Assembly agreed to pay the costs incurred by physicians who attended the indigent Indians. The bills began to come in with alarming frequency. Consequently, when Babey presented himself as a "phisician, Chemist, and Alchemist" in a petition to the house on 19 Feb. 1852 and asked for compensation such as the "white men who pretend to give any assistance to the poor Indian receives," the members were not receptive. Babey claimed to have followed his vocation for over 25 years, ministering to Indians and, occasionally, whites, without pay. He used remedies extracted from plants, roots, and herbs because they "renovate the System, give Vigour to the frame, and have a tendency to prolong life." In contrast, white doctors employed "minerals and noxious medicines calculated to destroy life." The house debated his petition, with "a good deal of interest and some merriment." After it was facetiously suggested that Babey be appointed physician to the assembly, providing he were of the right party, the house did nothing.

On 16 Jan. 1855 Babey presented a second petition, deploring the "rapid numerical decrease of his people" as increased settlement caused the "means by which [his] forefathers obtained a livelihood [to] disappear." Claiming that he could no longer assist them because he lacked the financial means and had been "labouring under disease premature age and decripitude, often occasioned by want of food and raiment, and other privations incidental to life in the woods," he asked that help be given to four Indians, each approximately 80 years of age, who were in a "sick state incapable of helping themselves." The matter was referred to the Indian committee which, following Babey's suggestion, agreed to send £4 for medicines to a clergyman in Liverpool to hold for Babey's use. Unfortunately, there is no further record of Babey.

In 1857 the House of Assembly resolved to end the payment of doctors' bills for attendance on Indians "except in cases of surgical operations or accouchements." Under the direction of the Indian commissioner, William Chearnley, funds were to be spent primarily on the annual distribution of blankets and greatcoats.

L. F. S. UPTON

PANS, MG 15, 3, no.74; 4a, no.126; 5, no.42. *Novascotian*, 1 March 1852. Upton, *Micmacs and colonists*.

BABY, FRANÇOIS, militia officer, politician, justice of the peace, businessman, and office holder; b. 16 Dec. 1768 in Detroit, son of Jacques Baby*, *dit* Dupéront, and Susanne Réaume (Rhéaume), *dit* La Croix; m. 5 Sept. 1795 Frances Abbott, and they had eight sons and four daughters; d. 27 Aug. 1852 in Windsor, Upper Canada.

François Baby belonged to the most powerful family in the Western District of Upper Canada, and his uncle François*, who supervised his education and that of his elder brother James*, was an influential member of the governing class in Lower Canada. Tall, ramrod straight, active in mind and body throughout his long life, and fluently bilingual, François possessed both personal qualities and family connections which made him a natural choice for political and civil office. His political career began in 1792 when James advised him to stand in Essex County for election to Upper Canada's first parliament. Since a Baby candidacy in Essex with its large French-speaking population would threaten the election chances there of Surveyor General David William Smith*, François was apparently persuaded to run in neighbouring Kent County instead. Duly elected to the House of Assembly for Kent with William Macomb, Baby may have been responsible for the order in 1793 to translate acts of the legislature into French "for the benefit of the inhabitants of the Western District." In July of that year he was one of 15 assemblymen who signed a private petition protesting "the great inconvenience" of the contract which awarded a monopoly on army provisioning to major merchants such as Robert Hamilton*. Their petition gave stature to the province-wide opposition to the contract. In 1794 James, who had become lieutenant of Kent County, appointed his brother lieutenant-colonel of the 1st Kent Militia. Two years later François received his first commission as justice of the peace for the Western District and served almost continuously in that capacity for more than 40 years.

The position of the Baby family, Roman Catholic and French Canadian, was unique in Upper Canada. At the centre of power locally, the family enjoyed good relations with successive administrations at York (Toronto), the provincial capital. Yet within the French-speaking settlement of the Western District, it was often regarded with suspicion. In 1795, after François had become Alexander McKee*'s deputy lieutenant for Essex County, the vicar general of Upper Canada, Edmund Burke*, granted him the pew in the church of Notre-Dame-de-l'Assomption reserved since the French régime for the highest ranking government official. When Baby took possession of the pew one Sunday shortly after his marriage to a non-French convert, the congregation objected and had the "distinctive pew" removed. Lieutenant Governor John Graves Simcoe* ordered that the respect "observed formerly towards the French Commandant" be maintained, but the controversy continued. Baby finally withdrew his claim in 1797 in order to avoid further confrontations.

Baby averred that his family's attachment to the British crown was the real reason for the opposition. Such "patriotic feeling and an anxiety to contribute his personal exertions toward the defence of the Province" would motivate Baby to join the British forces at Amherstburg when war broke out in 1812. As an assistant quartermaster general he saw action at the battles of Detroit, Frenchtown (Monroe, Mich.), and Fort Meigs (near Perrysburg, Ohio). In the fall of 1813 he accompanied Major-General Henry Procter*'s retreat from the Western District after the defeat at Moraviantown and later was to testify at his court

Baby

martial. Baby saw action again on the Niagara frontier in December 1813 and was commended by Lieutenant-General Gordon DRUMMOND for being "useful and indefatigable" in embarking troops at Black Rock (Buffalo, N.Y.). On 31 Jan. 1814 he was captured by an American raiding party led by Andrew Westbrook* on the Thames River, "shamefully and inhumanely tied with cords," and removed to the United States. His fate was a matter of some concern since American citizens (as Detroit-born Baby was considered to be) taken in arms against the United States were to be referred directly to President James Madison. A remonstrance to the United States government, however, resulted in his return.

In 1812 Baby's property at Sandwich (Windsor) and his newly built house had been occupied by Brigadier-General William Hull's invading army. Baby sought damages from the enemy of £2,450, a measure of his financial well-being, but without effect. It was not until 1824 that he received compensation of £444 from the British government. More galling to his pride was the government's decision to give him a grant of land based on the rank of captain he had held as an assistant quartermaster general, rather than on his pre-war rank as colonel of militia, conferred on him in 1807 when he acted for three months as lieutenant of Essex County in place of Alexander Grant*. Baby received 800 acres and petitioned the government repeatedly over the years – to no avail – for the additional 400 acres.

With his election to the House of Assembly in 1820 as one of the two members for Essex, Baby resumed his political career. Advocating positions perhaps unexpected for the brother of a well-known member of the "family compact," who had himself repeatedly received appointments to government office, François became increasingly reform-minded. He voted against the expulsion of reformer Barnabas Bidwell* from the assembly in 1822 and the following year affirmed Marshall Spring Bidwell*'s eligibility to run for election in his father's stead. He strongly opposed the union of Upper and Lower Canada, a move which he thought "would prove fatal to both Provinces & perhaps to the Mother Country." His own political efforts seem to have been punctuated by failure. Attempts in 1824 to secure the offices of surrogate court judge and registrar of Essex County were unsuccessful, and in the general election of that year he tied for second place with the result that the attending magistrate, William Hands, returned only one member for Essex. Baby protested, a new writ of election was issued, and Baby was returned to the assembly the following year. He was elected once again in 1828, but the re-emergence of discord in the parish, this time over church finances and the failure to provide suitable housing for the girls' school, begun by Sister Marie-Clotilde Raizenne* and supported by

the Babys, contributed to François's political undoing in 1830. When in late October Baby was defeated at the polls, he blamed the local priest, Joseph Crevier, *dit* Bellerive, and the pastor at Amherstburg, Louis-Joseph Fluet, and tried to have both removed. Baby's defeat was a source of outrage for the vicar general, William John O'Grady*, and for Bishop Alexander McDonell*, who described Baby as "the most independent, and most upright, and . . . the most honest member" who ever sat in the assembly.

Crevier, however, had strong support from his congregation, which resented Baby's boast that he had more influence with the bishop than "all the parishioners put together" and which feared that he would use that influence to have Crevier replaced by an "English priest." These fears were realized in November 1831 when the bishop's nephew Angus MacDonell was appointed to the predominantly French-Canadian parish. But Baby's troubles were far from over. His refusal to turn over the deeds to the church which O'Grady had entrusted to him in 1830 caused the bishop to listen more sympathetically to local complaints. The result was a bill passed in the assembly in February 1834 which allowed removal of the deeds from trustees such as Baby, "whose views and intentions were hostile to the interest of the Catholics of Sandwich, and their Religion." Friction between Baby and Angus MacDonell continued until the latter was replaced by Pierre Point in 1843.

Baby lived as a gentleman on his inherited wealth and the income derived from his property. He had, however, made some efforts to acquire more land. In 1799 he patented a grant for 1,200 acres in Yarmouth Township and that same year received 360 acres in Malden Township. But his most important holdings were in Sandwich Township, lots 79 and 80 in concessions 1 and 2 which he received from his mother in 1800 and their extensions in concession 3 granted in 1805. In 1836 he received the adjacent water lots on the Detroit River to build wharfs for the village being developed there. His land holdings were thus relatively modest in scale; however, in qualitative terms his Sandwich property was most significant since the village there was to become the future city of Windsor. On 4 Dec. 1838 the so-called battle of Windsor was fought in Baby's orchard. Critical of the summary executions ordered by Colonel John Prince* for the first five Americans captured in the abortive Patriot invasion, Baby and his son-in-law, James Dougall*, were among those who cancelled their subscriptions to the Sandwich *Western Herald, and Farmers' Magazine* for its support of Prince.

During the 1840s Baby operated a government-leased ferry service to Detroit and ran an inn. He maintained his reform party contacts and in 1843 was recommended for a seat in the Legislative Council by Louis-Hippolyte La Fontaine*. Though not appointed, he remained influential in local politics, chairing a rally at which Malcolm Cameron* spoke in 1849 and serving as a conduit for party patronage right up until his death three years later. A raconteur, Baby had regaled the American historian Francis Parkman* in 1845 with tales of his father's friendship with the Ottawa war chief Pontiac*. Parkman left a vivid description in his journals of Baby's "fine old brick house" (now the Hiram Walker Historical Museum), referring to its "waste and picturesque air – books, guns, neglected tables, old clocks, chests of drawers, and garments and Indian equipment flung around" as well as to "the little Negro girl, and the strange-looking half breed, who were sunning themselves among the hens and hogs in the back yard." Perhaps the life and comportment of this Upper Canadian gentleman was best captured by his grandson: François Baby "lived in a feudal sort of way and was very proud and, I might say, arrogant."

JOHN CLARKE

AO, MS 392, 20-11 (Baby family); 20-135 (G. F. Macdonald papers); MS 498; RG 22, ser.155, will of François Baby. Archdiocese of Detroit, Chancery Office, Reg. des baptêmes, mariages et sépultures de Sainte-Anne (Detroit), 2 févr. 1704–30 déc. 1848 (transcripts at Detroit Public Library, Burton Hist. Coll.), 17 déc. 1768. Arch. of the Archdiocese of Toronto, Ser.1, AB03, 09, 20–21, 36, 39, 45, 47–49, 58; AC21–23; CA01–2; CB07, 10. Arch. of the Diocese of London (London, Ont.), Assumption Church (Sandwich [Windsor, Ont.]), Reg. of baptisms, marriages, and burials, 5 Sept. 1795, 28 Aug. 1852. AUM, P 58. MTL, Robert Baldwin papers; W. W. Baldwin papers. PAC, RG 1, L1; L3; RG 5, A1: 2668–69, 20799–811, 31701–3, 35694–95, 35704–10, 36398–99; RG 8, I (C ser.); RG 68, General index, 1651–1841. PRO, CO 42/317: 189. *The John Askin papers*, ed. M. M. Quaife (2v., Detroit, 1928–31). "Journals of Legislative Assembly of U.C.," AO *Report*, 1909: 23; 1914: 152–53, 314–15. Francis Parkman, *The journals of Francis Parkman*, ed. Mason Wade (2v., New York and London, 1947). *The Windsor border region, Canada's southernmost frontier* . . . , ed. E. J. Lajeunesse (Toronto, 1960). *Canadian Correspondent* (York [Toronto]), 25 Jan., 8 Feb. 1834. *Colonial Advocate* (York), 1 May 1828; 7 Oct. 1830; 17, 24 July 1834. *Upper Canada Gazette*, 3 June 1824.

Armstrong, *Handbook of Upper Canadian chronology*. P.-B. Casgrain, *Mémorial des familles Casgrain, Baby et Perrault du Canada* (Québec, 1898). [A. J. Dooner], named Brother Alfred, *Catholic pioneers in Upper Canada* (Toronto, 1947). E. J. Lajeunesse, *Outline history of Assumption parish* (n.p., [1967]). J. E. Rea, *Bishop Alexander Macdonell and the politics of Upper Canada* (Toronto, 1974). F. H. Armstrong, "The oligarchy of the Western District of Upper Canada, 1788–1841," CHA *Hist. papers*, 1977: 87–102. John Clarke, "The role of political position and family and economic linkage in land speculation in the Western District of Upper Canada, 1788–1815," *Canadian Geographer* (Toronto), 19 (1975): 18–34. R. A. Douglas, " 'The Battle of Windsor,' " *OH*, 61 (1969):

137–52. C. C. James, "The second legislature of Upper Canada – 1796–1800," RSC *Trans.*, 2nd ser., 9 (1903), sect.II: 167–68.

BAGNALL, JAMES (often incorrectly **James Douglas**), printer, publisher, politician, and office holder; baptized 16 Nov. 1783 in Shelburne, N.S., son of Samuel Bagnall and Elizabeth Whitehouse; m. 22 Aug. 1815 Anna Matilda Gardiner in Charlottetown, and they had at least three sons and four daughters; d. 20 June 1855 in Bedeque, P.E.I.

James Bagnall's parents, loyalists from New York, went from Shelburne, where James was born, to St John's (Prince Edward) Island probably in 1787. Unable to get an expected land grant, Samuel, a carpenter and cabinet-maker, settled his family in Charlottetown where from 1788 to 1795 he was deputy sheriff and jailer, the jail being in his own house. There were no proper schools and so young James had a limited opportunity for education. When his brother-in-law, William Alexander Rind, king's printer for the Island, returned with his family to his native Virginia in 1798, the 15-year-old Bagnall went with them as Rind's apprentice. There he gained experience on two newspapers Rind published, one in Richmond, Va, the other in Georgetown, D.C.

Bagnall returned with a press in 1804 to set up shop on an island with fewer than 7,000 inhabitants, many of whom could not read, distributed over wilderness land in small communities. Appointed king's printer on 25 December by Lieutenant Governor Edmund Fanning* with a salary of £60, he began publishing his first newspaper, the *Royal Herald*, a month later. Because money was scarce he announced that "country produce and furs will be taken as payment from those who cannot make it convenient to pay cash." In November 1805 he printed the House of Assembly's current *Journal*, the first printed on the Island since 1797. Meanwhile, when an expected shipment of paper failed to arrive from England, he reduced the size of his already small newspaper, and then stopped printing it for three months. It ultimately proved unprofitable and ceased publication entirely early in 1806. Late that year, Bagnall, whose arrangement with Fanning had been vague, successfully worked out a more business-like agreement with Lieutenant Governor Joseph Frederick Wallet DesBarres*, specifying that he would receive extra payment and paper for printing laws that had been passed before his appointment.

Bagnall, who "felt a strong desire" to promote the Island's settlement and prosperity, ran for a Georgetown seat in the general election of November 1806. He attributed the successful result to the influence of the Loyal Electors, a political society formed during the election. Although many of the founding members were loyalists or their descendants (Samuel Bagnall

Bagnall

was its first president and meetings were held in his tavern), its principal organizer was James Bardin Palmer*, an Irish attorney who had come to the colony in 1802 and who was also elected to the 1806 assembly. Palmer appreciated the value of a printing-press and was a major influence on the younger, less educated Bagnall for the next 22 years.

Bagnall served in the spring of 1808 on a committee of the assembly that reported it was necessary to print a revised set of all the colony's laws including those printed by Rind and his predecessor James Robertson*. During the same session an act was passed, to be in force for two years, placing a tax on sugar and tobacco to meet the expense of "printing, publishing and collecting the Acts of the General Assembly." Until the money was raised, the government was reluctant to proceed. The delay in printing the laws coupled with the government's refusal to increase by £15 a salary Bagnall found inadequate led him to look for a more profitable opportunity.

That summer, leaving his press in Charlottetown in the hands of his brother Samuel and their nephew James Douglas Haszard*, Bagnall moved to Halifax and began publication, probably in January 1809, of his second newspaper, the *Novator and Nova Scotia Literary Gazette*. A sensational event in Halifax during the fall of 1809 was the trial of Edward Jordan and his wife, Margaret, for piracy and murder on board the schooner *Three Sisters*. In March 1810 Bagnall published a 59-page report of this trial, compiled by Charles Rufus Fairbanks* and Andrew William Cochran*. It included Jordan's dying confession and would have been popular reading material in its time. Both the *Novator* and its printer, who also published two almanacs, enjoyed a promising start. Nevertheless, Bagnall, whose brother Samuel had negotiated a salary of £100 on his behalf while he was away, was back in Charlottetown by September 1810 when he issued his third newspaper, the *Weekly Recorder of Prince Edward Island*. The *Journal* of that summer's assembly, hastily printed after his return, noted that James Bagnall had resigned his seat.

The *Weekly Recorder* was immediately involved in the controversy surrounding the Loyal Electors who by 1810 had grown in influence. Several by-elections had increased the rancour and suspicion that existed between a long-established group of government officials, allied with land speculators and their agents and known to their political enemies as the "cabal," and the Loyal Electors, spokesmen for the interests of the settlers. In his paper Bagnall vigorously defended the "Loyal and respectable Society," hoping that publicity would dispel charges of secrecy and disloyalty. Though he made a self-conscious effort to print both sides of the controversy, his membership in the society left him vulnerable to charges by Attorney

General Charles Stewart*, leader of the so-called "cabal," that the Loyal Electors controlled the press.

Bagnall had returned from Halifax under the impression that the laws were ready for printing. But a cumbersome division of responsibility in the committees for revision of the laws and the acrimonious dispute surrounding the Loyal Electors had prevented any effective organization for printing them. Both factions were, however, anxious to have the laws printed, and early in the assembly of 1812 unanimous support was given to an act appointing commissioners empowered "to contract with Mr. James Bagnall for printing the laws." A year later, in November 1813, the contract was signed.

For Bagnall the next four years were a desperate struggle to keep his printing business alive. The Island's temporary administration, directed by William Townshend*, had informed him in December 1812 that his salary as government printer would be discontinued in the spring. Charles Douglass SMITH, the newly appointed lieutenant governor, not only repeatedly refused to restore the salary, but when Bagnall was unable to complete the contract for the laws in the specified time withheld payment on accounts owed for other government printing. Bagnall, in debt for paper and printing supplies, explained in long memorials to the autocratic lieutenant governor that it had taken him a year of repeated applications to two of the commissioners, Palmer and Attorney General William Johnston*, to get corrected revised copies of the manuscript laws. He claimed he would be "subject to inevitable ruin" unless the accounts owed him were paid. The only concession Smith made was to authorize the treasurer, Robert Gray*, another of the commissioners, to pay Bagnall ten per cent of the old debt each time it was certified that the printing of the laws was proceeding. While Bagnall was engaged in this printing, shortage of paper and lack of time and money forced him to discontinue publication of his *Prince Edward Island Gazette*, the newspaper which had replaced the *Weekly Recorder* in the spring of 1814. The next year he produced the first almanac printed on the Island, the *Prince Edward Island calendar for town and country*. By the end of 1817 the colony had its first printed volume since 1789 of the revised laws and Bagnall was able to resume publication of the *Prince Edward Island Gazette*. The official proclamations and announcements along with business advertisements printed in the newspaper brought revenue to the editor, whose salary as king's printer was still denied. Unlike his other Island newspapers, the *Gazette* did not designate Bagnall as king's printer, that title now being reserved for use in official publications such as the assembly *Journal* and in the printing for the militia which also added to his income. The paper reported proceedings in the law courts and the assembly, and local economic, educational, and moral concerns were discussed by the editor and his correspondents. Bagnall's official printing continued with proclamations and announcements posted in public places and distributed to magistrates and other officials.

Bagnall's problems as a government printer were compounded by his interest in political action. Although he had lost in the hotly contested general election of 1812 he won a by-election in 1813. An active member during the next session of the assembly, in 1817, Bagnall was defeated in a general election the following year. He was chosen clerk of the assembly in 1818, a position he retained in the brief session of 1820, which was the last on the Island during Lieutenant Governor Smith's term of office. The successful and popular movement organized by John Stewart* to remove Smith was resisted by Bagnall's political friends Palmer and Angus Macaulay*. When Smith's successor John Ready* called an election for the fall of 1824 Palmer was defeated and Bagnall was left with few friends in the new assembly. Attending the January 1825 session as clerk of the former assembly, Bagnall found himself not only displaced as clerk, a position which had paid well, but also replaced as printer of the assembly *Journal* by his former apprentice J. D. Haszard, who had supported the movement for Smith's recall.

In an attempt to reinforce his nebulous position as king's printer, a title he retained, Bagnall started publication in 1826 of the *Royal Gazette and Prince Edward Island Recorder* (the *Prince Edward Island Gazette* had ceased publication, probably for financial reasons, in 1822). Issued in opposition to Haszard's *Prince Edward Island Register*, which had been publishing regularly since July 1823, Bagnall's paper appeared only sporadically until June 1827 and had little financial support either official or private.

In 1828 Bagnall printed his last newspaper, the *Phenix*, the first attempt on the Island by a group of private citizens to sponsor a newspaper. Although its ostensible purpose was to give opponents of measures being pursued in the assembly an alternate voice to that of Haszard's *Register*, its real purpose was to gather support for Palmer in his effort to regain his seat in the assembly from which he had been expelled in March. The paper, containing many well-written letters to the editor, must have gained some support because, after Palmer's defeat in the by-election, ambitious plans were announced to enlarge and extend it; but Bagnall's press was worn out and deficient in type and the plans never materialized.

Bagnall was dismissed as king's printer in August 1830, a formality, since he had received no government support for three years. He operated a small bookstore in his house and printing-shop but there is no reliable record that he continued long as a printer. He maintained his interest in the political

struggle of the tenant farmers against absentee landlords and their agents, advocating at district meetings constitutional and lawful means for escheat. He was defeated in the 1838 general election when the more radical element of the movement led by William Cooper* gained the popular mandate. Some time after 1848 Bagnall moved from his farm, Oatium, in Charlottetown Royalty to another leasehold farm at Bedeque (Central Bedeque), where his eldest son Samuel James Bagnall and daughter Caroline Charlotte Augusta Baker lived.

Though James Bagnall had been a conscientious member of the assembly working for the interests of the people, his major accomplishment was as a printer who kept the small colony informed of the issues that influenced its life by printing the assembly *Journal*, the laws, and his newspapers.

MARIANNE G. MORROW

The journals of the Prince Edward Island House of Assembly are important to a study of James Bagnall and the following were most useful: 1805 (consulted in PRO, CO 226/20: 81); 1806 (in PAPEI, Acc. 2702/935: 1); 1808 (in CO 229/3: 59, 73); 1810 (in CO 229/3: 132–33); 1812 (in CO 229/4: 100, 103, 117–18); 16 Nov., 18 Dec. 1813; 6–7 Jan. 1814 (in PAPEI, RG 3); 1817 (in Acc. 2702/938: 1, 8); 1818–19 (in Acc. 2702/939: 5); 1820 (in CO 226/36: 111); 1825 (in CO 229/5: 171–72, 218); 1828 (in CO 229/5: 271); and the published *Journal* for 1833: 107–8.

PAPEI, Acc. 2702/527, 2702/531a–b, 2702/533, 2702/535–36, 2702/538, 2702/546–47, 2702/839; Acc. 2849/124–27, 2849/129–30; RG 5, Minutes, 4 May 1789; 20 April, 29 Sept. 1790; 2 Aug. 1796; 5 Feb., 26 Aug. 1805; 13, 16 Oct. 1806; 2 May 1808; 16 Oct. 1809; 18 March 1811; 15 Dec. 1812; 24 July, 6 Nov. 1813; 4 Jan., 5 April, 7 June 1814; 9 May 1815; 3, 13 March, 7 April 1818; 4 Aug. 1830 (mfm. at PAC); RG 8, Warrant books, 1812–47, especially 1812–24; RG 18, 1848: 39. PRO, AO 13, bundle 11: 151–54 (mfm. at PAC); CO 226/20: 49; 226/21: 87; 226/22: 165–67; 226/24: 52–53; 226/26: 9, 189, 234, 238; 226/28: 4; 226/39: 422. St Paul's Anglican Church (Charlottetown), Reg. of marriages, 22 Aug. 1815 (mfm. at PAPEI). Shelburne County Museum (Shelburne, N.S.), Christ Church, Shelburne, reg. of baptisms, marriages, and burials, 16 Nov. 1783 (mfm. at PANS). Supreme Court of P.E.I. (Charlottetown), Estates Division, liber 1: f.23 (will of Samuel Bagnall); file 48 (estate of James Bagnall) (mfm. at PAPEI).

Colonial Herald, and Prince Edward Island Advertiser (Charlottetown), 8 April 1843. *Prince Edward Island Register*, 17 Jan., 18, 29 Dec. 1824; 21 Feb., 30 May 1826; 24 June 1828; 14 July 1829. *Royal Gazette* (Charlottetown), 26 July, 20 Sept., 24 Oct. 1836; 6, 13 Nov. 1838; 1 April 1845. *Royal Herald* (Charlottetown), 16 Feb., 16 March, 2 Nov. 1805. *Weekly Recorder of Prince Edward Island* (Charlottetown), 17 Sept., 13 Oct., 24 Dec. 1810; 16 Feb., 16 March, 4 May, 21 Aug., 26 Dec. 1811. Marie Tremaine, *A bibliography of Canadian imprints, 1751–1800* (Toronto, 1952), 287–88, 521, 668–69. [T. B. Akins], *History of Halifax City* (Halifax, 1895; repr. Belleville, Ont., 1973).

Baillairgé

Canada's smallest prov. (Bolger), 66–94. D. C. Harvey, "The Loyal Electors," RSC *Trans.*, 3rd ser., 24 (1930), sect.II: 101–10.

BAILLAIRGÉ, THOMAS (baptized **François-Thomas**), architect, wood-carver, and politician; b. 20 Dec. 1791 at Quebec, son of François Baillairgé*, a master painter and wood-carver, and Josephte Boutin, and grandson of Jean Baillairgé*, a master carpenter and architect; d. there 9 Feb. 1859.

Thomas Baillairgé belonged to a renowned family of craftsmen who had been settled at Quebec since 1741. According to his father's diary, Thomas began to attend the English school at the age of eight. Then he probably studied at the Petit Séminaire de Québec while his father taught him the rudiments of wood-carving and architecture. Young Thomas was undoubtedly in some degree a disciple of Jérôme DEMERS, a teacher of science and architecture at the Petit Séminaire. Demers, as superior of the seminary and vicar general of the diocese with responsibilities such as supervising the construction of religious buildings in the name of the bishop of Quebec, subsequently granted his patronage to Baillairgé whom he termed the "leading architect in the whole of Lower Canada." As for his apprenticeship, historian Émile Vaillancourt* points out it is not unlikely that Baillairgé worked with René Beauvais*, *dit* Saint-James, in Louis Quévillon*'s workshop around 1810. But, since this assertion is not based on documentary evidence and Baillairgé's whole career tends to invalidate it, it must be called into question. He may, however, have worked with wood-carver Antoine Jacson* in his father's atelier.

According to Georges-Frédéric Baillairgé, the family's biographer, Thomas started in the trade in 1812. That year he entered "into full possession of the workshop of his father, [who had been] appointed treasurer of the city." But in fact it was in 1815 that he really began his career as an architect and wood-carver at Saint-Joachim, near Quebec, where in partnership with his father and under the guidance of Demers he undertook to decorate the interior of the village church.

Baillairgé made his mark primarily as an architect. From 1815 to 1848, the year he retired, he drew up the plans for a considerable number of churches, presbyteries, public buildings, and houses. In the field of religious architecture Baillairgé enjoyed a commanding position because of both the scarcity of French Canadian and Roman Catholic architects and the close relations he maintained with the diocese of Quebec. Yet he did not succeed in gaining recognition in the Montreal region, where he attempted only two ventures: in 1824 when he presented a proposal for the reconstruction of Notre-Dame, which was rejected, and in 1836 when he drafted the plans for the church of Sainte-Geneviève. On the other hand, there is hardly a religious building in the eastern part of the province erected between 1820 and 1850 that does not bear his mark, either because he drew up the plans or because it was constructed by a contractor on the model of one of his churches.

Baillairgé built three types of churches. First, there were small parish churches that followed the architectural tradition inherited from the French régime. They are designed in the form of a Latin cross, with a semicircular apse and a bell tower rising above a façade ornamented only by niches, windows, and portals. In collaboration with Demers, he drafted the plans for a church of this kind at Sainte-Claire in 1823. This building seems to have been a significant accomplishment, since he repeated the design frequently – in 1830 at Lauzon, in 1839 at Saint-Pierre-les-Becquets (Les Becquets), and in 1845 at Saint-Anselme, to mention only a few examples; there were, of course, variations, for no two of Baillairgé's buildings were exactly alike. On the other hand, several rural parishes wanted a more majestic church incorporating a façade with two bell towers. In 1828 Baillairgé and Demers proposed at Charlesbourg a plan that could satisfy these expectations. At Grondines (Saint-Charles-des-Grondines) in 1831 and at Sainte-Croix in 1835, Baillairgé revived this type successfully: a screened façade enhanced a building that in other respects was rather traditional. But, beginning with the construction of St Patrick's at Quebec in 1831, Baillairgé developed an entirely new model linked more tenuously with architectural tradition. The nave was divided into three spaces by pillars supporting lateral galleries, and the formal treatment of the façade heralded the new layout of the interior. The architect used this model with some variations at Deschambault in 1833 and Sainte-Geneviève in 1836.

In among these three types of church, a number of other edifices show Baillairgé's never-ceasing quest for renewal of tradition: for example, the church of Sainte-Luce built in 1836 and that of L'Ancienne-Lorette erected the following year, in which the façade became more monumental even though a central bell tower was retained. But it was primarily through interior architecture that other intermediate variations were characterized. After completing the plans for the interior décor of the church of Saint-Joachim in 1815, Baillairgé repeated the semicircular retable (the structure housing the altar) on several occasions, at Lauzon, Saint-Antoine-de-Tilly, and Saint-François on the Île d'Orléans for instance. Yet, when the retable he carved in 1824 at Lotbinière in the form of a triumphal arch was a success, he proposed the same style for various other churches, notably one at Charlesbourg in 1833 and another at Sainte-Luce in 1845. Lastly, the kind of interior architecture found in

St Patrick's Church occurs again at Deschambault in 1841, at Lévis in 1850, and in the nave of the church of Pointe-aux-Trembles (Neuville) in 1854. But the last two instances must be listed as the work of his school, since the master had retired, making way for his pupils.

Baillairgé also drafted the plans for a number of public edifices, the first and most important undoubtedly being the parliament building begun in 1830 on the present site of Montmorency Park. This was in fact a more elaborate version of the architecture employed for the Séminaire de Nicolet in 1826. Similarly, a simplified form of the bishop's palace at Quebec, for which the plans were delivered in 1844, can be seen in the convent of Saint-Roch and the Collège de Sainte-Anne-de-la-Pocatière.

In addition to churches and public buildings, Baillairgé drew up the plans for several houses. Research into this aspect of his work has only begun, however, and since neither the plans nor the accompanying contracts are signed, only the architect's rather unusual penmanship makes it possible to detect that the plans are his. The houses so far identified were principally on Rue Saint-Louis and Rue Sainte-Ursule, but this does not rule out the possibility that similar houses were built in other adjoining parts of old Quebec.

Baillairgé followed the dominant style of his age, neoclassicism. This movement, which equally affected America and Europe at the beginning of the 19th century, was marked by a return to the principles underlying classical architecture and drew inspiration from the new science of archaeology. At the same time, there was growing interest in history, in the epochs which have in turn left monuments on the architectural landscape. That Baillairgé absorbed the neoclassicism introduced into Lower Canada by British architects, treatises, and books with illustrations of models, is clear from his library, which contained Colin Campbell's *Vitruvius Britannicus*, James Gibbs's *Book of architecture*, and Jacques-François Blondel's *Cours d'architecture*. Baillairgé also watched new buildings going up, and it is quite clear that the work of such men as Henry Musgrave Blaiklock*, Frederick Hacker, Richard John Cooper, and George Browne* had an influence on him. But beyond these new developments Baillairgé took into account the architectural heritage of Lower Canada, and it is a synthesis of new influences and acquired knowledge that he expresses in designs and also in techniques and materials. This synthesizing endeavour gives Baillairgé's architectural production a familiar image that maintained continuity in development, and so distinguishes his work that he can be considered the creator of an original style: the neoclassicism of Quebec.

If the edifices constructed according to his plans testify to this classical renewal, Baillairgé's style of draftsmanship also represents a development within the architectural profession. By following the precepts in the manual on architecture written by Demers, Baillairgé compels recognition as an architect rather than a master builder. Demers had affirmed that architecture drew its principles from the observation of nature, but that these "natural rules" were little respected in Lower Canada at the beginning of the 19th century. Accordingly, Baillairgé endeavoured to become the architect representing order, an indispensable element in architecture. He prepared more and more drawings, increasingly precise and detailed, to guide the work on site, thus depriving builders and contractors of freedom of choice and hence noticeably weakening the influence of tradition on the evolution of forms and techniques. Between the drawing he completed in 1829 for a house to be built for the Hôtel-Dieu of Quebec and the plans used in 1841 for the construction of the École Mgr Signay in Près-de-Ville at Quebec, this development is clearly discernible. It marked the true beginnings of the architectural profession.

This evocation of order was particularly evident when Baillairgé carried out the interior décor of a church. For example, as early as 1815 at Saint-Joachim, in collaboration with his father, he presented a wholly new decorative scheme, conceived as a unified whole. From then on the architect took the place of the usual ateliers of wood-carvers who scattered their ornamentation throughout the churches. At Saint-Joachim all the carvings are subordinate to an architectural framework that dictates the general arrangement, to fulfil the architect's desire for a coherent effect. It is not surprising that Baillairgé's aesthetic notions led him to advocate the use of plaster for ornamental motifs, and that figurative wood-carving declined perceptibly as his career advanced. The interior architecture of St Patrick's Church was executed in plaster in 1831, with the architect excluding all carved ornamentation.

Baillairgé was, however, a highly skilled wood-carver. The bas-reliefs depicting *La foi* and *La religion* in the church of Saint-Joachim, and the statues of *La foi* and *L'espérance* in the church of Saint-Louis at Lotbinière, are amongst the great achievements in wood-carving. By using a style of antique inspiration with folds cut closely and deeply, Baillairgé gave evidence of a coherent approach in his neoclassical aesthetics. But there is more to it than this. His art suggests a clear intention to escape from a vision of faith relying on narrative or anecdote. His restrained style dispenses with figurative references; he uses themes which are theological in character and he carefully avoids the descriptive episodes of the Old and New Testaments. He increasingly retained in his plans only non-figurative carving, in particular

Baillairgé

symbolic ornaments (trophies and instruments of the Passion, for example). In this respect his art was linked with the concerns of the church in Lower Canada, which around 1830 was seeking to reaffirm its position, within a traditional society facing disintegration, by preaching a return to doctrine and to the gospel message. The interior architecture of Baillairgé's churches was in tune with this reorientation of the church; at least it expressed this intention in the religious iconography employed. The renewal in architectural style, combined with the new iconology, gave significance to interior architecture despite the absence of carved figures, and conferred on Baillairgé a quite special position. Thus it is easy to understand why the church thought so highly of him that it treated him, in effect, as the diocesan architect.

But at the same time Baillairgé was a victim of his own success. Tied to his drawing-board, as much by the volume of work and the care he devoted to it as by his determination to separate himself professionally from those who engaged in construction, he took to giving very liberal and varied interpretations to his plans. As he did not visit the sites and follow the progress of buildings, the work was often quite out of his hands from the moment the structure was begun. At Deschambault the façade was not completed, and at Grondines the bell towers were scaled down. Elsewhere, contractors, who were skilful but insensitive to the aesthetics of the master, cut down his plans to adapt them to parish needs and resources. Baillairgé also showed far too little concern for the developing urban setting. For example his bishop's palace faces the stables of Notre-Dame and turns its back on the street.

Baillairgé had a number of pupils and as a result he enjoyed unquestionable influence. In his workshop the tasks were specialized, as Georges-Frédéric Baillairgé pointed out: Louis-Thomas Berlinguet excelled in colonnades and architecture in general, Joseph Girouard in large-scale constructions, Louis-Xavier Léprohon, André PAQUET, *dit* Lavallée, and Thomas Fournier in the interior ornamentation of churches, André-Raphaël Giroux* in the making of wooden models, Léandre Parent in figures of Christ, and Charles Baillairgé* in the boldness of his conceptions. Of all these pupils it was Thomas's second cousin Charles who was to leave the strongest imprint on the second half of the 19th century, but at the price of an unavoidable break with the aesthetics of his master. On the other hand, Giroux and Paquet carried on Baillairgé's work after his retirement, but by 1845 they had been forced out of Quebec by the emergence of Victorian architecture in the urban environment. If Quebec architects such as Charles Baillairgé, François-Xavier Berlinguet, Joseph-Ferdinand Peachy*, David Dussault, and David Ouellet* mostly continued in the vein of Thomas Baillairgé's work until about 1920, it was precisely because of the renewal that Baillairgé had brought to the profession in preferring the workshop to experience on site, and the plan to the building. But this prolonged survival of French Canadian architects unchanged in an environment subjected to North American eclecticism also caused a distinct sclerosis, since at the turn of the century Quebec was still training architects as Baillairgé had, whereas schools of architecture had sprung up everywhere. And by and large this state of things gave Quebec its image as a traditional city, despite the amount of new construction undertaken in the second half of the 19th century.

Baillairgé was an all-round artist. Like his father, he engaged in architecture and to a lesser degree in wood-carving. He occasionally gave his attention to painting but, like his uncle Pierre-Florent*, apparently preferred music. At least this is a plausible explanation for an interest in organs which led him for some years to serve as the tuner for the organ in the cathedral of Notre-Dame, and also to build himself a similar instrument in his dwelling.

A sober, reserved, pious man, Baillairgé led an uneventful bachelor's life entirely devoted to his work. He made only one journey, in 1846, during which he stayed a short time in Montreal and then visited his cousin, the notary Jean-Joseph GIROUARD, at Saint-Benoît (Mirabel). He seems at one point to have been attracted to public life, since on at least two occasions, in 1834 and 1835, he was elected to the municipal council of Quebec representing Séminaire Ward. It is known that he engaged in several land transactions. In 1815 he and his father received a grant of land in Upper Town belonging to the Ursulines. A series of deals he subsequently concluded makes it evident that he was comfortably off, even if he occasionally resorted to loans. Although Baillairgé did not enrich himself through his work, several of his pupils, including Paquet, who worked as contractors, acquired sizeable fortunes.

When Baillairgé retired in 1848 to make way for his second cousin Charles, he drew up his will. He divided his properties among his closest relatives and bequeathed his money to the Hôpital Général in Quebec and to the Quebec Education Society. However, he took care to leave his library, tools, and instruments to three of his pupils, Charles Baillairgé, Giroux, and Parent. He died on 9 Feb. 1859 at Quebec, at the age of 67. There, two days later, he was buried without ceremony in the crypt of the cathedral, the building which was the major achievement of his grandfather and his father, and for which in 1843 he himself had created the façade.

LUC NOPPEN

[More detailed information on the life and work of Thomas Baillairgé can be found in the author's thesis "Le renouveau architectural proposé par Thomas Baillairgé au Québec, de 1820 à 1850 (l'architecture néo-classique québécoise)" (thèse de PHD, univ. de Toulouse-Le Mirail, Toulouse, France, 1976), a copy of which has been deposited in the rare book section of the library at Laval Univ., Quebec.   L.N.]

AC, Rimouski, Minutiers, J.-B. Pelletier, 8 sept. 1845. ANQ-BLSG, CN1-5, 19 janv. 1838. ANQ-Q, CE1-1, 9 janv. 1787, 21 déc. 1791, 11 févr. 1859; CN1-17, 22 déc. 1845; CN1-27, 28 juin, 10 août 1830; CN1-60, 1er nov. 1824; CN1-61, 5 oct. 1841; CN1-80, 22 avril 1834, 1er avril 1835, 24 juill. 1837, 13 mai 1841, 11 févr. 1843, 11 févr. 1847, 5 août 1848; CN1-102, 26 déc. 1838; CN1-116, 20 mars 1832; CN1-155, 16 oct. 1837; CN1-188, 16 juin 1831, 12 nov. 1832; CN1-208, 11 févr. 1825; 5 nov. 1830; 22 mars, 26 avril 1831; 3 mai 1834; 26 mai 1845; 16 févr. 1852; CN1-212, 17, 21 mai 1828; 7 juill., 28 oct., 21 nov. 1829; 30 nov. 1830; 14 mars 1832; 19 nov. 1833; 10 juin 1840; 8 mai 1841; CN1-213, 14 mars 1845; CN1-219, 12 juill. 1841; CN1-230, 5 févr. 1811, 17 oct. 1815; CN1-253, 27 mai 1831; CN1-255, 10 mai 1856; CN1-267, 6 juin 1828, 22 juill. 1830. ASQ, MSS-M, 1040a. MAC-CD, Fonds Morisset, 1, 2695, 1–3; 2, B157/T454. *Le Journal de Québec*, 12 févr. 1859. G.-F. Baillairgé, *Notices biographiques et généalogiques, famille Baillairgé* . . . (11 fascicules, Joliette, Qué., 1891–94), 3: 71–86. David Karel *et al.*, *François Baillairgé et son œuvre (1759–1830)* (Québec, 1975). Raymonde [Landry] Gauthier, *Les tabernacles anciens du Québec des XVIIe, XVIIIe et XIXe siècles* ([Québec], 1974). Luc Noppen, *Notre-Dame de Québec, son architecture et son rayonnement (1647–1922)* (Québec, 1974). Luc Noppen *et al.*, *Québec: trois siècles d'architecture* ([Montréal], 1979). Luc Noppen et Marc Grignon, *L'art de l'architecte: trois siècles de dessin d'architecture à Québec* (Québec, 1983), 76–82, 87–106, 192–93, 200–1, 210–13, 216–17. Luc Noppen et J. R. Porter, *Les églises de Charlesbourg et l'architecture religieuse du Québec* ([Québec], 1972). Émile Vaillancourt, *Une maîtrise d'art en Canada (1800–1823)* (Montréal, 1920), 85. G.-F. Baillairgé, "Biographies canadiennes," *BRH*, 20 (1914): 348–51. Marius Barbeau, "Les Baillairgé: école de Québec en sculpture et en architecture," *Le Canada français* (Québec), 2e sér., 33 (1945–46): 243–55. Alan Gowans, "Thomas Baillairgé and the Québecois tradition of church architecture," *Art Bull.* (New York), 34 (1952): 117–37. Marc Grignon, "Architectes et architecture . . . dans l'ordre," *Habitat* (Montréal), 2 (1983): 29–33. Gérard Morisset, "L'influence des Baillairgé," *Technique* (Montréal), 26 (1951): 307–14; "Thomas Baillairgé, 1791–1859, architecte et sculpteur," 24 (1949): 469–74; 26: 13–21, 245–51; "Une dynastie d'artisans: les Baillairgé," *La Patrie*, 13 août 1950: 18, 42, 46. Luc Noppen, "L'architecture intérieure de l'église de Saint-Joachim de Montmorency: l'avènement d'un style," *RACAR* (Montréal), 6 (1979): 3–16; "Le rôle de l'abbé Jérôme Demers dans l'élaboration d'une architecture néo-classique au Québec," *Annales d'hist. de l'art canadien* (Montréal), 2 (1975), no.1: 19–33. A. J. H. Richardson, "Guide to the architecturally and historically most significant buildings in the old city of Quebec with a biographical dictionary of architects and builders and illustrations," Assoc. for Preservation Technology, *Bull.* (Ottawa), 2 (1970), nos.3–4: 73.

BAIRD, EDMOND (Edmund), cabinet-maker and upholsterer; b. 9 July 1802 in Stirling, Scotland; m. 21 Dec. 1833 Anne Robinson, in Montreal, and they had several children; d. there 22 Feb. 1859.

Edmond Baird was almost certainly related to James Baird, a Scottish cabinet-maker seven years his senior who preceded him to Montreal and who, when Edmond arrived at the beginning of the 1830s, was in partnership with John Hilton*. In the spring of 1833 the elder Baird and Hilton dissolved their partnership. Before the end of May, Edmond Baird had become Hilton's new partner. This partnership meant that Baird had early achieved recognition in his occupation, for Hilton was, even in the 1830s, becoming the acknowledged head of the cabinet trade in Montreal and one of the most prominent cabinet-makers in the Canadas. Baird was associated with him during a crucial period in Hilton's advancement.

Hilton and Baird advertised furniture in the "modern style" and of workmanship unsurpassed by "any other house in the trade." In 1833, when they made this announcement, "modern style" invariably included the Grecian style, but later in the decade the partners undoubtedly turned to Gothic and Elizabethan styles, both in demand in Montreal by the beginning of the 1840s. Much of the work produced in their workshop was executed in either rosewood or mahogany, imported woods which they also sold to other cabinet-makers.

The reputation which Hilton and Baird made for themselves quickly spread beyond Montreal. Although there were competent cabinet-makers at Quebec, the Quebec merchant J. Benjamin ordered his custom-made furniture from them. Another customer was Abraham Joseph*, the Quebec representative of the firm of H. Joseph and Company. Not even two fires, deliberately set by an arsonist on 4 and 13 Feb. 1843 and causing damages estimated at £600, impeded Hilton and Baird's progress.

By 1845 Hilton was anxious to bring his son William into partnership. On 17 May, therefore, the partnership with Baird was terminated. Baird retained the premises on Place d'Armes and launched into business on his own. He had sufficient work on hand by July to warrant advertising for "Several good CABINET MAKERS."

One of Baird's first important commissions was from the Christian Unitarian Society of Montreal. For its church, opened in 1845 (the first Unitarian church in Canada), the society entrusted Baird with the pew linings, the drapery behind the pulpit and organ railings, and a large wall hanging. The work was carried out in drab moreen and crimson damask, both colours and materials being considered the height of good taste at the time and an effective contrast with the white walls of the church's interior. In his advertise-

Baird

ments Baird made much of the fact that he kept constantly on hand fine English and French satins, brocatelles, and other upholstery and curtain materials, all in "the latest fashions."

Baird's own religious affiliation was Methodist. In this he was in company with many of the principal cabinet-makers of Victorian Montreal. Like John Hilton, he attended St James Street Methodist Church and was a major contributor to that church's building fund. One of Baird's daughters, Emmaline Edmond, married in 1860 the Reverend Edward Bradshaw Ryckman, who became a distinguished Methodist clergyman.

Though Edmond Baird's career was cut off comparatively early, he had already achieved success as a leader in a highly competitive trade, first as the partner of the outstanding John Hilton and later while conducting his own business. He left a number of descendants; a grandson, Edward Baird Ryckman, was federal minister of public works in 1926 and minister of national revenue from 1930 to 1933.

ELIZABETH COLLARD

Arch. of the Mount Royal Cemetery Company (Outremont, Que.), Reg. of burials, 22 Feb. 1859. PAC, MG 24, I61, U, 25 April 1845; RG 31, A1, 1842, Montreal, St Lawrence Ward. St James United Church (Montreal), Reg. of baptisms, marriages, and burials, 21 Dec. 1833. *Bible Christian* (Montreal), June 1845. *Montreal Gazette*, 30 May, 27 Aug. 1833; 7, 14, 23 Feb. 1843; 22 April, 21 May 1845. *Montreal Transcript*, 22 April 1845. *Pilot* (Montreal), 5 July 1845, 15 April 1848. *Quebec Mercury*, 21 Feb. 1846. *Times and Daily Commercial Advertiser* (Montreal), 23 April 1845. *Canada directory*, 1851, 1857–58. *Montreal directory*, 1842–58. G. E. Jaques, *Chronicles of the St. James St. Methodist Church, Montreal, from the first rise of Methodism in Montreal to the laying of the corner-stone of the new church on St. Catherine Street* (Toronto, 1888), 90. Elizabeth Collard, "Montreal cabinetmakers and chairmakers, 1800–1850: a check list," *Antiques* (New York), 105 (January–June 1974): 1132–46.

BAIRD, JOHN, soldier and schoolmaster; b. 1795 in Graffa (Republic of Ireland), son of William Baird and Susan Teel; m. first 30 March 1817 Annie Diggin (1798–1836) of Dublin, and they had two sons and two daughters, including William Teel Baird*, military officer and author; m. secondly 1836 or 1837, and by that marriage had six children; d. 1858 near Tobique (Sisson Ridge), N.B.

John Baird was educated at Graffa and later in the town of Monaghan, before entering the Seminary for School Masters in County Kildare. In 1817 the 74th Foot was stationed there and the commander, Colonel Sir Robert Trench, visited the seminary in hopes of persuading one of the student teachers to join his regiment, which was about to sail for British North America. Baird volunteered and was signed on for seven years as a teacher. He was given the pay and rank of sergeant and was promised 200 acres of crown land, probably along the upper Saint John River valley, when his term expired. In 1818 the regiment left for New Brunswick and was stationed at Fredericton, where Baird completed his service conducting a school for the children of the men of the regiment. The poor children from the town, including blacks, who were not admitted to white schools, also attended as free students. Baird's wife, Annie, taught a school for young ladies.

Baird was released from the army in 1823 and in March of that year he took his wife and three children by sleigh about 100 miles up the Saint John River to the parish of Kent, where he had been given a grant of land in an area in which other disbanded soldiers had been settled earlier. For two years Baird farmed during the summer and taught during the winter. He was joined by a number of his relatives from Ireland, who later founded the settlement of Bairdsville.

In the spring of 1825 Baird returned to Fredericton to become principal of the Madras or National School, which had been established there in 1820. Similar schools were being founded throughout the province, chiefly through the efforts of Lieutenant Governor George Stracey Smyth*, to provide facilities for children whose parents could not afford to pay for their education. These schools were supported by the Society for the Propagation of the Gospel, the National Society in England, the Church of England, and the New Brunswick government. In order to keep costs to a minimum, a system of monitors was used by which a large number of students could be taught by a few teachers. The instructors worked directly with the older children who then passed on the lessons they had learned to the younger ones. Although there was some concern over the control exerted by the Church of England in these schools, it was the most effective educational system in the province prior to the passage of the Common Schools Act of 1871. Madras schools were to remain in operation in New Brunswick until 1900.

Baird's original schoolhouse, the old guardhouse, was destroyed along with much of Fredericton in the disastrous fire of October 1825. For the next few years classes were held in the old Market House and once again Baird taught both white and black children together as well as conducting a night-school. For a time he was assisted by his wife. Baird was a great success as a teacher for some years, but in February 1836 his wife and two daughters died of consumption and shortly afterwards the members of the Madras School Board expressed some dissatisfaction with the way the school was being operated. They ordered an investigation in July 1836 to determine whether or not the master should be replaced. Nothing happened for two years, but in May 1838 the board decided that

Baird's services would no longer be required as of 1 October. They later reconsidered the decision and his appointment was continued until May 1839 when he was replaced.

Two years later Baird left Fredericton and moved to land he had purchased near Tobique on the upper Saint John River. He lived quietly there, farming and teaching, until his death. Baird was one of the pioneer teachers who helped the Madras board provide many poor children with an education at a time when few such opportunities existed for them.

WILLIAM A. SPRAY

PANB, RG 2, RS8, Education, 2/59; RG 4, RS24, S45-P138. *The New Brunswick census of 1851 for Victoria County*, comp. D. F. Johnson (Perth-Andover, N.B., 1979). "The genealogical scrapbook," comp. D. F. Johnson (typescript, Perth-Andover, 1978; copy in PANB, MC 2), 10–11. W. T. Baird, *Seventy years of New Brunswick life* ... (Saint John, N.B., 1890; repr. Fredericton, 1978), 1–29. *Canadian education: a history*, ed. J. D. Wilson *et al.* (Scarborough [Toronto], 1970). "Historic homes of Fredericton," *Daily Gleaner* (Fredericton), 7 Jan. 1931.

BAKER, HUGH COSSART, businessman and politician; b. 1818 in England, eldest son of George William Baker and Ann Cole; m. 18 Nov. 1845 Emma Wyatt at Wellington Square (Burlington), Upper Canada, and they had two sons and four daughters; d. 2 March 1859 in Savannah, Ga, and was buried in Hamilton, Upper Canada.

Hugh Cossart Baker's father, a Royal Artillery captain on half pay, immigrated with his family to Upper Canada in 1832 and settled at Bytown (Ottawa), where two years later he became postmaster. Hugh first worked with his father in the post office but about 1838 found employment as a clerk with the Bank of the People in Toronto. While there, he became secretary of the Home District Mutual Fire Insurance Company. When the Bank of Montreal, which had absorbed the Bank of the People in 1840, opened a branch in Hamilton three years later, Baker was appointed its first manager.

In 1845, the year he married, Baker decided to insure his life. The nearest agency in Canada offering such insurance was at Quebec, so he chose to deal with the New York office of a British firm which, because of his asthmatic condition, forced him to take a medical examination there. Although he was issued a policy, the agency required him to pay an extra one per cent premium because of the "hazard" of the Canadian climate. In addition to the costs of exchange, he was probably subjected to the British practice of charging "40 per cent more than was necessary" to arrange coverage in the absence of actuarial data for Canada.

These difficulties convinced Baker that an opportunity existed to form a Canadian-based life insurance company. Declaring the "purest motives of humanity" and possessed of "great mathematical ability," he maintained that such a company, by assembling detailed actuarial tables and by directing its funds into profitable Canadian investments, could operate more efficiently than British or American companies and could pass on savings to policy-holders in the form of lower premiums. From his experience in banking and fire insurance, he also realized that an insurance company was a good vehicle for mobilizing investment capital. In 1846 he took steps to organize a mutual insurance company in which little initial capital was required from the promoters, no shares were to be issued, and assets would be owned by the policy-holders. The plan won support from a number of leading businessmen in Hamilton, including Sir Allan Napier MacNab* and John Young*, and the following spring they petitioned the provincial legislature for incorporation. Members of the legislature, however, feared that too much of the risk of this new type of business would be placed on the policy-holders and consequently the petition was rejected.

In August 1847, undaunted and without a charter, Baker organized the Canada Life Assurance Company as a joint-stock company with a capital of £50,000 in shares of £100. The firm's petition for incorporation met with greater support in the assembly the following year, although some questions were raised. The inspector general of public accounts, Francis Hincks*, cautioned that, unlike the charters of English life insurance companies, which made each shareholder liable for the full value of a company's capital, Canada Life's charter limited the shareholder's liability to the value of his shares. This, Hincks feared, might tempt the directors to take chances with the assets of the company. To protect policy-holders, he wanted to limit its investments to what he considered safe and tangible assets (real estate and mortgages), and he moved an amendment to the bill of incorporation which would prevent Canada Life from investing capital in the stock of chartered banks and established companies. The original bill, however, was successfully defended by MacNab and Henry SHERWOOD, and incorporation was granted in 1849.

As president, general manager, and actuary, Baker ran Canada Life almost single-handed and devoted enormous energy to its promotion. One of his first tasks was to overcome public resistance to life insurance, a reaction based partly upon common ignorance of the economic principles involved and partly upon traditional dependence on private wealth and bequests. In spite of opposition from some directors, Baker initiated an aggressive marketing campaign. Advertisements were placed in newspapers across the province, literature was distributed, and lectures extolling the "great moral and social benefits

Baker

of Life Assurance" were delivered by Baker and his brother George William, who had been hired as a general agent to promote the company. By 1848 Canada Life had issued 117 policies and had established a network of agents from Saint John, N.B., to Port Sarnia (Sarnia), Upper Canada. Most of these agents represented various insurance companies as sidelines to mercantile businesses, legal practices, or administrative positions.

Baker, whose "business abilities were of no ordinary order" according to the Hamilton *Times*, spent much time in the gradual revision of British actuarial tables for use in Canada. In a speech given to the Hamilton Mechanics' Institute in 1848 (and published that year as *A lecture on life assurance*), he reported that no mortality rates or valuations on life "had been made in Canada, other than the calculations of the comparative health of British troops quartered in the wide-spread colonies of the Empire." Baker was the first British North American to be recognized for his work by the Institute of Actuaries of Great Britain and Ireland, which elected him corresponding member in 1851 and fellow a year later. He undoubtedly found this professional contact useful and by the late 1850s had gained a reputation for his "voluminous calculations in connection with premiums, reserves and bond values."

The early and mid 1850s in Canada were years of optimistic speculation and booming real estate values. With its policy premiums invested by Baker in municipal debentures and, increasingly, in mortgages, Canada Life grew steadily, a situation facilitated by the lack of serious competition. Some observers, however, after witnessing the collapse of the land market and the fall in real estate values in 1857, during which Canada Life's assets depreciated accordingly, felt that Baker could have exercised greater caution. To protect the company during the ensuing recession, Baker took steps to reduce the rate of default on payments by policy-holders.

Canada Life's problems in the late 1850s were largely occasioned by the economic conditions of the time, but in 1862 Allen Good, a Brantford-area farmer with experience in banking and insurance, voiced the opinion that Baker had simply undertaken too much. Besides Canada Life, he was a founder of the Ontario Marine and Fire Insurance Company in 1849 and continued to manage the Bank of Montreal in Hamilton until 1850. He was involved in the formation and operation of the Hamilton Building Society, the Gore District Building Society, and the Western Building Society. As well, he was a director of the Hamilton Gas Light Company and of the Gore Bank, vice-president of the Hamilton and Port Dover Railway, and a prominent shareholder of the Great Western Railway. A member of various business organizations, he served as secretary-treasurer of the Hamilton Board of Trade and as a member of the Board of Arts and Manufactures of Upper Canada.

Baker's reputation as president of Canada Life was impugned by an incident which came to light only after his death. When the company took over the Hamilton and Gore District Savings Bank in 1856, Edward Cartwright Thomas, John Young, and William Paterson McLaren* (who were directors of both institutions) sought Baker's complicity in concealing the embezzlement of $30,000 by the bank's treasurer, Richard Porter Street. Thomas, Young, and McLaren intended to make good the loss from property assigned to them by Street but, in the depressed market after 1857, this was not possible. Although Baker did not actively participate in the cover-up, a shadow of suspicion fell upon his presidential record in 1863 when worried shareholders sued the three directors to make them responsible for the balance of the defalcation.

Although the Hamilton *Times* believed that his "reserved habits and close application to business caused him to be less generally known than many of his less eminent fellow townsmen," Baker took his social and public responsibilities seriously. He was a member of the Hamilton Mercantile Library Association, president of the mechanics' institute, vice-president of the St George's Society, treasurer of the City Tract and Missionary Society, and a warden of the Church of the Ascension, Hamilton. "Few, with the exception of his most intimate friends," the Hamilton *Times* revealed following his death, "were aware of the large sums constantly expended by him in benevolent and Christian objects." In 1857, following service as a city alderman, he was selected by the local tory machine to contest the provincial seat recently vacated by MacNab; reputedly dubbed "an insurance agent with a d—d amount of assurance," he was defeated by a commercial rival, Isaac Buchanan*.

Despite his energy and capacity for hard work, Baker wore himself out. Like his brother George, who had died of bronchitis in 1853, he had a history of respiratory problems and succumbed to tuberculosis in 1859 while returning from a period of convalescence in Florida. He was succeeded as president of Canada Life by John Young and as manager by Alexander Gillespie Ramsay, former secretary of the Scottish Amicable Assurance Society of Glasgow.

DAVID G. BURLEY

Hugh Cossart Baker is the author of *A lecture on life assurance, delivered before the Mechanics' Institute of Hamilton, on the 5th April, 1848 . . .* (Hamilton, [Ont.], 1848).

AO, RG 22, ser.204, H. C. Baker. HPL, Clipping file, Hamilton biog. PAC, MG 24, D16, 107: 70785–88; I9, 3: 944–45; MG 27, III, C1, 25, file 3, letter-book, 1861–71, Allen Good to A. D. Parker, 11 Oct. 1862; RG 5, A1:

114272–73. *Assurance Magazine, and Journal of the Institute of Actuaries* (London), 2 (1851–52): 302; 3 (1852–53): 89–90. Can., Prov. of, Legislative Assembly, *App. to the journals*, 1850, app.H; 1851, app.I; 1852–53, app.R; 1854–55, app.EE; 1856, app.5; 1858, app.8; 1859, app.13; *Statutes*, 1849, c.109, c.166, c.168. *Debates of the Legislative Assembly of United Canada* (Abbott Gibbs *et al.*), 6: 910, 1198; 7: 295, 311, 484, 492; 8, pt.I: 41; pt.II: 1400–2. Great Western Railway, *Proceedings at the annual general meeting of shareholders . . . and report of the directors* (Hamilton), 1852: 3; 1853: 26. Hamilton & Port Dover Railway, *Report of the president and directors to the shareholders* (Hamilton), 1856: 16. *Dundas Warder* (Dundas, [Ont.]), 16 April, 8 Oct. 1847; 21 April 1848. *Globe*, 25 Nov. 1845. *Ottawa Citizen*, 28 May 1853. *Sarnia Observer, and Lambton Advertiser*, 10 March 1859. *Semi-Weekly Spectator*, 5 March 1859. *Times* (Hamilton), 3 March 1859. *Canada directory*, 1851: 95, 99. *Canadian biog. dict.*, 1: 721. *Hamilton directory*, 1858: 24, 30.

M. F. Campbell, *A mountain and a city: the story of Hamilton* (Toronto and Montreal, 1966), 97–98. Denison, *Canada's first bank*, 2: 24, 59. C. M. Johnston, *The Head of the Lake; a history of Wentworth County* ([2nd ed.], Hamilton, [1967]), 195, 216–17. *Since 1847: the Canada Life story . . .* ([Toronto, 1967?]). J. D. Barnett, "An election without politics – 1857 – I. Buchanan," *OH*, 14 (1916): 153–62. Saturday Muser [Richard Butler], "Reminiscent of Hugh C. Baker," *Hamilton Spectator*, 5 Feb. 1921: 10. L. M. Shaw, "The Baker family of Hamilton," *Wentworth Bygones* (Hamilton), 3 (1962): 30–34.

BALDWIN, ROBERT, lawyer and politician; b. 12 May 1804 in York (Toronto), eldest son of William Warren Baldwin* and Margaret Phœbe Willcocks; m. 31 May 1827 Augusta Elizabeth Sullivan, and they had two sons and two daughters; d. 9 Dec. 1858 near Toronto.

Robert Baldwin grew up in an extended, and somewhat closed, world of Willcockses, Russells, and Sullivans. Few institutions were as important to Upper Canadian society as the family, and the Baldwins' relationships were especially close and affectionate. Unfortunately, the few documents surviving offer only glimpses into Robert's childhood and adolescence. It is clear, however, from his conduct and utterance as an adult that his character was forged in boyhood under the influence of his urbane and talented father and perhaps more important his mother, whom he once described as "the master mind of our family" and who was probably responsible for Robert's earliest education.

Robert was formally educated in York by John Strachan*. In 1818 William Warren said he was "as forward in point of education as our school here advances boys of his age. I shall keep him yet two years more at school . . . – I intend please God to bring him up to the bar." It was, however, the expectations and standards of his parents, especially their exhortation to goodness and correct conduct, which remained

with Robert. If anything, their hopes increased after the deaths of his younger brothers Henry (d. 1820) and Quetton St George (d. 1829). The legacy of principled life and uncompromised action defined Robert Baldwin in his public life, and it hobbled his spirit even as a young man. For he was, as he later put it, "a sceptic – may God forgive me though I hope not wholly an unbeliever." Moreover, he was melancholic, sickly, and intensely emotional.

The defining characteristic of the teenager embarking on a career in his father's legal office in 1820 was his idealization of women and his yearning for perfect love. He had few friends. His closest acquaintance was another young man of delicate and refined spirits, James Hunter Samson*, who had moved from York to Kingston early in 1819 and with whom he corresponded, though irregularly. They began a debate that year on the merits of love and friendship. Baldwin was adamant: love between a man and woman was nobler than the friendship of two men.

Some of Baldwin's leisure time went to poetry. He and Samson exchanged their work and offered criticism. In June 1819 Baldwin dropped a planned epic in favour of an "Ode to Tecumse," which Samson admired. For Baldwin, poetry was an important means of expressing the thoughts and emotions that dominated him. One recurring theme was love – much of the poetry was dedicated to women, individually or collectively. Another theme was virtue. He admired Tecumseh* as one more "Resolved to perish than to yield." In his early correspondence Baldwin also exhibits a frailty in health that would be his companion through life. His mental health was equally vulnerable. Yet the public world, and probably his own family, knew little of the doubts and demons tormenting young Robert.

His greatest yearning – for perfect love – was satiated early in 1825. He fell in love with his first cousin Augusta Elizabeth Sullivan. Robert's recently discovered private correspondence with her reveals a man of unsuspected passions, fervidly romantic. Admittance to the bar in April 1825 was secondary to his new-found love. When the families discovered it that same month, Eliza was shunted off to relatives in New York. For Robert, their love was a bittersweet experience. Eliza was the only one to whom he could reveal his innermost longings. In his letters he unfettered his emotions – his pervasive melancholy, his fear of professional failure, and his sense of the fleetingness of happiness. He was to go through life acutely aware of human mutability and its most extreme form, mortality. At last able through his relationship with Eliza to plunge into his unexpressed emotions, he was almost self-absorbed. Eliza became "the sweetest source of my future happiness and the kindest soother of my future disappointments." Love for Baldwin was not fancy; nor was it simply passion.

Baldwin

It was more elevated, pure and spiritual. Small wonder he had a predilection for novels extolling the virtues of domestic life. His favourite was Fanny Burney's *Camilla*, a panegyric to domesticity and matrimony.

Baldwin was called to the bar on 20 June 1825; three days later he was presented to the court by his father, treasurer of the Law Society of Upper Canada. The true meaning of the occasion was shared only with Eliza: "When I reflect how much of our happiness depends on my success in my profession . . . I own I almost tremble with anxiety." Yet, despite his preoccupation with Eliza, during their separation Baldwin gained proficiency in the law. He travelled on circuit, probably throughout the western and central districts of the province, and was "more successful" than he expected. In the late summer of 1825 John Rolph*, who had his own law practice, offered to assist him in his. Robert agreed, presumably to gain experience, and found himself immersed in Rolph's "causes." In a case before Judge William Campbell*, Rolph, assisted by Baldwin, opposed James Buchanan MACAULAY. Rolph unexpectedly ordered Baldwin to address the jury. Baldwin demurred, but finally rose. "Never was I in a more distressing situation," he wrote Eliza; all he could think of was "what passed between us" on a night seven months earlier. Then he proceeded, gaining in confidence as he went along. Macaulay spoke highly of Baldwin in his summary; "it was a moment of great happiness," he told Eliza. A capital case came next and Baldwin won an acquittal. Late in 1825 he finished his first tour of the assizes circuit. His friends judged him a success and, he confided to Eliza, thought a certain speech "affords a prospect of my one day not being altogether undistinguished in my profession – I have a horror of not rising above mediocrity." Baldwin was "trembling anxious" since "without commanding respect from my profession I never would be worthy of you I never could make you happy." The brief experience of professional life had been profoundly revealing for the introspective young man. It had, for instance, illuminated his obsession with being right and its concomitant effects upon him – mental anguish and procrastination. In May 1826 he wrote to Eliza: "When a person acts only on their own Judgment they are always fearful of being wrong. . . . Not that I admire indecision on the contrary I dislike it much[.] I know however it is one of my own faults & it pervades more or less everything I do."

By the end of a year of separation from Eliza, Robert was pleased with his professional progress. One of his clients was a former chief justice, William Dummer Powell*. In May 1826 John Strachan, about to leave for England, called on Baldwin to ask if he wanted his name entered at Lincoln's Inn. Baldwin declined. Love had overtaken a bachelor's plan for the future. In due course Eliza returned and with a few close friends and many relatives present, she and Robert were married on 31 May 1827. If their correspondence is an accurate indicator, they attained matrimonial bliss. The law practice thrived. Baldwin often cooperated on cases with his father, with his brother-in-law Robert Baldwin SULLIVAN and, from 1831, frequently with Rolph. Yet life still had its worries. His health was poor and Eliza suffered from continued sickness during her first pregnancy. He fussed over her incessantly, reminding her that Providence had "ordered that few of those maladies with which your sex are visited at such a period should be dangers – they are however all troublesome & call for a husbands care & a husbands fondness."

Eliza had an abiding effect on her husband. She was only 15 when their courtship began, and she died before turning 26. Although she was of gentle birth and educated to her station, her early letters are somewhat kittenish; later correspondence displays a greater measure of maturity. What attracted Baldwin was not her appearance, which was plain, but her character and opinions, of which we know little. Still, his expectations could only be met by a rare woman. They read the Bible together, his scepticism giving way to unshakeable faith. He came to believe that the body was but a temporary dispensation and the Christian horizon was eternity. He wanted to be with her *never* to part," even after death. The fear of death was removed, "for guilt alone need make us fear our hereafter."

Between 1825 and 1828 the administration of Sir Peregrine MAITLAND came under increasing attack from opposition critics, including William Warren Baldwin and Rolph. Matters came to a head in 1828 and, with personal and professional ties to two leading players, Robert was drawn in. On 17 June, John Walpole Willis* delivered in court an opinion that the Court of King's Bench was illegally constituted. He was dismissed by the governor and the Executive Council on 26 June, by which time the Baldwins had become involved in a collective protest against the court's legality and refused to argue before it. The affair prompted the Baldwins, no doubt in collaboration with Rolph and Marshall Spring Bidwell*, to launch the first popular campaign for responsible government in the history of the province.

A general election gave the imbroglio political overtones, especially in York and vicinity. Accepting nomination "in this important and alarming crisis," Robert ran in the county of York. Late in July the riding was taken by Jesse Ketchum* and William Lyon Mackenzie*, Baldwin coming in last in a four-man race. The election did nothing to put out the fire of protest ignited by the Willis affair. At a meeting on 15 August, at which a petition was adopted which included a plea for responsible government, the

Baldwins played leading roles, Robert moving key resolutions. It was, as he put it, a time when colonial policy had become important because of "the misrule of Provincial administrations." Maitland defended his administration in a dispatch to London; in it he referred to the Baldwins as the only gentlemen associated with the opposition.

On 13 November, Robert was named to the committee to prepare an address to the new lieutenant governor, Sir John Colborne*. Through the fall and winter of 1828–29 Baldwin participated in meetings and committees protesting Willis's removal, presenting other grievances, and urging the attention of parliament. In a by-election in December 1829, after John Beverley Robinson* had been appointed chief justice and resigned his seat for the town of York, Baldwin defeated James Edward Small*. In his victory speech Baldwin pronounced himself "a whig in principle, and opposed to the present administration." The writ of election had been improperly issued, however. In a new election Baldwin was opposed, unsuccessfully, by William Botsford Jarvis*. On 30 Jan. 1830 he took his seat in the assembly.

Baldwin was a regular participant in its affairs but not a dominant figure. He chaired several committees and gave evidence before others, including one headed by Mackenzie on the currency. A stockholder of the Bank of Upper Canada, Baldwin took exception to its administration, which he linked to the provincial executive. The following June he led a group of stockholders in an attempt to have an independent director elected to the board. Nominated himself he was defeated by an administration supporter, Samuel Peters JARVIS. With the death of George IV in June 1830, parliament was dissolved and a new general election called. Baldwin was defeated by W. B. Jarvis and dropped from the political scene. In September 1835 Colborne suggested the Baldwins for the Legislative Council if the secretary of state considered it "expedient." Neither was appointed.

Robert disliked politics. More important, he was preoccupied with his practice and family. He worried about the health of Eliza, increasingly delicate, and the daily routine of his expanding family in their Yonge Street home. The birth of Robert Baldwin Jr on 17 April 1834 by surgical means was a blow to Eliza's health. In May the following year she journeyed to New York with her father-in-law to recuperate. On the eighth anniversary of their marriage, Baldwin longed to join her but refrained: "it would be inconsistent with *duty* And I know my Eliza too well not to know that she could never wish me to sacrifice it to inclination." Eliza returned home but never recovered. She died on 11 Jan. 1836. Baldwin was devastated. His brief happiness had ended almost as he had foreseen it. "I am left to pursue the remainder of my pilgrimage alone – and in the waste that lies before me I can expect to find joy only in the reflected happiness of our darling children, and in looking forward, in humble hope, to that blessed hour which by God's permission shall forever reunite me to my Eliza."

What soon happened to Baldwin publicly takes on added meaning in the light of what is now known of his personal life. The new lieutenant governor, Sir Francis Bond Head*, arrived in Toronto on 23 Jan. 1836. Expectations were high among opposition groups that Head would attempt conciliation and reform, as he had been instructed. Maladministration by the Executive Council had been an opposition target since the days of Joseph Willcocks*. By 1828 reform of its administration, by responsible government, had become the issue associated with the Baldwins, father and son. Up to 1836 there were a variety of opinions about the most efficacious means of reform: responsible government was only one. Now the opposition looked to the composition of the council for a sign of Head's intentions.

The three executive councillors (Peter Robinson*, George Herchmer Markland*, and Joseph WELLS) were anxious for new appointments. Head's first choice was Robert Baldwin, whom he considered "highly respected for his moral character – being moderate in his politics, and possessing the esteem and confidence of all parties." Robert stated obstacles to Head. First, a council could not support the crown unless it possessed the assembly's confidence; thus, further appointments would have to be made. Secondly, although Baldwin was "on perfectly good terms" with the present councillors "in private life," he had "formerly . . . denounced them . . . as politically unworthy of the confidence of the country – and therefore . . . felt that [he] could not take office with them."

Having consulted his father and Rolph, Baldwin declined a seat. At a second interview he asked that his father, Marshall Spring Bidwell, John Henry DUNN, and especially Rolph, be appointed. Head consulted with Bidwell before again offering Baldwin a seat on the understanding that, if he accepted, Rolph and Dunn would be appointed. In spite of support from his father, Rolph, and Bidwell, Robert refused because Head was unwilling to dismiss the old councillors. When Rolph felt it wrong to continue the negotiations without a concession, Robert gave "a most reluctant consent"; he, Rolph, and Dunn would take office "as a mere experiment" without pressing for the retirement of Robinson, Wells, and Markland. Head agreed to write to Robert indicating that "no preliminary conditions" had been imposed by either side. The new councillors were sworn in on 20 February.

The note, however, was not received until after the ceremony. Head wrote, "I shall rely on your giving me your unbiassed opinion on all subjects, respecting which I may feel it advisable to require it." This

Baldwin

limitation was, according to Baldwin, not in a draft read to him and was unacceptable. On 3 March the council drew up a representation to Head arguing that only responsible government was consistent with the constitution. It was adopted the following day. Head's reply on 5 March disagreed with the interpretation of the constitution and reminded the councillors they had agreed to avoid important business until familiar with their duties. The councillors convened to consider Head's reply and on the 12th all six resigned. The assembly, led by Peter PERRY, reacted forcefully, treating Head's action as a violation of the "acknowledged principles of the British constitution." On 15 April it voted to withhold supplies. The dispute escalated within and without parliament until it was dissolved. By resigning, the council set Upper Canada's political underbrush on fire.

How responsible was Baldwin, who had been out of politics for more than half a decade and who had just been devastated by his wife's death? Emotionally and mentally spent, he had accepted office as his duty. Always reluctant to take it lest he be seen as compromising, he was equally ready to resign at the possibility of a taint upon his reputation. A gentleman, a man of propriety, and a political and religious moderate, he constituted an effective symbol for reformers of various political hues, but he was not a gifted organizer. It is impossible now to reconstruct exactly the events between 20 February and 12 March that led to the resignation of the council, but it seems unlikely, as Head and subsequent historians would have it, that Baldwin was the prime mover, capable of winning Robinson, Markland, and Wells to his side. Bidwell, the speaker of the assembly, was undoubtedly one of the two key players in any manœuvres; the other was Rolph, who had been persuasive enough to get Robert Baldwin to enter the council. Without Baldwin, it is unlikely that Head would have accepted the others. Years later Rolph's wife claimed: "I Know well that it was not Mr. Baldwin who wrote the remonstrance [3 March] to Sir F. B. Head with respect to Responsible Government"; it was her husband.

Baldwin departed the scene quickly. He left for England on 30 April 1836, bearing letters of introduction from Strachan. He made an unsuccessful attempt to plead for redress at the Colonial Office, then went to Ireland. In England he had mostly been a tourist visiting Windsor, Richmond, and Hampton Court. In Ireland he undertook research into his ancestry. He felt at home in "this dear land of my parents and of my own Eliza and if it makes me a worse philosopher I shall be satisfied if it makes me a better Irishman." On 10 Feb. 1837 he returned home. Once again he refrained from politics. He had, as Mackenzie asserted years later, no foreknowledge of the rebellion. Still, however, a major figure, he was called upon by Head to carry a flag of truce to the insurgents on 5 December. In the aftermath Baldwin defended several accused rebels, including Thomas David MORRISON. In March 1838 Sir George ARTHUR succeeded Head and two months later the Earl of Durham [Lambton*] became governor-in-chief. The Baldwins had a brief interview with him in 1838 and later submitted detailed comments, principally on responsible government. Despite his resignation and the non-official nature of his report, published early in 1839, Durham's recommendation of responsible government and union carried enormous force in the Canadas. The certainty of union and the weight attached to an altered role for the Executive Council ensured Baldwin would remain important to reform. That status was enhanced by his reputation as a man of principle. Francis Hincks*, a neighbour, intimate friend, and banker to Baldwin, was now principal strategist of the Upper Canadian reformers and saw the necessity of Baldwin's leading them and of forming close links with their Lower Canadian counterparts.

Architect of the union was Governor Charles Edward Poulett Thomson*, later Lord Sydenham. The importance of a new and pragmatic relationship between governor and Executive Council had been set out in the famous dispatch of Colonial Secretary Lord John Russell to Thomson 10 Oct. 1839. Such was its impact that William Warren Baldwin was initially persuaded that responsible government would be established. Russell, in fact, had urged only conciliation and harmony in relations with the assembly. The focal point of this thrust was a reconstituted Executive Council. Thomson, convinced of the value of Robert Baldwin in the realignment of politics in the Canadas, sought him for the new council. Again with extreme reluctance and want of confidence in his colleagues on council, Baldwin accepted, becoming solicitor general in February 1840 but without a seat on council.

When union was proclaimed in February 1841, at which time Baldwin entered council, he faced a dilemma. Reformers were divided over whether he should remain as solicitor general and he himself was ambivalent. He forced the issue of responsibility that month by declaring to Sydenham his "entire want of confidence" in most councillors. Yet he retreated when confronted by Sydenham and accepted his vague commitment to the unclear principles of Russell's dispatch. The episode confirmed Sydenham's belief that, as he wrote Arthur, Baldwin was "such an ass!" Sydenham held the upper hand in the general election of March 1841. Although the French party captured nearly half the Lower Canadian seats, corruption and intimidation assured election of pro-government members in Upper Canada. Only six independent or ultra-reformers, including Baldwin, were returned.

Baldwin had withdrawn as a candidate for Toronto

when defeat seemed certain but was elected for Hastings and 4th York, choosing to sit for Hastings. The immediate task was to revitalize the party. With French Canadian liberals dispirited and divided over whether to cooperate with Sydenham's government, Baldwin reconfirmed his commitment. When taking the oaths as an executive councillor in May, he refused the oath of supremacy; denying any foreign prelate had authority in Canada, it denied the rights of the pope and the Roman Catholic Church. An irritated Sydenham agreed to forgo the oath but complained to Russell that Baldwin was "the most crotchety impracticable enthusiast I have ever had to deal with."

Sydenham and his solicitor general met on 10 June. Baldwin demanded four cabinet posts for French Canadians and warned that on a vote of confidence he would have to oppose the government. Sydenham had had enough. What is usually treated as Baldwin's resignation was no more than a veiled threat by him during the conversation, but Sydenham used it as an excuse. He wrote on 13 June to accept the resignation Baldwin had not offered. It was a coup which, Sydenham was convinced, would end Baldwin's career. For some weeks, Baldwin wrote his father, he felt he was not "at all calculated" for politics. But, with the firm support of his family, he determined to fight on for his principles.

Yet there was much to the self-analysis. He was not a natural politician. A poor orator, and a less frequent contributor in parliament than other spokesmen, he even lacked the appearance of a leader. Of above average height, he had a pronounced stoop which made him look shorter, as did the heaviness of his body. His pallid complexion and dull, expressionless eyes gave him a funereal bearing. It was his character which made him outstanding. Baldwin lived the rhetoric of his times: he was a gentleman, morally courageous, utterly genuine in his willingness to sacrifice his interests to those of the institutions he revered – the constitution, the law, the church, property, and the family. His political opinions were essentially Whiggish, which meant a commitment to popular government and individual rights, and an adherence to the values of a landholding class and a social structure rooted in the family and traditional forms of mutual obligation. Other politicians, such as Robert Baldwin Sullivan and Sir Allan Napier MacNab*, who talked of honour knew it might have to take second place to other considerations. They paid deference to a man for whom there were rarely other considerations. To contemporaries as disparate as Wolfred Nelson* and Malcolm Cameron*, Baldwin was known for his honesty, integrity, and disinterested views.

Central to the idea of a gentleman was service. Baldwin's station in life thrust on him the responsibility to serve and he accepted it, despite his discomfort in office, his intensely private personality, and the disruption of his family life. Baldwin readily admitted he wished to exercise power but he disliked the politics of winning it and would sacrifice neither principle nor party to gain it.

When the first parliament of the Canadas met in Kingston on 14 June 1841, Baldwin faced challenges from a friend. Francis Hincks found Sydenham's business-like government ever more attractive. By July his *Examiner* was sympathetic to the ministry, by August he was voting with it on important measures, by Christmas he was urging the reform party to merge with the administration. Dazzled by dreams of economic progress under Sydenham, Hincks rejected Baldwin's alliance with the "unprogressive" French Canadians. But throughout the session Baldwin himself opposed the expansionist economic programs of Sydenham and Hincks. He and the French Canadians blocked the scheme for a "bank of issue," intended to provide sound paper money for Canada, and even opposed, unsuccessfully, the British loan guarantee of £1,500,000, intended for canal construction, which had done so much to lure Upper Canada into the union.

Baldwin combined British passion for liberty with insistence upon justice for French Canada, although he thereby endangered his popularity in Upper Canada. The most practical expression of concern was his arranging for the election in 4th York of the French party's leader, Louis-Hippolyte La Fontaine*. The least practical was pushing biculturalism to an absolute balance. In August he opposed a popular bill to provide municipal government for Upper Canada because it did not create parallel institutions in Lower Canada. However, Baldwin's contribution to French-English cooperation was one of his most important legacies to Canadian politics. It was characteristic that he sent all his children to francophone schools in Lower Canada and that he felt acute embarrassment over his own unilingualism.

Baldwin's major concern, responsible government, was raised several times in the assembly during the session. The most important occasion brought his much mythologized action of 3 Sept. 1841. The standard account says that Baldwin introduced resolutions intended to make the assembly and the ministry define a position on the principle of executive responsibility, and that Samuel Bealey Harrison*, on behalf of the ministry, countered with his own resolutions, which had to embody much of Baldwin's text to gain a majority. In reality, events were more confused and Baldwin's ideas less triumphant. He had prepared resolutions as had the ministry. Baldwin was shown the ministerial version and agreed, the cabinet thought, to introduce it in a gesture of constitutional harmony. Through misunderstanding or excessive zeal, however, he broke the agreement. In the house

Baldwin

he accepted the thrust of Harrison's resolutions but insisted on presenting his own, convinced that only his formulation was fully acceptable. In the end, his version was defeated and Harrison's adopted, Baldwin voting for every one of its resolutions, against predominantly tory opposition. Baldwin had attempted to establish, beyond argument, the practice of responsibility, particularly by insisting on the assembly's right to hold executive councillors responsible for government action. His precise wording gave way to Harrison's carefully ambiguous text. It probably did not matter. In years to come reformers would seize on the Harrison resolutions as a sanction and the subtleties would be submerged in politics.

For the moment it appeared Sydenham had again dammed up constitutional protest. That dam was breached when he died on 19 September. With him went his so-called régime of harmony, based on his personal political ability and ruthlessness. Baldwin could not take advantage of the removal of the Sydenham yoke because of the continuing public split with Hincks and the business-minded reformers Hincks represented. Despite public attacks in the *Examiner*, Baldwin kept lines open to Hincks, even defending him in May 1842 in a libel suit initiated by Archibald McNab. With Sydenham gone, reformers began to wander back into the fold. By the early summer even the tories were listening to Baldwin's proposals for a temporary alliance to defeat the government.

The new governor, Sir Charles Bagot*, had neither the strength nor the inclination for Sydenham's ruthless style. Although Hincks became inspector general of public accounts on 9 June, ministerial drift continued. In July, Attorney General William Henry Draper* and Harrison advised Bagot the ministry could not survive: he must bring in the leaders of the French Canadians and that meant inviting Baldwin as well. Draper, who considered Baldwin a traitor for resigning the previous year, was nevertheless prepared to make way for him. Although under instructions from Britain to keep Baldwin and the French out, when the legislature convened in September and it was apparent the reformers had a majority, Bagot had to ignore his instructions and call on La Fontaine. The talks nearly foundered on the governor's refusal to include Baldwin but he finally conceded. On 16 September, La Fontaine agreed to enter the ministry, with Baldwin.

Although Bagot and Baldwin would eulogize the triumph of responsible government in what Bagot dubbed his "great measure," the achievement was considerably less. Six previous ministers were joined by five reformers, but there was no prior agreement on policy and no commitment to cabinet solidarity. That they worked as a cabinet, and that Hincks rehabilitated himself as a solid party man, owed more to

personalities and politics than principle. In October, Bagot prorogued parliament. Forced to seek re-election with the other new ministers, by virtue of their appointments, Baldwin was defeated by Orange mobs in Hastings and 2nd York. He gratefully accepted a Lower Canadian seat. On 30 Jan. 1843 he was returned by acclamation in Rimouski, forging another link between east and west.

During his first term as attorney general west, (September 1842–November 1843), Baldwin showed his strengths and weaknesses. He was liberal in his leniency towards all but the most hardened criminals and his support of individual rights against arbitrary exercise of police and judicial power. His effectiveness as a law officer was not matched in his role as political manager. Attacked by critics for operating a spoils system and by supporters for leaving too many tories in office, faced by quarrels even within cabinet over appointments, he found patronage "the most painful and disagreeable" of political concerns.

Baldwin valued friendship but found it difficult to reach out to maintain it. Friends, including La Fontaine, commented on his elusiveness and his failure to reply to letters. Most contemporaries ascribed his peculiarities to his "reserve" or to overwork. But by 1843 he was showing symptoms of a severe depressive illness which would worsen as he grew older. By his second term as attorney general, after 1848, he would be incapacitated for extended periods by depressions, unable to represent the crown on the assizes. He claimed the press of political affairs required his presence in Montreal. However, he did not attend some ten meetings of the Executive Council for the first six weeks of the new government. Similar difficulties in business and absences from council marked the last three years of the government, 1849–51. In 1850 he confined himself to home from early January until mid March. The only known visitors outside the family were La Fontaine and Provincial Secretary James Leslie*. The former was shocked by the fluctuations of Baldwin's disorder, especially the headaches torturing him year after year.

When his government was threatened in 1850 by the radical Clear Grit revolt in its ranks [see Peter Perry], Baldwin's growing incapacity weakened it further. A friend and party organizer, William Buell*, wrote to him in June that confidence in him was waning; his critics, Buell related, saw him as a spent force, as "the finality man." It was a suspicion Baldwin himself nurtured. His need to isolate himself was expressed in his frequent desire to resign.

Since his wife's death in 1836 Baldwin's obsession with her had deepened into a cult in which she was more real than living people. The anniversaries of her death and their wedding were annual rites. Robert's father died on 8 Jan. 1844, leaving him grief-stricken, contemplating retirement from politics. For the introspective son, left to carry on his father's work of achieving responsible government without his father's flamboyant personality, the heritage was onerous. It heightened Robert's well-developed sense of family and feeling of responsibility for it. Unfortunately, he could more easily express this responsibility than the affection behind it. His granddaughter, Mary-Jane Ross, described Baldwin as the only source of affection his children knew and yet he was more venerated than loved: he was "a schoolmaster" to them. This man of ancient griefs and loves would have been unrecognizable to the political world, where he was so controlled and reserved. It is a measure of his force of character that he played out his role in politics for so long and so well, carrying the weight of oppression in his own mind. However, the reputation he had won for determination in pursuing responsible government must be balanced by his tendency to retreat through abdication. Duty and his father's mission prevented him from doing so permanently, but for a few months each year depression brought isolation.

Still, he was a dominating figure in parliament. After Bagot fell ill in November 1842, Baldwin and La Fontaine had a free hand – the first real premiers of the province. In March 1843 a new governor, Sir Charles Theophilus Metcalfe*, arrived with instructions to check the "radical" government. He expected confrontation, convinced only the tories were loyal. He saw Baldwin as fanatical and intolerant and, curiously, as one who took pleasure in conflict. Baldwin, in fact, was conciliatory. He allowed Metcalfe an involvement in the working of cabinet and administration that Bagot had never claimed, and urged reformers to avoid criticism of the governor. So unaware was Baldwin of Metcalfe's motives that he did not press on with the government's program before the governor could muster support against it.

In May, Baldwin persuaded Metcalfe to withdraw sanctions against his old friend and leader, Marshall Spring Bidwell. He was disappointed that Bidwell did not choose to return to Canada. While Britain was reluctant to grant a general amnesty to those implicated in the rebellions, Metcalfe was permitted to pardon exiles individually. A threat by La Fontaine and other Lower Canadian ministers to resign forced an amnesty for Louis-Joseph Papineau*. Baldwin, in contrast, nursed old grievances and made no direct effort for W. L. Mackenzie.

The reformers began a session on 28 Sept. 1843 which was to be, in many ways, a triumph. Hincks and Baldwin cooperated on legislation strengthening the financial base for Upper Canadian schools and providing for separate schools for religious minorities. A motion was passed demanding control for the assembly over the civil list. And, despite the opposition of some Upper Canadian reformers, the

ministry acted to move the capital from Kingston to Montreal. Baldwin, although a landowner, strongly supported Hincks's bill to tax wild land, and himself drafted a bill to create the non-sectarian University of Toronto. Both bills died when the government resigned in November.

Relations with Metcalfe had, however, deteriorated. Baldwin had moved to control violence by the Orange order, proceeding by the method followed in Britain: a parliamentary address to the crown asking for action against Orangeism. Metcalfe insisted on legislation. After a violent debate, bills were passed restraining party processions and banning secret societies. Baldwin's family paid a price: on the night of 8 November an Orange mob burned effigies of Baldwin and Hincks outside the Baldwin home in Toronto. Yet, Metcalfe reserved the very legislation, the Secret Societies Bill, he had insisted Baldwin introduce. The bill disappeared into the Colonial Office, to be disallowed in March 1844.

The government might well have resigned over this reservation, but it was patronage that precipitated the crisis. Metcalfe had instructions to control appointments. His practice of that control, without consulting his ministers, made a mockery of responsible government and forced their hands. Following a stormy interview with Metcalfe, Baldwin and La Fontaine met the executive councillors and all but Dominick Daly* resigned on 26 Nov. 1843. There was excited debate in parliament on the 29th, highlighted by Baldwin's lucid defence of the ministry and responsible government. The house adjourned three days later.

Baldwin clearly understood the resignation to be one of principle, necessary to resolve the constitutional issue. La Fontaine, on the other hand, expected it to force Metcalfe's recall and the ministry's return. The following year Hincks was reported as saying "we did not believe our resignation would have been accepted." Hincks and La Fontaine, it appears, hoped to use the threat of resignation to gain the upper hand on a recalcitrant governor. The election campaign of September 1844 went badly for Baldwin. Metcalfe cried loyalty to the crown: while the French party won a majority in Lower Canada, Baldwin was returned with only 11 followers in Upper Canada. Even Hincks was defeated in Oxford.

Baldwin soon rose from defeat. In the session of 1844–45, he gave the strongest performance of his career. He used debates, whatever the subject, as opportunities to lecture on responsible government. His other major theme was nationalism. Control of the civil list was only partly a constitutional question, it was also a demand that Canadians manage Canadian affairs. His affection for things British took second place to his Canadian nationalism. In March 1846, during a debate on the militia, he insisted it was

Baldwin

capable of defending the province without British help: "We want no foreign bayonets here. . . . He loved the Mother Country, but he loved the soil on which he lived better."

The tory government of William Henry Draper and Denis-Benjamin Viger* was weak, especially after the dying Metcalfe was replaced by the more neutral Lieutenant-General Charles Murray CATHCART, as adminstrator in November 1845 and as governor the following April. But the reform alliance was rickety. Many French Canadians listened to overtures from the tories. With even La Fontaine teetering in 1845, Baldwin could do little but remind his colleagues of the tory record on French Canadian rights. In the end, all negotiations foundered and the reform party remained intact.

Baldwin reduced his private involvements to concentrate on politics. A relative, Lawrence Heyden, was hired in 1845 to manage the extensive family property. This was salutary because Baldwin found it difficult to resist pleas for loans and could be extremely lenient with some debtors. He withdrew from active participation in his law practice by 1848, leaving it largely to his partner Adam Wilson*. The practice had been made difficult by his other partner, cousin Robert Baldwin Sullivan, who was likeable and clever but drunken and irresponsible.

The reformers' prospects had improved considerably after the arrival of Lord Elgin [Bruce*] as governor in January 1847. He carried instructions endorsing ministerial responsibility and strict neutrality for the governor. The weak tory ministry avoided controversial legislation in the session of 1847, and Baldwin's major differences were with his allies. He led the successful opposition to William Hamilton Merritt*'s bill to permit the formation of general partnerships with only limited liability, "on the old fashioned principle that men were bound in conscience, and ought to be bound in law to pay all their debts." He attacked the attempts of modernizers in both parties to reduce the dower rights of women. A bill by Solicitor General John Hillyard Cameron* would have permitted a husband to dispose of property without his wife's consent. Baldwin contended that "the main object of this Bill was THE INJURY OF WOMAN, *and to despoil them of the trivial rights they now held.*" He ignited the house and defeated it. His concern, however, was primarily with rights of property and the traditional economy which was being revolutionized by corporations, mining companies, and railways. On dower, as on other issues of 1847, he sought to prevent what he called, in debates on primogeniture, "the evil of subdivision of properties." He was not sympathetic to expansion of women's legal rights, and in 1849 his government took away the virtually unused right of Upper Canadian women who met the property qualification to vote.

Parliament was prorogued on 28 July 1847 with every expectation of an election. Baldwin chose his issues carefully. The university question, an emotional cause in Upper Canada, was kept at the forefront by a broadly based committee which supported Baldwin's University Bill of 1843. Baldwin was forced to attend to his own re-election in York North, formerly 4th York, where his campaign was directed by the leader of the Children of Peace, David Willson*, his manager in 1844. His opponent was the editor of the *British Colonist*, Hugh SCOBIE, whose manager, tory William Henry Boulton*, waged a scurrilous campaign. Baldwin's canvass of the riding was successful and he carried the election, which ended in January 1848. The Baldwinites took 23 of Upper Canada's 42 seats while their allies in Lower Canada captured 33 of 42. It was an overwhelming majority and Baldwin worried whether it could be kept together and reform expectations of immediate and sweeping change could be met. In February he warned the eastern Upper Canadian chieftain, John Sandfield Macdonald*, that if reformers insisted on extreme changes before a proper reorganization of government, they would have to find another leader and would wander in the wilderness until they learned "more practical wisdom." This gloomy prognosis in victory was characteristic of the depressive Baldwin, but it was also an accurate prediction of the troubles of the reform ministry.

When the house met on 25 February the tories clung to office. Baldwin's amendment to the reply to the throne speech constituted an expression of non-confidence in the government. It was passed 3 March: 54 to 20. The ministry resigned the next day. La Fontaine was called by Elgin on 10 March and Baldwin and the other ministers were sworn in on 11 March; they held their first cabinet meeting on the 14th. In negotiating the cabinet's composition with the two leaders, Elgin noted that Baldwin "seemed desirous to yield the first place" to La Fontaine.

Baldwin began with a short housekeeping session. It was a wise strategy, administratively, for it allowed the new ministers to master their departments and sort out the disorder after four years of weak government. Politically, it was a mistake to disappoint the faithful, especially when many would disapprove of the cabinet's composition. Robert Baldwin Sullivan and René-Édouard Caron*, traitors to many reformers, were included. As bad was the fact that 4 of the 11 new ministers did not secure seats and were thus removed from scrutiny in the house, a curious situation for the first responsible government. Only one member, Malcolm Cameron, came from the radical wing, in a newly invented post with no apparent function, assistant commissioner of public works. Baldwin had done little to meet the party's expectations and taken long strides towards alienating the radicals.

The times were not auspicious for the new government, which came to be known as the "Great Ministry." The economic depression dragged on and the provincial accounts were running a deficit. Hincks was again inspector general but despite promises of retrenchment, the deficit grew dramatically in the ministry's first year. Faced with political reality, the reformers pushed expenditures from £474,000 in 1848 to £635,000 in 1851. The fortuitous return of good times in 1850 with an increase in customs revenue produced a surplus of £207,000 in 1851. The surplus did not satisfy many reform partisans who had a powerful ideological commitment to retrenchment and smaller government. Baldwin's administration was bedevilled in the house by back-bench revolts over expenditures and warnings from followers that the increase in the size of government was threatening to rupture the party and as one reformer, Daniel Eugene McIntyre, lamented, create "a precious mess."

Hincks's ethics were often in doubt; his financial expertise was not. In England in 1849 he persuaded major financial houses to support provincial debentures and railway projects. The results allowed Baldwin and the government to press on with their reforms. Otherwise, Baldwin, who showed little understanding of economic affairs, was not much interested in the fine points of Hincks's financial dealings. He was also unenthusiastic about the grand financial schemes and retrenchment programs of William Hamilton Merritt who joined the cabinet 15 Sept. 1848. However, one economic issue could unite all reformers – reciprocity with the United States. Some liberals responded to British free trade by becoming doctrinaire free traders and others, notably Robert Baldwin Sullivan, called for Canada to develop a policy of protection, but all could agree on the advantages of freer trade with the United States. Baldwin, essentially pragmatic on tariffs and cool to free trade dogma, could join with the *laissez-faire* men on the interrelated issues of reciprocity and free navigation. On 18 May 1848 the Executive Council had attacked continuance of the British navigation acts, which limited colonial trade to British ships. In January 1849 Baldwin and Hincks moved an address to the queen for the immediate repeal of the acts. It passed unanimously. The offending acts had by year's end passed into the history of empire.

The La Fontaine–Baldwin government pursued freer trade with the Maritimes in 1849 and 1850, only to founder on Nova Scotian suspicions. Always reciprocity was the major goal. Baldwin told Elgin in 1848 that he feared for the British connection if it meant Canadian farmers had to accept less for their grain than American counterparts. His solution was an agreement offering the Americans free navigation of the St Lawrence River in return for free trade in natural products. It was a perceptive suggestion, for these were the lines of the reciprocity settlement achieved in 1854, after Baldwin's retirement. He played a major role in keeping the issue alive, in part through correspondence with reciprocity's chief protagonist in the American Congress until 1850, Senator John Adams Dix, a relative.

International diplomacy began to be part of Canadian politics as La Fontaine, Sullivan, and Hincks were separately dispatched to Washington between 1848 and 1851 to seek reciprocity, but patronage, closely connected to Baldwin's conception of responsible cabinet government, loomed larger. Baldwin had always recognized its importance in breaking the tory hold. But, as in 1842–43, he found patronage distasteful and difficult to manage, and by mishandling it he stirred reform discontent. Hincks named a tory, Robert Easton Burns*, a judge without Baldwin's knowledge. Baldwin himself damaged the party in the Henry John Boulton* case. Once a compact tory, Boulton now claimed to be a loyal reformer. When it was revealed in 1849 Baldwin had promised Boulton a judgeship, the Toronto *Globe* angrily attacked the would-be judge. Baldwin retreated in January 1850, claiming he had never guaranteed Boulton the job. Boulton soon joined the Clear Grit radicals as a vigorous and troublesome critic of the government.

A lasting legacy of Baldwin's second term as attorney general was the reform of the Upper Canadian judicial system in 1849. A new Court of Common Pleas and a Court of Error and Appeal were created; the Court of Chancery was reformed and expanded from one to three justices. Hincks later said Baldwin had laid out the basics of the reforms and given them final shape, while Solicitor General William Hume Blake* had helped in the drafting. Baldwin himself, not one to take credit for others' work, stated that he and Blake had worked together but Blake had drafted the Chancery Bill. Ironically, it was chancery which stirred controversy and helped drive Baldwin from politics in 1851.

Baldwin had to deal with two other difficult issues, the penitentiary question and amnesty. A commission to investigate charges of corruption and brutality at Kingston Penitentiary was dominated by its secretary, *Globe* publisher George Brown*. The report was lost in excitement over the rebellion losses crisis in April 1849, but its cruel rationalism about prison discipline, adapted from American models, would not have appealed to Baldwin. He delayed legislating about the prison until 1851 and then only improved its administration, thus souring his relations with Brown.

On taking office in 1848, Baldwin insisted Britain must grant a general amnesty for the rebels of 1837–38. Britain acceded in 1849. However, Baldwin was unable to satisfy three prominent exiles.

Baldwin

With Robert Fleming Gourlay*, expelled from Upper Canada in 1819, he could not reach an agreement. Marshall Spring Bidwell, despite Baldwin's promises to establish him in a legal career, seemed unwilling to come back with anything less than a guarantee of political leadership. By 1849 he too was complaining to disaffected reformers of Baldwin's ingratitude. The complaints were more justified with W. L. Mackenzie. He had had to wait for the general amnesty. His demands for compensation for parliamentary salary and committee expenses owed him from 1837 were dismissed contemptuously by Baldwin, who had a special hostility for Mackenzie the smasher. Baldwin effectively drove him from the party and made him a dangerous, indeed a lethal, enemy.

The La Fontaine–Baldwin government took office amid extraordinary unrest. Economic depression, the Irish famine migration, and revolutions in Europe helped stimulate riots by the Orange and the Green, Toronto tories furious over Mackenzie's return, angry sailors at Quebec, discontented railway navvies, and thousands more. From 1846 to 1851 rural French Canada saw arson and rioting against attempts to impose a centralized school system on the parishes [see Jean-Baptiste Meilleur*]. The "Great Ministry" is often seen by historians as committed to rapid progress, operating in a society sharing the same values. Clearly large numbers did not share a sanguine view of progress and Baldwin himself was racked with doubts. It was a time of transition and the movement from a traditional to a capitalist economy was not accomplished without opposition, often violent.

The most serious threat to the government arose from the rebellion losses crisis of 1849, when tory fury was directed against alleged French domination of the province and especially against La Fontaine. Baldwin took little part in the debate, fuelling opposition speculation that he did not support the government's proposal. Indeed, he seems to have had doubts about compensation for those convicted of treason and only assumed leadership when the legislation was amended to exclude convicted rebels. Taking a hard line with the opposition, he kept the house in session through the night of 22–23 February until the resolution was passed.

During the riots in Montreal after the signing of the bill by Lord Elgin on 25 April, Baldwin's boardinghouse was attacked by a mob, but there is no indication he was within. He was a member of the Executive Council committee which took responsibility for policing the city and made the potentially disastrous decision to swear in French Canadians as constables and arm them. Only a promise to withdraw these constables placated the tory mob and prevented a blood-bath. Baldwin moved quickly on the political front, urging reformers in Upper Canada to mount pro-government rallies and petitions, and personally financing petition campaigns in rural Upper Canada. He was instrumental in the cabinet's decision to move the capital from Montreal to Toronto in October 1849.

When the disgruntled tories turned to annexation to the United States as the solution to Canada's problems [see George Moffatt*], Baldwin with ruthless efficiency weeded annexationists out of public offices. He was equally firm with the reform party. Peter Perry, suspected of being an annexationist, was the candidate for the radical reformers in a by-election for York East to take place in December. Baldwin quickly set him straight. On 4 October, in a letter widely published in the reform press, he warned Perry "all should know therefore that I can look upon those only who are for the Continuance of that [British] Connexion as political friends, – those who are against it as political opponents." Perry publicly pledged not to discuss annexation and the party was steadied.

The crisis of 1849 helped obscure the government's continuing accomplishments. Just as surely has the achievement of responsible government, confirmed when Elgin signed the Rebellion Losses Bill, diverted attention. Baldwin was seen, by the *Examiner* and others since, as the man of one idea who had little to offer once responsibility was gained. In fact, the government, and Baldwin in particular, had a lengthy list of important reforms.

The Municipal Corporations Act provided the efficient system of local government reformers had been crying for since Durham had emphasized the need in his report. The act replaced the unwieldy districts with counties and allowed for incorporation of villages, towns, and cities, with each receiving an elected council (as did the townships). The act has been seen by some historians as a grand extension of democracy and as Baldwin's creation. By providing elected councils, it gave the municipalities a measure of independence from provincial control. However, it retained three restrictions: division of financial authority between provincially appointed magistrates and county councils, a property qualification for municipal voters, and appointment by the province of key county officials, including the registrar, sheriff, and coroner. Attacked in the house in 1850 by Peter Perry over these undemocratic remnants, Baldwin, unrepentant, argued the crown's prerogative was of the essence of a monarchical system, and officers in the administration of justice must be appointed by the crown. He also argued qualifications for voters and office holders were necessary. Hincks should share some credit for the act. A memorandum of December 1848 called for stronger municipalities with taxing and borrowing powers, and his concerns were embodied in the act, which permitted councils to issue debentures. When Baldwin and Hincks clashed in 1851 over railway financing by local governments, Hincks pointed to the act for authority. Baldwin seemed unaware of these provisions, which suggests he did not draft the act alone.

The University of Toronto was unarguably Baldwin's creation. His October 1843 bill on the university question died with the government in December [see John Strachan]. Baldwin was determined to settle the issue, to end the connection of church and state in higher education, and to destroy King's College as a visible symbol of Anglican privilege and class favouritism. Soon after taking office in 1848 he had asserted government control. In July he established a commission of inquiry into the finances of the college, which was supported by public lands. Controlled by reformers, the commission documented financial mismanagement and the need for reform. These findings laid the base for the University Bill of 1849, which Baldwin introduced on 3 April. His measure stripped the Church of England of its power in higher education and eliminated denominationalism at the university. To be called the University of Toronto, it would be secular, centralized, government controlled. The denominational colleges in Upper Canada, Methodist Victoria, Presbyterian Queen's, Roman Catholic Regiopolis and Bytown (University of Ottawa), could affiliate, but would lose the right to confer degrees, except in divinity, and have no share of the endowment. Baldwin did not accomplish all he had hoped. The denominational colleges did not give up their independence and indeed, over Baldwin's opposition, Bishop Strachan obtained a charter for an Anglican college, Trinity. Still, Baldwin had presaged the pattern of development for higher education in Ontario.

Baldwin also contended with his church over the clergy reserves. His efforts were hampered by reluctance among French Canadian liberals, including La Fontaine, who feared that if Upper Canadian radicals were encouraged by abolition of the reserves, they would attack the religious institutions of Lower Canada. Nevertheless, under pressure from his left wing, Baldwin tried a compromise. On 18 June 1850 James Hervey Price* introduced 31 resolutions in the assembly, the key one asking Britain to give the Canadian parliament power to dispose of clergy reserves revenue. This compromise, at best a modest advance, was adopted but, with the Anglican hierarchy opposed, the British government took no action.

The pressure to settle the reserves question, like the annexation controversy, pointed to one of the most serious threats to the Baldwin government, the increasing impatience of the radical wing. Buoyed by Perry's election, the Clear Grits adopted a separate platform in March 1850 far in advance of Baldwinite reform in espousal of democracy and voluntarism. The seriousness of the challenge was indicated by the desertion to the Clear Grits of the *Examiner*, now published by James Lesslie*. During the 1850 session, they behaved more as members of the opposition than as critics within the party.

Baldwin showed neither sympathy for nor understanding of the new liberalism. Indeed, through his mistakes, he fostered it. The token radical in the cabinet, Malcolm Cameron, was assigned in the spring of 1849 to draft amendments to the Common Schools Act of 1841. It was a typical case of Baldwin's preoccupation with private torments and great public issues while details of political success were forgotten. Baldwin allowed the bill to be introduced without reading it, so he was unaware Cameron was proposing a radical restructuring of the Upper Canadian school system. It passed the assembly in May 1849. Its democratic and decentralizing provisions outraged Egerton Ryerson*, superintendent of schools, who threatened to resign. Baldwin capitulated, though it involved the humiliation of suspending his own government's act. The inevitable result was the resignation on 1 December of Cameron, who became another rallying point for left-wing discontent. He soon campaigned vigorously for Caleb Hopkins*, a Clear Grit, against John Wetenhall, who had replaced him on the Executive Council. Baldwin, suffering from depression, was disconsolate at Wetenhall's defeat and resulting insanity, and was widely rumoured to be ready to resign.

The last year of the La Fontaine–Baldwin government was an extended retreat under continual harassment by critics to the left. The extremism released by the rebellion losses and annexation crises and Baldwin's loss of authority had weakened moderation in politics. The long commercial depression ending in 1850 had increased the attractiveness of economic success in the United States, not only to the Clear Grits but to the tories as well. To Baldwin's dismay, discussion of such constitutional change as fixed times for meetings of parliament and for elections occurred during the session of 1850. These were, to Baldwin, "part of a plan to change, bit by bit, our present constitution." He beat back each initiative, but there were always new ones.

Constitutional change was also winning advocates within Baldwin's cabinet. He had long opposed one panacea, an elected Legislative Council, as an innovation which would destroy the British connection. He was shocked when his cabinet determined it should be given to the radicals as a sop. On 10 April 1850 he wrote to Elgin to tender his resignation: he had no alternative but to leave a government committed to so disastrous a policy. His quiet terrorism worked and there was no more talk of the obnoxious reform from the cabinet. However, he heard a good deal from the house. On 3 June 1850 Henry John Boulton and Louis-Joseph Papineau

Baldwin

initiated a debate on constitutional change, including an elected council. With a bizarre twist of opportunism, tories such as Henry SHERWOOD expressed interest. Baldwin struck back. The innovators were republicans, advocates of independence from a generous mother, guilty of "black ingratitude." He prevailed and the Boulton–Papineau motion failed, but he had had to threaten resignation, and his defences of the constitutional *status quo* in the house were becoming shriller.

The opposition also hounded Baldwin on retrenchment, the means favoured by free traders and liberals to achieve smaller government. Its attacks gained force after 21 Dec. 1850, when the popular William Hamilton Merritt resigned from the cabinet, angry that the government would not adopt his sweeping reductions. The rebels found another cause in anti-Catholicism, stimulated by a wave of religious prejudice in England in 1850–51. The chief reform newspaper, the *Globe*, led the crusade. Its alienation from Baldwin, who was considered too closely allied to French Catholics, was completed in April 1851 when George Brown lost a by-election in Haldimand to W. L. Mackenzie, a defeat Brown ascribed to Catholic votes and lack of support from Baldwin.

An element in Baldwin's decline was continued conflict with Hincks over economic policy, and the increasing influence of his inspector general. The lines of division were as they had been in the 1840s, given greater point by the emergence of the railway. Although in April 1849 Baldwin supported Hincks's Railway Guarantee Act, he was suspicious of over rapid development and the financial probity of some companies. That month he unsuccessfully opposed the incorporation of the Toronto, Simcoe and Huron Union Rail-Road, whose money-raising plans sounded to him like "a lottery scheme" [*see* Frederick Chase Capreol*]. The following year he was alarmed by legislation to permit municipalities to acquire stock in the Great Western but failed to convince the house of the dangers. Hincks moved an amendment to permit municipalities to invest in all railways, not just the Great Western. In the vote, Baldwin found himself in a minority of eight, with six French Canadians and an English liberal from Lower Canada. It seemed he was back where he had begun in 1841, a lonely voice in a house of modernizers.

Hincks was never reluctant to express his differences. In October 1849, angered by disagreements over patronage and crown lands, and by what he perceived as softness towards annexationists, he told Baldwin the country was disgusted with the ministry's "vacillating policy" and with "you in particular." Baldwin's slowness in making cabinet changes led Hincks to snarl, "I could myself complete the administration on a permanent and satisfactory footing in 24 hours." A clear break did not come until 1851, when Hincks proposed in cabinet an extension of the powers of municipalities to support railways. Baldwin had fought it for months in council. On 30 April, Hincks, certain he had a cabinet majority behind him, wrote to La Fontaine to complain about Baldwin's obstruction and said he was prepared to resign. Baldwin, who also had been threatening resignation, had to back down. Saving face, he insisted to La Fontaine he was not "concurring" in the proposals, he was simply "acquiescing" in them.

The traditional economy based on landed property, whose values Baldwin adhered to, was being superceded by a capitalist economy. The constitution, which he thought he had settled by responsible government, was under increasing attack. The reform party, his instrument for achieving constitutional purity and French-English unity, was splintering. Religious tensions were transformed into an Upper Canadian outcry over "French domination" within the Province of Canada, and anti-French feeling had become a potent force as the clergy reserves question remained unresolved and Brown's *Globe* set itself up as the Protestant critic. The basics of Baldwin liberalism seemed to be losing their constituency.

Robert's mother had died in January 1851. Personal and political disappointment produced the usual response. Baldwin lapsed into depression, and was seriously ill in May and June. Continued radical harassment drove him deeper within himself. His class, landed proprietors and professional men, was being rejected by capitalist modernizers and radical agrarians. The greed of lawyers and the elaborate legal system became the focus of discontent. J. Reed, a reformer from Sharon, in Baldwin's own riding, wrote to W. L. Mackenzie in May 1851: "The watchword is to be no lawyers, more farmers and machinists." The assault gained strength in the 1851 session. Baldwin's mood was not lightened when, on 26 June, Mackenzie moved for a special committee to draft a bill for abolishing the Court of Chancery and conferring equity jurisdiction on the courts of common law. Baldwin pleaded with the house to give the judicial reforms a chance to prove their value. The house was not listening. Even the solicitor general west, John Sandfield Macdonald, confessed the courts were too expensive and complicated. Mackenzie's motion was lost 30 to 34. But a majority of Upper Canadians had voted for it, 25 against 8 opposed.

The next day Baldwin wrote to La Fontaine that, after analysing the vote, he had concluded "the public interests will be best promoted by my retirement." On 30 June he rose in the house to announce his resignation. He explained the vote had left him no choice. In a house where a major reform was given only two years' trial, he felt himself "an intruder." Although he had been urged by his colleagues to reconsider, he felt he could be of more aid to them out of office. His emotionally charged address isolated the main theme of his concern: "the consequences of that reckless disregard of first principles which if left unchecked can lead but to widespread social disorganization with all its fearful consequences." Saying a final word of thanks to the Lower Canadian liberals for their support, Baldwin took his seat with tears running down his face.

The same day La Fontaine announced that he, too, would leave. Hincks could now create a new and peculiar alliance, joining his modernizing reformers with the Grits and with the French party under Augustin-Norbert Morin*. Baldwin watched with discomfort. As a party man he felt that he owed Hincks help, but in September he urged his son-in-law, John Ross*, to avoid taking office in the new ministry if he could. Yet Baldwin himself could not avoid the call of duty. He ran in York North in the ensuing general election. It was a disastrous decision. The Grits nominated Joseph HARTMAN, who recruited Mackenzie to campaign for him. The old rebel dogged Baldwin's heels, following him from meeting to meeting to refute his every claim. Baldwin received only a third as many votes as Hartman. Never an effective organizer at the constituency level, as R. B. Sullivan had observed as early as 1828, Baldwin now had lost touch altogether with local interests. His failure to recognize that a coalition with traditional agrarian interests had been possible allowed the triumph of their common enemy, the modernizing reformers. Baldwin nevertheless remained an important political symbol, a subject of excited rumour whenever political liberalism was in difficulty. Such a rumour in 1853 had him returning to lead the shaky Hincks–Morin government. In 1854 Baldwin broke his political silence to urge support of Hincks's coalition with Augustin-Norbert Morin, which, he said, although far from perfect, deserved public sympathy. In 1856 Auditor John Langton*, viewing the tottering ministry of Sir Allan Napier MacNab and Morin, saw Baldwin as the only alternative to John A. Macdonald* in reconstructing the government. As late as the summer of 1858 reformers were appealing to him to save the party. Even after his death some moderate reformers, including those led by John Sandfield Macdonald, used the name Baldwinites to distinguish themselves from Brown's more radical supporters. In 1871, in another twist, Brown resurrected the Baldwin tradition and name in urging Catholics to join the Grits in the "reunion of the old Reform Party."

Baldwin's relationship with Hincks was not always friendly. A major issue was the University of Toronto. In September 1852 Hincks proposed the abolition of its convocation, which shared government with its senate, and its medical faculty, leaving medical education to private schools such as that founded by

Hincks's ally John Rolph. As well, the senate would include representatives from the unaffiliated colleges, who could obstruct the smooth functioning of the university. It was at this time, on 25 November, that the convocation elected Baldwin chancellor. To accept, he wrote to Professor Henry Holmes Croft*, "would imply less hostility than I entertain to the course adopted by the present Government." His rejection was also motivated by his need to isolate himself. He refused all offers to remain in public life, rejecting judgeships twice, as well as places on commissions and requests to stand for electoral nominations. He narrowed his life to its basics: home, family, and memories. Only the Law Society of Upper Canada, the law as institution, could draw him out. He served as treasurer of the society from 1850 until his death and as its representative on the senate of the University of Toronto 1853–56. The other partial exception was the Church of England. He had become, he told John Ross in December 1853, "rather a High Churchman as I understand the distinction between High and Low Churchman, though I trust without bigotry or intolerance." His concern was with maintaining the traditional internal government of the church, in contrast to his pragmatic views on its separation from the state, a reform he had argued was necessary to prevent it from becoming a political football. He did not approve of any democratization of the church. He worked with both high and low churchmen as president of the Upper Canada Bible Society until 1856.

A few honours came his way. On 3 April 1853 the Canadian Institute at Toronto publicly recognized his role as one of its founders. In 1854 he was made a CB. For the most part, however, his was a private existence. He took an interest in improving the property at Spadina, the family homestead, to which he had moved in 1850 or 1851. In summer the garden was a major preoccupation, in winter his past correspondence and the transcribing of his wife's letters filled the hours as he looked out over the family cemetery. To outsiders he was a ghostly figure, only occasionally venturing out into the streets or receiving friends.

After his retirement his health had grown worse. Debilitating illnesses, real and psychological, tortured him. He had temporary problems with motor control and visual perception, shown by shaky handwriting, misspelling, and repetition of words. Depression remains the most likely diagnosis. His reserve deepened into alienation and self-isolation. The most striking evidence of his deterioration was the letter he wrote to La Fontaine on 21 Sept. 1853, refusing his invitation to join him and his wife on an expedition to Europe. He had been ill since May, "seldom free for two consecutive days from the disagreeable rumbling noise in my head." He felt giddy, easily worried, and

Baldwin

excited. His fear of travel had been fuelled by the death of Barbara Sullivan, his aunt and mother-in-law, who had expired with no warning in 1853. He had a curious preoccupation with his body. As he told La Fontaine, "My organs are too powerful . . . I manufacture blood and fat too rapidly." This preoccupation contributed to his obsessive thoughts of death. Its nearness had been with him at least since 1826 and especially after Eliza died. The man who had co-ruled Canada was now reduced to pathos, living, his daughter Eliza said, "in dread of another attack." The family gathered round the invalid; taking care of the great man was a shared burden. Since he refused to leave Spadina, Eliza and John Ross had to move from Belleville to Toronto. The greatest weight, however, fell on the elder daughter, Maria – housekeeper, entertainer, and adviser to her father. To ensure she remained at home, he refused his permission when the scion of a compact tory family, Jonas Jones Jr, and an American professor both wished to marry her. Her father's prohibitive demands left Maria an embittered and unhappy spinster.

Baldwin's other daughter had a happier fate. Eliza was married to the much older Ross at Spadina on 4 Feb. 1851. Some of the family were dismayed but Baldwin liked Ross, had sponsored his legal career, and, perhaps, recalled family disapproval of his own romance with another Eliza. Baldwin's boys were less successful. The elder, William Willcocks, married in 1854 Elizabeth MacDougall, to whom Robert was devoted, but she died in 1855. According to his younger daughter, her death "seems to have broken him down completely . . . he says to him it is like a second widowhood." Willcocks remarried in 1856 but he was unsuccessful in his career and, probably because of his father's memory, in 1864 he was given a sinecure at Osgoode Hall. His fiscal irresponsibility forced him to sell his father's beloved Spadina in 1866. The other son, Robert, a young adventurer who went to sea in 1849, was stricken with polio in 1858 and had to live at home, crippled.

By the summer of 1858 there was little left for Baldwin but his dead Eliza. Headaches had become constant and when he could sleep he was tormented by "harassing and perplexing dreams." His memory was so unreliable he could not do his law society business at Osgoode Hall. His agony was increased by a last, ill-considered venture into politics in 1858. On the urging of George Brown, now leader of the party, Baldwin agreed to stand for the York divisional seat in the newly elective Legislative Council. It was a nice irony, given that he once had preferred leaving politics to seeing the council become elective. He soon realized he was unfit, physically and psychologically, for public office and on 12 August withdrew.

The family would trouble his last days. By early December 1858 it was clear he was dying, suffering from what the *Globe* described as "neuralgia in the chest" which had become "a severe case of inflammation of the lungs." He tried for several days to make his will, tormented by his son Willcocks, who believed incorrectly that Lawrence Heyden was conspiring to have Baldwin reduce his share of the estate. The will, completed on 9 December, distributed the proceeds of a prosperous law practice and the inherited family properties, both commercial and agrarian, in Toronto and throughout the province. They had made him one of the wealthiest men in Upper Canada. The same afternoon, Baldwin died at Spadina. One of the largest funeral crowds in the history of the province came to honour the dead statesman on 13 December. Baldwin was laid to rest. Or so the mourners thought.

The obsession of Baldwin's later years was his lost wife. His nostalgic love, grief, and guilt that Eliza had died as a result of childbirth were codified in a bizarre document designed to ensure that he would be reunited with her. The nine requests included that certain of her possessions and her letters be buried with him and their coffins be chained together. Most important, he asked that his body be operated on: "Let an incision be made into the cavity of the abdomen extending through the two upper thirds of the linea alba." It was the same Caesarean section as Eliza had suffered.

The instructions were left with the faithful Maria. She saw to most of them but, perhaps in a last act of rebellion, did not have the operation performed and apparently told no one in the family of the request. A month after Robert's death, when Willcocks was sorting his father's clothes, he found in a pocket an abbreviated version, carried there in case Robert died away from home. The old man pleaded with whoever found the note that "for the love of God, as an act of Christian charity, and by the solemn recollection that they may one day have themselves a dying request to make to others, they will not . . . permit my being inclosed in my coffin before the performance of this last solemn injunction." Willcocks heeded this injunction. One bitter January day in 1859, Dr James Henry Richardson, Lawrence Heyden, William Augustus Baldwin (Robert's brother), and Willcocks entered the vault and obeyed his request. It was a suitably strange end for one whose public persona and private agony were the sum of a man few understood, few loved, but all honoured.

By his own standards he was a failure. Compelled into politics by a profound sense of Christian duty, he had striven to preserve the rule of gentlemen and all it entailed. By the time he was driven out of politics, what he stood for had been eclipsed by the march of progress and the rise of the men of capital and machines. His accomplishments, none the less, were legion, most important among them the genius of responsible government and the centrally important heritage of a bicultural nation. That he did so much, at such personal cost, was the real measure of the man. It was fortunate that Robert Baldwin had his Eliza, in life and in death, the one immutable element in a world of puzzling change.

MICHAEL S. CROSS and ROBERT LOCHIEL FRASER

[The authors gratefully acknowledge the cooperation of J. P. B. Ross and Simon Scott, who allowed access to their hitherto unused papers. References to Robert Baldwin may be found in almost all the private manuscripts and government collections of the period. The most important sources are the various collections of Baldwin papers at the MTL; and the Baldwin papers (MS 88), attorney general's records (RG 4, A-1), and Mackenzie–Lindsey papers (MS 516) at the AO. The Coll. La Fontaine in BNQ, Dép. des MSS, MSS-101 (copies in PAC, MG 24, B14), and the recently acquired Baldwin–Ross papers at the PAC (MG 24, B11, vols.9–10) are indispensible, as is the private collection of Ross–Baldwin papers belonging to Simon Scott.

There are several collections of published documents worth noting: the *Arthur papers* (Sanderson); the *Elgin–Gray papers* (Doughty); and the *Debates of the Legislative Assembly of United Canada* (Abbott Gibbs *et al.*). The best newspapers are the Montreal *Pilot* (1844–51); the *Montreal Gazette* (1841–58); and the Toronto *Examiner* (1840–51) and *Globe* (1844–58). Of the biographies, G. E. Wilson, *The life of Robert Baldwin; a study in the struggle for responsible government* (Toronto, 1933) is an early treatment; R. M. and Joyce Baldwin, *The Baldwins and the great experiment* (Don Mills [Toronto], 1969) is useful, as is Stephen Butler Leacock*'s early study *Baldwin, Lafontaine, Hincks: responsible government* (Toronto, 1910); and J. M. S. Careless's "Robert Baldwin," in the volume he edited on *The pre-confederation premiers: Ontario government leaders, 1841–1867* (Toronto, 1980), 89–147, is the best. Of the periodical literature, M. S. Cross and R. L. Fraser, "'The waste that lies before me': the public and the private worlds of Robert Baldwin," CHA *Hist. papers*, 1983: 164–83, provides a re-evaluation. M.S.C. and R.L.F.].

BALLENDEN, JOHN, fur trader, justice of the peace, and office holder; b. *c.* 1812 in Stromness, Scotland, son of former HBC officer John Ballenden and Elizabeth Gray; m. 10 Dec. 1836 Sarah McLEOD in the Red River settlement (Man.), and they had eight children; d. 7 Dec. 1856 in Edinburgh.

John Ballenden is representative of the class of well-educated young gentlemen, mainly from Scotland, recruited by the Hudson's Bay Company in the early 19th century to administer its vast fur-trade empire. Ballenden entered the company's service as an apprentice clerk in 1829 and was described that year by James Hargrave* of York Factory (Man.) as "a fine modest & intelligent young fellow." Governor George SIMPSON felt that Ballenden promised especially well for the "Counting House or Depot business" and, after serving at both York Factory and

Red River, he was promoted accountant at Upper Fort Garry (Winnipeg) in 1836.

That December Ballenden's marriage to Sarah McLeod, a daughter of Chief Trader Alexander Roderick McLeod*, was a significant social event in Red River since it meant that HBC officers still considered acculturated mixed-blood women desirable wives, despite the recent introduction of British wives into fur-trade society. In 1840 Ballenden moved with his family to take charge of the HBC depot at Sault Ste Marie, Upper Canada; in 1844 he was promoted chief trader and assumed responsibility for the Lake Huron district as well. Apart from supplying provisions for the Lake Superior and Lake Huron districts, the company depot at the Sault also included a provisions shop for the growing number of settlers in the area. Ballenden participated in the development of Sault Ste Marie, serving as its first postmaster from 1846 to 1848 and as justice of the peace for the Western District of Upper Canada from April 1844. In the mid 1840s he invested in and acted as agent for the Montreal Mining Company, which was developing mining locations on the north shore of Lake Superior. Along with Governor Simpson and other HBC officers, he also invested in the Montreal and Lachine Rail-road.

In 1848, with his promotion to chief factor, Ballenden was placed in charge of the Lower Red River district, with headquarters at Upper Fort Garry. On the canoe trip west that August, he suffered a stroke which resulted in partial paralysis. Although he recovered, his weakened condition put him at a disadvantage in confronting the problems at Red River where the HBC's fur-trade monopoly was seriously threatened by the growing free-trade movement. Feeling that a stand had to be taken, Ballenden ordered the arrest of the Métis trader Pierre-Guillaume Sayer* and three others for trafficking illegally in furs. Sayer was tried and found guilty but no sentence was imposed, and the Métis population took this outcome as a vindication of free trade [*see* Adam Thom*]. As a result of this decision, Ballenden recognized that the HBC could best counteract its rivals and secure its trade by offering competitive prices. No sooner had Ballenden begun to get the company's affairs in order, than he became embroiled in a social scandal centring on his wife.

In June 1850 Ballenden left the settlement to attend the annual meeting of the Council of the Northern Department, and during his absence Mrs Ballenden found herself ostracized by the Red River society for reputedly committing adultery. Ballenden returned to witness a sensational trial in which his wife's slanderers were found guilty of defamatory conspiracy. The strain, however, was such that he temporarily relinquished his charge and went on furlough in the fall of 1850. As a result of the continuing scandal

Ballenden

surrounding his wife, who had remained in Red River, Ballenden did not take up his charge again but was posted instead to Fort Vancouver (Vancouver, Wash.) in 1851 to administer what was left of the HBC's Columbia district. Ballenden's health continued to deteriorate and, after suffering another attack of what was likely apoplexy, he went on furlough again in 1853. That fall he was reunited with his family in Edinburgh, shortly before his wife's death in December. The next year he was once again placed in charge at Red River, where the company now faced a "swarm" of free traders, but ill health forced his return to Scotland the following season. He retired officially on 1 June 1856 and died in Edinburgh on 7 December. Over the years, Ballenden had sent all of his children to Scotland for their education, and upon his death the five youngest were entrusted to the guardianship of their aunt Eliza Bannatyne. His eldest daughter had previously married HBC officer William McMurray.

A man of integrity and loyalty, John Ballenden was well liked by his contemporaries and pitied in his misfortune.

SYLVIA VAN KIRK

GRO (Edinburgh), Heriot and Warriston, reg. of baptisms, marriages, and burials, 13 Dec. 1856. PAC, MG 19, A21; RG 68, General index, 1841–67: 80, 265. PAM, HBCA, D.5. PRO, PROB 11/2257/667. *HBRS*, 3 (Fleming); 19 (Rich and Johnson). Van Kirk, *"Many tender ties."*

BALLENDEN, SARAH. *See* McLEOD

BARBIER, LOUIS-MARIE-RAPHAËL, physician, surgeon, militia officer, office holder, justice of the peace, politician, and landowner; b. 11 March 1792 in Berthier-en-Haut (Berthierville), Lower Canada, son of Raphaël Barbier, a farmer, and Josephte Tellier; m. first 21 Jan. 1815 Elizabeth Walker at William Henry (Sorel), Lower Canada, and they had three children; m. secondly 23 Aug. 1826 in Lanoraie, Lower Canada, Elizabeth Cairns, daughter of Alexander Cairns, the agent of the Berthier seigneury; d. 29 April 1852 in Berthier-en-Haut.

Louis-Marie-Raphaël Barbier studied at the Séminaire de Nicolet from 1805 to 1807. In 1808, at the age of 16, he began his medical training under James Walker of William Henry, where he settled upon being admitted to the medical profession in 1812. He served as a surgeon in the Saint-Ours battalion of militia, and then was transferred to the Voltigeurs Canadiens in 1814 with the title of assistant surgeon. He resigned from this post in January 1815. That year he left William Henry and took up residence at Berthier-en-Haut, where he practised medicine until his death.

Barbier soon took an interest in local questions. He

served as commissioner for roads and bridges in Warwick County in 1817. In 1821 he was named a justice of the peace for the district of Montreal, an appointment renewed in 1826, and was also appointed commissioner for the summary trial of small causes at Berthier-en-Haut, a post from which he resigned on 13 Aug. 1837. He was active as well in politics. In 1823 he served as president of the constitutional committee of Warwick County. The following year he was elected for the riding of the same name to the House of Assembly, in a contest in which he had to combat the political influence of Ross Cuthbert*, the owner of Berthier seigneury. Soon after the election Barbier wrote a letter thanking Barthélemy Joliette*, the owner of the neighbouring seigneury of Lavaltrie, for his support during the campaign. He kept his seat until 1827.

Barbier made himself known through his interest in public instruction, as well as through his brief entry into politics. In 1827 he founded the Society of Education at Berthier to "see to the means of spreading the benefits of education to the young people of all classes and beliefs in the parish of Berthier and its environs." The society opened a non-denominational school which was run on grants from the assembly. In May 1827 the Académie de Berthier, which later became the Collège Saint-Joseph, had 50 pupils. However, the society ceased to exist in 1833, and in 1846 Barbier made over the building that housed the college to the school commissioners of Berthier parish.

Barbier seems to have been quite well off. He owned some lots in and around Berthier-en-Haut, and in 1830 built his residence in the village; it subsequently became known as the "doctors' house." The 1851 census listed three servants in his household, and reported that he owned about 130 acres under cultivation.

Louis-Marie-Raphaël Barbier's career illustrates well the activity of the professional element in the French Canadian petite bourgeoisie of the 19th century, and especially the political and social role it played on the regional scene in Lower Canada.

JEAN-CLAUDE ROBERT

ANQ-M, CE3-1, 21 janv. 1815; CE5-1, 11 mars 1792, 1er mai 1852; CE5-4, 23 août 1826; CN1-134, 14 nov. 1838; CN3-35, 28 juin 1836, 10 févr. 1846. PAC, MG 24, L3: 10137, 10211; MG 30, D1, 3: 249; RG 31, A1, 1851, Berthier; RG 68, General index, 1651–1841: 196, 255, 350, 358. L.C., House of Assembly, *Journals*, 1825, 1830. *La Minerve*, 6 mai 1852. *Montreal Gazette*, 6 May 1852. *Le Pays*, 7 mai 1852. F.-J. Audet, "Les législateurs du Bas-Canada." Desjardins, *Guide parl. Mariages du comté de Joliette (du début des paroisses à 1960 inclusivement)*, Lucien Rivest, compil. (4v., Montréal, 1969). *Officers of British forces in Canada* (Irving), 105, 185. Arthur Kittson,

Berthier, hier et aujourd'hui (Berthier, Qué., 1953). Meilleur, *Mémorial de l'éducation* (1860), 88. Yves Champoux, "Sur la route de Berthier," *Le Nouvelliste* (Trois-Rivières, Qué.), 14 oct. 1972: 9. DuVern [Richard Lessard], "Ls.-N.-Raphaël Barbier, médecin," *L'Écho de Saint-Justin* (Louiseville, Qué.), 12 déc. 1935: 1. Édouard Fabre Surveyer, "James Cuthbert, père et ses biographes," *RHAF*, 4 (1950–51): 88. "La Société généalogique," *Le Mois généalogique* (Montréal), 2 (1949): 18.

BARCLAY, GEORGE, Baptist minister, farmer, and office holder; b. 1779 or 1780 in Cupar, Scotland; m. Janet Tullis, and they had nine children; d. 10 Aug. 1857 in Pickering Township, Upper Canada.

Little is known of George Barclay's early life. He grew up in Cupar, graduated from the University of St Andrews in Fife, and became a Baptist minister. In 1816 or 1817, when in his mid to late thirties, he brought his family to Pickering Township. Whatever he had done during the intervening years, he seems to have saved some money, because in 1819 he was able to buy the rear 100 acres of the farm at Pickering owned by the mother of Peter Matthews*, along with livestock and implements.

Barclay's subsequent career appears to have been rather nomadic. He was the minister at First Baptist Church in neighbouring Markham Township in the early 1820s, an area previously served by Elijah Bentley*, but his stay at the church was apparently short and contentious. A section of the congregation split off in 1821 over the question of paying Barclay a salary, and it formed the First Pickering (later Claremont) Baptist Church to accommodate Pickering and Whitchurch townships. During this period and afterwards Barclay served as a travelling preacher, ministering also in Whitby and Uxbridge townships. No record remains that he ever held a pulpit again on a permanent basis.

Perhaps the need to look after his farm and other property in the area – he had purchased additional land in 1835 and 1839 – occupied much of his time. He certainly must have been there for much of the period between 26 Aug. 1836 and 13 Dec. 1837, when he worked as the first postmaster of Brougham. That he was appointed to this position indicates he had some standing in the community. That he was removed in the general purge of postal officials whose loyalty was deemed suspect following the rising of 1837 indicates that his behaviour caused concern among more than members of his congregation.

Barclay was an outspoken critic of the policies of the "family compact," which he had experienced as a Baptist minister; his was one of those sects forbidden to carry out marriages prior to 1831. Peter Matthews's wife insisted after the rebellion that it was George Barclay's attitude towards reform which had persuaded her husband to join the rebels. Two of Barclay's sons, George and William, also participated in the uprising.

Barclay's latter years were spent quietly on the farm, which was a prosperous one providing a good living for himself and some of his children. At his death he was buried in the cemetery of the church at Claremont (Pickering), among the graves of those who had disagreed with him in 1821 and had founded this congregation.

RONALD J. STAGG

[The records of the First Pickering (later Claremont) Baptist Church (Claremont, Ont.) are to be found in the Canadian Baptist Arch., McMaster Divinity College (Hamilton, Ont.). George Barclay's will is in AO, RG 22, ser.264, and Whitby (Ontario County), reg.A, no.138 (mfm.). Records of his land dealings are in Durham Land Registry Office (Whitby, Ont.), [Ontario County], North Pickering Township, Abstract index to deeds, vol.A (1798–1958) (mfm. at AO, GS 4835). The Barclay–Matthews connection is discussed in PAC, RG 1, E3, 33: 61–63. There are several references to Barclay and his family in W. A. McKay, *The Pickering story* ([Brougham, Ont.], 1961), and some rather inaccurate information in R. A. Miller, *The Ontario village of Brougham; past! present! future?* (Brougham, 1973). R.J.S.]

BARNSTON, JAMES, physician, botanist, and professor; b. 3 July 1831 at Norway House (Man.), eldest child of HBC fur trader George Barnston* and Ellen Matthews; m. 5 May 1857 Maria Anne McDonald, daughter of HBC fur trader Archibald McDonald, in St Andrews (Saint-André-Est), Lower Canada, and they had one child; d. 20 May 1858 in Montreal.

Named after Hudson's Bay Company clerk James Hargrave*, a close friend and colleague of his father, James Barnston benefited early in life from the elder Barnston's professional advancement and social connections. Educated first at the Red River settlement (Man.) from 1840 to 1845 and then privately for two years at Lachine, Lower Canada, James began medical studies at the University of Edinburgh in 1847. He showed considerable promise both as a physician and as a botanist. He passed his medical examinations in 1851 while still too young to practise, and received his diploma in the spring of 1852. Specializing in midwifery, he was house-surgeon at the Royal Maternity Hospital and also assisted a physician with an extensive practice at Selkirk, Scotland. In 1852 he spent a year visiting hospitals in Europe, principally in Paris and Vienna, to broaden his medical experience, and returned to Edinburgh in 1853 with the highest certificates of merit from the medical directors under whom he had worked.

During his sojourn at Edinburgh, Barnston also deepened the love of natural history he shared with his father. A prize-winning student of botany, he was

Barss

greatly influenced by the teachings of John Hutton Balfour, dean of the medical faculty at the University of Edinburgh and one of the foremost British botanists of the day. Balfour impressed upon Barnston not only the importance of the study of natural history, especially botany, but also the vital roles played by scientific associations, by the presentation of lively formal lectures supplemented by popular field excursions, and by the use of the microscope in the successful pursuit of scientific studies.

Barnston returned to Canada in October 1853 and established a medical practice in Montreal. Convinced that the province was "rich in Plants yet to be made known," he started also to collect and catalogue a herbarium, beginning with plants found on Mount Royal but aiming ultimately for a complete Canadian collection by extending the work begun by Andrew Fernando HOLMES. Dismayed by the lack of general interest in natural science in Montreal, in 1854 Barnston started lobbying for a chair in natural history to be established at McGill College. By the summer of the following year he had also begun organizing the Botanical Society of Montreal under the auspices of the Natural History Society of Montreal, with hopes not only of completing the herbarium but also of establishing a museum of Canadian vegetable products and of publishing a circular for the new society. Barnston was encouraged by influential acquaintances such as William Edmond Logan*, the provincial geologist and a former schoolmate of his father, and by John William Dawson*, principal of McGill and later president of the Natural History Society of Montreal. During the winter of 1855–56, Barnston delivered a well-attended series of lectures on structural botany in Montreal.

In 1857 Barnston was appointed the first professor of botany at McGill. He was increasingly active in the Natural History Society, delivering papers on botany and serving as curator and librarian. He was also "the most active member" of the editing committee of the *Canadian Naturalist and Geologist*. But before the end of his first course of lectures to both arts and medical students at the college, he was "prostrated by a severe and lingering illness" from which he never recovered; he died within a year. The untimely loss of the "quiet, unassuming, gentle" young physician, not yet 27 years old, was a tragic one for Canadian science. Barnston had made brilliant beginnings in the reinterpretation of the flora of the Canadian wilderness as a unique and orderly environment with much of both intellectual and practical value to offer even the amateur observer. He was buried on the side of Mount Royal, which he had so often traversed in search of botanical specimens.

SUZANNE E. ZELLER and JOHN H. NOBLE

James Barnston is the author of "General remarks on the study of nature, with special reference to botany," "Hints to the young botanist, regarding the collection, naming and preserving of plants," "Introductory lecture to the course on botany, delivered before the students of arts and medicine, McGill College, session, 1857," and "Catalogue of Canadian plants' in the Holmes' herbarium, in the cabinet of the University of McGill College," in *Canadian Naturalist and Geologist* . . . (Montreal), 2 (1857): 34–40, 127–35, 335–45, and 4 (1859): 100–16 respectively.

PAC, MG 19, A21, ser.1. Royal Botanic Gardens (Edinburgh), J. H. Balfour corr., 2, 7 Sept. 1853; 30 Oct. 1854; 4 March 1855; 4, 29 Dec. 1856. Royal Botanic Gardens (London), North American letters, 64: 16, 269. *Pilot* (Montreal), 31 March 1858. *Montreal Transcript*, 8 May 1857, 21 May 1858. A. N. Rennie, "Obituary: James Barnston, M.D.," *Canadian Naturalist and Geologist* . . . , 3 (1858): 224–26.

BARSS, JOHN, ship's captain, businessman, politician, justice of the peace, judge, and office holder; b. 14 Sept. 1778 in Liverpool, N.S., second son of Joseph Barss and Elizabeth Crowell; m. 16 Dec. 1802 Sarah Collins, and they had one son and two daughters; d. 12 May 1851 in Liverpool.

John Barss was born to one of the original families of Liverpool. His early life appears to have been spent on merchant vessels, probably those of his father, where he became proficient in the ways of the sea. He gained a body of knowledge not uncommon to Nova Scotian sea captains of his day, knowledge which would allow him secure passage on the Atlantic seaboard from Labrador to the West Indies. The various cargoes carried by Barss included all the commodities that are so often associated with Nova Scotian trade with the other North American colonies and the Lesser Antilles – dry and pickled fish, rum, sugar, staves, shingles, coffee, lumber, indigo, salt, and plaster of Paris. On 1 April 1811, during the Napoleonic Wars, his brig, the *Caroline*, was taken by a French brig in the West Indies.

Subsequent to this loss Barss traded his master's cabin for a merchant's office and entered into a business partnership with his brother James. He put to work his invaluable knowledge of trading patterns along the Atlantic seaboard. With the outbreak of the War of 1812 he associated himself with James and others, including their brother-in-law Enos Collins*, as a shareholder in several privateers: the *Liverpool Packet* (commanded for a time by his brother Joseph*), the *Sir John Sherbrooke*, and the *Wolverine*. During the course of his mercantile career, John Barss carried on a substantial business "by himself" and also had occasion to fashion many minor partnerships in a wide variety of enterprises.

As with so many other prominent merchants in Queens County, such as Simeon Perkins* and Snow

Parker*, Barss combined his business activities with public service. He represented Queens County in the House of Assembly from 1813 to 1820 and from 1826 to 1830. On 28 Dec. 1837 he was offered appointment to the Legislative Council but declined to accept. In addition he served the law as justice of the peace from 1819 and as a judge of the Inferior Court of Common Pleas. A prominent member of the Church of England, he was associated with the British and Foreign Bible Society and with the establishment of Trinity Church parish in 1821. He served Queens County as a school commissioner from 1826 and as a member of the board of health from 1832.

It is apparent that at the time of his death Barss had acquired a fairly healthy estate. In his will he left £500 each to his wife and daughter and £400 to his granddaughter, as well as ten shares in the Bank of Nova Scotia to both his daughter and his granddaughter. His son, Edward Collins Barss, was executor of the estate and inherited the residue. His property in Liverpool was extensive and included not only several acres of town lands and appropriate buildings, but wharfs, stores, and vessels as well.

Barss was not an exceptional Nova Scotian, but he was one of that hardy Bluenose breed who may be said to have been exceptional in their own communities. A man of some foresight and no small ability, he belonged to that significant class of Nova Scotians upon whom the province's golden age secured a firm foundation. And lest he leave a patrician image, it might perhaps be useful to view the temper of the man through an entry in Simeon Perkins's diary on 30 May 1811: "Late in the Evening a fray happened near the House of Mrs. Hopkins between Capt. John Barss and Mr. Edward Dewolf – the Latter Cryed Murder on which a considerable concourse gathered and the fray was Soon Over. I understand the Occasion was Some altercation having happened Some time ago between Mr. Dewolf and the wife of Capt. Barss and Dewolf was Suspected to have written some Defameatory piece Called an Acrostick." It is perhaps not surprising that a man of such warm temper should have energies which would in his more mature years be put to work in business and community affairs.

JOHN G. LEEFE

PANS, MG 1, 819; MG 100, 176, no.20; Places: Liverpool, Genealogies of Queen's County families (mfm.); RG 1, 173: 450; 174: 97, 279–80, 320, 337; 175: 85, 177, 204; 214½F: 192; 245, no.113. Queens County Court of Probate (Liverpool, N.S.), Book 2: 178 (mfm. at PANS). N.S., House of Assembly, *Journal and proc.*, 1827: 14, 18–19, 22, 44–45, 49, 59, 62, 107, 114–16, 119, 123, 127; 1828: 193; 1829: 375, 383, 417, 452, 557; 1830: 601, 608–9, 618–19, 628, 630, 679, 691. Simeon Perkins, *The diary of Simeon Perkins, 1797–1803, 1804–1812*, ed. C. B. Fergusson (Toronto, 1967; 1978). *Directory of N.S. MLAs.* J. F. More, *The history of Queens County, N.S.* (Halifax, 1873; repr., Belleville, Ont., 1972). G. E. E. Nichols, "Notes on Nova Scotian privateers," N.S. Hist. Soc., *Coll.*, 13 (1908): 111–52.

BARTLETT, WILLIAM HENRY, illustrator; b. 26 March 1809 in Kentish Town (London), second son of William and Ann Bartlett; d. 13 Sept. 1854 off Malta and was buried at sea.

William Henry Bartlett, the son of middle-class parents, attended a boarding-school in London from 1816 to 1821 and in 1822 was apprenticed to the architect and antiquarian, John Britton, whose establishment in the parish of St Pancras (London) offered the boy an education that was both theoretical and practical. Bartlett studied and copied architectural drawings of the past and present and, with Britton, visited noted ruins in England from which he made detailed sketches to be engraved for some of Britton's own publications. At first these sketches were purely architectural, as drawings in the last volume of Britton's five-volume *The architectural antiquities of Great Britain* (London, 1807–26) attest. Later, the quality of Bartlett's sketches and his interest in landscape, especially obvious in some of the water-colours which he did about 1825 of Thomas Hope's home at Deepdene, Surrey, led Britton to undertake publication of *Picturesque antiquities of the English cities* (London, 1836).

Bartlett continued to work for Britton as a journeyman after his apprenticeship ended in 1829, although he also provided sketches for other London publishers. On 6 July 1831 he married Susanna Moon and thereafter his career was increasingly directed towards providing a livelihood for himself, his wife, and their five children. One of his first major assignments was to supply illustrations for Dr William Beattie's *Switzerland illustrated* (London, 1836), published by George Virtue. He sent 108 sketches in pen, pencil, and sepia wash to engravers who had been trained by the artist Turner, and they etched them on steel plates for Virtue. The thousands of prints made from these plates are proof of Bartlett's success in catering to the popular taste for picturesque landscape and the sublimity of mountain scenery. For the rest of his life Bartlett's travels were extensive and continuous, and they led to illustrations for works on Syria, the Holy Land and Asia Minor, the Mediterranean coast, northern Italy, the Netherlands and Belgium, Scotland, Ireland, the coastal areas of Britain, the Bosphorus, the Danube, the United States, and Canada. Bartlett became an accomplished traveller.

According to Britton and Beattie, Bartlett visited North America four times: 1836–37, 1838, 1841, and 1852. From the summer of 1836 to July 1837 he was in

63

Bartlett

the United States acquiring illustrations for Nathaniel Parker Willis's *American scenery* (1840), and in the summer and autumn of 1838 he was in the Canadas sketching for Willis's *Canadian scenery illustrated* (1842).

Although little is known about Bartlett's itinerary in North America, a map in *American scenery* suggests that his travels during 1836–37 began in New York City and took him north to the White Mountains, N.H., west to Niagara Falls, N.Y., and south to Washington, D.C. His itinerary in the Canadas in 1838 and the observations he may have made also remain obscure because none of his letters from this period has been found. His route appears on a map in *Canadian scenery illustrated*: he seems to have travelled from Quebec City westward to Niagara Falls, and then by way of the Erie Canal to visit Willis at Owego, N.Y., before sailing for England in December 1838. No written record survives of Bartlett's visit to the Maritimes. The dates of the engravings in *Canadian scenery illustrated* seem to indicate that he went there in 1841 after another visit to the United States.

Willis's texts for the two volumes are undistinguished, a major portion of the book on British North America having been drawn from the works of authors such as Pierre-François-Xavier de Charlevoix*, George Heriot*, James Pattison Cockburn*, and Catharine Parr Traill [Strickland*]. However, the five-by-seven-inch sepia sketches which Bartlett provided have remained popular. Their popularity owes much to Bartlett's attention to architectural detail as a result of his training in England, to his experiences during his travels, and to his own penchant for the picturesque and sublime in landscape. His was an art which appealed to viewers content to be passive spectators of engravings of scenes easily recognizable from their own experience or reading. It was an art which, reflecting the theories of William Gilpin and Edmund Burke, emphasized the irregular and rough, light and shadow, ruined buildings and vast mountains, wild river reaches and towering crags.

Above all, Bartlett's landscapes were readily identifiable. All but 6 of the 120 engravings in *Canadian scenery illustrated* have a specific geographic location. As a result, Bartlett's sketches have considerable historical value, for they depict the country and its people as they appeared in 1838 to one with an eye for the picturesque. Nearly 100 of the engravings show rivers, lakes, rapids, and waterfalls, and many of them capture the daily life of the Canadian people: the growth of settlement; the presence of British army units; travel by canoes, sailing boats, and early steamships; the timber trade with rafts on the Ottawa River; mills on the Rideau River and at Sherbrooke, Lower Canada; fish markets

and waterfronts; the excavation for the Cornwall Canal; and, especially, the homes of the people, from the pioneer log shanty in Upper Canada to Judge Thomas Chandler Haliburton*'s comfortable frame bungalow in Windsor, N.S. As with *Canadian scenery illustrated*, Bartlett's sketches had ensured the popularity of *American scenery*. The illustrations in the latter are similar in style; their content, distinctively American, shows the economic advance of the eastern United States over Upper and Lower Canada.

Bartlett was both author and illustrator of numerous other works, including two books about the United States for which he undertook a fourth visit to North America in 1852. *The Pilgrim Fathers* (1853) contains steel engravings and woodcuts, and *The history of the United States* (1856), completed by Bernard Bolingbroke Woodward after Bartlett's death, has 31 steel engravings, all of which had appeared in *Canadian scenery illustrated* or *American scenery*. The first of these works is more scholarly, containing original chronicles of the Pilgrims. Bartlett's contribution to the second is an elementary textbook which pays scant attention to identification of source material or analysis of cause and result. His own travels in America, however, enabled him to describe locations with facility and to sustain a realistic narrative. His prose is workmanlike and often effective, demonstrating the effects of his employment from 1849 to 1852 as editor of *Sharpe's London Magazine*. He continued to accept commissions for illustrations from his London publishers and died during his return from a sketching trip in Turkey and Greece, probably of cholera.

William Henry Bartlett was a warm-hearted, sensitive, rather reserved Englishman who was devoted to his family and to a small number of intimate friends among whom was his biographer, William Beattie. Because he was willing to subordinate his artistic talent to the needs of his major publisher, George Virtue, and to the contemporary taste for picturesque topographical illustration, Bartlett failed to achieve significant standing as an artist. Consequently his art seems inferior when compared with the best work of Cockburn, Heriot, or James D. Duncan*. But his skill in sketching architectural detail, his love for picturesque landscape, and his interest in the life of the people of Canada gave to his illustrations in *Canadian scenery illustrated* – and also in *American scenery* – a historical importance that merits their survival.

ALEXANDER M. ROSS

[William Henry Bartlett's drawings are housed at the PAC, Art Gallery of Ontario (Toronto), National Gallery of Canada (Ottawa), McLaughlin Library, Univ. of Guelph

Basquet

(Guelph, Ont.), and in England at the British Museum (London), Minet Library (London), Northampton Public Library (Northampton), and Victoria and Albert Museum (London). Engravings done from his drawings depicting North American scenes were published in N. P. Willis, *American scenery; or land, lake and river illustrations of transatlantic nature, from drawings by W. H. Bartlett . . .* (2v., London, 1840) and in *Canadian scenery illustrated, from drawings by W. H. Bartlett* (2v., London, 1842; repr. Toronto, 1967). Bartlett himself wrote and illustrated 12 books, including *The Pilgrim Fathers; or, the founders of New England in the reign of James the First* (London, 1853), as well as the first three sections of the first volume of *The history of the United States of North America; from the discovery of the western world to the present day* (3v., New York, [1855–56]), the remaining sections of which were completed by Bernard Bolingbroke Woodward. A full list of the books written or illustrated by Bartlett can be found in A. M. Ross, *William Henry Bartlett, artist, author, and traveller . . .* (Toronto, 1973), which also republishes the biography of the artist written by his contemporary, William Beattie, *Brief memoir of the late William Henry Bartlett . . .* (London, 1855). A.M.R.]

John Britton, *The autobiography of John Britton . . .* (3v., London, 1849–50). *DNB.* Harper, *Early painters and engravers.* Michel Brunet et J. R. Harper, *Québec 1800, W. H. Bartlett: un essai de gravures romantiques sur le pays du Québec au XIXe siècle* ([Montréal], 1968). Gérard Morisset, *Peintres et tableaux* (Québec, 1936). Janice Tyrwhitt, *Bartlett's Canada; a pre-confederation journey,* intro. H. C. Campbell (Toronto, 1968). John Britton, "Mr. William Henry Bartlett," *Art-Journal* (London and New York), 1 (1855): 24–26.

BASQUET, PIERRE (also known as **Pierre** and **Peter Basket**), captain of the Restigouche band of Micmacs; fl. 1841–52.

According to Micmac tradition, Pierre Basquet was a Frenchman who lived with the Malecites before joining the Micmacs in the Restigouche area. However, in 1852 Moses Henry Perley*, New Brunswick's commissioner of Indian affairs, described him as a Malecite by birth. Apparently forced to flee his home at Tobique in the upper Saint John River valley for some prank, he had arrived in Restigouche known only as Pierre. His knowledge of basket making, supposedly learned from the Malecites and subsequently taught to the Micmacs, earned him the surname Basquet. Because of his "dexterity, voluability and readiness for anything," he was soon adopted into the band and became a leader, exercising considerable influence over the Indians on the Restigouche River, particularly the principal chief, Joseph Malie* (Tkobeitch).

In 1841 Perley, accompanied by two army officers, visited the various Indian reserves in New Brunswick collecting information for the government. One of the officers, Captain Henry Dunn O'Halloran, studied the Micmac language and did some translation into it. He apparently suggested that Malie go to England to present grievances concerning the salmon-netting practices of the whites on the Restigouche, encroachment on Micmac lands, and changes in the method of distributing presents to the Indians of the region, as well as to appeal for aid in the construction of a new chapel for the Restigouche Indians. With letters of introduction to Colonial Secretary Lord Stanley from O'Halloran, Malie sailed on a timber ship accompanied by two of his captains, François Labauve and Pierre Basquet. They arrived in Liverpool in December 1841.

The three had travelled to England without first seeking the approval of Lieutenant Governor Sir William MacBean George Colebrooke*. The British authorities were embarrassed when they arrived in Liverpool and, at the expense of the mayor of that city, they were forwarded to London. There they were met at the railway station by a police inspector who found lodgings for them. Although there was some confusion over what they wanted, they were received cordially and were allowed to make their complaints to Stanley in January. They had wanted to see Queen Victoria, but this was not permitted and instead they were given medals in the name of the queen and sent home as quickly as possible. On the boat between Saint John and Fredericton, Basquet and his friends were accused of an "indulgence of intemperance" which led to a charge by the master of the vessel for damages committed by them. O'Halloran received an official reprimand for his involvement from Colebrooke, who had been cautioned against allowing other Indians to follow suit.

When Malie, Basquet, and Labauve returned to the Restigouche in April 1842, they had acquired considerable prestige from the band for their journey. In 1851 Basquet reappeared in England, where he caused even more confusion than he and his friends had ten years earlier. Officials at the Colonial Office believed he had come to apply for a writ of *quo warranto* so that a new chief justice could be appointed in New Brunswick. Unable to make sense of his request, they assumed that Basquet either was after the position himself or wanted the power to appoint a chief justice for the Indians.

Basquet was supported by an eccentric army officer, and he appeared in the High Court of Chancery dressed in European garb with several medals on his breast and wearing a red sash around his waist "from which were suspended a long constable's staff." He was introduced as a Malecite chief (a position he never attained) and as the constable of the Micmac nation, who was asking for the appointment of a chief justice for New Brunswick and "for a writ of quo warranto, to [be issued] on behalf of the Indians." The court could not understand his demand and the lord chancellor, who was presiding, asked him to return later. Basquet did not return, however, and the

65

Baudrand

Colonial Office insisted that he travel back to New Brunswick as quickly as possible. Lieutenant Governor Sir Edmund Walker Head* was then asked for some explanation of this most unusual visit. Head consulted Perley, who in his report of 18 Feb. 1852 described Basquet as being "notorious for unscrupulous trickery and mischief." Perley suggested that instead of a writ of *quo warranto* Basquet might have been requesting a "writ of worromontagas," which as far as he could determine was "an ancient missive of extraordinary power" that enabled the holder "to seize goods in a place where they are not – to arrest a man in a place where he never was and in fact, to do things readily which it is impossible he can perform." In Perley's opinion, Basquet believed that if such a writ were issued, the Indians could appoint a chief justice for New Brunswick.

Basquet returned to Restigouche and nothing more was heard of him. He had considerable influence over the Indians in the area and was gifted with a smooth tongue and a vivid imagination. His two visits to England without an interpreter may confirm band tradition that he was a white man. Whatever the case, these visits caused both the British authorities and the lieutenant governor of New Brunswick considerable embarrassment.

WILLIAM A. SPRAY

[I would like to thank Alphonse Metallic of the Restigouche Institute of Cultural Education, Restigouche Indian Band (Restigouche, Que.), for supplying information on Basquet from band tradition. w.a.s.]

PAC, MG 24, L6, 2, no.15. PANB, RG 1, RS345, A1: 119–20, 271–72, 274–76, 283. PRO, CO 188/76: 286–87; 188/80: 295–96, 303, 412–18, 442, 444–47; 188/107: 302–6; 188/116: 55–60; CO 189/16: 197–99, 268–69. *New-Brunswick Courier*, 29 Jan. 1842. *St. John Morning News, and General Advertising Newspaper* (Saint John, N.B.), 25 April 1842.

BAUDRAND, FLEURY (baptized **Jean-Fleury**), Roman Catholic priest and Oblate of Mary Immaculate; b. 9 March 1811 in Vienne, France, son of Jean-Fleury Baudrand, a farmer, and Madelaine Faure; d. 1 Oct. 1853 in Galveston, Texas.

Nothing is known of Fleury Baudrand's childhood or education. He was ordained priest at Grenoble on 16 July 1837 by Bishop Philibert de Bruillard, and on 31 October entered the noviciate of the Oblates at the Maison du Calvaire in Marseilles. Here on 1 Nov. 1838 he professed his perpetual vows. That year he began his service at the sanctuary in Notre-Dame de l'Osier as a preaching missionary and priest to those on pilgrimages, offices he held until 1841.

On 13 August of that year the founder of the Oblates, Bishop Charles-Joseph-Eugène de Mazenod, accepted the invitation of Bishop Ignace Bourget* to send some members of his community to the diocese of Montreal. Baudrand volunteered and was selected for the first group going to Canada. On 2 Dec. 1841 he arrived in Montreal along with fathers Jean-Baptiste Honorat*, Pierre-Antoine-Adrien Telmon, and Lucien-Antoine Lagier* and lay brothers Basile Fastray and Pierre-Jean-Louis-François Roux.

Baudrand took up residence in Saint-Hilaire parish (at Mont-Saint-Hilaire), where he became curate on 4 December. In August 1842 he moved to the Oblates' new house at Longueuil, where he remained nearly four years. He spent some of his time preaching retreats in the parishes, convents, and colleges of the Montreal region; in addition he worked hard to establish temperance societies and the Congrégation des Filles de Marie-Immaculée, a community of pious women. He also devoted his energies from 1843 to 1845 to the arduous work of ministering in the Eastern Townships, travelling an immense territory whose principal centres were Granby, Stanbridge, Dunham, and Stanstead. He stayed at Bytown (Ottawa) in 1846 and 1847 to help his confrères who were wrestling with a typhus epidemic.

Baudrand returned to Longueuil the following year and in 1849 and 1850 served as superior of the house. When the Oblates gave up their residence in the latter year, he went to the Maison Saint-Pierre-Apôtre in Sainte-Marie Ward, a working-class area of Montreal; in 1850 and 1851 he was the superior of the house, where he continued to live until 1853. In addition to undertaking ministry in the chapel, which was open to the public, and preaching, he supervised the construction of the magnificent church of Saint-Pierre-Apôtre. Enjoying Bourget's confidence, he accompanied the bishop to the first provincial council of Quebec in 1851 as a theologian.

A scholar with a good grasp of English and a man of high principle, Baudrand was sent as a missionary to Galveston, Texas, in April 1853. On his arrival in May, he was chosen superior of the future college at Brownsville and he supervised the construction of its buildings, which were completed under his successor, Julien Baudre, on 1 Jan. 1855.

Fleury Baudrand had been in Texas but a few months when he was stricken with yellow fever; he died on 1 Oct. 1853 after an illness of only three days. Although the doctor had advised him to leave the area where the epidemic was raging, he refused, being determined to remain at his post and not wanting to be accused of cowardice in the face of danger. Baudrand was buried at the entrance to the cathedral in Galveston. He was remembered as a good, charitable priest with a humble heart.

GASTON CARRIÈRE

ACAM, RLB, II: 438. AD, Isère (Grenoble), État civil, Vienne, 10 mars 1811. Arch. du diocèse de Grenoble (Grenoble, France), HEB 1342, J43c/3 (copie aux Arch. hist. oblates, Ottawa). Arch. générales O.M.I. (Rome), Dossier Fleury Baudrand; C.-J.-E. de Mazenod, *Journal* (copies aux Arch. hist. oblates). Arch. provinciales O.M.I. (Montréal), *Codex historicus*, Saint-Hilaire; Longueuil; Saint-Pierre de Montréal (copies aux Arch. hist. oblates). C.-J.-E. de Mazenod, *Lettres aux correspondants d'Amérique, 1841–1850* (Rome, 1977). Allaire, *Dictionnaire*, 1: 28. *Notice historique et statistique sur la Congrégation des missionnaires oblats de Marie-Immaculée et compte rendu de l'année 1853–1854* (Marseille, France, 1854), 41. *Notices nécrologiques des membres de la Congrégation des oblats de Marie-Immaculée* (8v., Paris, 1868–1939), 6: 325. Tanguay, *Répertoire* (1893), 233. Gaston Carrière, *Histoire documentaire de la Congrégation des missionnaires oblats de Marie-Immaculée dans l'Est du Canada* (12v., Ottawa, 1957–75), 1: 198; 11: 144. Bernardo Doyon, *The cavalry of Christ on the Rio Grande: a historical study of the Oblate missions in Texas and Mexico, 1849–1883* (Milwaukee, Wis., 1956), 39–40, 156–57, 236. Jacques Grisé, *Les conciles provinciaux de Québec et l'Église canadienne (1851–1886)* (Montréal, 1979), 33, 53. P.-F. Parisot, *The reminiscences of a Texas missionary* (San Antonio, Tex., 1899), 6, 8.

BAYNE, JOHN, Presbyterian minister; b. 16 Nov. 1806 in Greenock, Scotland, son of the Reverend Kenneth Bayne, minister of the Gaelic Chapel, Greenock, and Margaret Hay; d. unmarried 3 Nov. 1859 in Galt (Cambridge), Upper Canada.

After attending the universities of Glasgow and Edinburgh, John Bayne moved to Edinburgh in 1827 and was licensed to preach in the Church of Scotland by the Presbytery of Dingwall on 8 Sept. 1830. It was about this time that he refused an offer of a church in South Carolina, evidently preferring to remain at home in the hope of receiving a call from a Scottish congregation. While in Edinburgh he acted as assistant to various ministers. The drowning of two sisters in the spring of 1832 seems to have had a lifelong effect on Bayne's work and character. Although death had been no stranger to his family (he had already lost his parents, a brother, and a sister), this unexpected loss prompted him to compose in secret several pious resolutions, found only after his death, that are thought to have henceforth governed his demeanour and actions. According to one account, these "heavy domestic afflictions" gave him "an appearance of gloom, that was often mistaken by strangers for absolute melancholy, and also tended to produce that comparative indifference to the world, and that undoubted piety which ever characterized him." Asked in later years why he never married, Bayne replied that "since my father died I have never felt that I had a home, and I have never cared to marry."

He moved to Shapinsay, in the Orkney Islands, in 1833 to serve as assistant to the Reverend John Barry. When the parish's lay patron denied a popular request to grant him a continuing position there, Bayne, "chafed with the hauteur of the patron as well as with the treatment the congregation received," decided to leave. He was accepted by the Glasgow Colonial Society to serve as a missionary to British North America and was ordained by the Presbytery of Dingwall on 3 Sept. 1834. Bayne transferred all his property to his surviving sisters and departed for Upper Canada, arriving about the end of 1834. He first served at St Andrew's in Toronto between the departure of William RINTOUL and the return from Scotland of his successor, William Turnbull Leach*. Late in 1835 Bayne accepted a call from the congregation of St Andrew's in Galt, whose minister, William Stewart, had left to accept a call to Demerara (Guyana). In Galt, with a congregation composed almost exclusively of "a respectable class of Lowland Scotch farmers" and businessmen, Bayne commenced a remarkable ministry that, for all his having decided to serve only temporarily in Upper Canada, lasted until his death. His services, sometimes exceeding three hours, were characterized by a forceful and eloquent pulpit style that soon attracted one of the largest Presbyterian congregations in Canada and made him one of the church's highest paid preachers. An observer said that in his pulpit prayers he talked "as if he were alone with God, and yet covered all public and congregational needs and aspirations." He also established seven new congregations in the Galt region, but his exhausting travels ruined his health with the result that he seldom attended presbytery and synod meetings. Nevertheless, he was chosen in 1842 to recruit clergy in Scotland for newly settled areas in the province.

Bayne was still in Edinburgh in May 1843 when the disruption of the Church of Scotland occurred as a reaction against state interference with church business. He returned to Canada in the summer believing that the absence of state interference with the colonial church would prevent a similar upheaval there. During the winter, when the developments in Scotland were widely discussed in British North America [*see* Robert Burns*], Bayne became convinced that to maintain the connection would be to share the Church of Scotland's "sin" of accepting the direct involvement of the state. Unlike the long-settled Presbyterians in the eastern part of Upper Canada, recent Scottish immigrants to the western districts strongly favoured a Canadian disruption. Moreover, because the separatists in Scotland who had formed the Free Church there promoted the Glasgow Colonial Society's mission in British North America, most of the society's missionaries, including Bayne, supported the split.

Bayne

When the Synod of the Presbyterian Church of Canada in connection with the Church of Scotland met at Kingston in July 1844 Bayne took the lead by presenting a motion for separation from the Church of Scotland, thus opposing the Reverend John Cook*. With 20 elders and 22 other ministers, including Robert Burns, Alexander GALE, and Mark Young Stark*, he helped create the Synod of the Presbyterian Church of Canada, popularly called the Free Church. Most of Bayne's congregation in Galt supported his action, although it cost them their church building. Those in Galt who remained with the Church of Scotland received the guidance of the Reverend Thomas Liddell*, principal of Queen's College, Kingston, in securing possession of their property. A year later Bayne and Liddell publicly debated the disruption at Galt, and it was generally conceded that Bayne won.

The Free Church was approached in 1844 by the Missionary Synod of Canada in connection with the United Associate Secession Church in Scotland with a view to union. Bayne, convenor of his synod's union committee, and most of his colleagues demanded acceptance of their doctrine of the state's obligation to support the church without exercising any control, whereas the members of the Missionary Synod, led by William PROUDFOOT, were voluntarists, believing in the separation of church and state. Union was delayed until 1861, after Bayne's death.

In 1846 Bayne was unanimously chosen moderator of his synod. The following year he returned to Scotland on behalf of Toronto's recently established Free Church college (later Knox College), and obtained the services of the Reverend Michael Willis* as professor of theology. In later years Bayne, because of his continuing poor health, repeatedly refused a teaching post in the college, including one made vacant by the death of Henry ESSON.

Bayne's popularity assured that his Free Church congregation in Galt, Knox's, would grow rapidly; by 1852 it comprised 298 families and had an average attendance of 890. Made a doctor of divinity in 1853 by Union College, Schenectady, N.Y., he took a leave of absence in 1855–56 after a serious illness to visit Britain and Europe, resuming his pastoral duties at the end of 1856. When his church needed two Sunday services Bayne "acknowledged that he was not equal to the undertaking" and in 1858 offered to resign. His congregation rejected the offer and instead hired the Reverend Archibald Constable Geikie as his assistant. "Conscious at the age of fifty that he looked old," Bayne, a heavy smoker who engaged in "ever-growing sedentary habits," suddenly became ill at his home on the morning of 3 Nov. 1859 and died that afternoon.

JOHN S. MOIR

[John Bayne left no diaries and few letters. According to one biographer, he "disliked greatly the mere act of using a pen . . . and he had, as a rule, as little to do with pen and ink work as was possible for one in his position." Under those circumstances it is surprising that he published at all. Some of his sermons and polemical writings appeared in pamphlet form during his lifetime, including *Report of the discussion on the late disruption in the Presbyterian Church, which took place in St. Andrew's Church, Galt, on Tuesday, May 27, 1845, between the Rev. Principal Liddell, D.D., of Queen's College, Kingston, and the Rev. John Bayne, minister of the Presbyterian Church of Canada, Galt* (Galt [Cambridge, Ont.], 1845). At the request of the newly formed Free Church synod, Bayne drafted a defence of the disruption as a pastoral address that was later expanded and published as *Was the recent disruption of the synod of Canada, in connection with the Church of Scotland, called for? An address to the Presbyterians of Canada who still support the synod in connection with the Church of Scotland* (Galt, 1846). Another work, *Is man responsible for his belief? A lecture delivered before the members of the Hamilton Mercantile Library Association, on the evening of the 18th of February 1851*, was published in Galt in 1851. Although plans to publish notes of his sermons posthumously were never pursued, fragments of his sermons appeared as "Outlines of four discourses by the Rev. John Bayne, D.D., late minister of Knox Church, Galt," in *Canada Presbyterian church pulpit, first series* (Toronto, 1871), 16–30.

Notices of Bayne's death appeared in *Ecclesiastical and Missionary Record for the Presbyterian Church of Canada* (Toronto), 16 (1859–60): 20–22, 54, in its *Minutes of the Synod* (Toronto), 1860: 37, and in the *Sarnia Observer, and Lambton Advertiser*, 18 Nov. 1859. A longer obituary is Robert Irvine's sermon, *"Where is the Lord God of Elijah?"; a discourse preached in Knox's Church, Hamilton, C.W., on Sabbath, November 13, 1859, with a view to improve the sudden demise of the late Rev. John Bayne, D.D., of Galt* (Hamilton, [Ont.], 1859).

The first biography was written by his friend, the Reverend George Smellie. Called *Memoir of the Rev. John Bayne, D.D., of Galt . . .* (Toronto, 1871), it republished Bayne's essay on man's responsibility for his belief (91–139), and also contains the only surviving sample of his poetry, in which sphere Bayne "had some confidence in his abilities." In part to provide more anecdotal information, and in part to correct a misleading statement in Smellie's biography that obviously rankled, the Reverend Archibald Constable Geikie wrote an excellent biography of Bayne called "A colonial sketch: Dr. John Bayne of Galt," originally published in the *British and Foreign Evangelical Rev.* (Toronto), 24 (1875): 488–504. It was republished in *Rev. Dr. John Bayne, D.D., minister of Knox's Church, Galt, 1835–1859* (Galt, 1935), edited by a namesake, John Bayne Maclean. This work and A. J. Clark, "Notes on the Galt churches," *OH*, 22 (1925): 18–19, reproduce a portrait of Bayne which in 1935 was still hanging in his former manse. The pious resolutions written on the drowning of his two sisters are printed in Geikie's biography and in the *Ecclesiastical and Missionary Record for the Presbyterian Church of Canada*, 16: 104. A short, uncredited biography entitled "The Rev. John Bayne, D.D." also appeared in the *Knox College Monthly* (Toronto), 2 (1883–84): 34–38. J.S.M.]

PCA, H. S. McCollum papers. UCA, Biog. files, John

Beardsley

Bayne, esp. A. B. Baird, "Biographical sketch: Rev. John Bayne, D.D., of Galt" (typescript). Croil, *Hist. and statistical report* (1868), 25, 28–29. Scott *et al.*, *Fasti ecclesiæ scoticanæ*, vol.7. Gregg, *Hist. of Presbyterian Church. Knox's: for the extension of the redeemer's kingdom; the story of the congregation of Knox's Presbyterian Church of Galt ... 1844–1969*, ed. C. E. Saunders ([Galt], 1969). N. G. Smith *et al.*, *A short history of the Presbyterian Church in Canada* (Toronto, [1965]). J. R. Blake, "The history of Knox's Church, Galt, Ont.," Waterloo Hist. Soc., *Annual report*, 1937: 266–72.

BEARDSLEY, BARTHOLOMEW CRANNELL, lawyer, politician, and judge; b. 21 Oct. 1775 in Poughkeepsie, N.Y., son of John Beardsley* and Gertrude Crannell; m. Mary Jenkins, and they had six sons and one daughter; d. 24 March 1855 in Oakville, Upper Canada.

Bartholomew Crannell Beardsley was the son of the chaplain to the Loyal American Regiment and the grandson of Bartholomew Crannell, a prosperous Poughkeepsie attorney, both loyalists who settled by the Saint John River (N.B.) following the American revolution. Young Beardsley studied law in Saint John at the office of Ward Chipman* and was admitted to the New Brunswick bar in October 1796. The following spring he headed for Upper Canada where he set up practice in Newark (Niagara-on-the-Lake). He attended the founding meeting of the Law Society of Upper Canada at Wilson's Hotel, Newark, on 17 July 1797 and became a bencher of the society two years later. Beardsley subsequently returned to New Brunswick, but, finding his prospects there "by no means flattering," by 1807 he had resumed his practice in Upper Canada. The people and events of this period in the history of the province would provide material for the novel *The victims of tyranny*, written 40 years later by his son Charles Edwin.

During the War of 1812 Beardsley assisted Judge William Campbell* as an officer of the court on two circuits of eastern and western Upper Canada. In the spring of 1814 Beardsley, John Ten Broeck, and William Birdseye Peters* served as defence counsel for prisoners such as Jacob Overholser* on trial for treason at the Ancaster "Bloody Assize." Beardsley developed a close acquaintance with William Lyon Mackenzie*, who, in May 1824, read the first issue of his *Colonial Advocate* "word for word to my worthy friend Mr. Beardsley ... who, as a whole, was pleased to approve it." A few weeks later the *Advocate* referred to Beardsley as the lawyer in 1819 for Bartemas Ferguson*, the editor of the *Niagara Spectator* accused of libel for publishing an article by Robert Gourlay*. Though he had been unsuccessful, Beardsley was praised by Mackenzie for standing up "on the side of liberal ideas and in behalf of the independence of the Canadian press."

With the *Advocate*'s enthusiastic backing, Beardsley was elected in the summer of 1824 as one of the four members for Lincoln in the House of Assembly. Riding on a wave of anti-government, economizing sentiment, he proposed legislation "to guard against corruption in the selection of juries" and opposed government financial support for the Welland Canal. As well, he supported the rights of religious minorities and advocated a more liberal policy for admission to the bar. Sympathetic to the grievances of American settlers who were denied full citizenship and whose land titles were put in jeopardy by the alien laws, he played a minor role in the reform agitation which eventually led to their repeal. His stand on these issues earned him the approval of Mackenzie and the *Canadian Freeman*'s editor Francis Collins* and the vilification of Andrew Heron's Niagara *Gleaner*, which considered Beardsley and his Lincoln colleagues John Johnston Lefferty* and Robert Randal* "a curse and a disgrace to the District."

Beardsley proved, on occasion, sufficiently independent to irk his colleagues as well as his opponents. His vote with the majority in January 1825 to withhold from Mackenzie the position of official reporter to the assembly provoked Mackenzie to comment that he had always denied that Beardsley was "a mere tool in our hands, to mould him as we please" and now "the event proves that we spoke truth." Early in 1828 Beardsley chaired the committee and wrote its report supporting Randal's grievances against Solicitor General Henry John Boulton* over land matters involving John Le Breton*. But just before the assembly was dissolved that March, Beardsley "abused and vilified" Randal "without cause." Beardsley attributed his defeat in the ensuing election "to the falsehoods and misrepresentations" of Mackenzie, Lefferty, and Randal, and bitterly refused to "interfere" in the agitation occasioned by the dismissal of judge John Walpole Willis* in June 1828, resolving "to meddle in political matters as little as possible." Two years later, however, he ran again with Mackenzie's grudging support: "Mr. Beardsley is sometimes out of humour, but we imagine his heart is in the right place for the country." Returned once more, he voted regularly with the Mackenzie faction, objecting to the restrictions of the Marriage Bill of 1829, favouring the vote by ballot, and again opposing public funding for the Welland Canal on the grounds that "Canalling ... was not so profitable as reported." By the end of March 1831 Beardsley's popularity in Lincoln was said to be at an all-time high. During the next session he fought against Mackenzie's expulsion from the assembly and even favoured the dissolution of parliament on the issue.

For some unknown reason Beardsley left Upper Canada in the fall of 1832 and relocated his practice in Woodstock, N.B. In 1834 he was appointed a judge of the Inferior Court of Common Pleas and judge of

Beechey

probate for Carleton County. That year he ran unsuccessfully for the House of Assembly, but he was elected three years later. Remarks made during the campaign about his "extremely liberal political principles" resulted in Beardsley's bringing an action for slander. Defeated in the elections of 1842 and 1846, Beardsley failed to receive the political appointment he had hoped for from Lieutenant Governor Edmund Walker Head* in 1848, and the next year he wrote to his old friend William Hamilton Merritt*, stating that he would willingly return to Upper Canada if he were offered a suitable job. He had made many public and private sacrifices for the cause of political reform, he reminded Merritt, and now that the reformers were in power he thought he had "a right to expect a portion of their patronage." No appointment was forthcoming.

Beardsley returned to Upper Canada, nevertheless, and opened a practice in Oakville where he had purchased land in 1847. In the spring of 1853 he was back in Woodstock for the funeral of his son Horace Homer, who had been one of the members of the New Brunswick legislature for Carleton. Though 77 years old, Beardsley was asked to complete his late son's term, but this gesture of respect came to naught when Charles Connell* unexpectedly declared his candidacy. Defeated in the by-election, Beardsley returned to Oakville. A resident there remembered the judge, as Beardsley liked to be called, for his "fine knowledge of men and events" and his many interesting stories of bygone days in Upper Canada. He also noted that Beardsley "had some peculiar ideas which were too advanced for his time." Beardsley remained active to the end of his life, riding on horseback to pick up his mail a day or two before his death.

H. V. NELLES

AO, MS 516, David Thorburn to Mackenzie, 29 March 1831; RG 22, ser.14-a, 30: 40–42; ser.125, 2: 45, 177; ser.134, 4: 156; ser.155, will of B. C. Beardsley. MTL, W. W. Baldwin papers, B. C. Beardsley to W. W. Baldwin, 1 Aug. 1828. PAC, MG 23, D1, ser.1, 66: 62–65; D2, 9; D5; MG 24, A20, 3: 9; E1, 23: 3812–13; RG 1, L3, 29: B3/31. PANB, "N.B. political biog." (J. C. and H. B. Graves), IX. C. E. Beardsley, *The victims of tyranny: a tale* (2v., Buffalo, N.Y., 1847). Levi Beardsley, *Reminiscences; personal and other incidents; early settlement of Otsewego County; notices and anecdotes of public men; judicial, legal and legislative matters; field sports; dissertations and discussions* (New York, 1852), 13, 165. "Early records of St. Mark's and St. Andrew's churches, Niagara," comp. Janet Carnochan, *OH*, 3 (1901): 41, 44. *The records of Christ Church, Poughkeepsie, New York*, ed. H. W. Reynolds (2v., Poughkeepsie, 1911–[?]), 2: 10. U.C., House of Assembly, *Journal*, 1825–28, 1831–32. *Canadian Freeman* (York [Toronto]), 1 Dec. 1825; 18 Jan. 1827; 17 July, 7 Aug. 1828; 27 Jan., 17 Feb., 3 March, 29 Dec. 1831; 2 Feb. 1832. *Christian Guardian*, 4 April 1855. *Colonial Advocate*, 10 June, 8 July, 5 Aug. 1824; 27 Jan. 1825; 8 Nov. 1827; 24 Jan., 9 Feb., 27 March, 10 April 1828; 7 Oct. 1830; 4 Nov. 1834. *Gleaner* (Niagara [Niagara-on-the-Lake, Ont.]), February, April, 28 May 1825; March, April 1828. *New-Brunswick Courier*, 27 Dec. 1834, 2 Feb. 1839. *Niagara Spectator*, 1819. *Royal Gazette* (Fredericton), 22 April 1835, 15 June 1836, 4 Oct. 1837. *Canadian almanac*, 1850: 68. H. P. Hill, *Robert Randall and the Le Breton Flats: an account of the early legal and political controversies respecting the ownership of a large portion of the present city of Ottawa* (Ottawa, 1919), 20, 56–57. Lawrence, *Judges of N.B.* (Stockton and Raymond), 203. Lindsey, *Life and times of Mackenzie*, 1: 64–65. Mary McLean, "Index to unofficial Hansard of Upper Canada, 1820–1832" (MA thesis, Univ. of Toronto, 1938), xxxi, lviii, lxix, lxxiii. H. C. Mathews, *Oakville and the Sixteen: the history of an Ontario port* (Toronto, 1953; repr. 1971). W. R. Riddell, *The legal profession in Upper Canada in its early periods* (Toronto, 1916); "The law of marriage in Upper Canada," *CHR*, 2 (1921): 239.

BEECHEY, FREDERICK WILLIAM, naval officer, artist, explorer, hydrographer, and author; b. 17 Feb. 1796 in London, son of Sir William Beechey and Phyllis Ann Jessup; m. December 1828 Charlotte Stapleton, and they had five daughters; d. 29 Nov. 1856 in London.

Frederick William Beechey came from an artistic family, his father being a well-known portrait painter and member of the Royal Academy of Arts and his mother an accomplished painter of miniatures. Two of his brothers became recognized artists and Frederick William applied his own talents in sketching to the illustration of his naval expeditions. The artistic tradition of the family was later carried on by one of Beechey's daughters, Frances Anne*, who spent a number of years in Canada. Beechey apparently had no formal schooling, but he probably received a certain artistic training from his family. At the age of ten he entered the Royal Navy under the direct patronage of the Earl of St Vincent, first lord of the Admiralty, and on 8 Jan. 1807 was rated midshipman. He served aboard several ships on foreign service and in January 1815 took part in the attack on New Orleans, distinguishing himself in a boat action against the American lines. In recognition of this service he was appointed lieutenant on 10 March 1815.

In 1818 the British navy renewed attempts to discover a northwest passage to the Pacific, suspended since the discoveries of James Cook*. In January of that year Beechey was appointed as second in command and chief draftsman to the brig *Trent*, commanded by Lieutenant John Franklin*. With the barque *Dorothea*, the *Trent* formed an expedition under Captain David Buchan* with orders from the Admiralty to search for a passage "by a northern course across the Pole." Simultaneously a second expedition was dispatched under Commander John Ross and Lieutenant William Edward PARRY to proceed through Baffin Bay. Leaving the Thames on 25 April, the *Trent* and the *Dorothea* sailed northwest of Spitsbergen as far as 80°34′N where they became jammed in the ice. After three weeks the two crews finally succeeded in freeing the vessels, and the expedition headed west towards Greenland. Unfortunately heavy gales forced the ships hard against the ice, seriously damaging the *Dorothea*; despite repairs, the expedition finally had to be abandoned. Both ships reached Deptford on the Thames safely on 22 October. Beechey later prepared a narrative of this expedition, *A voyage of discovery towards the North Pole* (1843), in which six reproductions of sketches he had done while in the Arctic were printed.

Because of his experience and demonstrated skills in navigation and sketching, Beechey was assigned to another Arctic expedition in January 1819, as second in command to Lieutenant Parry in the bomb *Hecla*. Parry's instructions called for the exploration of Lancaster Sound (N.W.T.) to determine whether or not it was enclosed by a series of mountains. Setting out from London in May 1819, the *Hecla* in company with the gun-brig *Griper* reached Lancaster Sound by the end of July. They quickly determined there were no mountains, and proceeded west. By the fall of 1819 the expedition had penetrated as far as Melville Island, having discovered and named Prince Regent Inlet, Barrow Strait, Wellington Channel, and the North Georgian (Parry) Islands. The vessels wintered in Winter Harbour, Melville Island, the first time such a feat had been carried out successfully in the high Arctic; the crews occupied themselves with the development of survival techniques, the taking of magnetic and meteorological observations, the care of the ships, and leisure activities. Beechey undertook the direction of theatrical productions intended to break the monotony of the long winter, the first of these, "Miss in her teens," being presented on 5 November. He was also a regular contributor to the *North Georgia Gazette, and Winter Chronicle*, a weekly newspaper edited by Captain Edward Sabine* aboard the *Hecla*.

In the summer of 1820 the expedition managed to proceed as far west as 113°48′22″W, discovering Banks Land (Island) to the south, sighted by Beechey, and Cape Dundas to the west, before being forced to turn back by the impenetrable ice. Heading east along the southern shore of Barrow Strait and Lancaster Sound, they charted the north coast of Somerset Island and then returned to Britain, arriving at Peterhead, Scotland, at the end of October 1820 [*see* Sir James Clark Ross*]. Beechey had played an important role in this expedition by assisting in navigation, taking observations, keeping notes, and drawing sketches of

the Arctic scenery, 26 of which were later published in Parry's personal narrative, *Journal of a voyage for the discovery of a north-west passage* (1821). During the years 1821 and 1822 Beechey was attached to a survey of the coast of northern Africa, an account of which he later published with his brother Henry William, a civilian member of the expedition. On 25 Jan. 1822, while on this survey, Beechey was promoted to the rank of commander.

In 1825 Beechey was made commander of the sloop *Blossom* and instructed by the Admiralty to explore uncharted areas of the Pacific, to pass through Bering Strait, and to attempt to make contact there with either an overland expedition from the Mackenzie River (N.W.T.) led by Franklin or a naval expedition from Prince Regent Inlet under Parry. During the summer of 1826 an advance party from the *Blossom* reached as far east as Point Barrow (Alaska) but did not meet either expedition. It was later discovered that the *Blossom*'s party had missed Franklin, who had come within 160 miles of Point Barrow, by only nine days. After wintering in the Pacific, Beechey once more headed north to the Bering Strait in the summer of 1827 but again failed to rendezvous with either Franklin or Parry. He then returned to the Pacific, explored and charted parts of it, and sailed home, reaching Britain in September 1828. An account of the expedition, *Narrative of a voyage to the Pacific and Beering's Strait*, published by authority of the Admiralty in 1831, brought him deserved fame.

Beechey had been appointed captain on 8 May 1827, and following his return from the Pacific remained ashore for a few years. He subsequently carried out other surveys for the Admiralty, in 1835 along the coast of South America and from 1837 to 1847 along the coast of Ireland. In the latter year Beechey was appointed superintendent of the marine department of the Privy Council committee for trade, and was named to the Arctic Council, an informal body of experienced navigators assembled to advise the Admiralty in the search for Sir John Franklin, lost in the Arctic since 1845. In 1854 Beechey was promoted to rear-admiral. A fellow of the Royal Society, he was elected president of the Royal Geographical Society in 1855, a position he held until his death.

The importance of Beechey as one of the first artists and explorers of Canada's Arctic regions is seen in the many sketches and observations he made of the territory during his voyages of exploration. Among the landmarks that bear his name is Beechey Point (Alaska), named by Parry in 1826. Contrary to popular belief, Beechey Island, off the southwest corner of Devon Island (N.W.T.), was named in honour of his father.

JIM BURANT

Bell

[Representative examples of the water-colours and pencil drawings of Frederick William Beechey are in the permanent collections of the Arctic Institute of North America (Calgary), the National Maritime Museum (London), and the Scott Polar Research Institute (Cambridge, Eng.), as well as in the archives of the Hydrographic Department of the British Ministry of Defence (Taunton, Eng.). A number of his drawings are found in W. E. Parry, *Journal of a voyage for the discovery of a north-west passage from the Atlantic to the Pacific; performed in the years 1819–20* . . . (new ed., New York, 1968); in the two accounts of Beechey's voyage, *Narrative of a voyage to the Pacific and Beering's Strait, to co-operate with the polar expeditions: performed . . . in the years 1825, 26, 27, 28* (2v., London, 1831; two further editions were published, one in London, 1831 (repr. New York, 1968), and the other in Philadelphia, 1832) and *A voyage of discovery towards the North Pole, performed in his majesty's ships "Dorothea" and "Trent" under the command of Captain David Buchan, R.N.; 1818* . . . (London, 1843); and in a work which he prepared in collaboration with his brother Henry William, *Proceedings of the expedition to explore the northern coast of Africa, from Tripoli eastward; in [1821 and 1822]* . . . (London, 1828).

The notes made by Beechey during his expedition to the Pacific and the Bering Strait in 1825–28 were published in two works, first in *A narrative of the voyages . . . of Capt. Beechey . . . to the Pacific and Behring's straits, performed in . . . 1825, 26, 27, and 28 . . . and of Capt. Back, to the Thlew-ee-Chola River and the Arctic Sea* . . . , comp. Robert Huish (London, 1836), and then in *The zoology of Captain Beechey's voyage; compiled from the collections and notes made by Captain Beechey . . . during a voyage to the Pacific and Behring's straits* . . . , comp. John Richardson *et al.* (London, 1839). Beechey also prepared a chapter on hydrography in a work published by the Admiralty, *A manual of scientific enquiry; prepared for the use of her majesty's navy: and adapted for travellers in general*, ed. J. F. M. Herschel (London, 1849; 2nd ed., 1851; 3rd ed., 1859). J.B.]

Gentleman's Magazine, January–June 1857: 108–10. Cooke and Holland, *Exploration of northern Canada. DNB*. Daphne Foskett, *A dictionary of British miniature painters* (2v., New York, 1972), 1: 159. O'Byrne, *Naval biog. dict.* (1849), 66–67. John Barrow, *Voyages of discovery and research within the Arctic regions, from the year 1818 to the present time* . . . (London, 1846). S. S. Bershad, "The drawings and watercolours by *Rear-Admiral* Frederick William Beechey, F.R.S., P.R.G.S. (1796–1856) in the collection of the Arctic Institute of North America, University of Calgary," *Arctic* (Calgary), 33 (1980): 117–67. A. M. Johnson, "Edward and Frances Hopkins of Montreal," *Beaver*, outfit 302 (autumn 1971): 4–19. R. I. Murchison, "Address to the Royal Geographical Society of London; delivered at the anniversary meeting on 25th May, 1857," Royal Geographical Soc., *Journal* (London), 27 (1857): xciv–cxix. G. L. Nute, "Voyageur's artist," *Beaver*, outfit 278 (June 1947): 32–36.

BELL, ANDREW, Presbyterian minister; b. 5 Sept. 1803 in London, eldest child of William BELL and Mary Black; m. first 1 May 1832 Christian Dalziel; m. secondly 21 Nov. 1833 Eliza Thomson, and they had two sons and one daughter; m. thirdly February 1840 Elizabeth Notman, and they had two sons and one daughter; d. 27 Sept. 1856 in L'Orignal, Upper Canada.

Andrew Bell led a peripatetic childhood. His early years were spent in London, and in 1810 his family moved to Scotland, living first in Rothesay and then in a series of temporary homes until 1817 when they emigrated to Perth, Upper Canada.

Brought up in an evangelical Presbyterian atmosphere by his Scottish parents, Andrew decided to follow his father into the ministry. In June 1823, after having received nearly all his education at the hands of his father, he sailed for Scotland to complete his studies. For the next three years he took courses at the University of Glasgow and at the Associate Synod of Scotland's divinity school. He found, however, that his years in the Canadas had so profoundly altered his outlook that Scotland now seemed an alien environment, and he longed to return to the freer society and clearer skies of Upper Canada. Without completing his theological studies, he returned home in April 1826 and took a post as private tutor to a family at Albion Mills (Hamilton). Still wanting to become a minister, he was taken on trial by members of the United Presbytery of Upper Canada, including William Jenkins*, and was licensed to preach on 25 Sept. 1827 at York (Toronto). Shortly after that he accepted a call to Streetsville (Mississauga) and was ordained on 15 July 1828. While there he embarked on an eight-week missionary tour of the region and prepared a lengthy report of his findings. In 1830 he moved to nearby Toronto Township, retaining the Streetsville charge until 1835 when he resigned it in favour of the Reverend William RINTOUL. He married in 1832 for the first time, but his wife, an invalid, died the same year.

Andrew Bell soon became a leading figure in his presbytery which, in 1831, had reorganized itself into the United Synod of Upper Canada. Convinced that Presbyterians would have to unite if they were ever to be a force within provincial society, he pressed his synod to merge with either the Canadian affiliates of the United Associate Synod of the Secession Church, among whom the Reverend William PROUDFOOT was a leading figure, or with the Synod of the Presbyterian Church of Canada in connection with the Church of Scotland. When the latter formally proposed union with the United Synod of Upper Canada in 1832, Bell was one of his group's negotiators. The talks, along with divisions over the validity of accepting government grants, shattered his synod. In the resulting confusion he and three other ministers, including James George*, joined the Presbyterian Church of Canada in 1834. Bell made an important contribution to it as an organizer, rarely proposing motions or leading debates, but sitting on numerous committees and assuming, from 1843 to 1856, the onerous job of clerk, a position he had filled in his former synod as well.

Bell remained with the Presbyterian Church of Canada synod following the disruption of 1844 when several of its members left to form what was popularly called the Free Church [see Robert Burns*]. After the Reverend Mark Young Stark*, minister at Dundas and Ancaster, joined the Free Church, his former congregations issued a joint call to Bell, which he accepted in February 1847. He stayed with them until October 1852 when, seeking a better salary and hoping that a change of environment would benefit his health, he moved to the long-vacant congregations of L'Orignal and Plantagenet.

A congenial colleague and devoted family man, Andrew Bell displayed no signs of his father's tempestuous personality or religious fervour. He was conscientious in caring for his congregations, and in all his posts he undertook the exhausting missionary tours common in that era. But his real enthusiasm was reserved for his hobby, geology, in which he became highly knowledgeable. In 1854 he served on a select committee of the Legislative Assembly to advise on the work of William Edmond Logan* and the Geological Survey of Canada, which Robert Bell*, his son, was later to direct. At his request, his extensive fossil and mineral collection was given to Queen's College, Kingston, after his death.

H. J. BRIDGMAN

[Andrew Bell wrote a lucid and well-received "Appendix to letters from Perth" for his father William's *Hints to emigrants; in a series of letters from Upper Canada* (Edinburgh, 1824), as well as compiling *A collection of such acts of the Synod of the Presbyterian Church of Canada, in connection with the Church of Scotland, as appear to contain standing laws and rules of the church* (Toronto, 1847). The main sources for his life are QUA, William Bell papers, and the Bell–Williamson correspondence in the Queen's Univ. letters; PAC, MG 24, H10 (photocopies); and the correspondence of the presbyteries and synods mentioned in the text. Further material is found in PAC, MG 9, D7, 4 and 25, and in Bell's folder in UCA, Biog. files. Contrary to the entry in *Union list of MSS* (Maurice), 1: 79, the UCA does not possess Andrew Bell correspondence. H.J.B.]

Canadian Christian Examiner, and Presbyterian Magazine (Toronto), 3 (1839): 302–4. *Canadian Miscellany; or, the Religious, Literary & Statistical Intelligencer* (Montreal), 1 (1828): 111. Croil, *Hist. and statistical report* (1868), 9, 48, 82, 99–100. *Presbyterian*, 1 (1848): 5; 5 (1852): 178; 9 (1856): 163, 178. *Bathurst Courier*, 10 Oct. 1856 [this obituary was written by his father, William Bell]. *Christian Guardian*, 18 Dec. 1830, 9 May 1832, 4 Dec. 1833. *The matriculation albums of the University of Glasgow from 1728 to 1858*, comp. W. I. Addison (Glasgow, 1913). Scott *et al.*, *Fasti ecclesiæ scoticanæ*, vol.7. Gregg, *Hist. of Presbyterian Church*.

BELL, HUGH, educator, businessman, office holder, politician, and philanthropist; b. 1780 in Enniskillen (Northern Ireland), only son of Samuel Bell and Ann Cross; m. first 5 Dec. 1808 Elizabeth Lain in Halifax, and they had five children; m. secondly 14 June 1815 Ann Allison, sister of Joseph Allison, at the Mantua Estate near Newport, N.S., and they had nine children; d. 16 May 1860 in Halifax.

Hugh Bell, the son of a veteran of the American Revolutionary War, was brought to Nova Scotia when he was about two years old. Because his father died when he was a boy, and his mother could not provide him with the limited schooling that was then available in Halifax, he was largely self-educated. His early passion for reading was apparently the source of the reputation he later enjoyed as a "concise and winning speaker" and as a "writer of pure English." Bell was to employ his speaking abilities both as a Methodist lay preacher who was much in demand on Sundays in Halifax and nearby settlements, and as a politician able to hold his own in debate with the most formidable members of the legislature; his reputation as a writer rested largely on the articles which he wrote for the *Acadian Recorder* during the 1830s. The quality of Bell's self-education is perhaps most decisively indicated by the fact that he was asked in 1843 to deliver a lecture on "Self-Improvement" at the Halifax Mechanics' Institute. His concern for learning was also reflected in his participation during the early 1840s in the establishment of a school connected with the Wesleyan Methodist Church and in his activity as a governor of Dalhousie College from 1840 to 1858.

After a brief period as a schoolteacher in Cumberland County at the turn of the century, Bell was employed as a bookkeeper with the firm of Lydiard and Nock, a Halifax brewery and candle-making concern. When the original partnership was dissolved a few years later he became a full partner in the reconstituted firm of Nock and Bell. The uneven fortunes of Bell's business enterprise reflect those of the Nova Scotian economy in the early part of the 19th century. The firm prospered during the War of 1812, struggled through the slump of the immediate post-war period, and by about 1818 was again strong enough to expand its operations with the building of a new brewery and a new soap and candle factory. During the recession of the 1830s Bell once more suffered financial difficulties, but these were apparently soon overcome for in 1838 he was able to move into Bloomfield, his large estate in the northern part of the city. Three years later he possessed sufficient confidence in the stability of his business to turn it over to his elder sons, William and Samuel, in order to devote himself more completely to public concerns.

Until he was 55, almost all of Bell's spare time had been given to church work, but thereafter he became increasingly interested in public affairs. Although he thus entered public life relatively late, he achieved substantial success as a politician and office holder. His public career began in 1835 when he was made a commissioner "for the Superintendence . . . of the Poor of the Town and Peninsula of Halifax" as part of the effort of Lieutenant Governor Sir Colin Campbell* to reform the municipal government in the wake of Joseph Howe*'s successful defence against the charge of libel after his publication in the *Novascotian* of a letter accusing the city magistrates of corruption [*see* Richard TREMAIN]. In the same year Bell was nominated by Howe as a candidate for the House of Assembly in a by-election in Halifax Township, and won by acclamation. He was re-elected in the general election of 1836. At this period polling took as long as two weeks, the poll being moved from place to place to the accompaniment of gambling, dancing, and heavy drinking. When the Halifax poll closed at St Margaret's Bay, the people mounted the "popular candidates on chairs and carried them for nearly a mile up and down the Bay amidst cheers." Howe, the successful Reform candidate for Halifax County, enjoyed the carnival atmosphere, but Bell did not, finding such proceedings "extremely distasteful." In this, as in his business and church activities, Bell lived up to Howe's characterization of him as a "fit representative" of the virtues of the "middling class." Although Bell declared in an election speech that he was "the Champion of no party," and did not always support the reform cause as strongly as Howe wished, he did regard himself as a champion of the middle class. As such, he showed himself a consistent and at times "zealous" supporter of the reform party's challenge to the supremacy of the Halifax merchanto-cracy, particularly in municipal affairs. Thus he participated in the movement for the incorporation of Halifax as a city with elected officials [*see* Thomas Forrester*], though he was in favour of restricting the elective principle by means of a high property qualification.

In 1840 Bell gave up his seat in the assembly and turned his attention to municipal politics. He ran successfully for alderman in the first municipal election held in Halifax, on 12 May 1841; he was re-elected in 1842 and 1843, and in October 1844 he was chosen by his fellow aldermen to be mayor of the city for the following year. In the mean time Bell's prominence as a spokesman for the burgeoning middle class of Halifax had brought him to the attention of the new lieutenant governor, Lord Falkland [Cary*], who appointed him to the Legislative Council in 1841. His political career culminated with his appointment in February 1848 to the Executive Council of the first responsible government in Nova Scotia. While a member of the ministry of James Boyle UNIACKE he held the office of chairman of the Board of Works and,

for a brief period, that of financial secretary; he was often appointed to committees concerned with financial matters and was a delegate to a conference of British North American governments regarding commercial policy which was held in Halifax in September 1849. He resigned from the Executive Council in 1854, but remained as chairman of the Board of Works until 1857 when he was forced out, at the age of 77, by a conservative election victory.

Bell's retention of the chairmanship of the Board of Works was motivated by his desire to realize the goal which had been "uppermost in his thoughts for more than a decade." When selected as mayor of Halifax in 1844 Bell made an unusual declaration: instead of expending the mayor's salary of £300 on official entertaining, "it was his design to appropriate the whole sum to the founding of a Lunatic Asylum in Halifax." It was probably as a poor-house commis-sioner that Bell was first exposed to the plight of the mentally ill in Nova Scotia for, in addition to the indigent, the aged, and orphans, the Poor's Asylum housed those mentally ill whose families were unable or unwilling to care for them. In the year that Bell was mayor, for instance, 40 residents of the poor-house were classified as insane. It was estimated, moreover, that there were at least 200 insane persons throughout the province, most of whom were kept in local jails. The prevalent view of mental illness as an incurable disease of the mind, or even as evidence of demonic possession, precluded any program of treatment other than one of forcible restraint. Bell made the alleviation of this situation the chief object of his public activity.

In 1845 Bell, as mayor of Halifax and with the support of the city council, petitioned the legislature for the construction of a hospital in which the insane could be cured instead of being treated "like inferior animals to be caged and chained and whipped into submission . . . as if the link which unites them to the human family were entirely dissolved." In response to this petition the government appointed a three-man commission consisting of Bell, Dr Alexander Frater Sawers, and Samuel Prescott Fairbanks* to examine the feasibility of a joint mental institution for the three Maritime provinces (an idea they eventually rejected) and to investigate various institutions in the United States. The report which they submitted in 1846 reflected the influence of two prominent figures in the history of the treatment of mental illness in the United States: Dr Luther Vose Bell, superintendent of the McLean Hospital for the Insane in Charlestown (Boston), and the philanthropist Dorothea Lynde Dix. Hugh Bell's close association with Dix brought his project within the orbit of the "moral treatment" movement in 19th-century psychiatry, a movement informed by the humanitarian notion that mental illness was attributable largely to environmental stresses and should be treated by individual therapy in combination with the appropriate physical setting and social influences provided by a hospital.

An act establishing such a hospital was finally passed by the Nova Scotia legislature in 1852, and within a year Bell was able to report to Dix that £15,000 had been appropriated for it by the government, on condition that another £5,000 be privately subscribed. The site for the hospital, across the harbour from Halifax (about two miles from Dartmouth), was selected by Dix. She was also influential in the adoption of a plan for the hospital which called for a three-storey brick structure designed to accommodate 120 patients; every floor was to contain six wards, each equipped with parlour, dining-room, clothes-room, and bathroom. Bell, as chairman of the Board of Works, was responsible for the construction of the hospital and the purchase of some of its equipment. A few months before he was ousted from the chairmanship by the conservatives, an editorial appeared in the *Acadian Recorder* objecting to the amount of public money "squandered" by the Board of Works "upon a Spree at the laying of the corner stone of the Lunatic Asylum [9 June 1856]. . . . We find that the Chairman of the Board of Works gave *carte blanche* to the person who acted as purveyor and master of ceremonies on that occasion. . . . Why should not the benevolent old gentleman, in founding his darling institution, do the thing handsomely, seeing that the Province would pay for it?" This editorial did not, however, express the general sentiment, which was one of gratitude to Bell for his role as the principal founder of the Provincial Hospital for the Insane (now the Nova Scotia Hospital). Although Bell was to die well before the hospital was fully completed in 1874, Howe expressed the view that it would "ever remain a monument to his memory." Bell's activity on behalf of the hospital certainly accords him a prominent place in any account of the development of treatment facilities for the mentally ill in Nova Scotia.

PHYLLIS R. BLAKELEY

PANS, Biog., Bell family, docs., 1817–97 (mfm.); MG 100, 110, doc.12; 235, nos.22–22e; RG 1, 175: ff.1–2, 229–34, 256–360, 371–75, 410, 440, 518, 558; 199–200, 1847–54; 411: 91b; RG 5, P, 44, 69–71, 73, 81, 121–22; RG 7, 1: 128A; RG 34-312, P, 10–15. N.S., House of Assembly, *Journal and proc.*, 1836–40; 1846, app.32; 1847, app.11; 1850, app.18, 72; 1851, app.74; 1851–52, app.24, 74; 1908, app.3A; Legislative Council, *Debates and proc.*, 1858–60; *Journal and proc.*, 1841–60. *Halifax Morning Sun*, 1 March 1848; 18, 21 May 1860. *Morning Chronicle* (Halifax), 5 Oct. 1844. *Novascotian, or Colonial Herald*, 26 Nov., 17 Dec. 1835; 17 Nov., 8, 15, 22 Dec. 1836; 2, 21 Feb., 25 Oct., 1 Nov. 1837; 8, 15 March 1838. W. P. Bell, *A genealogical study* (2v., Sackville, N.B., 1962). J. S. Bockoven, *Moral treatment in American psychiatry* (New York, 1963). D. A. Sutherland, "The merchants of Halifax, 1815–1850: a commercial class in pursuit of metropolitan status" (PHD thesis, Univ. of Toronto, 1975). Francis Tiffany, *Life of Dorothea Lynde Dix* ([6th ed.], Boston and New York, 1891). W. [P.] Bell, "A Halifax boyhood of one hundred and twenty years ago . . . ," N.S. Hist. Soc., *Coll.*, 28 (1949): 108–11, 119, 129; "Hon. Hugh Bell, founder of the Nova Scotia Hospital," *Nova Scotia Medical Bull.* (Halifax), 31 (1952): 61–71. M. H. L. Grant, "Historical background of the Nova Scotia Hospital, Dartmouth and the Victoria General Hospital, Halifax," *Nova Scotia Medical Bull.*, 16 (1937): 314–19, 383–85.

BELL, JOHN, Wesleyan minister; b. 19 Oct. 1788 in Kingston upon Hull, England, son of Robert and Sarah Bell; m. Mary Ann ——; d. 26 Oct. 1855 in England.

The son of Episcopalians, John Bell was confirmed a Methodist at age 14. He was received as a local preacher in 1809, was ordained two years later, and then travelled for five years on the home circuit. In 1816 he was the senior of six missionaries dispatched to Newfoundland by the British Wesleyan Conference. With two of these men, George Cubit* and Richard KNIGHT, he left Poole, Dorset, on 1 August, arriving at Carbonear on 4 September. The Newfoundland mission had been part of the Nova Scotia District since 1787, but in 1815 it was constituted a separate district and William Ellis* was named the first chairman. Bell had been designated Ellis's successor by "his English brethren" and assumed the post on his arrival. Affectionately known as "the Bishop," Bell retained the chairmanship until he returned to England in 1823. While in Newfoundland, he first served in the circuit of Lower Island Cove and Perlican, then in St John's, Harbour Grace, and Port de Grave.

With the arrival of the missionaries in 1816, the Newfoundland District increased its circuits from five to eleven, spread along the coast from Bonavista in the northeast to Grand Bank in the south, with the main concentration in the Conception Bay area. At this time there were approximately 500 adherents on the island. As well as the Methodists, there were seven Roman Catholic priests, three Church of England clergymen, and one Congregational minister in Newfoundland, most of whom were "settled" in and around St John's. Only the Wesleyans braved the natural dangers of all seasons and faced "wild beasts and wilder men" to cover vast areas four and five times annually. Bell reported at his first district meeting on 3 June 1817 that during the past year he had visited all the circuits except Burin and Grand Bank.

From 1816 to 1818 Newfoundland suffered from a serious economic depression which had followed

Bell

several years of buoyancy as a result of the Napoleonic Wars. The economic disruption caused by the fires of 1816, 1817, and 1818 in St John's, as well as the poor returns from the cod and seal-fisheries, and the loss of markets, had forced many church members out of the city in order to find work. The beginning of a renewed prosperity came in 1818, the year Bell replaced Cubit in St John's, but Bell's newly acquired congregation had been scattered and those who remained were saddled with an intolerable debt. Under Bell's strong leadership, and with the assistance of the British conference, the debt was nearly liquidated by mid 1819 and Bell was spearheading a drive for funds to construct a parsonage; known as the Wesleyan Mission House, it would thereafter serve as a focal point for Methodism on the island. On a visit to England in March 1820 Bell raised an additional £350 for the Newfoundland District but was unsuccessful in an attempt to persuade his colleagues to appoint an assistant to the St John's circuit so that the Methodists in the adjacent coves could also receive the ministrations of a clergyman.

Bell was a very neat and precise person, an excellent pastor and administrator. Although not a great preacher, he delivered his sermons simply and powerfully. However, he might have had some assistance in writing them. According to the historian Philip Tocque*, "Mr Cubit sold Bell 30 or 40 of his MS sermons which was the making of Bell as a preacher." After seven fruitful years in Newfoundland, Bell returned to England in 1823 where he served in several pastorates over the next 28 years. Growing infirmities obliged him to accept a supernumerary retirement in 1851. He died peacefully four years later in the 45th year of his ministry, survived by his wife who passed away the following year.

CALVIN D. EVANS

Holy Trinity Parish Church (Church of England) (Hull, Eng.), Reg. of baptisms, 3 (1689–1792): 152. *Wesleyan-Methodist Magazine* (London), 39 (1816): 954–55; 42 (1819): 75–76; 79 (1856): 843–44. *Newfoundland Mercantile Journal*, 25 March, 11 Nov. 1819; 4 April 1822. *When was that?* (Mosdell), 9. *A century of Methodism in St. John's, Newfoundland, 1815–1915*, ed. J. W. Nichols (n.p., [1915]), 29. G. G. Findlay and W. W. Holdsworth, *The history of the Wesleyan Methodist Missionary Society* (5v., London, 1921–24), 1: 273–76. D. G. Pitt, *Windows of agates; a short history of the founding and early years of Gower street Methodist (now United) Church in St. John's, Newfoundland* (St John's, 1966), 41–44. T. W. Smith, *Hist. of Methodist Church*, 2: 35–40. William Wilson, *Newfoundland and its missionaries ... to which is added a chronological table of all the important events that have occurred on the island* (Cambridge, Mass., and Halifax, 1866), 234–37. *Daily News* (St John's), 26 March 1960.

BELL, WILLIAM, Presbyterian minister; b. 20 May 1780 in Airdrie (Strathclyde), Scotland, eighth and last child of Andrew Bell and Margaret Shaw; m. 13 Oct. 1802 Mary Black in Leith, Scotland, and they had eight sons and one daughter; d. 16 Aug. 1857 in Perth, Upper Canada.

William Bell came from a background of agriculture and minor rural trades. His father was a severe, patriarchal Presbyterian and William, thirsting for freedom, ran away from home twice, the second time to London in June 1802. There he worked for a number of carpenters and cabinet-makers before becoming a building contractor in 1805.

Although he had spent only some random months in school, he was a voracious reader and had always longed to be a minister. In 1808, against the wishes of his wife and family, he sold his business and entered the Congregational Church's Hoxton Academy in London to train for the ministry. He was licensed to preach by the Middlesex Congregational Court on 18 Feb. 1809, but, hoping to become a Presbyterian minister, he returned to Scotland in 1810. While teaching school at Rothesay to support his wife and children, he studied at the Associate Synod of Scotland's seminary at Selkirk, and, from 1812, attended classes at the University of Glasgow as well. In May 1814 he moved his family to Airdrie and devoted himself full time to finishing his studies. On 28 March 1815 he was licensed to preach by the Associate Presbytery of Glasgow.

Unpopular as a preacher and of a prickly disposition, he was unable to find a congregation and was obliged to work as an itinerant relief preacher. After months of constant travelling he decided in 1816, despite his wife's protests, to accept the Colonial Office's proposal of a land grant and a £100 salary to serve as minister to the government-assisted Scottish settlers at Perth, Upper Canada. Bell was ordained by the Associate Presbytery of Edinburgh on 4 March 1817, and a month later sailed with his family for the Canadas.

They arrived at the end of June to find Perth in an uproar, the immigrant families, disbanded soldiers, and half-pay officers having come only the year before. Seeing all around him what he believed to be rampant moral decay and social anarchy, Bell turned his considerable energies to organizing a congregation, teaching school, conducting pastoral visits, and building a church (First Presbyterian). Over the next decade he saw the village stabilize and his congregation quadruple.

In 1817 the Presbyterian church in the Canadas was in a very early stage of development; the four ministers in Lower Canada and the nine in Upper Canada operated without a permanent presbyterial organization. Before leaving Scotland, Bell had been approached by members of the Associate Synod of Scotland asking him to attempt to form a presbytery in the colony that could be allied to their synod. Within a month of his arrival, he and three other ministers, William Smart*, William Taylor, and Robert Easton*, applied to the Scottish synod for authority to organize a presbytery in Canada. Bell, initially arguing that they should obtain prior approval from Scotland before acting, split with his colleagues when they decided in January 1818 to establish an independent body, the Presbytery of the Canadas. He soon changed his mind, however, and joined them the following July when organizational details were worked out, including, at Bell's suggestion, acceptance of the principle that the new presbytery recognize "the doctrines, discipline and worship of the Church of Scotland." The presbytery experienced a number of mutations, ultimately evolving into the United Synod of Upper Canada in 1831. Bell took a keen interest in its proceedings, but his bitter quarrels with most of his colleagues, particularly those of Irish extraction, more often than not hindered progress.

The Church of Scotland forces in the colony were on the rise by the late 1820s and part of his congregation in Perth joined them in 1830, securing the services of the Reverend Thomas C. Wilson, and, in 1832, building St Andrew's Church. Bell, too, longed for the respectability of membership in the Church of Scotland and had often publicly argued for a union of all Scottish ministers in the Canadas, but he felt it should be done in an organized, official way. He was happy when merger negotiations opened in 1832 between the United Synod of Upper Canada and the Synod of the Presbyterian Church of Canada in connection with the Church of Scotland. However, disagreement over this question and over a government grant in 1833 shattered the United Synod. Eight members withdrew the following year and, in October 1835, amid much acrimony, Bell also left, joining the Church of Scotland affiliate. Although elected moderator in 1845, he played a minor role in his new synod. On most issues he aligned himself with the more evangelical members; unlike them, however, he did not leave the church as a result of the disruption of 1844, considering the fight to be a solely Scottish affair [*see* Robert Burns*].

Bell found it difficult to fit into a diversified society, believing as he did that the minister held a unique position in the community and should be recognized as the unquestioned arbiter of all moral standards. His intense sense of divine mission coupled with an irascible disposition and sanctimonious temperament led him into repeated clashes with most of his neighbours and associates. Yet his indefatigable energy and missionary zeal did much to keep the Presbyterian faith alive among the settlers. He

established temperance societies, Sunday schools, and Bible classes, and helped found congregations in Beckwith Township, Lanark, Smiths Falls, and Richmond.

He had good reason to be proud of his family. A younger son, the Reverend George Bell, was a student of Alexander GALE and became one of the first alumni of Queen's College, Kingston, later serving as its registrar and librarian. Another son, ANDREW, also joined the ministry and faithfully served a number of congregations before predeceasing his more robust father by some 11 months. William*, whose intemperate habits embarrassed his father, had died in 1844 at the age of 38. Shortly before his own death, William Bell ended the long-standing rivalry between the Presbyterians in Perth by bringing about the reunion, in May 1857, of his congregation and that of St Andrew's.

H. J. BRIDGMAN

[William Bell extensively rewrote his letter-book and 17 diaries (QUA, William Bell papers) late in life. Autobiographical information and comments on the church at Perth also appear in his *Introduction to pastoral letters from the Rev. Wm. Bell to the members of the Church of Christ under his care* (Lanark, [Ont.], 1828), 2–7, and in his "History of the first Presbyterian Church in U. Canada, 10 July 1840" (QUA, Bell papers). His more immediate responses to issues appear in the numerous pugnacious letters he sent to Upper Canadian newspapers, his *Hints to emigrants; in a series of letters from Upper Canada* (Edinburgh, 1824), and the records held by the UCA and QUA of the relevant sessions, presbyteries, and synods. H.J.B.]

St Andrew's (Presbyterian) Church (Perth, Ont.), Perth Presbyterian Church, reg. of baptisms and marriages: 2 (photocopy at PAC). UCA, Biog. files. Croil, *Hist. and statistical report* (1868), 83, 86–88. *Presbyterian*, 10 (1857): 131, 144. *Bathurst Courier*, 21 Nov. 1843, 21 Aug. 1857. *Christian Guardian*, 20 Aug. 1831. *Globe*, 25 Aug. 1857. *Kingston Chronicle*, 30 Oct. 1830, 10 Sept. 1831. *Annals and statistics of the United Presbyterian Church*, comp. William MacKelvie *et al.* (Edinburgh, 1873), 672. *Encyclopedia Canadiana*. Scott *et al.*, *Fasti ecclesiæ scoticanæ*, vol.7. Gregg, *Hist. of Presbyterian Church*. V. H. Lindsay, "The Perth military settlement: characteristics of its permanent and transitory settlers, 1816–1822" (MA thesis, 2v., Carleton Univ., Ottawa, 1972), 1: 1, 8–10, 12–13, 27; 2: 38–39, 46. C. G. Lucas, "Presbyterianism in Carleton County to 1867" (MA thesis, Carleton Univ., 1973). Isabel [Murphy] Skelton, *A man austere: William Bell, parson and pioneer* (Toronto, 1947). *CHR*, 29 (1948): 86–87.

BELLENGER, JOSEPH-MARIE, Roman Catholic priest, missionary, and journalist; b. 15 April 1788 at Quebec, son of Joseph Bélanger, a master furrier, and Marie-Catherine Manisson (Malisson), *dit* Philibert; d. 6 May 1856 in Longue-Pointe (Montreal).

Bellenger

Joseph-Marie Bellenger received a classical education at the Petit Séminaire de Québec from 1800 to 1808, and he continued his studies at the Grand Séminaire from 1810. Having been ordained priest on 13 March 1813, he became curate of Saint-Joachim at Châteauguay; that autumn he was appointed to a similar post at Saint-Laurent, on Montreal Island. Priests were then in such great demand that a curacy lasted barely long enough to provide pastoral training. In 1814, at the age of 26, Bellenger was sent as a missionary to Restigouche, on the Baie des Chaleurs, where he worked among the Micmacs for five years.

As a student, Bellenger had shown particular aptitude for versification and linguistics, and he now began to study the Micmac language. At the invitation of Bishop Joseph-Octave Plessis* of Quebec, who gave him manuscript notebooks left by Abbé Pierre Maillard*, the great apostle of the Micmacs, he set to work in 1817 on a Micmac alphabet, an outline of a grammar, and a collection of prayers; the following year he wrote a catechism.

In 1819 Bellenger was appointed parish priest of Saint-Paul (at Joliette), where he proved an able minister and gave particular attention to the pioneers of Rawdon Township, who for the most part were poverty-stricken Irish immigrants. He was parish priest of Saint-Pascal in 1829 and 1830, and of Saint-François-du-Lac from 1830 to 1833. The latter was the most important parish he served because the responsibilities also involved working as a missionary among a group of Indians. On his arrival, Bellenger set to work countering the initiatives of the Abenaki schoolmaster Osunkhirhine (Pierre-Paul Masta), who was introducing Protestantism to his people at the Saint-François-de-Sales (Odanak) mission, which was attached to Bellenger's parish. Masta, while a student at Dartmouth College in Hanover, N.H., had been an adherent of the Congregational Church. Since 1829 he had been employed by the Indian Department as a schoolmaster among the Abenakis of Saint-François-de-Sales, and was teaching some 40 children. He used, among other aids, an Abenaki-English vocabulary which he had put together and had had printed in Boston in 1830; furthermore, the Congregational Church was taking steps to provide his school free of charge with the books it needed, including a Protestant catechism.

To forestall "heretical" instruction Bellenger, with the agreement of his bishop, Bernard-Claude Panet*, had the short catechism of the diocese of Quebec translated into the Abenaki language, undertaking the work with the help of Masta himself. The book was revised by a Catholic Abenaki and published at Quebec in 1832 under the title *Kagakimzouiasis ueji uo' banakiak adali kimo' gik aliuitzo' ki za plasua*.

Masta, however, was becoming increasingly bold. With the agreement of his Abenaki assistant,

Jacques-Joseph Annance, *dit* Kadnèche, who had also studied at Hanover, he had invited a Protestant minister of Trois-Rivières to preach in the village and was putting pressure on the government for a resident minister. In May 1832 Bishop Panet came to urge the Abenakis to desert Masta. The visit over, Masta preached more fervently than ever in an attempt to dissuade them from obeying the bishop.

In order to meet the needs of the parish of Saint-François-du-Lac and the mission, Bellenger suggested that a new church be built in the centre of the village. The proposed church would be easier for the inhabitants of the seigneury of Pierreville to reach and would be opposite the Abenaki mission, which Bellenger could then keep an eye on more readily. His plan was opposed by a number of parishioners who did not want a church built on another site and threatened to take the matter to court. On the advice of the new bishop of Quebec, Joseph Signay*, Bellenger agreed to shelve his plan until some more favourable time.

In June 1832 Bellenger asked the village chiefs to sign a petition to have Masta relieved of his post, but to no avail. The chiefs were "of the opinion that no man can prevent [Masta] from explaining the Bible, since in so doing he is acting according to his conscience and is teaching valuable things." Kadnèche had interceded strongly on the schoolmaster's behalf and considered him the pastor of the Abenakis. The chiefs, however, were soon to change their opinion about Masta, when they realized that he was seeking to assume control of the village. Masta went so far as to insult them by claiming that the commissions granted to Simon Obomsawin, as first chief, and to the other chiefs of the Abenakis of Saint-François-de-Sales were not worth "the tassel on a corn cob." The new deputy superintendent of the Indian Department, Colonel William McKay*, was informed of the situation; he obtained a letter from the governor-in-chief, Matthew Whitworth-Aylmer*, threatening to strike Masta off the list of the department's officials if he continued to spread discord among his people. But McKay died suddenly during the cholera epidemic in Montreal that year and the government postponed making a decision.

While at Saint-François-du-Lac, Bellenger had asked three times to be relieved of his responsibilities. On 21 Oct. 1833 Bishop Signay accepted his resignation. At the bishop's request, the vicar general of the diocese, Louis-Marie Cadieux*, authorized Bellenger on 22 Feb. 1834 to act as assistant priest of Saint-Michel at Yamaska, where he remained until August 1835. Shortly thereafter he was sent to the Collège de Chambly, and on 12 October was made parish priest of Saint-François-d'Assise at Longue-Pointe. On 14 December he was given the same post in Saint-Esprit, a position he retained until 1846.

Bellenger also gained a reputation as a linguist, man

of letters, and journalist. The outline of Micmac grammar which he had prepared in 1817 with the help of Abbé Maillard's notebooks was to be used in 1864 in *Grammaire de la langue mikmaque*, published in New York by John Dawson Gilmary Shea; Shea had obtained the manuscript through Jean-Baptiste-Antoine Ferland*, a history professor at the Université Laval at Quebec. Bellenger was one of the first members of the Literary and Historical Society of Quebec, and with Michel BIBAUD was an active contributor to *La Bibliothèque canadienne* during its existence from 1825 to 1830. This journal's aim was to "spread knowledge of the sciences, arts, and letters, and bring out the unknown or unacknowledged talents of dead or living compatriots, make known literary movements, highlights of history, [and] memorable events, and impart them to the young and the general public." In it Bellenger showed himself conversant with poetry, agronomy, and mathematics.

At the beginning of February 1846 Bellenger and André-Toussaint Lagarde took charge of the diocesan newspaper *Mélanges religieux*. The two new owners and editors were particularly anxious to have their paper carry what they considered to be worthwhile items from other papers or periodicals and from letters and documents sent to them for publication. Strictly speaking, they did not write editorials or articles but confined themselves to publishing the material they had chosen. Bellenger devoted his attention to the ecclesiastical news of the diocese of Montreal and beyond. He worked with Lagarde at *Mélanges religieux* until June 1846, and then alone until September 1847 when he gave up his post.

Little is known about Bellenger's later years except that he no longer performed pastoral duties. In the absence of specific information it may be presumed, however, that Bishop Signay had forbidden him to carry on his ministry, since Bellenger had apparently not been altogether above reproach in his handling of money entrusted to him by his former parishioners. He is known to have lost his ecclesiastical powers in 1848, perhaps because he had been at fault or had been sick. Whatever the case, in the course of his life Bellenger had shown himself to be a cultured man, with a concern for truth and a mind open to various fields of knowledge.

LUCIEN LEMIEUX

AAQ, 12 A, G: ff.202, 224; H: ff.12, 34, 41; 210 A, VIII: 303–5, 377–80, 472–77; IX: 34–41, 109–11, 192–94, 254–56, 439–40; XII: 207, 538–39; XIV: 314–16; 26 CP, VII: 7a; T, Papiers J.-B.-A. Ferland, corr. ACAM, RLB, I: 92–94, 227–28; RLL, III: 163–64, 168–71; IV: 413–15; VIII: 220–21. ANQ-M, CE1-51, 8 mai 1856. ANQ-Q, CE1-1, 16 avril 1788. Arch. de l'évêché de Joliette (Joliette, Qué.), Cartable Saint-Paul-de-Joliette, I: 1825-5; Cartable Saint-Esprit, I: 1837-1, 4, 5, 1838-8, 9; Cartable Saint-Lin, I: 1837-4, 1838-1. Arch. de l'évêché de Nicolet (Nicolet, Qué.), Cartable Saint-François-du-Lac, I, 24 oct., 15 nov. 1830; 28 nov. 1831; 10 avril, 28 mai, 27 juin, 7, 16 juill., 13 août, 1er, 22 sept., 17 déc. 1832. ASQ, Fichier des anciens. *Grammaire de la langue mikmaque*, J.-M. Bellenger, édit. (New York, 1864). *Kagakimzouiasis ueji uo'banakiak adali kimo'gik aliuitzo'ki za plasua* (Québec, 1832). *Mélanges religieux*, 6 févr. 1846, 14 sept. 1847. Allaire, *Dictionnaire*, 1: 41. F.-M. Bibaud, *Le panthéon canadien* (A. et V. Bibaud; 1891), 20. Caron, "Inv. de la corr. de Mgr Signay," ANQ *Rapport*, 1936–37: 222, 241, 270; 1937–38: 53, 72. Le Jeune, *Dictionnaire*, 1: 170. J. C. Pilling, *Bibliography of the Algonquian languages* (Washington, 1891), 41, 539. P.-G. Roy, *Fils de Québec*, 3: 41–42. Tanguay, *Dictionnaire*, 5: 479; *Répertoire* (1893), 176. T.-M. Charland, *Histoire de Saint-François-du-Lac* (Ottawa, 1942), 233–50; *Histoire des Abénakis d'Odanak (1675–1937)* (Montréal, 1964), 179–80, 193–218. Meilleur, *Mémorial de l'éducation* (1876), 305–6. "Les disparus," BRH, 32 (1926): 59.

BELLOT, JOSEPH-RENÉ, naval officer, explorer, and author; b. 18 March 1826 in Paris, one of about seven children of Étienne-Susanne-Zacharie-Brumaire Bellot, a smith and farrier, and Adélaïde-Estelle Laurent; d. unmarried 18 Aug. 1853 in Wellington Channel (N.W.T.).

The Bellot family moved from Paris to Rochefort when Joseph-René was five years old. He did well in school and his teacher, impressed by his talent, persuaded the mayor that the municipality should subsidize his entry into the college at Rochefort, where he received an education that would have been beyond his father's limited means. The city of Rochefort continued to support him financially when, on 10 Nov. 1841, he entered the École Navale at Brest. He passed out from there on 1 Sept. 1843 and spent the following six months aboard vessels in the port of Brest.

In June 1844 Bellot embarked as naval cadet on the corvette *Berceau* for a voyage to the Indian Ocean. During this tour of service he was seriously wounded in a joint Anglo-French naval strike against the port of Tamatave in Madagascar on 15 June 1845, and for his part in this action he was nominated a knight of the Legion of Honour on 2 Dec. 1845. After a brief service aboard the frigate *Belle-Poule* in 1846, Bellot returned to France and was promoted sub-lieutenant on 1 Nov. 1847. Following a two-year tour of duty aboard the corvette *Triomphante* he returned to Rochefort on 25 Aug. 1850.

During a period of inactivity following his return to France, Bellot developed an interest in the search for Sir John Franklin*, lost in the Arctic since 1845. Until 1850 the search efforts had been sustained exclusively by the English-speaking world and Bellot felt that the concern of the French, and of seamen everywhere, should also be demonstrated. In mid March 1851 he wrote letters to Lady Franklin [Griffin*], who was

Bellot

then organizing her second private search expedition, and to William Kennedy*, the Canadian fur trader who was to command it, expressing his sympathy and volunteering his services. His application, though strongly supported by his own superiors and by the French ambassador in London, was at first opposed by Lady Franklin's advisers at the Admiralty, who had misgivings that the presence of a foreign officer on a British ship might lead to problems of discipline and rank. Kennedy, on the other hand, favoured Bellot's appointment, if only for his skills as a navigator. Finally, on 1 May, shortly before the search vessel, *Prince Albert*, was due to sail, he and Lady Franklin sent Bellot a cautious invitation to meet them.

Bellot impressed Lady Franklin at once and she confirmed his appointment after their first interview. Moreover, by the time the ship sailed from Stromness, in the Orkney Islands, on 3 June 1851, he had won the confidence and affection of all around him. Franklin's niece, Sophia Cracroft, wrote that "we are really *very* fond of him – his sweetness & simplicity & earnestness are most endearing."

The apprehension voiced by Lady Franklin's advisers was further dispelled when the expedition reached the Arctic, for Bellot had an early opportunity to demonstrate his authority over the British crew in Kennedy's absence. On 9 September Kennedy took a small landing party ashore at Port Leopold, on the northeast coast of Somerset Island (N.W.T.), and during his absence the ice carried the ship away to the south. Failing in his efforts to hold the ship in the vicinity of Port Leopold, Bellot was forced to put into Batty Bay, about 50 miles to the south, from which point he immediately set out on foot with a rescue party. Bad weather forced him to return to the *Prince Albert*, where preparations were made for another attempt. After a second failure Bellot finally led a successful rescue party overland to Port Leopold and back in mid October.

Kennedy began his sledging operations on 5 Jan. 1852. Bellot accompanied him on a preliminary outing to Fury Beach, and they were again together on the expedition's main sledge journey, leaving on 25 February. This trek of 1,100 miles was one of the longest accomplished during the Franklin search. They travelled south to Brentford Bay, where they discovered Bellot Strait, separating Somerset Island from Boothia Peninsula. Having reached Peel Sound, Bellot and Kennedy continued west and crossed Prince of Wales Island before making their way back to Peel Sound and heading north to Cape Walker. Returning to the *Prince Albert*, they followed the north and east coasts of Somerset Island back to Batty Bay, arriving on 30 May. This journey, particularly the discovery of Bellot Strait which revealed the northernmost point of the American continent, was the highlight of the expedition. On 6 August they set sail for Great Britain. Having made a brief stop at Beechey Island, the *Prince Albert* arrived safely at Aberdeen on 7 October.

The voyage had entirely vindicated Kennedy's initial support for Bellot. He had brought with him all the "vivacity, intelligence & good humour of a French officer" for which Kennedy had hoped, and their combined skills in sledge travel and navigation had made them excellent travelling companions. Bellot's participation in the expedition was also widely acclaimed as a symbol of Anglo-French friendship; he was named a foreign corresponding fellow of the Royal Geographical Society and upon his return to France he learned of his promotion to lieutenant, dated 3 Feb. 1852. From Paris he maintained a regular correspondence with Lady Franklin, whom he now regarded with almost filial affection, telling her of his efforts to persuade his own government to send out a search expedition. Those efforts having failed, he sent Lady Franklin a request, on 1 April 1853, to join Captain Edward Augustus Inglefield's *Phoenix* expedition and upon her recommendation was accepted by the Admiralty without question.

Inglefield was to deliver supplies and dispatches to Sir Edward Belcher*'s search expedition of five ships, then wintering at various sites in the Arctic. The *Phoenix* reached one of the ships, the supply vessel *North Star*, at Beechey Island on 8 Aug. 1853, and four days later Bellot set off on foot with four men to deliver messages to Belcher, then in Wellington Channel. On 17 August Bellot and two of the men drifted away from the shore on an ice floe. They made a shelter for the night and the next morning Bellot went out to examine the ice. One of the men went out to join him, but found only his stick on an adjacent floe; Bellot had apparently fallen between floes and drowned.

During Bellot's short period of Arctic service, his simple kindness and energetic devotion to a foreign cause had inspired the deep affection of Lady Franklin, the admiration of Kennedy, and the trust and friendship of all his shipmates. When news of his death reached Europe, that same affectionate esteem was demonstrated by a much wider community. Subscribers on both sides of the Channel, led by the personal initiative of Emperor Napoleon III, contributed to the financial relief of his impoverished family; the city of Rochefort erected a memorial to him; and his many admirers in Britain raised an obelisk in his honour outside Greenwich Hospital, on the south bank of the Thames. Bellot's narrative of the 1851–52 expedition, *Journal d'un voyage aux mers polaires*, was published posthumously in 1854 and was followed, in 1855, by an English translation.

CLIVE HOLLAND

Joseph-René Bellot is the author of *Journal d'un voyage aux mers polaires exécuté à la recherche de sir John Franklin, en*

1851 et 1852 . . . précédé d'une notice sur la vie et les travaux de l'auteur par M. Julien Lemer (Paris, 1854; nouv. édit., Oxford, 1907), an English translation of which was published under the title *Memoirs of Lieutenant Joseph René Bellot . . . with his journal of a voyage in the polar seas, in search of Sir John Franklin*, [ed. Julien Lemer] (2v., London, 1855). Another French edition later appeared under the title *Voyage aux mers polaires à la recherche de sir John Franklin . . .* , intro. Paul Boiteau (Paris, 1880).

Scott Polar Research Institute (Cambridge, Eng.), MS 248/107, 1 March–30 May 1851; MS 248/247/23, 30 May–4 June 1851; MS 248/348/1–5, 1852–53; MS 248/349, 30 Oct. 1852; MS 887; "Encyclopedia arctica," ed. Anne Fraser and Mical O'Maher (MS, Ann Arbor, Mich., 1974) (mfm.). G.B., Parl., Command paper, 1854, 42, [no.1725]: 101–331, *Papers relative to the recent Arctic expeditions in search of Sir John Franklin and the crews of H.M.S. "Erebus" and "Terror."* William Kennedy, *A short narrative of the second voyage of the "Prince Albert," in search of Sir John Franklin . . .* (London, 1853). *Memoir of the late Lieutenant Bellot . . . to accompany his engraved portrait; from the original picture, painted expressly for Lady Franklin, by Stephen Pearce, and engraved by James Scott* (London, 1854). Maurice Hodgson, "Bellot and Kennedy; a contrast in personalities," *Beaver*, outfit 305 (summer 1974): 55–58. Mary Kennedy, "Lieutenant Joseph René Bellot, knight of the Legion of Honour," *Beaver*, outfit 269 (June 1938): 43–45. F. J. Woodward, "Joseph René Bellot, 1826–53," *Polar Record* (Cambridge), 5 (January 1947–July 1950): 398–407.

BENEDICT, ROSWELL GARDINIER, civil engineer and businessman; b. 9 Dec. 1815, possibly in Saratoga Springs, N.Y., son of Daniel Davis Benedict and Phoebe Hedges; d. 5 Feb. 1859 in New York City.

Roswell Gardinier Benedict began his career as a civil engineer about 1833 and like other engineers of the period obtained practical training by working on numerous railways in New York and Ohio. About 1847 he moved to Upper Canada and secured a position with the reconstruction of the Welland Canal. On this project he met Samuel ZIMMERMAN, a Pennsylvanian contractor who was building several locks and an aqueduct. From this meeting developed a professional association that would last until Zimmerman's untimely death in 1857. Benedict also participated in surveying a route for a railway from Toronto to Georgian Bay (probably the Toronto, Simcoe and Huron Union Rail-Road) and in 1847, in addition to his connection with the Welland Canal, he became assistant to Charles Beebe Stuart, the American-born chief engineer of the Great Western Rail-Road.

Following Stuart's return to New York as state engineer in January 1848, Benedict acted in his stead on the Great Western, resurveying the line and rerouting some sections. During a temporary suspension of operations that summer, he worked briefly on a railway between Lockport and Rochester, N.Y. He nevertheless retained his job on the Great Western. Although he was well known to leading American

railway financiers such as Erastus Corning and Lewis Benedict, a distant relative, it was his position within the tightly knit group of American contractors and engineers then operating in Canada that proved most crucial in his relations with the Great Western.

In 1849 he was instrumental in persuading its board of directors to grant the building contract for the railway's eastern division to the firm of James Oswald and Samuel Zimmerman. Construction began in 1851 and later that year, largely through Zimmerman's fast-growing influence and Benedict's own enthusiastic promotion of the railway, Benedict was named chief engineer. His appointment effectively assured Zimmerman's control in a key department, as payments to contractors were contingent on the chief engineer's estimates. Although this sort of sympathetic association was almost standard practice in the construction of early North American railways, it angered the few Canadian engineers who felt qualified for the post but were overlooked. Walter Shanly*, particularly piqued, stated that "as to serving under the auspices of Roswell Benedict – alias Sam Zimmerman –it is absurd, and never can be so long as I could obtain a Rodmans berth any where else." Within months of Benedict's appointment, he had brought into his department several American engineering friends, including Ira Spaulding, with whom he shared a house in Hamilton, Charles L. McAlpine, and Silas Wright Burt.

As chief engineer, Benedict had control over employment policies, estimates, supply purchases, the letting of contracts (which left quantities and costs unspecified), and matters that were strictly engineering. By December 1851 the degree of managerial power held without accountability by Benedict and shared by Zimmerman was attracting mounting critical attention from Peter BUCHANAN and the Great Western's board of directors. The slow pace of construction eventually prompted American investors to push for the appointment of a supervisory commissioner and for an inquiry into Benedict's department. The inquiry exposed the slipshod nature of Benedict's engineering work and the extent of control actually wielded by Zimmerman, to whom he had shifted the contract for building the central division. In a bid to gain control, Isaac Buchanan* and other shareholders and directors forced Benedict's resignation in November 1852, ostensibly for his gross underestimation of costs, and Charles John Brydges* was named managing director.

Benedict nevertheless remained in demand as an engineer. In the spring of 1853 he was engaged as chief engineer by the Hamilton and Toronto Railway, which had been organized by a number of Great Western directors to provide a connection with the Grand Trunk at Toronto. Benedict, who seems to have made some amends to Canadian engineers by hiring Francis Shanly* for this railway, did not stay long

Bennett

with it. Within months he had moved to the London and Port Stanley, where he was joined by the contracting firm of Moore and Pierson, which had worked for him on the Great Western. By that fall he had also been named chief engineer to the Woodstock and Lake Erie Railway and Harbour Company, which soon engaged Zimmerman as contractor. Although construction was terminated in 1854, Benedict probably remained with this company until 1856.

By the mid 1850s he had purchased a house in Clifton (Niagara Falls), the eastern terminus of the Great Western and the crossing point to New York, and had become involved in two business ventures with former railway associates. In 1856 he and Ira Spaulding purchased a large portion of Zimmerman's extensive land holdings in Clifton. With Charles Pierson they formed R. G. Benedict and Company, which subsequently developed the property, donating land for a public market, a town-hall, and several churches. Benedict and Pierson were partners as well in 1857 at Niagara (Niagara-on-the-Lake) in the "Niagara car factory," which evidently specialized in the production of railway cars.

Benedict, who apparently never married, died in a New York City hotel in 1859 after being in poor health for some months. His will, which specified the disposition of his Clifton estate, reveals much about him. Among the possessions left to various members of his family were his technical books and instruments; sporting equipment and trophies; a large collection of photographs, prints, and genre paintings by Cornelius Krieghoff*; testimonial plate from the Great Western; a "life preserver" travelling case; and two seal-rings, one inscribed "Let her rip" and the other "I range free."

CHRISTOPHER ALFRED ANDREAE

AO, MU 2756; RG 22, ser.289, R. G. Benedict. McKinney Library, Albany Institute of Hist. and Art (Albany, N.Y.), Erastus Corning coll., Forbes to Corning, 11 Sept. 1852. PAC, MG 24, D16, 3: 1564; 5: 2823–31; 14: 11927–28; 31: 25789–92; 94: 65441–67; D80, 1, 4; MG 29, B6, 1: 2, 7. S. W. Burt, "An engineer on the Great Western: a selection from the personal reminiscenses of Silas Wright Burt," ed. A. G. Bogue and L. R. Benson, Western Ontario Hist. Nuggets (London), no.17 (1952): 4. Can., Prov. of, Legislative Assembly, App. to the journals, 1849, app.QQQ, examination of R. G. Benedict regarding Great Western Railway. Daylight through the mountain: letters and labours of civil engineers Walter and Francis Shanly, ed. F. N. Walker ([Montreal], 1957), 83, 177–78. Daily Spectator, and Journal of Commerce, 19 March 1857. Hamilton Gazette, and General Advertiser (Hamilton, [Ont.]), 26 Dec. 1853, 23 Jan. 1854. Mail (Niagara [Niagara-on-the-Lake, Ont.]), 9 Feb. 1859. Weekly Dispatch, St. Thomas, Port Stanley, and County of Elgin Advertiser (St Thomas, [Ont.]), 25 Aug. 1853. H. M. Benedict, The genealogy of the Benedicts in America (Albany, 1870), 313. Canada directory, 1857–58: 102, 177, 472. P. A. Baskerville, "The boardroom and beyond; aspects of the Upper Canadian railroad community" (PHD thesis, Queen's Univ., Kingston, Ont., 1973). Walter Neutel, "From 'southern' concept to Canada Southern Railway, 1835–1873" (MA thesis, Univ. of Western Ont., London, 1968). G. R. Stevens, Canadian National Railways (2v., Toronto and Vancouver, 1960–62), 1: 105. P. [A.] Baskerville, "Professional vs. proprietor: power distribution in the railroad world of Upper Canada/Ontario, 1850 to 1881," CHA Hist. papers, 1978: 47–63. R. D. Smith, "The early years of the Great Western Railway, 1833–1857," OH, 60 (1968): 205–27.

BENNETT, WILLIAM, Wesleyan Methodist minister; b. c. 1770 in or near Manchester, England; m. first 20 Feb. 1806 Elizabeth Allison (d. 1825) in Horton, N.S.; m. secondly 12 Oct. 1826 Sophia Sargent (d. 1839) in Barrington, N.S.; m. thirdly c. 1840 a Mrs Grant of Liverpool, N.S.; he had 11 children; d. 7 Nov. 1857 in Halifax.

Little is known of William Bennett before 1800 when he was received by the British Wesleyan Conference on probation and sent as a missionary to Nova Scotia. In a letter written in 1804 he mentioned that he had become a member of the Manchester Society in 1794, a class leader in 1796, and a local preacher in 1798. He evidently had attended good schools and gained a thorough knowledge of Wesleyan theology and polity. With three other recruits, including Joshua Marsden*, he sailed from Liverpool in late August 1800. The weather was stormy and he suffered much before landing in Halifax on 4 October.

He soon appeared in Liverpool, where he preached twice in the Methodist chapel. Simeon Perkins* heard him and wrote, "He is a good Speaker, is very Distinct, and methodical. . . . His doctrine Sound, & Scriptural." Bennett spent the winter at Shelburne, where conditions were not encouraging. Many of the loyalist settlers had left and he had to make long journeys by boat or on foot to minister to little groups along the coast. Back in Liverpool in April 1801 he seemed to enjoy a good year, though lack of heat in the chapel in winter and trips as far west as Sable River must have been irksome.

At the Nova Scotia District meeting in 1802 it was decided that Bennett would go to New York for ordination. His next ten years were spent on most of the circuits in Nova Scotia and New Brunswick, where a great deal of travel was called for and living conditions were most primitive. About 1804 he was made secretary of the district, a new position which enabled him to share the work of Superintendent William Black*. When Black retired in 1812, Bennett was made superintendent of all the Wesleyan Methodist work in eastern British America. In addition to his circuit duties he was required to keep in touch with the preachers and to visit missions with problems. In 1814 he crossed to Charlottetown where he arranged for the retirement of James Bulpit and the building of the first chapel. Returning from Montreal in 1815, he was nearly shipwrecked. His most important assignment was his attendance in 1816 along with Black at the American general conference in Baltimore where an effort was made to settle the jurisdiction of preachers from the United States and England in the Canadas. This matter took him again to Montreal the following year, where he almost died of pleurisy and liver trouble. Severely weakened, he was forced to seek retirement, which was granted in 1821.

Bennett purchased a farm near Avondale, N.S., with funds left to his wife, and continued to assist in local and district work as he was able. As a special honour, the British Wesleyan Conference financed his return to England in 1840 and welcomed him at its gathering. After this trip, he moved to Halifax and served for a time as chaplain of the provincial penitentiary. Following a painful illness he died in 1857 "in perfect peace" and was buried in Camp Hill Cemetery.

Bennett is regarded as one of the most dedicated and helpful workmen of his day in leading people to Christ. He was thorough in all he did, and to the end of his days felt that those trained in English institutions were superior to native sons. He believed wholeheartedly in the Methodist Church and saw it grow to a great power in the Maritimes. His running feud with the missionary committee over a better deal for married preachers with families bore fruit not only for him but in various amenities for all ministers. As an admirer, Matthew Richey*, put it, his "name will be transmitted to posterity as one of the most faithful missionaries that ever laboured in the Provinces."

E. A. BETTS

Six letters written by William Bennett between 1809 and 1821 are preserved in the MCA, five in the Duncan McColl papers and one, addressed to the members of the Methodist Church in St Stephen's, in the William Black papers; microfilm copies of both collections are available at the UCA. Some 65 further letters, written to the Wesleyan Methodist Missionary Society between 1802 and 1821, are among the North American correspondence in the SOAS, Methodist Missionary Soc. Arch.; these are also available on microfilm at the Maritime Conference Arch. and the UCA. A few of them were edited and then printed in the organ of the Wesleyan Methodist Church in Britain, the *Methodist Magazine* (London), 25 (1802)–44 (1821).

A portrait of Bennett appears opposite page 120 of the *British North American Wesleyan Methodist Magazine* (Saint John, N.B.), 1 (1840–41), accompanied by a short biographical note on page 160.

MCA, Halifax Methodist Soc., reg. of baptisms and marriages, 20 Feb. 1806; Wesleyan Methodist Church, Eastern British America Conference, minutes, 1812–21; Nova Scotia and New Brunswick District, minutes, 1804–21. William Croscombe, "The late Rev. W. Bennett," *Provincial Wesleyan* (Halifax), 19 Nov. 1857. "The late Rev. Wm. Bennett," *Provincial Wesleyan*, 12 Nov. 1857. Joshua Marsden, *The narrative of a mission to Nova Scotia, New Brunswick, and the Somers Islands; with a tour to Lake Ontario . . .* (Plymouth Dock [Plymouth], Eng., 1816; repr. New York, 1966). Simeon Perkins, *The diary of Simeon Perkins, 1797–1803*, ed. C. B. Fergusson (Toronto, 1967). Matthew Richey, *A memoir of the late Rev. William Black, Wesleyan minister, Halifax, N.S., including an account of the rise and progress of Methodism in Nova Scotia . . .* (Halifax, 1839); *A sermon on occasion of the death of Rev. William Bennett, preached at Halifax, N.S. on Sunday Dec. 27 [1857]* (Halifax, 1858; copy at PANS). Wesleyan Methodist Church, *Minutes of the conferences* (London), 2 (1799–1807)–5 (1819–24), minutes for 1800–21. *The Barrington Sargents*, comp. H. L. Doane (typescript, Truro, N.S., 1916; copy at PANS), 23. L. A. Morrison, *The history of the Alison, or Allison family in Europe and America, A.D. 1135 to 1893; giving an account of the family in Scotland, England, Ireland, Australia, Canada, and the United States* (Boston, 1893). E. A. Betts, *Bishop Black and his preachers* (2nd ed., Sackville, N.B., 1976). French, *Parsons & politics*. G. O. Huestis, *Memorials of Wesleyan missionaries & ministers, who have died within the bounds of the conference of Eastern British America, since the introduction of Methodism into these colonies* (Halifax, 1872). D. W. Johnson, *History of Methodism in eastern British America, including Nova Scotia, New Brunswick, Prince Edward Island, Newfoundland, and Bermuda . . .* ([Sackville], n.d.). T. W. Smith, *Hist. of Methodist Church*.

BERCZY, CHARLES ALBERT, businessman, office holder, and justice of the peace; b. 22 Aug. 1794 in Newark (Niagara-on-the-Lake), Upper Canada, son of William Berczy* and Jeanne-Charlotte Allamand*; m. 21 June 1828 Ann Eliza Finch in Amherstburg, Upper Canada, and they had at least one son and seven daughters; d. 9 June 1858 in Toronto.

Charles Albert Berczy was born in the midst of his father's attempts to establish a settlement in Markham Township, north of York (Toronto). The Berczys settled in York in 1794 and remained there until 1798, when the failure of the settlement scheme prompted them to move to Montreal. The family returned to York in 1802 but from 1804 lived in Montreal and Quebec. When the War of 1812 broke out Charles became a clerk in the British commissariat at Montreal. Between 25 Dec. 1814 and 24 April 1816 he served as acting deputy assistant commissary general, a position which no doubt aided his advancement in Canadian society. By 1818 he had settled at Amherstburg, in the Western District of Upper Canada, and soon entered into business there with his brother, William Bent*. William later claimed that their shipment of tobacco in 1821 was the first ever exported from Upper Canada.

Within a few years Berczy found favour with the

Berczy

district's official oligarchy. He received his first commission as a justice of the peace in September 1826 and five years later was appointed to the lucrative position of postmaster at Amherstburg. As a prominent office holder he gradually ascended within the provincial hierarchy and also gained considerable knowledge of political activities in Kent and Essex counties. In 1835, because of his postal experience and friendship with Thomas Allen Stayner* (deputy postmaster general of Upper and Lower Canada), Berczy was appointed to the newly created position of post office surveyor, or inspector, stationed in Toronto and responsible for all of the territory west of Kingston.

During the rebellion of 1837–38 and its aftermath in Upper Canada Berczy was secretly employed by Lieutenant Governor Sir Francis Bond Head* "to maintain a Correspondence throughout the Province to the designs of Foreign & Domestic Enemies." He was responsible for the surveillance of postmasters such as Joseph Watson of Lloydtown, whom he dismissed in 1837 for treasonous activity, and in 1838–39 he coordinated the secret service activities of at least 13 agents. In April 1838 Berczy was appointed postmaster of Toronto, replacing James Scott Howard*, who had been suspected of being too close to the rebel cause. Once settled in the capital, he gave political advice and assistance to Head's successor, Sir George ARTHUR. Feeling that he still had "influence enough" in the Western District, at Arthur's request Berczy tried, unsuccessfully, during the election of 1841 to persuade Joseph Woods to withdraw from the campaign in Kent in order to secure the return of Samuel Bealey Harrison*. As a result of such activity and his management of the large Toronto post office, Berczy gained increasing influence in the political and business world of Toronto. In 1840 John Strachan* had regarded him as "an officer of great merit – he is attentive to his duties which he discharges in a manner highly satisfactory to all concerned," although, according to William Henry Griffin*, the post office's eastern surveyor, he never "distinguished himself particularly in any way."

Berczy soon became involved in numerous entrepreneurial activities. He was a director of the Bank of Upper Canada (1840–43), a president of the Toronto Building Society, and a founder and major shareholder of the Toronto, Simcoe, and Lake Huron Union Rail-Road Company. In 1848 he became first president of the newly created Consumers' Gas Company of Toronto. Three years later he headed a joint-stock company that bought the City of Toronto Gas Light and Water Company from Albert Furniss, a transaction that proved overly ambitious. The firm defaulted on its mortgage payments and was repossessed in 1853.

It was at this point that Berczy's influence began to

wane for in the same year he lost his postmastership (the reasons are unclear) and in 1856 his directorship in Consumers' Gas ended. This series of set-backs and disappointments took their toll, shrouding a man who, in 1847, had been described as "an inveterate snuff user, very nervous, irritable and gloomy." By 1858 Berczy's circumstances had evidently become unbearable and on 9 June he committed suicide at his Carlton Street home in Toronto. Though he left a modest estate of £10,000 (a postal employee had described him as "extremely parsimonious"), he died a broken man, devoid of most of the positions and honours that had once dominated his life.

ERIC JARVIS

Two portraits of Charles Albert Berczy painted by his father are reproduced in John Andre's *William Berczy*, cited below; the earlier of these, an oil portrait done around 1798 (plate facing p.72), depicts him as a small child; a later water-colour (facing p.105) portrays him in his teens.

AO, MS 35, letter-books, 1827–41: 86; MS 526, W. H. Griffin to W. D. LeSueur, 16 April 1874; RG 22, ser.155, will of C. A. Berczy. Canada Post Corporation, Southwestern District (London, Ont.), Amherstburg Post Office records, information cards concerning postmasters; Toronto Metropolitan District (Toronto), Public Affairs Branch records. PAC, RG 1, E3, 9A: 172–75; 10: 115–39; 46: 153–58; 89: 183–96; L3, 40: B11/199; 44: B13/24, 78; 60: B20/48; RG 5, A1: 28427–33, 31446–47, 49704–7, 49915–17, 59082–93, 75469–70, 84221–24, 94096–98, 103299–302, 103696–98, 103854–58, 103968–74, 104205–6, 105239–43, 107721–23, 107869–71, 109255–60, 109906–12, 112387–89, 113870–71, 114660–63, 114706–9, 114779–81, 114824–25, 114846–47, 114859–62, 114891–97, 115013–14, 116288–91, 118167–72, 118200–1, 118637–43, 118648–50, 118958–66, 119889–90, 119973–76, 120980–84, 121341–43, 122691–95, 123952–53, 124186–89, 126973–77, 142253–54; RG 68, General index, 1651–1841: 458. St James' Cemetery and Crematorium (Toronto), Record of burials. *Arthur papers* (Sanderson), 3: 1590–92. Can., Prov. of, Legislative Assembly, *App. to the journals*, 1846, app.F; *Statutes*, 1842, c.27; 1848, cc.14, 16; 1849, c.196. *Globe*, 10 June 1858. *Leader*, 10 June 1858. *Loyalist* (York [Toronto]), 5 July 1828.

"Calendar of state papers," PAC *Report*, 1936: 583. Morgan, *Sketches of celebrated Canadians*, 113. "State papers – U.C.," PAC *Report*, 1943: 150–51, 184–85. *Toronto directory*, 1850–51: xlvi. John Andre, *William Berczy, co-founder of Toronto; a sketch* (Toronto, 1967). E. C. Guillet, *Toronto from trading post to great city* (Toronto, 1934), 158, 244. Middleton, *Municipality of Toronto*, 1: 230, 261, 300–1; 2: 782. W. H. Pearson, *Recollections and records of Toronto of old . . .* (Toronto, 1914), 176. *75th birthday: 1848–1923, the Consumers' Gas Company of Toronto*, comp. E. J. Tucker (Toronto, 1923). William Smith, *The history of the Post Office in British North America, 1639–1870* (Cambridge, Eng., 1920), 46–47, 171. C. C. Taylor, *Toronto "called back" from 1886 to 1850 . . .* (Toronto, 1886), 66. F. H. Armstrong, "The oligarchy of the Western District of Upper Canada, 1788–1841," CHA

Hist. papers, 1977: 87–102. Elwood Jones and Douglas McCalla, "Toronto waterworks, 1840–77: continuity and change in nineteenth-century Toronto politics," *CHR*, 60 (1979): 300–23.

BETHUNE, ANGUS, fur trader and politician; b. 9 Sept. 1783 on Carleton Island (N.Y.) in Lake Ontario, son of the Reverend John Bethune* and Véronique Waddens, daughter of Jean-Étienne Waddens*; m. Louisa McKenzie, mixed-blood daughter of Roderick McKenzie*, and they had six children; also fathered at least two children by Indian women; d. 13 Nov. 1858 in Toronto.

Angus Bethune was the eldest son in an illustrious family; his brothers included Alexander Neil*, Donald*, James Gray*, and John*. As a child he moved with his family from Carleton Island to Montreal, and then in 1787 to Williamstown (Ont.). At an early age he joined the North West Company. In 1804–5 he served at the post on the Whitemud River, near the south end of Lake Manitoba, and the following year he was listed as a clerk at Lake Winnipeg. Attached to the brigade of Alexander Henry* the younger in September 1810, Bethune accompanied Henry to Rocky Mountain House (Alta). Late in the fall of 1810 David THOMPSON arrived at this post and Bethune helped him to set off on his expedition across the Rocky Mountains. As part of the NWC strategy to establish a transpacific trade from the northwest coast, Thompson had been instructed to reach the mouth of the Columbia River ahead of the Pacific Fur Company's party, sent out by ship from New York. Bethune himself figured prominently in the NWC plans for the Pacific, and in 1812 or 1813 he was designated "as the Person to go to China to learn the Business & act as supercargo."

In the fall of 1813 he arrived with John George McTavish* at Fort Astoria (Astoria, Oreg.), where he acted as a witness in the sale of the post by the PFC to the NWC. He became a partner in the NWC in July 1814 and later that month embarked with a cargo of Columbia furs on the company vessel *Isaac Todd* for Canton (People's Republic of China). From China the ship sailed to England with a lading of tea for the East India Company, leaving Bethune in Canton to await the arrival of a second company vessel. In March 1815 he boarded the NWC ship *Columbia* as supercargo and returned to Fort Astoria, renamed Fort George by the NWC. He made trading voyages to Monterey (Calif.) and Sitka (Alaska), as well as another round trip to China, before leaving the vessel at Fort George in August 1816. These commercial ventures proved disappointing and expensive, and the NWC abandoned its attempt to employ its own vessels and personnel in the China trade, deciding instead to contract with the Boston firm of J. and T. H. Perkins for this sector of their business.

In April 1817 Bethune left Fort George headed for Montreal via Fort William (Thunder Bay, Ont.) with an overland party including Duncan McDougall*, Joseph McGillivray, Alexander McTavish, and Ross Cox. The journey, which was later chronicled by Cox, was marked by perils, hardships, and death. Bethune left the party in June 1817 at the English (upper Churchill) River, and his whereabouts are not known until November 1818 when, according to James KEITH, he unexpectedly turned up at Fort George with an "unusual accession of Gentlemen of one kind or other." Bethune likely remained at Fort George until the following spring.

He spent the winter of 1819–20 at Île-à-la-Crosse (Sask.), where in February he welcomed members of Captain John Franklin*'s overland expedition to the northern coast of North America. At this post he was faced with strong opposition from John CLARKE of the Hudson's Bay Company, and at the close of the season it became evident that Bethune had lost considerable ground to the aggressive Clarke.

In July 1820, at Fort William, Bethune and Dr John McLOUGHLIN were deputized by a group of 18 wintering partners to pursue negotiations towards an agreement with the HBC, in defiance of the NWC Montreal agents under the direction of William McGillivray*. To this purpose, the pair left for England in the fall of 1820. The impact of their representations on the coalition agreement, signed on 26 March 1821 by William and Simon* McGillivray and Edward Ellice* for the NWC, and by William Smith for the HBC, is difficult to assess; both, however, were named chief factors in the new HBC by the terms of the deed poll which followed. Bethune sailed to New York with HBC director Nicholas GARRY, and then continued on to Fort William for the July meeting of chief factors and traders to assign posts for the coming winter. At this gathering of former NWC partners and HBC employees he was insulted and ostracized.

His first appointment as chief factor was to Moose Factory (Ont.) in the Southern Department. In the summer of 1822 he became superintendent at Fort Albany and in 1824 was placed in charge of the provision depot at Sault Ste Marie. From all of these posts he waged a running battle by correspondence with the Southern Department governor, William Williams*, and contributed to the unruliness of the department council which led to the amalgamation, under Governor George SIMPSON, of the Northern and Southern departments. Simpson was more adept at managing Bethune, but nevertheless was as unimpressed by him as Williams had been, judging him "a very poor creature, vain, self sufficient and trifling" in his 1832 character book.

In the summer of 1832 Bethune was appointed to Michipicoten (Michipicoten River, Ont.), in charge of

Betzner

the Lake Superior district, to fill a vacancy caused by the illness of Chief Factor George KEITH. Under some protest, he returned to the Sault in June 1833, and later that year had the Lake Huron district added to his responsibilities while Chief Factor John McBean was on furlough. During this season he quarrelled bitterly with the Church of England missionary at Sault Ste Marie, William McMurray*. After a furlough in 1834 Bethune was reappointed to Michipicoten and then, in 1836, obtained a year's leave of absence because of "serious indisposition." In 1837 he again took charge of the Lake Huron district and was stationed at Fort La Cloche (Ont.), where he remained until his retirement from active service in 1839. He officially retired from the company in 1841.

Bethune settled in Toronto in 1839 or 1840, where he became a director of the Bank of Upper Canada. He also took an interest in municipal politics, and in the Toronto City Council election of 1845 defeated the incumbent alderman for St David's Ward, Dr Alexander Burnside. During the two years that Bethune sat on council he clashed with fellow St David's Ward alderman Henry SHERWOOD. It is reported that in 1845 Bethune met the painter Paul Kane* and, providing him with a chilling account of the inhospitality of HBC officers, nearly deterred Kane from his journey to the northwest coast.

Having lapsed into senility towards the end of his life, Bethune died in Toronto at the age of 75. His estate was valued at more than $56,000 and included two houses, stocks, mortgages, and 1,500 acres left to him by his father. His son, Dr Norman Bethune*, served as executor. In spite of the prominent positions Angus Bethune attained during his many years in the fur trade, his long career, which was full of adventure, turbulence, and controversy, was not crowned by many personal successes.

HILARY RUSSELL

AO, MS 107, Reg. of baptisms and marriages, 7, 9 Sept. 1783; MU 129; RG 22, Court of Chancery, case files, city suits, no.129/1878; ser.302, Angus Bethune. PAC, MG 19, A21, ser.1, 17–18; E1, ser.1, 9, 18, 21, 23–24, 28–31 (copies); MG 24, L3, 15–16 (copies). PAM, HBCA, B.3/a/127–128; B.3/b/51b–53; B.3/e/8–11; B.129/a/16–19; B.129/b/6–11; B.129/e/9–13; B.135/k/1; B.194/a/1–8; B.194/b/1–10; B.194/e/1–8; D.1/4–10; D.2/1; D.4/1–71; 88–108; D.5/1–15; F.3/2; F.4/4–10. Peter Corney, *Voyages in the northern Pacific; narrative of several trading voyages from 1813 to 1818, between the north west coast of America, the Hawaiian Islands and China . . .*, ed. W. D. Alexander (Honolulu, Hawaii, 1896). Ross Cox, *The Columbia River; or scenes and adventures during a residence of six years on the western side of the Rocky Mountains . . .*, ed. E. I. and J. R. Stewart (Norman, Okla., 1957). *Docs. relating to NWC* (Wallace). Gabriel Franchère, *Journal of a voyage on the north west coast of North America during the years 1811, 1812, 1813, and 1814*, trans. W. T. Lamb, ed. and intro. W. K. Lamb (Toronto, 1969). Nicholas Garry, "Diary of Nicholas Garry, deputy-governor of the Hudson's Bay Company from 1822–1835: a detailed narrative of his travels in the northwest territories of British North America in 1821 . . . ," ed. F. N. Garry, RSC *Trans.*, 2nd ser., 6 (1900), sect.II: 73–204; new ed., *The diary of Nicholas Garry, deputy-governor of the Hudson's Bay Company: a detailed narrative of his travels in the northwest territories of British North America in 1821*, ed. W. J. Noxon (Toronto, 1973). G.B., Foreign Office, *Certain correspondence of the Foreign Office and of the Hudson's Bay Company copied from original documents, London 1898*, ed. [O. J. Klotz] (Ottawa, 1899). J. J. Hargrave, *Red River* (Montreal, 1871; repr. Altona, Man., 1977). *HBRS*, 2 (Rich and Fleming); 3 (Fleming). Paul Kane, *Paul Kane's frontier, including wanderings of an artist among the Indians of North America*, ed. J. R. Harper (Toronto, [1971]). *New light on early hist. of greater northwest* (Coues). Simpson, "Character book," *HBRS*, 30 (Williams), 151–236. *British Colonist* (Toronto), January 1845–January 1846. Middleton, *Municipality of Toronto*. Rich, *Hist. of HBC*. P. [A.] Baskerville, "Donald Bethune's steamboat business: a study of Upper Canadian commercial and financial practice," *OH*, 67 (1975): 135–49. T. C. Elliott, "Sale of Astoria, 1813," *Oreg. Hist. Quarterly* (Salem), 33 (1932): 43–50. F. W. Howay, "A list of trading vessels in the maritime fur trade, [1805–1819]," RSC *Trans.*, 3rd ser., 26 (1932), sect.II: 43–86; 27 (1933), sect.II: 119–47. Marion O'Neil, "The maritime activities of the North West Company, 1813 to 1821," *Wash. Hist. Quarterly*, 21 (1930): 243–67. Hilary Russell, "The Chinese voyages of Angus Bethune," *Beaver*, outfit 307 (spring 1977): 22–31.

BETZNER, SAMUEL D., settler and district constable; b. 1 March 1771 in Lancaster County, Pa, a son of Samuel Betzner (Bezner) and Maria Detweiler; m. before 1798 Elizabeth Brech, and they had a son and a daughter; d. 10 Aug. 1856 near Flamborough (West Flamborough), Upper Canada.

A native of Württemberg (Federal Republic of Germany), Samuel D. Betzner's father immigrated to North America in 1755 and settled in Franklin County, Pa. In the fall of 1799 Samuel D. and his brother-in-law Joseph Schörg left that county for the Jordan area of the Niagara district of Upper Canada, where a number of other Mennonites from Pennsylvania had already settled. Betzner spent the winter in Ancaster and that spring set out with Schörg to explore the valley of the Grand River, which had been recommended to them as being attractive for settlement by Jacob Bechtel, an earlier visitor. Proceeding by way of Brant's Ford (Brantford) they came to block 2 (Waterloo Township), which had been purchased in 1796 from the Six Nations Indians by Richard Beasley*, James Wilson, and John Baptist Rousseaux* St John.

In August 1800 Betzner bought from them land adjacent to the site of the village of Blair. A disastrous fire at Ancaster had destroyed most of his possessions but despite this misfortune he took steps to establish a farm on his chosen lot by clearing land and erecting buildings. Joseph Schörg settled near by, on the east bank of the Grand, and these two men are credited with being the first to establish homes in the area which became Waterloo County in 1850. They were followed by other Pennsylvania Mennonites who sought not only reasonably priced land for farms for their sons but also the continuation of the exemption from military service they had received under British rule before the American Revolutionary War. Most purchased their land from Richard Beasley, who had bought out the interests of Wilson and Rousseaux.

Early in 1803 it was reported that the land these later settlers had bought had been mortgaged by Beasley, Wilson, and Rousseaux to trustees for the Six Nations in 1798 and therefore the settlers would not be able to secure clear title. Betzner and Jacob Bechtel were engaged to go to Niagara (Niagara-on-the-Lake) where they learned to their consternation that the report was true. The matter was resolved when Beasley agreed in 1803 to sell to the Mennonites a parcel of 60,000 acres of land in block 2 for the sum of £10,000 to pay off the mortgage. The settlers sent representatives back to Pennsylvania, where they eventually persuaded a group of affluent co-religionists and other investors to form a joint-stock company, the German Company, to raise the purchase money. A number of the early settlers, including Betzner, who did not have the mortgage problem remained on their original lots and had no financial interest in the German Company.

A leading member of the Mennonite community, he was made a constable for the Home District in 1800 and was a charter member of the church formed by Benjamin EBY in 1813. In 1817, however, Betzner sold his farm in Waterloo Township and settled on lot 3, concession 1, in West Flamborough Township, where he spent the rest of his life. In 1828–29 he transferred title on this farm to his son, David.

Perhaps Betzner's only claim to recognition is as one of the earliest settlers in Waterloo County, where heavily forested lands were reached by trails that could scarcely be called roads. He is, nevertheless, representative of those pioneers who, through perseverance and industry, overcame disasters and hardships in order to establish productive farms for succeeding generations of their families.

GRACE SCHMIDT

PAC, RG 1, L3, 33: B6/45; RG 31, A1, 1851, Flamborough (West) Township: 45 (mfm. at AO). Waterloo North Land Registry Office (Kitchener, Ont.), Abstract index to deeds, Waterloo Township, Beasley's old survey, concession 1, lot 5 (mfm. at AO, GS 3023); West Flamborough Township, concession 1, lot 3 (mfm. at AO, GS 1472). "Minutes of the Court of General Quarter Sessions of the Peace for the Home District, 13th March, 1800, to 28th December, 1811," AO Report, 1932: 44. *Berlin Chronicle and Provincial Reformers' Gazette* (Berlin [Kitchener]), 27 Aug. 1856. Laura Betzner Edworthy, *The Betzner family in Canada: genealogical and historical records, 1799–1970* (n.p., n.d.; copies at AO and Kitchener Public Library). E. E. Eby, *A biographical history of Waterloo Township . . .* (2v., Berlin, 1895–96); repub. as E. E. Eby and J. B. Snyder, *A biographical history of early settlers and their descendants in Waterloo Township*, with *Supplement*, ed. E. D. Weber (Kitchener, 1971), 1. A. B. Sherk, "The Pennsylvania Germans of Waterloo County, Ontario," *OH*, 7 (1906): 98–109.

BIBAUD, MICHEL, teacher, journalist, author, office holder, and justice of the peace; b. 19 Jan. 1782 in Côte-des-Neiges (Montreal), son of Michel-Ange Bibaud, a farmer, and Cécile-Clémence Fresne; m. 11 May 1812 Élizabeth Delisle, daughter of Joseph Delisle, a master cooper, in Montreal, and they had nine children; d. there 3 Aug. 1857.

Michel Bibaud came from a family of nine children and spent his childhood and adolescence at Côte-des-Neiges. At 18 he entered the Collège Saint-Raphaël in Montreal, where he studied until 1806; he then became a tutor. In 1813, while still in Montreal, he began a career as a journalist, working for *Le Spectateur* under its editor, Charles-Bernard Pasteur. Combining his new trade with the role of educator, he published *L'arithmétique en quatre parties* in 1816. The following year he went into partnership with Joseph-Victor Delorme to start *L'Aurore*, a political, scientific, and literary weekly. The paper merged with *Le Spectateur canadien* in 1819, of which Bibaud became editor in July. In October he accepted the same position with *Le Courrier du Bas-Canada*, a reform weekly recently founded by Delorme; the paper lasted only until December. Bibaud continued to write for *Le Spectateur canadien* until it ceased publication in 1822. He then concentrated mainly on teaching.

Bibaud embarked in 1825 on a new journalistic venture by founding *La Bibliothèque canadienne* and becoming its editor. This monthly journal featured historical, scientific, and literary articles. Bibaud allotted generous space to his own writings on the history of Canada and to the work of his contemporaries, particularly Jacques VIGER, Jacques Labrie*, and Jean-Baptiste Meilleur*. He replaced *La Bibliothèque canadienne* in 1830 with *L'Observateur*, a reform weekly of a somewhat more political cast. However, this publication, which was both a gazette and a literary journal, did not become popular and ceased to appear in July 1831.

The preceding year saw Bibaud publish his *Épîtres, satires, chansons, épigrammes et autres pièces de vers*, the first collection of poetry by a French Canadian to appear in Canada. Neither contemporary nor 20th-century critics have been disposed to acclaim

Bibaud

the work. Bibaud attempted to enlighten his audience about their misfortunes, to use irony in disclosing their defects and wrongdoings, and to present national and foreign heroes as ideals to emulate. But his poetry was moralizing, severe, bitter, and pessimistic, and it lacked originality, spontaneity, and warmth. A disciple of Horace and Boileau, whom he imitated slavishly, he was considered a third-rate classicist; according to Séraphin Marion, he composed his poems "like a lumberjack putting up his cottage."

Bibaud launched a new reform monthly, the *Magasin du Bas-Canada*, in January 1832; its content was similar to the literary and scientific articles in *La Bibliothèque canadienne*. However, the journal did not clear the difficult hurdle of the first year and ceased publication in December. That year Bibaud published his *L'arithmétique à l'usage des écoles élémentaires du Bas-Canada*, as well as *Quelques réflexions sur la dernière élection du Quartier-Ouest de la cité de Montréal*, which was drafted under the auspices of the Constitutional Association and in collaboration with his brother Pierre.

In 1833 Bibaud accepted from the government the posts of clerk of the market and inspector of weights and measures in Montreal. Four years later he was appointed justice of the peace and that year he published his *Histoire du Canada sous la domination française*. Journalism continued to attract him, and in 1842 he started *L'Encyclopédie canadienne*, a monthly through which he hoped to further the arts, letters, and sciences. The experiment once again proved disappointing, and *L'Encyclopédie canadienne* ceased to appear in February 1843. As well, Bibaud became a translator for the *Canadian Agricultural Journal* in 1843, and for the Geological Survey of Canada, directed by William Edmond Logan*, in 1844. His *Histoire du Canada, et des Canadiens, sous la domination anglaise* was also published in 1844.

For nearly 30 years Bibaud had worked tirelessly to raise the cultural level of his compatriots, whom he exhorted to intellectual effort. Despite unremitting work, repeated complaints, and sometimes severe reprimands, he never managed to capture the public's interest. His harsh, unpolished, dry style and the often moralizing tone of his writings, as well as his monotonous and slipshod way of presenting information in his weighty periodicals, no doubt put readers off and explain his lack of success.

As for Bibaud's *Histoire du Canada*, although it broke new ground, it was received with disparagement and indifference. The chronological, factual narrative, written in a tedious style, was based to a large extent on the writings of Pierre-François-Xavier de Charlevoix* and William Smith*. Bibaud found it difficult to describe the development of Canadian political life. Biased as an historian, he wrote history from the British point of view. Calling himself a true reformer, he pronounced in favour of a constitutional monarchy while advocating responsible government. He was rather servile in his approval of the colonial government, but displayed extreme severity towards French Canadians, and in particular towards the Patriote party, which he considered incompetent, obsessed with wild doctrines, and caught up in a chimerical struggle.

Bibaud's partisan spirit made him unpopular with his contemporaries. He had prepared a third volume of his history covering events from 1830 to 1837; nevertheless, because of the stands he had previously taken and the possibility of reprisals from the Patriote party, he refrained from publishing it. His son Jean-Gaspard brought it out in 1878, and the work was given a harsh reception by the critics. Little known, if not unknown, Bibaud's *Histoire du Canada* sank from sight. Quebec historian Guy Frégault* calls it "biased history, antiquated history," and considers it fortunate for Bibaud that oblivion saved him from ridicule.

Bibaud seems to have been a serious-minded, stern, surly man, given to moralizing. Frégault, who had little regard for him, finds his poetry shapeless, insipid, and pretentious, and his history shallow, derivative, and lacking in truth. He describes the man himself in unflattering terms: "His head was not exactly cast in the mould of Mirabeau's. A wig, heavy – and symbolic – set askew on a flat skull, small but bright eyes, an outsize nose, puffy cheeks, a rough-hewn mouth, a protuberant chin." Séraphin Marion compares him to "a pot-bellied bourgeois or a fussy bureaucrat," while Camille Roy* speaks of his scornful and contemptuous manner.

Bibaud was withdrawn and apparently had a very disagreeable nature. Conscientious and persevering, he contented himself with what he earned by hard work. He seldom went out, and was satisfied to keep a few close friends with whom he sometimes played whist. But as a general rule he shut himself up in his room to write. His son François-Maximilien* said that he was a good and affectionate father, but he stressed that his imposing and serious demeanour was a barrier to intimacy.

After the second volume of his *Histoire du Canada* was published, Michel Bibaud continued to work as a translator until he was stricken with paralysis in 1856. His son Jean-Gaspard took him into his house, where he died on 3 Aug. 1857. He was buried two days later in the Côte-des-Neiges cemetery.

CÉLINE CYR

Michel Bibaud is the author of a number of works, all published in Montreal: *L'arithmétique en quatre parties, savoir: l'arithmétique vulgaire, l'arithmétique marchande, l'arithmétique scientifique, l'arithmétique curieuse; suivie d'un précis sur la tenue des livres de comptes* (1816);

Épîtres, satires, chansons, épigrammes et autres pièces de vers (1830), an abstract of which was printed in the *Magasin du Bas-Canada*, 1 (1832): 21–31; *L'arithmétique à l'usage des écoles élémentaires du Bas-Canada* (1832); *Quelques réflexions sur la dernière élection du Quartier-Ouest de la cité de Montréal* (1832); *Histoire du Canada sous la domination française* (1837; réimpr., New York, 1968; 2e éd., Montréal, 1843); *Histoire du Canada et des Canadiens, sous la domination anglaise*, [1760–1830] (1844; réimpr., East Ardsley, Angl., et New York, 1968); and *Histoire du Canada et des Canadiens, sous la domination anglaise*, [1830–37], J.-G. Bibaud, édit. (1878). He also edited Gabriel Franchère*'s *Relation d'un voyage à la côte du nord-ouest de l'Amérique septentrionale dans les années 1810, 11, 12, 13 et 14* (Montréal, 1820).

ANQ-M, CE1-51, 20 janv. 1782, 11 mai 1812, 5 août 1857. AUM, P 58, A2/63. *Le Journal de Québec*, 6 août 1857. *Le Pays*, 4 août 1857. Beaulieu et Hamelin, *La presse québécoise*, 1: 29–30, 34–35, 39, 42, 49–53, 67–69, 72–74, 81, 120, 127, 146, 188. *DOLQ*, 1: 216–18, 345–47. Réginald Hamel *et al.*, *Dictionnaire pratique des auteurs québécois* (Montréal, 1976), 65–66. Pauline Perrault, "Bio-bibliographie de Michel Bibaud, journaliste, poète, historien" (thèse de bibliothéconomie, univ. de Montréal, 1951). J. [E.] Hare, *Anthologie de la poésie québécoise du XIXe siècle (1790–1890)* (Montréal, 1979). Lareau, *Hist. de la littérature canadienne*. Gérard Malchelosse, *Michel Bibaud* (Montréal, 1945). Frère Marcilien-Louis, "La pensée didactique de Michel Bibaud, versificateur (influences prépondérantes du XVIIIe siècle)" (thèse de MA, univ. d'Ottawa, 1949). Séraphin Marion, *Les lettres canadiennes d'autrefois* (9v., Hull, Qué., et Ottawa, 1939–58), 3: 167–202. Camille Roy, *Nos origines littéraires* (Québec, 1909). Fernande Roy-Chalifoux, "1837 dans l'historiographie québécoise des années 1840–1850" (thèse de MA, univ. du Québec, Montréal, 1975). L.-W. Sicotte, *Michel Bibaud* (Montréal, 1908). [F.-]M. Bibaud, historien loyaliste," *L'Opinion publique*, 6, 13, 20, 27 déc. 1877; 3 janv. 1878. Bernardine Bujila, "Michel Bibaud's *Encyclopédie canadienne*," *Culture* (Québec), 21 (1960): 117–32. Albert Dandurand, "Littérature canadienne," *L'Enseignement secondaire au Canada* (Québec), 11 (1931–32): 541–47. Guy Frégault, "Michel Bibaud, historien loyaliste," *L'Action universitaire* (Montréal), 11 (1944–45), no.2: 1–7. Jeanne d'Arc Lortie, "Les origines de la poésie au Canada français," *Arch. des lettres canadiennes* (Montréal), 4 (1969): 38–40. É.-Z. Massicotte, "La famille de Michel Bibaud," *BRH*, 45 (1939): 100–2. "Ouvrages publiés par Michel Bibaud," *BRH*, 19 (1913): 350–51. "Les revues de Michel Bibaud," *BRH*, 13 (1907): 156–59. V. L. Schonberger, "Le journalisme littéraire de Michel Bibaud," *Rev. de l'univ. d'Ottawa*, 47 (1977): 488–505. Claude Tousignant, "Michel Bibaud: sa vie, son œuvre et son combat politique," *Recherches sociographiques* (Québec), 15 (1974): 21–30.

BIBB, HENRY WALTON, lecturer, abolitionist, author, and newspaperman; b. 10 May 1815 in Shelby County, Ky, son of James Bibb and Milldred Jackson, a slave; m. first 1833 Malinda ——, and they had two children, one of whom died in infancy; m. secondly June 1848 Mary Elizabeth Miles, a Quaker from Boston; d. 1 Aug. 1854 in Windsor, Upper Canada.

Henry Walton Bibb, born into slavery, worked for at least three masters in Kentucky and Louisiana. He made several bids for freedom. On one of these he spent a few months in Canada in 1838, but when he returned to Kentucky in an attempt to free his first wife and their daughter he was caught and sold to a group of gamblers. He finally made his way alone to Detroit in December 1840. There he joined the anti-slavery movement, travelling across Michigan, Ohio, and the northeastern states lecturing upon the evils of slavery. In 1850, two years after his marriage to Mary Elizabeth Miles, a member of the Anti-Slavery Society in Boston, the passage by the American Congress of the Fugitive Slave Act compelled Bibb and his wife to cross the Detroit River and settle in Sandwich, Upper Canada. Bibb related the full story of his years in slavery and his efforts to escape in an autobiography published that same year in New York.

Bibb began publication of the *Voice of the Fugitive*, the first black newspaper in Upper Canada, at Sandwich on 1 Jan. 1851. A bi-weekly, the *Voice* militantly attacked racial bigotry, advocating the immediate end to chattel slavery everywhere and the complete integration into Canadian society of the black refugee by a devotion to temperance, education, and agriculture. The newspaper opposed annexation to the United States because of the institution of slavery in that country, and was utterly opposed to the introduction of black separate schools, through the Common Schools Act (1850), because Bibb felt that the future of the blacks in Canada depended upon their being part of an integrated community. Unlike its counterpart the *Provincial Freeman*, edited by Samuel Ringgold Ward* and Mary Ann Shadd*, the *Voice* greatly admired Josiah Henson*, the elder statesman and somewhat controversial leader of former slaves in Upper Canada.

Bibb was also a founding director of the Refugee Home Society, a black colonization project established in Detroit in May 1851 to help meet the needs of an estimated 25,000 to 35,000 fugitive slaves living in Canada. The society, supported by donations from American and Canadian anti-slavery groups, purchased land located in scattered blocks at Maidstone, Puce, Belle River, and elsewhere around Windsor from the Canada Company for resale to refugee blacks who had no personal property and lacked the means to buy land privately. Each settler received 25 acres, five of which would be free if the land was cultivated within three years and the remainder of which was to be paid for in nine instalments. Any profits from the land sales were to be used by the society to purchase more land, build schools, and pay teachers. In January 1852 the *Voice of the Fugitive* was made the official organ of the society, to publish its constitution and bylaws and to report regularly on its affairs.

Support for the society, however, was not unani-

Bird

mous among the black community. Within months of its incorporation, Mary Ann Shadd and her supporters attacked the practice of "begging" for funds and clothing from Canadian and American philanthropic associations. The society's opponents also accused the administrators of inept management, the fraudulent use of funds for personal gain, and land jobbing for the benefit of Detroit land speculators. None the less, with the assistance of the American Missionary Association, the society enjoyed a modest success, settling 150 refugees before it was disbanded at the end of the civil war.

Bibb was also closely associated with the antislavery movement in Canada. At Toronto on 11 Sept. 1851 he was elected chairman of the North American Convention of Colored Freemen, a general meeting of delegates from England, Jamaica, the free American states, and Upper Canada. The convention was called to renew the public and constitutional fight against American slavery, to encourage black slaves to resettle in Canada, and to unite all North American blacks into an agricultural union with the power to sway legislation. A year later, on 21 Oct. 1852, Bibb was elected president of the Windsor Anti-Slavery Society, a branch of the parent Toronto society.

From June 1852 Bibb had had an editorial assistant, James Theodore Holly, and this allowed him to resume an active schedule of speaking engagements promoting the work of the Refugee Home Society and soliciting subscriptions to his newspaper. The *Voice of the Fugitive* continued in print until a fire on 9 Oct. 1853 destroyed Bibb's printing office. Thereafter, Bibb published a one-page newsletter until his premature death at Windsor on 1 Aug. 1854.

JOHN K. A. O'FARRELL

[Henry Walton Bibb compiled two brief accounts of slave uprisings under the titles *Slave insurrection in 1831, in Southampton County, Va., headed by Nat Turner; also, a conspiracy of slaves, in Charleston, South Carolina, in 1822* (New York, 1849) and *Slave insurrection in Southampton County, Va., headed by Nat Turner, with an interesting letter from a fugitive slave to his old master: also a collection of songs for the times* (New York, 1850). Bibb's autobiography, *Narrative of the life and adventures of Henry Bibb, an American slave . . .*, published in 1850 in New York with an introduction by Lucius D. Matlack, was included in a collection entitled *Puttin' on ole massa: the slave narratives of Henry Bibb, William Wells Brown, and Solomon Northup*, ed. Gilbert Osofsky (New York, 1969), 51–171. Bibb also published a second anthology of anti-slavery songs in *The anti-slavery harp* (Windsor, [Ont.], 1852), but no surviving copy of this collection is known. A photograph of Bibb in the possession of the Ont. Dept. of Travel and Publicity is reproduced on p.201 of D. G. Hill's study, cited below. J.K.A.O'F.]

Private arch., Alvin McCurdy (Amherstburg, Ont.), Research notes; D. G. Simpson (London, Ont.), Research notes. *Liberator* (Boston), 4 March 1853, 11 Aug. 1854. *Provincial Freeman* (Toronto), 12 Aug. 1854. *Voice of the Fugitive* (Sandwich [Windsor]; Windsor), 1 Jan. 1851–October 1853. D. G. Hill, *The freedom-seekers: blacks in early Canada* (Agincourt [Toronto], 1981). A. L. Murray, "Canada and the Anglo-American anti-slavery movement: a study in international philanthropy" (PHD thesis, Univ. of Pa., Philadelphia, 1960). J. K. A. Farrell [O'Farrell], "The history of the negro community in Chatham, Ontario, 1787–1865" (PHD thesis, Univ. of Ottawa, 1955). W. H. Pease and J. H. Pease, *Black Utopia: negro communal experiments in America* (Madison, Wis., 1963). D. G. Simpson, "Negroes in Ontario from early times to 1870" (PHD thesis, Univ. of Western Ont., London, 1971). J. W. St G. Walker, "'On the other side of Jordan': the record of Canada's black pioneers, 1783–1865" (paper read before the CHA, London, 1978). R. W. Winks, *The blacks in Canada: a history* (Montreal, 1971). Fred Landon, "The negro migration to Canada after the passing of the Fugitive Slave Act" and "Henry Bibb, a colonizer" in *Journal of Negro Hist.* (Washington), 5 (1920): 22–36 and 437–47; "The work of the American Missionary Association among the negro refugees in Canada West, 1848–64," *OH*, 21 (1924): 198–205. Alvin McCurdy, "Henry Walton Bibb," *Negro Hist. Bull.* (Washington), 22 (1958): 19–22.

BIRD, JAMES (sometimes called **James Curtis**), fur trader, justice of the peace, office holder, and politician; b. *c.* 1773 probably in Acton (London); d. 18 Oct. 1856 in the Red River settlement (Man.).

James Bird joined the Hudson's Bay Company as a writer, by the terms of a contract signed in London on 23 April 1788, and left for York Factory (Man.). In 1792, after a four-year apprenticeship, probably served at York Factory, he accompanied William Tomison*, the HBC chief inland, to Cumberland House (Sask.), Manchester House (near Standard Hill, Sask.), and Buckingham House (near Lindbergh, Alta). The following year he was placed in charge at South Branch House (near Batoche, Sask.) to succeed William Walker* and in 1794 he established a post at Nepawi (Nipawin, Sask.) to compete with a nearby North West Company post. From 1795 to 1799 he was in charge at the newly built Carlton House (near Fort-à-la-Corne, Sask.) before being sent to Edmonton House (near Fort Saskatchewan, Alta) in 1799. There he directed the HBC's move farther up the North Saskatchewan River to build Acton House near their NWC rivals at Rocky Mountain House (Alta). He also organized the 1799 expedition led by Peter Fidler* north to the Beaver River and Lac la Biche, where Greenwich House was established. The London committee of the HBC found Bird's efforts to extend HBC trade "most pleasing" and in 1803 he was placed in charge of the inland posts in the Saskatchewan, from Cumberland House to the Rocky Mountains, to succeed Tomison. This was a time of intense competition in the fur trade and in 1810–11, under Bird's direction, Joseph HOWSE led

90

the first HBC expedition into the NWC trading territory west of the Rocky Mountains. Bird was based at Edmonton House until 1816 and spent the season of 1816–17 at Carlton House.

Following the death in June 1816 of the company's governor of Rupert's Land, Robert Semple*, Bird acted in his place until the arrival of the new governor, William Williams*, in 1818. He continued to oversee the trade of the Saskatchewan district until 1821 when, after the union of the HBC and the NWC [see Simon McGillivray*], he was named chief factor in charge of the Lower Red River district. In the summer of that year he accompanied the visiting HBC director, Nicholas GARRY, from Fort William (Thunder Bay, Ont.) to Norway House (Man.). After a furlough in 1822 and then a year's posting as chief factor for the Upper Red River district, Bird retired from the company in June 1824, deciding to stay in the Red River colony. With two other retired HBC officers, Thomas Thomas* and Robert Logan*, Bird occupied an influential position in the social élite of the small settlement. Considered by HBC governor George SIMPSON as a "principal settler," Bird received a company grant of 1,245 acres on the east side of the Red River.

During the HBC campaign against the NWC leading up to the merger, Bird had been appointed a justice of the peace for the Indian territories in 1815. Later, in Red River, he served from 1835 to 1845 as receiver of import and export duties and justice of the peace. A member of Governor Semple's council in 1815 and of the council of the HBC Northern Department from 1822, he was appointed councillor of Assiniboia in 1839 and held this position until shortly before his death in 1856.

As a fur trader James Bird had been a key figure in the HBC's success in the Saskatchewan district and in 1819 Colin Robertson* noted that Bird had "more knowledge of the internal arrangements of this country than all the officers put together." Nevertheless, a high opinion of his own importance and a strong sense of self-interest, together with excessive caution and vindictiveness, marred both his career and his retirement. In 1820, in what was not an isolated incident, the London committee found fault with Bird, noting that "jealous feelings – and fancied slights and injuries" had clouded his better judgement. At Red River, in spite of his social prominence, he was not held in high regard. He was known to have physically chastised an elderly servant, to have harshly dismissed and sued for breach of contract an indiscreet serving maid, and to have demonstrated an absence of charity when called upon to contribute to the relief subscription raised for the retired Reverend David Thomas Jones*, minister at Red River from 1823 to 1838.

Bird had married, according to the custom of the country, more than one Indian woman, possibly polygynously, before marrying an Indian, Elizabeth, at Red River on 30 March 1821. With his Indian wives he had had a large number of children, many of whom, including James*, are mentioned in the parish registers of the Red River colony. Elizabeth died in the fall of 1834 and was buried on 1 November. Like many of his fur-trade colleagues in retirement, Bird sought an English wife and, in what seemed to some indecent haste, he married Mrs Mary Lowman, the widowed governess of the Female Seminary at Red River, on 22 Jan. 1835. Mrs Lowman received a grant of £2,500 in trust from Bird before this marriage, for reasons that remain obscure. At his death Bird left an estate, excepting real property, valued at under £4,000, the bulk of which was left to his daughter and son by his last marriage, Eliza Margaret and Curtis James*. The village of Birds Hill, on or near the Bird property and northeast of Winnipeg, takes its name from James Bird.

JOHN E. FOSTER

PAC, MG 19, A21, ser.1, 5: ff.956–58; 6: f.1294; E1, ser.1, 24: 87 (copies); MG 25, 62. PAM, HBCA, A.6/10: f.23; A.6/16: f.126d; A.6/18: ff.40, 105d; A.6/23: ff.121d–22, 171–71d; A.31/1; A.32/3: f.202; A.36/16: f.43; A.44/3: f.110; B.27/a/1–3; 6; B.49/a/34; B.60/a/5–16; B.148/a/1; B.197/a/1; B.205/a/8; D.4/8: ff.3–17d; D.5/5: ff.306–7; D.5/7: ff.183–84; D.5/12: f.157d; E.6/2: f.139; MG 2, B4-1, 1844–51: ff.66–68; MG 7, B7-1, Reg. of baptisms, 1 Feb. 1838; Reg. of marriages, 30 March 1821, 22 Jan. 1835; Reg. of burials, 1 Nov. 1834, 24 Oct. 1856; MG 9, A78-3: 321–22. *Canadian North-West* (Oliver). [Robert Clouston], "A Red River gossip," ed. E. A. Mitchell, *Beaver*, outfit 291 (spring 1961): 4–11. Nicholas Garry, "Diary of Nicholas Garry, deputy-governor of the Hudson's Bay Company from 1822–1835; a detailed narrative of his travels in the northwest territories of British North America in 1821 . . . ," ed. F. N. Garry, RSC *Trans.*, 2nd ser., 6 (1900), sect.II: 73–204. *HBRS*, 1 (Rich); 2 (Rich and Fleming); 3 (Fleming); 26 (Johnson). *Journals of Samuel Hearne and Philip Turnor*, ed. J. B. Tyrrell (Toronto, 1934; repr. New York, 1968). Mactavish, *Letters of Letitia Hargrave* (MacLeod). David Thompson, *David Thompson's narrative, 1784–1812*, ed. R. [G.] Glover (new ed., Toronto, 1962). Van Kirk, *"Many tender ties."*

BIRDSALL, RICHARD, land surveyor, militia officer, justice of the peace, politician, and office holder; b. 1799 in Thornton-le-dale, England, son of Francis Birdsall; m. first 23 Oct. 1821 Elizabeth Burnham in Cobourg, Upper Canada, and they had four daughters; m. secondly 8 July 1836 Charlotte Jane Everett of Belleville, Upper Canada, and they had two sons and two daughters; d. 21 Jan. 1852 at Graham's Inn (Bailieboro), Upper Canada.

Richard Birdsall was raised in Yorkshire and educated, at his family's wish, for a career as an officer in the Royal Navy. At the end of the

Napoleonic Wars such prospects were dim, however, and possibly in response to this realization Birdsall immigrated to Upper Canada in 1817 with his older brother William. The brothers received land in Edwardsburgh Township, Johnstown District, but settled in Vaughan Township, Home District, instead. Richard taught school in adjacent York Township before qualifying for his licence as a deputy land surveyor in 1819. That summer he was hired to survey Otonabee Township in the interior of the Newcastle District and from that moment his life became intimately linked with the district.

Between 1819 and 1826 Birdsall surveyed a number of townships in the area as well as the future town-site of Peterborough in 1825. In 1823 Frances Stewart [Browne*], who with her husband Thomas Alexander Stewart* had settled in Douro Township the previous year, reported seeing the "very smart young Englishman" pass by her window with "a blanket about his shoulders, a pair of snowshoes in his hands, and a small fur cap," looking "ragged and weatherbeaten" after two months in the woods surveying the township. These surveys had been contracted for by Zacheus BURNHAM, a prominent citizen of Hamilton Township, whose daughter Birdsall married in 1821 and from whom he purchased 920 acres of land in Asphodel Township on the shores of Rice Lake. Birdsall had performed the survey of the latter township himself in 1820 and had named it after the abundant trilliums which reminded him of the asphodels of England. By 1827 he had cleared and cultivated 40 acres and built a substantial frame-house there, still occupied by his descendants. But his wife's accidental death that same year must have represented a severe set-back. His young daughters were looked after elsewhere for several years.

In the 1830s Birdsall completed several major surveys including those of Smith Township, Wilmot Township, and, with William Hawkins, the northern boundary of the Huron Tract. He was also employed as a land agent for the Canada Company and as an inspector for clergy and college reserves responsible for leasing and lumber licensing. A captain in the 2nd Regiment of Northumberland militia from 1822, during the rebellion of 1837–38 he served as a captain in the 4th Regiment and helped raise and equip at his own expense the 7th Provisional Battalion of Peterborough militia in 1838–39. A resourceful leader in the local community, he was first appointed a justice of the peace for the Newcastle District in 1827 and a coroner in 1828. His position as magistrate involved him in litigation such as that resulting from riparian flooding above the dam constructed in 1838 at Crooks' Rapids (Hastings) as part of the Trent Canal. His own property was affected, as was that of John GILCHRIST. In 1842–43 Birdsall represented Asphodel on the Colborne District Council. After the passage of the Municipal Corporations Act of 1849, he became the first reeve of Asphodel and sat on the Peterborough County Council in 1850 and 1851. His attempts to move into politics on the provincial level were unsuccessful. He withdrew his candidacy in 1844 for the sake of party unity, but in the general election of 1847–48 he split the conservative vote with John Langton*, allowing reformer James Hall to win for Peterborough.

By the late 1840s Birdsall had acquired more than 4,000 acres of land in scattered parcels. He developed his Asphodel farm, sold timber, and constructed a wharf on Rice Lake at Birdsall's Landing. Early in 1852, while on a business trip, he contracted pneumonia and died a few days later, an untimely end for a man whose diligence and skill had fostered permanent settlement and progress in Peterborough County.

ALAN G. BRUNGER

AO, MS 211; RG 1, A-I-6: 5721, 5748; RG 21, Newcastle District, Asphodel Township, census and assessment rolls, 1820–46; RG 22, ser.155, will of Richard Birdsall. St Peter's Anglican Church (Cobourg, Ont.), Reg. of baptisms, marriages, and burials, 1817–37. Frances Stewart, *Our forest home, being extracts from the correspondence of the late Frances Stewart*, ed. E. S. Dunlop (2nd ed., Montreal, 1902), 36. *Valley of the Trent* (Guillet). *Correspondent and Advocate* (Toronto), 3 Aug. 1836. *Weekly Despatch* (Peterborough, [Ont.]), December 1847, 10 Feb. 1852. *Land surveys of southern Ontario: an introduction and index to the field notebooks of the Ontario land surveyors, 1784–1859*, comp. [R.] L. Gentilcore and Kate Donkin (Toronto, 1973). J. L. Graham, *Asphodel: a tale of a township* ([Hastings, Ont.], 1978). Helen McGregor, "Richard Birdsall," *Peterborough, land of shining waters: an anthology* ([2nd ed.], Peterborough, 1967), 86–91. T. W. Poole, *A sketch of the early settlement and subsequent progress of the town of Peterborough, and of each township in the county of Peterborough* ((Peterborough, 1867; repub. 1941, 1967).

BLACK, GEORGE, shipbuilder, politician, and justice of the peace; b. *c.* 1778; m. 26 July 1817 Jane Gilley at Quebec, and they had nine children; d. there 19 May 1854.

George Black was a leading shipbuilder in the port of Quebec during the early 19th century. A ship's carpenter in 1817, he seems to have gone into business in 1819, and from then until 1846 he built at least 54 vessels for a total registered tonnage of 23,645. His shipyard was located at Cape Cove (Anse du Cap), below the monument to James Wolfe* on the Plains of Abraham, and specialized in the building of full-rigged vessels and, to a lesser extent, barques. Black's ships were of a high quality and of the larger class of contemporary shipping. Almost all were awarded the highest rating, A1, by *Lloyd's register of shipping*.

Therefore, by virtue of the quality and quantity of his shipbuilding, Black is a notable figure in Canadian economic history. He also engaged in ship-repairing, apparently an active sideline for shipbuilders at Quebec because of the hazards peculiar to the St Lawrence. Unlike his contemporaries, such as John MUNN, for whom five of Black's first six vessels were built, he seldom built on his own account. With the exception of two steamers, a schooner, and a brigantine, the vessels he built were destined for owners in the United Kingdom, and the bulk of them were employed, at least initially, in the British trade to the West Indies, Africa, and Australia.

Black is said to have been a partner of John Saxton CAMPBELL, a Quebec merchant and shipowner, but although there were numerous business transactions between them involving at least 15 vessels, no indication of an actual partnership has been located. The most extensive evidence of association between Black and Campbell is for 1829, the year in which Black launched the most vessels. A barque, a brig, and five ships were completed, for a combined registered tonnage of 2,433, two and a half times greater than that of his nearest competitor. Thereafter, Black's rate of construction slackened, and can be distinguished from the rising pace of the other major builders at Quebec. James and John Jeffery, John James Nesbitt, John* and David Gilmour, John Munn, and especially Thomas Hamilton Oliver, often surpassed and occasionally doubled Black's production of 1829.

Black has been awarded a measure of fame, singular for a Canadian shipbuilder, because of a vessel he built with Campbell in 1831, the paddle-steamer *Royal William*. The vessel was constructed for the Quebec and Halifax Steam Navigation Company which included Black, Samuel Cunard*, and numerous prominent Lower Canadian businessmen among its shareholders. As a steamer, the *Royal William* was untypical of Black's production, but her steam voyage from Pictou, N.S., to Cowes, England, in late summer 1833 was widely and repeatedly claimed decades later by Canadians to have been the first across the Atlantic. This assertion, made, ironically, in the late 19th century, when the eminence of Canada's mercantile marine was fast ebbing with the decline of the sailing ship, has not found acceptance outside Canada.

Active in municipal politics, Black was elected councillor for Saint-Laurent Ward in 1835. When the city reverted to a system of administration by justices of the peace between 1836 and 1840, he served as one of the justices. After a new charter provided for the appointment of a mayor and councillors [see René-Édouard Caron*], Black was appointed city councillor for Champlain Ward for 1840–42. The positions on the city council again became elective in 1842 but

he declined to stand for office although he continued to act as a justice of the peace until at least the late 1840s. A Presbyterian, he was also a member of the local St Andrew's Society.

During a strike by shipwrights in 1840, 800 members of the Société amicale et bienveillante des Charpentiers de Vaisseaux de Québec [see Joseph Laurin*] presented Black with an address thanking him "for your generous and disinterested conduct towards them in opening your shipyard and offering them a reasonable wage for their labour . . . notwithstanding the opposition and censure which you must have experienced from the master shipbuilders of Saint-Roch." In reply, he criticized the unjust conduct of the shipbuilders towards their employees and promised the shipwrights his continued support.

Like many other successful Canadian shipbuilders, Black capped his career with his largest ship, constructing the 1,278-ton *Omega* in 1846. On 1 May of that year he leased the shipyard, together with its "Two Floating Docks, Houses, wharfs, slips, grid Irons, Booms, Beaches and Deep water Lots," to his son George Black Jr for £800 per year and probably retired. An inventory taken three days later revealed that the shipyard contained building materials worth approximately £472, household furniture to the value of £35, as well as tools and other articles valued at £310. The business was carried on by Black Jr until his death three years later. Black Sr then leased the shipyard to another Quebec shipbuilder of note, William Henry Baldwin*.

IN COLLABORATION

ANQ-Q, 30076, George Black et famille (microfiches); CE1-66, 26 juill. 1817, 21 mai 1854; CN1-49, 22 avril, 6 nov. 1846; CN1-67, 27 mars 1851; P1000-11-203. PRO, BT 107/473–74, 476, 478, 480, 482, 484, 488, 490, 493, 495, 497, 499, 501, 503, 506, 508, 510, 514, 518, 522, 524, 527, 531, 535, 539, 542, 545, 549, 552, 555, 558, 561, 565, 568, 571, 574. *Le Canadien*, 21, 28 déc. 1840. *Globe*, 16 May 1876. *Lloyd's List* (London), 10, 13 Sept. 1833. *Morning Chronicle* (Quebec), 20 May 1854, 16 Jan. 1884. *Quebec Gazette*, 28 April 1831. *Lloyd's register of shipping* (London), 1819–50. *Quebec directory*, 1847–48. Chouinard et Drolet, *La ville de Québec*, vol.3. Merrill Denison, *The barley and the stream: the Molson story; a footnote to Canadian history* (Toronto, 1955). Marcel Plouffe, "Quelques particularités sociales et politiques de la charte, du système administratif et du personnel politique de la cité de Québec, 1833–1867" (thèse de MA, univ. Laval, Québec, 1971). Rosa, *La construction des navires à Québec*. F. W. Wallace, *Wooden ships and iron men: the story of the square-rigged merchant marine of British North America, the ships, their builders and owners, and the men who sailed them* (New York, [1924]). Archibald Campbell, "The *Royal William*, the pioneer of ocean steam navigation," Literary and Hist. Soc. of Quebec, *Trans.* (Quebec), new ser., 20 (1891): 29–62.

Blackman

BLACKMAN, CHARLES, Church of England clergyman and school administrator; b. *c.* 1798 in England; m. Julia Williams of Newfoundland, and they had four children, including the Reverend Thomas John Mark Willoughby; d. 16 March 1853 in St John's.

Charles Blackman arrived in Newfoundland in 1819 as tutor to the son of Governor Sir Charles Hamilton*. When he decided to seek ordination he encountered difficulties: Newfoundland, which did not yet have a Church of England bishop, was under the authority of Robert Stanser*, bishop of Nova Scotia, who was in England for reasons of health, and Jacob Mountain*, bishop of Quebec, refused to ordain Blackman in 1821 because he did not have letters dimissory. Nevertheless, Blackman read services in the St John's outharbours during the winter of 1821–22. Early in 1822 he returned to England and was admitted to the ministry on 1 June. He then travelled back to Newfoundland as a missionary of the Society for the Propagation of the Gospel. Although he was assigned the district of Ferryland at that time, he spent the winter at Torbay, north of St John's. In August 1827 he requested a transfer; he had first sought Harbour Grace, but he agreed to go to Port de Grave.

A man of considerable ability and eloquence, Blackman confidently expected promotion and applied for a variety of positions, such as the Harbour Grace mission in 1827, a schoolmaster's post in St John's in 1834, and the archdeaconry in 1840. To help secure these offices, he tried to use the influence of aristocratic relatives in England, such as his niece's husband, Lord Rayleigh, but it was to no avail. In 1839 he was even passed over as successor to Frederick Hamilton Carrington*, the incumbent at St John's, in favour of the Reverend Thomas Finch Hobday BRIDGE, of whom he later said, he "will be helped and the services of others will be kept most studiously in the background."

In 1841, however, Bishop Aubrey George Spencer* did make Blackman principal of the newly formed Theological Institute in St John's which was intended to provide professional training for missionary candidates recruited in England and Newfoundland. On 7 July of the following year he was also appointed perpetual curate to St Thomas' Church, a function he had been fulfilling since 1838, and garrison chaplain. With the translation of Spencer to the Jamaican see in 1843 because of his health, Blackman renewed his campaign for promotion in an attempt to succeed to the bishopric. Once again he failed. The new bishop, Edward Feild*, soon decided Blackman was incompetent and a liar, and declared to Ernest Hawkins*, secretary of the SPG, "he does not enjoy my confidence in any way." Feild complained about the administration of Blackman's church and he thought the theological students were unsuitably trained and undisciplined. He found Bridge more competent and congenial.

Blackman, an evangelical, was antagonized by Feild's tractarian principles and soon became involved in an open conflict with the bishop. He first tried to achieve financial independence of episcopal control by obtaining from the government a land grant as a reward for his duties as garrison chaplain. Then, when Feild dismissed him as principal of the Theological Institute in 1847, in spite of the fact that he had recently obtained a Lambeth MA, Blackman openly began to espouse causes of which the bishop disapproved. He supported the British and Foreign Bible Society, which Feild condemned on the grounds that it was not exclusively a Church of England institution. In addition, when Feild quarrelled with the Newfoundland School Society, an organization of his own church but one which permitted Wesleyans to teach in its schools, Blackman proceeded to become a member. He also opposed Feild's scheme to increase the funds of the Newfoundland Church Society to the level of self-sufficiency, largely because he feared that such an action would make the church less dependent on the merchants, many of whom were evangelical in sympathy, and more dependent on Feild and the church society. What was perhaps Blackman's most obvious revolt occurred in the late 1840s and early 1850s when Feild was leading a campaign to have government funding for Church of England schools separated from the general Protestant grant. Blackman and others lobbied members of the House of Assembly against Feild's plan.

Blackman died in 1853 after a prolonged illness, during which the Reverend Johnstone Vicars had performed his duties. He had always seen himself as an evangelical persecuted by tractarians such as Feild, and his attitude at various times may have stemmed partly from his support of pan-Protestant causes and his distrust of episcopal power. Disappointed ambition was clearly another potent motive and it led him to extremes. Well connected in both England and Newfoundland (his wife's brother-in-law was the merchant Robert John Pinsent*), he had the opportunity to be a leader in the Anglican community. His church, which he served conscientiously, soon became a place of refuge for opponents to Bishop Feild. By helping alienate the conservative merchants from an equally conservative bishop, Blackman facilitated the efforts of those forces which, with the backing of the Roman Catholic clergy, were campaigning for responsible government in Newfoundland.

FREDERICK JONES

PRO, CO 194/117–40. USPG, C/CAN/Nfl., 4–7; D9A; D9B. [Edward Feild], *An address to the congregation of St Thomas's Church by the Bishop of Newfoundland* (St John's,

94

n.d.; copy in USPG, D9A). *Times and General Commercial Gazette* (St John's), 13 July 1850; 26 Feb., 4 March 1851. Frederick Jones, "The early opposition to Bishop Feild of Newfoundland," CCHS, *Journal*, 16 (1974): 30–41; "Religion, education and politics in Newfoundland, 1836–1875," CCHS, *Journal*, 12 (1970): 64–76.

BLAKE, DOMINICK EDWARD, Church of England clergyman; b. 1806 in Kiltegan (Republic of Ireland), eldest child of the Reverend Dominick Edward Blake and Anne Margaret Hume; m. Louisa Jones, and they had two sons; d. 29 June 1859 in Toronto.

Dominick Edward Blake was of the Anglo-Irish gentry for whom education at Trinity College, Dublin, was customary. In 1823, two years after his father died, he entered the college and remained there until he graduated with a BA in the spring of 1829. Ordained deacon by the archbishop of Tuam on 17 Oct. 1830, he served a curacy at Westport, County Mayo, and became a priest on 20 May 1832. But the arduous work at Westport endangered his health and, in any case, the future was uninviting. That was probably why in the summer of 1832 Blake and his wife joined the rest of the family, including his brother William Hume*, and a number of friends from the university in emigrating to Upper Canada. After being licensed by Bishop Charles James Stewart* he was initially appointed to Caradoc Township in Middlesex County. One year after arriving in the province, however, Blake, accompanied by his wife, mother, and two unmarried sisters, was established in nearby Adelaide, a charge that was to have gone to Benjamin Cronyn*. Blake's home church, St Anne's, was built in 1833.

The prospects for an able, young clergyman were much brighter in Upper Canada, but Blake faced a financial problem on his arrival at Adelaide that, as it turned out, remained with him for the rest of his life. In the early 1830s the British government, under mounting pressure in the House of Commons, began to discontinue grants to the colonial church. The result, despite heated protests by the Society for the Propagation of the Gospel, was that unless local government could make up the deficit, clerical salaries were substantially reduced. Blake was one of the clergy affected, accumulating salary arrears of £840 during his 12 years at Adelaide. Although he seems not to have suffered actual poverty, the loss was serious enough to impel him to mount a lengthy campaign to secure payment. At times his determination embarrassed and annoyed Bishop John Strachan*, and it was without result: the arrears were still unpaid when Blake died.

In 1840, to supplement his income, Blake agreed to supply the SPG with a detailed journal of his missionary activities. The society had found that the appearance of such journals in its annual reports served to maintain public interest in the spiritual welfare of Upper Canada's British settlers. Because preparing a journal required additional efforts from the clergyman, the society was prepared to pay for it. Blake kept the record for over a year and its entries reveal him as a zealous and conscientious clergyman whose unsparing exertions sometimes reduced him to exhaustion and illness. He was the township's first Church of England cleric and he found newly settled Anglicans and potential converts scattered over a wide territory. He organized them into four congregations which he visited regularly and, before he left the area, had the satisfaction of seeing each of them erect a church.

By the mid 1840s his efforts began to win recognition. In February 1844 Blake was appointed superintendent of common schools for Adelaide Township. But just as he began his new duties the Reverend George Mortimer* of Trinity Church in Thornhill died and Bishop Strachan offered Blake the opportunity of succeeding him, which he accepted. Thornhill was a settled and thriving community located on Yonge Street north of Toronto. Trinity Church, completed in 1830, was the first of any denomination in the area and in 1840 had had to be enlarged to accommodate the rapidly growing congregation. There he continued to demonstrate that he was, in Strachan's words, "an excellent clergyman." Six years later, therefore, when the bishop appointed rural deans as agents of diocesan centralization, Blake was his choice for the Home District. Holding that position through the 1850s, Blake acted as a liaison between Strachan and the other clergy of the area.

The appointment involved him in the administrative details of the diocese as did his participation in the activities of the Church Society, of which he was an enthusiastic member from its beginning. But it was the inauguration of the diocesan synod in the early 1850s that allowed Blake to move closer to the centre of affairs. From the outset he took part in the discussions of synodical business, and his interest and ability were recognized by appointment to the synod's executive committee when it was organized in 1856. Blake was a member of that body when it drafted a constitution for the diocese and defined for the first time the procedure for episcopal elections. In 1858, again as a member of the executive committee, he produced a controversial paper on clerical discipline, and in the same session of synod it was his amendment that initiated a debate on the diocesan canon concerning parishes. That August he wrote and had printed a statement on the legal position of the Canadian church challenging a report on church canons prepared by a synod committee under James Beaven*.

By the spring of 1859 Blake could look back on more than 25 years of labour for the church in Canada. It was only through the efforts of such men as he that the complex institutions of Europe could be brought

Blanchet

intact across the ocean. Perhaps some sense of satisfaction with the part he had played was in his thoughts on the evening of 29 June as he addressed the annual dinner meeting at Trinity College, Toronto. In his speech he referred to the occasion as one of his happiest experiences in several years. After resuming his seat at the head table, he was suddenly overcome by pain and withdrew from the room. Dr James Bovell* was quickly summoned from his place in the hall but he could do nothing. Blake died within minutes.

H. E. TURNER

Dominick Edward Blake is the author of *A few brief observations upon the report of the committee on canons, &c., &c., addressed to the members of synod* (Thornhill, [Ont.], 1858); a copy is among his papers in AO, MU 138, ser.A-3.

AO, MS 35, letter-books, 1839–43, especially p.63 (John Strachan to D. [E.] Blake, 26 Aug. 1840, enclosing letter from the Upper Canada Clergy Soc.); "to societies," 1839–66; 1844–49; 1854–62; unbound papers, Blake, reports on the Home Rural Deanery, 9 April 1851, 3 June 1858; MU 138, ser.A-3. USPG, C/CAN/folder 370; X7: 489–92, 521–26, 580–93 (mfm. at PAC). *Canadian Ecclesiastical Gazette* (Toronto), 6 (1859): 89. J. D. Sirr, *A memoir of the Honorable and Most Reverend Power Le Poer Trench, last archbishop of Tuam* (Dublin, 1845), 773. *Church*, 3 Jan. 1850. *Daily British Whig*, 15–17 Sept. 1858. *Echo and Protestant Episcopal Recorder* (Toronto), 28 July 1859. *Globe*, 14 Oct. 1853; 3 May 1856; 19 June 1857; 8 June, 1 July 1859; 13 June 1860. Dora Aitken, *A history of St. Ann's Church and Adelaide* (n.p., [1967]). D. M. FitzGerald, *A chronicle of the parish of Trinity Church, Thornhill, 1830–1955*, ed. S. A. R. Wood ([Thornhill?, 1955]). D. M. FitzGerald et al., *Thornhill, 1793–1963: the history of an Ontario village* (Thornhill, 1964).

BLANCHET, JEAN (baptized **Jean-Baptiste**), physician, surgeon, professor, militia officer, and politician; b. 17 May 1795 in Saint-Pierre-de-la-Rivière-du-Sud, Lower Canada, son of Joseph Blanchet, a farmer, and Marie-Euphrosine Cloutier; d. 22 April 1857 at Quebec.

Little is known about Jean Blanchet's childhood and the family setting in which he grew up except that his parents seem to have been quite prosperous farmers. He received his classical education at the Petit Séminaire de Québec from 1810 to 1813. At the age of 17 he began to study medicine with his uncle, the celebrated Dr François Blanchet* of Quebec. Five years later, in 1818, he decided to go to Europe to finish his medical training. After several months in London he went to Paris to take the courses given by the famous surgeon and pathologist Guillaume Dupuytren at the Hôtel-Dieu and by Dominique-Jean Larrey at the Hôpital du Gros-Caillou. Returning to London he went to teaching sessions given by Astley Paston Cooper and Sir William Blizard. In 1820 he passed the examination set by the Royal College of Surgeons of London and obtained his certificate of fellowship as a qualified surgeon.

On his return to Quebec, Blanchet went into practice with his uncle and former mentor, François Blanchet. Their partnership lasted until 1823 when Jean Blanchet began to teach anatomy at the recently founded Emigrant Hospital (which merged with the Marine Hospital in 1834 to become the Marine and Emigrant Hospital). When François died in 1830 Jean inherited his practice and took up residence in his house on Rue du Palais, and it was not long before he became as famous as his uncle. Because of the sound surgical training he had received in Europe, he was also soon regarded as one of the most skilful obstetricians in the city. He had many patients and they came from all walks of life, according to François-Xavier Garneau*, who was one of them. His devotion to the underprivileged even earned him the nickname the "poor man's doctor."

Nor was it long before Blanchet acquired recognition among the members of his profession. For more than 15 years, between 1831 and 1848, he sat on the Medical Board of Examiners for the district of Quebec. He was an active member of the Quebec Medical Society, of which his uncle had been a founder, was its vice-president several times during the 1830s and 1840s, and also gave lectures before it. He was surgeon to Quebec's 2nd Militia Battalion in 1845, and that year, as a zealous advocate of medical education in the province, he helped found the Quebec School of Medicine. Blanchet taught clinical surgery there from the time it opened in 1847 until it became affiliated with the Université Laval in 1852. He also gave clinical instruction at the Marine and Emigrant Hospital as a permanent visiting doctor, a post to which he was appointed on 27 Dec. 1847 and which he gave up in 1854 in order to run for election to the legislature.

In addition, that year, as a result of plans to open a faculty of medicine at the Université Laval, Blanchet accepted an offer made to him by the council of the Petit Séminaire de Québec to become dean of the new faculty and to give courses in general pathology and physiology. The faculty was officially inaugurated in September 1854 and on that occasion he received from the university the honorary degree of doctor of medicine.

Blanchet was above all a doctor, but he also played a subsidiary role on the political stage. He had represented Quebec County from 22 Nov. 1834 to 27 March 1838, and during this difficult period he backed the majority in the assembly. In 1854 he was elected to represent Quebec City, and he supported the government of Augustin-Norbert Morin* and Sir Allan Napier MacNab* during the fifth parliament of the

Province of Canada. However, a serious illness soon forced him to abandon his political duties almost entirely. On 16 March 1857 he finally handed in his resignation for reasons of health; five weeks later, on 22 April, he died.

Jean Blanchet never married. On his death he left his practice and part of his fortune to his nephew and former pupil, Hilarion Blanchet, with whom he had been in partnership since 1852.

Jacques Bernier

ANQ-Q, CE1-22, 25 avril 1857; CE2-6, 17 mai 1795. ASQ, Polygraphie, XXXVI: li. F.-X. Garneau, *Voyage en Angleterre et en France dans les années 1831, 1832 et 1833*, Paul Wyczynski, édit. (Ottawa, 1968). *Le Canadien*, 23 oct. 1823. *Le Journal de Québec*, 28 sept. 1854. Morgan, *Sketches of celebrated Canadians*. *Quebec directory*, 1852. Cornell, *Alignment of political groups*. C.-M. Boissonnault, "Histoire de la faculté de médecine de Laval," *Laval médical* (Québec), 17 (1952): 1108–19. "Le Docteur Jean Blanchet, premier doyen, 1795–1857 – 1853–1856," *Laval médical*, 9 (1944): 460–62. J.-C. Taché, "Le Dr Jean Blanchet," *Journal de l'Instruction publique* (Québec et Montréal), 1 (1857): 113–14.

BLINKHORN, THOMAS, pioneer settler, farmer, justice of the peace, and office holder; b. 3 May 1806 in Sawtry, England, eldest son of Thomas and Ann Blinkhorn; m. 9 Aug. 1827 Ann Beeton of Great Gidding, England, and they had one son and two daughters; d. 13 Oct. 1856 in Metchosin (B.C.).

Thomas Blinkhorn was one of the small number of early settlers on Vancouver Island independent of the Hudson's Bay Company, which in 1849 had been granted a lease of the crown colony in return for its colonization. Possessed of "a mind of wide range, and well tried by experience," Blinkhorn had been "up and down the world somewhat," and from 1837 to 1849, it would appear, he had been stock-raising in Australia. He reached Vancouver Island from England on 9 May 1851, having formed a partnership aboard the *Tory* with a fellow passenger, James Cooper*, a former captain in the HBC maritime service now returning to Fort Victoria (Victoria) as a free merchant and landowner.

Cooper took up over 300 acres of land at Metchosin, 9 miles from the fort by sea, 15 miles by Indian trail through the forest, and the partners were soon engaged in various enterprises. Cooper himself traded between Vancouver Island, San Francisco, and Hawaii, leaving the management of his Metchosin farm in Blinkhorn's capable hands. Son and grandson of a miller, he had been a farmer in his native Sawtry and he had married a farmer's daughter. In the five years before his untimely death in 1856 he cleared and brought under cultivation some 60 acres and established a dairy herd. Unfortunately the HBC chief factor in charge at Fort Victoria, James Douglas*, considered some of Cooper's trading activities an infringement of the company monopoly. Consequently the partners joined with the other 13 independent settlers in an unsuccessful petition against the appointment of Douglas to succeed Richard Blanshard* as governor of Vancouver Island.

In March 1853 Blinkhorn, along with the three HBC farm superintendents, received a commission as "magistrate and justice of the peace," Governor Douglas considering him "the only independent settler with a sufficient degree of education" to qualify for the office. By December, Douglas had found his appointees so ignorant of the law that he had been obliged to restrict them to "their proper duties of Conservators of the Peace" by establishing a Supreme Court of Civil Justice, under his brother-in-law, David Cameron*. In February 1854 Blinkhorn and his fellow justices were among the 70 settlers who petitioned the queen, without success, against Cameron's appointment as chief justice.

"The most energetic settler on the island," Blinkhorn now added to his responsibilities at Metchosin the management of William Fraser Tolmie*'s farm at Cloverdale, 15 miles away, and proceeded to carry out his various commitments in a most conscientious manner. The road from Fort Victoria had still not reached Metchosin and so his visits to Cloverdale and his monthly attendance at the Court of Petty Sessions involved him in strenuous travel in all weathers. On one occasion he "got to the river walking across the ice and fell in, had to come back and change his things Tryed to get a canoe could not get one the Indians would not go it was Snowing very fast and very thick." Frequently he caught cold, "sitting in the canoe on the water going to the Fort." Soon his lungs were seriously affected and on 13 Oct. 1856 he died. He was buried in the graveyard adjoining the Victoria District Church, now Christ Church Cathedral, and on 4 November an auction sale, at which "the stock sold remarkably well," was held at the Metchosin farm.

Blinkhorn Island (Peninsula) in Johnstone Strait (named by Captain George Henry Richards* in 1861), Blinkhorn Lake and Mount Blinkhorn, both in Metchosin, perpetuate the name of this widely experienced and successful farmer, loved and respected by family and friends, and, within the limits of his scanty legal knowledge, the faithful holder of a minor office in the judicial system of Vancouver Island.

Dorothy Blakey Smith

PABC, A/C/20, Vi 2; C/AA/10.1/2; C/AA/10.4/1; E/B/B62.3. PRO, CO 305/5 (mfm. at PABC). M. C. Ella, "The diary of Martha Cheney Ella, 1853–1856," ed. J. K. Nesbitt, *BCHQ*, 13 (1949): 91–112, 257–70. G.B., Parl.,

Bobbeie

House of Commons paper, 1857 (session II), 15, nos.224, 260, *Report from the select committee on the Hudson's Bay Company*; 1863, 38, no.507: 523–38, *Correspondence with the governor of Vancouver's Island, relative to the appointment of Chief Justice Cameron. . . . HBRS*, 32 (Bowsfield). Walbran, *B.C. coast names*. H. H. Bancroft, *History of British Columbia, 1792–1887* (San Francisco, 1887). W. K. Lamb, "Early lumbering on Vancouver Island, pt.I: 1844–1855," *BCHQ*, 2 (1938): 31–53. S. F. Tolmie, "My father: William Fraser Tolmie, 1812–1886," *BCHQ*, 1 (1937): 227–40.

BOBBEIE, PETER. *See* BABEY, PETER PAUL TONEY

BOND, GEORGE, politician, millowner, and Baptist minister; b. *c.* 1790 in England; d. 8 Jan. 1852 in Saint John, N.B.

Born and raised in England, George Bond was brought to Saint John in 1819 as superintendent of the Carleton Tidal Power Mills, located on the Saint John harbour and owned by William Black*. Bond was to occupy this position for 18 years. Following Black's retirement in 1837, Bond obtained control of the milling complex and operated it until his death. It was one of the oldest and largest of its kind in southern New Brunswick, containing up-and-down saws, lathes, a shingle-mill, and grist-mills. During the 1840s Bond would have been one of the chief beneficiaries of the growing market in deals and sawn lumber. None the less he remained a man of modest means. Like most men of his class he was never able to participate in the export function of the city and never made the transition from manufacturer to merchant; apparently he did not own any vessels or engage in transatlantic trade. His operation entailed buying timber, milling it, and then selling it either on the domestic market or to timber merchants for export. By the 1850s, however, these merchants had begun to construct their own mills in the Saint John area, thereby offering stiff competition to Bond and other millowners in his position.

Bond, like Thomas HARDING and John McNeil Wilmot*, was one of a small but influential group of religious evangelicals who played a dominant role in the civic life of urban centres in New Brunswick in the mid 19th century. Bond was first elected to the Common Council of Saint John as alderman for Guys Ward in 1825 and was to survive 21 annual elections. He was prominent in the affairs of the council, particularly during the critical decade of the 1840s when the city went bankrupt. This period is marked by struggles between the various sections of the city for preferential treatment from the council. Bond's voting record reveals a cautious businessman primarily concerned with procuring benefits for the inhabitants of the Carleton side of the harbour and with protecting the concerns of the city's business community. Thus in 1843 he favoured efforts to tax the citizens of the Portland side of the harbour to support the Saint John Water Company, promoted by such powerful figures as Ward CHIPMAN, and also agreed to allow the prominent merchant John Robertson* to acquire control of considerable city leasehold at reduced rentals. Despite these biases, Bond's council career marks him as a mild reformer in most civic issues. As a sitting member for the west side, he was able to bring an objectivity to the many matters concerning the city proper. Similarly, his British background left him with little sense of deference to such colonial sacred cows as the city's charter, which was revered by many as the creation of the loyalist founders of New Brunswick. He persistently advocated reform of the administrative structure of Saint John, particularly in regard to the hiring of a permanent civil service, and supported efforts to revise the charter in the interests of public safety and order.

As well as sawmills and politics, religious concerns dominated Bond's life. He was prominent during the formative years of the British and Foreign Bible Society and the Saint John and Carleton temperance societies. But he was best known as a leading Baptist layman, local preacher, and, after 1840, minister. He owned the land on which the Carleton Baptist Meeting House was built, he provided most of the necessary financing for its construction, and he conducted services there during the last years of his life. As he had retained the title to the property, he was able to will both land and building to his stepdaughter.

Although he achieved neither the wealth of a merchant nor the status of a member of the House of Assembly, Bond was one of the comfortable burghers who was able to direct much of the public life of the city. Within his ward he exercised almost unchallenged political and economic authority.

T. W. ACHESON

City Clerk's Office (Saint John, N.B.), Common Council of Saint John, minutes, 14 Oct. 1839; 8, 9 Feb., 3 Oct. 1843; 19 May 1847. PANB, RG 7, RS71, 1852, George Bond. *New-Brunswick Courier*, 10 Jan. 1852.

BOOKER, ALFRED, Baptist minister; b. 14 March 1800 in Nottingham, England; m. first 1824 Sophia Varnham, and they had eight children; m. secondly 1846 Mrs Ann Gardner in Hamilton, Upper Canada; d. 12 March 1857 near Hamilton.

In his youth, Alfred Booker imbibed infidel opinions. Although he had little formal academic training, he was able to educate himself by reading widely, and in the process learned the French language. One evening, at the age of 17, he went to a chapel of ease in Nottingham to meet a friend attending a service. Booker heard a sermon there that led to his conversion and, later, his baptism in the city's General Baptist Chapel. Unable to keep his new-found faith to himself, he spoke of it with such enthusiasm that others, recognizing his ability in this direction, encouraged him to preach. In 1830 he was ordained and installed as the pastor of Park Street Baptist Church, and he also ministered to the Bethesda Meeting House.

Booker was among the many English Baptists of the time who were moved by Eustace Carey's accounts of Baptist missionary labours in India to respond to the needs of missions in general. Because Booker knew French he felt Providence calling him to America to preach to the French Canadians, and in 1842 he set out with his family for Montreal. No record of his work there has been found. That winter he wrote to "The Baptists of Hamilton, Canada West," appointing himself their pastor and inviting them to hold prayer meetings until his arrival. He was not the first to organize a Baptist church in that community. An earlier effort had lasted from 1834 to 1836, and was followed about three years later by the establishment of a black Baptist congregation, one with which Washington Christian* was later involved. When Booker's letter was received in Hamilton the postmaster decided that it was not intended for the black congregation and gave it to a boot merchant, Philo Warner Dayfoot, who followed Booker's instructions. Within a few weeks of his arrival on 1 May 1843, Booker had established a congregation that met first in the police station and then in Patrick Thornton's schoolhouse before building a meeting-house in 1846. Initially called First Baptist, the church was later named Park Street after its location. The congregation grew from 10 in 1843 to 59 in 1846.

Despite the church's growth and the financial assistance of Baptists from the nearby towns of Beamsville and Dundas, there was little money to pay the pastor. Booker, whose wife had died in 1845, helped support himself by selling Nottingham lace throughout the countryside while soliciting contributions to the Hamilton church. At his followers' request in 1847 he gave up the business, and they applied to the American Baptist Home Mission Society for £50 to assist in his support; there is no record that the grant was ever made. The congregation none the less continued its aid to bible and missionary societies, including the Grande-Ligne mission in Lower Canada [see Henriette Odin*], and local benevolences. Sir Allan Napier MacNab* later made a generous gift to the church that eased Booker's financial problems.

Booker was a leader in organizing the Baptists in Canada. In 1844 he took part in the first annual meeting of the Canada Baptist Union, and in 1848 became a vice-president of a convention that sought the union of Regular (closed communion) Baptist churches in Canada. Unfortunately, it was around this time that controversy disrupted the congregation he had founded. In 1847 he had participated in the considerable discussion that took place about the method of hymn singing and the new tunes being used. This sort of dissension grew, and in 1849 a new deacon, Thomas Haines, sought Booker's removal from office. When the attempt failed, Haines led a small exodus in June 1850 to form the John Street Baptist Church. Because the new church was also active in the Regular Baptist cause, Park Street cut back on its denominational commitments. Though personality rather than theology seems to have caused the split, one Park Street member was excluded for heresy.

Despite the controversy, the Park Street Baptist Church was able to expand its activities. In 1857 it undertook missionary work and Booker began to preach in Wellington Square (Burlington) once a week. On 12 March he was returning to Hamilton by train when he was killed in the accident at the Desjardins Canal bridge [see Samuel ZIMMERMAN]. A collection taken during an interdenominational service held at Knox Presbyterian Church in Hamilton paid for his grave-marker. The pastor of the John Street church died in the same year as Booker, and the two congregations united that July.

A good-looking, learned man, with strong opinions, Booker had the support of most of his congregation and won the respect of his fellow ministers. Of his children, one son, Theophorus, joined the ministry, and another, Alfred*, had a distinguished career in business and in the militia.

RICHARD E. RUGGLE

A portrait of Alfred Booker is reproduced in F. K. Anderson's history of the James Street church, cited below.

Canadian Baptist Arch., McMaster Divinity College (Hamilton, Ont.), James Street Baptist Church (Hamilton), records, Park Street Baptist Church minutes, 1843–78. PRO, RG 4/1718, 1831–37 (photocopies at Canadian Baptist Arch., McMaster Divinity College). T. L. Davidson, *A funeral sermon, preached in the Park Street Baptist Chapel, Hamilton, March 22nd, 1857 . . . occasioned by the death of the late Rev. Alfred Booker . . .* (Hamilton, 1857). *Minutes of the convention of associational delegates convened at St. George's, 6th & 7th September, 1848, to effect a union of the Regular Baptists of Canada; and of a convention of delegates of churches held at the same place, September 7* (London, [Ont., 1848]). *Register* (Montreal), 18 Jan., 18 April, 16 May 1844. *Weekly Spectator*, 11 July 1850, 19 March 1857. *The Canadian Baptist register* (Toronto), 1857, 20–21. *DHB*. F. K. Anderson *et al.*, *A history of James St. Baptist Church: 125th anniversary edition, 1844–1969* (Hamilton, 1969).

BOUCHER DE BOUCHERVILLE, THOMAS-RENÉ-VERCHÈRES (baptized **René-Thomas**, he added **Verchères** to his name later in life), fur trader,

Boucher

merchant, militia officer, justice of the peace, seigneur, and author; b. 21 Dec. 1784 in Boucherville (Que.), son of René-Amable Boucher* de Boucherville and Madeleine Raimbault de Saint-Blaint; d. there 13 Dec. 1857.

Thomas-René-Verchères, the tenth of 11 children, was a descendant of Pierre Boucher* and was born into one of the province's leading families. His father was seigneur of Boucherville and his mother was an heiress to the seigneury of Verchères. In 1792 he entered the Sulpician Collège Saint-Raphaël in Montreal and six years later began his *cours classique*. Although a prize-winning student, he left the college in 1799 before completing his studies. The next few years were spent in Boucherville where, as he later admitted himself, he was involved in various "foolish pranks." In 1803 his father obtained a post for him as clerk in the New North West Company (sometimes called the XY Company) under Sir Alexander Mackenzie*. In the spring of 1803, on a seven-year contract as a clerk, he left Lachine in a canoe bound via Lake Nipissing (Ont.) for Grand Portage (near Grand Portage, Minn.). From there he continued to Fort Dauphin, on Lake Dauphin (Man.), where he wintered in 1803–4 under Thomas McMurray. A youth on his first long journey away from his family, he was at first desperately homesick, but the lively journal he later wrote shows that he soon began to enjoy his new life. The rigours of winter travel involved in the collection of furs from the neighbouring Indians, however, brought on high fever and inflammation of his legs. In May, suffering from continued aching of the legs, which he possibly exaggerated because of a desire to return home and his dislike of his occupation, he left the service of the New North West Company and returned to Lower Canada.

In October 1804 he was employed by the French royalist *emigré* Laurent Quetton* de Saint-Georges, a close business connection of Boucher de Boucherville's brother-in-law Louis-René Chaussegros* de Léry, and went with him to York (Toronto) to serve as clerk. The business dealt in general merchandise at York and Niagara (Niagara-on-the-Lake), and also conducted a trade in furs with local Indians. Boucher de Boucherville often made the short visits to the Mississauga villages that this trade necessitated. Quickly gaining Quetton de Saint-Georges's confidence, he was sent to Amherstburg in 1806 with £2,500 worth of merchandise to open a branch. The new store prospered and two years later Quetton de Saint-Georges sold it to him. A warm friendship had developed between the two men and when in 1811 American customs officials impounded $58,000 of goods belonging to Quetton de Saint-Georges at Lewiston, N.Y., under the terms of the Non-Intercourse Act, Boucher de Boucherville undertook to return his former employer's kindness. According

to his own account, he hurried to Niagara and with the connivance of the garrison at Fort George he successfully led an armed nocturnal raid on the Lewiston custom-house and absconded with the shipment, saving his friend from bankruptcy.

When the War of 1812 erupted, Boucher de Boucherville served as a volunteer on the Detroit frontier and saw action under Major-General Isaac Brock*. For his service at the capture of Detroit he was awarded a medal and clasp. Meanwhile, his business had been badly disrupted by his absence and the hostilities. After a visit to Boucherville in early 1813, he rashly made his way back to Amherstburg carrying £1,348 worth of general merchandise in four canoes. The only merchant to have brought in new stock, he succeeded in selling most of what he had in a very short time and at high prices; during the first three days alone he recorded sales of £4,800. However, the defeat of Commander Robert Heriot Barclay* by an American naval force on Lake Erie in September 1813 forced the abandonment of Amherstburg. Boucher de Boucherville later claimed for losses of £1,271 on his stock, of which £500 was recognized. Fleeing with his money, he was near the site of the battle of Moraviantown when the British under Major-General Henry Procter* were defeated and he hastened on to Montreal. There, as he notes in his journal, he gave a report on the battle to the commander-in-chief of the British forces, Sir George Prevost*. After a short rest at the family home in Boucherville, he joined his regular militia unit, the Boucherville battalion of militia, then at Châteauguay, serving as adjutant with the rank of captain. He was not, however, involved in the battle of Châteauguay and returned to Boucherville for the winter of 1814–15.

After the war, Boucher de Boucherville tried briefly to re-establish his business in Amherstburg, but soon arranged to liquidate his stock. He then unsuccessfully imported merchandise on joint account with Quetton de Saint-Georges and attempted to set up a business in Boucherville and once again tried Amherstburg. He returned to Boucherville in September 1816 and retired from business.

Boucher de Boucherville's later career presents a complete contrast to his restless youth. He settled at Boucherville, becoming a justice of the peace and a major in the militia. On 17 May 1819 he married Joséphine Proulx, daughter of Louis-Basile Proulx, a Montreal bourgeois, and they had five children. By 1829, through inheritance from both sides of the family, he was co-seigneur of Boucherville and Verchères. It was in 1847 that he wrote his journal, a lively account of his fur-trade adventures and wartime experiences intended for his children, which was eventually published in 1901.

FREDERICK H. ARMSTRONG

Thomas-René-Verchères Boucher de Boucherville is the author of "Journal de M. Thomas Verchères de Boucherville . . . ," *Canadian Antiquarian and Numismatic Journal* (Montreal), 3rd ser., 3 (1901): 1–167. The journal was translated by W. S. Wallace* and published under the title *A merchant's clerk in Upper Canada; the journal of Thomas Verchères de Boucherville, 1804–1811* (Toronto, 1935); a second English translation, "Journal of Thomas Verchères de Boucherville," was printed in *War on the Detroit; the chronicles of Thomas Verchères de Boucherville and the capitulation, by an Ohio volunteer*, ed. M. M. Quaife (Chicago, 1940), 3–178.

ANQ-M, CE1-22, 22 déc. 1784, 16 déc. 1857. ASTR, 0032, Louis Dugas, "Généalogie Boucher," 70–77. PAC, RG 19, 3754, 4356–57. F.-M. Bibaud, *Le panthéon canadien* (A. et V. Bibaud; 1891). *Officers of British forces in Canada* (Irving), 189–91. P.-G. Roy, *Inv. concessions*, 2: 283, 300; 3: 33–34. Maurault, *Le collège de Montréal* (Dansereau; 1967). "Les disparus," *BRH*, 34 (1928): 622. J.-J. Lefebvre, "Jean-Moïse Raymond (1787–1843), premier député de Laprairie (1824–1838), natif du comté," *BRH*, 60 (1954): 111–12.

BOXER, EDWARD, naval officer, office holder, and politician; b. 27 Feb. 1784 in Dover, England, son of James and Kitty Boxer; d. 4 June 1855 on board the *Jason* near Balaklava (U.S.S.R.).

Edward Boxer, one of three brothers who served in the British navy, began his career in 1798 and, after long, eventful service in the English Channel, West Indies, and Mediterranean, won promotion to lieutenant on 8 Jan. 1807 and commander on 1 March 1815. On half pay until he received command of the sloop *Sparrowhawk* on the Halifax station in September 1822, he became post captain on 23 June 1823, and went to England as inspecting commander of the coastguard in July 1824. From 1827 to 1830, while commanding the fifth-rate *Hussar*, he served as flag-captain to the commander-in-chief of the American and West Indies squadron, Sir Charles Ogle. In 1827 Boxer began a survey of the capes, coves, and shoals in the Gulf of St Lawrence which he later presented to Ogle. At the same time the government of Lower Canada was considering the establishment of a series of navigational aids to provide greater safety for maritime traffic in the area. Consulted by Canadian authorities about possible sites, Boxer was able to make a significant contribution. He suggested the construction of lighthouses at several dangerous points, including places on the coasts of Newfoundland, Prince Edward Island, Anticosti Island, St Paul Island, N.S., and on the banks of the Miramichi River, N.B. The majority of his recommendations were accepted, but construction of lighthouses and lightships, the beginnings of a network of such aids, proceeded slowly from the 1830s to the 1860s.

Commander of the *Pique* from 1837 to 1841, Boxer was again active in Lower Canada when in 1838 he brought troops to reinforce the Quebec garrison. In 1840 he played an important part in the bombardment of St Jean d'Acre (Akko, Israel), for which he won a Turkish gold medal and was made a CB, before returning to the West Indies.

On 26 Oct. 1841 Boxer was named harbour-master of Quebec and captain of that port by the governor general, Lord Sydenham [Thomson*], partly because Sydenham wanted professional naval advice and partly because Boxer would be "ready at a moment's notice to take command of the Lakes" should it become necessary. His duties involved the enforcement of harbour regulations, including those relating to pilots, wharfage, and tonnage. Boxer's previous naval experience, more extensive than that of his predecessors, John Lambly, François Boucher*, and James Frost*, served him well in his new post. Although his work was seasonal, from the opening of navigation on the river in May to the close in December, he was none the less responsible for a busy port which, during his tenure, registered the arrivals and departures of upwards of 1,000 vessels a year. He submitted an elaborate plan for the improvement of the harbour to the provincial secretary, James Leslie*, in November 1848 and shortly afterwards presented a more detailed plan to the city council for docks and piers at the mouth of the Rivière Saint-Charles and along the St Lawrence. The project was again put forth, unsuccessfully, by Quebec mayor Ulric-Joseph Tessier* in 1853.

In 1845 Lieutenant-General Richard Downes Jackson* appointed Boxer to a commission with Lieutenant-Colonel William Cuthbert Elphinstone Holloway to investigate Canada's defences against the United States. Boxer, assisted by Lieutenant Hampden Clement Blamire Moody of the Royal Engineers, examined the lines of communication leading to the west, and then set off with another assistant, David Taylor, former master attendant at the naval dockyard at Kingston, Upper Canada, to visit American ports on the Great Lakes. Boxer's reports, developing the idea that "the defences of a country should keep pace with its prosperity," emphasized the importance of improving canals and railways. He argued in favour of a revived naval establishment on the Great Lakes. In 1864, after Anglo-American relations had again deteriorated, Captain Richard Collinson*, RN, submitted his report on Canada's defences and, by basing his own examination almost entirely on Boxer's conclusions, confirmed their validity.

In the course of his travels Boxer made particularly caustic remarks about the Welland and Beauharnois canals and the channel through Lac Saint-Pierre, accusing the provincial Board of Works of being costly and inefficient. He urged the appointment of an engineer from England "free from the trammels of local associations and interests." Much to Boxer's professed surprise Hamilton Hartley Killaly*, chair-

Boyle

man of the Board of Works, resented these aspersions on his department and the engineering projects with which he had been associated and complained to the Colonial Office. Boxer's subsequent disclaimer of ill-feeling towards the board minimized the controversy. By 1853 his attention had turned to the defence of trade in the event of war between Great Britain and other powers.

Boxer is remembered for his efforts, together with those of Lieutenant-General Jackson, Astronomer Royal George Biddell Airy, and the Quebec Board of Trade, to establish an observatory in the city during the late 1840s. His interest in transportation, communication, and defence may also have led him to become a director from 1847 to 1849 of the British North American Electric Telegraph Association, founded in 1847 to provide a telegraphic link between Quebec and Halifax, and prompted him to serve on the local committee of the Halifax and Quebec Railway early in 1849. On 6 Feb. 1849 he was elected to represent Saint-Louis ward on the Quebec City Council, where he sat until 1851. He was also a member of the board of health from 1848 to 1851, a particularly active post because of the frequent outbreaks of cholera.

Promoted rear-admiral on 5 March 1853, Boxer left Quebec on 14 July. During the Crimean War he became admiral superintendent at Balaklava and tackled the disastrous confusion of the harbour with his customary energy but at the cost of his life. He died of cholera on board the *Jason* outside the harbour on 4 June 1855.

A thoroughgoing professional, Boxer left few traces of his private life. According to the *Gentleman's Magazine* of 1855, his wife Elizabeth had died on 25 June 1826, but the place of burial cannot be determined. His will named Elizabeth Boxer, probably a second wife, as the legatee. He had a large family; one of his daughters had married the Quebec businessman Charles E. Levey.

W. A. B. DOUGLAS

[The author wishes to express his appreciation to Roch Lauzier of Quebec for his assistance in the preparation of this biography. W.A.B.D.]

Arch. of Christ Church Cathedral (Canterbury, Eng.), Reg. of baptisms, marriages, and burials for the parish of St Mary, Dover. PAC, RG 8, I (C ser.), 31, 60, 76, 175, 222, 308, 827, 860, 938, 1008. Ports Canada Arch. (Quebec), Trinity House, Quebec, minute-books, IV: 204–8; VII. PRO, ADM 1/1586 (copies at PAC); ADM 7/624 (copies at PAC); ADM 107/31; PROB 11/2215: f.587; WO 1/552–59 (copies at PAC). Can., Prov. of, Legislative Assembly, *App. to the journals*, 1849, app.MMM. *Gentleman's Magazine*, July–December 1855: 95–96. *Quebec Gazette*, 3 Nov. 1841; 3, 7 Feb. 1849. *DNB*. G.B., Admiralty, *The commissioned sea officers of the Royal Navy, 1660–1815*, [ed. D. B. Smith et al.] (3v., n.p., [1954]). Morgan, *Sketches of celebrated Canadians*, 483–85. O'Byrne, *Naval biog. dict.* (1849), 109–10. *Quebec directory*, 1847–49. Chouinard et Drolet, *La ville de Québec*, vol.3. J. M. Hitsman, *Safeguarding Canada, 1763–1871* (Toronto, 1968). J. M. LeMoine, *The port of Quebec: its annals, 1535–1900* (Quebec, 1901), 78–79. E. F. Bush, "The Canadian lighthouse," *Canadian Hist. Sites: Occasional Papers in Archæology and Hist.* (Ottawa), no.9 (1974): 5–107. "L'observatoire de Québec," *BRH*, 42 (1936): 16–18. "Un conseiller de ville de Québec amiral britannique," *BRH*, 38 (1932): 641–42.

BOYLE, ALEXANDER, physician, surgeon, and army officer; b. 1771 in Aberdeen, Scotland; m. 11 Feb. 1818 Cornelia Jane Boyd of Saint John, N.B.; d. 14 April 1854 in Saint John.

Little is known of Alexander Boyle's early life. He received his MD from Marischal College (University of Aberdeen) and then as a young man entered the British army. Stationed in Saint John from 1817 to 1822, he became a personal friend of Lieutenant Governor George Stracey Smyth*. In 1818, with Smyth's support, he established the Provincial Vaccine Establishment in Saint John, which was supervised by his father-in-law, Dr John Boyd Sr. At that time concern was being expressed throughout the province over the care of sick and disabled seamen. When many sick immigrants arrived in 1818 and 1819 the overseers of the poor complained that many seamen and immigrants were being cared for in almshouses, at the expense of the parishes, whereas they should be treated in hospitals. As a result, in March 1820, the House of Assembly passed an act to provide for the care of seamen: a duty of one penny per ton was to be imposed on all vessels over 60 tons entering the province's ports and the money was to go to the overseers of the poor in the parish where it was collected. The following March the act was amended to allow excess funds collected in one port to be transferred to the overseers in another parish where they might be required. However, the problem was not solved, and Boyle and others urged the establishment of a marine hospital.

In April 1822 Boyle announced in the newspapers that he intended to retire from the army and set up a practice in Saint John. This statement came one month after the House of Assembly passed an act providing for the creation in Saint John of the province's first marine hospital as well as a pest-house. Duties collected under the earlier acts would be transferred to a board of commissioners, which was to have five or more members appointed by the lieutenant governor. The first board consisted of William Black*, president, Thomas Heaviside, secretary treasurer, Edward James JARVIS, Zalmon Wheeler, and Boyle. The commissioners were empowered to hire a building for use until proper facilities could be erected and Boyle took up the search. In June he rented one for

£70 per annum. Boyle also drew up the first regulations for the hospital, which was called the Kent Marine Hospital. A number of seamen were transferred immediately to this building; immigrants too were to use the hospital for several years.

The question of a medical officer was also discussed in June 1822. At a meeting which Boyle did not attend, it was decided that he should be offered the position at a salary of £180 per year, and he subsequently accepted it. No one at the time considered it irregular that the board should appoint one of its own members to the position. In 1823 Boyle went to Fredericton to attend Smyth in his last illness and he was named an executor of the governor's will. Shortly after Smyth's death, a committee of the House of Assembly decided that Boyle's salary as medical officer was too high and that it was improper for a member of the board also to be its employee. The board of commissioners disagreed, claiming that under the act of 1822 they had the right to appoint whomever they pleased and that they could set the salary of the medical officer just as they regulated all other expenditures of the hospital. They said they had already reduced the salary to £150, pointed out how valuable Boyle's services had been in establishing the hospital, and maintained "that they should have looked in vain for such aid elsewhere in the Province." The implication was that Boyle was irreplaceable.

The commissioners also claimed they were responsible to the lieutenant governor and not to the assembly. While Smyth had been alive, this arrangement had worked well. However, the new lieutenant governor, Sir Howard Douglas*, sided with the house. It was soon obvious that Boyle could be replaced and in September 1824 the position was offered to his brother-in-law, Dr John Boyd Jr, at a salary of £100. He accepted and continued to hold the position until his death in 1857.

During the squabble between the board and the assembly, Boyle had tactfully withdrawn from the province. He returned to Scotland and in 1826 was elected a fellow of the Royal College of Physicians of Edinburgh. Later the same year he returned to Saint John where he continued to practise medicine until his death. Little is known about his activities as a medical practitioner after his return, but he had no further connection with the hospital. He was described as a "reserved and courtly gentleman who had a habit, when walking, of throwing his head back as if gazing at heaven." He was generally respected as a physician and surgeon and during the 1830s served on examining committees which licensed physicians to practise in the province.

WILLIAM A. SPRAY

N.B. Museum, Elizabeth Innes, notebooks: 27; Marine Hospital, minute-book, 1822–27; Reg. of marriages for the city and county of Saint John, book A (1810–28): 112. N.B., *Acts*, [1786–1836], 1820, c.15; 1821, c.9; 1822, c.27. *Morning News* (Saint John, N.B.), 17 April 1854. "Provincial chronology," *New Brunswick Magazine* (Saint John), 2 (January–June 1899): 229. W. B. Stewart, *Medicine in New Brunswick . . .* (Moncton, N.B., 1974). A. D. Gibbon, "The Kent Marine Hospital," N.B. Hist. Soc., *Coll.* (Saint John), no.14 (1955): 1–19. J. W. Lawrence, "The medical men of St. John in its first half century," N.B. Hist. Soc., *Coll.*, 1 (1894–97), no.3: 292–93. Observer [E. S. Carter], "Linking the past with the present," *Telegraph-Journal* (Saint John), 30 April 1930: 4; 1 Dec. 1930: 4.

BRADLEY, MARY. *See* COY

BRIARD, MARIE-HENRIETTE LEJEUNE, *dit.* *See* LEJEUNE

BRIDGE, THOMAS FINCH HOBDAY, Church of England clergyman; b. 20 Dec. 1807, second son of Captain Thomas Bridge, RN, of Harwich, England; m. 1835 Sarah Christiana Dunscombe, daughter of John Dunscombe, aide-de-camp to Governor Sir Thomas John Cochrane*, and they had nine children; d. 28 Feb. 1856 in St John's.

Born into a family with a long-standing naval affiliation, Thomas Finch Hobday Bridge was unable to continue in the tradition because of health problems. He was educated at Charterhouse, London, and then at Christ Church College, Oxford, where he "found his work too easy and was too much in society." Graduating with an undistinguished BA, he studied law at Lincoln's Inn, London, but changed his mind about a profession in 1831 and was ordained a Church of England clergyman. After serving in Norfolk as a curate, Bridge went to Newfoundland in 1832 as chaplain to Cochrane and tutor to his son.

When Cochrane left in 1834, Bridge stayed behind in St John's because he had received a promise from the Reverend Frederick Hamilton Carrington* that he would succeed to Carrington's church there, if he accepted an appointment meanwhile as curate. Already a member of the conservative Society for Promoting Christian Knowledge, Bridge now joined the more evangelical Temperance Society and the Bible Society, giving the appearance of becoming a thoroughly low church clergyman. When Carrington died in 1839, Bridge, supported by a petition from the congregation, successfully applied to Bishop Aubrey George Spencer* for the vacancy. Late in 1840 Spencer sent Bridge to England to raise funds for the projected cathedral in St John's, the cost of which was estimated to be £4,000. In the approximately six months Bridge spent there he collected close to half that sum. Not occupied solely with soliciting money, he also received his MA from Oxford and preached a sermon at Islington (London) on behalf of the

Brien

Newfoundland School Society; his sermon was published in the *Pulpit* (London), one of the most important evangelical journals in England at that time.

Returning to Newfoundland early in 1841, Bridge became Spencer's principal assistant, assuming the positions of examining chaplain, vicar general, and ecclesiastical commissary. When the bishop gained control of the Newfoundland School Society later that year, Bridge became its superintendent, a post he was to hold until 1849. In 1843 Spencer visited Bermuda, the other area included in his diocese, and he left Bridge in charge in Newfoundland. Upon Spencer's translation to the see of Jamaica later that year, Bridge applied for the Newfoundland bishopric, alleging that he would follow the "Scriptural principles of the Reformed Church of England" which Spencer had professed. He also warned officials of the Society for the Propagation of the Gospel of the intrigues of his rival Charles BLACKMAN, principal of the Theological Institute and incumbent of St Thomas' Church. In spite of his application, Governor Sir John HARVEY and Spencer believed that he was trying to secure not the bishopric but the post of archdeacon. In any case, Edward Feild* was appointed bishop.

Arriving in Newfoundland in 1844, Feild quickly came to dislike Blackman and Bridge, two of the most prominent Anglican clergymen on the island, believing they were "both selfish and self seeking." Feild felt that his tractarian ideas caused Blackman to oppose him and that Bridge favoured him because of self-interest, but he also was well aware that both men were capable of altering their position to suit any situation. However, as Bridge was efficient and industrious, with ideas which became increasingly similar to those of the new bishop, Feild eventually came to acknowledge his position as principal assistant. As chairman of the committee which ran the Newfoundland Church Society, Bridge worked hard collecting funds. These were distributed among the clergy on the island according to need, thereby reducing their direct financial dependence on their congregations and establishing some independence for the church from the SPG. These activities, and his public defence of moderate tractarian doctrines, made him the obvious choice for archdeacon in 1850.

During the early 1850s Bridge became tired of Newfoundland and declared in letters home that he had to leave because the climate and excessive work were exhausting him. A holiday in England paid for by his congregation enabled him to remain in the colony but he persisted unsuccessfully in seeking other situations. The burden of work increased. He became chairman of the Protestant education board of St John's, a director of the Church of England Academy, and remained as chairman of the church society with responsibility for diocesan finances. He took a prominent part in the conflict between Feild and Governor Ker Baillie* Hamilton over what Feild saw as excessive government interference in church affairs. Moreover, as rector of the Cathedral of St John the Baptist, he had to perform his parish duties and to conduct four services and preach three sermons every Sunday, all without the aid of a curate. When a cholera epidemic struck St John's in 1855–56, Bridge worked among the sick, but he was so weakened by strain and financial worries (the SPG had cut his salary to a level inadequate to support his large family), that he caught a cold early in 1856 while hauling wood. He died after performing the evening service on 28 February.

Repenting of his earlier judgement, Feild praised Bridge as the "most fond, faithful and efficient archdeacon that ever any Bishop was served by" and called him his "Iron Bridge." The St John's *Newfoundlander* spoke of his work among the poor, and John Kent*, the Roman Catholic politician who became premier in 1858, lauded his non-sectarian works of charity. Large silent crowds gathered for his funeral, the House of Assembly was adjourned, flags were flown at half-mast, and shops were closed. Historian Daniel Woodley Prowse* describes Bridge as the "most beloved Anglican minister that ever set foot on our soil; his place has never been filled." Bridge was certainly one of the most influential clergymen of the Church of England in Newfoundland: under both Spencer and Feild he played a major part in establishing the Anglican diocese on a solid foundation.

FREDERICK JONES

Thomas Finch Hobday Bridge is the author of *A letter to Peter Winser, Sr., esq., in reply to his reasons for leaving the church of his fathers and of his baptism* (St John's, 1847), a copy of which is preserved in USPG, C/CAN/Nfl., 5, and *The two religions: or, the question settled, which is the oldest church, the Anglican or the Romish? A sermon . . .* (London, 1841). His sermon on behalf of the Newfoundland School Society appeared in the *Pulpit* (London), 38 (1840): 444–50.

PRO, CO 194/117–42. USPG, C/CAN/Nfl., 5; D9A; D9B. *Newfoundlander*, 3 March 1856. *Public Ledger*, 4 March 1856. Prowse, *Hist. of Nfld.* (1896). Frederick Jones, "The early opposition to Bishop Feild of Newfoundland," CCHS, *Journal*, 16 (1974): 30–41.

BRIEN, *dit* DÉROCHER (Desrochers), URBAIN.
See DESROCHERS

BROUSE, GEORGE, farmer, businessman, office holder, justice of the peace, politician, and militia officer; b. 1790 in Matilda Township (Ont.), son of Peter Brouse and Eliza ——; m. Catherine Carman, and they had two sons and five daughters; d. 12 Feb. 1860 in Iroquois, Upper Canada.

George Brouse's father, a resident of Stone Arabia, N.Y., served during the American revolution as a private in the King's Royal Regiment of New York [*see* Sir John Johnson*]. Discharged in 1783, he and other members of the regiment settled a year later in Township No.5 (Matilda) on the St Lawrence River. When he died in 1810, George, his elder son, inherited the west half of the "homestead" (lot 22, concession 1 of Matilda Township). Acquiring more land in the area over a period of years by grant, as the son of a loyalist, and by purchase, George eventually owned at least 900 acres. He farmed extensively, raising livestock and growing a variety of crops including apples and vegetables. During the War of 1812 he suffered losses of livestock, farm equipment, and personal effects on two occasions: in 1813 at the hands of the invading army of Major-General James Wilkinson, and in 1814 from a party of British seamen en route west.

Brouse's property included part of an area on the shore of the St Lawrence known as Point Iroquois. A settlement, first called Matilda and later Iroquois, grew up there around a general store opened by Brouse evidently after 1814. In the 1820s he began building a steam-driven mill complex, which comprised a flour- and grist-mill, a sawmill and shingle factory, and a woollen-mill. His enterprises made him a prosperous and prominent figure in the area. He built one of the village's largest houses, and reputedly employed a black servant and kept a racehorse.

In 1810 Peter Brouse had converted George and his brother Peter to Methodism but according to John Saltkill Carroll* "merchandize cooled George's heart till the great revival in 1822, when he was restored, and became a life long steward of the Church." Brouse also occupied a number of local offices. On 5 July 1828 he was appointed postmaster, a position he held for at least 20 years. He sat with Peter Shaver for one term (1828–30) as a member of the provincial assembly for Dundas but does not appear to have had a strong political orientation prior to the 1828 election. William Lyon Mackenzie* listed him under "political sentiments not known" in the *Colonial Advocate* of 26 June 1828, although in the house Brouse voted consistently with the reform majority. His local prominence was enhanced by his appointment as captain in the 2nd Regiment of Dundas militia on 30 Jan. 1839, and in 1847 he received his first commission as a justice of the peace.

The growth of both the village of Iroquois and Brouse's business, which from 1847 included a telegraph office in his store, was stimulated by the completion of the Point Iroquois Canal (1847) and the Grand Trunk Railway (built between Montreal and Brockville in 1854–55). Brouse was influential in having Iroquois incorporated as a village in 1857 and served as its first reeve. His sons, George William and Guy Carleton, inherited and continued his farming and mercantile activities in Matilda Township. One

daughter, Abigail Ann, married William Patrick*, a reform member of the Legislative Assembly.

J. K. JOHNSON

AO, RG 22, ser.198, George Brouse. BLHU, R. G. Dun & Co. credit ledger, Canada, 14: 42. PAC, MG 25, 14; RG 1, E3, 8: 10; L3, 37: B10/52; RG 9, I, B5, 6; RG 19, 3746, claim 409. Can., Prov. of, Legislative Assembly, *App. to the journals*, 1846, app.F. "Land board minutes, etc.," AO *Report*, 1905: cxxxv. "Settlements and surveys," PAC *Report*, 1891, note A: 5, 13, 17. "Surveyors' letters, notes, instructions, etc., from 1788 to 1791," AO *Report*, 1905: 463. U.C., House of Assembly, *Journal*, 1829–30. *Colonial Advocate*, 26 June 1828. *Ottawa Citizen*, 17 Feb. 1860. Armstrong, *Handbook of Upper Canadian chronology*, 69, 80. *Canada directory*, 1857–58; 1864–65. "1828 Upper Canada election results table," comp. R. S. Sorrell, *OH*, 63 (1971): 68. *Illustrated historical atlas of the counties of Stormont, Dundas and Glengarry, Ont.*, comp. H. Belden (Toronto, 1879; repr. Owen Sound, Ont., 1972). W. D. Reid, *The loyalists in Ontario: the sons and daughters of the American loyalists of Upper Canada* (Lambertville, N.J., 1973). A. L. Burt, *The old province of Quebec* (2v., Toronto, 1968), 2: 89–90. Carroll, *Case and his cotemporaries*, 1: 8, 207, 209. J. S. Carter, *The story of Dundas . . .* (Iroquois, Ont., 1905; repr. Belleville, Ont., 1973), 171, 347–48, 351, app.B. J. G. Harkness, *Stormont, Dundas and Glengarry: a history, 1784–1945* (Oshawa, Ont., 1946), 154.

BROWN, PAOLA (Paoli, Paole, Peole), town-crier and handyman; fl. 1828–52.

Tradition has ascribed to Paola Brown, who was born in Pennsylvania around 1807, the status of a runaway slave from a southern plantation. However, his first name, possibly derived either from a town near Philadelphia or from the famous liberator of Corsica (Pasquale Paoli, who died in 1807), combined with the fact that he claimed to be literate, suggests that he was probably an indentured urban servant or freeman rather than a rural slave.

Brown surfaced in Upper Canada in late 1828 as a peripatetic leader of scattered black families between Niagara (Niagara-on-the-Lake) and Dundas. He prepared two petitions to secure land for a settlement that would draw together black families from Niagara to Waterloo. The first petition claimed that the black settlement designated by the government for Oro Township was too distant and appealed for a more conveniently located grant. The Executive Council rejected this petition early in December, insisting that the blacks settle in or near Oro Township. The second petition followed shortly and asked for approval to form a company to purchase a block of clergy reserve land on the Grand River where the petitioners planned to cultivate tobacco. On 17 Jan. 1829 the council rejected this petition, stating that the desired block of land had not yet been surveyed and was not for sale at that time.

Browne

One reason why the petitioners pleaded for special consideration was a perceived need for self-protection: cases of blacks being kidnapped and returned to the United States were cited in the petitions. Moreover, racially inspired petty violence had occurred in Upper Canada and, not long after his petitioning, Brown himself was a victim. In May 1829 George Gurnett*, the publisher of the *Gore Gazette* of Ancaster, was accused of "violent assault and battery upon one Paoli Brown, a man of colour."

Unable to establish a new settlement but retaining his passionate interest in black welfare in the Niagara and Gore districts, Brown gravitated to Hamilton. The flourishing state of Hamilton in the late 1820s and during the 1830s attracted a small black community, in which Brown assumed a leadership role. After 1833 he marshalled the area's blacks during annual celebrations on 1 August commemorating the abolition of slavery in the British empire. He also continued to be involved in petitions on behalf of blacks. In 1837 he signed one from the black community appealing for a fair extradition hearing in the case of runaway slave Jesse Happy. Five years later his name heads a list of 170 "coloured persons of Hamilton and its vicinity" who petitioned Sir Allan Napier MacNab* to protest the forcible return of Nelson Hackett* from Sandwich (Windsor) to slavery in the United States.

During his years in Hamilton, Brown supported himself and his wife by working as a handyman and by acting as town-crier and crier for an auctioneer. Local accounts describe him as unusual and popular; Laura B. Durand noted, in a later anecdotal and condescending remembrance, that "his vanity and affectation were as typical of his race as his good nature and volubility." As crier, dressed in white trousers and a white top hat in warm weather and a large military cape in winter, he exercised his "deep and sonorous" voice aided by a large handbell. Some citizens, however, were less than pleased by these activities, and insults and demands for silence reached Brown. By 1849 enough of them considered him a nuisance that a by-law was passed which, if strictly enforced, would have prevented him from shouting his messages and ringing his bell.

Brown's interest in education and religion was a source of cruel amusement and inspired the "sporting youths" of Hamilton to make him the butt of jokes. Although he claimed that the "great authors of antiquity" were his "constant companions," Durand alleged that he was "absolutely uneducated." His carrying a book in hand would prompt sarcastic questions about how he was getting on with his studies. In turn, the community's behaviour reinforced a fatalism in Brown that must have made his pronouncements about the evils of the day a bitter outpouring rather than a humorous display from an amiable local character.

In 1843 a major Adventist movement, led by William Miller, swept over western New York proclaiming that the world was beyond secular rescue and that the second coming was at hand. Many of the leaders of this movement, which was strongest in Rochester, were prominent abolitionists, and they described a world in which violence and corruption were growing stronger. Brown, an adherent and proselytizer, was a member of the tabernacle in Hamilton and was one of those who assembled on 22 Oct. 1844 in the hope of being taken to heaven; that the appointed time passed without incident must have only exacerbated the cruelty already evident in Hamilton.

Early in 1851 more than 200 citizens invited Brown to lecture on the evils of slavery. On 7 February a large crowd assembled but he was barely into his address when a practical joker extinguished the lights and precipitated a panic. Brown's speech, published that year, fused in prophetic rhetoric his passion for black freedom in the United States and his vision of divine justice. The message was clear: "Slaveholders, I call God, I call Angels, I call Men, to witness, that your destruction is at hand, and will be speedily consummated, unless you repent."

The 1852 census notes that Brown lived in the basement offices of Hugh Bowlby Willson*, a prominent Hamilton lawyer and land speculator. Paola Brown disappears thereafter and it has been alleged that he died a pauper.

JOHN C. WEAVER

Paola Brown is the author of *Address intended to be delivered in the City Hall, Hamilton, February 7, 1851, on the subject of slavery* (Hamilton, [Ont.], 1851). A report of the speech and its disruption appeared as "Lecture of Paola Brown, Esq., on slavery," *Weekly Spectator*, 13 Feb. 1851.

HPL, Hamilton census and assessment rolls, 1837, 1840–41; Scrapbooks, H. F. Gardiner, 215: 43; 216: 51; 273: 109. McMaster Univ. Library (Hamilton), Research Coll. and Arch., Hamilton Police Village minutes (typescript). PAC, RG 1, E3, 35: 225–27; L3, 50: B15/115; RG 5, A1: 50676–78. *Canadian Freeman* (York [Toronto]), 5 Jan. 1832. *Hamilton Spectator, and Journal of Commerce*, 25 July 1849. *DHB*. G. E. French, *Men of colour: an historical account of the black settlement on Wilberforce Street and in Oro Township, Simcoe County, Ontario, 1819–1949* (Stroud, Ont., 1978). D. G. Hill, *The freedom-seekers: blacks in early Canada* (Agincourt [Toronto], 1981). L. B. Durand, "'Peole' Brown: town crier; an incident of 1843," *Canadian Magazine*, 50 (November 1917–April 1918): 291–94. C. R. McCullough, "Head of the Lake: a review of an old-time address" and "Colourful characters of bygone years," *Hamilton Spectator*, 1 Nov. 1941: 15, and 14 Sept. 1946: 5.

BROWNE (Brown), TIMOTHY, Roman Catholic priest and Augustinian; b. *c.* 1786 probably in New Ross (Republic of Ireland); d. 9 Oct. 1855 in Galway (Republic of Ireland).

106

Timothy Browne studied for the priesthood at New Ross under his uncle Philip Crane, an Augustinian priest, and the celebrated James Warren Doyle of the same order, who was later bishop of Kildare and Leighlin. Reported to have "superior ability," Browne was professed as an Augustinian monk in 1808 and ordained to the priesthood on 29 June 1810 in Waterford.

Browne, a member of the Irish province of the Order of St Augustine, left Ireland in 1811 to serve in Newfoundland. Initially a curate to Bishop Patrick Lambert* in St John's, he was soon appointed, probably in 1815, pastor of the Ferryland district to replace Father Ambrose Fitzpatrick, whose scandalous conduct had forced his resignation. Covering the coast south of St John's from Bay Bulls to Trepassey and the whole of St Mary's Bay, Browne's extensive parish contained some 3,500 Catholics. His first headquarters seem to have been at Bay Bulls, perhaps because the house and chapel at Ferryland were "in ruins."

In 1819 the shortage of priests of his order in Ireland caused his Augustinian superiors to threaten Browne's recall, despite his own preference to stay in Newfoundland. To prevent his removal, Bishop Thomas Scallan*, Lambert's successor, went so far as to seek Rome's intervention. Not only did he stress that Browne's departure would even further decrease the already sparse Newfoundland clergy, but he maintained that Browne was his most outstanding priest, "the greatest glory and pride of this mission." This appeal had effect, and the Roman authorities saw that Browne was allowed to remain.

Scallan's enthusiasm for Browne soon waned. In reporting to Rome in 1822 he mentioned that Browne, although a worthy priest and an excellent preacher, was a poor manager of his personal affairs and heavily in debt. Browne was nevertheless one of three priests recommended by Scallan in 1827 as his possible successor. However, Michael Anthony Fleming*, Scallan's first preference, eventually received the appointment as coadjutor bishop in 1829.

Scallan's death and Fleming's succession in 1830 marked a turning-point in Browne's career. From the beginning Fleming considered Browne a liability to the church and within a few months had described the Augustinian to Rome as "lacking prudence and religion." Although Browne had previously served his mission alone, in 1834 Fleming assigned to him as curate James W. Duffy, one of a number of priests recently arrived from Ireland. In so doing, Fleming probably hoped to undermine Browne's position in the parish. Browne disliked Duffy intensely; technically Duffy's superior, he held aloof from the legal difficulties Duffy was involved in after 1835 as a result of the destruction of fishing premises at St Mary's.

By 1835 even Governor Henry Prescott* noted that Browne was "in bad odour" with the new bishop and "diametrically opposite in disposition and conduct to him – and the rest of the clergy." Open hostility soon divided Catholics into supporters or opponents of Fleming. In St John's the latter were denounced by Father Edward Troy*, who publicly taunted them as "Mad Dogs." Browne supported one of those Catholics against whom reprisals had been taken in a formal complaint to government. At the same time Browne began to receive favourable notice from Henry David Winton, Fleming's arch-antagonist, in the columns of the St John's *Public Ledger*.

Fleming acknowledged differences with "two or three" of his clergy, ascribing them to his subdivision of existing missionary districts and the resulting loss of income to the incumbents. Browne, although not mentioned by name, had been especially affected by this reorganization, since by 1837 two new parishes (St Mary's, given to Duffy, and Bay Bulls) had been carved from his district. In that year, without particular reason, Fleming stripped Browne of all his priestly faculties, except the permission to say mass privately. Local clergy were even forbidden to hear Browne's confession. Totally estranged from his bishop, Browne had recourse only to Rome; in 1838 he denounced Fleming in a letter to the Sacred Congregation of Propaganda for having made Newfoundland Catholicism "inhuman, irreligious, and bigoted."

In June 1841 Browne, aided by some £200 collected from both Catholics and Protestants, left Newfoundland for Rome as agent for the Catholic opposition to Fleming. An unedifying quarrel followed. Browne accused his superior of abuse of his episcopal authority, and Fleming alleged in turn that Browne had neglected his spiritual duties, caused division in his parish by his involvement in litigation, and appropriated church property for private use. Indeed, Fleming insinuated that Browne and his brother and cousin were in Newfoundland solely for personal gain. Catholic opposition to himself, Fleming put down to a renewal in Newfoundland of rivalries between two areas in Ireland, Leinster and Munster; most of his adversaries, he noted, were from Leinster. Although Browne's charges made some impact in Rome, Fleming was able to counter them with success and by late 1843 Browne's cause was clearly lost. He left Rome for Ireland in 1844. Details of his later career there are few but it appears to have been unremarkable. In July 1855, while attending a chapter of his order in Galway, he became ill and died.

Browne was a respected pastor and deserves credit for his concern for the harmony of the Newfoundland community. Yet his early promise went unrealized, and secular affairs became a growing preoccupation with him. Still, Fleming's contention that Browne's unworldliness lay at the root of their differences was unjust. Nor was theirs simply a clash of subordinate with superior. Newfoundland Catholicism of the

Bruneau

1830s wore a new and more militant aspect than Browne was accustomed to, and perhaps his real difficulty was that he was unable, or unwilling, to adapt to it.

RAYMOND J. LAHEY

AAQ, 10 CM, IV: 30; 30 CN. AASJ, Fleming papers; Scallan papers. Archivio della Propaganda Fide (Rome), Scritture riferite nei Congressi, America Settentrionale, 2 (1792–1830); 5 (1842–48). PRO, CO 194/57, 194/86, 194/90, 194/94–95. M. A. Fleming, *Relazione della missione cattolica in Terranuova nell'America settentrionale* . . . (Rome, 1837). *Newfoundlander*, 26 Sept. 1833, 5 Nov. 1855. *Public Ledger*, 23 June, 29 Sept. 1835; 4 May, 21, 24 June 1836; 22 May 1840; 22 June 1841; 23 March 1843. *Royal Gazette and Newfoundland Advertiser*, 4 March, 23 Feb. 1815. Howley, *Ecclesiastical hist. of Nfld.*

BRUNEAU, FRANÇOIS-PIERRE, lawyer, seigneur, businessman, and politician; b. 24 July 1799 in Montreal, son of François-Xavier Bruneau, a dealer in pelts, and Thérèse Leblanc; d. unmarried 4 March 1851 in Saint-Bruno-de-Montarville, Lower Canada.

François-Pierre Bruneau, who came from a family of Montreal merchants and was a cousin of Louis-Joseph Papineau* by marriage, was the first of his lineage to study law. He trained under Louis-Michel VIGER, and was called to the bar on 25 June 1822, about three years before his brother Jean-Casimir and seven before his cousin Théophile. He then took up residence at Montreal; after practising there for a few years, he joined with Henri Desrivières in purchasing the Montarville seigneury, where he planned to put money into developing mills.

The site was an advantageous one and the terms of purchase were favourable, since the seigneur, René Boucher de La Bruère, was particularly anxious to secure a life annuity for himself. Hence the transaction was concluded expeditiously, and on 8 Aug. 1829 Bruneau obtained three of the six lots in the fief for £2,150, to be paid in equal instalments by 1 Jan. 1850. Desrivières, who had already inherited two lots from his mother, was to obtain the remaining one, together with the title of premier seigneur, for £650, payable under the same terms. On 8 Aug. 1829 the two new partners also signed a ten-year agreement under which they shared equally all costs attached to the properties comprising the seigneury, in order to build and operate mills. Bruneau was to supply the initial capital, on condition that Desrivières oversaw the construction and running of the mills and repaid to Bruneau, by 1 Jan. 1834, his share of the capital including the legal interest of six per cent payable annually. A month later, on 7 and 8 Sept. 1829, arrangements were made to build the first mill; however, owing to delays in installing the machinery, it was not yet finished when Bruneau rendered fealty and homage on 27 Sept. 1830.

It is not possible to estimate the revenues produced by the seigneury at this time, but judging by the partners' real estate transactions they appear to have been substantial. The seigneurs sought to have new title-deeds issued, bought and resold lots to make higher profits, and claimed the arrears owed to the previous owner, Boucher de La Bruère, which they had acquired by their deed of purchase, including the benefits that would eventually result from actions brought by the former seigneur against some of his *censitaires*. According to Joseph Bouchette*, after the French régime the lots in this seigneury had been "more heavily rated than those of an older date." In short, the venture would pay off provided the seigneury received proper attention! For his part, Bruneau thought it at least as lucrative as the real estate market in Montreal, where he was attempting to acquire several sites to resell, particularly around Rue Notre-Dame and the old citadel.

It may also have been at this time that Bruneau embarked on manufacturing conveyances which *La Minerve* of 9 Dec. 1847 termed "Bruneau Sleighs." Nothing is known about the development of this enterprise, but it appears to have been profitable, since *La Minerve* called Bruneau the originator of this kind of vehicle in the province.

In 1839 Bruneau apparently was the owner of the Pierreville seigneury, and for a while refused to take part in the building of the new church there. That, at least, is the gist of a letter Pierre Béland, the local parish priest, sent to Bishop Joseph Signay* on 28 October: "Mme de Montenach [Marie-Élisabeth Grant] has just sold her seigneury to a certain M. Pierre-François Bruneau, who seems in no way to favour the construction of the church. . . . The said seigneur having appeared only once in the parish, I have not had the occasion to see him. . . . The new seigneur of Pierreville refuses to deliver without payment the stone and the wood that Mme de Montenach had promised." Since this letter closely followed Bruneau's appointment on 8 July 1839 as a commissioner for the building and repair of churches and presbyteries, it is possible that he is the person referred to in it, and that he took advantage of his office, with the information it afforded about future sites for such buildings, to expand the scope of his investments in property.

On 9 June 1841, only a few months after the Act of Union came into effect, Bruneau was elevated to a much more prestigious post, a life appointment to the Legislative Council. He then divided his time between the Montarville seigneury, where he was engaged in developing the village of Saint-Bruno-de-Montarville, and Kingston in Upper Canada, where the first parliament of the united Canadas had just convened. Considered a conservative, he joined the other legislative councillors in opposing the transfer of parliament to Montreal in 1844. What especially drew the sharp criticism of reform circles upon him was his agreement on 8 Dec. 1847 to join the government of Henry SHERWOOD as a member of the Executive Council and as receiver general. However, the appointment, which came at the very moment when the governor, Lord Elgin [Bruce*], dissolved parliament and called a general election, gained Bruneau nothing, since on 3 March 1848 the government that had appointed him was brought down on a vote of non-confidence.

Bruneau then retired to his Montarville seigneury, where he died on 4 March 1851. He was buried four days later at Saint-Bruno-de-Montarville. His estate went to his two brothers, Jean-Casimir, a judge of the Superior Court since 1849, and Olivier-Théophile, known particularly as one of the first professors of McGill College's faculty of medicine. Mont Saint-Bruno and the village of Saint-Bruno-de-Montarville perpetuate the name of the seigneur of Montarville.

SERGE COURVILLE

ANQ-M, CE1-16, 8 mars 1851; CE1-51, 25 juill. 1799; CN1-270, 1829–31. ANQ-Q, P-240, boîte 33. *Le Canadien*, 11, 16 juin 1841; 10 déc. 1847. *La Minerve*, 6, 9, 20 déc. 1847; 13 mars 1848; 6 mars 1851. Joseph Bouchette, *A topographical dictionary of the province of Lower Canada* (London, 1832). J.-J. Lefebvre, "Tableau alphabétique des avocats de la province de Québec, 1765–1849," *La Rev. du Barreau*, 17 (1957): 286. Joseph Bouchette, *A topographical dictionary of the province of Lower Canada* (London, 1832). *Political appointments, 1841–65* (Coté; 1866). Turcotte, *Le Conseil législatif*. Buchanan, *Bench and bar of L.C.* T.-M. Charland, *Histoire de Saint-François-du-Lac* (Ottawa, 1942). J. C. Dent, *The last forty years: Canada since the union of 1841* (2v., Toronto, [1881]). J.-E. Roy, *L'ancien Barreau au Canada* (Montréal, 1897). *Saint-Bruno de Montarville, 250e anniversaire* (Saint-Bruno, Qué., 1961). L.-P. Turcotte, *Le Canada sous l'Union, 1841–1867* (2v., Québec, 1871–72). Montarville Boucher de La Bruère, "Le 'livre de raison' des seigneurs de Montarville," *Cahiers des Dix*, 4 (1939): 243–70. J.-J. Lefebvre, "La vie sociale du grand Papineau," *RHAF*, 11 (1957–58): 483–84. É.-Z. Massicotte, "Les seigneurs Bruneau," *BRH*, 32 (1926): 517.

BUCHANAN, ALEXANDER, lawyer, judge, and justice of the peace; b. 23 April 1798 in Gosport, England, son of John Buchanan and Lucy Richardson; d. 5 Nov. 1851 in Montreal.

John Buchanan, Alexander's father, came from an old Scottish family established in Ireland; he immigrated to Canada in 1802 with his young family when the 49th Foot, to which he was attached as surgeon, was sent out on a tour of duty. After his wife's death the following year, he took up residence at Quebec, becoming surgeon to the staff of the garrison in that town. Young Alexander, the eldest of three children, was sent like others of his social background to the school run by the Reverend Daniel WILKIE.

In 1814, a year before his death, John Buchanan apprenticed Alexander to his friend Andrew Stuart*, a lawyer, who made a contractual agreement to see to the boy's education for five years and to facilitate his call to the bar. After his father died, Alexander remained with his mentor, who now became his guardian; the other members of the family were entrusted to the care of Joseph-François Perrault*, a well-known protonotary in the district of Quebec.

Having reached his majority in April 1819 and after being called to the bar in May, Buchanan without more ado used his inheritance to embark on a long trip that took him to England, Ireland, Scotland, and France. He returned to Lower Canada in the autumn of 1820, and from then on could concentrate on his career. It was at Montreal, where he subsequently lived, that in 1821 he defended his first case before the Court of King's Bench. The next year he went into partnership with his mentor's brother James STUART, a renowned lawyer who had been solicitor general. When Stuart left for Quebec upon his appointment as attorney general in 1825, Buchanan joined a lawyer equally well known in the province, Charles Richard Ogden*, son of judge Isaac Ogden* and solicitor general. In the spring of 1824 Buchanan had married Mary Ann Buchanan, daughter of James Buchanan, the British consul in New York, and sister of Alexander Carlisle Buchanan*. Despite the demands of his profession Buchanan found time to lead an active life in society. A member of St Paul's Lodge and of St Patrick's Society in Montreal, he helped found the Advocates' Library and Law Institute of Montreal in 1828. In a report submitted to the institute, he suggested that its members play a part in training candidates for the bar by giving courses and lectures on the law and jurisprudence. He later undertook this role himself, and was several times president of the institute between 1836 and 1843.

An important stage in Buchanan's career was reached on 17 June 1835 when he was made a king's counsel. A few months later he was asked to replace a member of the commission established to work with a corresponding body in Upper Canada to determine the boundary between the two provinces. On 30 Nov. 1838, after the rebellion had been crushed by force of arms, he was made chairman of a commission of inquiry concerning the prisoners being held in the Montreal jail.

In 1839, at the conclusion of the trials, Governor Sir John Colborne* rewarded Buchanan for his services by appointing him judge of the Court of Requests (a circuit court limited to small causes) for the district of Montreal and justice of the peace to the Court of Quarter Sessions. Considering this double office too onerous and underpaid, Buchanan resigned in 1841; he did, however, subsequently agree to act as justice of the peace in the district court. Resuming his practice, he went into partnership with a succession of

Buchanan

well-known lawyers, including Henry Ogden Andrews, nephew of his second partner, Francis Godschall Johnson*, subsequently chief justice, and John Bleakley.

In addition to these numerous occupations, Buchanan was made chairman of two important commissions of inquiry in 1842. The first was set up to revise the acts and ordinances of Lower Canada. Buchanan's report, which was presented in three sections from 1843 to 1845, incorporated the previously scattered laws into one volume; it recommended that these laws, which were in both French and English, be codified and translated to promote their dissemination. The second commission was to inquire into the system of seigneurial tenure in Lower Canada. In this period of economic and political change many people were demanding that it be abolished or at least reformed. The report, laid before the Legislative Assembly of the province of Canada on 4 Oct. 1843, took note of the divergent opinions of various representatives of French Canadian and English Canadian interests. Nevertheless it came down on the side of those opposing seigneurial tenure, accepting their criticisms: a true relic of "barbaric ages," this system of servitude was disastrous for agriculture and industrial development, no longer met the needs of the population, and must be abolished. Freehold tenure, encouraging competition, would on the other hand help the population attain a more advanced stage of civilization and bring progress to the whole colony. This report helped prepare the way for the 1854 act abolishing the seigneurial system [see Lewis Thomas Drummond*].

Alexander Buchanan would not live to see the result. On 5 Nov. 1851, soon after being appointed to the council of the Montreal bar (incorporated in 1849), and to the post of governor of the association administering the Montreal General Hospital, he died at his new residence, Cornwall Terrace, on Rue Saint-Denis in Montreal. His son, George Carlo Vidua, followed in his footsteps and became a judge.

JACQUES BOUCHER

The reports of the last two commissions of inquiry directed by Alexander Buchanan are reproduced in Can., Prov. of, Legislative Assembly, App. to the journals, 1843, app.FF, app.OO.

ANQ-M, CE1-63, 5 nov. 1851. ANQ-Q, E17/18, no.1119; E17/29, no.2189; E17/31, no.2423; E17/35, no.2772; E17/40, no.3191. La Minerve, 6 nov. 1851. P.-G. Roy, Les avocats de la région de Québec; Les juges de la prov. de Québec. Buchanan, Bench and bar of L.C.; The Buchanan book; the life of Alexander Buchanan, Q.C., of Montreal, followed by an account of the family of Buchanan (Montreal, 1911); Later leaves of the Buchanan book (Montreal, 1929). "Le Docteur John Buchanan," BRH, 17 (1911): 100–3.

BUCHANAN, PETER, merchant; b. 25 July 1805 in Glasgow, third son of Peter Buchanan and Margaret Buchanan; d. 5 Nov. 1860 at Adamton House, near Monkton, Scotland, and was buried in Glasgow.

Peter Buchanan began his mercantile training in 1820 in the office of his father, a Glasgow merchant. Following his father's death in 1826, Peter took charge of the family and liquidated his father's business, which had lost heavily in the Caribbean trade. At the same time he entered the drysaltery business of Robert Laing in Glasgow. In 1834, after touring Upper Canada and the northern United States, Peter agreed to buy the wholesale dry goods firm of William Guild Jr and Company of Toronto with his younger brother Isaac*, who was a partner in the business. The firm was reorganized to form Peter Buchanan and Company in Glasgow, which handled finances and supply, and Isaac Buchanan and Company in Toronto, which managed distribution and sales. Peter, from his base in Glasgow, began withdrawing his funds from the Laing firm in 1834 and forced Isaac to retrieve his other investments in Upper Canada so that all their capital could be brought into the new business. It subsequently earned high profits, other lines of goods were added, and new branches were opened. In 1840, in a bid to control trade in western Upper Canada, Isaac and his partner Robert William Harris* compelled Peter to acquiesce in the formation of Buchanan, Harris and Company in Hamilton, which soon became in his opinion the largest mercantile house in the province. Branches were opened in Montreal in 1841 and in New York four years later.

Although Isaac was nominally his equal, Peter Buchanan was increasingly the business's leading figure. It required large amounts of capital to support goods in transit and to cover debts due on sales, and Peter's most important function was the management of its complex financial affairs in Britain. For the Buchanans' fast-growing business much of the capital was borrowed. On the basis of his character and reputation Peter skilfully lined up credit from suppliers, banks, and mercantile middle men such as shipping agencies. He drew on these sources to make payments and used remittances from Canada, which tended to be seasonal and linked to the vicissitudes of the grain trade there, to repay business debts. Buchanan also sold the business's produce consignments, supervised its buyers, and oversaw the shipment of goods from Britain. In contrast to Isaac, Peter generally advocated caution in business and pressed for the consolidation of gains, but he was undoubtedly ambitious and alert to new opportunities. The value of his capital in the business, initially £7,500, grew at an exceptional rate, exceeding £190,000 (Halifax currency) in 1856.

In 1838–39 and again in 1841–43 Buchanan lived

in Toronto to direct Canadian business operations while Isaac handled affairs in Britain. During these years Peter actively spoke out on commercial matters, and joined Isaac's social clubs and the local militia. Business brought Peter back to Canada a number of times thereafter, his longest stay being from May to October 1860, when the business was reorganized. Through Buchanan, Harris and Company, and his visits to Canada, he became the most eminent British businessman interested in, and known in, Hamilton, where the business's operations were concentrated following the closure of the Toronto store in 1844. To assist Hamilton and his trade, Peter acted as London agent from 1845 to 1855 for Canada's most successful early railway, the Great Western [*see* Charles John Brydges*]. Buchanan had no previous experience with railways, but he fast became an important figure in the company and handled financial negotiations with decisive ability. His greatest contribution came in 1849–52, when, with Robert S. Atcheson, an influential English businessman, he committed the railway company to an imaginative but calculated scheme for raising funds on the London market, traditionally suspicious of unbuilt colonial projects. The successful sale of convertible bonds, which appealed to British investors, enabled the Great Western to move rapidly ahead. As the company developed its own reputation and staff after 1853, Buchanan's role as agent diminished, although in 1854 he joined the Great Western's newly formed London board of directors.

In 1852 Buchanan had also been appointed agent for the Hamilton and Toronto Railway, a subsidiary of the Great Western, and, with prominent Londoners associated in the Great Western, he raised the funds for that line. The group sought large profits from this promotion and accusations of jobbery followed. Largely as a result of this criticism, construction was delayed for so long that sharply rising costs consumed the anticipated profits. To protect his interests Buchanan remained active in the management of the Hamilton and Toronto until it was completed and merged in 1856 into the Great Western, from which he then withdrew immediately.

During the period of his railway agencies Buchanan effectively utilized his high credit standing on behalf of other Canadian companies seeking credit. In the late 1840s he assisted the Upper Canada Trust and Loan Company in its search for British backing. As well he helped to secure better British banking connections for the Commercial Bank of the Midland District, which handled some of the Buchanan business. A reserved man, who never married, Buchanan was little known outside British business circles, where he did, however, receive recognition. He was a director of both the Buchanan Society (1849–52), a prestigious charitable and genealogical

organization, and the Merchants' House of Glasgow (1849–53). In 1860 he was elected a director of the Union Bank of Scotland.

Peter Buchanan's mercantile standing cushioned somewhat the heavy impact of the commercial crisis of 1857 upon the Buchanans' business enterprises in Canada and the failure that year of leading credit sources in Britain. Confronted with the business's precarious position, he nevertheless moved to correct immediate financial and accounting problems, notably the low remittances received from the Hamilton branch under Isaac. In 1860 Peter's implementation of drastic and often ruthless measures for reorganizing the business was abruptly halted by his untimely death. While hunting in Scotland he was accidentally shot in the leg by a nephew and subsequently died of tetanus.

The career of Peter Buchanan exemplifies with particular clarity the private mercantile links between Britain and Canada that were so important in the rapid development of the Canadian business system in his era.

DOUGLAS MCCALLA

HPL, M. H. Farmer, "Calendar of the Buchanan papers, 1697–1896 . . ." (typescript, 1962). PAC, MG 24, D16; RG 30, 1–2, 5, 10–11, 19, 361. SRO, RD5/1113: 165–81. Williams & Glyn Bank Ltd. (London), Glyn Mills & Co., corr. received (mfm. at PAC). *Daily Spectator, and Journal of Commerce*, 22, 26 Nov. 1860. *Times* (London), 21 Feb.–12 April 1861. *Glasgow directory*, 1826–60. *Notes on the members of the Buchanan Society, nos.1–366 (1725–1829)*, comp. R. M. Buchanan (Glasgow, 1931), no.131. P. A. Baskerville, "The boardroom and beyond: aspects of the Upper Canadian railroad community" (PHD thesis, Queen's Univ., Kingston, Ont., 1973). Douglas McCalla, "The Buchanan businesses, 1834–1872: a study in the organization and development of Canadian trade" (DPHIL thesis, Univ. of Oxford, 1972); "Peter Buchanan, London agent for the Grand Western Railway of Canada," *Canadian business history; selected studies, 1497–1971*, ed. D. S. Macmillan (Toronto, 1972), 197–216; *The Upper Canada trade, 1834–1872: a study of the Buchanans' business* (Toronto, 1979); "The Canadian grain trade in the 1840's: the Buchanans' case," CHA *Hist. papers*, 1974: 95–114.

BULGER, ANDREW H., soldier, office holder, and colonial administrator; b. 30 Nov. 1789 in Newfoundland, son of John Bulger and Catherine Foran; d. 2 March 1858 in Montreal.

Andrew H. Bulger was appointed ensign in the recently established Newfoundland Regiment of Fencible Infantry on 26 Oct. 1804, and within two years he received his commission as lieutenant. He served with his unit, which became the Royal Newfoundland Regiment in 1806, in Newfoundland, Nova Scotia, and Lower Canada until the outbreak of war with the United States in 1812 when he was sent to

Bulger

the Niagara frontier in Upper Canada to serve under Major-General Isaac Brock*. He was present at the capture of Detroit in August 1812, and that fall he was attached to the naval force which harassed the enemy along the upper St Lawrence. He also participated in the battles of Fort George (Niagara-on-the-Lake, Ont.) and Stoney Creek [see John Vincent*] in May and June 1813 and in the battle of Crysler's Farm in November. As adjutant to Lieutenant-Colonel Robert McDouall*, Bulger was with the reinforcements sent to Fort Michilimackinac (Mackinac Island, Mich.) in 1814. The force of 10 officers and some 200 men left Kingston in early February, and after a difficult winter trek by way of Lake Simcoe to Georgian Bay they proceeded by boat, arriving at the fort on 18 May. The repulse of an American attack on 4 August, coupled with the daring capture of the American schooners *Tigress* and *Scorpion* in early September [see Miller Worsley*], ensured British supremacy on the upper Great Lakes for the duration of the war. Bulger was prominent in both of these engagements and was slightly wounded during the boarding of the *Tigress*.

In October Bulger, with the local rank of captain, was appointed commandant of Fort McKay, at Prairie du Chien (Wis.) on the upper Mississippi River, an American fort captured in July by William McKay*, commander of the Michigan Fencibles, a provincial corps. The situation at Fort McKay was both dangerous and delicate, but through determined leadership Bulger preserved the security of the 200 French Canadian inhabitants of the area and maintained the Indians' allegiance to the British flag. In early January 1815 he suppressed a near mutiny among the Michigan Fencibles, stationed at the fort, by convening a general court martial and having the three worst offenders summarily flogged.

Bulger also had an ongoing quarrel with Robert Dickson*, agent and superintendent to the Western Indians, stationed at Prairie du Chien, over relations with the Indian allies. In his instructions Bulger was given jurisdiction over the distribution of provisions and gifts to the Indian families, and the young officer refused to allow the Indian agent to interfere with his authority. Dickson was finally recalled to Michilimackinac early in 1815. In spite of this unfortunate power struggle, Bulger's general conduct was endorsed by the inhabitants of Prairie du Chien in an address of 15 Jan. 1815 thanking him for his leadership and protection. McDouall was equally complimentary and praised him for his "judicious, manly, and energetic conduct."

News of the peace settlement signed at Ghent (Belgium) on 24 Dec. 1814 reached Prairie du Chien in April 1815. Bulger succeeded, with some difficulty, in convincing the Indian allies on the upper Mississippi to ratify the treaty, which recognized American sovereignty over the area south of the lakes.

Then on 24 May, after distributing food and gifts among them, he burned the fort and abandoned the area to American occupation. He proceeded by way of Michilimackinac to Quebec where he learned to his "mortification" that he had not received the captaincy to which McDouall had recommended him in late 1814. The Royal Newfoundland Regiment was disbanded in June 1816 and he was placed on the half-pay list as lieutenant. Bulger spent most of the next few years in England where he attempted to gain remuneration for his services during the war, a military appointment, and promotion to half-pay captain. Although his several applications were always fully supported by senior British officers, it was not until 1820 that he finally succeeded in obtaining a compensation of £500 and military allowance equal to the half pay of a captain.

In the winter of 1821–22 Hudson's Bay Company director Andrew Colvile, upon the recommendation of Sir Gordon DRUMMOND and on behalf of the executors of the estate of Lord Selkirk [Douglas*], offered Bulger a three-year appointment as secretary and registrar for the Red River settlement (Man.). He was also to form and train a militia force of 100 settlers. Bulger accepted the offer and, in order to bolster his authority in the colony, he was made governor locum tenens of Assiniboia, at a salary of £250. He arrived at Red River on 28 June 1822 and within a few weeks he was so thoroughly disillusioned with his "life of slavery and of exposure to the insults and threats of some of the most worthless of God's creatures, in one of the most miserable countries on the face of the earth," that he submitted a year's notice of his intention to retire. Bulger also deplored the lack of a military or police force to provide him with the power to maintain order within the colony and to preserve it from the constant threat of attack from the Sioux.

The HBC's chief factor at Fort Garry (Winnipeg), John CLARKE, quickly antagonized Bulger by officially serving notice to him that he was prohibited from trafficking in furs, and as a consequence any hope of cooperation between Bulger as civil governor and Clarke as the company's chief representative vanished. This situation contributed to the poor state of health from which Bulger suffered for most of the winter of 1822–23. Much of the difficulty he experienced in managing the colony arose from the ill-defined relationship between the settlement and the fur trade and from the confusion surrounding the rights of the settlers, given the fur-trade monopoly granted to the HBC by its charter. Nevertheless, after learning of the dispute between Clarke and Bulger, in May 1823 the London committee of the HBC exonerated the governor and condemned their own officer as "imprudent and indiscreet," and on some counts "preposterous and indecorous."

Bulger had written a lengthy letter to Colvile in December 1822 about the state of the colony. He recommended that a system of courts and magistrates be set up, that a company of troops be sent to the colony to enforce the laws and keep the natives in order, that the settlers be allowed to purchase provisions and skins for clothing from the Indians and Métis, and that money be circulated. He also asked Colvile to find a market for the colony's surplus grain. "If these things cannot be done," he warned, "spend no more of Lord Selkirk's money upon Red River." Although his recommendations concerning provisions and currency were implemented by return post, the appeal for troops and markets remained unsatisfied for many years. Bulger left Red River in August 1823 and returned to England. Although he had made enemies in the colony and was later criticized by HBC governor George SIMPSON as wasteful and extravagant, he had inspired confidence and loyalty in his councillors and was appreciated by the settlers who credited him with bringing peace and prosperity to the settlement. In the summer of 1825 Bulger sailed for Quebec to become principal and confidential clerk to the military secretary. His health, never again robust, continued to deteriorate. He was none the less conscientious and industrious in the service of Quebec's various military secretaries. In 1839 he moved with the civil administration to Montreal, where he continued to serve faithfully until his death in March 1858. He would appear to have been survived by his wife, Alicia.

Bulger reached the height of his career at an early age, and his service after 1823 was largely uneventful. Bold, dedicated, and guided by a rigid code of honour and duty, he was also at times pompous, easily affronted, and intolerant of any challenge to his authority. In later life Bulger was prone to glorify his achievements in the War of 1812, but even he seemed not to recognize the fine service he had rendered the Red River settlement in its struggle for life.

ROBERT S. ALLEN and CAROL M. JUDD

Andrew Bulger's papers, which include documents on his military career from 1810 to 1815 and on his administration in the Red River Colony, are in PAC, MG 19, E5. His correspondence concerning events at Prairie du Chien during the War of 1812 is printed in Wis., State Hist. Soc., *Coll.*, 13 (1895): 10–153, and one letter, *Last official letter from Captain Bulger to Lieutenant Colonel M'Douall* (n.p., n.d.), was issued as a pamphlet. Bulger prepared a short autobiography which was published several years after his death by the 10th Regiment of the British Army serving in India, under the title *An autobiographical sketch of the services of the late Captain Andrew Bulger of the Royal Newfoundland Fencible Regiment* (Bangalore, India, 1865). The regiment also printed Bulger's *Papers referring to Red River settlement, Hudson's Bay territories* (Bangalore, 1866).

ANQ-M, CE1-81, 5 mars 1858. PAM, HBCA, D.4/87: f.1. *Canadian North-West* (Oliver). *Officers of British forces in Canada* (Irving). C. [M.] Livermore, *Lower Fort Garry, the fur trade and the settlement at Red River* (Can., National Parks and Hist. Sites Branch, *Manuscript report*, no.202, Ottawa, 1976). R. S. Allen, "The British Indian Department and the frontier in North America, 1755–1830," *Canadian Hist. Sites: Occasional Papers in Archæology and Hist.* (Ottawa), no.14 (1975): 5–125. A. E. Bulger, "Events at Prairie du Chien previous to American occupation, 1814" and "Last days of the British at Prairie du Chien," Wis., State Hist. Soc., *Coll.*, 13 (1895): 1–9; 154–62. B. L. Dunnigan, "The battle of Mackinac Island" and "The Michigan Fencibles," *Mich. Hist.* (Lansing), 59 (1975): 239–54; 57 (1973): 277–95. G. F. G. Stanley, "British operations in the American North-east, 1812–15," Soc. for Army Hist. Research, *Journal* (London), 22 (1943–44): 91–106.

BURN, WILLIAM SCOTT, merchant, accountant, justice of the peace, militia officer, teacher, and author; b. 8 March 1797 in the parish of Inveresk, Scotland, son of David Burn, timber merchant, and Helen Scott; m. with at least one son and two daughters; d. 30 Sept. 1851 in Toronto.

William Scott Burn studied arts at the University of Edinburgh in 1811–13, after which he may have acquired training in accountancy in Edinburgh, a leading centre for that profession. By 1825, however, he had established himself as a timber merchant in nearby Leith. In 1833 he immigrated to Upper Canada, bearing a letter from John George Shaw-Lefevre, the parliamentary under-secretary in the Colonial Office, to Lieutenant Governor Sir John Colborne* which introduced him as a "gentleman of experience in mercantile and agricultural pursuits." The following year he settled in Barton Township near Hamilton and reputedly became involved in the grain trade, in addition to other business enterprises. He was made a director of the Gore Bank in 1836 and about a year later he became a trustee for a proposed road from Hamilton to Brantford. In 1838 he was commissioned as a justice of the peace and was appointed a militia paymaster. Though baptized in the Presbyterian church, he acted as secretary for the Anglican congregation in Barton.

By late 1839, for reasons which are not clear, Burn was in serious financial difficulty. During the early 1840s his work as an accountant and his other ventures were not lucrative. He was forced to put up for sale, through assignees (David Burn in 1842 and later Judah George JOSEPH of Toronto), his house and farm, called Chedoke. Some time in the following year he moved to Toronto. A handful of accountants worked in the city but there was not enough professional business to engage any of them full time so most practices combined accounting with bankruptcy and general financial agency work. Burn's practice developed slowly, if at all, for in the spring of 1844 he declared bankruptcy. In 1844–45 he temporarily replaced James Duffy, an English master at Upper Canada College.

It was evidently for the college's course in bookkeeping, which Burn presumably taught, that he prepared *The principles of book-keeping*, one of the earliest textbooks on accounting written in Canada [*see* Joseph Laurin*]. This work, which remained in use at the college until after 1856, provided a straightforward introduction to basic bookkeeping, with a heavy emphasis on procedural aspects. Designed for use in the classroom, it contained sample transactions with space in which the student could work. Burn's principles were in no way revolutionary although he did propose a simplification of ledger-balancing routines.

In 1845 his introductory text was followed by *The principles of book-keeping, by double entry; exemplified in their application to real business*. This text came in two parts, with some notes on teaching methods, a subject which interested Burn. The first part was a standard practice set, dealing with retail business, for students who had progressed beyond the primary level. It was in the second part that Burn introduced innovations. He argued that by making changes to the structure of the cash-book, notably the insertion of additional columns, it was possible to take all the transactions of a business and account for them in the cash-book by the double-entry system of recording. But for all his innovations Burn was more important as a popularizer than as a theorist. In 1846 the *Cobourg Star* praised *Principles* as "the best and most lucid work on the subject with which we are acquainted. Mr. Burn is evidently not only an experienced practical merchant, but a man of no ordinary philosophical depth and literary accomplishment, whilst he possesses the happy talent of rendering his subject matter interesting and level to the most ordinary capacity. When one reflects on the loss of money and loss of time which occurs to men in business from ignorance of a clear and correct system of book-keeping, a little volume such as Mr. Burn's, becomes invaluable." Most business transactions, both commercial and personal, were based on credit. Sloppy bookkeeping was therefore not just inconvenient but also potentially disastrous.

Like other Victorian accountants, Burn had the conviction that business and commerce formed the foundation upon which rested all the wonders of 19th-century British civilization. In 1845 he read to the Literary and Historical Society of Toronto two papers on the subject, which were published that year as a pamphlet. Expounding on the social utility of commerce, he claimed: "With the full development of society comes the diffusion of wealth, with wealth comes the desire of luxurious ease, and luxurious ease

passes naturally into indolence. . . . But here the commercial spirit steps in and arrests the progress of decay; it keeps society in constant motion, elevating the low and depressing the lofty, filling every rank with new claimants for distinction."

Burn's reputation as an accountant rests on the work he did in the building society movement in Toronto [*see* Joseph Davis Ridout*]. Developed in England in the early 19th century, the building society was a financial intermediary for the secure investment, in real property or mortgages, of the relatively small monthly contributions of its members. The society was also a source of loan capital. When enough contributions had been accumulated, members could borrow from the society upon first mortgage security, to finance construction projects or acquire real estate. Such loans were limited to the amount of the shares the members had subscribed. When contributions and earned profits were sufficient to pay up the shares, usually in eight to ten years, the society would terminate. The investing members would receive their contributions plus accumulated profits while borrowing members had their debts discharged. Because of its various interests and the large number of transactions involved, the accounting for building societies was complex. The terminating building society movement was particularly strong in Upper Canada. At least 30 societies existed, 7 of them in Toronto, and probably 1 in 12 urban adult males was a shareholder.

Burn became a consultant to the Church of England and Metropolitan Building Society, one of the societies incorporated in Upper Canada after enabling legislation had been passed in 1846. By 1848 Burn was also acting as an auditor for the Toronto Building Society; in March 1850 a group which included Joseph Curran Morrison* and Judah George Joseph formed the County of York Building Society and named Burn as secretary-treasurer, a position he held until his death. In announcing his appointment, the *British Colonist* credited him with designing the accounting system in general use by such societies. The building society positions probably gave Burn a steady income with which to cover the overhead expenses of his accounting business. Among his professional clients, in 1850, was the Toronto, Simcoe, and Lake Huron Union Rail-Road Company, for which he and other leading Toronto accountants reported on the financial forecast contained in the company's prospectus.

During most of the years he worked in Toronto, his wife and daughters ran a Berlin-wool and fancy-work establishment. This operation was an artistic success, for Mrs Burn took a prize in Berlin work at the mechanics' institute show of 1851, but whether her shop achieved equal success commercially is not known. William Scott Burn died in Toronto of stomach cancer on 30 Sept. 1851 and was buried in St James' Cemetery.

PHILIP CREIGHTON

William Scott Burn is the author of *The principles of book-keeping; explained in an address to a student of Upper Canada College; and an elementary course of book-keeping by double entry* (Toronto, 1844); *The principles of book-keeping, by double entry; exemplified in their application to real business: in two sets, consequent to the elementary set already published . . .* (Toronto, 1845); and *The connection between literature and commerce; in two essays, read before the Literary and Historical Society of Toronto* (Toronto, 1845).

CTA, RG 5, F, St George's Ward, 1844, no.169; 1846, no.195 (mfm. at AO). Edinburgh Univ. Library, Special Coll. Dept., Matriculation records, 1811–13. GRO (Edinburgh), Inveresk, reg. of births and baptisms, 8, 20 March 1797. HPL, Clipping file, Hamilton biog., Land family: 990; Scrapbooks, Historic houses in Hamilton, 1: 55. PAC, RG 1, L3, 473: S21/46; RG 5, A1: 71741–42, 97813–14, 98654–57, 104081, 106217, 108022–24, 110347, 110917–20, 113177, 114300–2, 115915–16, 119152, 119526–27, 122798–800, 123275–79, 125378–80, 128514–18, 128519–28, 129528–31, 136872; RG 31, A1, 1842, Barton Township (mfm. at AO); RG 68, General index, 1651–1841: 571. St James' Cemetery and Crematorium (Toronto), Record of burials, 30 Sept. 1851. Wentworth Land Registry Office (Hamilton, Ont.), Abstract index to deeds, Barton Township, concession 4, lot 19 (mfm. at AO, GS 1408). *Canada Gazette*, 13 April 1844: 1222. *The roll of the pupils of Upper Canada College, Toronto, January, 1830, to June, 1916*, ed. A. H. Young (Kingston, Ont., 1917), 46, 50, 146. Toronto Building Soc., *Annual statement of the funds and effects of the Toronto Building Society* ([Toronto]), 1850/51–1853/54; *The Toronto Building Society; incorporated in accordance with an act of the provincial legislature, in 1846 . . .* (Toronto, 1846). *British Colonist* (Toronto), 19 June 1846; 21 Dec. 1849; 19 March, 4 June 1850; 14 Oct. 1851. *Church*, 23 Sept. 1842. *Cobourg Star*, 17 June 1846. *Globe*, 7 Oct. 1851. *Herald* (Toronto), 20 March 1848. *Toronto Patriot*, 7 May 1844. *A compilation of the laws and amendments thereto relating to building societies, loan companies, joint stock companies, and interest on mortgages, and other acts pertaining to monetary institutions . . .*, comp. N. S. Garland (Ottawa, 1882). *DHB*. *Edinburgh and Leith directory*, 1825–26. W. H. Smith, *Canada: past, present and future*, 1: 48. *Toronto directory*, 1846–47: 10; 1850–51: xlvi, 19. V. Ross and Trigge, *Hist. of Canadian Bank of Commerce*, 1: 179.

BURNET, DAVID, businessman and politician; b. *c.* 1803; m. *c.* 1831 Mary Ann Forsyth; d. 2 June 1853 at Quebec.

David Burnet was a merchant at Quebec for 30 years, and was noteworthy for the extent and diversity of his undertakings. The date and place of his birth are unknown, and there is no information about the early years of his career. By 1823 he apparently was working for his brother Peter, a rich merchant on Rue Saint-Pierre who was a landowner and a director of the Bank of Montreal at Quebec. David became his partner a few years later. The Burnet brothers engaged in the lumber business and in the importing of merchandise, and they owned beaches and a shipyard on the Rivière Saint-Charles at Quebec which they rented to shipbuilders. It was probably there that David had two ships built in 1825.

When Peter moved to London around 1830, David succeeded him on the board of directors of the Bank of Montreal at Quebec, which included such influential businessmen as Mathew Bell*, the lessee of the Saint-Maurice ironworks, and James Bell Forsyth*, a leading timber merchant whose sister David married around 1831. Burnet often had business dealings with the two men, particularly in the purchase of property. They jointly held great stretches of land on the Saint-Charles for speculative purposes. The interest Burnet and Forsyth shared in the timber trade also led them to become co-owners of the timber cove that Burnet set up at La Canardière on the north shore of the Saint-Charles in 1837. Moreover, Burnet sat on the board of directors of the Canada Marine Insurance Company, which was founded that year and which had Forsyth as its president.

From 1838 Burnet took a considerable interest in marine transport. In addition to buying shares in at least one ship, he had the 389-ton *Mathew Bell* built in 1838 and the 802-ton *Cataraqui* in 1840. The next year he joined businessmen from Kingston in Upper Canada, Quebec, and Montreal in founding the Quebec and Upper Canada Forwarding Company, which planned to transport timber and merchandise between Kingston and Quebec by barge. The company owned nine barges and one steamship in 1843. During this time Burnet made a number of investments in small industries. With Francis Harris Stuart of Montreal he had financed the building and operation of a distillery at Saint-Hilaire (Mont-Saint-Hilaire) in 1838, and in the summer of 1842 he set up a textile-mill at La Canardière, with equipment including "carding machinery, a spinning machine, and two weavers' looms."

All through the 1830s Burnet enjoyed a prominent position at Quebec in organizations relating both to business and to the English and Protestant communities. During this period he was administrator for the Quebec Committee of Trade [*see* John Jones*], and was at various times on the management committee of the Quebec Exchange. On 7 Nov. 1832 he was appointed a warden of Trinity House in Quebec [*see* François Boucher*]. He was socially influential through his service on the management committees of philanthropic, educational, and religious bodies such

Burnham

as the Quebec Emigrant Society, the British and Canadian School Society of the District of Quebec, the St Andrew's Society, the Quebec Auxiliary Bible Society, and the Quebec Male Orphan Asylum. As a member of the committee of the Quebec Constitutional Association, Burnet opposed the plan to unite the two Canadas put forward by Lord Durham [Lambton*] following the events of 1837–38.

A well-known and respected figure, Burnet decided to run for Quebec City in the 1841 elections. Although his political views had led him to champion the cause of those opposing union, he nevertheless stressed in his campaign speech the necessity of complying with the law and endeavouring to turn the new régime to good advantage. He also promised to further the proposals for canals on the St Lawrence as a means of ensuring the prosperity of Quebec. Burnet won an easy victory on 29 March, unlike his running mate Louis-Joseph Massue*, who was defeated by Henry Black*. Burnet's parliamentary career was brief, however, for heavy financial losses incurred at the beginning of 1843 forced him to declare bankruptcy and resign his seat on 26 August.

In order to make his investments Burnet had had to run heavily into debt. According to a balance sheet drawn up on 22 March 1843 he owed £65,658 to a large number of creditors. However, an impressive list of property holdings amounting to some 10,000 acres in various places in Lower and Upper Canada and even in New York State served as security for part of the loans.

Distressed by his financial difficulties, David Burnet was much less active during the last ten years of his life. After selling his timber cove in 1848, he apparently concentrated on running a business involving various types of merchandise, while continuing to buy and sell landed property at Quebec.

PIERRE POULIN

ANQ-Q, CE1-74, 3 juin 1853; CN1-49, 24 avril, 8 déc. 1828; 1ᵉʳ déc. 1831; 17 août 1834; 5 avril, 25 nov. 1836; 27 juill. 1837; 22 sept., 21 nov. 1838; 1ᵉʳ févr. 1840; 22 mars, 15, 22 nov. 1842; 22 mars 1843; 14 janv. 1845; 17 nov. 1846; 3, 5 févr., 12 mai 1847; 31 août 1853; CN1-116, 31 mai 1839, 13 janv. 1840, 21 janv. 1848, 13 mai 1851; CN1-208, 14 mars 1824, 6 déc. 1839. *Le Canadien*, 29 mars 1841, 19 août 1842, 21 août 1843, 3 juin 1853. *Morning Chronicle* (Quebec), 3 June 1853. *Quebec Gazette*, 10, 29 March 1841, 31 March 1843. F.-J. Audet, "Les législateurs du Bas-Canada." E. H. Dahl et al., *La ville de Québec, 1800–1850: un inventaire de cartes et plans* (Ottawa, 1975), 184, 215, 238, 250, 275. Desjardins, *Guide parl.* [J.-C. Langelier], *Liste des terrains concédés par la couronne dans la province de Québec de 1763 au 31 décembre 1890* (Québec, 1891), 16. *Quebec almanac*, 1823–40. *Quebec directory*, 1826, 1844–45, 1847–50, 1852. Chapais, *Cours d'hist. du Canada*, 5: 288. Rosa, *La construction des navires à Québec*.

BURNHAM, ZACHEUS, farmer, land speculator, militia officer, justice of the peace, office holder, politician, and judge; b. 20 Feb. 1777 in Dunbarton, N.H., son of Asa Burnham and Elizabeth Cutler; m. 1 Feb. 1801 Elizabeth Choate, and they had one son and five daughters; d. 25 Feb. 1857 in Cobourg, Upper Canada.

Raised in New Hampshire, Zacheus Burnham came in 1797 to central Upper Canada, a move facilitated by his cousin Aaron Greeley, an agent for the settlement of the Newcastle District under the township land grant scheme initiated by Lieutenant Governor John Graves Simcoe*. Arriving first in Haldimand Township, Zacheus soon moved to nearby Hamilton Township where several of his brothers would eventually settle. Like many of the New England immigrants who poured into Upper Canada during the 1790s, Burnham had a passion for acquiring land. Much of the most desirable land in the townships along Lake Ontario, however, had been granted by 1801 when he brought his bride back with him from New Hampshire. The following year he and his brother Asa leased lot 21 in concession 1 of Hamilton Township, but it was not until 1805 that Zacheus obtained land of his own when he purchased the adjoining lot and established Amherst House, the farm near the site of present-day Cobourg which he occupied until his death.

Burnham thus began a process of land acquisition which would make him one of the largest land owners in the area, a process marked by favourable treatment from the provincial land authorities as well as shrewd and aggressive action on his own part. Indeed in 1819 he was cited by the Reverend John Strachan* as an Upper Canadian success story: "Mr Zaccheus Burnham had perhaps one hundred dollars or £25, when he began about twenty years ago . . . and has accumulated property worth 20,000 dollars, or £5,000." By 1821 he held 1,780 acres in Hamilton Township. Large holdings in the interior of Newcastle District were acquired when he bid successfully in 1818 for the contract to survey the townships of Alnwick, Otonabee, Asphodel, Douro, Dummer, and parts of Smith and Percy. His reward for these surveys, which were carried out by his future son-in-law Richard BIRDSALL, consisted of a percentage of the land within each township, amounting to just under 13,000 acres. In the 1830s Burnham acquired additional land at tax sales, through purchase, and through the lease and purchase of crown lands. In this way he amassed a large and scattered land empire that assured him considerable financial gain through land sales with the influx of immigrants into the area during the 1830s and 1840s.

As a resident speculator familiar with the region, Burnham was quick to recognize the strategic advantage of potential mill-sites and townsites. The village of Ashburnham, directly across the Otonabee River from Peterborough, was located on land owned by Burnham as were portions of the village of Amherst (now part of Cobourg). In support of his Amherst interests, he played a critical role in preventing the court-house from being moved to nearby Cobourg in 1829. He also promoted the building of sawmills and grist-mills in the interior such as those in Keene, Lakefield, and Warsaw. Unlike some speculators Burnham took an active part in the economic development of the Newcastle District. With James Gray Bethune* and Charles Rubidge* he petitioned to have Cobourg made a port of entry in 1829, and he supported the development of road and ferry connections with the Peterborough back country during the early years of its settlement. Later he was a subscriber in the Cobourg Rail Road Company chartered in 1834 to build a railway from Cobourg to Peterborough, and served as one of the commissioners appointed to implement Nicol Hugh Baird*'s proposed canal route between Rice Lake and Lake Simcoe. Along with Henry Ruttan* and others he sought to establish the Newcastle Banking Company, a joint-stock bank founded in 1835 and chartered in 1837 as the Bank of the Newcastle District.

In addition to his many other activities, Burnham maintained a farm which far exceeded in size and standard of production those typical of early Upper Canada. At a time when most settlers were struggling to acquire and clear enough land to support their families, Burnham farmed commercially and provided the area with a local source of foodstuffs and livestock. As early as 1810 he had cleared 100 acres of land and kept a dozen head of cattle; by 1831 he kept 20 milk cows, 100 neat cattle, 150 sheep, 70 pigs, and 10 horses on a farm that spanned 1,000 acres. His farm remained one of the largest, most productive, and prosperous in the area before 1850. Unable to manage it personally because of other concerns, he employed a farm manager and a large labour force. Yet Burnham took a lively interest in his farm and was active in local agricultural affairs as befitted his role as a local squire. He was instrumental in having market fairs established in Port Hope and Cobourg in 1821. A director of the Northumberland Agricultural Society upon its founding in 1828, he later served as a show judge and as president of the society.

Literate, ambitious, and a firmly established land owner, Burnham soon rose to prominence in local militia and political affairs. First mustered as a private in 1801, by the beginning of the War of 1812 he had risen to the rank of captain, and during the war he guided the movement of government stores along Lake Ontario. He remained active in the 1st Regiment of Northumberland militia and as colonel led a large force to Toronto in response to news of the rebellion in December 1837. Burnham became a road commis-

sioner for the Newcastle District in 1811 and two years later received his first of several commissions as justice of the peace. He was appointed district treasurer in 1815, a position he held until 1851. From 1817 to 1820 Burnham represented the riding of Northumberland and Durham in the House of Assembly, which was grappling with the problem of getting the province moving again after the unsettling war. His contribution was dutiful and workmanlike, resting with issues such as road improvements, the establishment of schools, and the adjustment of property assessment laws. When Burnham returned to the assembly in 1825, he found himself in a political arena that rapidly became polarized and contentious as the vexing alien question dominated the affairs of the house. American-born yet not a loyalist, he nevertheless aligned himself with the tory side, voting for the Naturalization Bill of 1827 [see Sir John Beverley Robinson*]. In 1831 he was appointed to the Legislative Council by Lieutenant Governor Sir John Colborne* and served there until 1841. In July 1839 he was made a judge of the district court for Newcastle.

Like many leading men in early Upper Canada, Burnham was involved in a variety of philanthropic and religious associations. During the 1830s and 1840s when Cobourg was one of the important immigrant entrepôts of the province, he was a leading figure in the Newcastle District Emigrant Relief Society and the Children's Friend Society. He was also active in the Newcastle committee of the Society for Promoting Christian Knowledge.

At his death in 1857 Burnham was one of the oldest residents of the district, a self-made man in a society of immigrants. During his 60 years in the province, an imposing wilderness had given way to a complex and prospering society, and he had played an important role in the process. "A powerfully built man, more than six feet high, with a fine, manly countenance, and a clear head," he exemplified for his contemporaries the human achievement of the new society, as excerpts from the funeral sermon by Archdeacon Alexander Neil Bethune* and a biographical sketch by his son-in-law Edward Ermatinger* acknowledge with ample heroic rhetoric.

Burnham left an estate still consisting principally of extensive land holdings. Because large sections had previously been ceded to his daughters it is difficult to appraise its full value; the contemporary estimate of a million dollars probably inflated his real worth. None the less Burnham had entered Upper Canada a young man without wealth; he died rich and respected. His son, Mark, attended John Strachan's Home District Grammar School, went on to Queen's College in Oxford, and was ordained an Anglican priest, serving as rector in St Thomas and later in Peterborough. Other relations populated the Newcastle District and

Burpee

were prominent in business and legal affairs throughout the remainder of the century.

PETER ENNALS

A striking portrait of Zacheus Burnham is reproduced in *Kawartha heritage: proceedings of the Kawartha conference, 1981*, ed. A. O. Cole and Jean Murray Cole (Peterborough, Ont., 1981), 56.

AO, MS 393, C-1; MU 2388; RG 1, A-II-6, 20–21; B-II, 7–17; C-I-8, 6; RG 21, Newcastle District, Hamilton Township, census and assessment rolls, 1804, 1810, 1821, 1831, 1842, 1856; RG 22, Newcastle District, Clerk of the Peace, reg. of lands sold for taxes, 1820–60; ser.7, 96–96G; ser.155, will of Zacheus Burnham; ser.187, 1–3. N.H. Hist. Soc. (Concord), Dunbarton cemetery records, 17. N.H. State Library (Concord), "Genealogy of Dunbarton, N.H., descendants, A–J," p.183 (mfm.; GS no.1003057); "Town records of Dunbarton, N.H.," 1: 184 (mfm.; GS no.15124). PAC, RG 1, E3, 26: 62, 100, 122, 151; 35: 138; L3, 85: B leaves, 1802–18/35; 222: G misc., 1794–1830/25½; RG 5, A1: 9739, 51236–38; RG 8, I (C ser.), 688A: 138; RG 31, A1, 1842, 1848, Hamilton Township. St Peter's Anglican Church (Cobourg, Ont.), Reg. of baptisms, marriages, and burials, 1817–37 (mfm. at AO).

Edward Ermatinger, *Life of Colonel Talbot, and the Talbot settlement* . . . (St Thomas, [Ont.], 1859; repr. Belleville, Ont., 1972). "Journals of Legislative Assembly of U.C.," AO *Report*, 1913. James Strachan [John Strachan], *A visit to the province of Upper Canada, in 1819* (Aberdeen, Scot., 1820; repr. Toronto, 1968), 93. "Upper Canada land book C, 11th April, 1797, to 30th June, 1797," AO *Report*, 1930: 159. "Upper Canada land book C, 29th June, 1796, to 4th July, 1796; 1st July, 1797, to 20th December, 1797," AO *Report*, 1931: 62. *Valley of the Trent* (Guillet). *Cobourg Star*, 31 May 1831; 18 April, 10 Oct. 1832; 18 Nov., 22 Dec. 1835; 8 Sept. 1841; 4 March 1857. P. M. Ennals, "Land and society in Hamilton Township, Upper Canada, 1797–1861" (PHD thesis, Univ. of Toronto, 1978). Guillet, *Lives and times of Patriots*. T. W. Poole, *A sketch of the early settlement and subsequent progress of the town of Peterborough, and of each township in the county of Peterborough* (Peterborough, 1867; repub. 1941, 1967), 140, 155, 175. D. E. Wattie, "Cobourg, 1784–1867" (2v., MA thesis, Univ. of Toronto, 1949).

BURPEE, RICHARD E., merchant, Baptist minister, and missionary; b. 1810 in York County, N.B., son of Thomas Burpee and Esther Gallop; m. Laleah Johnston, niece of James William Johnston*, and they had at least two sons; d. 26 Feb. 1853 in Jacksonville, Fla.

Of New England planter stock, Richard E. Burpee became a general merchant in Fredericton. There he was converted and baptized on 21 Nov. 1829, joining the Brunswick Street Baptist Church. Burpee quickly became a leading member of that congregation, where he was greatly influenced by the ministry of the Reverend Frederick W. Miles*, a keen advocate of foreign missions. Feeling himself called to the ministry, he was licensed to preach in 1836 or 1837. Then, on 7 Sept. 1837, he was ordained as the first minister of St George's Baptist Church (western branch).

As early as 1814 the Baptists of Nova Scotia and New Brunswick had expressed concern for "the poor heathen" in foreign lands. During the next two decades the Baptist denomination in the Maritimes grew significantly and so did interest in the oversea mission field. In June 1838 the Nova Scotia Baptist Association, "having taken into serious consideration the lamentable condition of the heathen world," asked its sister association in New Brunswick to join with it in "pledging themselves and the Churches to the adequate education and maintainance of some one suitable person as a Missionary in some foreign field." The New Brunswick association warmly endorsed the proposal, and by the following year that "one suitable person" had been found.

Richard Burpee was 29 years old when he responded to the appeal in 1839. The next year, in preparation for service overseas, he entered the newly established Queen's (after 1841 Acadia) College in Wolfville, N.S. Before graduating with a BA in 1844, he spent his summers fostering interest in the foreign missions throughout the Maritimes. By 1845 all the necessary arrangements had been made. Since the Baptists of the Maritimes did not have a mission station and could not afford one initially, it was arranged that Burpee and his wife would go as missionaries of the American Baptist Board of Foreign Missions, with Maritime Baptists committed to pay half of the expenses. After a very emotional farewell, the Burpees left Halifax on 20 April 1845, sailing to Burma via Boston.

The years in Burma, spent mostly at Mergui, among the Karens, were less successful than expected, although by 1848 Burpee had baptized his first converts. His health had begun to fail soon after his arrival and by 1849 he was forced to abandon the missionary enterprise. After his return to New Brunswick in 1850 his health continued to decline. He died three years later, probably of tuberculosis, in Florida, where he had gone for the climate.

However small his actual accomplishments in the mission field, to Maritime Baptists Burpee was the symbol of their brave new venture, the first of hundreds of such missionaries sent by that denomination. "Burpee" became a cherished, if unusual, Christian name given to generations of Baptist males. In addition, the desire to support Burpee and other Baptist mission endeavours was one of the most important factors bringing about, in 1846, the union of the New Brunswick and Nova Scotia Baptist associations to form the Baptist Convention of Nova Scotia, New Brunswick and Prince Edward Island (now the United Baptist Convention of the Atlantic Provinces).

BARRY M. MOODY

ABHC, Fredericton, Brunswick Street United Baptist Church, membership lists to 1868; minutes, 1814–44; Edward Manning, corr., vol.8; journals. *Baptist Missionary Magazine of Nova-Scotia and New-Brunswick* (Saint John and Halifax), 1 (1827–29)–3 (1833); new ser., 1 (1834)–3 (1836). N.B. Baptist Assoc., *Minutes* (Fredericton; Saint John; Fredericton), 1835–38, 1844. N.S. and N.B. Baptist Assoc., *Minutes* (Saint John), 1814. N.S. Baptist Assoc., *Minutes* (Halifax), 1838. *Christian Messenger* (Halifax), 20 Oct. 1837; 19 July, 6 Sept. 1844; 1848–50. *The Acadia record, 1838–1953*, comp. Watson Kirkconnell (4th ed., Wolfville, N.S., 1953). Bill, *Fifty years with Baptist ministers*. Eaton, *Hist. of King's County*. Levy, *Baptists of Maritime prov.* R. S. Longley, *Acadia University, 1838–1938* (Wolfville, 1939). E. M. Saunders, *History of the Baptists of the Maritime provinces* (Halifax, 1902). E. C. Wright, *The loyalists of New Brunswick* (Fredericton, 1955; repr. Moncton, N.B., 1972).

C

CALDWELL, FRANCIS XAVIER, militia officer, politician, office holder, justice of the peace, and businessman; b. 4 May 1792 in Detroit, son of William Caldwell* and Suzanne Baby, daughter of Jacques Baby*, *dit* Dupéront; m. 10 Jan. 1831 Mary Frances Réaume, widow of Francis Baby, and they had a son; d. 5 June 1851 in Malden Township, Upper Canada.

Francis Xavier Caldwell was raised in the Roman Catholic faith and educated in either Detroit or Amherstburg, Upper Canada, where his family had settled in 1782 or 1783. At the age of 20 he joined his father (a former captain in Butler's Rangers) and two brothers to serve with the British army in the War of 1812. Promoted ensign in the 1st Essex Militia on 12 July 1812, Francis participated that year in the capture of Detroit and in 1813, as an officer in a ranger corps commanded by his father, in several major battles on the western frontier: Frenchtown, Miamis River, Fort Meigs, and Fort Stephenson. Retreating from Amherstburg with Major-General Henry Procter* when the fortunes of war were reversed, the Caldwells escaped death or capture at Moraviantown in October 1813 but were then faced with the realization that they could not return home again as long as the American occupation of the western part of Upper Canada continued. The Caldwell name – associated in the decade following the American revolution with border warfare and the instigation of Indian atrocities in the Ohio country – was still so odious to Americans that the family property in Amherstburg was put to the torch and William Caldwell Sr pronounced a hunted man. Francis served as a volunteer with the British army's Right Division in late 1813 in the capture of Fort Niagara (near Youngstown), Lewiston, Black Rock (Buffalo), and Buffalo, all in New York state. The Caldwells fought together again in 1814 as volunteers in the Right Division at the battle of Longwood (near Thamesville, Ont.), after which the elder Caldwell was appointed to replace Matthew Elliott* in the Indian Department. The family was reunited later in 1814 in the fighting at Lundy's Lane and at the siege of Fort Erie.

Returning to post-war Amherstburg, Francis Caldwell engaged in farming and watched his father receive shoddy treatment from the government as the Indian Department was reduced to its peace-time level. Though elevated to captain in the Essex militia in 1819, Francis felt similarly treated when promotions for others led to a minor revolt in the regiment. With others he resigned in a huff. He was as quick to react to a supposed slight or injustice, but apparently Adjutant-General Nathaniel Coffin* was able to satisfy all concerned. The resignations were withdrawn a year later and peace was re-established.

Upon his father's death in 1822, Caldwell inherited a substantial amount of property, including water-lots on the Detroit River in front of the family homestead. To this property he added loyalist and militia grants, amassing nearly 2,500 acres of land in the Western District. He also became involved with his brothers in improving the so-called Pike Road, which ran into Amherstburg across Caldwell property, and in the late 1830s he secured the rest of the water-lots fronting his property. In 1831 he had married Mary Frances Baby, a widow with two sons, and, aided perhaps by his close association through birth and now marriage with the prestigious Baby clan, the growth in his stature continued. Appointed collector of customs for Amherstburg in 1831 and a magistrate two years later, by 1834 Caldwell was ready to enter politics.

The Upper Canadian political arena in the mid 1830s was increasingly dominated by the reform politics of William Lyon Mackenzie*, which seemed to threaten the structure of society. Responding to the call from the *Canadian Emigrant* of Sandwich

Caldwell

(Windsor) for "independent and loyal representatives of tried patriotism," Caldwell ran in 1834 for the House of Assembly in the two-seat riding of Essex, winning easily with John Alexander Wilkinson, an incumbent. The same journal accepted them as "staunch loyalists, friends of internal improvement and rational reform," qualities certain to make them "worthy of conspicuous place in Mackenzie's Black List." After reviewing their initial activities in the assembly, the *Canadian Emigrant* boasted that Caldwell and Wilkinson were "unanimous in their opposition to Mackenzie" and the reform press branded them tories.

Elected as an independent, Caldwell proved himself to be in reality a moderate tory. He opposed the secret ballot, a measure enthusiastically advocated by the reformers, but in 1839 he voted against the reactionary tory element's demand for an unequal union of the Canadas wherein Upper Canada would dominate over the lower province. Although he supported the secularization of the clergy reserves, with proceeds to go to general education, Caldwell was one of the small group which had joined Archdeacon John Strachan* in his demand in 1835 for a religious test in the appointment of staff for King's College (University of Toronto). Usually protective of the crown and its agents, Caldwell could yet be pugnacious in promoting the payment of claims for losses suffered during the War of 1812 and in arguing that land should be granted to loyalist descendants and militia claimants without the required settlement duties. Caldwell was a strong supporter of public improvements as well. Roads, lighthouses, and harbours within his constituency benefited from his diligent advocacy in parliament. His major legislative disappointment was his failure to persuade the home government to reduce the imperial duty on Canadian-grown tobacco, of which the Western District was a major producer.

In January 1838, following the outbreak of rebellion, Caldwell was commissioned to raise and command a force for frontier service, the Amherstburg Volunteers. The situation had become very tense when, as a result of the *Caroline* affair in December 1837 [see Andrew Drew*], border skirmishes with such Patriots as Edward Alexander THELLER threatened to escalate into open hostilities with the United States. Caldwell evidently attended parliament in Toronto during the most intense period of activity, but he doubted whether the Americans would attack Canada, adding characteristically, "Let them Come if they Dare." By the summer of 1838 border activity had subsided and the Amherstburg Volunteers were disbanded. Regular military units were moved into the area and, when the Patriots again threatened invasion in the fall of that year, the local militia was strengthened to defend the area. Caldwell played no part in the fighting which occurred in the orchard of François BABY in Windsor in December 1838, remaining at his parliamentary duties while the flamboyant John Prince*, who had been elected along with Caldwell for Essex in 1836, returned to lead the defence of the Western District. For the election of 1841 Essex was limited to one representative and Caldwell lost to Prince, whose unhesitating execution of five Patriot prisoners in 1838 had gained him extraordinary popularity.

It was in business that Caldwell suffered his greatest disappointment. In July 1835 he had invested heavily in village lots near the Colborne Iron Works in Gosfield (North and South Gosfield) Township, Essex County, which had been founded four years earlier by Eleakim Field* and Benjamin Parker Cahoon and probably named for Lieutenant Governor Sir John Colborne*. Caldwell may have been encouraged both by the report of a Toronto founder, Amos Horton, that Colborne iron was the best in the country and by government support for an improved southern road between the Detroit and Niagara rivers, to run through the Colborne site and be some 60 miles shorter than the traditional Thames River–Chatham route. When ground was broken in April 1838 at Sandwich for the Niagara and Detroit Rivers Rail Road, the charter of which Caldwell had fought for in the assembly, the ironworks' success seemed assured. It was not to be, however. A combination of the financial panic of 1837 [see John Henry DUNN], opposition from such railway promoters as Sir Allan Napier MacNab*, and the disruption caused by the rebellion prevented the successful development of the ironworks and the town of Colborne (Olinda). As well, Caldwell assumed liability for a portion of Cahoon's debts, expecting that the sum "would when due be fully paid."

Cahoon failed and fled to the United States in 1839 and, when the trusteeship arranged to clear his debts also failed as a result of fraud and mismanagement, Caldwell found himself liable. He was subsequently sued by the Michigan Farmers and Mechanics Bank for £500. Although he was able to meet his obligations, he never recovered from the financial loss. In 1842 he was forced to mortgage some of his extensive lands. Five years later, after his hope of profiting from the properties in Chicago of his late stepbrother, Billy*, proved fruitless, Caldwell found himself even deeper in debt, owing more than £900. A consolidation loan in 1847 from Thomas Fletcher Park, an Amherstburg merchant, allowed Caldwell to meet his several debts but he had to pledge all his land as collateral. He died in 1851 without clearing up this mortgage and much of his property consequently went over to the Park family. His son, William, managed to retain the family homestead but he soon went to sea in a vain attempt to recoup his family's fortunes. William always blamed Cahoon for the misfortune of his father, charging bitterly that before Francis became acquainted with Cahoon "he was in easy circumstances and well off."

Despite his reversal of fortune, Francis Caldwell had remained a respected member of the community, reaping the prestige of the family's fighting tradition, which continued to grow over the years. Local accounts may have exaggerated or confused some of his feats, but Caldwell had time and again risked his life for his country. In a testimonial to his services, signed by 89 of the area's most illustrious personages upon his retirement from politics in 1841, this "gallant and brave" man was honoured with the supreme compliment of his time: "always in the forefront in the field."

LARRY L. KULISEK

AO, MS 392, 20–135 (G. F. Macdonald papers) (mfm. at Hiram Walker Hist. Museum, Windsor, Ont.); MU 1771, 6: 855–56; RG 22, ser.310, reg.D: 20–22 (will of William Caldwell); ser.311, no.199 (F.-X. Caldwell). Can., Parks Canada, Fort Malden National Hist. Park (Amherstburg, Ont.), Arch. coll., Caldwell family papers; Francis Caldwell papers; H. M. Stancliff papers; Information files, Caldwell family; roads. Essex Land Registry Office (Windsor), Abstract index to deeds, Gosfield Township, concession 5, lot 22 (mfm. at AO, GS 894); Malden Township, concession 5, lots 3, 22, 26, 101 (mfm. at AO, GS 936). PAC, MG 24, B147; RG 1, L1, 35: 322, 349; L3, 114: C18/174; 117: C19/31; 120: C20/145; RG 5, A1: 60472; RG 8, I (C ser.), 84: 320; 255: 139–40; 257: 150–62; 258: 80–81, 86, 89–89a; 678: 19; 1202: 2; 1219: 61–68; RG 9, I, B1, 11, Essex folder; 42: 289–92; B2, 3–4; B5, 8; RG 68, General index, 1651–1841: 182, 482, 501.

William McCormick, A sketch of the Western District of Upper Canada, being the southern extremity of that interesting province, ed. R. A. Douglas ([Windsor], 1980). Mich. Pioneer Coll. (Lansing), 23 (1893): 42–43. John Prince, John Prince: a collection of documents, ed. and intro. R. A. Douglas (Toronto, 1980). U.C., House of Assembly, Journal, 1831–40. Canadian Emigrant, and Western District Weekly Advertiser (Sandwich [Windsor]), 19 April, 18, 25 Oct. 1834; 7, 16 Feb. 1835. Western Herald, and Farmers' Magazine (Sandwich), 31 March 1841. Commemorative biographical record of the county of Essex, Ontario, containing biographical sketches of prominent and representative citizens and many of the early settled families (Toronto, 1905), 121–22. Christian Denissen, Genealogy of the French families of the Detroit River region, 1701–1911, ed. H. F. Powell (2v., Detroit, 1976), 1: 26–27, 176; 2: 985. Officers of British forces in Canada (Irving). D. P. Botsford, "The Caldwell family of Fort Malden," Essex County Hist. Assoc., Radio sketches of periods-events-personalities from the Essex–Detroit area: transcriptions ([Windsor], 1963), broadcast of 30 July 1960. F. H. Armstrong, "The oligarchy of the Western District of Upper Canada, 1788–1841," CHA Hist. papers, 1977: 87–102. John Clarke, "The role of political position and family and economic linkage in land speculation in the Western District of Upper Canada, 1788–1815," Canadian

Geographer (Toronto), 19 (1975): 18–34. J. I. Poole, "The fight at Battle Hill," London and Middlesex Hist. Soc., Trans. ([London, Ont.]), 4 (1913): 7–61.

CALOOSÀ. See KALLIHIRUA

CAMERON, JOHN DUGALD, fur trader; b. c. 1777 in the province of Quebec; d. 30 March 1857 in Grafton, Upper Canada.

John Dugald Cameron was probably born in the loyalist town of Sorel, Quebec, where his family settled while his father fought for the British during the American revolution. Little is known of his upbringing, except that his education was minimal. In January 1794 he followed in the footsteps of his brother Ranald and entered the fur trade, signing on with David and Peter Grant, and by the following year he was a clerk for the North West Company. He served for more than a decade in the Nipigon country (Ont.), during which time he married à la façon du pays an Ojibwa woman, who was later baptized Mary. Cameron undoubtedly owed much of his fluency in Ojibwa and his outstanding skill as an "Indian Trader" to the aid and influence of his wife.

In 1813, after having managed the Lake Winnipeg department for two years, Cameron was made a partner in the NWC. He was credited with being the first person in the northwest to construct a flour-mill, located at his headquarters at Bas-de-la-Rivière (Fort Alexander, Man.). During the conflict with the Hudson's Bay Company in the Red River settlement, Cameron staunchly defended the Nor'Westers' rights. He felt that the colony established by Lord Selkirk [Douglas*] must be disbanded and he was responsible for transporting a large group of its settlers to Upper Canada in the spring of 1815. Cameron was stationed next at Sault Ste Marie (Ont.), but he also served at Île-à-la-Crosse (Sask.) before the NWC's merger with the HBC in 1821.

As an experienced and respected fur trader, Cameron became a chief factor upon the union and was placed in charge of the Columbia district until the appointment of John McLOUGHLIN in 1824. He then served at Rainy Lake (Ont.) for almost a decade, where he was noted for his ability to keep the Indians loyal in the face of increasing competition. In 1830 Cameron renamed the Rainy Lake post Fort Frances in honour of the visit of Governor George SIMPSON's young English bride, Frances Ramsay SIMPSON. From 1832 to 1834 Cameron was given his former charge at Bas-de-la-Rivière. During this time he made several trips to the Red River settlement, where on 5 June 1833 he and his Indian wife were formally married in the Anglican church. After a furlough spent in both Upper and Lower Canada in 1835, Cameron served the remainder of his career in the Southern Department, from 1836 to 1839 at Michipicoten (Michipi-

Campbell

cotin River, Ont.) and from 1839 to 1844 at Fort La Cloche. Because of ill health, he settled with his wife and daughter Margaret near Grafton in 1844, although he did not officially retire from the HBC until 1846. He invested his fortune in land as well as in growing Canadian enterprises such as the Bank of Montreal and several railway companies.

John Dugald Cameron had a distinguished fur-trade career, being widely admired by colleagues and Indians alike for his integrity, affability, and generosity. Simpson, with whom he maintained a warm correspondence, described him as "a very good well meaning steady man." Of abiding religious faith, Cameron also thirsted for knowledge and largely educated himself by reading "almost every Book that ever came within his reach." Finally, he was a devoted family man, remaining loyal to his Indian wife during a time of increasing racial prejudice and showing considerable concern for the education of his children, of whom there were at least four sons and three daughters.

SYLVIA VAN KIRK

PAC, MG 19, A21; B1, 1: 20; E1. PAM, HBCA, A.36/4; E.4/1a, 1b; D.4; D.5. *HBRS*, 2 (Rich and Fleming). Simpson, "Character book," *HBRS*, 30 (Williams), 151–236.

CAMPBELL, ALEXANDER (baptized **Alexander Colvin**), shipbuilder, businessman, militia officer, justice of the peace, judge, politician, and office holder; baptized 9 Feb. 1795 in Pictou, N.S., son of William Campbell and Margaret Henderson; m. 10 March 1825 Mary Archibald, and they had four sons and four daughters; d. 13 April 1854 in Tatamagouche, N.S.

Alexander Campbell began his career in the employ of Edward Mortimer* at Pictou. After the latter's death in 1819, Campbell continued with the company of William Mortimer, Edward's nephew, and George Smith, moving about 1823 to Tatamagouche to manage the firm's timber contracts with the mills controlled by Wellwood Waugh*. The next year Mortimer, Smith and Company began shipbuilding at Tatamagouche, with Campbell supervising construction of the 91-ton schooner *Elizabeth*. In 1826 the firm expanded in a significant new direction, with the 281-ton brig *Devon* built on speculation for sale in Britain. Although small coastal vessels had been built locally since at least 1804, this marked the beginning of an industry which was to be Tatamagouche's economic mainstay for some 50 years.

Some time after the construction of the 133-ton brig *Mary* in 1827, Campbell left Mortimer, Smith and Company to continue shipbuilding. Beginning in 1831, several vessels, with which Alexander was probably involved, were registered in the names of his brothers James and William. From 1834 ships were registered in Alexander's name and he continued to work at times with his brothers and later with his nephew John Millar. Alexander's forceful ambition apparently precluded any long-term, harmonious partnerships, but he nevertheless rapidly became the most productive local builder, and the only one successful in the risky overseas market.

Involved as he was in a purely speculative business, he none the less found himself responsible for Tatamagouche's economic continuity. After new premises were opened on the French River about 1840, the yard, which frequently employed 200 to 300 men, became Tatamagouche's dominant economic force. Although he normally did not pay salaries *per se* and inextricably controlled his employees through the company store barter system, his large work-force had no desire to return to their marginal farms in an era of agricultural recession. As well as building some 90 vessels in his lifetime, Campbell founded a sawmill, grist-mill, oat kiln, and mercantile establishment as commercial adjuncts.

Although Campbell appeared to be a successful entrepreneur, maintaining an elegant home, servants, and a high profile in the community, his financial position was never secure. His chief difficulty was insufficient capital. Financing for vessels came from prospective buyers in England, or sometimes in Halifax, Pictou, and Charlottetown, with repayment dependent upon successful sale. Hull timber and plentiful labour were available locally, but sails and hardware had to be purchased elsewhere at considerable expense. Brokerage and interest fees were high, the demand for certain types of vessels fluctuated, and the yard did not always provide a high quality product. Campbell continually courted financial disaster, but he survived, even through years which ruined other builders. Although tempted to retire on his occasional profits, he was compelled by economic responsibilities to continue.

Campbell's local prominence and ability were early recognized. In 1826 he was appointed a justice of the peace; he also served in the local militia, being commissioned captain in 1823 and second major in 1829. In 1837 he was appointed judge of the Inferior Court of Common Pleas for Colchester County, a position which he reputedly held with ability, and the following year he was nominated to the Legislative Council in Halifax. He also served as *custos rotulorum* for Colchester County from 1848, was named school commissioner for Stirling District in 1850, and was a strong supporter of the area's secession Presbyterian church. In addition, he was the local agent for the estate of Joseph Frederick Wallet DesBarres*, and used this position to accumulate gradually a portfolio of prime Tatamagouche property.

It was inevitable that his prominence and forceful character would eventually fuel local dissension. Beginning in 1840 Campbell sided against the Reverend Hugh Ross in a church dispute over doctrinal interpretation, and the conflict was continued into the Colchester County by-election the next year. Campbell strongly supported the liberal candidate, Thomas DICKSON, ensuring his victory by personally appearing at the poll. Ross, who did not attend or vote but who did support the conservative opponent, bitterly denounced "the nefarious wickedness of . . . such a polluted scene" and railed against the interference of "Baillie Bottle Nose." Ross was forced from Tatamagouche in 1842, after having been burned in effigy, an incident in which Campbell was again reputedly involved.

Although such actions undoubtedly stemmed from strong religious and political convictions, they did little to enhance Campbell's reputation. Following his sudden death in 1854, he was remembered as capable, energetic, and honest. According to author Israel Longworth, "He was a true-hearted and good man; and many a youth blesses his memory for words of encouragement and deeds of substantial kindness." Nevertheless, a young Tatamagouche resident called him "a cross old bugger," and it was conceded that few dared to challenge him, since he was domineering and intolerant of opposition. His death signalled the end of an era in Tatamagouche, for he had been regarded as the father of local shipbuilding as well as the foundation of the town's economy. The settlement of his estate was lengthy and complicated and, although his sons David and Archibald salvaged the yard and continued building into the 1880s, the decline of sail power denied them any real success.

LOIS KATHLEEN KERNAGHAN

Colchester County Court of Probate (Truro, N.S.), Estate papers, no.416 (mfm. at PANS). PANS, MG 4, James Presbyterian Church (New Glasgow, N.S.), reg. of baptisms, 9 Feb. 1795 (mfm.); RG 1, 174: 126; 175: 49, 66–70, 362; 176: 11; 214½F: 189; RG 22, 26: 299, 354. Univ. of King's College Library (Halifax), Israel Longworth, "A history of the county of Colchester" (MS, 2 pts., Truro, 1866–78; typescript at PANS), pt.1. *Presbyterian Witness, and Evangelical Advocate* (Halifax), 7 (1854): 63. *Mechanic and Farmer* (Pictou, N.S.), 17 Feb. 1841. *Observer* (Pictou), 22 March, 12, 19 April, 3, 17 May, 7 June 1842. F. H. Patterson, *The days of the ships, Tatamagouche, N.S.* (Truro, 1970); *A history of Tatamagouche, Nova Scotia* (Halifax, 1917; repr. Belleville, Ont., 1973); *Tatamagouche, N.S., 1771–1824* (Truro, 1971).

CAMPBELL, JOHN SAXTON, businessman, justice of the peace, and seigneur; b. *c.* 1787, son of Archibald Campbell, a merchant, and Charlotte Saxton; m. first 11 March 1817 Jane Hamilton in London; m. secondly Mary Carne Vivian; d. 25 April 1855 in Penzance, England.

John Saxton Campbell was apparently not born at Quebec, for his birth is not recorded in the parish registers of the town. But since his younger brother Archibald* is listed there as born in 1790, he was probably at Quebec from the age of two or three. Campbell came from a well-to-do family. His father, a loyalist who had immigrated to the province of Quebec after the American revolution, prospered in the timber trade. In light of the attractive prospects at that time for the export of Canadian forest products from Quebec to England, Campbell decided in 1811 to assume the management of his father's business. By 1808 he was active in business and had become an inspector of staves at the port of Quebec.

Around 1815 Campbell went into partnership with his brother-in-law William Sheppard* to trade in timber. They first set themselves up at Wolfe's Cove (Anse au Foulon), and then bought Anse Woodfield from Mathew Bell* in 1816, a short distance upstream from Quebec. There they received the timber which was then loaded on ships bound for Great Britain. For unknown reasons the partnership was dissolved in 1823. In 1824 and 1825 Campbell worked for John Caldwell* as agent in charge of his sawmills near Chutes Etchemin at Saint-Nicolas, on the south shore of the St Lawrence.

At the beginning of 1825 Campbell transferred his base to Anse des Mères, closer to the town; there, as well as fitting out wharfs for loading ships, he built a steam-driven sawmill and a shipyard. Since 1816 he had been investing in the purchase and construction of ships, and had already registered two ships, two brigs, and a barque at the port of Quebec. His involvement in this activity expanded considerably between 1825 and 1835, when he registered 24 vessels: 14 brigs, 9 sea-going ships, and a two-master. Several of them had been built by George BLACK, but the exact nature of the business relationship between Campbell and Black is not known. It seems that Campbell financed the building of ships and placed his shipyard at the disposal of Black and other shipbuilders. His vessels were sometimes sold to local merchants, but more often he dispatched them to England with a cargo of timber. In these same years Campbell had connections with several merchants in Upper and Lower Canada who routed to his cove large quantities of white and red pine, either squared or sawn. The measuring and grading that determined the price of timber often gave rise to disputes between buyers and sellers. Campbell was closely concerned with this problem, and from 1823 to 1837 served on a board of examiners set up to ensure that candidates were accepted as cullers impartially.

In 1831 Campbell was one of the original shareholders of the Quebec and Halifax Steam

Carey

Navigation Company [see Sir Samuel Cunard*]. It was at his shipyard that the company built the *Royal William*. Once again the work of George Black, this 618-ton steamer was equipped with a 200-horsepower engine installed by the Bennet and Henderson Ironworks of Montreal. Its launching on 27 April 1831 "was so important that a public holiday had been proclaimed. The governor general [Whitworth-Aylmer*] and Lady Aylmer presided at the ceremonies, and the participants included a guard of honour and the band of the 32nd Foot." From the top of Cap Diamant, which jutted out over the shipyard, the painter James Pattison Cockburn* recorded the event in a fine water-colour.

At that time Campbell was one of the important figures in the town. From 1826 to 1828 he had served as an adviser to the Quebec Committee of Trade [see John Jones*]. Like other prosperous merchants, he was interested in the field of banking. Elected a director of the Quebec Bank in 1828, he remained in this office until 1831. He also sat on the board of directors of the Quebec Savings Bank in 1829 and 1830 and from 1835 to 1841. On 14 Oct. 1830 he had received a commission as justice of the peace which was renewed three years later. Campbell lived on a vast estate on the Grande Allée, just opposite that of the well-known timber merchant William Price*. In his spare time he took an interest in literature; moreover, he was listed as one the founders of the Literary and Historical Society of Quebec in the royal charter incorporating it in 1831.

From 1835 Campbell progressively relinquished his business ventures at Quebec. On 19 January he acquired by auction the seigneury of Îlet-du-Portage at Saint-André, which he shrewdly sensed had potential value for timber, water-power, and harbour facilities. He built a magnificent manor-house there, a number of other buildings around it, a sawmill, and a great wharf a quarter of a mile long, with an extended 200-foot pier to allow large vessels to dock. In order to make these investments, he put up for sale some 20 properties in various townships of Upper and Lower Canada. In January 1837 he also divested himself of the holdings he had acquired at Anse du Cap around 1829; the majority of them were bought by George Black for £5,437. Campbell maintained business relations with Black, according to a document dated 1838 which mentions the existence of a company called Campbell and Black. In 1840 they were joint owners of a ship. Apparently at the behest of his second wife, John Saxton Campbell decided around 1842 to leave the colony and go to England. He settled at Penzance, and continued to purchase ships built in North America.

The varied and changing nature of Campbell's undertakings well illustrates the kind of economic activity characteristic of the timber merchants in 19th-century Lower Canada.

PIERRE POULIN

ANQ-Q, CE1-61, 1er août 1790, 19 avril 1809; CN1-49, 2 juill. 1824; 5 mars, 28 juill., 4 déc. 1825; 20 juin 1826; 22 déc. 1827; 1er août, 11 oct., 5 nov. 1829; 13 janv., 10 juill. 1830; 21 juin 1831; 11 juin, 24 nov. 1832; 18 sept., 12 oct. 1833; 3, 22 avril, 24 juin, 15 juill. 1834; 17 janv., 18 mars, 4 juin 1835; 16 janv., 12 avril, 17 juin, 14 déc. 1836; 3 févr., 26 oct., 9 nov. 1838; 23 mai, 22 juill. 1840; CN1-67, 14 mars, 25 avril 1840; CN1-116, 24 janv. 1837, 23 oct. 1840; CN1-212, 20 août 1832; CN1-230, 27 nov. 1815, 21 sept. 1816. *Morning Chronicle* (Quebec), 15 May 1855, 18 July 1862. *Quebec Gazette*, 19 May 1808; 5 July 1810; 2 May 1811; 20 Feb., 12 May 1823. E. H. Dahl *et al.*, *La ville de Québec, 1800–1850: un inventaire de cartes et plans* (Ottawa, 1975), 125, 159, 212. *Quebec almanac*, 1828–41. *Quebec directory*, 1822; 1826. Christina Cameron et Jean Trudel, *Québec au temps de James Patterson Cockburn* (Québec, 1976), 33, 38–39. J. M. LeMoine, *Monographies et esquisses* (Québec, 1885), 276. Rosa, *La construction des navires à Québec*. J.-E. Roy, *Hist. de Lauzon*, 5: 144. Georges Desjardins, "Un chantier naval à la Pointe-Sèche de Kamouraska," SGCF *Mémoires*, 21 (1970): 215.

CAREY, JOHN, farmer, newspaperman, brewer, and printer; b. 1780 in County Westmeath (Republic of Ireland); m. *c.* 1806 Margaret ——, and they had at least two sons and six daughters; d. 28 Dec. 1851 in Springfield on the Credit (Erindale), Upper Canada.

Little is known of John Carey's early life. He himself once claimed that he was bred as a lawyer. On the recommendation of Samuel Whitbread, a member of the House of Commons, he was appointed a clerk in the commissariat in 1813, serving in British North America, England, and the West Indies. Although he returned to England after the general reduction in 1816, he soon immigrated to New York City, where he became a tobacconist and his family conducted a school. In 1818 he came to Upper Canada with a letter of introduction from Colonial Secretary Lord Bathurst, deeds for 500 acres in the Perth military settlement that he had bought from an army officer in New York, and a quantity of tobacco seed. His family arrived the following year, when the yellow fever epidemic in New York broke up their school.

Carey soon discovered that the land near Perth had been forfeited by his army acquaintance, but he was granted 300 acres as a military claimant, got another 300 on the direction of Lord Bathurst, and was eventually given land in lieu of the properties he had bought in New York. He was unsuccessful, however, in getting the locations he wished. His intention of cultivating tobacco was given up, although he may have maintained some interest in the business: in 1826 Francis Collins* recommended that he "stick to Cigar making," and three years later George Gurnett* referred to his "profitable trade in smuggling segars."

After spending some time farming near Kingston and then on the Sixteen Mile (Oakville) Creek in Trafalgar Township, Carey moved to York (Toronto) in 1820 and reported the House of Assembly debates for the *Upper Canada Gazette*. He acquired the press and types of the *Upper Canada Phoenix*, formerly published in Dundas, and on 22 May 1820 he founded the *Observer*, the first newspaper in York that was not an official organ of government. Although Gurnett claimed in 1829 that the *Observer*'s publisher worked his press and delivered his newspapers himself, Carey was employing at least three printers in 1826. Much of his income came from job printing, especially for the government. William Lyon Mackenzie*, Collins, and Carey constantly quarrelled over the division of this work and its payment. Carey's most ambitious printing job was Thomas Taylor's *Reports of cases . . . in the Court of King's Bench* (York, 1828), which contains almost 800 pages.

Carey published the *Observer* until 1831. In May 1832 he began to edit a new paper, the *Sapper and Miner*, published by G. W. Thompson, but his interest in farming was again aroused when he was finally granted the land he wanted on the Credit River at Dundas Street. The *Sapper and Miner* ceased publication before the end of the year, and Carey moved to Springfield on the Credit where he had a farm and a small brewery which burned down in 1835. Here he lived for the rest of his life, except for about a year in 1840–41, when he returned to publish another newspaper, the *Globe*, beginning on 28 March 1840.

Although Carey published weekly newspapers for almost 13 years, few issues have survived, and so it is necessary to depend on other sources for information about them. Henry Scadding* described the *Observer* as "a folio of rustic, unkempt aspect, the paper and typography and matter being all somewhat inferior." In July 1820 Governor Lord Dalhousie [Ramsay*] called Carey "a scurrilous scribbler" who was "unworthy of notice"; 20 years later the lieutenant governor of Upper Canada, Sir George ARTHUR, called him "a vagabond . . . who richly deserves to be punished." The surviving issues of his papers are innocuous, but his journalism was probably characterized by the personal vituperation usual in the period. He himself was viciously attacked by Charles Fothergill* in the *Upper Canada Gazette* during much of 1822 and by Gurnett in the *Gore Gazette* in 1829. Both called him the "Prince of Liars," as did Samuel Peters JARVIS, and accused him specifically of fabricating speeches in his reports of assembly debates.

Many of Carey's political views were similar to those of Mackenzie and Collins. He was against union with Lower Canada in 1822 and 1841 [*see* John Beverley Robinson*] and supported Barnabas* and Marshall Spring* Bidwell on the alien question, Collins in his libel case, and Judge John Walpole Willis* in his dispute with the executive. He was a member of Robert BALDWIN's committee in a by-election of 1829; he voted for Baldwin in 1830 and for Mackenzie in 1836. Although he took no part in the rebellion of 1837–38, he assisted in the legal defence of those taken prisoner and in the preparation of their petitions. He was a faithful prison visitor of the rebels, as he had been with Collins ten years earlier, and even went to see Mackenzie in prison in Rochester, N.Y. He vehemently opposed what he considered the corrupt principles and dictatorial methods of Governor Lord Sydenham [Thomson*]; he also attacked those who cooperated with him, calling Robert Baldwin "a trimmer of the very worst description."

Like Mackenzie and Collins, Carey was keenly interested in the commercial development of the province and wrote long letters proposing improvements in agriculture, milling, commercial relations with Lower Canada, roads, railways, and canals. His pamphlet *Observations on the state of the colony* (1821) contains many such suggestions. It also demonstrates the typical inconsistency of his thought and the illogicality of his arguments. More important, it shows the two themes that remained constant throughout his life.

His main criticism in the *Observations* was directed at the land granting system, which he thought misleading, dilatory, and expensive, and thus a source of great hardship for the poor immigrant. His concern for the poor and the sick was very real. Many of his schemes for their welfare were obviously too costly for the state of the colony, but most of them were eventually implemented. He had a deep compassion for all the unfortunate in Upper Canada; in a sectarian age he ignored denominational distinctions. He himself was a Roman Catholic for most of his life, but he died an Anglican.

Unlike Mackenzie and Collins, he rarely attacked the lieutenant governor or governor (except for Sydenham), or their senior advisers. To Carey, the enemy was the lower echelon of government – the magistrates, militia officers, sheriffs, postmasters, and so on – whose "ignorance and insolence" he found intolerable. His longest and most vitriolic feud was with the Magrath family on the Credit, who represented everything he most disliked in Upper Canada. In this regard Carey differed from Mackenzie and Collins, who were more concerned with the iniquities of the central government and the Colonial Office.

All three journalists were erratic, but Carey

Carmichael

exceeded the others in eccentricity. He probably had less influence than the others, but in his concern for the poor and his aversion to the petty local tyrant, he represented the views of many of the people of Upper Canada.

EDITH G. FIRTH

[Patricia Lockhart Fleming, in the course of her research for a forthcoming bibliography of Upper Canadian imprints, discovered the only known copy of John Carey's *Observations on the state of the colony* (York [Toronto], 1821) among a large collection of uncatalogued pamphlets in a turret at the Library of Parliament (Ottawa). E.G.F.]

AO, MS 78; MS 516; RG 1, A-I; A-II. MTL, Robert Baldwin papers; W. W. Baldwin papers; York, U.C., minutes of town meetings and lists of inhabitants, 1797–1822. PAC, RG 1, L3; RG 5, A1; RG 31, A1, 1851. PRO, CO 42. St Peter's (Anglican) Church (Erindale, Ont.), Reg. of burials, 1851–73 (mfm. at AO, MS 360). *Arthur papers* (Sanderson), vol.3. Can., Prov. of, Legislative Assembly, *Journals*, 1841–51. J. K. Dean, *The sayings and doings of the self-styled royal family, the Magraths of Mackenzie's Castle, Springfield* (Toronto, 1844). *Town of York, 1815–34* (Firth). U.C., House of Assembly, *Journal*, 1825–40; Legislative Council, *Journal*, 1828–40. *Canadian Freeman* (York; Toronto), 1825–34. *Colonial Advocate*, 1824–34. *Examiner* (Toronto), 7 Jan. 1852. *Globe* (Toronto), 1840–41 [this newspaper is not related to the paper begun on 5 March 1844 by George Brown*]. *Gore Gazette, and Ancaster, Hamilton, Dundas and Flamborough Advertiser* (Ancaster, [Ont.]), 14 Feb. 1829. *Observer* (York), 1820–31. *Sapper and Miner* (York), 1832. *Upper Canada Gazette*, 1820–41. *Dict. of Toronto printers* (Hulse). *Early Toronto newspapers* (Firth). Patricia [Lockhart] Fleming, *A bibliography of Upper Canada imprints, 1801–1841* (forthcoming) [research notes and work in progress consulted]. Charles Durand, *Reminiscences of Charles Durand of Toronto, barrister* (Toronto, 1897), 126. Scadding, *Toronto of old* (1873), 269–70.

CARMICHAEL, JAMES, militia officer, businessman, justice of the peace, and office holder; b. 29 Jan. 1788 in Fishers Grant (Pictou Landing), N.S., eldest son of James Carmichael and Ann ——; m. January 1812 Christian McKenzie, and they had eight children; d. 1 June 1860 in New Glasgow, N.S.

James Carmichael's father was born in Aberdeen, Scotland, and came to North America in 1778. In all probability he was the Sergeant James Carmichael of the 82nd Foot who received a 200-acre grant at Merigomish, N.S., in 1785. It is unlikely that James Carmichael, subject of this biography, received much formal education, given the general lack of teachers and schools in the recently settled Pictou region. As a young man he was subject to militia duty and by 1807 he was a lieutenant in the Pictou Regiment. That year, following the Chesapeake affair [see Sir George Cranfield Berkeley*], the British government decided

to call out the militia in its North American colonies, and Carmichael took a small detachment to Halifax where he remained until the early spring of 1808 working on the fortifications. By the 1820s he had become a major, and when the Pictou Regiment was divided in January 1828 he was appointed lieutenant-colonel of the second battalion, a post he retained until his retirement about 1846.

Carmichael's advances in the militia reflect his rise in community status, which took place slowly and with some effort. He had begun a business career in 1809 and two years later he and George Argo purchased from Alexander McKay an acre lot on the East River, at the future site of New Glasgow. The two men built a store there and began to trade in ton timber for the British market. Before the year was finished fire had destroyed both the store and the stock, but Carmichael re-established the business on his own. Although he had selected a good site, the fall of timber prices following the close of the Napoleonic Wars and the uncertainties of British tariffs on timber were serious blows. He survived, however, and continued to develop his local business, chiefly with hardware and general supplies imported from Liverpool and Aberdeen. He was assisted in 1827 when the General Mining Association began to develop large-scale coal mining at the nearby Albion Mines (Stellarton). The community of New Glasgow expanded until by 1837 it had some 750 residents.

As his business developed, Carmichael was able to build his own schooners for local trade. His first venture, in conjunction with his brother-in-law George Rogers McKenzie*, was the 14-ton schooner *James William*, constructed in 1821. The following year Carmichael, with brother-in-law John McKenzie and John Johnston, built the *Perseverance*. This 77-ton brigantine was intended for the West Indies trade but was lost on its maiden voyage. The loss, particularly severe because the Halifax agent had pocketed the money intended for insurance, apparently slowed down Carmichael's expansion since it was not until 1828 that he and John McKenzie built the 139-ton brig *Two Sisters*. This vessel was sold quickly, but at the same time Carmichael began to develop a regular coasting trade with the 45-ton schooner *Mary Ann*, also built in 1828. By 1832 this vessel regularly carried oxen and agricultural products to the Richibucto and Miramichi regions in New Brunswick and brought back to Pictou timber and salt for the fishing industry. The salt was probably obtained from the Jersey merchants who brought it as ballast in the ships with which they controlled the fishing trade in the Gulf of St Lawrence. The merchants represented in these partnerships of the 1820s and others with whom Carmichael had dealings such as James MacGregor, his future son-in-law, and

Thomas Graham, a large New Glasgow shipbuilder, constituted a significant network of relationships for the area.

Throughout the 1830s Carmichael apparently concentrated on trade but in 1840 he began once more to engage in shipbuilding. In addition to such schooners as the *Alert* (53 tons), *Gem* (73 tons), and *Georgina* (107 tons), he built the barques *Hyndeford* (510 tons) and *John Geddie* (391 tons) as well as the ship *Janet Kidston* (889 tons). One of the last ships he constructed was the barque *Lulan* (472 tons), again with his brother-in-law George McKenzie.

An intriguing glimpse into Carmichael's code of business ethics is provided by events surrounding a trip he made in the *Lulan* of which he and McKenzie were co-owners. The ship arrived in Glasgow in August 1848 and was due to return to Pictou. McKenzie, the captain of the ship, contracted with a proprietor's agent to transport 127 impoverished Gaelic-speaking immigrants to Pictou for £3 10s. 0d. each; they wanted ultimately to go to Cape Breton Island and Prince Edward Island. Although the trip was relatively brief, three passengers died of smallpox and when the vessel arrived in Pictou it was placed in quarantine. Carmichael and some members of his family were passengers. Soon impatient to take on contracted cargo, he had temporary wooden sheds built on the beach outside Pictou Harbour to house the settlers. There they remained, ill fed and poorly housed, and without means to move on, until they were finally taken to their original destinations in early December at public expense. Carmichael, who had been forced to pay the costs incurred in the care of the immigrants, petitioned the legislature for compensation for erecting the wooden sheds. In rejecting his request, a committee, which included Thomas Killam*, condemned the callousness and deceit shown by Carmichael, who had a reputation for compassion where his own family and community were concerned.

Apart from his interest in the militia and his business affairs, Carmichael took an interest in education which at the time was at the heart of a number of religious and political quarrels. He was appointed school commissioner for the district of Pictou on 28 May 1828 and retained the post for two or three years. He was a supporter of the Pictou Academy and he sent his sons to be educated there. He did not, however, take any active role in the management of the institution until 1841, by which time it had been remodelled into a high school. This participation apparently ended in 1845, the year when new provincial legislation removed any denominational test in the school. Carmichael does not seem to have taken any role in this particular controversy over the academy. He resumed his formal tie with the school

system in 1851 when he was appointed a commissioner for schools for the south district of Pictou County. Carmichael's involvement in educational issues indicates that although he was not a leader he was prepared to meet the responsibilities incumbent on the "respectable" element of society. Thus in the 1820s he became a justice of the peace and in 1834, after helping to obtain an act establishing a commission of streets for New Glasgow, he served as a commissioner for some years.

Early in his life Carmichael joined the congregation of James Drummond MacGregor* which worshipped in James Church. As a member, and then an elder of this church, Carmichael was obviously allied with the anti-burgher Presbyterian faction, which was deeply involved in politics in the early part of the century. Although he was not particularly active in politics, his strong connection with the church may have led him to help organize the anti-burgher forces in the infamous "Brandy Election" of 1830 which was marked by open conflict [see Enos Collins*]. As a supporter of the Presbyterian Church of Nova Scotia and a trustee of James Church, Carmichael took seriously the mandate to help spread the Gospel and in 1834 he helped establish, and became the first president of, the Lower Settlement East River Evangelical Society, intended to promote missionary activities in the Maritimes as well as to extend the influence of the Presbyterian Church "to Heathen, Mahomedan and Anti-Christian Countries." The next year he promoted a petition requesting that regulations concerning the issue of licences to sell liquor be tightened. As a merchant Carmichael might well have been more in favour of temperance than of total abstinence, a cause very strong in New Glasgow at the time.

By 1837 Carmichael, as treasurer of James Church, was involved in attempts to place its finances on a more regular basis. These efforts contributed to a dispute within the congregation, which also arose because some members disliked changes introduced by the new minister, the Reverend David Roy. The controversy was instigated, in large part, by James MacGregor, a son of the Reverend James MacGregor and a son-in-law and occasional business associate of Carmichael. The dissension was obviously a severe test of Carmichael's loyalties. In 1845 he was one of the 18 members who officially broke away. This group, in recognition of their insistence on basic religious practices, named their new church the Primitive Church; it remained within the Synod of the Presbyterian Church of Nova Scotia. Carmichael's involvement in church affairs increased, particularly as his sons, John Robert and James William, assumed a greater role in the family business. By March 1854 it was operating under the name of J. W. Carmichael and Company. The firm continued to construct ships,

Caron

maintain ownership in several vessels in whole or in part, export lumber, and act as an importer. The two Carmichaels also became involved in developing an iron industry through the Acadia Foundry Company. James Carmichael's active career ended in 1857 when he was thrown from his wagon. He subsequently suffered a painful illness until his death on 1 June 1860.

Carmichael died a man of moderate wealth, leaving about £7,000 in cash as well as real property of a somewhat arbitrarily assessed value of £2,000. He had established a business that was ably continued by his sons and, more significant, he played a steady, if inconspicuous, role in the development of New Glasgow. It was therefore quite appropriate that he had the largest funeral in the neighbourhood for some years and that all places of business in the New Glasgow area were closed.

KENNETH GEORGE PRYKE

PAC, RG 8, I (C ser.), 1321–22, 1324, 1335–36; RG 42, ser.I, 294–96. PANS, MG 2, 1250, no.12 (J. H. Sinclair, "Alexander Fraser and his dissatisfaction with David Roy, D.D., and the organization of the Primitive Church of New Glasgow, 1845"); MG 4, James Presbyterian Church (New Glasgow, N.S.), reg. of baptisms, marriages, and burials (mfm.); RG 1, 446, 448–50. Pictou County Court of Probate (Pictou, N.S.), Will of James Carmichael (mfm. at PANS). PRO, CO 218/24, 218/28 (mfm. at PAC). *Christian Instructor, and Missionary Reg. of the Presbyterian Church of Nova Scotia* (Pictou), 5 (1860): 223–24. T. C. Haliburton, *An historical and statistical account of Nova-Scotia* (2v., Halifax, 1829; repr. Belleville, Ont., 1973). *Colonial Patriot* (Pictou), 1827–34. J. M. Cameron, *The churches of New Glasgow, Nova Scotia* (n.p., [1961]); *More about New Glasgow* (n.p., 1974); *The Pictonian colliers* (Halifax, 1974); *Ships and seamen of New Glasgow, Nova Scotia* (New Glasgow, 1959). J. P. MacPhie, *Pictonians at home and abroad: sketches of professional men and women of Pictou County; its history and institutions* (Boston, 1914). *One hundred and fifty years in the life of the First Presbyterian Church (1786–1936), New Glasgow, Nova Scotia . . .*, ed. J. M. Cameron and G. D. Macdougall (Toronto, 1937). George Patterson, *A history of the county of Pictou, Nova Scotia* (Montreal, 1877). *Proceedings at the centennial celebration of James Church Congregation, New Glasgow, September 17th, 1886 . . .* (New Glasgow, 1886). J. H. Sinclair, *Life of James William Carmichael and some tales of the sea* (Halifax, n.d.). H. B. Jefferson, "Mount Rundell, Stellarton, and the Albion Railway of 1839," N.S. Hist. Soc., *Coll.*, 34 (1963): 79–120.

CARON, CHARLES (oddly enough he signed **Charle Caront**), farmer and politician; b. 3 Jan. 1768 in Saint-Roch-des-Aulnaies, Que., son of Michel Caron and Marie-Josephte Parent; d. 30 Jan. 1853 in Yamachiche, Lower Canada.

Charles Caron was still a youth when his father went to the seigneurial manor-house at Yamachiche to request 800 acres of land from Elizabeth Wilkinson, who would later be the usufructuary heiress of Conrad Gugy*, seigneur of Grandpré, Grosbois-Ouest, and Dumontier. The transaction was completed on 21 July 1783 for £22,000; Michel Caron paid this sum in less than four years, making the final instalment on 19 Feb. 1787. The lots he obtained were in the parish of Sainte-Anne, at Yamachiche, to the west of Des Vide-Poche concession, in what would soon be the village of the Carons. Here Charles Caron settled, as did eight of his brothers, and he devoted the early years of his life to clearing and developing the family estate.

Not much is known, however, of Caron's activity as a farmer, except that when he married Marie-Françoise Rivard at Yamachiche on 24 Feb. 1794 he owned 100 acres. In the 1831 census he declared that he owned about 232 acres which he apparently worked with his son Barthélemy, who held 43 acres near by. Together they produced 426 *minots* of wheat and 600 of oats, and raised 22 cattle, 49 sheep, 18 pigs, and 5 horses; they were among the largest producers in the county. Some 10 or 15 years later Caron gave up farming and handed over his operations to Barthélemy and to François Ferron, the son of a neighbour.

Like several members of his family, Caron allowed himself to be tempted into politics. For him, however, the venture came late and was short-lived. No doubt spurred by the example of his father-in-law, Augustin Rivard (Rivard-Dufresne), who in 1792 became one of the first two representatives of Saint-Maurice in the House of Assembly, as well as by that of his two brothers, Michel* and François, members for the same constituency from 1804 to 1814 and from 1810 to 1814 respectively, he decided at age 56 to stand as a candidate. He was successful in the general elections held in the summer of 1824, running with Pierre Bureau*, a merchant from Trois-Rivières, but was defeated in the October 1830 elections by notary Valère Guillet of Trois-Rivières. As a member of the assembly, Caron had experienced one of the worst political crises of the time, connected with the abuses of the administration of Lord Dalhousie [Ramsay*]. His stance during the rebellion of 1837–38 in Lower Canada is not known; perhaps he confined himself to attending the county meeting held on 26 July 1837 under the chairmanship of his brother François. Whatever the case, he apparently retired from all political activity that year.

In addition to Barthélemy, Caron and his wife had seven children. Charles-François (1795–1862) was ordained priest in 1822 and later became chaplain to the Ursulines of Trois-Rivières; Marie-Françoise (1810–88) joined that order in 1833 and was twice elected superior general; Victoire married André

Gérin-Lajoie, and their son Charles Gérin-Lajoie became a member of parliament at Quebec from 1863 to 1867 and then at Ottawa from 1874 to 1878.

Charles Caron had received some training in music at the school run by Charles Ecuier*, the parish priest of Sainte-Anne in Yamachiche from 1802 to 1820, and for nearly 50 years he belonged to the "Chantres de Machiche." Beloved and widely respected, he died on 30 Jan. 1853 after suffering briefly. He was interred four days later in the parish church, and was the subject of a long and moving obituary in *La Minerve*.

SERGE COURVILLE

ANQ-MBF, CE1-52, 24 févr. 1794, 3 févr. 1853; CN1-60, 21 juill. 1783, 14 févr. 1794. AP, Saint-Roch-des-Aulnaies, Reg. des baptêmes, mariages et sépultures, 4 janv. 1768. *La Minerve*, 8 févr. 1853. F.-J. Audet, *Les députés de Saint-Maurice (1808–1838) et de Champlain (1830–1838)* (Trois-Rivières, Qué., 1934). Raphaël Bellemare, *Les bases de l'histoire d'Yamachiche, 1703–1903* . . . (Montréal, 1901). F.-L. Desaulniers, *Les vieilles familles d'Yamachiche* (4v., Montréal, 1898–1908).

CARRIER, MICHEL, Roman Catholic priest; b. 27 Aug. 1805 at Quebec, son of Michel Carrier and Catherine Bleau; d. 15 Jan. 1859 in Baie-du-Febvre (Baieville), Lower Canada.

The son of a tanner of the *faubourg* Saint-Roch at Quebec, Michel Carrier, having "fallen on hard times," was taken under the wing of Joseph Signay*, then the parish priest of Quebec. After classical studies at the Petit Séminaire de Québec from 1814 to 1824, Carrier passed through the various stages leading to the priesthood. Ordained priest on 1 March 1828, he was immediately appointed curate of the parish of Notre-Dame at Quebec, and he served there for four years. In 1832 a cholera epidemic raged in the city, and Carrier was assigned to help the victims. To carry out his mission, he had to accept an irksome quarantine; he went out only to visit the sick and he even had to receive his food through a wicket. Although not stricken with the disease himself, he emerged from this ordeal almost bald, and worn down by an extreme weariness that left permanent after-effects: from then on the smallest inconveniences became major dramas.

To reward Carrier for his devotion, in the autumn of 1832 Bishop Bernard-Claude Panet* of Quebec entrusted him with the important parish of Saint-Édouard at Bécancour. From the time he arrived the new incumbent attracted attention by the great eloquence of his sermons. While remaining priest of Saint-Édouard, he accompanied Signay, now bishop of Quebec, as a preacher on his episcopal visit in 1835 and 1836.

This parish served as a stepping-stone for Carrier, for on 8 Oct. 1836 he was appointed priest of the parish of Saint-Antoine-de-Padoue at Baie-du-Febvre to replace Charles-Vincent Fournier*. Knowing his reputation for eloquence, the parishioners were delighted to have him come. But by March 1837 Carrier was confronted with his first difficulty. When the annual accounts were done it was discovered that money had been stolen from the safe of the *fabrique*. An extremely sensitive man, Carrier found himself in charge of a parish that had been robbed of 12,000 *livres*, at a time when the church and the presbytery required enlargement and repairs. Bishop Signay, who knew the priest's timorous nature, offered him a steady stream of advice and encouragement.

From 1845 Carrier had to wrestle with problems arising from the financing of schools. Despite the fact that legislation in 1841 provided for schools to be financed directly from public funds [*see* Jean-Baptiste Meilleur*], some of the churchwardens put pressure on the *fabrique* to support the local schools. Carrier was opposed because the presbytery and attached buildings were in a dilapidated state and the work carried out on the church since 1839 had not yet been paid for. He was so upset by the situation that he became seriously ill, and in 1847 had to take a rest at the Hôtel-Dieu at Quebec. The vicar general, Thomas Cooke*, made his concern known to Bishop Signay in January, noting that Carrier "needs to be cheered up. Solitude is bad for him."

In addition to his parish duties at Baie-du-Febvre, Carrier, who became archpriest in 1849, played a role in the settlement of the Bois-Francs region and the Eastern Townships. He was associated with the founding of the parishes of Saint-Louis in Saint-Louis-de-Blandford, Saint-Félix in Saint-Félix-de-Kingsey, Saint-Pierre in L'Avenir, Saint-Germain-de-Grantham and Saint-Bonaventure-d'Upton in Saint-Bonaventure, Saint-Jean in Wickham, and Saint-André in Acton-Vale. Cooke, who became bishop of Trois-Rivières in 1852, charged him with the most delicate tasks, even in matters concerning the appointment of parish priests, and instructed him to check the validity of requests for the creation of new parishes. Imbued with the spirit of social justice, Carrier discharged these duties most conscientiously, but he always needed support and encouragement from his bishop. Thus, when the question of dividing the parish of Saint-Guillaume-d'Upton in Saint-Guillaume arose in 1856, he asked Cooke for advice, since the division threatened to split fine properties; freed from the responsibility of making a decision, he wrote to Cooke, "Thank you for relieving me of the painful burden that weighed upon my shoulders."

Despite his morbid propensity to worry, Carrier continued to be renowned for his eloquence. For more than ten years he was the official preacher on Signay's episcopal visits. He excelled in the form of preaching popular at the time called the *conférence*, a theological discussion between two priests, one, usually Carrier, playing from the chancel the part of sinner or devil's advocate, the other, from the pulpit, being God's advocate. He put his eloquence to particular use during the rebellion of 1837–38 in order to restore calm amid the tension and excitement. He led an energetic preaching campaign against the Patriotes of the Nicolet region.

Michel Carrier's last years were trying; the slightest setbacks took on the proportions of insoluble problems. A succession of anxious letters were sent to the bishop's palace in Trois-Rivières. Overwhelmed, Carrier felt he no longer had the strength to run his parish. In December 1858 he told Cooke, "You do not know the state I am in; if you did, you would not abandon me . . . I am quite beside myself. I have reached the point where I can apply myself neither to the affairs of my ministry nor to my own affairs. I can hold out no longer." He did not hold out for long, since he died on 15 Jan. 1859. He left part of his estate to his family, in particular to his father who lived with him, and made a donation of "a sum of five hundred *livres*, one-half to the diocese and the other half to the Séminaire de Nicolet." He was buried on 19 January by the bishop of Trois-Rivières in the chancel of the church at Baie-du-Febvre. Many of his parishioners regarded him as a saint, and provided themselves with relics in commemoration of him. An energetic man even though his health had been undermined by his dedication during the the cholera epidemic at Quebec, Carrier can rightly be considered one of the architects of Yamaska County.

MICHEL MORIN

AAQ, 12 A, C: f.58v; 1 CB, XII: 27. ANQ-M, CE3-2, 19 janv. 1859. ANQ-Q, CE1-1, 27 août 1805. Arch. de l'évêché de Nicolet (Nicolet, Qué.), Cartable Baie-du-Febvre, 15 janv. 1849. Arch. de l'évêché de Trois-Rivières (Trois-Rivières, Qué.), Boîte Carrier–Cooke, corr., 5 janv., 19 oct. 1856. ASN, AO, Séminaire, IV, 26 févr. 1855; AP-G, L.-É. Bois, G, 8: 175. "Les dénombrements de Québec" (Plessis), ANQ *Rapport*, 1948–49: 194. Allaire, *Dictionnaire*, 1: 100. Caron, "Inv. de la corr. de Mgr Panet," ANQ *Rapport*, 1933–34: 268, 313, 357, 382; 1935–36: 266; "Inv. de la corr. de Mgr Plessis," 1932–33: 219; "Inv. de la corr. de Mgr Signay," 1936–37: 153, 162, 183, 294; 1937–38: 51, 128, 132; 1938–39: 216, 233, 240, 258, 279, 293, 301; "Inventaire des documents relatifs aux événements de 1837 et 1838, conservés aux Archives de la province de Québec," 1925–26: 223. P.-G. Roy, *Fils de Québec*, 3: 120–22. Tanguay, *Répertoire* (1893), 199. J.-E. Bellemare, *Histoire de la Baie-Saint-Antoine, dite Baie-du-Febvre, 1683–1911* (Montréal, 1911), 183, 197–275. Chabot, *Le curé de campagne*, 125. Douville, *Hist. du collège-séminaire de Nicolet*, 1: 451–52. L.[-H.] Fréchette, *Originaux et détraqués: douze types québecquois* (Montréal, 1943), 48–49. C.-É. Mailhot, *Les Bois-Francs* (4v., Arthabaska, Qué., 1914–25), 1: 182.

CARTIER, CLAUDE, tailor, soldier, innkeeper, militia officer, and lighthouse-keeper; b. *c*. 1787 in the parish of Saint-Michel-d'Yamaska in Yamaska, Que.; he and his wife Anne had 11 children (one drowned in 1847); d. 9 July 1855 in Chatham, Upper Canada.

Claude Cartier's initial occupation was tailoring, a trade which he learned as a youth at Quebec and pursued until his mid forties. In 1810, however, he enlisted in the Canadian Fencibles, an infantry regiment raised in Lower Canada for service in North America. During the War of 1812 he was present at the capture of Ogdensburg, N.Y. (receiving a severe leg wound which later affected his health), at the Lacolle mill affair in Lower Canada, and at the battle of Crysler's Farm in Upper Canada [*see* Joseph Wanton Morrison*]. When his regiment was disbanded in 1816, Cartier, who had attained the rank of sergeant, received his discharge. He subsequently spent a few months in Ohio, where he resumed his labours as a tailor.

Moving to Upper Canada in 1817, he plied his trade for a while at York (Toronto); on 17 Aug. 1819 he took the oath of allegiance to the crown. He later settled in Simcoe, married, and about 1830 moved farther west to the small undeveloped village of Chatham. The next year Cartier purchased a parcel of land alongside the Thames River from Peter Paul Lacroix. Cartier may have been attracted to the region by the large number of French-speaking settlers already there, notably in the area of Paincourt and in the township of Tilbury West.

One of Chatham's pioneer citizens, Cartier soon became a highly successful innkeeper. His log tavern, originally known as the Chatham Hotel, opened about 1831 and played a prominent part in the early life of the village. Located on busy shipping and stage-coach lines, this popular inn was famous for its three-cent drinks of corn whiskey, its inexpensive meals, and the "splendid balls" held there on New Year's Eve. Following the 1835–36 celebration, one guest reported that "the gaiety of the numerous attendants, the management and arrangement of the room, the music, and unremitting attention of Mr. Cartier, would do credit to any place of ten times the age of Chatham." To serve an increasingly larger clientele, Cartier expanded the inn, which by 1834 had been renamed the Steamboat Hotel. Township meetings were held there and occasionally it served as a meeting-place for local groups and organizations such as the Chatham Vigilant Society for the Suppression of Felony.

Upon opening his inn, Cartier had become active

in local affairs. In 1831 he was named a member of Chatham's first board of common school trustees, and between 1831 and 1837 he served terms as a constable for the village and for Chatham and Harwich townships. In January 1838 he was chosen ensign of a company of Kent County volunteers dispatched to Sandwich (Windsor) to prepare for an anticipated invasion by the Patriot army which had gathered on American soil. The Kent volunteers do not appear, however, to have taken part in the resulting capture of the schooner *Anne* or in the skirmishing at Bois Blanc Island [*see* Thomas Jefferson SUTHERLAND; Edward Alexander THELLER].

Cartier's leg injury made it increasingly difficult for him to continue the active life of an innkeeper, and he sought a less strenuous occupation. In 1837 he had petitioned the provincial government for appointment as keeper of the lighthouse then under construction on Lake St Clair at the mouth of the Thames. The following year he became keeper, charged with maintaining and operating the light, and in 1840 he took up permanent residence at the lighthouse, which soon became a landmark of the region. Cartier retained the post until 1855 and successive generations of his family kept the light until the death of William C. Cartier in 1950.

RONALD G. HOSKINS

AO, RG 22, ser.103, 1–2. Kent Land Registry Office (Chatham, Ont.), Deeds, Reg. book E: ff.14, 381. PAC, RG 1, L3, 102: C12/170; 113: C18/105; 300: L5/56; RG 5, A1: 66157–60, 81766–71, 81961–68, 82002–4, 82805–6; C1, 6, file 655; RG 31, A1, 1851, Tilbury West Township (mfm. at AO). *Chatham Gleaner*, 10 Aug. 1847. *Western Semi-Weekly Planet* (Chatham), 12 July 1855. *Chatham directory*, 1885–86. W. L. Baby, *Souvenirs of the past, with illustrations: an instructive and amusing work, giving a correct account of the customs and habits of the pioneers of Canada . . .* (Windsor, Ont., 1896). F. C. Hamil, *The valley of the lower Thames, 1640 to 1850* (Toronto, 1951; repr. Toronto and Buffalo, N.Y., 1973), 166, 181, 207, 217, 345. C. E. Beeston, "The old log school house," Kent Hist. Soc., *Papers and addresses* (Chatham), 1 (1914): 30–39. *Chatham Daily News* (Chatham), 14 May 1928, 24 Nov. 1950. "His lamp is out: the late Thos. Cartier, light-keeper of the Thames," *Chatham Weekly Planet* (Chatham), 28 Oct. 1880: 1.

CARY, GEORGE MARCUS, agriculturalist, politician, and justice of the peace; b. 1795 in Ireland; d. 4 Feb. 1858 in London Township, Upper Canada.

Little is known about George Marcus Cary's family or childhood. He apparently entered the British army as a volunteer and served in Spain at the battle of Salamanca on 12 July 1812. In October he was commissioned lieutenant in the 95th Foot. He then saw action at Vittoria (Italy), in the Pyrenees, and at Nice, Orthez, and Toulouse in France. Decorated for his services, he was placed on half pay with the rank of captain on 25 Dec. 1818.

Cary probably resided in France during the early 1830s. At some time in this period he may have married Anne Eliza and begun a family. In 1836 he signed a memorandum of agreement to serve a term of five years as manager of an experimental farm to be established at the Red River settlement (Man.) by the Hudson's Bay Company. The third and most ambitious of the company's experimental farms, this one was intended to be an example for the settlers, to assist them in the adaptation of modern agricultural practices, and eventually to produce crops appropriate for an export trade.

HBC governor George SIMPSON had high hopes for Cary, describing him as "a Gentleman who understands both the theory and practise of those branches of agriculture" to be implemented at the farm. Red River resident and historian Alexander Ross saw Cary as "a person of active business habits, sober, intelligent, and prepossessing in his manners" and "in all respects a gentleman of amiable qualities," but he felt that his "agricultural knowledge consisted in theory alone." In Ross's pointed opinion, Cary was "more of a florist than agriculturalist."

Despite considerable investment, the farm was not a success. No one single factor led to its demise. Although Cary had the necessary ability and knowledge, the 10 to 20 English servants sent out by the HBC to assist him proved to be "unmanageable" and "comparatively useless." Since Cary's agreement with the company stipulated that he was to receive one-third of the export profits, the inadequacy of the servants must have been particularly frustrating. The farm's success was also handicapped by the opposition of the Red River settlers, who claimed that by supporting the farm the HBC was seeking to displace them in the supply of provisions for the fur trade. Against these odds, it was not surprising that Cary failed to achieve an export trade in wool and flax although "the Country and climate are well adapted."

In 1841 the experimental farm was abandoned and Cary was allowed to take over part of it as a private concern. He continued to cultivate this property, adjacent to Upper Fort Garry (Winnipeg) on the Assiniboine River, on a modest scale. In 1843 he had 8 horses, 26 cattle, 12 pigs, 100 sheep, and 60 acres of cultivated land. While not a successful agriculturalist, Cary did play a prominent role in the public life of Red River. From 1837 to 1847 he was a member of the Council of Assiniboia, serving on its board of public works, committee of economy, and committee of finance. He was also appointed justice of the peace for the upper district in 1837. Cary was kept busy providing for his family which, by the 1840s, had grown to three sons and five daughters.

Case

Cary retired from the Red River settlement to London Township, Upper Canada, in the spring of 1847, homesteading on the fifth concession until his death. A practising member of the Church of England, he was buried in St John's churchyard, London Township.

GREGORY THOMAS

PAM, HBCA, A.11/95: ff.9d, 10; B.235/z/3: ff.548a, 548b; D.4/22: ff.53, 53d; D.4/58: f.147; D.5/4: ff.160–61; D.5/5; D.5/7: f.185; MG 2, B3, 1843; MG 2, C3. *Canadian North-West* (Oliver), vol.1. Alexander Ross, *The Red River settlement: its rise, progress and present state; with some account of the native races and its general history, to the present day* (London, 1856; repr. Minneapolis, Minn., 1957, and Edmonton, 1972).

CASE, WILLIAM, Methodist minister; b. 27 Aug. 1780 in Swansea Township, Mass.; m. first 4 May 1829 Hester Ann Hubbard*, and they had one daughter; m. secondly 28 Aug. 1833 Eliza Barnes, and they had one daughter; d. 19 Oct. 1855 in Alderville, Upper Canada.

William Case was the eldest son of George Case, a farmer of English descent, whose family had immigrated to Massachusetts in the 17th century. Probably the Cases were Baptists and they must have shared the New England concern for literacy. "After years of religious impressions, and a sinful course," William Case was converted in February 1803. Two years later he was admitted on trial as an itinerant minister by the New York Conference of the Methodist Episcopal Church and appointed to the Bay of Quinte circuit in Upper Canada.

The Methodist Episcopal Church was one of the most aggressively evangelical denominations in the United States. At a very early stage it responded to the pleas of former citizens of the northern states now resident in Upper Canada, and by 1805 the Upper Canada District was well established. For this area, as for the church as a whole, the Methodist bishops recruited young men who had demonstrated a deep commitment to Methodist teaching and the ability to evoke conversion experiences in their followers. Justification by faith was the initial step on the way to Christian perfection, which could be achieved only through a disciplined life. The Methodist system thus depended on the careful selection of many evangelists and a smaller number of those who could administer the itinerancy and foster the quest for holiness in this life.

From the outset, Case must have been identified as a man of promise. Described by Nathan Bangs* as about "five feet, eight inches high, and every way well-proportioned," he had "a pleasant expression of countenance, while yet there was an air of solemnity about him, that could hardly fail to leave the impression that his mind was chiefly fixed upon the interests of the world to come." A thoughtful reader and student, Case was also an assiduous and ardent preacher who was determined "to spend all my time, my talents & property, yea my life in the service of God." Bangs noted that his voice was clear and that he "spoke easily and fluently." His preaching "was rather practical and experimintal than doctrinal" and he was successful in part because "he was one of the most guileless, friendly and obliging of men." He thought nothing of travelling 2,500 miles and preaching 360 times in one year. His journal for 1808–10 reveals a diffident, humble personality, homesick for his family, frequently beset with self-doubt about his ability and his vocation, and urged on and comforted by ecstatic spiritual reflections. This combination of qualities and his fondness for singing, in and out of the pulpit, endeared him to his congregations and enhanced his appeal to the sceptical and the disaffected. His preaching skill, loyalty, and careful attention to detail were recognized quickly by his colleagues and his superiors.

Case was ordained deacon in 1807 and elder in 1808. After a year on the Ancaster circuit (1808–9), he was asked to revive the work begun by Bangs in 1804 and to develop a new circuit in the remote lower Thames valley. In 1810 he became presiding elder of the Cayuga District in the newly created Genesee Conference. He never returned to the circuit itinerancy. He remained as a presiding elder in the United States during the war years, 1812–15, returning to Upper Canada in 1815 as presiding elder of the Upper Canada District, which embraced the area from Detroit to Kingston. For the rest of his career, Case lived and worked in the Canadas.

Despite the wartime disruption, Canadian Methodism revived quickly after 1815, but it was beset by conflict between the Methodist Episcopal ministers and Wesleyan missionaries from the British Wesleyan Conference. As an American and a leading figure in the Genesee Conference, Case was labelled vindictively and probably inaccurately as a "republican Methodist." Elected to the general conference of 1820, he had some part in easing the tension between the two churches. He recognized, however, that the association between the Methodist societies in Upper Canada and the parent body in the United States was changing. At the general conference of 1824 he promoted successfully the formation of a separate conference in Upper Canada. As a presiding elder in the new conference, and its secretary from 1824 to 1827, he helped to contain the attack on the conference by his former friend and colleague, Henry Ryan*, which was engendered in part by continued dissatisfaction with the conference's American ties. In conformity with decisions taken at the 1824 general conference, the independent Methodist Episcopal

Church in Canada was established in 1828 with the consent of the church in the United States. William Case was elected general superintendent *pro tempore* and superintendent of the conference's Indian missions. He was also named to a committee with George Ryerson* and James Richardson* created to foster friendly relations with the British Wesleyans.

Doubtless the Canadian Methodists intended to perpetuate the American Methodist version of the episcopacy and expected to confirm their most popular preacher as general superintendent or bishop. The evidence suggests that Case did not have the requisite stature, self-confidence, or ambition. In any event, although he was elected general superintendent *pro tempore* annually until 1833, by 1828 his overriding concern was to promote the welfare of the Indian missions of which he was the effective founder, and to which he would devote the rest of his life.

In 1820 several thousand Indians were living in Upper Canada, including the majority of the Six Nations on their Grand River lands, a number of Ojibwa groups, and some tribal remnants from the United States. These people had been exposed in varying degrees to the impact of European business, social mores, cultural values, and religion. With few exceptions they had not become assimilated to western culture; rather they had become demoralized and partly disillusioned with their social and religious convictions. They were being pushed back relentlessly along the frontier of settlement, a process symbolized by the land cessions which they made regularly. Probably most white inhabitants assumed that eventually they would retreat into the wilderness or disappear from view altogether.

Fortuitously, one of Case's first circuits was in the Ancaster area, where he met the Mohawk chief Henry [Tekarihogen*] and some of the Six Nations group. From the outset, unlike many Europeans, he seems to have regarded the natives as human beings who were open to Christian teaching and in grave need of salvation. In 1822, stirred by the support of the general and Genesee conferences, he stressed that "my mind recently has been impressed with the importance of our trying to better their [the Indians'] condition and I have spoken to several of our brethren about the matter." In June 1823 his determination was strengthened immensely by the conversion, at a camp meeting where he preached, of Peter JONES. "Now," Case exclaimed, "is the door opened for the work of conversion among his nation!" Peter Jones was received on trial for the itinerancy in 1827 and became the first Indian minister in the Canada Conference. The collaboration between the two men, begun shortly after Jones joined the Methodist community, continued until Case's death.

Case believed that "the Indian character . . . has been but little understood. . . . Let these people possess the advantages of Christian example and instruction and they are as capable of instruction and good impressions as any nation." Thus, with the help of Jones, other Indian converts including Peter Jacobs [Pahtahsega*], and some of his ministerial brethren, he began a systematic program of missionary expansion through which all the Indian groups in Upper Canada were exposed to Methodist teaching. Convinced as he was that Christianization and westernization were integral parts of the same process, he and his collaborators sponsored translations of the New Testament and hymns, established schools, and instructed the natives in the rudiments of European agriculture and technology.

Case assumed, moreover, that the Indians should be enabled and encouraged to come together in permanent settlements in which secular and religious instruction could be provided for them. To this end, in 1826 he secured two islands in the Bay of Quinte, on one of which, Grape Island, houses were built, agricultural implements were collected, and the Indian women were instructed in housekeeping and other crafts. Both of the women Case would marry, Hetty Hubbard and Eliza Barnes, taught at the settlement. Case travelled throughout the northern United States to raise money to support the community and to secure additional teachers. Religious services were held regularly and the Indians were urged to attend quarterly and camp meetings. By 1828 there were at least 79 converts, who were learning with Peter Jones's help to plant gardens and to live in a European style. Case would write optimistically two years later from Grape Island "of the stability and perseverance of most of all who have embraced the Gospel." One of the original Indian settlers, John Sunday [Shah-wun-dais*], went on to become a Methodist preacher himself.

In 1832 the conference, confronted with the prospect of rivalry with representatives of the British conference, agreed to adopt a proposal from John Ryerson* to unite with the latter, despite Case's passionate advocacy of independence. The next year the Wesleyan Methodist Church in Canada was created and the Upper Canadian missions came under the control of Wesleyan superintendent Joseph Stinson*. Case was relegated to the role of "General Missionary to the Indian tribes" and charged to "pay attention to the Translation of the Sacred Scriptures into the Indian languages."

His missionary zeal was not diminished; from his base at the Credit Mission (Mississauga) he continued his visitations of the missions. In 1836 he was again elected secretary of the conference and over the next two years he established a new model settlement at Alderville near Rice Lake, where he lived until his death. In this new planned community each native family had a 50-acre farm, house, and garden, and the

Cathcart

men were instructed in carpentry and agriculture. A day-school and a coeducational boarding-school that emphasized domestic skills were established in 1839. Late in 1848 a new three-storey building was opened with 26 students and room for 100. By 1852 the Alderville Industrial School had 43 boarders and 35 day students; arithmetic and rudimentary science were taught and woollen cloth and knitwear were manufactured. The success of this venture had led to the establishment in 1849 of the Mount Elgin Industrial Institution under Samuel Dwight Rice*. Both were sponsored jointly by the British Wesleyan Missionary Society and the provincial government and partly supported by subsidies from the Indians' annuities. Here the missionaries could act on their belief in "the necessity of an entire separation" of the children "from their friends and relatives and a continued non-intercourse with them until they are made emphatically new creatures."

Despite his preoccupation with transforming the Indians into "new creatures," Case did not lose contact with the wider interests of Canadian Methodism. When the union between the Canadian and British conferences was dissolved in 1840 at a special session of the Canada Conference over which he presided, his concern for the Indian missions led him to espouse the cause of the Wesleyans, to whom he believed that God had "committed the conversion of the Indian tribes in British North America." In the lengthy negotiations that preceded the reunion of the two conferences in 1847 he played a cautious role, largely because he distrusted Egerton Ryerson*, whose guileful advocacy had undermined his own position in 1832. In 1847 Case declared that "before there was any 'hugging and kissing' there should be some 'confession,'" but he joined in the post-reunion rejoicing. In 1852, aged 72, he was given permission to work part time. His last public act was to deliver his jubilee sermon at the 1855 session of the conference on the text "All the paths of the Lord are mercy and truth unto such as keep his covenant and his testimonies." In this he recalled incidents in his long career as an intinerant and urged his brethren not to be diverted "from the work of God in the *growth of grace* and the advancement of pure and undefiled religion throughout the land!"

William Case died on 19 Oct. 1855 of injuries sustained in a fall from his horse, and he was buried in Alderville amidst the Indian people whom he loved and served in his own way. His death marked the end of the first phase of Canadian Methodism, which was characterized largely by simple evangelical preaching and an intense determination to bring the Gospel to every settlement in Upper Canada. Case's style and teaching epitomized the qualities of the Methodism of his time. He took the lead as well in reaching out beyond the European community to the demoralized Indian tribes and bands. His acceptance of the natives

as human beings and his concern for their material, moral, and spiritual needs gave them a renewed sense of pride and hope which ultimately may have had some effect on their will to live as autonomous societies. It was fitting that his brethren should testify that for the Indians "he lived and died" and that they could not forget "his works of faith and abundant labours of love for half a century."

G. S. FRENCH

[Many of William Case's letters were printed in the *Christian Guardian*, the *Methodist Quarterly Rev.* (New York), and its predecessors, the *Methodist Magazine* (1818–28) and the *Methodist Magazine and Quarterly Rev.* (1830–40); his *Jubilee sermon delivered at the request of and before the Wesleyan Canada Conference, assembled at London, C.W., June 6th, 1855* was published in Toronto by the Wesleyan Book Room in 1855. His manuscript diary from April 1808 to August 1809 is in the UCA, as is a microfilm copy of SOAS, Methodist Missionary Soc. Arch., Wesleyan Methodist Missionary Soc., corr., North America, which includes numerous manuscript letters.

The UCA also possesses copies of various official publications of the conferences to which Case belonged in the United States and Canada, including the following annual reports of their missionary societies, which contain much information on his activities: the Methodist Episcopal Church, Canada Conference (1825–29), the Methodist Episcopal Church in Canada (1829–31), and the Wesleyan Methodist Church in Canada, (1833–55), all published in York or Toronto. A complete collection of the minutes of the Wesleyan Methodist Church in Canada and its predecessors from 1824 is available in *The minutes of the annual conferences . . . from 1824 to 1845 . . .*, a one-volume compilation published in Toronto in 1846, and in the *Minutes [of the annual conference]* (Toronto), 1846–55.

The individual conference and district minutes of the Methodist Episcopal Church to which Case belonged prior to the formation of the Canada Conference in 1824 are not at the UCA, but his career from 1805 to 1823 can be traced in the collected *Minutes of the Methodist conferences, annually held in America; from 1773 to 1813, inclusive* (New York, 1813), and in the annual compilations of *Minutes taken at the several annual conferences* (New York) for 1820, 1822–23. The minutes for 1814–19 and 1821 are not available.

The principal biography of Case is Carroll, *Case and his cotemporaries*, which includes many of his letters. Case also figures largely in G. F. Playter, *The history of Methodism in Canada: with an account of the rise and progress of the work of God among the Canadian Indian tribes, and occasional notices of the civil affairs of the province* (Toronto, 1862), and appears frequently in Peter Jones, *Life and journals of Kah-ke-wa-quo-nā-by (Rev. Peter Jones), Wesleyan missionary,* [ed. Elizabeth Field and Enoch Wood] (Toronto, 1860), and French, *Parsons & politics.* G.S.F.]

CATHCART, CHARLES MURRAY, 2nd Earl CATHCART, army officer and colonial administrator; b. 21 Dec. 1783 in Walton-on-the-Naze, England, son of William Schaw Cathcart, 10th Baron Cathcart,

134

and Elizabeth Elliot; m. 30 Sept. 1818 Henrietta Mather, and they had six children; d. 16 July 1859 in St Leonards (East Sussex), England.

Charles Murray Cathcart carried on a family tradition of military service dating back to at least the 16th century. Educated at Eton College, he joined the 2nd Life Guards, of which his father was colonel, as a cornet and sub-lieutenant in 1799. He served, chiefly in staff appointments, in Holland in that year, in Naples and Sicily (Italy) in 1805–6, under his father at the siege of Copenhagen in 1807, and at Walcheren (Netherlands) in 1809. After a short bout of "Walcheren fever," he joined Lord Wellington's army in the Iberian peninsula as a lieutenant-colonel and assistant quartermaster general in 1810, and fought there at the battles of Barrosa, Salamanca, and Vitoria. He filled a similar post in the army of occupation in Holland, his service in the struggle against Napoleon culminating at the battle of Waterloo in 1815, where he had three mounts shot from beneath him. He received several medals and in 1815 was made a CB.

Cathcart, who was known by the courtesy title of Lord Greenock after his father's elevation to the rank of earl in 1814, continued in senior quartermaster-general appointments at home and abroad after 1815. In 1823 he took command of the Royal Staff Corps at Hythe (Kent), where aspects of the work awakened a passion for science, and more particularly for geology and mineralogy, which he never relinquished. On 22 July 1830 he was promoted major-general and went into semi-retirement in Edinburgh, where he pursued his scientific interests. He attended lectures at the university, read and published papers, and became a valued member of the Highland Society of Scotland and a fellow of the Royal Society of Edinburgh. His next military appointment, as governor of Edinburgh Castle and commander of the forces in Scotland from 1837 to 1842, permitted him to stay on in Edinburgh. In 1840 near Port Glasgow he discovered a new mineral, a sulphide of cadmium which became known as greenockite.

In mid June 1845 Cathcart, who had been promoted lieutenant-general in 1841 and had succeeded his father as 2nd Earl Cathcart and Baron Greenock in 1843, assumed command of the forces in British North America. His predecessor as commander-in-chief, Sir Richard Downes Jackson*, died as Cathcart was arriving. The threat of war with the United States over the Oregon boundary, which the British government considered serious, was almost certainly the reason for Cathcart's appointment. He was available at short notice, holding no full-time military employment, and his military credentials were impeccable. A 15-gun salute and guard of honour welcomed him to his headquarters in Montreal on 17 June 1845.

When a painful cancer forced the governor-in-chief, Sir Charles Theophilus Metcalfe*, to resign, Cathcart became administrator of the Province of Canada on 26 November. The imperial government saw the advantages of uniting the highest executive powers, civil and military, in the same person at a time of crisis in Anglo-American relations. Cathcart's instructions were dispatched on 3 Feb. 1846 and he formally took office as governor on 24 April. He seemed unlikely to succeed. Retiring in his habits and conversation, he was inexperienced in politics and ignorant of constitutional practice. His instructions, which preached the necessity of harmony between the executive and the assembly, and yet set Metcalfe as a shining example, provided little guidance. Cathcart's speech from the throne on 20 March 1846, while he was administrator, warmly and perhaps naïvely commended his predecessor, much to the consternation of Robert BALDWIN and some of his more extreme colleagues in the assembly. James Johnston*, the Conservative member for Carleton, expressed dissatisfaction in the house at this step backwards into the age of the military governor. Soon thereafter, Cathcart had to be admonished from London for improperly entering into correspondence with the speaker of the House of Assembly in Prince Edward Island, Joseph Pope*, concerning petitions to be forwarded to London.

Cathcart's brief tenure as governor, however, was marked by none of the rancour and controversy of the previous decade. Despite invitations from William Henry Draper* and his friends, Cathcart was astute enough not to become involved in day-to-day politics. He was a hard and conscientious worker who did not shrink from the exercise of his constitutional responsibilities. "He is certainly neither a handsome, nor pleasing looking person," wrote Registrar Richard Alexander Tucker*, but he quickly won a reputation as "an attentive & intelligent man of business, & a straight forward Politician."

Cathcart concentrated on defence. He championed a redrafting and consolidation of the militia laws and signed the Militia Act of 1846, the first of the united province [see Sir Étienne-Paschal Taché*]. He travelled more than 2,000 miles to examine the borders and defences of his domain and studied reports such as the one by Captain Edward BOXER on naval strength in the Great Lakes. Disagreeing with the assessment that all territory south of the St Lawrence River would have to be abandoned in the event of war with the United States, he was bitterly disappointed that the British government seemed unaware of the pressing need to spend more money, particularly on new works.

The Oregon Boundary Treaty, signed on 15 June 1846, made Cathcart instantly dispensable. By the end of July the new administration of Lord John Russell moved to extract two regiments from Cathcart's command and to replace him as governor with Lord Elgin [Bruce*]. Cathcart was "a mere soldier," Colonial Secretary Lord Grey said later; there was "extreme danger" in leaving him as governor. Characteristically, Cathcart found it easier to accept the loss of his position than the reduction of his army. He was asked to continue as commander-in-chief, but refused. He had realized from the beginning how vulnerable a soldier-governor was, how "very precarious" his tenure would be. Once he had held the highest office, however, he would not revert to a lesser one. Again this decision was in character: it was made not for his own sake but for that of his office. Cathcart stayed on as governor until Lord Elgin arrived on 30 Jan. 1847 and as commander-in-chief until May. Elgin's first speech from the throne contained no praise for his predecessor.

Cathcart returned to England to command the Northern and Midland district. His active service ended on 20 June 1854, when he became a full general. In 1858 he fell ill, and did not recover. He died at his seat in Sussex the next year, shortly after having been made a GCB. His beloved Royal Society of Edinburgh published a generous tribute to "a long and useful life" of goodwill, service, and achievement.

O. A. COOKE and NORMAN HILLMER

AO, MS 78. PAC, MG 24, A28; RG 7, G1, 109–15; G12, 64–65; G14, 17–18; RG 8, I (C ser.), 31, 35, 1194B. Private arch., Alan Cathcart, 6th Earl Cathcart (London), Cathcart papers. *Debates of the Legislative Assembly of United Canada* (Abbott Gibbs *et al.*), vols.5–6. *Gentleman's Magazine*, July–Dec. 1859: 306–7. *A list of the officers of the army and Royal Marines on full, retired, and half-pay . . .* (London, 1829). J. C. Dent, *The Canadian portrait gallery* (4v., Toronto, 1880–81), 4: 166–67. *DNB. Hart's army list*, 1841–55. Morgan, *Sketches of celebrated Canadians*, 448–57. *The Scots peerage, founded on Wood's edition of Sir Robert Douglas's peerage of Scotland . . .*, ed. J. B. Paul (9v., Edinburgh, 1904–14). [Charles] Neaves, "[Opening address]," Royal Soc. of Edinburgh, *Proc.* (Edinburgh), 4 (1857–62): 222–24.

CAZENEUVE, LOUIS-JOSEPH-CHARLES, farmer, businessman, doctor, militia officer, and educator; b. 16 Feb. 1795 in L'Assomption, Lower Canada, son of Louis-Amable Cazeneuve, apothecary and doctor, and Esther Daguilhe, daughter of notary Joseph Daguilhe of L'Assomption; d. there 29 Nov. 1856.

Louis-Joseph-Charles Cazeneuve received his classical education at the Petit Séminaire de Montréal from 1806 to 1814; he was considered a good pupil in Latin, Greek, and rhetoric. On leaving the college he began an apprenticeship with a doctor in his village,

thereby continuing a family tradition that went back four generations. However, prior to obtaining his licence to practise medicine, on 8 July 1818, he remained uncertain about what career to follow. Between 1816 and 1818 he described himself in turn as apothecary, botanist, farmer, and merchant, stating a preference for the last-named occupation.

In 1815 Cazeneuve had inherited from his mother a substantial sum of money, a farm that was "virtually all arable" with a house, cowshed, and outbuildings, as well as property on Rue Saint-Étienne in L'Assomption, on which stood a fine wooden house, stable, dairy, cowshed, and piggery. From then on he seems to have obtained some income from selling agricultural produce.

On 9 Jan. 1816 Cazeneuve married Charlotte Cormier, daughter of François Cormier, *dit* Malouin, an important farmer at L'Assomption. The young couple, who were to have four children, went to live in the house on Rue Saint-Étienne, a residence eminently suitable for the future doctor since it was large enough to provide for a consulting room and was located on the main business thoroughfare where the bourgeoisie of L'Assomption was concentrated. Cazeneuve made his home there until 1843, when he decided to occupy a two-storey building on Rue Notre-Dame.

At the outset of his medical career Cazeneuve recruited patients from his father's large and varied clientele, and thus received invaluable help at a time when competition was keen. While Jean-Baptiste Meilleur* looked after the villagers of L'Assomption, Cazeneuve shared the practice in the countryside with Truman Sterns (Starnes) and Thomas-Edmond d'Odet* d'Orsonnens. Cazeneuve extended so much credit to rural patients that when he died they owed him 8,000 *livres*; his heirs judged that nearly a quarter of this sum was unrecoverable.

Like a number of his colleagues, however, Cazeneuve did not live solely on professional fees. He drew income from the produce of his land, the sale of lots, and several loans made at the legal rate of six per cent. Endowed with an inexhaustible capacity for hard work, he succeeded in enlarging his estate. At the time of his death he owned three properties that were for the most part arable, together with their outbuildings, as well as a tract of standing timber and a number of lots in the village on some of which there were buildings.

In the small community in which he lived Cazeneuve was a figure of distinction. In 1827 he became surgeon to the 1st Battalion of L'Assomption militia, a position he retained until 1834. He was elected churchwarden of the parish in 1829, and the following year the taxpayers chose him as a trustee for the newly established parish schools. He sat on the council for these schools with the parish priest, François Labelle, and Jean-Baptiste Meilleur, among others. From then on Cazeneuve maintained an interest in the progress of education in his region. Despite the hostility of several leading citizens of the area, he joined forces with Labelle and Meilleur to set up the Collège de L'Assomption in 1832. He devoted a great deal of his energy to this institution. He was a life member of its board of trustees and on occasion served as prefect of studies and science teacher.

A fervent believer in education, Cazeneuve had a library well stocked with scientific, medical, historical, geographical, musical, and even gastronomical works. He passed on to his pupils his passion for reading, and ordered books for them from Édouard-Raymond FABRE in Montreal.

Cazeneuve belonged to the diocesan council of the Society for the Propagation of the Faith from its foundation in 1838 by Bishop Jean-Jacques Lartigue*. He passed for a moderate Patriote, and declared his support for "an economic war fairly waged against England." He died at L'Assomption on 29 Nov. 1856.

GILLES JANSON

AC, Beauharnois (Valleyfield), Minutiers, Godefroy Chagnon, 1er juin 1827, 24 mai 1830, 3 juin 1846; Joliette, Minutiers, Camille Archambault, 26, 29 déc. 1856. ACAM, RLB, III: 349. ANQ-M, CN5-3, 15, 21 janv., 27 mai, 1er juin, 21 juill., 8 sept., 27 oct. 1835; 29 janv., 1er août 1836; 17 avril, 6 mai 1837; 19 août 1839; 29 avril 1842; 21 févr., 15 nov. 1843; 19 avril 1845; 7 juill. 1847; 18 janv., 5 avril 1848; 26 mars 1849; 15 janv., 20 avril, 18 mai, 25 août 1850; 15 janv., 19 mars, 26 juin 1851; 6 mai, 1er juill., 7 sept. 1854; 28 mars 1855; CN5-18, 27 avril, 30 mai, 17, 20 nov. 1815; 7, 14 janv., 21 mars, 4 avril, 14 juin 1816; 13 août, 19 oct. 1822; 29 sept., 28 déc. 1824; 10 juin, 26 juill., 23, 25 sept., 1er oct. 1826; 26 juin 1827; 9 oct. 1830; CN5-24, 10 juin, 30 sept. 1816; CN5-37, 21 sept. 1789; CN5-42, 6 oct. 1832, 15 mars 1842. ANQ-Q, P-69/1. AP, Assomption-de-la-Sainte-Vierge (L'Assomption), Reg. des baptêmes, mariages et sépultures, 16 févr. 1795, 9 janv. 1816, 2 déc. 1856. AUM, P 58, C2/203; U, Cazeneuve à Drummond, 11 mars 1845. *Biographie et oraison funèbre du Rév. M. F. Labelle, et autres documents relatifs à sa mémoire, ainsi qu'à la visite de Philippe Aubert de Gaspé au collège de L'Assomption* (Montréal, 1865). Can., Prov. of, *Statutes*, 1841, c.68. Arthur Dansereau, *Annales historiques du collège de L'Assomption depuis sa fondation* (Montréal, 1864). *Le 19 janvier 1865 au collège L'Assomption* (Montréal, 1865). *La Minerve*, 3 déc. 1856. *Le Spectateur* (Montréal), 12 août 1813. *Liste de la milice du Bas-Canada pour 1828* (Québec, s.d.). *Liste de la milice du Bas-Canada pour 1832* (Québec, s.d.). Anastase Forget, *Histoire du collège de L'Assomption; 1833 – un siècle – 1933* (Montréal, [1933]). Meilleur, *Mémorial de l'éducation* (1876). Pierre Poulin, *Légendes du Portage*, Réjean Olivier, édit. (L'Assomption, 1975), 41–42. C. Roy, *Hist. de L'Assomption*.

CHABOT, JEAN, lawyer, politician, and judge; b. 15 Oct. 1806 in Saint-Charles, near Quebec, son of Basile Chabot, a farmer, and Josephte Prévost; m. 1 July 1834 Hortense Hamel at Quebec; they had no children; d. there 31 May 1860.

Jean Chabot attended the Petit Séminaire de Québec from 1820 to 1828, and then from 26 Feb. 1829 studied law in the office of Elzéar Bedard*, who became the first mayor of Quebec in 1833. Chabot was called to the bar on 27 Feb. 1834 and quickly acquired a reputation as an eminent lawyer. In September 1843 he agreed to run in the by-election for the riding of the city of Quebec and was elected by acclamation. He was a supporter of Louis-Hippolyte La Fontaine* and, because the political conduct of Governor Sir Charles Theophilus Metcalfe* had resulted in the resignation of the government of La Fontaine and Robert BALDWIN in November and the formation of a new one the following month by William Henry Draper* and Denis-Benjamin Viger*, Chabot had to settle for working in the opposition.

In the general election of 1844 he campaigned on the theme of ministerial responsibility and was returned by acclamation. Although not a great orator, he possessed real ability for parliamentary work; he was acknowledged especially to have the qualities of an excellent jurist and a gift for a biting reply. As member for the city of Quebec, he made a particular attempt, along with his colleagues Pierre-Joseph-Olivier Chauveau* and Thomas Cushing Aylwin*, to obtain the government's cooperation in solving the problems overburdening his constituents. The major ones stemmed from the fires that raged in the city in May and June 1845. Although he supported some of the government initiatives, in particular the education act of 1845, Chabot was profoundly dissatisfied with the government. On 23 June 1847 he gave a dismal assessment, in the assembly, of its accomplishments, denouncing its favouritism towards Upper Canada and condemning as ineffective the measures passed to help the victims of the fires at Quebec.

In the same period Chabot took an active part in establishing the Society of St Vincent de Paul of Quebec [see Joseph PAINCHAUD]. On 19 Nov. 1846 he was asked to be chairman of the Quebec conference of this philanthropic society, the first conference in the Province of Canada, and on 7 Feb. 1847 he was also appointed president of the Quebec council; he retained both responsibilities until 1850. Although he was aware of the problems facing the working class, he none the less did not approach them from the standpoint of social inequality. A man of his time and his milieu, Chabot appealed to charitable sentiments, at the same time holding that the poor were "for the most part depraved, idle, [and] improvident," as he stated in a letter to the citizens of Quebec signed on 31 Dec. 1847.

Perceived as a solid defender of the interests of Quebec, Chabot was again re-elected by acclamation in December 1847. This election, which led to the return to power of the coalition of La Fontaine and Baldwin in March 1848, also sent Louis-Joseph Papineau* back to the house. Papineau's position on the union of the Canadas divided the liberals; for his part Chabot was firmly opposed to repeal of the union, a step Papineau was demanding, and reiterated his confidence in the reform policy of La Fontaine. Called upon to chair the public meeting held when Papineau came to Quebec on 11 May 1848, Chabot must have been aware of the enthusiasm of the French-speaking population there for the former Patriote chief, but he warned the meeting that despite his admiration for Papineau he was against repeal. This loyalty to La Fontaine's party earned him appointment as commissioner of public works on 13 Dec. 1849, at the time of the reshuffle in the government due to the retirement of the speaker of the Legislative Council, René-Édouard Caron*. It was, however, largely through the influence of the secretary of the diocese of Quebec, Charles-Félix Cazeau*, his first cousin, that he was appointed. According to historian Jacques Monet, Cazeau proposed Chabot's name to Joseph-Édouard Cauchon* and La Fontaine, who heeded his recommendations. Before assuming office, Chabot was obliged to seek a new mandate from his constituents, and had to campaign against annexationist Rouges and their candidate Joseph LÉGARÉ. With Cauchon's support and Cazeau's assistance this re-election posed no problem. But Chabot held office only a few months; an inveterate drunkard, he was obliged to resign in March 1850 after spending a night in jail in Toronto. Even before Chabot had been officially appointed, Lewis Thomas Drummond* had warned La Fontaine that he "possesses neither the personal dignity nor the political status that will be necessary," and for his part Cauchon admitted to his leader on 15 December that he would need to have "a strong motive of public interest to support Chabot."

Probably fearing the effect of these incidents on his popularity at Quebec, Chabot sought re-election in 1851 in Bellechasse and was successful. Following the speech from the throne he declared his support for the new government of Francis Hincks* and Augustin-Norbert Morin* and drew up a list of the things he expected it to accomplish: construction of roads to facilitate access to the new lands being opened up and thereby reduce emigration to the United States, abolition or at least reform of the Legislative Council, building of the Quebec–Halifax railway, codification of the laws, and above all abolition of seigneurial tenure to which he gave much attention. In September 1852, following the resignation of the commissioner of public works, John Young*, and the refusal of George-Étienne Cartier* to take the office, Chabot once again accepted it. In this capacity he would be closely involved in the first phase of expansion of the Canadian railway system, marked by the building of

the Grand Trunk, although his role was primarily to back up the work of Hincks, the prime mover in these matters. From 20 Nov. 1852 to 26 Jan. 1855 Chabot sat as government representative on the board of directors of the Grand Trunk. He was also involved personally in various railway projects. In 1850 he was a director of the Quebec and Melbourne Railway, and in 1854 his name appeared on a petition presented to the assembly on behalf of the Northern Pacific Railroad. Chabot also took an interest in improving communications between Quebec and Lévis during the winter season, and in 1853 he managed to get a committee of the house to study the feasibility of using steam-powered ferries rather than an ice bridge.

In 1854 Jean Chabot stood as a candidate in both Bellechasse and the city of Quebec. He won easily in each and decided to represent Quebec. He kept his post as commissioner until January 1855, when Morin resigned and Sir Allan Napier MacNab* and Étienne-Paschal Taché* formed a new government. He was excluded from the cabinet but his services were retained from 19 June 1855 under the Seignorial Tenure Act as commissioner to draw up the land registers in each seigneury. Chabot remained member for Quebec until he was appointed on 20 Sept. 1856 as judge of the Superior Court with residence at Montreal. The following year his residence was transferred to Quebec, where he worked for the last three years of his life.

Pierre Poulin

ANQ-Q, CE1-1, 1er juill. 1834, 2 juin 1860; CE2-4, 15 oct. 1806. ASQ, Fichier des anciens. PAC, RG 68, General index, 1841–67. Debates of the Legislative Assembly of United Canada (Abbott Gibbs et al.). Le Canadien, 18 sept. 1843; 2 oct. 1844; 15, 22 déc. 1847; 12 mai 1848; 14 déc. 1849; 28 janv. 1850; 24 sept. 1852; 10, 12, 24 juill. 1854; 1er juin 1860. Le Journal de Québec, 22 juill. 1854. F.-J. Audet, "Commissions d'avocats de la province de Québec, 1765 à 1849," BRH, 39 (1933): 587; "Les législateurs du Bas-Canada." Desjardins, Guide parl. I.-J. Deslauriers, Juges de la cour supérieure de 1849 à 1978 (s.l., 1978). Morgan, Sketches of celebrated Canadians. Quebec directory, 1847–60. P.-G. Roy, Les juges de la prov. de Québec. Monet, La première révolution tranquille. [Henri Têtu], Les noces d'or de la Société de Saint-Vincent de Paul à Québec, 1846–1896 (Québec, 1897). L.-P. Turcotte, Le Canada sous l'Union, 1841–1867 (2v., Québec, 1871–72).

CHANDLER, WILLIAM, lawyer, office holder, and judge; b. 17 Sept. 1804, probably in Amherst, N.S., son of Charles Henry Chandler and Elizabeth Rice; m. 28 Jan. 1834 Ruth Roach Smith, and they had nine children; d. 22 Aug. 1856 in Richibucto, N.B.

The seventh of eight children, William Chandler was the product of the influential Church of

England–loyalist community that dominated so much of the political and judicial life of early 19th-century Nova Scotia and New Brunswick. Through family marriages he was related to many of the prominent families, including those headed by his uncles Joshua Upham* and Amos Botsford*. His grandfather, Joshua Chandler, had been a member of the Connecticut legislature before he immigrated to Nova Scotia in 1783. His father was sheriff of Cumberland County and was succeeded in that office by William's brother, Joshua. A first cousin, James Watson Chandler*, was judge of probate in Charlotte County and a member of the New Brunswick legislature. Edward Barron Chandler*, William's elder brother, became probate judge for Westmorland County, a member of the assembly and of the legislative and executive councils, and eventually lieutenant governor of New Brunswick. William's wife was the daughter of a loyalist doctor much respected in the Chignecto area.

William was educated in the Amherst public school system. The legal profession had attracted many of his family, and so William, following in the footsteps of his brother Edward Barron, articled with his cousin William Botsford* at Westcock, N.B. In the fall of 1828 he was admitted to the New Brunswick bar as an attorney and early in 1831 as a barrister. He chose to set up his office in Liverpool (Richibucto), the shire-town of the newly created jurisdiction of Kent County along the east coast of New Brunswick. Liverpool was an ideal place to start a new practice: in 1831 there were only two other attorneys in the county.

It was not long before Chandler's legal capabilities were recognized locally. Most of his practice was devoted to land transactions, boundary disputes, and civil infractions. He also assumed an active role in county administration. In 1829 he was appointed county treasurer; two years later he became both a commissioner for taking affidavits to be read in the Supreme Court and a judge of probate for the county of Kent. By 1840 William's generation of Chandlers held important local judicial offices in three New Brunswick counties.

Chandler never entered provincial or municipal politics. He seems to have been happy to serve his county as a lawyer and legal administrator, and to be involved in extensive land dealings. Shortly before his death he arranged a complicated purchase involving 624 acres in the parishes of Dundas and Moncton for £156. However, payment, as his widow discovered, was never made, and it was not until 1865 that the transaction was concluded in the courts to the satisfaction of the original seller.

On 22 Aug. 1856 Chandler died after a week's illness. His obituary in the Saint John *Morning News* reported that the cause of his death was "erysipelas,

and gastric fever and prostration of the nervous system," or what would be known today as typhoid fever. Although he was a probate judge, Chandler died intestate, leaving an estate valued at £11,000.

DELLA M. M. STANLEY

Anglican Church of Canada, Diocese of Fredericton Arch., Richibucto Parish, N.B., reg. of baptisms, 1815–1955 (mfm. at PANB). Fort Beauséjour National Hist. Park (Au Lac, N.B.), Westmorland County, N.B., reg. of marriages, 1790–1835 (mfm. at PANB). Kent County Registry of Deeds (Richibucto), Index to record books A–Y (1827–80); books B–G, especially book B, no.77 (mfm. at PANB). N.B. Museum, Ralph Hewson, "Chandler family" (typescript). PANB, "N.B. political biog." (J. C. and H. B. Graves); RG 18, RS150, A1–2. St Mark's (Anglican) Church (Westmorland), Reg. of marriages, 1823–1917 (photocopies at Mount Allison Univ. Arch., Sackville, N.B.). *Morning News* (Saint John, N.B.), 25 Aug. 1856. *Royal Gazette* (Fredericton), 12 Feb. 1834. *N.B. almanac*, 1830; 1831; 1834; 1854: 27. J. H. Stark, *The loyalists of Massachusetts and the other side of the American revolution* (Boston, 1910). E. L. Gallagher, *History of old Kingston and Rexton* ([Hampton, N.B., 1948?]). Lawrence, *Judges of N.B.* (Stockton and Raymond). G. E. Rogers, "The career of Edward Barron Chandler; a study in New Brunswick politics, 1827–1854" (MA thesis, Univ. of N.B., Fredericton, 1953). Howard Trueman, *The Chignecto isthmus and its first settlers* (Toronto, 1902; repr. Belleville, Ont., 1975). E. C. Wright, *The loyalists of New Brunswick* (Fredericton, 1955; repr. Moncton, N.B., 1972).

CHAPERON, JOHN (baptized **Jean**), notary and office holder; b. 1 April 1825 in La Malbaie, Lower Canada, son of Michel Chaperon, a merchant, and Constance Simard; d. 13 Nov. 1851 in Rivière-du-Moulin (Chicoutimi), Lower Canada.

John Chaperon belonged to a family that had come from Berne, Switzerland, and settled in the Charlevoix region. He went to the primary school in La Malbaie, but apparently did not receive a classical education. Around 1842 he entered the office of Laughlan Thomas Macpherson at Quebec to train as a notarial clerk. Chaperon received his commission from the Quebec Board of Notaries on 2 Dec. 1847, at the age of 22. On 18 Jan. 1848 at Quebec he married Aurélie-Rosalie Bolduc, the daughter of Henri Bolduc, a notary of that city; they were to have three children. A few months later he moved with his young wife from Quebec to Rivière-du-Moulin, near Chicoutimi.

Chaperon was the first notary to settle in the Saguenay region, where he drew up his first deed on 18 April 1848. Peter McLeod, then the undisputed lord of the region, lost no time in making him his regular notary. A Montagnais on his mother's side and an associate of William Price* of Quebec in the timber trade, McLeod insisted on his status as a native son, claiming he was entitled to all rights to the lands and

Chartier

forests in the Chicoutimi area. An analysis of Chaperon's minute-book makes clear McLeod's stubborn determination to defend his rights, ambitious claims which embroiled him in numerous altercations with local settlers. Of the 378 notarized documents Chaperon drew up, 66 were at the express request of McLeod. There were a good many protests (18) and admissions of judgement in favour of McLeod (17). Then, in order of importance, come receipts, loans, powers of attorney, transfers of debts, and, lastly, a cancellation of sale.

Chaperon's minute-book in its own way provides a picture of the anonymous mass of ordinary people, the men who primarily worked in the forest but surprisingly called themselves farmers. Against this background of struggling people, certain individuals stand out by adding the imposing title "master" before their occupation: navigators, stevedores, timber cullers, and blacksmiths, not to mention, of course, the baker, shoemaker, and furniture maker. In this Chicoutimi society, which had a well-defined structure based on occupation, the higher level was the bourgeois class, represented by the manager McLeod, Chaperon's brother-in-law Dr Pierre-Cyrille-Adolphe Dubois, agent general George Forest, and parish priest Jean-Baptiste Gagnon. Also included were the foreman, bookkeeper, schoolmaster, store clerks, and bailiffs.

As the local notary, Chaperon fitted into this social hierarchy at the top, just below McLeod. Yet his income, drawn from his professional practice, was by no means excessive. At the end of each year he drew up his balance-sheet carefully. In 1848 he entered 84 instruments, which earned him £54 4s. 0d. He reached a peak in 1849: 163 for £104 17s. 6d. The following year he had to face competition for clients from a newcomer to Chicoutimi, Ovide Bossé. A number of people immediately ceased doing business with him and in 1850 he drafted only 79 instruments, which brought him a modest £46 17s. 6d. On 31 October of that year he was appointed clerk of the circuit court of Chicoutimi, and the additional revenue from his new duties was welcome in the circumstances. In 1851 he drew up only 52 documents, and he was not to have time to account for the last, dated 21 October. On 13 November his life ended prematurely at Rivière-du-Moulin, when he was 26. He was buried two days later in the cemetery of Saint-François-Xavier parish in Chicoutimi.

Primarily known as the first notary of the Saguenay region, John Chaperon left a minute-book that, although not large, none the less furnishes valuable information on the economic, political, and social life of this corner of Lower Canada in the late 1840s when it was changing from a purely lumbering area into an agricultural settlement.

JEAN-PAUL SIMARD

John Chaperon's minute-book, containing instruments notarized between 1848 and 1851, is held at the ANQ-SLSJ as CN1-3.

ANQ-Q, CE1-1, 18 janv. 1848; CE4-3, 1er avril 1825. ANQ-SLSJ, CE1-2, 15 nov. 1851. Arch. de la Compagnie Price Limitée (Chicoutimi, Qué.), no.699. PAC, RG 68, General index, 1841–67: 35. *Le Canadien*, 24 nov. 1851. Frère Éloi-Gérard [Talbot], *Recueil de généalogies des comtés de Charlevoix et Saguenay depuis l'origine jusqu'à 1939* (La Malbaie, Qué., 1941), 118. J.-E. Roy, *Hist. du notariat*, 3: 175. Léonidas Bélanger, "Les notaires du Saguenay," *Saguenayensia* (Chicoutimi), 8 (1966): 128–30.

CHARTIER, ÉTIENNE, journalist, lawyer, educator, Roman Catholic priest, school administrator, and Patriote; b. 26 Dec. 1798 in Saint-Pierre-de-la-Rivière-du-Sud, Lower Canada, son of Jean-Baptiste Chartier and Marie-Geneviève Picard Destroimaisons; d. 6 July 1853 at Quebec.

Étienne Chartier was the son of a farmer, and the sixth in a family of ten. His childhood was spent in an environment firmly rooted in the values of rural society and the religious traditions that were part of it: work in the fields, close relations between neighbours and exchanges of information about the crops, strict observance of religious practices, and the strong moral authority of the parish priest. At Saint-Pierre-de-la-Rivière-du-Sud, where they had settled shortly before 1760, the Chartiers were considered difficult, quarrelsome, and formidable as neighbours. On occasion they would take issue with the priest. In 1803 for example, when the *curé* of Saint-Pierre-du-Sud, Joseph-Michel Paquet, decided to abolish the patronal feast-day, which was accompanied by celebrations with all kinds of excesses, Chartier's father openly showed his disapproval. The hostility of the Chartiers towards the British was also well known. This attitude was scarcely suprising in a family in which paternal and maternal grandfathers had joined with the Bostonnais during the American occupation in 1776 to repulse the British troops that had moved into the parish. Consequently, from childhood Chartier had learned to curse British tyranny, and had begun to develop a spirit of independence which he would increasingly manifest as he grew up.

Chartier could have followed in the footsteps of his father and brothers. But since he was not robust his parents thought he would not make a good farmer, and decided to send him to the Latin primary school in Saint-Pierre-de-la-Rivière-du-Sud, at which the principal teacher was M. Lavignon, the former sacristan of the Jesuits' chapel at Quebec. Among other things, Lavignon initiated him into an austere piety, thus playing a crucial role in nurturing Chartier's earliest religious beliefs. After a year of Latin in 1810–11, Chartier went directly into the second form at the Petit Séminaire de Québec in September 1811. Quebec, with its House of Assembly, the scene of parliamentary debates and numerous political struggles, strengthened the country lad's sense of belonging to the nationalistic milieu in which he had been brought up. Chartier felt drawn to the French Canadian cause. He no doubt was able to discuss these questions with his classmate Elzéar Bédard*, son of Pierre-Stanislas*. When he reached the higher forms, he took even greater interest in public life, which fascinated him. Like his colleagues, he closely followed the career of Louis-Joseph Papineau*, at the time when Papineau was emerging more and more clearly as the new leader of the French Canadians. He was a fervent admirer of Papineau, and was a witness to the signing of his marriage contract in April 1818.

That year Chartier successfully completed his studies at the Petit Séminaire de Québec. An exceptionally gifted student, he stood among the first in his class, and at the end of the year was awarded most of the prizes on the honours list. He was drawn to the priesthood, and formed friendships with classmates who shared the same aspirations. During his years at the seminary he probably spent more time with Ignace Bourget*, later bishop of Montreal, than with anyone else. However, the two young men apparently did not have much influence on each other, for their personalities were already very different.

At the end of his studies, Chartier decided to become a priest, and then, changing his mind, chose a legal career. His choice hardly seems surprising: it corresponded to the vogue for the liberal professions among classical college graduates at the beginning of the 19th century. With the advent of the parliamentary régime and the decline of the seigneurial class, men in the liberal professions commanded respect in French Canadian society by their outstanding qualities and leadership. By the same token, they assumed the direction of their compatriots' nationalism, articulating French Canadian interests, values, and themes. Some of them were even persuaded to the ideals of republicanism, democracy, and secularism. Once out of the seminary and the certainty of its universe, Chartier felt in harmony with the ideals of the new professional class, the beginning of an important shift in his thinking.

In the autumn of 1818 Chartier decided to stay at Quebec and study law. He began his training under Louis Lagueux*, who was to become member for Dorchester in the House of Assembly in 1820. A nationalist of liberal bent, Lagueux received Chartier courteously, and secured lodgings for him with his father, Louis. Chartier was a young newcomer in a law office, without money or support, but he had a liking for ideas and books. Everything interested and excited him. At the beginning of the 1820s, when the question of providing for the civil establishment was the focus of political conflict, Chartier was consumed with desire to intervene in the debate, and it was in all probability to this end that he accepted the position of editor for *Le Canadien*, which had been revived by

François Blanchet*. There he met Augustin-Norbert Morin*, his associate in taking over the direction of the paper. He got on very well with Morin, who was young, nationalistic, and intellectual, and they established a lasting friendship. Both of them wrote leading articles: Chartier was interested in the question of education and Morin gave his attention to the granting of supplies. However, in 1821, a year after their appointment, the two young journalists resigned because of ideological differences with the owners over the orientation to be given the paper.

His hopes dashed, Chartier decided that year to resume legal studies under Denis-Benjamin Viger* at Montreal. Viger's law office was undoubtedly the best that Chartier could have chosen for his training in this professional milieu. At that time at least six students were articled to Viger, who, next to Papineau, was the most prominent leader of the Canadian party. Chartier continued his apprenticeship in an environment that stimulated him and kindled his enthusiasm. He was in contact with young men who were passionately nationalistic and steeped in liberal ideals. On 31 Dec. 1823 he was given his lawyer's commission by the governor-in-chief, Lord Dalhousie [Ramsay*], and thus joined the crowded professional ranks. Montreal already had at least 50 lawyers, and in this field the English-speaking lawyers were giving relentless competition. Burdened with debts contracted while articling, for which his creditors threatened to sue, Chartier was at a disadvantage when he took up practice.

In January 1825 Rémi GAULIN, the priest of Saint-Pierre-du-Portage (parish of L'Assomption-de-la-Sainte-Vierge) at L'Assomption, invited him to set up a *fabrique* school there. When he left Montreal that month, Chartier felt the need for a period of reflection and still had only vague plans about his vocation. As soon as he had settled in the parish, he lost no time in bringing the neighbourhood children together to begin classes. Until then Chartier had been well received by the clergy as a whole and had encountered no difficulty with his superiors. On 25 Dec. 1825 Jean-Jacques Lartigue*, Quebec's auxiliary bishop at Montreal, conferred the tonsure on him in Saint-Jacques church. Yet Chartier remained preoccupied and anxious about his priestly vocation. In the final period it became harder and harder for him to be clear about his own intentions. Sometimes he did not have the courage to respond to a vocation growing steadfastly for more than a year; at other times he declared that he would become a priest when the clergy paid his debts. He even accused Jacques-Guillaume Roque*, his confessor, of having hastened his tonsuring. His ambivalence about his vocation would surely heighten the inner vacillation that would dog his ministry. It was obvious that priesthood would not bring peace to this unstable, passionate man. For this reason and others that are unknown, various

Chartier

ecclesiastical authorities opposed his entering the Grand Séminaire de Québec. But they soon changed their minds, for the dioceses of Quebec and Montreal were short of priests, the clergy was ageing, and there were few recruits.

In the autumn of 1826 Chartier entered the Grand Séminaire de Québec, a few weeks after his brother Pierre had agreed to make him a loan so he could repay his debts. Chartier thus complied with the rule that all candidates for the subdiaconate be free of debts. During his stay at the seminary he was engaged largely in teaching and supervision and like his colleagues had little time to devote to his theological training. He indeed was quite satisfied with this state of affairs, since his theological studies struck him as inferior and humdrum. In February 1828 a brief illness forced him to take a rest. He seized this opportunity to read works on education. Learning of his research, Charles-François Painchaud*, the priest of Sainte-Anne parish at Sainte-Anne-de-la-Pocatière (La Pocatière), contemplated making him principal of the new Collège de Sainte-Anne-de-la-Pocatière, and invited him to submit a proposal outlining the educational scheme that he would set up there. Chartier applied himself resolutely to the task.

Imbued with liberal ideas, Chartier centred his report on the concept of liberty, and made himself the voice of reason. At the college corporal punishment would be abolished, close friendships would be tolerated, certificates of confession would be forbidden, and confession and communion would not be obligatory, even at Easter. For all practical purposes discipline would be replaced by the student's sense of responsibility and feelings of honour and loyalty. Political education would take the same direction. As in the community at large, the students would be invited to choose their representatives; they would also have their own newspaper, and the authorities would not be involved in it. A tribunal consisting of a jury of duly elected students and chaired by the principal would be responsible for reprimanding those who committed offences. Such a political apprenticeship would also serve as a powerful means of imparting a patriotic education. The college would become, as it were, a large city in which each person would discharge his duties but also exercise his rights. As for specific teaching methods, the teachers would emphasize reasoning and systematically reject memorization as a learning process. Chartier was by no means alone in proposing reforms in education. From the beginning of the century various members of the liberal bourgeoisie had been denouncing the discipline prevailing in the colleges and advocating a fresh pedagogical approach. Whether he was aware of it or not, Chartier wrote his proposal in a period of unrest and discontent. A tireless worker, he also started on a short analytical French grammar for use in the college.

Chartier took the final steps to the priesthood at the end of 1828. On 8 December he received the diaconate, and three weeks later was ordained priest in the cathedral of Quebec. However, he had to wait another eight months before the Collège de Sainte-Anne-de-la-Pocatière accepted him. In the mean time the bishop of Quebec, Bernard-Claude Panet*, appointed him curate of Saint-Gervais parish, near Quebec. At that period of his life Chartier was still a priest known only in the restricted milieu to which he devoted himself. His own ideas were slowly maturing but he avoided expressing them openly. It was at the college that he would have the chance to communicate them. Chartier was officially appointed principal at the beginning of September 1829 and on his arrival he was invited to deliver the inaugural address for the college. In the presence of local dignitaries and Joseph Signay*, the coadjutor to the bishop of Quebec, he used the occasion to attack the British oligarchy, which he held responsible for the woes of the colony. In his speech he also condemned some of his compatriots as propagandists of doctrinaire liberalism. These last assertions might suggest that he had finally rejected liberalism and moved closer to his ecclesiastical colleagues on this issue. However, other statements would later show that he had not rejected any of his earlier liberal ideas.

Chartier's comments caused an outcry. The English-language papers in Lower Canada seized on the affair and demanded his dismissal. The French Canadian press riposted and applauded his attacks on British officialdom. The incident assumed the proportions of a state crisis. The matter was brought up in the British House of Commons. At the beginning of November the administrator of Lower Canada, Sir James KEMPT, and the bishop of Quebec summoned him and insisted on an explanation for his conduct. Chartier was not relieved of his office, but he remained none the less hurt and shaken. Furthermore, after this incident his educational plan met with a poor reception. He was increasingly regarded as an intruder and, at that, one who liked to make trouble. The curé Painchaud and the young teachers did everything they could to drive him out of the Collège de Sainte-Anne-de-la-Pocatière. It was insinuated, among other things, that he had corrupted some of the students, and this rumour spread like wildfire through ecclesiastical circles. During the summer of 1830 Chartier became increasingly vulnerable because of the tension caused by the reactions to his speech and the many rumours of sodomy being spread about him. Brought up to date on the affair, Bishop Panet placed him in a closed retreat at the Grand Séminaire de Québec. By now Chartier was a priest with a stigma, condemned for ever by the ecclesiastical authorities. His early beginnings would be mirrored in his enduring experiences through countless ups and downs.

In March 1831, after six months of seclusion, Chartier was appointed priest of Sainte-Martine parish near Châteauguay. In this heavily populated community where, however, settlement was widely scattered, he was charged with a difficult ministry, made more burdensome by constant travelling. He carried out his duties honourably but did not manage to rid himself of debts contracted after his ordination. Despite his difficult experience at Sainte-Anne-de-la-Pocatière, his political convictions had not changed. He continued to read *La Minerve*, and corresponded with Ludger Duvernay, who had been imprisoned at the beginning of 1832. His frequent trips to Montreal also led him to maintain a steady connection with the Patriote circle. Consequently he quickly awakened Bishop Lartigue's distrust and the two soon came into conflict.

The difficulty began when Chartier opposed the churchwardens' use of parish funds for the restoration and decoration of the church vaulting. Chartier thought that the *fabrique* of Sainte-Martine had insufficient resources to assume such expenses. The churchwardens, with the support of prominent parishioners, then declared open war on him. In the circumstances, Bishop Lartigue sought to avoid the worst by offering Chartier another parish. The incident was minor, given that in this period a number of priests met a similar fate in the course of their careers. But Chartier refused to submit to the decision, and asked to meet the bishop of Quebec in the hope of obtaining a parish in that diocese. Lartigue was annoyed and reprimanded him vehemently. A rift was created between them which with time would widen into a chasm. The conflict was temporarily resolved when the two bishops agreed to appoint Chartier priest of Saint-Pierre-les-Becquets (at Les Becquets), a parish no priest wanted, in which the diocesan authority placed priests offering "few guarantees."

Indeed, for some ten years this parish had been caught up in violent quarrels provoked by the problem of getting its church built. Two factions had split the community along classic lines: the first, which included the seigneur, small merchants, and professional men, insisted that the church be erected in the village; the second, composed of farmers, wanted to have it built a little farther out, in the countryside. Chartier arrived at Saint-Pierre-les-Becquets at the end of 1833 when the crisis reached its peak. The affair burst into the newspapers, and one of the factions launched a lawsuit. The new parish priest hesitated to take a stand at the outset; then he changed his mind and lent his support to the farmers' group. He met with resentment everywhere for having backed it. The village notables approached the new bishop of Quebec, Joseph Signay, and demanded that Chartier be dismissed from the parish. Once again his bishop sacrificed him and assigned him to another charge.

Chartier could never reconcile himself to having been abandoned by the bishop of Quebec, and seems to have been more affected by the attitude of Signay in 1834 than by that of Lartigue the year before. These transfers, which he considered ill timed, led him perforce to criticize a system which gave parish priests no certainty of tenure. According to Chartier, this system had made the clergy in Lower Canada effectively dependent upon their bishops. Consequently he demanded the application of the Tridentine right, which guaranteed permanent tenure to the incumbents of parishes. In this respect Chartier happened to be reviving on his own account the rumblings of discontent which especially in the past ten years or so had been disturbing the lower ranks of the French Canadian clergy. Nevertheless, it was not the only claim he articulated against episcopal authority. His difficult experience as a rural priest made him also much more critical of the institutional and disciplinary arrangements of the church, so that his curiosity was directed to problems often overlooked: the locus of decision-making within the church, the priesthood as a career, and the use of sanctions against the most refractory clergy. Quite clearly it was the whole edifice of the ecclesiastical hierarchy, with its decision-making processes and its modes of participation, that Chartier was inclined to call in question. Of course his individual action failed to carry the day at a time when the diocesan authorities had succeeded in re-establishing ecclesiastical discipline and put an end to a disputatious trend in the church. Left to himself, Chartier was carried along more and more swiftly towards disaster.

During the autumn of 1834 Chartier also ventured to challenge the political authorities, and rallied the Patriote party on the question of the Jesuit estates [*see* Antoine-Nicolas Braun*] and the issue of meetings of the *fabriques* [*see* Louis Bourdages*]. From then on Chartier began to associate regularly with the principal leaders of this party. He took an active part in the election campaign in Nicolet riding, and passionately defended the objectives of the 92 Resolutions. In the same year he insisted that the clergy should not stay out of political struggles. Despite the division that developed between the clergy and the members of the assembly during debate on the bill concerning *fabrique* meetings, he urged his colleagues to give their support to the Patriote party. Chartier's latest stand meant open conflict with his superiors. At the end of 1834 the bishop of Quebec officially dismissed him as priest of the parish of Saint-Pierre-les-Becquets and assigned him to the wretched parish of Saint-Patrice (at Rivière-du-Loup). In the months that followed Chartier did not alter his convictions in the slightest, and defended them with the same determination. But the weight of his debts continued to plague him and made it necessary for him to seek a better

Chartier

parish. During the summer of 1835 Bishop Lartigue refused point-blank to grant Chartier a parish in his diocese. Then he changed his mind and agreed to appoint him *curé* of Saint-Benoît parish (at Mirabel), on condition that he cease to fight against the Executive Council and abandon his views on the permanent tenure of parish priests and on the *fabrique* meetings. After the 1837–38 rebellion, when his relations with Lartigue were extremely strained, Chartier would even accuse his bishop of having driven him into a trap in giving him Saint-Benoît.

In 1836 Saint-Benoît was already one of the principal centres of political agitation. Numerous public meetings were held there; several leaders of the Lac des Deux-Montagnes region, notably Jean-Olivier Chénier* and Jean-Baptiste Dumouchel*, came to preach revolution. In this partisan setting, Chartier lost no time in becoming extremely active in local Patriote circles. He sat on the committees, attended the meetings, and took part in nearly all the popular demonstrations in the county. He likewise made himself conspicuous by the violence of his comments, particularly in his sermons, in which he raged against the British government and the colonial régime. He continued also to attack his superiors, always with the same vigour and persistence as in earlier years. Any excuse sufficed to fight against Bishop Lartigue, who distrusted his temperamental excesses and considered him "wrong-headed."

For their part, the Patriote leaders had a high regard for Chartier and increasingly sought his support to establish broad public trust. In May 1837 he was invited to take part in Ludger Duvernay's election campaign in Lachenaie riding. At a meeting in Saint-Scholastique (Mirabel) in June, Chartier harangued his fellow-citizens and introduced Papineau as "the country's saviour." In the autumn he preached several sermons inciting his parishioners to armed revolt. Always active and impassioned, he even visited the neighbouring parishes in an endeavour to rally the farmers to the Patriote cause. At the end of October Lartigue's pastoral letter gave him another opportunity to support the revolutionary aims of the Patriote movement and to attack the church's official stand on the rebellion. Chartier reproached Lartigue primarily for having adopted in this letter the theory of theocratic absolutism, which identifies as the only authority in human society the power of sovereigns appointed by God and destined to rule in an absolute manner over mankind. There are, he said, "cases where a sovereign may lose his authority, namely when he oppresses the religion of his people or when he violates the fundamental laws of his state."

No other parish priest had dared to criticize the pastoral letter from this angle. Furthermore, most priests blindly followed their superiors' directives and condemned the revolutionary movement in violent language. Like their bishop, these priests idealized the *ancien régime* and divine right monarchy, ardently defended obedience to the civil authority, and affirmed their fierce hostility to any revolution. In fact Chartier was the only priest who engaged himself in the revolutionary movement. On the eve of the battle of Saint-Eustache on 13 Dec. 1837, he went to this parish to harangue the armed forces in the village. On the same day he attended an important meeting at the headquarters of the Deux-Montagnes battalion of militia. He was still in the parish when fighting broke out, but he soon realized the cause was hopeless and fled to the United States. His participation in the battle of Saint-Eustache gave rise to the gravest conflict so far. On 27 Jan. 1838 Bishop Lartigue committed himself to institute proceedings against him under canon law and suspended him from his parish charge. The British government offered a reward of £500 for his capture.

Once he was settled in the United States, Chartier established contact with the principal Patriote leaders who had taken refuge near the border. On 9 Jan. 1838 he attended a meeting at Swanton, Vt. Robert Nelson* and Cyrille-Hector-Octave Côté* won those assembled to their views and proposed to draw up a plan to invade Lower Canada. Chartier certainly subscribed to these objectives, but at the time he wanted above all to find himself a new parish. Hence his role among those who had fled Lower Canada remains difficult to determine. He certainly did not take part in the attempted invasion in February. After the meeting at Swanton he went directly to Pennsylvania, settling first in Clearfield and then a few months later at Philadelphia. There he met the bishop of the diocese, Henry Conwell, who entrusted him with St Augustine parish. He got on very well with Conwell, who drew his warm admiration, for in Chartier's eyes he personified the democratic, liberal prelate. Chartier then urged Conwell to use his influence with Lartigue to get him to restore his right to serve as a priest. In August 1838, through the good offices of the bishop of Philadelphia, Lartigue agreed to a compromise: Chartier could exercise his ministry in the United States but could not resume his duties in the Montreal region. Chartier made an even more direct approach to John England, the bishop of Charleston, S.C., who was the papal legate to the United States, with the intent, basically, to prepare for a fresh struggle against Lartigue's pastoral letter of October 1837.

Chartier did not remain idle in Philadelphia. He gave his attention to St Augustine parish, where he was amazed to find men and women won over to liberalism, who admired democratic institutions and were sworn enemies of the British monarchy. In his writings he expressed on many occasions the firm hope of seeing the two Canadas become independent. In July 1838 Papineau stayed in Philadelphia for a few weeks. Chartier was able to meet the Patriote leader and introduce him to the bishop of Philadelphia. Although he did not at that time exercise a direct influence on the revolutionary endeavour, Chartier none the less remained in touch with some of the refugees. At the beginning of October he learned that plans were being readied near the Canadian-American border for a new insurrection. Without the slightest hesitation he left Philadephia, and he managed to obtain a new parish at Salina near Syracuse, N.Y. From there he journeyed regularly to Plattsburgh, Swanton, and St Albans to maintain communication with the refugees. He even joined personally in the preparations for a rising in November, making clear in this way his unconditional support for the radical group under Côté and Nelson. Gradually, through his role within the revolutionary structure, he assumed as important a place in it as he had occupied in 1837.

After their failure in November 1838, the insurgents turned more and more against Papineau. Meetings at Swanton on 24 Jan. 1839 and at Corbeau, N.Y., on 18 March reflected this state of mind. During the deliberations, Chartier unhesitatingly gave his support to Nelson and Côté. He had idolized Papineau too much to refrain from calling him to account for his role and his participation in the rebellions of 1837–38. He was one of those who, although not accepting the radicals' ideology, were ready to reject Papineau and embark on a new revolutionary adventure, telling themselves that ideological differences would moderate after victory. With Nelson, Côté, Édouard-Élisée Malhiot*, and several other associates, he urged Papineau to go to France, for his passive, even disapproving attitude was causing considerable harm to the movement. It was he who approached Julie Bruneau, Papineau's wife, asking her to try to influence her husband's decision. Subsequently, with Nelson and Côté, he attempted unsuccessfully to devise several plans for the invasion of Lower Canada. In 1839 he went there incognito, with the hope of rallying farmers anew to the revolutionary cause.

But conflicts quickly arose between Chartier and Nelson's group. While remaining very much a partisan of independence, the revolutionary priest continued to profess a moderate form of liberalism. He could not bring himself to accept the social program of the radicals, who demanded in particular separation of church and state and abolition of both the tithe and seigneurial rights. Disillusioned, he turned against them and decided to support Papineau once more. In November 1839 he wrote Papineau a long letter reproaching him for his cowardice and inviting him to place himself at the head of a new revolutionary movement. He also denounced his conduct before and during the rebellion. In February 1840 the revolutionary committee, probably to get rid of Chartier, sent

him to France where he was to evaluate Papineau's success in finding political allies. He was instructed to replace Papineau if that proved necessary. The task, which required him to deal directly with the former Patriote leader, suited Chartier, for he wanted to know Papineau's real intentions with regard to the revolutionary movement. It also gave him an opportunity to plead his case in Rome against Bishop Lartigue. In Paris Chartier met Papineau, who was ill disposed to cooperate and not anxious to seek support for organizing another revolt. Chartier declared him "purely and simply a demagogue, and in no way a statesman." He was bitterly disappointed. In his distress and discouragement he began to have doubts about his mission. With the death of Lartigue in April 1840 a trip to Rome was pointless, and he embarked for the United States in August. In these few months all he had gained from his actions was the hostility of Papineau and of Nelson's radical group. On his arrival he settled in Indiana, where Célestin de La Hailandière, the bishop of Vincennes, made him priest of the parish of Madisonville (Madison).

As a result of the numerous disappointments he had experienced in the Patriote milieu, and the void left by the failure of the rebellion in 1837–38, Chartier decided to abandon the revolutionary movement. In 1841 he returned to Lower Canada, to ask pardon publicly of Bishop Bourget, Lartigue's successor. On 10 December he published a long letter in *Le Canadien* disavowing his previous activities. Bourget persuaded him to remain for a period of time in the United States, so that people in Lower Canada would forget their image of him as a revolutionary. In March 1842 Chartier settled once more in Madisonville; he subsequently proposed to enter the community of the Brothers of St Joseph. He seems to have abandoned this plan, since in 1843 he was appointed principal of the Catholic seminary at Vincennes. Then in 1844–45 he was in Louisiana, where he served the parish of Avoyelles at Marksville. His passionate fondness for travel was certainly a factor in these journeys, although the real motives remain somewhat obscure. In any case, Chartier could not miss such a fine opportunity to learn more about American society. However, the plight of the blacks and of the French minority soon aroused his indignation. In these circumstances, the annexation of Lower Canada to the United States no longer seemed a valid means of preserving the institutions and language of his compatriots. Following his difficult experience in Louisiana, Chartier wanted to return home. At the end of 1845, after several fruitless approaches to the bishops of Quebec and Montreal, he finally got Bourget to grant him Saint-Grégoire parish (at Mont-Saint-Grégoire).

On his return from exile, Chartier openly adopted the moderate ideas of the group around Louis-

Chartier

Hippolyte La Fontaine* and categorically rejected those of his former Patriote friends. The rancours, past frustrations, and innumerable denunciations led him increasingly to keep his distance from his new superiors. In his parish he again displayed unbounded energy: he gave consolation and comfort, and saw to it that his parishioners regularly received the sacraments. Eager to gain Bourget's confidence, he openly led a struggle against the Protestant proselytizing that was spreading in the Dorchester (Saint-Jean-sur-Richelieu) region [see Henriette Odin*]. In 1849 La Fontaine's moderate group, fearing the strength of the Rouges and the consequences of Papineau's return from exile, approached Chartier and urged him to publish in the papers his famous 1839 letter addressed to Papineau. Unaware of what lay behind this move, Chartier agreed, believing that in this way he was working for the emancipation of his compatriots. His action brought down upon him the fury of various papers and of former Patriote friends. In fact this was his last foray into politics; bitterly disappointed by those around him, he never again experienced any desire to involve himself in public affairs.

In 1850, as a result of conflicts with some parishioners, Chartier asked to be transferred to the parish of Sainte-Philomène (at Mercier). There he again found himself at the centre of a quarrel provoked by the problem of repairs to the church. Fearing the worst, he urged the bishop of Montreal to send him as a missionary to Arichat, N.S. A year later he asked to be brought back into the diocese of Quebec and was made priest of the parish of Saint-Gilles near Quebec. He was a broken man who had almost no contact with the politicians and priests around him. He was still in debt and in 1852 claimed £455 from the Rebellion Losses Commission for possessions pillaged by the volunteers at Saint-Benoît. He died at the Hôpital Général at Quebec on 6 July 1853 from the after-effects of a liver complaint, and was buried at Saint-Gilles. Only one member of his family and two priests from the Séminaire de Québec were present at his funeral.

Throughout his adult life, Étienne Chartier as a parish priest was totally different from his colleagues. He was a man of his time, who took close interest in the problems of his contemporaries and adopted stances that condemned him to isolation. In his day Chartier was a catalyst of strong passions, which unfortunately made sport of him and finally reduced him to the state of victim, spurned, detested, and scorned by all.

RICHARD CHABOT

[Étienne Chartier is the author of essays dealing primarily with educational issues. His writings include a descriptive curriculum for the Collège de Sainte-Anne-de-la-Pocatière (La Pocatière, Qué.) prepared in 1828 as well as a short analytical French grammar for the students and an educational plan for the college produced in 1829. The curriculum and the educational plan are held in the Arch. du collège de Sainte-Anne-de-la-Pocatière, in Collège, 112-II and 51-VI respectively.

There is a great deal of material relating to Chartier in various archival collections. For documents concerning his childhood, youth, and education, see: ACAM, 355.114, 826-3; ANQ-M, CN1-28, 18 sept. 1821; Arch. de l'évêché de Sainte-Anne-de-la-Pocatière, Saint-Pierre-du-Sud, corr. J.-M. Paquet; corr. M. Vallée; and PAC, RG 4, B8, 21: 7659-62.

For his career in the priesthood, the following sources should be consulted: AAQ, 210 A; 26 CP, VI: 45; ACAM, 420.048; RLL; RLB; Arch. de l'évêché de Sainte-Anne-de-la-Pocatière, Sainte-Anne (La Pocatière), Chartier à C.-F. Cazeau, 12 juill. 1830, and Saint-Patrice (Rivière-du-Loup), corr. Étienne Chartier; Arch. du collège de Sainte-Anne-de-la-Pocatière, Collège; Fonds Painchaud; ASN, AP-G, L.-É. Bois, G, 6: 348; 8: 40-42; 10: 235; 12: 291-96; ASQ, Séminaire, 9, no.84; ASSH, F, Fg-2. See also the following collections of Chartier correspondence: Arch. de la chancellerie de l'évêché de Saint-Hyacinthe (Saint-Hyacinthe, Qué.), XVII.C.33; Arch. de la chancellerie de l'évêché de Valleyfield (Valleyfield, Qué.), Sainte-Martine, and Sainte-Philomène (Mercier); Arch. de l'évêché de Nicolet, Saint-Pierre-les-Becquets (Les Becquets); Arch. de l'évêché de Saint-Jérôme (Saint-Jérôme, Qué.), Saint-Benoît (Mirabel), V1A20K.

For Chartier's activities as a Patriote and revolutionary, it is necessary to turn to different collections. The ANQ-Q undoubtedly offers the richest source material for this aspect of his life. Relevant collections here include the Papineau family papers (P-417), the Ludger Duvernay papers (P-68), and the papers concerning the events of 1837–38 (E17/6–52). The Viger–Verreau collection at the ASQ, which contains numerous documents on his political activities, is also useful, as are the extensive Ægidius Fauteux papers deposited at the BVM-G. The PAC also holds several documents on Chartier and his participation in the rebellion of 1837–38, notably in the Papineau papers (MG 24, B2), the Perrault papers (MG 24, B37), and the L.-É. Bois papers (MG 24, K36). The Univ. of B.C. Library (Vancouver), Special Coll. Division, has a letter from Chartier to Robert Nelson, written in July 1839. Chartier's birth and burial records are in ANQ-Q, CE 2-6, 26 déc. 1798, and CE 1-1, 8 juill. 1853, respectively.

The most important of the published studies of Chartier are: F.-J. Audet, "L'abbé Étienne Chartier," Cahiers des Dix, 6 (1941): 211–23; Ægidius Fauteux, "Les carnets d'un curieux: Étienne Chartier ou les avatars d'un curé révolutionnaire," La Patrie, 9 déc. 1933: 36–37, 39–40; Pascal Potvin, "L'aumônier des patriotes de 1837," Le Canada français (Québec), 2e sér., 25 (1937–38): 417–32. See also "Un document important du curé Étienne Chartier sur les rébellions de 1837–38: lettre du curé Chartier adressée à Louis-Joseph Papineau en novembre 1839, à St Albans, Vermont," Richard Chabot, édit., Écrits du Canada français (Montréal), 39 (1974): 223–55; Chabot, Le curé de campagne; "Le rôle du bas clergé face au mouvement insurrectionnel de 1837," Cahiers de Sainte-Marie (Montréal), 5 (1967): 89–98. R.C.]

Child

CHILD, MARCUS, businessman, office holder, justice of the peace, school administrator, and politician; b. December 1792 in West Boylstone, Mass.; m., probably in 1819, Lydia F. Chadwick of Worcester, Mass., and they had two children who survived infancy; d. 6 March 1859 in Coaticook, Lower Canada.

In 1812 Marcus Child moved to Stanstead, Lower Canada, from Derby Line, Vt, where he had been clerking for a merchant uncle the previous year. In Stanstead, Child prospered as a druggist, and began to take an interest in politics. He was one of the few residents of the Eastern Townships to speak out against the proposal of 1822 for the union of Upper and Lower Canada, and in 1829 he was elected to the House of Assembly as a reformer for the newly created two-member constituency of Stanstead. In 1830 he became postmaster for Stanstead and commissioner of the peace for the districts of Montreal and St Francis. Citing the long absences from his family as the reason, he declined to defend his seat in the general election that year.

Child was a school visitor from 1815 to 1840 and a trustee of the local school of the Royal Institution for the Advancement of Learning from 1822 to 1829. His major contribution during the session of 1829 was to acquire financial aid for the founding of Stanstead Seminary and Charleston Academy, the first two secondary schools in the Eastern Townships. During the 1830s he became a trustee and secretary of the seminary, as well as secretary of the Stanstead County Bible Society.

Deciding to return to politics, Child presented himself as a candidate for Stanstead in a by-election held in December 1833. Although the returning officer declared Wright Chamberlin the victor on the grounds that many of Child's supporters were not qualified to vote, this decision was overturned by the assembly and Child took his seat in February. He only had time to vote for the 92 Resolutions drafted by Augustin-Norbert Morin* before appearing on the radical ticket for Stanstead in the fall general election. A friendly newspaper, the *St. Francis Courier and Sherbrooke Gazette*, claimed that he was "by no means a polished orator, or calculated to shine in debate, as but few men are, but is capable of expressing himself with ease, force and clearness." His opponents, Chamberlin and Elisha Gustin, ran as moderate reformers but Child and his running mate, a Hatley farmer named John Grannis, nevertheless received the majority of votes.

During the sessions of 1835–36 Child was appointed a member of the assembly's permanent committee on education and schools, established to inquire into the state of education in the province. He continued to give active support to Louis-Joseph Papineau*, attacking the British American Land Company formed in 1834 and heading an inquiry in 1836 which condemned the conduct of Sheriff Charles Whitcher, a member of the Tory clique surrounding landowner William Bowman Felton* of Sherbrooke. Unfortunately for Child, however, the region's ardour for the Patriote party was cooling. In 1835 the assembly had seized upon a technicality to reject a petition for a vital project which Child himself had been promoting – a railway from Boston through the district of St Francis to Montreal. Moreover, a pronouncement by Papineau about an extension of the seigneurial system into the townships led to repeated predictions in the Tory press about the implications for Anglo-Protestant farmers. Residents of the townships became acutely aware of their dependency upon the French-speaking, Catholic majority in the assembly. The report in May 1836 of a special commission of inquiry, headed by Lord Gosford [Acheson*] and charged with investigating the conflict between the assembly and the executive, shrewdly observed that the radical representatives of Stanstead and Missisquoi were not elected to defend the "feudal system" and the French language, or to object to the establishment of land registry offices, but to oppose a government "which neglects or regards with disfavour" settlers from the United States.

In January 1837 a by-election was held to replace Grannis. Despite the unpopularity of the crown's land policies, the assurances of Edmund Bailey O'Callaghan* that the French Canadians were opposed to the seigneurial system, and Child's pledge that he would consider the vote a test of confidence, the radical candidate was decisively defeated by Moses French Colby*. Child, however, not only refused to resign but persisted in his political allegiance. In late November of that year he apparently even assisted some Patriotes to cross the border secretly. His dismissal as postmaster shortly thereafter, however, seems to have shaken him: one of the Patriote organizers in the United States, John B. Ryan*, wrote in January 1838, "He worships his property too much to jeopardize his safety by doing anything or even saying anything to advance the interests of the sacred cause." Nevertheless, Child refused to take the oath of allegiance, on the grounds that he had already done so in the fall of 1837, and in November 1838, after being discharged as commissioner of the peace, he fled to Vermont to avoid arrest.

Child's exile was brief, and during the early 1840s he became a merchant, potash manufacturer, and carding-mill operator in the village of Coaticook, although he remained a resident of Stanstead. Child defeated Colby in the election of 1841, and in the assembly of the united Province of Canada he actively promoted agricultural policies. At one time a leading proponent of free trade, he was forced by the American tariffs of 1842 to switch to protection for

147

Chipman

Canadian agricultural produce. Attacking the timber trade as morally debilitating, he favoured the extension of the agrarian frontier by the construction of good colonization roads and the improvement of municipal government. He also obtained protection for spawning maskinonge and salmon in Stanstead, Sherbrooke, Missisquoi, and Shefford counties, though the legislative committee did not recommend extension of this legislation to all freshwater fish in Canada, opting rather for local initiative. Such a recommendation was consistent with Child's *laissez-faire* liberal philosophy, as was his support in principle for free tuition while he opposed provincial taxation of those municipalities refusing to tax themselves for school purposes. But he was not so opposed to the centralization of power when it came to his personal interest. He lobbied to have the Post Office Department made directly answerable to the Executive Council. He was not motivated simply by political principle; he was also seeking revenge against his dismissal in 1837 by Postmaster General Thomas Allen Stayner*. In fact, a growing conservatism can be discerned in Child's conversion from Methodism to Anglicanism and in his defence of Canadian textbooks in lieu of the popular American imports which had "injurious effects" because of their support for republicanism and democratic ideas. It is not surprising, therefore, that he pledged his allegiance to Governor Sir Charles Theophilus Metcalfe* when Robert Baldwin and Louis-Hippolyte La Fontaine* resigned over the issue of responsible government in November 1843. His constituency was not appeased, however, for in 1844 it elected John McConnell, an uncompromising government supporter, by a strong majority.

Child nevertheless became senior magistrate for Stanstead County as well as inspector of schools for the district of St Francis in 1845, holding the latter position until his death. He controlled local patronage after the Baldwin–La Fontaine victory of 1848, but suffered a crushing defeat at the hands of lawyer Hazard Bailey Terrill when he appeared on their slate in 1851. This was the last time he ran for public office. His interests in Stanstead remained important enough for him to support a railway through that village in 1852, but after Sherbrooke and Coaticook won the route for the St Lawrence and Atlantic Rail-road, he joined the migration to the latter town in 1855. In 1859, after a short illness, he died there of inflammation of the lungs.

J. I. LITTLE

ANQ-E, CE1-41, 9 mars 1859. PAC, MG 24, B1, 7; B2; MG 30, D1, 8; RG 4, A1; RG 68, General index, 1651–1841: 290, 394, 421. Private arch., Roger Jean-Marie (Coaticook, Qué.), B. N. Robinson, "The early history of Coaticook, from its foundation down to 1902" (MS, 1933).

Stanstead County Hist. Soc., Colby-Curtis Museum (Beebe, Que.), Marcus Child papers. Can., Prov. of, Legislative Assembly, *Journals*, 1852–53. *Debates of the Legislative Assembly of United Canada* (Abbott Gibbs *et al.*), vols.1–3. L.C., House of Assembly, *Journals*, 1834–36. *Missiskoui Standard* (Frelighsburg, [Que.]), 1835–39. *Montreal Gazette*, 3, 10 Dec. 1829; 19 Jan. 1837; 17, 20 Nov., 6 Dec. 1838; 27 March, 1 April 1841; 5 Oct., 7, 9 Nov. 1844. *St. Francis Courier and Sherbrooke Gazette* (Sherbrooke, [Que.]), 2 Oct. 1834. *Stanstead Journal* (Rock Island, [Que.]), 4–18 Dec. 1851, 4–11 Feb. 1858, 10 March 1859. *Vindicator and Canadian Advertiser* (Montreal), 17, 20 Nov. 1829; 31 Jan.–25 Feb., 10 Oct., 14 Nov. 1834; 7–27 Jan. 1837. *Cyclopædia of Canadian biog.* (Rose and Charlesworth), 2: 647–48. Fauteux, *Patriotes*, 178–79. Albert Gravel, "Marcus Child" (paper delivered before the Stanstead County Hist. Soc., Beebe, 1963). B. F. Hubbard, *Forests and clearings; the history of Stanstead County, province of Quebec, with sketches of more than five hundred families*, ed. John Lawrence (Montreal, 1874; repr. 1963). "An address by Marcus Child," Stanstead County Hist. Soc., *Journal* (Stanstead, Que.), 6 (1975): 16–24. "The story of Stanstead College since 1817," Stanstead County Hist. Soc., *Journal*, 3 (1969): 49–56.

CHIPMAN, ELIZA ANN (Chipman), diarist and teacher; b. 3 July 1807 in Cornwallis Township, N.S., daughter of Holmes Chipman and Elizabeth Andrews; m. 24 May 1827 William Chipman at First Cornwallis Baptist Church, and they had 12 children; d. 23 Oct. 1853 in Pleasant Valley (Berwick North), N.S.

The first milestone in Eliza Ann Chipman's life occurred at the age of 16, when she "passed through . . . a sound conversion." Following the declaration of her faith, she was baptized on 6 June 1824 by her influential pastor, Edward MANNING, and was accepted as a member of the First Cornwallis Baptist Church. At age 19, after much soul-searching, she married her cousin William Chipman, a prosperous merchant and farmer, a prominent deacon in the Baptist church, and a 46-year-old widower with eight children, two of whom were older than Eliza herself. Despite such obstacles, the marriage proved stable and mutually supportive. In addition to her ready-made family, Eliza was to have 12 children, 8 of whom survived infancy. A year after their wedding, William decided to enter the ministry, and 1829 saw Eliza and her family, including her first baby, newly established in Pleasant Valley, where William was installed as the first pastor of the Second Cornwallis Baptist Church. Since this was a new and relatively small congregation, the Chipman family was forced to pioneer a farm in order to support its growing number, with all the attendant financial and physical hardships. Eliza lived the remaining 24 years of her life in the parsonage of Pleasant Valley, dying at 46, following a severe bowel disorder, three years after the birth of her last child.

She had begun a spiritual journal on 20 July 1823, at

148

the age of 16, probably at the suggestion of Manning; her last entry was on 6 Aug. 1853, less than three months before her death. Three days before she died she revealed the existence of her diary to her husband in the hope that the perusal of it might be profitable to him and to her friends. In compliance with her desire, in January 1855 he published *Memoir of the life of Mrs. Eliza Ann Chipman, wife of the Rev. William Chipman, of Pleasant Valley, Cornwallis.*

Although she never travelled outside her native western Nova Scotia, Eliza exhibited a broad spiritual and intellectual outlook that belied her parochial situation. Her diary is couched in the religious expression common to her day and is essentially concerned with pious introspection, but it clearly reveals honest self-examination and a keen mind of literary bent. Manning wrote of her while she was yet in her teens that she possessed "powers of mind of some considerable promise." Striving for a Christ-like existence was her first priority, but after marriage her concern for those in her care caused her to sacrifice many private spiritual aspirations, creating a constant tension in her life. However, far from being a mere appendage to her husband and family, Eliza remained a strong individual. Her awesome involvement in her church and community was based on personal conviction: besides caring for her large family, she organized and led women's prayer groups, taught Sabbath school, maintained a hospitable hearth for ministers on circuit, established a day-school in her own home, and became a surrogate mother for lonely students at Horton Academy and Acadia College in Wolfville. At the same time she coped with 12 pregnancies, several severe illnesses with a resultant diminution of hearing, and extended absences of her husband on preaching tours. Little wonder that she confided in secret to her diary, "My body is so worn down with fatigue and care that I get no time for rest or reading."

One of Eliza's greatest concerns and spheres of influence was education – both secular and spiritual. She and her husband became vigorous supporters of Baptist educational institutions, namely Horton Academy and Acadia College. Her own children were sent there, her stepson Isaac Logan Chipman became one of Acadia's first professors, and her daughter-in-law Alice Theodosia Shaw Chipman became a pioneer in women's education at Grand Pre Seminary in Wolfville. With a woman of Eliza's calibre to provide leadership and a model for younger women in the community, it is no surprise that her denomination played such a prominent part in female education.

Eliza Ann Chipman earned the attention of posterity primarily through the posthumous publication of her diary, which spanned virtually her whole adult life. A study of her life reveals not only that she left an intimate literary portrait of a 19th-century Nova Scotian woman, but also that she exerted a quiet, but definitive, influence on the social and intellectual development of her native province.

CAROL ANNE JANZEN

Eliza Ann Chipman's journal was published under the title *Memoir of the life of Mrs. Eliza Ann Chipman, wife of the Rev. William Chipman, of Pleasant Valley, Cornwallis* (Halifax, 1855). Three copies are preserved in the ABHC; an original letter from George Armstrong to Mrs Chipman, dated 26 Jan. 1839, is affixed to the inside front cover of copy 1. Two entries from the *Memoir* appear in *Pioneer and gentlewomen of British North America, 1713–1867*, ed. Beth Light and Alison Prentice (Toronto, 1980), 60–61.

ABHC, William Chipman, day-book, 1837–57; Edward Manning, journals, 1812–45; D. O. Parker, "Berwick, its people and institutions as I knew them about sixty years ago" (scrapbook of clippings of articles by Parker in the *Register* (Berwick, N.S.), 1897). Bill, *Fifty years with Baptist ministers*. J. D. Davison, *Eliza of Pleasant Valley: her family, church, and community in nineteenth century Cornwallis Township, Kings County, Nova Scotia* (Wolfville, N.S., [1983]).

CHIPMAN, WARD, lawyer, office holder, judge, and politician; b. 10 July 1787 in Saint John, N.B., only child of Ward Chipman* and Elizabeth Hazen; m. 24 March 1817 Elizabeth Wright; there were no children of this marriage; d. 26 Nov. 1851 in Saint John.

At birth Ward Chipman became heir apparent in one of the most important families in colonial New Brunswick. His father, a prominent loyalist lawyer with close ties to the Fredericton establishment, had married the daughter of William Hazen*, a partner in Hazen, Simonds, and White, the oldest and most respected mercantile firm in Saint John. Chipman Sr doted on his only child, whom he described in 1789 as "fat, noisy and ungovernable." But while parental discipline was lightly applied, "little Chip" was carefully groomed for his role as patriarch to a web of families, including numerous Hazens and Botsfords and their kin, who would dominate many areas of public life in the colony well into the 19th century. A precocious child, the younger Chipman was learning to spell before he was three. By five he had begun to read and at ten he had sufficiently mastered the classics to be ready for college. However, because of his youth, he was sent to an academy in Salem, Mass., where he lived with his father's sister, the wife of a wealthy merchant. From there he proceeded to his father's alma mater, Harvard College, receiving an AB in 1805 and an AM in 1808. Although his talents were, as even his father admitted, not "uncommonly great," Chipman was industrious and studious and he sufficiently distinguished himself at Harvard (which was to award him an honorary doctorate in 1836) that he was asked to give "the English oration" at

Chipman

commencement. Having received "the best education which America could afford," according to his father, he returned to Saint John "a genteel, sensible, well informed young man."

Unfortunately there were limited opportunities for such young men in early 19th-century New Brunswick. For several decades after 1784 the colony languished and many loyalists drifted back to the United States. Few of the loyalist office holders joined this exodus but for the children of those who remained the prospects were bleak. The élite was small but still larger than the colony could accommodate. Some of these sons of the gentry dirtied their hands and engaged in trade, a few entered the clergy or the military, and a much larger number, including the younger Chipman, were directed toward the legal profession, a career which, in time, might lead to public office. But the critical problem was to earn a livelihood while waiting for the older generation of officials to die off. There were lawyers aplenty in Saint John and too little work to support them all in the style of life to which the children of the gentry aspired. Chipman Sr was acutely aware of the problem, and saw two solutions. The more desirable one was to send his son to London to acquire superior qualifications in law. But the expense of this training was more than he could afford. The alternative was to send Chipman Jr to practise where the competition was less ferocious and advancement less uncertain. Fortunately, two of his former students, Jonathan* and Stephen* Sewell, had established successful practices in Quebec and Montreal respectively and were prepared to assist his son. Yet Chipman Sr was reluctant to lose his only child and he continually found excuses for delaying his departure. Chipman Jr therefore began to study law in his father's office and in July 1808, on coming of age, he became an attorney. But his father's practice did not generate enough business to support two lawyers and young Chip began to study French in preparation for his move.

Chipman was saved from a painful separation from his parents by the death in 1808 of two New Brunswick judges, Joshua Upham* and George Duncan Ludlow*. His father succeeded to one of the vacancies in 1809 and Chipman inherited his father's law practice and replaced him as advocate general and clerk of the crown. By borrowing money, he was able to go to London in 1810 to study in the office of the noted English lawyer George Sowley Holroyd. Chipman was admitted to the society of the Inner Temple on 20 April 1811 and in due course, on 22 Nov. 1822, to the English bar. Returning to Saint John in November 1813, he resumed his practice and became surrogate general. Two years later he was appointed recorder for the city of Saint John, another post previously held by his father. His practice, concerned almost entirely with commercial and real

estate transactions, grew steadily and in 1820 he was elected a director of the Bank of New Brunswick.

In 1814 Chipman's grandfather Hazen died, leaving a vast estate which was to be the subject of complicated litigation among the heirs for half a century. As executor of the estate, Chipman was able to purchase at low cost land owned by Hazen in the Portland area of Saint John, which soared in value as the city expanded. After his own death Chipman's executorship was challenged in the courts. Although the charges were dismissed, no one denied that he had profited handsomely from his speculations in the Hazen estate. By 1817 Chipman felt he was sufficiently prosperous to take a wife and on 24 March he married Elizabeth, daughter of Henry Wright, collector of customs for Saint John. The marriage was childless, but theirs was apparently a close relationship and the connection with Wright, who had considerable patronage at his disposal, expanded Chipman's influence.

Also useful in promoting Chipman's interests was his appointment to the British commissions established under the Treaty of Ghent of 1814 to locate the northeastern boundary between the United States and British North America. Chipman Sr was selected as the agent to prepare the British case and he persuaded the imperial government to allow his son to act as co-agent. Chipman assisted his father during the successful negotiations in 1816 which resolved the British ownership of a number of islands in Passamaquoddy Bay and the Bay of Fundy. He also assisted in the continued negotiations between 1817 and 1821 over the location of the border between Maine and New Brunswick above the St Croix River. When these negotiations ground to a halt, largely because Chipman Sr had been able to disguise the weakness of the British position, Chipman Jr was sent to London to advise the British government. He continued to act as agent, at a generous salary for what had become by 1821 virtually a sinecure, until the commission was formally terminated in April 1828.

Inevitably, Chipman was also drawn into provincial politics. He was elected to the House of Assembly in June 1820, topping the poll in Saint John County. During the sessions of 1821 and 1822 he actively supported the agitation against the policies of Lieutenant Governor George Stracey Smyth*, who had antagonized the loyalist-merchant élite of Saint John by distributing patronage to non-loyalists and by introducing stricter regulations for cutting timber on crown lands. None the less, through his influence at the Colonial Office, Chipman secured the post of solicitor general while in England early in 1823. Smyth died that March and for nearly a year Chipman Sr, who was the most senior councillor both capable and willing to assume responsibility, served as administrator of the colony. With his father's support

Chipman Jr was easily elected speaker of the assembly in January 1824, replacing his uncle, William Botsford*. But, unlike his more gregarious father, Chipman never enjoyed politics and after his father's death in February 1824 he lost much of his drive. The new lieutenant governor, Sir Howard Douglas*, acknowledged Chipman's abilities but recommended that he succeed to the vacancy on the bench created by his father's death so that the speaker's chair could be filled by the more aggressive Robert Parker*.

Chipman took his place on the bench on 17 March 1825. As a judge he also inherited a seat on the Council and he continued to act as an adviser to Douglas and to assist in drafting legislation. Between November 1828 and July 1830 he was in London to aid in the preparation of the British submission to the king of the Netherlands, who had been chosen to determine the location of the boundary between Maine and New Brunswick. Chipman won high praise from Douglas and from officials in London for his careful and diligent research, and it was partly because of his efforts that the award in 1831 was so favourable to the British claim that the American government refused to accept it. During Chipman's absence public pressure mounted in New Brunswick for the removal of the judges from the Council but Chipman advised the Colonial Office that their presence was "a most important barrier against popular follies and encroachments." By 1831, however, it had become clear that the Whigs were prepared to yield to the pressure and so Chipman resigned from the Council. For his work on the boundary question and his loyalty to the Colonial Office, Chipman was amply rewarded. In 1830 he was presented to the king of England and in 1833, as in 1825, he received exorbitant fees for serving as an arbitrator in the negotiations between the two Canadas over the division of customs revenue collected in Lower Canada. On 4 Oct. 1834 he was promoted to the position of chief justice of New Brunswick over the heads of the other puisne judges.

As chief justice, Chipman automatically became president of the Legislative Council (which had been separated from the Executive Council in 1833) and he presided over its deliberations from 1835 to 1842. For much of this period the assembly and the council were at loggerheads, particularly during the lieutenant governorship of Sir Archibald Campbell*, who with the council resisted the efforts of the assembly to obtain control of the administration of crown lands and the casual and territorial revenues of the crown. Chipman supported Campbell's policies but "uniformly" supported the more conciliatory policies of his replacement, Sir John HARVEY, who reported that "Chief Justice Chipman did not hesitate in placing himself by my side." A continuing issue in New Brunswick during the 1830s was the boundary question, which brought the United States and Britain

close to war. Chipman wrote extensively on this subject, acted as an adviser to both Campbell and Harvey, and played an important part in convincing the British government of the justice of New Brunswick's claims. In fact, by upholding what was in reality a dubious legal interpretation of the terms of the Treaty of Paris of 1783, Chipman stiffened the resolve of British officials both in the colony and in London; he thus indirectly helped prepare the way for the compromise reached in the Webster–Ashburton Treaty of 1842, which gave to New Brunswick less than it wanted but probably more than it was entitled to. The *New-Brunswick Courier* correctly declared that to the two Chipmans the province "may feel much indebted for having sustained so little injury" from the treaty of 1783. Harvey recommended that, for his diligent labours in both domestic and international affairs, Chipman should, during his visit to London in 1840, become the first native of New Brunswick to be given a knighthood. Unfortunately Chipman had to return to the colony before the distinction could be awarded.

Although Chipman loyally served the imperial government and its representatives in the colony, there were limits to his subservience to the executive. When the Colonial Office selected James Carter*, an English lawyer, to succeed to a vacant judgeship in 1834, Chipman vigorously protested against this slight to the New Brunswick bar. In 1842 he again found himself in opposition, this time protesting the municipal incorporation bill sponsored by the lieutenant governor, Sir William MacBean George Colebrooke*, and the latter's efforts to secure for the executive control over the initiation of money bills. Chipman voted against Colebrooke's measures in the Legislative Council and declared that it was "impolitic," when the people were content, "to change the whole frame work of their Civil polity, and open the door to such agitation and political strife as would . . . weaken their attachment to Monarchical Institutions, and pave the way for Institutions altogether elective and Republican." None the less, when the Colonial Office supported Colebrooke, Chipman resigned from the council on 7 Oct. 1842 rather than continue the struggle. Failing health provided an additional legitimate excuse for his decision to withdraw entirely from political activity. For the next decade he was too ill to go on circuit or to take a significant part in lengthy trials, although he continued to prepare many of the written judgements of the Supreme Court. By 1845 he was ready to resign but the assembly would not grant him, or any of the judges, a pension. Finally he could continue no longer and on 17 Oct. 1850 he retired without a pension. On 26 November of the following year he died, leaving an estate conservatively estimated at £50,000.

Chipman was probably of limited significance as a

Chipman

politician, but he did make an important contribution in the settlement of the boundary question and an even more valuable one to the evolution of the colony's legal and judicial system. "My profession," he truthfully declared in 1834, "has been the favourite pursuit of my life." He trained a number of students in his law office, including brothers Robert and Neville* Parker and apparently he trained them well. At a meeting held on 21 Feb. 1825 Chipman was involved in the creation of a law library and the first barristers' society in the colony, and in the 1830s in the preparation of comparatively strict criteria for admission to the bar. In 1831 he helped formulate a series of provincial acts which, following similar acts already adopted in Britain, greatly mitigated the severity of the criminal code and drastically reduced the number of offences for which the punishment was death. He strongly advocated, and drafted, regulations for the establishment of a provincial penitentiary system. He chaired the special inquiry of 1832 into the administration of justice, which modified the court system, and the first compendium of *The acts of the General Assembly of New Brunswick* [1783–1836] was prepared by George F. S. Berton under his direction. In the 1840s he assisted Colebrooke in a further revision of the colony's criminal code. His written judgements formed the basis for future decisions long after his death.

Yet there is a less attractive side to Chipman's achievements. As a lawyer he drew his practice almost exclusively from the colonial élite and as a judge he was primarily concerned with protecting the interests of the property-owning class. When humanity and the protection of property clashed, he sided with the latter. In 1828 he caused a public outcry when he sentenced an 18-year-old youth to death for a relatively trivial offence. Although prepared to introduce the more lenient aspects of the criminal code which had already been adopted in Britain, he insisted that in those cases where the death penalty was still applicable it should be vigorously enforced even when there were mitigating circumstances. Chipman's approach to other aspects of legal reform was also very cautious. The special inquiry of 1832, over which he presided, consciously presented a more conservative report than its British counterpart; for example, it recommended that arrest and imprisonment for debt should not be abolished in New Brunswick. In these areas he was no more insensitive or less compassionate than the majority of his colleagues on the bench and at the bar, virtually all of whom were drawn from the same social group. But in other respects Chipman was more conservative, prepared to uphold, for example, outmoded laws of libel designed to stifle criticism of the government even when public opinion – and many of his colleagues – no longer believed in their utility.

Moreover, Chipman's reforming zeal was tempered by a strong dose of self-interest and a desire to defend the status of the legal profession. One of his reasons for serving on the 1832 commission was "to defeat a scheme for Summary Proceedings in small actions in the Supreme Court," which would have substantially reduced the costs of litigation. When he became chief justice he sought to dismiss the clerk of the Supreme Court, George SHORE, ostensibly because Shore had no legal training, but in reality so that he could give the post to a relative. He vigorously defended the salaries and fees received by the judges although public opinion, as voiced in the press and in the assembly, was convinced that the judges were overpaid in comparison to other provincial officials. He thus contributed to the unpopularity of what the Saint John *Morning News* vituperatively described as the colony's "legal gentry." Of course, self-interest is not necessarily a vice and Chipman was hardly unique in his pursuit of it. The original loyalists had always assumed that they should be rewarded for their loyalty and Chipman believed it was his duty to live in the grand style of the English country gentleman. None the less, he did acquire a reputation for excessive meanness and there was something distasteful about his relentless search for a style of life so vastly superior to that of the poor wretches with whom he dealt so harshly in court.

While still a youth, Chipman was described as a "true son" of his father. Indeed, although he rose to greater heights on the bench, his career followed an almost identical pattern to his father's and his political and social philosophy was largely shaped by his parents' teachings. At the age of ten, when asked by his uncle in Salem whether he would consider becoming an American citizen, young Chip replied that "no, no, no, he never will desert, the British cause, or Government." The conservatism of the scions of the loyalist élite in New Brunswick may have been less rigid, less vehement, and less emotional than that of their Upper Canadian counterparts. More secure in their control over the institutions of the colony, they adjusted more easily to a rapidly changing universe. However, their commitment to what Chipman described in 1833 on the 50th anniversary of the landing of the loyalists as the "principles of their Fathers" was real and abiding. Indeed, over time, and particularly after the War of 1812, the anti-Americanism of the New Brunswick élite hardened and their anglophilia became more pronounced.

None the less, the influence of the second-generation loyalist gentry was receding in the face of large-scale non-loyalist immigration and of changes both within New Brunswick society and in the policies of the imperial government. In politics Chipman and his kind fought to preserve the constitutional structure

152

established by their fathers. They lauded the English constitution as "better adapted to secure all the great ends of civil society than any form of Government which the wit of man has yet produced" and condemned "organic changes." Their ideal was to preserve a constitutional balance in which the powers of the popularly elected assembly would be curtailed by a strong and independent executive authority and an appointed second chamber representing the colony's élite. But gradually during the 1830s power shifted into the hands of the assembly, where the influence of the gentry, while still important, was in decline. The ultimate irony was that Chipman could do little to oppose this development after the appointment of Harvey without attacking the imperial government whose policies the governor was implementing. Only when Colebrooke sought to revitalize the executive by a series of reforms, which would have further weakened the Legislative Council and established a closer link between the executive and the assembly, did Chipman speak out. He allied himself with the conservative forces in the assembly who wished to preserve the decentralized nature of the New Brunswick constitution and to resist the growing pressure for some form of responsible government. But loyalty again conflicted with principle: Chipman withdrew from a confrontation with the imperial authorities and passively left others to carry on the struggle to preserve the *status quo*.

In religion, too, Chipman was engaged in a kind of holding action. Although the original loyalists had been prepared to extend toleration to dissenters, they had sought to establish the primacy of the Church of England and to give that church control over education. Chipman was not a zealot but he was "warmly attached" to the "doctrine and discipline" of the established church. He regularly attended the parish church in Saint John. Indeed, he owned the land on which it was situated and through his influence with successive governors could control the selection of ministers. Chipman recognized that the Church of England could not indefinitely rely upon public support and he gave generously of his time and, in his will, of his private fortune to assist the church. He left £10,000 to be invested for the support of the "missionary objects" of the Diocesan Church Society of New Brunswick, and gave his own church the land on which the building stood and an annual income for the minister. He also bequeathed £5,000 for the establishment of Madras schools in Saint John and Fredericton [*see* John BAIRD]. But undoubtedly his greatest concern was to preserve the integrity of King's College (University of New Brunswick), Fredericton. He served for many years on its governing body and while he supported the efforts of Douglas and Harvey to remove the most restrictive provisions in the charter of the college, he was

determined that it would remain firmly under the control of Anglican churchmen. Yet by the time of his death the final assault upon the remaining privileges of the Church of England was already well under way.

Perhaps the most discouraging feature to Chipman of New Brunswick society by mid century was the emergence of a class system based upon the possession of capital rather than the ownership of land. However, it would be wrong to draw too stark a dichotomy between the capitalist and landowning groups. Intermarriage was common and in Saint John the two groups blended together to some extent. But wealth *per se* did not guarantee entry into the social circle in which the Chipmans moved and it did not automatically confirm one's status as a gentleman, the occupation by which Chipman listed himself in the 1851 census. Significantly, Chipman invested almost all of his money in land; he operated a farm, published articles in the newspapers on agriculture, and publicly deplored the dependence of the colony on the timber trade. Unlike many other second- and third-generation loyalists, he never really adjusted to the economic, and increasingly the new political and social, realities of life in colonial New Brunswick. In later life he became more and more an aloof figure, respected but not loved, fighting to preserve a system of values that was becoming unpopular and irrelevant. In part, this failure to adjust explains his passionate devotion to his profession, for the bench and the bar were the last preserves of the loyalist gentry. And by the 1850s even these were under siege. Chipman had no son to succeed him. But since, to achieve prominence, that son would have had to adjust to a New Brunswick quite different from that envisaged by his father and grandfather, perhaps Chipman would not have been sorry to see his family name disappear with his death.

PHILLIP BUCKNER

[The bulk of Ward Chipman's papers were apparently destroyed after his death but the remnants can be found in the Lawrence collection, PAC, MG 23, D1. Also very useful are the references and letters in the Sewell correspondence, PAC, MG 23, GII, 10; the Winslow family papers in UNBL, MG H2, the most important of which were published in the *Winslow papers, A.D. 1776–1826*, ed. W. O. Raymond (Saint John, N.B., 1901); and the H. T. Hazen coll.: Ward Chipman papers in the N.B. Museum. Letters to or from Chipman may also be found at the PAC in the papers of Sir Howard Douglas (MG 24, A3), E. J. Jarvis (MG 24, B13), Sir John Harvey (MG 24, A17), Sir William M. G. Colebrooke (MG 24, A31), Sir Edmund Walker Head (MG 24, A20), Sir Archibald Campbell (MG 24, A21), and Amos Botsford (MG 23, D4), and in the Saunders papers at UNBL, MG H11.

The other major primary source for this study was the New Brunswick correspondence in the PRO, especially CO 188/39: 376–79; 188/41: 284–85; 188/42: 158–61;

Christie

188/43: 99–102; 188/45: 84; 188/47: 236–38; 188/49: 242–44; 188/50: 4–8, 11, 205–6; 188/52: 10, 12–17, 19–23, 169–70, 288–90, 291–93, 367–70; 188/56: 371–72, 427–29; 188/59: 261; 188/60: 311–15; 188/66: 70–72; 188/68: 136–41; CO 189/13: 48–49; 189/16: 294–99; CO 323/154: 201–4, 232–35, 253; 323/158: 270–71; 323/172: 193. There are also numerous references to Chipman in the New Brunswick newspapers. The most useful were the *New-Brunswick Courier*, 2, 9, 23 Feb. 1828; 26 Nov. 1830; 15 Jan. 1831; 14 Jan. 1832; 4 Nov. 1837; 18 Jan., 29 Nov. 1851; and an item in the *Saint John Globe*, 27 July 1907: 8. Official publications containing information about Chipman include *Copy of the report made to his Excellency, the Lieutenant Governor of the province of New-Brunswick by the commissioners appointed to inquire into the judicial institutions of the province* (Fredericton, 1833); N.B., *Acts*, [1786–1836]; House of Assembly, *Journal*, 1821–24; and Legislative Council, *Journal*, 1831–42. Useful PANB holdings include the probate records for his estate in RG 7, RS71, 1852, and the N.B. Barristers' Soc. papers, MC 288. There is also valuable material in the N.B. Museum, W. F. Ganong scrapbook no.1: 99.

The only good study of Chipman is Lawrence, *Judges of N.B.* (Stockton and Raymond), 301–70, but there is some useful general information in Ann Gorman Condon, "'The envy of the American states': the settlement of the loyalists in New Brunswick: goals and achievements" (PHD thesis, Harvard Univ., Cambridge, Mass., 1975); J. W. Lawrence, *Foot-prints; or, incidents in early history of New Brunswick, 1783–1883* (Saint John, 1883); MacNutt, *New Brunswick*; and P. A. Ryder, "Ward Chipman, United Empire Loyalist" (MA thesis, Univ. of N.B., Fredericton, 1958). On the northeastern boundary dispute the major sources are *International adjudications, ancient and modern: history and documents . . . modern series*, ed. J. B. Moore (6v., New York, 1929–33), 6; W. F. Ganong, "A monograph of the evolution of the boundaries of the province of New Brunswick," RSC *Trans.*, 2nd ser., 7 (1901), sect.II: 139–449; and R. W. Hale, "The forgotten Maine boundary commission," Mass. Hist. Soc., *Proc.* (Boston), 71 (1953–57): 147–55. P.B.]

CHRISTIE, ROBERT, militia officer, lawyer, office holder, journalist, historian, and politician; b. 20 Jan. 1787 in Windsor, N.S., second son of James Christie and Janet McIntosh; m. 24 Feb. 1812 Monique-Olivier Doucet, and they had at least one son who probably died in early childhood; d. 13 Oct. 1856 at Quebec.

Robert Christie's father, a shoemaker, immigrated to Nova Scotia from Scotland. He held considerable land and minor posts in Windsor, where Robert attended King's College, graduating some time before 1803. Robert is supposed to have started out in business in Halifax but, following a career pattern common at that time, he left for Quebec in 1805. There he was indentured by his father as clerk and apprentice to lawyer Edward Bowen* for five years. He was commissioned advocate and attorney on 3 Oct. 1810. During the War of 1812 he served as captain in Quebec's 4th Militia Battalion.

Turning to journalism in the spring of 1816, Christie established and edited a weekly newspaper, the *Quebec Telegraph*. The paper, one of the first commercial newspapers at Quebec, also carried agricultural reports and foreign news. Its reporting of events in the House of Assembly foreshadowed Christie's later writings on Lower Canadian politics. Aiming for both English and French readers, it was published from the beginning in the two languages. In late November 1816 Robert-Anne d'Estimauville* became its editor but the arrangement lasted only a few weeks; he and Christie quarrelled in mid December and d'Estimauville left. Management problems continued to plague the paper until it ceased publication in July 1817.

Meanwhile, on 26 Jan. 1816 Christie had been appointed law clerk by the House of Assembly, with responsibility for framing bills; the appointment was confirmed by a government commission in March 1817. In 1819 he was also appointed registrar to a commission, consisting of Jean-Thomas Taschereau*, Michel-Louis Juchereau* Duchesnay, and George Waters Allsopp*, established to determine Gaspé land claims, and thus began his long association with the Gaspé region. During his early involvement in Lower Canadian politics, Christie was an admirer of the Canadian party under James STUART. The latter, also an alumnus of King's College, may have had considerable influence on Christie. But Christie's opposition to the government was short-lived and, after finding favour with the governor, Lord Dalhousie [Ramsay*], he began to support the executive. He received other government appointments and contracts and served as law clerk until about 1827.

On 15 Oct. 1827 Christie was elected to the assembly as the member for Gaspé, a district with a substantial English-speaking population. In the same year he was appointed chairman of the Court of Quarter Sessions for the district of Quebec, but his partisanship on behalf of the executive and the governor brought him into conflict with the assembly. He followed instructions of the government in that year to prepare a new list of magistrates for the province, deleting those members of the assembly who had opposed Dalhousie. The commissions of several Quebec magistrates, including John Neilson*, François Blanchet*, and François Quirouet*, together with those of others from Montreal, were not renewed. The judges of the Court of King's Bench, James Kerr*, Taschereau, and Christie's former mentor, Bowen, refused to accept the new list when it was submitted to them for approval, but Christie failed to heed this warning not to allow any tampering with the judicial system. The assembly was determined to establish the independence of the judiciary and the matter came to a head with the report in 1829 of its select committee established to investigate methods for appointing justices of the peace. The report contained accounts of Christie's hot-tempered responses as well as his clashes with Louis Bourdages* and other politicians with whom he had discussed the list. Christie was not allowed to speak in his own defence and he may also have suffered from his association with Dalhousie's secretary, Andrew William Cochran*, his former classmate at King's College.

Christie's salary was dropped from the next civil list, but the matter was not as simple as the firing of a minor official. As a result of the report of its committee, the assembly expelled Christie from the house on 14 Feb. 1829. However, Gaspé continued to re-elect him and he was expelled five times in all from 1829 to 1832. His opponents, especially Neilson and Bourdages, claimed Christie's expulsion constituted a legal disqualification which only the assembly could lift. Supporters of Christie's right to his seat, including Andrew Stuart*, Charles Richard Ogden* and Jean-François-Joseph Duval, argued that accepting this claim would place the assembly above the expressed wishes of the people. When the matter was referred to the British government, the Whig colonial secretary, Lord Goderich, seeing British precedents and a certain parallel with the case of John Wilkes, upheld Christie's right to his seat. The later stages of the controversy were complicated by Christie's espousal of a movement in Gaspé to break away from Lower Canada and to be annexed to the province of New Brunswick. The Gaspé electors were enraged by what they perceived as denial of their right to representation and were also interested in the recent attention by New Brunswick to the timber trade and the management of crown lands in the Miramichi area. The movement, like others before it, came to nothing in 1833 when John Le Boutillier* was elected for Gaspé. Christie temporarily retired from politics, returning as member for Gaspé in 1841.

For some years Christie had pursued another and perhaps more important career, as historian of Lower Canada. In September 1816 the *Quebec Telegraph* began printing excerpts from his account of the governorships of Sir James Henry Craig* and Sir George Prevost* covering the years 1807 to 1815. The work was published in full at Quebec in 1818. From then until 1829 Christie published accounts of the administrations of successive governors from Sir Gordon DRUMMOND to Dalhousie. These accounts were later included in his six-volume work, *A history of the late province of Lower Canada* (1848–55). Christie's writing style is too ornate to commend his work as literature but it is of historiographic importance for its detailed, impartial chronicling of events and its presentation of documents, some no longer extant in their original form. Compared to the two-volume work by William Smith*, *History of Canada; from its first discovery, to the peace of 1763* (Quebec, 1815), which was a polemic against the tyranny of French rule, Christie's writings were well balanced. Even Louis-Joseph Papineau* conceded that Christie's history was supportive of his role in the events of 1837, although wrong in some details. The next comprehensive history of Canada to be written in English would be *The history of Canada* by William Kingsford*, published in ten volumes at Toronto from 1887 to 1898, but Kingsford would not rely extensively on original documents to prepare his work. Christie may also be considered a bridge from the historians of his generation to those of the romantic era of Francis Parkman*, for one of the last events of his life was to introduce Parkman to Papineau.

Christie was convinced that "the history of a people is part of their public property," and during his second term of office, as member of the legislature for the Province of Canada, he pressed for government responsibility in the collection, preservation, and publication of historical documents and public records. In 1844–45 he moved the establishment of, and chaired, the committee appointed to inquire into the condition of the archives and public records of New France, the province of Quebec, and Lower Canada. The committee was to adopt measures for the collection, arrangement, and preservation "from all accessible sources whatsoever, of such ancient and authentic records and documents relating to the first settlements of Canada, as . . . may cast light upon or be conducive to a full knowledge of its early history." Subsequently, under the auspices of the government and the Literary and Historical Society of Quebec, colonial documents of New France were copied in Albany, N.Y., and France. In 1846 Christie chaired the committee appointed to inquire into the state of the judicial and parliamentary records in Lower Canada and it presented a conservation report on the often deplorable condition in which the records of both Upper and Lower Canada were kept. Again in 1849 Christie pressed the legislature for funds to preserve a variety of documents, this time those relating to the civil and military government of the province before 1791 and to the Jesuits prior to their suppression in that year, which were scattered throughout various government departments. Canadian historians are indebted to Christie for his efforts.

Christie kept his seat in the legislature from 1841 until 1854. As before, he upheld the interests of Gaspé, especially in questions of land claims, administration of justice, and registration of marriages, all areas where problems arose from settlement preceding the organization of government in the area. He was a strong advocate of economy in government spending and of control of finances by the legislature; his role as critic gave him some claim to be

Chubb

called the "Canadian Hume." He was not an advocate of the union of the Canadas. It was he who introduced the motion in 1842 to move the capital from Kingston, complaining that the location was not central for the majority of the population. Though conservative in nature and sceptical about "responsible government," he was not a party man, tending to vote for the issue. He was a frequent contributor to newspapers and from 1848 to 1850 edited the conservative *Quebec Mercury*. He had an opinion on every issue before the assembly and his erratic performance and frequent comments drove the *Globe* to describe him as a "driveller." Always quick of temper, he grew more irascible with age, at one point challenging a member of the legislature to a duel. In the 1840s, however, he was reconciled with a former adversary, John Neilson. Papineau, also once a keen opponent, became a close friend at the end of Christie's life and Christie championed attempts to have Papineau's pre-1837 salary as speaker of the assembly paid to him. He acquired a reputation for incorruptibility because of his outspokenness and obvious honesty.

Christie's health began to fail in 1854. He hoped to be appointed to the committee studying the abolition of seigneurial tenure in Lower Canada, a favourite cause of his, but he was defeated by Le Boutillier in the elections of that year. He died suddenly of a heart attack on 13 Oct. 1856.

SHIRLEY C. SPRAGGE

Robert Christie is the author of *Memoirs of the administration of the colonial government of Lower-Canada, by Sir James Henry Craig, and Sir George Prevost, from the year 1807 until the year 1815, comprehending the military and naval operations in the Canadas during the late war with the United States of America* (Quebec, 1818), also published under the title *The military and naval operations in the Canadas during the late war with the United States, including also the political history of Lower Canada during the administration of Sir James Henry Craig and Sir George Prevost, from 1807 until 1815* (Quebec, 1818; repr. New York, 1818); *A brief review of the political state of Lower-Canada, since the conquest of the colony, to the present day, to which are added, memoirs of the administrations of the colonial government of Lower Canada, by Sir Gordon Drummond, and Sir John Coape Sherbrooke* (New York, 1818); *Memoirs of the administration of the government of Lower-Canada, by Sir Gordon Drummond, Sir John Coape Sherbrooke, the late Duke of Richmond, James Monk, esquire, and Sir Peregrine Maitland; continued from the 3d April, 1815, until the 18th June, 1820* (Quebec, 1820); and *Memoirs of the administration of the government of Lower Canada, by the Right Honorable the Earl of Dalhousie, G.C.B., comprehending a period of eight years, vizt: – from June, 1820 till September, 1828* (Quebec, 1829). These volumes were integrated into a work issued under the title *A history of the late province of Lower Canada, parliamentary and political, from the commencement to the close of its existence as a separate province* ... (6v., Quebec and Montreal, 1848–55; 2nd ed., Montreal, 1866).

ANQ-Q, CE1-61, 24 févr. 1812, 16 oct. 1856; P1000-22-399. Hants County Court of Probate (Windsor, N.S.), Will book, I (mfm. at PANS). PAC, MG 24, B2; MG 30, D1, 8: 314–16; RG 68, General index, 1651–1841. Can., Prov. of, Legislative Assembly, *App. des journaux*, 1844–45, app.HH; 1846, app.KK. *Debates of the Legislative Assembly of United Canada* (Abbott Gibbs et al.), vols.1–2. *Docs. relating to constitutional hist., 1791–1818* (Doughty and McArthur). L.C., House of Assembly, *Journals*, 1828–29, app.DD. *Memoranda respecting King's College, at Windsor, in Nova Scotia* ... (Halifax, 1836). L.-J. Papineau, "Lettres de L.-J. Papineau à Robert Christie," *BRH*, 34 (1928): 296–320, 347–77. *Gleaner*, 4–11 Sept. 1832, 25 Oct. 1856. *New-Brunswick Courier*, 1, 8, 29 Dec. 1832; 9, 16 Feb., 6 April 1833. *Quebec Gazette*, 27 June 1805, 11 Oct. 1810, 20 March 1817, 6 May 1819, 14 Oct. 1856. *Quebec Telegraph*, 29 April 1816–14 July 1817. *Royal Gazette* (Fredericton), 5, 26 Dec. 1832. Beaulieu et Hamelin, *La presse québécoise*, 1: 32–33. Morgan, *Bibliotheca Canadensis*, 75–76; *Sketches of celebrated Canadians*, 357–58. John Archer, "A study of archival institutions in Canada" (PHD thesis, Queen's Univ., Kingston, Ont., 1969). J.-G. Barthe, *Souvenirs d'un demi-siècle ou mémoires pour servir à l'histoire contemporaine* (Montréal, 1885). Jules Bélanger et al., *Histoire de la Gaspésie* (Montréal, 1981). J.-M. LeMoine, *Monographies et esquisses* (Québec, 1885). Taft Manning, *Revolt of French Canada*. "Obituary notice of the late Robert Christie, esq.," *BRH*, 44 (1938): 9–12. "Robert Christie," *BRH*, 20 (1914): 338, 351–52. P.-G. Roy, "Les expulsions de Robert Christie," *BRH*, 43 (1937): 349–50.

CHUBB, HENRY, printer, militia officer, newspaper publisher, businessman, politician, and justice of the peace; b. 1787 in Saint John, N.B., son of John Chubb and Mary ——; m. 14 July 1816 Jane Lugrin, sister of printer George Kilman Lugrin*, and they had three sons and three daughters; d. 20 May 1855 in Saint John.

Henry Chubb's father and mother immigrated to British North America from Philadelphia in 1783. As a loyalist, John Chubb was granted a lot in Parrtown (Saint John) where he worked as a cordwainer and also served in the militia. In 1802 Henry Chubb began his apprenticeship at the offices of Jacob S. Mott*, king's printer and publisher of the Saint John *Royal Gazette and New Brunswick Advertiser*. After Mott's death in 1814, Chubb managed the paper for his widow until she had to discontinue publication in 1815. On 2 May 1811 Chubb had begun his own newspaper, the *New-Brunswick Courier*. He formed a partnership with William Durant at some point but it was dissolved on 1 June 1822. For years the *Courier* consisted of advertisements, marine intelligence, and news items reprinted from foreign papers. By 1841, when his premises were destroyed by fire, Chubb's News Room had become a popular meeting place. In 1842 Chubb formed a partnership with his eldest son, Henry John, and Samuel Seeds, who for many years acted as editor of the *Courier*. The enterprise was moved into a new brick building in 1846 on what is still known as "Chubb's Corner." Since the late 1840s stocks, securities, and land have been auctioned outdoors on the corner, and until the 1860s the Chubb offices maintained their predominance as the business information centre in the city.

In 1831 Chubb had hired George Blatch to report the House of Assembly debates, and within two years the *Courier* had become the "organ for a popular feeling that was rapidly crystallizing into a political party with a clear objective": the reform of imperial land policy, and in particular of the Crown Lands Office under Thomas Baillie*. From November 1832 to April 1833 the *Courier* published a series of satirical letters attacking Baillie by John Gape, the pseudonym of Robert Gowan*. After 1837, when the province began receiving large revenues from the sale of crown lands, and until 1848, with the advent of responsible government, the *Courier* also pressed for reforms in government expenditures, arguing that the assembly's appropriations committees should give control of the budget for province-wide improvements to the Executive Council, which was now composed of elected members of the assembly. One of these improvements was railways and the *Courier* insisted that the price of New Brunswick's support for the route along the northeast coast of the province, linking Halifax with the Canadas, should be a branch line from Shediac to Saint John.

Over the years the paper also encouraged reform in the treatment of Indians, campaigned for a standard provincial common-school system, cautiously supported the temperance movement, and pressed for reorganization of King's College, Fredericton, as the non-denominational University of New Brunswick. The *Courier* approved of Lord Ashburton's peaceful settlement of the New Brunswick–Maine boundary dispute in 1842, and it supported the Reciprocity Treaty of 1854 because American markets were becoming increasingly important for natural products as imperial free-trade policies destroyed the colony's protected position in the timber trade. After Chubb's death the *Courier* continued to be concerned with markets for New Brunswick products. Even before the treaty ended in 1866, the newspaper, encouraged by the 1864 conferences at Charlottetown and Quebec, supported Samuel Leonard Tilley*'s plans to bring New Brunswick into confederation. It argued for the retention of local legislatures, to be subsidized by the federal government in any new arrangement.

In 1833 Chubb had been a founder of the Merchants' Exchange, Saint John, and a shareholder in the New Brunswick Mining Company; in 1854 he bought stocks in the Saint John Fire Insurance Company which was established that year. He helped organize the Saint John Orphan Benevolent Society in 1840, and seven years later he and his wife donated property for the erection of a marine hospital. He served in the militia, acted as justice of the peace, and

was the last mayor of Saint John (1850–53) to be appointed by the New Brunswick government.

Henry Chubb's office was the training-ground for a generation of journalists, including the New York publisher Robert Sears and the New Brunswick editors Robert Shives* of the *Amaranth* and James Hogg* of the *New Brunswick Reporter and Fredericton Advertiser*. According to the obituary Hogg published in the *Reporter*, "Mr. Chubb has long been designated 'the Father of the Press' by his brotherhood of the craft." After Chubb's death, his surviving sons, Thomas and George James, continued the paper with Seeds, who died in 1864. The *Courier* was discontinued in July 1865 and George remained sole proprietor of the firm's printing and bookselling operations until the great fire of 1877. In 1825 his father had printed Hogg's *Poems; religious, moral and sentimental* and, in partnership with James Sears, produced Peter Fisher's *Sketches of New-Brunswick*. George carried on the tradition of encouraging local literary activity by printing and underwriting George Stewart's *Stewart's Literary Quarterly Magazine* from 1867 to 1872. All the Chubb children died without issue.

GEORGE L. PARKER

N.B. Museum, E. B. Chandler papers, Henry Chubb to Chandler, 23 Sept. 1836; Chubb family papers; F51, no.32; Marine Hospital, CB DOC.; Misc. index relating to biog., geneal., and hist. N.B. subjects; N.B. Hist. Soc. papers, packet 8, no.70; Reg. of marriages for the city and county of Saint John, book A (1810–28): 77; Tilley family papers, H. Chubb & Co. to S. L. Tilley, 30 April 1858. PAC, MG 23, D1, 61, book 6; 68, book 90; MG 24, A20, 3: ff.211–12, 243–46, 675; RG 8, I (C ser.), 1883: 57; 1884: 32, 38, 64, 73, 88; 1885, Nathaniel Vernon, muster rolls, 25 Oct.–24 Dec. 1781, 24 Feb.–24 April 1782. [Peter Fisher], *Sketches of New-Brunswick . . . by an inhabitant of the province* (Saint John, N.B., 1825), reprinted as Peter Fisher, *The first history of New Brunswick* (Saint John, 1921; repr. Woodstock, N.B., 1980). N.B., *Acts*, [1786–1836], 1833, c.12; *The revised statutes of New Brunswick . . .* (3v., Fredericton, 1854–55), 3: 447, 689–90. *New-Brunswick Courier*, 5 Feb. 1831; 20 March 1841; 3 Sept. 1842; 7 Feb. 1846; 1 Jan., 19 Feb. 1848; 17 March 1855; 24 Sept., 10 Dec. 1864; 7 Jan., 15 July 1865. *New Brunswick Reporter and Fredericton Advertiser*, 25 May 1855. *Novascotian, or Colonial Herald*, 5 Feb. 1835.

J. R. Harper, *Historical directory of New Brunswick newspapers and periodicals* (Fredericton, 1961), xiv. W. G. MacFarlane, *New Brunswick bibliography: the books and writers of the province* (Saint John, 1895). Lorenzo Sabine, *The American loyalists, or biographical sketches of adherents to the British crown in the war of the revolution . . .* (Boston, 1847), 209. George MacBeath, *Historic Chubb's Corner* (Saint John, [1966?]; copy at N.B. Museum). MacNutt, *Atlantic prov.*; *New Brunswick*. *St. John and its business: a history of St. John . . .* (Saint John, 1875), 179–80. George Stewart, "The history of a magazine," in his *Essays from reviews: 2nd series* (Quebec, 1893), 126. P. B. Waite, *The life and times of confederation,*

Chubbee

1864–67: politics, newspapers, and the union of British North America (Toronto, 1962). E. C. Wright, *The loyalists of New Brunswick* (Fredericton, 1955; repr. Moncton, N.B., 1972), 269. J. R. Armstrong, "The Exchange Coffee House and St. John's first club," N.B. Hist. Soc., *Coll.* (Saint John), 3 (1907–14), no.7: 60–78. Dorothy Dearborn, "It takes style to run a good auction," *Telegraph-Journal* (Saint John), 8 Dec. 1973: 13. D. R. Jack, "Acadian magazines," RSC *Trans.*, 2nd ser., 9 (1903), sect.II: 173–203, especially 179; "Early journalism in New Brunswick," *Acadiensis* (Saint John), 8 (1908): 250–65. J. S. Martell, "The press of the Maritime provinces in the 1830's," *CHR*, 19 (1938): 24–49.

CHUBBEE, WILLIAM. *See* TUBBEE, OKAH

CLARKE, JOHN, fur trader; b. 1781 in Montreal, son of Simon Clarke, innkeeper, and Ann Waldorf; m. first about 1812, according to the custom of the country, Josephte Kanhopitsa, and they had one daughter; m. secondly Sophia (Sapphira) Jacobina Spence (d. 1824), daughter of HBC clerk Joseph Spence, a fur-trade alliance entered into in or before 1816 and solemnized on 9 Nov. 1821 in Montreal; m. thirdly by 1822 Marianne Trustler (Tranclar, Trutter), a country marriage solemnized in Montreal on 26 Oct. 1830, and they had four sons and four daughters; d. 19 Dec. 1852 in Montreal.

John Clarke joined the North West Company as an apprentice clerk on 17 Jan. 1800, and that spring he journeyed from Montreal to Grand Portage (near Grand Portage, Minn.) in the same NWC party as Daniel Williams Harmon*. After three hectic weeks at Grand Portage, Clarke left for Athabasca in July with John Finlay and Alexander Henry* the younger. In 1802 he established the NWC post at Pierre au Calumet (north of Fort McMurray, Alta) on the Athabasca River; he served at Fort Vermilion (near Fort Vermilion, Alta) on the Peace River in 1804–5 and in 1809 was placed in charge of Fort St John (near Fort St John,, B.C.), farther up the river. This promotion, however, did not work out successfully, and Clarke left the NWC, returning to Montreal in the spring of 1810. A colleague, George KEITH, wrote shortly afterwards that "latterly, his conduct in this country was rather reprehensible. . . . A little elevation is apt to dazzle and make us sometimes forget the previous footing we were on."

Later that year, possibly aided by maternal ties with John Jacob Astor*, Clarke became a partner in Astor's Pacific Fur Company and in October 1811 he was in charge of the PFC party, including Ross Cox, that left New York aboard the *Beaver*, reaching Fort Astoria (Astoria, Oreg.) in May 1812. Late in June he and a small party travelled up the Columbia River to build a post in opposition to the NWC's Spokane House (near Spokane, Wash.) on the Spokane River, and that winter the competition for furs between Clarke and the

NWC clerk, James McMILLAN, was fierce. Clarke also ran into difficulties with the Indians. During the return trip to Fort Astoria with his furs in the spring of 1813, he hanged an Indian for stealing a silver goblet, thus obliging his party to flee from attackers seeking revenge.

The instability of American control on the Pacific northwest coast during the War of 1812 forced the sale of the entire PFC operation based at Fort Astoria to the NWC in October 1813, a transfer negotiated by Duncan McDougall*, an Astorian and former Nor'Wester. Clarke spent the winter of 1813–14 in the employ of the NWC at Fort Astoria (renamed Fort George), under the command of John McDonald* of Garth. The following summer he travelled overland with the NWC brigade to the Canadas in company with two other former Astorians, Donald McKENZIE and Gabriel Franchère*.

Clarke turned down a commission with the Indian Department before accepting a handsome contract with the Hudson's Bay Company in 1815. Colin Robertson* recruited him, at an initial salary of £400, for the HBC expedition aimed at countering the NWC's trading activity in the Athabasca country. The party left Terrebonne, Lower Canada, for the interior in May and, after Robertson retired from the expedition at Jack River House (Man.) in July, Clarke was chosen as his replacement by HBC officers Thomas Thomas* and James BIRD. From early fall the HBC party faced difficulties. A skirmish with the Nor'Westers at Cumberland House (Sask.) was followed by an amicable exchange of prisoners. Food ran short beyond Île-à-la-Crosse as the NWC diverted Indian provisioners from Clarke's path. In October he established Fort Wedderburn on an island in Lake Athabasca, across from the NWC's Fort Chipewyan (Alta). He then took five canoes up the Peace River hoping to winter near Fort Vermilion, but NWC men John McGILLIVRAY and William McIntosh* succeeded in cutting off his supplies. After three men died of starvation at Loon River (Alta) and another 13 while trying to make their way back to Fort Wedderburn, Clarke was obliged to surrender his goods to McIntosh in exchange for provisions. Although Fort Wedderburn survived what Clarke labelled the NWC's "starving system," there were no returns to compensate for the great expenses incurred.

The Athabasca campaign of 1816–17 was also obstructed; a large NWC force at Lake Athabasca kept the HBC party immobile at Fort Wedderburn by threats and seizures of men and goods. Finally, on 23 Jan. 1817, NWC partner Archibald Norman McLeod*, exercising his authority as justice of the peace, imprisoned Clarke and seized the HBC fort. Clarke's subsequent detention at Great Slave Lake (N.W.T.) and later at Fort Vermilion destroyed any chance of his organizing a new expedition the next season. Meanwhile, Clarke's HBC colleagues had begun to find fault with his conduct. In July 1816 Robertson, while praising Clarke's courage, had noted that "the heroic manner he bore his misfortunes covers a multitude of sins" and in 1818 commented that "his inordinate vanity is such that the management of John Clarke is as arduous a task as that of opposing the N.W.Co." James Bird at Edmonton House (Edmonton) was equally critical.

Robertson took command of the HBC enterprise in Athabasca in 1818 and sent Clarke up the Peace River where, after a skirmish at Fort Vermilion, he established St Mary's Fort (near Peace River, Alta). In June 1819 Clarke was with HBC governor William Williams* at the Grand Rapids (Man.) to help with the arrest of the Nor'Westers, Benjamin Joseph Frobisher*, John George McTavish*, and others. After serving two seasons at Île-à-la-Crosse, Clarke was appointed chief factor in the 1821 union of the HBC and the NWC [see Simon McGillivray*], despite Governor George SIMPSON's opposition, and was granted a year's leave of absence before taking charge of Fort Garry (Winnipeg). Clarke's overbearing assertion of company authority in the Red River colony earned him the deep dislike of both Governor Andrew H. BULGER and the settlers. Particularly at issue were his strictures against the settlers' conducting any trade with Indians, even for needed provisions, in a narrow-minded effort to protect the HBC fur trade.

Severely criticized by the HBC London committee in 1823, Clarke was removed to the charge of the post at Lesser Slave Lake (Alta) for the years 1824–26 and from there went to Fort Pelly (Sask.) where he competently managed the Swan River district until 1830. Convinced that "to the joint efforts of Mr Robertson and myself are the HB Coy in a great measure indebted for the splendor & importance of their rank & standing in the great Commercial World," he visited London in 1831 to seek company recognition for his past services. But, in Simpson's words, "the committee treated him with the contempt he deserved." In his 1832 "Character book" Simpson portrayed Clarke as "a boasting, ignorant low fellow" showing "total want of every principle or feeling, allied to fair dealing, honour & integrity. . . . He is in short a disgrace to the 'Fur Trade.'" Although effective in opposition, commanding in appearance, and able to control Indians and servants by his strength of personality, he lacked the social qualities and character favoured in the new generation of officers.

From 1831 to 1833, Clarke served at Mingan, Lower Canada, where he soon came into conflict with James KEITH, his superior in charge of the Montreal department. A furlough from 1833 to 1835 was followed by retirement to Montreal where he died in 1852.

JENNIFER S. H. BROWN

ANQ-M, CE1-63, 26 oct. 1830; CN1-29, 17 janv. 1800. PAC, MG 19, E5, 2. PAM, HBCA, A.36/4: f.182; MG 2, A5. PCA, St Gabriel Street Church (Montreal), reg. of baptisms, marriages, and burials, 9 Nov. 1821. *Les bourgeois de la Compagnie du Nord-Ouest* (Masson), vol.2. *Catholic Church records of Pacific northwest* (Munnick). Cox, *Adventures on the Columbia*. *Docs. relating to NWC* (Wallace). Harmon, *Sixteen years in the Indian country* (Lamb). *HBRS*, 1 (Rich); 2 (Rich and Fleming). A. Ross, *Adventures on the Columbia; The fur hunters of the far west; a narrative of adventures in the Oregon and Rocky mountains* (2v., London, 1855). Simpson, "Character book," *HBRS*, 30 (Williams), 151–236; *Fur trade and empire* (Merk; 1968). Campbell, *Hist. of Scotch Presbyterian Church*, 125. Adèle Clarke, *Old Montreal, John Clarke: his adventures, friends and family* (Montreal, 1906). J. S. Galbraith, *The little emperor; Governor Simpson of the Hudson's Bay Company* (Toronto, 1976). J. J. Hargrave, *Red River* (Montreal, 1871; repr., Altona, Man., 1977), 491–96. A. S. Morton, *A history of the Canadian west to 1870–71, being a history of Rupert's Land (the Hudson's Bay Company territory) and of the North-West Territories (including the Pacific slope)*, ed. L. G. Thomas (2nd ed., Toronto [and Buffalo, N.Y., 1973]). J. U. Terrell, *Furs by Astor* (New York, 1963). J. R. Anderson, "John Clarke of Athabasca," *Family Herald* (Montreal), 12 July 1933: 19–20.

CLARKE (Clark), SEPTIMUS D., farmer; b. 1787; m. and he and his wife had at least five children; d. 15 Jan. 1859 in Preston, N.S.

Septimus D. Clarke was one of more than 2,000 former slaves who were brought to Nova Scotia following the War of 1812. Having escaped from plantations in the United States, they travelled along its eastern seaboard in British naval vessels, and in 1815 the majority of the refugee blacks were settled in Preston Township. Preston was a township of stones, an infertile land with widely scattered patches of soil and trees and long, damp winters to which the new settlers were not accustomed. The blacks became subsistence farmers.

On or before 19 Nov. 1816 Clarke, his wife, and their four children were established on a ten-acre farm by Theophilus Chamberlain*. The family endured numerous hardships and in December 1819 Clarke, now the father of five children, petitioned Lieutenant Governor Lord Dalhousie [Ramsay*] for more land. In support of his claim he reported that he and his family had produced "one hundred twenty bushels of potatoes besides other vegetables" and, having cleared most of the land he was licensed to occupy, he feared becoming "destitute of wood for fuel." The petition requested 250 additional acres but Dalhousie suggested that he be given 100. A note on the petition signed by Surveyor General Charles Morris states, "I think 50 acres in addition to what he has got, is as much as can be well afforded unless he is content to go some miles into the interior." Clarke did not receive his additional grant, of only a further ten acres, until

Claude

1841, the same year in which he finally obtained clear title to his original farm. The petition reveals Clarke and his family as diligent farmers, and he also became active in community service.

Clarke was involved in three major black organizations in Nova Scotia in the 19th century: the African Friendly Society, which encouraged black communities in Halifax County to provide mutual aid; the African Abolition Society, working for the "universal abolition of Slavery and the Slave Trade"; and the African Baptist Association, whose aim was to seek continuity among black worshippers by ensuring there would be black clergy to attend and officiate at services, thus providing the essential element of a free black community. These organizations all encouraged black leadership and the advancement of blacks in Nova Scotia and elsewhere. From 1846 Clarke acted in various capacities with these organizations. At the time of his death he was treasurer and secretary of the African Friendly Society, president of the African Abolition Society, and clerk of the African Baptist Association. In 1855, at the request of his good friend Richard PRESTON, Clarke preached the introductory sermon at the second session of the association.

In politics Clarke supported the reformers who, under Joseph Howe*, were proponents of legislation granting blacks land ownership. Following the general election of 1840 he acted as vice chairman at a political dinner where he toasted those who carried the banners of reform: William Annand*, Thomas Forrester*, James McNab, and Howe. In legal matters Clarke, a man without formal education, relied upon the honesty of his white neighbours. They spoke highly of him. What he had to offer was his faith, and his devotion to duty, family, and the collective destiny of his people. He had learned that a price must be paid to keep the freedom he and his family enjoyed, and he paid it with the community service in which he was engaged until his death in Preston. His funeral service was held in the African Chapel in Halifax.

FRANK S. BOYD JR

PANS, RG 20A, Clarke, Septimus, 1820; RG 20C, 88, no.169. African Baptist Assoc. of N.S., *Minutes* (Halifax), 1854–59. *Novascotian*, 28 June 1832; 21 Jan. 1841; 24 Aug., 23 Nov. 1846. *Belcher's farmer's almanack*, 1859: 77. A. P. [Borden] Oliver, *A brief history of the colored Baptists of Nova Scotia, 1782–1953; in commemoration of the African United Baptist Association of Nova Scotia, Inc.* ([Halifax, 1953]). C. B. Fergusson, *A documentary study of the establishment of the negroes in Nova Scotia between the War of 1812 and the winning of responsible government* (Halifax, 1948), 11–13. [P. E.] McKerrow, *McKerrow: a brief history of the coloured Baptists of Nova Scotia, 1785–1895*, ed. F. S. Boyd, assisted by M. I. Allen Boyd (Halifax, 1976).

CLAUDE. *See* GLODE

CLEMO, EBENEZER, author, businessman, and inventor; b. *c.* 1830, probably in London; d. *c.* 1860, probably in Morristown, N.J.

Ebenezer Clemo undoubtedly came from England. His family name is of Cornish origin; in his writings he mentions his arrival in Canada and calls himself "a British subject." In a brief biographical sketch which is the chief source of information about Clemo, a contemporary, Henry James Morgan*, says that he was "a native of London, England, who came to Canada in 1858." Clemo had received a good education. He described himself as a chemist and the novels attributed to him show a familiarity with the works of many British writers.

According to Morgan, Clemo, who was destitute upon his arrival in Canada, sought work "as a message boy" with the Montreal publisher John Lovell*, but "knowing his acquirements, [Lovell] engaged him to write a couple of books on Canadian life." *The life and adventures of Simon Seek; or Canada in all shapes*, by Maple Knot, was published by Lovell in December 1858 and attributed to Clemo by his contemporaries. The story of poor Londoners who immigrate to Canada, *Simon Seek* probably reflects Clemo's own experiences. In the same year Lovell launched a vigorous campaign to sell the second novel attributed to Clemo, *Canadian homes; or the mystery solved.* He advertised it in several newspapers, most of which reviewed it favourably. Henri-Émile Chevalier* prepared a translation, *Le foyer canadien ou le mystère dévoilé* (1859), that was also widely advertised and reviewed. Lovell's announcements claimed that he had printed 30,000 copies in English and 20,000 in French for sale at 25 cents each, half the price of *Simon Seek*.

Canadian homes was the story of another group of English immigrants, who arrived in Toronto in mid winter only to find that, because of the lack of a protective tariff to encourage Canadian manufacturing, there were no jobs. Lovell's efforts on the novel's behalf underlined its importance as a publication. "Printed at Montreal, from Types, manufactured by . . . the Montreal Type Foundry" and on paper made in Lower Canada, *Canadian homes* was a thesis novel, part of a campaign mounted by Lovell, William Weir*, and others for the adoption of a protective tariff to help wrest Canada from its "great commercial distress" by "the establishment and encouragement of her home manufactures." In addition to publicizing Clemo's novels, Weir, who was secretary of the Tariff Reform Association established in Toronto in 1858, formed a partnership with him. By mid December 1858 Clemo had moved to Toronto and in the following year Weir and Clemo, "commission brokers and manufacturers' agents," were located at 18 Wellington Street West. Since Weir, publisher of the *Canadian Merchants' Magazine*, noted in the issue of June 1859 that "an able writer" had contributed to the journal "during the past few months," Clemo may have assisted in this enterprise as well.

By January 1860, however, both the magazine and the business had folded and the partners had returned to Montreal. On 10 January Clemo petitioned the governor-in-chief, Sir Edmund Walker Head*, for letters patent for "a new process of manufacturing PULP, for the manufacture of paper and parchment, from straw and other vegetable substances," the description of the "invention" being witnessed by Weir. The patent was granted on 27 January. Apparently Clemo left again for Toronto shortly after.

On 18 June Clemo swore an oath in New York City that he was the "first inventor" of the "process" he had already patented in Canada. Then he left for Washington, D.C., where, on the following day, his application for an American patent was received. On 22 June he amended its specifications as requested by the United States Patent Office, which issued a patent on 10 July. Giving his mailing address as care of George Brown* in Toronto, he then left Washington.

Clemo's activities afterwards cannot be verified. Since a Canadian patent was issued to Weir on 2 October for what appears to be an improvement on Clemo's invention, Clemo was probably dead by then. Morgan says that he died in 1860, at age 30, in Morristown, N.J., where he was "erecting machinery for the manufacture of . . . paper." Another contemporary writer, Andrew Learmont Spedon, in his work *Rambles among the Blue-Noses* (1863) also noted "poor unfortunate" Clemo's death.

Unfortunate or not, Ebenezer Clemo had connections with "Celebrated Canadians" of his day. He invented a paper-making process which was considered promising enough to be patented in two countries. Although now forgotten as a novelist, he made two interesting, albeit somewhat idiosyncratic, contributions to mid-19th-century Canadian fiction. Finally, in his exploration of "mysteries" such as the protective tariff he discussed issues and debated theories still relevant to Canadian economic thought.

MARY JANE EDWARDS

Ebenezer Clemo wrote, under the pseudonym of Maple Knot, *The life and adventures of Simon Seek; or Canada in all shapes* (Montreal and Toronto, 1858) and *Canadian homes; or the mystery solved, a Christmas tale* (Montreal and Toronto, 1858); the latter was translated into French by Henri-Émile Chevalier and published as *Le foyer canadien ou le mystère dévoilé, nouvelle du jour de Noël* (Montréal et Toronto, 1859).

Canada Patent Office Library (Ottawa), Canada Patent 1045, Ebenezer Clemo, 27 Jan. 1860; 1148, William Weir, 2 Oct. 1860. National Arch. (Washington), RG 241, Patented application file, no.29059. *Daily British Whig*, 14 Dec. 1858, 6–17 Jan. 1859. *Daily Spectator and Journal of Commerce*, 14, 30 Dec. 1858. *Montreal Gazette*, 29 Dec. 1858–4 Jan. 1859. *L'Ordre* (Montréal), 17 déc. 1858–14 janv. 1859. *Le Pays*, 11 déc. 1858–25 janv. 1859. *Quebec Mercury*, 4–8 Jan. 1859. *Transcript* (Montreal), 11–29 Dec. 1858. *Cyclopædia of Canadian biog.* (Rose and Charlesworth), 2: 349. Morgan, *Bibliotheca Canadensis*, 77; *Sketches of celebrated Canadians*, 766. *Toronto directory*, 1859–60. A. L. Spedon, *Rambles among the Blue-Noses; or reminiscences of a tour through New Brunswick and Nova Scotia, during the summer of 1862* (Montreal, 1863). William Weir, *Sixty years in Canada* (Montreal, 1903). "A new Canadian novel," *Canadian Merchants' Magazine and Commercial Rev.* (Toronto), 3 (April–December 1858): 476. M. J. Edwards, "The case of *Canadian homes*," *Canadian Literature* (Vancouver), no.81 (summer 1979): 147–54. "To our readers," *Canadian Merchants' Magazine and Commercial Rev.* (Toronto), 4 (January–June 1859): 400–1.

CLENCH, JOSEPH BRANT, Indian Department official, militia officer, justice of the peace, and office holder; b. *c*. February 1790, probably in Niagara (Niagara-on-the-Lake, Ont.), eldest child of Ralfe Clench* and Elizabeth Johnson, granddaughter of Sir William Johnson*; m. before June 1816 Esther Serena Joseph Leon, and they had at least five sons and three daughters; d. 22 Feb. 1857 in London, Upper Canada.

Early in 1811 Joseph Brant Clench, who lived in Niagara Township, took the oath of allegiance and successfully petitioned for a 200-acre grant as the son of a loyalist. In the tradition of the maternal side of his family, on 25 Oct. 1813 he entered the Indian Department, as a clerk in charge of Indian stores at Fort George (Niagara-on-the-Lake). During the War of 1812 he conducted himself with "bravery" and "zeal" in action on the Niagara frontier, on the Grand River, and at Amherstburg; his "military talent" led to his employment on secret service by Major-General John Vincent*, Lieutenant-Colonel Christopher Myers, and Major John Bachevoye Glegg.

In 1816 Lieutenant-Colonel John HARVEY tried unsuccessfully to have Clench appointed to the vacant post of superintendent of Indian affairs at Amherstburg, but, through the efforts of Lieutenant Governor Francis GORE and Clench's great-uncles Sir John Johnson* and Colonel William Claus*, the position went instead to John Askin Jr. On 24 Aug. 1817 Clench was reduced to "writingout" clerk at Fort George, responsibility for Indian stores having been transferred to the office of the storekeeper general. In addition to this position within the Indian Department, Clench, like his father, played an active role in local government. By 1818 he had been appointed district court clerk for Niagara and in 1823 he received his first commission as a magistrate. On several occasions he was unanimously elected chairman of the Court of Quarter Sessions for the Niagara District.

During the 1820s, though officially a clerk, Clench served the Indian Department as an interpreter and also performed most of the duties of Alexander McDonell, the assistant secretary at Fort George. In

Clench

these capacities he visited Kingston, Richmond, Belleville, and the Trent River in 1824 and again in 1825. During the winter of 1825–26 Clench was bitterly disappointed when, despite McDonell's assurances, he did not succeed him following the assistant secretary's transfer to York (Toronto). However, on the strength of his service within the department and his need to support and educate his ever-growing family, in January 1826 Clench successfully petitioned Henry Charles Darling*, the deputy superintendent general of Indian affairs in the Canadas, to have his stipend increased to 4s. 8d. a day. As well, he was employed for a time at Amherstburg on what he described as "very important duty" under the special orders of Lieutenant Governor Sir Peregrine MAITLAND.

In 1828–29 he attempted, with varying results, to secure additional positions. A member of the Church of England, he applied to Charles James Stewart*, bishop of Quebec, to be made secretary to the Upper Canada Clergy Corporation, but in November 1828 he learned that George Herchmer Markland* had already been appointed to the office. Clench was further disappointed that year when his presumed kinsman, John Brant [Tekarihogen*], was appointed superintendent of the Six Nations rather than himself. By 1829, however, Clench had been transferred to York as a clerk and was receiving £1 sterling a day.

Early in 1829 he attained the superintendency of the Mohawks and the Mississaugas of the Bay of Quinte and Rice Lake, at a salary of £185 14s. 4d. a year. In April 1830, as a result of the departmental reorganization recommended by Lieutenant Governor Sir John Colborne* the previous year, Clench was named superintendent of Indian affairs in Delaware and Caradoc townships in Middlesex County. The new duties of superintendents included bringing the Indians together in villages, and Clench was directed to "select an eligible spot for a village" for "the Chippewas and Munceys, now residing on the River Thames." The location he selected was either the existing settlement of Muncey Mission or the site of Upper Muncey, a short distance upstream, in Caradoc.

In 1833, while living in Caradoc, Clench was appointed a magistrate for the London District and he later served as chairman of the district's Court of Quarter Sessions. By November 1834 he had become lieutenant-colonel of the 5th Regiment of Middlesex militia. In the aftermath of the uprising led by Charles Duncombe* during December 1837, Clench was foreman of the grand jury which found bills leading to the indictment of "a great number of Persons Charged with High Treason and misprison of treason." But, so convinced was he that a greater crisis was impending – he believed that rebels planned to hang him and murder the Indians under his charge – that he wrote late in June 1838 to Samuel Peters JARVIS, chief superintendent of Indian affairs for Upper Canada, begging that he and the Indians be armed so "that we may die like Men!" On 6 December, two days after the so-called battle of Windsor [see John Prince*], Clench was directed by Lieutenant-Colonel John Maitland of the 32nd Foot "to cause 150 of the most active Indians to be in readiness to move" with that regiment to the west. He was further informed that "one hundred Stand of Arms will be taken from here to equip such of them as may not at present be provided with efficient Arms." On the 8th he was appointed to the court martial which, under Judge Advocate Henry SHERWOOD, tried some 44 prisoners, including Joshua Gwillen Doan* and Elijah Crocker Woodman*, between 27 December and 19 January.

As a result of the reorganization begun within the Indian Department in 1844 [see Sir James Macaulay Higginson*], Clench was placed in charge of the entire Western superintendency, comprising the reservations within the London and Western districts. At the same time he was named visiting superintendent of the Grand River superintendency, while David Thorburn became superintendent. In 1845, by which time Clench had moved to the town of London, he was also appointed agent for conducting the sale of Indian lands in the Western and London districts. Though he diligently sought to safeguard and promote the interests of the Indians, he generally believed that he knew what was best for the various bands under his charge, regardless of their views. In the spring of 1847, when the Credit River Mississaugas were preparing to settle on land donated by the Six Nations on the Grand River, he cautioned the Reverend Peter JONES that the young people at the Grand were the "next thing to worthless" and warned him to ignore the demands of the poor there.

In London the Clench family was not part of the inner circle, despite invitations to various military and civilian balls and dinners. Clench, however, did enjoy some prominence and in March 1847 he was called upon by John Duggan, a Toronto lawyer, to use his support and influence to help him win a seat in a London by-election. Between 1839 and about 1848 Clench served as inspector of shop, still, and tavern licences for the London District. It was probably his knowledge of the adverse effects of alcohol that led him, as inspector, to draw up in about 1842 a memorandum advocating tighter controls and increased taxes on its sale. He appears to have been president of the temperance society in London in 1852. The following year his daughter Victorine Leon married Francis Evans Cornish*, a future mayor of the city.

But, at the height of his career, things began to sour for Clench. The late 1840s had seen the breakup of the marriage of his daughter Caroline and her committal to an insane asylum. His wife, a native of Germany and probably the first Jewess to settle in the London District, was beginning to have increasingly expensive tastes in clothes and furnishings, and their son Leon Moses was, by 1852, known by Clench to be appropriating, for himself and his mother, monies entrusted to Clench from the sale of Indian lands.

In the early 1850s, and evidently before that, Clench's "want of success and apparent inertness" in conducting his duties as Indian land agent were censured by successive superintendents general Thomas Edmund Campbell* and Robert Bruce. Early in September 1854 Superintendent General Laurence Oliphant directed Thomas Worthington and C. E. Anderson to investigate the "seeming irregularities" in Clench's capacity as agent and his "refusal to afford any explanation thereof." A month later they recommended that he be suspended. Clench's "state of health" was one "almost amounting to imbecility" and he was confined to bed. Monies sent through the mails to his house were not reaching his hands and might never have been known to him. Accordingly, he was removed from office on 9 October, and in December departmental policy was revised, requiring that all payments to the department be deposited in a chartered bank.

At the court of inquisition held in London in August 1855, it was learned that Clench's wife and two of his sons, Leon and Holcroft, had purchased properties with monies belonging to the Indian Department. It was subsequently estimated that, with interest, some £9,000 had been embezzled. Of this, £5,950 had been recovered and £1,207 15s. 6d. had been secured in mortgages and in cash. During the investigation, which had led to the tarnishing of his good name, Clench himself refused to name his sons and wife as the persons directly responsible for the defalcation.

The strain of the disclosure of the embezzlement led to alienation between him and his family and to further deterioration of his health. Possibly as a result of the strain, Clench resigned as lieutenant-colonel of the 6th Battalion of Middlesex militia in December 1855. Leaving London, he retired to Caradoc Township. His death in 1857, from an apoplectic fit, occurred while he was temporarily staying at the Western Hotel in London. The *London Free Press and Daily Western Advertiser* in its obituary described him as "an upright, good, and just man" and, while viewing him as "the victim of others villany," saw a tragic flaw in "his want of firmness and discretion." At the time of his death he still owed the Indian Department more than £6,950.

DANIEL J. BROCK

PAC, RG 1, L3, 98: C10/16; 99: C11/133, 150; RG 8, I (C ser.), 266, 268, 270; RG 10, B8, 802; CI, 2, vols.446–47, 570; 10017; RG 68, General index, 1651–1841: 451, 477. Private arch., F. H. Armstrong (London, Ont.), Elida Clench to Armstrong, 19 Feb. 1969, containing genealogical information. UWOL, Regional Coll., Middlesex County, Ont., Chancery Court records, 1838–1912, cases, 1859, *Gibson, E. v. Clench, L.M.*, doc.3. U.C., House of Assembly, *App. to the journal*, 1839–40: 1, pt.II: 143–44. *London Free Press and Daily Western Advertiser*, 24 Feb. 1857. *Canadian biog. dict.*, 1: 589–90. *The roll of the regiments (the Sedentary Militia)*, comp. H. M. Jackson (n.p., 1960), 37. Elizabeth Graham, *Medicine man to missionary: missionaries as agents of change among the Indians of southern Ontario, 1784–1867* (Toronto, 1975). *Hist. of Middlesex*, 20, 74, 151, 269.

CLINGERSMITH (Clinglesmith). *See* KLINGENSMITH

CLITHEROW, JOHN, army officer, politician, and colonial administrator; b. 13 Dec. 1782 in Essendon, England, eldest son of Christopher Clitherow and Anne Jodrell; d. 14 Oct. 1852 at Boston House, Brentford, England.

Descended from Sir Christopher Clitherow, lord mayor of London in 1635, John Clitherow entered the British army on 19 Dec. 1799 as ensign in the 3rd Foot Guards, which in 1831 became the Scots Fusilier Guards. He served in the Egyptian campaign of 1801 and on the expeditions to Hanover (Federal Republic of Germany) in 1805 and to Walcheren, Netherlands, in 1809, and was wounded twice in the Peninsular War. He attained the rank of colonel on 25 July 1821, major-general on 22 July 1830, and lieutenant-general on 23 Nov. 1841.

Clitherow arrived in British North America in March 1838 as commanding officer for the military district of Montreal. Four months later he was asked by Lord Durham [Lambton*] to serve on the Special Council after Durham had dismissed the members appointed by Sir John Colborne* and chosen men from his own civil and military entourage. Durham expressed the need for councillors free of local party ties and formed the new council largely for the purpose of sanctioning measures proposed by him to deal with the aftermath of the rebellion of 1837. Clitherow, like the four other military men on the eight-member council (including Major-General James MACDONELL), felt some uneasiness at being involved, even nominally, in the civil legislative process. Durham insisted, however, that were Clitherow or the other military men to withdraw, he would be unable to carry on and, under those circumstances, Clitherow sat on the council from 9 July until 2 Nov. 1838, the day after Durham's departure for England.

In early September 1838 Clitherow became alarmed at the frequency and nature of intelligence reports from the area near the United States border concerning intended disturbances. To ascertain the accuracy of the reports himself, he visited Île aux Noix and returned to Montreal convinced that they were greatly exaggerated. It may have been his appraisal of the area south of the St Lawrence that led Colborne, commander-in-chief of the forces in the Canadas, to underestimate the danger of insurrection at that time.

When the second uprising broke out on 3 Nov. 1838, Clitherow commanded the left wing of the army of 3,000 regulars that marched on the rebel headquarters at Napierville. Clitherow's brigade, consisting of the 15th and 24th Foot, converged on the village on the morning of 10 November at the same time as a second brigade commanded by Macdonell. However, the rebels had dispersed before the troops' arrival and Clitherow's brigade proceeded to Saint-Jean (Saint-Jean-sur-Richelieu) by way of Henryville while the second brigade returned to Montreal by way of Clarenceville, a sweeping movement designed to impress upon the disaffected the futility of continued resistance.

Clitherow was more at ease in performing these purely military operations, yet when called upon to assume civil and judicial duties he did so without giving offence. As senior military officer of the Montreal district, he presided at the general courts martial assembled in November 1838 to try the 108 men charged with treason in connection with the insurrection. Although these courts martial were conducted in English, which few of the prisoners understood, Clitherow appears to have acted impartially and with goodwill towards the accused. These trials engendered contemporary criticism. Some loyalists condemned them as too lenient towards the insurgents, others such as Lieutenant-Colonel Charles Grey found fault with the way they were prosecuted. During the debate on the Rebellion Losses Bill in 1849, Attorney General Louis-Hippolyte La Fontaine* challenged their legality. More recent scholarship has reiterated this challenge. Yet in his work on the rebellions, Gérard Filteau considers that "the military judges accomplished their duty in a spirit of justice and even . . . benevolence."

Clitherow remained in Montreal until July 1841 when he took command of the forces in Upper Canada, with headquarters at Kingston. In his capacity as senior military officer, he was made deputy governor by Lord Sydenham [Thomson*] on 18 Sept. 1841 and prorogued the first session of the first parliament of the Province of Canada the day before Sydenham died. Clitherow continued to act as deputy governor for six days until the appointment of Sir Richard Downes Jackson* as administrator.

Little is known of Clitherow's immediate family. In January 1809 he married Sarah Burton, and John Christie Clitherow of the Coldstream Guards, who appears to have been the only child of this marriage,

served as his father's aide-de-camp when the latter was stationed in the Canadas. Clitherow remarried in 1825, taking as his wife Millicent Pole of Gloucestershire. He inherited the family estate at Boston House when his cousin James Clitherow died in October 1841 and he returned to England in June 1842. He was succeeded as commander of the forces in Upper Canada by Sir Richard ARMSTRONG. In January 1844 he became colonel of the 67th Foot, an appointment he held until his death. He was made a knight of the Crescent in 1845.

Clitherow was, above all, a military man, concerned about the administration, efficiency, and image of his command, so much so that officers were glad to move their regiments south of the St Lawrence River to get away from his close scrutiny. His duties on Durham's Special Council, as president of the general courts martial, and as deputy governor were largely nominal. In Montreal he and his wife went beyond the call of duty in cultivating social links. For instance, they attended a service in the Spanish and Portuguese Synagogue, probably a gesture from the military towards the Montreal Jewish community which had rallied so swiftly to the loyalist coalition under Colborne during the insurrections.

ELINOR KYTE SENIOR

PAC, MG 30, D1, 8. PRO, WO 17/1542; 17/1544–46. G.B., Army, *Report of the state trials, before a general court martial held at Montreal in 1838–9: exhibiting a complete history of the late rebellion in Lower Canada* (2v., Montreal, 1839). *Gentleman's Magazine*, January–June 1853: 200. [Charles] Grey, *Crisis in the Canadas: 1838–1839, the Grey journals and letters*, ed. W. G. Ormsby (Toronto, 1964). Daniel Lysons, *Early reminiscences, with illustrations from the author's sketches* (London, 1896). *Montreal Gazette*, 13 Nov. 1838. *Montreal Transcript*, 21, 28 Sept. 1841. *Quebec Gazette*, 16 March 1838. *Times* (London), 16 Oct. 1852. Boase, *Modern English biog.*, 1: 652. Desjardins, *Guide parl. DNB.* G.B., WO, *Army list*, 1838. Morgan, *Sketches of celebrated Canadians*, 406. Filteau, *Hist. des Patriotes* (1938–42). Elinor Kyte Senior, *British regulars in Montreal: an imperial garrison, 1832–1854* (Montreal, 1981). B. G. Sack, *History of the Jews in Canada, from the earliest beginnings to the present day*, [trans. Ralph Novek] (Montreal, 1945). F. M. Greenwood, "L'insurrection appréhendée et l'administration de la justice au Canada: le point de vue d'un historien," *RHAF*, 34 (1980–81): 57–93.

COBBEYALL. See GLODE, GABRIEL

CODNER, SAMUEL, ship's captain, businessman, and philanthropist; baptized 16 Feb. 1776 in Kingskerswell, England, son of Daniel Codner and Joan ——; d. 5 Aug. 1858 in Dartmouth, England.

Although Samuel Codner was born in Weston-super-Mare on the west coast of England, his family came from Kingskerswell, Devon, in a region with a

Codner

long-standing tradition of involvement in the New-foundland cod fishery. Not surprisingly, at the age of either 12 or 13 he began a seafaring career by joining his father, uncle, and two brothers at St John's. At this time his family owned three ships: a 92-ton brigantine and a 118-ton brig used in the fishery, and a 46-ton vessel employed in transporting passengers to New-foundland as well as in fishing occasionally on the Grand Banks. Samuel rose quickly to the rank of ship's captain and by 1794 he was acting as agent in St John's for Daniel Codner and Company.

After his father's death in 1799, the firm continued as Daniel Codner and Company until Samuel's mother died in 1811. At that time the administration of the estate and the management of the firm fell to Samuel, who returned to England where he was to set up his permanent residence. His sea captains and various partners, including Robert Alsop of Newton Abbot, England, and William Bond, assumed direction of the company in Newfoundland. For the next eight years the firm was variously styled Samuel Codner and Company and Codner, Alsop and Company, with some of Samuel's relatives and colleagues such as Alsop as principal shareholders. In 1819, however, Codner began to conduct trade on his own account, initially from Teignmouth and then, after 1828, from Dartmouth.

The early stages of Codner's career had been marked by extreme fluctuations in trade. The price of cod, which had collapsed in 1790–92, recovered somewhat during the French revolutionary wars, a period when Codner made two significant adjustments in his Newfoundland ventures. First, he followed the lead of several other prominent firms, such as John Slade and Company and Noble and Pinson, by setting up a fishery on the Labrador coast and, secondly, he took advantage of the increasing resident population of Newfoundland by becoming a major importer of provisions, clothing, and fishing gear. Despite various set-backs, such as the loss of nine ocean-going vessels between 1806 and 1815, Codner sustained his interest in Newfoundland trade, including the cod and salmon fishery in Labrador, until 1844. From 1815 to 1844 his main commercial activities were centred in St John's from whence his ships carried salt fish to Spain, Portugal, and the West Indies, and brought salt and coal from England and wheat, bread, and biscuits from Germany. From the 1820s, however, Codner specialized in importing "Bridport goods," sailcloth, ropes, nets, and twines from west Dorset, and cloth goods from Devon. While building this lucrative business in St John's, Codner retained his share of the Teignmouth coastal trade.

Even though Codner's firm was one of St John's leading mercantile establishments for more than three decades, he made his mark in Newfoundland history by founding the Newfoundland School Society, an institution which had a profound effect on the island's educational and cultural development. Undoubtedly his experience as a resident of St John's from 1801 to 1811 gave Codner a clear understanding of the need for schools and cultural institutions; in 1804 he had contributed to the support of the St John's Charity School [see Sir Erasmus Gower*]. Apart from the charity schools, and a few establishments supported by the Society for the Propagation of the Gospel in some of the larger outports, the growing number of resident islanders had no opportunity to acquire the rudiments of a formal education. An explanation for Codner's interest in promoting schools in Newfoundland comes from a story about an experience he had in crossing the Atlantic to England: his ship encountered a violent storm and Codner is said to have vowed to devote himself to humanitarian work if he were safely delivered. Certainly religious conviction played a part. He was a supporter of the evangelical movement within the Church of England and was a member of the British and Foreign Bible Society. Another explanation of his concern for schools has it that at a meeting of the bible society in London in 1822 he was inspired by an address by Lord Liverpool, the prime minister, who reminded his audience of its obligation to circulate the Scriptures among Britain's "extensive colonies and foreign possessions."

Codner immediately set about organizing support and collecting subscriptions for schools in Newfound-land and over the next few years exerted unflagging energy to establish and diffuse the school movement. He circulated a leaflet entitled *Schools in Newfound-land*, which asserted that a large proportion of the 70,000 inhabitants were without access to instruction. He gained the support of several prominent merchants in the England–Newfoundland trade, including Mar-maduke Hart*, as well as of evangelicals within the Church of England.

In 1823 Codner set up a provisional committee and issued a prospectus which stressed the strategic and commercial importance of Newfoundland to British interests and at the same time deplored the lack of moral culture among its inhabitants. Liverpool approved the objectives of the proposed Newfound-land Society for Educating the Poor at an inaugural meeting in London on 30 June and agreed to act as vice-patron. The colonial secretary, Lord Bathurst, became president, with Codner taking the office of secretary. Codner immediately petitioned the British government for land grants for buildings, free passage on naval ships for teachers, and assistance from the government in St John's for the construction of schoolhouses. Despite the opposition of Newfound-land's governor, Sir Charles Hamilton*, who held that the level of education provided by the charity and SPG schools was adequate and also maintained that the low church evangelicals were sectarian enemies operating within the Church of England, the requests were granted. In 1824 the British government gave £500 for the construction of a central school in St John's and £100 for the salary of a schoolmaster. Codner then made a second circuit of the most important towns and cities in England, Ireland, and Scotland, evidently at his own expense, to solicit both donations and the assistance of political and ecclesiastical leaders in founding branch societies. Through private subscription in 1825–26 he raised £1,871, and secured the patronage of such persons as Sir John Gladstone in Liverpool and the archbishop of Dublin.

After his association with the school society during its formative years, Codner's participation is difficult to assess. He held the office of honorary secretary until the 1830s, by which time the movement was well established. Apparently he did not visit Newfoundland in connection with the society but rather confined his efforts to the British Isles. Nevertheless, his business agent in St John's, William Bond, acted on his behalf and Codner himself maintained a personal interest in the society until his death.

The first school opened in St John's in September 1824 with an enrolment of 75. Two years later it had moved to a larger building to accommodate 450 students. By 1829 eight principal schools, located in the larger settlements, were in operation; they were staffed by society teachers, recruited and trained in England. There were also 15 branch schools in smaller communities. Following the principles of the Bell or Madras systems, the classes were conducted by monitors who were directed by teachers in the principal schools. By 1836 the society had expanded into most of the main settlements. Its 46 schools were located as far north as Twillingate, along the south coast, and up the west shore to St George's Bay. The society claimed to have provided instruction for approximately 16,500 students, both children and adults, which equalled slightly less than 25 per cent of the total population.

Commonly known as the Newfoundland School Society, the organization underwent several official name changes through the years; when first established it was known as the Newfoundland Society for Educating the Poor (1823), then the Newfoundland and British North America Society for the Education of the Poor (1829), the Church of England Society of the Poor of Newfoundland and the Colonies (1846), the Colonial Church and School Society (1851), and the Colonial and Continental Society (1861). The latter name was retained until 1958 when the organization became known throughout the world as the Commonwealth and Continental Church Society.

Although originally interdenominational, the schools run by the Newfoundland School Society became increasingly identified with the Church of England, and in 1923 they were merged into a denominational school system known as the Church of England schools. The existence of the society, indeed, was one of the influences in the evolution of a denominational school system in Newfoundland. The teachers sent out in the society's early years were well trained and highly regarded as leaders within the communities in which they lived, and they usually served as catechists or lay readers as well. A considerable number later elected to become ordained as Anglican priests and furnished the Newfoundland church with one of its main sources of clerics during the 19th century. Regarding themselves as missionaries as well as pedagogues, they strove to inculcate the virtues of hard work, regular habits, sobriety, and the observance of Sunday as a day of rest.

Codner certainly possessed some personal qualities which helped ensure the success of the movement. He was clearly a persuasive speaker and a good organizer, and he held strong convictions. He was also a highly respected member of both the mercantile community and the Church of England evangelicals, and thus was well placed to gain support from both groups. Codner was able to sway the merchants by arguing that a more literate population in Newfoundland would also be a more moral population. Merchants, like himself, who did not reside in Newfoundland but conducted trade through agents, would then have less need to fear for the safety of their property from "fraudulent and improper practices."

The idea of social control through education was equally palatable to the evangelicals and the British government. To the evangelicals, Newfoundland was, or was about to become, one of the heathen areas needing conversion and redemption, and the British government was forced to face the fact that by the 1820s it could no longer be regarded as a transient station for British fishermen. Indeed, the government had already committed itself to some improvements, and the support of schools aimed at making the indigenous population "industrious" and "moral" complemented their policy of cautious reform [*see* Sir Richard Goodwin Keats*]. In this respect Codner's school movement can be seen as one of a series of reforms which led to the granting of colonial status and representative government to Newfoundland in 1832.

On 6 Dec. 1820 Codner had married Selina Cave Browne, daughter of John Cave Browne of Stretton, England. The social connections of his spouse probably aided the school mission project he would begin two years later. When he retired from the Newfoundland trade in 1844 at the age of nearly 70, he sold his St John's premises to the firm of Wilson and Meynell. Codner died in Dartmouth and was interred in St Petrox Church. A memorial erected there in his honour bears the inscription: "Newfoundland Merchant who in 1823 founded the Society which became the Colonial and Continental Church Society."

Was Codner a "self-sacrificing, humanitarian" as Frederick William Rowe describes him, or was he an agent of cultural imperialists, acting on behalf of the vested interests of the groups who promoted the school movement, as he has been portrayed by Phillip McCann? If the former, he stands in marked contrast to the mercantile community, which has been represented as the root of every evil afflicting Newfoundland's development and the main obstacle to every cultural improvement. If he was indeed elected by fate and circumstances to instigate social reform, he must be regarded as a wise choice and as an individual who promoted positive change in Newfoundland's social, cultural, and educational life.

W. GORDON HANDCOCK

Centre for Nfld. Studies, Memorial Univ. of Nfld. Library (St John's), "D'Alberti papers" (transcripts of corr. between the Colonial Office and the governor's office of Newfoundland, 1780–1825, from various PRO, CO files), comp. Amalia and Leonora D'Alberti (34v., typescript). Devon Record Office (Exeter, Eng.), 53/6 (Kingskerswell parish, docs. relating to land), box 34, will of Daniel Codner, 1798; assignment of Joan Codner and children of houses, lands, and shares in 5 vessels, 1798; administration of estate of Joan Codner, 1811; box 53, marriage settlement of Samuel Codner and Selina Cave Browne, 6 Dec. 1820; 1528 A (St Nicholas, Shaldon, parish records); 3119 A/PR1 (Kingskerswell parish, reg. of baptisms, marriages, and burials), 16 Feb. 1776; 3289 S/1–6 (Exeter shipping reg., 1786–1847). Hunt, Roope & Company (London), Hunt, Newman, Roope & Company, Oporto, letter-books, letter of Samuel Codner, 29 May 1833 (mfm. at MHGA). MHGA, Codner, William; Codner, Samuel, name files. PANL, GN 5/2; P4/17, Misc., box 17, file 10. PRO, CO 194/44. Phillip McCann, "The Newfoundland School Society, 1823–1836: missionary enterprise or culture imperialism?" (lecture to the Nfld. Hist. Soc., St John's, 1976). W. Pilot, "The Church of England in Newfoundland," in Prowse, *Hist. of Nfld.* (1895), supp., 7–9. F. W. Rowe, *The development of education in Newfoundland* (Toronto, 1964), 40–50.

COGSWELL, HENRY HEZEKIAH, lawyer, financier, office holder, politician, and philanthropist; b. 12 April 1776 in Cornwallis Township, N.S., son of Mason Cogswell and Lydia Huntington; m. June 1805 Isabella Ellis in Windsor, N.S., and they had ten children; d. 9 Nov. 1854 in Halifax.

Henry Hezekiah Cogswell emerged from rural Nova Scotia to become a leading Halifax entrepreneur, ranking with Enos Collins* and Samuel Cunard* in material wealth. The Cogswell family had come to Cornwallis Township from Connecticut in 1761, occupying land formerly held by Acadian settlers. Henry's father developed the farm to the point where it ranked within the top five per cent of township holdings. Three of Mason Cogswell's sons stayed on the land but Henry, the second eldest, was selected for a professional career. Sent to King's College in Windsor in 1789, shortly after its establishment, young Cogswell received the rudiments of a higher education. Equally important, he made connections, both with fellow students and with faculty, which probably contributed decisively to his gaining admission to the Halifax oligarchy.

After graduation Cogswell moved to Halifax, where he underwent legal training as a clerk in the office of Richard John Uniacke*, solicitor general of Nova Scotia. Admitted to the bar in 1798, Cogswell appears to have quickly built up a flourishing law practice, benefiting from a scarcity of professional competition as well as from the bustle of business created by litigation concerning prizes of war which occupied the Halifax courts during the Napoleonic Wars. In June 1805 he married Isabella Ellis, daughter of an Anglican clergyman, and the first of their ten children was born five months later. As he progressed in society, Cogswell gradually abandoned Presbyterianism in favour of the more socially desirable membership in the Church of England. Conformity to oligarchic norms was important, since very early Cogswell displayed a desire for an official position. Frustrated in efforts to obtain the position of clerk to the House of Assembly, he studiously cultivated connections within the legal fraternity until, in 1812, the intervention of Chief Justice Sampson Salter Blowers* resulted in his appointment as deputy provincial secretary. This position, which Cogswell held for the next six years, carried an annual income, including fees, of over £1,000. More important, it gave the incumbent daily access to the lieutenant governor, the key source of government patronage.

It would appear that after 1812 Cogswell never returned to personal law practice, being able to draw an ample income from a combination of his official positions and private investments. In 1818 his tenure as deputy provincial secretary ended but as compensation he was named registrar of the Court of Chancery, a position which he apparently had held on an acting basis since 1814. A contemporary later observed that the post yielded an annual income of from £500 to £600; moreover, it allowed Cogswell to retain regular contact with the lieutenant governor. By now Cogswell was also well on his way towards building up a substantial investment portfolio, mainly in the form of freehold and mortgages. He had also engaged in entrepreneurial speculation, which included playing a leading role in founding two of Halifax's earliest corporate ventures, the Halifax Fire Insurance Company (1809) and the Halifax Steam Boat Company (1815). After the Napoleonic Wars he complemented his other activities with a brief venture into politics, winning election to the House of

Cogswell

Assembly from Halifax Township in 1818. As a member of the assembly he displayed an enthusiasm for money matters, advocating an increase in the supply of provincial paper money, seeking to expand the credit available to farmers, and urging incorporation of a bank in Halifax. These measures, designed to alleviate the post-war economic depression in Nova Scotia, all failed to pass the assembly. Cogswell's position on banking may have contributed to his electoral defeat in 1820, since key members of the Halifax merchant community feared that such an institution would compete with their activities as private bankers.

His interest in banking persisted, however, and in 1825, after repeated failures to secure a charter from the legislature for a joint-stock public bank, he joined with Enos Collins, Samuel Cunard, William PRYOR, and four other prominent Halifax merchants to form the Halifax Banking Company, an unincorporated partnership capitalized at £50,000. This was Nova Scotia's first true bank, an institution organized to receive deposits, issue bank notes, and extend short-term credit to local businessmen. Without a charter, the partners remained fully liable for the bank's debts and lacked the security of a legal monopoly within the province. Nevertheless, sustained by a long-term growth in Nova Scotian trade, the bank prospered. Within a decade, the partners were earning a return of 20 per cent on their investment. Cogswell, who had subscribed one-fifth of the original capital, was elected the first president of the bank, a post which he retained until his death. As officer presiding over the weekly meetings of directors, before long he was known as "Lord Hezekiah," who, according to Joseph Howe*, ruled the community with a "rod of paper," exploiting the "labour and sweat of the people."

Antagonism towards Cogswell and his associates grew as they achieved even greater integration of economic and political power within the province. In 1831, for example, Cogswell secured appointment to the Council, which meant that five of its twelve seats were held by members of the Halifax Banking Company. At the same time, the bank, which as yet had no formal competition, held more than one-third of the provincial debt, Cogswell alone holding over ten per cent. It was a situation ready-made to foster suspicions of conflicts of interest, especially in light of Enos Collins's questionable behaviour during the so-called "Brandy Dispute" of 1830. Suspicion turned into accusation in 1832 when the Council imposed obstacles in the way of efforts to establish a second bank in Halifax through incorporation by public charter. The new Bank of Nova Scotia did obtain its charter in 1832 but the conflict had further compromised the reputation of Cogswell and his partners. Public dissatisfaction mounted to new heights over the

next four years as competition between the two banks threw credit into disarray and contributed to a wave of bankruptcies among small businessmen. Under such circumstances "old Coggy" was subjected to vehement denunciation. Joseph Howe complained that "every species of property was raised or depressed in value at the nod of the wily President. Whatever the Bankers wanted to buy suddenly fell, and whatever they wanted to sell, as suddenly rose."

Cogswell made an obvious target for any emerging reform movement, since he possessed a prominence in community affairs that went beyond his role as banker and councillor. By the mid 1830s he held a multiplicity of public offices: head of the Halifax Street Commission, and thereby responsible for expenditures on major public works; commissioner of the Vice-Admiralty Court and of the Halifax Commons; president of the Halifax Board of Health; and member of the Revenue Commission, a body charged with supervision of the public treasury. In addition, Cogswell was a pervasive personality in the business world, functioning as president of both the Albion Fire and Life Insurance Company and the Annapolis Iron Mining Company and as director of the Nova Scotia Marine Insurance Company, the Nova Scotia Whaling Company, and the Halifax Hotel Company. Ironically, Joseph Howe was personally indebted to Cogswell for £1,200 at the time he launched his campaign for responsible government in the general election of 1836.

Reform agitation steadily gathered strength from 1836 and gradually brought about Cogswell's withdrawal from public affairs. In 1838 he was obliged to step down from the newly separated Legislative Council and two years later he found himself excluded from the Executive Council. Incorporation of Halifax as a city in 1841 deprived him of his municipal offices. The process climaxed in 1843 when Lieutenant Governor Lord Falkland [Cary*] dismissed him from the Revenue Commission after he had attempted to prevent Howe from being appointed collector of excise. In the course of demanding a hearing from the colonial secretary, an infuriated Cogswell complained that reform had so wrecked "constitutional principles" that the local constitution bore "a strong resemblance to that of Turkey where to satisfy clamorous agitators or to gratify the caprices of a Bashaw, heads are thrown over the wall." Neither rhetoric nor copious amounts of money, allegedly channelled into the pockets of such conservative politicians as James William Johnston*, enabled Cogswell to prevent the coming of responsible government. The defeat, however, was one which proved more damaging to his ego than to his vital interests.

Other than a short-lived refusal to entrust public funds to the Halifax Banking Company, the ascendant reformers carried out no vendetta against Cogswell.

Their moderation stemmed in part from respect for his activities as a public benefactor, for Cogswell ranked as Halifax's leading philanthropist. He was a member of the local Poor Man's Friend Society; vice-president of the Nova Scotia Bible Society and the Diocesan Church Society of the Church of England; president of the Royal Acadian Society, the Association for the Aid of the Colonial Church Society, and the Halifax Library Committee; and director of the Halifax Agricultural Society. He also supported the Halifax Mechanics' Institute by making donations and by providing its meeting place with a fire-escape. In addition, he helped organize the King's College Alumni Association, and gave donations to the college on a scale which secured him an honorary DCL in 1847. All of this activity, which may have derived from an evangelical element in Cogswell's character, helped to alter his image as the rapacious head of Halifax's monied interests. Perhaps more decisive in prompting the victorious reformers to seek an accommodation with Cogswell, however, was their need of his support in the pursuit of economic development.

The one major topic on which Howe and Cogswell were in approximate agreement concerned the introduction of railways into Nova Scotia. In the mid 1840s both men became caught up in the enthusiasm for a rail link between Halifax and Quebec. Cogswell served as chairman of a Halifax-based business lobby, organized to convince the assembly that public funds should be allocated for railway construction. The effort produced few immediate results but Cogswell remained convinced of the importance of the new technology as a stimulus to economic growth. In 1852 he issued a pamphlet, *View: relative to the construction of a railway from Halifax to Quebec*, which called on the imperial government to provide more generous financial support for the intercolonial line. Cogswell argued that the project was beyond the capacity of private enterprise, but rather than entrust the work to local colonial governments he favoured establishment of a British North American federation wherein leadership would presumably be entrusted to men guided by something more than parochial considerations of patronage. He also stated that construction of the railway could be carried out by a mass of immigrants supervised by British army officers and subject to "military order and control."

The railway pamphlet, an expression of tory élitism and entrepreneurial ambition, was Cogswell's last public gesture. He died two years later; despite his business acumen, he left no will. An appraisal of his estate revealed assets of £116,905. More than £40,000 consisted of mortgage holdings, freehold real estate accounted for another £30,000, and the remainder was made up of cash, stocks, and bonds. Although an advocate of local industrial development,

Cogswell had confined his investments largely to real estate and commercial ventures. Moreover, almost 20 per cent of his savings had gone into American bank securities. All of this wealth went to a half-dozen children and grandchildren. Two of his children, Isabella Binney Cogswell* and James Colquhoun Cogswell, achieved prominence in 19th-century Halifax, the one as a philanthropist and the other as a merchant-banker who eventually succeeded to the presidency of the Halifax Banking Company.

Three men can be said to have dominated the business community of early Victorian Nova Scotia – Enos Collins, Samuel Cunard, and Henry Hezekiah Cogswell. Despite the difficulty of penetrating his mask of humourless probity, Cogswell probably had a more complex personality than either of his two peers. A blend of rigid toryism, business vision, and community stewardship made him a memorable expression of his times.

DAVID A. SUTHERLAND

H. H. Cogswell is the author of *Views: relative to the construction of a railway from Halifax to Quebec, by the British government* . . . (Halifax, 1852).

BLHU, R. G. Dun & Co. credit ledger, Canada, 11: 239. Halifax County Court of Probate (Halifax), Estate papers, no.564 (mfm. at PANS). Halifax County Registry of Deeds (Halifax), Deeds, 58: f.322 (mfm. at PANS). Kings County Court of Probate (Kentville, N.S.), Book 2: f.148 (will of H. H. Cogswell) (mfm. at PANS). PANS, MG 1, 797B, no.29; MG 100, 123, nos.15–16; RG 1, 117: f.90; 231, no.106; 237, no.172; 289, no.122; 308, no.41; 311, no.11; 412, no.50; 413, nos.23, 37. PRO, CO 217/101: 172; 217/183: 153; 217/203: 372. Alumni of King's College, Windsor, N.S., *Annual report* (Halifax), 1852. N.S., House of Assembly, *Journal and proc.*, 1818–20. *Acadian Recorder*, 20 June 1818; 24 May, 15 Dec. 1832. *British Colonist* (Halifax), 18 Jan. 1849, 14 Nov. 1854. *Colonial Patriot* (Pictou, N.S.), 22 May 1830. *Halifax Morning Post & Parliamentary Reporter*, 11 Nov. 1845. *Journal* (Halifax), 4 Nov. 1811, 29 May 1820. *Novascotian*, 25 Aug. 1831; 8 March 1832; 11 July 1833; 4 Sept. 1834; 1 Jan., 5 March 1835; 16 Aug. 1838; 10 Aug. 1842; 1 Dec. 1845; 14 Sept. 1846; 13 Nov. 1854. *Nova-Scotia Royal Gazette*, 25 April 1809, 30 Oct. 1811, 24 May 1815. *Belcher's farmer's almanack*, 1824–54. *The calendar of King's College, Windsor, Nova Scotia* (Halifax), 1878–79: 44–62. E. O. Jameson, *The Cogswells in America* ([Boston, 1884]), 234–35. Eaton, *Hist. of Kings County*, 481–84. V. Ross and Trigge, *Hist. of Canadian Bank of Commerce*, vol.1.

COMEAU, MARIE-HENRIETTE. *See* LeJeune

CORRIGAN, ROBERT, farmer; b. 1816 or 1817 in County Tyrone (Northern Ireland), fourth of eight children of Patrick Corrigan and Grace McNult, all born in Ireland; m. Catherine Mortin (Moreton), and they had two sons and a daughter; d. 19 Oct. 1855 in

Corrigan

Saint-Sylvestre, Lower Canada, and was buried 27 October in Leeds, Lower Canada.

Patrick Corrigan immigrated to Canada in 1831 and was later joined by his family. They were Catholic, but Robert Corrigan converted to Anglicanism at an unknown date. He acquired a lot and in 1852 or 1853 set up as a farmer on the Sainte-Marguerite concession in the eastern sector of Saint-Sylvestre, an area largely populated by Irish Catholics. In 1851 Saint-Sylvestre's population of 3,733 included 2,872 Catholics; the majority of these were Irish, but there were 1,061 French Canadians, some English and Scots, and about 10 Germans.

Despite dissimilar ethnic and religious origins, the people lived in comparative harmony. The Irish, however, were conspicuous for unruliness. Being more numerous, they presumed to make demands in respect to the parish buildings (the chapel, church, and presbytery), which the French Canadians were quick to find outrageous. Earlier, in the years 1846–50, the Irish of Saint-Sylvestre, like those of several other places in Lower Canada, had proved "the worst agitators" during a famous but inglorious episode in the annals of education known as the *guerre des éteignoirs* [*see* Jean-Baptiste Meilleur*]. To these local conflicts were added far more serious ones originating in the native countries of the immigrants, Great Britain and Ireland. For example, there was strife between Catholics and Protestants, and between the Ribbonmen, a secret society of Irish Catholics at Saint-Sylvestre, and the Orangemen of nearby Leeds.

Shortly after his arrival at Saint-Sylvestre, Robert Corrigan made enemies within the Irish Catholic clan. Quarrelsome and exceptionally strong, he challenged his adversaries to tests of strength, thereby fanning a dislike that was fuelled by sectarian prejudice. He was accused of being a "convert who had abandoned the Catholic church." Corrigan attended the Anglican church in Saint-Sylvestre, and had at least two of his children baptized there by the minister, William King. He was also reproached for having presumed to ridicule the religious observances of those whose beliefs he had once shared; in the opinion of John Caulfield O'Grady, parish priest of Saint-Sylvestre, this scorn "roused their exasperation with him to an extreme point."

His neighbours, therefore, were waiting for the chance to pick a fight with him, and the opportunity came at an agricultural fair on 17 Oct. 1855. Corrigan was acting as judge for a class of animals and a decision he made aroused protest in the Irish clan. Seven or eight people armed with sticks suddenly broke away from the group and rushed Corrigan, who was savagely beaten and knocked to the ground. He was unable to get up and two days later he died.

He had evidently been murdered, but who were the guilty parties? The Quebec police were unable to track them down. The Catholic element of the population totally refused to cooperate; worse, it made preparations to thwart the inquest to be conducted by the district of Quebec's coroner, Jean-Antoine Panet, one group even proposing to intercept him and make off with the corpse in order to destroy all trace of the murder. When Panet finally reached Saint-Sylvestre, he was told that he had to go to Leeds, where Corrigan's body had been transported on 22 October, escorted along the Craig road by some 300 Protestants with rifles at the slope for all to see. The inquest was held at Leeds from 23 to 27 October. The 4 Catholic and 16 Protestant jurors, recruited at Leeds and Saint-Sylvestre, unanimously agreed that 11 Irish Catholic suspects of Saint-Sylvestre should be indicted for murder.

William Harrison, the bailiff of Leeds, was given the responsibility for executing the coroner's warrant of arrest. He carried out repeated searches in Saint-Sylvestre and the adjoining parishes in an effort to apprehend the accused, but because the inhabitants hid them he was unable to make any arrests. On 20 November the government of Lower Canada offered a reward of $800 for their arrest, but nobody succumbed to the temptation, even when the government raised the amount to $400 for the arrest of each of the accused. By December the police did not have even one arrest to their credit. Determined to succeed where the police had failed, the government then sent military detachments totalling 130 men from Montreal and Quebec, but all to no avail. Finally, several of the accused, notably Richard Kelly, gave themselves up around 10 Jan. 1856, no doubt feeling sure that they would escape punishment since it would be impossible to identify clearly the person or persons who had struck the fatal blow. They were taken to Quebec under escort, and their trial took place before the Court of Queen's Bench, presided over by Judge Jean-François-Joseph Duval. In the face of contradictory evidence from the English-speaking witnesses, the jury acquitted the seven Irish Catholic defendants on 18 February.

The Corrigan affair had political repercussions. The verdict roused a wave of indignation among a great many Protestants in Upper Canada. John Hillyard Cameron*, a conservative member for Toronto, made himself the spokesman of the protesters in the Legislative Assembly. On 7 March 1856 he presented a resolution demanding the publication of the "irregular" charge Duval had made to the jury. The resolution was passed and it put the coalition government of Sir Allan Napier MacNab* and Étienne-Paschal Taché* in a difficult position. Having been forced to obtain a vote of confidence, the government refused to resign or to furnish the text of Duval's charge. Nevertheless, divided and under attack from Cameron as well as from George Brown*,

170

the Grits, and the Rouges, MacNab's government was breaking up. He was obliged to resign as premier in May and John A. Macdonald*, the leader of the conservatives in Upper Canada, formed a new coalition ministry with Taché.

The Corrigan affair, like the riots marking the visits of Italian revolutionary Alessandro Gavazzi to Quebec and Montreal in June 1853, which had also not resulted in the instigators being punished, led many Protestants in Upper Canada to think that their co-religionists would never obtain justice where there was a predominance of Catholics. Subsequent incidents brought to fever pitch the prejudices, and indeed the hatred, that the Orange Order did its best to arouse, especially when two of its members were directly involved: Thomas Scott*, who was executed at Fort Garry (Winnipeg) on 4 March 1870, and Thomas Hackett, who was killed during a riot in Montreal on 12 July 1877. Eight years later, with the execution of Louis Riel* in Regina, Orange sectarianism had its long-awaited revenge.

PHILIPPE SYLVAIN

[This biography summarizes the material in the author's article "L'affaire Corrigan à Saint-Sylvestre" in *Cahiers des Dix*, 42 (1979): 125–44.

A typescript of Gertrude Corrigan's study, "The genealogy of the Corrigan family, from county Tyrone, Ireland, beginning about 1782" (Newton Centre, Mass., 1965), is available at the ANQ-Q. This 62-page work includes a list of Patrick Corrigan's children. It is probably significant that the author gives no details concerning the fourth child, Robert. The ANQ-Q also holds the burial record of William Corrigan, Robert Corrigan's eldest son (CE5-13, 31 juill. 1861), and the baptismal records of John and Henrietta Corrigan, his other children (CE1-91, 13 mars 1849, 16 nov. 1854). The first of these bears the father's mark; the third is signed, but in an illiterate's hand. The Anglican minister William King has spelled the name of the children's mother differently in the two baptismal entries: Mortin and Moreton.

Two documents shed full light on the details of the Corrigan affair: Can., Prov. of, Legislative Assembly, *App. to the journals*, 1857, app.45; and *District of Quebec, depositions of witnesses severally taken and acknowledged at Leeds in the county of Megantic in the district aforesaid, on the 24th day of October . . . , one thousand eight hundred and fifty five . . . , touching the death of Robert Corrigan before Me Jean Antoine Panet, esquire, her majesty's coroner for the said district, or an inquisition then and there taken on view of the body of the said Robert Corrigan then and there lying dead* ([Quebec], 1855).

The main secondary sources consulted in preparing this biography were Arthur Caux, "Le recensement de 1851 dans la seigneurie de Beaurivage, St-Gilles, St-Sylvestre," *BRH*, 58 (1952): 87–92, and "Une exposition agricole qui tourne mal, meurtre de Corrigan à S. Sylvestre en 1855," 56 (1950): 229–34. These articles contain interesting information, but because Caux did not examine the essential sources concerning the Corrigan affair, he presents a flawed study,

giving the victim's name as Hugh and describing him as a "notable Leeds Orangeman." These errors have been repeated by amateur historians writing the local histories of Saint-Patrice-de-Beaurivage, Saint-Sylvestre, and Leeds. Donald Swainson devoted part of his article on John Hillyard Cameron in *DCB*, 10, to the political repercussions of the affair; Hereward Senior, in *Orangeism: the Canadian phase* (Toronto, 1972), 51, 55, 75–77, discusses its religious consequences. P.S.]

COSTER, GEORGE, Church of England clergyman and professor; b. 29 Nov. 1794 in Newbury, England, son of George Nathaniel Coster, a clergyman, and Anne Allen; m. Eleanor Hansard, and they had nine daughters and one son; d. 8 Jan. 1859 in Fredericton.

George Coster was the eldest of three brothers who served as missionaries of the Society for the Propagation of the Gospel, and who all eventually settled in New Brunswick. Educated at Charterhouse, London, and St John's College, Cambridge (BA in classics and mathematics, 1816; MA 1829), he was ordained priest by the bishop of London in 1819. Although he had expressed a wish to work in the Canadas, that year he went to Bermuda to become head of a college; it proved unsuccessful and he stayed on as rector of a parish. In 1822 he became a missionary of the SPG. Coster was not satisfied with the response to his efforts among the poor blacks in the parish, but apparently his superiors were impressed by his talents, for in June 1825 he was transferred to Newfoundland as bishop's commissary and that colony's first archdeacon. He resided at Bonavista and personally served that very large outport parish. He travelled extensively by boat and is credited with leading his parishioners in building their first three miles of roads. Living so far from the capital gave him an appreciation of outport life but made it difficult to carry out his responsibilities as archdeacon. He had firm ideas on the pastoral duties of missionaries and on the teaching of church doctrines in the schools. These beliefs led to disagreements with the governor, Thomas John Cochrane*, and with the Newfoundland School Society. Coster felt the governor was "too" liberal and "conciliating" in encouraging "Parsons, Priests and Dissenting 'Clergymen'" to meet on an equal footing at Government House, and in issuing licences to unqualified persons so that they could perform marriages. Also objecting to the governor's criticisms of clergymen, he argued that the outharbours required a "humbler description" of men than the gentlemen of talents, attainments, and polished manners that the governor and the Council were seeking. Coster's objection to the school society was based on his belief that it was more concerned with religious zeal than with Church of England principles.

In October 1829 Coster was appointed to succeed the Reverend George Best* as archdeacon of New

Brunswick and rector of Fredericton. He arrived in Fredericton the following July. When recommending the transfer, John Inglis*, bishop of the diocese of Nova Scotia (which included both Newfoundland and New Brunswick), had written of the "immense good" that Coster had been effecting in Newfoundland and of "the plans of improvement which thro this arrangement might be left unfinished." He was nevertheless concerned to remove Coster "to a situation of superior advantage and comfort" in view of his ill health. He was also anxious to have his own man in New Brunswick, for he saw the archdeacon as "the confidential agent and *Eye* of the Bishop." Inglis had moved vigorously to assert his right of nomination to the archdeaconry in order to head off the appointment of Benjamin Gerrish GRAY, rector of Saint John, the favoured candidate of Lieutenant Governor Sir Howard Douglas* who had the right to nominate the rector of Fredericton. Gray did not share the bishop's high church ideas of episcopal authority. Coster did.

In passing over Gray, Inglis unwittingly divided the Church of England in New Brunswick. Gray refused to acknowledge Coster's authority and, when Coster did intervene, attacked the archdeacon's ideas and friends from the pulpit and through the newspapers. As a result, Coster's influence did not extend into the city of Saint John, though his point of view was effectively expressed on the other side of its harbour by his combative brother Frederick, the rector of Carleton.

In the polarization of evangelicals and high churchmen within the Church of England, Coster was firmly with the latter party. Until his arrival, the more prominent clergymen had all been evangelicals: Best; the Reverend Edwin Jacob*, the new principal and vice-president of King's College (after 1859 the University of New Brunswick); and the influential Gray. In Coster's eyes, a fondness for "vital religion," which they shared with Methodists and Baptists, led to their paying too little attention to some important teachings of the church. There was also laxity in the supervision of SPG funds intended for the support of parish schools, often referred to as the Madras or national schools [*see* John BAIRD]. In a number of places schoolmasters who did not belong to the Church of England were being employed. Since the New Brunswick assembly was generous in making funds available for the parish schools, Coster saw it as his duty to ensure that SPG funds were used to support only those teachers who taught the full catechism and instilled church principles. However, being mild-mannered and conciliatory, he moved gradually in making changes. His thorough, careful, and lengthy appraisals, and his downright assessments of the character and competence of teachers, show his concern to weed out incompetence and to improve the general quality of education in the province.

In 1832 Coster chaired a meeting at which it was suggested that there should be an annual convention of clergy, open to lay delegates, for the purposes of encouraging local support of the church in New Brunswick, then still largely maintained by funds and priests sent from England. Initially, Bishop Inglis disapproved but in 1836 he gave his permission, "if we can make all of its parts harmonize with the two great Church Societies [the SPG and the Society for Promoting Christian Knowledge] whose objects must form our limits." Otherwise, he noted, "we shall be in danger of running wild." According to Ernest Hawkins*, the SPG secretary, the establishment of the Church Society of the Archdeaconry of New-Brunswick (Diocesan Church Society of New Brunswick) in 1836 was "the *first* systematic attempt made in a British colony for the more full and efficient support of its own Church." The society placed emphasis on providing funds for missionary work in remote parts of the province, on assistance to church building, on aiding candidates for the clergy, and on the training of schoolmasters and schoolmistresses. Its central figures, until the arrival of Bishop John Medley* in 1845, were Archdeacon Coster and his brother Frederick. The society grew to have such pivotal importance to churchmen in New Brunswick that it became known as "the Parliament of the Church." On Coster's recommendation, annual reports were published from the beginning, helping to provide Anglicans throughout the province with a new sense of identity and purpose.

Although Coster was cautious in making innovations, he showed persistence and skill in looking after the interests of the church in its relations with the government of the colony. Particularly noteworthy was his success in gaining title, in the name of Church of England institutions, to public lands set aside for the support of religion and education. In most cases the title went to parish corporations, but they were difficult to control and, just before responsibility for crown lands was transferred from the Colonial Office to the assembly in 1837, Coster arranged that the property the church had yet to receive should be placed under a board of trustees of church lands, made up of prominent officials.

In the two decades before 1837, the Colonial Office had used part of the public revenues it controlled to support an Anglican system of education. Coster feared that when it surrendered those revenues to the province the church's influence would be undermined. However, in 1838 the reformers in the assembly failed either to carry proposals for amending the charter of King's College or to make changes in the Madras School Board. The house did pass an appropriation for the support of a Baptist seminary in Fredericton, but this was rejected in the Legislative Council by a large majority. "The only point that they [the anti–Church of England group] have gained against us," Coster wrote in a report to the SPG offices on 6 March 1838, "is an extension of the right to celebrate marriage among parties not of their own denomination; which before they did not hesitate to do whenever they had the opportunity." For the time being at least, he was encouraged, and noted, "Our Churchmen are evidently awakened to the necessity of exerting themselves in defence and support of the Church."

The attacks on King's College, which persisted until 1859, were of particular concern to Coster, because from 1829 to 1845 the archdeacon of the province was its unpaid president under the terms of the royal charter. Day-to-day administration was in the hands of the vice-president, Edwin Jacob, with whom his relations were never cordial and Coster's formal duties were confined to chairing meetings of the council. However, in 1841–42 when Jacob was on leave in England, he went up to the college every day to supervise its operations and to teach Jacob's classes in divinity. On Jacob's return, Coster continued to hold a weekly tutorial for prospective clergymen, emphasizing "the peculiar position of the Church and her positive dogmatic teaching." This, in the words of William Quintard Ketchum, a former student writing many years later, "was far from a popular course; the tide was all the other way."

Evangelical hopes reached their high point in New Brunswick during the régime of Lieutenant Governor Sir John HARVEY. They were to ebb with the appointment in 1844 of one of the highest of high churchmen, John Medley, as the first bishop of Fredericton. Coster wrote of his nomination, "We want such a man exactly as he is represented to be." Earlier, when Harvey had urged the appointment of Jacob, a low churchman, Coster had himself reluctantly agreed to be a candidate if the appointment was to go to a clergyman already in the colony. Medley brought youth, vigour, and new ideas to the church in New Brunswick; even more essential to his success, however, were the financial resources and the support of his tractarian friends in England. In the presence of this powerful figure, Coster faded into the background.

The four years before Medley's arrival were probably the happiest of Coster's life. Lieutenant Governor Sir William MacBean George Colebrooke* was his friend and the Costers went "often to make music at Government House": the archdeacon was a fine musician and his wife, son, and several of their daughters were singers. Whereas his letters to the SPG in the late 1830s had been pessimistic about the future of the church in the colony, they were now full of hope, with reports on the excellence of candidates for the ministry, on the greatly improved condition of the national schools, and on the success of his ideas within

the church and of the church within the community, even though newspapers and political figures alike seemed often to be "friendly to dissent."

In handling his own parish Coster was very cautious. He insisted on adhering strictly to the rules of the prayer book with reference to the celebration of Holy Communion and holy days, but the only significant innovation introduced was the institution in 1835 of evening services at the direction of Bishop Inglis. The parish vestry was a conservative body which maintained the church as a bastion of privilege, discouraging the attendance of the poor by refusing to provide free seating. The advent of Medley disturbed this cosy situation. He decided that the site of the parish church was the most suitable that could be found for his new cathedral. This decision required either the removal or the demolition of the old church building. In 1846 the vestry voted to cooperate with the bishop, but popular agitation arose against the incorporation of the parish church into the cathedral; eventually, in 1853, it was agreed to split the parish and cathedral properties. The upsetting of old social customs and the proposal to make the cathedral seating free probably had more to do with the popular feeling against the union than anything else. Throughout the controversy Coster adhered rigidly to the old church principle "Nothing without the Bishop," obeying even when ordered to hold services in the cathedral instead of in the parish church. Finally, to Coster's relief, his parish congregation was reconstituted at St Anne's, an attractive stone church in the Gothic revival style, which Medley had had erected as a chapel of ease. When collections in the new church proved to be inadequate, Coster himself paid most of the costs of poor relief that had previously been met by the congregation: the sum amounted to more than £70 annually. The last months before his death were to be disturbed by yet another action of the bishop; his brother Nathaniel, the rector of Gagetown, received what Coster considered to be a harsh condemnation for striking a parishioner.

In 1831, the year following their arrival in Fredericton, the Costers had lost most of their possessions, suffering two house fires in five months. The vestry then constructed a fine brick parsonage for them. In this house the poor were received with Christian charity. There were also pleasant parties, with Eleanor Coster "always ready for a rattling discussion." And there was music, both sacred and popular. In the evenings there were readings: "The best plays of Shakespeare he knew by heart. No one enjoyed more the fun and wit of Dickens and Thackeray, or felt more deeply their beauty and pathos."

The household became a centre for the British community in Fredericton. James Robb*, a young Scottish medical doctor who was professor of chemistry and natural history at the college, was converted to Anglicanism by Coster and married his eldest daughter. Other sons-in-law included James Carter*, the chief justice; Edward Barron Chandler*, member of a prominent political family; and Frank WILLS, the architect of Christ Church Cathedral in Fredericton and a pioneer among the architects of the Gothic revival in North America. Coster's son, the Reverend Charles, was a master in the collegiate school in Fredericton.

The archdeacon was "a good staunch Tory" who defended the privileges of the church and, in particular, opposed efforts to make King's College a more secular institution. He had little sympathy with the emergence of popular politics and was unhappy about the coming of responsible government, with the accompanying decline of families whose fortunes depended on high official salaries and life tenure in public offices. In his later years he suffered severely from asthma, and frequent illnesses curtailed his public activities. He was, in any event, essentially a man of the study and of the pulpit, not of the active political world.

Coster's few published sermons are models of clarity. Bishop Medley described them as distinguished for conciseness and purity of style with considerable force of expression. On his death the bishop wrote, "The Church has lost in him an able and accurate scholar. . . . The poor will feel the loss of a very kind friend."

D. MURRAY YOUNG

Anglican Church of Canada, Diocese of Fredericton Arch., Christ Church Anglican Church (Fredericton), records (mfm. at PANB). Guildhall Library (London), MS 9532A/2 (Diocese of London; bishop's act-book, 1809–28). Lambeth Palace Library (London), Fulham papers. PAC, MG 24, A17; RG 7, G8 B, 10, no.23. PANB, MC 58; MC 211, MS4/5/1 ("Notes on the history of Fredericton parish church . . ." (typescript, 1922)); 4/5/2 ("Manuscript notes on the Fredericton parish church"); 4/5/3 ("The present (Fredericton) parish church" (typescript, 1922)); MC 300, MS4/9 ("A calendar of the S.P.G. . . . ," intro. Lillian Maxwell (typescript, [1940?])); "Ven. Archdeacon George Coster, 1829 to 1844," comp. E. M. Chapman (typescript, 1936)); RG 7, RS75A, 1859, George Coster. PRO, CO 188 (mfm. at PANB). USPG, C/CAN/folder 253; C/CAN/NB, 6, nos.4, 7, 10, 12–13, 23, 33, 36, 39, 42, 56, 62, 65, 68–69, 71, 74; D11: 225–30, 397–402, 493–94 (mfm. at PAC). UNBL, MG H1, "Old Fredericton and the college: town and gown as described in the letters of James and Ellen Robb," ed. A. G. Bailey (typescript, 1973). Church of England, Diocesan Church Soc. of N.B., *Report* (Saint John), 1837–59. Ernest Hawkins, *Annals of the diocese of Fredericton* (London, 1847). [John Inglis], *A journal of visitation in Nova Scotia, Cape Breton, and along the eastern shore of New Brunswick, by the lord bishop of Nova Scotia, in the summer and autumn of 1843* (3rd ed., London, 1846). Robb and Coster, *Letters* (Bailey). SPG, [*Annual report*] (London), 1822–59.

W. J. Clarke, "An introduction to the constitutional history of the Church of England in British North America" (MA thesis, Univ. of N.B., Fredericton, 1944). G. E. Fenety, *Political notes and observations; or, a glance at the leading measures that have been introduced and discussed in the House of Assembly of New Brunswick* . . . (Fredericton, 1867). I. L. Hill, *Fredericton, New Brunswick, British North America* ([Fredericton?, 1968?]). W. Q. Ketchum, *The life and work of the Most Reverend John Medley, D.D., first bishop of Fredericton and metropolitan of Canada* (Saint John, 1893). G. H. Lee, *An historical sketch of the first fifty years of the Church of England in the province of New Brunswick (1783–1833)* (Saint John, 1880). MacNutt, *New Brunswick*. C. F. Pascoe, *Two hundred years of the S.P.G.* . . . (2v., London, 1901). J. E. Pinnington, "Anglican reactions to the challenge of a multiconfessional society, with special reference to British North America, 1760–1850" (2v., PHD thesis, Univ. of Oxford, 1971). J. D. Purdy, "The Church of England in New Brunswick during the colonial era, 1783–1860" (MA thesis, Univ. of N.B., 1954). Douglas Richardson, "Canadian architecture in the Victorian era: the spirit of the place," *Canadian Collector* (Toronto), 10 (1975), no.5: 20–29.

COUILLARD-DESPRÉS, EMMANUEL, surveyor, seigneur, militia officer, builder, and farmer; b. 22 May 1792 in L'Islet, Lower Canada, son of Emmanuel Couillard-Després and Marie-Françoise Robichaud; d. 15 July 1853 in Saint-Aimé (Massueville), Lower Canada.

Emmanuel Couillard-Després was a sixth-generation descendant on his father's side of Guillaume Couillard* de Lespinay, son-in-law of Louis Hébert*. His great-great-grandfather, Jacques Couillard, son of Geneviève Desprez (Després), had been the first in the family to add his mother's name to his own, which then became Couillard-Després. In 1732 his great-grandfather, Jean-Baptiste Couillard-Després, had rendered fealty and homage as co-seigneur of L'Islet. Around 1793 his father had abandoned the seigneury, which he had inherited, to settle with his wife in Saint-Hyacinthe, where the fertile lands of Delorme seigneury were then being opened. A few settlers from Saint-Thomas parish (in Montmagny), including some of the Couillard-Després family, had already come. He bought several lots so that he could establish his family, and he himself took up a piece of land in the second concession of the seigneury.

The eldest of ten children, Emmanuel Couillard-Després attended the Séminaire de Nicolet from 1810 to 1815. At the end of his studies, believing that he had a religious vocation, he began training for the priesthood. He offered his services to Antoine Girouard*, the priest of the parish of Saint-Hyacinthe, who had founded the Collège de Saint-Hyacinthe in 1811. The young man became the first teacher of mathematics there. After four years, realizing that he had been mistaken about his vocation, he gave up the religious life. Because he had a liking for numbers he took up the study of civil engineering, and on 25 July 1821 he received his commission as a surveyor.

Couillard-Després began to practise his profession at Saint-Hyacinthe in 1824. On 18 May of that year, at Saint-Denis on the Richelieu, he married Louise-Esther Bourdages, the daughter of Louis Bourdages*, the great orator, who represented the riding of Buckingham in the House of Assembly. The marriage was celebrated with great solemnity by Girouard, a personal friend of the bridegroom, in the presence of all those prominent in the parish and in neighbouring parishes. Shortly afterwards the young couple settled in Saint-Hyacinthe. On 8 November Couillard-Després undertook to provide his parents with an income, and thus inherited his father's estate. He was appointed a captain in the 1st Battalion of Saint-Hyacinthe militia on 10 Feb. 1831. Having lost his wife that year, he devoted most of his energies to his work.

Couillard-Després ran in a by-election in 1832 for the riding of Saint-Hyacinthe but was defeated by Louis Poulin, as was Thomas Boutillier*. In August Couillard-Després was given the job of surveying the land on which the church of the new parish of Sainte-Rosalie, near Saint-Hyacinthe, was to be erected. He put up the first court-house in Saint-Hyacinthe in 1835, and a decade later had to reinforce it with iron rods and chains which kept the building standing until it burned down in 1859.

In 1836 Couillard-Després engaged in land transactions. On 3 May he sold the property on the second concession of Delorme seigneury to François Morel for 4,500 *livres* on terms obliging the purchaser to pay the vendor's parents the income he had previously paid them. Also in 1836 Couillard-Després staked out for himself a huge seigneurial land grant – 10 *arpents* by 30 – to the west of Saint-Hyacinthe and stretching beyond the present site of the municipal aqueduct.

When the rebellion broke out in 1837 Couillard-Després, as a captain in the Saint-Hyacinthe militia, did not see eye to eye with the Patriotes. Because he disapproved of their acts of violence, he had to endure all kinds of annoyances. The Patriotes took revenge on him by raising a ruckus on numerous occasions, smashing doors and windows and doing considerable damage to the interior of his home.

During the next 15 years Couillard-Després continued his career as a surveyor. In 1853 he decided to move to Sainte-Rosalie, and then went to Saint-Aimé; in both places he took up farming. He died at Saint-Aimé on 15 July 1853 at the age of 61, and was buried three days later in the vault of the cathedral at Saint-Hyacinthe.

Emmanuel Couillard-Després did a good deal of work as a surveyor, to judge by the seven volumes of reports that he wrote in the course of his 29 years in practice. He and his wife had only one son, Emmanuel-Louis-Rémi, who became the first secretary-treasurer of the town of Saint-Hyacinthe. A street there is still called Després, a reminder that "Village Després" was the name given in the 1860s to a group of houses spread across part of the former Couillard-Després land grant.

JEANNE D'AIGLE

The surveyor's reports of Emmanuel Couillard-Després for 1821–53 are in ANQ-M, CA1-17.

ANQ-M, CE2-1, 18 juill. 1853; CE2-12, 18 mai 1824; CN2-22, 3 mai 1836; CN2-80, 18 mai, 8 nov. 1824. ANQ-Q, CE2-3, 22 mai 1792; P-52. ASSH, F, Fg-41, Dossier 5.2. PAC, MG 30, D1, 9: 69–71; RG 68, General index, 1651–1841: 665. *Le Courrier de Saint-Hyacinthe* (Saint-Hyacinthe, Qué.), 19 juill. 1853. *Liste de la milice du Bas-Canada pour 1832* (Québec, s.d.). Allaire, *Hist. de Saint-Denis-sur-Richelieu*, 212. J.-B.-O. Archambault, *Monographie de la paroisse de Sainte-Rosalie* (Saint-Hyacinthe, 1939), 47–48. Choquette, *Hist. du séminaire de Saint-Hyacinthe*, vol.2; *Histoire de la ville de Saint-Hyacinthe* (Saint-Hyacinthe, 1930), 51, 98–99, 209, 414–15. Azarie Couillard-Després, *Histoire des seigneurs de la rivière du Sud et de leurs alliés canadiens et acadiens* (Saint-Hyacinthe, 1912), 79–84, 200, 206–8, 308–10, 374–80; *La première famille française au Canada, ses alliés et ses descendants* (Montréal, 1906), 306–7. Douville, *Hist. du collège-séminaire de Nicolet*.

COX, ROSS, fur trader and author; b. 1793 in Dublin, son of Samuel Cox and Margaret Thorpe; m. 1819 Hannah Cumming; d. 1853 in Dublin.

The details of Ross Cox's youth and his arrival in North America remain obscure. Having left Ireland at an early age, he was in New York in 1811, when John Jacob Astor*'s Pacific Fur Company was making arrangements for its second supply ship, the *Beaver*, to be sent to the northwest coast. Cox, who was "captivated with the love of novelty, and the hope of speedily realising an independence in the supposed *El Dorado*" of the northwest fur trade, signed on as clerk with the company at a salary of $100 per year. In October 1811 he sailed with a party under John CLARKE aboard the *Beaver* for Fort Astoria (Astoria, Oreg.). The vessel arrived in May 1812 and, at the end of June, Cox left with Clarke and three other clerks for the Spokane River to set up a post near the North West Company's Spokane House (near Spokane, Wash.). The journey was long and hazardous, and Cox, a small and somewhat corpulent man, had difficulty maintaining the pace set by the more experienced Clarke. Near the junction of Cow Creek and the Palouse River he was separated from the other members of the group, who, following an unsuccessful search, continued on to the Spokane River. After wandering for 14 days on foot, he found his way to this river where, hungry and dangerously exhausted, he rejoined the party.

Cox passed the summer months at the new PFC post, Spokane, slowly regaining his strength. In October he left with another clerk for a trading

Coy

expedition in the Flathead country to counter the NWC activity at Saleesh House (near Thompson, Mont.). He returned to Spokane where he spent the winter and then, at the end of May 1813, made the journey back to Fort Astoria with the party carrying the produce of the winter's trade. The fort was short of provisions and because of the state of war between Great Britain and the United States its position was seriously threatened by both British naval control of the west coast and the aggressive competition of the NWC, trading under the British flag. In the face of these difficulties, on 25 June 1813 the company partners at Astoria offered to cancel the contracts of Cox and two other clerks if they could find employment elsewhere. Cox apparently took advantage of this proposition to secure a position with the NWC, and early in July he left with Joseph Larocque* to provision the NWC posts at Spokane House and in the Okanagan. The party returned to Fort Astoria in the fall and Cox was there when John George McTavish* negotiated the NWC's purchase of all of the PFC's holdings.

In the employ of the NWC, Cox made a number of trips up the Columbia River accompanying Finan McDonald, James KEITH, Alexander Stewart, James McMILLAN, and other NWC servants, before being given the charge of Fort Okanagan (Wash.) in April 1816. Towards the end of that summer, however, he submitted his resignation and in April 1817, after having spent the winter at Fort Okanagan, he left with the overland party, which included Angus BETHUNE and Duncan McDougall*, for Fort William (Thunder Bay, Ont.), and then continued on to Montreal. After unsuccessfully soliciting a position in the Hudson's Bay Company through the influence of Colin Robertson*, Cox returned to Dublin late in 1818 or early in 1819 where he found employment as a clerk in the main police office. He also worked as the Dublin correspondent for the *Morning Herald* (London) up to 1837 and remained in Ireland until his death in 1853.

In 1831 Cox published his *Adventures on the Columbia*, the second narrative prepared by an employee of the PFC on the northwest coast, Gabriel Franchère*'s *Relation d'un voyage à la côte du Nord-Ouest de l'Amérique septentrionale* having appeared in 1820. Cox's account was an immediate success and re-editions soon appeared, both in London and in New York. Written in a journalistic style, his tale is thrilling and at the same time very human. However, prepared many years after the events, and constructed from memory and hearsay, the account often credits Cox with an importance out of proportion to his position and is chronologically inaccurate in places. He was not, for instance, as his narrative would suggest, present at Fort Astoria when the lone survivor of the ill-fated *Tonquin* arrived in August 1813 to relate the massacre of the crew by Indians in June 1811

[*see* Jonathan Thorn*]. Yet in spite of its factual weaknesses, there is much of value in the work. He presents a day-to-day account of the operations of both the PFC and the NWC in the early years of the trade west of the Rocky Mountains. His descriptions of the Indians and of the country, as well as his vivid portrayal of the life of the traders, its hardships, boredom, and dangers, remain of interest.

ERIC J. HOLMGREN

Ross Cox is the author of *Adventures on the Columbia*, which also appeared under the title *The Columbia River; or, scenes and adventures during a residence of six years on the western side of the Rocky Mountains, among various tribes of Indians hitherto unknown; together with a journey across the American continent*, ed. E. I. and J. R. Stewart (Norman, Okla., [1957]).

Docs. relating to NWC (Wallace). Gabriel Franchère, *Relation d'un voyage à la côte du nord-ouest de l'Amérique septentrionale, dans les années 1810, 11, 12, 13 et 14*, Michel Bibaud, édit. (Montréal, 1820). *HBRS*, 2 (Rich and Fleming). A. Ross, *Adventures on the Columbia*. David Thompson, *David Thompson's narrative, 1784–1812*, ed. R. [G.] Glover (new ed., Toronto, 1962). H. H. Bancroft [and H. L. Oakes], *History of the northwest coast* (2v., San Francisco, 1884), 2. Rich, *Hist. of HBC*. Robert Rumilly, *La Compagnie du Nord-Ouest, une épopée montréalaise* (2v., Montréal, 1980). W. S. Wallace, "A note on Ross Cox," *CHR*, 14 (1933): 408.

COY, MARY (Morris; Bradley), farmer's wife, shopkeeper, and author; b. 1 Sept. 1771 in Grimross (Gagetown, N.B.), eighth of 11 children of J. Edward Coy (McCoy) and Ama Titus; one of Mary's brothers, Amasa*, was a prominent Fredericton merchant; m. first 15 Feb. 1793 David Morris (d. 1 March 1817); m. secondly 30 June 1819 Leverit Bradley; there were no children from either marriage; d. a widow 12 March 1859 in Saint John, N.B.

Mary Coy, except for the fact that she did not bear children, is representative of most women of her time and place. Her only distinguishing characteristic was a strong lifelong interest in religion, particularly in the revivalist phenomenon that came to be known as the Great Awakening. That interest may not have been atypical, but it was unusually intense. Certainly her expression of it, in a memoir entitled *A narrative of the life and Christian experience of Mrs. Mary Bradley, of Saint John* (published in 1849), is remarkable given that she had had only a few months of formal schooling. Her aim, she announced in the preface, was "to promote the glory of God and the good of my fellow creatures," and she recommended the book to Wesleyan ministers for "gratuitous distribution."

Mary and her husband David Morris lived first in Maugerville Township, and then on 1 May 1800 took up a farm at Portland Point (Saint John). Five years later they moved to Saint John itself, where they kept a store in their home until 1816. David's ill health, which had prevented their remaining on the farm, was also responsible for the closing of the shop. Two years after his death in 1817 Mary remarried, and she remained in Saint John for the rest of her life. A witness of the fire of 14 Jan. 1837, which destroyed more than 100 buildings in Saint John, Mary Bradley recorded that she had believed "the kind hand of the Almighty would stop the progress of the flames, before they should reach us: I prayed earnestly that he would do so." She felt the combined efforts of "the praying members of the church" and of the many ministers of her Wesleyan faith who were in town caused the wind shift that saved the meeting hall and her home.

Throughout her life, Mary pursued her faith aggressively. In her youth, filled with spiritual fervour, she spoke out in church and was sharply reprimanded by the Congregational elders for her outburst. She was also refused permission to pray aloud at meetings because "the Scriptures forbid females praying in public." Nevertheless she persisted, attending church services and prayer meetings, and denouncing the occasional backslider. She constantly strove to find a church in which she was comfortable in her faith. Although born a Presbyterian, she associated with the Congregationalists and the New Light Baptists before joining the Wesleyan Methodists in January 1803. Her constant need to speak out and her self-assurance culminated in the publication of her memoir, by which she added to an evangelical literature that included the efforts of Henry Alline* and John Wesley.

In her *Narrative*, Mary Bradley describes a series of religious experiences, from attacks of hysteria to the more prosaic overcoming, through prayer, of a fear of bears when as a young woman she was required to fetch the family cows. "I was conscious of a two-fold strife; life and death were set before me, and . . . evil being the food my fallen nature craved . . . but when my mind centred in God and his word . . . I was enabled, after due consideration, to set up a firm and settled resolution, no longer to neglect my salvation."

Also recorded in the *Narrative* are the comings and goings of a host of ministers who worked in New Brunswick during Mary's lifetime. "Henry Allen," presumably Alline, visited her community in Maugerville Township when she was nine. In 1788 Lady Huntingdon, a prominent English religious philanthropist, sent bibles and tracts, as well as two ministers from her own connection, to the settlements in the area. One became the local preacher but was later removed from the ministry because of drunkenness. Other ministers followed, including the Reverend William Black*, a Wesleyan from Nova Scotia. For the years when she was living in the Saint John region, Mary Bradley mentions in her journal a number of visiting clergymen such as the Wesleyan missionary Joshua Marsden* and the Methodist ministers Enoch Wood* and Albert Des Brisay.

Above all else, Mary Bradley was a consumer of the religious revival known as the Great Awakening. In her will she placed the bulk of her approximately £1,800 estate in trust, with the interest to be used to hire an "Itinerant or Travelling Wesleyan Methodist Minister to teach the Gospel at Grand Lake and New Cannan," an area she described as her "native place." She also bequeathed £100 to assist in the construction of a Wesleyan chapel in Saint John. The rest of her substantial estate was to be divided among a number of her nephews and nieces. She died at 87 years of age, having borne, according to an obituary in the Saint John *Morning News*, "the infirmities of her great age with patience, and her last illness with resignation. Her end was eminently peaceful."

JO-ANN CARR FELLOWS

Mary [Coy] Bradley is the author of *A narrative of the life and Christian experience of Mrs. Mary Bradley, of Saint John, New Brunswick, written by herself; including extracts from her diary and correspondence during a period of upwards of sixty years* (Boston, 1849).

PANB, RG 7, RS69A, 1795–96, J. E. Coy; RS71, 1859, Mary Bradley; RS75, 1838, Amasa Coy. J. M. Bumsted, *Henry Alline, 1748–1784* (Toronto, 1971), 52.

CRAIG, JOHN, artisan, artist, art gallery owner, and politician; b. 1804 in Ireland; m. Charlotte ——, and they had one daughter, Mathilda (b. 1847); d. 25 March 1854 in Toronto.

Little is known of John Craig's early life. He probably arrived in York (Toronto) early in 1828. By July of that year he was advertising his services in the *Colonial Advocate* as a painter of portraits, fancy signs, and heraldry. Forced by economic circumstance to ply a varied trade, he soon extended his business to include coach, sign, and house painting. His most notable commission was to design painted altar windows for the second St James' Church, erected 1831–33 [*see* Thomas ROGERS]. Executed by William Schofield, a glazier and sign-painter, these windows received much local praise; however, according to the more sophisticated eye of Anna Brownell Jameson [MURPHY], they were "in a vile, and tawdry taste." Unfortunately this early example of Craig's ecclesiastical work was destroyed by fire in 1839.

Craig's career, which peaked in the 1840s, developed with the architectural growth of Toronto. Through his role as master artisan his name can be linked with most major public buildings erected during that time. He was frequently involved in various aspects of the interior decoration of many

Craig

buildings designed by John George Howard*, such as Christ Church (Tyendinaga, 1843) and the Bank of British North America (Toronto, 1845). Along with Edward Claxton Bull, Craig executed stained glass windows for Henry Bowyer Joseph LANE's Church of St George the Martyr (Toronto, 1844). He was responsible for the decoration and stage scenery for John Ritchey's Royal Lyceum Theatre which opened its doors to Toronto audiences in 1848, and he supervised painting the interior of St Michael's Cathedral, Toronto (erected 1845–48 on a design by William THOMAS). Also included among his designs were coats of arms for several provincial court-houses as well as banners for many local Orange and masonic lodges, and for Toronto's "national societies," such as the St Andrew's, St George's, and St Patrick's benevolent societies.

Craig was one of Toronto's earliest picture dealers, operating from his "Painting Room" at 229 King Street during the early 1830s. He was a member of Toronto's first art society, the short-lived Society of Artists and Amateurs. He did not, however, submit any works to its one and only exhibition, held in the legislative buildings in July 1834. He later belonged to the Toronto Society of Arts and contributed works to its two exhibitions, in 1847 and 1848. His design for a model water-wheel was featured in the October 1848 exhibition sponsored by the local mechanics' institute.

Craig, a tory, was elected a councilman for St George's Ward in 1834, the year Toronto was incorporated, which may account for his not having submitted works to the 1834 exhibition. Shortly thereafter, he and fellow councilmen George Gurnett* and John Doel* formed a committee to oversee production of a design for the city seal. Craig, in all likelihood, produced the actual design; the engraving of the seal was awarded for a fee of £10 to William Connell, a local engraver, tinsmith, and fellow Irishman. Perhaps as a result of Craig's influence, Connell's impressions were displayed at the 1834 exhibition. According to reviews in the Patriot, the committee's choice of engraver had met with some opposition from Mayor William Lyon Mackenzie*, who would have preferred that the commission be awarded to someone other than an Irish Catholic.

As a political figure, Craig seems to have maintained a low profile, choosing the role of mediator rather than instigator. He voted faithfully with fellow tory Gurnett throughout his lengthy tenure as councilman from 1834 to 1849. Craig and Gurnett, assisted by Ritchey who was also a member of council, were instrumental in securing the position of city surveyor for John George Howard in May 1843. Craig was, as well, an early member of the St Patrick's Benevolent Society and of the Emigrant Society of Upper Canada.

Craig died in 1854 of pneumatic gout. Shortly after his death, his widow presented a petition to city council requesting a remission from taxes. This, and the fact that his burial costs went unpaid, suggest that he had died heavily in debt. Although Craig's achievements seem modest when compared with those of many of his contemporaries, he clearly made significant contributions to art, architecture, and local politics. An obituary in the Globe described him as an "old and respected inhabitant."

CAROL LOWREY

[John Craig's artistic career can be traced through reviews and notices of his designs published in Toronto newspapers. His name appears regularly in the J. G. Howard papers (MTL) with respect to various designs in stained glass, coats-of-arms, and painted interiors produced for Howard's buildings. Comments on his windows for the second St James can be found in Murphy, Winter studies and summer rambles, 1: 274. Craig's participation in Toronto's early art societies is recorded in the Soc. of Artists & Amateurs of Toronto, Catalogue of the first exhibition . . . (Toronto, 1834; [rev. ed., 1848?]), and in the Toronto Society of Arts: first exhibition, 1847 . . . and second exhibition, 1848 . . . , probably published in Toronto in 1847 and 1848. Connell's impressions of the city seal are mentioned in reviews of the 1834 exhibition which appeared in the Patriot (Toronto), 11 July 1834. For further details see also CTA, Information file, city seal.

Two examples of Craig's work are known to survive. Three of four stained glass windows designed for Duncan Campbell's house (now the Lynnwood Arts Centre) in Simcoe, Ont., have been identified as his (see British Colonist (Toronto), 4 Nov. 1851, for a contemporary description). Another work, the Arms of George IV at the Middlesex County Court-house (London, Ont.), is described in MacRae and Adamson, Cornerstones of order, 98.

The most useful sources for Craig's political career include the City Council minutes, CTA, RG 1, A, especially 8 April, 2 Oct., 22 Nov. 1834; 16 April 1849; 18 April, 1 May 1854; B. D. Dyster, "Toronto, 1840–1860: making it in a British Protestant town" (1v. in 2, PHD thesis, Univ. of Toronto, 1970); and the local newspapers.   C.L.]

ACC-T, Little Trinity Church (Toronto), reg. of baptisms, 1844–61, no.173. MTL, Carfrae papers, scrapbook; Toronto, Mechanics Institute papers, D25 (Exhibitions, 1847–49: accounts and exhibits). St James' Cemetery and Crematorium (Toronto), Record of burials, 28 March 1854. British Colonist (Toronto), 27 June 1845, 29 Dec. 1848. Colonial Advocate, 5–17 July 1828; 30 Jan., 13 Feb.–27 March 1834. Correspondent and Advocate (Toronto), 11 Dec. 1834. Courier of Upper Canada (Toronto), 5 May 1835. Globe, 30 Dec. 1848, 30 March 1854. Loyalist (York [Toronto]), 6–27 Dec. 1828. Toronto Patriot, 24 May 1833, 5 March 1841. Toronto Star, 20 Nov. 1844. Harper, Early painters and engravers. Toronto directory, 1837–51. W. [G.] Colgate, Canadian art; its origin & development (Toronto, 1943; repr. 1967). MacRae et al., Hallowed walls, 148. Robertson's landmarks of Toronto, 1: 336. Scadding, Toronto of old (1873). C. D. Lowrey, "The Society of Artists & Amateurs, 1834: Toronto's first art exhibition and its antecedents," RACAR (Montreal), 8 (1981): 99–118.

Crandall

CRANDALL, JOSEPH, Baptist minister and politician; b. *c.* 1761 in Tiverton, R.I., son of Webber Crandall and Mercy Vaughan; d. 20 Feb. 1858 in Salisbury, N.B.

Joseph Crandall immigrated with his parents to Chester, N.S., in the early 1770s. His later recollections of these pioneering days emphasized the absence of schools, the death of his mother when he was about 13, and the subsequent appearance of Henry Alline*, called by the people of the area a "New Light" and described by Crandall as a "strange man that was preaching in Windsor and adjoining places." Crandall apparently never met Alline – although his father heard him preach – but he did listen to a succession of evangelicals, such as John Sargent and Harris HARDING, without being visibly affected. His only bow to religion in these early years, one which he later regretted, was to be "sprinkled" by a Presbyterian minister.

After the death of his father, Crandall went to Liverpool to engage in the cod fishery and subsequently worked freighting lumber from Shubenacadie to Windsor. Like most of the "founding fathers" of the Baptist denomination in the Maritimes, he eventually experienced an adult crisis conversion, in his case at about 35 years of age. In July 1795 he entered a private house in Chester where Harding and Joseph Dimock* were preaching, and he later recalled: "My hard heart was at last, broken, and I had such a view of a perishing world lying in ruin as I never could express. To the great surprise of all present I began to speak and try to tell what I felt and saw. . . . I saw mercy so connected with the justice of God, that they were both one, that what God had done in the person of Christ was alone sufficient to save all that came to God for mercy through Jesus Christ." After a summer in Newport, Crandall returned to Chester and joined Dimock's open communion church. Although he yearned to preach publicly, he held himself back because he lacked formal schooling. Late in 1795, however, he had a dream in which he was told to wade into a raging river "and save all the people I could." Baptized by immersion that day by Dimock, Crandall soon afterwards accompanied Harding to Liverpool, where he began his preaching career.

Crandall preached his way back and forth across Nova Scotia for a few years and eventually went to New Brunswick, which he was to make his evangelical territory for the remainder of his life. After considerable soul-searching while clearing a farm in Salisbury, Westmorland County, Crandall found that "the cloud of darkness that had for so long obscured my mind" had lifted and he decided to enter the ministry. On 8 Oct. 1799 he became the first regularly ordained Baptist minister in the province when he was set apart as a pastor at the Sackville church by Edward MANNING, Theodore Seth Har-

ding, and Dimock. A year later he organized a church at Salisbury with which he maintained a connection until his death. He had married the eldest daughter of Jaimy Sherman of Salisbury in 1797, and they had six children. After the death of his first wife Crandall married Martha Hopper of Sackville, and the couple had eight children.

Crandall was active in the Nova Scotia Baptist Association from its founding in 1800. When a separate New Brunswick association was organized in July 1822, he was appointed the first moderator and seems to have filled that position regularly until the 1840s. He served for many years as a missionary of the Nova Scotia organization in eastern New Brunswick, and throughout his long career continued to itinerate in both colonies; "steady pastoral guidance, in connection with an individual church," commented Ingraham Ebenezer Bill*, one of his successors, "was not his *forte*." He seems to have thrived on the trials and discomforts of backwoods travel, and, like many of his contemporaries, regarded both money and a regular stipend with considerable disdain. He attempted to exercise spiritual supervision over all the Baptists in Westmorland and Albert counties, and served as pastor to a number of different churches in the area at various times during his life. As the denomination grew and flourished in the 1840s, and as the province became more densely populated, Crandall's itinerant leanings, so well suited to the church's formative years, came into disfavour. Although in 1821 there had been only six ordained ministers serving a scattered membership of 506, by 1847 the number of communicants had increased to 4,806, served by 48 regular preachers. There came to be objections to the unintentional by-products of Crandall's itinerancy, which were "to unsettle young pastors, and to induce in the people the love of change."

In 1818, when the Baptist Church was attempting to achieve legal recognition and equality with the established Church of England, Crandall was elected to the New Brunswick House of Assembly for Westmorland County. He was forced to resign his seat, however, when the assembly declared all clergymen ineligible to sit in the house. Crandall always regarded this action as unfair, but he refused to confront the government over it. For many years thereafter he used his authority in the county to ensure that its representatives in the assembly supported civil and especially religious liberty. In 1836 he was elected president of the New Brunswick Baptist Education Society, serving in that post until his death.

Undoubtedly the most influential and venerated Baptist leader in New Brunswick during the first years of the 19th century, Crandall has left little written evidence of his importance. His sermons were almost all extemporaneous and thus were never published or

179

Crandall

preserved. But several generations of New Brunswickers in the scattered settlements of the back country remembered him fondly as a commanding pulpit presence, whose invariable topic – typically evangelical – was Christ and the crucifixion. He wrote but one brief and tantalizing autobiographical fragment, cast in the form of a spiritual memoir. It is impossible to calculate the number of individuals he converted, or baptized, but he was always successful. Active until the end, Crandall, supported in the pulpit by two of his deacons, preached his last sermon in Salisbury six weeks before his death at the age of 97. He died, as he had lived, "with his armour on."

J. M. BUMSTED

Joseph Crandall's spiritual memoir has been edited by J. M. Bumsted and published as "The autobiography of Joseph Crandall" in *Acadiensis* (Fredericton), 3 (1973–74), no.1: 79–96.

Bill, *Fifty years with Baptist ministers*. Levy, *Baptists of Maritime prov.* MacNutt, *New Brunswick*.

CRANDALL, REUBEN, Baptist clergyman; b. 24 March 1767 in Northeast Township, Dutchess County, N.Y., believed to be the son of Laban Crandall and Molly Seein; m. first *c.* 1786 Lida (Lydia) Mace, and they had seven children; m. secondly December 1813 Julia Smith, widow of Joseph Beemer, and they had two children; d. 28 Sept. 1853 near Aylmer, Upper Canada, and was buried east of Aylmer in the Burdick Cemetery.

Reuben Crandall was converted to the Baptist faith at the age of 16 and shortly thereafter was licensed to preach by the Baptist church in his native township or by some other congregation located nearby. In June 1794 he immigrated to Hallowell Township, Prince Edward County, Upper Canada, and immediately began to conduct religious services around West Lake. Unable to support himself entirely through preaching, he obtained a grant in 1796 of lot 28, concession 2, Cramahe Township, Northumberland County, where he farmed. Upon his arrival there he began travelling extensively throughout the district as a missionary preacher while working to build a congregation near his home. In 1798 he was instrumental in organizing a church with branches in Cramahe and Haldimand townships. Formally ordained at the church in Hallowell by a council of fellow Baptists on 27 Oct. 1799, Crandall appears to have enjoyed considerable success. In 1804 a visiting American missionary wrote that "Elder Crandall had had a comfortable season in the year past. The church is increasing in members, and we thought in graces likewise."

Ordination permitted Crandall to apply for the right to perform marriages in his district. That privilege had been restricted to clergy of the Church of England until a statute of 1798 extended it to clergy of certain other denominations. On 9 April 1805 the Court of Quarter Sessions, meeting in Haldimand Township, granted Crandall the authority to perform marriages in the Newcastle District.

The following August he joined Joseph Winn and Abel Stevens* in ordaining another Baptist preacher, Elijah Bentley*. For the next seven years Crandall continued to serve the church in the central part of the province. In 1812 he relinquished his oversight of the Cramahe and Haldimand congregations and moved to the area west of Lake Ontario where he and his wife became members of the church at Boston in Townsend Township. While there, Crandall took frequent missionary tours through the newly opened districts along the Lake Erie shore. It was shortly after his move to Townsend that Crandall's first wife died. His subsequent remarriage within a year was viewed as a scandalous act by the conservative members of his church. Crandall, however, refused to acknowledge that the church had any right to question him on the matter and the issue was quietly dropped. He then apparently settled for a brief time in Oakland; by 1816, however, he had made his permanent residence in Malahide Township near the present town of Aylmer. Here he led in the organization of a Baptist church which was established in October of that year with a charter membership of 12. Aylmer was to remain the focus of his future activities.

In 1820 Crandall was arrested and tried at the spring assizes of the London District for illegally performing marriages. He had been granted permission to conduct such services in the Newcastle District, but that authorization was not valid in other areas. Following Crandall's conviction Attorney General John Beverley Robinson* noted in a letter to the lieutenant governor's secretary, Major George Hillier*, that Crandall had not only performed marriages without permission but, unlike the Methodist clergyman Henry Ryan*, had "solemnized matrimony in a manner that could not have been legal whatever his authority." Robinson further stated that the judge was obliged by the statute to impose the full punishment – banishment for 14 years. Crandall, however, was contrite. According to Robinson he "urged" in his own defence that "Preacher tho' he was, he could scarcely read and could not write," and claimed that he had broken the law in ignorance. Given the situation and evidence of Crandall's good character, Judge D'Arcy Boulton* decided to recommend clemency. The decision was supported by the grand jury and a full pardon was ultimately granted by Lieutenant Governor Sir Peregrine MAITLAND.

In the early 1820s Crandall gave up his pastorate at Aylmer but retained a permanent home in Malahide. He returned for a brief while to minister at Cramahe, and then moved to Southwold Township in the southwestern part of the province where he stayed approximately three years. By 1832 he was ministering to the church in Dumfries (North and South Dumfries) Township, and his address was given as Galt (Cambridge). He is also said to have worked in nearby Blenheim and Zorra (East and West Zorra) townships. Some time in the late 1830s Crandall retired to Malahide and there lived frugally until his death.

Sources clearly show Crandall to have been a sincerely devout, humble yet determined minister of the Christian gospel. A notation in the minute-book of the Aylmer church dated 28 Sept. 1853 shows the loving respect in which he was held: "Elder Reuban Crandall, who has been a member of this church from its commencement, died to-day at the age of 86. Mark the perfect man and behold the upright, for the end of that man is peace." By his life and work, Crandall is a superlative example of the evangelistic Protestant clergymen who did so much to develop church and community life in the rural environs of early Ontario.

DOUGLAS L. FLANDERS

Canadian Baptist Arch., McMaster Divinity College (Hamilton, Ont.), Aylmer Baptist Church (Aylmer, Ont.), church minute-book, June 1848–January 1888; Biog. file, Reuben Crandall, especially certificate to Crandall, 9 April 1805. PAC, RG 5, A1: 24133–42. David Benedict, *A general history of the Baptist denomination in America and other parts of the world* (New York, 1848), 899. S. Read, "A memoir," *Christian Messenger* (Brantford, [Ont.]), 23 April 1857. *Toronto Christian Observer*, 3 (1853): 173. J. C. Crandall, *Elder John Crandall of Rhode Island and his descendants* (New Woodstock, N.Y., 1949), 105. Z. M. Hotson, *Pioneer Baptist work in Oxford County* ([Innerkip, Ont., 1939]), 26, 36. Stuart Ivison and Fred Rosser, *The Baptists in Upper and Lower Canada before 1820* (Toronto, 1956). Rev. Dr. Davidson, "Rev. Reuben Crandell, Aylmer: the pioneer preacher," *Canadian Baptist* (Toronto), 1 Feb. 1866.

CRANE, SAMUEL, businessman and politician; b. 1794 in Massachusetts; m. before 1827 Eunice ——, and they had two sons and eight daughters; d. 13 Nov. 1858 in Prescott, Upper Canada.

Nothing is known of Samuel Crane's early life but by May 1820 he had moved to Lower Canada and had joined Levi Sexton, Cornelius A. Van Slyck, and Alpheus Jones as a partner in a forwarding firm at Lachine, Montreal's western outport. The partnership was involved in shipping between Montreal and ports along the upper St Lawrence River and on Lake Ontario. It had offices in Upper Canada at Prescott and in New York State at Genesee River and Ogdensburg. Until 1824, through a monopoly granted by the state of New York, only American steamships could stop at ports in that state, and the partners' ability to serve both sides of the border was vastly improved by their part-ownership of the *Ontario*, the first American steamship on the Great Lakes. The firm was thus well equipped to take advantage of the increasing volume of traffic on the river. Since the War of 1812 there had been a steady growth in imports of merchandise into Upper Canada and exports of agricultural produce from that province.

Over the following years Crane was involved in a number of other partnerships, most notably that formed in 1822 with W. L. Whiting of Prescott, which, situated at the head of the Galops Rapids, had developed since the war as an important port for the trans-shipment of freight from river-boats to lake-boats. These early years of the forwarding trade were characterized by frequently changing partnerships and business connections. At the same time, however, as more and more steamboats were brought into the trade, there was a movement towards consolidation in order to control competition and to cope with rapidly increasing overhead costs. By early 1828 Crane had moved to Prescott, possibly to become resident partner in John Macpherson and Company which, with John Macpherson of Kingston as its senior partner, operated establishments at Prescott and Montreal. Crane certainly became a partner some time before January 1831, when the firm was dissolved. Immediately, however, he and Macpherson formed a new firm. After several years of transitory business connections, Crane had finally found a stable partnership, which would be known variously as Macpherson and Crane, Macpherson, Crane and Company, and S. Crane and Company. The firm prospered and dominated the forwarding trade for the next 22 years. In the process the partners acquired a reputation as enterprising and reliable businessmen. Crane became known as an incessant worker who, in the estimation of an agent for R. G. Dun and Company, made "a perfect slave of himsf" in the pursuit of his work. So single-minded was this pursuit that he earned a name for being "cold, almost to repulsion," according to the *Journal of Education for Upper Canada*.

The reasons for the partners' success are obscure, but a step taken early in their association played an important role. On 15 Dec. 1836 they formed a partnership with the Ottawa and Rideau Forwarding Company, which controlled access to the recently completed Rideau Canal by means of its ownership of the lock at Sainte-Anne-de-Bellevue, near the junction of the Ottawa and St Lawrence rivers. By thus assuring themselves of easy access to the Rideau route, Macpherson and Crane secured an important competitive advantage over their rivals, who had to continue using the hazardous St Lawrence or towing their boats through Sainte-Anne's Rapids. Crane and

Crane

his partner protected this vantage when, in 1837, they made an agreement with all other major forwarding firms to charge common freight rates. A public lock at Sainte-Anne-de-Bellevue was completed in 1842 but the monopoly held by Macpherson and Crane and the Ottawa and Rideau company had ended the year before when the latter agreed to tow rival barges through its lock.

The pre-eminence of Macpherson and Crane as forwarders was well established by 1841, when they controlled 12 of the 20 steamers engaged in the Montreal to Kingston trade. In addition they owned 40 barges and 5 schooners for transport on the Great Lakes. Major warehousing facilities were maintained at Montreal, Bytown (Ottawa), Kingston, and Prescott. Large ship-building yards were kept running at Montreal, Prescott, and Kingston. To operate these various concerns more than 650 men were employed by Macpherson and Crane. They maintained their leading position throughout the 1840s, adding establishments at the western Upper Canadian ports of Hamilton, Port Stanley, and Amherstburg. As well, in 1850 they expanded into Lake Champlain to provide a connection with Boston and New York. During his rise as a forwarder, Crane had personally devoted some time to other business pursuits. In 1833 he was elected a director of the Saint Lawrence Inland Marine Assurance Company. Three years later he and others attempted without success to secure a charter for a bank at Prescott; in 1837 Crane became a director of the Commercial Bank of the Midland District. By 1852 he had as well acquired or built a distillery and a steam grist-mill in Prescott.

Despite the advances made by Crane's firm, in the spring of 1853 it sold several of its vessels and withdrew completely from the passenger business. Later that year, on 21 December, Macpherson and Crane sold most of their remaining vessels and terminated their long involvement in the forwarding trade. This turn of events may have a number of explanations. The previous year David Lewis Macpherson*, a partner in the firm since 1842, became heavily involved in railway construction and apparently withdrew from the partnership. His corresponding withdrawal of capital may have necessitated the sale of passenger vessels. Furthermore, the imminent completion of the Grand Trunk Railway, with its threat of year-round competition, must have made the future of marine shipping seem precarious. This prospect was the more ominous since Macpherson and Crane had already suffered through two losing years. Yet another factor may have been the devastating fire which destroyed their warehouses and wharf at Kingston on 12 Nov. 1853; their notice to sell appeared shortly thereafter.

Crane continued his partnership with Macpherson for they still shared a variety of business interests.

They had some assets left to sell, including several vessels and barges, and numerous accounts to settle and collect. Their major debtor was the firm of Henderson and Holcomb, which had purchased the bulk of their business. When the latter firm failed in 1857, it still owed Macpherson and Crane upwards of £20,000. This staggering loss led in turn to the bankruptcy of Macpherson and Crane and to the dissolution of their partnership on 10 Nov. 1857. The failure devastated Crane and, it was believed, contributed to his failing health and death the following year.

Although almost exclusively concerned with forwarding and other business interests, Crane had made a brief venture into politics. A reformer, he entered a by-election in Grenville in 1838 but withdrew over the issue of the poll's distant location, in Merrickville. Elected for Grenville in the general election of 1841, he sat until 1844 but evidently did not take an active part in parliament. He was appointed to the Legislative Council on 16 Jan. 1849 but again he does not appear to have played a significant role. On 17 March 1858 his seat was declared vacant because of absence.

HARRY PIETERSMA

ACC-O, St John's Church (Prescott, Ont.), reg. of baptisms, 20 March, 29 April 1827; 4 March 1830; 6 March 1833; 22 June 1834; 27 May 1835; 21 April 1837; 29 Jan. 1839; 21 Jan. 1841; 30 Aug. 1842; 25 Dec. 1846; reg. of burials, 15 Nov. 1858, 8 Dec. 1863. AO, RG 21, United counties of Leeds and Grenville, Prescott, census and assessment rolls, 1828. BLHU, R. G. Dun & Co. credit ledger, Canada, 15: 202, 213. PAC, RG 31, A1, 1842, 1848, 1851, Prescott. QUA, Macpherson, Crane and Co., letter-books, 1845, 1857. Can., Prov. of, Legislative Assembly, *App. to the journals*, 1841, app.EE. "The forwarding interest," *Canadian Merchants' Magazine and Commercial Rev.* (Toronto), 1 (April–September 1857): 332–34; 3 (April–December 1858): 238–40. "The Honorable Samuel Crane," *Journal of Education for Upper Canada* (Toronto), 12 (1859): 27–28. U.C., House of Assembly, *Journal*, 1832–33, app.: 90–101. *Brockville Recorder*, 17 Jan. 1833; 19 Dec. 1834; 31 Oct., 7 Nov. 1837; 2 April 1846; 24 July 1851; 4 Feb., 25 Nov. 1858. *Canadian Courant and Montreal Advertiser*, 22 Nov. 1820. *Chronicle & Gazette*, 29 June 1833, 26 Nov. 1836, 7 June 1837, 8 Dec. 1838, 27 May 1840. *Chronicle and Weekly Advertiser* (Merrickville, [Ont.]), 23 Oct. 1857. *Church*, 11 Aug. 1853. *Daily British Whig*, 6 Feb., 7 March 1850; 12 April, 12, 30 Nov., 23 Dec. 1853; 22, 27 April 1854; 7, 14 April 1855; 23 April 1856. *Kingston Chronicle*, 26 March 1819; 17 March 1820; 13 April 1821; 3 May 1822; 28 March 1823; 25 May 1827; 6 March 1830; 22 Jan., 9 April 1831. *Montreal Gazette*, 28 Feb., 28 March 1823. *Montreal Transcript*, 10 Oct. 1839. *Prescott Telegraph, and Counties of Grenville and Dundas Advertiser*, 3 May 1848, 1 May 1850, 5 Nov. 1851. *Statesman* (Kingston), 15 Nov. 1843. *Political appointments, 1841–1865* (Coté; 1866). D. D. Calvin, *A saga of the St. Lawrence: timber & shipping through three generations* (Toronto, 1945). H. C. Klassen, "L. H. Holton: Montreal businessman and politician, 1817–1867" (PHD thesis, Univ. of Toronto, 1970). Duncan McDowall, "Kingston, 1846–1854: a study of economic change in a mid-nineteenth century Canadian community" (MA thesis, Queen's Univ., Kingston, 1974). *Prescott, 1810–1967*, comp. J. A. Morris (Prescott, 1967). R. B. Sneyd, "The role of the Rideau waterway, 1826–1856" (MA thesis, Univ. of Toronto, 1965). G. N. Tucker, *The Canadian commercial revolution, 1845–1851*, ed. H. G. J. Aitken (Toronto, 1964). Tulchinsky, *River barons*. A. L. Johnson, "The transportation revolution on Lake Ontario, 1817–1867: Kingston and Ogdensburg," *OH*, 67 (1975): 199–209.

CRANE, WILLIAM, merchant, justice of the peace, judge, and politician; b. 15 Feb. 1785 in Horton Township, N.S., sixth child of Colonel Jonathan Crane and Rebecca Allison; m. first 1813 Susannah Dixon (d. 1830) of Amherst, N.S., and they had one daughter; m. secondly 25 Oct. 1838 Eliza Wood of London, and they had four daughters and two sons; d. 31 March 1853 in Fredericton.

After attending school in Horton, William Crane moved to Westmorland County, N.B., some time during the first decade of the 19th century. He commenced business as a merchant in Westcock but soon transferred his interests to the larger centre of Sackville. There, in partnership with Bardin Turner, he traded for almost a decade, until 1819. He then joined his younger cousin, Charles Frederick ALLISON, in a business venture which was to endure until Crane's death. The firm of Crane and Allison was a typical enterprise of its day, exchanging local staples for a variety of goods imported from Britain, Halifax, the United States, and Lower Canada. A branch house was established at Miramichi to engage in the important transatlantic trade in timber from that port and to supply the lumbermen of northern New Brunswick with agricultural surpluses from Westmorland County [*see* Alexander RANKIN]. Despite the firm's extensive trading connections, its business was loosely structured, being conducted on credit through agencies in distant ports. Wooden vessels, owned by Crane and Allison, and built and manned locally, sought markets for New Brunswick timber in British ports, and endeavoured to make paying voyages, often sailing on return by way of New England. Family links were important to the firm's business. Crane's nephew Thomas came to Sackville to work in the store; another William Crane ran a schooner on the firm's account in Northumberland Strait; and the Halifax business was handled, in part, by William B. Fairbanks and John C. Allison, successors to the company run by Enos Collins*.

As the firm of Crane and Allison prospered and expanded, its principals assumed leading roles in the Westmorland community. Crane's rising status is effectively revealed in local marriage and probate records. Signatures he appended as a witness to several documents show him as "William Crane" in 1809, "William Crane . . . merchant" in 1810, and "William Crane *Esquire*" by 1819. He held the offices of justice of the peace, justice of the quorum, and judge of the Inferior Court of Common Pleas for the county of Westmorland; he was prominent in the local agricultural society, and a leading proponent of improved farming and marshland drainage. The store on "Crane's Corner" became a Sackville landmark, and the family home near by, built of stone in the late 1830s, was one of the finest in the county. Settlers throughout the Chignecto area looked to Crane for assistance in dealing with distant officialdom in Fredericton, whether for help in securing land grants and timber licences, or for assurance that the line of the "Great Road" would not be altered to the "infinite injury of the County." Credit at the Crane and Allison store allowed many an individual to acquire everyday necessities which might be paid for with timber in the spring, butter or stock in the fall, or periods of work when circumstances allowed. And Crane provided mortgage financing for settlers from Moncton to Shediac and Baie Verte.

Elected to the New Brunswick House of Assembly in a by-election in 1824, Crane retained his seat in four general elections but was defeated in 1842. He held the speaker's chair from 1831 to 1835, and was a member of the Executive Council between December 1837 and March 1843. In December 1843 Crane was appointed to the Legislative Council of New Brunswick, but he resigned in 1850 and in July of that year was re-elected to the assembly, where he sat until his death. Crane was again appointed speaker of the house in January 1852, but ill health forced his resignation in March of the following year.

In 1836 the House of Assembly appointed Crane and Lemuel Allan Wilmot* as its delegates to the Colonial Office. The assembly wanted to acquire complete control of the public domain and the resulting revenues [*see* Thomas Baillie*]. Previous representations to Britain, voicing grievances against the colonial administration, had failed to win acceptable terms, but economic expansion in New Brunswick in the mid 1830s and the appointment of the conciliatory Lord Glenelg as colonial secretary, spurred a further submission to the British government. The house chose its delegates for their temperate attitudes on the issue, and in August and September 1836 Crane and Wilmot settled terms for the provincial legislature's control of New Brunswick crown lands. Opposition to the transfer of power by Lieutenant Governor Sir Archibald Campbell* and Solicitor General George Frederick STREET, who carried his case to England early in 1837, delayed implementation of the arrangements and sent the two

Creedon

delegates to England a second time. But Campbell had been succeeded by Sir John HARVEY, and in July 1837 approval of the civil list gave control of the province's ungranted lands and the cash assets of the Crown Lands Office to the legislature. New Brunswick thus became solely responsible for the support of its internal government.

At Crane's death, his financial worth exceeded £120,000. Approximately one-tenth of his estate was in bank and other stocks; almost £7,000 derived from scattered real estate holdings – Crane's own purchases and properties acquired through foreclosures on mortgages. But the greatest part of his wealth lay in debts owing, a reflection of the extent to which Crane's credit underpinned the cash-scarce, and essentially subsistent, local economy. Crane was a pivotal figure in his developing community. Representative, arbitrator, financier, supplier, employer, and leader in church and community affairs, he became a virtual patriarch in the local society. The mediator between local interests and remote, impersonal bureaucratic and market forces, Crane was a focus of community consciousness, and a prop of the disparate local population's sense of place in the new and fluid environment of early-19th-century Chignecto.

GRAEME WYNN

N.B., Legislative Library (Fredericton), Card file, members of the N.B. legislature. N.B. Museum, Crane family, CB DOC; N.B. Hist. Soc. papers, Crane & Allison corr., 1834–52; William Crane corr., 1824–52. PANS, MG 3, 300. J. F. W. Johnston, *Notes on North America, agricultural, economical, and social* (2v., Edinburgh and London, 1851), 2: 83–90. N.B., House of Assembly, *Journal*, 1824–53. *New-Brunswick Courier*, 1830–53. *New Brunswick Reporter and Fredericton Advertiser*, 1844–53. *Royal Gazette* (Fredericton), 1836–44. W. C. Milner, *History of Sackville, New Brunswick* (Sackville, 1934). Graeme Wynn, "The assault on the New Brunswick forest, 1780–1850" (PHD thesis, Univ. of Toronto, 1974); "Industrialism, entrepreneurship, and opportunity in the New Brunswick timber trade," *The enterprising Canadians: entrepreneurs and economic development in eastern Canada, 1820–1914*, ed. L. R. Fisher and E. W. Sager (St John's, 1979), 5–22. W. S. MacNutt, "The politics of the timber trade in colonial New Brunswick, 1825–40," *CHR*, 30 (1949): 47–65.

CREEDON, MARIANNE (Mary Ann), named **Mother Mary Francis (Frances)**, member of the Congregation of the Sisters of Mercy, mother superior, and educator; b. 1811 in County Cork (Republic of Ireland), daughter of John Creedon and Ellen ——; d. 15 July 1855 in St John's.

On 4 July 1839 Marianne Creedon entered the Congregation of the Sisters of Mercy which in 1831 had been established in Dublin by the Irish heiress Catherine Elizabeth McAuley (Sister Mary Cather-

ine). She received her religious habit as Sister Mary Francis on 27 Feb. 1840 and was professed on 19 Aug. 1841, becoming the 50th Sister of Mercy. Prior to entering the order, she had lived for some years in St John's with her sister, Ellen Maria, whose husband John Valentine Nugent* was one of Newfoundland's more prominent reform politicians. During her stay she became acquainted with Bishop Michael Anthony Fleming* and was to renew her friendship with the bishop in Ireland in 1841 when he negotiated the establishment of a mission of the Sisters of Mercy in St John's. Sister Mary Francis offered her services to the bishop, who had been instrumental in having her make her novitiate with the congregation as part of his plan for the mission.

In keeping with his determination to establish a "proper system of religious education for my congregation," in 1833 Fleming had arranged for four sisters from the Order of the Presentation of Our Blessed Lady to come to Newfoundland and oversee the education of poor females [*see* Miss KIRWAN, named Sister Mary Bernard]. This work had expanded rapidly and soon the more affluent families were also sending their daughters to the Presentation schools. Fleming then saw the need for separate schools designed to accommodate the "children of the more wealthy classes, who were both able and anxious to pay for their education." It was these schools that Sister Mary Francis and "such other ladies as should be inspired to accompany her" were to staff, and they were to serve a dual purpose. Not only were the students to be taught "the elegant and fashionable accomplishments of the day" but they were also to have "their young minds properly imbued with the principles of religion."

Sister Mary Francis and two other volunteers left Ireland on 2 May 1842. In June they began their work in the colony, visiting and caring for the sick in their homes; they opened their first school with 42 pupils in attendance in May 1843. Sister Mary Francis was officially appointed superior of the Newfoundland mission in November. The two nuns who had accompanied her returned to Ireland that month and she was left with only one postulant, Maria Nugent, sister of John Valentine. Eventually she became Sister Mary Joseph, the first Sister of Mercy professed outside the British Isles. Her short religious career ended in June 1847 when she succumbed to typhus contracted while nursing. Mother Mary Francis was again left alone.

Resisting all importunities from the motherhouse in Dublin to return home, Mother Mary Francis remained, determined to carry on the overseas mission, the congregation's first in the New World. Compelled to close the school, she devoted herself to nursing the sick, caring for the elderly, and attending to the needs of the poor, while maintaining her religious life. Although she must have pondered the advisability of either returning to Ireland or joining the Presentation Sisters, who were staying with her at the Mercy Convent after losing theirs in the fire of June 1846, she saw the will of God in her own life and in the establishment of a Congregation of the Sisters of Mercy in Newfoundland. Nothing could induce her to abandon the mission and after some months her faith was rewarded. Her niece, Agnes Nugent, joined her and was professed on 8 Dec. 1850, taking the name Sister Mary Vincent, and earlier that year a young novice had arrived from Ireland. The congregation had finally begun to establish a solid foundation, and continued working in education with sisters from both Ireland and Newfoundland.

Mother Mary Francis lies buried in St John's at Belvedere, the Franciscan monastery bequeathed by Bishop Fleming to the Sisters of Mercy to be used as an orphanage. She had surmounted all obstacles to bring to the people of her adopted country the advantages of education and refined living. A woman of indomitable faith, she had shown a zeal, pertinacity, and loyalty to her calling which marks her as one of the outstanding women in Newfoundland history.

SISTER M. PERPETUA BOWN

[Mother Mary Teresa Austin [M. A.] Carroll], *Leaves from the annals of the Sisters of Mercy, by a member of the Order of Mercy* (4v., New York, 1881–95), 3. Paul O'Neill, "Mother Francis Creedon," *Remarkable women of Newfoundland and Labrador* (St John's, 1976), 8–9. Mother [Mary] Teresa Austin [M. A.] Carroll, *Life of Catherine McAuley, foundress and first superior of the Institute of Religious Sisters of Mercy* (St Louis, Mo., [1866]). Sister [Mary] Bertrand Degnan, *Mercy unto thousands; life of Mother Mary Catherine McAuley, foundress of the Sisters of Mercy* (Westminster, Md., 1957). Sister Mary James Dinn, *Foundation of the Presentation Congregation in Newfoundland* (St John's, 1975). Howley, *Ecclesiastical hist. of Nfld.* O'Neill, *Story of St. John's.*

CROOKS, JAMES, businessman, militia officer, office holder, justice of the peace, and politician; b. 15 April 1778 in the parish of Kilmarnock, Scotland, son of William Crooks, shoemaker, and Margaret Ramsay; m. 8 Dec. 1808 Jane Cummings, and they had eight sons and five daughters; d. 2 March 1860 in West Flamborough Township, Upper Canada.

In 1791 James Crooks immigrated from Scotland to join his half-brother Francis, who about 1788 had established a mercantile concern at Fort Niagara (near Youngstown, N.Y.) at the mouth of the Niagara River. In 1792, about which time Francis probably left a partnership with Robert Hamilton* to set up Crooks and Company, they were joined by James's brother William. As a result of British plans in 1795 to improve the defensive works at Fort Niagara, the

company's premises were apparently expropriated, forcing the Crookses to move across the river to Newark (Niagara-on-the-Lake), Upper Canada, where they resumed business. After Francis died in the West Indies in 1797, the brothers formed W. and J. Crooks, which became competitively engaged in numerous enterprises, particularly military provisioning, the shipment of grain and flour to Lower Canada, brewing and distilling, and the production of potash. To facilitate these operations the brothers chartered vessels, and in 1811 they had built at Niagara (Niagara-on-the-Lake) the schooner *Lord Nelson*, the principal vessel in their carrying business.

James Crooks quickly gained prominence within the local élite, which included many Scots merchants and office holders. Between 1794 and 1807 he rose from ensign to captain in the 1st Lincoln Militia. In 1797 he became postmaster at Newark. Three years later he campaigned with other Niagara merchants, notably Robert Hamilton and John Warren*, to secure the election of two mercantile candidates, Samuel Street* and William Dickson*, in Lincoln and of the influential Surveyor General David William Smith* in the riding of Norfolk, Oxford and Middlesex. In 1808 Crooks's position within the community was strengthened when he married a daughter of a loyalist and former member of Butler's Rangers, Thomas Cummings, of nearby Chippawa.

In the Niagara District after 1800 industrial and mercantile activities which were related to local agricultural needs and to the export trade in Lower Canada became increasingly important. In 1809, in an attempt to break Thomas Clark*'s domination of milling in the district, Crooks petitioned for mill-sites on islands near Chippawa, without success. As a result he looked elsewhere: he bought land in 1810 along the Trent River, in the Newcastle District, and the next year he purchased 400 acres at the head of Lake Ontario in West Flamborough Township from Elizabeth Russell*, sister and heiress of Peter Russell*, a former customer of W. and J. Crooks.

The War of 1812, in which Crooks fought, precipitated the collapse of his Niagara operations and had an indelible effect on his political outlook. On 5 June, 13 days before the declaration of war, the *Lord Nelson* had been commandeered on Lake Ontario by the American navy and later armed for service under the name *Scourge*. During the American occupation of Niagara between May and December 1813 invading troops seized or destroyed Crooks's nearby homestead, Crookston, and his buildings and goods in Niagara; for these losses, as well as for those sustained in the sinking of the *Lord Nelson* during a storm that year, he later submitted claims totalling more than £9,700. Though allowed £4,450 on his losses at Niagara, he never fully recovered from these severe financial setbacks.

Crooks

As a captain in the 1st Lincoln he commanded a flank company at the battle of Queenston Heights on 13 Oct. 1812, for which action he was commended by Major-General Roger Hale SHEAFFE. Crooks later claimed that he had been authorized to recruit for a majority in the proposed incorporated militia during the winter of 1812–13 but the promotion was never officially recognized. Following the capture of York (Toronto) by the Americans in April 1813, Crooks and other men of standing in the Niagara peninsula petitioned Brigadier-General John Vincent* to institute strict measures to quell civil disaffection. Crooks later served on the grand jury which found true bills against Jacob Overholser* and others accused of treasonous activity. On 26 May 1813 the Crooks family, with James probably in the lead, had fled from the frontier. They resided for a time in Thorold, where James's second son was born in July. During this period he remained on active military duty.

In November 1814, when Crooks again petitioned unsuccessfully for mill-sites in the Niagara River, he was still hoping to restore his Niagara base. By that time, however, he had settled in West Flamborough, no doubt conscious of that locale's relatively secure position in the event of future hostilities and of its commercial potential. Within four years, in a remarkable display of energy and resilience, he had constructed there along Spencer Creek a grist-mill, sawmill, carding-mill, general store, cooperage, and blacksmith's shop, forming a complex and small community later known as Crooks' Hollow (near present-day Greensville). In 1818 he was granted a quay lot in Coote's Paradise (Dundas) on Burlington Bay (Hamilton Harbour), a few miles from his prospering entrepôt. He quickly became active in district and provincial affairs. First commissioned as a justice of the peace in 1814, he was later named chairman of the Gore District Court of Quarter Sessions, in which office he was soon known for his vehement interest in removing the district seat from Hamilton to Dundas. In 1818 Crooks, Thomas Clark, Joseph Papineau*, and George Garden* formed a joint Upper and Lower Canadian committee on the improvement of navigation on the St Lawrence River. They recommended the construction of canals comparable in size to those in New York State. Crooks was elected in 1820 to the House of Assembly along with William Chisholm to represent the riding of Halton and two years later he became colonel of the 1st Regiment of Gore militia.

As an industrialist Crooks was woefully aware of the shortage of working capital in Upper Canada and he opposed any impediments thrown in the way of private enterprise. For development to occur, he believed, private and public interests must dovetail. Probably because of his strong commercial background and conservative inclinations, he was named

in 1822 to the first board of directors for the Bank of Upper Canada [see William ALLAN]. In the assembly he energetically promoted both domestic manufacturing and the development of transportation systems, upon which the functioning of the province's economy depended. In 1823 he sponsored the bill authorizing the construction of the Burlington Bay Canal, for which he became a commissioner [see James Gordon Strobridge*]. That year, to encourage the production of exportable goods, he also tabled a bill permitting the duty-free importation from the United States of hemp mills and other machinery. As well, he chaired a parliamentary committee on legislation for appropriating funds for the improvement of inland navigation.

Crooks apparently did not run in the general elections of 1824 and 1828, perhaps because of his preoccupation with the expansion of his commercial and industrial operations. In 1822 Robert Gourlay* had speculated that "Half the farmers of Halton probably have their names standing on the books of James Crooks . . . for goods furnished to them when prices were high." During the 1820s, as before the war, Crooks operated a number of vessels in the carrying trade between Montreal, Niagara, and the head of the lake, notably for the export of flour and potash. In 1825–26, encouraged by an expanding domestic market, the British government's imposition of a high tariff on paper imported into Canada from the United States, and the £125 prize offered by the provincial assembly, he established Upper Canada's first paper-making mill, his most ambitious and innovative enterprise. Its inception was keenly supported by William Lyon Mackenzie*, for whose newspaper Crooks had been an agent. As well, by 1825 he had amassed more than 1,000 acres along the Trent River, where about 1828 he erected a grist-mill at what became known as Crooks' Rapids (Hastings). By 1834 he had built mills on the Speed River, in the region west of Dundas, and his complex on Spencer Creek had been enlarged to include, among other manufactories, a tannery, distillery, potashery, agricultural implement factory, woollen-mill, and oil-mill.

To permit this industrial expansion, between 1827 and 1835 he secured mortgages on his West Flamborough property totalling £23,500, most of it from the Bank of Upper Canada and the trustees of the Montreal firm of Maitland, Garden, and Auldjo. Possibly because of the resulting financial burden, he spent much time lobbying and petitioning for half pay on his claimed majority during the war and for a settlement of his remaining war loss claims, including that for the *Lord Nelson*. (Only in 1930 was any compensation received by Crooks's heirs for the loss of that ship.) He travelled to England at least once, in 1831, and to Washington twice to pursue his various claims. To generate capital on a larger scale, Crooks, whose reputation as a major land-holder was known even to "capitalists" in England, advertised in 1832 the sale of no less than 45,000 acres which he owned throughout the province.

During the late 1820s and 1830s he continued to be a highly visible proponent of schemes for developing the region around the head of the lake and of a mercantile system conducive to that development. In 1826 he promoted the linking of Burlington Bay and the Grand River by canal. Four years later he was chosen first president of the newly formed agricultural society for the Gore District and was a director of the Desjardins Canal Company [see Peter Desjardins*]. He was an initiator in 1833 of a grand proposal to join Dundas by railway to other commercial centres in western Upper Canada. In January 1830, at a public meeting in Hamilton which he organized and chaired, he had forcefully defended against American encroachment the monopoly held by the Canadas, under British statute, in trade with the British West Indies and in mercantile navigation on the St Lawrence River. Four years later in the *Gore Balance* he vigorously supported Upper Canada's connection with Britain on the grounds that imperial protective tariffs provided the province's produce with a "decided advantage" in British markets.

In 1830, when he was returned to parliament for Halton, Crooks was clearly in the upper realms of the province's social and industrial hierarchy. A year later he was appointed to the Legislative Council, a position he held until his death. Much of his energy in politics continued to be expended on commercial matters aimed at economic development. In 1831, for example, he supported the bill of incorporation for the Commercial Bank of the Midland District; six years later, with Absalom Shade*, Crooks managed to get substantial funds voted for the improvement of the Dundas and Waterloo road, along which they owned property.

As for the partisan issues which most inflamed Upper Canadian politics, Crooks rejected not only radicalism but the extreme toryism of the controlling, largely Anglican élite led by the Reverend John Strachan*. In the early 1820s what Crooks and William Lyon Mackenzie saw as tory misgovernment had drawn them together in a close but short-lived liaison. Crooks's position was largely defined, however, by his long association with William MORRIS, another moderate tory and the leading spokesman for Scottish interests in Upper Canadian politics. In 1821 Crooks had supported the movement led by Morris and John Beverley Robinson* to prevent the American-born reformer Barnabas Bidwell* from sitting in the assembly. Two years later Crooks joined Morris in moving the passage of a highly contentious bill calling for the recognition in Upper Canada of the

Church of Scotland as a state church, along with the Church of England, and for its right to share equally in funding from the clergy reserves. The bill pitted Morris and Crooks decisively against the Strachanites. Yet he steadfastly refused to advance the Kirk's claims to the point of interfering with those of other denominations. In 1822–23, for example, he voted in favour of extending the legal right to solemnize marriages in Upper Canada to churches other than his own or the Church of England. His position on church-state affairs could not have been made easier by the marriage in 1827 of his daughter Jane Eliza to the Reverend Alexander Neil Bethune*, an adherent of Strachan.

Following his appointment to the Legislative Council, Crooks frequently and eloquently enunciated a view of that body as the bulwark in Upper Canada for the defence of the British constitutional balance of executive, appointive, and elected elements. Canadians, he proclaimed in the *Western Mercury* in 1834, must "cling to the connection with the Mother Country as to the ark of our safety" against American expansionism, whether overtly military or political. He disliked both majoritarian democracy, which he perceived many reformers to be advocating, and oligarchical tyranny, which he feared the élite behind Strachan was trying to impose, especially in the reactionary wake of the civil disorders of 1837–38. In January 1837 Crooks had opposed Strachan on the bill to amend the charter of King's College (University of Toronto) because, Crooks believed, both the disproportionate allocation of school lands to that institution and provisions for the support of district schools were detrimental to the establishment of a system of "free Grammar Schools." These he contended would best foster open competition and opportunity in society. More indicative of his status as a squirearch than of his political views was Crooks's enrolment of four sons, including Adam*, at Upper Canada College between 1839 and 1845.

By the end of the 1830s Crooks's political prominence had reached its peak. Opposition to Strachan by the so-called "Scotch party" in council, led by Crooks and Morris (who had become a legislative councillor in 1836), continued in 1839 over the Clergy Reserves Bill, a contentious piece of legislation which proposed the denominational division of the reserves, a principle accepted by Crooks. Passed in the assembly by a bare majority, the bill was opposed in council early in May only by John Simcoe MACAULAY and Strachan, whose defeat greatly gratified Crooks. During the same session, however, the moderate faction on council lost a struggle to have him appointed to a joint committee on education in Strachan's stead when, on an amended motion, Macaulay was substituted.

Though Crooks, like so many others, publicly

Crooks

condemned the factionalism which permeated the ranks of tories and reformers alike, he was repeatedly drawn into political alignments within the Legislative Council. In 1839 he agreed with the view expressed in the report of Lord Durham [Lambton*] that the cause of political unrest in Upper Canada was monopolistic control of government by the "family compact," but he disagreed with the proposed remedy, responsible government. He preferred instead the fine-tuning of existing constitutional checks and balances by drawing executive members from all parts off the province and by making their number equal to assemblymen, introducing a court for the impeachment of government officials, and providing for joint addresses from the assembly and the Legislative Council. The institution of responsible government, he felt, would be merely an exchange of one constitutional disequilibrium for another, in which the assembly would control the executive. A committee composed of Crooks, John Simcoe Macaulay, and Adam Fergusson*, another Scottish associate, was formed in council in April 1839 to consider the Durham report. On 11 May, the last day of the session, Macaulay deviously submitted a report without ever having consulted Crooks or Fergusson. The moderates' motion in council to have this procedure investigated was defeated, but Crooks, William Morris, Fergusson, Peter Adamson, John McDONALD, and Alexander FRASER entered a dissenting opinion on this decision on 9 December.

Though he professed support for political union with Lower Canada, Crooks harboured a strong disdain for French Canadians, a sentiment which pervaded proposals he put forward on union later in December: the location of the seat of government in Upper Canada, the use of English alone in parliamentary debates and proceedings, and the creation of electoral divisions in Lower Canada which would assure a "due proportion of the representation in the United Legislature to the British inhabitants" of that province. He was, nevertheless, appointed to the Legislative Council of the united provinces in 1841. In the post-union era he was past his prime as a politician. He viewed developments such as the appointment of a reform majority in council in 1843, during debate over the move of the seat from Kingston to Montreal, as an erosion of executive authority and hence a diminution of the imperial tie. In November 1843, to protest the reform majority's repeal of resolutions blocking the change of capital, Crooks, Adam Fergusson, William Henry Draper*, Levius Peters Sherwood*, Thomas McKAY, Peter Boyle DE BLAQUIÈRE, and seven others took unprecedented action by walking out of council. Six years later Crooks, citing his role in the War of 1812 in maintaining the province as a British colony, deplored the Rebellion Losses Bill [see James Bruce*] as a device for compensating treasonous activity and as evidence of the constitutional imbalance inherent in responsible government.

Queenston Heights had been the ultimate testing ground for Crooks's fervid sentimental attachment to the motherland. During the 1850s he enthusiastically supported the Upper Canadian militia and championed unequivocal loyalty, principally by trying to keep memories of the war alive in the public consciousness. In council in 1851 he supported the issue of medals to living veterans of the battles of Queenston Heights, Ogdensburg, and Lundy's Lane. Two years later he wrote his recollections of the war, which he submitted to Thomas Maclear* for possible publication in the *Anglo-American Magazine* as a supplement to the articles on the war written by Gilbert Auchinleck. In 1857 Crooks was still promoting compensation for militia officers who had served in the war.

Concurrent with his belief in British patriotism as essential to social and political well-being was his constant, statesmanlike support for efforts to achieve social, religious, and political harmony, a pragmatic approach he had set forth on numerous occasions since the 1830s. Like Egerton Ryerson*, the superintendent of education who was also a political moderate, he opposed denominational schools, maintaining in council in 1855 that the "settled policy of every Government is to provide that all its subjects live in amity . . . , and that whatever difference may exist among them, as to forms of Religion, or any other matter, it is deemed good policy that the youth, . . . be brought together at Public Schools of Education at an early period of Life." Unity and fellowship, he repeatedly maintained, were urgent goals in a young colony that had experienced foreign invasion, bitter political and religious feuding, and armed insurrection.

Crooks remained active in business until the early 1850s, by which time water supplies at Crooks' Hollow had diminished and industrial competition in the region had increased substantially, largely as a result of railway development. In 1851 Crooks's complex contained four mills, a clothing works, distillery, tannery, cooperage, and machine-shop. Later that year, however, at the age of 73, he sold both his paper-mill and his mills at Crooks' Rapids. In 1860 he died at his home in Crooks' Hollow. All that remains of his once mighty commercial estate on Spencer Creek is the skeletal ruin of a solitary grist-mill.

DAVID OUELLETTE

James Crooks is the author of *Statement of the seizure of the British schooner "Lord Nelson," by an American vessel of war, on the 5th June, 1812, 13 days before the late war with* the United States, published anonymously in Hamilton, [Ont.], in 1841. His account of the battle of Queenston Heights, along with a covering letter to Thomas Maclear, dated 17 March 1853, is in PAC, MG 24, G39, and photocopies are available in the AO's Miscellaneous coll., MU 2144, 1853, no.14. The account was later published under the title "Recollections of the War of 1812, from manuscript of the late Hon. James Crooks," Niagara Hist. Soc., [Pub.] (Niagara-on-the-Lake, Ont.), no.28 (n.d.): 28–41.

AO, MS 75; MS 148, no.3 (corr. concerning *Lord Nelson* claim); no.4 (misc.), Crooks family genealogy; MS 392, 20–108 (Hands family papers); MS 393, A-6-a, box 14, letter of James Crooks, 3 July 1841; MS 503; MS 516; RG 21, Gore District, Flamborough West Township, census, 1842; RG 22, ser.155, will of Francis Crooks. GRO (Edinburgh), Kilmarnock, reg. of births and baptisms, 16 April 1778. HPL, Clipping file, Dundas biog., Crooks family papers, the *Lord Nelson* matter. Ont., Ministry of Citizenship and Culture, Heritage Administration Branch (Toronto), Hist. sect. research files, Hamilton–Wentworth RF.18 ("Upper Canada's first paper mill, 1826"); Northumberland RF.3 ("Founding of Hastings"). PAC, RG 1, L3, 89: C1/87, 89; 90: C2/42; 97: C9/38; 100: C11/153; 104: C13/77; 109: C16/10; RG 5, A1: 3784–86, 3848–49, 11290–93, 11376–79, 12207–8, 12747–52, 14333–35, 18432–34, 18677–79, 19487–89, 20353–55, 25583–85, 26313–14, 26983–91, 28159–61, 28438–41, 28466–67, 28520–21, 29004, 30268–69, 31245–47, 31439–41, 31949–52, 32077–93, 32381–82, 33478–79, 34476–78, 34716–18, 35012–20, 35804–21, 36076–78, 36218–48, 38305–8, 38312–13, 38980–86, 39570–72, 40059–90, 40717–18, 41833–34, 41918–20, 42216–17, 43116–18, 43653–60, 45441–51, 46517–20, 46524–25, 46533–36, 46766–8, 46976–78, 46988–91, 49028–31, 49413–16, 50132–33, 51944–46, 54631–32, 58460–62, 60028–30, 61825–38, 62732–40, 62857–61, 63539–43, 70710–12, 72591–95, 73804–6, 74011–14, 76003–4, 77373–77, 77465–67, 83120–25, 96573–78, 96771–74, 98428–35, 120949–50, 122401–6, 128653–56, 134076–78, 139726–29, 141645–46; RG 8, I (C ser.), 108: 102–3; 112: 72; 115B: 202; 115E: 101, 189, 212; 115F: 94, 98, 103, 179, 254, 257; 272: 85–87; 274: 21, 23–24; 372: 163; 1701: 11; 1702: 2, 288–91; RG 9, I, B5, 5: 48; RG 19, 3740, claims 7, 8, 12; RG 31, A1, 1851, Flamborough (West): 26; RG 68, General index, 1651–1841: 425, 510. PRO, CO 42/378: 257–62; 42/393: 248–49; 42/395: 168–213; 42/473: 113–16; 42/474: 92–95. QUA, William Morris papers. Wentworth Land Registry Office (Hamilton), Abstract index to deeds, West Flamborough Township, concession 2, lot 5 (mfm. at AO, GS 1472).

Can., Prov. of, Legislative Council, *Journals*, 1844–45: 52, 167; 1851: 92; 1855: 499; 1857: 241. *Canadian Christian Examiner, and Presbyterian Magazine* (Toronto), 3 (1839): 157–58. *The correspondence of Lieut. Governor John Graves Simcoe . . .*, ed. E. A. Cruikshank (5v., Toronto, 1923–31), 3: 49, 69–70, 174; 4: 132. "Death of Hon. James Crooks," *Daily Spectator, and Journal of Commerce*, 8 March 1860. "District of Nassau; letter book no.2," AO *Report*, 1905: 324, 329, 331–32. *Doc. hist. of campaign upon Niagara frontier* (Cruikshank), 2: 325; 4: 18, 72, 131, 215; 5: 7, 222. "Grants of crown lands in U.C.," AO *Report*, 1929: 135. "Journals of Legislative Assembly of

U.C.," AO *Report*, 1911: 368, 479; 1913: 34–35, 78; 1914: 37, 219, 274, 279, 282–83, 306–7, 347, 400, 409, 412–13, 415, 475, 547, 552, 560–61, 650, 665, 668. "Names only, but much more," comp. Janet Carnochan, Niagara Hist. Soc., [*Pub.*], no.27 (n.d.): 23–24. *Presbyterian*, 1 (1848): 12. Presbyterian Church of Canada in connection with the Church of Scotland, *Minutes of the Synod*, [1831–36] ([Toronto], n.d.), 1831. "Records of Niagara, 1805–1811," ed. E. A. Cruikshank, Niagara Hist. Soc., [*Pub.*], no.42 (1931): 79–80, 92. Thomas Rolph, *A brief account, together with observations, made during a visit in the West Indies, and a tour through the United States of America, in parts of the years 1832–3; together with a statistical account of Upper Canada* (Dundas, [Ont.], 1836), 223. *Select British docs. of War of 1812* (Wood), 1: 607, 631; 3: 615. *Statistical account of U.C.* (Gourlay; ed. Mealing; 1974). U.C., Legislative Council, *Journal*, 1836–37: 101–2; 1839: 75–76; 1839–40: 15–16, 26. "Upper Canada land book B, 19th August, 1796, to 7th April, 1797," AO *Report*, 1930: 8, 104. "Upper Canada land book C, 11th April, 1797, to 30th June, 1797," AO *Report*, 1930: 137. *Valley of the Trent* (Guillet), 153, 264–65.

British Colonist (Toronto), 22 Nov. 1838, 2 Oct. 1839, 29 Jan. 1840, 7 Nov. 1843, 9 Feb. 1844. *Dundas Warder* (Dundas), 23 Aug. 1846. *Gore Balance* (Hamilton), 21 Jan., 15 May, 22 July, 14, 28 Oct. 1830. *Mackenzie's Toronto Weekly Message*, 17 March 1860. *Montreal Transcript*, 17 May 1849. *Toronto Patriot*, 14 Jan. 1840. *Upper Canada Gazette*, 11 Oct. 1797. *Western Mercury* (Hamilton), 17 Feb. 1831; 22 March, 27 Dec. 1832; 28 Nov. 1833; 28 June, 14 July 1834. Janet Carnochan, "Inscriptions and graves in the Niagara peninsula," Niagara Hist. Soc., [*Pub.*], no.19 ([2nd ed.], n.d.). *Death notices of Ontario*, comp. W. D. Reid (Lambertville, N.J., 1980). J. C. Dent, *The Canadian portrait gallery* (4v., Toronto, 1880–81), 2: 139–40. *DHB*. Morgan, *Sketches of celebrated Canadians*, 314–15. W. H. Smith, *Canada: past, present and future*, 1: 249.

V. B. Blake et al., *Spencer Creek conservation report, 1962: history* (Toronto, 1962), 103–4, 106. Emily Cain, *Ghost ships: "Hamilton" and "Scourge"; historical treasures from the War of 1812* (Toronto, 1983). Janet Carnochan, *History of Niagara . . .* (Toronto, 1914; repr. Belleville, Ont., 1973), 36, 252. Craig, *Upper Canada*. Johnson, *Hist. of Guelph*, 54, 61, 85. C. M. Johnston, *Head of the Lake* (1967), 125–27, 133–34. J. S. Moir, *Church and state in Canada West: three studies in the relation of denominationalism and nationalism, 1841–1867* (Toronto, 1959), 30, 39. W. J. Rattray, *The Scot in British North America* (4v., Toronto, 1880–84), 2: 349–50. *Township of West Flamboro, province of Ontario, 1850–1950: centennial celebration . . .*, comp. G. R. Jackson et al. (Dundas, [1950]), 15–16. B. G. Wilson, "The enterprises of Robert Hamilton: a study of wealth and influence in early Upper Canada, 1776–1812" (PHD thesis, Univ. of Toronto, 1978). J. E. Wodell, "The Fools' College," *Pen and pencil sketches of Wentworth landmarks . . .* (Hamilton, 1897), 105. N. L. Edwards, "The establishment of papermaking in Upper Canada," *OH*, 39 (1947): 63–74. "Escarpment 'wonder man' built 19th century empire," *Cuesta* (Georgetown, Ont.), 5 (1981): 33–35. Helen Marryat, "Hon. James Crooks first settler on land, part of which is village of Hastings," "James Crooks taken prisoner in War of 1813 when Americans invaded Niagara," "Hon. James Crooks describes

Crooks

War of 1812 and Battle of Queenston Heights," and "Pioneers claimed bushel of buckwheat only grist turned out by Crooks' mill," *Examiner* (Peterborough, Ont.), 11 Jan. 1947: 5, 10; 18 Jan. 1947: 5, 11; 25 Jan. 1947: 5, 13; and 15 Feb. 1947: 5, 14 (photocopies of clippings available at AO, MU 3815).

CROOKS, RAMSAY, fur trader; b. 2 Jan. 1787 in Greenock, Scotland, son of William Crooks, a shoemaker, and Margaret Ramsay; m. 10 March 1825 Marianne Pelagie Emilie Pratte, and they had five sons and four daughters; d. 6 June 1859 in New York City.

Ramsay Crooks immigrated to the Canadas in 1803 with his widowed mother and some siblings; two of his brothers, including the eldest, JAMES, and a half-brother had come to Upper Canada in the previous decade. Upon his arrival he was briefly employed by a Montreal mercantile firm before going west to Michilimackinac (Mackinac Island, Mich.) as a clerk for fur trader Robert Dickson*. The formative period of his career, between 1805 and 1810, was spent on the Missouri River "learning the arduous routines, picayune details, and ruthless rivalries" of the trade. He wintered on the Missouri River for Robert Dickson and Company in 1805–6 and 1806–7. After an unsuccessful partnership with Robert McClellan (McLellan), trading on the Upper Missouri, Crooks was persuaded by Wilson Price Hunt to join the overland expedition to the mouth of the Columbia River proposed by John Jacob Astor* of the American Fur Company. On 23 June 1810, together with Astor, Duncan McDougall*, Donald McKENZIE, Alexander MacKay*, Hunt, and others, he became a founding partner in the Pacific Fur Company. During the overland journey, which began shortly afterwards, Crooks was forced by illness to remain behind in the Oregon country while the rest of the expedition continued on, and he finally reached Astoria (Oreg.) in May 1812. A few days later, exhausted by the demands of the expedition, he relinquished his interest in the PFC. On his return journey from Astoria, he crossed South Pass (Wyo.), one of the first white men to do so.

Evidently impressed by the young man's capabilities, in 1813 Astor offered Crooks a one-third interest in a venture in the Michilimackinac area, then under British control, to secure furs belonging to the South West Fur Company, a firm formed in 1811 by Astor's American Fur Company and the North West Company [see William McGillivray*]. Using Michilimackinac as his base of operations, Crooks travelled extensively during the next five years, gradually assuming more responsibility for the AFC concerns around the Great Lakes. He became one of the company's principal agents in 1817 after Astor purchased the NWC's interest in the South West Fur Company. Astor's confidence in such a young and relatively inexperi-

enced man testifies to Crooks's natural aptitude for commerce, his managerial ability, his honesty, and his reliability.

With Astor often abroad, Crooks assumed leadership in directing the affairs of the AFC, spearheading a policy of expansion into the west. In 1827 he secured a partnership with Bernard Pratte and Company of St Louis (headed by his father-in-law), which meant equal shares for both companies in the trade on the Mississippi River below Prairie du Chien (Wis.) and along the Missouri River. In the same year he also directed a consolidation with the Columbia Fur Company, active around the Great Lakes, the Mississippi, and especially the upper Missouri. According to the new agreements, Bernard Pratte and Company assumed control of the AFC's Western Department, and the AFC's newly created subdepartment, the Upper Missouri outfit, was directed by former Columbia Fur Company employees. Wherever possible, Crooks favoured absorbing rivals or coming to terms with them rather than competing. "I prefer peace," he wrote in 1828, "if to be obtained on equitable terms." He took out naturalization papers in 1830.

On 3 June 1834 Crooks and three other stockholders purchased the Northern Department of the AFC from Astor and retained use of the company name. Crooks was elected president and soon afterwards moved the headquarters from Michilimackinac to La Pointe on the Apostle Islands (Wis.). The Western Department was purchased by Pratte, Chouteau and Company, but business ties, reinforced by familial bonds, remained close. Under Crooks's rigorous leadership, the AFC diversified its enterprises after the collapse in the beaver market and fought a ruthless battle for control of the Ohio valley furs. A tireless competitor, he refused none the less to lower his ethical standards to obtain an advantage, cautioning his field captains against using unscrupulous tactics and forbidding the use of liquor in trade. "If we cannot beat [our competitors] on principles that will bear the strictest scrutiny, we prefer abandoning the contest," he wrote in 1840. Overextended and facing a glut in the European market, the AFC suspended payment in 1842. Salvaging what he could, Crooks continued to operate the business as a clearing house for furs in New York City until his death. Ever the practical business man, Crooks's motto was "Half a loaf is better than none."

A prolific writer, Crooks left voluminous correspondence which reveals his kindly personality and the reasons for his success. Plagued by chronic ill health, he never spared himself in attending to his responsibilities. He was an unusually gentle person, and the only faults he ever found in others were indolence, inefficiency, and impertinence. Through his daily correspondence, he was informed of the current prices of furs in Europe and of the minute details of conditions at remote posts. A master of the pen, with it he endeavoured to win political favours for the company and its employees. He was both tactful and precise, earning the respect and friendship of his associates.

Though perhaps a bit drab and humourless, Crooks did not lack warmth. He cherished his family, "the only true solace of my existence," but was often separated from them during lengthy business trips. He carefully provided for the education of a daughter, Hester, born in 1817 of a woman of Chippewa and white descent, and was a loving and devoted grandfather to her children. Historians have endorsed Crooks's reputation as a man of unimpeachable integrity, and James LeRoy Clayton referred to him for the years 1820–40 as "the most important fur merchant in the history of the American fur trade during its period of greatest eminence."

TANIS C. THORNE

Minn. Hist. Soc. (St Paul), Biog. file, Ramsay Crooks and family. Mo. Hist. Soc. (St Louis), Chouteau coll., American Fur Company letter-books, 1 (1816–20); letters of Ramsay Crooks, John Jacob Astor, and the American Fur Company, 1813–1846 (typescript, 1918); miscellaneous letters of Ramsay Crooks. *DAB*. A. T. Andreas, *History of Chicago, from the earliest period to the present time* (3v., Chicago, 1884–86), 1. H. L. Carter, "Ramsay Crooks," *The mountain men and the fur trade of the far west . . .* , ed. L. R. Hafen (10v., Glendale, Calif., 1965–72), 9: 125–31. J. L. Clayton, "The American Fur Company" (PHD thesis, Cornell Univ., Ithaca, N.Y., 1964). Washington Irving, *Astoria; or, anecdotes of an enterprise beyond the Rocky Mountains* (rev. ed., New York, 1882). D. [S.] Lavender, *The fist in the wilderness* (Garden City, N.Y., 1964); "Ramsay Crooks's early ventures in the Missouri River: a series of conjectures," Mo. Hist. Soc., *Bull.* (St Louis), 20 (1963–64): 91–106. G. L. Nute, "The papers of the American Fur Company: a brief estimate of their significance," *American Hist. Rev.* (New York and London), 32 (1926–27): 519–38; "Wilderness Marthas," *Minn. Hist.* (St Paul), 8 (1927): 247–59. J. W. Ruckman, "Ramsay Crooks and the fur trade of the northwest," *Minn. Hist.*, 7 (1926): 18–31.

CROOKSHANK, GEORGE, office holder, politician, and businessman; b. 23 July 1773 in New York City, son of George Crookshank and Catherine Norris; m. there 19 July 1821 Sarah Susanna (Susan) Lambert, and they had a daughter and two sons, one of whom died in infancy; d. 21 July 1859 in Toronto.

The Crookshanks came from the island of Hoy in the Orkneys, north of Scotland. The family became involved in mercantile ventures and George Crookshank Sr was the owner-captain of a merchantman sailing out of New York City during the American Revolutionary War. George Jr was educated at Shrewsbury, N.J., and then emigrated to Saint John, N.B., with his family after the war. He began his career as a supercargo on the ships of his uncle, John Colville, on the run to Jamaica, where he spent a winter for his health.

Following the appointment in 1796 of John McGill*, husband of his sister Catherine, as commissary general of Upper Canada, Crookshank and another sister, Rachel, who was to marry Dr James Macaulay*, also went to the colony. In December of that year he was appointed to the commissariat. Crookshank was highly regarded by Lieutenant Governor John Graves Simcoe* and his wife, Elizabeth Posthuma Gwillim*, and also by Simcoe's Scottish successor, Peter Hunter*. Work in the commissariat involved organizing the military supplies for Fort York and other garrisons around the colony, making use of imports from England or local supplies. Crookshank was employed at York (Toronto), where he built his home about 1800, and was also commissary for such posts as Fort Erie. During the War of 1812 he was charged with building a road connecting Lake Simcoe with Georgian Bay at Penetanguishene. At the fall of York in April 1813 he accompanied the retreating British troops to Kingston and his looted house became American General Henry Dearborn's headquarters and was used as a hospital.

In December 1814 Crookshank was promoted assistant commissary general. The next year he refused transfer to another colony, possibly Sierra Leone. In October 1816 he retired on half pay of 7s. 6d. per diem. New appointments had nevertheless followed his refusal to leave Upper Canada. In December 1815 he was gazetted one of the four commissioners to receive claims for war losses. In 1820–21 he was on the local committee to build a hospital in York (the beginnings of the Toronto General Hospital). His most important appointment was in 1819, as receiver general of the province succeeding McGill. This appointment was not confirmed by the Colonial Office; instead John Henry DUNN took over in October 1820. Crookshank was disappointed, but somewhat relieved for the responsibilities were great. Possibly as a compensation, he was appointed to the Legislative Council in January 1821, which gave him a designation as "Honourable," and he remained a member until the union of Upper and Lower Canada in 1841.

Finance and investment already occupied much of his time and after his appointment to the council he concentrated on his business affairs. In 1822 he was elected one of the first directors of the Bank of Upper Canada and might have been elected president instead of William ALLAN had he not been out of the colony. Crookshank remained on the board until 1827, serving as president in 1825–26 and as a government appointee in 1826. He did not, however, find the bank a profitable enterprise; as he wrote in 1825, it was "a great deal of trouble with little thanks and less pay."

Crosskill

Like most of the province's élite, Crookshank engaged in land speculation from the time he came to Upper Canada. In 1797 he had received a crown grant of 1,200 acres, of which part became the Crookshank estate of some 330 acres west of Crookshank's Lane (Bathurst Street). He owned another farm of about the same size at Thornhill, some 10 miles north of York, and a third still farther north at Newmarket. In York itself he purchased a large number of properties which he rented out.

Crookshank also made investments through the commercial house of his brother Robert William in Saint John, but his main involvement outside Upper Canada was in New York City. After the War of 1812 he made regular visits to deal with financial matters for himself and his sisters. It was in New York that he met his wife, whose brothers ran the house of Lambert and Company, headed by David Rogers Lambert. Crookshank was justly suspicious of their means of operation; as he wrote to Samuel F. Lambert in 1826, "I must say that my money concerns from the first with your House has been a great source of uneasiness and loss to me." He attempted to cover his advances to the firm by securing mortgages on their properties in New York City and Harlem. However, when David Lambert was murdered in 1825 while returning from a party, the business folded quickly and, partly as a result of misappropriations by one of the other brothers, Crookshank became involved in litigation which lasted until at least 1830. This must have had the effect of removing him temporarily from Upper Canadian financial activities. By the time affairs were wound up he had acquired considerable holdings, some of which he did not want: property at Rochester, N.Y.; a marble quarry at Kingsbridge, N.Y.; considerable land and some houses at Wilton, Conn.; the Lambert home; and above all two valuable stores on Pearl Street in the commercial heart of New York City, which he rented out.

Basically a kindly man, whose quick temper blew itself out equally quickly, he assumed responsibility for the Lambert family and helped members of it when they needed assistance as he also helped his brother Robert after his fortune was lost. At York he lived on an opulent scale, enlarging his home after his marriage and employing eight servants to keep it up. He travelled constantly, often in his own carriage, to New York and Wilton, and he exchanged visits with Robert in Saint John. When his wife's health began to fail, several years before her death in 1840, his sister-in-law, Julia Maria Lambert, came to manage his household; her letters tell us a great deal about Toronto society. Crookshank's son, George, who trained in the law, seems to have been something of a man about town, owning an expensive yacht and leaving two illegitimate sons when he died suddenly in 1853. His daughter, Catherine, married Stephen Heward Jr, member of another old Toronto family.

Much of Crookshank's time in his later years was spent in managing his Toronto properties and in sorting out the tangled estate of his friend Alexander Wood*, who died in 1844. He had also become one of the first directors of the City of Toronto and Lake Huron Rail Road in 1837 and when the Bank of British North America was established that year he was appointed to its Toronto directorate. A member of the Church of England, he supported St James' Cathedral and in 1850 gave $500 towards founding Trinity College. During the last decade of his long life his health failed badly and he played little part in the city of which he was now the oldest inhabitant. By 1853, when westward expansion was reaching his Bathurst Street property and his son had died, he began to sell off lots for development. The probate of his will shows his property in Upper Canada, aside from real estate, as valued at £40,986.

Crookshank's career demonstrates how a man of ability could make a fortune despite the economic fluctuations of the early 19th century. It shows, moreover, something of the world view of the élite of the era, who, far from being immersed in a provincial town, often had business and personal connections in other colonies, in the United States, and in Great Britain.

FREDERICK H. ARMSTRONG

AO, MS 6; RG 22, ser.305, will of George Crookshank; will of J. M. Lambert. MTL, William Allan papers, letter-book recording letters written by Allan as commissioner of the Canada Company. PAC, RG 1, L3, 91: C3/27, 33; 93: C5/16; 99: C11/79; RG 8, I (C ser.), 115B–D, 116. Walter Barrett [J. A. Scoville], *The old merchants of New York City* (5v., New York, 1862), 2: 308–16. J. [M.] Lambert, "An American lady in old Toronto: the letters of Julia Lambert, 1821–1854," ed. S. A. Heward and W. S. Wallace, RSC *Trans.*, 3rd ser., 40 (1946), sect.II: 101–42. *Town of York, 1793–1815* (Firth), 220, 222, 314–15; *1815–34* (Firth), 45, 184. *Globe*, 22 July 1859. *Patriot* (Toronto), 21 Feb. 1837. Armstrong, *Handbook of Upper Canadian chronology*. D. S. Macmillan, "The 'new men' in action: Scottish mercantile and shipping operations in the North American colonies, 1760–1825," *Canadian business history; selected studies, 1497–1971*, ed. D. S. Macmillan (Toronto, 1972), 85, 93–94. Scadding, *Toronto of old* (1873), 62–63, 80, 148, 287, 356. T. W. Acheson, "The great merchant and economic development in St. John, 1820–1850," *Acadiensis* (Fredericton), 8 (1978–79), no.2: 3–27.

CROSSKILL, JOHN HENRY, publisher, militia officer, newspaperman, and office holder; b. 4 March 1817 in Halifax, son of Henry Crosskill and Catherine Charlotte Weeks; m. 30 Sept. 1847 Sarah Ann McIntosh of Halifax, and they had three children; d. there 13 Feb. 1857.

John Henry Crosskill was born into a prominent Nova Scotia family. His maternal great-grandfather John Fillis*, a Halifax merchant, was a member of the first provincial House of Assembly in 1758. His paternal grandfather, John Crosskill*, founded Bridgetown, N.S. John Henry, whose own father was a sportsman and boxer, was apprenticed to William Gossip* and John Charles Coade of the *Times* (Halifax), published one issue of a literary magazine in October 1837, and served as a militia officer beginning in 1839. In 1838 he had compiled and published in Halifax one of the province's first textbooks, *A comprehensive outline of the geography and history of Nova Scotia*, whose 1,000 copies, he claimed in the preface to the second edition (1842), were sold out in "several months." Based on Thomas Chandler Haliburton*'s *An historical and statistical account of Nova-Scotia* (Halifax, 1829), it emphasized the province's cultural and economic potential.

On 1 Oct. 1840 Crosskill launched the *Halifax Morning Post & Parliamentary Reporter*. It was the second penny paper and, from October 1844, the first daily in Nova Scotia. With plenty of news arriving on the ocean steamers recently inaugurated by Samuel Cunard*, and aided by a power press, the *Post* introduced a new type of journalism which Daniel Cobb Harvey* has described as having had "no principle except catering to the public and no policy but increase of circulation." He also published from 1843 to May 1844 the *Olive Branch*, a newspaper associated with the temperance movement.

In January 1844 Crosskill published in the *Post* reformer George Renny YOUNG's anonymous satire of the lieutenant governor, Viscount Falkland [Cary*], "The prince and his protégé." Then, in February, when John Sparrow Thompson* resigned as queen's printer on a matter of principle, Crosskill accepted this post, which included the editorship of the *Royal Gazette*. He apparently agreed to turn the *Gazette* into an organ for Falkland and the conservatives led by James William Johnston*. That summer Crosskill declared himself "a Great Neutral," but he now engaged in violently partisan journalism, at a time when the reformers were preaching the cause of responsible government. Their leader in this struggle, Joseph Howe*, had resumed editorship of the *Novascotian* in May, and outflanked Crosskill.

In the *Post* and the *Gazette* Crosskill was accustomed to defame his enemies and justify his own erratic behaviour. But he himself was mercilessly ridiculed in the *Novascotian*. Its columns for 1844 and 1845 present a whole series of events in his personal life. A dying servant girl ambiguously hinted that "Posty" (Crosskill) had given her arsenic, but he was discharged at the coroner's inquest in 1844. The next year he pulled a dagger on an officer who complained about Crosskill's public criticism of his manners. In court on this charge Crosskill insulted the mayor, Hugh BELL, and council, who then forced him to apologize publicly. Meanwhile, Crosskill himself took a man to court over a New Year's Day scuffle

caused by Crosskill's increasing attentions to the man's wife. William Young*, the speaker of the assembly, hauled Crosskill into court for libelling the Young brothers in their business transactions; Crosskill was defended by Johnston, who was the attorney general. In 1846 Falkland was recalled. Crosskill was then quoted in the *Novascotian* as heaping insults on him and praising his successor, Sir John HARVEY, probably in hopes of keeping his appointment. The *Novascotian* also gave coverage to what was perhaps Crosskill's most notorious gaffe: his accusation that William WALSH, the bishop of Halifax, advised Roman Catholics from the altar of St Mary's Cathedral not to vote tory in the 1847 election; the liberals won it handily.

Because of criticism from reform newspapers concerning his sympathies with the tories and Falkland, Crosskill in the mid 1840s apparently tried to hide his connections both with the *Post*, which he edited until 1846, and with the *Morning Courier*, where he served as editor from October to December 1848, by having his employees pretend to be their proprietors. When he was forced to resign as queen's printer in June 1848, the recently married editor found himself in poor financial shape. Although many years later George Edward Fenety*, a liberal newspaperman, accused Crosskill of having taken the appointment because "the shekels were of more importance to him than political principles," Crosskill claimed that printing for the government had ruined him because in each session of the assembly his payment was reduced. In fact, Crosskill overcharged and a committee of both parties in 1847 and 1848 reduced his price scales to those Thompson had used. Journalism wore him out "body and soul," and his ventures thereafter verged on collapse. From October to December 1848 he ran the *New Times* and the *Courier* as separate papers, and then in 1849 he merged them as the *Times and Courier*, publishing it at least until June. His next paper, the *British North American*, planned for the summer of 1849, was postponed until July 1850, and lasted until about the end of 1855. During that time the *Novascotian* on 7 Jan. 1850 published his letter on the province's impending ruin, which he believed was the result of British free trade and American protection; the only remedy would be colonial representation in the imperial parliament. In 1849, 1852, and 1854 he petitioned, successfully, for old printing claims, and when he declared bankruptcy in 1854 the assembly appointed him official reporter at a salary of £100. This task he performed diligently until his death.

Crosskill contributed to provincial literature by publishing G. R. Young's *On colonial literature, science and education . . .* (1842), John McPherson*'s prize temperance poem *The praise of water* (1843), and Samuel Douglas Smith Huyghue*'s historical romance *Argimou: a legend of the Micmac*

Crysler

(1847). In private, as in a poem to his wife on their eighth anniversary, he appears kindly and affectionate. A good printer and a talented reporter, Crosskill had the misfortune to be satirically exploited by his enemies, and the dubious honour of being one of the first recipients of patronage as practised in the party system of the 1840s. The *Novascotian* on 28 Sept. 1846 accused the "government pet" of ruining the character of the press by his connection with Falkland's "scurrillous organ" and its "semi-barbarous warfare." Unfortunately for Crosskill's reputation, it is Howe's own savage and demeaning view of him that has prevailed.

GEORGE L. PARKER

John Henry Crosskill published one issue of the *Literary and Hist. Journal* in Saint John, N.B., in October 1837. He is also the author of *A comprehensive outline of the geography and history of Nova Scotia; from the discovery of America to the reign of Queen Victoria I . . .* (Halifax, 1838), a second edition of which, covering the period *to the sixth year of the reign of Queen Victoria I . . .* , was published there in 1842; and of a poem "To my wife, on the anniversary of our marriage day," which appeared in the *British North American* (Halifax), 15 Oct. 1855. He is the compiler of *A complete narrative of the celebration of the nuptials of Her Most Gracious Majesty Queen Victoria, with His Royal Highness Prince Albert of Saxe Co[b]urg and Gotha, by the Nova Scotia Philanthropic Society, with introductory remarks on similar celebrations by the other charitable societies in Halifax, and by the people of Nova Scotia generally* (Halifax, [1840]).

BLHU, R. G. Dun & Co. credit ledger, Canada, 11: 222. PANS, MG 1, 544; MG 100, 128, no.18; RG 1, 175: 297–98, 368, 516; RG 5, GP, 2, petition of J. H. Crosskill, 1 March 1852; RG 22, 26: 1, 14–15. Joseph Howe, *Joseph Howe: voice of Nova Scotia*, ed. and intro. J. M. Beck (Toronto, 1964), 100–5, 110. N.S., House of Assembly, *Journal and proc.*, 1848: 168; app.82; 1849: 266, 294, 316, 385, 395; petition 46; 1852: 190; petition 64; app.79: 383–86; 1854: 503, 512, 541; app.23: 205; app.67: 304–5. *Acadian Recorder*, 14 Feb. 1857. *British Colonist* (Halifax), 14 Feb. 1857. *New-Brunswick Courier*, 9 Oct. 1847. *Novascotian*, 4, 11 March, 13 May, 17, 24 June, 1, 22 July, 5 Aug. 1844; 9, 16, 30 June, 7 July, 11 Aug., 15, 22 Dec. 1845; 17 Aug., 28 Sept. 1846; 2 Aug. 1847; 7 Jan. 1850; 16, 23 Feb. 1857 [the obituary notices of February 1857 were seen in bound copies at PANS, a different edition than that available on CLA mfm.; wording differs slightly]. J. R. Harper, *Historical directory of New Brunswick newspapers and periodicals* (Fredericton, 1961), 68. *An historical directory of Nova Scotia newspapers and journals before Confederation*, comp. T. B. Vincent (Kingston, Ont., 1977), nos.25, 59, 65, 89, 96, 108, 130. Beck, *Joseph Howe*. G. E. Fenety, *Life and times of the Hon. Joseph Howe . . .* (Saint John, 1896), 24. W. R. Livingston, *Responsible government in Nova Scotia: a study of the constitutional beginnings of the British Commonwealth* (Iowa City, 1930). MacNutt, *Atlantic prov.*, 227–28. D. C. Harvey, "Newspapers of Nova Scotia, 1840–1867," *CHR*, 26 (1945): 279–301.

CRYSLER, JOHN, businessman, politician, justice of the peace, office holder, and militia officer; b. 24 July 1770 in Schoharie, N.Y., son of John Crysler (Johannes Krausler) and Dorothy Meyers; m. first June 1791 Dorothea Adams (d. 1803) in Williamsburgh Township (Ont.), and they had three sons and four daughters; m. secondly 20 Nov. 1803 Nancy Loucks, and they had two sons; m. thirdly 19 April 1808 Nancy Finkle, and they had six sons and four daughters; d. 18 Jan. 1852 in Finch Township, Upper Canada.

Prior to the American revolution John Crysler lived in New Dorlach (Sharon Springs), N.Y. In 1777 his father joined the British army at Fort Stanwix (Rome, N.Y.) and served under Sir John Johnson*. Crysler himself served as a drummer with Lieutenant-Colonel John Butler*'s rangers and arrived in the province of Quebec in 1779. He was discharged in 1784 at the age of 14 and settled with his father in Township No.4 (Williamsburgh). In 1801 the younger Crysler was granted tavern and shop licences in the Eastern District of Upper Canada and imported liquor, tobacco, and salt from Lower Canada. Between 1806 and 1810 he bought more than 4,600 acres of timber-rich land in Finch and Mountain townships, 2,500 acres of which he sold in September 1810 to John Richardson* of the Montreal firm of Forsyth, Richardson and Company. In 1808 he had received a licence to cut timber and was under contract to supply masts for the Royal Navy. During his early life, it is reported, Crysler "amassed a large property" and erected several grist-mills and sawmills.

Crysler had entered public life in 1804 when he was elected to the House of Assembly for Dundas. During the sessions from 1805 to 1808 he established himself as a supporter of the government, though in 1807 he joined Robert Thorpe* and David McGregor Rogers* in opposing the bill "to establish Public Schools in each and every District" of the province. The following year Crysler returned to his business pursuits in Williamsburgh. In addition, he had been appointed a justice of the peace for the Eastern District in 1806; until the outbreak of the War of 1812 and for more than 30 years thereafter he regularly attended the district Court of Quarter Sessions.

In 1812 Crysler was a lieutenant in the 1st Dundas Militia. He was promoted captain the following year and saw active service throughout the war. On 11 Nov. 1813 he was present at the battle of Crysler's Farm. This battle, which halted an American advance on Montreal, was fought on his land in Williamsburgh Township, and the British commander, Lieutenant-Colonel Joseph Wanton Morrison*, used Crysler's farmhouse as his headquarters. Crysler himself carried the dispatches containing news of the victory to Montreal. His farm had sustained heavy damage during the battle, however, and further damage resulted from the subsequent use of his farmhouse and outbuildings as a hospital and barracks. By early 1816 Crysler had received £400 in compensation.

Crysler also served in the assembly from 1812 to 1820, continuing to vote with the majority on most issues. Re-elected in 1824, for this, his last term as the member for Dundas, he supported the administration's spokesman, Attorney General John Beverley Robinson*. After 1825, however, his attendance gradually declined, probably because of his increasing commitments in the Eastern District. He had been collector of customs for Cornwall since at least 1818, and in 1826 he received a government contract to survey concessions 7, 8, and 9 of Osnabruck Township. Crysler had been promised a percentage of the land surveyed but, on completion of the survey, the government discovered that, since most of the land had already been granted, it could not uphold its part of the contract.

There are other indications that the 1820s were difficult years for Crysler. His deputy collector of customs was found guilty of "misconduct and neglect" and in 1822 a special act of the legislature was passed "for the relief of John Crysler," allowing him to continue to collect his percentage from the revenues which were to be paid back as restitution to the government. In February 1825 Crysler's workmen were jailed and fined by Sheriff John Stuart of the Johnstown District for cutting timber on clergy reserves. That May Stuart also seized a load of Crysler's timber bound for Montreal under a contract for a new Roman Catholic church there, a claim having been made that the timber was suitable for masts for the Royal Navy. Crysler may have been experiencing financial problems as early as 1820. In that year Allan Napier MacNab* obtained a £3,000 judgement against him for debt. Though Crysler paid this judgement in 1824, two others in 1834 to different creditors amounting to just over £3,000 remained unsatisfied. In all, 28 judgements worth in excess of £12,000 were registered against him in the Court of King's Bench between 1820 and 1835. One reason for these difficulties may have been Crysler's business methods. In 1830, for instance, John Strachan* wrote an angry letter concerning land Crysler had sold him in 1819. Strachan had discovered that 1,200 of the 1,400 acres were "under water or barren rocks," which "surprised and disappointed me . . . as I neither purchased water nor rocks." It was commonly believed that Crysler's lavish hospitality and generosity also contributed to the change in his fortunes.

Despite the state of his enterprises Crysler remained a prominent man in Dundas County. Supporting his claim to land for services during the War of 1812, judge Archibald McLean* described him in 1837 as "one of the oldest and most loyal Inhabitants of the Province." On 1 Nov. 1838 Crysler was appointed lieutenant-colonel of the 1st Regiment of Dundas militia and later that month, at the age of 68, he led his

regiment against the Patriots at the battle of the Windmill near Prescott [see Plomer Young*]. In 1843 he moved to Finch Township in the northern part of Stormont County. The village of Crysler at the site on the South Nation River where he operated a sawmill and a grist-mill is named after him. He died there in 1852. His oldest surviving son, John Pliny Crysler, represented Dundas in the Legislative Assembly from 1848 to 1851 and from 1854 to 1857 and was county land registrar between 1867 and 1881.

C. J. SHEPARD

Anglican Church of Canada, Diocese of Ottawa Arch., United Anglican Missions of Williamsburg, Matilda, Osnabruck and Edwardsburg, Ont., reg. of baptisms, marriages, and burials (mfm. at AO). AO, MS 35; MS 451, Stormont County, Finch Township, Crysler cemetery records; MU 500; RG 1, A-I-5, 8: 68; C-I-3, 14: 460; 15: 486; RG 8, ser.I-1-H, 2: 14; RG 22, ser.47, 2: 173, 190, 304, 314; ser.131, 1, 4. MTL, Sir George Prevost papers, memorial book, 154–56. PAC, RG 1, E3, 15: 15 (mfm. at AO); L3, 97: C9/39; 120: C20/163; 122: C21/135; 123: C22/12; RG 5, A1: 2994, 37350–51, 38255–59, 38423–25, 40622–23, 123920–24; RG 8, I (C ser.); RG 31, A1, 1851, Finch Township; RG 68, General index, 1651–1841. PRO, CO 42/381: 280–84. Stormont Land Registry Office (Cornwall, Ont.), Abstract index to deeds, Finch Township, 1: 225, 227–28, 252–53, 283–84 (mfm. at AO, GS 5580); Deeds, Finch Township, vol.A: 27, no.26 (mfm. at AO, GS 5582). United Counties of Stormont, Dundas and Glengarry Court-house (Cornwall), Road petitions, Finch Township, no.6 (mfm. at AO, MS 40).

"Accounts of the receiver-general of Upper Canada from the year 1801 . . . ," AO Report, 1914: 746, 758, 770, 777. Arthur papers (Sanderson). "District of Luneburg: Court of Common Pleas," AO Report, 1917: 401, 406. "Journals of Legislative Assembly of U.C.," AO Report, 1911; 1912. Statistical account of U.C. (Gourlay), 2, app.B: xcv. "United Empire Loyalists: enquiry into losses and services," AO Report, 1904: 481. U.C., House of Assembly, Journal, 1825–28; Statutes, 1822, c.23. Armstrong, Handbook of Upper Canadian chronology. H. C. Hilliker, Crysler and Chrysler history and family trees (1v. and supplement, n.p., 1974–81). Places in Ont. (Mika). Political appointments, 1841–65 (Coté; 1866). Rolls of the Provincial (Loyalist) Corps, Canadian command, American revolutionary period, comp. M. B. Fryer and W. A. Smy (Toronto, 1981), 59. James Croil, Dundas, or a sketch of Canadian history . . . (Montreal, 1861; repr. Belleville, Ont., 1972). J. F. Pringle, Lunenburgh or the old Eastern District; its settlement and early progress . . . (Cornwall, 1890; repr. Belleville, 1972). R. L. Way, "The day of Crysler's Farm," The defended border: Upper Canada and the War of 1812 . . . , ed. Morris Zaslow and W. B. Turner (Toronto, 1964), 61–83.

CUTHBERT, WILLIAM, farmer, businessman, justice of the peace, office holder, militia officer, and politician; b. 1795 in Alloway, Scotland; m. March 1832 Christiana Montgomery in New Richmond,

Cuthbert

Lower Canada, and they had one daughter; d. 3 Aug. 1854 in Rock Ferry, England.

William Cuthbert came to Lower Canada in the second decade of the 19th century. It is not known under what circumstances he settled at New Richmond, in the Baie des Chaleurs region, but a local account states that the young man was poor. There is no record of the name Cuthbert prior to the 1825 census. It is next mentioned in 1828, when he shipped more than 300 barrels of cod from Gaspé harbour to Quebec. In the 1831 census Cuthbert, who is listed as a farmer, was clearly the most important person in New Richmond. He had 50 acres under cultivation, and the previous year had harvested 40 *minots* of wheat, 400 of oats, 20 of barley, and 450 of potatoes. In addition he kept some 30 animals.

From then on Cuthbert was involved in all sectors of the region's economy. In partnership with his brother Robert, of Greenock in Scotland, he formed William Cuthbert and Company, which specialized at first in the import trade. From its New Richmond store it supplied clothing and foodstuffs, as well as a variety of equipment. To further its trade with Great Britain the company soon went into the lumber trade. It obtained grants of land in New Richmond and Maria townships, in particular along the Rivière Cascapédia where it brought in Scottish and Irish settlers to work at felling trees under sub-contractors.

In 1833 Cuthbert built a "splendid" sawmill at the mouth of the Petite Cascapédia, and there pine, fir, and birch logs were made into boards, shingles, and laths. He also owned other facilities in the region, including a flour-mill and a sawmill to the east of Bonaventure harbour, which he leased out. In March 1832, by his marriage with Christiana, the daughter of Donald Montgomery, a member of the House of Assembly of Prince Edward Island, he had acquired business allies on the south shore of the Baie des Chaleurs, since two of his brothers-in-law, Hugh and John*, were also involved in lumbering and shipbuilding at Dalhousie, N.B. Like the other local contractors, Cuthbert paid little attention to strict observance of cutting restrictions in his licences. This seems to have caused him no difficulties, particularly since he was the close friend of the land agent Étienne Martel, of New Carlisle.

Cuthbert is thought to have built 14 ships at New Richmond, but it is not known whether they were for his own use or for sale. On several occasions he also bought boats from other local shipbuilders. The skilled craftsmen of William Cuthbert and Company came from Scotland, where Robert Cuthbert saw to their recruitment.

William Cuthbert was one of the major landowners in the Baie des Chaleurs region. In addition to land granted by the government or bought from individuals or at public auctions, he acquired a large number of properties for non-payment of debts. In effect he practised a credit system common to other lumbermen and to fishing companies on the Gaspé peninsula. His employees were paid in kind, and, as the value of these supplies invariably exceeded their wages, they ran into debt and mortgaged their land, which after a period of time often went to Cuthbert. In 1854 he owned 46 properties, some with dwellings, which were concentrated in New Richmond and Maria townships. A form of capitalism based on land transactions seems therefore to have been an important source of his wealth. But he was also owed money, and that year mortgage obligations, accounts, and doubtful and bad debts amounted to £22,211, contracted by 597 persons.

Cuthbert purchased crops from local inhabitants and apparently engaged in the fishing trade. Great Britain was both his source of supplies and his principal market; even after his partnership with his brother Robert ended on 29 Oct. 1849, Greenock remained his preferred port of entry. In North America, he made use of Quebec, Halifax, and St John's.

Cuthbert was an influential man in his own region, and on 3 May 1828 was appointed justice of the peace for the district of Gaspé; his commission was renewed on 31 Dec. 1831. On 9 May 1829 he was appointed commissioner for improving the road from Bonaventure to New Richmond. At this period he joined in the conflict between the Protestants of New Richmond and the Catholic missionary, Louis-Stanislas Malo, over the construction of school houses. He became a militia captain on 8 Jan. 1833, and was later promoted lieutenant-colonel of the Bonaventure County militia.

In 1848 an association of influential men in Bonaventure riding urged Cuthbert to run for the Legislative Assembly of the province of Canada. Their antipathies were directed against John Robinson Hamilton, a New Carlisle lawyer, who had been campaigning since his defeat by John Le Boutillier* in 1844. A third candidate, John Meagher, a merchant and personal friend of Cuthbert, was persuaded to enter the contest by the Carleton missionary, Félix Desruisseaux, who wanted a Catholic as member. Thanks to the division of votes and to overwhelming support in New Richmond, Maria, and Restigouche, Cuthbert was elected on 17 January, with a majority of 225 over Hamilton. The election was contested, since Cuthbert apparently did not meet the statutory qualifications and polling in Mann Township had not been supervised by a scrutineer. But by various ploys Robert CHRISTIE, member for Gaspé, managed to forestall the protest. Cuthbert was present in the assembly only during the session of 1848 and never made a speech. Until 1851 it was Christie who presented the petitions from Bonaventure. Cuthbert was kept at home by ill health and in June 1850 handed in his resignation. However, the speaker of the house, Augustin-Norbert Morin*, refused to take immediate action, and Cuthbert remained officially a member until the end of his term on 6 Nov. 1851.

Suffering from erysipelas of the neck, Cuthbert landed at Liverpool on 13 July 1854, having come by way of Greenock. He was taken to the house of a nephew, a doctor in Rock Ferry, where he made his will on 3 August. He died that day and was buried six days later in Greenock cemetery. He had been one of the most important figures of the Gaspé peninsula and northern New Brunswick, as the inventory of his assets, carried out from 22 Sept. to 10 Oct. 1854, makes clear. His estate, consisting of an immense residence, two cattle sheds, a dairy, a house, and a forge, was evidence of his wealth. In his wardrobes were the finest clothes and in his cellar the best spirits. All told, he left his wife and their only child, Ann, a fortune worth £38,500, including more than £13,000 in cash. As his wife was bequeathed only the usufruct, Cuthbert's business passed to the firm of Hugh and John Montgomery and Company.

YVES FRENETTE

AC, Bonaventure (New-Carlisle), Cour supérieure, Vieux dossiers, 7 avril 1851; Minutiers, J.-G. Lebel, 5 déc. 1833; 22 janv., 12 mars, 29 avril 1834; 30 mars, 19 mai, 3 juill. 1835; 3 avril, 23 oct. 1837; 17 nov. 1838; 15 juill. 1839; 29 janv., 13 juin 1840; 3 févr. 1841; 15, 23 avril, 1er sept. 1842; 22 sept.–10 oct. 1854; Martin Sheppard, 3 mars 1828, 1er févr. 1831. Arch. de l'évêché de Gaspé (Gaspé, Qué.), Boîte Carleton, corr., 1794–1870, 24 août 1831; 3 juill., 3 août 1832. PAC, MG 30, D1, 9: 572–647; RG 4, B15, 2; B28, 134; RG 9, I, A5, 14; C1, 2; RG 16, A1, 97; RG 31, A1, 1825, 1831, New Richmond; RG 42, ser.I. Can., Prov. of, Legislative Assembly, *App. to the journals*, 1842, app.T. *Debates of the Legislative Assembly of United Canada* (Abbott Gibbs *et al.*), vols.7–10. L.C., House of Assembly, *Journals*, 1835–36, app.BB. *Rapport sur les missions du diocèse de Québec . . .* (Québec), no.17 (avril 1866). *Mélanges religieux*, 21 janv. 1848, 10 mai 1850. *Quebec Gazette*, 26 Jan. 1848. F.-J. Audet, "Les législateurs du Bas-Canada." Jules Bélanger *et al.*, *Histoire de la Gaspésie* (Montréal, 1981). J.-B.-A. Ferland, *La Gaspésie* (Québec, 1877; réimpr., 1879). J. M. LeMoine, *The chronicles of the St Lawrence* (Montreal, 1878). P.-L. Martin *et al.*, *La Gaspésie de Miguasha à Percé: itinéraire culturel* (Québec, 1978). F.-J. Audet, "William Cuthbert (1795–1854)," *BRH*, 41 (1935): 112–13. Raymond Gingras, "Le district de Gaspé en 1833: qui en était responsable?" *Rev. d'hist. de la Gaspésie* (Gaspé), 9 (1971): 231–32.

D

DALCROMBIE. *See* MCGILLIVRAY

DALRYMPLE, GEORGE R., apothecary, businessman, and politician; b. in Scotland, probably in 1790; m. 14 Sept. 1825 Eliza Webster, and they had one child; d. 6 Feb. 1851 in Charlottetown.

George R. Dalrymple drifted to Prince Edward Island in 1821 after wandering extensively in America. A hardworking Presbyterian Scot and trained apothecary, he opened a "Cheap Medicine Store" in Charlottetown and married the daughter of an early Island resident and proprietor, John Webster. In 1827 he petitioned for a grant of land at the head of the North River creek (probably Ellens Creek) in Charlottetown Royalty to run a carding-mill, opened it in 1828, and later added a fulling-mill, a flour-mill, and a kiln, thereby creating an establishment known as Dalrymple's Mills. He incurred great expense in bringing his machines in and remained in the forefront of Islanders working toward the improvement of local agricultural and business practices.

Dalrymple regarded political reform as a natural extension of his commitment to progress. In 1828 he took an uncontested by-election for a Kings County seat in the House of Assembly. Avoiding "the malignant influence of party spirit," he ran on a platform of "public utility" which stressed the need for agricultural improvement and tenant relief. Dalrymple lost his seat in the general election of 1830 but was returned in an 1831 Queens County by-election. From 1828 to 1830 he had laboured to promote and pass such reform measures as bills for the relief of Roman Catholics and for the establishment and support of schools, and by 1830 the assembly's progressive members were deferring to him as their leader. While directing the agitation for the secularization of glebe lands and the reduction of the assembly's term from seven to four years, Dalrymple avoided public demonstration or mob violence, resting content with patience, respect for the law, and adherence to constitutional principle. These methods were slow but effective: a quadrennial bill was passed in 1833, followed four years later by royal assent for an 1835 act allowing for the sale of glebe lands.

As the 1830s progressed, politics on the Island focused on the single issue of escheat, whose advocates desired the establishment of a court to investigate whether the conditions of the original land grants of 1767 had been met. Because practically all landholders had failed to meet these conditions the result would have been the redistribution of land from large, mostly absentee, proprietors to the local tenant

Dalton

farmers. Dalrymple proposed a bill to establish a court of escheat in 1832 because he felt that the rights of private property had been forfeited by the implied breach of contract. He took some time to realize that escheat was not just another in a series of reforms but was nothing short of a social revolution. His methods of patience and constitutional propriety were unlikely to satisfy the tenants' violent discontent and were probably incapable of achieving concessions from the proprietors. Loath to adopt radical measures, Dalrymple lost his leadership of the reformers to William Cooper*, who was only too willing to use tenant agitation "out of doors" to influence British policy by usurping the power of the assembly. Dalrymple won re-election in 1834 and was chosen speaker – under the circumstances an appropriate post.

The Hay River tenant meeting of 1836, at which Cooper advised tenants to withhold payment of rent, led to Dalrymple's open break with the escheat leader and his followers. Convinced that "one of the best causes has been ruined by the violence and ignorance of its pretended friends," Dalrymple fell out of step with electors and lost his seat in the November 1838 election. His last duty as speaker had been to act as one of the Island's delegates (along with Thomas Heath Haviland* and Joseph Pope*) to the meeting Lord Durham [Lambton*] convened at Quebec in September 1838 to discuss a federation of British North American colonies.

Dalrymple was appointed in March 1839 to the Legislative Council after Lieutenant Governor Sir Charles Augustus FitzRoy restructured it and he sat there until his death. These were frustrating years for Dalrymple because he continued to work for progressive measures and for the assembly's rights in a body which demonstrated little sympathy for either. He found more fulfilment as a member of the Island's Board of Education (appointed 1834), a trustee of the Central Academy in Charlottetown (appointed 1834), and president of the Highland Society (elected 1841). He also lectured on scientific topics before the Charlottetown Mechanics' Institute, of which he was president in 1839. Perhaps satisfied to concentrate on his political and social activities as well as on his store in Charlottetown, Dalrymple sold his mills in 1844.

Although, while acting as agent for the Greenwich estate in 1830, he had threatened to use "coercive measures" to collect unpaid rents, he maintained a moderate and constitutional approach to reform and escheat which was legitimately consistent with his role as a friend to improvement. When Cooper's methods had been tried and failed, Dalrymple may have gained a measure of satisfaction from observing the moderate and dogged pace of the new age of Island Reformers led by George Coles*.

M. Brook Taylor

PAPEI, RG 1, Commission books, 15 May 1834; RG 5, Petitions, 21 July, 6 Oct. 1827; RG 16, Land registry records, conveyance reg., liber 29: f.205. PRO, CO 226/39: 16. St Paul's Anglican Church (Charlottetown), Reg. of baptisms, marriages, and burials (mfm. at PAPEI). P.E.I., House of Assembly, *Journal*, 3, 11 Feb., 6 April 1831; 26 Jan. 1835; Legislative Council, *Journal*, 1839–51. *Prince Edward Island Gazette*, 22 Aug. 1821. *Prince Edward Island Register*, 10 June, 20 Sept. 1825; 12 June, 14 Aug., 30 Oct. 1827; 3 June, 1, 29 July, 5 Aug. 1828; 10, 17, 24, 31 March, 7 April 1829; 23 March, 6, 13, 27 April, 22 June 1830. *Royal Gazette* (Charlottetown), 3, 10, 24 Jan., 7, 14 Feb., 3 April 1832; 15, 29 Jan., 5, 19, 26 Feb., 19 March, 2 April, 21 May, 25, 26 Nov. 1833; 1 April, 13 May, 23 Sept., 25 Nov., 9, 23 Dec. 1834; 27 Jan., 31 March 1835; 14 Feb. 1837; 3 April, 27 Sept., 20 Nov. 1838; 8, 29 Jan., 12 March 1839; 11 Feb., 21 April 1840; 21 Sept. 1841; 14 Feb. 1843; 30 April, 14 May, 3 Sept. 1844; 15 June 1847; 11 Feb. 1851. *Canada's smallest prov.* (Bolger), 95–114. D. C. Harvey, "Glebe and school lands in Prince Edward Island," CCHS, *Journal*, 10 (1968): 120–47.

DALTON, CHARLES, Roman Catholic priest, Franciscan, and vicar general; b. 1786 near Thurles (Republic of Ireland); d. 17 June 1859 in Harbour Grace, Nfld.

Charles Dalton is known to have been a student at St Kieran's College, County Kilkenny (Republic of Ireland), in 1813–14. By 1819 he had become a Franciscan priest. Closely associated thereafter with the Clonmel friary, of which he was guardian from 1824 to 1831, Dalton was noted for his reacquisition of the medieval Clonmel abbey, which had been in Protestant hands since the Reformation. Recruited for the Newfoundland mission by the new bishop, Michael Anthony Fleming*, Dalton arrived in St John's on 2 June 1831. He was actually one of eleven priests, including Edward Troy* and James W. Duffy, who were brought from Ireland between 1831 and 1833. Fresh from the victory of Catholic emancipation, this group markedly changed the character of the priesthood in Newfoundland. Dalton served in St John's with Troy as a curate to Fleming until September 1833, when he succeeded Thomas Anthony Ewer* as parish priest of Harbour Grace.

Although lately reduced in size by the creation of the new parish of Brigus, Harbour Grace was still a populous parish, encompassing a large part of Conception Bay. With two assistant priests, it was next in importance only to St John's, and Fleming's choice of Dalton to be its pastor was a mark of his confidence. Indeed, Fleming and Dalton seem to have enjoyed an excellent relationship. Dalton was Fleming's vicar general for a time in the 1830s and he was also the bishop's companion on several lengthy voyages, including the episcopal visitations of the north and south coasts in 1834 and 1835 respectively and a recuperative trip to Ireland in 1845. In 1843 Dalton was named an executor of Fleming's will.

Active participation in Newfoundland politics was a trait of many of Fleming's clergy, and Dalton was no exception. During the general election of 1836 he openly favoured the four Liberal candidates who were victorious in Conception Bay and led a procession supporting two of them, Robert PACK, a Protestant, and James Power. The success of Edmund Hanrahan* in the 1840 by-election there was also attributed to his influence. Dalton was never accused of intimidation, however, and he had no part in the violence that ended both campaigns. Nor is there any evidence that he or his curates had even remotely encouraged the vicious attack in his parish on Henry David WINTON in 1835, despite Governor Henry Prescott*'s attaching blame to the Catholic priesthood. In 1852 Dalton unsuccessfully attempted to recruit Thomas Ridley* and John Munn*, both Protestants, as local candidates.

As a school board member appointed under Newfoundland's first education act (1836), Dalton was a principal in the dispute which led to denominational schools. This act, which Roman Catholics supported, provided for public education in non-denominational schools. Nevertheless, at its first meeting, the Conception Bay board adopted the King James version of the Bible as a school text, to be read without comment outside regular hours to "children of the parents who desire it." Catholic board members unanimously objected to the use of this Bible as discriminatory and threatened to resign unless the governor overturned the provision. Prescott thereupon requested that Conception Bay adopt instead the St John's by-law, which provided for the withdrawal of children from school for religious instruction. This failed to carry, since to most Protestant members of the board it was equivalent to a vote for the removal of the Bible. Dalton and the other Catholics once again demanded that the original provision be overturned, making it clear that otherwise Catholic children would not attend the new schools. When the governor acquiesced, the non-Catholic majority maintained that they could not in conscience allocate funds where the Bible was excluded. This impasse was finally resolved only by the establishment of separate Protestant and Catholic boards in 1843.

Dalton was an ardent Irish nationalist and a devoted admirer of Daniel O'Connell. A staunch foe of union in Ireland, he publicly expressed the view that O'Connell would be instrumental "in raising our degraded country from a province to that place in the scale of nations which her natural position entitles her to." Dalton assiduously promoted the collection in Newfoundland of "repeal rent," contributions to the campaign for the dissolution of the union between Ireland and England, and was a generous personal donor to it. In 1844 he was prominent in the protest movement against O'Connell's imprisonment.

Dalton was a strong supporter of Irish philanthropic causes. He made substantial personal donations to the restoration of the Clonmel abbey, to the Irish Franciscan monastery in Capranica di Sutri, Viterbo (Italy), and to the victims of the Irish potato famine even when his own parish was suffering from the same blight. This personal largesse may have been made possible by his ownership of a fishing schooner.

Dalton did much for the development of his own parish. In the tradition of the Irish priests of his day, he was especially active in church building. He had churches constructed in Carbonear by 1836 and in Spaniard's Bay by 1844. His major undertaking, however, was the erection of a new stone church at Harbour Grace to companion the cathedral under way at St John's. Dalton had appealed for funds as early as 1844 and went to Ireland the following year to procure stone for the work. Financial difficulties ensued, and construction did not start until 1852. The new church, accommodating 1,200, was officially opened the next year. Enlarged and embellished by his successors, it became the core of the first cathedral of Harbour Grace, which burned in 1889.

The first Newfoundland convents outside St John's owed much to Dalton's encouragement. As early as 1839, he had purchased a house and land at Harbour Grace for convent use. However, not until 1851 was a convent of the Order of the Presentation of Our Blessed Lady established there. A second foundation, at Carbonear, followed in 1852 [see Miss KIRWIN, named Sister Mary Bernard]. The convent schools meant improved educational facilities for young women and complemented the 11 Catholic schools already in existence in the parish.

A new diocese of Harbour Grace was established in 1856. Dalton's advanced age and poor health precluded his being considered for the office of bishop, but the appointment went to John Dalton*, his nephew and charge from youth, who was curate in Carbonear. The senior Dalton became the diocese's vicar general.

Charles Dalton ably served both his bishops and his parishioners during the 25 turbulent years of his ministry. At a time when religion and controversy were nearly synonymous, he had friends of every class and denomination. His benevolence, his simplicity, and his hospitality towards all were the characteristics that most impressed those who knew him.

RAYMOND J. LAHEY

Father Dalton may well have served as the model for Father Terence O'Toole, the inoffensive pastor of "Bay-Harbour," in Robert Traill Spence Lowell*'s novel, *The new priest in Conception Bay* (2v., Boston, 1858; repr. in 1v., Toronto, 1974).

AASJ, Fleming papers; Mullock papers, diaries, 1851–52, 1856. Archivio della Propaganda Fide (Rome), Scritture riferite nei Congressi: America Settentrionale, 5 (1842–48).

Dalton

Basilica of St John the Baptist (Roman Catholic) (St John's), St John's parish, reg. of baptisms. Cathedral of the Immaculate Conception (Harbour Grace, Nfld.), Reg. of baptisms (mfm. at PANL). M. A. Fleming, *Relazione della missione cattolica in Terranuova nell'America settentrionale* ... (Rome, 1837). *Liber Dubliniensis: chapter documents of the Irish Franciscans, 1719–1875*, ed. Anselm Faulkner (Killiney, Republic of Ire., 1978). J. T. Mullock, *The Cathedral of St John's, Newfoundland, with an account of its consecration* ... (Dublin, 1856). Nfld., House of Assembly, *Journal*, 1848–49; Legislative Council, *Journals*, 1837. *Newfoundlander*, 9 June 1831; 14 Feb., 18 April, 29 June, 8 Aug., 21 Sept., 7 Nov. 1833; 27 March, 17 April, 26 June 1834; 31 May 1845; 15 July, 5 Aug. 1847; 7 June 1852; 1 Dec. 1853; 20 June, 1 Aug. 1859. *Newfoundland Indicator* (St John's), 17 Feb., 18 May, 10, 27 July 1844; 4, 11, 18 Jan., 31 May 1845. *Patriot* (St John's), 1 Sept. 1835; 12 Jan., 8 Oct. 1836; 24 July 1844. *Pilot* (St John's), 28 Feb. 1852. *Public Ledger*, 28 Oct., 1, 4, 8, 22 Nov. 1836; 30 Oct., 17 Nov., 1, 11, 29 Dec. 1840; 17 May, 29 Aug. 1843. *Sentinel and Conception Bay Advertiser* (Carbonear, Nfld.), 19, 26 Feb., 12 March 1839. *Times and General Commercial Gazette* (St John's), 6 July 1836. *Weekly Herald and Conception Bay General Advertiser* (Harbour Grace), 27 Oct. 1847, 28 June 1848, 2 June 1852, 30 Nov. 1853. Peter Birch, *St. Kieran's College, Kilkenny* (Dublin, 1951). *Centenary of the diocese of Harbour Grace, 1856–1956*, [ed. R. J. Connolly] (St John's, 1956). Howley, *Ecclesiastical hist. of Nfld*. Patrick Power, *Waterford & Lismore; a compendious history of the united dioceses* (Dublin, 1937).

DALTON, SOPHIA. *See* SIMMS

DART, ELIZABETH (Eynon), Bible Christian preacher; b. April 1792 in Marhamchurch, England; m. 18 March 1833 John Hicks Eynon*, and they had one daughter, who died at birth; d. 13 Jan. 1857 in Little Britain, Upper Canada.

Elizabeth Dart has been called the best missionary that her denomination sent to Canada. Her parents belonged to the Church of England, but were not deeply religious. Sometimes her invalid mother talked to her about "spiritual matters"; her father was more interested in his farm crops and livestock. She read the Bible as a child, and at times her thoughts of Christ were so intense that she could see Him on the cross. In 1811, at the age of 19, she joined the Wesleyan Methodist Church, but four years later was one of 22 men and women who met at a farm house in Shebbear on 9 October to form a new society, later called the Bible Christian Church. In 1816 she became its first itinerant preacher under the founder, William O'Bryan. By 1819 there were 29 itinerants, 15 men and 14 women.

Elizabeth had spoken in public before the new society began, although like most 19th-century women preachers she began hesitantly and reluctantly. At first it was difficult for her even to lead in prayer, but she kept on because of her effectiveness. She often spoke three times on Sunday and once every day except Saturday. She preached to mobs; she was pelted with rotten eggs; she walked 14 miles some days. In Bristol she began a society, and was responsible for the movement's success in Wales, although she travelled mainly around Devon and Cornwall. She was an outstanding speaker, intelligent, and fond of books. She was well liked and was said to possess a "simplicity of character, a quaintness of manner and a power of sympathy."

In 1833 Elizabeth married the itinerant John Hicks Eynon, who had been converted nine years earlier through her preaching in Redbrook, Wales. That May, as missionaries posted to Upper Canada, they boarded the small brig *Dalusia* with six other settlers, and after a stormy 42-day crossing landed at Quebec on 17 June. They reached Cobourg, where a number of emigrants from the West Country had settled, on 6 July, and immediately began their ministry. Among the colleagues who later joined them in Upper Canada were Philip JAMES and Ann Robins [VICKERY].

Elizabeth preached her first sermon in Cobourg on 10 July 1833. Later that month she set out alone on a 45-mile trip to Whitby Township to preach in a large barn in the woods. Often she and her husband went their separate ways on a 200-mile circuit, speaking in fields, woods, homes, or schools. Elizabeth rode in a one-horse carriage or walked. She took part in protracted meetings in the winter: at Cobourg for four weeks in 1838, and at Bowmanville in 1840 and 1842. In the summer of 1842 she also preached at field meetings in Bowmanville and Peterborough, and at a revival at Dummer Township. On her missions Elizabeth felt afraid and inadequate, but trusted in the power of the Lord. "I walked about six miles through the woods; on entering which, I was tempted that fear would overcome me; but after I proceeded some distance, I felt not the least fear, and my soul was so filled with heaven and God, that I felt all within was joy and love. . . . I could truly say I had fellowship with the Father, Son and Spirit." She was sensitive to her environment, recording in her journals the beauty of the woods and the waters. "I delight to see on the one hand the woods showing forth their beauty in so many shades of green; and on the other, the large Lake runs by Cobourg, shewing its fulness. These things lead me to reflect on the power of the Creator, and the valuable purposes they serve. The wood to make fire to communicate warmth in this icy climate, and the water for navigation to convey the necessaries of life to the inhabitants in its vicinity."

John suffered from the long journeys, hot summers, and severe winters. He was bedridden for several months in 1839, and Elizabeth took over his ministry in addition to her own. In 1848, both exhausted from their missionary work, they returned to England for a visit that lasted a year. Elizabeth had been plagued with ill health as a young woman, and was asthmatic for the last 20 years of her life. Yet, after returning from their visit, she remained active in the Cobourg church until her death in 1857.

ELIZABETH MUIR

Elizabeth Dart's journals and letters were published during her lifetime along with those of other Bible Christian missionaries in the *Bible Christian Magazine* (Shebbear, Eng.), 12 (1833)–36 (1857). Excerpts from the journals comprise the bulk of an uncredited biography, "Delayed but not forgotten: Elizabeth Dart Eynon," which appeared in a later organ of the Bible Christian Church in Canada, the *Observer* (Bowmanville, Ont.), 28 March–9 May, 23, 30 May, 25 July, and 1 Aug. 1883.

Bethesda Cemetery (Bowmanville), Tombstone of John Eynon and Elizabeth Dart Eynon. UCA, Bible Christian Church in Canada, minutes of the elders' meetings, Cobourg, 1849–55 (mfm.). Bible Christian Church in Canada, *Minutes of the annual conference* (Bowmanville), 1876–83. Bible Christians, *Minutes of the annual conference* (Stoke Damerel, Eng.), 1819. *Canadian Statesman* (Bowmanville), 22 Jan. 1857. *Cobourg Star*, 3 July 1833. F. W. Bourne, *Bible Christians; their origins and history, 1815–1900* ([London], 1905). William Luke, *The Bible Christians: their origins, constitution, doctrines, and history* (London, 1878). Methodist Church of Canada, General Conference, *Centennial of Canadian Methodism* (Toronto, 1891). *Canadian Statesman*, 24 March, 4 April 1888. W. Kenner, "Memoir of Rev. J. H. Eynon," *West Durham News* (Bowmanville), 20 April 1888: 1. Elizabeth Muir, "Petticoats in the pulpit: three early Canadian Methodist women," Canadian Soc. of Church Hist., *Papers* (Toronto), 1984. *West Durham News*, 23 March 1888.

DAULÉ, JEAN-DENIS, Roman Catholic priest and author; b. 18 Aug. 1766 in Paris, son of Firmin Daulé, a servant, and Marie-Madeleine Mireux; d. 17 Nov. 1852 in L'Ancienne-Lorette, Lower Canada.

Jean-Denis Daulé belonged to a family of modest means, originally from Picardy. At the time of his birth his parents were employed as servants in a large house on Rue Saint-Eustache in Paris. Treated generously by their master, they lived respectably. In his childhood Jean-Denis was free to go to Les Halles, the market, every day or to pray for a while in the church of Saint-Eustache and listen there to the choir of Saint-Sulpice, which was renowned for its glorious singing. It was one of the few places in Paris where concerts of religious music were still given.

Impressed by his remarkable memory and diligence, Daulé's first teachers helped him gain admittance to the Séminaire des Pauvres, where he received his classical education and began theological studies. In a moment of fervour, at the end of his two-year Philosophy program, he sought refuge in the Trappist monastery at Sept-Fons. But his exuberance disqualified him from admission into such an austere religious order. He returned to the seminary and

resumed the study of theology. On 30 March 1790, at the age of 23, he was ordained priest.

On 1 Oct. 1791 the French Constituent Assembly required all priests to take an oath to abide by the Civil Constitution of Clergy. Like many of his colleagues, Daulé refused. On 26 Aug. 1792 the Convention adopted a Draconian decree stipulating that any non-juring priest must leave France within a fortnight on pain of deportation to Guiana. To avoid the worst, Daulé fled from Paris; he went to Rouen, then to Calais, and from there crossed to England in October. In so doing he joined the large number of his fellow-countrymen who had already settled in London. A Catholic by the name of Winter took the refugee priest into his home; Daulé taught him French and learned English from him. It was not long before a fund was launched to assist impoverished ecclesiastics, and Lower Canada was identified by the English relief committee as a suitable asylum for many of these unfortunates. Daulé applied to go as soon as he learned of the committee's wishes.

On 26 June 1794, carrying only his breviary and his violin, Daulé landed at Quebec, together with Jean-Baptiste-Marie Castanet*, François-Gabriel Le Courtois*, and Louis-Joseph Desjardins*, *dit* Desplantes. On arriving they offered their services to Jean-François Hubert*, the bishop of Quebec, who welcomed them with open arms, for at that time Lower Canada badly needed priests. Daulé spent the summer in Saint-Joachim at the country home of the Séminaire de Québec as a guest of the superior, Henri-François Gravé* de La Rive. On 1 October he went to stay at the Jesuit college, where the last member of this order in Lower Canada, Jean-Joseph Casot*, lived. For one year he held the position of assistant priest in the parish of Notre-Dame at Quebec.

At the request of Pierre Denaut*, the new bishop of Quebec, Daulé assumed responsibility for the parish of Saint-Jean-Baptiste at Les Écureuils (Donnacona) on 15 Aug. 1795. The parish was experiencing great difficulties. It had been without a *curé* from 1766 to 1786, being served sporadically by priests from Sainte-Famille at Cap-Santé or Saint-François-de-Sales at Pointe-aux-Trembles (Neuville). Daulé's predecessor, Auguste-Pascal Tétreau, had been the victim of spite on the part of parishioners. Furthermore, the operation of a flour-mill on the banks of the Rivière Jacques-Cartier by George Allsopp*, a Protestant merchant of Cap-Santé, created problems. Nearly 200 men, mostly immigrants, worked at this mill. They were the only ones in the area to be paid in hard cash every Saturday, and most of them considered Sunday a day of pleasure, when they could do what they liked with their money. The prospect of wages attracted labourers from the parish, who turned away from agricultural work, and both family life and religious observance felt the effects. The new parish priest, an astute, diplomatic man who also spoke English, made repeated visits to the Allsopp residence and thus earned the goodwill of this influential family. In addition, Daulé spared no effort to attract the faithful to church: he delivered homilies interspersed with canticles which he composed and taught to his parishioners, and he played the violin so well that even the most hardened of them were won over.

On 13 June 1806 Daulé was appointed chaplain to the Ursulines of Quebec. He felt immediately at ease in his new office. He had an innovative mind, and gave the pupils in the convent a part in liturgical ceremonies; he himself trained them to sing the canticles he had set to music for them. It was at this time that Daulé undertook to produce a collection of canticles for religious services, in grateful acknowledgement of the warm welcome accorded him in Lower Canada. He secured the collaboration of Colonel Joseph-François-Xavier Perrault, the bandmaster of the Voltigeurs Canadiens, who provided him with songs of bygone times which he turned into canticles. Marie-Félicité Baillairgé, the daughter of Pierre-Florent*, herself an excellent musician and a former pupil of the Ursulines, composed much of the music for the collection. The work was published at Quebec in 1819 under the title *Nouveau recueil de cantiques à l'usage du diocèse de Québec*.

In 1815 and 1816, while performing his duties as chaplain, Daulé had ministered to the mission of Notre-Dame-de-Foy at Sainte-Foy. During the 1820s his sight grew progressively worse as a result of the many hours he had devoted to preparing his collection. By the spring of 1832 he was almost blind and was forced to resign as chaplain. On 14 May, with much regret, he left the Ursuline convent and was sent to the new parish of Saint-Roch, where he worked as a preacher and confessor. Then he spent a few months in Trois-Rivières. Finally he retired and went to live at L'Ancienne-Lorette, first in the home of Joseph Laberge, the parish priest of Notre-Dame-de-l'Annonciation, and then in a residence built for him by his protégé, the schoolmaster François-Xavier Gilbert, who spent the next 20 years in close association with him.

Jean-Denis Daulé died at L'Ancienne-Lorette on 17 Nov. 1852, at the age of 86. This refugee French priest had distinguished himself particularly by the collection of canticles he had prepared during his long years of service with the Ursulines of Quebec. French Canadians vied with one another in eagerness to sing these verses, which they adopted as their own, for they found in them their own feelings and aspirations expressed in a language of which they were proud. Daulé's talent as an author had enabled him to make a smooth transition from a classicism that had outlived its day to a romanticism that was to give individuality to poetry. In his own way, he had laboured for the survival of the French spirit in Lower Canada.

SUZANNE PRINCE

Jean-Denis Daulé is the author of *Nouveau recueil de cantiques à l'usage du diocèse de Québec* . . . and *Airs notés pour servir au "Nouveau Recueil de cantiques à l'usage du diocèse de Québec"* . . . , both published at Quebec in 1819.

AAQ, 20 A, II: 141, 218. AD, Paris, Etat civil, Saint-Nicolas-des-Champs, 18 août 1766. ANQ-Q, CE1-2, 19 nov. 1852. Arch. du monastère des ursulines (Québec), Annales, II: 94–95, 243, 327–28. ASN, AP-G, L.-É. Bois, G, 4: 125. ASQ, Polygraphie, XIII: 81. *L'Abeille*, 25 nov. 1852. *Le Journal de Québec*, 20 nov. 1852. Allaire, *Dictionnaire*, 1: 145. F.-M. Bibaud, *Le panthéon canadien* (A. et V. Bibaud; 1891), 66. *Encyclopedia of music in Canada* (Kallmann et al.), 253–54. Tanguay, *Répertoire* (1893): 159. G.-F. Baillairgé, *Notices biographiques et généalogiques, famille Baillairgé* . . . (11 fascicules, Joliette, Qué., 1891–94), 3: 87. [Catherine Burke, named Saint-Thomas], *Les Ursulines de Québec, depuis leur établissement jusqu'à nos jours* (4v., Québec, 1863–66), 4: 453–57. P.-B. Casgrain, *Mémorial des familles Casgrain, Baby et Perrault du Canada* (Québec, 1898), 181–82. N.-E. Dionne, *Les ecclésiastiques et les royalistes français réfugiés au Canada à l'époque de la révolution, 1791–1802* (Québec, 1905). Ernest Gagnon, *Choses d'autrefois, feuilles éparses* (Québec, 1905), 173. Ernest Myrand, *Noëls anciens de la Nouvelle-France* (Québec, 1899), 40–52, 171–78. Mère Sainte-Sophie-Barat [Suzanne Prince], "Jean-Denis Daulé et son époque (1765–1852)" (thèse de MA, univ. d'Ottawa, 1963), 47–49. L.-É. Bois, "L'Angleterre et le clergé français réfugié pendant la révolution," RSC *Trans.*, 1st ser., 3 (1885), sect.I: 82–83. G. du Chevrot, "Le père Daulé," *BRH*, 8 (1902): 345–47. "Les disparus," *BRH*, 36 (1930): 248. Ernest Gagnon, "Les prêtres français réfugiés au Canada pendant la révolution," *BRH*, 5 (1899): 187. Ernest Myrand, "Le père Daulé," *BRH*, 10 (1904): 253–54. H.-A. Scott, "Notre-Dame de Sainte-Foy," *BRH*, 6 (1900): 75.

DAVIDSON, ALEXANDER, teacher, author, journalist, businessman, politician, and office holder; b. 1794 in Downpatrick (Northern Ireland), son of Thomas Davidson; m. Mary —— (b. in Ireland), and they had at least one son and one daughter; d. 23 Feb. 1856 in St Catharines, Upper Canada.

Details about Alexander Davidson's childhood and youth are not known. He came to Upper Canada in 1821 under the auspices of Lord Castlereagh, secretary of state for foreign affairs, and obtained a 400-acre grant in Douro Township. The land, however, was "not at all fit for Agriculture," and the following year he began teaching school. Davidson disliked the extensive use of American textbooks in Upper Canadian schools. He noted in June 1828 to George Hillier*, the civil secretary at York, that in his experience nine out of ten books in use were from the

United States. In fact in his neighbourhood, he reported, "for several years past no English Books could be procured . . . so that I am led to believe that the supply from England is precarious, and not at all equal to the growing demands of the Province." In any case, spelling-books from England, Davidson was to assert in 1840, were "to *us* necessarily defective, not being suited to our scenery and other localities." But "books of a foreign origin [i.e. American] are liable to more serious objections." He complained to Hillier in July 1828 that, "unless some proper elementary books be got into general circulation, common school education will continue to be little better than a mere farce, and an useless expenditure of public money."

Intent upon correcting this lack, Davidson decided to write his own speller and in 1829 while resident in Port Hope he completed "The Upper Canadian spelling book." He made many efforts to gain government support in aid of publication but all came to naught. Finally in 1840 he succeeded in getting the manuscript published in Toronto by Henry Rowsell* under the title *The Canada spelling book*, the first copyrighted book in Upper Canada. The lessons in his speller were illustrated by references to Canadian places, and the necessary connection between religion and education was maintained by ensuring that each reading lesson would "subserve the interests of religion and morality." It was common for spellers of the day to provide moral lessons. When Egerton Ryerson* was appointed superintendent of schools for Upper Canada in 1844, Davidson tried to persuade him to adopt *The Canada spelling book* for use in the expanding common school system. Although Ryerson shared Davidson's concern about the widespread use of American textbooks in the colony's schools and praised the Canadian speller, he had decided to have published in Upper Canada the impressive Irish National Series. Therefore he wanted to give no encouragement to other publications which might interfere with general acceptance of his own scheme. None the less, by 1847 Davidson could enthusiastically report that 43,000 copies of the book had been sold, and by 1856 that figure had tripled. Although these figures were probably exaggerated, clearly the book was being widely used even without official government support and approval. Davidson added to his educational publications with *An introduction to the spelling book* (1843) and *The progressive primer* (1846). In 1847 he published *The domestic receipt book*, which was advertised as "A useful Compendium for Families."

A prominent layman in the Wesleyan Methodist Church, Davidson was the first Methodist class leader in Port Hope, conducting a mid-week study session beginning in 1824, and was named "Visitor" (inspector) to the newly founded Upper Canada Academy in Cobourg in 1836. He later compiled a tunebook entitled *Sacred harmony*, published and distributed in 1838 by the Wesleyan Methodist conference office in Toronto. One of the most comprehensive and influential of the pre-confederation tunebooks published in Canada, it was intended to be used as a book of praise and as a textbook for singing schools, a popular social movement in what is now eastern Canada, led by itinerant singing masters who taught harmony and choral singing to volunteer classes. *Sacred Harmony* contained a short introduction to the rudiments of music theory and composition and a selection of British and American tunes, many of which were arranged for three voices with the melody set in the tenor line following the American custom. A few of the tunes, for example "Toronto," were original pieces composed by Davidson himself. In its 1845 edition, *Sacred Harmony* was the only Canadian tunebook ever published using the tonic sol-fa system of shape notes.

By January 1837 Davidson was settled in Niagara (Niagara-on-the-Lake) as postmaster. From the post office he ran a bookshop where he sold a wide assortment of books, including his own, as well as stationery, hardware, and garden supplies. His position in Niagara was enhanced by a career as a municipal office holder which included seven years on the Niagara town council; frequent re-election as a trustee of the grammar and common schools; and several terms on the board of health, directing the accommodation of Irish immigrant families in the Niagara area. In 1849 he served as president of the Niagara Board of Police and in January of the following year was named the town's first mayor, serving a one-year term.

Davidson was also involved in the newspaper business, becoming publisher and editor of the *Niagara Mail* in April 1846. A reform paper, the *Mail*, according to a later local history, was in these years "marked by wit, vivacity, originality, [and] literary ability." In 1847 Davidson passed the editorial post on to his son, James Alexander Davidson, who, assisted by his father and Francis M. Whitelaw, also published a short-lived temperance newspaper known as the *Niagara Fountain*. Shortly thereafter Alexander Davidson attracted attention to himself and the *Mail* by supporting the free school system that Ryerson was promoting, thus challenging the conservative views of the "aristocracy of the Town." By October 1849 local opposition to him was such that Davidson appealed to government leader Robert BALDWIN for a fair hearing in the event that "a combination against me on account of my political opinions" should threaten his coveted job as postmaster. For a few months in late 1851 and early 1852 the *Mail* was published by the younger Davidson in nearby St Catharines, "the centre of political influence," but the paper had returned to Niagara, "for family convenience," by March 1852. Davidson and his son sold the paper in June 1853 to their editorial assistant, William Kirby*.

Davidson died on 23 Feb. 1856 at the American Hotel in St Catharines. The *Mail*, for some unexplained reason, gave him only a one-line obituary. The *St. Catharines Journal* was more generous in space and praise: "He was a man of superior talent, as many articles of his plainly demonstrated: could grapple with most subjects, and evinced an acute and logical mind in their treatment."

J. DONALD WILSON

[Although Alexander Davidson compiled the manuscript of his spelling-book in 1829, his first publication was *Sacred harmony: consisting of a variety of tunes, adapted to the different metres in the Wesleyan-Methodist hymn book; and a few anthems and favourite pieces; selected from the most approved authors, ancient and modern* (Toronto, 1838). It was republished at Toronto in 1845 with a supplement of tunes and anthems selected by Toronto musician E. W. Bliss from works by well-known European composers. Subsequent editions appeared in 1848, 1856, and 1860, published in round notation. *The Canada spelling book, intended as an introduction to the English language, consisting of a variety of lessons, progressively arranged in three parts, with an appendix containing several useful tables; the outlines of geography; a comprehensive sketch of English grammar, with morning and evening prayers for every day of the week; the words divided and accented according to the purest mode of pronunciation* (Toronto, 1840) was also reissued several times by various Toronto publishing houses in 1842, 1845–48 inclusive, 1856, and 1864. At Niagara (Niagara-on-the-Lake, Ont.), Davidson published a collection of school texts under the series title Colonial School Books which included *An introduction to the spelling book* (1843) and *The progressive primer* (1846). He also published a household guide entitled *The domestic receipt book* (Niagara, 1847). J.D.W.]

AO, MS 74, package 22, Alexander Davidson to W. H. Merritt, 5 Sept. 1854, 7 March 1855; RG 1, A-I-6: 6542–44. MTL, Robert Baldwin papers, Alexander Davidson to Baldwin, 6 Oct. 1849. PAC, RG 1, L3, 156, pt.1: D13/52; RG 5, A1: 49113–15, 49576–77; B11, 3, file 196; 4, file 520. Can., Prov. of, Legislative Assembly, *App. to the journals*, 1846, app.F. *Doc. hist. of education in U.C.* (Hodgins), 2: 127; 6: 172, 240, 285–86. *Christian Guardian*, 5 March 1856. *Niagara Fountain*, March 1847. *Niagara Mail*, 1 April 1846–15 June 1853; 27 Feb. 1856. *St. Catharines Journal* (St Catharines, [Ont.]), 28 Feb. 1856. Nathanael Burwash, *The history of Victoria College* (Toronto, 1927), 491. Janet Carnochan, *History of Niagara* ... (Toronto, 1914; repr. Belleville, Ont., 1973). W. A. Craick, *Port Hope historical sketches* (Port Hope, Ont., 1901), 19, 71–72, 84. *Historical sketch of Methodism in Canada and Port Hope* (Port Hope, 1925), 12–14. C. B. Sissons, *Egerton Ryerson: his life and letters* (2v., Toronto, 1937–47), 1: 218–19. W. R. Riddell, "The first copyrighted book in the Province of Canada," *OH*, 25 (1929): 405–14.

J. D. Wilson, "Common school texts in use in Upper Canada prior to 1845," Biblio. Soc. of Canada, *Papers* (Toronto), 9 (1970): 36–53.

DE BLAQUIÈRE, PETER BOYLE, militia officer, politician, office holder, and university official; b. 26 April 1783 in Dublin, fifth son of Sir John Blaquiere and Eleanor Dobson; m. first 13 Sept. 1804 Eliza O'Brien (d. 1814) of Newcastle (Newcastle West, Republic of Ireland), and they had four sons and three daughters; m. secondly 26 Nov. 1818 Eliza Roper of Rathfarnham Castle, County Dublin (Republic of Ireland), and they had three sons and five daughters; d. 23 Oct. 1860 in Yorkville (Toronto), Upper Canada.

Peter Boyle de Blaquière's Canadian career clearly owed much to the reputation and rank of his father. John Blaquiere, son of a French *émigré* who had settled in London, became secretary of legation in France and accompanied Lord Harcourt to Ireland as chief secretary on the latter's appointment as lord lieutenant in 1772. When Harcourt resigned four years later, Blaquiere remained in Ireland. He was elected to the Irish parliament, was made a baronet in 1784, and was created Baron de Blaquiere of Ardkill, County Londonderry (Northern Ireland), in 1800. His eldest son, John, succeeded him to the peerage in 1812. Thus, when Peter Boyle de Blaquière emigrated to Upper Canada in 1837, he was the son and brother of a peer and the prefix "Honourable" was attached to his name in his own right. A half-century later his grandson William would inherit the family title, which became extinct in 1920.

Yet little is known of the first half-century of de Blaquière's life. He served in the Royal Navy as a midshipman on the *Director*, commanded by Captain William Bligh of *Bounty* fame. During the mutiny at the Nore in May and June of 1797, Bligh and three midshipmen, including de Blaquière, were forced off their ship, but they were able to return and were present at the battle of Camperdown that October when the Dutch fleet was destroyed. After de Blaquière left the navy, he maintained a residence in Southampton, where baptismal, marriage, and other records from the 1820s and 1830s relating to him and his family survive. He served as an honorary burgess, was an active tory in both local and national politics, strongly supported the Church of England, and was interested in railway promotion. In these respects his Canadian career was foreshadowed.

In Upper Canada de Blaquière was received as a person of considerable consequence. He came in 1837 with his large family, apparently with some means, and bought property in the recently founded village of Woodstock in Oxford County. Here he was in the midst of a remarkable settlement of gentry, half-pay officers from Great Britain who had begun taking up land earlier in the decade and had acquired influence over all aspects of local government. Among the best known of his neighbours were former naval officers Rear-Admiral Henry Vansittart and Commander Andrew Drew*. The latter called upon de Blaquière within months of his arrival to collect pikes for the attack on the *Caroline*. As lieutenant-colonel of the 3rd Regiment of Oxford militia, de Blaquière himself played an active role in suppressing the rebellion. Held high in local regard, in 1838 he was selected churchwarden at St Paul's, the first Anglican congregation in Woodstock [see William Craddock Bettridge*], and in 1842 he was appointed warden of the Brock District.

In 1837 Sir Francis Bond Head* had recommended that de Blaquière be appointed to the Legislative Council. The lieutenant governor described him as "a very intelligent man, a good speaker," adding, "he is besides almost the only Irishman I can name" (undoubtedly a reference to de Blaquière's social standing and tory views). He did in fact become a legislative councillor in 1839, and two years later he was continued in the Legislative Council of the United Province of Canada. In the council de Blaquière appears not to have been a figure of the first importance. A man of strong tory instincts, he found it difficult to accept the transition to responsible government although he was on good personal terms with reform leaders Robert BALDWIN and Francis HINCKS*. Perhaps his convictions were too firm to allow him to engage in the game of party politics and to approve the policy of bringing French Canadians into the government. At any rate, he was passed over by Governor Sir Charles Theophilus Metcalfe* both for the speakership of the Legislative Council in 1843 [see René-Édouard Caron*] and for a place in the Executive Council the following year. In 1850 Lord Elgin [Bruce*] wrote that de Blaquière had "maintained a kind of huffy seclusion for the last four years because Lord Metcalfe did not make him Speaker of the Legislative Council." The journals of the council reveal that for several years after 1844 de Blaquière was frequently absent, sometimes for an entire session. In 1856, however, he made a point of being present to lead ten members in a dissent against the measure to make the council elective, since it would give "undue preponderance to the popular element" and tend to "the separation of Canada from the Parent State." Yet near the end of his life he voted in favour of making the speakership of the council elective. The Toronto *Globe* suggested in 1860 that de Blaquière had been "an exception to the rule" that men become more conservative with age.

Although a prominent and unswerving layman of the Church of England, de Blaquière was quite prepared, if necessary, to break a lance with the redoubtable bishop of Toronto, John Strachan*. On 31 Jan. 1850, from Rockwood, his residence near Kingston where he had moved when the provincial capital was located there, de Blaquière wrote a public letter proposing a drastic reorganization of the Church of England: election of two more bishops and triennial convocations in which the clergy and laity would share power with the bishop. At the same time he submitted a draft bill on the subject which he proposed to introduce in the Legislative Council. For de Blaquière to make this public proposal without consulting the bishop was regarded as outrageous, and a storm of abuse descended upon him. In fact, as events in the next half dozen years would show, the church was moving in this direction. In 1856, when Strachan was ready to ask for enabling legislation to prepare the way for synodical government, he asked de Blaquière to pilot the bill through the council.

A much more serious difference between the two men arose out of the university question. In 1849 the legislature passed a bill transforming the Anglican-oriented King's College into the secular University of Toronto and transferring the substantial endowment of the former to the latter. Bishop Strachan regarded this action as a monstrous act of betrayal and spoliation. He expected faithful members of the Church of England to support him in his denunciations of the "godless" University of Toronto and in his efforts to raise money, in Canada and England, to found a new church university, Trinity College. It was soon clear, however, that not all Anglicans in Canada supported the bishop; in particular, when the first senate of the University of Toronto was announced early in 1850, the list of 25 names was headed by that of the Honourable Peter Boyle de Blaquière. Soon afterward the convocation of the university proceeded to the election of a chancellor and, when Chief Justice James Buchanan MACAULAY declined the honour, it was offered to and, on 4 May 1850, accepted by de Blaquière. He had recently moved from Kingston to Toronto "for the express purpose of affording to my son the inestimable advantage of academical education," and he was to reside just north of the city in Yorkville for the remainder of his life.

Meanwhile the 72-year-old Strachan had sailed for England where he spent several months raising money, seeking a royal charter for Trinity College, and denouncing the University of Toronto as "Anti-Christian" and "Impious." Word of the bishop's activities led Chancellor de Blaquière into vigorous and lengthy defences of the university, and on Strachan's return the two men engaged in a bitter exchange of views which was published in the newspapers. Strachan insisted that the Church of England had a right to form, with its own funds, a church university to replace the "suppressed" King's College. With equal vehemence, de Blaquière insisted that there must be but one university in Upper Canada receiving public support, and that the Church of

Deblois

England should limit itself to the founding of a divinity school. He further charged that Strachan had acted without consulting "our Church, as such," and Strachan retorted that de Blaquière, "in a most unkind spirit," had issued "a slanderous Paper."

To some extent, the contest was a draw. The establishing of Trinity College in 1851–52 shook but did not destroy the University of Toronto. A half-century later the college federated with the university. As for de Blaquière, he resigned the chancellorship in October 1852 in protest against Francis Hincks's bill, made law in 1853, that reorganized the University of Toronto along lines similar to the University of London.

Peter Boyle de Blaquière was obviously not a typical Upper Canadian of his time, but he was an outstanding representative of a fairly large number of upper class and upper middle class emigrants from the "Parent State" who offered political, educational, and social leadership in the land of their adoption.

G. M. CRAIG

[The assistance of Miss S. D. Thomson, City Archivist, in providing information on Peter Boyle de Blaquière from records held in the Southampton City Record Office (Southampton, Eng.) is gratefully acknowledged. G.M.C.]

AO, MS 35; MU 2863, Andrew Drew to [de] Blaquière, 23 Dec. 1837. MTL, Robert Baldwin papers. PAC, RG 7, G14, 9: 3986–96. *Arthur papers* (Sanderson). Can., Prov. of, Legislative Council, *Journals*, 1841–61. *Doc. hist. of education in U.C.* (Hodgins), vols.9–10. *Elgin–Grey papers* (Doughty). *British Colonist* (Toronto), 1839–40. *Chronicle & Gazette*, 5 Oct., 21 Dec. 1839; 25, 29 Jan. 1840; 2, 23 Feb., 28 Sept. 1842; 30 Sept., 18 Oct. 1843; 25 May 1847. *Church*, 14, 21 Feb., 14 March, 25 April, 6, 27 June, 4 July 1850. *Cobourg Star*, 4 May 1859. *Globe*, 1 May 1850; 7, 9, 11 Jan. 1851; 25 Oct. 1860. *Pilot* (Montreal), 12 Aug. 1844. *DNB* (biog. of John Blaquiere). L. G. Pine, *The new extinct peerage, 1884–1971: containing extinct, abeyant, dormant & suspended peerages; with genealogies and arms* (London, 1972). Brian Dawe, *"Old Oxford is wide awake!" pioneer settlers and politicians in Oxford County, 1793–1853* (n.p., 1980). J. A. Froude, *The English in Ireland in the eighteenth century* (3v., New York, 1873–74). George Mackaness, *The life of Vice-Admiral William Bligh, R.N., F.R.S.* (2v., Sydney and London, 1931; rev. ed., 1v., 1951). Read, *Rising in western U.C.* Arthur Sweatman, *A sketch of the history of the parish of Woodstock* ([Woodstock, Ont., 1902?]).

DEBLOIS, JOSEPH-FRANÇOIS, militia officer, lawyer, businessman, politician, and judge; b. 22 April 1797 at Quebec, son of François Deblois, a merchant, and Marie-Geneviève Létourneau; d. there 10 Aug. 1860.

Joseph-François Deblois entered the Petit Séminaire de Québec in 1810 and studied there until 1813. In the autumn of 1812, after war had broken out with the United States, he was serving as an ensign in Quebec's 1st Militia Battalion. At the time of his father's death in January 1814 the family business was doing reasonably well and, since Joseph-François was the eldest son, he gave his mother a hand in running the store. He received legal training in the office of Louis Lagueux*, a Quebec lawyer, from 1821 to 1826, while continuing to work part time for his mother. He was called to the bar on 1 April 1826.

To help his mother, who was being pursued by various creditors for more than £980, Deblois in May released her from the obligation to repay a substantial sum she owed him, and along with his brothers gave up his rights of inheritance. With others, he also stood surety for her. Since her creditors had granted an extension of time for payment, Deblois decided to try his luck in the district of Gaspé, "which he had heard much about." After visiting the region, he thought he had found an effective way to solve the family's financial problems and returned to Quebec to make the preparations and purchases for operating a large herring fishery at Baie de Cascapédia in the Baie des Chaleurs. At the end of August 1826 he was back in the Gaspé with his brother François-Xavier, who was to manage the store established in New Richmond. However, the results of the fishery were meagre and Deblois incurred liabilities that included wages and food for the workers and rent for the sheds. In addition, the boats, nets, and fishing tackle suffered damage. The business therefore showed financial losses in the autumn of 1826.

Concurrently with this venture, Deblois began to practise as attorney and lawyer for the Provincial Court in the district of Gaspé. Thus he became one of the first lawyers to engage in his profession on a permanent basis in the Gaspé. On 28 July 1827 he purchased a farm and two lots at New Carlisle, a small loyalist village which was the chief administrative and judicial centre of the region. François-Xavier soon joined him, as did his mother and younger brother. Deblois acquired two other properties at New Carlisle in December 1828, and another in April 1830. Around 1830 the farm had a few animals, which were tended by a hired hand.

In the autumn of 1834 Deblois ran for the House of Assembly in Bonaventure, a riding with two members. He was elected on 5 December with another lawyer, Édouard Thibaudeau*, who was returned for a second term. *Le Canadien* called both men "reformers," and ascribed the defeat of the previous member, John Robinson Hamilton, to his vote against the 92 Resolutions. Deblois seems to have benefited from the help of the missionary based at Carleton, Louis-Stanislas Malo, whose territory included the western part of the constituency.

Meanwhile, it seems that Deblois's financial position had not really improved. On 13 Sept. 1834 he borrowed money from Amasa Bebee, the clerk of the

Provincial Court in the district of Gaspé, and mortgaged his five properties and farm at New Carlisle. On 15 April 1835, a few months after his arrival in Quebec for the assembly session, he learned that Bebee was suing him for £64, and that a judgement against him for non-payment of debt had been delivered in the Provincial Court in the district of Gaspé during his absence by Judge John Gawler Thompson. Hamilton, a lawyer at New Carlisle and Thompson's nephew seems to have been behind both this action and another launched by Peter Du Val, a merchant of Île Bonaventure, around the same period.

On 16 Nov. 1835 Deblois called in the house for the dismissal of Judge Thompson. Deblois accused Thompson of incompetence and of "high crimes and misdemeanors," of being "partial, capricious, arbitrary and vindictive," of frequent drunkenness while exercising his office, and of having meddled in the last election in Bonaventure along with "the declared enemies of the liberties of the People." This affair, which had begun with two rival groups in conflict at the local level, quickly moved onto the provincial stage, with successive clashes between the assembly and the Executive Council. At the same time the Patriote members were also protesting against the appointment of Samuel Gale* in 1834 to the Court of King's Bench in Montreal. During this debate on government appointments, it became known that Thompson was, in fact, a friend of Lord Dalhousie [Ramsay*], the former governor, and of Robert Christie, an erstwhile member for Gaspé.

The charges by Deblois were laid before the assembly's standing committee on grievances, on which he sat. On 12 March 1836 the committee declared that it endorsed them, and it recommended to Governor Gosford [Acheson*] that Thompson be suspended from office, pending dismissal. The house approved a resolution on the matter by 37 to 4. However, Gosford was unwilling to reach a decision before hearing Thompson. In the autumn of 1836 the latter, along with a number of his supporters, assured the governor that Deblois was contradicting himself, for he had previously defended the judge when complaints were levelled against him in 1827 and 1828; they suggested that Deblois had resented the competition from Hamilton and wanted to be appointed to the judiciary in Thompson's place. Gosford referred the question to Lord Glenelg, the colonial secretary, who turned it over to the Judicial Committee of the Privy Council. The governor decided not to dismiss Thompson before receiving a reply from London. The decision apparently was favourable to Thompson for he continued to hold office.

Following the outbreak of rebellion and the suspension of Lower Canada's constitution, parliament was dissolved on 27 March 1838. Deblois none

the less remained at Quebec, where he continued to practise law. He was also a captain in Quebec's 1st and 2nd militia battalions (in the 1830s he had been an adjutant of militia in the Gaspé).

Deblois was appointed one of two circuit judges for the district of Gaspé on 9 July 1849, and took up residence at Percé on 6 August. His circuit also included the Îles de la Madeleine. The second magistrate was none other than Judge Thompson, who was stationed at New Carlisle. As magistrate, Deblois was sought after in many ways by the inhabitants of the peninsula. On 27 Feb. 1852, for instance, he became the president of the Société d'Agriculture de Gaspé. His financial problems apparently had been settled, for he often gave or lent large sums to various *fabriques* of Gaspé County, especially to help with the construction of churches at Grande-Rivière and Cap-d'Espoir and of a school at Percé. In 1857 he lent £300 to the archdiocese of Quebec. He had entrusted the administration and management of his affairs at Quebec to notary Michel Tessier. Between 1852 and 1857 he had purchased a piece of land and two building sites at Saint-Lazare, near Quebec, on which he set up his brother François-Xavier.

In June 1857 the post of circuit judge was abolished by act of parliament, and Deblois was not assigned to any other office. It had been suggested that he seek retirement, to avoid appearing to have been dismissed. He thus obtained a pension equivalent to one-third of his salary as judge. In May 1858 he moved to Quebec, where he died on 10 Aug. 1860 after a few days of illness.

MARC DESJARDINS

AAQ, T, D. AC, Bonaventure (New-Carlisle), Minutiers, J.-G. Lebel, 25 janv., 10 oct. 1835; Martin Sheppard, 28 juill. 1827, 12 nov. 1830. ANQ-Q, CE1-1, 22 avril 1797; CN1-261, 6 juin, 26 juill. 1859; P1000-27-505. ASQ, E, 4. PAC, MG 30, D1, 10: 94–96; RG 4, B8, 22: 8018–27; RG 9, I, A5, 13–16; A6, 1–3; A7, 18. Bas-Canada, Chambre d'Assemblée, *Journaux*, 1835–36: 143–44, 500–1, 693–94, app.EE, app.OO. Can., Prov. of, Legislative Assembly, *App. to the journals*, 1841, app.W. *Le Canadien*, 7 janv. 1835. *Le Courrier du Canada*, 13, 15 août 1860. *La Gazette de Québec*, 7 janv. 1835. F.-J. Audet, "Les législateurs du Bas-Canada." *Quebec almanac*, 1826–41. *Quebec directory*, 1847–50. P.-G. Roy, *Les avocats de la région de Québec*; *Fils de Québec*, 3: 79–81; *Les juges de la prov. de Québec*, 153. J.-G. Barthe, *Souvenirs d'un demi-siècle ou mémoires pour servir à l'histoire contemporaine* (Montréal, 1885), 169–80. Jules Bélanger et al., *Histoire de la Gaspésie* (Montréal, 1981). Christie, *Hist. of L.C.* (1848–55), 4: 205–8. "Les disparus," *BRH*, 32 (1926): 172.

DECOW (DeCew, DeCou), JOHN, businessman, office holder, and militia officer; b. 3 Feb. 1766 in New Jersey, probably in Sussex County, son of Jacob

DeCow

DeCow, a loyalist; m. 9 Aug. 1798 Catherine Docksteder, and they had five sons and six daughters; d. 25 March 1855 in DeCewsville, Upper Canada.

John DeCow came to the Niagara peninsula in 1787. After extensive exploration, including service with a survey crew in 1788, he acquired a mill-site on the Beaver Dams branch of Twelve Mile Creek in Thorold Township. There, in 1792, DeCow built one of the first sawmills in the Nassau District of Upper Canada. Later efforts to secure other sites near the Niagara River failed but, aided by Queenston merchant Robert Hamilton*, DeCow added a grist-mill and probably a linseed-oil mill. Located on a principal road, DeCew Falls quickly became an important milling centre in the region. (DeCew Falls, like other places named after the subject, employs a popular variant later adopted by the family.) Between 1799 and 1835 DeCow also served frequently as an assessor, collector, and warden for Thorold. A founding member in 1800 of the Niagara Library, the province's first circulating library, he also served as a director of the Niagara Agricultural Society in 1804.

During the War of 1812 DeCow, a commissioned militia officer since 1797, commanded a company of the 2nd Lincoln Militia. His stone house, located on a major stream which, with the adjacent escarpment, constituted a strategic defensive line, was occupied as a British headquarters and stores. It was in this house in June 1813 that Laura Secord [Ingersoll*] warned James FitzGibbon* of the planned American attack at Beaver Dams (Thorold). DeCow himself, while returning to his home in the British retreat from Fort George (Niagara-on-the-Lake), had been captured on 29 May 1813 and was eventually incarcerated in an infamous Philadelphia prison, the "Invincible." He escaped on 20 April 1814 and, aided en route by Quakers, he vigilantly journeyed to Lower Canada despite being painfully retarded by a broken foot. That June he reached the Niagara front, where he rejoined his regiment for the duration of the war.

Although DeCow remained in the militia until 1823, he restored and expanded his milling and farming operations following the war. Plagued by an irregular supply of water for the mills, he responded favourably to the proposal of another mill-owner, William Hamilton Merritt*, to stabilize supply and improve transportation by means of a canal linking Twelve Mile Creek and the Chippewa (Welland) River. In 1818 the initial route was charted via DeCew Falls and six years later DeCow joined with others to form the Welland Canal Company. Subsequent route changes, with the resulting diversion of water-power from DeCow's mills, completely alienated his support and in 1825 he withdrew his company stock. Only after repeated petitioning between 1830 and 1836 did he receive any compensation for losses at his mills. DeCow's plans to establish a less vulnerable industry

in the area, a window-glass manufactory, collapsed when the company's bill of incorporation failed to obtain Legislative Council approval in 1829.

In the provincial election of 1832 Merritt's candidacy in Haldimand attracted DeCow's vindictive opposition. DeCow's Methodism, hatred of the canal, and association with William Lyon Mackenzie*'s reform politics, then rampant throughout the peninsula, were scathingly attacked by Colonel John Clark as the "frontier interest," but DeCow was only narrowly defeated. He continued to assail the canal company, and in 1834 supported the reform challenge by David Thorburn in another Niagara riding. Although DeCow led Thorold Township petitioners in condemning the provincial administration in 1836, he took no apparent part in the rebellion of 1837–38.

About 1834 a frustrated DeCow had relocated on former Indian land in the Haldimand County township of North Cayuga, where he soon erected a sawmill. He failed to secure ferry and bridge rights across the Grand River but, as one of the earliest promoters of glass production in Upper Canada, he again pushed to establish a glassworks. The report of a Pennsylvania glass-man confirmed the suitability of his property for a works and in 1835 the Cayuga Glass Manufacturing Company was incorporated. The disruptive effect of the rebellion reportedly led to the charter's expiry. In 1845 the defeat of a new bill for incorporation finally forced DeCow to abandon any plans for actual production.

DeCow's industrial pursuits were sustained by his milling, farming, and lime kiln operations, which stimulated the growth near by of a small hamlet, DeCewsville. Although DeCow had apparently retired by 1851, he remained keenly interested in politics. Mackenzie's victory as an independent reformer in the Haldimand by-election of that year rekindled his anti-government hostility. Three of his sons, John, Robert, and William, openly supported Mackenzie's damning investigation of government affairs. Writing of his father's good health in 1853, William conveyed DeCow's final sentiment to the ageing radical: "He has you fresh in his memory and often enquires where you are, wonders why he cant get to see you oftener, and rejoices at the downfall of Toryism."

DAVID ROBERTS

[Indispensable for any study of John DeCow are Ernest Green's excellent article "John DeCou, pioneer," *OH*, 22 (1925): 92–116, and *The genealogy of the De Cou family, showing the descent of the members of this family in America from Leuren des Cou of the Sandtoft colony, a Huguenot settlement in Lincolnshire, England, founded about 1630,* comp. S. E. and J. A. DeCou ([Philadelphia, 1926]; repr. Ann Arbor, Mich., 1978). A compilation of John DeCow's reminiscences, prepared by his sons Edmund and Robert, was first published in the *Haldimand Advocate* (Cayuga, Ont.) of 1888. The relevant issues could not be located, if they exist, but Green quotes frequently from the reminiscences, presumably from the 1888 compilation. Differing versions and extracts also appear in *Jubilee history of Thorold Township and town from the time of the red man to the present*, [comp. M. H. S. Wetherell] (Thorold, Ont., 1897–98), and in [Edmond DeCew], "Reminiscences of Captain DeCew," ed. E. Munro, Niagara Hist. Soc., [*Pub.*] (Niagara [Niagara-on-the-Lake], Ont.), no.36 (1924): 84–92. Because of John DeCow's advanced age, and apparent errors in transcription or printing, the reminiscences are inaccurate on several details. D.R.]

AO, MS 74, package 59, no.41; package 60, no.68; MS 516, John DeCew [Jr.] to Mackenzie, 14 May, 16 June 1851; Robert DeCew to Mackenzie, 18 June 1851; William DeCew to Mackenzie, 22 Nov. 1853; indenture, announcing Mackenzie's election in Haldimand, 21 April 1851; petitions, electors of Haldimand to Mackenzie, 11 Aug. 1851; RG 1, A-I-6: 11430–32; A-II-2, 1: 91; C-I-1, petitions of John DeCow, 20 April 1819, 4 June 1834; John DeCew, 19 Sept. 1841; C-IV, Cayuga Township, concession 1 (north), lot 40; Thorold Township, concessions 1 and 2, lot 16; RG 22, ser.256, ser.260, John DeCew. PAC, MG 24, E1, 11; I8, 28: 87–92; RG 1, L3, 149: D1/74; 150: D2/16, 84; 152: D6/36, D7/1, 2; 153: D10/34c, d; 154: D11/16; 269: K5/29; RG 5, A1: 19664–67, 20915–16, 39353–54, 47923–24, 69768–70, 70089–91, 71736–40, 76261–63, 81460–63, 84729–31, 137460–63; RG 8, I (C ser.), 679: 140–41; 684: 179; 688C; 116; 688E: 229; 690: 124; 692: 44, 267; RG 9, I, B1, 1: 223, 225; 3: 11; 22: 322–28; B2, 30: 253. Can., Prov. of, Legislative Assembly, *Journals*, 1841, 1843–45. "District of Nassau; letter book no.2," AO *Report*, 1905: 335; "District of Nassau; register of the lots in the townships of that district; book no.3," AO *Report*, 1905: 345. *Doc. hist. of campaign upon Niagara frontier* (Cruikshank), vols.1–6. "Grants of crown lands in U.C.," AO *Report*, 1929: 78. U.C., House of Assembly, *Journal*, 1829–31, 1833–36. "Upper Canada land book B, 19th August, 1796, to 7th April, 1797," AO *Report*, 1930: 50. *British American Journal* (St Catharines, [Ont.]), 17 June, 10 Aug., 4 Dec. 1834; 29 Jan. 1835. *British Colonial Argus* (St Catharines), 28 Sept., 6 Oct. 1833. *Cobourg Star*, 7 Nov. 1832. *St. Catharines Journal*, 31 May 1834; 4 Aug., 8 Dec. 1836; 17 May 1840; 20 Jan., 17 March 1842; 20 Feb. 1845. J. N. Jackson, *St. Catharines, Ontario; its early years* (Belleville, Ont., 1976). J. P. Merritt, *Biography of the Hon. W. H. Merritt . . .* (St Catharines, 1875). R. L. Gentilcore, "The beginnings of settlement in the Niagara peninsula (1782–1792)," *Canadian Geographer* ([Ottawa]), 7 (1963): 72–82. H. V. Nelles, "Loyalism and local power; the district of Niagara, 1792–1837," *OH*, 58 (1966): 99–114. J. W. Watson, "The changing industrial pattern of the Niagara peninsula; a study in historical geography," *OH*, 37 (1945): 49–58.

DELPHINE, MARIE-ANTOINETTE FONT-BONNE, named **Sister.** *See* FONTBONNE

DÉMARAY, PIERRE-PAUL, notary, office holder, justice of the peace, militia officer, Patriote, and politician; b. 8 Oct. 1798 in Trois-Rivières, Lower Canada, son of Pierre Démarest, a carpenter, and Louise Patrie; m. 15 June 1825 Marie-Jovite Descombes-Porcheron, widow of notary Roger-François Dandurand, in Laprairie (La Prairie), Lower Canada, and they had one son; d. 17 Sept. 1854 in Saint-Jean (Saint-Jean-sur-Richelieu), Lower Canada.

Nothing is known of Pierre-Paul Démaray's early years. After studying for a while he decided to become a notary, and from 1819 to 1824 worked as a clerk under Pierre Lanctôt and Laurent Archambault at Sainte-Marguerite-de-Blairfindie (L'Acadie), and Jean-Emmanuel Dumoulin at Trois-Rivières. He was admitted to the notarial profession on 17 April 1824 and began his career at Dorchester (Saint-Jean-sur-Richelieu). He soon built up a substantial practice, which eventually included landowners and local merchants such as GABRIEL, Louis, and François Marchand.

Closely associated with the founding of the parish of Saint-Jean-l'Évangéliste, Démaray acted as first secretary-treasurer of the *fabrique* from 16 Nov. 1828 until his resignation on 4 May 1834. On 25 Dec. 1829 he was elected churchwarden of the parish and, although 1832, when he held the post of chief warden, was the last year of his term, he did not render his accounts until 2 June 1833. In this period Démaray also obtained other public offices, such as those of commissioner for the construction of the high road between Dorchester and Laprairie (1831), commissioner for the trial of small causes (1832), and justice of the peace (1833). He also carried out the duties of postmaster in Dorchester and served as a lieutenant in the 3rd Militia Battalion of Chambly County.

In 1837 Démaray attracted attention by his zeal for the Patriotes' cause. After attending the Assemblée des Six Comtés at Saint-Charles-sur-Richelieu on 23 October, he took part on 5 November in the meeting at Saint-Athanase (Iberville), where he moved a resolution calling for the abolition of seigneurial tenure. The next day he resigned as justice of the peace and as militia lieutenant in protest against the "tyrannical" administration of Governor Lord Gosford [Acheson*]. Then on 10 November, with Joseph-François Davignon, a doctor from Dorchester, he led a group of Patriotes which attacked a cavalry troop returning from a reconnaissance to Saint-Athanase.

On the eve of the rebellion, Démaray, who was considered the leader of the Patriotes at Dorchester, was among those against whom a warrant of arrest for high treason was issued. During the night of 16–17 November a detachment of the Royal Montreal Cavalry under Charles Oakes Ermatinger Jr burst into the homes of Démaray and Davignon and took them prisoner. Learning that they were being taken to the Montreal prison, Bonaventure Viger* ambushed the detachment on the Chambly road several hours later

Demers

with a handful of men and managed to free the two prisoners. Shortly after, Démaray and Davignon fled to the United States. On 29 November Lord Gosford issued new warrants for the two Patriotes and offered a reward of £100 each for their capture. When the new governor, Lord Durham [Lambton*], proclaimed an amnesty on 8 June 1838, he specifically excluded Démaray. During his exile Démaray lived at St Albans, Vt, and then at Keeseville, N.Y., and for his livelihood opened a grocery store at Plattsburgh in partnership with his compatriot, Médard Hébert, a notary from Laprairie.

Taking advantage of a subsequent amnesty, Démaray returned to Lower Canada and resumed notarial practice in Dorchester on 9 May 1841. There he began to create difficulties for his parish priest, Charles La Rocque*. He criticized the clergy for the attitude they had adopted at the time of the rebellion and subjected La Rocque to numerous trials.

Démaray took up municipal politics in 1845. On 28 July he was elected the first mayor of Saint-Jean-l'Évangéliste and he retained this office until the parish municipality was abolished in 1847. During his term the inhabitants of the village of Dorchester presented him with a plan to seek municipal incorporation for their community. However, Démaray did not deign to take action. On 1 Sept. 1847 the government of the Province of Canada decided to abolish parish municipalities and replace them by county municipalities. Under the new law the parish of Saint-Jean-l'Évangéliste, incorporated into Chambly County, was entitled to two representatives on the county council. Démaray did not run in the elections for these new posts, which were held on 14 September at Dorchester, but with Pierre-Moïse Moreau he apparently carried out the duties of election agent for Samuel Vaughan and Louis Marchand. In this capacity Démaray and Moreau unsuccessfully contested the election of James Bissett and Henry Larocque as councillors.

Démaray began campaigning as a candidate in a by-election for Chambly in December 1847, but was defeated in January 1848 by Dr Pierre Beaubien*. He returned to the municipal scene two years later and on 9 July 1850 managed to get himself elected councillor for the village of Saint-Jean (incorporated in July 1848). He succeeded Benjamin Burland as its third mayor on 11 Aug. 1851. Under his administration the village's first police corps was created. On 11 July 1853 Démaray gave up the mayoralty and again became a councillor. Then on 22 August he was appointed one of the two delegates to represent the parish of Saint-Jean-l'Évangéliste at the Anti-Seigniorial Tenure Convention called in the Montreal district; he was elected to represent Chambly County on the central committee of this large gathering, which was held at Montreal on 1 September.

Pierre-Paul Démaray remained a councillor until the end of his term of office in July 1854. He died at Saint-Jean that September at age 55, after a month's illness. One of the most active public figures of his day in that community, he was still serving at the time of his death as a notary and a justice of the peace. His passing was deeply regretted by his fellow-citizens, who had always seen him "in the forefront of those who had at heart the progress of the little town of which he was one of the most outstanding members." He was mourned by his widow and his son, Pierre-Octave, who pursued a career as a lawyer in Saint-Jean and Montreal.

LIONEL FORTIN

Pierre-Paul Démaray's minute-book, containing instruments notarized between 1824 and 1854, is held at ANQ-M, CN4-16.

ANQ-M, CE1-2, 15 juin 1825; CE4-10, 20 sept. 1854; CN1-12, 10 mai 1822; CN4-15, 26 mars 1819. ANQ-MBF, CE1-48, 8 oct. 1798; CN1-6, 17 janv. 1824. ANQ-Q, E17/6, nos.50–70; E17/7, nos.131–32, 134; E17/8, no.262; E17/15, nos.853–54; E17/34, nos.2755a, 2756; E17/37, no.3035. AP, Saint-Jean-l'Évangéliste, livres des délibérations de la fabrique, 16 nov. 1828, 25 déc. 1829, 25 déc. 1832, 2 juin 1833, 4 mai 1834. Arch. de la ville de Longueuil (Longueuil, Qué.), Fonds Brais, "Retour de l'élection de James Bissett et Henri Larocque, écuiers, comme conseillers de la paroisse Saint-Jean l'Évangéliste dans la municipalité du comté de Chambly (13 et 14 septembre 1847)." Arch. de la ville de Saint-Jean-sur-Richelieu, livres des délibérations du conseil municipal, 7 sept., 8 nov. 1846; 30 juin, 13 déc. 1847; 13 mars, 12 juin 1848. PAC, MG 30, D1, 10: 302–8; RG 4, B8, 6: 1985–2005; RG 68, General index, 1651–1841: 206–7, 257, 376. La Minerve, 6, 9 nov. 1837; 23 déc. 1847; 17 janv. 1848; 25 août, 3 sept. 1853; 19 sept. 1854. Le Patriote canadien (Burlington, Vt.), 21 août 1839. Le Populaire (Montréal), 22, 29 nov. 1837. Fauteux, Patriotes, 204–5. Les maires et les conseillers de Saint-Jean, Qué.-août 1848 à février 1956 ([s.l.], 1956), 21, 28. J.-D. Brosseau, Saint-Jean-de-Québec; origine et développements (Saint-Jean[-sur-Richelieu], 1937), 213–15. Christie, Hist. of L.C. (1866), 4: 443, 451–54. Filteau, Hist. des Patriotes (1975), 312–15. Lionel Fortin, Le maire Nelson Mott et l'histoire de Saint-Jean ([Saint-Jean-sur-Richelieu], 1976), 31–38, 50–51, 57, 103. [Jean Foisy-Marquis], "Arrêtés, Davignon et Démaray sont délivrés par les patriotes," Le Canada français (Saint-Jean-sur-Richelieu), 17 févr. 1971: 23. Lionel Fortin, "Le notaire Pierre-Paul Démaray," "Pierre-Paul Démaray, notaire et patriote enterré avec ses chaînes," and "Démaray fut le premier maire de la paroisse Saint-Jean-l'Évangéliste" in Le Canada français, 23 déc. 1974: 28–30; 31 oct. 1979: 68–69; and 18 juin 1980: 12. J.-J. Lefebvre, "Les De Couagne (Decoigne)," SGCF Mémoires, 25 (1974): 214–27. Victor Morin, "La 'République canadienne' de 1838," RHAF, 2 (1948–49): 505.

DEMERS, JÉRÔME, Roman Catholic priest, author, architect, educator, and vicar general; b. 1 Aug. 1774 in Saint-Nicolas, near Quebec, son of Jean-Baptiste Demers, farmer and notary, and Geneviève Loignon; d. 17 May 1853 at Quebec.

Jérôme Demers was a fifth-generation descendant of Jean Demers, who came to New France around 1650. Jérôme's father had two brothers who were Recollets, Father Louis* and Brother Alexis, and apparently it was from Alexis that he received the instruction necessary to carry out his duties as a militia captain and notary. Jérôme himself is thought to have benefited from the good offices of his uncle Louis. A sturdily built man with somewhat rough manners, Jérôme probably would have made an excellent farmer. But from childhood he showed so strong a bent for study and such an earnest turn of mind that his father had no hesitation in sending him in 1785 to the Petit Séminaire de Québec.

Demers found adjustment so difficult that he had to repeat his second year. As a result, his father later decided to send him to the Recollet friary in Montreal, where he may have been in attendance by 1788. Louis and Alexis Demers were then at this institution, as was Pierre-Jacques Bossu*, *dit* Lyonnais, a theology student. Louis Demers and Bossu were greatly interested in science and strong in mathematics. Under these two tutors Jérôme could not help but develop his own skills. The lessons given by the Recollets did not deter him from enrolling, probably that same year, as a pupil in the Collège Saint-Raphaël (which in 1806 became the Petit Séminaire de Montréal). In January 1789 he was monitor of the second year (Syntax), according to the class list recording the competition results and prizes. The following year he was in the third-year class (Method). He is thought to have finished his classical studies in 1794, having probably taken the Philosophy program, which covered that subject and science, with his uncle Louis and Bossu rather than at the college, where this course had not yet been established.

When he returned to Quebec, Demers, pursuing his interest in mathematics, enrolled in the surveying course given by Jeremiah McCarthy*. But in 1795 he abandoned mathematics and entered the Grand Séminaire de Québec. After a year and a half of theology he gave up his training for the priesthood and returned to live with his father, who immediately put him to work clearing the land. One week of this régime and he was back in the Petit Séminaire de Québec. In September 1796 he began teaching third-year classes there while continuing theological studies. In accordance with Jesuit tradition Demers followed his pupils into the higher classes. He was ordained priest on 24 Aug. 1798 and made a member of the seminary the next year. In the autumn of 1800 he became a teacher in the Philosophy program, which comprised two years of study, the first devoted to philosophy, the second to physics and mathematics. The same teacher taught philosophy one year and science the other.

Demers thus discovered his double vocation as priest and teacher. Indeed he was to spend his whole life at the Séminaire de Québec, returning only once to Saint-Nicolas, on the occasion of his father's death. During the 53 years he devoted to education he taught grammar and the humanities from 1796 to 1800, philosophy and science from 1800 to 1835, philosophy from 1835 to 1842, and theology from 1842 to 1849. Moreover, he performed all the duties related to managing the institution. He was a directing member of the community for 49 years and of the Petit Séminaire for 7; a director of the Grand Séminaire for 1 year, he served as procurator for 9 and superior for 18. His final term as superior ended in 1842.

Virtually nothing is known about how Demers conducted his grammar and humanities classes. His career can be followed, however, from the time he became a teacher of philosophy, thanks to the testimony of his former pupils and the direct evidence of the course notes he left. It was not yet common pedagogical practice to use printed textbooks. Ever since the Renaissance, teachers had written out their own courses and either dictated them or had students copy them. Thus it was not, as invariably alleged, the scarcity of books after the conquest that prompted college teachers to write out their courses, but an age-old custom brought over by the Jesuits. At Quebec, teachers drafted their courses, explained them in class, and gave them to their students, who copied them into exercise books. Rhetoric, philosophy, and science lent themselves to this type of teaching. Philosophy, like rhetoric, was given in Latin, with the course notes being written in that language. After 1830 French textbooks replaced notes in Latin, except for philosophy, a subject for which the majority of classical colleges continued to use Latin textbooks until after 1950.

Demers taught philosophy in this manner for 29 years during the period from 1800 to 1842, his duties as procurator and superior sometimes obliging him to find a replacement. At that time there were four divisions in philosophy: logic, metaphysics, ethics, and physics (the philosophy course itself dealt with the first three). Demers committed this course to paper in 1802, 1808, and 1818. He published the last version in 1835 with numerous additions, and this in fact constituted the first philosophy textbook produced in French Canada. In the prospectus Demers justified its printing on the grounds that pupils wasted too much time copying the teacher's notes and that French texts were too costly and "gave little or no explanation on certain topics of which young Canadians would find it extremely useful to have some knowledge, in view of their moral and religious environment." His intention was not to produce a catalogue of the errors of the human mind but to present a clear, precise, and methodical manual calculated to recall the principles and laws of sound reason, and the nature and duties of man as a thinking, moral being. He was prompted not only by a practical need, but also by the necessity to

Demers

provide young people with a sure guide through the debates taking place in these years of intellectual and political ferment.

The *Institutiones philosophicae ad usum studiosae juventutis* presented logic, metaphysics, and ethics in Latin, and to them Demers added a treatise in French, "Preuves de la religion révélée," taken from the *Philosophie de Lyon* published in 1823. What is important to note is the discussion of political philosophy in the section dealing with ethics. The country was on the verge of a rebellion which Demers could see was coming; he even endeavoured to dissuade Louis-Joseph Papineau* from becoming embroiled in it. Convinced that men do not possess political equality even if they are equal, Demers rejects the argument of the social contract and of a pact which established primitive communal living. In his view, God is the source of all power, and He confers it on those who exercise it on earth. Respect and obedience must therefore be rendered to authority. To revolt against the civil power is to revolt against God. Insurrection is never permissible; moreover, it spawns more serious ills than it can correct. The philosophy teacher was indeed anxious to be involved in the discussions of his time. He drew much of his inspiration from the authors of the counter-revolution, such as Jean-Baptiste Duvoisin, the Comte de Frayssinous, the Vicomte de Bonald, and the La Mennais of the *Essai sur l'indifférence en matière de religion* (Paris, 1817).

Publication of the philosophy textbook, used in all the classical colleges except Montreal's, which was under strict French and Sulpician obedience, was to be followed by that of a physics manual, it was announced. But Abbé John HOLMES, who was in Paris in August 1836, told Demers in a letter that physics treatises went out of date as fast as they appeared, because of the increasing speed of scientific advance. Demers then realized that he would have to give up his publishing activity, just as in 1834 he had left the teaching of physics, chemistry, and mathematics to three young priests, keeping for himself only "speculative philosophy." In the teaching of science Demers had also been an innovator.

From the 16th century to the middle of the 18th, French classical colleges had expounded the old Aristotelian physics. It was only after 1750 that pupils were taught the fundamental discoveries of the age of Descartes. For their part, the Jesuits of Quebec had provided sound teaching in mathematics before 1750, but only to the students of the École royale de Mathématiques et d'Hydrographie [*see* Joseph Des Landes*]. Once the Jesuit Collège de Québec had closed, the seminary took over that task in 1756, and instruction in science was provided ten years later. The teachers' notes for the courses make it clear that until 1800 they followed what was done in France.

Pedagogy was still based on the scholastic method by which physics theories were presented, discussed, and defended or refuted with the aid of the *Institutiones philosophicae ad usum seminarii Tullensis* (5v., Toul, France, 1769) by abbés Gigot and Camier, or the *Abrégé latin de philosophie, avec une introduction et des notes françoises* (2v., Paris, 1784) by Abbé Hauchecorne. The seminary library owned the most widely known works on physics and mathematics, written by the best authors of the time. There were also a few pieces of physics apparatus, but they belonged to the teacher and were used only outside class.

Having been well prepared by his Recollet uncle, by Bossu, and by the lessons of McCarthy, Demers had begun teaching science during the academic year 1801–2, and his first course notes were dated 1804. The material was divided into three parts – mathematical, systematic, and experimental physics – according to a plan derived from the *Dictionnaire de physique* ... (3v., Avignon, France, 1761) by Aimé-Henri Paulian. He also drew upon the works of Mathurin-Jacques Brisson, Jean Saury (Sauri), Nicolas-Louis de La Caille, and Joseph-Jérôme Lefrançois de Lalande, as well as from the *Histoire du galvanisme et analyse des différens ouvrages publiés sur cette découverte, depuis son origine jusqu'à ce jour* (4v., Paris, 1802–5), published by Pierre Süe. His physics course, based on mathematics and informed by the latest advances, was already good but in 1809–10 he prepared a new one, organized on the plan of Brisson's *Traité élémentaire ou principes de physique fondés sur les connaissances les plus certaines, tant anciennes que modernes, et confirmés par l'expérience* (3v., Paris, 1789). With 18 chapters and 970 articles, Demers's course goes from the general properties of bodies to galvanism. Magnetism, electricity, and galvanism are the subjects of three successive chapters that are informed by the latest discoveries and most recent publications. Starting in 1817 Demers drafted a third course, using the same outline and enlarging his notes with corrections and additions. In 1833 he undertook a final revision for publication, which was halted by the letter from his colleague Holmes.

From the beginning Demers had wanted to set up a physics laboratory by putting together a few instruments himself with the help of the seminary's craftsmen, and at the same time bringing in other equipment from England. In 1806, he and Félix Gatien* opened a "museum," which eventually became a physics laboratory. Thanks to Demers's knowledge of mathematics and physics, philosophy students, not only at the Séminaire de Québec but also at the Séminaire de Nicolet, the Collège de Saint-Hyacinthe, and the Collège de Sainte-Anne-de-la-Pocatière, where his course notes were used, received first-class scientific instruction.

His knowledge was also useful to the diocese of Quebec as a whole, where parishes were increasing in number and churches were needed. Demers, who had ties with the Baillairgé family and was a great friend of THOMAS, had been involved in the work of these architects and wood-carvers since 1815; for ten years before he became vicar general in 1825, he was consulted by parish priests and *fabriques* and was called upon to give his opinion on plans of proposed churches. As in philosophy and science, he felt an imperative need to draw on the best sources: Jacques-François Blondel, architect and professor, Augustin-Charles Daviler, and Giacomo da Vignole. He later decided to add to his science course lessons on architecture, which he began in 1828. His "Précis d'architecture pour servir de suite au Traité élémentaire de physique à l'usage du séminaire de Québec," which was illustrated by Flavien Baillairgé, comprises 19 chapters and 414 articles whose simple, coherent text shows his mastery of the theory of classical architecture. By 1828 a copy had been sent to the Séminaire de Nicolet, and the "Précis d'architecture" was being used in six classical colleges. Through it, parish priests would acquire a better knowledge of the builder's art. As an architect, Demers not only gave his opinion on plans of churches in the diocese but also prepared or altered several of them. He produced plans for the church in his village, Saint-Nicolas, for the cathedral of Saint-Boniface (Man.), and for the Séminaire de Nicolet, the masterpiece of Quebec monastery architecture.

Although preoccupied by teaching philosophy and science, Demers played an important role in the religious and social spheres of his day. He was appointed vicar general in 1825, and was also director of the Society for the Propagation of the Faith, a member of the episcopal council, vice-president of the Quebec Education Society, and counsellor and patron of the Baillairgés and the painter Antoine Plamondon*. Nor was Demers indifferent to the political struggles that took place from 1822 to 1837. When his friend John Neilson* was approached in 1822 about going to London to fight the plan to unite the Canadas, he asked Demers to help him choose the Canadian assemblyman who would accompany him. Demers suggested Louis-Joseph Papineau, to whom he hastened to write: "I entreat you not to abandon our poor country until we have emerged advantageously from the terrible struggle in which we are engaged." Less than three weeks later he urged Papineau not to leave, on the grounds that the speaker of the house could not desert his post, and he expressed regret that he had forgotten this aspect of the question at the time of his first letter. In 1831 Louis Bourdages* introduced a bill to have prominent citizens in addition to the churchwardens admitted to the meetings of *fabriques*. The clergy intervened vigorously with a petition accompanied by a statement thought to have been drafted by Bishop Jean-Jacques Lartigue*. Demers wrote in December to Charles-François Painchaud*, the parish priest of Sainte-Anne-de-la-Pocatière (La Pocatière, Que.), using a line of reasoning closely resembling that of the statement, in order to give the priest arguments for the articles he was publishing in the *Quebec Gazette* under the pseudonym La Raison. John Neilson took the advice Demers gave on the question and declared himself against the bill. Bourdages, having been supported by Papineau and the members from the Patriote party, succeeded in having his bill passed by the House of Assembly on 23 Dec. 1831. But the Legislative Council, which on this occasion had only one Catholic member present, deferred the bill for six months, in other words, indefinitely. In the same letters he wrote to Painchaud that month Demers also stated that several politicians had come to see him about this matter. It was quite impossible for a Canadian priest of that period to accept a democratic element in parish administration.

In August 1832 Demers wrote to Neilson urging him to enter the Legislative Council and assuring him not only that the people's welfare required it but also that, if he accepted, his "Montreal friend will accept also" – undoubtedly an allusion to Papineau. If Neilson refused, there would be unrest and disturbance for a long time. The vicar general added that in speaking to Neilson in this way he was adding his voice to the wishes of many highly reputable people, two of whom had instructed him to see Neilson on this score. Neilson replied that though Demers was a friend in whom he had complete confidence, he did not in this instance agree with him about the conduct of public affairs. Furthermore, Neilson, then a member of the assembly, said that he was not convinced he could be of service to the country in the position Demers was discussing. He concluded by pointing out that the office he was refusing was less important than the one the vicar general had himself earlier declined, the bishopric of Quebec. The few pieces of evidence such as these that have been preserved are valuable indications of the role that Demers no doubt played for more than a quarter of a century as a discreet counsellor and as spokesman for the diocese.

A man of rare intelligence, Demers assimilated with disarming ease mathematics and physics, philosophy, and the builder's art. He knew how to adapt all of them to his time and country, whether as teacher, superior and procurator of the seminary, or as adviser to the bishop, politicians, and parish priests, or to builders, artists, and his former pupils. He was blessed with uncommon physical strength and robust good health. He would rise at three in the morning, and stay up late preparing sermons or refining his comments on the plan of a church. Somewhat high-strung, he studied zealously and intently, according to one pupil. All those who knew or met him stressed his goodness, gentleness, uprightness, and unfailing kindness towards everyone, especially the young. He was pre-eminently the friend of youth. As someone observed, although he had the sensitivity of a child, he had to be firm as the director of his pupils. But incapable as he was of causing distress, he tempered this firmness with great tolerance. Uncompromising on principles and scrupulous to excess in regard to his own actions, he pardoned the boys their scatter-brained and irresponsible behaviour, knowing full well that they were far away from their parents and sometimes found the austere life of the seminary hard to bear. None has described better than Papineau – writing nearly half a century later – the "tenderness" that was one of the master's qualities.

The consideration for others which Demers preached and which he displayed as often to his servants as to his colleagues was equalled only by his modesty. Unconcerned about his appearance yet most distinguished in his bearing, he never spoke of himself or of his family, and seemed to live only for others. He would not allow his portrait to be painted, even though his friend and protégé Antoine Plamondon had once surreptitiously sketched his features. He is thought to have destroyed shortly before his death all his writings of the preceding four years, and hence to have deprived posterity of an exceptional legacy. His contemporaries stated that he twice refused the episcopacy, once at the death of Bishop Joseph-Octave Plessis* in 1825 and again when Bishop Bernard-Claude Panet* died in 1833. After the death of Plessis, Demers told his friend Charles-François Painchaud that he was unworthy of the office and incapable of bearing its weight. In 1825 Ignace Bourget*, who would later be bishop of Montreal, stated that it was the parish priests of the district of Quebec who "elected" him unanimously. Demers is said to have justified his refusal by explaining "that the bishops were wrong to attack the rights of the seminary and that he did not want to follow suit." On his deathbed Plessis is believed to have suggested that Demers, not a favourite of his, would not accept the high office if it were offered to him. It certainly cannot be said that the two priests did not get on well together, but it is quite possible that the bishop had suffered from having Demers so close at hand. Plessis was very gifted intellectually and had a knowledge of classical culture that few of his priests had been able to attain. But Demers clearly surpassed him in the sciences and arts. One incident was created when Plessis, seeing the lights on in the senior students' study room in the Petit Séminaire at a late hour, drew this to the superior's attention. But the students in question, Papineau among them, were Demers's pupils, and had

been given his permission to continue studying after others stopped, in order to satisfy their desire to read. Plessis had once tried to keep late hours in order to improve his knowledge, but not having the stamina of Demers had been obliged quite soon to curtail these excesses. In religious matters Plessis's tendency was to centralize everything and to make all decisions himself. The important place occupied in the diocese of Quebec by the seminary since the time of Bishop François de Laval* must have sometimes proved awkward for the bishop, especially one who came from Montreal. Bishop Pierre Denaut*, the immediate predecessor of Plessis, had remained in the parish of Longueuil, near Montreal, leaving his coadjutor, none other than Plessis, to take care of administration at Quebec. The considerable reputation that Demers had quickly acquired as superior of the seminary and as adviser to parish priests, politicians, and the bishop himself, certainly could have offended Plessis.

Demers was a distinguished and original person who disdained affectation and preferred to use simple language. However, he excelled in the pulpit, where he expressed himself with extraordinary eloquence. When he preached on hell, the Last Judgement, or eternity he even became vehement, gaining mastery of the conscience of all present by persuasion, and subjugating them by terror, as a contemporary recalled. The oration he delivered at Plessis's funeral was long remembered. He possessed all the gifts of a great teacher: strong powers of reasoning, clarity of exposition, a liking for teaching and an affection for the young, whom it was his pleasure to introduce to mathematics, logic, and astronomy. He even inspired his pupils with his enthusiasm for genius, for example when he explained the discoveries of Copernicus, Kepler, and Newton. He admired Napoleon, of whose faults he was not unaware, and advised his pupils to respect men of genius of every age and place.

He not only kept his door wide open to penitents from outside, as the saying then went, who came to seek spiritual and moral comfort, but he also had many good friends, among them Pierre-Stanislas Bédard*, Louis Moquin, Andrew Stuart*, Joseph-Rémi Vallières* de Saint-Réal, John Neilson, and Louis-Joseph Papineau himself. The latter wrote in 1860, "He has remained my friend, my counsellor, my comforter in moments of profound grief."

A claim is sometimes made that Jérôme Demers was one of the founders of the Université Laval, an assertion also made about Abbé Holmes. It does not seem that they had a direct part in setting up the institution early in the 1850s, since both had been ill and in retirement for some years. But there is no doubt that the university could not have come into being when it did without the substantial work undertaken by Demers at the seminary. As superior and procurator he had for 27 years directed in masterly fashion the foundation of Bishop Laval. He breathed new life into it, raising the standard of teaching to the level of excellence, thanks to his intelligence and skills as an educator, and to his choice of such men as Holmes, with whom he effected important changes in the programs of study and in pedagogical practices during the period from 1830 to 1835. He was also able to keep at the seminary young priests of talent – Louis-Jacques Casault* and Elzéar-Alexandre Taschereau*, to name only two – who would be in a position to take up the challenge of a university. The active part he played in building churches was an example of the quality of service the diocese received from the seminary. His role as the discreet adviser to administrators and public figures earned him the respect of those in politics. It was Demers who enabled the venerable institution to keep abreast of the times, through his innovations and unremitting toil, and through his concern to involve himself in the problems of his society. Pierre-Joseph-Olivier Chauveau* could rightly say that rarely did a man as modest exercise a more sovereign influence. Jérôme Demers was one of the most remarkable men in Lower Canada during the first half of the 19th century.

CLAUDE GALARNEAU

[Jérôme Demers is the author of the first philosophy text published in Lower Canada. *Institutiones philosophicae ad usum studiosae juventutis* (Québec, 1835) fully reveals the philosophy professor's interest in keeping up with the issues of the day and demonstrates his extraordinary store of knowledge. C.G.]

AAQ, 12 A, G: f.13; K: f.7v; 210 A, XIV: 209; 26 CP, IV: 124. ANQ-Q, CE1-1, 17 mai 1853; CE1-21, 1er août 1774; P1000-28-541; P1000-31-572. Arch. du collège de Joliette (Joliette, Qué.), Jérôme Demers, "Précis d'architecture," 1857, 1860, 1863. Arch. du collège de l'Assomption (Montréal), Jérôme Demers, "Précis d'architecture," 1854, 1877. Arch. du collège de Montréal, Cahiers de la congrégation. Arch. du collège de Sainte-Anne-de-la-Pocatière (La Pocatière, Qué.), Jérôme Demers, "Précis d'architecture," 1837, 1844; "Précis de physique et d'astronomie," 1818; Fonds Painchaud, 2-33, -40, -46, -53, -64, -70–71; 3-7-8, -11, -20, -22, -31, -35–37. ASN, Jérôme Demers, "Précis d'architecture," 1828, 1835, 1838. ASQ, Fichier des anciens; Lettres, S, 125; T, 18, 118; MSS, 34, I, 10–18 mai 1853; 437; MSS-M, 15–16b, 66, 84, 86, 105, 109–10, 115, 129, 131, 144, 160–61, 186, 189–92, 195, 197–98, 214–15, 219, 232, 266–67, 1014–15, 1040–40a; Polygraphie, VIII: 19; XXVIII: 7b; XLII: 22a; XLIII: 1, 1a, 1d, 1e, 1i, 1m; Séminaire, 5, no.9b; 57, no.46; 72, no.9. ASSH, Jérôme Demers, "Précis d'architecture," 1837; "Traité élémentaire de physique," 1834; F, Fp-4. BNQ, Dép. des doc. spéciaux, Jérôme Demers, "Précis d'architecture," 1839. PAC, MG 24, B1, 1: 402–4; 7: 87–89, 92–93, 413–14; 12: 398–99; 18: 75–82. L.C., House of Assembly, *Journals*, 1835–36. *L'Abeille*, 19 mai 1853. *Le Canadien*, 12 mars 1834, 16 févr. 1835. *Le Journal de Québec*, 19, 31 mai 1853. [L.-A. Huguet-Latour],

Annuaire de Ville-Marie, origine, utilité et progrès des institutions catholiques de Montréal . . . (2v., Montréal, 1863–82). Univ. Laval, *Annuaires* (Québec), 1893: 94–99; 1894: 110–25. N.-E. Dionne, *Galerie historique, VII; une dispute grammaticale en 1842, le G.-V. Demers vs le G.-V. Maguire, précédée de leur biographie* (Québec, 1912). Maurice Fleurent, "L'éducation morale au petit séminaire de Québec, 1668–1857" (thèse de PHD, univ. Laval, 1977). Claude Galarneau, *Les collèges classiques au Canada français (1620–1970)* (Montréal, 1978). Labarrère-Paulé, *Les instituteurs laïques.* Lambert, "Joseph-Octave Plessis." Yvan Lamonde, *La philosophie et son enseignement au Québec (1665–1920)* (Montréal, 1980). Marc Lebel et al., *Aspects de l'enseignement au petit séminaire de Québec (1765–1945)* (Québec, 1968), 31–60. Maurault, *Le collège de Montréal* (Dansereau; 1967); *Marges d'histoire; l'art au Canada* ([Montréal], 1929), 93–113. Luc Noppen et J. R. Porter, *Les églises de Charlesbourg et l'architecture religieuse du Québec* ([Québec], 1972). É.-T. Paquet, *Fragments de l'histoire religieuse et civile de la paroisse Saint-Nicolas* (Lévis, Qué., 1894). J.-E. Roy, *Souvenirs d'une classe au séminaire de Québec, 1867–1877* (Lévis, 1905). J.-A. Gagné, "The teaching of chemistry at Quebec City before 1852," *Chemistry in Canada* (Ottawa), 4 (1952): 36–37. Yvan Lamonde, "L'enseignement de la philosophie au collège de Montréal, 1790–1876," *Culture* (Québec), 31 (1970): 109–23, 213–24. Gérard Morisset, "Une figure inconnue: Jérôme Demers," *La Patrie*, 22 mars 1953: 36–37. Luc Noppen, "Le rôle de l'abbé Jérôme Demers dans l'élaboration d'une architecture néo-classique au Québec," *Journal of Canadian Art Hist.* (Montreal), 2 (1975), no.1: 19–33. Jonathan Rée, "Philosophy as an academic discipline: the changing place of philosophy in an arts education," *Studies in Higher Education* (Oxford), 3 (1978): 5–23.

DÉROCHER. *See* DESROCHERS

DE ROTTERMUND, ÉDOUARD-SYLVESTRE DE ROTTERMUND, COUNT. *See* ROTTERMUND

DESAGONDENSTA. *See* JONES, PETER

DES BRISAY, ALBERT, Methodist minister and school administrator; b. 24 July 1795 in Stanhope, P.E.I., son of Theophilus Desbrisay* and Margaret Stewart; m. Margaret B. McLeod, and they had two sons and one daughter; d. 24 May 1857 in Charlottetown.

A member of a large and cultured family, Albert Des Brisay was converted in 1815 under the ministry of the Reverend John Hick, one of the Methodist missionaries sent from England to British North America after 1800 by the Wesleyan Methodist Conference. In 1822 Des Brisay volunteered to become a candidate for the ministry and was received on trial by the Nova Scotia District. He was stationed initially in New Brunswick on the Petitcodiac section of the huge Cumberland circuit.

From the outset, and in contrast to some of the Wesleyan missionaries, Des Brisay appears to have

Des Brisay

been an intensely evangelical minister. He found his circuit, served earlier by William Black*, full of people ignorant of and opposed to Methodism. To overcome their hostility he travelled some 3,000 miles in his first year and preached so effectively that in the second year a revival occurred. Doubtless the fact that he was a native of the eastern colonies enabled him to reach his people more effectively than some of his English colleagues.

Having served the customary four years, Des Brisay was admitted to full connection in 1826 at the first meeting of the New Brunswick District. He was stationed on the Sheffield circuit, and subsequently on the Annapolis, the Miramichi, and other circuits. His assiduous "public preaching" frequently led to revivals. These efforts may well have been the cause of the poor health which began to plague him in the 1830s. He was alert, however, to the importance of strengthening Methodist institutions in the Maritimes, and as early as 1833 he joined two of his brethren in urging the establishment of a Methodist seminary, a matter which had been first raised by the Nova Scotia District in 1828.

In 1839 Charles Frederick ALLISON, a Sackville merchant and a fervent Methodist who believed firmly that great social benefit could be derived from the establishment of schools in which "*Pure Religion* is not only taught, but *Constantly* brought before the youthful mind," offered to establish one such institution for the eastern provinces. His proposal was accepted gratefully by the New Brunswick District and subsequently at a joint meeting that year of the Nova Scotia, Newfoundland, and New Brunswick districts under the chairmanship of the Reverend Robert Alder*. The missionary secretaries, whose attitude toward such initiatives had hitherto been ambivalent, were distracted by the rising tide of dissension in the Wesleyan connection and failed at first either to help or to block the plan. The New Brunswick District decided that "we must now try and help ourselves." Humphrey Pickard* was appointed principal of Mount Allison Wesleyan Academy in Sackville, and Des Brisay became governor and chaplain in 1842.

The academy received its first students in January 1843. The early years of its growth were as difficult as those of similar institutions in British North America. Its survival owed much to Pickard, "a thorough gem" in his field. Des Brisay, however, was not a success. He was unable to manage the student residence and had no administrative skill. Indeed, Enoch Wood*, the key figure on the academy's board, remarked in a letter to Alder in 1846 that, in light of Des Brisay's background and mature years, he was "the smallest man we could have." In 1844 Des Brisay lost most of his administrative functions; according to Wood, he now had only "to attend to religious duties, with the exception of a General oversight of the Buildings and Grounds, an engagement most suitable to his habits and talents."

Doubtless to his surprise, in his role as chaplain Des Brisay initially involved the academy in controversy and embarrassment. A member of the New Brunswick Council, Amos Edwin Botsford*, made an accusation on 5 March 1845 that Des Brisay had instigated a revival among the students that winter in an attempt to convert them to Methodism. Some of the students, in the words of fellow councillor Edward Barron Chandler*, "would pray aloud in the lecture room at the close of the day when all the scholars as also Mr. DesBrisay were present. This led to further prayers and exhortations and an invitation by Mr. DesBrisay for all who *wished* to come forward to the *Altar* . . . many, in fact nearly all went forward and professed to be moved." Des Brisay reported in his defence to the district meeting in May that he wished "to record the loving-kindness of the Lord in visiting the Institution during the past winter with the awakening influences of the Holy Spirit arousing attention of many of the youth to serious concern for salvation." His brethren, of course, could not repudiate his action or his concern; they sought to maintain an evangelical atmosphere in the academy but were fearful that Des Brisay's efforts would enable its critics to describe it as a narrowly denominational institution. This charge was made, but there was no proof that he was attempting to recruit Methodists as opposed to converts to Christian teaching, and the academy continued to receive grants from the governments of New Brunswick and Nova Scotia. Moreover, Des Brisay along with Pickard ensured that the academy became a place in which the students were reminded continually of "the superior claims which Religion ought always to have upon their attention."

Albert Des Brisay, after being replaced by the Reverend Ephraim Evans*, retired from his chaplaincy in 1854 and returned the next year to Charlottetown where, despite ill health, he was "most industriously employed" and "his efforts in doing good closed only with his life." He was "a man of prayer. In imitation of the benevolence of his Divine Master, the law of kindness was upon his lips, while the spirit he breathed toward the suffering and the erring was that of tenderness and love." One of the earliest native-born Wesleyan Methodist ministers in the eastern provinces, Des Brisay in his zeal, simplicity, and evangelical spirit was reminiscent of an earlier Methodist generation; his tireless ministry helped to lay strong foundations for his church in New Brunswick and Nova Scotia.

G. S. FRENCH

Albert Des Brisay is the author of "Wesleyan Academy: report of the religious state of the students, &c., presented to the district meeting," *British North American Wesleyan*

Methodist Magazine (Saint John, N.B.), 4 (1845–46): 62–63.

P.E.I. Museum, File information concerning the Des Brisay family, especially geneal. chart. SOAS, Methodist Missionary Soc. Arch., Wesleyan Methodist Missionary Soc., corr., North America, 1815–46 (mfm. at UCA). Wesleyan Methodist Church of Eastern British America, *Minutes* (Halifax), 1857: 7–8. *Islander*, 29 May 1857, 5 Sept. 1862. Cornish, *Cyclopædia of Methodism*, vol.1. G. O. Huestis, *Memorials of Wesleyan missionaries & ministers, who have died within the bounds of the conference of Eastern British America, since the introduction of Methodism into these colonies* (Halifax, 1872). J. G. Reid, *Mount Allison University: a history, to 1963* (2v., Toronto, 1984), 1. T. W. Smith, *Hist. of Methodist Church*, vol.2. *Stanhope: sands of time*, ed. Evelyn Simpson (Stanhope, P.E.I., 1984). *Examiner* (Charlottetown), 8 Sept. 1862, 13 March 1876.

DÉSILETS, AIMÉ, lawyer, newspaper editor, and translator; b. 2 Aug. 1826 in Bécancour, Lower Canada, son of Isidore Désilets, a farmer, and Marie Morasse (Perenne de Moras); d. 4 March 1860 at Quebec.

Aimé Désilets received his classical education at the Séminaire de Nicolet from 1839 to 1844. In 1842 he helped form at the seminary a literary society which had been conceived by Abbé Jean-Baptiste-Antoine Ferland* and which later became known as the Académie. After studying law under Pierre-Benjamin DUMOULIN and Joseph-Georges-Antoine Frigon, lawyers in Trois-Rivières, Désilets was called to the bar on 13 Sept. 1848. He practised law in partnership with Joseph-Édouard Turcotte* until January 1853.

On 9 Dec. 1852 the first issue of *L'Ère nouvelle* was published at Trois-Rivières, with Désilets and Napoléon Bureau as editors. In their editorial the two contemplated "with great pride the present state of [their] district in comparison with its past," and they asserted that "a new era had just opened" for the region. "A dynamism and spirit of enterprise that had never been seen there before" were now manifest, and the editors proposed to take a particular interest in commercial and industrial development. They further planned to give the paper a reform slant, and to discuss the abolition of seigneurial tenure, payment of jury members, increased parliamentary representation, an elected legislative council, and the settlement of the townships.

Désilets contributed to *L'Ère nouvelle* until 20 Jan. 1853, when he resigned as editor because of "grave and unforeseen circumstances." Joseph-Édouard Turcotte, owner of the *Journal des Trois-Rivières*, had been attacked in an article in *L'Ère nouvelle* and was suing its editors and printer for £500 in damages. This action, which marked the end of the partnership of Turcotte and Désilets as lawyers, is also thought to have caused the latter's resignation from the newspaper. Désilets returned to the practice of law, moving into an office previously occupied by lawyer Louis-Eusèbe Désilets on Rue Saint-Joseph. On 16 Aug. 1854 Désilets agreed to resume his post at *L'Ère nouvelle*, not without some hesitation, for in his opinion it entailed a heavy burden which no one who had not held such a position could appreciate.

L'Ère nouvelle argued constantly in favour of building a railway on the north shore of the St Lawrence between Montreal and Quebec so that the Trois-Rivières region would not be isolated and disadvantaged in comparison with other parts of the province. In 1853 Désilets was secretary of the local committee at Trois-Rivières to promote the north shore railway, and he was among those seeking the incorporation of a company to build it [*see* Joseph-Édouard Cauchon*].

Désilets left *L'Ère nouvelle* and Trois-Rivières in May 1855 to devote his efforts to practising law in the Bois-Francs region. At this time, on 31 May 1855, his marriage to Élize Dumont was solemnized at Yamachiche. The couple had one daughter. During the summer Désilets opened a law office at Stanfold (Princeville) and another at Saint-Christophe-d'Arthabaska, where he took up residence. He became the first secretary-treasurer of the latter municipality on 4 August and of the council of Arthabaska County on 10 October.

In 1856 Aimé Désilets went to Toronto to carry out new duties as translator for the Legislative Assembly of the Province of Canada. On 4 March 1860, just after a session opened at Quebec, Désilets died at the age of 33 following "a brief illness." He was buried in Trois-Rivières, where he owned a residence. Soon afterwards, lawyers from the Arthabaska district assembled to pay homage to one who, as the first lawyer to live and practise in the Bois-Francs region, was a pioneer in his profession.

JEAN-MARIE LEBEL

ANQ-MBF, CE1-4, 2 août 1826; CE1-52, 31 mai 1855; CN1-11, 30 mai 1855; CN1-19, 29 sept. 1849; CN1-47, 21 août 1849, 23 mars 1860; CN1-62, 6 avril 1850, 19 avril 1851, 26 août 1852. PAC, MG 30, D1, 10: 621–22. *Le Courrier du Canada*, 5 mars 1860. *L'Ère nouvelle*, 1852–55, 5 mars 1860. Douville, *Hist. du collège-séminaire de Nicolet*, 1: 299; 2: 160. Alcide Fleury, *Arthabaska, capitale des Bois-Francs* (Arthabaska, Qué., 1961), 12, 191, 224, 228. Albert Tessier, *Trois-Rivières: quatre siècles d'histoire, 1535–1935* (2ᵉ éd., [Trois-Rivières], 1935). Nive Voisine, *Louis-François Laflèche, deuxième évêque de Trois-Rivières* (1v. paru, Saint-Hyacinthe, Qué., 1980–), 1: 68. "Quelques journaux trifluviens," *BRH*, 42 (1936): 723–25. Léon Trépanier, "*L'Ère nouvelle* des Trois-Rivières," *La Patrie*, 4 févr. 1951: 100.

DESPRÉS. *See* COUILLARD-DESPRÉS

DESROCHERS (Dérocher; Brien, *dit* **Dérocher; Brien,** *dit* **Desrochers), URBAIN** (baptized **Pierre-**

Desrochers

Urbain), wood-carver; b. 22 Jan. 1781 in Varennes, Que., son of Joseph Brien, *dit* Dérocher, and Marguerite Rive; d. 19 Aug. 1860 at Quebec.

Nothing is known about the early years of Urbain Desrochers. He probably began to learn wood-carving with Louis Quévillon* around 1798, when Quévillon was working on the decoration of the church in Varennes, but no trace of an apprenticeship contract has been found. On 7 Feb. 1809 Desrochers married Marie-Josephte Rocan, *dit* Bastien, at Saint-Vincent-de-Paul (Laval); his master, Quévillon, and Jessé Brien, *dit* Dérocher, also a carver, attended the ceremony. The couple had three children: Zoé, Pierre-Urbain, and Vital. Both sons followed in their father's footsteps to become wood-carvers.

Desrochers had settled permanently in Pointe-aux-Trembles (Montreal) by 1809, but his contracts with various parishes obliged him to travel. From 1809 to 1813 he was engaged in wood-carving and gilding at the church in Saint-Henri-de-Lauzon (Saint-Henri); Quévillon had begun carving there by 1803. Since this church was demolished in 1879 no trace of their work remains. A note in the account-books of Saint-Michel (at Saint-Michel-de-Bellechasse) suggests that at the same period Desrochers did part of the ornamental carving carried out by Quévillon in the parish church. From 1810 to 1818 Desrochers also decorated the church in Varennes. Only fragments of this work are left; two reliefs depicting evangelists, which came from the pulpit, are held at the National Gallery of Canada. On 15 June 1812 Desrochers contracted to decorate the base of the altar and the cornice, pilasters, stalls, and candelabra of the church of Saint-Grégoire (Bécancour). These carvings, which still exist, give some idea of the artistic quality of his work; they constitute the first church decoration that Desrochers executed without the collaboration of Quévillon. Since there is no subsequent record of collaboration, it may be conjectured that the two artists had by then ceased to work together, perhaps because of a conflict over the Bécancour contract.

From 1813 to 1819 Desrochers received several payments for decorative carving at the church of Saint-Denis, on the Richelieu River. At that time Pierre-Léandre Daveluy, an apprentice wood-carver, signed an agreement with Desrochers to help him in his work for six years. No trace of what Desrochers did remains in this parish, although part of the pilasters and some ornamental motifs are preserved in the collection belonging to the Congregation of Notre-Dame at the Ferme Saint-Gabriel in Pointe-Saint-Charles (Montreal). On 18 Feb. 1819 Desrochers contracted with the parish of Sainte-Trinité in Contrecœur to carve the vault, the retable (the structure housing the altar), the tabernacles, the base of the altars, and the pulpit, as well as to do several pieces of carpentry and wood-carving. He received payments from the churchwardens until 1830, and worked closely with the carpenter Ambroise Aubry and possibly with Louis Nerbonne.

Desrochers's workshop seems to have been quite important during the 1820s, since the carpenter Louis Marion, the journeyman wood-carver Joseph Goupil, and the apprentice Charles Dauphin worked there. Desrochers's son Pierre-Urbain served his apprenticeship there as well, and in 1830 also called himself a master wood-carver. From 1834 to 1838 Desrochers and his son worked on the carvings for the vault, pulpit, baldachin, and retables of the church at L'Assomption. Desrochers carried out a number of wood-carving assignments at the church of Saint-Sulpice near Montreal from 1835 to 1839, receiving several payments from its churchwardens.

No information on Desrochers's activity during the next 21 years has been located. He apparently retired to Quebec, for he died in that city on 19 Aug. 1860, at the age of 79, and was buried there two days later.

Gérard Morisset* considered Desrochers "the most talented wood-carver of his time." It is, however, difficult to judge his work, since much of it has been destroyed by fire or by demolition. The size of his contracts suggests that, along with other artists from Quévillon's workshop, he was one of the important figures in the first half of the 19th century doing religious carving in the Montreal region.

Nicole Cloutier

ANQ-M, CE1-5, 2 sept. 1810, 14 déc. 1813, 20 avril 1816, 20 juill. 1829, 19 juin 1830; CE1-10, 19 juin 1775, 22 janv. 1781, 23 sept. 1799; CE1-59, 7 févr. 1809; CN1-23, 21 févr. 1838; CN1-68, 7 janv. 1818, 6 août 1822, 16 mars 1825; CN1-110, 14 déc. 1820; CN1-134, 20 janv. 1822; CN1-143, 18 févr. 1819, 31 déc. 1820, 2 août 1822, 14 juin 1825; CN1-167, 24 janv., 4 mars 1809; CN1-295, 24 mars 1814, 22 juin 1825, 25 oct. 1831; CN1-326, 3 mars 1824; CN1-384, 23 mai 1812; CN5-3, 19 janv., 2 déc. 1834. ANQ-Q, CE1-1, 21 août 1860. MAC-CD, Fonds Morisset, 2, B853.5/P662.97. Montreal Museum of Fine Arts, ms, 1971, Rodrigue Bédard *et al.*, "Catalogue des biens de la ferme Saint-Gabriel." National Gallery of Canada (Ottawa), Files 9977, 15381. *Le Journal de Québec*, 21 août 1860. Mariette Fréchette-Pineau, "L'église de Saint-Grégoire de Nicolet (1802)" (thèse de MA, univ. de Montréal, 1970), 56–57. Harper, *Early painters and engravers*, 88–89. Olivier Maurault, *La paroisse: histoire de l'église Notre-Dame de Montréal* (2e éd., Montréal, 1957), 51. Morisset, *Coup d'œil sur les arts*, 37–38; *Les églises et le trésor de Varennes* (Québec, 1943), 17–21. Luc Noppen, *Les églises du Québec (1600–1850)* (Québec, 1977), 45, 212, 232–34, 272. J. R. Porter, *L'art de la dorure au Québec du XVIIe siècle à nos jours* (Québec, 1975), 81–82. Jean Bélisle, "Le retable de Saint-Grégoire de Nicolet et le problème de la contrainte architecturale dans les ensembles sculptés québécois," *Journal of Canadian Art Hist.* (Montreal), 5 (1980), no.1: 18–32. François Cormier, "Le chandelier de monsieur Raimbault," *Les Cahiers nicolétains* (Nicolet, Qué.), 2

De Witt

(1980): 55–62; "Saint-Grégoire de Nicolet: une paroissse, une église (1637–1812)": 105–89.

DE WITT, JACOB, businessman, politician, and justice of the peace; b. 17 Sept. 1785 in Windham, Conn., son of Henry De Witt, a hatter, and Hannah Dean; m. 12 Jan. 1816 in Dunham Township, Lower Canada, Sophronia Frary of Montreal, and they had at least four children, one of whom was living in Iowa at the time of his father's death; d. 23 March 1859 in Montreal.

The De Witt family can be traced back to around 1650, the period of Dutch colonization, when an ancestor, Tjerck Claessen De Witt, is thought to have taken up residence at New Amsterdam (New York). It is not known when the family left the United States for Lower Canada. But according to Louis Richard, the author of a particularly well-documented biographical account of Jacob De Witt, his family settled in Montreal around 1802.

Little is known of De Witt's early training. In 1802, when he had just turned 17, he was probably serving an apprenticeship with his elder brother Jabez in their father's hat business in Montreal. However, De Witt entered the hardware trade, apparently seizing the opportunity to reap substantial profits during the War of 1812. In 1814 he went into partnership with hardware merchant George Busby Willard, but the two men terminated their association at the end of three years. In 1819 the Doige directory described De Witt as a hardware merchant located on Rue Saint-Paul and living on Ruelle des Fortifications. De Witt was long identified with the hardware trade and was to make his nephew Benjamin Brewster a partner.

While attending to his commercial concerns, De Witt became involved in various other business activities. He soon took an interest in navigation upstream from Montreal, probably for reasons not unconnected with his business. In 1816 he bought a 50-ton steamship, the *Montreal*, which sailed between Lachine, Châteauguay, and Annstown (Beauharnois). Four years later he invested in the steamship *Car of Commerce*. In 1825 he was one of the 50 or so large landowners of Montreal, and around 1829 he purchased a sawmill and 130 acres in Godmanchester Township, in Beauharnois County. He acquired in 1833 the steamship *Chateauguay*, which plied between Lachine and Saint-Joachim parish at Châteauguay. It seems therefore that in the mid 1830s De Witt's fortune rested on a solid and varied foundation.

One of the charter members of the Bank of Canada in 1822, De Witt collaborated in 1833 with Thomas Storrow Brown* in petitioning for the establishment of the City Bank in Montreal. Two years later De Witt and Louis-Michel VIGER formed Viger, De Witt et Cie, otherwise known as the Banque du Peuple. This new bank corresponded to the desire in reform circles of the time to put an end to the Bank of Montreal's monopoly on credit in Lower Canada and to create an institution more open and responsive to the economic needs and aspirations of the colony's petite bourgeoisie. It is easy to account for De Witt's decision to launch such an undertaking. He had become a member of the Lower Canadian House of Assembly in 1830, and because of his sympathies for the struggles of the French Canadian members against the governor and the Executive and Legislative councils he leaned towards the Patriote party. His American origins, and some dissatisfaction with the politics of the British upper middle class in Montreal, as well as rivalries in the world of business, may have determined his action. To Viger, the chief promoter of the venture, De Witt seemed the ideal man to help set up and direct it. He was an experienced businessman, with a solid fortune, the high regard of business circles, good connections, and sound credit; it was on him that the success of the project would partly depend. His prudence was needed to prevent the bank from foundering during the events of 1837–38, for in some circles it was regarded as an organization intended to subsidize the rebellion. Despite difficult circumstances the bank prospered, and in 1843 Viger and De Witt decided to seek a charter for it, which was granted the following year. De Witt was the principal partner and contributed a substantial part of the bank's initial capital; in 1845 he became its vice-president and, on Viger's death ten years later, succeeded him as president. He held this office for the rest of his life.

De Witt had a lengthy political career. From 1830 to 1838 he was the member for Beauharnois. Defeated in the 1841 elections, he was returned the next year by acclamation for Leinster, which he represented in the Legislative Assembly of the Province of Canada until 1847. The following year he was re-elected in Beauharnois, a seat he held until 1851. Then he served as member for Châteauguay from 1854 to 1857. Being strongly attached first of all to Beauharnois, doubtless because of his physical presence in the region, he strove to retain this riding despite the ups and downs of contemporary political struggles.

Although De Witt was identified with the party of Louis-Joseph Papineau*, he did not follow him during the rebellion of 1837–38. Clearly prompted by staunch liberalism, he was quite ready to cooperate in any undertaking of a reform nature, but as a prudent businessman he refused to take risks. After the rebellion De Witt was to be seen in the ranks of the moderate reformers, and was associated with the group centring around Louis-Hippolyte La Fontaine*. According to the newspaper *Le Pays*, he was not a brilliant politician, being "neither an impassioned speaker, nor an outstanding publicist, nor a profound legal expert." None the less, he did involve himself in

De Witt

certain matters, such as the seigneurial question and the question of the right of nonconformist Protestant churches to keep parish registers. In 1853 he assisted in organizing the Anti-Seigniorial Tenure Convention, of which he was to become chairman. His interests as a businessman were never far from his mind when he made his political choices. In 1849 he held the office of vice-president of the Association for the Encouragement of Home Manufactures. That year also he signed the Annexation Manifesto, thus making common cause with the business circles of Montreal. As well, in 1849 and 1850 he advocated protectionist measures to stimulate small manufacturing. Indeed, he contined to take an interest in tariffs until the end of his life.

De Witt was also involved in municipal politics. On the expiry of the charter of the city of Montreal in 1836, he was appointed a judge in the Court of Special Sessions of the Peace, which was given responsibility for administering that municipality. He discharged this duty for four years. Then he unsuccessfully ran for election as a councillor in Queen Ward in 1842 and Sainte-Anne ward in 1851.

The affairs of the Banque du Peuple, along with political life, absorbed all De Witt's energy, and he gradually detached himself from his hardware business, handing over management to Brewster. This did not prevent De Witt from taking part about 1846 with John Young* and Ira Gould in an operation to put to profitable use the water power produced by the new improvements in the Lachine Canal. In 1852 De Witt also participated in setting up the Montreal and Bytown Railway Company. Thus he was amongst those who played a role in the rapid expansion of industry in Montreal in the mid 19th century.

A convinced Presbyterian, De Witt belonged to the St Peter Street Church. He was one of the group of Americans who in 1822 refused to accept the appointment of Scottish pastor John Burns [see Robert Easton*], and who formed the American Presbyterian Church between 1822 and 1824. In the latter year he became almost an official member of the committee responsible for its temporal affairs, and in 1830 was ordained an elder. His participation earned him the designation of "Grand Old man of the Church." He also gave time to the Montreal Auxiliary Bible Society and the Montreal Temperance Society. He sat on boards of charitable organizations such as the Montreal General Hospital, the house of industry, and the Immigration Committee of Montreal. People were quick to appeal to him on behalf of good causes. He was one of the founding directors of the Montreal City and District Savings Bank in 1846.

Jacob De Witt's career as a businessman illustrates well the way the economic life of Montreal developed in the first half of the 19th century. The son of a craftsman and merchant, he went into the hardware business, prospering from the opening of Upper Canada to settlement; then, diversifying, he became involved in the transportation and lumber industries, as well as in real estate; finally, from the mid 1830s, he took an increasing interest in banking. It may be revealing that on his death certificate he is called a "banker." Like many middle-class men of his time, De Witt was very much a part of his society. His participation in political life and in religious affairs, which always bore the stamp of liberalism, is the principal evidence, and it had a natural extension in the role he played in charitable organizations.

JEAN-CLAUDE ROBERT

ANQ-E, CE2-38, 12 janv. 1816. ANQ-M, CE1-115, 25 mars 1859; CE1-126, 19 mars 1827, 8 févr. 1828; CN1-134, 23 juill. 1816, 8 juill. 1831, 10 mai 1833; CN1-187, 3 août 1820; CN1-213, 4 avril 1859. ASQ, Fonds Viger–Verreau, Carton 46, no.9. BNQ, Dép. des MSS, MSS-101, Coll. La Fontaine (copies at PAC). McCord Museum, Jacob De Witt papers, Jacob De Witt to Thomas Lyon, 3 Nov. 1817. PAC, MG 24, B2; K2, 13: 190–92; L3; MG 30, D1, 11: 34–46. "The annexation movement, 1849–50," ed. A. G. Penny, *CHR*, 5 (1924): 236–61. Can., Prov. of, *Statutes*, 1843, c.66; 1852–53, c.103. L.C., *Statutes*, 1821–22, c.27; 1832–33, c.32. *Le Courrier du Canada*, 28 mars 1859. *Montreal Gazette*, 9 Feb. 1849, 13 Sept. 1853. *Montreal Herald*, 24 Dec. 1840. *Le Pays*, 31 mars, 2, 5 avril 1859. *Pilot* (Montreal), 6 March 1851; 8 June 1852; 19 Feb., 18 July 1853. F.-J. Audet, "Les législateurs du Bas-Canada." Desjardins, *Guide parl. Montreal almanack*, 1830. *Montreal directory*, 1819. Terrill, *Chronology of Montreal*.

J.-P. Bernard, *Les Rouges: libéralisme, nationalisme et anticléricalisme au milieu du XIXᵉ siècle* (Montréal, 1971). Campbell, *Hist. of Scotch Presbyterian Church*, 254–55. R. S. Greenfield, "La Banque du peuple, 1835–1871, and its failure, 1895" (MA thesis, McGill Univ., Montreal, 1968), 9, 38–39. *Hist. de Montréal* (Lamothe et al.), 202. E. A. [Kerr] McDougall, "The American element in the early Presbyterian Church in Montreal (1786–1824)" (MA thesis, McGill Univ., 1965). D. C. Knowles, "The American Presbyterian Church of Montreal, 1822–1866" (MA thesis, McGill Univ., 1957), 10–22, 231. G. R. Lighthall, *A short history of the American Presbyterian Church of Montreal, 1823–1923* (Montreal, 1923), 4, 32, 36, 38. H. E. MacDermot, *A history of the Montreal General Hospital* (Montreal, 1950), 4. Monet, *La première révolution tranquille*. Ouellet, *Bas-Canada*, 364; *Histoire économique et sociale du Québec, 1760–1850: structures et conjoncture* (Montréal et Paris, [1966]). Robert Rumilly, *Histoire de Montréal* (5v., Montréal, 1970–74), 2: 204. S. B. Ryerson, *Le capitalisme et la confédération: aux sources du conflit Canada–Québec (1760–1873)*, André d'Allemagne, trad. (Montréal, 1972), 221. T. T. Smyth, *The first hundred years: history of the Montreal City and District Savings Bank, 1846–1946* (Montreal, [1946]), 14, 161, 163. Tulchinsky, *River barons*, 230, 276. P.-A. Linteau et J.-C. Robert, "Propriété foncière et société à Montréal: une hypothèse," *RHAF*, 28 (1974–75): 45–65. Louis Richard, "Jacob De Witt (1785–1859)," *RHAF*, 3 (1949–50): 537–55.

DICKERSON, SILAS HORTON, printer, journalist, publisher, office holder, and politician; b. 12 May 1799 in New Jersey; m. 1 Sept. 1822 Mary Price in Montreal, and they had seven children; d. 23 Oct. 1857 in Stanstead-Plain, Lower Canada.

Silas Horton Dickerson must have immigrated to Upper Canada when quite young, since at 14 he was a printer's apprentice in Kingston. He later worked in Montreal as a typographer for Nahum Mower, owner of the *Canadian Courant and Montreal Advertiser*. In the spring of 1823 he settled in Stanstead, where he began publishing the weekly *British Colonist and St. Francis Gazette*, the first newspaper printed in the Eastern Townships.

Dickerson's venture had a difficult beginning. The region served by his paper was extensive and without adequate roads; his subscribers were poor and scattered. He often had to accept payment in kind. In the early years the *British Colonist*, as well as reprinting news from American papers, took a particular interest in religious questions. Dickerson gave a good deal of space to articles on religion and morals, and to letters from missionaries, especially Methodists. Thus he duplicated in the Eastern Townships the endeavours of his former employer, Nahum Mower, who was now encouraging in Montreal the publication of Protestant periodicals. From 1826 Dickerson regularly opened his paper to local correspondents who, writing under various pseudonyms, demanded improvements in the area's highways and administrative structures.

Because he published comments from a number of his readers on the conduct of John Fletcher*, a judge in the Saint-François district, Dickerson was ordered by Fletcher to appear in court on 25 March 1826, was arrested, and was fined £5. The author of an article to which exception had been taken, Francis Armstrong Evans of Kingsey, whose name Dickerson had been obliged to disclose to the judge, was also arrested, imprisoned for three months, and then released on suspended sentence and bail of £200. Dickerson thought that Fletcher's attitude threatened freedom of the press in the region. Consequently, on the advice of a lawyer in Sherbrooke, Pierre-Joseph Cressé, he decided to sue the judge in the Court of King's Bench at Trois-Rivières for illegal proceedings. This move initiated a series of legal skirmishes involving Fletcher and Dickerson, his lawyer, and his incriminated correspondents, which went on for more than two years. Between September 1826 and June 1828 Dickerson was arrested on four occasions, found guilty of contempt of court three times, and imprisoned for several weeks. The fines and bail he had to pay totalled more than £600. Finally, in 1828, the court of Trois-Rivières declared the matter beyond its jurisdiction.

Despite these legal and financial reverses, Dicker-son continued to publish his newspaper, which displayed an increasingly definite political commitment. Late in 1828 he filed a petition against Fletcher before the House of Assembly at Quebec, and the house set up a special committee to inquire into the case. The committee concluded in 1829 that the judge had exceeded his rights and acted arbitrarily toward several persons, and it asked the governor-in-chief, Sir James KEMPT, to relieve him of office. Its recommendations, like those of other select committees of the house in 1831, 1832, and 1836 dealing with the judge's conduct and other matters, remained a dead letter. Dickerson was neither exonerated nor compensated, but to the province's progressive circles he had become a martyr for freedom of the press.

Hoping to make political capital out of this situation, Dickerson ran in the 1829 election for the new constituency of Stanstead. He obtained only a handful of votes, but his paper came out more and more strongly in favour of the reform majority in the house, and in 1834 publicized its firm support for the 92 Resolutions, which set forth the assembly's principal grievances and demands. The growing acceptance of the *British Colonist*'s ideas among those in the Eastern Townships who were of American origin, and the forum it provided the member for Stanstead, Marcus CHILD, who had openly joined the reformers, worried loyalist circles which were headed by Sherbrooke's prominent citizens Edward Hale*, John Felton, Samuel Brooks, and Hollis Smith*. Taking advantage of Dickerson's heavy debts, some Sherbrooke merchants had his printing-press sold in June 1834. Ironically the press, when brought to Sherbrooke, was used to print a tory paper, the *Farmer's Advocate and Townships Gazette*.

Although deprived of his paper, Dickerson went on fighting for his beliefs. As president of his riding's reform association in 1834, he received Louis-Joseph Papineau* when he came to Stanstead to celebrate the victories of reformers Marcus Child and John Grannis in the elections of that year. During the insurrection of 1837 he took refuge in the United States, and for several years there is no trace of him. He returned, however, to Stanstead, and in 1854 was appointed collector of customs. In January 1857 he became the first mayor of the village of Stanstead-Plain. He died there some months later of lung congestion.

JEAN-PIERRE KESTEMAN

ANQ-E, CN1-23, 12 oct. 1833; CN1-24, 27 avril 1835; T12-501, 1826, no.245; 1832, no.109. ANQ-M, CE1-63, 1er sept. 1822. L.C., House of Assembly, *Journals*, 1828–29, app.MM; 1830; 1831, app.CC; 1831–32, app.W; 1835–36, app.EE. *British Colonist and St. Francis Gazette* (Stanstead, Que.), 1823–31. *Stanstead Journal* (Rock-Island, Que.), 29 Oct. 1857. *St. Francis Courier and Sherbrooke Gazette* (Sherbrooke, Que.), 1834. *Vindicator*

Dickson

and Canadian Advertiser (Montreal), 1829–35. Beaulieu et Hamelin, *La presse québécoise*, 1: 46–47, 64–65, 71–72, 144–45. Morgan, *Sketches of celebrated Canadians*. B. F. Hubbard, *Forests and clearings; the history of Stanstead County, province of Quebec, with sketches of more than five hundred families*, ed. John Lawrence (Montreal, 1874; repr. 1963). Maurice O'Bready, *De Ktiné à Sherbrooke; esquisse historique de Sherbrooke: des origines à 1954* (Sherbrooke, 1973). J.-P. Kesteman, "Les premiers journaux du district de Saint-François (1823–1845)," *RHAF*, 31 (1977–78): 239–53.

DICKSON, THOMAS, lawyer, politician, and office holder; b. 8 July 1791 in Onslow, N.S., fifth son and tenth child of Charles Dickson and Amelia Bishop, both emigrants from Connecticut; m. 24 Jan. 1818 Sarah Ann Patterson, and they had nine children, most of whom, including their only son, predeceased him; d. 13 Feb. 1855 in Pictou, N.S.

Thomas Dickson studied law under his brother-in-law Samuel George William Archibald* and about 1816 began a practice in Pictou, where such notables as Jotham Blanchard* would article under him. He maintained some connection with the region around Onslow, however, since in 1820 he owned a mill in Truro reputed to have been the first to grind oatmeal in Nova Scotia.

Family tradition and connections brought him to politics. His father had been a member of the House of Assembly. Two of his brothers (Robert and William), a relative of his wife (Edward Mortimer*), and a brother-in-law (Archibald) all sat in the assembly with him. He represented Sydney County (now Guysborough and Antigonish counties) from 1818 to 1836. He did not enter the 1836 election, won a by-election in Pictou County two years later, lost that seat in 1840, and won a Colchester County by-election in 1841. In 1843 he retired to Pictou after being appointed registrar of probate on 8 Nov. 1842. He had served as collector of impost and excise for the district of Pictou since 6 May 1833; on 21 March 1843 he petitioned the assembly to grant him a further extension on paying duties he had owed since 1844.

Dickson's electoral battles were seldom dull. He won his first victory in 1818 over John George Marshall*, who complained of outside interference; Mortimer's comment; "I started the boys that fixed it," might explain the massive backing Dickson received in Antigonish. In 1820 Dickson's opponent, John Ross, charged that the sheriff closed the poll and fled the village when informed that electors were rowing up Country Harbour to vote. Despite reports that he would be beaten, Dickson won re-election in 1826 and again in 1830 in spite of some violence at the poll in Antigonish. That he did not contest the 1836 election might in part be a result of the criticism which John Young*, his fellow representative for Sydney County, had directed his way. His 1838 by-election victory in

Pictou, over the Reverend Kenneth John McKenzie, a staunch foe of Pictou Academy [see Thomas McCulloch*], was a typical political-religious confrontation, and Dickson's defeat in 1840 was engineered by the dividing and sub-dividing of farms to obtain freeholder privileges for his opponent's supporters. The Colchester by-election of 1841 was described in a letter to the Pictou *Observer* as a scene of "drunkenness, perjury, bribery and corruption," and only the active participation of Alexander CAMPBELL at the Tatamagouche poll enabled Dickson to carry the day.

Dickson was a reformer in politics and the first native-born Nova Scotian to represent Pictou in the assembly. Tall, good looking, he was, in his quiet manner, a power in the assembly. He frankly admitted he was better known for his deeds that his words. When McCulloch became president of Dalhousie College in 1838, he was warned by Dickson, "It is our duty, if we can't forget, at least to forgive." Dickson supported Joseph Howe* on most of the major issues from 1838 to 1843, but he candidly admitted, "As for reform in our House, it is only from the teeth out."

Dickson emerges as a quiet, almost stoic, figure, drawn to the political scene more by connection than conviction. Inherent in the determined spirit and gentle dignity of Dickson, and others of like political persuasion, were the seeds which bore fruit in 1848 when Nova Scotia became the first overseas colony in the British empire to obtain responsible government.

ALLAN C. DUNLOP

PANS, RG 1, 174: 391; RG 5, E, 3; P, 1; 124, no.69. *Mechanic and Farmer* (Pictou, N.S.), 18 Nov. 1840. *Observer* (Pictou), 1842. *Dickson, Scotch-Irish: Connecticut, 1719; Nova Scotia, 1761; California, 1865; descendants of Charles and Amelia Bishop Dickson of Onslow, Nova Scotia*, [comp. E. M. Dewey] ([Boston], 1953). A. C. Jost, *Guysborough sketches and essays* (Guysborough, N.S., 1950). J. S. Martell, "Origins of self-government in Nova Scotia, 1815–1836" (PHD thesis, Univ. of London, 1935). F. H. Patterson, *The days of the ships, Tatamagouche, N.S.* (Truro, N.S., 1970).

DIONNE, AMABLE, merchant, militia officer, politician, and seigneur; b. 30 Nov. 1781 in Kamouraska, Que., son of Alexandre Dionne, a farmer and militia captain, and Magdelaine Michaud; m. 10 June 1811 Catherine Perreault, niece and adopted daughter of the local seigneur, Jacques-Nicolas Perrault*, in Rivière-Ouelle, Lower Canada, and they had 13 children; d. 2 May 1852 in Sainte-Anne-de-la-Pocatière (La Pocatière), Lower Canada.

A descendant of a family that was among the first to settle at Kamouraska, Amable Dionne attended school there for about a year and a half. In 1802 he signed an employment contract with Pierre Casgrain*, a merchant of Rivière-Ouelle, becoming his clerk, and in 1811 was made his partner. A year later Dionne and his wife moved from Rivière-Ouelle to Kamouraska; there, in a house owned by his partner, he became a merchant for Casgrain et Dionne. The partnership was dissolved in 1818 by mutual agreement and Dionne set up on his own account.

Dionne's talents, and the discipline that went with his highly authoritarian character, were not the sole reasons for the financial success he achieved. His business was located at the centre of a seigneury with a rapidly growing population; around 1820 it had some 5,000 inhabitants. There had been an extraordinary jump of about 300 per cent since 1790, prompted perhaps as much by immigration as by natural increase. Moreover, according to surveyor Joseph Bouchette*, between 1815 and 1820 six schooners transported to the Quebec market substantial quantities of fish, wood, wheat, and butter of a quality renowned in the capital. The volume of trade with external markets ensured net receipts of currency that could be used for the purchase of consumer goods. This development was the source of the prosperity enjoyed by leaders in commerce, medicine, and law at Kamouraska, who in prestige and power could hold their own with the residents of the presbytery.

Dionne's political career began in 1830 when he was elected to represent Kamouraska in the House of Assembly. Re-elected in 1834, he was a signatory to the 92 Resolutions drafted that year by Augustin-Norbert Morin* which outlined the main grievances and demands of the assembly. Dionne, none the less, eventually dissociated himself from Louis-Joseph Papineau*'s position and rallied to the defence of order during the rebellion of 1837. He was appointed to the Legislative Council in August 1837 and sat there until March 1838. In April he was summoned to the Special Council, on which he remained until February 1841. Then he was a legislative councillor from August 1842 to May 1852.

At the time Dionne entered politics he also undertook a series of transactions by which he became owner of the seigneuries of La Pocatière and Grande-Anse. He entrusted management of them to agents. During the 1830s Dionne had substantial liquid assets and landed property at his disposal, and over the years he also accumulated the symbolic capital of social esteem and respectability. His status was demonstrated, for example, by the rank he held in the militia. Appointed captain in the militia battalion of Rivière-Ouelle in 1818, he was promoted major on 10 Aug. 1830. He showed he could use the combined assets of his financial success and his prestige to set in motion matrimonial schemes befitting his status. The $8,000 dowry that each of his eight daughters received sufficiently indicates the overriding influence of the

merchant in the choice of his sons-in-law. They would include a notary, Olivier-Eugène Casgrain, who owned the seigneury of L'Islet and was the son of Dionne's former partner; a lawyer, Pierre-Elzéar Taschereau*, colleague of Dionne in the assembly; a Quebec printer and publisher, George-Paschal Desbarats*; Jean-Thomas Taschereau*, son of Judge Jean-Thomas Taschereau*; a merchant, Jean-Charles Chapais*; Dr Ludger Têtu and businessman Cirice Têtu, sons of a friend of Dionne. After Dionne's death his two sons, who had practised law for a few months, abandoned legal concerns and settled down on their estates.

As well as distributing various assets to his children during his lifetime, Dionne assumed certain responsibilities with regard to his relatives. A particularly painful family drama involved an adoption. In 1821 one of Mme Dionne's sisters lost her husband, and the Dionne family decided to take over the care of her son Charles-Paschal-Télesphore Chiniquy*. Chiniquy was turned out of the house four years later because he was thought to have made indecent advances to one of his adoptive sisters, and he vowed a deep and undying hatred towards his uncle. In his memoirs published in 1885 he claimed that Dionne "had made a colossal fortune" at the expense of the parishioners of Kamouraska: "The Rev. Mr. [Jacques] Varin, who was always in his debt, was also forced by the circumstances, to buy everything, both for himself and the church, from him, and had to pay, without a murmur, the most exorbitant prices for everything." Yet the record also shows Dionne settling a pension in 1824 on his wife's natural father, Michel Perrault, a school-teacher who was no longer able to work. When one of Dionne's sisters left her drunken, brutal husband, she took refuge in the Dionne household and spent a good part of her life there. A grandson, whose mother died in 1838, was also brought into Dionne's home.

Amable Dionne remained at Kamouraska until 1849, when he had his manor-house at Sainte-Anne-de-la-Pocatière made ready for occupation. He lived in it only three years, however, for he died on 2 May 1852, leaving his wife an estate worth $150,000. The funeral took place on 6 May, with some 2,000 people from the neighbouring area in attendance. His body was interred in the parish church following a funeral service sung by pupils of the Collège de Sainte-Anne-de-la-Pocatière, of which he was a benefactor.

SERGE GAGNON

AP, Notre-Dame-de-Liesse (Rivière-Ouelle), Reg. des baptêmes, mariages et sépultures, 10 juin 1811; Sainte-Anne (La Pocatière), Reg. des baptêmes, mariages et sépultures, 6 mai 1852; Saint-Louis (Kamouraska), Reg. des baptêmes, mariages et sépultures, 30 nov. 1781. P.-B. Casgrain,

Disbrow

Mémorial des familles Casgrain, Baby et Perrault du Canada (Québec, 1898). [C.-P.-T.] Chiniquy, *Fifty years in the Church of Rome* (Toronto, 1886). Alexandre Paradis, *Kamouraska (1674–1948)* (Québec, 1948). Henri Têtu, *Histoire des familles Têtu, Bonenfant, Dionne et Perrault* (Québec, 1898). F.-J. Audet, "Membres du Conseil spécial," *BRH*, 7 (1901): 82–83. Serge Gagnon, "Le clergé, les notables et l'enseignement privé au Québec: le cas du collège de Sainte-Anne, 1840–1870," *Social Hist.* (Ottawa), no.5 (April 1970): 45–65. W. J. Price, "Aux origines d'un schisme; le centenaire d'une réconciliation avortée," *RHAF*, 12 (1958–59): 519–20. P.G. Roy, "Trois hommes de bien," *BRH*, 34 (1928): 28–31.

DISBROW, NOAH, businessman, politician, and justice of the peace; b. 10 July 1772, probably in Norwalk, Conn.; m. first May 1793 Isabella Chillis, and they had four sons and five daughters; m. secondly 15 Feb. 1827 Amelia Canby of Saint John, N.B., and they had one daughter; d. there 19 April 1853.

Information about Noah Disbrow's background is scanty. He came to Saint John in 1785 with his widowed mother and her loyalist family whose name was Stanton. His father had died under mysterious circumstances in Boston harbour while on board a ship returning from England. Noah's paternal grandfather, who apparently did not have loyalist sympathies, enjoyed less than cordial relations with his daughter-in-law's family, but at the time of his death he did leave his grandson some property. As the Connecticut Disbrows were reputedly a family of means, this inheritance may have helped provide the financial foundation for Noah Disbrow's later success in business. By mid century he employed two Irish servants, a reflection not only of 19th-century immigration patterns to New Brunswick but also of the household of a wealthy merchant. Others who might have shared Disbrow's status were Thomas Millidge*, William Black*, and Lauchlan Donaldson.

Disbrow's commercial involvement was typical of his time and his position in the mercantile community. He was engaged in trading, owned at least two vessels and probably had shares in others, and had a warehouse on Water Street near his own wharf. He also operated as a general dealer in dry goods, liquors, salt, and provisions, selling out of his Market Square store which fronted the city's main thoroughfare. Among his real estate holdings was the first brick building in the city, erected in 1817 at the corner of Germain and Church streets. From 1818 to 1823, the *Duke of Wellington*, owned by Disbrow, was the principal packet on the Saint John to New York City run, carrying both mail and passengers. In 1832 Noah Disbrow's name was one of the amalgam of pre-loyalist, loyalist, and Scottish surnames representing the business and political élite of the city which appeared on the act of incorporation of the Saint John Water Company. This company built the first waterworks for the city.

Like his commercial peers George BOND and Thomas HARDING, Disbrow participated in municipal government, serving from 1821 to 1827 as alderman for Queens Ward. In March 1830 he was appointed a magistrate for the city and county of Saint John, a position he held for the rest of his life. By the time of his death, Disbrow had ceased to be an active member of the Saint John business community. The probate record reveals that his wealth was concentrated chiefly in his sizeable real estate holdings throughout the city. These properties were divided among his surviving children and his grandson. Essentially, however, both the Disbrow name and its high profile in business affairs disappeared with the demise of Noah Disbrow. Although Disbrow had apparently not been a regular communicant of any denomination, two of his sons became Church of England clergymen. The only child of his second marriage, Caroline Amelia, became the wife of William Brydone Jack*, president of the University of New Brunswick (Fredericton) from 1861 to 1885.

ELIZABETH W. MCGAHAN

City Clerk's Office (Saint John, N.B.), Common Council of Saint John, minutes, 1821–27 (mfm. at PANB). N.B. Museum, C8: 11, col.1; C19: 7 ("Saint John 100 years ago"); Noah and Amelia Disbrow family Bible; Reg. of marriages for the city and county of Saint John, book A (1810–28): 487. PANB, MC 7; RG 2, RS6, A3: 347; RG 7, RS71, 1853, Noah Disbrow. Saint John Regional Library (Saint John), "Biographical data relating to New Brunswick families, especially of loyalist descent," comp. D. R. Jack (4v., typescript), 2. "Inscriptions from the old burial-ground, Saint John, N.B.," N.B. Hist. Soc., *Loyalists' centennial souvenir* (Saint John, 1887), 107. *The New Brunswick census of 1851: Saint John County* (2v., Fredericton, 1982), 1: 194. H. F. Walling, *Topographical map of the counties of St. John and Kings, New Brunswick, from actual surveys under the direction of H. F. Walling* (New York, 1862) (copy in PANB, H2-203.1-1862). *New-Brunswick Courier*, 24 May 1823, 3 Sept. 1825. *New Brunswick vital statistics from newspapers, 1784–1815, 1824–1828*, comp. D. F. Johnson et al. (Fredericton, 1982; 1983). D. R. Jack, *Centennial prize essay on the history of the city and county of St. John* (Saint John, 1883), 74, 114–15. E. W. McGahan, *The port of Saint John . . .* (1v. to date, Saint John, 1982–). MacNutt, *New Brunswick*.

DOAK, ROBERT, businessman, farmer, office holder, and justice of the peace; b. 4 April 1785 in Ochiltree, Scotland, third of eight children of Robert Doak and Agnes ——; m. 3 Oct. 1808 Jean Kirkland, and they had three sons and three daughters; d. 5 April 1857 in Doaktown, N.B.

Nothing specific is known about the youth, education, or financial background of Robert Doak. In

1815 he and his family left Scotland intending to settle in Kentucky. However, inclement weather forced their ship into the port of Miramichi, N.B., and the passengers were landed there. Doak remained in the colony at Newcastle and by 1817 had established himself as an innkeeper in nearby Nelson Parish. The next year his elder brother, James, arrived with his wife and three children, and both brothers entered into partnership with Alexander MacLaggan to operate a mill in Blackville. By July 1822 the Doaks had sold out to MacLaggan and moved approximately 20 miles farther up the Southwest Miramichi River to the present site of Doaktown; there they were joined by their father, who had recently emigrated from Scotland. On 1 April 1825 Robert Doak Jr purchased lot 45 from the Ephraim Wheeler Betts estate (having earlier obtained two adjacent lots for farmland) and his brother James and his family settled in close proximity.

In conjunction with his son James Andrew, whose family was to share the homestead, Doak soon had constructed and was operating a carding-mill, grist-mill, and kiln, and later built a sawmill and oatmeal mill, the latter serving the whole of Northumberland County. The mills were operated by water-power; there was a brook-fed mill-pond at the rear of the property which provided a constant source of water. Doak also farmed and, according to family tradition, "raised as many as one hundred hogs every year which they salted down or smoked to be sold. The cellar used to look like a wholesale grocery at times."

Shortly after his arrival in upper Miramichi, Doak became involved in local government. In 1822 he was appointed overseer of the poor, town clerk, and clerk of the market. The following year he became overseer of highways for the district and in this capacity he supervised the construction of the road between Fredericton and Newcastle. The Miramichi fire of October 1825 affected Doak and his enterprises, although not as disastrously as it did many of the earlier established settlers. Claiming a loss of £20, he petitioned the relief committee set up by the provincial government and received half the amount. In the same year he was appointed a justice of the peace for the county. Unlike most other men after 1800, Doak had managed to bypass many of the lesser municipal offices such as overseer of fisheries and fence viewer: the normal pattern was to hold two or three of the more minor positions before becoming a magistrate. In 1826 he became a school trustee, a post which ten years later enabled him to force long-term squatters from a school reserve lot adjoining his own property and to have the land granted to himself later that year for "safe-keeping." A school was eventually built on the site. Appointed acting coroner for the area in 1829, he was still holding inquests as late as 1844.

Until the mid 19th century, the settlement had remained nameless, at times being referred to as part of Ludlow and after 1830 as Blissfield Parish. Following the completion of the highway and the establishment of a post office, the village was designated Doaktown, because Doak was the most politically influential and the most affluent resident. When in 1847 the first bridge was built across the Miramichi at the village, Doak, who admired a large elm tree standing directly in line with the road, persuaded the road supervisor, for £5, to place a slight crook in the highway.

Doak's career was not without blemishes. At a special session of the county council in 1819, he was accused of keeping a gambling house. In 1830 he was fined for the unlawful selling of spirituous liquors – a common offence of the times, yet unbefitting his position. And from 1837 to 1840 he was a key figure in an unpleasant domestic lawsuit between himself and his son-in-law William Robinson, "an absconding debtor"; at the same time he served as a presiding magistrate at the trial.

Doak, commonly known as "the Squire," was noted for his benevolent spirit; he contributed generously to the religious and educational life of the community, with gifts of land for a Baptist church (although the family was Presbyterian) and the local school.

WILLIAM R. MACKINNON

[Information concerning Robert and Jean Kirkland Doak was kindly supplied by a descendant, the Reverend Douglas Earle of Halifax, from a family Bible in his possession. W.R.MACK.]

Anglican Church of Canada, Diocese of Fredericton Arch., Ludlow Parish, N.B., reg. of baptisms, 1818–24. Central Miramichi Hist. Soc. (Doaktown, N.B.), "Notes on the Doaks." GRO (Edinburgh), Ochiltree, reg. of births and baptisms, 10 April 1785; reg. of marriages; Sorn, reg. of marriages, 3 Oct. 1808; Stair, reg. of marriages. Northumberland Land Registry Office (Newcastle, N.B.), Registry books, 25: 279 (mfm. at PANB). PAC, RG 31, A1, 1851, Blissfield. PANB, MC 216/46; MYY 262; RG 4, RS24, S38-P42; RG 5, RS55, 1840, *Doak* v. *Hutchison*; RG 7, RS68, 1856, Robert Doak; RG 10, RS108, Robert Doak, 20 July 1822, 18 Feb. 1836; RG 18, RS153, 1817, 1822–23, 1826, 1829–30, 1843–44; 17. St Thomas United Church Cemetery (Doaktown), Tombstones of Robert and Jean Kirkland Doak. SRO, RS14/55/206, 14 Feb. 1807. UNBL, A. H. Ross Foster [Hanley] coll., A. H. Ross [Foster] Hanley, "Some account of the families of James Ross, Donald McDonald, Joseph Story, James Doak and their descendants" (typescript, 1959). N.B., Postmaster General, *First report of the Postmaster General of New Brunswick, General Post Office, Fredericton, 31st December 1856* ([Fredericton, 1857]), xx. W. A. Spray, "Early Northumberland County, 1765–1825; a study in local government" (MA thesis, Univ. of N.B., Fredericton, 1963), 113. Margaret Doak, "Squire Doak – and Doaktown," *Atlantic Advocate* (Fredericton), 58 (1967–68), no.1: 29–33. "Doaktown," *Gleaner* (Fredericton), 21 May 1887:

Dodd

3. Mrs Frank Swim, "History of Doaktown," *Doaktown Rev.*, 28 March 1902.

DODD, CHARLES, ship's captain and fur trader; baptized 29 Nov. 1808 in New Buckenham, England, son of John Beck Dodd, surgeon, and Mary Cobbold; m. 22 Nov. 1842 in Fort Vancouver (Vancouver, Wash.) Grace McTavish, daughter of John George McTavish* and Nancy McKenzie, and they had seven children; d. 2 June 1860 in Victoria.

Charles Dodd apparently first went to sea in 1827. Although little is known of him for the next few years, he seems to have gained the experience necessary to sign on with the Hudson's Bay Company brig *Nereide* as second mate in May 1833. The vessel arrived at the HBC's Columbia district headquarters at Fort Vancouver in April 1834, carrying orders to conduct a maritime trade along the northwest coast. In defiance of these instructions Chief Factor John McLoughlin ordered the ship back to England with a cargo of lumber and salmon. In 1835 Dodd was assigned as second mate to the recently built steamship *Beaver*, under Captain David Home, sailing from London in August for Fort Vancouver. This vessel was the first steamship on the north Pacific and was destined to play important and varied roles in the history of British Columbia. Promoted first mate upon arrival in April 1836, Dodd was initiated that summer into the HBC trade as the *Beaver* undertook its first trading cruise along the northwest coast.

From 1837 to 1840 Dodd served as first mate aboard the *Nereide*. Plagued with mutinous crews and frequent desertions, the ship carried supplies to forts Simpson (Port Simpson, B.C.) and McLoughlin (near Bella Bella, B.C.), sheep for the farms at Fort Nisqually (near Tacoma, Wash.), and lumber to the Sandwich (Hawaiian) Islands. Dodd's next appointment was as first mate on the barque *Cowlitz*. In December 1841 Sir George Simpson, governor of the HBC, boarded this vessel for a tour of the northwest coast as part of his journey round the world and was impressed by the character and ability of Dodd. When the vessel arrived at Fort Stikine (Alaska) in April 1842 it was discovered that the officer in charge, John McLoughlin, son of Chief Factor McLoughlin, had been fatally shot in a drunken fray. After order was restored and the sale of spirits discontinued, Simpson placed Dodd in charge, on a three-year contract to begin 1 June. Dodd, a teetotaller, had no qualms about enforcing the ban on liquor. Early in 1843 David Manson* was sent to take command of the post. Dodd remained as assistant but was once again placed in charge following Manson's transfer in early 1844.

In the spring of 1845 Dodd was relieved of his land assignment and placed in command of the *Beaver* which, as a result of Simpson's 1842 decision to close forts McLoughlin and Taku (Alaska), played an important role in the collection of furs from the northern Indians by the company. In addition, the steamer carried supplies for Fort Simpson and conducted an exchange of furs with the Russian American Company at Sitka (Alaska). Dodd, therefore, was doing double duty – commanding a ship and trading in furs. None the less, although highly respected for his "zeal and judgement" by his superiors, such as Chief Factor James Douglas*, he was not adequately compensated for his services. In 1851, owing to lack of promotion and difficulties in obtaining good crew members because of the gold finds in California, he resigned from the HBC and settled in Victoria with his wife and family. The HBC, however, had considerable difficulty in finding qualified officers for its now all-important marine service, those available being either "drunkards or incapables," and Simpson persuaded Dodd to return to the *Beaver* early in 1852, promoting him to chief trader in June.

Dodd stayed with the *Beaver* until 1859, when he was transferred to the larger, newly built steamship *Labouchere*, and continued to serve in the HBC coasting trade. In January 1860 he received an official expression of gratitude from the Legislative Assembly of the territory of Washington for recovering the scalp of Colonel Isaac N. Ebey who had been murdered in August 1857 on Whidbey Island (Wash.) by northern Indians in reprisal for the murder of a chief by American naval forces the previous autumn. After two years of careful searching, Dodd had finally succeeded in locating and purchasing the scalp, for six blankets and other items, and it was then returned to the Ebey family.

Promoted chief factor in February 1860, effective 1 June, Dodd did not live long to enjoy his honours. On 2 June he died of a kidney infection at Victoria. Dodd Passage and Dodd Rock, near Port Simpson, B.C., as well as Dodd Narrows at the south end of Vancouver Island, are named in his honour.

SHIRLEE ANNE SMITH

PAM, HBCA, A.6/20: f.294; A.6/25: f.96; A.6/35: f.30; A.11/72: f.46d; A.12/5: f.346d; A.32/28: ff.33, 35; B.223/b/20; 27; C.1/208; 243; 257; 610; C.3/14: f.15d; D.4/43: f.38d; D.4/71: ff.340, 346d; D.5/31: ff.221–221d; Charles Dodd file. *Catholic Church records of Pacific northwest* (Munnick). *HBRS*, 4 (Rich); 6 (Rich); 7 (Rich). Helmcken, *Reminiscences of Helmcken* (Blakey Smith and Lamb). George Simpson, *Narrative of a journey round the world, during the years 1841 and 1842* (2v., London, 1847). *British Colonist* (Victoria), 5 June 1860. Walbran, *B.C. coast names. Lewis & Dryden's marine history of the Pacific northwest; an illustrated review of the growth and development of the maritime industry . . .*, ed. E. W. Wright (2nd ed., New York, 1961). Derek Pethick, *S.S. "Beaver": the ship that saved the west* (Vancouver, 1970). Rich, *Hist.*

of HBC. W. K. Lamb, "The advent of the *Beaver*," *BCHQ*, 2 (1938): 163–84. B. A. McKelvie, "Colonel Ebey's head," *Beaver*, outfit 287 (summer 1956): 43–45. Sylvia Van Kirk, "Women and the fur trade," *Beaver*, outfit 303 (winter 1972): 4–21.

DOLLARD, WILLIAM (sometimes written as **Dullard**), Roman Catholic priest and bishop; baptized 29 Nov. 1789 in Ballytarina, County Kilkenny (Republic of Ireland), son of Michael Dollard and Anastasia Dunphy; d. 29 Aug. 1851 in Fredericton.

Little is known of William Dollard's background or of the influences which may have shaped his character. Kilkenny was a relatively stable part of Ireland during his youth, not much affected by the bloody rebellion of 1798 and its aftermath in the neighbouring counties. He was first educated in a hedge-school (an unauthorized school which served the Roman Catholic population) but entered St Kieran's College, just outside the town of Kilkenny, possibly as early as 1804. By 1812 he was listed as a student of theology.

Between 1812 and 1815, Joseph-Octave Plessis*, bishop of Quebec, made three tours of the missions of the Maritimes. He found that the recent migrations of Scots and Irish had left thousands of Roman Catholics without adequate spiritual care, and in 1813 he attempted to recruit missionaries or theology students who spoke either Irish or Scottish Gaelic. One of the schools he canvassed was St Kieran's, and one of those who responded was William Dollard.

In 1816 Dollard took passage for Quebec City, where he completed his training. After being raised through the minor orders, he was ordained by Plessis on 12 Oct. 1817. Ten days later he was posted to Arichat, where he shared with Abbé François Lejamtel* the burden of ministering to the whole of Cape Breton. In the next few years, Dollard, who assumed responsibility for the Scots and the Micmacs, was constantly on the move. Often sleeping in the open, even in winter, he seems to have managed his difficult task despite poor health. He served as many of his scattered parishioners as possible and learned Scottish Gaelic in the process. One of the many people he befriended was Lawrence Kavanagh*, the influential St Peters merchant who successfully challenged the laws which barred Roman Catholics from public office in Nova Scotia. In 1822, just as Kavanagh was beginning his struggle, Dollard was sick at his house, stricken with pleurisy. Plessis was forced to recall him to Quebec where he entered the ecclesiastical society for a needed rest.

The next year Dollard was sent back to the Maritimes, to serve the growing community on the Miramichi in New Brunswick. The timber trade had brought thousands of Irish and Scots to the north shore of the colony, and the ports of Chatham and Newcastle had a turbulent immigrant population controlled by merchants who practically wrote their own laws [*see* Alexander RANKIN; Joseph Cunard*]. The single parish church, at Bartibog, had been built in 1800, but the centre of population had moved upriver. The Irish were now concentrated in the parish of Nelson, where they used a small chapel built in 1769, and in 1825 Dollard opened a new church in Nelson (Nelson-Miramichi) dedicated to St Patrick. Although the disastrous fire that swept the settlement that year stilled ethnic and religious antagonisms for a time, Dollard's greatest problems were the rivalry between the Irish and Scottish Catholics, and the stiff competition he faced from aggressive evangelist missionaries such as the Baptist preacher Joseph CRANDALL. His disposition earned the respect of all parties, including his Protestant rivals and his strongly Scottish superior, Bishop Angus Bernard Mac-Eachern* of Charlottetown. Civil authorities demonstrated their admiration by appointing him to the local boards of health and education.

In 1833 Dollard was summoned by MacEachern to the episcopal residence at St Andrews, P.E.I., where he apparently lectured in the small seminary and served as vicar general of the diocese. The bishop's death two years later led to the first of a series of feuds over episcopal succession among the French, Scots, and Irish in the Maritimes. Dollard's role in this dispute is obscure, but he seems to have supported Bernard Donald MACDONALD, the man chosen in 1837 to be MacEachern's successor. In 1836 Dollard was appointed to the mission at Fredericton and the following year was again named vicar general by the new bishop.

Although Fredericton was less rowdy than the Miramichi, having both the lieutenant governor's entourage and a garrison, Dollard's new duties were no less challenging. His parish covered all of central New Brunswick, and he had to serve a scattered Roman Catholic population of French, Indians, and Irish. Because there were only a few small chapels, his first task was to provide suitable churches, which he promptly did at Woodstock and Kingsclear. Although nowhere was this need as pressing as in the capital itself, the demands on Dollard's time kept him from replacing the small chapel there for some years. In response to a growth in the Catholic population throughout his mission as well as to ethnic jealousies, ecclesiastical jurisdictions in the Maritimes were reorganized in September 1842. Halifax was elevated to an archiepiscopate with responsibility for the Maritimes, and a diocese for New Brunswick was carved out of the diocese of Charlottetown. The choice of bishop for New Brunswick rekindled old flames. Abbé Antoine Gagnon*, who worked in the northern section of the colony, had more seniority, but Dollard apparently had better connections. After

Donlevy

Bishop Macdonald had been given his choice of diocese and had decided to stay on the Island, William Dollard was given New Brunswick.

Dollard was consecrated bishop of Fredericton by Pierre-Flavien Turgeon*, coadjutor bishop of Quebec, on 11 June 1843. He never used that title, preferring "Bishop of New Brunswick." Had an Irish Catholic bishop styled himself after the very British capital of a British and Anglican province, there might have been problems. Perhaps Dollard also wished to avoid any confrontation with the Church of England (which in any case soon sent John Medley* as its own bishop to assume the Fredericton title). With a sense of urgency, probably created by his consecration, he immediately set about building a new church in Fredericton. It was reported that he collected as much money from Protestants as from Catholics. One donation came from the British government in exchange for free pew space for the Catholic soldiers in the garrison. The provincial government was not so generous. Beginning in 1844, Dollard attempted to have the diocese incorporated so that he need not own church property as a private citizen. Twice the House of Assembly passed the enabling legislation, and twice it was rejected by the Legislative Council. On the third attempt, the council relented, and the diocese was incorporated on 6 July 1846. During the previous year the new church, diplomatically dedicated to an appropriate Englishman, Saint Dunstan, had been opened, although it was far from completed. In the next few years gifts of altar furniture arrived from Lower Canada and Ireland, until Dollard and his new charge had one of the finest wooden churches in the province.

Even before it was finished, more important events drew Dollard away from his principal church. The Irish famine had driven thousands of immigrants to New Brunswick, and he felt he could be of more use in the port city of Saint John. By 1848 he had shifted his residence there. Alleviating starvation, disease, and poverty was more urgent to Dollard than maintaining the prestige of a bishop in the capital. It was also imperative that he do all in his power to ameliorate relations between the suspicious and often hostile resident communities and the bitter and angry Irish newcomers. In 1847 a serious clash had occurred in Woodstock, and two years later a far more serious confrontation took place in Saint John. Dollard's role was to advocate moderation. The bishop's attempt to organize and settle the immigrants meant almost continuous travel and a return of poor health. On Friday, 29 Aug. 1851, while on a visit to Fredericton, Dollard died, possibly of diabetes. On the following Sunday, he was quietly and fittingly interred under the altar of St Dunstan's. (A century later, the altar-boy descendants of his immigrant charges, including the undersigned, were to assure one another in hushed and reverent tones that the holy water of the baptismal font dripped onto his forehead, ensuring eternal communion with the Catholic community he had done so much to create.)

To describe William Dollard merely as a missionary and bishop is to ignore the tremendous impact this man had on the growing and unstable society that was New Brunswick during the first half of the 19th century. In his quiet and benevolent, yet diligent manner, Dollard was a pioneer who contributed as much as those, including some of his fellow missionaries, who achieved a fleeting notoriety through opposite qualities. He was universally seen as an honest broker who could bridge the gaps created by ethnic and denominational rivalry. Even the most virulent critics of the Irish or the Roman Catholics could still cite him as the exception to the rule. No hostile reference to him as a person has survived, if such ever existed. Given the New Brunswick of the time, what better epitaph.

PETER M. TONER

Arch. of the Diocese of Saint John (Saint John, N.B.), Dollard papers. [Robert Cooney], *The autobiography of a Wesleyan Methodist missionary, (formerly a Roman Catholic), containing an account of his conversion from Romanism, and his reception into the Wesleyan ministry; also reminiscences of nearly twenty-five years' itinerancy in the North American provinces* ... (Montreal, 1856); *A compendious history of the northern part of the province of New Brunswick, and of the district of Gaspé, in Lower Canada* (Halifax, 1832; repub. Chatham, N.B., 1896). A. A. Johnston, *Hist. of Catholic Church in eastern N.S.* J. G. McDonald, "Nucleus of Saint John diocese centred in pioneer mission work of Jesuits 300 years ago," *Official historical booklet, Diocese of Saint John*, ed. B. P. McCafferty (Saint John, 1948). C. A. Nugent, "A study of the Right Reverend William Dollard, D.D., first Catholic bishop of New Brunswick" (typescript essay, 1964, formerly at N.B. Museum but withdrawn, 1983). W. J. Osborne, "The Right Reverend William Dollard, D.D., first bishop of New Brunswick," CCHA *Report*, 9 (1941–42): 23–28.

DONLEVY, CHARLES, newspaperman and office holder; b. in 1812 or 1813 in Ballymote (Republic of Ireland), probably the son of Dr Patrick Donlevy; m. 26 Oct. 1846 Mary Walsh in Brockville, Upper Canada, and they had at least one child, a son; d. 22 July 1858 in Toronto.

Nothing is known of Charles Donlevy's whereabouts from the time of his immigration to British North America in 1831 until he settled in Toronto in the mid 1830s. After serving as an apprentice to John and Michael Reynolds, printers and newspaper publishers, he quickly became a prominent member of the city's Irish Catholic community. Besides publishing the *Toronto Mirror*, a journal that in the pre-confederation period was one of the most important voices of Irish Catholic reformers in Upper Canada, Donlevy was a leading figure in the St Patrick's Benevolent Society, the Total Abstinence Society, and the Catholic Institute, as well as the Catholic Colonization Society, which had as its object the settlement of the province's urban Irish, a group suffering from "the miseries and wretchedness of city life," on the "unshaken soil." During the administration of Governor Sir Charles Theophilus Metcalfe*, he was on the general board of the Reform Association of Canada, a province-wide organization pledged to the defence of the principle of responsible government. In 1843 he was a driving force behind the creation of the Loyal Irish Repeal Association of Toronto, which, as its name suggests, called for the dissolution of the union of 1800 between Great Britain and Ireland; in the late 1840s he was a member of the general board of a relief organization established to alleviate the suffering caused by the Irish famine; and in 1853 he was elected as a separate school trustee for St James's Ward and served as chairman of the Toronto separate school board.

Without question, the most historically significant feature of Donlevy's life was his long association with the *Mirror*. This weekly journal was founded by Donlevy and Patrick McTavey in 1837 and was the sole reform paper to survive the rebellion without folding at least temporarily. A few years later, in 1843, McTavey launched a newspaper of his own, the *Constitution*, and Donlevy became the *Mirror*'s sole publisher. Despite a fire that destroyed its office in 1849, the *Mirror* prospered under Donlevy's direction, gaining a large readership not only in Toronto but in every section of the province. However, by the time of his death in July 1858 the *Mirror* was evidently in financial difficulty, for the following month his widow, acting as the executrix of his estate, announced in the paper that "the receipts of late have gone very much below the actual expenses; and unless a prompt remittance from defaulters take place, the value of the paper must sensibly diminish." The *Mirror* was able to survive this crisis and continued publication under Patrick A. O'Neill until about 1866. As for Donlevy himself, there is reason to believe that his personal income in the 1850s was seriously reduced as a result of the *Mirror*'s financial problems. When he died he left debts, and at a special high mass the officiating priest noted that his financial contributions to the cause of religion were all the more praiseworthy in light of his "late limited means."

It is difficult to say whether Donlevy wrote the *Mirror*'s editorials: in 1838 A. K. Mackenzie, writing to William Lyon Mackenzie*, described one McSweeney as "the late editor of the Mirror," and for a brief period in 1843 C. P. O'Dwyer was listed in the *Mirror* as the paper's editor. Even so, Donlevy was the *Mirror*'s publisher, and he undoubtedly made sure

that his views were accurately reflected in its pages. Thus, for example, Donlevy's concern over the state of Ireland under British rule was also a main preoccupation of the *Mirror* from the time of its foundation. In countless editorials, all revealing a spirit of fervent Irish patriotism, the *Mirror* denounced Britain's oppression of the Irish people and emphasized the need for immediate dissolution of the union of 1800, a tangible symbol of "the galling chain of proud England's despotism." Most of these editorials categorically rejected the notion of armed resistance against British persecution and instead urged Irishmen to give their whole-hearted support to the peaceful, constitutional agitation of Ireland's "liberator," Daniel O'Connell. However, after the outbreak of the Irish famine, the *Mirror* adopted a more belligerent stance. In October 1846 it described Ireland's absentee landlords as "ruthless, beastly, incorrigible" and expressed the hope that these "tyrants" would be crushed into "non-entity" by the "starving multitudes." Some years later, in 1851, another *Mirror* editorial praised those Young Ireland rebels of 1848 who, "maddened to desperation by the groans and tears of their starving fellow countrymen, flung their banner to the breeze and summoned an expiring race to fight for their lives, for their liberty, for their country."

On the domestic front, the *Mirror*'s political position cannot be fully understood unless viewed in relation to the Irish Catholic experience in Upper Canada. Unlike Ireland, where the indigenous population was oppressed and exploited, Upper Canada offered full civil and religious equality to the Catholic Irish. As a result, the radical tradition of Irish politics – a radicalism that frequently boiled over into open rebellion – was entirely absent in Upper Canada. This is not to say that all was well for the colony's Irish; most Irishmen in Upper Canada, at least those in urban centres, were mired in poverty and for many years their penchant for violence, drunkenness, and crime of all sorts created severe social problems. Nevertheless, it is striking that the turbulence of the Irish never translated itself into a direct assault on the social and political order. It is also significant that leaders of the Irish Catholic community, with the exception of such renegades as William John O'Grady*, rejected radicalism in favour of the politics of moderate reform. To them, defending the basic fabric of Upper Canadian society was primarily a matter of common sense: however difficult the Irishman's lot in Upper Canada, conditions in Ireland were far worse. At the same time, their fundamental conservatism reflected an intuitive grasp of the realities of Upper Canadian life. As they saw it, if Irish Catholics were to make a place for themselves in their new home, they would have to be scrupulously careful not to arouse suspicions about their political loyalties.

Donlevy

In this context, the politics of the *Mirror* reveal much about Donlevy himself and the Irish Catholic community generally. When rebellion broke out in December 1837, the *Mirror* denounced the "deluded men" responsible, reminded Catholics of their obligations to show "a respectful obedience to the laws of the land," and asserted unequivocally that the severance of the imperial tie would result in the "eternal annihilation" of the Canadas. The last note rang oddly for a paper that was so bitterly hostile towards British rule in Ireland, but the fact remains that for most of its life the *Mirror*'s loyalty to the British connection was beyond reproach. During the 1840s the *Mirror* adhered to a moderately reformist political position, standing side by side with the reform party led by Robert BALDWIN and Louis-Hippolyte La Fontaine* in the struggle for responsible government. The *Mirror* argued that responsible government, by giving the Province of Canada complete control over its internal affairs, would reinforce the emotional ties that linked the colony with the parent state. With the winning of responsible government in 1849, the *Mirror* was exultant and it singled out for praise Governor Lord Elgin [Bruce*] who, "by his unswerving adherence to constitutional principles," had "done more to strengthen the bond of connexion between this Colony and the mother country than all his predecessors." After the publication of the Annexation Manifesto in Montreal in 1849, the *Mirror*'s loyalty showed signs of wavering, but even then the paper was remarkable for its cautious, moderate tone. In an editorial in October the *Mirror* claimed that annexationism should be resisted with calm reason, not hysterical tirades, while adding its opinion that an "interminable prolongation" of the British tie was neither likely nor desirable. The following month it retreated slightly, asserting that annexation "savours somewhat of the spirit of vassalage."

In the early 1850s Donlevy's *Mirror* devoted itself to defending the brand of moderate reformism epitomized in Upper Canada by Baldwin and Francis Hincks*. Although it too supported the extension of the elective principle, especially with regard to the Legislative Council, the *Mirror* argued that the impatience of the Clear Grits [*see* George Brown*] to see radical changes implemented might destroy the reform party. The *Mirror* frequently lashed out against the racial and religious intolerance both of the Clear Grits and of George Brown, a man it described as "a nuisance to society and a traitor to his party." Demands for representation by population and a repeal of the union, in the *Mirror*'s view, were inspired by irrational francophobia and threatened to engulf the Canadas in a civil war. As for the "no-popery" agitation, the *Mirror* angrily announced that this kind of religious bigotry was an unbearable affront to all Catholics, the very people who had always been the bedrock of the reform party in Upper Canada. As it gradually became apparent that the Brownites and Clear Grits were gaining control of Upper Canadian reformism, the *Mirror* went so far as to indicate that the Catholic community might be forced to change its political allegiance. Catholics were "insulted day after day by the press of that very party for which they had done so much," the *Mirror* lamented in October 1851, "their religion and their religious pastors . . . reviled and calumniated. . . . Better, a thousand times better, support Tories or Orangemen or any other political class, than continue to be kicked and spat upon by such infamous vagabonds."

Another issue – that of separate schools – was just as troublesome and eventually left the *Mirror* without any clear sense of political direction. In the early 1850s it joined forces with Bishop Armand-François-Marie de Charbonnel* and the rest of the Roman Catholic hierarchy in campaigning for an improved system of separate schools. At first, the paper was generally supportive of the reform party's efforts to deal with this question, but by mid decade it had grown restive and was urging Catholics to withhold their electoral support from all candidates, reformers or tories, who were opposed to more generous separate school legislation. When the liberal-conservative ministry of Sir Allan Napier MacNab* and Augustin-Norbert Morin* took office in late 1854, the *Mirror*'s commitment to separate schools – as well as its unhappiness over the "no-popery" crusade – prompted it to come out in support of the new government. As it happened, however, this situation was only temporary. In 1856 a separate school bill introduced by John George Bowes* was shelved by the government of John A. Macdonald* and Étienne-Paschal Taché* at the urging of the superintendent of education in Upper Canada, Egerton Ryerson*. Denouncing this "treacherous" action, the *Mirror* asserted that "it is high time that the existing demoralizing political alliance in which we find ourselves betrayed and disgraced should begin to have an end."

Yet, if it was obvious that a new sort of political alliance was necessary, it was by no means clear who the Irish Catholics were supposed to ally with. The Baldwin–Hincks variety of liberal reformism was now a rare commodity in Upper Canada and, in any case, most moderate reformers and conservatives were supporters of the MacNab–Morin ministry. At the other end of the political spectrum, Brown and the Grits were certainly a powerful force, but their ultra-Protestantism made them anathema to Irish Catholics. The *Mirror* attempted to solve the dilemma by calling on all opponents of the government to bury their differences and establish a new reform party.

230

When this union of reformers did not materialize, the *Mirror* swallowed its pride and resumed its support of the Macdonald–Taché ministry. Declaring its loyalty to something it called the true "Liberal" party of Upper Canada, the *Mirror* stated in April 1858 that the government, now under the leadership of Macdonald and George-Étienne Cartier*, was not "absolutely the best" but was nevertheless "the best that we can obtain under present circumtances."

Mirror editorials thus make it clear that by the late 1850s Donlevy was a man without a political home. His political wanderings from the time of the rebellion reveal the confusion of one Irish Catholic in the changing conditions of the 1850s. They also reflect broader currents in the Irish Catholic community. Although it would be going too far to equate Donlevy's views with the views of all Irish Catholics, it does seem safe to say that the *Mirror*'s editorials expressed the chief concerns of its readership. From this perspective, the paper's doubts about party allegiance may well indicate that the Irish Catholic community, because of rampant religious bigotry and the difficulties posed by the separate schools issue, was no longer certain either about its political loyalties or about its place in Upper Canadian society.

Donlevy's death in 1858 – he was then only in his mid 40s – came suddenly. A report published in the Toronto *Leader* stated that Donlevy, who had "for some time been subject to fits," was eating dinner with his wife on 22 July when he "fell back in his seat and immediately expired." His funeral was held in St Michael's Cathedral on 31 July, and on 2 August he was buried in its crypt. As an indication of his prominent position in Toronto's Irish Catholic community, his name is included on a plaque in the cathedral honouring that church's leading "benefactors."

CURTIS FAHEY

AAT, St Paul's Church (Toronto), reg. of baptisms, 27 July 1849. AO, MS 516, 11 May 1838; RG 21, York County, Toronto assessment rolls, 1834–40, St David's Ward, Richmond St., south side; RG 22, ser.155, administration of Charles Donlevy estate. *Herald* (Toronto), 16 Nov. 1846. *Leader*, 23 July 1858. *Toronto Mirror*, 28 Oct. 1837–13 Aug. 1858. *True Witness and Catholic Chronicle* (Montreal), 30 July 1858. *Dict. of Toronto printers* (Hulse), 85, 177. *Early Toronto newspapers* (Firth), 13. Middleton, *Municipality of Toronto*, 1: 418, 421. Wallace, *Macmillan dict.* J. M. S. Careless, *Brown of "The Globe"* (2v., Toronto, 1959–63; repr. 1972), 1. J. J. Lepine, "The Irish press in Upper Canada and the reform movement, 1828–1848" (MA thesis, Univ. of Toronto, 1946). F. A. Walker, *Catholic education and politics in Upper Canada: a study of the documentation relative to the origin of Catholic elementary schools in the Ontario school system* (Toronto and Vancouver, 1955; repub. Toronto, 1976). P. F. Cronin, "Early Catholic journalism in Canada," CCHA *Report*, 3 (1935–36): 31–42. F. A. Walker, "The political opinion of Upper Canadian Catholics," CCHA *Report*, 22 (1955): 75–86.

DOUCET, NICOLAS-BENJAMIN, notary, office holder, justice of the peace, militia officer, and author; b. 19 Feb. 1781 in Trois-Rivières, Que., second of 12 children of Jean Doucet and Magdeleine Mirau; d. 27 May 1858 in Montreal.

Nicolas-Benjamin Doucet's forebear Germain Doucet de La Verdure, who was probably a native of La Touraine, France, came to Acadia in 1632. He served there as master at arms at Pentagöuet (Castine, Maine), and a few years later as commander at Port-Royal (Annapolis Royal, N.S.). Charles Doucet, Nicolas-Benjamin's grandfather, had to leave Acadia at the time of the deportation and took refuge with his family in Trois-Rivières, where his son Jean married in 1778 and settled to carry on his trade as a baker. Jean Doucet soon became one of the leading figures in the district and held the offices of trustee and justice of the peace. Several of his sons chose to follow professions, and his daughters formed ties with people of their own station.

It was within this family, which was comfortably off and well known in Trois-Rivières at the end of the 18th century, that Nicolas-Benjamin grew up. In 1799, his studies behind him, he began his legal training in Trois-Rivières under Joseph Badeaux*. Doucet received his commission as a notary on 17 March 1804 and signed his first notarial act three days later, the day he took his oath of office. On 5 Aug. 1807 he married 18-year-old Marie-Euphrosine Kimber, the eldest daughter of René Kimber*, a prominent merchant in Trois-Rivières, and the sister of René-Joseph Kimber*, who would become a physician, member for Trois-Rivières in the House of Assembly, and legislative councillor. The ceremony was performed by the bishop of Quebec, Joseph-Octave Plessis*.

With such good connections, in a society where prestigious offices were rare, Doucet soon took part in the affairs of the district of Three Rivers, becoming an assistant clerk of the peace and then in 1811 justice of the peace. He might have continued his rise in society in this uneventful way, but preparations for the War of 1812 gave him an unexpected chance to bring his talents to the attention of the colonial authorities. He was asked to assist the military as a commissioner for taking oaths from half-pay officers on 11 March 1812, for issuing licences in the district on 20 March, and for taking oaths of allegiance on 30 June. In addition, he was given commissions as captain and second major in the 3rd Select Embodied Militia Battalion of Lower Canada on 25 May 1812 and 25 Sept. 1813 respectively. In these capacities he proceeded with his men to Fort Lennox on Île aux Noix, and to Lacolle

Doucet

and Plattsburgh, N.Y., where hostilities were largely concentrated. Doucet was in command of various operations there, sat on a court martial, and took part in the famous battle of Châteauguay [see Charles-Michel d'Irumberry* de Salaberry]. He was decorated in 1813 for his service in the war.

Once the American threat was over, Doucet returned to Trois-Rivières. In 1815 he left to take up permanent residence at Montreal in a house on Place d'Armes, where he resumed working as a notary. However, he kept some assets at Trois-Rivières; in addition, his wife later inherited some of her father's properties. A daughter had been born to them in 1814, and they were to have five more children, two of whom died in infancy.

Upon arrival in Montreal, Doucet, through his contacts with government circles, was appointed on 30 Oct. 1815 secretary and treasurer of the commissions of inquiry into the state of the roads and into the construction of a prison. On 21 June 1821 he was given the post of agent for the Indian Department on the Caughnawaga (Kahnawake) Reserve, and on 10 Feb. 1823 similar posts on the Saint-Régis Reserve near the New York border and the Lac-des-Deux-Montagnes Reserve (Oka). A well-known notary who was sought out for his thorough knowledge of the law, Doucet led a social life which brought some honorary offices; although few in number they were relatively important, a fact that probably indicates his influence. For example, he was elected churchwarden of the parish of Notre-Dame in Montreal in 1820 and president of the notaries' association in the district of Montreal in the 1840s. For unknown reasons, possibly of a professional nature, he is believed to have refused the office of justice of the peace of Montreal in 1830, and to have declined in 1842, like his colleagues George VANFELSON and John Samuel McCord, a post as commissioner to inquire into the operation of the laws on seigneurial tenure in Lower Canada.

At the end of the 1830s Doucet prepared *Fundamental principles of the laws of Canada, as they existed under the natives, as they were changed under the French kings, and as they were modified and altered under the domination of England*, his most important accomplishment. Registered at the Court of Queen's Bench of Montreal on 14 Feb. 1840 and published by John Lovell* from 1841 to 1843, probably in instalments, the work, which was intended for law students, describes the origins and history of laws and institutions. Written in English, it represents an immense effort of compilation and erudition. In the first volume Doucet mentions the Hebraic laws contained in the Bible, goes on to Roman law and to that of the barbaric tribes, particularly the Anglo-Saxon ones, and devotes the major portion to the history of English law from the Norman conquest to 1774. In the second volume he gives a brief account of laws of the American Indians and then elucidates the principal parts of the Code Napoléon, which, although without official standing in Lower Canada, was then in use among legal practitioners and judges there. The volume concludes with a bilingual version, without commentary, of the Coutume de Paris. In sum, this is a work of encyclopaedic pretensions but little originality which is almost wholly devoted to English law before the conquest and to the Code Napoléon; its merit probably lies in making accessible in English a body of English and, above all, of French laws in current use in Lower Canada at the beginning of the 19th century. Commenting on the work, the *Montreal Gazette* of 27 March 1841 noted: "It is, we must confess, a new thing to find a native French Canadian of this Province devoting so much time and labour, as this work required, to the instruction of those who intend to prosecute the study of our laws, and, throwing aside all native and national prejudices, giving it to the public in the English language."

Doucet gave up the profession of notary in 1855, after 51 years in practice, leaving one of the most voluminous minute-books extant – it contains more than 30,000 notarized instruments – to the Palais de Justice in Montreal. His son Théodore, who had been his partner since 1839, followed in his footsteps. Nicolas-Benjamin Doucet died on 27 May 1858 in Montreal at the age of 77. Joseph-Edmond Roy* calls him "one of the outstanding figures in the professional and social life" of Montreal in the first half of the 19th century.

JACQUES BOUCHER

The minute-book of Nicolas-Benjamin Doucet, consisting of instruments notarized between 1804 and 1855, is in ANQ-M, CN1-134. He is also the author of *Fundamental principles of the laws of Canada, as they existed under the natives, as they were changed under the French kings, and as they were modified and altered under the domination of England* . . . (2v. in 1, Montreal, 1841–43).

ANQ-M, CE1-51, 29 mai 1858; CN1-68, 1er mars 1826; CN1-69, 29 sept. 1845; CN1-122, 4 nov. 1834; CN1-270, 10 mars 1823. ANQ-MBF, CE1-48, 2 févr. 1778, 20 févr. 1781, 5 août 1807; CN1-38, 1er mars 1799. AUM, P 58, U, Doucet à Louis Guy, 7 févr. 1812; Doucet à J.-G. de Tonnancour, 4 mars, 20 juin, 10 oct., 13 nov. 1820; 10 mars 1821; 21 janv. 1822; 16 juill. 1828; Doucet à Mme Dufresne, 18 sept. 1821; 11 juill., 24 sept. 1823; 8 juill. 1824; 4 janv. 1825; 13 juin, 27 sept. 1826; Doucet à Joseph Masson, 28 juin 1826; lettre de Doucet, 8 sept. 1841. PAC, MG 30, D1, 11: 242–45; RG 4, B8, 2: 507–12; RG 68, General index, 1651–1841: 279–80, 341–42, 368; 1841–67: 343. *La Minerve*, 29 mai 1858. *Montreal Gazette*, 27 March 1841. E. A. Cruikshank, *Inventory of military documents in the Canadian archives* (Ottawa, 1910), 54–56. "Marguilliers de la paroisse de Notre-Dame de Ville-Marie de 1657 à 1913," *BRH*, 19 (1913): 276–84. Morgan, *Bibliotheca Canadensis*, 107. *Officers of British forces in Canada* (Irving), 111, 125,

157. [J.-E. Roy], "Bibliographie notariale," *La Rev. du notariat* (Lévis, Qué.), 2 (1899–1900): 225–29. A. W. P. Buchanan, *The Buchanan book; the life of Alexander Buchanan, Q.C., of Montreal, followed by an account of the family of Buchanan* (Montreal, 1911), 123–24. Lareau, *Hist. de la littérature canadienne*, 398–99. J.-E. Roy, *Hist. du notariat*, 2: 234; 3: 82, 97. Sulte, *Mélanges hist.* (Malchelosse), 3: 100; 10: 93–94; 18: 61. F.-J. Audet, "Un jurisconsulte dans notre administration: Nicolas-Benjamin Doucet, sa carrière et les diverses fonctions qu'il occupa dans le Québec," *La Presse* (Montréal), 12 août 1933: 29. "La famille Jékimbert ou Kimber," *BRH*, 21 (1915): 201–5. J.-J. Lefebvre, "Une dynastie acadienne de notaires québécois: les Doucet (1804–1917)," *La Rev. du notariat* (Québec), 58 (1955–56): 474–81, 521–31. É.-Z. Massicotte, "Un record notarial," *BRH*, 24 (1918): 104. Henri Têtu, "L'abbé André Doucet, curé de Québec, 1807–1814," *BRH*, 13 (1907): 3–22. [Yvonne Yon] Mme L.-J. Doucet, "Généalogie des familles Doucet: souche acadienne," SGCF *Mémoires*, 6 (1954–55): 371–88.

DOUGLAS, JAMES, merchant and office holder; b. 1789 in Annan, Scotland, son of John Douglas, a labourer, and Sarah Hunter; d. unmarried 31 Oct. 1854 in St John's.

James Douglas arrived in Newfoundland as a young man. Although he may have come to join his brother Hugh R. in a haberdashery and tailoring business, he was probably in the employ of one of the large Scottish mercantile houses based in Greenock which were involved in the St John's trade. First mentioned in 1818 as co-owner of a vessel, he was a typical independent trader with diversified interests; at various times during his life he was active in the importing and exporting field, a newspaper, a retail store, and a drugstore in partnership with Thomas McMurdo. In 1846 his business reached its peak with his ownership of four sealing vessels, but it soon declined when his premises in St John's were destroyed by the fire in June of that year which ravaged the city and when some of his ships were lost in the great gale that swept the coast of Labrador three months later. Most of Douglas's investments were of a high-risk nature and, according to his contemporaries, by 1848 he was dependent on the annual salary of £200 that he received as commissioner of roads for the central district, although he continued to outfit a sealer until 1850.

Douglas's first recorded political activity occurred in 1831 when he signed a petition urging that representative government be introduced in Newfoundland. Some time after April 1833 Douglas and William Carson* supported Robert John Parsons* in the founding of the reform *Newfoundland Patriot* but Douglas severed his connection with the paper in 1835. In that year he was chairman of a group including Patrick DOYLE, Thomas Bennett*, and James William Tobin* which petitioned the British government to dismiss Chief Justice Henry John Boulton* for using the bench to protect the interests of Conservative politicians. Boulton was eventually removed from his post by Lord Glenelg, the colonial secretary, in 1838. After the reform victory in the election of 1837 Douglas had been appointed to the board of road commissioners for the central district by Governor Henry Prescott*, a move which was interpreted by some as a token gesture to the reformers. In 1843 he was nominated chairman of the board by Sir John HARVEY. The board had veto power over the local commissions in all decisions concerning the dispensing of funds for the construction of roads in the district. Like Governor Harvey, Douglas was most interested in building and improving truck roads which would facilitate the transportation of foodstuff to the capital. By using winter road crews he also provided work and wages for some of the seasonally unemployed in the city. Although the post of chairman was potentially the most lucrative of any in the colony, allowing the holder to dispense patronage almost at will, Douglas seems to have filled it in an efficient and business-like manner. He was reappointed to the post every year until his death.

During the 1830s Roman Catholic reformers dominated the House of Assembly and Protestant Conservative merchants, the group usually favoured by the governors, had control of the Council. In a move that defied the religious polarity of the island's politics, the Presbyterian Douglas entered a May 1840 by-election under the Liberal banner in the predominantly Catholic district of St John's. Shortly before the election, however, the Roman Catholic bishop, Michael Anthony Fleming*, urged his parishioners to "support their religion" by voting for one of Douglas's nominators, Laurence O'Brien*, a Roman Catholic who had consented to run. O'Brien was subsequently elected by eight votes in a hard-fought and often vicious campaign.

In December 1841 Douglas became one of the founding members of the Agricultural Society, formed to encourage and improve husbandry. The society was patronized and encouraged by Harvey and his successor, John Gaspard Le Marchant*. Under its direction, production in the colony doubled over the next few years and, through the distribution of seed potatoes, the population was saved from the worst effects of the potato blight during the depression of 1846–49. Douglas belonged to the closely knit Scottish-Presbyterian community of St John's and he served on the non-sectarian board of the St John's Hospital. As well, he was appointed to the Fire Relief Commission in 1846, was supervisor of streets for St John's, and was instrumental in establishing a new water supply system for the city following the fire.

Subsequent to his appointments to the roads commission and the Agricultural Society, Douglas in

Doyle

the early spring of 1843 demonstrated his political independence by opposing Governor Harvey in his dispute with Chief Justice John Gervase Hutchinson Bourne*, a fellow Presbyterian; however, his action does not appear to have affected his future as a public servant. In 1848 Douglas again entered active politics, running in St John's during the general election as an independent against four Catholic Liberal candidates. He came fourth in the three-member constituency. Two years later he made his third and last attempt to gain elective office, standing, once again as an independent, in the St John's by-election called after O'Brien had taken a seat on the Legislative Council. He, like many other older politicians in these years, was defeated by a member of the new political generation: in Douglas's case, it was Philip Francis Little*, a future prime minister of Newfoundland.

Douglas, a Scottish Presbyterian and a 19th-century liberal, was forced to run as an independent when the predominantly Roman Catholic Liberal party refused to support him. His political opponents did not attack his character during elections nor did they aim charges of corruption at the man who, during his tenure as roads commissioner, used highway construction as a means of providing employment for the poor. When he died, Douglas left an estate valued at less than £1,200.

GERTRUDE CROSBIE

MHGA, Douglas name file. *Morning Courier and General Advertiser* (St John's), 1844, 1846, 1848, 1850–54. *Newfoundlander*, 1827–34, 1837–49, 1851. *Newfoundland Mercantile Journal*, 1825–27. *Patriot* (St John's), 1836–37, 1840–45, 1848–50, 1854, October–December 1855. *Public Ledger*, 1827–28, 1830, 1834–38, 1840, 1843, 1848, 1850, 1852, 1854. *Royal Gazette and Newfoundland Advertiser*, 1810–16, 1828–35, 1838–40, 1844, 1848–49, 1854. *Times and General Commercial Gazette* (St John's), 1832–43. *Nfld. almanack*, 1849, 1853. R. H. Bonnycastle, *Newfoundland in 1842: a sequel to "The Canadas in 1841"* (2v., London, 1842), 2. Gunn, *Political hist. of Nfld.* C. E. Hillier, "The problems of Newfoundland from discovery to the legislative sessions of 1847" (MA thesis, Acadia Univ., Wolfville, N.S., 1963). R. B. Job, *John Job's family; a story of his ancestors and successors and their business connections with Newfoundland and Liverpool, 1730 to 1953* (2nd ed., St John's, 1954). Keith Matthews, *Lectures on the history of Newfoundland: 1500–1830* (St John's, 1973). R. G. Moyles, *"Complaints is many and various, but the odd divil likes it": nineteenth century views of Newfoundland* (Toronto and New York, 1975). Prowse, *Hist. of Nfld.* (1895). Malcolm MacDonell, "The conflict between Sir John Harvey and Chief Justice John Gervase Hutchinson Bourne," CHA *Report*, 1956: 45–54.

DOYLE, PATRICK, ship's captain, businessman, justice of the peace, politician, and judge; b. 1777 in Newfoundland; m. Mary ——; they had no children; d. 4 June 1857 in St John's.

During his lifetime Patrick Doyle pursued a number of careers, the first being that of ship's captain. From 1803 to 1809 he was captain of the snow *Rover*, sailing between Newfoundland and Bristol, England, and by 1818 he had become sufficiently wealthy to own a 46-ton sealing schooner, the *Elizabeth*, which he sold that year to finance his expanding commercial interests. By 1819 he had acquired considerable mercantile property along the St John's waterfront, and he was importing basic foodstuffs and fishery supplies as well as an assortment of luxury items. He was also the owner and operator of the Globe Tavern, with its public house, meeting hall, theatre, and tenement building.

Doyle's mercantile premises were destroyed in the city fire of 1819, but by 1828, the year in which he formed a partnership with Stephen Lawler, he was once more doing a thriving importing business. For unknown reasons the partnership was dissolved on 1 Oct. 1831 and Doyle again resumed sole ownership of the firm. Although he auctioned off the Globe Tavern shortly thereafter, he still retained his wharf and two large stores, the rent from which, combined with that of a number of tenement buildings, afforded him a comfortable living until his death. His estate, not including "lands, tenement houses and premises," was valued at £4,600.

In addition to his commercial interests Doyle was actively involved in the political life of Newfoundland. During the period of the colony's struggle for representative government, between 1820 and 1832, he was a member of the political committee of the reform movement led by Dr William Carson* and Patrick Morris*. As a member of this committee, Doyle was chiefly concerned with the administrative and organizational work of the movement, such as the planning of public meetings, the implementation of decisions reached at these meetings, and the preparation and forwarding of petitions to the British government. In November 1820 he was one of a committee of 13 which had been appointed at a public meeting to draw up a petition calling for the abolition of the surrogate court system and appealing the flogging sentences given to Philip Butler and James Lundrigan*, two Conception Bay fishermen who were found in contempt by local surrogate magistrates. During the mid and late 1830s he also protested the unconstitutional and politically biased activities of Chief Justice Henry John Boulton*.

In the 1836 election, which was subsequently invalidated, and again in 1837 Doyle was elected to the Newfoundland House of Assembly as a Liberal representative for the district of Placentia–St Mary's. Although not one of the political leaders of his day, he nevertheless played a very important role in the day to day affairs of the house: he was often called upon to chair the committee of the whole house, to sit on the various committees of inquiry, and to serve on the numerous assembly delegations which met with either the Council or the governor. Since many of these conferences were intended to settle major disputes between the branches of government, it is obvious that Doyle must have been an able negotiator, possessing tact and diplomacy as well as firmness and determination. In 1838 Governor Henry Prescott* considered appointing Doyle, Morris, and Robert PACK to the Council in the hope that enlarging it to include members or former members of the assembly would help reduce tension between the two bodies. This proposal was not adopted because the Colonial Office was reluctant to make any changes in Newfoundland's constitution.

Rather than seek re-election at the end of his legislative term in 1842, Doyle accepted the position of police magistrate for St John's. This was a natural choice since he had been a grand juror for a number of years, and had been made a justice of the peace in 1834. In 1845 Doyle was appointed stipendiary magistrate of the Court of Sessions, a position he retained until his death in 1857.

A Roman Catholic, Doyle was involved in the work of the Benevolent Irish Society, a local organization dedicated to the alleviation of poverty and the encouragement of education. As a member of this highly respected and influential society, he held a number of offices: first assistant 1818–22 and 1827; treasurer 1830–32; and vice-president 1835–40. His most important contribution was his piloting through the House of Assembly of two bills (1839 and 1841) aimed at incorporating the society. Although ultimately unsuccessful in his efforts – the British government disallowed both bills – Doyle nevertheless spent the greater part of his legislative career pursuing this goal, as well as promoting the interests of the poor and disadvantaged in general. He also helped supervise the construction of the Orphan Asylum Schools in 1827, and was one of the closest advisers of Bishop Michael Anthony Fleming* when the latter was trying to secure a building site for the new Roman Catholic cathedral. Doyle was also involved with the non-denominational Charity School Society, the Sons of Old Ireland Society, the Natives' Society, and the Agricultural Society.

Throughout his life Patrick Doyle contributed much of his time and energy toward the improvement of the lot of his fellow countrymen. As a merchant he generated wealth and prosperity and used that wealth to promote culture and refinement. As a political agitator and politician he helped bring democratic institutions to Newfoundland and then helped make those institutions more responsive to the popular will. And finally, as a member of various civic organizations he contributed much toward the relief of economic hardship, the promotion of education, and

the fostering of religious expression. His passing was greatly mourned by all classes and sectors of society and by the highest officials of church and state.

DEREK BUSSEY

PRO, CO 194; CO 195/17 (mfm. at PANL). Supreme Court of Nfld. (St John's), Registry, will of Patrick Doyle, probated 1 June 1857. *Dr William Carson, the great Newfoundland reformer: his life, letters and speeches; raw material for a biography*, comp. J. R. Smallwood (St John's, 1978). Nfld., House of Assembly, *Journal*, 1837–42. *Newfoundlander*, 1827–31, 1837–42. *Newfoundland Mercantile Journal*, 1819–22. *Patriot* (St John's), 1835, 1845, 1857. *Public Ledger*, 1827–28, 1831–32. *Royal Gazette and Newfoundland Advertiser*, 1815, 1818, 1820, 1828–31, 1834, 1842, 1845, 1847. *The register of shipping* (London), 1803–9. *When was that?* (Mosdell). *Centenary volume, Benevolent Irish Society of St. John's, Newfoundland, 1806–1906* (Cork, [Republic of Ire., 1906?]). Devine, *Ye olde St. John's*. Gunn, *Political hist. of Nfld.* Howley, *Ecclesiastical hist. of Nfld.* O'Neill, *Story of St. John's*, vol.1. J. C. Pippy, "The Benevolent Irish Society," *The book of Newfoundland*, ed. J. R. Smallwood (6v., St John's, 1937–75), 2: 273–87. Prowse, *Hist. of Nfld.* (1895). F. W. Rowe, *The development of education in Newfoundland* (Toronto, 1964). J. M. Kent, "The Benevolent Irish Society," *Newfoundland Quarterly* (St John's), 1 (1901–2), no.4: 13–16.

DROUIN, PIERRE (baptized **Pierre-Étienne**), furniture-maker; b. 22 Sept. 1810 at Quebec, son of Pierre Drouin, a merchant, and Marie-Louise Fraise; m. 21 Nov. 1843 Marie Paquet, widow of Simon Forgues, at Saint-Michel, Lower Canada; d. 27 May 1860 at Quebec.

By 1843 Pierre Drouin was in partnership at Quebec with François Drouin, with an establishment at 24 Rue des Fossés (Boulevard Charest) in the *faubourg* Saint-Roch. The firm made all kinds of furniture, including cots, cradles, sofas, love-seats, chairs, tables, and buffets, and it assured clients that in their manufacture solidity was combined with elegance. The next year, on 5 June 1844, the entire stock of household furniture was sold by auction. After the company's demise on 11 June, Pierre notified his debtors that he alone was authorized to receive payments on account. He remained in business on his own at 27 Rue des Fossés.

In 1845 Drouin did not escape unscathed in the fire that ravaged part of the *faubourg* Saint-Roch, but he carried on with his work and invited the public to visit his workshop. In 1847 he advertised furniture in "good condition" and exquisite taste, particularly "a large stock of straw-bottomed chairs painted in a fanciful style, and others of wood alone." Probably in 1854, Drouin moved to 45 Rue des Fossés. No sooner had he set up shop there than journalists became keenly interested in the items he was making for the universal exposition in Paris in 1855. However, there were no entries by Drouin among the Canadian pieces displayed. Two or three years later he formed another partnership, probably with François Roy, a furniture-maker who had come to the province in 1854. The firm of Drouin et Roy attracted numerous customers and interested enquiries. The partners manufactured furniture in the styles current in Paris and London, and sold it at lower prices. As master furniture-makers, they advertised that they personally supervised the manufacturing and employed only the best workers. Unfortunately, the premature death of Pierre Drouin at 49, from a "heart ailment," put an end to this promising partnership.

JOCELYNE MILOT

ANQ-Q, CE1-1, 23 sept. 1810; CE1-22, 30 mai 1860; CE2-5, 21 nov. 1843. Can., Prov. of, Legislative Assembly, *App. to the journals*, 1856, app.46. *Le Courrier du Canada*, 28 mai 1860. *Le Journal de Québec*, 13 mai 1843; 1er, 15 juin, 8 août 1844; 28 nov. 1846; 4 déc. 1847. *Quebec directory*, 1848–58. P.-L. Martin, *La berçante québécoise* (Montréal et Québec, 1973). Morisset, *Coup d'œil sur les arts*.

DRUMMOND, Sir GORDON, army officer and colonial administrator; b. 27 Sept. 1772 at Quebec, youngest of five sons of Colin Drummond of Megginch and Catherine Oliphant of Rossie; m. 17 Oct. 1807 Margaret Russell, daughter of William Russell of Brancepeth, at Brancepeth Castle, England, and they had two sons and one daughter; d. 10 Oct. 1854 in London.

Gordon Drummond was born into an old landed family of Perthshire, Scotland. His father, the Quebec agent for the London firm of Fludyer and Drummond and a business partner of Jacob Jordan*, served as deputy paymaster general to the forces in the province of Quebec and as a legislative councillor. The family left Quebec four years after Colin Drummond's death in 1776, and Gordon received his education in Britain. On 21 Sept. 1789 he entered the British army as an ensign in the 1st Foot. Thereafter he rose rapidly in rank even by the standards of the time, becoming lieutenant in the 41st Foot in March 1791, captain in January 1792, major in the 8th Foot on 28 Feb. 1794, and junior lieutenant-colonel in the 8th the next day. Drummond saw his first active service during the Netherlands campaign of 1794–95, in which he distinguished himself at the siege of Nijmegen, and he led his regiment throughout the reconquest of Egypt in 1801. On 1 Jan. 1798 he was promoted colonel in the army.

Following garrison duty in the Mediterranean, in 1804 Drummond was appointed brigadier-general for staff duty in Britain, and became a major-general the

following year. After serving as second in command at Jamaica for two years, he returned to his birthplace in July 1808 as a subordinate to Sir James Henry Craig*, commander of the forces in British North America. Advanced to lieutenant-general on 4 June 1811, he was commander of the forces in the Canadas between the tenures of Craig and Sir George Prevost* that year, before leaving in October to take charge of a military district in northern Ireland.

Drummond was still in Ireland when the War of 1812 broke out. In August 1813 he left for North America after being appointed president of the government and commander of the troops in Upper Canada, the principal seat of the war. His previous service in the Canadas was probably an important reason for his selection, which came in the wake of Prevost's disenchantment with Sir Roger Hale SHEAFFE, who had in the mean time been replaced by Francis de Rottenburg*. When Drummond reached his headquarters at Kingston on 3 December, he found the province in considerable disarray. The Detroit and Niagara frontiers were in American hands, and the southwest part of the province had been evacuated following the British defeats on Lake Erie and at Moraviantown [see Robert Heriot Barclay*; Henry Procter*]. Moreover, the population was dispirited, and some were actively aiding the enemy [see Joseph Willcocks*]. Both civilians and the armed forces were suffering from a shortage of food.

All was not lost, however. The American force in Fort George (Niagara-on-the-Lake) and its vicinity had been much weakened by the withdrawal of troops to other regions. Early in December, apparently in response to Drummond's order to advance from their positions on Burlington Heights (Hamilton), British troops pushed up the Niagara peninsula. The movement caused the Americans to evacuate Fort George and the neighbouring village of Newark (Niagara-on-the-Lake), which they burned on 10 December. Drummond himself arrived on the frontier on the 16th and immediately decided to attack Fort Niagara (near Youngstown), N.Y. He threw a force across the river which stormed the fort on the morning of the 19th and captured 344 Americans as well as an immense quantity of munitions and supplies. The same day more troops under Major-General Phineas Riall* crossed over, and during their operations the town of Lewiston was destroyed. Eleven days later a force under Riall undertook another raid, during which it routed some American militia at Buffalo. The towns of Black Rock (Buffalo) and Buffalo were burned to avenge the destruction of Newark; also burned were some vessels of the American Lake Erie fleet and large amounts of supplies. This brief but decisive campaign restored control of the Niagara frontier to the British and greatly improved the confidence of the army and the people of Upper

Canada. Drummond himself showed great personal energy in advancing to the frontier and considerable daring in attacking Fort Niagara, the strongest position in the region.

In February 1814 Drummond presided over the session of the provincial legislature at York (Toronto). The political climate of Upper Canada had changed considerably since the beginning of the war, for the security offered by Drummond's campaign and the bitterness over the American ravages contributed to a much more suspicious and intolerant attitude towards American sympathizers. Drummond thus had little difficulty in persuading the legislature to pass bills which suspended habeas corpus and which provided for the more effective trial and punishment of those accused of treasonable activities. These measures were linked to the apprehension of persons accused of treason over the winter of 1813–14 and to the issuing of a special commission by Drummond on 14 Dec. 1813 to try those taken. In May and June 1814 some 20 persons were tried at Ancaster, eight being executed and others sentenced to be transported [see Jacob Overholser*].

On a different issue Drummond received little cooperation. Because of a chronic lack of provisions and forage in the Kingston garrison, on 22 Nov. 1813 Rottenburg had proclaimed martial law in the Johnstown and Eastern districts in order to force the sale of food to the army. The legislature had protested strongly, and one of Drummond's first acts as president was to repeal the proclamation. But he soon found that farmers continued to withhold provisions, and although he tried to persuade the legislature to authorize him to declare martial law, he was rebuffed. Nevertheless, the problem was so acute that on 12 April 1814 he reimposed martial law, this time throughout the province, in order to allow the army to purchase supplies at a fixed rate once the needs of individual farmers were met. Both his superior, Prevost, and the legislature were strongly critical, but Drummond maintained martial law until the end of the war. In his defence it must be said that he insisted on fair prices and kept a rigid control over the operation of the purchasing system.

Military affairs, however, were of paramount importance. An advance planned on Amherstburg and Detroit in the winter had to be cancelled because of the mildness of the weather, but at Kingston Drummond discussed the coming campaign for 1814 with Sir James Lucas Yeo*, naval commander on the lakes. Both men agreed that control of Lake Ontario was essential before men and supplies could be conveyed efficiently from Kingston to the Niagara peninsula, the expected scene of operations. To this end, in April Drummond and Prevost considered the possibility of an attack on the main American naval base of Sackets Harbor, N.Y., to destroy the enemy fleet. Drum-mond's plans were feasible, but Prevost refused his repeated requests for reinforcements from Lower Canada which he felt were necessary for success. Drummond and Yeo therefore decided to attack the less strongly held depot at Oswego, N.Y., where supplies for the American vessels being built at Sackets Harbor were being assembled. A successful attack took place on 6 May under Drummond's personal leadership. The large quantity of supplies was especially valuable because of the continuing shortage of food in Upper Canada. Nevertheless, the raid failed to capture the principal equipment for the American vessels. When it was learned that this material was to be sent by water to Sackets Harbor, Yeo dispatched a force of gunboats to intercept it, but they were defeated and captured in Sandy Creek, N.Y., on 30 May.

Drummond's efforts in the land campaign of 1814 were concentrated almost exclusively on the Niagara frontier. Initially he was thrown on the defensive. American plans envisaged an advance on Burlington Heights, and on 3 July some 4,000 men under Major-General Jacob Jennings Brown crossed the Niagara River and captured Fort Erie. Phineas Riall, commanding the British forces in the peninsula, attacked the American advance guard at Chippawa (Niagara Falls) two days later, but was heavily defeated and forced to retreat to Fort George. The British position was now critical, for the Americans might easily have captured forts George and Niagara had their navy delivered the heavy artillery Brown needed to reduce the works. But for various reasons their squadron remained in Sackets Harbor and, while Brown's army sat for two weeks awaiting the guns, Drummond rushed reinforcements to the frontier from York and Kingston. He himself sailed from York on 24 July, determined to drive Brown out of the province.

The following day the armies clashed in the battle of Lundy's Lane, near Niagara Falls. The action began about six o'clock in the evening with only part of each force present; reinforcements subsequently increased the Americans to about 3,000 and the British to about 2,800. Believing himself to be badly outnumbered, Drummond remained on the defensive and held off attacks on his position until about nine o'clock, when his artillery was captured and his line forced back several hundred yards. During the next three hours he led three unsuccessful counter-attacks, in the course of which he was wounded in the neck, and he twice had to beat off American columns attempting to outflank his line. Finally, at midnight, when the Americans were withdrawing in exhaustion, a party of British light infantry recaptured the guns. Each side suffered over 850 casualties in this extremely confused action, the bloodiest of the war fought on Canadian soil, but it was ultimately to be a British

Drummond

victory. Crippled by wounds, Brown had turned over command to Brigadier-General Eleazar Wheelock Ripley, who ordered a retreat to Fort Erie the following day.

When Drummond advanced early in August, he discovered that the Americans had enclosed their army in a hastily erected fortified camp adjacent to Fort Erie. Reasoning that it would be easier to starve them into surrender than to assault, on 2 August he sent a force to raid the supply depots at Black Rock and Buffalo. Unfortunately, the British were observed crossing and had to withdraw after skirmishing with American troops sent to intercept them. Drummond was thus compelled to undertake a formal siege under unfavourable conditions. The American squadron had seized control of Lake Ontario at the beginning of August, which prevented him from receiving the artillery and ammunition he needed to succeed. Nevertheless, he erected a battery of four guns and opened a bombardment on 13 August. William Dunlop*, a British army surgeon, thought that the fire of the guns was completely inadequate but by the 15th Drummond considered that enough damage had been done to warrant an assault. One column of 1,500 troops was to attack the southern end of the camp, while two more totalling 1,600 men were to attack the fort at its northern end. Despite the dangers inherent in the widely separated positions of the columns, Drummond had planned well: he refrained from showing troops to the west and south so that the Americans would not expect an attack from that direction, and he launched the southern column first to give it the best chance of achieving surprise.

Unfortunately for Drummond, the American commander, Colonel Edmund Pendleton Gaines, had suspected a British attack and had made sure his men were prepared. As the southern column neared its objective, it was met with "one broad uninterrupted sheet of light" as the defenders fired. Most of De Watteville's Regiment, which comprised the majority of the column, immediately fled, taking the remainder with it. Some troops rallied and returned to the attack, but were beaten off in the end. The northern columns were also met with a heavy fire, but succeeded in breaking into the fort and held their ground for several hours against enemy counter-attacks. At dawn, however, a stock of ammunition exploded, blowing many of the British to pieces, and the rest fled in panic to their own lines.

Although the attack had proved Drummond's daring, it had ended in a brutal defeat, 906 men being lost as against 84 Americans. Reinforcements soon arrived, but Drummond still lacked enough artillery and would have been wise to withdraw after the failure of the assault. Moreover, sickness and desertions were increasing and supplies diminishing. None the less, he persisted. During the remainder of August and into

September he constructed two more batteries, and joined all three by rows of fortifications. In the mean time, Brown had assumed command at Fort Erie, and immediately began to plan a sortie. By boating New York militia across the Niagara at night, Brown assembled nearly 3,000 men in the camp by 17 September. Drummond had 3,500, all of them regulars, but only one-third served in the lines; the rest were in a camp to the rear. Drummond welcomed deserters' reports of an impending attack because it would spare him from having to make a second assault on the fort, but he failed to reinforce his front line, and so exposed himself to being defeated in detail.

The Americans attacked in a rain storm on 17 September. One column advanced to roll up the British siege works from the right flank, another attacked head-on. They succeeded in capturing two of the batteries before Drummond led up reinforcements from the camp and drove them back into the fort. The British suffered 609 casualties in this engagement while inflicting only 511 on the enemy. Moreover, the Americans wrecked three of the siege guns and destroyed much of the ammunition. These losses, together with a worsening shortage of food and continuing bad weather, forced Drummond to abandon the siege on 21 September and retreat behind the Chippawa River.

The campaign remained at a standstill until 1 October, when Brown was joined by 3,500 regulars under Major-General George Izard. The combined American forces advanced to the Chippawa and fought a number of inconclusive skirmishes with Drummond's troops, who were partially ensconced behind field works. Drummond was saved from a pitched battle by Yeo's squadron, which reached the mouth of the Niagara on the 18th with supplies and reinforcements. When the Americans learned of Yeo's arrival, they withdrew to Fort Erie and then to their own side of the river. On 5 November they blew up Fort Erie and the adjoining camp, thus abandoning their last hold on the Upper Canadian bank of the Niagara. No action took place on the frontier during the winter, and in March 1815 news of the end of the war was received.

At the same time Drummond learned of his appointment as administrator and commander of the troops in the Canadas, Prevost having been recalled to explain his conduct of the Plattsburgh campaign of 1814. Drummond's entry into his new position was inauspicious: Prevost left Quebec some hours before Drummond arrived on 3 April 1815, and he was deprived of any possible advantages from a personal discussion. Soon afterwards he received orders from the British government to send home the large majority of the troops in the Canadas to meet the threat posed by Napoleon's return from Elba. Drummond also inherited the arrangements for implementing the

Treaty of Ghent, and he therefore supervised the handing over of captured posts to the Americans. Because Michilimackinac (Mackinac Island, Mich.) was returned, he ordered surveys for a new British fort in the region, and settled on a site on Drummond Island (Mich.).

In the political sphere, Drummond took little action of his own. The British government informed him that the Privy Council had exonerated the Lower Canadian judges Jonathan Sewell* and James Monk* from charges laid by their house of assembly, and ordered him to dissolve the assembly should it show any inclination to revive the charges. This Drummond duly did in February 1816. But as he reported, there was little chance that a new assembly would be more cooperative since those members most critical of the judges were likely to be re-elected.

Because he thought that his appointment was temporary, Drummond had asked to be relieved as soon as possible, citing ill health and urgent family matters which required his presence in Britain. He was upset to learn that he would have been made lieutenant governor of Nova Scotia had he not made this request, and realized that he was now cut off from future advancement. His temper was not improved when his successor, Major-General John Wilson, arrived some months later than expected, and again when he and Wilson had an "extremely unpleasant" disagreement about the date of the handing over of the administration.

Drummond left Quebec for the last time on 20 May 1816, and on his return to England settled into the normal life of a peace-time soldier. His services in North America had been recognized with the award of a KCB on 2 Jan. 1815, and on 11 March 1817 he became a GCB. Promoted general on 27 May 1825, he held in succession the colonelcies of the 97th Foot (8 Feb. 1814), the 88th Foot (11 March 1819), the 71st Foot (16 Jan. 1824), the 49th Foot (21 Sept. 1829), and finally his old command, the 8th Foot (24 April 1846). At the time of his death he was the senior general in the British army.

Gordon Drummond was an experienced infantry officer who was clearly more aggressive and ruthless than either Sheaffe or Rottenburg. In his relations with Prevost he was polite and respectful, but perhaps because of his rank and experience he was more willing to continue to press his arguments than his predecessors had been. For Prevost's part, his letters to Drummond have the character of advice rather than command. Drummond also worked well with Yeo, although he was infuriated by Yeo's lack of cooperation in transporting men and supplies to the Niagara peninsula during the fall of 1814.

As a commander, Drummond was uniformly successful for a long period. The reverses he suffered in the second half of the campaign of 1814 must be partly attributed to Prevost's refusal to let him attack Sackets Harbor in the spring, for Drummond had realized that he could not succeed on the Niagara frontier unless the American Lake Ontario squadron was destroyed. Much of the campaign he was subsequently forced to fight is testimony to the frustration an intelligent and aggressive officer must suffer under the orders of a more timorous one. After the defeat at Chippawa in July, he used the remaining period of British naval superiority effectively to reinforce and supply the troops in the Niagara peninsula and then led them to victory at Lundy's Lane. It was the decisive battle of the campaign, and it was won by Drummond's persistence no less than that of his troops. At Fort Erie he lacked the means to succeed, and this seems to have left the normally self-confident soldier in a quandary. He was suffering from stomach trouble, and this, together with the wound he had received at Lundy's Lane, may have contributed to his mistakes. Whatever the case, the mistakes he made were severe and he showed himself inferior to his opponent Brown in both energy and skill.

KENNETH STICKNEY

PAC, RG 8, I (C ser.), 682–86, 1222–23. PRO, CO 42/162, 42/163, 42/166. *Doc. hist. of campaign upon Niagara frontier* (Cruikshank), vols.7–8. *Gentleman's Magazine*, July–December 1854: 625–26. *Select British docs. of War of 1812* (Wood), vol.3, pt.I. DNB. G.B, WO, *Army list*, 1790–1854. E. A. Cruikshank, *The battle of Lundy's Lane, 25th July 1814: a historical study* (3rd ed., Welland, Ont., 1893); *Drummond's winter campaign, 1813* (2nd ed., [Welland, 1900]); *The siege of Fort Erie, August 1st–September 23rd, 1814* (Welland, 1905). *A military history of Perthshire, 1660–1902*, ed. [K. M. Ramsay Stewart-Murray], Marchioness of Tullibardine (2v., Perth, Scot., 1908). E. A. Cruikshank, "Sir Gordon Drummond, K.C.B. . . . ," *OH*, 29 (1933): 8–13. W. M. Weekes, "The War of 1812: civil authority and martial law in Upper Canada," *OH*, 48 (1956); 147–61.

DUCHAÎNE, AMABLE-DANIEL, educator, scientist, inventor, and author; b. 27 May 1774 in Yamachiche, Que., son of Jean-Baptiste Duchaîne, a seigneur, and Marie Paquin; d. 14 Nov. 1853 in Montreal.

Amable-Daniel Duchaîne was related, on his father's side, to the Lesieur-Duchêne (Duchaîne) family that towards the end of the 18th century had inherited part of Grosbois seigneury near Trois-Rivières. He received a classical education at the Collège Saint-Raphaël in Montreal from 1792 to 1800. His scientific bent was encouraged when science began to be taught there towards the turn of the century by the French Sulpicians Claude Rivière, Jean-Baptiste-Jacques Chicoisneau*, and Antoine-

Duchaîne

Jacques Houdet*, who brought from Europe works on physics, chemistry, mathematics, electricity, and the natural sciences. On leaving the college Duchaîne started his theology, and he was tonsured by Pierre Denaut*, the bishop of Quebec, on 23 Sept. 1800. He was never ordained priest, but because he continued to wear a cassock and bands people became accustomed to calling him Abbé Duchaîne. From 1804 to 1806 Duchaîne taught with Jean-Baptiste ROUPE in a Latin school in Nicolet which had been opened in 1803 by its priest, Alexis-Basile Durocher, and he may have continued his theological studies as well. In 1806 this school became a classical college, but Duchaîne is not listed among its first teachers.

Nothing further is known of Duchaîne's career until 1821. That year he drafted a plan for elementary education and a prospectus for a university, securing approval for his proposals from several people whose names he did not disclose. In his scheme Duchaîne made a distinction between general education for those who would become farmers, artisans, and labourers, and comprehensive education for those preparing to take up public office or a profession. For general education he outlined a primary program of instruction in French, English, religion, sacred and secular history, geography, arithmetic, and science. In addition to covering these subjects, his comprehensive education provided a classical program, without Latin except for those who would need it; it included jurisprudence and the study of the country's laws, as well as all branches of philosophy and science, their enumeration displaying his erudition. What Duchaîne had in mind was a university. This university, located in a small town or in the countryside, would not be a residential institution; the students would be housed with local people, and the neediest would receive free instruction. Under the patronage of the government, which would provide financial assistance, and that of friends of education, who would become subscribers, the university would be directed by a corporation consisting of the principal, professors, prominent persons, and priests and ministers of the various creeds, with no restrictions being placed on either professors or students. In this respect, the institution resembled the military school that Captain Anthony Gilbert Douglas* had wanted to set up at Trois-Rivières some years earlier. But if the diverse religious and cultural elements could not coexist, there would be two universities, one for French Canadians and the other for English Canadians. Duchaîne's proposals constituted a criticism of the teaching given in the classical colleges and of the physical, intellectual, and religious constraints placed on their students.

In 1837 Duchaîne had this plan printed in booklet form. The publication was roundly denounced that same year by someone he identified as a schoolteacher of foreign origin acting as spokesman for a clerical clique. He republished the plan in L'Aurore des Canadas in 1841 and L'Encyclopédie canadienne in 1843, and in the latter year Michel BIBAUD also expressed some reservations about it.

In the 1820s Duchaîne, according to contemporaries, had taught theology in Upper Canada and appears to have had some connection with Iona College in St Raphael (St Raphael West); outside the classroom he concentrated his attention on the exact sciences. Around 1830 he was in Montreal and made the acquaintance of Pierre Beaudry, a manufacturer producing soap, pearl ash, and candles on a large scale. Beaudry turned Duchaîne's scientific knowledge to such good account that in return he gave him free accommodation in two furnished rooms in one of his houses and by his will in 1843 ensured Duchaîne possession of them for the remainder of his life. There Duchaîne gave private courses to pupils, and translated and wrote texts on grammar, belles-lettres, history, logic, mathematics, and physics. During this period he worked for La Minerve, preparing the astronomical calculations and tables required for a calendar that was the first of its kind in the French language to be published in Lower Canada; for several years he also drafted an almanac. In January 1832 he discovered a new method of building wooden bridges; by being supported only at the ends, they would withstand flood waters, violent currents, and the spring break-up. The government of Lower Canada granted him letters patent for and exclusive rights to his invention, which probably represented another source of income for him.

In the same month Bishop Bernard-Claude Panet* of Quebec informed Bishop Jean-Jacques Lartigue*, his assistant in the district of Montreal, that he would not ordain Duchaîne priest. Noting that "this abbé is 58 years old," Panet asserted, "he will soon be unfit and can only be a burden to the bishops." Duchaîne later remarked, "If I have not done [religion] greater service, everyone knows well that it has not been my fault, and that it is because human injustice has stood in my way."

In 1837 Duchaîne published an article on lightning-rods and how to install them. The article, which appeared in various journals and then in the Mélanges religieux in 1841, provoked a brief controversy. Following Benjamin Franklin, Duchaîne asserted that the tip of a lightning-rod drew the electric "fluid" from the clouds. Under the pseudonym of Un Ami des Sciences, Isaac-Stanislas Lesieur-Désaulniers* retorted, on the authority of François Arago, that being charged with electricity from the ground the tip of the lightning-rod instead neutralized the electricity of the clouds. Jean-Baptiste Meilleur*, who had become a friend of Duchaîne, joined in the argument with another theory based on Newton's laws. Lesieur-

Désaulniers, the only real physicist of the three, ridiculed this view. Duchaîne snapped back: "To keep abreast of one's time, there is no need to pour scorn on the theories of past ages, to adopt without due consideration, out of love of novelty or as a fad, every conceivable new hypothesis and theory. . . . Besides, it is a known fact in this country and even in foreign countries that I have made many discoveries not previously known in this century; I am therefore a little ahead of my time." Duchaîne, whose encyclopaedic but superficial and outdated knowledge dazzled his contemporaries, was nothing if not conceited.

Amable-Daniel Duchaîne continued to teach with indisputable success for a few more years, but he was apparently confined to his house by illness from around 1845. Pierre Duchaîne, a relative, ran errands for him and helped him in several other ways. He was in straitened circumstances at the end of his life, and died on 14 Nov. 1853, at the age of 79, in the Hospice Saint-Joseph run by the Sisters of Charity of Providence. The parish records of Notre-Dame in Montreal mention that he was buried in the ruins of the cathedral of Saint-Jacques, which had been destroyed during the great fire of 1852. The inventory of his possessions after his death shows that he owned a library of about 250 volumes; it was well stocked in works on theology, as compared with some 30 volumes closely or distantly related to science. His friend Meilleur declared that his literary writings were "numerous and long-winded."

LÉON LORTIE

Amable-Daniel Duchaîne is the author of *Nouveau plan d'éducation ou plan d'établissements littéraires adaptés aux besoins du pays* (Montréal, 1837).

AAQ, 12 A, F, f.56. ACAM, 450.904; RLL, V: 218–20; VI: 204; XV: 4–6. ANQ-M, CE1-51, 16 nov. 1853; CN1-32, 4 sept. 1843. AP, Sainte-Anne (Yamachiche), Reg. des baptêmes, mariages et sépultures, 27 mai 1774. *L'Aurore des Canadas* (Montréal), 28 août 1841. *L'Encyclopédie canadienne* (Montréal), janv.–févr. 1843. *Mélanges religieux*, 16 juill., 6, 13, 20 août 1841. *La Minerve*, 30 janv. 1832, 17 juill. 1837, 15 nov. 1853. Allaire, *Dictionnaire*, 1: 183. F.-M. Bibaud, *Le Panthéon canadien* (A. et V. Bibaud; 1891). Morgan, *Sketches of celebrated Canadians*, 422. J.-G. Barthe, *Le Canada reconquis par la France* (Paris, 1855), 289. Hector Berthelot, *Montréal, le bon vieux temps*, É.-Z. Massicotte, compil. (2v. en 1, 2e éd., Montréal, 1924), 2: 121. Napoléon Caron, *Histoire de la paroisse d'Yamachiche (précis historique)* (Trois-Rivières, Qué., 1892). Choquette, *Hist. du séminaire de Saint-Hyacinthe*. Douville, *Hist. du collège-séminaire de Nicolet*, vol.2. Lionel Groulx, *L'enseignement français au Canada* (2v., Montréal, 1931–[33]), 1: 152, 270. Maurault, *Le collège de Montréal* (Dansereau; 1967). Meilleur, *Mémorial de l'éducation* (1876). L. K. Shook, *Catholic postsecondary education in English-speaking Canada: a history* (Toronto, 1971), 18. E.-Z. Massicotte, "L'industriel Beaudry et le savant Duchaîne," *BRH*, 47 (1941): 156–58.

DUCHARME, CHARLES-JOSEPH, Roman Catholic priest, educator, and founder of the Petit Séminaire de Sainte-Thérèse; b. 10 Jan. 1786 in Lachine, Que., son of Dominique Ducharme, a militia captain, and Marguerite Charlebois; d. 25 March 1853 in Sainte-Thérèse-de-Blainville (Sainte-Thérèse), Lower Canada.

Charles-Joseph Ducharme was enrolled by his parents in the Collège Saint-Raphaël at Montreal in October 1798, but he became disenchanted with studying and returned home after only a few weeks. In 1801 he apparently was engaged as a clerk by Denis Viger*, a Montreal businessman, for whom he worked for three years. He joined the Congrégation des Hommes de Ville-Marie in 1802 or 1803. In October 1804 he decided to return to the Collège Saint-Raphaël (which two years later became the Petit Séminaire de Montréal) and he proved a brilliant classical scholar. With a lively mind and a prodigious memory, Ducharme distinguished himself by his literary accomplishments and he also showed a talent for music. At the end of his course in 1811 he decided to become a priest and entered the Grand Séminaire de Québec, where he studied theology for three years. Among his fellow-students were Rémi GAULIN, Joseph-Norbert PROVENCHER, Thomas Cooke*, and Antoine Manseau*. While pursuing his studies he acted as a regent and instructed the young students at the seminary, one of whom was Ignace Bourget*, later the bishop of Montreal. On 9 Oct. 1814 Ducharme was ordained priest by Joseph-Octave Plessis*, the bishop of Quebec, for whom he felt a devotion marked by respect and fascination. Despite his eagerness to remain at the seminary as a teacher, he was sent to Saint-Laurent, on the Île de Montréal; on 24 October Plessis had appointed him curate there to assist François-Joseph Cazeneuve, the parish priest, who was confined to bed because of illness. Ducharme carried out his duties with great diligence. After he left the parish two years later he was remembered as an excellent speaker, and indeed his congregation unsuccessfully petitioned the bishop for permission to keep such a "worthy priest."

Bishop Plessis decided to name Ducharme priest of Sainte-Thérèse parish at Sainte-Thérèse-de-Blainville in October 1816. Ducharme agreed to go there but retained a strong desire to become a member of the community of the Séminaire de Québec, or failing that, of the Séminaire de Montréal. He reminded his bishop regularly of his wish, and even expressed the fear that he could not ensure his salvation if he stayed in contact with the world, but Plessis did not yield. From the beginning Ducharme attended to his parish and also engaged in an intensive drive to promote the

Ducharme

education of children. Primary schooling was then in a deplorable state in Lower Canada: the shortage of competent, qualified teachers, the dearth of textbooks, and the indifference of parents towards schools kept the population in a fairly general state of illiteracy. In 1824, for example, Antoine PARANT, the superior of the Séminaire de Québec, asserted that in several parishes "scarcely five or six people are able to express their thoughts acceptably in writing or do the most common arithmetical operations, about a quarter of the population knowing how to read tolerably well, [and] a tenth at most able to write their names, in rather sorry fashion if the truth were told." Aware of this pressing need, Ducharme was also spurred on by fear of Protestant proselytizing and of government control over education secured through the Education Act of 1801, which had established the Royal Institution for the Advancement of Learning [see Joseph Langley Mills*]. His views coincided with those of Bishop Plessis, who commented: "I advise you very strongly to do all you possibly can to set up a school that will be answerable to you alone, even if you have to increase your debts in order to manage this. And now Protestant ministers are beginning to visit the royal schools set up in the parishes. It is a galling sight for our parish priests to have to witness. Spare yourself this humiliation."

In 1817 Ducharme built a house which was to serve as a primary school for the boys of the parish. He also asked for some sisters of the Congregation of Notre-Dame in Montreal to be sent as teachers for the girls, but he had to wait his turn and the nuns did not arrive until 1847. Meanwhile Ducharme started two classes in his school, one for girls and the other for boys. He hired teachers at his own expense. He did move forward but not without arousing opposition. In 1822 Janvier-Domptail LACROIX, the seigneur of Blainville, who was sympathetic to the Protestants, brought an action against the priest, claiming that he had been insulted by the refusal of one of the churchwardens to recognize his seigneurial rights during mass at the village church. Lacroix blamed Ducharme for this insult, but Ducharme disclaimed responsibility and defended his churchwarden. The affair lasted for several months and was finally settled by mutual agreement through the intervention of a mediator. However, Ducharme, who was sensitive to public opinion, was disheartened and asked for a transfer, saying that he had taken a dislike to his parish. The bishop then appointed him priest of Saint-Joachim parish at Châteauguay, but Ducharme changed his mind and admitted to "no longer having any reasons to leave." Two years later a Scotsman of Sainte-Thérèse-de-Blainville, Thomas Porteous*, sued Ducharme, seeking £1,000 in damages for insults to his son James. This affair was also settled out of court, in Ducharme's favour; James apologized

to Ducharme, saying that he had been misinformed about him.

Despite these obstacles Ducharme continued his endeavours. During the next few years he concentrated on founding a Latin school where the classical course would be offered. His first aim was to prepare candidates for the priesthood, but he also wanted to train competent young schoolteachers. The opening of a royal school run by Thomas Porteous and attended by a few Catholics prompted Ducharme to act quickly. On 25 Feb. 1825 he brought six children together at the presbytery to teach them the rudiments of Latin. Thus the Latin school was started and the foundations of what would become the Petit Séminaire de Sainte-Thérèse were laid. Two of the children, Basile and Pierre Piché, were the verger's sons. For three years Basile, with his brother's help, had been teaching French, mathematics, and catechism in Ducharme's classes for boys. Their four fellow students in the Latin school were sons of farmers. In 1826 the Latin school had 13 pupils. However, it was not until 1837 that the first class completed the full eight-year course, from Latin elements to philosophy.

During the day Ducharme gave his attention to his numerous parishioners while the two Piché boys taught the village children. Around 4:00 P.M. they met with the other classical scholars in the presbytery, where Ducharme gave the lessons in Latin, natural sciences, mathematics, geometry, literature, history, and geography. He had no textbooks, except the French and Latin grammars of Sulpicians Antoine-Jacques Houdet* and Claude Rivière, which had recently been published in Montreal. For the rest, he drew upon the notes he had made as a schoolboy, filling in as he went along. He modelled his courses on those of the Petit Séminaire de Montréal. In 1841 the regulations of the Petit Séminaire de Sainte-Thérèse would specify that in the classes on grammar, classical literature, and rhetoric, Cicero, the fables of Phaedrus, Cornelius Nepos, Ovid, the elegies of Tibullus, Horace, Virgil, Catullus, and Caesar would be studied. The pupils learned to translate and comment on these authors; they themselves wrote verse or prose, and even conversed in Latin for Ducharme. In the philosophy classes they learned logic, metaphysics, and ethics, as well as physics and mathematics. The teaching of philosophy was based on a work published in France from 1726 to 1728, Charles Rollin's *De la manière d'enseigner et d'étudier les belles-lettres, par rapport à l'esprit et au cœur*, to which everyone was then turning. According to Rollin, logic made it possible to understand "the various operations of the mind in order to know truth and refute error." Metaphysics was strongly oriented ideologically towards the refutation of atheism and the demonstration of the proofs of God's existence and His attributes, and then towards the knowledge of man's soul, his origins, his indivisible and spiritual nature, and his immortality. Finally, ethics was centred upon duties, and taught "what qualities are necessary for our actions to be good and virtuous."

Ducharme coordinated as best he could the slow, arduous process of building his institution. Having no external resources he drew upon the French classes for the best candidates to serve as teachers in the Latin classes; as the latter classes progressed, he selected from them the best candidates who in turn taught the younger pupils, supervised them in their school work, and enforced discipline. In 1836, of some 60 Latin students more than 20 were boarders. One was Joseph Casavant*, a 29-year-old native of Saint-Hyacinthe who had come two years earlier to learn music under Ducharme and who on his advice was studying the workings of the organ.

The year 1837 marked the initial consolidation of the endeavour Ducharme had been closely involved in for 20 years. Bourget, the new coadjutor to the bishop of Montreal, made himself the official protector of the institution. In paying tribute to his former teacher in a letter of 4 July 1837 Bourget observed: "I have a special reason to be interested in your work, [and] that is the personal knowledge I have of the zeal with which you have always sought to give young people a true and sound education. I have not forgotten the care you took to train us in the ways of virtue, and the pleasant hours we spent listening to the lessons about them that you gave to all your pupils." In the same year four students finished the two-year philosophy program, three of whom wanted to become priests. Bourget confirmed to Ducharme that they were acceptable, but added, "It is good for you to know that your pupils, like those of other educational establishments, will not be ordained priests without living for at least one year in a regular seminary." Ducharme protested to the bishop. He succeeded in keeping two seminarists, Joseph Duquet and Georges Thibault, with him, but the third, Pierre-Jérémie Crevier, went to the Grand Séminaire de Montréal to study theology.

In September 1838 Ducharme had 120 children under his care; 55, including 35 boarders, were enrolled in the classics program. Times were difficult: incomes were low, crops were poor, and the tithes were not coming in. The construction of a building of adequate size was delayed, even though the school was housed in cramped quarters. On 18 Dec. 1841 Bourget, now bishop of Montreal, issued orders for the canonical erection of the Petit Séminaire de Sainte-Thérèse. To be admitted, boys "must be at least 12 years old, be born of a legitimate marriage, be able to read and write well, and have a character and turn of mind which would give reason to hope that they will always remain attached to the priestly ministry." That year 26 of the 60 Latin students intended to become priests. They had to wear cassocks and this caused

conflict in the establishment for it apparently gave the impression that those wearing them benefited from favouritism. The following year it was accepted that those without an explicit intention of embracing the priesthood should also be admitted to the seminary, as was the case in other classical colleges.

On 17 March 1845 the Legislative Assembly of the Province of Canada passed a bill incorporating the Petit Séminaire de Sainte-Thérèse and creating a corporation to run it. This act marked the end of the period when the work was shaped by the force of Ducharme's personality. The task of defining regulations and standards, of assigning responsibilities, and of establishing structures became a source of perpetual conflict for him and led to his gradual withdrawal. The seminary's founder was by now nearly 60 years old and felt that he was being left behind. He no longer had the energy to respond to the new needs of the institution. He found it increasingly difficult to keep control of his pupils. He was often at odds with his colleagues over discipline, over the way to run the seminary, and over educational concepts, and his decisions were being challenged. On 7 July 1845 the corporation set up a council which conferred on him the office of superior but gave him as assistants three of his former pupils who were now priests: Duquet was appointed procurator, Jean-Baptiste Berthiaume bursar and assistant director, and Louis Dagenais prefect of studies. In 1847 a start was made on the construction of a stone building which would house more than 150 boarders. On 9 March of that year two sisters of the Congregation of Notre-Dame of Montreal came to Sainte-Thérèse-de-Blainville to look after the girls' education. In November the Brothers of the Holy Cross took charge of the village school, but they left in 1848.

At that period Ducharme still wanted to look after everything, but in February 1848 he suffered a paralytic stroke that gravely undermined his health. Bishop Bourget then intervened, advising him to reduce his activity and let his subordinates assume their full responsibilities. He urged Ducharme to put his affairs in order and guaranteed him a pension of £150 from the time he felt obliged to leave his office. Bourget asked the Society of Jesus to strengthen the seminary's work by putting it on a stable legal footing and by improving its staff and its training program. Thus in September Louis-Césaire Saché was appointed principal and Charles Cicaterri professor of philosophy and theology. Although Ducharme remained titular superior of the seminary, his role was confined to presiding at the council's deliberations and to "important" activities.

This was all that Ducharme needed to feel rejected. He had always been very sensitive to criticism and prone to feeling persecuted; even as a young parish priest he had written strong letters to Bishop Plessis

Ducharme

protesting his good intentions. His life had been one of the utmost austerity, wholly devoted to his parish and the education of the young; he had few friends, took no holidays, and was afraid to invite people to his home, so meagre was his daily fare. He was deeply convinced that he was being betrayed, abandoned, and persecuted by his own kind. He complained to Bourget pathetically: "In speaking to me about my idea of taking a trip you said, but for heaven's sake where are you going in such a hurry? I answer, where my suffering will take me. . . . How many slanders have been insinuated in the last two years to persuade the laity that I was a bad priest? M. Dag[enais] and M. Duq[uet] have brought everything into play that could set people against me, and have obtained all they wanted at my expense, and have not ceased to hound me. They had no desire for my possessions, they said, and the letter that M. Dag[enais] wrote to a so-called friend shows what he had in mind, and it compromised Your Excellency while insulting me. In short all of their conduct towards me was designed to do me outrage, to ridicule me, to make me suffer, in a word to rob me of everything, and Your Excellency has been sympathetic to them." Ducharme's entire correspondence with Bourget expresses the feeling of abandonment and betrayal that beset him.

Ducharme resigned as priest of the parish of Sainte-Thérèse in 1849 but continued to live in the presbytery. That year Duquet, the seminary's new superior, persuaded him to leave the presbytery and take a room in the seminary, in order to protect him from solitude and a tendency to alcoholism. Ducharme spent the last years of his life there but his health gradually worsened. He often travelled, to Lachine and to Bytown (Ottawa) and Plantagenet in Upper Canada, as well as to Saint-Laurent and Sault-au-Récollet (Montreal North), seeking a measure of peace among his few friends.

He became a victim of increasingly frequent strokes and died on 25 March 1853 – Good Friday – in his room at the Petit Séminaire de Sainte-Thérèse. Bishop Bourget came to officiate at Ducharme's funeral, which took place three days later in the presence of a large crowd from Sainte-Thérèse and the adjoining parishes. During the ceremony Bourget delivered a moving oration recalling Ducharme's virtues and the service he had rendered to religion and to his community. Ducharme was buried in the vault of the church of Sainte-Thérèse, where he had been priest for 33 years.

BERNARD DENAULT

AAQ, 12 A, H, f.89. ACAM, RLB, I: 12, 40, 47, 187, 250, 254, 277, 288, 303, 343–44, 348, 351; III: 511, 526–27, 533; IV: 4, 388–90, 410–11, 451, 484–86, 536, 540–41, 561–62; V: 4, 259–60, 300–1, 312–13, 356; VI: 200, 217–18, 241–44, 255; RLL, II: 154–56; IV: 76, 164; V: 186, 270, 347, 360; VI: 147, 186–87, 203; VII: 667; VIII: 190–91, 324–25, 327, 374; IX: 49, 71, 83, 85–86, 98, 111, 115, 202, 211, 215, 233. ANQ-M, CE1-8, 11 janv. 1786; CE1-37, 23 févr. 1784; CE6-25, 28 mars 1853; CN1-114, 15 nov. 1850. Arch. de l'évêché de Saint-Jérôme (Saint-Jérôme, Qué.), 332.176; 814.100. Can., Prov. of, *Statutes*, 1844–45, c.100. [C.-J.] Ducharme, "Lettres de M. Ducharme," J.-B. Proulx, édit., *Annales térésiennes* (Sainte-Thérèse, Qué.), 3 (1883): 247–50, 282–86. *La Minerve*, 7 avril 1853. Allaire, *Dictionnaire*, 1: 183. L.-P. Audet, *Histoire de l'enseignement au Québec* (2v., Montréal et Toronto, 1971), 1; *Le système scolaire*, 6: 37–38, 52–54. *Cahiers historiques: histoire de Sainte-Thérèse* (Joliette, Qué., 1940). [Louis Dagenais], *Souvenirs du 4 novembre 1864, dédiés aux anciens élèves du séminaire de Ste. Thérèse* (Montréal, 1865). Émile Dubois, *Le Petit Séminaire de Sainte-Thérèse, 1825–1925* (Montréal, 1925), 9–135; *Souvenirs térésiens* (Québec, 1927), 7–44. Labarrère-Paulé, *Les instituteurs laïques*, 21–23, 99. Yvan Lamonde, *La philosophie et son enseignement au Québec (1665–1920)* (Montréal, 1980). Meilleur, *Mémorial de l'éducation* (1876), 136–39. Antonin Nantel, *Pages historiques et littéraires* (Montréal, 1928), 29–49, 85–113. Pouliot, *Mgr Bourget et son temps*, 1: 46. É.-J.[-A.] Auclair, "Un éducateur d'il y a cent ans: M. le curé Charles-Joseph Ducharme, fondateur du séminaire de Sainte-Thérèse," *Rev. canadienne*, nouv. sér., 25 (1920): 321–45; "Les origines de Sainte-Thérèse de Blainville et de son séminaire," RSC *Trans.*, 3rd ser., 34 (1940), sect.i: 1–19. Pantaléon Hudon, "Le capitaine Dominique Ducharme," *Rev. canadienne*, 15 (1878): 420–30. J.-B. Proulx, "La jeunesse de M. Ducharme," *Annales térésiennes*, 1 (1880): 69–78; "M. Ducharme et le séminaire," 2 (1882): 236–43, 300–8; "M. Ducharme, vicaire," 3 (1883): 137–44. J.-B. Saint-Germain, "Notice biographique de Messire Joseph Charles Ducharme, archiprêtre, fondateur du séminaire de Ste. Thérèse, mort le 25 mars 1853," *L'écho du cabinet de lecture paroissial* (Montréal), 6 (1864): 357–60.

DUCHARME, DOMINIQUE (baptized **François**), fur trader, militia officer, office holder, and justice of the peace; b. 15 May 1765 in Lachine, Que., second son of Jean-Marie Ducharme* and Marie-Angélique Roy, *dit* Portelance; d. 3 Aug. 1853 in Lac-des-Deux-Montagnes (Oka), Lower Canada.

Dominique Ducharme came of a distinguished family that had been present in New France from the mid 17th century. Residing at Lachine, a centre of recruitment for the western fur trade, the Ducharmes naturally became involved in that activity at an early date. Dominique's father made a comfortable living from the business, which enabled Dominique to attend the Collège Saint-Raphaël in Montreal from 1780 to 1786. But the boy possessed his father's independence of spirit, and, his course completed, he too entered the fur trade. By 1793 he had at least one clerk, William McKay*, in his service on the Menominee River, which flows into Green Bay (Wis.), and possibly a second, his elder brother, Joseph. The following year, at La Baye (Green Bay), he brought out his younger brother Paul from Montreal also to act as a clerk. In 1793 Ducharme had paid two barrels of rum to two Indians for land on both sides of the Fox River at the Kaukauna rapids, thus gaining control of the portage around them and of the lower Fox. He built a house on the land and settled there. In 1794 he and another trader, Jacob Franks, obtained from the Menominee Indians "for value received," a 999-year lease on a total of 1,200 acres on both sides of the Fox at La Baye; at the time Ducharme already possessed a concession on one side of the river beside one of the leased lots. He may have continued to engage in the fur trade in the west for the next 15 years; certainly he acquired a working knowledge of several native dialects.

Ducharme eventually returned to the Montreal area, settling at Lac-des-Deux-Montagnes. On 26 June 1810 he married Agathe de Lorimier, daughter of Claude-Nicolas-Guillaume de Lorimier*, resident Indian agent at Caughnawaga (Kahnawake). On 21 July 1812, after war broke out with the United States, Ducharme was commissioned a lieutenant in the Pointe-Claire Battalion of Militia. A cousin, also named Dominique, became an ensign in the same unit the following day, and it was possibly his uncle Dominique who had been appointed a captain at Lachine in the 2nd Battalion of Montreal Militia in 1811. In May 1813 Ducharme was ordered to the Niagara frontier, Upper Canada, in command of a party of Six Nations Indians from Lac-des-Deux-Montagnes and Saint-Régis. On 24 June, after Laura Secord [Ingersoll*] had informed Lieutenant James FitzGibbon* of a planned American attack on his outpost at Beaver Dams (Thorold), Ducharme's scouts located the American force of some 500 men. Ducharme, by then a captain, reported its position to FitzGibbon and, with 300 of his Indians, joined later by about 100 Mohawks under Captain William Johnson Kerr*, he attacked the Americans from woods in the rear of their position. After three hours of fighting an enemy they could not see, and terrified by the war whoops issuing from the woods, the Americans surrendered to FitzGibbon on his arrival with just 46 men as reinforcements. According to Ducharme's later account, confirmed in large part by FitzGibbon, it was his warriors, not Kerr's Mohawks or FitzGibbon, who had engineered the victory.

Returning quickly to Lower Canada, Ducharme was placed under the command of Lieutenant-Colonel Charles-Michel d'Irumberry* de Salaberry; for his participation in the battle of Châteauguay on 26 October he was later awarded a medal and clasp. His relations with the rigorous Salaberry were not always happy. On one occasion, according to the journalist Pantaléon Hudon, Ducharme's Indians tracked down and captured six deserters from Salaberry's unit; they were court-martialled and, on the lieutenant-colonel's orders, shot. Ducharme, who regarded such punishment as too severe for amateur soldiers with family and farm concerns in the area, never forgave Salaberry and told him that he would have helped the men to escape had he known the fate that awaited them.

After the war Ducharme returned to Lac-des-Deux-Montagnes, where, about 1816, he was appointed interpreter for the Indian Department, with all the duties of a resident agent. In November 1819 he received a commission of the peace, subsequently renewed until at least 1828. In November 1821 he was appointed commissioner for the trial of small causes at Lac-des-Deux-Montagnes. As political tensions in Lower Canada rose steadily in the 1820s and then dramatically in the 1830s [see Louis-Joseph Papineau*], he became increasingly alarmed by the possibility of armed revolt, which he considered pure folly. In 1837 he was sent to Saint-Benoît (Mirabel) to inspect the militia, a delicate task under the circumstances. After the inspection he breakfasted with the men, but the friendly tone of the conversation deteriorated over politics. When one man branded him a *chouayen* (a term of derision applied by the Patriotes to government supporters) for not giving up his commissions, Ducharme, who had a fiery temper even at 72, challenged him to a duel, but the challenge went unanswered. In late November a contingent of Patriotes, led by Amury Girod* and Jean-Olivier Chénier*, arrived at Lac-des-Deux-Montagnes to commandeer muskets and cannon. After the force had found only a few small arms and powder in a Hudson's Bay Company storehouse and had been denied arms by the Indians, it confronted Ducharme, who angrily refused to produce any weapons and urged the insurgents to return to their homes. Two weeks later, however, upon learning of the rebel defeat, Ducharme's humane concern again came to the fore, and he made his way to Saint-Eustache, where he evidently helped some of the rebel survivors escape. He was clearly content with the political *status quo*, but was not prepared to see men he knew, even though they had attempted the violent overthrow of legitimate authority, arrested for treason.

Ducharme's last years were spent in the quiet obscurity of Lac-des-Deux-Montagnes, where he continued as interpreter, reporting to the secretary of the Indian Department, Duncan Campbell Napier*. Ducharme's active career had spanned nearly 70 years. A small, wiry man of great physical strength, he was representative of a whole generation of Indian Department employees in the early 19th century, men who, by their involvement in the Indian trade, usually

Duffy

spoke several dialects and acquired an understanding of native customs. They linked Britain's military and trade policies of the 18th and early 19th centuries with the peace-time priorities of the post-1815 period.

DOUGLAS LEIGHTON

PAC, MG 24, B2; RG 4, B37, 1; RG 8, I (C ser.), 230, 257, 688b, 825, 1168, 1171, 1202, 1695; RG 10, A3, 495; RG 68, General index, 1651–1841: 255, 262, 281, 349, 354, 357, 362, 639. *Quebec Gazette*, 30 July 1812. F.-J. Audet, *Les députés de Montréal (ville et comtés), 1792–1867* ... (Montréal, 1943), 344, 346–50. *Officers of British forces in Canada* (Irving), 170–71, 214, 217–18. Wallace, *Macmillan dict.* Pierre Berton, *Flames across the border, 1813–1814* (Toronto, 1981). Maurault, *Le collège de Montréal* (Dansereau; 1967), 189. Benjamin Sulte, *Histoire de la milice canadienne-française, 1760–1897* (Montréal, 1897). "La bataille de Beaver-Dam," *BRH*, 11 (1905): 341–44. Pantaléon Hudon, "Le capitaine Dominique Ducharme," *Rev. canadienne*, 15 (1878): 420–30, 531–44. Joseph Tassé, "Un épisode de la guerre de 1812," *Rev. canadienne*, 7 (1870): 753–55.

DUFFY, JAMES W., Roman Catholic priest, farmer, and office holder; b. *c.* 1798 in County Monaghan (Republic of Ireland); d. 1 Dec. 1860 in Charlottetown.

A curate in Ireland, James W. Duffy was brought to Newfoundland by Bishop Michael Anthony Fleming*. He arrived in St John's on 21 Sept. 1833 and remained there until early the next year when the bishop named him to Ferryland. As assistant to Timothy BROWNE, with whom he did not get along, Duffy apparently served only that part of the parish from Fermeuse, where he resided, through Trepassey to St Mary's Bay. Actually, so bad was the relationship between the two that Browne thought Duffy "detestable and immoral." Nevertheless, Fleming, who disliked Browne, found Duffy "a zealous and indefatigable teacher" and especially praised his efforts in building churches.

At St Mary's two earlier churches had been toppled by wind, and in December 1834 Duffy decided to build anew on low ground near the beach. There was opposition from John Wills Martin*, the local agent for Slade, Elson and Company, which had extensive premises near by, but Duffy found Martin's alternative site unsuitable and proceeded with his plans. Martin, one of four non-Catholics in St Mary's, had recently erected a large fish flake which impeded access to the new church and he refused to remove it despite protests that tradition had made the beach a public right of way. However, although he considered that the building of the church warranted civil action for trespass, he merely instructed his clerk, William Lush, not to do business with Duffy. Lush refused to fill the priest's order for brandy, and, Martin claimed,

on 13 Jan. 1835 Duffy led some 80 persons from the church to dismantle and burn as a public nuisance that part of the flake extending beyond the property of Slade, Elson. The remainder was similarly destroyed soon afterwards. Charges were laid against Duffy and nine others.

Although the circuit court sat at St Mary's that summer, no action was taken until November, and then in the Supreme Court of Newfoundland at St John's. Duffy was arrested in Fermeuse on criminal charges and two constables brought him to Ferryland, where he posted bail. He understood that his case would be heard in the winter session of the court but when he and another man, who had voluntarily gone to St John's, appeared on 30 December he found the attorney general, James Simms*, and the chief justice, Henry John Boulton*, unready to proceed. Meanwhile at St Mary's a government brig attempted to arrest the eight remaining men charged with Duffy but the authority of the constables was questioned and, fearing violence, they withdrew. Governor Henry Prescott* was outraged. In May 1836 he readied a warship and by proclamation demanded the surrender of the accused. However, an appeal from Bishop Fleming reached St Mary's first, whereupon the men journeyed to St John's and gave themselves up. The absence of prosecution witnesses meant further delay. By December 1836, when Duffy appeared for a third time, the case already had obliged him to travel more than 1,300 miles. Only in May 1837 did the crown abandon its prosecution; Duffy and his co-defendants finally were freed of the charge. Father Duffy's Well, a Newfoundland provincial park, now marks his resting place on his many journeys between St Mary's and St John's.

The contest between officialdom and a Catholic priest ensured Duffy becoming a hero to many and Boulton an arch-villain. Indeed, the liberal *Newfoundland Patriot* of St John's charged that Boulton himself had instigated the prosecution to discredit his Catholic opposition. The chief justice's personal direction of a misdemeanour case, his seemingly prejudiced statements, and the undue prolongation of the proceedings in the Duffy case all lent substance to this charge. Undoubtedly the case had some influence in Boulton's eventual dismissal in 1838.

Duffy became the first parish priest of St Mary's in 1837, a parish which had been formed from part of Browne's district. At St Mary's he became a pioneer of Newfoundland agriculture, and his premises there – 25 acres cultivated, a large number of livestock, and even two fishing rooms – were an example of self-sufficiency to his parishioners.

By 1841, however, Duffy was again embroiled in controversy, this time as commissioner of roads for St Mary's, an office he had held since 1837. The cause was the replacement of his former co-commissioners

246

by new appointees, one of whom was Lush. Duffy announced that he would never sit with the new board and effectively halted road work in the area. At the time, agitation for his removal from the parish was resisted by Fleming, but it may have contributed to his replacement by Kyran Walsh* in 1843. The following year Duffy auctioned his farm and on 4 September left St John's for Cork (Republic of Ireland). For the next six years his whereabouts are unknown.

Duffy arrived in the diocese of Arichat, N.S., in 1850, seeking a parish from Bishop William FRASER, who was initially reluctant. By Easter 1851, however, he had given Duffy temporary charge of Notre-Dame Cathedral, Arichat, and before the bishop's death later that year Duffy was assigned to the parish of St Ann's in the town of Guysborough. A dispute with the pastor, James D. Drummond, soon resulted in his assuming sole charge and Drummond's appointment elsewhere. Duffy's administration of Guysborough was a stormy one throughout, culminating in the exclusion of Bishop Colin Francis MacKinnon* from the church. Duffy had left the parish by July 1857.

In November 1858 Duffy migrated to Prince Edward Island, becoming assistant at St Dunstan's Cathedral in Charlottetown. In February 1859 he went as parish priest to Kelly's Cross. Duffy was noted here again for instructing the people and constructing churches, and now, additionally, for his advocacy of temperance. Unfortunately, he suffered from a severe cold throughout the spring and summer of 1860 and by September, in Charlottetown on business, he was too ill to return to his parish. He died at the house of Bishop Peter MacIntyre* and was buried on 3 December in the cemetery at Kelly's Cross.

Fleming wrote of Duffy at St Mary's that, whatever his foibles, it was usually admitted "his instruction and example made the people of that District the most virtuous and industrious in the island." Duffy typified, almost to caricature, the traits requisite of a rural Canadian clergyman of his day: an endurance of hardship, a dauntless spirit, a concern for the political and economic (as well as the religious) needs of his people, and a sturdy independence. The last, no doubt, he had to excess.

RAYMOND J. LAHEY

AAH, William Walsh papers (mfm. at PANS). AASJ, Fleming papers; Mullock papers. Archivio della Propaganda Fide (Rome), Scritture riferite nei Congressi, America Settentrionale, 5 (1842–48). Assumption of the Blessed Virgin Mary (Roman Catholic church) (St Mary's, Nfld.), Reg. of baptisms, 1843 (mfm. at PANL). Basilica of St John the Baptist (Roman Catholic) (St John's), St John's parish, reg. of baptisms, 1833–34 (mfm. at PANL). PANL, GN 2/1, 40; GN 2/2, 1835–36. PRO, CO 194/94–95; CO 195/18. M. A. Fleming, Relazione della missione cattolica in Terranuova nell'America settentrionale . . .
(Rome, 1837). J. B. Jukes, Excursions in and about Newfoundland during the years 1839 and 1840 (2v., London, 1842), 2. Nfld., House of Assembly, Journal, 1837. Examiner (Charlottetown), 10 Dec. 1860. Newfoundlander, 26 Sept., 27 Oct., 7 Nov. 1833; 14 Aug. 1834. Patriot (St John's), 12 Jan., 2 Feb., 5 April, 14, 21, 28 May, 11 June, 26 Nov., 10, 17, 24 Dec. 1836; 8 April, 20, 27 May, 10 June, 15 July, 10, 21, 28 Oct., 25 Nov., 16 Dec. 1837; 20 Dec. 1843; 3 Jan. 1844. Public Ledger, 1, 12 Jan., 16 Feb., 25 March, 12 April, 17, 27 May, 4 Nov., 13, 16 Dec. 1836; 6 Jan. 1837; 9 Nov. 1841. Royal Gazette and Newfoundland Advertiser, 22 Dec. 1835, 20 Dec. 1836. Times and General Commercial Gazette (St John's), 6, 13, 20 Jan., 11 May 1836; 11 Sept. 1844. Gunn, Political hist. of Nfld. Howley, Ecclesiastical hist. of Nfld. A. A. Johnston, Hist. of Catholic Church in eastern N.S., vol.2. Michael McCarthy, "History of St Mary's Bay, 1597–1949," Winning entries in the Newfoundland government sponsored competition for the encouragement of arts and letters, etc., 1971 (St John's, [1972?]), 63–116. J. C. Macmillan, The history of the Catholic Church in Prince Edward Island from 1835 till 1891 (Quebec, 1913). T. J. Gough, "Rev. James Duffy's well: R.I.P.," Newfoundland Quarterly (St John's), 26 (1926–27), no.3: 23–24.

DULLARD. See DOLLARD

DUMOULIN, JEAN-GASPARD, lawyer and office holder; b. 19 April 1832 in Trois-Rivières, Lower Canada, son of Pierre-Benjamin DUMOULIN and Hermine Rieutord; m. 10 Jan. 1855, in Saint-Norbert-d'Arthabaska (Norbertville), Alida Pacaud, daughter of Philippe-Napoléon Pacaud*, a notary, and they had three children; d. 25 July 1860 in Trois-Rivières.

Nothing is known of Jean-Gaspard Dumoulin's childhood. He received his classical education at the Séminaire de Nicolet from 1842 to 1846, and then at the Petit Séminaire de Montréal from 1847 to 1851. In 1849, when he entered the two-year philosophy program, he began training as a law clerk under Louis-Charles Boucher* de Niverville in Trois-Rivières.

Dumoulin was called to the bar of Lower Canada in 1853 and went into practice at Trois-Rivières. He moved to Saint-Christophe-d'Arthabaska (Arthabaska) later that year. The first lawyer to settle in this locality, he was appointed clerk of the Circuit Court of Arthabaska on 2 September. On 10 Oct. 1855 the council of the county of Arthabaska, which had been created by the partitioning of Drummond County, was installed in a ceremony held at Dumoulin's house. The mayors of several municipalities in the county took part in the first session of this council, when Saint-Christophe-d'Arthabaska was chosen as the county seat. On 6 March 1858 the governor-in-chief, Sir Edmund Walker Head*, appointed Dumoulin protonotary of the Superior Court and clerk of the Circuit Court in the new district of Arthabaska, which had been set up the year before.

Dumoulin

Dumoulin had also taken a hand in municipal affairs. On 27 Feb. 1856 he had been appointed secretary-treasurer of the board of school commissioners for the parish of Saint-Christophe-d'Arthabaska, an office he retained until 1858. To serve in this capacity he had to provide guarantees, which he did by mortgaging a property he owned in Saint-Maurice Township, near Trois-Rivières. In addition, the mayor of the municipality and warden of the county, Adolphus Stein, as well as the county registrar, Édouard-Modeste Poisson, answered for Dumoulin's good conduct in the administration of the school board.

Jean-Gaspard Dumoulin died prematurely on 25 July 1860 in Trois-Rivières at the age of 28, and was buried three days later in the crypt of the cathedral there. He had engaged in a number of real estate transactions at Saint-Christophe-d'Arthabaska; however, fortune apparently did not favour him, since on his death his widow renounced her inheritance, considering it too heavy a liability. Dumoulin was also survived by three children. His son Philippe-Benjamin became cashier (manager) of the Banque du Peuple at Quebec around 1885.

ALCIDE FLEURY

AC, Arthabaska, État civil, Catholiques, Saint-Christophe (Arthabaska), 11 mars 1917. ANQ-MBF, CE1-48, 20 avril 1832, 28 juill. 1860; CE2-72, 10 janv. 1855; CN1-19, 15 août 1849; CN1-25, 17 janv. 1855, 15 févr. 1861; CN2-15, 26 févr. 1856; 14 avril, 16 juill. 1860; CN2-26, 17 janv. 1855. Arch. de la Corporation des commissaires d'écoles de la paroisse Saint-Christophe-d'Arthabaska (Arthabaska), Livres des délibérations, 14 déc. 1858. ASTR, 0184; 0296. PAC, MG 30, D1, 11: 739–40; RG 68, General index, 1841–67: 35, 314. L'Écho du Saint-Maurice (Trois-Rivières), 12 mars 1858. L'Ère nouvelle, 26 juill. 1860. F.-J. Audet, Les députés des Trois-Rivières. P.-G. Roy, Les avocats de la région de Québec. Le Centenaire d'Arthabaska ([Arthabaska], 1951), 37, 85, 91, 93, 95, 97, 159, 169. Douville, Hist. du collège-séminaire de Nicolet. Alcide Fleury, Arthabaska, capitale des Bois-Francs (Arthabaska, 1961), 164–65, 188, 190, 228. Maurault, Le collège de Montréal (Dansereau; 1967). Robert Cannon, "Les Trois-Rivières et les familles Dumoulin et Cannon," BRH, 40 (1934): 109–16.

DUMOULIN, PIERRE-BENJAMIN, lawyer, seigneur, politician, justice of the peace, office holder, land speculator, and judge; b. most probably in January 1799 in Trois-Rivières, Lower Canada, son of François Dumoulin and Louise Cressé; m. there 2 May 1825 Hermine Rieutord, only daughter of François Rieutord, a surgeon, and they had 11 children, of whom 6 reached adulthood; d. there 24 Sept. 1856.

Pierre-Benjamin Dumoulin belonged to a typical family of the petite bourgeoisie which was making its presence felt in Lower Canada towards the end of the 18th century. His father, who came from the canton of Bern in Switzerland, declared himself in official documents to be a businessman living in Sainte-Anne-de-Bout-de-l'Île (Sainte-Anne-de-Bellevue), Lower Canada, in 1796. His mother, the sister of Pierre-Michel Cressé*, had inherited one-third of the seigneury of Courval after her father's death in 1764; she and François Dumoulin acquired the remaining two-thirds from Pierre-Michel in 1796. They relinquished the seigneury eight years later. Two brothers of Pierre-Benjamin were based in Trois-Rivières, Jean-Emmanuel as a notary and Louis-François as a merchant. Another brother, SÉVÈRE, was to become a missionary in the Red River colony (Man.) with Joseph-Norbert PROVENCHER, and then priest of the parish of Sainte-Anne at Yamachiche in Lower Canada.

Having studied from 1810 to 1815 at the Séminaire de Nicolet, in 1816 Pierre-Benjamin became a clerk in the office of Pierre Vézina, a lawyer in Trois-Rivières. He was called to the bar on 21 July 1821 and decided to practise his profession there. Around the middle of the 1820s Dumoulin acquired part of the seigneury of Grosbois-Est; as a result, from 1825 he derived rents from his *censitaires* and granted mortgage loans.

In 1826, when he was just 27, Dumoulin went into politics, and ran against Charles Richard Ogden*, the attorney general of Lower Canada, in a by-election in Saint-Maurice for the House of Assembly. Despite the personal support he received from Charles-Elzéar Mondelet* and Ludger DUVERNAY through L'Argus, the "journal électorique," he was defeated. He stood again the following year for Trois-Rivières and was elected; he retained his seat until his resignation in 1832. According to Thomas Chapais*, Dumoulin apparently distinguished himself when in 1831 he opposed a bill to reduce the powers of priests in administration of parishes, a measure which was defended by Louis-Joseph Papineau* and Louis Bourdages*. Chapais also reports that during the summer of 1837, in the face of the growing radicalism of some members of the Patriote party, Dumoulin spoke out strongly "against the doctrines preached at various protest meetings and against the resolutions passed by them."

On 13 Jan. 1838, shortly after the outbreak of rebellion, Dumoulin was made a QC, and on 16 January he was named a justice of the peace, a commission renewed on 2 July 1839. On 24 April 1839 he was appointed a commissioner of the Court of Requests and on 7 Sept. 1840 a bankruptcy commissioner. His accession to the magistracy underlines the fact that he had found favour with the Special Council. However, the Court of Requests was

Dumoulin

abolished in December 1841 and Dumoulin returned to practising law. In 1843 he was divested of his QC and relieved of his duties as bankruptcy commissioner on a complaint made against him as a magistrate by Colonel Bartholomew Conrad Augustus Gugy*. He was in disgrace for a decade.

This did not preclude Dumoulin's becoming involved again in public life after an absence of 13 years when Trois-Rivières was incorporated as a municipality in 1845. He was elected its first mayor and was elected again in 1853 to hold office for one year. Meanwhile, it is probable that the advent of ministerial responsibility prompted his return to provincial politics. In the elections of 1848 he ran against Antoine Polette*, a lawyer in the city, for the riding of Trois-Rivières, but was defeated. A year later he joined other members of the bar of the region in denouncing a bill on the administration of justice entailing, among other things, the elimination of the judicial district of Three Rivers. In December 1851 he was elected for Yamaska to the Legislative Assembly of the Province of Canada, where he sat until June 1854. As member for Yamaska, Dumoulin took a stand in 1852 favouring the construction of a railway to link Trois-Rivières with Saint-Christophe-d'Arthabaska (Arthabaska).

He regained the trust of his colleagues and of the authorities in 1853; on 7 May he was appointed *bâtonnier* of that district, a title he retained until his death. On 5 July 1853 the governor of the Province of Canada, Lord Elgin [Bruce*], reappointed him a QC. Finally, on 6 March 1856, Dumoulin was chosen as chief judge of the Court of Quarter Sessions at Trois-Rivières.

When the property of the Saint-Maurice ironworks was broken up in 1845, Dumoulin seized the opportunity to go beyond making mortgage loans and take up land speculation. In 1846 he divested himself of the seigneury of Grosbois-Est, bought the Saint-Maurice seigneury, and speculated on the resale of the lots it contained. His purchase was roundly denounced by James Dickson, a merchant of Trois-Rivières, who also wanted to buy the seigneury. The transaction put the Dumoulin family on a sounder economic basis.

Pierre-Benjamin Dumoulin died in Trois-Rivières on 24 Sept. 1856 at the age of 57 and was buried three days later in the cathedral. He left a highly respected family, including Sévère, a lawyer, an MLA, mayor of Trois-Rivières in 1865, and sheriff of the district of Three Rivers from 1869 to 1882; JEAN-GASPARD, a lawyer and protonotary of Arthabaska; Pantaléon-Benjamin, a notary of Trois-Rivières; and Charles, a lawyer and sheriff of Trois-Rivières after Sévère. After Dumoulin's death at least two of his sons, Charles and Pantaléon-Benjamin, followed his lead in land speculation. They were identified with the

purchase and sale of lots which accompanied the first wave of urban expansion at Trois-Rivières from 1850 to 1880.

BENOÎT GAUTHIER

ANQ-M, CE6-11, 23 févr. 1784. ANQ-MBF, CE1-48, 2 mai 1825, 27 sept. 1856; CN1-27, 4 févr. 1853; CN1-56, 1er mai 1825. ASTR, 0368. BE, Trois-Rivières, reg. B, 1, no.17. PAC, RG 31, A1, 1825, 1831, Trois-Rivières; RG 68, General index, 1651–1841: 10, 77, 221, 393, 401, 540; 1841–67: 312, 317. *L'Argus* (Trois-Rivières, Qué.), 30 août 1826. *L'Ère nouvelle*, 31 janv., 25 sept. 1856. *La Gazette des Trois-Rivières*, 28 janv. 1847. *Journal des Trois-Rivières*, 1849; 6 mars 1852; 7 mai, 9 juill., 6 août 1853. *Le Journal des Trois-Rivières*, 12 août, 21 oct. 1872; 6, 31 août 1874. F.-J. Audet, *Les députés des Trois-Rivières*; "Les législateurs du Bas-Canada." Desjardins, *Guide parl. La Mauricie et les Bois-Francs: inventaire bibliographique, 1760–1975*, René Hardy et al., édit. (Montréal, 1977). P.-G. Roy, *Les juges de la prov. de Québec*. Raphaël Bellemare, *Les bases de l'histoire d'Yamachiche, 1703–1903* ... (Montréal, 1901), 58, 72–74. Napoléon Caron, *Histoire de la paroisse d'Yamachiche (précis historique)* (Trois-Rivières, 1892). Chapais, *Cours d'hist. du Canada*, 3: 252; 4: 150. Douville, *Hist. du collège-séminaire de Nicolet*, vol.2. Albert Tessier, *Les forges Saint-Maurice, 1729–1883* (Trois-Rivières, 1952). Robert Cannon, "Les Trois-Rivières et les familles Dumoulin et Cannon," *BRH*, 40 (1934): 109–16. "Les disparus," *BRH*, 31 (1925): 479. Benjamin Sulte, "Anciens journaux des Trois-Rivières," *BRH*, 7 (1901): 282–84. Albert Tessier, "Un curé missionnaire: l'abbé S.-N. Dumoulin (1793–1853)," *Cahiers des Dix*, 16 (1951): 117–31.

DUMOULIN, SÉVÈRE (baptized **Sévère-Joseph-Nicolas**), Roman Catholic priest, missionary, and author; b. 5 Dec. 1793 in Sainte-Anne-de-Bout-de-Île (Sainte-Anne-de-Bellevue), Lower Canada, son of François Dumoulin and Louise Cressé; d. 27 July 1853 in Trois-Rivières, Lower Canada.

Sévère Dumoulin's father was Swiss and Protestant by origin, but he married as a Roman Catholic when he took a daughter of Louis-Pierre Poulin* de Courval Cressé to be his wife. She had already inherited a third of the Courval seigneury after her father's death in 1764, and became its sole owner in 1796 when her brother Pierre-Michel Cressé* assigned his share to her. The Dumoulins took up residence among their *censitaires*, and later moved to Nicolet where three of their sons would attend the seminary; Sévère completed his classical and theological studies between 1807 and 1816, PIERRE-BENJAMIN attended from 1810 to 1815, and Jean-Emmanuel was a pupil from 1810.

Sévère Dumoulin was ordained priest on 23 Feb. 1817 and appointed curate of Notre-Dame cathedral at Quebec. In 1818 Bishop Joseph-Octave Plessis* sent him and Abbé Joseph-Norbert PROVENCHER to set up

Dumoulin

a mission in the Red River colony (Man.). Although the missionaries were eagerly awaited by Lord Selkirk [Douglas*] and the settlement's Catholic population, they had been instructed to make Christianizing the Indians "the primary object" of their labours.

Dumoulin left Quebec on 24 April 1818, and after a few days visiting his family reached Montreal on 8 May. There he was delayed by organizational difficulties and still more by latent, unresolved quarrels between the Hudson's Bay Company, in which Lord Selkirk was a shareholder, and the North West Company. The "apostolic canoe" carrying the three ecclesiastics – seminarist William Edge accompanied the two priests – left Montreal on 19 May and reached Red River on 16 July. A naturally resourceful man with no "excess of fat," Dumoulin easily endured the discomforts and fatigues of the long journey. He had also made his first contact with the Indians, and had already formed the conviction – from which he never really deviated – that their conversion would be easier "if one could manage to gather them into villages." This view ran counter to that of Provencher and Plessis, who believed that a missionary should adapt to the Indians' way of life and if necessary travel with them to preach the Gospel.

Although Dumoulin started his work by ministering to the colony's whites and Métis, he also began studying Indian languages. On 13 Sept. 1818 he went with Edge to Pembina (N.Dak.), which he made his principal place of residence. There he encountered a large population of Indians, Métis, and whites, attracted by the herds of buffalo near by. Despite some unforeseen obstacles – two attempted murders by a disgruntled Indian, the arrival in 1820 of a Protestant minister, John West*, and the lack of "presents" – he managed to create a lively Christian community. On his arrival Dumoulin opened a school with Edge as teacher; it soon had about 60 pupils. Not long afterwards he sent a young French Canadian, one Legacé, to teach the children in the buffalo-hunting camps at some distance from the village. Provencher informed Plessis in a letter written in February 1819 that Legacé, who was spending the winter on the plains, had even more pupils than Edge. Dumoulin helped establish Pembina as a settled and permanent community by building a presbytery, a school, and a chapel which was opened in 1821.

In the summer of 1819 Dumoulin had gone on a three-month evangelizing journey which took him to Rainy Lake (Ont.), and the following summer he set off again for seven weeks, this time reaching Hudson Bay. These trips produced little result; like his visits to the parish of Saint-Boniface created by Provencher at Red River, they were only interruptions to his work in the Pembina mission. There, up to June 1821, Dumoulin recorded 326 baptisms, 56 marriages, and 31 burials, and was delighted to be able to note: "I have succeeded this year in getting a good many Indians to plant crops [and they] have formed small villages." But even by 1818 the future of Dumoulin's mission had been compromised: a treaty signed that year settling the frontier between American and British territory to the west of Lake Superior had placed Pembina in the United States. With Selkirk's death in 1820 and the instructions given by John HALKETT, the administrator of his estate, to abandon Pembina and bring its people back to Red River, Provencher was forced to recall Dumoulin in 1823. Unhappy with this decision, Dumoulin sought permission to return to Lower Canada and, despite the disappointment of Provencher and Plessis, he left the northwest in 1823 to the regret of his converts.

On returning to Lower Canada, Dumoulin was given the parish of Saint-François-de-Sales (at Saint-François-de-Montmagny), but he retained his interest in the missions he had left. In 1824 he published *Notice sur les missions de la Rivière-Rouge et du Sault Ste-Marie*; in it he supported Provencher's appointment as bishop of Juliopolis and coadjutor to Plessis for the northwest, and answered the criticisms of some of the Lower Canadian clergy. At the same time he set up a fund for the missions which brought in more than £600. He put his missionary experience at the service of Bishop Joseph Signay* in 1837–38 and 1840, agreeing to work among the Têtes de Boules at Weymontachingue, on the upper reaches of the Saint-Maurice River.

Dumoulin in October 1825 became the ninth parish priest of Sainte-Anne at Yamachiche, where he remained until he died. His administration was marked by various developments: the division of the parish, which had become over-populated, and the creation of two new parishes, Saint-Barnabé in 1835 and Saint-Sévère in 1850; the impetus he gave to parish institutions in rebuilding the church and presbytery; the founding of a convent under the Congregation of Notre-Dame in 1852 and of a boys' school entrusted to the Christian Brothers in 1853; and, finally, a renewed devotion to the parish's patron saint, St Anne.

During the summer of 1853 Sévère Dumoulin felt ill. He left the parish to stay with his brother Pierre-Benjamin, a lawyer at Trois-Rivières, and to place himself under the care of a local doctor. He died there on 27 July at the age of 59. One account noted that "his funeral service was the most solemn ever sung in the church at Yamachiche," and for a long time his parishioners continued to venerate Dumoulin as a saint and to attribute to him certain signal favours they received.

NIVE VOISINE

250

The correspondence of Sévère Dumoulin is found, for the most part, in AAQ, 330 CN, I–II, and in Arch. de l'évêché de Trois-Rivières (Trois-Rivières, Qué.), Paroisses, Sainte-Anne (Yamachiche). His letters from the Red River Colony have been edited by G. L. Nute and most were published in *Documents relating to northwest missions, 1815–1827* (St Paul, Minn., 1942). Copies of the majority of the letters sent to Dumoulin are in AAQ, 210 A, IX–XXI.

His pamphlet, *Notice sur les missions de la Rivière-Rouge et du Sault Ste-Marie* (Saint-Pierre-de-la-Rivière-du-Sud, Qué., 1824), has been reprinted under the title *Notice sur la Rivière-Rouge dans le territoire de la baie d'Hudson* (Montréal, 1843). The manuscript text of the *Notice*, entitled "Exposé naïf sur la mission de la Rivière-Rouge suivi d'une souscription" and dated 19 Feb. 1824, is available in ASN, AP-G, L.-É. Bois, D, 14, no.67.

J.-E. Bellemare, *Histoire de Nicolet, 1669–1924* (Arthabaska, Qué., 1924). Napoléon Caron, *Histoire de la paroisse d'Yamachiche (précis historique)* (Trois-Rivières, 1892). J.-É. Champagne, *Les missions catholiques dans l'Ouest canadien (1818–1875)* (Ottawa, 1949). Georges Dugas, *Monseigneur Provencher et les missions de la Rivière-Rouge* (Montréal, 1889). Marcel Giraud, *Le Métis canadien; son rôle dans l'histoire des provinces de l'Ouest* (Paris, 1945). A.-G. Morice, *Histoire de l'Église catholique dans l'Ouest canadien, du lac Supérieur au Pacifique (1659–1905)* (3v., Winnipeg et Montréal, 1912). J.-A. Pellerin, *Yamachiche et son histoire, 1672–1978* ([Trois-Rivières], 1980). Antoine d'Eschambault, "La Compagnie de la baie d'Hudson et l'effort missionnaire," SCHÉC *Rapport*, 12 (1944–45): 83–99. Albert Tessier, "Un curé missionnaire: l'abbé S.-N. Dumoulin (1793–1853)," *Cahiers des Dix*, 16 (1951): 117–31.

DUNN, JOHN HENRY, office holder, politician, businessman, and militia officer; baptized 26 Feb. 1792 on St Helena, son of John Charles Dunn and Elizabeth Bazette; m. first 4 May 1820 Charlotte Roberts (d. 1835), and they had six sons and two daughters; m. secondly 9 March 1842 Sophie-Louise Juchereau Duchesnay at Quebec, and they had a son and a daughter; d. 21 April 1854 in London.

John Henry Dunn's father, a surgeon and native of Northumberland, England, is believed to have occupied a position with the East India Company. He was wealthy enough to ensure that his son received a proper English education and to marry his daughter, Mary Ann, to Francis William Ogilvie-Grant, later the 6th Earl of Seafield. It is not entirely clear though how John Henry, in his late twenties, secured the life appointment of receiver general of Upper Canada. He himself attributed it to the influence of Charles Grant (later Lord Glenelg), the chief secretary of Ireland and a relative of Mary Ann's husband.

Dunn was appointed receiver general on 12 April 1820. By that summer he and his 19-year-old bride, from a wealthy Sussex family, had left England for their new home at York (Toronto), Upper Canada. He was sworn in on 18 October and within a month had received the office's money, bonds, accounts, and ledger-books from the acting receiver general, George CROOKSHANK.

Dunn's duties involved the collection of the casual and territorial revenue, including the funds derived from the crown lands and clergy reserves, all of which was subject to the control of the crown through its representative, the lieutenant governor. The receiver general also served the provincial House of Assembly by collecting the customs duties, tolls, and other local imposts under its control. Dunn's dual role was reflected in his salary: he received £200 annually for administering funds controlled by the executive, a three per cent commission on all collections made in Upper Canada, and three and a half per cent on customs revenue collected in Lower Canada. Shortly after his appointment, the Upper Canadian legislature sought to replace his commission with a fixed salary of £550. Dunn initially objected but, although the British Treasury upheld the province's right to pay him in any way it wanted, the appropriate legislation never received royal assent. Only in July 1831 did the legislature establish a fixed annual salary, £700, which along with Dunn's £200 as a crown officer and £200 for collecting funds for the Canada Company, enabled him to maintain the annual return of £1,100 he had attained under the old arrangements.

Although his books received an initial audit in Upper Canada, Dunn always claimed that as receiver general he was ultimately responsible to the British Treasury. In 1824, because of this belief, he labelled as "unwarranted" the criticism by Attorney General John Beverley Robinson* and Chief Justice William Dummer Powell* of his collection of a fee on a provincial loan he had negotiated. When an assembly committee on public accounts, chaired in 1829 by Thomas Dalton*, condemned both the disproportionate costs of the receiver general's office (caused largely by his emoluments) and its inefficient accounting, Dunn rejected as "impossible" the "great many mistakes" found in his accounts. Equally sensitive to criticisms by British officials of his salary and accounting procedures, Dunn continually sought to use his dual accountability to evade his responsibility to, and establish a degree of independence between, both his provincial and his imperial masters. His early successes in resolving the province's financial difficulties would allow him gradually to widen his discretionary powers as receiver general. It was not until Upper Canada faced bankruptcy that its executive and legislature would successfully assert control over their financial officer.

Dunn had arrived in Upper Canada shortly after a dispute had arisen between the upper and lower provinces over their agreement to share the duties collected at Lower Canadian ports. As a result of this

Dunn

controversy, Upper Canada had not received any portion of its share since July 1819, an annual loss of nearly "four-fifths of the whole revenue" of the upper province, according to the report made in 1821 by the commissioners representing Upper Canada in the negotiations between the two provinces, William Claus*, Thomas Clark*, and Allan MacLean*. Faced by such financial difficulty, the legislature sent Attorney General Robinson to England in 1822 to enlist the aid of the imperial government. In the mean time Dunn faced the immediate problem of dealing with the temporary shortfall in revenues. He pressed customs inspectors in Upper Canada for funds they were owing, thereby increasing the amount collected from £6,000 in 1820 to £9,500 a year later. More significantly, Dunn sought private funds to finance public activities. In 1821 the legislature authorized him to borrow money to pay arrears in the pensions due militia veterans of the War of 1812. That fall the Niagara district firm of Thomas Clark and Samuel Street* lent the government £20,000 at six per cent, the maximum rate allowed under the British usury act. The loan was to be paid off in instalments over the next three years. Because the public revenues were insufficient to cover the amount, however, the government permitted the Bank of Upper Canada to take up the debentures as they fell due, thus borrowing from one source to pay another.

The eventual resolution of the dispute with Lower Canada did not relieve the financial difficulties of Upper Canada. The imperial parliament's Canada Trade Act of 1822, in failing to give Upper Canada effective control in the division of the duties collected at the major port of Quebec, limited its ability to raise revenues to meet its escalating expenditures on public works. Revenue received from the Canada Company after it began operations in 1826 [see John Galt*] would help to defray the government's expenses, but, as the province sought to improve roads and waterways in the 1820s, its receiver general resorted to borrowing to finance these improvements. By 1830, through the issue of provincial debentures, Dunn had secured loans for upwards of £90,000.

Dunn was personally involved in one private transportation project which increasingly absorbed government revenues. In 1824 William Hamilton Merritt*, a mill-owner with an ambitious plan to link lakes Ontario and Erie, persuaded him to purchase stock in the newly formed Welland Canal Company and asked him to serve as its first president [see George KEEFER]. Dunn's initial decision to decline the position was no doubt influenced by the lack of either official or unofficial enthusiasm in York for Merritt's project. The following year, however, he accepted the presidency, a decision that coincided with an amendment to the company's charter which made a directorship dependent on the subscription of

at least £250, thus virtually ensuring majority representation by the York élite on the company's board. Although Merritt simply hoped that the receiver general's name would help promote the sale of company stock, Dunn proved to be a personal friend and a valuable ally within government circles. In New York City he personally disposed of 6,000 shares worth £75,000 and assisted Merritt in a successful application for £25,000 in aid from the House of Assembly, which the company received early in 1826. Financial problems, precipitated by the failure of a fellow director, Solicitor General Henry John Boulton*, to sell the £100,000 worth of shares reserved for the London market, prompted the company to seek further government assistance. In his role as financial adviser to the government, Dunn maintained that it could safely subscribe for £50,000 in shares without seriously embarrassing provincial revenues, and it did so in 1827. At the same time, Lieutenant Governor Sir Peregrine MAITLAND forwarded to the Colonial Office a scheme outlined by Dunn proposing an imperial loan of £50,000 sterling for the canal project. Merritt followed up this initiative in 1828 by visiting England, where he secured the loan.

In March 1833 the canal was completed, but Dunn was no longer president. He had resigned in February, refusing to bow to pressure from other directors to be made personally liable for a loan needed to pay several contractors. The following year, relations between Dunn and Merritt were severely strained when the receiver general, fearing excessive depreciation, refused to release £50,000 in debentures for the Welland Canal, though Merritt had already negotiated a loan against their anticipated sale. In the end, the government repaid the loan and cancelled the debentures, adding the loss to a growing public debt.

As demands mounted for the government to support the Welland Canal and other transportation projects, and as debenture issues fell due, Dunn became a central figure in the province's efforts to secure its financial position. In March 1830, in order to cancel the public debt, the House of Assembly empowered him to negotiate a long-term loan in England, where, it was convinced, he could get better terms than were available within the province. Dunn unsuccessfully applied to a number of London firms whose principal business was the financing of British trade with North America. He tried the London market again three years later, by which time he had been able to raise, in Upper Canada, only a little more than £10,000 of the £250,000 required for the improvement of navigation on the St Lawrence River, the construction of roads and bridges, the reduction of the public debt, and the payment of compensation to those who had suffered losses in the War of 1812. This time the responses to Dunn's request for a loan were more favourable. One firm, Thomas Wilson and Company, expressed some interest in offering a long-term loan of £200,000 sterling. Lieutenant Governor Sir John Colborne* granted Dunn permission to go to England, where he arrived in early September 1833, and by October he was back in Upper Canada, having succeeded in his negotiations with the Wilson firm.

After the agreement was sanctioned by the legislature on 6 March 1834, the strains on the provincial funds were considerably eased. By the end of the year, however, the loan was exhausted. Public expenditures continued to outstrip regular revenues, particularly as work proceeded on the St Lawrence canals. On 16 April 1835 the assembly, eager to exploit its new source of finance, expressed its support for all future loans negotiated in London and authorized Dunn to procure a loan for £400,000 sterling. Arriving in London during a stock-market boom in which North American securities were highly valued, Dunn succeeded that winter in negotiating the whole of the loan on favourable terms, dividing it between Baring Brothers and Thomas Wilson and Company. Despite the tremendous (and perhaps unconstitutional) authority granted to Dunn to carry out these negotiations outside the province, as well as the possible repercussions of continually refinancing the public debt on the London market, success muted criticism of the receiver general's policy. William ALLAN, president of the Bank of Upper Canada, seems to have been alone in questioning Dunn's fiscal practices. Responding to Allan in 1834, Dunn simultaneously defended his own practices and revealed his discontent with Allan's conservative banking policy: "I have advocated borrowing foreign instead of domestic Capital first because money is got upon more easy and certain terms and secondly it leaves the Private resources of the Province to Private enterprise."

At the height of his career, in 1836, Dunn received an honour which he had long desired. Although he had been made a member of the Legislative Council on 1 March 1822, he had been unable to secure an appointment to the Executive Council, in spite of his sister's efforts in 1822 and Colborne's recommendation in 1834. When the new lieutenant governor, Sir Francis Bond Head*, considered expanding the council from three to six members, Colonial Secretary Lord Glenelg reminded him that, on the recommendation of his predecessor in the Colonial Office, Dunn had been assured a seat. Seeking to broaden representation in council to include reformers, Head was likely relieved to hear that Dunn's appointment, alongside those of John Rolph* and Robert BALDWIN, would be supported by the reform-dominated assembly. The three were sworn in on 20 Feb. 1836. Head's conciliatory gesture, however, turned into a fiasco when he refused to consider a document signed by all six councillors asking that they be consulted on all matters relating to the government of the province. Head demanded that they abandon either their principles or their positions. Although Dunn, George Herchmer Markland*, Peter Robinson*, and Joseph WELLS were prepared to retract their names, they resigned on 12 March along with Baldwin and Rolph. In less than three weeks Dunn had lost an appointment he had sought for 16 years.

Angered by this incident, Head was enraged by his receiver general's subsequent behaviour. In April Dunn was asked by the assembly to join Marshall Spring Bidwell* and Peter PERRY, two of Head's most outspoken critics, in meeting with Louis-Joseph Papineau* and two other Lower Canadian reformers, evidently to discuss the development of the St Lawrence. Instead of declining the offer in the firm language that the lieutenant governor had directed him to use, Dunn replied, either naïvely or to spite Head, that however much he might desire to, he could not accept the "Honour" conferred on him by the assembly because of his other duties and because he did not have the approval of the lieutenant governor. Though Dunn claimed throughout this affair that he was only interested in promoting improvements to the St Lawrence, an infuriated Head unsuccessfully demanded that Glenelg dismiss him. Head considered him to be sympathetic to the "revolutionary party" and stories appeared in George Gurnett*'s tory newspaper that Dunn was a member of the "cabal" which had met at John Rolph's house and that he was donating money to the radical Canadian Alliance [see James Lesslie*]. Dunn publicly denied these accusations.

Dunn's political affiliations before 1841, by which time he had clearly emerged as a moderate reformer, are difficult to determine. Socially, he held positions of the sort associated with members of the tory élite in Toronto. He did not admit to being wealthy: in 1834 he confided to William Hamilton Merritt that only the family income of his wife, Charlotte, kept him out of debt and during the 1840s he claimed to be living on her bequest to their children. But he held a senior government post for which he received a sizeable annual salary, lived on a spacious estate known as Dunstable, sent his eldest son to Upper Canada College, and was a member of and conspicuous donor to St James' Church. He participated with prominent tories as well as reformers in numerous other community bodies during the 1820s and 1830s: as a trustee of both the general hospital and the Home District Grammar School, member of the Board for the General Superintendence of Education, president of the Upper Canadian Temperance Society and of the Auxiliary Bible Society, director of the Bank of Upper Canada and the British America Fire and Life Assurance Company, colonel of the 2nd Regiment of West York militia, treasurer of the masonic lodge of

Dunn

Upper Canada, patron of the York Mechanics' Institute, and member of the Upper Canada Club (Toronto Club). Yet he never seems to have been a member of the social or the political élite. Shortly before the outbreak of rebellion in 1837 [see William Lyon Mackenzie*], he informed Lord Glenelg that much mischief was resulting from "party spirit" in Upper Canada. He insisted that he was of no political party and that he had always tried to mediate between the two conflicting factions. Two years later he wrote Lord John Russell a lengthy memorandum, in which he argued: "Union will break up [the] parties etc. which have brought this province into its present deplorable condition, and these parties are becoming more and more opposed. Both are highly capable and equally wrong." Regardless of his attempts to be non-partisan, Dunn clearly had no sympathy for the "violent party" of tories into whose hands Head had fallen. Although he had backed down during the Executive Council incident of 1836, his name continued to be linked with Rolph and Baldwin.

Though Dunn's differences with the lieutenant governor did not lead to his dismissal as receiver general, they complicated his ability to deal with the financial impact on Upper Canada of the international commercial crisis of 1836–37. Late in 1836 the booming market in Britain for North American securities, which had allowed him to borrow with relative ease, slowed considerably. Rumours abounded in Upper Canada about the imminent collapse of both Thomas Wilson and Company and Baring Brothers, in which firms the province had an estimated £147,000 sterling on deposit. In April 1837 Dunn asked to be sent to London as a provincial agent to protect the revenues and public works of Upper Canada against the bankruptcy of the British firms. Head refused and appointed Solicitor General William Henry Draper* to go instead, although Dunn was granted a personal leave of absence in order to accompany him.

By the time they arrived in June, the Wilson company had suspended all payments, including an estimated £80,000 sterling to Upper Canada. Draper pressed the Colonial Office to issue a writ of extent on behalf of the province, which would give the crown priority over the firm's private creditors in bankruptcy proceedings but which might have ruinous implications for any Canadian banks or companies represented by the Wilson firm. Glenelg, who was upset because he had not known of the past loans to the province, questioned the political wisdom of issuing an extent and thus offending private creditors. In the mean time, Dunn, who was liable for loss of provincial funds on deposit in England, learned that another London firm, Glyn, Halifax, Mills and Company, had approached the Colonial Office and

agreed to assume, beginning in July, the interest payments due on the provincial debentures held by Thomas Wilson and Company. Through Robert Gillespie*, a merchant familiar with Canadian affairs, Dunn was introduced to the firm and, on his own authority, accepted the proposed assignment, thereby eliminating the possibility of an extent being issued and preventing the province from defaulting on interest payments. He was later criticized for this agreement because an extent might have resulted in more money being recovered to the province. It was never clear, however, whether the imperial parliament would have agreed to Draper's request for an extent and what effect such a step might have had on Upper Canada's credibility on the London market. Glenelg informed Head in August of Dunn's action and reserved judgement on the wisdom of his agreement, preferring to question the soundness of allowing one person to control Upper Canada's finances: "Mr. Dunn claims, and very probably possesses, the right to make on behalf of the Province pecuniary arrangements of vast extent in the adoption of which he acts upon his own single judgement." Though touchy about his initiative with Glyn, Halifax, Mills and Company, Dunn had nevertheless felt justified in July in petitioning for a knighthood, which he never received. He returned to Canada in September.

Dunn's negotiations in London had introduced no new capital into Upper Canada, in spite of the fact that the assembly was seeking £654,250 for public works, including the proposed construction of two railways. In the climate of continued financial depression, provincial bonds were unsaleable in London. The province's credit was further weakened by Head's decision during Dunn's absence to sell £138,000 in debentures, payable at Baring Brothers but without the firm's knowledge, and by the rebellion of 1837–38. On two occasions, once in 1839 and again a year later, Dunn returned to London, ostensibly on personal business but also in an attempt to negotiate a loan to reduce the province's burden of debt, which had forced the restriction or cancellation of various works. Both times he failed. It took the union of the Canadas, with improved provincial revenues, and an imperial-guaranteed loan of £1,500,000 sterling to bring financial stability back to Upper Canada.

The receiver general's credibility within the government was undermined by his resistance to administrative reforms in his office. In the fall of 1839 Head's successor, Lieutenant Governor Sir George ARTHUR, acting on a request from the assembly, established committees of investigation into the conduct of various executive departments. Dunn, always sensitive to criticism, was probably even more reluctant to cooperate with the committee investigating his office since it was chaired by his most persistent critic, William Allan, who months earlier had attacked Dunn's broad discretionary powers as receiver general.

The report of Allan's committee harshly condemned the practices of Dunn's office, as well as his resistance to the investigation. The casual and highly personal administration of the office was no longer suited to its complex operations, including its responsibility for large sums of public money. The committee found that of the £41,496 owed to the public by the office, only the £4,666 deposited in the Bank of Upper Canada and the office vault could be accounted for. Dunn claimed that £10,560 had been forwarded to Glyn, Halifax, Mills and Company to cover part of the interest payments on the provincial debentures, but he could not immediately provide any evidence of this transaction. The remaining £26,270, he explained, was available on demand from his personal agent in Montreal, Forsyth, Richardson and Company, where money was, and always had been, held at Dunn's private risk. There was nothing improper in this arrangement, for which Dunn had posted bonds (themselves a matter of some question). His responsibility as receiver general was to produce the funds he had collected when and as required by the government, which, he emphasized, he was always prepared to do. Conscious of his previous disagreements with Allan on fiscal policy, Dunn defended his use of Montreal agents, the Bank of Montreal and Forsyth, Richardson and Company, for handling matters of colonial finance and exchange. He argued that the money was deposited in Montreal rather than Toronto so that the receiver general, and therefore the public, could continue to benefit from the superior market there for purchasing exchange.

Dunn failed to see that the commingling of private and public finance, once traditional to many British departments, was outmoded. In 1833 the Audit Office in London had noted that, under the existing system, Dunn could derive personal benefit from the funds deposited with his Montreal agents, an argument which had been used in the debate to restrict his emoluments. Still, there was no evidence, and not much likelihood, that he had risked speculating with funds in his possession. In 1835, before William Lyon Mackenzie's committee on grievances, Dunn had offered to cooperate with any measure to create a purely public, interest-bearing account, provided that he be released from his securities. But Arthur informed Governor Charles Edward Poulett Thomson* in 1840 that Dunn regarded every criticism and every effort at reform as "an affront – a doubt of his integrity." A feud broke out that year between Dunn and John MACAULAY, the inspector general of public accounts, who had been instructed by Thomson to implement reforms in the auditing of the receiver general's accounts. Thomson, later Lord Sydenham, eventually intervened on Macaulay's behalf and ordered Dunn to make quarterly statements showing government revenues and expenditures and the exact locations where provincial funds were deposited. The governor thus ensured that Dunn would not have "the unlimited control he wishes" over the government's money.

Despite Dunn's resistance to reform, Sydenham was able to pressure him into obeying his instructions; in October 1839 the Colonial Office had ended the practice of life tenure in various colonial offices, including Dunn's. Late in 1840 he coyly let it be known that he would run as a pro-union candidate in Toronto in the upcoming general election, provided that Sydenham appoint him receiver general for the united provinces. The governor realized the value of such a popular candidate but set his own conditions on Dunn's candidacy. He was sworn in as receiver general on 27 Feb. 1841, prior to the election and only after he had agreed to continue to respect Sydenham's instructions concerning the handling of the province's finances, if elected, and to resign, if defeated.

Although his official future rested on electoral success, the political novice almost backed out of the heated campaign on three occasions, once when his running mate, Robert Baldwin, resigned, again after Baldwin was replaced by the politically aggressive Isaac Buchanan*, and yet again as a result of Sydenham's decision to make Kingston, rather than Toronto, the new capital. Sir George Arthur, who played a backstage role in the elections, described Dunn to Sydenham as a "weak man, influenced by the impulse of the moment, and wayward to the extreme." With good reason he complained, "It is terrible work to sustain in a public contest a person of this temperament." Francis Hincks*, editor of the reform *Examiner* and a candidate in Oxford, was even blunter in his assessment: "Dunn is a weak man *who does not understand politics* but is anxious to act with Baldwin & the reformers." In the end, Dunn and Buchanan defeated their tory opponents, George Monro* and Henry SHERWOOD, and paraded triumphantly through the streets on 21 March. Dunn's first and last electoral victory was marred by partisan violence that day when a man was killed in a riot.

Dunn's career for the next three years was unspectacular. In the new era of public finance after the union, Dunn was largely eclipsed in matters of revenue by Francis Hincks, who, as inspector general of public accounts, castigated his outdated methods of bookkeeping and his concept of public accountability. Dunn, in response, did not hesitate to voice his opinion, in conversations with other officials, that Hincks had been "implicated in the insurrections of 1837." Sydenham's successor, Sir Charles Bagot*,

Dunn

considered Dunn to be incompetent and would not entrust to him the negotiation of the £1,500,000 loan which had been guaranteed by the British government.

During these years Dunn's commitment to the reform cause, and to Robert Baldwin and Louis-Hippolyte La Fontaine* in particular, intensified. On 26 Nov. 1843 Dunn resigned along with all the other members of the Baldwin–La Fontaine coalition, except Dominick Daly*, to protest the refusal of the new governor, Sir Charles Theophilus Metcalfe*, to consult the Executive Council over patronage. Dunn vacated the office of receiver general early the following January and was replaced by Bernard Turquand as acting receiver general. Briefly elated at being free of the office, Dunn remained in Canada, reportedly to support the cause of reform and responsible government. In April he rejoiced over La Fontaine's decisive victory in a by-election in Montreal and denounced the "insolence and arrogance of those rabid Tories." Still, as a result of his public disappointments since 1836, he maintained a bitter ambivalence about his prospects in Canada.

Having lost the post he had held for 23 years, Dunn was "like a fish out of water," one contemporary observed, and could scarcely believe the country could go on without him. Forgotten or ignored in the changing political and financial world of the union, he intended to return to England. He nevertheless ran as the reform candidate in Toronto in the general election of 1844 but was defeated. The following year he left Canada for London with his 23-year-old French Canadian wife and most of his surviving children. In England after an absence of 25 years, with no pension and no expectation of receiving another position from the Colonial Office, he hoped to find "some employment . . . through my friends who have Interest." In the fall and winter of 1845–46 he complained to his Canadian friends of the high taxes and of the "horrible wretched climate" in London. He expressed a desire to live in Montreal if ever he could afford it. He waited in vain to be recalled when Baldwin and La Fontaine returned to power in 1848. Though he retained some land in Canada, he does not seem to have returned to the country he had come to regard as his real home. In the spring of 1848 he attempted to serve the Canadian government in a familiar role when Hincks asked him to negotiate a loan with Baring Brothers, but he was unsuccessful. Four years later Toronto's mayor, John George Bowes*, approached him with a request to sell bonds on the London market on behalf of the city. Dunn remained in the country he claimed to detest until he was "called to his last audit" in London on 21 April 1854. Despite his many expressions of financial destitution during his lifetime, he left an estate valued at more than £86,200. He had not lived to see his son

Lieutenant Alexander Roberts Dunn become the first Canadian-born recipient of the Victoria Cross for his valour on 25 Oct. 1854 in the charge of the Light Brigade.

William Lyon Mackenzie, in an obituary in *Mackenzie's Weekly Message*, remembered the former receiver general as a "faithful guardian of the public purse" who was a powerful supporter of the Welland Canal, the St Lawrence canals, and other public improvements. Yet Dunn was not simply a promoter of provincial development. Between the passage of the Canada Trade Act and the Act of Union, he had tried to ensure that projects received funding despite the financial constraints on the province. During that period, he later claimed, he had kept Upper Canada "from Bankruptcy by my own Personal exertions." But borrowing on the London market was a temporary expedient which could not resolve the fundamental fiscal problems facing a developing province. Nevertheless, because Dunn's actions facilitated an intensification of government involvement in the economy and a strengthening of the connection between Canadian economic development and British capital, his tenure as receiver general had a lasting impact in the realm of public finance in Canada.

KEN CRUIKSHANK

ANQ-Q, CE1-1, 9 mars 1842. AO, MS 74; MS 78; MS 500; RG 22, ser.155, will of J. H. Dunn. BNQ, Dép. des MSS, MSS-101, Coll. La Fontaine (mfm. at PAC). Diocese of St Helena (St Helena Island), St Helena, reg. of baptisms, 26 Feb. 1792. MTL, William Allan papers; Robert Baldwin papers; S. P. Jarvis papers, B67 (Bank of Upper Canada papers). PAC, MG 24, B18, 8 (copies); B101 (transcripts); RG 1, E1, 51–57; E3, 21–103; RG 5, A1; RG 19, 1130–75. PRO, CO 42/365–517 (mfm. at PAC). *Arthur papers* (Sanderson). "Journals of Legislative Assembly of U.C.," AO *Report*, 1914. "The journals of the Legislative Council of Upper Canada . . . [1821–24]," AO *Report*, 1915. *Town of York, 1815–34* (Firth). U.C., House of Assembly, *App. to the journal*, 1836, 3, no.90; 1837–38, 1: 77–131; 1839–40, 2: 27–36; *Journal*, app., 1825–26: 5–9; 1830: 21–48, 67; 1833–34: 113–20; *Statutes*, 1802, c.3; 1831, c.14; 1834, c.53; 1838, cc.51–52. *British Whig*, 1834–38, 1847. *Chronicle & Gazette*, 1833–44.

Burke's peerage (1970), 2394. "Calendar of state papers," PAC *Report*, 1936: 399–598. "State papers – U.C.," PAC *Report*, 1943. G. E. Cokayne, *The complete peerage of England, Scotland, Ireland, Great Britain and the United Kingdom, extant, extinct, or dormant* (new ed., ed. Vicary Gibbs et al., 13v. in 14, London, 1910–59). *Toronto directory*, 1833–34, 1837. H. G. J. Aitken, "The Family Compact and the Welland Canal Company," *Historical essays on Upper Canada*, ed. J. K. Johnson (Toronto, 1975), 153–70 (republished from the *Canadian Journal of Economics and Political Science* (Toronto), 18 (1952): 63–76); *The Welland Canal Company: a study in Canadian enterprise* (Cambridge, Mass., 1954). Careless, *Union of the*

Canadas. Craig, *Upper Canada*. D. [G.] Creighton, *The empire of the St. Lawrence* (Toronto, 1956). J. L. Field, "The Honourable John H. Dunn (1794–1854): a Canadian receiver general" (MA thesis, Queen's Univ., Kingston, Ont., 1947). W. D. LeSueur, *William Lyon Mackenzie: a reinterpretation*, ed. A. B. McKillop (Toronto, 1979). M. L. Magill, "John H. Dunn and the bankers," *Historical essays on Upper Canada*, 194–215 (republished from his article, written under the pseudonym John Ireland, in *OH*, 62 (1970): 83–100). J. R. Robertson, *The history of freemasonry in Canada from its introduction in 1749 . . .* (2v., Toronto, 1900), 2: 183–86. *Robertson's landmarks of Toronto*, 1: 264, 504, 506; 3: 110. P.-G. Roy, *La famille Juchereau Duchesnay* (Lévis, Qué., 1903), 395–96. Scadding, *Toronto of old* (Armstrong; 1966). Adam Shortt, *Lord Sydenham* (Toronto, 1908). "Hon. J. H. Dunn," *Mail and Empire* (Toronto), 22 June 1935: 6. J. K. Johnson, "The U.C. Club and the Upper Canadian elite, 1837–1840," *OH*, 69 (1977): 151–68. George Murray, "Dunn descendants," and "Hon. John Henry Dunn," *Mail and Empire*, 15 June 1935: 6; 29 June 1935: 6.

DU VAL, PETER (baptized **Pierre**), ship's captain, privateer, merchant, and justice of the peace; b. 11 Oct. 1767 and baptized 14 Oct. 1769 in St Brelade, Jersey, son of Jean Du Val and Marie Piton; m. Elizabeth Hubert, and they had three sons; d. 12 Feb. 1851 on Île Bonaventure, Lower Canada.

Popular Gaspé legend suggests that the ancestors of Peter Du Val were French Calvinist refugees exiled in the Channel Islands. He was strongly influenced by the Jersey aristocracy, with its usufructuary system of landed entailments, its desire for a base of independent wealth, and its adherence to a chivalric military tradition.

By the 1790s the partners of a transatlantic company trading in cod and staple commodities, Philip, Francis, and John* Janvrin of Jersey, engaged Du Val as a master mariner. Serving in this capacity for more than 20 years, Du Val developed a reputation as a daring captain. During the Napoleonic Wars, letters of marque and reprisal were issued for ships under his command, including in 1806 letters of marque directed against the Batavian Republic (Netherlands) for the *Young Phoenix*. On a voyage from Jersey to Arichat, Cape Breton, in the spring of 1813 the *Young Phoenix* was seized and plundered by the *Paul Jones*, a licensed American privateer. The *Orpheus*, a British naval vessel, captured both ships in the harbour of New London, Conn. All three vessels made port at Halifax, where an inquiry took place before Alexander Croke*, judge of the Vice-Admiralty Court. The *Young Phoenix* was returned to its owners after they guaranteed payment of the expenses incurred in the salvage of the ship.

In 1814 Du Val had leased a lot near Dundee, Cape Breton, which was granted to him in 1818. He continued to work for the Janvrins until about 1818,

buying fish at Arichat, at Havre Boucher and Tracadie in Nova Scotia, and in the Gaspé region, and trading in Mediterranean and Baltic ports as many as three times per season. Having acquired the capital necessary to engage in his own commercial ventures, by 1819 Du Val was established on Île Bonaventure. The partners in his new fishery, Peter Du Val and Company, were his brother Nicholas, John Perrée Sr, Philip Godfrey, and Philip Le Gresley. Du Val's son Peter John purchased the company on 8 Oct. 1825 and proceeded to expand its operations, constructing additional fishing stations at Havre de Gaspé and Newport, Lower Canada, and at Caraquet, Miscou Island, and Shippegan, N.B., although he seems to have made Spain, and later Guernsey, his main residence and place of business. By the late 1820s his father, established as a merchant on Île Bonaventure in partnership with Amice Du Val of St Helier, Jersey, also began to acquire fishing stations, at Île Bonaventure, Anse à Beaufils, and Cannes-de-Roches. He also acted as agent for his son, and father and son may have jointly operated some fishing stations. In 1830 either the father or the son, or perhaps both, owned three vessels involved in the codfish trade. In 1833 Peter John sold his interests at Shippegan to his financial backers, five Jersey merchants, for £1,000. That year father and son sold assets on Île Bonaventure and water lots at Havre de Gaspé to the Jersey merchants to cover their debts to them of more than £978; they retained the use of the land and the right of redemption for five years. Deteriorating relations with John Fauvel, who replaced John Le Boutillier* as agent at Percé for the company of Charles Robin*, the most important fishery in the Gaspé and northern New Brunswick, seriously affected their business. In 1835, on arriving at Île Bonaventure from Jersey, Peter John found the sheriff auctioning some of his property. He died shortly afterwards.

Peter Du Val, as tutor to his grandchildren, assumed responsibility for his son's business affairs and, with some reluctance, attempted to collect outstanding debts by prosecuting local fishermen. By 1838 the losses he had sustained prevented him from redeeming the property but the agreement with the Jersey merchants, now the firm Bertram, Godfray, Gray and Company, was renewed for another five years on the understanding that Du Val would pay 800 quintals of "good dry merchantable cod fish" to them. Du Val anticipated that he would be unable to meet this second commitment. He transferred his son's estate together with his personal property in entail to his grandson, now 21, in an effort to provide his descendants with a lasting inheritance. After challenging this settlement, Bertram, Godfray, Gray and Company took over the unredeemed property in 1843, discharging the debts to the company of both Du Val

Duvernay

and his son's estate. Du Val then leased the fishery from its new owners for two years.

Throughout his career, Du Val was active in community life. He received a commission in the Jersey militia in 1812 and was appointed centenier in 1829 at St Brelade. Yet his interest in Jersey gradually lapsed and it was to Lower Canada that he looked for the future of his grandchildren. From 1831 to 1838 he received four appointments as justice of the peace on Île Bonaventure, where because of a lack of notaries he was called upon to draw up and witness deeds for the transfer of property. The documents he prepared display an intimate knowledge of property conveyance. Tradition attributes to him the cultivation of literary talent and credits him with having written an account of his family.

Peter Du Val's career has been confused in secondary sources with that of his twin brother, John, a British naval officer, and with that of his son Peter John. As well, the body of myths surrounding his privateering days has obscured his importance as a mariner for the Janvrin firm, as the mainstay of his own and his son's international commerce, and as a minor rival to Charles Robin and Company, which exercised a near monopoly in the maritime fishery.

ALDO BROCHET

AC, Bonaventure (New-Carlisle), minutiers, Martin Sheppard, 3 avril, 2 juin, 2 juill. 1832; 22 juill. 1833; 1er, 3 août 1835; Gaspé (Percé), État civil, Anglicans, Protestant Episcopal Congregation (Gaspé), 13 févr. 1851. BE, Gaspé (Percé), reg. A, 1, no.130; reg. B, 1, nos.14–16, 26, 244, 263. Gloucester Registry Office (Bathurst, N.B.), vol.1, no.511. PAC, MG 24, D9, 1; MG 28, III18; MG 55/24; RG 1, L7, 79; RG 4, A1, 37: 71, 73; RG 8, IV, 134, *Young Phoenix*; RG 68, General index, 1651–1841: 382, 389, 397, 643. PANS, RG 20B, petitions, nos.569, 1896. Soc. jersiaise (Saint-Hélier, Jersey), Saint-Brelade, reg. des baptêmes, 1769, 1822. J.-C. Pouliot, *La grande aventure de Jacques Cartier* (Québec, 1934). Thomas Pye, *Canadian scenery: district of Gaspé* (Montreal, 1866). Donat Robichaud, *Le grand Chipagan: histoire de Shippagan* (North Beresford, N.-B., 1976). Joan Stevens, *Victorian voices; an introduction to the papers of Sir John Le Couteur, Q.A.D.C., F.R.S.* ([Saint-Hélier], 1969). M. G. Turk, *The quiet adventurers in Canada* (Detroit, 1979).

DUVERNAY, LUDGER, printer, newspaperman, office holder, politician, and Patriote; b. 22 Jan. 1799 in Verchères, Lower Canada, son of Joseph Crevier Duvernay and Marie-Anne-Julie Rocbert de La Morandière; d. 28 Nov. 1852 in Montreal.

Ludger Duvernay's forebear Christophe Crevier, a native of Normandy, immigrated to New France in the mid 17th century and settled at Trois-Rivières. His son, Jean-Baptiste Crevier, adopted the surname Duverné, which with time became Duvernay. On 26 June 1748 his grandson Jacques Crevier Duvernay was granted a commission as royal notary by the intendant Gilles Hocquart* authorizing him to practise in the *côtes* of Verchères, Varennes, Saint-Ours, and along the Rivière Chambly (Rivière L'Acadie). One of Jacques's sons, Pierre Crevier Duvernay, also served as a royal notary in 1762, and another, Ludger's father Joseph, was a master carpenter at Verchères. Joseph drowned on 21 Aug. 1820 while crossing the St Lawrence from a point opposite Saint-Sulpice. Ludger's mother was descended from an illustrious family. Her father, François-Abel-Étienne Rocbert de La Morandière, who had been a lieutenant in the colonial regulars, captain of a battalion dispatched against Pontiac*, and military engineer, was the grandson of Étienne Rocbert* de La Morandière, the keeper of the king's stores at Montreal in the early decades of the 18th century.

Ludger is thought to have had the advantage of being taught by schoolmaster Louis Labadie*, who, after teaching in various villages in Lower Canada, ran a school at Varennes, near Verchères, from 1805. Some of his pupils came from the neighbouring parishes and boarded near his school. In 1813 Labadie took up residence in Verchères, where with keen interest he followed Duvernay's first steps in the printing world. On 3 June *Le Spectateur* of Montreal, owned by Charles-Bernard Pasteur, advertised for an apprentice for its printing house: "a young boy well brought up and of a respectable family" able to "read and write the French language." Duvernay, who was then 14, applied and was selected. The young apprentice proved reliable and diligent. A resident of Verchères assured his parents that their son reasoned "not like a parrot but like a man of good sense." He finished his apprenticeship in 1815 and, with Labadie's support, became an employee of the Pasteur printing house. Labadie had strongly advised Duvernay to make a career in printing, emphasizing that "in this calling you could not fail to be an enlightened man." Duvernay won Pasteur's confidence and held an increasingly important place within the establishment. It was Duvernay who was entrusted with running the business when his employer was away.

Duvernay left Montreal in 1817 to open his own printing house at Trois-Rivières. He is thought to have chosen this spot because of the lack of competition there, and he was probably urged on by Denis-Benjamin Viger* who was helping printers and newspaper owners by providing financial assistance and renting them premises. On 12 August, with some degree of recklessness, he launched *La Gazette des Trois-Rivières*, the first Lower Canadian newspaper to be published outside Quebec and Montreal. The first issue attracted a crowd to the doors of the shop, and Duvernay received many flattering comments. He had previously outlined the responsibilities of a newspaper

258

in his prospectus for *La Gazette des Trois-Rivières*. A "periodical paper" should on the one hand stress and praise "good actions" but on the other should denounce oppression "so as to arouse [the] salutary fear that gives support and protection to the weak by acting as a brake upon the ill-intentioned." He declared also that he would do his utmost to publish literary works in order to enliven "the seriousness of business with the pleasures of literature." Throughout his career as a publisher, Duvernay deviated little from this approach. *La Gazette des Trois-Rivières* is thought to have ceased publication in February 1821.

Duvernay had also published, from June to September 1820, a religious monthly, *L'Ami de la religion et du roi*, of which the unofficial editor was the priest of the parish of Trois-Rivières, Louis-Marie Cadieux*. Jean Raimbault*, the curé of Nicolet and superior of the local seminary, also contributed to the newspaper, and the numerous royalist priests in the Trois-Rivières region, who had been exiled from France after the revolution, publicized it. On 11 March 1823 Duvernay began publishing *Le Constitutionnel*, a newspaper which in presentation and content resembled the defunct *Gazette des Trois-Rivières*. It is believed to have lasted until the autumn of 1824. Despite his fruitless attempts, Duvernay persevered in trying to keep a newspaper going at Trois-Rivières. In August 1826 he took advantage of a by-election in the riding of Trois-Rivières to launch another one. *L'Argus* appeared for three months, and as its subtitle, *"journal électorique,"* indicates, its contents were mainly devoted to the progress of the campaign. Its editors, brothers Dominique* and Charles-Elzéar* Mondelet, supported candidate Pierre-Benjamin DUMOULIN, but he was unsuccessful.

At his establishment on Rue Royale, Duvernay also printed a few books and pamphlets and maintained a small bookstore as well as a bindery. Even though he was young, he had soon begun to play an important part in the affairs of Trois-Rivières. He was the superintendent of highways and the inspector of bridges and roads for the town. He was also inspector of the Fire Society from 1819 to 1826. During his years in Trois-Rivières, in addition to familiarizing himself with the various aspects of the printer's trade, Duvernay showed initiative and a sense of organization. But Trois-Rivières did not yet have the resources to sustain a newspaper and its printer.

In December 1826 Duvernay was approached by the *Canadian Spectator* of Montreal, which had been without a publisher since the departure of John Jones. Duvernay accepted the offer and was back in Montreal by the beginning of January 1827. On 18 January, in the presence of notary Jean-Marie Mondelet*, he signed an agreement to publish the paper, which was intended particularly for the Irish in the Montreal

region, and to rent Jean-Dominique Bernard's printing workshop on Rue Saint-Jean-Baptiste. On the same day he purchased for £7 10s. 0d. *La Minerve*, a newspaper which had been launched on 9 Nov. 1826 by Augustin-Norbert Morin*, when he was a law student. Morin had stopped publishing the paper on 29 November because of a lack of subscribers, but at the time of its sale he promised to remain editor for six more months. In December 1828 Jocelyn Waller*, the editor – and moving spirit – of the *Canadian Spectator*, died. Duvernay took his place as editor and continued to publish the paper until its demise in February 1829. In August he acquired the printing house of James Lane, at the corner of Rue Saint-Paul and Rue Saint-Gabriel, where he remained until 16 Nov. 1837. *La Minerve* was thus produced in the heart of the business quarter in Montreal, and it supplied the various kinds of printed material useful to businessmen, members of the liberal professions, and officials. From 1829 to 1837 Duvernay was the principal producer of books and pamphlets in the city. School textbooks, devotional works, and political pamphlets were printed on the newspaper's presses. A number of printing and sales agreements linked Duvernay and bookseller Édouard-Raymond FABRE. The almanacs of *La Minerve*, with several thousand copies printed of each issue, were sold by rural merchants in the Trois-Rivières and Montreal regions. Other than devotional manuals, the almanac was often the only book that most of the rural population and city dwellers could afford to buy. In 1836 and 1837 a work that Duvernay had reprinted without authorization at the suggestion of Amury Girod* stirred up a great deal of controversy. The book, *Les paroles d'un croyant* by Hugues-Félicité-Robert de La Mennais, had been published in Paris in 1834 and been condemned by Pope Gregory XVI the same year. The Patriotes used the work of La Mennais to justify their struggles. Bishop Jean-Jacques Lartigue*, auxiliary bishop at Montreal and a long-time disciple of La Mennais, in compliance with the pope's decision opposed the dissemination of the book.

Under Duvernay's leadership *La Minerve* soon gained recognition as one of the principal newspapers of Lower Canada. At the time he purchased it in 1827 it had 240 subscribers and by 1832 there were about 1,300, a respectable circulation for the period. According to Morin, it had become "the national newspaper." As a supporter of the ideas of the Patriote party, Duvernay had placed his paper at the service of this political group. *La Minerve* had the benefit of financial assistance from Viger and Fabre. Duvernay himself seldom wrote for it, being content to contribute occasional short news items on various topics. However, when he considered himself under attack he could produce scathing pieces. Antoine Gérin-Lajoie*, who was employed for two years in the

Duvernay

office of *La Minerve*, acknowledged that Duvernay was very effective at "crushing someone through insults [and] offensive personal remarks." However, he usually left it to a member of the staff to defend the paper's views. Morin remained as editor longer than the six months originally agreed upon, but after he was elected to the House of Assembly for Bellechasse in October 1830 he had less and less time to devote to the paper and Léon Gosselin* may be considered its real editor from 1831 to 1834. After that Hyacinthe-Poirier Leblanc* de Marconnay, James Julien Theodore Phelan, Gérin-Lajoie, and Raphaël Bellemare served successively as Duvernay's editors. A very demanding man, Duvernay constantly imposed his own point of view, and he quarrelled frequently with his employees. Gosselin, Leblanc de Marconnay, and Phelan all left the establishment on bad terms with him. The salaries he paid were low or downright meagre. If someone complained, Duvernay accused him of wanting to accumulate money at his expense. In Gérin-Lajoie's words, "To put anything by or to economize was a foolish, indeed a monstrous thing to him."

As the articles in *La Minerve* and the *Canadian Spectator* were usually anonymous, it was Duvernay who assumed responsibility for them. In 1828 he was arrested and put in jail, along with Waller of the *Canadian Spectator*, on a charge of libel. In January 1832 Duvernay and Daniel Tracey*, the publisher of the *Vindicator* (later the *Vindicator and Canadian Advertiser*), were summoned before the bar of the Legislative Council of Lower Canada, accused of having maintained that the council was a "great nuisance." The two guilty parties were reprimanded by the speaker, Jonathan Sewell*, and kept in the jail at Quebec until the end of the session. This second imprisonment of Duvernay incensed the Patriote press and made a hero and martyr of him. When he was released, he received congratulations in numerous villages on his way back to Montreal. In that city triumphal arches had been erected in his honour. He was presented with a medal bearing the inscription, "The freedom of the press is the palladium of the people." But in 1836 he was once again behind bars. In March of that year *La Minerve* had accused the sheriff, Louis Gugy*, of appointing a jury favourable to a jailer charged with responsibility for the death of a prisoner who had succumbed to privation and cold in the Montreal jail. Duvernay was prosecuted for contempt of court and in September was sentenced to 30 days imprisonment. He was led to jail in an impressive triumphal procession of Patriotes which included the mayor of Montreal, Jacques VIGER.

A few months earlier Duvernay had defended the honour of his newspaper in a duel with lawyer Clément-Charles Sabrevois* de Bleury, who had been elected as a Patriote to represent Richelieu in 1832.

When he was severely attacked by *La Minerve* for leaving the Patriote party and later joining the more moderate members from the Quebec region, Sabrevois de Bleury challenged the proprietor to a duel. The encounter took place on 5 April 1836 behind Mount Royal. The lawyer, a militia officer who was a skilful shot, wounded Duvernay just above the right knee. "The blood he was determined to shed," retorted Duvernay in *La Minerve* two days later, "does not efface what has been written, and saltpetre and sulphur do not whiten what is black!"

In March 1834 Duvernay had joined with George-Étienne Cartier*, Louis-Victor Sicotte*, and other Patriotes in founding the society called Aide-toi, le Ciel t'aidera (God helps those who help themselves), and had been elected its president. Every member of the secret society was to produce and read an essay on politics or literature. Duvernay then conceived the idea of giving French Canadians an annual patriotic festival to be celebrated on 24 June. From ancient times, the summer solstice had been an occasion for rejoicing. The church had taken over this pagan celebration, transforming it into the feast of St John the Baptist. A "Midsummer Night's bonfire" had been held in New France as early as 1646, and the custom of celebrating Saint-Jean-Baptiste Day had been carried on, particularly in the Lower Canadian parishes dedicated to Saint-Jean (Saint-Jean-Port-Joli, Saint-Jean on the Île d'Orléans, and others), before Duvernay decided to make it a French Canadian national festival. He saw to the preparations for a banquet that took place on 24 June 1834 in the garden of lawyer Jean-François-Marie-Joseph MacDonell*'s property (now the site of Windsor Station). Nearly 60 guests, including several influential members of the Patriote party, joined in the celebration, which was primarily a political demonstration. Some time earlier the Patriote party had adopted the 92 Resolutions, and it was gradually becoming more aggressive towards the government of the colony. Those attending the banquet paid tribute to the people, the "primary source of all legitimate authority," and to the reformers of Lower and Upper Canada and of Ireland. They gathered around Duvernay again in 1835, 1836, and 1837. The rebellion was to interrupt this custom for a few years.

Duvernay had long wanted to make a career in politics but had never had the opportunity. He ran in a by-election for Rouville in February 1833 but was defeated by François Rainville. Several people dissuaded him from standing at the general election of November 1834 because he was then thought to be much more useful at the helm of *La Minerve*. He himself insisted on being allowed to run in 1837, and was elected by acclamation for Lachenaie on 26 May. The session began on 18 August but was prorogued on the 26th by the governor, Lord Gosford [Acheson*], who was unhappy about the attitude of the members belonging to the party of Louis-Joseph Papineau*. Hence Duvernay sat in the assembly for only a few days.

During the autumn of 1837 recourse to arms by the Patriotes appeared increasingly likely and indeed inevitable. On 23 October more than 5,000 people attended the Assemblée des Six Comtés at Saint-Charles-sur-Richelieu. On the evening of 6 November there was a violent confrontation in Montreal between members of the Doric Club and the Fils de la Liberté. The printing house of the *Vindicator and Canadian Advertiser*, the Patriote newspaper then under the editorship of Dr Edmund Bailey O'Callaghan*, was sacked and Duvernay's establishment was threatened with a similar fate. On 16 November Lord Gosford issued warrants for the arrest of 26 influential Patriotes including Duvernay. Duvernay had been warned that his arrest was imminent and had fled by the time the bailiffs made their appearance at the printing house of *La Minerve*. Before leaving Montreal he entrusted his newspaper to Phelan and to the printer François Lemaître, but only one issue came out after his departure.

Duvernay was appointed an officer of a small Patriote battalion and took part in the battle of Moore's Corner (Saint-Armand-Station) on 6 Dec. 1837. The Patriotes, who were too few in number to face up to their adversaries, abandoned their two cannon and their rifles and fled. Duvernay found refuge in the United States, where he lived in turn at Swanton and St Albans, Vt, Rouses Point, N.Y., and Burlington, Vt. Although he encountered numerous difficulties in obtaining the necessary printing equipment, he managed to start a newspaper at Burlington in 1839. "We declare in advance that we shall spare no one," he announced in a prospectus. The first issue of *Le Patriote canadien* came out on 7 August. One of Papineau's sons, Louis-Joseph-Amédée*, contributed a few articles to the paper. As he did not receive authorization from the new governor, Charles Edward Poulett Thomson*, to distribute his paper by mail in Lower Canada and as the exiles were poor, scattered, and dwindling in number, Duvernay was forced to cease publication on 5 Feb. 1840. Exile then became harder and harder for him to bear. He had always been partial to liquor and now began to drink to excess. "I sometimes consign to the devil the whole business of politics and all those who have plunged us into this abyss," he confided to his Montreal colleague, printer Louis Perrault*, who had returned to Lower Canada from exile the year before. During the summer of 1840 he even considered going to work for the American Board of Customs. At the beginning of May 1841 Ignace Bourget*, the bishop of Montreal, travelling to New York, met him at Burlington. As spokesman for the exiles, Duvernay requested that French Canadian

priests be sent to minister to them. The bishop replied that he was edified by the religious sentiments of Duvernay, who prior to the rebellion had none the less agreed to publish anti-clerical writings. In October 1841 it was the turn of Charles-Auguste-Marie-Joseph de Forbin-Janson*, the bishop of Nancy and Toul in France and a famous preacher, to pay him a visit. Soon afterwards Duvernay presided at the meeting of the French Canadians of Burlington to discuss the possibility of building a Catholic church in that town. At a time when most of the exiles had returned home, Duvernay, despite the advice of a number of people, insisted on remaining in the United States. "You can . . . rest assured," he claimed, "that nothing prevents my returning to Canada, except a sense of honour that must come before personal interest." In fact, however, he was delaying more for financial reasons than political ones. He had lost everything. The venture of *Le Patriote canadien* had proved disastrous. The printing shop of *La Minerve* had suffered a good deal of pillaging. Joseph Lettoré had disclosed to him that within a few days of his departure from Montreal "people were vying with one another to see who could steal the most." Furthermore, those responsible for collecting money owing to him had met with scant success.

Louis-Hippolyte La Fontaine* was emerging as Papineau's successor, and he could not manage without the support of a newspaper. His organizers therefore contacted Duvernay, recognized for his talent and ability to run a newspaper, and invited him to revive *La Minerve*. After some evasive delays, Duvernay accepted the offer and returned to Montreal in 1842. On 9 September *La Minerve* again appeared, proclaiming that it would not deviate from its former principles but would adapt to the circumstances in which the country found itself. Protesting against some injustices in the Act of Union, the paper supported La Fontaine's reform party and the principle of ministerial responsibility. Duvernay no longer produced books in his shop, which was now at the corner of Rue Sainte-Vincent and Rue Sainte-Thérèse. He concentrated on producing *La Minerve*, which became once more the most important and influential French paper in Montreal, as well as on organizing the Association Saint-Jean-Baptiste. At the beginning of 1843 he was asked to re-establish this society, but in fact there is no record that one had existed before the rebellion. Duvernay had instituted a national celebration and organized a banquet, not a society, in 1834. However, Montrealers spoke in 1843 of reorganizing a society, and, on Duvernay's initiative, the Association Saint-Jean-Baptiste de Montréal was constituted on 9 June during an impressive meeting held at the Marché Sainte-Anne. Duvernay was appointed coordinating commissioner, a key post which put the responsibility for current

Duvernay

matters in his hands and allowed him to give the society its guidelines and objectives. The charter, obtained in 1849, stipulated that this charitable organization had been established with the object of aiding and helping people of French origin and contributing to their moral and social progress. The Association Saint-Jean-Baptiste de Montréal counted in its ranks most prominent French Canadians, many of whom had been Patriotes in 1837 and had later come over to La Fontaine's party. Some young people, who were more radical, found that they could not promote their ideas within Duvernay's society and decided in 1844 to create the Institut Canadien [see Jean-Baptiste-Éric Dorion*].

By 1848 Papineau, still loyal to the principles he had defended before the rebellion, had become a nuisance to La Fontaine and his supporters, who were endeavouring to extract all possible advantages from the new institutions set up when the Act of Union came into effect. Duvernay shared Papineau's admiration for the "republican elective institutions" of the United States but he was also much more conciliatory and no longer approved of the "radicalism" of the Patriote party's former leader. "We do not like the Union, but we prefer it to devastation," declared La Minerve, which termed Papineau a "great agitator." In 1849, during the debates on a proposal for the annexation of Canada to the United States, the attitude of La Minerve was somewhat ambiguous. Duvernay admired the American people and their institutions. "The American is proud of his country and he has reason to be," he had stated in 1838 during his exile. In 1849 he still held that view. La Fontaine's reform party was opposed to the annexation advocated by the Rouges of the Institut Canadien, and Duvernay, an "annexationist at heart," to use Hector-Louis Langevin*'s expression, was placed in an untenable position. He did not wish to displease La Fontaine and was unable to ally himself with the radical members of the Institut Canadien and of the newspaper L'Avenir. La Minerve was slow in speaking out openly on the question. On 12 July 1849 Duvernay's paper finally declared, "Annexation has never frightened us." La Fontaine was not pleased. A few days later, as a result of various pressures, La Minerve retracted, now stating, "We did not claim to make ourselves the apostles of annexation." Needing the financial support of La Fontaine's party, Duvernay had temporarily retreated because the survival of his business was at issue. He continued, subtly, to publish articles stressing the prosperity of the United States.

Duvernay's long exile had not mellowed him completely. Divergences of political views and commercial rivalry set him against Joseph-Guillaume Barthe*, the publisher of L'Aurore des Canadas. Barthe and his paper were supported by the government of William Henry Draper* and Denis-Benjamin Viger, while Duvernay and La Minerve defended the positions taken by La Fontaine's party. Moreover, La Minerve and L'Aurore des Canadas competed strenuously for advertisers, and Duvernay took with ill grace the fact that the rival paper was awarded the advertising of official notices. On 25 July 1844 he challenged his competitor to a duel. Barthe brought an action against him and Duvernay was forced to give assurances to a magistrate that he would keep the peace for six months. But the affair was by no means closed. When the two ran into each other on a Montreal street in 1845, Duvernay took a stick to Barthe and beat him up, an incident for which he was sentenced to four days in jail. Duvernay was also involved in a lengthy quarrel with Louis-Antoine Dessaulles* of the Institut Canadien. In 1848 La Minerve accused Dessaulles of atheism and perjury, and the ensuing lawsuit in December 1849 became a cause célèbre, for it pitted the supporters of La Fontaine against those of the Institut Canadien. Duvernay's lawyers claimed that Dessaulles must prove that he practised "some religion or other." But, being unable to substantiate his charge of perjury, Duvernay had to pay Dessaulles £100 in damages.

In the last two years of his life Duvernay was troubled by "sharp pains in the chest" and an increasingly severe cough. On 2 June 1851, he was none the less elected president of the Association Saint-Jean-Baptiste de Montréal, an honorary post he held until his death. He passed away during the night of 28 Nov. 1852, at the age of 53. Bishop Bourget officiated at his funeral, which took place on 1 December in Notre-Dame in Montreal. La Fontaine, Fabre, and Romuald Trudeau* had agreed to act as pallbearers. Papineau, who never forgave Duvernay for abandoning him, did not come to the funeral. Three years later, on 21 Oct. 1855, Duvernay's remains were transferred from the cemetery on Rue Saint-Antoine to the new cemetery of Notre-Dame-des-Neiges. In an impressive ceremony which attracted more than 10,000 people, Cartier, as president of the Association Saint-Jean-Baptiste de Montréal, and Thomas-Jean-Jacques Loranger* delivered a funeral oration in his praise.

On 14 Feb. 1825 Duvernay had married Reine Harnois, the daughter of Augustin Harnois, a captain, at Rivière-du-Loup (Louiseville). They had nine children, four of whom died in infancy. Their two daughters received a good education and learned to play the piano; Marie-Reine-Joséphine married Charles Glackmeyer, a lawyer who was assistant clerk and then clerk of the city of Montreal, and Marie-Adèle-Victorine married Dr Ovide Pelletier. Impressed by the career of the American printer and politician Benjamin Franklin, Duvernay gave the name Franklin to a son who was born and died while he himself was in exile. On 19 Nov. 1852 he had bequeathed his business to his eldest son, Louis-Napoléon, but probably because of protests from his other son, Ludger-Denis, he altered his will on 24 November in order to leave the assets to both sons, while stipulating that they must give a pianoforte to each of their sisters.

Ludger Duvernay's many remarkable deeds made him one of the best known and most popular figures in Montreal. He was "cheerful and good-natured" by disposition, but he had a quick temper and became belligerent when politics were involved. In his activities as a journalist he was impulsive and, unlike his contemporary Étienne Parent*, quite incapable of adopting a detached attitude. Parent was, moreover, afraid that Duvernay would compromise the Patriotes' cause by "idiocies." Obstinate and uncompromising, he defended his ideas stubbornly and became involved in innumerable disputes; he was jailed four times and forced into exile. Yet through the ups and downs of his tumultuous career it is possible to discern in many of Duvernay's actions an ideal that guided him from the day he published his first newspaper: education of the people. Some of his writings reveal his acute awareness that his responsibilities as a journalist and printer enabled, indeed obliged, him to play the role of educator. This ideal can also be found in some of the objectives of the Association Saint-Jean-Baptiste, which he founded, and in the motto he gave it: *Rendre le peuple meilleur* (For the improvement of the nation). In 1849 he suggested to its members that they should establish a reading-room in order to provide the working classes with the advantages enjoyed by the "business and literate classes." Devoted to his trade, he launched newspapers at Trois-Rivières, Montreal, and Burlington under conditions that were often difficult and unfavourable. One of the outstanding figures in journalism and printing in Lower Canada during the first half of the 19th century, Duvernay made *La Minerve* into the first great French-language newspaper in Montreal and a respected institution that outlasted him by nearly half a century. As he once remarked, "I have sacrificed my time, my work, my meagre earnings, my future and that of my family, and the best years of my life, all for *La Minerve*."

JEAN-MARIE LEBEL

[A portrait of Ludger Duvernay, painted by Jean-Baptiste Roy-Audy* in 1832, hangs in the Maison Ludger-Duvernay, the head office of the Société Saint-Jean-Baptiste de Montréal.

Duvernay is the author of "Liste des journaux publiés dans le Bas-Canada depuis 1764," which appeared in *La Canadienne* (Montréal), 22 oct. 1840: 3–4. This article is considered to be the first bibliographic essay on the Lower Canadian press. J.-M.L.]

ANQ-M, CE1-26, 22 janv. 1799; CE1-51, 1ᵉʳ déc. 1852; CN1-32, 6 mai 1837; 19, 24 nov. 1852; CN1-192, 4 oct. 1833; CN1-295, 18 janv. 1827, 27 août 1829, 27 févr. 1834, 23 avril 1835, 30 mars 1837; CN1-312, 7 déc. 1843; 21 juin,

2 juill. 1844. ANQ-MBF, CE1-15, 14 févr. 1825. ANQ-Q, P-68. Antiquarian and Numismatic Soc. of Montreal, Ludger Duvernay, 1799–52 (mfm. at PAC). Arch. de l'Assoc. Saint-Jean-Baptiste de Montréal (Montréal), Procès-verbaux des assemblées générales, 1843–52. BVM-G, MSS, Ludger Duvernay, 11 sept. 1836, 14 janv. 1845. PAC, MG 24, C3; L3: 10781–82, 10868–69, 10879–80, 11169A–70, 11217–18, 11451, 11480–81, 11632–33, 11726–27, 12850, 31807, 33031, 33034–35, 33465. Can., Prov. of, *Statutes*, 1849, c.149. "Papiers de Ludger Duvernay," L.-W. Sicotte, édit., *Canadian Antiquarian and Numismatic Journal* (Montreal), 3rd ser., 5 (1908): 167–200; 6 (1909): 1–33, 87–138, 151–86; 7 (1910): 17–48, 59–96, 106–44, 178–92; 8 (1911): 21–48, 76–96. Amédée Papineau, *Journal d'un Fils de la liberté, réfugié aux États-Unis, par suite de l'insurrection canadienne, en 1837* (2v. parus, Montréal, 1972–   ), 1: 13, 15, 18, 31; 2: 67, 152, 191–92. *L'Ami de la religion et du roi* (Trois-Rivières, [Qué.]), 1820. *L'Argus* (Trois-Rivières; Montréal), 1826–28. *Le Constitutionnel* (Trois-Rivières), 1823–24. *La Gazette des Trois-Rivières*, 1817–21. *La Minerve*, 1827–37; 1842–52; 3 déc. 1852. *Le Patriote canadien* (Burlington, Vt.), 1839–40. Roland Auger, "Essai de bio-bibliographie sur Ludger Duvernay, imprimeur, journaliste et fondateur de la Société Saint-Jean-Baptiste" (thèse de bibliothéconomie, univ. de Montréal, 1953). Ivanhoë Caron, "Papiers Duvernay conservés aux Archives de la province de Québec," ANQ *Rapport*, 1926–27: 145–252. Fauteux, *Patriotes*, 36, 58, 148, 150, 210, 366–67. *Montreal directory*, 1824–54.

H.-R. Casgrain, *Œuvres complètes* (2ᵉ éd., 4v., Montréal, 1896), 431–542. David, *Patriotes*, 9, 43, 72–73, 77. Ægidius Fauteux, *Le duel au Canada* (Montréal, 1934), 172–73. Filteau, *Hist. des Patriotes* (1975). J.-L. Gagner, *Duvernay et la Saint-Jean-Baptiste* (Montréal, 1952). J.-M. Lebel, "Ludger Duvernay et *La Minerve*: étude d'une entreprise de presse montréalaise de la première moitié du XIXᵉ siècle" (thèse de MA, univ. Laval, Québec, 1982). Thomas Matheson, "Un pamphlet politique au Bas-Canada: *Les paroles d'un croyant* de La Mennais" (thèse de L. ès L., univ. Laval, 1958). Monet, *La première révolution tranquille*. R.-D. Parent, *Duvernay, le magnifique* (Montréal, 1943). J.-L. Roy, *Édouard-Raymond Fabre*, 42, 84–85, 92, 127–28, 135–36, 146, 156–57. P.-G. Roy, *La famille Rocbert de La Morandière* (Lévis, Qué., 1905). Robert Rumilly, *Histoire de la Société Saint-Jean-Baptiste de Montréal: des patriotes au fleurdelisé, 1834–1948* (Montréal, 1975); *Papineau et son temps*. Sulte, *Mélanges hist.* (Malchelosse), vol.15. F.-A. Angers, "Qui était Ludger Duvernay?" *Action nationale* (Montréal), 71 (1981–82): 82–94. F.-J. Audet, "Ludger Duvernay," *La Rev. nationale* (Montréal), 7 (1925): 133–36. Montarville Boucher de La Bruère, "La Société 'Aide-toi, le Ciel t'aidera,'" *BRH*, 34 (1928): 107–11. Michel Brunet, "Ludger Duvernay et la permanence de son œuvre," *Alerte* (Saint-Hyacinthe, Qué.), 16 (1959): 114–20. Ivanhoë Caron, "Le Patriote canadien," *Le Devoir* (Montréal), 27 oct. 1927: 1, 10. É.-Z. Massicotte, "Comment Ludger Duvernay acquit *La Minerve* en 1827," *BRH*, 26 (1920): 22–24. Robert Rumilly, "Quand la Société Saint-Jean-Baptiste a-t-elle été fondée?" *RHAF*, 1 (1947–48): 237–42. Yves Tessier, "Ludger Duvernay et les débuts de la presse périodique aux Trois-Rivières," *RHAF*, 18 (1964–65): 387–404, 566–81, 624–27.

E

EASSON. *See* ESSON

EASTSTAFF (Eastaff), THOMAS GEORGE WILLIAM, army officer, surveyor, and draftsman; b. in England, probably in 1772; m. Elizabeth (Eliza) ——, and they had seven children; d. 13 Aug. 1854 at Quebec.

Following training at the Royal Military Academy in Woolwich (London) from 1787 to 1793, Thomas George William Eaststaff served in several places as a royal military surveyor and draftsman with the Board of Ordnance. In 1795 he left for Newfoundland where he was employed as a military surveyor and draftsman with the Royal Engineers in St John's. He also accepted a lieutenant's commission in the Royal Newfoundland Fencible Regiment commanded by Thomas Skinner*, remaining with it until 1800. It was during this period that he accepted the part-time but important position of civil surveyor.

Eaststaff began his duties as surveyor at a time when St John's was undergoing considerable change. Principally a fishing community, military strong point, and naval station in the latter part of the 18th century, the town was then confined to the immediate area of the harbour, with land set aside for fishing rooms, defence works, and an Ordnance wharf. By the turn of the century European wars had increased its strategic importance; at the same time, growth in its population and commercial activity placed new demands upon available land. As early as 1804 it became evident, not only to the residents but also to the governor, Sir Erasmus Gower*, that new areas for residential settlement were needed. Eaststaff was to play an important role in the subsequent planning. His first major project was to complete a survey of St John's and mark out a new road dividing several large properties and opening up new areas for settlement. By 1807 the road, Gower Street, had been laid out and a plan for the town drawn up. The latter represented the first attempt by government to develop St John's based on civil rather than purely military and naval considerations. It remained until the 1840s as the principal plan of the town.

Under Governor Sir John Thomas Duckworth*, a further demand for land led in 1812 to the leasing of fishing rooms for commercial and residential construction. Because of frequent encroachments on crown land, in 1814 Eaststaff was instructed by Governor Sir Richard Goodwin Keats* to undertake a survey to re-establish the boundaries of government property. An accompanying register of deeds and grants which Eaststaff prepared enabled the govern-ment to develop a record of legal grants and to determine what land was available for future allocation.

Eaststaff's abilities were recognized in 1815 when he was appointed surveyor of lands for the colony; he continued, however, to work for the Ordnance department. With the end of the Napoleonic Wars his service in Newfoundland was abruptly terminated. In 1817 he was ordered to return to England, where he was placed on half pay pending reappointment. While in St John's he had played an active role in the Congregational Church and served as secretary of the church's auxiliary missionary committee.

For a brief period Eaststaff and his family waited in London for an appointment. Though strongly recommended by Governor Francis Pickmore* for the new permanent post of surveyor of crown lands in Newfoundland, a position he apparently expected to receive, he was ordered to Quebec in May 1817 to serve with the Ordnance office. He accepted the appointment "from extreme necessity." A man with a large family, he had found the period on half pay financially ruinous and had been obliged to sell land acquired in Newfoundland. He took up his appointment in the summer of 1818. His work at Quebec differed markedly from that in St John's: most of the assignments he received involved surveys and drafting directly related to military construction. Before 1830 he was employed on defence works at Quebec; after that date, when the military importance of the city began to decline, his activities shifted to defence projects elsewhere in the Canadas. At the same time an organizational change in the Ordnance department created a civil establishment for the Royal Engineers in Quebec, and Eaststaff was placed in charge of it. His work was now more varied, but it is impossible to determine the extent of his contribution to the numerous plans and surveys that bear, or include, his signature. It is more than likely that he simply compiled them on the basis of field-work and notes of others.

Nothing is known of Eaststaff's activities after his retirement from the Ordnance service in 1839. He died at Quebec on 13 Aug. 1854, three years after his wife. It is perhaps a measure of the man and of his life's work that his obituary appeared in the papers of Quebec, Montreal, and St John's.

DAVID R. FACEY-CROWTHER

PAC, RG 8, I (C ser.), 381–495. PANL, GB 2/1, 1805–14, 1827–29; P8/A/11 (Congregational Church, St John's, reg.

of baptisms, 1773–1857) (transcripts). PRO, CO 194/44, 194/55–57, 194/59–60, 194/62–63. SOAS, Methodist Missionary Soc. Arch., Wesleyan Methodist Missionary Soc., corr., Nfld. (mfm. at PAC). *Morning Chronicle* (Quebec), 14 Aug. 1854. *Newfoundland Express* (St John's), 23 Sept. 1854. *Royal Gazette and Newfoundland Advertiser*, 26 Sept. 1854. *Sun* (Montreal), 18 Aug. 1854. *Times and General Commercial Gazette* (St John's), 23 Sept. 1854. E. H. Dahl *et al.*, *La ville de Québec, 1800–1850: un inventaire de cartes et plans* (Ottawa, 1975). *Quebec almanac*, 1820–39. *The book of Newfoundland*, ed. J. R. Smallwood (6v., St John's, 1937–67), 2. O'Neill, *Story of St John's*. Charles Pedley, *The history of Newfoundland from the earliest times to the year 1860* (London, 1863). D. W. Thomson, *Men and meridians; the history of surveying and mapping in Canada* (3v., Ottawa, 1966–69), 1. D. A. Webber, *Skinner's Fencibles: the Royal Newfoundland Regiment, 1795–1802* (St John's, 1964).

EBY, BENJAMIN, farmer, Mennonite minister, bishop, educator, and author; b. 2 May 1785 at a homestead on Hammer Creek, Lancaster County, Pa, son of Christian Eby and Catharine Bricker; m. first 25 Feb. 1807 Mary Brubacher (d. 1834), and they had eight sons and three daughters; m. secondly Magdalena Erb, widow of Abraham Erb*; they had no children; d. 28 June 1853 in Berlin (Kitchener), Upper Canada.

Benjamin Eby, the sixth son and eleventh child of German-speaking Mennonites, "received a fair common school education" while working on the farm and in his father's cooperage. He was among the minority of Mennonites in Pennsylvania who were unhappy at the prospect of remaining under American rule in the aftermath of the revolutionary war, and in 1806 visited Upper Canada to inspect the land in Waterloo Township that fellow Mennonites Daniel Erb and Samuel Bricker had purchased from Richard Beasley* on behalf of the German Company. After claiming lot 2 of the Beasley Tract he went back to Pennsylvania to marry and then, in the company of other settlers, returned to Upper Canada, reaching his homestead on 21 June 1807. The role he played as a founder and leading citizen of the community was reflected in its being named Ebytown, or Ben Eby's, in his honour.

Although farming was always to be the chief source of Eby's livelihood, soon after his return to the province he became involved in the affairs of the pioneer settlement. After being ordained first as minister (27 Nov. 1809) and then as bishop (11 Oct. 1812) at ceremonies presided over by his brother Peter, a bishop from Pennsylvania, he was instrumental in erecting in 1813 the village's first meeting-house for religious worship, and two years later a frame annex to serve as a schoolhouse. Ben Eby's Church, as it was known during the bishop's lifetime, began with a membership of some 150. As the years went by he donated some of his own land to expand the

church's holdings, including its first cemetery. As bishop he left his mark not only on the town but on the whole county, where all Mennonite congregations were under his supervision. He was a leader of the church conferences which emerged in the province during his lifetime. When the Niagara and Markham districts were without bishops he presided over the election of new ones and officiated at their ordinations. A family tradition that Benjamin's parents had decided he should become a teacher seems to have been fulfilled in the winter of 1818–19 when he began a teaching career that, with some interruptions, was to last until the early 1840s.

Eby made a major contribution to the Mennonite church and to the preservation of German-language education in the province through a number of published works. In 1836, in an effort to enrich the church's worship and congregational life in general while respecting the various traditions of its adherents, he compiled a hymn-book called *Die Gemeinschaftliche Liedersammlung*. Reprinted several times in both Canada and the United States, it was in use until the end of the century. His first original work was a primer, *Neues Buchstabir- und Lesebuch*, published in 1839. Other works of a religious and educational nature followed, including his most important book, *Kurzgefasste Kirchen Geschichte* (1841), a study of the Mennonite church's history and doctrine.

Apart from his roles as family man and farmer, and as preacher and teacher, Eby was a promoter of the general good. He was frequently called on to offer his counsel and he occasionally adjudicated community disputes. Business involvements included the donation of some of his own land to two men in need of a property on which to establish a furniture factory, generous support of the printer Heinrich Wilhelm PETERSON, and the sale of land in 1833 to Friedrich GAUKEL for an inn. That sale was among the first on record to refer to the town as Berlin, a change of name traditionally attributed to the bishop.

Eby also found time to look beyond his community by corresponding with church leaders in Europe, as well as in America, and thereby establishing and cultivating international connections. His biggest contribution, however, was in his own community where he raised a large family (his son Christian succeeded him as minister), promoted a diversified economy, established a broadly based religious worship, introduced elementary school education, and inaugurated a literary tradition which served many generations.

FRANK H. EPP

[Benjamin Eby's work as educator and clergyman is reflected in his publications. He wrote *Neues Buchstabir- und Lesebuch* . . . (1st ed., Berlin [Kitchener, Ont.], 1839); a speller entitled *Fibel zu den ersten Lese-Uebungen* (Berlin,

Edmundson

[1839?]), a second edition of which was published there in 1843; *Kurzgefasste Kirchen Geschichte und Glaubenslehre der Taufgesinnten-Christen oder Mennonisten* (Berlin, 1841); and a second primer, *A B C- Buchstabir- und Lesebuch, zum Gebrauch fuer Deutsche Schulen in Canada* (2nd ed., Berlin, 1842). In addition to compiling *Die Gemeinschaftliche Liedersammlung* . . . (1st ed., Berlin, 1836), he published an edition of a popular German Mennonite catechism, [Gerhard Roosen], *Christliches Gemüths Gespräch* . . . (Berlin, 1839). He subsequently arranged for the first English edition of this work, which was published under the title *Christian spiritual conversation on saving faith* . . . (Lancaster, Pa., 1857), and may even have been the translator. His correspondence with churchmen abroad resulted in the publication of some of their letters to him in *Briefe an die Mennonisten Gemeine, in Ober Canada, mit einer Zugabe* (Berlin, 1840) and *Zweyter Brief aus Dänemark an die Mennonisten Gemeine in Canada* (Berlin, 1841). F.H.E.]

AO, RG 22, ser.211, Benjamin Eby. *Guelph Advertiser* (Guelph, [Ont.]), 7 July 1853. E. E. Eby and J. B. Snyder, *A biographical history of early settlers and their descendants in Waterloo Township*, with *Supplement*, ed. E. D. Weber (Kitchener, 1971). *The Mennonite encyclopedia: a comprehensive reference work on the Anabaptist-Mennonite movement* (4v., Hillsboro, Kans., 1955–59). F. H. Epp, *Mennonites in Canada, 1786–1920: the history of a separate people* (Toronto, 1974). J. B. Cressman, "Bishop Benjamin Eby," Waterloo Hist. Soc., *Annual report*, 1941: 152–58; "History of the First Mennonite Church of Kitchener, Ontario," *Mennonite Quarterly Rev.* (Goshen, Ind.), 13 (1939): 159–86. *Daily Telegraph* (Berlin), 19 May 1906: 1–2. M. [L]. Gingerich, "Mennonite leaders of North America: Benjamin Eby (1785–1853)," *Gospel Herald* (Scottsdale, Pa.), 58 (1965): 178. I. D. Landis, "Bishop Peter Eby of Pequea, 1765–1843," *Mennonite Quarterly Rev.*, 14 (1940): 41–51.

EDMUNDSON, WILLIAM GRAHAM, farmer, businessman, and publisher; b. *c.* 1815, son of James Edmundson and Margaret Graham; d. 19 Oct. 1852 near Nauvoo, Ill.

In 1841 William Graham Edmundson, a young farmer in the Home District of Upper Canada, considered launching an agricultural publication in Toronto. The appearance that year of the *Canadian Farmer and Mechanic* in Kingston, however, caused him to defer his plan and he gave his support to the new journal. The paper soon encountered financial difficulties and its editor, A. B. E. F. Garfield, left Kingston in the fall of 1841 and began another newspaper in Syracuse, N.Y. His partner, a Mr Good, transferred the subscription list, exchange papers, correspondence, and unpaid bills (£100) to Edmundson and John Eastwood who began publishing the *British American Cultivator* in Toronto in January 1842. Its first editor, William EVANS, worked out of Montreal until April 1843 when financial constraints and the expense and inconvenience of sending material from Montreal forced Edmundson to take on

the editorial work. His monthly paper dominated agricultural journalism in the province until December 1847, providing a model which later, more stable journals used successfully.

The *British American Cultivator* was decorated with an ornate mast-head and displayed a lofty motto: "Agriculture not only gives riches to a nation, but the only riches she can call her own." Some issues carried detailed woodcut illustrations by Frederick C. Lowe of livestock and implements. The articles, many of which were reprinted from American papers, tended to be theoretical and esoteric. Topics included better livestock management through cross-breeding with imported pure-bred stock, improved methods of soil cultivation, and hardier strains of seed. The journal encouraged the advancement of agricultural education through farmers' clubs, libraries, model farms, classes in agriculture in the common schools, and a chair of agriculture at King's College (University of Toronto). It also gave its full support to the work of local agricultural societies and published reports from their meetings and from local agricultural fairs. Edmundson repeatedly pressed for the formation of a province-wide association to coordinate the activities of scattered local societies and to organize a provincial exhibition. His efforts bore fruit in August 1846 when the Provincial Agricultural Association (renamed the Agricultural Association of Upper Canada in 1847) was formed. Edmundson received an appointment to the executive committee and the *Cultivator* was made its official journal. Letters to the editor from such men as Adam Fergusson* show that circulation was restricted mainly to the "older" parts of the province and that the majority of the subscribers were well-established, often well-to-do farmers. The *Cultivator* reflected the development of agriculture and agricultural journalism in the 1840s, but it also showed the hazards involved in such ventures.

By the latter half of the decade Edmundson's problems were becoming more numerous and serious. He had always had financial difficulties, in his opinion because of the reluctance of many readers to pay for their subscriptions and because of a disappointing circulation which was about 5,000 copies at best. In November 1845 he complained that in four years he had not received any money for his work and, to make matters worse, had sustained a loss of £500 cash. In an attempt to make ends meet, by May 1843 he had moved with his wife and son to a farm in Whitchurch Township, 27 miles from Toronto. Owing to the distance involved, this enterprise not only failed to augment his resources satisfactorily but also interfered with his writing. Therefore, in 1846 he opened the Provincial Agricultural Warehouse in Toronto, where he sold farm implements and operated a land and patent agency office. The rural population evidently was not yet ready to use the advanced equipment which he offered for sale. By late 1847 he found himself in another losing venture and closed the business. That same year Edmundson and George Buckland*, his co-editor, also published the *Provincial Advertiser*, "a monthly newspaper dealing with Domestic Manufacturers, Emigration, Internal Improvements, Trade and Commerce." It was intended to provide information on topics other than agriculture, perhaps in response to requests from readers of the *Cultivator* for a greater variety of news.

Edmundson's temperament may well have played a large role in the difficulties he encountered during his career. His inability to form lasting associations is evident in the fact that no fewer than four printers produced the *British American Cultivator* during its existence from 1842 to 1847. His stormy relationship with William McDougall*, who had acted as a travelling agent for the *Cultivator* in 1842 but went on to publish a competing journal, the *Canada Farmer*, in partnership with Charles Lindsey*, provides further evidence of this characteristic. Throughout 1847, when the two papers coexisted, Edmundson and McDougall sniped at one another through their editorials, each accusing the other of provoking the attacks. In April McDougall accused Edmundson of using funds from the agricultural society to buy advertising space in the *Provincial Advertiser*. On 22 May McDougall stated, most unfairly, that Edmundson could not "write a single sentence of English correctly" and that his journal, "save a few extracts, would be a disgrace to the literature of any country." Despite this condemnation, the two publishers amalgamated their papers to form the *Agriculturist & Canadian Journal*, which appeared in January 1848. This partnership lasted only until the following August and ended bitterly with McDougall accusing Edmundson of not doing his share of the work and also of receiving money which he failed to record in the books or use for payment of expenses. The sheriff seized and sold Edmundson's interest in the paper to pay his personal debts, whereupon Edmundson left with the subscription lists which he kept until an injunction from the Court of Chancery compelled him to return them.

Edmundson's service from 1846 to 1848 as secretary treasurer of the agricultural society he had helped to establish turned out to be yet another unfortunate undertaking. He handled the society's funds unwisely, purchasing books and charging them to the association's account, presumably without authorization since the other officers took action against him for settlement. According to its financial report, the Agricultural Association of Upper Canada eventually received £120 marked "Edmundson's Securities" in March 1850.

In the fall of 1848, after Edmundson's break with McDougall, a paper named the *Farmer and Mechan-*ic, with the characteristics of Edmundson's work, had appeared in Toronto for a short period; its last issue was dated April 1849. No further articles written by Edmundson can be found in any Canadian papers. He appears to have left Canada in disgrace some time that year and gone to the United States. In January 1852 the *Cultivator*, published in Albany, N.Y., contained a piece signed "W.G.E." discussing the cultivation of wheat on the upper Mississippi. This may well have been the last contribution he made to agricultural journalism before his death.

Edmundson's downfall is evident in the treatment Canadian papers gave the news of his death. The *Canadian Agriculturist*, the official publication of the Agricultural Association of Upper Canada at the time, customarily carried obituaries of leading agriculturists but it ignored Edmundson's passing. A brief notice appeared in the *Globe* on 25 Nov. 1852 which stated that Edmundson had died of inflammation of the brain after only nine days' illness. There was no reference to his family, only to a "large circle of friends and acquaintances."

ANN MACKENZIE

[Mention of William Graham Edmundson seems to be found almost exclusively in the agricultural journals of Upper Canada in the 1840s. The most extensive collection of these exists in UWOL. The collection was the work of the late Professor Fred Landon, whose early study, "Agricultural journals of Upper Canada," *Agricultural Hist.* (Chicago), 9 (1935): 167–75, brought Edmundson to light. In addition to many American journals, the collection contains the following Canadian publications which pertain directly to Edmundson: *Canadian Farmer and Mechanic*, published in Kingston (Ont.), 1841; and *British American Cultivator*, 1842–47, *Canada Farmer*, 29 Jan.–4 Dec. 1847, *Agriculturist & Canadian Journal*, January–November 1848, *Farmer and Mechanic*, 1848–49, and *Canadian Agriculturist*, 1 (1849)–15 (1863), all of which were published in Toronto. The prospectus of the *Canadian Farmer and Mechanic*, dated 16 Nov. 1841, with a letter written by Edmundson on the back, is in the David Barker Stevenson papers, AO, MU 2884. A.MACK.]

AO, MU 2128, 1906, no.13 (V. M. Roberts, "The Canadian National Exhibition, 1768–1906," typescript); MU 2884, W. G. Edmundson to D. B. Stevenson, 4 Sept. 1841; Edmundson to Stevenson, 8 June 1842; MU 2885, John Eastwood to Stevenson, 31 Jan. 1846. MTL, Robert Baldwin papers, A43, nos.71–79 (Baldwin corr., February 1843–March 1849). PAC, RG 31, A1, 1842, Toronto, St Andrew's ward. York North Land Registry Office (Newmarket, Ont.), Deeds, Whitchurch Township, 3, no.37646 (mfm. at AO, GS 6424). *Cultivator* (Albany, N.Y.), new ser., 9 (1852). *Provincial Advertiser* (Toronto), 1847. U.C., Board of Agriculture, *Journal and Trans.* (Toronto), 1 (1851–56). *Globe*, 25 Nov. 1852. *Toronto directory*, 1843–47. R. L. Jones, *History of agriculture in Ontario, 1613–1880* (Toronto, 1946; repr. Toronto and Buffalo, N.Y., 1977). Ann MacKenzie, "Animal husbandry in the

Egan

1840s as reflected in the agricultural journals of Canada West," *OH*, 66 (1974): 114–28. J. J. Talman, "Agricultural societies of Upper Canada," *OH*, 27 (1931): 545–52.

EGAN, JOHN, businessman, office holder, justice of the peace, militia officer, and politician; b. 11 Nov. 1811 in the town-land of Lissavahaun near Aughrim, County Galway (Republic of Ireland); m. 13 Aug. 1839 Anne Margaret Gibson in Bytown (Ottawa), and they had three sons and five daughters; d. 11 July 1857 at Quebec and was buried in Aylmer, Lower Canada.

Shortly after emigrating from Ireland in 1830, John Egan became the depot clerk for Thomas Durrell, a leading lumberman in Clarendon Township, Lower Canada, on the upper Ottawa River. As clerk he was in charge of purchasing supplies and handling administrative duties. After gaining experience in the square-timber trade and developing a network of friends, he struck out on his own, first by opening a store in Aylmer to supply lumbermen and then by entering the trade himself. In March 1836 he helped found the Ottawa Lumber Association at Bytown and that winter he was cutting red pine on the Rivière Schyan in Lower Canada. In 1837 he purchased the farm of James Wadsworth at the "Fourth Chute" on the Bonnechere River in Upper Canada, which he later developed as the village of Eganville. At this time, when he was still supplying more than three dozen other producers, Egan began building dams and timber slides on the Bonnechere River and on Herd's Creek in order to get out his own timber. By early 1837 he had formed John Egan and Company at Aylmer in association with Henry LeMesurier* (a leading timber exporter at Quebec), William Henry Tilstone, and Havilland LeMesurier Routh.

Genial and gentlemanly, Egan was no crude lumberman on the rise. In the summer of 1838 he fought an affair of honour with Andrew Powell, a barrister in Bytown. No one was injured in the exchange of shots, but Powell withdrew his accusation that one of Egan's intimate friends was "no gentleman."

Up to the mid 1840s Egan dealt primarily in red pine, a scarcer but more profitable commodity than white pine. Though general depression brought his business to a near standstill in 1842, it quickly recovered. In 1844 he was rafting two and a half million feet of square timber to Quebec, less than one-fifth of which he reported as coming from crown land. Some of his timber was supplied by small producers and some by settlers as payment for land. To facilitate his operations he began to spend considerable sums on the construction of more dams and timber slides in both Upper and Lower Canada, primarily on the Quyon, Petawawa, and Madawaska rivers but also on a series of tributaries. In the late 1830s he had spent about £1,300 annually on river

improvements; in 1847 the figure, his highest, was £9,456. Leading producers such as Egan and his close friend Ruggles Wright frequently cooperated in use of these private facilities. In 1852 Egan joined with Daniel McLachlin*, James Skead*, and others to build a wagon road from Arnprior to the head of the Long Rapids on the Madawaska.

Egan had begun to diversify his business interests by the late 1840s. In 1846 he built a large sawmill, with 14 saws, and a grist-mill at Quyon, Lower Canada. Three years later, he erected two smaller sawmills on the Bonnechere and Little Bonnechere rivers, plus a grist-mill at Eganville. He even purchased a carding- and fulling-mill in Lochaber Township, Lower Canada. In 1853 he completed a very large sawmill near Quyon at the foot of the Chats Falls rapids, which was, in the estimate of historian H. R. Morgan, "perhaps the most extensive establishment of the kind on the Ottawa with machinery of the latest pattern."

Chats Falls became the focal point of a transportation system established by Egan to compete with the line of steamboats operated by Jason Gould. In 1845 Egan and Joseph-Ignace Aumond* contracted for two prefabricated iron steamers from the shipyards of John MOLSON in Montreal, and during the winter the sections were hauled up over the ice of the Ottawa. The *Emerald* was launched at Aylmer in the spring of 1846 and served between there and Chats Falls. The *Oregon*, launched on the Mississippi River, ran from above the falls to Arnprior. That year Egan, along with Aumond and Ruggles Wright, formed the Union Forwarding Company to operate these vessels and transport passengers and goods around the falls by means of a short, horse-drawn tramway, the Union Railroad.

In the early 1850s the fortunes of John Egan and Company were at their peak. In 1851 the firm employed 2,000 men throughout the Ottawa valley and it gave work to hundreds of farmers, who provided the supplies including the 1,600 oxen and horses which it used. The following year Egan's timber limits, which covered an area of more than 2,000 square miles, were unmatched by those of anyone else on the Ottawa except perhaps Allan* and James Gilmour. Egan's carefully integrated company was employing 3,500 men in 100 lumber camps throughout the valley in 1854 and its cash transactions exceeded $2 million. It had been Egan, in the opinion of the *Canadian Merchants' Magazine and Commercial Review* of Toronto, "who first gave a systematic business character to the lumber trade of the Ottawa, . . . before his day, lumbering on the Ottawa was nothing more than a wild venture."

Besides being the dominant square-timber king on the Ottawa River – the *Canadian Merchants' Magazine* later described him as the "Napoleon of the

Ottawa" – Egan was an active participant in the civic life of Aylmer and the region. He was the first warden in 1841 of the Sydenham District, served as a justice of the peace, and in 1847 became the first mayor of Aylmer. An Anglican, he helped found Christ Church there in 1843. In 1846 he was appointed major in the battalion of Ottawa militia commanded by Ruggles Wright, and later he served as lieutenant-colonel of the 4th Battalion. As well he was a committee-member of the Bytown Emigration Society, of which Thomas McKay was president.

Egan viewed political office as a means for promoting the welfare of the Ottawa valley generally and lumbermen specifically. In 1841 he and others had supported the election in the Lower Canadian riding of Ottawa of Charles Dewey Day*, a tory and a former counsel for several timber barons, whom Egan viewed six years later as the "only man connected with the Government in whom I have the slightest confidence." Following the retirement of Denis-Benjamin Papineau, Egan ran successfully in the general election of 1847–48 in Ottawa, "unpledged to any party" but with strong reform sympathies. Re-elected to the Legislative Assembly by acclamation in 1851, he was returned three years later for the newly created constituency of Pontiac. He held the seat comfortably until his death, a situation attributable to his wide popularity and to the fact that he had timber limits on most of the unoccupied lands in Onslow, Bristol, and Clarendon and owned extensive blocks of land in those townships.

Egan frequently spoke with considerable "passion" in the assembly on matters pertaining to the Ottawa valley, which, he believed, the government neglected. Early in 1852 he helped organize and lead the movement to have the timber dues on red pine reduced from a penny to a halfpenny per cubic foot. After the fee was reduced in September by provincial order-in-council, Egan and others faced allegations in the assembly that they had "put the screws on" the government by threatening to oppose it in votes on the clergy reserves issue unless the duty was reduced. In 1853 he used his influence with Francis Hincks* to persuade the government to vote $50,000 for the construction of a small canal, roughly parallel to the Union Railroad, at Chats Falls. Plagued by labour shortages and problems in excavation, this highly political project, which Egan had promoted as a public work despite its clear value to his own business and that of Ruggles Wright, was suspended in November 1857 after almost half a million dollars had been spent.

Outside the assembly Egan was a central figure in the promotion of a series of internal improvement schemes, especially those which would benefit the lumber industry. He was an early supporter of the Bytown and Prescott Railway because, he claimed in 1848, it would open "a profitable market for manufactured timber" in the United States. He and Joseph-Ignace Aumond helped recruit Walter Shanly* in 1851 to build the railway. In 1852 Egan was a founder of the Bytown and Pembroke Railway Company. He was first president of the Bytown and Aylmer Union Turnpike Company, which had completed a road between the two towns in 1850. In addition he supported the government's construction in 1852–54 of a colonization road between the Ottawa River and Opeongo Lake, believing that it would help lumbermen as well as settlers. In 1853 he joined James Bell Forsyth*, Malcolm Cameron*, and others in founding the Cap-Rouge Pier, Wharf and Dock Company, which operated near Quebec.

Despite his public and commercial standing, Egan had suffered "severe reverses of fortune" by 1855. The red pine market had declined steadily after 1847, with both exports and prices falling 30 per cent by 1852. Late in 1855 it was widely rumoured, according to the Perth *Courier*, that he had failed and the cause was attributed to his heavy involvement with an English firm, Delisle, Janvrin and Company, which had collapsed. At this time his health was failing and his death at Quebec two years later was not unexpected. The personal property in his estate was worth only about £5,000. In 1867 his rich timber limits on the Madawaska River were bought for $45,000 by John Rudolphus Booth* but his executors were unable to dispose of John Egan and Company until 1868, when it was sold to James Bonfield, a former bookkeeper in the company, and Robert Turner.

RICHARD REID

AO, MU 1957, John Egan to Daniel McLachlin, 29 March 1849; McLachlin *et al.* to subscribers, 18 May 1852; RG 8, ser.I-6-A, 1: 32; RG 22, ser.155, will of John Egan. Ottawa, Hist. Soc., Bytown Museum Arch. (Ottawa), ABUS 79–80. Ottawa Public Library, Ottawa Room, H. T. Douglas, "Bits and pieces, that's all: ten thousand words concerning Ottawa and the Ottawa area" (typescript, 1969), 49–51; Ottawa hist. scrapbook, 5: 48–50. PAC, MG 24, D8, 30, 37; D66, 2, 5–6; RG 1, L3, 182B: E7/7½, 7½B; 183: E8/5; RG 5, A1: 94333–34, 141297. Renfrew Land Registry Office (Pembroke, Ont.), Abstract index to deeds, Grattan Township, concession 21, lots 19–22 (mfm. at AO, GS 5246); Wilberforce Township, concession 8, lots 18–19 (mfm. at AO, GS 5312). Can., Prov. of, Legislative Assembly, *App. to the journals*, 1844–45, app.00; 1852, app.AAA; 1853, app.MMMM, app.QQQQ; 1856, app.31; *Statutes*, 1852, c.137, c.257. *Canada Gazette*, 19 May 1855: 678. *Daylight through the mountain: letters and labours of civil engineers Walter and Francis Shanly*, ed. F. W. Walker ([Montreal], 1957), 186. *Debates of the Legislative Assembly of United Canada* (Abbott Gibbs *et al.*), vols.4–7. "The Honorable Samuel Crane," *Journal of Education for Upper Canada* (Toronto), 12 (1859): 27–28. "The late John Egan,"

Ellis

Canadian Merchants' Magazine and Commercial Rev. (Toronto), 1 (April–September 1857): 500–2. J. A. Macdonald, *The letters of Sir John A. Macdonald*, ed. J. K. Johnson and C. B. Stelmack (2v., Ottawa, 1968–69), 1: 335, 337. *Muskoka and Haliburton, 1615–1875; a collection of documents*, ed. F. B. Murray ([Toronto], 1963), 160. *Bathurst Courier*, 23 Oct. 1855. *British Whig*, 19 Jan. 1837, 3 Aug. 1838. *Bytown Gazette, and Ottawa and Rideau Advertiser*, 14 Aug. 1839. *Chronicle & Gazette*, 5 Jan., 18 June 1842. *Ottawa Citizen*, 15 April 1854. *Packet*, 18, 26 June, 4 Sept., 29 Nov., 18 Dec. 1847; 23 Jan., 8 July, 10 Oct. 1848. F.-J. Audet, "Les législateurs du Bas-Canada."

Eric Acland *et al.*, *Christ Church, Aylmer, Quebec, 1843–1968* (Aylmer, 1968), 2, 5. Cornell, *Alignment of political groups*, 24 [incorrectly refers to Egan as a "conservative" in 1847]. M. S. Cross, "The dark druidical groves: the lumber community and the commercial frontier in British North America, to 1854" (PHD thesis, Univ. of Toronto, 1968), 31, 311. R. L. Jones, *History of agriculture in Ontario, 1613–1880* (Toronto, 1946; repr. Toronto and Buffalo, N.Y., 1977), 110–12, 291–92. C. C. Kennedy, *The upper Ottawa Valley* (Pembroke, 1970), 188–90. E. L. Lake, *Pioneer reminiscences of the upper Ottawa Valley, commemorating triple centennial years of St. John the Evangelist Church, Eganville, Ontario* ([Ottawa, 1966]). Robert Legget, *Ottawa waterway: gateway to a continent* (Toronto and Buffalo, 1975), 149, 168, 173. A. R. M. Lower, *Great Britain's woodyard; British America and the timber trade, 1763–1867* (Montreal and London, Ont., 1973); *Settlement and the forest frontier in eastern Canada* (Toronto, 1936), 51. *Quyon–Onslow, 1875–1975: souvenir of centennial* (Quyon, Que., 1975). A. H. D. Ross, *Ottawa, past and present* (Toronto, 1927), 49, 155. "John R. Booth's death closes rich chapter of Canada's life," *Ottawa Farm Journal*, 11 Dec. 1925. H. R. Morgan, "History of early Ottawa," *Ottawa Farm Journal*, 12 June 1925; "Steam navigation on the Ottawa River," *OH*, 23 (1926): 370–83.

ELLIS, WILLIAM, shipwright and shipbuilder; b. 1774 (baptized 23 August), probably in Monkleigh, England, second son of Robert Ellis and Mary Handford; m. 1796, and had at least nine children; d. 25 Dec. 1855 in Port Hill, P.E.I.

William Ellis came of a north Devon family which had migrated inland to Monkleigh from the maritime parish of Northam in 1725. Ellis returned to tide-water to work as a shipwright in yards on the Bideford River, and also in the royal dockyard at Devonport (Plymouth), before settling down in 1813 to become master shipwright, and possibly also some kind of business partner, of Richard Chapman, a famous north Devon shipbuilder of the time. In 1818 Chapman fell ill and the yard was taken over by John Evans of Bideford. Ellis then became interested in an expedition mounted and financed by Thomas Burnard, Bideford's leading merchant and shipowner. Burnard's plan was to establish a colonizing and shipbuilding venture on the Goodwood (Bideford) River at the eastern end of Lot 12 in Prince County, P.E.I. Ellis agreed to be the project's master

shipwright, and in the summer of 1818 he set sail for the Island in the polacca brigantine *Peter & Sarah* of Bideford.

The first vessel built, the *Mars*, was launched in 1819 and sailed to Bideford with a load of lumber. For the next eight years one or two ships were launched each year at the settlement, New Bideford (later Bideford), culminating with the *Superb* of 1826, a very large merchant vessel for her time, with a cargo capacity of about 900 tons. She was Ellis's greatest single shipbuilding achievement. In the same year the shipbuilding enterprise and the leases on the settlements which had been established at New Bideford and at Port Hill on Lot 13 were transferred by the Burnard family to Thomas Burnard Chanter*, a son of Thomas Burnard's sister. Chanter in turn disposed of the property and all rights, including the considerable uncollected debts due to the enterprise from local settlers, to Ellis on condition, *inter alia*, that he complete two further vessels for Chanter.

Unfortunately for Ellis, James Yeo*, also a former employee of Thomas Burnard, was settled at Port Hill and over some years he appears vigorously to have collected the debts owed to Ellis and to have kept the proceeds. Yeo thereby built up capital with which he gradually established himself, among other endeavours, as the colony's principal shipbuilder. In due course he bought out Ellis's land holdings and business interests, and the latter was reduced to working for Yeo as master shipwright on the building of vessels financed by his former colleague, though he retained, and farmed, a small landholding on Lot 13 for the rest of his life.

Because of the way builders' names were recorded in contemporary documents it is not possible to say with certainty how many ships Ellis was responsible for building in Prince Edward Island, but it certainly ran into scores. He was a great traditional craftsman who played an important pioneering role in the establishment of an industry which was to prove vitally important in the development of the Island between 1818 and the early 1870s. The shipbuilding traditions he established and the skills he taught were his memorial: these, and the small tragedy of the loss of his inheritance to the more dynamic but less principled James Yeo. The story of the slow reversal in fortunes of these two contrasted men became an enduring myth on the Island.

BASIL GREENHILL

[Beginning in 1750 the parish registers of St George's Church (Church of England) in Monkleigh, Eng., contain records of the baptisms, marriages, and burials of the Ellis family. William Ellis's career as a shipbuilder in Britain is traceable through the Bideford Custom House registration of shipping docs. in the Devon Record Office (Exeter, Eng.),

3319 S/1, and to a smaller extent through the Reports of Lloyd's surveyors of the port of Bideford in the National Maritime Museum (London), LYY (mfm. at PAC). His years as a shipbuilder and landholder on Prince Edward Island can be followed in PAPEI, Port Hill papers, Acc. 2685; RG 16, Land registry records, conveyance reg.; in PAC, RG 42, ser.I, 150–59; and in the files of the P.E.I. Museum. There are also a number of references to him in the Charlottetown press, including issues of the *Islander* for 1844–56; the *Prince Edward Island Register*, 1823–29; and the *Royal Gazette*, 1830–44. His obituary appears in the *Islander* of 4 Jan. 1856. Basil Greenhill and Ann Giffard, *Westcountrymen in Prince Edward's Isle: a fragment of the great migration* (Newton Abbot, Eng., and [Toronto], 1967; repr. Toronto and Buffalo, N.Y., 1975), gives details of his career on the Island. B.G.]

ENSLIN, CHRISTIAN (Emanuel Christian Gottlieb), bookbinder, newspaperman, notary, and office holder; b. 4 Feb. 1800 in Württemberg (Federal Republic of Germany); m. Julia ——, and they had one child; d. 29 March 1856 in Berlin (Kitchener), Upper Canada.

Christian Enslin came from Württemberg to North America about 1830. One of the early German immigrants to the Waterloo area, he arrived in Berlin some time before 1833 with all his possessions in a carpet-bag. He first supported himself as a daily labourer, but soon began to practise his trade as a bookbinder, travelling from house to house until he could establish a small bindery. There he bound books for customers such as Bishop Benjamin EBY and Heinrich Wilhelm PETERSON. Some time later Enslin expanded his business to include a bookstore, where he sold not only books but also patent medicines, eyeglasses, school supplies, and other specialized articles.

In December 1837 Enslin began an active role in journalism, working for almost a year as the associate editor of Peterson's *Canada Museum, und Allgemeine Zeitung*. When Peterson decided to stop publishing it, Enslin and Heinrich Eby, a son of Bishop Eby and a former apprentice at the *Canada Museum*, purchased the newspaper plant from him in December 1840. A month later Peterson's two former employees founded *Der Deutsche Canadier und Neuigkeitsbote*. Following the demise in September 1841 of *Der Morgenstern*, a short-lived German weekly published in Waterloo, Enslin and Eby acquired a subscription list and perhaps also some equipment from its publisher Benjamin Burkholder. The sole German-language newspaper published in British North America from 1841 to 1848, the *Deutsche Canadier* was more successful than its first rival, the *Morgenstern*, and it continued in print until January 1865.

Enslin, editor of the *Deutsche Canadier* from its first issue until he was succeeded by Johann Jakob Ernst in January 1850, proudly boasted that his reform journal was "a staunch advocate of Responsible and Constitutional Government." The paper did not publish much local news, but it did support instruction in German in county schools. Enslin concentrated instead on reports of political unrest in Europe and reprinted literary extracts from various continental journals. Despite its popularity the *Deutsche Canadier* was never free from the threat of bankruptcy. With tongue in cheek Enslin warned his readers early in 1844 that, "inasmuch as the end of the world is to come on the 22nd of March, according to Miller's prophecy, we respectfully request all our readers who are in arrears with their subscriptions to call and settle at once, otherwise it will go hard with them on Judgment Day."

Enslin, a convert to the religious views of Emanuel Swedenborg, was instrumental in the formation of a Swedenborgian congregation in Berlin, later known as the Church of the New Jerusalem or the New Church. For some time before the cooperative Free Church, which was used by a number of denominations, was opened on 25 Dec. 1842, Enslin's group met for services in his orchard in the summer and in his bindery in the winter. A circulating library of religious books, most of which were Swedenborgian, operated out of his bookstore under the auspices of the New Church Society of Berlin. Enslin was also one of the organizers of the second Mennonite Sunday school in the county, established in April 1841.

During his career Enslin held a number of civic offices. As a bilingual notary he assisted many German farmers in their land transactions and, according to an obituary in the *Berlin Chronicle and Provincial Reformers' Gazette*, "he wrote more public documents than any other man in Canada." He was appointed commissioner to the Court of Queen's Bench, responsible for taking affidavits for use in local court sessions, and from 1853 to 1855 he served as the first clerk of the Surrogate Court in Waterloo County. He became the second treasurer of the county a few months before his death from consumption on 29 March 1856.

TOM EADIE

AO, RG 1, A-I-6: 23046–48; RG 22, ser.155, will of Christian Enslin. PAC, RG 31, A1, 1851, Waterloo Township, pt.4: 180–81. *New Jerusalem Magazine* (Boston), 28 (1856): 623–24. *Berlin Chronicle and Provincial Reformers' Gazette* (Berlin [Kitchener, Ont.]), 2 April 1856. *Canada Museum, und Allgemeine Zeitung* (Berlin). *Der Deutsche Canadier und Neuigkeitsbote* (Berlin), 1 Jan. 1841–December 1849. *Der Morgenstern* (Waterloo, [Ont.]), 8 June 1839–16 Sept. 1841. M. B. Block, *The New Church in the new world: a study of Swedenborgianism in America* (New York, 1932; repr. 1968). A. E. Byerly, *The beginning of things in Wellington and Waterloo counties . . .* (Guelph, Ont., 1935). H. K.

Esson

Kalbfleisch, *The history of the pioneer German language press of Ontario, Canada, 1835–1918* (London, Ont., and Münster, German Federal Republic, 1968). Gottlieb Leibbrant, *Little paradise: the saga of the German Canadians of Waterloo County, Ontario, 1800–1975* (Kitchener, 1980). W. V. Uttley, *A history of Kitchener, Ontario* (Kitchener, 1937; repr. [Waterloo, 1975]).

The Waterloo Hist. Soc. (Waterloo) has published a number of articles relating to Christian Enslin's life in its *Annual report*, including: Salome Bauman, "First Mennonite Church, 1813–1963," 1963: 19–26; Michael Bird, "The Swedenborgian community in Waterloo County: two religious approaches to culture," 1975: 69–74; W. H. Breithaupt, "[Address at the dedication of the Waterloo County Pioneers' Memorial Tower, 28 Aug. 1926]," 1926: 220–25, "Some German settlers of Waterloo County," 1913: 11–15, and "Waterloo County newspapers," 1921: 152–60; A. E. Byerly, "Henry William Peterson," 1931: 250–62; D. Johnson, "The Church of the Good Shepherd," 1943: 39–43; D. N. Panabaker, "President's report," 1932: 298–308; and Jacob Stroh, "Reminiscences of Berlin (now Kitchener)," 1930: 175–207; 1931: 274–84.

A brief account of Enslin's life was published a few years after his death in "Minutes of the meeting of the Association of the New Church in Canada," *New Jerusalem Magazine*, 36 (1864): 210–11.

ESSON, HENRY (baptized **Hary Easson**), Presbyterian minister, educator, and author; baptized 7 March 1793 in Balnacraig, Aboyne and Glentanner parish, Scotland, son of Robert Easson; d. 11 May 1853 in Toronto.

Henry Esson was the youngest son of an Aberdeenshire farmer. He studied for the ministry of the Church of Scotland at Marischal College, Aberdeen, entering in 1807, winning prizes for academic excellence, and graduating MA in 1811. Six years later the Scotch Presbyterian Church in Montreal, later known as the St Gabriel Street Church, true to traditional ties with the Church of Scotland, wrote a letter of procuratory to the Reverend John Stuart, professor at Marischal College, declaring "their anxious desire of forming a more intimate connextion with their Mother church," and requesting that a clergyman ordained by the Church of Scotland and "sent out to America under [its] particular sanction and authority" be selected to assist their present minister, the Reverend James Somerville*. The salary offered was substantial, £400 per year, not including fees received, but was guaranteed for only four years. Stuart selected Esson, his former pupil, who accepted the position. On 15 May 1817, eight days after it had licensed him to preach, the Presbytery of Aberdeen ordained Esson for the overseas charge.

By the fall of 1817 Esson had settled in Montreal, was familiar with the city and its Presbyterian inhabitants, and was becoming recognized by the members of his church's affluent congregation as both an exceptionally gifted scholar and a brilliant conversationalist. He was also being drawn into the leadership of the church in the Canadas. Rallying his fellow clergymen in opposition to a plan of Canadian secessionist Presbyterian ministers to unite all branches of Presbyterianism in the Canadas, he attempted instead to form "a more intimate connexion" with the Church of Scotland. Dr Duncan Mearns of Aberdeen, moderator of that church's General Assembly, informed Esson in 1821 that he despaired of the Canadian church effecting a formal connection with its mother church until it found a permanent source of financial support. With other clergy and laymen Esson undertook a long and fruitless campaign to obtain recognition of his church's claims to co-establishment with the Church of England and to a share of the revenue from the clergy reserves. They encountered stiff opposition, especially from Archdeacon John Strachan*. Esson vented his frustration in the June issue of the *Canadian Miscellany*, a short-lived religious journal he published between April and August 1828: "Wherever we turned – through whatever channel – with whatever secrecy – we made, or thought we made, our representations to His Majesty's Government, still the Archdeacon of York – like our evil genius – stood prepared to oppose us."

Esson was more successful in the field of education. He had opened the Montreal Academical Institution with the help of the Reverend Hugh Urquhart in 1822. By the end of the following year the school had 78 students, 58 of whom were studying the classics. In 1836 Esson was elected a member of the management committee of the École Normale de Montréal, and he was the only clergyman of his affiliation among the founders of the High School of Montreal in 1844. He was also active in protesting efforts to make McGill College an exclusively Church of England institution [*see* John Bethune*].

Esson's personal life was marred by troubles and disappointments. His 24-year-old wife, Maria Sweeny, whom he had married on 7 July 1823, died in 1826, and his two sons, Campbell Sweeny and Henry Robert, died in childhood. He did not remarry until 1842, taking as his second wife Elizabeth Campbell of Edinburgh. Moreover, Esson's ministry was beset by problems. In 1822, while his contract was being renegotiated, his congregation arranged for Somerville's retirement with pension and called another minister, the Reverend Edward Black*. Black's evangelical style appealed to a group within the congregation which perceived Esson as cold and intellectual. Within a few years, realizing the impossibility of supporting the three ministers, the management committee suggested that either Black or Esson resign. A vicious struggle between the clergymen which distracted and divided the congregation deadlocked the church. On one occasion members of the faction supporting Black barricaded themselves inside the church while those supporting Esson tried to break down the door. Aspersions, later discovered to be completely unfounded, were cast on Esson's character. The quarrel probably hastened the formation of a superior church body in the Canadas, the Synod of the Presbyterian Church of Canada in connection with the Church of Scotland, in June 1831. A synodical committee dictated the solution: that Esson remain at the St Gabriel Street Church and that Black go elsewhere. Esson's prestige remained undamaged – in 1842 he was elected moderator of the synod – and his travail seems to have mellowed him. His contemporaries observed changes in his theological views; his concern for people and their problems intensified and he began to preach with evangelical fervour.

In 1844 the disruption among Canadian adherents of the Church of Scotland occurred, triggered by the disruption in the mother church [see Robert Burns*]. Esson supported the Free Church, perhaps as a result of his increasingly evangelical views, and he began to develop the strong voluntarist position later demonstrated in his pamphlet *A plain and popular exposition of the principles of voluntaryism* (1849). In November 1844 he accepted an appointment to teach history, literature, and philosophy at a college (later Knox College) established by the Free Church in Toronto. The atmosphere in Esson's Toronto dwelling must have reminded him of his Montreal home. Two or three teachers and ten or more students had lived with him in Montreal and his several Toronto residences formed the nucleus of Knox College. His nephew, the Reverend Alexander GALE of Hamilton, joined the staff in 1846. Late in 1851 Esson applied for the newly constituted chair of civil history and English literature at the University of Toronto but he died before an appointment was made. His body was taken to Montreal and buried in Mount Royal Cemetery near those of his first wife and sons.

Esson's outstanding achievement was without doubt his work as an educator. Shortly after his death, the Reverend Michael Willis*, principal of Knox, paid tribute to his scholarly and contemplative nature, as well as to the "noble simplicity and ingenuousness of his temper and manners, united with an ardour of spirit which he carried into his professional pursuits."

ELIZABETH ANN KERR MCDOUGALL

Henry Esson is the author of *An appeal to the ministers and members of the Presbyterian Church, under the jurisdiction of the Synod of Canada, on the question of adherence to the Church of Scotland as by law established* (Montreal, 1844); *Answer of the Rev. Henry Esson, to the charges and statements of a committee of the session of St. Gabriel Street Church, Montreal . . .* (Montreal, 1832); *A plain and popular exposition of the principles of voluntaryism, in*

opposition to the misapprehensions of those who have imputed to them an infidel tendency; being an humble essay, to mediate between the advocates and antagonists of the establishment principle, and to promote generally the catholic unity of evangelical churches (Toronto, 1849); "Review of a speech of the venerable John Strachan, D.D., archdeacon of York, in the Legislative Council," *Canadian Miscellany: or, the Religious, Literary & Statistical Intelligencer* (Montreal), 1 (June 1828), no.3: 65–85; *Statement relative to the educational system of Knox's College, Toronto; with suggestions for its extension and improvement* (Toronto, 1848); *Strictures on the present method of teaching the English language and suggestions for its improvement* (Toronto, 1852); and *Substance of an address explanatory and apologetic, in reference to the late disruption of the Synod of Canada, in connexion with the established Church of Scotland, delivered to the congregation of Saint Gabriel Street Church, on Tuesday, the 20th of July, 1844* (Montreal, 1844).

GRO (Edinburgh), Aboyne, reg. of baptisms, marriages, and burials, 1773–93. PAC, MG 24, D16, 25: 21544–50; I3, 8. PCA, St Gabriel Street Church (Montreal), reg. of baptisms, marriages, and burials, 7 July 1823–9 Dec. 1830. QUA, Presbyterian Church of Canada in connection with the Church of Scotland, Synod papers, overtures, 1836–38; reports, 1821. UCA, Biog. files; Montreal–Ottawa Conference (Montreal), St Gabriel Street Church, parish records, box II. *Testimonials of literary and educational qualifications, in favour of the Rev. Henry Esson, A.M., professor of mental and moral philosophy, Knox's College* (Toronto, 1851). *Fasti Academiae Mariscallanae Aberdonensis: selections from the records of the Marischal College and University, [1593–1860]*, ed. P. J. Anderson (3v., Aberdeen, Scot., 1898), 2. Scott *et al.*, *Fasti ecclesiæ scoticanæ*, 7: 632–33. Campbell, *Hist. of Scotch Presbyterian Church. The centenary of the granting of the charter of Knox College, Toronto, 1858–1958* (Toronto, [1958]). Gregg, *Hist. of Presbyterian Church.* "Death of the Rev. Professor Esson," *Ecclesiastical and Missionary Record for the Presbyterian Church of Canada* (Toronto), 9 (1852–53): 117. "The following is the minute of Synod with reference to the lamented deaths of Professor Esson, Mr. John Burns of Toronto, and Mr. John Fraser of London," *Ecclesiastical and Missionary Record for the Presbyterian Church of Canada*, 9 (1852–53): 152.

ESTCOURT, JAMES BUCKNALL BUCKNALL, army officer and surveyor; b. 12 July 1802 in London, second son of Thomas Grimstone Bucknall Estcourt, MP, and Eleanor Sutton; m. there 15 Aug. 1837 Caroline Pole Carew; they had no children; d. 24 June 1855 near Sevastopol (U.S.S.R.).

James Bucknall Bucknall Estcourt was a scion of an old Gloucestershire family and received his education at Harrow. He entered the army on 13 July 1820 as an ensign in the 44th Foot and then transferred to the 43rd Foot on 7 June 1821. He was promoted lieutenant in 1824 and captain the following year. His early service included garrison duty in Ireland from 1821 to 1825, at Gibraltar from 1825 to 1830 (except for a stint with the British army expedition to Portugal in 1827–28),

Estcourt

in England from 1830 to 1831, and back in Ireland until 1834. In January 1835, as second-in-command to Colonel Francis Rawdon Chesney, Estcourt set out with an expedition to survey the valleys of the Tigris and Euphrates rivers. He distinguished himself in his direction of the magnetic experiments and by his arduous efforts before the expedition returned to England in September 1836. On Chesney's recommendation he was promoted major on 21 Oct. 1836 and brevet lieutenant-colonel on 29 March 1839.

Following his return to England, Estcourt was granted leave of absence until 31 March 1838. His regiment had been ordered to New Brunswick in June 1834 and had made a renowned overland trek to Lower Canada in December 1837 to reinforce Sir John Colborne*'s troops during the rebellions of 1837–38. In March 1838, accompanied by his wife, Caroline, Estcourt left England on board the *Pique* for Halifax. After their arrival in June, they proceeded to La Prairie, Lower Canada, where the 43rd was temporarily stationed, and then in July travelled via the Ottawa River, the Rideau Canal, and Lake Ontario to the Niagara frontier in Upper Canada. In August they settled at Lundy's Lane, not far from regimental headquarters at Drummondville (Niagara Falls). During the latter part of 1838 and in 1839, besides fulfilling his regimental duties, Estcourt busied himself conducting road surveys, particularly of the Cayuga Road from Niagara Falls to London, the poor condition of which he drew to the attention of military authorities. He and Caroline also engaged in the social life of the Niagara frontier, participating in sleighing parties, visiting Toronto on occasion, and sketching local scenery, particularly Niagara Falls. In late summer 1839 he was ordered to rejoin the depot companies of the 43rd at Portsmouth, England, and by September the couple had left the Canadas.

Estcourt remained in England until 1843. On 31 March the foreign secretary, the Earl of Aberdeen, appointed him British boundary commissioner in fulfilment of article 6 of the Webster–Ashburton Treaty, signed with the United States in 1842, which had determined the American border with New Brunswick and Lower Canada. Estcourt's instructions enjoined him not only to demarcate the line but also to examine the possibilities of defending it. The delineation of this boundary had been a bone of contention since 1783 when the Treaty of Paris, ending the American revolution, had broadly defined it. A joint commission set up in 1796, on which Britain was represented by Thomas Henry Barclay* and before which Ward Chipman* pleaded the British case, had determined the boundary from Passamaquoddy Bay to the source of the St Croix River. From 1816 to 1821 Barclay and Chipman replayed their roles and first Joseph Bouchette* and then William Franklin Odell* acted as chief surveyor on the British

side when another commission struggled unsuccessfully to define the line between New Brunswick and Lower Canada on the one hand and Maine, Vermont, New Hampshire, and New York on the other. In 1830 the dispute was arbitrated by Willem I, King of the United Netherlands, but his award was rejected by the United States. Over time jurisdictional conflicts between Maine and New Brunswick authorities [*see* Ward Chipman; Sir John Harvey] and border disputes elsewhere led to the formation in 1842 of the Webster–Ashburton commission, which produced a treaty settling the boundary from the head of the St Croix to the St Lawrence and providing for a joint survey to demarcate the line.

Five days after his appointment Estcourt embarked for Boston, where he landed on 19 April 1843. The same day he met with the American boundary commissioner, Albert Smith. In this and subsequent meetings, in Bangor, Maine, on 1 May and in Houlton on 1 June, Estcourt and Smith planned the year's work of making the astronomical survey and cutting the boundary line from the source of the St Croix to the intersection of Hall's Stream with the 45th parallel. Estcourt's permanent staff included a secretary, a surveyor, three Royal Engineers, and six non-commissioned officers of the Royal Sappers and Miners. To these he added a local surveyor, John Wilkinson*, and perhaps as many as 120 local axe-men and foremen. By the end of the 1843 season most of the work on the north line, from the source of the St Croix to the Saint John River, as well as the settling of the Saint John River boundaries, had been completed. The arrival of winter, the failure of needed equipment to appear, and problems in verifying earlier surveys all delayed the running of the astronomical surveys, however. Aberdeen commended Estcourt on his work and, in response to a request from him, dispatched an additional 14 sappers, to hasten progress in 1844; that year Estcourt would employ 500 foremen and axe-men.

Although Estcourt and Smith had agreed in December 1843 on the American and British roles during the 1844 season, failure by the American Congress to grant necessary appropriations left the British alone in the field. Having arranged in the spring to lay in supplies at strategic points along the highlands line, which stretched from the source of the southwest branch of the Saint John River to the head of Hall's Stream, Estcourt agreed with Smith in June that the British would cut all boundary lines until the Americans arrived, but that the lines thus determined would be considered exploratory until confirmed by a joint survey. As a result the British surveyed the entire highlands boundary and cut 140 miles of exploratory lines from the Kennebec Road to Hall's Stream in addition to those from the southwest branch of the Saint John to the Metgermette Portage. The Americans cut the intervening line, between the Kennebec Road and the Metgermette Portage, when they came into the field later in the summer.

The season's work over, in January 1845 Aberdeen again approved Estcourt's management, but, commenting on the heavy expenses, he reiterated a desire to see Estcourt's establishment reduced. Estcourt had already removed from duty ten sappers and a Royal Engineer in anticipation of winding up operations in 1845. That season the two parties determined astronomically the 45th parallel and jointly surveyed the southwest and south lines from Lac Pohénégamook, Lower Canada, to the southwest branch of the Saint John River, the highlands line to Hall's Stream, and the west line along the 45th parallel to the St Lawrence. Since the British had done most of the work in 1844, the Americans cut and marked with iron reference monuments the 45th from Hall's Stream to the St Lawrence. By 10 July 1845 Estcourt was able to report that all the work had been completed, except for the placing of iron markers, which was to be done by the Americans. The commissioners met in Washington in October to finalize surveys, maps, and other details. They had directed work over 670 miles of boundary from the St Croix to the St Lawrence, of which only 179 miles were formed by rivers; almost all the remainder had had to be cut through wilderness. The cutting operations had been preceded by astronomical survey measurements of remarkable accuracy; on one occasion two cutting parties separated by 64 miles of forest arrived within 341 feet of each other. In addition the entire operation had been conducted in a spirit of utmost cooperation, and Estcourt was praised in the House of Commons in 1845 by Sir Howard Douglas* for his work on the commission which, in effect, demarcated definitively a boundary that had long bedevilled Anglo-American relations. He returned to England in 1846, and the next year the commission's final report was tabled.

Estcourt had gone on half pay from his regiment in August 1843 in order to take on his duties as boundary commissioner. He continued on half pay after his return to England, and in February 1848 he entered the House of Commons as Conservative MP for Devizes, the family borough. He did not seek re-election in 1852, and on 21 Feb. 1854 he received a staff appointment as adjutant-general with the rank of brigadier-general in the British expeditionary force to the Crimea. He performed his duties diligently and efficiently, and was promoted major-general on 12 Dec. 1854. However, Estcourt and Major-General Richard Airey, Lord Raglan's chief staff officers, were savagely criticized for the terrible suffering experienced by the British force in the winter of 1854–55. Raglan strongly defended their conduct, and they were not replaced. Estcourt continued to throw himself into his work, but on 21 June 1855 he was struck down by cholera, and in spite of the care devoted to him by Caroline, who had accompanied him throughout the campaign, he died on 24 June. Caroline survived until 17 Nov. 1886.

Estcourt was described by his contemporaries as a man of the world, of good nature and judgement, and a perfect gentleman. In recommending him to the post of boundary commissioner, John Gellibrand Hubbard, later Lord Addington, had praised his temper, energy, and integrity. The contemporary historian Alexander William Kinglake called him "a man greatly loved by Lord Raglan, by all his friends at headquarters, and indeed by all who knew him." Had he lived, he was to have been appointed a KCB, in spite of the problems in the Crimea; instead Caroline was made a KCB's widow by special patent in 1856. Viewed in perspective, Estcourt emerges as a competent, if not spectacular, peace-time staff officer. His work on the boundary commission, although generally well executed, exhibited logistical shortcomings which were later magnified in his tragic Crimean experience.

JIM BURANT

[James Bucknall Bucknall Estcourt is the author of a report which appeared as G.B., Commission for running and tracing the boundary line between her majesty's possessions in North America and the United States under the Treaty of Washington, 1842, North American boundary: narrative of the survey . . . (n.p., n.d.). His correspondence as British boundary commissioner, published as G.B., Foreign Office, Correspondence respecting the operations of the commission for running and tracing the boundary line . . . , under the VIth article of the treaty signed at Washington, August 9, 1842 . . . (London, [1845]), was reprinted with other documents in G.B., Parl., Reports, correspondence, despatches, and papers relating to the boundary between the British possessions in North America and the United States of America (Shannon, Republic of Ireland, 1969).

A volume in the MTL contains a copy of each of these publications and another report bound together with two pencil sketches and two water-colour drawings of scenes near the boundary done by Estcourt. He and his wife, Caroline, were amateur artists, and a large collection of their water-colours and drawings of the areas of the British North American colonies that they visited is preserved in the PAC. The couple are portrayed in a print depicting the sleigh club of the 43rd Foot at Niagara (Niagara-on-the-Lake) in 1839. J.B.]

Gloucestershire Record Office (Gloucester, Eng.), Estcourt papers (mfm. at PAC). PAC, MG 24, A10, 7: 55; RG 8, I (C ser.), 277: 104; 675. PRO, WO 17/1542: 95, 103, 135, 140; 17/1543: 173; 17/2384. Gentleman's Magazine, 1800: 589; 1802: 683; July–December 1837: 302; July–December 1855: 189. United Service Gazette, and Naval and Military Chronicle (London), 8 Nov. 1845. DNB. G.B., WO, Army list, 1820–55. R. G. A. Levinge, Historical records of the Forty-Third Regiment, Monmouthshire Light Infantry, with a roll of the officers and their services from the *period of embodiment to the close of 1867* (London, 1868). *Roll of officers of the Corps of Royal Engineers from 1660 to 1898 . . .*, ed. R. F. Edwards (Chatham, Eng., 1898), 24–26. H. G. Classen, *Thrust and counterthrust: the genesis of the Canada–United States boundary* (Don Mills [Toronto], 1965), 89–92. International Boundary Commission, *Joint report upon the survey and demarcation of the boundary between the United States and Canada from the source of the St Croix River to the St Lawrence River . . .* (Washington, 1925). A. W. Kinglake, *The invasion of the Crimea: its origins and an account of its progress down to the death of Lord Raglan* (8v., Edinburgh and London, 1863–87).

EUART. *See* EWART

EVANS, FRANCIS, Church of England clergyman and educator; b. 1 Jan. 1801 in Lough Park, an estate near Castlepollard, County Westmeath (Republic of Ireland), son of Francis Evans; m. *c.* 1825 Maria Sophia Lewis, and they had six sons and six daughters; d. September 1858 in County Westmeath, and was buried in Castlepollard.

Francis Evans, a graduate of Trinity College, Dublin, arrived in Lower Canada in 1824, intent on entering the Anglican ministry. His decision to emigrate may have been influenced by the presence in the Canadas of his uncle, Thomas Evans*, a soldier. Shortly after arriving he went back to Europe to marry, and then returned to the colony. On 11 Nov. 1826 he became a deacon, was appointed curate two days later to the Reverend Robert Quirk Short* at Trois-Rivières, and was ordained priest on 27 Oct. 1827 by Bishop Charles James Stewart*. Evans, unlike a predecessor, the Reverend Leger-Jean-Baptiste-Noël Veyssière*, did well at Trois-Rivières, reporting in 1827 that his congregation had grown by one-third since his arrival even though there had been no increase in population. Nevertheless, he accepted a missionary posting to Upper Canada sponsored by the Society for the Propagation of the Gospel and resigned his charge to the Reverend Samuel Simpson Wood*. In October 1828 he took his young, growing family to Norfolk County where St John's, near the village of Simcoe in Woodhouse Township, became his home church.

He was the first Anglican clergyman to settle in Woodhouse, even though his parishioners, largely United Empire Loyalists and their descendants, had built the church some years before in anticipation of a permanent appointment. The residents had previously known only occasional visits by Church of England ministers, including Robert Addison* and Robert Lugger*. Like most Anglican clerics, Evans concentrated his efforts by ministering regularly to a few settled charges. He attempted, however, to preach occasionally in "every place that it is in my power to visit." He found his labours well received. In 1830 he

reflected, "It is particularly gratifying to perceive that the prejudices against our Establishment which were very prevalent are disappear[ing] most rapidly."

None the less, the privileged position of the Church of England ensured it and its servants a host of enemies. William Lyon Mackenzie*, for one, twice publicly portrayed Evans as unfeeling and uncaring, characteristics allegedly typical of Anglican clergymen. In 1836 Evans found himself in the public eye again when Lieutenant Governor Sir John Colborne* responded to the critics of the church's claims to establishment by endowing 44 Anglican rectories, one of which went to Evans. The rectories, and Anglican pretensions generally, certainly helped bring about the Upper Canadian rebellion, which affected Evans dramatically.

In December 1837 Charles Duncombe* and Eliakim Malcolm, responding to rumours that rebels had taken Toronto, mustered some 400 to 500 insurgents southwest of Brantford. On the night of 12 December Evans led a little loyalist band bearing messages through rebel lines to Brantford. The next day the rector bravely went to the insurgent camp "to expostulate," as a fellow priest recorded, "with the deluded schismatics." Evans brought news of the governor's proclamation promising pardon for those returning peacefully home. For his efforts, he was detained. Fortunately, release came soon when the rebels dispersed upon discovering that Mackenzie had been defeated in Toronto and that forces, led by Allan Napier MacNab*, were marching against them. But Evans could not escape controversy. In the trials that followed he testified against several prominent insurrectionists, thereby earning further ill will. On 2 Oct. 1838 a mob occupied the Congregational church in Burford Township to prevent his preaching there.

Eventually the clamour faded, and Evans settled back into an all too penurious routine. As was the custom with other clerics he had to supplement his meagre income by teaching. He first operated a boarding-school and began teaching at the district grammar school in Simcoe when it opened in 1839. As a teacher he took special interest in aspiring clergymen. He also laboured earnestly at his regular pastoral duties, establishing some 14 congregations in the surrounding district. He toiled for the Upper Canada Bible Society and spread the temperance message. In the 1850s he helped establish the diocese of Huron and campaigned in 1857 for the election of fellow Irish evangelical Benjamin Cronyn* as its first bishop. Evans and others then organized the Church Society of the new diocese. That same year Trinity College, Toronto, awarded him a DCL. At the time of his death he was an archdeacon and rural dean of Norfolk County.

These toils exhausted Evans. In 1855 Bishop John Strachan*, who thought him "an active and zealous

Missionary," warned him that a continuance of his "usual labours" would be too much for him, and he was right. In a futile effort to recover his health Evans holidayed in Ireland in 1858 but died there between 5 and 7 September after spending only a week with a brother and sister. In Canada he left a monument of solid if unspectacular work and a large, well-educated family. Fittingly, his son William B. Evans later became the rector of Woodhouse.

COLIN FREDERICK READ

ACC-Q, 71: 91–93 ([Francis] Evans, Woodhouse, U.C., parish report, 1833) (typescript at Anglican Church of Canada, Diocese of Huron Arch.). Anglican Church of Canada, Diocese of Huron Arch. (London, Ont.), Incorporated Church Soc. of the Diocese of Huron, minute-book, 1858–64, 2, 6, 16. AO, MS 35, letter-books, 1839–43: 107, 235, 245, 260, 263; 1844–49: 134, 306; 1852–66: 18; 1853–54: 312; 1854–62: 13, 20, 49, 92, 174; unbound papers, letters missive authorizing the bishop of Quebec to institute the Reverend Francis Evans to the parsonage in the township of Woodhouse, 16 Jan. 1836; Evans to [John Strachan], 29 Feb. 1848. PAC, RG 5, A1: 99167, 112558–61, 112570–73, 112663, 112665, 112674–75, 112706–6A, 112709–12, 114638–41; RG 9, I, B1, 45, G. W. Whitehead to James Winniett, 19 Oct. 1838, enclosed in Winniett to Colonel Bullock, 22 Oct. 1838; RG 31, A1, 1851, Woodhouse Township: 113. Trinity College Arch. (Toronto), Degree-book, 1852–1904, entry for Francis Evans. USPG, C/CAN/folder 474; X7: 158–70 (mfm. at PAC). UWOL, Regional Coll., William Wood diaries, pp.22–33 (typescript). *Church*, 3 Nov. 1838: 78–79. W. L. Mackenzie, *Sketches of Canada and the United States* (London, 1833), 128–29. SPG, [*Annual report*] (London), 1829: 141. A. H. Crowfoot, *Benjamin Cronyn, first bishop of Huron* ([London, Ont.], 1957), 65–66, 68, 76. A. E. E. Legge, *The Anglican Church in Three Rivers, Quebec, 1768–1956* ([Russell, Ont.], 1956). Millman, *Life of Charles James Stewart*. E. A. Owen, *Pioneer sketches of Long Point settlement . . .* (Toronto, 1898; repr. Belleville, Ont., 1972), 417–18. Read, *Rising in western U.C.* Historicus, "Pioneer clergy of the diocese of Huron, II," *Huron Church News* (London), 1 Jan. 1952: 6 [contains a portrait of the subject]. Henry Johnson, "St. John's Church, Woodhouse," *Western Ontario Hist. Notes* (London), 14 (1957–58), no.1: 11–20.

EVANS, WILLIAM, farmer, agronomist, journalist, and author; b. 22 Nov. 1786 in County Galway (Republic of Ireland); m. secondly Jane Stephens (d. 1842) in Vaudreuil, Lower Canada, and they had one child; m. thirdly 19 Feb. 1844 Selina Wood in Montreal, and they had at least one child; d. 1 Feb. 1857 in Côte-Saint-Paul (Montreal).

William Evans arrived in Lower Canada in 1819, and soon settled at Côte-Saint-Paul to run a farm. At 33 he was already experienced, since in Ireland he had for some years managed a specialized operation to fatten livestock. Unfortunately nothing else is known about his early training and background. Until his death the pursuit of agriculture remained an important activity – Evans apparently never gave it up for long. He was one of the most dynamic farmers in the Montreal region. All of the 150 acres he owned at Côte-Saint-Paul in 1851 were under cultivation and he apparently also farmed about 40 additional acres in the same region. The abundance of his production, which was varied and included a certain amount of seed grain, placed Evans clearly above the average farmer at that time. In addition, the farm had 22 head of cattle, which he and his eldest son, William, looked after, no doubt with hired help since the household included five servants. He regularly put his theories into practice and carried out experiments; according to Pierre-Joseph-Olivier Chauveau*, his was a genuine model farm.

Evans apparently was not to have any significant source of income but farming. His other activities as agronomist and writer cost him more than they earned, to judge by the petitions he submitted to the Legislative Assembly of the Province of Canada in the 1840s and 1850s to obtain money. Towards the end of his life he persuaded William to start a business in seed grain and agricultural implements. However, the extent to which he shared financially in this undertaking is unknown.

Evans began to gain renown from the time of his appointment as secretary of the Agricultural Society of the District of Montreal, which probably occurred in 1830. During the first half of the 19th century the reform of agriculture in Lower Canada was left to such bodies. The first, the Agricultural Society of Canada, had been founded in 1789, and in time a decentralized structure had developed with district organizations in Montreal, Quebec, Trois-Rivières, the Gaspé, and Saint-François. Having originally attracted for the most part merchants or gentlemen farmers, these bodies then tried to reach ordinary farmers through county associations. According to historian Vernon Clifford Fowke, the main problem of these societies was their failure to have much impact on the bulk of the farmers. This failure was probably attributable to several factors: the members were of British origin and, because of various barriers such as language and farming practices, their endeavours did not reach French Canadian farmers. As secretary-treasurer of the Montreal society, Evans soon sought to promote the creation of county associations. According to the *Journal du cultivateur et Procédés de la Chambre d'agriculture du Bas-Canada*, he was the first to suggest that in agricultural competitions there should be a separate class for French Canadians. The division of competitions into three categories – "Canadian practical farmers," "British Canadians," and "all competitors" – was necessary in order to attract French Canadian entrants, who had no chance of winning when competing with farmers of British origin. The organizing of these competitions was considered the agricultural societies' prime task; it was thought that in this way emulation would be fostered, and thus, in the members' view, progress would be achieved. Evans held his office for as long as the Montreal organization lasted, and then performed the same duties in the Agricultural Society of Lower Canada, which was founded in 1847. This society in turn disappeared, and Evans in 1852 became secretary-treasurer of the new Board of Agriculture of Lower Canada.

In addition to these activities of a quasi-official nature, Evans worked at various other levels. Because of his concern for the progress of agriculture, he turned to writing and in the 1830s tried his hand at agricultural journalism. In this period there was no periodical devoted to agriculture. He therefore contributed to the *Montreal Gazette* and the *Montreal Courier*, before attempting to launch his own publication. In May 1838 he began publishing the *Canadian Quarterly Agricultural and Industrial Magazine*, but because of a dearth of readers the journal ceased in August with the second issue. In 1842, while remaining in Montreal, Evans became the editor of the *British American Cultivator*, a monthly published in Toronto by William Graham EDMUNDSON and John Eastwood. He occupied this post until April 1843, when financial problems forced Edmundson to take over as editor. In January of that year Evans had begun to publish in Montreal the *Canadian Agricultural Journal*, which included a French edition at irregular intervals and which under various titles lasted until 1868.

Evans also expressed his interest in agriculture through the publication of treatises. His first work, *A treatise on the theory and practice of agriculture*, came out in 1835 at Montreal. It consisted of five parts: the first surveyed the history of agriculture; the second, which was more theoretical, focused on the "science of agriculture"; the third and fourth dealt with the cultivation of various plants; and the fifth examined cattle raising. In this work as in others, Evans reiterated the necessity of systematic experimentation when making any innovation. In his opinion farmers should first try new ideas on a small scale before adopting them.

The assembly had voted funds for a French translation of his treatise, which appeared the next year. Evans provided a sequel in 1836 but this *Supplementary volume*, which completed his examination of questions related to the establishment of new farmers on their land, as well as of the conditions governing the development of agriculture in general, was not translated. The following year he published a further study dealing with instruction in farming, a matter of great importance in his view. *Agricultural*

improvement by the education of those who are engaged in it as a profession took the form of a collection of 12 letters, which sought to demonstrate the interest that the farming community would have in better training. Finally, under the title *Review of the agriculture of Lower Canada, with suggestions for its amelioration*, Evans in 1856 published a series of his articles taken from the *Montreal Gazette*. These articles constituted a survey of Lower Canadian agriculture, and included suggestions for its improvement. His works bear the mark of a cultivated and well-informed mind. The authors he quoted in his treatise, from the economist Adam Smith to the English agronomist William Marshall, give eloquent testimony to his erudition. His repeated references to English, French, and American examples further show that he was familiar with the latest agricultural developments in other countries.

In Evans's writings there is always a double preoccupation: the advancement of farming and the constant concern for placing agriculture in a wider socio-economic context. Thus the *Supplementary volume* contains not only a description of the British North American colonies, but also discussions about the price of land, problems of land clearance, transportation systems, and other subjects more directly related to farming.

A harsh observer of farm practices yet indulgent towards farmers, Evans never missed an opportunity to criticize what he saw as deficiencies in Lower Canada. His attitude may have been dictated by his conviction that agricultural production was basic to all economic development in the colony. By 1835 he had passed severe judgement on what would be called in the 20th century subsistence farming: "A farmer who systematically consumes each year the production of his land without establishing for himself any reserve of produce, useful improvements, or money, makes no kind of contribution to individual or national wealth." In his treatise he also attacked the routine, persistent attachment to growing wheat, even though the harvests were by then meagre. He suggested that farmers should sow other cereals and vary their rotation of crops.

On 8 Aug. 1850 Evans testified before the select committee set up by the Legislative Assembly to inquire into the state of agriculture in Lower Canada. He listed the principal weaknesses in agricultural techniques as inadequate drainage, ineffective use of manure, shallow ploughing, insufficient weed control, and poor pasturage. In his 1856 collection of articles he again made mention of these elements, adding the problems of raising cattle and a few others of lesser magnitude. He also proposed that a network of small model farms be created, and suggested that the Province of Canada should follow the British government's lead in instituting a system of loans to farmers to enable them to undertake major drainage projects. It can thus be seen that Evans was sound in his criticism of agriculture and that his notions of improvements were not impracticable. He fully realized that many transformations would come about in the long run, but for him this was no reason not to make a start on them.

Unfortunately, Evans's influence was limited. Despite the constant care not to give offence to French Canadian farmers shown in all his writings, he did not succeed in changing farming practices. It may well be thought that, given the situation at the time, publishing treatises and newspaper articles was not the best way to reach the great majority of farmers. Evans himself was under no illusions, for shortly before his death he expressed serious doubts about the effects of his endeavours. However, his action was not futile, for agriculture in Lower Canada would enter upon a period of profound change during the second half of the 19th century. Evans did play an important role in the development of agronomy in Lower Canada. At a time when initial, halting steps were being taken in this discipline, he was a pioneer in gleaning knowledge and shaping practice.

JEAN-CLAUDE ROBERT

William Evans is the author of *A treatise on the theory and practice of agriculture, adapted to the cultivation and economy of the animal and vegetable productions of agriculture in Canada; with a concise history of agriculture; and a view of its present state in some of the principal countries of the earth, and particularly in the British Isles, and in Canada* (Montreal, 1835). A French translation was prepared by Amury Girod* as *Traité théorique et pratique de l'agriculture, adapté à la culture et à l'économie des productions animales et végétales de cet art en Canada; avec un précis de l'histoire de l'agriculture et un aperçu de son état actuel dans quelques-uns des principaux pays, et particulièrement dans les Îles britanniques et le Canada* (Montreal, 1836–37). Evans also wrote a *Supplementary volume to "A treatise on the theory and practice of agriculture, adapted to the cultivation and economy of the animal and vegetable productions of agriculture in Canada"* (Montreal, 1836), as well as *Agricultural improvement by the education of those who are engaged in it as a profession; addressed, very respectfully, to the farmers of Canada* (Montreal, 1837); *Suggestions sur la subdivision et l'économie d'une ferme, dans les seigneuries du Bas-Canada, avec divers plans et dessins* (Montréal, 1854), also published in English as *Suggestions for the sub-dividing and management of a farm in the seignories of Lower Canada, with plans and description of a farm, dwelling house, dairy, farm yard, and farm buildings; prepared for the local exhibition at Montreal, March, 1855* (Montreal, 1855); and *Review of the agriculture of Lower Canada, with suggestions for its amelioration* (Montreal, 1856).

ANQ-M, CE1-63, 26 déc. 1842, 19 févr. 1844, 1ᵉʳ févr. 1857; CE1-67, 27 janv. 1842. PAC, RG 31, A1, 1825, Montreal, city; 1851, Montreal, parish. Can., Prov. of,

Legislative Assembly, *Journals*, 1844–45, 1848, 1849, 1850; Special Committee on the State of Agriculture in Lower Canada, *Report* (Toronto, 1850). *Debates of the Legislative Assembly of United Canada* (Abbott Gibbs *et al.*), vols.4, 7–9. *Farmer's Journal and Transactions of the Lower Canada Board of Agriculture* (Montreal), March, September 1857. J. F. W. Johnston, *Notes on North America, agricultural, economical, and social* (2v., Edinburgh and London, 1851), 1. *Le Journal de Québec*, 5 févr. 1857. *Montreal Gazette*, 3 Feb. 1857. *Montreal Transcript*, 5 Feb. 1857. Beaulieu et Hamelin, *La presse québécoise*, vol.1. Borthwick, *Hist. and biog. gazetteer*. Le Jeune, *Dictionnaire*. *Montreal almanack*, 1829–31. *Montreal directory*, 1842–57. Morgan, *Bibliotheca Canadensis*; *Sketches of celebrated Canadians*. Terrill, *Chronology of Montreal*. Wallace, *Macmillan dict.* V. C. Fowke, *Canadian agricultural policy; the historical pattern* (Toronto, 1978). Firmin Létourneau, *Histoire de l'agriculture (Canada français)* (Montréal, 1959). Fernand Ouellet, *Histoire économique et sociale du Québec, 1760–1850: structures et conjoncture* (Montréal et Paris, [1966]). M.-A. Perron, *Un grand éducateur agricole: Édouard-A. Barnard, 1835–1898; essai historique sur l'agriculture de 1760 à 1900* ([Montréal], 1955). Normand Séguin, "L'histoire de l'agriculture et de la colonisation au Québec depuis 1850," *Agriculture et colonisation au Québec; aspects historiques*, Normand Séguin, édit. (Montréal, 1980). P.-J.-O. Chauveau, "William Evans, l'agronome," *Journal de l'Instruction publique* (Québec et Montréal), 1 (1857): 33–34.

EWART, JAMES BELL, businessman, justice of the peace, office holder, politician, and gentleman farmer; b. *c.* 1801 in Surrey, England; m. 23 May 1832 Mary Margaret Crooks, daughter of James CROOKS, and they had at least two sons and two daughters; d. 17 Dec. 1853 in Dundas, Upper Canada, and was buried at nearby Crooks' Hollow (near present-day Greensville).

In 1817 James Bell Ewart immigrated to Upper Canada, where he accepted a clerkship in the large mercantile firm of Thomas Clark* and Samuel Street* at Niagara (Niagara-on-the-Lake). Three years later, while still in their employ, he opened a general store in Coote's Paradise (Dundas), near the head of Lake Ontario. He did not move there, however, until 1825, when he left Clark and Street and purchased the Dundas Mills from the estate of Richard Hatt*.

Ewart quickly dominated business at Dundas. Although his success was based on a diversity of enterprise, his principal activities were grain trading and milling at various locations throughout the western regions of the province. Besides the grist-mill at Dundas, with its ancillary cooperage, distillery, and blacksmith shop, he owned mills in Waterloo Township, Galt (Cambridge), Dawn Mills, St George, and Ayr. In partnership with John Gartshore, Ewart financed the establishment of the large Dundas Foundry in 1838. As part of his early mercantile activity he also operated a private bank; then, from

Ewart

1832 to 1844, he held the Dundas agency of the Commercial Bank of the Midland District, of which he was president in 1841. He took up the agency in Dundas of the Bank of British North America in 1844, possibly because of that institution's more extensive operations in the western section of Upper Canada.

Like many general merchants of the period, Ewart acted as a land agent for non-resident clients and business associates. A major landowner in Dundas, he also built up extensive property holdings throughout Upper Canada, notably in Waterloo, West Oxford, and Puslinch townships. Shortly before his death he had begun his most ambitious real estate venture, the development of land on Lake Simcoe (now the village of Bell Ewart) into a major port and a depot on the Ontario, Simcoe and Huron Union Rail-road.

Ewart actively supported transportation projects which would enhance the commercial position of Dundas and facilitate his grain trade. A shareholder in the Desjardins Canal Company [see Pierre Desjardins*], he was also a founding director of two road companies: the Guelph and Dundas (incorporated in 1847) and the Dundas and Paris (1850). He was an early promoter of the London and Gore Rail Road (1834) and a director of its successor, the Great Western Rail-Road. Ewart and Sir Allan Napier MacNab* travelled to Great Britain in 1845, at the height of its boom in railway shares, to arrange financing for the Great Western. They were joined in this effort by Peter BUCHANAN of Glasgow and Malcolm Cowan, a London solicitor. The collapse of the boom that year panicked investors, but Ewart remained sanguine and urged cautious progress on the line which, he maintained, was "no doubt the best in British North America."

As Dundas's leading businessman of the period, Ewart was highly visible in the community's social and political life. He belonged to the St Andrew's Society, keenly supporting its curling club, and was an active member of the Church of England. The holder of a number of offices and appointments, he was first commissioned a justice of the peace in 1833; from 20 Dec. 1837 to his death he served as postmaster of Dundas. He led the movement for its incorporation as a town in 1847 and two years later succeeded John PATERSON as president of the town council.

For most of his career Ewart was a wealthy man; in 1845 his financial worth was estimated at £100,000. His commercial and public success permitted him to enjoy the role of a gentleman farmer at his beloved Carfin Farm, near Dundas, where he raised prize-winning cattle. The farm, which he bequeathed to his eldest son, James Bell, was the part of his estate for which Ewart left the most carefully detailed instructions in his will in 1852, at which time his other interests were suffering. He had experienced heavy losses in the wheat market and in 1846 both Galt Mills

and Gartshore's founding shops in Dundas had burned. Although he was able to finance the reconstruction of both facilities, he was forced to assume a heavy burden of indebtedness on mortgages (£5,000) against his Dundas property alone. At his death the mortgages had not been retired and his creditors were compelled to sue his estate.

DAVID G. BURLEY

AO, MS 35, letter-books, 1839–43: 128; 1844–49: 109; RG 22, ser.155, will of J. B. Ewart. BLHU, R. G. Dun & Co. credit ledger, Canada, 25: 155. Dundas Hist. Soc. Museum (Dundas, Ont.), Richard Hatt, folder no.2, indenture between J. B. Ewart and Hatt estate, 28 Dec. 1830. PAC, MG 24, D16, 25: 21558–61; RG 31, A1, 1851, Waterloo Township, pt.5: 288; Galt Village: 19; RG 68, General index, 1651–1841: 474, 511. Simcoe Land Registry Office (Barrie, Ont.), Abstract index to deeds, Innisfil and Medonte townships: 68–70, 273 (mfm. at AO, GS 5437). Can., Prov. of, Legislative Assembly, App. to the journals, 1846, app.F. Cobourg Star, 30 May 1832. Dundas Warder, 13 Nov. 1846; 2 July, 8 Oct. 1847; 7 April 1848; 21 Aug. 1851; 23 Dec. 1853; 31 March 1854. Dundas Weekly Post, 25 Aug., 8 Dec. 1835; 19 Jan. 1836. Western Mercury (Hamilton, [Ont.]), 17 March 1831, 18 Oct. 1832, 18 July 1833. Canada directory, 1851: 74. The history of the town of Dundas, comp. T. R. Woodhouse (3v., [Dundas], 1965–68). Johnson, Hist. of Guelph, 86. Douglas McCalla, "Peter Buchanan, London agent for the Grand Western Railway of Canada," Canadian business history; selected studies, 1497–1971, ed. D. S. Macmillan (Toronto, 1972), 198–99. R. D. Smith, "The early years of the Grand Western Railway, 1833–1857," OH, 60 (1968): 205–27.

EWART (Euart), JOHN, architect, builder, and businessman; b. 31 Jan. 1788 in Tranent, Scotland, son of William Euart and Margaret Dobson; m. 1810 Jane Wilson of the parish of Cranston, Scotland, and they had 11 children; d. 18 Sept. 1856 in Toronto.

By 1810 John Ewart had completed his apprenticeship in the building trade and had qualifed as a free craftsman. Presumably he was employed on construction projects in Edinburgh's New Town but after 1811, like many other ambitious Scottish builders, he moved to London, possibly in the hope of securing lucrative commissions or recognition as an architect. The death there of two of his children, and the building recession which followed the Napoleonic Wars, may have led to his decision to emigrate with his family to New York City about 1816. Within three years the Ewarts had moved to York (Toronto), Upper Canada. Although the town's building needs following the War of 1812 had attracted "many good tradesmen," Ewart was quickly recognized as a builder of some accomplishment and found work almost at once. His first recorded building contract was for the York Hospital (1819–20), a plain, Georgian-style structure which was well within his competence as a designer, but it was almost certainly planned in consultation with Dr William Warren Baldwin*, a prominent physician and lawyer.

The following decade, the most creative of Ewart's career in Canada, marked his development as York's first architectural designer of merit. In 1822 he was commissioned to design and to build the town's first Roman Catholic church, St Paul's, on Chapel (Power) Street [see William John O'Grady*]. Carefully adapted to the scale of surrounding buildings, it was a modest but elegantly proportioned Regency interpretation of the baroque idiom long favoured in the Canadas by the Roman Catholic church but inspired here by Scottish churches known to Ewart, notably the parish church of St George in Glasgow (1807). Built of brick, which was less expensive than stone and a natural building material in muddy York, St Paul's was described in 1824 by James Baby*, a prominent parishioner, as "the neatest Building of the kind in U: Canada – to this may be added also the cheapest."

The provincial parliament building of 1818, the hospital, and St Paul's constituted the capital's few scattered monuments in 1824. (The wooden Anglican church and outlying Fort York, built largely of log and brick, counted for little.) As an urban complex the town fell miserably short of London, England, whose architectural panache Ewart remembered so well. Dignified buildings, particularly a concentration set in public space, were needed, and, in William Warren Baldwin, he found an influential townsman who shared his conviction and sometimes helped him to realize it.

The Home District court-house and jail were planned by Ewart in 1824 (with some features based on Baldwin's legal experience) and erected as a pair of pedimented brick buildings, set back from King Street and toward either side of a square bounded by King, Toronto, Newgate (Adelaide), and Church streets which had been laid out by Ewart. The architectural quality of the two buildings and the siting suggest that Ewart anticipated the construction of a majestic central edifice, a version of which was later designed by John George Howard* but never built. The northern face of the square was soon completed by the erection of two churches of harmonious form: Robert Petch's Newgate Street Methodist Chapel, backing on to the jail's yard, and St Andrew's Church, designed in 1830 by Ewart, a member of that Presbyterian congregation, and set behind the court-house. For this design, executed in time for the arrival of the Reverend William RINTOUL, he evidently used architectural features derived from the Regency work of John Soane in Britain: tall pilasters, untrimmed window openings, crisply incised linear panelling of the exterior walls, and, at roof level, stilted acroteria (some of which contained chimneys). The square was a brave attempt to combine law and order, religion, and urban amenity in the commercial heart of the town.

Ewart's second court-house, designed in 1827 for the London District of Upper Canada, differed markedly from its counterpart in York. An open and uneven site located between the proposed town of London and the Thames River suggested a feudal ambience and hence the use of stone, but economy dictated brick. Financed by the mercantile firm of Thomas Clark* and Samuel Street*, the court-house was a Regency Gothic building, reminiscent of James Wyatt's Royal Military Academy in Woolwich (London), England, which had been newly built when Ewart arrived there. The court-house, a rectangular building with a buttressed, octagonal tower at each corner, was and still is a picturesque but functional structure, designed to complement a rustic setting by one who understood the Romantic prelude to the Victorian Gothic revival in architecture.

In 1826 Ewart had made an unsuccessful bid for a much debated architectural plum: designing a replacement for the parliament building, which had burned two years earlier. Plans were submitted by Ewart, Baldwin, John Ford, and Joseph Nixon, who won the competition – an empty triumph as plans were later provided by Thomas ROGERS of Kingston. The nature of Ewart's design is not known but, as a builder, he retained an interest in York's grandest public building; following the failure of the contractor, Matthew Priestman, Ewart and Thomas Parke* became the first overseers of construction for the complex, which opened in 1832.

The plans which Ewart apparently provided for Upper Canada College, built at York in 1829–30, are lost. His last known commission, a complex of three pavilions named after William Osgoode*, was undertaken in 1829 for the Law Society of Upper Canada; one pavilion, a parapetted brick building, was built and the following year a lateral dormitory was added. Although most of Osgoode Hall's Regency features were subsequently masked by the remodelling and additions of Henry Bowyer Joseph LANE and the firm of Cumberland and Storm, Ewart's smooth, spare trim still curves around the original entrance. Trim of the same plasticity, so characteristic of his work, also informs the doorway of the Bank of Upper Canada, begun at the corner of Duke (Adelaide) and George streets in 1825. This was probably another result of the successful collaboration between Ewart, who understood the design of buildings, and Baldwin, who recognized the architectural needs of York.

After 1830 Ewart abandoned active design work. The architectural styles best known to him were becoming increasingly unfashionable and he may have begun to suffer from the bane of many builders, hardening of the leg arteries (he was to die of gangrene). He nevertheless maintained a building yard and a wharf until his death. His highly lucrative construction trade was probably carried out by subcontractors, an arrangement which evidently enabled him to return frequently to Great Britain and to New York on business. In Toronto he remained prominent in several institutions and enterprises, and within the city's architectural community. He was a life-long trustee of the York General Burying Ground (laid out in 1826), first president of the York Mechanics' Institute in 1830, a founding member six years later of the benevolent St Andrew's Society of Toronto, and president in 1840 of the Toronto Cricket Club. An extensive property owner and proponent of Toronto's development as a major transportation terminus, he was a founding director in 1837, along with William ALLAN and others, of the City of Toronto and Lake Huron Rail Road Company, with which he was involved for some ten years; in 1843 he prepared experimental designs for road-beds. In 1841 Ewart, Robert Sympson JAMESON, Dr William Charles Gwynne*, and William Botsford Jarvis* were named to a board to superintend the province's temporary lunatic asylum [see William Rees*]. Four years later, with a group of other builders and architects (including Henry Bowyer Joseph Lane, Thomas Storm, and William THOMAS), he also served on a committee chaired by William Henry Boulton* to form a building and loan society.

Of John Ewart's eleven children, seven lived to maturity; none followed him as a builder or as a designer. Two sons, John and George, took up mercantile activities in Toronto, much of their backing coming from their father. Following Ewart's death his financial worth was estimated at £100,000. His mantle of public service fell to a daughter, Jane, the wife of Sir Oliver Mowat*, and to a grandson, John Skirving Ewart*, a distinguished lawyer and author who died in 1933.

MARION BELL MACRAE

An unsigned study of shops for Market Lane, Toronto, attributed to John Ewart, is preserved in MTL, J. G. Howard papers, sect.III, architectural plans, no.410.

AAT, Ser.1, AB01.07. AO, RG 22, ser.155, will of John Ewart. BLHU, R. G. Dun & Co. credit ledger, Canada, 26: 64, 350. GRO (Edinburgh), Tranent, reg. of baptisms, 31 Jan., 10 Feb. 1788. MTL, William Allan papers, City of Toronto and Lake Huron Rail Road Company papers, John Ewart, reports to the president and directors, 1 Aug., 6 Dec. 1845; J. G. Howard papers, sect.II, diaries, 19 July 1841; 3, 8 May 1843; 18 April–2 May 1845. PAC, RG 5, A1: 41612–14, 54861–62, 57196–211, 58629–41, 69561–67, 69814–18, 73396–97, 74105–10, 77624–26, 87344–46, 119540–41. Private arch., Janet Fitzgerald (Toronto), Ewart family papers and records. Toronto Necropolis and Crematorium, Reg. of burials. UWOL, Regional Coll., Vertical file, no.412 (London, Court-house and gaol, corr. and accounts relative to building, 1826–28). *Town of York, 1815–34* (Firth), 41–42, 324n. U.C., House of Assembly, *Journal*, 1831–32, app.: 96–99; *Statutes*, 1836, c.5. *Examiner* (Toronto), 9 Sept. 1840, 6 Oct. 1844. *Globe*, 2 Dec. 1845. *Leader*, daily ed., 20 Sept. 1860. *Toronto Patriot*, 28 Feb., 21 Aug. 1840; 10 Aug. 1841; 15 Oct. 1844. Alfred Sylvester, *Sketches of Toronto, comprising a complete and accurate description of the principal points of interest in the city, its public buildings . . .* (Toronto, 1858), 23, 29, 36, 56–57. *Toronto directory*, 1833–34: 11; 1846–47: 24, 36. [G. P. Ure], *The hand-book of Toronto; containing its climate, geology, natural history, educational institutions, courts of law, municipal arrangements, &c.&c, by a member of the press* (Toronto, 1858), 171, 268.

Eric Arthur, *Toronto, no mean city* ([Toronto], 1964), 65. C. K. Clarke, *A history of the Toronto General Hospital . . .* (Toronto, 1913). *Hist. of Middlesex*, 91. Law Soc. of U.C., *Osgoode Hall: a short account of the hall, issued by the Law Society of Upper Canada, 1832–1932* (Toronto, 1932), 8. MacRae and Adamson, *Cornerstones of order.* MacRae et al., *Hallowed walls*, 85. Middleton, *Municipality of Toronto*, 1: 440; 2: 746–47. *Robertson's landmarks of Toronto*, 4: 121. C. T. Campbell, "The beginning of London," *OH*, 9 (1910): 73.

EYNON, ELIZABETH. *See* DART

F

FABRE, ÉDOUARD-RAYMOND (baptized **Raymond**), bookseller, Patriote, and politician; b. 15 Sept. 1799 in Montreal, son of Pierre Fabre and Marie-Anne Lamontagne; d. there 16 July 1854.

Édouard-Raymond Fabre came from a family of humble origins. His forebear Raymond Fabre, a master ironsmith from Montpellier, France, immigrated to New France in 1745. Little is known about Édouard-Raymond's parents. His father, a carpenter in Montreal towards the end of the 18th century, was married there in 1794. Eight children were born, but

only the four eldest, Josephte, Julie, Sophie, and Édouard-Raymond, reached adulthood.

Apart from a few sentimental reminiscences suggesting a happy childhood, Édouard-Raymond Fabre is silent in his writings about the first 20 years of his life. It is known, however, that the path he chose for himself soon separated him from his family, although he remained staunchly loyal to them all his life. The Fabres were not well off but they were not among the large number of poor to be found in Montreal throughout the first half of the 19th century.

Consequently Pierre Fabre was able to send Édouard-Raymond to the Petit Séminaire de Montréal, where he studied from 1807 to 1812. The following year, at the age of 14, the boy became a clerk in the hardware store of Arthur Webster, who ran one of the biggest commercial establishments in Montreal; he worked there for nine years. In this firm he familiarized himself with all aspects of business practice: bookkeeping, credit, financing, and management for profit.

Fabre's interest in business was diversified through his contacts with Hector Bossange, whose father, Martin, was a famous Parisian bookseller. Hector, after a brief stay at Quebec, settled in Montreal and in 1815 opened the Bossange bookstore as a branch of the Galeries Bossange in Paris, then considered among the largest firms in the business. Shortly after arriving in Montreal, Bossange began to visit the Fabres, and in 1816 he married Julie, who was both friend and confidante to her brother Édouard-Raymond.

In 1822 Fabre left Montreal for Paris, where in the course of a year he acquired a working knowledge of the bookseller's trade at the Galeries Bossange. His going to France showed that he liked change, enjoyed taking risks, and had a conscious desire for independence. In "the world's premier city," which he would visit again in 1843, Fabre learned about the complex financial, commercial, and cultural aspects of the trade he would take up on his return to Montreal. He was to be the first real bookseller in Lower Canada.

Back in Montreal in 1823, Fabre purchased from Théophile Dufort the goodwill of a bookstore that had belonged to the Bossange firm and had been acquired by Dufort in 1819. Fabre soon added to its modest stock through the good contacts he had made in France. From 1823 to 1828 this store was known as the Librairie Française or Librairie Édouard-Raymond Fabre. During this period Fabre married, on 2 May 1826 in Montreal, Luce Perrault, the daughter of Julien Perrault. In this way he became allied to a family that, according to Laurent-Olivier David*, was one "of the oldest and most highly esteemed in [the] country." Because of difficulties in choosing stock for his French Canadian clientele Fabre terminated the special relations he had maintained with the Bossange firm, and in 1828 went into partnership with his brother-in-law Louis Perrault*, a printer. The two men did business under the name Librairie Fabre et Perrault until 1835. To improve his services, on several occasions Fabre sent Perrault to Europe on buying trips. The initial plan was that Perrault would "establish himself in Paris," since Fabre wanted to have a permanent agent there to conduct his business more efficiently and avoid costly middlemen. In 1835 Fabre and Perrault dissolved their partnership, and the bookstore resumed the name Librairie Française or

Librairie Édouard-Raymond Fabre, with Fabre announcing that the business would remain in operation under his name alone.

That year Fabre hired Jean-Adolphe Gravel, the son of his sister Sophie, as a clerk. His bookstore occupied the first floor of a large stone dwelling at the corner of Rue Saint-Vincent and Rue Notre-Dame. The house was owned by the Perrault family and was rented by Fabre until 1844, when he bought the property, and there fitted up "a magnificent shop in the French style, 20 feet by 60." In the same year he took Gravel, only 24 at the time, into partnership, and the Société Fabre et Gravel was set up. The description of the assets put in by uncle and nephew indicates that Fabre invested £3,755 12s. 0d. in the company, and Gravel contributed his time, industry, and talents. The partners at first shared profits and losses unequally but after a time split them on an equal basis. Until his death in 1854 Fabre remained in the book trade with Gravel. In the course of his 31 years in business Fabre was thus involved in three partnerships with a common element: all three partners were, in varying degrees, his relatives.

The clientele of the Fabre firm consisted of members of the clergy and the liberal professions, teachers, students, and businessmen. The 1830, 1835, and 1837 catalogues show the predominance of, and progression in, religious texts. This evolution is a significant one. Religious knowledge and change in styles of devotion and piety were fostered in Lower Canada by numerous printed works, which no doubt decisively influenced the expansion and maintenance of the new trends.

The firm's inventories also demonstrate an obvious decline in literary and philosophical works as compared with religious and school texts. The catalogues of the 1830s included the chief philosophical and literary works of the time, as well as the great writings of ecclesiastical authors such as St Augustine, Bourdaloue, Abbé François, François de Sales, Fénelon, and Bossuet, but the 1854–55 catalogue was no longer of this exceptional quality.

The increase in the quantity of pedagogical texts, which was linked with the great strides being made in primary education, was a major factor in the development of Fabre's business. This increase occurred at the expense of jurisprudence, history, and politics, and, surprisingly enough, of technical subjects and trades. The first catalogues presented a whole body of works related to apprenticeships (the 1837 one offered theoretical and practical manuals for 38 different trades) which apparently were of interest to quite a large clientele, but they virtually disappeared from the shelves of the Librairie Fabre et Gravel, judging by the 1854–55 inventory.

It is difficult to be precise about the changing nature of the merchandise carried by the Fabre firm.

Fabre

According to advertisements in *La Minerve*, before his trip to Paris in 1843 Fabre was offering, besides a fairly wide range of volumes, such items as envelopes, account-books, ledgers, visiting cards, pens, sketching pencils, and paper suitable for writing, drawing, and printing. In addition, the store sold books of worship, religious pictures and engravings, lithographs, maps, school supplies, and gift-books. The Librairie Fabre was the repository of official documents in Montreal, including provincial statutes and ordinances and acts of the imperial parliament relating to Lower Canada. From 1830 it carried various objects used in worship: chalices, ciboria, monstrances, holy-water basins, altar cards, pascal candlesticks, stations of the cross in soft cloth, and basins for baptismal fonts.

As a result of Fabre's trip to Paris in 1843, the merchandise offered by his firm was modified substantially. The volume of transactions he had carried out in France can be surmised from the announcement he made in *La Minerve* on his return. It states that Fabre was waiting for "about 80 cases and bales" containing in part goods traditionally sold in his bookstore but in addition an entirely new category of merchandise, including perfume, gloves, shoes, umbrellas, suspenders, ties, champagne, absinth, and gruyère cheese.

From 1828 to 1835 Fabre et Perrault owned a printing shop which was extremely active, publishing at least five titles a year. There were many ways to finance publishing in Lower Canada at that time: by subscription or agreement in advance to purchase, by association between a bookseller and a printer in return for exclusive rights of sale, or by agreements between booksellers. As an example, the Fabre firm and that of John Neilson* in Quebec concluded agreements concerning exchanges of works published by either house. In all, 49 publications have been found with which the Fabre firm was associated between 1827 and 1854.

The company's operations as a whole – publishing, book-binding, and importing books and various types of goods – ensured Fabre's financial success. Behind this success can be seen his ability to balance the goods offered with the main areas of demand, and to establish stable, diversified relations with publishers and booksellers in France. As a businessman he showed himself able to adapt to changing circumstances concerning power and resources. He knew how to turn to account the rising forces of conservatism and clericalism.

Although Fabre devoted tremendous energy to ensuring the success of his business, he found the great political debates of his time no less absorbing. By 1827 he was moving in the Montreal Patriote circles frequented by his brother-in-law and friend Charles-Ovide Perrault*, who was then a clerk

working for Denis-Benjamin Viger*, the cousin of Louis-Joseph Papineau*. According to his biographer, Joseph Doutre*, Fabre first became involved in political developments during both the general elections that year and the mission of Viger, Neilson, and Augustin Cuvillier* in England in 1828. He was soon strongly influencing the actions of public figures, and his office became the daily meeting-place for the leaders of the Patriote party. It was in this context that Fabre consolidated his business and gradually began to take a part in the public affairs of Lower Canada prior to the rebellion of 1837.

From 1832 to 1837 Fabre held offices and exerted an influence of prime importance in the institutions set up by the Patriotes. In 1832 he was a founding member of the Maison Canadienne de Commerce. He was secretary of this group's first meeting, held at the Nelson Hotel, gathering there with his friends Côme-Séraphin Cherrier*, Pierre-Dominique Larocque, Dominique Mondelet*, and Pierre-Dominique Debartzch*. The Maison Canadienne de Commerce sought to draw French Canadian business circles together, to ensure that they worked their way "into big business," and to set up warehouses for imported goods from which retail merchants could obtain supplies without having to go through the large British houses. This initiative embodied the clearly expressed intention of an élite mainly composed of Montreal reformers to channel and control the savings of ordinary people, with a view to using them as a powerful weapon in its struggle against the colony's government. In 1834 Fabre signed the act of association for the creation of the Banque du Peuple with, among others, Louis-Michel Viger, Jacob De Witt, and Joseph Roy. He was appointed treasurer of the bank, and received subscriptions for it at his offices. The Banque du Peuple opened in 1835.

That year Fabre took part with Denis-Benjamin Viger, De Witt, Roy, Augustin-Norbert Morin*, Edmund Bailey O'Callaghan*, Léon Asselin, and André Ouimet in the founding of the Union Patriotique in Montreal. The aims of this association were to spread knowledge, obtain responsible government, improve means of communication in the colony, secure the prompt and cheap administration of justice, and oppose by all means undue intervention by the Colonial Office, the Treasury, or the War Office. These goals were exactly those of the Patriote party as succinctly expressed in a letter sent in 1834 by the Patriote leaders of the Montreal region to those of the Quebec region. Fabre was made treasurer of the Union Patriotique. Besides his simultaneous responsibilities at the Maison Canadienne de Commerce, the Banque du Peuple, and the Union Patriotique, in 1835 he was a member of the group that owned the steamship *Le Patriote*. In April of that year he was elected secretary-treasurer of the general management committee of this group and of its executive committee. He was also closely connected with the new Association Saint-Jean-Baptiste, being one of its most active organizers in Montreal.

Fabre gave considerable financial help to the information and publicity agencies of the Patriote party. He made sure that *La Minerve*, Ludger DUVERNAY's newspaper, was kept going. When in 1832 Duvernay was jailed for libel, Fabre immediately intervened, promising the editor on his arrest that he would "put [his] affairs in order." In 1836 Duvernay was in jail again for libel. Fabre launched and chaired a great fund-raising drive "to compensate M. Duvernay for his imprisonment." Fabre had also purchased in 1832 the *Vindicator and Canadian Advertiser*, an English-language paper of Patriote allegiance which his friend O'Callaghan was to run.

Having become a friend of Papineau, for whom he had unbounded admiration, Fabre served as his adviser before the rebellion. He accompanied Papineau to the principal meetings that preceded the outbreak of the rebellion. On 15 May 1837 he participated in the one at Saint-Laurent, where he was elected a delegate to the Convention Générale, a sort of estates general of the Patriotes, and a member of the permanent committee to attend to the political interests of Montreal riding. On 28 June he chaired the great protest meeting in Montreal, where Papineau in effect launched the insurrectionary movement. Fabre opened proceedings by invoking the rights of the people and warning of the looming dangers of a tyranny.

A few hours before the rebellion broke out on 23 Nov. 1837, Fabre appeared at Saint-Denis on the Richelieu to persuade Papineau and O'Callaghan to flee to the United States. He himself did not leave Lower Canada, but he had to absent himself from Montreal for seven months. He stayed in hiding at Contrecœur, Lavaltrie, or neighbouring villages. Besides having to endure separation from his family and friends, Fabre was upset by his wife's state of health following a miscarriage, as well as by the death of his brother-in-law, Charles-Ovide Perrault, in the battle of Saint-Denis. He was finally arrested and sent to jail in Montreal on 12 Dec. 1838; according to Doutre, the authorities, lacking evidence, were forced to release him a month later. Considering his activity before November 1837, it is amazing that he was not arrested sooner. His imprisonment must therefore be attributed to the attempted invasion of Lower Canada under Robert Nelson* and Cyrille-Hector-Octave Côté*.

Once the rebellion was over, Fabre did not ignore the plight of the French Canadians in exile. At first he served as an intermediary between Lower Canada and some of the refugees, particularly Papineau and Duvernay. During Papineau's exile Fabre still remained his friend. In 1843 he went to Paris for reasons of business but also to see "his very dear friend." Fabre began to dream of the return of Papineau, whom he saw as French Canada's only saviour. Duvernay had already benefited from Fabre's support during his imprisonment, and in exile could still count on Fabre's being in Montreal and on his readiness to help. When Duvernay returned, D.-B. Viger and Fabre assisted in reorganizing *La Minerve*.

However, Fabre's action on behalf of the exiles went well beyond the small circle of his Montreal connections. On 19 Dec. 1843 *La Minerve* published an address which included a proposal to found the Association de la Délivrance. Fabre was appointed treasurer of the new body, and in this capacity played an outstanding role in solving the problem of the exiles' return. He left no stone unturned to secure their repatriation. By 1846 the last of them were back "in the homeland," and Fabre could congratulate himself on having completed his task.

As soon as Papineau returned in 1845, Fabre passionately wanted the former leader of the Patriote party to resume his place in the political arena. No matter what others thought, he was sure that Papineau's presence in the assembly would by itself re-establish his leadership. In the 1847–48 elections, which brought the overwhelming defeat of Denis-Benjamin Viger's government and the spectacular come-back of Louis-Hippolyte La Fontaine*, Papineau won a seat. He re-entered the Legislative Assembly in April 1848, but hopes soon fell: Papineau did not "create a sensation" in the house or regain his influence.

Increasingly isolated, the little group around Papineau, which included Fabre, had been worried since Viger's defeat about its bad relations with the press. Duvernay's *La Minerve* did not approve of the former Patriote leader's radicalism. But *L'Avenir*, as the mouthpiece for the Rouges of the Institut Canadien, had supported Papineau's views, particularly on annexation to the United States, and was becoming more radical. It clashed with the *Mélanges religieux*, the unofficial organ of the diocese of Montreal, over the delicate matter of relations between the religious and political authorities. Fabre had backed *L'Avenir*, but he severed his ties with it and in January 1852 started *Le Pays* with Jacques-Alexis Plinguet. This moderating intervention in the liberal press by Fabre was probably related to a need to pay attention to a certain clientele and institution – the church – whose growing strength was having important economic repercussions for his bookstore.

Fabre's commitment to public affairs led him at that time to take up municipal politics. In 1848 he yielded to urgent pleas from voters and stood as a candidate. He was easily elected councillor for the East Ward, and was nominated alderman and chairman of the finance committee of the council. In 1849 he was elected mayor of Montreal. It seems that Fabre's success as chairman of the finance committee explains his election, which came unsought. During his first term of office Fabre worked steadily to reorganize the city's finances under extremely difficult economic circumstances. He got the municipal council to adopt measures to suppress the riots which had led to the burning down of the Parliament Buildings in Montreal after the passing of the Rebellion Losses Act. He further applied himself to increasing protective and preventive measures to counter the cholera epidemic raging in the city that year. Re-elected by acclamation in 1850, against his own wishes he became mayor for a second term. In his farewell address on 28 Feb. 1851, he thanked the councillors and aldermen for their cooperation and used the occasion to sum up the achievements of the past two years of his administration. A close reading of this speech suggests that he exerted on the 11 departments and on the officials running them an influence that no mayor of Montreal had ever exercised before. In 1850 Fabre had also been elected president of the Association Saint-Jean-Baptiste de Montréal, an office he held for a year, at a time when his business and political activity, in the context of prevailing economic difficulties, left him scant opportunity to give attention to this "national" society.

Despite the demands of business and his constant participation in public affairs, Fabre was very involved in family life. Luce ran the household with a firm hand but regularly consulted her husband, who kept an eye on everything and in particular on the children's education. Of their 11 children, Édouard-Charles* became the first archbishop of Montreal, Hector* was the first representative of the Canadian government in Paris, and Hortense married George-Étienne Cartier*, whom Fabre described as "one of the most eligible bachelors of Montreal."

In 1854 Fabre again ran for mayor of Montreal, against Wolfred Nelson*. The election campaign was extremely violent. Fabre failed in his attempt and, exhausted, was stricken with cholera on 11 July and died five days later. On learning of his death, Papineau expressed the same friendship and admiration for Fabre that the Montreal bookseller had shown towards him. In a letter written a few days later he spoke of his deep feelings for this "constant and warm friend, comrade in arms during the constitutional struggles, [and] noble-hearted brother" who, with "unshakeable patriotic faith, abundant generosity and liberality, . . . rendered outstanding services to the country."

JEAN-LOUIS ROY

ACAM, 576, F; 902.002; RCD XXIX. ANQ-M, CE1-51, 15 sept. 1799, 2 mai 1826, 17 juill. 1854; CN1-135; CN1-295, 8 mai 1826; CN1-311, 25 oct. 1854–31 mars 1855; CN1-312, 17 mars 1842. ANQ-Q, P-9; P-68; P-69; P1000-37-694; P1000-76-1540. Arch. de la ville de Montréal, Doc. administratifs, commissions, 1843–54; divers, 1843–54; procès-verbaux du conseil municipal, 1843–54; règlements, 1843–54. McGill Univ. Libraries, Dept. of Rare Books and Special Coll. (Montreal), MS coll., "Livre de notes d'É.-R. Fabre" (Paris, 4 mai 1843–Montréal, 7 juill. 1843); lettre d'É.-R. Fabre. PAC, MG 24, B1, 1; B6, 1–5; B37, 1–2; B46, 1; B50; C3; RG 4, B37, 1–5. L'Avenir, juill. 1847–déc. 1854. Mélanges religieux, 1848–52. La Minerve, 1826–37, 1842–54. Montreal Gazette, 1849–54. Le Pays, janv. 1852–déc. 1854. Vindicator and Canadian Advertiser (Montreal), 1832–35. Montreal directory, 1842–54. Hector Berthelot, Montréal, le bon vieux temps, É.-Z. Massicotte, compil. (2v. in 1, 2ᵉ éd., Montréal, 1924), 2: 24–26. J. D. Borthwick, History of the Montreal prison from A.D. 1748 to A.D. 1886 . . . (Montreal, 1886), 67. David, Patriotes, 73–75. Joseph Doutre, "Notice biographique sur feu Édouard R. Fabre, écr. . . . ," Institut canadien en 1855, J.-L. Lafontaine, édit. (Montréal, 1855), 117–49. Antonio Drolet, Les bibliothèques canadiennes, 1604–1960 (Ottawa, 1965), 77. Hist. de Montréal (Lamothe et al.). Maurault, Le collège de Montréal (Dansereau; 1967). J.-L. Roy, Édouard-Raymond Fabre. Marcel Trudel, L'influence de Voltaire au Canada (2v., Montréal, 1945), 1: 128. Cabrette [É.-Z. Massicotte], "Les disparus," BRH, 30 (1924): 232. Alfred Duclos De Celles, "La maison canadienne," BRH, 11 (1905): 220. Édouard Fabre Surveyer, "Charles-Ovide Perrault (1809–1837)," RSC Trans., 3rd ser., 31 (1937), sect.I: 151–64; "Édouard-Raymond Fabre d'après sa correspondance et ses contemporains," 38 (1944), sect.I: 89–112. É.-Z. Massicotte, "Cinquante ans de librairie à Montréal," BRH, 49 (1943): 103–7; "Nos anciens présidents: Édouard-Raymond Fabre, président en 1850," La Rev. nationale (Montréal), 7 (1925): 283. Léon Trépanier, "Figures de maires: Édouard-Raymond Fabre," Cahiers des Dix, 24 (1959): 189–208.

FARIBAULT, JEAN-BAPTISTE, fur trader, militia officer, office holder, and farmer; b. 19 Oct. 1775 in Berthier-en-Haut (Berthierville), Que., son of Barthélemy Faribault* and Catherine-Antoine Véronneau; d. 20 Aug. 1860 in Faribault, Minn.

The son of a notary, Jean-Baptiste Faribault did not pursue his father's profession, although three of his brothers, including JOSEPH-ÉDOUARD, did so. Instead, at the age of 16 he left school to take employment as a clerk in one of the commercial houses at Quebec. After two years with a certain Monsieur Thurseau, he was engaged by a second firm, probably that of brothers John* and Mathew Macnider which conducted a retail trade on Rue de la Fabrique. Like many young men, Faribault was restless and longed for adventure, and much to the dismay of his family and friends he often talked of becoming a sailor. Family pressure kept him from accepting a commission in the 7th Foot, stationed at Quebec from 1791 to 1793. Prince Edward* Augustus, fourth son of George III and commanding officer of the regiment, had been pleased with some sketches Faribault had made of his troops and had apparently invited him to enlist. In 1798, despite his family's objections, Faribault left for Fort Michilimackinac (Mackinac Island, Mich.) to enter the fur trade. He was probably in the employ of the Montreal firm of Parker, Gerrard, and Ogilvy [see Samuel GERRARD; John Ogilvy*], whose representative, George Gillespie*, was Faribault's agent at Michilimackinac. Faribault obtained a permit to trade in the American Northwest Territory from the territorial secretary, William Henry Harrison, and spent the winter of 1798–99 at Kankakee (Ill.). During the following two seasons he traded among the Sioux on the Des Moines River, and in 1802, after mastering the Sioux language, he was placed in charge of the post at Little Rapids on the St Peter (Minnesota) River. While at this post, he took Pelagie Hince, daughter of Joseph Hince (Hanse), as his country wife. The marriage was formalized on 30 April 1817 at St Gabriel's, a Roman Catholic church in Prairie du Chien (Wis.); the couple were to have eight children.

In 1809 Faribault severed his ties with the Montreal traders, now united under the North West Company, and began trading for furs on his own account at Prairie du Chien. He also traded in lead, buying the mineral from Julien Dubuque and selling it in St Louis (Mo.). At the outbreak of the War of 1812 the inhabitants of Prairie du Chien, the vast majority of whom were French Canadians, remained loyal to Great Britain. Sir George Prevost*, governor of the Canadas and commander in chief of the British forces, placed the defence of the region under the direction of Robert Dickson*, deputy superintendent of the Indian Department. Away from the village when American troops captured the settlement in June 1814, Faribault refused to join the force led by William McKay* which was sent to regain control and he claimed to have been held prisoner by Captain Thomas Gummersall Anderson*. Although Prairie du Chien was easily retaken by McKay's troops, the area none the less reverted to the United States by the terms of the peace settlement signed at Ghent (Belgium) on 24 Dec. 1814. After the war Faribault became an American citizen and served as militia officer and coroner while rebuilding his fortunes at Prairie du Chien.

By 1819, when Colonel Henry Leavenworth passed through Prairie du Chien on his way west to establish a military installation among the Sioux, the town was losing its importance as a trading centre. Leavenworth learned of Faribault's ability to deal with the Indians and urged him to open a trading post near the projected fort. Faribault left Prairie du Chien to join Leavenworth in the fall of 1819 and helped to negotiate the 1821 treaty by which the Sioux sold the land needed for the military reservation, Fort Snelling (St Paul, Minn.), completed in 1823. This treaty also gave

Pike's Island, at the confluence of the St Peter and Mississippi rivers, to Faribault's wife. Although the treaty was signed, it was never ratified by the United States Senate, leaving ownership of the land in doubt. In 1822 the military took possession after Faribault was driven off the island by a flood, and he was unsuccessful in his attempts to gain compensation for the loss of this land. Another flood four years later destroyed his home on the banks of St Peter River, so Faribault moved to the village of St Peter's (Mendota, Minn.); for many years he farmed there during the summer and traded in furs at Little Rapids during the winter. While at Little Rapids in 1833 he was stabbed in the chest by an Indian to whom he had refused credit. He never fully recovered from this wound.

Faribault remained active in the fur trade, doing business with the American Fur Company, until 1853, when he retired to Faribault, the town founded by his son Alexander as a fur-trading post in 1826. He died there in 1860 at the home of his daughter Emily. Faribault had been a successful trader and later in life settled down as one of Minnesota's earliest farmers. Respected by his neighbours, he had been elected periodically to minor public offices in Prairie du Chien and Mendota. It was in part through his influence that the United States had been able to negotiate treaties in 1821, 1841, and 1851 with the Indians of the upper Mississippi by which they gave up much of their land. Faribault's home in Mendota, built in 1837, has been reconstructed as a historic site.

PAUL TRAP

AP, La Visitation (Berthierville), Reg. des baptêmes, mariages et sépultures, 29 oct. 1775. Minn. Hist. Soc. (St Paul), Alexis Bailly papers; H. H. Sibley papers; Stephen Jewett, "After eighty-four years" (1910). Wis., State Hist. Soc. (Madison), Platteville MSS V, 1; P. L. Scanlan papers. "Prairie du Chien documents, 1814–'15," Wis., State Hist. Soc., Coll., 9 (1882): 262–65. The territorial papers of United States, comp. C. E. Carter and J. P. Bloom (28v. to date, Washington, 1934– ; vols.1–26 repr. in 25v., New York, 1973), 28: 160–61, 303–5. DAB. Tanguay, Dictionnaire, 4: 9. W. W. Folwell, A history of Minnesota (4v., St Paul, 1921–30), 1. Joseph Tassé, Les canadiens de l'Ouest (2v., Montréal, 1878), 1: 310–31. H. H. Sibley, "Memoir of Jean Baptiste Faribault," Minn. Hist. Soc., Coll. (St Paul), 3 (1880): 168–79.

FARIBAULT, JOSEPH-ÉDOUARD, notary, businessman, justice of the peace, militia officer, politician, and office holder; b. 4 May 1773 in Berthier-en-Haut (Berthierville), Que., son of Barthélemy Faribault*, a notary, and Catherine-Antoine Véronneau; d. 3 Aug. 1859 in L'Assomption, Lower Canada.

Joseph-Édouard Faribault was a clerk in his father's office by the age of 15 and received his commission as

Faribault

a notary on 12 Feb. 1791. He opened an office at Berthier-en-Haut but a few months later went to practise in L'Assomption. There on 24 Nov. 1794 he married Marie-Anne-Élisabeth Poudret, the daughter of merchant Antoine Poudret and Marie-Apolline Spagniolini. Faribault carried on his profession until 1849. His minute-book contains 9,622 notarized instruments. Notaries who trained in his office include his elder brother Jean-Marie, nephew Barthélemy Joliette*, and sons Narcisse and Jacques-Eugène. Another son, Norbert, studied law under Jean-Roch Rolland* in Montreal, and a younger one, Adolphe, studied medicine in Paris, where he died in 1851.

Faribault had a good business sense, and from the time he went into practice he obtained land grants, bought lots and buildings, leased out land for farming, and made mortgage loans at six per cent or in return for annuities. But his chief occupation was to rent, build, and operate sawmills and flour-mills. Directly or indirectly he controlled almost all the mills in the vicinity, and according to Christian Roy, who wrote a history of L'Assomption, he was "the most influential man in L'Assomption between 1800 and 1845." In addition he looked after the affairs of Paul-Roch Saint-Ours, who in 1805 chose him as attorney and agent for his seigneuries. He was the recognized administrator of the Lavaltrie seigneury for ten years from 30 June 1812. He also built up a sizeable fortune for his daughter Aurélie, whose estate he managed; in 1837 she inherited part of the seigneuries of her first husband, Charles Saint-Ours, the seigneur of L'Assomption and of the Bayeul fief, and on the death of her second husband, Louis-Michel VIGER, whom she had married in 1843, she inherited in 1855 the seigneury of Repentigny.

Faribault took part in the public life of his region. From 18 June 1808 to 2 Oct. 1809 he held the seat for Leinster in the House of Assembly. According to the classification of members drawn up by the newspaper *Le Canadien* in October 1809, he was among the supporters of the government, but he did not participate in any of the recorded votes of the 1809 session. In the election the following year Faribault was scrutineer for Leinster. On 2 April 1838, at the behest of Sir John Colborne*, he was appointed to the Special Council responsible for governing Lower Canada while the 1791 constitution was suspended. This council, which was dissolved by Lord Durham [Lambton*] on 1 June 1838, was re-established by Colborne in November, and Faribault, who received new commissions as a councillor on 2 Nov. 1838 and 19 Jan. 1839, remained on it until its work was completed on 10 Feb. 1841. It should be noted that he was absent when the vote approving the union of the two Canadas was taken in November 1839. Later he was active on the municipal scene, first as warden of Leinster District in 1841 and 1842, and then as mayor of L'Assomption from 1846 to 1848.

In addition to political offices Faribault held various other posts: justice of the peace for the district of Montreal (first commission in 1803), commissioner for the taking of oaths of allegiance (1812), commissioner in Leinster County for the improvement of internal communications (1817) as well as for the census (1825), and commissioner for the summary trial of small causes (1821, 1826, 1831). He was secretary of his *fabrique* from 1796 to 1830, and a member of the council set up at L'Assomption in 1825 to open a public primary school. However, no doubt because he was extremely cautious in business matters, he opposed the idea of founding a college put forward by Jean-Baptiste Meilleur*, and even resigned as secretary of the *fabrique*. Despite this reservation, in 1838 he unhesitatingly offered a substantial sum to assist the Collège de L'Assomption, which had opened five years before. Faribault served as well in the Lavaltrie battalion of militia. In 1805 he was a captain and adjutant. He was subsequently promoted major and then lieutenant-colonel, and he took part in the War of 1812; for his service he received land grants in Kilkenny Township in 1823. Some time between 1815 and 1820 he became lieutenant-colonel in command of his battalion.

In the course of his career Joseph-Édouard Faribault amassed a considerable fortune. At the time of his first wife's death in 1828 his assets amounted to 106,332 *livres*, a sum he had to share with his children. On 1 Nov. 1845 he took as his second wife Geneviève Fauteux, the widow of Norbert Hénault, a merchant of Saint-Cuthbert. Stricken with apoplexy, Faribault passed away on 3 Aug. 1859 after four years of illness. He died intestate, leaving an inheritance valued at 82,216 *livres*, of which almost 80 per cent consisted of mortgage loans. The settlement of his estate gave rise to a long dispute between his second wife and his children which had to be resolved by arbitration. Faribault was reputed to have been a learned man, with a good legal mind, and to have had sound judgement and rare sagacity.

MARTHE FARIBAULT-BEAUREGARD

Joseph-Édouard Faribault's minute-book, containing instruments notarized from 1791 to 1849, is held at ANQ-M, CN4-19. An oil portrait of Faribault by an unknown painter is in the possession of Claude Faribault of Outremont, Que.

AC, Beauharnois (Valleyfield), Minutiers, Godefroid Chagnon, 17 août 1826, 2 juin 1830, 24 juill. 1833, 4 janv. 1836; Joliette, Minutiers, J.-Z. Martel, 2 oct. 1877, 29 mars 1880. ANQ-M, CE5-1, 4 mai 1773; CE5-12, 25 sept. 1837; CE5-14, 24 nov. 1794, 10 févr. 1820, 18 oct. 1824, 28 juin 1828, 10 sept. 1843, 1er nov. 1845, 6 août 1859; CE5-16, 30 mai 1855; CN1-216, 22 janv. 1861; CN1-312, 2, 14 nov. 1859; 25 sept. 1861; CN1-313, 17 oct. 1855; CN2-29, 20 avril 1795; CN2-73, 15 mars, 6 sept., 11 nov. 1817; CN5-3, 1er nov. 1845; CN5-11, 30 juin 1812; 24 juill. 1832; 25 avril, 10 sept. 1843; CN5-24, 10 févr. 1820; CN5-30, 1er juin

1814; CN5-36, 1er nov. 1801, 1er juill. 1804. 13 janv. 1810. ANQ-MBF, CN1-60, 12 juin 1788. ANQ-Q, CN1-99, 18 oct. 1824. ASSM, 8, C, 12 juin 1797. AUM, P 58, U, Faribault à sa nièce, 20 nov. 1813. PAC, RG 1, L3L: 995, 41096–97; RG 4, B8, 1, 12 févr. 1791; 20: 7319–29; RG 8, I (C ser.), 704: 264; RG 9, I, A5, 4: 122; RG 11, A1, 10: 10–11; RG 68, 5: 58; 6: 276–77, 376, 379–80; 8: 270–71; 13: 103, 107; 16: 7–8; 17: 66–67. Émélie Berthelot-Girouard, "Les journaux d'Émélie Berthelot-Girouard," Béatrice Chassé, édit., ANQ *Rapport*, 1975: 31. *Quebec Gazette*, 2 June 1808, 12 July 1810, 22 May 1817, 24 Sept. 1821. F.-J. Audet, "Les législateurs du Bas-Canada." Caron, "Inv. de la corr. de Mgr Denaut," ANQ *Rapport*, 1931–32: 165, 172, 181; "Inv. de la corr. de Mgr Panet," 1934–35: 403; "Inv. de la corr. de Mgr Plessis," 1932–33: 89, 131. Louise Dechêne, "Inventaire des documents relatifs à l'histoire du Canada conservés dans les archives de la Compagnie de Saint-Sulpice à Paris," ANQ *Rapport*, 1969: 218, 249, 256. Desjardins, *Guide parl.*, 80, 132. *Officers of British forces in Canada* (Irving), 183. *Quebec almanac*, 1805: 29, 52; 1810: 33, 63; 1815: 58, 97; 1820: 49, 56, 99; 1821: 49, 57, 115. L.-P. Audet, *Histoire de l'enseignement au Québec* (2v., Montréal et Toronto, 1971), 2: 32. Chapais, *Cours d'hist. du Canada*, 4: 209–10, 278–79. Christie, *Hist. of L.C.* (1866), 5: 51. Anastase Forget, *Histoire du collège de L'Assomption; 1833 – un siècle – 1933* (Montréal, [1933]), 48–49, 62. Marcel Fournier, *La représentation parlementaire de la région de Joliette* (Joliette, Qué., 1977), 21, 141. Hélène Lafortune, "La situation de la profession notariale à L'Assomption entre 1800 et 1850" (thèse de MA, univ. de Montréal, 1981). J.-C. Robert, "L'activité économique de Barthélemy Joliette et la fondation du village d'Industrie (Joliette), 1822–1850" (thèse de MA, univ. de Montréal, 1971). C. Roy, *Hist. de L'Assomption*. J.-E. Roy, *Hist. du notariat*, 3: 18, 28. P.-G. Roy, *La famille Faribault* (Lévis, Qué., 1913), 18–28. F.-J. Audet, "Membres du Conseil spécial," *BRH*, 7 (1901): 82–83. "La famille Faribault," *BRH*, 19 (1913): 65–75. Jacques Rainville, "Vers notre tricentenaire, la famille Faribault," *Le Courrier de Berthier* (Berthierville, Qué.), 9 mai 1968. J.-C. Robert, "Un seigneur entrepreneur, Barthélemy Joliette, et la fondation du village d'Industrie (Joliette), 1822–1850," *RHAF*, 26 (1972–73): 376–77, 382.

FASSIO, GEROME (often spelled **Fascio**, but he signed **G. Fassio**; some sources, without proof, put **Giuseppe** as his given name), painter, lithographer, and teacher of painting and drawing; b. in all likelihood in 1789 in Italy, probably in Rome; d. 1 Jan. 1851 in Bytown (Ottawa).

Gerome Fassio began doing portraits at Montreal late in the spring of 1834. At that time he was about 45 years old and had a son, Eugenio, who had been born in 1825 or 1826. Claiming that he had recently arrived from Italy, in the advertisements he placed in newspapers Fassio made much of the professional experience he had acquired in Europe and New York. In that city, where he had practised his art for at least a year on Broadway, he painted the portrait of a well-to-do citizen of Trois-Rivières, believed to have been Moses HART. When Fassio came to Montreal he got in touch with Hart, and after spending some time

there painting miniatures he went to Trois-Rivières, where he was working in 1835. Some sources suggest that he was then living with Hart; if so, it could not have been for long, since Fassio went to Quebec in August.

The visit to Quebec, like all Fassio's activity in the Canadas, was characteristic of itinerant portraitists of that era in America. To attract the curious, he exhibited "a collection of choice pieces of the Italian School." His work was launched with the backing of anonymous eulogies in *Le Canadien* concerning both the painter's character and his art: "When people from abroad, instead of bringing us their vices, their woes, and their afflictions, dispense among us the benefits of science, the arts, and industry, and the amenities and gracious living that accompany them, they have a right to our full consideration." The admirer continued on the subject of Fassio's work: "What subtlety of colour, what deft shading! what faultless draftsmanship!" The writer in *Le Canadien* let it be known that Fassio was ready to spend the winter at Quebec "if he receives encouragement," apparently at that time a virtual certainty. Towards the end of 1835, acknowledging the "encouragement he is receiving," Fassio proposed to give "courses in painting in miniature and drawing" to young ladies and gentlemen. In the spring, however, he announced he was leaving at the end of May, and he reappeared in Montreal in August 1836. Hoping to deserve the "eminent encouragement that he so liberally enjoyed during his first stay," he followed the formula that had been successful at Quebec and held separate classes for young ladies and for young gentlemen. But the town of Montreal was not destined to become the painter's chosen ground, perhaps because of competition from other miniaturists. At Quebec Fassio could count on the support of the press and on undisputed professional pre-eminence.

Fassio was back at Quebec some time before the summer of 1838, when he left his lodgings on Rue Saint-Jean to move into the residence of the chief justice, Jonathan Sewell*. He received clients there, but no longer advertised painting and drawing lessons. To earn money with his brush, Fassio in 1839 executed and exhibited at Joseph LÉGARÉ's picture-gallery an ambitious work on the theme of Great Britain and Canada; a sympathetic reporter described it as a "superb allegorical picture in miniature, on a large scale." Lots were to be drawn for it, with tickets on sale at the painter's house. The experiment cannot have proved successful, for Fassio never repeated it. The picture's fate is unknown.

Fassio was drawing-master at the Petit Séminaire de Québec for the academic year 1839–40. Nothing is known of his activities during 1841, but he probably remained at Quebec. In May of the following year, while he was living on Rue Sainte-Hélène (Rue McMahon), he announced he was opening a new

Fassio

school of "classical drawing" that respected "the rules of art, and the practices of the great schools of Italy." His fame attracted Michel BIBAUD to Quebec in October; Bibaud, however, did not have enough time to meet the painter of the miniature portraits he had admired in Montreal.

In the autumn of 1843 Fassio tried his hand at lithography, putting his name to a portrait of Pope Gregory XVI which was dedicated with permission to the bishop of Quebec, Joseph Signay*. One critic noted "distinct progress in the country's lithography," while regretting that Fassio had "failed to give to Gregory XVI's face the expression of kindliness and quiet contentment that . . . all the [other] likenesses of him convey." Numerous copies of the lithograph must have been sold, for it continued to be advertised in *Le Castor*, which printed it, until about the beginning of March 1844, when the paper's presses were destroyed by fire. This reverse must have been the more trying for Fassio because on 21 December he had been "stripped of all he possessed" when his house on Rue de la Fabrique burned down. At the end of February, recalling this calamity, he protested that he had "lost everything but [his] life." The public does not seem to have been moved by the painter's predicament. In addition, facing a new rival, the daguerreotype, Fassio was forced to cut his prices almost in half.

When *Le Castor* obtained a new press, Fassio hastened to turn it to good account; in June 1844 he produced a new lithographed portrait, of Louis-Joseph Papineau*, this one also printed by *Le Castor*. The paper's editor, Napoléon Aubin*, himself an artist, was apparently encouraged by the success of these portraits, and published a prospectus in August announcing a "Galerie des illustrations canadienne," to be sold by subscription. This was to be a collection of lithographed portraits "of a size convenient for framing or keeping in a notebook," each accompanied by "a printed biographical notice." Fassio's portrait of Bishop François de Laval* was the first to appear. It was followed by ones of Joseph-François Perrault*, Bishop Charles-Auguste-Marie-Joseph de Forbin-Janson*, and Robert BALDWIN; of these, Aubin did the first but it is not known which of them did the other two. Aubin abandoned the project towards the end of the year, no doubt because of a lack of subscribers.

After his son Eugenio had signed on as a sailor in training in July 1843, Fassio may have contemplated returning to his native land. He left Quebec early in 1845 but returned at the end of the summer. He recommenced teaching and painting, the latter at the same reduced prices, so that his art might be within everyone's reach. None the less, Fassio seems to have maintained the quality of his portraits, witness the claim made in an article written in February 1846: "If his talent had not already brought him so far [along the road] to perfection, truly we would say he had made new conquests."

Towards the end of 1847 Fassio made plans to return to Italy. His son was to have completed his apprenticeship in July of that year and to have become a navigator or pilot. Fassio now offered his clients the opportunity to avail themselves of his talents "for the last time" before his departure, which was arranged for the spring. He set his price at "four piastres" a portrait, but in February 1848 he lowered it to three, a sum that hardly seems remunerative in light of the ten days he required to complete a miniature portrait of Jean-Baptiste Godin. The painter's plan to leave was frustrated, as he observed in October, "by unfortunate circumstances." It may plausibly be assumed that he was referring to the political situation in Italy rather than to the cholera epidemic then raging in Lower Canada. He again took up residence at Quebec and planned to teach "the drawing of flowers and other elements of the same art" to adults.

Fassio left for Italy late in June 1849. Unfortunately the situation there was too precarious for him to consider a lengthy stay. Consequently, in October 1850, after an absence of less than 16 months, Fassio was back again at Quebec, some two months before his death. By a strange coincidence the issue of the paper carrying news of his return also announced the establishment at Quebec of "a new Canadian daguerreotype undertaking," that of L.-A. Lemire, which seems to have been the first firm concerned solely with this art to be located at Quebec. Having exhausted his prospects in the two cut-rate campaigns he had launched before departing for Italy, the miniaturist was forced to settle elsewhere.

He chose Bytown, where he advertised for the first time at the end of November, describing himself as an Italian artist straight from Rome. He again adopted the formula he had developed over the years, which included painting lessons for small groups of young people and for adults on an individual basis. According to him, "a good education can never be complete without possessing a knowledge of this art." To attract pupils Fassio noted that he had "taught with much success in different courts in Europe." While the notice was still running, Fassio died of a severe illness on the morning of 1 Jan. 1851.

Fassio was a miniaturist in the true sense of the word, for the full precision of his brushwork can only be appreciated with a magnifying glass. He was also an excellent colourist, unrivalled in the province during his lifetime. His landscape *Genève vu des Paquis* reveals the measure of his two talents. The pigment is applied in minute dots in a well-ordered composition that is not unlike the work of Georges Seurat. But this static style gives the figures in his portraits a rigid air, so that they lose in vivacity what the work gains in style. Herein lies the painter's weakness. As a European portraitist, Fassio was primarily concerned with the aesthetic requirements of his painting, however tiny it might be. In his miniatures on ivory he created the likeness of his subject, but the line is refined as if the image, instead of being painted, is engraved. There is a lack of expression in the faces, a flaw rightly identified by contemporary critics in the portrait of Gregory XVI.

The available sources imply that Fassio was a prolific artist. How many portraits in miniature he executed during his years in the Canadas and who posed for him are questions that cannot be answered precisely, but given the considerable esteem he enjoyed it may be conjectured that he often painted the portraits of prominent people, as he intimated at the end of his life. That the impecunious artist finally had to open his studio to humble folk suggests that his portraits could provide an interesting testimony to the ordinary life of his time.

DAVID KAREL

[The author wishes to thank John R. Porter for having located Eugenio Fassio's apprenticeship contract (ANQ-Q, CN1-49, 21 juill. 1843). D.K.]

A number of Gerome Fassio's paintings are held at the BVM, the Musée du Québec (Québec), the Musée du Séminaire de Chicoutimi (Chicoutimi, Qué.), and at the National Gallery of Canada (Ottawa).

ASQ, MSS, 433: 215–17. MAC-CD, Fonds Morisset, 2, F249/G537.5. *L'Ami de la religion et de la patrie* (Québec), 6 oct. 1848–25 juin 1849. *Le Canadien*, 31 août, 11, 14 sept., 14 déc. 1835; 8 janv., 2 mai 1836; 20 juill., 31 août, 5 sept. 1838; 15 nov. 1839; 9 mai 1842; 4 sept., 22 déc. 1843; 8 janv. 1844; 30 oct. 1848; 14 oct. 1850. *Le Castor* (Québec), 7 nov. 1843–25 nov. 1844. *Le Journal de Québec*, 7 sept. 1843; 29 févr. 1844; 6 janv., 7, 13 févr., 6 déc. 1845; 7 févr. 1846; 4 déc. 1847. *Mélanges religieux*, 15 sept. 1843. *La Minerve*, 19, 23 juin, 7 juill. 1834; 29 août 1836. *Packet*, 30 Nov. 1850–4 Jan. 1851. *Quebec Mercury*, 18 Aug. 1835; 30 April, 2 May 1836; 2, 11 Jan. 1844; 30 Sept. 1845. Gérard Morisset, "Giuseppe Fascio le miniaturiste," *La Patrie*, 9 avril 1950: 26, 38.

FEATHERS. See A-CA-OO-MAH-CA-YE

FENOUILLET, ÉMILE DE (at birth named **Hypolite-Joseph Mille**), journalist and teacher; b. 9 March 1807 in Hyères, France, son of Hypolite Mille, a mason, and Claire-Sophie Bonnet; d. 25 June 1859 at Quebec.

Hypolite-Joseph Mille did his legal studies in France and defended a thesis on 8 Aug. 1828. Afterwards, he made his home in Montpellier and subsequently in Paris. The fall of Louis-Philippe and the 1848 revolution apparently ruined him. In September 1851 Mille was living in Cologne (Federal Republic of Germany), but later that year he settled in Bonn. From there he sent to *L'Univers*, the ultramontane daily in Paris edited by Louis Veuillot, a series of articles on art and on religious questions which he signed E. de Fenouillet.

Fenouillet went to Lower Canada in 1854, reaching Quebec at the end of October. He was immediately taken on staff at the *Journal de Québec* by the owner, Joseph-Édouard Cauchon*. The following year Fenouillet became editor in place of Cauchon, who had recently been appointed commissioner of crown lands for Lower Canada. He handled the literary section and wrote numerous articles dealing primarily with art, literature, and religion. In January 1856 he was attacked by a journalist of the Montreal paper *Le Pays*, who claimed that "this man [who is] so profoundly religious and moral lost no opportunity to spend his Sundays on public platforms or even in taverns, where he no doubt collects his thoughts for his lessons on religious morality [presented] for others to use." Fenouillet retorted that this was "a scurrilous fabrication . . . a veritable lampoon full of lies and slander." Nevertheless, upset by this acrimony, he left the *Journal de Québec* soon afterwards.

In May 1857, through the patronage of Pierre-Joseph-Olivier Chauveau*, superintendent of the Board of Education, Fenouillet was appointed a teacher of literature, French grammar, history, and philosophy (including logic and ethics) at the École Normale Laval, which had recently been founded at Quebec. He was a competent, talented, enthusiastic, and devoted teacher, who commanded the admiration of his pupils, inspiring their respect and affection.

That year Fenouillet contributed to the *Journal de l'Instruction publique*, a periodical newly launched by Chauveau. He wrote articles on a variety of subjects: two paintings of Christ, one in the chapel at the Séminaire de Québec and the other in Notre-Dame cathedral at Quebec; Christ as traditionally portrayed in the fine arts; the authorship of the *Imitation de Jésus-Christ*; the university in Bonn; and the Swiss historian Johannes von Müller. In addition he gave a number of lectures at the Institut Canadien of Quebec dealing with Blaise Pascal and *Les Provinciales*, Port-Royal by Charles-Augustin Sainte-Beuve, Mme de Sévigné, and Hugues-Félicité-Robert de La Mennais.

Seriously ill at the start of the school year 1858–59, Fenouillet asked for an assistant, and Napoléon Lacasse was appointed to help him in his teaching duties. Fenouillet found it so difficult to teach that in 1859 he gave only one course. He died on 25 June of that year, leaving two daughters and a son. Cauchon, François Évanturel*, and Jacques* and Octave* Crémazie attended his burial in the Saint-Charles cemetery. The *Journal de l'Instruction publique*, announcing the death of this "good and courageous teacher," noted that he had been one of "the most able contributors" to the paper. The *Journal de Québec* also devoted a short article to this "scholarly, honourable, and good man." For his part, Octave Crémazie paid homage to him in a long and stirring poem entitled *À la mémoire de M. de Fenouillet*.

CÉLINE CYR

Ferguson

AD, Var (Draguignan), État civil, Hyères, 10 mars 1807. ANQ-Q, CE1-22, 28 juin 1859. *Journal de l'Instruction publique* (Québec et Montréal), 1 (1857)–3 (1859). *Le Journal de Québec*, 1856. *Le National* (Montréal), 18 janv. 1856. *La Patrie*, 22 févr. 1856. *Le Pays*, 22 janv. 1856. Beaulieu et Hamelin, *La presse québécoise*, 1: 123. Octave Crémazie, *Œuvres*, Odette Condemine, édit. (2v., Ottawa, 1972); *Œuvres complètes de Octave Crémazie publiées sous le patronage de l'Institut canadien de Québec*, H.-R. Casgrain et H.-J.-J.-B. Chouinard, édit. (Montréal, [1882]). Labarrère-Paulé, *Les instituteurs laïques. Les noces d'or de l'école normale Laval, 1857–1907* (Québec, 1908). P.-G. Roy, *À propos de Crémazie* (Québec, 1945), 214–15. C.-J. Magnan, "Éducateurs d'autrefois: anciens professeurs de l'école normale Laval," *BRH*, 47 (1941): 357–62.

FERGUSON, ROBERT, businessman, justice of the peace, judge, office holder, and militia officer; b. 17 April 1768 in Logierait, Scotland, son of Adam Ferguson and Marjory Connacher; m. 11 Dec. 1806 Mary Adams, the first English child born on the Restigouche River, N.B., and they had eight sons and three daughters; d. 10 Aug. 1851 in Campbellton, N.B.

Robert Ferguson came to the Restigouche area in 1796 as chief clerk for the mercantile firm established at Martin's Point (Campbellton) in 1794 by his brother Alexander. Upon Alexander's death in 1803 Robert took over the business. By 1805 he was the leading merchant and exporter of fish on the Restigouche and was shipping approximately 1,400 barrels of salmon a year. In later years this branch of the business declined slightly but it was still profitable and during the 1840s Ferguson continued to ship about 1,200 barrels per annum. In 1812 he purchased more than 2,000 acres of land, a sawmill, and several fishing lots from the widow of his former rival, Samuel Lee*, thus becoming the largest landowner in the region. Operating the only grist-mill and sawmill on the river, by the 1820s the firm was buying and exporting square timber.

About 1812, at the village now called Atholville, Ferguson had begun building his own ships to carry his fish and timber to market and, although there are few records of his activity in this sphere, it is known that he built at least three barques, a brig, and two schooners. During the War of 1812 two of his vessels were captured by American privateers and Ferguson, a passenger on one of them, spent some time as a prisoner in Salem, Mass. Shortly after his return, he built an impressive residence, Athol House, and a store which became the business centre of that part of the Restigouche.

In 1813 Ferguson was made a justice of the peace for Northumberland County and in 1827, on the advice of Hugh Munro*, the leading magistrate, he was appointed a justice of the peace as well as a justice of the Inferior Court of Common Pleas for the newly created county of Gloucester. He was to retain these posts until his death. In 1826 he had advertised for sale town lots which eventually formed part of the settlement of Campbellton. One of the founders of the Gloucester Agricultural and Emigrant Society in 1828, and of the Restigouche Agricultural Society in 1840, he served as president of both organizations for many years. In 1831 Ferguson was one of the commissioners charged with laying out the first highway between New Brunswick and Lower Canada. He was colonel of the 1st battalion, Restigouche Regiment, in the 1840s, and a member of the county's first board of health, which was established in 1840. A religious individual, he provided the land for the earliest Presbyterian church on the Restigouche.

Ferguson was a friend of Hugh Munro and the two men belonged to the old guard in the northern part of the province. This group was composed of loyalists and early Scottish settlers who controlled the trade and commerce of the region; they virtually ruled the Acadians in the period 1790–1830, and were also unpopular with the new immigrants, mostly Irish, who began to arrive after the Napoleonic Wars. Their authority was first seriously challenged when William End* assumed the position of county clerk in 1827. End became the champion of the Irish and the Acadians, and Ferguson and Munro tried to have him removed from office. In the Gloucester County elections of 1830, End ran successfully as county clerk against Munro. When End called a meeting of the Court of Quarter Sessions the following year, however, Ferguson (whom End had referred to as "a perjured old villain") and the other magistrates refused to attend. End then appointed new magistrates but Ferguson, Munro, and their colleagues persuaded the government to remove him from his post on the grounds that he was not a resident of the county. Their victory was short-lived; on 1 July 1831 Lord Goderich, the colonial secretary, ordered that he be reappointed. Goderich also directed End to move from Newcastle to Bathurst and to apologize to Ferguson and the other magistrates for having exceeded his authority in replacing them.

Conditions in the northern part of the province were changing in the 1830s and the pre-eminence of men such as Ferguson and Munro was coming to an end as immigration increased. To combat this decline, Ferguson began organizing meetings in 1836 to press for the creation of a new county, one in which he could retain his prominent position. Gloucester County was divided in 1837 and the new county of Restigouche was established. Ferguson continued to be an influential man there and during the 1840s he was known as "the founder and father of Restigouche." From his home, he operated one of the largest farms in the area and all visiting dignitaries, including Lieutenant Governor Sir William MacBean George

Colebrooke*, were entertained there. Ferguson, the leader of the business community on the Restigouche from the first decade of the 19th century until his death in 1851, was to be followed by his sons who also occupied prominent positions in the region.

WILLIAM A. SPRAY

N.B. Museum, F64, no.36; Ferguson family, CB DOC. Northumberland Land Registry Office (Newcastle, N.B.), Registry books, 10: 90–95 (mfm. at PANB). PANB, RG 10, RS108, James Butters *et al.*, 1817; Robert Ferguson Jr., 1817. Robert Cooney, *A compendious history of the northern part of the province of New Brunswick, and of the district of Gaspé, in Lower Canada* (Halifax, 1832; repub. Chatham, N.B., 1896). N.B., House of Assembly, *Journal*, 1850, app.: clix–x. *Gleaner* (Chatham), 25 Oct. 1831, 19 Jan. 1836, 28 Jan. 1840, 26 Jan. 1841, 18 Oct. 1842, 3 Jan. 1844, 25 Aug. 1851. *Mercury* (Miramichi, N.B.), 12 Dec. 1826, 29 May 1827, 19 Feb. 1828. G. B. MacBeath, *The story of the Restigouche: covering the Indian, French, and English periods of the Restigouche area* (Saint John, N.B., 1954). MacNutt, *New Brunswick*. J. C. Henderson, "Sketches in Restigouche history," *Daily Sun* (Saint John), 7 Feb. 1883.

FERRIE, COLIN CAMPBELL, businessman, justice of the peace, politician, and office holder; baptized May 1808 in Glasgow, son of Adam Ferrie* and Rachel Campbell; m. 8 Dec. 1830 Catherine Priscilla Beasley, daughter of merchant Richard Beasley*, and they had two sons; d. 9 Nov. 1856 in Hamilton, Upper Canada.

The eldest son of a Glasgow textile merchant, Colin Campbell Ferrie arrived in Montreal in 1824 with William Cormack, a partner in the wholesale and forwarding firm of Ferrie, Cormack and Company, newly established there by Colin's father. As a result of Cormack's subsequent mishandling of the business, the partnership was dissolved in 1826 but under Colin's management the firm recovered. In 1829 he entered into partnership with his brother Adam* and his father. The latter settled in Montreal and agreed to supply the wholesale and retail store established by his sons in the boom town of Hamilton under the name of Colin Ferrie and Company. Between 1830 and 1833 branches of the Hamilton store were set up at Brantford, Preston (Cambridge), Nelson (Burlington), Dundas, and Waterloo, centres which figured prominently in the rapid expansion of Hamilton's commercial hinterland.

Colin Ferrie's firm supplied rural merchants who, lacking sufficient credit, were unable to buy directly from forwarding companies in Montreal. Credit was likewise extended to retail customers. Further risk was incurred when produce was accepted on account, for fluctuations in market prices and shipping problems often upset anticipated returns. The business had a seasonal rhythm which began after the opening of navigation in late spring with the arrival of customers as well as supplies from Adam Ferrie Sr in Montreal. During the following winter, when bulky country goods owed on account could be transported by sleigh and delinquent clients were less likely to flee, Colin tried to settle debts. Clerks, such as Jasper Tough Gilkison*, were frequently sent out to make collections and, if that failed, debtors were brought to court. In 1833, for example, more than 20 summonses were issued on Ferrie's behalf. Some clients fled, others paid, and a few were sent to the Gore District jail, which Ferrie supplied. Appointed a justice of the peace in 1833, he made use of his powers to arrest those who stole from his store.

Legal recourse helped to shore up Colin's mercantile affairs, but he also sought to stabilize Hamilton-based trade by promoting local transportation facilities and financial institutions. As secretary of a joint-stock company formed to operate a steamboat out of Hamilton, he helped raise the capital that led to the launching of the *Constitution* in the summer of 1833. That November Ferrie and other district businessmen, including Andrew Steven*, submitted a petition for a chartered bank at Hamilton which resulted in the incorporation of the Gore Bank two years later. Ferrie succeeded James Matthew Whyte* as its president in 1839 and held the position until his death.

Throughout the 1830s Ferrie's mercantile, legal, and civic interests pervaded Hamilton. Unlike the brash parvenu Allan Napier MacNab*, he appears to have taken up public office as a duty and not simply as an opportunity. He occupied many local positions, but in a quiet fashion that lacked partisan zeal. During the cholera epidemic of 1832 he chaired the board of health and a year later was a member of the town's first board of police. In 1839 he helped to organize the Hamilton and Gore Mechanics' Institute and the local St Andrew's Society. He had resigned his position as a returning officer three years earlier to run successfully in the provincial election for Hamilton, which he represented in the House of Assembly until 1841. A moderate tory, Ferrie, like his father, did not respond vindictively to the rebellion of 1837–38 and, in fact, appeared as a defence witness at the trial of Solomon Lossing, the London District magistrate who was charged with treason but found not guilty. In the assembly, Ferrie's most noteworthy position was as a member of the select committee which investigated the financial crisis of 1837 [*see* Sir Francis Bond Head*].

Despite Ferrie's many positions, his affluence, prestige, and confidence were drastically reduced by the collapse brought on by this financial crisis. He had shunned the prudent counsel of his father, who had warned Colin and Adam against excessive ambition and had specifically denounced the extravagance of Westlawn, the £7,000 Hamilton estate which Colin

Ferrie

had given his wife as a wedding present. The cost appears later to have forced an auction of some of his stock holdings at a large loss. He nevertheless survived the depression of 1837, in which many country clients defaulted, by selling off branch stores and sacrificing real estate. As well, the suppression of the rebellion brought hard currency to loyal businessmen such as Ferrie, who outfitted the 3rd Regiment of Gore militia with clothing, gunpowder, shot, camp ovens, and whisky.

Ferrie never quite regained his early mercantile paramountcy. While other merchants detected a general return of prosperity in 1840, a commercial rival, John Young*, regarded him as a spent force whose "old debts will be worse and worse to collect." Besides old accounts, Colin and Adam Ferrie Jr had additional burdens. The milling and distilling complex at Doon Mills (Kitchener), begun by Adam in 1834, needed costly repairs after a dam collapsed in 1840. Their father was unable to render much aid since two Montreal forwarding firms in which he was involved failed in 1841 and he lost heavily the following year on shipments of produce to Britain. Meanwhile, Isaac Buchanan* had established a large wholesale firm in Hamilton in 1840 and noted later that Colin Ferrie's business began to decline "when exposed to superior competition."

During the 1840s Ferrie turned to banking and real estate speculation on a major scale. The struggling Gore Bank required his increasing attention, particularly as it meshed with his business and land activities. From the outset it was undercapitalized and constantly denied the government business which benefited the Bank of Upper Canada and the Commercial Bank of the Midland District. Ferrie himself was part of the problem since investors and potential clients distrusted the involvement of a reduced merchant in a new bank. In early 1842 Gore Bank shares traded at a discount when it became known that Ferrie, as president, had borrowed about £17,000. The bank purchased property from him in 1844 for a new building directly beside his firm's store, making tangible his strong financial connection with the bank. Apart from his bank shares and his interest in the store and warehouse, his assets were tied up in real estate, which came into his firm's possession as payment from customers and increasingly through speculative investment. As early as 1835 he had advertised farms and urban lots for sale and by 1851 the firm had land valued at over £36,000.

The shock of nearly complete financial collapse after 1839 and persistent business troubles during the early 1840s eclipsed Ferrie's other local interests and shook his youthful confidence. His expansion had a public side, involving the promotion of the town and joint-stock companies, but over-extension, retrenchment, and survival were private matters. Thus for several years he withdrew from public life in order to scramble to meet his obligations, but gradually, as his business recovered, he re-entered civic affairs. He was a founding member of the Hamilton board of trade in 1845 and two years later became first mayor of the newly incorporated city of Hamilton. During his year in office he concentrated on fiscal affairs, which included civic financing by the Gore Bank and an appeal to the provincial government for aid to help the city provide hospital accommodation for the anticipated wave of impoverished Irish immigrants. Ferrie also became involved again in the promotion of joint-stock ventures. Realizing that the enlargement of the Lachine Canal between 1843 and 1848 would permit the operation of large vessels between Montreal and Lake Ontario, he served as chairman of the Burlington Bay Dock and Ship-Building Company, founded in 1847. Although he worked to finance a dockyard and a foundry for the company, no facilities appear to have been built before the company's reorganization in 1858.

The financial crisis of 1848–50, generated in Canada by an international tightening of credit, precipitated Ferrie's final withdrawal from public life. The failure in 1847 of Reid, Irving and Company, the Gore Bank's British agent, had caused the loss of several thousand pounds. Negotiations for a merger with the Bank of Upper Canada were dampened by the Reid, Irving collapse and by the consequent run on the Gore Bank. Persistent merger rumours, however, continued to concern Ferrie, whose easy access to Gore Bank financing was at stake. Once again he had to squeeze debtors, clear off stock, and mortgage property, and in this difficult period he quarrelled with family members over business affairs. Robert Ferrie, the brother who had taken over the management of Doon Mills in 1847, encouraged him to exercise more caution when extending credit and to sell off lots from Westlawn. Perhaps this preoccupation with teetering finances explains Colin's minimal involvement in a major local concern, the Great Western Railway. In 1834 he had been a charter supporter of its predecessor, the London and Gore Rail Road Company, but later seems to have lost much of his enthusiasm. He did join other local businessmen, however, in a bid to consolidate Hamilton's dominance in the vast area north and west of Guelph by supporting the construction of a Great Western feeder from Galt (Cambridge) to Guelph and another branch between Preston and Berlin (Kitchener) which would pass near Doon Mills.

In spite of commercial problems Colin and his father directed the reorganization and expansion of the family business in 1848. Of particular importance was their success in securing control of the Doon Mills from Adam, then in failing health. Following his death the next year, the Hamilton firm was re-formed by Colin with his brothers, John and Robert. During the railway boom in Canada West between 1852 and 1857, the firm appeared to regain much of its initial prestige. An agent for R. G. Dun and Company nevertheless questioned the brothers' ability to "underst[an]d the pres[en]t mode of conduct^g bus[iness] as well as many others in the town." In addition, the stress inherent in rebuilding and protecting the family business undermined Colin's health and in 1855 a new series of crises struck his firm. Winter collections turned up an unusual number of bad accounts, two vessels carrying company goods sank on Lake Ontario, and a banking panic similar to that of 1842 broke when Ferrie was rumoured to have had a capital flow problem. At the time, his firm owed the Gore Bank £50,000. Colin met challenges from some of the bank's directors to his management of the bank by having the family purchase more shares, an intricate and, to some, suspicious credit arrangement, especially as family partnerships, under Adam Sr at Montreal and Colin at Hamilton, guaranteed the bills of exchange of each other.

The compounded difficulties were soon offset by general prosperity but the anxiety visibly affected Ferrie. In November 1856, after a meeting with directors of the Gore Bank, he collapsed and within days had died of "an enlargement of the heart." His business interests were continued by John and Robert Ferrie.

JOHN C. WEAVER

AO, MS 497; RG 20, Hamilton court records, 1830–40; ser.F-15, 1, 1833–40; RG 22, ser.155, will of C. C. Ferrie. BLHU, R. G. Dun & Co. credit ledger, Canada, 25: 111; 26: 13. GRO (Edinburgh), Glasgow, reg. of births and baptisms, May 1808. HPL, Arch. file, Ferrie family papers. PAC, MG 24, D16, 63, John Young to Peter Buchanan, 21 Oct. 1840; Isaac Buchanan to Young, 11 May 1840; 64, Isaac Buchanan to Peter Buchanan, 22 Oct. 1840; D80, 1, memorandum of Isaac Buchanan, 2 April 1845; memorandum on contract for rolling stock, 20 April 1852; memorandum on contract for locomotives, [1852]; RG 5, C1, 202, file 16782; RG 19, 1138, 1141–42. Adam Ferrie, *Autobiography, late Hon. Adam Ferrie* (n.p., n.d.; copy at MTL). U.C., House of Assembly, *App. to the journal*, 1835, 1, no.21; 1837–38, 1: 77–131; 1839–40, 1, pt.II: 31–41. *Daily Spectator, and Journal of Commerce*, 8, 29 Sept. 1847; 11 Nov. 1856. *Hamilton Gazette, and General Advertiser* (Hamilton, [Ont.]), 12 Dec. 1835, 6 April 1836. *Western Mercury* (Hamilton), 13 June 1833; 10 April, 20 June 1834. C. M. Johnston, *The Head of the Lake* (1967), 326. V. Ross and Trigge, *Hist. of Canadian Bank of Commerce*, 1: 172–80. P. R. Austin, "Two mayors of early Hamilton," *Wentworth Bygones* (Hamilton), 3 (1962): 1–9.

FITZROY, Sir CHARLES AUGUSTUS, colonial administrator; b. 10 June 1796 in England, the eldest son of General Lord Charles FitzRoy, second son of the 3rd Duke of Grafton, and Frances Mundy, who died a year after he was born; m. first 11 March 1820 Lady Mary Lennox (d. 1847), eldest daughter of the 4th Duke of Richmond and Lennox [Lennox*] and Charlotte, daughter of the 4th Duke of Gordon, and they had three sons and one daughter; m. secondly 11 Dec. 1855 Margaret Gordon Hawkey, *née* Milligan; d. 16 Feb. 1858 in London.

Charles Augustus FitzRoy went to Harrow and in April 1812 a commission was purchased for him as an ensign in the Royal Horse Guards. After promotion to lieutenant in October 1812 he served at Waterloo and then accompanied the Duke of Richmond to Lower Canada in 1818. Born into one ducal house, FitzRoy, by marrying Richmond's daughter Lady Mary Lennox in March 1820, connected himself to two more. The following month he became a captain and in June 1825 a major, but was then placed on half pay. In October 1825 he became a lieutenant-colonel and was appointed to the Cape of Good Hope as deputy adjutant general of the forces. He also held a number of minor posts at the Cape and for a time edited the *Cape of Good Hope Government Gazette* (Cape Town). He liked South Africa but went deeply into debt after his position as deputy adjutant general was abolished. In 1831 he returned to England and was elected to the House of Commons for Bury St Edmunds, a seat controlled by the Duke of Grafton, and one his father had held. Beyond voting for the Reform Bill of 1832 he appears to have played little part in politics and gave up the seat that year when it was required for his brother-in-law. In 1833 he retired from the army, probably selling his commission to pay off his debts, and waited for his connections to find him employment. They succeeded on 19 March 1837 when he was appointed lieutenant governor of Prince Edward Island. Prior to his departure he was given the KH (civil division) and was knighted by William IV at St James's Palace.

FitzRoy arrived in Prince Edward Island and assumed control of the government from the administrator George Wright* on 25 June 1837. Although he was aware that the colony had been disturbed by a popular movement which wanted the confiscation by the crown of the vast proprietorial estates into which the Island had originally been divided, FitzRoy had been led by the dispatches of his predecessor, Sir John HARVEY, to believe that the agitation was subsiding. He was soon disillusioned. In parts of the Island it was increasingly difficult to collect rents. The situation in the northern section of Kings County was particularly disturbing. During the summer of 1837 the sheriff was twice prevented from seizing the property of recalcitrant tenants and he was "driven off by a body of armed persons, who cruelly mutilated his horses." News of this incident reached FitzRoy while he was on an extended tour of the Island

FitzRoy

and he promptly repaired to Bear River in Kings County where he received a petition from a large public assembly recommending escheat.

FitzRoy's response was predictable. Scion of one of the great aristocratic families of England, even if only a poor cousin, he set his face against escheat "upon the broad basis of the security of all property." The existing assembly, which met in January 1838, was opposed to wholesale escheat, and both in his opening and in his closing addresses to the legislature FitzRoy reiterated his opposition to any measure which threatened to deprive the landlords of their property. Sir John Harvey had toyed with the idea of establishing a court to investigate the proprietors' titles, but FitzRoy rejected this proposal as "holding out hopes which could not be realized, and thereby increasing the discontent." He strongly supported a revised election law passed in 1838 dividing the counties into smaller units and increasing the number of seats because he hoped it would frustrate the Escheat party. In fact, the party swept to victory in the 1838 elections winning 18 of the 24 seats in the assembly, and William Cooper*, its leader, was elected speaker.

While maintaining good relations with the new assembly FitzRoy assiduously worked behind the scenes to undermine the Escheat party. When Cooper carried a petition to the Colonial Office in 1839, FitzRoy ensured that it was rejected "in decided terms." In dividing the appointed council into separate executive and legislative bodies in March 1839 he selected a number of men for both councils who were not associated with the local compact, but he also packed both bodies with men opposed to escheat. For the next three years virtually every measure passed by the assembly was opposed or mutilated beyond recognition by the Legislative Council. Shrewdly, FitzRoy also appointed to the latter "the only man of Education" among Cooper's supporters, Charles Young, thus removing him from the assembly and limiting his effectiveness as an advocate of escheat. Partly because of FitzRoy's actions the Escheat party collapsed in the elections of 1842.

None the less, it would be wrong to see FitzRoy as concerned simply with protecting the interests of the landed proprietors. He frequently condemned the "unfortunate policy" of alienating the whole Island to proprietors and he probably understood the tenants' problems more clearly than did any of the governors of the period. He pointed out that, although rents in Britain might be higher, "this Rent bears much more heavily upon the Tenant in this Island" since "it is the labour alone of the settlers which renders Wilderness land of any value." The Charlottetown *Royal Gazette*, reflecting the expectations of the colony's élite, hailed FitzRoy as "not likely to be biased by fear or favour, or by any of the proprietors" and anticipated that "through his own family and connexions" he would be able to act at the Colonial Office as a countervailing influence to the absentee landlords. FitzRoy did his best to live up to these expectations. In October 1837, shortly after the Bear River meeting, he issued a circular letter to the proprietors which criticized them for not offering longer leases and lower rents to their tenants. The letter, published without FitzRoy's approval in the *Royal Gazette*, unleashed a storm of protest from the proprietors. But FitzRoy did not retreat and ultimately he persuaded a number of the proprietors that it was in their own interest to deal with their tenants more leniently. When the proprietors advanced a claim to the fishery reserves attached to coastal lots he insisted that these reserves should be opened to the public. In 1837 the assembly's land assessment bill, designed to encourage settlement and raise funds for the colony, prompted intense opposition from the Prince Edward Island Association, which represented a number of the absentee landlords in Britain. Nevertheless, in 1838, FitzRoy, with the assistance of Lord Durham [Lambton*], persuaded the Colonial Office to allow the bill to go into effect and reproached his superiors in London for delaying its implementation. The following year he even suggested both an imperial loan to allow the local government to purchase undeveloped estates and a severe penal tax on wilderness land to coerce the landlords into selling. Neither suggestion was approved by Lord John Russell, the colonial secretary.

In the short run FitzRoy's actions, particularly his circular letter of 1837, may well have encouraged the escheat movement, as several of the proprietors and their agents claimed. But over the longer run his efforts at ameliorating the conditions under which the tenants laboured helped to defuse a potentially explosive situation. Escheat was, as FitzRoy maintained, a "hopeless" cause because it advocated a policy to which the British government would never agree. By encouraging their followers to withhold the payment of rent and to resist the enforcement of the law, the escheat leaders, whether aware of the implications of their actions or not, were encouraging a confrontation with the government. Fortunately, FitzRoy acted circumspectly. While insisting that "Loyalty implies obedience to the laws, and resistance with violence is an act of rebellion," and while increasing the size of the provincial garrison, he warned the proprietors in his circular letter not to "expect that, in the remote parts of the Island, the Government can be prepared at all times, and on all occasions with an armed force to support your officers."

Prince Edward Island was on the verge of a serious outbreak of violence by 1838 but FitzRoy did not over-react. Although he was determined to see that the law was "promptly and duly supported," he used only the modicum of force that was essential to maintain order. To some extent FitzRoy was simply acting as an astute representative of the land-owning class, maintaining the *status quo* by using his authority circumspectly and by tempering force with benevolence. But compassion should never be dismissed so cynically. FitzRoy, the most aristocratic governor ever sent to Prince Edward Island, was distinctly unsympathetic to proprietors who seemed to regard their estates solely as an investment and who refused to accept the social obligations that to a true scion of the aristocracy were assumed to accompany the ownership of property. His sympathy for the tenants was genuine; he was motivated by altruism, or at least by a deep-rooted sense of paternalism, as well as by self-interest. Moreover, his compassion extended both to individuals and to distressed groups such as the Indians, whose survival had become precarious [*see* Thomas Irwin*]. Because he was concerned to convince the people of Prince Edward Island that "the Crown takes an interest in their Welfare," violence on the Island continued to be a localized phenomenon, directed against land agents and the proprietors rather than against the government. FitzRoy's personal popularity never waned, particularly among the Island's resident élite. Many of the latter, although opposed to escheat, shared FitzRoy's disdain for those proprietors who had failed to populate their estates and who wished to avoid contributing to the development of the colony. FitzRoy particularly relied for advice and support upon officials such as Thomas Heath Haviland* and Robert Hodgson*, whose claims for advancement he promoted.

As a reward for his effective service FitzRoy was appointed lieutenant governor of the Leeward Islands and departed for Antigua on 28 Sept. 1841, leaving George Wright as administrator until the arrival of Sir Henry Vere Huntley*. In Prince Edward Island FitzRoy, who enjoyed the good life but lacked a private income, had bitterly complained of the inadequacy of his salary and had fallen once again into debt, but in the Leewards, where his salary was more substantial and his expenses lower, he was able to pay off his creditors. Lord Stanley, the colonial secretary, in 1845 offered him the post of governor of New South Wales, which he assumed in August 1846. On 7 Dec. 1847 FitzRoy's wife, who had been a perfect consort on Prince Edward Island, managing Government House and participating in charitable activities in the community, was killed in a carriage accident while he was driving. After her death he acquired a reputation as a philanderer, became the subject of continuous gossip, and seems to have lost some of his vitality as an administrator. Nevertheless, in 1851 he became the first governor general of the Australian colonies and in 1854 he was appointed a KCB. He returned to England in 1855 and married Margaret Gordon Hawkey, the widow of an Australian land agent, on 11 December, in London, where he died on 16 Feb. 1858.

In Australia FitzRoy had presided over a number of important developments. He was an effective conciliator and a competent administrator, although the colonial secretary, Lord Grey, objected to several of his decisions and described him as "a most incapable Governor of so important a Colony." He was less than outstanding when compared to his successor, Sir William Thomas Denison, and has frequently been dismissed as an aristocratic idler. This judgement is unfair, as is that of James Stephen, permanent under-secretary at the Colonial Office, who compared FitzRoy to his ancestor, Charles II, to whom FitzRoy apparently bore an uncanny physical resemblance: "indolent, good humoured, rather pleasant, & having ready credit for talent." The historian John M. Ward has concluded that FitzRoy was "at least the equal of any Australian governor of his time"; the same and more could be said of him during his earlier career on Prince Edward Island.

PHILLIP BUCKNER

PAC, MG 24, A17, ser.II, 3: ff.384–87, 477–87; 4: ff.1371–78; B13, 1: ff.1286–339. PRO, CO 226/54–62; CO 227/8; CO 229/9–10; WO 25/758: 125. Australia, Parl., *Historical records of Australia* (ser.1, 26v., Sydney, 1914–25), 25: ix–xiv; 26: v–xvii. *Royal Gazette* (Charlottetown), June 1837–September 1841. *ADB*. Boase, *Modern English biog.*, 1: 1063. *Burke's peerage* (1967), 1076. *DNB*. *Dictionary of South African biography*, ed. W. J. de Kock *et al.* (4v. to date, Pretoria, South Africa, 1968–   ), 2: 238–39. *Canada's smallest prov.* (Bolger), 107–14. S. G. Foster, *Colonial improver: Edward Deas Thomson, 1800–1879* (Melbourne, Australia, 1978), 84–106. J. M. Ward, *Earl Grey and the Australian colonies, 1846–1857; a study of self-government and self-interest* (Melbourne, [1958]), 281. T. J. Barron and K. J. Cable, "The diary of James Stephen, 1846," *Hist. Studies* (Melbourne), 13 (1969): 518.

FLEMING, ANN CUTHBERT. *See* RAE

FLEMING, PETER, civil engineer and author; fl. 1815–52.

Peter Fleming was of British origin, according to comments made by Thomas Coltrin Keefer* while addressing the Canadian Society of Civil Engineers in 1888. He was the author of two pamphlets on surveying published in Glasgow in 1815 and in 1820. The first traces of his work as a civil engineer are found in 1829, the year in which he wrote from Albany, N.Y., to the governor of Lower Canada, Sir James KEMPT, seeking preferment. Fleming had been employed on the construction of the Mohawk and Hudson Railway and was still committed to the railway company, but he preferred a post in the Canadas. The report he enclosed for the governor on a proposed canal and railway between Saint-Jean

Fontbonne

(Saint-Jean-sur-Richelieu) and Chambly to carry goods and passengers past the rapids on the Rivière Richelieu contained detailed drawings which are still useful for information on wooden-track, metal-shod horse-railways. In the same year he recommended that the Richelieu be dredged so as to avoid the building of a lock and dam at Saint-Ours. He was appointed superintending and consulting engineer for the dredging, begun in 1830.

In 1829–30 Fleming made survey plans and estimates for the construction of the Chambly Canal. Work was begun in 1831, but not under Fleming's supervision since he had had a falling out with Kempt and the commissioners responsible for the canal. In 1830 Fleming had also made a plan of the port of Montreal at the request of the commissioners appointed to execute improvements.

Fleming became consulting engineer on the Williamsburgh and Cornwall canals on the St Lawrence River in 1834. In that year he also made recommendations concerning the rapids at Chute-à-Blondeau on the Ottawa River downstream from Hawkesbury, Upper Canada. He designed a number of road bridges in the period immediately before the union of the Canadas: two near Coteau-du-Lac, one at Cap-Rouge, and one over the Rivière Saint-Maurice in 1839, as well as others at Sainte-Anne-de-la-Pérade (La Pérade) and Bout-de-l'Île in 1840. In the latter year he designed improvements to the lock at Sainte-Anne-de-Bellevue on the Ottawa River and made a chart of the St Lawrence River between Île Sainte-Hélène and Île Saint-Paul (Île Des Sœurs). Fleming then designed improvements for the basin of the Lachine Canal at Montreal in 1841. Appointed superintending engineer in 1843 for the construction of bridges between Montreal and Quebec, some of which he had planned earlier, he appears to have done little work for the government after that date. In 1845 he petitioned the Legislative Council for professional employment in the government service. A few days later he petitioned the Legislative Assembly, complaining that he had been neglected by the government and the Board of Works, that his plans had been monopolized, and that he had in consequence suffered much financial loss. He asked for an investigation of his grievances. The matter was referred to a select committee and there it seems to have died. Fleming designed improvements to the harbour at Port Hope, Upper Canada, in 1846 but they were not implemented.

Fleming was an early promoter of a major railway line through the Canadas. In a letter published in the *Quebec Mercury* in December 1830 he had proposed the construction of a railway from Montreal to Lake Huron, arguing that railways were a less costly, faster, and more efficient means of transportation than canals. A map by Fleming dated 1851 illustrates a proposed trunk line joining Montreal, Bytown (Ottawa), and Kingston, with extensions to Georgian Bay, Goderich, and Windsor, anticipating the construction of major trunk lines in Canada which was beginning in the period.

Fleming had again turned his attention to writing. Author of a pamphlet on the St Lawrence canals in 1849, he was also interested in mathematics, publishing two works on the subject, in 1850 and in 1851. In 1852 Peter McGill presented a petition by Fleming to the Legislative Council for assistance to enable him to publish a work he had prepared on the mathematical sciences. After this, no further traces of him have been found.

Peter Fleming was one of many engineers who came to the Canadas in the 1830s. He worked for more than a decade, planning, designing, and supervising works in Upper and Lower Canada. After 1843 he seems to have fallen into disfavour and to have devoted his time to other activities.

COURTNEY C. J. BOND

Peter Fleming is the author of *A system of land surveying and levelling; wherein is demonstrated the theory, with numerous practical examples, as applied to all operations, either relative to the land surveyor, or civil and military engineer* (Glasgow, 1815); *New method of finding the true length of a base line for trigonometrical surveys* (Glasgow, 1822); *Report to the president and directors of the Mohawk and Hudson Railway Company* (New York, 1829); *On the St. Lawrence Canals and gradual diminution of the discharge of the St. Lawrence* (Montreal, 1849); *Geometrical solutions of the quadrature of the circle* (Montreal, 1850); and *Geometrical solutions of the lengths and division of circular arcs, the quadrature of the circle, trisection of the angle, duplication of the cube, and quadrature of the hyperbola* (Montreal, 1851).

PAC, National Map Coll., H1/312-1840; H2/300-1829; H3/300-1839; V1/440-1846; RG 4, A1, 216: 70–71; RG 8, I (C ser.), 58: 204; RG 11, A1, 56: 11/56-3. Can., Parl., *Sessional papers*, 1891, 10, no.9. Can., Prov. of, Legislative Assembly, *Journals*, 1844–45: 303, 313; Conseil législatif, *Journaux*, 1844–45: 108; 1852–53: 164. *Quebec Mercury*, 7 Dec. 1830. Morgan, *Bibliotheca Canadensis*, 126. S. J. Gillis, *The Chambly canal: a structural history of the locks* (Can., National Hist. Parks and Sites Branch, *Manuscript report*, no.170, Ottawa, 1975). [T. C. Keefer], "President's address," Canadian Soc. of Civil Engineers, *Trans.* (Montreal), 2 (1888): 9–44.

FONTBONNE, MARIE-ANTOINETTE (sometimes incorrectly Jeanne-Marie), named **Sister Delphine**, first superior and founder of the Congregation of the Sisters of St Joseph in the United States and Canada; b. 24 Dec. 1813 at Bas-en-Basset, France, eleventh child of Claude Fontbonne, vine-dresser, and Marie-Françoise Pleynet; d. 7 Feb. 1856 in Toronto, and is buried in St Michael's Cemetery.

Trained from youth in a pious manner and educated by the Sisters of St Joseph, Marie-Antoinette Fontbonne entered that community in Lyons in June 1832, taking the name Sister Delphine. A few years later, in response to a plea from the bishop of St Louis, Mo., for help in spreading the faith, she and her elder sister Antoinette, another member of the congregation and known as Sister Fébronie, offered their services as missionaries. Their superior, Mother Saint-Jean, who was also their aunt, gave her approval and in 1836 the two sisters, joined en route by their brother, Father Jacques, and four other members of the community went to the United States. After studying English for a short time, Sister Delphine was appointed superior that year of a log cabin convent in Carondelet (St Louis), the congregation's first motherhouse in the United States. Several years of service in that area followed. In 1850 she was appointed superior of a noviciate and orphanage in Philadelphia.

Mother Delphine might have spent her entire career in the United States had it not been for the visit to Philadelphia in 1851 of Toronto's Bishop Armand-François-Marie de Charbonnel*, whose father had helped Mother Saint-Jean re-establish the order following the upheavals of the French revolution. When Bishop Charbonnel, persistent in his efforts to bring religious to Toronto, learned of the presence in Philadelphia of a member of the Fontbonne family trained in France in the original spirit of the order, he immediately asked her bishop that she be released to look after an orphanage in his diocese. In accordance with his wish, Mother Delphine, Sister Mary Martha [Maria Bunning*], and two other sisters arrived in Toronto on 7 Oct. 1851 to take their place alongside the Loretto sisters [see Ellen Dease*] who had arrived in 1847. The Sisters of St Joseph immediately took charge of the institution established by John Elmsley* to care for orphaned children, many of whom had lost their parents in the epidemics that had visited Upper Canada. One contemporary account records: "Hardly had they placed their bonnets and shawls in the front room, when the Superior was inspecting, arranging, ordering, from dormitory to cellar. It was not long before a complete transformation was effected, and one of the front rooms on the ground floor turned into a most inviting chapel."

But the sisters did not restrict their apostolic activities to the care of orphans and the needy in Toronto. As early as 1852 Mother Delphine, at the request of Vicar General Edward John Gordon*, sent her friend and former teaching companion Sister Mary Martha to found another orphanage in Hamilton, and two sisters began teaching at St Patrick's School in Toronto. Within a year of its establishment in Toronto the community had welcomed its first Canadian-born member, Margaret Brennan*, named Sister Teresa. The sisters assumed responsibility for two more separate schools in 1853 and established a mission in Amherstburg. In 1854 they responded to a request to care for men injured in a train wreck in Chatham, and built a new motherhouse near St Paul's Church in Toronto. Next year, at the request of Bishop Charbonnel, Mother Delphine undertook her most significant accomplishment, the planning of the House of Providence, in which anyone in need was to be received. But she was not to see the building completed.

At the close of 1855 Toronto was struck by another typhus epidemic and, as always, the clergy responded selflessly to the needs of the victims. Untiring in her efforts to care for the orphans, for her sisters, and for a woman distraught at the death of her husband, Mother Delphine witnessed the death of two of her nuns before herself contracting the disease. After an illness of only two weeks she died on 7 Feb. 1856, leaving a community of 38 members to mourn her. At the early age of 42, Mother Delphine, by her desire to help the poor and develop the minds and hearts of the neglected, had left a splendid example of love of God and love of neighbour.

Bishop Charbonnel dispatched a letter to France to inform her brother and to express his appreciation of Mother Delphine's worth: "This excellent and worthy niece of his saintly aunt, Mother Saint-Jean, in five years had established in Toronto a noviciate, an orphanage, and a house of temporal and spiritual succour, and several other [establishments] in the diocese. . . . Very sensible and wise, she . . . possessed sound judgement, perceptiveness, and foresight. She was industrious, active, and provident."

MARY BERNITA YOUNG

Arch. de la Congrégation des Sœurs de Saint-Joseph de Lyon (Lyon, France), Reg. Arch. municipales, Bas-en-Basset, France, Descendance des époux Fontbonne–Pleynet (photocopy). Sisters of St Joseph of Toronto, *Community annals*, [1851–1956] (3v. to date, [Toronto, 1968–]), 1: 6–7. D. M. Dougherty *et al.*, *Sisters of St. Joseph of Carondelet* (St Louis, Mo., 1966), 55, 62, 70. *Jubilee volume, 1842–1892: the archdiocese of Toronto and Archbishop Walsh*, [ed. J. R. Teefy] (Toronto, 1892), 221–23, 230–31. [Agnes Murphy], named Sister Mary Agnes, *The Congregation of the Sisters of St. Joseph: Le Puy, Lyons, St. Louis, Toronto* (Toronto, 1951). J. Rivaux, *Vie de la révérende Mère Saint-Jean . . .* (Grenoble, France, 1885), 394–95. M. B. Young, *The dawn of a new day: a sketch of the life and times of Sister Delphine Fontbonne, 1813–1856* (Toronto, 1983).

FOREMAN, JAMES, businessman, judge, justice of the peace, politician, and philanthropist; b. 21 Dec. 1763 in Coldstream, Scotland, son of John Foreman; m. 1791 Mary Gardner, and they had seven daughters and six sons; d. 25 Oct. 1854 in Halifax.

Foreman

James Foreman's career originated in the close commercial linkage between London and Nova Scotia late in the 18th century. Little is known of his family background other than the fact that his father was a merchant in Coldstream; presumably James found in trade his best opportunity for advancement. He apparently had connections to draw upon since, on coming to London, he obtained employment with a leading firm in the colonial trade, the house of Brook Watson*. Watson dominated the export trade to Nova Scotia, ranked as creditor and confidant of most Halifax merchants, and had the ear of the imperial government on British North American affairs. In a move designed to consolidate his position in the Nova Scotian trade, he sent Foreman and another young Scot, George Grassie, to Halifax in 1789. There they established the firm of Foreman and Grassie, which functioned as a branch operation for Watson, receiving consignments from Britain, supervising the distribution of goods throughout Halifax's hinterland, and engaging in the various colonial staples trades. During the protracted hostilities with France, Foreman and Grassie acted as agent for several Royal Navy vessels in the sale of captured enemy and neutral ships. By the first decade of the 19th century the firm had established itself as the second largest importer on the Halifax waterfront, surpassed only by William Forsyth*'s company. The partners acknowledged their prominence by making very generous donations to local philanthropic campaigns, and in 1801 Foreman joined several other notables in an ultimately unsuccessful attempt to establish what might have been British North America's first chartered bank.

Foreman's association with Grassie (and apparently also with Watson's surviving partners) ended in 1812. Foreman continued in trade, taking in his friend Thomas Leonard as partner, and over the next few years Foreman and Company ranked as one of Halifax's leading merchant houses. In 1814, for example, it imported British dry goods valued at £26,312, along with 61,246 gallons of wine and spirits. The firm's Long Wharf premises on Water Street had an assessed value in 1819 of £4,500, considerably more than the rating for George Grassie and Company. Foreman's commercial success was such that he could retire the following year, his future assured by an annual rental income of from £400 to £500 derived from land holdings in both Halifax and Scotland. Foreman had contributed only marginally to institutional development within Halifax business. He served as a director of the Halifax Fire Insurance Company and, in 1819, joined with Michael Wallace* and others to defeat incorporation of a local bank. This action, which contradicted his earlier advocacy of a bank, grew out of factional rivalries within the Halifax merchant community. Although all might endorse the principle of institutionalized banking, divisions appeared when the discussion turned to the creation of a chartered monopoly. The disagreement, combined with rural suspicion of urban moneyed interests, meant that Nova Scotia would not acquire its first chartered bank until 1832.

Community affairs occupied a fair proportion of Foreman's time. He had joined the North British Society in 1790 and served three terms as president. In the realm of philanthropy he belonged to the Halifax Humane Society, helped Walter Bromley* provide education for the poor, and served as director of the Nova Scotia Bible Society. In 1810 he was commissioned a justice of the peace and a justice of the Inferior Court of Common Pleas for Halifax County. He came forward as a candidate for the House of Assembly from Halifax County in 1820 but then withdrew in favour of Simon Bradstreet ROBIE. With this exception, his involvement in politics was confined to the municipal level. He held several offices within Halifax's civic administration, most notably serving as chairman of the board of magistrates from 1828 to 1835. Shortly before resigning as a magistrate, Foreman joined with Richard TREMAIN to bring Joseph Howe* to trial for having allegedly libelled the municipal authorities. This confrontation eventually led to the granting of corporate city status to Halifax in 1841, a reform vigorously opposed by Foreman and most of his business peers.

In retirement Foreman established himself as a respected eccentric. He read extensively, delighting in French and Spanish novels, and would spend days poring over mathematical puzzles. Well into old age he took a daily sea-bath, even when that necessitated breaking through the harbour ice. Foreman also attracted comment by changing his clothes two or three times a day and by going on fasts of bread and water for weeks at a time. He enjoyed company, was a good host, and sang a Scottish folk ballad only hours before his death.

Foreman left a considerable estate: the Halifax portion alone had a value of £10,000. Bequests went to his two surviving brothers in Scotland as well as to his wife and a combination of eight children and grandchildren. The principal beneficiary was his eldest son, James, the first cashier (general manager) at the Bank of Nova Scotia.

DAVID A. SUTHERLAND

GRO (Edinburgh), Coldstream, reg. of births and baptisms, 4 Jan. 1764. Halifax County Court of Probate (Halifax), Estate papers, no.560 (mfm. at PANS). PANS, RG 1, 140: f.319; 173: f.169; 175: f.113; 252, no.3; 314, no.26; RG 31-104, 9, 1814. *Glimpses of Nova Scotia, 1807–24, as seen through the eyes of two Halifax merchants, a Wilmot clergyman and the clerk of the assembly of Nova Scotia*, ed.

C. B. Fergusson (Halifax, 1957), ii. *Journal* (Halifax), 15 May, 25 Dec. 1820. *Novascotian*, 5 Jan. 1832, 6 Nov. 1854. *Nova-Scotia Royal Gazette*, 21 May 1806; 1 Sept. 1807; 6 Jan., 11 Aug. 1813; 12 Oct. 1814. *Royal Gazette and the Nova-Scotia Advertiser* (Halifax), 5 May, 29 Sept. 1795. *Annals, North British Society, Halifax, Nova Scotia, with portraits and biographical notes, 1768–1903*, comp. J. S. Macdonald ([3rd ed.], Halifax, 1905), 14, 150. *Belcher's farmer's almanack*, 1824–54. *Halifax almanack*, 1819. Beamish Murdoch, *A history of Nova-Scotia, or Acadie* (3v., Halifax, 1865–67), 3: 205.

FORETIER, MARIE-AMABLE (Viger), humanitarian; b. 2 Aug. 1778 in Montreal, 11th of 14 children of Thérèse Legrand and Pierre Foretier*, businessman and landowner; m. there 21 Nov. 1808 Denis-Benjamin Viger*, and they had one daughter, who died in infancy; d. there 22 July 1854.

Marie-Amable Foretier lost her mother when she was five and her father remarried four years later, taking as his wife Catherine Hubert, widow of Thomas Baron. Marie-Amable and her four sisters, the only surviving children of the first marriage, grew up in comfortable circumstances in the large home which her mother's parents had ceded to her father in 1778. Pierre Foretier was a man with a penchant for amassing extensive landed property and he also possessed a large library of books and maps. In this atmosphere Marie-Amable may have been introduced to the administrative skills she would use in later life.

In 1808, at 30, Marie-Amable married Denis-Benjamin Viger, a lawyer with some financial ability, who would inherit considerable property in Montreal in 1823. During her husband's sojourns in England in 1828 and from 1831 to 1834, Mme Viger, who had been granted power of attorney, managed the leases on the land and buildings. From 1816 to 1842 she, her husband, and other members of the family would be involved in a prolonged legal battle over the settlement of her father's estate. Among the clauses of Foretier's will which the legatees refused to accept was one which placed Mme Viger's share of the inheritance under the management of the executor, Jean-Baptiste-Toussaint Pothier*, until the death of her husband, so as to exclude Denis-Benjamin Viger from exercising any control over the legacy.

Often left alone after her marriage, because of her husband's frequent absences as a member of the House of Assembly and later as a member of the Legislative and Executive councils, Marie-Amable turned to the aid of the less fortunate as a way of giving meaning to her life. During the 1820s and 1830s Montreal began to experience an increase in population as a result of emigration from Great Britain. Realizing that few charitable institutions existed to meet the needs of the destitute, Angélique Blondeau*, widow of Gabriel Cotté*, challenged the women of Montreal in December 1827 to seek means of easing the suffering of the poor. Members of the Association des Dames de la Charité, founded as a result of Mme Cotté's initiative, chose different fields of concentration for their efforts: young women in trouble, orphans, or the aged and infirm. Mme Viger, through the generous use of her wealth, her administrative ability, her social position, and the political influence of her husband, offered sustained support to all of these concerns.

Mme Viger was also among the women who petitioned the assembly for the incorporation of the Charitable Institution for Female Penitents in 1833. She served as president of the institution from 6 Oct. 1836 until the Sisters of Our Lady of Charity of the Good Shepherd assumed charge in 1846. In that same year, continuing her support for the work, she donated a property on Rue Sherbrooke to the institution. In January 1841 she had been elected president of the Association des Dames de la Charité. She served as president of that association's home for orphans, the Roman Catholic Orphan Asylum of Montreal, from its incorporation in 1841 until her death. She also served until her death as a member of the corporation of the Montreal Asylum for Aged and Infirm Women founded by Émilie Gamelin [TAVERNIER]. It may have been his wife's influence that led Denis-Benjamin Viger to introduce the bill for incorporation of this asylum in 1841 and to lend his support to both it and the bill to incorporate the orphanage. In addition, from the beginnings of the Association des Dames Bienveillantes de Saint-Jacques in July 1828, Mme Viger had served on the executive committee overseeing the society's work for the education of poor girls. On 15 Nov. 1828 she was elected treasurer and assistant of the association, a position she held until 23 July 1831.

According to historian Joseph Royal*, Marie-Amable Viger deserved the title "mother of the poor" of Montreal. Louis-Joseph Papineau* wrote, "How inclined she was to believe the best of a person and how ready to do good; how far removed she was from thinking evil possible, and how incapable of speaking ill of anyone at all." Papineau's description coincides with the impression given by a portrait of this gentle person. The small painting by an unknown artist reveals a pleasant, self-assured woman with intelligent eyes, a woman who might well merit the confidence of her friends and associates in work for the unfortunate.

EDYTH B. BORTHWICK

ACAM, 525.107, 835-1; 846-3. ANQ-M, CE1-51, 3 août 1778, 21 nov. 1808, 1er déc. 1813, 7 juill. 1814; CN1-134, 22 janv. 1816, 22 nov. 1827; CN1-295, 19 nov. 1808, 4 févr. 1828, 7 mai 1831. AP, Notre-Dame de Montréal, reg. des baptêmes, mariages et sépultures, 24 juill. 1854. Arch. des

Fortier

Sœurs de la charité de la Providence (Montréal), Assoc. bienveillante Saint-Jacques, reg. des procès-verbaux, 1828. PAC, MG 24, B46, 1: 95–98. Can., Prov. of, *Statutes*, 1841, c.62, c.67. L.C., *Statutes*, 1832–33, c.35. *Mémoire de Denis Benjamin Viger, écuyer, et de Marie Amable Foretier, son épouse, appellants; contre Toussaint Pothier, écuyer, et autres intimés, à la Cour provinciale d'appel, d'un jugement de la Cour du banc du roi de Montréal, pour les causes civiles, du 20 février 1827* (Montréal, 1827). *La Minerve*, 25 juill. 1854. M.-C. Daveluy, *L'orphelinat catholique de Montréal (1832–1932)* (Montréal, 1933). Joseph Royal, "Biographie de l'hon. D. B. Viger," *L'Écho du cabinet de lecture paroissial* (Montréal), 3 (1861): 68–71.

FORTIER, NARCISSE-CHARLES, Roman Catholic priest; b. 1 Dec. 1800 at Quebec, son of François Fortier, a trader, and Marie Poulin; d. 3 Feb. 1859 in Saint-Michel, Lower Canada.

Narcisse-Charles Fortier received his classical education at the Séminaire de Nicolet from 1811 to 1818. On 4 Oct. 1818 Bishop Joseph-Octave Plessis* tonsured him in Notre-Dame cathedral at Quebec. Fortier then taught at the college just founded by Plessis in Saint-Roch parish and at the same time served as the bishop's secretary. In the latter capacity he was principally responsible for carrying out decisions concerning the temporal administration of the diocese: erecting new parishes and dividing old ones, appointing priests to new posts, building churches, and replying to the various requests of parishioners. He received the minor orders on 16 June 1821 and the diaconate on 15 March 1823, and was finally ordained priest on 12 June of the following year.

After the death of Plessis in 1825, Fortier continued his duties as secretary to the new archbishop of Quebec, Bernard-Claude Panet*. Four years later he became parish priest at Saint-Michel on the south bank of the St Lawrence, where he took over from Antoine Gosselin. Charles-Félix Cazeau* replaced him as Panet's secretary.

At Saint-Michel, Fortier had some difficult moments, especially from 1836. That year, with the support of the churchwardens, he decided to rent or sell the church pews to the highest bidders. The decision, far from being unanimously accepted by the parishioners, gave rise to heated discussion that dragged on for years. Indeed, the conflict was not resolved until 1849, when Archbishop Joseph Signay* informed the parishioners by letter that the pews in the nave would be sold as they became vacant and those in the rood-loft would be rented.

During the disturbances of 1837–38 Fortier, like his colleagues in Rivière-Ouelle and L'Islet, Louis-Marie Cadieux* and François-Xavier Delage, had disapproved of armed revolt and given a warm welcome to a military detachment en route from New Brunswick to Montreal.

In 1853 Fortier founded the industrial college of Saint-Michel, placing it under the direction of François-Xavier Toussaint*. It was one of some 15 such colleges which were set up between 1846 and 1856 in Lower Canada. The curriculum, which was quite flexible and depended on the skills of the faculty, focused on commercial courses. At Saint-Michel in 1854, three teachers gave courses in both English and French to about 130 students.

Narcisse-Charles Fortier died at Saint-Michel on 3 Feb. 1859 and was buried five days later in the sanctuary of the parish church. In his will he had bequeathed to the church the organ, which belonged to him, and to the school commissioners the land on which the college had been built.

CÉLINE CYR

ANQ-Q, CE1-1, 1er déc. 1800; CE2-5, 8 févr. 1859. ASQ, Lettres, T, 128, 133. Allaire, *Dictionnaire*, vol.1. Caron, "Inv. de la corr. de Mgr Briand," ANQ *Rapport*, 1929–30: 76; "Inv. de la corr. de Mgr Panet," 1933–34: 263–64, 275, 285, 295, 304, 306, 331, 355, 371–72, 384–86, 391, 403, 408, 414, 418; 1935–36: 174, 188; "Inv. de la corr. de Mgr Plessis," 1928–29: 155, 203; 1932–33: 139, 175, 188, 197, 205, 215, 219; "Inv. de la corr. de Mgr Signay," 1936–37: 161, 353, 355, 362, 369, 433; 1938–39: 346. L.-P. Audet, *Histoire de l'enseignement au Québec* (2v., Montréal et Toronto, 1971), 2: 136–37. Chabot, *Le curé de campagne*. Douville, *Hist. du collège-séminaire de Nicolet*. Henri Gingras, *Saint-Michel de Bellechasse* (Saint-Romuald, Qué., 1977). Lambert, "Joseph-Octave Plessis." Père Marie-Antoine, *St-Michel de la Durantaye (notes et souvenirs), 1678–1929* (Québec, 1929).

FRASER, ALEXANDER, army officer, militia officer, office holder, justice of the peace, politician, and farmer; b. 18 Jan. 1786 in Glendoemore, near Fort Augustus, Scotland; m. first Catharine Grant (d. 1818); m. secondly Ann McDonell, daughter of Archibald MacDonell (Leek), and they had two sons and four daughters; d. 12 Nov. 1853 in Fraserfield, near Williamstown, Upper Canada.

In 1803 Alexander Fraser joined the Canadian Fencibles in Scotland and was one of the non-commissioned officers to be retained when most of the regiment was discharged the following year. He accompanied the staff to Quebec in September 1805 and shortly thereafter assumed command of the regiment's recruiting department at Montreal. Four years later he became quartermaster and served in that capacity throughout the War of 1812. Placed on half pay in 1816, he established himself in Charlottenburgh Township, Glengarry County, where he purchased lot 40, north of the Raisin River, from his first wife's family. He was to build the 200-acre farm, which he called Fraserfield, into a 1,281-acre estate by 1851. His acquisition of other property through purchases and grants, including his wives' loyalist claims, had given him "a large stake" in the county as early as 1820.

Unlike many of those prominent in Glengarry, Fraser was not connected with the fur trade (though his brother Paul was). But he occupied a position in Glengarry society equal to that of the great fur traders such as Simon Fraser* and William McGillivray*, with whom he founded the Highland Society of Canada in 1818; Alexander Fraser served as the society's treasurer until 1825. Though a Scottish Catholic, he became close friends with the Presbyterian lay leader and former fur trader John McGillivray (Dalcrombie) and with the Reverend John McKenzie of St Andrew's Church, Williamstown. Fraser's experience with public office seems to have been less smooth. In spite of a strong recommendation from legislative councillor Neil McLean*, he was not appointed county registrar in 1819. The registry office was kept at Fraserfield, however, and for some time Fraser served as deputy registrar. His innumerable letters dealing with land transactions reveal a deep if paternalistic concern for the problems of the early settlers. In 1820 Fraser received his first of several commissions as justice of the peace for the Eastern District. Later that year, despite his lack of militia connections, he was recommended by Alexander McDonell* (Collachie) to command the 1st Regiment of Glengarry militia. His appointment over senior militia officers such as Duncan Macdonell (Greenfield) was the source of considerable friction within the county. Fraser's feud with the powerful Greenfield Macdonells lasted for several years and culminated in the winter of 1825–26 with a petition to the House of Assembly drawn up by Duncan's brother, sheriff Donald Macdonell*, accusing Fraser of "Unconstitutional and Unofficer like conduct." The outcome of the petition is not known, but Fraser clearly emerged unscathed. He was elected with Alexander McMartin to the assembly for Glengarry in 1828 and continued to serve there until 1834, supporting the conservative cause and, especially, the interests of his friend Bishop Alexander McDonell*.

In the 1830s Fraser devoted his energies to acquiring more land, avoiding his creditors, improving Fraserfield (mentioned by Thomas Rolph in 1836 as "a fine farm, well cultivated, with a handsome residence on it"), and seeking appointment to local office. He was made registrar of Glengarry County in the winter of 1836–37 and held that position until his death. During the rebellion of 1837–38 Fraser was commended by Sir John Colborne* for his role in "dispersing the rebels" in Lower Canada. He and his regiment were stationed at Saint-Philippe-de-Laprairie in February and March 1838. That November, with fighting breaking out anew, they made a foray into Beauharnois. Although the action was brief, the subsequent pillaging forced even Fraser to admit that his men were "looked upon as savages." Many of his

Glengarries, it was said, had "marched out . . . as infantry . . . and returned as cavalry" on "stray French ponies."

On the recommendation of Lieutenant Governor Sir George Arthur, who described him as "a farmer and possessed of large real estate," Fraser was sworn in as a member of the Legislative Council in December 1839. There he supported the moderate, pro-union position of Governor Charles Edward Poulett Thomson* (soon to become Lord Sydenham) and Attorney General William Henry Draper*. For the 1841 elections to the first Legislative Assembly of the united provinces, Fraser and his fellow legislative councillor John McGillivray selected John Sandfield Macdonald* as their candidate for the single Glengarry seat, thus launching the future first premier of Ontario on his long political career. Although Sandfield Macdonald would desert his patron politically the following year when Robert Baldwin and the reformers replaced Draper in the government, he and Fraser kept up their deep personal friendship and their mutual concern for Glengarry.

In June 1841 Fraser became a legislative councillor for the province of Canada. As such he supported Sydenham's bill to divide the annual proceeds from the clergy reserves among several denominations. Yet his moderate political position was severely tested when Sydenham and Draper successfully pushed through a bill to replace the old courts of quarter sessions, dominated by appointed justices of the peace, with elected councils. Fraser joined hard-line tories in vainly opposing a measure which would have undermined his local power. He also opposed the government's bill to make the naturalization of Americans easier. Draper could ill afford to alienate Fraser; he quickly had him named the first warden of the Eastern District, the only appointed position on the new district council. Thus placated, Fraser was able to adjust to the new age and to secure control over elections to the council. He held the wardenship until early 1850 when it too ceased to be an appointed office.

After 1843 Fraser made only rare appearances in the Legislative Council. He was there in 1845 to support Draper's unsuccessful attempt to establish a federated university structure which would guarantee financial support to the various denominational colleges. Indeed Fraser's main political thrust involved support for education, especially state aid for schools in the Eastern District. Many local schools benefited greatly from these efforts. Fraser often worked with reformers on matters of local interest. In 1848 he and Sandfield Macdonald each put up a £500 surety to enable Fraser's brother-in-law Donald Aeneas MacDonell*, a defeated Stormont reform candidate, to be appointed district sheriff. The following year they succeeded in preventing the Eastern District from being split into separate county jurisdictions under the Municipal

Fraser

Corporations Act. The district kept its integrity as the United Counties of Stormont, Dundas and Glengarry. But the Rebellion Losses Bill of 1849 was too much for the old soldier to swallow. Though Sandfield Macdonald's newspaper, the Cornwall *Freeholder*, praised Governor Lord Elgin [Bruce*] for his deep grasp of responsible government, Fraser made two rare appearances in the upper house that spring to denounce the "disastrous advice" tendered the governor over the bill. To show his displeasure with the reformers Fraser ran for election to one of the five seats on the newly established Charlottenburgh township council in 1850, despite attempts by Sandfield Macdonald to dissuade him. He secured election but came fourth, well behind Macdonald and his own son-in-law, reformer Dr Daniel Eugene McIntyre. When the full council of the united counties met, it was McIntyre, not Fraser, who was chosen warden. An era had ended.

Nevertheless Fraser remained a central figure in local society. In 1846 he was appointed lieutenant-colonel of the 1st Battalion of Glengarry militia, in the newly organized regiment of the Eastern District, precursor of the Stormont, Dundas and Glengarry Highlanders, and in 1851 he was elected president of the Highland Society. He and his wife saw their children marry into prominent families on both sides of the political and religious divide and continued to hold court at Fraserfield. In the late 1840s two wings had been added to the square core of the large and imposing mansion, which is still standing, and the farm was a model of diversified agriculture, in the vanguard of dairy farming for the region. Fraserfield was mortgaged, however, and codicils in Fraser's will provided for the sale of much of his remaining property to pay off his debts. In May 1853 an ailing Fraser made his last appearance in parliament to speak in favour of a reform-sponsored bill increasing representation in the assembly. His sons-in-law Daniel McIntyre and Donald Alexander Macdonald*, at the instigation of the latter's brother Sandfield, had persuaded the old man to make the difficult trip to Quebec. "If anything happened, the little woman will never forgive Donald and myself," McIntyre wrote. Fraser died that November. His body was piped from Fraserfield to his well-attended funeral in Williamstown.

BRUCE W. HODGINS

A portrait of Alexander Fraser is reproduced on p.51 of *A history of Glengarry*, cited below.

AO, MS 266; MU 1968. MTL, Robert Baldwin papers. PAC, MG 24, B30; I3, 10; RG 1, E3, 70: 46–48; L3, 189: F10/40, 62; 190: F12/84, 107; RG 5, A1: 24580–81, 25579, 40733–36, 67384–93, 69719–21, 70631–34; RG 31, A1, 1851, Charlottenburgh Township: 211–12. *Arthur papers* (Sanderson). Thomas Rolph, *A brief account, together with observations, made during a visit in the West Indies, and a tour through the United States of America, in parts of the years 1832–3; together with a statistical account of Upper Canada* (Dundas, [Ont.], 1836), 139. *Montreal Gazette*, 16 Nov. 1853. [J. F. Pringle], *The genealogy of Jacob Farrand Pringle and his wife Isabella Fraser Pringle* ([Cornwall, Ont., 1892]). John Fraser, *Canadian pen and ink sketches* (Montreal, 1890). B. W. Hodgins, *John Sandfield Macdonald, 1812–1872* (Toronto, 1971); "The political career of John Sandfield Macdonald to the fall of his administration in March, 1864: a study in Canadian politics" (PHD thesis, Duke Univ., Durham, N.C., 1964). Royce MacGillivray and Ewan Ross, *A history of Glengarry* (Belleville, Ont., 1979). J. F. Pringle, *Lunenburgh or the old Eastern District; its settlement and early progress . . .* (Cornwall, 1890; repr. Belleville, 1972). Elinor [Kyte] Senior, "The Glengarry Highlanders and the suppression of the rebellions in Lower Canada, 1837–38," Soc. for Army Hist. Research, *Journal* (London), 56 (1978): 143–59.

FRASER, RICHARD DUNCAN, fur trader, merchant, militia officer, farmer, justice of the peace, politician, and office holder; b. *c.* 1784 in the province of Quebec, probably in Montreal, third son of Thomas Fraser* and Mary MacBean; m. by January 1812 Mary McDonell, and they had at least two sons and three daughters; d. 1 April 1857 in Fraserfield, Grenville County, Upper Canada.

Richard Duncan Fraser's father, a captain in Edward Jessup*'s Loyal Rangers during the American revolution, settled in Township No.6 (Edwardsburgh) after the war and became a prominent landowner in eastern Upper Canada. Richard Duncan spent his early years in Edwardsburgh Township and was said to have been educated by John Strachan*. From 1802 to 1806 he worked for the North West Company as a clerk under Duncan Cameron* at Lake Nipigon. On his return to Edwardsburgh in 1807 he received a 200-acre land grant as the son of a loyalist and settled in the village of Johnstown. There he operated as a merchant until the outbreak of the War of 1812.

A lieutenant in the 2nd Grenville Militia, Fraser was attached to an artillery company at Prescott. Then, during the fall of 1812, he commanded a light gunboat on the St Lawrence. In late February 1813, after having rejoined the artillery, he was in charge of a field gun during the capture of Ogdensburg, N.Y. [*see* George Richard John Macdonell*] and shortly afterwards was promoted captain in the 1st Dundas Militia, of which his father was lieutenant-colonel. On the orders of Lieutenant-General Sir George Prevost* but using his own funds, he recruited a troop of light dragoons which he led that November in the battle at John CRYSLER's farm. Described in 1814 by the inspecting field officer of militia, Lieutenant-Colonel Thomas Pearson, as "an active and zealous officer," Fraser was appointed assistant quartermaster general in February 1815. Before he could benefit from this position, however, news reached Canada that the war had ended.

After the war Fraser did not return to his mercantile pursuits, but was "obliged to have recourse to farming" to support himself and his family. In addition he made several unsuccessful attempts during the next 15 years to obtain a government position. The only appointment he received, however, was in 1816 as a justice of the peace for the Johnstown District. Fraser's difficulty in obtaining office despite support from his influential father may have been a result of his hot-tempered, violent behaviour. Before 1812 he had been convicted and fined on three separate assault charges, one involving an attack on Charles Jones* of Brockville. In 1813, as a militia officer, he had been charged with trespass, assault, and false imprisonment, and a judgement was made against him for civil damages in 1814. When Fraser applied for funds from the government to pay this two years later, William Campbell*, who had presided at the civil trial, reported that Fraser's conduct had been "most violent and brutal" and refused "to offer any opinion, as to how far the interference of the Government . . . may comport with its honour and interest."

In 1818 Fraser was again before the Court of Quarter Sessions at Brockville, this time charged with an assault against Robert Gourlay*. When Gourlay had arrived at Johnstown on his eastern tour of the province, Fraser called him "a Liar and a Blackguard" and proceeded to beat him in public with "a rod of correction." Supporters of both men arrived and a small riot ensued. Unsuccessful in his attempt to disrupt Gourlay's meeting by force, Fraser exercised his authority as a magistrate and arrested him on charges of seditious libel. In response Gourlay charged Fraser with assault. At the assizes, held that August at Brockville, Gourlay was acquitted on a reduced charge of libel; Fraser was tried before a sympathetic local court and assessed a small fine.

Given such a background, it was unlikely that an official post of any importance could be risked on Fraser. For the next several years he seems to have modified his behaviour; there were no further charges of assault. Finally in 1832 his persistence was rewarded with an appointment as collector of customs for Brockville. This came slightly more than a year after his election as a member for Grenville in the House of Assembly. In December 1831, during the session that resulted in the first expulsion of William Lyon Mackenzie* from the house, Fraser had chiefly distinguished himself by threatening to horsewhip Mackenzie. In the general elections of October 1834, Fraser withdrew his candidacy before the opening of the polls. During a by-election for Leeds in the spring of 1836 he allied himself with Ogle Robert Gowan*, but the two tory candidates were defeated by reformers William Buell* and Mathew H. Howard.

Until the rebellion of 1837–38, Fraser had to content himself with his duties as magistrate and as customs collector.

In January 1838, with the threat of a Patriot invasion, Fraser as colonel of the 2nd Regiment of Grenville militia was stationed at Prescott. Four months later he was aboard the steamship *Sir Robert Peel* when it was attacked and pillaged by William Johnston*, Donald M'Leod*, and other Patriots. In November he commanded the left flank in the so-called battle of the Windmill near Prescott [*see* Plomer Young*]. During this period of tense relations between Upper Canada and the United States, Fraser became involved in a minor diplomatic incident when in May 1839, as customs collector, he seized the American schooner *G. S. Weeks* at Brockville for failure to declare a cannon as part of its cargo. Lieutenant Governor Sir George ARTHUR conducted a personal inquiry and condemned the behaviour of both American and Canadian participants in the affair. Arthur considered that Fraser had been "popularity-hunting" and that his ill-considered and unauthorized actions in seizing the vessel and subsequently releasing it had laid the foundation "for all the mischief that followed."

By this time Fraser was also in trouble with the government because of his failure to pay over his customs duties. In September 1838 he had been questioned about the default and, when the government persisted in its demands despite his claim that the money had been lost with the *Sir Robert Peel*, he offered to make partial payment that December. It is apparent that Fraser was, at the least, unable to manage the funds he received through his official positions. Certainly his business abilities appear to have been poor. By 1840 he owed £4,000 in outstanding civil judgements to creditors amongst whom were the Bank of Upper Canada, the Bank of Montreal, and the Commercial Bank of the Midland District. The combination of his mismanagement of government funds with the lack of judgement demonstrated during the *Weeks* affair as well as his virulent toryism left him with few allies powerful enough to assist him when the reformers came to power in 1842. Fraser was replaced as customs collector in January 1843. That September Brockville reformer William Buell Richards* claimed that Fraser's decisions as a magistrate were "far from satisfactory" and recommended his removal from a position that he was "totally incompetent to fill." The following month Fraser's name was struck from the district commission of the peace.

Retaining only his position as militia colonel, Fraser retired to Fraserfield in Edwardsburgh Township, the farm fronting on the St Lawrence which he had inherited in the early 1820s from his father and his brother John. Although Fraser seems to have left

Fraser

active politics after the 1830s, he reappeared briefly during 1849 as a delegate to the convention of the British American League [*see* George Moffatt*] in Kingston. He died eight years later at Fraserfield.

C. J. SHEPARD

AO, MS 35, alphabetical list of students, 26 Nov. 1827; RG 8, ser.I-1-H, 2: 42; ser.I-1-P, box 4; RG 21, United counties of Leeds and Grenville, Edwardsburgh Township, census and assessment rolls, 1811–20, 1848; RG 22, ser.12, 1: 190, 225, 233; 2–6; ser.14, boxes 2–3; ser.131, 1, 4; ser.134, 4; ser.155, will of Thomas Fraser; ser.179, John Fraser; Mary Fraser. MTL, Robert Baldwin papers; R. D. Fraser, "Journal, from Edwardsburgh to Nipigon and other places in the North or Indian country." PAC, RG 1, E3, 30A: 224–35; L3, 188: F9/8; 189: F10/37, F11/77; RG 5, A1: 11450–62, 12127–30, 12465–68, 13982–83, 25948–50, 30952–53, 49558–59, 51281–83, 52468–70, 93132–38, 103272–73, 108363–64, 114278–81; C1, 14, file 1748; RG 8, I (C ser.); RG 31, A1, 1851, Edwardsburgh Township; RG 68, General index, 1651–1841, 1841–67. PRO, CO 42/390: 188–91; 42/460: 144–54; 42/518: 70–75. *Arthur papers* (Sanderson). *Docs. relating to NWC* (Wallace). *Elgin–Grey papers* (Doughty). U.C., House of Assembly, *Journal*, 1831–34. *Brockville Recorder*, 22 Dec. 1831, 10 Oct. 1834, 9 April 1857. *Kingston Gazette*, 7 July–22 Sept. 1818. Armstrong, *Handbook of Upper Canadian chronology*. Duncan Fraser, *William Fraser, Senior, U.E., and his descendants in Fulton County, New York, and Grenville County, Ontario* (Johnstown, N.Y., 1964). *Officers of British forces in Canada* (Irving). Patterson, "Studies in elections in U.C."

FRASER, WILLIAM, Roman Catholic priest and bishop; b. 1778 or 1779 in Glenn Cannich, Scotland, eldest of 12 children of John Fraser and Jane Chisholm; d. 4 Oct. 1851 in Antigonish, N.S.

William Fraser attended the seminary at Samalaman in Moidart, Scotland, after having gone to elementary school in his own district. In January 1794 he began his studies for the priesthood at the Royal Scots College in Valladolid, Spain. Ordained there on 8 Jan. 1804, he soon returned to Scotland, where his cousin Bishop John Chisholm put him in charge of all the missions of Lochaber. For a decade he ministered to the small but scattered population and then spent eight years directing the College of Killechiarain, the seminary for the Highlands, at Lismore. Fraser adapted well to both missionary and academic life and was loved and respected by his parishioners and students. His talents were recognized when his was among the names proposed to the Sacred Congregation of Propaganda to succeed another cousin, Æneas Chisholm, bishop of Lismore, who died in 1818. He was not selected but such recognition placed him in good standing for future appointments.

Throughout his years at Lismore, Fraser had expressed a strong desire to follow some of his fellow Highlanders who had immigrated to Nova Scotia. The Roman Catholic Church in Nova Scotia had its origins with missionaries from France and New France who came to minister to the Acadian population during the 17th and 18th centuries. After the colony became part of Great Britain in 1763, a few priests were permitted to come and serve Roman Catholics among the native and Acadian populations as well as among the growing number of Irish and Scottish immigrants. The activities of the church in the Maritimes came under the jurisdiction of the diocese of Quebec and since 1787 had been governed by a local vicar general appointed by the bishop of Quebec. By 1815 Propaganda in Rome had decided that the area covered by the diocese was becoming too large and in 1818 Father Edmund Burke*, vicar general for Nova Scotia, was consecrated titular bishop of Sion and vicar apostolic of Nova Scotia. In June 1821 Father Angus Bernard MacEachern* was consecrated titular bishop of Rosen and was appointed vicar general of Cape Breton Island, Prince Edward Island, New Brunswick, and the Îles de la Madeleine.

Before Bishop Burke died in 1820, he had offered Fraser a mission near Antigonish but it was not until 1822 that Fraser was able to obtain permission to move to Nova Scotia. When he arrived in August, the church had yet to appoint a successor to Burke. Father John Carroll, parish priest at Halifax, was serving as administrator. Bishop MacEachern, a Scot, introduced Fraser to the Highland Scots of Cape Breton Island and the area around Antigonish. Fraser was soon appointed to a mission at Cape Mabou on Cape Breton and in less than a month received responsibility for the Bras d'Or Lakes missions. In January 1824 he was given charge of St Ninian's parish, centred in Antigonish, where he was to remain for the rest of his life.

Fraser's ability and dedication to the missions resulted in his being recommended as a worthy successor to Burke as early as December 1823. After a concerted effort to find an Irishman for the post, on 7 Dec. 1824 Pope Leo XII approved Fraser's appointment as titular bishop of Tanen and vicar apostolic of Nova Scotia. He was consecrated at Antigonish on 24 June 1827 by his good friend MacEachern. Fraser's vicariate, covering all of mainland Nova Scotia, comprised a substantial Highland Scottish population in the east, Acadians in the southwest, and an active and growing Irish community in and around Halifax. In September 1830 Cape Breton, with its large Scottish population, was added and, six years later, the island of Bermuda came under his jurisdiction. Fraser himself estimated that by 1831 the Catholic population of the province numbered at least 50,000, of whom over half were Scots and only about one in ten was Irish.

From the day of his appointment, Fraser found the

Irish in Halifax, who were disappointed that an Irishman had not been named bishop, a particularly onerous responsibility. In choosing to remain at Antigonish, where as a Gaelic-speaking missionary he felt he was needed, Fraser alienated the Halifax Irish who believed that the see of the diocese should have been located in the largest community. The departure of Carroll from the province late in 1827 left Halifax without a parish priest and Fraser's choice as a successor, Father John Loughnan, although an Irishman, was to bear the brunt of the Irish resentment towards Fraser. In 1839, with the assistance of Archbishop Daniel Murray of Dublin and after repeated representations from Halifax, Fraser was able to obtain the services of two Irish priests, Lawrence Joseph Dease and Richard Baptist O'Brien. They proved popular with the Halifax Irish but did not get along with Loughnan, who felt that they were working too closely with the "rich and powerful" and were subverting his authority as the representative of Bishop Fraser.

Fraser's difficulties in Halifax did not go unnoticed by Propaganda in Rome. After a visit to Halifax in 1840, Bishop John England of Charleston, S.C., provided Archbishop Murray in Dublin with a first-hand account of the situation there. Murray then wrote to Rome urging the cardinals to appoint an Irish coadjutor bishop with right of succession to assist Fraser. In a letter dated 19 Oct. 1840 a similar recommendation was made by Father Vincent de Paul [MERLE], superior of the Trappists in Nova Scotia and a friend of Fraser's. The situation worsened by late 1841 when a dispute arose over the departure of Dease. A committee of wardens and electors of St Mary's Cathedral petitioned Fraser to allow Dease to remain. Accusing them of meddling in ecclesiastical affairs, Fraser curtly rejected their petition, stating that "any future application . . . will meet with . . . unqualified and well-merited contempt." In support of Fraser, Father Hugh O'REILLY, parish priest at Pictou, penned a series of letters to a local newspaper under the name Hibernicus, attacking "the conduct of the Irish Catholic Schismaticks of the Capital." These anonymous letters brought the conflict into public view and put further pressure on Rome to resolve the issue.

On 9 Jan. 1842 Pope Gregory XVI approved a recommendation from Propaganda to raise the status of the vicariate apostolic of Nova Scotia to that of a diocese and to appoint an Irish priest, William WALSH, as coadjutor to Fraser with the right of succession. Throughout all their discussions, officials in Rome had neither been in contact with nor heard from Fraser. He learned of Walsh's appointment from an article in a Halifax newspaper and in a letter from Walsh written after the latter's consecration in May 1842. Fraser had some justification in feeling that he

had been treated unfairly, and he was annoyed that a few dissidents among the 60,000 Catholics in the province had been able to provoke such drastic action by officials in Rome. He was supported by 21 of the 23 priests of the diocese who, on 27 May 1842, sent a petition to Cardinal Giacomo Filippo Fransoni, prefect of Propaganda, urging the pope to cancel Walsh's appointment and expressing their loyalty and support for Fraser. Thirteen of these priests also wrote to Walsh stating their opposition to his appointment and to the Halifax "faction" which had provoked the situation.

The arrival of Walsh in Halifax in October 1842 further polarized the pro- and anti-Fraser forces. A coadjutor traditionally can act only when his bishop so authorizes and Fraser was reluctant to give Walsh any authority until he received official confirmation of the appointment from Rome. He did, however, instruct Walsh to assume responsibility for the temporal affairs of the church in Halifax from the wardens and electors of St Mary's, a body that he felt had instigated many of his difficulties. He also left Loughnan in his post as vicar general, a decision that was to cause an open rift between Walsh and Loughnan. For almost a year and a half both sides flooded Rome with memorials. Finally, in March 1844, Walsh set off for Rome to seek a final resolution of the matter. It seemed to most observers that the only solution was to divide the diocese along ethnic lines: the Scots in one diocese and the Irish in another. Fraser had suggested this course of action in May 1842 before he knew of Walsh's appointment. Walsh agreed with the plan but felt that part of the problem was Fraser's inability to administer and govern a diocese no matter how small and that even if Fraser were put in charge only of the Scottish areas he would still require a coadjutor to assist him.

The debate continued, with Fraser and Walsh and their supporters placing their respective cases before the cardinals, who, on 2 Sept. 1844, decided that the diocese was to be divided. Fraser's diocese, officially created on 22 September, included Cape Breton and the area that is now Antigonish and Guysborough counties. On 20 July 1845 Walsh became bishop of Halifax and Fraser bishop of Arichat. Despite the fact that the see of the diocese was Arichat, Fraser chose to remain in Antigonish, a decision that was later to cause problems with the Acadians in Cape Breton similar to those with the Irish in Halifax.

Fraser had lost the battle but won the war: the Irish "faction" in Halifax was no longer his concern and for the next six years he concentrated on his first love – developing the missions within the diocese through the construction of schools and churches for his fellow Scots. His difficulties with Halifax had arisen for a number of reasons, not the least of which was the historic antagonism between the Scots and the Irish.

Frémiot

The personality of Loughnan and the determination of the Irish Catholics in Halifax to participate in church matters were also factors, but ones that Fraser could have handled. His lack of administrative ability prevented him from resolving the problem before it got out of hand. He remained in Antigonish and ultimately the decision making was left to others.

Although the jurisdictional battle marked his term as bishop, Fraser did accomplish much in the field of education. In 1838 he had reluctantly agreed to a proposal from the Irish-Catholic community in Halifax to establish a college there, incorporated on 29 March 1841 as St Mary's College. In Arichat he began St Andrew's Grammar School, the precursor of St Francis Xavier University in Antigonish. He also encouraged the establishment of a number of temperance groups throughout the diocese.

When Fraser died at Antigonish on 4 Oct. 1851, it was not his administrative shortcomings that were remembered. Instead he was described as a "profoundly learned, . . . venerable prelate [who] was ever singularly affable, honest and unobtrusive," who "never cared for human applause," and who "won the attachment and respect of all classes." He shunned riches and lived simply among the people he served. It may be said of him that he was a good missionary and one whose talents lay more in the basic ecclesiastical virtues of his calling than in the administrative and political aptitudes required of a bishop of the church. He was succeeded by Colin Francis MacKinnon*.

DAVID B. FLEMMING

AAH, William Fraser papers; William Walsh papers. Hibernicus [Hugh O'Reilly], The letters of Hibernicus: extracts from the pamphlet entitled "A report of the committee of St. Mary's, Halifax, N.S.," and a review of the same (Pictou, N.S., 1842). G. M. Haliburton, Clansmen of Nova Scotia (Halifax, 1979). A. A. Johnston, Hist. of Catholic Church in eastern N.S. D. J. Rankin, A history of the county of Antigonish, Nova Scotia (Toronto, 1929). J. E. Burns, "The development of Roman Catholic church government in Halifax from 1760 to 1853," N.S. Hist. Soc., Coll., 23 (1936): 89–102. A. A. Johnston, "The Right Reverend William Fraser, second vicar apostolic of Nova Scotia, first bishop of Halifax, and first bishop of Arichat," CCHA Report, 3 (1935–36): 23–30; "A Scottish bishop in New Scotland: the Right Reverend William Fraser, second vicar apostolic of Nova Scotia, first bishop of Halifax, and first bishop of Arichat," Innes Rev. (Glasgow), 6 (1955): 107–24. Mason Wade, "Relations between the French, Irish and Scottish clergy in the Maritime provinces, 1774–1836," CCHA Study sessions, 39 (1972): 9–33.

FRÉMIOT, NICOLAS-MARIE-JOSEPH (baptized **Nicolas-Joseph**), Roman Catholic priest, Jesuit, and missionary; b. 5 Oct. 1818 in Bellefontaine, dept of Vosges, France, son of Joseph Frémiot and Marie-Jeanne Didier; d. 4 July 1854 near present-day Blind River, Ont.

After five years of training with the Society of Jesus in France, Nicolas-Marie-Joseph Frémiot was ordained subdeacon in September 1846 and priest one year later. He departed at once for the Canadian mission field to which the Jesuits had only recently returned after a long absence [see Jean-Pierre Chazelle*], and spent his first winter in the Montreal region. On 20 May 1848 he set out for Sandwich (Windsor), Upper Canada, site of the most westerly Roman Catholic parish at that time. Only after his arrival was he informed that he and Father Jean-Pierre Choné were to establish a mission at Pigeon River at the west end of Lake Superior. From Sault Ste Marie, Frémiot travelled west with Father Choné and Brother Frédéric de Pooter. At Pigeon River, near the newly determined international boundary, they ministered to the region's Northern Ojibwa Indians. Father Choné was the senior in age and in experience, already familiar with the Ojibwa language that Frémiot had yet to learn, so that in the first year of their association Choné had to undertake most of the journeys from the Pigeon River mission while Frémiot studied to prepare himself for his later work. At different times in his ministry Frémiot made good use of the Ojibwa grammars written by fellow missionaries George-Antoine Bellecourt* and Frederic Baraga*.

In 1849, a year after their arrival, Choné and Frémiot decided to move their headquarters to the Kaministikwia River near Fort William (Thunder Bay), and Frémiot spent the fall there in charge of building the new Mission de l'Immaculée-Conception. During the next four years the two priests divided duties between them, one remaining at Fort William, the other travelling to the smaller Hudson's Bay Company posts and to the mining locations at Isle Royale in Michigan and at Prince Bay. As time went on Frémiot undertook most of the extended journeys while Choné concentrated on the area near the mission and on the school for Indian children that he had begun. It was Frémiot, for example, who established a mission at Nipigon in February 1852. Later the same year the two men parted in amity with no hint of the disharmony that sometimes existed between Choné and his assistants, and Frémiot set out for his new headquarters, Wikwemikong on Manitoulin Island, where Jean-Baptiste Proulx*, a fellow missionary, had previously laboured. Given a roving commission, he usually travelled among the Ottawas, the Potawatomis, and the Saugeens (a mixed group of Ojibwas, Potawatomis, and Ottawas), about whom his previous experience had taught him little. But, on his final journey along the north shore of Lake Huron, he again encountered the Northern Ojibwas.

While performing the many arduous tasks demanded of a pioneer missionary, Frémiot wrote a number of lengthy and detailed letters to his colleagues in Canada and abroad. These letters are particularly important as a counterbalance to contemporary accounts by John

McLean* and Thomas Gummersall Anderson* of the region and its native peoples. Frémiot assessed Indian life from a point of view far removed from that of those who sought economic advantage or the expansion of Canadian political power, and his horror at many of the customs he described was tempered by his sympathy for the individuals he met. He perceived that most of the young Indians owed their livelihood to the HBC, and he questioned the effect on them of both the long journeys undertaken to secure furs and the company's practice of paying with merchandise, some of it worthless. As a witness to the discussions held in 1849 between Canadian representatives, led by Anderson, and the Indians around Fort William prior to the treaty concluded the next year by William Benjamin Robinson*, Frémiot had a rare oportunity to record contacts between Indians and whites and the resulting misunderstandings. At first, he was inclined to view the treaty as acceptable, if only because it seemed preferable to American contemporary practice, which included pushing the Indians to the area west of the Mississippi River, but, observing its effects, he came to regard it as a shameful bargain that reduced the Indians to poverty.

Frémiot's experience and influence were largely restricted to the small groups he served at his missions and on his travels. For most of his missionary career he was far removed geographically from the centres of institutional power; in the Thunder Bay region he had little contact with government officials or with missionaries of other faiths, and the mines he visited were closing down rather than expanding their operations. His own training, moreover, had left him completely isolated from the pressures and prejudices of contemporary politics. His was the voice of the European humanist in the Canadian wilderness.

In a letter dated 2 Feb. 1851 Frémiot described his many missionary trips as involving "at one and the same time the greatest hardships and dangers, but also the greatest consolations and, perhaps, the greatest rewards." He fell victim to those very dangers some three years later when he drowned in the Mississagi River while on a journey among the Ojibwas. He was buried at Wikwemikong.

ELIZABETH ARTHUR

Valuable material relating to Nicolas-Marie-Joseph Frémiot is held in the Arch. de la Compagnie de Jésus, prov. du Canada français (Saint-Jérôme, Qué.).

AD, Vosges (Épinal), État civil, Bellefontaine, 5 oct. 1818. *Lettres des nouvelles missions du Canada, 1843–1852*, Lorenzo Cadieux, édit. (Montréal et Paris, 1973). *Thunder Bay district, 1821–1892: a collection of documents*, ed. and intro. [M.] E. Arthur (Toronto, 1973). M. A. Norton, *Catholic missionary activities in the northwest, 1818–1864* ... (Washington, 1930). [M.] E. Arthur, "Le Père Frémiot à Thunder Bay, de 1848 à 1852," *RHAF*, 25 (1971–72): 205–23.

G

GAGE, JAMES, farmer and businessman; b. 25 June 1774 in Greenbush, N.Y.; m. 1796 Mary Davis, and they had four sons and six daughters; d. 15 Feb. 1854 in Hamilton, Upper Canada.

Although there is some controversy surrounding the identity of James Gage's father, it appears certain that he was James Gage, a private in the New York militia who was killed in 1777 fighting the British at the attack on forts Clinton and Montgomery, N.Y. About 1790 his widow, Mary, moved with her two children to the head of Lake Ontario, where her brother, Augustus Jones*, was already working as a surveyor. The Gages took up land at Stoney Creek in Township No.7 (Saltfleet) and began farming. Though the homestead remained in Mary Gage's name until 1835, James gradually took over responsibility for the family and in 1796 married Mary Davis, a member of a loyalist family from North Carolina.

Gage's "commodious" farmhouse became the principal stopping-place for travellers by land between Niagara (Niagara-on-the-Lake) and York (Toronto). Over the years prominent Methodists, including Elizabeth Field* and itinerant preachers such as James Coleman, William CASE, Joseph Sawyer, and Nathan Bangs*, were welcomed particularly warmly by Gage, a devout Methodist. His farming activities and reception of visitors were interrupted by the War of 1812, during which he and his son Andrew served with the 5th Lincoln Militia. In June 1813 the adjoining farms of James and his uncle William Gage were the scene of the decisive battle of Stoney Creek, in which the American forces were halted by Lieutenant-Colonel John HARVEY. James's house was occupied as a barracks by the British; as a result of American and British depredations, by the end of the war he had suffered extensive losses of crops, flour, whisky, livestock, timber, and fencing, for which he received some compensation in 1823. The Gage residence is now a museum known as Battlefield House, and the farm a park.

Following the war Gage resumed farming but he also developed other interests. In 1810 he had bought 338½ acres at the northern end of Burlington Beach from Augustus Jones and Catherine Brant [Ohtowaʔkéh-

Gale

son*], the trustees of the estate of Joseph Brant [Thayendanegea*]. Gage is credited with laying out the first town-site in that part of the Brant tract. Known as Wellington Square (Burlington) after 1815, the settlement prospered; Gage built a sawmill, a shingle factory, lath and stave mills, a warehouse and wharf, and, elsewhere in Nelson Township, flour and feed mills. He sold land to his employees for houses and supplied them with building materials and flour. His sons, notably James Philipse, managed these business ventures while their father remained at Stoney Creek, where he had established a general store.

In 1835 Gage moved to Hamilton in order to pursue his business affairs with greater ease. Among these was the Gore Bank, of which he was a stockholder and a director in the 1840s and 1850s. He was fully aware too of the commercial potential at another flourishing port, Oakville, and his entry into business there was probably facilitated by his relation through marriage to the influential Chisholm family (his wife's sister had married John Chisholm, a collector of customs and brother of William). Gage set up a general store in Oakville in 1841 and, concentrating on buying and shipping grain, entered into partnership with Benjamin Hagaman, an American merchant. The firm opened a branch at nearby Bronte (now part of Oakville) the following year, traded extensively in the United States through Hagaman's connections in Oswego, N.Y., and quickly became one of Oakville's largest retailers and grain handlers. Gage and Hagaman were joined by the latter's cousin Worthington Ely Hagaman in 1852; on Gage's death two years later his interests were taken over by his son James.

In a lengthy obituary in the *Christian Guardian*, the Reverend John Saltkill Carroll*, a family intimate, observed that "though a man of safe judgement in matters of business and of industrious habits," Gage "was by no means a bustling man of the world." Carroll regretted above all that the church had lost a true and valuable "friend," one who had been famous for his hospitality and liberal contributions to Methodist institutions. On 2 April 1854 a memorial sermon to Gage was preached by the Reverend William Ryerson*.

Gage was highly respected as a pioneer and as a useful citizen, but he lived quietly, did not seek public office, and was content to exercise his talents in commercial dealings which served the needs of a developing society.

KATHARINE GREENFIELD

AO, RG 22, ser.204, James Gage. Halton Land Registry Office (Milton, Ont.), Abstract index to deeds, Nelson Township, vol.B: 52 (mfm. at AO, GS 3387). HPL, Clipping file, Hamilton biog. PAC, RG 1, L3, 203: G1/34, G3/34; RG 19, 3746, claim 447. Victoria Univ. Library (Toronto), Peter Jones coll., Eliza[beth Field] Jones Carey papers, diary, 13 Sept. 1834. Wentworth Land Registry Office (Hamilton, Ont.), Abstract index to deeds, Saltfleet Township, concession 4 (mfm. at AO, GS 1627). *Christian Guardian*, 26 April 1854. *Daily Spectator, and Journal of Commerce*, 17 Feb. 1854. "Gage families, part two: the English–Irish–early American and Canadian families," comp. C. V. Gage (typescript, Worcester, N.Y., 1965; copy in AO, MU 3298, no.11). *Genealogical and historical records of the Mills and Gage families, 1776–1926; 150 years*, comp. Stanley Mills (Hamilton, 1926). *Westbrook–Gage miscellany: a souvenir of the Westbrook–Gage reunion, Stoney Creek, Ontario, July 1, 1909* ([Thamesville, Ont.], 1911). Carroll, *Case and his cotemporaries*, 1: 42–43; 2: 304. Claire Emery and Barbara Ford, *From pathway to Skyway: a history of Burlington* (Burlington, Ont., 1967). C. M. Johnston, *Head of the Lake* (1967). H. C. Mathews, *Oakville and the Sixteen: the history of an Ontario port* (Toronto, 1953; repr. 1971). V. Ross and Trigge, *Hist. of Canadian Bank of Commerce*, 1: 216. *Saltfleet – then and now: 1792–1973* (Fruitland [Stoney Creek], Ont., 1975). Stanley Mills, "The Gage family," Wentworth Hist. Soc., *Papers and Records* (Hamilton), 9 (1920): 17–18.

GALE, ALEXANDER, Presbyterian minister and educator; baptized 18 Dec. 1800 in Logie Coldstone, Scotland, son of John Gale and Jean Esson; m. 9 Aug. 1836 Margaret Scarth of Kirkwall, Scotland, and they had at least two daughters and one son; d. 6 April 1854 in Albion Mills (Hamilton), Upper Canada.

Eldest child of a middle-class farming couple, Alexander Gale was born and raised in the rural parish of Logie Coldstone, deep in southern Aberdeenshire. After attending the local parish school he went on scholarship in 1815 to Marischal College (University of Aberdeen), graduating with an MA in 1819. He then began theological training in Aberdeen and was licensed to preach by the Church of Scotland's Presbytery of Kincardine O'Neil. But without influence it was difficult to find ministerial posts in Scotland and in the spring of 1827 he sailed for Montreal to join his uncle the Reverend Henry ESSON, who had been serving there since 1817.

During his first year in the colony he assisted Esson and coordinated a survey by the home church's colonial committee of the Scottish Presbyterian community in the Canadas. In the fall of 1828 he moved to Amherstburg, Upper Canada, where he formed a school and a congregation and was, it seems, ordained. But plagued by what contemporaries described as malarial fever, he decided to try a change of environment. In July 1831, no doubt with his uncle's assistance, he was assigned to the Lachine Free School by the Royal Institution for the Advancement of Learning. The Presbytery of Quebec simultaneously appointed him missionary to the area, replacing both Esson and Edward Black*, and by the following year he had succeeded in organizing a congregation there. He resigned both posts in 1833 to accept a call from Hamilton, Upper Canada, where he was to remain for the next 13 years.

Although Gale helped found the Presbytery of Hamilton in 1836, was elected moderator of synod the following year, and created the home missions committee in 1841, he rarely played a dominant role in church affairs. Mild, urbane, he was a voice of moderation, counselling conciliation and tolerance both within and without the church. He urged, for example, ongoing negotiations for union with other Presbyterian bodies and the distribution of state support to a wider range of Protestant groups. It was his compromise motion that held the Canadian synod together in 1843 when the established church in Scotland was experiencing widespread defections, but moderation could not succeed in the Canadas the next year and Gale reluctantly sided with the breakaway evangelical Synod of the Presbyterian Church of Canada, commonly called the Free Church. Recognizing the pressing needs of the new church, he became more active, assuming, among other duties, the editorship of the *Ecclesiastical and Missionary Record* from 1844 to 1846 and again briefly in 1853.

Gale was not particularly at home in the pulpit. Unassuming and infinitely patient, he made teaching his first love. He warmly advocated the training of ministerial candidates in the Canadas and with the synod's approval oversaw their instruction at Hamilton from 1837 until Queen's College, Kingston, opened in 1842. When the Free Church synod in 1846 offered him the dual appointment of professor of classics at its college in Toronto (after 1858 Knox College) and principal of Toronto Academy, the proposed boarding- and day-school intended to raise prospective students of the college to seminary level, he accepted with alacrity. With the creation of the University of Toronto in 1849 it was no longer necessary for the college to offer his courses so it abolished Gale's professorship, allowing him to devote his full energies to the academy. Converted into a private institution, it flourished under his astute management. In 1853 his synod elected him moderator in acknowledgement of his services, but poor health forced him to retire that year to Logie, his farm at Albion Mills, where he advertised the opening of a select boarding-school. A year later, in April 1854, he died, survived by his wife and two children.

H. J. BRIDGMAN

[Primary sources relating to Gale's life are fragmentary. Records of the relevant sessions, presbyteries, and synods outline his career; further details appear in PAC, MG 9, D7, 27 and MG 24, D16; QUA, William Morris papers; the Lee papers in the National Library of Scotland (Edinburgh), MSS 3436/270, 3437/68; McGill Univ. Arch. (Montreal), Royal Institution for the Advancement of Learning, letter-books and salary returns; and in the Gale files in the UCA and PCA. The *Ecclesiastical and Missionary Record for the Presbyterian Church of Canada* (Toronto) carries advertisements for and commentary on the Toronto Academy. *See also* E. A. [Kerr] McDougall, "The Presbyterian Church in western Lower Canada, 1815–1842" (PHD thesis, McGill Univ., 1969), and *The Presbytery of Hamilton: 1836–1967*, comp. T. M. Bailey *et al.* (Hamilton, Ont., 1967).

Two works bearing Gale's name, *Address of the commission of the Synod of the Presbyterian Church in Canada, in connection with the Church of Scotland, to the members of that church* (Toronto, 1838) and *Address of the commission of Synod . . . to the people under their charge* (Toronto, 1838), are official statements of the church published over his signature as moderator and, as such, should not be considered his publications. In his official capacity as moderator he also addressed a protest on behalf of the church to Lieutenant Governor Sir George ARTHUR; it was published as a broadsheet under the title *Protest by the moderator of the Synod of Upper Canada, against the rectories established by Sir John Colborne* (Hamilton, 1838); a copy is available at UCA.   H.J.B.]

GRO (Edinburgh), Logie-Coldstone, reg. of births and baptisms, 18 Dec. 1800; reg. of marriages, 23 Feb. 1800. SRO, CH1/2/150, 27 Oct. 1827. UCA, James Croil papers, diary, 1866–67: 56, 199. Croil, *Hist. and statistical report* (1868), 13, 56–57. *Ecclesiastical and Missionary Record for the Presbyterian Church of Canada*, 4 (1847–48): 32; 5 (1848–49): 163–64, 184; 6 (1849–50): 25, 168, 183, 190; 9 (1852–53): 25, 113–14, 160; 10 (1853–54): 102–3. "Rev. Alex. Gale, M.A.," *Knox College Monthly* (Toronto), 2 (1883–84): 65–70. George Sheed *et al.*, "Memorial on the state of religion in certain districts of Upper Canada," Glasgow Soc. (in Connection with the Established Church of Scotland), for Promoting the Religious Interests of the Scottish Settlers in British North America, *Annual report* (Glasgow), 1831: 28–32. *Daily Spectator, and Journal of Commerce*, 10 April 1854. *Fasti Academiae Mariscallanae Aberdonensis: selections from the records of the Marischal College and University, [1593–1860]*, ed. P. J. Anderson and J. F. K. Johnstone (3v., Aberdeen, Scot., 1889–98), 2: 423. *Handbook of the Presbyterian Church in Canada, 1883*, ed. A. F. Kemp *et al.* (Ottawa, 1883). Scott *et al.*, *Fasti ecclesiæ scoticanæ*, 7. William Campbell, *A history of Knox Presbyterian Church, Hamilton, Ontario* ([Hamilton], 1967), 2–3. Gregg, *Hist. of Presbyterian Church*.

GAMACHE, LOUIS (also known as **Louis-Olivier**), sailor, merchant, settler, and legendary figure; son of Michel-Arsène Gamache and Marie-Reine Després, *dit* Disséré (Dicere); fl. 1808–52.

The story of Louis Gamache's life has been handed down through oral tradition. Since few official records of this legendary figure of Île d'Anticosti remain, it is almost impossible to verify the available biographical information.

According to tradition, Gamache's ancestors came from the French village of Saint-Illiers-la-Ville. They immigrated to New France in the 17th century and after a number of years on the Beaupré heights they

Gamache

went across the St Lawrence to settle on the south shore. Some accounts say that Gamache was born around 1784 at L'Islet, the village where his parents lived. At the age of 11 he enlisted in the British navy as a cabin-boy. He spent several years sailing around the world, and the ups and downs of this tough existence gave a keen edge to his adventurous nature and strong personality. His parents died while he was away and on his return Gamache found himself alone. Tradition has it that he then went directly to Rimouski to set himself up as a merchant. But a fire, which completely destroyed his store, put an end to this undertaking.

On 11 Jan. 1808 Gamache married Françoise Bacelet, *dit* Casirtan (Cassista), of Rivière-Ouelle. The marriage was solemnized there and on that occasion Gamache described himself as a sailor. Does this description mean that the event took place before the Rimouski episode? Or that, disappointed by the set-back at Rimouski, he no longer considered himself a merchant and resumed his previous occupation? Unfortunately there is no way of knowing. However, it was with his wife and at least one child, Pierre-Louis, that around 1810 Gamache crossed the St Lawrence to Anticosti, which was then one of the most desolate regions in North America.

Gamache chose a spot at the head of Baie Ellis, the island's only natural port. There he put up a house and outbuildings which resembled a fort. To defend himself, he apparently kept a large number of weapons and plenty of ammunition handy. Gamache found here the kind of life that best suited his independent temperament and his longing for freedom. He lived virtually alone on his part of the island, with his wife, children, and one or two companions. He hunted, fished, and engaged in shipping and the fur trade. Probably to prevent the authorities from searching his premises, he soon styled himself seigneur of the island, claiming he had bought it from a man named Hamel. But no evidence of this property transaction has been found, and it could only have been a subterfuge on the part of this odd individual – who, moreover, had no hesitation in detaining at his house for a whole winter a bailiff come to claim payment of a debt.

Gamache's wife and his daughter Christine both died at L'Isle-Verte, apparently of smallpox. They were buried there on 10 July 1836. The couple had had nine children. In 1837, it is thought, Gamache married Catherine Lots of Quebec, and they had three children. Gamache's second wife is believed to have died on the island around mid November 1845. At the time, she was alone with her children, of whom the eldest, a girl, was six; Gamache was away hunting. On his return, after an absence of several days, he found her dead and gave her a rough-and-ready burial, which was all he could manage.

Anticosti was cut off from the rest of the world during the long winter months, but in summer it was visited by seamen seeking shelter, provincial administrators, and adventurers. Relations between these visitors and Gamache were not always cordial, even though he was the keeper of the supply depot set up on the island to help shipwreck victims. Problems sometimes arose. For example, on 6 Oct. 1824, two Inuit brought an action for theft against Gamache. In his turn, on 7 Sept. 1830, he felt compelled to complain about the "continual pillage that occurs on the island of Anticosti" and to ask for "the appointment of justices of the peace on this island"; he even added that he himself was "duly qualified under the law to be a justice of the peace."

Faced with the various dangers threatening him and his family, Gamache surrounded himself with a double protection, of both a physical and a psychological nature. The numerous weapons at his disposal could be useful against wild beasts and equally against humans bent on theft or prying. He also built up a rather disturbing reputation and deliberately cultivated it to inspire fear. He was shrouded in mystery and, according to legend, assumed a number of weird characters: pirate, sorcerer, ogre, intimate of the devil, werewolf, and will-o'-the-wisp.

Abbé Jean-Baptiste-Antoine Ferland* paid a visit to Gamache in 1852. In the accounts of his travels he recorded some of the legends surrounding this man. Gamache was said to have been seen standing on a seat in his boat and ordering the devil to bring a favourable wind. Moments later his boat was running before the wind with full sails while other vessels lay becalmed. Or, alone with invisible companions, he allegedly massacred whole crews and seized rich cargoes. He encouraged these stories by playing practical jokes. Thus one day when he was hungry he ordered two meals in a private room in a Rimouski hotel, letting it be understood that he maintained close ties with the devil. When the innkeeper asked him who was expected for dinner, he replied that this was none of her business. After he had eaten both meals, he summoned her in, and she almost fainted, for two chairs were drawn up to the table, both sets of dishes and cutlery had been used, and one man could not have eaten all the food served. "The next day," recounted Ferland, "the whole township was informed that Gamache had spent the day before with the devil." Not content with this response, Gamache repeated the exploit the following day, with even more fanciful refinements. In this way he acquired the reputation of being the "sorcerer of Anticosti island." The will-o'-the-wisp legend derives from an incident involving a ship of the company which held a monopoly on trade with part of the north shore. While trying to escape arrest for smuggling, Gamache lit a fire on a small raft and set it adrift. When the ship neared what its crew thought was Gamache's boat, they found only a "small fire which seemed to feed on the waters of the sea." They concluded that the devil had come to Gamache's aid by transforming him into a will-o'-the-wisp.

Louis Gamache is thought to have died on 11 Sept. 1854 on Anticosti, but no record of his burial has been found. Tradition has it that he died alone, and that a trapper named Goudreau found him several days after his death and buried him beside his second wife.

The stories surrounding Gamache far outlived the man himself. Even in the 20th century the residents of the island still recount the real or imaginary exploits of Gamache. An unpublished version of 1948 describes him as an agent of the government or a go-between in its contacts with the island's Indians. In 1976 another facet was added to his personality, that of a wrecker of ships, and he was portrayed as a dwarf with a bent, stunted body.

His rough appearance concealed a generous nature. Those who knew Louis Gamache reported that he readily gave substantial presents to people upon whom he had played tricks confirming his legendary powers. They also quoted as his favourite saying, "The devil isn't as black as he's painted."

CATHERINE JOLICŒUR

ANQ-Q, CE2-3, 8 avril 1801, 21 févr. 1807. AP, Notre-Dame-de-Liesse (Rivière-Ouelle), Reg. des baptêmes, mariages et sépultures, 11 janv., 29 nov. 1808; Saint-Jean-Baptiste (L'Isle-Verte), Reg. des baptêmes, mariages et sépultures, 10 juill. 1836. Centre d'études sur la langue, les arts et les traditions populaires (Québec), Coll. Luc Lacourcière, enregistrement 3858. PAC, MG 30, D1, 13; RG 4, A1, 230, 241, 335, 368, 434, 544. Private arch., Catherine Jolicœur (Carleton, Que.), enregistrement 5197, 18350. Le Pays, 17 déc. 1859. Robert Choquette, Le sorcier d'Anticosti et autres légendes canadiennes (Montréal, 1975). E. A. Collard, Canadian yesterdays (Toronto, 1955). [J.-B.-A.] Ferland, Opuscules: Louis-Olivier Gamache et le Labrador (Montréal, 1912). M. J. U. Gregory, Récits de voyages en Floride, au Labrador, sur le fleuve Saint-Laurent (Montréal, 1913). Damase Potvin, Le Saint-Laurent et ses îles; histoire, légendes, anecdotes, description, topographie (Québec, 1945). P.-G. Roy, Les petites choses de notre histoire (7 sér., Lévis, Qué., 1919–44), 7: 98–101. J.-P. Drapeau, "Le sorcier de l'île d'Anticosti," Le Soleil, perspectives (Québec), 1er mars 1975: 8–11. P.-G. Roy, "Les légendes canadiennes," Cahiers des Dix, 2 (1937): 76–79.

GAMELIN, ÉMILIE. See TAVERNIER

GAMELIN, PIERRE (baptized **Pierre-Ambroise**), army and militia officer, notary, and office holder; b. 31 May 1789 in Saint-Vincent-de-Paul (Laval), Que., son of Pierre Gamelin and Marianne Lemaître-Lamorille; d. 14 April 1856 in Iberville, Lower Canada.

Pierre Gamelin's earliest Canadian forebear was surgeon Michel Gamelain* de La Fontaine, who was seigneur of Sainte-Anne-de-la-Pérade in the latter half of the 17th century. Gamelin's father, a highly respected man, had served against the Americans in 1775 as captain in the Canadian militia under François-Marie Picoté* de Belestre, and had helped defend Fort St Johns (Saint-Jean-sur-Richelieu). He held the office of justice of the peace in the district of Montreal towards the end of the 18th century.

After receiving his schooling, Pierre Gamelin trained as a notary under Joseph-Bernard Planté* at Quebec in 1804 and 1805, and then under Louis Chaboillez* in Montreal from 1805 to 1811. However, once his studies for the notarial profession were completed, he joined the Canadian Fencibles, obtained the rank of ensign, and saw service in the War of 1812. He married Jane Sophia Walker at Christ Church, the Anglican church in William Henry (Sorel), on 14 May 1813. In 1814 he left the regiment with the rank of lieutenant because of ill health.

On 26 July 1815 Gamelin petitioned Sir Gordon Drummond*, the administrator of Lower Canada, for admission to the notarial profession. His request was granted, and on 25 August he obtained his commission. Unable to settle anywhere for long, over the ensuing 40 years he practised as a notary in many places: Saint-Philippe-de-Laprairie from 1815 to 1817; Sainte-Marie-de-Monnoir (Marieville) in 1817 and 1818; Montreal from 1818 to 1821; La Prairie from 1821 to 1832; Napierville from 1832 to 1841; Dorchester/Saint-Jean (Saint-Jean-sur-Richelieu) from 1841 to 1852; and finally Christieville (Iberville) from 1852 to 1855.

In 1837, while at Napierville, Gamelin served as captain in the 1st Battalion of L'Acadie militia. During the Patriote uprising in his village in November he remained loyal to the colony's government, and was forced to hand over his commission as militia captain to the local Patriote leaders. In November 1838, when the rebels gathered at the large camp in Napierville which was under the command of Robert Nelson*, he was arrested by Patriotes and held in the county jail. After the rebellion had failed, Gamelin made four depositions on these events, in particular against Cyrille-Hector-Octave Côté*, who represented L'Acadie in the House of Assembly and was one of the leaders of the Patriote movement at Napierville, and against Charles Huot, a fellow notary of that village who had been the camp quartermaster.

Gamelin had just settled at Dorchester in 1841 when he was appointed clerk of the district municipal council, created by an ordinance of the government in 1840. He served until 1 July 1845, when this first type of municipal institution was abolished. However, on 28 July 1845 he was appointed secretary-treasurer for the municipal council of the parish of Saint-Jean-

Garry

l'Évangéliste, an office he retained until 1 Sept. 1847. Gamelin was also secretary to the board of health, which that council set up in June 1847 as a result of the raging epidemic of typhus brought in by Irish immigrants.

Pierre Gamelin died on 14 April 1856 in Iberville, at the age of 66. He was buried two days later in the cemetery of the Church of England congregation there, to which he belonged. He had probably become a convert to Anglicanism, but it is not known when. His wife had died on 7 Dec. 1855 and they apparently had had no children.

LIONEL FORTIN

Pierre Gamelin's minute-book, containing instruments notarized from 1815 to 1855, is held in ANQ-M, CN4-20.

ANQ-M, CE1-59, 15 sept. 1785, 31 mai 1789; CE3-1, 14 mai 1813; CE4-28, 16 avril 1856; CN1-269, 1er déc. 1805. ANQ-Q, CN1-60, 5 sept. 1804; E17/7, no.122; E17/11, no.512; E17/32, no.2544; E17/33, no.2647. PAC, MG 30, D1, 13: 703–15; RG 4, B8, 4: 1276–87; B36, 5: 1541. *Quebec Gazette*, 19 March 1812. Lionel Fortin, *Le maire Nelson Mott et l'histoire de Saint-Jean* ([Saint-Jean-sur-Richelieu, Qué.], 1976), 31–39. J.-J. Lefebvre, "Les De Couagne (Decoigne)," SGCF *Mémoires*, 25 (1974): 214–27.

GARRY, NICHOLAS, deputy governor of the HBC; b. *c.* 1782, son of Isabella Garry; m. 4 Aug. 1829 Phoebe Vesey in the parish of St George, Hanover Square, London, and they had at least one son; d. 24 Dec. 1856 in Claygate, Surrey, England.

Nicholas Garry was probably the illegitimate son of Nicholas Langley, a London merchant, who in 1783 was paying for his upbringing. Langley also left £1,000 in trust for the child by the terms of the last codicil to his will, drafted only a couple of weeks before his death in October 1783. Raised by Langley's brother and sister-in-law, Thomas and Sarah Langley, Garry was well educated and learned to speak German, French, and Russian fluently. It would appear that for some time prior to 1811 he conducted a mercantile business in the Baltic timber port of Riga (U.S.S.R.) and in 1815 the London directory lists him as a member of the firm Garry and Curtis, trading between Russia and Great Britain. Thomas Langley had been appointed a director of the Hudson's Bay Company in 1807, and ten years later Garry joined him on the London committee as a director. He does not seem to have taken a major role in the company's affairs, which at this time included the preliminary discussions that led to the merger of the HBC and the North West Company. When an agreement was arrived at in early 1821, it became apparent that a representative from each company would have to meet with the wintering partners at Fort William (Thunder Bay, Ont.), explain the new trade arrangements,

obtain the partners' concurrence, and visit the united company's posts from Fort William through to the Red River colony (Man.), Norway House, and York Factory. In February, Garry, the only unmarried member of the committee, volunteered for this "mission of adjustment and conciliation." By the terms of the merger agreement signed on 26 March, the trading activity of the new HBC was divided into two jurisdictions, each to be directed by a governor and council. The Northern Department was to include the territory to the west of Rainy Lake (Ont.) and Fort Albany, and the Southern Department that to the east including Fort William. On 28 March the London committee appointed Garry president of the Council of the Northern Department, granting him the authority to do what was necessary to implement the merger agreement. Simon McGillivray*, formerly of the NWC, received a similar commission, on the understanding that he could exercise its powers only in Garry's absence.

Accompanied by former NWC partner Angus BETHUNE, Garry left London on 29 March 1821 and from this date kept a detailed diary of his journey. Another NWC partner, John McLOUGHLIN, joined them in Liverpool and on 31 March the three men sailed for New York aboard the American packet *Amity*. From there, Garry departed for Montreal with McGillivray, who had arrived by another vessel. In his diary Garry noted with irony that but a few months earlier McGillivray had been known to him as "the most active and strenuous Opposer of the Interests of the Company I came out to represent." In Montreal Simon's elder brother, William*, joined the party and, travelling in a 36-foot birchbark canoe manned by 12 French Canadian voyageurs, Garry and the two McGillivrays made the trip to Fort William in 18 days, arriving on 1 July. The elder McGillivray delivered a frank explanation of the merger agreement to the NWC wintering partners gathered there; despite their initial indignation at the terms of the amalgamation, he persuaded them to sign the agreement and accept their commissions as chief factors or chief traders, which they did on 11 July. The distribution of posts was the next item to be considered. Garry, however, discovered that his commission and the powers of the Council of the Northern Department were only valid in Rupert's Land and as a consequence he had no real authority to exercise his mandate at Fort William. The postings were nevertheless settled although, at least according to Colin Robertson*, this jurisdictional anomaly permitted Simon McGillivray to have his way in most of these selections. Garry's diary, which on the whole is a descriptive and sensitive account of the people he met and the land he saw, is disappointingly silent on business matters such as these talks, reading simply: "Tuesday the 10th July [to] Saturday 14th. Discussions without end." Garry proceeded to verify NWC inventories, lists, and accounts prior to their dispatch to London and on 21 July he left with Simon McGillivray for York Factory.

For this stage of the journey each commissioner travelled in his own canoe with a crew of eight men and, as Garry noted in his journal, the competition between the two canoes was keen: "Mr. McGillivray's Crew consisting of Pork Eaters or Montreal Men (as he intends returning to Montreal) there was much Emulation between the two Crews. . . . but our Men had so much the Advantage that Mr. McGillivray was obliged to take an additional Man at Rainy Lake." They met with an Indian council there and Garry gave assurances that "though the two great rival Companies had coalesced, . . . this Union would be in no way injurious to them, on the contrary . . . the active and good would be benefited." The party travelled across the Lake of the Woods and down the Winnipeg River to the Red River colony where Garry noted the need for strong measures "or the Colony must become the Receptacle of a lawless Banditti and a most dangerous Thorn in the Side of the Hudson Bay Company."

On 11 August at Norway House Garry presided over the first Council of the Northern Department, which endorsed the appointments made at Fort William and, despite Simon McGillivray's objections, formally abandoned the Montreal–Fort William supply route in favour of the route from Hudson Bay through York Factory. The party then proceeded down the Nelson River to York Factory where on 23 August they were greeted by HBC governor William Williams*. Because of the animosity built up between Williams and the NWC during the bitter struggle preceding the union, McGillivray insisted that he be excluded from the governorship of the Northern Department. Garry, however, in a manœuvre designed to assert HBC authority over that of his fellow commissioner, decided to wait until after McGillivray's departure for Montreal on 29 August to resolve the issue. He did, nevertheless, come to the conclusion that, for the sake of better relations with the former NWC men now conducting much of the trade, it would be more appropriate to place Williams in charge of the less important Southern Department. Pleased to learn that Williams himself preferred the latter position, Garry placed the junior governor, George SIMPSON, at the head of the Northern Department. With this final matter satisfactorily taken care of, Garry embarked upon the *Prince of Wales* and left York Factory for England on 13 September.

In 1822 Garry became deputy governor of the HBC. His role in the company from this date is obscure, although he does seem to have been interested in trade with Russia and China and in religious affairs. He was still deputy governor in July 1835 when, declared of unsound mind, he was relieved of his functions. He died 21 years later, never having recovered his sanity.

During his mission to North America in 1821 Nicholas Garry had proven himself a tactful and humane diplomat. In his handling of the HBC–NWC merger, he had seized upon the company's need for efficiency in the unified trade and realized that success lay in accommodating to a certain degree the former NWC men who would be counted upon to conduct much of the inland business. Pleased with Garry's shrewdness and influence in handling these matters, in 1821 Williams reported "universal satisfaction, confidence, and unanimity." In September Simpson noted that "our old opponents no longer received us as enemies but met us as aquaintances which I think will soon assume the character of Friendship. . . . Mr. Garry's handsome and impartial conduct acted like Majick in removing all sort of jealousy, he was open and easy of access with the nicest observance of strict honor integrity and impartiality and so different in all these respects from his travelling companion Mr. Simon McGillivray." The new HBC fort built at the Red River settlement in 1822 was named Fort Garry (Winnipeg) to commemorate Garry's visit of 1821.

JOHN McFARLAND

The diary written by Nicholas Garry during his visit to North America in 1821 was edited by his grandson Francis N. A. Garry and published in RSC *Trans.*, 2nd ser., 6 (1900), sect.II: 73–204, under the title "Diary of Nicholas Garry, deputy-governor of the Hudson's Bay Company from 1822–1835: a detailed narrative of his travels in the northwest territories of British North America in 1821. . . ." Garry is also the author of a short publication on the commerce between Great Britain and Russia entitled *The origin and early history of the Russia or Muscovy Company . . .* (London, 1830).

GRO (London), Death certificate, Nicholas Garry, 24 Dec. 1856. Hampshire Record Office (Winchester, Eng.), Reg. of baptisms, marriages, and burials for the parish of Lymington, 18 Oct. 1783. PAM, HBCA, A.1/51: f.82; A.1/56: f.92; A.9/4: ff.13–17; A.10/2: f.307; Nicholas Garry file. *HBRS*, 1 (Rich); 2 (Rich and Fleming); 3 (Fleming); 10 (Rich). *London directory*, 1815. Rich, *Hist. of HBC* (1960), vols.2–3. Glyndwr Williams, "Highlights in the history of the first two hundred years of the Hudson's Bay Company," *Beaver*, outfit 301 (autumn 1970): 46–47, 63.

GAUKEL, FRIEDRICH (Frederick), farmer and businessman; b. 7 June 1785 in Württemberg (Federal Republic of Germany); m. first c. 1813 Polly Kaufman (d. 1827), and they had four sons and three daughters; m. secondly Maria Roschang (d. 1834 of cholera); m. thirdly Dorothea Weikmillar; d. 8 Nov. 1853 in Berlin (Kitchener), Upper Canada.

Friedrich Gaukel's name appears among those of the German immigrants who arrived at Philadelphia from Holland aboard the *Rebecca* on 27 Aug. 1804. Along with other Württemberg natives, he may have been attracted to America by the publicity attending

Gaulin

the exodus to Pennsylvania at this time of members of the charismatic sect led by the German lay preacher and weaver John George Rapp. According to a short biography published by Gaukel's grandson Jacob Stroh, he served for his passage money as a redemptioner on a farm near Philadelphia. He continued farming after his release from the indenture and by 1815 lived near Johnstown, Pa.

About 1820 Gaukel, a Lutheran, heard of the Mennonite migration from Pennsylvania to Upper Canada and decided to move there. After a trip of four weeks he arrived with his family in Waterloo Township, where he worked in a distillery until he bought a small farm near Bridgeport (Kitchener) and began operating a distillery of his own. After 1826 increasing numbers of Germans arrived in the region directly from Europe and settled largely in four townships: Wilmot, Waterloo, Woolwich, and Wellesley. Thus when the settlement of Ebytown began to expand, Germans, as well as Mennonites, were prominent in its development as a commercial centre. On 2 Nov. 1833 Gaukel purchased property from Joseph Schneider* and from Benjamin EBY and moved into the settlement. The deeds for these transactions are the first on record referring to the community as Berlin.

Gaukel operated a tavern while awaiting the completion of a larger building which would meet the demands of the growing village. A public-spirited member of the community, he subscribed to the establishment of Heinrich Wilhelm PETERSON's newspaper *Canada Museum, und Allgemeine Zeitung* in 1835, the year in which Gaukel's Inn (later known as the Commercial Hotel) opened to the public. For many years Gaukel and his third wife, also a native of Württemberg, hosted, in addition to the inn's daily commercial activities, various civic and political meetings, markets, and other public gatherings in this predominantly German-speaking community. The wide veranda of the inn was a favourite tribune for political candidates who addressed the citizenry assembled in the street.

In 1841 and 1846 Gaukel acquired additional property and as one of Berlin's leading landowners he took an active interest in its municipal development. He donated the land on which Waterloo Township Hall was built in 1848–49. Together with his friend Joseph Schneider and other early citizens, he had campaigned for the organization of Waterloo County, which took place in 1850, and he was much involved in promoting Berlin's selection as county seat in 1852. He provided land that year for the construction of a county court-house. In recognition of Gaukel's contributions, a grateful community named two of its early streets after him.

KLAUS WUST

AO, RG 22, ser.214, Friedrich Gaukel. Kitchener Public Library (Kitchener, Ont.), "Gaukel family notes" (typescript). PAC, RG 31, A1, 1851, Waterloo Township, pt.4: 178. Waterloo North Land Registry Office (Kitchener), Abstract index to deeds, Berlin (mfm. at AO, GS 2958); Waterloo Township (mfm. at AO, GS 3023, GS 3027). *Der Deutsche Canadier* (Berlin [Kitchener]), 10 Nov. 1853. R. B. Strassburger, *Pennsylvania German pioneers: a publication of the original lists of arrivals in the port of Philadelphia from 1727 to 1808*, ed. W. J. Hinke (3v., Norristown, Pa., 1934), 3: 147. Gottlieb Leibbrandt, *Little paradise: the saga of the German Canadians of Waterloo County, Ontario, 1800–1975* (Kitchener, 1980), 36, 38–51. Bill Moyer, *Kitchener: yesterday revisited; an illustrated history* (Burlington, Ont., 1979), 19–21, 27. W. V. Uttley, *A history of Kitchener, Ontario* (Kitchener, 1937; repr. [Waterloo, Ont., 1975]), 35, 37–38, 40–41, 71, 80, 83, 85, 88. Jacob Stroh, "Frederick Gaukel," Waterloo Hist. Soc., *Annual report*, 1928: 86–87; "Reminiscences of Berlin (now Kitchener)," Waterloo Hist. Soc., *Annual report*, 1930: 175–207; 1931: 274–84.

GAULIN, RÉMI (as bishop he signed **Remigius**), Roman Catholic priest and bishop; b. 30 June 1787 at Quebec, son of François Gaulin, a cooper, and Françoise Amiot; d. 8 May 1857 in Sainte-Philomène (Mercier), Lower Canada.

After classical and theological studies at the Séminaire de Québec and, from 1807 to 1810, further theological studies at the Séminaire de Nicolet, Rémi Gaulin served as secretary to Bishop Joseph-Octave Plessis* on a pastoral visit to the Îles de la Madeleine and New Brunswick in June and July 1811. On 13 October he was ordained in Quebec by Plessis, who immediately named him curate to the Reverend Alexander McDonell* in Glengarry County, Upper Canada. The young priest was very contented there. Described by his superiors as a sensible and likeable man, he ministered to the Catholics in Kingston during the early months of 1812 and made preparations for a church to be built. From June 1812 until the spring of 1815 he was in charge of the parishes at St Raphael (St Raphael West) and St Andrews. He saw service during the War of 1812 as a military chaplain. Having worked with McDonell for nearly four years, Gaulin, despite the desire expressed by Catholics in Kingston to have him placed in their parish, went back to Quebec in May 1815 in order to accompany Bishop Plessis on a pastoral visit to the missions on the Gulf of St Lawrence.

The bishop's arrival at Arichat, Cape Breton Island, on 3 July 1815, attracted a number of the region's clergy, including François Lejamtel*, Antoine Manseau*, Alexander Macdonell*, and Angus Bernard MacEachern*. The next day Plessis assigned Gaulin to be the first resident pastor of St Ninian's parish in Antigonish, N.S., with responsibility for Margaree and Chéticamp, Cape Breton. He set out immediately, taking, he later wrote, nothing but "my soutane and my breviary." In serving Antigonish, Gaulin was following in the footsteps of his great-granduncle Antoine*, who had ministered to the same locale nearly 100 years earlier. In anticipation of the establishment of a vicariate apostolic in Nova Scotia [see Edmund Burke*], Gaulin transferred to Chéticamp and by October 1816 was serving the Acadians of that community and of Margaree, and the Scots living in the Bras d'Or Lake district. In July 1819 he took charge of the Arichat mission, reporting to Plessis at the end of 1821 that the Catholic population there totalled 2,704.

Gaulin seems to have been unhappy in the Maritimes. He experienced continuing financial problems that included indebtedness to a fellow priest; he encountered "the most consummate ignorance" of religion throughout the Scots settlements he served and was frustrated by his inability to instruct these Catholics in their Gaelic language. Compounding his problems was a lengthy illness that began in February 1816 and lasted several months. It may be for these reasons that Gaulin asked to be allowed to return to Quebec. In October 1817 Plessis granted permission for him to depart the following summer, stating that he would probably be posted to Upper Canada where Alexander McDonell ardently sought his return. Although Plessis repeated his permission in April 1818, nothing came of the request until September 1822 when, following the arrival of his successor, Hyacinthe Hudon*, Gaulin returned to Quebec, probably taking with him the ailing William DOLLARD.

Perhaps to compensate Gaulin for lengthy service in remote missions, or simply to make use of his command of English, his superiors then placed him in a number of parishes around Montreal. In November 1822 he was assigned to serve Saint-Luc on the Rivière Richelieu and, a month later, to minister as well to Saint-Athanase (in Iberville). Gaulin was transferred to L'Assomption in January 1825, where he had responsibility for four outlying missions. He returned to the Rivière Richelieu in October 1828 to replace Augustin-Magloire Blanchet* at Dorchester (Saint-Jean-sur-Richelieu) and, some two years later, was also given the new parish at nearby Saint-Valentin. In October 1831 he was assigned to Sainte-Scholastique (Mirabel), and then moved a year later to Sault-au-Récollet (Montreal North). Gaulin performed a variety of duties during these years, including teaching theology to Étienne CHARTIER. He impressed his superiors and was popular with his parishioners. Bishop Bernard-Claude Panet* stated that Gaulin preached with grace and dignity and, later, that he had refused the request of parishioners from Saint-Jean seeking Gaulin's return. Clearly, here was someone with promise.

Meanwhile, Alexander McDonell, Gaulin's first superior, had been appointed bishop of Kingston in 1826. His long and frustrating search for a coadjutor to help him administer a diocese comprising the whole of Upper Canada had involved the resignation of Thomas Weld in 1830 and the refusal of Thomas MAGUIRE, John LARKIN, and Joseph-Vincent QUIBLIER to accept the post. Renewing his efforts, McDonell in 1832 again requested a coadjutor, citing his infirmities and advanced age, and he invited his episcopal colleagues to find him a worthy candidate. In order to reduce friction within his diocese, McDonell sought a French Canadian rather than a Scots or Irish candidate. Bishop Jean-Jacques Lartigue* recommended Antoine Manseau and Gaulin, preferring the latter because of his proficiency in English and, ironically as it was soon to prove, because of his superior health. McDonell welcomed Gaulin's candidacy with enthusiasm since Gaulin was well acquainted with Upper Canada as a result of having worked there for nearly four years. He had also acquired some facility in Gaelic while in the Maritimes. Accordingly, on 20 Oct. 1833 Gaulin was consecrated bishop of Thabraca in Numidia and made coadjutor to McDonell with right of succession. The ceremony, which took place in Montreal, was performed by Lartigue, with the assistance of Louis-Marie Cadieux* and Jacques-Guillaume Roque*.

Over the next several years Gaulin occupied himself with the many problems peculiar to a young, pioneer diocese of vast size. On one of his extensive pastoral trips he visited Penetanguishene and, convinced that a pious and zealous missionary might accomplish much good there, he assigned Jean-Baptiste Proulx* in 1835 to work in that region. At the end of 1835 McDonell ceded to Gaulin the entire administration of the diocese, which was then estimated to consist of 32 missions, 22 pastors, and some 60,000 Catholics. Among the vexing difficulties Gaulin faced were the lack of clergy, laxity among both priests and laity in observing the faith, and clerical insubordination, especially that of William John O'Grady*.

Gaulin succeeded to the bishopric in 1840 when McDonell died. The next year, however, marked the beginning of a decline in physical and mental health that dogged him until his death, although his illness did not entirely prevent him from functioning, at least initially. Among his early achievements in office were the establishment in Kingston in 1841 of the sisters of the Congregation of Notre-Dame [see Marie-Françoise Huot*, named Sister Sainte-Gertrude]; the creation of the diocese of Toronto the same year and the consecration of its first bishop, Michael Power*, on 8 May 1842; preparations in the summer of 1842 for the commencement of work on Kingston's cathedral; and the beginning of classes at Regiopolis College the same year. Gaulin also continued to make extensive pastoral visits throughout his diocese.

Gaulin

Nevertheless, despite Gaulin's initial successes, deteriorating health soon made his position untenable. Bishop Ignace Bourget* tried to help by letting Gaulin rest in Montreal during the summer of 1841. It was apparently not enough, for that September Kingston's vicar general, William Peter MacDonald*, wrote directly to the authorities in Rome demanding a replacement for the physically and mentally ailing bishop. The following August Father Jean-Charles PRINCE stated that Gaulin "is no longer able to look after any matters," a sentiment echoed by Bishop Power two months later. Another priest gave a detailed description of Gaulin's behaviour in letters written in the summer of 1843: "A constant watch must be kept because he goes out of his bedroom with no clothes on, calls for people never heard of, refuses to eat, closes his doors. . . . Imagine how painful and shameful it is to have someone of his rank [about] in the centre of the town." In another letter he added: "He can only be approached at his own pleasure; he spends whole days taking no food; he leaves his room all of a sudden and shows up at the kitchen without being decently dressed. . . . And then [imagine] when he became infuriated. . . ." His condition at times even required a strait-jacket. There was no doubt that decisive action was necessary. Despite Gaulin's wish for a further division of his diocese rather than an assistant, the Canadian episcopate moved vigorously to secure a coadjutor and in the spring of 1843 Bourget informed Gaulin that Patrick PHELAN had been chosen for that office.

While waiting for the pontifical bulls to arrive, Bishop Power decided to take charge of the diocese of Kingston. In June 1843, taking advantage of a temporary tranquillity in Gaulin's condition, he secured the sick man's signature to a letter transferring all his powers to the bishop of Toronto. Power noted that Gaulin was unsympathetic to Phelan, and he expressed the view that Gaulin was "completely insane, believing himself in the Orient and wanting his poor housekeeper to explain to him the manner and route by which she had conveyed herself from Kingston to the Holy Land to bring him soups." Within weeks Bourget was in Kingston where he successfully persuaded Gaulin to return with him to Montreal. Phelan received his bulls in July and was consecrated in August. Gaulin, although by then in Lower Canada, remained the bishop of Kingston and only gradually relinquished control of his diocese to Phelan. Bourget aided the transition by appointing Gaulin vicar general of the diocese of Montreal, president of the corporation of the Collège de L'Assomption (October 1844), and then, for the second time in his career, curé of L'Assomption (September 1845).

For several years Gaulin was well enough to be of considerable assistance to Bourget in furthering the work of the Montreal diocese. He took an active interest in the college, built a convent in L'Assomption, and ordained or conferred minor orders on a number of people, including François-Maximilien Bibaud*, Joseph-Julien Perrault*, John Farrell*, and Albert Lacombe*. He also participated in the consecrations of bishops Augustin-Magloire Blanchet and Joseph-Bruno Guigues*. But Gaulin never really lost interest in his own diocese and between 1849 and 1852 attempted to regain control of it; the result was turmoil that repeatedly involved the church's hierarchy in both the Canadas and Rome.

Gaulin returned to Kingston late in 1849 and, to the confusion of the diocese's clergy, the following February appointed Patrick Dollard* and others to his own administrative council prior to beginning work on a number of projects. The bishops in the Canadas reacted swiftly, reminding Gaulin that Phelan possessed full episcopal authority and that Rome had left him the title bishop of Kingston only to let him retire with honour. They advised him to give up administrative responsibility for his diocese. Although in April he agreed to do as his fellow bishops counselled, by June he had reversed his decision. Gaulin, despite the fact that Rome had renewed Phelan's office without reference to him, convened and chaired a meeting of the episcopal council that he had appointed. The council passed resolutions affirming that Gaulin was fit once more to administer his diocese, and this responsibility he indeed resumed. In December 1850 the bishops of the ecclesiastical province of Quebec issued another declaration on the Gaulin affair, but he remained intransigent: "As long as I am not to be canonically removed from my see, I will act as bishop of Kingston." In April 1851 Gaulin received a letter from Cardinal Giacomo Filippo Fransoni, prefect of the Sacred Congregation of Propaganda in Rome, emphasizing that Phelan alone governed the diocese of Kingston. Visibly affected, but convinced that most of the clergy preferred him to Phelan, Gaulin declared that he would continue to intervene in diocesan matters when necessary. One priest expressed the view that the clergy would opt for Phelan not from affection, but to avoid a greater evil.

The troubles were by no means over. During the first provincial council of Quebec, the assembled bishops persuaded Gaulin to bow to the pope's will, which he did in a letter dated 26 Aug. 1851. Two days later Bishop Pierre-Flavien Turgeon* sent a circular letter to the clergy in the diocese of Kingston reminding them that Phelan had sole responsibility for the administration of the diocese. The solution turned out to be short-lived. Gaulin recanted and in December 1851 Pope Pius IX himself had to warn him not to meddle with the governance of his diocese in the future. His health broken, Gaulin retired to Sainte-Philomène, Lower Canada. Although calm was gradually restored in the ensuing months, he continued to be an encumbrance to Phelan until the day he died, on 8 May 1857. His remains were transferred to Kingston and buried on 13 May in St Mary's Cathedral, where a likeness of his mitred head was later carved.

J. E. ROBERT CHOQUETTE

Rémi Gaulin's report of 25 Sept. 1838 describing a missionary journey in western Upper Canada was printed in the *Annales de la Propagation de la Foi* (Lyon, France, et Paris), 12 (1840): 425–32, under the title "Lettre de Mgr. Gaulein, coadjuteur de Kingston, à son évêque," and in the Assoc. de la Propagation de la Foi, *Rapport* (Montréal), no.3 (1841): 53–58, as "Mission chez les sauvages du Haut-Canada." The version published in the *Annales* is followed on page 432 by "Extrait d'une lettre du même au Conseil central de Paris," an excerpt from Gaulin's letter of 14 April 1840 requesting two missionaries to serve at Lake Superior. Gaulin's other letters to the society are held in the Arch. de la Propagation de la Foi (Paris), F 178, microfilm copies of which are available at the Centre de Recherche en Hist. Religieuse du Canada, Saint Paul Univ., Ottawa.

In addition to the archives cited below, source material relating to Gaulin's episcopacy is held at the AAT. Those holdings and their inventory, "Documents and letters relating to the history of the Catholic Church in the western part of the Diocese of Upper Canada prior to the establishment of the Diocese of Toronto, December 17th, 1841," comp. G. A. Bean (Toronto, 1970), are also available on microfilm at the AO.

Likenesses of Gaulin include the carving referred to in the text, and a painting in the bishop's residence at Kingston reproduced in L. J. Flynn, *Built on a rock; the story of the Roman Catholic Church in Kingston, 1826–1976* (Kingston, Ont., 1976).

AAQ, 301 CN, I: 36–61. ACAM, 255.102, 832-3, -4; 833-7–8; 834-2, -7; 835-1, 837-7; 838-1; 839-5; 840-4; 842-8–11; 843-6–7; 849-1; 850-11–12; 851-2, -8, -19; 255.104, 842-3–4; 843-7, -9; 295.101, 850-48. ANQ-Q, CE1-1, 30 juin 1787. Arch. of the Archdiocese of Kingston, AI (Alexander MacDonell papers, corr.), 1C13-5, -7; 1C15-1; 2C1-19–20, -23; 2C7-16; 3C3-9–13; 5ED1-1; 5ER1-16; B (Remigius Gaulin papers), especially I (corr.), 1C8-1; CI (Patrick Phelan papers, corr.), 1C10-3; 2C3-2; 2C6-14; 3C14-12, -14; 4CL1-1; 4ED1-4; 4ER1-5; 4ER2-1, -9, -11. ASQ, Fonds Viger–Verreau, Sér.O, 0139–52. PAC, RG 5, A1: 73255–57. *Daily British Whig*, 12–15 May 1857. *Toronto Mirror*, 13 Oct. 1848; 15, 22 May, 12 June 1857. Allaire, *Dictionnaire*, 6: 297. F.-M. Bibaud, *Le panthéon canadien* (A. et V. Bibaud; 1891). Caron, "Inv. de la corr. de Mgr Panet," ANQ *Rapport*, 1933–34, 1934–35, 1935–36; "Inv. de la corr. de Mgr Plessis," ANQ *Rapport*, 1927–28, 1928–29, 1932–33; "Inv. de la corr. de Mgr Signay," ANQ *Rapport*, 1936–37, 1937–38. L.-A. Desrosiers, "Correspondance de Mgr Ignace Bourget . . . ," ANQ *Rapport*, 1945–46, 1946–47, 1948–49; "Inv. de la corr. de Mgr Lartigue," ANQ *Rapport*, 1941–42, 1942–43, 1943–44, 1944–45, 1945–46. Le Jeune, *Dictionnaire*. Léon Pouliot et François Beaudin, "Correspondance de Mgr Ignace Bourget," ANQ *Rapport*, 1955–57, 1961–64, 1965, 1966, 1967, 1969. Tanguay, *Dictionnaire*, 4: 201. Douville, *Hist. du collège-séminaire de Nicolet*, 2: 3–5. A. A. Johnston, *Hist. of Catholic Church in eastern N.S.* Lemieux, *L'établissement de la première prov. eccl.* C. Roy, *Hist. de L'Assomption*, 221–22.

GAUTRON, *dit* **Larochelle, SIMÉON,** carder, businessman, and inventor; b. 24 April 1808 in Saint-Vallier, Lower Canada, son of Michel Gautron and Marie-Louise Bolduc; m. 13 Oct. 1829 Sophie Vachon, *dit* Pomerleau, in Sainte-Marie-de-la-Nouvelle-Beauce (Sainte-Marie), Lower Canada; m. there secondly 19 Feb. 1849 Henriette Proulx; seven children were born of these marriages; d. 23 June 1859 in Saint-Anselme, Lower Canada.

The forebears of Siméon Gautron, *dit* Larochelle, came to New France from La Rochelle, France, in 1673 and founded a family at Saint-Vallier, where Siméon was born. Little is known about Siméon's life before he was about 20, when he decided to move to Saint-Anselme. He is said to have offered his horse – all he had to his name – for the services of an itinerant teacher. Having been taught to read and write, he went to Sainte-Marie-de-la-Nouvelle-Beauce and learned the rudiments of carding. He married there in 1829, and then returned to Saint-Anselme. Once he had settled down he acquired a property on the east side of the Rivière Etchemin, beside the falls, and built a carding-mill, which was in operation by 1830. He proved a skilled machinist, and in 1832 the seigneur of Sainte-Marie, Pierre-Elzéar Taschereau*, invited him to build a carding-mill in partnership with him on the Rivière du Domaine, and to share his privileges in respect of mill rights.

That year Larochelle installed near the first carding-mill a sawmill with vertically reciprocating blades, to which he added a carpentry workshop in 1844. Around 1837 Sir John Caldwell*, the seigneur of Lauzon, who had always refused to allow competition on his estates, nevertheless encouraged Larochelle to grind the grain grown by the farmers on his seigneury, after millstones had been installed in Larochelle's sawmill. He added a forge for making iron tools in 1838, and he was so successful that in 1844 the forge was replaced by a foundry, which remained in operation for a long time. Over about 15 years Larochelle had assembled various facilities which, although part of Saint-Anselme, really constituted a new village, Larochelle.

To promote the settlement of land at the back of the seigneuries and no doubt also to make his own business profitable, Larochelle organized a cooperative for erecting a bridge over the Rivière Etchemin. The bridge was opened in 1849 and linked Saint-Anselme to the fertile region of the Beauce. In 1853 Larochelle added to his facilities a factory for making cloth, putting under one roof the machinery needed for

319

Germain

successive operations: carding, spinning, weaving, and shearing. That year he also made a printing-press for *Le Canadien* at Quebec.

In addition, from 1835 Larochelle had taken numerous steps to get a railway built linking the Beauce region to Lévis via Saint-Anselme. This particular objective was part of an ambitious project to construct a railway line running from Lévis to the Maine border which would link with another from the Atlantic coast. However, the project foundered on innumerable obstacles. The charter of the Belfast and Quebec Railroad was obtained in 1836 and renewed in 1845, yet no construction was undertaken despite Larochelle's pleas. In 1853 the St Lawrence and Atlantic Rail-road was built, but from Montreal to Portland, Maine, via Sherbrooke. When the Grand Trunk system joined this line the following year, the city of Quebec had its first railway connection, although an indirect one, with the United States. Far from resting content with this achievement, the people of the Beauce region joined Quebec citizens in presenting a petition in 1854 to the Legislative Council and the assembly. As the result of a second one, given legislative sanction in 1855, the Quebec, Chaudière, Maine and Portland Railway Company was incorporated, with Larochelle as one of the 16 directors. No further trace of this company has been found. Finally, ten years after Larochelle's death, another plan was carried through: the Levis and Kennebec Railway Company was formed in 1869 and the railway reached Scott, in the Beauce region, in 1875. Among its directors was his son, Louis-Napoléon*, who made himself the principal promoter of the undertaking.

Siméon was endowed with remarkable energy, initiative, and inventiveness, talents which contemporary accounts hailed as the mark of genius. The principal newspapers of Lower Canada spoke highly of the extraordinary cannon he had invented. Their descriptions and commentaries indicate that he had designed a weapon which "fires from 10 to 12 rounds a minute." In 1836 he asked the assembly to grant him the means to give it extensive trials. This request was rejected by the casting vote of the speaker, Louis-Joseph Papineau*, who considered the invention "a machine for killing." Ten years later Larochelle obtained the support of the governor-in-chief, Charles Murray CATHCART, but the artillery commander Colonel J. Campbell thought his cannon was "too complicated and expensive for the service." In the face of this set-back, Larochelle had to content himself with putting his cannon on show at Montreal and Quebec.

Stricken with paralysis, Siméon Gautron, *dit* Larochelle, died on 23 June 1859 at Saint-Anselme. One of his sons, Anselme-Hyppolite, had inherited his mechanical skills. Louis-Napoléon took over his business. A daughter, Marie-Louise, married Dr Cyrille Vaillancourt, and their son Cyrille-Émile gained distinction on the board of the Fédération des Caisses Populaires Desjardins.

MADELEINE FERRON

The cannon invented by Siméon Gautron, *dit* Larochelle, is in the Musée du Québec at Quebec.

L.C., House of Assembly, *Journals*, 1835–36. *Le Canadien*, 14 août, 2, 16 sept. 1846. *Le Journal de Québec*, 8 août, 5, 12, 17 sept. 1846. *La Minerve*, 7, 14 sept. 1846. Ernest Arsenault, *La paroisse "St-Anselme"* ([Saint-Anselme, Qué.], 1975), 17, 167–68, 249–50, 262–63. Honorius Provost, *Chaudière Kennebec; grand chemin séculaire* (Québec, 1974); *Sainte-Marie de la Nouvelle-Beauce; histoire civile* (Québec, 1970). J.-E. Roy, *Hist. de Lauzon*, vol.5. P.-G. Roy, *Toutes petites choses du Régime anglais*. Léon Trépanier, *On veut savoir* (4v., Montréal, 1960–62), 3. "Les Disparus," *BRH*, 39 (1933): 761. Léa Pétrin, "M. J.-Adélard Bégin a ressuscité l'entreprise de Siméon Larochelle à St-Anselme, Dorchester," *Le Soleil* (Québec), 22 août 1948: 7.

GERMAIN, AUGUSTIN-RENÉ LANGLOIS, *dit.*
See LANGLOIS

GERRARD, SAMUEL, fur trader, businessman, militia officer, justice of the peace, politician, and seigneur; b. 1767 in Ireland, possibly in County Kilkenny; m. 11 Nov. 1792, in Montreal, Ann Grant, daughter of John Grant and granddaughter of Richard Dobie*; they had three sons and two daughters; d. 24 March 1857 in Montreal.

Samuel Gerrard, son of a prosperous Anglo-Irish family, came to Montreal as a young man. As early as 1785 he was established there as a merchant, specializing in the fur trade of the Timiskaming region. In 1791 he became a partner with his future brother-in-law William Grant* and Étienne-Charles Campion* in Grant, Campion and Company, a leading firm in the fur trade southwest of Michilimackinac (Mackinac Island, Mich.), around the Great Lakes, and in the Timiskaming region. Gerrard was the company's accountant and received a quarter of the profits. By 1795 he appears to have owned a one-third interest in the partnership. The declining health of his two associates and the uncertain nature of the fur trade in what might soon become American territory led to the dissolution of the firm in November 1795. Probably anticipating this dissolution, Gerrard had signed a partnership agreement the previous month with William Parker and John Ogilvy* to establish the firm Parker, Gerrard, and Ogilvy for the fur trade south and west of Michilimackinac. When the new firm began to trade north and west of the Great Lakes as far as the Athabasca region in the late 1790s, it met with stiff competition from the North West Company [*see* Simon McTavish*].

Parker, Gerrard, and Ogilvy was also involved in relatively new staples trades, buying and selling wheat and flour and possibly timber and potash. The partnership continued to expand and by 1800 counted seven partners: Parker and John Gillespie in London; John Mure* in Quebec; Gerrard, George Gillespie*, and Thomas Yeoward in Montreal; and Ogilvy, the wintering partner. Sir Alexander Mackenzie* joined the firm, now Parker, Gerrard, Ogilvy and Company, in 1803. Mackenzie, Ogilvy, and Mure were also involved in the New North West Company (sometimes called the XY Company) on their own account, and Parker, Gerrard, Ogilvy and Company acted as suppliers for the XY Company. In 1805, a year after the absorption of the XY Company by the NWC, Gerrard's firm held the fourth largest interest in the NWC; by 1814 it was worth £38,500. The firm was one of the fur-trade partnerships that established the Michilimackinac Company in 1806 [*see* John Ogilvy]; Gerrard himself still held shares in that company as late as 1832. Parker, Gerrard, Ogilvy and Company was dissolved in 1812 but the outbreak of war delayed the settlement of the firm's affairs until 1814. Afterwards, Gerrard seems to have been less directly involved in the fur trade.

Gerrard had formed a partnership with Yeoward and Robert Gillespie* in 1812. Gerrard, Yeoward, Gillespie and Company continued to maintain links with Sir Alexander Mackenzie, Gillespie, Parker and Company, the English firm which had looked after the London affairs of Parker, Gerrard, Ogilvy and Company. In 1817 Gerrard entered into partnership with Robert Gillespie, Robert Strachan, Jasper Tough, George Moffatt*, William Finlay*, and William Stevens to export wheat and timber and import general merchandise for the wholesale or retail trade. This arrangement created three firms: Gillespie, Gerrard and Company in London; Gerrard, Finlay and Company at Quebec; and Gerrard, Gillespie, Moffatt and Company in Montreal. Thus, for the first time, Gerrard had a share in the profits of the European end of the business. The Montreal firm sent nearly 100 boatloads of general merchandise to Upper Canada in 1817. In December 1821 Gerrard sold his share in the three firms to his partners for £40,000.

Gerrard's business activities were not limited to his partnerships. He was a major shareholder in a shipping company, and a shipowner in his own right. In addition, he speculated in real estate and acted as an estate executor. He was also a business and legal representative as well as a collector of debts for individuals or companies based in the Canadas, England, France, and the United States, activities which continued to occupy him until his death.

After 1821 Gerrard's major interest shifted from trade to finance. Both privately and through his firms, he had been involved for some time in extending credit, making loans, discounting bills, and transferring funds. The shift in focus was therefore less abrupt than might at first appear. As early as June 1810 Gerrard attended a meeting of bank stockholders, probably of the Canada Banking Company, a project proposed by John Richardson* but never realized. Gerrard was in England from October 1816 to the spring of 1818 and thus, unlike his partner Moffatt, he was not a signatory of the Bank of Montreal's articles of association in 1817, but he was involved with its affairs from the beginning and served as its president from 1820 to 1826. He was deposed in a coup led by Moffatt, despite the support of the older directors who had their origins in the fur trade, such as John Forsyth*, George Garden*, and Peter McGill. The basis of the dispute was the charge that Gerrard had exceeded his powers as president and had made loans on the basis of favouritism. As a result, the bank faced potential losses, particularly in the failure of McTavish, McGillivrays and Company and McGillivrays, Thain and Company. Gerrard, a personal creditor of Simon McGillivray*, was one of the trustees appointed to administer the liquidation of the firms. Despite Moffatt's victory, Gerrard remained on the board of directors of the bank and continued to be active in its affairs. At an important shareholders' meeting in June 1826 Moffatt lost a vote to have Gerrard reimburse the bank.

Gerrard was a founder of the Montreal Savings Bank, established in 1819 and closely allied with the Bank of Montreal, sharing the same quarters and often the same officers. In 1822 he authorized loans for the bank, in 1826 he was a director, and in 1856, as its president, he suggested that it be absorbed by the Bank of Montreal and become the latter's savings department. The absorption took place that year. He was also a substantial shareholder in the Bank of Canada, which was taken over by the Bank of Montreal in 1831. In addition to his banking interests, Gerrard supervised the Canadian affairs of the Alliance British and Foreign Life and Fire Assurance Company of London from 1831 until well into the 1840s. In 1841, as administrator of the bankrupt estate of Jean-Baptiste-Toussaint Pothier*, Gerrard purchased the seigneuries of Lanaudière and Carufel in order to facilitate their resale to a third party. When two attempts to resell the seigneuries failed, he held on to the properties, eventually bequeathing them to his heirs.

Gerrard took an active interest in political questions, particularly when they impinged on his economic activities. He was appointed by Lord Durham [Lambton*] to the Special Council, holding office from 2 April to 1 June 1838 and from 2 Nov. 1838 to 10 Feb. 1841 and playing a prominent role in the council's deliberations. In 1831 he had succeeded Richardson as Edward Ellice*'s agent in North America and in that capacity offered and received political advice. Gerrard was a confirmed monarchist, an anti-democrat, and a defender of imperial ties. He was a virulent critic of Louis-Joseph Papineau* and the Patriotes for their opposition to banks, land companies, and immigration. In July 1838 Ellice felt it necessary to remind him that "an English Ministry . . . can never propose the permanent establishment of arbitrary government." For his part Gerrard described the French Canadians as "all rebels at heart," advised against conciliatory measures after the uprising of 1837–38, and lamented the failure to hang a dozen of its leaders. The union of Upper and Lower Canada in 1841 safeguarded Gerrard's economic investments and his involvement in politics declined.

Gerrard was active in a variety of organizations consistent with his political and business interests. He was a major in the militia; justice of the peace in 1821; director of the Montreal Library; member of the Committee of Trade; treasurer, life governor, vice president from 1835 to 1837, and president from 1837 to 1857 of the Montreal General Hospital; treasurer of the Provincial Grand Lodge; warden of the Montreal Protestant House of Industry and Refuge; and president of both the British and Canadian School Society of Montreal and the Montreal Auxiliary Bible Society.

Gerrard and his wife had two daughters, who married British army officers and left Lower Canada, and two sons who became officers in the British army and also left Montreal. A third son, Richard, became the Canadian agent for the Alliance British and Foreign Life and Fire Assurance Company in 1843 with his father's recommendation and guarantee. Gerrard's wife died in Montreal on 18 Oct. 1854.

Samuel Gerrard was a prominent Montreal businessman during the early period of the city's transformation from fur-trade centre to commercial metropolis. Like many of his contemporaries, Gerrard lived a life dominated by his business interests, as was illustrated in the Christmas wish he offered to his former partner Parker in 1814, "that pepper, cheese, tobacco and every other delicacy of your choice speculations may rise in value and yield tenfold increase."

PETER DESLAURIERS

ANQ-M, CE1-63, 11 nov. 1792. Antiquarian and Numismatic Soc. of Montreal, Samuel Gerrard papers, 1805–51 (mfm. at PAC). AUM, P 58, A3/85; A5; C2; G1; G2; U. PAC, MG 24, A2; B2; RG 68, General index, 1651–1841. Can., Prov. of, Legislative Assembly, *App. to the journals*, 1854–55, app.ZZZ. *Docs. relating to NWC* (Wallace). *Quebec Gazette*, 19 Jan. 1818. Denison, *Canada's first bank*, vol.1. E. A. Mitchell, *Fort Timiskaming and the fur trade* (Toronto and Buffalo, N.Y., 1977). Charles Drisard, "L'Honorable Samuel Gerrard," *BRH*, 34 (1928): 63–64. R. H. Fleming, "The origin of 'Sir Alexander Mackenzie and Company,'" *CHR*, 9 (1928): 137–55. Thomas O'Leary, "Ramble through St. Paul Street in the year 1819," *Montreal Daily Star*, 24 May 1920: 18.

GIBB, JAMES, businessman and seigneur; b. 22 April 1799 in Carluke, Scotland; m. 8 May 1822 Marion Torrance in Montreal, and they had nine children; d. 10 Oct. 1858 at Quebec.

Nothing is known of James Gibb's childhood or of the circumstances bringing him to Lower Canada. He arrived at Quebec in 1814 at the age of 15 and went to work as a clerk for William Torrance who, like his brothers John* and Thomas of Montreal, traded in foodstuffs, wines, and spirits. Gibb was given board and lodging by Torrance, and received £30, £40, and £50 for his first three years of service. As well as teaching him trade practices, the Torrances played an important role in Gibb's life and his initial endeavours in business. He became linked by marriage to this family, which had a strong hold on commercial operations in Lower Canada. In 1815 his sister Isabella married William Torrance, and seven years later Gibb himself married one of William's sisters. Like the Torrances, he was to make his fortune by the importing of foodstuffs and liquor, a trade he engaged in all his life at Quebec.

During the course of his career Gibb joined a number of companies. In 1821 Torrance took him on as a partner at Quebec. Initially financed solely by Torrance, the business was managed by Gibb until 1827. Then Gibb formed a partnership with his own brother Thomas under the name Thomas Gibb and Company, and around 1830, in a desire to branch out, he started a second business, James Gibb and Company, with Elisha Lane as his partner. Thomas Gibb and Company was dissolved at the beginning of 1835, when Thomas made over his shares to Robert Shaw. The new company, incorporated as Gibb and Shaw, had a capital of £17,702 and lasted until 1840. However, Gibb took no part in its daily management, and devoted his time mainly to James Gibb and Company.

By the end of the 1830s Gibb had become an influential merchant at Quebec. He was the principal financial backer of James Gibb and Company, which was reorganized in 1837 with Thomas Gibb joining as a third partner. In addition to his capital share of £4,900, Gibb had advanced £24,675 at six per cent interest. The shortage of agricultural products in Lower Canada during this decade provided him with attractive prospects, and his firm played an important part in the trade in comestibles. As well as liquor and grocery items, he imported large quantities of pork, beef, flour, and wheat bought from suppliers in New York, Oswego, and Rochester, N.Y., whom he had gone to the trouble of visiting personally. The market sought was huge; circulars were printed in 1838 and business cards in 1840, and these were distributed all over the Canadas and in the United States. Furthermore, James Gibb and Company also operated a sawmill, acquired in 1838, on the Rivière du Chêne, in the village of Deschaillons.

In January 1844 Gibb left the business, making over to his partners for £15,900 his share of the capital and profits, as well as the sawmill and other properties. According to a balance sheet drawn up on 18 December, the company had assets of more than £70,000. Thomas Gibb and Elisha Lane continued to run the business under the name Gibb and Lane. James set up a new firm with John Ross, a nephew he had formerly employed, with whom he had a profitable association until his own death. The New York commercial information agency R. G. Dun and Company considered Gibb and Ross the largest importer of wines and foodstuffs in Quebec during the 1850s. James Gibb Ross*, John's younger brother, became the third partner of the firm in April 1858.

Gibb also retained substantial interests in lumbering. In August 1843 he invested in the construction of a sawmill on the Rivière Portneuf, and also secured the services of Alexis TREMBLAY, dit Picoté, a former sawmill manager in the employ of William Price*, who directed operations until 1849. Some one hundred employees are thought to have done the felling and sawing. The mill experienced slow-downs in production during the 1850s because of fluctuations in the timber market.

Gibb also played a prominent part in both the financial sector and transportation. In 1832 he became a director of the Quebec Bank, where he held the posts of vice-president from 1839 to 1842 and president from 1842 until his death. In addition, he sat quite regularly on the board of the Quebec Savings Bank from 1831, and periodically on that of the Quebec Fire Assurance Company in the 1840s and 1850s. His interests in the importing and distribution of merchandise naturally led him to assist the Quebec bourgeoisie in its efforts to develop means of transportation. Gibb was one of the founders and shareholders of the Quebec and Halifax Steam Navigation Company (1831) and of the Quebec Forwarding Company (1843), being particularly active in the latter. The Quebec Forwarding Company, a firm that emerged from the winding up of the Quebec and Upper Canada Forwarding Company of which David BURNET of Quebec was a principal owner, had several barges and a number of steamboats carrying merchandise and passengers between Quebec and the Great Lakes, without calling at Montreal. Later Gibb was one of the incorporators of the Quebec and Trois-Pistoles Navigation Company (1853) and the Quebec, Chaudière, Maine and Portland Railway Company (1855). He

also took an interest in public utilities such as the Quebec Gas Light and Water Company, which he helped to found in 1842, and the Quebec Turnpike Roads Company, of which he was president from 1852 to 1855.

Gibb was one of the group of businessmen seeking the incorporation of the Quebec Board of Trade in 1841, and was elected a member of its first board. An influential man, he also worked as a volunteer for a number of philanthropic associations. However, he had no success in politics. He was known as a staunch supporter of the union of Upper and Lower Canada, and ran for the city of Quebec in the 1841 elections, campaigning with Henry Black* against Burnet and Louis-Joseph Massue*. Noting that he had little support, he stood down on the fourth day of voting.

Gibb's landed property and real estate, valued at about £15,000 in 1855, constituted an important part of his investments. In 1837 he had acquired the Jolliet seigneury in the Beauce. As for his places of residence, they were among the most magnificent at Quebec. Towards the end of the 1830s, like other prominent citizens, he moved to the suburbs, fleeing the unsanitary streets of Lower Town. He first lived on the estate of Bellevue at Sainte-Foy, which he made over to his brother Thomas in 1848 in exchange for the estate of Woodfield on the Chemin Saint-Louis at Quebec.

An energetic entrepreneur, James Gibb, having made a favourable marriage and established a diversity of business relations, succeeded in making the most of the commercial prospects at Quebec in the first half of the 19th century. The fortune he left more than sufficed to ensure that his descendants would be well-to-do. By the terms of the will he drafted a few weeks before his death, Gibb, among other things, left Woodfield to his wife, £15,000 to each of his seven remaining children, and £500 to each of two Protestant institutions.

PIERRE POULIN

ANQ-M, CE1-126, 8 mai 1822. ANQ-Q, CE1-67, 14 oct. 1858; CN1-49, 7 déc. 1814; 6 mai 1815; 7 mars 1821; 26 juin 1829; 7 sept. 1832; 27 oct. 1835; 15 juin, 6 juill., 9 déc. 1836; 9 nov. 1839; 16 janv. 1840; 5 janv. 1844; 16 oct. 1846; CN1-67, 15 sept. 1858; CN1-116, 5 mai 1842, 21 janv. 1845; CN1-178, 6 sept. 1823; CN1-197, 2 févr., 24 oct. 1835, 11 déc. 1837, 20 mai 1839, 2 août 1843, 9 déc. 1845, 14 sept. 1846, 22 mars 1847. BLHU, R. G. Dun & Co. credit ledger, Canada, 5: 53. Can., Prov. of, Statutes, 1841, c.92; 1842, c.23; 1849, c.192; 1852–53, c.247; 1854–55, c.196; 1858, c.69. Le Canadien, 22 févr., 29 mars 1841. Quebec Gazette, 10, 29 March 1841; 22, 31 March 1843. Cyclopædia of Canadian biog. (Rose and Charlesworth). Quebec almanac, 1830–41. Quebec directory, 1822, 1826, 1845, 1847–58. J. M. LeMoine, L'album du touriste . . . (2e éd., Québec, 1872); Monographies et esquisses (Québec, 1885). Monet, Last cannon shot, 73, 76.

Gibotte

Fernand Ouellet, *Histoire de la Chambre de commerce de Québec, 1809–1859* (Québec, 1959), 103.

GIBOTTE. *See* GUIBOCHE

GILCHRIST, JOHN, physician, surgeon, militia officer, businessman, office holder, justice of the peace, and politician; b. 5 Feb. 1792 in Bedford, N.H., eldest son of Samuel Gilchrist, a farmer and mill-owner, and Sarah Aiken; m. 1818 Lucretia Gove, a niece of Zacheus BURNHAM, and they had nine children; d. 15 Sept. 1859 in Port Hope, Upper Canada, and was buried in nearby Cobourg.

One of four brothers who became doctors, John Gilchrist entered the medical school of Yale College, New Haven, Conn., in 1815. There he attended the lectures of such famous medical and scientific educators as Nathan Smith and Benjamin Silliman, who regarded Gilchrist as a "gentleman in every respect." His education was completed at Dartmouth College, Hanover, N.H.; Smith also lectured at Dartmouth and on 11 Dec. 1816 certified Gilchrist's "qualifications for the degree of M.D." Although Gilchrist did not graduate, he apprenticed in Goffstown, N.H., probably with Dr Jonathan Gove, his future father-in-law, who later recommended him as "a wise-knowing & well inform'd Practioner on whose knowledge fidelity prudence & Care any person or persons may with Confidence & safety rely."

Gilchrist came to Hamilton Township, Upper Canada, about 1817 and on 5 Jan. 1818 he took the oath of allegiance to the crown. On 5 Jan. 1819 he appeared before the newly established Medical Board of Upper Canada and the following day received its first licence to practise "Physic Midwifery and Surgery." One of the Cobourg area's earliest physicians, he was gazetted surgeon in 1822 to the 1st Regiment of Northumberland militia and in 1847 became surgeon with the 7th Battalion of Peterborough militia.

Gilchrist moved north to the Indian River in Otonabee Township, where in 1825–27 he erected a sawmill and a grist-mill in association with Zacheus Burnham and Dugald Campbell, a merchant. The mills soon formed the nucleus of a small settlement, Gilchrist's Mills, which also became known as Keene after a village near Gilchrist's childhood home. Regarded as the settlement's founder, he opened the first general store in 1829 and a distillery in 1831. Although he leased his operations that year in order to resume full-time medical practice in Cobourg, he continued to improve his grist-mill. It was rebuilt in 1833–34 to house a second run of stones and "good flouring machinery." In 1838 the water supply from the Indian River was increased by cutting a channel from Gilchrist Bay on Stony Lake to the river's headwaters; Gilchrist was aided in this endeavour by Burnham, who owned a mill on the river at Warsaw, and Thomas Choate, the miller at Warsaw.

Gilchrist's businesses apparently prospered until 1839, when he experienced the first in a series of set-backs. A large dam constructed at Crooks' Rapids (Hastings) affected high water levels at Keene and disrupted his milling operations at peak periods. Compensation from the government was slow to come and in 1846 Gilchrist's petition was still under investigation. Other set-backs resulted in the serious diminution of his landholdings. Between 1825 and 1845 he had purchased some 1,000 acres of land in the Keene area, and in 1834 had begun to sell village lots. In 1840 he was forced to mortgage his mills and surrounding acreage in order to compensate his Lower Canadian agents, Forsyth and Bell of Quebec and Forsyth, McGill and Company of Montreal, for a £1,000 advance and his non-delivery of wheat and lumber. In 1843 more land was tied into a mortgage for nearly £3,500 from his brother-in-law, Mark Burnham of Port Hope, who foreclosed in 1856. Gilchrist's remaining land was sold by 1846, although his son John remained active at Keene in the lumber trade.

Gilchrist had a colourful career as an office holder and politician. Early in 1831 he was elected a director of the Cobourg Harbour Company. As building committee chairman he laid the cornerstone on 7 June 1832 of Upper Canada Academy in Cobourg. Appointed coroner for the Newcastle District on 3 Jan. 1833, he received his first commission of the peace for that district on 9 Jan. 1835. In October 1833 Gilchrist had closed his medical practice in Cobourg but in 1834 re-established it in Peterborough. Claiming no "pretensions to oratory," he was narrowly elected that year on a reform platform to the House of Assembly for the riding of Northumberland; its second seat went to Alexander McDonell*, the constitutional candidate.

In the assembly Gilchrist was a conscientious member and supported reform positions except on the issue of banking; he favoured the establishment of more banks throughout the province. He was an effective member of many committees, one of which deliberated the "most eligible route for a Canal to connect Lake Simcoe and Rice Lake." As well he supported most petitions relating to the Peterborough area, including that which led to the formation of the Colborne District in 1838 with Peterborough as the district town. Gilchrist lost the 1836 election, probably a victim of the strong loyalty vote which resulted in the defeat of other reform candidates. He was accused of disloyal behaviour during the rebellion of 1837 and was arrested that December. Drinking and cheering at his Keene "Still House" on 9 December had preceded a small riot, but charges against him were dropped. In 1841 Gilchrist was elected for the north riding of Northumberland in the united province's first election.

Apparently an independent and well-respected member, he had always demonstrated a strong interest in local government issues and chaired legislative assembly committees on public improvements, the petition of Robert Fleming Gourlay*, the review of bank charters, and the incorporation of religious societies – interests also shared by William Lyon Mackenzie*. Although Gilchrist did not run for re-election in 1844, he served as a district agent for the Crown Lands Department until 1845, and as Colborne District treasurer from 1842 to 1845.

In 1849 Gilchrist moved from Peterborough to Port Hope, where he practised until his death. It is not clear that he ever worked with his brothers, Hiram and Samuel in Port Hope or James Aiken in Cobourg. John Gilchrist's accomplishments in medicine and politics were real, and Keene remains an enduring reminder of his talents.

ELWOOD H. JONES

Academy of Medicine (Toronto), MS 67; MS 137. AO, MU 2553; RG 1, A-I-6, 22–24; C-IV, Otonabee Township, concession 6, lots 12–13; RG 22, ser.191, John Gilchrist. BLHU, R. G. Dun & Co. credit ledger, Canada, 22: 93. BNQ, Dép. des MSS, MSS-101, Coll. La Fontaine (copies at PAC). Can., Parks Canada, Ont. Region (Cornwall), Trent Waterway papers, file F06, Hastings (Crooks Rapids), general, 1, Gilchrist to F. Hall, 17 Oct. 1843. PAC, RG 1, L3, 214A: G2/34, 47–48; 222A: G misc., 1794–1830/97; 221: G leases, 1832/139; RG 68, General index, 1651–1841: 165, 168–70, 490, 503. Peterborough Centennial Museum (Peterborough, Ont.), MG 1-24; MG 1-34; MG 1-77, C-5X; MG 2-6. Peterborough Land Registry Office (Peterborough), Abstract index to deeds, Otonabee Township (mfm. at AO). Debates of the Legislative Assembly of United Canada (Abbott Gibbs et al.), vols.1–3. U.C., House of Assembly, Journal, 1834–36. Valley of the Trent (Guillet), 239, 297–300, 328. Cobourg Star, 8, 15 Oct. 1834. Tri-weekly Guide (Port Hope, [Ont.]), 17 Sept. 1859. Canada directory, 1851, 1857–58. Canadian biog. dict., 1: 560–61. DAB (biogs. of Eli Ives, Benjamin Silliman, Nathan Smith). Illustrated historical atlas of Peterborough County, 1825–1875 (Toronto, 1975), 62–63. Port Hope directory, 1856–57. Canniff, Medical profession in U.C., 38–39, 69–75, 382–85. Cornell, Alignment of political groups. Dave DeBrou, "Political alignments of the Upper Canadian members of the Legislative Assembly: first parliament, 1841–43" (undergraduate essay, Trent Univ., Peterborough, 1975). Forest to farm: early days in Otonabee, ed. D. G. Nelson (Keene, Ont., 1975), 46, 79–80, 114–15. C. M. Godfrey, Medicine for Ontario: a history (Belleville, Ont., 1979). E. C. Guillet, Cobourg, 1798–1948 (Oshawa, Ont., 1948), 238. J. J. Heagerty, Four centuries of medical history in Canada and a sketch of the medical history of Newfoundland (2v., Toronto, 1928), 1: 241. Historical sketch of the township of Hamilton, comp. Walter Riddell (Cobourg, Ont., 1897). Fred Landon, Western Ontario and the American frontier (Toronto, 1941; repr. 1967), 54. John Langton, Early days in Upper Canada: letters of John Langton from the backwoods of Upper Canada and the Audit Office of the province of Canada, ed. W. A. Langton (Toronto, 1926). Lindsey, Life and times of Mackenzie, 2: 376. Bernard McAllister, Reminiscenses of Cobourg (Cobourg, 1918), 80. [F. N. Pickford], "Two centuries of change": United Counties of Northumberland & Durham, 1767–1967 (Cobourg, 1967). T. W. Poole, A sketch of the early settlement and subsequent progress of the town of Peterborough, and of each township in the county of Peterborough (Peterborough, 1867; repub. 1941, 1967). J. H. Elliott, "John Gilchrist, J.P., L.M.B.U.C., M.D.: a pioneer New England physician in Upper Canada," Bull. of the Hist. of Medicine (Baltimore, Md.), 7 (1939): 737–50 [includes a photograph of Gilchrist].

GILDERSLEEVE (Gilderslieve), HENRY, shipbuilder, ship's captain, businessman, and justice of the peace; b. 8 Nov. 1785 in Gildersleeve (Portland), Conn., son of Philip Gildersleeve and Temperance Gibbs; m. 28 Jan. 1824 Sarah Finkle, and they had five sons, two of whom died in infancy, and three daughters; d. 1 Oct. 1851 in Kingston, Upper Canada.

Henry Gildersleeve came from a family of shipbuilders: both his father and his grandfather, Obadiah Gildersleeve, were ship-carpenters. Henry learned the trade in a shipyard in Gildersleeve before immigrating to Upper Canada in 1816. He obtained employment at Bath in the yard operated by Lucretia Finkle, widow of Henry Finkle, a loyalist and founder of the business. Gildersleeve helped in the construction of the *Frontenac*, which was built at the Finkle yard by Henry Teabout and James Chapman of Sackets Harbor, N.Y., where Gildersleeve is reputed to have worked as a shipwright about 1815. Launched in September 1816 by a group of merchants from Kingston and York (Toronto), the *Frontenac* was the first Canadian-built steamboat to ply Lake Ontario, beginning service between Kingston and Niagara (Niagara-on-the-Lake) on 5 June 1817. (An American steamboat, the *Ontario*, built at Sackets Harbor, began service on the lake early in 1817 [see Samuel CRANE]. The first steamboat built in the Canadas, the *Accommodation*, had been constructed in Montreal in 1809 for John Molson*.)

Gildersleeve was master builder as well as part-owner of the second steamboat from the Finkle yard, the *Charlotte*, but was not a member of the committee which sponsored its construction. He acted as purser on this vessel while qualifying for his captain's certificate, and in 1821 he became its captain. From 1818 to 1827 the *Charlotte* ran between Prescott, on the St Lawrence River, and Carrying Place, on the Bay of Quinte. The *Sir James Kempt*, which replaced the *Charlotte* on this run in 1828, was built under Gildersleeve's supervision. He was a

Gildersleeve

stockholder of the ship and served as its captain for many years before becoming its agent. His identification with these steamers and others that later plied the same route led to Gildersleeve's designation by Edwin Ernest Horsey, a Kingston historian, as "the father of steam navigation on the Bay of Quinte and the upper St. Lawrence."

Over the years Gildersleeve was involved both as a shareholder, in association with others (mainly Kingston businessmen), and sometimes as building superintendent, in the construction and operation of a succession of steamboats: *William the Fourth* (Gananoque, 1831), *Commodore Barrie* (Kingston, 1834), *Henry Gildersleeve* (Kingston, 1840), *Prince of Wales* (Kingston, 1841), and *New Era* (Kingston, 1848). Of these, the *Prince of Wales* plied the Bay of Quinte exclusively, while the others ran on that bay, on Lake Ontario, or on the St Lawrence. Gildersleeve also had interests in other steamboats. Along with Robert Drummond*, Donald Bethune*, and others he had been on the committee formed to build the *John By*, intended for the Rideau Canal but run instead on Lake Ontario. He became a shareholder in and later the agent for the *Kingston*, built by John G. Parker in 1833. In 1847 he purchased the *City of Kingston*, which had been built on Garden Island as the *Prince Edward* in 1841 by Dileno Dexter Calvin*, John Counter*, and others. Finally, Gildersleeve may have projected the construction of the *Bay of Quinte*, which was built under the direction of his son Overton Smith* in 1852.

Competition between steamboat operators became increasingly intense as the number of vessels multiplied. A bitter exchange of letters took place in the *Kingston Chronicle* in May 1830 between Gildersleeve and Archibald McDonell, whose ship *Toronto* had begun running on the Bay of Quinte. Gildersleeve also faced opposition there from Donald Bethune's *Britannia*. To counteract the effects of competition, operators began coordinating their schedules and establishing joint undertakings. Gildersleeve, for instance, arranged for cooperation in the schedules of his *Commodore Barrie* and the American steamer *Oswego* in 1835. At various times, he chartered the *Commodore Barrie*, the *Henry Gildersleeve*, and the *New Era* to John Hamilton* of Kingston for service on his lines.

Gildersleeve had married a daughter of Henry and Lucretia Finkle in 1824, and by 1826 he and his wife had settled in Kingston, where he built a substantial stone house in 1825–26. He became a prominent citizen, known not solely as a shipbuilder but also as a man active in many business and community affairs. He was a stockholder of the Ottawa and Rideau Forwarding Company, which provided passenger and freight service between Kingston, Bytown (Ottawa), and Montreal via the Rideau Canal. With others, notably John Counter, he promoted and was an original stockholder of the Kingston Marine Railway Company, founded in 1836 and incorporated two years later. For many years Gildersleeve was a director and president of this firm, which built and repaired ships of all kinds at its marine railway and shipyard on the Kingston waterfront. He was a director and, later, treasurer of the Kingston Gas Light Company, and was a promoter of the Kingston Waterworks. As well, Gildersleeve was a founder and vice-president of the Kingston Provident and Savings Bank, president for several years of the Kingston Building Society, and vice-president of the Kingston Fire and Marine Insurance Company. As an investor, he held shares in both the Commercial Bank of the Midland District and the Bank of Upper Canada.

In response to early proposals for Upper Canadian railways, which threatened Kingston's role as a trans-shipment centre, Gildersleeve and other enterprising businessmen conceived the idea of developing the city as the centre of a railway linking Toronto, Kingston, and (via Wolfe Island to the south of Kingston) Cape Vincent, N.Y., where it would connect with American railways. The Wolfe Island, Kingston and Toronto Rail-road Company was incorporated in 1846 but the railway was never built. An attempt to revive the plan, with the added feature of a canal across Wolfe Island, led to the incorporation in 1851 of the Wolfe Island Rail-way and Canal Company, of which Gildersleeve was named a director. He did not live to see the failure of this project, for he died in October of that year.

Gildersleeve participated in various other aspects of life in Kingston. He sat on the grand jury for the Midland District Assizes for several years and became a magistrate in 1842. The previous year he had served on the committee set up by the local board of trade to assess available accommodation for the use of the Canadian government after its scheduled move to Kingston. In religion he was an active member of St George's Church (Anglican).

In 1828 the *Kingston Chronicle* described Gildersleeve as "well known for the urbanity of his manners." A benevolent man, of strong character and firm integrity, he was above all a shrewd and far-sighted businessman and an enterprising pioneer in shipbuilding in Upper Canada. At his death he left a large estate, consisting of steamboats, real estate, and cash, to his son Overton Smith. Another son, Charles Fuller*, and a grandson, Henry Herchmer Gildersleeve, gained prominence as managers of major shipping firms on the Great Lakes and the St Lawrence.

RUTH McKENZIE

ACC-O, St George's Cathedral (Kingston, Ont.), reg. of marriages, 1824. AO, MS 78, Henry Gildersleeve to John Macaulay, 24 May 1837, 28 Feb. 1843; MU 610, no.61

Gilkison

(cash-book of steamer *Sir James Kempt*, 1836). Kingston Public Library (Kingston), E. E. Horsey, "The Gildersleeves of Kingston – their activities, 1816–1930" (typescript, Kingston, 1942; copy at QUA). PAC, MG 24, D24: 236–44, 280–86; RG 5, A1: 20075–78; RG 42, ser.I, 205: 71. Can., Prov. of, Legislative Assembly, *App. to the journals*, 1857, app.11, nos.7–8; *Statutes*, 1846, c.108; 1848, c.13; 1849, c.158; 1850, c.139; 1851, c.149. U.C., *Statutes*, 1837–38, c.30. *British Whig*, 13 May 1834–25 March 1848. *Chronicle & Gazette*, 27 July 1833–10 May 1845. *Daily British Whig*, 1 Oct. 1851. *Daily News* (Kingston), 8 Oct. 1851. *Kingston Chronicle*, 1 June 1827–26 Nov. 1831. *Kingston Gazette*, 14 Sept. 1816–8 June 1818. *Weekly British Whig*, 6 July 1849; 29 March, 5 April 1850; 30 July 1852.

Canada directory, 1851: 119–29. *Cyclopædia of Canadian biog.* (Rose and Charlesworth), 1: 586–87. W. H. Gildersleeve, *Gildersleeves of Gildersleeve, Conn., and the descendants of Philip Gildersleeve* (Meriden, Conn., 1914). *Heritage Kingston*, ed. J. D. Stewart and I. E. Wilson (Kingston, 1973), 155, 164–65, 170. *Pioneer life on the Bay of Quinte, including genealogies of old families and biographical sketches of representative citizens* (Toronto, 1904; repr. Belleville, Ont., 1972), 332, 339. *Canada and its prov.* (Shortt and Doughty), 10: 493–502, 506–14, 536–40. E. E. Horsey, *Kingston, a century ago; issued to commemorate the centennial of Kingston's incorporation* (Kingston, 1938). *To preserve & defend: essays on Kingston in the nineteenth century*, ed. G. [J. J.] Tulchinsky (Montreal and London, 1976), 1–14 (editor's intro.), and J. K. Johnson, "John A. Macdonald and the Kingston business community," 141–55. A. G. Young, *Great Lakes saga; the influence of one family on the development of Canadian shipping on the Great Lakes, 1816–1931* (Owen Sound, Ont., 1965). Dorothy Geiger, "A history of the Kingston waterfront and water lots," *Historic Kingston*, no.19 (1971): 3–16. A. L. Johnson, "The transportation revolution on Lake Ontario, 1817–1867: Kingston and Ogdensburg," *OH*, 67 (1975): 199–209. Duncan McDowall, "Roads and railways: Kingston's mid-century search for a hinterland, 1846–1854," *Historic Kingston*, no.23 (1975): 52–69. R. A. Preston, "The history of the port of Kingston," *OH*, 46 (1954): 201–11; 47 (1955): 23–38.

GILKISON, DAVID, businessman, office holder, and college clerk; b. *c.* 1803 in Sandwich (Windsor), Upper Canada, eldest son of William Gilkison* and Isabella Grant; m. 10 June 1835 Margaret Geddes, and they had at least seven children, three of whom survived infancy; d. 8 May 1851 in Toronto.

David Gilkison was born in Upper Canada, where his Scottish father had commanded a schooner and from 1811 engaged in the forwarding business. David probably received most of his education in Glasgow after his father took his family to Scotland in 1815 in order to further the education of his sons. Returning to Upper Canada in 1827, David entered business by opening the first general store in the fledgling community of Guelph, founded in April of that year by John Galt*, a close friend and cousin of his father and superintendent of the Canada Company.

Gilkison apparently came equipped with some capital and he entered into partnership with William Leaden, a retired army officer, to form D. Gilkison and Company. This business benefited from the cash trade provided by the Canada Company, which purchased supplies for the considerable number of its employees who were clearing the townsite and building company facilities, as well as for some destitute immigrants. Gilkison and Leaden also took advantage of the potential for water-power on the Speed River at Guelph. Their proposal to rent and eventually to purchase a grist-mill, to be built by the Canada Company, was rejected by the company's directors in London, England, but in August 1827 they purchased a good mill-seat for less than £10 and built a dam and a sawmill. Lumber was in great demand in the boom-town atmosphere and the mill operated day and night. But the town's rapid growth depended on the Canada Company's continued stimulation, which came to a sudden halt following Galt's dismissal in early 1829. The result was a severe local depression in which a number of businesses, including Gilkison's, failed. Although his store seems to have been continued by Leaden, the firm's remaining assets were seized by creditors.

For a few years following his unsuccessful venture in Guelph, Gilkison worked as a clerk at the store in West Flamborough Township of James CROOKS, another associate of his father. An upturn in David's fortunes took place when his father decided to return from Scotland in 1832. He was unable to rescue his son's sawmilling operation, but he did purchase about 14,000 acres in Nichol Township in the fall of 1832 and at a superb mill-seat about ten miles northwest of Guelph he founded the town of Elora. William's sudden death in April 1833 put David, as the eldest son, in charge of the settlement project even though his father had planned to make a younger son, Jasper Tough*, the manager. Their father's property was divided equally among six surviving sons, but David seems to have sold land for all of them.

In superintending the development of the settlement, Gilkison provided a community infrastructure intended to make the village and the surrounding agricultural land desirable to potential purchasers of land. He appears to have settled in Elora about May 1833 and the combined house and store in which he first lived served as a community centre for religious and social occasions; he was later involved in the erection of an Anglican church. He also acted as a township commissioner and oversaw the building of some of the area's roads. He took a considerable interest in those to whom he sold land. George Elmslie, a member of a group of Scottish settlers who purchased land for a settlement named Bon-accord in the northern part of the township, wrote of his "kindness and attention" and that "his father's purchase here and his own exertion undoubtedly gave the first impulse to the settlement of this flourishing part of Canada West." Gilkison nevertheless decided

327

to leave Elora, perhaps because of the slowness of land sales, and in 1837 he auctioned off his farming equipment and some property, leaving his father-in-law, Andrew Geddes, in charge of his land interests. By September 1838 he was reported to have resettled in Elora, but soon thereafter he attempted, apparently without success, mercantile ventures in Queenston, Upper Canada, and Genesee (Geneseo), N.Y. Because of his wife's poor health, he had moved to Toronto by October 1841 but as late as 1842 he and his brothers still owned more than 3,000 acres of uncleared land and 40 cleared acres in Nichol Township.

Although Gilkison's financial situation must have been extremely precarious when he settled in Toronto, he and his wife were able to associate with other Anglicans in intellectual and musical circles. In 1845 he obtained a position as second clerk in the bursar's office of King's College (University of Toronto). His wife became a well-known singing teacher and the organist of St James' Cathedral but was plagued by chronic ill health. Her reputedly delicate condition was probably related to the fact that the Gilkisons lost four children in infancy, including twin boys, between 1846 and 1849.

Gilkison's career, marked by his constant wandering, fluctuating circumstances, and attempts at many tasks, seems to have been representative of entrepreneurial life on the frontier in his day. Although he was able to take advantage of Scottish connections in a variety of business ventures, commercial activity in Upper Canada was fraught with uncertainty and his efforts failed more often than they succeeded.

GILBERT A. STELTER

AO, MS 497; MS 564, Corr., Thomas Smith to John Galt, 15 Nov. 1828; RG 1, A-I-6: 17525–29; RG 21, Wellington County, Nichol Township assessment rolls, 1842 (mfm. at Wellington County Museum, Wellington County Arch., Fergus, Ont.). Brant County Museum (Brantford, Ont.), Gilkison papers, William Gilkison corr. MTL, Canada Company papers. Private arch., Charles Corke (Guelph, Ont.), William Gilkison letters. St James' Cemetery and Crematorium (Toronto), Record of burials, 12, 14 May 1847; 18 Jan. 1849; 10 May 1851. Univ. of Toronto Arch., A68-0010, I/A/3, 45: 2. UWOL, Regional Coll., Canada Company, records and papers; William Gilkison papers, diary (transcript). Wellington County Museum, Mary Grant, Nichol Township map, 1948; Map of Elora, 30 Nov. 1832. [L. W. V.] Smith, *Young Mr Smith in Upper Canada*, ed. M. L. Smith (Toronto, 1980). *British Colonist* (Toronto), 9 May 1851. *Toronto directory*, 1846–47: 27; 1850–51: lix. C. A. Burrows, *The annals of the town of Guelph, 1827–1877* (Guelph, 1877). J. R. Connon, *"Elora"* (n.p., 1930); repub. as *The early history of Elora, Ontario, and vicinity*, intro. Gerald Noonan (Waterloo, Ont., 1974). A. D. Ferrier, *Reminiscences of Canada and the early days of Fergus; being three lectures delivered to the Farmers' and Mechanics' Institute, Fergus* ... (Guelph, 1866; repr. Fergus, 1923). Johnson, *Hist. of Guelph*. A. I. G. Gilkison, "Captain William Gilkison," *OH*, 8 (1907): 147–48.

GINGRAS, ÉDOUARD (baptized **François-Édouard**), wheelwright and master coach-builder; b. 3 June 1806 at Quebec, son of Pierre Gingras, a merchant, and Marguerite Gaboury; m. there 3 July 1827 Louise Contremine, *dit* Jolicœur, and they had 11 children; d. there 22 Sept. 1857.

Édouard Gingras, the seventh of a family of ten, was married at the age of 21 in a ceremony which both his father and his brother LEON attended. By then Gingras was a recognized wheelwright, and he soon opened his own workshop in the town, probably on Rue d'Aiguillon. In 1833 notarized acts designated him master coach-builder; he had a number of employees, among them blacksmith François Ratté, who had joined him the preceding year and remained in his service for at least 13 years.

Gingras sought to improve his technique and to give a finish of higher quality to his vehicles. He imported many of the parts he used, as witness his prosecution in 1835 for refusing material from Ireland because he considered the price too high. Gingras was conscientious in his work; as a master in his trade and owner of a workshop he continually had to alter the designs of the various models offered to his clients: vehicles for outings, coaches, and sleighs. Every year the fashion changed and techniques became more refined. Gingras responded with imagination and efficiency. For example, aware that there were problems related to the suspension system used for carriages, on 16 Sept. 1843 he patented a "New method of making springs for vehicles." Gingras in 1839 had become the owner of a three-storey stone house at 36 Rue Sainte-Ursule, in which he had already lived for nine years. He bought another one on the same street in 1850 and installed his equipment there. The census of the following year shows that he had ten employees.

In 1851 the Canadian government participated in the Great Exhibition in London, sending, among other products, three vehicles manufactured by Joseph Saurin of Quebec and two built by Clovis Leduc of Montreal. Within four years, in both quality and financial yield, Gingras succeeded in catching up with his competitor Saurin, whose workshop on Rue Sainte-Anne employed 20 people. The two men took part in the universal exposition held in Paris in 1855. Gingras sent a de luxe four-wheeled vehicle, Saurin a de luxe sleigh. That the two were chosen undoubtedly proves the excellence of their work, since by 1851 Lower Canada had 584 coach-builders and wheelwrights and Upper Canada 1,789. The author of a work published in Paris on the exposition spoke highly of the Canadian entries: "These vehicles are elegant in form, and the mountings in particular have been treated with great care; they speak well for the taste of the builders." Afterwards the vehicles of Gingras and Saurin were sent to the Crystal Palace at Sydenham, southeast of London.

Gingras's workshop at Quebec continued to produce vehicles and sleighs, and his fame steadily grew. But he died on 22 Sept. 1857, the very day that he learned he had won first prize at an exhibition held in Montreal. A master coach-builder who was concerned about the quality of his products, Gingras had also proved able to set up a business dealing in superior finished articles and to run it successfully. His son Édouard, who worked with him, took over the business, and in partnership with his father-in-law, Charles Hough, increased its importance. By 1871 the undertaking was by far the largest coachmaker's establishment in Quebec County. In that year the 23 employees produced 407 winter and summer vehicles, most of them with silver fittings.

ANNE BERNATCHEZ

ANQ-Q, CE1-1, 3 juin 1806, 3 juill. 1827, 25 sept. 1857; CN1–138, 30 juill. 1835; CN1-219, 22 mars 1833, 22 janv. 1845. AVQ, VII, E, 1, quartier Saint-Louis, 1830–56. PAC, RG 31, A1, 1851, 1871, Quebec. [J.-C. Taché], *Le Canada et l'exposition universelle de 1855* (Toronto, 1856). *Journal of Education for Lower Canada* (Montreal), 1 (1857): 138.

GINGRAS, LÉON, Roman Catholic priest, educator, seminary administrator, and author; b. 5 Aug. 1808 at Quebec, son of Pierre Gingras, a tavern-keeper, and Marguerite Gaboury and brother of ÉDOUARD; d. 18 Feb. 1860 in Paris.

Léon Gingras went through the various stages of classical studies at the Petit Séminaire de Québec from 1820 to 1828. According to a friend's statement in *L'Abeille*, the seminary's newspaper, he was a brilliant student and was often awarded the first prize at the end of the year. Because of his piety, the young man was drawn to the priesthood and from 1828 to 1831 he studied theology at the Grand Séminaire de Québec. He was ordained priest on 21 Aug. 1831. His liking for intellectual work and teaching kept him at the seminary, inclining him to the studious life of a teaching priest rather than to parish ministry.

At first Gingras was assigned the task of teaching the fourth form (Versification), but in 1832 he was made professor of theology and in 1833 was appointed in addition principal of the Grand Séminaire; he carried out these responsibilities until 1840. He was principal of the Petit Séminaire and prefect of studies from 1840 to 1842, and from 1842 to 1844 he again occupied the post of principal of the Grand Séminaire.

Exhausted from hard work and illness, Gingras left for Europe on 18 May 1844 with a friend (possibly Narcisse Bélanger). He was fulfilling a wish cherished from the time of his introduction to the life of the mind: "I had but begun my education when my thoughts and desires turned to the diverse countries where the great deeds of ancient and modern history have come to pass." After a 34-day crossing, Gingras and his companion hastened to Paris, where he paid a visit to one of the authors whose books had delighted him as a young student, François-René de Chateaubriand. Six years earlier Chateaubriand had left the villa adjoining the Infirmerie Marie-Thérèse, an establishment run by his wife to care for aged priests, and moved to 120 Rue du Bac. It was there that, as Gingras noted, "the immortal author of *Les martyrs* deigned to honour us with his welcome." From Paris, travelling through Lyons and Marseilles in France, and Milan, Venice, Assisi, and Rome in Italy, the two made their way to Sicily, to the island of Malta, and then to Egypt, where they landed at Alexandria.

Europe did not hold Gingras's attention for long: "The Orient alone engaged my thoughts; it alone absorbed them completely." Having joined a caravan, Gingras and his companion journeyed from Egypt to Mount Sinai, which they reached on 25 Feb. 1845. The Quebec priest climbed it Bible in hand. "Everything about this mountain," he later wrote, "confirms Moses's account; no prejudices, no scepticism, can hold up in the face of so many testimonies to truth." Continuing on their way, the pilgrims reached Jerusalem on 14 March; the faithful reader of Chateaubriand explored the city, tracing the footsteps outlined in *L'itinéraire de Paris à Jérusalem*. On Easter Day he celebrated mass in the Church of the Holy Sepulchre: "The fact of my being a Canadian, together with the thought that I was the first priest from Canada to whom it had thus far been given to offer the holy mysteries in the tomb of Jesus Christ, contributed in no small measure to my already vivid impressions."

From Jerusalem, the travellers crossed Galilee and went to Beirut, where they embarked on 3 April for Smyrna, Istanbul, and Athens. They came back through Austria, Germany, and Belgium, to Liverpool in England, and reached Quebec in July 1845.

Shortly after his return Gingras resumed his duties as principal of the Grand Séminaire, a post he held along with that of professor of philosophy and theology from 1845 to 1849. The following year he was appointed to the council of the bishop of Quebec, with, among others, his colleague Antoine PARANT; Gingras kept this office until his death. He once more discharged the duties of principal of the Grand Séminaire from 1854 until May 1859, when he again set off for Europe to recover his health. But he was overcome by illness in Paris and died at the Infirmerie Marie-Thérèse on 18 Feb. 1860. His remains were buried in the cemetery of Montparnasse but were later brought back to Quebec and interred on 28 Aug. 1863 in the vault of the seminary chapel.

Girouard

In 1847 Gingras had published at Quebec *L'Orient ou voyage en Égypte, en Arabie, en Terre-Sainte, en Turquie et en Grèce*, a two-volume work. After more than a century, the 1,028 pages can still be read with interest. Gingras had gathered his material with great care, as is evident from the authors he quotes. As well as the work of Chateaubriand, he mentions in a number of places the *Pèlerinage à Jérusalem et au mont Sinaï*, published in Paris between 1834 and 1836 by Baron Ferdinand de Géramb, a Trappist; Jean-Joseph-François Poujoulat's *L'histoire de Jérusalem*, a work brought out in 1841 which he noted was "of the greatest use" to him; the geographical publications of Conrad Malte-Brun; and Alphonse de Lamartine's *Voyage en Orient*. Gingras deeply regretted that the celebrated poet had set out on his journey as a Christian and had returned a deist.

Gingras, a Catholic priest of Lower Canada in the 19th century, naturally shared the prejudices of his time, of those of his station in life, and of the authors in whom he put his trust. It is far too easy, at more than 130 years' distance, to write as Jean Ouellette did in an analysis of his work that, although Gingras showed "considerable sympathy towards the Jews and Jewish religion," by contrast, "towards the other ethnic or religious groups that made up the Palestinian society of the time" he "displayed in general a crass intolerance and did not even seek to disguise his hostile feelings." These lines are over harsh in their judgement, but Ouellette speaks with greater equanimity and justice in observing that Gingras's testimony "is not devoid of interest for Orientalists in search of data experienced at first hand in a region of the world which is now in the spotlight."

Léon Gingras expressed himself in a language that was usually correct. His long familiarity with the best French writers of the day gave his style elegance, variety, and precision. Consequently, comments by critic Edmond Lareau* on "the defects of style and the inadequacy of the form" that he believes he discovered in Gingras's work reveal a manifest lack of sympathy or even of simple fairness.

PHILIPPE SYLVAIN

Léon Gingras is the author of *L'Orient ou voyage en Égypte, en Arabie, en Terre-Sainte, en Turquie et en Grèce* (2v., Québec, 1847).

AAQ, 12 A, K, f.171v. ANQ-Q, CE1-1, 5 août 1808, 28 août 1863. ASQ, MSS 437: 225–27. *Le Séminaire de Québec: documents et biographies*, Honorius Provost, édit. (Québec, 1964). *L'Abeille*, 15, 22 mars 1860. Allaire, *Dictionnaire*, 1: 242. *DOLQ*, 1: 555. Morgan, *Sketches of celebrated Canadians*, 411–12. P.-G. Roy, *Fils de Québec*, 3: 142–44. Tanguay, *Répertoire* (1893), 207. Lareau, *Hist. de la littérature canadienne*, 168–70. "Les disparus," *BRH*, 36 (1930): 365. Jean Ouellette, "La Palestine au XIXᵉ siècle vue par un voyageur de Québec," Centre de recherche en civilisation canadienne-française, *Bull.* (Ottawa), 19 (déc. 1979): 15–22.

GIROUARD, JEAN-JOSEPH, militia officer, notary, politician, Patriote, portrait painter, and philanthropist; b. 13 Nov. 1794 at Quebec, son of Joseph Girouard and Marie-Anne Baillairgé; d. 18 Sept. 1855 in Saint-Benoît (Mirabel), Lower Canada.

Jean-Joseph Girouard's forebear, François Girouard, came to live in Acadia during the 1640s. Following the deportation, a small number of his descendants, including Jean-Joseph's grandfather, Joseph Girouard, went to Quebec, settling there during the Seven Years' War. In his youth Jean-Joseph's father was apprenticed to Jean Baillairgé*, a master carpenter. He worked subsequently as a shipbuilding contractor at Quebec. There he married Baillairgé's youngest daughter, Marie-Anne, in 1793, and they had three children: Jean-Joseph, Angèle, and Félicité. From his paternal ancestors Jean-Joseph retained an instinctive and lasting distrust of England. From his mother he inherited the artistic tradition of the Baillairgé family.

In September 1800, at the age of five, Jean-Joseph lost his father, who was drowned while sailing off Wolfe's Cove (Anse au Foulon). After Joseph's death the boy, his mother, and his two sisters were given shelter in his maternal grandfather's house, where he remained from the age of six until he was ten. It was during this period that the young boy learned something of the skills of the Baillairgé family, whose name was already well known at Quebec. In the diary that he kept later with his second wife, he described how he learned from his grandfather "the rules of finding cubic content." He also recalled seeing his uncles François* and Pierre-Florent* busy at their saw-horses while he tried his own hand, almost in fun, at the various tasks undertaken in the Baillairgé workshop.

After her father's death in 1805 Mme Girouard met Jean-Baptiste Gatien, one of his close friends, who was priest of the parish of Sainte-Famille on the Île d'Orléans. Gatien proposed that she become the housekeeper in his presbytery and bring her children to Sainte-Famille. She agreed, and Gatien looked after their material needs; he also assumed responsibility for the children's intellectual and religious instruction. He could find no praise great enough for his young pupil Jean-Joseph, whom he thought exceptionally talented. None of the subjects he studied – music, painting, architecture, physics, or mathematics – gave any trouble to Jean-Joseph's gifted mind. The boy was also well behaved, thoughtful, and reflective, as the portrait painted by François Baillairgé suggests.

Mme Girouard and her children followed Gatien when he was sent to take charge of the parish of Sainte-Anne at Sainte-Anne-des-Plaines in 1806, and again in 1811 when he became priest at Saint-Eustache. Having assimilated the general knowledge imparted by his tutor, in 1811 Girouard began training as a notarial clerk under Joseph Maillou at Sainte-Geneviève (Sainte-Geneviève and Pierrefonds), on Montreal Island. At the beginning of the War of 1812 he was too young to be called up for militia service but became a volunteer in a corps at Lachine. When Maillou was called to the colours, Girouard left the corps and continued his training under Pierre-Rémi Gagné at Saint-Eustache. In November 1812, having reached enlistment age, he served at Montreal as an adjutant in the Lavaltrie Battalion of militia under Lieutenant-Colonel Joseph-Édouard FARIBAULT. After his return to Saint-Eustache at the end of the war he finished his clerkship and took his examinations. On 13 June 1816 he received his commission as a notary, and that year settled in Saint-Benoît, a village adjoining Saint-Eustache, where he spent the rest of his life.

That a man such as Girouard was to become a rebel can be explained only by the environment in which he lived. Girouard opened an office in the house of Jean-Baptiste Dumouchel*, a merchant in the village with whom he soon became friends. On 24 Nov. 1818 he took as his first wife Dumouchel's sister-in-law Marie-Louise Félix, whose brother Maurice-Joseph was the priest of the parish of Saint-Benoît. Through his marriage the young notary quickly secured entry to the small circle of village society and sealed his friendship with Dumouchel by family ties. From then on, enjoying the high regard of the townspeople and possessing undeniable talents as a notary, Girouard attracted numerous clients, the most regular being Dumouchel, and eventually acquired a sound reputation in his profession.

In the autumn of 1821 Governor Lord Dalhousie [Ramsay*] appointed Girouard a captain in the Rivière-du-Chêne battalion of militia, a position he retained until the beginning of 1828. On 7 March 1827 Dalhousie decided to adjourn the House of Assembly because of the conflict which had developed between it and the Legislative Council. During the electoral campaign the following summer, Girouard travelled through York riding with the Patriote party candidate, Jacques Labrie*, and Jean-Olivier Chénier*. In July several Patriote supporters, in particular Dumouchel, Joseph-Amable Berthelot, and Labrie, all three close friends of Girouard, were dismissed as militia officers because they had taken part in election meetings. As a token of protest against these unjust dismissals, Girouard resolutely returned his commission as a militia captain to the governor in January 1828.

Meanwhile, Girouard and Chénier had none the less succeeded in getting Labrie elected, in a climate of violence heralding the stormy years before the rebellion.

Following Labrie's death in 1831 Girouard was chosen by acclamation as member in the assembly for the new constituency of Deux-Montagnes, which had been part of York riding. He set to work soon after arriving at Quebec in January 1832 and became a keen supporter of Louis-Joseph Papineau* and a close friend of Augustin-Norbert Morin*. He had not been blessed with oratorical gifts, however, and rarely contributed to the fiery debates in the assembly. He preferred to sit on committees studying matters such as municipal affairs, regulations governing the notarial profession, and education. In 1834 he supported unreservedly the 92 Resolutions, which outlined the principal grievances and demands of the assembly.

General elections had been planned for the autumn of that year, and it was anticipated that the struggle would be extremely fierce. In these circumstances Girouard, who had a gentle and timid disposition, was reluctant to rush into the political arena, but he finally agreed to run as a Patriote party candidate along with William Henry SCOTT, the other member for Deux-Montagnes. The English party decided to contest the seat, James Brown* and his brother-in-law Frédéric-Eugène Globensky campaigning as candidates. The electoral struggle, as foreseen, gave rise to violence: in riots at St Andrews (Saint-André-Est) numerous people were hurt, including Scott and Dumouchel, and a veritable street battle developed at Saint-Eustache. As a result of the incidents at Saint-Eustache, Stephen Mackay, the returning officer who was also a brother-in-law of Globensky, quickly stopped the voting, in order, he said, to put an end to the violence constantly erupting around the polling-booth. Fearing that the English party candidates would be defeated, he resorted to a subterfuge. He declared Girouard and Scott elected, although they had 30 votes fewer than Brown and Globensky, the hope being that the English party could contest the election results. However, Girouard and Scott resumed their seats in the assembly and kept them until 1837; no one ever ventured to raise an objection.

On the eve of the outbreak of the rebellion in November 1837, Girouard, who had taken an active part in Patriote meetings at Saint-Benoît and the neighbouring villages during the preceding three years, was regarded by the authorities as a leader of the resistance movement in the Lac des Deux-Montagnes region, along with Chénier and Luc-Hyacinthe Masson*. His name was on the list of outlaws, beside the names of Papineau and Morin. There was a price on his head and a reward of £500 for

Girouard

anyone who turned him in. On 13 December Sir John Colborne* and his troops left Montreal and headed for Saint-Eustache and Saint-Benoît, to arrest in particular Chénier, Amury Girod*, Dumouchel, and Damien and Luc-Hyacinthe Masson, as well as Girouard. At Saint-Eustache, Chénier and his supporters decided to go down fighting. At Saint-Benoît, on the other hand, Girouard persuaded the villagers to lay down their arms and surrender, while the outlawed leaders sought refuge in flight. He himself made his way to Rigaud, where he found shelter with a habitant. Meanwhile Colborne and his troops, along with the volunteers from neighbouring villages, sacked and set fire to Saint-Benoît. Girouard hid for some days at Coteau-du-Lac, but soon learned in his hide-out that his supporters had been arrested and put in jail at Montreal. Rather than pursuing his plan to reach the American border, he decided to give himself up to Colonel John Simpson*, who was stationed at Coteau-du-Lac, and to place his legal knowledge at the disposal of his friends who were accused of high treason.

Girouard was taken to Montreal and imprisoned on 26 Dec. 1837. He continued to be active behind bars. He managed to acquire a small table for a desk, and Adèle Berthelot, the wife of Louis-Hippolyte La Fontaine*, got pencils and drawing paper for him. There he maintained a notarial "office" and a painter's studio. Friends came to ask him to paint their portraits and he executed these with the skill of a master. He frequently gave advice and wrote letters, including personal letters to the families of those in custody in which he often included a portrait of the prisoner.

Girouard was quickly reassured as to the prisoners' lot. After initially harsh treatment, discipline within the jail became much less severe. He was no longer worried about his fate or that of his friends. He kept up correspondence with La Fontaine, who had reached England and who sent encouraging news to the French Canadian Patriotes. Moreover, Girouard's temperament led him always to attribute kind intentions not only to his friends but even to his enemies. He radiated serenity, a serenity which spread to the other prisoners.

With the arrival of Lord Durham [Lambton*] in May 1838, a general amnesty was expected. Before settling the fate of the prisoners, however, Durham sent Simpson to the jail in Montreal to extract confessions from the chief prisoners. Girouard objected to this procedure and refused to sign any document containing an admission of guilt. In addition he used his influence to dissuade his companions from agreeing to any statement, however honourable in appearance, attesting to their responsibility in the revolutionary movement. Despite Girouard's advice, eight prisoners signed a confession of guilt and were condemned to be deported to

Bermuda. Girouard was released on 16 July, only a few days after Lord Durham's amnesty, on bail of £5,000. He was imprisoned again at Montreal following the second uprising, because of his past record, and released on 27 December. When he recovered his freedom, Girouard had nothing left: his large house had been burned down, as had another dwelling he owned in the village of Saint-Benoît; his notarial minute-book, his books, and his physics and astronomical instruments had been either looted or burned. His wife had not been harmed, thanks to the charity of her brother-in-law Ignace Dumouchel of Rigaud. Girouard was no longer young. At 44 he could count only on relatively good health and his great personal and professional qualities.

Profoundly embittered by the British army's attitude at the time of the sacking of Saint-Benoît, and disappointed with his fellow man and with political action, Girouard went back to his village, where he decided to devote himself to his profession as a notary and to the study of science and philosophy. When a group of political leaders of the Province of Canada, notably Simpson, René-Joseph Kimber*, Frédéric-Auguste Quesnel*, Joseph-Édouard Turcotte*, Louis-Michel VIGER, Étienne Parent*, and Étienne-Paschal Taché*, literally besieged his Saint-Benoît retreat to persuade him to participate in the new ministry proposed by Governor Sir Charles Bagot* in September 1842, they met with a polite but dignified and emphatic refusal. At the risk of offending La Fontaine, the former member for Deux-Montagnes sent the governor a letter of refusal in which he pleaded reasons of health for declining. Girouard was not ill, but he took refuge behind a lofty and contemptuous attitude betraying his scorn for the idea of collaborating with those whom he considered of little faith and integrity. He continued to lead an active professional life centred on his office. Moreover, he was often called to Montreal, Rigaud, and the parishes south of Montreal to deal with estate matters, in which he had become highly skilled. It was he who settled the difficult estates of seigneurs Joseph Masson* of Terrebonne and Charles de Saint-Ours*.

On 2 April 1847 Girouard lost his wife; they had had no children. On 30 April 1851 he took as his second wife Émélie Berthelot, the daughter of his long-standing friend Joseph-Amable Berthelot, a notary of Saint-Eustache. They had two daughters, one of whom died at birth, and two sons. Émélie Girouard had always dreamed of becoming the founder of an almshouse. She realized this dream with the help of her husband, who fully shared her enthusiasm for the project. In one of her three diaries, Mme Girouard devoted many pages to describing the ups and downs that she and her husband experienced in building the Hospice Youville in Saint-Benoît. Girouard allocated all the income from the indemnity he had received in

January 1853 for his losses during the rebellion, £924 (he had claimed £2,424 7s.), to the construction of a convent for the education of girls and the care of the elderly. In addition to endowing this establishment, he and his wife personally shared in the work, carrying out as many tasks as they could. Girouard, the grandson of Jean Baillairgé, designed the hospice and the decoration of the chapel himself. He donated the land for the building, hired the contractors, and with his wife's help supervised the construction work.

Girouard and Émélie truly put their hearts and souls into the building of the Hospice Youville, which they considered the crowning achievement of their lives. When Bishop Joseph La Rocque*, the administrator of the diocese of Montreal in the absence of Bishop Ignace Bourget*, came on 9 Nov. 1854 to preside at the opening of this convent, which was committed to the care of the Sisters of Charity of the Hôpital Général in Montreal, it was indeed a supreme moment for the couple. For Mme Girouard this event seemed a mystic consecration of her union with her husband. The building still stands; instruction is no longer given to young girls, but it does provides a home for the elderly.

Girouard died, most likely of pulmonary tuberculosis, on 18 Sept. 1855 in Saint-Benoît, at the age of 60. He was buried three days later in the chapel of the hospice he had founded. He might be judged to have had a narrow existence because he confined his talents to his family and his parish, when everything destined him for a brilliant political career. In public life he never had any title higher than that of member for his riding in the House of Assembly. Yet this likeable figure deserves a place in the historical record for several reasons, as notary and Patriote, as portrait painter and artist, and as the philanthropist who endowed his parish with a home for the elderly. From all these points of view Girouard is memorable. But he himself would have liked his name to be remembered especially for his charitable works. After his death, to honour his memory, the habitants in the Lac des Deux-Montagnes region called Girouard "the father of the poor."

BÉATRICE CHASSÉ

Jean-Joseph Girouard's minute-book was destroyed by fire during the sack of Saint-Benoît in December 1837, and only part of its index has been preserved. This document, which lists the titles of 4,025 instruments notarized by Girouard from 27 June 1816 to December 1830, is held at the ANQ-M, CN1-179.

Girouard is the author of *Relation historique des événements de l'élection du comté du lac des Deux Montagnes en 1834; épisode propre à faire connaître l'esprit public dans le Bas-Canada* (Montréal, 1835; réimpr., Québec, 1968). He is also the co-author, along with his second wife, of the "Journal de famille de J.-J. Girouard et

d'Émélie Berthelot," composed between 1853 and 1896. This 193-page journal is full of minor incidents in the life of the Girouard family. The first 23 pages are in Girouard's hand. The second part of the journal, pages 23 to 193, is entirely the work of Émélie Berthelot, who after the death of her husband in 1855 continued the account of family events. This document forms part of the Coll. Girouard in ANQ-Q, P-92.

Girouard drew a portrait of the Patriotes who were held in the Montreal jail on charges of high treason at the end of 1837 and the beginning of 1838. In 1846 he also presented a carefully detailed inventory of the losses he had suffered in the looting of Saint-Benoît to the Rebellion Losses Committee, established to compensate the victims of 1837. These documents were published by Paul-André Linteau in "Documents inédits," *RHAF*, 21 (1967–68): 281–311, 474–83.

Girouard also sketched a great many portraits, especially during the period when he was a member of the House of Assembly of Lower Canada, and while he was behind bars in the Montreal jail. A collection of 102 of these pencil sketches is now in the possession of his great-grandson, Pierre Décarie, of Dorval, Que., and consists for the most part of portraits of Patriotes imprisoned in 1837–38 and of several members of the Baillairgé family. Girouard's artistic works also include a view of the ruins of Saint-Benoît, a plan of the Montreal jail, a self-portrait, a magnificent portrait of Louis-Hippolyte La Fontaine, and the plans for the Hospice Youville in Saint-Benoît.

ANQ-M, CE6-9, 24 nov. 1818, 21 sept. 1855; CE6-11, 30 avril 1851; CN6-15, 29 avril 1851. ANQ-Q, CE1-1, 5 févr. 1793, 14 nov. 1794; E17/12–14, nos.646–840; P-52/13. Arch. de l'Institut d'hist. de l'Amérique française (Montréal), Coll. Girouard. Arch. des Sœurs Grises (Montréal), Dossier Saint-Benoît, historique. PAC, MG 11, [CO 42] Q, 239: 373; 259-2: 265–66; MG 24, A27, 34; A40, 27; B2, 32; B4, 8: 525; RG 4, B8, 4: 1386–88; B20, 2. R.-S.-M. Bouchette, *Mémoires de Robert-S.-M. Bouchette, 1805–1840* (Montréal, 1903). Alfred Dumouchel, "Notes d'Alfred Dumouchel sur la rébellion de 1837–38 à Saint-Benoît," *BRH*, 35 (1929): 31–51. Placide Gaudet, "Généalogie des Acadiens, avec documents," PAC *Rapport*, 1905, 2, IIIᵉ part.: 60. Amury Girod, "Journal tenu par feu Amury Girod et traduit de l'allemand et de l'italien," PAC *Rapport*, 1923: 408–19. "Lettre de M. Girouard à M. Morin, sur les troubles de '37 dans le comté des Deux Montagnes," *L'Opinion publique*, 2 août 1877: 361–62. *Rapports des commissaires sur les pertes de la rébellion des années 1837–1838* (s.l., [1852]). *L'Aurore des Canadas* (Montréal), 28 août 1841. *Le Canadien*, 1831–37. *La Gazette de Québec*, 1821–38. *La Minerve*, 1827–37; 29 déc. 1855. F.-J. Audet, "Les législateurs du Bas-Canada." F.-M. Bibaud, *Le panthéon canadien* (A. et V. Bibaud; 1891). Desjardins, *Guide parl.* Fauteux, *Patriotes*, 253–56. *Quebec almanac*, 1822–27. P.-G. Roy, *Fils de Québec*, 3: 71–73. G.-F. Baillairgé, *Notices biographiques et généalogiques, famille Baillairgé . . .* (11 fascicules, Joliette, Qué., 1891–94), 1–2; 6. Auguste Béchard, *Galerie nationale: l'honorable A.-N. Morin* (2ᵉ éd., Québec, 1885). L.-N. Carrier, *Les événements de 1837–38* (2ᵉ éd., Beauceville, Qué., 1914). Béatrice Chassé, "Le notaire Girouard, Patriote et rebelle" (thèse de D ès L, univ. Laval, Québec, 1974). Christie, *Hist. of L.C.* (1866). David, *Patriotes*, 53–64, 79–90. Émile

Glode

Dubois, *Le feu de la Rivière-du-Chêne; étude historique sur le mouvement insurrectionnel de 1837 au nord de Montréal* (Saint-Jérôme, Qué., 1937), 61–62, 66, 118–19. [Albina Fauteux et Clémentine Drouin], *L'Hôpital Général des Sœurs de la charité (Sœurs grises) depuis sa fondation jusqu'à nos jours* (3v. parus, Montréal, 1916–   ), 3: 25–34. Filteau, *Hist. des Patriotes* (1975). Désiré Girouard, *La famille Girouard en France* (Lévis, Qué., 1902). [C.-A.-M. Globensky], *La rébellion de 1837 à Saint-Eustache avec un exposé préliminaire de la situation politique du Bas-Canada depuis la cession* (Québec, 1883; réimpr., Montréal, 1974). A.[-H.] Gosselin, *Un bon Patriote d'autrefois, le docteur Labrie* (2e éd., Québec, 1907). Laurin, *Girouard & les Patriotes*, 5–20. Meilleur, *Mémorial de l'éducation* (1876), 295. Monet, *Last cannon shot*. P.-G. Roy, *La famille Berthelot d'Artigny* (Lévis, 1935). R.-L. Séguin, *Le mouvement insurrectionnel dans la presqu'île de Vaudreuil, 1837–1838* (Montréal, 1955). Taft Manning, *Revolt of French Canada*. André Vachon, *Histoire du notariat canadien, 1621–1960* (Québec, 1962). F.-J. Audet, "Les députés de la vallée de l'Ottawa, John Simpson (1788–1873)," *CHA Report*, 1936: 32–39. L.-O. David, "Les hommes de 37–38: Jean-Joseph Girouard," *L'Opinion publique*, 19 juill. 1877: 337–38. Bernard Dufebvre [Émile Castonguay], "Une drôle d'élection en 1834," *Rev. de l'univ. Laval* (Québec), 7 (1952–53): 598–607. [Désiré Girouard], "La famille Girouard," *BRH*, 5 (1899): 205–6. Léon Ledieu, "Entre nous," *Le Monde illustré* (Montréal), 5 nov. 1887: 210–11. "Quelques Girouard," *BRH*, 47 (1941): 350–51. [Arthur Sauvé], "Évocation d'un passé plein de gloire: les trois Girouard," *Le Journal* (Montréal), 10 févr. 1900: 5.

GLODE (Gloade, Glower, Claude), CHARLES, Micmac chief and farmer; married and had at least one son and two daughters; d. 1852 in Annapolis County, N.S.

On 2 Dec. 1822 Charles Glode and three other Indians, John Glode, Francis Glode, and Malti Paul, petitioned Lieutenant Governor Sir James KEMPT for lands in Annapolis County along the line of a new road being opened between Annapolis Royal and Liverpool. The road was to run through their principal hunting-grounds and would destroy a good part of their livelihood and thus, they claimed, they had to start planting crops immediately. Their application was supported by Abbé Jean-Mandé Sigogne*, who explained to Thomas RITCHIE, the local MHA, that he had often exhorted Indians to take up farming yet few had had the courage to do so and that, if these men were to succeed, others might follow their example. The board of land commissioners for the eastern district of Annapolis County was sceptical of the Indians' ability to farm but, in deference to Kempt's well-known wish to help the Indians, it consented to taking the unusual step of granting land to the petitioners as individuals. Orders were issued in March 1823 for the laying out of 200-acre lots on a ticket of location for each of the four men.

Charles Glode was the only one to make a sustained attempt to farm. In March 1827 he accompanied Thomas Chandler Haliburton*, who had replaced Ritchie as MHA for Annapolis Royal, on a visit to Kempt and was reimbursed for the expenses of the grant and some basic farm supplies. The visit came at an opportune time, for Kempt had just delivered a special message to the legislature calling upon their help to establish each Indian on his own "potatoe plantation."

A year later, on 12 Feb. 1828, Haliburton introduced Glode at the bar of the House of Assembly with a petition to prohibit the sale of rum to the Indians. Handsomely dressed and speaking in halting English, Glode explained "that himself and friends were led to trouble the House from having daily witnessed the disgrace and misery which spirituous liquors spread among the Indians." The result of this appeal was a law passed in 1829 that left to the discretion of local magistrates the banning of liquor sales to Indians. The initiative also won Glode a measure of fame among whites. On 13 Aug. 1830 Joseph Howe* editorialized in the *Novascotian, or Colonial Herald* on the "loathsome" appearance of many Indians, but reminded his readers that for contrast "we should allow the eye to rest on such men as Gload." From distant London, the Quaker philanthropist Samuel Gurney sent for information about him.

Glode added to his landholdings on 1 Nov. 1839 with the purchase of 100 acres from a white settler for £15. On 10 Feb. 1840 he petitioned for a freehold grant to his original holding so that he might pass his land on to his family. This request was first met with the usual argument that a freehold grant would simply be an invitation for some unscrupulous white to cheat a reckless Indian out of his land, but for once the objection was overruled and a freehold grant was issued on 22 February.

The government still hoped that the four original grantees would develop the area into what they optimistically called the "Glode settlement." Lieutenant Governor Lord Falkland [Cary*], reporting to the colonial secretary in 1841, described Glode as a "sober industrious man" with a good farm of 20 or 30 acres under cultivation and several head of livestock. These resources, together with those gained from Glode's excellence as a hunter, provided a comfortable living. But none of the other Indians had developed their holdings.

Glode tried to bring others in, requesting seed potatoes for seven families; four, he said, had already cleared land and the rest planned to do so. Howe, the first provincial Indian commissioner, visited the settlement in October 1842. Glode was away hunting and had left two young daughters in charge; with some effort Howe persuaded them to allow him to stay overnight. He fully approved of the accomplishments of Glode, who had a well-chosen site, a large barn with its lofts full of hay, a clean threshing floor, good stables, potatoes stored in a root-house, tolerable fences, and a plough. Here indeed was "the most successful farmer of any of the Indians of the west." The house itself, however, was not up to standard, and Howe left a message offering help to build a proper one. On his return Glode readily accepted the offer and eventually received £10 from the government. He had a frame-house completed by 1846. In February of that year he bought another piece of land, described as part of a mill lot, after he had successfully petitioned the assembly for the £2 purchase price.

If Glode was an ideal Indian from the white point of view, he was not so well regarded by his own people. He styled himself at various times "Chief" or "Governor" of the Indians of the western part of the province, and in 1835 he claimed to have 415 Indians under his jurisdiction. His brother Jack had been chosen chief in the early 1830s, only to hand the office over to the more ambitious Charles; but the other Micmacs refused to recognize the transfer and continued to regard Jack as their chief. In the opinion of Andrew Henderson*, a local white, Charles was "the more active and intelligent, but Jack the more sagacious and manly." Howe caught the essence of Charles Glode: "shrewd and intelligent, though his own people accuse him of selfishness – not a bad trait in an Indian."

Charles Glode died in 1852. On 8 April an administrator was appointed for his estate, and within a year it was sold for £25 10s. 0d. to pay his debts. Glode had the distinction of being one of the few Indians to be granted freehold land in the province, and to have left an estate to be administered. He was singular proof to officials that an Indian could become a successful farmer and, in gratitude, they freed him from the legal restrictions that prevented Indians from owning, buying, and bequeathing land as individuals. These achievements won him little praise from his own people, however, for he had chosen the path leading to assimilation into white society.

L. F. S. Upton

AAH, Edmund Burke papers, no.39 (T. C. Halliburton to Sigogne, 10 March 1827). Annapolis County Registry of Deeds (Bridgetown, N.S.), Deeds, 33: 400; 38: 278; 44: 186; 45: 95–96 (mfm. at PANS). N.S., Dept. of Lands and Forests (Halifax), Crown land grants, book U: 46 (mfm. at PANS). PANS, MG 1, 979, William Bowman to Peleg Wiswall, 20 Jan. 1829; MG 15, 3, no.89; RG 1, 430, no.188; 432: 21, 115–18, 127–31, 262; RG 20A, Glode, Charles, 1840. PRO, CO 217/178: 91. N.S., Acts, 1829, c.39; House of Assembly, Journal and proc., 1826–27: 74–75; 1828: 208 [subject cited as Charles Glower]. Acadian Recorder, 16 Feb. 1828 [subject cited as Charles Glower]. Novascotian, or Colonial Herald, 13 Aug. 1830. Upton, Micmacs and colonists.

GLODE, GABRIEL (also known as **Cableal Groad** and **Chief Cobbeyall**), Micmac guide and settler; fl. 1842–57 in Nova Scotia.

When Joseph Howe*, Nova Scotia's first Indian commissioner, visited Queens County in October 1842, he hired as his guide Gabriel Glode, a Micmac whom he described as "a sober Indian of good character." From 16 to 21 October they travelled from Ponhook Lake to Kejimkujik Lake and back again. On the journey they visited one settlement, later called Greenfield, where trouble was brewing between the Indians and whites. The Micmacs were convinced that the area had been allocated to them as a reserve and they complained that the whites were destroying the fishery. They were most incensed by the threat to their burial-ground in a two-acre clearing known locally as Indian Gardens.

Howe was so impressed with their arguments that he thought he would try to evict the whites as squatters. When he consulted his surveys, however, he found that the reserve set aside for the Micmacs in that county lay ten miles away, close to the settlement then known as Brookfield. He thereupon told Glode to persuade the Indians to settle there and offered his help if Glode would be the first to move.

Together Howe and Glode returned to Greenfield to break the news of a reserve that neither the whites nor the Micmacs had heard of previously. Howe stood in the middle of a circle of impassive Indians and gave a lengthy speech explaining why they would have to give up the land at Greenfield, and how their burial-ground would be safe from desecration. After he had finished, Glode rose and with great emphasis and deliberation replied, "Howe, I believe you lie."

The negotiations nevertheless continued. Howe and Glode jointly guaranteed that, in exchange for fencing the burial-ground, the white settler on the land would be forever free of any further Indian claims. Howe also purchased one-third of an acre along the river to ensure that the Micmacs had access to the fishery, and ordered it put in trust for Gabriel Glode and his descendants.

The story of Glode's confrontation with Howe was treasured by generations of Greenfield settlers. Howe, so it was said, smoked the Micmac's pipe in friendship and then inadvertently took it away with him. He eventually sent Glode a dollar, but kept the pipe. The official records merely show that Glode received £1 for his services.

About 1846, Glode settled on 40 acres of crown land on Lamoony Island (Big La Mouna Island) in

Gore

Molega Lake. He was convinced, he later said, "that a steady home is the sure way to approach civilization." He petitioned the House of Assembly in 1856 for money to erect a frame-house, and received £5. The following year he requested a freehold grant of the land so that he could hand it on to his heirs, but no grant was issued. That November he was very ill, and was twice visited by a physician at considerable public expense. The treatment included bleeding: it is not known whether he survived it.

L. F. S. UPTON

PANS, MG 15, 5, no.77; 6, nos.19–20, 48; RG 1, 432: 86–94, 96–97. N.S., Legislative Council, *Journal and proc.*, 1843, app.7: 24. Upton, *Micmacs and colonists.*

GORE, FRANCIS, colonial administrator; b. 1769 in Blackheath (London), England, son of Francis Gore and Caroline Beresford; m. 1803 Annabella Wentworth, sister of Sir John Wentworth*; they had no children; d. 3 Nov. 1852 in Brighton, England.

The Gores were a cadet branch of the family of the earls of Arran; the Beresfords, of the marquises of Waterford. Both families had a history of court military appointments: Francis Gore's father, before receiving a West Indian lieutenant governorship in 1763, had served as aide-de-camp to Queen Charlotte's brother in the Portuguese campaign of 1761. Francis entered the army in June 1787 directly from school at Durham as an ensign in the 44th Foot. Promoted lieutenant in September 1793, he transferred to an independent company and then, the following year, to the 54th Foot, with which he saw his only active service, in the Duke of York's abortive Flanders campaign of 1794. The next year, a captain in the cavalry regiment that became the 17th Light Dragoons, he went to Ireland as aide-de-camp to the new lord lieutenant, Earl Camden. Camden left Ireland in 1798, but he was to hold cabinet office for 10 of the next 14 years and to prove an influential patron. Gore returned to regular duty in June 1798 and was promoted major the following year. He retired from the army in July 1802 after the Treaty of Amiens. When the war against France resumed in 1803, he served briefly as an inspector of volunteers with the temporary local rank of lieutenant-colonel, but thereafter held no military commission.

He secured more active employment in 1804, when Camden became secretary of state for war and the colonies in William Pitt's second administration. Gore was appointed lieutenant governor first of Bermuda and then in 1806 of Upper Canada. He went to that province directly from Bermuda and was sworn in at York (Toronto) on 25 August. He would hold his new office for 11 years. Allowed leave to go back to England in 1811, he departed from York on 8 October and did not return until 29 Sept. 1815, after the end of the War of 1812. He left the province for good early in June 1817.

Gore came to Upper Canada with the expectation of being a peacemaker. His predecessor, Peter Hunter*, had left an administration reformed in its procedures but divided by resentment at his reliance on the advice of a few officials and at the directness of his efforts to improve the efficiency of subordinates. Hunter had also paid some of the expenses of civil government out of funds – the revenues from local taxation and from the province's share of the customs duties collected at Quebec – that the legislature had been accustomed to control. He had not consulted the House of Assembly, which raised the question with Alexander Grant*, administrator of the province during the year between Hunter's death and Gore's arrival. On 1 March 1806 the assembly moved a formal address of protest. Warned in advance of this double disharmony and supposing it to involve little beyond personal animosities, Gore proposed to cure it by the application of tact and social prestige.

With three peerages among their family connections, the Gores offered Upper Canada more social prestige than it had yet seen. They were zealous in the performance of their ceremonial duties. Their ball at Niagara (Niagara-on-the-Lake) on 4 June 1807 to celebrate the king's birth was hailed by the *Upper Canada Gazette* for "a splendour and magnificence hitherto unknown in this country" and became the standard by which such affairs were judged for 20 years. Gore was a ready patron of worthy causes, although not always effective in carrying through good intentions: he seems never to have paid the £25 he promised to St James' Church, York, for a new pulpit, and the relief fund that he sponsored in 1815 for war sufferers, still unexpended when he left the province, was ultimately diverted to other purposes. He attached importance to the small change of polite society: being careful to leave calling cards, issuing invitations according to status rather than personal preference, and making sure that no guest was ignored and no invitation unacknowledged. The York élite responded with praise of his manners and amiability. His tact was not infallible. In the interests of harmony he tried to end the ostracism of Elizabeth Small, who was suspected of not actually being the wife of John Small*, clerk of the Executive Council; but his attempt only ruffled feathers that his own wife had to smooth. She was an undoubted social success, able to maintain lasting friendships with such diverse people as the Cartwrights, the Powells, John Strachan*, and Thomas TALBOT. In the narrow circle of official society she was praised more extravagantly than her husband for her poise, kindness, and fashionable sensibility. The death in March 1808 of her favourite dog seems to have occasioned more expressions of

Gore

regret than that six months later of Peter Russell*, a member of the Executive Council. On 25 March 1816 the assembly gave formal recognition of the Gores' popularity. In what Robert Gourlay* was to ridicule as the "Spoon Bill," it voted £3,000 to present them with a service of plate.

Gore's personal initiatives in the administration of government, while less evident and less systematic, were sometimes equally effective. He began with a proclamation on 31 Oct. 1806 reopening the United Empire Loyalist list, a move which had been in contention for years [see Peter Hunter]. Most of the time, however, he responded more readily to the claims of individuals than to general issues. He persuaded William Jarvis*, the provincial secretary, to drop a law suit against Chief Justice Thomas Scott* in return for adjustments to Jarvis's fees and a grant from the imperial government that saved him from bankruptcy. Gore cut across the land-granting regulations, lately amended, to have patents made out to the settlers of Joseph-Geneviève de Puisaye*, Comte de Puisaye. He ignored those regulations altogether in favour of Thomas Talbot, whom he also supported against his Executive Council in a dispute in 1811 with the surveyor Simon Zelotes Watson over land claims along the Talbot Road. The following year, when Gore was absent, the council ordered Talbot to submit a return of his locations on that road. He claimed 5,400 acres, having brought in only 27 settlers. By the time of Gore's return, however, Talbot had brought in more than 100 settlers; and the lieutenant governor was able in February 1816 to have his grants on the Talbot Road east confirmed at 200 rather than the standard 100 acres per settler. Gore further exerted himself to have Talbot appointed to the Legislative Council, without ever being able to obtain his attendance. In June 1817 he at last agreed, reluctantly, that Talbot's land-granting agency should be ended, on terms that would secure his title to 20,000 acres. Gore found a much more active ally in John Strachan, whom he had urged to move from Cornwall to York and for whom he eventually got a regular seat on the Executive Council, effective in July 1817. In such interventions Gore was unquestionably rewarding favourites, but he was also trying to strengthen his government.

Particularly from the beginning of his second tour of duty, Gore was obliged to find new advisers. Of those Hunter had relied on most, only John McGill* remained in office, as acting receiver general. Henry Allcock* had long ago gone to Lower Canada where he had died, and his successor as chief justice, Thomas Scott, retired in 1816. Gore required subordinates who shared his tory opinions, but he insisted on ability and must be allowed to have been a good judge of it. According to David McGregor Rogers*, an oppositionist and member of the

assembly, loyalists had complained that "all appointments of consequence are made and given to persons favourites of those in power in Europe," residents of the province being neglected. Gore's practice was to recommend men established in Upper Canada and experienced in its adminstration. In 1808, against the wishes of the governor-in-chief at Quebec, Sir James Henry Craig*, he had restored to the Indian Department the disgraced superintendent Matthew Elliott*, who was out of favour for misuse of public funds but whose influence among the western Indians was not in question. Gore persisted, despite the reservations of Colonial Secretary Lord Bathurst, in recommending the York lawyer Henry John Boulton* as solicitor general. To replace Scott he secured the promotion in 1816 of Judge William Dummer Powell*, who became speaker of the Legislative Council as well as chief justice. John Beverley Robinson*, already solicitor general, Gore had promoted to attorney general in February 1818. Powell and Strachan became his most frequent and influential advisers, but he never allowed either to occupy the sort of grand vizier's position that Allcock had for a time under Hunter or that Robinson was to have under Gore's successor, Lieutenant Governor Sir Peregrine MAITLAND. The men Gore singled out for his confidence were to form the nucleus of the group, later known as the "family compact," which controlled the government of the province for the next generation.

On most issues of civil administration he himself had few plans and little inclination to assume responsibility. He did show a real interest in education and saw four school bills enacted, in 1807, 1808, 1816, and 1817. These produced a system of district grammar schools and another of common schools assisted by provincial grants. The first, however, owed more to Strachan's enterprise and ideas than to Gore's, and the second was the result of initiatives from the assembly introduced by John WILLSON. He was also concerned to foster the Church of England in Upper Canada, particularly to improve the lot of its clergy. His circular of 11 Oct. 1809 asked for details of their tenure, duties, and stipends. Although Strachan later praised his "invaluable" energy as "a great Friend to the Church," Gore did not make much use of this information. His hope was that leases of the clergy reserves would soon bring in revenue. He and Receiver General Prideaux Selby* persuaded the Executive Council to increase the rents by a third in April 1811. There were few leases, however, and the rents continued to be in arrears. Gore wrote personally to the sheriff of the Western District, William Hands, who had set a record by making no returns of rent at all for eight years. He was nevertheless reluctant to give sheriffs authority to compel the payment of rents, just as he refused to decentralize the granting of leases.

Gore

Nor would he approve of harsh measures to stop the illegal cutting of timber on reserved lands. By the end of his term, Anglican clergy were nominally receiving £527 a year from 96 leases, but most of the rents were unpaid. Just before leaving, Gore was considering, as a way to finance the church, the adoption of a clergy corporation for managing the reserves, similar to that operating in Lower Canada [see Jacob Mountain*].

Upper Canada was a rapidly growing province: during Gore's administration its white population almost doubled, from 46,000 in 1806 to 83,000 in 1817. Yet he showed only a narrow concern for its economic development. He was content to make no revisions to Hunter's land-granting system, which he accepted in spite of continuing complaints. The Heir and Devisee Commission, formed by an act of the assembly to untangle claims resulting from transfers of land before deeds had been issued, was a measure begun before his arrival. So was the province's road building program, much of the initiative for which passed during his term of office into the hands of the assembly. Bills of 1808, 1809, and 1816 authorized a total expenditure of £34,200 for public roads. Gore did take an active interest in the northward extension of Yonge Street, especially in the prospect of its use by the North West Company as an alternative to the established route of the fur traders, via Niagara and Detroit. He agreed in 1811 to the company's petition for 4,200 acres on Lake Simcoe and Georgian Bay. The lands in question were part of a crown purchase from the Ojibwa Indians which he had just arranged but which was not confirmed until November 1815. At the request of York merchants he lobbied for the route while in England, but he laid as much stress on its military as on its commercial advantages. In reserving the bank bill of 1817, as his instructions required, he did point out the province's dependence on American paper money and the claim by York merchants, particularly William ALLAN, that a central bank with the power to issue local currency was therefore necessary. He did not, however, commit himself to the arguments that he reported, and the incorporation of the Bank of Upper Canada had to wait until 1821. When no proposals for economic development were made to him, he seldom had any of his own. The vexed question of sharing the customs duties with Lower Canada was twice debated in the assembly, in 1811 and in 1817; he forwarded reports of both debates, offering no solutions but asking for instructions. When in 1815 there was some question of moving the government offices to Kingston, as a safer place than York, he based his reservations entirely on the inconvenience and loss that officials would suffer. Directed to report on the state of the province, he did so promptly on 17 Oct. 1815, but his survey made no more than general reference to economic problems or growth. Perhaps the only independent suggestion he

ever made on economic policy was for a tax on vacant lands, and there his concern was as much about government revenue as about absentee ownership.

When satisfied that his responsibility was clear and on subjects with which he felt comfortable, Gore was by no means an inactive governor. During his first period in Upper Canada he paid much attention to its defence. In the fall of 1808 and again a year later he protested forcibly to Washington, through the British ambassador, over American attempts to enforce a claim to Carleton Island (N.Y.), in the St Lawrence River. At the same time, during the period of tension which followed the Chesapeake affair of June 1807 [see Sir George Cranfield Berkeley*], he inquired into the supply of rations to Indians and their readiness to help defend the province. On 11 July 1808 he addressed a council of 1,000 warriors at Amherstburg. He met Tecumseh* there, finding him "a very shrewd intelligent man" and receiving the chief's message that western Indian support against the United States could be expected "if we show ourselves in any force to join them," but not otherwise. In 1809 he protested to Washington again, over an incident in which American troops sought out and killed on Canadian soil Isaac D. Underhill, a deserter from the United States Army living at Elizabethtown (Brockville).

Although the militia of Upper Canada received 4,000 stands of arms in December 1807, Gore was disturbed by its lack of training and organization. He shepherded three bills through the assembly. The first, in 1808, gave authority for militia units to serve outside the province in time of war or insurrection. In 1809 a second made arrangements for their provisioning. Two years later the third consolidated earlier militia acts and revised the regulations for service and training. Gore's expectations of the militia were not high. He did not think the province defensible against anything more than a "partial or sudden incursion," although he felt it his duty, he had told Craig in January 1808, to conceal that opinion "from Persons of almost every description in this colony, for there are few People here that would act with Energy were it not for the purpose of defending the lands which they actually possess." When he came back to Upper Canada after the War of 1812, he acknowledged the service of the militia. Persuaded that a 50-acre grant to militia privates was too small, he had it doubled.

The responsibility that Gore saw most clearly was to defend the political tranquillity and British allegiance of the province. Soon after being sworn into office, he had become convinced that both were threatened by the malcontent judge Robert Thorpe*. Setting himself up as a spokesman for popular grievances, Thorpe succeeded, in spite of Gore's objections, in being elected to the assembly in December 1806. He found enough support there to disrupt the government's order of business, but his most active allies were two other officials: his fellow Irishman Joseph Willcocks*, sheriff of the Home District, and the surveyor general, Charles Burton Wyatt*. On 31 Oct. 1806 an interview with Thorpe, planned by Gore to be conciliatory, had led him to believe that Thorpe was seditious as well as mischievous. "What grievances he alludes to, I do not know," Gore reported to Colonial Secretary William Windham, "the most respectable persons, with whom I have conversed, do not complain of any." Thorpe was alleged to have campaigned under the banner of the rebellious Society of United Irishmen, and his references to the American revolution were in themselves "almost Treasonable." Gore was not alone in thinking that Thorpe's aim was, as a newspaper correspondent put it, "to fill one class of subjects with enmities against another . . . and to destroy the original confidence so necessary to the existence of civil society." He neither understood nor believed Thorpe's claim to be a loyal reformer, and his equation of opposition with demagoguery and republicanism aroused some resentment. "We know no discontented Demagogues nor if we did could not be deluded by them," a meeting chaired in York by William Willcocks* resolved; "many of us have fought, bled & sacrificed our families & properties for the British Government." Gore's toryism was conventional and unimaginative: he recognized no clear line between the opposition of the discontented and that of the disaffected. He simply did not think it possible that there could be legitimate opposition to a legally established colonial government, or that a government could tolerate organized dissent without inviting revolution.

Thorpe's tactics in opposition were obstructive and abusive, increasingly directed towards discrediting the lieutenant governor with the imperial government. Gore, for his part, felt justified in intercepting his opponents' mail, even bribing postmasters in the United States. With "Anarchy and Republicanism in league" against him, he denied them access to the pages of the province's only newspaper, the *Upper Canada Gazette*. He collected reports (including one from the wife of Charles Burton Wyatt, who was believed to have locked her in a cellar for punishment) that their private conversations were seditious. The most direct challenge to his authority came from Wyatt, who submitted his accounts as surveyor general to an investigative committee of the assembly without getting executive permission and who had been forwarding official papers to England secretly and for the "purposes of misrepresenting the acts of the late Government." As well, he had altered a land location book in his own favour. Gore suspended him and dismissed Joseph Willcocks; finally, in July 1807, he suspended Thorpe, just before receiving official instructions to do so.

The quarrel did not end there. Thorpe appealed his suspension, without success. His supporter John Mills Jackson* had more influential connections in British politics than Thorpe had, and so did Wyatt. In 1809 Jackson condemned Gore in a pamphlet released in England, to which the lieutenant governor had to make a long and careful reply, but still his conduct was questioned in the House of Commons that year. In August 1810 Gore asked for leave to defend himself. The threat of an inquiry had in fact already receded, and his prolonged stay in England was probably due more to the American war than to his continuing dispute with subordinates. Upper Canada, facing invasion, needed a soldier; and Gore had never commanded anything larger than a company in action. In England he found that Upper Canada's attorney general, William Firth*, angry at his lack of promotion and at his share of legal fees, had joined the attack on him. Firth, too, was able in 1815 to have an inquiry demanded in the Commons, where Gore was accused of "simple despotism." He never did have to face a parliamentary inquiry, but his opponents were not utterly defeated. His counter-attacks had gone too far: in 1816 Wyatt, and two years later Thorpe, were awarded damages in the libel suits that they had brought against him.

The bitterness of this long dispute did not poison Gore's relations with the assembly, which remained cordial until the very end of his governorship. He did want to strengthen the Legislative Council, as "a counter poise to the Rashness of the House of Assembly," but his first acquaintance with assembly-men, at the session which opened in February 1807, was a pleasant surprise. More than half the members were loyalists, and he identified only two American immigrants. There was a loose coterie of six generally anti-executive members, but they did not follow Thorpe's lead. In fact the assembly withdrew the formal protest it had made in 1806 to Alexander Grant, concerning Peter Hunter's appropriations from the provincial treasury, and in 1808 it jailed Joseph Willcocks for accusing its members of having lost their independence by accepting land grants. The new assembly elected that summer was even more satisfactory: of the old opposition members only David McGregor Rogers and Joseph Willcocks were returned, and Gore at last saw Hunter's and Grant's expenditures ratified. After returning from leave he met a third assembly, in 1816. It showed a mind of its own over common schools, but was otherwise cooperative as well as industrious. In addition to the "Spoon Bill," it passed 40 acts, among them one creating the post of provincial agent for Gore's secretary, William Halton.

This harmony was disrupted soon after the general election of 1816, which saw several of the old oppositionists, including James Durand* and Peter

Gore

Howard*, returned with a new sense of grievance. Gore had instructions from the colonial secretary, Lord Bathurst, to check American immigration. Since the time of John Graves Simcoe*, Americans had been granted land on taking the oath of allegiance, the legal requirement of seven years' residence being enforced only for the right to vote. Concerned though he was about the near prospect of an American majority in the province, Bathurst probably intended merely that the seven-year rule should apply to land grants. Gore's action, which he did not think beyond his instructions, was more drastic. His circular of 14 Oct. 1815 forbad commissioners to administer the oath of allegiance to anyone, office holders and loyalists' children excepted, without express permission from his office. This effectively limited the acquisition of land to British subjects. The circular also ordered sheriffs to compile lists of resident aliens. Since they could be deported simply by the order of any magistrate, Gore was posing a threat to the security of most new settlers. His action was unacceptable to anyone hoping either to buy or to sell land, especially to the land speculators of the growing Niagara District. The circular also compounded the difficulty of meeting claims for war-time damage to private property, because such claims were to be met by selling the confiscated estates of traitors. William Dickson*, a legislative councillor, Niagara magistrate, and major landowner, openly disobeyed the circular. When the new assembly met, early in 1817, its attack on Gore's policy was led by Robert Nichol*, another Niagara landowner, one of the biggest war claimants, and until then a cordial supporter of the lieutenant governor.

The assembly went into committee of the whole on the state of the province and found fault with a wide range of government action or inaction: the inadequacy of the post office and of roads, the retention of crown reserves, the limitation of revenues from the clergy reserves to the support of Anglican clergy, the scale of land fees, the neglect of war claimants, and the lack of progress in allotting land to the militia. Above all, the assembly questioned the wisdom of restricting immigration from any source and the legality of Gore's circular. On 5 April 1817, by a vote of 13 to 7, it resolved that he had contravened British statutes passed to encourage settlement in British North America; it drew back from the claim that those statutes were still in force by a single vote. All this was much more polite than Thorpe and Wyatt had been, but harder to deal with. Nichol had other resolutions drafted and could not be persuaded by John Strachan to withdraw them. On 7 April Gore prorogued the assembly, the only way he could think of to avoid an open challenge to what he regarded as imperial policy.

He had had enough of being a colonial governor. The province to which he had meant to bring harmony had rejected him. He had not only survived but had ended the squabbles in officialdom with which his term began; and, if his talents for civil government were not conspicuous, he had always applied them conscientiously. Neither his charm nor his patronage, however, could enable him to manage an assembly dissatisfied with his administration. His rigid toryism, while it prevented him from compromising with or even respecting political opposition, was not foreign to Upper Canada. Yet the limited range of his interest and his lack of active concern for economic growth kept him out of touch with all but a narrow circle of the people he had been sent to govern.

Despite his popularity, he left curiously little personal impression behind him. He was both extravagantly praised and extravagantly damned for reasons which, having nothing to do with his character, reveal nothing about it. It is no longer possible to say whether his character was really enigmatic or whether it has merely been obscured by the polemics he encountered.

Within Upper Canada the memory of his early successes was soon obscured by that of his final clash with the assembly. Later reformers were to look back on the session of 1817 as a flagrant and calculated attack on the rights of the assembly by an arbitrary governor defending his own maladministration. This partisan writing of history began with Robert Gourlay's *Statistical account* in 1822, followed by the critiques of William Lyon Mackenzie* and John Rolph*. In the reform tradition of Upper Canada, Gore became a tory ogre. Since he had himself demonstrated that it was safer to complain of a former governor than to attack a present one, he may be said to have invited the caricature. It was only in 1885 with *The story of the Upper Canadian rebellion . . .* by John Charles Dent* that the full weight of reform disapproval shifted to his equally tory successors.

Gore left the province in June 1817 by the quickest route, through New York City, disillusioned and worried by his wife's failing health. But there was no bitterness in the correspondence that he maintained with Canadian friends. He exchanged his lieutenant governorship in 1818 for the more comfortable post of deputy teller to the Exchequer and held that until he was awarded a pension on its abolition in 1836. His wife died in August 1838. A member of the Athenaeum Club and active on its managing committee until disabled by paralysis and dropsy, he spent the rest of his life in the fashionable and aristocratic society that he had exemplified for Upper Canadians.

S. R. MEALING

[Gore left no private papers, so that his official correspondence, most of it in PRO, CO 42/341–61, is the main source of information about his life and career. There are scraps at the AO in the Strachan papers (MS 35) and the Macaulay papers (MS 78), and at the MTL in the papers of William Dummer Powell and Peter Russell. His letters during the Thorpe affair have been printed, with an introduction by Douglas Brymner* (pp.vii–x), under the title "Political state of Upper Canada in 1806–7," PAC *Report*, 1892: 32–135. Four contemporary pamphlets survive: [John Mills Jackson], *A view of the political situation of the province of Upper Canada, in North America . . .* (London, 1809); Robert Thorpe, *Appendix to the case of Robert Thorpe, esq., L.L.D., elicited by a letter from Viscount Goderich to Joseph Hume, esq., M.P.* (London, 1828); an anonymous pamphlet, *A letter on Canada in 1806 and [1807], during the administration of Governor Gore* ([London], 1853), attributed to an E. Magrath and to James Macaulay* but more likely by John Beverley Robinson; and [Richard Cartwright], *Letters, from an American loyalist in Upper Canada, to his friend in England; on a pamphlet published by John Mills Jackson, esquire: entitled, "A view of the province of Upper Canada"* (Halifax, [1810]). The longest and most partisan attack on Gore's administration is in *Statistical account of U.C.* (Gourlay), 2: 234–538; an abridged one-volume edition was prepared by S. R. Mealing for the Carleton Library series (Toronto, 1974). An obituary notice entitled "Lieutenant Governor Gore and Upper Canada" appeared in *Fraser's Magazine for Town and Country* (London), 47 (January–June 1853): 627–39; it is the source of the personal details in the biography of Gore by David Breakenridge Read* in *The lieutenant-governors of Upper Canada and Ontario, 1792–1899* (Toronto, 1900), and of those given by William Kingsford* in *The history of Canada* (10v., Toronto and London, 1887–98), 8: 87–114; 9: 193–207. s.r.m.]

AO, MS 522, memorandum respecting the District School Bill, 5 March 1808. PAC, RG 1, L7, 24; RG 10, A1, 2; A2, 11. *Docs. relating to constitutional hist., 1791–1818* (Doughty and McArthur). *Gentleman's Magazine*, July–December 1838: 338; July–December 1852: 661. G.B., Parl., *Parliamentary debates* (London), [ser.1], 31 (1815): 905–12. "Journals of Legislative Assembly of U.C.," AO *Report*, 1911, 1912. John Strachan, *The John Strachan letter book, 1812–1834*, ed. G. W. Spragge (Toronto, 1946). *Ten years of Upper Canada in peace and war, 1805–1815; being the Ridout letters*, ed. Matilda [Ridout] Edgar (Toronto, 1890). *Town of York, 1793–1815* (Firth). *Morning Herald* (London), 21 June 1809. *York Gazette*, 13 June, 31 Oct. 1807.

G.B., WO, *Army list*, 1791–1801. John Wentworth, *The Wentworth genealogy, comprising the origin of the name, the family in England, and a particular account of Elder William Wentworth, the emigrant, and of his descendants* (2v., [Boston], 1870), 2: 325. Cowdell, *Land policies of U.C.* Craig, *Upper Canada*. F. C. Hamil, *Lake Erie baron: the story of Colonel Thomas Talbot* (Toronto, 1955). David Mills, "The concept of loyalty in Upper Canada, 1815–1850" (PHD thesis, Carleton Univ., Ottawa, 1982). S. G. Roberts, "Imperial policy, provincial administration and defence in Upper Canada, 1796–1812" (D PHIL thesis, Oxford Univ., 1975). J. B. Walton, "An end to all order: a study of Upper Canadian Conservative response to opposition, 1805–1810" (MA thesis, Queen's Univ., Kingston, Ont., 1977). H. C. Wilkinson, *Bermuda from sail to steam: the history of the island from 1784 to 1901* (2v., London,

1973), 1: 226–27. [G.] A. Wilson, *The clergy reserves of Upper Canada, a Canadian mortmain* (Toronto, 1968). R. J. Burns, "God's chosen people: the origins of Toronto society, 1793–1818," CHA *Hist. papers*, 1973: 213–28. W. L. Morton, "The local executive in the British Empire, 1763–1828," *English Hist. Rev.* (London), 78 (1963): 436–57. P. J. Robinson, "Yonge Street and the North West Company," *CHR*, 24 (1943): 253–65.

GRANT, CUTHBERT, fur trader, Métis leader, farmer, office holder, justice of the peace, and politician; b. *c.* 1793 in Fort de la Rivière Tremblante (near Kamsack, Sask.), son of Cuthbert Grant*, fur trader, and a Métis woman, probably of Cree and French descent; m. according to the custom of the country first Elizabeth MacKay, secondly Madelaine Desmarais, and perhaps thirdly an unnamed woman; m. 1823 Marie McGillis in St Boniface (Man.); he had by these marriages at least three sons and six daughters; d. 15 July 1854 in White Horse Plain (St François Xavier, Man.).

Cuthbert Grant, effectively bilingual, was the first educated Métis to wield a profound influence over the fate of his people. He was largely responsible for implanting in their minds the concept of a Métis nation that played such a vital role in the Red River uprising of 1869–70 and the Northwest rebellion of 1885. Yet Grant was no rebel. Throughout his career he was a staunch supporter of the authority he knew, first that of the North West Company and, after 1821, that of the Hudson's Bay Company, and he made his violent mark in history not as an insurrectionist but as a partisan in a private war between two trading companies struggling within the great political vacuum of the early northwest.

Grant was virtually born into the NWC; his father was a long-time employee and a wintering partner from 1795, and his uncle Robert Grant, in association with William Holmes*, was among the original group of Montreal fur traders who formed the NWC in 1779. He spent his early childhood in various NWC fur-trading posts along the Assiniboine River. The elder Cuthbert Grant died in 1799, having provided in his will for the education of his two sons, Cuthbert and James, and having named William McGillivray*, the NWC's Montreal agent, as their guardian. In 1801 McGillivray took young Cuthbert to Montreal, where he was baptized on 12 October in the Scotch Presbyterian Church, later known as St Gabriel Street Church. Despite conjecture that he followed his brother to Scotland for his schooling, he would appear to have been educated in Montreal under McGillivray's supervision.

Grant entered the company's service, probably about 1810 to work in the Montreal offices, and in 1812 he travelled to Fort William (Thunder Bay, Ont.) with the annual brigade. At the meeting of Montreal and wintering partners that summer, he was assigned as clerk to the Upper Red River department. He was posted to Fort Espérance (Sask.) on the Qu'Appelle River under John PRITCHARD, where he was put in charge of a small outpost.

By this time the fur-bearing animals in the Qu'Appelle region had been almost exterminated by hunting and Fort Espérance had become to all intents and purposes a victualling post whose primary functions were the organization of the buffalo hunt and the supply of pemmican to sustain the trade in the Athabasca country. By 1812 also the struggle between the NWC and the HBC for control of the fur trade was building towards violence. That summer the tension was heightened by the arrival of the first contingent of Scottish settlers whom Lord Selkirk [Douglas*], a director of the HBC, was proposing to establish in the Red River valley – right across the routes by which the Nor'Westers transported both furs and pemmican. The HBC claimed prior rights over the territory by virtue of its charter to Rupert's Land granted in 1670; the NWC claimed rights of access as successor to the French fur traders and explorers, and particularly to Pierre Gaultier* de Varennes et de La Vérendrye, who had established Fort Maurepas on the Red River in 1734.

The arrival of the settlers, led by Miles Macdonell*, the recently appointed HBC governor of Assiniboia, created a strain on the food resources of the region. They arrived too late in the season to put in crops and during the winter of 1812–13 were forced to rely on buffalo meat, provided by friendly Saulteaux Indians, and on pemmican. The following year the colony was still far from self-sufficient and on 8 Jan. 1814 Macdonell issued a proclamation forbidding the export of pemmican from the Red River area without his permission, an act which endangered the source of supplies for the NWC's trade in the fur-rich Athabasca country.

Grant was still serving in the Upper Red River department when the NWC partners Alexander Greenfield Macdonell*, a second cousin of the governor, and Duncan Cameron* were placed in charge of it in July 1814. Both were convinced that the survival of the NWC trade could only be secured through aggressive opposition to the proclamation. Furthermore Macdonell and Cameron, as well as the NWC Montreal agents Simon* and William McGillivray, realized that to succeed in any struggle against the Selkirk colony, backed by the HBC, they would have to gain the allegiance of the only available force in the region outside the Saulteaux, who had already shown themselves favourable to the settlers. This force was the Métis, with their traditions of frontier warfare combining Indian tactics with European weapons and skills. Though many of the Métis were employed by the NWC, some had attached themselves to the HBC, and the community as a whole, which as yet lacked a sense of identity and recognized leaders, had taken no decisive position in the dispute between the companies.

To gain the support of the Métis, the Nor'Westers proceeded to cultivate, and in fact were the first to voice, the idea of a Métis nation with aboriginal rights to the land and special interests as hunters, at variance with the claims of the HBC colony. In doing so they were exploiting ill-defined sentiments of Métis identity and giving them shape and direction. Alexander Greenfield Macdonell and Cameron looked among their mixed-blood clerks for the leaders they could use to channel the energy and provoke the anger of the Métis on behalf of the NWC. To this end, Grant, William Fraser, Angus Shaw, and Nicolas Montour were appointed "captains of the Métis" by Cameron in the fall of 1814. It was soon evident that Grant possessed the qualities of daring and resourcefulness that made him the best choice among the candidates, and by March 1816 he was singled out, again by Cameron, as "Captain-General of all the Half-Breeds." There is little doubt that Grant allowed himself to be used by the Nor'Westers, and that he did so partly because of the vanity that was one of his abiding weaknesses and partly because of his desire for advancement in the company's hierarchy of officers. There is nothing to suggest that before 1814 he saw the Métis as a nation, or gave any thought to their cause, or even identified himself with them.

Grant's persuasion and the promise of reward appear to have won over a considerable number of Métis to the NWC cause and, between 1814 and 1816, in his new role as military leader of an irregular Métis cavalry, Grant had many opportunities to show his zeal. He arrived with Cameron at Fort Gibraltar (Winnipeg) on 30 Aug. 1814 as one of Cameron's uniformed officers and was active in persuading many of the Selkirk settlers to accept the NWC's offer of transportation out of the colony to the Canadas. In March 1815, after HBC men had arrested Peter Pangman (known as Bostonais by the Métis) on a charge of assault, Grant at the head of 27 Métis seized four colonists as hostages. On this occasion, there was an exchange of prisoners, but as the year went on the pressure applied by the Nor'Westers to the colonists increased and Grant was in the thick of the action. On 7 June he established a Métis camp on the west bank of the Red River, four miles downstream from Point Douglas, the colony's headquarters, to cover the departure in NWC canoes for Canada of 42 colonists. Grant's men began to harry the settlement, stealing horses and ploughs, and there were exchanges of fire between the Métis and the remaining settlers. In such an encounter at Fort Douglas (Winnipeg) on 10 June, one of Governor Macdonell's men was killed. On 17 June the governor gave himself up to the Nor'Westers who sent him down to the Canadas under arrest. But the attacks on the colony did not end, settlers continued to flee, and on 25 June Peter Fidler*, left in charge of the colony after Macdonell's departure, capitulated under an agreement on which Grant's signature appears as one of the "chiefs of the Half-breeds." Fidler consented to the complete evacuation of the colony. Nobody signed the agreement on behalf of the NWC. The Métis – and Grant – were being made to appear responsible for actions intended to further the company's interests.

Grant returned to the Qu'Appelle River after Fidler's surrender, but that incident did not mean the end either of the Selkirk colony or of the HBC's presence on the Red River. In August 1815 Colin Robertson*, a former Nor'Wester who had joined the HBC, arrived with a group of about 50 of the departing settlers who had asked him to lead them back, and in November Robert Semple* arrived as governor-in-chief of the HBC territories to take over the administration of the settlement.

Grant reacted with calculated hostility to Semple's approaches. On 8 May 1816, two months after he had been named captain-general by the NWC, he set out with a troop of 60 Métis horsemen on an expedition clearly intended to prevent a resurgence of the rival power on the Red River. First they ambushed the HBC boats, under Pierre-Chrysologue Pambrun* and James Sutherland, bringing pemmican down the Qu'Appelle. Joined by Alexander Greenfield Macdonell and the NWC boats, Grant then escorted the pemmican down the Assiniboine, and at the Souris River he and his men captured and ransacked the HBC's Brandon House, commanded by Fidler. He then proceeded to Portage la Prairie from which point he left on 18 June with a supply of pemmican for the NWC brigades waiting on Lake Winnipeg.

On 19 June Grant reached a point about three miles from the fork of the Assiniboine and Red rivers and turned inland, hoping to circle unseen the now stockaded Fort Douglas, but his party was discovered. Governor Semple, at the head of a small group of armed men, went out to meet them at Seven Oaks (Winnipeg). It is not clear how the fighting began; the first shot may indeed have been fired by Semple's men. But certain facts are evident. The encounter would never have taken place if Grant and his men had not set out with the hostile intent demonstrated in their ambushing of the HBC pemmican boats and their capture of Brandon House. As soon as firing began Grant shot at Semple and broke his thigh, rendering him a helpless victim for the Métis or Indian who killed him. The skirmish degenerated into a gruesome massacre in which about 20 of Semple's party and one of Grant's were killed in the space of 15 minutes. The wounded were ruthlessly slaughtered and most of the dead were mutilated. Grant either could not or would

not prevent the massacre; he certainly used it to frighten the remaining colonists into departing, so that once again the NWC was ascendant on the Red River.

In August 1816 Grant was at the NWC post Bas-de-la-Rivière (Fort Alexander) on Lake Winnipeg and, because of his association with Archibald McLellan, he was later reported to have been implicated in the murder of HBC officer Owen Keveny* on the Winnipeg River the following month. When he learned of the capture by Selkirk of the NWC depot at Fort William, Grant retreated to Red River and then in October returned to Fort Qu'Appelle. After the re-establishment of the colony and the arrival of William Bacheler Coltman* as commissioner from Lower Canada to inquire into the conflict in the northwest, Grant, in August 1817, gave himself up. Coltman recorded his deposition on the events of 1815 and 1816, and then took him to Montreal to face charges of murder, theft, and arson. Grant arrived there about the end of October and was held in the common jail while awaiting his hearing on the first of the charges, that of the murder of Keveny. In this case his guilt was indeed doubtful and he was released, but in the spring of 1818 true bills were found against him and other NWC men at York (Toronto) for theft and pillage of HBC property and for the murder of Semple and the colonists killed at Seven Oaks. Grant jumped his bail and fled in a light canoe to the northwest. The law officers in the Canadas, where the Montreal-based NWC was favoured over the London-based HBC, were unenthusiastic about pursuing the matter. After Grant's lieutenant at Seven Oaks, François-Firmin Boucher, was acquitted of the murder of Semple, the charges against Grant were quietly shelved.

Grant was present at the last major encounter between the two companies, when in June 1820 the HBC brigade from the Athabasca country, headed by Robertson, was ambushed by NWC men at the Grand Rapids (Man.). A year later the conflict came to an end with the union of the two companies under the HBC charter. Old scores surfaced and Grant was allowed to cool his heels, excluded from employment in the new company. George SIMPSON, the new governor of the HBC's Northern Department which included Red River, met him in February 1822 and decided that Grant had been made "a party tool" in the late conflict. Simpson was astute enough to recognize malleability when he saw it, and to realize that Grant's recent exclusion from the service could only have increased his prestige with the Métis who had themselves suffered from the union of the companies. The Métis were an increasingly unstable element in the Red River region. A man who could control them on the HBC's behalf would be very useful. In July 1823 Grant was appointed clerk at Fort Garry (Winnipeg) and made a special constable. His presence in the settlement, however, was a provocation to those who

Gray

remembered his role in the events of 1815–16. After being assaulted by a group of settlers led by Alexander McDonell*, Grant retired from the company in 1824.

He was encouraged to settle near the colony and was granted land at White Horse Plain on the Assiniboine River. There, with about a hundred Métis families, he founded the village of Grantown (St François Xavier) in the spring of 1824. By 1827 he had 34 acres under cultivation and looked upon himself as seigneur of White Horse Plain, though he had no legal claim to such a title. He transported goods for the HBC on contract from York Factory to the Red River, and from the winter of 1824–25 was allowed to trade as an independent under licence from the company. This trading, like that conducted by Andrew McDermot*, was designed to keep American fur traders out of the territory covered by the HBC charter by providing a company-controlled market for furs not directly taken by the HBC.

In July 1828 the HBC Council of the Northern Department appointed Grant warden of the plains of Red River, at an annual salary of £200, to prevent "the illicit trade in Furs within that District." He had transferred his loyalties to the new masters, and his value was recognized. He was still sufficiently respected by the Métis to be elected captain of the annual buffalo hunts. In 1835 the Council of Assiniboia, which had taken over the administration of the colony after the settlement reverted to the HBC from the Selkirk estate in 1834, commissioned Grant as a justice of the peace. He was invited to attend council meetings and in March 1839 was officially appointed councillor, as well as sheriff of Assiniboia with Alexander Ross. From 1840 the Métis and the Sioux were fighting a kind of guerrilla war over infringement of tribal buffalo-hunting territories, and Grant, as "Chief of the half-breeds and warden of the Plains," negotiated a peace settlement in 1844. This peace did not last, since by 1851 the two peoples were again in violent conflict.

By the 1840s Grant's influence among the Métis had waned. A new generation of young and rebellious men had appeared and a French element led by men such as the elder Louis Riel* began to take leadership away from the Scots half-breeds such as Grant. The crucial issue was freedom of trade; in defiance of the HBC monopoly, the Métis were beginning to trade furs with Americans at Pembina (N.Dak.) and St Paul (Minn.), following the example of McDermot, whose HBC licence was not renewed in 1843, and James SINCLAIR. Here Grant, as warden of the plains, magistrate, and sheriff, was on the side of the company. When Pierre-Guillaume Sayer* was tried for illicit trading in 1849, Grant was on the bench as one of the magistrates. With a large body of armed Métis vociferously supporting Sayer in the court-room and proclaiming Sinclair as their leader, Sayer was found guilty of trading furs but went unpunished. The verdict was heralded in the colony as the end of the HBC monopoly.

Grant's usefulness to the company had ended, and he was relieved of the office of warden of the plains. A division now appeared between the militant Métis of the Red River settlements and the people of White Horse Plain, who remained under Grant's conservative influence. His followers, such as his son-in-law Pascal Breland*, became leaders of the moderate Métis who held aloof from Louis Riel* in 1870 and were opposed to Gabriel Dumont*'s activism.

Grant's final years were relatively inactive. His decline as a leader of the Métis had undermined his usefulness to the HBC and his role was reduced to that of host to the rich travellers who began to visit the Prairies. In the late spring of 1854 he fell from his horse. He did not recover from his injuries and died on 15 July. On 16 July he was buried, inside the church of St François Xavier which he had built at Grantown after his conversion to Roman Catholicism.

GEORGE WOODCOCK

PAC, MG 25, 62. *Canadian north-west* (Oliver), vol.1. *Docs. relating to NWC* (Wallace). *HBRS*, 2 (Rich and Fleming); 3 (Fleming). Alexander Ross, *The Red River settlement: its rise, progress and present state; with some account of the native races and its general history to the present day* (London, 1856; repr., Minneapolis, Minn., 1957; repr., Edmonton, 1972). *Quebec Gazette*, 19 March 1818. Marcel Giraud, *Le Métis canadien; son rôle dans l'histoire des provinces de l'Ouest* (Paris, 1945). J. M. Gray, *Lord Selkirk of Red River* (Toronto, 1963). M. A. MacLeod and W. L. Morton, *Cuthbert Grant of Grantown; warden of the plains of Red River* (Toronto, 1974). C. [B.] Martin, *Lord Selkirk's work in Canada* (Oxford, 1916). J. P. Pritchett, *The Red River valley, 1811–1849: a regional study* (New Haven, Conn., 1942). Margaret Complin, "The warden of the plains," *Canadian Geographical Journal* (Montreal), 9 (Aug. 1934): 73–82. M. A. MacLeod, "Cuthbert Grant of Grantown," *CHR*, 21 (1940): 25–39.

GRAY, BENJAMIN GERRISH, Church of England clergyman; b. 22 Nov. 1768 in Boston, eighth child of Joseph Gray and Mary Gerrish, daughter of Joseph Gerrish*; m. Mary Thomas, and they had one son; d. 18 Feb. 1854 in Saint John, N.B.

Benjamin Gerrish Gray inherited considerable property in Nova Scotia upon the death in 1772 of his great-uncle Benjamin Gerrish*. When Gray was eight, his family moved to Halifax where it had close ties to the inner circle of pre-revolutionary families. After being educated in England and in Nova Scotia at King's College, Windsor, he returned to Halifax and eventually married. At his ordination as deacon in the Church of England on 25 Sept. 1796, Lieutenant Governor Sir John Wentworth*, one of his wife's connections, acted as his sponsor. Wentworth subsequently appointed him king's chaplain to the 400–500 Jamaican maroons, descendants of escaped slaves who had been deported to Nova Scotia and settled near Preston. He had also to supervise their schoolmaster. Gray had some success among the maroons, many of whom were not Christians, but at least one observer was critical of his preaching and asserted that he was unable to communicate effectively. In 1797 he had been admitted to priest's orders and inducted as a missionary of the Society for the Propagation of the Gospel, remaining at Preston. From 1799 to 1800 he was also grand chaplain of the provincial grand lodge of the masonic order in nearby Halifax.

Following the departure of the maroons in 1801, Gray was employed as English master in the academy of King's College, where he was also a fellow of the college and its librarian. Five years later he became the SPG missionary at Sackville, near Halifax, and from there moved into Halifax itself. This move does not seem to have had official sanction and for a time Gray's status with the society was somewhat in question. It appears that in 1817, when the authorized missionary was unable to carry out his duties, Gray began to preach regularly in St George's Church. Founded by German-speaking Lutherans, the church had been served since the 1750s by Anglican clergymen, although the congregation had not yet entered into full conformity. Under Gray's ministry the distrust between the Church of England authorities and the congregation subsided, and in 1827, two years after his departure, St George's became a separate parish fully integrated into the church establishment.

On 16 Dec. 1824, by order of Michael Wallace*, the administrator of the province, Gray inducted Robert Willis* to succeed John Inglis* as rector of St Paul's Church, Halifax. The ceremony took place outside the locked doors of the church, because the churchwardens, on behalf of the parishioners, were challenging the right of the government to nominate their minister. Patronage in the church went to persons who stood in good stead with the authorities and Gray thus came down on the side of the bishop, Inglis, and the government in a quarrel that deeply divided the Anglican community. He was named rector of Trinity Church in Saint John, N.B., in June 1825. There, as at St Paul's, the parishioners had a claim to the right of nomination, but since their favoured candidate was Gray's son, John William Dering*, they did not object, especially when the younger Gray was brought to Saint John to be his father's assistant the following year. Both enthusiastic evangelical Christians, they appear to have worked well together, enjoying the support of the lieutenant governor, Sir Howard Douglas*, and the archdeacon of the province, George Best*.

Gray, a man of action, was, in his own words, "very inattentive" in his communications with the SPG. There are, however, a few breathless, vigorous letters covering his early years in Saint John. These indicate that he cultivated good relations with the congregation of a Methodist chapel and employed its minister in an Anglican school. He also told of building new churches at Portland (Saint John) and at the neighbouring communities of Loch Lomond and Musquash and described how he had taken over a large vacant building for services on Sunday evenings in order that "the poor, the poorer sort of the middling classes who cannot afford to pay Church rates, Servants, and many others who from various causes cannot avail themselves of the day services, may benefit from the ordinances of religion. As all the seats are free, the plan succeeds, even beyond our expectations." He continued as well to carry on full morning and evening services in both Trinity Church and St John's Church (commonly referred to as the Stone Church). The Grays were successful in keeping within the Church of England in Saint John sections of the community that in other parts of eastern North America tended to become Baptist or Methodist.

Within a decade of moving to Saint John, Gray Sr suffered two severe blows. The first was to his pride: in 1829 he was passed over for the office of archdeacon, which went to George COSTER. The second, and more serious blow, came in November 1833, when his wife and a female servant died in a fire which destroyed the rectory. Gray's long-felt wish to retire in favour of his son was granted in 1840, the regulation against a son succeeding in his father's parish being set aside. Gray continued as chaplain to the forces, a position he had held since his arrival in Saint John.

It is impossible to delineate the separate roles of the two Grays in their shared ministry. The younger Gray appears to have been in the forefront of the interdenominational Saint John Religious Tract Society. Father and son worked together in founding the Temperance Society in 1831, with the elder Gray taking the chair at its early meetings. Gray Sr was also involved in the organization of the volunteer health association formed to combat cholera in 1832, and his name appears in connection with both the Portland Merciful Society and the Female House of Industry. He is known to have supported the establishment of a penitentiary and to have signed a petition against the prohibition of secret societies or Protestant associations, a move which suggests that he was in favour of the formation of Orange lodges. He also strongly attacked theatrical performances.

In order to make it possible for Gray's son to be brought to Saint John, Inglis had dismissed Frederick Coster, younger brother of George, from his position as assistant missionary. Coster moved across the harbour to Carleton, the newest, smallest, and poorest parish in the province. Over time he built up a strong Anglican church there. Inglis described him as "a very acute person, perhaps the most gifted in the Maritimes"; he, like Gray, showed great concern for the poor, but to Gray's theology of personal salvation and zeal for vital religion Coster opposed his own rigorous high church principles, with emphasis on Anglican exclusiveness in politics and education. Until 1829 evangelical piety was in the ascendant in the province, and on the death of Best that year Lieutenant Governor Douglas, almost certainly encouraged by Charles SIMONDS, took steps to ensure its continuance by having Gray made archdeacon. The bishop, however, was determined to keep the appointment out of the hands of the governor, and he arranged for the transfer to New Brunswick of George Coster, who had been archdeacon of Newfoundland since 1825. In the conflict between the Grays and the Costers there was personal animosity and some pettiness on both sides, but the basic cause of the dispute was their differing views of the nature and purposes of the church. At times there was great bitterness. It was made clear to George Coster that he was not welcome in Saint John, and on one occasion, in 1831, Gray publicly opposed the archdeacon in a sermon. Writing privately to the SPG, Coster expressed doubts about Gray's sanity and also about his orthodoxy; according to reports reaching him, Gray had developed scruples about baptism by sprinkling and was contending from the pulpit for immersion. In an unusual outburst of pique Coster referred to him as "this ordained Baptist." In 1837 a quarrel broke out between high and low churchmen over the newly organized Church Society of the Archdeaconry of New-Brunswick. Gray's parish refused to participate in it, and one of his opponents accused him of having a "vindictive unchristianlike and low persecuting spirit."

As a young man Gray had shown considerable talent in drawing and sketching. In 1803 he prepared an illustrated catalogue of the King's College library for Sir John Wentworth. According to Dr Fenwick William Vroom, a leading historian of the college, "this Catalogue, containing 840 entries, is itself a work of art, not only because it is a model of graceful penmanship, but because it is illustrated with heraldic designs in India-ink, and several water-colour sketches which show the College as it appeared at that date." In 1805 Wentworth sent one of Gray's sketches to Thomas Moore, the Irish poet. Another picture commissioned by Wentworth, a drawing of Fort Cumberland (near Sackville, N.B.), hangs in the library of King's College (now located in Halifax). King's College, Fredericton, awarded Gray a DD in 1830, the first advanced degree granted by that institution. In 1846 he attended the meeting at which the alumni association of King's College, Windsor, was founded.

A portrait of Gray reproduced in the *History of Trinity Church* shows him, in middle age, with a strong handsome face, but there is a restlessness about him which is quite at variance with the character depicted in a portrait of his son in the same volume. In his old age, when anti-Catholicism was rife, he was remembered as the "beloved parson Gray, founder of the Protestant faith in Saint John." His memorial tablet in Trinity Church reads, "Sound in Doctrine / In Labours abundant / a Father to the Poor."

D. MURRAY YOUNG

PAC, MG 23, D8; MG 24, A3, 3–4. PANB, MC 58; RG 4, RS24, S43-P24, -P36; S45-P149; S53-P132; S57-P258; RG 7, RS71A, 1854, B. G. Gray. PRO, CO 188 (mfm. at PANB). Trinity Anglican Church (Saint John, N.B.), Minutes of the wardens and vestry (mfm. at PANB). USPG, C/CAN/NB, 4, nos.492, 496–97, 501; C/CAN/NS, 3, nos.284–87 (mfm. at PAC). Church of England, Diocesan Church Soc. of N.B., *Report* (Saint John), 1837–59. R. C. Dallas, *History of the maroons, from their origin to the establishment of their chief tribe at Sierra Leone . . .* (2v., London, 1803; repr. 1968), 2: 223–24. Ernest Hawkins, *Annals of the diocese of Fredericton* (London, 1847). *Church Times* (Halifax), 4 March 1854. *City Gazette* (Saint John), 22 April, 10 June 1829; 29 Jan. 1831. *Loyalist and Protestant Vindicator* (Fredericton; Saint John), 1845–50. *Morning Chronicle* (Halifax), 7 March 1854. *New-Brunswick Courier*, 17 March, 10 May, 14, 28 July, 11, 18 Aug. 1832; 11 Sept., 5 Oct. 1833; 26 July, 2, 9 Aug. 1834; 11 March 1837; 17 March 1838. Art Gallery of N.S., *[Robert Field, 1769–1819]; an exhibition organized by the Art Gallery of Nova Scotia, Halifax, October 5 to November 27, 1978* (Halifax, 1978). A. W. H. Eaton, *The Gerrish family (family of Capt. John Gerrish)* ([Boston], 1913), 9. E. A. Jones, *The loyalists of Massachusetts: their memorials, petitions and claims* (London, 1930; repr. Baltimore, Md., 1969), 274–75.

[T. B. Akins], *History of Halifax City* (Halifax, 1895; repr. Belleville, Ont., 1973), 234. Judith Fingard, *The Anglican design in loyalist Nova Scotia, 1783–1816* (London, 1972). R. V. Harris, *The Church of Saint Paul in Halifax, Nova Scotia: 1749–1949* (Toronto, 1949). H. Y. Hind, *The University of King's College, Windsor, Nova Scotia, 1790–1890* (New York, 1890). *History of Trinity Church, Saint John, New Brunswick, 1791–1891*, comp. [F. H. J.] Brigstocke (Saint John, 1892). M. J. [Lawson] Katzmann, *History of the townships of Dartmouth, Preston and Lawrencetown, Halifax County, N.S.*, ed. Harry Piers (Halifax, 1893; repr. Belleville, 1972), 165. G. H. Lee, *An historical sketch of the first fifty years of the Church of England in the province of New Brunswick (1783–1833)* (Saint John, 1880). MacNutt, *New Brunswick*. C. F. Pascoe, *Two hundred years of the S.P.G. . . .* (2v., London, 1901). J. E. Pinnington, "Anglican reactions to the challenge of a multiconfessional society, with special reference to British North America, 1760–1850" (2v., PHD thesis, Univ. of

Oxford, 1971). J. D. Purdy, "The Church of England in New Brunswick during the colonial era, 1783–1860" (MA thesis, Univ. of N.B., Fredericton, 1954). J. H. Stark, *The loyalists of Massachusetts and the other side of the American revolution* (Boston, 1910), 334–37. C. W. Vernon, *Bicentenary sketches and early days of the church in Nova Scotia . . .* (Halifax, 1910), 226–28. F. W. Vroom, *King's College: a chronicle, 1789–1939; collections and recollections* (Halifax, 1941). R. W. Winks, *The blacks in Canada: a history* (Montreal, 1971). [Francis] Partridge, "The early history of the parish of St. George, Halifax," N.S. Hist. Soc., *Coll.*, 7 (1891): 73–87. H. G. Ryder, "Stone church," *Canadian Antiques Collector* (Toronto), 10 (1975), no. 3: 63–65.

GRIEBEL, FERDINAND (Frederick), violinist, composer, and teacher; b. *c.* 1819 in Berlin, youngest son of Johann Heinrich Griebel; m. Johanna——, and was survived by five children; d. 18 Feb. 1858 in Toronto.

Ferdinand Griebel's father was a bassoonist, and his elder brothers Heinrich and Julius played oboe and cello in the Prussian court orchestra which performed for both the royal opera and the national theatre. All three achieved fine reputations. Ferdinand studied the violin under Léon de Saint-Lubin, concert-master of the Königstadt theatre from 1830 to 1847, and eventually joined its orchestra. He later had lessons from two famous violinists, Charles-Auguste de Bériot, probably during a visit to Berlin in 1838, and Heinrich Wilhelm Ernst, who appeared in Berlin in 1841 and 1842. In the latter year Ferdinand and his elder brother Julius, the cellist, undertook a successful concert tour of Denmark, Sweden, and England. On 18 Jan. 1843 the *Allgemeine Musikalische Zeitung* of Leipzig (German Democratic Republic) praised Griebel's recent performance of a violin concerto by Ferdinand David as that of a talented and skilled musician.

The political turmoils of 1848 set back cultural life in Europe but indirectly provided an impetus to music in North America. Marie-Hippolyte-Antoine Dessane* and Charles Sabatier [Wugk*] came from France to settle in Quebec and Montreal respectively, followed by Griebel and, later, by Theodor August Heintzmann* from Berlin. Early in 1848 Griebel had joined a group of some 25 musicians in Berlin who formed an orchestral cooperative, the Musik-Gesellschaft Germania or Germania Musical Society, for the purpose of settling and performing in the United States. In the original group Griebel was head of the first violin section. After a farewell concert on 4 May 1848 the group left Berlin, arriving in New York in September. The players gave several hundred concerts of high calibre during the next six years, performing in Toronto, Kingston, Montreal, and Quebec in 1850. The following year some members of

the orchestra joined Jenny Lind for concerts in New England. Griebel was later reported to have visited Toronto with Lind's concert troupe in October 1851, but his first documented appearances in the city took place in May 1852 with the troupe of the Irish soprano Catherine Hayes. On this occasion he performed a solo of his own composition and Paganini's "Carnaval de Venise." It is not known precisely when Griebel left the Germania orchestra but by the end of 1853 he had settled in Toronto.

Documentation exists for 36 public appearances by Griebel as a resident musician from January 1854 until 9 Feb. 1858, nine days before his death. Nearly all were at St Lawrence Hall. In concerts featuring an orchestra, notably the Toronto *première* of Handel's *Messiah* presented on 17 Dec. 1857 by the Toronto Philharmonic Society, Griebel usually was the concert-master. On other occasions he played solos, of which his own composition on "Airs from *Linda di Chamounix* [Donizetti]" and "Carnival de Berlin" are typical examples. He also played more serious music, for example de Bériot's Violin Concerto no.1 and "Concerto militaire," and led a string quartet with Augustin Noverre, second violin, Mr S. Childs, viola, John Ellis*, cello. Griebel gave lessons at his Church Street address but no record of his pupils is known.

Griebel may be considered the first fully professional violinist to have settled in Canada. Even 20 years after his death his reputation survived as that of "the greatest violinist ever resident in this city. He was equally skilful in playing a solo, in leading the orchestra, or in interpreting chamber music, and had a remarkable talent for directing amateurs in their performances." Yet Griebel's income was inadequate for his family's needs and his widow and children were left destitute. A subscription fund for their support was soon raised by such prominent citizens as George Duggan*, Abraham Nordheimer*, and James Dodsley Humphreys*, and three benefit concerts were organized, in 1858, 1861, and 1865. In the last a daughter, Alice Griebel, participated as a pianist. Mrs Griebel, a piano teacher, eventually moved to New York City, where she is said to have died about 1890.

HELMUT KALLMANN

AO, RG 22, ser.302, petition by Johanna Griebel for guardianship, 17 Jan. 1862. *Allgemeine Musikalische Zeitung* (Leipzig, [German Democratic Republic]), 45 (1843): 43. *Globe*, 19 Feb. 1858. *Leader*, 19, 23 Feb. 1858. Carl [Ledebur], Freiherr von Ledebur, *Tonkünstler-Lexicon Berlin's . . .* (Berlin, 1861; repr. Tutzing, German Federal Republic, and Berlin, 1965), 207–8. Hermann Mendel, *Musikalisches conversations-lexikon . . .* (11v. in 6 and supplement, Berlin, 1870–83), 4: 358–59. *The new Grove dictionary of music and musicians*, ed. Stanley Sadie (20v., London, 1980). *Toronto directory*, 1856. Helmut Kallmann,

Grigor

A history of music in Canada, 1534–1914 (Toronto and London, 1960). W. H. Pearson, Recollections and records of Toronto of old . . . (Toronto, 1914). D. J. Sale, "Toronto's pre-confederation music societies, 1845–1867" (MA thesis, Univ. of Toronto, 1968). C. C. Taylor, Toronto "called back" from 1886 to 1850 . . . (Toronto, 1886). F. E. Dixon, "Music in Toronto, as it was in the days that are gone by forever," Daily Mail and Empire (Toronto), 7 Nov. 1896: 9. H. E. Johnson, "The Germania Musical Society," Musical Quarterly (New York), 39 (1953): 75–93. "Music and the drama," Daily Mail and Empire, 14 Nov. 1896, pt.II: 8. "Music in Toronto," Mail (Toronto), 21 Dec. 1878, suppl.

GRIGOR, WILLIAM, doctor, office holder, and politician; b. 1798 in Elgin, Scotland; m. 14 April 1827 Catherine Louisa Foreman, fourth daughter of James FOREMAN, in Halifax, and they had nine children; d. there 24 Nov. 1857.

William Grigor was born and educated in Scotland. Like many of Nova Scotia's early physicians, he received his medical training at the University of Edinburgh, reputed at that time to be the finest medical school in the empire. In 1819, shortly after receiving his MD, Grigor emigrated to Nova Scotia. He practised medicine at Antigonish and Truro before taking up permanent residence in Halifax in 1824.

Grigor quickly set out to raise the standard of medical treatment in Halifax. Between 1827 and 1832 he served without remuneration as assistant to Charles Wentworth Wallace, the health officer of the city. When Wallace resigned in 1832 Grigor's services were dispensed with. In the mean time Grigor and his colleague John Stirling had established in 1829 the first Halifax dispensary to provide medical aid to the poor and indigent, supplying it with their own surgical instruments. From their offices in the rear of St Matthew's Church (Presbyterian), Grigor and Stirling gave medical advice, administered medicine, and performed surgical operations. In the summer of 1831 alone they vaccinated 464 poor children. The House of Assembly provided some support, but the success of the dispensary was largely dependent upon the personal sacrifices of the two doctors.

In addition to maintaining a large private practice and working in the dispensary, Grigor laboured from 1848 to 1857 as Halifax County coroner. In that capacity, however, not everyone seemed pleased with his efforts. The Novascotian of 3 March 1849 reported that "in the office of coroner he is said to act so very uncourteously and selfishly towards his professional brethren, that they intend to question his right to preside and play the part of medical witness too, at inquests."

Grigor's marriage in 1827 to the daughter of a successful Halifax merchant propelled him into the energetic mercantile and professional élite of Halifax, which in the 1820s and 1830s looked to the future with purposeful optimism. Like many of his contemporaries during this period of Nova Scotia's awakening, Grigor became involved in a number of organizations concerned with social improvement. An early promoter and first president of the Halifax Mechanics' Institute on its establishment in 1831, he favoured a less theoretical education for tradesmen and workers than did Joseph Howe*, calling for a vocational and scientific orientation to their education. Grigor and his wife were interested as well in painting, both contributing works to the 1831 Halifax exhibition; in 1836 he gave a lecture to the mechanics' institute on the "Philosophical view of art." At its first annual meeting on 5 Oct. 1854, he was elected president of the Halifax Medical Society, a province-wide organization of physicians and surgeons that represented a restructuring of the Medical Society of Halifax which had been established ten years earlier. He was also a governor of Dalhousie College.

On 21 Feb. 1849 Lieutenant Governor Sir John HARVEY had appointed Grigor to a seat in the Legislative Council, describing him as a "gentleman in large practice in Halifax and of considerable literary and scientific acquirements, and disposed to give the administration a fair and generous support." The new member had earlier belonged to The Club, a group of Joseph Howe's associates whose political satire was featured in the Novascotian between May 1828 and June 1831 [see Laurence O'Connor Doyle*]. In the Legislative Council, although a liberal and Howe's personal physician, Grigor quickly demonstrated an independence of mind in politics that was potentially embarrassing to the liberal administration. Soon after his appointment he voted against the bill to abolish the permanent grant to King's College, an action which led many to question why "the Government have heaped a load of honors on Dr. Grigor within the past twelve months."

Grigor seems to have avoided further political controversy, while continuing his painstaking efforts to improve the quality of medical treatment in colonial Nova Scotia. Although the dispensary was reorganized at various times after his death, it continues even today to provide out-patient treatment at the Izaac Walton Killam Children's Hospital in Halifax.

COLIN D. HOWELL

Edinburgh Univ. Library, Special Coll. Dept., Medical matriculation records, 1814–16. Halifax County Court of Probate (Halifax), Estate papers, no.755. PANS, RG 1, 120: 260; 182: 82; RG 5, P, 80. St Paul's Anglican Church (Halifax), Reg. of marriages, 14 April 1827 (mfm. at PANS). N.S., House of Assembly, Journal and proc., 1830–31, app.14; 1832, app.44; Legislative Council, Journal and proc., 21 Feb. 1849. Acadian Recorder, 3, 10 March 1849. Liverpool Transcript (Liverpool, N.S.), 3 Dec. 1857. Novascotian, 26 Feb., 3, 12 March 1849; 22 Aug. 1853. DCB, vol.9 (biog. of F. W. Morris). M. W. Fleming,

"The Halifax Visiting Dispensary – 100 years ago," *Nova Scotia Medical Bull.* (Halifax), 36 (1957): 106–9. Patrick Keane, "Joseph Howe and adult education," *Acadiensis* (Fredericton), 3 (1973–74), no.1: 35–49. D. S. McCurdy, "Growth of the medical profession in Truro," *Nova Scotia Medical Bull.*, 44 (1965): 163–67. K. A. MacKenzie, "Founders of the Medical Society of Nova Scotia," *Nova Scotia Medical Bull.*, 32 (1953): 240–41; "Nineteenth century physicians in Nova Scotia," N.S. Hist. Soc., *Coll.*, 31 (1957): 119. H. L. Scammell, "The legacy of Pictou County Scots to medicine, 1767–1914," *Nova Scotia Medical Bull.*, 53 (1974): 71–73.

GROAD, CABLEAL. *See* GLODE, GABRIEL

GUIBOCHE (Gibotte), LOUIS, also known by the Indian name of **Nemisses (Minissis)** and the nickname **Little Pigeon (Petit Pigeon),** fur trader and interpreter; b. *c.* 1785 in Rupert's Land; d. before 13 Oct. 1859 in the vicinity of the Red River settlement (Man.).

Louis Guiboche represents the first generation of Métis in the northwest descended from the fur traders and the Indians of the trading regions. Although his origins cannot be precisely identified, presumably he was born of a French Canadian father and an Indian mother. In March 1779 Philip Turnor* of the Hudson's Bay Company met a trader named "Gibosh" employed by Jean-Étienne Waddens*, in the area around Upper Hudson House (near Silver Grove, Sask.) on the North Saskatchewan River. Some years later, in May 1788, a Louis Guiboche of Berthier-en-Haut (Berthierville), Que., was taken on as middleman paddler by McTavish, Frobisher and Company, a co-partner in the North West Company. Both references may well be to Louis Guiboche's father. On the other hand, the Louis Guiboche working for the NWC in the Lower Red River department in 1799 is equally likely to have been the subject of this biography or his father.

Guiboche is known to have been employed in 1804 as an interpreter by the NWC in the English (Churchill) River department. Its accounts for 1805 show that his contract had three years to run and that he owed the company 1,487 *livres*, while his wages totalled only 500. It may have been this situation that prompted him to leave the company and enter the service of its rival, the HBC, around 1810.

From 1815 to 1818 Guiboche was an interpreter for the HBC at Lesser Slave Lake (Alta), and in 1818–19 he was in the Athabasca country. The following year he seems to have settled in the Red River colony, but during the 1820s he travelled regularly for the HBC to York Factory, on Hudson Bay, as well as in the English River district. Guiboche had a special role during these years. With Cuthbert GRANT, he was an independent merchant who contracted to carry the company's trade goods and supplies between the colony and Hudson Bay. George SIMPSON, the HBC's governor, appealed to Guiboche and Grant in 1826 to stem the opposition to the company's monopoly mounted by the American fur traders from the south. The two were fitted out by the company and authorized to trade in the region between Turtle Mountain (Man.) and the Qu'Appelle River, with the object of acquiring the furs coveted by the independent traders. Probably in recognition of the success of this venture, Guiboche was appointed interpreter-clerk for the Winnipeg district in 1828. The following year he held the position of postmaster and winterer at Netley Creek, but in 1831 he retired and returned to the Red River settlement.

When the colony's first census was taken in 1827, Guiboche had declared himself married and the father of seven; a census in 1832 showed that his possessions included a house, four horses, seven oxen, four carts, and two canoes, but that he did little farming, and this suggests that his livelihood came mainly from hunting and transporting goods. He owned properties on the Assiniboine River west of the colony, and near the fork of the Red and Seine rivers. However, around 1835 he began to dispose of these, keeping only one lot for himself at St Boniface, where he lived. Meanwhile, his work obliged him to travel. Nothing further is known of his pursuits until 1859, when a note in the colony's records dated 13 October states that Guiboche had died and that his sons wished to sell his land.

There is little information about Guiboche as a person, except that he was a decent and conscientious employee. Governor Simpson, not normally lavish with his compliments, said in 1830 that he was "very steady and correct, well qualified as Postmaster." His role as an interpreter for the Indians was considered indispensable by those running the HBC and, during the period of rivalry between that company and the NWC before 1821, his ability was such that in 1820 the NWC wished to secure his services "at any price."

DIANE PAULETTE PAYMENT

ANQ-M, CN1-74, 3 mai 1788. PAC, MG 19, C1, 55. PAM, HBCA, A.16/52–53; A.32/30: f.180; A.34/1: f.25; A.34/2: f.52; B.4/d/22: f.12d; B.235/a/6: f.9; B.235/d/60: f.33; D.4/7: ff.196–96d; D.4/90: f.30; E.5/1; E.6/2: f.137; E.24/4; MG 2, B3; MG 7, D8. *Les bourgeois de la Compagnie du Nord-Ouest* (Masson), vol.1. *HBRS*, 2 (Rich and Fleming); 3 (Fleming). *Le Manitoba* (Saint-Boniface), 14 août 1883. É.-Z. Massicotte, "Répertoire des engagements pour l'Ouest . . . ," ANQ *Rapport*, 1942–43; 1944–45. G. C. Davidson, *The North West Company* (Berkeley, Calif., 1918; repr. New York, 1967). Marcel Giraud, *Le Métis canadien; son rôle dans l'histoire des provinces de l'Ouest* (Paris, 1945). H. A. Innis, *The fur trade in Canada: an introduction to Canadian economic history* (rev. ed., Toronto, 1956).

Haldane

H

HALDANE, JOHN, fur trader; b. *c.* 1775 in Scotland, son of George Haldane, manufacturer, and Katharine Murray; d. 11 Oct. 1857 in Haddington, Scotland.

John Haldane's fur-trade career would appear to have started on the Saskatchewan River in 1798. He was probably in the employ of the New North West Company (sometimes called the XY Company) for four years and then in 1802 he joined the firm as a wintering partner. That year he was at the New North West Company post on Lake Athabasca, in competition with Peter Fidler* of the Hudson's Bay Company at Nottingham House (Alta) and James MacKenzie* of the "old" North West Company at Fort Chipewyan. When the two North West companies amalgamated in 1804, John Forsyth* signed the agreement on behalf of Haldane, who entered the NWC as a winterer with one share. He was present at the annual meeting of wintering partners and Montreal agents at Kaministiquia (Thunder Bay, Ont.) that year, and at the meeting of 1808 he was appointed to a committee with, among others, Roderick McKenzie and Donald McTavish*, to investigate the financial arrangements of the company. From 1805 to 1811 he was in charge of the Monontagué department, to the west of Lake Nipigon, where he conducted the NWC's trade campaign against the HBC. This competition was at times particularly violent and in one incident, in 1809, a Nor'Wester, Aeneas Macdonell, was killed in a clash with HBC men at Eagle Lake.

Haldane replaced Pierre Rastel* de Rocheblave as proprietor at Pic (Ont.) in 1812, and then took charge of the Athabasca River department in 1813 and the Saskatchewan River department in 1814. He spent 1815–16 in Great Britain on a long-deferred leave and then, in 1819, with Peter Skene OGDEN, he made his first trip beyond the Rocky Mountains. When the HBC and the NWC merged in 1821, he became a chief factor and, with John Dugald CAMERON, assumed command of the Columbia district.

Haldane's career with the HBC was highlighted by a power struggle over the administration of the North American fur trade, and he soon became involved in a dispute with George SIMPSON, the newly appointed governor of the HBC's Northern Department. The two men met for the first time at Norway House (Man.) in 1822. At the Northern Department council meetings of that year, there and at York Factory, Haldane and James BIRD were seen as the leaders of a group of traders who attempted to block Simpson's plans for company management which included a reduction in salaries and allowances. Haldane was granted leave for 1822 and it was clear that Simpson wanted to be rid of him permanently from the councils of the Northern Department, where "he devotes himself more to Legislating than to business and he has the entire lead of [John McDonald*, George KEITH, and James Leith*], his old XY partisans." After his furlough Haldane was appointed to the Lake Superior district of the Southern Department and Governor William Williams* was delighted to get a man of "known abilities." There does not appear to have been any difficulty between Williams and Haldane such as had developed with Simpson, who noted that this was because Haldane ruled "both Williams and the southern department."

In 1826 Simpson was appointed governor of both departments, and it was perhaps not surprising that in August 1826 Haldane tendered his resignation, ostensibly for health reasons, to be effective in 1827. When the two men met at Michipicoten (Michipicoten River, Ont.) in September 1826, Simpson was pushing to reduce expenses and to institute new transport arrangements which Haldane opposed. But, now that he had decided to resign, Haldane chose to be "smooth as oil," and Simpson reported privately to John George McTavish* that "from the teeth outward we were excellent friends." Haldane retired to Scotland, taking up residence in Haddington, and in 1827 received £2,665 9s. 0d. from the HBC for his interest in the company.

Early in his career Haldane had taken as his country wife Josette Latour, when she was "turned off" by William McKay* on his retirement in 1808. For nearly twenty years she was recognized as Haldane's wife *à la façon du pays* and on one occasion was credited with saving his life. Before leaving Michipicoten in 1827 Haldane had, according to Keith, promised to provide his wife with an annuity of £60. Over the years, however, he chose to forget this responsibility and Josette, who survived into the 1850s, suffered real hardship. Other old fur traders, such as Keith and Charles McKENZIE, were enraged by his callousness and recounted exaggerated stories of his wealth and style of living. Protests on her behalf seem to have resulted in the severing of long-time contacts. By the end of his life Haldane's links with his associates from the North American fur trade had virtually ended. On 11 Oct. 1857 he died of jaundice in Haddington.

Haldane's fur-trade career was marked in particular by his conflict with Simpson, and at the height of his influence he became known for self-indulgence and a propensity for intrigue. The manner in which he turned his back on his country wife at his retirement stands as an unfortunate example of the fate of Indian and Métis women. Both of these circumstances have combined to create for Haldane an unenviable place in the history of the North American fur trade.

ELIZABETH ARTHUR

GRO (Edinburgh), Haddington, reg. of deaths, 11 Oct. 1857. PAC, MG 19, A21, ser.1, 17. PAM, HBCA, A.44/3: f.116; B.107/a/2; B.135/k/1; B.231/e/3; B.239/c/1: ff.292, 330–30d; D.1/5: f.5d; D.2/1; D.4/8: ff.27–28; D.4/82: f.46d; D.4/86: f.27d; D.4/89: ff.22–22d, 69d, 105–5d; D.4/92: ff.1–57; D.5/1: f.219; D.5/6: f.85; D.5/8: f.142; D.5/13: f.71; D.5/20: f.307d; D.5/43: f.225. Andrew Amos, *Report of trials in the courts of Canada, relative to the destruction of the Earl of Selkirk's settlement on the Red River; with observations* (London, 1820). Cox, *Adventures on the Columbia*. *Docs. relating to NWC* (Wallace). Harmon, *Sixteen years in the Indian country* (Lamb). *HBRS*, 2 (Rich and Fleming); 3 (Fleming); 26 (Johnson). Mactavish, *Letters of Letitia Hargrave* (MacLeod). R. A. Pendergast, "The XY Company, 1798–1804" (PHD thesis, Univ. of Ottawa, 1957). Simpson, *Fur trade and empire* (Merk; 1968). James Tate, "James Tate's journal, 1809–1812," *HBRS*, 30 (Williams), 95–150. Van Kirk, *"Many tender ties."*

HALKETT (Wedderburn), JOHN, HBC director and author; b. 27 Feb. 1768 in Pitfirrane, Scotland, third son of John Wedderburn and his second wife, Mary Hamilton; m. first 1794 Anna Todd (d. 1805); m. secondly 1815 his cousin Lady Katherine Douglas, sister of Thomas Douglas*, Earl of Selkirk; d. 12 Nov. 1852, and was buried in Petersham (London).

John Wedderburn assumed the name of Halkett in 1779 when, upon the death of his cousin Sir Peter Halkett, he succeeded to the baronetcy of Pitfirrane. His son John apparently matriculated to the University of St Andrews (Scotland) in 1786, and was admitted to the Scottish bar in Edinburgh in August 1789. During the years 1797–1801 he was secretary of presentations to his cousin Alexander Wedderburn, 1st Baron Loughborough, who was then lord chancellor of England. In 1801 he was appointed governor-in-chief of the Bahamas and in 1803 captain-general and governor-in-chief of Tobago. On his return to London he was appointed first chief commissioner of West Indian accounts.

With two other cousins, Andrew Wedderburn, who in 1814 changed his name to Colvile, and Lord Selkirk, Halkett became interested in the Hudson's Bay Company. Selkirk began buying shares in the company in 1808, as did Halkett and Wedderburn the next year. Halkett was appointed a member of the HBC's London committee in November 1811, a few months after the company had granted a large tract of

land around the Red River to Selkirk for the establishment of a colony. By training and temperament Halkett was eminently suited to become the main British defender of Selkirk's efforts in North America, and he spent most of the years 1815 to 1820 trying to counteract what he considered misleading and false statements circulated by the North West Company about Selkirk's character and his work. Given the indifference of the colonial secretary, Lord Bathurst, and the arrogance of the influential under-secretary, Henry Goulburn, it was a disheartening period. Bathurst regarded the violent acts of 1815–16 at Red River, which culminated in the ruin of the colony [see Cuthbert GRANT], as simply quarrels between the two rival fur-trading companies, while Halkett sought unsuccessfully to impress upon him that justice was being denied British settlers. He wrote a number of pamphlets and long explanatory letters to Bathurst, based on judicious arguments and accompanied by affidavits and depositions, in efforts to prove that, despite their self-righteous attacks on Selkirk, the Nor'Westers had been the instigators in these events. His letters were dispassionate in tone, outlining point by point the inconsistencies in the various statements made by the NWC. He frequently had reason to be provoked by the curt replies he received from the under-secretary, but his calm judgement always prevailed.

In 1817 Halkett published, for private circulation, the unsigned *Statement respecting the Earl of Selkirk's settlement*, in which he blamed the destruction of the colony on the NWC and its agents. The NWC reply was not long in coming: later the same year a rebuttal entitled *A narrative of occurrences in the Indian countries of North America* was released. The book was unsigned but has been attributed to NWC employee Samuel Hull Wilcocke*. In 1818 Halkett reprinted his pamphlet and included a reply to the NWC publication. In the end, however, Halkett and Selkirk's few other supporters were out-manoeuvred by the Nor'Westers. The NWC's Montreal agents Simon* and William* McGillivray cultivated leading judicial and political leaders in England and the Canadas, and they succeeded in bringing these officials more or less to their point of view. This favourable disposition, joined with legal technicalities and delays in the Canadian courts, enabled the NWC men to escape punishment for their violent acts. Halkett's statement to Bathurst in 1819, that Selkirk had been "treated with marked and signal injustice," appears in retrospect to be justified.

Selkirk died in 1820 and in the fall of 1821 Halkett travelled to Montreal as an executor of the estate. Two former NWC men, disgruntled by Halkett's treatment of them in print, enlivened his visit. On 18 October Alexander Greenfield Macdonell* met him outside his hotel and threatened him with a horsewhip. Halkett

Halkett

had him arrested and as a precaution armed himself with a pair of pistols. That evening Jasper Vandersluys attacked him and struck him twice with a whip before Halkett fired, wounding his assailant. Vandersluys charged him with "assault with intent to kill" but the charge was later withdrawn.

After a visit to Washington in connection with that part of the Selkirk grant in American territory, Halkett returned to Montreal in May 1822. He was determined to visit the Red River settlement and give it a fair trial. He set off by canoe, with John McLOUGHLIN and the new governor of the colony Andrew H. BULGER, on 15 May, arriving in the settlement in late June. He found the settlers demoralized and some of them mutinous. Grasshoppers had destroyed the previous year's crops, bison were scarce, and the Sioux had murdered a number of people in the vicinity of Pembina (N.Dak.) to the south. Halkett assured the settlers that the promises made by Lord Selkirk would be upheld. These included a supply of farm animals and fixed prices for goods and grain. He also arranged for a reduction in interest payments and for concessions in rent. To promote the prosperity of the Red River settlement, he closed the administrative buildings and the HBC post at Pembina, and asked Bishop Joseph-Norbert PROVENCHER to close the Roman Catholic mission there. Provencher described Halkett as haughty in his dealings with the Catholic missionaries and stated that his visit had done more harm than good. This criticism was unfair. The proposal to abandon the settlement at Pembina was responsible, since its inhabitants were outside the jurisdiction of British law and the Sioux had already killed ten people in the area. Father Sévère DUMOULIN was recalled from Pembina, and the mission closed, in 1823.

Halkett made a short tour of the country to the west of the settlement and then embarked by canoe for York Factory (Man.) where he presided over a meeting of the HBC Northern Department council on 20 Aug. 1822. Resolutions were passed regarding education and the granting of land to mixed-blood fur-trade families at the Red River settlement. Halkett's liberal views and ardent support of the colony did much to ease the frustrations of the settlers and, indeed, without his interest and his influence within the HBC the colony would probably have lost most of its settlers to the Canadas and the United States, thus rendering Selkirk's project a failure.

As a director of the HBC Halkett retained his interest in British North America after his return to England in 1822. He had been favourably impressed by the kindness extended towards the colonists by the Saulteaux chief Peguis* and his band. He had a high regard for the Indian people but, with the events of 1815–16 in mind, he held the Métis in contempt, referring to them as "Banditti." He was critical of the HBC for its trade in spirits with the native people and recommended its prohibition. These views were given a favourable hearing by the London committee, dominated by men with strong humanitarian views, and it is to the committee's credit that the trade in spirits was gradually suppressed. In 1825 Halkett published *Historical notes respecting the Indians of North America: with remarks on the attempts made to convert and civilize them*. It is a sympathetic account based on the writings of Claude-Charles Le Roy* de La Potherie, *dit* Bacqueville de La Potherie, Pierre-François-Xavier de Charlevoix*, and others, with Halkett's suggestions for the "civil and religious advancement" of Indians. He recommended a more sympathetic approach to the native way of life and emphasized that changes should be made slowly and cautiously, attitudes which have only recently been adopted in relationships with Indians. His interest in North American native culture is also reflected in his collection of aboriginal artifacts.

In the spring of 1848 Halkett retired from the HBC's London committee. When he died four years later, leaving four sons from his second marriage, there were signs that the Red River settlement, which he had helped to nurture, was beginning to think of itself as the metropolis of western British North America.

SHIRLEE ANNE SMITH

John Halkett is the author of several works dealing with the controversy surrounding the events at Red River in 1815 and 1816. In 1817 he published his *Statement respecting the Earl of Selkirk's settlement of Kildonan, upon the Red River, in North America; its destruction in the years 1815 and 1816; and the massacre of Governor Semple and his party* in London. He subsequently published an expanded version of this work, *Statement respecting the Earl of Selkirk's settlement upon the Red River . . . with observations upon a recent publication, entitled "A narrative of occurrences in the Indian countries, &c."* (London, 1817; New York, 1818; repr. East Ardsley, Eng., and New York, 1968, and [Toronto, 1970]), which was translated into French as *Précis touchant la colonie du lord Selkirk, sur la rivière Rouge, sa destruction en 1815 et 1816, et le massacre du gouverneur Semple et de son parti . . .* (Montréal, 1818). He is also the author of *Postscript to the statement respecting the Earl of Selkirk's settlement upon the Red River, in North America* (Montreal, 1818). A series of his letters appeared in London, probably in 1819, as *Correspondence in the years 1817, 1818, and 1819, between Earl Bathurst, and J. Halkett, Esq. on the subject of Lord Selkirk's settlement at the Red River, in North America*. His reflections on the native peoples of North America are included in *Historical notes respecting the Indians of North America: with remarks on the attempts made to convert and civilize them . . .* (Edinburgh and London, 1825). In addition, there is a collection of his correspondence from the period when he was in the British West Indies: [*Ten holograph letters and two enclosures from John Halkett, governor of the Bahamas, to Admiral, Sir J. T.*

Duckworth, commander-in-chief at Jamaica] (New Providence, Bahamas, 1802–4).

PAC, MG 19, E1, ser.2 (mfm. at PAM). PAM, HBCA, A.1/50: f.47; A.1/53: ff.25d–26; A.8/1: ff.14–14d, 19–19d; A.10/4: f.393; A.10/9: f.408; A.43/7: f.2; A.44/3: f.80; copies, letters Red River settlement, VII, 160a: 1030–33, 1051b–67, 1083, 1085–86, 1090, 1094–96. *HBRS*, 1 (Rich); 3 (Fleming). [S. H. Wilcocke], *A narrative of occurrences in the Indian countries of North America . . .* (London, 1817; repr. East Ardsley, Eng., and New York, 1968). Andrew Wedderburn, *The Wedderburn book: a history of the Wedderburns . . . 1296–1896* (2v., n.p., 1898). J. M. Gray, *Lord Selkirk of Red River* (London, 1963). C. [B.] Martin, *Lord Selkirk's work in Canada* (Oxford, 1916). Rich, *Hist. of HBC*.

HALL, WILLIAM, businessman and gentleman farmer; b. 1767; m. Helenore Gowen, and they had ten children; d. 6 Dec. 1854 in the parish of Saint-Joseph (at Lauzon), Lower Canada.

Nothing is known of William Hall's life until 1791, when he opened a hat shop on Rue Saint-Jean at Quebec, facing the Palais gate. Hall's first child was born in 1793 and, like his other children, is listed in the registers of the Scotch Church at Quebec. Around 1801 he owned a second shop, at Trois-Rivières. As well as selling hats retail at his two establishments, he sold them wholesale to the small tradesmen of Quebec and the surrounding countryside. His Quebec store was moved in 1797 from Rue Saint-Jean to Rue de la Fabrique, across from the Upper Town market.

Hall soon became the owner of substantial properties. In 1792 he and his uncle Henry Juncken, a businessman, had petitioned for a grant of ten square miles in the Beauce, behind the parishes of Saint-Joseph and Sainte-Marie. On 18 August of that year they secured permission to have a survey done of their land grant, which was then called Broughton Township. In order to comply with a notice published on 17 Jan. 1795 in the *Quebec Gazette*, the two partners entered into association in 1796 with a number of farmers from the two parishes, and with some artisans from Quebec, in accordance with the system of township leaders and associates [*see* James Caldwell*]. The associates each received 1,200 acres, and then ceded 1,100 of them to Juncken and Hall as compensation for the costs related to obtaining the concession. On 26 Oct. 1800 a proclamation of the governor officially established Broughton Township and granted a third of it – 22,000 acres – to Juncken, Hall, and their associates. When Juncken died on 10 Oct. 1802 Henry Hall, William's brother, inherited their uncle's share in the township. Within two years Henry was dead, and William became sole owner of 18,300 acres.

Hall none the less had maintained his activities at Quebec. On 1 Jan. 1810 he went into partnership with his brother-in-law Hammond Gowen. In addition to engaging in the hat trade, the firm of Hall and Gowen dealt in lumber and foodstuffs. During the War of 1812 the partners sold hats and uniforms to the military. For a while Hall was interested in public works, and in 1812 he obtained a contract to repair Rue Saint-Jean. He terminated his partnership with Gowen on 1 Jan. 1815, and two years later formed a new company with his son Charles Henry under the name William Hall and Son. This partnership was dissolved on 3 March 1819.

In April 1817 Hall was chosen to participate in the work of a commission dealing with transportation in Dorchester County and in that part of Buckingham County within the district of Quebec. As well, on 23 April he published a notice in the *Quebec Gazette* of his intention to petition the legislature for a licence to erect a toll-bridge at Saint-Henri, on the Rivière Etchemin. When the assembly granted his request in 1818, Hall brought Gowen, merchant Robert Melvin, and three inhabitants of Saint-Henri into the project. Construction began in the spring of 1820.

That year Hall received a prize from the Agriculture Society in the district of Quebec for his harvests of the previous year. At this period it was his son Charles Henry, not he himself, who was living in the spacious residence (known locally as Broughton Manor) that he had built on his estate, located on lot 12, concession 4. Hall also owned a flour-mill and a sawmill on lot 10, concession 5.

On 6 Dec. 1821 Hall put his property on Rue de la Fabrique up for sale or rent, announcing that he wanted to retire to his estate in Broughton the following spring. The property consisted of three stone buildings, each with three storeys: a house, a large building with chimneys used as a hat factory, and, behind it, a warehouse. Legal difficulties during the next two years ended in the sale of the property by sheriff's auction. Hall abandoned the hatter's trade for good in 1824. It is not known whether he did so to avoid bankruptcy in the immediate or near future, or to pursue his growing interest in the Broughton properties. Whatever the case, he instructed merchant Joseph Cary to liquidate his Quebec operation.

For the 1831 census Hall declared that he occupied 600 acres in the Beauce and farmed 200 of them. That year he harvested 300 *minots* of wheat and 500 of potatoes. His livestock included 40 horned animals, 5 horses, 50 sheep, and 12 pigs. Hall continued to operate his flour-mill and sawmill. Twelve people, four of them servants, lived on the Broughton farm. The township's population went from 55 in 1825 to 111 in 1831, when a group of Irish settlers arrived, and to 612 by 1851.

William Hall succumbed to a haemorrhage of the throat on 6 Dec. 1854 in the parish of Saint-Joseph, where he had been living for a short time. He was then 87 years old and owned 17,150 acres in Broughton

Halliburton

Township and a number of lots in Stoke and Shipton townships. His son Charles Henry inherited the manor-house and the lot on which it was built. His other children shared the remainder of his landed property.

MICHEL MONETTE

No baptismal or marriage certificates have been found for William Hall. His burial is registered at ANQ-Q, CE1-75, 8 déc. 1854.

ANQ-Q, CE1-66, 4, 7 avril 1793; CN1-178, 10 févr. 1796; 23 mai, 20 août 1804; CN1-232, 25 juin 1856; CN1-253, 4, 8 juin 1812; 24 févr. 1813; 5 avril, 20 mai 1820; 27, 30 sept. 1822; 6 avril 1824. *Quebec Gazette*, 1 Dec. 1791; 31 March 1803; 11 May 1815; 30 Jan., 1 May 1817; 8 March, 2 April 1818; 24 Feb. 1820; 6 Dec. 1821; 5 June 1822. *Quebec Mercury*, 11 Dec. 1809, 16 July 1810, 6 May 1811; 1812. J.-A. Lapointe, "William Hall," *BRH*, 42 (1936): 431–36.

HALLIBURTON, Sir BRENTON, army officer, lawyer, judge, and politician; baptized 27 Dec. 1774 in Newport, R.I., son of John Halliburton and Susannah Brenton; m. 19 Sept. 1799 Margaret Inglis, and they had four sons and five daughters; d. 16 July 1860 in Halifax.

Raised in a clerical family of Scottish descent, Brenton Halliburton's father served on a British frigate during the Seven Years' War and afterwards started a medical practice in Newport. The Halliburtons and Brentons were among the leading loyalist families there and, during the American Revolutionary War, John Halliburton had to flee the town after the rebels obtained control. Settling in 1782 in Halifax, where a brother-in-law, James Brenton*, was an assistant judge on the Supreme Court, he became head of the Royal Navy's medical department and resumed private practice. When Brenton was about 12, his father took him to join his elder brother John, who was being educated in Scotland, but Brenton was placed instead at the school of the Reverend Mr Shaw at Enfield (London), England. After his brother's death in 1791, he was brought back to Halifax, where he began to study law in the office of his brother-in-law James Stewart, a loyalist from Maryland.

At the commencement of war with France in 1793, Halliburton joined the Royal Nova Scotia Regiment, but two years later was transferred as a lieutenant to the 7th Foot, the regiment of Prince Edward* Augustus, commander of the forces in Nova Scotia and New Brunswick. While in command of York Redoubt, at the entrance to Halifax Harbour, Halliburton was thanked by the prince in public orders for his endeavours to rescue part of the crew of a wrecked frigate, the *Tribune*. In 1798 he was posted to a company in the 81st Foot, but Prince Edward transferred him back to the 7th. The next year he married a daughter of Charles Inglis*, the Anglican bishop of Nova Scotia. His marriage, and his belief that the Treaty of Amiens in 1802 ended the war with France, made Halliburton decide to return to law. He resumed his studies with James Stewart, who had become solicitor general; Halliburton signed the roll as an attorney on 12 July 1803 and was admitted as a barrister on the same day. He began practice as an assistant in Stewart's private office and most of his early cases, in the Vice-Admiralty Court, concerned shipping.

The Halliburton family, through its position in Halifax's social élite, was able to assist Brenton's career. On 10 Jan. 1807, following the death of his uncle Judge James Brenton, Lieutenant Governor Sir John Wentworth* appointed him a puisne judge of the Supreme Court, a position Brenton thought would be less detrimental to his health than being confined in an office. Upon being sworn in, "I . . . returned home and prostrated myself before the Almighty to thank him for this instance of goodness to me." Chief Justice Sampson Salter Blowers* was pleased with the appointment because former puisne judges had not had legal training. In 1819 Lieutenant Governor Lord Dalhousie [Ramsay*] described Halliburton as a judge "highly respected in publick & private life, a loyal subject, & a morally good man . . . peculiarly distinguished by great fluency of conversation, & a loud & vulgar laugh at every word." In the opinion in 1887 of Peter Lynch, a Halifax lawyer and historian, Halliburton's "law was not very extensive, but like his wine it was of the best quality."

The Supreme Court travelled regularly on circuit throughout the province to try a variety of cases: debt, trespass, theft, assault, stabbing, rape, murder, arson, and casting away a vessel for the insurance. On circuit, Halliburton, in the opinion of a fellow judge, Peleg Wiswall, was "a very pleasing associate." A spectator in a Windsor courtroom described him as "a small, delicate, light complexioned man." Though good-humoured and sociable (he enjoyed public dinners and Scottish reels), he disliked the arduous journeys which circuits to Cape Breton involved. In 1825 he wrote, "I by no means wish to repeat my visit to that Island, oftener than my tour of duty calls upon me to do so – out of the four circuits which the Supreme Court has travelled thither, I have performed three, and I have taken the easy circuit to the Westward but once during these last seven years, altho my private business had compelled me every year, to visit that part of the Country, after returning from the eastward." Yet he recognized that by travelling the circuits as frequently as possible, he could in later life, as he admitted to Peleg Wiswall in 1833, "remain at home with a better grace when I shall feel it necessary to do so."

After several years on the bench, Halliburton was made a member of the Council by Lieutenant Governor Sir John Coape Sherbrooke*; his appointment took effect on 20 June 1815 and he took his seat on 26 October. The appointment solidified his position at the centre of an emerging "family compact." Between 1816 and 1837 he attended the Council faithfully. He was frequently appointed with others to manage joint conferences with the House of Assembly when it sat, and he served on committees dealing with legal matters, roads and bridges, fisheries, and schools. After Inglis died in February 1816, Halliburton maintained his father-in-law's moderate position on sectarian issues, in opposition to such extremist members of the Council as Attorney General Richard John Uniacke*. Thomas McCulloch* and Edward Mortimer* applied to Halliburton in 1816 to aid them in obtaining an act to incorporate an academy in Pictou for Presbyterians. Halliburton responded that "being himself a Churchman, and as warmly attached to his Church as they were to theirs, he would not concur in any measure that would establish a common centre for all Dissenters to rally round, but as a member of the Legislature in a Country where Dissenters formed so large a part of the population," he promised his support "in their endeavour to establish a Seminary for the education of their own youth." The bill, which passed that year with an amendment proposed by Halliburton, allowed Anglicans as well as Presbyterians to become trustees and teachers of the academy. Along with the other political moderates on the Council, Surveyor General Charles Morris*, James Stewart, and Simon Bradstreet ROBIE, Halliburton continued to support Pictou Academy until 1827. The four moderates all had strong ties outside of the capital and had offices which made them more responsive to provincial interests. In February 1827, however, Halliburton reversed his position on Pictou Academy because of the open disputes between McCulloch, its first president, and Bishop John Inglis*, Halliburton's brother-in-law, and the opposition of the Church of Scotland, as an established church, to both the academy and secessionist McCulloch. Halliburton's provincial perspective, or his basic tory inclinations, led him to write an anonymous pamphlet in 1828 attacking Thomas Chandler Haliburton*, who had made sweeping criticisms of Council members as "pensioned old ladies," most of whom "think all the world is contained within the narrow precincts of Halifax."

Until the late 1820s Halliburton had acquiesced in Attorney General Uniacke's ambition to succeed Sampson Salter Blowers as chief justice. As Uniacke "gradually retired from the labours of the Bar and approached the decline of life," Halliburton informed him that "the idea almost gradually arose in my mind that I should myself have claim to the office." In 1829,

at 54 years of age, he was the youngest man on the bench but had long been the senior puisne judge. As well, a financial crisis caused by his sisters' entitlement to monies from his father's estate, which he had used for a new house, probably sharpened his desire for the greater emoluments of the chief justiceship. In memorials to the Colonial Office he claimed that he had been recommended for the position by four successive lieutenant governors: Sherbrooke, Dalhousie, Sir James KEMPT, and Sir Peregrine MAITLAND. He had carried on the duties of chief justice without extra pay, he pointed out in 1832, for Blowers, "who was an aged man when I went upon the Bench, has never travelled a circuit since my appointment and as his advanced years have long rendered him unable to attend the Courts, I have presided there, for the last ten years."

Contention for the chief justiceship was to enter into the fierce "Brandy Election" of 1830. The main reason for the election was the dispute between the assembly and the Council over the control of taxes [see Enos Collins*]. But the rivalry which developed between Halliburton and Solicitor General Samuel George William Archibald* over the chief justiceship and their constitutional differences in the Council on revenue matters were both major factors. A manifesto published by the Council in 1828, but written by Halliburton, maintained that the Council had the legal right to reject money bills. In January 1831 Maitland intervened in the contest between Halliburton and Archibald when he sent the former to England, ostensibly to object to the reduction of imperial duties on foreign timber imported into Great Britain. Though he would handle other matters of provincial business there, including support for a provincial bill on the incorporation of dissenting congregations, many, such as Judge Lewis Morris Wilkins*, clearly recognized the trip as "a fine opportunity" for Halliburton "to exert his interest to procure the reversion of the Chief Justice's appointment." In Wilkins's estimate, "Halliburton is strong and swift, and may have good bottom, but all must at time yield to superior Judgeship. . . . I wish success to Archibald; he is a mild, gentlemanly man and would make a pleasant Chief, and his legal abilities are quite equal to, if not superior to the other, who I think has a little tyrannical blood in him." As a result of Halliburton's trip, Archibald was forced to launch his own lobby in England. Halliburton's absence from the bench became a matter of some concern when his stay dragged on for months since he refused to return until Archibald did. "We miss [him] very much," William Blowers Bliss*, a Halifax lawyer and MHA, informed his brother Henry*, "and need him at the Court which is filled by ignorance and prejudice and is going to the deuce." By December he was back in Halifax.

During his absence, Halliburton's views on consti-

Halliburton

tutional change apparently altered, the result perhaps of his reaction to Lord John Russell's Reform Bill and of at least one interview with Lord Goderich, the colonial secretary. In 1830, in response to Lieutenant Governor Maitland's request for his opinion on an enlargement of the Council, Halliburton had recommended, in radical fashion, the formation of a separate legislative council and an increase in the number of seats in the assembly. However, writing from London in March 1831 to Simon Bradstreet Robie about the issue of popular representation, notably an elective legislative council, he noted that "there is little danger at present of the hasty adoption of any mischievous measures relative to Nova Scotia. I think they will leave us as we are, or make trifling alterations." A strong tory, one who had experienced the effects of the American and French revolutions, Halliburton distrusted democracy.

On 4 Dec. 1832 Lord Goderich announced that, following the retirement of Blowers, the chief justice was to be Halliburton, "who has for many years discharged the principal part of that office." His commission, dated 13 Jan. 1833, was announced to the Council the following month by the provincial administrator, Thomas Nickleson Jeffery*. The influential *Novascotian*, which was edited by Joseph Howe*, the leader of Nova Scotia's emerging reform movement, reported "great diversity of opinion respecting the propriety of the choice." On the legal side it blamed Halliburton for allowing the bar "to discuss points long since settled, talk against time, and . . . spend whole days in the discussion of causes that ought to be settled in a few minutes." Halliburton's appointment as chief justice brought him directly into the developing dispute over judicial independence. In 1830 Lord Goderich had instructed Maitland not to admit any more puisne judges to the Council, a move which had come out of the growing desire within the assembly to have judges excluded from political bodies. Three years later, when Halliburton received his appointment, the *Novascotian* argued that the chief justiceship "should have been filled . . . from England – by a perfect stranger to our local parties and political contentions – a man trained in the higher tribunals." Further, evidently in reaction to Halliburton's position within the "family compact," it condemned his partisan activities. In its reply to an address by the assembly, however, the Council claimed that the presence of the chief justice in its midst was compatible with British practice. Nevertheless, in 1837 the British government decided that none of the judges in Nova Scotia, including the chief justice, should sit in a restructured council. On 23 Dec. 1837, when Halliburton's withdrawal took effect, members of the Council presented him with an address.

Also of consequence to him during the 1830s was the debate over the transfer of casual revenue to the provincial legislature in return for a permanent civil list, a controversial matter involving the abolition of judicial fees, which had traditionally formed a substantial supplement to the income of the chief justice. In 1839 the Colonial Office directed the lieutenant governor to pay the judges set salaries and abolish fees. Halliburton accepted the proposal, though the resulting financial loss probably exacerbated his difficulties in meeting the expenses of a large family and maintaining his social position in Halifax.

Halliburton owned two estates in Halifax as well as valuable lands in Pictou and in the Annapolis valley. During his rise to prominence as a lawyer and judge, he had taken part in many of Halifax's social and religious organizations, including the Hand-in-Hand Fire Company, the Turf Club, and the Provincial Agricultural Society. A leading Anglican, he was a zealous member of the diocesan Church Society, the Bible Society, and the Sabbath Alliance, and he served as a trustee of the Halifax Grammar School, the National School, and the Royal Acadian Society [see Walter Bromley*]. In 1833, at the request of the colonial under-secretary, Robert William Hay, he helped raise funds in Nova Scotia to purchase the Scottish home of Sir Walter Scott for his heirs.

Though Halliburton was removed from the Council in 1837, he remained active as chief justice. His career in that office, from 1833, was to cover 27 years. Only in 1853 were records and papers of the Supreme Court covering the period 1834–41 collected and edited by James Thomson, so that the documentary record of Halliburton's service is not full. The cases heard by him during the years reported, which included charges of trespassing, breaking and entering, defaulting on promissory notes, and breach of promise of marriage, often necessitated judgements on rules of evidence, marine insurance, and land titles. Though Halliburton presided at Joseph Howe's trial for libel in 1835 and voiced his opinion that the outspoken editor was guilty, Howe described him in 1851 as a "capital judge." According to Halliburton's obituary in the Digby *Acadian*, he was "an industrious and thorough legal student" who "made himself perfectly conversant with every new treatise of value upon law; and he was familiar with the improving practice and accumulating decisions of the English Courts." On occasion he also quoted American legal precedent. In the case of *Lessees of Lawson et al.* v. *Whitman* in 1851, for example, he introduced into Nova Scotia law the American doctrine of constructive possession of land. The defendants cited American authorities for allowing a squatter, for a period of 20 years, entitlement not only to the land he occupied but also to all the land described in the title under which he claimed to hold the land, whether it was occupied by him or not. Halliburton observed, "The situation of lands in this Province resembles that of those in the United States so much more than those old and cultivated lands in the Mother Country that we may frequently consider with advantage the view which their courts have taken of questions of this nature."

During his career as chief justice, Halliburton performed various related judicial functions. In 1851 the legislature appointed him to a commission to study the possible abolition of the Court of Chancery. Partly because they took so long in studying chancery reform in England, the commissioners were unable to agree by the time the commission was to end and in March 1852 they submitted individual reports, followed early the next year by further commentary on British legislation. Charles James Townshend*, a judge on the province's Supreme Court, later wrote that Halliburton's views reflected long experience and thorough acquaintance with the whole subject and were expressed in vigorous and clear language. Halliburton pointed out that, if abolished, the Court of Chancery would have to be re-established, which it was in 1864 as the Court of Equity under Judge James William Johnston*.

Advancing age and infirmity prevented Halliburton from going on circuit during the 1850s but he attended court in Halifax until as late as January 1859. That year Queen Victoria bestowed a knighthood upon him. Though increasing blindness must have caused difficulties, he took it for granted, even in his 85th year, that he would remain chief justice until his death. After enduring a long illness which reduced him "to the proportions of a child," he died on 16 July 1860 and his burial three days later was conducted by Bishop Hibbert Binney*. Halliburton was succeeded as chief justice by William Young*.

PHYLLIS R. BLAKELEY

Sir Brenton Halliburton published a number of pamphlets anonymously during his lifetime, including *Observations upon the importance of the North American colonies to Great Britain, by an old inhabitant of British America* (Halifax, [1825]), another edition of which, entitled *Observations on the importance of the North American colonies . . .* , was published in London in 1831; *Report of Mr. Bull's jury, ex-officio, on the late conduct of his servants, in a certain public establishment* ([Halifax], 1829), a copy of which is available at PANS; and *Reflections on passing events; written prior to the termination of the late war with Russia, by an octogenarian* (Halifax, 1856). The last of these is included in a collection of three works published after his death in two private editions: the first, *John Bull and his calves (written previous to the Canadian rebellion); Addressed to Louisa Collins, who died at Margaretville, 16th of Oct., 1834, aged 1 year and 5 months; Reflections on passing events,* appeared as an appendix to G. W. Hill*'s biographical *Memoir of Sir Brenton Halliburton, late chief justice of the province of Nova Scotia* (Halifax, 1864), and the second, *John Bull and his calves; Address to a mother, on*

the death of a young child; and Reflections on passing events, was published separately. Neither edition of *John Bull* bears a date or place of publication, but they were most likely also published in Halifax in 1864. Hill's *Memoir* also appears in two editions, alike except that one includes the *John Bull* pamphlet as a separately paged appendix, while the other does not. In addition, some of Halliburton's writings appear within the *Memoir* itself, including a republication of the *Observations on the importance of the North American colonies* on pages 121–43, and a satirical essay, "Critical state of the Bull family," on pages 143–57.

A full-length oil portrait of Halliburton, painted in 1820 by Albert Gallatin Hoit, hangs in the courtroom of the Nova Scotia Supreme Court in Halifax.

Halifax County Court of Probate (Halifax), Estate papers, no.926 (mfm. at PANS). Newport Hist. Soc. (Newport, R.I.), Trinity Church, reg. of baptisms, 27 Dec. 1774. PANS, MG 1, 226, nos.31–32, 37, 40, 42, 44, 48–49; 334; 805, no.10: 24; 979–80; 1490, no.3; 1596, 1598–99; RG 1, 173: 402; 293, doc.110; 304, no.91; RG 5, A, 15, 16 Dec. 1808; P, 69, 1828, 1830; RG 8, 1, no.2; RG 39, J, 14–16, 39, 120, 122, 131; M, 45. PRO, CO 217/149: 168–77; 217/153: 471–72; 217/154: 397–401. Joseph Howe, *The speeches and public letters of Joseph Howe . . .* , ed. J. A. Chisholm (2v., Halifax, 1909). *Letters and papers of Hon. Enos Collins*, ed. and intro. C. B. Fergusson (Halifax, 1959), 14–16, 23–34. N.S., Supreme Court, *Law reports: containing decisions . . . between 1834 and 1841* (Halifax, 1853). PANS, *Report of the Board of Trustees* (Halifax), 1955: 18. Ramsay, *Dalhousie journals* (Whitelaw), 1: 54, 66, 104–5, 111, 166–71, 188–89, 191–95.

Acadian (Digby, N.S.), 24 July 1860 (copy in PANS, MG 1, 334, no.98). *Acadian Recorder*, 24 June 1826, 20 Feb. 1830. *British Colonist* (Halifax), 17 July 1860. *Colonial Patriot* (Pictou, N.S.), 20 Aug. 1833. *Liverpool Transcript* (Liverpool, N.S.), 9 June 1859. *Novascotian*, 13 July 1826; 14–15 April 1830; 7, 21 Feb., 4 March 1833; 10 Jan. 1848. Beck, *Government of N.S.* Brian Cuthbertson, *The old attorney general: a biography of Richard John Uniacke* (Halifax, [1980]). Judith Fingard, *The Anglican design in loyalist Nova Scotia, 1783–1816* (London, 1972). S. W. Spavold, "Nova Scotia under the administration of Sir Colin Campbell" (MA thesis, Dalhousie Univ., Halifax, 1953). *The Supreme Court of Nova Scotia and its judges, 1754–1978* (n.p., n.d.). C. J. Townshend, "Historical account of the courts of judicature in Nova Scotia," *History of the Court of Chancery in Nova Scotia* (Toronto, 1900), 3–60. A. W. H. Eaton, "Bishop Charles Inglis and his descendants," *Acadiensis* (Saint John, N.B.), 8 (1908): 191–94, and "Correction," 335. Peter Lynch, "Early reminiscences of Halifax – men who have passed from us," N.S. Hist. Soc., *Coll.*, 16 (1912): 196–97. Norah Story, "The church and state 'party' in Nova Scotia, 1749–1851," N.S. Hist. Soc., *Coll.*, 27 (1947): 33–57.

HAMILTON, ROBERT DOUGLAS, physician, author, and militia officer; b. 16 Jan. 1783 at Muirhead, in the parish of Dalserf, Scotland, son of John Hamilton and Isabella Torrance; d. 2 April 1857 in Scarborough Township, Upper Canada.

The son of a stonemason turned farmer, Robert Douglas Hamilton attended schools at Lesmahagow

Hamilton

and Stonehouse (Strathclyde) and later received a "classical and philosophical education" at the universities of Glasgow and Edinburgh without obtaining a degree from either institution. From 1805 to 1808 he took medical courses, including military surgery, at the University of Edinburgh. Between April 1808 and November 1809 he served as assistant surgeon on the naval hospital ship *Tromp*, stationed at Falmouth, England. He subsequently practised medicine at nearby St Mawes. In 1812, during the Peninsular War, Hamilton returned to military service as an army staff surgeon in Spain and Portugal. After the war he settled in Scotland at Lesmahagow.

Hamilton immigrated to the United States in 1827 and continued his practice at New York City and at Hunter, N.Y. Three years later he moved to Scarborough Township, near York (Toronto), Upper Canada. Hamilton was Scarborough's first resident physician and he gradually attracted a wide clientele. Reputedly he did not own a horse and had to be called for and returned home when his services were needed. Although Hamilton was a member of the Medical Board of Upper Canada (1838–39) and the College of Physicians and Surgeons of Upper Canada (1839–40), he attended few meetings of either body.

Hamilton was an accomplished writer on both medical and political topics. His chief medical work, *The principles of medicine*, appeared in London in 1822. In this textbook on fevers and inflammatory diseases Hamilton expounded a mechanistic view of biology and discarded contrary views with the emphatic and ironic eloquence that can also be recognized in his political writings. He was a conservative practitioner, opposed to the use of obstetrical forceps and convinced of the usefulness of heavy bleeding to relieve a wide variety of disorders.

Hamilton's conservatism in medicine carried over to his political views as expressed in the letters and articles he wrote for local newspapers and periodicals under the pseudonym of Guy Pollock, the name of a Scarborough blacksmith. In 1832, aggravated by growing reform agitation in the province, Hamilton sought to demonstrate in the *Courier of Upper Canada*, a strong tory journal, "that the people of Upper Canada, instead of complaining of grievances, have more abundant causes for being satisfied with the government under which they live, than any other people on the face of the earth." He came to public notice most prominently through letters published in the Toronto *Palladium* in 1838, in the aftermath of the rebellion of 1837. Plunder was the chief motive behind the rebellion, he claimed, and no one spoke of reform in Upper Canada "without harboring a lurking wish for a revolution." Coupled with this reactionary fervour was a contempt for the United States which prompted Hamilton to characterize Americans as cowardly braggarts. In 1836 he had served as

lieutenant-colonel of the 3rd Regiment of East York militia and he may have accompanied the militiamen who marched from Scarborough to Toronto on 5 Dec. 1837. Hamilton's political interests, which included support for an established church, led him in 1839 to contest, unsuccessfully, the provincial by-election held in 3rd York riding, when the sitting member, Thomas David MORRISON, was unseated for his part in the rebellion.

The wide variety of literary works published by Hamilton in Britain and Upper Canada also attracted attention. A diligent search has so far failed to turn up copies of the novel, poetry, and essays reported by British contemporaries, nor have his voluminous unpublished writings come to light. In Upper Canada, Hamilton, along with such other British-trained littérateurs as William Dunlop* and Susanna Moodie [Strickland*], contributed to the short-lived *Canadian Literary Magazine*, launched in 1833 by George Gurnett*. Hamilton was a founder and first president (1834) of the Scarborough Subscription Library. The *British American Journal of Medical and Physical Science* regarded him in 1847 as "one of the few literary men which Canada possessed." His writings were marked, in the later opinion of the Reverend Henry Scadding*, "by an elevation of thought and culture beyond the ordinary, and by a good style."

Hamilton apparently retired from medical practice before 1852, "after a long career of active exertion and professional usefulness," and returned to Scotland. He did not remain, for the "beloved physician" died in Scarborough "after a painful and lingering illness." He was buried there in the cemetery of St Andrew's Presbyterian Church. "Rather eccentric and quite self-independent," Hamilton had never married.

CHARLES G. ROLAND

Robert Douglas Hamilton is the author of *The principles of medicine, on the plan of the Baconian philosophy; volume first: on febrile and inflammatory diseases* (London, 1822). Under the pseudonym of Guy Pollock he published numerous articles and letters, including: "A chapter on craniology" and "A description of the falls of Niagara written for the information of a friend in England, during the month of August, 1830" in *Canadian Literary Magazine* (York [Toronto]), 1 (1833): 101–4 and 24–31 respectively; "Preservation of potatoes from winter frost," *Canadian Emigrant, and Western District Commercial and General Advertiser* (Sandwich [Windsor, Ont.]), 3 Nov. 1835; "War with the United States," "Nature of political liberty," and "Nature of political grievances" in *Palladium of British America and Upper Canada Mercantile Advertiser* (Toronto), 24 Jan., 7 Feb., and 7 March 1838; and "Mr. George's sermon, preached on the late Thanksgiving Day," *British Colonist* (Toronto), 26 July 1838.

AO, RG 22, ser.155, will of R. D. Hamilton. PAC, MG 29, D61, 10: 3652–56. Sarnia Public Library (Sarnia, Ont.), Henry Jones diaries, 25 April 1839. *British American*

Journal of Medical and Physical Science (Montreal), 3 (1847–48): 222. *Upper Canada Journal of Medical, Surgical and Physical Science* (Toronto), 1 (1851–52): 60. *Courier of Upper Canada* (York), 29 Feb. 1832. *Palladium of British America and Upper Canada Mercantile Advertiser*, 4 April 1838. G. C. Boase and W. P. Courtney, *Bibliotheca Cornubiensis . . .* (3v., London, 1874–82), 3: 1215. Morgan, *Bibliotheca Canadensis*, 174–75. Canniff, *Medical profession in U.C.*, 107, 113, 126, 139, 409–10. T. B. Higginson, "*Scarborough Fair," part II* (Scarborough [Toronto], 1979), 2–3, 5. *A history of Scarborough*, ed. R. R. Bonis ([2nd ed.], Scarborough, 1968), 104, 119–20. *History of Toronto and county of York, Ontario . . .* (2v., Toronto, 1885), 1: 112. *The township of Scarboro, 1796–1896*, ed. David Boyle (Toronto, 1896), 206–8, 233. T. B. Higginson, "Dr. Robert Douglas Hamilton, 'the beloved physician,'" *Scarborough Hist. Notes & Comments* (Scarborough), 1 (1976–77), no.1: 2–4. Henry Scadding, "Some Canadian noms-de-plume identified: with samples of the writings to which they are appended," *Canadian Journal* (Toronto), new ser., 15 (1876–78): 263–64. J. J. Talman, "The newspapers of Upper Canada a century ago," *CHR*, 19 (1938): 19–20.

HANNA, JAMES GODFREY, silversmith, businessman, militia officer, and seigneur; baptized 9 Nov. 1788 at Quebec, son of James G. Hanna* and Elizabeth Saul; m. 25 Oct. 1812 Margaret Roberts Eckart, and they had four daughters; d. 19 Dec. 1851 in the seigneury of Saint-Charles-de-la-Belle-Alliance, Lower Canada.

James Godfrey Hanna's father arrived at Quebec from Dublin about 1763 and two years later had established himself as a clockmaker, watchmaker, silversmith, and merchant at "the sign of the Eagle and Watch," 15 Rue de la Fabrique. There he trained James Godfrey to follow him as a craftsman and merchant, and in 1803 he took his son into partnership, gradually withdrawing from the business himself. After his death in 1807, James Godfrey continued the business along the lines established by his father. From England he imported jewellery, cutlery, plated ware, Britannia metal, clocks and watches, fishing tackle, pistols, money scales, and a wide variety of fashionable goods, as well as some general merchandise on consignment. In addition, he produced objects in gold and silver, repaired clocks and watches, and purchased gold, silver, and copper.

Hanna developed an active interest in community affairs. He was commissioned lieutenant in the Île d'Orléans battalion of militia and during the War of 1812 served as adjutant-major under Lieutenant-Colonel Jacques Voyer*. In April 1813 he was elected to the committee of the Quebec Fire Society and in the same month was a subscriber to the Loyal and Patriotic Society of the Province of Lower Canada.

By 1815 Hanna's business was prosperous enough for him to advertise, although apparently without success, for two apprentices to the silversmith's trade.

The following year he operated a second shop at 16 Rue de la Montagne. He also entered into partnership with Quebec silversmith François Delagrave, perhaps in order to have someone who could assist him in managing two stores but also to enable him to devote more time to other business interests. Hanna owned property in Trois-Rivières, Rivière-du-Loup, and Kamouraska. In 1816–17 he began to buy and sell real estate at Quebec in the *faubourg* Saint-Roch and on Rue Saint-Jean, but he does not seem to have made substantial profits from the transactions. In addition, he owned a quarry on Rue Saint-Jean which he leased in 1817. Hanna also began to develop the seigneury of Saint-Charles-de-la-Belle-Alliance in the Beauce region, which his wife had inherited from her father. In 1817 he purchased 3,000 acres in the area, probably near his wife's property, and in the same year he announced his intention of petitioning the House of Assembly for permission to build a toll-bridge over the Rivière Famine in the parish of Saint-François (at Beauceville).

Hanna's partnership with Delagrave and other plans were abandoned early in 1818 when he went bankrupt. In February, Louis Gauvreau*, John Reinhart, and Anthony Anderson were elected trustees and they asked for payment of all debts owing to Hanna, whose bankruptcy seems to have been a personal one. Hanna's stock was sold by the sheriff on 4 May. Later that month the *Quebec Gazette* announced the September sale by public auction of some of his properties, including a two-storey and a three-storey house on Rue de la Fabrique; two additional lots, both with houses; land in the Lower Town on Rue de la Montagne; and two plots of land in the *faubourg* Saint-Roch. All were to be sold at the suit of Samuel Dumas, a Montreal merchant from whom Hanna had borrowed £1,100 early in 1816. On 23 Dec. 1819 the sheriff advertised the imminent sale of two more properties owned by Hanna, in Kamouraska and in the seigneury of Rivière-du-Loup, this time to satisfy the claims of Kamouraska merchant Jean-Baptiste Chamberland. There were no further seizures and public sales of Hanna's property, but his bankruptcy had brought to an end the family's association of more than 50 years with the silversmith-merchant trade of Quebec. Among the few remaining pieces identified as being his work, either alone or in partnership with Delagrave, are a snuff-box, soup-spoons, serving spoons, and a skewer.

Hanna probably left Quebec soon after his bankruptcy. He settled on his wife's property in the Beauce where he attempted to live the life of a seigneur. He is said to have brought numerous settlers from England or northern Ireland around 1820 to colonize the seigneury. The venture was an expensive one and hardly profitable since many of the settlers moved on to other areas. By 1825, however,

Harding

approximately 25 families of northern Irish origin had settled in the region and were manufacturing cloth and sewing thread. In that year they sold 700 yards of high-quality linen on the Quebec market and expected to produce 1,500 yards the following year. Little else is known of the seigneury or of Hanna's life at Saint-Charles-de-la-Belle-Alliance. He appears to have stayed there until his death in 1851.

JOHN E. LANGDON

ANQ-M, CN1-353, 28 juin 1849. ANQ-Q, CE1-61, 25 oct. 1812, 3 oct. 1813, 31 août 1817, 19 sept. 1819; CE1-66, 9 nov. 1788; CN1-49, 25 févr. 1814; 10, 21 juin, 8, 31 oct. 1817; CN1-230, 26 mai 1812; 10, 26 janv., 13 mai 1816; 16 janv., 10 févr. 1817; CN1-262, 28 janv., 3–4, 23, 25–26, 30 avril 1817. MAC-CD, Fonds Morisset, 2, H243/J27.5/2; H243.1/J27.5/2. *Quebec Gazette*, 5 July 1764; 19 Feb. 1807; 6 July 1809; 5, 29 April 1813; 27 Nov. 1817; 19 Feb., 30 April, 21 May 1818; 15 June, 23 Dec. 1819; 1 Aug. 1825; 31 Dec. 1851. *Quebec Mercury*, November 1815–August 1816. *Quebec Telegraph*, 21 May 1816. *Officers of British forces in Canada* (Irving). P.-G. Roy, *Inv. concessions*, 5: 22–23. Philippe Angers, *Les seigneurs et premiers censitaires de St-Georges-Beauce et la famille Pozer* (Beauceville, Qué., 1927). J. E. Langdon, *Canadian silversmiths, 1700–1900* (Toronto, 1966), 81. J.-E. Roy, *Hist. de Lauzon*, 5: 63–64. P.-G. Roy, *Toutes petites choses du Régime anglais*, 2: 92–93.

HARDING, HARRIS, educator and Baptist minister; b. 10 Oct. 1761 in Horton, N.S., son of Israel Harding and Sarah Harris; d. 7 March 1854 in Yarmouth, N.S.

Although born in Nova Scotia in the early years of New England planter settlement of the province, young Harris Harding returned to Connecticut in the 1770s with his parents, among the many who decided that "Nova Scarcity" was not as attractive as they had been led to believe. According to John Davis*, his later associate and biographer, Harding served during the American revolution on a rebel boat conveying goods from New York to Boston, and on one occasion was held briefly by the British as a suspected spy. Whatever the truth of such stories, Harding returned to Horton in 1783 with his father, who received a land grant from the British government. His years in Connecticut meant that Harris had received a better education than most of his later Baptist colleagues, and he kept school in Cornwallis for several years after his return.

Since his parents were Anglicans, it is not surprising that Harding was drawn to the Methodists (who claimed to be reforming the Church of England); he later remarked that they taught him to "*work hard for salvation instead of believing heartily for it.*" Finally converted around 1786 by the New Light preacher John Payzant* in a highly emotional

experience, Harding soon after began exhorting and preaching in Kings and Hants counties. From 1790 he used Liverpool as a base for preaching forays to such places as Yarmouth and Shelburne (where he spoke in David George*'s chapel). On 16 Sept. 1794 he was ordained by Joseph Dimock* to an "open communion" church (of paedobaptists and antipaedobaptists) at Onslow. Joseph CRANDALL experienced his emotional conversion the following July in a private house in Chester in which Harding and Dimock were preaching. Gradually in the mid 1790s Harding began to spend increasing amounts of time in Yarmouth, where he had helped to organize a church in 1790. In May 1797 his church at Onslow sent a letter calling him home, but he decided to remain in Yarmouth as pastor at a small meeting-house near the hamlet of The Mills (Milton). Scandal had touched his life the previous year when, after publicly confessing to having impregnated Mehitable Harrington of Liverpool, he married her on 28 September, six weeks before their child was born. When Harding preached a sermon in Liverpool in 1797, Simeon Perkins* noted: "I think it not too much to the Honor of the Town to allow a man of His Character & principles to preach in a publick Meeting House."

At the first general meeting of New Lights and Baptists in Cornwallis in June 1798, Harding was charged with "new dispensationism," which denied the necessity of structured churches with formal rules and stressed the direct relationship between God and mankind [*see* Edward MANNING]. At this time he acknowledged his faults and confessed his errors and was admitted to the association. Baptized himself by James Manning on 28 Aug. 1799, Harding, like most of his fellow evangelical ministers in the Maritimes, had been brought to believer's baptism by immersion by the end of the 18th century but, although his church moved to the same position in 1806, it continued to allow occasional communion to paedobaptists. As the Baptists gradually took over the association, which became the Nova Scotia Baptist Association in 1800, they began moving to exclude the older "open communion" churches from their ranks. The final break came in 1809, when, almost immediately upon Harding's completion of the opening sermon, the association voted "to withdraw fellowship from all the churches who admit unbaptised persons to what is called occasional communion and consider themselves a regular close communion Baptist Association." The Yarmouth church at once withdrew from the association, and did not return for almost 20 years.

Although he gradually became more sedentary and travelled less on the revival trail, Harding had the satisfaction of stirring several major awakenings within his own community. The first and most impressive had come in 1806, when 150 new converts were made and most of his congregation were baptized by immersion. Another less intense revival occurred in 1812–13, and they happened sporadically throughout Harding's pastorate of nearly 60 years.

Harding and his church went through a number of bad times as well as good ones. He lost ground to the Methodists under the Reverend Robert Alder* around 1816 and, in his last years, there was much trouble with associate pastors, such as Davis, who were intended to aid the aged minister. Like most of the pioneer evangelicals in the Maritimes, Harding eschewed a fixed stipend, insisting "I do not wish to be a hireling." As a result he and his family frequently suffered from extreme poverty.

Although not a great pulpit preacher, Harding was an effective one, offering extemporaneous sermons richly studded with biblical citations. As Davis observed: "Mr Harding kept no journal. He wrote few letters. His labours from year to year and from one season of revival to another, were marked by but few varieties. The recollections of survivors are but vague and indistinct." Unlike many of his colleagues, however, Harding was good at pastoral work and visitation. Much of his most effective work was done on such occasions. As Harding grew older he became extremely portly, so that "his length and breadth seemed to be so nearly equal as to suggest ideas of the square and cubical." Instead of turning him into a comical figure, however, his size and gravity made him extremely impressive and he was one of the beloved figures of his denomination.

J. M. BUMSTED

Simeon Perkins, *The diary of Simeon Perkins, 1790–1796* and *1797–1803*, ed. C. B. Fergusson (Toronto, 1961 and 1967). Bill, *Fifty years with Baptist ministers*. John Davis, *The patriarch of western Nova Scotia: life and times of the late Rev. Harris Harding, Yarmouth, N.S.*, intro. J. W. Nutting (Charlottetown, 1866). Levy, *Baptists of Maritime prov.*, 70–71. G. A. Rawlyk, "From Newlight to Baptist: Harris Harding and the second great awakening in Nova Scotia," *Repent and believe: the Baptist experience in Maritime Canada*, ed. B. M. Moody (Hantsport, N.S., 1980), 1–26.

HARDING, THOMAS, tanner, politician, and justice of the peace; b. *c.* 1786 in Saint John, N.B., fifth son of Captain William Harding and Leah ——; m. 15 Oct. 1808 Mary Johnson, and they had seven sons, two of whom became doctors, and four daughters; d. 7 April 1854 in Saint John.

Thomas Harding's father, a loyalist, arrived in Parrtown (Saint John) in 1783 and became a respected sea captain in the city's merchant marine. As a young man, Thomas was apprenticed to a Saint John tanner, and enrolled as a freeman tanner of the city in 1808. He subsequently established his own tannery, which he operated until mid century. Although he owned the largest tannery in the city, and by the early 1840s was employing steam engines in his enterprise, the firm remained a craft-oriented operation. In the late 1840s he most probably had a dozen journeymen and apprentices, including his second son, Thomas.

Harding was one of a small group of religious evangelicals, mostly from non-conformist traditions, who came to dominate the civic life of mid-19th-century Saint John. In 1805 his younger brother, George, had brought Edward MANNING to Saint John, the first white Baptist preacher to visit the town [*see* David George*]. As a result of the services he held, several members of the Harding family were converted to his New Light–Baptist faith. The rest of the family (including Thomas) were baptized a short time later by another Baptist visitor, Joseph CRANDALL. Thomas became not only a leading Baptist layman, in a community in which Baptists were a scorned minority into the 1840s, but also a prominent supporter of more broadly based evangelical organizations such as the British and Foreign Bible Society and the Saint John Total Abstinence Society.

Another factor which shaped the perceptions of the young Harding was the district of the city in which he lived. Dukes and Sydney wards comprised the southern half of the main peninsula of Saint John. Its centre was the Lower Cove, inhabited by tradesmen, labourers, and soldiers, an area which had provided the popular opposition to the pretensions of the loyalist aristocracy in the famous contested election of 1785 [*see* Elias Hardy*].

Harding's initiation into public life came with his election as assistant alderman for Dukes Ward in 1815. He was returned to that office the following year and in 1817 successfully contested the aldermanic seat. Between 1817 and 1851 he was elected alderman 30 times, in most cases by acclamation. In an age of tumultuous open elections and sometimes violent civic politics, Harding proved himself to be a successful political campaigner. In 1851 the lieutenant governor, Sir Edmund Walker Head*, agreed to surrender to the Common Council his prerogative of naming the city's mayor, and Harding was unanimously elected to that office by the Saint John council. In his acceptance speech, he announced that he planned to serve for only one term. He retired from public life in 1852.

As one of the city's six aldermen, Harding held a commission as a justice of the peace and sat as a magistrate on both the Inferior Court of Common Pleas and the county Court of Quarter Sessions. As a function of their civic and judicial offices, the aldermen also controlled the appointment of most parish officers in the city and county. In addition, through the committees of council, the aldermen personally directed virtually every aspect of municipal life, frequently negotiating agreements and contracts, supervising the construction of public works, and employing both casual and contract labour. Harding's seniority after 1830 gave him a place on the principal committees, notably those concerned with finance and public safety.

Harding spoke for the tradocracy (tradesmen and retailers) and the religious dissenters, two influential but unprivileged groups in Saint John society. His responses to a number of issues which accompanied the urban expansion of the 1830s and 1840s provide an insight into the perception of the imperial system held by this middling, second generation, religious dissenter of colonial American origins. Harding was convinced that the constitutional settlement made in the royal charter granted to Saint John in 1785 provided the commonalty of the city with the best possible government. On any issue involving the prerogative rights of the Common Council, he remained a stalwart defender of the council's position. Most of his other political positions flowed from this one. He particularly feared the centralizing tendencies of the lieutenant governor and the Executive Council, the pretensions of the official elements, and the demands of the great commercial interests for the protection which broader executive powers and stronger provincial institutions could provide. These prejudices led him both to oppose the efforts of Saint John's leading timber interests to obtain control of the city's largest potential power source, and to resist strongly the bid by John Robertson*, one of the province's major merchants, to obtain long-term leases at unusually low rents on a substantial part of the city's land bordering the harbour.

The principal struggle of Harding's career followed the great fire of 19 Aug. 1839 when the provincial legislature, at the instigation of Lieutenant Governor Sir John HARVEY, passed a bill to widen the streets through the burnt-out district. The cost of expropriating the required land from the city's largest landowners was to be borne by the citizenry at large. Led by Harding and Gregory Van Horne, a group of councillors met this challenge to the city's autonomy with a petition to the crown. They were opposed in their resolve by the mayor, Robert Fraser Hazen, and the city recorder, William Boyd Kinnear*, both crown appointees. In the ensuing struggle the dissidents, who were a majority on the council, took control over the mayor's objections, put their resolution through, and went on to attack the recorder for his support of Harvey's position. At the height of the debate, Harding placed his right arm on the council table and declared his willingness to cut it off before surrendering any of the city's prerogative rights. An irate Harvey at first berated the aldermen, and then agreed to forward their petition to London accompanied by his objections. The British government subsequently overturned the provincial legislation.

It is not surprising that Harding opposed any attempt to modify the city charter despite the changing urban conditions of the mid 19th century. Most of the proposed changes involved efforts on the part of the provincial government and the city's merchant community to restrict the franchise, increase the property qualifications for the office of alderman, and create a permanent civil service to replace the tradition of public administrators who volunteered or were co-opted in return for fees. Harding was also a leading opponent of the efforts made by the House of Assembly to deprive the Common Council of its judicial authority through the creation of a stipendiary magistracy responsible for the administration of justice and the maintenance of order within the city [see Benjamin Lester PETERS].

Harding's position on these issues led both tories and advanced reformers to view him as a parochial figure concerned only with ward politics and with the influence which derived from his aldermanic position. Inevitably, his concerns focused on his ward where his political authority rested on a complex system of formal and informal patronage which had developed over the years. But much of this criticism emerged from his willingness to use public money to meet human needs in the city and from his tendency to accept the wishes of the "mob." In periods of economic recession, for example, Harding was always willing to use large numbers of unemployed labourers for public works. In the main he was an able and effective civic leader. He was involved with committee meetings, the supervision of public works of all kinds, the negotiation of contracts, dealing with miscreants, personal supervision of police, and fortnightly court sittings, and to these civic duties he devoted hundreds of hours every year.

T. W. ACHESON

[There are no secondary sources dealing with Thomas Harding apart from brief references to his mayoralty found in several studies of the city of Saint John, N.B. The best sources for his activities are the minutes and supporting papers of the Common Council of Saint John; the former are found in the City Clerk's Office, the latter in PANB, RG 18, RS427. Of particular value are the minutes for 15 Nov. 1836; 14 Oct., 7, 21 Nov. 1839; 9 Feb., 3 Oct. 1843; 10 Jan. 1844; 26 Feb. 1845; 19 May 1847; and 29 Jan. 1849. T.W.A.]

Morning News (Saint John), 10 April 1854. *New-Brunswick Courier*, 10 May 1851. *Saint John Chronicle and Colonial Conservative*, 14 April 1854. *Biographical review: this volume contains biographical sketches of leading citizens of the province of New Brunswick*, ed. I. A. Jack (Boston, 1900), 112–14. I. E. Bill, *The Baptists of Saint John, N.B.; two sermons on the rise and progress of the Baptist church in Saint John, New Brunswick* (Saint John, 1863), 5. MacNutt, *New Brunswick*.

HARGRAVE, LETITIA. *See* MACTAVISH

HARPER, CHARLES, teacher, Roman Catholic priest, and seminary administrator; b. 7 Jan. 1800 in Sainte-Foy, Lower Canada, son of Lewis Harper and Charlotte Bleau (Blaut); d. 7 April 1855 in Nicolet, Lower Canada.

Charles Harper was the fifth in a family of nine children. His childhood and youth were influenced by the good example of his father, the most upright of men, and the edifying conduct of his deeply religious mother. At an early age Charles gave signs of superior intelligence, and his parents spared no effort to get him an education that would enable him to earn his own living despite the handicap of a club foot. As a pupil he lived up to their expectations, being remarkably successful at the school run by the Reverend Daniel WILKIE at Quebec. In 1815 the *Quebec Gazette* announced that Harper had taken first prize in Latin, English grammar, French, bookkeeping, algebra, and geography.

On 30 April 1818 Harper obtained from the government the post of "Schoolmaster at the free school of the Royal Institution [for the Advancement of Learning] established at Cap Santé," which had recently been set up at the request of the villagers. He taught reading, writing, and arithmetic to about 36 pupils in both English and French, for an annual salary of £45. He seems to have carried out his duties satisfactorily, since his appointment was renewed regularly until 30 April 1822, when he gave up his post.

Harper then entered the Séminaire de Nicolet, where from 1822 to 1824 he completed his classical and philosophical studies. From 1824 to 1828 he took his theology, and at the same time taught the students of the seminary. He was ordained priest on 7 Sept. 1828, becoming the second in his family to choose the priesthood: his brother Jean had been ordained in 1824, and another, Jacques, would be ordained in 1835.

Harper's career as a priest was spent at the Séminaire de Nicolet. Things might have turned out quite differently, however, for in 1831 Bishop Joseph-Norbert PROVENCHER was eager to have him come to the Red River settlement (Man.) as a teacher. Despite the bishop's repeated efforts Harper remained at Nicolet.

As bursar and procurator of the seminary from 1828 to 1853 (except for the years 1836–40 when he taught theology), Harper won and retained the confidence of Bishop Joseph Signay*, who relied upon him in all matters related to the seminary's administration. Among other tasks, Harper had to supervise the construction of a larger building, begun in 1828. In performing his duties as bursar and procurator Harper was often, rightly or wrongly, subjected to complaints and criticism, especially about food and heating. However, thanks to his tenacity, administrative abilities, and faith in the future, he managed on various occasions to save the seminary, whether from ruin, a transfer to Trois-Rivières, or sale to the government.

The history of the Séminaire de Nicolet bears testimony to the services rendered by Charles Harper, and identifies him as a benefactor. To recognize his merit and to reward him, the seminary's board of trustees in 1853 bestowed upon him the office of superior. But Harper did not hold this position long, for he died in 1855.

WILFRID BERGERON

ANQ-MBF, CE1-30, 10 avril 1855. ANQ-Q, CE1-20, 8 janv. 1800. ASN, AO, Polygraphie, IV, nos.69–148; Séminaire, IV, nos.36–53. *Quebec Gazette*, 24 Aug., 22 Dec. 1815; 18 May 1818. Allaire, *Dictionnaire*, 1: 265. L.-P. Audet, *Le système scolaire*, vols.3–4. Douville, *Hist. du collège-séminaire de Nicolet*, 1: 405–9; 2. Claude Lessard, *Le séminaire de Nicolet, 1803–1969* (Trois-Rivières, Qué., 1980). Lucien Brault, "Charles Harper, maître d'école au Cap Santé," *BRH*, 43 (1937): 31–32. Raymond Douville, "Les trois abbés Harper," *Cahiers des Dix*, 13 (1948): 143–57. Yvon Thériault, "Histoire de trois célèbres Écossais de la région," *Le Nouvelliste* (Trois-Rivières), 26 août 1950: 11.

HART, AARON EZEKIEL, lawyer, militia officer, and office holder; b. 24 June 1803 in Trois-Rivières, Lower Canada, son of Ezekiel Hart* and Frances Lazarus; m. 1 Nov. 1849 his cousin Phoebe David, daughter of Samuel David and Sarah Hart, and they are thought to have had four children; d. 26 Sept. 1857.

The record shows that, at the age of 21, "Aaron Ezekiel Hart of the City of Quebec, Esquire, hath passed his Trials and was found to be qualified to the practice and profession of the Law as Advocate, Barrister, Attorney, Solicitor, Proctor and Counsel in all His Majesty's Courts of Justice in Lower Canada, according to the certificate signed by the Lieutenant-Governor on November 6, 1824." Hart was thus the first Jew to be called to the bar in either of the Canadas. His singular position was short-lived, however, since the following month a distant cousin, Thomas Storrs Judah (1804–95), was similarly called, as was Thomas's brother Henry Hague Judah (1808–83) four years later. His cousin Aaron Philip Hart, son of Benjamin HART, was admitted to the profession in 1830, his future brothers-in-law Eleazar David David* in 1832 and Moses Samuel David in 1837, and his own brother Adolphus Mordecai Hart* in 1836.

All of these men were of comparable merit, but Aaron Ezekiel had the advantage of being the first. His biography affords the opportunity for some description of this group of lawyers, who were all third-generation Canadian Jews. Aaron Ezekiel began

Hart

to familiarize himself with both business and the practice of law when he entered the service of his uncle Moses HART in 1824. He first filed claims against some *censitaires* of the seigneury of Bélair, and then from 1825 to 1833 frequently worked as counsel for Moses Hart in court. In 1832 he asked his uncle's advice, "having it in contemplation to get up a Life Assurance Company [at Trois-Rivières] upon the principle of a joint stock company." There is no indication that this plan was carried out.

Concurrently with his legal career, Hart was interested in the army. On 21 Dec. 1826 he became an ensign in Quebec's 3rd Militia Battalion; he was made a lieutenant in the 2nd Battalion of Quebec County militia on 17 March 1831, and then captain on 4 June. Finally, on 1 April 1857 he was appointed major of the 1st Battalion of Saint-Maurice militia. The American Jewish Historical Society has a record of his admission to the Société pour l'Encouragement des Sciences et des Arts en Canada on 14 June 1827 and to the Literary and Historical Society of Quebec on 17 March 1831.

Hart was evidently quite a prominent lawyer at Quebec. Archivist David Rome considers it "a measure of Aaron Ezekiel Hart's acceptance into Quebec Society" that in 1836 he transmitted the challenge to a duel from Clément-Charles Sabrevois* de Bleury, a member of the House of Assembly for Richelieu, to Charles-Ovide Perrault*, the young member for Vaudreuil, who would lose his life the following year at the battle of Saint-Denis on the Richelieu.

Hart took great interest in the political struggles of the 1830s. With his brother Samuel Becancour he played a major role, particularly as legal adviser, in the effort to get a bill "to declare persons professing the Jewish Religion entitled to all the rights and privileges of the other Subjects of His Majesty in this Province" passed during the 1831–32 session. But this act was to give rise to varying interpretations. Thus in a letter dated 31 May 1833 Aaron Philip Hart advised his father and Moses Judah Hayes* to decline the office of justice of the peace, on grounds that there might be ambiguities about taking the oath of abjuration. Those who had had faith in this law felt somewhat foolish, particularly Samuel Becancour Hart, a new justice of the peace, who had taken his oath privately before notary Joseph Badeaux*. To clarify the situation, the assembly decided to set up a special committee under René-Joseph Kimber* to study the rights of Jews in Lower Canada.

Aaron Ezekiel presented his testimony in February 1834 with vigour and self-assurance. After replying to some questions, he read a statement which he had carefully prepared. In his view the law passed in 1724 (10 George I, c.4) had guaranteed the Jews equal rights, since it provided that the litigious words " 'upon the true faith of a Christian' should be omitted whenever a person professing the Jewish Religion presents himself to take the oath of abjuration." Even if it were demonstrated that this statute had lapsed, "there is not one legal enactment," he stated, "which excepts Jews from holding office in this Country" including the 1740 law on naturalization. In his opinion this law had been "improperly construed, and incorrectly comprehended," not, however, by "the Law Officers of the Crown," but "by a young man who has scarcely been admitted but two years to the practice of the Law, and who is far from being celebrated for the consistency of his opinions, and for the solidity of his judgment." The reference was evidently to Aaron Philip Hart, whom in his argument Aaron Ezekiel expressly criticized for seeking to restrict to naturalization a law which was of more general intent, and which contained the same terms as the 1724 law on the oath of abjuration. Aaron Philip's error, he explained, was that he did not read the law of 1740 in its entirety but confined himself to the title. On the question as a whole, the special committee declared Aaron Ezekiel to be right.

The attitude of the Patriote members in the matter of the rights of Jews was certainly gratifying for the Hart clan of Trois-Rivières. At the appropriate time Aaron Ezekiel and his three brothers were not unmindful of it. In 1837, while he and Ira Craig joined wholeheartedly in the meetings which were held at Quebec mainly to denounce the resolutions of Lord John Russell, Adolphus Mordecai and Samuel Becancour were active at Trois-Rivières. They spoke at public meetings and denounced the Executive Council's assertion of absolute authority. In July and August 1837, they served on liaison committees to coordinate the action of adjacent parishes.

Nevertheless, the Jews of that period, including the Harts who lived at Montreal, generally supported the government. So too did Benjamin Hart and his eldest son Aaron Philip. But the latter, although unwilling to join in the rebellion, distinguished himself as one of the most ardent defenders of Patriotes' rights. In December 1838 he was at the side of Joseph-Narcisse Cardinal*, who had to defend himself alone before a court martial. On 6 December Aaron Philip and his colleague Lewis Thomas Drummond* obtained permission to "make a commentary" in public on the proceedings in court. The speech of young Hart, who was only about 27, was remarkable, for after a long exposition he undertook to refute each of the solicitor general's arguments. The court sentenced four defendants to death but recommended them to the clemency of the Executive Council, which in turn demanded that the judgement be reviewed. Finally, 10 of the 12 prisoners on trial were condemned to death. On 20 Dec. 1838, the day before notary Cardinal and his clerk Joseph Duquet* were to be executed, lawyers

Drummond and Hart made a final approach to Governor Sir John Colborne*. In their opinion, "the proceedings followed in regard to the prisoners were illegal, unconstitutional, and unjust." The governor turned a deaf ear.

Aaron Ezekiel Hart had none of the taste for business shown by his brothers Ira Craig and Samuel Becancour, nor of the venturesomeness of Adolphus Mordecai, nor of the panache and hot-headedness of his cousin Aaron Philip, but he won respect as a man of law. After practising at Quebec he settled in Trois-Rivières. In July 1852 Chief Justice John Beverley Robinson* of Toronto appointed him commissioner for receiving affidavits in Lower Canada. He was very attached to his father, Ezekiel, as well as to the Jewish community, and he was a faithful member of the Montreal synagogue, to which he gave financial support.

DENIS VAUGEOIS

[The American Jewish Hist. Soc. Arch. (Waltham, Mass.) holds records relating to Aaron Ezekiel Hart's appointments, as well as an official note from from the grand lodge, dated 14 Nov. 1826, admitting him as a freemason. Hart had previously been made a member of Merchants' Lodge No.77 at Quebec, which was listed in the grand register of the United Grand Lodge of England on 12 Dec. 1825 (see "On the early Harts," comp. David Rome, Canadian Jewish Archives (Montreal), no.18 (1980): 415).

The report of the select committee of the House of Assembly, chaired in February 1834 by René-Joseph Kimber, notes the views expressed by Hart (L.C., House of Assembly, Journals, 1834, app.GG). There are numerous references to Hart in the new series of publications of the Canadian Jewish Archives, but some of the statements are contradictory. "On the early Harts, their contemporaries," no.20 (1981), states on p.153 that "he died on Sept. 27, 1853, at the age of 54, and was buried in the Prison St. cemetery at Three Rivers, but, his remains were reinterred, stone still intact, in the cemetery of the Spanish and Portuguese Jews in Montreal, in 1909," but in no.23 (1982), p.113B, David Rome suggests a death date of 1857. Again, in "Samuel Bécancour Hart and 1832," no.25 (1982), Aaron Ezekiel Hart is mentioned at least twice, at pp.62 and 75, with the dates 1803–57. In no.18, p.414, Hart's birth date is given as 24 June 1803 and death date as 6 Sept. 1857.

The collection Montarville Boucher de la Bruère (0032), fonds Pierre Boucher, at the ASTR contains 36 letters written by Aaron Ezekiel Hart as legal counsel for Moses Hart in the period from 1824 to 1833. The fonds Hart (0009) lists 83 different attorneys.

On Aaron Philip Hart's role in the case of Joseph-Narcisse Cardinal, see Le Boréal express, journal d'histoire du Canada (Montréal, 1962), pp.542–43; part of the proceedings of the trial were published as Procès de Joseph N. Cardinal, et autres, auquel on a joint la requête argumentative en faveur des prisonniers et plusieurs autres documents précieux ... (Montréal, 1839). See also P.-G. Roy, Les avocats de la région de Québec and J.-J. Lefebvre, "Tableau alphabétique des avocats de la province de Québec, 1765–1849," La Rev. du Barreau, 17 (1957): 289. D.V.]

HART, BENJAMIN, businessman, militia officer, and justice of the peace; b. 10 Aug. 1779 in Montreal, eighth surviving child and fourth son of Aaron Hart* and Dorothea Judah; d. 27 Feb. 1855 in New York City.

The son of a prominent merchant of Trois-Rivières, Benjamin Hart was educated privately, first in Philadelphia, where at age 11 he was placed under the supervision of Benjamin Jonas Phillips, and then, three years later, in New York under the care of Eleazar Levy. Although Aaron Hart may have considered a medical career for his son, by 1798 Benjamin had returned to Trois-Rivières to assist his brothers and aged father with the family's extensive business. Two indictments for assault and one for rioting laid against him that year suggest a combative nature. Benjamin held a one-tenth share in the family firm, his father four-tenths, and his brothers Ezekiel* and MOSES three- and two-tenths respectively, while another brother, Alexander (Asher), operated on his own in Montreal. Among Benjamin's assignments was that of travelling salesman for the family brewery.

When Aaron died in December 1800 he left to Benjamin the Harts' main store in Trois-Rivières and a two-storey stone house in the commercial heart of Montreal. Benjamin continued operations in the former and opened a mercantile business in the latter, both in copartnership with Alexander, with whom he had allied himself in the prolonged and acrimonious family litigation that preceded settlement of his father's estate. In 1802 Benjamin went to England to make arrangements with Aaron's former suppliers, including the Ellice empire, recently taken over by Edward Ellice*. Advertising themselves as commission merchants, brokers, auctioneers, and cashiers ready to lend money, sell or purchase land and goods, or store merchandise, Benjamin and Alexander Hart traded in anything from pearl ash and lumber to cotton and earthenware, and as far away as Kingston in Upper Canada, Boston, New York, and Belfast. In Montreal they operated as Alexander Hart and Company and in Trois-Rivières, where Benjamin directed the business, as Benjamin and Alexander Hart and Company.

On 1 April 1806, in New York, Hart made an advantageous marriage with Harriot Judith Hart, daughter of Ephraim Hart, a wealthy stockbroker. From her father she brought to the marriage a trust fund of $5,000, provided immediately; Benjamin promised a fund of $3,000 within three years. The couple had 16 children, of whom 8 survived.

Ambitious, hard-working, independent, and aggressive, in the first decade of the 19th century Hart consolidated his position in Trois-Rivières society. He became a grand juror soon after 1800, and in 1811 he was treasurer of the Fire Society. He also joined the early struggles for Jewish civil liberties. In 1807 he urged his elder brother Ezekiel to contest the seat for Trois-Rivières in the House of Assembly and, when the seat was won but Ezekiel prevented from taking it on religious grounds, Benjamin encouraged him to seek re-election. In February 1811 Benjamin petitioned the government for a commission in the Trois-Rivières battalion of militia, but was opposed by Colonel Thomas Coffin*, the unit's commander, who argued that Christian militiamen would not wish to serve with or under a Jew. In response Hart sent to Governor Sir George Prevost* favourable affidavits from leading residents of the town, including Judge Louis-Charles Foucher*, who was lieutenant-colonel under Coffin, Roman Catholic vicar general François Noiseux*, and the Anglican priest at Trois-Rivières, Robert Quirk Short*, as well as 47 militiamen. Given Coffin's influence, it is doubtful whether Hart would have received a commission while he remained in Trois-Rivières. In 1812 he lent the military £1,000 to permit immediate establishment of a garrison at William Henry (Sorel), and during the War of 1812 he served as a private in Captain John Ogilvy*'s company of light infantry in the Montreal Incorporated Volunteers. Benjamin believed that Coffin's opposition to him had been personal, and that religion had been merely a pretext. Whatever his motives, Coffin's religious objections were eliminated when Ezekiel joined his unit as a lieutenant around 1813.

Although Benjamin's partnership with Alexander had been dissolved on 1 April 1812, he continued in business in Trois-Rivières as a commission merchant, auctioneer, and broker. That year he seems to have had a short-lived partnership with Jesse Joseph, and in 1813 he was in association at Trois-Rivières with Nicholas Osborne and again with Alexander under the name of Nicholas Osborne and Company. The dissolution of this company in September 1813 may have occurred in a period of financial difficulties; from late 1813 to early 1815 Benjamin was obliged to seize the properties of three debtors, one of whom was Ezekiel.

In 1818 Benjamin moved to Montreal to start up a new business as a general agent and commission merchant, eventually selling everything from sherry to shovels; he retained his business in Trois-Rivières, however, until May 1820. His fortunes did not improve immediately. Defaulting debtors – from 1820 to 1822 he seized the properties of five in the Trois-Rivières area – worsened his situation to a point where, in May 1821, Ezekiel had the sheriff seize 15 lots in Melbourne Township belonging to Benjamin. The death of Benjamin's father-in-law in 1825 and the inheritance of a considerable sum of money by Benjamin's wife seem to have given him the capital necessary to refloat his sinking business. In October 1829 he was among eight men requesting incorporation of the Montreal Savings Bank, founded ten years

earlier. By 1831 he also held some 18,000 acres of land in 12 townships of Lower Canada. The following year he held shares in the Champlain and St Lawrence Railroad, at a time when investment in railways was just beginning. He was also a shareholder in the Île Saint-Paul (Île Des Sœurs) toll-bridge and owned interests in ships, one of which, built at Quebec in 1839, bore his name.

The expansion of Hart's business was accompanied by increasing social prominence. In October 1820 he was promoted from ensign to lieutenant in Montreal's 1st Militia Battalion. He contributed generously to the house of industry, founded in 1818, and to the Montreal General Hospital, established the following year. In 1829 he was appointed to the Montreal Board of Examiners of Applicants to be Inspectors of Pot and Pearl Ashes, and the same year he was a director of the Montreal Committee of Trade.

Persistent in his advocacy of Jewish civil liberties, Benjamin contributed to the pressure that produced a law, passed in 1831 and sanctioned the following year, giving Jews equality of civil liberties. Consequently, he, Samuel Becancour Hart, and Moses Judah Hayes* were offered appointments as justices of the peace in 1833, but because the recent legislation had provided only for a Christian oath of office, Benjamin and Hayes refused to accept the appointments until 1837 [see Aaron Ezekiel HART]. The two men were not long in office before the rebellion of 1837 broke out, and Hart, who was an active constitutionalist and had made no secret of his antipathy to the Patriote cause, claimed to have played a prominent role as a magistrate in receiving intelligence, suppressing violent activities, and warranting the arrest of suspected rebels; indeed, he was suspected by rebel leaders of issuing blank warrants. According to author John RICHARDSON, rumour spread in November 1838 that a rebel plan had been found calling for the disposal of the principal loyal merchants and the proscription of all Jews – "Mr Benjamin Hart, a wealthy merchant of that persuasion, was to have been elevated to a gibbet." Not the least intimidated, in 1838 Hart privately and then publicly campaigned, in vain, to obtain appointment to the Special Council set up to govern the colony in the wake of the 1837 rebellion.

In addition to promoting Jewish civil rights, Hart, whose religious orthodoxy was often scandalized by the heterodox beliefs and practices of his brother Moses, spent much time and money trying to revitalize Montreal's Jewish congregation. Its last resident minister, Jacob Raphael Cohen*, had departed in 1782, and in 1825 the land on which Shearith Israel Synagogue stood reverted to the heirs of David David*, depriving the Jews of their place of worship. In July 1826 Hart made a passionate printed appeal to his co-religionists of the city to reorganize

Shearith Israel. A trustee of the congregation, he initiated a subscription campaign to finance construction of a new synagogue and was himself the third largest contributor to it. Meanwhile, he opened a room adjoining his home for religious services. In 1830 the congregation obtained government authorization to hold civil registers. The construction of the new synagogue was not completed until 1838. By-laws were adopted by the congregation at a meeting on 3 July over which Hart presided. At his insistence they provided that the Sephardic ritual, traditional in the congregation, would be observed even though the membership, including the Hart family, was largely of Ashkenazic origin.

By 1840 Hart was among the leading Jews in Montreal. He was the city's agent for Minerva Life of London in 1843. Benjamin Hart and Company was one of Montreal's more active import firms in 1844, and by that year Benjamin's energetic son Theodore* had joined it as a partner. In the late 1840s, however, the company may have been caught up in a general trade collapse, which Benjamin, like other Montreal merchants, blamed on British trade policies; in 1848 he declared bankruptcy at the same time as his wife sued him for the financial support guaranteed by their marriage contract. His disappointment at not obtaining public favours for his loyalty in 1837–38 festered; as early as 1840 in Liverpool, England, he had published a broadside ridiculing former governor Lord Gosford [Acheson*] for presenting to the House of Lords a mammoth petition from Lower Canada against the union of the Canadas. The Rebellion Losses Bill of 1849 [see James Bruce*] was the last straw. That year Hart signed the Annexation Manifesto, advocating economic and political union with the United States. When, in consequence, he was stripped of his magisterial and militia commissions (by 1846 he had become lieutenant-colonel, commanding Montreal's 3rd Militia Battalion), he moved to New York, in failing health. In this city, where his wife had property inherited from her father, Hart lived out his last years in retirement near his son Arthur Wellington. He died in 1855 in St George's Hotel on Broadway.

CARMAN MILLER

ANQ-M, CL, 1827–29, 13 mai 1828; CN1-175, 10 juill. 1837. McCord Museum, Gerald Hart papers, folders 1, 7, 14, 15. PAC, RG 68, General index, 1651–1841: 60, 296, 392, 644. L.C., House of Assembly, *Journals*, 1828–29, app.EE; *Statutes*, 1831–32, c.58, art.1. "Benjamin Hart and 1829," comp. David Rome, *Canadian Jewish Arch.* (Montreal), no.24 (1982): 4–6. William Berczy, "William von Moll Berczy," ANQ *Rapport*, 1940–41: 39, 42. "On the early Harts – their contemporaries, part 5," comp. David Rome, *Canadian Jewish Arch.*, no.23 (1982): 92, 98, 100–4, 111, 113–15, 117. "On the Jews of Lower Canada and 1837–38," comp. David Rome, *Canadian Jewish Arch.*, nos.28–30 (1983): 284. [John] Richardson, *Eight years in Canada, embracing a review of the administrations of Lords Durham and Sydenham, Sir Chas. Bagot and Lord Metcalfe, and including numerous interesting letters from Lord Durham, Mr. Chas. Buller and other well-known public characters* (Montreal, 1847), 62. "Samuel Becancour Hart and 1832," comp. David Rome, *Canadian Jewish Arch.*, no.25 (1982): iii, 34–36, 38, 40, 51–53, 55–64, 69–71, 73–74, 79, 82, 89. *Montreal Gazette*, 3 April 1834. *Montreal Transcript*, 23 Feb. 1837. *Quebec Gazette*, 13 June 1799; 11 June, 13 Aug. 1801; 4 Nov. 1802; 26 Nov. 1807; 14 Dec. 1809; 7 Feb. 1811; 9 Jan., 23 April, 4 June, 12 Nov. 1812; 14 Oct., 2 Dec. 1813; 12 Jan., 9 Feb. 1815; 16 Jan. 1817; 14 May, 30 July 1818; 13 April, 18 May, 17, 20 July, 10 Aug., 7 Sept., 26 Oct., 28 Dec. 1820; 3 Jan., 24 May, 2 Aug., 13 Sept., 8 Nov. 1821; 20 June, 19 Dec. 1822; 27 March 1823. *Quebec Mercury*, 9 Dec. 1805. Ivanhoë Caron, "Inventaire des documents relatifs aux événements de 1837 et 1838, conservés aux Archives de la province de Québec," ANQ *Rapport*, 1925–26: 271; "Papiers Duvernay conservés aux Archives de la province de Québec," ANQ *Rapport*, 1926–27: 152, 181, 186, 188. *Montreal directory*, 1842–44; 1850–51. "The record book of the Reverend Jacob Raphael Cohen," ed. A. D. Corré and M. H. Stern, *American Jewish Hist. Quarterly* (New York), 59 (1969): 36. Terrill, *Chronology of Montreal*. S. E. Rosenberg, *The Jewish community in Canada* (2v., Toronto and Montreal, 1970–71), 1: 37–38. G. J. J. Tulchinsky, "Studies in the development of transportation and industry in Montreal, 1837 to 1853" (PHD thesis, Univ. of Toronto, 1971), 480. Raymond Douville, "Années de jeunesse et vie familiale de Moses Hart," *Cahiers des Dix*, 23 (1958): 198–201, 213–14. Gérard Malchelosse, "Les Juifs dans l'histoire canadienne," *Cahiers des Dix*, 4 (1939): 184. Albert Tessier, "Deux enrichis; Aaron Hart et Nicolas Montour," *Cahiers des Dix*, 3 (1938): 232.

HART, MOSES, businessman and seigneur; b. 26 Nov. 1768 in Trois-Rivières, Que., eldest son of Aaron Hart* and Dorothea Judah; d. there 15 Oct. 1852.

Moses Hart lived just short of 84 years and participated in nearly all the fields of activity of his time, often with extravagance and, except for politics, almost always with success. He was first and foremost a businessman, and in this respect was able to benefit from the valuable experience of his father. In 1786 Aaron Hart, who was closely tied to Trois-Rivières, entrusted him to the care of his brother Henry, a merchant at Albany, N.Y. Moses soon decided to push on to New York City, where he quickly exhausted his money in the social round and in "lavish tips to hotel barmen." According to the diary he kept at his father's request, he learned as much about life as about business. Nevertheless he made some useful contacts which he maintained throughout his life.

When he returned to Quebec, Hart took his first initiatives at Nicolet, which he was pleased to call Hartville. However, it was at William Henry (Sorel)

Hart

that his career began in earnest. In this strategic post located at the start of the road to New York – in times past, the commercial fief of Samuel Jacobs* – he ran a general store. His trade was with England as well as with the United States. He remained there for nearly a decade, until his father's death in 1800. That year he returned to Trois-Rivières to take up residence. Before doing so he had travelled a great deal, particularly in the United States, and had gone at least once to Europe, in 1792.

Undoubtedly prompted by his father, Hart had taken repeated steps to be granted land in the region of William Henry, following in this the example of the many loyalists who had settled there. On 10 May 1795 he received a negative reply: the lands sought were reserved "for Emigrants from Europe." Hart was disappointed but tenacious. He refused to accept being treated differently from the newcomers, and at that time conceived the notion of getting himself elected to the House of Assembly. In 1796 he issued an appeal to the voters in William Henry. His father was worried and tried to get him to change his mind: "what I do not like is that you will be opposed as a Jew" and the cost of staying at Quebec had to be considered. Whatever transpired in this instance, Hart never gave up his desire for a political career. In 1809 he attempted to succeed his brother Ezekiel* in the riding of Trois-Rivières but had to concede the election to Mathew Bell* and Joseph Badeaux*. He ran again in Saint-Maurice in 1819 and in Upper Town, Quebec, the following year. Finally, at the age of 75, he made a new attempt in Trois-Rivières against Edward Grieve, and then another in Nicolet against Antoine-Prospère Méthot; both times he was beaten and contested the election of his opponents.

Having failed to get elected, Hart tried to secure appointment to the Executive and Legislative councils. Hence his numerous letters to political leaders such as Louis-Hippolyte La Fontaine* and to governors such as Sir Charles Theophilus Metcalfe*, to whom he wrote on 6 Dec. 1843: "I am the oldest English Canadian in Canada and the largest land-holder in this district [Trois-Rivières]."

Looking beyond honours, Hart aspired to bring about numerous reforms. He found a number of laws intolerable, and in his letters often took exception to a "wretched Code of Civil justice made up of a medley of the worst parts of the french edicts" or to a house of assembly with 50 members, four-fifths of them French Canadians "led by lawyers [who] have on occasion evinced strong symptoms of illeberality, and mischief, [being] inimical to change and english customs." If French laws sometimes revolted him, Hart was equally critical of the place of the French language in public affairs.

Year after year, his letters to various correspondents included precise details about possible reforms, and he even drafted a code of laws. He also worked out a proposal for a penitentiary, preparing a budget to cover construction and operational costs and an outline of regulations. He sometimes proposed the reduction of certain punishments (for example, in cases involving rape), suggested the appointment of "several English magistrates," and denounced legal costs he thought too high. His innumerable grievances against the legal system in general did not, however, prevent him from making extensive use of the courts. A partial list established for the period 1799–1824 shows that judicial decisions were pronounced every year for cases in which he was concerned. In 1822 and 1823 he obtained at least 28 different judgements against people of various origins and professions, even including members of his own family.

Hart was a difficult man to do business with. The same held true in personal and family matters. In 1799 he married his cousin Sarah after a stormy courtship punctuated by squabbles with her father, Uriah Judah. Three children, Areli Blake, Orobio, and Louisa Howard, were born of their rather fragile union. In 1807 Sarah went back to her parents' home and obtained a monthly pension of £4 3s. 0d. After getting Hart to agree to drive out his "two women," she returned to him and remained for about five years. But in 1814 she again denounced his conduct and dissolute life, and in the end obtained on 15 March 1816 an annual pension of £300.

Hart had an astonishing number of fairly short affairs. He would finish his days with Mary McCarthy (the widow of one Peter Brown), who, along with some of his legitimate and illegitimate children, was to inherit part of his assets. Hart already had at various times acknowledged and even lent assistance to a number of his other illegitimate children.

Profoundly affected by his matrimonial rebuffs and influenced by his reading of foreign philosophers, Hart began writing discourses – as yet unpublished – in which he attacked the Catholic faith, and then finally proposed a new religion. In 1815 he had a 60-page pamphlet entitled *General universal religion* printed in New York; he took up his treatise again in 1824 under the title *Modern religion*. He made use of his business connections to circulate his texts and his ideas, and on occasion made himself available to give lectures to promote his religion which, he said, was relevant to both Jews and deists. He also kept up a correspondence with American deists, among them William Carver.

From 1825 or 1826 Hart seems to have recovered a degree of equanimity in his personal life. No doubt having Mary McCarthy by his side was a factor. From then on he concentrated on his numerous concerns and took a greater interest in political questions than in religious ones.

Paradoxically, at the same time as he denounced Christianity he agreed to help many religious institutions. The Ursulines of Trois-Rivières, as a result of loans he made to them without interest, at one time counted him among their generous benefactors. Hart also financed numerous parishes and made possible the building or restoration of churches, including those of Saint-Michel-d'Yamaska (Yamaska), Saint-Stanislas, William Henry, Saint-Apollinaire, Saint-Charles-des-Grondines, Baie-du-Febvre (Baieville), and Deschaillons.

Hart was beyond doubt eccentric, but he was a shrewd businessman. Between 1795 and 1835 he had dealings with 21 large English firms (12 in London, 4 in Liverpool, and the rest in Bristol, Stourbridge, Wolverhampton, Leeds, and Birmingham) and also with a company whose head office was in Glasgow. He traded in a wide range of items. He imported raw sugar, coffee, woollen goods, fabrics, and Jamaica rum, among other things, and he exported mainly potash and grains. Until his father's death, Hart used the firm of Aaron Hart and Sons as his usual middle man. But after 1800 he established relations with a network of British agents and avoided the agents at Montreal, Quebec, New York, and Halifax. He also frequently used personal friends, and he took advantage of his family ties with his uncle George Joel from 1807 to 1818 and with his cousin Judah Joseph from 1803 to 1834.

Hart was interested in everything, but especially in banks. When the Bank of Montreal was created in 1817, the promoters found only 12 subscribers outside Montreal, two of them at Trois-Rivières: Moses and his brother Ezekiel. Moses' original investment was £150 and on four occasions in the next year he purchased new shares, for £480, bringing his total to 124 shares. In 1819–20 he purchased at least £520 in shares and from 1828 to 1830 he added several further blocks. When the Quebec Bank was started in 1818, the two brothers were again among the shareholders. Archival records contain numerous notes exchanged from 1824 to 1847 between Moses Hart and Noah Freer, who was its cashier (general manager). In 1824 alone, Freer offered Hart three blocks of shares valued at £950. The Bank of Canada was also founded in 1818, in Montreal, and on 18 June Hart obtained 20 shares for £100. Two months later he acquired another 20 shares, for which he paid £150, and in February 1819 a further 20 shares for £50. In 1820, 1821, and 1823 respectively he bought 15, 30, and 45 additional shares. By 1819 he was also a customer of the bank. When the City Bank opened its subscription register at Montreal in 1833, Hart figured among the shareholders, and he was soon directing part of his business to it, at least from 1835 to 1840. In 1835 Louis-Michel VIGER and Jacob DE WITT founded the Banque du Peuple, and in January of the following year the partnership agreement was signed by nine French Canadian merchants. Hart transacted business there immediately.

When a bank crisis occurred in the United States in 1837 and many banks suspended payments in cash, the Canadian banks followed suit. Faced with a shortage of ready money, some of the larger merchants reacted by issuing their own currency [see William Molson*]. This was the moment if ever there was one for Hart to realize an old family dream. On 9 May 1839 he requested a licence to operate "a private Bank . . . for the convenience of this town." He reported that certain notes were already in circulation and gave a brief outline of his financial situation, estimating his real estate at £15,000 and his secured credits at the same amount. There is every indication, however, that the licence was never granted and that the notes were progressively redeemed by the Harts.

Steam navigation fascinated Hart as much as banking. Even during his time in William Henry he had been interested in navigation on the St Lawrence. First a rival of the Molsons of Montreal in the manufacture of beer, he is reputed to have quickly decided to compete with the steamship *Accommodation*, which they had launched in 1809. Legend has it that by 1810 a steamship christened *Hart* began to provide a service between Montreal and Quebec. The *Hart*, although slower than the *Accommodation*, sailed a straighter course, according to its owner. Contemporary records, however, do not mention this ship. In any case, with steam navigation becoming increasingly important, in 1824 Hart offered to buy from John Molson* the *Telegraph*, a ship belonging to John Molson and Sons [see William Molson]. Molson considered the proposal absurd, but when Hart insisted, he demanded £2,150 for the boat and its engine and Hart's agreement to refrain from any activity that would put him in competition with the Molsons! But there were other ships. In May 1833 Hart and John Miller bought for £1,070 the *Lady Aylmer*, built in the port of Quebec in 1831. Hart made over his shares in the ship, amounting to 50 per cent, on 30 May 1833 to Alexander Thomas Hart, one of his adopted sons. The relations between Alexander and Miller proved difficult, and several differences between the joint owners in 1834 and 1835 brought them before the courts. Hart and his son then acquired another vessel, the steamship *Toronto*, valued at £2,500. They rented it to interested parties in 1839 and operated the *Hart*, "a 45-horsepower steamship," which they built in 1840 and sold by auction on 27 March 1845. The Hart family papers mention more than 50 steamships that were plying the St Lawrence in that period. In partnership with his son Alexander Thomas, for a time "master of the Steamboat Hart," and with his nephew Ira Craig Hart, Moses remained active in the shipping business and from time to time in shipbuilding.

It was, however, as a landed proprietor that Hart really asserted himself and made a mark. In the early 1820s he owned a good many properties in almost all

Hartman

the townships behind the seigneuries on the south shore of the St Lawrence. More important were the fiefs and seigneuries belonging to him totally or in part. Around Quebec he owned the seigneuries of Grondines, Bélair, and also Gaspé, which was on the south shore behind the seigneury of Tilly. His holdings in the immediate vicinity of Trois-Rivières were obviously the largest: the Sainte-Marguerite and Carufel seigneuries, the "marquisat Du Sablé," the Vieuxpont fief, and on the south shore the Godefroy, Dutort, and Courval seigneuries. Each of these domains naturally had its own history: one had come to him by inheritance, another had been acquired by auction, another had been seized.

The ambitious side of Hart dreamed of one day acquiring the Chutes Shawinigan, or looked enviously towards the Jesuit estates. The philanthropic side responded to appeals for building a school at Bécancour or agreed to give a piece of land at Rivière-du-Loup (Louiseville) for the construction of an Anglican church. He was ruthless and quarrelsome but he always selected his victims with care. Thus, throughout his life, he kept his distance from Mathew Bell, the other giant who lived in the same small town as he did and who died in 1849 at the age of 80. They seldom had any connection in business or politics; except for the 1809 elections, they appear to have avoided each other carefully.

Evidently Hart was a demon for work and something of an elemental force. A meticulous person, he kept his own accounts and scrupulously filed all documents received, together with copies of his own letters. Despite his stormy existence and his fleeting impulses for religious reform, Hart progressively re-established closer ties with the religion of his forefathers. Occasionally he made donations to the Shearith Israel congregation of Montreal and New York. At his death he was given a Jewish burial.

"Moses was born temperamental, undisciplined," writes historian Raymond Douville, who has studied the Hart family thoroughly; "he lived unrepentant and did not greatly lament it. If he had curbed his passions more, he might have left a more enduring testimony. But he was one of those who are bent on pleasures that pass away. He has passed away with them." Surely a severe judgement, and an excessive one. Moses Hart was more complex.

DENIS VAUGEOIS

[Moses Hart is the author of a 60-page pamphlet entitled *General universal religion*, 500 copies of which were printed in New York by Van Winkle and Wiley in 1815 and another 250 copies three years later. Hart reworked his treatise in 1824 and published it as *Modern religion*, also printed in New York, this time by Johnstone and Van Norden.

The Hart papers in ASTR, 0009, constitute the principal documentary source for this biography. In addition, Raymond Douville wrote two essays, published in *Cahiers des Dix*, "Les opinions politiques et religieuses de Moses Hart," 17 (1952): 137–51, and "Années de jeunesse et vie familiale de Moses Hart," 23 (1958): 195–216, and also devotes a sizeable portion of his *Aaron Hart: récit historique* (Trois-Rivières, Qué., 1938) to Moses Hart. However, Douville confuses him with his father, especially at pages 98–99 and 140.

In 1966, Denis Vaugeois presented a paper to the SCHÉC on "Les positions religieuses de Moses Hart," which was published in the *Sessions d'études*, 33 (1966): 41–46. American historian Jacob Rader Marcus also became interested in Moses Hart in *Early American Jewry* (2v., Philadelphia, 1951–53) and "The *Modern religion* of Moses Hart," *Hebrew Union College Annual* (Cincinnati, Ohio), 20 (1947): 1–31. Mention must also be made of the important work of David Rome who has published a number of texts relating to the Hart family entitled "On the early Harts" in *Canadian Jewish Arch.* (Montreal), 15–18 (1980). As numerous studies address the religious ideas of Moses Hart, the present biography, which includes unpublished material in other areas, only touches upon them. D.V.]

HARTMAN, JOSEPH, farmer, educator, and politician; b. 16 Jan. 1821 in Whitchurch Township, Upper Canada, son of John Hartman and Mary Webb; m. 1 June 1843 Mary Ann Cosford, and they had three sons and three daughters; d. 29 Nov. 1859 in Whitchurch.

Joseph Hartman's Quaker parents emigrated from Columbia County, Pa, to Upper Canada in 1807, settling on a farm in Whitchurch Township where Joseph was born and raised. Not strong in health, he became a school teacher and in 1844, at the early age of 23, was named superintendent of education for the township. He continued to farm, however, and in 1848 was able to purchase 160 acres in Whitchurch which his father had leased shortly after arriving in Canada.

Hartman entered local politics in 1847 and served on the Home District Council for three years. His political ascent began in 1850 with the reorganization of local government brought about by the Municipal Corporations Act [see Robert BALDWIN]. Elected to the township council, he was chosen Whitchurch's first reeve, an office he held until his death, and as reeve he sat on the county council. In 1853 he became warden of the United Counties of York, Ontario, and Peel. He did not stand for office in 1854 but was selected warden again in 1855, this time for the United Counties of York and Peel, and served for four subsequent terms, one of the longest wardenships in the history of the province.

It was this solid base of local influence that facilitated Hartman's move into provincial politics. In the general elections of 1851 he decisively defeated tory Hugh SCOBIE and Baldwin himself in the riding of York North, the old constituency of the recently resigned co-leader of the great reform coalition. Hartman's margin of victory over James Hervey Price* in 1854 was a much narrower one, but he was returned again in 1857 with an overwhelming majority.

Hartman also gained support by aligning himself with the radical Clear Grits, now developing as a potent electoral force. One of the Grits who supported Francis Hincks* and Augustin-Norbert Morin*, Hartman crossed over to the opposition when their government failed to introduce legislation secularizing the clergy reserves. A New Connexion Methodist, he vigorously opposed state aid to religious bodies and sectarian school legislation. In May 1855 when Étienne-Paschal Taché*'s school bill was introduced in the assembly late in the session after many Upper Canadian members had returned home from Quebec, Hartman joined forces with George Brown* in an unsuccessful attempt to recommit the bill for six months. The Taché bill, which allowed any 10 Roman Catholic freeholders in Upper Canada to elect trustees to manage a separate school in their district, was passed by Lower Canadian votes, with most of the westerners still present voting against it. That summer Hartman called for dissolution of the union. He was eventually won over to Brown's political solution, representation by population, and in 1857 participated in the Toronto Reform Convention, further allying himself with Brown, the emerging leader of a new reform party.

Above all else, Hartman reflected the concerns of his constituency; he addressed temperance meetings, advocated retrenchment, and proposed legislation on a number of minor municipal reforms. Himself a farmer representing a predominantly agricultural district, he was involved in various unsuccessful efforts to improve transportation in his riding. In 1855 he presented a bill to incorporate the Port Perry and Whitchurch Junction Railway Company, of which he was a shareholder, and in 1856 he helped found the Toronto and Georgian Bay Canal Company. A year later he was appointed chairman of a parliamentary committee to study the canal's feasibility and the possibility of government aid. Perhaps not surprisingly, Hartman's committee, which consisted of two fellow shareholders, Angus Morrison* and John William Gamble*, and four others through whose ridings the proposed canal would run, favoured the plan. Their involvement, which by later standards would constitute a conflict of interest, is fairly typical of situations that could easily arise in a developing Upper Canada at mid century.

Another aspect of Hartman's life which typifies the era was of a more tragic nature. His family had a long history of consumption or tuberculosis, for which there was then no cure. Joseph contracted the disease years before his death and was forced to wage a long debilitating struggle against its effects before finally succumbing at age 38.

ERIC JARVIS

AO, MS 451, York County, King and Whitchurch township cemeteries, Aurora cemetery record; RG 8, ser.I-6-A, 11: 122; RG 22, ser.305, Joseph Hartman; ser.94, 8–9. PAC, RG 1, L3, 232: H14/186; 554: 12. York North Land Registry Office (Newmarket, Ont.), Deeds, Whitchurch Township, 3, nos.33135–36 (mfm. at AO, GS 6424). Can., Prov. of, Legislative Assembly, *App. to the journals*, 1857, app.61; *Journals*, 1857: 26, 138, 190; *Statutes*, 1854–55, c.195; 1856, c.118. *Doc. hist. of education in U.C.* (Hodgins), vols.11–13. Jaradiah, the scribe [Joshua Winn], *Chronicles of the north riding of York, giving a brief historical account of the late parliamentary contest* (Newmarket, 1854). *The legislation and history of separate schools in Upper Canada: from 1841, until the close of the Reverend Doctor Ryerson's administration of the Education Department of Ontario in 1876: including various private papers and documents on the subject*, ed. J. G. Hodgins (Toronto, 1897), 69, 94–95, 110. *Examiner* (Toronto), November–December 1851, July 1854. *Globe*, 23 July 1855; 30 Nov., 2, 3 Dec. 1859. *New Era* (Newmarket), 1852–59. *North American* (Toronto), 4 Nov. 1851. *North York Sentinel* (Newmarket), 1856. *Commemorative biographical record of the county of York, Ontario . . .* (Toronto, 1907). *History of Toronto and county of York, Ontario . . .* (2v., Toronto, 1885), 2: 438, 454. J. M. S. Careless, *Brown of "The Globe"* (2v., Toronto, 1959–63; repr. 1972). *Historical sketch of Whitchurch Township: centennial celebration of municipal government, 1850–1950* ([Stouffville, Ont.], 1950]). James Johnston, *Aurora: its early beginnings* (Aurora, Ont., 1963). C. B. Sissons, *Egerton Ryerson, his life and letters* (2v., Toronto, 1937–47). Eric Jarvis, "The Georgian Bay Ship Canal; a study of the second Canadian canal age, 1850–1915," OH, 69 (1977): 125–47.

HARVARD, WILLIAM MARTIN, Methodist minister; b. *c*. 1790 in England, probably in the London area; m. 23 Nov. 1813 Elizabeth Parks in London, and they had five sons, two of whom died in infancy; d. 15 Dec. 1857 in Richmond (London).

William Martin Harvard was evidently trained as a printer. In 1810 he became a probationer for the ministry in the Wesleyan Methodist Conference and in 1813 volunteered to join the Reverend Thomas Coke and others in establishing Methodist missions in India and Ceylon (Sri Lanka). As a prospective foreign missionary Harvard was ordained in 1813 in London. Subsequently, Coke performed Harvard's marriage ceremony. In December Coke and his companions sailed from Portsmouth on the long voyage to India, but Coke's contributions to the missionary enterprise of the conference ended when he died at sea. Harvard conducted the funeral service, and the party proceeded to its destination. He remained in the India–Ceylon mission until 1819 when ill health forced his return to England. His well-written but discursive account of the inception and growth of the mission to India was published in 1823, the year his wife died.

Harvard regained his health at home, and between 1819 and 1835 he was stationed on several circuits in southern England. In 1836 he was appointed president of the Canadian conference, an office he held until

Harvard

1838, and chairman of the Lower Canada District. He arrived in Montreal on 16 October and immediately assumed his duties there. A year later he moved to Toronto. John Saltkill Carroll* described him as "commanding in person, almost the *fac simile* of General Washington; dignified in his carriage; polite in his manners; pre-eminently Christian in his spirit; and unusually faithful as a minister." At first he impressed the Canadian ministers much more favourably than had his predecessor, the Reverend William Lord.

Harvard's appointment as president came at an unpropitious juncture in the relationship between the English and Canadian conferences. The two had united in 1833 to form the Wesleyan Methodist Church in Canada. In the mean time, in England, the Wesleyan Methodist Conference had come to be defined as a church, with a ministry ordained by the imposition of hands, whose authority could not be shared with local preachers or class leaders, and in which the conference was sovereign. The church's leaders accepted the established church and were intensely hostile to those —usually the same persons — who promoted disestablishment and radical politics. Harvard evidently shared these views and was slow to learn that the conference in Upper Canada was not wholly of the same mind.

By 1836 some members of the latter conference were becoming disillusioned with the union. Two years earlier the union had precipitated a secession led by disgruntled local preachers who established a new organization, the Methodist Episcopal Church in Canada. Within the conference, the Wesleyan sympathizers urged that the *Christian Guardian* become a solely religious journal, supportive if necessary of the political *status quo*, and that the conference accept a share of the clergy reserves income, were a division of the reserves to occur. The Canadian leaders, and probably the majority of their followers, were dubious at best, or outright opposed to the Wesleyans' position. As for Harvard, in a letter to the Reverend Robert Alder* in January 1837, he commented that the Methodists could use a share of the clergy reserves for chapels, schools, and parsonages. "The Scotch people," he wrote to the Reverend Egerton Ryerson* in May, "are making a grand effort for the clergy reserves. We might find a slice of the loaf highly helpful for our Parsonage houses, Supernumerary Preachers, and students for the ministry at Cobourg. . . . I should be unutterably vexed to be disinherited of our just ground of expectation." Harvard doubtless had some part in framing the equivocal resolutions adopted by the conference in 1837, in which the exclusive claims of Anglicans and Presbyterians were condemned and the conference's willingness to accept a share of the reserves "for the religious and educational improve-

ment of the Province" was indicated. Not surprisingly, he continued to press for the payment of the government grant to the Wesleyan Methodist Missionary Society.

Given his conservative proclivities, Harvard was intensely agitated by the disturbances in the colony in December 1837. He believed that if the rebels had succeeded, all pro-British citizens would have been massacred, and he was cheered by the support for the government in Toronto and elsewhere. This support, he concluded, "would tend greatly to tranquillise the public mind and thus to forward the cause of godliness in this Province." In contrast, in March 1838, the Reverend John Ryerson* exclaimed: "Never were the prospects of the friends of Civil & Religious liberty so gloomy & desperate as they now are; & Harvard & [Ephraim Evans*] love to have it so. Mr. H is a *weak high-church despot* & Evans is his *intire tool*."

Harvard would provide confirmation of this assessment with the publication the next month in the *Guardian* of a pastoral letter to the ministers in Upper Canada of the Wesleyan Methodist Church. Having learned that there were Methodists who had "not done honour to their christian profession, during the late unnatural rebellion," he thought it imperative to state that "some opinions . . . so involve the very vitals of morality as that they are never found associated in the same bosom with fervent piety and deep devotedness to God." In "a question of loyalty to the Sovereign of an Empire, the Government may well say, in the words of our adorable Saviour, '*He that is not with me is against me.*'" Thus he instructed the district chairmen to require every minister to scrutinize the loyalty of all members. "Should there be a single individual, for whose christian loyalty the Preacher cannot conscientiously answer to his brethren, . . . such individual should be dealt with, kindly and compassionately, but firmly, according to the provisions of the Book of Discipline." He reminded his brethren that in Britain the Methodists were known for their "faithful attachment" to the crown.

Perhaps to Harvard's surprise, his statement stirred up sharp controversy among the Methodists. "Last night," he reported to Alder, "I was rather rudely arrested by one of our Leaders and a local preacher who termed my letter a bull — that I was acting like a Pope." In a later issue of the *Guardian* he insisted that he did not intend to take away church membership from anyone "merely on account of party politics." Doubtless he was distressed to learn from Egerton Ryerson that he had read the letter "with great pain and regret." Ryerson stressed that disaster would result "if the undoubted constitutional right of individual judgment and discussion on political matters is not fully understood and mutually acknowledged by all." Ryerson's private letter was accompanied by the publication in the *Guardian* of a lengthy statement entitled "What is Christian Loyalty?" in which he recalled that John Wesley "gives the right hand of fellowship to those who differ from him in opinion on many points . . . , nor can we with any reason or propriety, allow less latitude and liberty of sentiment on doctrines and measures of government."

Undaunted, Harvard asked Ryerson, "How can we keep our Methodist stage from going deeply again into Radical mud . . . but to keep well off from the ditch while we turn this corner?" Harvard wished "to see Canadian Wesleyan Methodism become more and more Wesleyan, and this will make it the glory of the land. It appears to me that to Americanize it will be to neutralize it." He presided with equanimity at the conference in June 1838. Many there, however, must have shared John Ryerson's opinion that "Mr. Harvard [is] a very dangerous man. . . . You would be surprised to see how he has been runing about [Toronto], fawning, bowing, smiling, eulogizing, flattering, etc. . . . to make proselites to himself & Mr. Evans." No doubt they were relieved to learn that the missionary society had decided already to station him in Quebec.

Harvard remained in the Lower Canada District until 1845, acting as chairman throughout that period. In the latter year he returned to Toronto as chairman of the Canada Western District which had been created after the dissolution of the union between the Wesleyan and Canadian conferences in 1840. During his tenure in Toronto as chairman, an appointment proposed by the Reverend Matthew Richey*, his role became that of helping persuade his recalcitrant brethren to accept the reunion of the two conferences in 1847. This must have been a difficult task, for he was not alone in considering the disruption of 1840 "a providential opening" for the establishment of a truly Wesleyan connection in Upper Canada. Throughout the pre-union negotiation, he urged that the Wesleyans and the Canadian Methodists should go their separate ways and "agree to differ." Reunion should be effected only on condition that the British conference secured supreme control over the Canadian conference. In the end the Wesleyans settled for less than Harvard thought wise, but he worked loyally with Alder to bring the Canada Western District into line. Clearly, however, his usefulness was at an end and in 1847 he was assigned to the Maidstone circuit in England.

At home, Harvard was appointed in succession to the Maidstone, Portsmouth, and Norwich circuits, and finally in 1855 he became house governor of the southern branch of the Wesleyan Theological Institution, in Richmond. He died in office in 1857, after experiencing a time of turmoil in the English conference over the status to be assigned to ordained ministers.

Harvard's brethren recorded that "his character was distinguished by lowliness and sanctity. . . . He was faithful in the exercise of his ministry; 'gentle' among the churches . . . esteemed and beloved by a multitude on both sides of the Atlantic." He epitomized much of the Wesleyan Methodism of his generation in his conviction that its polity, missionary zeal, loyalty to British institutions, and conservatism made it a form of Methodism superior to all others. His kindly temper and courtesy enabled him to persuade many that the unadventurous Methodism he proclaimed was the one most likely to succeed in his time.

G. S. FRENCH

William Martin Harvard's writings include *The Gospel warning: a sermon occasioned by the death of Private J. Jenny . . .* (London, 1818); *The faith of departed saints: an unperishable monument of instruction and admonition to survivors; a funeral sermon, occasioned by the lamented death of his late most gracious majesty, George III, of religious and blessed memory, preached at the Wesleyan Methodist Chapel, Duke Street, Deal, on Wednesday, Feb. 16, 1820, being the day appointed for the interment of his late majesty* (Deal, Eng., 1820); *A narrative of the establishment and progress of the mission to Ceylon and India, founded by the late Rev. Thomas Coke, L.L.D., under the direction of the Wesleyan-Methodist Conference . . .* (London, 1823); *The substance of a funeral sermon, delivered in the Wesleyan Chapel, St. James Street, Montreal, on Sunday, August 13, 1837, on occasion of the lamented demise of his most gracious majesty, William the Fourth* (Montreal, 1837); *Remarks and suggestions, respectfully offered, on that portion of the clergy reserve property, (landed and funded,) of Upper Canada, "not specifically appropriated to any particular church"; in a letter addressed to His Excellency Sir George Arthur, K.C.B., governor, and commander-in-chief . . .* (Quebec, 1838; 2nd ed., 1839); *Defence of protracted meetings: special efforts for the souls of men justified, and observers of such efforts admonished, in a discourse delivered in St. Ann Street Chapel, Quebec,* a second edition of which, published at London and Quebec during the 1840s, is available at the UCA; *No honesty separate from veracity; the unrighteous monopoly, (by an intolerant party in the Church of England,) of "whatever Christian knowledge Canada possesses," examined, exposed, and rebuked; to which is added: a defence of the Wesleyan Methodists, and other orthodox churches in Canada, against the "unchristian bitterness," "violent dealing," and misrepresentation, of the theological professor of M'Gill College, Montreal* (Montreal, 1845); *Facts against falsehood: the false allegations . . . made by the "Christian Guardian," (the official organ of the Upper Canada Conference,) against the missionaries of the British Wesleyan Conference, in Western Canada . . . fully and forcibly disproved . . .* (Toronto, 1846; copy at UCA); and *Five defensive letters in behalf of the British Wesleyan Conference and their missionary society . . . against the attacks of the Canada Conference Journal* (Toronto, 1846). He is also the author of *Memoirs of Mrs. Elizabeth Harvard, late of the Wesleyan mission to Ceylon and India; with extracts from her diary and correspondence,* a biography of

Harvey

his wife prepared following her death in 1823; a copy of the 3rd edition (London, 1833) is at the UCA.

SOAS, Methodist Missionary Soc. Arch., Wesleyan Methodist Missionary Soc., corr., North America, 1837–47 (mfm. at UCA). Jabez Bunting, *Early Victorian Methodism: the correspondence of Jabez Bunting, 1830–1858*, ed. W. R. Ward (Oxford and New York, 1976). Wesleyan Methodist Church, *Minutes of the conferences* (London), 5 (1819–24): 102; 8 (1836–39): 47; 10 (1844–47): 198, 466; 13 (1855–57): 26; 14 (1858–62): 8–9. Wesleyan Methodist Church, *The minutes of the annual conferences ... from 1824 to 1845 ...* (Toronto, 1846), 168. *Wesleyan-Methodist Magazine* (London), 42 (1819): 714; 60 (1837): 72. *Christian Guardian*, 30 Nov. 1836; 15 Nov. 1837; 18, 25 April, 9 May 1838. Cornish, *Cyclopædia of Methodism*. Carroll, *Case and his cotemporaries*, 4: 131. French, *Parsons & politics*. J. E. Sanderson, *The first century of Methodism in Canada* (2v., Toronto, 1908–10), 1: 390–91, 393, 398, 404, 413, 420. C. B. Sissons, *Egerton Ryerson: his life and letters* (2v., Toronto, 1937–47), 1: 379, 433, 471, 473.

HARVEY, Sir JOHN, army officer and colonial administrator; b. 23 April 1778 in England; m. 16 June 1806 Lady Elizabeth Lake, and they had five sons and one daughter; d. 22 March 1852 in Halifax.

Unlike most of his contemporaries in the higher ranks of the British army and the colonial service, John Harvey was not born to the purple; he described himself as the child of an obscure Church of England clergyman of modest means who had persuaded William Pitt the younger to give his son a commission in the army. On 10 Sept. 1794 Harvey became an ensign in the 80th Foot. He was fortunate. The regiment had been raised by Henry William Paget, the future Marquess of Anglesey, a distinguished cavalry officer whose family was part of a widespread and influential military network to which Harvey was to owe much of his future advancement. Yet because he lacked the private resources that would have enabled him to rise through the ranks by purchase, Harvey's progress was slow and was achieved primarily by hard work, talent, and that quality most prized in the 18th-century British army – personal courage in the face of danger. From 1794 to 1796 Harvey saw active service in the Netherlands and along the coast of France, in 1796 at the Cape of Good Hope, from 1797 to 1800 in Ceylon (Sri Lanka), and in 1801 in Egypt. From 1803 to 1807 he served in India during the campaigns against the Marathas where by an unusual act of daring he brought himself to the attention of the commander-in-chief, Lord Lake, and was invited to join his staff. While in India he married Lake's daughter, making another connection that would prove useful in later years. Lady Elizabeth also proved to be the perfect consort for a colonial governor. She was a gracious hostess and actively involved herself in charitable activities. Harvey was affectionately described by one of his friends as a "Soldier of Fortune," and to the extent that his life was to be spent in a perennial search for a high station in an aristocratic society the description is an apt one. Since he lacked private means, Harvey had to live with financial insecurity, but thanks to his wife his domestic life was relatively stable and untroubled.

Harvey returned to England in September 1807. On 15 July 1795 he had become a lieutenant and on 9 Sept. 1803 a captain; on 28 Jan. 1808 he was promoted major. From January to June 1808 he was employed in England as an assistant quartermaster general and in July 1808 he joined the 6th Royal Garrison Battalion in Ireland under the command of the Earl of Dalhousie [Ramsay*]. On 25 June 1812 he was raised to the rank of lieutenant-colonel and appointed to Upper Canada as deputy adjutant general to John Vincent*. In his haste to reach his new post he travelled overland on snowshoes across New Brunswick in the depth of winter and arrived in Upper Canada early in 1813.

For the duration of the War of 1812 Harvey played a conspicuous part in the campaigns along the Niagara peninsula. His greatest triumph was at the battle of Stoney Creek, one of the most decisive encounters of the war. In May 1813 a large American force of more than 6,000 men landed at Fort Niagara (near Youngstown, N.Y.) and drove the British from Fort George (Niagara-on-the-Lake), Upper Canada. Vincent, with 1,600 infantry, retreated to Burlington Heights (Hamilton), pursued by about 3,500 Americans who camped at Stoney Creek on 5 June. Vincent's position was precarious since his opponents could expect reinforcements and he could not. As senior staff officer, Harvey was responsible for reconnaissance and he suggested a surprise attack at night to disperse the Americans before they could be reinforced. At 2:00 A.M. he led out about 700 men. Fortunately, the night was dark, the American pickets were bayoneted before they could give the alarm, and the enemy encampment was poorly organized. Although the battle rapidly degenerated into confused fighting in the dark, Harvey was able to withdraw his men in an orderly fashion before dawn. Among their prisoners were the two American generals, and the enemy force, lacking an experienced commander, retreated. Harvey owed much to luck, but he had taken a calculated risk and he had succeeded. If he had failed, the whole of the Niagara district might have fallen to the Americans; his success greatly raised the morale of the British forces throughout Upper Canada. It also established him as an officer of unusual "zeal intelligence & gallantry." His reputation was enhanced in November 1813 at the battle of Crysler's Farm, where he earned a medal, and at Oswego, Lundy's Lane, and Fort Erie in 1814. Despite numerous acts of bravery and the loss of several horses shot from under him, Harvey was wounded only once, at the siege of Fort Erie on 6 Aug. 1814.

As deputy adjutant general, Harvey also had onerous administrative responsibilities. He negotiated terms for paroles and prisoners of war with his American counterpart, Colonel (later General) Winfield Scott, and the two men formed a continuing friendship. Harvey acted as a liaison with Britain's Indian allies, was responsible for collecting intelligence, and assisted in organizing the provincial militia. Bravery was not an unusual quality among British officers of the period but administrative competence was less common. Harvey's talents were recognized and he was clearly marked out for future advancement. Unfortunately for him, in December 1814 the war came to an end and a few months later so did the war in Europe. Harvey was now simply one of hundreds of young officers who faced an uncertain future in a period of retrenchment. Promotion was slow because it was by seniority. Although Harvey became a colonel in May 1825, he would not reach the rank of major-general until January 1837 and lieutenant-general until November 1846. Since he had little *"Parliamentary* Interest" and most of the patronage within the army was distributed by the Duke of Wellington to those who had served under him in Spain or at the battle of Waterloo, Harvey's chances of employment were slim. Moreover, though awarded a KCH and knighted at Windsor, England, in 1824, he was not given the KCB, to which he felt entitled, because his rank in the army was too low. It is not surprising that in 1829 he proclaimed to Dalhousie that "no Credit was to be gained in Canada."

With the conclusion of hostilities in Canada, Harvey had moved to Quebec City, where he continued to act as deputy adjutant general. In 1817 he was placed on half pay and in 1824 he returned to England. His timing, once again, was fortunate. The Colonial Office had decided to appoint a five-man commission to evaluate the price at which crown land should be sold to the recently formed Canada Company [*see* John Galt*] and Harvey was selected as one of the two government appointees. The members sailed for Upper Canada late in December 1825 and remained until June 1826 when they returned to present a report which immediately became the focus of a bitter controversy. It recommended the sale of waste lands to the company at a price critics claimed was too low. The Colonial Office ordered a second investigation which concluded that the first commissioners had performed their work hastily and inadequately. Ironically, Harvey had been the only commissioner to advocate a higher price, but for the sake of unanimity he had signed the report. Despite his efforts to dissociate himself from it, he was censured along with his fellow commissioners and his prospects for employment in the colonial service receded.

Finally, in 1828, owing to the influence of Anglesey, Harvey was appointed inspector general of police for the province of Leinster (Republic of Ireland). He assumed his post at a critical moment. Ireland had remained unusually calm during the struggle for Catholic emancipation in the 1820s, but between 1830 and 1838 it was caught up in disturbances over the collection of tithes by the Church of Ireland. The centre of agitation was Leinster and, although Harvey did everything in his power to promote compromise and prevent violence, one of the bloodiest incidents of the period took place within his district: on 14 Dec. 1831, 13 policemen were killed and 14 wounded during a riot. Yet Harvey's own reputation emerged unscathed. He was popular both with Dublin Castle and with Irish Roman Catholics and in 1832 he was called as a witness before the House of Commons select committee on tithes in Ireland, where he recommended the solution to the problem that was adopted six years later. None the less, he continued to seek employment in the colonies and in April 1836 he was appointed lieutenant governor of Prince Edward Island.

Harvey found himself confronted on Prince Edward Island by problems not dissimilar to those he had faced in Ireland. All of the British North American colonies entered a period of turmoil in the 1830s, but the Island was unique in one respect. Most of it was owned by absentee landlords in Britain, who were as unpopular as their counterparts in Ireland. By 1836 a popular movement led by William Cooper* was demanding that they be dispossessed for not fulfilling the original conditions of their grants. Although the leaders of the Escheat party hoped to achieve their goals without violence, they encouraged tenants to withhold rents. As in Ireland, the efforts of the government to enforce laws which were considered unjust would lead to civil disobedience and ultimately to retaliation against the property of the landlords and their agents. Yet the pressure upon the government to enforce the collection of rents was growing stronger in Britain. Many of the original grants were passing into the hands of land speculators, who were able to purchase lots at low prices, or were now managed by agents in England and Scotland determined to secure an income from estates long ignored. Conscious that the rising tide of immigration to British North America was increasing the value of colonial properties, and frequently involved in land speculation elsewhere, these men were not interested in the prestige that the possession of large estates might bring but in maximizing profits. Led by David and Robert Bruce Stewart, two London merchants who had purchased large tracts of land on the Island, and by the agents of some of the largest proprietors, such as William Waller and Andrew Colvile, they organized the Prince Edward Island Association to act as a lobby in London.

Harvey

Before departing for the Island in July 1836, Harvey met with representatives from the association who assured him that, if the escheat issue were resolved, they would deal leniently with their tenants and invest more capital in the colony. But, as Harvey discovered upon his arrival on 30 August, the escheat movement was gaining momentum. Because of an early frost, the Island's potato crop partially failed in September and the distress thus occasioned, as well as a shortage of hard currency, strengthened the resolve of the tenants. Although Harvey optimistically predicted that he could restore the Island to "a state of perfect tranquillity," an escheat meeting in Kings County attracted 1,300 people. At Harvey's request the colonial secretary, Lord Glenelg, prepared a dispatch ruling out escheat and Harvey published it in October. But on 20 Dec. 1836 another mass meeting was held at Hay River, attended by Cooper and two other MHAS, John MacKintosh* and John Windsor LeLacheur. The meeting not only demanded escheat but encouraged the tenants to withhold their rent.

This meeting convinced Harvey that more vigorous measures had to be taken to open "the eyes of the deluded Tenantry." He dismissed from office the magistrate who had chaired the meeting and stripped Cooper of several minor governmental posts. But Harvey placed his greatest faith in the assembly, which was dominated by an élite sympathetic to some of the complaints made against the proprietors but also determined to uphold the rights of property. Working through the speaker of the house, George R. DALRYMPLE, and councillors Thomas Heath Haviland* and Robert Hodgson*, two of the Island's most influential politicians, Harvey persuaded the assembly to adopt a series of resolutions condemning the Hay River meeting. Indeed, in its enthusiasm it committed the three MHAS who had attended the meeting to the serjeant-at-arms and they remained in custody for two full sessions until the assembly was dissolved. Publicly Harvey predicted that these measures would lead to a "moral revolution" and claimed that the question of escheat had been "settled & *forever*." Privately he confided that by arresting Cooper and his fellow escheators the assembly might turn them into martyrs. Harvey quickly realized that the escheat issue would not disappear so easily. In March 1837 he prepared a dispatch requesting permission to establish a special commission to discover which proprietors had not fulfilled the conditions of settlement imposed in 1826. Although he did not send it until the eve of his departure in May, rumours that he was in favour of at least partial escheat circulated freely on the Island.

The major reason why Harvey delayed his dispatch was his desire to convince the absentee landlords that the escheat agitation would end if they offered more lenient terms to their tenants. He had toured much of Prince Edward Island in 1836 and what most impressed him was "how exact an Epitome this Island in some respects is, of the Island . . . which I have so recently left." Because the proprietorial system diffused settlement and large blocks of wilderness lands hindered development, communications on the Island were primitive. Many landlords would give only short leases and would not compensate tenants for improvements. Rents were high and frequently had to be paid in hard currency, which was in short supply. Thus many tenants owed substantial arrears which they could never hope to pay. Moreover, the Island élite, many of whom owned property or were agents of the proprietors, had limited sympathy with the absentees, who contributed little to development in the colony. Harvey was opposed to the "extreme & unjust Proposition of extinguishing vested Rights for the non fulfillment of impracticable conditions," but he admitted that his ideas had "undergone some change since my arrival here" and he supported the introduction of "a very moderate 'Penal Assessment' " on unsettled lands to raise funds for internal development. He also appealed to the landlords in February and March 1837 to grant longer leases with lower rents, to accept the payment of rent in kind, and to abandon the arrears already due. To a friend he had written in January 1837: "Between the Proprietors & the tenants I have had a somewhat difficult card to play but I hope to satisfy both."

This was a noble objective, but impracticable. Although the assembly passed the Land Assessment Act in April 1837, the proprietorial lobby in London delayed its implementation until 12 Dec. 1838. They also did not respond to Harvey's request to deal leniently with the tenantry. In fact, several proprietors announced in March 1837 their determination to force the tenants to live up to the terms of existing leases. Harvey considered this action "illtimed & premature," yet he was bound to enforce their legal rights. Anticipating violence, he asked that the garrison on the Island be strengthened. In his dispatches Harvey continued to give the impression that the Island was basically tranquil, and it is true that while he remained in the colony he was able to maintain order. But the failure of the proprietors to follow Harvey's advice inevitably aided Cooper and the Escheat party. By May 1837, to take the initiative out of the hands of Cooper, Harvey had decided to send the dispatch recommending partial escheat.

Of Harvey's influence over the assembly there can be little doubt. Among the numerous measures passed during the 1837 session at Harvey's request were not only an act levying a moderate assessment on all land in the colony to be used to erect a public records repository, but also bills to create a more effective system of elementary education and to improve the administration of justice. None the less, Harvey overestimated his influence on "the honest, warm-hearted, simple minded People of this Island." Far from disappearing, the escheat agitation continued to gain momentum and Cooper's party would form the majority in the next assembly. Fortunately, Harvey did not have to witness this event. He was promoted to New Brunswick and on 25 May 1837 he left Prince Edward Island, to be replaced by Sir Charles Augustus FitzRoy.

On the surface the turbulence of New Brunswick politics resembled that elsewhere in British North America during the 1830s; in reality, the struggle was one for power and place between different factions within the provincial élite. Harvey's predecessor, Sir Archibald Campbell*, had distributed patronage almost exclusively to a handful of the colony's leading families, mainly resident in Fredericton and mainly members of the Church of England. He had thus created a bureaucratic élite at least as inbred as its counterpart in Upper Canada in the 1820s. But the Upper Canadian élite was motivated by ideological considerations that simply were not present in New Brunswick, where the politically articulate population was relatively homogeneous in ethnic background and in social and political attitudes and united in its commitment to the imperial connection. Since New Brunswick was divided into a series of communities, each of which was concerned to advance its own immediate self-interest, factionalism was endemic, but party divisions were therefore slow to develop and political rivalries were muted by the existence of a consensus upon fundamental principles. None the less, those excluded from official patronage or resentful of government policies did combine in the mid 1830s to form a coalition that controlled the assembly. Led by the wealthy timber merchants and by the representatives of the dissenting interests, including Charles Simonds, they demanded control over the rapidly increasing crown revenues and over the policies of the Crown Lands Office, headed by the immensely powerful and equally unpopular Thomas Baillie*. When the reformers succeeded in convincing the British government of their moderation and extracted from Glenelg a series of major concessions, Campbell proffered his resignation.

Harvey, as historian James Hannay* has noted, was "a man of a very different spirit" from Campbell. Although basically conservative, Harvey's patron Anglesey was a member of the Whig ministry and Harvey recognized that the winds of change were sweeping across Britain and into British North America. In 1837 he warned an old friend in Upper Canada, Solicitor General Christopher Alexander Hagerman*: "You deceive yourself – the spirit of real, downright, *old Style* Toryism being extinct, dead, defunct, defeated and no more capable of revisiting the Nations of the Earth than it is possible for the sparks to descend or the stream to flow upwards."

While on Prince Edward Island, Harvey had applauded the "equitable, just & liberal principles, upon which the Colonial Policy of England is now happily conducted" and had criticized the "anomolous & defective composition" of the Island's Legislative Council. Immediately upon his arrival in Fredericton on 1 June 1837 he embarked upon the policy of conciliation that Campbell had refused to implement. In July he hastily convened the assembly to present it with a bill surrendering the revenues of the crown for a permanent civil list. He also sought to end "the dissatisfaction which has long & I fear so justly prevailed, throughout the whole colony, regarding the conduct & management of the Crown Land Department." But although he was able to limit "the undue, uncontrolled, almost irresponsible Financial Powers" exercised by Baillie, he could not suspend him from office until 1840, after Baillie had become insolvent. Indeed, Baillie's refusal to retire upon terms that the assembly would accept was the one issue that threatened to disrupt Harvey's harmonious relationship with the house.

This harmony was based on more than just the concession of crown revenues and the reorganization of the Crown Lands Office. Adjustments were necessary in the personnel of the government to place power in the hands of those having the confidence of the assembly. In New Brunswick, since the challengers resembled the existing ruling class in background and attitude, all that was required was the distribution of patronage upon a less exclusive basis. Thus Harvey appointed a number of reformers as justices of the peace and he selected "men of Liberal opinions" such as Lemuel Allan Wilmot* and William Boyd Kinnear* as queen's counsels "for the purpose of counter balancing the Barristers of opposite Politics who had been previously preferred." He also expanded the Legislative Council to include those speaking for the "*Dissenting* Interests" and areas of the colony long underrepresented. Among the latter was the city of Saint John. Unlike many of the aristocratic and military governors of the 1830s Harvey did not look down upon commercial men. He sought to ally his government with the entrepreneurial leaders of the colony and frequently visited Saint John and promoted urban reforms.

Harvey's most important decision, however, was to bring into his Executive Council the leading figures in the assembly, especially Simonds, the speaker of the house. It is frequently asserted that Harvey established a form of responsible government in New Brunswick. If one uses that term in its broadest sense, as it had been used in Britain for more than a century, then Harvey did indeed introduce into New Brunswick, as historian William Stewart MacNutt* has claimed, "the essential ingredients of the British system, an executive responsible to the elected representatives of the people." But this was not responsible government as it was later understood. Harvey did not turn the Executive Council into a cabinet of ministers and he did not feel that he had to follow the advice he was given. Neither Harvey nor his superiors in London wished to introduce into the colony a system of party government similar to that which had evolved at Westminster by the early 19th century. The New Brunswick assembly clearly indicated in its resolutions of 29 Feb. 1840 that it wanted "an efficient responsibility on the part of the Executive officers to the Representative Branch of the Provincial Government," but in the absence of a coherent party system there could be no demand for party government. Harvey's Executive Council was thus a coalition of the leading political figures in the colony, who felt free to disagree among themselves. The absence of parties allowed Harvey to initiate policies and to control patronage.

Although Harvey did not intend to exclude from his Executive Council the leaders of the old official party, their stubborn resistance to his policies left him little choice. William Franklin Odell*, George Frederick STREET, and Baillie, all interrelated by marriage, were sufficiently influential in Fredericton to be able to embarrass the lieutenant governor on several occasions; he therefore welcomed the arrival of Lord John Russell's famous dispatch of 16 Oct. 1839 announcing a change in the tenure of public office in the colonies and circulated it to the leading officials in New Brunswick. Those opponents of his régime whom he could not conciliate, he could now at least silence.

Yet, as Harvey clearly understood, there were distinct limits to his authority and influence. One of the fundamental principles to which the members of the assembly were committed was their right to decide how the provincial revenues would be distributed and they would support the government only upon this condition. Undeniably, this system could be abused and to a considerable extent the colony's financial resources were frittered away on purely local projects. But Hannay was right to stress that "a glance at the statute books [during the Harvey years], discloses the fact that there was great activity in many lines of enterprise." Much of this activity was in response to private or local pressures and frequently served merely to advance the interests of a particular community, a specific interest group, or even an individual entrepreneur. None the less, this decentralized system made sense in a colony divided by geography into a series of distinct communities which had little contact with one another. Harvey's successor, Sir William MacBean George Colebrooke*, would discover in the 1840s that he could not artificially create a provincial mentality. Until the railway era, perhaps even later, such a mentality did

not exist, at least outside limited circles in Fredericton and Saint John. In any case, a system of party government and executive centralization, as the history of the Canadas in the 1850s shows, would not have prevented the government from becoming the agent of particularistic interests in an age when the pursuit of private gain was considered the most effective way to advance the public interest. Brokerage politics was an inevitable development in a pre-industrial society where the scope of government was extremely limited and the vast majority of the population was only intermittently affected by government activities. To criticize Harvey, as MacNutt has done, for acquiescing in the uncontrolled expenditures of an assembly "whose political horizons were for the most part limited by the parish pump" is to apply anachronistic standards. Indeed, by yielding to pressures which were too strong to resist, Harvey did help preserve a respect for the imperial authority that to a limited degree would persist into the industrial era. During his administration he initiated or supported, with varying degrees of success, major reforms in the colony's legal system, revisions in public and higher education, improved communications, the first geological survey of the province, by Abraham Gesner*, the development of agriculture, a revitalized militia, and an improved system of support for paupers and the insane. These objectives he was to pursue in all the colonies in which he served.

Much of Harvey's time was devoted to military affairs. Within 24 hours of his arrival he was embroiled in the Maine–New Brunswick boundary dispute by the arrest of Ebenezer Greeley, a census taker from Maine who had been working in the territory claimed by the British government. With Maine threatening to retaliate by occupying the disputed area, Harvey sent troops to Woodstock and Grand Falls and personally visited the area. His main objective was to deter American encroachments before they led to a confrontation that would engulf Britain and the United States in another war. Although the possibility of conflict receded during the autumn of 1837, the following spring Maine renewed its efforts to establish control over the area. Harvey was now placed in an awkward position. Because of the rebellions in the Canadas, New Brunswick was denuded of troops, and he was forbidden by Sir Colin Campbell*, military commander for the Atlantic region, from stationing troops, when they did arrive, in positions above Fredericton on the Saint John River. Yet between December 1837 and the spring of 1839 Harvey was responsible for conveying overland five regiments and two companies of British troops to Lower Canada, and the security of the route became his major concern. For this reason he sought to reduce tensions with Maine by releasing Greeley from prison, entering into a personal correspondence with the governor of Maine, John Fairfield, and turning a blind eye to Maine's encroachments into the valley of the Aroostook River. In March 1839, however, Harvey decided that another show of strength was necessary and re-established a British force in the disputed territory, but he warned the officer in charge to retreat at the first sign of real danger. He eagerly assented to an agreement with the governor of Maine, negotiated by General Winfield Scott representing the American federal government, to withdraw the force if Maine would remove her troops.

By these actions Harvey prevented the "Aroostook war" from evolving into a serious confrontation at a moment when Britain was ill equipped for one. Harvey's personal prestige was never higher than during this period. Not only had he pacified New Brunswick but the colony volunteered men and money to put down the Canadian rebellions. Harvey was in charge of the New Brunswick mission to meet with Lord Durham [Lambton*] in 1838, the year in which at long last he received his KCB, and he was fulsomely praised in the Durham report. Charles Edward Poulett Thomson*, later Lord Sydenham, visited New Brunswick in 1840 and described Harvey as "the Pearl of Civil Governors." Although his relationship with Sir Colin Campbell had gradually deteriorated into open hostility, Harvey had persuaded the military authorities in London to give him command of the troops in New Brunswick in July 1837, to place him on the staff as a major-general in November, and to grant him the pay and allowances of his rank in November 1839. In September 1840 Harvey replaced Campbell as commander of the troops in the Atlantic provinces and moved the headquarters to New Brunswick.

Harvey's personal affairs were on a more secure basis in the late 1830s. In Ireland he had gone into debt, in Prince Edward Island his salary had not been sufficient to meet his expenses, and shortly after his arrival in New Brunswick he had been forced to negotiate a loan from the Bank of British North America. But owing to the generosity of the New Brunswick legislature, which not only increased his salary but also made special grants for the upkeep of Government House and for a private secretary, and to the allowances and patronage attached to the military command, Harvey was on his way to solvency. Since he had no estates, he had provided for his sons in the only way that he could, by securing them commissions in the army and the navy. With considerable military patronage at his disposal, he was able to reunite his family under his roof in Fredericton. His only daughter married his aide-de-camp in 1839 and they lived at Government House. The death of his eldest son, on 22 March 1839, was the only tragedy to mar what Harvey would afterwards recall as the happiest years of his life.

Yet Harvey had already set in motion the train of events that would lead to his recall. He believed that the agreement with Maine would serve to maintain the territorial *status quo* until the British and American governments could reach a final settlement of the boundary. But negotiations moved slowly during 1839 and 1840 and Maine gradually extended its authority in the area under dispute by building roads and establishing new settlements. Although Maine had agreed in March 1839 to withdraw its troops from the disputed territory, it retained an armed civil posse which established a small base at the mouth of the Fish River during the summer. These actions did not break the 1839 agreement, but they were clearly contrary to its spirit, and Harvey gradually came to realize that he had underestimated Maine's determination and had signed an agreement which left the initiative in its hands. In November 1840 Harvey decided that Britain must reassert her authority and he asked Sydenham to dispatch a substantial force to Lake Temisquata (Lac Témiscouata, Que.) on the edge of the disputed territory. After reconsidering this request, Harvey appealed to Sydenham to rescind the order but the troops were already on the march. Foolishly, Harvey then assured the governor of Maine that they would soon be withdrawn. For this indiscretion he was dismissed by Lord John Russell, the British colonial secretary, who was persuaded by Sydenham and by a bellicose Lord Palmerston, the foreign secretary, that Harvey's action would encourage Maine's transgressions.

For once, Harvey had totally misjudged the political situation. With Canada pacified and with an enormous British force stationed in the North American colonies, the balance of power, at least temporarily, had shifted in favour of Britain and the British government was determined to force the United States to agree to a negotiated settlement of the boundary dispute. Harvey did not realize until too late that his policy of appeasement was no longer in line with government policy. When the overseas mail arrived in Fredericton in February 1841, the first letter that Harvey opened was from his friend Sir Charles Theophilus Metcalfe* predicting that Harvey would some day be appointed governor of Canada. The second letter was from George W. Featherstonhaugh, another friend, who had been deputed by Russell to inform Harvey of his dismissal. The blow, being quite unexpected, came as a tremendous shock to Harvey and his family. He had good reason to despair. Without a private income, he would be ruined. Fortunately, his advocate, Anglesey, persuaded Russell to appoint Harvey to Newfoundland in April 1841.

After a brief visit to London, Harvey arrived in Newfoundland in September 1841. Both before and after the introduction of representative government in

Harvey

1832, Newfoundland politics had been disrupted by sectarian animosities and by bitter disputes between the wealthy merchants of St John's, who were frequently transients, and the representatives of the rapidly growing resident (native) population, which was engaged in the fisheries. Harvey's predecessor, Henry Prescott*, had sought to mediate between the rival factions in the colony, but had succeeded only in dissatisfying virtually everyone. During the general elections in November and December 1840 this dissatisfaction led to considerable violence and when the Newfoundland legislature met in 1841 the assembly and the council disagreed over nearly every measure, including the annual supply bill. By the autumn of 1841 the British government had reached the conclusion that substantial changes would have to be made in the constitution of Newfoundland and, while considering the nature of the reforms to be introduced, it suspended the existing constitution. To some extent these developments worked to Harvey's advantage. Many of Newfoundland's political and religious leaders had been shocked by the escalation of violence and were prepared to cooperate, at least for the moment, with a governor who sought to heal old wounds. Harvey, as the members of the St John's Natives' Society noted, had already established a reputation as a "political physician" and James Stephen at the Colonial Office believed that he was "more likely than any man I know to allay the storms which have so long agitated Society in Newfoundland." None the less, the traditional enmities in island politics had not disappeared and Harvey's task was a formidable one.

Potentially the most disruptive force in Newfoundland, as elsewhere in British North America, was religion. Given his background, it is hardly surprising that Harvey was a committed supporter of the Church of England. Indeed, he conscientiously attended services, gave generously from his meagre private resources, and consistently sought to advance the church's interests. His sympathies lay with the low-church party and he formed a close friendship with Aubrey George Spencer*, the bishop of Newfoundland, a friendship cemented by the marriage of his youngest son to one of the bishop's daughters. Harvey assisted the bishop in acquiring the land upon which a cathedral was eventually erected in St John's.

In both Prince Edward Island and New Brunswick, while actively supporting the Church of England, Harvey had, however, endeared himself to dissenters by extending government patronage to their institutions. He was less successful with the various Protestant sects in Newfoundland. In 1843 an education bill was introduced in the assembly by Richard Barnes*, member for Trinity Bay, which provided for an equal distribution of funds between Catholic and Protestant elementary schools. Harvey strongly supported the bill, but only with great difficulty was he able to convince the dissenting sects that it did not unduly favour the Church of England schools. Harvey also aroused the suspicion of the dissenters by appointing Bryan Robinson*, an outspoken advocate of the Church of England, to the Executive Council in 1843. Robinson, a prominent lawyer, had become involved in a bitter personal controversy over the functioning of the Supreme Court with Chief Justice John Gervase Hutchinson Bourne*, and Harvey became unavoidably entangled in the dispute when he sought to mediate between the two men. Harvey ascribed Bourne's refusal to abandon the controversy to the chief justice's alliance with "a certain party of Dissenters" who bitterly assailed "our venerable Church establishment."

Harvey maintained his efforts on behalf of the Church of England, but in 1844 he supported the founding of an academy which would be free of religious instruction and in 1845 he advocated a policy of assisting all religious groups in the construction of churches. These policies were frustrated by Spencer's successor, Edward Feild*, who had high-church leanings. In New Brunswick, Harvey had vainly tried to liberalize the charter of King's College, Fredericton; in Newfoundland, too, he was unable to convince his co-religionists of "the mischievous consequences of clothing Educational institutions with too exclusive a character."

These difficulties were overshadowed, however, by the problem of convincing the colony's Roman Catholics of the good intentions of the government. Prescott had entered into a vitriolic debate with Bishop Michael Anthony Fleming* and had alienated almost the entire Catholic population. Like most of his contemporaries, Harvey was suspicious of the Catholic Church in general and of non-Anglo-Saxon Catholics in particular. While serving in Prince Edward Island, he had attempted to prevent the appointment of an Irish or French Canadian Catholic to a vacant bishopric, because their clergy "meddle too much with Politics." He also subscribed to the popular stereotype that the Irish were excitable and easily misled by their religious leaders. None the less, having seen both in the Canadas and in Ireland how discrimination and bigotry led to religious and political conflicts, he had actively and consistently sought the cooperation of Catholic clergy in Ireland, Prince Edward Island, and New Brunswick.

From the moment of his arrival in Newfoundland in September 1841 Harvey sought to end sectarian conflicts and conciliate Catholics. As an initial "act of leniency," he released several prisoners arrested during the election riots of the previous December and he withdrew the garrison stationed in Carbonear. He then secured a promise from Fleming to withdraw from politics, a promise which the bishop kept. Harvey's share of the bargain was to administer the government impartially and this promise was also kept. Despite Protestant outcries, he appointed the first Catholic magistrate in St John's. In December 1842 he censured a Protestant magistrate for arresting the prominent Catholic politician John Valentine Nugent* during an election. Harvey wanted the Education Act of 1843, which placed Catholics and Protestants on an equal footing in the distribution of funds, to include provision for both a Catholic and a Protestant inspector of schools. When the assembly made provision for only one position, he alternated the appointment on an annual basis. His Executive Council was "composed fairly & impartially of Protestants & Catholics." According to Catholic politician John Kent*, Harvey's "conciliatory conduct & strict impartiality" persuaded leading Catholics William Carson*, Laurence O'Brien*, and Patrick Morris* to serve on this council. Even when some of them attended an Irish repeal meeting in St John's, and thus incurred the censure of the British government, Harvey defended their actions in July 1844 in his report to the Colonial Office.

Catholic support was critical for Harvey. The constitution introduced in 1842 by the Newfoundland Act, partly at Harvey's request, had been imposed against the wishes of the Catholics who dominated the reform party. Harvey realized that without reform support the amalgamated legislature of 15 elected and 10 appointed members would work no more efficiently than the old. Although he had encouraged the Colonial Office to try the experiment, he indicated to the reform leaders that it was to be only a temporary expedient. In theory, under the new constitution, the lieutenant governor, by controlling the initiation of money bills, would be able to exert a commanding influence upon the development of the colony. In practice, Harvey allowed the members of the Amalgamated Legislature to distribute the funds according to their perception of the requirements of the colony. Under these conditions the reformers were prepared to assist in making the legislature work. By 1846, however, even Harvey could not persuade the reformers to accept a renewal of the amalgamation bill when it was to expire the following year. In February 1846 the legislature voted by ten to nine for a series of resolutions, moved by Kent, advocating responsible government. Nine of the ten votes in favour were by Catholics and the tenth was by a Protestant dependent upon Catholic support. None the less, even Kent remained ready to defend Harvey's administration.

More remarkable is the fact that Harvey consolidated Catholic and reform support without antagonizing the Conservatives, whose leadership was drawn largely from the Protestant, mercantile community of St John's. Along with its rural areas the city represented nearly 40 per cent of the island's population, and Harvey quickly realized that he had to show its leading citizens they could expect concrete improvements from his government. During his tenure of office he vigorously supported the ambitions of the St John's Chamber of Commerce by advocating more efficient postal service and steamship communications with the outside world and by protesting "the French invasion of our Fisheries." He also sought to improve the appearance of St John's and the quality of health and public services within the city. It is ironic that in his efforts at beautification he may have contributed, by removing some of the natural fire-breaks, to the damage caused by the great fire of June 1846, which "suddenly swept away three fourths of this so lately wealthy and prosperous City." By appointing the candidate of the St John's Chamber of Commerce, William Thomas, to the Executive Council in 1842, by consulting frequently with the merchants, and by devoting himself "heart and soul to the local and general improvement of the country," Harvey reconciled the merchant élite to the reintroduction of the old representative system. "His Excellency arrived amongst us," Charles James Fox Bennett* proclaimed in 1846, "at a period when the country had been torn and distracted by political animosities, when disorder and confusion had reigned on every side, and when the framework of our political existence had been disjointed and severed; but no sooner had he placed his foot upon our shores than he, as if by the touch of a talismanic wand, restored order, peace and happiness to the country."

This claim is exaggerated. Harvey had no magic wand, and he could not make ethnic, religious, and socio-economic rivalries disappear. None the less, whenever the opportunity presented itself, he sought to persuade the various groups within the community to focus upon the issues that united rather than those that divided them. He founded Newfoundland's first Agricultural Society at St John's in 1841, partly to provide an association to which both Catholics and Protestants could belong. He attempted to persuade the religious leaders of both to unite in a temperance crusade in 1844, and he became patron of the Natives' Society because he felt it was an organization that promised to transcend other loyalties. Yet many Protestants bitterly resented Harvey's efforts to distribute patronage to Catholics, and reformers and Conservatives remained at odds over the direction in which the colony should develop. Harvey did not remove the sources of friction, but he did create an atmosphere in which differences of opinion could be resolved peacefully.

Despite this achievement, Harvey did not enjoy his sojourn in Newfoundland. Like his close friend Sir Richard Henry Bonnycastle*, he found the "siberian" winters nearly unbearable. He was also plagued by

Harvey

financial difficulties. His sudden removal from New Brunswick had occurred before he had paid off his debts and it left him virtually destitute. He had already disposed of most of his household effects in New Brunswick at a heavy loss before he learned of his appointment to Newfoundland and he had had to request an advance to meet the charges on his commission and to purchase Prescott's furniture. The annual salary of £3,000 was £1,000 less than in New Brunswick, St John's was an expensive city in which to live, and Government House was costly to maintain. Shortly after his arrival in the colony, the Bank of British North America demanded payment of his outstanding debts and Harvey was compelled to borrow money from his colonial secretary, James Crowdy*. During the prolonged controversy with Bourne, this arrangement was brought to the attention of the Colonial Office. Ultimately, Harvey was exonerated of any wrongdoing, but he was reprimanded for indiscretion. It is not easy to feel much sympathy for a man who earned more in a year than most labourers could earn in a lifetime, who travelled with a retinue of servants, and who entertained lavishly. But Harvey must be judged by the standards of the age in which he lived. He was expected to maintain a standard of living which, without a private income, he simply could not afford, and "the exercise of hospitality" was, as he claimed, one of the means by which a governor cultivated a "good understanding" in a colony. He did give generously to charities and other worthy causes. If he lived beyond his means and engaged in activities that justifiably led to charges of conflict of interest, he really had little choice.

It was more than harsh climate and financial worries that led to Harvey's dissatisfaction. His youngest son fell ill in Newfoundland and died early in 1846. His other sons were forced to seek employment elsewhere and his daughter was with her husband in Halifax. Harvey wished to reunite his family under one roof, and when the lieutenant governorship of Nova Scotia became vacant he eagerly applied for it. With almost unseemly haste, and to the consternation of the Colonial Office, he departed from Newfoundland in August 1846 as quickly as he could after receiving the appointment.

When Harvey arrived in Nova Scotia late in August 1846, he was hailed by the *Yarmouth Courier* as the man who could "check that spirit of discord which has been rife throughout this province for some years." Certainly Harvey hoped that by applying to Nova Scotia the methods that had worked so successfully elsewhere he could restore "this distracted Province to that condition of political & social tranquillity which I really believe to *be desired by all*." But those methods had only limited success in Nova Scotia. Both the Conservatives and the Liberals were now relatively cohesive political parties. Although the Conservatives had a majority of seats in the house, Harvey sought to create a calmer political atmosphere than the one he had inherited from his predecessor, Lord Falkland [Cary*], who had ostracized the leading Liberals and identified himself with the Conservatives [see George Renny YOUNG]. By friendly gestures to the leaders of the Liberal party and by inviting "the influential of all parties" to dine at Government House, Harvey succeeded in reducing tensions.

Yet, despite repeated efforts, Harvey could not persuade the Liberals that they should join with the Conservatives in a coalition government. Indeed, so confident were the Liberals of success in the approaching election that they only reluctantly abandoned their demand for an immediate dissolution and agreed to refrain from obstructing the final session of the legislature in 1847. Although these concessions in themselves represented a major victory for Harvey, they did not result in the formation of a coalition. Harvey's failure led Earl Grey, who had recently become secretary of state for the colonies, to enunciate in two important dispatches his willingness to accept party government in the larger British North American colonies. But Harvey continued to hope that he could bring about "a fusion of parties" in Nova Scotia after the forthcoming general election.

On 5 Aug. 1847 the Liberals were victorious at the polls. After a final, but unsuccessful, effort to construct a coalition, Harvey was left with no option but to accept the first administration based on party in British North America. But until the assembly met in January 1848 and carried a vote of non-confidence by a margin of 29 to 22, Harvey had to carry on with a government that refused to resign until the house had pronounced its verdict. During this period he was able to persuade the Conservatives not to recommend appointments that he could not approve and the Liberals to restrain their impatience for office.

The transfer of power formally took place on 2 Feb. 1848, when James Boyle UNIACKE became premier of "the first formally responsible ministry overseas." But the transition was neither as simple nor as harmonious as many historians, particularly Chester Martin*, have implied. A rudimentary system of cabinet government had been introduced into the Province of Canada in 1841, but in Nova Scotia the Executive Council did not consist of officials holding ministerial positions and the Liberals were determined to restructure the council into a cabinet of ministers. Harvey thus had to force into retirement the provincial secretary, Sir Rupert D. George, who had held office for 25 years, and to dismiss Samuel Prescott Fairbanks*, who had been appointed provincial treasurer for life in 1845. He also agreed to the creation of several new ministerial posts. Lord Grey had already agreed to the principle of responsible party government, but he had hoped to limit to the barest minimum the number of ministerial positions that would change, and he was only reluctantly persuaded by Harvey of the necessity of converting the Executive Council into a cabinet on the British and Canadian models.

Harvey sincerely tried to persuade his new advisers to compensate generously with pensions those who were displaced, but he was only partially successful and a stream of petitions were sent to the British government complaining of the changes. The Conservative press in Nova Scotia began to abuse him for yielding to Liberal demands and James William Johnston*, who had been forced to resign as attorney general, moved a resolution in the assembly to reduce the lieutenant governor's annual salary from £3,000 to £2,500. The crown revenues in Nova Scotia had not been surrendered for a permanent civil list and the Liberals had frequently condemned the high salaries paid to officials, many of whom were owed several years' arrears because of the inadequacy of the crown's revenues. Johnston's motion was designed to embarrass both the lieutenant governor and his advisers and the government hastily introduced a civil list bill which gave Harvey £3,500 per annum (£1,500 more than his successors were to receive), reduced the salaries of most other officials, and disallowed the arrears that had been accumulating since 1844. To Harvey's dismay Lord Grey refused to assent to the act and reprimanded Harvey for placing his own claims before those of other officials who were owed arrears or whose salaries had been reduced. Although Harvey ultimately persuaded the Liberal government to agree to Grey's terms, he was forced to abandon his claim to a higher salary. Harvey felt badly treated, but by foolishly consenting to the initial bill he had brought upon himself Grey's censure and given credence to the charge that he had "bargained with his Council, to promote his pecuniary interests."

During 1849 Harvey again became the subject of Conservative criticism when he agreed to a wholesale revision of the commission of the peace. Although it is frequently asserted that the reform ministers of this period withstood the pressure from their supporters for the introduction of the spoils system, in 1849 scores of Conservative justices of the peace were dismissed and several hundred Liberals were appointed. Believing that Harvey had become "a regular partizan of his present advisors," Grey vigorously protested against the change in the commission. Harvey was able to persuade his ministers to restore some of the dismissed magistrates to office, but he defended his government and correctly pointed out that there were limits to his influence. Party control over patronage was an inevitable concomitant of party government and Harvey at best could moderate the extension of this principle to Nova Scotia. Ultimately, he forced Grey to accept this fact and, without any prospect of Colonial Office support, the Conservatives of Nova Scotia began to adjust to the new system, although the attacks on Harvey continued.

Much of the criticism directed against Harvey was, as he claimed, motivated by nothing more than the frustrations and pique of those dismissed from office, but it is clear that he reacted to the criticism by identifying himself more closely with his Liberal advisers and by relying upon them to defend him in the assembly. Indeed, Harvey did not think that he would be able to remain in Nova Scotia if the Conservatives were returned to office. He also came to play only a minor role in the governmental process. To some extent this was an inevitable development, as his Executive Council increasingly demanded that "the introduction & management" of bills "should be left in their hands." But Lord Elgin [Bruce*] in Canada and Sir Edmund Walker Head* in New Brunswick were able to show that a governor could continue to influence the course of events, even after the introduction of party government. However, these were men in the prime of health. Harvey was over 70, ill, and by 1850 without much energy to resist or to question the advice he was given. He did espouse a number of important causes after 1848: he was an outspoken proponent of imperial aid for railways, defended the principle of public ownership for both railways and telegraph lines, and promoted intercolonial free trade and British North American federation. But on all these issues his views were largely shaped by others, particularly Joseph Howe*, the colony's provincial secretary, with whom he formed a friendship that went deeper than mere political convenience.

Harvey suffered a shattering blow when his wife died on 10 April 1851, and his health rapidly deteriorated. On his doctor's advice he began a six months' leave of absence in May but, even though his health improved, he was partially paralysed and on his return to the colony in October he was scarcely capable of performing even the routine functions of his office. Pathetically he appealed to Grey to transfer him to a warmer climate, but he was to die in Nova Scotia on 22 March 1852 and was buried in the military cemetery in Halifax beside his wife.

Although Harvey served in more colonies in British North America than any other governor and was successful in all of them, his fame was strangely ephemeral. In part, his fate reflects the central Canadian bias of our historiography. Although he played a conspicuous part in the evolution of the system of responsible government, he worked on the periphery and thus was never accorded the same status as Durham, Sydenham, and Elgin. But there is another reason why Harvey is little known. Most of what has been written about pre-confederation Canada has been Whiggish in approach. From this perspective (the colony-to-nation perspective), governors are interesting only in so far as they produce colonial discontent which leads to demands for autonomy and reform. Thus it is the unsuccessful governors – Sir

Hawkins

Peregrine MAITLAND, Lord Dalhousie, Sir Archibald Campbell – who occupy the centre stage, whereas governors who reduce tensions and minimize conflict are relegated to the wings. And no one performed these tasks better than Harvey. His career belies the cliché that military men necessarily made poor civil governors. Of course, in one critical respect Harvey differed from the other military governors of the period. He came from a family that had neither aristocratic connections nor a tradition of military service and he had no private fortune to fall back on. Harvey was frequently accused of being motivated by personal and financial considerations and these accusations were not entirely unfounded. Yet it would be wrong to dismiss Harvey as a man devoid of principle who governed through what James Stephen, the under-secretary at the Colonial Office, described as "a system of blandishments." Because his origins were comparatively humble, he did not find exile among the colonists as tedious as did most governors. "Never have I known a man so tolerant, so placid and so affable to all who approach him, high or low, rich or poor," Bryan Robinson declared in 1846. That was the ultimate secret of Harvey's success. He was flexible and he was tolerant. He was, as he described himself in one letter, a "Peace maker" and thus the ideal person to govern four colonies during a difficult period.

PHILLIP BUCKNER

[The major primary sources for this study were the Colonial Office records, especially PRO, CO 188/56–71, 194/112–27, 217/193–208, and 226/53–55; the Executive Council minutes and the journals of the assemblies of Prince Edward Island, New Brunswick, Newfoundland, and Nova Scotia; the Harvey papers in the PAC, MG 24, A17; the Harvey letter-books in PANB, RG 1, RS2/14–15, and in the N.B. Museum, the Harvey letter-books and correspondence in the W. F. Ganong coll.; Harvey's correspondence with Lord Dalhousie in the Dalhousie papers, SRO, GD45/3/543–44; the Howe papers, PAC, MG 24, B29 (mfm. at PANS); and the Russell papers, in PRO, PRO 30/22, 3B–4B, 7C. Also useful on Harvey's military career were PRO, WO 25/578, 25/746, G.B., WO, *Army list*, 1816–52, the *United Service Gazette, and Naval and Military Chronicle* (London), 10 April 1852, and PRO, CO 42/151; on the Canada Commission PRO, CO 42/396, 42/398, 42/400, 42/405–6; on Ireland PRO, HO 100/240 and the evidence given in the *Report from the select committee on tithes in Ireland*, G.B., Parl., House of Commons paper, 1831–32, 21, no.177: 1–244. There are numerous references to Harvey in the newspapers of the period but especially useful were the *Daily Sun* (Halifax), 23, 29 March 1852, *New-Brunswick Courier*, 27 March 1852, *New Brunswick Reporter and Fredericton Advertiser*, 18 April 1851, *Novascotian*, 14, 21 April 1851, 29 March 1852, and the *Times* (London), 10 April 1852.

Correspondence from or about Harvey can also be found in the *Arthur papers* (Sanderson); John Strachan, *The John Strachan letter-book, 1812–1834*, ed. G. W. Spragge (Toronto, 1946); and [C. E. P. Thomson, 1st Baron] Sydenham, *Letters from Lord Sydenham, governor-general of Canada, 1839–1841, to Lord John Russell*, ed. Paul Knaplund (London, 1931). Useful contemporary printed sources were R. H. Bonnycastle, *Canada, as it was, is, and may be . . .* , ed. J. E. Alexander (2v., London, 1852); James Carmichael-Smyth, *Precis of the wars in Canada, from 1755 to the treaty of Ghent in 1814, with military and political reflections* (London, 1826; repub., ed. James Carmichael, 1862); William James, *A full and correct account of the military occurrences of the late war between Great Britain and the United States of America . . .* (2v., London, 1818); *Official letters of the military and naval officers of the United States, during the war with Great Britain in the years 1812, 13, 14, & 15 . . .* , comp. John Brannan (Washington, 1823); and [Winfield] Scott, *Memoirs of Lieut.-General Scott, LL.D., written by himself* (2v., New York, 1864).

The most valuable secondary sources were Beck, *Government of N.S.; Canada's smallest prov.* (Bolger); C. [B.] Martin, *Empire & commonwealth; studies in governance and self-government in Canada* (Oxford, 1929) and *Foundations of Canadian nationhood* (Toronto, 1955); Gunn, *Political hist. of Nfld.*; James Hannay, *History of New Brunswick* (2v., Saint John, N.B., 1909); Malcolm MacDonell, "The conflict between Sir John Harvey and Chief Justice John Gervase Hutchinson Bourne," CHA *Report*, 1956: 45–54; W. S. MacNutt, *Atlantic prov., New Brunswick*, and "New Brunswick's age of harmony: the administration of Sir John Harvey," *CHR*, 32 (1951): 105–25; H. F. Wood, "The many battles of Stoney Creek," *The defended border: Upper Canada and the War of 1812 . . .* , ed. Morris Zaslow and W. B. Turner (Toronto, 1964), 56–60. Also useful were H. S. Burrage, *Maine in the northeastern boundary controversy* (Portland, Maine, 1919); D. R. Facey-Crowther, "The New Brunswick militia: 1784–1871" (MA thesis, Univ. of N.B., Fredericton, 1965); Frances Firth, "The history of higher education in New Brunswick" (MA thesis, Univ. of N.B., 1945); Garfield Fizzard, "The Amalgamated Assembly of Newfoundland, 1841–1847" (MA thesis, Memorial Univ. of Nfld., St John's, 1963); Charlotte Lenentine, *Madawaska: a chapter in Maine–New Brunswick relations* (Madawaska, Maine, 1975); W. R. Livingston, *Responsible government in Nova Scotia: a study of the constitutional beginnings of the British Commonwealth* (Iowa City, 1930); D. F. Maclean, "The administration of Sir John Harvey in Nova Scotia, 1846–1852" (MA thesis, Dalhousie Univ., Halifax, 1947); E. D. Mansfield, *Life and services of General Winfield Scott, including the siege of Vera Cruz, the battle of Cerro Gordo, and the battles in the valley of Mexico, to the conclusion of peace, and his return to the United States* (New York, 1852); M. R. Nicholson, "Relations of New Brunswick with the state of Maine and the United States, 1837–1849" (MA thesis, Univ. of N.B., 1952); R. B. O'Brien, *Fifty years of concessions to Ireland, 1831–1881* (2v., London, [1883–85]); Prowse, *Hist. of Nfld.* (1895); J. M. Ward, *Colonial self-government: the British experience, 1759–1856* (London and Basingstoke, Eng., 1976); [G.] A. Wilson, *The clergy reserves of Upper Canada, a Canadian mortmain* (Toronto, 1968). P.B.]

HAWKINS, ALFRED, merchant, author, publisher, and office holder; baptized 10 Oct. 1792 in Bridport, England, second of six children of George

Hawkins

Hawkins and Elizabeth Ellery; m. 2 Oct. 1819 Martha Paterson at Quebec, and they had four children, two of whom survived infancy; d. there 30 June 1854.

In January 1817 Alfred Hawkins, a wine merchant from Dorset, England, advertised in the *Quebec Mercury* and the *Quebec Gazette* that he was entering into partnership with John Leland Maquay. The firm of Hawkins and Maquay, wine and brandy merchants, operated from Rue du Sault-au-Matelot in Lower Town until March 1818 when a move was made to the office and vaults of the Quebec Freemason's Hall in Upper Town. Both men were active in the social and economic life of the city. For several years during the period 1818 to 1824 Hawkins was treasurer of a social organization called the Quebec Assembly which held dances and banquets during the winter months. In 1819 he was acting secretary and treasurer of the Quebec Exchange. He was appointed director of the Quebec Bank on several occasions from 1822, and was also a member of the Quebec Fire Society.

The Hawkins–Maquay partnership was dissolved on 1 March 1820 and Maquay left the province the following year. Hawkins moved his business to Rue Saint-Pierre in Lower Town. In March 1821 he rented a house in Upper Town and from some time before 1824 he occupied a "central and pleasantly situated" house and office on Rue du Parloir.

During the 1830s Quebec was experiencing a period of political, economic, and social turbulence, but there was also a surprising degree of literary activity and interest in the history of the colony. Hawkins had become a keen collector of Canadiana, and after eight years of research *Hawkins's picture of Quebec*, dedicated to the Earl of Dalhousie [Ramsay*], was printed by the firm of Neilson and Cowan in 1834. In the preface he acknowledged the assistance of journalists John Charlton Fisher* and Adam Thom*. His association with these two men is an indication that politically he identified with the English party in Quebec.

According to the review of the book in the *Montreal Gazette*, Hawkins had "indomitable perseverance in the acquisition of information, a taste refined by an extensive acquaintance with the best ancient and modern authors, and an ardent love for his subject." The work contains a history of Quebec from its discovery to the founding of the city, accounts of the various sieges, and histories of the religious establishments and the important buildings. The final chapter, which deals with the geology of the area, was contributed by Lieutenant Frederick Henry Baddeley* of the Royal Engineers. The book is illustrated with 14 plates lithographed by Robert Auchmuty Sproule* from sketches by several artists.

In 1835 Hawkins issued a *Plan of the city of Quebec*, engraved by William Cumming Smillie. The plan was reprinted in 1840, and five years later it was brought up to date by the city surveyor, Joseph Hamel.

In April 1837 Hawkins founded the *Morning Herald and Commercial Advertiser*, which was published in Quebec until the following March. The *Morning Herald* was predominantly a commercial paper and politics occupied little space. Hawkins's *Plan of the military & naval operations under the command of the immortal Wolfe & Vice Admiral Saunders before Quebec* was published in London by James Wyld in 1841. The London *Sun* commented that Hawkins "omitted not one single point, however minute, that may serve to explain the proceedings of the attacking and defending parties . . . all these various explanatory details are delineated with a skill and accuracy that is truly astonishing."

Hawkins next compiled two directories for the city. W. Cowan and Son printed 1,000 copies of the *Quebec directory* in 1844. The second part of this work was printed separately in the same year as *Hawkins' historical guide to Quebec and its environs*. Following two disastrous fires which almost destroyed the city in 1845, the second part was reissued as *Hawkins' guide to Quebec and its environs for 1845, with a plan of the city and burnt district*. The second directory appeared in 1847; because of problems with W. Cowan and Son it was printed in Montreal at the office of the *Canada Gazette*. Both directories were similar in format to the Montreal directories being compiled by Robert Walter Stuart MACKAY. Hawkins was at this time residing at Mount Pleasant (Sillery), and his collection of material on Quebec was available to the public.

On 14 Aug. 1847 Hawkins was appointed shipping master of the port of Quebec, the chief lumber port in British North America and an important shipbuilding centre. From that year destitute Irish immigrants were pouring through the port, bringing with them first typhus and then cholera. Seven years later Hawkins died at age 62, a victim of one of the cholera epidemics. A son, Alfred George, became a customs employee at Quebec.

Hawkins's picture of Quebec is today mainly of interest to antiquarian book-dealers, but his *Plan of the city of Quebec* and his two directories remain of value to the antiquary, the historian, and the genealogist.

Dorothy E. Ryder

Alfred Hawkins is the author of *Hawkins's picture of Quebec; with historical recollections* (Quebec, 1834); *This plan of the city of Quebec is respectfully inscribed to the Mayor R. E. Caron Esqr. by his obedient servant Alfred Hawkins* (n.p., 1835; repr., 1840; new ed., 1845); and *Plan of the military & naval operations under the command of the immortal Wolfe & Vice Admiral Saunders before Quebec* (London, 1841). He compiled the *Quebec directory* for 1844 and 1847; the second part of the *Directory* for 1844 was also published as *Hawkins' historical guide to Quebec and its environs* (Quebec, 1844) and as *Hawkins' guide to Quebec* and its environs, for 1845, with plan of the city and burnt district (Quebec, 1845). For more information about the directories and guides published by Hawkins, see D. E. Ryder, Checklist of the Canadian directories, 1790–1950 (Ottawa, 1979). Hawkins was also the founder of the Morning Herald and Commercial Advertiser (Quebec), which was published from April 1837 to March 1838. There is a portrait of Hawkins at the Hôtel de Ville in Quebec.

Cathedral of the Holy Trinity (Quebec), reg. of baptisms, marriages, and burials, 2 Oct. 1819, 1823–28, 1 July 1854. Dorset Record Office (Dorchester, Eng.), P196/RE4–5 (reg. of baptisms, marriages, and burials, 1754–1806). PAC, RG 68, General index, 1651–1841. Quebec Gazette, 1817–34, 1 July 1854. Quebec Mercury, 1816–20, 1853–54. Beaulieu et Hamelin, La presse québécoise, 1: 95. Morgan, Bibliotheca Canadensis, 179. Quebec directory, 1852. "Alfred Hawkins," BRH, 41 (1935): 747–48. "Le Bureau de poste de Québec," BRH, 5 (1899): 247–49. J. M. LeMoine, "Alfred Hawkins," Le courier du livre (Québec), 1896: 89–91.

HAWLEY, WILLIAM FITZ, author and office holder; b. 1804, probably in La Prairie, Lower Canada; d. there January 1855.

Information about William Fitz Hawley is scant, and comes largely from his two printed volumes. In the earlier of these, published at Montreal in 1829, he refers to his writing as being done "amidst the turmoil of business" but the nature of that business is not known. The only other evidence of an occupation is his appointment as registrar for Huntingdon County on 31 Oct. 1850. Interest in Hawley lies in his activity as one of a number of authors of prose and verse during the 1820s, some of whom were published locally, especially in the newspapers.

Across the St Lawrence from La Prairie, Montreal was experiencing in this decade an initial flurry of literary activity in English. Canadian imitations of the great British literary journals were provided by the Scribbler (1821–27), the Canadian Magazine and Literary Repository (1823–25), and the Canadian Review and Literary and Historical Journal (1824–26). Hawley is said to have written extensively for local periodicals, but few of his contributions have been identified.

He began by collecting manuscripts and papers for a history of the Canadas. The collection was destroyed by fire and, according to Henry James Morgan*, the project was "reluctantly abandoned." Then Hawley turned to what he described as "irregular effusions of early life." These poems were gathered into his first book, Quebec, the harp, and other poems, printed at the Montreal Herald. A second volume, The unknown, or lays of the forest, was ready shortly afterwards and was published in Montreal early in 1831.

"The harp," which won for its young poet an honorary medal from the Société pour l'Encouragement des Sciences et des Arts en Canada, at Quebec, showed the path of poetry he hoped to follow. In its

lines it soon became apparent that Hawley was one for whom "blest sounds of music" were to issue from "The Western Harp's yet untun'd strings" and that a colonial "Harp of the West" might attempt to emulate the celebrated songs and romances of the "Harp of the East" (the Near East) and of "the North" (Great Britain). In this first volume the poem "Quebec" was Hawley's show-piece for "native numbers." The technique for his elevated review of heroic events along the St Lawrence River was borrowed, with, as Richard Ernest Rashley has pointed out, only "a partial bridging of the gap" between "the old world art" and the expression of "new world experience." The book was apparently received "in a flattering manner" by the contemporary public.

Hawley named his Old World masters in the preface to his second volume: Thomas Campbell, Lord Byron, Thomas Moore, and Ossian. There too he cited Arabian nights' entertainments and Moore's Lalla Rookh, an oriental romance as examples of how a series of independent tales could be linked, a structure he himself adopted for The unknown. He sets four eastern romances (told "in the forest") in the framework of a narrative about "the Stranger," a young Frenchman who comes to Lower Canada to convert the Indians to a "civilized" way of life. Into this framework Hawley incorporates some accurate description in prose and verse of the manners and homes of French Canadians, apparently observed at first hand, and of the Rivière Saint-Maurice and the Chutes Shawinigan.

Hawley was proud of Quebec's Indian-French-British history and, while he indulged in songs and narratives in the Byronic romantic fashion, he also "essayed faithfully to delineate [Quebec's] unknown scenery, together with the dark traits of its early history, and to cheer the fire-side of our long winter evenings with 'the deeds of days of other years.'"

CARL F. KLINCK

William Fitz Hawley is the author of Quebec, the harp, and other poems (Montreal, 1829) and The unknown, or lays of the forest (Montreal, 1831).

Montreal Gazette, 12 July 1830. Morgan, Bibliotheca Canadensis, 179–80. Norah Story, The Oxford companion to Canadian history and literature (Toronto and London, 1967), 349–50. L. M. Lande, Old lamps aglow; an appreciation of early Canadian poetry (Montreal, 1957), 145–49. Lareau, Hist. de la littérature canadienne, 75. Lit. hist. of Canada (Klinck et al.; 1976), 1: 144–45. R. E. Rashley, Poetry in Canada; the first three steps (Toronto, 1958), 17–22. Benjamin Sulte, "The unknown," RSC Trans., 2nd ser., 6 (1900), sect.I: 117–20.

HAWS, JOHN, shipbuilder, justice of the peace, and office holder; b. c. 1798 in the Highlands of Scotland; m. 18 Oct. 1823 Calista Calvert, youngest daughter of

Richard Calvert, a merchant of Saint John, N.B., and they had four sons and four daughters; d. 11 Dec. 1858 in Liverpool, England.

Little is known of John Haws's early life except that he grew up in Halifax, N.S. Haws, who spoke Gaelic as well as English, apparently acted as a translator and interpreter among the Scots and Irish coming to the colony. He probably worked for a few years at the naval dockyards in Halifax. Following the War of 1812 he spent some time trading in the West Indies and then, in 1819, settled in Portland (Saint John), N.B. Five years later he began to build ships. Esther Clark Wright has determined that between 1824 and 1848 Haws constructed 32 vessels representing 15,896 tons of shipping.

Like most Saint John shipbuilders of the period, Haws began producing vessels under contract for local shippers such as John McNeil Wilmot* as well as for shippers in Liverpool. Only rarely before 1840 did he build for himself; Wright records but one instance. After 1840, however, he did construct ships mainly for his own use: sometimes he acted as a broker on specific sales to British shippers and at other times he used the vessels for several years before selling them. According to some sources a partnership was created in 1853 between Frederick Smith and John Haws but the latter was most likely John Haws Jr.

Haws joined the masonic order while he was still living in Halifax and went on to become a prominent freemason in Saint John. From some point in the early 1840s he served as a magistrate for Saint John County, and he also acted in the capacity of firewarden for the Portland area. While travelling to England in 1858 he suffered a stroke on 1 December and died ten days later of paralysis in Liverpool at the age of 61.

His estate was valued at more than £20,000. The assets included a shipyard worth approximately £4,000, a brick house and lot in Saint John which brought a further £4,500 to the estate, other real estate in the town valued at £2,100, and the ship *Calista Haws*, which sold for £8,000. His will provided that a trust of £6,000 be invested for the benefit of his daughters, who were to receive the interest through their lifetimes and also were to have the power to distribute the trust by will at their deaths. The remainder of the estate was divided equally among his sons.

The family continued its close links with the shipping trades. Three of Haws's daughters married shipbuilders or ships' officers and all four of his sons were associated with shipping. His two eldest sons, John Jr and Richard Calvert, eventually moved to Liverpool, probably because of the depressed condition of the shipbuilding industry in New Brunswick in the early 1860s. In Liverpool, Richard was to establish the Haws (Diamond H) Line.

T. W. ACHESON

BLHU, R. G. Dun & Co. credit ledger, Canada, 9: 31. GRO (London), Death certificate, John Haws, 11 Dec. 1858. Liverpool Record Office (Liverpool, Eng.), Toxteth Park Cemetery, reg. of burials, no.5008. N.B. Museum, Reg. of marriages for the city and county of Saint John, book A (1810–28): 312 (mfm. at PANB). PANB, RG 7, RS71; 1859, John Haws. G. W. Haws, *The Haws family and their seafaring kin* (Dunfermline, Scot., 1932). E. C. Wright, *Saint John ships and their builders* (Wolfville, N.S., 1976).

HENRY, JOHN, author and spy; b. *c.* 1776 in Dublin; m. *c.* 1800 Miss Duché of Philadelphia, and they had two daughters; d. 1853 in Paris.

In 1807 Montreal society was enlivened by the arrival from the United States of John Henry, then about 30 years old. Henry was perceived by his new circle – the McGills, Frobishers, Richardsons, and McGillivrays of the Beaver Club, as well as government officials visiting from Quebec – to be handsome, charming, learned, and articulate. A particular attraction for this group lay in the fact that he professed a fervent monarchism, despite having grown up a Roman Catholic in Dublin and having lived for more than ten years in the American republic. He was also a man of the world. After having immigrated to the United States to seek his fortune about 1796, Henry had successively edited a newspaper and managed a wine business in Philadelphia, been an active propagandist for the Federalist party in Cambridge, Mass., and run a farm in Vermont, where he had also studied law, given speeches, and written articles in the Federalist cause. His wife, who had died not long after their marriage, had been the daughter of a prominent Episcopalian clergyman of Philadelphia. Henry's marriage had brought him some money but he had no patrimonial fortune of his own. He estimated his income in 1807 to be £400 a year, half of which derived from real estate in the United States.

Henry assiduously cultivated his new-found friends in Lower Canada by writing anonymous letters to the *Montreal Gazette* in October and November 1807 defending the North West Company against sundry charges of monopolizing the fur trade, of stirring up the Indians against the United States, and of relying almost exclusively on liquor to obtain furs. He was probably also the author of a letter printed by the *Canadian Courant* on 3 November denouncing President Thomas Jefferson's proposed embargo on trade with Great Britain and France. The leading merchants of Montreal were quick to reciprocate. Later that month they wrote Lieutenant Governor Francis GORE of Upper Canada recommending that Henry be appointed to the judgeship vacated by the dismissal of Robert Thorpe*. They later organized their London associates to memorialize the colonial secretary, Lord Castlereagh, in the same vein. This energetic campaign failed, probably because Gore

Henry

remained unimpressed with Henry's credentials, describing him as "an Irish Adventurer – not even called to the Bar, and . . . a citizen of the United States."

Soon after his arrival in Montreal, Henry appears to have met and favourably impressed that arch-intriguer for patronage, the civil secretary, Herman Witsius Ryland*. They soon became fast friends. When, in October 1807, Henry wrote to Ryland communicating the view of his correspondents in the United States that war with Britain would lead to a "dissolution of the Confederation," the civil secretary foresaw the possibilities. Henry could speedily gain high favour by employing his political experience and talents in the interests of Lower Canadian and imperial security. His opportunity came early in 1808 when he was called to Boston on private business.

Henry wrote Ryland a series of letters describing political opinion in Vermont, Boston, and other points in New England. It was a time of ferment. Commercial interests in New England were particularly hard hit by Jefferson's newly proclaimed embargo and, in any case, tended to support the conservative Federalist opponents of the Jefferson administration. In all Henry's correspondence the message was the same: the embargo was outraging opinion and, should hostilities ensue, disloyalty in New England could easily be exploited by Britain. In a letter written after his return to Montreal, Henry concluded that "in case of a war, the States on our borders may be detached from the Union." Finding these letters to be of interest, Governor Sir James Henry Craig* forwarded them to Castlereagh, who in July 1808 instructed Craig that Henry, "a person of good information and discretion," deserved "encouragement."

By early 1809 Craig, doubtless influenced by Ryland, decided to dispatch Henry on an official undercover mission to Vermont and Massachusetts. Issued instructions dated 6 Feb. 1809 and marked "Most secret and confidential," Henry was to obtain accurate information on the strengths and weaknesses of the two political parties and on public opinion concerning the probability of war with Britain. It was especially urgent that he carefully estimate whether the Federalists of the eastern states would be able to exert influence "to bring about separation from the general Union" and to what extent "they would look up to England for assistance or be disposed to enter into a connexion with us." If Henry succeeded in contriving "an intimacy" with any leading Federalists, he was authorized to open a secret correspondence between them and the governor. To convince such persons of his bona fides, he was issued a letter of credence from Craig, but was to exercise extreme caution in communicating it. His letters to Craig were to be sent under cover to an executive councillor, John

Richardson*, with only a private mark to indicate that they should be forwarded to the Château Saint-Louis. Henry's expenses would be paid by the government, but he was promised no reward.

From 14 February to 22 May 1809 Henry wrote Craig 14 letters which in due course were forwarded to Castlereagh. In them he included much detail on elections, political parties, and anti-war sentiment. He reported conversations with leading Federalists, whom he invariably portrayed as potentially disloyal to the United States but whom he was unable to quote to this effect. Indeed, he appears to have gathered his information from newspapers, coffee-house chatter, and dinner parties. He uncovered no plot of secession and did not dare reveal his letter of credence. Nevertheless he confidently concluded on 6 April that in the event of war the Federalist "Junto of Boston" would, as a preliminary to separation and an alliance, make "application to the Governor General of British America for aid . . . which would protect the seaport towns." Soon after Britain and the United States appeared to have reached an agreement exempting the former from the embargo, Henry was recalled. He arrived in Montreal on 11 June.

During and immediately after Craig's "reign of terror" in March 1810, Henry supported the government's position. On 19 March, the very day that Pierre-Stanislas Bédard* and two other leaders of the Canadian party, François Blanchet* and Jean-Thomas Taschereau*, were arrested on suspicion of treasonable practices, a letter by Henry, signed Camillus, was published in the *Quebec Mercury*, arguing that the assembly was run by men who had everything to gain and nothing to lose by revolution. In April and May extracts from a chapter of a proposed book by Camillus appeared in the *Courant*. The author then decided to publish the entire chapter as a pamphlet. *An enquiry into the evils of general suffrage and frequent elections in Lower Canada* was Henry's attempted synthesis of many of the ideas of the governing clique. As long as the French Canadians retained their language and customs they were a potential threat to security. The ignorance and national prejudices of the habitants made them easy prey to designing demagogues such as the professional men of the Canadian party. The real fault lay in the Constitutional Act of 1791 which had given the vote to almost every male head of household and did not enact property qualifications for members of the assembly. The inevitable result was an elected house entirely in the control of "attornies and attornies' clerks, country clowns, dram sellers and bankrupts." Henry's solutions were commonplace among the governor and his advisers although he avoided several controversial questions. He suggested that a member of the assembly should be able to read and write his vernacular tongue, understand English well enough to render it into his own tongue, and meet certain income or property qualifications. Voting should be restricted to those who met other income or property requirements. After a few years, English should become the sole language of the law courts and the assembly. English schools should be established in every parish containing 100 families. Henry was confident that these and other measures would ultimately lead to the anglicization of the French Canadians. Then and only then would the colony be a safe and useful appendage of the British empire.

As his activities in Lower Canada indicate, Henry expended much energy to gain the favour of the powerful. But, fundamentally, he was a lazy man, driven by a profound need to feel important. Henry would not take Ryland's advice to qualify for the bar, finding it impossible to associate with the "miserable creatures," ignorant of Justinian's science, "who crowd and disgrace the profession" in Lower Canada. There was, indeed, "no private pursuit" which could offer "adequate inducement to even more humble abilities than mine." He was, however, prepared to act as judge advocate of the militia and army or to improve the deplorable quality of the Montreal magistrates' bench by becoming chairman of the Court of Quarter Sessions at £500 a year. He succeeded in gaining neither post. Henry had applied in September 1809 for the position of sheriff of Montreal, to take effect upon the death of the 66-year-old incumbent, Edward William Gray*. When, in the summer of 1810, Ryland was sent to England by Craig, Henry hastened after his patron. This may have been an error, for when Gray died later that year, Craig felt obliged to appoint a replacement, Frederick William Ermatinger*, immediately.

While in London, Henry appears to have helped William McGillivray* prepare a pamphlet entitled *On the origin and progress of the North-West Company*. The pamphlet emphasized the role played by the NWC in stimulating British manufacturing and in keeping the Indians loyal, outlined the perils of American competition, and asked for a charter granting the company a monopoly of trade in the Columbia River country. No doubt Henry expected a favour in return. But whatever influence the London merchants and Ryland may have exercised in his interest, it was not sufficient. Nor was his extravagant portrayal of the espionage mission. In a memorial to Castlereagh's successor, Lord Liverpool, Henry claimed that Craig had promised him public employment at more than £1,000 a year. He would, however, settle for a post at £500 a year. In a second petition, Henry described his indefatigable efforts in 1809 to strengthen and organize the Federalists, asserting among other things that he had drafted most of the resolutions of assemblies in New England denouncing the embargo. No doubt sceptical, Liverpool confined his enthusi-

asm to a general recommendation in Henry's favour, addressed to Sir George Prevost*.

On board ship during his return voyage, Henry fell in with an engaging rogue, then posing as Édouard, Comte de Crillon, knight of Malta, and scion of a famous noble family of mixed Spanish and French origin. Crillon was in reality a notorious swindler named Soubiran, wanted by the French police. He soon convinced Henry that he had suffered intolerable injustice at the hands of the British and that he should sell his papers to the government of the United States. In Washington, Crillon opened negotiations on Henry's behalf with the secretary of state, James Monroe. The times were propitious: war fever was spreading through the country, save New England, and President James Madison had adopted a policy of brinkmanship. Madison saw in the Henry disclosures a perfect opportunity to unite the country for war and to discredit the Federalist opposition. The bargain was struck on 7 Feb. 1812. In return for the papers, Henry would receive the princely sum of £18,000 ($90,000). The entire secret service budget voted by Congress, $50,000, was paid to him. The remainder, $40,000, would be made up by Crillon, who in a flourish of generosity deeded to his friend an ancestral estate, "St. Martial," in Gascony and in his capacity as knight of Malta made Henry his squire. Crillon was to be reimbursed later by the government of the United States, a scheme which miscarried when the American minister to France uncovered the imposture. Crillon did, however, receive from Henry a gift of $1,000 and a loan of $6,000.

The papers sold included Craig's secret instructions, copies of Henry's letters to the governor while on the mission, and copies of his two memorials to Lord Liverpool. Henry doctored the papers by making erasures or in some cases rewriting segments. The names of Federalist friends were omitted and the extravagant claims made in the second memorial were deleted. A few additions suggesting Henry had become privy to seccessionist plotting were included. On 9 March Madison submitted the papers to Congress. They revealed, he stated, that while the United States was negotiating in good faith with Britain, the latter had employed a secret agent to intrigue with the disaffected for the purpose of destroying the union. The immediate effect was sensational, but when the innocuous nature of the letters came to be understood and it was learned that the entire secret service budget had been spent, Madison's strategy backfired. War fever was not, for the moment, further aroused, the government appeared to be run by fools, and in New England sympathy for the Federalists grew. It is therefore incorrect to suggest, as is sometimes done, that public reaction in the United States to the Henry papers contributed to the War of 1812.

Henry

Henry had prudently sailed for France before the papers were made public. Soon after landing, he learned that he had been swindled. Not only was the sole heir of the Crillon family living in Paris and "St. Martial" non-existent, but the securities Crillon had given Henry for the loan proved worthless. There was doubtless some satisfaction to be found when Soubiran landed near Bayonne in the summer of 1812 after being deported from England and was promptly arrested for impersonation.

Information on Henry's later life comes from an interview between the American historian Samuel Eliot Morison and Henry's granddaughter in Paris in 1913. According to her, the "Colonel" had lived in Paris as a gentleman of fortune until his death in 1853, drawing his income from vast estates in Ireland. When asked why Henry had never returned to the United States she answered naïvely that the "Colonel always said . . . the climate of America did not agree with him." No doubt the "Colonel" had included Lower Canada in the term "America."

F. MURRAY GREENWOOD

[The *Montreal Gazette*, in October and November 1807, and the *Canadian Courant and Montreal Advertiser*, on 3 Nov. 1807, published anonymous letters which were probably written by John Henry. A letter signed Camillus appeared in the *Quebec Mercury* on 19 March 1810, and Henry used this pseudonym when he published *An enquiry into the evils of general suffrage and frequent elections in Lower Canada* (Montreal, 1810), extracts of which had already appeared in the *Canadian Courant*, April–May 1807. This pamphlet was reprinted in part in *Ideas in conflict; a selection of texts on political, economic, and social questions in Lower Canada (1806–1810)*, ed. J. [E.] Hare and J.-P. Wallot (Trois-Rivières, Que., 1970). Henry was probably, with William McGillivray, editor of Duncan McGillivray*'s *On the origin and progress of the North-West Company of Canada, with a history of the fur trade as connected with that concern . . .*, published in London in 1811. F.M.G.]

PAC, MG 11, [CO 42] Q, 109; RG 4, A1: 30609–1009, 34095–533. "Anticipation of the War of 1812," PAC *Report*, 1896: 38–64. [Duncan McGillivray], "Some account of the trade carried on by the North West Company," PAC *Report*, 1928: 56–73. *DAB*. I. N. Brant, *James Madison* (6v., Indianapolis, Ind., 1941–61). E. A. Cruikshank, *The political adventures of John Henry: the record of an international imbroglio* (Toronto, 1936). S. E. Morison, *By land and by sea; essays and addresses* (New York, 1953). Bradford Perkins, *Prologue to war: England and the United States, 1805–1812* (Berkeley and Los Angeles, Calif., 1961; repr. 1963), 369–72. P. C. T. White, *A nation on trial: America and the War of 1812* (New York, 1965), 110–11. Henry Adams, "Count Edward de Crillon," *American Hist. Rev.* (New York and London), 1 (1895–96): 51–69. C. S. Blue, "John Henry, the spy," *Canadian Magazine*, 47 (May 1916): 3–10.

HENRY, ROBERT, fur trader, businessman, justice of the peace, and office holder; b. *c.* 1778 in Albany, N.Y., son of Robert Henry and nephew of Alexander Henry* the elder; m. 2 Nov. 1817 Christine Farrand, *née* Bethune, and they had two daughters; d. 10 May 1859 in Cobourg, Upper Canada.

Robert Henry was the son of a merchant-trader in Albany who, during the American revolution, provided the Continental Army with supplies brought from the province of Quebec. These supplies were procured with specie and when he was not repaid in full he faced financial ruin. Following the war, the Henry family moved to Montreal, where Robert was educated. He entered the North West Company as a clerk in 1806 and subsequently worked on the English (upper Churchill) River under Donald McTavish* and John Duncan Campbell*. Henry became a company partner in 1810, at which time he was trading on the Churchill River. Between 1810 and 1815 he served in the Athabasca department, and upon coming back to Montreal in 1815 was elected to the Beaver Club.

In the spring of 1816 Henry returned to the northwest, where he played a minor role in asserting the interests of the NWC as tension grew between it and both the Hudson's Bay Company and the Red River settlement [*see* Thomas Douglas*]. He was called upon in June to lead a group of Indians from Fort William (Thunder Bay, Ont.) to the Red River as a show of force; in late 1816 he participated in the harassment of HBC men who had built Fort Wedderburn on Lake Athabasca [*see* John CLARKE; Archibald Norman McLeod*]. The strain which Henry felt during this period of hostility prompted him to remark in August 1816 that he was "much inclined to leave this rascally Country for ever." Because trade was sagging, the company needed every man in the field and Alexander Henry persuaded him to remain another winter.

Robert Henry retired from the fur trade in 1817 and settled at Hamilton (Cobourg), Upper Canada. With James Gray Bethune*, he purchased property there that September and erected a grist-mill. Under Henry's management, the operation came to be the principal mill in the Newcastle District. Two months after the purchase of the property, Henry married Bethune's sister Christine and thus became the brother-in-law of ANGUS, another NWC partner, and Alexander Neil*, who became the Church of England rector at Cobourg in 1827.

After selling the mill for £6,000 in 1831, Henry operated a private bank in his house in Cobourg and by 1832 had become agent there for the Commercial Bank of the Midland District. Despite later efforts by others to charter a Cobourg bank, Henry's was the only one in the community. This enterprise made him a target of the celebrated "Cobourg conspiracy," one of the Patriot-inspired border incursions launched from the United States in the aftermath of the rebellion of 1837–38. In late July 1839 a group of dissidents led from New York by Benjamin LETT and Samuel Peters

Henry

Hart conspired to rob and murder Henry and to attack other area residents, including George Strange Boulton* and his nephew D'Arcy Edward Boulton (prominent Cobourg tories), Maurice Jaynes (a wealthy farmer), and Sheppard McCormick (a participant in 1837 in the capture of the Patriot supply ship *Caroline*). The attack was presumably designed to spark both an invasion by other filibusterers and an uprising in an area where several Hunters' Lodges, formed to change Canada into a republic, had appeared. As the conspirators hatched this plot, one of their number, Henry J. Moon, became agitated by the murderous intent of the band and revealed the plan to an intended victim, D'Arcy Edward Boulton. A force was mounted and the conspirators were stopped before they could carry out their attacks. During the ensuing trial, at which Boulton acted for the defence, the conspirators and two local sympathizers were found guilty. Henry was described by the prosecution as one of Cobourg's "most respectable and inoffensive inhabitants."

Henry served as a justice of the peace from 1818 until the late 1830s, and as Cobourg's first treasurer in 1837 after its establishment as a police village. Although aligned by social standing with Cobourg's oligarchy of political leaders, American-born businessmen, and British half pay officers, he was less active than many in local institutions and politics, nor did he invest in local improvement schemes. He presumably preferred conventional investments, which included bonds and securities, and the poor record of such local ventures as the Cobourg and Peterborough Rail-way vindicated his caution.

Although Henry prospered he did not die an exceptionally wealthy man; his estate totalled $28,000. It is possible that he lost money covering some of the debts of James Gray Bethune, who had suffered bankruptcy in 1834. Henry nevertheless lived quietly in his old age surrounded by a number of former NWC and HBC fur traders such as Jacob Corrigal, William Nourse, and John Dugald CAMERON who had also chosen the Cobourg area for their retirement.

PETER ENNALS

ACC-T, Church of St Peter (Cobourg, Ont.), reg. of baptisms, burials, and marriages, 1819–37 (mfm. at AO). AO, RG 22, ser.191, Robert Henry. PAC, MG 19, B3: 55, 95; E1, ser.1, 6: 2378; 22: 8729–32 (transcripts); MG 23, B3, CC 41/4: 33–38; RG 1, L3, 231: H14/2; RG 4, B46, 1: 434; RG 68, General index, 1651–1841: 431, 502. West Northumberland Land Registry Office (Cobourg), Abstract index to deeds, Cobourg: 216 (mfm. at AO, GS 4172). *Docs. relating to NWC* (Wallace). Frances Stewart, *Our forest home, being extracts from the correspondence of the late Frances Stewart*, ed. E. S. Dunlop (2nd ed., Montreal, 1902), 18–19, 23–24, 52, 64–65, 70, 72, 128. *Valley of the Trent* (Guillet), xliii, 49, 59. *Cobourg Star*, 18 Sept. 1839. *Montreal Herald*, 15 Nov. 1817. Armstrong, *Handbook of Upper Canadian chronology*, 201. Guillet, *Lives and times of Patriots*, chap.17. D. E. Wattie, "Cobourg, 1784–1867" (2v., MA thesis, Univ. of Toronto, 1949). Jennifer Brown, "Ultimate respectability: fur-trade children in the 'civilized world,'" *Beaver*, outfit 308 (spring 1978): 53. A. H. Young, "The Bethunes," *OH*, 27 (1931): 559.

HENRY, WALTER, army officer, surgeon, author, and sportsman; b. 1 Jan. 1791 in Donegal (Republic of Ireland), first son of John Henry, merchant; m. first 6 April 1831, in Montreal, Charlotte Todd (d. 1833); m. secondly 2 July 1834 Leah Allan Geddes in Kingston, Upper Canada, and they had four sons and two daughters; d. 27 June 1860 in Belleville, Upper Canada.

Walter Henry was born of what he described as a "respectable" family. An avid reader, he received a classical education and, possibly influenced by his uncle, a Donegal physician, he pursued medicine at Trinity College, Dublin, at the University of Glasgow, and at hospitals in London. Upon completing his studies in 1811, Henry passed the regimental surgeon's examination set by the Royal College of Surgeons of London and he immediately entered the army as a hospital mate on general service. In December 1811 he became an assistant surgeon in the 66th Foot, with which he served throughout the Peninsular War, participating in numerous actions including Badajoz, Vitoria, and Nivelle. Henry was posted to India and Nepal in 1815 with the regiment's first battalion, which was recalled in 1817 to join the second battalion in garrisoning the south Atlantic island of St Helena, where Napoleon was confined. He found the former French emperor "unsightly and obese"; in 1821 he kept the official notes made during Napoleon's autopsy. Subsequently he served with the 66th in Ireland (1822–27), and in 1826 was made regimental surgeon.

In 1827 Henry arrived in the Canadas with his regiment, which was stationed at Quebec (1827–30 and 1835–39), Montreal (1830–31), Kingston (1831–33 and 1834–35), and York (Toronto) (1833–34). Promoted surgeon to the army medical department in 1839, he remained at Quebec until 1841, when he was posted to Halifax where four years later he became a deputy inspector general of military hospitals. He returned to England in 1848 but in 1852 came back to Quebec as inspector general in charge of military medical services in British North America. His career seems not to have had medical distinction. Nevertheless his memoirs leave little doubt of his surgical competence, and his courage was exemplary both in battle and while performing equally dangerous work such as during the cholera epidemics.

Henry was an alert and witty man who must have enlivened the social scene in the towns to which he was posted. Through his second wife, the daughter of

Henry

James Geddes, a Kingston physician, and grand-daughter of John Gamble, a loyalist surgeon, he was probably known to many established families in Upper Canada. Long peace-time service gave him the opportunity to pursue, with much enthusiasm, his varied recreational and literary interests.

Fishing, which for Henry included detailed bi-ological study, was a hobby in which he had engaged ardently since boyhood. This activity and his writing talent first merged in an 1837 article on the habits of the salmon family and its conservation. Under an appropriate *nom de plume*, Piscator, four long letters were published by Henry between 1839 and 1842 in the *Albion*, the weekly journal of the British emigrant community in New York City. In these he declared his eagerness to pursue "scientific, exciting, absorbing, glorious, imperial salmoncide." The accounts of fishing expeditions on Lake Ontario, the fast-flowing Rivière Jacques-Cartier near Quebec, and Nova Scotia's plentiful Gold River are entertaining and gripping despite his addiction to a baroque luxuriance of language. Henry's medical writings, neither numerous nor innovative, nevertheless reflect his common sense and powers of clear observation, and are marked by the absence of cant. As well as a commendatory article on medical education at McGill College, Montreal, he published papers on traumatic emphysema and malaria, and a statistical study of delirium tremens among the military in Canada from 1824.

In his writings on the rebellion of 1837 and politics, Henry was intensely conservative and sympathetic to the crown, as one might anticipate given his background of service. In a detailed account of the Lower Canadian rebellion, written for the *Albion* under the pseudonym Miles, Henry expressed con-tempt for both Louis-Joseph Papineau*, whose radical course he expected would lead him to the gallows or a lunatic asylum, and Wolfred Nelson*, whom he identified as an "opulent distiller" rather than a fellow physician. The account betrays the xenophobia displayed by many of Henry's British contemporaries. Henry described the typical French Canadian as ignorant and slothful, but not inherently vicious; he was eloquent in blaming Papineau for encouraging his compatriots to resistance and crime. Early in 1844, again for the *Albion*, he contributed a series of articles on Nova Scotia politics under the name of Scrutator. He vigorously attacked the effrontery of Joseph Howe*'s "Liberals," whose "utopian" interests in responsible party government and evident identifica-tion with the reform politics of Robert BALDWIN and Louis-Hippolyte La Fontaine* in Canada appalled Henry.

In addition to his published articles and letters, Henry produced an autobiography, *Trifles from my port-folio*, published in Quebec in 1839 and reissued in London in 1843 as *Events of a military life*. It remains his chief literary contribution. A stylist, and of an adventurous and romantic nature, he produced one of the most colourful accounts written by a soldier while in the Canadas. The Canadian portion of *Trifles* provides many valuable and entertaining observations on life before 1839. Henry is most interesting when he describes Kingston's depressing appearance during the 1832 cholera epidemic, his regiment's headquar-ters in York (where he hunted snipe to stimulate a failing patient's appetite), and the "oppressive feeling of melancholy" encountered in "passing through the gloomy recesses of a Canadian forest."

Henry nevertheless admired Upper Canada's "high-ly moral and respectful" nature; as early as 1844 he wished to settle permanently in British North America. After retiring from the medical department in 1855, Henry lived out his life in Belleville, evidently to be near members of his wife's family there and in Kingston.

CHARLES G. ROLAND

Walter Henry is the author of *Trifles from my port-folio, or recollections of scenes and small adventures during twenty-nine years' military service* . . . (2v., Quebec, 1839), republished as *Events of a military life* . . . (2v., London, 1843) and again as *Surgeon Henry's Trifles: events of a military life*, ed. Pat Hayward (London, 1970). The 1839 edition was published under an anonym, A staff surgeon, and extracts from the 1843 edition were published in the *Albion* (New York), 23 Sept., 7 Oct., 11 Nov. 1843. "Dr Walter Henry's account of the post-mortem examination" of Napoleon Bonaparte is found in James Kemble, *Napoleon immortal: the medical history and private life of Napoleon Bonaparte* (London, [1959]), 282–83. He published the following medical papers in the *Medical Chronicle* (Mont-real): "Malaria," 3 (1855–56): 121–27; "Medical education at the McGill University, Montreal," 3: 289–92; "Statistics of delirium tremens amongst the troops in Canada for the last thirty years, with some observations on the disease," 1 (1853–54): 321–27; and "Traumatic emphysema," 1: 193–96. Under the anonym Scrutator he wrote the following political articles in the *Albion*: "Nova Scotia – political changes," 13 Jan. 1844, and "Politics of Nova Scotia," 23 March, 13 July, 14 Sept. 1844. Under the anonym Miles he wrote "Narrative of the late revolt in Lower Canada," *Albion*, 23 Dec. 1837, 20 Jan. 1838. Henry's "Observations on the habits of the salmon family" appeared under his own name in Literary and Hist. Soc. of Quebec, *Trans.* (Quebec), 3 (1832–37): 346–64. The following articles written by Henry under the anonym Piscator appeared in the *Albion*: "The salmon fisher," 18 July 1840; "Salmon fishing in Canada," 13, 20 April 1839; and "Salmon fishing in Gold River, Nova Scotia," 18 June 1842.

ACC-O, St George's Cathedral (Kingston, Ont.), reg. of burials, 25 Jan. 1833; reg. of marriages, 2 July 1834. ANQ-M, CE1-65, 6 April 1831. PAC, MG 29, D61, 11: 3898–900; RG 8, I (C ser.), 36: 250, 305–6. PRO, WO 17/1544: 4; 17/1545: 75; 17/1556: 62, 68; 17/1559: 73; 17/2388: 67; 17/2389: 2; 17/2393: 15; 17/2395: 125 (mfm. at

PAC). Univ. of Glasgow Arch., GUA 19057; 19089: 33; 26678: 361; 26680: 69. *Hastings Chronicle* (Belleville, [Ont.]), 11 July 1860. G.B. WO, *Army list*, 1813: 284; 1827: 242; 1839: 370; 1849–50: 413; 1853: 431; 1857–58: 554; 1859–60: 631. *The matriculation albums of the University of Glasgow from 1728 to 1858*, comp. W. I. Addison (Glasgow, 1913), 225. Morgan, *Bibliotheca Canadensis*, 182–83. R. L. Blanco, *Wellington's surgeon general: Sir James McGrigor* (Durham, N.C., 1974). Canniff, *Medical profession in U.C.*, 378, 382. *Lit. hist. of Canada* (Klinck et al.; 1965), 128–29, 142. *Canada Lancet* (Toronto), 5 (1872–73): 106. C. G. Roland, "Walter Henry – a very Lilyputian hero," *New England Journal of Medicine* (Boston), 280 (January–June 1969): 31–33.

HERTEL DE ROUVILLE, JEAN-BAPTISTE-RENÉ, militia officer, seigneur, and politician; b. 20 June 1789 in Montreal, son of Jean-Baptiste-Melchior Hertel* de Rouville and Marie-Anne Hervieux; d. 3 Jan. 1859 in Boucherville, Lower Canada.

Like many of his forebears Jean-Baptiste-René Hertel de Rouville took up a military career early in life. He was only 18 when he obtained a commission as a lieutenant in the militia, and at 22, on 15 April 1812, he was made a captain in the Voltigeurs Canadiens. The following year he took part in the battle of Châteauguay under the command of his brother-in-law, Charles-Michel d'Irumberry* de Salaberry. He was promoted lieutenant-colonel in the Chambly battalion in 1815 and in 1816 assumed its command, replacing his father. On 3 Sept. 1816, at Boucherville, he married Charlotte de Labroquerie (Boucher de La Broquerie), who brought him a dowry of 10,000 *livres*. They were to have at least five children.

A little over a year after his marriage Hertel de Rouville inherited the seigneury of Rouville and part of the seigneury of Chambly under the terms of his father's will, dated 24 Sept. 1814. The will stipulated that the properties would not pass to him until the death of his mother, which occurred on 25 Jan. 1819. Hertel de Rouville was the first seigneur in his family who chose to live on the seigneury of Rouville. He began immediately to put his manor-house into good shape, and about two years later he undertook to draw up his register of landed property. Meanwhile, he initiated negotiations for the construction of a church to replace the chapel built by his father at the end of the 18th century. The chapel had created a great deal of dissension among the *censitaires* of three concessions – Des Hurons, Des Étangs, and Du Bord-de-l'Eau – who disapproved of the seigneur's visions of development. But the circumstances were different this time. The burning down of the church at Belœil in 1817 had unexpectedly obliged the neighbouring population to attend services in Hertel de Rouville's parish. He made repeated appeals to the ecclesiastical authorities alleging that the church was too small.

However, the *censitaires* apparently nursed their old grudges, for Hertel de Rouville did not get his way until 24 Feb. 1827, when consent was finally given for the canonical erection of Saint-Hilaire parish (at Mont-Saint-Hilaire). Even then he had to wait several years for the church to be built and the first resident parish priest to be appointed. Indeed, the parish was not incorporated until 10 July 1835.

Like his father, Hertel de Rouville could not resist the lure of politics. Elected to the House of Assembly at the age of 35, he represented Bedford riding from 28 Aug. 1824 to 2 Sept. 1830, and the new constituency of Rouville from 26 Oct. 1830 until he resigned on 10 Nov. 1832. During his first term the Quebec and Montreal voters decided in the winter of 1827–28 to send petitions to the king denouncing the abuses of the government led by Lord Dalhousie [Ramsay*]. The submission from Montreal was particularly bitter, for the first part contained a long series of charges against the head of the executive, followed by an urgent demand for his recall. Torn between his responsibilities as a soldier and as an assemblyman, Hertel de Rouville none the less decided to sign the petition. The response was immediate: on 25 Feb. 1828 he learned through the newspapers that he had been stripped of his rank by a general militia order, as had four other officers likewise compromised by the petition. The incident was heatedly discussed on 6 March at a meeting of county committees of the Montreal region. It resolved to denounce this new abuse of power by the governor and to inform the province's agents in England so they could make the matter known to the king. The affair was not settled until the summer of 1828, with the departure of Lord Dalhousie.

Hertel de Rouville was appointed to the Legislative Council, where he sat from 22 Aug. 1837 to 27 March 1838. This honour did not prevent him from being attacked by the parish priest of Saint-Jean-Baptiste-de-Rouville, Louis Nau*. Nau issued a sworn statement on 8 Nov. 1838 that accused him not only of supporting rebel activity in his region, but also of provoking new disturbances, and even of supplying "one hundred and fifty *louis* to provide the revolutionaries with arms." On 5 Oct. 1839 Nau told the rebellion losses commissioners, who were examining Hertel de Rouville's claims, it was his duty to inform them that the day before "an address and several statements and another authentic document *which prove the disloyalty* of the said De Rouville were presented to His Excellency, with a view to assisting the just and honest progress of His Majesty's government." To such testimonies was added that of the police magistrate William Foster Coffin*, who had no sympathy for the seigneur of Rouville.

These statements seem to have had a decisive influence on the British authorities, who from then on were guarded in their attitude towards Hertel de

Rouville. Yet he had unhesitatingly provided board and lodging for the troops in the county; moreover, in his correspondence with British officers he continued to offer his services and to testify to his loyalty. For example, in a letter to Major Thomas Leigh Goldie dated 14 June 1839 he asserted, "Although my name and Christian names are French or Canadian, . . . I am and . . . I have always been as good, and perhaps a better, subject of His Britannic Majesty than all those who have names with O and Mac [in them], and all other English, Irish and Scottish names. . . . I am far from being the man people have tried . . . to persuade [the governor] that I was and that he believes I am."

But Jean-Baptiste-René Hertel de Rouville would never be the same again. He was uneasy, tense, and withdrawn, which made his relations with those around him very difficult. Furthermore, his business affairs were going badly. Soon, having fallen ill, he instructed his son-in-law Dr Jean-Baptiste Brousseau of Belœil to sell the seigneury of Rouville, and he left his manor-house and went to live with his son, Jean-Baptiste-René-Jacques, at Sorel. The sale to Major Thomas Edmund Campbell* was completed on 16 April 1844 for 17,000 *livres*. On 1 Feb. 1855, after his wife's death, Hertel de Rouville, who was ill again and in debt, sold the seigneury of Lac-Mitis to three English-speaking businessmen: Alfred Gill of Hartford, Conn., Cartland Starr of Boston, and Samuel Eastman Crocker. He is believed to have made his home with his daughter Marie-Anne-Charlotte at Belœil in 1858. According to the burial certificate, Hertel de Rouville died at Boucherville on 3 Jan. 1859 and was interred there five days later.

SERGE COURVILLE

AC, Beauharnois (Valleyfield), Minutiers, Ovide Leblanc, 16 avril 1844. ANQ-M, CE1-22, 3 sept. 1816, 8 janv. 1859; CE1-51, 20 juin 1789; CN1-43, 24 sept. 1814; CN3-29, 1er févr. 1855. ANQ-Q, E17/44, nos.3564, 3595–96, 3597–98a, 3599–600; E17/45, nos.3601, 3603a. Caron, "Inv. de la corr. de Mgr Panet," ANQ *Rapport*, 1933–34: 293, 322, 341, 344, 347–48; 1934–35: 397, 401, 406–7; 1935–36: 170, 172–73, 233, 260. Desrosiers, "Inv. de la corr. de Mgr Lartigue," ANQ *Rapport*, 1944–45: 182, 209. Turcotte, *Le Conseil législatif*. Armand Cardinal, *Histoire de Saint-Hilaire; les seigneurs de Rouville* (Montréal, 1980). P.-G. Roy, "Biographies canadiennes," *BRH*, 21 (1915): 53–54.

HILL, THOMAS, newspaperman, playwright, and publisher; b. 13 June 1807 in Cornwall, England; d. 13 Oct. 1860 in Fredericton.

The only evidence concerning Hill's early years is his testimony during a libel trial he had initiated in 1858. He stated that he had come to Montreal in 1831, but left the city shortly thereafter to settle temporarily in Grand Falls, N.B., before moving to Maine. Among his occupations at that time were those of a joiner and a musician. According to his further testimony, he had married and had three children before he relocated in Woodstock, N.B., in the late 1830s, having left his family behind. Some believed that while in the United States Hill had joined the army, from which he subsequently deserted. In fact, it was a charge of desertion which appeared in a letter printed in James Hogg*'s *New Brunswick Reporter and Fredericton Advertiser* on 12 March 1858 that led to the libel suit. Although Hill argued that he had been a civilian who had so strongly opposed the American position in the "Aroostook war" [see Sir John HARVEY] that he had voluntarily left the United States, the court ruled in favour of Hogg.

By 1842, in partnership with James Doak, a printer, Hill was the editor of the weekly Saint John *Loyalist*; during the next ten years, the newspaper, which adopted several banners, moved to Fredericton for approximately three years before returning to Saint John. On 25 May 1844 Hill set out a statement of principles, advocating a conservatism which would preserve British constitutionalism and a hereditary monarchy and opposing radicalism and republicanism. Under Hill's editorship the *Loyalist* was an outspoken champion of the imperial connection and Orangeism, and an opponent of responsible government.

Two editorials by Hill on the debate in the House of Assembly about responsible government appeared in the *Loyalist* on 23 Feb. 1844. The first questioned the loyalty of those in the house who had spoken in favour of it and the second directly attacked one of the movement's leaders, Lemuel Allan Wilmot*, in the following words: "Let [those members] at the next election tell the hound who fawningly crept into their confidence and then bit the hand which fed them that they have no further need of his services – that being loyal themselves they will no longer be represented by a rebel and a coward, and drive him back to the kennel from which he emerged to poison with his foetid breath the atmosphere of New Brunswick." Hill and Doak sent copies of the paper to the house to be placed on the desks of the members, who were scandalized. In a motion of 26 February, which made use of the term "libellous," they called Hill and Doak to the bar of the house to answer for their editorials. The representatives decided to imprison the partners "during pleasure" by using a speaker's warrant, and it was a week before they were released on a writ of habeas corpus by Judge James Carter*.

Doak and Hill immediately returned to the galleries of the assembly, which roused the ire of the legislators. The house committee on privileges met straight away in response to their release, but the next issue of the *Loyalist* continued the attacks. On 26 March the committee issued a report reaffirming the assembly's right to imprison those responsible for such flagrant contempt. But it took no further action.

Meanwhile Hill and Doak had begun a court action against John Wesley Weldon, the speaker, and George Gardner, the serjeant-at-arms, for false imprisonment. At a jury trial on 16 Oct. 1845 the case was resolved in favour of Hill and Doak, who were awarded more than £220 in damages. The Supreme Court upheld the decision, stating that the House of Assembly had acted beyond its powers. In effect, through the efforts of Hill and Doak, freedom of the press from parliamentary control was established in New Brunswick.

The relationship of Hill and Doak had its difficult times. In February 1845 Hill, presumably drunk, broke into Doak's house "with all the ferocity of a savage" and beat his partner until he was exhausted. Their association was dissolved on 25 February, but apparently all was forgiven and in July 1846 the partnership was resumed.

Hill's publishing interests were not confined to the *Loyalist*. In September 1842 he had initiated the tri-weekly *Aurora* (Saint John), but it died after one issue. Three years later, in Fredericton, he and Doak started the *Wreath*, which also lasted for only one issue. In 1846 they were planning to issue a children's publication, the *Young Aspirant*, but in the end it was Hogg who produced it. Hill was involved in Saint John with the *Commercial Times* in 1847, the *Satirist* in 1848, and the *Lancet* in 1849; in each case either publication did not occur or only one issue appeared. During the 1840s Hill was the key legislative reporter in the province. Reports from the House of Assembly which appeared in newspapers other than the *Loyalist* were often credited to him. Moreover, in this decade published reports of assembly debates frequently carried the imprint of Doak and Hill, publishers.

Hill's desire for further publications took him temporarily to Boston, where in 1851 he planned to produce a monthly dealing with the Maritime provinces. It was to be entitled the *British American Review*, but there is no record that it ever appeared. In 1852 came the demise of the *Loyalist*. Two years later Hill started the semi-weekly *United Empire*, which lasted for four months and advocated an imperial federation. Hill then spent the remainder of his life on the editorial board of the Fredericton *Head Quarters*.

In 1845 Hill wrote a play entitled the *Provincial Association: or, taxing each other*. Billed as a tragi-comedy, it took its theme from the recently founded Provincial Association which had been formed to combat government policy on free trade. At the planned opening on 31 March in Saint John, supporters of the association prevented its showing. In fact performance of the play was disrupted several times before it was actually presented. Once it was staged, the controversy it stirred up carried over into the newspapers. Hill published the play, but no copy of it exists today.

While in Fredericton Hill compiled two other works. The first, in 1845, was *The constitutional lyrist, a collection of national songs . . . adapted to the use of the loyalists of New Brunswick* and the second, five years later, of which one copy exists, was entitled *A book of Orange songs*. Although active in the Orange order, having been a founding member of the provincial grand lodge in 1844, Hill is rumoured to have married, possibly bigamously, the daughter of Roman Catholic innkeepers Jane and John McDowal in the late 1840s.

Hill lived in a controversial period of New Brunswick's history, during which he often fuelled controversies with his own editorials and writings. He was an adept writer with strongly held and ably articulated opinions. It is unfortunate that so much of his material has been lost. He had, in the words of William Godsoe MacFarlane, given "evidence of a nature of fire that flamed at times into vivid flashes of genius and again into the consuming fires of debauchery." In October 1860 he died in Fredericton and was given a pauper's burial.

ERIC L. SWANICK

Thomas Hill is the author of two poems which appeared in New Brunswick newspapers. "The bluenose boys" was printed anonymously in his *Loyalist and Conservative Advocate* (Fredericton) on 18 July 1844, and "The emigrant's Christmas song" was published under his name in the *New-Brunswick Courier* on 26 Dec. 1844. His play, *Provincial Association: or, taxing each other*, issued as a pamphlet in Fredericton in 1845, is lost, but copies of the two song collections which he compiled, *A book of Orange songs* (Fredericton, [1850]) and *The constitutional lyrist . . .* (Fredericton, 1845), appear to have survived. All three are cited in W. G. MacFarlane, *New Brunswick bibliography: the books and writers of the province* (Saint John, N.B., 1895).

Enough issues of Hill's main newspaper, the weekly *Loyalist*, survive to allow us to trace most of its publishing history. The paper appeared in Saint John from May 1843 to May 1844, and continued in Fredericton under the title *Loyalist and Conservative Advocate* between 1844 and 1845 and once again as the *Loyalist* around 1846. After ceasing publication for a time, it returned to Saint John from 1848 until its demise in 1852 under the title *Loyalist and Protestant Vindicator*. The other newspapers and journals that Hill initiated, many of which died in the planning stages or saw only a single issue, are listed in J. R. Harper, *Historical directory of New Brunswick newspapers and periodicals* (Fredericton, 1961). The Fredericton *Head Quarters* is the only one of which copies are known to have survived.

N.B. Hist. Soc., N.B. Hist. Soc. papers, J. E. Sereisky, "The mystery of Thomas Hill" (typescript, n.d.). *Hill* v. *Hogg*, [1858] 9 N.B.R. 108. *Hill* v. *Weldon*, [1845] 5 N.B.R. 1. N.B., House of Assembly, *Journal*, 1844: 103–4, 110; app., 231–40. *New Brunswick Reporter and Fredericton Advertiser*, 1844–60. James Hannay, *History of New Brunswick* (2v., Saint John, 1909), especially 2: 95–97.

Hoerner

D. K. Hazen, "The development of freedom of speech and freedom of the press in New Brunswick" (typescript, n.d.; formerly at N.B. Museum, but since withdrawn). MacNutt, *New Brunswick*. M. E. Smith, *Too soon the curtain fell: a history of theatre in Saint John, 1789–1900* (Fredericton, 1981). J. E. Veer, "The public life of Lemuel Allan Wilmot" (MA thesis, Univ. of N.B., Fredericton, 1970). Edward Mullaly, "Thomas, we hardly knew ye . . . ," Assoc. for Canadian Theatre Hist., *Newsletter* (London, Ont.), 6 (1982–83), no.1: 17–18.

HOERNER, OLYMPE (Tanner), educator and Protestant missionary; b. 3 Oct. 1807 in La Chaux-de-Fonds, Switzerland, daughter of David-Balthazar Hoerner and Marguerite Chanel; m. 1838 Jean-Emmanuel Tanner, probably in France; d. 4 Nov. 1854 in Pointe-aux-Trembles (Montreal).

Olympe Hoerner, whose father was a pharmacist of German origin, came to the Red River colony (Man.) in 1821 with her parents, her five brothers and sisters, and other Swiss families. These settlers had been recruited at the suggestion of Lord Selkirk [Douglas*] as reinforcements for the colony, but in the face of innumerable difficulties many left the region, either to settle on American soil or to return home. The Hoerner family may have chosen the latter course, for Olympe took a position in London, England, as a governess. In this capacity she accompanied Lord Barham's family to France; there she met a Swiss compatriot, the Reverend Jean-Emmanuel Tanner, and they were married in 1838. A son, Charles Augustus, who was to become a Presbyterian minister in Canada, was born in April 1839. Olympe apparently first worked as an evangelist in France, but only briefly, because in 1841 her husband was forced to return to Geneva for reasons of health, and there he obtained an offer to join in evangelizing French Canadians.

Interest in the Canadian missions had been awakened in Switzerland around 1830, through the London Missionary Society. A few Swiss evangelists, among them Henriette Feller [Odin*] and Louis Roussy*, began working in the Montreal region in 1835, and the anticlerical demonstrations during the 1837–38 rebellion stirred hopes of converting some French Canadians to Protestantism. Taking advantage of the circumstances, a dozen English-speaking Montrealers of various religious denominations met on 13 Feb. 1839 to found the French Canadian Missionary Society. Its objects were to recruit pastors, teachers, and evangelists whose native tongue was French, as well as to establish centres for worship and schools. Their action was in keeping with the search for unity being pursued as an ideal by the Protestant churches. The society's constitution contained the rudiments of a common profession of faith, and specified that the evangelists who were appointed must put their denominational ties in second place.

From the start the attempt at unification ran into serious difficulties. Church of England ministers refused to cooperate, and the French-speaking Protestant community of Grande-Ligne under Mme Feller declined to join.

The year the society was founded, its officers sent James Court and William Taylor* to Europe to enlist evangelists and collect funds. At the end of 1840 four lay recruits arrived in Lower Canada. They were stationed in the Montreal region on the north shore of the St Lawrence, at Belle-Rivière, Petit-Brûlé (Mirabel), and Sainte-Thérèse-de-Blainville (Sainte-Thérèse), for there was an understanding with the Protestants of Grande-Ligne that they alone should proselytize on the south shore. The choice of localities was based in part on the prospects of success, but especially on the proximity of Protestant English-speaking families in sympathy with the cause.

The society as yet had no pastor to administer the sacraments. In response to its request, the committee that had been set up in Geneva to assist with recruitment recommended Tanner and his wife, who arrived at Montreal in August 1841. After working for a few months in the city, the Tanners settled in Sainte-Thérèse-de-Blainville, where the resignation of evangelist Henri Provost had thrown the little Protestant community into confusion. Mme Tanner opened a school in their house which became a target for the hostility of Catholics. On one occasion people trespassed on their property and the windows of the house were broken. The incident gave the Tanners a chance to show their goodness of heart by asking that the sentence given to the offenders be suspended. Despite this gesture, the school was attended by only "a small number of children."

Meanwhile Jean-Emmanuel Tanner had been entrusted with coordinating the work of the evangelists. In the spring of 1843 he was asked to move to Montreal and settle in a house large enough to accommodate missionaries passing through the city. His wife made use of the space to start a French class for English-speaking girls. The society encouraged her endeavour, although it stressed that its objectives would be more swiftly attained if she concentrated solely on evangelizing French Canadians.

At the end of 1843 Mme Tanner accompanied her husband to Europe on a recruiting trip. They returned on 7 June 1844 with six evangelists. She then resumed her French class, which apparently had continued without interruption while she was away. It is possible that her sister, Mme Higgs, who occasionally helped the missionary society, took it over in her absence. Probably in deference to the executive body of the society, Mme Tanner gave up the French class in 1845 to devote her time to educating French Canadian girls. She took in three girls as boarders, and taught them academic subjects, homemaking, and the Bible; this was the beginning of the institute for girls which officially opened its doors to nine boarders in May 1846 in the Tanners' Montreal residence.

With the arrival of the evangelists recruited by the Tanners, the society had 17 missionaries, including wives. It could therefore undertake to enlarge its field of action, particularly since the recruits included Louis Marie, an agricultural specialist hired to work on its model farm at Belle-Rivière adjoining the institute for boys. The executive then decided to relocate the main establishments of the society at Pointe-aux-Trembles on a recently purchased farm, and to erect a building there which could accommodate the students. It asked Tanner to become the principal of the boys' school. In May 1847 Mme Tanner's school was in its turn transferred to Pointe-aux-Trembles, no doubt to allow the Tanners to live together, but also as an economy measure, for the same teachers would teach both boys and girls, and the girls would get practice in domestic chores.

French Canadian students at Pointe-aux-Trembles received free board and education because the French Canadian Missionary Society counted on this generosity to further its mission. English-speaking students had to pay, and were admitted only on accepting the same regulations as the French-speaking students. The program kept the pupils busy from 5:00 A.M., when they got up, to 9:00 P.M., the appointed bed-time. The boys and girls received separately about six hours of instruction daily; as well as mathematics, French grammar, history, natural sciences, and geography, they learned singing or music and studied the Bible. Two or three hours were devoted to study and about two hours to manual training, farm work for the boys and housework for the girls. The latter suspended their studies on Monday afternoons and Saturdays to do the laundry and mending for the schools.

During the early years these schools were on average attended annually by about 50 boys and just under 20 girls, ranging in age from 9 to 23. In February 1849 the executive reported that, since they had opened, the institutes at Pointe-aux-Trembles had helped to train 112 boys and 62 girls, from 78 families and 21 places in Lower Canada. They were sometimes obliged to refuse students or to send the pupils home for a few weeks because there was no money for board and lodging. But the development of the institute for girls was hampered particularly by cramped premises.

When Mme Tanner moved to Pointe-aux-Trembles, she set up her school and her residence in an old farmhouse adjoining the institute for boys. The building could barely accommodate the 15 to 18 female students housed there in addition to the Tanner family and no doubt also Mme Higgs and her daughter, both of whom taught in the school and assisted its principal. In 1848 an auxiliary committee

of English-speaking Montreal women tried without success to collect enough money to build a new school. The sums contributed were sufficient to allow a small structure to be put up, but it apparently did not meet the needs of the Tanner family, whose size is unknown.

Dissatisfied with their working and living conditions, and probably also with their salary, the Tanners resigned in June 1849, intending to settle in Montreal, where they proposed to continue evangelizing and to open a French school for English-speaking students. The executive could not accept the idea of losing their services and engaged in frantic negotiations. Tanner first suggested that he be given a plot on the Pointe-aux-Trembles farm so that he could build his dwelling there and set up a French school which his wife would run. Finally the committee settled the disagreement by adjusting their stipend. The Tanners were given an annual salary of £75, which was £5 more than the salaries of the other married evangelists. An annuity of £15 sterling, bearing interest, was established in their names to take care of their retirement. In addition to their stipend, at the end of 1851 they were granted free board and lodging. The implication doubtless was that they would be better housed, and in fact at the beginning of 1852 the society took fresh steps towards building the girls' school and the principals' residence. Despite financial help from the ladies' auxiliary committee, the Tanners had to go to the United States in the summer of 1853 to raise funds. The new building was completed that September. Shortly afterwards Mme Tanner was stricken with a serious illness which led to her death on 4 Nov. 1854, at the point when she might have begun to enjoy the fruits of her labour.

As the years passed, the churches belonging to the French Canadian Missionary Society decided one by one to set up their own organizations to spread the gospel among French Canadians. Thus in 1880 the society had to wind up its operations. For his part, Tanner had joined the Presbyterian church in 1861. Olympe Tanner may have had an inconspicuous career, living as she did in the shadow of her husband. She none the less exerted a considerable influence on the destiny of the French Canadian Missionary Society, since much of its evangelizing work was based on the education of the young.

RENÉ HARDY

ANQ-M, CE1-92, 6 nov. 1854. Arch. de l'État (Neuchâtel, Switzerland), La Chaux-de-Fonds, reg. des baptêmes, 16 janv. 1808. UCA, Biog. files, C. A. Tanner; J.-E. Tanner; French Canadian Missionary Soc., General Committee, minutes, 1848–61 (mfm.). French Canadian Missionary Soc., *Occasional Papers* (Montreal), 1842–44; *Reports* (Montreal), 1842–53. *Feuille religieuse du canton de Vaud* (Lausanne, Switzerland), 1830–60. *Missionary Record*

Hoffmann

(Montreal), November 1842–December 1848. E. H. Bovay, *Le Canada et les Suisses, 1604–1974* (Fribourg, Switzerland, 1976). R.-P. Duclos, *Histoire du protestantisme français au Canada et aux États-Unis* (2v., Montréal, [1913]). Paul Villard, *Up to the light; the story of French Protestantism in Canada* (Toronto, 1928). René Hardy, "La rébellion de 1837–38 et l'essor du protestantisme canadien-français," *RHAF*, 29 (1975–76): 163–89.

HOFFMANN, MATTHIAS FRANCIS, surgeon, naval officer, militia officer, and office holder; b. *c.* 1780; d. 3 April 1851 in Halifax.

Nothing is known about Matthias Hoffmann's background except that he was probably born in Trieste (Italy) and that he was related to local nobility. He joined the Royal Navy about 1797 and in 1804 was assigned as a medical assistant to a prisoner-of-war camp in Jamaica. After service on various vessels he was appointed surgeon on the frigate *Endymion*, which was stationed in the Mediterranean until it was paid off in February 1809. A few months later Hoffmann joined the 64-gun *Inflexible* as surgeon just before it sailed for Halifax. Once there he was transferred to the sloop *Driver*, which performed convoy duty and coastal patrols before being paid off in England in 1811.

The posting to the sloop, which followed so quickly upon several promotions, marked a definite eclipse in his naval career. Hoffmann decided after 1811 to abandon any further service at sea. At his own request he was made surgeon to the prisoner-of-war depot on Melville Island near Halifax. His interest in returning to Halifax was due at least in part to his engagement to Charlotte Mansfield, daughter of a Halifax loyalist. They were married by Robert Stanser* on 21 Sept. 1811 and subsequently had six daughters and two sons. The closing down of the Melville Island depot in 1815 marked the end of Hoffmann's naval service. Later he was to serve as surgeon of the 2nd Halifax Volunteer Artilllery Company and in 1843 he was appointed surgeon general of the Nova Scotian militia, an honorific position he held until his death.

After Hoffmann left the navy he established a private practice in Halifax. He had succeeded sufficiently well by July 1816 to be able to move to larger quarters on Granville Street near St Matthew's (Presbyterian) Church. In 1831 he assumed public prominence when, with doctors Samuel Head* and John Stirling, he operated a lazaret on Melville Island to deal with an outbreak of smallpox in Halifax. It had been established by the local magistrates, the first occasion on which they had recognized any direct responsibility for providing medical services, and was an effort to prevent a repetition of the epidemic of 1827 which had disrupted the Halifax economy and had resulted in some 800 deaths. Their enthusiasm for the temporary hospital was not shared by the poor, and

the three doctors treated only sixteen patients. The failure of the lazaret to attract many of the ill in Halifax was compounded for the three doctors when they received from the legislature but a third of the fees requested for their work. Hoffmann did not have the financial resources to donate his services and so he was reluctant to serve as a medical attendant in 1832 when temporary hospitals were once more considered to deal with an anticipated outbreak of cholera.

At the same time two provincial statutes were passed to give effect to an aggressive policy of quarantine and of public sanitation. A central board of health was established in Halifax to coordinate health measures in the province; it also served as the local board of health for Halifax, a function it retained until 1841 when the newly established city council assumed that responsibility. Hoffmann was appointed a health warden for St Paul's district, one of the ten divisions created in the city. The extensive duties of the wardens ranged from supervising the cleaning of yards to the removal of the ill to the cholera hospitals. The enthusiasm with which the board set about its affairs, and its plan to establish temporary hospitals, including one in the governor's residence and another at Dalhousie College, created considerable animosity. Much of the initiative behind these preventive measures, fortunately not needed in 1832, came from Sir Peregrine MAITLAND, the lieutenant governor, who overrode the well-established views of the legislature against concerted action to deal with health crises. Once the fear of an epidemic abated, a public reaction set in. Maitland left Nova Scotia in October 1832 and, when cholera did break out in August 1834, the city was unprepared. Hoffmann and the other doctors in Halifax had to deal with it as best they could. Although some 400 died during the epidemic, many people continued to oppose any radical changes in public policies concerning infectious diseases.

It was not until 1839, with the arrival of immigrant vessels carrying typhus, that a firm sentiment developed in the legislature that provision must be made by the province for immigrants ill with contagious diseases. The government reorganized the central board of health by appointing several doctors, including Hoffmann, to it. On 6 Aug. 1840 he was appointed health officer after the incumbent, William Bruce Almon*, died of typhus.

As health officer Hoffmann was expected to enforce the quarantine regulations whenever they were proclaimed by the lieutenant governor in order to prevent the general spread of contagious diseases into Halifax from vessels arriving in port. The government was, however, reluctant to enforce quarantine on ships other than those arriving from Great Britain with immigrants, lest the colony's trade be disrupted. In 1832, the only previous occasion on which the regulations had been systematically applied, the merchants had been vehement about the shipping delays and consequent expenses. No government would willingly repeat the experience. Moreover, several doctors, including some on the central board of health, accepted contemporary theories of miasma, and concluded that quarantine was ineffective. Hoffmann, believing in the older theory of contagion, accepted the necessity of quarantine. His official duties and his professional beliefs thus met with opposition from his colleagues, which became a source of continuous frustration during his term as health officer. Yet it was probably because the government believed the post of health officer not to be onerous that it appointed the 60-year-old Hoffmann to it. His appointment was an act of patronage intended to recognize his long career in the Royal Navy and in Halifax, as well as a means of providing some slight financial compensation. Hoffmann rarely collected more than £50 a year in fees from his duties as health officer, and he probably needed the money since he had a large family and only a limited medical practice. Moreover, unlike the two unsuccessful candidates, who were identified as reformers, Hoffmann took no part in politics and regarded public debates as unseemly. He was thus unlikely to create any political controversy unless strongly provoked.

Just at the time Hoffmann joined the central board of health, the *Edward*, out from Cork (Republic of Ireland), put into Halifax with fever on board. Existing legislation provided not only for quarantine but also that commissioners of the poor were bound to provide medical aid and support in the poor-house for all immigrants who were ill. When the *Edward* arrived, the commissioners of the poor-house decided not to accept any immigrants. The central board of health insisted that some facility was needed on shore for those who had contagious diseases. Following negotiations with the government a temporary facility was established at Waterloo Farm near the corner of Robie and South streets. Known as Waterloo Hospital, it was separate from the poor-house but under the administration of the commissioners of the poor, and it operated for two months until the immediate danger was past.

In the fall of 1840 Hoffmann helped convince the government that a permanent facility was needed to deal with contagious diseases among immigrants and sailors. Otherwise, Hoffmann argued, he would have no means of preventing such persons from becoming a constant source of infection in the crowded boarding-houses of the city. The commissioners of the poor, who controlled the poor asylum and were responsible for providing for the poor, were most unwilling to admit liability for such persons. However, in January 1841, faced with the care of a large number of recently arrived immigrants, they agreed to reopen Waterloo Hospital and allow Dr Hoffmann to attend the ill.

According to the agreement, the hospital remained under the jurisdiction of the commissioners and the inmates were to be legally classified as paupers, but they would be admitted and treated by Hoffmann who would receive £2 per diem for his services. Jealous of their jurisdiction over the asylum, the commissioners terminated their arrangement with Hoffmann in September 1842 and declared that only surgeons officially attached to the poor asylum could provide treatment in their facilities. They continued to admit immigrants into Waterloo Farm but, when faced with a serious outbreak of contagious diseases in Halifax in 1846, they returned to their earlier position that they had no liability for treating immigrants. Thus no facility remained for the treatment of immigrants, and the government refused to take any action because it believed that an adequate hospital would merely serve to attract more immigrant vessels in distress.

The government was forced into action again in May 1847 when Hoffmann was suddenly confronted with 279 passengers, many of them ill with typhus, on board the barque *Mountaineer* bound for New York from Cork. Authorized to open a lazaret in a small house in Richmond (Halifax), Hoffmann soon moved from this filthy and damp location to Melville Island, the site of the former naval base, but both these makeshift arrangements were totally inadequate and he was unable to cope properly with the emergency. Lieutenant Governor Sir John HARVEY, sharing the belief that an adequate hospital would attract more immigrant ships, remained adamant that no provision should be made for the treatment of their passengers and ordered the disposal of all medical equipment purchased in 1847 for the lazaret. None the less, a commitment remained to provide at least minimal care for immigrants. When the survivors of a shipwreck, many of them ill with typhus, were brought into Halifax Harbour in March 1848, Hoffmann was expected to deal with them. Unable to find any facility in Halifax on short notice, the city council, acting in its role as a board of health, opened a lazaret in Dartmouth. This action was met by a storm of opposition from local residents who feared, all too rightly, that typhus would spread throughout the town.

Hoffmann received some harsh criticism for his handling of the immigrants in 1848, but his basic difficulty was the lack of equipment, staff, and facilities. As early as 1832 some doctors had begun advocating the creation of a general hospital, separate from the poor asylum, which could also serve as a teaching institution. In 1839, however, the agitation for a permanent hospital began to focus on the need for dealing with the resident poor, rather than with destitute, sick immigrants. Hoffmann, shortly after his appointment as health officer in 1840, lent his support for a hospital which would deal with infectious diseases. The proposal for a hospital was thus a complex issue, touching as it did on such controversial issues as poor relief and revealing differences in view between public authorities and doctors concerned about medical care. In 1848 when the city council and the legislature did endorse the construction of a hospital, the proposed facility was intended to deal only with immigrants and sailors and not residents of the province. The campaign for a hospital in the 1840s, however, held back partly by a continuing suspicion of the medical profession, had made the doctors realize that to improve their influence and status they would have to cooperate more among themselves. Thus, in October 1844 they formed the Medical Society of Halifax, of which Hoffmann was a vice-president until his death in 1851.

Difficulties with the enforcement of quarantine regulations continued to be a preoccupation for Hoffmann. He was particularly hard pressed to deal with vessels bound for other ports which arrived in Halifax with a serious outbreak of disease on board. The quarantine act of 1839 had allowed him to inspect only those ships carrying ten or more steerage passengers from Europe. On several occasions Hoffmann pointed out that coastal vessels, especially from Newfoundland, also brought disease into the city and he insisted on inspecting some vessels which were outside his jurisdiction. This procedure brought protests from shipowners who objected to the added expense and delay, and the quarantine regulations proclaimed in 1847 by Harvey made no concession to Hoffmann's arguments.

Hoffmann's political impotency was particularly evident when he attempted to inspect cabin passengers on board Cunard steamships. Although Hoffmann argued that the respectable classes could be infected by the lower classes, Samuel Cunard* persuaded Harvey to order Hoffmann to confine his inspection to steerage passengers. Social bias and political pressures thus prevented Hoffmann from carrying out any meaningful quarantine policy.

Unlike health officers in other colonies Hoffmann, moreover, had no regular salary, no office, and no boat. His frustrations were brought to a head in November 1847 when his small rented craft capsized in the harbour and he almost drowned. Hoffmann indignantly informed the mayor "that I never go aside a man of war, a foreign vessel or one of our merchantmen that I do not feel that our flag and the authority of our province are disgraced by my boarding such vessels in a fishing boat or a flat boat besides endangering my life." He also contended that he should receive a salary instead of depending upon fees from ships inspected, which brought him only £40 to £50 a year and encouraged captains to evade inspection. His requests for a boat, office, and salary

were brushed aside by the legislature. Indeed the reform ministry led by James Boyle UNIACKE, which took office in February 1848, began to question seriously the utility of any quarantine regulations.

As health officer Hoffmann was thus quite unable to make improvements in the enforcement of quarantine regulations, the care of sick immigrants, or his own position. He deserved better treatment by the legislature and the administration, particularly as critics in 1848 were intensifying their condemnation of the central board of health for failing to keep contagious diseases out of the city. Despite his age, the frustration, and the indignities suffered by his vanity, Hoffmann continued in office, probably because he needed money to support his family. His estate was to consist of but £675 in currency and £1,625 in real property. The hazards of his office were fully realized in March 1851 when the immigrant ship *Infanta*, bound for New York from Liverpool with typhus on board, tied up to a Halifax wharf. The mayor, Andrew MacKinlay*, became enraged by Hoffmann's refusal to quarantine the ship because he was cautious about exercising his powers as health officer; but before MacKinlay could take action against him, Hoffmann had contracted typhus while treating the passengers. He died on 3 April at the age of 71.

KENNETH GEORGE PRYKE

Halifax County Court of Probate (Halifax), Estate papers, no.391. PANS, RG 1, 214½C–G; RG 25, sect.3, 1–2, 5; RG 34-312, P. PRO, ADM 1/1732–33; ADM 24/65; ADM 36/1094, 36/15879, 36/16939; ADM 37/11, 37/781, 37/1093, 37/2392; ADM 51/1563, 51/1804, 51/1975, 51/2276; ADM 99/77. N.S., *Acts*, 1832, especially c.14; 1839; 1848; House of Assembly, *Journal and proc.*, 1804–51, especially 1832. *Acadian Recorder*, 29 May, 4 June 1831. *Nova-scotian*, 1824–51. *Nova-Scotia Royal Gazette*, 1812. Geoffrey Bilson, *A darkened house: cholera in nineteenth-century Canada* (Toronto, 1980). S. L. Morse, "Immigration to Nova Scotia, 1839–1851" (MA thesis, Dalhousie Univ., Halifax, 1946). C. E. Saunders, "Social conditions and legislation in Nova Scotia (1815–1851)" (MA thesis, Dalhousie Univ., 1949). D. A. Sutherland, "Gentlemen vs. shopkeepers: urban reform in early 19th century Halifax" (paper presented to the CHA annual meeting, Montreal, 1972). D. A. Campbell, "Pioneers of medicine in Nova Scotia," *Maritime Medical News* (Halifax), 16 (1904): 195–210, 243–55, 519–27; 17 (1905): 8–17. M. H. L. Grant, "Historical background of the Nova Scotia Hospital, Dartmouth, and the Victoria General Hospital, Halifax" and "Historical sketches of hospitals and alms houses in Halifax, Nova Scotia, 1749–1859," *Nova Scotia Medical Bull.*, 16 (1937): 250–258 and 17 (1938): 229–38, 294–304, 491–512. M. H. L. and H. G. Grant, "An epidemic of cholera in Halifax, Nova Scotia, 1834," *Nova Scotia Medical Bull.* (Halifax), 14 (1935): 587–96. W. F. Hattie, "The first minute book," *Nova Scotia Medical Bull.*, 8 (1929): 155–63. A. E. Marble, "A history of medicine in

Nova Scotia, 1784–1854," N.S. Hist. Soc., *Coll.*, 41 (1982): 73–101. "The Medical Society of Nova Scotia: synopsis of steps leading to its organization," *Nova Scotia Medical Bull.*, 6 (1927), no.3: 21–22.

HOGAN, JOHN SHERIDAN, printer, newspaperman, lawyer, and politician; b. *c*. 1815 near Dublin; d. 1 Dec. 1859 in Toronto.

Son of a hospitable but poverty-ridden family, John Sheridan Hogan came to York (Toronto) to live with an uncle in 1827. He ran away to Hamilton, where he worked successively as newsboy, printer, foreman, and writer on A. K. Mackenzie's *Canadian Wesleyan* which was published from 1831 to about 1835. Hogan probably had little formal education, although he convinced Samuel Thompson*, who later employed him, that he had "distinguished himself at college." By 1837 he was working in the law office of Allan Napier MacNab*, and on 29 Dec. 1837 was involved with his employer in the burning of the Patriot supply ship *Caroline*. Nevertheless, after the acquittal of Alexander McLeod*, who had been tried in October 1841 for his involvement in the *Caroline* affair, Hogan was a key figure in an attempt to keep the Patriot flame alive. Early in 1842, following a plan by his former employer A. K. Mackenzie, Hogan agreed to enter the United States and have himself arrested for harming American citizens during the *Caroline* affair. The intention was to stir up hostilities between the Canadian and American governments and thus aid the Patriot cause. He did cross the border and was arrested in Lockport, N.Y.; however, the warrant against him was found to have been made out improperly and, on the advice of William Lyon Mackenzie* (who had opposed the scheme), he returned to Canada. But Mackenzie soon changed his mind and another attempt was arranged. Mackenzie had Edward Alexander THELLER arrest Hogan in Rochester on 31 March but once more the court decided that it could not properly try him. At this point, in the face of growing cordiality between the two countries following the arrival in April of Lord Ashburton, who defused the situation diplomatically, the affair petered out entirely. The motives and actions of both Hogan and A. K. Mackenzie are not clearly understood and some historians have suggested that they may have been serving the loyal faction as double agents.

In the late 1830s Hogan had suspended his law studies and in 1840 had become clerk and bookkeeper to Allan Macdonell*, sheriff of the Gore District. In 1841, however, he returned to a Hamilton law office and was called to the bar two years later. By 1849 he had shifted to political journalism and was parliamentary correspondent for several journals, developing a "bold, bitter, and unsparing style." His strength as a political writer appears in three able articles published in *Blackwood's Edinburgh Magazine* in 1849–50, two entitled "Civil revolution in the Canadas" and one "Civil revolution in the Canadas – a remedy." He argued that, as a British colony, Canada could exceed the United States as a field for British development but that want of internal accord was destroying the confidence of British capitalists in Canadian capabilities. The articles were reprinted and circulated in London and were widely referred to in Canadian newspapers. In 1850 *Blackwood's* had also published Hogan's New Year's poem "Canadian loyalty." Two years later he was associated with Samuel Thompson in establishing the *United Empire*, a semi-weekly journal published in Toronto. The *United Empire* attacked Francis Hincks* for pro-American sympathies, commented on the clergy reserves question, and urged the British to grant the colonies representation in the imperial parliament. Curiously, in view of Hogan's death, the 19 June 1852 edition contained, along with a rich mixture of economic and political comment, two items on drownings and a court report of the trial of one James Brown who was charged by his mother with beating his sister. Hogan had presented his ideas on politics and economics in more permanent form the previous month in his essay *The Canadas*. Using statistics showing trade with Britain declining, he concluded that free trade was disastrous for the Upper Canadian farmer. British garrisons appeared as "the last remains of expensive furniture in a ruined house."

After Thompson bought the *Daily Colonist* in 1853, Hogan moved to that paper, as assistant editor and Quebec correspondent, and took up cudgels against Hincks and his "crop of corruption," while continuing to report and comment on sensational murders as well as politics. The *Colonist*, which according to Thompson was "an exact counterpart of the *London Times*" in typographical appearance, size of page and type, style of advertisements, and above all, in independence of editorial comment and fairness in its treatment of opponents," eventually claimed a weekly circulation of 30,000. In 1854 Hogan decided to enter politics but, running as a moderate reformer for the York East seat in the Legislative Assembly, he was defeated by Amos Wright*, an ultra reformer.

Hogan pulled his ideas together the following year in an essay submitted to the contest for the universal exposition in Paris; it won first prize and was published by order of the government in both English and French. A history of the two Canadas, it traces the rise of towns, self-government, and capital, all in relation to trade, banking, immigration, and education. Sober statistics are converted into a panegyric on a land of "quiet plenty" and the essay is an important reflection of mid-19th-century assumptions about progress through industrial development. It included a detailed map of railway development in Canada and

Hogsett

the northern United States, reflecting an interest shared with his old colleague MacNab.

In 1856 Hogan became editor-in-chief of the *Daily Colonist* but the following year he left the paper to run again for parliament and this time he was elected for Grey. He was regarded, with Oliver Mowat* and Thomas D'Arcy McGee*, as one of the coming men among the new members. Tall, spare, and agile, he was admired for his writing and wit, and respected for his independence. Hogan, an Independent Liberal, voted against the ephemeral Liberal ministry of George Brown* and Antoine-Aimé Dorion* on 2 Aug. 1858, though he "continued to favour the Liberal side of questions." When John A. Macdonald*, whom Hogan had admired as a young politician, and George-Étienne Cartier* returned to power that same month, he did not hesitate to attack their ministry. Active involvement in politics had not, however, ended his writing, and a political pamphlet appeared in November 1859.

Then, as December 1859 began, he disappeared. Although he had married Madeline Wharton Metcalf at Christ's Church (Anglican) in Hamilton on 18 Nov. 1847, he apparently was living alone at this time. He resided at Toronto's Rossin House hotel and intermittently supported a Mrs Laurie and her children. His movements were often erratic and his absence caused no alarm for two months, when an unsuccessful search for him was launched in the United States. More than 16 months after his disappearance, his body was found in Toronto's Don River. A police informer said she had seen Hogan attacked and robbed by James Brown, Jane Ward, John Sherrick, and two other members of the notorious "Brooks' Bush Gang," terrorizers of east end citizenry. The melodramatic trial of Ward and Sherrick revealed that Hogan had left Mrs Laurie on 1 Dec. 1859, stopped in at the *Colonist* office, and then proceeded east on the Kingston road. Flashing an unusually large roll of money on the Don bridge, Hogan was beaten when he offered to pay a usual "toll" to the gang members. Unfortunately he recognized one of the attackers, whom he called by name, whereupon a member of the gang "put a stone in a handkerchief and brained him." Ward and Sherrick were acquitted but at a later trial James Brown, though he swore his innocence to the end, was convicted; despite a retrial, he was executed at a public hanging on 10 March 1862.

Ardent and loyal yet reform-minded, Hogan had in his life as a journalist and politician helped direct Canadian hopes of maintaining, while liberalizing, the British connection. Like McGee, he contributed a controversial note to political and literary life in the 1840s and 1850s but, unlike his distinguished compatriot, he was murdered not by a political assassin but by a gang of roughnecks. His death, like the minor columns of his papers, revealed the seamy life on the edges of Toronto society in the mid 19th century.

ELIZABETH WATERSTON

John Sheridan Hogan is the author of *The Canadas: shall they "be lost or given away?" A question to be decided by the people of England in cho[o]sing between free trade or protection; an essay . . .* (Toronto, 1852); *Canada: an essay: to which was awarded the first prize by the Paris Exhibition Committee of Canada* (Montreal, 1855), which was also published as *Le Canada: essai auquel le premier prix a été adjugé par le Comité canadien de l'Exposition de Paris* (Montréal, 1855); and *A review of the proceedings of the Reform Convention, held in the St. Lawrence Hall, Toronto, 9th November, 1859 . . .* (Toronto, 1859). Hogan published anonymously in *Blackwood's Edinburgh Magazine* (Edinburgh and London) a series of articles entitled "Civil revolution in the Canadas," 65 (January–June 1849): 727–41 and 67 (January–June 1850): 249–68, and "Civil revolution in the Canadas – a remedy," 66 (July–December 1849): 471–85. Hogan's poem, "Canadian loyalty: an ode, written at sunrise on New-Year's morning of 1850, at the head of Lake Ontario, in western Canada," was published anonymously in *Blackwood's Edinburgh Magazine*, 67: 345–46.

AO, MS 516, 15 Feb.–18 April 1842. *British Colonist* (Toronto), 1849–50. *Daily Colonist* (Toronto), 1851–58. *United Empire* (Toronto), 1852–53. *Marriage notices of Ontario*, comp. W. D. Reid (Lambertville, N.J., 1980), 214. Morgan, *Bibliotheca Canadensis*, 192; *Sketches of celebrated Canadians*, 764–65. Cornell, *Alignment of political groups*, 37, 45, 48. L. F. [Cowdell] Gates, *William Lyon Mackenzie: the post-rebellion years in the United States and Canada* (Ithaca, N.Y., 1978). N. F. Davin, *The Irishman in Canada* (London and Toronto, 1877), 645–51. L. S. Fallis, "The idea of progress in the Province of Canada: a study in the history of ideas," *The shield of Achilles: aspects of Canada in the Victorian age*, ed. W. L. Morton (Toronto and Montreal, 1968), 169–83. Guillet, *Lives and times of Patriots; Toronto from trading post to great city* (Toronto, 1934), 224–25. O. A. Kinchen, *The rise and fall of the Patriot hunters* (New York, 1956). Samuel Thompson, *Reminiscences of a Canadian pioneer for the last fifty years: an autobiography* (Toronto, 1884; repub. Toronto and Montreal, 1968). W. S. Wallace, *Murders and mysteries; a Canadian series* (Toronto, 1931), 255–71; "The periodical literature of Upper Canada," *CHR*, 12 (1931): 4–22.

HOGSETT, AARON, public servant; b. *c.* 1777 in Cookstown (Northern Ireland); d. 14 Aug. 1858.

Nothing is known of Aaron Hogsett's family or early education. In 1808 he became a clerk in the Royal Navy. Two years later he was appointed second accountant at the important naval victualling depot on the island of Minorca, where he executed much of the financial business connected with the provisioning of some 20,000 seamen as well as the transport service for the land forces on the coast of Catalonia, Spain.

As a result of the reduction in naval services at the close of the Napoleonic Wars, Hogsett returned in

1815 to England, where he accepted an appointment as clerk to the secretary of Vice-Admiral Sir Richard Goodwin Keats*, newly appointed governor of Newfoundland. In 1818 Vice-Admiral Sir Charles Hamilton*, the next governor, named him waiter and searcher in the customs department at St John's, but within a year he was superseded in this post by an appointee of the treasury office.

Hogsett returned to the lesser post of clerk to the governor's secretary until 1821 when he was appointed a deputy naval officer, responsible for such tasks as overseeing the maintenance and revictualling of naval vessels, collecting customs duties, and recording incoming and outgoing vessels. In 1825 Hogsett found himself without employment for a third time when the naval establishment was moved from St John's to Halifax. However, within a year or so, he was appointed deputy sheriff of the central district of Newfoundland with a yearly stipend of £252. On 1 Sept. 1835 his undoubted ability eventually secured for him the post of high sheriff of Newfoundland with a salary of £513.

As deputy sheriff, Hogsett was largely responsible for enforcing the new rules set up in 1833–34 by Chief Justice Henry John Boulton*. These rules related to empanelling juries, issuing writs of attachment against fishermen's boats and tackle, and other innovations in the legal processes. Hogsett, Boulton, and members of the Council were attacked by the leaders of the dominant group in the House of Assembly, the reformers, particularly Dr William Carson*, and by Robert John Parsons*, editor of the *Newfoundland Patriot* of St John's. One newspaper article was so vicious that Hogsett sued Carson and Parsons for libel. He won a partial victory; although he had claimed £300 in damages, he was awarded only £10 and court costs.

In contrast to the hostility shown by Carson and Parsons, Hogsett had a close association with Patrick Morris*, the Roman Catholic leader of the reformers. By 1834 Hogsett was a vice-president of the Benevolent Irish Society, of which Morris had been president since 1822 and under whose tutelage the originally non-denominational society had become almost wholly Catholic in character. Whether Hogsett had converted from the Church of England to Roman Catholicism in the 1830s is uncertain, but in the attacks made upon him by the Protestant leaders of the liberal group, he was charged with apostasy. Morris, on the other hand, championed Hogsett's appeal to the British government for a post in 1833, describing him as "competent to fill any civil situation" and one whose "character stands very high with the distinguished officers under whom he has served in the Navy; in the Colony it stands equally high."

After the controversies of the 1830s Hogsett appears to have had an uneventful public life. He was married, and he and his wife had at least four children. His second son, George James*, rose to prominence in the Liberal party, becoming attorney general in 1858, the year his father died on board the *Spray* while returning home from a trip to Liverpool, England.

Skill in accounting and administrative ability helped Aaron Hogsett overcome the difficulties he thrice faced when deprived of work through no fault of his own. As a key man in the judicial process, he was included in the abuse heaped on leading office holders by members of the popular party in the 1830s, though he himself kept aloof from political involvement. At various times he served in St John's as coroner, clerk of the peace, customs collector and controller, Spanish vice-consul, and secretary to the city's board of health.

ELINOR KYTE SENIOR

Private arch., Lawrence Lande (Montreal), H. J. Boulton papers, G.B., Parl., Report of the committee of the whole house on the present state of the administration of justice in Newfoundland, 15 Oct. 1837, 9–44. PRO, CO 194/86: 198–209; 194/103: 83. *Newfoundlander*, 6 Sept. 1858. *Patriot* (St John's), 18 March 1834, 21 June 1869. *Public Ledger*, 7 Sept. 1858. *Times and General Commercial Gazette* (St John's), 4 Sept. 1858. *When was that?* (Mosdell). R. H. Bonnycastle, *Newfoundland in 1842: a sequel to "The Canadas in 1841"* (2v., London, 1842), 2: 88–89. Howley, *Ecclesiastical hist. of Nfld.* Prowse, *Hist. of Nfld.* (1895). Philip Tocque, *Newfoundland: as it was, and as it is in 1877* (Toronto, 1878).

HOLMES, ANDREW FERNANDO (Ferdinando), physician, professor, college administrator, author, and scientist; b. 17 March 1797 in Cadiz, Spain, second son of Thomas Holmes, a businessman, and Susanna Scott; m. Juliet Wadsworth, and they had three daughters and one son; d. 9 Oct. 1860 in Montreal.

Andrew Fernando Holmes was born at Cadiz because the vessel in which his parents and his brother, Benjamin*, sailed from the British Isles had been captured by a French frigate and taken to Spain as a prize. The family did not reach British North America until 1801, settling first at Quebec for a few years and then moving to Montreal.

Holmes received his preliminary education at the school of Alexander Skakel*. In 1811 he was articled to Dr Daniel Arnoldi* and five years later he received his licence from the Montreal board of medical examiners. At that period many men would have been satisfied with this qualification and would have immediately begun medical practice. Holmes set his sights higher. He went to Scotland, where he obtained his diploma from the Royal College of Surgeons of Edinburgh in 1818 and his MD from the University of Edinburgh in 1819. His graduation thesis, in Latin,

Holmes

was entitled "De tetano." After completing his studies, he visited London and Dublin, and spent a short time in Paris before returning to Lower Canada.

In 1819 Holmes entered into partnership for five years with his former instructor, Arnoldi, and then practised alone until his death in 1860. With the opening of the Montreal General Hospital in 1822, he joined its medical staff, a connection he retained for the rest of his life; he was a member of the active attending staff for more than 20 years and on retiring became a consultant. Holmes and his colleagues at the Montreal General Hospital wished to teach medicine as well as practise it. As early as 1822 Holmes was giving a course in chemistry at the home of Skakel, and Dr John Stephenson*, with whom he had studied in Great Britain, was lecturing on anatomy and physiology at the hospital. Not content with these informal arrangements, Holmes and Stephenson drew up a memorandum setting forth the arguments in favour of establishing a medical school. After approval by their colleagues at the hospital, the memorandum was sent to the governor, Lord Dalhousie [Ramsay*], together with a letter suggesting that the medical licensing body be remodelled to consist of the medical officers of the Montreal General Hospital. Dalhousie expressed his approval of both plans, thus giving the future staff of the medical school authority to license as well as teach their students (a situation which provoked criticism and eventually led to new legislation regulating medical licensing). The medical officers of the hospital rented a house on Rue Saint-Jacques near Place d'Armes and provided it with chemical apparatus, anatomical and pathological specimens, and a library. Opening its doors to students in the autumn of 1823, the Montreal Medical Institution was the first medical school established in Canada. Instruction was given both at the institution and at the Montreal General Hospital. Holmes taught chemistry, pharmacy, and botany, and was in charge of the library. The terms pharmacy and materia medica seem to have been used interchangeably; in 1826 he was described as professor of chemistry and materia medica.

The Montreal Medical Institution had applied for a royal charter in 1823 but its application was rejected by the Colonial Office in 1828 because it had no affiliation with an educational institution. The officers then approached McGill College which had obtained a royal charter in 1821 but, because of prolonged litigation over the bequest of James McGill*, existed only on paper. In 1829 the problem of erecting a university with more than a nominal existence was neatly solved by "engrafting" upon McGill College the flourishing Montreal Medical Institution, which then became the McGill College Medical Faculty. The medical staff of the institution, William Caldwell*, William Robertson*, Stephenson, and Holmes, became the founding members of the faculty with Robertson, the senior member, as official head.

Apart from bestowing the power to grant academic degrees, the change was, at first, little more than one of name. As the school grew, however, Holmes relinquished some of his earlier responsibilities and assumed more senior duties. Dr Archibald Hall* took over materia medica in 1835 and chemistry in 1842. In 1845 Dr Lactance Papineau relieved Holmes of the teaching of botany. In 1843 Holmes had been appointed professor of the principles and practice of medicine, succeeding Robertson, and he therefore became official head of the faculty with the title of secretary. In 1854 this title was changed to dean. Like his professorship, Holmes occupied the deanship until his death. He continued in charge of the library throughout his life and, in addition, donated his private library to the college.

The recollections of his students indicate that Holmes was a conscientious but not a brilliant teacher. His lectures were said to be too detailed and exhaustive to be attractive, his voice was weak, and his delivery was wanting in animation. But there is no doubt that his teaching was based on the most careful, even laborious, preparation and, as one of his former students recalled, every word was worthy of being noted.

Holmes's medical work was by no means confined to university teaching and administration. As well as maintaining an active practice, he made a number of original contributions to medical journals on topics such as diseases of the heart (including a description of an unusual congenital malformation), gunshot wound of the heart, congenital malformation of the oesophagus and trachea, cholera, uterine tumour, obstruction of the vermiform appendix, jaundice, and the use of chloroform as an anaesthetic. He was one of the founders of the Montreal Medico-Chirurgical Society in 1843 and was its first president. He served as a member of the board of governors of the College of Physicians and Surgeons of Lower Canada and was elected to a three-year term as its president in 1853.

Holmes's interests ranged far beyond medicine. As a chemist he confined himself to teaching by lectures and highly successful demonstrations, but as botanist, mineralogist, and geologist he did much more. From his early sojourn in Edinburgh he brought to Canada an extensive herbarium of plants and a large collection of minerals and geological specimens to which he added from sources in Canada and the United States. His collection of the flora of Montreal Island and vicinity is especially noteworthy. In the field of mineralogy his reputation was enhanced by the naming of a form of brittle mica after him. He had submitted specimens to Dr Thomas Thomson, Regius professor of chemistry at the University of Glasgow. Thomson wrote, "This mineral being obviously new, I

Holmes

have given it the name of *Holmite* as a small tribute to Dr. Holmes of Montreal, to whom I am indebted for so many new and curious minerals from Canada and the United States of America." Unfortunately, the name did not last long. Shortly after Thomson's paper was published, holmite was found to be identical with seybertite, which had already been described, and the name holmite was dropped. Another mineral specimen submitted by Holmes was a relatively rare feldspar collected near Bytown (Ottawa), which Thomson named bytownite. In 1856 Holmes's collection of minerals was purchased by McGill and, at the same time, he presented it with his herbarium. Thus Holmes served McGill not only as a teacher and administrator, but also as a discriminating collector of plants and minerals. His outstanding contributions were recognized in 1859 when McGill awarded him an honorary LLD.

In view of his wide and varied interests, it is not surprising to find that Holmes was a founding member of the Natural History Society of Montreal in 1827, and that he took an active part in all its work. He catalogued the minerals and geological specimens in the society's cabinets and was a curator of its museum. From 1827 to 1836 he was corresponding secretary of the society, and then, from 1836 to 1841, its president.

Finally, Holmes was a devout supporter of the Church of England and a member of the Montreal Auxiliary Bible Society. An appreciation published after his death stated that "in every sense of the word he was a Christian gentleman" and this was his "most striking characteristic."

Holmes's death in 1860 was sudden and unexpected, and caused widespread dismay. The McGill medical faculty wore mourning for a month and their students erected a memorial tablet which is still on display at the university. In 1865 the school established the Holmes medal, awarded annually to the student graduating with the highest total marks in the different branches of the medical curriculum. It remains today as the senior award for scholastic achievement in the medical undergraduate program. A portrait of Holmes, painted in 1819 by Scottish artist John Watson (later Sir John Watson-Gordon), was presented to the medical faculty by Holmes's daughter. It was destroyed by fire in 1907 but, using a photograph of the portrait as a model, Robert Harris* painted another, which now hangs in the medical sciences building of McGill University.

EDWARD HORTON BENSLEY

Andrew Fernando Holmes is the author of numerous articles on medicine published in the *Trans.* (Edinburgh) of the Medico-Chirurgical Soc. of Edinburgh in 1824, the *New York Medical and Physical Journal* in 1826, the *Boston*

Medical and Surgical Journal in 1833, the *Montreal Medical Gazette* in 1844, the *British American Journal of Medical and Physical Science* (Montreal), 1 (1845–46), 2 (1846–47), 3 (1847–48), and 6 (1850–51), and the *Medical Chronicle* (Montreal), 2 (1854–55) and 3 (1855–56). His mineral collection, which was purchased by McGill College, is at the Redpath Museum (McGill Univ., Montreal), and his herbarium is part of that at Macdonald College in McGill University. James BARNSTON prepared a catalogue of the section of the herbarium that concerns the Montreal region, which was published as "Catalogue of Canadian plants' in the Holmes' herbarium, in the cabinet of the University of McGill College," *Canadian Naturalist and Geologist . . .* (Montreal), 4 (1859): 100–16.

ANQ-M, CE1-68, 13 oct. 1860. Arch. of the Mount Royal Cemetery Company (Outremont, Que.), Reg. of burials, 13 Oct. 1860. McGill Univ. Arch., McGill College Medical Faculty, minute-book, 1842–52; Montreal Medical Institution, minute-book, 1822–24. McGill Univ. Libraries, Blacker-Wood Library, Montreal Natural Hist. Soc. Arch. Univ. of McGill College, Faculty of Medicine, *Annual announcement* (Montreal), 1852–61. *Montreal Gazette*, 11 Oct. 1850. Borthwick, *Hist. and biog. gazetteer.* Morgan, *Bibliotheca Canadensis*; *Sketches of celebrated Canadians*, 485–86. Abbott, *Hist. of medicine.* S. B. Frost, *McGill University: for the advancement of learning* (2v., Montreal, 1980–84). Archibald Hall, *A biographical sketch of the late A. F. Holmes, M.D., LL.D. including a summary history of medical department of McGill College* (Montreal, 1860). R. P. Howard, *A sketch of the late G. W. Campbell . . . being the introductory address of the fiftieth session of the medical faculty of McGill University* (Montreal, 1882). H. E. MacDermot, *A history of the Montreal General Hospital* (Montreal, 1950). M. E. [S.] Abbott, "Andrew F. Holmes, M.D., LL.D., 1797–1860," *McGill Univ. Magazine* (Montreal), 4 (1905): 176–81; "An historical sketch of the medical faculty of McGill University," *Montreal Medical Journal*, 31 (1902): 561–672; "Early American medical schools: the faculty of medicine of McGill University," *Surgery, Gynecology and Obstetrics* (Chicago), 60 (1935): 242–53. E. H. Bensley, "The Holmes medal," *McGill Medical Journal* (Montreal), 34 (1965): 3–7; "The Holmes mineral collection," *Montreal General Hospital News*, 27 (1983), no.1: 10. D. C. MacCallum, "Reminiscences of the Medical School of McGill University," *McGill Univ. Magazine*, 2 (1903): 124–48. R. W. Quinn, "The four founders," *McGill Medical Undergraduate Journal* (Montreal), 5 (May 1936): 5–11.

HOLMES, JOHN (rebaptized **Jean**), Roman Catholic priest, educator, and school administrator; b. 7 Feb. 1799 in Windsor, Vt, son of John Holmes, shoemaker and farmer, and Anna Bugbee; d. 18 June 1852 in L'Ancienne-Lorette, Lower Canada, and was buried 21 June in the chapel of the Séminaire de Québec.

The story of John Holmes, whom his contemporaries as well as later generations considered one of the great educators of the 19th century, was unusual for French Canada. His parents, who were Protestants, left Windsor soon after his birth to settle in the

405

Holmes

neighbourhood of Hanover, N.H. They enrolled John in Moor's Indian Charity School, a Congregational establishment founded in 1769 to give Indians a Christian education. After 1800 this school had many more sons of white Americans than of Indians. Since teaching was carried out under the supervision of neighbouring Dartmouth College, young Holmes embarked upon a serious program of classical studies at a school of good standing. There is to be a minister of religion became evident. In 1814 his father decided to buy a property for farming in Colebrook, near the border with Lower Canada. Needing labour, he informed his son in August 1815 that his studies were finished and that he was thenceforth to stay on the farm. Distressed, John decided after a few days' reflection to leave home without notifying his parents. He crossed the border and went to Hyatt's Mill (Sherbrooke) in Lower Canada, where he became an apprentice to the tanner Samuel Willard* until he could resume his schooling.

In the autumn of 1815 or the winter of 1816 Stephen Burroughs, a former student at Dartmouth who had become a Catholic schoolmaster at Trois-Rivières, met Holmes at Willard's home. The latter agreed to let Holmes leave with Burroughs, who took him into his school at Trois-Rivières as an assistant. During an examination session in May 1816 the parish priest of Yamachiche, Charles Ecuier*, met Holmes and invited him to take up residence at his presbytery, promising he would allow him to continue his Latin studies. Even though the young American was as Protestant as ever – according to tradition he wanted to destroy the images and statues of the church at Trois-Rivières on his arrival – he accepted the priest's offer. Holmes set to work with dispatch, and his studies made good progress under the guidance of Ecuier, a classical scholar. He experienced as swift a change in religion for he embraced Catholicism. On 3 May 1817 he received baptism and communion in the church at Yamachiche, and adopted a new Christian name, Jean. In the autumn Ecuier sent him to take the final part of the classical program, Philosophy, at the Petit Séminaire de Montréal, which was run by emigrant French Sulpicians. Antoine-Jacques Houdet* was its regular teacher. As Holmes's course notes show, in the first of his two years he devoted himself to philosophy, studying logic, metaphysics, and ethics; in the second, following Houdet's textbook, he took mathematical, systematic, and experimental physics.

Holmes decided to become a priest, and the bishop of Quebec, Joseph-Octave Plessis*, assigned him to the Séminaire de Nicolet. He was to teach there while pursuing theological studies, in accordance with the European custom already established at Quebec and Montreal. His studies were paid for by the diocese. In 1819–20 he taught the Philosophy program, and in the following year the fourth-year class (Versification).

From 1821 to 1823 he was again with the Philosophy class, and taught philosophy and science using Houdet's treatise. It was probably while studying theology that he learned Greek on his own, to judge by a book in his library, signed and dated 1820. Holmes was ordained priest on 5 Aug. 1823. In October Bishop Plessis appointed him assistant priest at Berthier-en-Haut (Berthierville, Que.) and missionary at Drummondville. In 1825 he was attending only to the latter post. He ministered to the faithful in the region between Drummondville and Sherbrooke, travelling constantly in both winter and summer. That year, visiting someone who was ill, he was drenched by icy rain and contracted rheumatism, from which he was to suffer for the rest of his life.

Whether Holmes had contact with his family over the years is no longer in doubt. Some assert that his father came to see him at Hyatt's Mill in the autumn of 1815. According to others, once he had reached Trois-Rivières Holmes wrote to his father. In 1904 his sister, an Ursuline nun called Mother Sainte-Croix, noted that Holmes had gone with another seminarist to Colebrook just before his ordination in order to see his family, which included several brothers and sisters born after he had left home. Thereafter he returned to Colebrook every summer. On one occasion he brought back his eldest sister, Delia, and placed her in the convent of the Congregation of Notre-Dame at Berthier-en-Haut to learn French. On another trip he is believed to have baptized one of his young sisters in the Catholic faith. In 1827, after directing a week's retreat at Saint-Michel-d'Yamaska (at Yamaska), he baptized Delia before the assembled parish. Just as much as the Protestants longed to snatch the Catholics from their idolatry, Holmes wanted to bring members of the reformed church back into the "true" religion.

The harshness of his missionary existence, made more miserable by his illness, prompted him to seek a new ministry, as did his love of study and attraction to teaching. Consequently, when Bishop Benedict Joseph Fenwick of Boston asked Bishop Bernard-Claude Panet* to send Holmes to him, the bishop of Quebec promised Holmes that he would secure a post for him in the Petit Séminaire de Québec if he stayed in the diocese. Holmes immediately applied for admission, which was granted on 3 March 1827. He arrived in August, was made responsible for the Philosophy class, and became a member of the community the following year. Since teaching proved demanding and his health was frail, in 1830 he was given instead the post of director of students and prefect of studies, in which he showed all his capabilities. He remained prefect until 1849, except during 1836 and 1837 when he was travelling in Europe. This appointment began an extremely fruitful phase of his career.

During his first three years at the seminary Holmes reflected on the gaps in the curriculum and the weakness of the programs. The syllabus included

Latin, French, a smattering of English, and science and mathematics only in the Philosophy class. He thought the history and geography offered were thin. Holmes introduced Greek in 1830, and then put mathematics into the course of study for all years, including the sixth (Rhetoric), a step amounting to a revolution. From 1834 the seminary had a philosophy teacher and two science teachers, one for physics and chemistry, the other for mathematics. English, history, and geography were taught from textbooks and still partly in English.

Using textbooks was an innovation. Until then their use had been confined to Latin grammar. Languages were learned through the study of Latin and French authors. According to a custom dating back to the Middle Ages, teachers drafted course notes for the other subjects, and pupils copied the notes. But enrolment was increasing, and copying written courses took the students a great deal of time. Holmes and his colleague Jérôme DEMERS prepared history, geography, and philosophy texts, and Holmes bought manuals for other subjects. In 1838 he also introduced the teaching of Canadian history, and he encouraged students to take up music, public speaking, and drama. A brass band was formed in 1833. The "learned prefect of studies," as Étienne Parent* called Holmes in *Le Canadien*, revised the end-of-year examinations to make them comparable to the literary exercises the colleges of France had been familiar with prior to 1760. Instead of having a day of examinations ending with an oration and a declamation, Holmes revived the great demonstrations held in the Jesuit and Oratorian colleges of the 17th and 18th centuries. For three days, in the presence of prominent local citizens, there was a feverish display of activity: each class was questioned by the audience on the subject-matter of the program and presented speeches, orations, fables, or dialogues. Gradually theatrical presentations were revived; extracts from plays of Racine and Molière were given in 1831, and from 1836 a complete sacred tragedy was presented, evidently by the students of Rhetoric. The pupils in the Philosophy program did chemistry and physics experiments; those in the first three classes (Latin elements, Syntax, and Method) dramatized geography by playing the roles of young travellers back from Asia and South America, wearing exotic costumes and bearing journals. This whole program was inspired, rehearsed, and often written by Holmes. It was also during his administration that the famous discussion circles, such as the Société Laval, were founded. The climate of emulation and animation, as well as the zest for study, never faltered during his 20 years as prefect.

Before Holmes, according to Pierre-Joseph-Olivier Chauveau*, the seminary had been a model of correctness, regularity, erudition, piety, and discipline, but not a very amusing place. Consequently the arrival in Bishop François de Laval*'s house of a young priest of most unusual background – an American and converted Protestant who had studied in Montreal and taught at Nicolet – might have been ill received, especially since he was considered to be an original, was enthusiastic, full of ideas, and not reluctant to criticize the curriculum's weaknesses. Evidently Jérôme Demers, the seminary's superior, and the other members of the council soon came to appreciate the new recruit, for they made him a member of the community as soon as he had completed his first year. Demers, Louis-Jacques Casault*, and Holmes quickly became inseparable colleagues, and they were joined after 1840 by Elzéar-Alexandre Taschereau*. Demers tempered the zeal of his two young associates, helped them overcome the resistance they occasionally encountered, and always gave them active and sympathetic support. He sometimes even had to act as a moderator between Casault and Holmes, since the first disliked publicity and the second believed in being visible.

His immense effort in the cause of classical education led many to assert that Holmes had taught all subjects. As a regent at Nicolet and at Quebec, before becoming prefect of studies, he taught the Philosophy program. From 1833 to 1835, at the invitation of the Ursulines of Quebec, he gave courses in the convent parlour to the most advanced nuns and students to help them prepare for their task as teachers. He also made himself available to students to furnish explanations on any subject or would go botanizing with a handful of pupils; in whatever he did he displayed the same pedagogical abilities.

Such a career in classical education alone would have sufficed to establish a solid reputation for Holmes. But circumstances were to demonstrate that he was as enthusiastic and knowledgeable about public education. An inquiry into education, instituted in 1835 by the standing committee of education and schools, revealed that one of the most important defects stemmed from the lack of training for teachers, and that it was necessary to set up normal schools. Jérôme Demers made this suggestion to the committee on 5 December. A bill was introduced on 25 Jan. 1836 and enacted on 21 March. It provided for two normal schools for men, in Montreal and at Quebec, each under a management committee of ten. Holmes was made a member of the Quebec committee. The two bodies asked him to obtain documentation on elementary instruction and teaching methods and on teachers' colleges in other countries, and also to hire directors for the normal schools. Holmes left Quebec for the United States and Europe on 12 May 1836, bearing a letter of introduction from the governor-in-chief, Lord Gosford [Acheson*], to the colonial secretary, Lord Glenelg.

He visited colleges in Albany, N.Y., and New York City, in Boston, Cambridge, and Andover, Mass., and in Hartford and New Haven, Conn., collecting

Holmes

material on their administrative, pedagogical, and financial aspects and on their systems of teaching. He then drafted reports and forwarded documents and books to the management committees. All this was accomplished between 16 May and 8 June, the day he left New York.

Having seen the best that the United States had to offer, Holmes went to Europe to gather information on the British, German, and French systems. He was accompanied by three seminarists who had almost come to the end of their studies: Elzéar-Alexandre Taschereau, who later became archbishop of Quebec, Édouard Parent, the brother of Étienne, and Joseph-Octave Fortier. In addition to his responsibilities for the management committees, Holmes was instructed by the seminary and by the Ursulines of Quebec to attend to the question of the property in France they had lost during the revolution, and in this connection to approach both the authorities in London and Jean-Baptiste Thavenet*, the agent in Europe for the Canadian communities. He was also to buy an organ for Nicolet, and instruments for physics and chemistry or books needed by eight colleges, religious communities, the House of Assembly, the normal schools, the Quebec Education Society, and Thomas Cary*'s bookshop. Arrangements were made for him to meet members of learned societies in various countries on behalf of the Literary and Historical Society of Quebec.

Holmes went to England, Scotland, Ireland, France, the Netherlands, Switzerland, and Italy to accomplish his objectives; he met ministers, rectors, and teachers of schools and universities, and members of the London and Paris academies; he bought books and instruments, and wrote letters at each stage of his journey describing his endeavours, his interviews, and his observations. He was uniformly successful in his missions, and he found two excellent teachers for the normal schools, Andrew Findlater in Scotland and François-Joseph-Victor Regnaud* at Montbrison in France. His three Canadian protégés, who had received the tonsure in Rome, sailed for home in mid August 1837. He himself did not leave Portsmouth until 1 October, after an extraordinarily busy year and a half of travelling. Reading the material he forwarded during those months, one wonders how he managed to see so many people, settle so many problems, make so many purchases, and write so many memoranda, reports, and letters to London, Paris, Rome, Quebec, and Montreal – all this from a man with a disease which caused him cruel suffering. He confessed, moreover, in letters to Jérôme Demers that he felt tired, indeed exhausted. On his return he made his report to the Montreal and Quebec committees. Findlater and Regnaud were already at their teaching posts and were to remain there until the schools were disbanded in 1842. Holmes resumed his position as prefect in August 1838 with the same zeal.

His inquiring mind was eager for knowledge; he studied and read a great deal. In Quebec he was a frequent client of the bookshops of Samuel Neilson* and William Cowan, Thomas Cary, Peter Sinclair, Gilbert Stanley, and Octave Crémazie*, and in Montreal that of Édouard-Raymond FABRE. An active member of the Literary and Historical Society of Quebec, founded in 1824, he chaired its arts committee from 1830. He had a hand in publishing the second volume of documents put out by the society in 1840, documents he himself had collected during his trip to France.

In the winter of 1848–49 Holmes gave a series of talks at Notre-Dame cathedral in Quebec. Published under the title *Conférences de Notre-Dame de Québec*, they are reminiscent of Henri Lacordaire's famous preaching in Paris and they evoke Holmes's own purpose as an apologist. The Catholics and Protestants in Quebec, who had known him for a long time, filled the church well before the appointed hour. He held his audience spellbound as he drew arguments from history, enlisted where necessary the help of science and scientists, and sought answers in nature, the monuments and arts of man, and the languages and customs of peoples. Liveliness of imagination, nobility of gesture, a resonant, harmonious voice, loftiness of thought, beauty of imagery: such gifts tradition associates with this religious orator. Chauveau, a pupil at the seminary before 1840, remembered the Easter and Christmas sermons, and those of the novena to St Francis-Xavier, true masterpieces no longer extant. The American who had become Canadian and mastered the French language was well loved; the converted Protestant whose words were as persuasive as they were subtle had won admiration.

Politically, Holmes was acknowledged as a true Canadian who was very interested in what was taking place in his adopted country. During his ministry in the Eastern Townships he had noticed that this region of Lower Canada needed an increase in population. Thus he encouraged the movement of settlers into the townships. After 1840 he is reported to have entertained the idea of a regrouping of the British territories in North America into a sort of customs union. Although he had well-articulated political notions, it cannot be said that he belonged to the Patriote party. Scattered remarks in his correspondence from Europe show that he too was marked by the counter-revolutionary spirit. A man of culture, equally interested and knowledgeable in politics and science or literature and the arts, Holmes also had the reputation of being well versed in Holy Writ. The erstwhile Protestant had not forgotten the Bible.

Throughout his life and despite all his occupations, John Holmes never neglected his family. Through his initiative, five of his six sisters studied under the Ursulines of Quebec, and the sixth under the nuns of

408

the Congregation of Notre-Dame at Berthier-en-Haut. In 1825 he helped one of his three brothers, George, enter the Séminaire de Nicolet. The latter became a doctor at William Henry (Sorel), but had to flee to the United States in 1839 under suspicion of murder. The drama, retold in 1970 by Anne Hébert in *Kamouraska*, was never referred to by members of the family. But this "great tribulation," as it was called at the time, caused inner sufferings which aggravated Holmes's physical infirmities. He gave up his office as prefect in 1849. To find rest, he went alternately to La Malbaie and Île aux Coudres, but returned to Quebec to instruct candidates for the priesthood on preaching. At Christmas 1851, finding his room at the seminary too cold, he went to L'Ancienne-Lorette to stay with one of his friends. It was there that death claimed him on the morning of 18 June 1852. The seminary recognized the contribution Holmes had made as an educator by inscribing his name as a founder of the Université Laval in the charter granted on 8 Dec. 1852.

CLAUDE GALARNEAU

[John Holmes wrote *Nouvel abrégé de géographie moderne suivi d'un petit abrégé de géographie ancienne à l'usage de la jeunesse* (Québec, 1831) in connection with his pedagogical work, and he also prepared the four subsequent editions (1832, 1833, 1839, and 1846). Taking his inspiration from the best authors, he drew attention to the latest discoveries, indicated political changes, and gave population figures, and, mindful that his readers would be school children, included useful, picturesque, and diverting details. The statistical tables on Lower Canada and the United States he included are unique for the period. The work was republished a number of times after Holmes's death, at first with no editor being named (1854, 1857, 1862, and 1864), and later under the direction of Abbé Louis-Onésime Gauthier (Montréal, 1870, 1877, and 1884). Holmes is also the author of *Conférences de Notre-Dame de Québec, première série* (Québec, 1850), a reworking of talks he gave in the winter of 1848–49; Alfred Duclos* De Celles published a second edition entitled *Conférences de Notre-Dame de Québec par Jean Holmes* (Québec, 1875). C.G.]

AAQ, 12 A, I: f.52v. ANQ-MBF, CE1-52, 3 mai 1817. ANQ-Q, CE1-1, 18 juin 1852. ASQ, MSS, 2, I, 16 août 1828; 12 nov. 1829; 19 mai, 2 déc. 1849; 25 mai, 29 sept., 25 déc. 1850; 18, 20, 21 juin 1852; 12: ff.71, 77–85; 437; MSS-M, 53, 155, 159, 162, 433, 676; Polygraphie, V: 55–55B; XIV: 7A; XXVIII: 2; XXIX; XLII: 15A, 21, 22E; XLIII: 1–1B, 1D–1E, 1I, 3L–3N; XLIV: 2, 2H, 3, 3B–3D, 4, 14A, 20–20B, 20D–20F, 21B–21C, 22F, 22I, 22K–22L; Séminaire, 9, nos.21–21E; 56, no.19; 75, nos.5–5B; 85, no.10B; 117, no.20B; 123, no.286. BVM-G, Coll. Gagnon, Corr., John Holmes à Mgr de Sidyme, 13 juill. 1850. *L'Abeille*, 23 juin 1842. *Le Canadien*, 10, 12 mars 1834; 18, 21 juin 1852. *Le Journal de Québec*, 19 juin 1852. *Mélanges religieux*, 24 juin 1852. Caron, "Inv. de la corr. de Mgr Panet," ANQ *Rapport*, 1933–34: 275–76, 300, 303, 322, 353; "Inv. de la corr. de Mgr Plessis," 1928–29: 170, 175, 182, 184–85, 191, 193, 207. L.-M. Darveau, *Nos hommes de lettres* (Montréal, 1873). L.-P. Audet, *Le système*

scolaire, 4: 126–63. Ginette Bernatchez, "La Société littéraire et historique de Québec (the Literary and Historical Society of Quebec), 1824–1890" (thèse de MA, univ. Laval, Québec, 1979). [Catherine Burke, named Saint-Thomas], *Les Ursulines de Québec, depuis leur établissement jusqu'à nos jours* (4v., Québec, 1863–66), 4. P.-J.-O. Chauveau, *L'abbé Holmes et ses conférences de Notre-Dame, étude littéraire et biographique* (Québec, 1876). Douville, *Hist. du collège-séminaire de Nicolet*. Claude Galarneau, *Les collèges classiques au Canada français (1620–1970)* (Montréal, 1978). Marc Lebel et al., *Aspects de l'enseignement au petit séminaire de Québec (1765–1945)*, 103–22. Maurault, *Le collège de Montréal* (Dansereau; 1967). Maurice O'Bready, *Panoramas et gros plans, le Sherbrooke d'avant 1850* (n.p., n.d.). J.-E. Roy, *Souvenirs d'une classe au séminaire de Québec, 1867–1877* (Lévis, Qué., 1905). Antonio Drolet, "Les éditions de l'*Abrégé de géographie* de l'abbé Holmes," *BRH*, 53 (1947): 160–61. A.[-H.] Gosselin, "L'abbé Holmes et l'instruction publique," RSC *Trans.*, 3rd ser., 1 (1907), sect.I: 127–72. [Joséphine Holmes, named Sainte-Croix], "An affectionate tribute to the memory of Abbé Holmes; a New England convert and Catholic priest," *Guidon* (Manchester, N.H.), 11 (1904): 10–12, 43–47. Sylvio Leblond, "Le drame de Kamouraska d'après les documents de l'époque," *Cahiers des Dix*, 37 (1972): 239–73. Maurice O'Bready, "Un pédagogue dynamique," *Le Devoir* (Montréal), 14 mars 1957: 24. Jacques Rousseau, "Grandeur et décadence des monts Watshish," *Saguenayensia* (Chicoutimi, Qué.), 2 (1960): 115–21. Mason Wade, "The contribution of Abbé John Holmes to education in the province of Québec," *Culture* (Québec), 15 (1954): 3–16.

HOWISON, JOHN, doctor and author; b. 10 May 1797 in Edinburgh, son of William Howison, a writer, and Janet Bogle; d. 8 Feb. 1859 in Brompton (London).

John Howison appears to have received some medical education; his writing indicates interest in "chemical, mineralogical, and zoological inquiry." He came to Lower Canada in 1818 and travelled from Montreal to York (Toronto), visiting Glengarry County, Prescott, and Kingston en route. He set up a medical practice in Shipman's Hotel in St Catharines, where he was on friendly terms with the family of William Hamilton Merritt*, receiving "unbounded hospitality" from them. During his two and a half years in the Canadas he became involved with Robert Gourlay* and attended one of his first meetings. Howison, influenced by friends in the Niagara District, later turned against the radical politics of his fiery fellow Scot. He knew John Norton*, whom he described as "the white person who appears to have most influence with the Indians," and was an interested observer of Indian affairs. Howison also travelled throughout the Niagara District and along the north shore of Lake Erie from Niagara (Niagara-on-the-Lake) to the Talbot settlement and beyond to Amherstburg, where Charles Stuart*, retired officer of the East India Company, was a justice of the peace. During this westward swing he received a commission

Howison

as an assistant surgeon with the East India Company's military service, and in mid June 1820 he "bade adieu" to Upper Canada.

On his return to Scotland, via the United States, the West Indies, and Cuba, Howison prepared to publish his *Sketches of Upper Canada, domestic, local, and characteristic: to which are added, practical details for the information of emigrants of every class* (Edinburgh, 1821), and between May 1821 and July 1822 a series of essays appeared in *Blackwood's Edinburgh Magazine*. The *Sketches*, favourably reviewed by John Galt* and many others, went rapidly into three editions, was translated into German, and became a standard source on Canadian conditions. It stood out above such contemporary works as those by Charles Stuart and John Strachan*.

Howison's book remains one of the most interesting of some twenty accounts of Upper Canada published in the 1820s. Although the reports by Gourlay, Edward Allen Talbot*, and John Mactaggart* are also of great value, Howison's Blackwood connections probably account for the great critical response to his work. The Edinburgh magazine described it as "by far the best book which has ever been written by any British traveller on the subject of North America," and praised his quiet and temperate view of "manners, occupations, and hardships, comforts, . . . set forth too in plain agreeable language . . . and totally free . . . from all prejudices, except a few, from which we hope English gentlemen will never be quite emancipated." Another critic, in the *Monthly Review*, was prompted to write, "In describing the Falls of Niagara, he has out-Heroded Herod, and beaten *Bombastes Furioso* out of the field." Howison encouraged later travellers to try unusual approaches to the great spectacle: "Darkness began to encircle me; on one side, the black cliff stretched itself into a gigantic arch far above my head, and on the other, the dense and hissing torrent formed an impenetrable sheet of foam, with which I was drenched in a moment." His major concern, however, was less with the picturesque than with the ordinary scenes of Upper Canada, which though "rather destitute of variety and interest" did provide opportunities for immigrants. The *Sketches* offer vignettes of life in Quebec City, Montreal, Prescott, Brockville, Glengarry, York, and the Talbot settlement.

At the end of 1821 Howison was posted to Bombay, where he worked for 20 years. He spent his army leaves travelling across India and Africa and wrote a number of books about their travel conditions, aboriginal peoples, medical care, and politics. From these experiences he wrote three other books: *Foreign scenes and travelling recreations* (1825), *Tales of the colonies* (1830), and *European colonies* (1834).

John Howison retired and drew a pension from the East India Company beginning 1 Oct. 1842. He also had a company annuity from 1851 until his death. In 1858, the year in which he gave *Blackwood's* permission to republish his early stories, *Nimmo's popular tales* also began reprinting his work. He died on 8 Feb. 1859 in Brompton, leaving an estate of under £8,000.

Howison's comments on the life he observed in the Canadas between 1818 and 1820 are lively and outspoken. Canadians, he said, "are hospitable, good-humoured . . . but have little vivacity of disposition, and their manners are somewhat abrupt, boisterous, and unconciliating." The young doctor, not notably conciliating in his own manners, remarked upon the indolence and ignorance of frontier farmers and the pretensions to style of young Canadian ladies; and he tucked into his account such anecdotes as the story of a backwoods doctor asked by a farmer, whose wife was afflicted by acute rheumatism, "Now, sir, can *you* raise that there woman?" The doctor left something to be infused into a pint of whisky and taken three times a day. "I guess I had as well take it four times a day," said the patient and the doctor rode off, with a promise of pay, not in money but in "plenty of good buck-wheat." Actually Howison in his *Sketches* never admits that he was a doctor.

In *European colonies*, published 14 years after his visit, and after extensive travels in India, Africa, and the Arctic, Howison still advised emigrants that Upper Canada was the best choice for agriculturalists. He had not changed his opinion of the population, however. The great mass consisted of "persons of the lower classes, who have emigrated from Europe." The conclusion of *European colonies* presents a chilling vision of British North America – "scenes of wildness, solitude, and sterility extend westward without interruption to the Pacific Ocean, and northward to the icy regions of the Pole."

ELIZABETH WATERSTON and J. J. TALMAN

John Howison is the author of *Sketches of Upper Canada, domestic, local, and characteristic: to which are added, practical details for the information of emigrants of every class; and some recollections of the United States of America* (Edinburgh, 1821; 2nd ed., 1822; 3rd ed., 1825); the 1821 edition has been reprinted twice ([East Ardsley, Eng., and New York], 1965, and Toronto, 1970). It was translated into German as *Skizzen von Ober-Canada . . .* (Jena, [German Democratic Republic], 1822). His other travel books include *Foreign scenes and travelling recreations* (2v., 1st and 2nd eds., Edinburgh, 1825; 3rd ed., 1834); *Tales of the colonies* (2v., London, 1830); and *European colonies, in various parts of the world, viewed in their social, moral, and physical condition* (2v., London, 1834).

Howison also wrote the following stories published in *Blackwood's Edinburgh Magazine* (Edinburgh and London): "Vanderdecken's message home; or, the tenacity of natural affection," "Adventure in Havana," "The fatal repast," and "The Florida pirate" in 9 (April–August 1821): 125–31,

305–12, 407–14, and 516–31; "Adventure in the North-West Territory," "The floating beacon," and "Vanderbrummer; or, the Spinosist" in 10 (August–December 1821): 137–44, 270–81, and 501–8; and "The nocturnal separation" in 12 (July–December 1822): 17–25. Two of his stories were subsequently reprinted in *Nimmo's popular tales . . .* (12v., Edinburgh, [1866–67]): "The nocturnal separation" appeared under the title "My trip to St Thomas's" in 2: 184–205 and "An adventure in Havana" in 5: 210–29.

British Library (London), India Office Library and Records, [East India House Arch.], IOR, L/AG/21/15/5–7 (Medical service pensions, 1825–59); L/AG/23/10/1, no.261 (ff.82v–83) (Madras Military Fund subscribers, 1808–62); L/MIL/9/261: f.40 (Cadet reg., 1819–20). GRO (Edinburgh), High Church, Edinburgh, reg. of births and baptisms, 20 March 1793, 1 Nov. 1796, 31 May 1797; reg. of marriages, 19 March 1792. NLS, Dept. of MSS, MSS 4007: ff.56–57; 4008: ff.300, 302, 304; 4036: f.106; 4131: ff.291, 293. Oliver and Boyd (Edinburgh), [George] Boyd to John Howison, 19 Oct. 1821; Howison to Boyd, 24 Oct. 1821. Somerset House (London), Probate Dept., will of John Howison, proved 7 March 1859. *Athenæum* (London), 21 June 1834: 470–71; 9 Aug. 1834: 585–87. *Edinburgh Rev.* (Edinburgh and London), 37 (1822): 249–68. "'An essay on the sentiments of attraction, adaptation, and variety,'" *Blackwood's Edinburgh Magazine*, 9: 393–97. [John Galt], "Howison's Canada," *Blackwood's Edinburgh Magazine*, 10: 537–45. William Howison, "An essay on the arrangement of the categories" and "A key to the mythology of the ancients," *Blackwood's Edinburgh Magazine*, 11 (January–June 1822): 308–14, 315–16. John Mactaggart, *Three years in Canada: an account of the actual state of the country in 1826–7–8 . . .* (2v., London, 1829). *Monthly Rev.* (London), ser.ii, 99 (September–December 1822): 171–85. *Statistical account of U.C.* (Gourlay). James Strachan [John Strachan], *A visit to the province of Upper Canada, in 1819* (Aberdeen, Scot., 1820; repr. Toronto, 1968). Charles Stuart, *The emigrant's guide to Upper Canada . . .* (London, 1820). E. A. Talbot, *Five years' residence in the Canadas . . .* (2v., London, 1824). *Niagara Spectator* (Niagara [Niagara-on-the-Lake, Ont.]), 6 Aug. 1818. *Times* (London), 12 Feb. 1859.

S. A. Allibone, *A critical dictionary of English literature, and British and American authors, living and deceased, from the earliest accounts to the middle of the nineteenth century . . .* (3v., Philadelphia, 1858–71), 1: 905. *Alphabetical list of the medical officers of the Indian army . . . from the year 1764 to the year 1838*, comp. Edward Dodwell and J. S. Miles (London, 1839). *A bibliography of articles in "Blackwood's Magazine," volumes I through XVIII, 1817–1825*, comp. A. L. Strout (Lubbock, Tex., 1959). *The East-India register and directory . . .* (London), 1820–42. *Edinburgh and Leith directory*, 1844, 1850–51. *Roll of the Indian medical service, 1615–1930*, comp. D. G. Crawford (London, 1930), 434. J. P. Merritt, *Biography of the Hon. W. H. Merritt . . .* (St Catharines, Ont., 1875), 45. B. M. Murray, "The authorship of some unidentified or disputed articles in *Blackwood's Magazine*," *Studies in Scottish Literature* (n.p.), 4 (1966–67): 146. A. L. Strout, "The authorship of articles in *Blackwood's Magazine*, numbers xvii–xxiv (August 1818–March 1819)," *Library* (London), 5th ser., 11 (1956): 198–99. J. J. Talman, "Candid pioneer," *Canadian Literature* (Vancouver), no.36 (spring 1968): 98–100; "Travel literature as source material for the history of Upper Canada, 1791–1840," CHA *Report*, 1929: 111–20.

HOWSE, JOSEPH, fur trader, explorer, and linguistic scholar; baptized 2 March 1774 in Cirencester, England, son of Thomas Howse and his wife Ann; d. there 4 Sept. 1852.

After ten years' fur-trading experience in the Saskatchewan district, Joseph Howse took part in the exploration of western North America as the first Hudson's Bay Company man to cross the Rocky Mountains; a pass, a peak, and a river bear his name. Howse also wrote the first grammar of the Cree language, placed next to "the labours of [John] Eliot, [David] Zeisberger[*], [John Gottlieb Ernestus Hackenwelder] Heckewelder, [Henry Rowe] Schoolcraft" by his contemporaries and still recognized as an outstanding document both of the Cree language and of early grammatical practice.

The name Howse has long been common in the Cirencester area. Although his father was a brazier there, Joseph Howse is consistently described, after his return from North America, as a "Gentleman"; the family, which came from nearby Ampney St Mary, belonged to the "yeoman" class of landholders. The handwriting on the contract with the HBC which Joseph Howse signed at the age of 21 is quite mature and differs little from that exhibited in his later correspondence. Aside from his own remark (in 1844) about "some knowledge of Latin, French, and Italian, acquired before I left England," no more is known about his youth than that he was "originally apprenticed to a bookseller and stationer" at Cirencester.

Following the example of Joseph Colen*, who had left Cirencester for Hudson Bay ten years earlier, Howse and Colen's nephew Thomas sailed from Gravesend on 5 June 1795. The HBC ship *King George* carried two other "writers" besides Howse and Thomas Colen and, presiding over this "literary company," there was Chief Factor Joseph Colen, "educated and articulate," who appears to have taken a special interest in Howse. When William Hemmings Cook*, another passenger on the voyage, reported to Colen (then in retirement at Cirencester) in 1811 on Howse's expedition across the Rocky Mountains, he referred to him explicitly as "your pupil."

On 28 Aug. 1795 the *King George* arrived at York Factory (Man.) where Howse spent the next two years. His own account suggests that he began his practical language studies without delay: "As long as it was requisite, I had the assistance of an Interpreter; but the absolute necessity of understanding and being understood by those among whom I was to live, made me diligent in endeavouring to learn their language." In one of his commissions for goods to be sent from

Howse

England there is a hint of an individual Cree tutor to whom Howse may have apprenticed himself; his order for 1799 not only reflects life in a settled condition but includes, in particular, several items (such as "6 Y^{ds} of printed Cotten – lively pattern") seemingly destined for a woman; the request for "2 p^r of red Shoes – for a Child of a year old" supports the inference of a household *à la façon du pays*. While there are no further glimpses of his domestic life in Hudson Bay, it is reasonable to suppose that Howse had ample opportunity to practise his Cree, and by 1798 he is described as a "good linguist." Nor did he, as his book orders show, neglect his other languages, and in 1808 there is a request for "1 pair of neat Spectacles with green glasses – to save the eyes when reading by candlelight – not to magnify at all."

Reading – and writing – dominate Howse's later life in England, but for most of his 20 years in North America intellectual endeavours had to yield priority to his duties as an inland trader.

The first stage of Howse's apprenticeship ended in December 1797 when as a writer and accountant he left York Factory for Gordon House on the Hayes River; he spent the rest of the season there and did not return to York Factory until 4 July 1798. Scheduled "to settle a House in the Bungee country near poplar River" for the 1798–99 season, Howse was, in the summer of 1799, characterized by John Ballenden as "being every way qualified and generally approved . . . fit" to take command of a post on the Prairies. Travelling to Cumberland House (Sask.) with James BIRD, he was sent to Carlton House on the Saskatchewan River, for the 1799–1800 season, where he was also responsible for the trade at Cumberland House. Howse remained at Carlton, now as master, for another winter, 1800–1. While his post during 1801–2 has not been ascertained, Peter Fidler*'s journal entries for Chesterfield House make it seem likely that Howse was stationed on the North Saskatchewan River. His financial records suggest that he stayed in the same region for a second winter, 1802–3, with his salary raised to £50, and when he took charge of Carlton House again in 1803–4, Howse was described as "Trader." In 1804–5 he was master at Chesterfield House on the South Saskatchewan River – that is, no longer among Cree speakers primarily – but he returned to the new Carlton House on the South Saskatchewan in 1805–6 and remained there (aside from the summers) until the spring of 1809. The letters Howse wrote during his first decade in the Saskatchewan district illustrate not only his personal style, epistolary as well as managerial, but also his enterprising attitude towards the affairs of the company.

As the HBC prepared to challenge the position of the North West Company in the Rocky Mountains, Howse joined Bird at Edmonton House (Edmonton) in 1809 and remained there until 1811. The itinerary of the HBC's first foray into the Rocky Mountains is, ironically, documented only in the journals of David THOMPSON of the NWC. Starting from their neighbouring posts of Edmonton House and Fort Augustus, the two explorers both set off on 18 July 1809. The HBC party consisted of Howse and three others, and its goal was obvious: in Thompson's words, Howse "went off for the Mountains to examine the Country &c&c." When Thompson and his party, preparing to winter in the mountains and thus encumbered with supplies and trading goods, reached Rocky Mountain House (Alta) on 26 July, Howse appeared to be several days ahead. The two parties did not meet until 9 August at the head of navigation, at the forks of the North Saskatchewan River, "when Mr Howse & the Indian with him" were already on their way back from the pass. Thompson gave Howse a letter for James Hughes at Fort Augustus, a clear indication that Howse intended no further exploration at this time. At next report, on 23 September, he was back on the Prairies.

A novice at exploration, Howse had crossed the continental divide without delay. That he had also explored a portion of the Columbia River is suggested by a final remark from Thompson's journal: on 19 August his advance party reported seeing "the Tracks of 2 Horsemen" where it had camped just below the present Lake Windermere (B.C.). Official recognition is expressed in the York Factory account-book for 1810 against the entry for Howse's current wages of £65: "hopes your Honors will allow him 80£ the readiness wth which this Gent^n undertook, the expedition across the Rocky Mountain, merits some attention."

When Howse returned to the Rocky Mountains in 1810–11, he stayed a full year. On 19 June 1810 Alexander Henry* the younger, NWC partner at New White Earth House (Alta), recorded the departure from the adjacent HBC post of "two canoes for the Columbia, with nine men. . . . They embarked four rolls of tobacco, two kegs of high wine, powder, several bags of balls, a bag of shot, pemmican, etc." Howse himself began his journey "by land"; as Henry noted on 20 June, Howse had left "with four Cree guides and hunters . . . the whole H.B.Co. Columbia expedition consists of 17 persons." This time, evidently, there was to be trade as well as exploration. The NWC took the challenge seriously; on 9 July James McMILLAN "set off for the Columbia to watch the motions of the H.B. in that quarter."

Opposition to both companies was mounted by the Peigans; at war with the Flatheads, they strove to block all trade across the mountains. While Thompson, travelling in October, chose to seek a more northerly route through Athabasca Pass (B.C.), Howse had reached the Cootana (Columbia) River by

20 August. There he remained some time "to gain further intelligence" in view of the threat the Peigan Indians posed to "him, or any white man" in the summer of 1810. According to one of his Cree guides, Howse was still on the Columbia on 1 September and on 22 October another guide, who had "just come across the mountains," specified his location to Henry as the "old" Kootenay House, at the head of the Columbia. The NWC's watch was still being kept, and McMillan did not leave until 12 December, at which time Howse was reported to be wintering on or near Flathead Lake (Mont.). When he returned to Columbia Lake (B.C.), Howse once more crossed paths with Thompson, who was told of Howse's presence on 14 May.

The only record of the journey by Howse's own hand is contained in a letter written to HBC governor Sir George SIMPSON in 1843. In sketching his itinerary Howse writes that he "crossed the Rocky Mount^s in the Summer and Autumn of 1810 by ye North Branch of the Saskatchewan – ascended the Kootoonay [Columbia] River – carried into the Flat-Bow (?) [Kootenay] River – descended by the most Southly Bight of it – crossed (Portage Poil de Custer) to Flathead River . . . where we built." He goes on to describe a further crossing of the continental divide in December 1810: "with a couple of my men I accompanied the Flat-heads to the head branches of ye Missouri – returned to our House – in Feby 1811."

Meanwhile the Peigan blockade continued in full force; according to Bird their chiefs "declared that, if they again met with a white Man going to supply their Enemies, they would not only plunder & kill him, but that they would make dry Meat of his body." Bird, consequently, had by the end of March sent two men "with horses and Pemican" to meet Howse at the Columbia River and in May five men were left at Acton House (Alta) "to conciliate the minds of the Indians, and to dispose them . . . to behave friendly towards Mr. Howse, and party."

In no small part thanks to Bird's prudent support, Howse reached Edmonton House by mid July 1811, the first HBC man to have followed the NWC into the land across the Rockies. The rewards were considerable: while the trading goods, stores, and wages for Howse's expedition had come to £576, the furs brought back were valued at £1,500. In spite of Bird's plans, however, and the HBC London committee's hopes to continue this trade, the declared hostility of the Peigans proved effective: no further expeditions across the Rocky Mountains were undertaken by the HBC until after its merger with the NWC in 1821. But Howse, "adventurous, tough and intelligent," had shown, as Edwin Ernest Rich has put it, that the HBC had men "who could rival the Nor'Westers in their ability to travel, to trade, and to manage Indians."

When William Hemmings Cook, the HBC officer

in charge at York Factory, wrote to Joseph Colen at Cirencester in the autumn of 1811, he claimed that Howse had "explored a Country that European feet had never trod." Unfortunately, as Colen noted with regret, Howse "was not provided with Astronomical Instruments" and thus, although he had "explored ye Country many hundred Miles," had not "laid down his track."

In 1811–12 Howse wintered at Paint Creek House (Alta) on the North Saskatchewan, and in September 1812, after a survey of the Nelson River from York Factory to Split Lake (Man.), he sailed for England on the *King George*. Aside from family matters, he met with the London committee whose plans for another expedition across the Rockies were well advanced. But whatever Howse's intentions may have been, he did not in fact undertake another journey into the Columbia. On his return voyage the *Prince of Wales*, leaving London on 1 June 1813, was late arriving at York Factory because of ship's fever which had broken out among the passengers under Archibald McDONALD bound for the Red River colony (Man.), forcing a month's delay at Churchill.

On 29 Sept. 1813 Howse left York Factory on a journey that turned into a *tour de force*: from Knee Lake (Man.) onwards, an early freeze-up forced his party to proceed on snowshoes to Vermilion River (Alta), "a distance *little* if any short of 1000 miles"; from there he went on "to Edmonton and back drawn by dogs – then . . . on horseback" to the Red River settlement and back, by August 1814, to York Factory.

While at Red River in the early summer of 1814, Howse found himself entangled in the affairs of the colony. Nor was this the first time: in September 1813 he had been among the HBC officers at York Factory who had opened and read letters from Lord Selkirk [Douglas*] to the colony's governor, Miles Macdonell*. Now, in June 1814, Howse was one of the men sent by Macdonell to seize supplies of pemmican held by the NWC at Fort La Souris on the Assiniboine River. On his way back to Red River, Howse was captured by the Nor'Westers and taken to Fort Gibraltar (Winnipeg); although he was not, in the event, sent to Montreal to be tried for "burglary," as had been threatened, Macdonell's demands for his release were ignored. Conciliation was achieved only upon the arrival of John McDonald* of Garth, who had been Howse's NWC "Neighbour" at Chesterfield House in 1804–5.

Howse's troubles, however, were not over. Hardly returned to York Factory, on 9 Aug. 1814 he is "just on the eve of another expedition": he was sent to Île-à-la-Crosse (Sask.) to re-establish the HBC presence at the threshold of the Athabasca country. His NWC opponent there was Samuel Black*, infamous for his ruthlessness, and a quarrel on 14 Feb.

Hoyle

1815 left several men dead. In the spring Howse left Île-à-la-Crosse; whether his retreat was "shameful," as Colin Robertson* described it two years later, or prudent, remains an open question. The events of 1814–15 may well have decided Howse to quit Hudson Bay. His appointment in May 1815, along with Thomas Thomas*, Bird, and others, as councillor to the governor-in-chief of Rupert's Land, Robert Semple*, may have been gratifying, but on 19 Sept. 1815 he left York Factory for the last time.

Howse's life in North America could hardly have been idle. Yet even in 1813–14, when he was forced to travel overland to the Saskatchewan only to become embroiled in the troubles of the Red River colony, he had been able to spare some time for scholarship. Now, at Cirencester, Howse led the life of a gentleman and scholar. But the calm of his country life was enlivened by frequent visits to London and by correspondence with "some of the most eminent men of the Continent from Rome to Berlin, as well as of the greater part of our Universities and even Ministers of our Government." None of these letters have come to light, and of those which Howse exchanged with his former associates at Red River, notably James Bird, only fragments survive.

Howse's advice was sought by the Royal Geographical Society, of which he had become a fellow by 1837, and the Church Missionary Society, which together financed the publication of his Cree grammar. Although the manuscript was almost complete in 1832, the addition of textual illustrations in Ojibwa and continuous revisions and printing difficulties held up publication until 1844. When *A grammar of the Cree language* finally appeared, it was not only praised but used and cited by linguists everywhere. By 1865 a reprint had become necessary. Now in his mid 70s, Howse travelled to London to read papers before the newly established Philological Society in May 1849 and again in February 1850. The papers contain material, notably in Kutenai and in several Salish languages, which he must have collected during his expedition of 1810–11.

Howse's will and death certificate suggest that he died a bachelor. But besides the child whose existence is implied in his York Factory commission of 1799, there is Jenny (probably an adolescent), baptized at Red River in 1824 as the "daughter of Joseph Howes supposed resident [in] England and an Indian woman," and Henry Howes (Howse), who married at Red River in 1830 and in 1831 gave his age as 23; his descendants were later to be found in Métis settlements from the Red River to the North Saskatchewan.

Joseph Howse lived in two worlds: in a frontier territory whose natural rigours were exacerbated by mercantile exploitation and competition, and in the placid country world of a 19th-century British gentleman-scholar. He left his mark in both. As a fur trader, he was justly appreciated for his effectiveness and judgement and as the first HBC man to match the exploratory vigour of the Nor'Westers. The fruit of his scholarly labours, the first *Grammar of the Cree language*, remains his lasting monument.

H. CHRISTOPH WOLFART

Joseph Howse is the author of *A grammar of the Cree language, with which is combined an analysis of the Chippeway dialect* (London, 1844; repr. 1865) and of two articles published in the *Proc.* (London) of the Philological Soc.: "Vocabularies of certain North American Indian languages" and "Vocabularies of certain North American languages," in 4 (1848–50): 102–22 and 191–206 respectively. Apart from the correspondence held in several public archives, the three works appear to be the only writings of Howse still extant. His maps, many of which were sent to British geographer Aaron Arrowsmith, have never been found. Some of his letters are published in *HBRS*, 26 (Johnson), and others will be included in a forthcoming biography by H. Christoph Wolfart, "Joseph Howse: a linguist's life."

AO, MS 25, 10, no.23; MU 2982. British and Foreign Bible Soc. Arch. (London), Foreign corr. inwards, 1832, no.3. British Library (London), Add. MSS 32440: f.42. Church Missionary Soc. Arch. (London), G, AC1/8; C.1/XIII. Gloucestershire Record Office (Gloucester, Eng.), Reg. of baptisms for the parish of Cirencester, 2 March 1774; Reg. of burials for the parish of Cirencester, 9 Sept. 1852 (transcript). PAC, MG 19, E1, ser.1–3, 42 (copies). PAM, HBCA, A.1/51; A.5/6; A.6/18; A.10/1; A.16/34; A.32/17; A.36/7; A.64/52; B.34/a/3; B.49/a/30; B.60/a/5–6, 8–9; 13; B.60/d/2b; B.89/d/2; B.239/a/99–101, 114, 118; B.239/b/71; B.239/d/128–29, 132, 147; C.1/398, 424, 779, 783; D.5/8; E.5/5; G.3/88; MG 4, D13; MG 7, B7. Royal Geographical Soc. Arch. (London), Council minute-book, 1830–41; Howse corr. Royal Soc. Arch. (London), Letters, 1800–30. *HBRS*, 2 (Rich and Fleming). *New light on early hist. of greater northwest* (Coues). David Thompson, *David Thompson's journals relating to Montana and adjacent regions, 1808–12*, ed. C. M. White (Missoula, Mont., 1950); *David Thompson's narrative*, ed. R. [G.] Glover (new ed., Toronto, 1962). J. P. Pritchett, *The Red River valley, 1811–1849: a regional study* (New Haven, Conn., 1942). A. B. Braunberger and Thain White, "Howse's house, an examination of the historical and archeological evidence," *Wash. Archeologist* (Seattle), 8 (April–July 1964): 2–89.

HOYLE, ROBERT, businessman, militia officer, justice of the peace, office holder, and politician; b. 16 Sept. 1781 in Lancashire, England; d. 15 Feb. 1857 in Lacolle, Lower Canada.

In 1806 Robert Hoyle emigrated from Great Britain to the United States and settled near Keeseville, N.Y. There he developed an estate, later claimed to be worth £30,000, which produced lumber for the market at Quebec. His prosperity was temporarily checked in 1812 when he declared his interests to be with Great

Britain and, abandoning his estate, fled northwards to Lower Canada. During the War of 1812 he and William Bowron were said to have obtained the contract to supply beef to the British garrison at Île aux Noix in the Rivière Richelieu. They made large profits by buying American cattle cheap, smuggling them across the border, and selling them at high prices to the British authorities.

Hoyle settled in the area near Lacolle and Odelltown in the Richelieu valley just north of the American border. He engaged in agriculture, the lumber trade, and other "business persuits," probably with his brother Henry, who became usufructuary seigneur of Lacolle. They apparently invested in land and developed sites for carding- and fulling-mills in Huntingdon County. Robert suffered a few set-backs in the 1820s. On 26 Aug. 1823 fire broke out in his store opposite Île aux Noix and, despite the efforts of the entire garrison which turned out to combat the blaze, the property was completely destroyed. It is not known if he rebuilt the store, but by 1825 he was operating a ferry service across the Richelieu at Noyan. Three years later he acquired Île aux Têtes (Île Ash), intending to cut a channel across the island, which blocked the ferry's most direct route. In 1825 his wife Pamelia Wright died, leaving him with three small children.

Because of his economic and social position, Hoyle rapidly became part of the community's élite. In 1820 he was appointed second major in the 1st Battalion of Townships militia and thus began a long career in the local militia. In 1821 he was named justice of the peace and in the following year commissioner for the summary trial of small causes. Ten years later he married Elizabeth B. Nye, whose brothers were important merchants in the Lacolle area. Hoyle had been elected to the House of Assembly in 1830 as one of the representatives for the new riding of L'Acadie. Though he was in a position to view the political strife in the assembly, his letters reveal a preoccupation with local interests and his business affairs, rather than with provincial politics. A tory, he voted in 1834 against Louis-Joseph Papineau*'s 92 Resolutions, thus incurring the displeasure of some of his constituents. He did support improvements which would benefit his riding, but was more concerned with obtaining a government appointment. In April 1834 he was named collector of customs for Stanstead in the Eastern Townships and therefore did not contest the general elections held later that year. In 1835 he was made joint county registrar for L'Acadie.

Hoyle's new positions did not fulfil his need for financial security and social standing. He moved to Stanstead, but his wife and children stayed behind in Lacolle, and he missed them, his friends, and his business activities very much. He had been promised 50 per cent of the custom duties he collected, up to a maximum of £100. Unfortunately, the assembly cut or abolished many duties and his salary never reached £100. He nevertheless continued in his support of the government, playing an active role in the Townships militia, especially during the unrest of 1837–38 when he raised two cavalry troops and was made a lieutenant-colonel.

Hoyle did not receive any additional posts after the union of the Canadas in 1841. The next year he sent a memorial to the government asking for a more "lucrative position" than his present one. Nothing came of the petition and he retired from public employment in 1844, returning to live in the Lacolle area. Almost nothing is known of his activities after this date, except that he continued in the militia. He was buried in Glenwood Cemetery, Champlain, N.Y.

LARRY S. MCNALLY

Brome County Hist. Soc. Arch. (Knowlton, Que.), Seignory of Beaujeux, bond to Michel Morin, 27 Oct. 1825. PAC, MG 8, F99, 14; MG 24, B141; MG 30, D1, 16: 117; RG 4, B58; RG 68, General index, 1651–1841: 181, 256, 258, 354. *Quebec Gazette*, 26 Oct. 1820, 8 Sept. 1823. Jules Romme, *Odelltown, 1823–1973* (Saint-Bernard-de-Lacolle, Qué., 1973). Robert Sellar, *The history of the county of Huntingdon and of the seigniories of Chateaugay and Beauharnois from their first settlement to the year 1838* (Huntingdon, Que., 1888). W. D. Lighthall, "The manor house of Lacolle," *Canadian Antiquarian and Numismatic Journal* (Montreal), 3rd ser., 12 (1915): 18–26.

HUNTINGTON, HERBERT, teacher, militia officer, businessman, surveyor, office holder, and politician; b. 27 July 1799 in Yarmouth, N.S., son of Miner Huntington and Martha Walker; m. there 20 July 1830 Rebecca Russell, *née* Pinkney, and they had five children; d. there 13 Sept. 1851.

A son of a Connecticut loyalist, Herbert Huntington grew up in the shipbuilding and seafaring town of Yarmouth. Situated at the western end of the Nova Scotian peninsula, relatively close to New England, Yarmouth became, early in its history, a citadel of pioneer democracy, individualism, and religious dissent. Next to nothing is known of Herbert's schooling, but he may have received some training from his father, who, as a land surveyor and protonotary, must have had some education. During the War of 1812, Joseph Howe* later recounted, Herbert mustered with the Yarmouth militia to repel the landing of an American vessel. As a young man, he taught school in Yarmouth for a time, served as a militia captain, and in 1822 became the first librarian of the newly formed Yarmouth Book Society. He was a farmer and, not surprisingly for Yarmouth, he held shares in one or more vessels and owned at least one ship, a wrecked brig, which he bought in 1833. As well, he served as a commissioner of sewers for

Huntington

Yarmouth Township and was a founder of the Yarmouth County Agricultural Society, of which he became secretary. In 1839 he succeeded to his father's positions of surveyor and protonotary.

Huntington was repelled by the inefficiency and rank partisanship of the justices of the peace on the courts of sessions, which, in his opinion, formed a "centre of political intrigue [where] Liberals could get neither justice nor courtesy." His antipathy to this abuse of political and judicial authority at the county level led him to attempt to strike at the root of the evil, the provincial government, which controlled the appointment of the justices. Indeed, Huntington later claimed that the authorities in Halifax, often heedless of the people's wishes, had placed their sycophants in "all offices worth holding in Town or Country . . . from the first settlement of the province."

His first essay into provincial politics was in 1830, when the voters of Shelburne County elected him and John Forman to the House of Assembly. Six years later, when Yarmouth County was carved out of Shelburne, Huntington became its assemblyman and would hold the seat until 1851, being opposed only once, during the crucial general election of 1847. From the beginning, the voters' confidence in him was amply justified. In 1834, aided by the efforts of Alexander Stewart*, he succeeded in having Yarmouth made a free port. He was a leader in the fight to abolish the legislation upholding two unpopular measures, quitrents and the General Mining Association's monopoly of coal mining [see Richard Smith*]. The rents were repugnant to a people who wanted free grants of land. Like the majority in the assembly in 1834, Huntington acceded, rather readily, to the demands of the colonial secretary that the rents be commuted for an annual payment of £2,000. Only John Young* and eight other assemblymen, backed by Joseph Howe in the *Novascotian*, protested Nova Scotia's acceptance of these terms. As for the mining monopoly, it hindered the development of new mines at a time when cheap coal was needed to augment increasingly scarce and dear supplies of firewood. Huntington also opposed protective duties on farm produce, partly from personal conviction and partly because he felt them to be an unfair burden on a fishing population. Only half in jest did he champion his home county against the pretensions of other assemblymen. "The inhabitants of the County of Yarmouth, poor as it is," he claimed in 1841, "could buy Colchester County all up, together with McLellan's shipbuilding establishment at Londonderry" [see Gloud Wilson McLELAN]. Even his vote against government aid to sectarian colleges, including the Baptist college, Acadia, did not alienate his constituents, most of whom were Baptists.

Huntington's combination of intellectual power, honesty, and political ability won him a commanding position in the assembly. No great orator, he was a blunt-spoken man with uncommon powers of questioning and summation. He played little part, however, in communicating the reformers' ideas to Nova Scotians outside of Yarmouth, in contrast to Joseph Howe, who entered the assembly in 1836 and became the leading spokesman for the reform cause. Caring little for power for its own sake – Huntington later said that a seat on the Council was "no better than that of a woodcutter" – he nevertheless accepted a place on the newly constituted Executive Council in early 1838, the only reformer to be appointed. Late in March it was discovered that the commission issued to the new governor-in-chief, Lord Durham [Lambton*], differed, in terms of the composition of the Executive and Legislative councils, from the instructions sent to the lieutenant governor of Nova Scotia, Sir Colin Campbell*. It was therefore necessary to reconstitute the councils with reduced numbers, and Huntington was not included in the new Executive Council. Though offered a seat later in the year, he resisted all Campbell's overtures, claiming that his acceptance would do nothing to further the reform cause.

Huntington was convinced that only a strong party, disdainful of coalitions, could wrest power from the ruling clique. His ideas were reinforced by those of Lord Durham, whom he called "the best friend these colonies ever had." To forestall unrest in the British North American colonies, Durham had made numerous recommendations to Westminster, notably the adoption of the principle of responsible party government, a goal Huntington had sought with unflinching determination in Nova Scotia. In an attempt to convince the Colonial Office that the province was ready for a large degree of self-government, Huntington and William Young* took the reform assembly's case to London early in 1839. There they made useful contacts with the likes of Charles Buller* and Colonial Under-Secretary Henry Labouchere, but they made little headway in securing constitutional change before their return that fall, in part because of the presence of the Legislative Council's delegates, Lewis Morris Wilkins* and Alexander Stewart. Still, the reformers came to believe that Lord John Russell, the colonial secretary, had opened the door to party government; his dispatch of 6 Oct. 1839 directed "colonial officers" to be appointed or dismissed on a political basis.

In October 1840, some months after the arrival in Halifax of Durham's successor, Lord Sydenham [Thomson*], Joseph Howe and two other reformers, James Boyle UNIACKE and James McNab, succumbed to the governor's blandishments and entered the Executive Council, in coalition with James William Johnston*. But Huntington, undazzled by the "king's wine," spurned the "inglorious" coalition in spite of

416

repeated invitations to join from Howe and Lieutenant Governor Lord Falkland [Cary*]. Again and again Huntington attacked the excessive powers, emoluments, and perquisites enjoyed by the lieutenant governor and the bureaucracy. In 1841 he carried a vote in the assembly against the government over its refusal to surrender the casual revenues to the province, a step which Huntington had constantly demanded, but he failed to get a vote of non-confidence then or in 1844. His efforts produced a cooling in his relations with Howe, for whom he had once acted as second in a duel with John Croke Halliburton, a son of Chief Justice Brenton HALLI-BURTON. In assembly debate in 1841 Huntington, along with William Young, Thomas Forrester*, and Henry Goudge, vigorously assailed Howe, who in turn became annoyed when he failed to impress upon Huntington the need for compromise. As a result of Huntington's partisan intransigence, Howe's *Novascotian* labelled him "disloyal," "traitor," and "democrat."

Huntington kept the reform party on the rails in Nova Scotia during the heated debates of the 1840s, in which few dared to cross swords with the champion of Yarmouth. Even the rabid tory journalists usually let him alone. In December 1843 Howe, McNab, and Uniacke resigned from the Executive Council, outraged by the controversial appointment of tory Mather Byles Almon* to the Legislative Council, and returned to the reform fold. The man from Yarmouth had been right all along: compromise was made impossible by the tories themselves. Reunited, the reformers provided formidable opposition. An editorial diatribe in the *Halifax Morning Post & Parliamentary Reporter* in April 1847 compared the party to a smithy: Howe was the "Master Blacksmith," always forging something, usually "patriotism" or "office"; Uniacke was a "big sledgehammer with no head"; but Huntington was a "strong pair of tongs, fit to grapple large work." And by 1847 the Colonial Office's opinion of party government had changed. During the general election of that year, which produced a reform victory and led to the first administration based on party in British North America [*see* Sir John HARVEY], the tories mounted a mighty offensive against Huntington in Yarmouth, but to no avail.

In January 1848 he had the supreme satisfaction of seconding William Young's motion of non-confidence, which toppled the administration of James William Johnston and brought in a Liberal government. Huntington entered the Executive Council without portfolio on 30 January, but only reluctantly did he accept the financial secretaryship in mid-June. His appointment was short-lived. Another falling out with Howe may have been a factor. According to the *British Colonist*, Huntington's belief in 1849 that

Howe had treated him badly over the issue of grants to sectarian colleges, which he and William Annand* had opposed unrelentingly and unequivocally, prompted Huntington to strike Howe in the face, evidently in the assembly, and to call him "the lowest and most opprobrious of the epithets among the inhabitants of Billingsgate." As well, study of Adam Smith's views on economics had made Huntington a convinced free trader; he opposed any public aid to the province's economy and he was dismayed by the government's expensive, Halifax-oriented railway policies. His dislike of a protective system, including intercolonial duties, was one reason for his early endorsement of a union of the British North American colonies. In failing health, he resigned from cabinet and left the assembly in December 1850. He died nine months later. Soon afterwards, the assembly unanimously resolved to erect a monument in Yarmouth in recognition of his strenuous public service. Only Joseph Howe has received a like honour from the province's legislature.

The salient features of Huntington's public career are easily set out, but his private life remains obscure, possibly by design. Plagued by recurrent heart trouble during his mature years, he found a haven from the stresses of public life in the austere, unobtrusive piety and plain living of his Congregational household. During his later years at least he became an advocate of temperance and even abstinence. This, of course, was in line with his high regard for the rational and intellectual side of human nature as opposed to the sensual.

It is clear, from the terms of his will (he left modest bequests to his wife and children) and from contemporary accounts, that Huntington was far from wealthy. But his rewards were of another kind: faithful public service, the respect of his friends, and quiet enjoyment of family life. And the achievement of political reform in his native province was largely brought about by his single-minded tenacity and political subtlety.

A. A. MacKenzie

PANS, MG 100, 166, nos.22, 24; RG 1, 115, doc.49: 114–15; 174: 225; 175: 181; RG 7, 7, May 1833. Joseph Howe, *Joseph Howe: voice of Nova Scotia*, ed. and intro. J. M. Beck (Toronto, 1964); *The speeches and public letters of Joseph Howe . . .* , ed. J. A. Chisholm (2v., Halifax, 1909), 1: 314. *British Colonist* (Halifax), 20, 22, 24 March 1849. *Halifax Morning Post & Parliamentary Reporter*, 8 April 1847. *Novascotian*, 11 March 1841; 17 Feb., 8 April 1842; 22 Sept. 1851. *Yarmouth Herald* (Yarmouth, N.S.), 3, 17 April 1841; 7 Jan. 1847; 20, 27 Sept., 18 Oct. 1851. *The Huntington family in America; a genealogical memoir of the known descendants of Simon Huntington from 1633 to 1915 . . .* (Hartford, Conn., 1915). Grace Lewis, "The Huntington family of Yarmouth" (typescript, 1958; copy at PANS).

Hurd

Nova Scotia vital statistics from newspapers, 1813–1822, comp. T. A. Punch (Halifax, 1978), no.1498; *1829–34*, comp. J. M. Holder and G. L. Hubley (1982), no.739. Beck, *Government of N.S.*; *Joseph Howe*, vol.1. J. G. Bourinot, *Builders of Nova Scotia . . .* (Toronto, 1900), 67. G. S. Brown, *Yarmouth, Nova Scotia: a sequel to Campbell's history* (Boston, 1888), 69, 314, 349, 351. J. R. Campbell, *A history of the county of Yarmouth, in Nova Scotia* (Saint John, N.B., 1876; repr. Belleville, Ont., 1972), 155. W. R. Livingston, *Responsible government in Nova Scotia: a study of the constitutional beginnings of the British Commonwealth* (Iowa City, 1930). M. E. McKay, "The first reform administration in Nova Scotia, 1848–1857" (MA thesis, Dalhousie Univ., Halifax, 1946). D. F. Maclean, "The administration of Sir John Harvey in Nova Scotia, 1846–1852" (MA thesis, Dalhousie Univ., 1947). C. [B.] Martin, "Nova Scotian and Canadian reformers of 1848," RSC *Trans.*, 3rd ser., 23 (1929), sect.II: 1–16. Gene Morison, "Herbert Huntington," N.S. Hist. Soc., *Coll.*, 29 (1951): 43–61.

HURD, SAMUEL PROUDFOOT, office holder, politician, and militia officer; b. 30 Nov. 1793 in Bermuda, son of Thomas Hurd and Elizabeth Proudfoot; m. first 2 Feb. 1815 Frederica Wynyard (d. 1824), and they had two sons and two daughters; m. secondly 18 Nov. 1837 Anne Mary Pratt, and they had one daughter; d. 10 Aug. 1853 in Toronto.

Samuel Proudfoot Hurd's father was an officer in the Royal Navy and hydrographer to the Admiralty from 1808 to 1823. Samuel joined the 1st Foot Guards as ensign in March 1814, served in the 1815 campaign against Napoleon, and was awarded the Waterloo medal. He went on half pay in 1817 as captain of the 60th Foot and retired completely in 1825, when he was appointed surveyor general of New Brunswick. In this capacity Hurd was responsible for allotting all locations of land, ordering the necessary surveys, and preparing plans and descriptions of the allotments. When Lieutenant Governor Sir Howard Douglas* asked for comments on a British parliamentary report on emigration, Hurd prepared an impressive memorandum, accompanied by a plan for laying out hamlets for emigrants, for the New Brunswick Agricultural and Emigrant Society. His memorandum was approved and forwarded to the Colonial Office, but no action was taken on it.

In 1826 Douglas appointed Hurd to the Council; however, the surveyor general's position was weakened the following year when the Colonial Office introduced a new land policy, designed to raise funds. Public land was to be sold by auction, though some grants would still be allowed. Douglas found the system impractical. Hurd disliked the new policy, for under it his fees were reduced while the increasing demands on his office necessitated additional staff whom he had to pay out of his own salary and emoluments. But the commissioner of crown lands, Thomas Baillie*, favoured the policy. Baillie, who

prior to Hurd's appointment had also been surveyor general, reported to the Colonial Office in 1828 that he had been handicapped by Hurd's neglect in issuing warrants for land sales and his delay in making surveys, and he suggested that the offices of crown lands commissioner and surveyor general should again "be performed by the same individual." On his part, Hurd submitted proposals to Douglas for improving the land disposal system, stating that capitalists would not be attracted by the current policy. These plans were not put into effect. Douglas returned to England in March 1829 and later that year the offices of surveyor general and commissioner of lands were reunited under Baillie. Hurd was transferred to Upper Canada to succeed its late surveyor general, Thomas Ridout*.

Hurd's new appointment was to begin on 1 Nov. 1829 but, unable to settle his debts in New Brunswick, he remained there two years more. Even then, because of a combination of circumstances (changes in shipping schedules, the difficulties of winter travel, and the illness of his children en route), he did not reach York (Toronto) until early in May 1832. Although the colonial secretary, Lord Goderich, had instructed Lieutenant Governor Sir John Colborne* to dismiss Hurd if he did not arrive by 1 January, Colborne accepted Hurd's explanations and issued his commission on 16 May 1832. Goderich decided to let the appointment stand.

Hurd's delayed arrival in Upper Canada, his lack of knowledge of the province and its land practices, and the dissatisfaction of some staff members over the appointment of an outsider did not bode well for his success. The acting surveyor general, William Chewett*, a surveyor of many years' experience whom Colborne had recommended to succeed Ridout, retired on Hurd's arrival. Hurd declared later that he was "considered as an Interloper."

Nor were his relations with Colborne as smooth as they had been with Douglas. Mistrustful of Hurd's ability to control speculation in loyalist and militia land grants and disturbed by complaints about the delay and "want of System" in the Surveyor General's Office, Colborne in February 1834 requested that the Executive Council investigate what steps, if any, might be taken to render the department "more efficient." In March the lieutenant governor wrote to the Colonial Office that Hurd's appointment had been "a sad mistake" and that he was "not fit for this very important post." Colborne limited Hurd's authority to locate lots, required him to report weekly on locations assigned, and ordered him not to give work to surveyors without the lieutenant governor's written instructions. Differences were aggravated that spring over a lithographic machine, used to speed up the reproduction of plans and maps. Colborne insisted that Hurd install in the Surveyor General's Office the press bought for that purpose which had been made available for use by lithographer Samuel Oliver Tazewell*. However, the senior draftsman, James Grant Chewett*, balked at operating the press, and the machine fell into disuse. Then in the fall of 1835 the senior clerk, John Radenhurst, was accused by a fellow clerk of conducting a private land agency, although an 1832 order-in-council forbade such activities. At Colborne's urging, Hurd questioned Radenhurst, who answered evasively. Concluding that Radenhurst did conduct an agency but only outside office hours, Hurd merely advised him to obey the order-in-council or risk suspension.

Shortly before he left the province in January 1836, Colborne complained to Colonial Secretary Lord Glenelg that he could not speak of Hurd's qualifications "without mortification and pain." Yet he did not discharge him. Colborne's successor, Sir Francis Bond Head*, lost no time in doing so. Within a week of taking office, Head suggested to Hurd that he retire or risk being dismissed. Hurd then requested a six-month leave of absence on grounds of ill health, with a view to retirement afterwards. But within three weeks Head appointed John Simcoe MACAULAY surveyor general. The lieutenant governor justified his removal of Hurd by saying he was incompetent and that, owing to his "unfortunate habit of drinking," he had latterly been unable to attend the office. Hurd was a man of honour and "very gentlemanlike," but, Head stated, he could not let his sympathetic feelings interfere with his "painful duty." The appointment of Macaulay, however, was unexpectedly opposed, mainly by friends of Radenhurst, who had applied for the vacant post. Macaulay submitted his resignation, which Glenelg accepted, though the colonial secretary supported Head in his refusal to reinstate Hurd or, because of his land agency, to appoint Radenhurst. In October 1836, John MACAULAY of Kingston was named surveyor general. Hurd, no longer able to hope for reinstatement, told Head that "the Injury I have received is incalculable." His request to the House of Assembly for a retirement allowance on the grounds that he was "totally destitute" was not granted. Head made one gesture: he appointed Hurd's 17-year-old son, Thomas Gladwin Hurd, second clerk in the office of the Executive Council.

Samuel Proudfoot Hurd never again held an important position. He did serve in the militia, as a major in the Queen's Rangers during the abortive Patriot raid at Short Hills on the Niagara frontier in June 1838 [see Linus Wilson Miller*] and briefly as deputy assistant quartermaster general in 1838–39. Although he owned some property, Hurd was in debt to various creditors and, two years before his death, he stated that he was "entirely dependent" on his family for support. His misfortunes were caused partly by circumstances – the merging of the two New Brunswick offices and his transfer to Upper Canada. He was, however, inefficient, a procrastinator, and a weak administrator. No doubt Hurd's alcoholism was an important factor in his incompetence. Letters from friends hinted at the "habits that have been the destruction of your prospects," "old charges," and "injurious rumours." The gentlemanly Hurd was apparently marked for failure: his career was disturbed to an extraordinary degree by bad luck, disappointment, and frustration.

RUTH MCKENZIE

Samuel Proudfoot Hurd's name appears on the pamphlet *Information, for the use of persons emigrating to Upper Canada; containing an explanation of the various modes of application for land . . .* (York [Toronto, 1832]), an official publication of the Surveyor General's Office of Upper Canada.

AO, RG 1, A-I-1, especially 66–71; A-I-2, 28–30; A-I-3, 1. PAC, MG 23, HI, 4, vols.5–6; MG 24, A3, 4; A40, 3–4 (mfm.); RG 1, L6B, 22; RG 5, A1, 96–204; RG 7, G1, 65, 67–69, 77–78; G8B, 2–4, 7–11. PRO, CO 42/388–438; CO 47/146–52; CO 188/32–41; CO 193/8–12 (mfm. at PAC). *Arthur papers* (Sanderson). U.C., House of Assembly, *App. to the journal*, 1839–40, 2: 201–47. *Daily Leader* (Toronto), 11 Aug. 1853. *Mackenzie's Weekly Message*, 18 Aug. 1853. *North American* (Toronto), 12 Aug. 1853. Cowdell, *Land policies of U.C.* Norman Macdonald, *Canada, 1763–1841, immigration and settlement; the administration of the imperial land regulations* (London and Toronto, 1939), 312–463. "Biographical sketch," Assoc. of Ont. Land Surveyors, *Proc.* (Toronto), 1897: 157–60. H. P. Gundy, "Samuel Oliver Tazewell, first lithographer of Upper Canada," *Humanities Assoc. Rev.* (Kingston, Ont.), 27 (1976): 466–83.

HUSTON, JAMES (baptized **Jacques**), typographer, journalist, office holder, and author; b. 17 Aug. 1820 at Quebec, son of William Huston, a carpenter, and Théotiste Audette, *dit* Lapointe; d. there 21 Sept. 1854.

While still young, James Huston became an apprentice in a printing-house at Quebec. He educated himself by reading on his own, and early manifested a concern to further the interests of French Canadians. On 19 June 1842 he was elected one of the secretaries of the Société Saint-Jean-Baptiste. On 10 October he and another typographer, Charles Bertrand, launched *L'Artisan*, a bi-weekly with reform leanings which was intended for the working class. However, the venture was not successful and publication ceased on 13 July 1843. Stanislas Drapeau* revived the paper in January 1844 but changed its contents substantially. Huston's brief sally into journalism did, nevertheless, make him known, and enabled him in 1846 to obtain the post of assistant French translator to the Legislative Assembly of the Province of Canada.

Huston

From then on he followed the government to its various capitals.

In Montreal he found a milieu favourable to the intellectual endeavours he had in mind. He took part there in the founding of the Institut Canadien, becoming an active member on 25 Jan. 1845. In August 1847 he delivered a lecture to it entitled "De la position et des besoins de la jeunesse canadienne-française," in which he denounced with singular courage the injustices suffered by educated young people in Lower Canada: "Since 1759 French Canadian youth have vegetated on [their] native soil, without hope, without a future, without receiving any support, any encouragement, any advice either from the men of their own race, or from the government." He spoke in the same vein as Pierre-Joseph-Olivier Chauveau*, who had just published in 1846–47 his "Charles Guérin, roman de mœurs canadiennes" in *Album littéraire et musical de la Revue canadienne* (Montreal) to stress identical problems.

Huston was elected president of the Institut Canadien on 4 Nov. 1847, and during his term of office the institute founded on 5 April 1848 the Association des Établissements Canadiens des Townships, which sought to halt the steady stream of emigration to the United States. Louis-Joseph Papineau*'s return to the political scene led to the formation of a radical wing within the reform party and the politicizing of the institute, moves that Huston refused to endorse. Huston's opponents, among whom were the leading figures of the newspaper *L'Avenir*, nominated Toussaint-Antoine-Rodolphe Laflamme* for the presidency of the institute. At the session of 4 May 1848 Huston was defeated by 36 votes. Antoine Gérin-Lajoie* contested the results, but a second ballot, held after several officers resigned, confirmed Laflamme's election. When the parliament buildings were set on fire in 1849, Huston left Montreal with the government; he stayed in Toronto for some time before returning to Quebec, where he died prematurely.

Huston is known primarily as the compiler of *Le répertoire national*, a collection, according to the prospectus published in *L'Avenir*, of the "best works of Canadian writers, now scattered in the numerous French Canadian newspapers which have been published for half a century." It was to comprise two 384-page volumes and to appear in 32-page instalments fortnightly from the date when 250 subscribers had signed up. The instalments began to reach readers on 26 Feb. 1848, appearing with some regularity until the end of the year. On 13 September *L'Avenir* published the introduction to *Le répertoire national*. The selections, presented chronologically, were not necessarily forgotten masterpieces, but in Huston's view their publication would "certainly do honour to the country and to its writers." The suggestions made in the newspapers, as well as by subscribers and friends, "to pass less rapidly over the different periods and be less severe in your choice," led Huston to publish two new volumes, whose instalments were spaced out until 1850. In 1853 Huston published in Paris a second collection entitled *Légendes canadiennes*, which brought together some short narrative pieces already in *Le répertoire national*.

Huston's decision to eliminate political writings from *Le répertoire national* placed him in an uncomfortable but understandable position. The majority of French Canadian authors were politicians who had taken sides at the time of the recent rebellion, and militant texts were legion. The compiler was not far enough away from the events to be able to make an impartial selection. Despite his unequivocal political convictions, Huston therefore chose not to touch the problem. He presented a watered-down selection and gave an incomplete idea of the period his work was supposed to represent. Napoleon Aubin*, the former editor of *Le Fantasque*, seems non-committal, a writer of nerveless prose; so does Joseph-Édouard Cauchon*, who had taken such categorical stands. Papineau, a dominant figure in the first half of the 19th century, does not even appear in *Le répertoire*. On the other hand, there are innumerable inoffensive and rather colourless pieces. Joseph Quesnel*, Joseph-Guillaume Barthe*, François-Magloire Derome*, and Pierre PETITCLAIR occupy an enviable place. Poems, chronicles, narratives, short stories, and lectures on innocuous and general topics give a very limited notion of the real literary production of the time. It would, however, be unfair to make no mention of the substantial texts included, such as the poems of François-Xavier Garneau*, the addresses of Étienne Parent*, and the "Essai sur la littérature" of Louis-Auguste Olivier, which were all without specific political orientation but clearly had a nationalist thrust.

Despite its bland character, *Le répertoire national* attained its object of preserving and disseminating Canadian writings. It may not have given an exact picture of French Canadian literature, because the most dynamic and living elements had been excised. But the majority of commentators, from Edmond Lareau* to Pierre de Grandpré, have held it in special regard as a reference work. These men have perpetuated an image to which James Huston, in his endeavour to avoid incurring political attack, had unintentionally lent credence.

MAURICE LEMIRE

James Huston is the author of "Visite à un village français, sur la frontière américaine: le cap Vincent," which appeared in the work he compiled, *Le répertoire national, ou recueil de littérature canadienne* (4v., Montréal, 1848–50), 2:

283–93. He also gave a paper before the Institut Canadien in Montreal on 12 Aug. 1847 which was published under the title "De la position et des besoins de la jeunesse canadienne-française" in *L'Avenir* on 21 Aug. 1847 and reprinted in *Le répertoire national*, 4: 122–55. Excerpts from *Le répertoire national* were published by Huston in Paris in 1853 as *Légendes canadiennes*. *Le répertoire national* was itself republished in 1893 by Adolphe-Basile Routhier*, and the original edition was reprinted in 1982.

ANQ-Q, CE1-1, 18 août 1820, 22 sept. 1854. PAC, MG 30, D1, 16. *L'Avenir*, 23 oct., 6, 13 nov. 1847; 4 mars, 6, 24 mai 1848. *Le Pays*, 3 oct. 1854. Beaulieu et Hamelin, *La presse québécoise*, 1: 121–22. *DOLQ*, 1: 650–52. Réginald Hamel *et al.*, *Dictionnaire pratique des auteurs québécois* (Montréal, 1976). P.-G. Roy, *Fils de Québec*, 4: 43–45. H.-J.-J.-B. Chouinard, *Fête nationale des Canadiens français célébrée à Québec en 1880: histoire, discours, rapport . . .* (4v., Québec, 1881–1903), 1: 27–28. J.-R. Rioux, "L'Institut canadien; les débuts de l'Institut canadien et du journal *L'Avenir* (1844–1849)" (thèse de DES, univ. Laval, Québec, 1967). D. M. Hayne, "*Le répertoire national* de Huston," *BRH*, 56 (1950): 49–51.

HWISTESMETXĒ'QEN (meaning "walking grizzly bear"; also known as **Shiwelean, Nicola, N'Kuala**, and various spellings of Nicholas), head chief of the Okanagans; fl. 1793–1859.

Much of what is known about Hwistesmetxē'qEn, who was called Nicola by the early fur traders, comes from the folklore and oral history of the Okanagan Indians, one of the Interior Salish people of present-day British Columbia. These legendary accounts, which preserve the Okanagan toponymy and appellation, have been collected by anthropologists and local historians and despite their lack of precision present a remarkably consistent portrait of the major events that marked his life. Nicola was descended from a long line of Okanagan head chiefs and, according to legend, was born at the fortified encampment established by his father, PElkamū'lôx (which means "rolls over the earth"), near the junction of the Similkameen and Okanagan rivers (Wash.). When Nicola was still a young boy PElkamū'lôx took his people north to Fish Lake (B.C.), where he settled near the band of his brother Kwolī'la at Chapperon Lake. PElkamū'lôx at times went to the plains through the Flathead country to hunt buffalo and the legends speak of his meeting two North West Company traders, Finan McDonald and a certain Lagacé, at Hell's Gate Pass (near Helena, Mont.). This meeting would have been some time after 1807, the year McDonald arrived in the Columbia region with David THOMPSON. For the Okanagan Indians the meeting was their first contact with whites, and PElkamū'lôx, known as a great orator, returned to his country to recount the story of men with white skins and blue eyes, of sticks that made thunder, smoke, and fire and that could kill birds in flight, and of an animal, the horse, that could run faster than the buffalo. At one of the feasts called to hear these tales a Lillooet chief declared that such things could not exist and that PElkamū'lôx was a liar. The head chief rose to defend his honour but was struck down by two arrows fired by his accuser. Before he died, PElkamū'lôx made his son Nicola head chief and confided him to the care of Kwolī'la, exhorting the young boy to avenge his death.

The exact date of PElkamū'lôx's death is not known. It would appear, however, that when the first party from the newly established Pacific Fur Company, led by David Stuart, arrived in the Okanagan during the winter of 1811–12, it found Nicola as head chief. Ovide Montigny, a member of the party, apparently met Nicola at the head of Okanagan Lake and, after a successful winter's trading, returned to the PFC's headquarters at Fort Astoria (Astoria, Oreg.), leaving the head chief to watch over the goods he was not taking with him. The legend tells how the young chief was rewarded by Montigny upon the latter's return the following autumn with a gift of ten guns, ammunition, some tobacco, and other goods. Reminded of his duty to avenge the murder of his father, he is said to have organized a party of some five hundred warriors from the Okanagan, Thompson, Shuswap, and Similkameen tribes, and to have attacked the Lillooet in their fishing territory on the Fraser River, killing three or four hundred of their people.

But there is another source that has to be taken into account in trying to work out the events of Nicola's life. The journal of the Thompson's River Post (Kamloops, B.C.) for November 1822, kept by John McLeod*, relates the murder of a leading Indian, supposedly PElkamū'lôx, who "was killed by the Fraser's River Indians and suffered a most cruel Torture by being left to linger for some days after his bowels were ript open." In January 1823 McLeod mentions Nicola's plans to "revenge his Father's Death."

During the early fur trade era in New Caledonia (B.C.), Nicola's influence was much appreciated by the traders of the NWC and the Hudson's Bay Company, and his generous welcome was largely responsible for the happy relationship between them and the Interior Salish people. In the late 1830s Chief Factor Samuel Black*, in charge at Thompson's River Post, lent him a plough so that he could grow potatoes and other vegetables at his summer camp on Nicola Lake; this first local effort at cultivation was soon imitated by other bands. Following the murder of Black by a young Shuswap warrior in 1841, Nicola calmed the HBC men, who feared a widespread uprising, by delivering a moving eulogy, reported by Archibald McKinlay, which called for the capture of the killer.

Jackson

In later years, however, Nicola was granted less respect by the HBC men at Fort Kamloops, as Thompson's River Post came to be known in the 1840s. John Tod* claimed in his old age to have thwarted a plot by Nicola to capture the post in the 1840s, though no hint of such an attack can be found in his journals. Chief Trader Paul Fraser noted a visit made by the chief at the end of 1851 in the following terms: "Arrived Neckilus from the Grand Prarie and as usual begging for supplies, this old Man is a Compleat nusance to this Establishment."

In the tradition of powerful and wealthy Salishan chiefs, Nicola had a large number of wives, perhaps as many as 17, and many children. Following his death, which was reported by the HBC in 1859, his body was temporarily laid to rest at the Kamloops post, and then later carried to the head of Okanagan Lake for burial. A monument to him is to be found in the Okanagan graveyard north of Vernon, B.C., bearing the name "Inkuala," and such place-names as Nicola Lake and Nicola River, in the Kamloops district, honour his memory.

MARY BALF

PABC, Add. MSS 505, 2, file 15: ff.12–15; Fort Kamloops, Journals, 3 Aug. 1841–19 Dec. 1843; 17 Aug. 1850–17 May 1852; September 1854–June 1855. PAM, HBCA, B.97/a/1: ff.9, 14, 14d; D.5/6: ff.466–68. *HBRS*, 10 (Rich); 18 (Rich and Johnson). Angus McDonald, "Angus McDonald: a few items of the west," ed. F. W. Howay *et al.*, *Wash. Hist. Quarterly*, 8 (1917): 188–229. John Tod, "Career of a Scotch boy," ed. Madge Wolfenden, *BCHQ*, 18 (1954): 222–24. Sophia Steffens, *The land of Chief Nicola . . .* (n.p., [1961]). M. S. Wade, *The Thompson country . . .* (Kamloops, B.C., 1907). M. H. Brent, "Indian lore," comp. Mrs Harold Cochrane, Okanagan Hist. Soc., *Report* (Vernon, B.C.), 30 (1966): 105–13. G. M. Dawson, "Notes on the Shuswap people of British Columbia," RSC *Trans.*, 1st ser., 9 (1891), sect.II: 26–28. J. A. Teit, "The Salishan tribes of the western plateaus," ed. Franz Boas, Bureau of American Ethnology, *Report* (Washington), 45 (1927–28): 265–78.

J

JACKSON, JAMES, Methodist minister; b. 1789 or 1790, probably in New York State; d. 6 July 1851 in Norwich, Upper Canada.

All that is known of James Jackson's background is that his father's family was in Potsdam, N.Y., during the War of 1812 and immigrated to Edwardsburgh Township, Upper Canada, following that conflict. At some later date Jackson may have served as presiding elder's supply assisting the Reverend Isaac B. Smith on the Yonge Street circuit, near York (Toronto), of the Methodist Episcopal Church, an American body that had missions in Upper Canada. In 1817 Jackson was recommended for its ministry and was sent to the Duffin's Creek circuit in Pickering Township, returning in 1818 to the Yonge Street charge. Ordained deacon in 1819, he was assigned to the Long Point circuit where he remained until 1821, an unusually long term of three years at a time when one-year appointments were the normal Methodist practice. From 1821 to 1824 he served on the Westminster and the Thames circuits near London.

Jackson was popular among the church's followers. John Saltkill Carroll*, a colleague, said that he "was certainly one of the most attractive preachers of that day," an assessment reflected in the success he enjoyed. During his last year at Long Point he reported an increase of 102 members from the 404 recorded in 1819, and at Westminster membership grew from 356 to 475. It was at this time, however, that conflict arose between Jackson and the church's leaders, including William CASE, and a major part of the 1822 session of the Genesee Conference was spent debating his status. A motion to expel him was reduced to a temporary suspension of his ministry and a reproof from the presiding bishop. Despite the questions raised about his temperament and style of ministry he was ordained a preacher in 1824 and reassigned to the Westminster circuit the following year.

In 1826 Jackson was superannuated because of poor health and began work as a mission school teacher in Westminster. His problems with the church continued, now largely relating to its association with the American parent. In his desire for independence he sided with Henry Ryan*, a fellow preacher, and agitated for the complete separation of the Canadian church. The two were not satisfied when that goal was achieved in 1828 and organized conventions to disrupt the new body, called the Methodist Episcopal Church in Canada. In 1829 Jackson was charged with making slanderous statements concerning certain preachers, and with the misuse of mission funds. He did not appear in his own defence and was expelled.

Jackson then assisted Ryan in organizing the Canadian Wesleyan Methodist Church, a "reformed and pure Church" whose government featured lay representation and an elective presidency. Although the Ryanites did succeed in attracting some members from the Methodist Episcopals, their numbers remained small, and in 1833 the movement received a major setback when Ryan died. Jackson, who had returned to the arduous labours of an active preacher, then assumed the leadership, serving as president of conference in 1835. His most urgent problem was the possibility of a general return of his members to the Methodist Episcopal Church in Canada following its union in 1833 with the Wesleyan Methodist Church. The merger with that British body had reduced the hostile feelings within his own group toward the Methodist Episcopals. To counter the threat he campaigned for union with the Methodist New Connexion Church, an English sect which was also an exponent of stronger lay representation in church government. He succeeded in 1841 when the 1,915 members of his church joined that group to form the Canadian Wesleyan Methodist New Connexion Church. Jackson, then serving on the Welland Canal circuit, became its first president. As Carroll commented, "This union put that body on a much more respectable footing than it had ever been before."

In 1843 the British parent body requested that the Canadian mission send a delegate to England to report on its work and to raise funds, and Jackson was chosen. The clergyman sent from England to be superintendent of the mission in Canada wrote a letter introducing Jackson to his counterpart in England. It provides clues to the difficulties Jackson encountered in his pastoral ministry: "Bro Jackson is a *sanguine go ahead* man he leaves consequences for other people to think about. In the management of business he is determined and persevering but lacks *prudence*. He is also very fond of controversy There is hardly a body in the Province but he has been at war with, less or more either with their doctrine or govt. . . . At the missionary services and in Revival meetings I think you will find him an acquisition. I hope our friends will bear with his American peculiarities." His tour was partially successful in that contributions to the missionary society of the English church increased by one-third, but his appeal for financial support to liquidate the Canadian church's debt was less rewarding. He then suggested a great Canadian bazaar: friends in England would donate goods to Canada where they could be sold and the proceeds applied toward a theological seminary, houses for ministers, and financial grants to missionaries. The plan was accepted and goods arrived from England, but no record of the outcome has been found.

After his return to Canada, Jackson served the Hamilton and Welland Canal circuits (1844–45) before becoming supernumerary minister at Waterford (1846), Malahide Township (1847), and Norwich (1849–50). Apart from serving a third time as president of conference in 1848, he rapidly declined as a leader in the united church. The dominant influence became the superintendent and preachers who were sent out from England. Jackson "labored till increas-

ing infirmities obliged him to retire." He died on 6 July 1851 at the age of 61. It is not known whether he ever married. The church he helped form and served at great personal cost barely exceeded 7,000 members at its peak and was the first of the smaller Methodist groups to unite with the Methodist Church of Canada in 1874.

ALBERT BURNSIDE

SOAS, Methodist Missionary Soc. Arch., Methodist New Connexion Church, Foreign and Colonial Missions Committee, corr., North America, John Addyman to W. Cooke, 25 July 1843; James Jackson to Cooke, 21 April 1844 (mfm. at UCA). UCA, Biog. files, James Jackson; Albert Burnside, "The Canadian Wesleyan Methodist New Connexion Church, 1841–1874" (typescript, 1967), 26, 148–49; "Relationships between the Methodist Church in the Canadas, the Methodist Episcopal Church in the United States, and the Wesleyan Methodist Society in England, 1791–1847" (typescript, 1959), 29–30. Canadian Wesleyan Methodist New Connexion Church, *Minutes of the annual conference* (Toronto), 1852: 7–8. Cornish, *Cyclopædia of Methodism*, 1: 43, 240, 468. Carroll, *Case and his cotemporaries*, 2: 95–96, 98–99, 306, 390–91; 3: 1, 3, 253–54, 295. [H.] O. Miller, *A century of western Ontario: the story of London, "The Free Press," and western Ontario, 1849–1949* (Toronto, 1949; repr. Westport, Conn., 1972), 21–23, 25–26. J. E. Sanderson, *The first century of Methodism in Canada* (2v., Toronto, 1908–10), 1: 141, 206, 226. Thomas Webster, *History of the Methodist Episcopal Church in Canada* (Hamilton, Ont., 1870), 228–29. D. J. Brock, "The confession: Burleigh's pre-hanging 'statement' mystery" and "That confession again: error leads to further probe, suggestion of Burley's innocence," *London Free Press* (London, Ont.), 10 April 1971: 8M and 24 April 1971: 8M respectively. H. O. Miller, "The history of the newspaper press in London, 1830–1875," *OH*, 32 (1937): 120–21.

JACQUIES, ADOLPHE, shopkeeper, printer, trade unionist, and newspaperman; b. *c.* 1798 in Bordeaux, France, son of Hilaire-Jacob Jacquies and Adélaïde Prahm; m. 10 June 1828 Catherine Ponsy at Quebec, and they had nine children; d. there 30 Jan. 1860.

Adolphe Jacquies arrived in Quebec shortly before 1826, and at first opened a confectioner's shop on Rue Saint-Jean. He became a typographer, and struck up a friendship with Napoléon Aubin*, for whom he printed from 1837 the weekly *Le Fantasque*, one of the most widely read newspapers in the city. Although moderate in its political leanings, the paper was distinguished by an ironical tone and lively satire. Not surprisingly, because of its articles criticizing the government and its acknowledged sympathy for the Patriotes of 1837, it drew the wrath of Quebec's chief of police, Thomas Ainslie YOUNG. When Aubin was arrested on 2 Jan. 1839, Jacquies was not spared; he was taken into custody, and his presses, paper, and type were seized. He was held in an unhealthy prison

James

without any charges being laid by the crown, and was released on bail on 22 February at the request of several doctors. The incarceration had a lasting effect, depriving him of the ability to move normally for the rest of his life. Several months later his presses and type were returned to him in damaged condition. In 1846 he claimed compensation from the government for the wrongs done to him on this occasion; in 1852 the rebellion losses commissioners appointed by the government granted him an indemnity of £100.

In July 1839, having recovered his presses, Jacquies decided to print and publish his own newspaper, the *Canadian Colonist and Commercial Advertiser*, an English-language bi-weekly. This paper consisted largely of advertisements and material reprinted from other newspapers but it also contained political articles by Jacquies. When the Act of Union came into effect, the paper immediately denounced the anti-democratic character of this measure, which deprived the inhabitants of Lower Canada of fair representation and established a sizeable civil list. In Jacquies's view the act constituted an impediment to democracy, "strik[ing] a fatal blow at Colonial liberty." The printer also protested against the dubious practices employed by the governor, Lord Sydenham [Thomson*], during the 1841 elections. Conscious that the timber trade was important for the Canadas, he opposed the advocates of free trade in England, noting that Canadians needed revenues protected by imperial preference to buy manufactured goods from Great Britain. Although the paper ceased publication in 1841, certain news items imply that Jacquies favoured Louis-Hippolyte La Fontaine*'s strategy of seeking a *rapprochement* between the reformers of Lower Canada and those of Upper Canada.

That year Jacquies became the owner of the *British North American*, a tory tri-weekly published at Quebec that he renamed the *Quebec Argus*. Unfortunately there are only two issues of this paper extant and it is impossible to follow the political direction pursued by its publisher. From 1844 to 1847 Jacquies put his presses at the disposal of the *Quebec Times*, a tory tri-weekly under the editorship of John Cordner* and John Henry Willan*. Nothing is known of Jacquies's career in later years, but it is possible that he took up residence at Montreal, for his wife died there in 1847.

More noteworthy than his activity as printer and newspaper editor is the interest Jacquies showed in unionizing the printers of Quebec. By 1827 they had started a union that apparently was short-lived. Under Jacquies's stimulus it was reorganized in 1836, under the name Canadian Typographical Union. Initially, this body had 66 members, and it set as its objectives "to promote good understanding between employers and workers, to establish a reasonable pay scale, to prevent competition often unfair to conscientious employers, to educate members, and to help the families of members stricken by illness." In 1839 it demanded a salary increase from the master printers, citing the higher cost of living. It is not known what attitude Jacquies adopted on this question, which was of direct concern to him since he was then a master printer. During the first half of the 19th century the idea of trade unions showed a good deal of originality; he probably had been persuaded to it in France.

One of the first to defend workers' rights, Adolphe Jacquies had also promoted liberal ideas in Lower Canada. Responsible government meant for him the political freedom of the people, while trade unionism represented his wish for economic democracy for the workers.

JACQUES ROUILLARD

ANQ-Q, CE1-1, 10 juin 1828. Can., Prov. of, Legislative Assembly, *Journals*, 20 April 1846. *Canadian Colonist and Commercial Advertiser* (Quebec), 16 Nov. 1840; 22 March, 12, 26 April 1841. *Le Journal de Québec*, 31 janv. 1860. Beaulieu et Hamelin, *La presse québécoise*, 1: 107–8, 118, 132. Fauteux, *Patriotes. Montreal directory*, 1842–60. *Quebec directory*, 1847–60. *100ᵉ anniversaire de l'Union typographique de Québec no. 302* (Québec, 1936). Charles Lipton, *Histoire du syndicalisme au Canada et au Québec, 1827–1959*, Michel Van Schendel, trad. (Montréal, 1976), 40–41. J.-P. Tremblay, *À la recherche de Napoléon Aubin* (Québec, 1969). F.-J. Audet, "Les Canadiens et la Guerre de Sécession," *BRH*, 46 (1940): 357–58. "L'imprimeur Adolphe Jacquies," *BRH*, 42 (1936): 540.

JAMES, PHILIP, Bible Christian minister; b. in Cornwall, England, around 1800; d. 1 March 1851 in Pickering Township, Upper Canada, and was buried at Columbus (Oshawa), Upper Canada.

Philip James experienced an evangelical conversion in 1820 on the St Ervan circuit, Cornwall, of the Bible Christian Church, a Methodist sect founded in the West Country five years earlier. The movement was characterized by revivalism, the ministry of women itinerants, and the plain dress of its adherents. In 1825 James was appointed an itinerant minister on trial and in 1828, after appointments to Buckfastleigh, Devon, the Forest of Dean mission, Gloucestershire, and Bristol, he was received as a minister in full connection. Additional one-year assignments followed, including postings in the Isles of Scilly, Penzance, and Guernsey, until 1834 when, "having had deep feelings on the subject," he offered himself as a missionary and was sent to assist the Reverend Francis Metherall* on Prince Edward Island.

His arrival, on 29 July 1834, allowed Metherall to expand the Bible Christian mission westward from its first outposts north and east of Charlottetown. James, assigned to serve the eastern area (including Gallas

Point, Rustico Road, and Wheatley River), found that most of the Island's inhabitants, chiefly Presbyterians and Roman Catholics in affiliation, were almost totally bereft of Christian preaching. In some communities people had only one or two opportunities annually to hear the Gospel preached, and one group he addressed had not been able to hear a sermon for over two years. James worked hard to meet the need, travelling the rough terrain on foot in all seasons. At New Bideford (Bideford), he formed a small class "composed of some of our friends from England," but regretted that he could be among them only at six-week intervals. He could not visit some preaching points as often as that. Clearly, the mission's resources were totally inadequate to minister to the Island's many communities, most of which lacked places of worship. James, who was highly devout, wrote in 1835 that he was frequently "destitute of a room in which to retire for prayer." Moreover, he felt that the church did not understand the conditions under which its missionaries laboured, in particular the severity of the Canadian winter, the need for warm clothing, the poor housing and isolation of its preachers, the scattered circuits, and the difficulties of transportation. After two years on the Island he wrote: "I should just like to have the Missionary Committee with me for a few days, *only a few days*, when I am tottering through the snow three or four feet deep, and over the ice, when the water and slush . . . takes me nearly to my knees for six or seven miles together, and then say, whether a horse be necessary."

One of the drawbacks of sporadic preaching was that its benefits were often lost before the preacher had the opportunity to return. As James described it, "A poor Irish woman told Brother Metherall, that I came among them so seldom, that although they felt under the word when I was there, they 'got wild again' before my return." He was convinced that if the church's leaders could see the spiritual destitution of some of the areas where he worked, they would exert themselves to the utmost to send the Gospel. A third missionary was just as necessary as the second had been. Help came in 1839 when Richard Cotton arrived to share the load, but James was not to benefit long from the additional assistance. The increased immigration to Upper Canada of people from Devon and Cornwall, where most supporters of the Bible Christian Church resided, meant that experienced missionaries were needed there. Accordingly, in 1841 he departed Prince Edward Island to join other colleagues, including John Hicks Eynon*, his wife, Elizabeth [DART], and, later, Ann Robins [VICKERY], in bringing the Gospel to their followers in Upper Canada.

James was first assigned to Cobourg, which received many Bible Christian immigrants before they passed through to other destinations. In 1842 he moved on to the circuit in Darlington and Whitby townships, another area with a large number of West Country immigrants, and returned to the Cobourg circuit in 1844. Two years later he was sent to Mitchell to minister to Bible Christians who had moved to the Huron Tract on the southeast shore of Lake Huron. By 1848, with the help of the Reverend Arthur Doble, James had gathered a circuit which extended 50 to 60 miles one way and 40 to 50 in the other, an area covering 12 townships. He found that 30 of the first 38 members of his congregation were English-born, and that some 11 or 12 had been Bible Christians in the old country. Unfortunately, for the want of Christian preaching and fellowship, many had fallen away from their faith; however, after a short time, he reported that most were "repairing their loss" and appeared "to be in full sail for Port Glory." The Huron Tract, with some of the worst roads in the province, made heavy physical demands upon him. Doble, writing in 1849, said, "I learn from the people that he has laboured very hard among them, more than his strength would rightly admit. He seems to be failing." But despite the concerns of his congregations, James reported that lay help was difficult to obtain because it was hard to persuade the people of their duty to sacrifice just one hour to attend to the business of the church.

James left the arduous Huron mission in 1850 and moved to the Pickering circuit, only to find that his new appointment also strained his declining strength. On the evening of 28 Feb. 1851, disregarding the advice of friends, he conducted a preaching service. Afterwards he had to be taken to a follower's home, where he said, "How well it is to be always ready, – If I live or die I am the Lord's." Despite medical attention, by noon the following day he was "enjoying eternal life." His superintendent, the Reverend Paul Robins, paid tribute to him by saying: "We have lost an efficient labourer. . . . He was greatly beloved . . . in every station where he laboured: was remarkably punctual in attending his appointments; and his straight-forward, open-hearted, and affectionate carriage won for him general esteem, confidence, and affection."

ALBERT BURNSIDE

UCA, Bible Christian Church in Canada, Annual conference and district meetings, minutes, 1847, sect.5, "Mitchell, Huron Tract." *Bible Christian Magazine* (Shebbear, Eng.), 14 (1835): 35–40, 106–9; 15 (1836): 49–50; 28 (1849): 43–44, 121–24; 30 (1851): 161–62, 204. Bible Christians, *Minutes of the annual conference* (Stoke Damerel, Eng.; Shebbear), 1828: 6; 1841: 6; 1851: 5–6. *United Methodist ministers and their circuits . . . 1797–1932*, comp. O. A. Beckerlegge (London, 1968). John Harris, *The life of the Rev. Francis Metherall, and the history of the Bible Christian Church in Prince Edward Island* (London and Toronto, 1883), 36, 38, 45, 47, 54–55, 109.

Jameson

JAMESON, ANNA BROWNELL. See MURPHY

JAMESON, ROBERT SYMPSON, lawyer, judge, politician, and office holder; baptized 5 June 1796 in Harbridge, England, son of Thomas Jameson and Mary Sympson; m. 1825 Anna Brownell MURPHY in London; they had no children; d. 1 Aug. 1854 in Toronto.

Of a modest but aspiring family, Robert Sympson Jameson was born in Hampshire and raised and educated at Ambleside in the Lake District. From childhood he was a close friend of Hartley Coleridge, son of Samuel Taylor Coleridge and himself a poet, who later dedicated three sonnets to him. Jameson was admitted to study law at Middle Temple, London, in 1818 and was called to the bar in 1823. For the next six years he worked in London as an equity draftsman and during this time he co-edited two volumes of bankruptcy case reports, but he continued his literary interests through an association with the *London Magazine* and the preparation of an edition of Samuel Johnson's *Dictionary of the English language*.

Jameson first met Anna Murphy in the winter of 1820–21. After a protracted and intermittent courtship, they began an unhappy marriage in 1825. The incompatible pair lived together until 1829 when Robert gained appointment in the West Indies as the chief justice of Dominica; Anna, already launched on a promising literary career, travelled to the Continent. Jameson's four years of "wearisome banishment" in the tropics brought frustration; he sought unsuccessfully to reform the judicial system which the powerful local slave owners manipulated to their personal advantage. Repelled by the West Indies, categorized by him as a "dismal, vulgar, sensual, utterly unintellectual place," he declined an offer of the chief justiceship of Tobago (Trinidad and Tobago) and returned to London in 1833. Possibly through the efforts of influential friends, he was promptly made attorney general of Upper Canada that March in place of Henry John Boulton*, who had been dismissed from office. He assumed his duties in York (Toronto) in June 1833, the last Upper Canadian attorney general to be appointed by the British government.

Jameson capably performed the large and varied business of his new office, handing down legal opinions, reporting on petitions, reviewing applications for licences and patents, and dealing with legislative, administrative, and judicial matters. Although an outsider, he soon found himself embroiled in the turbulent provincial politics of the 1830s. During the election of 1834, he and Ogle Robert Gowan*, the ever-active leader of the Orange order, ran successfully as "Constitutional" candidates for the riding of Leeds; however, their reform opponents, William Buell* and Mathew H. Howard, proved their charges that voters had been intimidated

by Gowan's supporters, and the results of the election were controverted. In an 1835 by-election, violence again nullified Jameson's victory, and he was not a candidate when yet another by-election was held the following year.

Anna finally consented to join her husband late in 1835 and set out for Toronto in the fall of 1836. She found provincial society insufferable, however, and left permanently after less than a year, having secured an annuity and a separation agreement from Robert and collected material for another travel book. *Winter studies and summer rambles in Canada* (1838) met with great success but Anna's husband, always anxious about his position, did not welcome her caustic account of the province.

With or without a wife, Jameson had secured a respectable niche in Upper Canada. In 1837 he was appointed vice-chancellor of the newly created and long overdue Court of Chancery, the chancellorship being nominally held by the lieutenant governor of the province. As vice-chancellor, he also became a member of the Court of Appeal. His training in English equity made him one of the few capable local candidates for the demanding post, the jurisdiction of which included cases of fraud, accident, and account; co-partnerships; and matters relating to trusts and mortgages. Although for more than a decade he handled the onerous load of the court alone and with dignity, some solicitors became impatient with his excessive caution and respect for precedent. Jameson's limited practical experience, the cumbersome procedures inherited from English equity, and the presence in the court of several outstanding lawyers such as William Hume Blake*, James Christie Palmer Esten*, and Robert Baldwin SULLIVAN, further complicated his task as vice-chancellor. A drinking problem, starting probably in Dominica, also progressively reduced his effectiveness.

During his years in Upper Canada, Jameson's official and social position drew him into many activities, often involving contentious political issues. He served as treasurer of the Law Society of Upper Canada during 1836–41 and 1845–46. He was a member of the Legislative Council for the province of Canada between 1841 and 1853, and its first speaker until 1843. He sat on the council of King's College (University of Toronto) from 1834 and was one of the first councillors of Trinity College when it was founded in 1851. In 1842 he became chief superintendent of education, though the actual work of the department was carried out by his deputy superintendents, Jean-Baptiste Meilleur* in Lower Canada and the Reverend Robert MURRAY in Upper Canada. Jameson also served on a number of important government commissions including those concerned with treason during the rebellion of 1837–38, with the operations of the Indian Department and the Inspector

General's Office in 1839, with the establishment of a lunatic asylum in Toronto in 1840 and with its superintendence from 1841 [*see* William Rees*], with the review and adjudication of claims to unpatented land grants between 1841 and 1848, and with the practices of the Court of Chancery in 1842 and 1843.

Other activities reflected his personal interests. As Henry Scadding* recalled years later, Jameson "was a man highly educated and possessing great taste, and even skill, in respect of art. He was a connoisseur and collector of fine editions. His conversation was charged with reminiscences and anecdotes of . . . the Coleridges, Wordsworths and Southey, with all of whom he had been intimate in his youth." Jameson helped to organize and served as president of both the Toronto Literary Club (1836) and the St George's Society (1839–41, 1848), and was a founding patron of the Toronto Society of Arts (1847). He also helped found the Anglican Church of St George the Martyr, Toronto, and was president of the British Emigrant Society of Upper Canada (1835) and of Thomas ROLPH's Canadian Emigration Association (1840). In 1845 he established a gold medal, which he designed himself, to be awarded for "proficiency in History and English Composition" at King's College.

By the late 1840s Jameson's position was declining. He had sought to retire from the vice-chancellorship as early as 1847, and in 1849 had to have a leave of absence from the Legislative Council because of his "shattered health." George Ridout* spoke for many members of the bar when he wrote to Attorney General Robert BALDWIN urging Jameson's retirement as vice-chancellor. With the reorganization and expansion of the Court of Chancery in 1849, William Hume Blake, who had piloted the reforms, became chancellor and James Christie Palmer Esten, senior vice-chancellor; Jameson was demoted to junior vice-chancellor. A year later, a broken man, he resigned on a government pension of £750 a year. He had already sold the house he had built for his wife to Frederick Widder* and seems to have been speculating heavily in land. In 1854 Jameson died of pulmonary consumption while in the care of the Reverend George Maynard, an eccentric master at Upper Canada College, and his wife Emma. To them and not to Anna, he willed his personal effects and his "property on Queen Street" in what is now the Parkdale section of Toronto. His burial at St James' Cemetery, Toronto, in the family vault of his late friend Lieutenant-Colonel Joseph WELLS, received little notice.

Jameson's life was marred by ruined ambitions and personal unhappiness; however, he served with dignity and self-sacrifice, if not always great distinction, in many important and constructive capacities for more than two decades. His efforts and contributions deserve more attention than they have received. This neglect is probably due in large part to the more renowned and colourful career of Anna Jameson, whose published letters give an all too sketchy and jaundiced view of Robert Sympson Jameson.

JOHN D. BLACKWELL

Robert Sympson Jameson is the editor of two volumes of *Cases in bankruptcy . . . containing reports of cases . . .* [1821–28]*; and a digest of all the contemporary cases relating to the bankrupt laws in the other courts*, the first co-edited with T. C. Glyn and the second with Basil Montagu (London, 1824–28); and two editions of *A dictionary of the English language . . . ; with the pronunciation greatly simplified, and on an entire new plan; revised, corrected and enlarged, with the addition of several thousand words*, compiled by Samuel Johnson and incorporating John Walker's pronunciation guide (London, 1827; 2nd ed., 2v., 1828). His publications also include various judicial decisions and reports of government commissions.

A miniature of Jameson as a young man is reproduced in *Anna Jameson: letters and friendships (1812–1860)*, ed. [B. C. Strong] Mrs Steuart Erskine (London, 1915); an oil portrait of the mature Jameson painted by John Wycliffe Lowes Forster around 1919 for the Law Soc. of U.C. (Toronto) appears in Clara [McCandless] Thomas, *Love and work enough: the life of Anna Jameson* ([Toronto], 1967).

AO, RG 22, ser.155, will of R. S. Jameson. British Library (London), Add. mss 38757: ff.238–43. Hampshire Record Office (Winchester, Eng.), Bishop's transcripts of Harbridge reg. of baptisms, marriages, and burials, 5 June 1796. Law Soc. of U.C., "Journal of proceedings of the Convocation of Benchers of the Law Society of Upper Canada" (8v.). MTL, Robert Baldwin papers; Henry Scadding scrap-books, 6: 14–15. Niagara Hist. Soc. Museum (Niagara-on-the-Lake, Ont.), Alma–Lauder–Hunter papers, R. S. Jameson to E. J. Alma, 11 Feb. 1847. PAC, RG 1, L3, 261a: J22/29; RG 5, A1, 127–75; C1; C2, 1–30. PRO, CO 42/492–93, 42/495–96 (mfm. at AO); CO 71/68, R. S. Jameson to Horace Twiss, 30 Jan. 1829; 71/74, Jameson to E. J. MacGregor, 22 Feb. 1832. St James' Cemetery and Crematorium (Toronto), Record of burials, 3 Aug. 1854. Toronto Land Registry Office (Toronto), General reg. of wills, no.445, will and estate papers of R. S. Jameson. *Arthur papers* (Sanderson). Can., Prov. of, Legislative Assembly, *App. to the journals*, 1841, app.LL; 1842, app.U; Legislative Council, *Journals*, 1841–55. *Canada Gazette*, 5 March 1842, 22 July 1843. Hartley Coleridge, "Sonnets addressed to R. S. Jameson," *London Magazine*, 7 (January–June 1823): 180–81. *Debates of the Legislative Assembly of United Canada* (Gibbs et al.), 1841–53. *Doc. hist. of education in U.C.* (Hodgins), vols.3–5. *Elgin–Grey papers* (Doughty). A. [B. Murphy] Jameson, *Letters of Anna Jameson to Ottilie von Goethe*, ed. G. H. Needler (London, 1939); *Winter studies and summer rambles*. U.C., House of Assembly, *App. to the journal*, 1839–40, 2: xii; *Journal*, 1833–40. William and Dorothy Wordsworth, *The letters of William and Dorothy Wordsworth*, ed. Ernest de Selincourt et al. (2nd ed., 5v., Oxford, 1967–79), 2–3.

Chronicle & Gazette, 1834–37, 1842. *Church*, 2 Aug.

Jarvis

1854. *Globe*, semi-weekly ed., 3 Aug. 1854. *Mackenzie's Weekly Message*, 4 Aug. 1854. *Upper Canada Gazette*, 15 July 1841. Armstrong, *Handbook of Upper Canadian chronology*. *Canada, an encyclopædia of the country: the Canadian dominion considered in its historic relations, its natural resources, its material progress, and its national development*, ed. J. C. Hopkins (6v. and index, Toronto, 1898–1900), 4: 360. *Political appointments, 1841–65* (J.-O. Coté). D. B. Read, *The lives of the judges of Upper Canada and Ontario, from 1791 to the present time* (Toronto, 1888). *Register of admissions to the Honourable Society of the Middle Temple, from the fifteenth century to the year 1944*, comp. H. A. C. Sturgess (3v., London, 1949), 2: 440. D. H. Akenson, *The Irish in Ontario: a study in rural history* (Kingston, Ont., and Montreal, 1984), 180–88. M. A. Banks, "The evolution of the Ontario courts, 1788–1981," *Essays in the history of Canadian law*, ed. D. H. Flaherty (2v., Toronto, 1981–83), 2: 492–572. Gerardine [Bate] Macpherson, *Memoirs of the life of Anna Jameson* (London, 1878). J. D. Blackwell, "William Hume Blake and judicial reform in the United Province of Canada" (MA thesis, Queen's Univ., Kingston, 1980); "William Hume Blake and the Judicature Acts of 1849: the process of legal reform at mid-century in Upper Canada," *Essays in the history of Canadian law*, 1: 132–74. Lucy Booth Martyn, *Toronto: 100 years of grandeur: the inside stories of Toronto's great homes and the people who lived there* (Toronto, 1978). J. C. Dent, *The last forty years: Canada since the union of 1841* (2v., Toronto, [1881]). E. L. Griggs, *Hartley Coleridge, his life and work* (London, 1929). Herbert Hartman, *Hartley Coleridge, poet's son and poet* (Oxford, 1931). R. B. Howard, *Upper Canada College, 1829–1979: Colborne's legacy* (Toronto, 1979). W. G. Ormsby, *The emergence of the federal concept in Canada, 1839–1845* (Toronto, 1969). Patterson, "Studies in elections in Upper Canada." W. R. Riddell, *The bar and the courts of the province of Upper Canada, or Ontario* (Toronto, 1928); *The legal profession in Upper Canada in its early periods* (Toronto, 1916). *Robertson's landmarks of Toronto*, vols. 1, 3–4. [Henry] Scadding, *Mrs. Jameson on Shakespeare and the Collier emendations* (Toronto, 1892). Raymond Vézina, *Théophile Hamel: peintre national (1817–1870)* (2v., Montréal, 1975–76), 1: 114. F. N. Walker, *Sketches of old Toronto* ([Toronto], 1965).

B. W. Connolly, "After 100 years – a Jesuit seminary," *Philosophers' Quarterly* (Toronto), May 1944: 4–6, 13; June 1945: 3–4, 13; December 1945: 11–12, 21–22; also issued as a separate pamphlet (copy in AO, Pamphlet coll., 1945, no.55). "Death of Vice-Chancellor Esten," *Upper Canada Law Journal* (Toronto), 10 (1864): 281. J. D. Falconbridge, "Law and equity in Upper Canada," *Canadian Law Times* (Toronto), 34 (1914): 1130–46. Clara [McCandless] Thomas, "Vice-Chancellor Robert Sympson Jameson, 1798–1854: memorial for a forgotten man," *OH*, 56 (1964): 5–15. G. H. Needler, "The Jameson medal," *University College Bull.* (Toronto), 1939: 47–51; also published as a separate pamphlet ([Toronto, 1939]). "Personal sketches; or, reminiscences of public men in Canada," *British American Magazine* (Toronto), 2 (1863–64): 234–48. W. R. Riddell, "Judges in the parliament of Upper Canada," *Minn. Law Rev.* (Minneapolis), 3 (1918–19): 163–80, 244–56. Hereward Senior, "Orangeism takes root in Canada," *Canadian Genealogist* (Toronto), 3 (1981): 13–22.

JARVIS, EDWARD JAMES, lawyer, notary, office holder, judge, and politician; b. 1788 in Saint John, N.B., youngest son of Munson Jarvis* and Mary Arnold; m. first 29 April 1817 Anna Maria Boyd, daughter of Dr John Boyd of Saint John, and they had eight children; m. secondly 12 Dec. 1843 Elizabeth Gray, daughter of Robert Gray* and Mary Burns, and they had three children; d. 9 May 1852 at Spring Park (Charlottetown), P.E.I.

Edward James Jarvis's father was a leading Connecticut loyalist who removed to New Brunswick in 1783, establishing a mercantile firm in Saint John and serving as a member of the provincial assembly and as vestryman of the local Anglican church. Edward received a BA in 1809 from King's College in Windsor, N.S., was admitted to the New Brunswick bar as an attorney at law on 12 Oct. 1811, became a notary public in Saint John on 22 Feb. 1812, and in January 1813 sailed from Saint John to continue his legal studies in London. He became a student of Joseph Chitty, and was admitted to the bar at the Inner Temple. While in London he met two other law students from his province, John Simcoe Saunders* and Ward CHIPMAN. Jarvis returned to Saint John in 1816 to resume practising law. His position within the town's élite was further strengthened by his marriage the following year to a member of another influential Saint John family active in commercial affairs, and he soon began to receive official attention.

Following the death in 1821 of George Ludlow Wetmore*, clerk of the House of Assembly, Lieutenant Governor George Stracey Smyth* appointed Jarvis on 22 Jan. 1822 to replace him. Shortly afterwards he was given a seat on the first board of commissioners of the city's marine hospital, where he served with Alexander BOYLE, his wife's brother-in-law, and on 16 March he replaced Chipman as recorder for the city of Saint John during the latter's absence in England. On 19 October, Smyth appointed Jarvis to an assistant judgeship on the Supreme Court left vacant when John Saunders* replaced Jonathan Bliss* as chief justice, and on 30 October made him a member of Council. The appointment to the bench encountered strong opposition from Solicitor General William Botsford* and his supporters, in particular Sir James KEMPT, lieutenant governor of Nova Scotia, who thought the post should have gone to the solicitor general. When London overturned Smyth's decision in the spring of 1823 and gave the office to Botsford, Jarvis went to England to lay his case before the government. In compensation, the authorities that July made him king's assessor (similar to the office of attorney general) in Malta. He remained in that post until the end of 1827 when it was eliminated as part of a cost-cutting exercise. His next appointment was to replace Samuel George William Archibald* as chief justice of Prince Edward Island.

When Jarvis was sworn into office on 30 Aug. 1828 he was the only professional jurist in Prince Edward Island. The post had had a troubled history there, including a series of singularly poor appointments. Several earlier chief justices, among them Thomas Tremlett* and Cæsar Colclough*, had been removed for their inability to walk the fine line separating the contending political and social interests. Jarvis, in contrast, put himself above politics, and he did know something about the law. In addition to his judicial duties, which at the outset lasted a fortnight thrice annually, Jarvis initially took his attendance at the Island's Council seriously. There he was a moderating and conciliating force.

His knowledge of the law revealed a number of problems in the administration of justice in the colony. On his arrival he found that members of the bar were "much given to habits of intemperance," and he apparently conducted his court in a strict and professional manner. When one barrister who had been suspended for unprofessional activity appealed to the Privy Council, Jarvis's concern over the success of the appeal was not that his decision had been overturned, but rather that his authority to improve the general character of the bar had been weakened. Although his court had several unpaid assistant judges, the burden of work in a jurisdiction where litigation was frequent and contentious fell upon the chief justice. He complained bitterly throughout his career about the workload, describing in 1830 a "very laborious sitting of the court – for ten successive days I did not get home till 8 in the evening & one day not until midnight." Two years later he observed that the solicitor general alone held 68 briefs for civil trials.

In 1831 the House of Assembly had struck a select committee to inquire into the state of the courts of justice and Jarvis was among those examined. The committee recommended that the Supreme Court sit in circuit, that courts of general sessions be established, and that provision be made for a salaried professional judge to sit as an assistant to the chief justice and serve as master of the rolls of the Court of Chancery. When it became clear that the measure would be opposed owing to the cost, Jarvis apparently offered to preside at the sittings of the circuit court if his travelling expenses were defrayed. Although the circuit courts were finally established in 1833 no provision was made for an additional judge and thus Jarvis was forced to travel extensively, for he sat in each of four districts twice yearly. As his wife reported angrily in July 1836, without an assistant judge Jarvis was "obliged to keep his mind so intent on the business that I really fear he will be worn out." He had to sit for days on end, often in excessive heat, and without relief. "Since the beginning of November last year," his wife noted, "there has been eight Courts held on the Island and Edward has charged seven Grand Juries, whereas

when he came first here there were also but three courts held during the year."

His first years on the Island were also full of uncertainty. Although he did not take entirely seriously rumours in 1832 of the annexation of Prince Edward Island to Nova Scotia, in which case he would lose his job, he was none the less hopeful of an appointment to New Brunswick that never came. Despite his complaints and ambitions, by 1833 Jarvis felt well enough established to begin development of an estate on land just outside Charlottetown. He intended the house to be of brick – not a typical building material on the Island but an understandable one for a man planning a family seat "for generations yet to come." Most material was imported from England, and the construction was not completed until 1835, at enormous expense, more than "one hundred per cent upon the original estimates and contracts." Furnishing was finished in 1836, and early in 1837 the Jarvises held a house-warming ball for 81 persons, although the private bedrooms had still not been painted. Mount Edward was a large, two-storeyed mansion, containing ballrooms and several other public rooms, a substantial number of bedrooms, two kitchens, and servants' quarters. Nor was its size merely a matter of ostentation. The Jarvises had public responsibilities for entertaining, as well as children anxious for amusement through balls and dances, in addition to a large family circle, mainly resident in New Brunswick. Mount Edward typically housed not only the immediate family, but a minimum of three live-in servants and a constant assortment of permanent and temporary house guests, both kin and friends: the problems of travelling to the Island made long visits essential, but they were standard practice everywhere in the 19th century. Even with the help of servants, running this establishment was a major responsibility and expense, and Jarvis was forced to abandon it in January 1848 for smaller quarters; his son would return to Mount Edward after his father's death.

By the late 1830s both Jarvis and his wife were in continued ill health, the chief justice suffering from what was perhaps an occupational hazard but certainly a serious professional disability: encroaching blindness made it difficult for him either to read or to write. In 1839 Lieutenant Governor Sir Charles Augustus FitzRoy wrote to the Colonial Office expressing concern about the "very precarious state" of the chief justice's eyesight and making his recommendation for a successor. Jarvis, however, did not resign. Despite his wife's health problems and continual worries about money – the family enterprises in New Brunswick upon which he relied to supplement his salary were not prospering – Jarvis was advised by Island doctors to travel to England to seek relief for his affliction. He left Halifax on his own in June 1841,

Jarvis

and two months later his wife suddenly died. She had not felt up to the journey, but had kept her pain from her husband. Upon his return to Charlottetown in November, Jarvis was on the verge of a nervous breakdown, with financial worries, family responsibilities, and guilt about leaving his wife intermixing to produce a severe depression. As he himself described it, "I cannot shake off the dreadful weight & oppression which hangs increasingly upon my spirits & the slightest exciting cause wholly overpowers me. . . . The utmost indifference to every passing event & occupation possesses me & I cannot overcome it." He carried on with his judicial duties – increasingly dependent on his salary for his livelihood – but without enthusiasm or commitment.

Although his eyesight temporarily improved, other ailments took their toll and he began to experience ever greater problems in administering the judicial system, particularly after his eyes again gave out in 1843. Despite his problems some rejuvenation came to Jarvis that year when he unexpectedly remarried. The decision was taken because his eldest daughter, who had been running the large household, decided herself to marry. "The want of eyesight, to read," Jarvis bemoaned, "makes me extremely helpless & forlorn." After marrying Elizabeth Gray, one of his first wife's closest friends and her own choice as her successor, Jarvis re-entered the Charlottetown social whirl, boasting proudly of his renewed ability to be at a ball until 3:00 A.M. and in his court-room a few hours later. For several years his public activity ebbed and flowed with his health and personal situation. When in September 1847 Elizabeth died giving birth to their third child, Jarvis again went into a deep depression, feeling "wholly unfit for any business" and anxious to "leave the Island for as long a time as I can remain absent." He continued to sit on the bench, but pressed the assembly with increasing urgency for an assistant judge, adding in one family letter, "Were it not that my children require my assistance, I think I would at once resign my office, if I could get any small retiring allowance." In 1848 the assembly finally provided a grant of £400 and passed a bill to appoint an assistant judge and master of the rolls, a measure first proposed in 1831. Jarvis's relief was short-lived, however, for his salary was one of those affected by the concessions involved in the granting of responsible government to the colony in 1851. The legislation greatly reduced the payments to Jarvis and exacerbated his financial problems. The salary reduction led to continual friction with the assembly and the Colonial Office until his death on 9 May 1852. He was succeeded by Robert Hodgson*.

Jarvis had always tried to remain politically neutral. When public opposition to Lieutenant Governor Sir Henry Vere Huntley* reached the point where the House of Assembly in 1846 censured him by a vote of 19 to 3, Jarvis observed, "I almost stand alone in having had no personal collision with His Excellency." On the whole, Jarvis's relative lack of involvement in Island politics, especially in his latter years, probably worked to his advantage. Although there were those who would have preferred a Supreme Court with a higher profile, most political factions on the Island were content to allow Jarvis to continue.

J. M. Bumsted and H. T. Holman

N.B. Museum, Jarvis family papers; Reg. of marriages for the city and county of Saint John, book A (1810–28): 94. PAC, MG 24, B13. PANB, MC 288, MS8a, 12 Oct. 1811; Trinity Term, 1820; RG 2, RS6, A3: 103, 150, 157–59; RG 18, RS538, B5, pt.1: 43, 63, 66. PRO, CO 158/36: 1287; 158/56: 2902; 159/5, 7–8; 226/54: 238. St Paul's Anglican Church (Charlottetown), Reg. of marriages, 12 Dec. 1843 (mfm. at PAPEI). Supreme Court of P.E.I. (Charlottetown), Estates Division, liber 5: f.191 (will of E. J. Jarvis). P.E.I., House of Assembly, *Journal*, 25, 26 April 1831; 14, 23 April 1841; 8 March 1848; 31 March 1851. *Royal Gazette* (Charlottetown), 10 May 1852. *The calendar of King's College, Windsor, Nova Scotia* (Halifax), 1880–81: 63. *The Jarvis family: or, the descendants of the first settlers of that name in Massachusetts and Long Island, and those who have more recently settled in other parts of the United States and British America*, comp. G. A. Jarvis et al. (Hartford, Conn., 1879), 28–29, 60. "Provincial chronology," *New Brunswick Magazine* (Saint John), 2 (January–June 1899): 285. *An Island refuge: loyalists and disbanded troops on the Island of Saint John*, ed. Orlo Jones and Doris Haslam (Charlottetown, 1983), 120–21. Lawrence, *Judges of N.B.* (Stockton and Raymond), 240, 270–79. J. M. Bumsted, "The household and family of Edward Jarvis, 1828–1852," *Island Magazine* (Charlottetown), no.14 (fall–winter 1983): 22–28. J. W. Lawrence, "The first courts and early judges of New Brunswick; read before the New Brunswick Historical Society, November 25, 1874," N.B. Hist. Soc., *Coll.* (Saint John), no.20 (1971): 8–34. W. O. Raymond, "New Brunswick schools of the olden time," *Educational Rev.* (Saint John), October 1894: 89–90.

JARVIS, SAMUEL PETERS, militia officer, office holder, and lawyer; b. 15 Nov. 1792 in Newark (Niagara-on-the-Lake), Upper Canada, eldest surviving son of William Jarvis* and Hannah Owen Peters*; m. 1 Oct. 1818 Mary Boyles Powell, daughter of Chief Justice William Dummer Powell*, in York (Toronto), and they had five sons and four daughters; d. 6 Sept. 1857 in Toronto.

Samuel Peters Jarvis enjoyed an initial advantage in the emerging colonial society of Upper Canada. His father, who had gained the patronage of Lieutenant Governor John Graves Simcoe*, was the first provincial secretary and registrar, and, while the Jarvis family was not wealthy, it did enjoy the comparative luxury of three servants to minister to household needs. Young Jarvis was educated along with many of his peers by the Reverend John

Strachan* at his Cornwall grammar school. In 1810 he was articled to Attorney General William Firth*, but his law studies in York were interrupted by the War of 1812. He joined Captain Stephen Heward's flank company in the 3rd York Militia which assisted Major-General Isaac Brock* at the capture of Detroit in August 1812 and at Queenston Heights in October. After that battle he acted as one of the pallbearers for Lieutenant-Colonel John Macdonell* (Greenfield) when he was interred with Brock at Fort George (Niagara-on-the-Lake). Jarvis later saw action in the engagements at Stoney Creek and Lundy's Lane. He also obtained several minor administrative posts during the war: in January 1814 he was commissioned to act as assistant secretary and registrar to his father, and that December, in the absence of John Powell, he was made clerk of the Legislative Council.

Jarvis was called to the bar in 1815. Two years later he was appointed clerk of the crown in chancery, an administrative post in the House of Assembly which he was to hold for the next 20 years. His real ambition, however, was to follow in his father's footsteps as provincial secretary and registrar, a position which he seemed to feel should be his by right of succession as the eldest Jarvis male. Circumstances and his own personality thwarted that ambition. Jarvis possessed a fiery temperament and an impetuous nature combined with a strong sense of family and personal honour. Such traits involved him in a number of incidents, most of which came to nothing. In 1817, however, the feud which had simmered for a decade between the Ridout and Jarvis families came to a head when Samuel quarrelled with 18-year-old John Ridout, a son of Surveyor General Thomas Ridout*. On 12 July Jarvis and Ridout, accompanied by their seconds Henry John Boulton* and James Edward Small*, confronted each other just north of the town of York, and Ridout was killed. The duel badly split the local élite: the Ridouts certainly never forgave Jarvis for his part in the affair. The timing of the duel was also unfortunate for the development of his career, since his father died that August while Samuel was in jail awaiting trial. Although the courts exonerated him in the fall, his position at the centre of controversy temporarily ruined his chances for preferment. Duncan Cameron was appointed to the coveted secretaryship, though Jarvis briefly filled the position in Cameron's absence. He also succeeded Cameron as civil and private secretary to the acting lieutenant governor, Samuel Smith*, and served in that capacity until August 1818.

During the summer of 1818 Jarvis moved to Queenston and pursued an active career in law there and later in Niagara. In 1824 he returned to York where, nearly a decade after the fatal duel, he again became enmeshed in a *cause célèbre*. On 8 June 1826, in response to the vitriolic and sometimes personal attacks of the *Colonial Advocate*, a group of tory young bloods invaded William Lyon Mackenzie*'s shop, damaging the interior and scattering his printing type. Mackenzie, who had been facing bankruptcy, received damages of £625 in the ensuing trial, and the award was collected by subscription from disgruntled senior members of the "family compact" and from York lawyer Samuel Peters Jarvis, now almost 34 years old, who on that June evening had led the group of young men in their late teens and early twenties. His hot temper and misplaced sense of pride had once again led to his involvement in a questionable affair with negative consequences for the cause he espoused. Despite this second blot on his public character he obtained the position of deputy provincial secretary and registrar through an involved rearrangement of government posts in 1827. The following year Lieutenant Governor Sir Peregrine MAITLAND pointed out in a memorandum to his successor, Sir John Colborne*, that although Jarvis's "very imprudent Act" had had "an effect injurious to the Government," Maitland did not feel that his past actions should interfere with his chances for advancement.

Jarvis occupied the position of deputy secretary until 1839, but he was not destined to succeed to the secretaryship itself. Instead, he had to content himself with the post of chief superintendent of Indian affairs for Upper Canada, to which Lieutenant Governor Sir Francis Bond Head* had on short notice seconded him in June 1837 when it had become evident that the Indian Department's aged incumbent, James Givins*, was growing senile. With the outbreak of the rebellion of 1837–38 a few months later, Jarvis was active in defending the established order and in hunting down suspected rebels. In December 1837 he raised and commanded a unit of militia volunteers named the Queen's Rangers and at the end of the month he witnessed Andrew Drew* and his men setting fire to the rebel steamer *Caroline* at Navy Island. On his return from Niagara early the following year he acted as commandant of the Toronto garrison and in March was president of the court martial which tried the American Patriot, Thomas Jefferson SUTHERLAND. That September, Provincial Secretary Duncan Cameron died. Jarvis's frustration must have been great when Lieutenant Governor Sir George ARTHUR refused to recognize his services or consider his pleas about the temporariness of his Indian Department position. The provincial secretaryship was granted to Richard Alexander Tucker*, the former chief justice of Newfoundland, who had recently arrived in Upper Canada; Jarvis remained chief superintendent of Indian affairs.

During Jarvis's term of office (1837–45) no government department was to be examined so closely or so often as Indian affairs. The first inquiry took place in 1839. Sir George Arthur commissioned Judge

Jarvis

James Buchanan MACAULAY to take over the inquiry begun by Tucker and act as a one-man board of investigation. Macaulay thought the department's chief problem was attracting "persons sufficiently diligent, active and zealous" to supervise its programs. His report of April 1839 was followed in January 1840 by a second one, composed as part of a general examination of all departments of the government which had been carried out by several committees. The Indian Department was reviewed by committee no. 4, whose three members, Macaulay, Vice-Chancellor Robert Sympson JAMESON, and William Hepburn, a former clerk in the department under Givins, congratulated Jarvis for the vigour with which he carried out his official duties. The chief superintendent appeared to have passed his first two tests with flying colours. These appearances, however, were deceptive: Jarvis was a close friend of Macaulay's, whose views were reflected in both reports. A third investigation was to have very different results.

In 1842 Governor Sir Charles Bagot* established a three-man royal commission to inquire into the structure of the Indian Department in the new province of Canada. Its first report, delivered in January 1844, was directly responsible for Jarvis's being stripped of his official rank in all but name that May and for his forced retirement the following year. Chaired by Rawson William Rawson, the governor's civil secretary, the commission found the department's administration chaotic and the chief superintendent incompetent and possibly dishonest. Indian Department accounts could not explain the whereabouts of more than £4,000, a sum which was later adjusted to an amount in excess of £9,000 and then again revised downwards. Jarvis's attempts to defend himself only resulted in new evidence being gathered against him. In contrast to the two previous inquiries, the commission found him evasive and uncooperative, a view that would be shared by Rawson's successor as civil secretary, James Macaulay Higginson*, who assumed responsibility for the Indian Department on 15 May 1844.

What had happened to the man who seemed to be a model administrator as late as 1840? It would be attractively simple to see Jarvis as merely a larcenous official who was found out. A more adequate explanation is that he was unfamiliar with mid-19th-century accounting techniques. He maintained both his private and his official department accounts at the Bank of Upper Canada, of which he was also a director, and juggled money back and forth between the two in the gentlemanly, informal, and confused manner of an earlier period. The Indian Department's bookkeeping had always been problematic: Jarvis was simply unfortunate enough to be the first chief superintendent asked to provide such a detailed accounting. In this regard he was utterly dependent upon his chief clerk, George Vardon, who may have had reasons of his own for wishing to see Jarvis discredited.

As chief superintendent, Jarvis was subjected to strains that would have been intolerable even for an individual whose competence was unquestionable. His official position embroiled him in the affairs of the Grand River Navigation Company, the interests of which were often antithetical to those of the Six Nations Indians on the Grand River Reserve. Indeed, he was president of the company in 1843–44, precisely at the time he was being forced to defend himself against the findings of the Bagot commission. Jarvis, who found the Indian Department confusing enough, was ill equipped to deal with all these matters simultaneously.

The office of chief superintendent was abolished on 1 July 1845 and Jarvis retired from the Indian Department in disgrace. He continued the attempt to clear himself of charges of peculation but seems never to have been successful. On the other hand, the government seems never to have forced him to restore the missing funds for which it claimed he was responsible, an indication that the issue of his corrupt behaviour was not as clear as it had first appeared to be. Right up until his death Jarvis was still trying to untangle his complex financial affairs. In order to pay off some of his debts he had hired John George Howard* during the summer of 1845 to subdivide for public sale the 100-acre park lot east of Yonge Street which he had received from his father in 1816. Two years later Hazelburn, the house he had built there for his family 23 years before, was torn down to make way for the street which still bears Jarvis's name. Yet despite his precarious financial position his last years were spent pursuing the activities of a socially well-connected, semi-retired man of private means: fishing trips to the Gaspé, hunting in the Bruce Peninsula, grand tours of Great Britain and the Continent. In the middle 1850s his health declined; he died in 1857 and was survived by his wife and seven of his children. His eldest son, Samuel Peters Jarvis Jr, had a distinguished career in the British army; other descendants took their places in the professional and business life of Toronto.

Samuel Peters Jarvis, attempting the life of an 18th-century tory squire, had become an anachronism. The mid 19th century with its growing emphasis on commerce and industry – and proper bookkeeping and procedures – was an age which he never fully understood. Along with his outdated attitudes went a mediocre intelligence that spelled disaster for him as an administrator. These factors were sufficiently powerful to neutralize the advantages he had enjoyed at the beginning of his career, so that he was left on the fringes of power in the small Upper Canadian community. In Jarvis's life can be seen a partial answer to the question of what became of the "family compact."

DOUGLAS LEIGHTON and ROBERT J. BURNS

Samuel Peters Jarvis wrote two works concerning his early misadventures: *Statement of facts, relating to the trespass on the printing press, in the possession of Mr. William Lyon Mackenzie, in June, 1826; addressed to the public generally, and particularly to the subscribers and supporters of the "Colonial Advocate"* published anonymously in Ancaster, [Ont.], in 1828 (another edition was issued at York [Toronto], probably in the same year); and *To the public; a contradiction of "The libel," under the signature of 'A relative,' published in the "Canadian Freeman," of the 28th February, 1828; together with a few remarks, tracing the origin of the unfriendly feeling which ultimately led to the unhappy affair, to which that libel refers* ([York], 1828). The "unhappy affair" is the Jarvis–Ridout duel of 1817; the matter was revived in a letter published in the *Canadian Freeman* (York) on 28 Feb. 1828 under the signature and title quoted by Jarvis. The original letter is republished on pp.3–8 of the pamphlet as a prelude to Jarvis's refutation.

AO, MS 35; MU 1127, McCormick–Dunsford–Jarvis–Read family tree; MU 1532–37; RG 22, ser.155, will of S. P. Jarvis. Law Soc. of U.C. (Toronto), "Journal of proceedings of the Convocation of Benchers of the Law Society of Upper Canada" (8v., MS), 1810. MTL, S. P. Jarvis papers. PAC, MG 19, F24; RG 10, A1, 6–7; A4, 47–77, 124–39, 498–509, 739, 748–49, 751; A5, 142–50, 510–12, 752–60; A6, 718–21; C2: 10017: 80–81. Can., Prov. of, Legislative Assembly, *App. to the journals,* 1844–45, app.EEE; 1847, app.T, app.VV. *Town of York, 1815–34* (Firth). *Montreal Gazette,* November 1846–February 1847. *Montreal Herald,* November 1846–February 1847. *Pilot* (Montreal), November 1846–February 1847. Armstrong, *Handbook of Upper Canadian chronology.* Chadwick, *Ontarian families. The Jarvis family: or, the descendants of the first settlers of that name in Massachusetts and Long Island, and those who have more recently settled in other parts of the United States and British America,* comp. G. A. Jarvis et al. (Hartford, Conn., 1879). R. J. Burns, "The first elite of Toronto: an examination of the genesis, consolidation and duration of power in an emerging colonial society" (PHD thesis, Univ. of Western Ont., London, 1974). J. D. Leighton, "The development of federal Indian policy in Canada, 1840–1890" (PHD thesis, Univ. of Western Ontario, 1975). Middleton, *Municipality of Toronto,* 1: 96–99. Scadding, *Toronto of old* (1873). A. S. Thompson, *Jarvis Street: a story of triumph and tragedy* (Toronto, 1980). R. J. Burns, "God's chosen people: the origins of Toronto society, 1793–1818," CHA *Hist. papers,* 1973: 213–28. [J.] D. Leighton, "The compact tory as bureaucrat: Samuel Peters Jarvis and the Indian Department, 1837–1845," OH, 73 (1981): 40–53.

JOBIN, ANDRÉ, notary, Patriote, justice of the peace, politician, militia officer, and office holder; b. 8 Aug. 1786 in Montreal, son of François Jobin and Angélique Sarrère, *dit* La Victoire; m. first 16 May 1808 Marie-Joseph Baudry; m. secondly 22 April 1816 Marie Archambault, widow of Louis Baudry, in Montreal; m. thirdly 16 Feb. 1824 Émilie Masson, sister of Marc-Damase Masson*, in Sainte-Geneviève (Sainte-Geneviève and Pierrefonds), Lower Canada; m. fourthly 27 May 1839 Marie-Élize Dorval in L'Assomption, Lower Canada; there were several children; d. 11 Oct. 1853 in Sainte-Geneviève.

After graduating from the Sulpician Collège Saint-Raphaël in 1805 and completing his articles, André Jobin was commissioned a notary on 24 Sept. 1813. He opened an office in Montreal, drafting his first deed on 24 October. He began slowly, averaging only a little more than a deed per week during his first year and drawing most of his clients from the ranks of labourers and artisans. A large proportion of his practice consisted of drafting agreements between masters and journeymen and paid substitutions for active militia service. By 1820 he was averaging more than a deed a day and had expanded his clientele to include merchants, builders, and real estate speculators. From the beginning, his work revealed a clarity of expression and a careful attention to detail.

By the late 1820s Jobin had become one of the more prominent Patriotes in the city. In 1828 he was elected to the committee which drew up instructions for John Neilson*, Denis-Benjamin Viger*, and Augustin Cuvillier*, the agents of the House of Assembly, sent to explain Lower Canada's grievances to the British parliament. Although commissioned a justice of the peace on 17 Aug. 1830, Jobin made no secret of his political allegiance during and after the riot in Montreal that preceded the election of Daniel Tracey*. On 21 May 1832 British regulars fired on a crowd, killing three French Canadians. Jobin and his colleagues Joseph ROY and Pierre Lukin were the only magistrates who had opposed the request for use of the military to maintain order. He pointedly attended the funeral of the victims and in September helped Roy gather new evidence which resulted in the arrest of the commanding officers for the second time. In November he was elected to a committee to protest the events of 21 May. For these activities the governor, Lord Aylmer [Whitworth-Aylmer*], struck Jobin from the list of magistrates in 1833, although he was restored to office by Lord Gosford [Acheson*] in 1837.

Jobin's dismissal did not alter his politics. In 1834, shortly after he had moved to Sainte-Geneviève on Montreal Island, he became a member of the committee established in the parish to foster political action on the basis of the 92 Resolutions. In November of the following year the popularity he had gained as a "martyr" in 1833 helped ensure his election by acclamation to the House of Assembly for the riding of Montreal County. In the house Jobin gave consistent support to Louis-Joseph Papineau*.

Jobin was a highly visible Patriote in the months prior to the rebellion of 1837. At a mass meeting in

Jobin

Montreal on 15 May, which became a model adopted in other parts of the colony, he moved the resolution accusing Lord Gosford of using a façade of conciliation to effect coercion. Jobin also served on the Comité Central et Permanent du District de Montréal, which coordinated the agitation throughout the district. In August he resigned his recently restored commission as justice in protest against Gosford's attempt to prohibit magistrates from attending political meetings. In his letter of resignation Jobin asserted that his commission meant nothing since it had not been conferred by the people, and he concluded on a dramatic and defiant note: "The sacrifice of my commission as a justice of the peace is too small a thing to be weighed against my most sacred right as a British subject (to discuss peacefully measures of interest to his country). I gladly renounce my commission . . . to preserve the title of free man." Jobin's act was applauded by the committee and the Patriote press, including the *Vindicator and Canadian Advertiser* and *La Minerve* which published the letter.

When the magistrates began to issue warrants for the arrest of leading Patriotes, Jobin went into hiding on 14 Nov. 1837 and remained there for more than five months. That period would forever remain a bitter memory. Faced with a rumour that the troops would burn the Jobins' house and any other building in which their property might be stored, his wife, Émilie, attempted to save the household effects by arranging a simulated auction sale by bailiff. The dishonesty of some of the purchasers caused the scheme to miscarry and Jobin's absence may have hastened his wife's death, which occurred at her father's house on 27 March 1838. On 27 April of that year the government issued a proclamation ending martial law. Jobin came out of hiding that day and was arrested on 3 May. Although charged with seditious practices, he was never tried, being released on a £1,000 bond on 7 July.

Jobin did not lose his taste for politics. In 1840, as notary for the Sulpicians, he travelled north of Montreal Island to organize opposition to the government's policy of gradually extinguishing the community's title to its vast seigneurial holdings. Some of his listeners at Saint-Benoît claimed that he passionately denounced the government and "the Scots" for having condoned pillage and arson during the rebellions and, now, for condoning theft of French Canadian lands. These alleged remarks, which a magistrate characterized as seditious, were vehemently, but not altogether convincingly, denied by Jobin.

Jobin ran as a reformer for Vaudreuil in the general election of 1841. The violent tactics of the supporters of his opponent, John Simpson*, helped bring about the defeat of Jobin, who barely escaped personal injury by jumping through a window. He was more successful in October 1843, winning a by-election in the riding of Montreal. In the election of 1844 on a platform of responsible government he trounced Viger, a leading ministerialist who had also been defeated in Richelieu. During his years as a member of the assembly from 1843 to 1851, Jobin voted with reform leader Louis-Hippolyte La Fontaine* on such major political issues as the bill outlawing secret societies, the status of the French language, and the Rebellion Losses Bill.

As a legislator Jobin devoted much of his energies to matters of a technical, legal nature such as land registration and the corporate powers of Roman Catholic religious orders. He was also active in the area of business law and commercial development, being one of the principal authors of statutes to regulate mutual life insurance companies (1845), to expand the turnpike road system near Montreal (1846), and to extend financial aid to railway construction (1849).

In 1849 Jobin introduced a bill to amend the act of 1847 establishing the notariate as a self-regulating profession. A storm of protest from the Montreal notaries, who had not been consulted, did not deter him. He succeeded in having his personal views written into law in the next session. The amending act of 1850 tightened the requirements for drafting and conserving deeds, provided for the financial autonomy of the boards of notaries in the districts of Montreal, Quebec, and Trois-Rivières through a system of mandatory dues, and restricted the supervisory jurisdiction of the courts to the few matters where it was needed, such as the suspension of notaries and the setting of fees.

During his last years Jobin enjoyed considerable prestige. He was named a director of the Montreal City and District Savings Bank in 1846 and a lieutenant-colonel of militia in 1847. In the latter year he was also elected the first president of the Montreal Board of Notaries, an office he resigned in disgust two years later during the dispute over his amending bill. In 1852 Jobin was named inspector of Roman Catholic schools for the city and county of Montreal. His standing among reformers was evident at the banquet to honour La Fontaine on his retirement from politics in 1851, when Jobin sat at the head table. Almost 50 years after Jobin's death, his memory was honoured by *La Revue du notariat*, which singled out his life to begin a biographical series on outstanding notaries.

Jobin was a man of diverse talents. He was respected in Sainte-Geneviève as a generous and effective patron of the schools and as a highly skilled arboriculturist. He also took a great interest in the geography of the Montreal area, probably as a result of his experience as a notary for the Sulpicians. That experience was put to good use in 1834 when he published an accurate map of the city and island which was used by the commission of inquiry headed by Lord Gosford in 1835–36. Jobin also drew a detailed plan of the Montreal prison during his incarceration. This plan was cited by *Le Devoir* in 1911 to refute the claims of *La Patrie* and the historian Laurent-Olivier David* that the Patriotes had been held in the dungeons of the old prison.

Jobin should be remembered, not only as a pioneer in the organization of the notarial profession, a useful legislator, and a successful politician, but also as a man who had the courage to act upon and suffer for his political principles.

F. MURRAY GREENWOOD

André Jobin's minute-book, containing instruments notarized from 1813 to 1853, is held by ANQ-M, CN1-215. The map of Montreal Island which Jobin drew up is at PAC, National Map Collection, H2/349-Montréal-1834 (1837). A copy of the plan of the Montreal jail is in the Fonds Ægidius Fauteux at the BVM-G.

ANQ-M, CE1-28, 16 févr. 1824, 14 oct. 1853; CE1-51, 16 mai 1808, 22 avril 1816. ANQ-Q, E17/6–52; P-316. PAC, MG 24, B2: 2901–3, 2925–28, 3608–11, 3875–82, 3993–98; RG 4, A1, 561. L.C., House of Assembly, *Journals*, 1832–33, app.M; 1835–37. *Elgin–Grey papers* (Doughty). *Debates of the Legislative Assembly of United Canada* (Abbott Gibbs *et al.*), 1843–51. "Document historique inédit sur la rébellion de 1837–38," *Le Devoir* (Montréal), 18 févr. 1911: 5–6. *Docs. relating to constitutional hist., 1819–28* (Doughty and Story). *La Minerve*, janvier–mars 1828; 1832–37; octobre–novembre 1844. *Vindicator and Canadian Advertiser* (Montreal), 1832–37. F.-J. Audet, *Les députés de Montréal (ville et comtés), 1792–1867* . . . (Montréal, 1943), 417–19. Fauteux, *Patriotes*, 275–76. *Quebec almanac*, 1832–37. J.-E. Roy, *Hist. du notariat*, 3: 147–70. André Vachon, *Histoire du notariat canadien, 1621–1960* (Québec, 1962). "André Jobin," *La Rev. du notariat* (Lévis, Qué.), 3 (1900–1): 25–28.

JOHNSTON, JAMES FINLAY WEIR, agricultural chemist, mineralogist, and author; b. 13 Sept. 1796 in Paisley, Scotland; m. 1830 one of the daughters of Thomas Ridley of Durham, England; d. 18 Sept. 1855 in Durham.

James Finlay Weir Johnston spent his childhood in Paisley and in Manchester, England, and Kilmarnock, Scotland. Although his formal education was sparse, he enrolled as a student of theology at the University of Glasgow in 1823, supporting himself by acting as a private tutor. He received an MA and a silver medal in philosophy in 1826 but continued on the rolls of the university until 1828. He operated a school in Durham from 1825 to 1830, when his marriage brought him a "competent income" that allowed him to abandon the school and pursue work in chemistry.

In 1833, after studying with the famous Swedish chemist, Jöns Jacob Berzelius, Johnston was appointed reader in chemistry and mineralogy at the newly founded University of Durham, a post he retained

until his death. A fellow of the royal societies of London and Edinburgh, Johnston was elected to fellowships in the geological and chemical societies; he also became an honorary member of the Royal Agricultural Society of England and a foreign member of the Royal Swedish Academy of Agriculture, and was chemist to the Agricultural Society of Scotland. Widely travelled and highly respected, Johnston sought to turn scientific knowledge to practical application and published many extremely popular works in agricultural chemistry. His *Catechism of agricultural chemistry and geology*, first published in 1844, went through 33 English editions in his lifetime, was translated into numerous languages, and was widely used in schools on both sides of the Atlantic. Among Johnston's other publications, *Lectures on agricultural chemistry and geology* and *The chemistry of common life* were influential. He also contributed articles and papers to the Royal Society, the British Association for the Advancement of Science, the Royal Agricultural Society, *Blackwood's Edinburgh Magazine*, and the *Edinburgh Review*.

In 1848, at the invitation of the New York State Agricultural Society, Johnston made plans to visit North America. New Brunswick, which was later added to his itinerary, was suffering a recession due to the reduction of Britain's preferential tariff on timber which had caused a decline in the staple trade of the colony, and there was considerable interest in revitalizing the province's economy. Well-worn arguments for agricultural self-sufficiency were reiterated, and the slowness of immigration to the province was lamented. Official and lay reports attributed this slowness to "a want of information as to [New Brunswick's] position and resources" in Britain. When news of Johnston's trip reached Saint John late in 1848, Moses Henry Perley* and other members of the local agricultural society recognized an opportunity to publicize the farming potential of New Brunswick, and asked Lieutenant Governor Sir Edmund Walker Head* to invite Johnston to the colony. The House of Assembly agreed to finance the venture and in June 1849, just weeks before his departure, Johnston agreed to report on the agricultural capabilities of the province.

Neither Johnston nor the provincial authorities clearly appreciated the implications of their arrangement. On his arrival, Johnston recognized that "the extent of the province, and the slow rate of travelling, would compel [him] . . . to devote some months longer to the work" than he had anticipated. The cost to the government ultimately amounted to £500, exclusive of travelling expenses incurred by Johnston and his provincial assistants James Robb* and James Brown*; Johnston's energy and vision, however, enabled him to accomplish the task with remarkable dispatch. Although most of September and early

October 1849 were given to his business in New York, he spent 53 days between August and November travelling some 2,000 miles of New Brunswick roads. In the six weeks before Christmas he wrote his sweeping yet detailed *Report*. The conviction that geological structure revealed agricultural potential was central to his interpretation of provincial capabilities. He devoted much effort to deciphering the still imperfectly known geology of New Brunswick and appended both geological and pedological maps to his report. But this deductive methodology was complemented by inductive empiricism. He sought responses to a series of questions which he had published in provincial newspapers, visited officials of local agricultural societies, talked with many farmers on his travels, and was an indefatigable observer of the landscapes through which he passed. Indeed, he saw the major virtue of his *Notes on North America, agricultural, economical, and social* (1851) in its presentation of the "matter-of-fact information" on the lower St Lawrence and New Brunswick revealed by his "agricultural eye."

Johnston's public appraisal of New Brunswick's agricultural potential, given in an address at Saint John in December 1849 and in his published *Report* (1850), was optimistic. The soils of New Brunswick were more productive than those in New York and Ohio, New Brunswick farmers achieved greater financial returns than did their counterparts in Upper Canada, and the land could sustain a population of perhaps four million. These conclusions were widely acclaimed within the province, where the sluggish economy seemed to deny conviction that progress and prosperity were possible. Sceptics who suggested that Johnston's information came from the most successful farmers on the best lands in the province were denounced, and the *Report*'s recommendations for a more scientific agriculture were commended to provincial settlers. Enthusiasm about agricultural matters grew. Soon after Johnston's arrival in the province James Robb had been instrumental in establishing the New Brunswick Society for the Encouragement of Agriculture, Home Manufactures, and Commerce. In 1851 a New Brunswick edition of *Elements of scientific agriculture* by Johnston's student, John Pitkin Norton, was published. The *Report* had gone into a second edition in 1850, with 10,000 copies intended for distribution in England. Thirteen years later, more copies of the *Report* were delivered by James Brown to communities in Britain to promote immigration to New Brunswick, and Johnston's *Catechism* was published at Saint John in 1861.

The immediate purposes of Johnston's visit to New Brunswick were served. His skill and experience infused energy into provincial proponents of improved agriculture and his writings helped publicize the colony in Britain. But in the long term, Johnston's impact was limited. Both immigration and scientific agriculture remained relatively uncommon in late-19th-century New Brunswick, and experience revealed that Johnston's appraisal of the province's agricultural potential was far too sanguine.

GRAEME WYNN

James Finlay Weir Johnston wrote extensively on the application of science to agriculture. The following works, originally published in Edinburgh and London, were among the most influential: *Lectures on agricultural chemistry and geology*. . . (1841), *Catechism of agricultural chemistry and geology* (1844), and *The chemistry of common life* (2v., [1853–55]), all of which went through many editions. The *DNB* and the *National union catalog* give some indication of the scope and popularity of his writings although neither work provides a comprehensive list.

Johnston's main North American publications are his *Report on the agricultural capabilities of the province of New Brunswick* (1st and 2nd eds., Fredericton, 1850) and the two-volume *Notes on North America, agricultural, economical, and social* (Edinburgh and London, 1851; also published Boston, 1851). In addition, his Saint John address was published under the title *The agricultural capabilities of the province of New-Brunswick, British North America; an address delivered before the Mechanics' Institute of the city of Saint John, New-Brunswick, on Friday evening, December 21st, 1849* (Saint John, 1850), as were two editions of his address to the New York State Agricultural Society. *Lectures on the general relations which science bears to practical agriculture, delivered before the New-York State Agricultural Society* (New York, 1850) apparently prints Johnston's own text; a version entitled *Lectures on the general relations of science to agriculture . . . delivered before N.Y. State Agricultural Society, January, 1850*, reported by Sherman Croswell (Albany, N.Y., 1850), was issued by the society.

The impact of Johnston's visit to North America is reflected by the popularity of a work by his student, J. P. Norton, *Elements of scientific agriculture* . . . , which was first published in Albany in 1850, went through many subsequent American editions, and appeared in a New Brunswick edition at Saint John in 1851, and by the publication of a 40th edition of Johnston's *Catechism of agricultural chemistry and geology* for use in New Brunswick schools (Saint John, 1861).

PANB, RG 2, RS7, 31–32; RG 3, RS13, A7. *Gentleman's Magazine*, July–December 1855: 545. Northumberland Agricultural Soc., *Report* (Miramichi, N.B.), 1849–50. "Professor Johnston's last work," *Blackwood's Edinburgh Magazine* (Edinburgh and London), 78 (July–December 1855): 548–61. Saint John Agricultural Soc., *Annual report* ([Saint John?]), 1848; *Proceedings at the annual meeting, with the report of the directors* (Saint John), 1850. *New-Brunswick Courier*, 1849–50. Graeme Wynn, "The assault on the New Brunswick forest, 1780–1850" (PHD thesis, Univ. of Toronto, 1974). C. A. V. Barker, "M. A. Cuming, V.S. (Edin.), M.R.C.V.S.: a biography and the inducement to settle in New Brunswick in 1852," *Canadian Veterinary Journal* (Ottawa), 17 (1976): 123–35.

JONES, HENRY, Owenite community founder; b. 21 or 22 May 1776 in the parish of Plympton St

Maurice, Devon, England, son of Richard Jones and Julia Maria Collier; m. first Elizabeth ——, and they had four sons and five daughters; m. secondly Susan ——; d. 31 Oct. 1852 in Maxwell (near Brights Grove, Ont.) and was buried in Plympton Township, Upper Canada.

Henry Jones, founder of Canada's only Owenite community and perhaps the earliest avowed socialist in British North America, came of an ancient Welsh landowning family which had been settled for some generations in Exeter and the surrounding countryside in Devon. He became a purser in the Royal Navy in 1794 and served in the Channel fleet during the Napoleonic Wars. By 1815 he had been retired on half pay. He subsequently lived with his wife, Elizabeth, in Bovey Tracey, enjoying perhaps the profits of what his brother the Reverend John Collier Jones called in 1818 "a fortunate adventure not many years since." In the early 1820s, like a number of military and naval officers with little to occupy them, Henry became interested in the ideas of the Welsh socialist Robert Owen and particularly in his proposals for "villages of unity and cooperation" – self-sufficient communities conceived as a solution to the problem of acute unemployment among the hand-loom weavers who were being replaced by machinery.

By the time the British and Foreign Philanthropic Society for the Permanent Relief of the Labouring Classes was founded in London in 1822 to establish cooperative communities, Jones was already sufficiently involved in the Owenite movement to become a member of the society's committee. Shortly afterwards, when the society sponsored a scheme for a community at Motherwell in Scotland, he made a loan of £5,000 (approximately a third of his assets and presumably the profits of his early "adventure") towards its funds. The sum was given to Archibald James Hamilton, a former army officer, who with Abram Combe was the leading organizer of the community. In later years the loan was to prove the cause of litigation that would consume much of Jones's time and energy.

The Motherwell community never came into existence. In its place, in 1825, Hamilton and Combe founded a community near Glasgow at Orbiston, the estate of Hamilton's father. Jones came to Scotland that year, subscribed towards the funds of the community, and became one of its auditors. In the summer of 1826, when Combe had to leave Orbiston temporarily because of illness, Jones took charge of it. But by 1827 the difficulties caused by the poor selection of members had made him apprehensive of its future. In a letter of 23 March he broached to Hamilton the matter of a return of his loan to the Motherwell community and accused him of an "Aristocracy of decision" in his "pronunciation respecting the identity of the friends of the New Views, – and the proper understanding of the

principles of the System." Nevertheless, Jones continued, "We may go on, seperately, to exert ourselves in what we believe will best advance the object which we profess to have in view, and where we can, conjointly." His forebodings were justified when the Orbiston community came to an end after Combe's death in August.

As early as April 1827 Jones had been planning to establish a new, agrarian community in British North America, influenced perhaps by Owen's purchase two years earlier of the New Harmony community in Indiana. In the fall of 1827 Jones set off with his valet, Alexander Hamilton, to seek a location. They sailed to New York and travelled, mostly by water, to Lake Huron, where Jones found suitable land for the community in Upper Canada near the mouth of Perch Creek, about 10 miles northeast of present-day Sarnia. Jones returned to Britain later that year. In 1828 he gathered together a group of settlers from the Glasgow area and secured from William Huskisson, the colonial secretary, authority to purchase a large tract of land. His plans to acquire land in Upper Canada were favoured by the appointment in August of Sir John Colborne* as the province's lieutenant governor. Jones's brother John Collier, who had become rector of Exeter College, Oxford, had married the sister of Lady Colborne, a Devon girl.

Jones invested a great deal of his remaining capital in the community, which he called Maxwell, reputedly after Robert Owen's residence at New Lanark, Scotland. He hoped eventually to settle between 50 and 100 families. The first contingent of 20 people, which arrived early in 1829 accompanied by a surgeon, consisted mostly of former members of the Orbiston community, almost all of whom were Lowland Scots and unemployed hand-loom weavers. In June, Charles Rankin was instructed to survey the tract Jones had selected in Sarnia Township and in November Jones secured patents on seven lots there, including the site of Maxwell. A log building was erected that year with Orbiston as a model, for there were individual family apartments and common kitchens and dining-rooms. A contemporary sketch shows the building, not entirely completed, occupying three sides of a rectangular green; there is a central, two-storey block and the wings are single-storeyed. Jones also established a store and a school on Owenite principles. The extent of his personal commitment was shown by the fact that in August 1830 his wife and five of his children joined him at Maxwell. His eldest son, Henry John (whose diaries tell much about the settlement's later life), became a crown lands agent at York (Toronto) and later at Chatham, but the rest of the family, and other relatives who arrived afterwards, stayed at Maxwell.

Not much is known of the day-to-day life of the community. About 50 acres were brought under cultivation during the first season and by 1830 Jones

Jones

had also established a lucrative fishery at Point Edward, which, surveyor Roswell Mount* observed in March, was being operated by Jones's "People." The wharfs and storehouses which he erected about this time in the nearby settlement of Port Sarnia (Sarnia) may have been related to this operation. Maxwell, however, suffered in its early days from the inexperience of its members in pioneering techniques and from the presence of ample land in the vicinity which could be bought for little and privately cultivated. The Methodist missionary Peter JONES reported that even before the end of 1829 the settlers were beginning to leave, although four years later Henry Jones claimed to have brought out a total of between 70 and 80 settlers.

The major crisis in the community came in 1834 after Jones had left on a trip to England and Scotland, in part to confirm the purchase authorization made by the Colonial Office six years earlier. On 17 May a fire started in the community house and, as Henry John Jones recorded, "in less than an hour Maxwell had disappeared – the greater part of the books and light furniture was saved." The few people remaining in the community after the fire lived in the barn and above the stables until a new building was erected. After Jones returned to Upper Canada in June he occupied himself with land matters, and in the general election that fall he unsuccessfully contested the constituency of Kent. By this time he had evidently consented to the revocation of his claim to lands in the Sarnia Township tract, which was bought a year later from the crown by Samuel Street*. Jones nevertheless retained his patented lots and a claim to additional land as the grant appropriate to his naval rank.

Jones sailed for England again in 1835 and stayed there and in Scotland for at least eight years. Archibald James Hamilton had died in 1834 and for several years Jones was involved in complex litigation to get back from Hamilton's estate the money he had advanced to the Motherwell community. But his time was by no means entirely spent in the courts. As Henry John Jones remarked in 1839, he became "further gone in Socialism than ever." He bombarded his reluctant relatives in Canada with letters suggesting that they should form a kind of "family community" with the few settlers who remained at Maxwell. He talked vacuously, his son recorded, "of bringing out another ragged regiment to form a community in case his own family shd fail to come to terms." The family's disinclination to further his wishes was certainly one of the reasons for the constant delays in his return.

At the same time Jones became involved in Britain in a series of schemes for ameliorating the lot of his fellow man there. In 1837 he suggested a "collegiate plan" (a kind of benefit society) for naval officers. Two years later, while he was trying to get employment as an emigration agent for Canada, he became involved in a "property tax association," which anticipated the arguments of Henry George, the American economic theorist, by suggesting that all existing taxes should be abolished and replaced by a single tax on land. In 1840 Jones was planning a "Society for the instruction of music" and in 1841 a "Domestic Benefit Club." Some time before 1840 he had encountered the phalansterian teachings of Owen's great communitarian rival, François-Marie-Charles Fourier of France. Jones appears to have been critical of some aspects of them from the beginning, as he had also become of some of Owen's theories, if one can judge from his poem "Collegiate life," which was published in the London *Era* in 1840. A didactic work in the Byronic manner (but without the Byronic sparkle), "Collegiate life" specifically mocks both Owen and Fourier for their more extreme eccentricities of theory and, while hailing the "social state," sees its achievements in voluntary associations of the well-to-do pooling their means. The type of association suggested by Jones seems to consist of freely organized groups modelled on colleges or "Clubs" and has a remote flavour of Rabelais's imaginary Abbey of Thélème. Jones calls for a practical Christianity, but since he decries charity and replaces mercy with justice, his attitude must be regarded as heterodox.

Thus, when Jones returned to Upper Canada some time after July 1843, he may have partly shed his Owenism and may have largely remained immune from phalansterianism. In 1840, after Owen's presentation to Queen Victoria had resulted in vigorous criticism of his principles, Henry John Jones had noted that his father seemed "a little ashamed of 'Socialism.'" He nevertheless appears to have remained a utopian thinker and planner and, in the sense of desiring a social change in the direction of voluntary association apart from the state, a kind of libertarian socialist. A surviving portrait by Field Talfourd, which probably dates from this period, shows an elderly, almost bald man with a lean aquiline profile, a straight narrow mouth above a firm chin, and the clear eyes of a sailor accustomed to distances – a face suggesting obstinacy and vision combined.

Jones's days of activity were in fact ended. He found that the few people at Maxwell who remained from the original settlement had established their own households and had no interest in forming a new community. The family home at Maxwell had been burnt down in 1839 but was rebuilt in 1842 and there Jones lived the rest of his life. Nobody in Canada was influenced by his utopian ideas, but he kept up an active correspondence, commenting on world affairs and sometimes reminiscing about his naval past, with those who shared his ideals. His death on 31 Oct. 1852 appears to have been sudden or the result of a very short illness, for letters written by him that month give no hint of sickness and suggest a man who was mentally active, morally upright, and sensitively aware of his surroundings as he praised the beauty of autumn and talked of his crops.

GEORGE WOODCOCK

Henry Jones is the author of "Collegiate life," a series of cantos published anonymously in the *Era* (London), 23 Feb., 1, 8, 15 March 1840.

AO, RG 1, A-I-6: 9735, 10750–51, 11729–32, 11852–53, 12673–77, 13112–14; A-II-2, 1: 27, 161, 365, 370–71, 382; C-I-1, petitions of Henry Jones, 12 Oct. 1833, 27 Nov. 1845; C-I-3, 124: 102. Lambton County Library (Wyoming, Ont.), H. J. Jones, diary, 1833. Lambton Land Registry Office (Sarnia, Ont.), Abstract index to deeds, Sarnia Township, concession 9, lots 4–5, 14–17; front concession, lot 71 (mfm. at AO, GS 1356). Motherwell District Council Library (Motherwell, Scot.), A. J. Hamilton papers, Henry Jones to Hamilton, 23 March 1827. National Library of Wales (Aberystwyth), MSS 12378B (A. C. Evans MSS, 23: letters and pedigrees). Ont., Ministry of Natural Resources, Surveys and Mapping Branch (Toronto), Field book no.614: Roswell Mount, 1829: 48–48A, 50A, 51. PAC, MG 24, A40, 2: 118–20; 21: 6102–3; 26: 7890–92 (mfm.); RG 1, L3, 259: J16/7; RG 5, A1: 52555–56, 55565–66, 78125–30, 78136–44. PRO, CO 42/424: 386–87; CO 384/20: 143–44. St George's (Anglican) Church (Sarnia), Reg. of burials, 1, no.7; 2, no.31. Sarnia Public Library, Henry Jones papers; Julia and J. H. Jones diaries. West Devon Record Office (Plymouth, Eng.), Plympton St Maurice, reg. of baptisms, 13 June 1776. Peter Jones, *Life and journals of Kah-ke-wa-quo-nā-by (Rev. Peter Jones), Wesleyan missionary,* [ed. Elizabeth Field and Enoch Wood] (Toronto, 1860), 244. *Motherwell and Orbiston: the first Owenite attempts at cooperative communities; three pamphlets, 1822–1825* (New York, 1972). *Canadian Emigrant, and Western District Commercial and General Advertiser* (Sandwich [Windsor, Ont.]), 17 Aug. 1833; 12 Sept., 3 Nov. 1835. *Lambton Observer, and Western Advertiser,* 8, 22 May 1856. *Sarnia Observer, and Lambton Advertiser,* 9 Sept. 1864. G.B., ADM, *Navy list,* 1815, 1823.

Arthur Bestor, *Backwoods utopias: the sectarian origins and the Owenite phase of communitarian socialism in America: 1663–1829* (2nd ed., Philadelphia, 1970). Nevil Burke, *St. John-in-the-Wilderness Anglican Church, Perche, Ontario, 1856: a history . . . , 1856–1972* ([Forest?], Ont., [1972?]). Alexander Cullen, *Adventures in socialism: New Lanark establishment and Orbiston community* (Glasgow and London, 1910; repr. [New York], 1971). Ian Donnachie, "Orbiston: a Scottish Owenite community, 1825–28," *Robert Owen, prince of cotton spinners,* ed. John Butt (Newton Abbot, Eng., 1971), 135–67. J. T. Elford, *A history of Lambton County* (Sarnia, 1967). J. F. C. Harrison, *Quest for the new moral world: Robert Owen and the Owenites in Britain and America* (New York, 1969). J. M. Wolfe, "Some early Canadian utopias" (paper read at the Soc. for Utopian Studies, Saint John, N.B., 1982). John Morrison, "'The Toon O'Maxwell' – an Owen settlement in Lambton County, Ont.," *OH,* 12 (1914): 5–12.

JONES, PETER (known in Ojibwa as **Kahkewaquonaby,** meaning "sacred feathers" or "sacred waving feathers"; also known as **Desagondensta,** in Mohawk, signifying "he stands people on their feet"), Mississauga Ojibwa chief, member of the eagle totem, farmer, Methodist minister, author, and translator; b. 1 Jan. 1802 at Burlington Heights (Hamilton), Upper Canada; m. 8 Sept. 1833 Elizabeth Field* in New York City, and they had five sons, four of whom survived infancy; d. 29 June 1856 near Brantford, Upper Canada.

Peter Jones was born in a wigwam on Burlington Heights, the second son of Augustus Jones*, a retired surveyor, and Tuhbenahneequay (Sarah Henry), the 22-year-old daughter of Wahbanosay, a Mississauga chief. Shortly after his birth he was given the name Kahkewaquonaby by Wahbanosay. Since Augustus was legally married to Sarah Tekarihogen (Tekerehogen), the daughter of the leading Mohawk chief, Henry [Tekarihogen*], he left the upbringing of Peter and his elder brother John* to Tuhbenahneequay. She raised them, teaching them the religion and the customs of her people, and they remained with her until 1816. Among the Mississaugas, Kahkewaquonaby learned how to hunt, fish, and canoe, and gained the reputation of being an excellent hunter.

Augustus Jones was interested in his sons' welfare. In 1805 he had obtained a deed from the Mississauga band for a two-square-mile grant for each of them at the mouth of the Credit River, but he failed in his attempt to secure the government's recognition of this transfer. Eleven years later, when he saw that the band at the western end of Lake Ontario was disintegrating (a result of declining population and scarcity of game), he took direct charge of his two Mississauga sons. He sent Kahkewaquonaby to a school near his farm at Stoney Creek. There the young Mississauga became known as Peter Jones, and learned to speak, read, and write in English. When Augustus moved with his Iroquois family to his extensive lands at the Grand River in 1817, he took Peter, now 15 and a strong youth, with him. On this farm Augustus taught him to care for his poultry and livestock, and to farm. Peter liked the Iroquois and he enjoyed his seven years among them. As a result of his stepmother's membership in an important Mohawk family, he was adopted by that tribe and given the name Desagondensta. At home with his father, stepmother, and eight half-brothers and -sisters, Peter spoke English and never learned Mohawk.

While he was still a young man, Christianity did not appeal to him, although at his father's request he was baptized in the Church of England in 1820. He later confessed, quite frankly, that one of the reasons that led him to accept baptism was the wish that "I might be entitled to all the privileges of the white inhabitants." By his own admission his baptism had no effect on his life, since he continued to be "the same wild Indian youth as before." At the age of 20 the ambitious Peter decided to return to school. Throughout the summer of 1822 he worked in a brickyard near Brantford to

Jones

obtain the money to pay his fees. After studying arithmetic and writing the following winter, he returned to his father's farm in the spring of 1823. Determined to succeed in the white man's world, he hoped eventually to enter the fur trade as a clerk. He might well have done so had not a Methodist camp-meeting changed his entire life.

Purely out of curiosity Peter, with his half-sister Polly, attended a camp-meeting of the Methodist Episcopal Church in June 1823. During the five-day gathering in Ancaster Township, Peter became a convert, his soul touched by the preachings of the evangelical Christians. At the end of the meeting the Reverend William CASE, seeing Peter rise to his feet to acknowledge his conversion, cried out with joy: "Glory to God, there stands a son of Augustus Jones of the Grand River, amongst the converts; now is the door opened for the work of conversion among his nation!"

When the Reverend Alvin Torry came to preach at the Grand River in 1823, he formed a native congregation around Chief Thomas Davis [Tehow-agherengaraghkwen*] and Peter Jones. The young Mississauga encouraged his people to settle near the chief's home, which became known as Davisville or Davis's Hamlet. Many of Jones's relatives came: his mother Tuhbenahneequay; his uncle Joseph Sawyer [Nawahjegezhegwabe*] with family, including Peter's cousin Kezhegowinninne*; his half-sister Wechi-kiwekapawiqua and her husband, Chief Wageezhe-gome [Ogimauh-binaessih*]. By the end of the year Jones had begun teaching Sunday school and in the spring of 1824 he helped build a regular chapel for the growing Christian community. That summer he vowed to devote his life to missionary work. By the end of the summer of 1825 he had converted over half of his band to Christianity. That fall Lieutenant Governor Sir Peregrine MAITLAND offered to build for the converts a village of 20 houses on the west bank of the Credit River, in what is now Mississauga. Jones moved there early in 1826 and the village, called the Credit Mission, was completed by the winter of 1826–27. He was received on trial for the Methodist itinerancy in 1827.

During the summer of 1826 Jones had persuaded almost all those band members who were not yet Christians to enter the Methodist church. The faith of many Mississaugas in their own culture and religion had been shaken, as the life of one of their chiefs, Kineubenae*, demonstrates. In one generation they had lost more than half of their population and almost all of their hunting and fishing grounds. In their anxious state they looked to Jones for direction, entrusting him entirely with the conduct and management of their affairs. The native Christians felt that only he and his brother John, both English speakers, could deal effectively with the white missionaries and

the Indian Department. In January 1829 the Credit band elected Peter one of their three chiefs, and he thus acquired a position of great influence, both in the band's council and as an official spokesman.

The work of teaching his people to farm and to lead a settled way of life proved difficult, but he did have allies. His brother John, who worked as the village schoolmaster, became his most valuable assistant. Whenever they felt the band's interests were threatened they went to York (Toronto) to petition the government. In 1825 they strongly urged that the white man's intrusion on the band's salmon fishing at the Credit River should end. When, the following year, the Indian Department failed to pay the band the full annuity owed under the terms of the land surrender by the Mississaugas in 1818 [see Kineubenae], they vigorously protested. Peter could also rely on his half-sister Polly, who lived at the mission, on John's Iroquois wife, Kayatontye (Christiana), who taught the Mississauga women housekeeping, and on the family of his niece Nahnebahwequay*. In the village, his uncle Joseph Sawyer, Chief Wageezhegome, Samuel Wahbuneeb, and the three Herchmer brothers (William, Lawrence, and Jacob) had all "occasionally lived among white people" and possessed a knowledge of farming. By the fall of 1827 each family in the village had begun to cultivate a quarter-acre plot around their home and shared in the cultivation of a 30-acre field. Within ten years the community had cleared another 850 acres.

The news of the success of Peter Jones and the Methodists at the Credit spread quickly through the white community. When Jones went on tours in Upper Canada to raise money for mission-work, many whites came to hear him. According to Samuel Strickland*, his sermons in English were "both eloquent and instructive." In response to his appeals, several white settlers gave individual contributions and as a group various churches gave presents. The Methodists of Vittoria, in Norfolk County, gave a stove to heat the schoolhouse, and those in York and on Yonge Street presented the band with a new plough.

Jones did not restrict himself to preaching to whites during his travels. In February 1826 he travelled to the Bay of Quinte, attracting Indian families from as far as 30 miles away, and the Methodists settled the resulting group of native converts on Grape Island. Among the Mississaugas led by Jones into the Methodist church from the Belleville and Kingston bands were Peter Jacobs [Pahtahsega*] and John Sunday [Shah-wun-dais*], both of whom became highly successful missionaries to the Indians. The stationing of capable white missionaries at the Credit, first Egerton Ryerson* in September 1826 and then James Richardson*, allowed Jones to carry out lengthier missionary tours to other Ojibwa bands.

The phenomenal success of the Methodists among the Mississaugas alarmed Lieutenant Governor Maitland and the province's Executive Council, who had hoped that the native converts could eventually be won over to the Church of England. But Jones refused to abandon the Methodists. When John Strachan*, the powerful Anglican archdeacon of York, promised to increase the salaries of Peter and John beyond whatever the Methodists could possibly afford to pay them, in return for the brothers' support, they both declined his offer.

Throughout the late 1820s Peter continued energetically with his missionary work. With the help of his brother John he prepared the earliest translations of the Bible into Ojibwa. He successfully led into his church the Mississaugas at Rice Lake, the majority of the Ojibwas at Lake Simcoe, many at the Muncey Mission (southwest of London), and several Ojibwa bands on the eastern shore of Lake Huron. To raise money for the missions he accompanied William Case and several native converts in 1829 on a tour of the northeastern United States. In early 1831, along with George Ryerson*, he left on a missionary tour of Britain, and it proved a complete success. As he wrote back to John, "When my Indian name, *Kahkewaquon-aby*, is announced to attend any public meetings, so great is the curiosity, the place is sure to be filled." During his year abroad he gave more than 150 addresses and sermons attired in his Indian costume, and collected over £1,000 for the Methodist church's mission-work. As well, he petitioned the Colonial Office on native land interests. He attracted great attention and on 5 April 1832, shortly before his return to Upper Canada, he had a private audience with King William IV.

On his English tour the celebrated Indian met Eliza Field, a pious Englishwoman who came to North America in 1833 to become his wife and lifelong companion in the mission field. She helped him copy out his translations of the scriptures into Ojibwa, taught the Indian girls how to sew, and instructed them in religion. Very supportive of her husband, who became a fully ordained Methodist minister on 6 Oct. 1833, Eliza worked to bring about the Europeanization of the Credit River band by giving them the skills and beliefs with which they could compete as equals with the whites. Peter and Eliza Jones believed unquestioningly that Christianity and European civilization represented man's highest form of existence.

In the late 1830s Jones and the Methodists, with their allies in Britain, Sir Augustus Frederick D'Este and Dr Thomas Hodgkin of the Aborigines Protection Society, resisted the proposal, first made by Lieutenant Governor Sir Francis Bond Head*, to remove the Credit band and other southern Indian groups to the barren Manitoulin Island. Behind Head's proposal lay the desire to protect the Indians by removing them

completely from white influences. But Jones and others knew that most of Manitoulin was too rocky to farm and that the Mississaugas would have to revert to hunting. On behalf of the Credit band, Jones went to England in late 1837. Because of the Colonial Office's preoccupation with the rebellion of 1837–38, he was unable to discuss either the issue of removal or Indian claims to land titles with Lord Glenelg, the colonial secretary, until the following spring. Glenelg, however, refused to approve Head's proposal. Impressed by the well-spoken native leader, he arranged a short audience for him with the young Queen Victoria in September 1838. With his wife, Jones returned to Upper Canada late that year.

Head had left the colony early in 1838 but the Methodists' mission-work was soon plagued by more direct threats. In 1840 the fragile union of the Canadian Methodists and the British Wesleyans dissolved [*see* Matthew Richey*]. Peter and the majority of the Ojibwa Christians remained with the Canadians, but William Case and several of the bands sided with the Wesleyans. The split hampered the advance of the Methodists among the Indians, the two Methodist churches remaining apart until their reunion in 1847. As well, at the Credit, opposition to Jones's leadership had arisen in the mid 1830s and continued through the following decade. Many Indians there objected to being made over into brown Englishmen. William and Lawrence Herchmer, in particular, fought to remain Indian as well as Christian. They protested against the harsh discipline imposed on the young. At issue too was Peter's personal claim, which William Herchmer disputed, to a portion of the grant conceded by the band to him and his brother John in 1805. As a result of this internal strife, departures from the village became a serious problem.

The 1840s proved a difficult decade for Jones. From 1841 to 1849 he was stationed at the Muncey Mission, a demanding post with three tribes under his charge, Ojibwa, Munsee Delaware, and Oneida, all speaking different languages. His health began to deteriorate, and, as a calotypic photograph of 1845 clearly shows, he had gained considerable weight. For months at a stretch he made no entries in his diary, which comprises a significant record of missionary work among the Indians of Upper Canada. As a young man, he had spent a great deal of his time taking notes for a history of his tribe, but now he gave his manuscript little consideration. Even his third missionary tour of Britain, in 1845, failed to revive his spirits. He again attracted huge crowds, particularly in Scotland, but the constant travelling began to depress him. On 23 October he wrote to Eliza from Glasgow, "I am getting heartily tired of begging." The British public was, it seemed to Peter, only interested in him as the exotic Kahkewaquonaby dressed out in his "odious"

Jones

native custom, and not as Peter Jones, the civilized Indian that he had worked so hard to become.

Despite his weakened state, he continued to work for his people. In 1840 the band council had begun to consider the relocation of the Credit village because of the increasing severity of problems later enumerated by Jones: the pressure of white settlement, the scarcity of wood, the inconvenience of the village arrangement for farming, and the uncertainty surrounding his people's claim to land at the Credit. Finally, in 1847, Jones led more than 200 band members to land donated by the Six Nations in the southwest corner of their reserve on the Grand River. He worked hard to ensure the early success of New Credit, as the reserve was named, and applied repeatedly to the government to have the funds from the sale of the Credit lands used for its development. As well, he frequently approached the Indian Department for support in securing farm supplies and erecting buildings. Probably through his initiative, a Methodist mission was established there by William Ryerson* in 1848.

After his people's resettlement, Jones's health failed to improve. Though in 1850 his physician ordered him to retire, forbidding him to travel or "to perform his clerical duties," he continued to make long trips: in 1852 to the northern missions on the upper Great Lakes, the following year to a missionary meeting in New York City, and in 1854 to a convention in Syracuse, N.Y., which, Jones reported, was attended by 300 to 400 Indians. In 1851, after a brief period of residence in London, Upper Canada, the Joneses had moved into Echo Villa, a fine brick house they had built about 20 miles north of New Credit, near Brantford. Born in a wigwam, Kahkewaquonaby spent his last years in a Classical Revival style country home. His final illness began in December 1855 and was brought about by one of his frequent visits to New Credit. After completing the tiring journey in a lumber wagon, he felt unwell, but he was determined to attend the council meeting the following day and refused to return to Brantford. When the meeting was over he rode home through a drizzling rain. As soon as he reached Echo Villa he had to lie down. Despite consultations with Dr James Bovell* in Toronto, he never recovered and died on 29 June 1856.

The attendance of whites and Indians at his funeral illustrates the respect in which both communities held him. In its obituary notice, the Toronto *Globe* noted that the funeral procession was the largest ever witnessed in Brantford and included "upwards of eighty carriages besides a great number of white people and Indians on foot." As Egerton Ryerson, a close friend for 30 years, stated in his funeral sermon, Jones had "enjoyed the esteem of, and had access to, every class of Canadian society." Under the terms of his will, he left to his wife Echo Villa and a £1,000

policy from the Canada Life Assurance Company. The Indian missionary's diaries were edited by Eliza and the Reverend Enoch Wood* and published in 1860 by Anson Green* as his *Life and journals*. Eliza edited his historical notes, which appeared in 1861 as *History of the Ojebway Indians*, an invaluable source for an understanding of the early Ojibwa converts in Upper Canada. In 1874 his third son and namesake, Peter Edmund (Kahkewaquonaby), a medical doctor, became a chief at New Credit.

In his lifetime Peter Jones accomplished much for his people. Before his conversion to Methodism, his Mississauga band had appeared to be on the verge of disintegration. However, as a result of his intervention and that of other native and white missionaries, the Credit River people and many other Ojibwa bands in southern Upper Canada successfully adjusted to the European presence.

DONALD B. SMITH

Manuscript material by or concerning Peter Jones is available in a number of repositories. His papers in the Peter Jones collection at Victoria University Library (Toronto) include his manuscript for *History of the Ojebway Indians . . .* , his personal notebook (entitled the "Anecdote book"), and his diaries for 1827–28, as well as incoming and outgoing correspondence, including a volume of letters written to his wife, Eliza, between 1833 and 1848, copied in her hand. The collection also includes the Eliza[beth Field] Jones Carey papers. The Jones papers at the UCA include a manuscript autobiography entitled "Brief account of Kahkewaquonaby, written by himself" and his diary for 1829; the Credit Mission record-book is also at the UCA. Other records for the mission, as well as the Credit Band Council minutes, are found in the Paudash papers in PAC, RG 10, A6, vol. 1011. Jones's will is at the AO, RG 22, ser.155.

The published works of Peter Jones are extensive; only a representative selection is provided below. Additional titles and editions are listed in the *National union catalog* and in J. C. Pilling, *Bibliography of the Algonquian languages* (Washington, 1891), which has been reprinted as volume 2 of his *Bibliographies of the languages of the North American Indians* (9 parts in 3 vols., New York, 1973).

Jones's diaries, edited after his death by Eliza Jones and Enoch Wood, were published as *Life and journals of Kah-ke-wa-quo-nā-by (Rev. Peter Jones), Wesleyan missionary* (Toronto, 1860). His *History of the Ojebway Indians; with especial reference to their conversion to Christianity . . .* , edited by Eliza, was issued posthumously in London in 1861.

The majority of Jones's work, however, was published during his lifetime. His article concerning the relocation of his band appeared in the *Christian Guardian* of 12 Jan. 1848 under the title "Removal of the River Credit Indians." Most of his other publications reflect his work as a clergyman and missionary. Numerous sermons and speeches given during his tour of Britain in 1831–32 went into print, and include the following pamphlets: *Report of a speech, delivered by Kahkewaquonaby, the Indian chief, in the Wesleyan Chapel, Stockton-on-Tees, September 20th, 1831* (Stockton-on-

Tees, Eng., 1831); *The sermon and speeches of the Rev. Peter Jones, alias, Kah-ke-wa-quon-a-by, the converted Indian chief, delivered on the occasion of the eighteenth anniversary of the Wesleyan Methodist Missionary Society, for the Leeds District . . .* (Leeds, Eng., [1831]); and *The substance of a sermon, preached at Ebenezer Chapel, Chatham, November the 20th, 1831, in aid of the Home Missionary Society* (Maidstone, Eng., n.d.), a copy of which is available at the UCA. Several others were reproduced in the *Wesleyan Preacher* (London), among them sermons delivered ". . . at the Welch Methodist Chapel, Aldersgate Street, on Sunday afternoon, January 22, 1832," in volume 1 (October 1831–April 1832): 265–70; ". . . at Ebenezer Chapel, King Street, Bristol, on Sunday evening, February 5, 1832": 422–27; and his "Farewell sermon delivered . . . at City Road Chapel, on Sunday evening, April 7, 1832, in aid of the funds of the Methodist Sunday schools," volume 2 (April–October 1832): 108–15. A letter by Jones, dated 20 July 1831, appears on pages 270–72 of volume 1.

Peter Jones was also responsible for translating many religious works into Ojibwa, sometimes in collaboration with his brother John. He edited John's translation of *The Gospel according to St. John* (London, 1831), and both brothers were involved in the translation of Matthew, published under the Ojibwa title *Mesah oowh menwahjem-oowin, kahenahjemood owh St. Matthew* (York [Toronto], 1831). Peter's translation of *The first book of Moses, called Genesis* was issued in Toronto in 1835. His translations also include *Part of the discipline of the Wesleyan Methodist Church in Canada* (Toronto, 1835), and a number of Ojibwa hymns, among them *Collection of hymns for the use of native Christians of the Chippeway tongue* (New York, 1829); *A collection of Chippeway and English hymns, for the use of the native Indians . . .* (Toronto, 1840); and *Additional hymns translated by the Rev. Peter Jones, Kah-ke-wa-qu-on-a-by, a short time before his death, for the spiritual benefit of his Indian brethren, 1856,* issued posthumously in Brantford, [Ont.], in 1861.

Miniature portraits of Peter and Eliza Jones, painted in 1832 by Matilda Jones, are in Eliza's papers in the Peter Jones collection at Victoria University Library. The 1845 photograph mentioned in the biography is one of several calotypes of him held by the Scottish National Portrait Gallery (Edinburgh).

PAC, RG 10, A1, 712. [Egerton] Ryerson, "Brief sketch of the life, death, and character of the late Rev. Peter Jones," *Christian Guardian*, 23 July 1856. Methodist Episcopal Church, Canada Conference, Missionary Soc., *Annual report* (York [Toronto]), 1826: 6; 1827: 12–13. Benjamin Slight, *Indian researches; or, facts concerning the North American Indians . . .* (Montreal, 1844). Samuel Strickland, *Twenty-seven years in Canada West; or, the experience of an early settler,* ed. Agnes Strickland (2v., London, 1853; repr. Edmonton, 1970), 2: 59. *Christian Guardian,* 25 Aug., 1 Sept. 1852; 13 April 1853; 18 Oct. 1854. *Globe,* 4 July 1856. *Western Planet* (Chatham, [Ont.]), 4 July 1856. "Calendar of state papers," PAC *Report,* 1935: 265–68; 1936: 572–73; 1937: 601–8. Mary Byers and Margaret McBurney, *The governor's road; early buildings and families from Missis-sauga to London* (Toronto and Buffalo, N.Y., 1982). Elizabeth Graham, *Medicine man to missionary: missionaries as agents of change among the Indians of southern Ontario, 1784–1867* (Toronto, 1975). Egerton Ryerson,

"The story of my life" . . . (being reminiscences of sixty years' public service in Canada), ed. J. G. Hodgins (Toronto, 1883). D. B. Smith, "The Mississauga, Peter Jones, and the white man: the Algonkians' adjustment to the Europeans on the north shore of Lake Ontario to 1860" (PHD thesis, Univ. of Toronto, 1975). Alvin Torry, *Autobiography of Rev. Alvin Torry, first missionary to the Six Nations and the northwestern tribes of British North America,* ed. William Hosmer (Auburn, N.Y., 1864). A. E. Kewley, "John Strachan versus Peter Jones," United Church of Canada, Committee on Arch., *Bull.* (Toronto), 16 (1963): 16–28. D. B. Smith, "The transatlantic courtship of the Reverend Peter Jones," "Eliza and the Reverend Peter Jones," "Peter and Eliza Jones: their last years," and "Historic peace-pipe," in *Beaver,* outfit 308 (summer 1977): 4–13; (autumn 1977): 40–46; (winter 1977): 16–23; and outfit 315 (summer 1984): 4–7.

JONES, ROBERT, draftsman, builder, merchant, office holder, farmer, and militia officer; b. 26 April 1778 in Hawkhead, near Paisley, Scotland, son of William Jones and Margaret Locke; m. 2 Aug. 1803 Hannah Simpson of West Kilbride (Strathclyde), Scotland, and they had eight children; d. 25 Nov. 1859 in Pownal, P.E.I.

Little is known about the early life of Robert Jones except that he served in the Royal Navy before spending seven years studying cabinet-making and drafting in the area around London. He immigrated alone to Prince Edward Island in 1809 and was reunited with his wife and four children two years later. Following his arrival he joined Edmund Waters in the general merchandising and shipping business in Charlottetown, continuing with the firm after Alexander Birnie became Waters's partner. Jones served as a bookkeeper, cabinet-maker, and builder; in 1812 he spent 58 days "surveying lumber and loading" the *Princess of Wales* and 44 days as a "joiner on board."

Jones, who was a freemason while he lived in Charlottetown, seems to have been a respected and practical man. He was appointed surveyor of timber for Prince Edward Island in 1813 and travelled frequently to the Pinette–Belfast area where he appears to have been an agent for Waters and Birnie. Two years later and with a business associate, Robert Patton, leased a mill on the Pinette River owned by Lord Selkirk [Douglas*]. Even though a total of 90 man-days were spent repairing the mill, William Johnston*, Selkirk's agent, informed the owner in 1815 that Jones and Patton were "behind the rent, altho' Jones is an industrious laborious man," and mentioned the "repeated breaking down of the dam which had been faulty in its original construction." Small wonder Jones gave up the lease the following year and moved to Pownal where he cleared some land, built a house, and began farming.

He then became involved in a number of public-spirited activities, first as a captain in the

Joseph

militia from 1820 to 1827, and then as surveyor of timber for townships 49 and 50 in 1821. Two years later he joined Paul Mabey*, Donald McDonald, John Stewart*, and others in petitioning High Sheriff John MacGregor to convene meetings that would enable Islanders to air their grievances against Lieutenant Governor Charles Douglass Smith, acting receiver general John Edward Carmichael*, and Ambrose Lane. In 1825 Jones was commissioner of highways for townships 48, 49, 50, and 55, and in 1826, 1829, and 1830 he served as fence viewer and constable. He was appointed a census taker in 1827; the only fragments of this census known to exist are from some of the lots he canvassed. That year he was also among those who joined Lieutenant Governor John Ready* in forming the Central Agricultural Society, one of whose goals was to obtain and distribute better seed grain and potatoes to all who were interested.

Despite the numerous public offices Jones held, he made his most lasting mark as a draftsman and builder. Although his plans for the new court-house in Charlottetown were rejected shortly after his arrival in favour of the design by John Plaw*, he constructed a number of buildings in the capital. His masterpiece, however, completed in the mid 1820s for John MacLennan, was St John's Presbyterian Church in Belfast, whose proportions and simple lines have been described as an architectural gem of "carpenter gothic." Its "crowning feature," the tower, was inspired by Sir Christopher Wren, whose churches Jones had seen in London. A public duty connected with his career as a builder was discharged in 1834–35 when he was appointed to inspect and report on the workmanship and the materials used in building Charlottetown's Government House and Central Academy.

A devout Baptist and staunch abstainer, Jones frequently conducted Sunday church services and was instrumental in forming a community church before Baptist churches were built in the Pownal area. In addition to continuing his trade by designing and building houses, furniture, sleighs, and wagons, he was often called upon to render advice and assistance to members of the community. When he was almost 70 years old he planned, and then helped his son build, the house that is still the Jones homestead in Pownal. His great-grandson, John Walter Jones*, was to become premier of the Island.

Orlo Louise Jones

The Robert Jones papers are in the possession of Mrs Wilbur Jones and Arthur Jones (Pownal, P.E.I.) (copy at P.E.I. Museum and Heritage Foundation (Charlottetown)).

PAPEI, RG 8, Warrant books, 1827–28, no.522; 1834–35, no.951; 1835–36, no.1064. P.E.I. Museum and Heritage Foundation, Charles Jones coll. *Islander*, 9 Dec. 1859. *Prince Edward Island Register*, 13 Sept. 1823; 23 April, 13 May 1825; 28 March 1826; 19 June 1827; 24 March 1829; 15 June 1830. *Weekly Recorder of Prince Edward Island* (Charlottetown), 27 June 1811. W. B. Hamilton, *Local history in Atlantic Canada* (Toronto, 1974), 171. M. A. Macqueen, *Hebridean pioneers* (Winnipeg, 1957), 42–43, 48–49, 78. M. R. Ross, "Pioneer builder of St. John's Church," *Historic sidelights, Prince Edward Island* ([Charlottetown, 1956]), 69–71. F. H. Sinnott, *History of the Baptists of Prince Edward Island* (n.p., n.d.).

JOSEPH, JOHN, public servant; b. *c.* 1801 in England; m. 19 July 1837 Anne Elizabeth Hagerman, daughter of Christopher Alexander Hagerman*, and they had one son; d. 28 or 29 May 1851 in Toronto.

John Joseph's early life is obscure though there is reason to believe that he was related in some way to Samuel Joseph, a well-known 19th-century English sculptor. As a young man John was befriended by the famous British abolitionist, William Wilberforce, who was in the habit of paying for the education of promising young men. Joseph probably lived with him for a time and served as a kind of private secretary to Wilberforce, who in old age was nearly blind. No doubt through the close relationship between Wilberforce and the Stephen family, Joseph obtained a clerkship in the Colonial Office, to which James Stephen was permanent counsel. William Lyon Mackenzie* visited the Colonial Office in 1833 and later recollected Joseph as "an awkward and loutish lad who opened the door and handed a chair."

In December 1835 Joseph resigned his Colonial Office position to accompany Sir Francis Bond Head* to Upper Canada as his private secretary and civil secretary of the province, his appointment dating from 25 Jan. 1836. Although his salary was only £208 per annum, he supplemented it by collecting "fees on Marriage, Medical, and Surveyor's Licences, Certificates, Commissions, and all Instruments, &c. under the Seal of the Governor's office," and he later estimated that he received "between nine and ten hundred pounds a year." He was a conscientious and industrious official who handled his work efficiently. He did not seek nor was he permitted by Head to take any important role in public affairs, but, with his good connections and "distinguished and gentlemanly appearance," he quickly became a part of the local political and social establishment through both his marriage and his close friendship with John Beverley Robinson* and his family.

When Head was recalled in 1838, Joseph was reappointed on 26 March as secretary by the new lieutenant governor, Sir George Arthur, on the recommendation of Stephen and the Wilberforce family. Joseph's relationship with Arthur was not as close and congenial as that with Head and, since the new lieutenant governor did not "see many things in the same light" as Head, Arthur found the relationship "productive of inconvenience & of some unpleasantry." Deciding he needed a secretary who was prepared to accept more independent responsibility, he arranged for Joseph to be transferred to the clerkship of the Legislative Council on 16 June 1838 and replaced him with John MACAULAY. Joseph was happy to accept. Although his income was to be less, the "calamity" of his wife's sudden death on 14 June led him to prefer a "more retired" situation.

At the time of the union of the Canadas in February 1841, Joseph found himself without a job, the clerkship of the Legislative Council of the new united parliament having been given to James FitzGibbon*. The new governor-in-chief, Lord Sydenham [Thomson*], promised Joseph a job as soon as a suitable position became available. This promise was repeated by Sydenham's successors, Sir Charles Bagot* and Sir Charles Theophilus Metcalfe*, but Joseph did not obtain a permanent appointment until 1847. In the mean time he was "dependent on precarious employment" as a clerk of assize, arranged by John Beverley Robinson. He accompanied Robinson on his judicial circuits throughout the province, while continuing his search for "justice" by writing numerous petitions and applying for a variety of vacant registrarships, collectorships, and other positions. Finally on 20 May 1847 Lord Elgin [Bruce*] appointed him clerk of the Executive Council at an annual salary of £500.

On 2 May 1851 he applied for two months' sick leave, which was granted, but his health deteriorated rapidly and he died later that month of "Chronic asthma." At the time of his death he was living at the home of John Beverley Robinson* Jr, who had married a younger sister of his deceased wife. Joseph's only son, Frank John, followed a similar career, serving as assistant law clerk of the Legislative Assembly of Ontario.

J. K. JOHNSON

ACC-T, St James' Cathedral (Toronto), Reg. of marriages, 19 July 1837. PAC, RG 5, C1, 107, file 5612; 195, file 15860; 322, file 675; 333, file 1246; C2, 7: 164. St James' Cemetery and Crematorium (Toronto), Record of burials, 31 May 1851. *Arthur papers* (Sanderson). *Constitution* (Toronto), 26 July 1837. Armstrong, *Handbook of Upper Canadian chronology*, 8, 37. *Toronto directory*, 1850–51. "Cars telescoped . . . ," *Globe*, 9 Feb. 1895: 13.

JOSEPH, JUDAH GEORGE (Gershom), businessman and craftsman; b. 1798 in Exeter, England; m. Rebecca ——, and they had two daughters and two sons; d. 17 May 1857 in Toronto.

The late 1830s and the 1840s saw the small Jewish population of Toronto augmented by the arrival of Jews from England, Germany, Lower Canada, and the United States. Primarily shopkeepers and skilled artisans – grocers, clothiers, jewellers, tobacconists – they sought to integrate themselves into the social and economic life of Toronto. Judah George Joseph, one of the most prominent members of this early community, was born of a family described as "highly respectably connected." Much of his early life had been spent in the Channel Islands of Guernsey and Jersey. He immigrated to the United States in 1829 and eventually established himself as a jeweller and optician in Cincinnati. He prospered but "his generous nature led him to become a victim of false friends" and he was swindled in business, losing most of his property. About 1840 Joseph reportedly moved with his family to Hamilton, Upper Canada. Possibly attracted by the mercantile prospects offered by Toronto, he settled there between 1842 and 1844 and opened a business on King Street near the St Lawrence Market, then the city's leading commercial district. In addition to his trade as a jeweller and optician, he produced silverware, timepieces, mathematical and drafting instruments, and scientific equipment. Joseph observed traditional Jewish practice and closed his shop on Saturday, the Jewish sabbath. He built a successful business, acquired property, and enjoyed considerable popularity as a result of his "cheerful, open-hearted and familiar" manner.

Joseph was instrumental in the formation of the Hebrew Congregation of Toronto, a small group which evidently performed no synagogal functions. In September 1849, however, Judah Joseph and Abraham Nordheimer* laid the foundation for Jewish community organization in Toronto by purchasing land for a cemetery from John Beverley Robinson*. This half-acre property, located in York Township east of Toronto (on present-day Pape Avenue), was to be held in trust for the Hebrew Congregation, which probably had the cemetery as its sole concern. In 1850 Joseph's young son, Simeon Alfred, was one of the first to be buried there and it is possible that the lad's illness may have motivated this purchase by Joseph who was "domestic and intensely attached to his family."

Joseph declined to join the city's first synagogue, Toronto Hebrew Congregation (Sons of Israel), when it was organized in 1856. The membership requirements may have seemed restrictive to Joseph; there also appears to have been a social, if not economic, gap between the cemetery trustees (established members of the city's society) and the synagogue's founders (many of whom, such as Lewis Samuel*, were recent arrivals). Nevertheless, as an observant Jew, Joseph continued his annual payments through the synagogue for the support of a ritual slaughterer, which was evidently a practical arrangement to facilitate his purchase of kosher meat. About 1859 the burial-ground was transferred to the synagogue (now

Juneau

Holy Blossom Temple), which Joseph's son, George, joined two years later.

The glowing obituaries occasioned by Joseph's death described him as "a good citizen and a sincere friend." His funeral, conducted at the Jewish cemetery in orthodox fashion, was attended by a large number of people and probably provided the first opportunity for local residents to observe a Jewish ritual. Following his death, Joseph's business was continued by his son-in-law Henry Joseph Altman of Birmingham, England, and Thomas Hawkins Lee of Toronto.

STEPHEN A. SPEISMAN

AO, RG 1, A-I-6, 25; RG 22, ser.305, J. G. Joseph; RG 55, ser.3, 1, nos.194, 255–56, 404, 1511–12. CTA, RG 1, A, 1853–57. Holy Blossom Temple Arch. (Toronto), RG 1(a): 8, 23–25, 29–31, 91, 94. Toronto Boroughs and York South Land Registry Office (Toronto), Deed no.69381. *British Colonist* (Toronto), 21 May 1857. *Leader*, daily ed., 19 May 1857; semi-weekly ed., 26 May 1857. *Toronto Mirror*, 29 May 1857. *Toronto directory*, 1846–47; 1850–51; 1856; 1862–63; 1866. *The Jew in Canada: a complete record of Canadian Jewry from the days of the French régime to the present time*, ed. A. D. Hart (Toronto and Montreal, 1926), 41. J. E. Langdon, *Canadian silversmiths, 1700–1900* (Toronto, 1966), 89. *Robertson's landmarks of Toronto*, vol.3. B. G. Sack, *History of the Jews in Canada, from the earliest beginnings to the present day*, [trans. Ralph Novek] (Montreal, 1945; [2nd ed.], ed. Maynard Gertler, 1965), 116, 152. S. A. Speisman, *The Jews of Toronto: a history to 1937* (Toronto, 1979), 12–13, 16–17, 23, 25. S. J. Birnbaum, "The history of the Jews in Toronto," *Canadian Jewish Times* (Montreal), 29 Nov. 1912, 24 Jan. 1913. David Eisen, "Jewish settlers of old Toronto," *Jewish Standard* (Toronto), 15 Dec. 1965, 1 Jan. 1966.

JUNEAU, LAURENT-SALOMON, fur trader, office holder, businessman, and politician; b. 9 Aug. 1793 in Repentigny, Lower Canada, son of François Juneau, *dit* Latulippe, and Thérèse Galarneau; m. probably 1818 or 1819 Josette Vieau, and they had 15 children; d. 14 Nov. 1856 in Shawano, Wis.

Laurent-Salomon Juneau was raised in L'Assomption, Lower Canada, and while still a teenager he left for the fur trade as voyageur for Louis Reaume (Eaume). He apparently traded for the Hudson's Bay Company some time later and then, in 1818, he signed on as a clerk with the American Fur Company at Fort Michilimackinac (Mackinac Island, Mich.). In early 1819 he took over the post run by his father-in-law, Jacques Vieau, at the mouth of the Milwaukee River on Lake Michigan. Juneau was a big man, standing over six feet two inches tall, and was well adapted by temperament to life as a fur trader. His neighbours and the Indians with whom he did business at the Milwaukee post trusted and respected him because of his generosity and honesty.

In 1832, following the defeat of the Fox and Sauk Indians led by Black Hawk, the area between Lake Michigan and the Mississippi River was considered safe for American settlement. Because of his long residence at the Milwaukee post, Juneau, who had become an American citizen in 1831, had pre-emptive rights to land on the east side of the river. In October 1833 he sold a half-interest in these rights to Morgan Lewis Martin, a resident of the Green Bay area since 1827, and made a claim for 132 acres in his name and 157 in the name of his brother Pierre, who had moved to Milwaukee some time before 1830. These claims were recognized by the United States government in August 1835 and purchased by Juneau and Martin for $361. That year they laid out a plan for the town of Milwaukee on this land.

From 1835 to 1839 Juneau and Martin expended a considerable sum of money on streets and public improvements. A post office for the new town was granted in 1835 and located on land belonging to Juneau, who was appointed postmaster, a position he held until 1843. At a cost of some $8,000 he built a court-house in 1836 so that the county seat would be located in his town, and the following year he set up a newspaper, the *Milwaukee Sentinel*, helped in the establishment of the Bank of Milwaukee, and with Martin built a hotel, the Milwaukee House. Speculation pushed the price of lots up, and by 1836 Juneau was reported to be worth more than $100,000 in the inflated "wild cat" bank notes circulating at that time.

Caught up in the excitement of speculation, he began buying back his lots at inflated prices and reselling them, guaranteeing the buyer that the lots would double in value within a year. In 1837 a financial panic brought on by President Andrew Jackson's specie circular of July 1836 put an end to speculation and the price of lots in Milwaukee fell sharply. Juneau, a poor money manager, had borrowed large sums for the civic improvements he had effected and for other projects such as the construction of the steamboat *Milwaukee*, completed in 1837. With the crash in land prices, he lost virtually everything he had. In 1836 he had been negotiating to buy the American Fur Company interests at Fort Michilimackinac, but by 1838 he could not even pay for his own trade goods.

Despite Juneau's financial losses and overwhelming debt, he retained the respect of the people of Milwaukee. In 1839 they elected him village president; seven years later, when the city of Milwaukee was incorporated, he was elected its first mayor and served for one term. In 1848 Juneau left Milwaukee and moved to Theresa, Wis., a town he organized on the Rock River and named for his mother. There he operated a store, served as postmaster, and ran a grist-mill.

The death of his wife in 1855 left Juneau a broken man and his health rapidly deteriorated. He was at Shawano on business in November 1856 when he died. His body was taken to Milwaukee for burial and 10,000 people lined the streets to pay their last respects. Today a street, a park, and a large monument honour Juneau as the founder of Milwaukee.

PAUL TRAP

Milwaukee County Hist. Soc. (Milwaukee, Wis.), Solomon Juneau papers. Wis., State Hist. Soc. (Madison), Juneau files, 1836–37; M. L. Martin papers. Wis., State Hist. Soc., *Coll.*, 1 (1855): 130–34; 11 (1888): 218–337, 385–407; 15 (1900): 458–69. *Daily Wisconsin* (Milwaukee), 28 Nov. 1856. *Milwaukee Sentinel*, 14, 18 Nov. 1856. *DAB*. Tanguay, *Dictionnaire*, 5: 38. J. S. Buck, *Pioneer history of Milwaukee* . . . (4v., Milwaukee, 1876–86). Isabella Fox, *Solomon Juneau; a biography with sketches of the Juneau family* (Milwaukee, [1916]). Joseph Tassé, *Les canadiens de l'Ouest* (2v., Montréal, 1878), 1: 213–37.

K

KAHKEWAQUONABY. *See* JONES, PETER

KALLIHIRUA (modern spelling Qalasirssuaq, also known as **Caloosà** and **Erasmus York**, baptized **Erasmus Augustine Kallihirua**), Inuit guide; b. probably between 1832 and 1835 in the Thule region of northwest Greenland, son of Qissunguaq (Kirshung-oak) and Saattoq (Sa-too); d. unmarried 14 June 1856 in St John's.

Kallihirua was encamped with a small group of Inuit at Cape York, Greenland, when Captain Erasmus Ommanney, commanding the *Assistance* and participating in Horatio Thomas Austin*'s expedition in search of Sir John Franklin*, called there in August 1850. He went on board the ship and consented to accompany the expedition as guide. The ship's company gave him the name Erasmus York after their captain and the cape where he was taken aboard. One of his first tasks was to help check the veracity of a story reported by Adam Beck, an Inuk from southern Greenland who had been employed by Sir John Ross to act as interpreter aboard the *Felix*, another vessel engaged in the Franklin search that year. According to Beck, natives of the Cape York region had told him of the massacre of two ships' crews, presumed to be Franklin's, near Cape Dudley Digges in 1846. Kallihirua took the *Assistance* north, past the cape to Wolstenholme Fjord and showed Ommanney where another search vessel, the *North Star*, and its crew had passed the previous winter in the company of his own band. Some members of both groups had died of sickness but there was no sign of a massacre and no sign of Franklin. Kallihirua stayed with the *Assistance* for the remainder of the expedition, wintering on board near Griffith Island in Barrow Strait (N.W.T.). During the return voyage there was no opportunity to land him back at Cape York, so he went with the expedition to England, arriving in the autumn of 1851.

In November, at the suggestion of the Society for the Propagation of the Gospel and by direction of the Admiralty, he was placed in St Augustine's College, a college for the education of missionary clergy of the Church of England, at Canterbury. There he was taught to read and write and was given religious instruction; for a year and a half he also spent five hours a day in the shop of a Canterbury tailor learning the trade. During 1852 and 1853 he helped Captain John Washington to revise his *Eskimaux and English vocabulary, for the use of the Arctic expeditions* (London, 1850). He was baptized Erasmus Augustine Kallihirua in St Martin's Church near Canterbury on 27 Nov. 1853, in the presence of, among others, Eleanor Isabella Gell (Sir John Franklin's daughter) and Captain Ommanney, who still maintained a fatherly interest in his welfare.

He left England in autumn 1855 for further religious training at Queen's College (formerly the Theological Institute) in St John's. Plans were made by the bishop of Newfoundland, Edward Feild*, for Kallihirua to accompany him on a trip to the coast of Labrador in the summer of 1856 where he was to begin missionary work among the Inuit. However, Kallihirua's health, which had been poor since he had left the Arctic, suddenly became worse and he died at the college before he could leave St John's.

Kallihirua was one of a small number of Inuit who, in the 19th century, won a degree of international fame through their association with polar expeditions. Even fewer had the experience of visiting the outside world; he was almost certainly the first of the Inuit of northern Greenland to do so. He appears to have adapted readily and cheerfully to his new life and to have won the affection and admiration of both Ommanney and his missionary colleagues, who had high hopes for his career before his premature death.

CLIVE HOLLAND

Kane

Cathedral of St John the Baptist (Anglican) (St John's), Reg. of burials, 17 June 1856 (mfm. at PANL). G.B., Parl., Command paper, 1852, 50, [no.1436]: 269–670, *Additional papers relative to the Arctic expedition . . .* , 603–4; House of Commons paper, 1851, 33, no.97: 195–307, *Arctic expeditions, return to an address of the Honourable the House of Commons, dated 7 February 1851; – for, copy or extracts from any correspondence or proceedings of the Board of Admiralty in relation to the Arctic expeditions . . .* , 297–301. W. P. Snow, *Voyage of the "Prince Albert" in search of Sir John Franklin: a narrative of every-day life in the Arctic seas* (London, 1851). *Times and General Commercial Gazette* (St John's), 18 June 1856. T. B. Murray, *Kalli, the Esquimaux Christian; a memoir* (new ed., London, [1857]). Aage Bugge, "Kallihirua, polareskimoen i Canterbury" and "Polareskimoen i Canterbury: supplerende oplysninger vedr. Kallihirua" in *Grønland* (Charlottenlund, Denmark), 1965: 161–75 and 1966: 17–22.

KANE, ELISHA KENT, surgeon, naval officer, explorer, and author; b. 3 Feb. 1820 in Philadelphia, eldest of six sons and one daughter of John Kintzing Kane, a distinguished jurist, and Jane Duval Leiper; d. 16 Feb. 1857 in Havana.

Having decided to pursue a career in civil engineering, Elisha Kent Kane entered the University of Virginia at Charlottesville in 1837. The following year, however, a severe attack of rheumatic fever forced him to withdraw and left him with a permanently damaged heart. A small, slight man, Kane possessed a courage and stamina which helped him to overcome this handicap and which served him well in later years. In the fall of 1839 he began the study of medicine at the University of Pennsylvania in his native Philadelphia, and after a residency in the hospital of the Blockley Almshouse he graduated in March 1842. On the advice of his father, Kane applied for service in the United States Navy and then, in May 1843, while awaiting his commission, he left for China as the physician attached to the diplomatic mission headed by Massachusetts statesman Caleb Cushing. Kane travelled extensively in the Orient and, after leaving the legation in June 1844, he conducted a hospital boat at Whampoa (Huang-pu), China, for six months before making his way back to the United States by way of Egypt and Europe, arriving at Philadelphia in late summer 1845. His naval commission as assistant surgeon had become official on 1 July 1843. During the next four years, Kane served on various peace-time postings off the west coast of Africa, in the Mediterranean, and along the eastern coast of the United States, besides seeing some action during the Mexican-American War.

In March 1850 Kane applied for service as surgeon to the proposed American expedition in search of Sir John Franklin*, lost in the Arctic since 1845, and received orders on 12 May to join the brig *Advance*, which, with the brig *Rescue*, was being outfitted for the mission by the New York merchant Henry Grinnell. Ten days later, under Lieutenant Edwin Jesse De Haven*, commander of the expedition, and Passed Midshipman S. P. Griffin, the two vessels sailed from New York with instructions to search in the vicinity of Barrow Strait (N.W.T.), northward in Wellington Channel, and westward to Cape Walker. The ships followed the south shore of Lancaster Sound to Port Leopold, and then turned north to Beechey Island where at the end of August they joined with the search expeditions of William Penny*, Sir John Ross, and Captain Horatio Thomas Austin*. Kane noted in his journal that on 28 August there were seven ships, under three different commands, "within hailing distance" of Beechey Island and that two other vessels under Captain Erasmus Ommanney were only 15 miles to the west, embedded in the ice. While Kane was at Beechey Island traces of Franklin's expedition were found, indicating that his two vessels, *Erebus* and *Terror*, had passed the winter of 1845–46 there. The *Advance* and the *Rescue* then continued westward to Griffith Island before turning back on 13 September. At the southern end of Wellington Channel the ships were beset in the ice and forced to winter in Arctic waters. Drifting with the ice, first north, then south and east out of Lancaster Sound into Baffin Bay, they were finally released in June 1851. After an unsuccessful attempt to find a route through the ice-pack that would take his ships north to continue the search, De Haven set sail for New York where the expedition arrived safely at the end of September.

Kane then applied himself to writing a narrative of the voyage, *The U.S. Grinnell expedition in search of Sir John Franklin*, and delivering lectures before various scientific bodies. A believer in the hypothesis of an open polar sea, he persuaded Grinnell, American financier George Peabody, the United States Navy Department, and several scientific societies to sponsor a second expedition to go north from Baffin Bay to the shores of the "Polar Sea" in search of Franklin. This expedition was unusual in that Kane, a medical officer, was assigned to command its only vessel, the *Advance*, and, because of the mixed crew of naval personnel and civilians, naval rules did not altogether apply. From the outset Kane faced problems of morale and discipline with the crew.

Leaving New York on 30 May 1853, the *Advance* stopped at the fishing port of Fiskenæsset, Greenland, at the beginning of July where the Inuit hunter Hans* Hendrik joined the crew. On 20 July Kane put in to Upernavik and engaged the Danish sledge driver and interpreter Johan Carl Christian Petersen. The *Advance* then proceeded up the west coast of Greenland and into the sound Kane named Peabody Bay (later renamed Kane Basin) where, by the end of August, its northward progress was stopped by the ice. While the vessel was being prepared in its wintering berth at

Rensselaer Harbour, boat and sledge excursions reached as far north as 79°50'. During a winter that saw temperatures drop to −70°F, 57 of the 60 dogs that Kane had acquired for his sledging operations died of Arctic canine hysteria and all members of the expedition suffered to a greater or less degree from scurvy and malnutrition.

In 1854 four sledge expeditions were sent out to explore Peabody Bay. Under Henry Brooks, first officer, eight men left on 19 March to lay supply depots for further exploration. With temperatures as low as −57°F, four of them suffered severely from frost-bite, two dying shortly after their return to the *Advance*. The ship's surgeon, Isaac Israel Hayes*, and a crew member made a survey to the southwest in May; James McGary, second officer, and Amos Bonsall headed north across Peabody Bay in June; and the steward, William Morton, accompanied by Hans Hendrik, continued from the point where McGary turned back and reached the northernmost point attained by the expedition, 81°22' at Cape Independence, Greenland. On 12 July 1854, fearing that the *Advance* would remain ice-bound, Kane and five men tried to reach Edward Belcher*'s squadron at Beechey Island by boat, but failed. Hayes, Petersen, and seven other crew members then decided to leave the vessel against Kane's counsel that they would be safer staying with the *Advance*. On 28 August they headed south in an effort to reach Upernavik on foot, but, having nearly perished, they returned to the ship on 12 December. Kane, who was not a stern disciplinarian, took no punitive action against the group and treated them more like patients than mutineers or deserters. In May 1855, facing the probability of yet a third winter in the ice, Kane abandoned the vessel. In a dramatic 83-day trek, the whole company travelled 1,300 miles on foot and by boat to Upernavik; they were then taken aboard a Danish vessel which carried them to Godhavn on Disko Island. In early September the American ships *Release* and *Arctic*, sent out in search of them, arrived at Godhavn and returned them to the United States. In light of the extreme hardship encountered during this expedition it is remarkable that all but three of the participants survived the ordeal − one crew member had died from malnutrition and two others from exposure.

In the course of Kane's extensive travels he had contracted a number of different maladies, including "rice fever" (cholera) in China, "plague" (typhoid fever) in Egypt, "coast fever" (bacterial septicaemia) in West Africa, and scurvy several times in the Arctic. On his return to the United States in 1855 he was in very poor health. He nevertheless rapidly completed his account of the expedition, *Arctic explorations: the second Grinnell expedition in search of Sir John Franklin*, and then visited England in late 1856. Proceeding next to Cuba, where he hoped to find relief

from his chronic illness, he died there on 16 Feb. 1857 after two severe strokes. Kane was given a grand public funeral in Philadelphia as America's first great Arctic explorer and was buried in Laurel Hill Cemetery. Although Kane was never publicly married, he had had a continuing association with the spiritualist Margaret Fox from 1855 to 1857 and after his death she claimed to have been his wife.

In his short lifetime Elisha Kent Kane had captured the imagination of America through his travels in the Orient, his brief but illustrious service in the Mexican-American War, and his two Arctic expeditions. Both of his books were well received, and still rank high for literary merit among works on Arctic exploration. His contribution to Arctic medicine could have been substantial if later explorers had paid heed. He stressed adaptation to the environment by means of shelter, clothing, and activity, and he showed that the Inuit way of life was important to survival. Above all he urged a diet of fresh meat as a preventive and cure for scurvy. The route that Kane had followed in 1853 was later favoured by other Arctic explorers, including Isaac Israel Hayes in 1860 and 1869, Charles Francis Hall* in 1871, Sir George Strong Nares* in 1875, Adolphus Washington Greely in 1881, Robert Edwin Peary in 1898, 1905, and 1908, and Donald Baxter MacMillan in 1913.

ROBERT E. JOHNSON

[Elisha Kent Kane is the author of a number of scientific articles, the first of which was his thesis in medicine, "Experiments on kiesteine, with observations on its applications to the diagnosis of pregnancy," published in *American Journal of the Medical Sciences* (Philadelphia), new ser., 4 (July 1842): 13–38. On his return from the 1850–51 Arctic expedition he put forth his theory of an open polar sea in a 24-page pamphlet, *Access to an open polar sea in connection with the search after Sir John Franklin and his companions* (New York, 1853). Four articles prepared from his notes on the 1853–55 expedition and edited by Charles Anthony Schott were published posthumously in *Smithsonian Contributions to Knowledge* (Washington): "Astronomical observations in the Arctic seas . . . ," 12 (1860), 2nd article; "Magnetical observations in the Arctic seas . . . ," 10 (1859), 3rd article; "Meteorological observations in the Arctic seas . . . ," 11 (1859), 5th article; and "Tidal observations in the Arctic seas . . . ," 13 (1860), 2nd article. The articles were later published as a monograph edited by Schott, *Physical observations in the Arctic seas . . .* (Washington, 1859–60). Kane's journal of the 1850–51 expedition, *The U.S. Grinnell expedition in search of Sir John Franklin: a personal narrative* (London and New York, 1853; new ed., 1854), was well received and was republished by Horace Kephart as *Adrift in the Arctic ice pack, from the history of the first U.S. Grinnell expedition in search of Sir John Franklin* (New York, 1915). Kane's account of the second Arctic voyage was also published several times under the title *Arctic explorations: the second Grinnell expedition in search of Sir John Franklin, 1853,*

Keefer

'54, '55; illustrated by upwards of three hundred engravings, from sketches by the author (2v., Philadelphia and London, 1856; new ed., 1857; new ed., London, 1861). These works were sufficiently popular to be translated and published in German as *Zwei Nordpolarreisen zur Aufsuchung Sir John Franklins*, trans. Julius Seybt (Leipzig, [German Democratic Republic], 1857), and *Kane, der Nordpolfahrer: Arktische Fahrten und Entdeckungen der zweiten Grinnell-Expedition zur Aufsuchung Sir John Franklin's in den Jahren 1853, 1854 und 1855 . . .*, trans. F. Kiesewetter (2v., Leipzig, 1859). Margaret Fox, in an attempt to prove that her relationship with Kane was in fact a common-law marriage, edited *The love-life of Dr. Kane; containing the correspondence, and a history of the acquaintance, engagement, and secret marriage between Elisha K. Kane and Margaret Fox, with facsimiles of letters, and her portrait* (New York, 1866), a collection of Kane's letters, including a few of disputed authenticity.

The American Philosophical Soc. Library (Philadelphia), E. K. Kane papers, includes his correspondence and writings, and the journals of his second expedition are in Pa., Hist. Soc. (Philadelphia), Ferdinand J. Dreer coll., and in Stanford Univ. Libraries (Stanford, Calif.), MS Division, M61. R.E.J.]

I. I. Hayes, *An Arctic boat journey, in the autumn of 1854* (Boston, 1860). Cooke and Holland, *Exploration of northern Canada. DAB.* G. W. Corner, *Doctor Kane of the Arctic seas* (Philadelphia, 1972). William Elder, *Biography of Elisha Kent Kane* (Philadelphia and Boston, 1858). Jeannette Mirsky, *Elisha Kent Kane and the seafaring frontier* (Boston, 1954). S. M. Smucker [Schmucker], *The life of Dr. Elisha Kent Kane, and of other distinguished American explorers . . .* (Philadelphia, 1858).

KEEFER (Kieffer), GEORGE, farmer, cabinet-maker, surveyor, militia officer, justice of the peace, and businessman; b. 8 Nov. 1773 near Newton, N.J., son of George Kieffer and Mary Cooke (Conke, Conck); m. first 6 Feb. 1797 Catherine Lampman, and they had nine children; m. secondly 8 June 1815 Jane Emory, *née* McBride, with whom he had seven children; m. thirdly 2 June 1836 Mary Swaize; m. fourthly 14 Nov. 1839 Esther Magdalen Secord; d. 27 June 1858 in Thorold, Upper Canada.

In about 1750 George Keefer's father, then 10 years old, went to live near Paulins Kill, Sussex County, N.J., with his stepfather, Frederick Saveraine, and his mother, Ann Waldruff (widow of Samuel Kieffer, an Alsatian Huguenot). Within a few years the family operated two farms and a distillery, and was sufficiently well off to own a household slave. George Kieffer married Mary Cooke and they had four children (George, Jacob, Samuel, and Mary) before the American revolution tragically intervened. He joined the Queen's Rangers to fight the rebels only to fall victim to army fever (probably typhus) in 1783. After the war Mary Kieffer remarried. She retained temporary possession of the family estate, but, on coming of age, her eldest son, George, faced the prospect of having it confiscated because of his father's loyalism.

In 1790 Keefer, his brother Jacob, and several other lads from Sussex County in similar circumstances set out for Canada to look for land on which to make new beginnings. The Keefers located and began clearing a tract near present-day Thorold and in 1793 guided their family and a small herd of cattle overland to their rude farm. Once again the family began to prosper, assisted by a generous land grant; in 1797 George married Catherine Lampman, who had also made the trek from New Jersey, and children began to arrive at about the rate of one every 18 months. In addition to farming he worked as a cabinet-maker and about 1807 was appointed a deputy provincial land surveyor.

George Keefer remained ardently loyal during the War of 1812, joining the 2nd Regiment of Lincoln militia as an ensign at the outbreak of hostilities. In 1813 his house was commandeered as a hospital by American occupation forces and his wife died of army fever. His 16-year-old daughter, Elizabeth, assumed the trying burden of caring for the other children while she performed nursing chores for the invaders (one of whom later returned to marry her). Keefer rose to the rank of captain early in 1814; his company was active on the Niagara frontier throughout that summer, seeing action in July at the battle of Lundy's Lane and in October at the engagement at Chippewa (Welland) River. He retained his captaincy in the 2nd Lincoln until 1828, when advancing age and declining interest led him to resign his commission.

After the war, Keefer opened a store, built a grist-mill on Twelve Mile Creek, and married Jane Emory, a widow with five children of her own. The future must have seemed promising for they had seven more children. In 1817 Keefer, who had become a justice of the peace three years earlier, and twelve of his neighbours replied with considerable satisfaction to the questionnaire of Robert Gourlay* on the state of settlement in Thorold Township. Its soil, they reported, could produce 15 to 30 bushels of excellent winter wheat per acre; crops of hay, oats, buckwheat, and barley were also good. The prospering township, their reply further revealed, had a population of 830 and contained a grist-mill, four sawmills, a linseed-oil mill, and several mercantile shops and taverns.

Keefer and John DeCow offered every encouragement when their friend and fellow mill-owner, William Hamilton Merritt*, proposed stabilizing the supply of water on Twelve Mile Creek by linking it to the Chippewa River, a project which developed into a plan to connect lakes Erie and Ontario by canal. Beginning in 1818 Keefer, DeCow, and Merritt conducted preliminary surveys, petitioned the provincial assembly for incorporation as a canal company, and organized local meetings to win public approval.

Merritt needed men like Keefer, whose influence among landowners along the proposed route of the canal (which required 30 acres of Keefer's own land) would help in the negotiation of the transfer of property rights. The Welland Canal Company was chartered in January 1824; Keefer subscribed for 25 shares and that summer, after Receiver General John Henry DUNN had refused the position, he was elected its first president. Merritt soon realized, however, that if he were to raise enough money in Canada and abroad to complete the canal, he would require someone with much greater prestige than Keefer at the head of the company. Dunn was again approached but did not immediately accept. Thus it fell to Keefer to let the first construction contracts and turn the first sod on 30 Nov. 1824. However, the growing scope of the scheme and its financial requirements quickly eclipsed such local notables as Keefer. Replaced by Dunn the following year, he drifted into the background, playing a minor financial role in support of Merritt and Dunn and attending board meetings regularly throughout the Niagara District but only infrequently at York (Toronto).

Keefer nevertheless made good use of the Welland Canal. Having obtained from the company free land opposite the site of what would become lock 34, he built a mill there in 1827 and waited for the canal to be completed – a bold declaration of faith and, for a time, a source of local amusement. Eventually the canal did arrive, providing upon its completion in 1829 essential water-power for the mill and a means of transportation.

Keefer was an enterprising, even-tempered, and widely respected patriarch who devoted himself to the formidable task of providing for a large, extended family. His last child was born when he was 52 and he was 60 when he lost his second wife in 1833. With several small children still at home, however, he remarried twice more. As he grew older he had the satisfaction of seeing his family well educated and firmly established in Canadian society as engineers, doctors, civil servants, and lawyers. The Welland Canal had captured the imagination of Keefer's boys and its construction, repair, and rebuilding provided them with unusually advantageous opportunities for technical training and employment: three sons (George, Samuel*, and Thomas Coltrin*) learned or practised their trade there as civil engineers. Under the patronage of William Hamilton Merritt, who never forgot Keefer's early support, they rose to places of distinction at the head of the emerging Canadian engineering profession. A fourth son, Jacob*, built one of the largest flour-mills in Canada on the banks of the canal at Thorold in 1845–47.

Like most of his contemporaries, George Keefer suffered greatly from events beyond his control. War made him a refugee and a soldier; it destroyed his patrimony and carried off his father, his first wife, and one of his sons. But in peace he prospered and his family flourished. Moreover, Keefer and his neighbours on Twelve Mile Creek possessed the vision and determination, if not the means, to improve their world with an ambitious scheme, the Welland Canal.

H. V. NELLES

AO, MS 74; MS 191. PAC, MG 24, E1; I33; K2, 15: 291–93 (transcripts); National Map Coll., H12/410-Welland Canal-1818; RG 9, I, B1, 3, 14; B7, 22, 25; RG 68, General index, 1651–1841: 24. *Arthur papers* (Sanderson), 3: 32, 325. "Grants of crown lands in U.C.," AO *Report*, 1929: 88. *St. Catharines Journal* (St Catharines, [Ont.]), 1 July 1858. Chadwick, *Ontarian families*, 2: 90–98. *Cyclopædia of Canadian biog.* (Rose and Charlesworth), 1: 226–28. Morgan, *Sketches of celebrated Canadians*, 648–50. H. G. J. Aitken, *The Welland Canal Company: a study in Canadian enterprise* (Cambridge, Mass., 1954). *The history of the county of Welland, Ontario . . .* ([Welland], 1887; repr. with intro. by John Burtniak, Belleville, Ont., 1972), 361, 363, 531. M. W. Keefer, *George Keefer* (London, Ont., 1931). Robert Keefer, *Memoirs of the Keefer family* (Norwood, Ont., 1935). T. C. Keefer, *The old Welland Canal and the man who made it* (Ottawa, 1911), 9; *Philosophy of railroads and other essays*, ed. and intro. H. V. Nelles (Toronto, and Buffalo, N.Y., 1972), editor's intro., vii–lxiii.

KEIR, JOHN, Presbyterian clergyman and educator; b. probably 2 Feb. 1780 in Bucklyvie, parish of Kippen, Scotland, and baptized in the same parish 4 Feb. 1781; eldest child of John Keir, a farmer, and Christian Wood; m. 2 Sept. 1808 Mary Burnet in Glasgow, and they had at least one son and two daughters; d. 23 Sept. 1858 in Truro, N.S.

John Keir was born into a family who were Presbyterian seceders, a group so called because of their origin in Ebenezer Erskine's separation from the Church of Scotland in 1733. Keir matriculated to the University of Glasgow in 1799 but did not graduate. He taught school before and during training in divinity, from 1803 to 1806, at the theological hall of the General Associate Synod in Whitburn. In 1807 or 1808 he was licensed by the anti-burgher Presbytery of Glasgow. Although the New Light controversy in Scotland had left a number of congregations there without preachers, Keir was attracted to the colonial missions, undoubtedly in part by his college companion the Reverend Peter Gordon, who had been serving in Prince Edward Island since 1806. In 1808 Keir formally offered himself for the Secession congregation in Halifax, and in September he sailed with his bride for Nova Scotia. Despite the application to Halifax, the Presbytery of Pictou assigned him to Prince Edward Island, where he wintered at Prince-

Keir

town (Malpeque). Gordon's death in April 1809 left Keir the only Presbyterian clergyman on the Island. Although he preached at both Halifax and Merigomish, N.S., during the summer, the presbytery approved his call in June 1809 from the Princetown congregation, and there he was ordained in June 1810. The ordination proceedings, attended by Duncan Ross* and Thomas McCulloch* among others, concluded with a sermon by the Reverend James Drummond MacGregor* in Gaelic, the language of the Argyllshire settlers of the district, but not of their new minister.

Apart from serving his widely dispersed congregation in west-central Prince Edward Island, Keir itinerated throughout the Island and even paid a missionary visit to the Miramichi region of New Brunswick in 1817. He largely escaped the disruptions experienced by his Pictou brethren in the 1820s as a result of territorial and jurisdictional disputes between the well-established Presbyterian Church of Nova Scotia and newly arrived Church of Scotland clergy. In 1825, when his adherents at New London proposed applying to the Church of Scotland's recently formed Glasgow Colonial Society for a Gaelic-speaking missionary, Keir persuaded them to remain with the Nova Scotian church. The following year the Reverend Hugh Dunbar, a Gaelic-speaking Nova Scotian, began work at New London, Cavendish, and New Glasgow, and the Reverend Robert S. Patterson, one of the first divinity graduates of the Nova Scotian church's Pictou Academy, settled at Bedeque. In 1848, 87 per cent of Keir's district still adhered to the Presbyterian Church of Nova Scotia, and it was claimed that 3,000 people attended the celebration of his jubilee in 1858.

In 1821 the settlement of the Reverend William MacGregor at Richmond (Malpeque) Bay and the Reverend Robert Douglas at St Peters had permitted the formation of a separate presbytery on the Island. Keir was its first moderator and frequently thereafter either its official moderator or its moderator pro tem. Already looked upon as the father of the Island's Presbyterian church, he was diligent in his attention to the disciplinary, instructional, and political issues which occupied the presbytery's numerous gatherings. Keir apparently penned many of its documents and acted regularly as its messenger to the Nova Scotian synod, of which he had been a member since its formation in 1817. Although he served as the synod's moderator in 1823, his participation in that body remained occasional until the mid 1840s, when his appointment as the synod's professor of divinity and his interest in the issue of establishing a foreign mission led to his greater involvement. Keir was a strong proponent of a larger union of adherents to the Westminster Confession, but he did not live to see the

union of his church and the Free Church of Nova Scotia in 1860.

Keir was also active in the promotion of education. As early as 1820 he supported Walter Johnstone*'s mission to encourage sabbath schools on the Island. By 1827 the Prince Town Female Society, which had been established two years previously in Keir's congregation and of which his wife was treasurer, was purchasing books for such schools. In October 1822 he had presided over the creation of a school at Princetown of which he was named rector. When the legislature provided provincial funds for education in 1825, Keir's school was recognized as the district grammar school. He is also said to have established a library for his parishioners. Keir worked in the 1830s to have the province's reserved glebe and school lands, claimed exclusively by the Church of England, appropriated for the general support of education. In the 1850s he was president of the Literary and Scientific Society, the first such organization on the Island, and a member of the provincial board of health. In 1852 he received an honorary doctorate in divinity from Amherst College in Massachusetts.

The synod's appointment of Keir as its divinity professor occurred following the death of McCulloch in 1843. From 1844 until the naming of the Reverend James Ross* as professor of biblical literature in 1846, Keir taught ministerial candidates in his own home and was the synod's sole professor. With Ross's appointment, the theological hall was relocated in West River (Durham), N.S., where, in 1848, the synod established a seminary under Ross's principalship. Two years later Keir resumed teaching in the six-week fall term at the West River seminary. His *Course of study in systematic and pastoral theology and ecclesiastical history, for students attending the Theological Seminary of the Presbyterian Church of Nova Scotia* was published in Charlottetown in 1857. The synod rejected his proffered resignation in July 1858 and that September Keir was at Truro for the opening of the church's new seminary there.

Himself a missionary to a foreign land, Keir provided essential support to John Geddie* in launching a foreign mission by the Presbyterian Church of Nova Scotia, apparently the first undertaken on the sole responsibility of a colonial church. Geddie's call to Cavendish and New London in 1837 formally introduced the issue on the Island. At his ordination a year later Geddie's dedication and enthusiasm inspired the formation of a bible and missionary society, over which Keir presided. Thereafter, while Geddie promoted his cause in the public sphere, Keir carried the issue formally in the Island presbytery and also in the synod, where a missionary society was formed in 1840 and a petition proposing the establishment of a foreign mission was introduced in 1843. When the synod directed that the proposal be further investigated the following year, Keir was named convener of the church's first Board of Foreign Missions, whose responsibility it became in 1845 to select a mission station and choose a missionary. After they had settled on Geddie and an island in the Pacific Ocean, Keir chaired the contentious synodical session which confirmed the decision. In November 1846 Geddie departed for the New Hebrides (Vanuatu). Keir remained a faithful supporter and a member of the Board of Foreign Missions until his death; his congregation was regularly the most generous contributor to the foreign mission fund.

Keir's contemporaries noted his meekness, his disinterested benevolence, and his untiring service. At his death it was claimed that "not one of the old Presbyterian congregations on the Island, whether in connection with the Scottish Establishment, the Free Church or the Presbyterian Church of Nova Scotia . . . did not to some extent enjoy his missionary labors, or experience his fostering care in its infancy."

SUSAN BUGGEY

John Keir is the author of *Course of study in systematic and pastoral theology and ecclesiastical history, for students attending the Theological Seminary of the Presbyterian Church of Nova Scotia* (Charlottetown, 1857).

Amherst College (Amherst, Mass.), Office of the Registrar, record of subject's DD degree, 1852. GRO (Edinburgh), Glasgow, reg. of marriages, 2 Sept. 1808; Kippen, reg. of marriages, 19 Nov. 1779; reg. of births and baptisms, 4 Feb. 1781. MCA, Presbyterian Church of N.S., Theological Seminary, Board of Superintendence, minutes, 1848–58, including *Bye-laws of the Theological Seminary of the Presbyterian Church of Nova Scotia* (n.p., 1852); Presbyterian Church of N.S. (United Secession), minutes of the Synod, 1 (1817–42)–2 (1842–60); Presbytery of P.E.I., minutes, 1 (1821–30); 3 (1836–47)–5 (1856–60); Prince Town Congregation (Princetown [Malpeque], P.E.I.), Prince Town Session, minutes, 1807–58. Univ. of Glasgow Arch., Matriculation records, 1799. *A brief sketch of the life and labors of the late Rev. John Keir, D.D., S.T.P.* (Pictou, N.S., 1859; annotated copy available in the George Patterson papers, PANS, MG 1, 742, no.18). Walter Johnstone, *Travels in Prince Edward Island . . .* (Edinburgh, 1824), 37, 113. *Missionary Reg. of the Presbyterian Church of Nova Scotia* (Pictou; Halifax), 1 (1850)–9 (1858). *Presbyterian Witness, and Evangelical Advocate* (Halifax), 11 (1858): 102, 106–7, 154, 169. "Rev. John Kier, D.D., Professor of Divinity to the Presbyterian Church in Nova Scotia," *Canadian United Presbyterian Magazine* (Toronto), 5 (1858): 352. James Robertson, *History of the mission of the Secession Church to Nova Scotia and Prince Edward Island, from its commencement in 1765* (Edinburgh, 1847). *Colonial Herald, and Prince Edward Island Advertiser* (Charlottetown), 24 March 1838, 30 March 1839. *Royal Gazette* (Charlottetown), 4, 25 March 1834.

P.E.I. calendar, 1855: 43, 47, 49–50; 1857: 44, 48. E. A. Betts, *Pine Hill Divinity Hall, 1820–1970: a history* (Halifax, 1970). Duncan Campbell, *History of Prince Edward Island* (Charlottetown, 1875; repr. Belleville, Ont., 1972). C. J. Crowdis, *The Prince Town United Church; until 1925, the Prince Town Presbyterian Church, Malpeque, Prince Edward Island* (Halifax, 1958). Gregg, *Hist. of Presbyterian Church. Life of Rev. Dr. John and Mrs. Geddie, and early Presbyterian history, 1770–1845*, comp. W. E. Johnstone (Summerside, P.E.I., 1975). George Patterson, *Memoir of the Rev. James MacGregor, D.D. . . .* (Philadelphia, 1859); *Missionary life among the cannibals: being the life of the Rev. John Geddie, D.D., first missionary to the New Hebrides; with a history of the Nova Scotia Presbyterian Mission on that group* (Toronto, 1882). D. C. Harvey, "Glebe and school lands in Prince Edward Island," CCHS, *Journal*, 10 (1968): 120–47. George McMillan, "A Canadian minister of a hundred years ago," *Presbyterian* (Toronto), new ser., 13 (July–December 1908): 767–69.

KEITH, GEORGE, fur trader; b. 29 Dec. 1779 at Netherthird in the parish of Auchterless, Scotland, son of James Keith, farmer, and Isabella Bruce; d. 22 Jan. 1859 in Aberdeen, Scotland.

With his younger brother JAMES, George Keith came to North America in 1799 as an apprentice to Forsyth, Richardson and Company, a partner in the New North West Company (sometimes called the XY Company). Until 1806 he served in the Athabasca country, joining the North West Company after its merger with the New North West Company in 1804. From 1806 to 1815 he was stationed in the Mackenzie River department, where he worked under John George McTavish* and then Simon Fraser*, becoming a partner in the NWC in 1813. Although few details of his life during these years are known, his observations on the geography of the area and the Athapaskan-speaking Indians around his post on the Liard River and, after 1810, at the west end of Great Bear Lake and on the Mackenzie River, have survived in a series of letters addressed to Roderick McKenzie*. His descriptions of the Beaver (Slave) and Long-Arrowed (Hare) Indians are literate and detailed.

From 1816 to 1821 Keith served at Fort Chipewyan (Alta), on Lake Athabasca, assuming charge of the Athabasca department in 1817. These years were marked by keen, and sometimes violent, competition with the Hudson's Bay Company men at nearby Fort Wedderburn, on Coal (Potato) Island. In late 1816 Keith was one of a party of Nor'Westers sent by Archibald Norman McLeod* to harass the HBC fort's fishery. While HBC officer Colin Robertson* was a prisoner at Fort Chipewyan during the winter of 1818–19, Keith confided in him about the strained relations between the NWC wintering partners and their Montreal agents, McTavish, McGillivrays and

Keith

Company. Keith and his brother James were, according to Robertson, among the few Nor'Westers with any "firmness of character" in that dispute: "A good dinner, a few fair promises would waltz the remainder about, to any tune the McGillivray's chose to strike up."

After the HBC–NWC coalition in 1821, Keith was named chief factor and given charge of the English (upper Churchill) River district, based at Île-à-la-Crosse (Sask.). Following a leave of absence in 1826–27, he was placed in command of the Lake Superior district, based at Michipicoten (Michipicoten River, Ont.). With the exception of another furlough in 1832–33, he remained at this post until 1835, when he was transferred to Moose Factory (Ont.). Keith returned to Michipicoten for the period 1839–43 before taking a two-year leave of absence and then retiring to Scotland in 1845.

Keith ranked among the more respected HBC officers of his time. In 1832 Governor George SIMPSON portrayed him as "a man of highly correct conduct and Character and much attention to his business; well Educated and respectably connected." He was "not wanting in personal courage when pushed," but considered to be "rather timid, nervous and indecisive on ordinary occasions."

Like many of his NWC and HBC colleagues, Keith took a country wife and had a large family during his fur-trade career. Between 1807 and 1838, six daughters and three sons were born to him and Nanette, the country daughter of James Sutherland, a NWC clerk. Keith was devoted to his family and in 1844, before sailing for Scotland, he formalized his marriage by Christian rite to protect their interests. His marrying and retiring with his fur-trade wife contrasted with the domestic behaviour of several of his contemporaries, such as William Connolly*, John George McTavish, George Simpson, and John Stuart*; it was unusual for fur traders to suffer the stress encountered in introducing their native wives to the "civilized world." The Keiths, however, survived the adjustment well. In 1847 Keith reported to Simpson that "the Gud-wife . . . has acquired a considerable smattering of the English language, together with some comparative degree of civilised polish" and the following autumn wrote that "all things considered I think she deserves some credit for acting or playing *her part* so well as she does." On the acre of land around their home, Morningside Cottage, near Aberdeen, Nanette tended a garden, selling produce and eggs; her native handicrafts were also admired. When, in 1850, Chief Factor Alexander Christie* brought his mixed-blood wife, Anne Thomas, to settle near Aberdeen, Nanette gained a close friend. After her husband's death in 1859, her whereabouts are not known, although it is thought that she may have returned to North America to live with

her daughter Betsey, wife of Chief Factor John Swanston.

JENNIFER S. H. BROWN

Aberdeen Univ. Library (Aberdeen, Scot.), James Keith papers (mfm. at PAC). Anglican Church of Canada, Diocese of Moosonee Arch. (Schumacher, Ont.), Moose Factory Anglican and Methodist mission records, 1780–1906, 22 June 1838 (mfm. at AO). PAM, HBCA, A.36/8: ff.9–30; A.44/4: ff.45–46; D.5/20: f.308; D.5/23: ff.88–88d; MG 7, B7 (mfm.). *Les bourgeois de la Compagnie du Nord-Ouest* (Masson), vol.2. *Docs. relating to NWC* (Wallace). *HBRS*, 1 (Rich); 2 (Rich and Fleming); 3 (Fleming). Simpson, "Character book," *HBRS*, 30 (Williams), 151–236. Sylvia Van Kirk, "The role of women in the fur trade society of the Canadian west, 1700–1850" (PHD thesis, Univ. of London, 1975).

KEITH, JAMES, fur trader; b. 12 March 1782 at Netherthird in the parish of Auchterless, Scotland, son of James Keith and Isabella Bruce; d. 27 Jan. 1851 in Aberdeen, Scotland.

The rural gentry of northeast Scotland gave the North American fur trade many able officers including James Keith and his brother GEORGE, sons of an Aberdeenshire tacksman and farmer. The Keiths were brought from Scotland with Edward Smith and A. Wilkie as apprentice clerks in 1799 by Forsyth, Richardson and Company, the principal partner in the New North West Company (sometimes called the XY Company). James proceeded to Grand Portage (near Grand Portage, Minn.) in 1800 and the following year he went to the English (upper Churchill) River department. He stayed on there after the merger of the New North West and the North West companies in 1804 [*see* Sir Alexander Mackenzie*], serving at various NWC posts, and was married by the custom of the country to the second daughter of Jean-Baptiste Cadot, a union he later described as "a much lamented though almost unavoidable consequence of the situation and Country." Two daughters were born of this marriage, Helen in 1811 and Mary in 1814. Both were apparently raised under the supervision of James's brother George.

In 1813 Keith was sent out to the Columbia River, with Alexander Henry* the younger and Alexander Stewart, to reinforce the NWC party on the Pacific coast, and he arrived at Fort George (Astoria, Oreg.) in November. He travelled east in early summer 1814 to Fort William (Thunder Bay, Ont.), where, at the July meeting of the company, he became a partner with four other clerks: Angus BETHUNE, Alexander Greenfield Macdonell*, John McLOUGHLIN, and Edward Smith. Keith was back in the Columbia department by the end of the year, and, after a second trip to Fort William in 1815, he was placed in charge of the NWC business on the Pacific coast from 1816 to

1821. The Columbia trade was hobbled by poor relations with the Indians, dissension among officers, unsuitable employees, and disappointing markets in China. None the less, William McGillivray*, the chief director of the NWC, held Keith blameless for these troubles. With the merger of the NWC and the Hudson's Bay Company in March 1821 [see Simon McGillivray*], Keith was named one of the 25 chief factors in the reorganized HBC, a commission he accepted on 11 July at the meeting of former NWC men and HBC officers at Fort William.

After a year's sick leave in England, Keith was given charge of the Severn district and posted to Fort Severn (Ont.). The following year he was transferred to Fort Chipewyan (Alta), in the Athabasca country. His annual reports from both places showed a lively interest in Indian character and in the social consequences of the fur trade. He deplored the familiarity between company men and the Indians, and at Severn drafted rules, which were adopted by the Council of the Northern Department, for "the more effectual civilization and moral improvement of the families attached to the different establishments and the Indians." In Athabasca he strove to change the natives' work habits and economic customs by raising the price of furs, slashing gifts and autumn advances, and curbing the use of the "exhilarating cordial." He acknowledged the "reverses and unsatisfactory results" which marked his trading activities in this district, but pointed to adverse circumstances and the company's conservation policies to explain low fur returns. He retained the confidence of Governor George SIMPSON and in 1826, with the administrative reforms that brought all of the HBC's North American activity under Simpson's control, his talents as a desk officer were recognized by a posting to Montreal.

As superintendent of the Montreal department, Keith ran the HBC office at Lachine, Lower Canada, from early 1827 to September 1835, and, after a furlough spent touring Great Britain and the Continent, from April 1837 to his retirement in September 1843. The business of the department consisted of the often unprofitable trade of the Ottawa valley and the king's posts, the hiring of winterers for the northwest, and a more remote supervision of the fur trade and fisheries of the lower St Lawrence and Labrador. Keith helped negotiate HBC leases of the king's posts in 1830–31 and 1841–42, and shared important aspects of his Lachine duties, including government correspondence, with Governor Simpson. His most demanding and rewarding work, however, was his semi-official handling of family business and private investments for fellow officers isolated inland.

Keith returned to Scotland in 1843, and his resignation from the HBC became effective 31 May 1845. On 8 July 1845 he married his second cousin Susan Angus, and they lived in Aberdeen until his death in 1851. His estate was valued at £15,000, securely invested in shares and debentures of English, Canadian, and Scottish public and private corporations, and was divided among his Scottish relatives and North American descendants.

Bureaucratic diligence and rigid integrity underlay Keith's success in the fur trade. Contemporaries stressed his intelligence, education, and at times stiff formality. Simpson's 1832 "Character book" described him as "a scrupulously correct honourable man of a serious turn of mind, who would not to save life or fortune, do what he considered an improper thing"; somewhat more colourfully, Keith's 1829–30 assistant at Lachine, Thomas Simpson, spoke of him as "a dried spider." Keith knew his limitations; contemplating retirement after a quarrel with the governor in 1834, he confessed that "I have been a martyr to low spirits and certain nervous affections during the greater part of my residence in the Indian Country, which have made me always appear and often feel very awkward and uncouth." This was a little harsh. His acerbic manner was balanced by his discretion, his invaluable service to colleagues while handling "private cash" accounts at Lachine, and his lifelong generosity to Scottish relatives and to the children and grandchildren of his brief country marriage. Keith belongs to that class of men who are remembered not for striking or colourful achievements, but for long and competent service in responsible though unspectacular positions.

PHILIP GOLDRING

Aberdeen Univ. Library (Aberdeen, Scot.), Davidson and Garden MSS, James Keith's estate trust papers. AUM, P 58. Can., Parks Canada, National Hist. Parks and Sites Branch (Ottawa), Nicholas Garry journal, 1821. GRO (Edinburgh), Auchterless, Reg. of births and baptisms, 20 March 1782. PAC, MG 19, A7; A41 (mfm.); B1; C1. PAM, HBCA, A.11/28: ff.18–171; A.36/8: ff.36–61d; B.134/b/1–9; B.198/e/6. Docs. relating to NWC (Wallace). HBRS, 2 (Rich and Fleming); 3 (Fleming). Alexander Ross, The fur hunters of the far west; a narrative of adventures in the Oregon and Rocky mountains (2v., London, 1855), 1. Simpson, "Character book," HBRS, 30 (Williams), 151–236. H. H. Bancroft [and H. L. Oak], History of the northwest coast (2v., San Francisco, 1884), 2.

KELLY, JEAN-BAPTISTE, Roman Catholic priest and vicar general; b. 5 Oct. 1783 at Quebec, son of John Kelly, a carter, and Marguerite Migneron; d. 24 Feb. 1854 in Longue-Pointe (Montreal).

As a boy, Jean-Baptiste Kelly was picked off the street by the parish priest of Quebec, Joseph-Octave Plessis*, and dispatched to primary school. He must have displayed potential for the priesthood, because in 1797 he was sent to the Petit Séminaire de Québec, where, according to a professor, he demonstrated

Kelly

"very great application in all things." In 1802 he was elected prefect of the students' Congrégation de la Bienheureuse-Vierge-Marie-Immaculée – the highest position in the fraternity; his assistants were Jacques Labrie* and Louis-Joseph Papineau*. From 1803 Kelly served under Plessis, then coadjutor bishop of Quebec, as assistant secretary, and from 1805 as diocesan secretary before being sent in August or September 1806 to assist Vicar General François Cherrier* at Saint-Denis, on the Richelieu. Cherrier quickly came to appreciate his "charming lieutenant vicar," whom Plessis, now bishop of Quebec, ordained priest on 9 Nov. 1806.

Two years later Kelly was sent to the arduous mission of Madawaska in New Brunswick. Plessis considered a three-year stint in the eastern missions excellent training and a severe test of character and discipline for mature young priests before they assumed responsibility for an established parish. On 16 Oct. 1808 Kelly reached Saint-Basile, N.B., a community of some 100 families to whom Plessis, through a pastoral letter, had expressed his displeasure "that your church is in ruins, that the presbytery is badly maintained, that the tithes are paid negligently, [and] that luxury, entertainment, and licentiousness reign among you." Alcohol was a major social concern; merchants and innkeepers sold liquor to the Indians at profits of 250 to 300 per cent. With such gains, "even my sexton wants to become an innkeeper," Kelly lamented, "and we already have nine!" Kelly was unable, despite constant efforts, to get the church rebuilt or the presbytery improved, and in 1809 he was obliged to seek refuge in an abandoned former presbytery, "open to the air on all sides." His problems only began at Saint-Basile, where he resided, for his mission included the Saint John valley south to Fredericton, and he made regular forays downriver which lasted as long as three months. In no community did he find complete facilities: chapel, presbytery, and communion silver. The Indians presented a particular challenge; they were Malecite and his dictionary was Abenaki.

Kelly had little time for study, but what leisure he had, he devoted to scripture and theology, as well as to English, French being his native tongue. Unlike most missionaries, he was not lonely; coming from a large, poor family, he had brought out four sisters, whom he supported. Moreover, the paternal Plessis counselled him regularly and in detail. Even so, Kelly suffered from the spiritual isolation that in the end bested most young priests sent to the missions. "I think," he wrote in January 1810, "that if St Jerome had had to go sixty leagues on snowshoe to obtain absolution and had needed confession as frequently as I, he would have given up the solitary life very quickly."

Kelly's ordeal ended in October 1810 when Plessis sent him to Saint-Denis to replace Cherrier, who had died the previous year. The promotion was a major one, for Saint-Denis was large, prosperous, and well disciplined, and it boasted a spacious and beautiful church. After piling up substantial surpluses in the parish treasury from 1810 to 1812, Kelly nearly emptied it between 1813 and 1817, on work inside the church by Urbain DESROCHERS and on the purchase of six paintings by European artists from a large collection sent to Lower Canada in 1816–17 by Philippe-Jean-Louis Desjardins*. In his selection of these paintings, Kelly displayed a refinement of taste in religious art uncommon among the clergy of his time. Trained under Plessis's influence, Kelly, unlike most of the older clergy, appreciated the importance of education, but his efforts to resuscitate a college established in the parish by Cherrier in 1805 were ultimately unsuccessful in the face of competition from another begun in 1809 at Saint-Hyacinthe by the Reverend Antoine Girouard*.

In addition to carrying a heavy parish charge, Kelly was employed by Plessis for diocesan affairs. In 1811 he accompanied the coadjutor bishop, Bernard-Claude Panet*, on a pastoral visit from La Malbaie to Quebec, and in 1816 he was with Plessis on another to Upper Canada. As well, Plessis consulted Kelly on the abilities and dispositions of the priests in parishes around Saint-Denis, a consultation he normally reserved for archpriests and vicars general.

By September 1817 Plessis felt Kelly was ready for a greater challenge. The parish of Saint-Pierre, in William Henry (Sorel), constituted a promotion in tribulation. Not only was it one of the five largest in the diocese and growing rapidly, it was tough. The soldiers in garrison were saintly in comparison to the *engagés* of the northwest fur trade, who raised boozing, brawling, and blasphemy to art-forms. In 1820 Kelly declined an invitation by Plessis to conduct a mission in the northwest. "I am so happy when spring comes to get rid of my voyageurs," he replied, "that I have no desire to meet them elsewhere." His income dropped, and his expenses rose from what they had been at Saint-Denis; his presbytery was declared structurally unsound about 1819; his church was old, dilapidated, and too small. The project that he initiated in 1822 to build a new church took ten years to complete and occasioned the usual disputes over location and assessment of the parishioners. Resourceful, Kelly used the stone from the old church to build a new presbytery.

An acute shortage of clergy obliged Plessis to add the charges of Île du Pads (Dupas) and Drummondville to Kelly's load. Kelly abhorred the latter, particularly because of its Irish population, but from 1818 to 1824 he faithfully struggled over the atrocious road to it. In 1822 he completed a small wooden church, Saint-Frédéric, that afforded a rare moment of joy. "The Protestants are jealous of it," he crowed, "theirs will never look as good as this one." In 1824 he was permitted to relinquish Drummondville to John HOLMES, but he continued to serve Île du Pads until 1831.

In William Henry as in Saint-Denis, Kelly promoted Catholic education. Following a policy instituted by Plessis, he boycotted the Royal Institution for the Advancement of Learning [see Joseph Langley Mills*], and by 1831 he had founded an English school; presumably one or more French schools already existed. In 1821 he had been a founding subscriber to the Association pour Faciliter les Moyens d'Éducation dans la Rivière-Chambly, formed to enable promising clerical prospects to attend the Collège de Saint-Hyacinthe.

Because the governor's summer residence was at William Henry, Kelly was able to keep Plessis and his successor, Panet, informed of the reactions of Lord Dalhousie [Ramsay*] to the controversial appointment in 1820 of Jean-Jacques Lartigue* as Plessis's auxiliary bishop at Montreal. Dalhousie's threats to subjugate the church to royal authority angered Kelly, who felt that the church should be an independent social power. He wrote to Panet in 1827: "I believe . . . we must not let ourselves be frightened by that man, that it will be necessary to bare our teeth. . . . We have a right to raise our voice and to make ourselves heard together at the foot of the throne. . . . Because we have been quiet spectators in politics it is thought that we feel nothing. It is quite clear that our enemies bear ill-will not only to the constitution of the country but also to its religion."

Although there was in Kelly a strain of French Canadian nationalism (which in part explains his repugnance for the Irish), he was as distrustful of the nationalist Canadian party, which dominated the House of Assembly, as he was of the colonial administration. When the assembly attempted to challenge the power of the clergy in parish administration by loosening the latter's control of the *fabriques*, Kelly urged Panet to intervene energetically: "It is time that a dike was erected against that body, ambitious and intoxicated by its success with the [British] ministers . . . it is trying to invade everything and take to itself not only the legislative and ecclesiastical power, but also the executive and judicial power." In 1834–35 he angered local nationalists led by Wolfred Nelson* when he refused to permit the erection in Saint-Pierre cemetery of a political monument to one of their followers, Louis Marcoux, slain during the elections of 1834. About 1837, as the government and the Patriote party moved steadily toward armed conflict, Kelly, who was convinced of the strength of the clergy's influence in Canadian society, urged Lartigue to speak out because his voice "at this time would be much more powerful than all the English bayonets in the country. . . . It

would be too late to wait for the government to strike several blows from which the factious would certainly profit to stir up the countryside. Once this impetus has been given, in vain will you try to make yourself heard; and the insidious would not fail to say that you were bribed by the government or that you came to its aid in your own interest." In William Henry, Kelly's own influence did much to brake the fervour of the rebellion movement.

In 1839 Kelly was suspected of having helped Dr George Holmes, murderer of Louis-Pascal-Achille Taché*, seigneur of Kamouraska, to flee to the United States. It is only certain, however, that he dissuaded Holmes from committing suicide. Holmes, a brother of John, was the lover of Taché's wife, Joséphine d'Estimauville, Kelly's relative by marriage, and he had for some time past been a favourite visitor to the presbytery. Two years after the murder, Kelly's testimony in favour of Joséphine at her trial for complicity probably helped obtain her acquittal.

By 1842 William Henry had exhausted Kelly. Ignace Bourget*, who had succeeded Lartigue, sent him and another ailing priest, Joseph-Sabin Raymond*, to Europe to restore their health and to try to resolve a number of issues facing the church. In Britain late that year they requested, in vain, the return to Lower Canada of the exiled rebels of 1837–38. A search for Irish priests to send to Montreal was scarcely more successful. In Paris they failed to persuade either the Filles de la Charité de Saint-Vincent de Paul or the Frères de Saint-Joseph to start communities in Montreal. Finally, in Rome, where they arrived in January 1843, they were unable to obtain the appointment of a coadjutor for Bourget or the creation of an ecclesiastical province in British North America. In both defeats Kelly detected the influential hand of the agent of the Montreal Sulpicians, Jean-Baptiste Thavenet*, with whom Kelly and Raymond also failed to settle the financial accounts of several Lower Canadian religious communities for which Thavenet was the European financial agent. The fruitless voyage destroyed several of Kelly's illusions. Still in ill health, he was dismayed to feel for the first time the inertia of old age and was thoroughly disenchanted with the quality of piety demonstrated by Parisians and Romans. "I am impatient to be back," he wrote to Bourget in March 1843, "for in the end, our country is as good as any other."

Kelly was in William Henry by August. Although his mission had been a failure, Bourget rewarded his efforts by naming him vicar general and a canon of the cathedral of Saint-Jacques, Montreal, the following month; the archbishop of Quebec, Joseph Signay*, who had made Kelly an archpriest in 1835, also appointed him vicar general. In the few months following his return, Kelly was troubled by a revolt of

Kempt

some parishioners who wished to retain his interim replacement, but their complete discomfiture in the election of wardens in December 1843 confirmed that he had imposed his authority on the parish. He did much to improve the welfare of his parishioners. In November 1843 Jean-Baptiste Meilleur*, deputy superintendent of education for Lower Canada, told him that his six schools were too many for the size of his population. In 1846 he founded a parish library containing 400 volumes. He had also founded a temperance society, and when in 1848 he blessed two bells purchased by the parish as a monument to temperance, an astonished Jacques VIGER commented, "It is a beautiful act of contrition and humility on the part of a parish formerly so – drunk!" That year Kelly began the establishment of an institution for the care of the poor and the sick and for the education of girls. In 1849, after he had built a new presbytery at his own expense, the old one was transformed into a college (to which he contributed £150) run by the Christian Brothers.

In the 1840s Kelly was gradually overcome physically by what Bourget described as his "immense task" at William Henry (renamed Sorel in 1845). By December 1849 he had retired to the Hospice Saint-Joseph at Longue-Pointe where he spent the next four years, increasingly infirm, mentally incapacitated, and in debt. He died there and was buried by Bourget in the church of Saint-Pierre, Sorel.

One of Kelly's parishioners, journalist Georges-Isidore Barthe*, described him as "a man of handsome and big stature, of very distinguished manners . . . admired for his knowledge and respected by all citizens, Catholic and Protestant." His historical significance lies chiefly in his having been, like Charles-Joseph DUCHARME, Thomas MAGUIRE, and Charles-François Painchaud*, an outstanding member of that generation of priests trained under Plessis who, by applying the bishop's principles, notably of parish ministry and education, contributed more than has been recognized to leading the clergy from its numerical weakness in the early 1800s to its position of independence and influence under Bourget.

JAMES H. LAMBERT

AAQ, 12 A, G: ff.53, 56v, 59, 79, 99, 140; H: f.3v; 210 A, VI: f.295; VII: ff.207, 275; IX: f.214; X: ff.77, 171, 357; XI: ff.23, 75, 437, 466–67; XIII: f.426; XIV: ff.195–96, 289–90, 446, 540–41; CD, Diocèse de Québec, I: 151; II: 111; 69 CD, III: 135; 311 CN, IV: 23–40; VI: 155; 26 CP, VIII: 129; H: 89–90. ACAM, 420.101, 843-1, 854-1; 901.017, 831-1; RC, I: ff.89, 90, 96v, 110–11v, 169–70; II: ff.104, 114, 142v, 146; III: f.186v; RLB, III: 158–59, 190–91, 300; RLL, V: 281, 339, 353–54. ANQ-Q, CE1-1, 27 mai, 5 oct. 1783; CN1-230, 20 févr. 1824. AP, Saint-Denis (Saint-Denis, sur le Richelieu), Livres des délibérations de la fabrique, 1791–1845; Livres de comptes, I (1775–1823). Arch. de la chancellerie de l'évêché de Saint-Hyacinthe (Saint-Hyacinthe, Qué.), XVII, C.25, 1810–17; C.66, 1817–50. ASQ, Fichier des anciens; Séminaire, 103, nos.42, 45; 178, nos.2, 148, 160, 163. "Les dénombrements de Québec" (Plessis), ANQ Rapport, 1948–49: 24, 49, 67. La Minerve, 25 Feb. 1854. Desrosiers, "Inv. de la corr. de Mgr Lartigue," ANQ Rapport, 1941–42: 399, 413; 1948–49: 346, 380–82, 389, 406, 416, 420–21, 445, 459, 473. Léon Pouliot et François Beaudin, "Correspondance de Mgr Ignace Bourget," ANQ Rapport, 1955–57: 183, 185, 195; 1965: 99; 1969: 39–40, 113, 117. Thomas Albert, Histoire du Madawaska d'après les recherches historiques de Patrick Therriault et les notes manuscrites de Prudent L. Mercure (Québec, 1920). Allaire, Hist. de Saint-Denis-sur-Richelieu. G. I. Barthe, Drames de la vie réelle, roman canadien (Sorel, Qué., n.d.). Chabot, Le curé de campagne. Chaussé, Jean-Jacques Lartigue. Azarie Couillard-Després, Histoire de Sorel de ses origines à nos jours (Montréal, 1926). Claude Galarneau, Les collèges classiques au Canada français (1620–1970) (Montréal, 1978). Lambert, "Joseph-Octave Plessis." Lemieux, L'établissement de la première prov. eccl. Pouliot, Mgr Bourget et son temps, 2. Côme Saint-Germain, Regards sur les commencements de Drummondville (Drummondville, Qué., 1978). F. M. Dufresne, "Le drame de Kamouraska," Québec-Hist. (Montmagny, Qué.), 1 (1972), nos.5–6: 72–76. Sylvio Leblond, "Le drame de Kamouraska d'après les documents de l'époque," Cahiers des Dix, 37 (1972): 239–73.

KEMPT, Sir JAMES, army officer and colonial administrator; b. c. 1765 in Edinburgh, son of Gavin Kempt and Miss Walker, the daughter of Alexander Walker of Edinburgh; d. unmarried 20 Dec. 1854 in London.

Nothing is known of James Kempt's early life, but in March 1783 he was commissioned as an ensign in the 101st Foot, becoming a lieutenant in August 1784. When the regiment was disbanded the following year, he was placed on half pay and remained so until 1794, when he was gazetted captain and then major in the newly raised 113th Foot. Following that regiment's disbandment he served for a while as inspecting field officer of recruiting at Glasgow but was reduced to half pay in 1796. Three years later, as lieutenant-colonel unattached, he was appointed aide-de-camp to Sir Ralph Abercromby, then commanding the troops in North Britain (Scotland), whom he accompanied with expeditionary forces to Holland and subsequently to the Mediterranean. On Abercromby's death in 1801 in Alexandria, Kempt was attached to the staff of Lord Hutchinson and was present throughout the Egyptian campaign. In 1803 he became aide-de-camp to General David Dundas, commander-in-chief of the Southern District in England, with headquarters at Chatham, and later that year he obtained the lieutenant-colonelcy of the 81st Foot, with which he went to the Mediterranean in 1805 under Sir James Henry Craig*. Between 1807 and 1811 Kempt was quartermaster general in British North America, and in 1809 he was promoted colonel. He was transferred in 1811 to the staff of the Duke of Wellington on the Iberian Peninsula, with the rank of major-general. Severely wounded in the assault on Badajoz, he fought with gallantry and distinction in the campaigns of 1813–14 in Spain and France. In the summer of 1814 he commanded one of the four brigades sent from Bordeaux to reinforce the British army in the Canadas; the forces under his command served in the Montreal District, on the Niagara frontier, and at Kingston. Recalled to Europe because of Napoleon's flight from Elba, he commanded the 8th Brigade at the battle of Waterloo.

For his distinguished service during the Napoleonic Wars Kempt received a succession of honours: the KCB and GCB in 1815, the GCH in 1816, and a clutch of foreign decorations. From 1813 he had held the lieutenant governorship of the garrison at Fort William, Scotland, and in 1819 he was appointed lieutenant governor of Portsmouth, England. He was successively colonel of the 60th Foot (1813), the 3rd West India Regiment (1818), the 81st Foot (1819), and the 40th Foot (1829). He was promoted lieutenant-general in 1825 and general in 1841.

Like so many of Wellington's officers, Kempt was to find employment after the Napoleonic Wars in the colonial service. In February 1819 he requested a military posting at Halifax, N.S., but that autumn he was offered the lieutenant governorship of Nova Scotia on the elevation of Lord Dalhousie [Ramsay*] to governor-in-chief of British North America. Unacquainted with Nova Scotia, its people, or its government, Kempt took advantage of his personal friendship with Dalhousie, with whom he had served in Spain, to write at once for information and advice. In June 1820, in a sketch of Nova Scotian politics that was to be followed by a decade of correspondence between the two men, Dalhousie warned Kempt of imminent political disharmony. His generally harmonious term in office had been marred during the last session of the assembly, when it had advanced claims to extend its rights, especially over the appropriation of crown revenues, at the expense of both royal prerogatives and the powers of the Council. Confronted with this challenge, Dalhousie's relations with the speaker of the assembly, Simon Bradstreet ROBIE, had deteriorated to the point where he had been determined not to accept again as speaker "an ill tempered crab, deeply tinctured in Yankee principles." In his journal, Dalhousie predicted that an unpleasant confrontation lay ahead "unless Sir Jas. Kempt begins with a firm hand, in the steps which I should have adopted had I remained here." Kempt, somewhat overawed by the magnitude of the task he had undertaken, professedly set out with the intention of following in Dalhousie's footsteps and taking his ideas and policies as the guide for his own conduct.

Fortunately for the harmony of his administration in Nova Scotia, and later in Lower Canada, as well as for his peace of mind, he adopted a more conciliatory stance than that instinctively assumed by his prickly, Presbyterian mentor when challenged by ambitious, wily local politicians. Though their notions of colonial government were not dissimilar, the contrasting temperaments of the two men made all the difference in practice.

One of Kempt's first tasks after he arrived in Nova Scotia on 1 June 1820 was to travel to Cape Breton in order to proclaim that colony's reunion with the mainland. The British government had decided on reannexation as the best means of eliminating the administrative chaos of recent decades and placing the island's government on a sounder and wholly legal basis [see George Robert Ainslie*]. Reunification also prompted new arrangements for leasing the coal mines in Cape Breton, and in 1826 all mineral rights in Nova Scotia were taken over by the General Mining Association of London to the eventual benefit of the provincial economy, if not of crown revenues [see Richard Smith*]. Financial questions were potentially controversial but, much to Kempt's relief and satisfaction, the annual meetings of the legislature during the early 1820s proceeded more temperately and harmoniously than he had been led to anticipate. Initially he attributed this conduct to the lecture Dalhousie had delivered to the assembly before his departure, but more decisive were Kempt's cordial relations with Speaker Robie in the transaction of public business. For several years the financial supplies were voted by the assembly without complaint or challenge to executive control over crown revenues, though Kempt did not expect this disposition to last. Writing to Dalhousie in January 1821, he recognized that "the temper of all such Bodies is very variable, and their unceasing aim is to grasp at power and to encroach upon the rights and privileges of the other Branches of the Legislature."

For the moment at least, the energies of the inhabitants seemed to be consumed in religious controversies. This was especially apparent in the matter of higher education, which involved both denominational and financial questions. King's College, the Anglican establishment at Windsor, was not only rent asunder by a long-standing and unseemly personal quarrel between its president, Charles Porter*, and its vice-president, William Cochran*, but the college's building was falling into an advanced state of dilapidation for want of funds. A sum of £30,000 was needed for a new edifice and additional teaching staff, and the Reverend John Inglis*, the ecclesiastical commissary, optimistically launched what Kempt described in December 1821 as a grand "begging scheme" to raise this vast amount in England. To break the Anglican monopoly of higher education, Dalhousie had been instrumental in inaugurating a non-sectarian college in Halifax, which bore his name but which lacked the financial resources to complete its building or even to obtain a royal charter of incorporation. By 1823 it was burdened with a debt of £5,000. A third institution, Pictou Academy, begun by the Reverend Thomas McCulloch* and the Presbyterians, also joined in the scramble for whatever funds might be available from crown revenues or by votes of the legislature. In 1821 the assembly had voted £1,000 towards the erection of Dalhousie College, and Kempt repeatedly urged the colonial secretary, Lord Bathurst, to authorize the grant of a further £1,000 out of the revenue received from the leasing of provincial coal mines. But Bathurst, a staunch churchman, stubbornly refused to sanction any payment to Dalhousie College. "Grieved and mortified" by the decision, Kempt blamed the intrigues of both the bishop of Nova Scotia, Robert Stanser*, "who is still at Home enjoying his Salary but living in a state of idleness as concerns the duties of his sacred office," and John Inglis, "one of the most *cunning* and *persevering* of Men."

Kempt soon reached the conclusion that the most effective and economical arrangement in these circumstances would be the unification of Dalhousie and King's colleges, though he could not yet see how it might be accomplished. Insufficient funds existed to finance separate institutions and Kempt considered one college, in Halifax, adequate to supply all the wants of Nova Scotia for years to come. Although some supporters of King's opposed its transfer to a populous metropolis, with its supposedly evil influences, by 1823 Inglis and the majority of the college's governors had come to favour amalgamation as a way out of their parlous straits. Representatives of the two academies hammered out a plan of union in 1824 which promised to safeguard their respective interests. Administration and instruction were to be placed in Anglican hands, but religious tests would apply only to students in divinity.

Kempt fully expected that so mutually acceptable and rational an arrangement would be endorsed by the colonial secretary and the archbishop of Canterbury, Charles Manners-Sutton. All parties, however, had not reckoned with the latter's assertive high-churchmanship. His veto was decisive. Kempt could do nothing, even by his presence in London, to temper "the abominable obstinacy or rather the bigotry of the Archbishop of Canterbury" or to convert Bathurst to a more sympathetic point of view. The failure of union, Kempt complained to Dalhousie in July 1825, "will be a great triumph to MacCulloch and his Gang," and it perpetuated rival denominational colleges in Nova Scotia at the expense of public education.

Between May 1824 and August 1825 Kempt was on leave of absence in England, attending to private affairs. By the time of his return to Nova Scotia, the British government had decided, against his cautionary advice, to ask the colonial legislatures in North America to vote a civil list covering the salaries of the leading officials for a period of years. In common with his councillors and the supporters of executive authority, Kempt doubted the wisdom of raising the highly contentious issue of financial appropriation. If the assembly's powers were thus increased and control over crown revenues surrendered in exchange for a civil list, the lieutenant governor and civil officers would become, in effect, dependent on the assembly for their salaries. The Colonial Office, Kempt predicted, would then experience ten times as much trouble in securing annual votes of supply and would excite in Nova Scotia disputes similar to those which were agitating the Canadas under Dalhousie's administration. At the same time, if the proposal was to be made at all, he maintained that it should be done only under circumstances which would ensure its favourable reception. In the session of 1826 members of the Nova Scotia assembly would be preoccupied with the impending general election and, as a result, would not treat such a controversial matter on its merits. With this in mind, Kempt did no more than allude briefly to the embarrassing subject in his speech opening the legislature in February 1826. "I *slipt* it in, in as *quiet* a way as I could," he informed Dalhousie. It was left to his successors to grapple with this uncomfortable issue.

As further justification of his cautious approach on financial matters, Kempt counselled delay until recent changes in imperial trade laws had produced their anticipated benefits for Nova Scotia's commerce. The relaxation in 1825 of restrictions on the British colonies' trade with the United States, Europe, and the West Indies was likely to give a positive fillip to Nova Scotia's economy, which was only now emerging from a prolonged post-war depression. When this recovery occurred, the province's assembly might be more receptive to granting a civil list. Certainly Kempt's term as lieutenant governor saw unmistakable signs of reviving commercial activity. The Halifax Banking Company was launched in 1825 by Henry Hezekiah COGSWELL and others, and construction began the following year on an ambitious and expensive project, the Shubenacadie Canal. Well might Kempt draw satisfaction from the growing mood of optimism. His time in Nova Scotia was an era of good feelings before the agitation over political reform began in the 1830s under Joseph Howe*. Kempt himself was universally liked and respected, being a man, Howe noted approvingly, who "had a passion for road making and pretty women." One of his aides-de-camp later recalled that "society, by the force of his example, was the most agreeable thing imaginable," but he was "perfectly astonished" by Kempt's abilities as a colonial administrator.

In the spring of 1828 Kempt was temporarily

engaged in a special military assignment, the presidency of a commission of inquiry into the building of the Rideau Canal in Upper Canada. With good reason, the authorities in London had become deeply worried about the mounting expense of the venture, the open-ended contracts made by its chief engineer, Lieutenant-Colonel John By*, and the projected cost of completing what military men still regarded as a valuable contribution to the defence of British North America. From what Dalhousie told Kempt confidentially about the enterprise, Kempt judged that the British government had sanctioned construction precipitately, before reliable estimates of its total cost had been received. If this were so, there could be no justification for blaming By because his expenditure far exceeded the careless preliminary calculations. Nor could Kempt see the point of assembling an investigative commission when By was quite capable of sending home whatever explanations were required. He also hoped to be spared the long, tiresome journey. His health had not been good, and because lameness resulting from an old wound had confined him to Government House for most of the previous winter, he complained in June that "my legs are by no means in *Campaigning Order*." But the commission was obliged to make a cursory inspection of the canal site that month. With as many as 17 hours a day spent traversing rough terrain between Bytown (Ottawa) and Kingston in sweltering temperatures, Kempt endured more misery and fatigue than during his soldiering days. *Thank God*," he exclaimed on reaching Kingston, "I am at last again in a Christian Country and out of the land of Swamps and Mosquitoes." In its report the commission made a number of recommendations which signally failed to check escalating costs and the lavishness with which By continued to spend the British taxpayers' money.

This task completed, Kempt expected to return to Nova Scotia to serve out peacefully the remainder of his gubernatorial term. But events in Quebec and London were soon to bring about his translation to Lower Canada. Since 1825, foreseeing the likelihood that he might be designated Dalhousie's successor as governor-in-chief, he had repeatedly told his superiors that he was comfortably placed in Halifax and had no desire at all to be moved to the Canadas. "I am grieved," he typically remarked to Dalhousie in March 1827, "seriously *grieved* to hear you *hint* at the possibility of my soon filling your shoes in Canada. . . . I do assure you most solemnly that a removal to Canada is the *last wish* of my heart." In the autumn of 1827 he wrote to the colonial secretary, William Huskisson, requesting that he might succeed to the chief military command in North America in the event of Dalhousie's rumoured transfer to India. Kempt's idea was to hold this senior military appointment in conjunction with the lieutenant governorship of Nova Scotia, by shifting the army's headquarters from

Quebec to Halifax. Objections from the military authorities in London ruled out this suggestion, but a rapid deterioration in Dalhousie's relations with the Lower Canadian assembly prompted Huskisson in May 1828 to consider the scheme of making Kempt the new governor-in-chief. That spring the assembly's weighty petitions of grievance arrived in Britain, embodying serious charges against Dalhousie's administration. When these, along with an accumulation of protests from Upper Canadian reformers, were taken up in the House of Commons by critics of the ministry of the Duke of Wellington, Huskisson thought it politic to concede a select committee of parliament to inquire into the civil government of the Canadas. In early 1828 Dalhousie was appointed to command the British forces in India and Kempt was invited to restore harmony and tranquillity to the distraught colony, a task he would commence late that summer.

Sir James did not greet the news of his appointment with enthusiasm. Although Dalhousie noted in his journal in July 1828, "I know well that he would have felt sore hit if any other had passed over him," Kempt did not regard the offer as a coveted promotion. Despite its grander title, the governorship, he argued, was in practice of no greater importance or pecuniary value than a lieutenant governorship. Moreover, the severity of the North American climate had adversely affected his health and he had grown weary of being a colonial administrator. He was now "anxious to get a couple of years *to myself* to take a ramble on the Continent" and fulfil a long-standing ambition to visit Switzerland and Italy. He reluctantly accepted the appointment only out of a sense of duty and with the warning that nothing would induce him to stay for more than two years at Quebec.

Certainly he was confronted in Lower Canada with a political crisis of formidable proportions and his predecessor gloomily forecast continued wrangling with an excitable, refractory legislature. For some years past the lower house had been trying to extend its political power at the expense of the executive by seeking to appropriate all revenues raised in the colony [see Denis-Benjamin Viger*]. Because the assembly would not agree to vote a permanent civil list, successive governors had fought not only to preserve the integrity of crown revenues but also to frame annual money bills in such a way that no tacit recognition was given to the assembly's claim to these revenues. During Dalhousie's absence on a visit to Britain in 1824–25, however, his deputy, Sir Francis Nathaniel Burton*, had accepted from the assembly a supply bill which merged crown and other revenues in one public fund and voted a lump sum to defray the expenses of government for a single year, thus vindicating a demand hitherto denied. The bill was endorsed by the Legislative Council and acquiesced in, after initial protests, by the authorities in London, and in 1826 a similar measure was presented to Dalhousie after his return. He rejected the bill as an infringement on crown rights. Having produced a deadlock on the matter of supplies, he illegally appropriated provincial funds to meet the deficit in the budget. His relations with the assembly were further soured by his vigorous, partisan interference in the election of 1827.

Despite the constitutional impasse produced by Dalhousie, Kempt approached his task with a degree of equanimity, if not sanguine confidence, which his predecessor considered most unrealistic. Although Kempt's "experience in these colonial Parliaments enables him to judge of the state of the quarrels here," the earl confided to his journal in July 1828, "yet he does not see clearly the difference that exists between a well adapted system in Nova Scotia with reasonable and sensible, and honourable men to deal with, from the state of these matters in Canada which I would at once pronounce to be the very opposite." Sir James hoped that fresh instructions from the Colonial Office would see him through his immediate difficulties and that the British parliament would soon provide a permanent settlement of the issues in dispute.

These expectations were to be disappointed, and throughout his brief administration Kempt was left very much to his own devices. Periodic instructions from London were couched in vague, contradictory terms, which reflected the bewilderment and indecision of British ministers when they pondered Canadian affairs. William Huskisson did at least acknowledge that Dalhousie's methods had been ill conceived and dangerous, and should not be emulated. "I am sure," he had explained to Kempt in May 1828, "that you must have seen too much of mankind not to be aware, that Governments, having a popular representation, are not to be manoeuvred like a Battalion upon the Parade." He stressed the imperative necessity of dealing with the Lower Canadian legislature in a conciliatory, tactful manner. Beyond that, Huskisson and his successor at the Colonial Office, Sir George Murray*, declined to send more explicit instructions until the select committee on Canada advised that ministry how best to resolve the present controversies. For this reason, too, in July Kempt was given a temporary commission as governor of Lower Canada and promised a new warrant and instructions as governor-in-chief once the committee had reported, a promise that was never fulfilled, much to his chagrin. In August 1828 he left Halifax, to assume his new duties following Dalhousie's departure for England early the next month.

Even after the select committee had completed its work later that summer, imperial policy continued to be paralysed by irresolution. Wellington's cabinet was not favourably disposed towards a report which, inconveniently, upheld the complaints of the colonists

on almost every point and made recommendations which, if implemented, would further undermine executive independence and transfer effective power to the assemblies, and thus, in the case of Lower Canada, to the Patriote party [see Louis-Joseph Papineau*]. At the same time, domestic political considerations precluded the ministers from openly repudiating the committee's findings, which had been greeted with approval in the House of Commons. Preoccupied by Catholic emancipation and other issues in Britain, they prevaricated, leaving Kempt to wrestle with the most baffling and meaningless instructions any governor ever received.

From the outset he saw his overriding task as that of keeping the peace by acting with prudence and forbearance. Learning from Dalhousie's mistakes, he abstained from expressing personal opinions and listened patiently to all parties, including Papineau. Eventually Kempt acted according to his own best judgement because there were no officials on whom he felt he could safely rely in a colony rent by political squabbles and personal animosities. "I find to my surprise and regret," he commented to Dalhousie in May 1829, "that scarcely any two Public Men entertain the same views and sentiments on any one Political Subject, or indeed on any matter of general interest!" In these circumstances, he had explained to Murray, "I am endeavouring to steer clear of all Parties, and to conciliate all . . . but no effectual reformation of any kind, I fear, can take place, until the Financial disputes are *finally settled*." He looked anxiously to British ministers to provide that settlement.

Until it occurred, temporary expedients and politic concessions were the order of the day in an attempt to keep the colony's government on an even keel and to preserve tolerable relations between councils and assembly. This was "very uphill laborious work," Kempt admitted to Dalhousie in February 1849, but "I have quite made up my mind not to Engage in a *personal* quarrel with either branch of the Legislature." He was aided in this endeavour by the current mood of both houses. Many members of the English party, such as Chief Justice Jonathan Sewell* and Herman Witsius Ryland*, concluded from the Canada committee's report that the unyielding conservatism traditionally evinced by the Legislative Council had fallen out of favour in England, and that prudential cooperation with the assembly was now necessary in order to maintain their influence. The assembly, too, was temporarily put into a more accommodating frame of mind by the unexpectedly favourable contents of the report and was prepared to work with a governor who commanded respect for his evident fair-mindedness.

When in November 1828 Kempt met the legislature, prorogued by Dalhousie "under very *peculiar circumstances* 18 months earlier, he devised a mutually acceptable formula for confirming Louis-Joseph Papineau as speaker of the assembly without re-election, even though he had previously been rejected by Dalhousie. When Sir George Murray subsequently pointed out that this procedure did not conform to his instructions, Kempt penned the first of several letters bemoaning the failure of his superiors to appreciate his efforts in trying circumstances. Greater controversy was soon sparked by the governor's acceptance of the supply bill for 1829. According to Murray's instructions of the previous September, the assembly was to be allowed, for one year at least, to frame a supply bill to defray the large proportion of the civil government's expenditure which could not be covered by crown revenues. The instructions also explicitly acknowledged the weakness of the governor's position in financial matters. "So long as the Assembly is called upon to provide for, & to regulate any portion of the Public Expenditure," Murray conceded, "it will virtually acquire a controul over the whole." Because of the insufficiency of crown revenues, the executive "cannot be relieved from a state of virtual pecuniary dependence upon the Assembly by any Constitutional means."

Fortified by this frank avowal, which Kempt was to cite when later accused of having disobeyed his instructions, the governor managed to secure a money bill from the assembly, the measure passing the Legislative Council through the extraordinary expedient of the chief justice, as speaker, exercising a double vote. Since the bill was similar in form to that of 1825, which the Colonial Office had deprecated, Kempt's action created dismay in London. Tory ministers exchanged anxious communications and there was talk of disallowing the act, but eventually cooler counsel prevailed and, with consolatory expressions of regret which fell short of outright censure, Kempt was authorized to accept a similar appropriation bill in 1830. In the short term the proceedings of 1829 and 1830 enabled Kempt to establish harmonious relations with the legislature in matters of finance. But acceptance of the assembly's view on the form that the appropriation bill should take merely encouraged that body to press a substantive and more contentious claim, control of the detailed expenditure of all crown revenues.

This financial arrangement was not the only unpleasant surprise that Kempt conveyed to his superiors. In 1829 the assembly unexpectedly decided to reform the inequalities in the system of representation in Lower Canada by redistributing seats in an enlarged house on the basis of population. Although the protests of English-speaking assemblymen went unheeded, the Legislative Council revised the bill on a combined principle of territory and population, and the lower house acquiesced in this alteration. Kempt welcomed the measure as the best that could ever be obtained from the assembly, but this colonial initiative on a controversial issue again caused consternation in London. Some ministers urged disallowance of the act because the English-speaking inhabitants of the Eastern Townships, though given seats for the first time, would be grossly underrepresented in an assembly whose membership, increased from 50 to 84, was certain to contain a greater proportion of French Canadians. At a special meeting of the British cabinet, however, the act was grudgingly approved and in August 1829 Murray informed Kempt of this decision.

By this time, if not before, Kempt had concluded that little useful guidance would be forthcoming from Britain to aid him in dealing with the Lower Canadian assembly. Many public dispatches remained unanswered and attempts to initiate private, confidential communications with Murray elicited only "a few hasty lines from the *Under Secretary* written apparently *without* the *least knowledge* of the subject on wh. he was treating!!!," Kempt confided to Dalhousie in August 1830. Meanwhile two parliamentary sessions had passed unproductively in Britain. Though a bill was introduced into the House of Commons in 1829 and again in 1830 to settle the financial dispute in the Canadas by surrendering to the two Canadian legislatures control over the revenues raised under the Quebec Revenue Act of 1774, in return for civil lists, the contents of the bill were wholly unknown to Kempt. Bereft of imperial aid or advice, he devoted his best endeavours to calming political passions as the assembly renewed in 1830 its violent attempts to secure judicial reform and elective councils [see Denis-Benjamin Viger]. "My Legislative Bodies are composed of such *inflammable* materials," the harassed governor declared in March, "that I feel myself seated on a *Barrel* of *Gunpowder* not knowing from one moment to another how soon an explosion may take place." He tried to act as a mediator, pursuing an independent course and keeping his temper. "My great object," he told Dalhousie, "has been to carry on the Government if possible without a reaction of any kind, and this I have in some degree accomplished." Anxious to escape from his uncomfortable thraldom, he reminded the colonial secretary in July of his desire to return to England that autumn at the latest. Murray attempted to dissuade him from resigning the governorship by appealing to his own interests as well as those of the public service. But having been a colonial administrator for more than ten years, and having passed almost the whole of his professional life overseas, Kempt asserted that "I have arrived at a *time of life*, when I am quite capable of judging what is best for my *personal interests*." No man, he believed, "ever relinquished an Office of £8,000 a year with greater satisfaction than I

Kempt

shall do." His release was granted and on 20 Oct. 1830 he handed over the government to Lord Aylmer [Whitworth-Aylmer*].

Well might Kempt have been satisfied with his term in office. He had managed the almost impossible feat of preserving a degree of harmony and good feeling in Lower Canada for two years. Although British ministers might grumble about his regrettable departures on several occasions from the letter of his instructions, he acquired the reputation of being the one governor who had handled Canadian affairs with a measure of success. This singular achievement can be attributed in part to qualities of character and personality and in part to a deliberately non-partisan approach to provincial politics. Though a dour Scot with at times a brusque, abrasive manner, he displayed sufficient tact and soundness of judgement to win a sympathetic respect from colonists of diverse interests and persuasions. Moreover, his lack of definitive instructions was far from a disadvantage, for it afforded him a latitude of discretion which he employed to good effect.

Kempt was also exceptionally lucky. He profited from the salutary effects in Lower Canada of the Canada committee's report, just as he benefited from the inevitably favourable contrast with his luckless predecessor. Perhaps these fortuitous circumstances distorted his achievement. When Kempt was again suggested as a candidate for governor of the Canadas in August 1837, Lord Howick, then secretary at war in Lord Melbourne's cabinet, remarked, "I have always thought him a man with a higher reputation than he deserves acquired I believe in a great measure for his having had the good fortune to leave Canada at the right moment & to have had both for his predecessor & successor persons who made him shine by comparison." There is some truth in this assessment. Certainly the "era of good feelings" which he and prevaricating Tory ministers conspired to produce in Lower Canada between 1828 and 1830 did nothing to resolve underlying disputes. On the contrary, the barren interlude stored up accumulating trouble for their respective successors in the early 1830s.

Kempt's dealings with Upper Canada in his capacity as governor-in-chief of British North America were slight and he was content to leave matters there in the care of the lieutenant governor, Sir John Colborne*, with whom he had served in the Napoleonic Wars. But his overall responsibility for defence and Indian affairs in both provinces led him to indulge an abiding enthusiasm for road building by constructing a military road from York (Toronto) to Penetanguishene and to work with Colborne in remodelling the structure and policy of the Indian Department, most notably by creating in 1830 a separate department for Upper Canada and transferring its supervision from the military to civil authorities [see James Givins*]. At a time when the British government was anxious to reduce its expenditure in the Canadas, Kempt argued that the costly practice of distributing presents and stores to Indian tribes in order to preserve their friendship could not yet be safely abandoned, but it might eventually be rendered unnecessary if the Indians could be encouraged to settle in villages. This move would promote their material welfare and long-term self-sufficiency as agricultural communities; it would also be the means of accomplishing their civilization through instruction in religion as well as in husbandry. Under the charge of a superintendent appointed for each district of the Indian Department, Kempt envisaged, the government would gather Indians together on cleared tracts of land and provide houses and initial supplies of agricultural implements and stock. He hoped to foster the activities of Anglican and British Wesleyan missionaries, who would also counteract the mischievous influence of American Methodists among the Indians [see William CASE]. Like many well-meaning contemporaries, Kempt believed that raising the Indians in the scale of civilization depended on permanent settlement and industrious labour, an assimilationist policy easier to espouse than to put into practice.

After his term in British North America, Kempt returned to England and became involved in domestic politics and military administration almost at once, following the advent of the Whigs to office in November 1830. They had great difficulty finding an experienced military man willing to become master general of the Board of Ordnance because most senior officers were Tories. Kempt accepted the post, with a seat on the Privy Council, on condition that he would not be required to enter the House of Commons or have anything to do with party politics. He thus became responsible for supervising the multifarious duties of the board: supplying the troops at home and overseas with arms and manufactured articles, erecting and maintaining military works and buildings, and administering the corps of artillery and engineers. In his capacity as master general he served on the royal commission appointed in 1834 to investigate the question of military punishments, which two years later produced a moderate defence of flogging in the army but recommended a wide range of salutary reforms in the conditions of army service.

More controversially, Kempt was a member of a royal commission set up in 1833 to examine the civil administration of the army. The following year its chairman, the Duke of Richmond, drafted a report which recommended a consolidation of the various civil departments involved in army affairs into an army board headed by a cabinet minister, and also a merging of the corps of artillery and engineers with the regular army. Because Kempt was known to be opposed to any change in the powers or status of the Ordnance department, he was not consulted about the draft report and he protested vigorously to Prime Minister Earl Grey. In 1835, when Lord John Russell criticized the decisive objections to administrative reform voiced by military men, he remarked that Kempt "was our great stumbling block before," though virtually all senior officers implacably opposed such a reorganization.

Kempt resigned as master general when the Whigs went out of office in December 1834 and he began a belated retirement from public life. His name was canvassed by Lord Aberdeen, the Tory colonial secretary in 1835, as one of the commissioners to be sent to the Canadas on a fact-finding mission. On the eve of the rebellion of 1837–38, when Whig ministers were discussing candidates to replace Lord Gosford [Acheson*] as governor, Kempt was again mentioned, though he would then have been more than 70 years of age. Thereafter he faded from the public scene.

In retirement he corresponded and socialized with old army friends, among them the Duke of Wellington and Lord Seaton [Colborne]. Kempt lived to see the outbreak of the Crimean War in March 1854 but was spared seeing the legendary Wellingtonian army humiliated. He died in London on 20 December; under the terms of his will gifts of money totalling £59,800 and £675 in annuities were left to various relatives, friends, and fellow officers, including Charles Stephen Gore* and the son of Sir Archibald Campbell*. Kempt's death, followed that winter by the passing of other Napoleonic War officers, was grievously lamented by John Charles Beckwith*, himself a veteran, whose opinion was undoubtedly shared by many comrades – "All these men I regard as the patriarchs of all that is solid in England."

PETER BURROUGHS

NLS, Dept. of MSS, Adv. MSS 46.8.8–15; MS 15029. PAC, MG 24, A52 (copies); B1, 6, 14–15; B16. PANS, RG 1, 63–66; 113–113½. PRO, CO 42/217–30; 43/27–28; 217/138–48; 218/29–30 (mfm. at PAC); PROB 11/2204: 392–93. SRO, GD45/3. Univ. of Durham, Dept. of Palaeography and Diplomatic (Durham, Eng.), Earl Grey papers. Christie, *Hist. of L.C.* (1848–55), vols.3, 6. *Doc. hist. of campaign upon Niagara frontier* (Cruikshank), 1: 175. *Gentleman's Magazine*, January–June 1855: 188–89. G.B., Parl., Command paper, 1836, 22, [no.59]: 1–556, *Report from his majesty's commissioners for inquiring into the system of military punishments in the army*; 1837, 34, pt.I, [no.78]: 1–200, *Report of the commissioners appointed to inquire into the practicability and expediency of consolidating the different departments connected with the civil administration of the army*. L.C., House of Assembly, *Journals*, 1828–30. N.S., House of Assembly, *Journal and proc.*, 1820–28. L.-J. Papineau, "Correspondance de Louis-Joseph Papineau (1820–1839)," Fernand Ouellet, édit., ANQ *Rapport*, 1953–55. *Select British docs. of War of 1812* (Wood), 1: 269; 3: 229, 344, 346. *Times* (London), 22 Dec. 1854. Boase, *Modern English biog.*, 2: 190–91. *DNB*. G.B., WO, *Army list*, 1783–1854. Morgan, *Sketches of celebrated Canadians*, 266–68. Wallace, *Macmillan dict.* Elizabeth Graham, *Medicine man to missionary: missionaries as agents of change among the Indians of southern Ontario, 1784–1867* (Toronto, 1975), 23–24. MacNutt, *Atlantic prov.* George Raudzens, *The British Ordnance Department and Canada's canals, 1815–1855* (Waterloo, Ont., 1979). G. C. M. Smith, *The life of John Colborne, Field-Marshall Lord Seaton . . .* (London, 1903), 327. H. [G. W.] Smith, *The autobiography of Lieutenant-General Sir Harry Smith, baronet of Aliwal on the Sutlej*, ed. G. C. M. Smith (2v., London, 1901), 1: 340–41; 2: 303, 396. Taft Manning, *Revolt of French Canada*.

KERBY (Kirby), JAMES, militia officer, businessman, justice of the peace, office holder, and politician; b. 1785 at Park Farm near Sandwich (Windsor, Ont.), son of John Kerby and Alison Donaldson; m. 1811 Jane Lambert, and they had three children; d. 20 June 1854 at Fort Erie, Upper Canada.

According to John Mackay Hitsman, before the War of 1812 the "acquisition of a militia commission was the first step towards a career in politics or a profitable position under the Crown." For James Kerby, however, it was much more. His interest in military affairs, which was to remain throughout his life and intertwine constantly with his civilian pursuits, was probably kindled by events during his early years which threatened the security of the Niagara peninsula [see John Graves Simcoe*]. In 1805 Kerby began working at Queenston as a clerk-bookkeeper for Thomas Clark*, who not only ran a series of profitable businesses but was also a senior officer in the militia. When Clark became commanding officer of the 2nd Lincoln Militia on 9 July 1809, Kerby was appointed regimental adjutant. In 1810 Kerby and another of Clark's employees, Robert Grant, launched their own shipping business. The outbreak of hostilities with the United States in the summer of 1812 disrupted trade along the frontier and ended the business activities of Grant and Kerby. Both men were immediately involved in militia affairs.

Kerby remained adjutant of the 2nd Lincoln and also commanded an artillery company in support of it. On the morning of 9 Oct. 1812 his company was manning the British batteries on the Niagara River opposite Black Rock (Buffalo, N.Y.) when it was ordered to open fire on the *Detroit* and the *Caledonia*, ships which had been captured by an American raiding party. In this, his first action under fire, Kerby seems to have performed well. After the death of Sir Isaac Brock* at Queenston Heights, the Americans mounted another offensive on 28 November. The attack was countered and, for his part in the action, Kerby

Kerby

received his first official commendation for service under battle conditions. Following the abortive offensive, the British continued to fire at troop movements on the opposite shore and during one such fire fight, on 2 Dec. 1812, "a twenty-four pounder gun" burst and Kerby was wounded severely in the right hand.

When winter ended a campaigning season, the militia usually returned to their homes, but the seriousness of the situation early in 1813 prompted the organization of the Volunteer Incorporated Militia Battalion, essentially a full-time organization composed of volunteers, which Kerby immediately joined on 25 March as a captain. In late May 1813 the Americans attacked and occupied Fort George (Niagara-on-the-Lake) and subsequently occupied the entire Canadian side of the river. Kerby accompanied the British forces as they withdrew before the Americans, and throughout the summer and autumn he commanded a small group of volunteers who joined the advance guard of Major-General John Vincent*'s division. By the end of the year, however, the British had reoccupied the frontier and in December captured Fort Niagara (near Youngstown) on the American side of the river. In this action, Kerby directed the embarkation of troops for the assault and was "the first person to land" on the American side. His activity in one of the storming parties was recognized in official dispatches and subsequently by the assembly which on 14 March 1814 voted that "a sword, value fifty guineas be presented to Captain Kerby."

At the beginning of July 1814 an invading force of Americans crossed the Niagara River at Fort Erie and moved towards Queenston. Kerby's battalion was hurriedly moved to the area and participated in the battle of Lundy's Lane which followed. Kerby had just been promoted major and, when his commanding officer, Lieutenant-Colonel William Robinson, was wounded, he assumed command of the battalion. It suffered 142 casualties but Kerby's handling of the force was commended by Lieutenant-General Gordon DRUMMOND. Kerby remained in command of the battalion during the siege of Fort Erie where he was wounded in both the shoulder and the hip, and was again singled out for honourable mention in dispatches. Disabled for several weeks, he resumed acting command of the incorporated militia on returning to duty. The battalion saw no more fighting, and the peace arranged in February meant that the incorporated militia could be disbanded. After two years of continuous military service, Kerby could attempt to resume his civilian career.

His business had been ruined by the war and his partner, who had been taken prisoner of war in July 1814, was not repatriated for several months. Kerby and Grant immediately began a series of memorials to the government asking for compensation for damages during the war, and Kerby began a series of petitions on his own behalf for a land grant and on behalf of the incorporated militia for half-pay. By late 1817, the year in which Kerby was appointed a justice of the peace, the business "had so far prospered that they planned the construction of a warehouse and wharf at Queenston of their own." In February 1820 Kerby and Grant purchased a grist-mill at "Fort Erie rapids" and two years later Kerby moved to the small village of Waterloo (Fort Erie) near the mill. In January 1823 Benjamin Hardison purchased one-third of the mill but died the following July, after which time Kerby "appears to have undertaken the management of the mill."

During his military service with the advance guard in 1813, Kerby had commanded a party which seized two horses from the home of an American sympathizer then residing in Upper Canada, and in 1824, while Kerby was visiting the United States, the man brought suit against him. After much legal wrangling, the case was eventually heard in circuit court. Kerby claimed that he would have been court-martialled had he disobeyed orders but the court found against him on 8 Jan. 1827. When the Supreme Court of New York upheld the decision, Kerby was quickly granted compensation for his costs by the Upper Canadian government.

Kerby had continued to devote substantial time to the militia, returning to the 2nd Lincoln following the disbandment of the incorporated battalion. In February 1822 he was gazetted major, in March 1823 he was promoted lieutenant-colonel, and that June he became regimental commander with the honorary rank of colonel. Kerby became the town warden of Bertie Township in 1826 and later the first postmaster in the township. Instrumental in establishing St Paul's Church (Anglican) in Waterloo, he remained a warden of the church until his death.

For reasons that are not altogether clear, Kerby dissolved his partnership with Robert Grant at the end of 1830, though he continued to operate the mill. In the 1830s Kerby was frequently bothered by ill health, which apparently interfered both with the profitable operation of his mill and with his service on the Legislative Council, to which he was appointed in 1831. On 20 Dec. 1837, shortly after the unsuccessful insurrection led by William Lyon Mackenzie*, Kerby was authorized to raise a special force from militiamen to resist any invasion Mackenzie might mount from American territory. Under Kerby's command this force became known as the Queen's Niagara Fencibles and served actively for a year and a half. From 5 April to 2 June 1838 Kerby was in command of all troops on the Niagara frontier, and throughout the summer and following winter he continued to play an important role in the courts martial and pacification which followed Mackenzie's rebellion.

In September 1834 Kerby had been appointed collector of customs at the port of Fort Erie, and his rigid application of the law aroused a good deal of hostility. In 1840 he also became the lessee of ferry rights at Fort Erie, which he hoped would substantially bolster his income. However, the combination of the two posts seems to have increased his problems, and his unpopularity, more than his income. According to one account he was "one of the most detested men on the Niagara frontier." Not only was he zealous in collecting duties but, in attempting "to provide a personal return badly needed and legally his, Kerby kept rival ferries constantly in custody and frequently up for sale."

In his later years Kerby seems to have been hard pressed for funds. In 1843 he sold his mill, though he retained his positions as postmaster and collector of customs. Illness continued to be a difficulty: he was frequently sick and in 1839 both his wife and his mother died; in 1846 his son died at 24 and the death of a son-in-law meant that one of Kerby's daughters and her small child became dependent on him. None the less, he remained active in the militia. With the reorganization resulting from the Militia Act of 1846 came the formation of the Welland Regiment. Kerby became commanding officer of the 1st battalion and remained the senior militia officer in the Niagara District. He was a member of the committee formed to superintend construction of a new memorial to Sir Isaac Brock, designed by William THOMAS. When the memorial cornerstone was laid, he acted as one of the honorary pallbearers for Brock's coffin. Kerby died on 20 June 1854, allegedly of cholera brought on by eating greens. He was buried at Fort Erie in St Paul's where a memorial window and tombstone commemorate him.

A. M. J. HYATT

AO, MS 500; MU 2109, 1845, no.7; MU 2110, 1846, no.8; RG 1, C-I-3, 32: 24, 47; 33: 68; 132: 14; C-I-4, 4: 100. PAC, MG 24, I31. *Doc. hist. of campaign upon Niagara frontier* (Cruikshank). "Journals of Legislative Assembly of U.C.," AO *Report*, 1912: 147–49. "The register of Saint Paul's Church at Fort Erie, 1836–1844," ed. E. A. Cruikshank, *OH*, 27 (1931): 77–192d. M. F. Campbell, *Niagara: hinge of the golden arc* (Toronto, 1958). E. A. Cruikshank, *A memoir of Colonel the Honourable James Kerby, his life in letters* (Welland, Ont., 1931). J. M. Hitsman, *The incredible War of 1812: a military history* (Toronto, 1965). B. A. Parker, "The Street–Clark business of Niagara to 1844: a study of a commercial dynasty" (MA thesis, Univ. of Western Ont., London, 1978). Janet Carnochan, "Inscriptions and graves in the Niagara peninsula," Niagara Hist. Soc., [*Pub.*] (Niagara-on-the-Lake, Ont.), no.19 ([2nd ed.], n.d.). R. K. T. Symons, "The Brock Monument and a visitors' book, 1829 and 1830," *OH*, 29 (1933): 72–75.

KERWAN (Kerwin). *See* KIRWAN

KIEFFER. *See* KEEFER

KIELLEY (Kielly), EDWARD, surgeon and naval officer; b. *c.* 1790 in St John's; m. there 13 June 1822 Amelia Jackson, and they had two sons and one daughter; d. there 8 March 1855.

Nothing is known of Edward Kielley's family or early life. He studied under Daniel Coughlan, a military surgeon at St John's, and in June 1814 became an assistant surgeon in the Royal Navy, serving on the hospital ship *Niobe*. In August of the following year he was promoted surgeon. His experiences in the navy during wartime may well have had a formative influence on his character; many years later he would recall with pride his visits to Russia and Greece, and he remained to his death strongly loyal to Britain. Kielley's cosmopolitan experience and military loyalty were factors which held him apart from other Roman Catholics in St John's, most of whom were Irish immigrants, and led him to identify and associate with the ruling Protestant establishment in the colony. By November 1818 Kielley was back in St John's practising as a surgeon. Six years later he was indicted by the grand jury for common assault and assault with intent to commit rape upon Mrs Eleanor Ann Shea of Twillingate. At the trial on 9 July 1824, prominent fellow surgeon William Carson*, who had known Kielley since arriving in Newfoundland in 1808, testified on his behalf. The verdict stated that "the Jury are unanimous in Honorably acquitting the Defendant, of charges brought ag[t] him in the *Disgusting* Action."

When Thomas John Cochrane* became governor of Newfoundland in 1825, Kielley found himself in official favour and in fact soon became Cochrane's friend. In 1826 he was appointed surgeon to the local jail, a salaried position under the government. It is possible that he would also have received the more lucrative post of district surgeon, had not both he and Cochrane been absent from the colony when the situation became vacant late in 1827. Instead, Carson received the appointment. Kielley had gone to England to try to secure his half pay from the navy, and to obtain permission to stay in Newfoundland while retaining his rank as surgeon. He in fact returned to full-time service, and was appointed surgeon to the *Barham*, on the Jamaica station. However, in May 1828 he was "invalided" at Jamaica and was obliged to return to Newfoundland "nearly in a dying state." The precise nature of the injury or illness is not known, but, according to his own statement, for some time afterwards he found himself in "embarrassed circumstances" owing to "periodical attacks, a debilitated constitution, and a total loss of my practice." Nevertheless, later that year he was back in St John's, where he resumed the office of jail surgeon.

Kielley professed a desire to stay away from

Kielley

political matters. In 1828 we find his name among petitioners for a representative legislature, and in 1829 he and John Kent* addressed a meeting of Roman Catholics who were pressing for the extension of Britain's Catholic relief act to Newfoundland. But in the late 1820s these were causes which the majority of sensible men were supporting. When reports circulated around St John's in 1830 that he had written a controversial letter on a Roman Catholic question, he wrote to Henry David WINTON's *Public Ledger* denying authorship and stating that he had never "either directly or indirectly, during my residence in this community, mixed myself with, or taken any part in, any dispute of a religious or political nature." Kielley was an active member of the Benevolent Irish Society until 1833, but when the society, led by Patrick Morris*, was drawn into partisan politics on the side of the reformers, he withdrew from it. However, the period 1832–38 was so charged with political and sectarian tensions that it was not possible for a prominent Catholic such as Kielley to remain untouched by events.

Although Carson was district surgeon, from 1827 Kielley was an occasional adviser to the local authorities on matters affecting public health. In 1832 he became a member of the newly established board of health and medical officer for the port of St John's. In giving Kielley this latter responsibility, Cochrane apparently overturned a decision of the chief justice, Richard Alexander Tucker*, who while acting as administrator some months earlier, had given the post to Carson's son-in-law, Joseph Shea. But Cochrane was determined to give Kielley an even greater boon. On 31 March 1834 he declared Carson's post of district surgeon "abolished," and shortly afterwards assigned the duties of the office to Kielley. The official appointment of Kielley as district surgeon followed on 1 July. It was a move which Carson deeply resented. Hereafter Kielley's government offices were a matter of contemptuous discussion in the reformers' newspaper, the *Newfoundland Patriot*, and of debate in the House of Assembly. Whether Kielley liked it or not, he was a public figure. In the event, his tenure as district surgeon was destined to be brief. Upon gaining control of the assembly in 1837, Carson and the reformers set about undermining his position, and in 1838 he was effectively forced out. In that year a supply act was passed providing for the appointment of four district surgeons for St John's and containing a provision prohibiting the jail surgeon (Kielley) from occupying one of the four positions. However, Kielley by then had sole charge of the St John's Hospital, a post which, though it initially brought him only a small income, by 1851 was providing him with a comfortable annual salary of £300.

In the heated political atmosphere of the 1830s Kielley, as a protégé of Cochrane, had soon been publicly identified as "a Tory of the first waters" and as an opponent of the pro-Catholic reform party. What kind of pressure was brought to bear upon him as a consequence is hard to determine with certainty. In 1838 Kielley complained to Cochrane about "the cruel system of persecution which thro' the influence of the Catholic priesthood has for the last four or five years been so industriously pursued against me," and which had affected him "most seriously in my professional practice." From this letter, Kielley seems to have been in straitened circumstances; yet John Valentine Nugent* described him the following year as "apparently affluent." At any rate, Kielley was making no effort to conceal his antipathy to the reformers in St John's and his public support for the candidates of the opposing interest in the elections of 1836. The openness of his political views is illustrated by his prominence at an extraordinary public occasion in March 1836. It was the custom of the Benevolent Irish Society to hold an annual celebration in honour of Saint Patrick. That year, Kielley presided at an opposition celebration on 17 March attended by "Orange Catholics" and certain of the Protestants whom the reformers most hated and feared, such as Winton, a particular friend of Kielley's, and Chief Justice Henry John Boulton*, one of his patients. Following a series of patriotic toasts, Kielley himself toasted Boulton and praised him for protecting citizens from the "tyranny of a mob." This was his most daring thrust at the reform party in Newfoundland. Antagonism towards Kielley was now so intense that in October the vicar general, Edward Troy*, refused to walk in a funeral procession in his company. The burial was delayed nearly an hour until Kielley was informed that his presence was causing embarrassment among the clergy. He withdrew. The funeral proceeded.

Kielley was a marked man. He was also a person of compassion and pride, "a plain man who spoke the feelings of his heart," as he once described himself, and the two sensational court cases in which he found himself embroiled in the late 1830s were provoked, in part, by his own outspokenness. The first of these cases was an action for defamation of character brought by Dr Samuel Carson, William Carson's son, against Kielley in May 1837. Kielley had been called to examine a female patient who had been attended by the younger Carson and another physician, John Rochfort*. The woman appeared to have been extensively mutilated in a surgical attempt to induce birth. On seeing her broken body and squalid circumstances, Kielley, who was known throughout his life, and with good reason, for his concern for the sick poor, exclaimed: "They have butchered the woman, and deserve to be hanged!" This opinion was widely circulated through St John's, allegedly to the injury of Samuel Carson's reputation. In the two-day trial in July which followed, Boulton, the presiding judge, openly sided with Kielley and denounced Carson for his shameful treatment of the woman. The child had died and, although the woman survived, Boulton stated that she was "a perfect cripple, and will most probably remain a wretched object all her life." When William Carson was called to testify, Boulton rebuked him scathingly and at length for conducting a painful, unauthorized, and intimate examination of the patient merely to be able to testify on his son's behalf. Boulton also took advantage of the occasion to remind "the lower orders of people" that they were not "to be treated like cattle" by physicians. The trial ended in a nonsuit. The *Public Ledger*, in commenting on the trial, pointed to the "combination which has so long existed among most of the medical men of this town" against Kielley. The elder Carson, the paper noted, was especially antagonistic towards him. In Winton's view, Kielley now stood "decidedly first among the civilian medical practitioners in this community."

In 1838 Kielley again found himself at the centre of furious controversy. On 6 August he and Kent quarrelled in the streets of St John's. Kielley allegedly called Kent a "lying Puppy" and threatened to beat him, whereupon Kent withdrew to the assembly and claimed that his privileges as a member of that body had been violated. After examining three witnesses, the house determined that Kielley should be arrested; a warrant was issued by the speaker, Carson, and the arrest was made by the serjeant-at-arms, Thomas Beck. Beck required the help of the messenger of the house, David Walsh, who later admitted in court that he was compelled to use "a little force" to get Kielley out of his home. Kielley, who later claimed he was arrested "with great force and violence," was kept in custody in Beck's home. On 7 August Kielley was brought before the House of Assembly and asked for an explanation of his conduct; he responded by calling Kent, in his seat, "a liar and a coward" and "other very many contumelious epithets," and was remanded in the custody of the serjeant-at-arms. On 9 August he was again brought before the house. A formal apology was demanded. He declined to make it. Warrants were then issued committing Kielley to the common jail, where he appears to have spent that night. On 10 August he was released by the sheriff on a writ of habeas corpus issued by George Lilly*, assistant judge of the Supreme Court. The house, on 11 August, ordered the arrest of the sheriff and Lilly, and both were taken into custody. Kielley, in the mean time, had gone into hiding. Two days later Governor Henry Prescott* prorogued the house and the immediate crisis was over. The house met again on 20 August. On entering the speaker's room shortly before it resumed, Carson was served with a writ by the sheriff on behalf of Kielley, claiming assault and false

imprisonment, and setting damages at £3,000. Similar writs were served on other members, including Kent and Peter Brown*, and on Walsh, whom Kielley tried to have arrested.

The case of *Kielley* v. *Carson* was a celebrated one in 19th-century Newfoundland legal history [*see* Sir Bryan Robinson*]. At issue was the House of Assembly's right to commit for contempt. This was by no means an inconsequential issue in the colony during the 1830s. It was "a restless and dangerous age"; if the house legitimately possessed the right claimed by its members, they were by no means ill disposed to use it. The indignation provoked by the behaviour of the assembly contained also an element of alarm. The case was tried by the Supreme Court of Newfoundland, and a decision favouring the House of Assembly was delivered on 29 Dec. 1838, with Lilly dissenting. Kielley then appealed to the judicial committee of the Privy Council in Great Britain. The case was argued before the committee in January 1841 and May 1842, and a decision reversing the judgement of the court was handed down on 11 Jan. 1843. Referring to the House of Assembly, the decision read: "They are a local Legislature, with every power reasonably necessary for the proper exercise of their functions and duties, but they have not what they have erroneously supposed themselves to possess – the same exclusive privileges which the ancient Law of England has annexed to the House of Parliament." The long delay in arriving at a decision caused tension and anxiety in Newfoundland. The verdict was important insofar as it defined a limitation in the power of colonial assemblies, and it thus had implications for the entire British empire. In Newfoundland it was believed that the affair was the cause of the suspension of the constitution of 1832. Certainly, it solidified the antagonism felt towards the assembly by the merchants and the press. Self-styled reformers summarily placing eminent citizens in custody was not likely to win esteem for the house. These same reformers in the assembly, said the Harbour Grace *Star*, "are the gentlemen who abhor oppression, who all along have been declaiming against our *arbitrary* Fishing Admirals, our *despotic* Governors, our *tyrannical* Judges, our *absolute* Surrogates, our *grinding* and *exactious* Merchants and *snarling* Officials." At the personal level, Kielley was vindicated and in 1844 the assembly agreed that Kielley's expenses in the lengthy litigation, nearly £1,000, should be paid out of public funds.

The rivalry between Kielley and Carson appears to have been professional and political rather than personal. In July 1841, at a public dinner in St John's, Carson proposed a toast to Kielley as "a happy specimen of Native talent, wisely and successfully exercised," and Kielley, to the surprise of the *Newfoundlander*, responded by complimenting Car-

Kimber

son as "his old and respected friend." The dinner was the "first festival" of the Natives' Society, an organization that was founded in June 1840 and soon attracted considerable notice. Kielley had originated the project of a natives' society in 1836. The idea arose, he said, "because strangers had been sucking the vitals of the country," while Newfoundlanders had been treated "as intruders in their Native Land." In 1840 he became the society's first president – an honour which he held to be "one of the proudest incidents of his life." The society held its first quarterly meeting on 12 September in a fish store in St John's. In an emotional speech, Kielley explained the objectives of the organization, and Robert John Parsons*, another native, followed by declaring: "This night we proclaim ourselves a people – we proclaim our nationality." The society professed to have "nothing to do with religion" and, as Kielley said in 1842, to belong to "no party."

Inevitably, however, the Natives' Society, like the Benevolent Irish Society, was drawn into the political squabbles of the day, and by 1845 was accused by Parsons of being "divided." When the natives met in July 1845 to protest the failure of Governor Sir John HARVEY to favour Newfoundlanders in making appointments, Kielley supported the move, apparently with some hesitation. He trusted, he said, "that the proceedings would be conducted with due respect to the Head of the Executive." Parsons, on the other hand, was now associating native rights with his campaign for responsible government and Daniel O'Connell's slogan of "Ireland for the Irish, and the Irish for Ireland." Such ranting must have made Kielley uncomfortable. In May 1845 the foundation stone for a Natives' hall was laid, but in a major storm of September 1846 a building erected on the site – a "miserable bundle of boards," according to Parsons – blew down, killing two people who had taken refuge in it. Subsequently interest in the society declined. A movement which might have done much to overcome religious and partisan bitterness in the colony had come to nothing.

Kielley's final years were passed in the comfort and comparative obscurity of professional employment. Unlike Carson, he had always taken a greater interest in medicine than in public affairs, and in a speech given in 1854 he expressed the hope that his health would enable him "long to enjoy the happiness of administering relief to suffering humanity."

Edward Kielley was a surgeon noted for his compassion. In politics, he was one of the few prominent Newfoundland Roman Catholics to side openly with the ruling Protestant élite and oppose the so-called "Catholic Party." He did not, however, seek publicity, and was drawn into prominence more by accident than by design.

PATRICK O'FLAHERTY

Benevolent Irish Soc. (St John's), Minutes (mfm. at PANL). NLS, Dept. of MSS, MSS 2276, 2278. PANL, GN 2/1; GN 2/2; GN 5. PRO, CO 194/61–146; CO 199/19. Supreme Court of Nfld. (St John's), Registry, 3: f.252 (will of Edward Kielley, probated 7 June 1855). *Kielley* v. *Carson* (1839), 2 Nfld. R. 91, *rev'd*. [1841–42] 4 Moore, P.C. 63–92; 13 E.R. 225; 2 Nfld. R. x (P.C.). Nfld., House of Assembly, *Journal*, 1833–55. *A record of the extraordinary proceedings of the House of Assembly of Newfoundland, in the arrest and imprisonment of Edward Kielley, esq., surgeon, &c. &c. and subsequent arrest of the Honorable Judge Lilly and the High-Sheriff (B. C. Garrett, esq.) for, (as the House has it!) "breach of privilege!!"* (St John's, 1838; copy in Memorial Univ. of Nfld. Library, Centre for Nfld. Studies, St John's). *Re Kielley* (1838), 2 Nfld. R. 72. *Newfoundlander*, 1827–34, 1837–43. *Newfoundland Express* (St John's), 1854–55. *Newfoundland Mercantile Journal*, 1816–27. *Patriot* (St John's), 1834–55. *Public Ledger*, 1827–55. G.B., ADM, *Navy list*, 1814–30. Gunn, *Political hist. of Nfld*.

KIMBER, TIMOTHÉE, physician, distiller, and Patriote; b. 11 Feb. 1797 at Quebec, son of Joseph Kimber and Josette Dabin; d. 6 Feb. 1852 in Chambly, Lower Canada.

Joseph-Antoine Jékimbert, a forebear of the Jékimberts or Kimbers, was a gardener originally from Aix-la-Chapelle (Federal Republic of Germany) who is thought to have come to New France as a soldier in the colonial regulars between 1750 and 1753. Some 12 or 15 years after his arrival, he adopted the spelling Kimbert or Kimber to give a more French form to his name. His son Joseph, the father of Timothée, served in Quebec's militia battalion in the winter of 1775–76 and probably helped repel the American invasion. He subsequently worked as a gardener in the town, like his father. In 1780 he married at Quebec.

Timothée Kimber was the eleventh in a family of twelve children. Despite his humble origin, it was possible to send him to school. He began classical studies at the Petit Séminaire de Montréal in 1806 and did not complete them until 1816. At the end of his schooling he remained in Montreal for a few years and decided to train as a doctor there. According to Laurent-Olivier David*, John Douglas Borthwick*, and Ægidius Fauteux*, in 1817 or 1818 Kimber's attention was attracted by young Jean-Olivier Chénier* – later the hero of Saint-Eustache – and he took the boy under his wing, making himself responsible for educating him. Kimber is believed to have gone to Europe in 1819, and the following year he studied medicine in Paris. No doubt he enjoyed being in France, where, as he attended courses, he probably absorbed the revolutionary philosophy of 1789.

Kimber returned to Lower Canada in 1821 and on 22 June was licensed to practise medicine, surgery, and obstetrics in the colony. He took up residence at

Chambly, near Montreal, and soon opened an office there. On 12 Nov. 1822, at Chambly, he married Emmélie Boileau, daughter of René Boileau*, a former member for Kent in the House of Assembly. By his marriage Kimber entered one of the old and distinguished French Canadian families in the Richelieu valley. Like his cousin René-Joseph Kimber* of Trois-Rivières, he was a skilful doctor and thus soon acquired a large practice. Because of his knowledge and ability he was also called upon to supervise the training of a number of medical practitioners, one of whom was Chénier. In 1831 Kimber was elected to the board of examiners for the district of Montreal, along with Robert Nelson*, Jacques Labrie*, and Wolfred Nelson*, among others. During the cholera epidemic the following year he was appointed a member of the Chambly board of health, which was chaired by the co-seigneur of Chambly, Samuel Hatt, a legislative councillor.

Kimber greatly admired Louis-Joseph Papineau*, the leader of the Patriote party. He also formed a friendship with Wolfred Nelson, one of Papineau's principal lieutenants in the Montreal region. Indeed, around 1830 he went into partnership with him to set up a distillery at Saint-Denis, on the Richelieu, which was burned down a few days after the battle in that village in November 1837. In 1834 Kimber was one of the principal Patriotes in Chambly County, and participated in the meeting held there that year which took a stand in favour of the 92 Resolutions.

By April 1837, following the British parliament's adoption of Lord John Russell's resolutions, the Patriote leaders decided to organize mass protest meetings [see Denis-Benjamin Viger*]. On 4 June Kimber participated in the one held in Chambly County, along with Louis-Michel Viger and Louis Lacoste*, Patriote members for Chambly in the House of Assembly. On 21 October he resolutely hoisted the tricolour over his house to salute Papineau as he passed on his way to Saint-Charles-sur-Richelieu where the Assemblée des Six Comtés was to take place. Two days later he himself attended this meeting; the day after, apparently well informed about deliberations that had already taken place amongst the Patriote leaders, he put forward a plan for an uprising: "As soon as the [St Lawrence] is taken, we will go with 40 or 50,000 armed men and take Montreal; all the habitants are well armed and well supplied with ammunition and very determined, and after Montreal we will take Quebec." Naturally his friend Nelson's proposal "to melt [our] spoons into bullets" had gained the enthusiastic support of Kimber, who had then dissociated himself from Papineau's moderate policy to side openly with the radicals and their advocacy of recourse to arms.

On 16 Nov. 1837 Kimber, considered the leader of the Patriotes in Chambly County, was on the verge of being arrested when a few of his supporters got to his house just in time to rescue him from the escort coming to take him prisoner. Historians are not agreed on what part Kimber played the next day in the Chambly road incident. According to Robert Christie, Kimber helped Bonaventure Viger* at the time of the ambush which Viger and a group of men set for a detachment of the Royal Montreal Cavalry in order to free Pierre-Paul Démaray and Joseph-François Davignon. But David asserts that Kimber only urged his supporters to go and liberate the two prisoners. Gérard Filteau and Fauteux make no mention of his participating in any way in the skirmish. Whatever the case, the Patriotes proposed soon after to seize Fort Chambly, and Kimber with François Barsalou, one of his assistants at Chambly, made preparations for the attack which was to be launched on the night of 18 November. However, that evening a large detachment of the 15th Foot and a number of volunteers arrived as reinforcements for the Chambly garrison and the plan had to be abandoned.

Eager to help with preparations for resistance, Kimber went to join Nelson at Saint-Denis, probably on 21 November. On the morning of the 23rd Nelson instructed Kimber to keep a watch on Lieutenant George Weir, who had been captured by the Patriotes the night before, but Weir was killed several hours later in circumstances which have never been completely cleared up. During the fighting at Saint-Denis, Kimber tended to wounded Patriotes and prisoners. Two days after the defeat at Saint-Charles-sur-Richelieu he fled from Saint-Denis. He was, however, arrested along with Siméon Marchesseault, Jean-Philippe Boucher-Belleville*, Rodolphe Desrivières*, and one or two other companions at Bedford on 7 December, before he could manage to cross the American border. He was held for a few days at Fort Lennox on Île aux Noix, and then taken on 12 December to the jail in Montreal, with, among others, Robert-Shore-Milnes Bouchette*. He was not set free until some days after the general amnesty granted by Lord Durham [Lambton*] on 11 July 1838. The authorities must have considered him a rebel of prime importance, since they required £10,000 bail for him; this figure was reduced to £5,000, the sum exacted for Jean-Joseph Girouard and William Henry Scott, after bitter arguments which, according to Fauteux, were the reason why Kimber and these two were not released at the same time as the other amnestied prisoners.

After his release Kimber returned to Chambly. It seems that he had no part in the second uprising, for the authorities must have kept him under close surveillance. He took up his profession again and practised medicine for the rest of his life. Kimber died at Chambly on 6 Feb. 1852, at the age of 54. He and his wife had had one son, Hector, who died in 1844.

Having come from a line of gardeners, Timothée

King

Kimber had risen in the social scale through his profession and his marriage with the daughter of a prominent family. As a member of the French Canadian middle class, which was assuming an increasingly important place in society, he played an active part in the struggle to reform the political régime, even joining those who resorted to armed uprising in 1837 to secure the triumph of the Patriote cause. Like many of his confrères, Kimber contributed in his way to the advancement, emancipation, and greater welfare of his compatriots in Lower Canada during the first half of the 19th century.

MICHEL DE LORIMIER

ANQ-M, CE1-39, 12 nov. 1822. ANQ-Q, CE1-1, 27 juin 1780, 11 févr. 1797; E17/15, nos.862–65; E17/22, nos.1485–86; E17/38, nos.3053–54. Arch. de l'univ. de Paris, Faculté de médecine, reg. des inscriptions, 1820. BVM-G, Fonds Ægidius Fauteux, notes compilées par Ægidius Fauteux sur les Patriotes de 1837–1838 dont les noms commencent par la lettre K, carton 6. PAC, RG 4, B28, 49: 822–24; 52: 1532–39. R.-S.-M. Bouchette, *Mémoires de Robert-S.-M. Bouchette, 1805–1840* (Montréal, 1903), 44. "Les dénombrements de Québec" (Plessis), *ANQ Rapport*, 1948–49: 15, 65, 114. *La Minerve*, 3 juill. 1832, 14 avril 1834, 12 juin 1837, 18 juill. 1844, 10 févr. 1852. F.-J. Audet, *Les députés des Trois-Rivières*, 53–55. Borthwick, *Hist. and biog. gazetteer*, 183. Fauteux, *Patriotes*, 174, 276–78. J.-J. Lefebvre, *Le Canada, l'Amérique: géographie, histoire* (éd. rév., Montréal, 1968), 142. Abbott, *Hist. of medicine*, 51. M.-J. et George Ahern, *Notes pour servir à l'histoire de la médecine dans le Bas-Canada depuis la fondation de Québec jusqu'au commencement du XIXᵉ siècle* (Québec, 1923), 318. Allaire, *Hist. de Saint-Denis-sur-Richelieu*, 346–47. Armand Auclaire, *Chambly: son histoire, ses services, ses associations, ses religions* (Chambly, Qué., 1974), 11–12. Chabot, *Le curé de campagne*, 111. Chapais, *Cours d'hist. du Canada*, 4: 197. Christie, *Hist. of L.C.* (1866), 4: 443, 451–54. L.-O. David, *Les gerbes canadiennes* (Montréal, 1921), 172–73; *Patriotes*, 28, 147. Filteau, *Hist. des Patriotes* (1975). Laurin, *Girouard & les Patriotes*, 68. Maurault, *Le collège de Montréal* (Dansereau; 1967). J.-B. Richard, *Les événements de 1837 à Saint-Denis-sur-Richelieu* ([Saint-Hyacinthe], 1938), 7, 30, 33. Rumilly, *Papineau et son temps*. Sulte, *Mélanges hist.* (Malchelosse), 9: 44–45. *Les Ursulines des Trois-Rivières depuis leur établissement jusqu'à nos jours* (4v., Trois-Rivières, Qué., 1888–1911), 1: 468. "Billets de la distillerie de Saint-Denis," *BRH*, 23 (1917): 346. C.-M. Boissonnault, "Histoire de la médecine: histoire des médecins canadiens," *Laval médical* (Québec), 17 (1952): 223–72. "La famille Jékimbert ou Kimber," *BRH*, 21 (1915): 201–5. Sylvio Leblond, "La médecine dans la province de Québec avant 1847," *Cahiers des Dix*, 35 (1970): 69–95. Gérard Malchelosse, "À travers notre histoire: un épisode de 1837," *La Rev. nationale* (Montréal), 3 (1921): 85–87. Fernand Ouellet, "Papineau dans la révolution de 1837–1838," *CHA Report*, 1958: 13–34. Damase Potvin, "D'autres médecins que les chefs des Patriotes furent moins directement mêlés aux troubles de 1837–38," *L'information médicale et paramédicale* (Montréal), 1ᵉʳ oct. 1957: 14. Benjamin Sulte, "La famille Kimber," *BRH*, 5 (1899): 252.

KING, WILLIAM HENRY, schoolteacher, homoeopathic physician, and convicted murderer; b. November 1833 in Sophiasburg Township, Upper Canada, eldest son of George King and Henrietta ——; m. 31 Jan. 1854 Sarah Ann Lawson of Brighton Township, Upper Canada, and they had one child, who died in infancy; d. 9 June 1859 in Cobourg, Upper Canada.

William Henry King, who from childhood "gave evidence of a very intellectual and persevering turn of mind," was sent to school in Sophiasburg at the age of five. His progress was so pronounced that the following year he was taken by his teacher to other schools "on exhibition days to speak pieces on the stage." In 1844 the family settled in Cramahe Township where William's father soon amassed "a considerable amount of property" and became "independent." After the 1851 harvest, William went to the Normal School in Toronto, which he attended during the winter months of the next two years. Married early in 1854, King moved to Toronto where he and his wife took in boarders while he studied for his first-class teaching certificate. After he obtained the certificate, they moved to Hamilton, again taking in boarders, and William taught school and began the study of homoeopathic medicine with a local doctor. In the fall of 1856 King entered the Homœopathic Medical College of Pennsylvania (Hahnemann Medical College and Hospital of Philadelphia), from which he received his diploma early in March 1858, and on St Patrick's Day he set up a practice in the small community of Brighton. His income was soon about $200 a month and he felt that he was "in a fair way to acquire both fame and wealth."

King's professional ascendancy was, however, offset by personal unhappiness. Three months after his marriage, he claimed, he had discovered that his wife "was not the virgin I married her for." Shortly thereafter his wife, now pregnant, accused her husband of "misusing" her and returned to her parents; during this time King wrote a number of letters accusing her of infidelity, for which he later apologized. Early in 1855 their child was born (to whom "it is said that he manifested much dislike") but it was to live only about a month. During King's stays in Philadelphia in 1856–57 and 1857–58, his wife had again removed to her parents' farm. It is perhaps not surprising that domestic tranquillity did not await him on his arrival in Brighton in the early spring of 1858.

Shortly after his return, King became involved with one of his patients, Dorcas Garrett. This relationship ended abruptly in the early summer when Miss Garrett threatened to make public a letter from King which entreated her not to marry too quickly since his wife was ill and would probably die. The doctor later claimed to have been ashamed of himself. His wife became pregnant again in June but that fall a further temptation entered his life. On 23 September he met Melinda Freeland Vandervoort, "a young lady of about 20 years, . . . well educated, of a rather . . . coquettish turn, though not what would be called handsome." She had apparently fallen in love with a photograph of King on a visit to his house and he was "completely intoxicated" by the beauty of her singing voice. They exchanged puerile love letters: one of his, addressed to "Sweet little lump of good nature" on 10 October, claimed that his wife was very ill. Four days later his wife "took sick." She suffered severely from vomiting until her death on 4 November. Despite the protestations of her parents, who attended her throughout most of the ordeal, King had resisted calling in other doctors when her condition did not improve. He had diagnosed her problem as ulceration of the womb and prayed that the medicine which he frequently administered, and always prepared in the privacy of his office, would "have its desired effect." On his wife's death he underwent "a paroxysm of grief" which was repeated at the funeral. None the less, by 8 November he was back to his practice, no doubt with an eye to the future and Miss Vandervoort. On returning from a professional visit that evening, however, his dreams were shattered. Before her daughter's death, his mother-in-law had found a likeness of Miss Vandervoort in the doctor's coat as well as some damaging correspondence, and the Lawson family had become suspicious. A coroner's inquest had been ordered and King was informed by his father-in-law that it was indeed in session at that very moment. The doctor panicked. He travelled immediately to the Vandervoort farm, persuaded Melinda to flee with him, and made for the border. Four days later he was apprehended by his brother-in-law and an American marshal near Cape Vincent, N.Y., and returned for trial.

On 4 April 1859 the "Wife Poisoning Case" opened in the court-house just north of Cobourg. It was estimated that "not less then fifteen hundred" had come to hear the trial and the court-room, which could "accomodate about four hundred, was filled to excess." Confident of acquittal during his incarceration, King, a man of "about 5 feet 11 inches, of a pale countenance, dark hair, with sandy whiskers, [and with] a small dark penetrating eye . . . that would seem to penetrate into the mind of his man," strode into the dock giving an impression that "much more bespoke a city gentleman than one who was about to be tried for the murder of his wife." The trial was heard before Judge Robert Easton Burns*; the chief crown counsel was Thomas Galt* and the defence was headed by John Hillyard Cameron*. The crown

established a solid case for arsenic poisoning, aided by the expert testimony of Henry Holmes Croft*, a professor of chemistry at the University of Toronto, and King's letter to Melinda as well as his actions upon hearing of the inquest sealed his fate. Nevertheless, when on the morning of 6 April the foreman of the jury pronounced him guilty, with a strong recommendation for mercy, the doctor "did not appear to have expected the verdict." Three days later King listened with composure as Burns sentenced him to be hanged on 9 June, but seconds after the judge had finished King's "lip quivered, and burying his face in his handkerchief he wept convulsively."

During his confinement while awaiting execution, King divided his time between prayers for salvation and tearful self-pity. He was visited by a steady procession of clergymen who prayed with him and also kept him informed as to the progress of his appeals for clemency. After all hope of commutation had vanished, King decided to confess. Later described as "a curious combination of self-revelation and sickening sentimentality," the confession, which blames early marriage, lust, his wife's infidelity, the devil, and just about everything possible save himself, was sent to the Toronto *Globe* for publication in May. The editor felt that this self-serving document was "abominable" and refused to print it. King, though offended, went on in pursuit of redemption and in the last days seemed convinced of his salvation.

As the execution approached, the *Cobourg Star* attempted to dissuade its readers from contributing to a public spectacle on the appointed day, wondering "that the boasted civilization of the nineteenth century has not taken away the opportunity of indulging such an unhealthy, such a prurient curiosity." None the less, a crowd estimated at between 5,000 and 10,000 gathered before the gallows on the morning of 9 June. King "ascended the ladder . . . with a very firm step," though "his face bore the mark of recent tears." He read his prepared address in a clear voice and was praying fervently when the drop fell and he was "launched into eternity." The Victorian civility of the crowd, which maintained "a respectful deportment befitting the solemnity of the occasion," was balanced by the fact that the rope was cut into pieces and distributed among certain interested persons. The appearance of polite reverence effectively masked the atmosphere of vengeance. Years later Edwin Clarence Guillet*, who inherited one of the pieces of rope, could observe: "Altogether, no one could want a better execution."

CHARLES DOUGALL

[Contemporary interest in King's case is indicated by almost verbatim accounts of the trial in the *Cobourg Star* and the Toronto *Globe* as well as by the publication in 1859 of at least four pamphlets containing the *Globe* reports along with information on King's life, imprisonment, and execution. The earliest of these pamphlets, written by R. De Courcey and shown to King for verification before his death, no longer survives. A second and fuller account by De Courcey, *Dr. King's life, trial, confession and execution, together with the journal, prison scenes and portrait, also the causes which led him to commit the awful crime*, was published in Brighton, [Ont.], in July 1859. The journal referred to was kept between 14 April and 9 June by Alexander Stewart, the special constable assigned to guard King until his execution. Stewart is thought to be the author of *The life and trial of Wm. H. King, M.D., for poisoning his wife at Brighton* (Orono, [Ont.], 1859), which contains the material found in De Courcey plus an account of the inquest. The fourth pamphlet, *Trial of Dr. W. H. King, for the murder of his wife, at the Cobourg assizes, April 4th, 1859, with a short history of the murderer* (Toronto, 1859), is a reprint of the *Globe*'s account of the trial with a summary of the addresses of counsel, not found in the other pamphlets. In 1943 E. C. Guillet wrote "The strange case of Dr. King; a study of the evidence in The Queen *versus* William Henry King, 1859," based on the above material, as the second volume in his "Famous Canadian trials" (50v., 1943–49). Only the first volume was published; the entire series is available in manuscript at York Univ. Arch. (Toronto), and five typescript copies were produced for distribution to major North American libraries, including MTL and the Thomas Fisher Rare Books Library at the University of Toronto. c.d.]

PAC, RG 31, A1, 1851, Brighton Township. *Cobourg Star*, 6, 13 April, 18 May, 8, 15 June 1859. *Globe*, 6–8, 14, 23 April, 24, 25 May, 10 June 1859. *Marriage notices of Ontario*, comp. W. D. Reid (Lambertville, N.J., 1980). E. C. Guillet, *Cobourg, 1798–1948* (Oshawa, Ont., 1948).

KIRBY. *See* KERBY

KIRWAN (Kirwin, Kerwin, Kerwan), Miss, named **Sister Mary Bernard**, member of the Order of the Presentation of Our Blessed Lady, mother superior, and educator; b. 1797 in Monivea, County Galway (Republic of Ireland), daughter of James Kirwan and Ann ——; d. 27 Feb. 1857 and was buried in Admiral's Cove (Port Kirwan), Nfld.

Nothing is known of Sister Mary Bernard Kirwan's early life and there is no record of her baptismal names. In 1823 she joined the Presentation Order, founded in 1775 in Cork (Republic of Ireland) by Honoria (Nano) Nagle, a religious and educator trained in France. Its special mission was to educate and instruct "young girls, especially the poor, in the precepts and rudiments of the Catholic Faith."

On 29 June 1833 Bishop Michael Anthony Fleming* visited the Galway Presentation Convent to recruit nuns to teach in Newfoundland. His object, he told Monsignor John Spratt of Dublin, was to establish "a system of education, that . . . would smooth the pillow of sickness, and soften the rigours of winter, by

the diffusion of true Christian feeling." He was especially concerned to separate "the female poor" from their male counterparts because their association, "in all the familiarity of school intimacy," was "by no means calculated to secure the acquirement of virtues, or to strengthen the morality of the female."

Previously established schools in Newfoundland had other defects as well. The St John's Charity School, though partially funded by the church, had never had a Catholic head, and the school operated by the North American School Society had sought to proselytize the children of Catholic parents. More surprisingly, the school run by the Benevolent Irish Society had opposed priestly instruction "*even after school hours*," though for some years there had been no Protestant students. Fleming's difference with this latter organization was part of a larger struggle over place and preferment in which he was engaged with some local Catholics. What Fleming wanted was a more exclusive and institutionally powerful church and his 1833 recruiting mission must be understood in this context.

Four nuns, including Mary Bernard Kirwan, volunteered to go to Newfoundland. The bishop agreed to provide a lump sum of £1,500 for the support of the sisters, a comfortable home while they awaited the building of a "suitable dwelling-house with a school for their use and accommodation," and £100 per annum for their support. The superior of the Galway Convent, Sister Mary John Power, also stipulated the right to recall the nuns after six years. These arrangements were approved by the bishop of Galway on 8 Aug. 1833, and Sister Mary Bernard Kirwan was named superior of the "intended convent" at St John's.

Accompanied by Fleming the nuns left Ireland on 11 August, arriving in St John's on 21 September. One month later they opened their first school. Living in a building formerly used as a tavern, they had two bedrooms and a small parlour which served "for choir, refectory, community and all," with the rest of the building and a nearby disused slaughterhouse for teaching. Although Fleming had apparently rented these premises for a year and spent nearly £500 on renovations, on 8 December the sisters moved into a house rented for £80 per annum, a payment the bishop described as "exorbitant." One of the sisters described the new convent as "quite retired from every house," with a garden and "a delightful view of the harbour."

Fleming then set about arranging for the construction of a school at a cost of more than £600. In 1844 he wrote that this institution had been attended daily for 11 years by more than one thousand children. The legislature voted £100 per annum in 1836 to support the school, an appropriation which no doubt brought welcome relief to Fleming's financial situation. The cost of bringing the nuns out and establishing them had forced him to lay aside many accustomed comforts. He had had to reduce the number of his domestics to "one general servant and a boy" and to subject himself "to a charge of parsimony" at the table. He had also given up his carriage and reduced his "stud to a single horse."

The nuns were agreeably surprised by the appearance of Newfoundland. "This country," Sister Mary Bernard wrote in her first letter home, "is by no means as dreary as we heard. The bay is beautiful and so is the country as far as we can see." Another of the sisters, Mary Magdalen O'Shaughnessy, was struck by the evident prosperity of St John's and the fondness of the children in the school for "dress-wear, necklaces, ear-rings, rings etc." "From their appearance," she wrote, "you would scarcely think you are teaching in a poor school. No such thing as a barefoot child to be seen here, how great the contrast between them and the poor Irish!" Nor were the nuns disillusioned by their first taste of winter, though Sister Mary Xavier Lynch was amazed to find stockings she had put out to dry "stiff as a board" and with "icicles hanging from them." "I suppose," she optimistically wrote in January 1834, "there is not a finer climate anywhere."

Local prices struck the nuns as very dear: cream and butter were luxuries and fresh meat "the greatest rarity in winter." The poor people were "very piously inclined," but Sister Mary Xavier told her Irish correspondent she would be astonished by their "simplicity and ignorance." Local priests had been asked whether the nuns would be sent to the outharbours to hear confession and whether they said mass for themselves. Some apparently thought that the nuns would live underground, and wondered whether they would ever speak or laugh.

The "Mode of Instruction" employed by the nuns was, initially at any rate, similar to that used in convent schools in Ireland. In 1848 they were offering instruction in spelling, reading, writing, English grammar, history (both sacred and profane), geography, arithmetic, natural history (taught from a book of the Irish National Schools), spinning, and needlework. As "lace mistress," Sister Mary Bernard had requested from her convent in 1833 "all the patterns of lace got since we parted and directions necessary for taking them off." In 1837 Fleming noted that the nuns had prepared 800 women of all ages for a confirmation service on 25 April 1836. In time the nuns also trained teachers.

In 1842 two others sisters came from Galway to St John's and in November of that year Fleming purchased a site for a new convent. The nuns moved to temporary accommodation in a former "ball-alley" on 31 Aug. 1843 and conducted school there until 14 Dec. 1844, when they moved into their new home. Here they taught in a few rooms and in the basement while work progressed on a school to accommodate at least 1,600 children. The total cost of the land, convent, and school was £4–5,000.

On 9 June 1846 the buildings were destroyed in the great fire that swept St John's. The nuns sought refuge at the convent of the Order of the Sisters of Mercy, established in 1842 [see Marianne CREEDON, named Mother Mary Francis], before moving that evening to a cottage on Fleming's farm outside the town. Sleeping "on the floor, four in a room," "teaching . . . on fine days in the open fields and in rough weather in the stables and outhouses," they remained there until November 1846. In the mean time they had been joined by two more recruits from Galway. Their next move was back to Mercy Convent, part of which was partitioned off for their use. This building, designed for 4 nuns, now housed 15, a circumstance, Fleming reasoned, "greatly calculated to militate against the health of the entire." In February 1847 he appealed to the colonial secretary, Earl Grey, for funds to offset the order's loss and to help the sisters continue their work in an efficient manner. No support was forthcoming but by February 1849 a petition was being circulated in St John's calling on the legislature to make a grant to the order. The nuns were now teaching in a temporary shed near Mercy Convent but their charges had "dwindled away to a mere handful, of poor children." No doubt the problems of the order were compounded by Bishop Fleming's long illness and his death on 14 July 1850.

Better times soon followed. On 23 Aug. 1850 Fleming's successor, John Thomas Mullock*, laid the foundation-stone for a new convent. The collection at mass that day was £300. The priests present contributed £50, though Denis Mackin and Charles DALTON, according to Mullock's diary, "escaped shabbily away." The nuns moved into the new convent, which was still under construction, on 20 Oct. 1851, taking formal possession on 2 July 1853. The cost of the new convent and school was £7,000, of which the legislature voted £2,000. In the mean time the order had expanded to other parts of the island, convents being opened at Harbour Grace in 1851, at Carbonear in 1852, and at Harbour Main in 1853.

The next party to be sent from St John's was headed by Sister Mary Bernard Kirwan. On 16 Sept. 1853 she led a group of four to found a convent at Admiral's Cove on the southern shore. They were accompanied by Mullock and the local priest, James Murphy. Since their convent was not yet finished, the nuns lived initially in Father Murphy's house. Sister Mary Bernard was appointed superior of the convent, her title being confirmed by Mullock on 23 June 1856. She died in this office less than a year later. According

Klingensmith

to the annals of her last convent, "she was remarkable for a peculiar sweetness of disposition, exalted piety, unbounded Charity, and a burning zeal for the glory of God and the good of her neighbour; her death was like her life most holy."

PETER NEARY

AASJ, Mullock papers, journals and diaries, 1850–69. Arch. of the Presentation Sisters in Nfld. (St John's), Annals of the Presentation Convent, Fermeuse, Nfld.; Annals of the Presentation Convent, St John's; Corr., Sister Mary Bernard Kirwan to Mother Mary John Power, [22 Sept. 1833]; Sister Mary Magdalen O'Shaughnessy to Mother Mary John Power, 22 Sept. 1833; Sister Mary Magdalen O'Shaughnessy to Sister Mary Augustine, 21 Nov. 1833; Sister Mary Xavier Lynch to Sister Ann, 6 Jan. 1834 (typescripts); "Mother Mary Bernard Kirwan" (typescript, n.d.). MHGA, Paula Moore, "History of the coming and spread of the Presentation Sisters' in Newfoundland education" (typescript, 1971). M. A. Fleming, "Bishop Fleming to the Very Rev. Mr. Spratt, of Dublin . . . , Sept. 24, 1834," *Catholic Magazine and Rev.* (Birmingham, Eng.), 6 (1835): v–xii; *Relazione della missione cattolica in Terranuova nell'America settentrionale . . .* (Rome, 1837); "To the Very Rev. Mr. Spratt, Dublin . . . , Oct. 8th, 1834," *Catholic Magazine and Rev.*, 6 (1835): lxxii–lxxxi. G.B., Parl., House of Commons paper, 1851, 36, no.679: 621–760, *Copies or extracts of the correspondence between the governor of Newfoundland and the secretary of state for the colonies in reference to the appropriation of the subscriptions raised for the relief of the sufferers at St. John's by the fire in 1846.* Nfld., *Blue book*, 1836; Legislative Council, *Journals*, 1848–49. *Newfoundlander*, 1833–73. *Patriot* (St John's), 1853. *Royal Gazette and Newfoundland Advertiser*, 1850. Louis Burke, "Some Irish contributors and contributions to Newfoundland education in the last century" (M.LITT. thesis, Univ. of Dublin, 1975). Sister Mary James Dinn, *Foundation of the Presentation Congregation in Newfoundland* (St John's, 1975). Gunn, *Political hist. of Nfld.* Howley, *Ecclesiastical hist. of Nfld*; "Operetta 'The Golden Jubilee' of the Presentation Nuns at St. John's Newfoundland," in his *Poems and other verses* (New York, 1903), 93–122. William Hutch, *Nano Nagle: her life, her labours, and their fruits* (Dublin, 1875). *Presentation Convent, Galway: sesquicentenary souvenir, 1965* (Galway, Republic of Ire., 1965). M. M. Byrne, "From acorn to oak, 1775–1975: the one thing necessary," *Monitor* (St John's), 43 (1975), no.12: 13. M. F. Howley, "The Presentation nuns in Newfoundland," *Irish Monthly* (Dublin and London), 12 (1884): 487–99. Paul O'Neill, "Around and about," *Monitor*, 43, no.12: 6.

KLINGENSMITH (Clingersmith, Clinglesmith), PETER, known as **White Peter**, settler; b. *c.* 1772 in Pennsylvania; m. Molly Ann ——, and they had several children (one daughter was adopted); d. 1855 or 1856 in Nanticoke, Upper Canada.

Members of the Klingensmith (originally Klingenschmidt) family were early settlers in Westmoreland County in western Pennsylvania. This region was subjected to Indian raids during the American revolution, and on 2 July 1781, as related by Colonel James Perry, a war party attacked the "small Garrison" assembled at the home of one "Philip Clinglesmith," several families having gathered there for protection. Most of the group were killed, including the immediate family of nine-year-old Peter Klingensmith, who was taken prisoner. The attack may have been made by Munsee Delawares from the upper Allegheny River in retaliation for the destruction of their town two years earlier by American troops under Colonel Daniel Brodhead. These loyalist Indians subsequently attached themselves to the Senecas of western New York and after 1784 settled with them on the Grand River, in what later became Upper Canada.

For a decade Peter's fate remained unknown. Then in 1791 members of the Hoover family, who had known the Klingensmiths in Westmoreland County, settled north of Lake Erie in Walpole Township. They apparently met White Peter (as he was then known) and discovered his original name. Traditions preserved in both Canada and Pennsylvania relate that they persuaded him to visit his former home, where relatives welcomed him but would not accept his wife, a member of one of the Six Nations tribes. According to a Westmoreland County historian, George Dallas Albert, who dated the visit to about 1800, Peter had hoped to claim his parents' property but was unable to prove his identity. Whatever the precise circumstances, he returned to the Grand River.

Although he evidently did not serve in the War of 1812, Klingensmith effectively supported the British cause. John Baptist Askin* later recalled that Klingensmith by his warnings, made "to the emenent danger of his own pate," had been "instrumental" in saving three militia officers (Thomas TALBOT, George C. Salmon, and Robert Nichol*) from the murderous depredations of a party of "vagabonds" led by John Dixon, a marauder who ravaged Long Point following the American invasion of the region in 1814. An "honest, peaceable and industrious Inhabitant," Klingensmith subsequently settled in Walpole Township on lot 4 of concession 1, where by 1827 he had erected "a good frame barn, and sheds – well shingled and weather boarded." Six years later he purchased the eastern half of lot 6, becoming the first settler on the site of present-day Nanticoke.

Although Klingensmith had a large family, only some of his children appear to have settled with him in Walpole. About 1825, according to his will, Sarah (Sally) O'Brian, a two-year-old girl, was left by her mother with the Klingensmiths and they raised her as their child. Peter's wife had apparently died before 1851, when the census return for Walpole listed Peter and six others as residing in a one-storey frame-house. The occupants included Sarah and her husband, John

476

Shuler, and Eliza Clingersmith, aged six. All seven were identified as Indians and as members of the Methodist Episcopal Church in Canada. Elsewhere in the township lived John Clingersmith, a 26-year-old labourer who was possibly a son or a grandson of Peter. Other probable children joined the Moravian Indian mission at New Fairfield (Moraviantown), on the Thames River in the western part of the province. Among these were a white girl from the Grand River, Pahellau, baptized in 1834 as Ketura and identified then as a member of either the Munsee or the Mahican nation (her mother's tribe), and her brother, also from the Grand River, Peter Clensmith (Klingersmith), who was baptized in 1844 as John Peter. He and his family thereafter used Peter as a surname. Other relatives, identified variously as Clingersmith, Clinansmith, Clingsmith, and Clinger, joined the mission at later dates.

Peter Klingensmith, a figure of more importance in the context of popular narrative than of history, died either in 1855, the date which appears on his grave marker at the Union Cemetery, Nanticoke, or early in 1856 (his will was registered on 13 February). He left his farm to Sarah Shuler and bequeathed a horse to his eldest son, "Fisjary (formerly called High flyer)."

WILLIAM A. HUNTER

AO, RG 1, C-IV, Walpole Township, concession 1, lot 4, J. B. Askin to Thomas Clarke, 13 June 1827. Haldimand Land Registry Office (Cayuga, Ont.), Abstract index to deeds, Walpole Township, 1, concession 1, lot 6 (mfm. at AO, GS 2771); Deeds, Walpole Township, 2: 731 (will of Peter Klingensmith) (mfm. at AO, GS 2776). Moravian Arch. (Bethlehem, Pa.), Indian mission records, box 166 (New Fairfield diaries, 1825–51); box 168, folder 4 (New Fairfield reg., 1870–1903); box 313, folder 8 (reg., including New Fairfield to 1870). PAC, RG 5, A1: 16395–98, 69624–30; RG 31, A1, 1851, Walpole Township (mfm. at AO). *Pennsylvania archives . . .*, ed. Samuel Hazard *et al.* (9 ser. in 119 vols., Philadelphia and Harrisburg, 1852–1935), 1st ser., 9: 240–41; 12: 155–58. U.S., Bureau of the Census, *Heads of families at the first census of the United States taken in the year 1790; Pennsylvania* (Washington, 1908), 262–63. *Pennsylvania German pioneers: a publication of the original lists of arrivals in the port of Philadelphia from 1727 to 1808*, comp. R. B. Strassburger, ed. W. J. Hinke (3v., Norristown, Pa., 1934; repr., 2v., Baltimore, Md., 1966), 1: 212–15, 678–81. G. D. Albert, "The frontier forts of western Pennsylvania," Pa., Indian forts commission, *Report of the commission to locate the site of the frontier forts of Pennsylvania* (2v., [Harrisburg], 1896), 2: 379–80. K. [N.] Brueton, *Walpole Township centennial history* ([Jarvis, Ont.], 1967]), 7–9. *History of the county of Westmoreland, Pennsylvania, with biographical sketches of many of its pioneers and prominent men*, ed. G. D. Albert (Philadelphia, 1882), 721. [I. D. Rupp], *Early history of western Pennsylvania, and of the west . . . by a gentleman of the bar . . .* (Pittsburgh, 1848), app., 259.

KNIGHT, ANN CUTHBERT. *See* RAE

KNIGHT, RICHARD, Methodist minister; b. 1788 in Devon, England; m. between 1818 and 1820 Mary Hosier in Bonavista, Nfld, and they had 11 children; d. 23 May 1860 in Sackville, N.B.

Raised as a devout member of the Church of England, Richard Knight converted to Methodism as a young man after an alarming dream and the death of a friend. Shortly thereafter he became a local preacher, serving for some time in England. He was accepted as a candidate for missionary work and was ordained by the British Wesleyan Conference in 1816. With five other carefully chosen men, including John BELL and George Cubit*, Knight was sent to Newfoundland in August of that same year. He was to have been stationed with Cubit at Carbonear but the colonial church, demonstrating its newly gained independence [*see* William Ellis*], posted both men to St John's where Knight served as Cubit's assistant for a few months. Knight was the first Wesleyan attached to the Fortune Bay circuit and, although his time of arrival is uncertain, he conducted his first wedding there in February 1817. For two years he served this vast area on the southwest coast, covering it three and four times a year to perform his duties. He became known to his parishioners as the "light bringer."

During his 17 years in Newfoundland, Knight worked on all 11 circuits. While he was stationed at Brigus in the summer of 1825 he went to Labrador with a merchant friend Charles Cozens to determine if a mission could be established there; the Wesleyans' first such attempt had been made the previous summer by Thomas Hickson. Knight spent the entire summer travelling some 300 miles along the coast, using Baie des Esquimaux (Hamilton Inlet) as his headquarters. He had a series of male and female interpreters who helped him in his preaching. Although he reported that he had difficulty in locating the main tribe and in interpreting their language, he concluded that the Indians of Labrador were of a superior class because of the Moravian influence [*see* Jens Haven*]. He praised their singing as the sweetest he had ever heard and concluded that a permanent Labrador mission should be established immediately. His vision became a reality the following year and he was instrumental in founding an institute to oversee the extension of this work.

Fortunately Knight was a man of great physical prowess and almost a stranger to sickness. He was thus able to endure the perilous winter travel overland and the equivalent hardships at sea. He also had to defend himself from both verbal and physical attacks: once, on the Grand Bank circuit, he was chastised for condemning dancing and drunkenness on Sundays and twice he was assaulted by Roman Catholics who had been encouraged by their priests. There is a popular story about Knight's attempt to stop a man from smoking during one of his services. After appeals to the local magistrate who was present failed, Knight personally threw the man out of the church. One version of the story says that the man became a Methodist shortly afterwards; the other, that he became one on the spot.

Knight was a man of commanding spiritual power, and extraordinary revivals accompanied his ministry. Indeed, during his stay on the island, Methodist membership quadrupled. He has been described as "the greatest man that God gave the church in Newfoundland," and his transfer from the district in 1833 was a heavy and permanent loss. He had already proved himself to be an excellent administrator with a fine business sense. This ability was demonstrated initially through his service as district secretary, probably in 1822, and in 1827 as secretary of the Newfoundland Methodist Missionary Society (its name was changed in 1840 to the Newfoundland Wesleyan Auxiliary Missionary Society).

Knight was transferred by the British conference to Nova Scotia, where he was immediately elected chairman of the east district. Exercising strong and judicious leadership, he opposed the immersionist theories and Universalist views which were prominent among Methodists in Halifax. Extensive revivals occurred shortly thereafter under his ministry and that of his colleague, Dr Matthew Richey*. During this period Knight curiously opposed the "assistant missionary" system, aimed at developing local preachers, in favour of the prevailing practice of sending them out from England. He feared that the new system was simply an expedient of the British Wesleyan Methodist committee to lessen their financial burden without contracting their sphere of influence. At Yarmouth in 1845 he unmasked and refuted the authors of an anonymous pamphlet signed Scrutator which charged Methodist preachers with misappropriation of public funds and dishonest collection policies. Later in the decade he was involved in establishing pensions for supernumeraries and ministers' widows patterned after the English model. Again demonstrating his administrative skills, Knight served as chairman of the Nova Scotia west district (including Prince Edward Island) as well as the New Brunswick district from 1849 to 1853 and he was general superintendent of missions for New Brunswick.

In July 1847 Dr Robert Alder*, who had succeeded in reuniting the conference in Upper Canada and the British Wesleyans, visited Sackville, N.B., to confer with the leading ministers of the maritime districts regarding union. Any action was postponed, but by the early 1850s the time appeared ripe to unite the Upper and Lower Canada districts and to draw the

maritime areas together in a separate conference. Knight played a key role in bringing the latter plan to fruition. In an attempt to secure the support of the reluctant Newfoundland district, Knight and Richey were sent to St John's in 1855: they met with marked success. The new conference was constituted in Halifax on 17 July of that year as the Conference of Eastern British America.

In 1857 Knight was sent by the conference to the Canada Wesleyan conference in Toronto as a fraternal delegate, and from 1857 until 1860 he served, with the full support of the British conference and of his own colleagues, as co-delegate of the Conference of Eastern British America. Although he possessed a fair education, Knight made no pretensions to extensive literary attainment but he did receive an honorary degree from Mount Allison Wesleyan Academy, Sackville, probably in 1857.

On Saturday, 12 May 1860, Knight travelled to Sackville to attend the meetings of the Mount Allison Academic Board. He preached there the next day and on Monday and Tuesday attended the institution's examination exercises. He became ill on Tuesday, however, and died peacefully on 23 May. In the 45 years of his ministry, Knight had never requested even a temporary retirement. It was predicted that, had he lived another year, he would certainly have been elected president of the conference.

CALVIN D. EVANS

Wesleyan Methodist Church of Eastern British America, *Minutes* (Halifax), 1860: 6–8. *Wesleyan-Methodist Magazine* (London), 48 (1825); 49 (1826): 131–34, 205–9; 83 (1860): 668. *Newfoundland Mercantile Journal*, 4 April 1822. *Public Ledger*, 28 Nov. 1828. Cornish, *Cyclopædia of Methodism*, 1: 389. *When was that?* (Mosdell), 71. *Who's who in and from Newfoundland* . . . (St John's, 1927), 38. *A century of Methodism in St. John's, Newfoundland, 1815–1915*, ed. J. W. Nichols (n.p., [1915]), 32. G. G. Findlay and W. W. Holdsworth, *The history of the Wesleyan Methodist Missionary Society* (5v., London, 1921–24), 1: 277, 330–38, 342–49, 480. G. O. Huestis, *Memorials of Wesleyan missionaries & ministers, who have died within the bounds of the conference of Eastern British America, since the introduction of Methodism into these colonies* (Halifax, 1872), 56–61. D. W. Johnson, *History of Methodism in eastern British America, including Nova Scotia, New Brunswick, Prince Edward Island, Newfoundland and Bermuda* . . . ([Sackville, N.B.], n.d.), 336–37. Charles Lench, *An account of the rise and progress of Methodism on the Grand Bank and Fortune circuits from 1816 to 1916* . . . (n.p., [1916]), 10–13, 22, 41–42; *The story of Methodism in Bonavista and of the settlements visited by the early preachers* . . . (2nd ed., St John's, 1919), 78–79. Jacob Parsons, "The origin and growth of Newfoundland Methodism, 1765–1855" (MA thesis, Memorial Univ. of Nfld., St John's, 1964), 66. D. G. Pitt, *Windows of agates; a short history of the founding and early years of Gower Street Methodist (now United) Church in St. John's, Newfoundland* (St John's, 1966), 30. T. W. Smith, *Hist. of Methodist Church*, 2: 31–37. Philip Tocque, *Newfoundland: as it was, and as it is in 1877* (Toronto, 1878), 198, 271–76. William Wilson, *Newfoundland and its missionaries . . . to which is added a chronological table of all the important events that have occurred on the island* (Cambridge, Mass., and Halifax, 1866), 227, 240–42, 298, 319, 343. *Daily News* (St John's), 6 Feb. 1960.

L

LACOSTE, LOUIS-RENÉ, notary; b. 10 Nov. 1823 in Boucherville, Lower Canada, son of Louis Lacoste*, a notary and politician, and Catherine de Labruère (Boucher de La Bruère); d. unmarried 7 Nov. 1854 in Boucherville.

From childhood Louis-René Lacoste lived among the leading citizens of the Boucherville region. His maternal grandfather, René Boucher de La Bruère, had been the seigneur of Montarville and a militia colonel. His father, an influential man in the lower Richelieu valley, was heavily involved in politics and a strong supporter of Louis-Joseph Papineau*. During the rebellion of 1837–38 young Louis-René saw his father imprisoned.

Lacoste's background led him to an interest in law, which he studied in Paris in 1844–45. He may well have chosen this city in hopes of finding a cure for a bad leg. On 24 May 1845, while still training to be a notary, he acknowledged receiving £150 from his father, which he used to pay for this study trip to Europe. He simultaneously made over to his father his rights of inheritance from his mother (who had died in 1832), including fishing rights on the Rivière Ouelle. In October 1845 his father gave him a £50 advance on his inheritance from him.

Having obtained his notary's commission on 25 Aug. 1845, Lacoste drafted his first minute on 28 October, on behalf of Louis-Hippolyte La Fontaine*, a family friend. On 23 Jan. 1847 he went into partnership with Octave Morin, and the two notaries established their office at the corner of Rue Sainte-Thérèse and Rue Saint-Gabriel in Montreal, where Louis had taken up residence a short while before. But Morin countersigned only 25 of the original copies of Lacoste's notarized instruments, for their partnership ended in May. In 1849 Lacoste had his own office on Rue Saint-Louis.

In 1846 Lacoste and his colleague Nicolas-Benjamin DOUCET had submitted a petition to the Legislative Assembly of the Province of Canada in the name of their fellow practitioners in Montreal, who were objecting to a bill to regulate the formalities of notarized instruments. That year a bill to organize the notaries of Lower Canada was presented by one of their number, Joseph Laurin*; an essential measure, it was passed on 28 July 1847. The act provided for the creation of three boards of notaries, at Quebec, Trois-Rivières, and Montreal, which would have authority to issue certificates to candidates and supervise professional practice. The first meeting of the Board of Notaries of Montreal took place on 28 Oct. 1847. Lacoste was elected a trustee, André JOBIN president, Henry Lappare secretary, and George Weekes treasurer.

Because of his profession and his activity in this body, Lacoste moved among both the business and the intellectual élite of Montreal. Still in his early twenties, he was one of the 40 active members of the important Société des Amis, which had been formed in 1842, two years before the founding of the Institut Canadien. Its members sought to become better acquainted with each other and to further their education in letters, the fine arts, law, jurisprudence, medicine, and economics. To exert some influence on the community, the society had started the *Revue canadienne* in 1845.

In January 1848 Lacoste published his "Essai de jurisprudence lu devant la Société des amis" in the *Revue de législation et de jurisprudence* (Quebec); the paper dealt with registration. In 1862, in the case of Rachel Boudrias, the wife of Antoine Couillard, versus John McLean, the judges of the Provincial Court of Appeal referred to this essay and praised Lacoste, terming him a "young legal expert." Louis-Amable Jetté*, who taught civil law at Université Laval in Montreal before he became lieutenant governor, always spoke highly of the young author to his new students. It was undoubtedly because of his ability that Lacoste was invited by notary Jean-Joseph GIROUARD to help him inventory the assets of Joseph Masson*, who had died in 1847, and was chosen by La Fontaine and Toussaint PELTIER as an arbitrator in a wrangle over a division of property in Montreal between the Hôtel-Dieu and the Séminaire de Saint-Sulpice.

On 19 July 1848, "wishing to leave the profession of notary to take up that of lawyer, counsel, solicitor and attorney," Lacoste undertook to article for five

Lacroix

years with Rouër Roy. He apparently did not finish his training for at his death he was still called a notary. In November 1850 Lacoste, who from the beginning of the year had been kept from sustained work by a fever, returned to live with his father. During the four years that followed he drafted no more than about 20 instruments, probably because of illness. He died in 1854 at the age of 30.

In 1851, in a letter written to a client who was slow in paying him, Lacoste had stated, "I have been ill for a year and a half, and I am very poor." The inventory of his assets after his death shows that his debts so far exceeded his accounts receivable that his father decided to renounce the estate he had left. Yet at the outset Louis-René Lacoste's career had been full of promise. In his history of the notarial profession, Joseph-Edmond Roy* reflects: "If this talented young man aroused the admiration of our greatest jurists and earned their praise, we wonder what he would have achieved had the experience of age been allied to the knowledge acquired by dint of study."

RAYMOND DUMAIS

Louis-René Lacoste is the author of "Essai de jurisprudence lu devant la Société des amis," *Rev. de législation et de jurisprudence* (Québec), 3 (1847–48): 121–42.

The ANQ-M holds the 467 notarial instruments drawn up by Lacoste between 1845 and 1854, under CN1-226. A photograph of him is in the possession of the ASTR.

ANQ-M, CC1, 8 nov. 1833; CE1-22, 11 nov. 1823, 10 nov. 1854; CN1-46, 12 janv. 1823, 11 avril 1834, 10 mai 1850; CN1-125, 24 mai, 13 oct. 1845; 21 sept. 1846; 23 janv., 25 mai 1847; CN1-237, 14 juill. 1847, 12 oct. 1848; CN1-304, 20 nov., 2 déc. 1854; CN1-315, 2 avril 1834; CN1-396, 19 juill. 1848, 26 mai 1849, 18 mai 1850; P-76; P-155. AUM, P 58, U, Lacoste à Delisle, 23 sept. 1851; P 79. *La Minerve*, 9 nov. 1854. *Montreal directory*, 1847–51. [Louis Lalande], *Une vieille seigneurie, Boucherville; chroniques, portraits et souvenirs* (Montréal, 1890), 211–20. J.-E. Roy, *Hist. du notariat*, 3: 147, 151, 218–19. "Les disparus," *BRH*, 41 (1935): 563. L.-A. Huguet-Latour, "La Société des amis," *BRH*, 8 (1902): 121–22. Marc Lacoste, "Rétrospective: l'honorable Louis Lacoste, notaire, premier maire de Boucherville 1857, Patriote, député du comté de Chambly, conseiller législatif et sénateur," *La Rev. du notariat* (Lévis, Qué.), 81 (1978–79): 304–17.

LACROIX, JANVIER-DOMPTAIL (baptized **Jacques-Janvier**), lawyer, militia officer, seigneur, and politician; b. 31 Jan. 1778 in Saint-Vincent-de-Paul (Laval), Que., son of Hubert-Joseph Lacroix* and Françoise-Pélagie Poncy; d. 15 July 1856 in Montreal.

Janvier-Domptail Lacroix, whose forebears came from the Netherlands, was the grandson of a doctor, Hubert-Joseph de Lacroix*. He studied law, probably in Montreal, and was called to the bar on 13 July 1801. Less than a year later, on 3 May, he married Marie-Anne Bouate, daughter of Jean-Baptiste Bouate, an infantry lieutenant, and Marie-Céleste Foucher. The marriage was solemnized at Notre-Dame in Montreal before several leading figures of the time, including the bride's uncle Louis-Charles Foucher*, a judge in the Provincial Court at Trois-Rivières, and Pierre-Louis Panet*, a judge in the Court of King's Bench at Montreal. These witnesses and the terms of the marriage contract, in which the spouses settled for separation of property, are evidence that Lacroix belonged to a privileged social group.

Like many of his compatriots Lacroix took part in the War of 1812. Appointed a captain in Montreal's 3rd Militia Battalion on 7 April 1812, he later transferred to the 5th Select Embodied Militia Battalion of Lower Canada. But he resigned on 16 March 1813 to concentrate on his legal career. A prominent attorney, on 30 June 1812 he had managed to secure appointment as a commissioner for the administration of oaths of allegiance. On 22 May 1818 he became a director of the House of Industry in Montreal, a charitable organization. He was appointed commissioner for the trial of small causes on 26 June 1821 and commissioner for the building and repair of churches and presbyteries in 1830.

Lacroix did not, however, experience uninterrupted success. For example, in February 1817 the House of Assembly, on a motion by Augustin Cuvillier*, found him guilty of bearing false witness when he appeared before a select committee charged with inquiring into the conduct of Judge Foucher, his wife's uncle. The assembly voted to have Lacroix appear before it, but to no effect since the deputy sergeant-at-arms was unable to locate him. The whole affair ultimately subsided after the governor referred the assembly's request to dismiss Foucher to the Colonial Office. By the time London ruled on the procedure to follow in such a case, two years had elapsed and the animosity felt towards Foucher and his over-accommodating attorney had cooled. Lacroix's reprieve was short-lived, however, because in March 1819 he found himself facing new difficulties, linked this time with his behaviour as seigneur of Blainville.

Earlier that year Lacroix had received from his father some of the seigneurial rights in Blainville and he proceeded at once to the seigneury to claim from the *censitaires* the arrears owed his father and to demand from the local parish priest, Charles-Joseph DUCHARME, the honours due his rank. This was all it took to arouse antipathy. A number of *censitaires* delayed paying their arrears, while the parish priest took the opportunity of the seigneur's first appearance in church to omit his sermon and thus avoid having to offer for Lacroix and his spouse the accompanying customary prayer for the seigneur. It was no ordinary Sunday: furious at this insult, Lacroix riposted by remaining standing from the sanctus to the communion, rather than kneeling as Ducharme had requested in conformity with the ritual established by Bishop Saint-Vallier [La Croix*]. A churchwarden, Martin Gratton, tried in vain to ensure compliance with the custom. The seigneur loudly replied that he knew what he had to do, and after the service he stalked out of the church, hat on head, threatening the church-warden and his parish priest with a lawsuit for *lèse-majesté* that would really create a stir.

The affair dragged on for two or three years, ending when Lacroix dropped his action after Ducharme finally agreed to accord him the honours he claimed as seigneur. Relations between the two later became more cordial, although in 1823 Ducharme was worried because the seigneur seemed inclined to support five Scottish families in their desire to set up a Protestant school in the parish. Nevertheless, in 1829 Lacroix backed the parish priest's request that his school, which was to become the Petit Séminaire de Sainte-Thérèse, should receive the same financial advantages from the government as the schools run by trustees.

One of Lacroix's chief concerns as seigneur of Blainville was to reconstitute his domain, and by 1822 he had purchased all the seigneurial rights belonging to his brothers and sisters. Thus, when he rendered fealty and homage on 16 Nov. 1829, he became as of right the sole holder of the seigneury of Blainville. From then on he adopted a tougher approach to management, seeking by all possible means to increase the profits from his fief. His practices resembled, nevertheless, those of most seigneurs at that time: refusal to make land grants in order to obtain higher returns from their estates; insistence on issuing new title deeds; and purchase of lots outside the seigneuries for resale at a profit.

Consequently it should come as no surprise that his *censitaires* displayed a lack of respect for Lacroix in his political struggles, in particular during a public meeting of 10 April 1834 at Sainte-Thérèse-de-Blainville. Reporting the event, *Le Canadien* stated that "the seigneur . . . M. J.-D. Lacroix . . . was obliged to withdraw in the general disorder." Lacroix, who supported the Executive Council, had denounced the 92 Resolutions, as he had in a speech given a few days before in Montreal, going so far as to advocate absolute loyalty to the government. He maintained this stand throughout the entire political crisis, prompting *Le Canadien* to observe on 17 Nov. 1837 that the appointment of Lacroix to the Legislative Council could not be regarded as that of a French Canadian. Lacroix performed the duties of councillor from 22 Aug. 1837 until the constitution was suspended on 27 March 1838.

Janvier-Domptail Lacroix sold his seigneury to George Henry Monk on 26 July 1846 for £4,500. Then living in Montreal and involved in municipal politics, he was critical of all those who, following the example of the strikers at Lachine, were a menace to social peace. He died on 15 July 1856 in Montreal, at the house of his daughter Marie-Henriette, who had married John Pangman, a legislative councillor and seigneur of La Chesnaye. Representative of an élite detested by the people for its political opinions, Lacroix was remembered as a man who had sacrificed everything to his climb up the social ladder.

SERGE COURVILLE

ANQ-M, CE1-51, 3 mai 1802, 15 juill. 1856; CE1-59, 1er févr. 1778. ANQ-Q, P-240, boîte 23. *Docs. relating to constitutional hist., 1791–1818* (Doughty and McArthur), 502–36. L.C., House of Assembly, *Journals*, 1817: 557–59. *L'Ami du peuple, de l'ordre et des lois* (Montréal), 12, 19 avril 1834. *Le Canadien*, 16 avril 1834, 17 nov. 1837. *La Minerve*, 7, 14 avril 1834. *Quebec Gazette*, 20, 27 Feb., 6, 20 March 1817. P.-G. Roy, *Inv. concessions*, 3: 276–78. Turcotte, *Le Conseil législatif. Cahiers historiques: histoire de Sainte-Thérèse* (Joliette, Qué., 1940). Chapais, *Cours d'hist. du Canada*, 3: 56–60. Émile Dubois, *Le petit séminaire de Sainte-Thérèse, 1825–1925* (Montréal, 1925). É.-J.[-A.] Auclair, "Les origines de Sainte-Thérèse de Blainville et de son séminaire," RSC *Trans.*, 3rd ser., 34 (1940), sect.I: 1–19. H. C. Pentland, "The Lachine strike of 1843," *CHR*, 29 (1948): 255–77.

LAGIMONIÈRE (Lagimodière, Lajimonière, Lavimaudier, Lavimodière), JEAN-BAPTISTE, fur trader and farmer; b. 25 Dec. 1778 probably in Saint-Antoine-sur-Richelieu, Que., son of Jean-Baptiste Lagimonière, a farmer, and Marie-Joseph (Josephte) Jarret, *dit* Beauregard; d. 7 Sept. 1855 in St Boniface (Man.).

Jean-Baptiste Lagimonière lived in Saint-Antoine-sur-Richelieu, and then at Maskinongé where his father had settled in 1790. Around 1800 he went into the fur trade in the northwest as a voyageur. He spent several years in the territory to the west of Grand Portage (near Grand Portage, Minn.), probably in the employ of the North West Company. It is believed that he married an Indian woman *à la façon du pays*, and that they had three daughters.

Lagimonière was back with his family in Maskinongé in 1805. There he met Marie-Anne Gaboury*, and they were married on 21 April 1806. Shortly after, he was again seized by the urge to travel, and set off with his new wife for the northwest. They reached Fort Daer (Pembina, N.Dak.) towards the end of August and spent the winter there; on 6 Jan. 1807 Marie-Anne gave birth to their first child, a girl they named Reine. In the spring the Lagimonières moved from Fort Daer to Fort Augustus (Edmonton) along with three French Canadians and their families. They lived in this area, where the Hudson's Bay Company and the NWC each maintained a trading-post, for four

Landmann

years. With his family, Lagimonière took part in numerous expeditions hunting buffalo and beaver, leading the life of a true "free man." He and others kept the French Canadian and British fur traders supplied with meat, in addition to providing furs that were properly prepared, thanks to a knowledge of trading standards not possessed by the Indians.

In 1811 the Lagimonière family set off for the forks of the Red and Assiniboine rivers, after learning that Lord Selkirk [Douglas*], a Scot and a shareholder of the HBC, planned to establish a farming settlement there. They spent the winter at Fort Daer, and in the spring of 1812 went to make a permanent home in the Red River colony (Man.). Lagimonière, however, continued to live a hunter's life, and between 1812 and 1815 was hired several times by Miles Macdonell*, the colony's governor, to supply the settlers with food. He spent the winters with his family on the Assiniboine, near Portage la Prairie.

During these years, the intense rivalry between the HBC and the NWC, which were both seeking to control the fur trade, led to violent clashes at Red River and to the eviction of the settlers on the impetus of the NWC in June 1815 [see Archibald McDonald]. After the settlers returned in August 1815, Colin Robertson*, the HBC agent in the colony, hired Lagimonière to carry dispatches to Lord Selkirk, who was in Montreal. On 17 Oct. 1815, accompanied by Bénoni Marier, an employee of the company, and by an Indian guide, he left the colony on foot. Venturing on a route mainly through NWC territory to the south of Lake Superior, he then proceeded by way of Sault Ste Marie (Ont.) and York (Toronto). On 10 March 1816, at the end of his 1,800-mile journey, he handed the dispatches over to Lord Selkirk. Armed with Selkirk's replies, he set out on the same route at the end of March. But this time the NWC principals were determined not to let him get through, and during the night of 16 June 1816 Lagimonière and his companions were seized near Fond du Lac (Superior, Wis.) by Indians acting on the orders of one of the partners, Archibald Norman McLeod*. They were stripped of their personal belongings and Selkirk's dispatches, escorted to Fort William (Thunder Bay, Ont.), and then released. Without provisions or the means to subsist, Lagimonière and his companions pushed on towards Red River. At the beginning of July they received help from Pierre-Paul Lacroix, who found them on a bank of the Rainy River to the west of Fort Frances (Ont.). Lagimonière then went to Red River, which he probably reached during the summer of 1816.

After this exploit, Lagimonière served as messenger for the HBC on many occasions, as did his sons. He also began to farm some land that Selkirk is said to have granted him for his services. It was on this land, which was at the mouth of the Seine River, that he built a home where he brought up his family of four girls and four boys. In 1844 his daughter Julie married a neighbour, Louis Riel*, and later that year gave birth to a son, Louis*, who was to become the principal leader of the Métis during the events surrounding the entry of Manitoba into confederation. In the 1830s and 1840s Lagimonière, with the help of his four sons, was one of the most prosperous farmers in the Red River settlement. He continued to engage in the fur trade, and with other settlers such as Cuthbert GRANT and Louis GUIBOCHE was also active in the carrying trade.

Jean-Baptiste Lagimonière's journey to Montreal in 1815–16 made him a celebrity, but he also deserves note as one of the first French Canadians to settle permanently in the northwest.

LYNNE CHAMPAGNE

ANQ-MBF, CE1-10, 21 avril 1806. AP, Immaculée-Conception (Saint-Ours), reg. des baptêmes, mariages et sépultures, 26 déc. 1778; Saint-Antoine (Saint-Antoine-sur-Richelieu), reg. des baptêmes, mariages et sépultures, 5 févr. 1776. Arch. de la Soc. hist. de Saint-Boniface (Saint-Boniface, Man.), Dossier Picton; Fonds Champagne. PAC, MG 25, 62. PAM, HBCA, E.5/1–6; E.6/10–11; E.8/6; MG 2, A1; MG 3, D1; MG 7, D8; MG 8, C1. *HBRS*, 2 (Rich and Fleming). *New light on early hist. of greater northwest* (Coues), vol. 2. Georges Dugas, *La première Canadienne du Nord-Ouest ou la biographie de Marie-Anne Gaboury . . .* (Montréal, 1883). Robert Gosman, *The Riel and Lagimodière families in Métis society, 1840–1860* (Can., National Hist. Parks and Sites Branch, *Manuscript report*, no.171, Ottawa, 1977). A. E. S. Martin, *The Hudson's Bay Company's land tenures and the occupation of Assiniboia by Lord Selkirk's settlers, with a list of grantees under the earl and the company* (London, 1898). A.-G. Morice, *Histoire de l'Église catholique dans l'Ouest canadien, du lac Supérieur au Pacifique (1659–1905)* (3v., Winnipeg et Montréal, 1912). *Petite histoire du voyageur*, Antoine Champagne, édit. ([Saint-Boniface], 1971).

LANDMANN, GEORGE THOMAS, army officer, military engineer, and author; b., probably on 11 April 1780, in Woolwich (London), son of Isaac Landmann; d. 27 Aug. 1854 in Shacklewell (London).

George Thomas Landmann was raised within the precincts of the Royal Military Academy at Woolwich, where his father was professor of artillery and fortification. He entered the academy as a cadet on 16 April 1793 and was commissioned as second lieutenant in the Royal Engineers on 1 May 1795. Two years later he was promoted first lieutenant, on 3 June, and was posted to the Canadas. Arriving in Halifax, probably in late October, he reached Quebec by 31 December. He was made welcome by some of the most prominent members of military and colonial society, including in Halifax, Prince Edward* Augustus, to whom his father was a well-known and respected figure. Young Landmann's carefree attitude and immaturity, however, were to mark his first posting in the Canadas and to create difficulties for his superiors.

In the spring of 1798 Landmann was posted to St Joseph Island in upper Lake Huron, the westernmost military post in Upper Canada, where he was to complete fortifications begun in 1797. He travelled there in canoes owned by the North West Company, the first year with William McGillivray* and the second year with McGillivray, Alexander Mackenzie*, and Roderick McKenzie*. When he took command of the works on 24 May 1798, one of his first tasks, assumed with others at Fort St Joseph, including the commander, Captain Peter Drummond of the Royal Canadian Volunteer Regiment, was to witness the deed of sale of St Joseph Island by the Ojibwa Indians to the British government on 30 June 1798.

Landmann, on instructions from commanding engineer Gother Mann*, was to construct a wharf, guardhouse, and temporary powder-magazine, and to surround the post with picketing. The work took longer than expected and was still not completed at the end of the second summer. Furthermore, whether through his youthfulness and inexperience or through the complex system of accounting, his books were not in order when the time came to leave the island. He arrived in Quebec in late November 1799 to find that the new commander-in-chief of the forces in the Canadas, Lieutenant-General Peter Hunter*, refused to accept his accounts. All work at St Joseph was suspended and he was ordered to return immediately to the island to correct his errors. Hunter's decision led to a further prolonged delay in the fortification of the island, major work not being resumed until 1804. Although the isolation of the post and the difficulties experienced in obtaining supplies may explain some of Landmann's problems, he must bear a share of the responsibility for the delay. While at St Joseph in 1799 he had been occupied for at least part of the summer in building a store and house for the use of the NWC. On his way back to the island in early 1800 he tarried until spring in York (Toronto), called on Peter Russell*, receiver general of Upper Canada, and purchased a block of land in Norwich. Leaving St Joseph in early July 1800, he reached Montreal in less than eight days, yet he did not report to Quebec until the following month.

After a winter in Quebec, during which time the problem of his accounts was resolved, Landmann was posted to the Cascades (near Île des Cascades), Lower Canada. Working under the direction of Captain Ralph Henry Bruyeres*, and following instructions laid down by Mann, a more mature Landmann

levelled and prepared the ground for the construction of a new canal at the Cascades and for the widening of the existing canal at Coteau-du-Lac. In 1802 he supervised the cutting of the canal at the Cascades, under the direction of Captain Robert Pilkington*. Promoted captain-lieutenant on 13 July of that year, he returned to England the following autumn.

Landmann shared with his contemporaries an active social life in both Quebec and Montreal. Despite a rather superior attitude as an affluent young officer with influential contacts, he exhibited a lively curiosity about the people and the customs of the country. These he depicted in *Adventures and recollections of Colonel Landmann*, published 50 years after he left the Canadas. The work follows his movements in detail and demonstrates that his interest stemmed not so much from intellectual or scientific curiosity as from the curiosity of youth for which each day offers a new adventure. One such event concerned the earliest known instance of vaccination against smallpox in the Canadas.

The British physician Edward Jenner had made public the use of cowpox matter for inoculation against smallpox in 1798 and the procedure was introduced into Newfoundland the same year by the Reverend John Clinch*. On 28 Nov. 1801, while stationed at Quebec, Landmann received a packet from England containing cowpox matter between two plates of glass, together with instructions for its use and drawings to illustrate the expected stages of reaction. In Landmann's own words, "no time was lost" in vaccinating the two children of a fellow engineer, Captain William Backwell. Although there is no confirming evidence, it is probable that other children were vaccinated and even, as Landmann later claimed, that medical men came from the United States to procure vaccine material from the Backwell children. However, the first formal promotion of vaccination in Lower Canada was undertaken by Dr George Longmore* in the spring of 1802.

Landmann's career advanced rapidly after his return to England. In December 1805 he was posted to Gibraltar where he was promoted captain on 1 July 1806. From Gibraltar he embarked for Portugal as commanding royal engineer in the summer of 1808. His services during the Peninsular War brought him recognition from the king of Spain and commissions in the Spanish engineers and the Spanish army. Wounded in Spain in 1811, he was forced to return to England. He was appointed lieutenant-colonel on 16 May 1814 and served as commanding engineer in the Thames and Yorkshire districts successively. He was granted leave of absence in 1819 and retired from the engineering corps by sale of his commission on 29 Dec. 1824. Between 1831 and 1845 he was responsible for engineering plans for several railways in Britain. He was elected a member of the Institution

Lane

of Civil Engineers in 1835, a position he held until his death.

It was his later military career that made George Thomas Landmann noted in England. In Canada he is remembered for his exuberance, his curiosity, and his youthful adventure as a pioneer vaccinator.

BARBARA R. TUNIS

George Thomas Landmann is the author of *Adventures and recollections of Colonel Landmann, late of the Corps of Royal Engineers* (2v., London, 1852), an autobiography based on a journal that has not been located. A listing of his publications is available in the *DNB* and some of his maps, plans, and drawings are listed in *The British Museum catalogue of printed maps, charts and plans: photolithographic edition to 1964* (15v., London, 1967), 8: 771.

ANQ-Q, CE1-61, 28 nov. 1801. Central Library, Royal Military Academy (Sandhurst, Eng.), Royal Military Academy, Woolwich, reg. of cadets. PAC, MG 19, B1, 1: 110–11; MG 23, GII, 17, ser.1, vols.17–18; RG 1, L1, 22: 478, 531; RG 8, I (C ser.), 38, 223, 252–53, 382–83, 512, 724, 1207–10, 1705; RG 10, D10, 661. *Gentleman's Magazine*, January–June 1855: 422–23. Harmon, *Sixteen years in the Indian country* (Lamb). Alexander Mackenzie, *The journals and letters of Sir Alexander Mackenzie*, ed. W. K. Lamb (Toronto, 1970). *Quebec Gazette*, 11 Aug. 1803. G.B., WO, *Army list*, 1793–1803. *Roll of officers of the Corps of Royal Engineers from 1660 to 1898 . . .*, ed. R. F. Edwards (Chatham, Eng., 1898). Abbott, *Hist. of medicine*. J. E. and E. L. Bayliss, *Historic St. Joseph Island* (Cedar Rapids, Iowa, 1938). J. J. Heagerty, *Four centuries of medical history in Canada and a sketch of the medical history of Newfoundland* (2v., Toronto, 1928). Whitworth Porter *et al.*, *History of the Corps of Royal Engineers* (9v. to date, London and Chatham, 1889– ; vols.1–3 repr., Chatham, 1951–54). Elizabeth Vincent, *Fort St. Joseph* (Can., National Historic Parks and Sites Branch, *Manuscript report*, no.335, Ottawa, 1978), 3–7, 78–95, 279–81. R. J. Young, *A comparative report and catalogue of blockhouses in Canada* (Can., National Historic Parks and Sites Branch, *Manuscript report*, no.155, Ottawa, 1973). R. C. Stewart, "Early vaccinations in British North America," Canadian Medical Assoc., *Journal* (Toronto), 39 (1938): 181–83. "Le vaccin à Québec," *BRH*, 44 (1938): 349.

LANE, AMBROSE, army and militia officer, politician, office holder, and judge; b. in County Tipperary (Republic of Ireland), probably in 1791, son of Colonel John Hamilton Lane; m. 19 Aug. 1817 Mary Smith, and they had six children; d. 7 Sept. 1853 in Charlottetown.

Ambrose Lane began his long military career in 1807 by joining the 99th Foot (renumbered 98th in 1815) as an ensign. He rose to the rank of lieutenant in 1811 and in 1812 was posted to North America. Four years later Lane was given command of a subaltern's detachment at Charlottetown. With the army reduction of 1818 he went on half pay and settled in Prince Edward Island where he took up the duties of captain in the militia and, in 1819, Charlottetown town major.

Lane quickly established his social and political position in Island society by marrying a daughter of Lieutenant Governor Charles Douglass SMITH. His father-in-law was a man of autocratic temperament engaged in a struggle to free himself from dependence on the House of Assembly. Lane shared both the lieutenant governor's acerbic disposition and his disdain for colonial politicians. In December 1818 Smith appointed Lane to the Council and used him, along with another son-in-law, John Edward Carmichael*, to provide his administration with the independence from political factions he desired. Local politicians objected to this nepotism, which not only reduced their own role in the government but also confirmed their suspicions of executive corruption. For example, as registrar (1818), examiner (1818), and master (1819) of the Court of Chancery, Lane was in the happy position of setting his own fees as registrar and then, as master, ruling on any complaints these fees aroused.

Frustrated by their inability to control the wilful lieutenant governor, Island worthies, including Paul Mabey*, Donald McDONALD, John MACGREGOR, and John Stewart*, formed a committee which held a series of public meetings in the spring and summer of 1823. The meetings resulted in the adoption and circulation of resolutions critical of the propriety and constitutionality of Smith's conduct. Lane's lack of qualifications for his judicial posts came under particular scrutiny as a blatant example of undue family influence. The result was the public spectacle of a rigged trial in the Court of Chancery which held the Island's attention throughout October and November of that year. The committee members who had framed the resolutions were charged with contempt of court for impugning Lane's behaviour as a court official; their real crime, of course, was political opposition. Smith, as chancellor of the court, found the defendants guilty. It was a Pyrrhic victory: London replaced him with John Ready* in 1824 and the defendants and their allies swept the election of that year.

Lane survived the retribution and inquiries which followed and adapted, not without some discomfort, to the new power of the local politicians. Although he lost his position as master in chancery in 1825, he retained his other military and judicial posts as well as his seat on Council. In fact, as he assimilated into the local élite he became a pillar of the new establishment which developed into the family compact of the 1830s and 1840s. From August 1828 to May 1829 he acted as the Island's colonial secretary and was appointed an unpaid assistant justice of the Supreme Court in November 1829 under Edward James JARVIS. In 1831 he was promoted to the temporary rank of captain on half pay in the regular army and became, with Coun Douly RANKIN, sub-inspector and district adjutant in the local militia, posts he held to his death.

In Council, Lane remained staunchly conservative, opposing advocates of escheat and responsible government and promoting proprietorial interests. When Lieutenant Governor Sir Charles Augustus FITZROY created separate Legislative and Executive councils in March 1839, Lane was excluded from both bodies, but by September, at FitzRoy's express request, he regained a seat in the Executive Council without loss of rank. From 1842 to 1853 he was the council's senior member and as such twice served as the Island's administrator, in September and October 1847 during a temporary absence of Lieutenant Governor Sir Henry Vere Huntley*, and from October 1850 to March 1851 between the terms of Sir Donald Campbell* and Sir Alexander Bannerman*. He also served on the Central Board of Health, was a trustee of the Central Academy, and became a founding member of the Central Agricultural Society.

A proud and irascible man, Lane made enemies as much by his character as by his political creed. None the less, as a man of talent and experience, not to mention social weight, he was never without important public office on an island often desperate for men with such qualities.

M. BROOK TAYLOR

PAPEI, Acc. 2552/46 ("Report of the committee on the state of the colony, 21 March 1825"); Acc. 2810/25; RG 1, Commission books, 2 Aug. 1828; 18 May, 16 Nov. 1829; RG 6, Court of Chancery, minutes, 27 June, 16 Sept. 1818; 26 May 1819; RG 16, Land registry records, 1814–53. PRO, CO 226/34: 164, 186; 226/36: 79; 226/58: 29–30. St Paul's Anglican Church (Charlottetown), Reg. of baptisms, marriages, and burials (mfm. at PAPEI). Supreme Court of P.E.I. (Charlottetown), Estates Division, liber 4: f.256 (will of Ambrose Lane, 3 Oct. 1853) (mfm. at PAPEI). P.E.I., House of Assembly, *Journal*, 1841: 151. *Islander*, 9 Sept. 1853. *Prince Edward Island Gazette*, 7 Aug. 1819. *Prince Edward Island Register*, 11, 25 Oct., 1, 15 Nov. 1823; 3, 17, 24 Jan., 18 May 1824; 5, 31 March, 11, 27 Oct. 1825; 19 June 1827; 22 April 1828; 22 June 1830. *Royal Gazette* (Charlottetown), 3, 24 Jan., 14 Feb., 3 April 1832; 2, 9 April, 14, 21 May 1833; 18 March 1834; 2 Dec. 1835; 12 March, 10 Sept. 1839; 15 March 1842; 28 Sept. 1847; 20 Aug. 1850. Duncan Campbell, *History of Prince Edward Island* (Charlottetown, 1875; repr. Belleville, Ont., 1972), 66–67, 108. *Canada's smallest prov.* (Bolger), 66–96. Frank MacKinnon, *The government of Prince Edward Island* (Toronto, 1951), 44–48. A. B. Warburton, *A history of Prince Edward Island from its discovery in 1534 until the departure of Lieutenant-Governor Ready in A.D. 1831* (Saint John, N.B., 1923), 336–43.

LANE, HENRY BOWYER JOSEPH, architect and water-colourist; b. 1817 or 1818 probably on Corfu (Kérkira, Greece), son of Captain Henry Bowyer Lane and Elizabeth Lacey; m. 9 May 1844 Lucy Anne Sharpe in Thornhill, Upper Canada; they had no known children; d. after May 1851, probably in England.

Henry Bowyer Joseph Lane's father, a Royal Artillery officer and veteran of the Peninsular War, was posted on Corfu between 1815 and 1819. The Lane family was prominent in Staffordshire and in Surrey although Henry spent much of his youth in Devon, where for a brief period in 1830–31 he attended Blundell's School at Tiverton. The balance of his schooling and his professional training in architecture are presumed to have taken place in England before he emigrated to Canada. He was in this country by 1841, living first in Cobourg, Upper Canada, and then in Toronto.

Although the boom years of the early 1840s saw many new buildings constructed in Cobourg, only two of Lane's commissions there are known: St Peter's (Anglican) parochial school (1841), which was also to house the Diocesan Theological Institution [see John Strachan*], and St Peter's Church (1843). This latter building was completed over a period of several years, all during the rectorship of the Reverend Alexander Neil Bethune*, and in the final phases of the work Lane's plans were modified by Kivas Tully*, the architect-in-charge.

Lane moved to Toronto in April 1842. There, during the 1840s, a spate of building activity resulted from a general sense that the city's architecture was no match for its emerging importance. This feeling of architectural poverty was summed up best by the *Toronto Star*: "We see the stiff, stale appearance of bygone days, vanishing like ugly phantoms and ARCHITECTURE in all its fair proportions, stealing coyly from the dark corner in which it has been confined, either by the niggardliness of propriety or stupidity of the building faculty." Shortly after Lane's arrival he prepared plans for Little Trinity Church (Anglican) in the eastern part of the city. He also submitted an entry in the 1843 competition, won by Thomas YOUNG, to design a replacement for the damaged monument to General Sir Isaac Brock* on Queenston Heights. In the following year, however, Lane emerged, at age 26 or 27, as a major figure when his plans were chosen for three significant buildings in Toronto: the market-house and city hall; the Anglican Church of St George the Martyr; and major additions to Osgoode Hall, the home of the Law Society of Upper Canada.

A classical building expressing the importance of common law, Osgoode Hall was clearly Lane's Canadian masterpiece. He was responsible for the entire west wing, for the impressive stone portico applied to John EWART's earlier east wing to create a balanced composition, and for a Palladian loggia and dignifying dome that dressed up an existing range of chambers between the wings. This central section was demolished in 1856, but the new lawcourts and Great Library built in its place to designs by Frederic

485

Lane

William Cumberland* and William George Storm* acknowledged Lane's choice of materials, massing, and style.

The balance of his short career in Canada produced only a few more known commissions of note: ecclesiastical furnishings for St Mark's Church (Anglican), Niagara (Niagara-on-the-Lake) (1845); plans for St Paul's Church (Anglican), Kingston (1846), which after a major fire in 1854 was rebuilt under the supervision of William Hay*; Holy Trinity Church (Anglican), Toronto (1846); and houses in that city for Colonel Arthur Carthew and George William Allan*, both begun in 1847. The competition to design Holy Trinity had resulted in the awarding of the premium to William THOMAS, a talented designer who had considerably more experience than Lane. Thomas's plans were set aside, however, and Lane was asked to prepare drawings with advice from a number of architects and others. It is likely that he had a hand in alterations made about that time to Dundurn, the Hamilton mansion of Sir Allan Napier MacNab*. While in Canada, Lane, who as an architect was also a competent artist, made a number of water-colour sketches, chiefly of places he visited. One of these sketches, of the Boulton family's Toronto home, the Grange, was shown in the 1847 exhibition of the Toronto Society of Arts. In 1845–46 Lane had entered, but did not win, competitions to design several Toronto structures – a new front for the old market buildings, the Commercial Bank of the Midland District, and St Michael's Cathedral (Roman Catholic) – as well as the combined district court-house, town hall, and market building in Niagara. In each case the first premium went to William Thomas. Lane's achievements were significant, none the less, and a remarkably large number of his buildings survive as evidence of his skill and his good fortune to arrive in Toronto at an appropriate time.

Lane came to Canada freshly trained in a wide variety of the Gothic Revival and classical styles which were current in England in the late 1830s. He was able, therefore, to inspire confidence that his designs were in fashion, while adapting his choice of architectural style to suit each situation. Little Trinity and Holy Trinity churches were "Domestic-Gothic," recalling the English parish churches of the Tudor period. On the other hand, the Perpendicular Gothic manner of St George the Martyr, considered the correct style by the emerging ecclesiological societies in England, pleased its well-informed and well-to-do congregation.

Some portion of Lane's success can be traced to the interest taken in his work by the influential Boulton family, to whom he was related through the marriage alliances of two of his aunts in England. In Cobourg, George Strange Boulton* and his nephew D'Arcy Edward Boulton (who had attended Blundell's School at the same time as Lane) clearly carried weight, although Lane, who was almost certainly the only professionally trained architect there at the time, would probably have secured some commissions in any event. At Niagara, James Boulton was in a position to be helpful. The Toronto field was more competitive, however, and Lane likely benefited from William Henry Boulton*'s membership on city council and on the building committees of St George the Martyr and Osgoode Hall. After enjoying this powerful patronage for more than six years, Lane left Canada in November 1847 for England and obscurity. In May 1851 he was living in Birchfield (now part of Birmingham) but details of his later life and death are unknown.

STEPHEN A. OTTO and MARION BELL MACRAE

[Surviving plans signed by Henry Bowyer Joseph Lane include drawings for the George William Allan house, 1847 (in the J. C. B. and E. C. Horwood coll. (uncatalogued), AO), and the Toronto City Hall (in the Henry Langley papers, nos.172–75, and the J. G. Howard papers, sect.III, architectural plans, no.415, MTL). Unsigned plans which can be attributed to him include one for Osgoode Hall (in the Horwood coll.), additional studies for City Hall (Howard papers, no.411; Langley papers, nos.170–71) and the Allan house (Howard papers, nos.90–91), and a damaged drawing for the Arthur Carthew house (in the John Fisken papers (uncatalogued), MTL), which is missing that part where a signature might originally have been. There are also three studies for City Hall in Howard's hand which were probably copied from drawings by Lane (Howard papers, nos.412–14).

Lane's written specifications for the Allan house, signed and dated 18 Aug. 1847, are also in section III of the Howard papers (box 2, misc. buildings, 1847–55). He is also the author of an architectural description of the newly completed "Church of the Holy Trinity," published anonymously in the *Church* (Toronto) on 15 Oct. 1847 and reprinted on the 19th in the *British Colonist* (Toronto).

Lane's sketch *The Grange* is listed in the Toronto Soc. of Arts catalogue, *Toronto Society of Arts: first exhibition, 1847* . . . ([Toronto?, 1847?]), no.155; the water-colour itself is now in the collection of the Art Gallery of Ont. (Toronto). The London Regional Art Gallery (London, Ont.) holds another of his sketches, *Quebec, Lower Canada*, painted around 1840, this being one of eight Lane water-colours of Canadian subjects and seventeen topographical and architectural sketches of English interest offered at two 1977 auctions in England. The illustration of Osgoode Hall facing page 195 of W. H. Smith, *Smith's Canadian gazetteer; comprising statistical and general information respecting all parts of the upper province, or Canada West* . . . (Toronto, 1846), is based on Lane's sketch; two other contemporary plates depicting his commissions may be seen in C. P. De Volpi, *Toronto, a pictorial record: historical prints and illustrations of the city of Toronto, province of Ontario, Canada* (Montreal, 1965), plates 13 and 22. S.A.O. and M.B.MacR.]

ACC-T, Church of St Peter (Cobourg, Ont.), vestry minute-books, 23 June 1851; Church of the Holy Trinity (Toronto) papers, T. A. Reed, "The Church of the Holy

Trinity" (typescript, n.d.), 11, 22; St George the Martyr (Toronto), papers, tenders for construction of church, 1844–45; finances for construction of church, 1842–51, especially W. H. Boulton to H. B. [J.] Lane, 1851, receipted by Lane, 8 May 1851. AO, Map coll., S. A. Fleming, "Plan of the town of Cobourg . . . ," 1848; MS 35, letter-books, 1844–49: 310; MU 296. Blundell's School (Tiverton, Eng.), Reg., 1830–31. CTA, RG 1, A, 10 Jan. 1843, 4 March 1844, 30 Jan. 1846; RG 5, F, 1842–47. Law Soc. of U.C. (Toronto), "Journal of proceedings of the Convocation of Benchers of the Law Society of Upper Canada" (8v.), 6, 10 Aug. 1844. MTL, John Fisken papers, papers concerning Arthur Carthew house, 1847–48, especially report, May 1848, [probably by William Robinson] (uncatalogued); J. G. Howard papers, sect.II, diaries, 15 April, 27 Aug. 1842; 31 July 1844; 29 Jan., 30 Oct. 1847. Univ. of Toronto, Thomas Fisher Rare Books Library, MS coll. 56 (A. N. MacNab papers), L. A. Sharpe to MacNab, 19 Sept. 1849. Sophia MacNab, *The diary of Sophia MacNab*, ed. C. A. Carter and T. M. Bailey (Hamilton, Ont., 1968), 65–66. "Town Hall and Market House in Niagara," *British Colonist* (Toronto), 21 July 1846, reprinted from *Niagara Chronicle* (Niagara [Niagara-on-the-Lake, Ont.]), 10 July 1846. *British Colonist*, 20, 27 Aug. 1844; 11 Feb., 27 June 1845; 27, 31 March 1846; 8 June 1847. *Church*, 21 April, 30 June 1843; 17 May 1844; 21 Nov. 1845; 17 April 1846; 27 Oct. 1847; 22 Feb. 1855. *Cobourg Star*, 30 June, 7 July 1841; 19 Jan. 1842; 7 June 1843; 24 April, 1 May 1844. *Examiner* (Toronto), 10 Jan. 1844. *Globe*, 2 Dec. 1845. *Herald* (Toronto), 27 July 1843, 11 April 1844, 18 May 1845, 2 July 1846. *Toronto Patriot*, 2 Feb. 1843, 7 May 1844. *Toronto Star*, 20 May 1841; 12 April 1842; 13 April, 20 Nov. 1844. John and J. B. Burke, *A genealogical and heraldic dictionary of the landed gentry of Great Britain and Ireland* (3v., London, 1849), 3: 123. MacRae and Adamson, *Cornerstones of order*. MacRae et al., *Hallowed walls*.

LANGEVIN, ANTOINE, Roman Catholic priest and vicar general; b. 7 Feb. 1802 in Beauport, Lower Canada, son of Antoine Langevin, a day-labourer, and Catherine Leclaire; d. 11 April 1857 in Saint-Basile, N.B.

Antoine Langevin entered the Séminaire de Nicolet in 1826. Four years later he was appointed prefect of studies, a post he held until 1833; he probably undertook studies in theology at the same time. On 29 Sept. 1833 he was ordained priest at Quebec, and shortly after he was appointed curate at Nicolet.

In 1835 Langevin became parish priest of Saint-Basile, in the Madawaska region of New Brunswick. This parish, founded in 1792, was the only one then established canonically in Madawaska. By the time Langevin came it boasted a chapel, sacristy, and presbytery in good condition. In addition he looked after two chapels, one at Saint-Bruno (Van Buren, Maine), 15 miles downstream from Saint-Basile, and the other at Sainte-Luce (St Luce Station, Maine), at the same distance upstream. Although the Madawaska mission, extending 70 miles along the Saint John River, was part of the diocese of Charlottetown (established in 1829), the bishop, Angus Bernard

MacEachern*, had left various administrative powers to the archbishop of Quebec. Thus it fell to Archbishop Joseph Signay* to appoint the French Canadian priests responsible for ministering to a population that by 1830 had risen to 2,612 settlers of Acadian and French Canadian origin. Langevin had to adapt to a rather primitive existence which none the less offered some compensations. As his predecessor, François-Xavier-Romuald Mercier, noted in 1834, "If the missionary at Madawaska has the misfortune to be isolated, he has on the other hand the joy of having a large number of virtuous settlers who love their religion and practise it faithfully."

In 1838 Langevin was appointed vicar general of the Madawaska mission by Bernard Donald MACDONALD, the new bishop of Charlottetown, in the course of a pastoral visit to New Brunswick. During his 22 years at Saint-Basile, Langevin was remarkably successful. He worked zealously and unremittingly in a number of spheres. His correspondence with Signay shows that, despite his energy and devotion to his widely scattered flock, he could not cope with the amount of work. Many of the faithful had to be satisfied with eight or nine visits annually from their parish priest, since more frequent visits could not be managed, given the distances and primitive means of transportation involved. Langevin repeatedly asked Signay to create other parishes with a resident priest. Thanks to his persistent requests, the parishes of Saint-Bruno and Sainte-Luce were founded in 1838 and 1843 respectively.

The Malecites of the region were also the object of Langevin's pastoral concern. He used his good relations with the lieutenant governor of New Brunswick, Sir John HARVEY, to obtain an annual sum of £50 from the government so that he could secure the help of a priest for his ministry at the Tobique Indian Reserve and at Saint-Bruno, where there were a number of Malecite families.

Langevin was reputed to be a good administrator. He made judicious use of the *fabrique*'s lands and of some properties in the region owned by the archbishop, renting them to farmers or cultivating them to make them profitable for their owners. During his years there the settlement of the Madawaska region made considerable progress. The population increased noticeably and the area prospered. Hence Langevin was able to replace the old presbytery with a new one of impressive size, and he started construction of a new church, which was still unfinished at the end of his life. He seems to have had enough money himself to lend funds at interest to various local people. From 1839 until his death he lent substantial sums (amounting to at least £1,700) to the Collège de Sainte-Anne-de-la-Pocatière.

In the field of education Langevin stood out as a leader. He encouraged the setting up of primary schools and bolstered the dedication of itinerant

Langlois

teachers. But his zeal was especially evident in the assistance he gave to the young men of the Madawaska area to enable them to pursue their studies at college, particularly at the Collège de Sainte-Anne-de-la-Pocatière. From 1839 Langevin, with Signay's permission, used the income from the lands belonging to the archbishop to pay the students' board, "in the hope of making ecclesiastics of them for this poor diocese . . . which needs them so badly." Part of his own income was put to the same purpose. Between 1855 and 1857 he gave the college donations totalling £2,000 for bursaries that are still offered. The college inherited his estate, estimated to be worth £3,079.

The vicar general's influence and action also extended to the political sphere. He maintained good relations with the authorities in New Brunswick, especially with Harvey, the lieutenant governor, who was Langevin's guest at the time of his visit to the Madawaska region during the quarrel between Maine and New Brunswick over the border between them. Langevin was an ardent defender of all things British, and it may have been because of his control over his parishioners that they remained quiet during the conflict. He continued to minister to the parishes which found themselves on the American side of the border when the Webster–Ashburton Treaty was concluded in 1842 [see James Bucknall Bucknall ESTCOURT]. Harvey wrote concerning Langevin: "The Madawaska region and the entire province of New Brunswick were fortunate in having such an enlightened guide in such a critical period of their history."

Although Langevin was generally esteemed during his years at Saint-Basile, his authoritarian, domineering, and sometimes uncompromising character occasionally aroused the displeasure, and even the hostility, of some parishioners. In 1849, for example, 44 of them signed a petition to Signay complaining about the conflicts between Langevin and the *fabrique* over control of parish funds, and stressing that they no longer had confidence in "a man whose daily conduct only tends to tyranny, and who takes pleasure in calling [us] morons and ranking [us] with brute beasts, whenever the opportunity arises." On the other hand, nine of the region's leading citizens wrote to Signay some months later that they were "perfectly satisfied" with their parish priest's behaviour.

These conflicts darkened the last years of Antoine Langevin's ministry. "A man with superior administrative ability," of "indomitable energy, unflagging perseverance, [and] an authoritarian character," to quote the Reverend Thomas Albert, the historian of Madawaska, Langevin stood out as one of the region's great benefactors and as a zealous priest who generously helped Madawaskans to weather one of the most difficult periods of their history. He died

prematurely in his parish on 11 April 1857, and was buried on 20 April in the church of Sainte-Anne-de-la-Pocatière (La Pocatière).

Guy R. Michaud

[The author wishes to thank Mgr Ernest Lang of Edmundston, N.B., for information on Antoine Langevin. G.R.M.]
AAQ, 311 CN, IV: 122–24, 127–34, 137–38, 140–42, 147–48, 150–54, 163; 60 CN, II: 88. ANQ-Q, CE1-5, 7 févr. 1802; CE3-12, 20 avril 1857; CN2-30, 29 mars 1841; 29 juill. 1842; 12, 21 mai 1852; 6 déc. 1856; 10 mai 1857. Allaire, *Dictionnaire*, 1: 302. Tanguay, *Répertoire* (1893), 214. Thomas Albert, *Histoire du Madawaska d'après les recherches historiques de Patrick Therriault et les notes manuscrites de Prudent L. Mercure* (Québec, 1920). H. G. Classen, *Thrust and counterthrust: the genesis of the Canada–United States boundary* (Don Mills [Toronto], 1965). Douville, *Hist. du collège-séminaire de Nicolet*. Wilfrid Lebon, *Histoire du collège de Sainte-Anne-de-la-Pocatière* (2v., Québec, 1948–49). Roger Paradis, "La bourse Langevin: une page de l'éducation des Acadiens au Madawaska," Soc. hist. acadienne, *Cahiers* (Moncton, N.-B.), 7 (1976): 118–30. "Une grande et noble figure de l'histoire du Madawaska, le grand vicaire Langevin, 1835–1857," *Le Brayon* (Edmundston), 3 (1975), no.2: 16–19.

LANGLOIS, *dit* **GERMAIN, AUGUSTIN-RENÉ**, bookseller and militia officer; b. 3 May 1770 at Quebec, son of Louis Langlois, *dit* Germain, and Catherine Sauvageau; m. there 24 June 1799 Marie-Josephte Laforce (Pépin, *dit* Laforce), and they had one child; d. 11 Sept. 1852 in Château-Richer, Lower Canada.

The father of Augustin-René Langlois, *dit* Germain, was an important merchant in the town of Quebec after the conquest. At his death he owned numerous properties, including a wholesale business on Rue de la Fabrique, a retail store on Rue Saint-Jean, and another in Saint-Cuthbert. After Augustin-René had studied at the Petit Séminaire de Québec from 1782 to 1791, he worked for his father. On the latter's death in 1798 he settled the estate under the supervision of Mathew Lymburner and Jean-Antoine Panet*, who were the executors as well as intimate friends of the family. He then opened a business at 10 Rue de la Fabrique and obtained his merchant's licence on 25 April 1800.

In the parish census of 1805 the priest listed Germain as a merchant living at 5 Rue de la Fabrique. The 1818 census, which gave his address as Rue Sainte-Anne, called him a bookseller, as did the *Quebec directory* of 1822 and 1826. His father had announced in 1764 that he was opening a circulating library – the first in the province – and he had sold hundreds of catechisms, novenas, and other devotional texts to parish priests. It is not known whether Augustin-René sold books before 1815, the year he

488

was in London to negotiate with Peter and William Wynne, who had imported books from France for him. His purchases, worth several hundred pounds, arrived at Quebec and were received by printer John Neilson* late in the summer. In early September a fire destroyed the warehouse storing the books, but they survived the disaster. On 2 Nov. 1815 Germain announced that they were on display on the second floor of the bishop's palace, but he did not succeed in selling all his stock.

In 1821 Germain published a catalogue containing 695 titles; 97 per cent of them were in French, the remainder in Latin. They included 262 books on religion and 177 on law, as well as volumes on science, the arts, history, and *belles-lettres*. The catalogue's title specified that these were books "recently arrived from France" and obtainable from Germain at Quebec and from Joseph ROY in Montreal. Germain received another imported collection in 1822, and published a second catalogue in 1826 on his return from a business trip to France. This time the books were for sale at Montreal through Isidore Malo's store rather than Roy's.

The second catalogue was the last; on 29 Dec. 1828 *La Minerve* announced that bookseller Théophile Dufort of Montreal had bought Germain's and Malo's stock. The transaction did not prevent the store on Rue de la Fabrique from later providing space to the Nouvelle Librairie and other booksellers. Germain was probably the first French-speaking bookseller at Quebec, long before Joseph and Octave* Crémazie.

The sale of Germain's book business occurred after the death in 1827 of his brother Pierre-Olivier, the parish priest at Château-Richer, of whom he and his brother Charles were joint heirs. Charles died the following year leaving Augustin-René sole heir to the properties of his father and Pierre-Olivier. The latter's estate included a house at Château-Richer, located on land a league deep fronting on the river, and a site near the church. Germain was consequently assured of an income that would enable him to maintain his family in reasonable comfort.

Germain continued a tradition begun by his grandfather and father of participating in Quebec public life. For 20 years he was a member of the Quebec Fire Society, and he was several times called to sit on its committee for Upper Town. In the 1808 elections Augustin-René ran for York constituency, as his father had done in 1792, but he was defeated. He tried again in Montmorency in 1832 only to be beaten by Elzéar Bédard*. He was promoted major in Quebec's 1st Militia Battalion in 1808, and at his death held the rank of colonel. Also in 1808, as a mark of esteem, he was granted the title *écuyer*.

Germain left Quebec permanently some time after 1832 to settle in Château-Richer. There he passed the time managing his properties in the town and on the Beaupré shore. In 1844, when ill health caused him some concern, he gave special powers of attorney for himself and his wife to Amable Berthelot*, a lawyer and assemblyman.

Augustin-René Langlois, *dit* Germain, had only one child, Augustin-Hyppolite, born 28 July 1805. After attending the Petit Séminaire de Québec for some years as his father and uncles had done, he is thought to have studied medicine in Chicago. Augustin-René's legacy was so strong that the premature death of Augustin-Hyppolite in 1829 did not prevent the latter's son from also carrying the title "gentleman farmer" at the time he married in Château-Richer.

CLAUDE GALARNEAU

ANQ-Q, CE1-1, 3 mai 1770, 24 juin 1799, 28 juill. 1805; CE1-6, 14 sept. 1852; CN1-230, 23 juin 1799; P-193, 1–35. ASQ, C 37–C 43; Fichier des anciens. PAC, MG 24, B1, 187: 2869–73. "Les dénombrements de Québec" (Plessis), ANQ *Rapport*, 1948–49: 164. *Recensement de la ville de Québec en 1818 par le curé Joseph Signaÿ*, Honorius Provost, édit. (Québec, 1976), 258. *Le Canadien*, 23 oct. 1822. *La Minerve*, 29 déc. 1828. *Quebec Gazette*, 2 Nov. 1815. *Catalogue de livres . . . à vendre chez M. Augustin Germain, à Québec, et chez M. Joseph Roi, à Montréal* (Québec, 1821). *Catalogue de livres . . . à vendre chez Mr. Aug. Germain, à Québec, et chez Mr. Isidore Malo, à Montréal* (Québec, 1826). *Quebec directory*, 1822, 1826. [Catherine Burke, named de Saint-Thomas], *Les Ursulines de Québec, depuis leur établissement jusqu'à nos jours* (4v., Québec, 1863–66), 4: 422.

LARKIN, JOHN, Roman Catholic priest, Sulpician, and educator; b. 2 Feb. 1801 in Ravensworth, England, second son of John Larkin, an innkeeper, and Elizabeth Jones; d. 11 Dec. 1858 in New York City.

John Larkin came from a family of Irish origin; he grew up at Newcastle upon Tyne and seems to have been taught first by a Protestant minister at Whickham. In 1808 he and his elder brother Charles Fox, who became a doctor and a champion of the Roman Catholics in England, entered St Cuthbert's College at Ushaw. The college had been started that year by teachers from the English college at Douai, France, who had been driven out by the French revolution. John had as his master John Lingard, a well-known English historian of the early 19th century, and one of his fellow students was Nicholas Patrick Stephen Wiseman, later the archbishop of Westminster and a cardinal. Larkin was reasonably successful, and in 1815 finished sixth in a class of 14. He believed he was called to the priesthood, but the college authorities dissuaded him, judging that he did not have the vocation.

On leaving the college, Larkin joined the navy; he

Larkin

went to sea several times and in particular visited India in 1816. When he came back he turned to business, and for a few years found work with firms at Newcastle upon Tyne and in London. In 1819 he met Mgr Edward Beda Slater, who had just been appointed vicar apostolic of Mauritius. Impressed by Larkin's manifest interest in the religious life, Slater made him his secretary and took him to the island. During his stay on Mauritius Larkin's call to the priesthood became clear, and in 1823 he decided to return to Europe. That year he entered the Séminaire de Saint-Sulpice in Paris, where he took the philosophy program and began his theology. He studied along with Henri Lacordaire, who was to become a Dominican and preacher at Notre-Dame in Paris. On 12 June 1824 he received the tonsure in Paris. Shortly afterwards he apparently informed the vice-president of the University of Baltimore, Michael Francis Wheeler, who was then visiting the seminary, of his desire to work for the Society of Saint-Sulpice in America. Late in the summer of 1825 he embarked for the United States with Wheeler, and they reached Baltimore on 9 September. Larkin finished his theological studies at St Mary's Seminary, where he was ordained priest for the vicariate apostolic of Durham, England, on 26 Aug. 1827. He had begun teaching in the seminary, but he was not to stay long at Baltimore.

The Petit Séminaire de Montréal, the only French-speaking establishment for secondary education in Lower Canada founded and run by the Sulpicians, had 4 priests, 5 or 6 regents, and 130 to 150 pupils, two-thirds of whom were boarders and 30 per cent English speaking. In 1827 the death of one of its teachers, Simon Boussin, left a void in the institution. Moreover, the seminary urgently needed an English-speaking priest. Candide-Michel Le Saulnier*, who was directing it in the absence of Jean-Henry-Auguste Roux*, therefore asked the director of St Mary's Seminary, Jean-Marie Tessier, to send Larkin to fill the vacant position. Tessier reluctantly agreed, and Larkin left Baltimore on 20 Nov. 1827, reaching Montreal nine days later. At the beginning of December he was appointed curate of the parish of Notre-Dame in Montreal, and in this capacity helped Sulpician Jackson John Richard* to minister to the English-speaking Catholics who met in the chapel of Notre-Dame-de-Bonsecours. He also became a teacher at the Petit Séminaire, a post he retained until 1840. From the start, Larkin enjoyed notable success as an instructor and as a preacher.

Under the guidance of the director of the Pétit Séminaire, Joseph-Vincent QUIBLIER, Larkin taught philosophy and classical studies. He exerted a strong influence on his pupils, and although at this period the Petit Séminaire was torn by internal quarrels, he adapted so well to teaching that in 1830 Quiblier

considered naming him as his successor. In 1832 Alexander McDonell*, the bishop of Kingston, asked for Larkin as his coadjutor, but Larkin refused outright, saying that he wished to live as an ordinary priest and teacher in a community where he could find fulfilment. In the ensuing period Larkin continued to teach, and in 1837 he published at Montreal a Greek grammar for the use of the college.

During his years as a student in Paris Larkin had been deeply affected by the ultramontane doctrines of Hugues-Félicité-Robert de La Mennais. The Canadian Sulpicians, who were traditionalist and opposed to the ideas of liberty spread by the French revolution, clung to the gallicanism prevalent under the *ancien régime*. In this matter they opposed Bishop Jean-Jacques Lartigue*, the auxiliary to the bishop of Quebec in the district of Montreal, and the teachers at the Séminaire de Saint-Hyacinthe. Because of Larkin's sympathies, Quiblier got the bishop of Quebec and the superior of the Séminaire de Saint-Sulpice in Paris, Antoine Garnier, to put pressure on him, and the advice of these men as well as the condemnations of La Mennais by Pope Gregory XVI in 1832 and 1834 proved stronger than Larkin's liberal tendencies. In the late 1830s the teachers of the Petit Séminaire were not of one mind, and the lack of authority of their director, Joseph-Alexandre Baile*, may not have been conducive to maintaining harmonious relations among the priests in the seminary. At that time Larkin had some differences of opinion with his confrères. In 1837 the Sulpicians in Baltimore asked the Canadian Sulpicians to allow him to return to work at St Mary's Seminary, but nothing came of the request.

In the summer of 1839 the bishop of Montreal's coadjutor, Ignace Bourget*, invited Jean-Pierre Chazelle*, the Jesuit rector of St Mary's College near Bardstown, Ky, to preach a retreat for his priests. From then on Larkin felt drawn towards the Society of Jesus, and confided his feelings to his superiors in Montreal and Paris. He gave up his membership in the community of the Séminaire de Saint-Sulpice in Montreal on 23 July 1840, and on 23 October he entered the noviciate of the Jesuits in Louisville, Ky. Subsequently he taught at St Mary's College, gave lectures, and preached in the Bardstown region. He even began to build a new college in 1845.

In the summer of that year all the Jesuits established in Kentucky moved to New York City to take over St John's College. This small institution, which was to become Fordham University, had 100 to 150 students. The following year, at the request of his superiors, Larkin opened a centre for teaching and spreading the faith in the heart of New York. For this purpose he converted a former Protestant church to accommodate more than 100 pupils. The centre opened in July 1847, but in January 1848 it was completely destroyed by fire. Refusing to be discouraged, Larkin found another house in the Bowery district where he could recommence the endeavour.

In February 1849 Larkin learned that the Canadian bishops had proposed to Rome that he be nominated bishop of Toronto. The bulls had been signed by Pius IX and all the authorities in Rome insisted that he should accept. In November Larkin went to France to ask the superior general to intervene with the pope and have his appointment cancelled. In the end Armand-François-Marie de Charbonnel* was appointed and Larkin concluded his training as a Jesuit by studying at the Laval theological college in France. On his return to the United States, he performed the duties of rector of St John's College from 1851 to 1854. A degree of permissiveness had slipped into this institution; Larkin corrected the abuses with a firm hand, and proved a remarkable educator. When a Jesuit exchange was arranged in 1854 Larkin went to England and Ireland for two years as a visitor, and devoted his activity to preaching. He also took the opportunity to see his family and friends once more.

John Larkin returned to New York in October 1856, and worked the following year as curate in the parish of St Francis Xavier. There, on 11 Dec. 1858, after a day spent in the confessional, he was stricken suddenly with apoplexy and died. Larkin's death in harness was fitting for a man who had led an active life wherever his apostolic zeal had taken him.

J.-BRUNO HAREL

John Larkin prepared a work for students beginning the study of the Greek language which contained selected pieces on mythology, and he also wrote *Grammaire grecque à l'usage du collège de Montréal* (Montréal, 1837).

AAQ, 210 A, XV: 56, 63. ACAM, 901.137, 832-1, -3, -17, -20; RC, VI: f.237v–238v; RLB, IV: 512, 547; V: 137, 169–71; VI: 11–15, 20–22; RLL, VI: 262–63; VII: 120. Arch. de la Compagnie de Jésus, prov. du Canada français (Saint-Jérôme, Qué.), A-1-7; D-7. Arch. de la Compagnie de Saint-Sulpice (Paris), Cahier des ordinations, Corr. avec le Canada, 12 juin 1824. Arch. of St Mary's Seminary (Baltimore, Md.), RG 24, boxes 7, 9. Arch. of the Archdiocese of New York (New York), St Francis Xavier Church, house history, 11 Dec. 1858. ASSM, 21; 25, Dossier 2. *Litteræ annuæ provinciæ franciæ Societatis Jesu ab octobri 1858 ad octobrem 1859* (Paris, 1861), 232–36. *Woodstock letters, a record of current events and historical notes connected with the colleges and missions of the Society of Jesus in North and South America* (Baltimore), [1869–1972], 3: 27–42, 135–50; 26: 268–80; 45: 364; 65: 192, 197, 201; 75: 132. *Mélanges religieux*, 22 mars 1850. *New Catholic encyclopedia* (17v., Toronto and San Francisco, 1966–78), 8: 385–86. Henri Gauthier, *Sulpitiana* ([2e éd.], Montréal, 1926). Tanguay, *Répertoire* (1893), 198. Louis Bertrand, *Bibliothèque sulpicienne, ou Histoire littéraire de la Compagnie de Saint-Sulpice* (3v., Paris, 1900), 2: 261. C. G. Herbermann, *The Sulpicians in the United States* (New York, 1916), 82–83. Lemieux,

L'établissement de la première prov. eccl., 404–6. Olivier Maurault, *Nos messieurs* (Montréal, [1936]), 90–91. J. W. Ruane, *The beginnings of the Society of St. Sulpice in the United States (1791–1829)* (Baltimore, 1935), 199–200. T. G. Taaffe, *A history of St John's College, Fordham, N.Y.* (New York, 1891), 86–93. "Les disparus," *BRH*, 36 (1930): 243. "Jesuit who was named second bishop of Toronto," *Catholic Reg. and Canadian Extension* (Toronto), 26 July 1934. Yvan Lamonde, "L'enseignement de la philosophie au collège de Montréal, 1790–1876," *Culture* (Québec), 31 (1970): 213–24. F. J. Nelligan, "Father John Larkin, S.J., 1801–1858," *Canadian Messenger* (Montreal), 67 (1957): 37–43, 103–10, 181–87.

LAROCHELLE, SIMÉON GAUTRON, *dit. See* GAUTRON

LARUE, FRANÇOIS-XAVIER, farmer, notary, office holder, politician, militia officer, and justice of the peace; baptized 29 Oct. 1763 in Pointe-aux-Trembles (Neuville), Que., son of Augustin Larue and Thérèse Delisle; m. 4 Oct. 1790 Marie-Magdeleine Hainse (Hains) (d. 1812), and they had 17 children, 11 of whom survived infancy; d. 13 July 1855 in Pointe-aux-Trembles.

François-Xavier Larue inherited farmland in the seigneury of Neuville, but in 1783 he entered into apprenticeship with Pierre-Louis Deschenaux*, a Quebec notary. He trained for the five-year term stipulated in an ordinance of 1785, the first law to regulate notarial practice under the British régime. Commissioned on 10 May 1788, he established his practice in Pointe-aux-Trembles, where he resumed farming and expanded his land holdings. In 1792 he served as returning officer for Hampshire County, which included Neuville, in the first provincial general election. Eight years later he was commissioned to receive affidavits in that county.

Between 1810 and 1814 Larue and François Huot* represented Hampshire in the House of Assembly. There, Larue, Louis Bourdages*, Joseph Papineau*, and Thomas Lee, all notaries, represented a professional group whose increasingly important political profile and influence were condemned by Governor James Henry Craig*. The electoral campaign of 1810 was dominated by the fervent nationalism of the Canadian party, by debates over provincial or imperial control of civil expenditure, and by Craig's grotesque fears of Napoleonic plots and Canadian democracy as well as his desperate repressive measures. A political moderate, Larue supported the Canadian party on critical partisan issues, notably the disqualification of judges as members of the assembly (a lingering issue directed originally against former member Pierre-Amable De Bonne*), local control of civil expenditure, and the unprecedented 1814 action of impeachment instituted by James STUART against two leading

Laurent

opponents of the party, chief justices Jonathan Sewell* and James Monk*.

Like many of his political associates, Larue participated actively in the War of 1812, serving as major in the Cap-Santé battalion of militia. During the war years he was a commissioner for the administration of oaths of allegiance. In 1815 Larue was appointed a justice of the peace for the district of Quebec. Four years later he also became parochial agent for the agriculture society in the region. During the 1820s and 1830s he continued to farm and to hold local offices, including census commissioner, parish commissioner for summary trial of small causes, roads and bridges commissioner, and school inspector. Between about 1832 and 1845 he acted as administrative and financial agent for the seigneur of Neuville, his grandson Édouard-Wilbrod Larue.

He was returned to the provincial assembly for Hampshire in the by-election of 1826 and represented that riding, renamed Portneuf in 1829, until 1838. In his nationalistic opposition to the administration, the Patriote political leader, Louis-Joseph Papineau*, relied heavily upon the support of such rural French Canadian constituencies. In 1834 Larue supported the assembly's overt bid to secure control of civil expenditure and voted to uphold the famous 92 Resolutions. With the Patriotes moving towards extremes of radical rhetoric and armed resistance, Larue and other members of the assembly from the Quebec area nevertheless urged the recall of the prorogued legislature in December 1837, in a failing effort to stem rebellion. During the same month, in the midst of the uprisings, Larue was appointed a commissioner for the administration of oaths of allegiance.

Following his retirement from politics, Larue continued to practise as a notary. He was to take an interest in the Association des Notaires du District de Québec, formed by 25 notaries on 7 July 1840 after previous unsuccessful attempts to organize the profession dating from 1824. Larue was not a founding member, but, as the district's senior notary, he was named president. He declined to assume the position because of his advanced age. Regarded as the "doyen" of the profession in the province and "one of the best notaries in the country," Larue performed his last notarial act on 20 Oct. 1843 but continued to oversee his farm until his death. He was buried at the parish church at Pointe-aux-Trembles on 16 July 1855.

DAVID ROBERTS

[The author wishes to thank Alice LaRue Grenier and the late Louis-Philippe Grenier of Neuville, Que., for information on François-Xavier Larue. D.R.]

François-Xavier Larue's minute-book for 1788–1843 is at ANQ-Q, CN1-147.

AP, Saint-Augustin (Saint-Augustin-de-Desmaures), Reg. des baptêmes, mariages et sépultures, 29 oct. 1763, 4 oct. 1790; Saint-François-de-Sales (Neuville), Reg. des baptêmes, mariages et sépultures, 25 nov. 1812, 16 juill. 1855. PAC, MG 24, B1, 32; B2, 2; RG 4, A1, 234: 134; 477: 158; 527: 87; B8, 1: 185–89; RG 9, I, A5, 4: 23; RG 31, A1, 1825, 1831, 1842, 1851, Pointe-aux-Trembles. L.C., House of Assembly, *Journals*, 1810–37. "Ordonnances édictées pour la province de Québec par le gouverneur et le conseil de celle-ci, de 1768–1791 . . . ," PAC *Rapport*, 1914–15: 168–72. *Quebec Gazette*, 24 May 1792; 11 Jan., 19 April, 3 May 1810; 27 April 1812; 30 Nov. 1815; 8 April 1819; 5, 9 July 1821; 3 April 1823. Desjardins, *Guide parl.* Ouellet, *Bas-Canada.* J.-E. Roy, *Hist. du notariat*, vols.2–3. Taft Manning, *Revolt of French Canada.* André Vachon, *Histoire du notariat canadien, 1621–1960* (Québec, 1962). Mason Wade, *The French Canadians, 1760–1967* (rev. ed., 2v., Toronto, 1968). P.-G. Roy, "La famille Larue," *BRH*, 45 (1939): 65–71.

LAURENT. *See* LOLA

LAVALLÉE, ANDRÉ PAQUET, *dit. See* PAQUET

LAVIMAUDIER (Lavimodière). *See* LAGIMONIÈRE

LAVIOLETTE, PIERRE (baptized **Pierre-Vincent**), teacher, seigneur, poet, and journalist; b. 4 March 1794 in Boucherville, Lower Canada, son of Jean-Pierre Guernier, *dit* Laviolette, a merchant and militia captain, and Charlotte Lenoir; d. 23 Aug. 1854 in Saint-Eustache, Lower Canada.

Pierre Laviolette, who came from an old Canadian family, seems to have received his elementary education in Boucherville, a village which then had a primary teacher for boys. After secondary studies at the Petit Séminaire de Montréal from 1808 to 1815, he took the priestly habit and taught there for a year. He then became a teacher at the Séminaire de Nicolet, where he taught the fifth form in the classical program (Belles-Lettres) in 1816–17 and the sixth (Rhetoric) the following year. He abandoned his plans to enter the priesthood in 1818.

From 1818 to 1824 Laviolette appears to have been engaged in teaching, probably at Saint-Eustache. It is known that in 1824 he was running a Latin school there, a sort of classical college, which he had set up himself. On 10 Jan. 1826 he married Elmire Dumont, daughter of Nicolas-Eustache Lambert Dumont*, owner of the seigneury of Mille-Îles and lieutenant-colonel of militia. Of their children, Godefroy*, Alfred, and Arthur are the best known. At his father-in-law's death on 25 April 1835, Laviolette became co-seigneur with Elmire's brother, Charles-Louis Lambert Dumont.

A man of letters, Laviolette composed short dramatic works for schoolchildren and articles which included the occasional piece of literary criticism. He was particularly skilful at writing verse in a pseudo-classical style. One of his songs appeared in a treatise on the humanities produced by the Petit Séminaire de Montréal. It was his song "O Nicolet qu'embellit la nature" that his contemporaries found most memorable. Influenced to some degree by social romanticism, Laviolette believed in the writer's mission, but he concealed his own identity under various pseudonyms, such as X, Le Frondeur, and ***. Some 50 pieces, largely of a poetic nature, have been identified and through them his thoughts on the concerns of his time can be discerned. They appeared in *L'Ami du peuple, de l'ordre et des lois*, *Mélanges religieux*, *La Minerve*, *Le répertoire national*, and elsewhere.

Laviolette attached great importance to education. His respect for Latin is revealed in a dialogue he composed, which was performed in August 1825 at the public examinations of the Latin school at Saint-Eustache. The Montreal and Nicolet seminaries were occasionally honoured in his poetry. In the sphere of economics, he exalted the benefits of industry and denounced somewhat simplistically the treachery of the Patriotes in holding industry and trade responsible for the country's woes. So far as politics was concerned, Laviolette condemned the union plot of 1822 [*see* Louis-Joseph Papineau*; Denis-Benjamin Viger*], and during the feverish decade preceding the union of the two Canadas in 1841 he campaigned as a moderate. An advocate of progress, in particular of political improvement, he extolled evolution and opposed revolution, always in the name of the rights of his compatriots. He was a correspondent for *L'Ami du peuple, de l'ordre et des lois* in 1833 and 1835, and fought against the radicals, who supported *L'Écho du pays* of Saint-Charles-sur-Richelieu and *La Minerve*. Without naming them, he criticized Papineau, William Lyon Mackenzie*, and the rhymesters James Julien Theodore Phelan, Joseph-Édouard Turcotte*, and Joseph-Guillaume Barthe*. He also had the Rouges in mind when he parodied the poetry of Joseph Lenoir*, *dit* Rolland.

Laviolette was a Catholic with a strong faith, who believed in a God transcending man but close to him, in the Word incarnate, and in the Christian understanding of the human condition. Deeply moved by the humanitarian enthusiasms of his century, he spoke glowingly of the material and spiritual regeneration then revitalizing Europe and Lower Canada.

Pierre Laviolette is forgotten today. In 1903 and even as late as 1934, however, he was recalled as one of the highly respected teachers of Nicolet and as a leading citizen of Saint-Eustache. A witness of the years 1830–50, he made a contribution of value to social, political, cultural, and religious thinking.

JEANNE D'ARC LORTIE

ANQ-M, CE1-22, 5 mars 1794, 30 sept. 1797. AP, Saint-Eustache, Reg. des baptêmes, mariages et sépultures, 10 janv. 1826, 25 août 1854. ASN, AO, Séminaire, V, no.79. *L'Ami du peuple, de l'ordre et des lois* (Montréal), 1833–38. *Mélanges religieux*, 1841, 1851. *La Minerve*, 1842–47. Douville, *Hist. du collège-séminaire de Nicolet*. Jeanne d'Arc Lortie, *La poésie nationaliste au Canada français (1606–1867)* (Québec, 1975). *Le répertoire national* (Huston; 1848–50), vols.1–2. "Les disparus," *BRH*, 31 (1925): 480.

LAWLOR. *See* LOLA

LE BLANC, NANCY. *See* McKENZIE

LE BOUTILLIER (Le Bouthillier), DAVID, businessman and politician; b. 14 Oct. 1811 in St John, Jersey, son of Josué Le Boutillier and Anne Amy; d. unmarried probably in 1854 in Paspébiac, Lower Canada.

David Le Boutillier came to Paspébiac in 1827. On his arrival, he began working as an apprentice clerk with Charles Robin and Company. William Fruing, the head clerk, taught him bookkeeping and current practices in the dried cod trade. In March 1838 Le Boutillier left the position of clerk and went into the trade for himself. In partnership with his brothers Amy and Edward, he created the firm Le Boutillier Brothers at Paspébiac. Appointed manager of the new venture, David immediately began building workshops, stores, and warehouses on the shore at Paspébiac, near his ex-employer's large establishment, and purchased a number of ships for transporting the cod.

During the 1840s the firm expanded rapidly under Le Boutillier's management, buying or setting up fishing stations on Île au Bois in the Strait of Belle-Isle, the Baie des Chaleurs, and Île Bonaventure in Lower Canada, on Miscou Island in New Brunswick, and at Forteau in Labrador. It hired on salary fishermen and others to work in its fishing rooms. They were generally recruited at Paspébiac and farther west in the Baie des Chaleurs area at Maria, Carleton, and Bonaventure. The catch was brought back to Paspébiac at the end of the season for a final drying, and exported from there to Mediterranean and West Indian markets.

In December 1851 Le Boutillier was elected to the Legislative Assembly of the Province of Canada for Bonaventure in a narrow victory over two other candidates, one of them being Clarence Hamilton, who had been backed by Charles Robin and Company. Le Boutillier played a rather inconspicuous part in the assembly, but he was a member of two of its select committees, one to inquire into the expediency of encouraging shipbuilding in the province, and another to inquire into the state of fishing in the Gulf of St Lawrence and on the Labrador coast, and he seized

Légaré

the opportunity to turn his ability to good account. In the second committee he stressed the disparity between government subsidies given to French Canadian fishermen and entrepreneurs working on the eastern shores of Lower Canada and the support that their foreign competitors from Jersey enjoyed. He decided not to run again at the end of his term in 1854.

David Le Boutillier died probably at Paspébiac in 1854, at the age of 42. After his death his brother-in-law, Daniel Carcaud, took over Le Boutillier Brothers; under his management the company continued to expand, and at the end of the 1850s opened two new fishing stations, at Magpie and Rivière-au-Tonnerre on the north shore of the Gulf of St Lawrence. Next to Charles Robin and Company, it was the largest fishing business established on the Gaspé peninsula, and around 1870 it was exporting annually some 20,000 quintals of dried cod, about one-third of its chief competitor's shipments abroad.

ANDRÉ LEPAGE

BE, Bonaventure (New-Carlisle), Reg. B, 6, nos.505, 592; B-B, 1, nos.4, 6; Gaspé (Percé), Reg. B, 2, no.982. PAC, MG 28, III18; MG 30, D1, 18: 129; RG 31, A1, 1861, Bonaventure. Soc. jersiaise (Saint-Hélier, Jersey), St John, reg. des baptêmes, 14 oct. 1811. Canada, Prov. of, Legislative Assembly, *App. to the journals*, 1843, app.6; 1853, app.JJJJ. Desjardins, *Guide parl.* Jules Bélanger *et al.*, *Histoire de la Gaspésie* (Montréal, 1981), 211, 285, 378. H. A. Innis, *The cod fisheries; the history of an international economy* (rev. ed., Toronto, 1978). André Lepage, *Le banc de Paspébiac, site commercial et industriel* (Québec, 1980), 76–88. Thomas Pye, *Canadian scenery: district of Gaspé* (Montreal, 1866); *Images de la Gaspésie au dix-neuvième siècle*, Jean Laliberté et André Lepage, trad. (Québec, 1980), 37, 60. Madeleine Bisson, "L'île Bonaventure à l'époque de la Cie LeBouthillier," *Gaspésie* (Gaspé, Qué.), 19 (1981), no.3: 16–23.

LÉGARÉ, JOSEPH, painter, glazier, landowner, seigneur, art gallery owner, politician, and justice of the peace; b. 10 March 1795 at Quebec, son of Joseph Légaré and Louise Routier; m. there 21 April 1818 Geneviève Damien, and they had 12 children, 7 of whom died in infancy; d. there 21 June 1855.

Joseph Légaré was the eldest of a family of six. His father initially worked as a shoemaker but by 1815 he had become a fairly prosperous merchant. In the autumn of 1810 young Légaré entered the first year at the Petit Séminaire de Québec. He was an indifferent student and probably terminated his studies in July 1811. Less than a year later, on 19 May 1812, he signed an apprenticeship contract with Moses Pierce, a painter and glazier who painted carriages, signs, and apartments, did gilding, and occasionally restored pictures. Légaré subsequently became a master

painter and glazier, and in this capacity on 24 June 1817 he hired an apprentice, Henry Dolsealwhite.

The arrival at Quebec that year of the canvases purchased by Abbé Philippe-Jean-Louis Desjardins* in France seems to have had a decisive influence on Légaré's career. There is an outside chance that Légaré helped restore some of them. In 1819 he hired Antoine Plamondon* as an apprentice. By then Légaré was beginning to execute large copies of religious pictures, some of which came from the Desjardins collection. His earliest known works date from 1820.

The claim made by some historians that Légaré went to Europe to study painting is unfounded. Contemporary documents that broach the matter all describe Légaré as a self-taught painter, and stress that he never set foot on the Continent. Furthermore, towards the end of his life the artist confided to collector Edward Taylor Fletcher that soon after his marriage he had refused the governor's offer to send him to Italy to improve his skills.

During the early years of his artistic career, Légaré did a great many copies of European religious canvases or engravings. This activity was a means of meeting the needs of parishes and religious communities, and at the same time enabled him to develop his gifts since it provided an opportunity to refine his pictorial techniques. Consequently it is not surprising that Légaré always retained an interest in painting copies of religious or secular works. In doing reproductions of the portraits of British monarchs George III, George IV, and Victoria, he also managed to make himself better known and to acquire more clients.

In 1828 Légaré was awarded a medal by the Société pour l'Encouragement des Sciences et des Arts en Canada, founded in Quebec, for his painting *Le massacre des Hurons par les Iroquois*. Despite obvious weaknesses, the canvas shows Légaré's clear determination to diversify his production and explore new avenues. He helped decorate the new Théâtre Royal at Quebec in 1832. A year later his career took a decisive turn: in addition to designing the first seal of the city of Quebec and the logotype of *Le Canadien*, Légaré was for the first time described as a "history painter."

From then on Légaré sought to turn to account even the most minor of his talents, and his production became increasingly varied. He took an interest in everything, as accounts of his exhibitions in Montreal and Quebec between 1842 and 1848 demonstrate. For example, in August 1842 the editor of Montreal's *L'Aurore des Canadas* could not contain his enthusiasm for "all the suppleness, all the diversity of talent and all the genius of the painter, who does as well in charmingly picturesque, or sylvan scenes as in solemn, pompous, or awe-inspiring ones," adding that "all types of painting appear to suit and be familiar to his palette."

At the outset of his artistic career Légaré had managed to purchase some 30 works from the Desjardins collection, and from this nucleus he developed a personal collection which by 1852 included 162 canvases. He took advantage of every opportunity to increase it, and in particular made several purchases from two Quebec merchants, John Christopher Reiffenstein* and Giovanni Domenico Balzaretti. Légaré began exhibiting his collection late in the 1820s, showing his work at the Union Hotel in premises lent by the government to the Literary and Historical Society of Quebec. In 1831, when the society received a royal charter, he was one of its most active members. Two years later he was appointed chairman of the arts class, and also was highly praised by the Reverend Daniel WILKIE during a lecture. Having had a new dwelling built on Rue Sainte-Angèle in 1833, he finally had enough room to house his entire collection of pictures and engravings. That year he invited the public to visit his gallery, the first in Lower Canada, a gesture that earned him the congratulations of the governor, Lord Aylmer [Whitworth-Aylmer*], and commendations from the newspapers. Légaré used all three storeys of his house for the collection, which was growing fast and already comprised some hundred pieces. His first gallery had to be closed in April 1835.

Three years later Légaré and lawyer Thomas Amiot opened the Galerie de Peinture de Québec in the building that Amiot had just built on the Place du Marché in Upper Town. Much was made at the time of its importance for artists eager to develop their skills. In 1838 as well, concerts were given in this "temple of fine arts," as it was called, and a school of drawing and painting was directed by Henry Daniel Thielcke. The gallery also exhibited "landscape views" and, the following year, a portrait of Queen Victoria by the American painter Thomas Sully and a painting by Gerome FASSIO. The arrangement between Légaré and Amiot dated back to 1836, when Légaré sold Amiot half of his collection which then included 134 pictures. In October 1838 Amiot came to an agreement with Légaré that he himself would go to Europe to sell part of their common collection. It is known that he found a purchaser for at least four pictures. Afterwards Amiot ran into serious financial difficulties and, because he was in Légaré's debt, in March 1840 he handed back to him the pictures still in his possession. The Galerie de Peinture de Québec probably closed that year, after having almost been destroyed by fire.

In 1841 Légaré lent his support to a plan for an institute to bring together all the learned societies of Quebec. This project had been put forward by Nicolas-Marie-Alexandre Vattemare*, an enthusiast for cultural exchanges. Although in the end the institute, with its projected museum of art and academy of drawing and painting, was not established, it seems that Vattemare's ideas had some influence on a plan for a national gallery developed in 1845. Eager to make use of a number of empty government buildings, Légaré and ten of his fellow citizens – among them Archibald Campbell*, Napoléon Aubin*, Daniel Wilkie, and Jean-Baptiste-Édouard Bacquet – suggested to the municipal authorities that such an establishment be set up at Quebec to foster interest in the fine arts in Lower Canada and to enable young people to study them. Since nothing came of this request, three years later Légaré temporarily exhibited some of his collection in the hall of the Parliament Building at Quebec. A letter in Le Canadien then blamed the government for failing to supply a suitable room, one large enough to house Légaré's whole collection. Tired of the situation, in 1851 Légaré had a spacious vaulted gallery fitted out on the top floor of his new house at the corner of Rue Sainte-Angèle and Rue Sainte-Hélène (McMahon). The following year he published a catalogue of his collection and made admission to the gallery free. In September he received a visit from Lord Elgin [Bruce*], who expressed great satisfaction. According to Fletcher, this gallery was a favourite meeting place for Quebec artists and painting enthusiasts.

Since Légaré had never been to Europe, he had to build his collection as best he knew how, drawing solely upon pictures that reached Quebec at this period. When these limitations are taken into account, the high quality of several works in his collection shows that he possessed remarkable flair. He was often consulted as an expert, for instance in 1853 when an inventory of Judge Bacquet's large collection was taken. This included 17 pictures jointly owned by Bacquet and Légaré, as well as 70 pictures and 12 engravings which were chiefly landscapes, seascapes, and still lifes. Towards the end of his career Légaré served on selection committees for industrial exhibitions that took place at Quebec. In 1854 he was even a member of the provincial committee set up in anticipation of the universal exposition to be held in Paris the following year.

It would seem that Légaré's many initiatives to promote the fine arts and foster interest in them did not produce all the results expected. In fact the only encouragement for his ventures came from some of the local élite. This limited success was due in large measure to the social and economic context of the period, and in some degree to the lack of tangible support from the government. Légaré was essentially

Légaré

a precursor whose initiatives went beyond the cultural needs of the society of his day. In this regard, there is keen insight in the observation that François-Xavier Garneau* made about Légaré the year he died: "The profound love he had for painting, one of the fine arts still so little known and so little appreciated in this land, where every thinking being is absorbed with material needs, made me regard him with sentiments of deep respect."

As an artist Légaré himself painted some 250 works, including about 100 religious pictures, a limited number of portraits, mostly of his own circle, several landscapes, episodes of contemporary life, some remarkable history paintings, as well as genre scenes, still lifes, allegories, and utilitarian commissions. His artistic production therefore presents a clear contrast to that of his most prolific contemporaries, such as Jean-Baptiste Roy-Audy*, Antoine Plamondon, and Théophile Hamel*, all artists who gave greater attention to portraits and religious pictures. By its variety and boldness, his work was often ahead of what clients of the period wanted. Légaré was able to paint the subjects he chose without always having to think of a future sale, but it was only because he had a degree of material comfort based on his real estate holdings. He had two residences in succession on Rue Sainte-Angèle, and purchased three income-producing houses on the same street, plus a fourth on Rue Saint-Jean. He was also seigneur of part of the fief of Saint-François from 1827 to 1841.

Landscape painting was one of the areas in which Légaré proved most innovative. The first landscape artist of French Canadian origin, he inherited from English topographical painters a distinct liking for waterfalls, rivers, forests, country houses, certain cityscapes, and, in general, picturesque views. It is known that his clientele of foreign residents, which included British officers garrisoned at Quebec, greatly appreciated this aspect of his work. Légaré also took an interest in the events of his day. Some of his paintings owe their origin to his social and political concerns. Examples include the drawing of the first seal of the city of Quebec, the logotype of *Le Canadien*, the banners he made for the Societé Saint-Jean-Baptiste of Quebec, and the paintings inspired by the cholera epidemic of 1832, the rock-fall at Cap Diamant in 1841, and the fires in the Saint-Roch and Saint-Jean wards in 1845. Other allegorical paintings, such as the *Paysage au monument à Wolfe* and the *Scène d'élections à Château-Richer*, have a more marked political connotation. A nationalist sensitive to the greatness of the past, Légaré interpreted in pictures several eloquent pages from the history of New France. Among his most remarkable history paintings are *Premier monastère des ursulines de Québec*, *Souvenirs des jésuites de la Nouvelle-France*, *Le martyre des pères Brébeuf et Lalemant*, and *La bataille de Sainte-Foy*. Légaré also painted a series of canvases depicting the customs of the Indians and portraying alternatively the concepts of the "noble savage" and the "barbaric savage." In these the artist perfectly mirrors the dilemma of his contemporaries in their thinking about the Indians.

Légaré did not hesitate to confront the social and political problems that marked his period. As a citizen of Quebec and as a nationalist, he became increasingly involved in public matters. His particular interest in his city and fellow citizens apparently began with the terrible cholera epidemic that struck Quebec in 1832. At that time he was a member of the Quebec Board of Health and of a relief committee to help afflicted and needy families. He was elected to the municipal council in 1833, and represented the Palais Ward until 1836. Appointed to the grand jury in 1835, he was among those suggesting that improvements be made to a penitentiary system judged inadequate. A year later, when municipal administration once again became the responsibility of justices of the peace, Légaré discharged the duties of this office from 22 August until he was dismissed on 8 Nov. 1837.

In 1842 he helped found the Societé Saint-Jean-Baptiste of Quebec, and until 1847 he was vice-president of the first of its sections within the city. After that he maintained close ties with the association as a member of its management committee. Taken up with questions of education, he became an advocate of schools for children and evening classes for adults, and also encouraged the establishment of the Christian Brothers and the creation of public libraries. He was a member of the Quebec Education Society from 1841 to 1849 and supported the mechanics' institute. Légaré in 1844 successfully directed a campaign for a fund to aid his friend Napoléon Aubin, the owner of *Le Castor* and *Le Fantasque*, whose printing works had burned down. Aubin's workshop was again destroyed by the fire in Saint-Jean Ward in June 1845, a month after the fire in Saint-Roch Ward. Légaré took an active part in numerous meetings of committees to assist the victims of the fires. In addition he participated in various collections for humanitarian purposes in 1846, 1847, and 1852.

Légaré was a justice of the peace almost continuously from 1843 to 1852, a member of the board of health from 1847 to 1849, a churchwarden of the parish of Notre-Dame from 1846 to 1848, and a member of the grand jury in 1843 and 1846. In 1849 he again recommended that the penitentiary system be improved, and he chaired a committee which sought changes in the charter of the city of Quebec. By 1845 he was fully aware of the commercial advantages of railways, and he eagerly promoted them in 1849 and 1852.

A respected citizen, Légaré was quick to take a stand on questions concerning the moral and material progress of his country. Despite the disappointments he encountered in this connection, he remained faithful to his principles and convictions. From 1827 he was an unwavering admirer of Louis-Joseph Papineau*. In 1834 he was among those who solicited signatures for a petition in favour of the 92 Resolutions, which outlined the main grievances and demands of the House of Assembly. Two years later he headed a delegation to Papineau in support of the action he and the Patriote members still loyal to him in the house had taken. He participated in 1837 in all the activities of the Quebec Patriotes, and became one of the directors of the reform paper *Le Libéral*, which was opposed to Étienne Parent*'s moderate *Le Canadien*. As a member of the Comité Permanent de Québec, Légaré was arrested and jailed on 13 November. He was set free on bail five days later to await a trial, which, in the event, never took place. He subsequently opposed the union of the Canadas, and supported the anti-unionists in several elections. He gave his backing to his friend Pierre-Joseph-Olivier Chauveau*, who ran successfully as a reform candidate in 1844.

Three years later Légaré became more involved with the political scene in Lower Canada. In 1847 he was elected deputy chairman of the Comité Constitutionnel de la Réforme et du Progrès, a political association chaired by René-Édouard Caron*. The following year one of the assembly members for the city of Quebec, Thomas Cushing Aylwin*, was appointed to the bench, and an election to fill the vacant seat was announced. At that time the ranks of politicians of liberal bent were divided. Two candidates stood, Légaré and the merchant François-Xavier MÉTHOT. Légaré, who supported the reformers in power but did not deny his sympathy for Papineau, won the majority of the French Canadian votes but was nevertheless beaten by Méthot, who had the backing of the *Quebec Mercury* and the tories. In 1850 Légaré ran again in a by-election, this time on the ticket of the Rouges who favoured annexation of the province to the United States. After many rebuffs, he was defeated by Jean CHABOT, the new commissioner of public works. During his two bids for election, Légaré had been subjected to attack by Joseph-Édouard Cauchon*, the member for Montmorency and owner of *Le Journal de Québec*. Consequently he supported Cauchon's opponent in the 1851 general elections, although the effort was in vain.

In the 1854 elections Joseph Légaré backed the reform candidates in the ridings of the city and county of Quebec, who were all elected. One of them, his friend Chauveau, entered the government, and it was on his recommendation that Légaré was appointed to the Legislative Council on 8 Feb. 1855, only a few months before his death.

JOHN R. PORTER

[At Joseph Légaré's death a large part of his work remained with his widow, and then in 1874 went almost in its entirety to the Université Laval in Quebec. That institution, which came under the Séminaire de Québec, acquired at the same time his important collection of European canvasses and engravings.

This biography summarizes the author's doctoral thesis, "Un peintre et collectionneur québécois engagé dans son milieu: Joseph Légaré (1795–1855)" (Univ. de Montréal, 1981), which is to be published and which is a companion piece to the author's descriptive catalogue of all Légaré's works, put out by the National Gallery of Canada, *The works of Joseph Légaré, 1795–1855* (Ottawa, 1978). The two works, the first to deal comprehensively with Légaré, shed a wholly new light on the subject. The more important items in the 70-page bibliography accompanying the thesis are listed here. J.R.P.]

ANQ-MBF, CN1-11, 2 mai 1839. ANQ-Q, CE1-1, 11 mars 1795, 21 avril 1818, 21 juin 1855; CN1-18, 3 avril 1843, 17 juill. 1852, 24 janv. 1853; CN1-62, 18, 26 avril 1853; CN1-80, 30 août 1851; CN1-116, 4, 31 déc. 1837; 29 nov. 1847; CN1-178, 19 mai 1812, 26 mars 1814, 14 sept. 1815, 7 avril 1837, 17 janv. 1838, 2 juill. 1841; CN1-208, 11 mai, 4 juin, 7 août 1830; 9 mars 1832; CN1-212, 1er mars, 8 juill. 1819; 20 juin, 27 juill., 12 nov. 1830; 29 juill. 1834; 8 oct. 1836; 7 déc. 1841; CN1-213, 8 janv., 3 avril, 27 juill. 1846; 13 déc. 1849; CN1-219, 31 mai 1843, 9 juin 1848, 14 août 1850, 15 août 1853; CN1-255, 25 juill. 1836; 9 mai, 19 oct. 1838; 11 janv. 1839; 23 mars 1840; 25 janv. 1848; CN1-260, 9 févr. 1842, 27 août 1852, 28 juill. 1854; CN1-261, 21 déc. 1827, 1er mars 1833; 13 avril 1835; 5, 6 août 1851; CN1-285, 12 mai 1834; CN4-9, 24 juin 1817; P-75. ASQ, C 28: 145; C 31: 355; C 66: 833; Fonds Viger–Verreau, carton 61, liasse 7, nos.4–6, 6, 13 déc. 1839, 22 févr. 1840; carton 62, no.227, 23 nov. 1839; Journal du séminaire, II: 563–64; Polygraphie, XXXI, no.19A; Séminaire, 12, no.41; 103, no.54. AVQ, II, 1, a. MAC-CD, Fonds Morisset. Montreal Museum of Fine Arts, J. W. H. Watts coll., 24 Dec. 1889. *La Bibliothèque canadienne* (Montréal), 6 (1827–28); 9 (1829). Can., Prov. of, Legislative Council, *Journals*, 1854–55: 273, 500. *L'Abeille*, janvier 1850. *L'Ami de la religion et de la patrie* (Québec), 1848–50. *L'Aurore des Canadas* (Montréal), 18 oct. 1839; 30 août, 24 déc. 1842; 26 juin 1845. *Le Canadien*, 25 déc. 1818; 13 mars 1822; 3 sept. 1823; 1833–55. *Le Castor* (Québec), 1843–45. *Le Fantasque* (Québec), 14 juill. 1838; 15 mars 1841; 30 juin, 1er juill., 13, 17, 21, 24 déc. 1842; 22 avril, 3, 20 juill. 1843; 17 juin, 8, 15 juill. 1848. *La Gazette patriotique* (Québec), 9 août 1823. *Le Journal de Québec*, 18 sept. 1847; 1848; 1850; 15 juin, 28 sept. 1852; 7 juin 1853; 21 juin 1855. *Le Libéral* (Québec), 1837. *Mélanges religieux*, 2 nov. 1849. *La Minerve*, 2 oct. 1828; 9 avril 1829; 1er nov., 9 déc. 1830; 18 avril, 5 sept. 1836; 1er juin, 24 sept. 1837; 15 mai, 7 sept. 1848; 25 juin 1849. *Le Populaire* (Montréal), 14, 16 juin, 17 nov. 1837; 17 août 1838. *Quebec Gazette*, 8, 15 April, 30 Dec. 1813; 22 Dec. 1814; 3, 24 Aug., 19 Oct. 1815; 9 April 1818; 22 April 1819; 5 June 1820; 16 April 1821; 29 May 1828; 23 Nov., 10

LeJeune

Dec. 1829; 14 Jan. 1830; 27 Nov., 13 Dec. 1833; 10 Nov. 1837; 27 June 1838; 30 May 1845. *Quebec Mercury*, 16 Sept. 1817; 1829–55. *Quebec Spectator, and Commercial Advertiser*, 6 Oct. 1848.

F.-M. Bibaud, *Le panthéon canadien* (A. et V. Bibaud; 1891). Joseph Bouchette, *The British dominions in North America; or a topographical and statistical description of the provinces of Lower and Upper Canada* . . . (2v., London, 1832), 1: 252. *Canada, an encyclopædia of the country: the Canadian dominion considered in its historic relations, its natural resources, its material progress, and its national development*, ed. J. C. Hopkins (6v. and index, Toronto, 1898–1900), 4: 355. *Catalogue of the Quebec gallery of paintings, engravings, etc., the property of Jos. Legaré, St. Angele Street, corner of St. Helen Street*, comp. E.-R. Fréchette (Quebec, 1852). P.-V. Charland, "Notre-Dame de Québec: le nécrologe de la crypte ou les inhumations dans cette église depuis 1652," *BRH*, 20 (1914): 313. *The encyclopedia of Canada*, ed. W. S. Wallace (6v., Toronto, [1948]), 4: 59. Fauteux, *Patriotes*, 33, 295–96. Harper, *Early painters and engravers*, 194. P.-G. Roy, *Fils de Québec*, 3: 67–70. Turcotte, *Le Conseil législatif*, 21, 155–56. Georges Bellerive, *Artistes-peintres canadiens-français: les anciens* (2 sér., Québec, 1925–26), 1: 9–24. H.-J.-J.-B. Chouinard, *Fête nationale des Canadiens français célébrée à Québec en 1880: histoire, discours, rapports* . . . (4v., Québec, 1881–1903), 1: 55, 58–59, 73, 597. Chouinard *et al.*, *La ville de Québec*, 3: 9, 15, 70–73. W. [G.] Colgate, *Canadian art; its origin & development* (Toronto, 1943; repr., 1967), 108–9. J. R. Harper, *La peinture au Canada des origines à nos jours* (Québec, 1966), 79–82. Barry Lord, *The history of painting in Canada: toward a people's art* (Toronto, 1974), 48–54. N. M. MacTavish, *The fine arts in Canada* (Toronto, 1925), 8. Morisset, *Coup d'œil sur les arts*, 62; *Peintres et tableaux* (2v., Québec, 1936–37), 1; *La peinture traditionnelle au Canada français* (Ottawa, 1960), 94–101. Edmund Morris, *Art in Canada: the early painters* ([Toronto, 1911]). *Painting in Canada, a selective historical survey* (Albany, N.Y., 1946), 27. D. R. Reid, *A concise history of Canadian painting* (Toronto, 1973), 46–49. A. H. Robson, *Canadian landscape painters* (Toronto, 1932), 18–20. [J.-C. Taché], *Le Canada et l'Exposition universelle de 1855* (Toronto, 1856), 8, 13. Claire Tremblay, "L'œuvre profane de Joseph Légaré" (mémoire de MA, univ. de Montréal, 1973).

Hormidas Magnan, "Peintres et sculpteurs du terroir," *Le Terroir* (Québec), 3 (1922–23): 347. Olivier Maurault, "Souvenirs canadiens; album de Jacques Viger," *Cahiers des Dix*, 9 (1944): 98. Gérard Morisset, "Joseph Légaré, copiste," *Le Canada* (Montréal), 12 sept. 1934: 2; 25 sept. 1934: 2; "Joseph Légaré, copiste à l'église de Bécancour," 12 déc. 1935: 2; "Joseph Légaré, copiste à l'Hôpital Général de Québec," 18 juin 1935: 2; "Joseph Légaré, copiste à Saint-Roch-des-Aulnaies," 4 juill. 1935: 2; "Une belle peinture de Joseph Légaré," 23 juill. 1934: 2. "Les peintures de Légaré sur Québec," *BRH*, 32 (1926): 432. J. R. Porter, "L'apport de Joseph Légaré (1795–1855) dans le renouveau de la peinture québécoise," *Vie des Arts* (Montréal), 23 (1978), no.92: 63–66; "L'architecture québécoise dans l'œuvre de Joseph Légaré," Conseil des monuments et sites du Québec, *Bull.*, 6 (mai 1978): 19–21; "Joseph Légaré, painter and citizen," National Gallery of Canada, *Journal* (Ottawa), no.29 (September 1978); "La société québécoise et l'encouragement aux artistes de 1825 à 1850," *Journal of Canadian Art Hist.* (Montreal), 4 (1977), no.1: 13–14; "Un projet de musée national à Québec à l'époque du peintre Joseph Légaré (1833–1853)," *RHAF*, 31 (1977–78): 75–82. Antoine Roy, "Les Patriotes de la région de Québec pendant la rébellion de 1837–1838," *Cahiers des Dix*, 24 (1959): 247.

LeJEUNE, MARIE-HENRIETTE (baptized **Marie-Tharsile**) **(Comeau; Lejeune,** *dit* **Briard; Ross),** midwife and nurse; baptized 13 Aug. 1762 in Rochefort, France, daughter of Joseph Lejeune and Martine Roy (LeRoy); m. first 17 Feb. 1780 Joseph Comeau in La Rochelle, France; m. secondly 26 Aug. 1786 at St George's Church (Anglican) in Sydney, Cape Breton, her cousin Bernard Lejeune, *dit* Briard; m. thirdly 18 Dec. 1792 James Ross, a disbanded loyalist soldier, and they had four children, two of whom died in infancy; d. May 1860 in North East Margaree, N.S.

Marie-Henriette LeJeune, subsequently remembered as "Granny" Ross, the Cape Breton midwife, remains a popular folk figure about whom little can be substantiated. Her reputation as a nurse and midwife was first established in the Little Bras d'Or area during a community smallpox epidemic when she reputedly inoculated many local inhabitants. She also had a cabin built in the nearby woods and used it as an infirmary where she successfully treated a number of victims. She and her family moved from Sydney, Cape Breton, about 1802, becoming the first settlers in the Northeast Margaree River valley; her reputation travelled with her, and as settlement increased in the area so did the demand for her services. Travelling on foot, by horseback, or on snow-shoes, with a pine torch to light the way at night, Henriette Ross worked unendingly in a locality where professional medical aid was non-existent. She was revered in the community for her selfless dedication, and even in extreme old age continued to work as a midwife. She eventually went blind, but did not allow this to impede her work; in summer her family transported her in a type of wheelbarrow, and in winter she was taken on a sled.

Known for her courage, determination, boundless energy, and love of adventure, Henriette Ross was a true pioneer woman. She was small with blue eyes and a dark complexion, and in her middle years thought nothing of walking 60 miles to Bras d'Or with her husband. In later life, although wizened with age, she could still easily walk the six miles to her granddaughter's home, a journey which included wading across a river. She displayed tact and ingenuity in dealing with local Indians, and boldness in killing two bears, one with a musket and one with a fire shovel.

The passage of time and countless retellings of the various versions of her tale have no doubt blurred the distinction between fact and fable; the strength of the surviving story in rural Cape Breton, however, suggests that "Granny" Ross, whatever her history, was a dynamic and devoted woman of the land.

LOIS KATHLEEN KERNAGHAN

The most up-to-date genealogical information on Marie-Henriette LeJeune is contained in "Granny Ross," *Contact – Acadie* (Moncton, N.-B.), no.5 (déc. 1984): 8–13.

Cape Breton Registry of Deeds (Sydney, N.S.), Deeds, vol.E: 162 (mfm. at PANS). PANS, RG 20B, petitions, nos.650, 2065, 3119. St George's Anglican Church (Sydney), Reg. of baptisms, marriages, and burials, 26 Aug. 1786, 18 Dec. 1792, 10 Sept. 1799 (transcripts at PANS). Clara Dennis, *Cape Breton over* (Toronto, 1942). E. E. Jackson, *Cape Breton and the Jackson kith and kin* (Windsor, N.S., 1971). J. L. MacDougall, *History of Inverness County, Nova Scotia* ([Truro, N.S.], 1922]). E. E. Jackson, "'The little woman': Granny Ross, her life and times," *Weekly Cape Bretoner* (Sydney), 29 Sept. 1956: 17. [Joseph] de La Roque, "Tour of inspection made by the Sieur de La Roque; census, 1752," PAC *Report*, 1905, 2, pt.II.

LEONARD, ELIJAH, ironmaster; b. 1 May 1787 in Taunton, Mass., son of Samuel Leonard and Sarah Williams; m. 13 Oct. 1811 Mary (Polly) Stone, and they had four sons and three daughters; d. 18 Dec. 1855 in London, Upper Canada.

Elijah Leonard's ancestors emigrated from Wales to Massachusetts about 1650, and he was a member of the sixth generation of the family to engage in the iron industry in North America. Leonard apprenticed in the iron-forging business at Taunton with his father but reputedly ran away before his apprenticeship was completed. He subsequently worked in various ironworks around Lake George and Lake Champlain in New York. Following his marriage in 1811 he settled on a farm near Syracuse, N.Y., but, dissatisfied with farming, he became involved in the operation of a furnace for smelting iron at Taberg, northeast of Syracuse. Leonard's later purchase of a furnace at Constantia, N.Y., led to a legal dispute with the former owner, a "New York firm"; the resulting proceedings, although decided in Leonard's favour, ruined him financially and he was forced to return to his farm.

Around 1829 Leonard was induced to join the firm of Joseph Van Norman*, co-owner of the ironworks and foundry in Charlotteville Township, Upper Canada, near which the village of Normandale soon developed. In this pioneer era the number of ironmasters in western New York was small and from his earlier involvement in the iron industry there Van Norman probably knew Leonard. Although the Normandale works had operated successfully for several years, an experienced furnace superintendent was apparently required and Leonard accepted that position. In 1830, with his eldest son Lewis, he returned briefly to Syracuse to arrange for the remaining family members to join them in Upper Canada.

Located at the mouth of a small creek on the shore of Lake Erie, the simple furnace which Leonard operated was typical of those used in the early 19th century. It consisted of a brick stack built on a hillside and charged from above with iron ore and charcoal. To facilitate the proper burning of the charcoal an air blast was supplied by a water-powered bellows. The resulting heat in the furnace reduced the ore to molten iron and slag which were drained off at the bottom of the furnace. According to his son Elijah*, who worked with him and learned the foundry trade at Normandale, Leonard's main responsibility was supervising the mixing of ore and charcoal in proper proportions.

The Leonards soon sought to establish their own foundry. Realizing that opportunities for developing a second operation at Normandale were limited, they looked elsewhere for a site. In 1834 Elijah Jr visited Hamilton for that purpose, but finding that there was a foundry at nearby Ancaster, he and his father decided instead upon St Thomas. On 7 May 1834 they formed a partnership with Philip Cady Van Brocklin (who had also worked at Normandale) to operate a foundry at St Thomas for the production of ironware. They did not manufacture pig-iron for this operation but for a while purchased it at Normandale. The partnership was short-lived, and the reasons for its dissolution on 4 September are not clear. Although the business was continued by his son, Leonard evidently retired at this time.

After 1834 he virtually dropped from sight. In 1840 Elijah Jr established a second, larger foundry in London, leaving his brothers Lyman and Delos in charge of the St Thomas operation. Through his father's efforts, Elijah secured a contract in 1853 to build 200 boxcars for the Great Western Railway. This was probably the last important business transaction in which Leonard was involved before his death in London.

CHRISTOPHER ALFRED ANDREAE

BLHU, R. G. Dun & Co. credit ledger, Canada, 19: 43. Old Colony Hist. Soc. (Taunton, Mass.), "James Leonard of Taunton, Massachusetts, ironmaster," comp. E. C. and G. M. Leonard (typescript). PAC, RG 1, L3, 298: L3/49. UWOL, Regional Coll., Leonard family papers; [R.] A. Trumper, "The business policy evolution of E. Leonard and Sons" ([1935?]). Woodland Cemetery (London, Ont.), Records of burials, December 1855. *Liberal* (St Thomas, [Ont.]), 18 Dec. 1834. *Annals of the Leonard family*, comp. F. L. Koster (New York, 1911). *Canadian biog. dict.*, 1: 594. W. R. Deane, *A genealogical memoir of the Leonard family; containing a full account of the first three generations*

Leroux

of the family of James Leonard, who was an early settler of Taunton, Ms., with incidental notices of later descendants (Boston, 1851; [new ed., 1853]). Vital records of Taunton, Massachusetts, to the year 1850 (3v., Boston, 1928–29), 2: 298. Hist. of Middlesex, 885. Elijah Leonard, The honorable Elijah Leonard: a memoir, [ed. F. E. Leonard] (London, [1894]), 3–5, 9–11. E. A. Owen, Pioneer sketches of Long Point settlement . . . (Toronto, 1898; repr. Belleville, Ont., 1972), 456–57. R. A. Trumper, "The history of E. Leonard & Sons, boiler-makers and ironfounders, London, Ont." (thesis, Dept. of Business Administration, Univ. of Western Ont., London, 1937). F. E. Leonard, "The Normandale furnace, 1829," OH, 20 (1923): 92–93. W. J. Patterson, "The Long Point furnace," Canadian Mining Journal (Gardenvale, Que.), 60 (1939): 547–49. Thomas Ritchie, "Joseph Van Norman, ironmaster of Upper Canada," Canadian Geographical Journal (Montreal), 77 (July–December 1968): 47.

LEROUX, LAURENT, fur trader, businessman, justice of the peace, militia officer, office holder, and politician; b. 17 Nov. 1759 in L'Assomption (Que.), son of Germain Leroux d'Esneval and Marie-Catherine Vallée, widow of Pierre Beaudin; m. before 1789, à la façon du pays, an Ojibwa in the Athabasca region, and they had at least four girls; m. secondly 20 June 1796 Marie-Esther Loisel in L'Assomption, and they had one daughter; d. there 26 May 1855.

Laurent Leroux was the son of a merchant, originally from Paris, who came to New France as a soldier during the War of the Austrian Succession and settled at L'Assomption probably in 1759, becoming one of its most prosperous inhabitants. Laurent received some instruction, for in July 1776 he could read, write, and do bookkeeping well enough to be hired as a clerk by Montreal merchant Pierre-Louis Chaboillez to go to Michilimackinac (Mackinaw City, Mich.). By 1784 he had become a clerk with Gregory, MacLeod and Company [see John Gregory*; Normand MacLeod*], an enterprise recently set up to trade in furs, principally at Michilimackinac (Mackinac Island, Mich.). However, on the initiative of fur traders Peter Pangman* and Peter Pond*, the firm soon directed its fur-trading activities towards the northwest, and became the chief rival of the North West Company. In the autumn of 1786, on the orders of his superior John Ross, Leroux set up a trading post in the name of Gregory, MacLeod and Company on the south shore of Great Slave Lake (N.W.T.), at the same time as Cuthbert Grant* was setting up an adjoining one for the NWC. The competition between the two groups became so intense that it resulted in the murder of Ross in 1787. This disastrous event led Gregory, MacLeod and Company to amalgamate with the NWC in the summer of that year to end the competition.

Leroux remained at Great Slave Lake, despite the NWC's decision to close this post because the partners considered it unprofitable. He reached Fort Chipewyan (Alta) in March 1789, and set off again at the beginning of June with Alexander Mackenzie* on the journey that was to take Mackenzie to the Arctic Ocean. They separated at Great Slave Lake, and Leroux took a more northwesterly route to trade furs at La Martre Lake before retracing his steps to meet Mackenzie, as agreed, on the return route. When they met at the end of August 1789, it was decided that Leroux should winter in the vicinity of Great Slave Lake. He then set up Fort Providence (Old Fort Providence) on Yellowknife Bay. At the beginning of June 1791 he was on his way to Grand Portage (near Grand Portage, Minn.), where in the summer he was rehired by the NWC to work in the Athabasca Department for five more years at £100 a year.

However, Leroux left Athabasca for good sooner than anticipated. After his father's death in July 1792 he decided to return to L'Assomption to take over his business concerns. He likely arrived at L'Assomption in 1794 or 1795, and in mid June 1796 he signed his marriage contract there. All the same, Leroux did not sever his contacts with the fur-trading world. For a number of years, along with Jacques Trullier*, dit Lacombe, a merchant in L'Assomption, he held the monopoly for the manufacture of the ceintures fléchées used by the NWC for trading purposes. In addition, on several occasions between 1801 and 1804 he recruited men for the New North West Company (sometimes called the XY Company) and for one of its co-partners, Sir Alexander Mackenzie and Company. He was also instrumental in getting his two nephews, François-Antoine* and Joseph* Larocque, into the service of the New North West Company.

Leroux did not confine himself to the trade in grain and foodstuffs he had inherited from his father. In 1798 he turned to the manufacture of potash, a product still little used but destined within a few years to become one of Lower Canada's principal exports. The undertaking must have proved lucrative, for in September 1806 he went into partnership with Pierre-Amable Archambault, another important merchant, and set up the Fabrique de Potasse de L'Assomption. Three years later Leroux further diversified his commercial activity by selling hardware produced by the Batiscan Iron Work Company: cauldrons, pots, kitchen kettles called bombs, and especially cast-iron stoves, then much in vogue. After the company closed down around 1812–13 he obtained his supplies from other producers.

Furthermore, by the late 1790s, Leroux adopted the practice of channelling some of his profits into real estate. He may have foreseen the considerable development that L'Assomption was to undergo at the beginning of the 19th century, when between 1800 and 1820 the number of householders tripled. Whatever the case, Leroux accumulated an impressive number of properties, mostly in the village, for rental purposes. This type of investment enabled him to assure the security of his capital and obtain a relatively good rate of return. It was probably for a similar motive that in 1817 he became one of the few French Canadian shareholders in the new Bank of Montreal.

Within the community Leroux restricted himself to a rather inconspicuous role, and held positions bringing relatively little prestige. He received a commission as justice of the peace in 1803 and again in 1810. He was a captain in the L'Assomption battalion of militia, assumed the post of aide-major during the War of 1812, and was promoted major in 1818. In April 1825 he was appointed treasurer of a council formed to establish and run a public primary school in L'Assomption. On 30 August of the following year he became a commissioner for the summary trial of small causes for Saint-Sulpice seigneury, conjointly with Joseph-Édouard FARIBAULT. During the month of September 1828 he sat as a grand juror on the Court of King's Bench for the district of Montreal. Leroux also tried his hand at politics. On 25 Aug. 1827 he became one of the two members for Leinster in the House of Assembly, where his son-in-law, Jean-Moïse Raymond*, had already represented Huntingdon for three years. At the opening of the session on 20 November, Leroux supported the candidature of Louis-Joseph Papineau* as speaker of the assembly. The choice of Papineau angered the governor, Lord Dalhousie [Ramsay*], who prorogued the house two days later. The assembly resumed sitting in November 1828, but Leroux took no further part in it, and when his term ran out on 2 Sept. 1830 he did not stand again. In any case, indifferent to honours, Leroux preferred to devote his leisure moments to reading historical works and travel accounts rather than to seeking the admiration of his contemporaries.

Leroux kept his hardware business until his death at the age of 95. He had been the first white man to explore Great Slave Lake. Later he succeeded in making good use of his father's estate because he had the acumen to identify sectors of the economy that were destined to develop and the willingness to take calculated risks. At the end of his life he was able in turn to leave his heirs a considerable fortune, and a rather uncommon bequest for a merchant at that time – a well-stocked library.

PIERRE DUFOUR

ANQ-M, CE5-14, 18 nov. 1759; CN1-313, 18 juin 1796; CN1-372, 13 juill. 1776; CN5-3, 3 juill. 1855. ASQ, Fonds Viger–Verreau, sér.O, 0521. Can., Parks Canada, Quebec Region (Quebec), Compagnie des forges de Batiscan, reg. de lettres, août 1807–juillet 1812. *Docs. relating to NWC* (Wallace). "État général des billets d'ordonnances . . . ,"

Pierre Panet, compil., ANQ *Rapport*, 1924–25: 229–359. *Journals of Samuel Hearne and Philip Turnor*, ed. J. B. Tyrrell (Toronto, 1934; repr., New York, 1968). L.C., House of Assembly, *Journals*, November 1827; 1828–29, app.R, EE; 1830, app.N. Alexander Mackenzie, *The journals and letters of Sir Alexander Mackenzie*, ed. W. K. Lamb (Toronto, 1970). Desjardins, *Guide parl. Historic forts and trading posts of the French regime and of the English fur trading companies*, comp. Ernest Voorhis (roneotyped copy, Ottawa, 1930). A.-G. Morice, *Dictionnaire historique des Canadiens et des Métis français de l'Ouest* (Québec et Montréal, 1908). *Officers of British forces in Canada* (Irving), 181. Wallace, *Macmillan dict.* Denison, *La première banque au Canada*, 1: 103–4. Anastase Forget, *Histoire du collège de L'Assomption; 1833 – un siècle – 1933* (Montréal, [1933]), 48–49. Marcel Fournier, *La représentation parlementaire de la région de Joliette* (Joliette, Qué., 1977), 20, 171. Pierre Poulin, *Légendes du Portage*, Réjean Olivier, édit. (L'Assomption, Qué., 1975). Christian Roy, *Histoire de L'Assomption* (L'Assomption, 1967). Sulte, *Mélanges hist.* (Malchelosse), 3. Ægidius Fauteux, "Les carnets d'un curieux: Germain Leroux ou l'art d'allonger son nom," *La Patrie*, 30 déc. 1933: 36–37, 41. J.-J. Lefebvre, "Jean-Moïse Raymond (1787–1843), premier député de Laprairie (1824–1838), natif du comté," *BRH*, 60 (1954): 109–20.

LETT, BENJAMIN, Patriot filibusterer; b. 14 Nov. 1813 in County Kilkenny (Republic of Ireland), son of Samuel Lett and Elizabeth Warren; d. 9 Dec. 1858 in Milwaukee, Wis., and was buried in Northville, Ill.

Benjamin Lett immigrated with his parents and family to Lower Canada in 1819 and they settled in Chatham Township on the Ottawa River. In 1833, nine years after Samuel Lett's accidental death, the family removed to Darlington Township on Lake Ontario and took up farming. Ben Lett did not participate in William Lyon Mackenzie*'s uprising at Toronto in 1837, but in its aftermath the Letts were forced to flee the colony when an armed band of local Orangemen sought Ben's arrest for refusing to join with them in terrorizing reform sympathizers. He subsequently joined the Patriot forces on the Niagara frontier while his family emigrated to Texas. Later, after his reputation as a fearless, vengeful enemy had grown to romantic proportions, stories were widely circulated that his hatred of the British stemmed from an earlier incident involving Orangemen, in which one of his brothers was shot and a sister sexually abused.

Patriot incursions along the Upper Canadian border in 1838 were marked by weak leadership, internal disunity, and a virtual absence of military planning and strategy. The result was an uninterrupted string of fiascos [see Thomas Jefferson SUTHERLAND]. Operating largely on his own in guerrilla fashion, Lett burned, killed, and destroyed for nearly four years, but the aims of the Patriots were not advanced. In November 1838 Captain Edgeworth Ussher, who had

Lévesque

piloted Allan Napier MacNab*'s boats across the Niagara River to burn the *Caroline*, was murdered in his home. A wave of outrage and indignation swept across the province discrediting the Patriot cause. Doubts were cast on the identity of the murderer, but provincial tories, convinced that it was the work of Lett, offered a reward for his capture. In January 1839 Lett made an unsuccessful attempt to burn the British ships anchored at Kingston. Six months later he joined Samuel Peters Hart and Henry J. Moon in raiding Cobourg for the purpose of robbing and murdering Robert HENRY, and abducting such area residents as Sheppard McCormick, a veteran of the attack on the *Caroline*. The authorities were informed, the raid failed, and Lett just managed to escape to the American side of Lake Ontario. In the wake of the "Cobourg conspiracy" Lieutenant Governor Sir George ARTHUR offered a £500 reward for Lett.

After the raid, every ugly incident in Upper Canada was attributed to the man armed customarily with four pistols and a bowie knife. The *Cobourg Star* described him as being "5 ft. 11 inches high, rather slim, sandy hair and whiskers, very red faced and freckled, light skinned, very large muscular hands, with round, long, and very white fingers. Eyes light blue, and *remarkably penetrating*." On 17 April 1840 Brock's Monument at Queenston Heights, built to commemorate the American defeat in the War of 1812 and a symbol of British power and domination, was badly damaged by an explosion of gunpowder. Though others may have been involved, Arthur held Lett primarily responsible for this vandalism. "It has been clearly brought to light," he informed Governor Charles Edward Poulett Thomson*, "that the wicked attempt to destroy the Monument was the deed of Benjamin Lett – the Rob Roy of Upper Canada – who is always prowling about Our frontier, devising and committing all manner of mischief." An attempt by Lett in June to burn the steamship *Great Britain* at Oswego, N.Y., led to his arrest by American authorities. Convicted that month of attempted arson and sentenced to seven years of hard labour, he escaped from the train conveying him to prison at Auburn, N.Y.

For the next year he was a fugitive from the law on both sides of the border. Finally captured in Buffalo, N.Y., in September 1841, he was taken to Auburn prison and thrown into solitary confinement. According to his brother Thomas, the guards "frequently fastened him (with his head drawn backwards) in stocks, and poured water on his face," risking his "almost instant death by strangling." In 1845, his health broken, Lett received a pardon from Governor Silas Wright and, after a period of recuperation under Dr Edward Alexander THELLER in Buffalo, he joined his brothers and sisters on a farm near Northville, Ill., where they had settled five years earlier. The Patriot

cause had long since been abandoned and Lett's border forays were now over.

In 1858, while en route to engage in a trading expedition on Lake Michigan, Lett died mysteriously of strychnine poisoning in Milwaukee – the work of tory agents, Thomas Lett later claimed. He was buried in the Lett Cemetery, Northville, where his tombstone inscription records Thomas's bitter grief over his brother's treatment at the hands of American authorities: "The records of American partnership in the case of Benjamin Lett – they are like a Christian hell without a Jesus Christ: NO ESCAPE."

ALLAN J. MACDONALD

AO, MS 516, Benjamin Lett to W. L. Mackenzie, 10 March 1839, 26 Aug. 1840; Thomas Lett to Mackenzie, 28 Dec. 1840, 16 Nov. 1845; MU 1881, no.4675. PAC, RG 5, A1: 121712–13, 121868–916, 123661–93, 123699–725, 123838–40, 124045–47, 124290–98, 125483–90, 125670–73, 126804–7, 127937–54, 132472–73, 132484, 134543–47, 142129–30. *Arthur papers* (Sanderson), 2: 207; 3: 46. *Cobourg Star*, 31 July 1839. A. B. Corey, *The crisis of 1830–1842 in Canadian-American relations* (New Haven, Conn., and Toronto, 1941). Guillet, *Lives and times of Patriots*. Thomas Lett, *The life, trial and death of Benjamin Lett, the Canadian Patriot of 1837–'38; together with the inscription on his monument* (Sandwich, Ill., 1876). R. B. Ross, "The Patriot war," *Mich. Pioneer Coll.* (Lansing), 21 (1892): 532, 541, 607–8.

LÉVESQUE, CHARLES-FRANÇOIS, lawyer, Patriote, and poet; b. 19 Oct. 1817 in Montreal, son of Marc-Antoine-Louis Lévesque, a protonotary, and Charlotte-Mélanie Panet; d. 3 Nov. 1859 in Sainte-Mélanie, Lower Canada.

Charles-François Lévesque, a grandson of judge Pierre-Louis Panet*, belonged to a bourgeois family of Montreal. In 1825 his father was stricken with paralysis, and his doctor recommended a stay in the country. The Lévesque family accordingly went to live in Berthier-en-Haut (Berthierville). The following year young Charles-François entered the Petit Séminaire de Montréal, where he received a classical education that he completed in 1834. That year he began his legal training under two prominent Montreal lawyers, Samuel Wentworth Monk and Robert Lester Morrogh; however, he had to break off his studies because of the rebellion.

As a fiery liberal, Lévesque espoused the nationalist philosophy in 1837 and even took a public stand in favour of the Patriotes. Believing that his safety was threatened, he thought it expedient to seek temporary refuge in the United States. A year later his brother Guillaume LÉVESQUE, who was two years younger, took an active part in the second uprising, was arrested, and was sentenced to death. Fortunately, through the intervention of his loyal friends, among them Philippe PANET, he was pardoned but nevertheless had to go into exile in France.

In 1839, when the situation had returned to normal, Charles-François came back to Lower Canada. He then resumed his studies and was called to the bar on 9 Jan. 1840. That year he decided to leave Montreal and take up residence at Berthier-en-Haut, where he opened a law office. There, on 14 June 1843, he married Mary Jessy Morrison, a young woman from the American west. From then on he divided his time between his wife, whom he adored, and his profession. But 11 months after their marriage his wife died while giving birth to a girl, Marie-Jessie-Béatrice. Lévesque was profoundly shaken by this loss: in an instant his whole world had collapsed. Under this traumatic shock he suffered a nervous breakdown that brought him to the edge of madness. He subsequently went to live with his mother at Sainte-Mélanie.

During the latter part of his life Lévesque, who was now stricken with neurasthenia, devoted himself entirely to his mother and daughter and to poetry, which became for him an indispensable refuge. From 1845 until the year of his death, he published some 50 poems in various newspapers and periodicals, including *La Revue canadienne*, *L'Aurore des Canadas*, *Le Canadien*, *Le Moniteur canadien*, and *La Minerve*, all of Montreal, and *L'Écho des campagnes* of Berthier-en-Haut.

Lévesque's poetry was strongly influenced by his state of mind. Suffering as he did from "romantic discontent," he was better able than most of his contemporaries to express this feeling in verse. He sought particularly to describe the evils and misfortunes of society, and to evoke death. But also, under the influence of his masters, Lamartine, Burns, and Longfellow, in the manner of *intimiste* poetry he celebrated pure love, tenderness, woman and her fine sensibilities, the joys and sorrows of life, and his own faith. His youthful experiences and romantic humanism led him also to write patriotic poetry, in which he sang the glory and grandeur of the Patriotes of 1837–38.

In the matter of form, Lévesque must be considered an innovator. First, modelling himself on Hugues-Félicité-Robert de La Mennais, he introduced poetry written in biblical verse form into French Canadian literature. Then, after the fashion of Gérard de Nerval, he crafted a number of charming poems in free verse in which he frequently alternated alexandrines and hexameters, his favourite lines, sometimes substituting octosyllabics for hexameters.

But in the midst of his preoccupations Lévesque continued to be haunted by the painful memory of his wife's death. On 3 Nov. 1859, having made up his mind to do away with himself, he gave as a pretext that he was going hunting in a nearby forest. There he put

an end to his life with a shot in the head. The jury charged with inquiring into the circumstances of his passing nevertheless returned a verdict of accidental death.

Charles-François Lévesque, an heir to the pre-romantic tradition represented in Lower Canada by the poet and historian François-Xavier Garneau*, succeeded in imparting a romantic direction to poetic themes and expression. As an innovator he gave fresh life to the rigid structures which too often had confined the stanza, in particular by using as a model the biblical verse form. Like his contemporaries Joseph Lenoir*, *dit* Rolland, and Octave Crémazie*, he prepared the way for the rich period of grandiloquent French Canadian romanticism in the 1860s.

GUY CHAMPAGNE

ANQ-M, CE1-51, 20 oct. 1817; CE5-1, 14 juin 1843, 17 mai 1844; CE5-8, 8 nov. 1859. Le Canadien, 14 nov. 1859. *Mélanges religieux*, 30 sept. 1851. La Minerve, 10 nov. 1859. F.-J. Audet, "Commissions d'avocats de la province de Québec, 1765 à 1849," *BRH*, 39 (1933): 589. *DOLQ*, 1: XXXIII–VII, 591–93. Fauteux, *Patriotes*, 301–2. J.-J. Lefebvre, "Brevets de cléricature des avocats de la deuxième quart du XIXᵉ siècle," *La Rev. du Barreau*, 14 (1954): 312. Michel Boucher, "Les œuvres de Charles Lévesque, écrivain oublié du dix-neuvième siècle (1817–1859)" (thèse de MA, Univ. Laval, Québec, 1972), iv–viii. Jeanne d'Arc Lortie, *La poésie nationaliste au Canada français (1606–1867)* (Québec, 1975), 291–302. Maurault, *Le collège de Montréal* (Dansereau; 1967). *Le répertoire national* (Huston; 1893), 4. P.-G. Roy, *La famille Panet* (Lévis, Qué., 1906). "Les Disparus," *BRH*, 32 (1926): 173. Marthe Faribault-Beauregard, "L'honorable François Lévesque, son neveu Pierre Guérout, et leurs descendants," *SGCF Mémoires*, 8 (1957): 24–25. J.-J. Lefebvre, "François Levêque (1732–1787), membre des Conseils législatif et exécutif," *BRH*, 59 (1953): 145. Jeanne d'Arc Lortie, "Les origines de la poésie au Canada français," *Arch. des lettres canadiennes* (Montréal), 4 (1969): 34, 47–48.

LÉVESQUE, GUILLAUME (baptized **Louis-Guillaume**), office holder, Patriote, lawyer, and author; b. 31 Aug. 1819 in Montreal, son of Marc-Antoine-Louis Lévesque, a protonotary, and Charlotte-Mélanie Panet, daughter of Judge Pierre-Louis Panet*; d. unmarried 5 Jan. 1856 at Quebec.

Guillaume Lévesque was a direct descendant of François Lévesque*, who had been a member of the first Legislative Council in 1775 and who died at Quebec in 1787. Guillaume was six years old when his father, who had been stricken with paralysis, had to take his doctor's advice to stay in the country for a period and moved with his family to Berthier-en-Haut (Berthierville). In 1830 young Guillaume joined his brother Charles-François LÉVESQUE at the Petit Séminaire de Montréal, where he studied for six years. He had not completed his program there when – in 1835, it appears – he was articled to Édouard-Étienne Rodier*, a Montreal lawyer; he continued his legal studies the following year with Hippolyte Guy. In May 1837 he was appointed a record clerk in the office of the sheriff of Montreal.

Caught up in the rebellion of 1837–38, Lévesque joined the Association des Frères-Chasseurs [see Robert Nelson*]. He also linked up with a group of Patriotes from Napierville. On 9 and 10 Nov. 1838 he took part in the attack on Odelltown, which ended with the defeat of the Patriotes. Arrested on 14 November, he was put in jail at Montreal. At the trial, which began on 24 December, he stood accused with 11 Patriotes, including Pierre-Théophile Decoigne* and Achille-Gabriel Morin*, "of having conspired with others in the parish of Saint-Cyprien to overthrow the legislative government established in Lower Canada," and was the only one to plead guilty. Witnesses for the prosecution, several of them leading citizens of Napierville, admitted at the court martial that they had recognized him among a group of Patriotes, but swore that he was not armed. Beginning on 29 December witnesses for the defence, in particular François-Roch de Saint-Ours, Jean-Roch Rolland*, and Pierre Rastel* de Rocheblave, testified in court "that they had known the accused and his family for a long time, that he had been well brought up and had always shown a quiet disposition. That his father, [being] ill, for many years had been unable to attend to the education of his children. That his family was one of the most respectable in the land." The court martial was unmoved: Lévesque was found guilty on 2 January and sentenced, like his companions, to death. He was again incarcerated in the Montreal jail, but through the influence of Philippe PANET, a relative who was an eminent supporter of the government, his sentence was commuted in September 1839 on condition that he leave the country, as his letter of thanks to Pierre-J. Beaudry, the clerk of the prison, confirms.

Lévesque then took refuge in France, initially with his father's relatives in Normandy, the Lévesque-Besselières and the Lévesque-Lemaîtres. From there he went to Paris where, under the assumed name of Guillaume d'Ailleboust de Ramesay, he entered the foreign ministry and worked for three years as a translator in the department dealing with Spanish and Portuguese affairs. He also took courses in medicine, anatomy, and law, and in 1843 worked at the Institut d'Afrique and the Société de Géographie de France. It is thought that for the rest of his life he remained a contributor to the annals of the latter learned society, and that some of his articles attracted attention although they went unnoticed in Lower Canada. Lévesque was pardoned in 1843, and returned to Lower Canada on 21 November of that year. He was called to the bar on 10 May 1844, but gave up practice to take a post as French translator in the Translation Bureau of the Legislative Assembly of the Province of Canada; he soon became its head, and he retained this position until his death.

Lévesque engaged in a great variety of intellectual activities. On 24 Nov. 1844 he helped found at Montreal the Société des Amis, and he served as its president in 1847 and 1848. Its members sought to "educate themselves and to encourage the arts and the sciences"; they had two meetings a week, and were required, on pain of a fine, to make a creative contribution each month to one of the four designated sections of the society. Lévesque made such a presentation at least once. On 1 Feb. 1845 he published in *L'Album littéraire et musical de la Revue canadienne*, established to disseminate the studies of the society's members, a text entitled "De l'habitude de saluer les passants." It was subsequently reprinted by James HUSTON in his *Répertoire national*, along with a speech Lévesque made on 29 Jan. 1848 to the members of the Institut Canadien in Montreal, "De l'influence du sol et du climat sur le caractère, les établissements et les destinées des Canadiens." Although there is no proof, it would not be surprising if Lévesque had collaborated with his friend Huston in selecting and compiling the texts in the *Répertoire national*. He published in *L'Écho des campagnes* at the end of 1846 and the beginning of 1847 a historical short story, "Vœux accomplis," set in the American revolution, and then on 18 and 25 Nov. 1847 "La croix du Grand Calumet," the first written version of the legend of one Cadieux, a voyageur who was abandoned on an island when his companions escaped from the Iroquois through the intervention of a white woman, and who died on the day he was discovered.

Guillaume Lévesque passed away suddenly on 5 Jan. 1856 at Quebec, at the age of 36. A funeral liturgy was sung two days later at the cathedral of Notre-Dame in the presence of numerous friends. He was buried on 11 January at Sainte-Mélanie, where his mother had gone to live on the death of her husband. *Le Canadien* reported on 7 January that Lévesque was "one of those men whose death is regretted as much because of their personal merit as by reason of the rare talents and distinguished works which gave lustre to their career." *Le National* of 8 January observed that he was "distinguished as much by his upright character, his talents, and his education, as by the trials amid which he was cast by the destinies of politics, and which he traversed with the dignity befitting courageous souls and generous hearts alike." If Lévesque can be reproached for not having written and published more, it must be acknowledged that he had a lively, sustained style, a polished, exact language, and a great love for his country and its inhabitants.

AURÉLIEN BOIVIN

Lewellin

[Guillaume Lévesque is the author of the essay "De l'habitude de saluer les passants," published first in *Album littéraire et musical de la Rev. canadienne* (Montréal) in 1845 and subsequently in *Le répertoire national* (Huston, 1848–50; 1893), and of a lecture given in 1848 at the Institut canadien de Montréal entitled "De l'influence du sol et du climat sur le caractère, les établissements et les destinées des Canadiens," also printed in *Le répertoire national*. In addition, Lévesque published two short stories, "Vœux accomplis" and "La croix du Grand Calumet," in *L'Écho des campagnes* (Québec), from 12 Dec. 1846 to 9 Jan. 1847 and on 18 and 25 Nov. 1847 respectively. The descriptive passages on the Ottawa River in "La croix du Grand Calumet" and on the crossing of the St Lawrence by canoe in December in "Vœux accomplis" merit inclusion in an anthology. A.B.]

ANQ-M, CE1-51, 31 août 1819; CE5-8, 12 janv. 1856. ANQ-Q, E17/31, no.2448; E17/32, nos.2502–4, 2543–44; E17/37, no.2969; E17/39, no.3114; E17/40, nos.3158, 3198; P1000-65-1291. Centre de recherche en civilisation canadienne-française (Ottawa), Fonds Guillaume Lévesque. PAC, MG 30, D1, 19: 106; RG 68, General index, 1841–67: 219. Guillaume Lévesque, "[Lettre de Guillaume Lévesque à Pierre Beaudry]," ANQ *Rapport*, 1926–27: 289. *L'Avenir*, 29 janv. 1848. *Le Canadien*, 7 janv. 1856. *La Minerve*, 27 janv. 1848. *Le National* (Québec), 8, 15 janv. 1856. F.-J. Audet, "Commissions d'avocats de la province de Québec, 1765 à 1849," *BRH*, 39 (1933): 592. *DOLQ*, 1: 261, 770–71. Fauteux, *Patriotes*, 302–3. J.-J. Lefebvre, "Brevets de cléricature des avocats de Montréal au deuxième quart du XIXᵉ siècle," *La Rev. du Barreau*, 14 (1954): 312. P.-G. Roy, *Les avocats de la région de Québec*, 279. Michel Boucher, "Les œuvres de Charles Lévesque, écrivain oublié du dix-neuvième siècle (1817–1859)" (thèse de MA, univ. Laval, Québec, 1972), iv–viii. Maurault, *Le collège de Montréal* (Dansereau; 1967). P.-G. Roy, *La famille Panet* (Lévis, Qué., 1906). Marthe Faribault-Beauregard, "L'honorable François Lévesque, son neveu Pierre Guérout et leurs descendants," SGCF *Mémoires*, 8 (1957): 13–30. Jacques Gouin, "La traduction au Canada de 1791 à 1867," *Méta* (Montréal), 12 (1977): 26–32. L.-A. Huguet-Latour, "La Société des amis," *BRH*, 8 (1902): 121–22. J.-J. Lefebvre, "François Levêque (1732–1787), membre des Conseils législatif et exécutif," *BRH*, 59 (1953): 143–45. Victor Morin, "Clubs et sociétés notoires d'autrefois," *Cahiers des Dix*, 15 (1950): 185–218.

LEWELLIN, JOHN LEWELLIN, farmer, land agent, politician, and author; b. *c.* 1781 in Wales; m. Mary Woodley, and they had four sons and two daughters; d. 16 April 1857 in Murray Harbour, P.E.I.

John Lewellin Lewellin had farmed for 16 years in England before he immigrated to Prince Edward Island in 1824 from Wiltshire. He was a friend of John Cambridge*, who had returned to Britain some ten years previously and who was the largest landowner on the Island. Before Lewellin left England, Cambridge and another proprietor, Laurence Sulivan, named him as their agent in the colony. The two proprietors owned a total of 13 lots of some 20,000 acres each, most of which were in the eastern part of the Island. Lewellin established himself at a farm on Lot 61 that he called Woodley Grove, and travelled extensively throughout the district in the course of his duties.

Lewellin ran for the House of Assembly in a by-election for Georgetown in 1827 against James Bardin Palmer*, a lawyer from Charlottetown, but lost by one vote. When the assembly met the following year, however, Palmer was prevented from taking his seat by the other members because of allegations that he had illegally oppressed a group of tenants through his activities in the Court of Chancery, and another by-election was called for June. Palmer contested the seat once again, and although Lewellin was reluctant to run against someone he saw as a promoter of the colony's agricultural interests, he finally agreed to oppose him and won by eight votes to seven. Lewellin sat for the two remaining sessions of the assembly and exhibited a concern for the commerce and industry of the Island, but he did not offer at the next election in 1830.

During a trip to England in December 1826 Lewellin had begun work on a pamphlet for emigrants concerning agriculture on the Island. His wish to have the work published in England before he left the following spring went unfulfilled. In 1828, when Lieutenant Governor John Ready* offered a prize for a "Manual of Agriculture," Lewellin solicited suggestions and additional information for a revised version of his manuscript, but there is no indication he submitted it for the prize. The competition was put into the hands of the Central Agricultural Society in 1832, and at the general meeting that year Lewellin presented the manuscript which was considered by a committee with a view towards publication. But when the work appeared later the same year under the title *Emigration; Prince Edward Island: a brief but faithful account of this fine colony*, it was not with the society's assistance, but by subscription. The volume was unfavourably reviewed in the *British American*, and the inability of the society to publish a "Husbandman's Manual" was noted in James Douglas Haszard*'s *Royal Gazette* as being a "miserable failure."

Lewellin's pamphlet contains the usual elements of an emigration tract of the period. He stresses the advantages of the colony – "Verily, this is a good poor man's country!" – but is critical of the lack of industry shown by its residents. Indeed, *Emigration* has a moralizing tone throughout. Even though two English editions followed the initial publication on the Island in 1832, Lewellin was better known during the period for his other contribution to the agricultural literature of the colony.

Almost from the time of his arrival he was an active contributor to the local press. Over his pen-name, Rusticus, appeared lengthy and detailed articles and letters on agricultural topics ranging from the

505

cultivation of flax to the establishment of a "farm seminary." Lewellin's early writings coincided with Ready's efforts to promote agricultural societies. The lieutenant governor suggested the advantages they would bring in his throne speech in 1827, and Lewellin attempted to form one in Three Rivers (the region around Georgetown) within the year, but it was not until 1831 that the Eastern Agricultural Society was founded. The Central Agricultural Society in Charlottetown also benefited from his efforts. In 1837 the society's secretary, Peter Macgowan, cited Lewellin as "the only person in the Colony capable of discharging the duties of a leading member of an Agricultural Society," and stated that he had been instrumental in the success of the organization. As a result the society made Lewellin an assistant vice-president and honorary correspondent.

Lewellin's writings, both *Emigration* and the newspaper articles, reflect his enthusiasm and optimism for the future of the colony. He was, however, far from being an ordinary farmer. As an agent he was placed in a superior position and probably carried on his own farming efforts as a supplement to his income. He was thus free to experiment in agriculture and no doubt used some of the improved methods of farming and stock-raising that he advocated in his writings. Although it is difficult to quantify the contributions made by Lewellin, his activity, at a time when agriculture on the Island changed from subsistence farming to the major industry, probably had a significant effect. He was also interested in the development of the colony's fisheries, but in spite of his promotion they continued to be neglected by the Islanders, and left to the Americans who flocked to the area each summer.

H. T. HOLMAN and BASIL GREENHILL

John Lewellin Lewellin is the author of *Emigration; Prince Edward Island: a brief but faithful account of this fine colony* . . . ; published first in Charlottetown in 1832 by James Douglas Haszard, it was reissued in London in 1833 and again in 1834. The original Charlottetown edition was republished with an introduction by D. C. Harvey* in his collection *Journeys to the Island of St. John or Prince Edward Island, 1755–1832* (Toronto, 1955), 175–213.

PAPEI, RG 16, Land registry records, conveyance reg., liber 31: f.250; liber 33: f.653; RG 18, 1841, Lot 61. P.E.I. Museum, File information concerning J. L. Lewellin. *British American* (Charlottetown), 9, 30 March 1833 (available at PAPEI). *Examiner* (Charlottetown), 4 May 1857. *Islander*, 22 Jan. 1847, 1 May 1857. *Prince Edward Island Register*, 29 May 1824; 15 July 1825; 21 Aug. 1827; 5, 12, 19 Feb., 2, 10, 24 June 1828; 24 Nov. 1829. *Royal Gazette* (Charlottetown), 12 Oct. 1830, 6 March 1832, 21 Jan. 1834, 17 Jan. 1837, 11 March 1845, 25 March 1846. Elinor Vass, "The agricultural societies of Prince Edward Island," *Island Magazine* (Charlottetown), no.7 (fall–winter 1979): 31–37.

LITTLE PIGEON. *See* GUIBOCHE, LOUIS

LOCKWOOD, ANTHONY, naval officer, hydrographer, surveyor, office holder, and politician; b. *c.* 1775 in England; he had one son, also named Anthony, who was born in 1804; m. 11 May 1819 Mrs Harriet Lee of Saint John, N.B.; buried 25 Jan. 1855 in Stepney (London), England.

Anthony Lockwood joined the Royal Navy in 1791, holding the ranks of midshipman and master's mate before being made a master of the *Jason*, on which he served from 20 May 1797 to 25 Feb. 1799. He was master of the *Crescent* between 25 April 1799 and 26 July 1801, during which time he surveyed Curaçao and part of the Spanish Main. Illness then interrupted his naval career until July 1804, but over the next two years he conducted surveys of Cap Ferrat, France, La Coruña, Spain, and Falmouth harbour, England, as well as making an incomplete survey of the Channel Islands.

On 1 July 1807 Lockwood was appointed acting master attendant at the naval yard in Bridgetown, Barbados, by Vice-Admiral Sir Alexander Forrester Inglis Cochrane. He retained this position until the beginning of 1814, when he commenced surveys on the coasts of British North America. During the next four years, sailing the sloop *Examiner* and based near Halifax, Lockwood made extensive marine surveys of Nova Scotia and Grand Manan Island, N.B., in addition to producing a chart of the Saint John harbour. His last Admiralty chart was certified at the Hydrographic Office in London on 25 March 1818.

Seeking post-war preferment, in 1818 Lockwood published in London, at his own expense, *A brief description of Nova Scotia, with plates of the principal harbors*, which contained fulsome dedications to the lieutenant governor of the colony, Lord Dalhousie [Ramsay*], and officers of its government, especially Surveyor General Charles Morris*, who had already employed Lockwood as a map-maker. On 25 Feb. 1819, with the written support of Commander Charles Bullen, Lockwood petitioned the colonial secretary, Lord Bathurst, for the position of surveyor general of New Brunswick. Seven weeks earlier, however, Lieutenant Governor George Stracey Smyth* had recommended George SHORE, then acting surveyor general, for the appointment. Receiving no reply, Smyth confirmed his recommendation by letter to Bathurst dated 25 March. This, too, Bathurst ignored, appointing Lockwood on 23 April 1819 – a fact unknown to Smyth until Lockwood presented himself in Fredericton that July.

While passing through Saint John en route, Lockwood had encountered a shipload of Welsh emigrants from the snow *Albion*, for whom he issued location tickets on his arrival in the capital. This action, taken even before he had introduced himself to

Smyth and his Council, proved to be a significant initiative in forming settlement policy in New Brunswick. By August, Lockwood had assisted in founding the Cardigan Society, to aid the Welsh settlement of that name; it was in turn quickly absorbed by the Fredericton Emigrant Society of which he became secretary.

Lockwood's exertions during his first months in New Brunswick were impressive. Before taking his oath for the Council, which he automatically joined as surveyor general, he had written to Bathurst advising that the province be surveyed into sections. He took his place on the Council on 13 October, and found time that same fall to conduct the first survey of a canal route through the Chignecto Isthmus, which evidently won him valuable support among the Saint John merchants. On 16 December he proposed to the Council that he run a new survey of the boundaries of Kings, Queens, and Westmorland counties. During 1820 he surveyed 84 lots for emigrants on Cape Tormentine and built them a road to the Gaspereau River, as well as surveying another road between the Nerepis and Oromocto rivers. On 22 July of that year the Council heard Lockwood's report on a land grant to the Micmac band on the Richibucto River. He submitted recommendations for further emigrant lots in Shepody Road at the Council meeting on 5 October.

After such a vigorous introduction, Lockwood apparently withdrew into the routine conduct of his office, though by June 1822, it appears, he was appointed receiver general of casual revenues in addition to the post he already held. Perhaps his periods of frantic activity followed by ones of relative inactivity were ominous. In the early fall of 1822 Lockwood first consulted Dr Thomas Emerson* of Fredericton and then received treatment from Dr Thomas Paddock of Saint John for mental illness of some sort. He had recovered sufficiently, nevertheless, to attend nine meetings of the Council between 18 Jan. and 13 March 1823, on the latter occasion presenting a plan of the Richibucto River, which displayed town reserves, and another for the Buctouche River. However, the political crisis following Lieutenant Governor Smyth's death on 27 March provided the occasion, if not the inducement, for Lockwood's spectacular descent into madness.

An interim president of the Council being required, George Leonard*, the octogenarian senior member, was first offered the position, which he declined on the grounds of age. Despite a challenge by supporters of Christopher Billopp, Ward Chipman* assumed the post of administrator on 1 April. The challenges continued however. Lockwood attended the Council meetings on 30 April and on 1 May. Thereafter he absented himself and for the next few weeks his whereabouts are uncertain. By 24 May he had persuaded Leonard to assert his right to the presidency

"in the hope that it would produce tranquillity in the province." Ostensibly to assist in that purpose, Lockwood appointed himself as Leonard's civil aide-de-camp and inspecting field officer, as well as acting secretary. On 25 May he attempted to disseminate Leonard's proclamation in Saint John – while at the same time writing a letter to Chipman offering terms for his, Lockwood's, support. From 25 to 30 May Lockwood behaved with erratic violence in Saint John: issuing threats, brawling, taking up residence in Government House, and gathering an appreciative mob. Dr Paddock attended him with scant success. By the time he returned to Fredericton on 30 May, Lockwood was approaching collapse; on the steamboat *General Smyth* he scribbled a desperate note to Chipman requesting release from his present public offices since his "ailment" was "subject to increase from confinement."

The Council considered Lockwood's state of mind at their meeting on 31 May, hearing depositions from the doctors who had treated him and from the mayor of Saint John. The following day Lockwood set up a table in Fredericton square, at which he drank coffee, issued proclamations, and reacted pugnaciously to the crowd, before taking horse and riding about the streets firing pistols and declaring himself called to assume the government of the province. By nightfall Lockwood had been arrested and placed in the Fredericton jail. The Council received further evidence from the sheriff of York County on 2 June and were "fully satisfied" of Lockwood's derangement. Chipman appointed a commission *de lunatico inquirendo* that day and by 5 June it had determined that Lockwood was legally mad, and had been since 19 May. On 7 June his wife and son petitioned for a committee of custody over his person and estate, which was immediately granted.

When George Shore, Lockwood's replacement, examined the surveyor general's office, he found confusion, mutilated documents, and disarray which would take "two extra employees five years to straighten out." Furthermore, the discrepancy between Lockwood's receipts as receiver general and the office's bank deposit amounted to more than £2,000. Although he was moved from the jail to what was, in effect, house-arrest in September, Lockwood and his family had to suffer the public sale of his real and personal estate as the custodial committee sought to recover the missing public monies.

Throughout his confinement Lockwood petitioned for his liberty. But it was not until 10 Nov. 1825 that a further commission of inquiry, appointed by Lieutenant Governor Sir Howard Douglas*, declared him "restored to his understanding." Soon after his release he returned with his wife to England, where he continued to receive a £150 annual pension from the government of New Brunswick until his death.

Lola

Anthony Lockwood's respite from suffering was only brief. "At times subject to fits of insanity" until 1836, he probably spent some of the last years of his life in the Bethnal Green Lunatic Asylum in London.

PETER THOMAS

Anthony Lockwood prepared *A brief description of Nova Scotia, with plates of the principal harbors; including a particular account of the island of Grand Manan* (London, 1818). His chart of Saint John harbour was published under the title *Mouth of the River St. John* ([London], 1818; a copy is available in the British Library (London), Dept. of Printed Books); a photograph of this chart is in the PANB's map collection, H2-203.29-1818.

N.B. Museum, W. F. Ganong, "New Brunswick biography," 133; W. F. Ganong coll., box 12, packet 3; H. T. Hazen coll.: Ward Chipman papers, corr., George Leonard to Chipman, [27 or 28 May 1823]; Anthony Lockwood to Chipman, 25 May 1823; Lockwood to Thomas Wetmore, 10 Sept. 1823; George Shore to Chipman, 14 June 1823; Ward Chipman papers, deposition of R. C. Minette, city surveyor, Saint John; memorandum, Bank of New Brunswick, 7 Oct. 1823; Reg. of marriages for the city and county of Saint John, book A (1810–28); SB 42: 72 (L. [M. B.] Maxwell, "History of central New Brunswick," column in *Daily Gleaner* (Fredericton), 1933). Old Loyalist Graveyard (Fredericton), Tombstone of Anthony Lockwood Jr. PANB, "N.B. political biog." (J. C. and H. B. Graves); RG 2, RS6, A2, 2 Oct., 16 Dec. 1819; 22 July, 5 Oct., 23 Dec. 1820; A3, 13 March, 30 April, 2 June 1823; RS8, Estates, 2/1, administration of Anthony Lockwood. PANS, RG 20A, 68, 1817. PRO, ADM 1/4822, Pro L, nos.224–25; 1/4824, Pro L, no.248; 1/4826, Pro L, no.261; 1/4849, Pro L, no.74; ADM 11/4, 11/6; ADM 36/14409; ADM 106/1560, 27 Oct. 1806; 106/1693, 31 Jan. 1814 (enclosure in 31 Jan. 1818), 25 March 1818; 106/2248: 398; 106/3517, 1 April 1822; CO 188/25, Lockwood to Lord Bathurst, 25 Feb. 1819; Smyth to Bathurst, 4 Jan., 15 March 1819. N.S., House of Assembly, *Journal and proc.*, 1820: 158. *New-Brunswick Royal Gazette*, 22 June, 6, 9 July, 7 Dec. 1819. *Nova-Scotia Royal Gazette*, 30 June 1819. *Acadian Recorder*, 12 Dec. 1896, supp.

LOLA (Laurent, Lawlor), NOEL (also known as **Newell Lolar**), Malecite hunter, guide, and legendary figure; d. before 1861 in Woodstock, N.B.

Noel Lola is listed, as an adult, in the 1841 and 1851 census records for the Tobique region. In the latter document, it is reported that he was married. His wife was probably Louise St Pierre (Sappier). In April 1852 their son, also named Noel, was baptized in Woodstock at the age of ten days.

According to the tradition of the Malecite band on the Woodstock Indian Reserve, by the late 1850s Lola, a hunting guide, was living there with a woman who was not his wife. Having been among the first to move to the newly established reserve [*see* Peter LOLA], Lola had selected a favourable site adjacent to the Saint John River. Because of his domestic arrangement and his increasing intemperance, the other Malecites chose to live some distance from the couple.

One evening about this time, two white men, strangers to the area, were spotted approaching Lola's camp. When neither he nor the woman with whom he lived were seen for several days, one of the residents of the reserve went to investigate. Lola was found dead and there was no sign of the two men or the woman. The resident Roman Catholic priest was asked to conduct a proper burial but he refused, saying Lola's sinful life prevented him from so doing. A grave was then prepared near Lola's camp. In time the Indians forgot about the burial and established homes around the unconsecrated grave.

After a while the Malecites became aware of a strange whooping which was heard prior to every death on the reserve. This sound was attributed to a *kéhtəkws* or ghost – in this case the apparition of a person denied a Christian burial – which portends a death by whooping. This forerunner of death was last experienced about 1938 or 1939. At that time a resident, excavating his cellar, disinterred a skeleton. When analysis suggested that the bones were of a male who had died 80 or 90 years earlier, the community agreed that they were probably Lola's. Once these bones were reinterred in consecrated ground by the local priest, the whooping was no longer heard.

Most of what has survived about Lola's life is a matter of legend, but the circumstances reflect the values and expectations of the Malecites who were his contemporaries. Strongly influenced by both official Catholic doctrine and by Irish and French folk traditions, they believed a person's soul could not find rest until the body had received a Christian burial. These influences are also evident in the tale of the Dungarvon Whooper. Whooping was said to occur sporadically at sunset in a remote lumber camp because of the unconsecrated burial about 1860 of an Irish murder victim. It continued until the body received a proper burial in 1912.

The Malecites had added a moralistic overtone to their legend which was missing in the Irish one. To them, if a person sinned, he or she could become a ghost, the soul never finding peace until it received official church forgiveness. But, perhaps even more significantly, the end of the whooping came at a time when the Malecites' belief in *kéhtəkws* began to decline. Increased levels of education and profound changes in ethical values in Indian and white communities precluded the continuance of moral sanctions based on such legends.

VINCENT O. ERICKSON

N.B. Museum, W. F. Ganong coll., box 38, item 10 ("Return of Indians at Tobique and Madawaska, June

1841"). PAC, RG 31, A1, 1851, Victoria, return for Tobique Indian Reserve; 1861, Woodstock, N.B. St Gertrude's Roman Catholic Church (Woodstock), St Malachy's Church, Woodstock, reg. of baptisms, marriages, and burials. *Handbook of North American Indians* (Sturtevant *et al.*), vol.15. Rayburn, *Geographical names of N.B.*, 98, 289. Carole Spray, *Will o' the wisp: folk tales and legends of New Brunswick* (Fredericton, 1979). Stuart Trueman, *Ghosts, pirates and treasure trove: the phantoms that haunt New Brunswick* (Toronto, 1975). V. O. Erickson, "The Micmac *Buoin*, three centuries of cultural and semantic change," *Man in the Northeast* (Rindge, N.H.), nos.15–16 (spring–fall 1978), 3–41. N. N. Smith, "Notes on the Malecite of Woodstock, New Brunswick," ed. K. H. Capes, *Anthropologica* (Ottawa), no.5 (1957): 1–39; "Premonition spirits among the Wabanaki," Mass. Archaeological Soc., *Bull.* (Attleboro, Mass.), 15 (1954): 52–56.

LOLA, PETER (also known as **Pierre** or **Peter Laurent**), Malecite leader, guide, and runner; b. probably *c.* 1815 in or near Medoctec (four miles upriver from present-day Meductic), N.B.; m. 31 Oct. 1837 Fanny (Françoise) Joseph, and they had two sons and two daughters; last known to be alive in September 1852.

Beginning with William Odber Raymond*'s account in 1890, the story of Peter Lola's foot-race with a stage-coach has become part of New Brunswick's folklore. Some time around 1840, when he was in Fredericton, Lola requested passage in a stage-coach bound for Woodstock, a distance of approximately 60 miles. Although he offered the customary fare, he was refused. Angered, he vowed to reach the destination before the four-in-hand. Both left around eight in the morning and, despite the efforts of the coach's driver, John Turner, Lola led the entire way over the rough New Brunswick roads. Raymond describes the conclusion of the race: "It was still early in the afternoon when the citizens of Woodstock were aroused in a manner entirely unexpected. The stage-coach came tearing into the town at the heels of an Indian who was yelling like a demon and running as for his life. . . . The finish was a close one, but the Indian was ahead."

Unfortunately for the Malecites of the middle Saint John region, they were winners only of foot-races. Around the same time as the race took place, the members of the band were becoming increasingly concerned over the number of settlers homesteading on the site of their traditional summer village, Medoctec. This area had been allotted by the Nova Scotia authorities on 15 Oct. 1784 to 120 men from De Lancey's Brigade, including Benjamin Peck Griffith and Robert Brown, but it was well into the 19th century before the number of permanent settlers became substantial.

In 1836, when Peter Fraser*, a Fredericton lawyer, drew up his will, he included a direction that a farm of some 200 acres, situated three miles south of Woodstock, be made a reserve for Medoctec's displaced Indians. Fraser felt that the band should be compensated for the land of which they had been "wrongfully deprived." The reserve was finally established on 22 May 1851, more than ten years after Fraser's death. On 6 October, Peter Lola was one of the eight Malecites who signed the release whereby the band gave up their claim to Medoctec. John Dibblee, who was the eldest son of the Reverend Frederick Dibblee* and who, like his father, had been acquainted for some time with the Indians in the area, verified Lola's long-standing residence at Medoctec and his right to sign the document. Lola and his family were among the old Medoctec community that moved either onto the Woodstock reserve or to a settlement at the mouth of the Meduxnakik (Meduxnekeag) River at Upper Woodstock.

An intrepid woodsman and effective guide, Peter Lola accompanied William Teel Baird* on a hunting and fishing trip in September 1852. A nostalgic account of their experiences is given in Baird's autobiography, *Seventy years of New Brunswick life*. This work provides an excellent description of adventures with "rod and gun" carried out under the tutelage of Baird's Indian guides on the lakes and rivers of central New Brunswick.

Although Peter Lola was not an important Malecite leader, the facts and legends which surround his life help to depict both the attitude of the English-speaking community of central New Brunswick towards the Malecites and the band's response to that attitude.

VINCENT O. ERICKSON

Arch. paroissiales, St-Bruno (Van Buren, Maine), Reg. des baptêmes, mariages et sépultures, vol.1. PAC, RG 31, A1, 1861, Woodstock, N.B. PANB, RG 2, RS7, 40: 207. St Dunstan's Roman Catholic Church (Fredericton), Reg. of baptisms, marriages, and burials, vol.2: 1837, no.26; 1840, no.192. *Canada, Indian treaties and surrenders . . .* [1680–1906] (3v., Ottawa, 1891–1912; repr. Toronto, 1971), 3: 1–3. W. T. Baird, *Seventy years of New Brunswick life . . .* (Saint John, N.B., 1890; repr. Fredericton, 1978). W. O. Raymond, *The River St. John: its physical features, legends and history from 1604 to 1784* (Saint John, 1910; [2nd ed.], ed. J. C. Webster, Sackville, N.B., 1943; repr. 1950).

LYON, GEORGE, army and militia officer, businessman, justice of the peace, office holder, and politician; b. 1790 in Inveraray, Scotland, son of George Lyon and Elizabeth Philips; m. 1812 Catherine Radenhurst, and they had at least six sons and four daughters; d. 26 March 1851 in Richmond, Carleton County, Upper Canada.

George Lyon was commissioned ensign in the 40th Foot on 4 Sept. 1806 and lieutenant two years later. In

Lyon

1809 he transferred to the 100th Foot, which had come to Canada in 1805, and in November 1810 he joined the regiment there. Serving in the War of 1812, he was present on 3 June 1813 at the capture of the American gunboats *Growler* and *Eagle* at Île aux Noix, Lower Canada, and was put in charge of the American prisoners who were removed to Montreal. On the Niagara frontier, he commanded the regiment's eighth company at the battle of Chippawa on 5 July 1814. During the British retreat on that occasion he was severely wounded but he recovered and continued to serve with the 100th (renumbered the 99th in 1816) until it was disbanded in 1818. He was placed on half pay on 25 November at the rate of 4*s*. 6*d*. per diem.

Former members of the 99th Foot were given the opportunity to take up land in Upper Canada at the government-sponsored military settlement of Richmond in the Rideau River area. Lyon was given an initial grant of 500 acres of land in Goulbourn and March townships and settled in the newly surveyed village of Richmond, where he was to spend the rest of his life. A member of the group of retired military officers which governed the settlement in its early years under the superintendence of George Thew Burke (a former captain in the 99th), Lyon played an active role in the village's development. In 1820 he entered into an agreement with the deputy quartermaster general's department to erect for the settlers a sawmill and a grist-mill at Richmond, for which he was to receive extra land in the village and in Goulbourn Township. He was later allowed to patent even more land to compensate for the property flooded by his mill-pond. Lyon's total land holdings in the area have been estimated at 11,000 acres.

Lyon claimed the mills cost £1,500 to build. The sawmill was erected about 1821 and by April 1826 the grist-mill was fully operational. To the mill complex he added a distillery, which began production early in 1827, a fulling-mill, a forge, and a store at which he sold spirits and other goods, and he engaged in the potash trade. The principal markets outside the local area for his flour, lumber, and whisky were Montreal and the Point (Ottawa), the bustling construction headquarters for the Rideau Canal. The legal matters which arose regularly from his businesses and land activities (including land transactions and suits, the conveyance of financial notes, and the arrangement of securities on the debts of many settlers to Lyon) were handled after about 1825 in Perth by his brother-in-law, Thomas Mabon RADENHURST. Lyon's young brother Robert, who immigrated in 1829 and apprenticed in Radenhurst's law office, died tragically in 1833 in a duel with John Wilson*.

Given his background it was natural that Lyon would hold several positions of prominence, including a commission in the local militia. Appointed captain in the 1st Regiment of Carleton militia on 2 Aug. 1821, he was promoted major on 25 May 1843. He received his first commission of the peace for the Bathurst District on 18 April 1825, and later served as an agent for the Crown Lands Department and as postmaster of Richmond. Several times a tory candidate for the riding of Carleton in provincial elections, Lyon experienced mixed success. In a by-election marked by a bitter struggle between the rival tory factions of the Richmond area and March Township, he was defeated by Hamnet Kirks PINHEY in 1832 but, when Pinhey was unseated for election irregularities, Lyon was declared elected on 16 Jan. 1833. He sat in the House of Assembly, along with John Bower Lewis, Carleton's other member, until 1834. Lyon introduced a bill that year which led to the incorporation of the Richmond Canal Company for making the Goodwood (Jock) River navigable. Defeated in the elections of 1836 and 1844, he became a member for Carleton a second time at a by-election on 23 June 1846 but lost his seat in the general election of 1847–48.

Lyon remained active in business almost until his death but he appears to have faced increasing financial strain. In 1841 he seriously considered renting out his mills and moving, and in 1849 he was forced to sell his half pay in order to discharge a property obligation. He was gazetted a lieutenant in the Royal Canadian Rifles that year but immediately sold his commission to another officer.

Three of George Lyon's sons achieved some degree of prominence. The oldest, George Byron Lyon Fellowes (his surname was changed in 1856 to permit him to acquire property from his wife's family), was a lawyer and a member of the Legislative Assembly for Russell (1848–61). Robert, also a lawyer, was a Carleton County court judge and William Radenhurst Richmond was first reeve of Richmond (1850–54). A fourth son, Thomas, continued his father's milling and distilling businesses.

J. K. JOHNSON

AO, MU 2367; RG 1, A-I-6: 21184–87; RG 22, ser.155, will of George Lyon; ser.224, G. B. L. Fellowes; Catherine Lyon; W. R. R. Lyon. BLHU, R. G. Dun & Co. credit ledger, Canada, 13: 187. PAC, MG 30, D1, 19: 502–4; RG 1, L3, 289: L14/9, 11; 296: L21/55; 296a: L22/49; 421; RG 8, I (C ser.), 405: 125; 684: 56; 695: 109; 772: 133; 1011: 93; 1017: 52; RG 9, I, B5, 2, 6; RG 31, A1, 1851, Richmond Village; RG 68, 8: 457; 11: 454; 38: 470; 41: 483. PRO, WO 17/1515. Can., Prov. of, *Statutes*, 1856, c.33. U.C., House of Assembly, *Journal*, 1832–34, 1836; *Statutes*, 1834, c.31. *Bathurst Courier*, 4 April 1851. *Bytown Gazette, and Ottawa and Rideau District Advertiser*, 16 June 1836. *Cobourg Star*, 10 April 1833. *Montreal Transcript*, 5 March 1842. *Ottawa Citizen*, 12 Aug. 1854. *Toronto Herald*, 7 April 1842, 31 Aug. 1843. Armstrong, *Handbook of Upper Canadian chronology*, 71, 79. *Canada directory*, 1851: 345, 1857–58. *Canadian biog. dict.*, 1: 748–49.

G.B., WO, *Army list*, 1806–49. *Illustrated historical atlas of the county of Carleton (including city of Ottawa), Ont.* (Toronto, 1879; repr. Port Elgin, Ont., 1971), xxxiii. *The service of British regiments in Canada and North America . . .*, comp. C. H. Stewart (Ottawa, 1962). W. H. Smith, *Canada: past, present and future*, 2: 353–54; *Smith's Canadian gazetteer; comprising statistical and general information respecting all parts of the upper province, or Canada West . . .* (Toronto, 1846; repr. 1970), 160, 263.

Cornell, *Alignment of political groups*, 17, 19, 23, 31, 38, 48. J. M. Hitsman, *The incredible War of 1812: a military history* (Toronto, 1965), 136–37, 195–96. Edward Shortt, *The memorable duel at Perth* ([Perth, Ont.], 1970), 16, 64. M. S. Cross, "The age of gentility: the formation of an aristocracy in the Ottawa valley," CHA *Hist. papers*, 1967: 105–17. "Death of Judge Lyon," *Free Press* (Ottawa), 26 March 1888: 2. "Death of Mayor Fellowes," *Free Press*, 15 March 1876: 2.

M

MACAULAY, Sir JAMES BUCHANAN, army and militia officer, lawyer, politician, and judge; b. 3 Dec. 1793 in Newark (Niagara-on-the-Lake), Upper Canada, second son of James Macaulay* and Elizabeth Tuck Hayter; m. 1 Dec. 1821 Rachel Crookshank Gamble in York (Toronto), and they had one son and four daughters; d. 26 Nov. 1859 in Toronto.

James Buchanan Macaulay was born in the fledgling loyalist settlement of Newark to parents recently arrived from England. His father, a British army surgeon, and his mother enjoyed the personal friendship of the province's first lieutenant governor, John Graves Simcoe*, to which the given names of James's older brother, John Simcoe MACAULAY, bear eloquent witness. In 1795 or 1796 the Macaulays followed the seat of government to York near which the doctor had been granted a park lot. This land, stretching north into the edges of uncleared forest, rapidly attained the tag of Macaulay Town and as York grew it became a considerable financial asset for the Macaulay family.

In 1805 James was sent off to join other sons of Upper Canadian professional men in the privileged coterie of the Reverend John Strachan*'s school at Cornwall; there he undoubtedly rubbed shoulders with a fair number of his colleagues in later public life, including three future judges: John Beverley Robinson*, Archibald McLean*, and Jonas Jones*. On 14 Dec. 1809, a few days after his 16th birthday, Macaulay was commissioned an ensign with the 98th Foot, then stationed at Quebec. Appointed lieutenant in the Canadian Fencibles during the winter of 1812, that June, as rumours of war with the United States grew stronger, he became a lieutenant and acted as adjutant in the provincially raised Glengarry Light Infantry Fencibles. Almost immediately he was thrown into battle, first on 19 July at Sackets Harbor, N.Y., where he was wounded in the left hip, and then in February 1813 at the battle of Ogdensburg, N.Y., where he led a gallant, if not entirely sensible, charge across the frozen St Lawrence into American artillery fire. For this action he received the commendation of his commanding officer, Lieutenant-Colonel George Richard John Macdonell*, and of Lieutenant-Colonel John HARVEY, deputy adjutant general of the Upper Canadian forces. Briefly in command of the garrison at York in June 1814, Macaulay again fought courageously at Lundy's Lane and Fort Erie later that summer. His military career had little future at the end of the war, however, and when his regiment was disbanded in the summer of 1816, he appears curiously enough even to have flirted with the notion of joining the new military settlement at Perth, Upper Canada, as a pioneer farmer. Instead he turned to that eminently attractive profession in the young province – law.

Macaulay entered his name on the books of the Law Society of Upper Canada in 1816, when he was 22, and began studying in the law office of Attorney General D'Arcy Boulton*. He was soon involved in the litigation following the incident at Seven Oaks (Winnipeg) in June 1816 [see Cuthbert GRANT] and prepared charges for the trials of 1817–18, which were held, coincidentally, before Boulton, who had recently been appointed one of the assize judges. Continuing his studies with Boulton's son Henry John Boulton*, Macaulay became an attorney-at-law in 1819 and served briefly in the office of John Beverley Robinson, who had succeeded the elder Boulton as attorney general. By the beginning of 1822 Macaulay had been called to the bar and had married a daughter of the late John Gamble, one of his father's medical-military colleagues. Three years later he was admitted to the professionally desirable ranks of the Law Society benchers.

Macaulay's industrious advocacy at the bar, revealed in the official law reports, and his impeccable social standing brought him to Sir Peregrine MAITLAND's attention as an obviously desirable addition to the province's ruling élite. On 5 May 1825 he was appointed to the Executive Council, an undoubted bastion of the "family compact," where he joined Chief Justice William Campbell*, James Baby*, and

Macaulay

John Strachan. His executive role was to be short-lived for his last appearance in council was on 2 July 1829. The intervening years were not exactly smooth for Macaulay but he weathered them with expected ease. As an executive councillor he had inevitably to suffer William Lyon Mackenzie*'s attacks in the *Colonial Advocate*, culminating in one on 18 May 1826 which described him as "a *stink-trap* of government." That attack had not been entirely unprovoked for earlier in the month Macaulay had issued a pamphlet (of which no copies survive) uncharacteristically replying in kind to Mackenzie's sniping. The next month, just prior to his official swearing-in as an executive councillor on 27 June 1826, Macaulay acted for Samuel Peters JARVIS, Henry SHERWOOD, and other young bloods from local society families whom he had seen toss Mackenzie's type into the harbour on the evening of 8 June. At their trial that October a jury found in favour of Mackenzie and shortly thereafter Macaulay paid to Mackenzie's lawyer the costs and damages assessed against his clients.

Macaulay was also party to the celebrated decision which removed Judge John Walpole Willis* from the Court of King's Bench in 1828. During the long acrimonious dispute over his dismissal, Willis characterized Macaulay as "a Lieutenant on half pay, who ceased to be a Judge in consequence of my appointment." In fact, when Judge Boulton had retired in 1827 prior to Willis's arrival in Upper Canada, Macaulay had been temporarily appointed puisne judge to officiate during the summer assizes and had returned to his law practice that September when his commission had ended. This experience made him "a most eligible" candidate to replace Willis the following year, but since Macaulay had recommended in council "the measure which had occasioned the vacancy," the appointment went instead to his brother-in-law, Christopher Alexander Hagerman*. Hagerman's appointment was not confirmed, however, and in July 1829 Macaulay was elevated to Willis's seat on the bench. That August he withdrew from the Executive Council in order to confine himself as much as possible "to duties exclusively Judicial."

During the previous three years, Macaulay had collected several of the commissions necessary for the discharge of justice. As one of the three King's Bench judges, he became enveloped in the sheer quantity of work both at sittings at York and on circuit when travelling conditions and weather permitted. Along with Chief Justice John Beverley Robinson, he presided over a welter of cases dealing principally, in the absence of a court of equity, with matters of civil litigation. Macaulay's judgements on the many cases before him in the 1830s cannot be easily categorized but the law reports reveal the majority to be fair if cautious and rather more sensitive to social considerations than those of his fellow judges. He tended to clemency in cases of murder, though he rarely advised it directly. Most apparent from extant reports is his painstaking analysis of a case and the almost extreme lengths he would go to in order to be seen to be fair. His rulings and later recommendations on Orange rioters in the Johnstown District in 1833 [*see* Ogle Robert Gowan*] and on the murder trial of John Rooney and James Owen McCarthy* at Hamilton in 1834 nicely demonstrate Macaulay's good sense and his understanding of human failings. A deep-seated concern for the orderly regulation of justice and for prison conditions is evident in his advocacy of provincial supervision of district jails during a charge to the grand jury at the Gore District Assizes on 17 Aug. 1835. With liberal sensibility Macaulay advised that "the Law is neither in a sealed book nor a dead letter" – a statement that might easily be hung as a label upon his legal career.

In 1838 Lieutenant Governor Sir Francis Bond Head*, writing to his successor, Sir George ARTHUR, highly recommended Macaulay as "most excellent – man & lawyer." More than 20 years later the writer of his obituary would note that "whether . . . as a soldier, a lawyer, a judge, or . . . a Christian, . . . in all his actions" can be traced "the same entire devotion to the calls of duty." As a devout Anglican and a warden of St James' Church for most of his adult life, Macaulay dealt with all sorts of parochial affairs including provision for poor relief. As a former army officer and militia colonel, he had directed the militia in the defence of Toronto during William Lyon Mackenzie's uprising in December 1837. As a provincial judge with a capacity for hard work and a reputation for clear thinking, he was asked by Lieutenant Governor Arthur in 1839 to complete an investigation of the Indian Department begun by the provincial secretary, Richard Alexander Tucker*.

During March and April of that year Macaulay, though professing uncertain health and overwork, rushed off a lengthy report on the economic and social plight of what he termed "the degenerate races." This long-winded survey (some 446 manuscript pages) reveals concern and indicts some past practices, but it offered very little for future improvements in handling Indian problems and appears to rely on an extension of "Christian charity" to cope with the "far greater numbers of destitute tribes" that "inhabit the remote regions of the North," beyond lakes Huron and Superior and certainly beyond the experience or knowledge of James Buchanan Macaulay. The hurried examination was well enough received, however, for he was appointed with Robert Sympson JAMESON and William Hepburn to a more formal examination of the Indian Department as part of the general investigation of provincial administration in 1839–40. Simultaneously he served as chairman of the committee investigating the workings of the Executive Council. Though Macaulay's insight into public affairs is not revealed in these departmental reports, Governor Lord Sydenham [Thomson*], who had known him only for a short time, had no compunction in recording early in 1841 that "in political matters I know of no one whose opinions I would rather consult for I esteem him highly."

Nevertheless, it was to judicial matters that Macaulay turned for the remainder of his life. Along with commissioners John Beverley Robinson, William Henry Draper*, and John Hillyard Cameron*, he embarked on the first revision of Upper Canadian statute law in 1840 and served on the commissions of 1842 and 1843 inquiring into the Court of Chancery. In 1843 he was appointed to the Court of Appeal and in 1849 he was clearly the most logical and desirable choice for the position of chief justice in the reconstituted Court of Common Pleas. Macaulay held this post until the pressure of unremitting daily work on and for the bench, together with a self-admitted hearing loss, forced him to retire in 1856. That April he received the title of Queen's Counsel and the following January he agreed to supervise yet another statute revision committee, this time for both Upper and Lower Canada. Fellow commissioner David Breakenridge Read* lauded Macaulay for his amazing attention to details of law and of language and for his refusal to accept any remuneration over and above his pension though he served as chairman for nearly two years. Despite Macaulay's failing health, another judgeship followed in the summer of 1857, a seat in the Court of Error and Appeal. The next year he was made a CB and on 13 Jan. 1859 he was knighted. That February the Law Society of Upper Canada, which Macaulay had shepherded and served for more than 35 years, conferred on him the office of treasurer, succeeding the late Robert BALDWIN. Quite fittingly, perhaps, in retrospect, it was at Osgoode Hall on the morning of his re-election to this position that his heart failed.

James Buchanan Macaulay ended his days in what the young attorney general, John A. Macdonald*, paying tribute to him at a retirement dinner in 1856, had called "an untiring assiduity." The *Upper Canada Law Journal* that year noted the "ample monuments" represented by Macaulay's judgements in the law reports and observed quite accurately that he was the sort of figure whom "men of all parties looked up to as a pattern of judicial purity." He had, in short, as that journal recorded at his death, quite simply "grown with the country." A shy, retiring man, hesitant in speech but fluent and eminently rational in his reports, charges, and judgements, Macaulay had developed vast experience in watching over and guiding the new society. His opinions and recommendations were sought on a wide range of issues affecting the

machinery of government, his citizenship and private life were exemplary, and his military youth suitably dashing. To his equally reticent wife, who survived him until 1883 when she died in England at the home of a married daughter, Macaulay left the family home in Toronto, Wykeham Lodge, and an estate worth $40,000. To the province he left a legacy of quiet public service and principled professionalism.

GORDON DODDS

A portrait of James Buchanan Macaulay in the robes of chief justice of the Common Pleas, c. 1854, artist unknown, hangs in the Law Society of Upper Canada's premises at Osgoode Hall, Toronto.

AO, MS 35; MS 78; MU 2197; RG 22, ser.305, J. B. Macaulay. Law Soc. of U.C. (Toronto), "Journal of proceedings of the Convocation of Benchers of the Law Society of Upper Canada" (8v.), I: 93; III: 516–21; Secretary's notes: 145. PAC, MG 29, D61: 5088–89; RG 1, E1, 52: 239–40, 529; 53: 220; 79: 128; RG 8, I (C ser.), 30: 8, 114; 220: 200; 228: 53; 678: 98–102; 682: 86; 1168: 177; 1170: 107–8; 1706: 62–63; RG 10, A6, 718–19; RG 68, General index, 1651–1841; 1841–67. PRO, CO 42/375: 85–86; 42/381: 34–35; 42/384: 110–13; 42/388: 55–60; 42/389: 124–31, 150–51; 42/390: 414; 42/423: 95–112; 42/427: 249–58. *Arthur papers* (Sanderson). "The Honourable James Buchanan Macaulay," *Upper Canada Law Journal* (Barrie, [Ont.]), 2 (1856): 38–39. "Sir James Buchanan Macaulay," *Upper Canada Law Journal* (Toronto), 5 (1859): 265–68. *Town of York, 1815–34* (Firth). U.C., Commission appointed to inquire into and investigate the several departments of the public service, *Report* (Toronto, [1840]). *Colonial Advocate*, April–May 1826. *Globe*, 28, 30 Nov. 1859. *Sarnia Observer, and Lambton Advertiser*, 2 Dec. 1859. *DNB*. D. B. Read, *The lives of the judges of Upper Canada and Ontario, from 1791 to the present time* (Toronto, 1888). W. R. Riddell, *The legal profession in Upper Canada in its early periods* (Toronto, 1916). Scadding, *Toronto of old* (1873).

MACAULAY (McAulay), JOHN, businessman, office holder, newspaperman, justice of the peace, militia officer, and politician; b. 17 Oct. 1792 in Kingston, Upper Canada, son of Robert Macaulay* and Ann Kirby*; m. first 23 Oct. 1833, in Montreal, Helen Macpherson (d. 1846), sister of David Lewis Macpherson*, and they had six daughters and one son; m. secondly 1 March 1853, in Kingston, Sarah Phillis Young, and they had one daughter; d. there 10 Aug. 1857.

Young John Macaulay wanted for none of the advantages early Upper Canadian society could offer. His father was a loyalist and one of the earliest merchants at Cataraqui (Kingston). After his father's death in 1800, John and his brothers, William* and Robert, were raised by their mother and uncle, John Kirby*, also one of Kingston's leading merchants. The family seems to have been very close and affectionate. The Macaulays were well-to-do and had

Macaulay

been left a decent inheritance and excellent connections. John's particular legacy, as the eldest son in a social set that believed in the virtues of primogeniture, was the expectations and strictures of his mother. Educated by John Strachan* at his grammar school in Cornwall, Macaulay bore the imprint of these early years for the rest of his life. On one occasion Strachan reminded him, "Every person can make more of being good – the practice of the virtues is in every ones power." In 1808 Ann Macaulay shipped John off to Lower Canada to improve his French. Although his letters to her are not extant, he was obviously unhappy and wished to return. His mother, however, was unwilling to indulge him and she upbraided the serious youth for being "whimsical and unsteady," cautioning him not "to misapply your time that ought to be spent in study to fit you for the commerce of the world."

One historian has suggested that Macaulay intended a career in law, like his school chums Archibald McLean*, Jonas Jones*, and John Beverley Robinson*. If true, it was not to be. By 1812 he had set up shop in Kingston as a general merchant and the following year was one of the 14 merchants who established, for the purpose of issuing bills in exchange for specie, the Kingston Association, the first, albeit rudimentary, bank in Upper Canada [see Joseph Forsyth*]. Macaulay became deputy postmaster at Kingston in 1815 and acted, as well, as ticket agent for the Kingston Amateur Theatre, agent for the Saint-Maurice ironworks, subscription agent for the *New York Herald*, land agent, and, in 1822, vice-president of the Kingston Savings Bank. Although little is known about the scope of his mercantile operations, he prospered; in 1834 Lieutenant Governor Sir John Colborne* described him as "opulent." He was, primarily, a man of business until his entry into the bruising world of public politics and civil administration in 1836. Unlike his compatriots, Macaulay was a late comer to this arena, although it was not for the want of urging. In 1824 Robinson had tried to ginger him up, "You are one of the *regularly bred*, and You owe the State some service." Temperamentally Macaulay was unsuited to the rough-and-tumble fray of electoral politics and he knew it. He had no ambition – or, more correctly perhaps, no liking – for such public exposure. But if his sense of his political role was circumscribed by that predisposition, it channelled him into other, and as important, activities.

Macaulay shared the conventional wisdom of the Upper Canadian élite on politics and society. Although there were periodic disagreements among them, there was consensus on the fundamentals. Macaulay was first drawn into political battle in reaction to Robert Gourlay*'s accusations of abuses by government and his calls for reform. In a letter published in Stephen Miles*'s *Kingston Gazette* during the summer of 1818, Macaulay expressed alarm at Gourlay's "novel and alarming steps" – the provincial convention and proposed petition to the Prince Regent. In most respects, the letter is undistinguished, simply the commonplace utterances of counter-revolutionary toryism reacting to a "visionary reformer" and the "wild schemes of turbulent and factious men." Naturally enough, Macaulay urged redress "in a regular and safe way" and preservation of the British constitution "in all its purity." More important than his tory waxings was the image he drew of Upper Canada as a cornucopia of nature's riches. Whether a full-scale myth or simply a metaphor for the province's prosperity and potential, Macaulay's statement that Upper Canadians were "the most happy people on the face of the globe, possessing a fertile country, which smiles like Eden in her summer dress, and a free Constitution of Government," gave symbolic utterance to an inchoate and unlimited faith in the bounty of the province. Farming, development, and prosperity were cardinal articles of the élite's tory faith. To be sure, it was a naïve belief, especially in one who could without trouble stub his toe on the outcrops of Laurentian granite north of Kingston. Indeed, reproach was not long in coming. Common Sense, most probably a pseudonym of Barnabas Bidwell*, derided Macaulay in the *Kingston Gazette* in July 1818 for his defence of a hierarchical society in which the "industrious poor" were bent under the yoke of the "rich and the affluent," and he hooted at Macaulay's image of the landscape, which was, in fact, a "teeming land choked with rank and poisonous weeds, and your oozy swamps."

The Gourlay agitation had a marked effect on Macaulay and not solely because of the Scot's charges of illegality in the running of the post office at Kingston. Gourlay's impact had demonstrated the potential of the press for fuelling, and confronting, extra-parliamentary agitation [see Bartemas Ferguson*]. Early in December 1818 Macaulay and Alexander Pringle purchased the *Kingston Gazette*, renamed it, and published the first issue of the *Kingston Chronicle* on 1 Jan. 1819. The newspaper brought Macaulay to the forefront of the provincial stage, in part by his publication of a torrent of letters from Strachan, Robinson, George Herchmer Markland*, and Christopher Alexander Hagerman* on a host of local and provincial issues. Macaulay, however, was no one's cipher. At the outset of his editorship he rebuffed Strachan's proffered pieces on land granting, the first evidence of a resolute, if at times quirkish, independence. On this occasion, Strachan recovered his poise and seduously fostered his former student by counsel and ministrations. Even so, further disagreements were in the offing. Macau-

514

Macaulay

lay had little use for the infamous Sedition Act of 1818 and the manner in which it was used against Gourlay, though he later took a harder line on the Scot.

The *Chronicle* was ostensibly an independent press – independence was the chief virtue of the politics of pre-industrial society regardless of political leanings. The journal soon became, as Robinson put it, a paper that gave the "highest satisfaction to every well-wisher of *Church & State*." It was the first so-called administration paper, Robert Stanton*'s *U.E. Loyalist* and Thomas Dalton*'s *Patriot* being later examples. Macaulay's paper lacked the rabble-rousing quality of the latter, which sought to popularize toryism and give it roots in the urban lower classes. But the particular interest of the *Chronicle* is not simply that it was the first. Macaulay had close ties to Robinson and Strachan – the rising stars in the administration of Lieutenant Governor Sir Peregrine MAITLAND – and by late 1820 Strachan, then a legislative and executive councillor, had mentioned the importance of the paper to the governor. Maitland was suitably impressed and felt it could be used for the publication of government accounts and advertisements. This favourable impression gave Macaulay direct access to the office of the lieutenant governor through his secretary, Major George Hillier*. By early 1821 Hillier was a conduit for the administration's views on any number of issues of provincial or local importance. He would, for instance, report to Macaulay on parliamentary activities "from time to time in this loose way" and leave it for him to "dish up for the public according to your own taste."

Privy to the confidential information of the small coterie of advisers to Maitland, Macaulay became the administration's advocate. Although he had no use for the public world, he soon became what historian Sydney Francis Wise has called a "back room boy." Publicly he decried the factionalism of politics yet he could be as partisan and manipulative as the men he inveighed against. During the election of 1820, for instance, Strachan was "much gratified" with Macaulay's squibs against Barnabas Bidwell, whose possible election in Lennox and Addington would be "a disgrace to the Province." Bidwell lost the election but was returned at a by-election on 10 Nov. 1821. Eight days later in a letter to Macaulay, Robinson suggested a petition against Bidwell. "I will say further," the attorney general noted, "that if you have reason to believe, as I firmly do that the old Vagabond has solemnly sworn to renounce fore all allegiance to the King of Great Britain & that proof can be obtained of it I will go your halves in the expence of procuring a certificate of it properly authenticated, but this is of course as Judge [D'Arcy Boulton*] says sub rosa." Macaulay must have worked quickly. Parliament met on 21 November and the following day Robinson moved for leave to bring up the petition of 126 freeholders of Lennox and Addington protesting Bidwell's election on moral and legal grounds. Macaulay had, in fact, sent an employee to Massachusetts to get the documents suggested by Robinson. The costs were shared by Macaulay, Robinson, Strachan, Hagerman, and Markland.

Bidwell was expelled from the assembly in January 1822 by the slimmest of majorities. In the *Chronicle* Macaulay was aghast that "this grand triumph of the cause of correct principle and sound morals" had not attracted greater support in the assembly. Almost a year earlier Robinson had warned him to be "cautious not to speak too freely of the motions or proceedings of the House in yr. Editorial Articles." Robert Nichol* moved a resolution condemning his editorial of 11 Jan. 1822 as a "malicious libel, and a breach of the privileges of this House." It was carried with only Hagerman, then an assemblyman for Kingston, in dissent. Hillier reassured Macaulay that there was nothing to fear from the resolution and the issue was held over until January 1823. Hagerman, however, withheld Macaulay's response to the speaker, explaining in February of that year, "I did not admire your style, it was more in justification than in excuse of your conduct and was therefore scarcely to be received as an apology." After a resolution had been passed to the effect that the house had asserted its privilege and the author acknowledged his impropriety, Hagerman secured an indefinite adjournment of the debate.

To the tory mind, order was essential to the tranquillity and security of society and that order had its foundation in a hierarchical social structure, a belief which Macaulay articulated in a series of editorials in the *Chronicle* between 1819 and 1822. The "enemies of tranquility and good order" – restless agitators such as Gourlay or suspected democrats such as Bidwell – had brought Macaulay into the political fray with much force. In an early editorial he defended the relationship between natural inequality and political inequality; in short, he upheld the primacy of the rule of gentlemen. An unapologetic élitist, he quoted Blackstone's amazement that only in "the science of legislation the noblest and most difficult of any" was "some method of instruction . . . not looked upon as requisite." The prime example of such folly was the United States, where, Macaulay believed, "even the common street beggar thinks himself qualified to give gratuitous opinions, on the science of legislation, though his abilities and judgment have been totally inadequate to the task of devising 'ways and means' for keeping himself from rags and starvation." Turbulence was natural to any society but organized agitation was essentially seditious and the work of unbalanced or disturbed minds. Casting a glance at Europe and the apparent widespread "love

515

Macaulay

for a constitutional government," he wished success where it could be gratified by "the blessings of rational liberty," but he feared the desire was "mixed up in many instances, [with] a spirit of Jacobinism or Radicalism, a sort of wild theory which can never be reduced to practice." In contrast, the balanced or mixed constitution of Great Britain hallowed rational liberty. But the key to its preservation was balance. Democracy, not monarchy or aristocracy, threatened Upper Canada and Macaulay had "no particular penchant" for it, even in its "most alluring shape." He was particularly alarmed by the tendency evident in some of the American states to push the elective principle to extremes and was chary of a constitution that allowed "all men except perfect vagrants and mendicants and slaves" to vote. Democracy meant that "the interests of the public are often sacrificed to the furtherance of private interests – and that there is too great a temptation for men in official situations, to profit by the passing opportunity of grasping at the publican loaves & fishes, of thus paying due respect to that venerable maxim which suggests the wisdom of making Hay while the sun shines."

Macaulay's defence of the balanced constitution was real inasmuch as he upheld the independence of each of its constituent parts, including the House of Assembly. He disapproved, for instance, of a suggestion to introduce executive councillors into that body as an "impolitic, unwise & odious innovation on the Constitution." He was concerned "that the democratical principles of our neighbours are making large inroads on the purer democratical principles of our constitution – & that consequently . . . the influence of the crown has diminished & is diminishing [and] it ought to be increased." Rejecting Jonas Jones's tag of "a *High Monarchy* man," he admitted to "being a little *aristocratical* in sentiment." He favoured longer parliaments (hence fewer elections) and a much higher property qualification for voters. "I take it as an axiom that no man in this country who is worth less than £500, is fit, to make laws, or to be trusted with a power of meddling with the Laws fixing the rights of property."

More important than Macaulay's defence of a balanced constitution was his use of the *Chronicle* as an organ for popularizing the idea, which had been taking shape in the Canadas since the 1790s, of economic improvement and development. The late 1810s ushered in economic depression, extraordinary concern over the commercial impact of a canal system in New York State, and the discontent of the Gourlay episode. These developments cohered in Macaulay's mind. As a merchant and resident of Kingston, which was more intimately connected to the Laurentian trade than York (Toronto), he had a more practical grasp of the mechanics of the Upper Canadian economy than a Strachan or a Robinson. He was the first to sense and

then to articulate the imperative of wedding prosperity to the constitution, and the relation of both to a contented polity. Here was a particularly British North American faith, a combination of British conservatism and American technology, first expounded in Upper Canada by Lieutenant Governor John Graves Simcoe* and given quintessential expression in Nova Scotia in Thomas Chandler Haliburton*'s Sam Slick novels. In the shadows of depression and discontent, Macaulay and his friends, particularly Strachan and Robinson, put forward, in a somewhat desultory fashion, a strategy for provincial economic development which became increasingly identified with the governing tory élite and which it quickly shaped into a legislative priority of first importance.

The underlying assumptions were straightforward. Upper Canada's economic character was fundamentally and immutably agricultural. Upon the province had been bestowed the rich bounty of providential dispensation; men had but to turn their hands to cultivation to reap prosperity. Macaulay and his set loathed what Macaulay called the "lonely forest and dreary wilderness," which indicated the absence, rather than the presence, of civilization. Viewing society as organic, he could despair of antagonisms between its various orders and argue that its fundamental harmony could be improved by agricultural societies. These, he believed, would not only introduce and promote new agricultural methods among farmers but would excite a "spirit of emulation and enterprise" among them and demonstrate "how far their interest is connected with that of commerce, & how much depends upon them for promoting the general prosperity of this new country and their own advantage at the same time."

The basic strategy for development was to link the agricultural regions bordering lakes Erie and Ontario to markets in Great Britain. The major obstacles were Niagara Falls and the rapids of the St Lawrence River. Thus, the chief requirement was canals connecting Prescott to Montreal and linking the two lakes, thereby opening up the province's economy. Much is made by historians of the anti-American impulses behind the toryism of Upper Canada, but men such as Macaulay were awed by American achievement, especially in the field of canal building. In his editorial of 29 Jan. 1819 he praised New York governor DeWitt Clinton for his remarks on the "grand internal improvements" of his state and hoped parliament would "make some efforts towards accomplishing the projected improvements on the navigation of the St. Lawrence."

In a series of long letters on internal improvement published in the *Chronicle* in March 1819 (probably written by Strachan), the drum beating for economic development began in earnest. The letters suggested an innovative and positive role for the press as promoter of improvement rather than harbinger of discontent. Later in the year a discursive essay on the "happy art of anticipation," attributed to Robinson, defined the progressive, commercial nature of American civilization. The Yankees regulated "all their schemes and plans, not according to what is, but to what they hope and suppose will be." Here was the path for Upper Canada. Heretofore "great designs and brilliant specifications" only elicited ill favour from the populace in a colony that offered "fair scope" for anticipation. "Those who venture to shew a little public spirit and rational enterprise, will assuredly not be disappointed in the result of what they undertake."

In editorial after editorial, Macaulay returned to this theme, offering a host of suggestions and policies on topics such as canals, imperial duties, manufacturing, farming, banking, provincial tariffs, and regulations on trade. Within the framework of tory assumptions, he put forward, in collaboration with his friends, a positive role for government in fostering prosperity by means of important public works and complementary statutes. The depression was only temporary and Macaulay, following the analysis of Clinton, looked to "the enterprising spirit of the country" supported by the provincial treasury for a quick and sustained recovery. A comprehensive program of internal public works – canals mainly – would provide the fundamental framework. The economy was essentially agricultural, but it must be diversified, the range of native manufactures increased, and the dependence on imports reduced. Such independence from the American republic was necessary for the prosperity so keenly sought.

In 1818 a joint Upper and Lower Canadian committee had recommended the construction of canals on the St Lawrence equal in size to those in New York State. Progress was slow, however, and Macaulay lamented the delays in completing the Lachine Canal, begun in 1821, "the want of which is so much felt by every person whose produce descends to the Montreal market." In 1821 the Upper Canadian assembly took a major, albeit fledgling, step to come to grips with the province's economic destiny when it formed a select committee to examine the agricultural depression and the collapse of British markets. The resulting report, probably the production of the committee's brilliant and mercurial chairman, Robert Nichol, provided a framework for economic development which would last a generation: the linking of agriculture, imperial markets, and canals. Yet although it set the strategy for the province in motion, its tone was less than hopeful in view of the "limited power and deficiency of pecuniary means of the Provincial Legislature, [which] almost preclude the possibility of legislating on the subject." Recommendations on the specifics of canals, the report stated, should be the purview of a commission on the improvement of internal navigation. An act providing for such a body was approved on 13 April 1821. It was an auspicious moment in provincial history. Maitland, in his remarks at the closing of parliament the next day, called it "the commencement of an important undertaking eminently calculated to advance the prosperity and greatness of Upper Canada." It was exactly this newly developed sense of economic possibilities and an increasingly interventionist government that provided an outlet for Macaulay's now evident abilities.

Within the limited political circles of Upper Canada, Macaulay quickly gained, and would long retain, a reputation as an authority on the economy and public improvement. In early December 1822 Strachan, a director of the newly established Bank of Upper Canada, offered him the job of agent at Kingston. He doubted whether it would be "wise to continue Your Paper" but stated, "We have so much confidence in you that we shall part with you with the greatest reluctance." Strachan took it "for granted" that his former student would accept and proceeded a week later to offer him another plum, the post of secretary to James Baby*, who had been appointed an arbitrator for the division of customs duties between Upper and Lower Canada. A gentleman of charm and affability, Baby was, according to Strachan, "rather slow of apprehension and will proceed entirely by your superior intelligence as you will communicate it in that modest unobtrusive manner which will still leave him in his place." Strachan urged him to accept the position, as "I have not seen a chance of bringing you forward in so honourable a way since I had any thing to say in the Govt. nor will such an opportunity soon offer again." Macaulay accepted both positions and at the end of 1822 gave up the editorship of the *Chronicle*, although he almost certainly retained a proprietary interest in it for a few more years.

Macaulay early showed a disinclination to remain a merchant. He yearned for independence and probably for the security of a fixed income. The bank agency would help but he had also sought the rumoured appointment of deputy postmaster general for Upper Canada. In March 1823, however, Strachan warned him that William ALLAN, the bank's president, had reportedly lost his fortune and "if Allans loss be what it is conjectured you are better off than he is." Meanwhile Macaulay offered his resignation as agent of the bank over a row with its head cashier, Thomas Gibbs Ridout*. Strachan intervened to mollify him, reminding him that a permanent office might soon be set up in Kingston and he would become cashier there. Allan offered the full backing of the directors; Macaulay withdrew his resignation. The support for Macaulay was not simply an act of favouritism. The young Kingstonian had enormous ability and both Hillier and Strachan intended to make full use of it.

Macaulay

Macaulay's work on customs arbitration, which lasted until the summer of 1823 and possibly later, was vital in the short term. His report to Maitland on the matter drew praise all round; Strachan pronounced it "simple clear and modest." A fervid advocate of union with Lower Canada as the cure for the upper province's financial ills, Macaulay did not think the Canada Trade Act of 1822 went far enough in expanding Upper Canada's jurisdiction in matters of revenue sharing with Lower Canada and economic development. Still, his report settled the issue of arrearages and established, for purposes of arbitration under the act, a new formula for revenue sharing.

Macaulay's work for the commission on internal navigation, to which he had been appointed in the spring of 1821, had a far greater impact on provincial policy. Ever concerned about propriety, Macaulay wondered about potential conflict with his work on the arbitration. Both Strachan and Hillier, who was "quite anxious" on the matter, assured him the two positions could be reconciled "very easily." By September, Macaulay had become president of the commission and hence directed its work. Its various reports, the first of which was published in 1823, were submitted in 1825 to a joint committee on internal navigation, co-chaired by Strachan and Robinson. It published all the reports a year later. The joint committee accepted them "as containing the best, and in truth, the only satisfactory information" as to the means of improving internal navigation and of establishing parliamentary priorities on which canals to proceed with and on what scale.

In the last issue of the *Chronicle* edited by Macaulay, on 27 Dec. 1822, he had reviewed favourably "the manifest improvements effected in the internal condition of Provincial affairs with the last four years," but found scant cause for celebration when he compared Canadian progress to public works under way in New York. In 1825 he marvelled at the change that had taken place in popular attitudes, a transformation that owed much to the efforts of Strachan, Robinson, and especially Macaulay. Surveying the past seven or eight years he pronounced in the commission's report that "within this short period . . . is to be dated the happy nativity of that spirit of public enterprise, which . . . is destined to guide and quicken our march in the highway of prosperity." Major concern about the ability of the province to finance large-scale public works disappeared, for a decade at least, after Nichol's death in 1824. Robinson, who later claimed "the *glory* of laying the foundation of our public debt," had broken the psychological limits with his 1821 bill providing for the deficit financing of arrearages in militia pensions. The province consequently backed into deficit financing and the use of debentures but, once adopted, they were allotted almost exclusively to the advantage of public works, particularly canals. A concrete manifestation of this change came in 1826–27 when the province lent £75,000 to the Welland Canal Company [*see* William Hamilton Merritt*]. A few years later the faith in canals became a mania. The man primarily responsible for the development of this climate of opinion was John Macaulay.

His influence, now that his newspaper was in the background, stemmed from his counsel on local and provincial matters, his proven capability and intelligence in handling committees and preparing reports, and his participation in local institutions. Hillier, for instance, often consulted him on matters such as the appointment of coroners and sought his aid in placing certain items in the *Chronicle*. Locally Macaulay was associated with a host of lay, benevolent, and religious organizations. He was, as well, a steward for the Kingston races, a trustee of the Midland District Grammar School, a leading magistrate and chairman for many years of the district's Court of Quarter Sessions, president of the mechanics' institute, a member of the building committee and later warden of St George's Church, and an officer in the local militia. His pursuits were all in addition to his business, the bank, the post office, and his work for the government. Moreover, Macaulay generally attended meetings regularly, participated actively, and offered clear, simple, and constructive suggestions.

In 1828 he suffered a bitter disappointment. The collectorship of customs at Kingston became vacant upon Hagerman's temporary elevation to the Court of King's Bench. That summer Macaulay anxiously solicited the appointment through Hillier, Robinson, and Strachan. He wrote to Robinson: "I have fagged for years in editing a paper – the only one which defended the administration at the time, & though I had great trouble, I had not profit – and on every occasion I have endeavoured to make myself useful – not particularly . . . from any idea of *reward*, for that I never did think of . . . as from a feeling that I was acting rightly. . . . The place in question peculiarly comports with my situation & views. . . . It is the only one I care about – My ambition rises no higher[.] If I am disappointed, it is for the life – and the mortification will be severe." It was. The new lieutenant governor, Sir John Colborne, gave the job to Thomas Kirkpatrick* and, more important, Robinson had been unable, for complicated but proper reasons, to support Macaulay's application. Robinson had reminded his friend of the burden "of being thought able to render services to my friends which are in truth beyond my power." Strachan pointed out to Macaulay in December 1828 that the reasons for his rejection had their origins in Maitland's administration: "Nothing could be worse in taste and heart than Sir P. or rather Perhaps Col Hilliers conduct for the last year in the way of appointment." Though

Maitland, in a letter to Colborne in March 1830, would describe Macaulay as "a gentleman . . . [of] superior talents and information . . . capable of rendering to the Province services of the highest order, and whose claims . . . I should . . . certainly have considered as irresistible," it was clear that a misunderstanding of Maitland's intentions had transpired.

In the aftermath of the political crisis wrought by the imbroglio surrounding Judge John Walpole Willis* and the election of radicals to the tenth parliament (1829–30), Macaulay became increasingly disgusted with politics. His friends wanted him at York and in one of the councils. Early in 1830 Hagerman, a favourite of Colborne, discussed with him Macaulay's elevation to the Legislative Council. In 1831 Colborne appointed 13 men to the council including Zacheus BURNHAM and James CROOKS. Strachan, who quickly fell from favour in Colborne's administration, reported to Macaulay that many people commented that he "would have been worth them all." Through the early 1830s Macaulay was dispirited yet entranced by the political trends of society in Europe, Great Britain, and the Canadas. He was certain that what seemed to be movements to separate religion and education, church and state, had proven that "infidel and democratic ideas are in unison and are spreading far & wide." Early in 1832 Strachan and Macaulay discussed the usefulness of sending a representative to England to discuss with authorities there the problems of the colony. Strachan judged him "better fitted" to perform the task than Robinson, Hagerman, or Jones; "the truth is you are the very best political writer in the Province," the archdeacon confided to Macaulay. In fact Strachan considered Hagerman and Jones unable to handle such a task satisfactorily either "singly or combined." Hagerman and Colborne discussed the council's composition again in April 1832 and the lieutenant governor stated his intention to recommend Macaulay before leaving office. Although the recommendation was not immediately forthcoming, Colborne had, nevertheless, changed his mind on the usefulness of Maitland's old advisers, at least Robinson and Macaulay. Returning to the public harness, Macaulay in December 1833 wrote to his wife that he had handed in reports on a lighthouse, the provincial penitentiary, and the Welland Canal, and was working on two more, a major report for the St Lawrence canals commission and one on the northern section of the boundary between Upper and Lower Canada. As well, he was assisting in the revision of the province's road laws.

By the mid 1830s the political temper of the province had changed considerably from that of a decade earlier. Macaulay had changed too. His ambition was no longer confined to Kingston. To accept high office entailed moving to Toronto and up

to this point in time he had been unwilling to do that, probably out of personal reserve and his close attachment to his mother and uncle. What had changed? First, he was now married with a family, who could and would accompany him. Secondly, he was keenly aware of Kingston's economic decline. His once breezy confidence in his beloved town's future was being eroded by the slow development of its hinterland and by the town's loss of commercial leadership to Toronto. Late in 1834 Macaulay had taken the lead in suggesting manufacturing as the basis for a prosperous municipal future, but he was all too aware that the possibilities were bleak. Finally, it is probable that the cholera epidemic of 1834 had brought home the vulnerability of human life. In short, he was by 1835 ready to make a change, unthinkable a decade earlier.

The move to Toronto took place in two steps. The first was Macaulay's appointment to the Legislative Council, which was announced in May 1835. The possibility of the surveyor generalship was mentioned indirectly but nothing happened initially. There were rumours that Macaulay might not take his seat "in Consequence of the Directors [of the Bank of Upper Canada] being against your absence from the office," but this obstacle was quickly scotched by William Proudfoot*, the bank's president. On 3 Oct. 1836 Macaulay was offered the surveyor generalship with a salary of £600 and a small fee schedule; he was, almost simultaneously, nominated a customs arbitrator for the province. Three days later he accepted both positions. Like others, including friends such as Robert Stanton, Macaulay was "never . . . more taken by surprise than on this occasion." To William Allan he explained that he was not an office hunter. He had no need of employment and would not gain financially by the move. Indeed, his major concern was financial loss. His present income was £650 to £700 and "I occupy my own House in a town where domestic expenses, are far more moderate." It would be a "trial" being separated from his home, family, and town. Still, political affairs had changed with the election of 1836, which produced a tory majority [see Sir Francis Bond Head*], and the "King's Service should always be looked up to as an Honourable Service, and be the object of proper ambition with all."

Macaulay set off immediately to take up his new duties. In spite of a demanding work schedule, to say nothing of finding permanent accommodation for his family, Macaulay was homesick. He had a busy social calendar, which he found somewhat tedious, but was buoyed up at discovering his income would be about £800. The state of affairs at the surveyor general's office was chaotic [see Samuel Proudfoot HURD] and he predicted it would "require my steady attendance during office Hours & some labour for many months to see arrears of work brought up & the office placed in

Macaulay

an efficient state." Indeed the magnitude of the problems was such that they interfered "much with my Legislative Duties. . . . I find that my life will be devoted to the remedying of the injuries inflicted on individuals by the careless work of the early Surveyors." A typical day when parliament was in session saw Macaulay rise before 8 o'clock, get to the office by 10, work till 3, go to the council chamber until adjournment, return to quarters about 5:30, then dine, write, and read until retiring between 11 and 12. He disliked the round of parties and entertainment that marked the gentle life of the capital; on some occasions he was not invited.

In March 1837 the Bank of Upper Canada wanted to know whether he would resign his cashiership at Kingston. He had put off making a decision on permanent residence in Toronto while awaiting confirmation of his surveyor generalship from London. Although his salary was greater, he discovered living expenses were higher in Toronto and his duties there were "far more responsible" than he had expected. The exigencies of the surveyor generalship, such as the need to supervise his six clerks constantly, made it "a disagreeable office" and his inability to take leave when he wanted to amounted to "gilded slavery." Both his mother and his uncle urged him to return to Kingston. None the less, he could not make up his mind and remained "in a state of great doubt and perplexity." A superb administrator and councillor, Macaulay found "on the other hand I am not cut out for a Courtier, & do not like attending at levees – or being liable to the intrigues & jealousies of a Provincial Metropolis." He remarked to his wife, "A *Medium* elevation we shall prefer to the tip *top* rank as well for comfort, as interest." He remained close, however, to Robinson, Hagerman, and Markland, but "several of the great men here have never called on me! . . . others are all *frigid*." By April he had decided to remain for the present, "I find every one recommends it." He was beginning "to take a fancy to the Employment & will probably in time *like* it." The surveyor generalship was nevertheless "a *sadness* & requires a thorough Reform." He hoped to set it right within a year or two, but it is not known if he ever achieved any administrative reform. Towards the end of April 1837 Macaulay decided to stay in Toronto. Even his mother had conceded that he could not give up his post with honour. At the end of the month he returned to Kingston and resigned his office with the bank. Committed to the administration, Macaulay was quickly burdened with more work. On 25 May he was named, along with John Solomon Cartwright* and Frederick Henry Baddeley*, to carry out the provisions of an 1836 statute to survey the country between the Ottawa River and Lake Huron.

During the summer of 1837 Macaulay was preoccupied with parliamentary affairs, particularly

Head's refusal to allow banks to suspend specie payments in response to the international commercial crisis of 1836–37. He was also discovering the "great expence" attendant upon living the gentle life. He gave up an "extensive and aristocratical premises" rented from John Henry DUNN for a "snug" brick house on College Avenue. In order to preclude suspicion that he had used his "office to my own advantage," he sold off, at a premium, land he had purchased on speculation. Finally, in mid September, he received confirmation of his appointment as surveyor general. Through the fall he busied himself with decorating and furnishing the family home. After almost a year of "bustle and discomfort, and expence" he looked forward to a respite. The political horizon, however, looked stormy and he confided to his mother that unless conservatism gained ground in England, "our general political prospects will become gloomy." What worried him was radicalism in Lower Canada. The only hope was to act decisively, annex Montreal to the upper province and the Gaspé to New Brunswick, and leave the French with a military governor and a council to make laws. The effect would be to "render Canada quite English at last."

Macaulay never expected an armed uprising in Upper Canada. When it came in December 1837 [*see* William Lyon Mackenzie*] he considered it "a worse than Catalinian rebellion." Its defeat was a narrow "escape from frightful miseries." In the immediate post-rebellion period he expected "great changes in the Government of these colonies." By this time too his unqualified faith in deficit financing and public debt had been transformed. He discerned "the elements of a new sort of opposition" in the assembly and, like William Allan, feared the government's "heedless" practices in money matters. A particular and prescient apprehension was his observation that "great political discontent will result from this heavy debt." The future was "uncertain" and the province "can never return to our former state of security & repose." He saw the debt driving the province straight into union with Lower Canada, an end which he now deplored.

Macaulay applauded the initial actions taken by Head's successor, Sir George ARTHUR, particularly the execution of Samuel Lount* and Peter Matthews* in April 1838. Arthur had retained Head's secretary, John JOSEPH, but felt the need for a new appointment. In May he broached the subject with Macaulay, who was reluctant. Meanwhile, George Herchmer Markland's hold on the inspector generalship was, as Robinson put it, "shaking in the wind," and Robinson urged Arthur to appoint Macaulay, the "best man" in the province, to that office. On 16 June, Macaulay was gazetted as Arthur's civil and private secretary, with Robert Baldwin SULLIVAN succeeding him as surveyor general. In spite of Markland's strong rearguard action to absolve himself, his homosexual activity brought him down. He resigned on 30 September and Macaulay acceded to the inspector generalship the next day. He was secretary for a year, the most able and powerful secretary since George Hillier. It is difficult to assess the extent of Macaulay's influence. What is certain is that he brought order and organization to the office, kept Arthur thoroughly briefed on all aspects of the administration, and may have given him the idea to initiate a parliamentary investigation in 1839 into the state of government offices.

Macaulay had "great dread" of the consequences of the much-touted remedies for the Canadian crisis – union and responsible government. None the less, he voted with the majority in the Legislative Council in favour of union on 12 Dec. 1839. There had always been a quirkish bent to his actions; his reasoning seemed odd to friends such as Robinson. With far less experience in government administration, Macaulay believed it "my duty to give up my own opinions, & do all in my power to forward the views of the Government whose Servant I am" – a view which contrasted sharply with Arthur's statement that crown officers in Upper Canada "were left by the Government at liberty to act as they pleased, in their Legislative Capacity." The age of gentleman administrators was over; Governor Charles Edward Poulett Thomson*, later Lord Sydenham, would bring them to heel if necessary, as he had Hagerman, and Macaulay knew it. His decision caused a rupture with Strachan, who thought "such a principle carried out would justify the Servants of Queen Mary in condemning Ridley Latimer Cranmer &c to the stake." One by one the boyhood friends who had been so close to power since the War of 1812 were deprived of their political influence. Jones, McLean, and Hagerman joined Robinson on the bench; only Macaulay retained office. Sydenham had understood the position of inspector general would evolve into that of "a kind of Finance Minister" and judged Macaulay to have "first claim to it, as well as from his Character . . . as a Man of business." But because of the new stipulation that ministers must have seats in the assembly, Macaulay resigned the post in June 1842, not wishing "to attempt to play a part for which neither art nor nature has qualified me." He retained his seat on the Legislative Council, however, until his death.

During the last months of Arthur's administration, in early 1841, Macaulay had prepared for his return to Kingston, the new seat of government, and eventually to private life. By January 1842 Arthur had forwarded Macaulay's last official report, a massive general report on Canada, to London and wrote concerning his future employment. Macaulay hoped at least for a pension following his resignation that June but was humiliated by Sir Charles Bagot*'s offer in August of the shrievalty of the Midland District. He continued to press his claim for some years and was finally rewarded with the collectorship of customs at Kingston on 31 Dec. 1845. A stipulation was added that he give up his seat on the council. Macaulay refused and resigned the customs office the following May.

Macaulay was independently wealthy and spent the remainder of his years superintending a large portfolio of investments and speculating in land. He was an agent for several companies and, for a few years in the 1840s, was president of the Commercial Bank of the Midland District. In spite of the comparative ease of his public life, his domestic life was a series of tragedies. His first wife was a carrier of tuberculosis. During the 1840s Macaulay lost his infant triplets, his wife, his daughter Naomi Helen, his uncle, and his mother. Early in 1852 he received a telegram from his eldest daughter's finishing-school in England asking him to take her home. Ann was too ill to stand the voyage back. The distraught father took a suite of rooms and watched his beloved daughter die. During this period he kept a diary which provides the only real glimpse of the repressed emotionalism that was John Macaulay's. This kind and loving man, once scolded by his mother for spoiling his daughter, sat at her bedside talking and reading the Bible to her. This man, so deeply conscious of propriety, could only find relief by running in the streets while she slept, until he dropped from exhaustion. Macaulay was sustained, although his spirit was blasted, by an unfaltering faith that "God will be the strength of my heart and my portion forever." The following year he married the daughter of Lieutenant-Colonel Plomer Young*, assistant adjutant general of the Kingston garrison. In October 1855 Macaulay suffered a stroke. Two years later he died in Kingston.

Macaulay's name rarely, if ever, appeared in the reform critiques of the so-called "family compact." Because he shunned the electoral world, he never acquired the prominence of Robinson, Hagerman, or Jones; because he avoided the councils for so many years, he lacked the profile of a Strachan or a Markland. Not a permanent resident in Toronto and not given to ostentatious living, he could not be compared to a Henry John Boulton* or Samuel Peters JARVIS. Indeed, men such as William Allan, who lacked Macaulay's political clout and presided over less important institutions, have been considered by most historians to be much more important. But Macaulay probably ranks close to Robinson and Strachan and certainly surpassed the others in terms of his ability. Possessed of an agile, analytical mind, a clear writing style, a genius for organization and administration, a conscientious temperament, and a capacity for hard work, he was an indispensable figure

Macaulay

who forged and popularized many of the key, and enduring, policies of successive administrations from Maitland to Arthur. His early and longstanding concern with the development of a provincial strategy for economic prosperity was an embodiment of the consensus that underlay the political, social, religious, national, and geographical solitudes of Upper Canada.

ROBERT LOCHIEL FRASER

[The major source of information on John Macaulay is the collection of his papers held in AO, MS 78. The Macaulay papers held at the QUA relate mainly to his business affairs. Other major archival sources include the Upper Canada Sundries (PAC, RG 5, A1); the Colonial Office correspondence (PRO, CO 42); the William Allan papers at the MTL; the Robinson and Strachan papers at the AO (MS 4 and MS 35 respectively); and the records of the Commission for Improving the Navigation of the St Lawrence (PAC, RG 43, CV, 1). Among printed primary sources, the *Arthur papers* (Sanderson), and the *Kingston Gazette* (1810–18), *Kingston Chronicle* (1819–33), and *Chronicle & Gazette* (1833–47), are especially useful.

Macaulay's official reports may be found in the appendices of the *Journal* of the House of Assembly of Upper Canada, the most important of which were also published separately as U.C., Commissioners of internal navigation, *Reports of the commissioners of internal navigation, appointed by His Excellency Sir Peregrine Maitland, K.C.B. &c. &c. &c. in pursuance of an act of the provincial parliament of Upper-Canada passed in the second year of his majesty's reign, entitled, "An act to make provision for the i[m]provment of the internal navigation of this province"* (Kingston, [Ont.], 1826). His statement on Kingston's economic ills was published in pamphlet form as *The address delivered by John Macaulay, esq., to the public meeting convened in Kingston, Dec. 2nd, 1834, to "consider the expediency of ascertaining by a survey of the country between Loughborough Lake and the town, and also between the town and the Rideau Canal, the practicability of establishing water privileges at Kingston"* (Kingston, 1834).

Genealogical and historical information on Macaulay's family is provided in Margaret [Sharp] Angus's article "The Macaulay family of Kingston," *Historic Kingston*, no.5 (1955–56): 3–12. S. F. Wise's seminal article, "John Macaulay: tory for all seasons," in *To preserve & defend: essays on Kingston in the nineteenth century*, ed. G. [J. J.] Tulchinsky (Montreal and London, 1976), 185–202, is a superb analysis and account of Macaulay's Kingston career. My own thesis, "Like Eden in her summer dress: gentry, economy, and society: Upper Canada, 1812–1840" (PHD thesis, Univ. of Toronto, 1979), emphasizes Macaulay's role as a promoter of a provincial strategy for economic development. R.L.F.]

MACAULAY, JOHN SIMCOE, businessman, politician, and militia officer; b. 13 Oct. 1791 in England, eldest child of James Macaulay* and Elizabeth Tuck Hayter; m. 2 July 1825 Anne Gee

Elmsley in Croydon (London); d. 20 Dec. 1855 near Strood, England.

As John Simcoe Macaulay's name indicates, his father, a British army surgeon, enjoyed the patronage of Lieutenant Governor John Graves Simcoe* even before leaving England for Upper Canada in 1792, where he rose in the service to become a deputy inspector general of hospitals. The family settled successively in the administrative centres of Newark (Niagara-on-the-Lake) and York (Toronto). Young Macaulay attended William Cooper*'s elementary school at York and the Reverend John Strachan*'s school at Cornwall before travelling to England about 1805 to enrol in the Royal Military Academy, Woolwich (London). He was commissioned second lieutenant in the Royal Engineers in July 1809, and was promoted second captain in January 1815 and captain in October 1829. During the Napoleonic Wars he served in the Iberian Peninsula between 1810 and 1813 and briefly at Genoa (Italy) in 1814. He was stationed at Gibraltar between 1813 and 1819 when, upon his corps' reduction in size, he was placed on half pay. He subsequently came home to Upper Canada and stayed there until 1821.

Returning to full pay in 1825, he served in Ireland and on the Trigonometrical Survey of England. In December 1827 he became instructor in fieldworks at the Royal Engineers Establishment, Chatham, and 12 months later was appointed professor of fortification at his old college at Woolwich, a post he held until his resignation early in 1835. While there he wrote his own textbook, *A treatise on field fortification*. Despite the book's long life (it reached its sixth edition in 1869) and his claim to have made improvements in the teaching of the subject, his superiors refused the application he made after his resignation for the brevet rank of major. A college commission of inquiry, indeed, recommended reversion to the syllabus on fortifications used before 1829.

Macaulay, his father long dead, settled in Toronto in 1835 to manage his inheritance. Simcoe had granted Dr Macaulay park lot 9 near the provincial capital and Chief Justice John Elmsley* the adjacent lot 10. The Macaulay grant occupied the northwest corner of the busy intersection of Yonge and Lot (Queen) streets. On J. S. Macaulay's marriage to Elmsley's eldest daughter in 1825 the two holdings had been reapportioned, so that Macaulay gained the Lot Street frontage to both lots. A crowded and largely working-class precinct known as Macaulay Town grew on his land behind the lucrative ribbon development where the two high roads intersected, and in the late 1830s Macaulay moved into the subdivision to occupy Elmsley Villa, the former residence of his brother-in-law, John Elmsley*. In 1835 Macaulay bought land in nine scattered townships from John Solomon Cartwright* of Kingston, another brother-in-law, and added other properties across Upper Canada in subsequent years.

In January 1836, a few months after Macaulay's return to Toronto, Sir Francis Bond Head* arrived as lieutenant governor. Four weeks later Head announced his first official appointments: a new Executive Council, of which the reformer Robert BALDWIN was a member, and a new surveyor general, John Simcoe Macaulay, to succeed Samuel Proudfoot HURD. Much real power lay with the surveyor general and his office for they were involved in all decisions whereby public land became private property; colonists therefore cared deeply who the surveyor general might be. Although Head and Macaulay, both royal engineers, had passed through Woolwich only a year apart, the lieutenant governor said in February that he had not met his appointee for at least a quarter century before arriving in Upper Canada. Macaulay qualified not through friendship, Head declared, but through professional experience, his family's standing (Head cited Judge James Buchanan MACAULAY, a brother), and his substantial stake in the province. One other candidate for the position, John Radenhurst, chief clerk in the Surveyor General's Office, was disqualified in Head's opinion because he had used his office to run a private land agency on the side. But Radenhurst also had powerful connections. Through marriage to a daughter of Thomas Ridout*, a former surveyor general, he could claim relationship with a number of prominent Toronto families. A speedily circulated petition, headed by Archdeacon John Strachan and signed by both tories and reformers, urged Radenhurst's case. In the face of such a strong public movement, on 22 February (only two days after his appointment had been gazetted) Macaulay offered to stand down.

The issue did not die; Head would not let it. It was caught up in a broader constitutional crisis, at the centre of which was the collective resignation of the new Executive Council led by Baldwin, on the claim that Head had consistently acted without its advice. Majorities in the Legislative Council and in the House of Assembly deplored, among other matters, Macaulay's candidacy, charging that he was not a bona fide resident of the province because he remained on the army's active list. Reformers added that the appointment was yet another job for the "family compact." Head retorted that his candidate's long absence from Canada freed him from party ties. He advised Macaulay to proffer his resignation directly to Lord Glenelg, the colonial secretary, in the naïve belief that Glenelg would sustain his lieutenant governor and graciously decline to accept it. But to both men's dismay Glenelg did accept it, particularly embarrassing Macaulay who had relinquished his commission in the Royal Engineers so as to qualify for colonial office. John MACAULAY of Kingston became surveyor

general in October 1836 and later that fall John Simcoe Macaulay personally appealed Glenelg's decision in England, but without success.

After William Lyon Mackenzie*'s rebellion in December 1837, Macaulay became commandant of the militia in Toronto, with the rank of colonel. His forthright distaste for democrats, republicans, and Americans could be given full vent. He pressed for pre-emptive sorties into the United States and advised on the fortification of the province, stressing the strategic value of the Welland Canal and of the proposed railway from Toronto to Lake Huron. At the time he was vice-president of the short-lived City of Toronto and Lake Huron Rail Road Company and was a government nominee on the board of the Welland Canal Company. Soon afterwards he became chairman of the canal company, on whose board official nominees formed a majority of three to two, but in 1840 one of the nominees, John WILLSON, switched his vote for chairman to a shareholders' representative, William Hamilton Merritt*, who thus won the position. The new lieutenant governor, Sir George ARTHUR, dismissed Willson but Governor Charles Edward Poulett Thomson* (later Lord Sydenham), seeking support for his government, applauded Merritt's victory and blocked any reversal of the vote. Later the same year Macaulay, a director of the Bank of Upper Canada between 1836 and 1842, unsuccessfully contested its presidency, held by William Proudfoot*.

Arthur had placed Macaulay on the Legislative Council in 1839, as Head had recommended two years earlier, but Sydenham failed to reappoint him to the upper house of the united province in 1841. He stood instead for the Legislative Assembly at that year's general election, contesting the riding of 3rd York, across the Don River from Toronto, where Sydenham's candidate was James Edward Small*. Arthur informed Sydenham that Macaulay was not popular "with any Party" and Small won, after the army had been sent in to ensure his victory. Macaulay was also Small's unsuccessful rival in a by-election in 1842.

In November 1841 Macaulay had entered Toronto City Council as an alderman for St Patrick's Ward, which included Macaulay Town. When council met in January 1842 to choose a mayor, his was the first name proposed. He had been led to believe that his elevation would be unanimous but he was rejected by 15 votes to 5 in favour of Henry SHERWOOD. Humiliated, Macaulay resigned from council after only seven weeks as alderman. At the general election of 1841 Sherwood and George Monro* had been the unsuccessful tory candidates in Toronto; two members of the local compact, Sheriff William Botsford Jarvis* and Clarke Gamble, had been forced by the tory faction which dominated city council to withdraw their names from the provincial contest in favour of

McCarey

Sherwood and Monro. At the Toronto by-election of March 1843 Sherwood was the official candidate. Jarvis and Gamble, however, nominated Macaulay to run against him in this by-election, supposedly as a true-blue tory opposing a trimmer and place-hunter. Some reform leaders leaned towards Macaulay because he would be a less capable opponent in parliament but his backers discouraged such support by stating that he would adhere to the uncompromising tory principles of Sir Francis Bond Head. Macaulay himself was quoted in a newspaper as saying: "I am a straightforward English gentleman and I glory in it." Sherwood won easily.

It was the last of many rebuffs dealt Macaulay by provincial power-brokers. He immediately began selling much of his property in Toronto and within months had realized £21,000 from sales in and around Macaulay Town. By 1845 he had retired across the Atlantic to live the life of a straightforward English gentleman. He revised his *Treatise* several times for re-editions. At Bishop Strachan's request, he came to an agreement at the end of 1845 with the principal purchaser of his Macaulay Town properties for a site to be reserved "in the middle of the Square" on which a church for the poor (Holy Trinity Church) could be built. The remaining portion of his holdings, roughly bounded by today's College, Yonge, and Wellesley streets and by Queen's Park, comprised the grounds of Elmsley Villa, which from 1849 to about 1851 served as the province's vice-regal residence. Macaulay had plans to subdivide the grounds into choice lots for villas, but by 1854 his agent had sold the entire estate to Dr A. M. Clark, who undertook the subdivision.

Macaulay might brood in England over his disappointments in Canada, but he could also look back on the patronage of lieutenant governors Head and Arthur, and particularly on that of his namesake, John Graves Simcoe, whose gifts of land to his father and father-in-law ultimately allowed him to retire wheresoever he chose. Macaulay died of "apoplexy" on 20 Dec. 1855 at his residence, Rede Court, and was survived by his wife, four sons, and four of his five daughters.

BARRIE DYSTER

John Simcoe Macaulay is the author of *A treatise on defilement: containing the problems relating to that subject, with their application to field works: also, the practical methods of defilading field works* (London, 1830); *Description of Chasseloup de Laubat's system of fortification as executed at Alessandria, by an officer of the Corps of Royal Engineers* (London, 1833; 2nd ed., 1851); and *A treatise on field fortification, and other subjects connected with the duties of the field engineer* (London, 1834; 2nd ed., 1847; 3rd ed., 1850; 4th ed., 1856; 5th ed., 1860; 6th ed., 1869).

AO, MS 525, J. S. Macaulay papers; RG 22, ser.155, will of J. B. Macaulay, and codicils; ser.305, Anne Gee Macaulay. Croydon Parish Church (London), Reg. of marriages, 2 July 1825. CTA, RG 1, B, J. S. Macaulay to Mayor [John Powell], 1 March 1838; Macaulay to Mayor [Henry Sherwood], 13 Jan. 1842. GRO (London), Death certificate, J. S. Macaulay, 20 Dec. 1855. Institution of Royal Engineers, Corps Library (Chatham, Eng.), Connolly papers, "Notitia historica of the Corps of Royal Engineers," comp. T. W. J. Connolly (17v.). MTL, William Allan papers, City of Toronto and Lake Huron Rail Road Company papers; Robert Baldwin papers, corr. of H. J. Boulton, Alexander Grant, George Ridout, and J. E. Small to Baldwin, February–March 1843; S. P. Jarvis papers, misc. corr., February 1843; "Memoranda re the crown grants of park lots in the city of Toronto based on the records in the registry office," comp. T. A. Reed (MS, 1926). PAC, RG 1, L3, 342: M12/409; RG 5, A1: 88683–87, 93145–47, 107726–29, 121594–99. PRO, CO 42/429: 243–51, 258; 42/430: 46; 42/431: 96–101; 42/434: 75; 42/435: 129–34; 42/436: 270–71 (mfm. at PAC). *Arthur papers* (Sanderson), 1: 31, 68–69, 125, 236–37, 321, 353, 450–52; 3: 32, 341, 374, 377, 382. G.B., Colonial Office, *Lord Glenelg's despatches to Sir F. B. Head, bart., during his administration of the government of Upper Canada* ... (London, 1839). *Records of the Royal Military Academy, 1741–1892*, ed. H. D. Buchanan-Dunlop (2nd ed., Woolwich, Eng., [1895]). *Town of York, 1793–1815* (Firth), 193, 222; *1815–34* (Firth), lxxxi. U.C., House of Assembly, *Journal*, 1836: 198, 291, 293, 303.

Examiner (Toronto), 3 June 1840; 17 Nov. 1841; 19 Jan., 15, 22 Feb., 1–15 March 1843. *Rochester Gazette* (Rochester, Eng.), 25 Dec. 1855. *Toronto Mirror*, 21 Jan. 1842, 10–24 Feb. 1843. *Toronto Patriot*, 26 Nov. 1841; 14 Jan. 1842; 10, 14 Feb., 2 June 1843. Armstrong, *Handbook of Upper Canadian chronology*, 25, 31, 35. G.B., WO, *Army list*, 1810–35. Canniff, *Medical profession in U.C.*, 480–89. William Dendy, *Lost Toronto* (Toronto, 1978), 148. Middleton, *Municipality of Toronto*, 2: 793. Whitworth Porter *et al.*, *History of the Corps of Royal Engineers* (9v. to date, London and Chatham, 1889– ; vols.1–3 repr. Chatham, 1951–54), 1: 270, 272. Scadding, *Toronto of old* (Armstrong; 1966), 288.

McCAREY, WILLIAM. *See* TUBBEE, OKAH

McCLELLAND. *See* McLELAN

McCORD, WILLIAM KING, lawyer, landowner, justice of the peace, office holder, and judge; b. 14 Dec. 1803 in Dublin, second son of Thomas McCord* and Sarah Solomons (Solomon); m. 24 Feb. 1827, in Montreal, Aurelia Felicite Arnoldi, daughter of Daniel Arnoldi*, and they had two children; d. there 20 Oct. 1858.

William King McCord was born while his mother and father were on a visit to Ireland; his father was already established at Montreal and returned there with his family in 1805. Thomas McCord was a merchant, a police magistrate, and above all a prominent Montreal landowner. He had John Samuel, his eldest son, and William King partly taught by tutors. William stayed in Trois-Rivières in 1816 and

1817, and from 1818 to 1819 he studied at the Petit Séminaire de Montréal. There is no clear trace of his career in the next years, but it is known that he went to Great Britain. He is believed to have studied at Cambridge, because a letter written by John Samuel in 1825 mentions debts that William had contracted for this purpose. Whatever the case, he returned to Lower Canada in 1823 and the following year began legal training in Montreal under John Samuel. He appears then to have had some misgivings about his future. None the less he continued his legal studies at Quebec under William* and John Walker in 1825, finishing them there with Samuel Ussher in 1829. He was called to the bar at Quebec on 7 February of that year.

Little is known of McCord's activity from the time he entered the profession until the rebellion of 1837–38. In 1828 he was apparently living in Saint-Joseph parish, in the village of Les Cèdres, where he began to practise as a lawyer a year later. From then on, he had difficulty with his creditors because he was slow to pay his accounts. In 1830 it seems that he was living at Quebec. After their father's death in 1824, he and John Samuel had inherited his rights to the sub-fief of Nazareth at Montreal, but William had quickly entrusted his interest in this estate to his brother, who acted as his proxy. In 1836 he made another trip to the British Isles.

Some time after his return to Lower Canada, McCord began his career as a magistrate, during the period when the rebellion was being suppressed. He was recommended for the post of commissioner for the summary trial of small causes in 1838, and on 18 May 1839 was appointed stipendiary magistrate in the district of Montreal; as magistrate, he was involved in the arrest of rebels in Sainte-Scholastique parish (at Mirabel). In 1840 he applied for the office of sheriff of a district court, but instead was given commissions as justice of the peace and as police magistrate at Montreal.

McCord continued to have financial problems. In 1843 he was faced with numerous protests and the following year was even prosecuted for a debt. He then decided to sell his rights in the sub-fief of Nazareth, which were purchased for £8,000 on 2 Dec. 1844 by John James Day, a Montreal lawyer. McCord seems to have had no further debts or prosecutions.

Meanwhile, on 25 April 1844, he was appointed a judge of the Circuit Court of the district of Quebec. He held this post until 6 Oct. 1845, when he became inspector and superintendent of police for the city of Quebec. His new duties led him to play a supervisory role in the maintenance of law and order in the Quebec region. In 1846 he was also given the responsibility of organizing the river police, in collaboration with certain directors of the Quebec Board of Trade. In this capacity he seems to have done some travelling; at any rate he obtained permission that year to go to the United States to gather information on police organization there. On 3 Dec. 1845 he had been appointed commissioner for the relief of shipwrecked and destitute seamen, but he resigned on 19 Jan. 1848 because of a difference of opinion with a colleague.

In the mean time, McCord was made a QC on 14 June 1847, a title reconfirmed on 16 Sept. 1848. Then on 30 July 1849 he received a new commission as inspector and superintendent of police for the city of Quebec. Finally, on 25 Nov. 1850 he acceded to the office of judge of the Superior Court of Lower Canada. In addition to his many other pursuits, he had been involved in a number of organizations. A founder of the Literary and Historical Society of Quebec in 1824, he was also a member of the Provincial Grand Lodge of Montreal and William Henry.

William King McCord died on 20 Oct. 1858 in Montreal, at the age of 54. He had been living in Aylmer, in the Ottawa River region. As a sign of respect for him the members of the Montreal and Quebec bars wore mourning for 30 days. His son Thomas was named judge of the Superior Court of Quebec in 1873.

JEAN-CLAUDE ROBERT

ANQ-M, CE1-63, 24 févr. 1827, 30 oct. 1828, 22 oct. 1858; CN1-7, 1er juin 1830, 18 janv. 1832; CN1-134, 28 juill. 1827; CN1-187, 26 juill., 8, 15 août 1843; 18 janv. 1844; 29 janv. 1845; CN1-192, 2 déc. 1844; CN1-332, 28 févr. 1828. ANQ-Q, CN1-188, 7 févr. 1824, 15 nov. 1825; E17/42, nos.3406–20; E17/43, nos.3421–53. McCord Museum, McCord papers. PAC, MG 24, B2; L3, 21; MG 30, D1, 20: 623–24; RG 68, General index, 1651–1841: 13, 627, 645, 679; 1841–67: 134, 137, 311–12, 316–17, 332–33, 346. *Le Journal de Québec*, 2 nov. 1858. *Montreal Transcript*, 22 Oct. 1858. *Le National* (Québec), 23 oct. 1858. *Quebec Gazette*, 22 Oct. 1858. Borthwick, *Hist. and biog. gazetteer*. *The centenary volume of the Literary and Historical Society of Quebec, 1824–1924*, ed. Henry Ievers (Quebec, 1924). Lefebvre, *Le Canada, l'Amérique*. P.-G. Roy, *Les juges de la prov. de Québec*. Elinor Kyte Senior, *British regulars in Montreal: an imperial garrison, 1832–1854* (Montreal, 1981).

McCUTCHEON, PETER. *See* McGILL

MacDHÒMHNAILL 'IC IAIN, IAIN (John MacDonald), also known as **Iain Sealgair,** Gaelic poet; b. 1795 in Lochaber, Scotland, eldest son of Donald MacDonald and Mary MacDonald; m. Mary Forbes; they had no children; d. 1853 in South West Mabou, N.S.

Before John MacDonald left Scotland he was employed as a civil engineer and deerstalker on the estate of an English landlord and acted as a guide or

McDonald

gillie to parties of hunters. According to family tradition he was presented with two valuable shotguns by his appreciative patrons shortly before he departed for Cape Breton in 1834. Here too he developed a reputation for expert marksmanship, and was alleged to be able to snuff out a candle with one shot. It was also said of him that he would never shoot at a stationary quarry but would startle it into action before felling it. His prowess with the gun earned him the designation Iain Sealgair (John the Hunter). It is believed that Hunter's Road near Mabou, which he may have surveyed, is named after him.

A well-educated man, John MacDonald seems to have begun composing Gaelic poetry when he was quite young. He belonged to the Bohuntin branch of the MacDonalds, a sept especially gifted in the composition of Gaelic poetry. The song "Oran a' Chnatain" (Song to the Head Cold) was written in Scotland when the poet was about 20 years old. He was seriously ill at the time and believed himself to be in danger of death. The song later became well known in Cape Breton.

When MacDonald, with his wife, brother Angus, and sister Christie, immigrated to Nova Scotia in 1834, he came on the ship *Seonaid* and landed at Ship Harbour (Port Hawkesbury), Cape Breton. These details along with a brief description of the ocean voyage are found in "Dh'fhàg sinn Albainn na stuc," a poem composed while he was crossing the Atlantic. He lived in Mabou Ridge before settling in South West Mabou.

John MacDonald was keenly disappointed with his new home. His first winter in Mabou, long remembered as "the winter of the big snow," was so difficult that he wanted to return to Scotland. Shortly after his arrival, he expressed his negative reaction in what was to become his most popular song "Oran do dh'America" (Song to America), a poem contrasting his comparatively easy life in the old country with the harsh circumstances confronting him in Nova Scotia. It was sung to the air "As mo chadal cha bheag m' airtneal." One verse runs, in translation:

Alas, Lord, that I turned my back
on my country of my own free will,
thinking that in the new world
not a penny would I need;
rather a right to property, gold, and riches
would be the lot of everyone there.
The true state of affairs was hidden from me,
and my presumption deceived me.

There is no indication that the poet ever suffered actual poverty. In fact, local tradition has it that he was quite wealthy and that two wooden buckets would not hold his money on his arrival in North America. John's cousin Allan MacDonald (Ridge) was upset by this

poem and he hastened to compose another in reply, sharply reminding John that life in Scotland was far from pleasant and that he had done well to emigrate.

Unlike many of his fellow countrymen who were more inured to hardship, John MacDonald was unprepared for pioneer life, and time does not seem to have softened his attitude towards his adopted home. Another poem, composed about six years after his emigration, is permeated with feelings of self-reproach and nostalgia. Only a few of John the Hunter's songs have been preserved, but these are sufficient to procure for him a place in the Gaelic literary tradition of Nova Scotia.

MAUREEN LONERGAN WILLIAMS

The Gaelic poetry of Iain MacDhòmhnaill 'Ic Iain is available in a number of anthologies, two of which remain in manuscript: the Ridge MSS, compiled by members of the MacDonald (Ridge) family, are held by the Special Coll. Dept. of St Francis Xavier Univ. Library (Antigonish, N.S.); the department also possesses a copy of the Beaton MSS, compiled by A. S. Beaton and held by members of the Beaton family of Port Hood, N.S. Published anthologies featuring his work include *Comh-chruinneachadh glinn'-a-bhàird: the Glenbard collection of Gaelic poetry* (abridged ed., Charlottetown, 1901), 351–53, and *The Gaelic bards, from 1825 to 1875* (Sydney, N.S., 1904), 40–43, both compiled by the Reverend Alexander Maclean Sinclair; *Failte Cheap Breatuinn: a collection of Gaelic poetry*, ed. V. A. MacLellan (Sydney, 1891; photocopy in St Francis Xavier Univ. Library, Special Coll. Dept.), 79–81; and *Mabou pioneers . . .*, ed. A. D. MacDonald and Reginald Rankin (2v., [Mabou, N.S., 1952?]–77), [1]: 581–85.

John MacDonald's poetry has also appeared in several other publications devoted to Gaelic literature, including the *Casket* (Antigonish), 12 Aug. 1852; 12 Sept. 1929; 13 March, 3 April, 21 Aug. 1930; 7 April 1932; *Mac-Talla* (Sydney), 11 (1902–3): 192; and *Guth na Bliadhna; the Voice of the Year* (Aberdeen, Scot.), 1 (1904): 250–54.

Margaret MacDonell's translation of "Oran do dh'America" may be found alongside the original Gaelic on pages 80–87 of her collection *The emigrant experience: songs of Highland emigrants in North America* (Toronto and Buffalo, N.Y., 1982); it is fittingly followed on pages 88–93 by Allan MacDonald's reply, "Chuir thu bòilich sìos 'us bòsd" (You have been loud and boastful).

Place-names of N.S. J. L. MacDougall, *History of Inverness County, Nova Scotia* ([Truro, N.S., 1922]). *Casket*, 27 March 1930: 8; 8 May 1930: 8.

McDONALD, ARCHIBALD, colonial administrator, author, fur trader, justice of the peace, and surveyor; b. 3 Feb. 1790 in Glencoe, Scotland, son of Angus McDonald, tacksman of Inverrigan, and Mary Rankin; m. first 1823, according to the custom of the country, the princess Raven (Sunday) (d. 1824), daughter of Chinook chief Comcomly, at Fort George (Astoria, Oreg.), with whom he had one son, Ranald McDonald*; m. secondly 1825, also according to the

526

custom of the country, Jane Klyne, a mixed-blood woman with whom he had twelve sons and one daughter; marriage confirmed by Christian rite 9 June 1835 in the Red River settlement (Man.); d. 15 Jan. 1853 in St Andrews (Saint-André-Est), Lower Canada.

Archibald McDonald was enlisted in early 1812 by Lord Selkirk [Douglas*] to serve as clerk and agent for the Red River settlement. In Scotland he assisted in the recruitment of the second group of settlers, who sailed in 1812. Originally designated to travel with this group, McDonald was held back by Selkirk for training and in 1812–13 he studied medicine and related subjects in London. In June 1813 he sailed from Stromness, Scotland, with a group of 94 Kildonan emigrants on the *Prince of Wales* for York Factory (Man.), as second in command to Dr Peter Laserre. Typhus broke out during the voyage and Laserre, who was among those infected, died on 16 August, leaving McDonald to take charge of the party. The captain of the ship was anxious to be rid of his passengers and landed them at Fort Churchill (Churchill, Man.), where they spent an uncomfortable winter, poorly equipped and short of provisions. In the spring McDonald led 51 of the settlers, most of them in their teens or early 20s, on snow-shoes 150 miles south along the shore of Hudson Bay to York Factory, a march of 13 days. They then travelled by boat up the Hayes River to Lake Winnipeg and arrived at the settlement on 22 June. The rest of the group reached Red River two months later.

Before his departure from Great Britain, McDonald had been appointed to the Council of Assiniboia, a body created by Selkirk to aid the colony's governor, Miles Macdonell*, and during the winter of 1814–15 he served as one of Macdonell's principal lieutenants. In the spring of 1815 Cuthbert GRANT and the Métis, encouraged by the North West Company, who were opposed to the establishment of the Selkirk settlement, openly harassed the colony, attacking the settlers and stealing livestock, until in June they forced the abandonment of the colony. McDonald proceeded with a group of the settlers to the north end of Lake Winnipeg where they were joined by Colin Robertson*, who took charge of the colonists and returned to Red River to re-establish the colony later that summer. McDonald returned to England to report on the fate of the settlement and while there prepared an account of the events leading up to the abandonment of the colony, which was published in London in 1816.

In the spring of 1816 McDonald joined Selkirk in Montreal. There he wrote four letters, published in the *Montreal Herald*, in reply to the Reverend John Strachan*, who had written *A letter to the right honourable the Earl of Selkirk, on his settlement at the Red River, near Hudson's Bay* (London, 1816),

highly critical of Selkirk and all those associated with the colony. In August he was at Fort William (Thunder Bay, Ont.) when Selkirk arrested several NWC partners, including William McGillivray*, and seized the post. McDonald then returned to Montreal and in the spring of 1817 took charge of the group of soldiers from the disbanded De Meuron's Regiment recruited by Lady Selkirk to reinforce the troops Selkirk had taken west with him the year before. After conducting this force to Fort William, McDonald turned back to Montreal and sailed for England in the fall. In 1818 he returned to the Red River settlement by way of York Factory to assist in the administration of the colony. In February 1819 he was among those, with Selkirk, indicted on charges of "conspiracy to ruin the trade of the North West Company" arising out of the events at Fort William three years earlier, but after many delays in the courts the charges were finally dropped.

In the spring of 1820 he joined the Hudson's Bay Company as a clerk and was posted to Île-à-la-Crosse (Sask.). The following year HBC governor George SIMPSON sent him to the Columbia district, on the Pacific northwest coast, under chief factors John HALDANE and John Dugald CAMERON. He was instructed to prepare an inventory of the goods at the NWC posts acquired by the merger of the NWC and the HBC in March 1821, and then he served as accountant at Fort George. In 1826 he took charge of Thompson's River Post (Kamloops, B.C.) and in the fall of that year he explored the Thompson River to its junction with the Fraser, accompanied by the Okanagan chief Nicola [HWISTESMETXĒ'QEN]. From his observations he prepared a map of the region which delineated for the first time drainage patterns and contours.

McDonald was promoted chief trader in January 1828 and travelled east with Edward Ermatinger* in the spring to attend the Northern Department council meeting at York Factory. On the return journey to the west coast, McDonald accompanied Governor Simpson, who was proceeding west for a tour of inspection. Typical of all of Simpson's travels, this voyage was completed in exceptional time: the 3,261-mile trip from York to Fort Langley (B.C.), following the northern route from Cumberland House (Sask.), across the Methy Portage (Portage La Loche, Sask.), down the Clearwater River, up the Peace, and finally down the Fraser River, was completed in 90 days. The party ran the treacherous rapids of the Fraser, including the lower section that Simon Fraser* had not attempted in 1808.

At Fort Langley, McDonald took over the direction of the post from James McMILLAN. He remained there until 1833, conducting a trade with the coastal Indians in competition with American maritime traders and diversifying the activity of the post by some agricultural production and by the drying and packing of salmon and the cutting of lumber, both for shipment to the Columbia district's headquarters at Fort Vancouver (Vancouver, Wash.). In 1833 he left Fort Langley and established Fort Nisqually (near Tacoma, Wash.) before heading east to York Factory in 1834 and then on to Great Britain for a year's furlough.

McDonald was back in the Columbia in 1835, and took charge of Fort Colvile (near Colville, Wash.). Built by John Work* in 1825–26, Fort Colvile was important for its farming operations. When McDonald took over, there were more than 200 acres under cultivation, and in 1837 he noted that the three cows and three pigs brought to the post in 1826 had multiplied to 55 and 150 respectively. He developed the farm on a large scale, contributing provisions for the HBC posts to the north and after 1839 for the Russian American Company, based at Sitka (Alaska). He was promoted chief factor in 1841.

In September 1844, plagued by ill health, McDonald set off for retirement in Lower Canada with his wife and six youngest children; another was born en route. They wintered at Fort Edmonton, where in May 1845, before resuming their journey, three young sons died of scarlet fever. McDonald and his family stayed in Montreal for three years and then, in 1848, settled on a comfortable farm by the Ottawa River, near St Andrews. McDonald played an active role in local affairs, serving as justice of the peace and surveyor, and in 1849 he led a delegation from Argenteuil protesting the provisions of the Rebellion Losses Bill to the governor-in-chief, Lord Elgin [Bruce*], in Montreal. In January 1853, after a few days illness, McDonald died at his home, Glencoe Cottage.

During his years in the Columbia district, McDonald had demonstrated a lively interest in the collection of scientific specimens. He corresponded with the British Museum, the Royal Horticultural Society, and Kew Gardens (London), sending botanical, geological, and animal specimens from the region. He met the British botanist David Douglas* at Fort Vancouver in 1825 and helped in the collection of the impressive selection of plants and seeds that Douglas carried back to England. Another botanist, the German Karl Andreas Geyer, passed the winter of 1843–44 in McDonald's company at Fort Colvile. In September 1844 McDonald discovered the silver deposit on Kootenay Lake which was later developed as the Bluebell Mine.

Alert, industrious, a man of broad interests, McDonald had a facile pen and left a large body of journals and correspondence which provides valuable information on the native tribes he lived among during his quarter century in the west. His descriptions of family life at remote fur-trade posts are among the few accounts available to social historians, and his papers are rich in documentation on plant and animal life as well as on the early efforts in agriculture, lumbering, and fisheries in the Pacific northwest.

JEAN MURRAY COLE

The Selkirk papers (PAC, MG 19, E1, ser.1, 1–2, 4, 8, 63, 69–70) contain several of Archibald McDonald's journals and much of his correspondence for the period when he was agent for the Red River settlement. Other journals and more of his correspondence, dealing in particular with his endeavours on the west coast, are at PABC, AB20, C72M, C72M.1, Ka3A, L2, L3A, and AB40, M142. His *Narrative respecting the destruction of the Earl of Selkirk's settlement upon Red River, in the year 1815* was published in London in 1816. That year the four letters which he wrote in reply to John Strachan and which were published in the *Montreal Herald* in May–June 1816 were brought out as a pamphlet entitled *Reply to the letter, lately addressed to the Right Honorable the Earl of Selkirk, by the Hon. and Rev. John Strachan, D.D., rector of York, in Upper Canada . . .* (Montreal, 1816). Lastly, his *Peace River, a canoe voyage from Hudson's Bay to Pacific, by the late Sir George Simpson (governor, hon. Hudson's Bay Company) in 1828; journal of the late chief factor, Archibald McDonald (hon. Hudson's Bay Company) who accompanied him*, ed. Malcolm McLeod (Ottawa, 1872), came out posthumously.

PAC, RG 4, B28, 134, no.789; RG 68, 19: 433–34. PAM, HBCA, B.97/a/2; C.1/778; D.4/116: ff.50d–51d. Royal Botanic Gardens (London), North American letters, 62: 99–100; 63: 313–16. Yale Univ. Library, Beinecke Rare Book and MS Library (New Haven, Conn.), Western Americana coll., Walker–Whitman papers. *Canadian North-West* (Oliver), 1: 53–54. *HBRS*, 1 (Rich); 7 (Rich); 10 (Rich). Simpson, *Fur trade and empire* (Merk; 1968). *Montreal Gazette*, 21 Jan. 1853. *Pilot* (Montreal), 20 Jan. 1853. *Quebec Gazette*, 11 March 1819. J. M. Cole, *Exile in the wilderness: the biography of Chief Factor Archibald McDonald, 1790–1853* (Don Mills [Toronto] and Seattle, Wash., 1979); "Exile in the wilderness; Archibald McDonald's ten years at Fort Colvile," *Beaver*, outfit 303 (summer 1972): 7–14. Olive and Harold Knox, "Chief Factor Archibald McDonald," *Beaver*, outfit 274 (March 1944): 42–46. W. S. Lewis, "Archibald McDonald: biography and genealogy," *Wash. Hist. Quarterly*, 9 (1918): 93–102.

MACDONALD, BERNARD DONALD, Roman Catholic priest, bishop, and school administrator; b. 25 Dec. 1797 at Allisary, St John's (Prince Edward) Island, one of ten children of Angus MacDonald and Penelope MacDonald; d. 30 Dec. 1859 at St Dunstan's College, near Charlottetown.

Through his paternal grandfather, one of the settlers brought to St John's Island in 1772 by John MacDonald* of Glenaladale, Bernard Donald Macdonald claimed kinship with the leading Scots Catholic families on the Island. In 1812 he and Ronald MACDONALD were selected by Father Angus Bernard MacEachern*, at the behest of Quebec's Bishop Joseph-Octave Plessis*, to study for the priesthood at the Grand Séminaire de Québec. His expenses defrayed by subscription among Island Catholics, Bernard passed ten years there, and on his ordination in June 1822 became the first native Island priest.

For the next 13 years Macdonald laboured in the priest-poor missions of Prince Edward Island: first, among the largely Acadian Catholics in the west, and from 1829, following the ordination on 28 July 1828 of Sylvain-Éphrem Perrey*, in Charlottetown and its attendant missions. For much of this period, only three, sometimes four, priests served the Island's Catholic community, which consistently numbered slightly less than half the total population. In the course of Macdonald's ministry, on 11 Aug. 1829, the episcopal see of Charlottetown was created, with MacEachern as its first bishop. Macdonald became his lieutenant and chosen successor, not only for his indispensable fluency in French, English, and Gaelic, but because, as MacEachern wrote on 21 March 1835 to Bishop Joseph Signay* of Quebec, "his uniform regularity of comportment and disengagement from everything but his own duty renders him dear and respected to this community." When MacEachern died on 22 April 1835, Macdonald, who had been appointed vicar general on 6 April, assumed temporary control of the diocese, and on 21 Feb. 1836 he was named diocesan administrator by the Holy See. Exactly one year later, despite his known timidity and Signay's concern that he might lack firmness, he was named bishop of Charlottetown and consecrated by Signay at Quebec on 15 Oct. 1837.

Macdonald's see initially encompassed New Brunswick, Prince Edward Island, and the Îles de la Madeleine. Much of it remained in a frontier state, primitive and poor, its want of clergy underscored by a sharply increasing population. When New Brunswick was detached in 1842 to form a separate diocese, Macdonald declined the opportunity to take it, preferring his original appointment; the new post then went to William DOLLARD.

Events during the first decade of his episcopacy proved an acid test of Macdonald's will. In September 1843 he recalled his cousin, Father John McDonald*, from the missions of eastern Kings County, where his effectiveness as pastor was being blunted by a worsening dispute with parishioners over his conservative views on the land question. When McDonald balked at his instructions to move by 1 November, the bishop temporized by not enforcing the deadline. Macdonald's equivocation made possible an angry confrontation between the priest and the dissident parishioners, led by John MacKintosh*, who were determined to remove him. His attempts at persuasion unavailing, the bishop was forced to suspend McDonald's priestly faculties to pry him loose from his parish in November 1844. Before taking permanent leave of the diocese in 1845, Father John accused

the bishop of conspiring against him. For Macdonald, the whole episode was acutely embarrassing.

Conflict between the two spilled over into educational matters. In 1831 Bishop MacEachern had established St Andrew's College at his residence in St Andrews at the head of the Hillsborough River, chiefly to provide pre-seminarial training for would-be clerics. Macdonald was vice-president of its first board of trustees in 1833, and then, as bishop, its president. Equally anxious to secure a succession of clergy, but convinced of the existing school's inadequacy, he purchased land in 1841 in Charlottetown Royalty, a more central location, intending to build a larger, better-equipped college. Meanwhile, financial and disciplinary problems multiplied at St Andrew's College. Moreover, by late 1843 the bishop faced strong opposition from two trustees – Father John and his brother, Donald McDONALD – who accused him of overstepping his authority as president, and his college staff of wilful mismanagement and conspiracy with Island escheators [see William Cooper*].

The cross-current of criticism likely hastened Macdonald's decision to close St Andrew's in July 1844, when construction had hardly begun on its successor. For the next decade the bishop bent his efforts towards its completion. Financed mainly by alms solicited from the Society for the Propagation of the Faith, a lay missionary society based in France, St Dunstan's College was built piecemeal, finally opening on 17 Jan. 1855. Even afterwards, its precarious fortunes continued to preoccupy the bishop and its first rector, Angus McDonald*.

Religious controversy shadowed the last years of Macdonald's episcopate. A misinterpretation of the liberal government's education policy prompted him to write in private to the Board of Education on 7 Nov. 1856 protesting what he mistakenly supposed was a decision to introduce compulsory Bible reading into the Island's public school system and its Normal School. In a religiously mixed education system, he warned, "godless" schools were a necessary evil. Government leader George Coles* quickly reassured him, but when Macdonald's letter was made public, militant Protestant reaction, cynically manipulated by Edward Palmer* and other tory politicians to gain office, helped precipitate a generation of political and religious discord over educational policy which split Island society along denominational lines.

Macdonald took little part in the escalation of animosities. Beginning in 1856 "chronic bronchitis," compounded by neglect and continued missionary duties, steadily undermined his constitution. He became progressively less capable of administrating, and made a request to the bishop of Quebec for assistance in fulfilling his mission to the Acadians; George-Antoine Bellecourt*, formerly a missionary

McDonald

in the northwest, accepted the call. Macdonald, conscious of impending death, moved in October 1859 to St Dunstan's College, where he died two months later. Peter MacIntyre* was appointed the following May to succeed him.

Bernard Donald Macdonald was a reluctant prelate. By nature shy and mild-mannered, he was genuinely distressed by his episcopal appointment, and at first tried to decline. Even as bishop he preferred to live in the rural Acadian parish of Rustico, rather than the rightful episcopal seat at Charlottetown, the colonial capital. Despite his marked diffidence, he successfully brought the diocese of Charlottetown through adolescence. Catholic population, economic status, and the number of churches and clergy all increased during his tenure. Various Catholic institutions were established: total abstinence societies were organized under his direction in 1841; a mutual insurance society for diocesan clergy was established in 1846; and in late 1857 four sisters from the Congregation of Notre-Dame were brought from Montreal to Charlottetown to open a ladies' school. Thus, under his rule, a mature diocese took shape.

Last of the Island's missionary bishops, Macdonald seemed more at home tending souls than exercising episcopal authority. He was not politically minded. Nor, as a private person become a public figure, was he an assertive spokesman for Catholic interests, though his inoffensive personality tended to disarm potential opponents among the Protestant majority. Given his personality and the currents stirring in Island society by the late 1850s it is doubtful, even had he lived, that Macdonald could have forestalled the religious factionalism that marred much of the following two decades.

G. EDWARD MACDONALD

Bernard Donald Macdonald has left behind no printed works, with the exception of a few pastoral letters located in the Arch. of the Diocese of Charlottetown, Pastoral letters, 1802–51, and in his papers there. Some of these were printed for circulation around the diocese. The Macdonald papers, a miscellany of uncatalogued file boxes, also contain correspondence and documents relating to his term as bishop, including a letter-book kept by Macdonald and his successor, Peter MacIntyre. One authentic portrait of Macdonald exists. Perhaps painted from a photograph, it is slightly damaged and is kept at the bishop's residence, Charlottetown.

AAQ, 310 CN, I–II, especially I: 38, 81, 85, 95, 113, 132, 134, 140 (mfm. at Charlottetown Public Library). Arch. de la Propagation de la Foi (Paris), F 172 (mfm. at PAC). Arch. of Scots College (Pontifical) (Rome), Vicars Apostolic, corr. of A. B. MacEachern and William Fraser to Paul MacPherson and Angus MacDonald (transcripts at Arch. of the Diocese of Charlottetown). Arch. of the Diocese of Charlottetown, John McDonald, [*Apologia*], 5–58 (incomplete copy of book published probably in 1845 by McDonald, reprinting documents, with commentary, con-

cerning his conflicts with John MacKintosh, B. D. Macdonald, and his fellow priests); St Andrew's College (St Andrews, P.E.I.), board of trustees, minutes, 1833–62. Archivio della Propaganda Fide (Rome), Scritture riferite nei Congressi, America Settentrionale, 2 (1792–1830)–7 (1857–61), especially 3 (1831–36), Joseph Signay to Cardinal Fransoni, 3 June 1836; 6 (1849–57), B. D. Macdonald to Cardinal Barnabo, 15 Jan. 1857 (photocopies in the possession of Allan MacDonald, Univ. of P.E.I., Charlottetown). Diocese of Charlottetown Chancery Office, St Dunstan's Univ. Arch., St Dunstan's Univ. (Charlottetown), abstracts of property deeds, college reg., and ledger, 1855–69. PAPEI, Acc. 2353/349, 30 Dec. 1859. Supreme Court of P.E.I. (Charlottetown), Estates Division, liber 6: f.50 (will of B. D. Macdonald, 10 Sept. 1859). Univ. of P.E.I. Library (Charlottetown), P.E.I. Coll., R. B. MacDonald, "MacDonalds in P.E.I." (typescript, *c*. 1892–94).

P.E.I., House of Assembly, *Journal*, 1832, app.C; 1841, app.; 1856, app.D; 1861, app.A. *Examiner* (Charlottetown), 22 Jan. 1855; 23 Feb., 2, 30 March, 12 Oct. 1857; 16 Jan. 1860. *Islander*, 13 Jan. 1860. *Protestant and Evangelical Witness* (Charlottetown), 21 Jan. 1860. *Royal Gazette* (Charlottetown), 18 May 1830; 20 Dec. 1831; 28 April 1835; 18 July, 19 Dec. 1837; 23 Feb., 6 April 1841. Caron, "Inv. de la corr. de Mgr Plessis," ANQ *Rapport*, 1932–33: 149–50, 175, 182, 187. *The Catholic Church in Prince Edward Island, 1720–1979*, ed. M. F. Hennessey (Charlottetown, 1979). J. C. Macmillan, *The early history of the Catholic Church in Prince Edward Island* (Quebec, 1905); *The history of the Catholic Church in Prince Edward Island from 1835 till 1891* (Quebec, 1913). I. R. Robertson, "Religion, politics, and education in Prince Edward Island from 1856 to 1877" (MA thesis, McGill Univ., Montreal, 1968). Léon Thériault, "The Acadianization of the Catholic Church in Acadia," *The Acadians of the Maritimes: thematic studies*, ed. Jean Daigle (Moncton, N.B., 1982), 271–339. I. R. Robertson, "The Bible question in Prince Edward Island from 1856 to 1860," *Acadiensis* (Fredericton), 5 (1975–76), no.2: 3–25.

McDONALD, DONALD, landowner and politician; b. 1795, probably on 25 October, at Tracadie, P.E.I.; d. 20 July 1854 at Quebec.

The second of five children and the eldest of four sons to issue from the marriage of Captain John MacDonald* of Glenaladale, a Roman Catholic landed proprietor on St John's (Prince Edward) Island, and Margaret MacDonald, Donald McDonald was educated by the Jesuits at Stonyhurst College in Lancashire, England. He eventually became owner of a portion of the family estate, and in 1852 described himself as proprietor of one-quarter of Lot 35 and one-half of Lot 36, adjacent townships in eastern Queens County. This claim would mean that he possessed some 15,000 acres; other family members, including the controversial priest John*, owned the remainder of the two lots.

Although socially prominent because of his family background – he inherited a leading position among Islanders of Scottish extraction – McDonald does not appear to have played a significant role in politics until the end of the 1830s. The sole documented exception was his participation, as one of a committee of seven local notables, in organizing a public campaign to remove Lieutenant Governor Charles Douglass SMITH in 1823. No doubt his activism on that occasion was related to an exemplary distress suddenly issued in January against his estate and that of John Stewart*. The action, for non-payment of quitrents, was launched under Smith's direction by his son-in-law John Edward Carmichael*, the acting receiver general of quitrents. That autumn, McDonald and his fellow committee members were charged before the Court of Chancery with contempt, on the complaint of Ambrose LANE, the court's registrar and another son-in-law of Smith. Given that the alleged contempt was in fact criticism of the way the chancellor, Smith himself, and Lane conducted the court, few could have been surprised when Smith found the defendants guilty. But, uneasily aware that popular reprisal was a possibility, he put off sentencing them; indeed, Smith did not return to the case before being recalled to London, and in October 1825, almost a year after his departure, the matter was finally officially dropped.

When separate legislative and executive councils were appointed in 1839 by Lieutenant Governor Sir Charles Augustus FITZROY, McDonald was the only Roman Catholic named to the former. His marriage around January 1819 to Anna Matilda Brecken, a member of the Church of England, made him a key figure in 1841 when the House of Assembly, then dominated by radicals led by William Cooper*, investigated the local family compact. The assembly's data, embodied in two resolutions, indicated that McDonald was closely related by marriage to two of his eleven fellow legislative councillors, and that he had close family connections, through birth or marriage, with five executive councillors and more distant family connections with three of the four remaining members of the executive. The strategic nature of his linkages was such that he was the only non-member of the Executive Council mentioned by name in the assembly's resolution concerning that body.

McDonald attended meetings of the Legislative Council quite regularly over 16 winters, but he did not contribute frequently to debate. He became president by seniority in 1853, succeeding his wife's first cousin Robert Hodgson*, who had been appointed chief justice in 1852 following the death of Edward James JARVIS. McDonald did not consider himself a partisan, but since he was fiercely protective of the rights of landed property, he was widely regarded as a tory. In the session beginning February 1854, to his chagrin, the home government, acting on advice tendered, in concert with the lieutenant governor, Sir Alexander Bannerman*, by the local liberals when they had been

in power, granted rank and precedence to Charles Young, a fellow councillor, making him senior member and thus president. During the same session liberals repeatedly expressed their surprise and sympathy at McDonald's exclusion from the conservative cabinet formed by John Myrie Holl* and Edward Palmer* in February; apparently the tories had left him out in the hope of avoiding the appearance of a government dominated by proprietors. When Young, with whom McDonald had exchanged sharp words several times over the years, joined the chorus, the provocation was too much for the irascible McDonald, who on 19 April accused Young of dishonesty in denying having played a role in his displacement as president. McDonald's words were taken down, the committee on privileges met, and on 21 April he was ordered to "make the most ample apology" and to acknowledge having acted "under erroneous impressions and highly irritated feelings." He responded by repeating his charge, refusing to withdraw it, and, according to the official reporter, "at the same time expressing his intention of resigning his seat in this House. The Hon. Mr. Macdonald then retired." He never returned to the council, and appears to have resigned.

Best known to his contemporaries as a landlord, McDonald was so thoroughly identified with his estate that he was frequently referred to by its name, Tracadie. Surviving documentation suggests that he was a mixture of paternalist and tyrant. He encouraged organizations promoting agricultural improvement, such as the Central Agricultural Society, an Island-wide body, and the Monaghan Farming Society, a local group of which he became founding president on 3 June 1840. He attempted to attract colonists and, according to testimony before a committee of the assembly in 1841 and a land commission in 1860, he was not overly scrupulous in the information and the terms he gave to prospective tenants. He offered short leases, and was reputed to be ruthless in using distraint and eviction, and to insist upon the payment of sterling rents at the going rate of exchange, rather than at the much smaller one-ninth premium on local currency customarily accepted by many Island landlords. Indeed, in 1852 Joseph Pope*, an executive councillor, cited McDonald's practices as evidence of the need for a statute regulating extraction of sterling rents.

McDonald had serious difficulties with his tenants, most of whom were Irish Roman Catholics. On 5 Feb. 1838, at the height of the escheat agitation, he wrote, "I cannot obtain a shilling [of rent] now and . . . I am Credibly informed they are Sworn to protect each other . . . I have been threatened by my own Tenants and warned not to attempt to collect my rents." A letter he wrote in 1844 to Bernard Donald MACDONALD, bishop of Charlottetown, indicates that he considered

McDonald

the Irish-born priest in the area, James Brady, who had been there since July 1838, responsible for much of the discontent on his estate. He even threatened to evict his co-religionists and replace them with Protestant settlers who would not be influenced by Brady or any other "escheating, leveling Priest." In 1850–51 the colony's first formally organized tenant league appeared in a part of eastern Queens County that included his estate, and almost certainly drew upon his tenants for support.

Fires set by one or more arsonists early in the morning of 21 July 1850 destroyed McDonald's unoccupied Arisaig Cottage on Lot 35 and three outbuildings belonging to him at Glenaladale on Lot 36. An advertisement he placed offering 200 acres of freehold land for discovery of the perpetrators within six months indicated that the burning of the cottage brought to four the number of houses on his property destroyed "at different periods" that summer. The fires led him to place armed watchmen on his premises, and in the darkness of late evening on 8 August, while standing at his door, he was mistaken for an intruder and shot; he sustained "severe" buckshot wounds to the head, one arm, and both legs, but recovered soon after. He apparently continued to have problems with fires set on his property, and although charges were eventually laid, no convictions ever resulted.

On the morning of 25 July 1851 McDonald was shot at the outer gate of his property as he left for Charlottetown, and was wounded in at least two places. An Englishwoman who visited the Island three years later was told that shots came from both sides of the road and that he "fell weltering in blood. So detested was he, that several persons passed by without rendering him any assistance. At length one of his own tenantry, coming by, took him into Charlotte Town in a cart, but was obliged shortly afterwards to leave the island, to escape from the vengeance which would have overtaken the succourer of a tyrant." Although Lieutenant Governor Bannerman offered a reward of £100 for information leading to conviction of the attempted assassins, he told the Colonial Office that "the occurrence . . . may be exaggerated," and he linked it to the proprietor's explosive temper. Subsequently, according to a dispatch by Bannerman dated 24 March 1853, McDonald was convicted of assault. The lieutenant governor believed that McDonald, who always went about his estate armed, "would not hesitate, at any moment of excitement to carry into execution any threat which after reflection might cause him to regret." It was this rashness which Bannerman cited to London as the reason the proprietor of Tracadie was "not exactly qualified to *preside* at the Legislative Council."

Donald McDonald was an extreme case of a certain sort of landlord in 19th-century Prince Edward Island, and the only one against whom assassination is known to have been attempted. Thus the incident in 1851 – which was never solved – ranks with the slaying of land agent Edward Abell by tenant Patrick Pearce in 1819 as the most serious recorded incidents of physical violence in the history of the Island's land question. McDonald appears to have evoked a singular spirit of vengefulness, and a visitor to the Island, who described him as "a high-minded man," wrote in 1853 that "a house which once gave him shelter was burnt to the ground immediately afterwards." McDonald's imperious nature, obstinacy, and hot temper were major factors in his unpopularity among his tenants, and these qualities were also evident in his family relations. A letter written by his brother John in 1821 indicates that they were on poor terms, apparently because of differences over money, and that Donald was in conflict with their mother. In later years he fell out with his youngest son, William Christopher* (later Sir William, the tobacco magnate), his second daughter, Helen Jane, who became a Protestant, and possibly the second of his three sons, Augustine Ralph. Yet there appears to have been a reconciliation when he visited William and Augustine in Montreal in the summer of 1854. Impressed with their success in business, he decided to dispose of his estate, which was encumbered by debt, and move to Montreal. However, he died a few days afterwards when he contracted cholera at Quebec, where he had gone to place the youngest of his four daughters in a convent school. He was survived by his wife, his sons, and two daughters. Had he lived, it is quite possible that he would have acted upon his plan, for by August 1851 it was known that he was considering leaving Tracadie and moving to Charlottetown or even off the Island. But the property remained within the family, and the outbuildings of his eldest son, John Archibald, who inherited his temperamental characteristics and continued many of his proprietary practices, became the target of arsonists during the agrarian disturbances of 1865.

IAN ROSS ROBERTSON

[There may have been more than one attempt to assassinate Donald McDonald: *see* B. W. A. Sleigh, *Pine forests and hacmatack clearings* . . . (London, 1853); 170; [I. L. Bird], *The Englishwoman in America* (London, 1856; repr. Madison, Wis., and Toronto, 1966), 46–47, 473; and William Henry Pope*, in an editorial note in the *Islander*, 30 June 1865. Contemporary evidence concerning the situation on McDonald's estate in 1850–51 will be found in *Examiner* (Charlottetown), 24 July, 10 Aug., 11 Dec. 1850; 13 May 1851; *Haszard's Gazette* (Charlottetown), 13 Jan. 1852; *Islander*, 2, 9, 27 Aug. 1850; 22 Aug. 1851; 30 Jan., 20 Feb. 1852; *Royal Gazette* (Charlottetown), 23, 30 July, 13, 20 Aug. 1850; 28 July, 4 Aug. 1851; 19 Jan., 9 Feb. 1852; PRO, CO 226/79: 212–16; PAPEI, RG 6, Supreme Court, minutes, 9, 12–13 Jan. 1852. The four indictments against alleged arsonists Fade and John Hayden, together with a record of acquittal survive in PAPEI, RG 6, Supreme Court, case papers, 1852.

Further information on McDonald as a landlord and colonizer will be found in P.E.I., House of Assembly, *Public documents on various subjects connected with the interests of Prince Edward Island* (Charlottetown, 1841), 75–76, a copy of which is available in the Palmer family papers, PAPEI, Acc. 2849; *Abstract of the proceedings before the Land Commissioners' Court, held during the summer of 1860, to inquire into the differences relative to the rights of landowners and tenants in Prince Edward Island*, reporters J. D. Gordon and David Laird (Charlottetown, 1862), 114–16, 212; *Report of proceedings before the commissioners appointed under the provisions of "The Land Purchase Act, 1875"*, reporter P. S. MacGowan (Charlottetown, 1875), 558, 584; Donald McDonald to Bernard Donald Macdonald, 11 Oct. 1843, 30 April 1844, in the latter's papers at the Arch. of the Diocese of Charlottetown, a source brought to my attention by G. Edward MacDonald; *Examiner*, 25 Sept. 1848; *Islander*, 6 Feb. 1852; *Prince Edward Island Register*, 27 Jan. 1829; *Royal Gazette*, 16 Feb. 1836; 29 Jan., "Extra," 1852; 21 Feb. 1853; 20 Feb. 1854; PRO, CO 226/39: 112–13; 226/56: 110–14; 226/82: 83, 108–10. McDonald died intestate, but papers of administration in the Supreme Court of P.E.I. (Charlottetown), Estates Division, give detailed information on his property, his financial situation, and the holdings and arrears of his tenants, together with John Archibald's estimates of the probability of collecting the arrears. His burial at Quebec on 22 July 1854 is recorded in ANQ-Q, CE1-1.

For McDonald's participation in various Scottish and agricultural organizations see *Royal Gazette*, 26 Jan. 1836; 29 Jan., 9 July, 10 Dec. 1839; 16 June 1840; 26 Jan. 1841; 4 April 1853; 2 Jan. 1854; and [A. A.] MacDonald, "Scottish associations in Prince Edward Island," *Prince Edward Island Magazine* (Charlottetown), 1 (1899–1900): 425–30.

Concerning McDonald's involvement in the political turmoil of 1823, see *Prince Edward Island Register*, 13 Sept., 4, 11, 25 Oct., 1, 8, 15 Nov. 1823; 6 March 1824; PRO, CO 226/39: 16, 26–27, 153–61, 191–99, 264–84, 414–23; *Petitions from Prince Edward Island . . .* (London, [1824]), especially 41, 50, 55; PAPEI, RG 6, Court of Chancery, minutes, 14, 16, 27 Oct. 1823; 3, 5 Oct. 1825; orders and commissions, 14, 16, 28, 30 Oct. 1823; and PAPEI, Acc. 2702/784, Ambrose Lane to John Edward Carmichael, 6 Jan. 1824. The author is deeply indebted to Mr H. Tinson Holman for making available his unpublished study of the Court of Chancery under Lieutenant Governor Charles Douglass Smith.

The basic sources for McDonald as a legislative councillor are the journals of the Legislative Council, 1839–54, and the reports of its debates which appeared in the *Royal Gazette*, 1844–49, 1851–53, and in the *Examiner*, 1854, particularly P.E.I., Legislative Council, *Journal*, 1839, 2nd session: 9; 1841: 96–97; 1845: 55; 1853: 43–44; 1854: 11–12, 18, 21, 48, 50–51; *Royal Gazette*, 26 March 1844; 29 April, 6 May 1845; 3 March, suppl., 21 April, 19 May 1846; 22 March, "Extra," 1849; *Examiner*, 27 Feb., 27 March, 10 April, "Extra," 15, 22, 29 May, 28 Aug. 1854. See also *Islander*, 21 April 1854; PRO, CO 226/69: 206; 226/80: 96–105; 226/81: 46–47.

Family information relevant to Donald McDonald will be found in the MacDonald family papers in the custody of Colin and Jean MacDonald of St Peters, P.E.I., docs.56, 60, copies of which are available in PAPEI, Acc. 2664; J. F. Snell, "Sir William Macdonald and his kin," *Dalhousie Rev.* (Halifax), 23 (1943–44): 317–30, and his *Macdonald College of McGill University: a history from 1904–1955* (Montreal, 1963), 6, 8, 222, 224; and handwritten copies of a letter from McDonald to his mother, dated 31 July 1813, and of a letter from McDonald to John Archibald, dated 13 July 1854, in the J. F. Snell papers, McGill Univ. Arch. (Montreal), MG 2007. McDonald's connections with other members of the "family compact" are detailed in *Royal Gazette*, 27 April 1841, and P.E.I., House of Assembly, *Journal*, 1841: 151. There is miscellaneous family information concerning the McDonalds of Tracadie on file at the P.E.I. Museum; included there are a genealogical chart, some of whose dates are incorrect, and a typescript copy of the marriage settlement between Anna Matilda Brecken and Donald McDonald, dated 22 Jan. 1819. The Land Registry records in PAPEI, RG 16, Conveyance reg., contain much information concerning land arrangements within the McDonald family. See also J. M. Bumsted, "Captain John MacDonald and the Island," *Island Magazine* (Charlottetown), no.6 (spring–summer 1979): 15–20; I. R. Robertson, "Highlanders, Irishmen, and the land question in nineteenth-century Prince Edward Island," in *Comparative aspects of Scottish and Irish economic and social history, 1600–1900*, ed. L. M. Cullen and T. C. Smout (Edinburgh, [1977]), 227–40; and J. C. Macmillan, *The history of the Catholic Church in Prince Edward Island from 1835 till 1891* (Quebec, 1913), 23–24, 64, 244–48.

Only two surviving numbers of Island newspapers contain notices of McDonald's death, and they are brief and identical; see *Islander*, 4 Aug. 1854, and *Haszard's Gazette*, 5 Aug. 1854. I.R.R.]

MacDONALD, JOHN. *See* MacDHÒMHNAILL 'IC IAIN, IAIN

McDONALD, JOHN, businessman, justice of the peace, office holder, and politician; b. 10 Feb. 1787 in Saratoga (Schuylerville), N.Y., fourth son of John McDonald and Amelia Cameron; m. 10 Feb. 1831 Henrietta Maria Mallory, daughter of Benajah MALLORY, and they had one son and four daughters; d. 20 Sept. 1860 in Gananoque, Upper Canada.

John McDonald spent his earliest years in Athol, N.Y., where his parents had eventually settled after emigrating from Blair Atholl, Scotland, in 1785. "At an early age," however, he left Athol for Troy, N.Y., eventually becoming involved in "commercial business." In 1809 his brother Charles* settled in Upper Canada at Gananoque on the St Lawrence River and gradually built up a prosperous mercantile business. During the War of 1812 John McDonald's business in Troy apparently suffered losses and in the post-war depression his prospects there may not have seemed promising. During a visit to Gananoque in September 1815 he was probably impressed by the thriving

McDonald

business carried on by his brother. In late 1817 he left Troy for Gananoque and in January joined his brother as a full partner in a new firm, C. and J. McDonald.

Formed primarily as a lumbering business, the company would take advantage of the expanding market for colonial timber protected by British preferential tariffs. During the 1820s the business, which held the water rights along the west side of the Gananoque River, rapidly expanded to control a greater part of the lumber trade on the river. In 1825 John McDonald acquired property on the east bank of the river, thus solidifying the firm's control of water-power on the river and assuring its growth.

When British trade preferences were extended to Canadian wheat and flour in 1825–27, the firm moved quickly to expand the grist-mill it had operated since the partnership was established. In 1825 the company, which became C. and J. McDonald and Company when younger brother Collin was taken into partnership that year, made plans to dam the river for increased water-power and to build a new flour-mill. By July 1826 the new mill, reportedly one of the largest in Upper Canada, had gone into operation with four run of stone. After the death of Charles on 7 October of that year control of the firm effectively fell to John. Wheat for the mills was purchased locally and by agents throughout the large region of the province around the upper St Lawrence. The brand of flour put out by C. and J. McDonald and Company became well known, as the "Gananoque Mills" gained for the firm a prominent position in the flour and wheat trade in Canada. When the Reverend William BELL visited the mills in August 1830 he reported that he "had never before seen an establishment so extensive, so ingenious, and so complete" and he was told that the mills were capable of producing 160 barrels of flour a day. Although he found the sawmills no less impressive, and reported that "many hands were employed in the river, rafting timber and plank, for the Quebec market," this side of the business appears to have been considered secondary to grist-milling. In 1831 the company sent to Montreal and Quebec 20,000 barrels of flour and 10,000 bushels of wheat, as well as the lumber from 10,000 logs.

As his business grew, McDonald became interested in the various schemes for canal improvements which proliferated in the Canadas during the 1820s and 1830s. In 1828, on a trip to Bytown (Ottawa) and Hull, he had been impressed by the works on the Rideau Canal, then under construction [see Thomas McKAY]. Eight years later his interest led to his involvement in two navigation projects.

On the local level, McDonald became involved in the Gananoque and Wiltsie Navigation Company, organized in 1836, which proposed to finance the construction of a series of locks and dams on the Gananoque River to make it navigable for commercial shipping as far upriver as Charleston Lake. In this way the cost of transporting wheat from the rear townships to the St Lawrence would be reduced. In September, McDonald, the company's president, hired as its engineer Nicol Hugh Baird*, who had prepared the initial report and estimates on the proposed waterway. Survey work began the same month but the project was never completed, reportedly because of the rebellion of 1837–38 and the subsequent "unsettled state of affairs."

Earlier in 1836 McDonald had become involved in another, much larger project. In March the president of the Commission for the Improvement of the Navigation of the River St Lawrence, Jonas Jones*, recommended him as a commissioner to replace John MACAULAY. Jones described McDonald as a "gentleman of high character and standing, great enterprise, experience and business talents" who had always taken considerable interest in canal works on the St Lawrence and in improvements generally. By the time McDonald had taken his seat in May, the commission had overcome initial labour problems and legal battles over lands appropriated for the canal system. Construction had already begun on the first project, the Cornwall Canal, and plans were underway to extend work to other sections of the river. After 1837, however, the prospects for the St Lawrence canals changed drastically. As a result of the depression of that year and the disruptions caused by the rebellion, the project sank into financial difficulties. In the midst of this crisis, in May 1838, McDonald replaced Jones as president. In addition to the commission's financial difficulties, McDonald found himself contending with divisions caused by internal bickering involving Philip VanKoughnet* and John Hamilton* and later by scandal within the commission itself. At the end of June 1838 he was informed that the government would supply no further funds for the project and that the works were to be suspended. The increasingly costly project had become too expensive and by June 1839 work had been halted.

McDonald's prominence in business was reflected in the local posts he held. Although American-born, McDonald had married the step-granddaughter of Colonel Joel Stone*, the early loyalist settler, and his loyalty was not in question. He received his first commission as a justice of the peace in 1828 when, as well, he was appointed postmaster for Gananoque, a position which carried with it the free mailing privileges of value to his business. During the general election of 1836 he was a deputy returning officer for Leeds County. In 1838 he became commissioner of the Court of Requests (an early small claims court) at Gananoque. Furthermore, in 1838–39 he supplied the government with information concerning Patriot movements in the Gananoque area and across the border in New York [see Daniel D. Heustis*].

Primarily a businessman, McDonald showed little interest in politics beyond its practical effect on business or on his local area. His early political association was with Jonas Jones, the ardent tory from Brockville. During the late 1830s, however, McDonald's political views, based on conservative instincts, seem to have moderated. As well, he may have become disillusioned with Jones in 1837–38 for his open attempts to resign from the St Lawrence canals commission in the midst of difficulty and for his inability or unwillingness, as member of parliament for Leeds, to help him alleviate the shortage of magistrates in the Gananoque area. In 1837 he turned for help to the influential Ogle Robert Gowan*, the county's other representative.

In 1839 McDonald received his first political appointment, to the Legislative Council under Lieutenant Governor Sir George ARTHUR. His general lack of interest in politics and his moderate conservatism are both borne out in his career as a legislative councillor. After serving on council during the tumultuous debates of the pre-union years, he was reappointed in 1841 to the new moderate Legislative Council of the united provinces under Lord Sydenham [Thomson*]. During the council's first session, when the government sat at Kingston, McDonald attended regularly but by 1843 his attendance was infrequent. Preoccupied with his business affairs and the St Lawrence canals, on which construction had resumed in 1842, he found little time to attend the legislative sessions in Montreal after 1843. In 1848 he forfeited his seat for non-attendance.

During the 1830s and early 1840s McDonald's business affairs had continued to flourish. In 1834 his nephew William Stone McDonald entered the firm as a partner. Collin McDonald withdrew from it in July 1839 and soon set up a business in Cleveland, Ohio, but this may have been an extension of C. and J. McDonald and Company, since he seems to have bought American wheat for shipment to the mills at Gananoque. Taking advantage of the Canada Corn Act of 1843, which allowed American wheat ground in Upper Canada to qualify for colonial preference, McDonald had Gananoque declared a free warehousing port in late 1845, thereby permitting his importation of an increasing volume of wheat for his mills to flour. The company's growth was based not only on business acumen but also on colonial preference and, when milling and lumbering businesses throughout the province suffered after the abolition of the corn laws and timber preference in 1846, C. and J. McDonald and Company was no exception.

In 1847 McDonald was 60 years of age – perhaps too old to deal with the new economic difficulties. By 1851 he had passed control of the firm to William Stone McDonald. When John McDonald died in 1860, he was still a wealthy man. After a large debt to Forsyth, Richardson and Company, his former forwarding agent, was paid, his estate left $600 annually to his widow and an extensive amount of property to be divided among his four surviving children. His substantial two-storey brick house, built about 1831–32, remains standing as Gananoque's town hall.

C. J. SHEPARD

AO, MS 393, E-3, box 17, "Other projects: Gananoque and Wiltse Waterway"; MS 519; MU 1760; RG 21, United Counties of Leeds and Grenville, Leeds and Lansdowne townships (front), census and assessment rolls, 1818–33; RG 22, Johnstown District, oaths of office, 1833–42, John McDonald, oath, 26 March 1836; affidavit, 13 Feb. 1838; ser.12, vol.7, 14 Nov. 1837; ser.176, John McDonald. BLHU, R. G. Dun & Co. credit ledger, Canada, 18: 89. Leeds Land Registry Office (Brockville, Ont.), Abstract index to deeds, Leeds Township (mfm. at AO, GS 4572). PAC, MG 23, HII, 1, vols.2–4; RG 1, El, 48: 650; E3, 31; RG 5, A1: 42136–37, 70768–70, 79083–86, 89181–84, 95115–19, 103043–44, 108211–14, 110327–32, 111482–83, 113408–11, 114452–58, 114772–75, 130974–78; RG 11, A2, 94: 276; RG 43, CV, 1; RG 68, 76: 323; General index, 1651–1841: 455, 462, 477, 516, 671. QUA, William Bell, diaries, 7: 77–78. Can., Prov. of, Legislative Assembly, *App. to the journals*, 1846, app.F; *Journals*, 1841–45. U.C., House of Assembly, *Journal*, 1828–40; *Statutes*, 1836, c.8. *Colonial Advocate*, 24 Feb. 1831. *Daily British Whig*, September 1860. *Kingston Chronicle*, October 1826. *Reporter* (Gananoque, [Ont.]), September 1860.

MACDONALD, RONALD, educator and newspaper editor; b. February 1797 in Priest Pond (Prince Edward Island), son of John Macdonald and Margaret MacKinnon; d. 15 Oct. 1854 at Quebec.

Nothing is known of Ronald Macdonald's childhood except that he came from a family of modest means. He was brought to Lower Canada as a result of Bishop Joseph-Octave Plessis*'s determination to give the English-speaking Roman Catholics of the Maritimes a sufficient number of clergy. Several "carefully chosen" youths were sent to study in the seminaries of Lower Canada at the expense of the ecclesiastical authorities. Angus Bernard MacEachern*, a missionary at St Andrews on Prince Edward Island, apparently recruited Macdonald and Bernard Donald MACDONALD and recommended them to Plessis. Ronald arrived at Quebec in October 1812 and entered the Petit Séminaire in a preparatory class, knowing not one word of French. From his first months there he attracted the attention of Plessis, who wrote to MacEachern: "Ronald is a student whose ability and progress [are] remarkable." A brilliant pupil, he advanced rapidly and in 1813 he went into the second-year class (Syntax). In the summer of 1816 he began the sixth-year class (Rhetoric), and in 1817 the philosophy program. After only five years he had finished his classical studies. He entered the Grand Séminaire de Québec in 1817 to become a priest, and received the tonsure on 5 October in the cathedral at Quebec. According to some sources Plessis, who was impressed with Macdonald's capabilities, wanted to make him his suffragan bishop at Halifax; however, his correspondence makes no mention of this matter. In any case, after less than a year at the Grand Séminaire, Macdonald decided to give up the soutane.

Having renounced the priesthood, Macdonald was faced with financial difficulties, since he no longer received assistance from Plessis. In the early 1820s the former seminarist took up the study of law, did a little translation, and taught at the English Catholic school in Saint-Roch. He also decided to establish a family of his own. On 16 April 1822, at Quebec, he married Louise Lavallée; the marriage certificate bears the notation "law student." They were to have four children, but their three sons died in infancy. Macdonald's wife and daughter perished when the Théâtre Saint-Louis at Quebec was destroyed by fire on 12 June 1846.

Immediately after his marriage, Macdonald, burdened with financial responsibilities and without means, had abandoned the study of law and decided finally to become a teacher at the English Catholic school in Saint-Roch. In 1824, in association with schoolmaster Germain Kirouac, he started a private school on Rue Sainte-Ursule; this partnership lasted two years. Soon after, in 1826, Macdonald went to Rivière-du-Loup (Louiseville) to take charge of the boys' class. He is thought to have stayed there three years.

At this point, the House of Assembly, having decided it was expedient to adopt measures "for procuring a master or Preceptor to instruct the Deaf and Dumb in this Province," approached Macdonald, whose career then took a dynamic new turn. On 2 March 1830 he appeared before a special committee of the house studying educational problems, and it was suggested that he go to the United States for training in the methods of teaching deaf mutes. Macdonald set down several conditions before accepting: he was to receive a grant large enough to cover the expenses of his move and to provide for his family, and on his return he was to be appointed head of an institution financed by the government. These terms were agreed to, and by a law enacted on 26 March 1830 he was granted the necessary £300.

In June, Macdonald went to Hartford, Conn., where the American School for the Deaf, America's first and most renowned establishment of its type, was located. The method taught was that of Abbé Roch-Ambroise Cucurron, *dit* Sicard, a French educator of the early 19th century. Instruction was given in French and English. In May 1831, after a year's study, Macdonald returned to Quebec armed

with the requisite certificates. On 15 June the Deaf and Dumb Institution, the first such establishment in Lower Canada, came into being when Macdonald, as a tutor, opened a school at Quebec. That year there were 408 persons in the province listed as deaf mutes. The initial sum allocated for setting up the school was quickly exhausted, and Macdonald had to present a report to the House of Assembly on 31 Jan. 1832 applying for a further grant. On 25 February "An Act to make temporary provision for the instruction of the Deaf and Dumb and for other purposes relating to the same object" received royal assent. Given the provisional nature of this statute, the institution in time found itself short of funds, and had to close in 1836. Macdonald's endeavours had again come to nothing, despite his devotion to this humanitarian cause.

Under the circumstances, Macdonald went back to regular teaching and at the same time took up journalism. He became a schoolmaster at Saint-Laurent, on Île d'Orléans, and there acquired a reputation as a scholar; but it is hard to understand why a man of such ability had to teach in a rural school for two years.

Macdonald's journalistic career began in 1836 when, according to Henry James Morgan*, he joined the staff of the *Quebec Gazette*. On 4 October that year he was working on John Lovell*'s *Montreal Daily Transcript*, with which his name continued to be associated until 1849. From 10 April 1837 to 16 March 1838 he was the printer, with Lovell, of Montreal's tri-weekly *Le Populaire*, a paper founded by Léon Gosselin*.

John Neilson*, a reformer who had been publishing the *Quebec Gazette* since the end of the 18th century, decided to bring out a French edition of his paper, and in 1842 Macdonald became editor of *La Gazette de Québec*. He presented his program in the issue of 2 May. He proposed to make *La Gazette* a complete newspaper, devoting space to scholarly, scientific, artistic, and political news. To avoid religious controversy Macdonald planned to rely on the clergy for the material to be published on religion. In all cases he would turn to sound sources, and would keep himself informed of developments in both America and Europe. The program was ambitious, but Macdonald's venture and the French edition itself lasted only until 29 Oct. 1842. The balanced thinking, correct style, reliable information on domestic and foreign politics, and the quality and elegance of the translations made *La Gazette de Québec* a paper that was read and well regarded by the clergy and educated classes.

Macdonald joined *Le Canadien* in November 1842, replacing Étienne Parent*, who had just been appointed clerk of the Executive Council. In an article published on 4 November Macdonald stated that he would be solely responsible for everything appearing in the paper. He proposed to uphold its motto: *Nos institutions, notre langue et nos lois.* At his request the proprietor, Jean-Baptiste Fréchette, agreed to expand the paper in order to include more information on religious matters.

Five years later Fréchette turned *Le Canadien* over to his sons. The new owners dismissed Macdonald, replacing him with Napoléon Aubin*. In February 1848 Macdonald joined *La Journal de Québec* for a brief stint, but during the year he went to the *Quebec Gazette*, where he remained until 1849. That year E.-R. Fréchette became sole owner of *Le Canadien* and lost no time reinstating Macdonald as editor. It was his last position. On 15 Oct. 1854 Ronald Macdonald, then 57, died at Quebec. *Le Canadien*, "bearing a black border," mourned its editor as a writer who was a "model of clarity of expression and good taste."

All Ronald Macdonald's contemporaries agreed that he was a great journalist, a competent school-teacher, a discriminating writer, and a conscientious and honest man. Among the writers who had come from outside Lower Canada to settle there, he was, as many stressed, one of those who had contributed the most to the awakening and appreciation of literature and the arts. He was French in heart and mind, not by duty, but by choice.

JOCELYN SAINT-PIERRE

ANQ-Q, CE1-1, 16 avril 1822, 15 oct. 1854. ASQ, Fichier des anciens. L.C., House of Assembly, *Journals*, 1830–32. *Le Canadien*, 31 mars 1832, 4 nov. 1842, 16 oct. 1854. *Quebec Gazette*, 2 May–29 Oct. 1842. Beaulieu et Hamelin, *La presse québécoise*, 1: 2–3, 16–17, 72, 86, 91, 93. F.-M. Bibaud, *Le panthéon canadien* (A. et V. Bibaud; 1891). Caron, "Inv. de la corr. de Mgr Plessis," ANQ *Rapport*, 1927–28: 297; 1932–33: 127–28. L.-M. Darveau, *Nos hommes de lettres* (Montréal, 1873), 273–74. Morgan, *Bibliotheca Canadensis*. *Quebec almanac*, 1824–26. I.[-F.-T.] Lebrun, *Tableau statistique et politique des deux Canadas* (Paris, 1833). Germain Lesage, *Histoire de Louiseville, 1665–1960* (Louiseville, Qué., 1961), 148. P.-G. Roy, *L'Île d'Orléans* (Québec, 1928), 419–21. A.[-E.] Gosselin, "Ronald MacDonald," *BRH*, 27 (1921): 319. "L'incendie du théâtre Saint-Louis," *BRH*, 5 (1899): 343–44. Lacertus [Richard Lessard], "Un instituteur d'autrefois," *L'Écho de Saint-Justin* (Louiseville), 1er mars 1926: 11. P.-G. Roy, "Le journaliste Ronald MacDonald," *BRH*, 42 (1936): 443–48. "Les sourds-muets en Canada," *Magasin du Bas-Canada* (Montréal), 1 (1832): 112–14.

McDONELL, ALLAN, fur trader and politician; b. *c.* 1776 probably in Glen Garry (Highland), Scotland, son of Donald MacDonell, seventh of Lundie, and his third wife, a Miss MacDonald of Islay; d. 16 June 1859 in Montreal.

Having lost his ancestral lands through impoverish-ment, Donald MacDonell immigrated to British North America with his family and settled at Martintown, Upper Canada. In February 1799 Allan, who signed his name McDonell, joined the Montreal fur-trading firm of Forsyth, Richardson and Company [*see* John Forsyth*; John Richardson*] as an apprentice clerk and was sent to the northwest. This firm was one of the partners in the New North West Company (sometimes called the XY Company), which was competing with the North West Company. After the union of these two companies in 1804 [*see* Sir Alexander Mackenzie*], McDonell served as clerk in the expanded NWC at Fort Dauphin (Man.) on Lake Dauphin, and two years later he accompanied the Nor'Westers Alexander Henry* the younger and Charles Chaboillez* on their expedition to the Mandan villages on the upper Missouri River. During the years of conflict between the NWC and the Hudson's Bay Company, he remained in the Fort Dauphin and Red River departments, becoming an NWC partner in 1816. In June of that year he was in the Red River area and was listed by HBC officer Peter Fidler* as one of the NWC men "looking on" while the group of Métis led by Cuthbert GRANT ransacked the HBC's Brandon House. Later that summer he was one of the NWC partners arrested by Lord Selkirk [Douglas*] at Fort William (Thunder Bay, Ont.) as accessories to the murder of Governor Robert Semple*, who had been killed with about 20 Red River colonists in a battle with Grant's men at Seven Oaks (Winnipeg) on 19 June. On 22 Oct. 1818, with 13 others, he was indicted by the grand jury at York (Toronto), but he and several others were never tried, apparently not being in custody. He does not seem to have been actively involved in the events at Seven Oaks, although the testimony of one witness, John Palmer Bourke, implied that he had a reputation for violence.

When the HBC absorbed the NWC in 1821 [*see* Simon McGillivray*], McDonell was made chief trader and placed in charge of the Swan River district at Fort Dauphin. One of the principal functions of this district was the collection and transport of provisions such as salt, sugar, and pemmican for the more remote northwestern posts. Each spring McDonell conducted these supplies down the Assiniboine River and up to Norway House (Man.). He did not take advantage of the furlough granted to him in 1823 and stayed in the Swan River district until 1826, when the Council of the Northern Department posted him to the Timiskam-ing district. Initially he shared the management of this district with Chief Trader Angus Cameron*; in 1827 he became sole commander and a year later he was promoted chief factor.

By 1834 HBC governor George SIMPSON was dissatisfied with McDonell's handling of his men and the Indians, and his methods for dealing with the independent traders who were moving into the area.

Macdonell

McDonell was therefore granted a year's furlough and was replaced by Cameron. In 1835 he was appointed to the Rainy Lake district; he stayed there until 1841 when he was allowed two years' furlough before officially retiring in 1843. While at Rainy Lake he had been appointed to the Council of Assiniboia on 20 March 1839.

After retirement from the HBC, McDonell settled on the mountain in Montreal with his wife and family. McDonell's wife, who was baptized Margaret at Red River in 1833, was the daughter of Æneas Cameron* of Timiskaming. Their house, Lundy Cottage, which overlooked the ruins of Simon McTavish*'s unfinished residence, was described by another retired fur trader, George KEITH, as "a splendid mansion, with a valuable altho small lot of land attached" and with "elegant accomodations and furniture." With Peter Warren Dease*, John CLARKE, and others, McDonell was among those retired ex-Nor'Westers whom Simpson deplored as "sauntering through the streets of Montreal & smoking away the remainder of the day in Sword's Barroom." Yet, although Angus Cameron's nephew Angus Cameron, a banker, did not consider McDonell's means well invested, being mostly in railway stock, he told his uncle that McDonell managed his affairs very economically. By 1848 McDonell was almost blind from cataracts, and two operations, in Montreal in 1851 and in London in 1852, did little to help. Nevertheless, in 1855 the younger Angus Cameron noted that he was still able to "see and tell the colours of brandy & Water from pure water." He died in Montreal at the age of 83 and was buried in the Roman Catholic cemetery Notre-Dame-des-Neiges on 18 June 1859.

The McDonells had at least seven children and Mrs McDonell was still living in Montreal in 1876. Governor Simpson characterized McDonell in 1832 as "a good rather than a clever fellow" and this opinion seems to have been shared by his other friends who, again like Simpson, also appreciated his kindness, generosity, and wit. He acquitted himself creditably in the Northern Department, where he spent most of his career, but had less success in Timiskaming with its largely Canadian servants and rapidly increasing opposition from Canada. Although deficient in education himself, he did his best for his children, one of whom, Angus, was educated to be a doctor, and another, John, became a Jesuit. Former colleagues as well as young Angus Cameron all spoke of him with affection, and Chief Factor Cameron nicknamed him "Sir Allan," perhaps a compliment to his Highland lineage.

ELAINE ALLAN MITCHELL

Æneas and Angus Cameron papers are in the possession of E. A. Mitchell of Toronto (mfm. at AO).

ANQ-M, CN1-29, 5 févr. 1799. Glengarry Geneal. Soc. (Lancaster, Ont.), E. A. Mitchell, "An aspect of one branch line of the Macdonells of Lundie." *Les bourgeois de la Compagnie du Nord-Ouest* (Masson), vol.1. *Docs. relating to NWC* (Wallace). Hargrave, *Hargrave corr.* (Glazebrook). *HBRS*, 2 (Rich and Fleming); 3 (Fleming). *Report of the proceedings connected with the disputes between the Earl of Selkirk and the North-West Company at the assizes, held at York, in Upper Canada, October 1818, from minutes taken in court* (Montreal, 1819). *Report of trials in the courts of Canada, relative to the destruction of the Earl of Selkirk's settlement on the Red River; with observations*, ed. Andrew Amos (London, 1820). Simpson, "Character book," *HBRS*, 30 (Williams), 151–236. J. A. Macdonell, *Sketches illustrating the early settlement and history of Glengarry in Canada, relating principally to the Revolutionary War of 1775–83, the War of 1812–14 and the rebellion of 1837–8 . . .* (Montreal, 1893). E. A. Mitchell, *Fort Timiskaming and the fur trade* (Toronto and Buffalo, N.Y., 1977).

MACDONELL, Sir JAMES, army officer and politician; b. in Inverness-shire, Scotland, 3rd son of Duncan Macdonell, 14th chief of the Macdonell clan of Glengarry, and Marjory Grant, daughter of Sir Ludovic Grant; d. 15 May 1857 in London.

Born into an ancient Highland clan, James Macdonell was probably educated at Douai, France, where most of the Roman Catholic Highland gentry sent their sons. He began his military career as ensign in an independent company in 1793. A year later he was promoted to lieutenant in the 78th Foot and on 1 Dec. 1795 was appointed captain in the 17th Light Dragoons in which he commanded a troop for nine years.

When the second battalion of the 78th was formed in 1804, Macdonell was appointed one of its majors, serving in the Kingdom of Naples and in Sicily. He continued with this regiment until 1809, distinguishing himself at the battle of Maida (Italy) and in the Egyptian campaign. After serving in Portugal on the staff of Arthur Wellesley (later the Duke of Wellington) for two years, he exchanged into the Coldstream Foot Guards as captain (with the rank of lieutenant-colonel in the army) and saw active duty with the regiment throughout the Peninsular War and in North Holland, Netherlands, in 1814.

The night before the battle of Waterloo, Wellington sent Macdonell with the guards to occupy the Château de Hougoumont. Macdonell held this key position against overwhelming French attacks during the early part of the battle. When French troops were forcing their way into the courtyard, Macdonell, aided by a sergeant, closed and held the gates by sheer physical strength. Chosen by Wellington for the award of £1,000 as the "bravest man in the British Army," Macdonell insisted upon sharing the sum with his sergeant.

Macdonell served with the Coldstream Guards until

1830 when, upon promotion to major-general, he was sent to Ireland. Created a knight bachelor in 1837, Macdonell remained in command of the troubled military district of Armagh (Northern Ireland) until 1838. After having been made a KCB in April, he was posted to Lower Canada in charge of the brigade of Guards sent over with Lord Durham [Lambton*] in May 1838.

Macdonell's posting to Canada at a time of civil unrest may partly have been the result of his clan connections, his religion, and his experience in Ireland during the 1830s. He had close personal and family ties with many of the Highlanders of Glengarry County, Upper Canada, some of whom had been recruited in 1794 by his brother, Alexander Ranaldson, chief of the clan, into the Glengarry Light Infantry Fencibles, the first Roman Catholic corps raised in the United Kingdom since the Reformation.

Within a month of his arrival at Quebec, as officer commanding the Quebec district, Macdonell was named by Durham on 28 June to the Special Council along with other military and naval officers to deal with the ordinance banishing Wolfred Nelson* and seven other Patriote leaders of the first rebellion to Bermuda. He remained a member of the council until after Durham's departure on 2 Nov. 1838. After his arrival Macdonell had lost no time in contacting his relative Bishop Alexander McDonell* of Kingston, who journeyed to Montreal at the end of June to visit him. Sir James entertained the bishop at Île Sainte-Hélène and introduced him to the military élite. In turn, with the bishop, Macdonell and other British officers visited various Roman Catholic institutions and dined with Joseph-Vincent QUIBLIER and other priests of the Séminaire de Saint-Sulpice in Montreal. In July, Bishop McDonell accompanied Sir James to Glengarry County where the general reviewed the four regiments of Glengarry Highlanders, addressing them in their native Gaelic.

When the second rebellion in Lower Canada broke out early in November 1838, Macdonell was ordered by Sir John Colborne* to Montreal with the Grenadier Guards to form part of the army marching south of the St Lawrence River on the insurgent headquarters at Napierville under the command of Robert Nelson*. Macdonell commanded the right wing composed of the guards, the 7th Hussars, and the 71st Foot, while Major-General John CLITHEROW commanded the left wing. After Napierville was invested, Macdonell's division marched through the neighbouring area capturing insurgents and burning the homes of known rebel leaders such as the Boyer brothers of Douglasburg (Coin-Douglas). Troopers of the Royal Montreal Cavalry were usually detailed by Macdonell to apply the torch to those houses slated for burning. Macdonell has been criticized by contemporaries and historians for not keeping a tighter rein on his troops.

The burning of homes of the rebel leaders was deliberate military policy, designed to intimidate those who contemplated further insurrection. Pillaging by troops under his command got out of control because of the initial orders by Colborne to have the troops live at free quarters, an invitation to plunder. Only after Lieutenant-Colonel George Cathcart told Macdonell that he could not "sacrifice the discipline of my men" by allowing them to live off the land, did Macdonell, who agreed with his view, forbid the practice. It was some time, however, before the pillaging ceased.

Macdonell remained in command of the troops south of the St Lawrence until February 1839 when he returned to his post in the Quebec district. He was offered the command in Upper Canada relinquished by Sir George ARTHUR in 1841, but declined it, preferring to remain in Quebec with the guards. He served in Canada until 1842 when, upon promotion to lieutenant-general, he returned to England where he subsequently became colonel of the 79th Foot and the 71st Foot.

Sir James Macdonell was more than a distinguished officer, renowned for his bravery and firmness. He was an exception, a Roman Catholic who had become a general officer, and his appointments to Ireland and Canada owed much to his religion and family connections as well as to his outstanding ability.

ELINOR KYTE SENIOR

PAC, MG 24, A40: 5554, 5581; B25, II: 136; J13; MG 27, I, E30, 5: 57. PRO, WO 17/1547: 102. *Arthur papers* (Sanderson), vols.2–3. *Gentleman's Magazine*, January–June 1857: 733. [Charles] Grey, *Crisis in the Canadas: 1838–1839, the Grey journals and letters*, ed. W. G. Ormsby (Toronto, 1964). *Montreal Gazette*, 13 Nov. 1838, 28 Sept. 1841. *Montreal Transcript*, 17 March, 7 Aug. 1838. Boase, *Modern English biog.*, 2: 587–88. Desjardins, *Guide parl. DNB*. G.B., WO, *Army list*, 1838, 1850. Filteau, *Hist. des Patriotes* (1938–42). Elinor Kyte Senior, *British regulars in Montreal: an imperial garrison, 1832–1854* (Montreal, 1981).

McDOUGALL, JOHN LORN, fur trader, farmer, businessman, office holder, and politician; b. 1800 on the Isle of Mull, Scotland, son of Samuel McDougall and —— MacLean, a daughter of the chief of the MacLean clan; m. 1 Sept. 1835 Catharine Cameron in Pointe-au-Chêne, Lower Canada, and they had five sons and four daughters; d. 17 May 1860 in Renfrew, Upper Canada.

Orphaned at an early age, John Lorn McDougall was raised by his MacLean aunts. On 8 Aug. 1820, at Inverness, Scotland, he joined the Hudson's Bay Company as a clerk and that year came to Lower Canada with John McLean*. After a brief stay in Montreal, McDougall was sent to the post at Lac des

McGill

Deux Montagnes, where he was reputedly initiated into the hardships of the trail by such veteran fur traders as Gabriel Franchère* and Dominique DUCHARME. From about 1825 to 1836 McDougall served at posts in the company's Ottawa River and Timiskaming districts. During that period, Governor George SIMPSON wrote in 1832, he proved to be a "very hardy rough active persevering Man" who was "exceedingly useful" in the HBC's vigorous competition with petty or free traders on the Ottawa River. Between 1836 and 1840 his account was with the post at Bonne Chere, one of the Ottawa valley posts superintended by Chief Factor James KEITH.

In 1837 and 1839 McDougall had purchased farms in the vicinity of the hamlet of Renfrew, on the Bonnechere River. He retired from the HBC in 1840, a major factor in this decision being, according to tradition, a long and rapid trek between Montreal and Lake Superior for reasons that remain unclear and for which he was not adequately thanked. He settled in Renfrew, opened its first general store, and later accumulated some 4,000 acres of additional land in the area. In 1855 he bought from Francis Hincks* a mill-seat in Renfrew at the "Second Chute" and built the community's first grist-mill, which was to become a museum in 1969.

McDougall was active in political affairs throughout the 20 years he lived in Renfrew. He sat on the Bathurst District Council in the 1840s and, between 1850 and 1857, served six terms on township council, frequently as reeve. Renfrew was incorporated as a village in 1858; though nominated for village council that year, McDougall was not elected until February 1860. As well he was elected to the Legislative Assembly for the riding of Renfrew in 1858 but resigned his seat almost immediately at the request of John A. Macdonald* to make a place for a defeated cabinet minister, William Cayley*. He subsequently became coroner for the United Counties of Lanark and Renfrew.

McDougall was described in a local history in 1919 as "shrewd, energetic, masterful, the most considerable man in the community." He sat in 1852 on a committee to set up a library and a mechanics' institute, and was a prominent member of the Sons of Temperance. A moving force behind the establishment of the Renfrew County agricultural society, he became in 1853 its first president, a post he held for several years. He kept around him a band of retainers and conducted his affairs in the autocratic fashion of a highland chief. While this style of life did not endear him to other members of the largely Scottish community, his hospitality was renowned. His last house, possessing what must have been the only ballroom in the area, was a centre for social activity in Renfrew. Catharine McDougall, who apparently exercised a moderating influence on her husband, was known to be "a model wife and mother."

McDougall died in Renfrew on 17 May 1860 "after a protracted illness," according to the *Perth Courier*. Of the surviving members of his family, his eldest son, John Lorn*, became Canada's auditor general in 1878.

JOHN LORN MCDOUGALL

ANQ-M, État civil, Presbytériens, Church of Scotland (Grenville), 1 sept. 1835. AO, RG 22, ser.164, reg.B: 88. PAC, RG 31, A1, 1851, Horton Township, including agricultural census; RG 68, General index, 1841–67: 53. PAM, HBCA, A.32/40: f.285; B.110/c/1: f.15d; B.134/c/9–41, especially B.134/c/31: f.242; B.134/c/41: ff.163–63d; B.134/g/2: ff.10d–11; B.134/g/3: ff.11d–12; B.134/g/4: ff.9d–10; B.134/g/5: ff.11d–12; B.134/g/6: f.8; B.134/g/7: f.13; B.134/g/8–15. J. A. Macdonald, *The letters of Sir John A. Macdonald*, ed. J. K. Johnson and C. B. Stelmack (2v., Ottawa, 1967–69), 1: 21, 335. John McLean, *John McLean's notes of a twenty-five year's service in the Hudson's Bay territory*, ed. W. S. Wallace (Toronto, 1932). Simpson, "Character book," *HBRS*, 30 (Williams), 223. *Perth Courier* (Perth, [Ont.]), 25 May 1860. *The John Rochester family in Canada . . .*, comp. L. B. Rochester (4th ed., Ottawa, 1976), 13–14, 22. W. E. Smallfield and Robert Campbell, *The story of Renfrew, from the coming of the first settlers about 1820* (Renfrew, Ont., 1919). H. J. Walker, *Renfrew and its fair: through 100 years* (Renfrew, 1953).

McGILL, PETER (known until 29 March 1821 as **Peter McCutcheon**), merchant, bank and company director, justice of the peace, and politician; b. August 1789 and baptized 1 September in Creebridge, Scotland, son of John McCutcheon and his second wife, Mary McGill; m. 15 Feb. 1832 Sarah Elizabeth Shuter Wilkins in London, and they had three sons, two of whom survived infancy; d. 28 Sept. 1860 in Montreal.

Peter McGill's career illustrates the limits to an understanding of the past that is possible through the biographical mode of historical writing. For his importance to the development of capitalism in Montreal has less to do with the man than it does with the many institutions in which he was active. He would owe much of that prominence to inherited wealth and a financially interesting marriage contract. Born to a family of apparently modest means, he arrived in Montreal from Scotland in June 1809, equipped with a grammar school education. His maternal uncle John McGill* was apparently instrumental in finding him a position as a clerk in the Montreal office of the large mercantile firm, Parker, Gerrard, Ogilvy and Company [see Samuel GERRARD]. John McGill had been an officer in the loyalist forces during the War of American Independence. Following the appointment of John Graves Simcoe* as lieutenant governor of Upper Canada, he moved to Niagara where Simcoe, his former commanding officer, appointed him commissary of stores. In a succession of official positions, McGill was active in the public administration and private appropriation that accompanied the establishment of the colony. His wife died in 1819 without leaving him an heir, so he bequeathed his substantial estate to his nephew, provided that McCutcheon adopt his family name. Although the name change became effective by royal licence on 29 March 1821, Peter McGill did not inherit the bulk of the estate until after the death of his uncle in 1834. In all likelihood, however, Peter's "much beloved uncle" helped him with contributions of capital in his early mercantile partnerships.

The first decade of McCutcheon's career in Montreal remains obscure. Both his obituaries and the hagiographical biographies published during the 19th century indicate that, after serving his clerkship at Parker, Gerrard, Ogilvy and Company, he was admitted to the firm as a junior partner. He may subsequently have become the junior Montreal partner in Porteous, Hancox, McCutcheon, and Cringan, an importing firm headed by Andrew Porteous* with offices in Montreal and Quebec, but no primary sources have been located to support the claim. In May 1820 McCutcheon entered into a partnership which would be the basis of his mercantile activities for the rest of his business career. The partnership initially consisted of Parker and Yeoward, timber brokers in London; William Price and Company of Quebec; and McCutcheon as the senior partner of a Montreal firm including Kenneth Dowie, known as McCutcheon and Dowie and later as McGill and Dowie. In 1823 there was a major realignment within the partnership. Nathaniel Gould and James Dowie, both of London, replaced Parker and Yeoward as the English partners with a 50 per cent interest in the firm. Kenneth Dowie left the firm and James Hetherington joined the Montreal office, which became Peter McGill and Company. The Montreal and Quebec offices each had a 25 per cent share in the business.

Mercantile partnerships of the early 19th century did not enjoy the legal protection of incorporation. Thus, the firm could be held responsible for claims against its partners for their activities outside the partnership itself, and merchants did frequently engage in business outside their partnerships. The activities of McGill's partnership were further complicated, for the evidence overwhelmingly suggests that, while the Quebec operations concentrated on the wood trades, the Montreal office was principally an import house.

McCutcheon had been working with Dowie prior to the establishment of the partnership, supplying local merchants and grocers. Between 1820 and 1826, 21 short-term credit arrangements involving either McCutcheon and Dowie or Peter McGill and Company were protested before a Montreal notary for non-payment. In all cases the firm had extended credit either to Montreal area merchants, grocers, and petty commodity producers or to mercantile firms in Upper Canada. The direction of these lines of credit indicates the role of the Montreal firm as a supplier of imported goods rather than an exporter of Canadian produce.

The cargo lists of imports and exports by sea through the St Lawrence valley in 1825 reveal that William Price and Company was a major exporter of wood products, responsible for 36 export consignments and only 6 import consignments in that boom year of the business cycle. The Montreal firm participated only 9 times in export shipments, while being responsible for 14 import consignments.

Peter McGill and Company's exports included potash, a by-product of land clearance and a staple trade of relatively minor value, controlled by Montreal mercantile firms. McGill's house was responsible for 1.56 per cent of the total exports of this commodity through the St Lawrence in 1825. The trade, however, was carried on with the English firm of Parker and Yeoward rather than with his partners, Gould and Dowie.

The apparent concentration by Peter McGill and Company on imports of British manufactured goods and on West Indian produce is further revealed by the firm's relations with its debtors in the years 1825 to 1829. Prior to filing for bankruptcy, a firm could reach agreement with its creditors and assign its assets to trustees, usually chosen from among the leading creditors, to wind up the business. December 1825 saw the first world-wide capitalist crash. Although his firm was not even a creditor of the large import house of Porteous and Nesbitt, the latter's creditors appointed McGill their trustee in the summer of 1825 to liquidate the assets in the first major assignment in Montreal: a clear indication of McGill's expertise in the import business. During the crisis years of 1825–29 Peter McGill and Company were involved as creditors in 14 assignments. There the pattern visible in the short-term credit arrangements continued. Grocers and spirit dealers such as Alexander and Lawrence Glass and Alexander Nimmo failed, each owing McGill more than the total value of his firm's annual potash exports.

The prominence of the import activities of the Montreal firm should not obscure the fact that the firm did have relationships with local commodity producers. In 1827 Peter McGill and Company handled the commercial distribution in the Canadas of over 15,000 gallons of locally produced liquor from the distillery near Courant Sainte-Marie owned by the Handyside brothers. Undoubtedly, some of this produce found its way into the army supply contracts that the firm undertook in that year.

Profiting from a one-quarter interest in William Price*'s growing wood trade and developing an important mercantile business, McGill's firm invested some of its profits in real estate. The company had been operating out of a leased commercial and

McGill

residential complex adjacent to the old market in Montreal. This two-storey stone structure was purchased by the firm in 1824, after the first year of an eight year lease. The following year the property was evaluated by Jacques VIGER as being worth £5,000.

Profit maximization for mercantile partnerships such as the one linking McGill, Price, Gould, and Dowie could best be achieved by ensuring that at least some of the vessels used in international trade were owned by the firm. McGill's direct involvement in shipping was limited. Jointly with Price he had the 226-ton brig *William Parker* built at Montreal in 1820; it was sold two years later in London. The full partnership had seven vessels, including schooners for the coastal trade and barques and brigs for the transatlantic business, built at Quebec, Saint-Jean-Port-Joli, and Sunderland, England, between 1824 and 1837. Most of the vessels were acquired after the world-wide collapse in the price of vessels which followed the crash of 1825. In contrast with Price, who had eight vessels registered in his own name during the same period, McGill never invested in ocean-going vessels on his own account, separate from the partnership, failing to capitalize on his involvement in the sector to build an independant base of wealth.

Thus, the *ex officio* head of the Montreal business community did not rise to prominence on the basis of staple trades. McGill would become involved in numerous ventures on his own account but few could be considered logical extensions of his activities in the moderately successful firm, described by its letter-head of the mid 1830s as "Importers of British Manufactures, East & West India Produce."

McGill's principal business activity outside the partnership was his long association with the Bank of Montreal. He became a member of the board of directors of the bank in 1819 and was elected vice-president in 1830 and president in 1834. For the next 26 years he served as the equivalent to the chairman of the board of the colony's single most important financial institution. When McGill joined the board, the president was Samuel Gerrard, McGill's former partner. By the mid 1820s Gerrard had come under increasing attack from within the bank for the manner in which he had managed its affairs. Joint-stock companies were rare in the British empire of the 1820s and, not surprisingly, Gerrard had been running the bank as if it were a mercantile partnership. He had hired personnel and lent the bank's money in his own name for a number of years. By the time of the crash, loans implicating up to 25 per cent of the bank's paid-up capital had been lent by Gerrard without any mention that he was lending in his capacity as president. It became evident that the bank would have serious difficulties acting in its own name to recover the outstanding debts. The situation provoked a revolt against the president by several members of the board. Led by George Moffatt* and James Leslie*, these directors tried to force Gerrard's resignation and to have a new series of rules and regulations drawn up which would ensure that the shareholders would be protected against a similar occurrence in the future.

In every important vote taken on the numerous issues relating to the crisis, McGill supported Gerrard in his struggle against reform. As Gerrard's protégé, McGill was the only younger member of the board to support the old guard consistently. The Moffatt faction eventually forced Gerrard to resign, but not before McGill managed to block legal actions against him. An industrialist, John Molson* Sr, was brought in as president in June 1826 to put the bank back on the tracks, and in the following year a new cashier (general manager), Benjamin Holmes*, was given enhanced powers but was to report to a committee of the board of directors rather than to the president. Following the premature deaths of Molson Sr's successors, John Fleming* and Horatio Gates*, McGill acceded to the presidency as the senior member of the board, with 15 years' experience. The resolution of the crisis provoked by Gerrard had resulted in the stripping of much of the power of the presidency. Ironically, these changes which McGill had fought against permitted him to serve for a longer term than any other president, and thus assured his place in history.

Despite the favourable treatment McGill has received from historians writing about the Bank of Montreal, there is little to suggest that he played a major role in the bank's continued expansion during his tenure. Indeed, in the key political episode involving its extension into branch banking in Upper Canada, which had been denied by its original charter, the bank obtained the gerrymandering of the Montreal electoral districts in 1841 to ensure that Holmes would be available to guide the necessary legislation through the new Legislative Assembly of the United Province of Canada. This, despite the fact that McGill had already sat on the Executive and Legislative councils before the union of the Canadas and would be reappointed to the Legislative Council in June 1841.

As vice-president of the bank in 1830, McGill had undertaken a trip to Great Britain on behalf of the institution in an attempt to secure a royal charter. The resultant charter was too restrictive to be of much use. While there, McGill married Sarah Elizabeth Shuter Wilkins. Sarah was the daughter of Robert Charles Wilkins, a partner in the important Canadian mercantile firm of Shuter and Wilkins which had been particularly active in the Bay of Quinte region of Upper Canada. She brought to the marriage a dowry of £10,000 in real estate, which was to be placed in a trust fund managed by McGill, with all proceeds accruing to him during their marriage. At his death the trust was to revert to his wife.

McGill reached the height of his career during the early 1830s. The mercantile partnership had survived the crisis years and he had begun to diversify his interests. By 1824 he had become involved in the Marmora ironworks in Upper Canada. Active in the hiring of skilled workmen for this early foundry, he soon limited his relationship with the firm to that of a *rentier* capitalist. The direct supervision and management was left to Anthony Manahan* and others. In the late 1840s McGill sold the works to Joseph Van Norman*.

On his trip to Great Britain, McGill had negotiated a long-term loan from the estate of George Stanfield to permit Moses Judah Hayes* to purchase and revamp the Montreal waterworks. In cooperation with John MOLSON Jr and other Bank of Montreal directors, McGill became active in the new steamboat monopoly on the Ottawa River. The Ottawa and Rideau Forwarding Company, a corporate restructuring of the Ottawa Steamboat Company, was to be McGill's only fruitful long-term investment. At his death in 1860, it was providing him with an annual revenue of £728.

As a member of the Legislative Council since January 1832, the Honourable Peter McGill – for members of council were all honourable men – was active in Lower Canada's largest land deal. Organized in 1832 by Russell Ellice and Nathaniel Gould, McGill's London partner, the British American Land Company was sold over a million acres in the Eastern Townships for the sum of £110,321 sterling, by the British government. It thus had a stranglehold on much of the undeveloped agricultural land in the colony. McGill, along with Moffatt, was appointed a commissioner in Canada for the company in 1834. The commissioners' most important duty, overseeing the purchase of 147 different tracts of land in the developed regions of the townships, was completed by June 1835, thus ensuring almost absolute control over the subsequent agricultural and industrial development of the region.

In 1831 McGill became the first chairman of the board of directors of the Champlain and St Lawrence Railroad, which ran from La Prairie to Saint-Jean (Saint-Jean-sur-Richelieu). Although he was probably only a minor shareholder in British North America's first railway (it used wood not only for the ties but for the rails as well), his prominence in the business community had given this early venture greater credibility than it would otherwise probably have merited. In 1845, together with John Alfred Poor*, Alexander Tilloch Galt*, Moffatt, and others, he was an early promoter of the St Lawrence and Atlantic Rail-road. He sat on the first board of directors of the railway which, when completed, would link Montreal and Portland through the Eastern Townships. Upon the railway's merger with the Grand Trunk in 1853, he went on to the new board.

McGill was not only an honourable man, but a religious man. A life-long member of the Church of Scotland, he and John Redpath* owned St Paul's Church in Montreal and only sold it to the trustees on condition that it and its associated school be kept free of the heresies of the "Great Disruption" or the Erskinites. Lest it be thought that this defence of Calvinist orthodoxy by McGill was evidence of a narrow-minded approach to religious matters, it should be stressed that Sarah, who was a member of the Church of England, brought up their sons, John Shuter Davenport and Sydenham Clitherow, as Anglicans, and McGill subsidized the construction of the Congregational church. It must be admitted that the latter was part of a larger real estate deal in which McGill was attempting to develop a number of lots, and the church would serve as a selling point. Be that as it may, he was a long-time president of the Montreal Auxiliary Bible Society (1834–43) and the Lay Association of Montreal (1845–60) and was elected elder of St Paul's in 1845.

McGill was also a community leader in matters social and mystical. The first president of the St Andrew's Society (1835–42), he went on to become the provincial grand superintendent of Royal Arch masonry for the Province of Canada. While holding that post from 1847 to 1850, he also served the almost mandatory term of president of the Montreal Board of Trade in 1848.

McGill had been a member of the Legislative Council from January 1832 to March 1838. In April 1838 he was appointed to the Special Council set up with dictatorial powers following the rebellion of 1837. He sat for two months and from November 1838 to 1841 was a member of both the Special and Executive councils. As president of the Constitutional Association of Montreal from 1836 to 1839, McGill had been the spokesman for the Anglo-Scottish mercantile community and he had advocated the union of Upper and Lower Canada as a solution to the colonies' problems. After the union in 1841, he was again appointed to the Legislative Council and remained a member until his death, serving as its speaker from May 1847 to March 1848. Concomitant with his term as speaker, he again served on the Executive Council, as a member of the conservative ministry of Henry SHERWOOD and Denis-Benjamin PAPINEAU until December 1847 and, after Papineau's resignation, in the ministry led by Sherwood alone. A justice of the peace for the district of Montreal since at least 1827, McGill had participated in the day to day running of the city in the years prior to its gaining a charter. He was therefore a politically safe person for the Colonial Office to appoint as the city's first mayor in 1840. He declined to seek elective office when the first mayoralty campaign took place in 1842. Thus, although McGill held high political office, it was always as an appointed official, a fact that bears witness more to the importance of his business

McGill

connections and those of the Bank of Montreal than to any particularly strong political character of the man himself.

McGill had gone heavily in debt to his partners as the result of a speculative mercantile venture in 1843. As late as 1859 he owed £40,981 in principal plus 16 years' back interest to his London partners. The situation was further complicated by his debt to the firm as a result of the £70,000 sterling that Price owed the London partnership, dating from 1853. McGill had acted as surety for Price's loan from the partnership. For the last 17 years of McGill's life, his business was in liquidation. It was only by mortgaging his wife's trust fund that he was able to borrow £30,000 from the Bank of Montreal in 1859. By borrowing from a bank of which he was president and by using his wife's dowry, McGill was able to reschedule his heavy debt load.

McGill's active career in a variety of fields necessarily leads to a distorted perception of its nature. But if the same criteria of profit and loss which are used to judge the success of a firm's operations are applied to the career of an individual mercantile capitalist, McGill was clearly a failure. After all outstanding debts had been settled, the estate McGill left to his two sons was a very modest one: each received only $36,174. The *ex officio* head of the Montreal business community failed to establish a fortune that would ensure the continuance of the McGills as a leading bourgeois family in the city. The reality behind the public image was an estate comparable to one a minor industrialist might have accumulated. Perhaps this explains his request that the funeral arrangements be of a "plain inexpensive and unostentatious manner." Yet, conscious of image to the end, McGill had asked to be buried in Mount Royal Cemetery in the presence of his domestic servants, all sporting mourning suits provided by the estate. The estate also paid for the publication of the sermon preached in his honour on the Sunday after his death.

McGill's failure is understandable when placed within the context of the profound changes in the organization of the Montreal economy. His career coincided with the industrial revolution and in a period when the leading bourgeois families of the city would increasingly owe their wealth to the control of the means of production, McGill, despite numerous opportunities in manufacturing and transportation, failed to take advantage of his situation. Unlike his colleagues Molson and Redpath, he remained essentially a mercantile capitalist in the new age of industrial capitalism.

ROBERT SWEENY

[In the absence of the records of Peter McGill and Company, the history of the firm must be reconstituted from the following materials: ANQ-M (CN1-295, 7 oct., 30 déc. 1826; 10 mars, 7 juin 1827); Montreal Business Hist. Project (Assignment cross-reference file; General agreement file; Monetary protests, nominal series); *Quebec Commercial List* (Quebec), 1825; and Joanne Burgess and Margaret Heap, "Les marchands montréalais dans le commerce d'exportation du Bas-Canada, 1815–1888" (paper delivered before the Institut d'histoire de l'Amérique française, Montreal, in 1978). R.S.]

ANQ-M, CM1, 1/17; CN1-7, 22 mars 1833; CN1-187, 8 sept. 1823, 22 févr. 1827, 16 janv. 1844; CN1-102, 2 févr.–17 juin 1835; CN1-134, 6 nov. 1824, 12 juin 1826, 11 oct. 1828; P1000-3-309. ASQ, Fonds Viger–Verreau, carton 46, liasse 9. McGill Univ. Libraries (Montreal), Dept. of Rare Books and Special Coll., MS coll., CH297.S257; CH377.S337; CH341.S301; CH423.OLS; CH441.RBR. PAC, MG 28, II2; RG 68, General index, 1651–1841, 1841–67. William Snodgrass, *The night of death; a sermon, preached on the 7th Oct., 1860, being the first Sabbath after the funeral of the Honourable Peter M'Gill* (Montreal, 1860). *Globe*, 3 Oct. 1860. *Montreal Gazette*, 28 Feb. 1828, 21 Feb. 1835, 1 Oct. 1860. William Notman and [J.] F. Taylor, *Portraits of British Americans, with biographical sketches* (3v., Montreal, 1865–68). Terrill, *Chronology of Montreal*. Denison, *Canada's first bank*. Albert Faucher, "La condition nord-américaine des provinces britanniques et l'impérialisme économique du régime Durham–Sydenham, 1839–1841," *Histoire économique et unité canadienne* (Montréal, 1970). Tulchinsky, *River barons*. Adam Shortt, "Founders of Canadian banking: the Hon. Peter McGill, banker, merchant and civic leader," Canadian Bankers' Assoc., *Journal* (Toronto), 31 (1923–24): 297–307.

McGILL, ROBERT, Presbyterian minister and editor; b. 21 May 1798 in Ayr, Scotland, son of William McGill; m. Catherine McLimont, and they had at least three children; d. 4 Feb. 1856 in Montreal.

Robert McGill, the third son of a schoolteacher, was born and brought up in Ayr, Scotland. Initially taught by his father, he went on to the University of Glasgow and then, aspiring to the ministry, entered divinity. He was licensed by the Church of Scotland's Presbytery of Glasgow but, unable to find a permanent post, he accepted the onerous job of relief preacher, substituting for ministers throughout the presbytery.

In 1829 the long-established Presbyterian congregation of Niagara (Niagara-on-the-Lake), Upper Canada, petitioned the Glasgow Colonial Society for a minister. The request was passed on to the Presbytery of Glasgow and McGill accepted the call with its promise of £150 per annum. After being ordained by the presbytery on 15 July 1829, he set sail for America, arriving at Niagara in October.

McGill, a powerful, fervent preacher and a conscientious pastor, enjoyed his years in Niagara. He began construction of a new church, St Andrew's, in 1831, erected a manse, organized a strong congregation, and became a leader in local affairs, in particular taking a keen interest in educational matters. Enthralled as he was by the beauty and immensity of the country, he was appalled by the paucity and isolation of its Church of Scotland ministers and incensed by the lack of government recognition of his church's claims to establishment. Full of enthusiasm, he set out to rectify the situation. It was to be his lifelong conviction that the solution lay in numbers, organization, and, during the early years, the close support of the Scottish church. He urged the Glasgow Colonial Society to send and initially support a constant stream of missionaries, since many areas were too poor to sustain a minister. Once in the Canadas, he maintained, they would soon find permanent posts.

At the same time he rallied those ministers interested in forming a colonial synod, and in June 1831 saw the foundation of the Synod of the Presbyterian Church of Canada in connection with the Church of Scotland. A born organizer, he played a vital role in the new body, heading or sitting upon innumerable committees and serving as synod clerk from 1831 to 1835 and as moderator in 1839. A leader of the negotiations begun in 1831 for union with other Presbyterian groups in the Canadas, he, with the prominent Presbyterian layman William MORRIS, was instrumental in bringing about the union of their church and the United Synod of Upper Canada in 1840. From an early date he recognized the need to train ministers locally, supporting first the demand for a Presbyterian theological chair at the proposed King's College, Toronto, and then the plan to found a separate Church of Scotland seminary. After the decision was taken to create Queen's College, Kingston, he was appointed senior member of the board of trustees, a post he held until his death.

McGill published regularly. In March 1837 he founded the *Canadian Christian Examiner, and Presbyterian Review*, a monthly periodical intended to maintain the faith in areas without a preacher, and edited the paper until shortly before its demise in December 1840. His major work was a collection of prayers and meditations for the young, printed in Niagara in 1842.

Noted for his talents as a conciliator, McGill had smoothed over many contentious issues among his colleagues in the 1830s. As tensions rose within the church over the nature of the relationship that should exist between their synod and the Church of Scotland, he was at the centre, heading various committees in an attempt to find a compromise solution. When, despite all efforts, the church split on the issue in 1844, McGill, fearful of jeopardizing its state aid, stayed with the Church of Scotland synod. Next year, after the death of the Reverend Edward Black*, the parishioners of St Paul's in Montreal asked McGill to become their pastor. He found the lure of the city irresistible. In November 1845 he was inducted into his new charge and quickly became involved in the local scene, championing various Protestant charities.

Upset by the split that had taken place within the

church in 1844, McGill tried, as convener of a series of committees on the problems arising out of the rupture, to avoid exacerbating the situation, even though he concluded, with regret, that for the time being reconciliation was impossible. He continued to press for better organization, more ministers from Scotland, and increased efforts to find local ministerial candidates. Reunion, though, remained his chief goal. In 1852 he raised the subject again, arguing for a merger of the various Presbyterian groups in the Canadas. Three years later, just months before his death, he went to New Brunswick as the chief delegate of his church to lay before the synod there the need for all branches of the Presbyterian faith in British North America to unite.

McGill's unceasing work on behalf of his church was recognized in 1853 when he was awarded an honorary DD by the University of Glasgow.

H. J. BRIDGMAN

An outline of McGill's career is contained at the QUA in the session, presbytery, and synod records of the Presbyterian Church of Canada in connection with the Church of Scotland, and in the UCA biog. files. He was the author of "A Canadian missionary," Glasgow Colonial Soc., *Report* (Glasgow), 1835: 56–57; *The love of country, a discourse preached in St. Andrew's Church, Niagara, on Tuesday, the 6th February 1838, (a day appointed for public thanksgiving, on account of our deliverance from the miseries of the late insurrection)* (Niagara [Niagara-on-the-Lake, Ont.], 1838); *Letter to the friends of the Presbyterian Church of Canada, on the establishment of a literary and theological college* (Niagara, 1839); *Prayers, and devout meditations, designed to assist the young Christian in the cultivation of a devout temper* (Niagara, 1842); *Brief notes on the relation of the synod of Canada to the Church of Scotland, (being the basis of an exposition of this subject to the Presbyterian congregation of Niagara, on Wednesday evening, March 6th, 1844)* (Niagara, [1844]); *Report on the part of the convener of the synod's committee to negotiate on the subject of reunion with the seceding brethren* (Niagara, [1844]); *Letters on the condition and prospects of Queen's College, Kingston, addressed to the Hon. William Morris, chairman of the board of trustees* (Montreal, [1846]); and *Discourses preached on various occasions, in the course of ministerial duty* (Montreal, 1853). Along with George Sheed and Alexander GALE, he also wrote "Memorial on the state of religion in certain districts of Upper Canada," Glasgow Soc. (in Connection with the Established Church of Scotland), for Promoting the Religious Interests of the Scottish Settlers in British North America, *Annual report* (Glasgow), 1831: 28–32.

The journal McGill edited appeared as the *Canadian Christian Examiner, and Presbyterian Rev.* (Niagara), 1 (1837)–2 (1838), and then continued in Toronto as the *Christian Examiner, and Presbyterian Magazine*, 3 (1839)–4 (1840).

ANQ-M, CE1-125, 1 nov. 1864. UCA, James Croil papers, diary, 1866–67: 51; Glasgow Colonial Soc., corr., 2 (1829–30), nos.153, 202; 5 (1834–35), no.201; 6 (1836–38), nos.119, 222, 282–83; 7 (1839–43), nos.76, 83. John

McGillivray

Cook, *A sermon preached on the occasion of the death of the Rev. Robert McGill, D.D., minister of St. Paul's Church, Montreal* (Montreal, 1856). Croil, *Hist. and statistical report* (1868), 11–12. Glasgow Soc. (in Connection with the Established Church of Scotland), for Promoting the Religious Interests of the Scottish Settlers in British North America, *Annual report*, 1829: 18; 1830: 13; 1831: 16. *Presbyterian*, 8 (1855): 98, 155; 9 (1856): 35–36, 130; 17 (1864): 358. *Montreal Gazette*, 5–6 Feb. 1856. *Montreal Transcript*, 5 Feb. 1856. *The matriculation albums of the University of Glasgow from 1728 to 1858*, comp. W. I. Addison (Glasgow, 1913). *A roll of the graduates of the University of Glasgow from 31st December, 1727, to 31st December, 1897 with short biographical notes*, comp. W. I. Addison (Glasgow, 1898), 372. Scott *et al.*, *Fasti ecclesiæ scoticanæ*, vol.7. Janet Carnochan, *Centennial, St Andrews, Niagara, 1794–1894* (Toronto, 1895). Gregg, *Hist. of Presbyterian Church*.

McGILLIVRAY (Dalcrombie), JOHN, fur trader, gentleman farmer, justice of the peace, office holder, landowner, and politician; b. *c.* 1770 in Strathnairn, Scotland, son of Farquhar MacGillivray of Dalcrombie and Elizabeth Shaw of Dores; m. first *c.* 1796 *à la façon du pays* an Indian woman, and they had one son and one daughter; m. secondly 23 Feb. 1819 Isabella McLean, daughter of Neil McLean*, and they had four sons and four daughters; d. 13 Oct. 1855 at his farm near Williamstown, Upper Canada.

John McGillivray was a child of the late 18th-century Highlands: born at a time of major economic change and social readjustment, he was familiar with both traditional Gaelic life and the modern commercial world. The Dalcrombies were a cadet branch of the McGillivray clan chiefs and had been active Jacobites. As a boy John learned the language of the community – Gaelic – and its songs, with which he later delighted Highlanders in Montreal, but he also received a good Scottish primary education in English. The Highlands offered little opportunity for promising young men, and so, when North West Company partner William McGillivray*, a distant cousin, visited Inverness-shire on furlough in 1793–94, John likely decided to go to North America with him.

The younger McGillivray was engaged as a clerk by the NWC on 18 July 1794 for a seven-year term. He served in the Lower English (Churchill) River department under the direction of Alexander Fraser* and was stationed at Rat River (Goose River, Sask.) in 1797, built a house at Pelican Lake (Sask.) in September 1798, and opposed the Hudson's Bay Company post at Sturgeon Lake (Cumberland Lake, Sask.) in the winter of 1801. The NWC offensive to protect the profitable Athabasca trade, opened up by Peter Pond*, was waged here in the Churchill and along the Saskatchewan River where the Canadians' stiff opposition kept the HBC fully occupied and out of the far west. In the Lower English River department, however, as Fraser acknowledged to Alexander Mackenzie* in 1799, NWC prospects were "not very favourable the English have got so fast a hold there." Relations between traders in the area were unfriendly. In the spring of 1798 McGillivray had reacted to the desertion of an NWC indebted servant to the HBC's Granville House (on Granville Lake, Man.) by seizing three packs of furs from its master Thomas Linklater. To accomplish this end, McGillivray, according to HBC trader William Auld*, "was obliged to give repeated orders to his men before any would obey & then he set them the example." Such actions reflected the private settling of grievances that was the NWC norm in the fur trade, one that imitated the traditional practice of Highland society.

McGillivray became a wintering partner in the NWC at Grand Portage (near Grand Portage, Minn.) in 1801; it was probably then that he transferred to Athabasca River, a small department south of the larger Athabasca department. Certainly from 1806 until 1810 he headed the smaller district from his post at Lesser Slave Lake. After a furlough over the winter of 1810–11, he moved to Fort Dunvegan (on the Peace River at 118°40′ W) and took charge of the important Athabasca department, succeeding Donald McTavish*. In 1815–16 the HBC mounted a large expedition to Athabasca under John CLARKE: McGillivray orchestrated the isolation of the HBC men from the Indians, eliminating the newcomers' trade and starving them into surrender.

Although not as well known as his explorer-colleagues David THOMPSON and Simon Fraser*, John McGillivray was an important figure in the bitter competition between the HBC and NWC. For more than 20 years he worked effectively in areas of rich returns and strong opposition. McGillivray was a righteous man convinced of his own probity and worth, and ruled by standards of "urbanity and decorum suitable" to a gentleman. His administration of Athabasca was, however, criticized by other NWC partners; Archibald Norman McLeod* claimed that he "would not have been left [there] so long . . . were his name not McGillivray." McLeod's comments that McGillivray was too slow and "unfit to conduct an opposition" suggest that he was not as ruthless as some of his colleagues, who could nevertheless not name a man better able to do the job.

On his arrival at Fort William (Thunder Bay, Ont.) on 20 Aug. 1816, two months after the massacre at Seven Oaks (Winnipeg) [*see* Cuthbert GRANT], McGillivray was taken prisoner by Lord Selkirk [Douglas*] and sent east under guard three days later to join the other NWC partners arrested earlier. McGillivray denied complicity in the Seven Oaks incident and pleaded his powerlessness as an individual to alter company practices. The charges against him were not pursued and McGillivray spent the ensuing winter in Great Britain. In 1817 George KEITH assumed charge of the Athabasca department. McGillivray returned as far west as Rainy Lake (Ont.) where he organized brigade departures, but, his health weakened by rheumatism, the ageing partner retired from the NWC in 1818 to settle in Upper Canada.

With his purchase of a farm for £1,450 near Williamstown and his marriage to Isabella McLean, McGillivray was drawn into the kin-based gentry of Glengarry County and successfully established himself as a leader in the Highland community there. The retired trader held a variety of local offices, including justice of the peace and commissioner of the court of requests. A Presbyterian, he was an influential member of St Andrew's Church [*see* John McKEN-ZIE] and was chosen an elder on 7 July 1822. McGillivray had property interests across the eastern part of Upper Canada and in 1840 advertised "very desirable locations . . . for sale" to emigrants. He also acted as financial adviser and agent to the Roman Catholic bishop, Alexander McDonell*. In Glengarry, McGillivray enjoyed the convivial and cultural meetings of the Highland Society of Canada, and his home was well known for its proverbial "kind highland welcome" to visitors.

Only two major episodes broke the calm of McGillivray's retirement. Appointed with his neighbour Alexander FRASER, he served as a member of Upper Canada's Legislative Council from December 1839 until its dissolution in February 1841. Dismayed by the "passion of self Interest" that ruled "some mighty would be Individuals" in Toronto, McGillivray was one of the moderate tories who supported the union of the Canadas and the compromise settlement of the clergy reserves [*see* William MORRIS]. In his own words, he willingly helped bring "Down the mighty Doves of . . . [that] place" who had "had their own time of the Loaves & Fishes." Then in 1852 he returned to Scotland briefly to claim the estate of Dunmaglass and recognition as chief of the McGillivray clan; this recognition was officially awarded to his son in 1857.

As was proper for a Highland gentleman, John McGillivray passed an active, even predatory, early adulthood, but later settled down to raise a Scottish family. Although McGillivray came from a different part of Inverness-shire than did most of the Glengarry settlers, his descent from a clan chief and his successful fur-trade career assured his position as a leader of the community. Men such as McGillivray and Fraser played a mediating role between the Gaelic-speaking county and the rest of Upper Canadian society. The inheritance of the traditional position of clan chief was a fitting seal to McGillivray's life.

MARIANNE MCLEAN

PAC, MG 19, A35; B1; C1; E1 (transcripts); MG 24, I3; RG 4, B46. PAM, HBCA, B.42/a/124; B.118/a/1; F.1/1 (mfm. at PAC). *HBRS*, 26 (Johnson).

MACGREGOR, JOHN, merchant, landowner, civil servant, politician, and writer; b. 1797 at Drynie, near Stornoway, Scotland, eldest son of David MacGregor and Janet Ross; m. 30 Jan. 1833 Anne Jillard in London, and they had no children; d. 23 April 1857 in Boulogne, France.

Young John MacGregor immigrated with his parents to Pictou, N.S., in 1803 aboard the Stornoway brig *Alexander*. Local tradition has it that his father took charge of the vessel when the captain died and the owner became sick halfway across the Atlantic. In 1806 the family moved to Covehead on Prince Edward Island and took up 50 acres on Sir James Montgomery's Lot 34. Apparently well educated, John's father, in addition to farming, served as a surveyor and school teacher, and John undoubtedly acquired both his general education and his penchant for statistics from his father in the Covehead school.

In 1819 MacGregor advertised in the *Prince Edward Island Gazette* that he intended "to commence Business in this Town [Charlottetown]" with stock from Halifax, largely gin, rum, and dry goods, "sold cheap for cash." As well as running this mercantile establishment he obtained several lots in Charlottetown from Montgomery's agent James Curtis*, served as Curtis's attorney, and in 1823 succeeded him as agent for the Montgomery interests on the Island.

On 7 May 1822 MacGregor had been appointed high sheriff of the Island, an onerous office held for a year as a civic duty by aspiring young politicians. A few months later he complained to Lieutenant Governor Charles Douglass SMITH that the Charlottetown jail was so decrepit he feared for his own and the various debtors' safety every time he employed it. Early in 1823, however, MacGregor became involved in more important business than arresting and housing debtors. Smith and a son-in-law, acting receiver general John Edward Carmichael*, had moved in 1822 to collect quitrents which were well in arrears but had not been demanded of proprietors for some time. In January 1823 legal proceedings were begun against two leading resident proprietors, Donald McDONALD and John Stewart*, and then were extended to a number of small proprietors in Kings County. A group led by Stewart presented a petition to MacGregor as high sheriff asking him to convene meetings in the several shire towns to consider grievances against Smith and Carmichael. Despite explicit orders to the contrary from Smith and the Council, MacGregor, who as a proprietor's agent himself was not without an interest in the proceedings, did convene the meetings. As a result he was summarily dismissed as high sheriff. The meetings none the less were held and MacGregor ostentatiously served on the committee which prepared the inevitable public petition calling for Smith's recall. MacGregor and others, including Paul Mabey*, were put on trial in October 1823 for their part in the petition affair, and then released [see Ambrose LANE]. Not surprisingly, MacGregor was subsequently elected an MHA for Georgetown in the general election of November 1824, the first under the newly appointed Lieutenant Governor John Ready*, and attended the assembly's opening session of 1825.

By June of 1826 MacGregor was publicly advertising that he was leaving the Island and that his business would be taken over by two of his brothers. His decision was probably unconnected with his political adventures except in the sense that they had confirmed that the Island was not a large enough stage for his ambitions. Whether he was in financial difficulty at this juncture is not at all clear, although he was accused of absconding with the funds for the Prince Edward Island subscription library he had helped to found [see Walter Johnstone*]. In any event he moved to Liverpool, England, in 1827 and set up as a merchant and general commission-agent; of this endeavour the London *Times* later wrote: "His mercantile speculations were there unfortunate, and, indeed, rarely at any period of life successful." So unfortunate were they that he ultimately offered his creditors seven and a half pence on the pound as an alternative to bankruptcy. His heart, clearly, was not in business but on other, more exciting, matters.

Having travelled extensively in British North America and between the colonies and Britain, often aboard the newly inaugurated steamships, and having talked at length with businessmen about commercial prospects and emigration, MacGregor decided to become a political economist and commercial expert, at first specializing in Britain's American colonies. He became acquainted with James Deacon Hume and other political economists and began a lengthy writing career which resulted in the publication of more than 30 titles, many of them multi-volume works. His output included several travel accounts, a number of compilations of commercial data, and an incomplete history of the British Empire which, in its first two volumes, managed to get to 1655.

Contemporaries were most unkind to MacGregor's writing, one commenting, "We do not imagine that any one except the printers ever read these works through; yet the true historical writer might find in them useful materials for his purpose." Although this assessment may apply to many of his later publications, his first works, published between 1828 and 1832, were and are worth reading from beginning to end. In them he was able to rely on his own observation and experience and, emphasizing publicity for the various provinces of British America to a

British audience, showed at his most attractive. Particularly interested in bringing the advantages of the "Lower Provinces" to the attention of the British, MacGregor concentrated upon the Atlantic region in these early writings. In *Historical and descriptive sketches of the Maritime colonies of British America* (1828) he devoted an inordinate amount of space to Prince Edward Island and Newfoundland, commending the former for its ideal climate and recommending a legislative government for the latter, arguing that Newfoundlanders "are better informed than the same class in the United Kingdoms." In *Observations on emigration to British America* (1829) he asserted: "The retention of our North American Colonies is an object of such importance, that the very idea of abandoning them cannot be for a moment defended on just or political principles." The colonies needed immigrants, but "to gentlemen educated for the professions of law, divinity, or physic, British America offers no flattering prospects." Farmers, artisans, and labourers, industrious and healthy, were what British North America required. He advocated a settlement of Highland Scots between Lower Canada and New Brunswick "for the purpose of forming a barrier of *distinct men* near the frontiers of the United States." In *British America* (1832) he insisted that most errors and blunders in colonial policy were a product of "the *meagre* information possessed by our government" rather than neglect, and he maintained that British North America was more valuable than ever in the age of steam because it possessed coal in such abundance. He prophesied that British America, including the land west of the Great Lakes, was "capable of supporting" a population of 50 million, and that those who held this territory would have the power for "the umpirage of the Western World." If Britain lost her North American colonies they would probably merge with the United States or at least form an alliance with the northern states which would tarnish Britain's magnificence and diminish her political consequence.

MacGregor, reflecting the conventional wisdom of the time, clearly preferred agriculture to lumbering, and thought timbermen were the scum of the earth. His later espousal of extreme free-trade doctrines included opposition to preferential timber duties and a distinct preference for the lower provinces over the Canadas. These opinions have given him something of a bad press among Canadian historians, but in his earliest writings he was an enthusiastic imperialist and friend of the colonies.

In 1832 he began a major study of international commercial statistics in collaboration with James Deacon Hume; by 1833 he was residing in London and over the next few years travelled extensively on the continent, often in the employ of the Foreign Office. He negotiated a series of commercial treaties on behalf of Great Britain, including those with Austria (1838), the Kingdom of the Two Sicilies (1839), and Prussia (1840). He succeeded Hume as one of the two joint secretaries at the Privy Council committee for trade in January 1840 and that May was a leading witness supporting free-trade doctrines before the famed select parliamentary committee on imports. One contemporary critic, trenchantly noting that the committee wiped out the old tariff system in ten days, commented: "The elation of Mr. McGregor thenceforwards knew no bounds. It made him often the laughing-stock even of his most intimate friends, and in later years he perambulated the clubs, unconscious of the general ridicule of his vain-gloriousness." A principal target of MacGregor's hostility to protectionist duties was the various timber duties favourable to British North America, and he constantly pressed for tariff reduction of considerable proportions, gradually achieved through the 1842 and 1846 budgets. Although he accepted that the colonies might require compensation in the form of removal of imperial restrictions on foreign trade, on the whole he thought the timber business was of dubious long-term value to British America because it deflected immigrants from clearing land for agriculture and encouraged an unstable, lawless society.

A strong Whig, MacGregor refused to resign from the Privy Council committee for trade in 1843 despite statements by the Tory ministry that it lacked confidence in him. He did offer to leave in 1845 if he could be assured of the vice-presidency of the committee in a Whig government; although these assurances were not given he did resign, relinquishing a salary of £1,500, to run for parliament from Glasgow. Elected in July 1847, he represented Glasgow until shortly before his death. Increasingly he acquired the reputation of an overly ambitious and conceited bore, which made it impossible for him to satisfy his enormous energy and achieve his ambitions – fame, respect, and a cabinet post, as well as more money. His writings became both more frequent and less digested.

MacGregor's downfall began in 1849 when he became first chairman of the Royal British Bank, a joint-stock bank organized in London on the Scottish system. It is doubtful whether he himself was an active promoter of the bank, but those who were behind it were promoters and confidence men of the worst sort. MacGregor, whose reputation in commercial circles provided the bank with an air of probity and respectability, was a party to the publication of misleading accounts and took out an unsecured loan for £7,362 to cover his debts. When the bank collapsed in 1856, MacGregor, who had resigned his position with it three years earlier, fled to France, prompting the *Times* to editorialize: "In the annals of commercial fraud we have never heard or read of more

outrageous acts of rascality than they [its promoters] have perpetrated against the customers and shareholders of the Bank." The editorial demanded action against MacGregor so that he could not "snap his fingers at the unfortunate persons whom he has so foully defrauded, and in too many instances reduced to ruin." According to the obituary in the *Times*, the reaction to the affair "overwhelmed a shattered body and a wounded spirit" and MacGregor soon died of a "bilious fever and paralytic affection." The article concluded: "Vanity was one of the passions which poor John M'Gregor, from an unfortunate nature and habit, could not control; and the abuse of it was, in truth, his worldly ruin."

Although MacGregor had a chequered career, few political figures in early Victorian Britain had his first-hand knowledge of British North America. As publicist and civil servant, he helped to shape economic policy in the transitional years from protectionism to free trade.

J. M. BUMSTED

[Works by John MacGregor (McGregor) of most importance to British North America are: *Historical and descriptive sketches of the Maritime colonies of British America* (London, 1828; repr. East Ardsley, Eng., and New York, 1968); *Observations on emigration to British America* (London, 1829); and *British America* (2v., Edinburgh and London, 1832; 2nd ed., 1833). The *National union catalog* and the *British Museum general catalogue* should be consulted for lists of his numerous other writings. It should be noted that the *DNB* article on MacGregor cites works that other catalogues attribute to another author. J.M.B.]

PAPEI, Acc. 2702/721, 2702/734; Acc. 2810/240c, f; 2810/249; RG 16, Land registry records, conveyance reg., liber 27: ff.255, 257; liber 31: f.93. PRO, CO 226/39. *Athenæum* (London), 2 May 1857: 569. D. E. Colombine, *A word to the shareholders and depositors in the Royal British Bank; containing a scheme for the arrangement of its affairs without litigation . . .* (London, [1856]). *Gentleman's Magazine*, January–June 1857: 735–36. *The suppressed pamphlet: the curious and remarkable history of the Royal British Bank, showing "how we got it up" and "how it went down,"* by one behind the scenes (London, [1857?]). *Prince Edward Island Gazette*, 8 Dec. 1819. *Prince Edward Island Register*, 4 Oct. 1823, 13 June 1826. *Royal Gazette* (Charlottetown), 16 April 1833. *Times* (London), 24 Sept. 1856, 27 April 1857. Lucy Brown, *The Board of Trade and the free-trade movement, 1830–42* (Oxford, 1958). *Canada's smallest prov.* (Bolger), 90–93. George Patterson, *A history of the county of Pictou, Nova Scotia* (Montreal, 1877).

McINTOSH, JOHN, militiaman, ship's captain, businessman, and politician; b. 4 March 1796 in Colarich, parish of Logierait, Scotland, eldest son of John MacIntosh and Ann Ferguson; m. first 27 Jan. 1824 Catherine Oswald Stewart (d. 1832), and they had at least two sons and two daughters; m. secondly

McIntosh

12 March 1833 Helen Baxter, widow of David Ferguson, and they had at least three sons and four daughters; d. 3 July 1853 in Toronto.

The MacIntosh family immigrated from Scotland to Quebec in 1800 or 1801, moving to York (Toronto) in 1803. As a militiaman in the War of 1812, John McIntosh saw action at Detroit and Queenston Heights and was captured during the American attack on York in April 1813 [see Sir Roger Hale SHEAFFE]. He later claimed to have piloted brigades of boats from York to Kingston on two occasions. After the war, he and his five brothers (Robert, James, Charles, William, and David) were active as captains, and sometimes as owners, of various vessels on the Great Lakes. Among those commanded by John was *The Brothers* (called *The Three Brothers* in some sources), a schooner launched at York by a joint-stock company early in 1820. Four years later McIntosh, a Presbyterian, married the daughter of Alexander Stewart, minister of the town's first Baptist congregation. In 1828 McIntosh received from his father several valuable town lots. Apparently the rental from these, together with the revenue from a farm he owned in the London District, allowed him to retire from sailing at an early age and gave him considerable time in the 1830s and 1840s to devote to reform causes, a political interest he seems to have inherited from his father.

Throughout his public life McIntosh was a close associate and supporter of William Lyon Mackenzie*, and his second wife, whom he married in 1833, was the sister of Mrs Mackenzie. But, since he did not embrace some of Mackenzie's outlandish ideas and was a respected businessman in the provincial capital, he was not perceived as being of the same ilk. For much of the 1830s he served as chairman of the Committee of Home District Reformers. As well, in 1832–33, when Mackenzie was in England fighting his expulsion from the House of Assembly, McIntosh acted as chairman of the Central Committee of One Hundred Freeholders of Upper Canada, which was charged with raising both support for Mackenzie and opposition to the policies of the provincial government. In 1834, and again two years later, he contested and won the fourth riding of York for the reformers. He chaired a meeting in 1837 at which a declaration was drawn up by Toronto reformers calling on Upper Canadians to form political unions to oppose the policies of the British government for the colony and those of the provincial administration. McIntosh was called to a meeting that fall of a few prominent reformers, to whom Mackenzie unsuccessfully proposed insurrection. Though aware too of Mackenzie's later plans for actual rebellion, in which he took no active part, McIntosh escaped the persecution suffered by many leading radicals [see David Gibson*], probably because of his reputation as a concerned but reasonable individual unlikely to be attracted to treasonous schemes. He always spoke with moderation on political issues and never confined himself solely to politics in matters of public interest. For example, in September 1836 he had headed the list of those calling for a meeting to establish a mutual fire insurance company in the Home District.

In 1841 McIntosh again presented himself for election in 4th York but this time Robert BALDWIN opposed him. Despite insisting that he would not run if McIntosh wanted to, Baldwin continued to campaign, arguing that it was the wish of the reformers in the riding, who had earlier asked McIntosh to run. William Lyon Mackenzie later maintained that Baldwin took this action in order to defeat McIntosh because of the latter's opposition to the union of Upper and Lower Canada. Whatever the case, it is true that Baldwin could have withdrawn in York (he was elected in another riding, Hastings) instead of staying on to defeat a respected reformer.

For the remainder of his life McIntosh continued to support the reform cause and Mackenzie in particular. In 1849 he gave refuge to Mackenzie when he returned from exile, causing a riot outside his own home on Yonge Street. He ignored some pressure at the time of the general election of 1851 to run in his old riding, deciding instead to support the reformer Joseph HARTMAN. In the last few years before his death in 1853 his activities were limited by illness.

RONALD J. STAGG

[There are numerous references to John McIntosh in the Mackenzie–Lindsey papers at the AO: the Mackenzie correspondence (MS 516) contains many entries, the most useful being several in 1841; in addition there is a small collection of biographical information on Mackenzie's relations in the C. B. Lindsey papers (MU 1947), and a little material in the Mackenzie clippings (MU 1855, no.2056). The obituary article "A memoir of John Mackintosh," which ran in *Mackenzie's Weekly Message* on 9 Feb. 1855, contains considerable material on him. McIntosh's will and codicil are contained in AO, RG 22, ser.155. The above sources are supplemented by material in several books: Lindsey, *Life and times of Mackenzie*; Scadding, *Toronto of old* (1873); and *Robertson's landmarks of Toronto*, vols.1–3. References to McIntosh's reform activities will also be found in the Toronto *Patriot*, 11 Nov. 1836, and *Constitution*, 2 Aug. 1837, and in the C. R. Dent papers at the AO (MU 837). R.J.S.]

AO, MS 2, baptisms and marriages performed by Presbyterian ministers in York, 1823–29, baptism of Catherine and A. J. McIntosh, 9 Feb. 1829. MTL, Robert Baldwin papers. PAC, RG 1, L3, 332: M6/57; 339a: M11/408. St Andrew's Presbyterian Church (Toronto), Reg. of marriages, 12 March 1833 (mfm. at AO). *Town of York, 1815–34* (Firth). *Patriot*, 20 Sept. 1836. *History of Toronto and county of York, Ontario . . .* (2v., Toronto, 1885), 2: 96–97. *Officers of British forces in Canada* (Irving), 209. *History of the Great Lakes*, [ed. J. B. Mansfield] (2v., Chicago, 1899; repr. Cleveland, Ohio, 1972), 1: 801.

550

McKay

MACKAY, ROBERT WALTER STUART, author, publisher, and librarian; b. *c.* 1809 in Scotland, son of Donald Mackay of the 42nd Foot; m. Christina ——, and they had at least one daughter; d. 9 Oct. 1854 in Montreal.

Robert Walter Stuart Mackay immigrated to British North America in 1840 and entered the publishing business as a book agent after his arrival. Between 1842 and his death in 1854 he was a prolific compiler of statistical works about the Canadas and their municipalities which constitute an invaluable source of information for their history. Unlike the personal narratives of travellers to the Canadas, such as that of Sir Richard Henry Bonnycastle*, which were principally concerned with relating to a foreign audience impressions of the prospects, customs, and physical conditions of the country, Mackay's works were factual and practical, compiled by a resident of the province for use by fellow residents, immigrants, and visitors.

Mackay's publications were primarily of two types: guide-books and directories. The former, copies of which are now quite rare, were often called strangers' or travellers' guides. Although some mention was made of the scenic or picturesque, their main concern was to list churches, educational institutions, municipal and provincial government departments, populations, and distances between cities. Most of the major communities in the Canadas were covered in one or more of Mackay's guide-books.

Mackay's most important and best-known works were the annual directories of Montreal, Quebec City, and the Province of Canada. The most significant was the *Montreal directory*, first published in 1842 and still being published. Although Thomas Doige had compiled *An alphabetical list of merchants, traders, and housekeepers, residing in Montreal . . .* in 1819 and a second edition in 1820, no other attempts to publish a yearly directory of the city appear to have been made until Mackay began his work. His original directory contained an alphabetical list of Montreal residents and a list of businesses arranged by type; subsequent issues contained separate lists of religious and charitable institutions, insurance companies, banks, and public offices. With the exception of 1846 and 1851, Mackay issued the directory annually until his death, and from 1855 until 1862–63 it was compiled by his widow, Christina. From 1863–64 to 1867–68 printer and publisher John Lovell*, who had assisted Mackay in publishing the first two directories and some of the guide-books, compiled and issued it, although Mrs Mackay retained ownership. Since 1868–69 Lovell's firm (later John Lovell and Son) has owned and published the directory. Mackay also published a *Quebec directory*, similar in format to the *Montreal directory*, during the years from 1848 to 1852. The *Canada directory* was compiled by

Mackay and published by Lovell in 1851, with a supplement published by Mackay in 1853, and was essentially a directory of businesses arranged by municipality and then by type. It also contained a list of institutions as well as numerous statistics on population, trade, and revenue. After Mackay's death Lovell issued both the *Canada directory* and the *Quebec directory* for a number of years.

Of Mackay's personal and professional life, few details are known. His own listing in the *Montreal directory* indicates that he moved frequently and that in 1845 he operated a circulating library on Rue Notre-Dame. Mackay deserves to be remembered, however, as a diligent compiler of statistical and factual information about mid-19th-century Canada. His works were of great value to contemporaries and they continue to be of use to historians for both the lists and the numerous advertisements they contain. For many types of research he provides the best, and frequently the only, source of information.

PETER F. McNALLY

Robert Walter Stuart Mackay compiled the *Montreal directory*, 1842–54; *Quebec directory*, 1849–52; *Canada directory*, 1851; and *A supplement to the Canada directory*, 1853. For more information on the directories compiled by Mackay and his wife *see* Dorothy E. Ryder, *Checklist of Canadian directories, 1790–1950* (Ottawa, 1979). Mackay also wrote and compiled the following guidebooks: *Statistical, commercial, judicial, legal, medical & travelling chart of Canada* (Montreal, [1851]); *The stranger's guide to the cities and principal towns of Canada, with a glance at the most remarkable cataracts, falls, rivers, watering places, mineral springs &c. &c.; and a geographical and statistical sketch of the province, brought down to 1854 . . .* (Montreal, 1854); *The strangers' guide to the cities of Canada, with a brief geographical and statistical sketch of the province* (Montreal, 1852); *The strangers' guide to the cities of Montreal and Quebec, together with sketches of the cities of Toronto, Kingston and Hamilton, and of the towns of Bytown, London, &c., and a glance at the most remarkable cataracts and falls, mineral springs and rivers of Canada; with a brief geographical and statistical sketch of the province* (Montreal, 1852); *The strangers' guide to the city of Montreal* (Montreal, 1843); *The stranger's guide to the island and city of Montreal, containing a brief description of all that is remarkable in either; illustrated by a map of the city, and numerous wood cuts* (Montreal, n.d.); and *The traveller's guide to the River St Lawrence and Lake Ontario* (Montreal, 1845).

ANQ-M, CE1-68, 12 oct. 1854. Arch. of the Mount Royal Cemetery Company (Outremont, Que.), Reg. of burials, 12 Oct. 1854. *Montreal Gazette*, 11 Oct., 20 Nov. 1854. *Montreal directory*, 1855–69. Morgan, *Bibliotheca Canadensis*, 240. Wallace, *Macmillan dict.*

McKAY, THOMAS, mason, architect, businessman, politician, justice of the peace, militia officer, and office holder; b. 1 Sept. 1792 in Perth, Scotland,

551

McKay

son of John McKay and Christina ——; m. 20 June 1813 Ann Crichton, and they had 16 children; d. 9 Oct. 1855 in New Edinburgh (Ottawa), Upper Canada.

On leaving school Thomas McKay was apprenticed to the mason's trade. Induced by the depression which followed the Napoleonic Wars, he and his wife immigrated to Lower Canada, arriving on 9 Sept. 1817 and settling in Montreal. McKay gained contracting experience on the Lachine Canal (1821–25), in partnership with a fellow Scot, John Redpath*, and on the fortifications at Île aux Noix (1821–26), in partnership with Peter Rutherford. McKay later contested the legality of that association, including any profit-sharing agreement, and in the resulting litigation, brought by Rutherford's executors in 1840, he was awarded judgement.

In 1826, attracted by the planning of the Rideau Canal, McKay came to the construction camp on the Ottawa River which within months was to be named Bytown (Ottawa). He soon formed a partnership with Redpath, Thomas Phillips*, and Andrew White* to execute various works on the canal, with McKay's responsibilities centring on the Bytown area. He was selected in the fall of 1826 by Lieutenant Colonel John By* to perform the masonry work on the spectacular tier of eight entrance locks, rising 81 feet from the Ottawa River to a canal basin. The work was to be finished in two years but delays were caused during excavation by underground springs and it was not completed until 1830. Stone for the locks was to have been transported across the river from Hull but McKay persuaded By to authorize the use at less cost of stone quarried at the site, resulting in enormous profit to McKay and his partners. Regarded by John Mactaggart* as a "good practical mason" who scorned "to *slim* any work," McKay was entrusted as well with the construction of the locks at Hartwells and, on the failure of the previous contractor, Walter Welsh Fenlon, with the locks at Hogs Back. In 1828, during a lull in construction at Bytown, he set his masons to work building the settlement's first Presbyterian church, St Andrew's, in Upper Town. He also built two of the seven spans of the Union Bridge across the fathomless, boiling cauldron of the Ottawa at the Chaudière Falls. By, who was pleased with the quality of his canal work at Bytown, celebrated its finish with a gala banquet, at which an ox was roasted whole and served in a standing position. On the completion of the formidable Rideau project in 1832, McKay and Redpath received an engraved silver cup from By in recognition of their services. According to John Glass Malloch, a Perth lawyer, in 1841, McKay made about £30,000 from his work on the canal.

Although McKay remained involved in various Montreal-based businesses, including the Ottawa and Rideau Forwarding Company, he had moved his family to Bytown in 1827. Two years later he began acquiring property near by at the falls of the Rideau River and by 1832 he had constructed a sawmill there. An extensive, water-powered flour-mill was built on the opposite bank in 1833 and a bakery was erected a year later. The lease of an island near the falls in 1836 and the acquisition of surrounding land over the next two years gave McKay complete control over the mill site. The five-storey flour-mill had a large productive capacity and served a wide region along the Ottawa River and the canal. In 1834 Edward John Barker* of Kingston observed that it was "presumed to be the best in Upper Canada," superior even to the mill at Gananoque of John McDonald, who competed with McKay in purchasing grain through agents along the canal. In 1837 McKay added a distillery and the first cloth factory on the Ottawa, in which he later installed power looms. Satinette from his factory won a medal for quality in 1851 at the Great Exhibition in London, England. In 1843 he had enlarged his timber resources by securing a limit on the Rivière Gatineau and about 1846 he formed a partnership with a son-in-law, John MacKinnon. A year later a new sawmill was built for the firm at the Rideau Falls site by Joseph Merrill Currier*. Within two years the sawmills were undergoing expansion to accommodate the production of shingles, doors, window sashes, and blinds. McKay and MacKinnon also actively promoted the first railway into Bytown, the Bytown and Prescott Railway, which was incorporated in 1850. Although they had sufficient influence to secure its terminus near their mills, the railway, largely financed by Boston interests, proved unsuccessful in diverting the flow of lumber from Montreal and Quebec. In 1852 the partnership with MacKinnon was dissolved.

As McKay's industrial complex developed on the east bank of the Rideau River, so did the surrounding settlement, which he laid out into lots about 1834 and named New Edinburgh. He was not only a highly successful contractor and entrepreneur but an architect of some distinction. Rideau Hall, completed in 1838 on a 65-acre estate at New Edinburgh, was a refined Regency-style villa, executed in limestone and freely adapted from a design by the British architect Sir John Soane. The stately mansion, also known as "McKay's Castle," contained more than 11 rooms, including a drafting-room and a parlour from which the skirling notes of the bagpipes played by the lord of the manor reportedly sounded through the surrounding woods of a summer's evening. The house and property were leased to the government in 1865 and purchased three years later to form the nucleus of the official residence of Canada's governors general. A second stone residence, built by McKay about 1854 for John and Annie MacKinnon, was purchased by Sir John A. Macdonald* in 1882 and named Earnscliffe.

McKay was as active in public life as in business.

McKay

He was a member of the municipal council formed at Bytown in 1828, became a justice of the peace in 1833, and a year later was elected to the House of Assembly for the Ottawa River riding of Russell, which he represented until 1841. A tory and an active member of the Constitutional Association in Montreal, he supported the legislative union of Upper and Lower Canada. An indication of his tolerance was his support in 1839 for a share by the Roman Catholic church in the apportionment of the clergy reserves. Concerning commercial matters, McKay prepared a report in 1836 on navigable communication from Bytown to Lake Huron [see Charles Shirreff*], urged public ownership of the Welland Canal, and served in 1837 on a select committee investigating navigation on the St Lawrence River. From 1841 until his death McKay served on the Legislative Council, in which office in 1849 he opposed the Municipal Corporations Bill, sponsored by the ministry of Robert BALDWIN and Louis-Hippolyte La Fontaine*, and the Rebellion Losses Bill [see James Bruce*]. In 1842 McKay was appointed first warden of the new district of Dalhousie, which he had promoted politically and for which he had built the court-house and jail at Bytown. He was involved as well in numerous organizations, including the St Andrew's Society of Montreal and the Bytown Emigration Society. A prominent elder in the Church of Scotland, he was a founding trustee of Queen's College, Kingston. He served as lieutenant-colonel of the 1st Battalion of Russell militia from 1838 to 1846, when he was transferred to the 4th Battalion of Carleton militia, replacing George LYON.

On 9 Oct. 1855 McKay died of stomach cancer at Rideau Hall. He was survived for many years by his wife but, with the early deaths of his sons without issue, his direct line died out. Three daughters, however, had married notable figures: John MacKinnon, Robert Mackay (a Montreal lawyer), and Thomas Coltrin Keefer*. The management of McKay's estate, which included the sale in 1866 of the New Edinburgh Mills to James* and John Maclaren, was assumed by Keefer, who, after the death of his wife, married MacKinnon's widow.

McKay's career was multifaceted. A man of diverse talents and abundant energy, he was very much a "self made man," in the opinion of the *Montreal Witness, Weekly Review and Family Newspaper*, and one who amassed much property and wealth but never lost the common touch. Known to one resident of New Edinburgh as "a ruddy faced, forceful man, who, when he had an objective, generally managed to reach it," McKay was also depicted, by Andrew Wilson in 1876, as a straightforward and honourable man who was accessible "even to the humblest" but who "knew his place as a gentleman." His obituary in the *Journal of Education for Upper Canada*, however, described his temperament as "neither cool nor certain" and rather uneven owing to his "humble" origins and rapid increase in wealth and social station.

E. F. BUSH

ANQ-M, CN1-7, 20 nov. 1831, 25 nov. 1833; CN1-175, 13 avril 1837; CN1-182, 17 nov. 1831; CN1-187, 31 mars, 1–2, 7 avril 1821; 21 janv., 21 févr., 20 mars, 21 juin 1822; 27 janv., 23 déc. 1824; 11 janv. 1826; 29 juin 1830; 9 févr. 1832. AO, MU 842, J. G. Malloch diary; RG 1, A-I-6, 24–25, 27; RG 21, Carleton County, Gloucester Township, assessment rolls, 1831–33; RG 22, ser.155, will of Thomas McKay. BLHU, R. G. Dun & Co. credit ledger, Canada, 13: 247. Carleton Land Registry Office (Ottawa), Gloucester Township, deeds, 1832–42, no.1147 (mfm. at AO, GS 3624). Ottawa, Hist. Soc., Bytown Museum Arch. (Ottawa), G. P. Drummond, "Bytown in the forties with glimpses of the thirties" (scrapbook of newspaper clippings). PAC, Library, Pamphlet coll., no.1944 (64) (J. E. Askwith, "Recollections of New Edinburgh" (typescript, n.d.)); MG 29, B6, 1: 13; MG 30, D1, 21; RG 1, L3, 320a: Mc6/115; RG 5, A1: 53657, 92907–13, 94457–63, 95611–12, 103045–47, 103554–55; RG 8, I (C ser.), 44: 83–84. St Andrew's (Presbyterian) Church (Ottawa), Reg. of burials, 1855 (mfm. at PAC). E. J. Barker, *Observations on the Rideau Canal* (Kingston, [Ont.], 1834). *Canada Gazette*, 2 July 1842. E. C. Frome, "Account of the causes which led to the construction of the Rideau Canal . . . ," *Papers on Subjects Connected with the Duties of the Corps of Royal Engineers* (London), 1 (1837): 73–102, with 4 plates. "The Honorable Samuel Crane," *Journal of Education for Upper Canada* (Toronto), 12 (1859): 27–28. John Mactaggart, *Three years in Canada: an account of the actual state of the country in 1826–7–8 . . .* (2v., London, 1829), 1. Gertrude Van Cortlandt, *Records of the rise and progress of the city of Ottawa, from the foundation of the Rideau Canal to the present time* (Ottawa, 1858).

Advocate (Bytown [Ottawa]), 4 Jan. 1848. *British Whig*, 20 May, 28 Oct., 11 Nov., 5 Dec. 1834; 7 March, 22 April 1837; 31 March 1838. *Bytown Gazette, and Ottawa and Rideau Advertiser*, 17 June, 18 Dec. 1841; 15 June 1843. *Chronicle & Gazette*, 11 Oct. 1828; 29 June, 16 Nov. 1833; 17 May, 17 June, 18, 26 Oct., 20 Dec. 1834; 18 April 1835; 17 Feb., 30 Sept., 7 Dec. 1836; 4 Jan., 11, 22 Feb., 4 March, 13 May, 21, 24 June 1837; 10, 13 June, 12 Jan., 30 March, 10, 27 April 1839; 12 Sept. 1840; 7 April, 12 June, 3 Nov. 1841; 12 Jan., 16 July, 17 Aug. 1842. *Montreal Witness, Weekly Rev. and Family Newspaper*, 17 Oct. 1855. *Ottawa Citizen*, 25 June 1853. *Packet*, 28 Nov. 1846; 15 May 1847; 15, 22 Dec. 1849. *Tribune* (Ottawa), 12 Oct. 1855. Lucien Brault, *Ottawa old & new* (Ottawa, 1946). E. F. Bush, *The builders of the Rideau Canal, 1826–32* (Can., National Hist. Parks and Sites Branch, *Manuscript report*, no.185, Ottawa, 1976). J. L. Gourlay, *History of the Ottawa Valley: a collection of facts, events and reminiscences for over half a century* (Ottawa, 1896). Robert Haig, *Ottawa, city of the big ears: the intimate living story of a city and a capital* ([Ottawa, 1970]). R. H. Hubbard, *Rideau Hall: an illustrated history of Government House, Ottawa; Victorian and Edwardian times* (Ottawa, 1967). Robert Legget, *Rideau waterway* (Toronto, 1955). Marion MacRae and Anthony Adamson, *The ancestral roof: domestic* architecture of Upper Canada (Toronto and Vancouver, 1963). Ont., Dept. of Energy and Resources Management, *History of the Rideau waterway* (Toronto, 1970). Tulchinsky, *River barons.* Harry Walker and Olive [Moffatt] Walker, *Carleton saga* (Ottawa, 1968). Andrew Wilson, *A history of old Bytown and vicinity, now the city of Ottawa* (Ottawa, 1876). F.-J. Audet, "The Honourable Thomas McKay, M.L.C., founder of New Edinburgh, 1792–1855," CHA *Report,* 1932: 65–79. G. R. Blyth, "Bytown, 1834, to Ottawa, 1854," Women's Canadian Hist. Soc. of Ottawa, *Trans.* (Ottawa), 9 (1925): 5–15. O.-S.-A. Lavallée, "Historic review of 'Bytown and Prescott Railway' as Ottawa observes centenary first rail service," *Spanner* (Montreal), no.209 (January 1955): 6–7. "Rideau Hall reminiscences," *Free Press* (Ottawa), 21 Oct. 1878: 4.

McKEAGNEY, HENRY, Roman Catholic priest; b. 15 June 1796 in Clogher (Northern Ireland), son of Patrick McKeagney and Catherine McCarney; d. 4 June 1856 in Sydney, N.S.

Henry McKeagney received his early education and perhaps some of his theological training in Ireland since he was a student at the Séminaire de Québec only from September 1820 until his ordination to the priesthood by Bishop Joseph-Octave Plessis* of Quebec on 30 Sept. 1821. McKeagney was then assigned to St Patrick's Church in Quebec, where he served until October 1822. During his period at the seminary he had met Bishop Angus Bernard MacEachern*, who as Plessis's suffragan was responsible for Prince Edward Island, New Brunswick, Cape Breton Island, and the Îles de la Madeleine. It was perhaps at MacEachern's request that McKeagney agreed to go to Cape Breton in 1822. He served with the Reverend Hyacinthe Hudon* at Arichat from November 1822 until January 1823 and then moved to L'Ardoise as its first resident priest. He evidently had a difficult time there, telling Plessis in 1823 that "ever since I came here I have suffered the utmost misery." MacEachern concurred that McKeagney was "half starved at L'Ardoise."

From his base on southern Cape Breton, McKeagney served a large Acadian population and some Irish Catholics as well as caring for the Micmac Indians at the historic Chapel Island mission. The missionary thought highly of his Acadian people and they in turn liked him as their pastor. He spent most of his first winter in the region on Chapel Island, informing Plessis that he did so because of inadequate accommodation at L'Ardoise. In reply, Plessis informed McKeagney that he was pleased with his work among the Indians but that his principal residence was to be at L'Ardoise. This conflict with the hierarchy was a foretaste of things to come.

Because of a scarcity of priests on Cape Breton Island, in October 1823 MacEachern asked McKeagney to take over the eastern district of the island. McKeagney, in a demonstration of independence for which he later became noted, did not wish to

move and argued that his obedience was due only to Bishop Plessis. He remained at L'Ardoise until Plessis ordered him to move in October 1824. When he finally made the transfer in January 1825 he was instructed to live at Low Point but chose instead to live at a boarding-house in Sydney, where he was the first resident pastor. Plessis had reservations about McKeagney's living in Sydney, believing that he would perform better in a rural setting. Among the places included in McKeagney's new mission were Sydney, Little Bras d'Or, and Main-à-Dieu.

Although dissatisfied with his appointment McKeagney was to stay in Sydney for the remainder of his active pastorate. His time there, however, was not particularly happy, for almost from the moment of his arrival he became involved in controversy with either his parishioners or his superiors. In 1828 he began the erection of a stone church, St Patrick's, but many years passed before it was completed. It was in connection with the building fund that some of his parishioners complained to both McKeagney himself and MacEachern. They claimed that those who contributed were not credited with the full amounts given. McKeagney was also accused of racing horses, buying shipwrecked foods at a public auction and selling them at a profit, threatening his congregation from the altar, disregarding his priestly duties, and obstructing the civic magistrates. MacEachern informed Bishop Bernard-Claude Panet* of Quebec that he had received many criticisms of McKeagney, but the Sydney pastor denied the charges and accused his detractors of lying.

Although he continued as pastor in Sydney until 1840, McKeagney still had his critics. In 1836 he was absent from his parish for several months and Bishop William FRASER, the vicar apostolic of Nova Scotia, had no knowledge of his whereabouts. Patient with McKeagney for a number of years, Fraser finally suspended him from his pastorate in 1840. McKeagney continued to reside in Sydney and made unsuccessful efforts to have the bishop restore him as pastor. According to Bishop William WALSH, after his retirement McKeagney became involved in court litigation in Halifax. He died in Sydney on 4 June 1856 and was buried in St Patrick's cemetery by the Reverend James Quinan.

Henry McKeagney worked effectively as a missionary priest but his tenure in Sydney cannot be described as completely peaceful. It may be that, like some other clerics from abroad, he found it difficult to adjust to pastoral life in a rugged environment. Certainly, he was not cast from the common mould.

RAYMOND A. MacLean

AAQ, 210 A, XI: 16, 209; 310 CN, I: 114; 312 CN, VII: 25, 39–40, 46, 333 (copies at Arch. of the Diocese of Antigonish, N.S.). Arch. of the Diocese of Antigonish, Files of the diocesan historian, A. A. Johnston, manuscript sketches, no.87 (A. B. MacEachern); no.114 (Henry McKeagney). Arch. of the Diocese of Charlottetown, A. B. MacEachern papers, Plessis to MacEachern, 1825 (copy at Arch. of the Diocese of Antigonish). T. C. Haliburton, *An historical and statistical account of Nova-Scotia* (2v., Halifax, 1829; repr. Belleville, Ont., 1973). *Cape Breton: a bibliography*, comp. and ed. Brian Tennyson (Halifax, 1978). David Allison, *History of Nova Scotia* (3v., Halifax, 1916). J. G. Bourinot, *Historical and descriptive account of the island of Cape Breton* (Montreal, 1892). Richard Brown, *A history of the island of Cape Breton, with some account of the discovery and settlement of Canada, Nova Scotia, and Newfoundland* (London, 1869). A. A. Johnston, *Hist. of Catholic Church in eastern N.S.* J. G. MacKinnon, *Old Sydney; sketches of the town and its people in days gone by* (Sydney, N.S., 1918).

MACKECHNIE, STUART EASTON, industrialist, farmer, and politician; b. 1816 or 1817 in Scotland; m. 30 Nov. 1848 Anna Maria Barbara Poore, and they had a son; d. 6 May 1853 in Cobourg, Upper Canada.

Stuart Easton Mackechnie toured widely in the United States and the Canadas in the 1830s, residing for a time north of Toronto before returning to Britain. During the next decade the increased pace of rural settlement and mercantile activity in Upper Canada led to intense rivalries between nascent towns which vied to capture the trade of common hinterlands. Nowhere was this more intense than in the struggle between Cobourg and Port Hope, on the north shore of Lake Ontario. In 1843 D'Arcy Edward Boulton, a Cobourg lawyer and town booster, persuaded a number of Scottish capitalists, including Mackechnie and John Sinclair Wallace, to establish in Cobourg. The following year, soon after arriving in Cobourg, Mackechnie purchased a grist-mill, which he sold in 1847. He retained the water rights, however, and constructed near by a large factory for the manufacture of woollens, known as Ontario Mills. In 1848 he secured a mortgage on the property for £7,960 from one Andrew Mackechnie. Three years later the factory was reportedly the largest in the province, turning out 800 yards of cloth a day and employing up to 175 people, many of them women. For Cobourg the works was the largest single source of tax revenue and the cornerstone of its economy.

Mackechnie had difficulty procuring adequate supplies of quality wool within the province. He repeatedly urged local farmers to improve their sheep and turn to the commercial production of wool, but by 1851 almost a quarter of his raw material was still being imported. To counter this problem of supply, he developed the largest sheep farm in the area, under the management of his brother Henry. The growing complexity of Mackechnie's operation and the need for additional capital led him to take Edward Sheldon Winans into partnership in February 1850. Mackech-

nie also had financial interests in the Cobourg Harbour Company, the Cobourg and Rice Lake Plank Road and Ferry Company, and the Cobourg and Grafton Road Company, and was on the board of management of the Colonial Life Assurance Company at Cobourg.

As a young man of wealth, he added lustre to Cobourg's self-conscious social élite. His marriage in Grafton in 1848 to Anna Maria Barbara Poore helped induce her brother, Sir Edward Poore, a former officer in the Scots Fusilier Guards, to settle near Cobourg. Both men shared a passion for steeplechasing, and meets were organized under their direction. Mackechnie's gentility was also evident in his stewardship at such social gatherings as the "Cobourg Assemblies" (1845) and in his large household staff (in 1851 a groom, four female servants, and a farm agent). His behaviour suggests that he was an early Victorian swell turned businessman but there is evidence that not everyone looked favourably upon him. In 1847 farmers claimed they could not get a fair price for their wool at his factory.

Mackechnie had interests other than business and society. He appears to have belonged in 1851 to the Cobourg branch of the Church Union, an Anglican association of prominent laymen pledged to the defence of the controversial system of clergy reserves in the province. Although his concern over tariff changes led him to be active as well in the British American League [*see* George Moffatt*], and to serve as a delegate to its second convention in November 1849, Mackechnie had shown no sustained interest in local politics. Thus, when he became mayor of Cobourg in early 1853 with no prior involvement in municipal politics, the editor of the *Cobourg Star*, Henry Jones Ruttan, warned office holders not to be self-serving and arrogant, citing the case of Lucius Aelius Sejanus, the Roman who had displayed great avarice in his drive to attain political power. However, Mackechnie's tenure as mayor was short for he died after only four months in office. The one lasting act of his administration was the commissioning of Kivas Tully* to design a new town hall. Not surprisingly, the resulting edifice, Victoria Hall, was the embodiment of mid-19th-century optimism and grand colonial pretension.

The cause of Mackechnie's death is unknown, but he had time in his final days to prepare a will and, on 28 April, to sell his interest in Ontario Mills to William Butler. Mackechnie died at age 36, leaving to his wife (who later remarried) an estate estimated to be worth about £10,000.

PETER ENNALS

AO, RG 22, ser.155, will of S. E. Mackechnie. Northumberland West Land Registry Office (Cobourg, Ont.), Abstract index to deeds, Cobourg, vol.1 (1802–1934) (mfm.

McKenzie

at AO, GS 4712); Hamilton Township (mfm. at AO, GS 4752). PAC, RG 31, A1, 1851, Hamilton Township. St Peter's Anglican Church (Cobourg), Reg. of baptisms, marriages, and burials (mfm. at AO). *Church*, 7 Dec. 1848. *Cobourg Star*, 24 Dec. 1845; 25 March, 24 June 1846; 20 May, 1, 8, 15 Sept. 1847; 19 Sept. 1849; 6, 13 Feb., 6 March 1850; 12, 26 March, 2, 9, 16, 23 July, 2 Oct. 1851; 18 Feb. 1852; 26 Jan., 16 Feb., 23 March, 6 April 1853. *Port Hope Commercial Advertiser* (Port Hope, [Ont.]), 14 May 1853. *Burke's peerage* (1970), 2148. W. H. Smith, *Canada: past, present and future*, vol.2. E. C. Guillet, *Cobourg, 1798– 1948* (Oshawa, Ont., 1948), 15, 28, 72, 252–53. G. A. Hallowell, "The reaction of the Upper Canadian tories to the adversity of 1849: annexation and the British American League," *OH*, 62 (1970): 41–56.

McKENZIE, CHARLES, fur trader; b. *c.* 1778 in Ferintosh, Scotland; m. some time before 1805, according to the custom of the country, and formally 6 March 1824 in Montreal, Mary McKay, a Métis, and they had one son and three daughters; d. 6 March 1855 in the Red River settlement (Man.).

Charles McKenzie was engaged as an apprentice clerk by McTavish, Frobisher and Company, one of the firms in the North West Company, for service in the fur trade by the terms of a contract signed in Montreal on 30 Dec. 1802. He proceeded in 1803 to the area around the Red and Assiniboine rivers where, in October 1804, NWC clerk Daniel Williams Harmon* met him at Fort Montagne à la Bosse (near Routledge, Man.). McKenzie was serving as clerk under Charles Chaboillez*, NWC partner in charge of the Fort Dauphin department, when on 11 November he was sent, with NWC clerk François-Antoine Larocque* and others, to trade with the Mandan Indians on the upper Missouri River. The party reached the Gros Ventre (Hidatsa) Indians, close neighbours of the Mandans on the Missouri, by the end of November and, discovering four Hudson's Bay Company men among these Indians, Larocque left McKenzie and another man with them to compete with the English company's traders. McKenzie passed the winter with the Gros Ventres, and both he and Larocque, who stayed in a nearby village, were in close contact with the American exploration party under Meriwether Lewis and William Clark which was wintering among the Mandans. McKenzie returned to the Assiniboine River in the spring of 1805, arriving at Fort Assiniboine (Man.) with Larocque on 22 May.

He made three other trading expeditions to the Missouri in 1805–6 and he was with the Gros Ventres when Chaboillez and Alexander Henry* visited the Mandans in the summer of 1806. McKenzie, who was at ease with the Indian way of life, was reproached by the two NWC proprietors for having adopted Indian dress. In his journal he wrote: "Let any man living with the Indians take the idea of 'Savage' from his mind and he will find their dress much more convenient. He can pass through the crowd, day and night, without exciting curiosity or draw a throng of children and barking dogs"; furthermore, he noted, their dress was "very light and cool in the warm season."

The Missouri trade had been found unprofitable, and was discontinued by the NWC in 1807. McKenzie was posted to the Monontagué department, near Lake Nipigon, Upper Canada, under John HALDANE, where he took charge of the relatively unproductive post on Lac Seul. He remained at this post after the union of the NWC and the HBC in 1821, and, except for a brief period from 1823 to 1827, was there until his retirement in 1854. In 1823 he resigned from the HBC, discontented with his salary and other arrangements. He accepted a position with the king's posts but when it proved to be unsatisfactory he returned to the HBC.

The journals of his ventures to the Missouri River were forwarded to Roderick McKenzie* of Terrebonne, Lower Canada, in 1842, and were eventually published in 1889–90. Those he kept at Lac Seul are more voluminous and more informative about his character. He was a strong advocate of Indian concerns, which often involved fur-trade policies he considered detrimental to their welfare; for example, he called the ready-barter system of trade "a most cold cold calculating system," because it prevented the Indians from obtaining in advance, on credit, the supplies upon which they had become dependent for hunting, trapping, and survival. He demonstrated a certain relativism towards Indian culture and he described, sometimes in detail, their hunting practices and other patterns of behaviour. He was very proud of his wife who had been raised as an Indian, and in his journal for 1831 he noted that "she hunts for her own pleasure, & tho' I pay her, as I would an Indian out of the Company's shop – wastes more in wear & tear than she gets & the only profit I see by it is she keeps herself in employment & her body in health." He also wrote extensively about events at the post, the habits of animals, and other natural phenomena. In the mid 1840s a series of epidemics killed many Lac Seul Indians and in August 1845, when the post was turned into a hospital, McKenzie himself became quite ill; his wife acted as nurse and comforter to the sick.

McKenzie remained a clerk until his retirement from the HBC, a fact that caused him much resentment. As early as 1827 Governor George SIMPSON had decided not to promote him, observing that "his best days are gone." McKenzie was convinced that promotions were based on favour and in November 1853 wrote to his son, Hector Æneas, who had himself been in the service of the HBC from 1839 to 1851, that "if there was any merit I would be ahead of most of their present Chief Factors." In his later years he suffered poor health, complaining of sore eyes and "decayed Bowels." Upon retirement he and his wife joined their son on his farm in the Red River settlement. McKenzie died there in 1855.

The record of McKenzie's long tenure at Lac Seul would indicate that he had managed the post well and had been generally liked by the Indians. The detailed and perceptive journals he kept during these years are his greatest contribution to history and science.

CHARLES A. BISHOP

The PAC has in MG 19, A44, a collection of letters exchanged between Charles McKenzie and his son as well as other members of the family for the years 1828–87. McKenzie's reports on the four expeditions to the Missouri River are published in "The Mississouri Indians: a narrative of four trading expeditions to the Mississouri, 1804–1805–1806" in *Les bourgeois de la Compagnie du Nord-Ouest* (Masson), 1: 315–93.

ANQ-M, CN1-29, 17 janv. 1800. PAM, HBCA, A.34/1: f.73; A.34/2: ff.38–38d; A.36/9: ff.186–87; A.44/3: 107; B.107/a/2, 6–31; B.107/b/1; B.107/d/1; B.107/e/3–5; B.107/z/1; Red River burial reg. Harmon, *Sixteen years in the Indian country* (Lamb). *New light on early hist. of greater northwest* (Coues). F.-A. Larocque, "The Missouri journal, 1804–1805," *Les bourgeois de la Compagnie du Nord-Ouest*, 1: 297–313. C. A. Bishop, *The Northern Ojibwa and the fur trade: an historical and ecological study* (Toronto and Montreal, 1974). [M.] E. Arthur, "Charles McKenzie, l'homme seul," *OH*, 70 (1978): 39–62.

McKENZIE, DONALD, fur trader and colonial administrator; b. 16 June 1783 near Inverness, Scotland, son of Alexander and Catherine Mackenzie; d. 20 Jan. 1851 in Mayville, N.Y.

At age 17, after receiving a good education, Donald McKenzie immigrated to the Canadas to follow his brothers Roderick*, Henry*, and James* into the fur trade. In March 1801 he became a clerk in the North West Company. Little is known of his experience with this company, but by 1809 he was disgruntled enough to contemplate switching to the rival Hudson's Bay Company, and he apparently collaborated with the ex-Nor'Wester Colin Robertson* in the latter's scheme to lead an HBC expedition into the Athabasca country. When this plan failed, McKenzie was attracted to the new enterprise of John Jacob Astor*, and in 1810, together with Ramsay CROOKS, Duncan McDougall*, Alexander MacKay*, Wilson Price Hunt, and others, he became one of the original partners in the Pacific Fur Company. McKenzie's considerable strength, courage, and experience were severely tested when he assisted Hunt with the command of the overland expedition that set out for the mouth of the Columbia River that summer. The party had to split up in order to survive and, according to Gabriel Franchère*, it was not until January 1812 that McKenzie and his men struggled into the newly

constructed Fort Astoria (Astoria, Oreg.) "with their clothes in rags." During the next season, McKenzie began his extensive trading and exploring journeys into the interior. One of the major tributaries of the Willamette River was named after him; as he himself declared, "The west of the mountains have everywhere been chequered by my steps."

In 1813, upon learning of the outbreak of war between Great Britain and the United States, McKenzie played a significant role in persuading the other PFC partners that, because of the tenuous nature of their position on the Columbia, they would be better off selling out to the NWC rather than risk capture. Upon the completion of the transactions and the formal transfer of Astoria to British hands, McKenzie returned east with the NWC brigade in the spring of 1814, conveying the papers connected with the Columbia negotiations to Astor in New York. Astor, feeling that he had been betrayed, had no further use for McKenzie, but the NWC and the HBC both tried to lure him into their service. Apparently McKenzie had some sympathy for the HBC and the beleaguered Red River settlement (Man.) under the governorship of Miles Macdonell*, but he cast his lot with the Nor'Westers and became a partner that year.

In the fall of 1816 McKenzie returned to the Columbia and for the next five years successfully managed the inland trade of the region, being primarily responsible for developing the arduous Snake River country expeditions. He gained a considerable reputation for being fearless and astute in his dealings with the turbulent tribes of the upper Columbia, and in 1818 he established Fort Nez Percés (Walla Walla, Wash.). With the union of the HBC and the NWC in 1821, he was made a chief factor in the HBC. On coming out to the annual meeting of the Council of the Northern Department at York Factory (Man.) the next year, the seasoned veteran had some thoughts of retirement. Instead, in the fall of 1822, with John ROWAND as his assistant, he was given charge of a large expedition to investigate the prospects of extending the HBC's trade south into the regions of the Bow and the South Saskatchewan rivers to check American competition.

Although the Bow River expedition demonstrated that trade in the region would not be profitable, McKenzie so impressed HBC governor George SIMPSON that he was sent in the fall of 1823 to restore order to the company's affairs in the Red River settlement after the removal of John CLARKE. The following year Simpson described him as "the fittest man in the Country for the Situation," being "a cool determined man, Conciliatory in his manners, economical & regular and privately attached to the Colony." McKenzie's heavy financial losses, resulting from the bankruptcy of McGillivrays, Thain and Company [see Thomas Thain*], contributed to his

McKenzie

decision to continue in the service. He was given additional responsibility in 1825 when he became the governor of Assiniboia. Throughout the 1820s McKenzie was praised for his management of the Red River colony. His "firmness, sound judgment and energy" were credited with mitigating the devastating effects of the flood of 1826, and in 1829 Simpson enthused: "His government is the most easy under the sun; he settles the most knotty points with a joke and a laugh, seated on a mortar opposite the gate of his fort, and is more beloved and respected by his subjects than words can tell; he is not so stout as he was, but much more healthy and looks as if he would live forever."

After spending the winter of 1830–31 in the settlement, Simpson radically revised his opinion of McKenzie. In his "Character book" he wrote a lengthy and damning sketch of McKenzie, denouncing his whole life as "one uniform system of art, deceit, falsehood, intrigue, suspicion, selfishness and revenge." Although McKenzie may have outlived his usefulness as governor by the 1830s, Simpson's assessment, written in a fit of spleen partially occasioned by domestic entanglements, should not be taken as a valid evaluation of his fur-trade career. McKenzie strongly opposed the callous action of Chief Factor John George McTavish* in casting off his country wife, McKenzie's niece Nancy McKEN-ZIE, in 1830 to marry a Scottish woman. He and John Stuart* obstructed Simpson's efforts to help settle his friend's affairs quietly. Simpson, in turn, had been critical of McKenzie's marital arrangements. Upon settling in Red River, McKenzie had divested himself of his own country wife, probably Mary MacKay, daughter of Alexander, but Simpson did not approve of his marrying, on 18 Aug. 1825, the governess he had hired to look after his three mixed-blood children. His new wife was Adelgonde Humbert Droz, the 18-year-old daughter of impoverished Swiss settlers. The children of the second marriage eventually numbered 13.

In the fall of 1832 McKenzie took an extended trip to the eastern United States, where he chose Mayville, N.Y., as his place of retirement. He returned to Red River in the summer of 1833 to collect his family, having been given leave of absence because of ill health until his official retirement in 1835. In Mayville he built a substantial brick house on his estate overlooking Chautauqua Lake. McKenzie invested heavily in land in the surrounding region. He died early in 1851, several months after being thrown from his horse while on a business trip.

During his wide-ranging career in the service of three different companies, Donald McKenzie earned a reputation as an intrepid explorer and bold trader. Although he had his faults, it is significant that in later years McKenzie regained Simpson's good opinion

and a cordial correspondence existed between the two families.

SYLVIA VAN KIRK

PAC, MG 19, A21, ser.1; E2, 3. Gabriel Franchère, *Journal of a voyage on the north west coast of North America during the years 1811, 1812, 1813, and 1814*, trans. W. T. Lamb, ed. and intro. W. K. Lamb (Toronto, 1969). *HBRS*, 2 (Rich and Fleming). Alexander Ross, *The fur hunters of the far west; a narrative of adventures in the Oregon and Rocky mountains* (2v., London, 1855). Simpson, "Character book," *HBRS*, 30 (Williams), 151–236. J. G. MacGregor, *John Rowand, czar of the Prairies* (Saskatoon, Sask., 1978). C. W. Mackenzie, *Donald Mackenzie: "king of the northwest"* . . . (Los Angeles, 1937). Ernest Cawcroft, "Donald Mackenzie: king of the northwest," *Canadian Magazine*, 50 (November 1917–April 1918): 342–49.

McKENZIE, JAMES, soldier, hotel-keeper, ship-owner, and shipbuilder; b. 28 Dec. 1788 in Duthil, Scotland; m. 29 April 1814 Elizabeth Cameron at York (Toronto), and they had seven children; d. 20 April 1859 at Quebec.

Nothing is known of James McKenzie's early years. He arrived in the Canadas, probably at Quebec in May 1813, as a private in the 2nd battalion of the 41st Foot, which took part in various battles in the Niagara region of Upper Canada until the end of the War of 1812. Back at Quebec in March 1815, the battalion was disbanded, and it was probably at this time that McKenzie settled at Pointe-Lévy (Lévis and Lauzon). At any rate it is certain that by the beginning of the 1820s he had become the keeper of the Hôtel Lauzon, then belonging to shipbuilder John Goudie*. In the spring of 1825, after Goudie's death, McKenzie rented the hotel from the Goudie estate, along with the steamship *Lauzon*, which he began operating as a ferry. In June 1828 he put into ferry service his own steamboat, the *New Lauzon*, built during the preceding winter. On 23 October he bought the Hôtel Lauzon cheaply at a sheriff's auction following its seizure. For some years thereafter McKenzie carried on the double undertaking of providing lodging and operating a ferry.

The Hôtel Lauzon, now known as the Hôtel McKenzie, was not only the most spacious on the south shore of the river across from Quebec but was also the best located. All the highways of Dorchester, Hertford, Devon, and Cornwallis counties converged at this spot and they were used by the farmers of some twenty neighbouring parishes to bring their supplies to the city of Quebec. In addition, in 1830 it also became the departure point for a road from Quebec to the United States via the Beauce region, and in the autumn of 1835 the Hôtel McKenzie was chosen as the terminus for a coach service linking Quebec and Boston.

Aware of the advantages of such a site, McKenzie had not hesitated in the summer of 1829 to invest in building a quay more than 100 feet long, adjoining the existing one on the land belonging to his newly acquired hotel. In September 1830 he had begun to operate a second ferry, the *Britannia*, which had paddle-wheels driven by horses. At this date three similar vessels were plying between Quebec and the south shore. The *Britannia*, however, had a distinct advantage over its competitors: the horses worked in a stationary fashion, walking on a drum rather than moving in a circle on the deck, so there was more space for passengers. Unquestionably, the combined undertaking of hotel trade and ferry service proved highly profitable for McKenzie.

But McKenzie was not content. In 1828, with his steamboat *New Lauzon*, he had also begun to tow to their moorings or anchorages the sailing ships which stopped at Quebec in ever-increasing numbers. He gradually concentrated his efforts on this new field, as well as on towing the lumber rafts that descended the river to Quebec, an enterprise that gave him the opportunity to transport goods as well as passengers. It was with this business in view that in 1837 he built for himself the new steamboat *Lumber Merchant* and rented his quay to another ferry owner, Jean Moreau. Three years later his new undertaking had grown sufficiently to worry its two most powerful Montreal competitors, the Molsons' St Lawrence Steamboat Company [*see* William Molson*] and the Torrances' St Lawrence Steam Tow Boat Company [*see* David Torrance*]. These companies in April 1840 undertook jointly to pay him £1,250 and to refrain from competing with him in towing timber rafts anywhere on the river, provided that McKenzie would refrain from using his steamboats and lighters on the Richelieu or on the river between Montreal and Quebec, or between the intermediary ports, for the transport of either foodstuffs or passengers. On the expiry of the agreement at the close of the 1840 shipping season, McKenzie proceeded to build a new steamboat, the *Pointe Levi*, which came into service the following spring. Subsequently he built two others, the *James McKenzie* in 1854 and the *Lord Seaforth* in 1855, to replace the *Lumber Merchant* and the *Pointe Levi*. In fact, until the end of his life, he maintained a fleet of four boats: two steamboats, normally under the command of his sons Charles and James, and two lighters. His decision not to increase the number may have stemmed from a judgement that he had attained an optimal level of profitability. He was not the sort of man to stake his capital on a single venture, however lucrative.

Thus, although he became involved in towing and river transport, McKenzie did not abandon the idea of using the crossing between Quebec and Pointe-Lévy to attract clients to his hotel. In 1842 he joined a partnership formed to operate a new steam ferry. When competition became stiffer, McKenzie and the others petitioned the Legislative Assembly of the Province of Canada in 1846 for the exclusive right to the crossing. Counting on a favourable reply, McKenzie had a new quay built in deep water near his hotel. Then in January 1847, with James Tibbits, Horatio Nelson Patton, James Motz, and Robert Buchanan, all directors of the Point Levy Steam Boat Ferry Company, he had a new steamship laid down, more powerful than those of his competitors. As the assembly had not, however, given a decision, McKenzie submitted a new petition in October 1852 which led to the enactment in June 1853 of a law regulating river crossings in Lower Canada. But McKenzie gained little from it because of the entry upon the scene of a new and much more powerful rival, the Grand Trunk.

This set-back, which was only a partial one, did not adversely affect the financial stability of McKenzie, who was both entrepreneur and shrewd investor. In fact he constantly reinvested the profits from his undertakings, making loans to people who offered sound guarantees or acquiring company shares and bonds. He advanced large sums to such prominent figures of the time as James STUART, James Douglas*, John James Nesbitt, Augustin Cantin*, William Drum, William and David Bell, Henry Dinning*, and Elizabeth Johnston Taylor, the widow of Allison Davie*. As for the shares and bonds he accumulated, they presented few risks, having been issued by the Bank of Montreal, the Bank of British North America, the City Bank (at Montreal), the Quebec Gas Company, the Montreal Harbour Loan, and the Montreal Road Trust.

At the end of his life McKenzie, who had always devoted his energies to his business ventures and his family while eschewing social or political activities, was able to leave his heirs an enviable fortune. He owned £40,000 in shares, bonds, and accounts receivable, as well as property valued at £50–60,000: his hotel, his fleet of boats, a spacious dwelling he had built in 1850 in Upper Town, and a three-storey stone building in the heart of Lower Town which was occupied at the time by Trinity House of Quebec.

In the eyes of his contemporaries, James McKenzie was an example of personal success. At a distance of more than a century, he seems to embody the entrepreneurial spirit which spurred many Scottish immigrants who had come to Lower Canada at the beginning of the 19th century, and which enabled them to play a decisive role in the economic development of their adopted country.

PIERRE DUFOUR and MARC OUELLET

McKenzie

AC, Québec, Minutiers, William Bignell, 2 mai, 28 sept. 1848; 16, 31 janv., 9, 16, 28 févr., 27 mars, 14, 25 juin 1850; 21 nov. 1851; 21 avril, 3 déc. 1852; 9 mai 1853; 20 mai, 13 août, 30 sept., 21, 28 nov. 1854; 19 janv., 20 févr., 1er mars, 11 mai, 16 juin, 9 juill., 14 déc. 1855; 10 juill., 4 oct. 1856; 14 janv., 24 févr., 3 mars, 15 mai, 8 oct. 1857; 18 janv., 1er, 3, 6 mars, 24 avril, 24 mai, 1er juin, 18 sept., 11 déc. 1858; 19, 25 févr., 4, 7, 9 mars 1859. ANQ-Q, CE1-66, 23 avril 1859; CN1-188, 21 sept. 1824; 24 mars, 10 août 1829; 21 juill. 1830; CN1-197, 22 mars, 30 juin 1825; 24 avril 1826; 22 nov. 1834; 30 mars, 18 avril, 22 sept. 1840; 23 mars 1841; 26 juin 1845; 23 avril, 8 mai, 30 nov. 1846; 19, 23 janv., 6 mars, 30 juin, 3 juill., 27 oct., 5, 26 nov., 27, 29 déc. 1847; 8, 17 juill., 26 déc. 1848; 11 mars 1854; 8 janv. 1855; 13 juin 1859; CN1-198, 7, 11 déc. 1848. PAC, RG 42, ser.I, 190: 108; 191: 194; 192: 97; 196: 148–50, 190; 198: 64–65; 267: 12. Ports Canada Arch. (Quebec), Trinity House of Quebec, minute-books, IV: 270–71. St James' Cathedral Arch. (Anglican) (Toronto), St James' Church, reg. of marriages, 29 April 1814. Can., Prov. of, Legislative Assembly, *Journals*, 1846. L.C., House of Assembly, *Journals*, 1830. *Le Canadien*, 28 janv. 1846. *Le Journal de Québec*, 21 avril 1859. *Morning Chronicle*, 23 April 1859. *Quebec Gazette*, 23 June 1828, 22 April 1859. *Quebec Mercury*, 13 Jan. 1846. P.-G. Roy, *Dates lévisiennes* (12v., Lévis, Qué., 1932–40), 1. Roger Bruneau, *La petite histoire de la traverse de Lévis* (Québec, 1983). Chouinard *et al.*, *La ville de Québec*, vol.2. George Gale, *Historic tales of old Quebec* (Quebec, 1923). J.-E. Roy, *Hist. de Lauzon*, vols.1–5. P.-G. Roy, *Profils lévisiens* (2 sér., Lévis, 1948); *Toutes petites choses du Régime anglais* (2 sér., Québec, 1946); *La traverse entre Québec et Lévis* (Lévis, 1942). "James McKenzie," *BRH*, 42 (1936): 384.

McKENZIE, JOHN, Presbyterian minister; b. 5 May 1790 in Fort Augustus, Scotland, eldest son of William McKenzie; m. Janet Fraser, and they had no surviving children; d. 21 April 1855 in Williamstown, Upper Canada.

John McKenzie, who came from a farming background, grew up in his native Inverness-shire and was educated at the local grammar school before going on to King's College (University of Aberdeen) as a bursary student in 1809. He received an MA on 26 April 1813 and, in order to support himself, became a schoolmaster in Urquhart. However, desirous of entering the ministry, he resigned his post in the winter of 1813–14 and enrolled in divinity the following spring. At the same time he set up as a teacher of English, writing, and arithmetic in Old Aberdeen.

By 1818 he found himself, at 28, a small, intense schoolteacher and licentiate of the Church of Scotland with no outstanding ability and little likelihood of ever finding a ministerial post in Scotland. Then, in July, members of the Presbytery of Aberdeen recommended that he accept a call from Williamstown, Upper Canada, whose congregation had been without a minister since the death of the Reverend John Bethune* three years earlier. He agreed. Passing his trials, he was ordained on 23 Dec. 1818 and by the summer of 1819 was ensconced in Williamstown.

When he arrived in the colony he was the sole Church of Scotland minister in Upper Canada and one of only a handful in the Canadas. His new charge, St Andrew's, was part of a community of United Empire Loyalists and disbanded soldiers of mixed background, Dutch, German, and English, but largely Highland and Lowland Scots. Able to speak Gaelic, he ministered to the Presbyterians among them and he conscientiously set out to organize congregations in the surrounding area and supply their needs until they could support ministers of their own.

For all his ministerial zeal, he took a minimal interest in the moves of his Canadian colleagues to gain state recognition in the early 1820s, doing little more than signing the petitions and letters forwarded to him. Similarly, he remained an observer of the efforts of Robert McGILL and others to form a synod later in the decade. Perhaps mistaking his lack of involvement for non-partisanship, and appreciative of his even-handed adjudication of two ministerial disputes, his colleagues awarded him the signal honour in 1831 of electing him the first moderator of the newly formed Synod of the Presbyterian Church of Canada in connection with the Church of Scotland. Little involved in church affairs, he often absented himself from the yearly synod meetings, although he was active throughout his life in sustaining the Presbytery of Glengarry, also formed in 1831. When he did appear at synod he was found on the reactionary edge of the church with men such as the Reverend Alexander Mathieson*, arguing in the 1830s, for instance, that ministers such as those in the United Synod of Upper Canada not trained by the Church of Scotland could not be admitted into their ranks. As might be expected he sided with the Church of Scotland forces during the disruption and was a bitter opponent of those who left its ranks in 1844.

His real contribution to the church lay in his parish work. Though a peppery man by nature, he endeared himself to those around him by his unusually keen concern for the poor and the distressed and by his tolerance, at a personal level, of other segments of the community. He lived to see his synod grow to six presbyteries and 80 ministers.

H. J. BRIDGMAN

[The 1,083 pages of material relating to McKenzie contained in the papers of the McGillivray family of Glengarry (PAC, MG 24, I3, 7–8) touch on his private affairs and illuminate his ministerial role from parish to synod. An appreciation of his career was published in the *Presbyterian*, 8 (1855): 66, 82–83. *See also* the McKenzie entry in UCA, Biog. files, and Presbyterian Church of Canada in connection with the Church of Scotland, *Minutes of the Synod* (Toronto), 1831–55. H.J.B.]

McKenzie

Croil, *Hist. and statistical report* (1868), 77. *Montreal Gazette*, 26 April 1855. *Officers and graduates of University & King's College, Aberdeen, [1495–1860]*, ed. P. J. Anderson (Aberdeen, Scot., 1893), 274. *Roll of alumni in arts of the University and King's College of Aberdeen, 1596–1860*, ed. P. J. Anderson (Aberdeen, 1900), 119. Scott *et al.*, *Fasti ecclesiæ scoticanæ*, vol.7. Gregg, *Hist. of Presbyterian Church*. *St Andrew's Presbyterian Church, Williamstown, Ontario; report of centenary celebration, August 25th to September 2nd, 1912* (Cornwall, Ont., 1916), 70.

McKENZIE, NANCY (McTavish; Le Blanc) (also known by the Indian name **Matooskie**), b. *c.* 1790, daughter of Roderick McKenzie*, NWC fur trader, and an unidentified Indian woman; d. 24 July 1851 at Fort Victoria (Victoria).

Nancy McKenzie was one of three children fathered by Roderick McKenzie during his service in the Athabasca country between 1789 and 1801. As was customary among Nor'Westers, McKenzie did not take his two daughters with him when he retired to Lower Canada in 1801, but entrusted them to the guardianship of fellow Nor'Wester John Stuart*. Matooskie, whose name would appear to mean "object of pity," was with Stuart when he went to New Caledonia (B.C.) to take charge of the department for the North West Company in 1809. In 1813 Stuart joined NWC partner John George McTavish* on the Columbia River and it was probably in that year that Nancy was married to McTavish, by the custom of the country. After the union of the NWC and the Hudson's Bay Company in 1821, McTavish was appointed chief factor in charge of York Factory (Man.) and during the 1820s his wife shared his social prominence as the *bourgeoise* of the fort. During these years they had as many as seven children, all of whom were daughters.

By the customs of fur-trade society, Nancy McKenzie was acknowledged as McTavish's legitimate wife. In 1830, however, while on furlough in Great Britain, McTavish, with the encouragement of HBC governor George SIMPSON, abruptly defied the norms of country marriage and legally married a Scottish woman. After travelling back to North America in company with Simpson and the governor's new bride, Frances Ramsay SIMPSON, McTavish did not return to York Factory but went directly with his wife to his new post at Moose Factory (Ont.), leaving his colleagues to break the news to Nancy. "The first blow was dreadful to witness," reported HBC clerk James Hargrave*, but "the poor girl is fast acquiring resignation." Nancy and several of her children were taken in temporarily at the HBC post Fort Alexander (Man.) by Stuart, who, with the injured woman's uncle Chief Factor Donald McKENZIE, were particularly vocal in denouncing McTavish for his cruel deception and demanded substantial compensation for

Nancy. Simpson, however, had decided that remarriage was the best means of providing for cast-off country wives and he had been delegated to settle McTavish's affairs. Despite Nancy's expressed wish that she not be forced to marry again, the dowry of £200 offered by McTavish soon enabled Simpson to arrange for her marriage to a respectable company employee, Pierre Le Blanc*, then in charge of building Lower Fort Garry (Man.). Nancy McKenzie was baptized and the couple were married in the Roman Catholic church at the Red River settlement (Man.) on 7 Feb. 1831.

Nancy McKenzie's life serves to illustrate the way in which native women were increasingly victimized by the changing mores of fur-trade society. The conduct of prominent officers such as McTavish and Simpson seriously undermined the legitimacy of marriage *à la façon du pays*, reducing the status of country wife to that of mistress. The arrival of British wives in Rupert's Land fostered the growth of racial prejudice and efforts were made to exclude native wives from "respectable" society. Simpson's young wife underlined Nancy's considerable loss of social position by describing her as "a complete savage, with a coarse blue sort of woollen gown without shape & a blanket fastened round her neck."

Nancy McKenzie's second marriage brought her further sorrow. Three children were born of this union, but Le Blanc became increasingly resentful of his role as stepfather to his wife's younger children by McTavish. In 1838 he was posted to the Columbia district on the Pacific northwest coast. The family crossed the Rockies with a party that included Catholic priests Modeste Demers* and François-Norbert Blanchet. Nancy McKenzie's name frequently identifies her as witness or godmother for the numerous baptisms they performed on the trip. In September, during the journey west, the Le Blancs' eldest daughter died. Then on 22 October a serious accident in the rapids at the Dalles on the Columbia River resulted in the drowning of Nancy's husband and their two other children. Nancy and her youngest daughter by McTavish, Grace, were given a home at Fort Vancouver (Vancouver, Wash.). In 1842 Grace married Charles DODD, captain of the steamship *Beaver*, and Nancy McKenzie lived with the Dodds for the rest of her life. After her death at Fort Victoria in 1851, her small estate was divided among her three surviving daughters by McTavish.

SYLVIA VAN KIRK

PAC, MG 19, A21, ser.1, 21. PAM, HBCA, A.36/8; B.4/b/1; B.135/c/2–3; B.235/z/3: f.547a; E.4/1a; E.24/4. *Catholic Church records of Pacific northwest* (Munnick). Van Kirk, *"Many tender ties."* J. A. Stevenson, "Disaster in the Dalles," *Beaver*, outfit 273 (September 1942): 19–21.

McKenzie

McKENZIE, RODERICK (generally known as Roderick McKenzie Sr), fur trader and politician; b. 1771 or 1772 probably in the parish of Assynt, Scotland; d. 2 Jan. 1859 at the Red River settlement (Man.).

It is likely that Roderick McKenzie, one of several fur traders bearing this name, was in the Timiskaming department as a clerk for the North West Company in the 1790s, but it was in the Lake Nipigon (Ont.) area that his reputation with the NWC was made, and after the union of the NWC and the Hudson's Bay Company in 1821 he was assigned to that district as a chief trader. In 1825 he assumed command of Fort William (Thunder Bay, Ont.). At this post his major preoccupations were competition from American traders and the difficulty of maintaining morale in a work-force sharply diminished by the HBC. McKenzie's promotion to chief factor in 1830 carried with it a transfer to the west, where, for the rest of his active life, he was in charge of the English (upper Churchill) River district, with headquarters at Île-à-la-Crosse (Sask.). Almost every year he made the trip to York Factory (Man.) with his furs and attended the HBC Council of the Northern Department. In 1839 he was also appointed to the Council of Assiniboia, formed by the HBC to govern the Red River colony, but he had little interest in such activities. Writing to James Hargrave* in 1839 he said, "I will not be at the Council in Red River – I can be of more use at my Post, in Trading a Skin; than at the Council, as Legislator I have no great ambition, to shine as an Orator, that I leave to young Gentlemen, better qualified."

The good returns McKenzie was able to maintain during his early years at Île-à-la-Crosse began to fall off in the early 1840s as the Chipewyan Indians who traded in this district moved into the plains region. McKenzie placed part of the blame for the desertion of his post by the Indians on the machinations of his neighbour in the Saskatchewan district, Chief Factor John ROWAND, and worried about the growing influence of the Roman Catholic missionaries at Fort Pitt (Sask.). Governor George SIMPSON commented upon the injurious rivalry existing between the two districts and, although his high opinion of Rowand was well known, he did not appear to play favourites. McKenzie's invitation to the Catholic missionary Father Jean-Baptiste Thibault* and the arrival of the latter at Île-à-la-Crosse prompted a rebuke from Simpson in 1845. McKenzie explained that his acceptance of missionaries was motivated by the desire of the Chipewyan Indians, who could be induced to trade where priests were to be found, and by the religious needs of the HBC employees, most of whom were Catholic. With the governor's consent priests were established at Île-à-la-Crosse in subsequent years, and during McKenzie's time two future bishops, Alexandre-Antonin Taché* and Louis-François Laflèche*, served in the area.

As early as 1832 Simpson had suggested that McKenzie, whose health was "broken and worn out so that his useful Days are over," ought to retire. In 1837 Thomas Simpson described him as a "well-meaning, warm-hearted but passionate and crabbed old Highlander," and by the early 1840s the opinion was widespread that he should take his retirement, especially after he broke his leg in 1843; but, limping and nearly blind, he stayed on, worrying about his finances and about finding a place where he could settle with his wife and family. He had married Angélique, an Ojibwa Indian of the Lake Nipigon area, by the custom of the country in about 1803, and they had raised a large family. In 1841 this marriage was apparently formalized by Christian rite. For his retirement McKenzie's preference was a remote location – Norway House (Man.), Sault Ste Marie (Ont.), or Cumberland House (Sask.). Ironically, by 1846 Governor Simpson seems to have changed his mind about McKenzie, urging him to stay at Île-à-la-Crosse: "While you continue healthy & that the business is not irksome and harassing to you, I see no reason for your retirement." This reassessment may, however, have been due more to the relative unimportance of the Île-à-la-Crosse district than to a genuine appreciation of McKenzie's usefulness. Finally, in 1850 McKenzie took a leave of two years at Fort Alexander (Man.) before retiring in 1852 and settling reluctantly in what he called "the civilized world of Red River." Like other HBC employees, McKenzie placed his savings, which in 1851 totalled £4,724, in Canadian investments such as the Bank of Montreal, the Montreal and Lachine Rail-road, the Bank of British North America, the Commercial Bank of the Midland District, and private loans. These investments, which provided his only link with the united Canadas, generally paid good returns of from six to eight per cent.

Among the old Nor'Westers he was known as "Captain of the Nipigon" and, unlike almost all the Scots of the fur trade, he never returned to his native land, even on furlough. Leaving a sizeable estate, he died at Caberleigh Cottage, Red River, surrounded by symbols of a distant Highland past, but committed to the Indian country he had adopted as his home. All seven of his sons served the HBC, one of them, Samuel, rising to the rank of chief trader; of his five daughters, one died unmarried and the other four married men in the company service.

ELIZABETH ARTHUR

Æneas and Angus Cameron papers, in the possession of E. A. Mitchell (Toronto), McTavish, Frobisher & Co. to Æneas Cameron, 3 Sept. 1799 (mfm. at AO). PAC, MG 19, A21, ser.1, 31. PAM, HBCA, A.31/9; A.34/2: f.8; A.36/10: ff.3–4; A.44/4: 67; B.89/a/14–27; B.129/b/1–11; B.129/e/1–13; B.149/a/11; B.162/a/1; B.231/a/7–9; B.231/e/5–6; D.4/18: ff.10d–11; D.4/31: ff.46d–47; D.4/32: ff.112, 217; D.4/42: ff.83, 159; D.4/84b: f.71; D.5/4: ff.152, 228, 229; D.5/7: f.199d; D.5/10: f.370; D.5/14: f.112; D.5/19: ff.15, 75; D.5/21: f.110; D.5/22: f.231; D.5/41: f.313; D.5/43: ff.169, 508. *Canadian North-West* (Oliver). *Docs. relating to NWC* (Wallace). *HBRS*, 1 (Rich); 3 (Fleming); 19 (Rich and Johnson). Hargrave, *Hargrave corr.* (Glazebrook). Mactavish, *Letters of Letitia Hargrave* (MacLeod). Simpson, "Character book," *HBRS*, 30 (Williams), 151–236. Van Kirk, *"Many tender ties."* Barbara Benoit, "The mission at Île-à-la-Crosse," *Beaver*, outfit 311 (winter 1980): 40–50.

MACLEAN, DUNCAN, merchant, farmer, politician, and newspaper editor; b. between 15 April and 8 Aug. 1799, probably in Scotland; d. 15 April 1859 in Charlottetown.

No record of Duncan Maclean's birthplace appears to have survived, but shortly after his death a contemporary, Edward Whelan*, referred to him as a "Scotchman." Although no precise information is available concerning his schooling, Maclean was generally credited with having had a good education, particularly in mathematics and science, which he described in 1843 as forming his "chief recreation and pleasure." In the same memorial he referred to himself as "a sworn surveyor." He is known to have married at least twice and to have had at least five children. According to his own account, also dated 1843, he immigrated to "the Colonies" around 1818. His destination apparently was the West Indies, where he was "exclusively engaged in commerce." As one of the "Colonial Dragoons" he took an active part in suppressing an 1831 slave revolt in Antigua. He moved to Montreal the following year, and was once again occupied as a merchant. His possible role in the rebellion of 1837–38 was later the subject of much recrimination in Prince Edward Island, and it appears, from his own account and the testimony of prominent Montrealers several years afterwards, that he was on the loyalist side. Nevertheless, on the Island the rumour persisted into the 20th century that he had been Louis-Joseph Papineau*'s secretary and that he had been a fugitive; this story, like one concerning an alleged bankruptcy in Montreal, may have originated in confusion between him and someone else of the same name.

Maclean had arrived in Prince Edward Island by late 1839, and his departure from Montreal appears to have had a dual motivation. He wanted "to exchange a commercial life for a rural one," and was "desirous of residing in what I then conceived to be a less disturbed colony than Canada." On 1 Nov. 1839, for £100 currency, he acquired from Charles WORRELL the improvements on a well-situated farm of 100 acres on the Cundall estate, at New London, Lot 20, in northwestern Queens County, with a 1,000-year lease at an annual rental of £5 sterling. His wife died on 30 March 1840 at age 20; when he married again at the end of 1844 his bride was Ann Smith of New London. He continued to farm over the years – in 1851 he stated that he had cleared more than 40 acres since his arrival – and resided on the same property until his death.

Finding that farming did not supply "my accustomed activity," Maclean in 1842 successfully contested a Queens County constituency that included New London. During the campaign he made a distinctly negative impression on the lieutenant governor, Sir Henry Vere Huntley*. When sending a list of assemblymen to the Colonial Office on 13 Aug. 1842, Huntley, as well as identifying Maclean as a land surveyor and conceding that he was "said to be clever, & educated," described his electoral card and speeches as "most violently revolutionary." More than once in later years Maclean expressed the opinion that the story, allegedly spread by his political enemies, that he had been a Lower Canadian rebel and fugitive had actually helped him to be elected. His conduct in the session of 1843, during which he made caustic remarks about the veracity of the lieutenant governor, provoked James Douglas Haszard*, editor of the *Royal Gazette*, to insert in the report of the debates a note regretting Maclean's behaviour. These verbal attacks further alienated Huntley, who informed London that Maclean was "a new member of little ability, but infinitely rancorous."

The political universe of Prince Edward Island had been convulsed throughout the 1830s by the land question, particularly the controversy over the proposed solution of escheat, whose advocates, led by William Cooper*, argued that landlords' titles should be forfeited for non-fulfilment of the terms of their grants, and the land given to tenants. The Escheators, who had won the election of 1838, lost that of 1842, a turn of events which pleased Huntley and the Colonial Office. However, the struggle against leasehold tenure continued in the countryside, and on 28 Feb. 1843 there was a public meeting at New London; James Scott, who had come to the Island with Maclean and was apparently residing with him, acted as secretary for the meeting. It resolved that the Island government was conducted "for the benefit of a couple of dozen of land Speculators, their connexions, dependents, and parasites." In March, Maclean took the report of the meeting to John Ings and James Barrett Cooper*, two newspaper publishers in Charlottetown; both refused to print it in full, and at least one provided the authorities with a copy of the offending resolution. After being advised by Attorney General Robert Hodgson* and Solicitor General James Horsfield Peters* that it was libellous, and that

Maclean

Maclean, by his actions, was legally responsible for circulating a libel, Huntley ordered that he be prosecuted. Even had the lieutenant governor wished to prosecute others, Scott had left the Island "very shortly after the meeting," and Maclean had taken the precaution of erasing the name of the chairman from the report of the meeting. Consequently, although Maclean had not been present, he was charged with libelling the government.

Maclean brought a substantial number of supporters from the New London area to attend his trial at the Supreme Court in Charlottetown at the end of June 1843; estimated at "about 160" by Huntley and at a minimum of 911 by Maclean, they filled the court-room and surrounded the court-house. In what was probably a further attempt to emphasize the political nature of the case, Maclean conducted his own defence before the presiding judge, Edward James Jarvis, although with the assistance of a lawyer, Charles Young, whose advice he rejected. These tactics did not save him from conviction by a special jury composed of persons with a higher than usual property qualification and empanelled at the request of the attorney general, Hodgson, who believed that the case "required a Jury of more intelligence than is to be found amongst that Class usually selected for Petit Jurors in this Island." None the less, Maclean escaped sentencing because Huntley, who, according to his own account, had commenced the action to discredit Maclean in the eyes of his followers, requested that sentence not be passed, to avoid creating a martyr while teaching a lesson about the legal limits of free speech.

Although the jury delivered its verdict on 30 June 1843, Maclean learned of Huntley's decision only when Hodgson announced it in court on 12 Jan. 1844. In the mean time, on 8 August, Maclean had written to the colonial secretary, Lord Stanley, soliciting the surveyor generalship, which was already occupied by George Wright*. Even though his memorial focused on Prince Edward Island, he also stated that, if asked to serve, he would go "*wherever* he may be ordered"; in a subsequent letter, he specified his willingness to do surveying in "the polar circle," Africa, or Australia. When forwarding the memorial, Huntley, whose own health had apparently suffered because of the climate while serving in western Africa, suggested that Maclean, who declared himself to be of vigorous constitution, be given a post there. Apart from the bizarre aspect of Maclean's request under the circumstances, the fact of his memorial must have prompted the suspicion that, with sufficient inducement, he could be removed from the reform camp. On 8 September an anonymous letter appeared in a conservative newspaper, purportedly from a reformer, challenging Maclean to disprove the report that he "has directly proposed to the home government to abandon us and agitation for an appointment worth 200 *l*. or 300 *l*. a year."

During his first term in the House of Assembly, Maclean usually voted with the minority, and although he was not a dominating figure in debate, his intemperate rhetoric, especially concerning the land question, led to heated exchanges with such tory leaders as Joseph Pope* and Edward Palmer*. But by 1847, when the leading issue in local politics was responsible government, he was voting with the tories in the most important partisan divisions. He absolutely refused to follow Alexander Rae and other reform leaders into their alliance of convenience with Huntley, who had fallen out with the family compact. He had never forgiven the lieutenant governor for his libel prosecution, and as recently as 8 April 1846 had declared in the assembly that he "felt nothing . . . but pity and contempt" for him.

Maclean had been re-elected later in 1846 on the basis of an electoral card in which he promised to support responsible government as a step towards abolition of leasehold tenure. He explained his behaviour by claiming that the reform leadership, in failing to insist upon the settlement of the land question as an indispensable condition for supporting Huntley, had abandoned principle in an opportunistic quest for office. Indeed, although Maclean's motives were suspect, and almost certainly included resentment at Rae's failure to follow his advice, he was justified in finding the new alignment strange. But even after Huntley had been replaced and his successor, Sir Donald Campbell*, had split with the reformers over responsible government, Maclean continued to support the tory leadership. During the sessions of 1848 and 1849 he contributed to debate infrequently, and in the election of February 1850 he was defeated. His career in electoral politics was over, and in 1853, prior to the next general election, he declined nomination.

In early March 1850 Maclean had become editor of the *Islander*, a tory newspaper owned by John Ings, one of the publishers who had testified against him at his libel trial. Although Ings had founded the *Islander* in 1842, it was only after he engaged Maclean that editorial articles on local themes began to appear regularly. During the 1850s Maclean's role in Island politics was that of leading journalistic spokesman for the tory party. He published column upon column of merciless attacks on the reform triumvirate of George Coles*, James Warburton, and Edward Whelan, in the form of editorials, signed open letters, and apocryphal accounts of their doings presented as "intercepted correspondence" between "Jarge Coals," "Jamie Wearbottom," and "Neddy." He also poured invective upon Sir Alexander Bannerman* and Sir

Dominick Daly*, the lieutenant governors under whom the liberals occupied office almost continuously from 1851 to 1859, accusing them of partisanship.

To the delight and entertainment of the reading public, Maclean carried on a running battle through the decade with the immensely talented Whelan, liberal editor of the *Examiner*. The local poet John LePage*, a contemporary, wrote, "Both trained to vigorous intellectual strife, / They WROTE – as Roman Gladiators FOUGHT – for life!" Maclean and Whelan had collaborated on the latter's first Island newspaper, the *Palladium*, founded in 1843, and they had enjoyed, in Whelan's words, a "long and very close friendship." But they eventually fell out and, as well as being political foes and journalistic rivals, became bitter personal enemies, reviling each other as "the Dirty-faced Urchin" and "Donkey Maclean," respectively. On one occasion Maclean successfully sued Whelan for libel, yet the token award of one farthing led the latter to crow that this was the value the judge placed on the plaintiff's character. None the less, despite all the abuse and taunts which passed between them, each appears to have had a genuine respect for the other as an antagonist worthy of serious attention.

Although Maclean managed a tory newspaper for a tory publisher, he maintained a measure of political independence. This was particularly evident in the late 1850s, when he adamantly refused to participate in the tory campaign for the "open Bible" in the schools. Skilled in the logical dissection of arguments, he insisted that, regardless of the declared intentions of Palmer and Thomas Heath Haviland*, the wording of their 1857 resolution in the assembly to bring the question forward entailed compulsion, and that compulsory use of the Bible in denominationally mixed schools would drive the large Roman Catholic minority out of the public educational system, thus dividing the colony along religious lines. This position was consistent with his strong criticism in the assembly during 1845 of a proposal to open the Central Academy, a publicly supported grammar school in Charlottetown, to the Bible. On that occasion he had declared that "when he was a boy at school, he had been compelled with others to read the Bible as a class book, and the effect produced on his mind was a dislike to the perusal of the Bible ever since." Indeed, Maclean was widely believed to be an "infidel," the contemporary Island term for atheist, agnostic, Unitarian, or apostate; in his own words, "I was known to entertain independent opinions in religion."

The controversy over putting the Bible into schools provided one of the few occasions in the 1850s when Maclean and Whelan, an Irish-born Catholic, found common ground and came to one another's aid. As an "infidel," Maclean was a prime target for the

Protector and Christian Witness of Charlottetown, an ultra-Protestant newspaper which supported the tory leadership on the issue. He became sufficiently estranged from his party that for a time Ings closed the editorial columns of the *Islander* to him with respect to the Bible question, forcing him to resort to signed letters and, on at least one occasion, to paid advertising in another conservative paper. Yet when the tories won the election of 1859 – primarily through effective exploitation of the Bible question – they decided to make him commissioner of public lands. In reviewing the appointment, Whelan pronounced him "quite competent to discharge its duties." Maclean did not live to assume the post, for on his way from New London to Charlottetown to be sworn in he caught a severe cold which led to pleurisy and inflammation, resulting in his unexpected death on 15 April 1859 after a week of illness. He was survived by his wife, Ann, and two sons and three daughters by their marriage. He died intestate, and one of two bondsmen in 1860 for the administrators of his modest estate, his widow and her new husband, was none other than Edward Whelan.

Duncan Maclean had been immersed in controversy throughout his public career in Prince Edward Island. Even his record in Antigua and Lower Canada became a subject of dispute. For years he bombarded the Colonial Office with memorials and complaints, sometimes rambling and abusive, written in a virtually illegible scrawl. When transmitting to London two of Maclean's letters in January 1857, Lieutenant Governor Daly stated that they led him to believe that "the doubts I have frequently heard expressed as to the sanity of their author, are not without foundation. Habits of intemperance, to which he has long been addicted, are producing their ordinary effects in his case, & he is without the slightest influence in this community." Daly went on to claim that Maclean lived 30 miles from Charlottetown "for the advantage of greater personal Safety from consequences that might follow upon his slanderous attacks on private character." In London, Arthur Johnstone Blackwood, a senior clerk in the Colonial Office, commented in 1857 concerning one of Maclean's letters that "a more slanderous low communication was never addressed to this Office – unless it may have been previously by himself." Such was the unflattering impression he created among many in authority: an extraordinarily combative, personally offensive, possibly unbalanced polemicist.

Yet among Maclean's contemporaries on the Island warm memories of his ability and logical powers as a writer, and of his epic battles with Whelan, lasted many years. Maclean's writings in the *Islander* reveal a curiosity about scientific matters in general, particularly astronomy, on which, although not an

McLearn

accomplished speaker, he gave several public lectures. Interested in science, a religious sceptic, and flagrantly disrespectful of authority, he seems to have contained the essential elements of a cranky 19th-century radical. Yet on the Island he soon left the radical camp and became a spokesman for conservatism. The reasons for his conversion – the sincerity of which Whelan frequently professed to doubt – are not entirely clear, and were probably a mixture of personal relations, political strategy, and future prospects: clashes with other strong personalities in the reform party, differences over the course to be followed when Huntley and the compact split, and the realization that the tories were abler than the reformers to provide him with security. As might be expected, he tended to play down the extent to which he changed – "of all the old liberal party D. Maclean alone has never wavered," he wrote in 1850 – and to account for his new allegiance by referring to alleged betrayals of the reform cause by Coles, Whelan, and Warburton, to whose party he gave the name "Snatchers," because of their supposed desire to snatch the emoluments of public office. Local tories used the epithet for many years, and Whelan retorted with the label "Snarlers," calling Maclean "Chieftain of the Snarler Clan."

Somewhat of an ideological enigma, a political turncoat, and a personal misfit, as well as an "infidel," Duncan Maclean, perhaps partially for these reasons, is almost entirely absent from the historical literature of Prince Edward Island. Yet he deserves to be remembered as a significant political and a major journalistic figure in the middle decades of the 19th century, particularly during the 1850s, when he edited the *Islander*, which he claimed had, by the latter half of the decade, the largest circulation of any newspaper in the colony. Eccentric and unrestrained as he was, he was also a force and a talent to be reckoned with.

IAN ROSS ROBERTSON

[Apart from material appearing in W. L. Cotton, "The press in Prince Edward Island," *Past and present of Prince Edward Island . . .* , ed. D. A. MacKinnon and A. B. Warburton (Charlottetown, [1906]), 115, and I. R. Robertson, "Religion, politics, and education in Prince Edward Island from 1856 to 1877" (MA thesis, McGill Univ., Montreal, 1968), chap. 1–3, and "The Bible question in Prince Edward Island from 1856 to 1860," *Acadiensis* (Fredericton), 5 (1975–76), no. 2: 13–15, 22, basic information about Duncan Maclean must come from primary sources.

Maclean's career as an assemblyman is documented in P.E.I., House of Assembly, *Journal*, 1843–49, and in the reports of debates which appeared in the *Royal Gazette* (Charlottetown), 1843–49. For 1845, however, reports which appeared in the *Islander* and *Palladium*, both of Charlottetown, should also be consulted. The *Islander* survives for the years Maclean was editor, 1850 through 1859; a note from the compositors complaining of his handwriting appeared in the issue of 19 Nov. 1852. The

journalistic rivalry with Edward Whelan is recalled in verse in John LePage, *The Island minstrel, miscellaneous papers* (Charlottetown, 1885), 13–17, and in prose in the *Island Argus* (Charlottetown), 21 Sept. 1875. Concerning his involvement with Whelan's *Palladium*, see *Examiner* (Charlottetown), 11 Sept. 1848, 18 June 1855, 31 Oct. 1859, and PRO, CO 226/83: 66. Obituaries will be found in the *Islander*, 15, 22 April 1859; *Examiner*, 18 April 1859; and *Monitor* (Charlottetown), 20 April 1859. A poetic tribute appeared in the *Islander*, 24 June 1859.

Over the years Maclean wrote many letters or memorials of complaint or self-justification in which he revealed something of his personal history. The most useful of these will be found in PRO, CO 226/66: 121–22, 154–62; in the *Islander* of 25 Jan. 1856 he alludes to a case of mistaken identity with a Montreal merchant of the same name. Statements signed by Montrealers attesting to Maclean's loyalty during the Lower Canadian rebellion can be found in PRO, CO 226/66: 123–24, 167–68.

The events and controversy surrounding Maclean's libel trial in 1843 can be followed in the *Islander*, 17 March, 30 June, 7 July, 25 Aug., 8 Sept., 3 Nov. 1843; 12 Jan. 1844; *Colonial Herald, and Prince Edward Island Advertiser* (Charlottetown), 1, 8 July, 4, 25 Nov. 1843; 13 Jan. 1844; *Palladium*, 16 Nov. 1843, 7 March 1844; PAPEI, RG 6, Supreme Court, minutes, 27–28, 30 June, 1 July, 31 Oct., 2 Nov. 1843; 12 Jan. 1844; PRO, CO 226/65: 195–235, 251, 256; CO 226/66: 125–26, 142–47.

Land transactions relevant to Maclean on the Island are documented in PAPEI, RG 16, Land registry records, conveyance reg., liber 47: f.48; liber 48: f.299; liber 77: f.188; liber 86: f.698. Papers of administration for Maclean's estate are in Supreme Court of P.E.I. (Charlottetown), Estates Division.

Other references to Maclean include: PRO, CO 226/64: 30–31; 226/65: 90; 226/80: 599; 226/88: 4–6, 9; *Examiner*, 11 April, 18 July 1859; *Islander*, 17 May 1850; 29 Aug. 1851; 18 Feb., 25 March 1853; *Protector and Christian Witness* (Charlottetown), 1 April, 15 July 1857 (copy at PAPEI). I.R.R.]

McLEARN, RICHARD, Baptist minister, college administrator, and merchant; b. 1804 in Rawdon Township, N.S., son of James McLearn and Elizabeth Fenton; m. 26 June 1838 in Sydney, N.S., Harriet Stout, youngest daughter of Richard Stout*, and they had four daughters; d. 17 Aug. 1860 in Dartmouth, N.S.

The son of an Irish Protestant immigrant, Richard McLearn attended the local school and then worked as a farmer and woodcutter. While still a youth he was caught up in the Baptist revival of the early 1800s inspired by such preachers as Edward MANNING and George Dimock, and by the age of 19 he had become a member of the Rawdon church. McLearn originally aspired to be a schoolteacher, but after feeling the call to preach he chose instead to "venture on the Lord." With the encouragement of Manning and Dimock he obtained his licence to preach in 1827, and on 8 March 1828 was ordained pastor of the church in Rawdon. The enthusiasm at his ordination ceremony was not unqualified, however. Afterwards Alexis Caswell, the first pastor of the Granville Street Baptist Church in Halifax and formerly a professor at Columbian College in Washington, D.C., wrote to Manning that although McLearn was obviously a young man of splendid natural abilities, he lacked the educational qualifications which a preacher should possess. At the time of McLearn's ordination no formal instruction was required for the Baptist ministry. The combination of zeal, experience, and self-education had served the church well in preachers such as Manning, but it was becoming clear that the further expansion of the Baptist denomination required a ministry with higher educational attainments. Caswell's call for the establishment of a theological seminary thus found a receptive audience among many of the Baptist clergy.

No one was more desirous of a better education than McLearn himself, and in July 1828 he went to Halifax to study English grammar with Caswell. After Caswell returned to the United States to become a professor at Brown University in Providence, R.I., McLearn was tutored by Lewis Johnston and Edmund Albern Crawley* of the Granville Street congregation. As well as taking steps to overcome his own lack of formal instruction, he took a leading part in the attempt to improve the level of education throughout the Baptist ministry. He became a director of the Nova Scotia Baptist Education Society when it was formed in 1828 to provide financial assistance to young men preparing for the ministry and to establish a seminary which would give instruction in English literature, classics, science, and other subjects "which usually comprise the course of education at an Academy." The initial outcome was the founding of Horton Academy at Wolfville in March 1829.

Owing to the small size of the Baptist congregation in Rawdon, McLearn was able in 1829 to add pastoral duties at the Windsor church, where he preached every second Sunday to a "large and very attentive congregation." Within a few years, after receiving letters from the eastern part of the province complaining of the "destitute condition" of the church there, McLearn decided to put his preaching abilities at the service of the Nova Scotia Baptist Home Missionary Board. These abilities were apparently exceptional: he was noted for his "clear and full" voice and, according to a contemporary, his "presentation of truth was searching as well as lucid." In 1832 McLearn embarked on an evangelical tour, spending about three months preaching throughout present-day Colchester, Pictou, Guysborough, and Antigonish counties before crossing over to Cape Breton for another three months. In addition to preaching and administering the ordinances of the church, McLearn encouraged the formation of female mite societies to raise funds for the Baptist mission to those "lying in pagan idolatry" in Burma. He also attempted to direct the attention of those he visited to their intemperate habits. His promotion of temperance societies was not always successful: one group of Gaelic-speaking immigrants in Cape Breton, to whom he spoke through an interpreter, did not "approve" of his reasoning when he "laboured to show the absurdity of expending the enormous sum of three hundred dollars in that poor little settlement for rum, while they neglected educating their children, and had not the gospel preached amongst them." This experience was apparently the source of his later proposal to the 1853 meeting of the Baptist Convention of the Maritime Provinces that a missionary be sent to minister specifically to the Gaelic-speaking population of Cape Breton. At the conclusion of his arduous six-month tour McLearn was able to report that he had "preached ninety-five times; administered the Lord's Supper fifteen times; attended eighteen conference meetings, besides prayer and temperance meetings; and baptized thirty-eight persons." Because of the hospitality of the people along the way his total expenses amounted to only 50 shillings.

While returning home from Cape Breton, McLearn received a request from the Nova Scotia Baptist Education Society to visit the churches throughout the Maritime provinces in order to collect funds for Horton Academy. This fund-raising activity took him in 1835 to the United States, where he spoke to Baptist congregations from Bangor, Maine, to Savannah, Ga. McLearn felt that the warm reception accorded him, particularly in the southern states, was partially attributable to his Irish descent: "This is in my favour, as they dislike the meddling English and Scotch more than the open-hearted honest Irish." By the end of his trip he had raised more than £400 for the academy and had received a promise from the Northern Baptist Education Society of New England to maintain five young Nova Scotians throughout a regular course of education for the ministry.

During the 1830s McLearn also continued his pastoral duties at Rawdon and Windsor. After 1834 he was responsible for the church at Windsor only, and he sought to strengthen the Baptist cause there in 1837 with a series of revival services conducted with Ingraham Ebenezer Bill*. The sudden loss of his voice, however, forced him to resign his charge at Windsor shortly thereafter. He wrote to his mentor, Edward Manning, in June 1838: "I have not been able to preach for nearly two months and I cannot converse much. . . . My complaint is called the laryngitis."

McLearn's affliction coincided with an event of great importance for higher education in Nova Scotia. In September 1838 Edmund Crawley was denied appointment as a professor at the newly established Dalhousie College in Halifax. Interpreting this decision by the Dalhousie board of governors as a deliberate attempt to place the college under the

McLelan

exclusive control of the Church of Scotland, Crawley and other prominent Baptists called for the establishment of a Baptist college. The Nova Scotia Baptist Education Society, meeting in Horton Academy two months later, passed a resolution "to establish and support a college in addition to the Academy." At this time McLearn was a member of the managing committee of the society and in 1839, when Queen's College (renamed Acadia College in 1841) came into operation on the same grounds as Horton Academy, he was made superintendent and bursar of both the college and the academy. His involvement in higher education did not end here. Still unable to resume preaching, he decided to use the extra time available to him to acquire the formal education he had always desired. The Church of England no longer required religious tests for entrance to King's College, Windsor, and McLearn took advantage of his residence there to enrol in 1838 in the BA program, from which he graduated in 1843.

McLearn had hoped that in the mean time his voice problem would be overcome, but by 1842 there was still no improvement. He therefore decided that same year to support himself by entering the mercantile business in Halifax in partnership with W. L. Evans; by 1849 he had taken over the business at the Commercial Wharf in his own name, importing flour, molasses, salt, and tobacco in his ships the *Actress* (59 tons) and the *Angelique* (31 tons). McLearn made his home across the harbour in Dartmouth where he was active as a trustee of the mechanics' institute and the Dartmouth Burial Ground, as president of the local temperance society, and as chairman of a public meeting organized to protest an increase in the price of ferry tickets made by the Halifax-Dartmouth Steamboat Company. He was also one of the founders of the Dartmouth Baptist Church in 1843, acting for several years as clerk and treasurer of the church as well as superintendent of the Sunday school, and administering the ordinances when there was no pastor available. Yet his involvement with the church was limited and it was with evident regret for his earlier preaching days that he wrote to Manning: "My life is spent in an office at Business and in my family except the few hours that are devoted to the meetings of the church. Though in a City I am solitary."

The financial and organizational experience derived from his business activity did, however, fit McLearn for a renewed role in education and missionary work, the areas where he had made his principal contribution to the expansion of the Baptist denomination in Nova Scotia. In the hope that he would be able "to control his secular business" sufficiently to devote himself to the organization of the home missionary enterprise, he was made secretary and chairman of the Home Missionary Board. Moreover, when the Baptist Convention of the Maritime Provinces decided in 1859 to set up provincial committees to raise funds for the support of those preparing for the ministry, McLearn was appointed chairman and treasurer of the committee for Nova Scotia. The convention's plans for McLearn were not to be realized, however, for a year later he was, in the words of his fellow committee members, "called to engage in a higher sphere of service."

PHYLLIS R. BLAKELEY

ABHC, Edward Manning, corr., Richard McLearn to Edward Manning. PANS, RG 1, 442, doc.11; RG 5, P, 70, 1834; 71, 1839; 72, 1835. *Baptist Missionary Magazine of Nova-Scotia and New-Brunswick* (Saint John and Halifax), 1 (1827–29)–3 (1833); new ser., 1 (1834)–3 (1836). *Christian Messenger* (Halifax), 2 June 1837, 21 April 1842, 22 Aug. 1860. *Morning Journal and Commercial Advertiser* (Halifax), 3, 15 June, 6 July 1859; 20 Aug. 1860. *Times and Courier* (Halifax), 18 Jan. 1849. Bill, *Fifty years with Baptist ministers*, 59, 66, 91, 96–98, 284–300, 399, 403, 628. Levy, *Baptists of Maritime prov.*, 93, 112, 117–42, 186.

McLELAN (McLellan, McClelland), GLOUD WILSON, businessman and politician; b. 18 April 1796 in Great Village, N.S., son of David McLelan and Mary Durling; m. 26 Dec. 1822 Martha Spencer in Londonderry, N.S., and they had a son, Archibald Woodbury*, and two daughters; d. 6 April 1858 in Halifax.

Gloud Wilson McLelan's grandfather, Peter McLelan, quite possibly came to North America from Londonderry (Northern Ireland) in the migrations supervised by Alexander McNutt* in 1761–62. By January 1770 Peter McLelan had settled in Londonderry Township, N.S. Gloud was casually educated, if indeed he was educated in any formal sense at all. His letters show decided aberrations in spelling, and he preferred to punctuate them with hard common sense. He early developed a mercantile business at Londonderry, and proceeded to invest the profits in a shipping business he established at Great Village, four miles away on the north shore of the Minas Basin. Eventually he took his son and his son-in-law John M. Blaikie into the firm with him.

In 1836 he was elected to the House of Assembly for Londonderry Township. McLelan was a reformer, and remained one all his life. He was re-elected in 1840 and again three years later, but was defeated in 1847 by John Wier, whom he had displaced in 1836. He subsequently occupied himself with his increasingly successful business, but in 1851 he returned to the assembly as member for Colchester County, which he represented until his death.

McLelan was a useful man in the assembly. Unschooled and rough, but capable, he was leaned on by men in his party who were obviously more sophisticated than he was. William Young*, the premier from 1854 to 1857, said of McLelan, "He had often hewn out of the rough material valuable ideas which had been polished into shape and form by other members of the House." McLelan was also a bear for work. He believed that MHAS were sent to Halifax to work for their constituents and to deal with every subject of legislation that came up. Thus he grappled manfully, if rather idiosyncratically, with the business of the house. In 1843, for example, in the contentious debate over government aid to sectarian colleges [see James William Johnston*], McLelan proposed a bill by which all educational grants would be wiped out and the whole question considered afresh. Like all reformers, he much favoured a non-sectarian college, centred in Halifax. His bill, however, failed to pass. More than once his quaint mannerisms provoked the assembly to laughter. He was a good party man, but his sturdy independence made it impossible to charge him with being too partisan. "Independent Reformer" is about right for him.

He retained some Presbyterian traits. He signed a petition about 1848 against the mail coach blowing its horn on Sunday. If it arrived in the middle of a church service, too many parishioners preferred their mail to their sermon. He was a member of the Sons of Temperance in the 1850s. He also had some anti-Catholic predilections that surfaced in 1857. Nevertheless, he made few enemies and his penchant for homely realities saved him from being abrasive.

He died suddenly in Halifax, there, as he always was, for the sittings of the house. Out walking on the evening of 3 April 1858, he was taken ill and died three days later. Not a great man, nor perhaps even a lovable one, he did his duty. The *Acadian Recorder* was a little hard in its assessment of McLelan, but it seemed to express a general view: "Of him it might be said, without detracting at all from his real merits, that we might have better spared a better man." One might remember him best by the sage advice he gave to Joseph Howe* and William Young in 1850 about attention to electoral business or, for that matter, any other kind of business, "One walk in spring is worth two in the fawl."

P. B. WAITE

[There are small collections of Gloud Wilson McLelan papers at Mount Allison Univ. Arch. (Sackville, N.B.), and in the following files at the PANS: Biog., McLelan, letters (a microfilm collection including several letters written to him between 1831 and 1844); MG 1, 1729 (mostly business papers, and including material connected with his son, Archibald Woodbury McLelan); and MG 100, 183, no.48 (his 1850 letter on election strategy). There are brief obituaries in the Halifax *Morning Chronicle*, 8 April 1858, and *Acadian Recorder*, 10 April 1858. Birth and marriage records are found in the Londonderry register book, p.46

(available on microfilm at PANS, under Places: Londonderry, Colchester County, township records, vol.II). Scattered references to him appear in *Great Village history: commemorating the 40th anniversary of Great Village Women's Institute, 1920–1960* ([Great Village, N.S., 1960]). Other useful secondary sources include Beck, *Joseph Howe*, vol.1, and A. W. H. Eaton, "The settling of Colchester County, Nova Scotia, by New England Puritans and Ulster Scotsmen," RSC *Trans.*, 3rd ser., 6 (1912), sect.II: 221–65. P.B.W.]

MacLENNAN (McLennan), JOHN, Church of Scotland minister, justice of the peace, and teacher; b. 1797 in Lochcarron, Scotland; m. 11 June 1823 Catherine MacNab in Laggan (Highland), Scotland, and they had ten children; d. 11 Feb. 1852 in Kilchrenan, Scotland.

Born among the mountains of Wester Ross and reared in the sunlight of the Reverend Lachlan MacKenzie's famous ministry, John MacLennan graduated MA from King's College (University of Aberdeen) in 1818. During the next four years he studied divinity at King's College and Marischal College (University of Aberdeen) and lived in Inverness-shire where he found his future bride. Licensed for the Church of Scotland ministry on 26 Nov. 1822, he was ordained on 15 April 1823 at Alvie "to qualify him for accepting of a Pastoral Charge in North America."

He had received a call, perhaps through the efforts of the Reverend James Drummond MacGregor* or the Reverend Donald Allan Fraser*, from a group of Scottish Presbyterians who had established "flourishing settlements" in the southeast corner of Prince Edward Island. These predominantly Gaelic-speaking communities were founded in 1803 by Highlanders whose immigration had been promoted by the Earl of Selkirk [Douglas*]. Their language and culture had largely isolated them from the pastoral care of the few Protestant ministers who came to the Island. By 1816–17 they could afford to support a minister of their own and they subscribed a bond for the maintenance of one "licensed and ordained by a Presbytery of the Church of Scotland." Not until MacLennan's arrival in 1823 were their hopes realized.

MacLennan landed in Nova Scotia and, with Fraser, John Martin, and Hugh MacLeod (all clergymen of the Church of Scotland), formed the Scotch Presbytery of Halifax at Truro on 18 Sept. 1823. Soon afterwards he reached Belfast, P.E.I., where he identified the need for a commodious, centrally located church. Fortunately, an able craftsman, Robert JONES, was already at hand; the main edifice of St John's Presbyterian Church, completed in the mid 1820s and featuring handwrought hardwood shingles, testifies to the skill of its builders.

From the Belfast area the pioneer minister's

569

McLeod

influence spread widely. He shepherded the Presbyterians around Charlottetown into a congregation which by 1829 had built a church, St James, that could seat more than a thousand. Cherishing the Highland settlements at New London, he visited them monthly for many years and officiated at the opening of their church in 1833. Although "every corner of the Island was known to him," he did not restrict his ministry to it. Robust and conditioned to arduous travel, he itinerated also in New Brunswick and Nova Scotia, visiting Cape Breton extensively in 1824, 1827, 1829, and 1831. Preaching and administering the sacraments to the thousands of Gaels who had settled there without a pastor, he took up their cause in correspondence with Scotland, most effectively with Robert Burns* of Paisley and with the Edinburgh Bible Society. Ministers were sent out, as were Gaelic and English Bibles, and in 1836 Cape Breton had its own presbytery.

His parishioners at Belfast, however, remained MacLennan's principal concern. He was appointed a justice of the peace in 1826 by Lieutenant Governor John Ready*, and later dispensed welfare payments to the feeble of his flock. Because the district lacked a doctor from the death of Angus Macaulay* in 1827 to the arrival of Angus MacSwain in 1841, MacLennan's pastoral care included nursing of the sick, first aid, and elementary medical treatment. Around 1839 he undertook responsibility for the school at Pinette, near his home, where he was an effective teacher of Latin as well as primary subjects.

During the 1840s Presbyterians outside Scotland were affected by conflicts in the homeland over spiritual freedom of the church, and the disruption in 1843 caused radical changes in the Maritimes. Most of the ministers in MacLennan's presbytery and synod either returned to Scotland or joined the Free Church. Several Island congregations which he had fostered also joined the Free Church but his own folk in Belfast and the Charlottetown congregation remained with him in the established church. Additional stress came in 1845 from the death in Newfoundland of his friend the Reverend Donald Allan Fraser, whose congregation at St John's MacLennan had then to look after for some months.

These events and the claims of his growing family determined his return to Scotland in 1849 for what he thought would be a temporary absence; his wish to return to Prince Edward Island was, however, never fulfilled. After a ministry of less than three years at the Gaelic Chapel in Cromarty he became parish minister of Kilchrenan and Dalavich, where he died on 11 Feb. 1852 of diphtheria contracted from a child he had been attending.

His missionary spirit, physical strength, and wide range of talents combined in helping to establish the Church of Scotland in Prince Edward Island, Cape Breton, Nova Scotia, New Brunswick, and Newfoundland. Sociable and peace loving, in the service of his Master he was the devoted servant of the whole pioneer community. His legacy to Canada also included the members of his gifted family who returned to make notable contributions in religion, education, the army, industry, and health services.

JEAN M. MacLENNAN

PAC, MG 9, C8, 5 (copies) (mfm. at PAPEI). Walter Johnston, *Travels in Prince Edward Island . . .* (Edinburgh, 1823). John MacGregor, *British America* (2nd ed., 2v., Edinburgh and London, 1833), 1: 541–42. *Prince Edward Island Register*, 1823–30. Scott *et al.*, *Fasti ecclesiæ scoticanæ*, 4: 93; 6: 369–71; 7: 7, 622. Gregg, *Hist. of Presbyterian Church*, 269, 271, 273, 275, 318, 323, 326. *The life and times of the Rev. Robert Burns . . . including an unfinished autobiography*, ed. R. F. Burns (Toronto, 1872), 172. J. M. MacLennan, *From shore to shore, the life and times of the Rev. John MacLennan of Belfast, P.E.I.* (Edinburgh, 1977). J. [M.] MacLeod, *History of Presbyterianism on Prince Edward Island* (Chicago and Winona Lake, Ind., 1904). M. A. Macqueen, *Skye pioneers and "the Island"* ([Winnipeg, 1929]), 35, 37, 44–45, 54. John Murray, *The history of the Presbyterian Church in Cape Breton* (Truro, N.S., 1921), 44. George Patterson, *Memoir of the Rev. James MacGregor, D.D. . . .* (Philadelphia, 1859), 413. Donald Sage, *Memorabilia domestica; or, parish life in the north of Scotland* (Edinburgh, 1889), 6, 228, 315, 435. A. B. Warburton, *A history of Prince Edward Island from its discovery in 1534 until the departure of Lieutenant-Governor Ready in A.D. 1831* (Saint John, N.B., 1923), 259, 275, 348, 357, 390.

McLEOD, PETER, timber contractor; b. *c.* 1807 most likely in Chicoutimi, Lower Canada, eldest son of Peter McLeod and a Montagnais woman; m. according to the custom of the country first Josephte Atikuapi and secondly Bélonie Siméon; two sons were born of these unions; d. 11 Sept. 1852 in Chicoutimi.

Except for a brief period of study, Peter McLeod spent his early years helping his father in the trade of various king's posts, where he later served as a clerk from 1834 to 1836. His father, who was born in Scotland around 1784, had settled in the Saguenay region and then on the north shore of the St Lawrence at the outset of the 19th century. Engineer, surveyor, and officer in the British army, he entered the service of the North West Company, and on its merger with the Hudson's Bay Company in 1821 he became the confidential agent of William Lampson, the lessee of the king's posts. He occupied this position until 1831, when the HBC secured the leasing rights.

It was during his time as Lampson's agent that McLeod Sr became interested in lumbering in the Charlevoix region. Acting virtually as a timber contractor, he built sawmills for rental in La Malbaie, served as a timber supplier, and obtained felling rights. From 1827 to 1836 he became one of the principal sources of timber for William Price*, who was then established at La Malbaie. In September 1836 he entrusted his eldest son with the responsibility for his facilities and commitments. But Peter's assumption of control evidently did not produce very satisfactory results. From 1837 to 1842 the McLeods' debts to Price continued to grow, and by the end of the latter year had reached £2,200. It is in the context of indebtedness, and also of Price's desire to be the first timber contractor established as far up the Saguenay as Chicoutimi, that the partnership between Price and the McLeods must be seen.

Price could not himself acquire the felling rights and the letters patent on mill sites or on land in the region because of the prerogatives over this territory granted to the HBC until 2 Oct. 1842, and its antagonism towards him. He therefore proposed to use McLeod Jr to push farther inland along the Saguenay. With the help of the Société des Vingt et Un [see Alexis TREMBLAY], McLeod had established himself between Tadoussac and Grande-Baie by 1837. Since, as a Montagnais on his mother's side, he had natural rights to circulate freely among the king's posts and to settle there, Price would be able, through him, to thwart the HBC and achieve his goal of exploiting the region's rich pine stands. This prospect prompted the agreement between Price and the McLeods.

The terms of the contract concluded before notary Laughlan Thomas Macpherson on 7 Nov. 1842 reveal a good deal about the intentions and interests of both parties. The assumption by the younger McLeod of managerial responsibility would discharge part of the debt he and his father owed Price. To wipe out the rest of it, Price agreed to purchase 20,000 deals from the McLeods' sawmill on the Rivière Noire for £1,200 and then to acquire the mill. McLeod Jr was to receive a £2,000 advance in equipment and cash, so that he could lay the foundations for sawmills on the Rivière du Moulin and the Rivière Chicoutimi. McLeod undertook to acquire from the crown the property rights at the entrance to these waterways and on their banks. The agreement specified that the new facilities were the joint property of the McLeods and Price, with profits and losses to be shared equally.

McLeod never managed to get title to the two mill sites, despite a request on 26 Oct. 1842 to Sir Charles Bagot* – the matter would not be settled until 1862, ten years after McLeod's death, when in the absence of a will or legal heirs, his estate passed to Price. But his lack of success did not stop him from setting himself up on the Rivière du Moulin and at Chicoutimi, and from launching the timber industry and settlement on the Saguenay. In August 1842, relying on his natural rights and eager to take advantage of the good season, McLeod, his wife

Josephte Atikuapi, and his son John had left the Rivière Noire with 23 men to begin construction on the Rivière du Moulin. The following winter he had the "building yards going," and he wrote to Price that lack of snow was delaying the transport of logs; he also explored Lac Kénogami and asked his partner to send him an engineer as well as equipment for building the conduit and the dam. By May, Price had met his request, and at the same time had sent him supplies for the store. A few months later, during the summer, as settlement proceeded on both banks of the Saguenay, McLeod gave permission for large areas to be cleared in the vicinity and on the slopes overlooking the settlement of Rivière-du-Moulin. He was thus able to begin sowing in the first year of his operation.

In 1844 McLeod shifted his attention to the Rivière Chicoutimi, to the west of the Rivière du Moulin. Better supplied with hydraulic power and better placed for harbour facilities, the Chicoutimi would accommodate a grist-mill and a sawmill, the first on the eastern slope and the second, set slightly back on the opposite slope, near the HBC trading post. The rivalry between the two companies and the proximity of their installations soon led to tension and clashes. Hence, to answer the HBC's claim that the lands were an integral part of its territory, McLeod wrote to Governor Charles Theophilus Metcalfe* on 27 March 1844. His petition explained that when he arrived in the area no use was being made of these lands, and that surveyor Duncan Stephen Ballantyne, under government orders to prepare the land register, had assured him personally that they were crown lands and would be divided up for occupancy. In conclusion, McLeod informed the governor that on the strength of these arguments and of his pre-emptive right, to which he added mention of his natural privileges as an Indian and his application to purchase in 1842, he intended to remain where he was and to continue the work already begun there.

The following month Price wrote to Sir George SIMPSON, the HBC governor, defending his partner and asking the company to end its opposition to the plan for the sawmill. Confronted with the swift development of this establishment, which was to become the major industrial centre of the Saguenay region and indeed one of the most important in Lower Canada, the HBC was forced to give in.

Through Ballantyne's report, drawn up in 1845, the progress of settlement and the detailed layout of the Price–McLeod establishments can be ascertained. At the Rivière du Moulin were clustered a sawmill, a wharf, a chapel, Peter McLeod's house, the general store, stables, and the smithy, and some 20 small log houses belonging to the company. At the Chicoutimi site were a sawmill, a wharf, a three-storey warehouse, a dozen resident landowners, the founda-

McLeod

tions of a grist-mill, some properties under cultivation, a dam, and the conduits for the mill-race to power the sawmill.

These establishments were designed to be self-sufficient. At a site called La Ferme, cattle, pigs, and poultry were raised and the grains to supply the lumber yards were processed. The one general store sold everything from flour and clothes to rosaries and lumbering tools. Every Saturday the settlers-cum-lumberjacks shopped for the basic needs of their families. From 1839 to 1878 merchandise was paid for with the customary tokens (a purchasing coupon issued to the bearer and exchangeable only at the store or in the company's office) or charged to the individual's account. The system of payment not only made it easy to run into debt and enabled the company to strengthen its hold on the local community, but also facilitated a double form of exploitation to the extent that the employer himself determined both the salary he paid and the price of goods. As manager of the Saguenay region, McLeod made sure that the system was applied and saw that his partner's instructions were obeyed, both in regard to tree felling and to discipline in the lumber yards.

An illustration of how rigorous the working conditions were is provided in McLeod's letter of 3 Dec. 1846 to Damase Boulanger, one of his foremen. After outlining at length the clauses concerning the hiring of workers, McLeod gave his agent directions as to the policy to be applied in the yards: "My orders are to charge those who lose time inopportunely on account of illness five shillings per day on amounts credited [to them]. . . . Any man who disobeys the orders of the one who is paid to direct him, [and] who does not give satisfaction, shall be dismissed immediately, and shall not receive a penny of his wages. . . . I want it also to be clearly understood that any repairing . . . shall be done in the evening, after the day's work is done. . . . Working time shall be from dawn until nightfall; the men must leave the yard before daybreak in order to be at their site as soon as it is light enough to work, and they shall not leave the site until it is too dark to continue."

It was precisely to improve the living conditions of these men and fight the stranglehold of Price and McLeod on the local population that Jean-Baptiste Honorat*, an Oblate priest, took up the cudgels for freedom. Given responsibility by his superiors to carry out missionary work in the Saguenay, he arrived at Grande-Baie on 15 Oct. 1844. In the first two weeks he had occasion to visit Rivière-du-Moulin where, to make possible his ministry to the approximately 600 residents, he advised the settlers to build a school, which could also serve as a chapel until a church was erected. Since McLeod had planned to make this place a Protestant fief, and had engaged the services of a pastor, he naturally took a determined stand against the notion of putting up buildings. At a public meeting

in December he attacked Honorat and the settlers, threatening them with reprisals if they persisted.

On 4 Jan. 1845 McLeod reversed his position. He offered to rent to Honorat and the village trustees for a five-year period the site chosen by them for the building, and quite unexpectedly even contributed £10 towards construction. An explanation for McLeod's volte-face emerged in the ensuing months. Informing his partner of the disturbing attitude of Honorat towards the power they had acquired at Chicoutimi, McLeod asked Price to approach the archbishop of Quebec, Pierre-Flavien Turgeon*, with a request to send secular priests to take the place of the Oblates of Mary Immaculate, and to allow the chapel at Rivière-du-Moulin to be replaced by a real church to be built midway between the two settlements of Chicoutimi and Rivière-du-Moulin; this site would, he thought, encourage the influx of new settlers and the development of a single village. In the spring of 1845 Price hastened to have a meeting with Turgeon on the matter. On 24 Feb. 1846, after negotiations with Honorat's provincial, Father Joseph-Bruno Guigues*, the archbishop gave his agreement to the request of Price and McLeod.

Honorat decided, in the face of the tactics being used to dislodge him and his community from the Saguenay, to "liberate" the settlers from the iron rule of Price and McLeod by giving them access to landed property. In May 1846, relying on European experience, he founded the mission of Grand-Brûlé (Laterrière). The plan to set up a free agricultural colony on the Saguenay quickly attracted the attention of the settlers and at the same time aroused the apprehension of Price and McLeod. The scheme contravened the interests of the two men because it involved displacing the population, was based on both agriculture and lumbering, and cut off the sawmills of the Rivière du Moulin and the Rivière Chicoutimi from their natural sources of timber. Since their monopoly in the Saguenay region would likely be jeopardized, they reacted swiftly.

On 3 March 1849 McLeod drew up a protest against Honorat before a notary, accusing him of having diverted some settlers of Grand-Brûlé from the contracts they had entered into with him. Subsequently, Price and McLeod developed a strategy designed to oust Honorat permanently from the Saguenay region. They also claimed that his undertaking was competing with their business and was leading the Oblates to certain failure. They accused him of taking too much interest in social questions and causing his community, the clergy, indeed the entire church, to be disliked because of his lack of consideration for the local Protestant élite. Thus they forced his superiors to recall him. In August 1849 Honorat quit the Saguenay in despair, leaving the people to the mercy of Price and McLeod.

Having no legal or political means to make

themselves heard, the settlers were once more submitted to McLeod's yoke. From 1848 to 1850 he maintained his control of the timber trade and devoted some of his energies to amassing wealth in the form of land. In return for mortgages on the settlers' lands, he advanced to them equipment and provisions from his general store; he used the law to expel settlers from the land they had cleared and sown when they did not hold a location ticket. On 29 Sept. 1849 McLeod's special attorney went before the government investigator, Jacques Crémazie*, to explain these dispossessions. In his report of 20 Feb. 1850 Crémazie pointed out the tactics used by McLeod, and made recommendations to correct the situation. These recommendations were not, however, put into effect until the next decade.

During the years 1849 and 1850 the Canadian timber trade enjoyed a strong recovery after the 1846 crisis precipitated by Britain's abolition of the tariffs protecting the colony, and by the slump in the market. On his partner's behalf, McLeod set up new sawmills as he took the first steps towards the conquest of the Lac-Saint-Jean region. But Price was alarmed about McLeod's health, and no longer felt that the 1842 contract was a sufficient guaranty, since there were no title deeds to the Rivière-du-Moulin and Chicoutimi establishments. Thus he decided in 1848 to undertake nothing further with McLeod unless a notarized contract was signed every autumn. On 21 Oct. 1850 Price submitted a request that the partnership with the McLeods be dissolved. On 2 November, as their debt to him was estimated at £4,520, he took a mortgage on the sawmill on the Chicoutimi and on the lands attached to it. When McLeod died suddenly on 11 Sept. 1852 and the legitimacy of his two sons, 16-year-old John and 5-year-old François, could not be established, Price, as creditor and trustee of the estate, became the sole owner of the establishments in the Saguenay and the largest timber merchant in Lower Canada.

Peter McLeod's acts of generosity, particularly towards Indians, which are occasionally noted in archival records, should not be forgotten. Nor should his influence and hold on the local population be underestimated. None the less, despite the legend surrounding him, he remains the figurehead of William Price, the partnership of 1842 condemning him to play second fiddle. Disadvantaged by the agreement that joined him to Price, he died more in debt than ever, leaving to his partner a booming industry and a region rich in resources to be developed.

GASTON GAGNON

ANQ-Q, CN1-197, 7 nov. 1842; CN4-9, 3 oct. 1828, 14 sept. 1829, 19 avril 1836; CN4-19, 25 juill. 1842; P1000-25-456. ANQ-SLSJ, P-2, Dossier 2, pièce 40; Dossier 3, pièce 14; Dossier 19, pièce 28; Dossier 645. Price Company Limited Arch. (Chicoutimi, Que.), Corr., Peter McLeod to William Price, 26 Jan. 1843, 27 Jan. 1844; Peter McLeod to C. T. Metcalfe, 27 March 1844; William Price to George Simpson, 16 April 1844. Arthur Buies, *Le Saguenay et le bassin du lac Saint-Jean; ouvrage historique et descriptif* (3e éd., Québec, 1896). Louise Dechêne, "William Price, 1810–1850" (thèse de licence, univ. Laval, Québec, 1964). Damase Potvin, *Peter McLeod, grand récit canadien inédit* (Québec, 1937). Arthur Maheux, "Le cas de Peter McLeod, jr.," *Concorde* (Québec), 6 (1955), no.5: 24. J.-P. Simard, "Biographie de Thomas Simard," *Saguenayensia* (Chicoutimi), 20 (1978): 4–7; "Onze années de troubles dans les postes du roi, 1821–1831," 10 (1968): 2–6.

McLEOD, SARAH (Ballenden), b. December 1818 in Rupert's Land, daughter of NWC fur trader Alexander Roderick McLeod* and a mixed-blood woman; m. 10 Dec. 1836 John BALLENDEN; d. 23 Dec. 1853 in Edinburgh.

Sarah McLeod was one of eight children born to Alexander Roderick McLeod and "an Indian woman of the half breed Caste" whom McLeod considered his legitimate wife since their union had been contracted according to the custom of the country. Alexander McLeod entered the Hudson's Bay Company as chief trader upon the union of the North West Company and the HBC in 1821. His daughter, raised at posts in the Mackenzie River and Columbia districts, was sent to the Red River settlement (Man.) for her education in the 1830s. Chief Factor John Stuart* acted as her guardian and gave his consent to her marriage, at the age of 18, to the promising HBC clerk John Ballenden. The bride received a dowry of £350 from her father, and the wedding, which was solemnized by the Reverend William Cockran*, was one of the social highlights of 1836 at Red River. It also indicated that, despite the example of Governor George SIMPSON and other HBC officers who introduced British wives into fur-trade society, attractive and acculturated young mixed-blood women could still aspire to social prominence through marriage to eligible young company officers. Ballenden was complimented on his choice by as severe a critic as Chief Trader James Hargrave*, who declared that Sarah was "a delightful creature" and that her husband had "every reason to consider himself a happy man."

As the wife of a rising young officer, Sarah Ballenden enjoyed life in Red River. Mixed-blood women were more readily accepted in society than they had been during Simpson's residence in the colony in the early 1830s. In 1837 this situation was underlined when Sarah named her first daughter Anne Christie, after the mixed-blood wife of Governor Alexander Christie*. The family moved to Sault Ste Marie, Upper Canada, in 1840, when John Ballenden was transferred, and Sarah was quite homesick there. She kept busy, however, entertaining visitors and caring for her growing family. Four children, a daughter who died in infancy and three boys, were born during the Ballendens' stay at the Sault.

McLeod

In 1848 Sarah Ballenden's delight in her husband's transfer back to Red River as chief factor was dampened when he suffered a stroke on the voyage west. That he made the recovery he did owed much to his wife's devoted nursing. Once installed as the chatelaine of Upper Fort Garry (Winnipeg), Mrs Ballenden began to play an active social role as befitted the wife of a chief factor. The christening in 1849 of a new daughter, Frances Isobel Simpson, named after Governor Simpson's wife, FRANCES, and her sister, was described by Letitia Hargrave [MACTAVISH] as "a splendid entertainment with abundance of champagne." Such was this vivacious young native woman's social success that, according to James BIRD, her friends predicted she was "destined to raise her whole Cast above european ladies in their influence on society here."

In 1850, however, Sarah Ballenden found herself at the centre of a scandal which had serious racial and social repercussions. What appears to have been an indiscreet flirtation on the part of Mrs Ballenden with Captain Christopher Vaughan Foss, an officer with the pensioners from the Royal Hospital, Chelsea (London), who frequented the HBC's mess table at Upper Fort Garry, provided fuel for gossip. By mid 1849 rumours were circulating that the relationship between Sarah and Foss was such that her husband would have grounds for divorce. Resentful newcomers to the colony including Anne Rose Clouston and Margaret Anderson, sister of the Anglican bishop David Anderson*, seized upon these rumours to bring about Sarah's downfall. Anne Clouston, who came out from Britain in the fall of 1849 to marry HBC clerk Augustus Edward Pelly, was piqued at having to give precedence to a woman who by race and reputation she did not consider her equal. She circulated gossip to discredit Sarah and demanded that the governor of Assiniboia, Major William Bletterman Caldwell*, censure her immoral conduct. When John Ballenden left the settlement briefly in June 1850 to attend the annual meeting of the Council of the Northern Department, Mrs Ballenden was subjected to a concerted effort to exclude her from respectable society, led by Caldwell, the Andersons, the Cockrans, as well as Chief Trader John Black* and his wife. Sarah Ballenden sought the aid of the recorder, Adam Thom*, and, when Pelly and Black persisted in public accusations, Captain Foss appealed to the courts "to clear the reputation of a Lady." He brought a suit for defamatory conspiracy against the Pellys and HBC mess steward John Davidson and his English wife, who had been at the origin of much of the gossip. The three-day trial, which began on 16 July 1850, brought into the open the racial tensions that had been growing in the colony's social élite between incoming whites and the acculturated mixed-blood community. In the words of Chief Trader Robert Clouston, Anne's brother, it seemed "a strife of blood." Numerous witnesses were called, but no truth could be discovered in the accusations of an adulterous relationship between Mrs Ballenden and Captain Foss. The jury decided in Foss's favour and the defendants were assessed heavy damages.

The Ballendens retreated to the quiet of Lower Fort Garry where they were sympathetically received by the newly arrived associate governor of Rupert's Land, Eden Colvile*. In spite of the outcome of the trial Mrs Ballenden's reputation was considerably tarnished and, according to Colvile, she continued to be shunned by "the 'nobs' of the womankind." Ballenden left his wife and younger children at the fort when he went to Scotland on furlough for medical treatment in the fall of 1850. The whole scandal blew up again when a note, allegedly from Sarah to Captain Foss inviting him to visit her at the lower fort, was intercepted and presented to Colvile. Mrs Ballenden was now cut by the Colviles, and Thom and her former champions turned against her. Although after some doubt her husband ultimately remained loyal to her, writing to Simpson that "there is no proof, notwithstanding Mr. Thom's opinion to the contrary," she was now vilified and shunned by Red River society. Her health deteriorated so badly after the birth of her eighth child in 1851 that she was unable to accompany her husband to his new posting at Fort Vancouver (Vancouver, Wash.). Alexander Ross, whose friendship for Sarah had not been shaken, noted sadly that, "if there is such a thing as dying of a broken heart, she cannot live long." After a wretched winter at Red River she sought refuge in 1852 at Norway House (Man.) with the family of Chief Factor George Barnston*. The following summer Ballenden gave instructions to his nephew Andrew Graham Ballenden Bannatyne* to take his family to Edinburgh where he was proceeding from the Columbia on furlough. Their reunion was brief, for Sarah Ballenden died on 23 Dec. 1853.

The personal tragedy of this woman, largely the result of rumour and innuendo, underscores the way in which the double standard punished women for any violation of the straight-laced moral code of the day. The controversy surrounding her fall from grace also reinforced the racial prejudice against native and mixed-blood women. According to Red River historian Joseph James Hargrave*, "probably no case ever brought before the Recorder's court . . . has given rise to so much bad feeling, and such deplorable sequences, as did this *cause célèbre*."

SYLVIA VAN KIRK

GRO (Edinburgh), South Leith, reg. of baptisms, marriages, and burials, 28 Dec. 1853. PABC, Add. MSS 635. PAC, MG 19, A21, ser.1. PAM, HBCA, A.36/10: ff.9–97; D.5;

MG 2, B4-1, 1844–51: ff.181–214. PRO, PROB 11/ 2257/667. *HBRS*, 19 (Rich and Johnson). J. J. Hargrave, *Red River* (Montreal, 1871; repr., Altona, Man., 1977). Van Kirk, *"Many tender ties."*

McLOUGHLIN, JOHN (baptized **Jean-Baptiste**), physician, fur trader, and merchant; b. 19 Oct. 1784 near Rivière-du-Loup, Que., son of John McLoughlin, a farmer, and Angélique Fraser, daughter of Malcolm Fraser*; d. 3 Sept. 1857 in Oregon City (Oreg.).

John McLoughlin's first choice of a career was influenced by his mother's brother Dr Simon Fraser. McLoughlin decided at an early age to study medicine; he was only 14 when he began an apprenticeship with Dr James Fisher* of Quebec, and was not yet 19 in May 1803 when he was granted a licence to practise in Lower Canada. But on 26 April of that year he had signed an agreement with McTavish, Frobisher and Company [*see* Simon McTavish*; Joseph Frobisher*], partners in the North West Company, to serve as physician and apprentice clerk for five years. The sudden switch to the fur trade appears to have been motivated by an incident involving an army officer that made it prudent for McLoughlin to leave the province. His NWC agreement was negotiated by Dr Fraser, whose brother Alexander* was a partner in the concern. McLoughlin contended later that it was Simon McTavish's virtual promise of exceptional prospects that induced him to accept a five-year engagement at the low stipend of £20 per year.

McLoughlin was sent first to the NWC depot at Kaministiquia (Thunder Bay, Ont.), where, contrary to his expectations, the departure of the medical officer, Henry Munro, made it necessary for him to act in that capacity. But he was soon spending winters at trading posts, since there was little need for professional services until the annual meeting. In 1806 he was at Rainy Lake and in 1807 he built a post at Sturgeon Lake in the Nipigon department where his winter companion was Daniel Williams Harmon*. McLoughlin's towering physique impressed the Indians and he proved to be a shrewd and effective trader, although he was probably of only average ability as a physician.

McLoughlin would have left the NWC in 1808, when his apprenticeship expired, if it had not been for the financial needs of his brother David, who was studying medicine in Edinburgh. McTavish had promised Dr Fraser that McLoughlin would be paid £100 a year if he were required to practise medicine, but McLoughlin was told that the promise was personal and had died with McTavish in 1804. After hard bargaining McLoughlin secured a three-year agreement for £200 a year from William McGillivray*, McTavish's nephew and successor as head of

the Montreal firm, renamed McTavish, McGillivrays and Company, and in 1811 he was able to make the promise of a partnership in 1814 a condition of the contract's renewal.

McLoughlin's whereabouts from 1808 to 1811 remain obscure. His first posting as a wintering partner, in 1814, was to the Lac la Pluie district, where he had been stationed since 1811, but in 1815 he moved to Fort William (formerly Kaministiquia). He was becoming concerned about the violence that marked the intense and costly rivalry between the NWC and the Hudson's Bay Company, and he was one of an NWC party which arrived "judiciously late" at the Red River settlement (Man.) in June 1816, thereby avoiding any active part in the attack on the colony that resulted in the massacre at Seven Oaks (Winnipeg) [*see* Cuthbert GRANT]. Nevertheless, McLoughlin was one of the partners arrested by Lord Selkirk [Douglas*] in mid August when he arrived with a military force and occupied Fort William. McLoughlin was not clear of the ensuing legal entanglements until he was found not guilty at a trial at York (Toronto) in October 1818.

Both before and after the trial McLoughlin continued to be stationed at Fort William. It was an excellent listening post and from what he saw and heard he became convinced that unless changes were made in management the battle with the HBC would result in the bankruptcy of the NWC. At the annual meeting of 1819 he was able to defeat William McGillivray's efforts to have the existing agreement between the wintering partners and the Montreal agents, McTavish, McGillivrays and Company, extended or renewed, and by the autumn he was prepared to come to terms with the HBC. Through Samuel Gale*, Selkirk's lawyer, he inquired anonymously in London whether the wintering partners "could obtain from the Hudson's Bay Company their outfits and supplies of goods & sanction to trade" if they agreed to send their furs to the HBC. The ascendancy McLoughlin had gained over the partners is evidenced by Gale's comment to Lady Selkirk that "the wintering partner" who posed the question possessed "influence to withdraw almost every useful member of the North West Association."

Shortly before the annual meeting of 1820 McLoughlin had an unexpected visitor. In 1817 Governor Sir John Coape Sherbrooke* had issued a proclamation calling upon both the HBC and the NWC to keep the peace, but violence had continued. Early in 1820 Lord Bathurst, the colonial secretary, instructed the HBC to require its servants to obey the proclamation. He also sent a similar message to the NWC to be delivered by the HBC. Both orders were carried to Lower Canada by George SIMPSON, newly appointed governor-in-chief locum tenens of HBC, and, with typical bravado, instead of handing

McLoughlin

Bathurst's communication to the NWC agents in Montreal, he decided to deliver it himself at Fort William. There on 28 May he and McLoughlin met for the first time. McGillivray complained later about the cordiality of McLoughlin's welcome, and in view of the critical importance of Simpson's influence on McLoughlin's later career, this first friendly encounter was of some significance.

At the annual meeting that followed, the wintering partners again refused to renew the agreement, and 18 of them authorized McLoughlin and Angus BETHUNE to proceed to London and negotiate with the HBC on their behalf. But Simon McGillivray*, representing the Montreal agents, also arrived in London for talks with the HBC. McLoughlin, apart from his presence, which evidenced the division in the ranks of the NWC, played no part of consequence in the negotiations that resulted in the coalition of the two companies in March 1821. He had been taken ill in London, and he spent the winter of 1821–22 in Europe, much of it under the care of his brother David in Paris. Back in North America, he attended the meeting of the Council of the Northern Department at Norway House (Man.) in July 1822. Simpson had previously intimated that McLoughlin's experience at Rainy Lake made him the officer best qualified to manage the Rainy Lake district and he was duly appointed its chief factor in 1822 and again in 1823.

The coalition had presented many problems to Simpson, now governor of the HBC's Northern Department, one being the policy that should be pursued in the Columbia district, a huge area west of the Rockies centring on the valleys of the Columbia River and its tributaries, in which the NWC had been active since 1813. Returns had been disappointing and in 1824 Simpson visited the Columbia district with a view to gauging its future. He had already decided that a change of command was essential; Chief Factor John Dugald CAMERON was transferred to Rainy Lake and McLoughlin was assigned to Fort George (Astoria, Oreg.), the district depot. With the departure in the spring of 1825 of Chief Factor Alexander Kennedy*, who was in charge of Fort George, McLoughlin would be the only chief factor in the entire district. He was probably chosen for the important post because the Columbia was vulnerable to American competition, and he had been successful in holding competing traders at check in the border district of Rainy Lake. Simpson overtook him en route and they arrived together at Fort George on 8 Nov. 1824.

McLoughlin assumed his new position at a difficult time, for in Simpson's view "mismanagement and extravagance" had been "the order of the day" in the Columbia. "Everything," he wrote, "appears to me . . . on too extended a scale *except the Trade*." The remedies Simpson proposed included drastic reductions in personnel and the substitution of home-grown produce for the costly provisions that had been imported from Europe. To complicate matters, the agreement between Great Britain and the United States concerning joint occupation of the area was due to expire in 1828, and it remained to be seen whether it would be extended. The HBC had already concluded that the Columbia River was the farthest south boundary that the American government was likely to accept, and recognized that it might well insist upon the 49th parallel. Throughout his years in the Columbia, McLoughlin would have to reckon with the possibility that the district might at any time be riven in two by a boundary settlement.

Important changes had already been made by the end of the five months Simpson spent in the area. A new post, Fort Vancouver (Vancouver, Wash.), which would become the district's headquarters, had been built 100 miles upstream on the north and, it was hoped, British side of the Columbia, in a country suitable for agriculture. James McMILLAN had been sent to explore the lower reaches of the Fraser River (B.C.) with a view to finding a possible site for a new district depot north of the 49th parallel. The activities of the Snake River expeditions which trapped far and wide south of the Columbia and its tributaries, were to be intensified, since the area was, in Simpson's words, "a rich preserve of Beaver and which for political reasons we should endeavour to destroy as fast as possible." Finally, McLoughlin took note of Simpson's remark that, to the company's shame, it was still "nearly totally ignorant" of the Pacific coast and the trading possibilities it probably presented.

Policy differences with Simpson were to play a determining role in McLoughlin's later career, but there was no sign of friction in 1825. Simpson had been impressed by McLoughlin and, in view of the remoteness of the Columbia and the many changes he was expecting, he departed from the usual HBC policy and instructed McLoughlin in 1825 to assume "a certain discretionary or controlling power" over "appointments, Outfits," and other important arrangements for all the posts and operations in the Columbia. McLoughlin thus became in effect, if not yet in name, superintendent of the district, a status he was to retain for nearly 20 years.

Simpson had developed a lively personal interest in the Columbia, which he was convinced could become a valuable property, both in itself and as a buffer area that would discourage American traders from penetrating to the district of New Caledonia to the north. He paid a second visit to the coast in 1828 and found that under McLoughlin's management a very marked improvement had taken place in the Columbia's affairs. Personnel had been reduced, the new farms at Fort Vancouver would soon make the district free of dependence on imported provisions, a flour-mill and a small sawmill were in operation, and salmon was being salted in some quantity. In 1827 the 70-ton schooner *Cadboro* had arrived. Although too small to make much of an impression in the coastal trade, it had enabled McLoughlin to establish Fort Langley (B.C.) on the lower Fraser and to send trial shipments of deals and spars to Monterey (Calif.) and Honolulu. McLoughlin's managerial capacity had perhaps been best shown in his reorganization of the Snake River trapping expeditions. The parties, formerly consisting mostly of freemen and Iroquois, had been reduced in size and made to include a much higher proportion of company servants. The cost of supplies advanced to the trappers on credit had been lowered and prices paid for furs had been increased, measures that discouraged desertion and the sale of furs to American traders encountered in the wilds. Routes to be followed were left to the discretion of the commander, who from 1824 to 1830 was the redoubtable Peter Skene OGDEN.

Two points of major importance had been settled by the time Simpson reached Fort Vancouver. Some months before, the joint occupation agreement between Great Britain and the United States had been extended indefinitely, and plans for the district could therefore be made on a long-term basis. Secondly, Simpson had come to the coast by way of the Fraser River, had found it useless as a travel route, and had therefore abandoned the idea of developing Fort Langley to replace Fort Vancouver as the district depot. McLoughlin, always firmly attached to Fort Vancouver, welcomed the decision and in 1829 rebuilt the fort on a larger scale on a more convenient site nearer the river.

Simpson had nothing but praise for McLoughlin's efforts. "Your whole administration," he wrote in March 1829 at the end of his visit, "is marked by its close adherence to the spirit of the Govr & Committees wishes and intentions, and is conspicious for a talent in planning and for an activity & perseverance in execution which reflect the highest credit on your judgement and habits of business."

Plans for the development of the coastal trade received much attention during Simpson's five-month stay. Although McLoughlin had been unable to participate in it effectively, he had learned a good deal about its nature. The famed sea otter, for long the only skin of much interest to traders, had become scarce. As a result, "anything and everything was included that might aid to make a paying voyage." Beaver and other land skins were collected, and most of them, brought to the coast by inter-tribal trading, originated in the interior, in what the HBC looked upon as part of its fur preserve. The ships frequenting the coast were American, and they usually depended on a supplementary activity, furnishing supplies and provisions to the Russians in Alaska, to make their voyage profitable.

Simpson and McLoughlin soon had two countermeasures in mind: the establishment of trading posts on the coast that would intercept the furs coming from the interior, and an effort to persuade the Russians to purchase their supplies from the HBC instead of from the American ships. The coastal trade would require ships, men, and supplies, and in March, shortly before Simpson left for the east, McLoughlin's hopes of having them available in 1829 were dashed when the supply ship *William and Ann* was wrecked on the Columbia bar, with the loss of its crew and cargo. The same day an American trading ship entered the river and it or its consort competed with the HBC for the next two years, forcing McLoughlin to pay higher prices for furs at the very time he was ill supplied with trade goods.

It was 1831 before he was able to see to the construction of the projected chain of coastal trading posts. The first, Fort Nass (B.C.), built by Ogden on the Nass River, was soon renamed Fort Simpson and in 1834 it was moved to Port Simpson, a better site on the coast. Fort McLoughlin (near Bella Bella), established by Chief Factor Duncan Finlayson*, his second in command, followed in 1833 and in the same year Fort Nisqually (near Tacoma, Wash.), intended to be a farming centre and depot for coastal shipping, was built by Chief Trader Archibald McDONALD. McLoughlin intended to build a post some distance up the Stikine River, the mouth of which was in Russian territory. But a preliminary survey in 1833 betrayed this intention, and neither the Russians nor the Indians wished to see their trade in furs disrupted. When Ogden arrived in the *Dryad* to build the post, he found that the Russians had blocked the river by establishing a fort of their own and by stationing a well-armed brig in its mouth. The importance of what later became known as the "*Dryad* incident" arises from a statement McLoughlin sent to London that estimated costs and losses arising from the affair at no less than £22,150 – a claim that was to play an important part in later negotiations with the Russians.

McLoughlin's experience with ships and sea captains was almost uniformly unfortunate. Shipbuilding at Fort Vancouver was not a success. The supply ships from London, arriving in the spring, were to engage in the coastal trade before sailing for London in the autumn, but wrecks, late arrivals, and drunken and uncooperative captains played havoc with the plan. From these circumstances sprang McLoughlin's strong prejudice against ships as opposed to trading posts. Ships, he contended, were expensive to maintain and required crews with special skills, whereas someone was always available who was capable of building a trading post and taking charge of it. He made his views clear in 1834 when the brig *Nereide* arrived, the intention being that she should remain on the coast and her captain, Joseph

McLoughlin

Millar Langtry, should become head of a marine department. In McLoughlin's view neither the ship nor the department was necessary, and he sent the *Nereide* and its captain back to England. In 1827, in what he doubtless later came to regard as a misguided moment, he had suggested that a steamboat, able to move about regardless of winds and currents, might be useful on the coast, but by the time the *Beaver* arrived in 1836, he looked upon it as an unnecessary and costly extravagance.

McLoughlin soon had to reckon with a marked increase in American interest in trade and settlement in the Columbia region. Late in 1832 Nathaniel Jarvis Wyeth arrived at Fort Vancouver, having travelled overland from Boston. He proposed to collect furs and cure salmon to send to market in ships that would bring him supplies both to meet his own needs and for sale to American trappers in the Rockies. Nothing came of this immediately, since Wyeth's first ship was wrecked. He spent the winter at Fort Vancouver, where McLoughlin gave him a friendly welcome. On his way eastward in the spring he sent a letter to the governor and the London committee of the HBC proposing a cooperative agreement. The committee refused, but in 1834, having established a post on the Snake on his way west, Wyeth was back at Fort Vancouver. There he renewed his proposal for a measure of cooperation, and McLoughlin finally agreed, to the displeasure of his superiors. His reasons for doing so were twofold: he was fearful that Wyeth would establish a supply line of his own if he refused, and he was confident that Wyeth's enterprise would fail.

The episode reveals a good deal about McLoughlin's character and trading strategy. He lacked the ruthless streak that was part of Simpson's make-up, and saw no reason why a trading rival should necessarily be regarded as a personal enemy. Nor did he always subscribe to Simpson's doctrine that opposition must be pressed relentlessly to the last skin. It was usually cheaper and equally effective to oppose a competitor only to the point at which his enterprise became unprofitable. This happened to Wyeth's venture: he sold out to the HBC in 1837.

When Wyeth first appeared McLoughlin suspected that in addition to furs and salmon he was also concerned with plans to bring American settlers to the attractive valley of the Willamette River (Oreg.), which flowed into the Columbia from the south, close to Fort Vancouver. The suspicion was unfounded, but when Wyeth reappeared in 1834 he was accompanied by the Reverend Jason Lee, the first of the Methodist missionaries who were to cause McLoughlin much trouble. Unlike the missionaries of other denominations, the Methodists took a marked interest in this world's goods, and when Lee returned to New England on a visit in 1838 he became a vigorous

advocate of immigration to the Oregon country. McLoughlin was not surprised; he had long been convinced that it was only a matter of time before the area would become part of the United States. Further evidence had come late in 1836 when William A. Slacum arrived, ostensibly to view the country and visit friends. McLoughlin suspected rightly that he was an American agent. He had indeed been sent by the secretary of state to spy out the land, and his glowing report on the Columbia stimulated interest in settlement there.

McLoughlin, firmly wedded to the Columbia, had declined hitherto to leave it on furlough, but in 1838 the governor and committee of the HBC called him to London, since a review of the district's affairs was clearly essential. He left Fort Vancouver on 22 March 1838 and returned on 17 October of the following year. The meetings were friendly and successful. Early in February 1839 the HBC concluded an agreement with the Russian American Company which gave the HBC a lease of the Alaskan panhandle. In return, the HBC agreed to supply the Russians with certain furs and commodities, including agricultural products. To provide the latter, the Puget's Sound Agricultural Company was to be organized [see William Fraser Tolmie*]. McLoughlin's authority was to extend to the company, and in view of these new developments he received a formal appointment "to the principal superintendence or management" of the Columbia district and was granted an additional £500 a year, over and above the sum due to him as chief factor.

James Douglas*, a recently promoted chief factor who had been in the Columbia since 1830, was sent in 1840 to conclude arrangements with the Russians at Sitka (Alaska), which included the take-over of Fort Stikine and the building of Fort Taku. But McLoughlin's cherished plans for his chain of coastal posts were to be rudely upset when Simpson, bound on a journey around the world, arrived at Fort Vancouver on 28 Aug. 1841. A week later he left in the *Beaver* to visit Sitka and the northern posts, and when he returned he informed McLoughlin that a complete reorganization of the coastal trade was called for; the agreement with the Russians had changed the entire trading picture of the region. All the northern posts except Fort Simpson, which would act as a northern supply depot, were to be closed, and Simpson was confident that the *Beaver* would "answer every necessary & useful purpose, in watching and collecting the trade of the whole of that line of Coast." McLoughlin was outraged, and contended that this decision had been made behind his back and without consultation, but Simpson was adamant. He and McLoughlin met subsequently at Honolulu, where an HBC agency had been opened in 1833, and the coastal trade was again discussed. McLoughlin had come armed with accounts that he felt proved the superiority of forts over ships (and especially over the *Beaver*), but Simpson held to his decision and instructed McLoughlin to begin by closing forts Taku and McLoughlin in 1843.

A further instruction that was not to McLoughlin's liking followed. For several reasons – the boundary question, again a very live issue, the dangers of the Columbia bar, upon which two supply ships had been lost, and the proximity of Fort Vancouver to the Willamette valley, where American immigrants were settling in some numbers – Simpson had decided that a new district depot farther north was essential. McLoughlin was therefore instructed to find a suitable site on the southern end of Vancouver Island, a decision that resulted in the founding of Fort Victoria (Victoria) in 1843.

From Honolulu, Simpson went to Sitka, but before sailing for Siberia he paid a second visit to Fort Stikine. He arrived on 27 April 1842, to find that McLoughlin's son John, who had been in command of the post, had been murdered by his men the previous week.

Simpson jumped to conclusions, in some measure understandable in view of his knowledge of young McLoughlin's past history. After making good progress in studying medicine in Paris, McLoughlin Jr had committed some unpardonable offence that forced him to leave France. Later he had become involved in the filibustering expedition led by the self-styled general James Dickson* which set out for Red River. A few stragglers, including McLoughlin, arrived there in December 1836. Simpson then intervened and offered him a clerkship. In June 1837 McLoughlin was assigned to the Columbia. There he seems to have done well. After serving at Fort Vancouver he was sent to Fort Stikine in 1840, and, owing to staff transfers, was left in sole charge of the fort in 1841. Simpson evidently assumed that young McLoughlin had simply reverted to type. He accepted the charges of terror, violence, cruelty, drunkenness, dissipation, and neglect of duty made by the men, took depositions to support them, and notified McLoughlin of the murder in a letter the wording of which was little less than brutal. He left Charles DODD temporarily in charge and continued his journey. Later he went so far as to remark to the governor and the London committee of the HBC that the murder had been committed "under circumstances that in my humble opinion, would in an English Court of Justice be pronounced justifiable homicide." Grief stricken and enraged, McLoughlin began a relentless effort to assemble evidence to refute Simpson's allegations, knowing much better than Simpson the turbulent character of the men who had been assigned to Stikine, "the worst characters among our men on the Coast." He succeeded, but he became obsessed with the matter and dealt with it at wearisome length in

letter after letter to the governor and committee. He also criticized several men under his command, including Donald Manson* and John Work*, for their lack of initiative in helping him bring the murderers to justice. Although McLoughlin substantially proved his case, Simpson was indispensable to the HBC and McLoughlin was warned that he must make up his quarrel with him or face transfer or retirement. He failed to do so, and by the spring of 1844 London had decided that "nothing" would then do "but McLoughlin's removal."

There were, of course, other factors involved. The general management of the district was being questioned; the profits were alleged to be only a fraction of those tabulated in McLoughlin's accounts. Differences over the merits of trading posts remained unresolved. McLoughlin's treatment of the American immigrants who were flowing into the Willamette valley was much criticized. He was a humanitarian at heart; he received the immigrants kindly and provided the needy with seeds, implements, and supplies, often on credit. By the spring of 1844 several hundred settlers had received advances totalling £6,600, a sum that alarmed the governor and the London committee. Both they and Simpson failed to realize that, apart from other considerations, McLoughlin's policy was realistic, for settlers were not likely to starve quietly with the well-filled warehouses of Fort Vancouver near by.

The falls on the Willamette River were the cause of further difficulties. McLoughlin had long considered them "the most important place in this country." He and Simpson had visited them in 1828 and in later years he sought to establish claims to properties adjacent to them, both on his own behalf and, on instructions from Simpson, on behalf of the HBC, thus clashing with the Reverend Alvan F. Waller, an aggressive Methodist missionary assigned to the nearby Willamette mission. Under American law which all realized would probably apply soon, foreign corporations could not pre-empt land and Waller believed that the interests of the HBC, and probably McLoughlin's as well, could be encroached upon with impunity. In 1842 McLoughlin had the properties at the falls surveyed and subdivided and laid out the town of Oregon City and in 1844 he was able to arrive at a settlement with the mission, when it was being closed. But disturbing developments had taken place in the interval. In 1843 a provisional government for Oregon had been organized, and in July it had adopted a law regarding land claims, a clause of which was aimed directly at McLoughlin and the HBC. McLoughlin concluded that the only way in which he could hope to protect the company's claims was to purchase them himself, and in March 1845 he sent Simpson bills to the value of £4,173 in payment. It is still a moot point whether McLoughlin intended this to be more than a

McLoughlin

pro forma transaction, but Simpson accepted the bills and they were charged to McLoughlin's personal account.

Simpson was well aware that this purchase would force McLoughlin's retirement, since he would have to move to Oregon City to take personal charge of the mills and properties there, but other steps to procure his retirement had already been taken. In November 1844 Archibald Barclay, secretary of the HBC, had written to inform McLoughlin that the governor and committee felt that the advantages they had anticipated from the Columbia being placed in the charge of one person had not been realized, and that his post of general superintendent and its supplementary salary would end on 31 May 1845. In June 1845 the Council of the Northern Department set up a three-man board of management for the Columbia, to consist of McLoughlin, Ogden, and Douglas.

It was assumed correctly that McLoughlin would react by going on furlough (Work was then added to the board of management). Humiliated and bitter, McLoughlin moved to Oregon City in January 1846, and on 26 March notified the HBC that he would not be returning to active duty. The company was not vindictive; the financial terms of his retirement were generous. After the year of furlough he was granted leave of absence for two years, and formal retirement was thus delayed until 1 June 1849. Thereafter he received his full share as a chief factor for another year, and a half share for five years. The bad debts incurred by immigrants were never charged to his account.

In spite of his friendliness with American settlers, McLoughlin was so closely identified with the HBC that he continued to be a victim of their violent prejudice against the company, even after he left its service. In 1846 the British government had accepted the 49th parallel as the boundary and two years later the Oregon Territory was created. McLoughlin applied as promptly as possible for American citizenship, granted finally in 1851, but this action did not safeguard his properties. In 1850 Samuel R. Thurston, Oregon's first delegate to Congress, sponsored the Oregon Land Donation Law, a clause of which reserved McLoughlin's holdings for educational purposes. McLoughlin was never dispossessed, but it was not until 1862, five years after his death, that the state legislature conveyed the bulk of his properties to his legatees upon payment of a nominal sum.

McLoughlin spent the last years of his life at Oregon City, where he was active as a merchant and mill owner, and engaged in an export trade in lumber and other commodities. He was for a short time mayor of the city. His youngest son, David, recalled in 1892 that, owing to his great shock of white hair, the Indians called him "Pee-kin – the White Headed Eagle of the Whites." Over the years the major role he had played for two decades in the early history of the

northwest was recognized and he has long been known as the father of Oregon. His home in Oregon City is now the McLoughlin House Museum, a national historic site, and he was one of the two pioneers chosen to represent Oregon in the National Hall of Statuary in the Capitol, Washington, D.C.

About 1810 McLoughlin had contracted a marriage according to the custom of the country with Marguerite Waddens, daughter of Jean-Étienne Waddens*, and previously the country wife of Alexander MacKay*, who was lost in the *Tonquin* massacre of 1811. They had two sons and two daughters, all born before McLoughlin went to the Columbia. They were formally married on 19 Nov. 1842 at Fort Vancouver by the Roman Catholic missionary François-Norbert Blanchet. Mrs McLoughlin died in 1860 at the age of 85. McLoughlin also had another son born some time before 1810.

In his famous "Character book," written in 1832 before any differences had arisen between them, Simpson described McLoughlin as "a man of strict honour and integrity but a great stickler for rights and priviledges" and commented upon his "ungovernable Violent temper and turbulent disposition." He added that McLoughlin "would be a Radical in any Country – under any Government and under any circumstances," an interesting remark in view of the sympathy McLoughlin showed a few years later for the rebels of 1837. William Stewart Wallace* has suggested that their contrasting stature was a contributing cause of the friction between McLoughlin and Simpson: "McLoughlin probably had for Simpson the almost instinctive dislike of the big man for the small man who is set over him." The remoteness of the Columbia was also a factor; it took almost a year to receive a reply from London, and many months even to hear from Norway House (Man.). As the man on the spot, McLoughlin often felt that he knew best, and at times he had to take action before he could receive advice or direction. But the deep differences that developed in 1841–42 over the coastal trade and his son's murder ultimately made him an impossible subordinate. In retrospect McLoughlin realized that those winter months had been the turning-point. In his last letter to Sir John Henry Pelly, governor of the HBC, written on 12 July 1846, he made the bitter comment: "Sir George Simpsons Visit here in 1841 has cost me Dear."

W. KAYE LAMB

[The principal archival collections consulted were PAM, HBCA, A.5; A.6; A.11; A.12; B.223/a/1–7; B.223/b/1–43; D.4; D.5; E.13/1; F.8–F.26. John McLoughlin's correspondence from Fort Vancouver to the governor and committee of the Hudson's Bay Company was published in *HBRS*, 4 (Rich), 6 (Rich), and 7 (Rich). Other letters were published in *Letters of Dr. John McLoughlin, written at Fort Vancouver, 1829–1832*, ed. B. B. Barker (Portland, Oreg.,

1948), and in *John McLoughlin's business correspondence, 1847–48*, ed. W. R. Sampson (Seattle, Wash., 1973). There is a mass of material relating to the McLoughlin family, including 118 letters from 1796 to 1857, in B. B. Barker, *The McLoughlin empire and its rulers . . .* (Glendale, Calif., 1959); 48 of these had already been published in "Letters of Dr. John McLoughlin," ed. J. L. Chapin, in *Oreg. Hist. Quarterly* (Salem), 36 (1935): 320–37, and 37 (1936): 45–75 and 293–300. Two articles, "McLoughlin proprietary account with Hudson's Bay Company" and "The estate of Dr. John McLoughlin: the papers discovered," both edited and published by B. B. Barker in *Oreg. Hist. Quarterly* (Portland), 45 (1944): 1–41 and 50 (1949): 155–85 respectively, were reprinted in *The financial papers of Dr John McLoughlin, being the record of his estate and of his proprietary accounts with the North West Company (1811–1821) and the Hudson's Bay Company (1821–1868)*, ed. B. B. Barker (Portland, 1949).

Dorothy Morrison and Jean Morrison, in "John McLoughlin, reluctant fur trader," *Oregon Hist. Quarterly*, 81 (1980): 377–89, discuss the circumstances under which McLoughlin joined the North West Company and print the agreement he signed in 1803. Another document, drafted by McLoughlin, is published as "McLoughlin's statement of the expenses incurred in the *Dryad* incident of 1834," intro. by W. K. Lamb, *BCHQ*, 10 (1946): 291–97.

The present author's three introductions in *HBRS*, 4, 6, and 7, are virtually a biography of McLoughlin. Earlier studies include F. V. V. Holman, *Dr John McLoughlin, the father of Oregon* (Cleveland, Ohio, 1907), long the standard reference; R. C. Johnson, *John McLoughlin: father of Oregon* (2nd ed., Portland, 1958); and R. G. Montgomery, *The white-headed eagle, John McLoughlin, builder of an empire* (New York, 1935). w.k.l.]

HBRS, 10 (Rich); 29 (Williams). Simpson, "Character book," *HBRS*, 30 (Williams), 151–236; *Fur trade and empire* (Merk; 1968). J. S. Galbraith, *The Hudson's Bay Company as an imperial factor, 1821–1869* ([Toronto], 1957). A. S. Morton, *A history of the Canadian west to 1870–71, being a history of Rupert's Land (the Hudson's Bay Company territory) and of the North-West Territories (including the Pacific slope)*, ed. L. G. Thomas (2nd ed., Toronto [and Buffalo, N.Y., 1973]). Rich, *Hist. of HBC* (1958–59), 2. C. H. Carey, "Lee, Waller and McLoughlin," *Oreg. Hist. Quarterly* (Salem), 33 (1932): 187–213. D. C. Davidson, "Relations of the Hudson's Bay Company with the Russian American Company on the northwest coast," *BCHQ*, 5 (1941): 33–51. T. C. Elliott, "Dr John M'Loughlin and his guests," *Wash. Hist. Quarterly*, 3 (1908): 63–77; "John McLoughlin, M.D.," *Oreg. Hist. Quarterly*, 36: 182–86; "Marguerite Wadin McKay McLoughlin," *Oreg. Hist. Quarterly*, 36: 338–47. Alice Greve, "Dr McLoughlin's house," *Beaver*, outfit 272 (September 1941): 32–35. "James Douglas and the Russian American Company, 1840," ed. W. E. Ireland, *BCHQ*, 5 (1941): 53–66. Charles Wilkes, "Report on the Territory of Oregon," *Oreg. Hist. Soc., Quarterly* (Portland), 12 (1914): 269–99.

McMAHON, PATRICK, Roman Catholic priest; b. 24 Aug. 1796, probably in Abbeyleix (Republic of Ireland), son of Patrick McMahon and Winifred Kelly; d. 3 Oct. 1851 at Quebec.

Patrick McMahon completed classical studies in Ireland, probably at St Patrick's College, Carlow, and around 1817 immigrated to Lower Canada with a large family group. By October of that year he had begun teaching English at the Collège de Saint-Hyacinthe, where he also studied for the priesthood and probably learned some French. Ordained in the cathedral of Notre-Dame at Quebec on 6 Oct. 1822, he was appointed curate there to serve the growing English-speaking, predominantly Irish, portion of the parish. On 25 May 1825 he was transferred to the mission at Saint John, N.B. Popular tradition suggests that he was sent there as punishment for his outspokenness, although no documentary evidence has been uncovered to support this conjecture. Despite his precarious health while in New Brunswick, he acquired a reputation for zeal and won the praise and admiration of his congregation.

By the time McMahon returned to Quebec in 1828 to resume his functions at Notre-Dame, Irish Catholic laymen, with Father Hugh Paisley as their curate, had taken the first steps towards obtaining a church of their own. John Cannon*, Gordian Horan, and Michael Quigley had formed the nucleus of a management committee of the "Catholics of Quebec Speaking the English Language" which had begun negotiations in 1827 with the trustees of the *fabrique* of Notre-Dame. Under McMahon, the discussions continued and construction of the new church, designed by architect Thomas BAILLAIRGÉ, began in 1831. On 7 July 1833 McMahon and the Irish Catholics rejoiced at the first mass in St Patrick's Church on Rue Sainte-Hélène (later named Rue McMahon in his honour). For the next 18 years McMahon, occasionally with the help of an assistant, ministered to that church, a succursal of Notre-Dame; by 1835 it served approximately 6,000 people.

During the 1830s and 1840s the port of Quebec received thousands of immigrants from the British Isles, most of them Irish Catholic. As a member of the executive of the Quebec Emigrant Society, McMahon worked closely with the emigration agent of the port, Alexander Carlisle Buchanan, and appeared with him before a committee of the House of Assembly inquiring into immigration in 1832. Moreover, McMahon's presence was often required by the Irish Catholics in the midst of the tragedies that struck Quebec. In 1832, 1834, 1849, and 1851 there were outbreaks of cholera. In 1841 rockslides killed scores of Irishmen working in the timber coves. In the summer of 1845 two serious fires levelled major dwelling areas of the city. In 1847–48 the quarantine station at Grosse Île under the direction of George Mellis Douglas* overflowed with typhus-stricken Irish immigrants and many ship passengers came to Quebec itself.

The Irish population of Quebec had taken an active part in politics as early as 1792 when Robert Lester* was elected to the first assembly. McMahon himself

McMartin

played a role in local political struggles. Reaction to a sermon preached by him on St Patrick's Day in 1835 served to polarize the existing factions in the parish and city. According to the *Quebec Gazette* he had "introduced with candor but proper reserve, some notice of the public institutions of the Province and of the respect and protection they afforded to all religions." The sermon was interpreted as a condemnation of the reformers. Responding to a rumour that French Canadian reformers had started a petition to Archbishop Joseph Signay* calling for McMahon's removal, a group from St Patrick's, principally anti-reformers, led 2,000 members of the congregation to sign a petition in support of their priest and presented it to the archbishop in a delegation of 21. Signay denied any knowledge of the reformers' petition and assured the men that he held McMahon in esteem. Shortly thereafter, Michael Connolly, John Teed, and Quigley, three known reformers who had been members of the delegation supporting McMahon, were dismissed from St Patrick's management committee, "for the peace and harmony of this committee." They were not reinstated until nine years later. Possibly pressure to remove the men had been brought to bear upon McMahon, perhaps by Signay, perhaps by members of the delegation such as Dominick Daly*, John Patrick O'Meara, or Patrick Lawlor, who belonged to the Quebec Constitutional Association which grouped Protestant, Catholic, English, and Irish anti-reformers. McMahon, chairman of the committee meeting that dismissed the reformers, exemplified the typical clerical reaction to reform at that period. He was also said to have thundered from the pulpit against the reformers in the elections of 1836. He had been chaplain of the garrison since 1831, and would later be lauded by Lieutenant-Colonel Robert Spark, its commander, for "his Loyalty and attachment to the British Government."

McMahon was to all intents and purposes a conservative, but politics did not form the most important facet of his career. He was essentially a builder, and his principal monument was the community he helped to establish. Through its various institutions, including the church itself, that community flourished. By 1846 renovations to St Patrick's were required to accommodate the substantial increase in the number of Irish Catholics. McMahon saw the boys of his congregation attending a school established by the Christian Brothers close to the church in 1843. He also supported the work of the Sisters of Charity of the Hôpital Général of Montreal who had arrived in Quebec in 1849, under the direction of Marie-Anne-Marcelle Mallet*, to care for the poor and the sick.

The silver jubilee of McMahon's ordination was celebrated in 1847. Among the gifts was a silver altar service executed by François Sasseville* and a portrait of McMahon by Théophile Hamel*, one of the few full-length portraits by the artist, depicting McMahon with his hand resting on the plans for St Patrick's Church. McMahon died at Quebec in 1851 and was buried under the pulpit of the church, after a large public funeral attended by the ecclesiastical, civil, and military authorities as well as by thousands of Irish Catholics.

MARIANNA O'GALLAGHER

Patrick McMahon is the author of *Copies of letters addressed by the Rev. P. McMahon, to the editors of "Le Journal de Québec," and "Le Canadien," containing the report of a conference, which took place, at his residence, in the month of April last, between him and two itinerant preachers* (Quebec, 1843).

AAQ, 61 CD, St Patrick's, 1: 16–17; 311 CN, II: 76; 60 CN, IV: 121; VII: 117. AP, St Patrick (Quebec), Committee of management, minute-book, 1829–35; Horan corr. L.C., House of Assembly, *Journals*, 1831–32. *Le Canadien*, 8 juill. 1833. *Quebec Gazette*, 18 March 1835. Caron, "Inv. de la corr. de Mgr Panet," 1933–34: 268, 272, 299, 307, 319, 377; "Inv. de la corr. de Mgr Plessis," 1928–29: 139, 160; 1932–33: 232. Desrosiers, "Inv. de la corr. de Mgr Lartigue," ANQ *Rapport*, 1941–42: 362, 378, 387, 391, 394. Tanguay, *Répertoire* (1868). Choquette, *Hist. du séminaire de Saint-Hyacinthe. Les Frères des écoles chrétiennes au Canada, 1837–1900* (Montréal, 1921). Marianna O'Gallagher, *Saint-Patrice de Québec: la construction d'une église et l'implantation d'une paroisse*, Guy Doré, trad. (Québec, 1979). J. M. O'Leary, *History of the Irish Catholics of Quebec: St. Patrick's Church to the death of Rev. P. McMahon* (Quebec, 1895). *Une fondatrice et son œuvre: Mère Mallet – 1805–1871 – et l'Institut des Sœurs de la charité de Québec, fondé en 1849* (Québec, 1939). J. A. Gallagher, "St. Patrick's parish – Quebec," CCHA *Report*, 15 (1947–48): 71–80. P.-G. Roy, "L'abbé Patrick McMahon," *BRH*, 45 (1939): 219–20.

McMARTIN, ALEXANDER, militia officer, businessman, politician, justice of the peace, and office holder; b. 1788 in Charlottenburgh Township (Ont.), son of Malcolm McMartin and Margaret McIntyre; m. 14 Jan. 1834 Mary Carlyle of Dumfriesshire, Scotland, and they had four sons and two daughters; d. 12 July 1853 in Martintown, Upper Canada.

Alexander McMartin's loyalist father settled in Charlottenburgh Township and in 1789 began acquiring land along the banks of the Raisin River. There he erected the mills from which the surrounding settlement would take its name. Alexander grew up in MacMartin's Mills (later known as Martintown) and by 1811 was running his father's general store. An ensign in the 2nd Glengarry Militia at the outbreak of the War of 1812, he was promoted lieutenant the following year and given command of a work party constructing a road from Long Sault in Stormont

McMillan

County through the interior of Glengarry County to the Lower Canadian border. McMartin remained active in the militia throughout his life. During the rebellion, as a lieutenant-colonel in the 1st Regiment of Glengarry militia, he was on duty in Lower Canada in February and March 1838 and that November helped disperse the Patriotes led by the Chevalier de Lorimier* at Beauharnois. When the regiment of the Eastern District was formed in 1846, McMartin was appointed lieutenant-colonel of the 3rd Battalion of Glengarry militia.

McMartin had taken over his father's growing sawmill, grist-mill, and carding-mill operations at Martintown in the 1820s. In 1827 he and a partner became involved in the construction of the Rideau Canal. Unsuccessful with their initial government tender, they later assumed Walter Welsh Fenlon's contract to clear a stretch of land 500 feet wide and 2 miles long, extending from the proposed site of the eighth lock to the rapids at Hogs Back. As work progressed, it became apparent that their costs were exceeding the project bid. McMartin confronted superintendent of works Colonel John By*, who, according to McMartin, admitted that the bid had been too low but advised him to continue the work. On the strength of By's verbal assurances that he would in the end sustain no loss, McMartin went ahead and mortgaged his entire property holdings to raise the money needed to meet the mounting costs. By 1830 the work was completed; saddled with debts in excess of £1,600, he submitted his claims to By, who denied that he had held forth any prospect of relief. Petitions for redress to the administrator of Lower Canada, Sir James KEMPT, and Colonial Secretary Sir George Murray* were dismissed. During the 1830s McMartin was pursued by his creditors, principally Peter Russell and Company and John Redpath*. By 1837, however, owing to a series of shrewd land deals, his fortunes had improved.

In 1812 McMartin had been elected to the House of Assembly for Glengarry along with John Macdonell* (Greenfield). A man of solidly conservative political views, he continued to serve in the house until 1824 when he lost to Duncan Cameron*. McMartin was returned in 1828 and again in 1830 but lost the general election of 1834 to Alexander Chisholm. Because of his standing in the community and his staunch support of the provincial government, McMartin also held numerous local public offices. He had received his first of several commissions as justice of the peace in 1820 and with Neil McLean* and Joseph Anderson administered the oath of allegiance during the 1820s in the Eastern District. He was appointed bailiff in 1827, postmaster of Martintown in 1828, and a commissioner of the district Court of Requests in 1833. Appointments to these offices were often hotly pursued and contested. In the winter of 1836–37 the

position of county registrar which McMartin had coveted went instead to Alexander FRASER of Fraserfield. The following year, however, he was chosen to replace Donald Macdonell* (Greenfield) as sheriff of the Eastern District with the support of Philip VanKoughnet* and of Fraser, who remarked that "hardly an individual in the District . . . would not hail his appointment with satisfaction." McMartin remained sheriff until 1847 when he was prevailed upon by William MORRIS and other conservatives to give up the post in order to oppose John Sandfield Macdonald* in the general election. McMartin ran and lost.

A pillar of the Presbyterian community, McMartin was a ruling elder of the congregation at Martintown and served for a time as president of the Bible Society and as a commissioner of the clergy reserve fund. When he died in 1853, he was eulogized in the local newspaper as a man "whose urbanity and warmth of heart endeared him to his fellow-men of all creeds and political opinions, and . . . whose place in society it will be difficult to fill."

ALLAN J. MACDONALD

AO, MU 1967–73, 3389–90; RG 22, ser.155, administration of Alexander McMartin estate. PAC, RG 5, A1: 94785, 110229–30, 110254–56. *Presbyterian*, 6 (1853): 130. R. C. M. Grant, *The story of Martintown* ([Gardenvale, Que., 1974]). W. L. Scott, "Glengarry's representatives in the Legislative Assembly of Upper Canada," CCHA *Report*, 7 (1939–40): 27–28.

McMILLAN, JAMES, fur trader, explorer, and farmer; b. *c.* 1783 probably in Glen Pean, Scotland, son of Allan McMillan and Margaret Cameron; d. 26 Jan. 1858 in Glasgow.

James McMillan joined the North West Company as a clerk in 1803 or 1804 and spent several years in the Fort des Prairies department (Sask.). In 1807 he accompanied David THOMPSON on his first expedition across the Rocky Mountains to the upper Columbia River. For the next three years he made trips back and forth across the mountains, wintering with Thompson at Kootenae House (B.C.) on the Columbia near Windermere Lake in 1808–9 and at Saleesh House (near Thompson, Mont.) in 1809–10. In the spring of 1810 he carried furs back to Fort Augustus (Fort Saskatchewan, Alta) and in July was dispatched to the Columbia with instructions to watch closely the activities of the Hudson's Bay Company trader Joseph HOWSE. During his remaining years with the NWC, McMillan stayed for the most part in the Columbia department, trading at the posts in Flathead country and at Spokane House (near Spokane, Wash.). He would seem to have established liaisons with several Indian women. By 1813 he apparently had three

McNab

country-born children – two in the Columbia and one in the Saskatchewan department and in about 1820 he took a Clatsop woman, Kil-a-ko-tah, as his country wife and with her had at least one daughter, Victoire, born in 1820 or 1821.

With the union of the NWC and the HBC in 1821, McMillan joined the reorganized HBC as a chief trader and was stationed in the Columbia district. After a furlough in 1823–24 spent in the Canadas, he was assigned to accompany HBC governor George SIMPSON on his trip from York Factory (Man.) to the Columbia. Simpson quickly came to appreciate McMillan as a "Staunch & Manly Friend and Fellow Traveller" and later noted that "it is Men of his Stamp the Country wants." At Fort George (Astoria, Oreg.) McMillan was sent to explore the lower part of the Fraser River and, although his party successfully completed its mission, he returned with misleading information concerning the river's navigability into the interior. On the basis of his report, Simpson recommended to the London committee that the HBC consider moving the Columbia depot to the mouth of the Fraser River. Fort Vancouver (Vancouver, Wash.) on the Columbia River was nevertheless established as the HBC west coast depot in 1824–25, under Chief Factor John McLOUGHLIN. After returning eastward in 1825, McMillan was placed in charge of Fort Assiniboine (Alta) with specific responsibility for surveying the alternative route to the headwaters of the Fraser in New Caledonia by way of the Yellowhead Pass. Appointed chief factor in March 1827, McMillan was again sent to the west coast. He was given the task of establishing Fort Langley (B.C.), at the mouth of the Fraser River, designed to secure the company's share of the coastal fur trade and to provide a depot if Fort Vancouver had to be abandoned. After a year at Fort Langley, McMillan once again travelled inland with Simpson, to the Red River colony (Man.), and was granted a year's furlough to return to Scotland. While in Scotland he married Eleanor McKinley.

In 1830 McMillan was appointed to establish an experimental farm for the company at Red River, where he was joined the following year by his wife and their infant daughter. The project did not prosper under McMillan's supervision and, frustrated by the farming operation and the "Backbitting and Slander" of Red River society, he was transferred to the Lake of Two Mountains district near Montreal in 1834.

McMillan retired from the HBC in 1839 and settled with his wife and eight children in Alexandria, near Perth, Scotland. His country-born children stayed in North America and the records of the Red River settlement indicate that three of them took up residence there. His daughter Victoire remained on the Pacific coast where she married John McLoughlin's son Joseph in 1839. From his Scottish retreat McMillan maintained contact with the fur trade through periodic meetings with other retired traders and through his correspondence with Governor Simpson, who had assumed control of his financial affairs in the Canadas. In the early 1840s Simpson asked McMillan for his commentary on some information about the fur trade west of the Rockies he planned to include in his *Narrative of a journey round the world, during the years 1841 and 1842*, published in London in 1847. After McMillan's death in 1858, his wife and family found themselves in rather serious financial difficulties and Simpson arranged for the extension of his company pension.

McMillan, whose career in the fur trade with both the NWC and the HBC spanned almost 40 years, was, in the words of Governor Simpson, "a very steady plain blunt man, shrewd & sensible of correct conduct and good character." He was influential in the expansion of the trade to the Pacific coast and McMillan Island in the Fraser River commemorates his contribution.

GREGORY THOMAS

PABC, Add. MSS 635. PAM, HBCA, A.33/4: ff.265, 267, 275; A.36/10: f.113; B.235/d/45: f.49; D.5/4; D.5/8; D.5/10; D.5/16; D.5/18; D.5/20–21; D.5/23–30; D.5/32; D.5/35–36; D.5/40–41; D.5/43; D.5/46–47; F.4/32: f.711. *Docs. relating to NWC* (Wallace). Hargrave, *Hargrave corr.* (Glazebrook). *HBRS*, 3 (Fleming); 4 (Rich); 6 (Rich); 7 (Rich); 10 (Rich). Simpson, "Character book," *HBRS*, 30 (Williams); *Fur trade and empire* (Merk; 1968). *Nor'Wester* (Winnipeg), 1 May 1861. Van Kirk, *"Many tender ties"*; "Women and the fur trade," *Beaver*, outfit 303 (winter 1972): 4–21.

McNAB, ARCHIBALD, 17th Chief of Clan MACNAB, colonizer, justice of the peace, and militia officer; b. *c.* 1781 in Bouvain, Glen Dochart, Scotland, only son of Robert MacNab and Anne Maule; m. *c.* 1810 Margaret Robertson, and they had six children, of whom two sons and two daughters survived infancy; he also had at least two illegitimate children; d. 12 Aug. 1860 in Lannion, France.

Until 1760 the Macnab clan of Glen Dochart had managed to weather the political changes of the centuries by close association with the Breadalbane branch of the powerful Campbell family. The 16th chief, Francis (d. 1816), Archibald McNab's uncle, was a man at odds with his times, living on a lavish scale as an old-fashioned Highland chieftain. He lacked a legitimate heir and Archibald knew from his early years that he was to be "The MacNab." His education was by Presbyterian schoolmasters; contrary to tradition, it was not completed at the Inns of Court, London, or in Paris. By 1806 he was living in London, well known among the sporting set of the capital as a drunkard, braggart, and whore-master. It was the nephew who introduced the uncle into London society in 1812, a visit which produced many, probably apocryphal, stories. Both were famous for their lack of money and touchy pride which could degenerate into uncontrolled rage if provoked.

When Archibald succeeded to the Macnab lands in 1816, he inherited an estate mortgaged beyond redemption, and debts of about £35,000 to be met on an annual income of £1,000 from property rentals. Aided by his uncle's old adviser and companion Dugald MacNab, he spent the next several years trying to stave off the inevitable collapse. Eventually minor creditors combined to secure a foreclosure on his lands and goods, threatening him with imprisonment by a writ of caption. The flight which followed, by way of England to Upper Canada, has a certain epic quality but the fact remains that he fled in disgrace, pursued by bailiffs, abandoning his wife and children in the process. He then proceeded to launch a highly controversial attempt to build a fortune upon the backs of settlers on the frontier of Upper Canada.

McNab arrived in the Canadas in 1822 intent on acquiring a free grant of land in the upper Ottawa valley and importing Scottish settlers, from whose improvements to the land he would profit. His flamboyant style quickly drew public attention. In the winter of 1822–23 articles in the *Kingston Chronicle* announced his reputed discovery in Glengarry County of the lost sword of Prince Charles, the Young Pretender, which he proposed to present to King George IV. By February 1823 McNab was in York (Toronto) petitioning that Torbolton Township on the Ottawa River be held vacant until the colonial secretary, Lord Bathurst, had reviewed his settlement scheme. Acting on the advice of Lieutenant Governor Sir Peregrine MAITLAND, who regarded the proposal as risky and a potential embarrassment to the provincial government, Bathurst refused to approve it. In October, however, McNab repeated his petition, expressing the hope of bringing his "people" to settle an unsurveyed township beyond Fitzroy Township. Though willing to be "personally responsible" for their conduct, he insinuated that he could avoid all "possibility of trouble" if he got them to sign indentures in Scotland. Under the agreement he would exact from each settler after three years, in return for his passage, an annual quitrent in the form of a bushel of wheat or its equivalent in flour for each cleared acre.

The petition went before the province's Executive Council, where the Reverend John Strachan* advised against accepting the scheme because of the danger of "leaving the Settlers & their descendants subject to a *perpetual* rent charge." They were not, he reasoned prophetically, "likely to remain content with a burthen which they could not, in any manner, shake off."

Though council saw the weakness of the scheme, it was so anxious to have the land settled that it approved the plan in November 1823. McNab was given a block grant of 1,200 acres at once and 3,800 additional acres later, as well as sole superintendence of the settlement of adjacent lands in the unsurveyed township, which was located at the junction of the Ottawa and Madawaska rivers. Once the settlers had performed the settlement duties required by the province and had met his claims on them for his costs, patents would be issued to them by the crown. The terms were to be explained to the settlers by McNab and embodied in agreements, copies of which were to be deposited in the government offices. He also had to submit a progress report within 18 months. The proposed township was surveyed and named McNab in 1824, the year in which he built Kinell Lodge, a log house at the mouth of the Madawaska.

McNab ignored council's conditions and for the next 15 years attempted to govern the township as his personal property. He was able to operate successfully for so long owing to the illiteracy and initial credulity of the settlers and to the trust and support of friends he had made both in York and in the Ottawa valley, including Alexander James Christie* and Hamnett Kirkes PINHEY. In dealing with settlers and government officials, McNab traded on his image as a chieftain, a trustworthy gentleman, and a frontier benefactor. His colourful but autocratic conduct stood out in the provincial society of Upper Canada. In the late 1820s John Mactaggart*, clerk of works on the Rideau Canal, described him travelling through the colony "dressed always in *full Highland costume*, the *piper* going before." He was, Mactaggart observed, "full of enthusiasm about Scotland: a thing rarely met with amongst people beyond the Atlantic." Henry Scadding* provides a description of McNab's visits to York on business, when he usually resided at the home of clansman David Archibald MacNab, brother of Allan Napier MacNab*: "Surrounded or followed by a group of his fair kinsfolk of York, he marched with dignified steps along the whole length of King Street, and down or up to the Kingston Road. . . . the Chief always wore a modified highland costume, which well set off his stalwart, upright form: the blue bonnet and feather, and richly embossed dirk, always rendered him conspicuous, as well as the tartan of brilliant hues depending from his shoulder after obliquely swathing his capacious chest; a bright scarlet vest with massive silver buttons, and dress coat always thrown back, added to the picturesqueness of the figure." Overbearing and offensive, McNab could also be charming and obliging. Joseph Bouchette*, Lower Canada's surveyor general, wrote that he had received in 1828 the "characteristic hospitality" of "the gallant chief," and during a tour of the province in 1836 Lieutenant Governor Sir Francis Bond Head* planned a special

McNab

visit with McNab at Bytown (Ottawa). In such social situations few, if any, ever saw his sordid side.

His thorough dishonesty in the Canadas began with the agreements concluded with his settlers, the first group of whom arrived from Scotland in 1825. They were made to acknowledge by deeds the excessive amounts charged but never fully expended by McNab for their passage to McNab Township. It is uncertain how many families he actually brought in. In 1839 he claimed to have paid the way for 29 families from Scotland and 36 families, of mixed national backgrounds, enlisted at Montreal. Yet of the 142 families then living in McNab, no more than 12 admitted to having come at his expense. Despite his interest in establishing his patriarchal control as a clan head, his system of quitrents was antiquated and untenable, and many settlers fell behind. His neglect of the township became notorious. Where there was progress before 1840, it was achieved by the settlers without contribution from McNab. Still, it would be difficult to prove that his unhappy rule retarded agricultural development, for cultivated acreage in the township rose by 65 per cent between 1840, when his power was at its height, and 1844, when he departed, by which time land grants in McNab were being made by the province in a fair and equitable manner.

McNab's downfall, though slow in coming, was engineered partly by his own folly in pursuit of greater financial return and partly by the capacity of the settlers to work together to apply pressure on the government. Trouble began as early as 1829 when 15 heads of families brought out from Scotland by McNab petitioned Lieutenant Governor Sir John Colborne* for help in having their agreements with McNab declared null and void. Now that they were "a little acquainted with the country, the usages and customs of the country and the nature of the soil," they found themselves saddled with a "grievous burden which none of his Majesty's subjects in this province are under or able to bear." The following year the government appointed Alexander McDonell*, crown lands agent for the Newcastle District, to investigate the township. Though he found that the settlers were unable to proceed with their clearances and could not supply the amount of wheat or flour demanded by their engagements, the government saw no reason to intervene.

The chief's inflexible nature led him to pursue many settlers for payment of arrears in the district court at Perth, a process facilitated by his powers as a justice of the peace since 1825. He used breach of covenant as the usual accusation. McNab frequently had proceedings drawn out, necessitating repeated trips to Perth, an entanglement which proved a considerable hardship for the settlers. His run of success in the court ended in 1835, at which time his attention turned to another source of revenue. He offered to give up his

claim to the 5,000 acres he had acquired in the 1820s in return for the right to cut or collect duties on the pine timber on unlocated lots in McNab. He claimed that little of the township's land was "fit for cultivation," so that if he was "to provide for his countrymen" – a typically perverse twist to the facts – he would need alternate income. His request was granted in 1836, despite Attorney General Robert Sympson JAMESON's concern that such an arrangement would form a "permanent obstacle" to the settlement of the lots affected. The grant sanctioned something McNab had been doing illegally since 1825. The value to him of this timber cutting is not known, but one settler, Dugald C. McNab, estimated that between 1825 and 1836 it was between £100 and £600 annually.

Emboldened by this success, McNab, who had patented 650 acres in his own name, exclusive of the block grant, secured 200 more in 1837. His bizarre manner of acquiring the land was utterly characteristic of the man. The lot was held by Duncan McNab, an illiterate who had arrived in 1832 at his own expense and had established a farm. Five years later he exchanged the lot for one thought to have better soil and occupied by Duncan Anderson, who wanted McNab's property for a tavern site. The chief intervened, asking the government to give the lot not to Duncan McNab but to himself, saying merely that it had been vacated by Anderson and was occupied by a squatter. He failed to add that he knew Anderson well, had taken in his sister-in-law as a housekeeper, and had had a child by her. How Duncan McNab had offended the chief is unclear, but the latter had his way and in 1840, after legal proceedings, Duncan and his family were turned out. With the help of neighbours Duncan petitioned the government for aid but, in spite of the view of Provincial Secretary Richard Alexander Tucker* that this appeared to be a genuine case of hardship, the Executive Council refused to interfere. After a continued legal battle and violence against Duncan by McNab, and despite strong public support for the former, council upheld the chief's claim in October 1841 on the technical ground that Duncan ought to have secured a new location ticket from McNab before moving.

However vital the issue of 200 acres was to Duncan McNab, the chief's attention between 1837 and 1841 had focused on larger matters. He tried unsuccessfully to increase his land holdings and hence his revenues. In 1837 he complained to Governor Lord Gosford [Acheson*] of the settlers' sale of lands and departure from the township. To prevent this continuing, McNab asked to be granted a trust-deed for the full 5,000 acres allotted to him in 1823, which he had forfeited in 1836. By restoring his direct control over a large area, the grant would supposedly enable him to make over lots only to those settlers who had discharged their obligations to him. Here was another example of his dissembling methods, for those of his settlers who wished to remain were certainly not offering their improved lots for sale and their number was relatively small. In June 1838 council accepted McNab's proposal but in October it reversed the decision. He was publicly humiliated during the rebellion of 1837–38 when some 80 militiamen from McNab refused to serve under his command in the 2nd Carleton Light Infantry because of their objections to their settlement agreements with him and because he had legally prosecuted many of them. No confusion marked council's deliberations in 1839 when McNab asked for the 5,000 acres outright with no mention of a trust-deed. He was again turned down.

Thereafter McNab sought compensation for his reputed losses in settling the township. In February 1839 he calculated them at £5,000 (the estimated value of the 5,000 acres he had forfeited) with an additional £4,000 for his expenses over 14 years. He secured the support in Toronto of Attorney General Christopher Alexander Hagerman* and of John Strachan who, though no longer on council, now believed that McNab had received little financial return on his scheme. Council nevertheless rejected his claim for the £5,000 but felt that a fund for compensating him could be created by having the settlers buy their land. Asked in July to submit an account of his actual outlay, McNab could only produce "loose estimates," so council fell back on his valuation of £4,000. By an order-in-council in September he was granted that amount, £1,000 of which was to be paid directly and the rest raised from the proposed sale of lands. At the same time, he was told to cease cutting timber in McNab by the end of the year except on his own 850 acres.

News that something important had happened in Toronto filtered back to the settlers, though the full contents of the order-in-council would not become known to them until 1842. By April 1840 a bitter petition had been submitted to Lieutenant Governor Sir George ARTHUR by 35 settlers, who denied the chief's claim of having underwritten their settlement expenses. They further asserted that McNab was still drawing income from timber duties as well as from land rents and sales. In response to their demand for an independent inquiry into the affairs of the township, the government authorized an investigation by Francis Allan, crown lands agent for the Bathurst District, who submitted his report that November.

McNab miscalculated seriously by failing to anticipate that the inquiry would fully endorse the settlers' position and paint a damning picture of his role. Roads were found to be in miserable condition. The one sawmill was owned by the chief, who blocked the erection of a grist-mill until late in 1840. The tax assessment for the township was less than £32. Even for an area with distinct disadvantages in the quality of its soil, this was a poor record. Most important, McNab was shown to have attempted to dominate the settlers in a thoroughly peremptory fashion. The report mentioned in particular Duncan McNab and John Campbell, a blacksmith whose tools the chief had seized and held for years after Campbell had refused to pay him rent or grant him a mortgage. In condemning McNab's affairs, Allan did not mince words: "The system of Rent and mortgage added to an arbitrary bearing and persecuting spirit seems to have checked all enterprise and paralyzed the industry of the settlers. . . . The devotion of Scotch Highlanders to their Chief is too well known to permit it to be believed that an alienation such as has taken place between McNab and his people could have happened unless their feelings were most grossly injured."

In the House of Assembly McNab still had friends, and it was reluctant to publish Allan's report, which became something of a political issue. As well, in June 1841 a further petition from the settlers went unheeded by the Executive Council, which moved instead to confirm the arrangements made in 1839. Consequently an order-in-council was passed giving McNab's settlers nine years to pay for their land and directing them to make their payments not to McNab but to the crown lands agent, thus cutting the chief off from direct access to his compensation. Then, in August, Francis Hincks*, the editor of the reform *Examiner* and a newly elected member of the assembly, seconded a motion by Malcolm Cameron* to have Allan's report tabled. The motion carried against the wishes of Sir Allan Napier MacNab, Stewart Derbishire*, and 17 others. A decision by the assembly to print the report was undermined by its referral to a committee of the house, but in 1842 it was published, embarrassing the government over its past involvement and causing a further loss of support for McNab.

Allan's progress through the township in the summer of 1840 had already roused the settlers, some of whom had sent details of their troubles to Hincks. Beginning in November 1840, Hincks began publishing in the *Examiner* accounts of McNab's mishandling of the township. The chief was moved to sue Hincks for libel, with damages set at £1,000. The case was heard in April 1842 in Toronto by Jonas Jones*, who had presided at the iniquitous persecution of Duncan McNab at Perth. Hincks, whose forthcoming appointment as inspector general was evidently brought into question, was represented by Robert BALDWIN, William Hume Blake*, and Adam Wilson*. Attorney General William Henry Draper*, Henry SHERWOOD, and John Willoughby Crawford* acted for McNab, who won the case but received only £5, a clear moral defeat. The proceedings, with all their revelations so damaging to McNab, were placed by an unremorseful Hincks before the reading public.

McNab

When the settlers in McNab learned early in 1842 of the obligatory purchase clauses in the orders-in-council of 1839 and 1841, there was further commotion. There were two more petitions, the first by settlers McNab had brought from Scotland and the second by those who had entered the township bearing their own costs. To the latter group the Executive Council merely replied, in March 1842, that as the settlers had never been promised free land they should not delay in paying the first purchase instalment for fear of seeing their lands sold. It was the last official word on that vexatious subject. In 1843, however, John Paris, who had fought McNab over the erection of a grist-mill in the township, succeeded in having him declared a public nuisance and fined by the Court of Quarter Sessions in Perth.

What was the effect of all this on McNab? Publicly his bearing remained unchanged. In August 1842 his presence at a drawing-room hosted by Lady Bagot in Kingston no doubt drew much comment. In an address to the Caledonian Society of Montreal in 1890 James Craig, an Ottawa valley lawyer, recalled talking "with some who knew the old Chief in the last days of his dying power and all unite in saying that he bore himself as of old, erect and dignified to the last. He still thought himself right and the settlers wrong. . . . And these friends . . . almost invariably said to me, 'Don't forget to tell how good the Chief was to the poor; how he doctored the people for nothing[,] how his house was always open to the passer on the highway, and how he never forgot his Highland home and the old, old Scottish customs; and oh dinna forget that though he was a hard man to some, yet he had a good warm Highland heart.'" Craig himself viewed McNab's arbitrary nature as the product of his "hereditary training" and family tradition. "I can well believe . . . he meant well," he concluded, "but the little tyrannies led to greater ones and the unlawful assertion of authority led to falsehood and cruelty to support it." The legend of the good-hearted but misguided highland chief on the banks of the Madawaska was thus elaborated.

The public record reveals McNab to have been a thoroughly unpleasant piece of work, dangerous even to his dependents and sycophantic to those more powerful than himself. His instability of character and purpose may have reflected a drinking problem, but such an explanation lacks evidence. He was not the only chief who attempted but failed to make the transition from clan monarch of the 18th century to serious landowner of the 19th. Driven by an ambition to erect a fortune in Upper Canada, he survived only at a modest level on a remote frontier, his frequent, almost relentless, excursions to Perth, Kingston, and Toronto notwithstanding. He proved himself a consummate liar and felon who by various means, at times sophisticated and subtle, robbed both the crown and the poor. He laid almost insupportable burdens on those who crossed him, pursuing them with great vigour in the courts. Ultimately his display of greed gave the settlers the means to uncover the real nature of his settlement scheme and to break his grip on McNab Township and drive him from his last home there, on the shores of White Lake.

In 1844, when he was still trying to collect his promised compensation from the government, he left for Hamilton, where he was financially supported by Sir Allan Napier MacNab. The chief's flair, however, never diminished. At a St Andrew's Day celebration in Kingston in 1847, Major James Edward Alexander was struck by his appearance and commanding presence. In 1848 McNab was presented by his estranged wife, Margaret, with the estate of Rendall in the Orkney Islands, Scotland, but he remained in Hamilton until as late as September 1851. Following his return to Britain he took up with Elizabeth Marshall, the daughter of a Leeds ironmonger, with whom he had a daughter. They moved to Passy (Paris), possibly in the winter of 1854–55, and subsequently to Lannion. There McNab died in 1860, leaving behind a legend in the Ottawa valley.

ALAN CAMERON and JULIAN GWYN

AO, MU 1978; MU 2598, no.37 (hist. sketch of Archibald McNab, photocopies of clippings from *Chronicle* (Arnprior, Ont.), 14 Dec. 1894–1 March 1895); RG 1, C-I-1, 33, McNab to John Davidson, 6 Oct. 1841; McNab to Metcalfe, 4 March 1844; F-I-8, 37: 7; RG 22, Perth (Lanark), District Court, case files, 1837–41; clerk account book, 1816–44; ser.75, 1: 259, 285. Court of the Lord Lyon (Edinburgh), Public reg. of all arms and bearings in Scotland, 40: f.133. Ont., Ministry of Citizenship and Culture, Heritage Administration Branch (Toronto), Hist. sect. research files, Renfrew RF.5. PAC, RG 1, E3, 53: 3–7, 60, 66–68, 75, 77, 89–92, 103–14, 117–18, 123–28, 135, 135v–w, 138, 141–48, 479–81; L1, 30: 477–79; L3, 307: Mc20/20, 23; 307a: Mc20/176; 308: Mc21/10, 56, 64; 308a: Mc21/94, 121; 310: Mc22/178; 311: Mc1/32–33, 64, 71; RG 5, A1: 29944–46, 31176–77, 33170–72, 103387, 125156–83, 135733–70, 139643–46; B3, 7: 686–89; B26, 3: 556, 569; 6: 236, 1097; 8: 1258; C2, 1: 95–96; RG 68, General index, 1651–1841: 454. SRO, GD50/119–20; GD112/43–46. Univ. of Toronto, Thomas Fisher Rare Books Library, MSS 5027, James Craig, "'The McNab' . . . address delivered at a meeting of the Caledonian Society of Montreal in 1890" (typescript, 1890). J. E. Alexander, *L'Acadie; or, seven years' explorations in British America* (2v., London, 1849), 2: 2. Can., Prov. of, Legislative Assembly, *App. to the journals*, 1841, app.HH, nos.1–2. Francis Hincks, *Reminiscences of his public life* (Montreal, 1884), 82–83. John Mactaggart, *Three years in Canada: an account of the actual state of the country in 1826-7-8 . . .* (2v., London, 1829), 1: 277–78.

Bytown Gazette, and Ottawa and Rideau Advertiser, 20 Dec. 1837. *Chronicle & Gazette*, 31 Aug. 1836; 9, 30 March, 30 April, 24 Aug. 1842; 27 April 1844. *Examiner*

(Toronto), 11 Nov. 1840. *Kingston Chronicle*, 20 Dec. 1822, 17 Jan. 1823. Joseph Bouchette, *The British dominions in North America; or a topographical description of the provinces of Lower and Upper Canada . . .* (2v., London, 1832), 1: 83. [J. B. Burke], *Burke's genealogical and heraldic history of the landed gentry*, ed. Peter Townend (18th ed., 3v., London, 1965–72), 2: 418–19, 670–71. "Calendar of state papers," PAC *Report*, 1935: 182. "State papers – U.C.," PAC *Report*, 1897: 168; 1898: 191–92. H. I. Cowan, *British emigration to British North America: the first hundred years* (rev. ed., Toronto, 1961). W. A. Gillies, *In famed Breadalbane; the story of the antiquities, lands, and people of a highland district* (Perth, Scot., 1938), 85–114. *The last laird of MacNab: an episode in the settlement of MacNab Township, Upper Canada*, ed. Alexander Fraser (Toronto, 1899). John McNab, *The clan Macnab: a short sketch* (Edinburgh, 1907). Marion MacRae, *MacNab of Dundurn* (Toronto and Vancouver, 1971). Richard Reid, "McMillan and McNab: two settlement attempts on the Ottawa River" (paper presented at Scottish conference, Univ. of Guelph, Ont., 1983). Scadding, *Toronto of old* (1873), 212–13. Roland Wild, *MacNab: the last laird* (London, 1938). M. J. F. Fraser, "Feudalism in Upper Canada, 1823–1843," *OH*, 12 (1914): 142–52. G. C. Patterson, "Land settlement in Upper Canada, 1783–1840," AO *Report*, 1920.

MacRAING. *See* RANKIN

MACTAVISH, LETITIA (Hargrave), letter-writer; b. 1813 in Edinburgh, eldest of nine children of Dugald Mactavish and Letitia Lockhart; m. 8 Jan. 1840 James Hargrave*; d. 18 Sept. 1854 in Sault Ste Marie, Upper Canada.

Letitia Mactavish spent most of her early life at Kilchrist House, the family home near Campbeltown, Scotland, where, as daughter of the sheriff of Argyllshire and granddaughter of the chief of the clan Tavish, she received a good education and the social training befitting her family's position. The name of McTavish (Mactavish) was renowned in the fur trade of British North America. Simon McTavish*, one of the principal partners in the North West Company and a distant relative, took Letitia's uncle John George McTavish* into the trade in 1798. After the union with the Hudson's Bay Company in 1821, John George became an influential officer, and three of Letitia's brothers, William*, Dugald*, and Hector, entered the HBC.

William was posted to York Factory (Man.) in 1834, under Chief Trader James Hargrave, and the two men became close friends. When Hargrave went to Scotland on furlough in the fall of 1837 he was warmly received at Kilchrist House. He was quickly convinced that he had found the ideal wife in Miss Mactavish but, before he had time to present his official suit, duty compelled him to return hastily to York Factory in March 1838. Both his proposal and Letitia's acceptance were conveyed by mail and

Hargrave returned to Scotland in the fall of 1839 for the marriage. After their January wedding the couple travelled in the spring of 1840 to London, where they were hospitably entertained by HBC governor George SIMPSON. Letitia formed a lasting friendship with Simpson's wife, Frances Ramsay SIMPSON, and her sister Isobel Graham Simpson*, the wife of Chief Factor Duncan Finlayson*. Between sightseeing and social engagements, Letitia selected furnishings, including "a 1st rate square piano, seasoned for any extremes of climate," to add to the comfort of life at York Factory.

The Hargraves sailed from Gravesend aboard the *Prince Rupert* on 6 June 1840, accompanied by Isobel Finlayson, and arrived at York Factory early in August. Although Letitia's first reaction to the bleak expanse of the factory was "to turn my back to the company & cry myself sick," her practical and optimistic nature enabled her to adapt readily to life on Hudson Bay. She wrote to her family as frequently as possible, describing her situation in lively detail. This unique collection of letters, written by one of the few white women living in the HBC territories in the 1840s, provides an intimate picture of the social life of the fur trade in the mid 19th century from a feminine point of view.

Despite the drawbacks of life at York Factory, notably the unhealthy climate and the isolation, Letitia was not subject to the toil and privation of many pioneer women. As the wife of the chief officer of the company's main supply depot, she enjoyed a privileged position. She was mistress of her own commodious, snugly furnished house and benefited from the services of a personal maid, Mary Clarke, who was an old family servant, as well as those of the company cook and butler. In the winter the gentlemen's mess was held in Letitia's dining-room, but during the hectic summer season, when Hargrave was so busy that his wife scarcely saw him, Letitia dined alone unless there were lady visitors. The fare, though monotonous and seriously lacking in greens, was plentiful, and even the women had prodigious appetites – a "usual dinner" for four ladies consisted of roast venison, three geese, four ducks, six plovers, a large Red River ham, potatoes, and mashed turnips or boiled lettuce. Letitia's fashionable gowns excited astonishment at York Factory, but she adapted her wardrobe to include Indian "leggins" and moccasins. Hargrave saw that his wife was well wrapped in furs when she went for an airing on the wooden walkways in the fort, called platforms, or for a ride in her elegantly appointed dog carriole.

As the only white woman at York Factory, Letitia was an object of curiosity to the native people. The Indian women called her "Hockimaw Erqua," meaning chieftainess, and often brought presents of berries and flowers. Letitia was much impressed by the cradle and moss bag in which the Indian women carried their babies and remarked on their great kindness to their children. It was difficult for a white woman to look with equanimity upon certain social customs of the fur trade, many men having taken an Indian or Métis wife "after the fashion of the Country." To her credit, Letitia realized that the too rigid enforcement of European morality could lead to unnecessary suffering. She strongly censured the Reverend John Macallum*, schoolmaster at the Red River settlement, for refusing to allow Métis children to visit their mothers if they had not had a church marriage. "This may be all very right, but it is fearfully cruel for the poor unfortunate mothers did not know that there was any distinction & it is only within the last few years that any one was so married."

In her private letters Letitia was often highly critical of people she met. With her sharp wit, she delighted in regaling her family with the gossip of the country, but her uncharitable remarks were usually motivated by her dislike of hypocrisy and affectation. Although she expected the deference due her social position, she did not shun the companionship of Métis women such as Harriet Vincent, wife of Chief Trader George Gladman* and godmother of the Hargraves' first child. In 1841 she met Dr William Fraser Tolmie* at York Factory and was impressed by his dedication and energy, both in his work for the company and in the classes in arithmetic and sacred music he offered to the inhabitants of the fort in the evenings. Another young doctor, John Sebastian Helmcken*, visited York as ship's surgeon in 1847 and formed a very favourable impression of Letitia. In his *Reminiscences* he described her as "one of those nice ladies, one occasionally meets with, kind and affable. Altho not handsome she had a decidedly nice face – and a very pleasing expression with a very good figure."

During her years at York, Letitia was chiefly concerned with the welfare of her growing family. The birth of her first son, Joseph James*, on 1 April 1841 created a sensation. The Indians flocked to see the new baby and the women were delighted to be able to kiss him, exclaiming "Very fat! Very white!" Letitia persuaded Hargrave to have a nursery, an unknown luxury at fur-trade posts, built on to their house with the advent of her second child. The death of the little boy shortly after his birth in December 1842 was a grievous blow. His mother found solace in the thriving health of her eldest and a daughter, Letitia Lockhart, born on 24 Oct. 1844.

By the mid 1840s Hargrave was hoping to move his family to a more congenial clime since both he and his wife suffered from ill health. In 1846 they went with their children to Scotland where Letitia received skilled medical treatment in Edinburgh, and returned to York Factory the following year. Letitia deeply missed her son, who had remained at school in

Scotland, but she was soon diverted by another daughter, Mary Jane, born 11 July 1848. With the anticipated transfer continually deferred, Letitia became despondent, seeing her husband worn out by his heavy duties at York Factory and the prospects of the trade fast declining. Before the birth of their fifth child, Dugald John, in September 1850, the Hargraves received confirmation of a transfer to the company depot at Sault Ste Marie, where more civilized amenities would be available. Hargrave left York for his new post in the summer of 1851 but considered the overland journey too strenuous for his family and arranged for them to leave on the HBC's fall ship to Britain. Letitia enjoyed the reunion with her family and placed her eldest daughter, "Tash," in school with Joseph James at St Andrews.

Hargrave wrote to her of the charms of the Sault, advising on purchases for their new home and for Letitia herself: "a fine silk velvet gown worthy of being worn by such a wife as you have been to me." Letitia and her two youngest children were met by her husband in New York in the summer of 1852. Two years later the Hargraves' domestic happiness was shattered when Letitia died of cholera, then epidemic. Hargrave left his post, without waiting for permission, to take her body to Toronto for burial at St James', the nearest consecrated cemetery.

SYLVIA VAN KIRK

The correspondence of Letitia Mactavish can be found in the Hargrave papers at PAC, MG 19, A21, ser.1, 27. Most of the letters have been published by the Champlain Society in *Letters of Letitia Hargrave*, intro. by M. A. MacLeod.

PAM, HBCA, B.239/a/154, 157, 161, 168, 179; D.5; E.12/5. Hargrave, *Hargrave corr*. (Glazebrook). Helmcken, *Reminiscences of Helmcken* (Blakey Smith and Lamb). I. [G. Simpson] Finlayson, "York boat journal," ed. A. M. Johnson, *Beaver*, outfit 282 (September 1951): 32–33. M. A. MacLeod, "Fur traders' inn," *Beaver*, outfit 278 (December 1947): 1–6; (March 1948): 28–31. A. A. W. Ramsay, "The letters of Letitia Hargrave," *Beaver*, outfit 271 (June 1940): 18–19; (September 1940): 37–39.

McTAVISH, NANCY. *See* McKENZIE

MADRAN, JEAN-MARIE (sometimes referred to as **Joseph**), Roman Catholic priest; b. 13 Feb. 1783 in Saint-Ours, Que., son of Jean-Baptiste Madran and Josephte Gamarre; d. 2 June 1857 in Petit-Rocher, N.B.

Jean-Marie Madran was one of ten children in a poor family left fatherless while he was still an adolescent. An intelligent and pious altar boy, he was brought to the notice of Abbé Pierre Fréchette, parish priest of Beloeil. Fréchette was to pay for his studies at the Séminaire de Québec, from 29 Sept. 1810 to 9 Feb. 1813. After ordination on 12 June 1813 at

Quebec, Madran served as assistant priest in Saint-Pierre on Île Orléans in 1813–14 and in Sainte-Famille at Cap-Santé in 1814.

His first posts as parish priest started well but ended with Madran desperate to leave. On 15 Oct. 1814, accompanied by one of his sisters, he arrived in the predominantly Acadian parish of Saint-Jacques-de-la-Nouvelle-Acadie (Saint-Jacques) north of Montreal [see Jacques Degeay*]. He quickly pacified quarrelling factions and persuaded the parishioners to complete the interior of the church. Madran himself donated 3,000 *livres* towards the total costs, which had mounted to approximately 28,500 *livres* and which the parish, in the midst of an agricultural crisis, was unwilling or unable to meet. But his conversion of a Protestant girl, Marie Brousse (Bruce), in July 1818 so outraged her father and caused such scandalous rumours that Madran asked Bishop Joseph-Octave Plessis* to transfer him. The continued goodwill of many parishioners was shown at a meeting when they voted the return of his 3,000 *livres*.

In the summer of 1819 Madran arrived in the Îles de la Madeleine, full of optimism: Plessis had considered the islanders model Catholics. But by September of that year Madran was complaining that outsiders had undermined native piety. Moreover, poverty compelled him to ask unsuccessfully for the additional parishes of Margaree and Chéticamp in Cape Breton and to consider the sale of dispensations. By 1821 quarrels between the Catholic inhabitants of Hâvre-Aubert and Hâvre-aux-Maisons, over who was to pay for the parish church and the chapel that they shared, combined with loneliness and poverty to drive Madran to despair. In a letter to Bishop Bernard-Claude Panet* of Quebec, he described this period as three years of misery and begged for a mainland post.

Madran went on to serve a number of parishes in succession: Saint-Joachim in Châteauguay, 1822–25; Saint-Patrice in Rivière-du-Loup, 1825–30; Saint-Georges in Saint-Georges de Cacouna, 1830–32; L'Assomption in Berthier-sur-Mer, 1832–34; and Saint-François in Saint-François-Montmagny, 1834–35.

He was to find a home in Petit-Rocher, N.B. On 26 Aug. 1835 he arrived and took charge of the parishes of Belledune and Petit-Rocher at Nepisiguit Bay. Madran built a new church in Bathurst and completed the chapel in Belledune. Although he found the life exhausting, he considered his parishioners to be people of goodwill and piety who respected him. While at Petit-Rocher, Madran bought several blocks of land and built a private house.

On 15 Jan. 1837 he became the parish priest at Caraquet with responsibility also for Tracadie. But parishioners disputing over church sites once again destroyed his early optimism. Around 1839 he was back in Petit-Rocher. A move to Shediac in 1848 was of an even shorter duration. Finding the church locked and the members of the congregation hostile, Madran quickly returned to Petit-Rocher without gaining the permission of Bishop William DOLLARD of New Brunswick. By June 1849 he was ill and asking for either retirement or a much quieter parish than Petit-Rocher. Dollard refused his request and sent him back to Shediac and Grande-Digue, where he served from 14 Oct. 1849 to 4 Nov. 1852. Throughout this period he was to be again plagued by contentious parishioners reluctant to pay their tithes.

From 1853 to 1857 Madran was officially the assistant to the priest in Richibucto, but by 1855, once again ill, he had returned to Petit-Rocher. There he was cared for until his death by Marcel Burgo and his daughter, the local schoolteacher, who in return were made heirs to his modest estate which included 140 acres of land, £300 in plate, and £60 of personal possessions. The community of Madran near Petit-Rocher was named in his honour.

A conscientious priest, Madran was anxious to confine himself strictly to spiritual duties. He tried to avoid the frequent controversies that other priests in Acadian parishes were encountering in trying to re-establish church control after the independence of the deportation period. His life provides an interesting contrast to those of contemporary Canadian priests such as François-Xavier-Stanislas Lafrance* and Antoine Gagnon* who sought a wider leadership role in Acadian society.

SHEILA ANDREW

AAQ, 311 CN (mfm. at PANB). Arch. de l'évêché de Trois-Rivières (Trois-Rivières, Qué.), François Aché à Thomas Cooke, 8 juin 1837; F2, J.-M. Madran à Cooke, 17 nov. 1835; F4, Madran à Cooke, 22 sept. 1835. Arch. of the Diocese of Saint John (Saint John, N.B.), Dollard papers, 22 Aug. 1848, 25 June 1849, 3 Jan. 1850. Arch. paroissiales, Saint-Pierre-aux-Liens (Caraquet, N.-B.), Reg. des baptêmes, mariages et sépultures (mfm. at PANB); Saint-Polycarpe (Petit-Rocher, N.-B.), Reg. des baptêmes, mariages et sépultures (mfm. at PANB). ASQ, MSS, 432: 284. PANB, RG 7, RS64, 1857, J.-M. Madran. *Gleaner* (Chatham, N.B.), 6 June 1857. Guy Courteau et François Lanoue, *Une nouvelle Acadie: Saint-Jacques de L'Achigan, 1772–1947* ([Montréal, 1949]). Robert Rumilly, *Les îles de la Madeleine* (Montréal, 1941; réimpr., 1951). Léon Thériault, "Les missionnaires et leurs paroissiens dans le nord-est du Nouveau-Brunswick, 1766–1830," *Rev. de l'univ. de Moncton* (Moncton, N.-B.), 9 (1976), nos.1–3: 31–51.

MAGUIRE, THOMAS, Roman Catholic priest, vicar general, author, and educator; b. 9 May 1776 in Philadelphia, son of John Maguire and Margaret Swite; d. 17 July 1854 at Quebec.

Thomas Maguire was the son of an Irish Catholic who had emigrated first to Philadelphia and then in

Maguire

1776 as a loyalist to Halifax, where he became commissary general. In 1788, possibly already destined for a sacerdotal career in the Maritime missions, Thomas was sent to the Petit Séminaire de Québec. A professor reported in 1791 that he was "very deserving of praise, gifted with a penetrating mind," zealous, and diligent. In 1794 he was prefect of the Congrégation de la Bienheureuse-Vierge-Marie-Immaculée, the highest student position in that fraternity. He seems to have entered the Grand Séminaire in 1795, and two years later he was appointed secretary of the diocese of Quebec, an important administrative post usually given to an ecclesiastic of potential so as to familiarize him with the diocese and its operation. He was ordained priest on 11 Oct. 1799 and about that time was named senior curate at the cathedral of Notre-Dame, Quebec, by Bishop Pierre Denaut*. There he would learn administration from the parish priest, Joseph-Octave Plessis*, recently named coadjutor bishop. Maguire became so essential to Plessis that Denaut left him at Notre-Dame for six years. In October 1805 he was sent to Notre-Dame-de-l'Assomption (at Berthier-sur-Mer), a small parish of some 350 communicants.

In February 1806 Denaut appointed Maguire to Saint-Michel, a prosperous agricultural parish about 20 miles downriver from Quebec, and to the subsidiary charge of Beaumont which he held until 1814; the total number of their communicants was triple that at Notre-Dame-de-l'Assomption. A few months after his arrival the church of Saint-Michel was gutted by fire but, building from the old walls, Maguire had his congregation worshipping in a new structure by August 1807. However, the building and decoration of the church, with paintings by Louis Dulongpré* and William Berczy* and European canvases from a collection sent to Quebec by Philippe-Jean-Louis Desjardins*, were not terminated until at least 1814. Despite the extraordinary expenses of rebuilding, Maguire finished every year from 1806 to 1817 with a surplus in the parish treasury. He was no less diligent in his pastoral duties, visiting his parishioners at least once a year, preaching regularly, and ferreting promising boys, such as Augustin-Norbert Morin*, out of his catechism classes for the priesthood. His parish was in general quiet, and he its undisputed master. In 1818 Edmund Burke*, newly appointed vicar apostolic of Nova Scotia, requested Maguire as his coadjutor; bulls were issued in October 1819, but he refused them.

Maguire was interested in education and felt that its development by the clergy would increase clerical vocations. In May 1821 Plessis named him to a committee at Quebec headed by Joseph-François Perrault* to draft the constitution of the Quebec Education Society. In 1822 he and several other priests launched the Société pour Encourager l'Éduca-

tion Ecclésiastique to finance the education of clerical candidates from poor families. He was probably the author of a memorandum, written about 1822, attributing to a faulty education the intellectual mediocrity, lack of urbanity, and rough-hewn language of most clergy as well as the loss "of that importance which assured our number, and above all that sovereign influence which we were able to turn not only to the good of religion but also to the temporal advantage of our flock, cruelly oppressed from all sides." A more secular curriculum would attract the professional and wealthy classes who were already drifting to non-denominational or even Protestant schools.

Throughout the 1820s Maguire engaged in polemical work. He supported Bishop Jean-Jacques Lartigue* in his struggle with the Sulpicians in the Montreal district. From about 1814 to 1824 he promoted the idea of a clerical newspaper but failed to rouse the interest of the clergy. In 1827 he replied anonymously in the *Quebec Gazette* to William Smith*'s *History of Canada* . . . (issued in 1826), which he saw as a continuation of "concerted and constant efforts of *prejudice* and *malevolence* to denigrate the Canadians, depress their institutions, and cast a pall over their religion." His anger with Smith was equalled only by his dismay that leaders of the Canadian party, such as Denis-Benjamin Viger* and Louis-Joseph Papineau*, did not make common cause with him on the basis of "the close connection that exists between our civil and religious institutions."

Maguire's educational and polemical activities were restricted by his incessant duties as parish priest of Saint-Michel. In September 1827 Plessis's successor, Archbishop Bernard-Claude Panet*, appointed him principal of the Collège de Saint-Hyacinthe, begun in 1809 by Antoine Girouard*. Maguire sought to raise the college's standards, encourage the theological studies of its regents, and improve its library. However, a number of disagreements with Lartigue, the college's superior, over administrative and philosophical questions prompted Lartigue to suggest to Panet in July 1828 that Maguire be removed as principal and made editor of an ecclesiastical newspaper. "His way would be to study and write," Lartigue felt, "which he could do advantageously if he were directed by someone who would moderate his hotheadedness and impetuous reasoning."

Panet ignored this suggestion, but in June 1829, on Lartigue's insistence, he sent Maguire and Pierre-Antoine Tabeau* on a mission to London and Rome. Their most important objectives were to stop a proposed transfer of the estates of the Séminaire de Saint-Sulpice in Montreal to the colonial government in exchange for a pension for the Sulpicians [*see* Jean-Henry-Auguste Roux*], to seek authorization for letters patent for the Collège de Saint-Hyacinthe, to negotiate a procedure for nominating the coadjutor bishops at Quebec and Montreal, and to obtain London's agreement to the creation of the diocese of Montreal. They failed in London, and in Rome their only success was to get suspended, but not revoked, an authorization previously accorded by Propaganda to the Sulpicians enabling them to transfer their estates.

In early 1830, on the return trip through Paris, Maguire published *Recueil de notes diverses sur le gouvernement d'une paroisse, l'administration des sacremens* to guide young priests through "the interminable labyrinth of our often contradictory customs . . . which trip us up at every step." The work was timely, for the liberal bourgeoisie in many parishes had begun an aggressive campaign to undermine the influence of the parish priest, particularly in the administration of the *fabrique*. Maguire's manual made the clergy aware of their rights. His attempts to consult with the bishops in Lower Canada while compiling the work had produced disappointing results and even some hostility on Lartigue's part over Maguire's treatment of certain topics, and the publication of the work in Paris without episcopal authorization from Quebec probably intensified ill feeling between the two men. Nevertheless, Maguire's book ultimately became the accepted manual of Roman Catholic parish administration in Lower Canada.

Maguire and Tabeau arrived back in Lower Canada in July 1830, and Maguire returned to Saint-Hyacinthe. He immediately drafted a program to restore the disastrous finances of the institution. By June 1831, according to a professor, Joseph-Sabin Raymond*, Maguire had "all the business of the house in hand" and was "placing things on a very good footing." However, his relations with Lartigue had deteriorated further, while those with the college's regents, for the most part theology students, had become increasingly strained. Maguire found them too immature and too poorly grounded in theology to be effective teachers but too busy teaching to progress as theology students. With enrolment at the college declining inexorably and rumours of impending student boycotts and revolts filling the air, Lartigue dismissed Maguire in August 1831. The principal believed himself a victim of those who opposed his reforms and was humiliated. "I leave heart-broken with pain, and God knows what will be the result of it; life is crushing me."

Maguire spurned Lartigue's face-saving offer of an honourable position in Montreal and accepted a temporary posting as professor of philosophy at the Séminaire de Québec. In April 1832 he was transferred to the chaplaincy of the Ursulines of Quebec, succeeding Jean-Denis DAULÉ. Meanwhile,

he collaborated with Joseph Signay*, Panet's coadjutor bishop, in the drafting of a diocesan ritual and of the clergy's reply to a bill introduced into the House of Assembly by the Canadian party aimed at reducing clerical influence in the *fabriques*. In July 1833 he published *Le clergé canadien vengé par ses ennemis*, an attack on a book entitled *Tableau statistique et politique des deux Canadas* (Paris, 1833) by French littérateur Isidore-Frédéric-Thomas Lebrun. Seeing in the work an attempt by Canadian liberals to introduce into Lower Canada, through Lebrun, French "irreligious liberalism and with it revolutionary fanaticism," Maguire warned against confiding the destiny of the colony to liberal politicians.

Lartigue was anxious to find a prestigious position for Maguire, preferably outside Lower Canada, and he had tried in 1830 to have him appointed coadjutor with the bishop of Kingston, Alexander McDonell*. He had warned Panet in September 1831 that Maguire's dismissal in apparent disgrace had produced complaints from many "who rightly esteem him." Panet and then his successor Signay refused Lartigue's suggestion that Maguire be sent back to Rome to defend the bishops' positions against Saint-Sulpice, which was energetically represented by Jean-Baptiste Thavenet*. In 1833 rumours that Rome intended to replace Signay's choice as coadjutor, Pierre-Flavien Turgeon*, with Jean-Baptiste Saint-Germain*, a priest allied with the Sulpicians, induced Signay to reconsider. On 16 Sept. 1833 Signay appointed Maguire his vicar general and procurator at the Vatican to obtain bulls for Turgeon, as coadjutor archbishop of Quebec, and to solve other problems.

Maguire arrived in Rome on 5 Dec. 1833. By day he pored over accounts with Thavenet, who was the financial representative in Europe for the Lower Canadian religious communities and with whom he had been authorized by several of them to arrive at a final audit. The two disagreed frequently because of the frightful state of the accounts and they finally came to an impasse in May 1834. Still Maguire had seen enough to estimate that during Thavenet's agency the communities had collectively lost between 150,000 and 160,000 francs in the bankruptcies of two large European financial houses. By night, often using information gleaned during the day from an unwary Thavenet, Maguire prepared his cases on other matters for the cardinals of Propaganda. Thavenet had immense influence with them but Maguire found an important exception: the prefect of Propaganda, Angelo Mai. Maguire lost almost all his cases in the formal deliberations of the cardinals but, by presenting vigorous memoranda to the pope through Mai who defended them, he succeeded in getting Propaganda's adverse decisions changed. Turgeon's bulls were issued and Maguire obtained a further suspension of Saint-Sulpice's authorization to alienate its estates. In addition, he negotiated a formula for determining future coadjutors at Quebec that blocked Saint-Sulpice's efforts to secure a determining voice. Finally, over Thavenet's opposition, he obtained bulls for Tabeau as auxiliary bishop and successor to Lartigue. Maguire failed only to persuade Rome to negotiate with London the creation of the diocese of Montreal. In his free moments Maguire went sightseeing, conducted research in the history and cartography of the French in North America for Georges-Barthélemi Faribault*, and acted as agent for Bishop McDonell.

Lartigue agitated to have Maguire remain permanently in Rome to oppose Thavenet, but Maguire insisted on returning, convinced that the task was done. In December 1834 he departed, leaving behind memoranda on the machinations of Thavenet and the Sulpicians. Maguire arrived in Montreal on 29 May 1835. He refused offers by Lartigue to become administrative assistant and vicar general at Montreal after Tabeau's untimely death but accepted Signay's invitations to become his vicar general and return as chaplain to the Ursulines. He had formed a strong mutual attachment with the nuns and their young charges. From Rome in 1834 he had assured "my children of the boarding-school" that, although the schoolgirls there appeared to him friendly and good, "I would not truck one of *mine* for a half dozen of them."

As chaplain, and in close collaboration with the superior, Marie-Louise McLoughlin*, named de Saint-Henri, Maguire addressed himself to the financial morass in which the Ursulines found themselves as a result of poor administration. He put the community's tangled financial and land records into such order as would enable the nuns to collect unpaid rents and other charges accruing from their properties. He launched a number of lawsuits and urged the community to seek the assembly's assistance in pressing the government to pay for the site of the citadel, which he claimed had been Ursuline property and was worth £111,000. In the 1840s and early 1850s he saw to the construction of buildings to bring in rental revenues. Under his astute and aggressive management, the Ursulines realized from 1837 to 1853 a total profit of £40,000. In about the same period they were able to add three wings to the convent.

Maguire also considerably enriched the spiritual life of the community. Having been struck by miracles he had witnessed in 1834 at the tomb of Sainte-Philomène in Naples, the following year he had constructed the chapel of Sainte-Philomène, in which thenceforth the Ursulines worshipped during winter. After a minute study of the documents, he relaxed their fasting practices in order to remove any danger to their health but fought a long and acerbic theological debate with the hierarchy to tighten observance of the cloister.

The Ursulines ran the premier female educational institution in the colony but, for reasons which included lack of both French textbooks and sisters capable of teaching in English, it had diminished in popularity with parents. Among the measures taken to restore the school's prestige was the establishment of the "Règlement des élèves du pensionnat des Dames Ursulines de Québec," drawn up by Maguire on Turgeon's orders and in consultation with Mother Saint-Henri and the teaching sisters. It codified existing practice and introduced ideas collected during visits to Ursuline convents at Lyons and Naples and to the major schools of Rome and Paris. Teaching at the convent was to be based on a number of fundamental principles: classes containing students of equal strength, encouragement of comprehension rather than rote learning, short lessons to maintain interest, unlimited patience with dull students, maintenance of discipline through promotion of goodness rather than scolding for misdemeanours, and interdiction of corporal punishment. His curriculum determined for decades the nature of education dispensed by the Ursulines to the girls of Quebec and reflected current views on the social role of women. When teaching arithmetic, instructors should "put aside all that can nourish a purely speculative curiosity" for "questions of real utility, of daily practice." On the other hand, the teaching of music "lends glory to the institution." Also taught were chemistry, physics, and natural history, all on a "purely elementary" level; composition, versification, and oral reading; English and French; needlework, calligraphy, drawing, and painting. Lessons in civility constituted "an essential part of careful education, especially of female persons."

History was a subject of predilection for Maguire, who corresponded frequently with Jacques VIGER on historical matters, acquired an invaluable collection of Ursuline manuscripts in Paris, and authored a fine manuscript history of the physical evolution of the Quebec convent. His curriculum called for non-controversial church history in regular classes, attended by Protestant as well as Catholic girls, but he insisted on points of controversy in the catechism classes he himself taught in order to counter what he perceived as a Protestant offensive in the colony. Secular history courses placed "in the first rank the history of our Canada," and included readings from the *Abrégé de l'histoire du Canada* . . . (4 vol., Quebec, 1832–36) by Joseph-François Perrault.

In the midst of his activities as chaplain, Maguire continued his polemical work. In 1838 he published *Doctrine de l'Église catholique d'Irlande et de celle du Canada, sur la révolte*, a collection of documents theologically justifying Lartigue's condemnation of armed rebellion in Lower Canada. Three years later

Maguire

appeared the *Manuel des difficultés les plus communes de la langue française*, destined for use in grammar schools. In it Maguire pleaded for the alignment of the French language in Lower Canada with that in France but his vigorous denunciation of numerous Canadianisms drew a strong rebuttal in the *Quebec Gazette*, probably from Jérôme DEMERS, superior of the Séminaire de Québec, who defended the idea of a correct Canadian French.

Although severely arthritic, Maguire enjoyed good health into the 1840s. In 1845, however, he described himself as "burdened with infirmities," and in March 1852 he asked two Ursulines to "pray *hard* for your old friend" when influenza nearly carried him off. In December 1853 he bequeathed almost his entire estate to Saint Louis University's mission to the Indians, in which he seems to have become interested only the year before. On 17 July 1854 he died of an inflammation of the lungs, complicated by cholera. Turgeon buried him the following day under the sanctuary of the Ursulines' chapel.

Thomas Maguire was a study in contradictions, a man capable of extremes of enthusiasm and self-discipline, agitated, passionate, yet tempered with a compassionate heart and a gift for cold analysis. However vehemently he had embraced the cause of the Canadian church and people, Lartigue wished to see him out of Lower Canada and the nationalist Viger considered him a foreigner; the cardinals in Rome, on the other hand, viewed him as a bothersome Canadian. An obituary described him as an active, virtuous, accomplished cleric for whom study served to demonstrate that learning and the ecclesiastical life were not incompatible. Achieving recognition for the social necessity of clerical education had indeed been Maguire's main object in life. His significance is broader, however, and would include his role in preparing the triumph of episcopal authority over Saint-Sulpice and his expression of social and political views increasingly distinct from those of the liberal Canadian bourgeoisie and the Protestant colonial government. In all these areas Maguire showed himself to be one of several protégés of Plessis, including Jean-Baptiste KELLY, Charles-François Painchaud*, and Jean Raimbault*, who were architects of the more assertive church that, under Bishop Ignace Bourget*, would fill the void left by liberal nationalists after the débâcle of 1837–38.

JAMES H. LAMBERT

[The author wishes to thank Christiane Demers for assistance in writing this biography. J.H.L.]

Thomas Maguire is the author of "Observations d'un catholique sur l'*Histoire du Canada* par l'honorable William Smith," published in *La Gazette de Québec*, 11 janv. 1827; *Recueil de notes diverses sur le gouvernement d'une*

paroisse, l'administration des sacremens, etc., adressées à un jeune curé de campagne, par un ancien curé du diocèse de Québec* (Paris, 1830); *Le clergé canadien vengé par ses ennemis ou Observations sur un ouvrage récent, intitulé "Tableau statistique et politique des deux Canadas"* (Québec, 1833); and *Manuel des difficultés les plus communes de la langue française, adapté au jeune âge, et suivi d'un recueil de locutions vicieuses* (Québec, 1841). He compiled *Doctrine de l'Église catholique d'Irlande et de celle du Canada; recueil de pièces constatant l'uniformité de cette doctrine dans les deux pays, et sa conformité avec celle de l'Église universelle* (Québec, 1838).

AAQ, 12 A, D: f.121; E: f.55v; F: f.157; G: ff.13, 20; H: f.155v; I: f.119v; K: ff.88v, 96, 164v; L: ff.20, 93–94, 161; 20 A, III: 170; VII: 5, 32; 210 A, IV: 138, 157, 159, 171, 210; XIII: 223, 319, 424, 535; XIV: 13, 20, 39–40, 46–47, 60–61, 65, 189, 360, 388, 424, 444, 446, 449, 519; XV: 185, 346, 413, 447, 463, 465–67; XVI: 163, 191, 273, 461; XVII: 38, 47, 59, 512; XXIII: 429, 579–80; XXV: 486; 22 A, VI: 361; 1 CB, V: 115, 117, 131; 61 CD, Saint-Michel, I: 21, 26, 30, 32, 34; 69 CD, III: 165–67, 180–81; VII: 118–19; VIII: 20; 81 CD, I: 48, 52, 57, 59–60, 76–78, 85–86; III: 1; CD, Diocèse de Québec, I: 141; IV: 169; VI: 34; VII: 2, 34–36, 39, 42, 44, 47, 55–61, 65–68, 70, 72, 74, 77, 79–80, 84–85, 87–90, 92–93, 95–96, 98–99, 101–12, 116–18, 121–24, 126–27, 131–34, 134–41, 147, 150–53, 155–56, 159, 169; 10 CM, III: 155; IV: 80, 95–96, 127, 199, 200, 202; 7 CM, I: 114; 90 CM, I: 18; 312 CN, IV: 136, 138; 320 CN, VI: 39; 60 CN, I: 30; II: 42; VI: 58; 26 CP, III: 177, C: 139, 141; EJ, I: 125–27; U, III: 1. ACAM, 901.017, 823-1; 827-1; 829-1, -9; 830-1, -5-7; 832-1; 833-1; 834-1-6, -8-11, -13, -15-17; 835-1; 901.028, 827-1; 830-2; RLB, I: 37; RLL, II: 218, 288; IV: 225–26, 281–82, 362–65; V: 34, 75, 228, 269, 306, 313, 342–43, 364, 378, 391; VI: 48–50, 52–53, 58, 69, 230–31; VII: 236, 439, 460, 491, 500, 595, 610, 703; VIII: 290. AP, Saint-Michel, Cahiers de prônes, 1810–36; Journal de recettes et de dépenses, 1809–26; Livre de comptes, 1776–1860; Travaux, 1757–1872. Arch. de la chancellerie de l'évêché de Saint-Hyacinthe (Saint-Hyacinthe, Qué.), XIII, B.8, 1827–31. Arch. du diocèse de Saint-Jean-de-Québec (Longueuil, Qué.), 1A/45; 5A/40, 6A/86, 117. Arch. du monastère des ursulines (Québec), Fonds Maguire. ASQ, Fichier des anciens; Lettres, Y, 3; MSS, 7: 35; Polygraphie, XV: 7; XXXIX: 21; XLII: 19f; XLIII: 1d; Séminaire, 48, nos.174, 178, 180; 49, nos.5, 7, 43; 56, no.44; 103, nos.30a, 30b; 178, no.2; XVIII: 77–78, 84, 88, 92, 95, 97–98, 101, 103, 105. ASSH, A, G, Dossiers 11–13. J.-O. Plessis, "Le journal des visites pastorales en Acadie de Mgr Joseph-Octave Plessis, 1811, 1812, 1815," Soc. hist. acadienne, *Cahiers* (Moncton, N.-B.), 11 (1980). *Le Canadien*, 9 oct. 1833, 24 juill. 1854. *Quebec Gazette*, 10 May 1821; 11 Jan. 1827; 3 Oct., 30 Nov. 1833. Chaussé, *Jean-Jacques Lartigue.* Choquette, *Hist. du séminaire de Saint-Hyacinthe.* N.-E. Dionne, *Une dispute grammaticale en 1842: le G.-V. Demers vs le G.-V. Maguire, précédée de leur biographie* (Québec, 1912). A. A. Johnston, *Hist. of Catholic Church in eastern N.S.*, vol.1. Lambert, "Joseph-Octave Plessis." Lemieux, *L'établissement de la première prov. eccl.* Père Marie-Antoine, *St-Michel de la Durantaye (notes et souvenirs), 1678–1929* (Québec, 1929). *Reminiscences of fifty years in the cloister, 1839–1889* . . . (Quebec,

Maitland

1879). T.-M. Charland, "Un projet de journal ecclésiastique de Mgr Lartigue," SCHÉC *Rapport*, 24 (1956–57): 39–53. Antonio Dansereau, "La mission de l'abbé Thomas Maguire à Rome, en 1833–1834," *RHAF*, 3 (1949–50): 9–29. André Lapierre, "Le manuel de l'abbé Thomas Maguire et la langue québécoise au XIXᵉ siècle," *RHAF*, 35 (1981–82): 337–54.

MAITLAND, Sir PEREGRINE, army officer and colonial administrator; b. 6 July 1777 at Longparish Hall, Hampshire, England, son of Thomas Maitland and Jane Mathew; m. first 8 June 1803 Louisa Crofton (d. 1805), and they had a son, Peregrine; m. secondly 9 Oct. 1815 Lady Sarah Lennox, daughter of Charles Lennox*, 4th Duke of Richmond and Lennox, and they had at least seven children, one of whom died in infancy; d. 30 May 1854 in London.

At the age of 15 Peregrine Maitland entered the British army as an ensign in the 1st Foot Guards. He quickly rose in rank, becoming a captain in 1794 and a lieutenant-colonel in 1803. During the Napoleonic Wars he served with his regiment in Spain, Flanders, and France. Promoted major-general in 1814, he was made a CB on 4 June 1815. Later that month he commanded the 1st brigade of the Foot Guards at the battle of Waterloo. He was subsequently placed in charge of the 2nd brigade, which formed part of the occupation force in Paris following the defeat of Napoleon. For this role he was created a KCB on 22 June.

While he was in Paris, his second marriage, to Lady Sarah Lennox, took place – an event to which both myth and romance have become attached. According to one story, recorded by both Henry Scadding* and David Breakenridge Read*, Maitland and Lady Sarah eloped because of her father's objections to Maitland's suit. It was thought there was too great a difference in their ages (he was 38, she was 23) and she had been expected to marry a man of higher station. Richmond's disapproval was overcome, it is said, through the intervention of the Duke of Wellington, at whose quarters in Paris the two were married. Maitland's marriage proved to be an advantageous one politically. There was, apparently, no lingering discord between him and his father-in-law, and when Richmond was appointed governor-in-chief of British North America in 1818, his influence was one factor in Maitland's appointment that year as lieutenant governor of Upper Canada, succeeding Francis GORE. Other factors were involved: Maitland was a personal friend of Lord Bathurst, the colonial secretary, and the British government wished to make places for its war heroes.

Maitland arrived in York (Toronto) on 12 Aug. 1818 and was sworn in the following day. He would remain in office for the next ten years, serving as well a brief term as administrator of Lower Canada from 17 March to 19 June 1820. The Reverend John Strachan*, who was to become one of his political allies during the 1820s, described him in December 1818 as "a most amiable and pious man, . . . most anxious to do all the good he can." He was a man "of great talent . . . much simplicity of manner and habit," and "at the same time firm and resolute," though extremely delicate in health. In June 1820 Lord Dalhousie [Ramsay*], the governor-in-chief, noted that he seemed to be "in rapid consumption." Henry Scadding recalled him as "a tall, grave officer, always in military undress; his countenance ever wearing a mingled expression of sadness and benevolence."

During his first year in office Maitland became "exceedingly popular from his quiet gentlemanlike manners, & the firm unassuming tone of his Government," as Dalhousie recorded after talking with William Dummer Powell*, speaker of the House of Assembly. Maitland was undoubtedly aided socially by his wife's "distinguished style." In York he was instrumental in setting up an elementary school on Lancasterian principles [see Joseph Spragge*], and he appointed a board of trustees for the proposed first general hospital [see Christopher WIDMER]. Confronted by the town's dreary streetscapes, he was confident in 1819 that a few public works would "induce a sentiment of national pride"; five years later he laid the cornerstone for the Home District's first court-house and jail, designed by John EWART.

But Maitland was never enamoured of the provincial capital. No doubt he considered it, as others did, an unhealthy site. During his stay in Upper Canada he built a 22-room summer house, Stamford Park, three miles west of Niagara Falls. In the opinion of Anna Brownell Jameson [MURPHY] in 1837, it was the only place in Upper Canada "combining our ideas of an elegant, well-furnished English villa and ornamental grounds with some of the grandest and wildest features of the forest scene." Maitland's dislike of York prompted him to investigate moving the provincial capital elsewhere. Between 1822 and 1826 he had properties purchased on the east shore of Lake Simcoe with a view to moving the capital there. In 1826 he suggested Kingston as a site. The locations were recommended by Maitland because both were more defensible than York, and Kingston had the potential for better accommodating government officials.

Soon after his arrival in Upper Canada in 1818, Maitland had conveyed to the Colonial Office reports that a man named Gourlay had been "perplexing" the province. A number of leading officials in Upper Canada, many of whom would be Maitland's advisers during his administration, must have considered this a temperate description of the situation in the province. Believing that the constitution was endangered, they viewed with alarm the colony's tendency to sedition under the influence of "turbulent and factious men."

Within a year Maitland informed the Colonial Office that reports of serious disturbances had been exaggerated.

At the centre of apprehension was Robert Gourlay*, a sincere but erratic and tactless Scottish radical, who had come to Upper Canada in 1817. Through his wife's relatives there and as a result of his tour of the western part of the province, Gourlay became aware that economic expectations following the War of 1812 had given way to dissatisfaction, which was particularly acute in the Niagara District. The war had been followed by economic depression; compensation to those who suffered war losses had not been made; land promised to militiamen had not been granted; capital necessary for development was inadequate; settlement remained scattered and there was little demand for land. Particularly frustrating to the large landholders was the continuation of a wartime prohibition on American settlement. In April 1817, shortly before Gourlay's arrival, Robert Nichol*, a member of the House of Assembly for Norfolk who had considerable property in the Niagara District, had secured the establishment of a legislative committee to investigate the state of the province. Full debate on its resolutions was prevented by Lieutenant Governor Gore, who had pre-emptorily prorogued the legislature. His reaction to what he considered a censure of the administration of the province would be reflected in Maitland's response first to Gourlay and then, during the 1820s, to sustained opposition within the assembly.

In 1817–18, through a series of newspaper addresses, questionnaires, and the promotion of township meetings of landowners and inhabitants, Gourlay condemned the administration. As well, he planned a provincial convention of township delegates, out of which would come a petition to the Prince Regent. When, instead, a petition was presented to Maitland by two members from the convention, held in York in July 1818, the new lieutenant governor refused to accept it, expressing his disapproval of the action by stating that the convention had been irregular and hostile to the spirit of the British constitution, since the people had lawful representatives in the legislature. A convention of delegates could not exist, said the Legislative Council in an address to Maitland, without danger to the constitution. He subsequently recommended legislation prohibiting "seditious" conventions and meetings such as Gourlay had organized; he dismissed from civil and military appointments, or denied them to, any who had supported Gourlay. In echoing Maitland's speech opening parliament in October 1818, the assembly accepted Maitland's recommendation and banned conventions "as highly derogatory and repugnant to the spirit of the Constitution."

Accounts of the emergence of a political opposition in Upper Canada in the 1820s and 1830s have asserted that members of the executive attempted to persuade successive lieutenant governors to accept their perception of executive authority as it should be exercised. Those in this influential group changed from time to time. The period of Maitland's administration saw the eclipse of Chief Justice William Dummer Powell as the chief legal adviser to the lieutenant governor and the rise of Attorney General John Beverley Robinson*. Along with Maitland's secretary, Major George Hillier*, Robinson and John Strachan were undoubtedly the most influential members of Maitland's administration. Hillier had served with Maitland in Europe and was a close friend as well as an adviser. He was an efficient and capable individual whose views coincided with those of Maitland and on whom the lieutenant governor relied in carrying out the routine business of administration and often in formulating reports and dispatches. At the end of 1818 Strachan, a member of the Executive Council and later of the Legislative Council, was not yet on terms of intimacy with Maitland but already he felt he had exerted some influence. "He arrived here," said Strachan in December, "with some ideas respecting the Executive Government not founded on sufficient evidence; but now he sees things more clearly."

In Maitland's case no conversion was necessary. He was of a decidedly conservative persuasion. His over-reaction to Gourlay and to public meetings or conventions reflected an intrinsic part of his political disposition and was directly related to the political unrest in Britain during 1816–19. At the time of his arrival in the province, response in Britain to economic dislocation following the Napoleonic Wars had led to demands for the reform of parliament, for universal suffrage, and for voting by ballot, all promoted by a post-war revival of political associations, mass meetings, and conventions. This revival became associated with the democratic excesses of the French revolution and led in 1817 and again in 1819 to legislation in Britain suspending habeas corpus and to a prohibition on public meetings, political clubs, and the sale of seditious literature. The suppression of public meetings and limitation of the freedom of the press were commended by Upper Canadian conservatives, who believed that public agitation was both dangerous and disloyal. Maitland concurred in this belief throughout the 1820s. The agitation by Gourlay aroused public discussion and interest in the affairs of the province, as he had intended. Maitland found himself increasingly in conflict with a group of oppositionists who were critical of his administration and of the conservative advisers with whom he surrounded himself.

Maitland did recognize that some of the grievances identified by Gourlay's agitation, as they related to the granting and distribution of land, were legitimate.

Maitland

Soon after arriving in Upper Canada he had informed Lord Bathurst of the harmful effects of absentee ownership of land. He subsequently made himself acquainted with the history of the land-granting system in Upper Canada and made a genuine attempt to curb abuses and to institute reforms. Yet he was not always free to determine land policies, being subject to joint control with imperial authorities. Many of his efforts were hindered by the influence of land speculators and by an agrarian-oriented assembly, which resisted the taxation of wild land. Even his critic William Lyon Mackenzie* recognized the problem of dealing with such vested interests and later gave Maitland credit for the limited improvements he had been able to effect. One of Maitland's first reforms was to bring some efficiency and energy to the work of the provincial land board, which had become a cause of constant complaint and which he accused in August 1818, the month of his arrival, of "sleeping over an office choked with applications." Within a month he was able to report to the Colonial Office that the derelict board had "brought up a long arrear of business."

Maitland had inherited the problems of an earlier policy of liberal and extensive grants of crown lands to loyalists, militia, pensioners, and officials – much of which remained unoccupied and uncultivated. Actual settlers complained it was their labour that increased the value of the lands of absentee owners and speculators. Despite strong opposition from a number of officials and the landowners, who argued that, in the existing state of Upper Canada's economy, it was unprofitable to lay out money on agriculture, a bill authorizing the taxation of uncultivated land was passed in 1819. Maitland believed the tax would induce owners to develop or sell their land. Since the Assessment Act of 1819 was a temporary measure, it was made permanent in 1824, despite the resistance of those members of the assembly and Legislative Council who, Maitland noted, "were the largest land proprietors." He believed that only his personal pressure in the Legislative Council, where W. D. Powell opposed the new act, secured its passage. In 1828, however, it was modified by the assembly to favour the owners of land who were tax-delinquent.

Maitland's criticism of the policy of liberal grants of crown land recognized that it had not been effective in settling the province, and settlement had been dispersed. Between 1818 and 1823 he recommended that grants be limited, that lands be used to produce revenue for supporting education and road-building, and that all grantees be forced to perform the settlement duties before receiving patents. By an order in council in 1819, he set up district land boards to examine applicants and make locations of land, thus relieving the provincial board of much of this work. To Maitland the land system of Upper Canada had a

political as well as an economic purpose. Lands should be used to develop support for the provincial administration and to make Upper Canada as attractive to immigrants as the United States. In achieving these ends it was essential for the executive to be financially independent from the assembly, which did not share his imperial enthusiasms. During Gore's administration, the assembly had demanded control of the revenue from crown lands and reserves, a trend which Maitland met head-on. Early in 1819 he informed the assembly that the casual and territorial revenue was not at its disposal. He nevertheless attempted to correct the province's financial problems by trying to make the land department self-supporting and to devise a method of making the crown reserves productive. In 1823, in a dispatch to the Colonial Office, he concluded that the only practical policy was to dispose of lands by sale instead of by grant, a proposal originally made by John Beverley Robinson to offset the province's growing financial burden [see John Henry DUNN].

In 1826 the reserves not leased or applied for in townships surveyed before March 1824 were sold along with the Huron Tract to the Canada Company, which on the basis of sales made an annual payment to the province. These payments supported the civil administration and helped to make it independent of the assembly. Though satisfied with this arrangement, Maitland experienced an irritating relationship with the Canada Company's agent in Upper Canada, John Galt*. Maitland considered him hostile to his administration and too sympathetic to his critics, including William Lyon Mackenzie, John Rolph*, and Marshall Spring Bidwell*. Galt's practice of communicating directly with the Colonial Office disturbed Maitland, who as lieutenant governor was justifiably concerned with maintaining executive control.

All of Maitland's efforts in the field of land reform were directed at the economic development of the province. He sought to discourage speculation and to promote actual settlement. He encouraged (in contrast to Lord Dalhousie) Peter Robinson*'s development of settlement in the Peterborough area and supported Thomas TALBOT in opening up much of the southwestern part of the province. He welcomed immigration schemes, such as the £10 deposit plan of 1818 [see Richard TALBOT], that would add to the British content of the population and thereby counteract American republican influences.

The question of the influence and status of the many American immigrants in Upper Canada was not a new one. It had been implicit in the community since its birth, but only took shape as a divisive issue in 1821–22 during the bitter debate surrounding the election to and expulsion from the assembly of Barnabas Bidwell*, a native of Massachusetts. He channelled the complex legal and moral arguments into a lasting accusation that he had been expelled by an administration intent on stripping all unnaturalized residents of their civil rights. The controversy over Bidwell's eligibility, and that of his son Marshall Spring at a by-election in 1822, suggested that a new doctrine was being established, under which many inhabitants who had come from the United States after the Treaty of Paris of 1783 would be considered aliens, unqualified to vote, ineligible to sit in the assembly, and incapable of legally owning lands. If carried into execution the doctrine would disenfranchise a large proportion of freeholders in every district of the province. Maitland and his supporters, believing that the growing opposition to the administration emanated from this portion of the populace, sought to limit its power in the assembly. Oppositionists, for similar political reasons, sought to force the recognition of the political and property rights of this group. Maitland had been aware of the problem for some years. In 1820 he had stated to Dalhousie that a "very large portion" of property in the province was in the hands of Americans "who had not complied with the terms of residence," and that if the laws of citizenship and naturalization were enforced "you would now unsettle more than half the possessions of the Colony."

In an atmosphere of tension and anxiety over the question of citizenship and naturalization, Maitland sought the advice of the Colonial Office in April 1822. He did not set out to dispossess the American-born of their property but he was firm in his desire to exclude from election to the assembly those whom he considered to be aliens. He believed exclusion was essential to the security of Upper Canada. The assembly, on the other hand, requested from the imperial government in 1823 an assertion that the American-born be guaranteed the rights of British subjects. The controversy over the Bidwells brought the alien question fully into the open as a highly charged political issue. Since a related case (*Thomas v. Acklam*) was pending in the British Court of King's Bench, no reply was received from the Colonial Office, though there was some indication that the imperial government subscribed to Maitland's point of view. Based on the court's decision in 1824, the British law officers ruled that both Bidwell and his son were aliens and could not sit in the assembly. Further, all inhabitants who had willingly stayed in the United States after 1783 and accepted American citizenship had forfeited their British allegiance. Recognizing that it would be advisable for the Upper Canadian legislature to pass an act naturalizing aliens and admitting them to the "civil rights and privileges of British subjects," Lord Bathurst authorized Maitland in July 1825 to have appropriate legislation prepared. In November the provincial government brought into

the Legislative Council a bill "to confirm, and quiet in the possession of their estates, and to admit to the civil rights of subjects, certain classes of persons." The assembly, however, rejected the government bill, which was vaguely worded and avoided specific mention of political rights for naturalized residents. As a result of the general election of late 1824, the assembly contained, for the first time, a clear-cut majority of anti-government members. Among these was John Rolph, the first man who could effectively stand up in the house to John Beverley Robinson, probably Maitland's closest adviser on the alien issue. In the session of 1825–26 an alternate bill was narrowly passed in the assembly, declaring that the parties affected had always been British subjects. This bill was unacceptable to the administration, but in January 1826 the opposition argued, correctly, that its bill only asserted what had been official doctrine until some time after the War of 1812 and had, moreover, constituted the understanding on which most of the colony's population had settled there.

In May the imperial parliament attempted to resolve the problem by passing a statute which empowered the Upper Canadian legislature to bestow, within the province only, all the rights and privileges of British subjects (including political rights). Bathurst then sent Maitland a dispatch outlining the terms of a provincial act that would be acceptable to the imperial authorities. They included provisions (in particular one that made naturalization conditional on the beneficiary's abjuration of his American allegiance) which were obnoxious to those affected. When the Naturalization Bill was brought in in 1827, it was accepted by the opposition only with great reluctance, under the threat that, if it were defeated, the parties affected would be unable to vote in the next general election. Opponents to the bill organized the Committee of the Inhabitants of Upper Canada and sent Robert Randal* to London with a petition asking that royal assent be withheld. To Maitland's dismay, Randal was successful. The imperial government rejected its former view that people could abjure their natural allegiance; consequently the Upper Canadian bill requiring resident aliens to do just that had to be disallowed. Annoyed and humiliated, Maitland was directed to prepare new legislation at the next session, failing which appropriate measures would be enacted at Westminster. He treated the task as a capitulation to his critics and, in his own defence, argued that both Upper Canada and the Colonial Office had been deliberately misled by malignant forces within the province and by radical elements in Britain.

In the session of 1828, as Maitland later viewed it, the members of the assembly were seeking issues "to sustain their popularity" in the expected election. Bitterness erupted when Maitland transmitted the Colonial Office dispatch directing new legislation and provoked the assembly by charging members with exciting "groundless alarm" among the inhabitants of the province. In retaliation, the members stated the necessity for them to reply to insults and to charges of misconduct and misrepresentation made by the lieutenant governor. Maitland, however, was fighting for a lost cause. The Colonial Office had decided against him and in 1828 the required Naturalization Bill was passed favouring the views of the anti-government forces. Throughout the debate Maitland repeatedly argued, in public and in dispatches to the Colonial Office, that the language of the act of 1828 was much like that rejected by the opposition in the bill of 1826. By ignoring the important differences of intent, particularly on political rights, Maitland may have been attempting, in an altogether devious manner, to discredit the opposition for needless rejection of the legislation of 1825. The alien question, though now closed, to the relief of many, left a legacy of enmity that served to intensify the antagonism between the assembly and the executive branch of the government. As an issue in the political education of the community it served to increase public awareness of the political process. John WILLSON, speaker of the assembly, remarked in February 1828, "It had been difficult to awaken the people from their slumber but they had at last been roused to save their liberties; their complaints were now heard."

The confrontation over the alien issue provided the assembly with an opportunity of by-passing the lieutenant governor in its criticism of the administration and its submission of petitions and resolutions to the Colonial Office. In the process the lieutenant governor was transformed from an impartial reporter of provincial events, for the information of the Colonial Office, to a spokesman for a faction, which was forced to compete with the opposition for the support of the colonial secretary. During the 1820s the assembly departed from traditional practice, deferral to the lieutenant governor on the speech from the throne, by criticizing and debating Maitland's addresses. Maitland considered this action an affront to his prerogative. In 1826, when the assembly did not adhere to the practice of forwarding petitions and resolutions through the lieutenant governor and with the concurrence of the Legislative Council, Maitland was annoyed. He did not wish to prevent the forwarding of petitions to London, but he was firm in his belief that they should be channelled through him. His military background and training made him, as a civil administrator, punctilious in matters of rank, position, and protocol. Temperamental and acutely conscious of his imperial position, he treated the action of the assembly as a "remarkable" departure, which exhibited disrespect for the representative of the crown and gave credence to grievances manufac-

tured by unprincipled agitators. In the last few years of his administration he became bitter in his criticism of the Colonial Office, which in his opinion was too inclined to accept censure of his administration by spokesmen whose opinions were not worthy of consideration without giving him an opportunity of stating his own case.

Soon after the 1825–26 session, Maitland had begun a tour of the province and in numerous communities he received addresses from the inhabitants. The tour seems to have been designed to create support for his policies, which had suffered a defeat in the alien issue. The universal tone of admiration for Maitland in the addresses and their approval of his administration lend credence to later charges, in the *Upper Canada Herald* and in the assembly, that John Strachan and John Beverley Robinson had organized and "manufactured" the tour.

Maitland's tour and his public criticism of the assembly excited widespread counter-criticism. In one district, notice was given that a petition would be presented to the legislature asking it to institute an inquiry into Maitland's charges accusing persons of sedition, of disaffection, and of an intention to overthrow the constitution of the province. In his opening speech to the 1826–27 session of the legislature, Maitland referred to his tour, during which, he said, he had found proof of advancement within the province and evidence of content. The spirited response in the assembly indicated the extent to which opposition members had been aroused by his actions. John Rolph led the attack, thrashing out at both Maitland and the pro-administration forces. He reproached the lieutenant governor for travelling through the province "purposely to libel and slander" members of the assembly and for "accepting slanders as loyal and affectionate addresses." One member, George Hamilton*, was reminded of the days of Robert Gourlay's agitation and noted the parallel between the organization of the townships by that critic and the organization of the townships by Maitland's supporters. Gourlay's attempt, however, had been treated as sedition.

During Maitland's tenure the claims of the Church of England, most notably in relation to the clergy reserves, emerged as a highly divisive political and religious problem, adding to the litany of grievances against Maitland. Under the Constitutional Act lands had been set aside for the support and maintenance of a "Protestant Clergy" by means of a leasing system. Prior to Maitland's arrival, it had been charged that the reserves, because of their chequered location throughout the townships, retarded settlement. Any attack on the reserves met with their spirited defence by John Strachan, who sought to make exclusive use of them for the benefit of the Church of England. In 1819 he had been instrumental in the development of the

Upper Canada Clergy Corporation, a body of members of the Church of England who would supervise and administer the lands. The same year, following the request of a Presbyterian church in the Niagara District for financial assistance, Maitland asked the Colonial Office to determine whether the Church of England, as Strachan claimed, had the exclusive right to the reserves under the Constitutional Act. The British attorney general and solicitor general were of the opinion that the clergy of the Church of Scotland could be included in the definition of "Protestant Clergy" under the act. Maitland was not in accord with this interpretation and attempted first to prevent the opinion of the law officers from becoming known in Upper Canada and then to evade its implication by suggesting that the Church of Scotland be limited to "occasional" assistance. Maitland had aligned himself with Strachan in the view that the state should have an established church and that, in Upper Canada, the established church was the Church of England. Any other view, in Maitland's opinion, would not be consistent with the British constitution. When the Church of Scotland pressed its claim, he asserted in 1824 that Strachan was "perfectly in my confidence" and was "fully in possession" of his views on the reserves.

Maitland, like Strachan, believed that only through support of the Anglican clergy and a system of education controlled by that clergy could Upper Canada overcome the dangerous republican ideas which, it was thought, were infiltrating the province through American Methodist clergymen and teachers. Because Methodists and Presbyterians formed such large, and vocal, segments of the population, the exclusive claims made by the Church of England could not escape becoming entangled in the political struggle between Maitland's administration and the anti-government opposition. Maitland became identified as an opponent by those forces that resisted the exclusive claims of the Church of England, sought the separation of church and state, and wished to see the revenue from the clergy reserves devoted to general education. Maitland was not prepared, he informed William Huskisson, the colonial secretary, in 1827, to see "the national church" degraded to a sect and all denominations "placed on a level." He admitted that Methodists "exceeded greatly" Anglicans and Presbyterians, but he did not accept finality in denominational attachments. Men who had been zealous Presbyterians in Scotland had become exemplary and active supporters of the Church of England in Upper Canada. Like Strachan, he believed that many who were only nominally attached to other denominations could be won over to the Church of England if it received the proper support.

Maitland's support of the Church of England and his identification with Strachan proved damaging to him personally and to his administration. Strachan had been pleased at Maitland's appointment in 1818 because the lieutenant governor was "exceedingly disposed to promote the cause of religion and education." As a result of William MORRIS's attempts in 1823 in the assembly to have the Church of Scotland recognized as a national church, the religious issue became a focus of public attention. Partly to divert the clamour and hoping to increase the revenue of the Church of England, Strachan, with Maitland's concurrence, went to London in 1826 to continue negotiations with the Canada Company for the sale of the clergy reserves. At the same time he sought to obtain a charter for a provincial university under the control of the Church of England. The establishment of a university had constantly been on Maitland's mind since his arrival in the province, the purpose being, he said, "to produce a common attachment to our constitution, and a common feeling of respect and affection for our ecclesiastical establishment." When Strachan went to London, Maitland wrote to the Colonial Office stating that nothing would gratify him more than to see Strachan's purpose implemented. While in London Strachan prepared an "Ecclesiastical Chart" that blatantly exaggerated the place of his church in the life of Upper Canada. Following his return to the province in the summer of 1827 he was easily challenged on his chart and denounced for his continuing derogation of the Methodists. The charter for a university was condemned. Even some of his fellow-churchmen were disturbed by his actions.

Though Maitland did not abandon his principles, he was upset by Strachan's zeal, which, he maintained, only served to inflame the debate on the claims of the Church of England. Reports circulated that a rupture between the two had developed, though no open manifestation of any change was detected. The bitterness the issue had aroused, Maitland said, was a result he had not anticipated. The debate on the chart and the university was a climax to one of the most acrimonious confrontations of the 1820s. Opponents rose up to challenge what they damned, in the *Upper Canada Herald* in October 1827, as an attempt to impose on the province an illiberal and exclusive "clerico-political aristocracy" alien to the Upper Canadian situation. In December, at a meeting in York, a petition, to which 8,000 signatures were obtained, was drawn up challenging Strachan's position on both the clergy reserves and the university [see George Ryerson*]. In March 1828 the assembly sent a petition to the Colonial Office requesting revocation of the university charter.

Toward the end of Maitland's administration Strachan's excesses had clearly become a liability. The lieutenant governor ignored Strachan's "Ecclesiastical Chart" and attempted instead to blame much of the agitation on those who misrepresented the Church

Maitland

of England and on the vacillations of the imperial government. But in the election of 1828 the province would register its disapproval of Maitland and his advisers. "There can be no question," Samuel Peters JARVIS wrote to W. D. Powell in December 1828, "that much of the odium, which has fallen to the share of many of those who were conspicuous in the late administration, was caused by his [Strachan's] uncompromising disposition."

By 1828 Maitland was being accused of authoritarian, vindictive, and Draconian measures. Charles Fothergill*, the king's printer, had been warned that the views expressed in his newspaper were unacceptable to Maitland. He was dismissed in 1826 for voting in the assembly against the administration and for being the "mover and conductor" of a "committee on grievances." He was replaced by Robert Stanton*, whose views were more in accord with those of the lieutenant governor and his advisers. In 1827 Maitland sent troops to remove an enclosure built on a government reserve by William Forsyth*, a Niagara Falls innkeeper. A committee of the assembly, made up of anti-administration men, supported Forsyth and reported the incident of military interference as one of a number of "unprecedented outrages perpetrated by the administration." The Colonial Office censured Maitland for his part in the incident. Judge John Walpole Willis*, who came to Upper Canada in 1827, associated with anti-government men. Maitland saw him as a man attempting to become a popular leader of an anti-administration cause. Aware that the retirement of Chief Justice William Campbell* was imminent, Willis sought the office, but Maitland strongly disapproved. When Willis challenged the authority of the Court of King's Bench, claiming that it was "incompetent" as a court in the absence of the chief justice, Maitland, after consulting the province's law officers, suspended him. William Lyon Mackenzie called the action "executive tyranny" and Willis became a hero to the anti-administration forces. A further example of the attacks on dissent came when Francis Collins*, editor of the *Canadian Freeman* and author of a pamphlet on the alien issue, was found guilty of libelling John Beverley Robinson in 1828.

The election of 1828 constituted a climax to the confrontation between Maitland's administration and the anti-government forces. The extent to which a polarization of attitudes had taken place was exhibited in the extreme partisanship of the electoral candidates. One, Thomas Dalton* in Frontenac, believed that Upper Canada needed to be saved from the oppression of the pro-administration group; another, Alpheus Jones in Grenville, withdrew from the election, believing that there was little hope of defeating the "radicals" who were hostile to Britain and whose purpose was to turn Upper Canada into a republic. Almost every political issue or incident of the 1820s

was a matter of electoral discussion – the clergy reserves, the university charter, Willis's removal, the treatment of Forsyth, and the alien question. The result was a thorough defeat of the pro-administration candidates and a more hostile reform assembly than that of the 1824–28 period. It was not, Maitland reported, "such as could be wished." He attributed it to "busy but obscure individuals" who had made use of the alien question. In characteristic fashion, he saw it as the victory of "notoriously disloyal" men, men of "detestable" character who "degraded the legislature by their presence."

Later in 1828 Maitland received another rebuff and experienced a further sense of betrayal by Britain. As a result of meetings held in York that summer, a petition was drawn up and sent to both the crown and the Colonial Office, listing a series of Upper Canadian grievances. Prominent in the list was the dismissal of Willis, the composition of the Legislative Council, the "practical irresponsibility" of the Executive Council, and (in direct reference to Maitland) the "total inaptitude of military men for civil rule in this province." The petition was occasioned by what the petitioners perceived to be the "liberal sentiments" expressed in the House of Commons and by the "favourable consideration" accorded Robert Randal's petition on the Naturalization Bill in 1827. Gratitude was expressed to two British radicals, Sir James Mackintosh and Joseph Hume who, the petition claimed, had been attentive to the rights of British subjects in Upper Canada. Early in January 1829 William Warren Baldwin*, chairman of the meetings at York, wrote to the prime minister, the Duke of Wellington, making references to the "misrule" that had crept into the administration of Upper Canada and recommending the adoption of the principle of a local "ministry" responsible to the "Provincial Parliament."

Maitland was infuriated by the petition, seeing it as a further censure of his actions. In September 1828, in a lengthy statement to Sir George Murray*, the colonial secretary, he refuted the charges made against him and belittled both the petition and the petitioners, whom, with the exception of Baldwin and his son ROBERT, he viewed as men of little social standing, men who had no character as gentlemen. They were "American Quack Doctors, a tanner, Shoemakers, Butcher and Penny postman." In Maitland's mind, that was sufficient to deny them and their opinions any serious consideration by the imperial government.

Prior to the debate on the York petition, the House of Commons, in response to petitions from Upper and Lower Canada, had appointed a committee of inquiry into the government of the Canadas. In its report, which reached Upper Canada in the autumn of 1828, many of the criticisms of the Maitland administration were accepted – judges should not be members of the

Executive Council (and thus politically involved as advisers to the lieutenant governor), clergy reserves retarded development and should be brought under cultivation, the Church of England should not have an exclusive right to the reserves and its control of the proposed university should be curtailed. The report was so favourable to the views of the opposition that Maitland was again compelled to express his frustration and anger at William Huskisson's liberal policy on colonial matters and the imperial government's readiness to accept the criticism which "any unprincipled partisan of faction" carried across the Atlantic. His supporters, already disturbed by the defeat suffered in the election of 1828, were equally enraged.

Maitland left office as lieutenant governor of Upper Canada on 4 Nov. 1828, a result, many believed, of the complaints against him. The extent of the reform domination of the assembly was clearly reflected in the vote, early in 1829, on the assembly address expressing dissatisfaction with Maitland's administration. In carrying the address, 37 to 1, the assembly administered a decisive rebuke to Maitland and his supporters. As a result, opposition men were hopeful that the appointment of Sir John Colborne* to replace Maitland would lead to further victories. They argued that opposition was legitimate; it was neither disloyal nor discourteous to the crown to criticize its representative in the province. Copying the words used in 1826 by John Cam Hobhouse in the House of Commons, John Rolph referred to himself as one of "His Majesty's faithful opposition." Hope was expressed that the new lieutenant governor would choose his advisers from the reform group that had a majority in the assembly. The assembly might then bring the lieutenant governor's advisers to account, which it had been unable to do while Maitland was in office. It was clear, however, that the British constitutional concept of responsible advisers was, for Upper Canada, not acceptable to the imperial authorities. The reform opposition's disappointment is evident in the assembly's response to the throne speech in January 1829, which noted that Colborne was "surrounded" by the same advisers who "so deeply wounded" the feelings and injured the best interests of the Country." Earlier, one of Maitland's harshest critics, William Lyon Mackenzie, had expressed a similar sentiment. Maitland, he said in 1824, was a religious, humane, and peaceable man "and if his administration had hitherto produced little good to the country, it may be it was not his fault, but the fault of those about him who abused his confidence."

Maitland had been sworn in as lieutenant governor of Nova Scotia on 29 Nov. 1828, with the added responsibility of commander-in-chief of the forces in the Atlantic region. Initially he was a far less controversial figure than he had been in Upper Canada. In May 1829 George Couper, Sir James KEMPT's military secretary, confided in Lord Dalhousie that Maitland's apparent apathy as lieutenant governor was generally condemned, but that he was popular as a man. Certainly his strongly moral conduct had an impact on Halifax's society. By insisting on walking to church, he effectively ended the garrison parades on Sunday, the city's major social event, and he publicly denounced the open market that day. In October his recurrent ill health forced him to move to the West Indies, leaving Michael Wallace* as provincial administrator.

Maitland resumed duty in June 1830, shortly after the rupture between the Council and the assembly over matters of revenue [see Enos Collins*]. He clearly understood that the dispute was exacerbated by the manœuvring for the chief justiceship of Solicitor General Samuel George William Archibald* and Judge Brenton HALLIBURTON (whom Maitland favoured). Maitland's inaction on the revenue issue, pending instruction from the Colonial Office, was resolved by the death of King George IV, which necessitated calling the "Brandy Election" that fall.

In the ensuing political calm of 1831, Maitland's manner of governing drew the early editorial criticism of Joseph Howe*, the spokesman of the emerging reform movement, who openly derided Maitland's shortcomings, including his lack of any gubernatorial achievement and his irresolution in handling the revenue crisis of the previous years. Maitland attempted to maintain a non-partisan position in the ongoing debates in 1831–32 over contentious matters of sectarian education; in 1832 he claimed some responsibility for the settlement reached for Pictou Academy [see Thomas McCulloch*]. In dealing with immigration and settlement, one of his major interests in Upper Canada, Maitland could act decisively. In 1831 he had lands laid out in Cape Breton at crown expense so that the 4,000 immigrants expected that year could be legally placed and systematically settled.

In October 1832 Maitland went to England on leave, presumably because of his health, and the government was placed in charge of Thomas Nickleson Jeffery*. Though he continued to conduct official correspondence from England, he never returned to North America and he was succeeded in Nova Scotia by Sir Colin Campbell* in July 1834.

For two years (1834–36) he was commander-in-chief of the British army in Madras; in 1843, at the age of 67, he became governor and commander-in-chief of the Cape Colony (Republic of South Africa). Arriving there early in 1844, he was well received by all elements of the colony's society (the heads of missionary societies were particularly impressed by his Christian devoutness and humanitar-

Maitland

ian interests). But by 1846 few considered him capable of dealing effectively with the difficult problems developing in relations with the Kaffir (Xhosa) and Griqua peoples and the Boers on the colony's frontiers. In the opinion of Lord Grey, the colonial secretary, Maitland had never been "a man of any great ability" and should have been retired. James Stephen, the colonial under-secretary, clearly recognized in 1846 that Maitland's administrative weakness was masked by the efficiency of his secretary, who wrote many of his dispatches. Promoted general in November 1846, several months after the outbreak of the Kaffir war, Maitland was replaced early in 1847, being considered too old and ineffective. He returned to London, where he lived in retirement until his death on 30 May 1854. In 1851, along with Sir John Colborne, he had been a pall-bearer at the funeral of the Duke of Wellington. The following year he was made a GCB.

As lieutenant governor of Upper Canada, the colony with which he has been chiefly identified, Maitland had the true interests of the province at heart. He worked with vigour and determination towards its growth and economic development. But in the view of his critics he merited censure. His administration was called a "reign of terror" by John Rolph; he had oppressed and harassed the people of the province. Such expressions were part of the inflammatory and highly personalized rhetoric of the political scene in Upper Canada. On his part Maitland was as guilty of over-reaction as his critics. With his military background and his conservative convictions he stood resolutely against those he considered his inferiors and who were thought to be enemies of the imperial connection. Despite his position during the alien issue, he could never see himself as partisan. In the British constitutional system, unlike that of the United States, there had to be an executive that stood above faction. His only duty, he said in 1821, was "to fulfil the wishes and expectations of my Sovereign." The assembly had a role in government, in achieving the checks and balances as defined in the British constitution, but Maitland could never accept the concept of dominance by an elected assembly.

The principles to which he held were not uncommon in the days of the Napoleonic period in Britain, when democratic ideas, it was feared, would lead to revolution, chaos, and mob rule, as they had in France. Maitland saw the same danger arising in Upper Canada, because of its proximity to the United States and the large American-born element in its population. In his administration he reflected the same fears as those of his native Upper Canadian advisers. He was as intransigent in his views as his critics, failing to appreciate that opposition was not necessarily disloyalty, and that the liberal winds blowing in Britain, which would bring about the Reform Act of 1832, would mark his authoritarian and hierarchical view of society as too inflexible. During his administration of Upper Canada the struggle between resolute and often rigid personalities forced the province to engage in organized political discussion to an extent unknown in the pre-Gourlay days. Debate and confrontation fostered the political education of the province through increased interest and participation in the political process. Upper Canadians had, as Gourlay wished, become activated.

HARTWELL BOWSFIELD

[Maitland's official correspondence, most of it in PRO, CO 42/361–90 and PAC, MG 11, [CO 217] Nova Scotia A, 169–79, is the main source of information on his life and career. There are some useful items in the AO, in the Macaulay papers (MS 78) and the Strachan papers (MS 35), and at the MTL in the papers of William Dummer Powell. A number of the important state papers are reproduced in *Docs. relating to constitutional hist., 1819–28* (Doughty and Story). The only full treatment of Maitland is F. M. Quealey's thesis, "The administration of Sir Peregrine Maitland, lieutenant-governor of Upper Canada, 1818–1829" (PHD thesis, 2v., Univ. of Toronto, 1968).

A copy of Sir William John Newton's portrait of Maitland is in the William Fehr Collection at The Castle, Cape Town, South Africa; a water-colour portrait is at the MTL.   H.B.]

AO, MU 2104, 1822, no.4. Hampshire Record Office (Winchester, Eng.), Longparish, reg. of baptisms, 29 July 1777. *Gentleman's Magazine*, July–December 1854: 300. "Journals of Legislative Assembly of U.C.," AO *Report*, 1913: 269. Ramsay, *Dalhousie journals* (Whitelaw), 1: 131, 139, 141; 2: 25, 72. *Town of York, 1815–34* (Firth). *Colonial Advocate*, 8 July 1824. *Kingston Chronicle*, 15 Dec. 1826; 2 Aug., 1 Nov. 1828; 24 Jan. 1829. *U.E. Loyalist* (York [Toronto]), 10 March 1826. *Upper Canada Gazette*, "Extra," 13 April 1825; 23 Feb.–30 March, 4 Nov., 5 Dec. 1826; 30 July 1828. *Upper Canada Herald* (Kingston, [Ont.]), 26 Dec. 1826; 9 Oct. 1827; 29 Jan., 26 Feb., 4, 11 March, 30 July 1828; 28 Jan. 1829. John and J. B. Burke, *A genealogical and heraldic dictionary of the landed gentry of Great Britain and Ireland* (3v., London, 1849). "Calendar of the Dalhousie papers," PAC *Report*, 1938: 9–12, 130. *DNB*. *Hart's army list*, 1853. Morgan, *Sketches of celebrated Canadians*, 244–45. "Nova Scotia state papers," PAC *Report*, 1947: 77–184. *Nova Scotia vital statistics from newspapers, 1813–1822*, comp. T. A. Punch (Halifax, 1978), no.1957; *1829–34*, comp. J. M. Holder and G. L. Hubley (1982), nos.785, 1159, 1794, 3076. D. B. Read, *The lieutenant-governors of Upper Canada and Ontario, 1792–1899* (Toronto, 1900), 117–18. "State papers – U.C.," PAC *Report*, 1900, 1901, 1943.

A. N. Bethune, *Memoir of the Right Reverend John Strachan* ... (Toronto, 1870). Peter Burroughs, *The Canadian crisis and British colonial policy, 1828–1841* (London, 1972), 28–42. Cowdell, *Land policies of U.C.*, 123. Craig, *Upper Canada*. J. S. Galbraith, *Reluctant empire: British policy on the South African frontier, 1834–1854* (Berkeley and Los Angeles, 1963). F. W. Hamilton, *The origin and history of the First or Grenadier Guards* ... (3v., London, 1874), 3: 10, 61. J. S. Moir,

604

Church and state in Canada West: three studies in denominationalism and nationalism, 1841–1867 (Toronto, 1959). Scadding, *Toronto of old* (1873; ed. Armstrong, 1966). G. McC. Theal, *History of South Africa, from 1795–1872* (5v., London, [1915–26]; repr. 1964), 2: 232; 3: 39–40. Peter Burroughs, "The administration of crown lands in Nova Scotia, 1827–1848," N.S. Hist. Soc., *Coll.*, 35 (1966): 98–99. E. A. Cruikshank, "Charles Lennox, the fourth Duke of Richmond," *OH*, 24 (1927): 323–51. B. C. U. Cuthbertson, "Place, politics and the brandy election of 1830," N.S. Hist. Soc., *Coll.*, 41 (1982): 16–17. J. B. Robinson, "Early governors: reminiscences by the Hon. John Beverley Robinson," *Daily Mail and Empire* (Toronto), 23 March 1895: 10. "Unveiling cairn at governor's cottage and tablet at ossuary at Niagara," *Mail and Empire*, 5 Oct. 1934: 12. Fred Williams, "They remember – in Lundy's Lane," *Mail and Empire*, 5 Oct. 1934: 8.

MALHIOT, FRANÇOIS-XAVIER (he also signed **Xavier**), army and militia officer, merchant, seigneur, and politician; b. 4 Dec. 1781 in Verchères, Que., son of François Malhiot* and Élisabeth Gamelin; d. 12 June 1854 in Boucherville, Lower Canada.

François-Xavier Malhiot was the son of a prosperous merchant in Verchères. In 1804 he and two of his siblings, François-Victor and Pierre-Ignace, were each given a share of their father's property. He then went into partnership with Pierre-Ignace to keep their father's business going. Some years earlier he had enlisted, like many of his compatriots, in the Royal Canadian Volunteer Regiment, specially formed for French Canadians by Lord Dorchester [Carleton*] in 1796. On 28 Oct. 1800 Lieutenant Malhiot was instructed to bring back to Montreal from Kingston, Upper Canada, a French agitator named Le Couteulx, who was suspected of spying. In 1802, having joined the militia, he was made a captain in the Saint-Ours battalion. Promoted major in 1812, he obtained the rank of lieutenant-colonel in the same battalion a year later. He held this command until 1828, when he was dismissed by Lord Dalhousie [Ramsay*].

The whole affair of Malhiot's dismissal caused a considerable stir at the time. He had been named chairman of a voters' meeting in Surrey riding held on 27 Dec. 1827 to "consider the necessity of making the state of the province known to the king and the two houses of the imperial parliament," and he had unhesitatingly supported several resolutions censoring the governor's high-handedness. He had even chaired the committee formed "to communicate with the general committees of the cities of Montreal, Quebec, and Trois-Rivières, in order to agree on the appointment of agents" to take the petitions to England. When several months later he was summoned to explain his conduct before the governor, he agreed to a private hearing on 14 June 1828 with

Dalhousie and Colonel George Heriot*. He refused, however, to go to Varennes on 20 June to justify his behaviour towards Lieutenant-Colonel Jacques Le Moyne de Martigny, who had been expelled from a meeting held at Verchères under Malhiot's chairmanship for attempting to defend the governor's position. Malhiot's refusal is the more understandable given that the meeting with Le Moyne de Martigny was to take place at the residence of his principal accuser. Dalhousie responded swiftly. He ordered the office of the adjutant general of the militia to revoke Malhiot's commission in the militia, as well as those of six other officers belonging to the battalions in Surrey and Richelieu counties. Dated 25 June 1828, the notice appeared in *La Minerve* on 30 June, just a week after the newspaper had published a long article on the Varennes affair, which it called a grotesque farce. The appearance of this notice was more than enough to fuel the debate. On 4 July Malhiot sent Ludger DUVERNAY, the printer of *La Minerve*, copies of two letters which made clear Le Moyne de Martigny's bad faith and the circumstances in which Malhiot had learned from Heriot about the complaint lodged against him. These letters were published on 7 July, and ten days later Colonel Charles de Saint-Ours*, under whose orders Malhiot had served, spoke well of him in public. The quarrel was not settled until Dalhousie left to assume command of the Indian army in 1829; his departure did not, however, stop Malhiot the following year from publishing a report on the dismissal.

In addition to distinguished military service, Malhiot participated with enthusiasm in politics. He was first elected to the House of Assembly at the age of 33, and represented the constituency of Richelieu from 8 March 1815 to 29 Feb. 1816. Running again after the crisis involving Dalhousie and the assembly, he was elected to replace Aignan-Aimé Massue in Surrey, which he represented from 30 Dec. 1828 to 2 Sept. 1830. He was elected a third time, after the Surrey riding became Verchères, and sat with Pierre Amiot* from 26 Oct. 1830 until he gave up his seat on 13 June 1832. Then he was appointed to the Legislative Council, retaining his seat until the constitution was suspended on 27 March 1838.

During the rebellion of 1837–38 Malhiot took a position similar to the one held by most council members, and refused to countenance any form of social upheaval or armed violence. He participated as a delegate from Verchères in the Assemblée des Six Comtés at Saint-Charles-sur-Richelieu on 23 Oct. 1837. He was with Siméon MARCHESSEAULT when the meeting turned sour. Marchesseault was roughed up, while Malhiot was kept off the platform by force for having tried to oppose the delegates' resolutions. In a deposition of 15 November, Malhiot stated that he had withdrawn from the platform of his own accord

Mallory

after hearing the call to arms made by Dr Cyrille-Hector-Octave Côté*, who asserted that "to hold meetings and pass resolutions at them was to demean oneself; what was necessary was to use bullets or to have recourse to the use of bullets."

Malhiot was not among those who valued social change. A merchant's son, he had succeeded through a fortunate marital alliance in joining one of the great seigneurial families of his day. On 27 May 1805 at Boucherville he married Julie Laperière, daughter of François Laperière (Boucher de La Perrière) and Marie-Charlotte Pécaudy de Contrecœur. Two years later, when his father-in-law died, Malhiot became one of the heirs to the seigneury of Contrecœur. In 1814 he had become the holder of part of the Saint-Jean fief in the seigneury of Saint-Ours and in 1816 the principal seigneur of Contrecœur, in right of his wife. His concern to maintain existing social relationships is thus understandable. The need became more imperative when on 16 Oct. 1821, again at Boucherville, he remarried, taking as his second wife Sophie Labruère, daughter of Charles Labruère (Boucher de La Bruère) and Josephte Labroquerie (Boucher de La Broquerie), who were both descended from great seigneurial families. Malhiot and his second wife had a number of children but only three survived childhood. In 1846, with the concurrence of his sons, François-Xavier Malhiot sold the seigneury of Contrecœur to John Fraser, a notary and merchant of Terrebonne, and retired to Boucherville. He lived there until his death on 12 June 1854, just a few months before the seigneurial régime was abolished in Lower Canada.

SERGE COURVILLE

François-Xavier Malhiot is the author of *Mémoire de Xavier Malhiot, écuyer, membre de l'Assemblée du Bas-Canada, sur sa destitution par lord Dalhousie, en juin 1828, de la place de lieutenant-colonel dans la milice du comté de Surrey* (Montréal, 1830).

ANQ-M, CE1-22, 27 mai 1805, 16 oct. 1821; CN1-295, 14 janv. 1804. *La Minerve*, 10 janv., 16, 23, 26, 30 juin, 7, 17 juill., 27 oct. 1828; 30 avril, 18 juin 1832; 30 oct. 1837. *Quebec almanac*, 1800–30. Fauteux, *Patriotes*, 30. *Officers of British forces in Canada* (Irving). P.-G. Roy, *Inv. concessions*, 2: 154, 159, 175. Turcotte, *Le Conseil législatif*. F.-J. Audet, *Contrecœur; famille, seigneurie, paroisse, village* (Montréal, 1940). Michel Bibaud, *Histoire du Canada et des Canadiens, sous la domination anglaise* [1760–1830] (Montréal, 1844; réimpr., East Ardsley, Eng., and New York, 1968). Azarie Couillard-Després, *Histoire de la seigneurie de Saint-Ours* (2v., Montréal, 1915–17), 2. Wolfred Nelson, *Wolfred Nelson et son temps* (Montréal, 1946). J.-J. Lefebvre, "Études généalogiques: la famille Malhiot, de Montréal et de Verchères," SGCF *Mémoires*, 12 (1961): 149–54.

MALLORY, BENAJAH, colonizer, businessman, militia officer, politician, justice of the peace, and army officer; b. *c.* 1764 in the American colonies; m.

first Abia Dayton, and they had five children; m. secondly Sally Bush, and they had no children; d. 9 Aug. 1853 in Lockport, N.Y.

Benajah Mallory may have been the son of Ogden Mallory, an early settler of Wells, Vt, where Benajah was living at the outbreak of the American revolution. He later enlisted in the local militia as a private and saw action in several battles. According to American historian Orasmus Turner, Mallory was the "first merchant" in the Genesee country of western New York State. He settled in the community founded there in the late 1780s by the followers of Jemima Wilkinson. He was drawn, no doubt, by an "anticipated" connection to the daughter of one of the sect's prominent members, though Mallory apparently never shared the religious tenets of the group. In 1792 he was listed as an ensign in the Ontario County militia. His father-in-law, Abraham Dayton, was interested in obtaining the grant of a township in Upper Canada near the Grand River lands of the Six Nations. In 1795 he and his associates, including Mallory, settled in Burford Township. Within a year Mallory had built a house and established a tan-yard, "at a great expence with other Improvements." Bedridden from the outset, Dayton died in 1797. Mallory assumed the leadership of the small community of 21 settlers and went to "much Expence towards opening and settling" the township. He hastened to report his intention to bring the number of settlers above the 40 required under the terms of the grant. It was, however, to no avail. Lieutenant Governor John Graves Simcoe* had become disenchanted with his experimental system of making township grants, and his successor, Administrator Peter Russell*, was determined to rescind them. The Burford Township grant reverted to the crown, but actual settlers were individually confirmed in their lands: Mallory was granted 1,200 acres and his wife was recommended for 200.

Within a regional population of nondescript, semi-literate, non-loyalist Americans, Mallory stood out. He had only cleared 15 acres by 1798, but he was a leader with both ambition and ability. During the reorganization of the region's militia that year Surveyor General David William Smith* successfully recommended him for the captaincy of a local company. Mallory's immediate interest, however, was land speculation, particularly within Burford Township. His claim to a lease of lands owned by the Six Nations occasioned a complaint to Smith by Joseph Brant [Thayendanegea*] early in 1798. By late 1801 Mallory had acquired stills, which he seems to have leased for some time since he did not possess a licence. On 2 April 1802 he took out a recognizance to maintain order in "his house of public entertainment." Soon after, he purchased 560 acres in Burford, an acquisition financed by mortgaging the property to the Kingston merchant Richard Cartwright*. Lord Selkirk [Douglas*], who visited Mallory in 1803, described him as possessing a "good frame house" and "a large stock of Cattle – 50 head or more." Mallory claimed at that time to have contracted to supply army garrisons with fresh beef and had sent "last year or before 20,000 lb from his own stock."

He had thus reinforced his early prominence with economic prosperity. The establishment of the London District in 1800 necessitated the appointment of local officials. For the most part, the positions went to loyalist officers such as Samuel Ryerse* and Thomas Welch*, rather than to the non-loyalist, largely Methodist Americans who comprised the majority of the new district's population. In May 1802 Smith had recommended Mallory to Ryerse as a likely candidate for the magistracy. Ryerse, "not being well acquainted with him myself," soon learned of two incidents that did not reflect "much honor on his character." In one case, Mallory had apparently demanded payment to divulge information relating to a robbery; in the second, he had, again apparently, arranged the robbery of one of his creditors, who was anxious to collect on a note. For his part, Mallory had become disenchanted with the officers of the local courts. In December 1802 he complained to Welch, clerk of the district court, about Welch's fees on suits filed by Mallory; at the same time, he criticized the fees taken by the judge, Ryerse. Criticism of this sort was a justifiable and common complaint, especially among small merchants and farmers. But Welch had obviously detected an unsettling quality in Mallory's charges; in his response, he offered the hope that "you do not mean . . . to advance your Popularity by impeaching the Conduct of the Judge of this District, and his Clerk." Such a course, he suggested, would be inconsistent with the conduct of the "Religious, the Humane Capt. Mallory."

Surveyor General Smith was the dominant influence in the area. His decision not to seek re-election to the House of Assembly opened the way for a formal political challenge to the office-holding élite. Mallory and Ryerse contested the riding of Norfolk, Oxford and Middlesex. In May 1804 Selkirk commented, "Electioneering seems here to go on with no small sharpness – his [Mallory's] adversaries threw out some allegations to which he replied by the Lie direct – and he alledges they pursued him with a view to assassinate." Mallory's victory, 166 votes to 77, only exacerbated factional strife, which soon erupted in the Court of Quarter Sessions. After shots had been fired into his home in January 1805, Mallory claimed the attempted assassination to be the work of Ryerse or John Backhouse, a justice of the peace; Ryerse, in turn, implied that Mallory had had the shooting staged. The affair degenerated into a skein of charge and countercharge, which spilled over from quarter sessions into the Court of Kings Bench, where ultimately the affair came to naught.

The unruliness of local life developed from concrete criticisms of the administration of the district's courts. In a small society, concern about such issues quickly acquired a personal dimension. When factionalism escalated into the political arena, the lines of division broadened. Thomas Welch denounced the Mallory-led group as seditious – Methodists bent on subverting "good Order." He noted that one of them had announced that Upper Canada would become "a very good Country after we have adriven out of it all the old Tories and Half Pay officers, and have a new Constitution like that of the United States."

Mallory's initial impact on the assembly was negligible; he was, at best, a secondary figure. His support of William Weekes*'s motion of 1 March 1805 to consider "the disquietude which prevails . . . by reason of the administration of Public Offices" indicated his attraction to the fragmentary opposition in parliament. In the session of 1806 he brought up a petition for the relief of Methodists in their want of full enjoyment of civil and religious rights. More important to him was Ryerse's charge that he had been "illegally and unduly returned," being "a preacher and teacher of the Religious Society or Sect called Methodists." In 1807 the charge was dismissed by the assembly for want of evidence: Ryerse had simply been unable to marshal his witnesses in York (Toronto). Some, however, such as Richard Cartwright, who was then a legislative councillor, claimed the charge was true.

Mallory had finally become a justice of the peace in December 1806; he was, as well, a captain in the 1st Oxford Militia. But he was identified with political opposition and symbolized the political beliefs frequently associated with the American settlers, whom Lieutenant Governor Francis GORE described as retaining "those ideas of equality & insubordination much to the prejudice of this Government." Welch claimed that nine out of ten settlers in Oxford County were Americans. The *Chesapeake* affair of 1807 [see Sir George Cranfield Berkeley*] led him to believe that, in the event of war with the United States, these people would become "internal enemies" and were therefore "very much to be dreaded." When in 1808 leadership of the opposition within the assembly passed to Joseph Willcocks*, Mallory became much more active in the day-to-day activities of the house and increasingly supported Willcocks's initiatives. He disagreed with Willcocks, however, on such issues as the bill to give salaries to judges in the Court of Common Pleas, which, although favourites of the opposition, were unpopular in the London District. Mallory was the sole opponent of an amendment to the District School Act because the "inhabitants were much dissatisfied with the law as it now stood."

In 1808 he was re-elected for Oxford and Middlesex. Throughout the fifth parliament (1809–

Mallory

12) the opposition became more cohesive. By 1811 Mallory was, with John WILLSON, one of Willcocks's foremost supporters. They worked together on a range of measures popular with the opposition; they unsuccessfully attempted, for example, to pass a bill restraining sheriffs from packing juries and another preventing government officials from sitting in the assembly. They cooperated too in adopting potentially popular positions on other measures: they opposed the bill to relieve creditors with absconding debtors, voted to reconsider the state of loyalist and military grants, and opposed changes to the Militia Act of 1793. On the one hand, it seems probable that Mallory was politicized by his career as an assemblyman. On the other, he himself felt harassed by members of a vindictive provincial administration. On 15 Jan. 1807 Richard Cartwright had won a massive judgement against Mallory for debt – £1,887 17s. 0d. and costs. No doubt the judgement had an effect on Mallory, for the following year he sought a lease of Six Nations land where he had discovered iron ore and planned to build an ironworks. He eventually leased about 1,460 acres, but nothing was erected. In 1810–11 he lost three cases involving debts, one for a staggering £1,000 and costs, and two parcels of his land were seized and sold to pay his debt to Cartwright. He was referred to in one case as "late of Burford, now a merchant and farmer." In 1810 he was acquitted of assaulting a sheriff. Mallory later claimed it had cost him "near" $2,000 just to defend himself; financially, he was ruined.

The greatest success of the opposition in the assembly occurred in early 1812 when Administrator Isaac Brock* attempted to put the province on a war footing. The resistance to changes in the Militia Act (notably the opposition's refusal to see an oath of abjuration incorporated in the act) was attributed to Willcocks and Mallory. Robert Nichol* reported in March 1812 that their efforts "to create apprehensions respecting the intended operation of the Militia Bill" had produced much alarm among young men at the head of Lake Ontario. A frustrated Brock dissolved parliament in May, hoping to secure, as Archibald McLean* put it, a new assembly "composed of well informed Men who are well *affected* to the Government."

The old élite had withered in the face of popular opposition. In the ensuing election Mallory was opposed by Mahlon Burwell*, a close associate of Thomas TALBOT, whose base of power was rooted in what amounted to a personal fiefdom. This alliance was determined to bring Mallory to heel. Years later Asahel Bradley Lewis* alleged that the hustings for Oxford and Middlesex in 1812 had been located in "an *entire wilderness*. So that Mallory and his friends were obliged to travel nearly 60 miles through the woods, to the poll, – there they found the '*Father of*

the Settlement' [Talbot], providing votes for his favourite . . . by furnishing all who were willing to support the claims of the Young Aspirant to office, and who were not already qualified – with LOCATION TICKETS." Mallory derided this tactic as "the most blackest and unConstitutional Designs" and urged electors to "Repell oppression accompanied with tyreney." His effort, however, proved futile and Burwell was returned.

Disaffection and treason are among the major themes of the War of 1812 and its effect upon Upper Canada. The population was overwhelmingly non-loyalist American; most, probably, were indifferent to the outcome. Some, such as Michael Smith*, returned to the United States while others, Ebenezer Allan* and Andrew Westbrook* among them, were immediately seditious; a few, such as Elijah Bentley*, sought the most propitious moment to declare their real loyalty. But the most sensational cases – Willcocks, Mallory, and Abraham Markle* – fall into none of these categories. Each man had had a record of political opposition, but only in the summer of 1813 did any one of the three become actively disloyal. Their treason then has to be understood in the light of changes taking place within the province at that time rather than by interpreting treason as the logical outcome of persistent opposition. Brock had used both Willcocks and Mallory as emissaries to the Six Nations; moreover, Willcocks had served at the battle of Queenston Heights in 1812. In 1829 Francis Collins* referred in the *Canadian Freeman* to a statement made in the assembly by Robert Nichol that Willcocks had been "forced from his allegiance by a vile conspiracy against his life." Collins reported that this "assertion was supposed by many" to mean the actions of Judge William Dummer Powell*. Like Willcocks and Markle, Mallory could argue that he too had been persecuted, but by none other than Nichol. At some point early in 1812 Mallory protested to Brock that "many caluminous reports has been advanced to you by a mr Robert Nicol and Some of his Coagiters loath against my Private and Public Character." The reports had accused him of disloyalty, of attending "Public Meetings for bad Purposes," and of having been prosecuted. Mallory denounced the charge of disloyalty but admitted that he had indeed been prosecuted. To him, however, the court actions, both civil and criminal, were tangible evidence of a persecution that had begun after his election in 1804. His public record as a magistrate and militia officer could not be impugned. He had, he said, encouraged the militia to adhere to the crown and offered to lead them "to Repel the Ravages or intrusion of an invading Enemy." But he was never given the chance. As concern for maintaining the rule of law withered before the civil élite's fear of disorder after the American occupation of York in the spring of

1813, the three leaders of opposition, one by one, crossed the border.

Willcocks went over to the Americans in July 1813 and offered to raise a corps of expatriate Canadian volunteers "to assist in changing the government of this province into a Republic." Mallory may have had some prior commitment to republicanism. Certainly what had begun 10 years previously as reaction to executive maladministration of government, when combined with his perception of military despotism in the summer of 1813, made him draw upon the only rhetoric of opposition that he knew, republicanism. Such language entailed a fundamental clash with the polity of Upper Canada.

Mallory's formal enlistment as a captain in the Company of Canadian Volunteers dates from 14 November; the same day he was reported to have been seen by Major William D. Bowen with a party recruiting on the Grand River. Following the burning of Niagara (Niagara-on-the-Lake) by the Americans and their retreat to Fort Niagara (near Youngstown), N.Y., Mallory was given command at Fort Schlosser (Niagara Falls), N.Y. In late December his detachment fought a spirited rearguard action against British troops advancing south after taking Fort Niagara. Mallory's men again distinguished themselves at Black Rock (Buffalo) as the British continued their drive towards Buffalo.

Mallory was outraged by the United States Army's obstruction of local generals and its resistance to establishing Willcocks's corps as a permanent force. In spite of the opposition of superiors, he continued to recruit and paid his men from his own resources. Finally, as a result of Willcocks's lobbying in Washington, the Volunteers were put on a permanent footing and on 19 April 1814 Mallory was promoted major. During the following summer the unit saw action at the battles of Chippawa and Lundy's Lane. In mid July Mallory barely escaped capture near Beaver Dams (Thorold). Despite their effectiveness, the Volunteers were disintegrating; on 24 August Mallory sought a transfer because of a lack of recruits and a surplus of officers. He hoped to remain on the Niagara frontier where, he explained to John Armstrong, the American secretary of war, "I have no Doubt from the Knowledge I Possess of the Country . . . I can be more usefull." Mallory urged a more aggressive military stance and the raising of 10,000 or 15,000 militia commanded by a "few Patriots." He was convinced that Americans now saw the "necessity of Exterminating British and Savage tyranny from the Demain of Canada I am Sattisfied our effort will be the Last Struggle of the British in Canada."

A transfer, however, was not forthcoming. Willcocks died in September and command devolved upon Mallory. He argued in vain for more arms and supplies. The Volunteers were hobbled by desertion and squabbling among the officers. On 15 November Markle and William Biggar, an ensign in the Volunteers and possibly Markle's son-in-law, charged Mallory with embezzlement and felonious conduct. He was suspended and Markle took command. Mallory attributed the accusations to "Malevolence and black Designs Proceeding from a black heart." The corps was disbanded on 3 March 1815 although Mallory continued to serve in the army in some capacity until 31 July.

In Upper Canada, Mallory had been convicted of treason at Ancaster in 1814 [*see* Jacob Overholser*] and his lands were later vested in the crown. He had sacrificed, as he put it, "both family & property." According to Joel Stone*, his mother-in-law's second husband, Mallory had joined the Americans "without the Knowledge or assent of his wife who was left in Canada with a family of five children." She remained "sincere – as to her Congugal vows" and later "followed him when Sent for." Mallory eventually settled in Lockport. On 1 Jan. 1829 a notice in York in the *Canadian Freeman* reported that he "has since figured in the Newspapers of his country as an adept in the art of converting the property of others to his own use, for which accomplishment he has been honoured with lodgings in a State Prison." A letter of 28 March 1832 in the *Western Mercury* reported that Mallory, "one of the basest of the human race," was "now lingering out his wretched existence in prison." His wife remained with him throughout, struggling to support their family, "until she found that her said Husband . . . was," according to Joel Stone, "if possible more criminally traitorous to herself than he had been . . . capable of being to both Governments." She renounced him and returned to Upper Canada with her two youngest daughters to live with Stone and her mother in Gananoque. Early in January 1838 Mallory offered his services to William Lyon Mackenzie* and "the brave Patriots" on Navy Island. He drew a parallel between the traitors of 1813 and the rebels of 1837: he "had once Suffred from my takeing the Same Stand In the british Parliament in opposing dispotic tyrants." Mallory later remarried and was baptized in Lockport in July 1853. He died there a month later.

ROBERT LOCHIEL FRASER

AO, MS 75, Thomas Welch to Russell, 31 Jan. 1805; MS 516: 1211–12, 1418–21, 1749–52; MS 522, memorandum respecting the District School Bill, 5 March 1808; MU 500, typescript letter-book, 258–61; MU 1836, no.491; RG 1, A-I-1, 55: 108–9; A-I-6: 2911; RG 4, A-1, box 2, file 30 May 1835; RG 22, ser.131, 1: f.153; 2: ff.7, 13–14; ser.134, 2: 272–73; 3, 13 Sept. 1804, 25 Sept. 1805; 4, 27 Sept. 1810, 19 Sept. 1811; ser.143, box 1, envelope 4 (*King v. Benajah Mallory*, 1814); ser.144, box 1, envelope 7. Brant Land Registry Office (Brantford, Ont.), Burford

Manning

Township, abstract index to deeds, ff.144, 183, 214, 216, 241, 245, 247, 271 (mfm. at AO, GS 1822); abstract of memorials, ff.1, 7–8 (mfm. at AO, GS 1821). Buffalo and Erie County Hist. Soc. (Buffalo, N.Y.), A439 (P. B. Porter papers), Mallory to Porter, 2 Sept. 1814. Conn. Hist. Soc. (Hartford), C. L. N. Camp papers, Mallory family genealogy. Eva Brook Donly Museum (Simcoe, Ont.), Norfolk Hist. Soc. Coll., Thomas Welch papers, 955, 957, 982–83, 1037, 1051, 1055–59, 1068–69, 1949–50 (mfm. at AO). MTL, W. D. Powell papers, B32 (general corr.): 70–71. National Arch. (Washington), RG 94, entry 125; RG 107, B284, I177, M73, W41, 281, 287, 300, 303; War of 1812, bounty land claim, Benajah Mallory; War of 1812, New York, Company of Canadian Volunteers, compiled service record, Benajah Mallory. Niagara County Surrogate Office (Lockport, N.Y.), will of Benajah Mallory, August 1854.

PAC, MG 23, HII, 1, pp.1141–42, 1208–9, 1273–75, 1306–8, 1379–80, 1404–5, 1558–60, 1573–74, 1579–80; MG 24, G3, Samuel Ryerse, letter, 6 Jan. 1803 (photocopy); RG 1, E1, 48: 109–11 (mfm. at AO); E3, 47: 117–23; E14, 10: 95–96; L3, 328: M2/83; RG 5, A1: 846–48, 1299, 1478, 2514–27, 2802–21, 2943–44, 4413, 4658–59, 15313–17, 15383–85, 15516–17, 16431–37, 139820–23; B9, 53, 56; B25, 3: 52; RG 8, I (C ser.), 681: 145; 1703: 83–86; RG 9, I, B1, 1: 408A; RG 68, General index, 1651–1841: 189, 418, 421. *Doc. hist. of campaign upon Niagara frontier* (Cruikshank), 1: 64–71; 4: 12–13; 8: 185; 9: 25, 118. [Thomas Douglas, 5th Earl of] Selkirk, *Lord Selkirk's diary, 1803–1804 ...*, ed. P. C. T. White (Toronto, 1958), 304–5. *Heads of families at the first census of the United States taken in the year 1790: Vermont* (Washington, 1907; repr. Baltimore, Md., 1966), 46. "Journals of Legislative Assembly of U.C.," AO *Report*, 1911; 1912; 1914: 749, 775. *Military minutes of the Council of Appointment of the State of New York, 1783–1821*, comp. Hugh Hastings and H. H. Noble (4v., Albany, N.Y., 1901–2), 1: 217, 337. "Minutes of the Court of General Quarter Sessions of the Peace for the London District ...," AO *Report*, 1933: 29, 32, 37, 60, 68, 70, 74, 76–77, 87, 94, 97, 113. *New England Hist. and Geneal. Reg.* (Boston), 7 (1853): 376. "Political state of Upper Canada in 1806–7," PAC *Report*, 1892: 43, 53, 90–92. *The Talbot papers*, ed. J. H. Coyne (2v., Ottawa, 1908–9), 2: 136–37. U.C., House of Assembly, *Journal*, app., 1830: 157. *Canadian Freeman* ([York] Toronto), 1 Jan. 1829. *Liberal* (St Thomas, [Ont.]), 29 Nov. 1832. *Rochester Daily Advertiser* (Rochester, N.Y.), 12 Aug. 1853. *Rochester Daily Democrat*, 23 July 1853. *Spectator* (St Catharines, [Ont.]), 14 Feb. 1817. *Upper Canada Gazette*, 27 Feb., 4 May 1811. *Western Mercury* (Hamilton, [Ont.]), 28 March, 5 April 1832. *Rolls of the soldiers in the Revolutionary War, 1775 to 1783*, comp. J. E. Goodrich (Rutland, Vt., 1904), 476. L. L. Babcock, *The War of 1812 on the Niagara frontier* (Buffalo, 1927), 126. Brian Dawe, *"Old Oxford is wide awake!" pioneer settlers and politicians in Oxford County, 1793–1853* (n.p., 1980). R. C. Muir, *The early political and military history of Burford* (Quebec, 1913). Patterson, "Studies in elections in U.C." Orasmus Turner, *History of the pioneer settlement of Phelps and Gorham's Purchase, and Morris' Reserve ...* (Rochester, 1851; repr. Geneseo, N.Y., 1976). H. A. Wisbey, *Pioneer prophetess: Jemima Wilkinson, the publick universal friend* (Ithaca, N.Y., 1964), 62–63, 84–85, 88–89, 100–1, 110–12, 116–17, 128–29,

182–83, 222–23. G. E. P. Wood, *A history of the town of Wells, Vermont, from its settlement, with family and biographical sketches and incidents* ([Wells, Vt.], 1955), 6, 17, 67, 88–94, 115–16, 130–31. E. A. Cruikshank, "Notes on the early settlement of Burford," *OH*, 26 (1930): 380–89. D. E. Graves, "The Canadian Volunteers, 1813–1815," *Military Collector & Historian* (Washington), 31 (1979): 113–17. R. C. Muir, "Burford's first settler, politician, and military man – Benajah Mallory," *OH*, 26 (1930): 492–97. W. R. Riddell, "Benajah Mallory, traitor," *OH*, 26: 573–78.

MANNING, EDWARD, Baptist minister; b. 16 Oct. 1766 in Ireland, third son of Peter Manning and Nancy Carroll; m. 25 June 1801 Rebecca Skinner, and they had three daughters; d. 12 Jan. 1851 in Upper Canard, N.S.

The family of Peter Manning came to Nova Scotia in 1769 or 1770 either directly from Ireland or, according to family tradition, after a stay in Philadelphia. The 1770 census lists him as a resident of Falmouth Township, at the head of a family numbering nine. Although born Roman Catholic, all the Mannings appear to have become at least nominal Protestants by the 1770s. In 1776 Peter Manning murdered a neighbour, the stepfather of the Reverend John Payzant*. For his crime he was tried, convicted, and hanged.

Little is known of the Manning family's life in the Falmouth area after the tragedy. Edward grew into a tall (6 feet 4 inches) and very strong young man, a good farmer, and an excellent woodsman; at the age of 16, armed only with a hatchet, he killed three bears. According to his own later account, he led a "riotous," wicked life, although it was probably a fairly normal one for the times.

The Great Awakening, begun in 1776 and led by another Falmouth resident, the charismatic preacher Henry Alline*, had a tremendous impact on Manning. For the rest of his life he retained a vivid picture of Alline, with tears flowing, begging him to flee from the wrath to come. It was not until 27 April 1789, however, that Manning was finally converted, through the ministry of Payzant. Clearly the single most important event of his life, his conversion was an intense experience that came at the culmination of a period of great anguish and would shape his entire future.

Shortly after his conversion, Manning joined Payzant's New Light Congregational church in Cornwallis and soon felt the "call" to preach to his fellow Nova Scotians. Although possessing little formal education, Manning began to itinerate in the Allinite tradition in 1789, preaching his first sermon in February 1790 at Onslow. He became part of a dynamic group of young men who had been "awakened" in the revivals that had swept the Maritime colonies since 1776. Over the next 20 years

610

they would do much to transform the religious life of the region. In the New England planter communities already stirred by Alline and in the newly settled and unstable loyalist areas, Manning, his brother James, Harris HARDING, Joseph Dimock*, Thomas Handley Chipman, and others carried revival to new heights – and extremes.

The move toward antinomianism was perhaps a logical development for some of these new religious leaders and their enthusiastic followers. Cornwallis, an area of early support for the Great Awakening, became the centre of the "new dispensation" movement, which insisted that the "new birth" was the means by which God spoke directly to mankind, thus placing the convert beyond church rules, ministerial leadership, or even scriptural injunctions. In 1791 this extreme position, championed by the Mannings, Harding, and Lydia Randall, split the Cornwallis church, and its influence spread rapidly outward from there. The following year, according to a distraught Payzant, the Manning brothers "came to the Church meeting, and began to dispute, and condemn the Church Rules, and say that all orders were done away, and that the Bible was a dead letter, and they would preach without it." The chaos and disorder – both doctrinal and social – brought on by this movement, and the uncontrolled excesses to which some of its people went, showed Manning and other would-be leaders that they had unleashed forces they could no longer control. Over the next few years there would be a rapid retreat by Manning from this extremist position. The "new dispensation" interlude greatly influenced the rest of Manning's life, forcing him in later years to seek stability and unity within the confines of a more structured church.

Manning attempted to return to full-time farming in 1792 but could not stay away from preaching. By 1793 he had moved beyond Nova Scotia and preached extensively in New Brunswick, especially in the Saint John River valley, laying the foundations for future Baptist development. There he was arrested for preaching without a licence from the government, but, according to tradition, the case was dismissed because the magistrate was so impressed by Manning's abilities. In his lifetime Manning would see major strides made toward the removal of such restrictions, making a significant contribution in this field himself.

On 19 Oct. 1795 Manning was ordained as pastor of the Cornwallis New Light Congregational Church, an uneasy alliance of "awakened" Congregationalists and Baptists. For the next few years Manning baptized adults and infants, by sprinkling or immersion, according to the wishes of those concerned.

The excesses of the "new dispensation" movement, the erratic and unorthodox behaviour of Harris Harding, and the continuing instability of the evangelical churches in the Maritimes led Payzant and

Manning in 1797 to urge the New Light clergy of Nova Scotia to form an association, its first full meeting taking place the following year. "The necessity of order and discipline" continued to be uppermost in the minds of the clergy, if not of their congregations, forcing them to consider a more formal organization by 1799. The late 1790s also saw an important movement toward the Baptist position of believer's baptism by immersion. Manning was convinced of the correctness of this stand and was himself baptized by immersion in 1798, although he continued to minister to his mixed congregation.

In 1800, at a meeting at Lower Granville, the association was transformed into the Nova Scotia Baptist Association, organized on the "mixed communion" plan. Although Manning is generally credited with engineering the move, it was actually Chipman who organized it, being opposed by Manning, who felt it dealt unfairly with their New Light–Congregational brethren, especially Payzant. Over the next few years, however, most of the New Light Congregational churches in Nova Scotia were transformed into Baptist churches. In a similar manner, most of the New Light clergy not only accepted the Baptist mode of adult baptism by immersion but also shifted their doctrinal stance away from the free-will approach of Alline and back to the Calvinism of their Congregational forerunners.

The difficulties of leading a church composed of both Baptists and Congregationalists became painfully apparent to Manning soon after 1800. In 1807 the rupture finally came and Manning, his wife, and seven followers left the Cornwallis New Light Congregational church and formed a separate Baptist church; Manning was ordained as a Baptist preacher the following year. Over the next few years the New Light Congregational church was virtually destroyed as more and more of its adherents left to join the dissidents.

It is not clear from the church records whether Manning was forced out or left of his own accord. It was perhaps no coincidence that his departure coincided with his acquisition of "some share of worldly property" (from an unspecified source) which enabled him to purchase his own farm and to be more or less financially independent for the rest of his life. He could now follow the dictates of his conscience without having to rely on the support of a large congregation. Whatever the cause or the occasion, Manning would remain, with one brief interruption, the pastor of the First Cornwallis Baptist Church until his death in 1851.

Manning served as pastor of a very large area – all of Cornwallis Township, Kings County. From his home in Upper Canard, he attempted to minister to an expanding population, mainly of New England origin. In spite of the claims of later Baptist historians, the

Manning

church records and Manning's own extensive diary make it clear that the relationship between congregation and pastor was often a rocky one. Manning himself created some of the difficulties through his inability to leave behind completely his itinerant beginnings. In addition, it clearly took far longer than has previously been assumed for the church to accept fully a settled minister and Baptist doctrine. Manning's years as pastor were tension filled, acrimonious, and at times debilitating, for both pastor and congregation.

Throughout his long ministry his congregation never managed to pay him an adequate salary, a problem common in most Maritime Baptist churches of this period. Although people frequently gave gifts to their pastor – usually in kind (turnips, a sack of grain, a load of wood), rarely in money – there was no organized attempt to provide for Manning's support. Forced at various times to farm on an occasional basis, to teach school, and to sell books, he was thus often prevented from devoting his entire time and energy to the spiritual welfare of his people.

More serious was the difficulty Manning had with his people over matters of doctrine. He himself, through his extensive study and fine intellect, had a clear understanding of Baptist doctrine. There is no indication that this understanding was shared by most of those who joined his church over the many years of his ministry. Whenever a popular speaker, of whatever doctrinal stripe, passed through the township, Manning's people flocked to hear him. At one stage he complained about "this flood of false fire, and doctrine that is prevailing among the people." Free-will preachers were especially welcomed, even by Manning's own deacons, suggesting that Alline's doctrinal impact was perhaps greater and longer lasting than has been generally recognized.

In later life Manning wrote that he had spent 35 years attempting "to protect the people from the various kinds of doctrine, and the cunning craftiness of subtle, and designing men." His frequent lack of success underscored the doctrinal confusion that persisted in the Baptist denomination long after its founding. The willingness of the Cornwallis people to follow new leaders – both Baptist and non-Baptist – and the frequency with which this took place, especially during Manning's absences or illnesses, would seem to indicate that at heart the people were not interested in doctrine at all. They were Baptists because Manning had given them forceful, dynamic leadership, and he was a Baptist. It was a commitment based on personality, not conviction. If he were not constantly on the spot, they would follow someone else, Baptist or non-Baptist, Calvinist or not. It is no wonder that, in drawing up a list of the things that bothered him about his people, he included as the fifth

and sixth items: "a neglect of reading the Scriptures and other good books, so they don't know when the truth is preached and when not" and "an itching of ears to hear strange preachers."

It was this instability within his own church, coupled with the lessons taught by the unfettered enthusiasm of the "new dispensation" movement, that led Manning to seek greater stability for the entire denomination. In this effort are to be found his greatest contributions to the growth and evolution of the Baptist movement. Nowhere is the influence more evident than in the field of education.

Although Manning possessed only minimal formal education himself, he clearly had a keen, incisive mind and was by no means an ignorant man. For his entire life his reading was both extensive and catholic. As the denomination grew and the number of ministers increased, he became more and more concerned that doctrinal diversity would tear the denomination apart. Education, he felt, was the key to unity for the denomination and to greater usefulness for the emerging clergy. He was really in the forefront of the movement that was transforming Maritime society in the first half of the 19th century. The move from the anti-intellectualism of the Great Awakening and its aftermath to the new zeal for education was not an easy or a rapid one, but the change was indeed being made. His interest in, and efforts on behalf of, education as early as 1819 led to an offer for him to move to Waterville (Maine), where he was to have helped with the development of Colby College, the Baptist college there.

In 1828 the steady influence of Edward Manning combined with the driving enthusiasm of Halifax Baptists such as Edmund Albern Crawley* and John Pryor* to force a rather surprised Nova Scotia Baptist Association to agree to the founding of a Baptist school as the first step toward providing potential Baptist leaders with the education that Manning so keenly felt they needed. He was elected president of the newly created Nova Scotia Baptist Education Society, a position he was to occupy for the rest of his life. The founding in Wolfville of Horton Academy, a boys' school that from the beginning was to be open to all denominations, followed immediately. On 15 July 1830 Manning proudly laid the cornerstone of the new academy building (Horton Academy remained in operation until 1959).

In 1838, in reaction to the exclusive nature of both King's College, Windsor, and Dalhousie College, Halifax, the education society, presided over by Manning, voted to proceed to the next step – a college. By January 1839 classes at Queen's (after 1841 Acadia) College had begun. On 16 July 1843 Manning, with his few years of formal education, presided over the first graduation exercises, for a class numbering four. He lived long enough to witness the very real impact that Horton Academy and Acadia College were to have on the denomination as a whole. Through his influence over younger clergymen, and his role in the establishment of Horton and Acadia, he contributed more than anyone else to the creation of a Maritime Baptist orthodoxy.

Manning was also keenly interested in strengthening the denomination by seeking the removal of some of the legal disabilities under which dissenters laboured in the Maritime colonies. The right to perform marriages by licence and the right to incorporate were two important "rights" sought by Manning and others. Beginning in 1819 he worked in concert with other Baptists, and with the Presbyterians led by Thomas McCulloch*, in an effort to secure equality with the Church of England, an aim finally achieved within his own lifetime.

Another contribution to the denomination made by Manning, with perhaps mixed results, was the successful wooing of a number of dissidents in Halifax's St Paul's Church (Anglican) in the mid 1820s. It was Manning, through his niece's husband, John Ferguson, who more than anyone else drew that significant group into the Baptist fold. James William Johnston*, Edmund Crawley, John Pryor, and others would add a new and at times discordant dimension to the denomination, with far-reaching implications, politically, socially, theologically, and educationally.

With Charles Tupper*, Manning was one of the first of the Baptist ministers to sense the significance of the temperance movement as it swept into the Maritime region from Maine in 1829. Immediately convinced of the correctness of the abstinence position, he led in forming a temperance society in Cornwallis and helped articulate the stand that became a virtual article of faith for many Baptist churches for nearly a century and a half.

He was also the first Baptist leader to take a conspicuous interest in the history of the denomination. As early as 1812 he wrote a short account of the Baptists in the Maritimes in response to questions sent him by the Reverend David Benedict of Rhode Island, who wished to publish a history of the Baptists in North America. It was probably his awareness of history that caused him to retain so carefully his voluminous correspondence and to keep so meticulous a diary, which together form the basis for any present-day understanding of the denomination in that period.

Manning also gave leadership in the move towards active participation in foreign missions. In 1814 he expressed his concerns for the "heathen in foreign lands" in a circular letter to the churches of the Baptist association, the first important plea for Baptist involvement in foreign missions. In this he was greatly influenced by his reading of American and British Baptist periodicals. He returned to this theme time after time, clearly wishing that he himself could go. His efforts led to the sending of the first Baptist missionary, Richard E. BURPEE, to Burma in 1845, the beginning of more than 140 years of involvement in foreign missions.

In the same important circular letter, Manning also expressed great concern for home missions. It would be at least partly through his influence and efforts that the denomination spread so rapidly in the Maritime region in the first half of the 19th century. As well as encouraging others, he himself travelled throughout the Maritime region and into Maine, founding new churches and reviving old ones. In addition to actual visits, he extended his authority throughout the Maritimes by a vigorous correspondence. When individuals or churches experienced difficulties, it was to Manning that they turned. It was he as well who kept the association in touch with Baptist development in the United States. In all of these matters, he sought to chart a moderate course for the denomination, avoiding what he saw as the twin dangers of excessive enthusiasm on the one hand and "dead formalism" on the other. Such stability as the denomination possessed by the mid 19th century was due in no small measure to Edward Manning.

It is ironic that he had more success in leading the denomination than he had with his own church or family. The Cornwallis church gave him endless trouble and his family was little better. Manning's wife, obviously disliking his frequent absences, became "ill" about 1815, suffering almost constantly from "palpitations of the heart" and "the glooms," as Manning called her afflictions. Mrs Manning was, however, still well enough 36 years later to walk in her husband's funeral procession. The constant fear of his wife's imminent death, the lingering deaths of two of his three daughters, and the frequent illnesses that he had to contend with as pastor caused him to become morbidly concerned with his own health. His diary is filled with references to his physical condition and his expected death. At times his own poor health (real or imagined) and that of his wife seriously hampered his effectiveness as pastor and denominational leader.

Manning's death in early 1851 marked the end of the formative years of Baptist development. The men of his generation had seen the movement in the Maritimes emerge out of the confusion and uncertainty following the Great Awakening and the American revolution to the position of a large and stable denomination. No one contributed more to that development than did Manning. The Baptist *Christian Messenger* paid tribute to this remarkable leader in the letters, articles, and editorials on news of his death. The final acknowledgement of his stature came when

Marchand

this paper, pointing out that "the history of his life is the history of the rise and progress of the Baptist interest in these Provinces," reported that no one was willing to take on the awesome task of writing the usual "memoir" of his life.

BARRY M. MOODY

An oil portrait of Edward Manning hangs in University Hall at Acadia (Wolfville, N.S.).

ABHC, Bennett coll.; Cornwallis, N.S., Congregational (Newlight) Church, records; Edward Manning, corr., journals, and "Reminiscences of his conversion"; N.S. Baptist Education Soc., papers; Upper Canard, N.S., Cornwallis First United Baptist Church, records. Kings County Court of Probate (Kentville, N.S.), M21 (will and inventory of estate of Edward Manning). Kings County Registry of Deeds (Kentville), Book 5: 260. Henry Alline, *The life and journal of the Rev. Mr. Henry Alline*, ed. James Beverley and B. [M.] Moody (Hantsport, 1982). *Baptist Missionary Magazine of Nova-Scotia and New-Brunswick* (Saint John and Halifax), 1 (1827–29)–3 (1833); new ser., 1 (1834)–3 (1836). N.B. Baptist Assoc., *Minutes* (Saint John; Fredericton), 1822–46. *The New Light letters and spiritual songs, 1778–1793*, ed. G. A. Rawlyk (Hantsport, N.S., 1983). N.S. and N.B. Baptist Assoc., *Minutes* (Halifax; Saint John), 1810–21. N.S. Baptist Assoc., *Minutes* (Halifax), 1822–46. N.S. Baptist Education Soc., *Report* (Halifax), 1832–51. John Payzant, *The journal of the Reverend John Payzant (1749–1834)*, ed. B. C. Cuthbertson (Hantsport, 1981). *Christian Messenger* (Halifax), 1837–51.

The Acadia record, 1838–1953, comp. Watson Kirkconnell (4th ed., Wolfville, 1953). M. W. Armstrong, *The great awakening in Nova Scotia, 1776–1809* (Hartford, Conn., 1948). Bill, *Fifty years with Baptist ministers.* J. M. Bumsted, *Henry Alline, 1748–1784* (Toronto, 1971). J. V. Duncanson, *Falmouth – a New England township in Nova Scotia, 1760–1965* (Windsor, Ont., 1965; repr., with suppl., Belleville, Ont., 1983). Eaton, *Hist. of King's County.* E. L. Eaton, "The Sheffield farm and other properties in Cornwallis Township" (typescript, 1961; copies at Acadia Univ. Library and PANS). Levy, *Baptists of Maritime prov.* R. S. Longley, *Acadia University, 1838–1938* (Wolfville, 1939). B. M. Moody, "Joseph Howe, the Baptists, and the college question," *The proceedings of the Joseph Howe Symposium, Mount Allison University*, ed. Wayne Hunt (Sackville, N.B., and Halifax, 1984). *Repent and believe: the Baptist experience in Maritime Canada*, ed. B. M. Moody (Hantsport, 1980). E. M. Saunders, *History of the Baptists of the Maritime provinces* (Halifax, 1902). B. [M.] Moody, "From itinerant to pastor: the case of Edward Manning (1767–1851)," Canadian Soc. of Church Hist., *Papers* (Montreal), 1981: 1–25. G. A. Rawlyk, "New Lights, Baptists and religious awakenings in Nova Scotia, 1776–1843," CCHS *Journal*, 25 (1983): 43–73.

MARCHAND, GABRIEL, merchant, militia officer, politician, justice of the peace, and office holder; b. 21 Nov. 1780 at Quebec, son of Louis Marchand, a ship's captain, and Françoise Roussel; d. 10 March 1852 in Saint-Jean (Saint-Jean-sur-Richelieu), Lower Canada.

Gabriel Marchand was a descendant of Jean Marchand, a native of Saint-Sauveur-le-Vicomte, near La Rochelle, France, who had taken up residence at Quebec under the French régime. During the siege of Quebec in 1759 his grandfather Nicolas Marchand served as a militia officer in the artillery and died after being struck by a cannon-ball. His father, who was well known at Quebec, was the captain of an ocean-going vessel and for many years sailed the high seas.

Following a year of study at the Petit Séminaire de Québec in 1790–91, Gabriel became a clerk in the large import firm of John Macnider*, on Rue de la Fabrique at Quebec. A man of initiative, he quickly rose to the position of manager. In 1803 he went into partnership with his employer and François-Xavier Durette to set up a business at St Johns (Saint-Jean-sur-Richelieu) under the name Gabriel Marchand et Cie. The same year he moved there and opened an office and warehouses for lumber which was shipped from Lake Champlain down the Rivière Richelieu to Quebec. Macnider, Durette, and Marchand decided to terminate their partnership in 1806, and Marchand continued to do business on his own account. He thus became one of the earliest merchants at Dorchester (as St Johns was now known) and a pioneer of the timber trade in the Richelieu region.

On 1 Jan. 1807, at Dorchester, Marchand married Amanda Bingham, the daughter of Abner Bingham, a loyalist from Hero Island (North Hero), near Plattsburgh, N.Y.; they had a daughter who died when she was just a month old. After his wife's death in 1809, Marchand married Mary Macnider, the daughter of his former employer, on 6 Oct. 1810 in the Cathedral of the Holy Trinity at Quebec; the couple were to have six children.

During the War of 1812 Marchand served as major and second in command in the 2nd Battalion of Beloeil militia. In 1816, two years after hostilities had ended, his two brothers, François and Louis, came to join him at Dorchester. Gabriel's business had expanded markedly and he had amassed a handsome fortune as a result of the heavy run on timber for shipbuilding, particularly during the years 1812–14. So he made over his business to François and retired to the countryside near Dorchester, to a fine farm on the banks of the Richelieu which he had bought and called Beauchamps. There he divided his leisure "between superintending his fields and a short walk he took every day to Saint-Jean" to keep an eye on the interests and progress of the village.

During the 1820s Marchand joined his brothers and other citizens of Dorchester in proposing that the parish of Saint-Jean-l'Évangéliste be created. He made every effort to secure a priest and collect money to build the church. With this goal in mind, on 21 Dec. 1826 he had been elected a trustee for its construction. The church building was finally opened in 1828, and that year Rémi GAULIN was appointed the first parish priest. The parish began to take shape with the initial organizational step of electing its first three church-wardens on 16 Nov. 1828. Surprisingly, Gabriel Marchand was not on the first council of the *fabrique*. Perhaps he was too modest and declined the honour. In any case, he was elected churchwarden at the end of 1833 and the following year was appointed secretary-treasurer of the parish, retaining these offices until 1837.

At the time of the rebellion, Marchand came out in favour of the Patriote cause. On 5 Nov. 1837 he participated in the meeting at Saint-Athanase (Iberville), proposing 24 reform resolutions that were passed. However, when the Patriotes decided to take up arms he declined to join them. To make clear his opposition to government policy, Marchand decided to refuse the post of legislative councillor to which he had been appointed on 22 Aug. 1837, as well as Governor Sir John Colborne*'s invitation on 31 March 1838 to join the Special Council.

In 1840 the government of Lower Canada created district municipalities, and on 23 Aug. 1841 Marchand was named to represent the parish of Saint-Jean-l'Évangéliste on the municipal council of the district of Saint-Jean. This body brought together representatives of some 20 localities in the Richelieu valley. Marchand carried out his duties as councillor with devotion and diligence until his term expired on 8 Jan. 1844.

Marchand was interested in the advancement of agriculture. In July 1845 he set up at Dorchester the Saint-Jean, Saint-Luc, and L'Acadie section of the Chambly County Agriculture Society, of which he was president until February 1847. He also took an interest in education, and was appointed chairman of the Saint-Jean-l'Évangéliste municipal school board, a post he retained until his death. In this capacity he helped found the Académie de Saint-Jean, which was incorporated in 1850.

According to his contemporaries, Marchand was a man whose "noble [yet] unassuming appearance inspired respect in all who saw him and conversed with him; and his manner and conversation had a remarkable urbanity that made his company extremely attractive." His personality could not but win him the confidence of the authorities who had appointed him to numerous public offices: justice of the peace in the district of Montreal (1815 and 1830), commissioner for receiving the oaths of public accountants (1823), for improving the road between Dorchester and La Prairie and for building the Chambly canal (1829), for macadamizing the La Prairie road and for receiving the oaths of certain public servants (1830), and for

administering the oath of allegiance (1837). A lieutenant-colonel of the 2nd Battalion of Belœil militia in 1827, Marchand was promoted colonel of the 3rd Battalion of Rouville militia three years later. On 1 July 1831 he resigned as colonel and as justice of the peace for the district of Montreal, because he was disgusted and insulted by the refusal of the governor, Lord Aylmer [Whitworth-Aylmer*], to appoint as magistrates the persons he had recommended in response to Aylmer's express request.

Gabriel Marchand died suddenly from an attack of apoplexy on 10 March 1852 at Saint-Jean. His unexpected death created a great stir in the small town, according to the obituary in *La Minerve*: "All Saint-Jean is grief-stricken because it has just lost one of those worthy and esteemed citizens who invariably leave behind them a void difficult to fill; and the parish in gratitude also recalls that it owes the benefit of existing as a parish and possessing a church largely to the efforts, perseverance, and particular sacrifices of the one it mourns." Marchand left his wife, who died three years later, and two sons, one of whom, Félix-Gabriel*, became premier of Quebec.

LIONEL FORTIN

ANQ-M, CE4-10, 15 mars 1852. ANQ-Q, CE1-1, 15 sept. 1778, 22 nov. 1780; CE1-61, 6 oct. 1810; CN1-262, 11 nov. 1806; P-174. AP, Saint-Jean-l'Évangéliste (Saint-Jean-sur-Richelieu), livre des délibérations de la fabrique, 25 déc. 1833, 4 mai 1834, 25 déc. 1836, mars 1837. Arch. du diocèse de Saint-Jean-de-Québec (Longueuil, Qué.), 14A/47, 112, 156. ASQ, Fichier des anciens. PAC, MG 30, D1, 20: 277–80; RG 4, B36, 5: 1500–611; RG 68, 4: 187–89; 7: 467–68; 10: 363–65; 11: 32–37, 228–29, 394–404; 12: 222–23; 15: 102–6; General index, 1651–1841: 199, 202, 213, 282–83, 285, 369, 638. Can., Prov. of, *Statutes*, 1844–45, c.53; 1850, c.124. *La Minerve*, 9 nov. 1837, 19 mars 1852. F.-J. Audet, "Les législateurs du Bas-Canada." *Officers of British forces in Canada* (Irving), 188. P.-G. Roy, *Fils de Québec*, 3: 5–7. Turcotte, *Le Conseil législatif*, 128–29. J.-D. Brosseau, *Saint-Jean-de-Québec; origine et développements* (Saint-Jean[-sur-Richelieu], 1937), 165–205. J.-J. Lefebvre, *Félix-Gabriel Marchand (1832–1900) notaire, 1855, premier ministre du Québec, 1897* (Montréal, 1978), 7–8, 29–30. J.-Y. Théberge, "Saint-Jean, 1848–1973: 125e anniversaire de l'érection du village" (typescript, [Saint-Jean-sur-Richelieu], 1973), 35. "La famille Marchand," *BRH*, 40 (1934): 40–42. "La mort de l'Hon. Félix-G. Marchand," *Le Canada français et le Franco-Canadien* (Saint-Jean-sur-Richelieu), 28 sept. 1900: 1.

MARCHESSEAULT (Marchessault), SIMÉON (baptized **Abraham-Siméon**), teacher, office holder, and Patriote; b. 18 Feb. 1806 in Saint-Ours, Lower Canada, and baptized the same day at Saint-Antoine-sur-Richelieu, son of Abraham-François Marchessaut, a master blacksmith, and Émélie

Marchesseault

Cormier; d. 8 July 1855 in Saint-Hyacinthe, Lower Canada.

Siméon Marchesseault was a descendant of Acadians on both sides of his family. His ancestor Jean Marchesseau had come to Acadia from Saint-Jary, near La Rochelle, France, probably around the beginning of the 18th century. Apparently Jean's grandson Christophe Marchessaut, who was Siméon's grandfather, had settled at Saint-Antoine-sur-Richelieu in the province of Quebec by 1770. Siméon Marchesseault's mother was from a family whose forebear Robert Cormier had begun living at Port-Royal (Annapolis Royal, N.S.) in 1654. Cormier's descendants had been driven from Acadia by the British at the time of the deportation.

According to Laurent-Olivier David* and Ægidius Fauteux*, Siméon Marchesseault reportedly studied for some years at the Petit Séminaire de Montréal but his name is not on the list of students at that institution; it does, however, figure in the record of those at the Collège de Saint-Hyacinthe for the year 1821–22. After his schooling Marchesseault went to work as a teacher at Saint-Denis, on the Richelieu, and then settled in the neighbouring village of Saint-Charles-sur-Richelieu, where he also taught, as did Jean-Philippe Boucher-Belleville*. On 22 Sept. 1829 he married Judith Morin there; they were to have three sons and five daughters. Marchesseault apparently found it difficult to support his family, for by 1837 he had abandoned his trade to assume the office of bailiff to the Court of King's Bench in the district of Montreal.

Intelligent, fervent, and energetic, Marchesseault had lost no time in joining the ranks of Louis-Joseph Papineau* and throwing himself into the constitutional struggle. With the assurance born of his education, experience as a teacher, and gifts as a speaker, he enjoyed a degree of "power over the people," according to David. He became one of the most vigorous defenders of the Patriote cause. In 1834, at a meeting held at Saint-Denis to protest against the Legislative Council's rejection of the 92 Resolutions, he was appointed a member of a committee "to promote the general welfare of the province." Two years later, he took part in the Saint-Jean-Baptiste celebrations in that village, during which a monument was dedicated to Louis Marcoux, a Patriote shot by members of the English party in the election campaign at William Henry (Sorel) in 1834; on this occasion he delivered a speech expressing republican sentiments.

Although he did not belong to a liberal profession, Marchesseault was one of the most influential Patriotes at Saint-Charles-sur-Richelieu in 1837. He attended all the large meetings in Richelieu County before the rebellion, roused the people against the government, and incited them to revolt by his fiery words. At the Saint-Ours meeting on 7 May, after Wolfred Nelson* and Cyrille-Hector-Octave Côté* had spoken, he condemned Lord John Russell's resolutions, terming them a "violation of the social contract," and expressed regret that French Canadians had not sided with the Americans in 1775. On 23 October he received at his home the delegates to the Assemblée des Six Comtés who had come together to draft its stirring resolutions; during the well-known meeting that followed he supported the resolution to create branches of the Fils de la Liberté in the six counties; he himself soon set up one in his village. On 5 November he protested at the doors of the church in Saint-Charles-sur-Richelieu against the first pastoral letter of the bishop of Montreal, Jean-Jacques Lartigue*, which called for obedience and submission to authority, and he urged his compatriots to continue to foment unrest.

When the rebellion broke out, Marchesseault was one of the first to take up arms. On 18 Nov. 1837, with the help of Thomas Storrow Brown*, Henri-Alphonse Gauvin*, and Rodolphe Desrivières*, three Patriote leaders who had come from Montreal to dodge warrants of arrest issued two days earlier, he set up a fortified camp at Saint-Charles-sur-Richelieu. The next day Marchesseault was appointed captain and became an aide-de-camp to General Brown. He took part in the battle at Saint-Denis on 23 November and in the one at Saint-Charles-sur-Richelieu two days later.

In the second battle he distinguished himself by taking over command after Brown left for Saint-Denis. With the energy born of despair he fought alongside some 100 men against three times as many well-trained troops under Lieutenant-Colonel George Augustus Wetherall*. According to Edward Alexander THELLER, he succeeded in bringing down the horse Wetherall was riding. But the camp was soon surrounded, cannon-balls shattered the ramparts, and Marchesseault had to flee to escape certain massacre. He spurred his horse into the midst of the British soldiers, and as he jumped over the fortifications narrowly escaped death from a bullet that penetrated a packet of papers in his jacket pocket. He then made for the village. To avoid being recognized, he mingled with the soldiers who had set fire to his house; through this ruse he managed to enter his dwelling, hunt out important documents, and then run to his stable and rescue his animals from the flames; finally, to evade pursuit by the volunteers he hid in the woods.

On 1 Dec. 1837 Marchesseault set out for the United States with Nelson and a few other Patriotes. But, separated from several of his companions following an alarm, he lost his way in the woods, and on 7 December, along with Boucher-Belleville, Desrivières, Timothée KIMBER, and one or two other comrades who had remained with him, was arrested at Bedford, near the American border. He was imprisoned in Fort Lennox on Île aux Noix, and then transferred on 12 December to the jail at Montreal, with Nelson, Desrivières, Gauvin, and Robert-Shore-Milnes Bouchette*. On 26 June 1838, with seven compatriots, he agreed to sign a confession of guilt in return for the amnesty granted to the other political prisoners. Two days later, by a proclamation issued by Lord Durham [Lambton*], he was condemned to exile. On 4 July he sailed on the frigate *Vestal* for Bermuda, where he arrived on 28 July.

Marchesseault was set free on 26 Oct. 1838 and went to the United States. Upon his arrival on 9 November he made his way towards the Canadian border, and stayed in turn at Swanton, Vt, Champlain, N.Y., and Burlington, Vt. From this last place he wrote to the attorney general, Charles Richard Ogden*, for permission to return to Lower Canada. But Ogden bluntly turned him down, fearing that he would again stir up trouble.

Meanwhile Marchesseault led a wretched existence. To keep body and soul together, he took on all kinds of jobs. At one point he spent a month ironing musk-rat skins at a Swanton fur merchant's establishment. In August 1840 he opened a grocery store with the help of a Burlington merchant who lent him 30 dollars' worth of merchandise, but his business yielded little profit and he soon had to liquidate it. When he had no work he engaged in smuggling; this activity led to his crossing the border into the Richelieu valley, where he was able to meet his family in secret.

In October 1840 Marchesseault was allowed to return permanently to Lower Canada. Soon after, he settled with his wife and children at Saint-Hyacinthe, where he once again carried out the duties of a bailiff. He died there on 8 July 1855, at the age of 49.

It was as a Patriote that Siméon Marchesseault became well known. At the time of the rebellion he had made his mark by his bravery and coolness on the field of battle, and he had displayed his sense of honour by accepting exile. Even though relegated to the ranks of the defeated, he could take pride that he had been one of those unafraid to take up arms in the endeavour to liberate the French Canadian people from British oppression in Lower Canada in 1837.

MICHEL DE LORIMIER

Siméon Marchesseault corresponded on a regular basis with his family and relatives while incarcerated in the Montreal jail, during his exile in Bermuda, and when he was in the United States after his release. Most of his letters are in the Siméon Marchesseault papers which form part of the Collection Montarville Boucher de la Bruère (0032) at the ASTR; these papers also contain his request for compensation for the damages suffered as a result of the burning of his house at Saint-Charles-sur-Richelieu. Two of Marchesseault's letters are held by the ANQ, one to René-Auguste-Richard Hubert, dated 7 Sept. 1838, describing the condition

of the Patriotes exiled to Bermuda (ANQ-M, P1000-34-805), and the other to his wife, dated 6 Dec. 1838 (ANQ-Q, E17/36, no.2873).

Montarville Boucher de La Bruère published several of Marchesseault's letters in "Un héros maskoutain de l'épopée canadienne, 1837–1838: les lettres de Siméon Marchesseault," *Le Clairon* (Saint-Hyacinthe, Qué.), 14 mars 1930: 1, 5, 8. Others were printed in "Documents inédits," Yvon Thériault, édit., *RHAF*, 17 (1963–64): 107–12, 424–32.

ANQ-M, CE1-3, 18 févr. 1806; CE2-1, 11 juill. 1855; CE2-10, 22 sept. 1829; CE3-12, 16 janv. 1804. ANQ-Q, E17/9, nos.345–46, 352, 355; E17/14, no.844; E17/15, no.862; E17/22, nos.1485–86; E17/37, no.2983; E17/40, no.3206a; E17/51, nos.4106, 4137, 4145. BVM-G, Fonds Ægidius Fauteux, notes compilées par Ægidius Fauteux sur les patriotes de 1837–1838 dont les noms commencent par la lettre M, carton 7. PAC, MG 30, D1, 20: 315–19. [L.-J.-]A. Papineau, *Journal d'un Fils de la liberté, réfugié aux États-Unis, par suite de l'insurrection canadienne, en 1837* (2v. parus, Montréal, 1972–   ), 1: 54. E. A. Theller, *Canada in 1837–38* . . . (2v., Philadelphia and New York, 1841). *Le Courrier de Saint-Hyacinthe* (Saint-Hyacinthe), 10 juill. 1855. *La Minerve*, 27 mars 1834; 4 juill. 1836; 11 mai, 30 oct., 13 nov. 1837. Fauteux, *Patriotes*, 313–15. Lefebvre, *Le Canada, l'Amérique*, 187. Allaire, *Hist. de Saint-Denis-sur-Richelieu*, 433. Bona Arsenault, *Histoire et généalogie des Acadiens* (éd. rév., 6v., [Montréal, 1978]). Chaussé, *Jean-Jacques Lartigue*. Choquette, *Hist. du séminaire de Saint-Hyacinthe*, 2; *Histoire de la ville de Saint-Hyacinthe* (Saint-Hyacinthe, 1930), 124, 368. Azarie Couillard-Després, *Histoire de la seigneurie de Saint-Ours* (2v., Montréal, 1915–17), 2: 227. L.-O. David, *Les gerbes canadiennes* (Montréal, 1921), 174; *Patriotes*, 103–4. G.-A. Dejordy, *Généalogies des principales familles du Richelieu* (2v., Arthabaska, Qué., 1927), 2: 106. Filteau, *Hist. des Patriotes* (1975). Labarrère-Paulé, *Les instituteurs laïques*, 48. Laurin, *Girouard & les Patriotes*, 84. Ouellet, *Bas-Canada*. Rumilly, *Papineau et son temps*. Mason Wade, *Les canadiens français, de 1760 à nos jours*, Adrien Venne et Francis Dufau-Labeyrie, trad. (2ᵉ éd., 2v., Ottawa, 1966), 1: 182. L.-O. David, "Les hommes de 37–38: Siméon Marchesseault," *L'Opinion publique* (Montréal), 21 juin 1877: 289.

MARCHILDON, THOMAS, farmer, shipbuilder, and politician; b. 27 Feb. 1805 in Batiscan, Lower Canada, son of Louis Marchildon, a farmer, and Victoire Alexandre; m. there 17 Jan. 1837 Marie-Philie Lefaivre, *dit* Despins; d. there 17 May 1858.

After a brief period in school Thomas Marchildon began farming at Batiscan, taking up what became a lifelong occupation. In partnership with one of his brothers he also ran a shipbuilding yard, which apparently proved profitable. It was his political career, however, that made him known across the province.

Marchildon first stood for election in 1851, on a liberal platform, and defeated his two opponents, Louis Guillet* and Jean-Baptiste-Éric Dorion*. He represented the riding of Champlain in the Legislative Assembly until 23 June 1854. He was re-elected that

Marcoux

summer this time as a Rouge, and he retained his seat until 28 Nov. 1857. In the elections of 1857–58 he was ousted by his first cousin Joseph-Édouard Turcotte*, the former representative for Saint-Maurice and Maskinongé, who won by 890 votes.

Like many other Rouges, Marchildon was strongly opposed to the building of railways and in particular to the construction of the North Shore Railway. In April 1853 *L'Ère nouvelle* reported some of the statements he made in the house. According to Marchildon, "railways are a punishment imposed by God" which "will be the ruin of dairying" and which "serve only to send the cattle stampeding through the fields, [when] there are no fences proof against oxen."

It seems that Marchildon became an object of derision because of the tenor of his words. In fact, his critics, whose ranks included journalists with *L'Ère nouvelle* [*see* Aimé DÉSILETS], spoke of his lack of stability, disordered mind, fanciful notions, and stupid pronouncements. His speeches were dismissed as gibberish. He was accused of using memorized statements and of imitating others. It was even claimed that Joseph-Hilarion Jobin, the member for Joliette, "drafts the resolutions and bills that M. Marchildon prints under his name." The voters of the constituency of Champlain were reproached for bringing shame upon themselves, and French Canadians were implored to stop electing individuals such as Marchildon and Noël Darche, the member for Chambly, if they wanted "to earn the respect of people of different origins." Others, however, credited Marchildon with doing his best to keep his electoral promises and having bridges and roads built.

On 17 May 1858 Marchildon was found drowned in his well. Rumours of suicide circulated widely but the coroner, Valère Guillet, returned a verdict of accidental death. The obituaries in some contemporary newspapers mention that Marchildon was believed to have suffered an attack of apoplexy while watering his livestock and so to have fallen into the well. He was mourned by his wife and nine children.

MIREILLE DUBÉ

ANQ-MBF, CE1-2, 28 févr. 1805, 17 janv. 1837, 19 mai 1858. ASTR, 0368, dossier Thomas Marchildon. PAC, MG 30, D1, 20: 320–34. Can., Prov. of, Legislative Assembly, *Journals*, 1852–55. *Le Courrier du Canada*, 19, 21 mai 1858. *L'Écho du Saint-Maurice* (Trois-Rivières, Qué.), 21 mai 1858. *L'Ère nouvelle* (Trois-Rivières), 17, 20 mai 1858. *Le Journal de Québec*, 16 déc. 1851; 13, 25, 29 juill., 5 août 1854; 10, 17, 26 déc. 1857; 5, 9, 12 janv., 20, 22 mai 1858. *Morning Chronicle*, 22 May 1858. F.-J. Audet, *Les députés de la région des Trois-Rivières (1841–1867)* (Trois-Rivières, 1934). [Prosper Cloutier], *Histoire de la paroisse de Champlain* (2v., Trois-Rivières, 1915–17), 2: 453–54. Cornell, *Alignment of political groups*. Labarrère-Paulé, *Les instituteurs laïques*, 190–93.

MARCOUX, JOSEPH (named **Tharoniakanere**, literally "one who contemplates heaven"), Roman Catholic priest, missionary, and author; b. 16 March 1791 at Quebec, son of Joseph Marcoux and Marie Vallière; d. 29 May 1855 on the Caughnawaga (Kahnawake) reserve, Lower Canada.

Joseph Marcoux was the son of a butcher who lived in Upper Town, Quebec, towards the end of the 18th century. He received his classical education at the Petit Séminaire de Québec from 1799 to 1808. A year later he began theological studies in that institution and, as was then customary, taught the junior classes at the same time. In 1812, having been made a subdeacon, he was placed under Jean-Baptiste ROUPE, the priest in charge of the Saint-Régis mission. Roupe prepared the young cleric for the priesthood and taught him the Mohawk language. During the War of 1812 Marcoux was at the mission station when the Americans attacked on 23 Oct. 1812. But unlike Roupe he managed to escape the invaders by hiding in a peat-house until they had withdrawn from the village.

Marcoux was ordained priest by Joseph-Octave Plessis*, the bishop of Quebec, on 12 June 1813 and five days later he received authorization to proceed to the Saint-Régis mission. There he succeeded Roupe, who had just been appointed priest in charge of the mission of Lac-des-Deux-Montagnes (Oka). Shortly after his return to the Saint-Régis mission, Marcoux was confronted with two adversaries. He had to struggle against the self-proclaimed heir to Louis XVI, Eleazer WILLIAMS, a Congregational preacher who was engaged in undermining the faith of the Indians in his mission and their loyalty to the British crown. He also had to struggle against American officers stationed on the New York state border who endeavoured to bribe the Indians with food. Some of the Indians could not resist the temptation of adding Marcoux's name to the list of petitioners without his knowledge, in order to obtain a larger share. In 1819 Marcoux presented a report about his conduct to the governor-in-chief, the Duke of Richmond [Lennox*], but the explanations he gave did not dispel the suspicions of the authorities concerning his loyalty and that of the Indians of his mission. To resolve the difficulty, at the end of the year Bishop Plessis appointed him priest in charge of Saint-François-Xavier mission at Caughnawaga.

During his ministry in this mission, Marcoux took effective steps to combat the scourge of alcoholism that was creating discord in the village of Caughnawaga; it had reached an alarming level following the arrival in the southern part of the Caughnawaga reserve of the quarrymen who had come to help build the Lachine Canal in 1823–24. In 1826 he managed to check the dissemination of a faulty translation of the gospels into Mohawk, a document "more likely to cast ridicule on religion than to spread it." Around 1821 the Indians had made a claim to a strip of land adjoining the village on the La Prairie side, and in 1828 and 1830 he intervened to get their demands satisfied, but to no avail. In these same years he resisted to the utmost the attempts made by certain Indian Department officials to lure, chiefly by offering them schools, his flock away from the Catholic religion. Fortunately, Lord Gosford [Acheson*], the governor-in-chief from 1835 to 1838, sided with him.

In 1840, however, one of Gosford's successors, Charles Edward Poulett Thomson*, asked Ignace Bourget*, the bishop of Montreal, to remove Marcoux from Caughnawaga, blaming him for the disorder that had been prevalent in the village and accusing him of having shown disloyalty towards the government during the rebellion of 1837–38. Bourget, convinced of Marcoux's innocence, kept him at his post, although he reproached him for labelling as "half-wits" several officials who were his opponents, notably James Hughes, Duncan Campbell Napier*, and Solomon Yeomans Chesley*, members of a commission to inquire into the attitude and conduct that he and the Indians of his mission had adopted in 1837–38. A very intelligent but impulsive man, Marcoux bristled like a porcupine when anyone attacked his flock. Despite Hughes's allegations, during the rebellion Marcoux had preserved the same stance taken by all the parish priests who remained obedient to their bishops. Thomas Leigh Goldie, the secretary to Sir John Colborne*, who was commander-in-chief of the armed forces in the Canadas in 1837–38, commented, "As for Mr Marcoux's conduct, His Excellency is in no doubt that he can rely on it."

From his first days at Caughnawaga, Marcoux had been concerned about the old mission church, which was "not respectable," and dreamed of building a new one. As a good missionary he quickly learned the art of soliciting gifts. In 1826 he obtained from the king of France, Charles X, three large pictures for his church. On two occasions, in 1842 and 1844, he received 1,000 francs from King Louis-Philippe to build a new church. By dint of knocking on countless doors, he managed to collect the necessary funds. The church was built in 1845 according to the specifications of Félix Martin*, an architect who was the superior of the Jesuits of Lower Canada. Seven years later, in response to his own discreet suggestions, Marcoux received from Napoleon III, emperor of the French, and Eugénie, his wife, liturgical vestments in cloth of gold, worthy of the fine temple he had erected, and a chalice engraved Donné par l'Impératrice.

A true linguist, Marcoux wrote remarkable works in the Mohawk language, among others a catechism, a book of prayers, extracts from the gospels, a volume of Gregorian chant with Indian words, the translation of a biography of Kateri Tekakwitha*, whose cult he strove constantly to promote, a grammar, and Mohawk-French and French-Mohawk dictionaries.

Joseph Marcoux died a victim of his zeal, at the age of 64, during an epidemic of typhoid. He was buried in the vaults of the church built through his efforts, among the Indians he had loved so well. His priestly life, consecrated to the Mohawks, had lasted 42 years, 36 of them spent in the Saint-François-Xavier mission at Caughnawaga.

HENRI BÉCHARD

The correspondence of Joseph Marcoux was published posthumously as Lettres de M. Jos. Marcoux, missionnaire du Sault, aux chefs iroquois du Lac des Deux Montagnes, 1848–49 (Montréal, 1869). His works are listed in Bibliography of the Iroquoian langages, comp. J. C. Pilling (Washington, 1888). There is a portrait of Marcoux in the room next to the sacristy in the church at the Saint-François-Xavier mission at Kahnawake.

AAQ, 12 A, H: f.46r; 26 CP, D: 24, 196; 210 A, VII: 411; IX: 464, 487; X: 9. ACAM, RLB, II: 155–57. ANQ-Q, CE1-1, 14 nov. 1786, 16 mars 1791. AP, Saint-François-Xavier (Kanawake), Reg. des baptêmes, mariages et sépultures, 30 mai 1855. Arch. de la Compagnie de Jésus, prov. du Canada français (Saint-Jérôme, Qué.), Boîte 1, nos.70, 82, 100, 167, 177; Boîte 2, no.236. Arch. du diocèse de Saint-Jean-de-Québec (Longueuil, Qué.), 3A/98, 131, 170, 216. ASQ, Fonds Viger–Verreau, Carton 25, no.212; Reg. du grand séminaire; Reg. du petit séminaire. "Les dénombrements de Québec" (Plessis), ANQ Rapport, 1948–49: 23, 73, 123. Doc. relatifs à l'hist. constitution-nelle, 1759–1791 (Shortt et Doughty; 1921), 2: 605. Lettres des nouvelles missions du Canada, 1843–1852, Lorenzo Cadieux, édit. (Montréal et Paris, 1973), 151, 447. Allaire, Dictionnaire, 1: 364–65. Handbook of American Indians (Hodge), 2: 953–55. Morgan, Bibliotheca Canadensis, 247. National union catalog. Tanguay, Répertoire (1893), 176. Henri Béchard, J'ai cent ans! L'église Saint-François-Xavier de Caughnawaga (Montréal, 1946), 16, 29. E. J. Devine, Historic Caughnawaga (Montreal, 1922), 283–84, 333, 345, 372. Pouliot, Mgr Bourget et son temps, vol.2. Jacques Viger, "La prise de Saint-Régis," J. M. LeMoine, édit., BRH, 5 (1899): 141–44.

MARTIN, GEORGE (known in Mohawk as **Shononhsé:se'**, meaning "he is of the long house" or "the house is too long for him"), Mohawk chief and interpreter; b. 23 Dec. 1767 in Canajoharie (near Little Falls, N.Y.); d. 8 Feb. 1853 in Salt Springs, near Brantford, Upper Canada.

Very little is known about George Martin's youth. In the early 1780s he married Catherine Rollston, who was alleged to be of Dutch ancestry and had been captured by the Mohawks when she was 13. She was brought to the Indian settlements on the Mohawk River, adopted by the prominent Mohawk family of Teyonnhehkewea, and given the name Wan-o-wen-re-teh (which means "throwing over the

Martin

head"). The Martins had one daughter, Helen, who later married John "Smoke" Johnson*, and possibly one or more sons.

Martin had participated, according to an obituary, in the American Revolutionary War, after which he and his wife moved with the Six Nations to the Grand River (Ont.). There, on a high bluff overlooking the river, they built a house, their lands becoming known as the "Martin Settlement." It was here, since Martin was an interpreter, that the British government's presents to the Six Nations, for their continued loyalty, were distributed each year. An anecdote recorded by the Martins' great-granddaughter Evelyn Helen Charlotte Johnson suggests that George had a fierce temper and that he had some influence within the community. Unlike his contemporary Joseph Brant [Thayendanegea*], however, he was not involved as a major spokesman in dealings with other Indian peoples or with the government, nor did he participate as a negotiator or signatory in any of the land surrenders involving the Six Nations. As an interpreter, he mediated between the Six Nations and government officials in various disputes, a position which almost invariably produced some resentment towards him.

Martin served as "Confidential Interpreter" to William Claus*, the deputy superintendent general of Indian affairs from 1799 until the latter's death in 1826. During the War of 1812, and likely earlier, he was an interpreter for the Indian Department, in whose service, Joseph Brant CLENCH later certified, he was "noted for zeal, bravery and general good conduct." Although he once conveyed a message from the Seneca chief Red Jacket [Shakóye:wa:tha?*] in New York State calling on some of the Six Nations in Upper Canada not to fight as allies of the British, he remained firmly loyal. At the urging of Joseph Willcocks*, he helped to persuade the Six Nations to send warriors to Amherstburg, Upper Canada, to take up arms with Major-General Isaac Brock* in the late summer of 1812. Martin was present, as an interpreter, for two British victories at least, Beaver Dams (Thorold), Upper Canada, in June 1813 [see William Johnson Kerr*] and Fort Niagara (near Youngstown, N.Y.) in December. In early January 1814, along with John Brant [Tekarihogen*], Henry Tekarihogen*, and others, he signed, as one of the Six Nations' chiefs, a petition to Claus suggesting that those Indians who, they alleged, had refused to fight for the British or had discouraged other warriors from fighting should not "receive presents of any description at the next distribution."

Although it is uncertain when Martin became a chief, he assumed new responsibility when he was appointed a war chief by a council held on 22 Feb. 1815. At the same time he was given the task of ensuring that non-Indians did not trespass upon the Six Nations' lands. He immediately acted upon this duty,

reporting in a letter to Claus that very day that Augustus Jones* and Kanonraron (Aaron Hill) – both "snaking and mean Fellows" – were attempting, along with Henry Tekarihogen, to get the Six Nations' chiefs to surrender their right to some salt-springs on the reserve. Martin continued to keep Claus informed of conditions on the Grand River in succeeding years. In September 1816 he wrote that his people were experiencing "very bad times . . . Corn most all dead some famalys want have nothing at all to eat this whinter." There was, however, in his view, little chance of "your friends" moving from the Grand unless the British government provided them with "better Country some where." Alluding to reports he could not substantiate, he believed it was only "those people that was not a friend of the Government" who were intending to move, possibly to the "Wabash" in the Ohio country or to western Upper Canada.

Martin was a staunch adherent of the Church of England. In December 1823 he reported to Claus on the activities of the "Mathodist Breacher," probably the Reverend Alvin Torry, who was attempting to convert members of the Six Nations. "I believe None of them join them [but] your friend Thomas Davis [Tehowagherengaraghkwen*] . . . and few famalys that lives round him So I am told and this few Massesawgas." One of the latter was Peter JONES. In 1830 Martin and others from the Mohawk Village (Brantford) petitioned Charles James Stewart*, the Anglican bishop of Quebec, to consecrate the Mohawk chapel, which they had helped raise money to restore. Stewart visited the settlement for that purpose and consecrated the chapel on 17 October of that year.

By the early 1840s Martin, then about 80 years of age, appears to have retired to his home. Since his friend William Claus was long dead and because resident superintendents were being appointed to work directly with the Six Nations, Martin's influence waned and his place as an interpreter was taken over by his son-in-law, John "Smoke" Johnson. Martin had reportedly been involved with other Six Nations Indians in supporting the government during the rebellion of 1837–38 in Upper Canada. He took no part, however, in the negotiations for the surrender in 1841 of the Six Nations' land on the Grand River, which was to be managed on their behalf by the crown [see Tekarihogen], or in other important matters affecting the Indians during the 1840s.

Martin, who was raised as a warrior in the Mohawk valley and experienced war as an ally of the British crown, was a man shaped by the 18th century, not the 19th. At his death in 1853, he was described by the Toronto Globe as "the last of the old warriors residing on the Grand River, that have taken part in the two great struggles between England and the United States." He left to his successors, John "Smoke" Johnson and his son George Henry Martin Johnson*, a legacy of loyalty to the crown in time of war and cooperation as an interpreter in peace-time, sometimes over considerable opposition.

DAVID T. MCNAB

PAC, MG 19, F1, 10: 25, 153–59; RG 1, L3, 377: M6/23. *Canada, Indian treaties and surrenders* . . . [1680–1906] (3v., Ottawa, 1891–1912; repr. Toronto, 1971), 1. *The valley of the Six Nations* . . . , ed. and intro. C. M. Johnston (Toronto, 1964), 193, 196, 203, 219, 248, 259, 284. *Globe*, 15 Feb. 1853. *Hamilton Gazette, and General Advertiser* (Hamilton, [Ont.]), 28 Feb. 1853. *Weekly North American* (Toronto), 10 March 1853. Betty Keller, *Pauline: a biography of Pauline Johnson* (Vancouver and Toronto, 1981), 4, 8, 15. Millman, *Life of Charles James Stewart*, 86. E. H. C. Johnson, "Chief John Smoke Johnson," *OH*, 12 (1914): 102–13; "The Martin settlement," Brant Hist. Soc., [*Papers*] (Brantford, Ont.), 1908–11: 55–64.

MARY BERNARD, Miss KIRWAN, named Sister. *See* KIRWAN

MARY FRANCIS, MARIANNE CREEDON, named Mother. *See* CREEDON

MASSEY, DANIEL, improver, farmer, and manufacturer; b. 24 Feb. 1798 in Windsor, Vt, son of Daniel Massey and Rebecca Kelley; m. January 1820 Lucina Bradley, and they had three sons and seven daughters; d. 15 Nov. 1856 in Newcastle, Upper Canada.

The founder of the Massey farm-implement business, Daniel Massey was a member of the seventh generation of Masseys to have lived in America since the emigration from England of Geoffrey Massy about 1630. Daniel was brought to Upper Canada between 1802 and 1807, when his father began farming in Haldimand Township, on the north shore of Lake Ontario, near the site of present-day Grafton. The reasons why this branch of the family moved to Upper Canada are not clear.

Daniel apparently was sent at an early age to live with relatives in Watertown, N.Y., where he received a few years of schooling. At age 14 he is said to have taken over the management of the family farm while his father worked as a teamster for the Upper Canadian militia. Daniel left home in 1817; within a year or two he was engaged in extensive land-clearing operations in the area. These involved buying wooded land, employing as many as 100 men (usually recent immigrants) to clear it, disposing of the timber, and then reselling the cleared farm-land. By 1830 he had cleared 1,200 acres and was known as an expert on the subject. About that time, however, he settled down to farm his own land in Haldimand and raise his growing family.

Massey's land-clearing operations and experience as an employer probably stimulated his interest in labour-saving machinery. In 1844 he turned the management of his farm over to his eldest son, Hart Almerrin* (b. 1823), and then spent much of his time in a small workshop he had built on the farm to repair implements. Many of his own early implements were brought back from visits to the United States. In January 1847 he sold his farm to Hart and moved with his family to the Newcastle vicinity, where he soon entered into partnership with Richard F. Vaughan, the owner of a small foundry and blacksmith shop. Vaughan left the partnership in 1849, the same year in which the business was moved to a new two-storey brick factory in Newcastle. Hart Massey joined his father in 1851, acting first as superintendent, then becoming an equal partner and manager in 1853, and finally buying out his father's interest in 1856, the year in which the elder Massey died.

Available sources contain only fragmentary information on the early years of what eventually became a great multi-national enterprise. Apparently known as Daniel Massey and Company, then H. A. Massey and Company, and later (or perhaps simultaneously) the Newcastle Agricultural Works and the Newcastle Foundry and Machine Manufactory, C.W., the business existed to manufacture farm implements and general machinery such as steam-engines. It was evidently Hart who, overcoming his father's inertia in the early 1850s, developed the important strategy of obtaining the rights to manufacture the latest American mowers and reapers in Canada. Earlier the firm may have served as sales agent for some American manufacturers. At the time of Daniel's death, the enterprise was apparently prosperous, but it was still a small local firm, one of dozens jostling to meet the demands of Upper Canada's flourishing farmers for ways of reducing the high cost of labour.

The Masseys were of Puritan background and Methodist persuasion. Daniel Massey was said by his son Hart to have been a strict, stern father, but also "the most tender-hearted man that ever breathed." He was reputedly an early temperance advocate who pioneered in abjuring the custom of giving free liquor to the men who cleared land for him; he also refused to take medicinal alcohol on his deathbed. Daniel Massey was not prominent in the life of his community. Nor was his business particularly outstanding during his lifetime. He was a founder, chief contribution to Canadian history lay in the genetic and cultural traits inherited by the Masseys who took over the family enterprise.

MICHAEL BLISS

AO, RG 21, United counties of Northumberland and Durham, Haldimand Township, census records, 1807–10. PAC, MG 32, A1; RG 1, L3, 379: M leases, 1798–1832/124. U.C., Board of Agriculture, *Journal and Trans.* (Toronto), 1 (1851–56): 594. *Christian Guardian*, 10 Dec.

Matooskie

1856. *Cyclopædia of Canadian biog.* (Rose and Charlesworth), 1: 774. *The Massey family, 1591–1961,* comp. M. [L.] Massey Nicholson (Saskatoon, Sask., 1961). *Pioneer life on the Bay of Quinte, including genealogies of old families and biographical sketches of representative citizens* (Toronto, 1904; repr. Belleville, Ont., 1972), 549–50. Merrill Denison, *Harvest triumphant: the story of Massey-Harris* (Toronto, 1948). *1847–1947: Massey-Harris, 100th anniversary* (n.p., n.d.). Mollie Gillen, *The Masseys: founding family* (Toronto, 1965). James Allen, "Address delivered by the Rev. James Allen, M.A., at the funeral service of the late Hart A. Massey, on Saturday, February 22," *Christian Guardian,* 11 March 1896: 162. "H. A. Massey dead . . . ," *Globe,* 21 Feb. 1896: 7.

MATOOSKIE. *See* McKENZIE, NANCY

MAYERHOFFER, VINCENT PHILIP (baptized **Vincent Ferrer**), Church of England clergyman; b. 22 Jan. 1784 in Raab (Györ, Hungary), eldest child of Michael Mayerhoffer and Catharina Lublé (Lliebb); m. 27 Aug. 1820 Caroline Stahl, and they had nine children; d. 15 Jan. 1859 in Whitby, Upper Canada.

Vincent Philip Mayerhoffer had an exotic early life that intrigued those who later learned of it. According to his autobiography, he was born to Roman Catholic parents and educated at the normal school and the gymnasium in Raab. After the death of his father, a city senator, Vincent was sent at age 13 to the gymnasium run by the Piarist order at Colocza (Kalocsa, Hungary). Financial problems, however, eventually forced Vincent's mother to apprentice him with a grocer in Pesth (Budapest) where he remained until difficulties with his master led him to move to Baja (Hungary) in September 1803 and become a baker's apprentice. But Mayerhoffer was encouraged by a former teacher to return to Colocza, and after a year he decided to enter the Franciscan novitiate at Bács (Bač, Yugoslavia) and seek ordination despite his mother's opposition. In February 1807 he sang his first high mass in Buda (Budapest), having received all seven ecclesiastical orders up to deacon and priest.

Following two curacies, Mayerhoffer became garrison chaplain at Peterwardein (Petrovaradin, Yugoslavia) and then, on 16 Oct. 1812, he was appointed chaplain of the 60th Infantry Regiment in the Austrian army. The following August he was captured by Napoleon's troops, only to escape at Mainz (Federal Republic of Germany) in January 1814 and rejoin the 60th to see service in France, Italy, and Switzerland. Mayerhoffer left the army on 31 Oct. 1816 and returned to parochial duties, serving at Klingenmünster (Federal Republic of Germany). In 1819 he immigrated to North America and was appointed a missionary in Pennsylvania but, after harrowing disputes with the Jesuits at Conewego, described in his autobiography, Mayerhoffer, long disillusioned with Roman Catholicism, left the church

on 20 March 1820. Although apparently without formal training, he opened in partnership a drug store in York, Pa, and "managed to pick up a living as a doctor." Believing celibacy a "hellish invention," he also married. After a two-year study of the Bible for guidance, Mayerhoffer decided to join "the German Reformed Church in Pennsylvania." In 1826 he moved to Buffalo, N.Y., to preach in German to four congregations, including one across the border in Upper Canada "on the Limestone Ridges" in Bertie Township.

Mayerhoffer was becoming convinced, however, that episcopalianism was more apostolic in doctrine and government than the Protestant denomination with which he was affiliated. Since his English was poor, he wrote in Latin to Anglican bishop Charles James Stewart* of Quebec requesting reception as a clergyman. Shortly after examination by the bishop on 14 June 1829 at York (Toronto), he was sent as a missionary to three German-speaking congregations north of the town in the townships of Markham and Vaughan. Unable to find a Lutheran replacement for their minister, who was on the point of retirement, these congregations had sought the aid of York's Anglican archdeacon, John Strachan*; after a few months Strachan considered that Mayerhoffer had begun "very successfully" in his new position. The peace and harmony that at first prevailed afforded Mayerhoffer the leisure to employ his talents in supplementing his meagre stipend; an advertisement appeared in the newspapers in 1832 for his newly invented "Wonder Salve" which "ought to be kept in every house, first for its inestimable goodness, and second because the [medicine] the older it gets the better it is."

Though there is a local tradition that Mayerhoffer allowed his parishioners to believe he was a Lutheran minister, he does not, in fact, appear to have disguised his Anglican convictions. There was potential for trouble, however, since the original land deed of St Philip's, Markham, stated that if ten years ever passed without a Lutheran pastor the property would be conveyed to the Church of England automatically. Furthermore, on 21 Jan. 1836 Mayerhoffer was among those Anglican clergy of the province granted a rectory by Lieutenant Governor Sir John Colborne*. The Colborne rectories infuriated those hostile to the concept of an established church and helped contribute to the political controversies about to engulf Upper Canada. These controversies were reflected in the developing split between reformers and tories among the congregations of Mayerhoffer, who was strongly opposed to William Lyon Mackenzie*. A meeting of Markham Lutherans in April 1837 resolved that since Mayerhoffer had "interfered in politics and other party proceedings" he should be removed and a Lutheran preacher found. On 4 May he was locked out of St Philip's; nine days later, on the advice of Attorney

General Christopher Alexander Hagerman*, he broke the locks and entered the church. The doors were locked and the locks broken repeatedly and then Mackenzie's supporters placed a sentry beside the church door. The guard was driven away in December, after the abortive rebellion, by Orangemen who accompanied "old Tory Mayerhoffer" back into the church. In 1839 a majority of the Lutheran trustees commenced legal proceedings. According to Mayerhoffer, the Court of Queen's Bench granted them possession three months before he could complete a ten-year ministry, though in fact it was not until 1843 that the Lutherans received the deed to St Philip's. Since flaws were also judged to exist in the Church of England's title to the lots of his other churches, he lost them as well; as he later recalled, "In this calamity I preached in schools and private houses." With land and money donated by his Anglican supporters, Mayerhoffer built St Stephen's in Vaughan and then St Philip's Church in Markham, across the street from its Lutheran namesake.

These embroilments embarrassed Bishop Strachan, who reported in March 1841 to the Society for the Propagation of the Gospel that Mayerhoffer, having fallen off his horse and ruptured himself, ought to be pensioned off. "He should never have been received into our Church," he added. Mayerhoffer, although still energetic, was less useful as a travelling missionary. Personal antipathy, however, appears to have figured in Strachan's continued search to find a pension for Mayerhoffer, who "tho' a moral & well meaning man is not in manners or qualifications calculated to build up the Church." He considered Mayerhoffer an "eye-sore and a great encumbrance."

By 1843 Mayerhoffer was working on a second church at Markham, in the village, where he was inducted by Archdeacon Alexander Neil Bethune* in the autumn of 1847. But the following year a replacement was found for Mayerhoffer and after some delays he was superannuated on 1 Jan. 1849, moving thereafter to Toronto with his family. In 1853 he took charge of a congregation in Perrytown but relinquished his post the following year, pleading ill health yet also under pressure from Strachan for being implicated in a bigamy case. Informed that never again should he function as a clergyman, he retired to Whitby where he finished his autobiography, appending a lengthy diatribe against the "putrid carcase" of Roman Catholicism. He died on 15 Jan. 1859 and was buried in the cemetery of St John's, Whitby, with full masonic honours. His fellow Anglican clergyman Henry Scadding* described Mayerhoffer as having "strongly marked and peculiar, perhaps Mongolian" features and characterized him as "a man of energy to the last: ever cheerful in spirit, and abounding in anecdotes, personal or otherwise."

CHRISTOPHER FERGUS HEADON

Vincent Philip Mayerhoffer is the author of *Twelve years a Roman Catholic priest, or, the autobiography of the Rev. V.P. Mayerhoffer, M.A., late military chaplain to the Austrian army, and grand chaplain of the orders of freemasons and Orangemen, in Canada, B.N.A., containing an account of his career as military chaplain, monk of the order of St. Francis, and clergyman of the Church of England in Vaughan, Markham and Whitby, C.W.* (Toronto, 1861).

AO, MS 35; MS 199, M. S. Gapper O'Brien, diaries; MU 2818. Österreichische Staatsarchiv-Kriegsarchiv (Vienna), "Schematismus der k.k. Militärgeistlichkeit," I: 99; Standestabellen des Infanterie-regiment 60, 1812: X; 1816: XI. PAC, RG 5, A1: 71036–40, 78344–47, 87623–25, 96875–82, 97031–42, 112017–20. PRO, CO 42/431: 329–31. USPG, C/CAN/folders 482a, 519; Journal of SPG, 39: 216–18; 40: 92–94. York County, Hist. Soc. (York, Pa.), "The registers of the First Moravian Congregation, York, Pennsylvania, 1751–1899," trans. H. J. Young (typescript, 1938), book II: 9. *Whitby Chronicle* (Whitby, [Ont.]), 27 Jan. 1859. J. L. H. Henderson, "John Strachan as bishop, 1839–1867" (DD thesis, General Synod of Canada (Toronto), Anglican Church of Canada, 1955). *Historical sketch of Markham Township, 1793–1950; centennial celebration of municipal government, 1850–1950* ([Markham, Ont., 1950]). *Markham, 1793–1900*, ed. Isabel Champion (Markham, 1979). Millman, *Life of Charles James Stewart*. G. E. Reaman, *A history of Vaughan Township; two centuries of life in the township* (Vaughan, Ont., 1971). Scadding, *Toronto of old* (1873), 454–56. M. C. Keffer, "The early days of Zion Evangelical Lutheran Church, founded 1806 at Sherwood, York County," *York Pioneer* (Toronto), 1960: 12–21. J. J. Talman, "From Moscow to Whitby, the romantic career of the first rector of Markham and Vaughan," *Canadian Churchman* (Toronto), 4 March 1937: 133.

MECHAM, GEORGE FREDERICK, naval officer and explorer; b. 1828 in Cove of Cork (Cobh, Republic of Ireland); d. 17 Feb. 1858 in Honolulu (Hawaii).

George Frederick Mecham entered the Royal Navy on 1 Sept. 1841 and after serving aboard various vessels attained the rank of acting lieutenant on 8 March 1849. On 5 March 1850 he was appointed third lieutenant of the barque *Assistance*. Under Captain Erasmus Ommanney, it was one of the four vessels assigned to the command of Captain Horatio Thomas Austin*. His expedition was instructed to proceed to the Arctic in search of the *Erebus* and *Terror*, commanded by Sir John Franklin* and missing since 1845. The *Assistance*, in the company of the barque *Resolute* and the two screw steamers *Pioneer* and *Intrepid*, sailed from London on 3 May 1850 and reached Beechey Island (N.W.T.) in Barrow Strait by the end of August, where the first traces of Franklin's 1845–46 winter quarters were found. At this time an unusual concentration of effort brought together in the vicinity of Wellington Channel a total of 11 vessels, from the five separate search expeditions under Austin, Sir John Ross, Captain Edwin Jesse De

Mecham

Haven*, William Penny*, and Commander Charles Codrington Forsyth. Austin's four vessels then continued westward in Barrow Strait and were beset by ice off the northeast coast of Griffith Island, where winter quarters were established. In October, Mecham travelled east by sledge, laying depots for further sledge operations the following spring, and came upon Ross's and Penny's winter station at Assistance Harbour (Bay) on Cornwallis Island. During the winter months Mecham contributed articles to the *Illustrated Arctic News* and *Aurora Borealis*, two periodicals produced aboard the vessels, and acted in various presentations of the Royal Arctic Theatre. These activities, and others, such as fancy dress balls, were designed to relieve the tedium of the Arctic winter.

Under the direction of Lieutenant Francis Leopold McClintock*, a number of sledge parties were organized in the spring of 1851 to search to the north, south, and west of the expedition's position in Barrow Strait. Two of these were conducted by Mecham. Setting out first on 15 April in company with another sledge under Captain Ommanney, Mecham and a crew of six men travelled as far south as Russell Island and the northern extremity of Prince of Wales Island before returning to the *Assistance* on 14 May, having covered a distance of 236 miles. On 27 May he took another party, once again heading south, and made a circuit of Russell Island; after mapping 75 miles of new shoreline he returned to the vessels on 19 June. When the ships were released from the ice on 8 August the expedition returned to England without having added any new information to the search for Franklin beyond what had been learned at Beechey Island in the summer of 1850. None the less, the sledging operations conducted during this voyage, which in total involved 103 men in 14 sledges and covered some 7,000 miles, had helped chart much previously unknown territory.

In 1852 the same four vessels were again commissioned by the Admiralty to search for Franklin, along with a fifth, the supply ship *North Star* [*see* William John Samuel Pullen*], and on 14 February Mecham was appointed first lieutenant of the *Resolute* under Captain Henry Kellett*. The expedition was commanded by Sir Edward Belcher* and left London on 15 April. Having arrived at Beechey Island, it separated into two divisions on 15 August; Kellett continued westward into Barrow Strait with the *Resolute* and *Intrepid* while Belcher took the *Assistance* and *Pioneer* north into Wellington Channel. The *North Star* was stationed at Beechey Island to serve as a supply depot. By mid September the western division was in winter quarters at Dealy Island, off the southern coast of Melville Island, and sledge parties were sent out to lay supplies for operations in the spring. Leaving on 21 September,

Mecham crossed Dundas Peninsula on Melville Island to Liddon Gulf where a depot was secured. During the return trip he stopped at Winter Harbour and found a dispatch left the previous spring by Lieutenant Robert John Le Mesurier McClure*, indicating the position of his ship, the *Investigator*, beset by ice at Mercy Bay, Banks Land (Island), since autumn 1851. Thanks to this fortuitous discovery, the crew of the trapped *Investigator* was later rescued and taken aboard the *Resolute* [*see* Bedford Clapperton Trevelyan Pim*].

The following spring Mecham set out, on 4 April 1853, across Melville Island to Cape Russell with a sledge party accompanied by a support sledge under George Strong Nares*, mate aboard the *Resolute*. On 3 May, after they had reached Eglinton Island, Nares returned to Dealy Island and Mecham continued on alone, exploring the southern and western coasts of Prince Patrick Island. At the sight of the pack-ice to the west he concluded that Franklin could not have gone in that direction. He then crossed the interior of Prince Patrick Island and, tracing the north shore of Eglinton Island, made his way back to the ships, where he arrived on 6 July. In 94 days, Mecham had travelled 1,006 miles and charted 680 miles of previously unknown shoreline.

The summer of 1853 being short and late in coming, the *Resolute* and the *Intrepid* were unable to rendezvous with the rest of the expedition at Beechey Island, and were forced to winter in Barrow Strait. In February 1854 Belcher ordered Kellett to abandon his ships and proceed to Beechey Island. Before executing these instructions, Kellett sent out three sledge parties: one under Lieutenant Richard Vesey Hamilton with reports for Belcher on the condition of the ships, and two others to the west, under the command of Mecham and Frederick J. Krabbé, master of the *Intrepid*. On 3 April, Mecham set out with orders to search in the vicinity of Prince of Wales Strait for signs of the *Enterprise* [*see* Sir Richard Collinson*], the vessel which had accompanied the *Investigator* from Bering Strait. In company with Krabbé's sledge he proceeded to Russell Point and from there continued alone down Prince of Wales Strait to the Princess Royal Islands (Amundsen Gulf). Here he found documents deposited by the *Enterprise* in the summer of 1852 indicating that the vessel had left the area, proceeding south and east. On the return journey Mecham stopped at Dealy Island on 27 May; there he found orders to head directly to the *North Star* at Beechey Island, the *Resolute* and *Intrepid* having been abandoned. In 152 travelling hours Mecham covered the distance to Beechey Island, where he arrived on 12 June. The complete sledge journey of 70 days remains one of the most impressive on record; averaging 19 miles a day the party covered a total of 1,336 miles.

Having ordered the abandonment of the *Resolute*, *Intrepid*, *Assistance*, and *Pioneer*, and taken under his charge the crew of the *Investigator*, Belcher decided to turn back to England. With the 263 men from these five vessels crammed aboard the *North Star* and two supply ships, the expedition arrived safely on 28 Sept. 1854. Mecham was one of the many officers of this group promoted upon its return, being raised to the rank of commander on 21 October. In 1855 he was assigned to the command of the steam vessel *Salamander*, stationed at Portsmouth, and two years later was transferred to the command of another steam vessel, the *Vixen*, for duty in the Pacific. While serving aboard this vessel Mecham was taken ill with bronchitis and suddenly, at the age of 30, died on 17 Feb. 1858.

As well as being an excellent navigator and seaman, Mecham was physically large and strong, and endowed with a warmth of personality which won him the admiration of his fellow officers and subordinates. In the field of Arctic exploration, he was, next to McClintock, probably the most skilful sledge operator and the extent of his travels during his two expeditions stands out as a notable achievement. In the Arctic two landmarks of note bear his name: Cape Mecham on the southern extremity of Prince Patrick Island and Mecham Island between Russell and Prince of Wales islands.

JIM BURANT

Arctic miscellanies; a souvenir of the late polar search; by the officers and seamen of the expedition (2nd ed., London, 1852). Edward Belcher, *The last of the Arctic voyages . . . in search of Sir John Franklin, during the years 1852–53–54 . . .* (2v., London, 1855). G.B., Parl., Command paper, 1852, 50, [no.1436]: 329–58, 548–58, *Additional papers relative to the Arctic expedition . . .*; House of Commons paper, 1851, 33, no.54: 13, *A return of all admirals, vice, rear, and retired, captains, commanders, and lieutenants in the Royal Navy, promoted on and since the 1st day of January 1848 . . .*; 1854–55, 35, no.1898: 537–39, 489–97, 499–539, 689–706, *Further papers relative to the recent Arctic expeditions in search of Sir John Franklin. . . .* Sherard Osborn, *Stray leaves from an Arctic journal; or, eighteen months in the polar regions, in search of Sir John Franklin's expedition, in the years 1850–51* (London, 1852). *Papers and despatches relating to the Arctic searching expeditions of 1850–51–52 . . .*, ed. James Mangles (2nd ed., London, 1852). *Illustrated Arctic News*, 14 March 1851. Cooke and Holland, *Exploration of northern Canada*. G.B., Adm., *Navy list*, 1848: 204; 1849: 254; 1851: 260; 1854: 282; 1858: 304. C. R. Markham, *The Arctic navy list; or, a century of Arctic & Antarctic officers, 1773–1873; together with a list of officers of the 1875 expedition and of their services* (London, 1875); *Life of Admiral Sir Leopold McClintock* (London, 1909). *Colburn's United Service Magazine* (London), 25 (December 1854): 623; 26 (December 1855): 628; 27 (October 1856): 320; 28 (February 1857): 140. R. I. Murchison, "Address to the Royal Geographical Society of London; delivered at the university meeting on the 23rd May, 1859," Royal Geographical Soc., *Journal* (London), 29 (1859): cxxxiii–iv.

MERLE, JACQUES, named **Father Vincent de Paul**, Roman Catholic priest and Trappist; b. 29 Oct. 1768 in Chalamont, France, son of Charles Merle and Louise Gagnon; d. 1 Jan. 1853 in Tracadie, N.S.

Jacques Merle was born into a devout Roman Catholic family. His father, a surgeon in Chalamont, sent him to a Jesuit college in nearby Lyons. Despite the outbreak of the French revolution in 1789, Merle began studies for the priesthood, apparently intending to enter the Order of Cistercians of the Strict Observance. This order, commonly known as Trappist, combined religious contemplation, prayer, and penance with manual labour in a secluded communal life. In 1790 religious orders were suppressed in France so Merle entered a monastery at Val-Sainte, Switzerland, which had been established by Dom Augustin de Lestrange and other French Trappists. Merle stayed six months; ill health prevented him from following the austere régime and he returned to France, where he secretly completed his theological studies. Ordained clandestinely on 7 April 1798 in Lyons, he worked as a catechist in that diocese until his arrest. He managed to escape and from 1799 taught rhetoric at seminaries in France. His health improved and, determined to enter the Trappists, he returned to Val-Sainte, probably in January 1804. He pronounced his vows on 13 Oct. 1805, taking the name Vincent de Paul. The following year, when Napoleon requested that the Trappists establish a hospice for French troops crossing the Alps into Italy, he and two monks founded a monastery-hospice at Montgenèvre. He remained there until 1811 when all Trappist monasteries were ordered closed by Napoleon because of the order's support of the papacy.

Trappists had searched throughout Europe, without much success, for a place where they might worship free from restriction. In August 1812 Vincent de Paul and two monks arrived in Boston with orders to establish a monastery near Baltimore; three other Trappists arrived the following year. They cleared the land, built log huts, and planted crops. By the summer of 1813 the marshes and the insects had taken their toll; all became ill and three died. Meanwhile, Lestrange summoned Vincent de Paul and other Trappists to join him in New York in a renewed effort to develop a monastic community in the New World. On hearing of Napoleon's abdication, however, Lestrange decided that they should return home. Leaving Vincent de Paul and six others to sell the property, he sailed for France.

Vincent de Paul and his companions left New York in mid May 1815 and arrived in Halifax 15 days later.

Merle

Edmund Burke*, vicar general of Nova Scotia, quickly formed a favourable impression of the pious and zealous Trappist. With Burke's help, Vincent de Paul secured passage to England for himself and the others. The group was obliged to wait two days for favourable winds and Vincent de Paul went ashore to secure extra provisions; when he returned, the boat had departed and all efforts to regain it were futile. In a strange country with little command of English and only a guinea and a worn-out cassock, he began a new sacerdotal career. Although he has been accused by Trappist historians of deliberately missing his passage because of his firm attachment to the North American missions, there is nothing to suggest the event was not an accident. Yet, throughout his career he demonstrated a talent for ignoring orders that did not suit his purpose and for turning to the advantage of himself and the Trappists the overlapping jurisdictions of French and British North American religious authorities. Burke was delighted to have another priest to aid the ailing Pierre-Marie Mignault*. In July Vincent de Paul met the bishop of Quebec, Joseph-Octave Plessis*, then on a pastoral visit to the Maritimes. Plessis saw in Vincent de Paul's misadventure a providential opportunity to develop a plan that he and Burke had long cherished, a central mission for the Micmacs of the province administered by Trappists living in a nearby monastery. Skilled in agriculture and accustomed to physical labour, the Trappists would be well suited to instruct the Micmacs and, as Plessis argued in a letter to the lieutenant governor of Nova Scotia, Sir John Coape Sherbrooke*, seeking the British government's approval, the self-sufficiency of the order would mean little cost to the government.

Plessis and Vincent de Paul had agreed that, while they awaited approval from both London and Lestrange, the Trappist would spend the winter with another French émigré priest, Jean-Mandé Sigogne*, in order to learn Micmac. Mignault's ill health prevented Vincent de Paul from leaving Halifax that winter, but he probably spent the winter of 1816–17 in Sigogne's mission among the Acadians of southwestern Nova Scotia. During most of 1815–17, however, he worked in the Halifax area, preaching, preparing a candidate for the priesthood, and ministering to the Micmacs there and in Shubenacadie as well as to the Acadians at Chezzetcook, whom he described as "ignorant, not very industrious, but naturally good." He also acted as doctor at Chezzetcook, perhaps drawing upon medical training he had acquired from his father. None the less, by 1817 government approval for his plans had not arrived and he was ordered by Lestrange to found a Trappist monastery or return to France. Although he longed for spiritual renewal in a cloistered monastery in France, he realized the need for Catholic priests in Nova Scotia.

His work among the Micmacs was progressing despite his having to speak through an interpreter, and he was concerned that in the absence of priests many Micmacs would fall under the influence of Protestants, especially Walter Bromley*. He also had hopes of founding a religious establishment at Chezzetcook, where he had purchased 50 acres. Searching for possible sites for a monastery, he made missionary visits to the northern mainland and, with the assistance of Father François Lejamtel*, to Arichat and Bras d'Or, Cape Breton. In late 1818 or early 1819, after frequent consultations with Plessis, he purchased 300 acres near Tracadie. "It is a long and deep valley in the middle of which a little river runs. . . . Two quite high mountains serve as ramparts, one on each side. The land here is excellent. We can have plenty of hay, wheat, potatoes, and all sorts of other vegetables. This property is only half a mile from the sea on a good site with good air." The nearby villages of Pomquet, Tracadie, and Havre Boucher, settled by Acadian, Scottish, and Irish families, might provide recruits for the monastery, and in May 1819 he wrote Plessis that a number of young people were interested in becoming novices.

Named parish priest for the three communities in 1818, Vincent de Paul soon realized that his impoverished parishioners were unable to pay the yearly tithe of one louis, and in general were less devout than the Micmacs. In 1821, during an unsuccessful trip to Lower Canada to raise funds for the monastery, he was disturbed by the pessimism of his host, Jean-Henry-Auguste Roux*, superior of the Sulpicians, concerning the possibility of establishing it on a sound footing. He persevered, despite a constant lack of funds, with a variety of projects, some only remotely connected with the monastery. While in Montreal, he arranged for the Congregation of Notre Dame to instruct without charge some young novices who would then be able to educate Nova Scotian girls for religious vocations; three girls from Pomquet and Tracadie left for Montreal in July 1822. A building large enough for 12 to 15 monks had been constructed by 1820, and another, attached to the church at Tracadie, was completed by 1821 to serve as a convent and a school for girls. The convent opened two years later when the three girls returned and took their vows as Trappistine sisters. Vincent de Paul also hoped to open a school for the children of some 30 black families in a community near the monastery and had set aside 50 acres to support a teacher. In addition to his duties as a parish priest, he served as a missionary to the Micmacs on the mainland and on Cape Breton Island. In 1822 he was named vicar general for the islands in the Gulf of St Lawrence that were in the diocese of Quebec, including, at that time, Cape Breton.

Vincent de Paul's major problem was a lack of

novices for the monastery. The few who entered did not stay and his appeals to France went unanswered. Alone, he could not continue his educational and missionary endeavours while pursuing the contemplative and communal life of a Trappist monk. Although he recognized the needs of the struggling communities in Nova Scotia, a letter written to his superior in France in June 1821 indicates his preference for the contemplative life. "I am most anxious to follow the [Trappist] rule entirely and now more than ever, long for retreat. . . . And although I have some inclination for the missions, I would not like to die there, but surrounded by our brothers, in the practice of the Holy Rule."

In 1823, in view of the precarious nature of his efforts in Nova Scotia, Lestrange ordered him to join a group of Trappists in Kentucky. Reluctant to abandon Tracadie and anxious to return to France to explain his problems to his superior, but fearing to disobey orders, the hesitant Trappist turned to Plessis. In a letter combining fatherly concern and ill-concealed exasperation at what seemed another example of Vincent de Paul's indecisiveness, Plessis supported his decision to return to France. Vincent de Paul sailed in October 1823, leaving his affairs in the hands of Hyacinthe Hudon*, parish priest at Arichat. While in France, besides consulting with Lestrange and other Trappist superiors, he wrote a memoir, which gave a brief account of his travels in the United States and Nova Scotia, emphasizing his work among the Micmacs and stressing the need for priests and funds. A short excerpt from the work was published in the *Annales* of the Society for the Propagation of the Faith in 1826, and the society granted him 1,500 francs for his mission.

Vincent de Paul returned to Nova Scotia in June 1825. With him on the voyage were four Trappists; two more would follow. At the suggestion of Plessis and Lestrange, he petitioned the lieutenant governor, Sir James KEMPT, to obtain government approval for the monastery and thus secure its future. No reply was received, but the new recruits gave the monastery, which he called Petit Clairvaux, some stability. Johann Baptist Kaiser, named François-Xavier, the only priest among the new arrivals, assumed the administration of the monastery while Vincent de Paul resumed his parochial duties and missionary work. He also had a grist-mill constructed in 1832 to serve both the monastery and the surrounding communities.

The 1830s and 1840s were difficult years for Petit Clairvaux. The death of Lestrange in 1827 had deprived it of a devoted superior and loyal protector. In 1834 a papal decree unified all Trappist orders in France and reverted to the rule in existence before Lestrange's reforms. Petit Clairvaux, unaffected by the decree, followed Lestrange's strict régime but was increasingly looked upon as an orphan by the French

Trappists. Anxious for replies to his appeals for assistance and new recruits, the 67-year-old Vincent de Paul returned to France in 1836. The vicar general of the order persuaded him to close Petit Clairvaux. Vincent de Paul seems to have fully accepted this advice and sent detailed instructions to that effect to Father François-Xavier. The monks themselves were to go to a monastery in England. After visiting England the restless Vincent de Paul returned to France to collect funds for the English Trappists, and perhaps also to obtain another opinion about Petit Clairvaux. He then journeyed to Rome to discuss the problem with ecclesiastical authorities. On 9 April 1838 a papal decree placed Petit Clairvaux, with its 10 to 12 monks, and the convent, with its 9 religious, under the jurisdiction of the vicar apostolic of Nova Scotia, Bishop William FRASER. At about that time Vincent de Paul received a letter from Fraser, asking that the Trappists remain in the province and that he return. Fraser's request was probably exactly what he was seeking. He justified his return in a letter to the vicar general of the Trappists in March 1840 on the grounds that he could not disobey his new superior, and sailed from France shortly afterwards. The French superior, in a letter written on 1 February to the parish priest at Arichat, Jean-Baptiste Maranda*, referred to Vincent de Paul as a "vagabond," thus arousing the ire of the Nova Scotian clergy who held the aged missionary in esteem. This letter is evidence of the strained relations between the two men as well as of their differing views of the role of a Trappist monk.

Vincent de Paul handed the administration of Petit Clairvaux to François-Xavier on his return and retired to the Trappistine convent. He none the less maintained an active interest in the affairs of the monastery. In February 1843 he wrote to Bishop William WALSH, requesting permission to collect funds in Halifax to complete a chapel which had been built with the generous assistance and labour of the people of Tracadie. A few weeks later he wrote again, explaining that on 19 February fire had destroyed a hostelry for visitors and the building containing the supplies for the monastery. The grist-mill, sawmill, cellar, and barn were saved as was the newest building, in which the monks resided.

After François-Xavier was unsuccessful in 1846 in another attempt to plead the cause of Petit Clairvaux in France, he, Vincent de Paul, and the ten remaining monks petitioned Rome for a decree affiliating them with one of the stricter Trappist monasteries in France which seemed willing to send them subjects. That plan fell through and the next year a second petition went unanswered. In 1848 an offer of Petit Clairvaux as a refuge to Trappists who might be obliged to leave France because of revolution received a polite refusal and then one final attempt at reconciliation by Vincent de Paul was ignored. After making arrangements

Méthot

which included bequeathing the property of the monastery and convent, held in his name, to the bishop of Arichat, Vincent de Paul died in 1853. The monastery would receive no recruits until 13 Belgian monks arrived in 1857–58 to usher in an era of prosperity. From 1903 to 1914 the monastery was again occupied by French Trappists, but it then remained empty until its purchase in 1937 by the Order of St Augustine, which continues to occupy it.

Vincent de Paul had readily discerned the spiritual, educational, and material needs of the small, dispersed communities in Nova Scotia, and his indefatigable work on their behalf, together with his saintly life of mortification and prayer, made him one of the most beloved and revered missionaries in the province. Miracles were attributed to his intercession and steps were taken in 1905, without success, for his beatification. In 1868 a settlement of Tracadie was renamed Merland in his honour. Throughout his missionary work, Vincent de Paul never lost sight of his original training as a Trappist and yearned for the life to which he had pledged himself. His correspondence reveals the many doubts he had about establishing a monastery, but also the many possibilities he envisaged in the New World. Although anxious to defer to his ecclesiastical superiors, he was accurately described by Trappist author Thomas Merton as "one of the most tenacious Trappists that has ever lived." His refusal to abandon his dream enabled him to succeed in establishing the first Trappist monastery in British North America.

PAULETTE M. CHIASSON

Jacques Merle, named Father Vincent de Paul, is the author of an autobiography, "Mémoire de ce qui est arrivé au P. Vincent de Paul, religieux de la Trappe; et ses observations lorsqu'il étoit en Amérique où il a passé environ dix ans avec l'agrément de son Superieur," published in *Relation de ce qui est arrivé à deux religieux de la Trappe, pendant leur sejour auprès des sauvages* (Paris, 1824). An English translation of Merle's account by A. M. Pope was published in Charlottetown in 1886 under the title *Memoir of Father Vincent de Paul, religious of la Trappe*.

AAH, Edmund Burke papers; William Walsh papers (mfm. at PANS); St Anselm's Roman Catholic Church (West Chezzetcook, N.S.), reg. of baptisms, marriages, and burials (mfm. at PANS). AAQ, 210 A, VIII: 346, 348, 351, 358, 529, 543; IX: 103, 143, 145, 398; XI: 41, 209; XII: 326; 31 CN, I: 130–130a; 312 CN, V: 89, 93–94, 97, 99–100, 103, 106–9, 111, 113, 115–19. AD, Ain (Bourg), État civil, Chalamont, 30 oct. 1768. Arch. de l'Abbaye cistercienne (Oka, Qué.), A 1000. PANS, MG 100, 239, no.22; 242, no.34; RG 1, 232: 41; 430: 153; RG 5, P, 51, no.109. N.S., House of Assembly, *Journal and proc.*, 1832: 157, 203, 249. J.-O. Plessis, "Le journal des visites pastorales en Acadie de Mgr Joseph-Octave Plessis, 1811, 1812, 1815," Soc. hist. acadienne, *Cahiers* (Moncton, N.-B.), 11 (1980). Caron, "Inv. de la corr. de Mgr Plessis," ANQ *Rapport*, 1927–28, 1928–29. Éphrem Boudreau, *Le Petit Clairvaux: cent ans de vie cistercienne à Tracadie en Nouvelle-Écosse, 1818–1919* (Moncton, 1980). André Coté, "L'ordre de Cîteaux et son établissement dans la province de Québec, depuis la Révolution française jusqu'à 1935" (thèse de MA, univ. Laval, Québec, 1971). A. A. Johnston, *Hist. of Catholic Church in eastern N.S.* L. J. Lekai, *Les moines blancs; histoire de l'ordre cistercien* (Paris, 1957). Lemieux, *L'établissement de la première prov. eccl.* [D.-A. Lemire-Marsolais, named Sainte-Henriette, et] Thérèse Lambert, named Sainte-Marie-Médiatrice, *Histoire de la Congrégation de Notre-Dame* (11v. in 13 to date, Montréal, 1941–), 7: 15–18. Thomas Merton, *Aux sources du silence*, Jean Stiénon du Pré, trad. (5ᵉ édit., Bruges, Belgium, 1955). Luke Schrepfer, *Pioneer monks in Nova Scotia* (New York, 1947). Éphrem Boudreau, "Le Petit Clairvaux (1825–1919)," Soc. hist. acadienne, *Cahiers* (Moncton), 7 (1976): 131–46. A. M. Kinnear, "The Trappist monks at Tracadie, Nova Scotia," CHA *Report*, 1930: 97–105.

MÉTHOT, FRANÇOIS-XAVIER, businessman, justice of the peace, office holder, politician, and militia officer; b. 10 Nov. 1796 in Pointe-aux-Trembles (Neuville), Lower Canada, son of Joseph Méthotte, a farmer, and Josephte Gouin; m. 8 Sept. 1829 at Quebec Dorothée Measam, daughter of William Measam, a fur merchant of that city, and they had three sons; d. there 6 Nov. 1853.

There is little information about the beginnings of François-Xavier Méthot's career. According to *Le Canadien*, he "went into business with no resources but his reputation, his intelligence [and] his love of work." He belonged to a family whose sons made their way quite satisfactorily in political and business circles. Louis, the eldest, became a merchant in Sainte-Croix, a member of the House of Assembly for Lotbinière, and later a legislative councillor, while Antoine-Prospère, the youngest, became a notary at Saint-Pierre-les-Becquets (Les Becquets) and a member of the assembly for Nicolet. Contrary to the assertions of such authors as Pierre-Georges Roy* and Horace Têtu, François-Xavier did not start his hardware business in 1808: he was then only 12 years old. A more reliable date is the year 1826, mentioned in Methot's obituary in *Le Journal de Québec*, probably written by the newspaper's editor, Joseph-Édouard Cauchon*, who knew him well.

Méthot settled in Quebec's Lower Town, and in the course of the 1830s made more and more of a name for himself in the wholesale and retail hardware business. By 1831 he had purchased buildings at the corner of Rue Saint-Pierre and Rue de la Montagne for £3,250 and had permanently located his business there. To extend his field of activity, he also began manufacturing a number of products. He set up a small mastic works in 1835; then around 1840 he established a factory to produce cut nails, known as the Moulin Ventadour, on three lots he had acquired in the seigneury of Notre-Dame-des-Anges at Beauport. It was described in 1842 as "the only large-scale factory of the kind existing in the District of Quebec." In the same period he also opened a small factory in Saint-Roch for making millstones to grind flour.

As a result of his success in these undertakings Méthot became an influential citizen. He served as a justice of the peace from 1836 to 1838, an auditor for the city in 1842, an alderman the following year, and a militia captain in 1848. He also took a close interest in the political events that followed the union of the two Canadas in 1841. In October 1840, with Augustin-Norbert Morin*, Étienne Parent*, and others, he had signed "L'adresse aux électeurs de toute la province," which stressed the necessity of electing throughout Lower Canada reform members determined to struggle against the injustices of the union. His patriotic ambitions also found expression in the Société Saint-Jean-Baptiste at Quebec, of which he was assistant treasurer in 1844.

Although Méthot did not feel drawn to the political limelight, the supporters of Louis-Hippolyte La Fontaine*, with Cauchon at their head, finally persuaded him to run in a by-election for the city of Quebec in June 1848, counting on his popularity and good name to win a contest that promised to be difficult. Incensed at being saddled with a share of the Upper Canadian debt and at having unequal representation in the assembly, Quebec voters were responsive to the campaign that had been launched by Louis-Joseph Papineau* the previous winter to repeal the union. When he passed through the city on 11 May, Papineau aroused the enthusiasm of a crowd of 4,000 at the Marché Saint-Paul, and thus won considerable support for Joseph LÉGARÉ, a candidate strongly advocating his policy. As a businessman anxious for the return of political stability, Méthot had no sympathy for this kind of agitation. He believed that change should be brought about by a moderate reform policy. No doubt his intellectual guide was Étienne Parent; Méthot was Parent's confidential agent at Quebec, and had been responsible for managing his real estate since 1843. In the end it was Méthot who won on 9 June, but without obtaining a majority of French Canadian votes. Historian Jacques Monet thinks that Méthot's election nevertheless marked an important step in the swing away from Papineau towards the party of La Fontaine. Although Méthot had ability and was not unpopular, he failed to obtain a second term in 1851, even with Cauchon's backing. The Quebec newspapers unanimously attributed his defeat to Cauchon's immoderate attacks on the government of Francis Hincks* and Morin.

During these years in politics, Méthot took care that his business maintained its initial impetus and did not go unsupervised. In the period 1845–50 he brought three of his nephews in turn into the management of his affairs: initially he took his former employee Guillaume-Eugène Chinic* into partnership and then added Georges-Honoré Simard*, and later Philéas Méthot in 1850. Financially sound, Méthot, Chinic, Simard et Cie was considered one of the best business houses at Quebec. Méthot gave up control of operations in May 1853. He died a few months later, leaving a "handsome fortune" to his three sons, who were still students at the Collège de Sainte-Anne-de-la-Pocatière. In the last years of his life, Méthot continued to hold a number of distinguished positions. He was a member of the board of directors of the Quebec Provident and Savings Bank (1847–53), an officer of Trinity House of Quebec (1850–53), and a member of the management committee for the aqueduct built by the city of Quebec (1850).

François-Xavier Méthot was one of the few French Canadians of his generation to make a mark in business, and for the liberal, professional middle class involved in politics he was a symbol of hope: the hope of a solution to the problem of his compatriots' economic inferiority. Parent, in a lecture delivered in 1852, urged his young audience to imitate the spirit of enterprise displayed by men such as Méthot, Joseph Masson*, Isidore Thibaudeau*, and a few others, and gave a rousing defence of them. On that occasion he affirmed: "You owe, we all owe [to these heads of business undertakings] a tribute of national gratitude. They have added lustre to the image of our race in the eyes of foreigners and of our compatriots by adoption, [and] at the same time they will be an example and an object of emulation for many of our own people . . . there are your models, your guides."

PIERRE POULIN

ANQ-Q, CE1-1, 8 sept. 1829; CE1-15, 10 nov. 1796; CN1-64, 15 oct. 1838, 11 juill. 1844, 16 sept. 1845, 3 févr. 1848; CN1-116, 9 mai, 10 déc. 1829; 28 nov. 1831; 29 mars 1832; 10 août 1843; 2 mai 1849; 21 juin 1853; CN1-208, 15 mars 1839, 6 déc. 1851, 21 févr. 1852, 2 mars 1853. *Le Canadien*, 19 août 1842; 5, 12, 19, 22, 29, 31 mai, 2, 9 juin 1848; 5 déc. 1851; 7 nov. 1853. *La Gazette de Québec*, 29 mars 1841. *Le Journal de Québec*, 29 nov., 6 déc. 1851; 8 nov. 1853. *Annuaire du commerce et de l'industrie de Québec contenant l'histoire et la statistique des établissements manufacturiers et du commerce de Québec, un essai sur la vallée de l'Outaouais, le commerce du Canada et beaucoup d'autres renseignements pour 1873*, J.-C. Langelier, édit. (Québec, 1973): 51, 62. Desjardins, *Guide parl. Quebec almanac*, 1836–38. *Quebec directory*, 1826, 1844, 1847–53. *Étienne Parent, 1802–1874; biographie, textes et bibliographie*, J.-C. Falardeau, édit. (Montréal, 1975), 227–43. Monet, *La première révolution tranquille*. P.-G. Roy, *Toutes petites choses du Régime anglais* (2 sér., Québec, 1946), 2: 268–69. Horace Têtu, *Résumé historique de l'industrie et du commerce de Québec de 1775 à 1900* (Québec, 1899), 6. *Une page d'histoire de Québec; magnifique essor industriel* (Québec, 1955), 40–44. "Les

Mille

Méthot," *BRH*, 39 (1933): 80–81. Léa Pétrin, "Industrie et commerce à Québec; un morceau du vieux Québec," *Le Soleil* (Québec), 21 sept. 1947: 7.

MILLE, HYPOLITE-JOSEPH. *See* Fenouillet, Émile de

MINISSIS. *See* Guiboche, Louis

MOLSON, JOHN, businessman, militia officer, justice of the peace, and politician; b. 3 Oct. 1787 in Montreal, eldest son of John Molson* and Sarah Insley Vaughan; m. 12 Oct. 1816 Mary Ann Elizabeth Molson at Quebec, and they had five sons; d. 12 July 1860 in Montreal.

The first reference to the career of the younger John Molson dates from the beginning of the 1800s. During the first decade of the century he learned the rudiments of business by working in the brewery his father had purchased at Montreal in 1785. He was so interested in the processes involved in making beer that when his father went on a trip to England in 1810 he left him to manage the undertaking. However, he gained his most valuable knowledge from engineer John Jackson, who taught him the principles and application of "steam power"; Jackson had been the partner of Molson's father and John Bruce, a shipbuilder, in a venture that had culminated in the launching in 1809 of the *Accommodation*, the first steamship built in Lower Canada.

In all probability Molson's engineering talents were quickly put to use in the shipping enterprise run by his father, especially since two new steamships, the *Swiftsure* and the *Malsham*, were added to the family firm's assets in 1812 and 1814. Fitted with powerful engines built in England at the workshops of Matthew Boulton and James Watt, these ships travelled between Montreal and Quebec in far less time than their predecessor the *Accommodation*, but it was still necessary to make numerous stops to load firewood for the steam-engines. The two boats were put into service during the War of 1812 to fulfil contracts for transporting and supplying troops in Lower Canada.

In that conflict Molson was appointed a cornet in the Royal Montreal Cavalry, a rank he would hold until 1821 when he was promoted lieutenant in this regiment. At the end of hostilities in 1815 he moved to Quebec, to supervise receipt of goods at the shipping company's wharf and warehouse below Cap Diamant. That year he went to England, apparently to settle a matter related to the building of the *Lady Sherbrooke* and the *New Swiftsure*, ships that would be launched in 1816 and 1817 respectively. It is thought that he met Mary Ann Elizabeth Molson, his first cousin, on this trip; her sister Martha married Thomas*, John's brother, in England in April 1816. The following month Mary Ann Elizabeth arrived at Quebec, and on 12 October she and John were married.

In December John went into partnership with his father and his two brothers, William* and Thomas, under the name John Molson and Sons. The new firm, created for a period of seven years, was to manage the family's total holdings (brewery, ships, wharfs, warehouses, and hotel); its assets of £69,550 came principally from the father. The younger John Molson now took charge of the shipping end of the business, largely because his share of £6,000 in the partnership consisted of the *Swiftsure*, which his father had recently given him. Despite the severe economic crisis in Lower Canada, he seems to have found navigation on the St Lawrence and the other activities of the family partnership profitable, since in 1819 his share had risen to a value of £16,783.

That year Molson moved back to Montreal. There he had to face the problem of competition engendered by over-investment in shipping, rival firms having launched several new steamships on the St Lawrence. The drop in the profit margin of his shipping business affected the general earning capacity of John Molson and Sons. It was therefore decided to transfer the assets of the shipping business to a joint-stock company – possibly one with limited liability – under the majority control of the Molson family. Thus in 1822 the St Lawrence Steamboat Company was founded [*see* William Molson], with John Molson and Sons holding 26 of the 44 shares, each valued at £1,000; the family firm contributed its three ships to the capital assets of the new company and was to manage it. Molson emerged from the arrangement with increased power and a freer hand to direct maritime activity.

The 1820s heralded an era of prosperity for the St Lawrence Steamboat Company; the growing influx of immigrants, the increased demand for lumber in Quebec and Montreal, and the general upsurge of economic activity gave fresh impetus to shipping on the St Lawrence. The company was called upon regularly by the British armed forces to transport freestone for the fortifications under construction during the 1820s at William Henry (Sorel), Île aux Noix on the Richelieu, and Île Sainte-Hélène on the St Lawrence. With lucrative contracts, the firm was able in 1827 to establish a towing service for ships and barges, and then to extend its operations to the Ottawa, Lac Saint-François, and the Richelieu. Around 1830 the St Lawrence Steamboat Company took over management of the Ottawa Steamboat Company, which shortly became the Ottawa and Rideau Forwarding Company. Thus the Molson firm secured control of shipping on the Ottawa, as well as on the Rideau Canal, which connected with Lake Ontario. Moreover, the St Lawrence Steamboat Company concluded an agreement on schedules and fares with John Torrance*, the owner of the St Lawrence Steam Tow Boat Company (better known as the Montreal Tow Boat Company), so that it could retain a virtual monopoly of shipping on the Richelieu. The two companies even built ships jointly. In 1827 the St Lawrence Steamboat Company had launched the *John Molson*, the most powerful of the tugs.

John, William, and their father had entered into a new partnership agreement (retaining the name John Molson and Sons) in 1824, at the time Thomas left for Kingston, Upper Canada. In 1828 some of the family business – the brewery, hotel, and wharfs – was transferred to the firm of John and William Molson, set up that year, in which William played a key role. Disappointed by this turn of events, the younger John Molson withdrew from the new company after only a year, to go almost immediately into the import-export business. On 1 May 1829 he went into partnership with the Davies brothers, George and George Crew, Quebec merchants, under the name of Molson, Davies and Company. But despite John's impulsive urge to be independent of the family enterprise, the new firm was to be financed largely by his father, as is evident from the numerous debts (one of £2,000) it owed him. Furthermore, in 1834 his father, who had previously made over some properties to him, agreed to give two of his warehouses to him in exchange for these properties. The company early specialized in trade in spirits, foodstuffs, hardware, and shipping equipment (cables, anchors, canvas, and sails). William and Thomas Molson sometimes turned to it for raw materials for their brewery and distillery; in 1836, for example, after disastrous harvests in Lower Canada, the firm won a contract to purchase on the European market the grain required for the brewery and the distillery. At that period it dealt with a large London agent, Henry Bliss*, who represented the principal merchants of Lower Canada. On 7 Sept. 1838 Molson put an end to Molson, Davies and Company by purchasing the shares of his partners, valued at £10,000. For reasons still unknown, he had decided to operate on his own in the field of commerce.

In extending his career as businessman and ship-owner, Molson took an interest in the financial sector, which was then expanding remarkably with the appearance of the first credit institutions in Lower Canada. In 1822 he bought 30 shares in the Bank of Montreal, worth £50 apiece. He was elected to the board of directors of this corporation in 1826, and sided with the faction represented by George Moffatt* which was critical of the irregularities in president Samuel GERRARD's management. In June, Frederic William Ermatinger* resigned from the board to let Molson's father join it and he soon became president. However, Molson himself resigned that month and was replaced by Ermatinger, who had been persuaded to rejoin the board. It was not until his father's death in 1836 that Molson again became a director. Meanwhile in 1831, with John Frothingham*, William RITCHIE, Stanley Bagg, William Lyman, and a number of

shareholders from New York State, he had helped found the City Bank (in Montreal), which served as a pocket of resistance to the Bank of Montreal's monopoly. Molson's financial activities were not, however, restricted to banking: for example, by 1842 he was the largest bondholder in Montreal, earning from them an annual income of £719.

Molson was involved in the transformation of Montreal as an urban community, making a particular contribution to the establishment of public services. In 1836 he was appointed president of the Montreal Gas Light Company, a recently created joint-stock company with a capital of £36,000. By the following year the main streets in the city were provided with gas lamps. After incurring financial deficits, the firm was taken over in 1848 by the New City Gas Company of Montreal, founded a year earlier by Thomas and William Molson. Having become a minority share-holder, John gradually lost interest in this field and around 1851 withdrew from the company.

In 1831 a group of Montreal businessmen had developed a plan to link La Prairie to Dorchester (Saint-Jean-sur-Richelieu), a distance of 20 miles, by a railway using wooden rails capped with an iron strip. The promoters thought such a line would offer two major advantages: a faster and shorter connection with New York and the encouragement of trade with Vermont and New York. United behind the two John Molsons, Peter McGILL, and George Moffatt, these businessmen set up the Champlain and St Lawrence Railroad with a capital of £50,000. The building of the railway involved such extensive unforeseen costs that the directors of the company had to mortgage their personal properties. In 1836, the year the line was inaugurated, Molson was named president of the company; his father, who died on 11 January of that year, had left him the £9,000 worth of shares that he had invested in the project. Despite the fragility of the tracks and the low engine power of the first locomotive, the *Dorchester*, which had been imported from Newcastle upon Tyne in England, the company carried more than 35,000 tons of merchandise and some 111,000 passengers from 1836 to 1840. Anxious to take advantage of this new means of transportation, the Molsons had built a wharf and a warehouse near the railway at La Prairie.

Until 1846 this company was the only one to provide transportation by wooden rails in the Montreal region or elsewhere in Lower Canada. However, with the advent of a competitor, the Montreal and Lachine Rail-road (which became the Montreal and New York Railroad four years later), the track linking La Prairie to Dorchester had to be improved to avoid losing too much of the land traffic on the south shore. Hence in the period 1848–51 the wooden rails were replaced by iron ones and the track was extended to Rouses Point, N.Y., on the line linking Boston to Ogdensburg, N.Y., on the upper St Lawrence. This attempt to

Molson

modernize the line required an investment of £141,560 in all, which increased the firm's indebtedness, in particular to the Bank of Montreal. Nevertheless, Molson remained an important financial backer of the railway link between Lake Champlain and the St Lawrence; in 1851 he was the second largest investor in the company, holding 179 of the 2,000 shares, valued at £50 apiece.

From the beginning of the 1820s, the technology of iron-making had been developing in Montreal through the efforts of American and British engineers, who were taking advantage of the boom in the building of the colony's first steamships. In spite of the small scale of its operation, the metallurgical industry had attained a level of competence and a flexibility permitting it to convert readily to meet the need for durable goods. It was under these circumstances that Molson acquired the St Mary's Foundry, which he inherited on his father's death in 1836. The year before he had begun to manage the establishment, which included a forge and a workshop where steam-engines were assembled. The account-books of the foundry show that there were no more than seven employees – an engineer, a machinist, three casters, and two apprentices. Presumably Molson's experience in the use of steam-power as well as in engineering in general had prepared him to take charge of the production process on his own. In the years 1835–40 the foundry built steam-engines not only for ships but also for a sawmill, a distillery, and an aqueduct. The engines were priced from £875 to £3,200, depending upon the horsepower and size requested by customers, and were delivered in three to nine months.

In 1840 Molson formed a partnership with William Parkyn, a civil engineer, under the name St Mary's Foundry Company. For reasons unknown the firm was dissolved in 1845, and the foundry's premises and equipment were rented to Parkyn for £500 annually. After five years Molson resumed management of the establishment and began to make coach wheels for railway companies, using a special technique. Following an action occasioned by a legal dispute, however, the patent for the invention was awarded to Samuel Bonner, a contractor of American nationality. This was probably the reason why Molson put the foundry's two foremen, Warden King and George Rogers, in charge of it in 1852, and then sold it to his nephew, John Henry Robinson Molson, five years later. During his time in the founding business Molson's involvement as an entrepreneur fluctuated with market changes.

The Molsons' tight grip on the wealth of Lower Canada associated them with an "oligarchy of money" against which the Patriote party took up the struggle during the 1830s. Molson participated in politics by affiliating himself first with the tory organizations in Montreal. As a member of the Constitutional Association he chaired the meeting that condemned the Montreal city council for supporting the 92 Resolutions in 1834. In succeeding years he urged Lower Canadian merchants to accept the union of the two Canadas. He was raised to the rank of militia colonel, took part in the military suppression of the 1837–38 rebellion, and is said to have been wounded on the Chambly road. He had remained loyal to the British empire and he received a commission as justice of the peace in 1838 and appointment to the Special Council when it was created that year. Backing the British government, he voted the following year for the plan of union. During its three years the Special Council enacted ordinances that suspended habeas corpus, suppressed the freedom of the press, allocated £47,344 on its own authority for the civil list, and saw to the reimbursement of £107,000 advanced by Great Britain. Molson's experience in business was put to good use when he steered through the ordinance renewing the charter of the Bank of Montreal. In the same period several financial groups, among them one including his brothers Thomas and William, were refused the legal status of a private bank. Molson again played a political role at the time of the unrest that led to the drafting in 1849 of the Annexation Manifesto [see James Bruce*]. Like the other signatories, he was subjected to penalties by the British government, which withdrew his commissions as justice of the peace and militia colonel.

At the beginning of the 1840s, Molson had resumed control of the family shipping business, which had run into difficulties during the economic recession of the 1830s. However, the rules of the game had changed; after his father's death he was forced to share management with his two brothers. Molson lost his desire to work for the company's advancement, especially since disputes about his father's estate had soured his relations with the family [see William Molson]. He preferred to carry on activities parallel to those of the shipping firm by engaging in ventures connected with maritime transport, in partnership with such men as mariner David Vaughan in 1841 and merchant Augustin Saint-Louis in 1842 and 1844. According to the correspondence of James Macaulay Higginson*, the private secretary of the governor-in-chief, Sir Charles Theophilus Metcalfe*, Molson had also set up a shipbuilding yard in the Montreal region.

Doubtless because of his involvement in shipping, Molson was appointed in 1832 and 1838 a warden of Trinity House in Montreal, which was responsible for regulating maritime traffic. As a member of this body, he took an interest in the improvements being undertaken on the St Lawrence waterway; in 1839, for example, he placed an order with David Vaughan for the building of a steamship (costing £1,975) specially equipped for dredging the river. He was also put on a commission to inquire into the strike in 1843 by workmen digging the Lachine Canal. In their report the commissioners attributed the disturbances to agitators, and concluded that there was no satisfactory civil authority able to command the respect of a large body of workers.

Meanwhile, the St Lawrence Steamboat Company, in which Molson kept his shares, had sold or rented out some of its ships. Moreover, from 1846 to 1854, he got rid of most of the ships that he had operated independently. Yet even if he lost money in some of his investments, he could easily refinance his debts through the real estate he had accumulated over the years. His holdings included an immense property at Côte à Baron, which he had acquired from Andrew Torrance in 1832; Belmont Hall, a luxurious residence at the corner of Rue Sherbrooke and Rue Saint-Laurent; several lots inherited from his father in the *faubourg* Sainte-Marie in Montreal; an estate on the Côte de la Visitation on Montreal Island; and Île Saint-Jean and Île Sainte-Marguerite at Boucherville, which together constituted a vast farming area. In addition he owned commercial buildings on Rue Saint-Pierre and Rue Saint-Paul in Montreal.

The beginning of the 1850s was marked by a reconciliation within the Molson family. On 3 Dec. 1853 John and William founded the Molsons Bank under the law governing private banks passed three years before. At first it primarily sought to attract savings deposits, at the same time engaging in short-term commercial discounting and issuing currency. In the latter activity John and William, with the participation of their brother Thomas, made use of their business deals with merchants of Upper and Lower Canada to circulate their own currency. The two had to face competition from the Bank of Montreal, whose principal strategy in dealing with them was to accumulate Molsons Bank notes for several days so that it could suddenly demand their conversion into cash, a manœuvre creating problems of liquidity for the bank. In 1855 the Molsons Bank was restructured through its incorporation as a chartered bank by the Legislative Assembly. Its authorized share capital was raised to £250,000, and the value of its issued notes would depend upon the sums put in by the investors. On 22 October the shareholders' meeting elected its five-man board of directors, which included John, William, and Thomas; at the board's first meeting, the next day, William was elected president and John vice-president.

Towards the end of his life John gradually withdrew from the business world in which he had been active for more than 40 years. In 1856 his shares in the Molsons Bank were worth £35,000 and yielded 8 per cent in dividends. In the will he drew up on 20 April 1860, less than three months before his death, he settled a substantial annuity upon his wife and each of his five children (John, George Elsdale, Alexander, Samuel Elsdale, and Joseph Dinham), in addition to the usufruct of such properties as Belmont Hall and the estate on the Côte de la Visitation. The will stipulated, however, that the heirs could not contest its terms without losing all rights under it. The remainder of his fortune (worth about £200,000 according to his contemporaries) was left in trust to his brother William until his grandsons, who were the principal beneficiaries, reached their majority.

Two aspects of Molson's life stand out particularly: first, the fragile nature of partnerships based on family capital and, secondly, the diversity of entrepreneurial activity. These were two characteristics of colonial society in the early days of capitalism. The family unit still played a predominant role in a period when capital was just being mobilized in such legal forms as the joint-stock company with negotiable shares and limited liabilities. However, there was a confusion of functions within the Molson family, and it was aggravated by Molson's disposition to assert his authority, particularly over his rebellious younger brothers; this situation continually threatened to cause economic, financial, and even emotional breakdowns. As for entrepreneurial diversity, Molson assuredly was in some sense involved in all important aspects of the economy: brewing, steam navigation, founding, railways, gas lighting for Montreal streets, the import-export trade, real estate investment, insurance, and banking. Yet one should not forget his political role, or his cultural and social concerns evidenced by his gifts to the Montreal General Hospital around 1829 and to McGill College in 1857. His associations were mainly with certain other families – among them the Torrances, McGills, Moffatts, Gerrards – it was as if the whole range of activities in this small colonial society was controlled collectively by a group of individuals who took the responsibility for its development upon themselves. They were not different from one another in any serious respect, and they were bound by a close community of interests. They demonstrated their cohesion through their approach to such issues as the future of the country, the conflict between membership in the empire and their feeling of attachment to North America, party affiliations, and policies for economic advancement; and there was no sign at the time – if indeed there ever would be – of a concentration of capital in business, real estate, industry, or banking.

ALFRED DUBUC and ROBERT TREMBLAY

The most important sources of information on John Molson Sr are the Molson's Brewery archives at PAC, MG 28, III57. ANQ-M, CE1-63, 7 août 1788, 15 juill. 1860; CN1-16, 19

Molt

oct. 1810; CN1-175, 12 juin 1837; 1er févr. 1851; 22 juill., 8 sept. 1852; 13 juin 1854; 20 avril 1860; CN1-182, 9 mars, 1er nov. 1832; CN1-187, 9 oct. 1819; 3 juin, 17 déc. 1822; 5 août 1823; 17 févr. 1824; 10 mars 1825; 3 mai 1827; 27 oct. 1829; 16 avril 1831; 25 avril 1832; 5 juin, 20 avril, 14, 20 déc. 1833; 12 mai 1834; 24 mars, 11 août 1835; 1er févr., 13 sept. 1836; 7 sept. 1838; 21 janv., 8 mars, 11 avril, 9 oct. 1839; 15 oct. 1842; 4 mai 1843; CN1-208, 25 août 1855; 2 juin, 18 déc. 1856; 27 mars, 25 avril 1857. ANQ-Q, CE1-61, 12 oct. 1816. McCord Museum, Molson family papers. McGill Univ. Libraries (Montreal), Redpath Library, John Molson and Sons papers. Montreal Board of Trade Arch. (Montreal), Minute-books, 1843–60. PAC, RG 68, General index, 1651–1841; 1841–67. Can., Prov. of, Legislative Assembly, *App. to the journals*, 1841, app.E; 1842, app.D; 1843, app.W; 1844–45, app.D; 1848, app.D; 1849, app.R; 1850, app.G; 1851, app.UU; 1852–53, app.I; 1854–55, app.FF; 1856, app.5, 13; 1857, app.6, 11; 1858, app.8; 1860, app.5; *Statutes*, 1841, c.98; 1854–55, c.202. L.C., Special Council, *Journals*, 1839–41; *Statutes*, 1831–32, c.58. Que., *Statutes*, 1874–75, c.93. *La Minerve*, 11 avril 1831. *Montreal Gazette*, 19 May 1845, 14 July 1860. *Montreal Transcript*, 14 July 1860. *Quebec Gazette*, 4 Jan., 29 April, 17 June, 5 Aug. 1819. André Giroux *et al.*, *Plans de l'architecture domestique inventoriés aux Archives nationales du Québec à Montréal* (Ottawa, 1975), 23–24. *Montreal directory*, 1842–60. Morgan, *Sketches of celebrated Canadians*. *Officers of British forces in Canada* (Irving), 163. *Quebec almanac*, 1812–41. Terrill, *Chronology of Montreal*. Merrill Denison, *The barley and the stream: the Molson story; a footnote to Canadian history* (Toronto, 1955); *Canada's first bank*. Alfred Dubuc, "Thomas Molson, entrepreneur canadien: 1791–1863" (thèse de PH.D., Univ. de Paris, 1969). Fernand Ouellet, *Histoire économique et sociale du Québec, 1760–1850: structures et conjoncture* (Montréal et Paris, [1966]). S. B. Ryerson, *Le capitalisme et la confédération: aux sources du conflit Canada–Québec (1760–1873)*, André d'Allemagne, trad. (Montréal, 1972), 247. B. K. Sandwell, *The Molson family, etc.* (Montreal, 1933). Tulchinsky, *River barons*. Alfred Dubuc, "Montréal et les débuts de la navigation à vapeur sur le Saint-Laurent," *Rev. d'hist. économique et sociale* (Paris), 45 (1967): 105–18. É.-Z. Massicotte, "Le palais de l'intendance après 1761," *BRH*, 49 (1943): 264–68; "Le premier théâtre royal à Montréal," *BRH*, 48 (1942): 169–72.

MOLT, THÉODORE-FRÉDÉRIC, teacher, author, organist, composer, inventor, and music dealer; b. *c.* 1795 in what is now the Federal Republic of Germany; d. 16 Nov. 1856 in Burlington, Vt.

Théodore-Frédéric Molt's childhood and formative years are mentioned in an article written by historian John K. Converse for *The Vermont historical gazetteer* in 1868. According to Converse, who was associated with him for more than 20 years, Molt received a sound basic schooling in the humanities and mathematics. It is believed that, shortly after he entered university, he was conscripted into Napoleon's army, serving as accountant and assistant paymaster in his regiment, and was a bystander at the slaughter on the day of the decisive battle at Waterloo.

On his return to his native land he is said to have decided to devote himself to music; apparently he had learned the rudiments in his childhood from his father and an elder brother.

Having pursued the study of music with the most eminent German masters, Molt came to Quebec late in the spring of 1822. He immediately announced that he would be available as a teacher of piano and music at the residence of Fred Hund on Rue Saint-Jean. The concerts given at the Union Hotel on 4 March and 26 Aug. 1824 by some of the young girls studying with him were a measure of his success in teaching. Reporting on the first concert, the *Quebec Gazette* noted that he had founded the Juvenile Harmonic Society. On 13 March 1823 Molt had contracted a marriage with Henriette, the daughter of Frédéric-Henri Glackmeyer*, a prominent musician at Quebec. They were to have at least nine children, only four of whom survived to adulthood.

In June 1825 Molt auctioned off his musical instruments and furniture and returned to Europe. During his stay of about a year he met such musical figures as Ignaz Moscheles, Karl Czerny, and, more important, Ludwig van Beethoven, and possibly Franz Schubert. On his return to Lower Canada the following year Molt claimed to have been their pupil. That Molt could have received lessons from all these prestigious musicians in such a short period is open to doubt. Whatever the case, his connections with Beethoven were more those of an admirer of the master's works than those of a pupil, and earned the "teacher of music at Quebec in America," as Molt called himself, the few bars of a canon on the words "Freu Dich des Lebens," written 16 Dec. 1825.

Molt returned to Quebec at the beginning of June 1826 and resumed work as a music teacher. Two years later he published at Quebec a pedagogical work entitled *Elementary treatise on music, more particularly adapted to the piano forte* and dedicated to his pupils. This bilingual theoretical work, the first of its kind printed in Lower Canada, showed his concern for imparting the latest knowledge and principles in an "absolutely simple and familiar" style. The originality of this teaching method stemmed from its approach, which was to engage the student in "joining theory to practice."

In 1833, a year after inventing a teaching instrument called a chromatometer, which Helmut Kallmann describes as one of the first such devices to be patented in Lower Canada, Molt left Quebec for Burlington, Vt. After a difficult start he was hired in May 1835 as a music teacher at the Burlington Female Seminary, recently founded by Converse. According to Converse, Molt spent 10 to 12 hours daily at that institution on private lessons, but was still able to find time to compose music for publication. Thus it may well have been there that Molt wrote his works for piano, in particular *Post horn waltz with variations*, and his pieces for voice and piano, which were published at Philadelphia, undated, after 1833.

In the summer of 1837 Molt left Vermont for Montreal. Between August and November of that year he put an announcement in *La Minerve* informing "the ladies and gentlemen of Montreal that he has taken up residence in that city and that he most respectfully offers them his services as TEACHER OF PIANOFORTE, ORGAN AND VIOLIN, teacher of SINGING and teacher of THOROUGH BASS." The announcement also says that "his plan of instruction on the pianoforte and on the organ is at once new and the result of several years' close study of the needs of the pupil; Mr. MOLT, through his courses of instruction, can complete in half the time that is generally presumed necessary the entire education of a pupil."

It is not known how long Molt remained in Montreal, but he does not seem to have succeeded in making a name there. That he shortly returned to Burlington cannot be ruled out in the light of a letter written there on 6 July 1841 but unsigned, which was sent by Ludger DUVERNAY to Louis Perrault*. The writer of the letter had been invited by Molt to "go into partnership with him to publish a monthly musical journal, containing accompaniments to sacred music as sung in churches in the United States." This project had evidently come to nothing, for in May 1841 Molt was back in Quebec.

In November, after six months' satisfactory service, the *fabrique* of Notre-Dame engaged Molt on the basis of his offer "to play the organ and form a permanent choir . . . for an annual salary of 100 pounds current." The contract further stipulated that he was responsible for tuning the reed-stops of the organ and "preparing and supplying at his own expense all the books, exercise books or sheets of music and song which he needs," these to be subsequently given to the *fabrique*. During the following years Molt looked after arranging and copying pieces of music – he estimated in 1846 that he had done some "6,000 sheets." Furthermore, in 1844 and 1845 he published two instalments of a work he had compiled and arranged, *Lyre sainte: recueil de cantiques, hymnes, motets, &c.* He also brought out at Quebec in 1845 *Traité élémentaire de musique vocale*, an 89-page manual dealing with fundamental concepts of music theory, sol-fa, and vocal technique.

Molt attracted public attention through his participation in the Saint-Jean-Baptiste celebrations, probably in 1847, as a choir director, and on this occasion received a silver snuff-box. The compilation of *La lyre canadienne: répertoire des meilleures chansons et romances du jour*, published anonymously that year, can also plausibly be attributed to him. It is known that as early as 1842 Molt had toyed with "publishing some time a collection of selected songs with music," and in a desire to stress the Canadian aspect of his book had invited all and sundry to supply him with songs or "newly composed couplets of Canadian origin." For the period 25 July 1847 to 25 March 1849 the Séminaire de Québec possesses various receipts which show that Molt was then teaching singing at the Petit Séminaire de Québec. Since the "lay choir" which he had contracted to direct in 1841 consisted largely of pupils from that institution, it is probable that he had begun to teach there that year.

A series of disappointments as well as manœuvres behind his back and a feeling of generally being misunderstood were, however, to prevent Molt from carrying on with his work. In July 1845 his creditors demanded that he transfer up to £84 of his earnings at the church. A week before the last payment was due, his wife and two of his sons, Frédéric-Félix and Adolphe-Alphonse, perished when the Théâtre Saint-Louis went up in flames on 12 June 1846. Finally, two years later, the churchwardens, who had in their possession a letter from Marie-Hippolyte-Antoine Dessane* with an offer to serve as organist, used what they described as Molt's excessive "indifference in executing the duties of his office," and the parishioners' dissatisfaction with him, as an excuse to dismiss him from his post. In fact, his discharge may have been prompted more by his marriage with Harriett Cowan on 14 June 1848 in the Anglican Cathedral of the Holy Trinity at Quebec, which ran counter to the spirit of the churchwardens' resolutions on the qualifications and duties of organist and chapel master as set out in a document dated 1837.

These events drove Molt away from Quebec, and around the middle of 1849 he moved back to Burlington with his family. During the last years of his life, as well as teaching at the Burlington Female Seminary he published a *New and original method for the pianoforte, 51 progressive lessons*, and *The pupil's guide and young teacher's manual, or the elements of piano forte playing*; an announcement that they were for sale by subscription appeared in 1854. However, Molt apparently did not break all ties with his first adopted city, since, according to the musician and journalist Nazaire Levasseur*, his name appeared in 1855 on the list of members of the Société Harmonique de Québec. Molt died at Burlington on 16 Nov. 1856, at the age of 61.

In his career, Théodore-Frédéric Molt concentrated on a professional standard of instruction in music that was marked especially by clarity, simplicity, and a methodical approach. This was the field of endeavour in which he most clearly distinguished himself, amongst such musicians as Frédéric-Henri Glackmeyer, John Chrisostomus Brauneis*, Jean-Chrysostome Brauneis*, and others with whom he maintained close relations during the first half of the

Moncoq

19th century in Lower Canada. Hence he himself liked to be thought of as a music teacher. At the end of his life, after more than 30 years of teaching in North America, Molt could take pride in his many pupils now dispersed throughout Lower Canada, some of whom had already assumed their master's role.

Lucien Poirier

Théodore-Frédéric Molt is the author of several works on teaching methods in music, the principal ones being *Elementary treatise on music, more particularly adapted to the piano forte* (Quebec, 1828); *Traité élémentaire de musique vocale* (Québec, 1845); *New and original method for the pianoforte* (Burlington, Vt., n.d.); *51 progressive lessons* (Burlington, n.d.); *The pupil's guide and young teacher's manual, or the elements of the piano forte playing* (Burlington, 1854). He also compiled and arranged two instalments of *Lyre sainte: recueil de cantiques, hymnes, motets, &c.* (Québec, 1844–45). He composed a number of works for the piano, principally songs and dances, and did more than 6,000 arrangements and harmonizations of sacred music; of these there remain fewer than 200 organ accompaniments for various liturgical pieces, inscribed in two manuscript notebooks at the National Library of Canada, and the 19 canticles, hymns, and motets included in *Lyre sainte*. The compilation of *La lyre canadienne: répertoire des meilleures chansons et romances du jour*, published anonymously at Quebec in 1847, can also be attributed to him.

ANQ-Q, CE1-1, 4 juin 1824, 16 juill. 1833; CE1-61, 14 juin 1848; CE1-66, 13 mars 1823; CN1-265, 5 nov. 1841, 11 juill. 1845, 14 avril 1846; P-68, no.510. AP, Notre-Dame de Québec, Livres des délibérations de la fabrique, 1837–48. ASQ, Fonds Plante, no.22; Polygraphie, XXVI: 21, 50; Séminaire, 218, nos.603–4. *Journal de l'Instruction publique* (Québec et Montréal), 3 (1859): 17. *Piano music I*, ed. Elaine Keillor (Ottawa, 1983). *Le Canadien*, 3, 24 mars 1845; 15 juin 1846. *Mélanges religieux, feuilleton*, 4 févr. 1842. *La Minerve*, 21 août 1837, 3 déc. 1856. *Quebec Gazette*, 21 April 1823; 18 March, 15 July, 2 Sept., 9 Dec. 1824; 13 June 1825. *Quebec Mercury*, 21 June 1822. *Catalogue of Canadian composers*, ed. Helmut Kallmann (2nd ed., Toronto, 1952; repr. St Clair Shores, Mich., 1972), 176. *Encyclopedia of music in Canada* (Kallmann et al.). *The Vermont historical gazetteer: a magazine, embracing a history of each town, civil, ecclesiastical, biographical and military*, ed. A. M. Hemenway (3v., Burlington, 1868), 1: 531–34. Willy Amtmann, *La musique au Québec, 1600–1875*, Michelle Pharand, trad. (Montréal, 1976), 294, 376–81. H.-J.-J.-B. Chouinard, *Fête nationale des Canadiens-Français célébrée à Québec en 1880: histoire, discours, rapports . . .* (4v., Québec, 1881–1903), 4: 521–22. Helmut Kallmann, *A history of music in Canada, 1534–1914* (Toronto and London, 1960), 79–82, 138. *Thayer's life of Beethoven*, ed. Elliot Forbes (2nd ed., 2v., Princeton, N.J., 1964), 2: 969–71. Helmut Kallmann, "Beethoven and Canada: a miscellany," *Les Cahiers canadiens de musique* (Montréal), 2 (1971): 107. Nazaire LeVasseur, "Musique et musiciens à Québec: souvenirs d'un amateur," *La Musique* (Québec), 1 (1919): 26, 52, 98, 110, 126. "Le recueil de cantiques de Molt," *BRH*, 46 (1940): 168. P.-G. Roy, "Le théâtre Saint-Louis, à Québec," *BRH*, 42 (1936): 174–88.

MONCOQ (Montcoq, Muncoq), MICHEL, Roman Catholic priest; b. 2 Aug. 1827 in Truttemer-le-Grand, dept of Calvados, France, son of Guillaume Moncoq and Marie-Anne Desmottes; d. 1 Jan. 1856 near Algonac, Mich.

Michel Moncoq was one of eight well-educated children: both his sisters became nuns, he and a brother priests, and his twin brother may have become a physician. He entered the Grand Séminaire de Caen around 1849 and at the end of 1851 was ordained deacon. In 1852, perhaps in response to a circular letter written by Toronto's Bishop Armand-François-Marie de Charbonnel* concerning the need for clergy in his diocese, Moncoq expressed a desire to serve as a missionary to the Indians in Canada. Released for service there, he embarked in 1852 in the company of the Reverend Jean-Mathieu Soulerin* and his fellow Basilians, one of whom later said that during the voyage Moncoq "gained every heart by the suavity of his manners, his modest deportment and his retiring disposition." He was ordained priest in Toronto by Charbonnel on 29 Sept. 1852, shortly after arriving.

Despite a severe shortage of clergy in Toronto, Charbonnel felt strongly enough about the need to provide for the Indians of his diocese, then comprising the entire western part of the province, that he released Moncoq from pastoral responsibilities to enable him to prepare for his missionary duties among them. Moncoq spent the next two years in Lower Canada studying Indian languages and customs and English. He studied first among the Algonkins and Iroquois in the Sulpician mission at Lac-des-Deux-Montagnes (Oka) and then, with the help of Father Joseph Marcoux, among the Iroquois at Caughnawaga (Kahnawake). Moncoq's active ministry began in 1854 when he left Caughnawaga for a brief stay at Penetanguishene, whose temporary pastor the previous winter had been the Reverend Nicolas-Marie-Joseph Frémiot. He then made a trip to Manitoulin Island to visit Father Dominique Du Ranquet*, who had served in the missions along the St Clair River to which Moncoq was appointed in October. He was assigned to serve both Indians and whites from Point Pelee to Penetanguishene.

Moncoq soon won them over by his affability, his linguistic skills, and, above all, by his zeal. His ministry to the Indians – mostly Ojibwas, Potawatomis, and Ottawas, whose languages were closely related to that of the Algonkins, and some Iroquois from Caughnawaga -- was especially effective. In Moncoq, according to a later account, the Indians once again had "a black-gown who would speak and pray and celebrate the mysteries of the Great Manitu in their own sweet language." His labours on their behalf, according to another commentator, were extraordinary: "It was no uncommon feat for him to celebrate Mass on the same day in widely distant missions. No Indian reserve was too remote to receive his frequent visits." But the Indians, whose spiritual welfare he had so much at heart, were not his only responsibility. In order to render better service to immigrants recently settled in the region Moncoq chose to reside in a central location, took steps to establish new parishes for the settlers, and bought property for a church in Owen Sound. Throughout his vast region he preached the Gospel in English, French, or whatever Indian language his congregation required. The Catholics of Owen Sound had hoped that he would become their pastor, but their wish was not to be granted.

Moncoq's zeal, which one observer later described as excessive, may have been the indirect cause of his death. On New Year's Day, 1856, Moncoq was at Babys Point when he was called to attend a sick Indian woman at Algonac, Mich. His guide across the frozen river was the woman's only son. For the return walk he dismissed his guide, missed a detour around a weak spot in the ice, and fell through it. One biographer wrote: "It seems that he struggled for a while. His cries were heard, but no one heeded them, thinking them to be the screams of some drunken Indian." His death ended an active ministry of only 15 months. Rumours that he had been murdered prompted a fellow priest to investigate, and in February he reported to Charbonnel that Moncoq's death was accidental. His body was found on the American side of the river in July and was brought to Babys Point for burial; in 1878 it was moved to Port Lambton where it rests beneath Sacred Heart Church.

In his personal life Moncoq was frugal, seldom accepting money from those he served, at times not drawing his salary. His piety was profound. Days before his death he is said to have written to Charbonnel that "he wished to bind himself by the vows of poverty and obedience that he might live the more mortified to himself, the more devoted to souls and the more united to God." His death brought to an end the era of Roman Catholic missionary service in what is now southwestern Ontario. The Indians would thenceforth be attended by the priests of neighbouring parishes with occasional visits from priests who spoke their language, possibly stopping while en route to or from Manitoulin Island.

ROBERT JOSEPH SCOLLARD

[Some of the principal sources for the life of Michel Moncoq are given below; a complete, annotated bibliography is in R. J. Scollard, *A young and holy priest: the life of Rev. Michel Moncoq, 1827–1856* (Toronto, 1979). Users of that bibliography should be aware that the second volume of Father Kelly's biographical notes (cited below) has now been found. R.J.S.]

AAT, Edward Kelly, "Biographical notes of some interest to me, probably not so to anybody else," 1: 203; 2: 125–27 (the latter reference notes that the entry for Moncoq continues on p.19 of a seventh volume, which has not been located). Arch. de l'évêché de Bayeux-Lisieux (Bayeux, France), Reg. du personnel. Arch. of the Diocese of London (London, Ont.), J. G. Mugan, "Historical notes and records of the parish of Corunna" (1901), 37–39 (this work was published in six weekly instalments in *Canadian Observer* (Sarnia, Ont.), under the title "The Mugan manuscript"; the last, on p.8 of the issue for 10 Sept. 1949, contains a biography of Moncoq). Private arch., Joseph Finn (Chatham, Ont.), R. H. Dignan, "History of the Diocese of London" (photocopy at Arch. of the Diocese of London), 72–77, 88, 90, 98, 105. St Joseph (Roman Catholic Church) (Corunna, Ont.), Reg. of baptisms, marriages, and burials. *Lambton Observer, and Western Advertiser*, 31 Jan. 1856. *Toronto Mirror*, 11 Jan. 1856. Félix Gauthier, "A monument to the memory of Father Moncoq," *Canadian Freeman* (Toronto), 20 May 1869. "Père Montcoq," *Sarnia Observer, and Lambton Advertiser*, 21 June 1878. "Rev. Father Moncoq: re-interment of his hallowed remains at Port Lambton," *Irish Canadian* (Toronto), 19 June 1878.

MORAND, PAUL (called **Hypolithe** in his youth), silversmith; b. 1782–83 or 1785, son of Laurent Morand, blacksmith, and Pélagie Massue; m. 29 Sept. 1845 Marie-Anne Dufresne, widow of François Bergevin, *dit* Langevin, in Montreal; d. there 11 July 1854.

There is no doubt about the identity of Paul Morand's parents, who are named in his marriage certificate. They were married in Varennes in 1771 and parish records have so far revealed 12 offspring born between 1772 and 1795 in Varennes, Pointe-aux-Trembles (Montreal), Saint-Eustache, and Sainte-Thérèse-de-Blainville (Sainte-Thérèse), but Paul is not one of them. On 28 April 1802 "Hypolithe" Morand, son of Laurent Morand and aged approximately 18, was apprenticed as a silversmith. Paul being an evident contraction for Hypolithe, it is reasonable to assume that, despite the hypothesis published by Gérard Morisset* in 1954, only one person is involved, and that, given the birth dates of the other 12 children, Paul was born either between September 1782 and June 1783 or between February and April 1785.

Morand's apprenticeship was to Pierre Huguet*, *dit* Latour, then a prosperous silversmith and merchant possessing one of Montreal's largest ateliers and most important stores. Huguet had had several apprentices. At the time of Morand's arrival, he was assisted by his son Pierre and apprentice Salomon Marion*. Morand no doubt worked closely with them. According to Marion's contract, his term expired in February 1803. Morand's own term expired when he reached the age of 21, presumably between September 1803 and April 1806. Huguet does not seem to have employed any other apprentices until 1810 when he engaged Alexander Fraser and signed a very important contract for several religious vessels to be made by Marion. Morand was probably also employed by Huguet at the completion of his apprenticeship: no silver has yet been discovered bearing his own mark before 1819. The first reference to Morand after his apprenticeship is as witness at Marion's marriage on 20 Oct. 1817, four months after Huguet's own death.

The few facts known about Morand are that he lived on Rue Saint-Vincent in 1819–20 and on Rue Viger (Rue Saint-Amable) from 1831 until his death. His marriage in 1845 seems to have been the major event of his life. In the following year he bequeathed all his belongings to his wife. He died on 11 July 1854 "at 5.30 p.m. after a lengthy illness, endured with the resignation of a true Christian. . . . He leaves in mourning an inconsolable wife and sister." In 1855–56 his widow was still living on Saint-Amable; in the following year she was not listed in the city directory.

Morand's first recorded works are a stoup and a ewer bought in 1819 by the parish of Sainte-Madeleine at Rigaud, the year in which he was first referred to as a silversmith in the Montreal city directory. From then until 1851 he received payment for religious vessels or repairs in 17 parishes; his silverware has also been found in several other locations. Morisset interpreted the records of these activities quite freely and almost abusively when he wrote that in 1817 "Salomon Marion . . . inherited many of his former master's religious clients and kept them until his death in 1830. Paul Morand, in turn, benefited from the premature departure of his colleague: henceforth, and until his death he was the usual supplier for the parishes in the Montreal region." Much of Morand's silverwork is identical to objects bearing Huguet's punch mark, PH; these pieces labelled and sold by Huguet may have been made by Morand.

In his article on Morand, Morisset discussed his styles and works, comparing them with others of the period. According to him, "The two censers of Varennes, fashioned in 1826 . . . are probably his masterpieces, at least the most perfect works he left behind." Morisset's criteria are debatable; he rejected every style that departed from "the best French Canadian tradition." He concluded, xenophobically, that all Anglo-Saxon influences on Montreal silversmiths were a cause of decadence and profound stylistic degradation. Morand's works are the best proof that these diverse influences were a source of evolution and of richness. His chalices, censers, baptismal ewers, and paxes were innovative in shape and decoration. Many of these objects, those in the

Henry Birks Collection of Silver for example, are far more interesting than the two Varennes censers praised by Morisset because they looked like those of Laurent Amiot* or François Sasseville*. It is true, however, that industrialization had a significant impact on aesthetics, and that some of Morand's designs suffered from his imitating commercialized objects executed in poor taste.

Numerous silver articles sold today as the work of local 19th-century silversmiths are in fact objects manufactured in such places as India or the Channel Islands. Styles and marks found on these pieces are very similar to those of Huguet, Morand, or Henry Polonceau, demonstrating the need for a stylistic analysis of Canadian colonial silversmithing in comparison with that of other British colonies. Morand's work, nevertheless, stands out as an important landmark in the evolution of religious silversmithing in Canada. Both the man and his work deserve a better understanding.

ROBERT DEROME and NORMA MORGAN

Works by Paul Morand are found in the Henry Birks Collection of Silver at the National Gallery of Canada (Ottawa), the Musée du Québec (Québec), the Montreal Museum of Fine Arts, the McCord Museum, and various churches in the Montreal area.

ANQ-M, CE1-10, 10 sept. 1771; CE1-51, 20 oct. 1817, 29 sept. 1845, 14 juill. 1854; CN1-32, 19 oct. 1846; CN1-74, 14 juill. 1812; CN1-128, 30 mars 1795, 25 sept. 1797, 23 juill. 1798, 28 avril 1802; CN1-243, 13 févr., 14 juin 1810. AP, Sainte-Madeleine (Rigaud), livres de comptes, 1819. MAC-CD, Fonds Morisset, 2, M829.2/P324. *La Minerve*, 2 oct. 1845, 22 juill. 1854. *Canada directory*, 1851–57. Groupe de recherche sur la société montréalaise au XIXe siècle, *Répertoire des rues de Montréal au XIXe siècle* (Montréal, 1976). *Montreal directory*, 1819. R. H. Mayne, *Old Channel Island silver, its makers and marks* (Jersey, 1969). Morisset, *Coup d'œil sur les arts*, 106–7. Ramsay Traquair, *The old silver of Quebec* (Toronto, 1940). W. R. T. Wilkinson, *Indian colonial silver: European silversmiths (1790–1860) and their marks* (London, 1973). Gérard Morisset, "L'orfèvre Paul Morand, 1784–1854," RSC *Trans*, 3rd ser., 48 (1954), sect.I: 29–35.

MORRIS, MARY. *See* COY

MORRIS, WILLIAM, businessman, militia officer, justice of the peace, politician, and school administrator; b. 31 Oct. 1786 in Paisley, Scotland, second child of Alexander Morris and Janet Lang; m. 15 Aug. 1823 Elizabeth Cochran of Kirktonfield, parish of Neilston, Scotland, and they had three sons and four daughters; d. 29 June 1858 in Montreal.

William Morris, champion of the Church of Scotland in the Canadas, was the son of a well-to-do Scottish manufacturer. He was brought up in comfort in Paisley where he attended the local grammar school. In the spring of 1801 the Morris family, encouraged by friends in Upper Canada and armed with a letter of introduction to Lieutenant Governor Peter Hunter*, set sail for Canada in search of increased wealth. After some hesitation William's father ventured his capital on the import-export trade between Montreal and Scotland. But in 1804 and 1805 he suffered severe financial reverses and shortly thereafter retired to a farm near Elizabethtown (Brockville), Upper Canada. There, amid heavy debts, he died in 1809. William, who had returned with the family to Scotland in 1802 and remained there with his mother, sister, and younger brother James* for nearly four years, had come back to Canada in the fall of 1806. With his elder brother Alexander, he set out to repay their late father's creditors and recoup the family fortunes. Not destitute, yet financially unable to engage in the transatlantic trade as importers or wholesalers, they opened a store in Elizabethtown. They became two more of those small merchants in Upper Canada who served as middlemen between the mercantile houses of Montreal and the Indians, loggers, and settlers peopling the edge of the wilderness.

On the outbreak of the War of 1812 William obtained a commission as ensign in the 1st Leeds Militia. He took part in a number of operations culminating in the battle of Ogdensburg, N.Y., in February 1813 when he was detailed by Lieutenant-Colonel George Richard John Macdonell* to lead the successful assault on the old French fort. The following year he resigned from the militia to return to the family business. The war had been an exciting interlude, one which convinced him that Canadians were fundamentally loyal to the crown and capable of defending their country.

The brothers, looking for new commercial opportunities, decided to open a second store in the proposed military settlement at Perth. In 1816 William left Alexander in charge of the store in Brockville and travelled to Perth where hard work, frugality, and a keen eye for business drove him up the ladder of success. It was not long before he was the largest merchant in town, and he was soon deeply involved in local real estate. In partnership with Alexander, then with their younger brother James, and by the late 1830s acting independently, William slowly and persistently expanded his speculation in land into the rest of eastern Upper Canada and then right across the province. Mindful of their father's problems, the Morris brothers were careful never to overextend themselves or to concentrate too heavily in any one enterprise. William wisely invested his excess capital from his land speculation and store in the new Canadian banking industry. Not all his ventures were to prove successful, however. Efforts to provide for navigation on the Tay River between Perth and the

Lower Rideau Lake culminated in 1831 in the incorporation of the Tay Navigation Company, behind which Morris was the leading spirit and chief stockholder. The first Tay Canal was opened in 1834, but the company was plagued by lack of funds, and the canal works ultimately fell into decay.

By the 1820s Morris had become a prominent figure in the Perth area. Commissioned a justice of the peace in 1818, he spearheaded the successful campaign the following year to obtain a seat in the House of Assembly for the Perth region. In the area's first general election in 1820 he was swept into office. A conscientious constituency man, he held the seat for Carleton and later for Lanark without trouble until his appointment to the Legislative Council in 1836 removed him from elective politics. Morris was named lieutenant-colonel of the newly formed 2nd Regiment of Carleton militia in 1822 and remained active in the militia for more than 20 years. During 1837–38, as senior colonel in Lanark County, he twice called out detachments to suppress rebellion and oppose invasion and on one occasion went in command himself. Successful businessman, militia colonel, and leader of the local conservative forces, William Morris was a man to be both courted and feared.

In the assembly Morris aligned himself with like-minded members such as John Beverley Robinson*, with whom he led the movement to expel the American-born reformer Barnabas Bidwell* from the house in 1821–22. An able parliamentarian and born tactician, he was one of the work-horses of the legislature who could be counted upon when the division bells rang. Although in time he became a leading force in the assembly, he never entered the charmed circle of "family compact" members who held official portfolios. Indeed, he came to have an intense hatred for them despite the many ideological assumptions they held in common.

Superficially, the reason for Morris's alienation from the predominantly Anglican conservative élite lay in his championship of the right of the Church of Scotland's colonial offshoots to a share in the clergy reserves. But his advocacy of the cause far exceeded his religious commitment. The clergy reserves for Morris, and for many other Scots, were the symbolic battleground in a struggle over whether the British empire would be uninational or binational in character. Until his death Morris publicly held steadfast to his triple belief that it was the Church of Scotland which gave form and substance to Scottish society, that the resultant Scottish nation was England's coequal partner in controlling and developing all parts of the empire acquired since the union of 1707, and that Scots Canadians were the heirs of this patrimony in the Canadas. It was this intense Scots nationalism that set him at loggerheads not only with many of his

Morris

fellow conservatives but also with the leaders of most other ethnic, religious, and political groups in the community.

The issue broke into the open late in 1823. That summer Morris had visited Scotland after an absence of 17 years, married, and established contact with the Reverend Duncan Mearns, the convener of the colonial committee of the Church of Scotland. On his return to Upper Canada, Morris introduced a bill calling for local recognition of the Church of Scotland as one of the two national churches of the British empire and for the equal funding of the two, if necessary, from the clergy reserves. Though narrowly defeated in the Legislative Council through the efforts of the Reverend John Strachan*, the bill was sent as an address to the king from the assembly in January 1824. What Morris had done was to take up an issue that had had, until then, little interest for any save a small group of Anglicans and a handful of Presbyterian ministers and thrust it into the public domain of the assembly, the newspapers, and, ultimately, the hustings.

For the next 17 years Morris led the political battle for what he saw as the rights of Scots Presbyterians. To demonstrate their numerical strength and to refute the opinions and statistics of Strachan's "Ecclesiastical Chart," he sought to have a religious census taken in 1827. What Morris lacked, at first, was the backing of a strong, effective colonial church since Presbyterians were a scattered, doctrinally diverse, and largely unorganized group. He therefore supported the colonial committee of the Church of Scotland and a few local ministers such as Robert McGill and John McKenzie in their efforts to form a synod. These efforts culminated in 1831 with the creation of the Synod of the Presbyterian Church of Canada in connection with the Church of Scotland. Morris also pressed the home church to send out more ministers in order to bolster the synod's importance.

In 1837 the synod, incensed over Lieutenant Governor Sir John Colborne*'s injudicious creation of 44 Anglican rectories the previous year, asked Morris to go to England to counter the seeming Anglican hegemony and to plead for equal and exclusive state recognition and funding for the two churches. Soon after arriving in London, however, Morris, sensing the reluctance of the government to ignore other Protestant groups, revised his stand and suggested that any government grant be divided into thirds, one part each for the Anglicans and the Scots Presbyterians, and the final third for any other Protestant groups thought deserving. Back in the Canadas he enthusiastically told the synod that the imperial law officers had declared the rectories illegal and that the Colonial Office and its secretary, Lord Glenelg, warmly supported the proposals he had put to them. His optimism proved premature; Lieutenant Governor Sir Francis Bond Head* seized on the vague wording of

Glenelg's public dispatches to oppose the synod's claims.

Over the next two years Morris consolidated support for his funding scheme among the clergy of his church, coordinated Scots Presbyterian pressure on the local administration and the British government, and attempted to weaken the confidence of the Colonial Office in Strachan and his allies. Settlement seemed near in 1839. The new governor-in-chief, Charles Edward Poulett Thomson*, determined to achieve the union of the Canadas and to resolve outstanding grievances in the colony, gathered around him a coalition of moderates, of which Morris was a key member. In return for Morris's political support in the Legislative Council and his influence among Presbyterians, the governor backed his campaign to bring about the merger of the two largest Presbyterian bodies in the Canadas, the United Synod of Upper Canada and the Synod of the Presbyterian Church of Canada in connection with the Church of Scotland. After intense negotiations, during which Morris held out the prospect of a clergy reserves settlement whereby all ministers belonging to the amalgamated church would benefit, the merger was finally accomplished in July 1840. The British parliament modified the proposals, however, and awarded the Church of England twice the amount granted to the Presbyterians, basing its decision on the census of 1839 which incorrectly recorded twice as many Anglicans as Presbyterians. Morris rationalized away his misgivings. The right of the two churches to equal funding had been acknowledged, and he persuaded his church to accept the Clergy Reserves Act of 1840 as a vindication, in principle, of their position.

The long bitter fight over Scottish rights in the British empire was not the only issue that set Morris outside the controlling élite. His views on education were a source of contention as well. Morris first became publicly involved in educational matters at Perth in 1822 as a member on a board of the Court of Quarter Sessions authorized to distribute funds to the Bathurst District grammar school. By the late 1820s he had become a recognized authority on the distressing state of schooling in Upper Canada. Convinced of the efficacy of education to produce a stable, prosperous society, he pleaded for a comprehensive, state-controlled system of free common schools capped in each district by a grammar school providing a classical education. He was opposed to plans to create a provincial university, believing that until the infrastructure had been laid a university was superfluous. Those in need of higher education could, he maintained, go to Great Britain. Moreover, the proposed university, King's College (University of Toronto), seemed destined under Strachan to become a bastion of Anglican power and yet another affront to his nationalism. When it became apparent in the mid 1830s that the college's 1827 charter would not be revoked, Morris argued for a non-sectarian university. Soon after, he compromised by suggesting that two state-funded chairs of Anglican and Presbyterian theology be added to the university, and Lord Glenelg gave some encouragement to this idea. However, by 1839 even these moderate proposals seemed unattainable, and Morris began to fear that Scots Presbyterians would be excluded from administrative and teaching posts at the university during Strachan's lifetime.

Just at this moment pressure within the Presbyterian Church of Canada in connection with the Church of Scotland for some form of local theological training had reached its bursting point. A committee of the synod under William RINTOUL asked Morris to obtain an act enabling it to establish a seminary. Morris turned from his frustrating struggle over King's to the more positive task of creating a new institution. Within a matter of weeks he had escalated the original proposal into a draft charter for a Presbyterian college complete with an arts and science faculty. By the winter of 1839–40 he was demanding that the proposed college, to be built at Kingston, be named Queen's College to emphasize its equality with King's and to demonstrate to Upper Canadians the parity of Scots and English in the empire. When it became known in January 1840 that the provincial government could not authorize the use of this title without the consent of the crown, Morris persuaded the synod to apply for a royal charter. Throughout the next two years, as chairman of the board of trustees, he bullied and cajoled his church into active efforts towards setting up the new college. By the time the royal charter was granted to Queen's in October 1841 it was clear that Morris, more than any other individual, was responsible for its foundation.

The battle had taken its toll. Morris never found it congenial to work with clergymen; he chafed at what he deemed their laziness and inefficiency and distrusted their apparent thirst for power. Continual clashes with his fellow trustees blunted much of his enthusiasm for Queen's, and the disastrous financial plight of the college further dimmed his initial ardour. In the harsh light of economic reality it was clear that Queen's would not, in the foreseeable future, be the great Scottish-style university he had envisaged. Disillusioned, he decided to send his eldest son, Alexander*, to Scotland to be educated. In February 1842 he stopped attending board meetings, and in July he resigned from his position as chairman.

This mood found Morris responsive to the suggestion put forward by the first principal of Queen's, Thomas Liddell*, and a number of board members that the college be moved to Toronto and amalgamated with King's. Morris quickly reverted to his earlier contention that in a new country where funds were scarce what was needed was one secular, state-supported university with two or more theological chairs. For the next half decade he advanced that

cause, fighting for the university bills sponsored in turn by Robert BALDWIN and William Henry Draper*. The disillusionment Morris felt over the Queen's experiment was further deepened by the disruption of 1844, when the Presbyterian church split into two factions. It seemed to him that the ministers, in their myopic way, threatened to undo all that he had achieved at such great effort.

Morris found solace in the world of politics. After the union of Upper and Lower Canada in 1841 he had been appointed to the new Legislative Council, and the following year he was made warden of the Johnstown District. When most of the Executive Council resigned over the patronage issue in 1843, Morris pledged his support to the governor-in-chief, Sir Charles Theophilus Metcalfe*, took part in strategy sessions, and then retired to Brockville, his home since 1842, to await events. In September 1844 he accepted the receiver generalship in the Draper government and in the following election stumped the province, successfully rallying conservative Presbyterians to the governor's banner. His astute business sense and eagle eye for economy made him a model receiver general, and in 1845 he moved to Montreal to be nearer his work. He later boasted that he had streamlined the department, introduced new procedures, and earned the government £11,000 of interest from his deposits of public money. In 1846 he accepted the post of president of the Executive Council and held both positions until May 1847 when he persuaded John A. Macdonald* to take over from him as receiver general. But illness dogged his footsteps, and he was not unhappy to use the opportunity afforded by the defeat of the government in 1848 to spend the next two winters in the West Indies in search of renewed health.

In 1851 the Presbyterian Church of Canada in connection with the Church of Scotland became alarmed by moves to expropriate their lands and revenues set afoot in the assembly the previous year by James Hervey Price*. They begged Morris to go to London to defend the share of the clergy reserves that he had won for them more than a decade earlier. Though a tired, ill man, he could not resist the call of his church and once again undertook the weary rounds of the Colonial Office. The old phrases and claims were dredged up, but this time the government was not receptive. Undaunted, Morris began to meld a strong opposition from a variety of disparate groups, including Anglican bishops and Scottish nationalists in the House of Lords and conservative politicians in the House of Commons. Faced with this hostile array and beset by myriad other difficulties, Lord John Russell's Whig government backed down. The Canadian proposal was shelved.

Heartened by this success, Morris became involved with Queen's again. For the next two years, until a stroke finally forced him into seclusion, he absorbed

Morrison

himself in its problems. Through the years he had kept a close watch over his business concerns, including his store at Perth. Though he sold out to John Murray in 1852, Morris, and later his son John Lang Morris, retained an active interest in the store. When Morris died in 1858, he left an estate worth £37,000 in land, cash, and securities.

William Morris had recognized many of the social and political forces at work in the Canadas and had, on occasion, modified his stands accordingly. None the less he always remained true to his fundamental belief in the equal rights of Scots and English in the empire. His strong Scots Presbyterian identity not only helped shape the causes he championed, but set him at odds with many of his fellow conservatives in Upper Canada and, indeed, helped undermine the position of the colonial élite.

H. J. BRIDGMAN

[Pamphlets by William Morris include *The correspondence of the Hon. William Morris with the Colonial Office, as the delegate from the Presbyterian body in Canada*, [ed. Alexander Gale (Niagara [Niagara-on-the-Lake, Ont.], 1838)]; *A letter on the subject of the clergy reserves, addressed to the Very Rev. Macfarlan and the Rev. Dr. Burns* and *Reply of William Morris, member of the Legislative Council of Upper Canada, to six letters, addressed to him by John Strachan, D.D., Archdeacon of York*, both published at Toronto in 1838; *Facts and particulars relating to the case of Morris* vs. *Cameron, recently tried at Brockville* (Montreal, 1845); and *Observations respecting the clergy reserves in Canada* (London, 1851). The "Journal of the Honourable William Morris's mission to England in the year 1837" has been edited by E. C. Kyte and published in *OH*, 30 (1934): 212–62, and his West Indian diary appears as "Twilight in Jamaica," *Douglas Library Notes* (Kingston, Ont.), 14 (1965), no.2.

The main source for Morris is the collection of his papers at QUA; the Alexander Morris papers in AO, MS 535 illuminate his land dealings. More fragmentary sources are the Edmund Montague Morris papers at PAC, MG 30, D6, and, at QUA, the William Bell papers, the Synod papers of the Presbyterian Church of Canada in connection with the Church of Scotland, and the Queen's Univ. letters.

A biographical sketch and photograph of Morris appear in William Notman and [J.] F. Taylor, *Portraits of British Americans, with biographical sketches* (3v., Montreal, 1865–68), 1. Two more modern treatments are found in H. [M.] Neatby, "The Honourable William Morris, 1786–1858," *Historic Kingston*, no.20 (1972): 65–76, and H. J. Bridgman, "Three Scots Presbyterians in Upper Canada; a study in emigration, nationalism and religion" (PHD thesis, Queen's Univ., Kingston, 1978). H.J.B.]

BLHU, R. G. Dun & Co. credit ledger, Canada, 17: 179. U.C., House of Assembly, *Journal*, 1821–35. *Montreal Gazette*, 10 July 1858. H. R. Morgan, "The first Tay Canal, an abortive Upper Canadian transportation enterprise of a century ago," *OH*, 29 (1933): 103–16.

MORRISON, THOMAS DAVID, clerk, physician, and politician; b. *c.* 1796, son of William Morrison;

m. 2 Sept. 1818 Effie Gilbert, *née* Patrick, in York (Toronto); d. 19 March 1856 in Toronto.

Thomas David Morrison was born at Quebec, where his father was senior clerk of works in the Royal Engineers department at the time of his death in 1842. During the War of 1812 the young Morrison served as a clerk in the purveyor's branch of the British army's medical department; following his reduction he became, by 1816, a clerk in the office of the surveyor general in York. In 1818 he married the sister of William Poyntz Patrick, a clerk in the House of Assembly and a prominent Methodist. Originally an Anglican, Morrison participated that year in the organization of the first Methodist church in York. In June 1822 he was dismissed by Surveyor General Thomas Ridout* for uttering "languages" and advancing "opinions very unbecoming a person employed in one of His Majesty's public offices." Some time after his dismissal he reputedly travelled to the United States to pursue a medical education. Returning to York, he was examined on 5 July 1824, by Christopher WIDMER, Grant Powell*, and Robert Charles Horne* of the Medical Board of Upper Canada, and was licensed to practise "Physic, Surgery and Midwifery."

Morrison prospered as a physician, establishing a large practice in the town as well as "in the country up Yonge Street." An active member of the profession, he served on the *ad hoc* board of health set up in York during the cholera outbreak of 1832, and was courageously involved in fighting the more virulent outbreaks of 1834. In 1832 he had joined his friends and fellow physicians William Warren Baldwin* and John E. Tims in administering the York Dispensary, which opened on 22 August. It lasted about eight months, during which time it prescribed and distributed free medicine to 746 patients, at a cost of £118 3*s*. 4*d*. In early 1836 Morrison was appointed to the Medical Board, a position he held until the winter of 1837–38. Active in other areas of the community, he served as vice president of the bible society, trustee of the York General Burying Ground, and common school trustee.

In politics Morrison played an important role in the reform agitation of the 1820s, though never with the driving spirit of William Lyon Mackenzie* or with the intellectual input of Baldwin, John Rolph*, or Marshall Spring Bidwell*. Morrison was a talented orator, and therefore much in demand in a highly politicized community where public meetings and demonstrations were occurring with increasing regularity.

Morrison first sought public office, for the town of York, in the provincial election of 1828, amid the furore caused by Lieutenant Governor Sir Peregrine MAITLAND's dismissal of Judge John Walpole Willis*. A committee of radical reformers, including Mackenzie, Jesse Ketchum*, and Francis Collins*, assembled in York in January to select a candidate to oppose Attorney General John Beverley Robinson*, a leading figure in the dismissal of Willis. Although some reformers put forward the more moderate Robert BALDWIN, Morrison was chosen. William Warren Baldwin, Robert's father and himself a candidate in Norfolk, nominated Morrison on the hustings, evidence perhaps of the solidarity and resolve of the reformers. Unfortunately, their exertions in York were to no avail: Robinson was declared elected by 110 votes to 93. The return was challenged by Morrison on the grounds of illegal votes and reputed irregularities on the part of the returning officer, William Botsford Jarvis*. Although Morrison's case was eloquently argued by the Baldwins, Robinson's election was upheld. The reformers, however, had won a majority of seats throughout the province, which they enjoyed until 1830 and again in 1834–36.

In the first municipal elections for the city of Toronto, held in 1834, Morrison was elected alderman for St Andrew's Ward on a reform-dominated council. During the negotiations within council over who would be mayor, he voted to support the nomination of Mackenzie. Having assumed the role of intermediary, however, he was chosen to read to council John Rolph's letter of resignation as an alderman because he had expected to become mayor. In the provincial election of 1834, in which the reformers swept the four ridings of York County, Morrison finally gained a seat, for 3rd York. Returned as an alderman in 1835 and again in 1836, when the reformers regained the majority in council they had lost the previous year, he was elected in January 1836 to a one-year term as mayor.

Although during Morrison's mayoralty, council spent some of its time on municipal business such as building a water-works and lighting the streets with gas, like previous councils it was preoccupied with provincial political controversies [see William Lyon Mackenzie]. In February 1836 Morrison, as mayor, signed an optimistic address of welcome to the new lieutenant governor, Sir Francis Bond Head*, who, it was hoped, would help secure reform. When John Rolph, John Henry DUNN, and Robert Baldwin resigned from the Executive Council the next month and Mackenzie was defeated in the provincial election in July (the result, he claimed, of the lieutenant governor's having "unduly interfered with the election"), the reformers once again used city council as a platform. Morrison himself had been re-elected to the House of Assembly that summer and he did not serve on city council again after the end of his mayoralty.

As the demands for reform intensified in 1837, Morrison continued to play a leading public role, especially in the assembly. Among the radicals, however, he was beginning to hold back. He attended the meeting of reformers at John Doel*'s brewery in July and seconded a motion by Mackenzie congratu-

lating the reformers in Lower Canada. Then, though hesitant, he signed the reform declaration drafted at that meeting and was made a member of the Central Vigilance Committee. He chaired a second meeting at Doel's brewery in October, at which time he refused to support Mackenzie's plan for revolt.

Morrison, like other leading reformers in the city such as Rolph, Bidwell, and William Warren Baldwin (with whom he probably consulted), was unwilling to participate openly in Mackenzie's plan to raise a force in the country and march on Toronto. According to Charles Lindsey*, he "remained in his house" during the abortive uprising. Upon the collapse of the rebellion, however, he was arrested by the militia on 6 December and held without bail, remaining in jail until his trial the following spring.

Morrison's trial for high treason opened on 24 April 1838 under the pall created by the executions of Samuel Lount* and Peter Matthews*, who had been hanged 12 days previously. Morrison was indeed fighting for his life. Moreover, his defence, led by Robert Baldwin, was exacerbated by Mackenzie's pronouncements from across the border and by the compromising evidence of Morrison's signature on the reform declaration of July 1837. In the end he was found not guilty, though the jury enquired about finding him guilty of misprision of treason, a lesser crime. The prospect of being tried on this charge terrified Morrison, who, according to John Ryerson*, believed that since "they were bent on his destruction & that they would accomplish it, he had better leave as Mr. Bidwell had done." On 29 April 1838 Morrison left Toronto for the United States.

He remained in exile for five years, settling in upstate New York near Batavia, where after some time he was able to establish himself in medical practice. But he was clearly not happy and toyed with the idea of moving to Michigan. In 1843, following the Canadian government's declaration of amnesty, he returned to Toronto and re-established his practice. Unlike Rolph, and later Mackenzie, he did not again seek public office. Instead he concentrated on his medical career, serving on hospital boards and lecturing at Rolph's Toronto School of Medicine. In 1851 Morrison was appointed to the reconstituted Medical Board as part of Rolph's machinations against the University of Toronto's medical faculty [see Christopher Widmer]. He died of palsy at his home on Adelaide Street on 19 March 1856.

Morrison's political career was inextricably connected with the fortunes of the provincial reform movement that was crushed in 1837. At the height of his career, in 1836–37, he played an important but not pivotal role in shaping events of the day. He was a respectable supporter of the great ones around him who, unlike Morrison, survived the defeat of December 1837.

VICTOR LORING RUSSELL

Mountain

Academy of Medicine (Toronto), MS 137: 45. AO, MS 78, Robert Stanton to John Macaulay, 20 Jan. 1827. CTA, RG 1, A, 1834–37; B, 1834–37; RG 5, F, 1834–37, 1843–56. MTL, Robert Baldwin papers. PAC, MG 24, B2: 1939–42, 2908–12; C10; RG 1, L3, 338: M11/234; 342: M12/365; RG 5, A1: 18146–47, 28885–95, 29098–99; B9, 14: 267. Toronto Necropolis and Crematorium, Reg. of burials, 14 May 1856, 29 Oct. 1882. J. C. Dent, *The story of the Upper Canadian rebellion; largely derived from original sources and documents* (2v., Toronto, 1885). *Town of York, 1815–34* (Firth). *Christian Guardian*, 23 Feb. 1853. *Colonial Advocate*, August 1832. *Toronto Herald*, 9 June 1842. *Toronto directory*, 1850–51, 1856. Geoffrey Bilson, *A darkened house: cholera in nineteenth-century Canada* (Toronto, 1980), 85–86. Canniff, *Medical profession in U.C.* Lindsey, *Life and times of Mackenzie*, 2: 326. W. H. Pearson, *Recollections and records of Toronto of old . . .* (Toronto, 1914), 284–85. *Robertson's landmarks of Toronto*, 1: 415. V. L. Russell, *Mayors of Toronto* (1v. to date, Erin, Ont., 1982–   ). C. B. Sissons, *Egerton Ryerson: his life and letters* (2v., Toronto, 1937–47), 1. E. S. Coatsworth, "The Toronto General Burying Grounds," *York Pioneer* (Toronto), 1971: 4–17.

MOUNTAIN, JACOB GEORGE, Church of England clergyman and educator; b. 14 Oct. 1818, son of the Reverend Jacob Henry Brooke Mountain, rector of Blunham, England, and Frances Mingay Brooke; m. 1854 Sophia Bevan; there were no children by this marriage; d. 10 Oct. 1856 in St John's.

Grandson of Jacob Mountain*, the first Church of England bishop of Quebec, nephew of George Jehoshaphat Mountain*, the third bishop of Quebec, and son of an Anglican minister, Jacob George Mountain too became an ecclesiastic. He was educated at Eton College, where he won the Newcastle medal, a high distinction in that school. In 1838 he attended Merton College, Oxford, as a postmaster, earning a 2nd class honours degree in classics. Mountain then returned to Eton where he was engaged as a private tutor. Some time later he was offered a mastership, a position of honour and great responsibility which was rarely proffered to anyone but a fellow of King's College, Cambridge. However, a desire to enter holy orders dominated his thoughts and he refused the post. Mountain was subsequently ordained deacon and became the assistant curate of Clewer, near Eton, so that he could complete his tutoring assignment.

Initially Mountain wanted to work in one of the many thickly populated areas in England neglected by the church; when no offer was made, he volunteered for the colonies. Although his uncle in Quebec could well have used his services, Mountain was attracted by the conditions in Newfoundland described by Bishop Edward Feild*, who had journeyed to England in 1846 to appeal for men to serve in the extremely isolated and spiritually neglected portions of his diocese. Mountain, a Tractarian like Feild, offered to

come as soon as he could. He set sail in April 1847, arriving the following month.

His ability and learning would have been invaluable to the Theological Institute at St John's, but Mountain insisted on being sent to a hard and destitute outport where he could work with the poor. That autumn he became the first rural dean at Harbour Breton in the mission of Fortune Bay and laboured there, without any companionship of mind, for seven years. The parish, which had a long, bare, and rugged coastline and covered approximately 200 square miles, contained some 40 tiny settlements, most composed of only three or four resident families along with the migratory West Country fishermen. They had to be reached by oar or sail and Mountain's task was made more difficult because he was never free from seasickness. As chairman of the board of education for the region, he established at least one government school on Brunette Island and had at least two schoolmasters brought out from England at his own expense.

In July 1854 Mountain journeyed to England where he married. Returning to Newfoundland that autumn, he assumed the post of principal at Queen's College (formerly the Theological Institute). While still retaining the charge of the college, at the end of February 1856 he replaced Thomas Finch Hobday BRIDGE, who had just died of fever, as chief minister of the parish and cathedral church of St John's and commissary to Feild. He also had in his charge two outports located near the capital. Seven months later Mountain, in an exhausted state caused by overwork, also became ill with fever and passed away on 10 October. In 1867 his widow married Bishop Feild.

G. H. EARLE

Jacob George Mountain is the author of *Some account of a sowing time on the rugged shores of Newfoundland*, published in London in 1857 as no.35 in the SPG's *Church in the colonies* series, and also as an offprint. A copy of the latter is preserved in Queen's College, now part of Memorial University of Newfoundland, St John's.

USPG, C/CAN/Nfl., 6–7. [Edward Feild], *Journal of the Bishop of Newfoundland's voyage of visitation and discovery, on the south and west coasts of Newfoundland, and on the Labrador, in the church ship "Hawk," in the year 1848* (2nd ed., London, 1851). *Times and General Commercial Gazette* (St John's), 15 Oct. 1856. H. W. Tucker, *Memoir of the life and episcopate of Edward Feild, D.D., bishop of Newfoundland, 1844–1876* (London, 1877).

MOWAT, JOHN, soldier, merchant, office holder, justice of the peace, politician, and college administrator; b. 12 May 1791 in Mey, Scotland, son of Oliver Mowat, a tenant farmer, and Janet Bower; m. 16 June 1819 Helen Levack in Montreal, and they had three sons, including Sir Oliver*, and two daughters; d. 4

Feb. 1860 in Kingston, Upper Canada, and was buried at nearby Waterloo (Cataraqui).

According to family accounts, John Mowat was intended for the ministry, but at 16 he joined the British army. Although his parents purchased his release twice, he re-enlisted once again in 1809 and with his regiment, the 3rd Foot, served in the Peninsular War. In 1814 the 3rd was sent to the Canadas for the duration of the War of 1812, during which it fought at the battle of Plattsburgh, N.Y. (11 Sept. 1814). When the regiment left the Canadas in June 1815, Mowat, who had attained the rank of sergeant, procured his discharge. He first tried farming near Kingston, but in 1816 moved into the town and became a merchant. By mid 1818 Mowat was in business with Joseph Bruce selling dry goods, groceries, crockery, and glassware.

When the partnership with Bruce was dissolved on 21 May 1822, Mowat bought the business and enlarged the shop. In 1841 he built a larger shop with two dwellings above, one of the impressive round-corner buildings designed by George Browne*, and three years later his second son, George, became his partner. In 1849, however, they sold the business and leased the store to John Carruthers. At the age of 58 John Mowat could devote his time to several new business interests such as his directorships for the Commercial Bank of the Midland District, Kingston Building Society, Mutual Fire Insurance Company of the Midland District, Kingston Waterworks, and Kingston Gas Light Company as well as to the board of trade and mechanics' institute. He also played a minor role in Kingston's civic affairs. Elected a township commissioner in 1836, he served as a justice of the peace, as a grand juror, and on the town's board of health. In 1846 he succeeded as alderman his life-long friend, John A. Macdonald*, who was becoming increasingly involved in provincial politics, but the next year was defeated by one vote.

Named one of the first elders of St Andrew's Presbyterian Church in 1822, Mowat was a fervent advocate of Church of Scotland rights. In 1825–26 he supported the Reverend John Barclay*, a Presbyterian, in his bitter dispute with Anglican archdeacon George Okill Stuart* over the rights of Presbyterians to be interred in the Kingston burial-ground according to the rites of their church. Although he sided politically with the tories, Mowat opposed high church Anglicans among them, especially on the questions of church establishment in Upper Canada, the clergy reserves and rectory endowments, and university control.

John Mowat's most notable contribution was in education. In 1829, dissatisfied with the Midland District Grammar School and its Anglican managers, he and other Kingston-area Scots had persuaded the Reverend John Cruikshank to open a school "for

classical and general education." Both John A. Macdonald and Oliver Mowat were students there. John Mowat's interest in higher education pertained particularly to opportunities for Presbyterians in Canada. One of the group that met in 1837 and 1839 to establish a college in Kingston, he was a member of the first board of trustees assembled at St Andrew's Church in May 1840. Under the influence of Mowat, William MORRIS, and others, the college evolved from the Presbyterian seminary first suggested to a true university on the Scottish pattern. Mowat's name is enrolled on the royal charter of Queen's College and amongst its first students in 1842 was his son John Bower. Intimately involved with the college for many years, Mowat was a member of a small group in Kingston (including the Reverend John Machar*, Alexander Pringle, and the Reverend Professor James Williamson*) upon whom much of the college's routine business fell. He was appointed in 1846 to a committee of general superintendence for student housing and he frequently arranged property rentals for the college. In 1853, with Andrew Drummond, he negotiated the purchase of Summerhill, George Okill Stuart's great country house, which still stands on the Queen's campus.

The relationship between Mowat and his sons was unusually close and informal. His letters to them, when they were away at school, are full of warmth and humour. He also gave his sons remarkable freedom in their choice of profession, perhaps because his own parents had been so strict. His obituary mentioned his "unbending integrity," benevolence, and public zeal, and noted that he possessed a "fervency of spirit which made him willing to spend himself and be spent in all that he undertook."

MARGARET SHARP ANGUS

AO, RG 1, C-IV, Richmond Township, concession 11, lots 18–19; RG 22, ser.159, John Mowat. GRO (Edinburgh), Canisbay, reg. of births and baptisms, 1791. PAC, RG 1, L3, 339a: M11/439; RG 8, I (C ser.), 55: 6–7; 274: 37–40; RG 9, I, B5, 5: 18; 6: 24; RG 68, General index, 1651–1841: 497, 505. QUA, Angus Mowat papers, "Genealogy and story of the Mowat family," comp. R. McG. Mowat, 1928; John Mowat, letters; Queen's Univ., Board of Trustees, letters. *Chronicle and News*, 27 March 1849. *Daily British Whig*, 6 Feb. 1860. *Daily News* (Kingston, [Ont.]), 7, 9 Feb. 1860. *Kingston Herald*, 23 April 1844. C. R. W. Biggar, *Sir Oliver Mowat . . . a biographical sketch* (2v., Toronto, 1905), 1: 4–7, 98–102. J. K. Johnson, "John A. Macdonald and the Kingston business community," *To preserve & defend: essays on Kingston in the nineteenth century*, ed. G. [J. J.] Tulchinsky (Montreal and London, 1976), 141–55. H. [M.] Neatby, *Queen's University: to strive, to seek, to find, and not to yield*, ed. F. W. Gibson and Roger Graham (1v. to date, Montreal, 1978–ﾠ), 1: 5, 21, 28–29, 56, 67–70. Margaret [Sharp] Angus, "The Mowats of Kingston," *Historic Kingston*, no.13 (1965): 41–49, 90.

Muir

MUIR, ANDREW, collier and office holder; b. *c.* 1828, probably in Ayrshire, Scotland, eldest son of John Muir* and Annie Miller; m. 31 Jan. 1854 Isabella Weir in Victoria, and they had one daughter; d. there 11 Jan. 1859.

Andrew Muir was about 20 years of age when in 1848 he signed on with the Hudson's Bay Company as a collier to work the coal deposits at Fort Rupert (near Port Hardy) on Vancouver Island. He sailed from Gravesend, England, aboard the HBC barque *Harpooner* on 5 December with a group of fellow miners – including his father, who was to be overman, three brothers, and two cousins – and their families. During the seven-month voyage across the Atlantic, round Cape Horn, and up the Pacific coast, Andrew Muir kept a diary in which he noted the many difficulties encountered, such as high seas, shortages of food, a mutinous crew, and conflicts among the passengers. After arriving at Fort Victoria (Victoria) on 1 June 1849, the party was put to work in the construction of a dockyard and in digging a well. At the end of August they embarked on the company brig *Mary Dare* for Fort Rupert.

At their destination the Muirs found undeveloped deposits, insufficient equipment, and primitive living conditions in place of the established mines they had been led to believe would be awaiting them. The local Indians, who were under contract to gather coal on the beach for the HBC, viewed the new operation as an intrusion and threatened the miners with violence. Digging pits as best they could, the Muirs soon discovered that there would be little yield from the proposed operation, and they were called upon to perform menial labour in and around the fort. Their complaints about these conditions, addressed to local company officials who placed a low priority on coal production, were met with indifference, and relations between the miners and the company men rapidly deteriorated. For a week beginning on 16 April 1850 the miners refused to work. George Blenkinsop, HBC manager at Fort Rupert, accused Andrew Muir of being "a rebellious person [who] kept the men off their duty," and after Muir and his cousin John McGregor stopped work for another week, Blenkinsop had the two arrested on 2 May and put in irons in the fort's bastion, where they were held for six days. They were released after a hearing before Blenkinsop, Captain William Henry McNeill*, Charles Beardmore, Captain Charles Dodd, and Dr John Sebastian Helmcken*. As Muir noted in his diary, he and his cousin were nevertheless "determined to make for some Christian place – since we could get neither rights nor privileges here."

The opportunity came at the beginning of July. Muir and McGregor left the fort on 2 July; six days later, with some of the other miners and their families, they boarded the brig *England*, which was carrying a load of coal, and sailed to San Francisco. All of the miners, except John Muir and his youngest son, Michael, eventually deserted the fort. Attracted by California's gold-rush, Andrew did not go any farther than San Francisco, where he took employment as a collier and deck-hand in the Sacramento River trade. Within months, however, he had moved again, this time to Astoria (Oreg.). He was back on Vancouver Island by late summer 1851, in time to present a written complaint about the treatment he had received at Fort Rupert to the departing governor, Richard Blanshard*. The London committee of the HBC later criticized Blenkinsop and the other officers at Fort Rupert for their actions.

With his cousin Archibald Muir, Andrew rejoined his family on the farm his father had purchased at Sooke. They conducted a logging and sawmilling operation on this property, supplying piles and square timber for the San Francisco market. Andrew, however, did not stay there very long and by 1853 he had relocated in Victoria, where he was appointed the town's first sheriff. Six years later, the day after his term as sheriff ended, he died intestate at age 31 of chronic alcoholism. He was buried in the churchyard of the Victoria District Church (Christ Church Cathedral) on 13 Jan. 1859, the same day that his only child, Isabella Ellen, was baptized.

Daniel T. Gallacher

Bancroft Library, Univ. of California (Berkeley), H. H. Bancroft, "British Columbia sketches," 13–18. PABC, Add. mss 520, 3, folder 1: 41; folder 3: 12; folder 6: 11; Andrew Muir diary, 9 Nov. 1848–5 Aug. 1850; Vert. file, Muir family. PAM, HBCA, A.6/29–30; A.11/72. G.B., Parl., House of Commons paper, 1857 (session ii), 15: nos.224, 260; *Report from the select committee on the Hudson's Bay Company*, 292–93. Helmcken, *Reminiscences of Helmcken* (Blakey Smith and Lamb). *Daily Colonist* (Victoria), 17 Jan. 1888. *Gazette* (Victoria), 13 Jan., 16 Aug. 1859. Derek Pethick, *Men of British Columbia* (Saanichton, B.C., 1975). Keith Ralston, "Coal miners' contracts with the Hudson's Bay Company, 1848–1858" (paper given at the B.C. Studies Conference, 1981). P. M. Johnson, "Fort Rupert," *Beaver*, outfit 302 (spring 1972): 4–15. W. K. Lamb, "The governorship of Richard Blanshard," *BCHQ*, 14 (1950): 1–40. B. A. McKelvie, "Coal for the warships," *Beaver*, outfit 282 (June 1951): 8–11.

MUNCOQ. *See* Moncoq

MUNN, JOHN, shipbuilder, shipowner, justice of the peace, and politician; b. 12 March 1788 in Irvine, Scotland, natural son of John Munn, a sailor, and Mary Gemmel; d. unmarried 20 March 1859 at Quebec.

John Munn Jr's father, a sailor, may have been the same John Munn who became a shipbuilder at

Quebec. Munn Sr, the shipbuilder, died in 1813 or 1814, leaving a will in which he referred to John (known until then as John Jr) as his "beloved son" and gave him two-thirds of the estate. Yet in the post-mortem inventory of John Sr's belongings, his widow declared that he had not "in this Province any natural heir"; moreover, John Jr was described by the notary as the deceased's "copartner under the style or firm of John Munn & Son," but not as his son. Despite the uncertainty of his parentage, John Jr was clearly related to the Munn shipbuilding family of Irvine; he was one of four members who immigrated to Lower Canada and became master shipbuilders. The three others, Alexander*, John Sr, and David were brothers, sons of the master shipbuilder John Munn (McMunn). During their lifetimes the four maintained close ties. John Sr arrived at Quebec in 1798, four years after Alexander, and set up his yard on the Rivière Saint-Charles in the *faubourg* Saint-Roch. David joined his brothers in or before 1803, but the following year established his own yard in Montreal. A fourth brother, James, was a Clyde shipbuilder for many years before moving to Sydney, Australia, in 1824.

John Munn Jr probably attended one of the several schools in Irvine, while effortlessly absorbing the maritime traditions and knowledge that life in a small town with two shipyards and a home fleet of 97 vessels would offer. In 1801, at age 13, he sailed for Quebec, where he presumably served an apprenticeship. By 1811 he had begun his career as a master shipbuilder in partnership with Munn Sr, during a time when shipbuilders were enjoying a measure of prosperity. The blockade of the Baltic had caused Britain to turn to British North America for timber, and additional tonnage was required to transport it. The Munns and other builders supplied vessels to British firms such as Mure and Joliffe and Whitfield, Coates. However, the Munn partnership was short-lived. John Sr died less than three years after its foundation.

John Jr did not immediately take over the Saint-Roch shipyard, although John Sr's widow had sold her one-third share to him. Instead, it was rented to other shipbuilders until 1821. Meanwhile, the War of 1812 made different demands for vessels on the shipbuilders. Munn went to Montreal and during the summer of 1814 built 30 bateaux for the government with men hired at Quebec. His services were then sought for the construction of two frigates at the Kingston dockyard in Upper Canada, but his tender was considered too high and his delivery date too late. He returned to Quebec to supervise the construction of a brig for David and his partner, Robert Hunter, at the Cap Diamant shipyard used by Alexander before his death in 1812.

The time had come for Munn to strike out on his own account. Working first with John Sr and later under David's wing, he had learned the ropes of shipowning as well as shipbuilding. After the launch of the brig built in 1815, he leased the Cap Diamant shipyard and began conducting business there. There is no record of any ships having been built by him at this time, although evidence suggests that he did undertake ship repairs. His decision to remain at Cap Diamant may have been taken because his own yard at Saint-Roch was unsuited to his activities. In 1821, after purchasing a 700-foot-wide beach lot with wharfs and sheds at Près-de-Ville, which afforded berths and other facilities for equipping, loading, and unloading vessels, he returned to his own shipyard.

At Saint-Roch the shipbuilding side of his career took on importance. Between 1821 and 1857 he built 32 fully rigged ships, 45 barques, and 16 brigs, ranging from 236 to 1,454 tons. The vessels built before 1830 were small, the largest measuring no more than 425 tons. After 1837 their considerably larger size reflected the changes in the shipping market. Yet, although Munn's 1,257-ton ship of 1839, *United Kingdom*, was hailed as the largest vessel to have been built at Quebec (with the exception of Charles Wood*'s two huge unorthodox square-timber craft), Munn showed no interest in breaking records for size. In fact, the opposite seems to have been true for he was not among those who in the 1850s built vessels of from 1,500 to more than 2,000 tons. He belonged perhaps to the school of opinion which held that such vessels exceeded the limits of the tree.

Almost all Munn's vessels were registered under his sole ownership and sent over to Britain where most of those not built to order were sold, many by his Liverpool agents and financiers, James, and later Duncan, Gibb. Some were operated by him for a number of years either on his own account or in partnership with others before being sold. Munn also had strong business connections with Glasgow through the firm Rodger Dean and Company, which at times provided financing in return for shares in the ships. In addition to shipbuilding and repairing, Munn occasionally bought stranded vessels for rebuilding and sale and, as a competent master shipbuilder, was solicited to carry out ship surveys for insurance and other purposes.

Munn was among the select group of Quebec shipbuilders whose high standards earned them recognition in Britain. When the *United Kingdom* arrived there in 1839, the *Liverpool Mail* wrote, "She looks most beautiful upon the water and her model and the symmetry of her proportions have been much admired by nautical men. . . . She was built by John Munn Esq. of Quebec, whose character, as a naval architect stands deservedly high in the Colonies." Training under Munn was a privilege, and several of his apprentices made their mark. George Taylor Davie*, the sole 19th-century shipbuilder whose yard

Munn

has survived, was sent to Munn to learn the trade. Aymerick Vidal, whose career began with great promise but was cut short by an accident, was his apprentice, as was William Simons, son of the Quebec master sailmaker Peter Simons and later warden of the port of Quebec.

Munn's efforts did not go without financial reward and by the 1840s he was wealthy. He increased the size and facilities of his shipyard, acquired various other properties, and became known for his charitable nature. A strong supporter of the independent evangelical Presbyterian congregation at Quebec orginally ministered to by Clark Bentom*, in 1823 he had been among those who guaranteed the minister's salary should the pew rents prove insufficient. Later he made a substantial contribution to the congregation's St John's Church. Yet his commitment to a church unconnected with the Church of Scotland did not prevent him from being one of the founders of Queen's College, Kingston, originally set up as a seminary to train Presbyterian ministers [see William MORRIS]. He was a trustee of the new Marché Saint-Paul in 1829 and 1830. In 1837 he was appointed a justice of the peace. That same year, as a candidate opposed to the policies of Louis-Joseph Papineau*, he was elected to the House of Assembly for the Lower Town, but he did not sit long since the house was prorogued in August and the constitution suspended the following spring. He then turned to municipal affairs, representing Saint-Roch on the city council from 1840 to 1842. He was also active in various community projects. In 1847 and 1848 he was on the committee of the British and Canadian School Society of the district of Quebec and the board of directors of the Quebec Provident and Savings Bank, and meetings of the Union Total Abstinence Society were held at his shipyard.

The 1840s, however, brought problems, beginning with the first general strike of shipyard workers in December 1840, which lasted for three weeks. It resulted from the builders' decision to lower the winter daily rate of pay to three shillings, a decision to which Munn was certainly an important party, and from the men's determination not to work for less than four shillings [see Joseph Laurin*]. The builders maintained that the only way they could remain in the falling shipping market was to cut either labour or material costs, and the latter could not be cut without sacrificing quality. They may have been justified, but the men did not see it that way. In fact, Le Fantasque referred to "a famine pact against the working class." Certainly, over the next two years the price of shipping declined even further and the men were grateful to have work, even at lower wages.

In May 1845 Munn suffered loss in the savage fire that gutted Saint-Roch. Afterwards, when the narrowness of the streets was held to be a cause of the extent of the fire, he offered to give the city 15-foot strips of land along three streets so that they could be widened, and to help finance the acquisition of land from other owners for the same purpose. He was fortunate to have safely launched the first steamboat built in his yard, the 115-ton paddle steamer Rowland Hill, and two sailing vessels earlier that month, although in retrospect he undoubtedly rued the day he entered the field of steam.

The Rowland Hill, the steamer Quebec launched from George BLACK's shipyard in 1844, and the 374-ton John Munn, built at Munn's yard in 1846, were all owned by the People's Line of Steamers, a group of grocers and chandlers headed by John Wilson. Munn's strong credit position had allowed him to borrow heavily from the Bank of British North America to finance the construction of the two ships. The People's Line, however, had been over ambitious. Even though the three vessels were heavily mortgaged to Munn, the line was unable to pay its way, and in 1849 an agreement was made whereby Munn, who had notes to meet at the bank, took over the steamboats and certain properties belonging to Wilson, together with all the debts of the company. Far from solving Munn's problems, before long the take-over and operation of the steamboats obliged him to sell off all his shipping and various properties in order to remain solvent. In debt to Duncan Gibb to the amount of £21,000, Munn finally handed over his shipyard to him in 1855 on the understanding that should Gibb sell it for a higher sum he would give Munn the difference. Fortunately, however, Munn's death spared him from seeing the sale of the yard that he had spent so many years building up.

At the end of Munn's career, his shipyard was very different from the modest one he inherited from John Sr. He had capped his acquisitions with the purchase of part of the yard belonging to his neighbour, John Goudie*, thus assembling the entire northeast corner of Saint-Roch, 11¼ acres with 1,650 feet of shoreline. A tide dock permitted timber to be floated to the premises, and four acres of booms supplemented his large timber and lumber yards. In all, six or eight vessels could be built in the double shipyard at the same time. The more important workshops – the forge, rigging-lofts, and mould lofts – were housed in large two-storey brick or stone buildings. One such building was almost entirely given over to a boilermaker's shop. Similar buildings with backyards and sheds provided accommodation for 52 workmen and their families. Many of these tenements were serviced with running water, and compared favourably with similar accommodation built by the shipbuilder William Denny in Dumbarton, Scotland, in 1853. Like those in Dumbarton, the homes were not intended for the higher paid skilled tradesmen but were occupied mostly by labourers. As was customary, the shipbuilder lived on the premises. His cousin Elizabeth Allan looked after the substantial residence on Rue Grant, with flower and vegetable gardens and an area partly planted with fruit-trees, that he shared with his apprentices. The stable, coach-house, and brick offices stood close by.

During Munn's long and active career, he built over 100 vessels, more than any other Quebec shipbuilder except Thomas Hamilton Oliver, but their 55,000 tons was exceeded by the production of Pierre-Vincent Valin*, Jean-Élie Gingras*, and Oliver, whose careers began at a date when the average tonnage of vessels was greater.

Throughout his life, Munn was close to the men who worked for him and is said at times to have laid down vessels to provide work for them even when there was no prospect of making a profit. As his assets melted away, he became concerned for the future of his cousin Elizabeth and "in consideration of her long and faithful services in the care and management of his household and family" gave her all the furniture in his residence, as well as a small shipyard property and house in L'Islet. The "family" to which Munn referred may have been the family of John, David Munn's son, who joined him in the shipyard at Quebec as a carpenter after his father's death.

Following Munn's death in 1859 his friends immediately established a fund for a memorial to him, and a fitting monument was erected on his grave at Mount Hermon Cemetery, Sillery, which bore the inscription: "To mark their respect for the modest values of an honest and good man Unassuming benevolent and liberal when in the possession of wealth Patient and uncomplaining When it took wings and Flew away." In 1880 Elizabeth was buried beside him.

EILEEN MARCIL

ANQ-M, CN1-74, 30 sept. 1807. ANQ-Q, CN1-16, 18 janv. 1809; 15 févr., 11 mars, 13 avril 1815; CN1-49, 9–13 juin 1812; 15 sept. 1814; 3 mars 1815; 22 déc. 1825; 21 juin 1832; 13 nov. 1848; 15 janv. 1849; 25 juill., 2, 15 nov. 1855; 29 mars 1856; 17 nov. 1857; CN1-116, 28 sept. 1849; CN1-197, 14 juill. 1821, 23 oct. 1823, 12 nov. 1831, 19 sept. 1834, 8 mars 1839; CN1-253, 8 févr., 8 août, 22 sept., 17 déc. 1814; 24 oct. 1823; CN1-256, 15 févr. 1794, 30 sept. 1798; CN1-285, 12 mai 1810, 25 janv. 1811. GRO (Edinburgh), Irvine, Reg. of births and baptisms, 1788. PAC, RG 8, I (C ser.), 734: 45; RG 42, ser.I, 183–203. Private arch., K. M. Richards and C. F. C. Seifert (Hamilton, Ont.), Information on the Munn family. SRO, RD5/161: 303. *Le Fantasque* (Québec), 10 déc. 1840. *Morning Chronicle* (Quebec), 23 March, 1 April 1859. *Quebec Mercury*, 12 Feb. 1821; 7 Nov. 1839; 2 June, 4, 15, 24 Dec. 1840; 23 Feb. 1843; 6, 8–9 May 1845. *Quebec directory*, 1858–91. F. W. Wallace, *In the wake of the wind-ships: notes, records and biographies pertaining to the square-rigged merchant marine of British North America* (Toronto,

1927). B. D. Osborne, "Dumbarton shipbuilding and workers' housing, 1850–1900," *Scottish Industrial Hist.* (Glasgow, Scot.), 3 (1980), no.1: 2–11. P.-G. Roy, "Le constructeur de navires John Munn," *BRH*, 39 (1933): 190–91.

MURPHY, ANNA BROWNELL (Jameson), writer, feminist, and traveller; b. 19 May 1794 in Dublin; m. 1825 Robert Sympson JAMESON; they had no children; d. 17 March 1860 in Ealing (London).

Anna Brownell Murphy was the eldest of five daughters of Denis Brownell Murphy, an Irish miniaturist and portrait painter. In 1798, just before the rebellion in Ireland, Murphy, a vociferous and therefore endangered patriot, immigrated with his English wife and daughter Anna to England. He settled in 1802 at Newcastle upon Tyne, where he prospered sufficiently to send for the two daughters who had been left behind in Ireland. By 1806, when he moved his family to London, there were five daughters and Murphy was enjoying a modest success as a miniaturist. In 1810, as "Painter in Enamel" to Princess Charlotte, daughter of the Prince and Princess of Wales, he began making miniature copies of Peter Lely's portraits of the ladies of the court of Charles II, hoping to sell these to his patroness. Princess Charlotte died in 1817, the miniatures were unsold, and Murphy's fortunes speedily waned.

Anna was the most precocious of the children, particularly clever in learning languages, always ambitious to excel, and, from an early age, anxious to assume a part of the responsibility for the family's welfare. For a time the Murphys could afford a governess, whom Anna remembered as "one of the cleverest women I have ever met." Before the family moved to London, however, she had gone; henceforth the sisters' education progressed with Anna in charge. In the words of her niece Gerardine Macpherson, she educated herself "chiefly at her own will and pleasure. ... She worked hard, but fitfully at French, Italian and even Spanish."

In 1810, when Anna was 16, she took up her first post as governess to the four small sons of the Marquis of Winchester, leaving in 1814. In 1819 she began an engagement with the Rowles family which was to lead to her first successful book. She accompanied them to the Continent in 1821, travelling in luxury "*à la Milor Anglais*" through the Low Countries and into Italy. She quickly became an avid traveller, a connoisseur of art galleries, and an intrepid sightseer: "I had an opportunity of witnessing a most magnificent spectacle, an eruption of Mount Vesuvius and ascended the mountain during the height of it." Back in England in 1822, and without the capital to start the school she had been planning, she became governess to the children of Edward John Littleton, afterwards 1st Baron Hatherton, a post she retained until her marriage to Robert Sympson Jameson of Ambleside in 1825. During these years she wrote two works for young children, "Much coin, much care," a drama (published 1834), and "Little Louisa," a vocabulary of useful words.

Robert Jameson had courted Anna Murphy since before her Continental trip in 1821. There was a strange intermittent incompatibility between them which both parties and Anna's family realized. However, there were also strong attractions, particularly a common love of literature and of literary society. Jameson encouraged his wife in the writing of her first travel book, published anonymously in 1826 under the title *A lady's diary* and then as *Diary of an ennuyée*. It was a romanticized and fictionalized version of her European trip ending with the death of its heart-broken narrator and heroine. Heavily influenced in plan and content by Mme de Staël's popular novel *Corinne* (1807), the book was a sentimental Childe Harold's journey for impressionable and adventure-hungry young ladies. It was a great success and when Mrs Jameson was shortly revealed as its author she became the "lioness" of the hour in London society.

By 1829, when Robert Jameson left England for an appointment as chief justice of Dominica, Anna was making no secret of unhappiness in her marriage. She was increasingly committed to a life of travel and writing. *The loves of the poets* was published in 1829 and *Memoirs of celebrated female sovereigns* in 1831. These books (*The beauties of the court of King Charles the Second*, with her text for her father's miniatures, was to follow in 1833) were designed for the growing numbers of women who were voracious in their appetite for entertaining and pleasantly improving reading material. From the beginning of her writing career Anna Jameson stressed the importance of better education for women. She was a determined, though conservative, early feminist, one of the many in her generation who were increasingly vocal about their rights in law and their needs and opportunities in society.

In 1832 her *Characteristics of women*, a discussion of Shakespeare's heroines, made her name on the Continent and in America as well as in England. On a trip to Germany after its publication she was the centre of an admiring group which included Johann Ludwig Tieck and August Wilhelm von Schlegel, and she began a lifelong friendship with Ottilie von Goethe, the poet's daughter-in-law. Her *Visits and sketches at home and abroad* (1834) is the record of a Continental trip taken in 1829, in the company of her father and Sir Gerard Noel Noel, a wealthy and eccentric aristocrat, and another in 1833. For it, as for all her future works, Anna Jameson was now assured of a reading public; she had become an established author.

In the fall of 1836 she reluctantly came to Toronto to join her husband who in 1833 had become attorney general of Upper Canada. Jameson was hoping to be appointed to the vice-chancellorship of the Court of Chancery, the highest legal post in the province. He had begun to build a house in which to receive his wife, and he wanted her presence to confirm his own social stability at this crucial time in his career. For Anna's part, she had long since accepted their emotional incompatibility; furthermore she thoroughly enjoyed the life of a successful writer and cosmopolitan traveller with many friends in England and on the Continent. Life in Upper Canada held no attractions whatever for her. She came grudgingly, only because both social and financial necessity dictated that she should. She had heavy responsibilities in the support of ailing parents and unmarried sisters. She needed Jameson's good will; had he wished, he could, by law, have claimed her earnings. She hoped instead for his financial assistance.

She sailed from London on 8 Oct. 1836, landed at New York in early November, and arrived in Toronto, after an arduous eight-day journey, in mid December. Her few weeks in New York, where she was much sought after and entertained by the literati, provided a radical contrast to her lonely arrival in Toronto. Her first journal entry in Upper Canada, dated 20 December, sets the tone of her wintry impressions: "A little ill-built town on low land, at the bottom of a frozen bay. . . . I did not expect much; but for this I was not prepared. . . . I see nothing but snow heaped up against my windows, not only without but within; I hear no sound but the tinkling of sleigh-bells and the occasional lowing of a poor half-starved cow." Jameson's appointment as vice-chancellor was confirmed and the couple moved in March into the house he had built. Anna remained in Toronto until early June 1837. Then she set out on a tour which took her through the southwestern part of the province – Niagara (Niagara-on-the-Lake), Hamilton, London, Port Talbot – and to Detroit – then by steamer to Michilimackinac (Mackinac Island, Mich.) and by open boat to Sault Ste Marie (Ont.), and back by way of Lake Huron and Manitoulin Island. She arrived in Toronto in mid August, reporting to her family that "the people here are in great enthusiasm about me and stare at me as if I had done some most wonderful thing; the most astonished of all is Mr. Jameson." In September 1837 she left Upper Canada, having arrived at a separation agreement with her husband. She spent some months in the United States, and after she had received and signed the final separation papers she sailed for England in February 1838.

Winter studies and summer rambles in Canada, published in London in 1838, is the record of both her winter in Toronto and her summer trip. In "Winter studies," written in the form of a journal to an absent friend, she intersperses notes on the frigidity of weather and society with lively characterizations of the few people, James FitzGibbon*, for instance, who took her fancy: "Colonel F. is a soldier of fortune – which phrase means, in *his* case at least, that he owes nothing whatever to fortune, but every thing to his own good heart, his own good sense, and his own good sword. He was the son, and glories in it, of an Irish cotter, on the estate of the Knight of Glyn. At the age of fifteen he shouldered a musket, and joined a regiment. . . . The men who have most interested me through life were all self-educated, and what are called originals. This dear, good F. is *originalissimo*." Her sharp and witty analysis of the current political factions, in those months rising toward the crisis of the rebellion, begins with a general indictment: "There reigns here a hateful factious spirit in political matters, but for the present no public or patriotic feeling, no recognition of general or generous principles of policy: as yet I have met with none of these. Canada is a colony, not a *country*." To offset her intellectual deprivation she determined to translate a manuscript volume of Johann Peter Eckermann's conversations with Goethe, and she included her musings on it in her journal.

In "Summer rambles" we see Anna at her best, an intrepid, adaptable, enthusiastic explorer, intensely interested in everyone she meets (Colonel Thomas Talbot being a lively example) and everything she experiences. She was delighted to be "the first European female" to shoot the rapids at the Sault, her companion a part-Indian friend, George Johnston. Escorted homeward down Lake Huron in a bateau rowed by four voyageurs, she was awestruck by the unspoiled beauty of the islands around her, "fairy Edens" as she called them: "I remember we came into a circular basin, of about three miles in diameter, so surrounded with islands, that when once within the circle, I could perceive neither ingress nor egress; it was as if a spell of enchantment had been wrought to keep us there for ever." She spiced her account of the tour with well-authenticated Indian lore gathered both from her reading and from her visit with Henry Rowe Schoolcraft and his family at Michilimackinac. The comparative position of women among whites and Indians is also a major theme, as is the need for women's education according to their various spheres of opportunity. Anna Jameson's is a vastly different account of Upper Canada from those of Susanna Moodie [Strickland*] or Catharine Parr Traill [Strickland*]: she was a bird of passage, a writer who already knew that she had a cosmopolitan audience for her work; the Stricklands were immigrant pioneers who wrote to instruct and, in Susanna's case, to warn others who would follow them.

The critical and popular success of *Winter studies and summer rambles* reinforced Anna's reputation as a writer – but Robert Jameson, she reported, was "displeased." In the last two decades of her life, her massive compendium of Christian art was her major work: *Sacred and legendary art* (1848), *Legends of*

the monastic orders (1850), *Legends of the Madonna* (1852), and *The history of Our Lord* (1864), the last completed after her death in 1860 by her friend Elizabeth Rigby, Lady Eastlake, the wife of Sir Charles Lock Eastlake, director of the National Gallery. The series was lavishly illustrated by her own drawings and etchings, and by those of Gerardine Macpherson, her niece. In 1855 Anna had given public lectures on working opportunities for women, and throughout her final years she acted as mentor and adviser to a group of young women, including Emily Faithfull, who began the *English Woman's Journal*, and Barbara Leigh Smith Bodichon, a founder of Girton College. Her close friendship with Robert and Elizabeth Barrett Browning was one of the mainstays of her later years. Shortly after her death Harriet Martineau, a well-known English traveller and author, referred to her as the "accomplished Mrs. Jameson . . . a great benefit to her time from her zeal for her sex and for Art." Her works, particularly the many editions of *Characteristics of women* and *Sacred and legendary art*, helped to form and direct popular taste in England and America, both in her own day and considerably beyond it. In Canada, *Winter studies and summer rambles* has remained a classic among our travel journals.

CLARA THOMAS

The popularity of Mrs Jameson's *Winter studies and summer rambles in Canada* is attested to by numerous Canadian and foreign editions; the original text (3v., London, 1838) was reprinted in Toronto in 1972. Further bibliographic information on her writings is available in the *National union catalog* and the *British Museum general catalogue*. The author's biography, *Love and work enough; the life of Anna Jameson* ([Toronto], 1967), includes a comprehensive list of sources. Some of Mrs Jameson's correspondence has been published, in *Letters of Anna Jameson to Ottilie von Goethe*, ed. G. H. Needler (London, 1939), and *Anna Jameson: letters and friendships (1812–1860)*, ed. [B. C. Strong] Mrs Steuart Erskine (London, 1915).

DNB. Gerardine [Bate] Macpherson, *Memoirs of the life of Anna Jameson* (London, 1878). Marian Fowler, *The embroidered tent: five gentlewomen in early Canada . . .* (Toronto, 1982). Ellen Moers, *Literary women* (Garden City, N.Y., 1976). A. M. Holcomb, "Anna Jameson: the first professional English art historian," *Art Hist.* (London), 6 (1983): 171–87. Clara [McCandless] Thomas, "Anna Jameson: art historian and critic," *Woman's Art Journal* (Knoxville, Tenn.), 1 (1980): 20–22. Leslie Monkman, "Primitivism and a parasol: Anna Jameson's Indians," *Essays on Canadian Writing* (Downsview [Toronto]), no.29 (summer 1984): 85–95.

MURRAY, ROBERT, Presbyterian minister, author, office holder, and teacher; b. *c.* 1795, probably the third son of John Murray of Banbridge (Northern Ireland); m. Jessie Dickson; they do not appear to have had any children; d. 30 March 1853 in Port Albert, Upper Canada.

Nelson

Robert Murray matriculated at the University of Glasgow in 1809, was ordained a minister of the Church of Scotland, and served a number of Scottish rural parishes as preacher and teacher. From 1824 to 1834 he was master of the Edinburgh Commercial and Mathematical Academy. During this time he published what was to be a very successful textbook on commercial arithmetic, later reprinted in Upper Canada. He then emigrated to the United States and in 1836 became pastor of the Church of Scotland congregation in Oakville, Upper Canada. Apparently a popular clergyman in his community though he took little part in the affairs of the Upper Canadian Kirk generally, he was unknown to a wider public except as the author of a pamphlet critical of temperance societies, which in 1839 had elicited a vigorous and vituperative rebuttal from Egerton Ryerson*.

During his ministry in Oakville he made a number of politically influential friends including his neighbour James Hopkirk and Samuel Bealey Harrison*. When the passage of a new school act in 1841 made the appointment of a chief administrative officer necessary, it was mainly these three men who promoted Murray's appointment. In April 1842 he became Upper Canada's first assistant superintendent of education, the provincial secretary being *ex officio* superintendent. His chief task was to administer the School Act of 1841. He had, however, no power to enforce uniformity on schools and trustees, and his job was made difficult not only because the act contained unpopular provisions but also because it was in many respects ambiguously worded and self-contradictory. Murray's efforts over the next two years were thus almost entirely devoted to making the best of a bad situation: explaining and interpreting the act, attempting to solve the problems it raised or ignored, and trying to convince the ministry of the need for better legislation. As part of his official duties he embarked on a tour of Upper Canada and, despite illness, managed to visit teachers and trustees throughout the province. Capitalizing on the tour and his extensive official correspondence, he submitted a report to the legislature in 1843 that summarized the inadequacies of the 1841 act and set out his proposed remedies: raise the quality of the teachers, improve the organization and selection of textbooks and the curriculum, and enlarge the powers of the superintendent.

The new school act brought in by the ministry in the fall of 1843, however, contained few of his recommendations and gave no greater powers to the superintendency. This in itself was a disappointment. As well, however, in early 1844 the new ministry of Sir Charles Theophilus Metcalfe* had decided that for political reasons Murray had to be replaced by Egerton Ryerson. Since Murray could not simply be dumped, another place for him had to be found, and a convenient resignation at King's College (University of Toronto) made it possible for Governor Metcalfe to arrange to have Murray appointed professor of mathematics and natural philosophy at that institution. The appointment was formally announced in September 1844.

Little is known of Murray's life from this point. He continued to officiate occasionally at his old congregation in Oakville and remained a professor at the university until his death at Port Albert in 1853 after a long illness. Murray's period of public life was brief, and his private life remains obscure. But as Upper Canada's first assistant superintendent of education, he implemented its first two school acts, established the Education Office, and worked for a stronger superintendency and improved teaching; he thus laid the foundations upon which his successor would build.

R. D. GIDNEY

[Robert Murray's popular textbook, *New system of commercial arithmetic . . . for the use of schools* (Edinburgh, 1830), was subsequently reprinted in Upper Canada; his controversial anti-temperance pamphlet, *A course of lectures on absolute abstinence; containing a refutation of the doctrines of the temperance society, advanced in the temperance volume; delivered before his congregation in Oakville, U.C.*, was published at Toronto in 1839. Murray's congregation publicized its support for his position in the *British Colonist* (Toronto), 28 Aug. 1839; Egerton Ryerson's editorials attacking the pamphlet appeared in the *Christian Guardian*, 18 and 25 Sept. 1839.

The present study is based primarily on my article, "The Rev. Robert Murray: Ontario's first superintendent of schools," *OH*, 63 (1971): 191–204. Additional sources include: H. C. Mathews, *Oakville and the Sixteen: the history of an Ontario port* (Toronto, 1953; repr. 1971), for information on Murray's life prior to 1836; PAC, RG 5, C1, 75, file 2195; 76, file 2273; his will (located at AO, RG 22, ser. 155); and the obituary notice in the *Journal of Education for Upper Canada* (Toronto), 6 (1853): 60.   R.D.G.]

N

NELSON, GEORGE, fur trader and author; b. 4 June 1786, probably in Montreal, eldest child of William Nelson* and Jane Dies; d. 13 July 1859 in Sorel, Lower Canada.

George Nelson's boyhood was spent initially in Montreal and then in William Henry (Sorel), where his father was a prominent schoolmaster. In 1802, when not quite 16, Nelson was apprenticed as a clerk for five years at £15 per year to the firm of Parker, Gerrard, and Ogilvy, which was associated with the New North West Company (sometimes known as the XY Company). His reminiscences of his first two seasons, spent in northwestern Michigan Territory (Wisconsin), reveal not only the anxiety and homesickness of a real greenhorn but also an early propensity for close observation of the Indians and their customs. During the fall of his second season, Nelson took his first Indian wife, the daughter of his guide, the Commis. This union was short-lived, however, because marriage according to the custom of the country was forbidden by the XY Company, and Nelson was forced to give up his wife when he came out to Grand Portage (near Grand Portage, Minn.).

In 1804, after being posted to Lake Winnipeg (Man.), Nelson became a clerk in the North West Company, the XY Company having been absorbed into the NWC. For the next nine years he served at various posts around Lake Winnipeg, principally on the Dauphin River (1807–11) and at Tête au Brochet (1811–13). In September 1807 he was seriously burned when a keg of gunpowder exploded while the brigade was encamped. His survival, apparently without much disfigurement, was credited to the application of native remedies: immediate submersion in the lake, a purgative recommended by the Ojibwa leader, Ayagon, and the treatment of his burns with swamp tea and larch-pine salve.

In the summer of 1808 at Bas-de-la-Rivière (Fort Alexander) Nelson married according to the custom of the country Mary Ann, an Ojibwa of the loon clan; this union was later formalized on 16 Jan. 1825 in Christ Church, William Henry. His new wife, who was related to the Ojibwa wife of NWC partner Duncan Cameron*, proved a valuable helpmate, especially after Nelson was given charge of a small outpost on Manitonamingan Lake (near Long Lake) in the Pic department, north of Lake Superior. By 1813 the competition with the Hudson's Bay Company had become severe, and Nelson's surviving journals present a fascinating picture of intrigue and harassment on the part of both companies and of the defection of some employees. Lamenting that "deep villiany is not the least essential part of a trader's attributes here," he himself had little stomach for the fight and in the summer of 1816 he took his wife and four daughters to William Henry. He had hoped to retire but financial need forced him to return to the NWC's service two years later. He was given charge of his old post Tête au Brochet in 1819 and was transferred the next season to the post at Moose Lake (Man.) in the Cumberland House department.

By 1820 Nelson, still an underpaid clerk, wrote to his superiors pressing his right to promotion. The partners had little time for his claims, however, since they were preoccupied with the pending coalition with the HBC. Nelson did not hear that the arch-rivals had

been united until June 1821. In a journal written in code, he freely gave vent to his anger at the way in which "old & faithful" servants such as himself had been betrayed; it galled him that the English company, with its muddled operations, should now have the upper hand. "Surely some secret power must aid & assist them otherwise how could they stand . . . out so long against us." In the fall of 1821 Nelson was placed in charge of distributing dry goods at Cumberland House (Sask.), but the next year he was given charge of Fort Lac la Ronge (La Ronge) in the Cumberland House department. There he penned his detailed and sympathetic record of Cree and Ojibwa legends, one of the finest early ethnographic documents of its kind. But although he was a "Good Clerk and Trader," the union had made him redundant, and he was forced to quit the HBC service in 1823.

Nelson's subsequent life in Lower Canada was marred by family tragedy and blighted hopes. In his absence, three of his eight children, one an infant whom he had never seen, had died. By 1831 his wife was dead, as were four other children. Nelson also became estranged from his brothers, especially Wolfred*, a leader of the rebellion of 1837. In his own account of the rebellion, George emphasizes that, in spite of their grievances, his brothers Wolfred and Robert* were not justified in resorting to treason against the British crown. Nelson had returned to the vicinity of William Henry and during the period 1825–36 he engaged in several business ventures, but all were failures. Ultimately he found solace in writing reminiscences of his days in the Indian country, which he worked on sporadically between 1836 and 1851. It was his intention "to inform" as well as "to charm," and one of his main purposes was to record his impressions of Indian society. His observations contain much philosophizing on the shortcomings of "civilization," which he contrasts unfavourably with the simplicity and egalitarianism of Indian life. Plagued by ill health through the 1850s, Nelson died in 1859, survived by one unmarried daughter, Jane.

Although George Nelson enjoyed little success as a fur trader, his writings, which consist of journals, letters, and reminiscences, make an outstanding contribution to the record of fur-trade life.

SYLVIA VAN KIRK in collaboration with
JENNIFER S. H. BROWN

George Nelson is the author of *A winter in the St. Croix valley; George Nelson's reminiscences, 1802–03*, ed. Richard Bardon and G. L. Nute (St Paul, Minn., 1948).

ANQ-M, CE3-1, 16 janv. 1825, 15 juill. 1859. AO, MU 842, George Nelson, Tête au Brochet diary. MTL, George Nelson journals. PAC, MG 19, E1, 22: 8638–40. Jennifer Brown, "Man in his natural state: the Indian worlds of George Nelson," and Sylvia Van Kirk, "George Nelson's 'wretched' career, 1802–1823," in *Rendezvous: selected papers of the Fourth North American Fur Trade Conference,*

Nemisses

1981, ed. Thomas Buckley (St Paul, 1984), 199–206 and 207–14 respectively.

NEMISSES. *See* GUIBOCHE, LOUIS

NICOLA (N'Kuala). *See* HWISTESMETXĒ'QEN

NOBILI, JOHN (baptized **Giovanni Pietro Antonio**), Roman Catholic priest, Jesuit, and missionary; b. 28 April 1812 in Rome, son of Domenico Nobili, lawyer, and Rosa Eutizi; d. 1 March 1856 in Santa Clara, Calif.

John Nobili entered the Society of Jesus in Rome in November 1828 and took his first vows in 1835. As a Jesuit scholastic, he taught humanities at several Jesuit colleges in Italy. After his ordination in 1843, Nobili volunteered for the Jesuit missions and in September of that year left Rome to join a group of missionaries being prepared for the northwest coast of North America by Father Pierre-Jean De Smet*. With De Smet, four other Jesuit priests (including Michael Accolti), one brother, and six sisters of Notre-Dame de Namur, Nobili sailed from Antwerp, Belgium, aboard the *Infatigable* on 9 Jan. 1844 and arrived at the Hudson's Bay Company's Fort Vancouver (Vancouver, Wash.) on 5 August, several days having been spent in crossing the dangerous bar of the Columbia River. During the voyage Nobili had begun to show evidence of pericarditis.

Nobili spent the next ten months in the area of the fort, ministering to the many French Canadian employees of the HBC, learning Indian dialects, and beginning his missionary career to the local Indians. In late June 1845 he left for New Caledonia, and while at Walla Walla (Wash.) in August he received instructions from De Smet to proceed north into the interior to visit as many Indian tribes as possible. No Catholic missionary, it seems, had ventured into this territory since the initiative taken by Father Modeste Demers* in 1841–43. The expedition came close to meeting a swift and tragic end when the HBC guide deserted Nobili and his companion, the novice brother Baptist (Battiste), taking with him their tent and provisions. This desertion appears to have been an isolated incident, for Nobili seems to have had excellent relations with the company. The missionaries were saved from death by two Cascades (Watlala) Indians.

Nobili none the less continued north, stopping to visit Fort Okanagan (Wash.) and Indians from the Siouxwaps (Shuswaps) and Thompson tribes. He arrived on 25 August at Fort Alexandria (Alexandria, B.C.) on the Fraser River, where he found the frame church built in the fall of 1842 during the Demers mission. By early September he was at Fort George (Prince George, B.C.), presumably among the Carrier Indians, and by the end of that month was at Stuart Lake. During the 11 days he spent at Stuart Lake he was pleased to have abolished "the custom of burning the dead and physically tormenting the widows or widowers." The hall where some of the medical (to him superstitious) practices had been taking place was turned into a church and solemnly blessed. He worked among the Chilcotins as well and wintered at Alexandria with the HBC trader Alexander Caulfield Anderson*. During this first of his missionary voyages he performed some 629 baptisms, most of Indians, including some chiefs; he estimated the total Indian population of the areas he visited at between 4,100 and 4,800.

Nobili reported to De Smet at Fort Colvile (near Colville, Wash.) in May 1846 and was instructed to continue his mission to the Indians of New Caledonia. His second trip, during which he had for a time the company of an HBC employee as well as a servant, began in July and took him as far as Fort Kilmars (near Babine, B.C.), close to the frontier with Russian Alaska. Turning south, he was at Fort George in mid December and by early March 1847 at Fort Alexandria. Speaking of these years in a letter dated 12 March 1852, Nobili stated: "I was there alone among 8 or 9 thousand Indians of different languages and manners. In all, I think I baptized and gave the other sacraments to nearly one thousand three or four hundred Indians, many of whom had the happiness to die soon after, including about five hundred children carried off by the measles." In May 1847 he selected a site for a residence, St Joseph's, among the Okanagans. Unfortunately, the location of this establishment, apparently the first permanent Jesuit mission in present-day British Columbia, is unknown. It seems most likely to have been on a creek near the head of Okanagan Lake, near the present-day O'Keefe railway station, on land apparently given to the missionary by Okanagan chief Nicola [HWISTESMET-XĒ'QEN]. A primitive house was built and, as was customary, a cross was raised.

The Jesuits decided at this time to leave New Caledonia to the diocesan clergy and concentrate on areas to the south, especially gold-rush California. Nobili was sent in the spring of 1848 to the Willamette valley (Oreg.) but his already frail health deteriorated and, much to his regret, he was ordered to California. After his final profession on 13 May 1849, he accompanied Father Accolti to San Francisco. In 1850 he served as assistant pastor in San Jose and the next year founded Santa Clara College (now the University of Santa Clara), the first Catholic college in California, in an abandoned Franciscan mission. While supervising construction in February 1856 he stepped on a nail and, having contracted tetanus, he died on 1 March. He was buried two days later in the mission church (now the chapel of the university).

CHARLOTTE S. M. GIRARD

Archivum Romanum Societatis Iesu (Rome), Nobili, Giovanni, 13, 14 Nov. 1828, 29 Aug. 1835; Missio M. Sax., 1001, IV, 27. Oreg. Prov. Arch. of the Soc. of Jesus (Spokane, Wash.), Corr. of John Nobili. PAM, HBCA, D.5/16: f.468. *Catholic Church records of Pacific northwest* (Munnick). P.-J. De Smet, *Cinquante nouvelles lettres du R. P. De Smet, de la Compagnie de Jésus et missionnaire en Amérique*, Édouard Terwecoren, édit. (Paris, 1858); *Life, letters and travels of Father Pierre-Jean De Smet, S.J., 1801–1873 . . .*, ed. H. M. Chittenden and A. T. Richardson (4v., New York, 1905); *Oregon missions and travels over the Rocky Mountains, in 1845–46* (New York, 1847); *Western missions and missionaries: a series of letters* (New York, 1863). W. N. Bischoff, *The Jesuits of old Oregon, 1840–1940* (Caldwell, Idaho, 1945). Gerald McKevitt, *The University of Santa Clara: a history, 1851–1977* (Stanford, Calif., 1979). Émilien Lamirande, "L'implantation de l'Église catholique en Colombie-Britannique (1838–1848)," *Rev. de l'univ. d'Ottawa*, 28 (1958): 460–66, 486. J. B. McGloin, "John Nobili, S.J., founder of California's Santa Clara College: the New Caledonia years, 1845–1848," *BCHQ*, 17 (1953): 215–22. Gerald McKevitt, "The beginning of Santa Clara University, 1851–1856," *San Jose Studies* (San Jose, Calif.), 3 (1977): 95–107; "The Jesuit arrival in California and the founding of Santa Clara College," American Catholic Hist. Soc., *Records* (Philadelphia), 85 (1974): 185–97.

NORMAND, FRANÇOIS (baptized **Nicolas-François**), wood-carver, carpenter, joiner, and architect; b. 8 Dec. 1779 in Charlesbourg, Que., son of Augustin-Nicolas Normand and Marie Lessard; d. 11 Oct. 1854 in Trois-Rivières, Lower Canada.

François Normand belonged to a family of craftsmen in wood who were living in the Quebec region at the end of the 1770s. The records provide no information about his childhood and training but, on examination, his works reveal a style and technique much closer to those of Louis Quévillon* than to those of François Baillairgé*. On 2 Feb. 1802 Normand married Claire Dufresne in Saint-Antoine-sur-Richelieu, where his parents then lived; the couple was to have three children. Normand's whereabouts suggest that he may have made contact with Quévillon, the master of the workshop at Les Écorres, who in 1801 was working at the village next to Boucherville with his students.

In 1803, having completed his apprenticeship, Normand was entrusted with a few minor pieces of wood-carving for the tabernacles of the church of Saint-Denis, on the Rivière Richelieu. Rather clumsy in his initial efforts, he confined himself to copying some of Gilles Bolvin*'s work. Normand rented a house at Trois-Rivières from Ezekiel Hart* in 1809, and when Jean-Baptiste Boucher de Niverville granted him land there in 1811 he lost no time in setting up his workshop. That year the *fabrique* of La Nativité-de-Notre-Dame at Bécancour contracted with him to supply the church with several pieces, including a retable (the decorated structure housing the altar), with payments extending to 1827.

It was not until the years just before and after 1820 that Normand produced his most notable work. In partnership with François Lafontaine, a joiner and wood-carver, he began in 1817 to decorate the interior of the church at Trois-Rivières with a large baldachin; he then panelled the entire nave, and produced two confessionals, a baptistry, all the balustrades, and three altars in Roman style. The work shows the influence of Quévillon. Normand carried out this contract over a four-year period during which he decided to settle permanently in Trois-Rivières.

Around the same time Normand also supplied several churches in the regions of Trois-Rivières and Quebec with decorative pieces and religious furniture: a vault, retables, a pulpit, and a churchwarden's pew for Gentilly (Bécancour) between 1817 and 1825; a cornice and baptismal fonts at Champlain from 1819 to 1823; a high altar at Batiscan around 1820; a vault and cornice for Pointe-aux-Trembles (Neuville) in 1826 and 1827; and a churchwarden's pew for Les Écureuils (Donnacona) in 1828. One of his sons, Hercule, whom he trained as a wood-carver and took on as a partner, helped him. François Normand had by then fully developed his own skills and did not hesitate to duplicate in broad outline some of the works produced by the team of François and THOMAS Baillairgé.

When commissions for wood-carving became scarce, Normand accepted contracts for carpentry and joinery which ensured him a good income. In 1818, for example, Normand, François Lafontaine, and François Routhier, a joiner, entered into an agreement with the Lower Canadian government to work on the interior of the court-house in Trois-Rivières.

From 1830 Normand's career apparently was on the decline. However, in 1840 the *fabrique* of Notre-Dame-du-Rosaire in Saint-Hyacinthe engaged him to undertake carpentry, joinery, and wood-carving projects for the new parish church. He completed work on the roof and belfry of the new church at Gentilly eight years later.

In 1853, knowing that his endeavours would be carried on in the Trois-Rivières region by his son Hercule, who was practising the trade of wood-carver there, he gave him his tools. François, his other son, had settled in Saint-Roch ward in Quebec, where he worked as a joiner. Normand died the following year at Trois-Rivières, at the age of 74.

It cannot be said that François Normand was a great innovator. None the less, he played almost the same role in the Trois-Rivières region as did François Baillairgé around Quebec and Louis Quévillon around Montreal. He managed to endow this part of Lower Canada with the kind of artistic works that already existed elsewhere in the province by the time he executed them.

RAYMONDE GAUTHIER

Nugent

ANQ-M, CE1-3, 2 févr. 1802; CN1-134, 28 mars 1808, 8 avril 1809, 1er mars 1811. ANQ-MBF, CE1-48, 13 oct. 1854; CN1-6, 21 oct. 1817; 15 oct., 1er, 18 déc. 1818; 25 janv., 5 oct. 1819; 12 déc. 1821; 18 mars 1823; 17 août 1832; CN1-7, 17 août 1832, 24 août 1835, 18 févr. 1838, 29 nov. 1853; CN1-19, 22 août 1836; CN1-32, 3 juill. 1816; 2 déc. 1817; 19 mai, 31 oct. 1818; 28 avril 1820; CN1-35, 3 juill. 1816; CN1-47, 19 oct. 1835; 3 févr., 14, 18 mars 1848. ANQ-Q, CE1-7, 8 févr., 8 déc. 1779; CN1-157, 27 déc. 1826, 3 nov. 1827. MAC-CD, Fonds Morisset, 2, N845/F825. *Quebec directory*, 1852. *Répertoire des mariages de Trois-Rivières, 1654–1900*, Dominique Campagna, compil. (Cap-de-la-Madeleine, Qué., [1963]), 339. [Prosper Cloutier], *Histoire de la paroisse de Champlain* (2v., Trois-Rivières, Qué., 1915–17), 2: 298–305. Lucien Dubois, *Histoire de la paroisse de Gentilly* (s.l., 1935), 109. Morisset, *Coup d'œil sur les arts*, 41–42. Luc Noppen, *Les églises du Québec (1600–1850)* (Québec, 1977), 152, 212. Jean Palardy, *Les meubles anciens du Canada français* ([2e éd.], Montréal, 1971), 281–82. J. R. Porter, *L'art de la dorure au Québec du XVIIe siècle à nos jours* (Québec, 1975), 94. *Sculpture traditionnelle du Québec* (Québec, 1967), 128. Sulte, *Mélanges hist.* (Malchelosse), 18: 72–73; 19: 82–83. Léon Roy, "Nos plus anciennes familles Normand et Normand, dit La Brière," *BRH*, 57 (1951): 9–16.

NUGENT, RICHARD, printer and newspaperman; b. May 1815 in Halifax, son of Patrick Nugent and Mary Hurley; m. 9 May 1837, in New York City, Elizabeth McFarlane of Halifax; d. 15 or 16 March 1858 in Flatbush (New York City).

Learning his trade with Joseph Howe* at the *Novascotian, or Colonial Herald* in the early 1830s, Richard Nugent was one of many apprentices whom Howe helped to educate at his home on Sunday evenings. Returning to the *Novascotian* after four years in the United States, Nugent took on increasing responsibilities as Howe became more heavily involved in politics: in 1840, manager of the office on a salaried basis; in 1841, printer and publisher on a rental basis; and, at the beginning of 1842, owner of the entire establishment. Until June 1842 he employed John Sparrow Thompson* as editor, but for the next year, although making "no pretensions to the experience and ability of the late editor," he wrote all but a handful of the *Novascotian*'s editorials and articles. In the spring of 1843 he began sharing editorial duties with Angus Morrison Gidney*, and this arrangement lasted until Nugent's tenure as proprietor came to an end that autumn.

In the case both of the *Novascotian* and of the newspapers he was to publish later in his career, Nugent emphasized that he intended them to be independent journals, wide-sweeping in character, covering politics, literature, humour, commerce, and general intelligence, always advocating "rational liberty, social order, and constitutional government." As issues arose, he almost invariably adopted a highly liberal stance, never averse, as a Catholic, to opposing the bishops and priests of his own church. Above all, he advocated a leading role for government in the promotion of public education, especially on the ground that ordinary people would cherish political rights more highly if they understood them better.

Freely admitting the difficulties of one who had few personal friends and no wealthy family connections, and having inherited "a host of bitter and powerful enemies" from Howe, Nugent, none the less, gave no quarter and experienced stormier times than any other Nova Scotia newspaperman. He began, between June and August 1842, by publishing anonymously the celebrated "Letters of a Constitutionalist." In these letters Howe demolished in barbarous fashion those extreme tories who were taking pot-shots at the tory-reform coalition government of which he was a member. Although the experienced Howe avoided anything that could be attacked as libellous in court, Nugent paid a penalty for printing the letters. Twice he had to defend himself in the streets, once from an attack by John Henry CROSSKILL. The second time he had James Colquhoun Cogswell convicted of assault.

Much more consequential was Nugent's part in intensifying Howe's difficulties with the Baptists, first for their failure to pay him for printing their newspaper, the *Christian Messenger*, and later for differences on the support of denominational colleges. In 1842 Nugent charged the *Messenger*'s editors, John Ferguson and James Walton Nutting*, with attempting to ruin Howe financially as "*the only mode of getting rid of him left to his political enemies.*" Because both had tory connections, he accused them all the more readily of engaging in a conspiracy to embroil Howe with the Baptists for political reasons. In 1843 Nugent took on the Reverend Edmund Albern Crawley* of Acadia College, who had not only charged Howe and his friends with seeking to destroy the denominational colleges but who had manifested his tory leanings by entering into the general political debate as well. Delightedly, Nugent replied with editorials headed "Professor Crawley turned politician" and "Parson Crawley's politics." Howe was horrified but powerless to restrain his *enfant terrible*. Eventually, however, he accepted Nugent's view of a planned tory-Baptist alliance and entered vigorously into a religious and political struggle which resulted in the loss of eight liberal seats in the province's Baptist belt in the elections of late 1843. It is at least arguable that Nugent played the leading role in these reverses and in the long-term alienation of the Baptists from the Liberal party.

At the same time, Nugent, at least nominally a Roman Catholic, was having troubles with Bishop William WALSH for opposing his decision to remove the control of the Total Abstinence Society from Father John Loughnan, the vicar general of the diocese of Nova Scotia and the rector of St Mary's Cathedral in Halifax. Even after 1,700 Catholics met to oppose the "calumnies" published in the *Novascotian* against their bishop, Nugent stated he would "disregard the threats of any faction" and print what he pleased on public matters. Because the tories tried to make political capital out of the episode by identifying the *Novascotian* as Howe's paper, the liberals sought Catholic good will by offering to nominate a Catholic for one of the Halifax seats in the election of 1843. But when none of the liberals' sitting members would withdraw, the Catholics showed their annoyance by staying away from the polls and thus permitted the tory Andrew Mitchell Uniacke to win one of the Halifax Township seats. The outcome, province-wide, was that the tories won one more seat than the liberals, and this result, in turn, led Lieutenant Governor Lord Falkland [Cary*] to appoint another tory to the Executive Council, an action which brought down the coalition in December 1843. For this train of events Nugent was at least indirectly responsible.

Meanwhile a crisis had developed in Nugent's personal fortunes. Because he had thought it his "duty to lay it before the public," on 10 Aug. 1842 he had published a letter by Joseph Fenwick Taylor, master of a British barque caught in the toils of the Vice-Admiralty Court. The letter described the Halifax city recorder and proctor of the court, William Q. Sawers, as "a rapacious attorney, doing a small business," who had pursued "a tortuous, pettifogging and vexatious course" to gratify "a spiteful malignity." On 9 Nov. 1842 Nugent printed another letter signed "Self Defence," which dealt harshly with a clique specializing in the wholesale slander of "private character" and singled out especially "*Councellor Skunkfeet*," whom Silas Livingston Morse of Annapolis County, because of specific allusions, identified as himself. Both Sawers and Morse proceeded against Nugent for civil libel.

In July 1843 a jury found for Sawers in the amount of £40 and costs; in October another found for Morse in the amount of £110 and costs. Although Nugent admitted to "imprudence, or impetuosity," his libels appear mild when compared with the steady diet of vilification served up by the newspapers in these years. He laboured, of course, under the difficulty that the special juries in libel cases were chosen from the grand jury panels, whose members, because of large property qualifications, were likely to be heavily tory in complexion. Moreover, Nugent appeared the victim of political enemies who, unable to contend effectively with the chief reform organ, sought to get rid of its impecunious editor by pursuing him mercilessly. Both trials were, in fact, political trials. At Annapolis the tory leader and attorney general, James William Johnston*, acted for Morse and spoke for more than three hours: "*passionate* – and [with] something very like *vindictiveness* towards us," wrote Nugent. In Halifax a second tory executive councillor,

Alexander Stewart*, joined Johnston in acting for Sawers, while two leading liberal lawyers, William* and GEORGE RENNY Young, defended Nugent.

Despite the two court defeats, Nugent vowed he would continue to hold up "*public* villainy to *public* execration." Laughingly he declared that Sawers's reputation was worth "the enormous sum of *forty pounds*," one twenty-fifth of what he claimed and "a sum too small to seriously injure us." But by November he was having second thoughts. Unable to make ends meet, he had earlier discussed the sale of the *Novascotian* to William Annand*. His editorial comments on Sawers's action had led to two further libel suits and the possibility that he might be mulcted in heavy damages and prevented from paying his creditors. Late in November came the news that he had made an assignment for his creditors' benefit and sold his establishment to Annand, who said with some truth that Nugent had been a victim of those seeking to "stifle free discussion, and suppress all wholesome censure of the conduct of public men." Though forced to languish in jail until he had met the £93 in damages and costs owing Sawers, Nugent was unrepentant: "I know of nothing with which to upbraid myself, – nor can I call to mind with regret a paragraph I have written." Vigorous in the Howe mould, Nugent in the years 1842–43 had been engaged in smaller publishing ventures – the *Colonial Farmer*, the temperance journal *Saturday Evening Visitor* (succeeded by the *Monthly Visitor* and the *Family Visitor*), and the literary *Gridiron* – but it was the heavy court fines and legal costs, not over-extended business ventures, that brought about his financial collapse.

After giving up the *Novascotian*, Nugent did editorial work with other Halifax newspapers for more than a year before he joined Alexander J. Ritchie, a friend since boyhood, to start the *Sun* on 17 March 1845. As its editor, Nugent suggested that "time and experience . . . may have subdued the almost boyish ardour of our earlier career" and hoped that no one would have "reason to complain of us that he was 'Sun-*struck.*'" But, although more careful to avoid libels, he had lost none of his zeal for liberal principles and continued to fight vigorously for responsible government. Still a favourite of Howe, he accompanied him on his trips to Lunenburg and the eastern counties in 1846, adding to his store of political knowledge and regaling his readers with stories of rising liberal fortunes.

Ritchie boasted, when he retired from the *Sun* in 1848, that "our little bark" had become "a good property." So much so that when Morse attached Nugent's household furniture in 1849 for the damages awarded him six years earlier, he did not endanger the existence of the *Sun*. In 1852 Nugent added the *Daily Sun* to the previous tri-weekly edition, and for a few years he also published a weekly edition, which he somewhat immodestly described as "the largest,

O'Brien

cheapest and best weekly Family Journal in the Lower Provinces." At the beginning of 1857 ill health compelled him to retire from the management of his papers. On his death the next year in New York, where he had been taken for medical treatment, it was reported that "for several years past, his mind, much too heavily taxed, became gradually impaired."

Nugent's role in the contest for responsible government and his influence on the future course of Nova Scotian politics have never received proper recognition. Undoubtedly, he was too independent, both for the leaders of his church and for his fellow reformers, whom he sometimes taxed with equivocation and backsliding, but, as an unswerving advocate of liberal principles, he had no superior, not even Howe himself.

J. MURRAY BECK

The Halifax newspaper begun by Richard Nugent and Alexander J. Ritchie in 1845 as the tri-weekly *Sun* continued under various other names: in 1850 the title was changed to *Halifax Sun*; during 1852 Nugent began publication of the *Daily Sun* and the *Weekly Sun*; and by the time of his retirement in 1857 it was being issued as the *Morning Sun*.

Harvard College Library, Houghton Library, Harvard Univ. (Cambridge, Mass.), MS Can. 58 (Joseph Howe papers) (mfm. at PANS). St Mary's Basilica (Halifax), St Peter's Roman Catholic Church, Halifax, reg. of baptisms, marriages, and burials. *Acadian Recorder*, 1842–43. *Morning Chronicle* (Halifax), 1844–58. *Novascotian*, 1840–58, especially 1841–43. *Times* (Halifax), 1842–43. *An historical directory of Nova Scotia newspapers and journals before confederation*, comp. T. B. Vincent (Kingston, Ont., 1977). G. E. N. Tratt, *A survey and listing of Nova Scotia newspapers, 1752–1957, with particular reference to the period before 1867* (Halifax, 1979). Beck, *Joseph Howe*.

O

O'BRIEN, JOHN, farmer; b. 1790, probably in Ireland; m. 29 Nov. 1823 Mary Darcy, in St John's, and they had at least four sons and two daughters; d. 1855 near St John's.

Some time between 1815 and 1820 John O'Brien began clearing land at Freshwater, an area two miles west of St John's which had been opened for settlement about 1800. Since no O'Briens or Darcys are recorded as sponsors or witnesses at their marriage and at the subsequent baptisms of their children, it is almost certain that O'Brien and his wife were recent immigrants who had arrived in Newfoundland on their own. The sponsors named came mostly from parishes in the south of County Kilkenny (Republic of Ireland), as did many St John's Roman Catholic Irish, and the O'Briens likely came from this region.

Between the years 1790 and 1815 St John's had been transformed from a small town of approximately 1,000 persons into the mercantile centre for the Newfoundland cod fishery with a population fluctuating between 8,000 and 10,000. Mainly because of the Napoleonic Wars, fish prices had soared in the European markets, and the related increase in wages had attracted large numbers of young Irish immigrants, women as well as men. During the 18th century much of the food consumed in the town, with the exception of fish, had come from either Britain or the North American mainland, but interruptions in the supply during the wars, and the growing resident population in St John's along with an increased military presence and the emergence of a middle class, all stimulated a demand for food that could be grown locally. Encouraged by Governor Sir Richard Good-

win Keats*'s relaxation of laws inhibiting the development of commercial agriculture in 1813, immigrants to St John's began to carve out small farms around the edge of the town and to produce such commodities as fresh milk and vegetables. By 1840 more than 400 farms were in operation, forming thin wedges of settlement along the new roads radiating from the town.

At the time of O'Brien's arrival virtually all of the workable land along the road and tributary paths between St John's and Freshwater was occupied by some 30 farmsteads and he pushed west beyond them. After trying one unsuitable site he moved to the slopes of Nagles Hill. There he began clearing on a level patch of glacial till near the eastern boundary of what was later officially demarcated as his farm lot, and built a tilt or temporary shelter.

Clearing the land was a formidable task. O'Brien was confronted by a dense cover of spruce and fir trees which stood between him and his farm, and the technology available was crude and primitive: light narrow axes and hatchets to hack away the trees and scrub, and then picks, crowbars, and makeshift wooden levers to prize out stubborn stumps. Larger roots were left to rot or were burned. Once a patch was finally stripped of its natural cover, O'Brien was faced with a shallow, stony soil from which rocks and stones had to be removed, a task no less laborious than clearing the forest. Some of this stone was taken to St John's and sold for ballast or used in harbour construction, but most was fashioned into the massive walls that helped define the fields within the farm.

By North American standards the rate of land

clearing was exceedingly slow. O'Brien had 14 acres improved and under cultivation in 1849, roughly three decades after initial occupancy. It is unlikely that he achieved even this much alone. Up to the 1840s many local farmers engaged immigrant Irish labourers, hungry for winter work after the summer fishery, to clear land and carve out paths and roads through the woods. These young men often worked for just food and shelter and O'Brien probably availed himself of this pool of cheap labour at least until his older sons could join him. Drier, elevated sites were first chosen for clearing, and then the wet hollows which had to be drained extensively before cropping. The deeper drift deposits in the hollows normally afforded a more fertile base for crops but generally the natural soil was no more than six inches deep and it took a generation of careful husbandry and intensive fertilizing to bring it to a satisfactory state.

Climate and soil precluded commercial grain farming. The short, cool, damp summers suited the growth of improved grasses and, like all Freshwater farmers, O'Brien adapted to these conditions and created a commercial dairy farm. He sold the milk to housewives and shopkeepers in the west end of St John's. The ultimate objective was the creation of a good meadow. A cow could consume more than two tons of hay through the long winter, and each spring two-thirds of the farm was reserved for this crop. Hayfields benefited from periodic cultivation and so a system of crop rotation evolved: an "old" meadow was planted with turnips and cabbage, then potatoes, and then oats and hayseed in the third year before the field was returned to hay for several years. These meadows, high on the southern slopes of Nagles Hill, were protected from the elements by broad strips of uncleared woodland.

O'Brien's farm stood on the fringe of the hinterland in Freshwater and was thus one of the most distant from the market. He cleared a path a half-mile past his nearest neighbour to his first home, deep in the woods. His second house, a much more substantial structure, was located close to his neighbours near the eastern boundary of the farm. Like other farmers, O'Brien could supply the expertise, technology, and basic materials for road construction, and procured small cash contracts from the government to open and maintain public roads and paths. One such contract, secured in the fall of 1844, fell through when the government experienced a shortage of capital; another, made in the summer of 1849, called for a road through a neighbour's uncleared land and ended in litigation which almost cost O'Brien his farm. He was fined £12 for assault and the sheriff attached his farm and advertised it for sale when O'Brien claimed he could not pay. This action drew an angry editorial from the *Newfoundland Patriot* of Robert John Parsons*, who regarded the proceedings as an unparalleled piece of oppression against one who "by

dint of persevering toil has succeeded in clearing fifteen out of some fifty acres of wild land from the Crown and has reared a large family during the process – calculating that . . . he could bequeath it to them as the produce of a life of labour and penury." Apparently nobody bid on the farm and O'Brien retained possession.

Little land was cleared on the original lot after 1850 but O'Brien's eldest son, with the family's assistance, established a farm and built a house west of his father's. The ancestral unit was bequeathed to the two remaining sons and shortly before his death O'Brien helped one of them build an impressive two-storey frame-house. This son acquired another farm on the edge of town and established a grocery store on the road to Freshwater, strategically located to capture the community's retail trade. Ultimately the youngest son obtained the ancestral farm, conforming to the pattern of an indivisible inheritance common in the area. One daughter joined the local exodus to Boston, the other worked with her brothers on the home farm or in the store. Two of the sons married recent immigrants from south Kilkenny, reinforcing cultural links with the homeland. John O'Brien and his wife died secure in the knowledge that their children had been well provided for by the standards of their time.

The O'Briens typified the experience of the Irish who came to St John's in the early 19th century and made a living off the land. Like many immigrants in rural British North America, O'Brien chose to live in a community dominated initially by people from the same region in his homeland. Although a few merchants of British Protestant stock later established summer cottages in the neighbourhood, as did some middle class Catholic Irish from St John's, Freshwater remained culturally homogeneous and socially egalitarian during O'Brien's lifetime. The vast majority of his neighbours worked small farms similar to his; some were also artisans and plied their trade in town to supplement their meagre income from the land. Life was hard and several families moved out within a generation. Despite the harsh environmental and economic conditions, O'Brien succeeded in striking deep roots and, four generations later, his descendants still work the land. Much of the 19th-century landscape survives, a document of his efforts to carve a farm out of the Newfoundland forest a century and a half ago.

JOHN MANNION

[The author gratefully acknowledges the assistance of Aly O'Brien, a great-grandson of John O'Brien, in the preparation of this biography. J.M.]

Basilica of St John the Baptist (Roman Catholic) (St John's), St John's parish, reg. of baptisms and marriages, 10 Sept., 29 Nov. 1823; 28 Jan. 1832; 17 Nov. 1834; 10 April 1837 (mfm. at PANL). Nfld., Dept. of Forest Resources and Land, Lands Branch (St John's), Registry of crown grants,

Ogden

geographical index to crown grants, vol.A (1813–23): 12 (typescript); grants, 27: f.63; 36: f.9; land titles, vol.A (1813–23). PANL, GN 2/1, 1806: 427–29; 1813: 310–14, 413–14; 1815: 342–46; 1816: 234–40; 1817: 25–29; 1818: 163–70; 1819–20: 3–5, 270–77; GN 2/1/A, 24 (1813): 3–9. PRO, CO 194/12–49. *Morning Courier and General Advertiser* (St John's), 11 Aug. 1849. *Patriot* (St John's), 1 Oct. 1845, 11 Aug. 1849. *Royal Gazette and Newfoundland Advertiser*, 30 Sept. 1834. R. A. MacKinnon, "The growth of commercial agriculture around St John's, 1800–1935: a study of local trade in response to urban demand" (MA thesis, Memorial Univ. of Nfld., St John's, 1981). J. J. Mannion, *Irish settlements in eastern Canada; a study of cultural transfer and adaptation* ([Toronto], 1974), 65, 143–45. *The peopling of Newfoundland: essays in historical geography*, ed. J. J. Mannion (Toronto, 1977), editor's introduction, 7.

OGDEN, PETER SKENE (baptized **Skeene**, he also signed **Skeen** and **Skein**), fur trader and explorer; baptized 12 Feb. 1790 at Quebec, son of Isaac Ogden*, jurist, and Sarah Hanson; d. 27 Sept. 1854 in Oregon City (Oreg.).

Peter Skene Ogden is one of the most energetic and controversial figures to have left his mark on the North American fur trade. At the age of four, he moved with his family to Montreal, where his father had been appointed puisne judge and where, with two brothers already lawyers, he grew up in a family wedded to the law. But late-18th-century Montreal was a city which derived much of its atmosphere from its vocation as the organizing centre of the Canadian fur trade and, although Ogden seems to have received some tutoring in law, the legal profession evidently held few attractions for him. After a brief spell with the American Fur Company in Montreal, he joined the North West Company as an apprentice clerk in April 1809. This was a critical period in the rivalry between the NWC and the Hudson's Bay Company and during the final years of turbulent competition before the coalition of 1821 the young Ogden earned an unenviable reputation for violence.

His first station was at Île-à-la-Crosse (Sask.), where soon after his arrival at the end of September 1810 he and fellow clerk Samuel Black* were involved in a fight with Peter Fidler* at the nearby HBC post. By 1814 Ogden was in charge of the post at the north end of Green Lake, about 100 miles south of Île-à-la-Crosse. What little is known of his activities during these years comes from HBC records, which note with growing disapproval the bully-boy tactics he and Black employed. In May 1816 Ogden crossed the boundary between physical assault, which had become a commonplace in the trade war, and killing, which had not. According to HBC officer James Bird, in charge at Edmonton House (Edmonton), Ogden and a small group of his men forced the HBC clerk at Green Lake, Robert McVicar*, to hand over to them a local Indian who had persisted in trading with the British company. When McVicar complied, the

Indian was "butchered in a most cruel manner" just a short distance from the fort. A year later Ogden dressed his violent behaviour in a legal guise for the benefit of a visiting Nor'Wester, Ross Cox: "In this place, where the custom of the country, or as lawyers say, the *Lex non scripta* is our only guide, we must, in our acts of summary legislation, sometimes perform the parts of judge, jury, sheriff, hangman, gallows and all." Cox found his host "humorous, honest, eccentric, law-defying . . . and the delight of all gay fellows," but to the HBC he was a dangerous man, whose actions were particularly to be deplored in light of his family background. In February 1818 an account of the incident at Green Lake was forwarded to Lord Bathurst, secretary of state for war and the colonies, by Governor Joseph Berens of the HBC, who pointed out that with a judge for a father Ogden "cannot surely shelter himself under the plea of not knowing right from wrong or grounding thereupon an excuse for murdering an Indian in cold blood, merely because the Indian was attempting to trade with [the HBC]."

An indictment against Ogden for murder was drawn up in Lower Canada in March 1818. To put Ogden out of reach of the HBC he was transferred to the Columbia department in 1818, and there he served variously at Fort George (Astoria, Oreg.), Spokane House (near Spokane, Wash.), and Thompson's River Post (Kamloops, B.C.). At about this time he took as his country wife Julia Rivet, a Spokan Indian, having left behind him at Green Lake the Cree woman who had borne his first child. The terms of the coalition agreement between the HBC and the NWC, signed in March 1821, excluded Ogden and Black, among others, from the new organization because of their violent conduct during the years of conflict between the two companies. Nevertheless, at the slightly abashed request of the HBC, Ogden remained in charge of Fort Thompson for the winter of 1821–22 before journeying east in 1822, first to the Canadas, and then to England, where he sought to persuade the company to reconsider its ban. A daguerreotype of Ogden, taken in London at this time, shows a firm-jawed, sturdy figure and hints at his physical strength and determination. Influenced by HBC governor George Simpson, who was concerned about the possible damage Ogden and Black might do in opposition and who on reflection considered that their behaviour in the period of competition had been no worse than that of others, the London committee of the HBC relented and in 1823 agreed that both men should be appointed chief traders. In July the HBC's Council of the Northern Department, meeting at York Factory (Man.), confirmed these appointments and posted Ogden to Spokane House with instructions to fit out a trapping expedition to the Snake River country for the spring of 1824.

Ogden's combative temperament was now to be

given full rein, for the Snake country, which covers a large area to the south of the Columbia River between the continental divide and the Pacific coast, was an area of grim natural hazards, menacing and unpredictable Indians, and rival American traders. After an initial expedition sent out under the direction of Alexander Ross, Ogden himself took charge of the HBC campaign in this country, which in 1818 Great Britain and the United States had declared temporarily open to joint occupation by the subjects of both nations in default of a permanent boundary agreement. Usage rather than geographical exactitude has given Ogden's activities here the title of "Snake country expeditions," for although they encompassed the Snake River that stream was only a starting point, and Ogden travelled, explored, and trapped a much wider area, covering present-day Oregon and Idaho, and parts of California, Nevada, Utah, and Wyoming, before returning to the Snake on his homeward run. Despite Spanish explorations from the south in the 1770s and the first hesitant American ventures following in the steps of Meriwether Lewis and William Clark, the geography of the Snake country was a bewildering puzzle of several different watersheds and drainage areas. Rumours of westward-flowing rivers and inland seas proliferated, but accurate maps were non-existent. It was this puzzle which Ogden now began to untangle, teasing out the knotted skeins one after another, and by 1830 he had a better, though still by no means faultless, knowledge of the area than any other explorer.

Geographical knowledge, however, was not his only, nor even his main, object and for the HBC it was clearly secondary to the task of trapping the country bare. Here the normal rules of company policy did not apply. If, as many believed, the region south of the Columbia was eventually to go to the United States, a careful trapping program of conservation would benefit only the Americans. Furthermore, the less profitable the Americans found this area, the less attracted they would be towards the established company trapping grounds farther north. At a meeting at Spokane House in 1824, Governor Simpson stated Ogden's task in bleak, unambiguous terms: "If properly managed no question exists that it would yield handsome profits as we have convincing proof that the country is a rich preserve of Beaver and which for political reasons we should endeavour to destroy as fast as possible."

On six separate expeditions between 1824 and 1830 Ogden did this, and more. The first expedition ran into trouble when Ogden lost many of his freemen, independent traders outfitted by the company, and their furs to a larger American group; the final expedition experienced tragedy near the end when 9 men, 500 furs, and Ogden's papers disappeared in the swirling cascades of the Dalles on the Columbia River. But between these misfortunes Ogden's returns

delighted Chief Factor John McLoughlin, his immediate superior, who wrote enthusiastically that the Snake country ventures were yielding 100 per cent profits. They were profits made at a cost, however, for even by tough fur-trade standards the hardships of the Snake country were exceptional. Men and horses fell sick and died, were killed by Indian arrows, froze in winter, and suffered from heat and fever in summer. In June 1827, as Ogden's party was heading northeast from Goose Lake (Calif.), a region where liquid mud was their only drink, he wrote that "this is certainly a most horrid life in a word I may say without exaggeration Man in this Country is deprived of every comfort that can tend to make existance desirable." Later that month the once-sturdy Ogden noted with disgust how illness, low rations, and excessively high temperatures had reduced him "to Skin and Bone." His journals, sometimes cynical in tone and often outspoken, give the overriding impression of a persistent and tenacious personality. With his men and horses Ogden discovered the Humboldt River (Nev.) and sighted Great Salt Lake (Utah). On his last expedition he probably reached the lower Colorado River and possibly the Gulf of California. Either to carry out exploration or to trap furs was an achievement over such terrain and to combine the two was a remarkable feat.

In July 1830 Ogden received orders transferring him to the northwest coast and in April 1831 he sailed north from Fort Vancouver (Vancouver, Wash.) to establish a new post near the mouth of the Nass River (B.C.). From this post, initially named Fort Nass and then renamed Fort Simpson, Ogden pursued a vigorous policy of competition against both American traders, active offshore up and down the coast, and the Russian American Company, based at Sitka (Alaska). Using the schooners *Cadboro* and *Vancouver*, he successfully countered the American maritime traders, but his attempt to found a post on the Stikine River in 1834 was thwarted by the opposition of the Russians and of the coastal Indians. Promoted chief factor in 1834, Ogden was given command of the New Caledonia district in 1835, to succeed Peter Warren Dease*. This move, strongly supported by Governor Simpson, is a more significant comment on the company's assessment of Ogden's worth than Simpson's oft-quoted entry in his confidential "Character book" of 1832. Recognizing Ogden's "conspicuous" services to the company, Simpson nevertheless foresaw trouble if he was promoted, describing him as "one of the most unprincipled Men in the Indian Country, who would soon get into habits of dissipation if he were not restrained by the fear of these operating against his interests, and if he does indulge in that way madness to which he has a predisposition will follow as a matter of course." But these dark hints are perhaps a reflection of Simpson's own state of mind, for although Ogden retained his

Ogden

reputation for boisterousness, there is little evidence in subsequent years of either the unscrupulousness or the instability conjured up by Simpson.

Ogden reached his new headquarters at Fort St James (B.C.) on Stuart Lake in 1835 where, for the first time in his fur-trade career, he was not faced with direct competition, though there was an echo of his Snake country experience in the company's determination to trap the country bare. As returns fell off as a result of this policy, Ogden worked at securing good relations and smooth trading arrangements with the local Carrier Indians. According to his "Notes on western Caledonia," prepared in 1842, he had as low an opinion of them – "a brutish, ignorant, superstitious beggarly sett of beings" – as he had of the Indians of the Snake country. In regard to the methods of trading, Ogden doubted whether the traditional system of allowing debts was preventing a seepage of furs from the Indians of the interior down to the coast.

Ogden left New Caledonia in 1844 for a one-year furlough, much of which he spent in England, where the HBC London committee was preoccupied with the looming Oregon question [see George Simpson]. On his return to Canada in 1845 he accompanied two British army officers, Mervin Vavasour* and Henry James Warre*, on their secret surveying trip from Lachine, Lower Canada, to the Columbia. In 1845 Ogden had also been appointed to the newly formed board of management for the Columbia district, with McLoughlin and James Douglas*, and after his arrival at Fort Vancouver in August he carried out his instructions to purchase Cape Disappointment at the mouth of the Columbia for the HBC. Regardless of this apparent claim to sovereignty, the Oregon Boundary Treaty of June 1846 fixed the frontier between British and American territory at the 49th parallel, placing the lower Columbia in the United States. Ogden, who together with Douglas and John Work* ran the Columbia district after the retirement of McLoughlin in 1846, now faced the problems of operating in an area which had passed under foreign control. Not least of these problems was the arrival of increasing numbers of settlers from the east, disrupting the stable relations with the Indians upon which the trading activities of the HBC depended.

In spite of the declared American sovereignty over the Oregon, the HBC remained for some time the recognized authority in much of the area. Ogden's decisive action in December 1847 following the Cayuse Indian attack on the mission at Waiilatpu (near Walla Walla, Wash.), in which 14 people were killed and 47 taken prisoner, served to underline this situation. With an American provisional government at Oregon City inexperienced in dealing with Indians and without the force capable of swift intervention to save the captives, Ogden left Fort Vancouver on 7 December, the morning after he had heard the news, and by 24 December had succeeded in negotiating the release of the prisoners. This was a triumph for Ogden's experience and judgement, and for the reputation of the HBC; as Ogden pointed out after receiving unstinted praise from George Abernethy, provisional governor of Oregon, and from the HBC directors in London, "without [the company's] powerful aid and influence nothing could have been effected."

Ogden's last years at Fort Vancouver were frustrating ones as he coped with the problems of a fast-changing environment in which settlers and prospectors were more in evidence than fur traders and Indians. In August 1854, in ill health, he left Fort Vancouver for Oregon City, where he died in September at 64 years of age. He died a man of some substance, and his will made careful provision for a division of land, cash, and bank stock between his children (one son from his first country marriage and seven from his second), his grandchildren, and other relatives. Unlike other fur traders such as McLoughlin, Ogden never formalized by Christian rite his country marriage with Julia and after his death his brother Charles Richard* and his sister Harriet Lawrence began legal proceedings to have Julia and the rest of Ogden's family disinherited. As one of the executors of the estate, Simpson worked towards a compromise by which the property was divided. Over the years Simpson's views on Ogden had changed. Mellower now than he had been, Simpson still did not give his friendship easily, and it was a measure both of Ogden's professional competence and of his personal qualities that the governor noted in November 1854, "Few persons I believe knew him so well or esteemed his friendship more highly than myself."

GLYNDWR WILLIAMS

The journals for five of the six expeditions led by Peter Skene Ogden into Snake country are held at PAM, HBCA. Those for the first two expeditions were published in *HBRS*, 13 (Rich and Johnson), while the one for the third appeared first as "The Peter Skene Ogden journals," ed. T. C. Elliott, Oreg. Hist. Soc., *Quarterly* (Portland), 11 (1910): 201–22, and then in a complete and annotated form as *HBRS*, 23 (Davies and Johnson). The last two journals are in *HBRS*, 28 (Williams). Ogden also wrote "Peter Skene Ogden's notes on western Caledonia," ed. W. N. Sage, *BCHQ*, 1 (1937): 45–56. He was likely the author of *Traits of American Indian life and character* (London, 1853), a work signed by "A fur trader." The events related in the 16 accounts that make up this volume correspond closely to Ogden's career.

ANQ-M, CN1-29, 27 avril 1809. ANQ-Q, CE1-61, 12 févr. 1790. PAM, HBCA, B.60/a/13: ff.14d–15d; B.60/a/15: ff.37d–38; B.89/a/2: ff.11, 13, 13d–14; E.8/5: ff.95–97d. *Catholic Church records of Pacific northwest* (Munnick). *Docs. relating to NWC* (Wallace). *HBRS*, 2 (Rich and Fleming); 3 (Fleming); 4 (Rich). Alexander Ross, "Journal of Alexander Ross – Snake country expedition, 1824," ed. T. C. Elliott, Oreg. Hist. Soc., *Quarterly*, 14 (1913): 366–88. Simpson, "Character book," *HBRS*, 30

(Williams), 151–236. *Quebec Gazette*, 19 March 1818. Archie Binns, *Peter Skene Ogden: fur trader* (Portland, 1967). G. G. Cline, *Peter Skene Ogden and the Hudson's Bay Company* (Norman, Okla., 1974). Van Kirk, *"Many tender ties."* T. C. Elliott, "Peter Skene Ogden, fur trader," Oreg. Hist. Soc., *Quarterly*, 11 (1910): 229–78. F. W. Howay, "Authorship of traits of Indian life," *Oreg. Hist. Quarterly* (Salem), 35 (1934): 42–49.

OLD SWAN. *See* A-CA-OO-MAH-CA-YE

ONWARENHIIAKI. *See* WILLIAMS, ELEAZER

OOLIGBUCK (Oolibuck, Ouligbuck, Oullibuck, Oulybuck, Ullebuck), Inuit hunter, interpreter, and guide; m. twice and had at least three children; d. 1852.

The first known reference to Ooligbuck is in May 1824, when he arrived at the Hudson's Bay Company post at Churchill (Man.). He was engaged by the officer in charge, Hugh Leslie, to accompany Captain John Franklin* on an overland expedition to the mouth of the Mackenzie River (N.W.T.). Ooligbuck, whose wages were 50 made beaver per annum, spoke no English but was to help with the hunt and be company for the Inuit interpreter Augustus [Tattannaaeuk*]. The expedition spent the winter of 1825–26 at Fort Franklin on Great Bear Lake (N.W.T.). Ooligbuck passed his time hunting but, unaccustomed to wooded country, he was not very successful. In the spring the expedition proceeded to Point Separation in the Mackenzie River delta where, on 4 July 1826, the party split into two groups, one under Franklin going west and the other under John Richardson* and Edward Nicolas Kendall* going east towards the Coppermine River. Ooligbuck accompanied Richardson, whom he impressed with his skill as a boatman as well as with his cheerful manner and excellent temper. His presence also reassured the Inuit encountered during this journey of 1,455 miles that the disposition of the exploring party was friendly. During the winter of 1826–27 the expedition made its way southeast overland to Norway House (Man.), where, in June, Ooligbuck and Augustus took leave of Franklin to return to Hudson Bay.

On his return to Churchill in September 1827 Ooligbuck entered the employ of the HBC, providing services which varied from hunting seals to weeding turnips in the company garden. In November 1829, having learned to speak English, he agreed to act as interpreter for a party being led by Nicol Finlayson* with instructions from HBC governor George SIMPSON to establish a fort at Ungava Bay, and on 23 November he left for Moose Factory (Ont.). After the Ungava Bay post, Fort-Chimo (Que.), was completed in the summer of 1830, Ooligbuck stayed on there as an employee of the company and he helped in opening up trade with the Inuit. Furthermore, since the food

supply was frequently precarious, his highly developed hunting skills were deeply appreciated by the men stationed at the fort.

In the autumn of 1837 Ooligbuck agreed to accompany another overland expedition to the Mackenzie and Coppermine rivers and to act as interpreter. Unable to join the group until 13 April 1839, he was none the less warmly greeted by Peter Warren Dease* and Thomas Simpson, the leaders of the party, who described him as a "valuable and unhoped for acquisition." During the summer of that year he accompanied the exploring party which descended the Coppermine River and surveyed the coastline as far east as the Castor and Pollux River, to the southeast of King William Island (N.W.T.).

When the expedition ended, Ooligbuck remained in the Mackenzie River district and in 1840 accompanied John Bell* up the Peel River to establish Fort McPherson (N.W.T.). Passing the winter of 1841–42 at the HBC fishing post at Big Island, Great Slave Lake, he did not return to Churchill until 1843. In 1846 both Ooligbuck and his son William were engaged as hunters and interpreters for the HBC expedition led by John Rae* to explore the northern coastline between the Castor and Pollux River and the Fury and Hecla Strait. It became apparent, however, that Ooligbuck's physical strength was weakening and he was unable to maintain the arduous pace of sledge exploration. Returning to Churchill on 31 Aug. 1847 with the expedition, he continued in the service of the company, despite Chief Trader William Sinclair*'s opinion of him as a "poor slow being in everything he does," until June 1848 when he left to live with his people. In January 1853 William Mactavish*, chief factor at York Factory (Man.), reported that Ooligbuck had died late in 1852.

Probably one of the most travelled Inuit of his time, Ooligbuck rendered important services to the explorers who charted the northern coastline of North America. During the first half of the 19th century there were probably fewer than ten Inuit capable of acting as interpreters, and Ooligbuck was among them. Furthermore, as a skilled guide and hunter he made life easier and safer for the explorers. None the less, he steadfastly maintained his identity as an Inuk despite his constant contact with the HBC. He refused to attend church at Churchill and, showing strong feelings of kinship, he demanded the company of at least one other Inuk during his travels. In 1961 Ooligbuck Point (N.W.T.) was named in his honour by the Canadian Board on Geographical Names.

SHIRLEE ANNE SMITH

PAM, HBCA, B.42/a/151: ff.32, 38; B.42/a/155: ff.11, 16d; B.42/a/156: f.1d; B.42/a/157: ff.6, 7d; B.42/a/179: f.14d, 3 Dec. 1843; B.42/a/185: f.4, 29 Nov. 1847; f.17, 7 June 1848; B.157/a/1: f.2d, 17 Aug. 1840; B.186/b/34: f.30;

O'Reilly

B.200/a/26: ff.6d, 9d, 28 Aug. 1841; B.200/b/13: f.16; B.200/b/16: f.6; B.200/b/17: ff.10, 10d, 30 July 1843; B.239/a/141: f.23, 2 Nov. 1829; B.239/b/104b: f.10, 22 Jan. 1853; B.239/c/3: 20 June 1837; D.5/5: f.133. R.M. Ballantyne, *Ungava: a tale of Esquimaux-land* (London, 1857). John Franklin, *Narrative of a second expedition to the shores of the polar sea, in the years 1825, 1826, and 1827* (London, 1828). Letitia Hargrave, *The letters of Letitia Hargrave*, ed. M.A. MacLeod (Toronto, 1947). *Northern Quebec and Labrador journals and correspondence, 1819–35*, ed. K.G. Davies and A.M. Johnson (London, 1963). John Rae, *John Rae's correspondence with the Hudson's Bay Company on Arctic exploration, 1844–1855*, ed. E.E. Rich and A.M. Johnson (London, 1953). Alexander Simpson, *The life and travels of Thomas Simpson, the Arctic discoverer* (London, 1845). Thomas Simpson, *Narrative of the discoveries on the north coast of America; effected by the officers of the Hudson's Bay Company during the years 1836–39* (London, 1843). Cooke and Holland, *Exploration of northern Canada*.

O'REILLY, HUGH (he also signed **O'Reilley, O'Reily, O'Riley, Reilly, Riely**), Roman Catholic priest and polemicist; b. *c.* 1794 in County Meath (Republic of Ireland); d. 22 or 23 June 1859 in North East Margaree, N.S.

Educated at the Irish College in Rome and at the Sorbonne, Hugh O'Reilly was ordained in Paris in 1819 or 1820. Although he served in Ireland for 15 years, nothing is known of him there other than Bishop William WALSH's later comment that in his homeland O'Reilly was generally regarded as insane and had had a violent quarrel with his bishop. He came to Nova Scotia in 1835–36 and had charge of Liverpool and Caledonia, Queens County, until the summer of 1841, when he took charge of Pictou County.

In his second posting, O'Reilly, who boarded in New Glasgow with a parishioner and held services in his home, had care of a large mission which included River John, Pictou, Albion Mines (Stellarton), New Glasgow, and Merigomish; he also ministered to the Micmacs of Pictou County. His responsibilities were lightened in 1850 when the town of Pictou and the northern part of Pictou County were transferred to the care of the Reverend Alexander MacSween. During O'Reilly's ministry, St Mary's Church, later renamed Our Lady of Lourdes, was built at Albion Mines. After leaving Pictou in 1858, O'Reilly had charge of North East Margaree on Cape Breton Island, where he died soon after his arrival that October. His headstone, besides giving Eugenius (the common Latinization of Hugh) as his Christian name, indicates that he died on 23 June 1859; an obituary gives the date of death as 22 June.

The tall and husky O'Reilly was a gifted linguist, but was singularly tactless. Residing in the Scottish Presbyterian town of Pictou, he kept three dogs and named them Luther, Calvin, and Knox. When he left Pictou after 17 years, his last words to his flock were, "You're rotten!" His love of a good fight is best revealed in an internecine dispute that afflicted his own church. During the 1830s relations between Bishop William FRASER, a native of Scotland, and the Catholics of Halifax, almost completely of Irish origin, deteriorated steadily. The Haligonians claimed that the bishop, who resided in Antigonish, was neglecting them and asked for more clergy in the town. Reluctantly the bishop agreed. The new priests, Lawrence Joseph Dease and Richard Baptist O'Brien, had been trained in Irish seminaries and thus felt closer to their countrymen than Fraser could. They were unacceptable to the bishop, however, and a power struggle of sorts developed. Most of the Irish Catholics of Halifax took sides against Bishop Fraser and his vicar in Halifax, the Reverend John Loughnan. O'Reilly threw his support behind Fraser. Under the pseudonym of Hibernicus, he published a series of letters in the Pictou *Observer* from 21 Dec. 1841 to 10 May 1842 in which he defended Fraser and attacked the Halifax Irish.

O'Reilly's reasoning was convoluted and tended to be repetitious. Its most outstanding quality was the generosity with which it employed name-calling, a practice of other clergy in this quarrel as well. Hibernicus claimed that the Irish were pretending they wanted the bishop to live in Halifax, when really it was the fact of his being a Scot that they disliked. He flayed the Haligonians by comparing them to the Pharisees for treachery and falsehood: "Since . . . the Scribes and Pharisees entered into a council to betray Christ, a more infamous gang was never assembled in the house of God than the leading Schismatics in the Capital of Nova Scotia." The Halifax Irish were, in O'Reilly's words, "the insolent, upstart, and low-bred *ci-devant* aristocracy," and "nothing more than mere coxcombs."

The new priests sent to Halifax came in for their share of O'Reilly's wrath. The Franciscan Dease, "venerable son of the lowly and humble St. Francis," moved about "in his easy car, clad in soft garments, so unlike those of his order." According to Hibernicus, Dease had followed up his apparent un-Franciscan behaviour by becoming "a willing aggressor on the episcopal rights" of Fraser. As for O'Brien, who had become principal of the newly founded St Mary's Seminary, Hibernicus sarcastically said that the people of Halifax "fell down before him, and worshipped with all the homage of heartfelt veneration and respect." O'Brien's school was accused of favouring Irish lads over Scots and of using corporal punishment unfairly. "We also fretted much to hear how the youths of the humble classes were treated, and how they were, from fear of the cat with nine tails induced to run wild through the country in all directions." All in all, Hibernicus considered the school "a Temple of Dunces" headed by "a mere nobody or nothing" (O'Brien) and "an ecclesiastical drone" (Dease).

Hibernicus suggested in his collected letters that Fraser had been a willing party to his partisanship on the bishop's behalf. Thus, he was able to quote from correspondence received by Fraser from Archbishop Daniel Murray of Dublin and could ask his readers to send in their letters of support to the bishop. The dispute was finally resolved in 1844, when the diocese was split in a manner which left Walsh responsible for Halifax.

The historical significance of Hugh O'Reilly, as Hibernicus, is slight, and his writings seem to have served no purpose at the time beyond inflaming an already troubled situation. He was one of those delicately balanced individuals who are often found on the edges of controversial situations: able neither to start nor to stop the quarrelling, but revelling in the middle of it by stoking the flames of passion and argumentation.

TERRENCE M. PUNCH

The letters written by Hugh O'Reilly under the pseudonym Hibernicus, originally published in the *Observer* (Pictou, N.S.), were also issued collectively as *The letters of Hibernicus: extracts from the pamphlet entitled "A report of the committee of St. Mary's, Halifax, N.S.," and a review of the same* (Pictou, 1842).

St Gregory's Roman Catholic Church (Liverpool, N.S.), Records of the parishes of Liverpool and Caledonia. Stella Maris Roman Catholic Church (Pictou), Records of St Patrick's Church. J. M. Cameron, *About New Glasgow* (New Glasgow, N.S., 1962), 57–58. A. A. Johnston, *Hist. of Catholic Church in eastern N.S.*, vol.2. T. M. Punch, "The Irish in Halifax, 1836–1871: a study in ethnic assimilation" (MA thesis, Dalhousie Univ., Halifax, 1977), 122–38.

OSGOOD, THADDEUS, Congregational minister and educator; b. 24 Oct. 1775 in Methuen, Mass., son of Josiah Osgood and Sarah Stevens; d. unmarried 19 Jan. 1852 in Glasgow.

The youngest in a large and pious family, Thaddeus Osgood grew up in obscure circumstances and became a tanner. During one of the evangelical revivals that swept over New England at the turn of the century he was inspired to "devote the remainder of his life to the service of his Redeemer." He attended Dartmouth College, Hanover, N.H., from 1799 to 1803, studied theology under various Congregational ministers, received a licence to preach in 1804, and was ordained a Congregational missionary in 1808 at North Wilbraham, Mass.

Osgood's early work as a travelling preacher brought him to the Canadas in 1807 and he adopted the two colonies as his main mission field for the rest of his life. He remained a Congregationalist but always stressed the non-denominational aspects of his work. His purpose was to teach the "plain truths of the Bible" to all, and especially to those lacking easy access to the message of salvation. Osgood pursued his goal by seizing upon a succession of plans adopted by 19th-century evangelicalism to promote the religious and moral improvement of mankind.

Though initially he concentrated on the distribution of religious tracts, his interests increasingly turned to the problem of illiteracy, and in 1812 he went to England to organize support for a plan to further colonial education based on the monitorial system [*see* Joseph Lancaster*]. He was remarkably successful, winning the aid of a cross-section of English evangelicals who sponsored his return to Quebec City in 1814 as agent of the Committee for Promoting the Education of the Poor in Upper and Lower Canada. Osgood's first step was to found the Quebec Free School on non-sectarian principles. Neither Catholic nor Anglican clergy, however, including bishops Joseph-Octave Plessis* and Jacob Mountain*, looked favourably upon schooling unaccompanied by denominational instruction. Together with competition from a newly established garrison school, their hostility put an end to the infant venture in 1817. Osgood helped organize a second school, opened in Kingston that year under the auspices of the Midland District School Society. The original non-sectarian plan, however, lasted only a year; after the first teacher departed the school gradually came under Anglican direction. Attempts to create other schools were even less successful.

For several years thereafter Osgood returned to the more conventional tasks of a missionary, although he also took up an interest in the growing Sunday school movement. In Stanstead, Lower Canada, and York (Toronto), he set up individual Sunday schools and, acting for the Sunday School Union Society of Canada, which he helped found in the early 1820s, he formed non-sectarian union societies in Quebec, Montreal, Kingston, York, and other communities. Day-schools remained a central concern, however, and in 1825 Osgood again crossed the Atlantic to seek support from English evangelicals. Once more he found powerful sponsors, and in 1826, accompanied by two teachers, he returned to the colonies, this time as agent of the Society for Promoting Education and Industry in Canada, which he had helped found in London.

In contrast to his earlier venture, Osgood's new design won over influential people in both Upper and Lower Canada, including the governor himself, Lord Dalhousie [Ramsay*]. At Kingston, however, the teacher whom Osgood installed was dismissed within the year for "improper conduct" and the school was closed. An attempt by the Montreal branch of the

Osgood

society to establish a non-sectarian school for the Indian children at Caughnawaga (Kahnawake) foundered on the undisguised opposition of the local priest, Joseph MARCOUX, and Bishop Jean-Jacques Lartigue*. A school at Châteauguay and a shelter in Montreal both operated for some time, but little else was achieved. Plans for day-schools, Sunday schools, circulating libraries, and houses of industry appealed to English enthusiasm but failed to take account of sectarian feeling or practical arrangements in the colonies. Osgood's particular brand of piety annoyed many colonists; he lacked an ability to implement his ideas effectively; he was less than scrupulous about accounting for public funds or using well-known names; but worst of all, his schemes were founded on a principle of united Christian action that was increasingly opposed by denominational sentiment.

Beset by difficulties in the Canadas, Osgood returned to Britain in 1829 where, among other activities, he began to raise money for various new colonial projects. Late in 1835 he was back and the next year in Montreal he founded the Friendly Union for "the suppression of vice and the promotion of useful knowledge." The growing problem of urban poverty and ignorance had become Osgood's new frontier of missionary endeavour.

Many of the city's dissenting ministers, including Henry ESSON, Robert L. Lusher*, William Taylor*, and Henry Wilkes*, wholeheartedly endorsed the Friendly Union. A building, sometimes called the Bethel, was erected in 1837 to accommodate religious services and a Sunday school, and within a year it harboured a small day-school, initially to combine non-sectarian education for the poor with simple manual work. Over the next decade and a half, however, the Bethel functioned primarily as a shelter from the city streets. For the rest of Osgood's life Montreal remained the focus of his work, though he also continued his preaching and fund-raising tours throughout Britain and North America. His death occurred at the outset of his seventh British campaign to secure funds for his Canadian mission.

Osgood's lifelong commitment to the well-being of his fellow man resulted in few permanent achievements. In part this was owing to his personal eccentricities and his penchant for leaping precipately from one good cause to another. However, his appeals to the conscience of 19th-century evangelicalism tapped a growing awareness in Britain and the colonies that religious feeling might legitimately be manifested in new forms of humanitarian action. His career, moreover, shows the variety of instruments to which 19th-century benevolence turned. The succession of philanthropic causes he adopted reflects the gradual development of institutionalized social concern within Canadian society.

W. P. J. MILLAR

[Thaddeus Osgood's principal works are *The Canadian visitor, communicating important facts and interesting anecdotes respecting the Indians and destitute settlers in Canada and the United States of America* (London, [1829]); *A brief extract from the journal of Thaddeus Osgood, minister of the gospel, with some anecdotes and remarks on men and occurrences, during a residence of six years in England . . .* (Montreal, 1835); and *A brief extract from the journal of Thaddeus Osgood, during his last visit to Great Britain and Ireland, with some interesting anecdotes and friendly hints* (Montreal, 1841). In addition to these he produced innumerable brief pamphlets and broadsides; like other primary sources concerning his life and work they are now scattered so thinly among a host of library and archival collections that it would be virtually impossible to list all of them. A few examples of such documents are a printed leaflet in the form of an open letter introducing himself and his mission on the occasion of his 1829 visit to Britain, dated Montreal, 1829 (a copy is available in UCA, London Missionary Soc., selected papers (mfm.)); *An affectionate appeal, on behalf of seamen and emigrants in Canada, by an agent of the Friendly Union of Montreal* (broadside, [Montreal, 1845]; copy at McGill Univ. Libraries (Montreal), Dept. of Rare Books and Special Coll., Lawrence Lande coll.); and *Canada must be protected or assisted, or lost to the British crown; the Queen and legislature are entreated to consider, what Lord Durham and others have said respecting that interesting colony* (London, n.d.; copy at PAC).

The principal manuscript collections used in researching Osgood's biography are: PAC, MG 24, B1, 2: 146–47, 225–26, 258–61, 358–59, 510–11; 3: 215–16; 11: 436–38; 29, Thaddeus Osgood, statement of receipts and expenditures, 16 May 1815; D8: 2998–99, 3019–24; RG 4, A1: 33593–95; 185: 45; 405: 10–11; B30, 4: 1; C1, 266, no.2691; 270, no.58; RG 5, C1, 112, file 6173 (an autobiographical account dated 28 July 1843); PRO, CO 42/210, Report of the meeting of the committee for promoting education and industry in Canada, 19 July 1826; 42/305, especially Osgood to Labouchère, 27 Feb. 1839; QUA, Midland District School Soc., Board of Trustees, minutes; SOAS, Council for World Mission Arch., London Missionary Soc., corr., Canada, folder no.8, 15 March, 20 May 1815; 14 Feb., 14 March 1816 (mfm. at UCA); SRO, GD45/3/82 (mfm. at UCA); and UCA, London Missionary Soc., selected papers, Soc. for Promoting Education and Industry in Canada, *An appeal from Canada* (printed leaflet, Montreal, 1829); *The Union Building of Canada, for the accommodation of the charitable and religious societies* (printed leaflet, Montreal, 1829) (mfm.).

Relevant printed primary sources include: Central Auxiliary Soc. for Promoting Education and Industry in Canada, *First* and *Second annual report . . .* (Montreal, 1827; 1829); *Doc. hist. of education in U.C.* (Hodgins), 1: 89–93; Joseph Lathrop, *Damnable heresies defined and described, in a sermon, preached at North Wilbraham, June 15, 1808; at the ordination of Rev. Thaddeus Osgood, to the office and work of evangelist* (Springfield, Mass., [1808?]); "Rev. Mr. Osgood, of Canada," *Christian Guardian*, 28 Jan. 1852, an item announcing his arrival in Britain just prior to his demise; and T. C. Orr, "Rev. T. Osgood," *Christian Guardian*, 25 Feb. 1852, a letter concerning Osgood's death. The most important references to Osgood in the colonial newspapers of the period include the *Pilot* (Montreal), 9 Nov. 1850, 21 Oct.

1851; *Quebec Gazette*, 19, 26 Oct. 1809; 5, 12 Oct., 28 Dec. 1815; 4 Jan. 1816; *Quebec Mercury*, 1805–29; and *Register* (Montreal), 6 Nov. 1845.

The only full-length treatment of Osgood is my article, "The remarkable Rev. Thaddeus Osgood: a study in the evangelical spirit in the Canadas," *Social Hist.* (Ottawa), 10 (1977): 59–76. Other secondary sources referring to him or treating some aspect of his life are: G. T. Chapman, *Sketches of the alumni of Dartmouth College, from the first graduation in 1771 to the present time, with a brief history of the institution* (Cambridge, Mass., 1867), 112–13; Judith Fingard, "English humanitarianism and the colonial mind: Walter Bromley in Nova Scotia, 1813–25," *CHR*, 54 (1973): 123–51; and "'Grapes in the wilderness': the Bible Society in British North America in the early nineteenth century," *Social Hist.*, 5 (1972): 5–31; Allan Greer, "The Sunday schools of Upper Canada," *OH*, 67 (1975): 174–75; B. F. Hubbard, "Materials for our church history; no.II," *Canadian Independent* (Toronto), 13 (1866–67): 282–86 (the details in this source agree with and expand on Osgood's version of his early life); G. W. Spragge, "Monitorial schools in the Canadas, 1810–1845" (DPAED thesis, Univ. of Toronto, 1935); and J. D. Wilson, "'No blanket to be worn in school': the education of Indians in early nineteenth-century Ontario," *Social Hist.*, 7 (1974): 293–305.   W.P.J.M.]

OUIMET, ANDRÉ, lawyer, Patriote, and politician; b. 10 Feb. 1808 in Sainte-Rose (Laval), Lower Canada, son of Jean Ouimet and Marie Bautron; m. 29 April 1839, in Montreal, Charlotte Roy, widow of Toussaint Brosseau, and they had two sons and one daughter; d. there 10 Feb. 1853.

André Ouimet was born into a farming family living at Sainte-Rose, on Île Jésus near Montreal, towards the end of the 18th century. He was the fifteenth of Jean Ouimet's 26 children and the seventh born of his second marriage. In 1823, at the age of 14, he was enrolled by his parents in the Petit Séminaire de Montréal, where he proved a brilliant classical student. On leaving the seminary in 1831, he became a clerk in the store of Joseph ROY, an important merchant in Montreal. While working there Ouimet decided to take up law, and in 1832 began legal training in his spare time, under Dominique* and Charles-Elzéar* Mondelet, prominent lawyers in Montreal. Two years later he was pursuing his legal studies in the office of his former fellow student, the young Montreal lawyer Charles-Ovide Perrault*. Called to the bar on 25 April 1836, Ouimet formed a partnership with Perrault and settled down in Montreal.

It was apparently during the period when he was in business and was preparing for the bar examination that he became involved in politics. Doubtless his employers exerted a strong influence on him. Roy was an intimate friend and long-time supporter of Louis-Joseph Papineau*, and he had become one of his inner circle. The Mondelet brothers broke with Papineau in 1832 but none the less remained moderate reformers. Perrault, a Patriote, was elected for Vaudreuil to the House of Assembly in 1834. Not surprisingly, Ouimet was among the group of young people who backed the French Canadian cause and regularly visited Édouard-Raymond FABRE's bookshop.

Proud, enthusiastic, and fiery, Ouimet quickly attracted attention by the part he took in the ongoing struggle against the government which engaged Papineau and his supporters. In 1835 he helped found the Union Patriotique, the governing body of which included Denis-Benjamin Viger* as president, Roy and Jacob DE WITT as vice-presidents, and Fabre as treasurer; Ouimet held the office of secretary. The association was committed to the Patriote party's goals, in particular to the attainment of responsible government and an elected Legislative Council. The following year Ouimet was among the first to respond to a campaign launched to provide compensation for incarceration to Ludger DUVERNAY, the publisher of *La Minerve*, recently imprisoned a third time for libelling the Legislative Council.

A young and highly gifted lawyer, Ouimet had just begun practising when he was caught up in the revolutionary upheaval. In April 1837 the Patriote leaders decided to organize large-scale meetings to protest the adoption of Lord John Russell's resolutions by the British parliament [*see* Denis-Benjamin Viger]. A permanent central committee was set up in Montreal, and Ouimet was one of the most regular in attending its meetings, which were held at Fabre's bookshop. At the end of the summer, when the political situation in the colony had gravely deteriorated, he threw himself without reservation into the resistance to the government. On 5 September, Ouimet met at the Nelson Hotel with a large group of young people, among them Papineau's son Louis-Joseph-Amédée*, Rodolphe Desrivières*, and Jean-Louis Beaudry*, to form the Fils de la Liberté. This quasi-political, quasi-military organization would have two sections, which in the words of Laurent-Olivier David* were to "work, the one by speeches and writings, the other by force of arms if necessary, for the advancement and triumph of the popular cause." Ouimet's patriotic fervour won him appointment as president of its political wing. During the meeting he made a scathing speech in which he displayed his qualities as a popular orator. On 4 October he was the first to sign the "Adresse des Fils de la liberté de Montréal, aux jeunes gens des colonies de l'Amérique du Nord," which appeared in *La Minerve* on 5 and 9 Oct. 1837; the manifesto spoke of "separation" and of "independent sovereignty" for the colony and proclaimed the intention "in our time to free our beloved country from all human authority except a fearless democracy established at its very centre."

As president of the political wing of the Fils de la Liberté, Ouimet drew the wrath of officialdom and the

667

Ouligbuck

condemnation of the authorities. During the clash between his association and the members of the Doric Club, on 6 November, he was wounded in the knee. Perhaps because his wound was a serious one he did not flee when warrants for arrest were issued ten days later. One of the first Patriotes to be taken in, he was immediately imprisoned on a charge of high treason. He spent nearly eight months in jail, and he was one of the last set free under the general amnesty of Lord Durham [Lambton*], on 8 July 1838 on £1,000 bail. The news of the tragic death of Perrault, his colleague and partner, in November 1837 at the battle of Saint-Denis on the Richelieu affected him profoundly, and his long days in prison significantly cooled his ardour.

After his release Ouimet kept away from politics for some time, and absorbed himself in his profession. According to Ægidius Fauteux*, he went into practice with Pierre-Georges Boucher* de Boucherville, who had been in the Fils de la Liberté. He soon became a highly competent lawyer. His dedication and integrity quickly brought him a sizeable clientele, chiefly farmers and artisans from rural parishes in the Montreal region. In his success he did not forget the debt he owed his parents, who had made sacrifices for his education; he undertook to protect his large family, which was in modest circumstances, and to provide them with the necessities. Among those he took on as law clerks were his young brother Gédéon*, later premier of Quebec, and Thomas-Jean-Jacques Loranger*. A few years later Ouimet practised in partnership with Louis-Victor Sicotte* and, according to David, René-Auguste-Richard Hubert. In that period he became widely known through the remarkable speeches he delivered before the Circuit Court of the district of Montreal, and he gained renown in the field of criminal law.

Ouimet had not lost all interest in public affairs, and in 1841, after the union of the two Canadas, he joined in supporting Louis-Hippolyte La Fontaine* and Robert BALDWIN in the struggle for responsible government. Ouimet also took an interest for some time in municipal politics. In 1848 he agreed to run in the Montreal municipal elections, and with Fabre was elected a councillor for the East Ward. He apparently did not take much pleasure in his duties, however, and refused to stand again for city council, of which he ceased to be a member in 1850.

Ouimet died at the peak of his legal career, in Montreal on 10 Feb. 1853, his 45th birthday. He was survived by his wife and children, as well as by brothers and sisters. He had proved a fervent defender of the rights of the French Canadian people on the eve of the 1837 rebellion. David notes that at the end of his life he was looked upon as "one of the most honourable and most brilliant lawyers at the [Montreal] bar."

MICHEL DE LORIMIER

André Ouimet left highly original memoirs recounting his impressions of life in prison; excerpts were published by Laurent-Olivier David in *Patriotes*, 145–46. Several letters written by Ouimet at the time of his incarceration were printed in "Papiers de Ludger Duvernay," L.-W. Sicotte, édit., *Canadian Antiquarian and Numismatic Journal* (Montreal), 3rd ser., 7 (1910): 59–96, 106–44.

ANQ-M, CE1-48, 3 mars 1783; CE1-51, 29 avril 1839, 14 févr. 1853; CE1-57, 21 oct. 1799, 11 févr. 1808; CN1-32, 27 avril 1839, 16 mars 1841; CN1-127, 1ᵉʳ déc. 1834; CN1-134, 21 févr. 1832; P1000-10-596. ANQ-Q, E17/6, nos.1–2, 6; P-68. BVM-G, Fonds Ægidius Fauteux, notes compilées par Ægidius Fauteux sur les Patriotes de 1837–1838 dont les noms commencent par la lettre O, carton 8. PAC, MG 30, D1, 23: 508–11; RG 4, B8, 26: 9690–94. "Papiers de Ludger Duvernay," L.-W. Sicotte, édit., *Canadian Antiquarian and Numismatic Journal*, 3rd ser., 5 (1908): 167–200. [L.-J.-]A. Papineau, *Journal d'un Fils de la liberté, réfugié aux États-Unis, par suite de l'insurrection canadienne, en 1837* (2v. parus, Montréal, 1972–), 1: 49–50, 52, 55, 56–65, 70. *La Minerve*, 29 mai 1835; 5, 9 oct., 9 nov. 1837; 11, 15 févr. 1853. *Le Pays*, 14 févr. 1853. F.-M. Bibaud, *Le panthéon canadien* (A. et V. Bibaud; 1891), 210. Fauteux, *Patriotes*, 125, 338–39, 349. J.-J. Lefebvre, "Brevets de cléricature des avocats de Montréal au deuxième quart du XIXᵉ siècle," *La Rev. du Barreau*, 14 (1954): 313; *Le Canada, l'Amérique*, 224. Le Jeune, *Dictionnaire*, 2: 393. *Montreal directory*, 1842–53. *Quebec almanac*, 1837–41.

Chapais, *Cours d'hist. du Canada*, 4: 168. David, *Patriotes*, 13–20, 145–46. J.-U.[-A.] Demers, *Histoire de Sainte-Rose, 1740–1947* ([Montréal], 1947), 116–17. Filteau, *Hist. des Patriotes* (1975), 117, 207–8. *Hist. de Montréal* (Lamothe et al.), 251. Laurin, *Girouard & les Patriotes*, 94. É.-Z. Massicotte, *Faits curieux de l'histoire de Montréal* (Montréal, 1922), 90–100. Maurault, *Le collège de Montréal* (Dansereau; 1967). Ouellet, *Bas-Canada*. J.-L. Roy, *Édouard-Raymond Fabre*, 122. Rumilly, *Papineau et son temps*. Mason Wade, *Les canadiens français, de 1760 à nos jours*, Adrien Venne et Francis Dufau-Labeyrie, trad. (2ᵉ éd., 2v., Ottawa, 1966), 1: 189, 194. F.-J. Audet, "Le Barreau et la révolte de 1837," RSC *Trans.*, 3rd ser., 31 (1937), sect.I: 85–96. L.-O. David, "Les Fils de la liberté," *L'Opinion publique*, 21 mai 1873: 241–43. É.-Z. Massicotte, "Coins historiques du Montréal d'autrefois," *Cahiers des Dix*, 2 (1937): 115–55. Victor Morin, "Clubs et sociétés notoires d'autrefois," *Cahiers des Dix*, 15 (1950): 185–218. Gustave Ouimet, "Au pays des souvenirs: épisodes," *La Minerve*, 11 févr. 1899: 3; 18 févr. 1899: 2. Léon Trépanier, "Figures de maires: Édouard-Raymond Fabre," *Cahiers des Dix*, 24 (1959): 189–208.

OULIGBUCK (Oullibuck, Oulybuck). *See* OOLIG-BUCK

OWEN, WILLIAM FITZ WILLIAM, naval officer, surveyor, landowner, politician, author, justice of the peace, and judge; b. 17 Sept. 1774 in Manchester, England, son of Captain William Owen* and perhaps Sarah Haslam; m. first January 1818 Martha Evans "of Bedfordshire," and they had two daughters; m. secondly 11 Dec. 1852 Amy Nichol-

Owen

son, *née* Vernon, in Saint John, N.B.; d. there 3 Nov. 1857.

Little of the future importance of William Fitz William Owen was to be noted in the first 30 years of his life. Illegitimate and orphaned at the age of four, he was boarded in foster homes in north Wales and knew nothing of family life and affection. However, he was an able scholar, best in mathematics and languages. His father's friend Sir Thomas Rich kept an eye on both Owen and his elder brother, Edward Campbell Rich Owen, and was their patron, introducing them into naval service. William embarked at 13 in Rich's ship, *Culloden*, and from that time shipboard was his universe. On shore and in civilian society he was, throughout his life, eccentric and out of his element. As midshipman he specialized in navigation and was latterly assistant master. Self-willed and boisterous, he was twice reduced to able seaman as a matter of discipline. Passing his Navy Board examination on 6 March 1794, he was appointed lieutenant on 24 October but tangled with his captain, was court-martialled at Cape Town (South Africa), and was dismissed from the service on 25 June 1795. The influence of his patrons was sufficient to bring him again into the service, for he was a midshipman in the *London* during the Spithead naval mutiny in May 1797. His reputation as a hard disciplinarian was already established: he was singled out by the mutineers as "too hard" and was confined in irons in the hold until he escaped with other officers. He was commissioned lieutenant a second time on 12 June 1797, commanding the gun vessel *Flamer*, and saw service under Lord Nelson in the English Channel till 1803.

Owen began to emerge as a seasoned naval commander of unusual energy and ability during the nine years of war service in the Indian Ocean that began in March 1804 on the *Seaflower*. He commanded in battle, led naval assault landing parties, and piloted fleets into action through uncharted waters. Captured with the *Seaflower* by the French southwest of Sumatra, he spent 21 months as a prisoner-of-war on Mauritius, during which time he was promoted commander. Following his release, he was quartermaster general in charge of loading troops and equipment for the British assault on Mauritius in October 1810 and the following May was promoted post captain.

Captain Owen had also begun to show evidence of his assurance in the art and science of naval surveying during his service in the Indian Ocean. Beginning in 1806 he completed a number of projections of ships' tracks and manuscript charts. Although some writers have speculated that Owen learned the intricacies of naval surveying from Captain Matthew Flinders, the surveyor of the Australian coasts and a fellow prisoner on Mauritius, neither man made any reference to such collaboration. Owen's independent interest in survey-

ing and his self-confidence were written into the log of the *Seaflower* on 7 Aug. 1807 as he meditated on the surveying methods of East India Company officers on the China coasts: "Give me my health, a Blue Coat Boy, a Boat of 70 tons, Twenty Men & a Cockle Shell Jolly Boat & I would do it all whilst they are preparing for it." On returning to England in 1813, Owen kept in touch with the hydrographic office of the Admiralty. In the following year it published his translation of Marino Miguel Franzini's book describing the coasts of Portugal.

Owen's first appointment specifically as a surveyor was to duty in the Canadas from May 1815 to August 1817 to act as an assistant to his brother. His Canadian service fell into two periods: a first rapid reconnaissance in the summer of 1815 to determine a number of urgently needed facts, followed by deliberate scientific surveying of the St Lawrence River and the Great Lakes. While crossing the Atlantic he began an "astronomical journal" which eventually contained the longitude and latitude of significant locations along the Canadian waterway from Quebec City to Penetanguishene on Georgian Bay. These fixed points set the general frame of the surveying that followed.

During his first summer in Upper Canada, Owen accomplished a number of urgent tasks. He confirmed the survey work already under way on Lake Ontario and the Grand River and examined both the mouth of the latter and the bay within Turkey Point in search of an appropriate site for a naval base. The international boundary at Saint-Régis near Cornwall was located and extensive soundings were taken in the Detroit River to provide data about the several channels which would be used in establishing the international boundary there. As well as a running survey of the north shore of Lake Erie, Owen began another of the east shore of Lake Huron and of Georgian Bay to near present-day Victoria Harbour: in the latter survey, land forms, timber resources, and navigational hazards were observed and again the site for a naval base was sought. The survey was hindered throughout the late summer when Captain Owen and his staff suffered from fever. A further hindrance arose from the heated tensions between British and Americans on the Detroit frontier. Lieutenant Alexander Thomas Emeric Vidal, a principal surveying officer under Owen, was arrested and detained at Detroit, which gave rise to time-consuming negotiations and protracted correspondence between British and American authorities. Yet the summer's work yielded a wealth of new understanding of virtually unknown shores.

Orders for the deliberate systematic survey of the St Lawrence River and lower Great Lakes were issued at Kingston on 5 Nov. 1815, envisaging work first in the region close to Kingston, and then in the upper lakes; time permitting, the frontier waters of Lake Champlain were to follow. The survey began on 1 Feb. 1816 with Captain Owen personally leading 7 officers and

Owen

some 50 seamen and marines out onto the ice about the Thousand Islands to measure survey baselines. In the following 69 days about 300 miles of baseline were surveyed in an area 80 by 30 miles, with some 10,000 angles and bearings being recorded. Owen believed the accuracy could not "err two inches in a mile." This episode, the beginning of accurate naval surveying in Canada, was typical of Owen, and his report breathes energy: in weather that reached −20°F, work took place "every day successively except the Sabbath from Eight O'Clock in the morning to six at night." Yet there were special pay, extra clothing, and double rum rations for the men. Thus a formidable surveying problem was solved while the naval garrison was relieved from the tedium of winter routine. Months later the Navy Board criticized the method of accounting, questioning the extra expenditure of £144 18s. for wages and the further item of £96 5s. for four horses "to replace those which were lost" in the river: Captain Owen had nearly drowned on the first day when the teams went through the ice.

A stone house in Kingston became the hydrographic office, supplying quarters for the officers of the survey, facilities for projecting their work, and a place for consultation and instruction. John Harris's young bride, Amelia [Ryerse*], lived there and breathed a special note of domesticity into their society, remembered fondly in the correspondence of the officers in later years. This experience probably prompted the captain to marry soon after returning to England. Through the spring and summer of 1816 the surveying progressed until Lake Ontario and the St Lawrence River to near Prescott were completed. Early in 1817 the Niagara River was surveyed. On 14 June Lake Erie lay before the surveyors when the establishment was closed down as a matter of peace-time economy. Lieutenant Henry Wolsey Bayfield*, who had first learned surveying on the ice in February 1816 under Owen's instruction, was left to complete the work when Owen returned to England in June 1817.

Captain Owen had also borne the considerable weight of day-by-day naval administration from 26 Oct. 1815 to 31 May 1816 when he was the senior naval officer on the Canadian lakes in the absence of both the commander-in-chief and the navy commissioner. Beyond administrative detail and the direction of surveying, he continued to deal with the overriding problems of strategic planning. He reported at length on the siting of naval bases above Niagara and lines of communication which would be secure in time of war. Surveying the western shores of Lake Ontario and the Grand River led to speculation about a route from Burlington Bay (Hamilton Harbour) to the Grand River and Lake Erie. He also reported at length on possible improvements in the established route between York (Toronto) and Lake Huron by way of the Nottawasaga River. In May and early June 1817 he traversed the Trent–Severn water route with a small party and Indian guides but found it less practicable because of the need for expensive works. He had laboured with great energy and insight and his findings helped in the understanding of numerous key geographical situations which had been unclear until that time. The 27 months of Canadian service had established him as a master of surveying and his work founded scientific hydrography in Canada.

Owen is best known for his surveys of the coasts of Africa in the years 1822–26. Sent to survey eastward from the Cape of Good Hope, he had his orders enlarged from time to time until his expedition had charted the entire east coast of Africa as well as southern Arabia, Madagascar, and several island groups in the Indian Ocean. On the return to England, long stretches of the west coast of Africa were examined and the Gambia River was carefully surveyed. In all, some 30,000 miles of coast were recorded and a chain of longitudinal distances extending from the British Isles to Bombay was established. The magnitude of the achievement placed Owen among the greatest British naval surveyors.

The expedition had, however, suffered staggering losses from tropical fever beginning in November 1822, which caught public attention and partly obscured the achievement in surveying. Captain Owen registered a ringing denunciation of medical practice to the Admiralty, rehearsing the uselessness of "copious bleeding" and "large doses of Calomel." In 1829, on the west coast of Africa, fever was again to dog his service. On the death of his surgeons he assumed control of treatment: by avoiding bleeding and energetic treatments, prescribing a purgative, rest, and fresh air, and administering quinine on remission, he proved to be well ahead of his time.

Owen's attention was not confined to surveying. He and his officers were appalled by the ravages of the slave trade and their testimony fuelled the anti-slavery movement in England led by Thomas Fowell Buxton. In two instances involving territories where political control was in dispute, Delagoa Bay (Mozambique) and Mombasa (Kenya), Owen accepted the temporary cession of the areas, pending his government's final decision. Although in both cases his arrangements were never made official, his actions were the basis for British claims in east Africa late in the century.

Hardly had the first expedition been paid off when Owen returned to Africa in 1827 to create on the island of Fernando Po (Bioko) a new settlement at which to relocate, from its unhealthy location at Sierra Leone, the international court which dealt with captured slave-ships. Although the court itself did not move, Owen's mission was completed with energy, innovation, and insight, and a colony was established. His professional career, however, was not advanced. His principal patrons at the Admiralty moved to other offices and he was involved in controversies with colonial officials, merchants of Sierra Leone, fellow naval officers, and a native ruler. Moreover, he used the advantageous location of Fernando Po to capture numerous slave-ships, although patrolling was not part of his responsibility, and the Admiralty suspected him of being lured by prize money. With these problems and the onset of fever, Owen became exhausted. Years of exacting service in the tropics had temporarily affected his temper and judgement. Sir John Barrow of the Admiralty, writing to Robert William Hay of the Colonial Office concerning Owen's refusal to accept the civil position of superintendent of Fernando Po, summed him up with grudging admiration: "I see you have as well as ourselves despatches from that half crack'd but clever person Owen, declining to accept. . . . I am sorry for it, as he is the man of all others for bringing forward a new settlement, and appears to have done wonders."

Owen served on the South American station from late 1829. He was originally intended to return to England by way of India, thus completing a connected chain of longitudes around the world, but, because his ship was not fit for a service of many months without a major refit, he was charged with transporting a large bullion shipment across the Atlantic. Arriving in England in August 1831 sick, exhausted, and out of favour, Owen spent a four-year interval there and on Jersey working up sailing directions based on the African surveys, settling accounts, and dealing with accumulated private and public business. He had been an early member of both the Royal Geographical Society and the Royal Astronomical Society and now he had the opportunity to attend both, providing material for the program of the former and donating instruments to the latter. After vain efforts to prepare a narrative of the 1822–26 surveys, he turned over his material to an editor, Heaton Bowstead Robinson, who brought out two volumes in 1833. The editing was faulty and confusing and by this time descriptions of the slave trade and of tropical fever had lost some of their novelty. The few reviews that appeared were unenthusiastic. Only in later years was the narrative, read in conjunction with his dispatches, discovered to be an invaluable primary source for knowledge of the African coasts.

Now 60 years old and with no prospect of a further naval appointment, Owen turned to settling with his family in British North America. He secured title to Campobello Island, N.B., which had been granted in 1767 to his father and several of his cousins, including David Owen*, and established residence there in September 1835. The island, with some 700 inhabitants, cried out for innovative leadership; its economy was dependent on fishing, there was little fertile land, and timber resources were limited by its size.

Investing his small capital, Owen made a strong attempt to realize the island's commercial potential, incorporating the Campobello Mill and Manufacturing Company on 1 June 1839 and planning to establish a bank. Neither project prospered, in part because of his own limitations of character and age and in part because of the economic circumstances of the time. An enthusiastic supporter of the St Andrews and Quebec Railway who had subscribed for shares and chaired its first public meeting in 1835, he served for years as a director on the revival of the company in 1846.

Owen was quickly attracted to questions of public policy. He was elected to the New Brunswick House of Assembly for Charlotte County in the general election of 1837, taking his seat on 27 Feb. 1838. Banking, commerce, the fisheries, defence, navigational aids, and a steam packet service to Campobello Island and Grand Manan occupied his attention in the house and in committees. He also pressed for the funding of local schools, roads, and lighthouses. For several years his experience and stature made him a very visible member. Defeated in the general election of late 1842, he was appointed on 30 Dec. 1843 to the Legislative Council which he continued to attend until 1851.

In 1841 Captain Owen published, privately and anonymously, *The Quoddy hermit; or conversations at Fairfield on religion and superstition*, which marked a climax in his growing concern with religious thought and practice. The "hermit" expounds Owen's religious views in a work which also contains considerable autobiographical detail and colour. He advocated Church of England practice, opposed Methodism, and was a self-confessed millenarian. In practice Owen was a licensed lay reader, leading services twice on Sundays. He expended money and much energy in regenerating the parish of Campobello and rebuilding the fabric of the church. At his urgent prompting the Society for the Propagation of the Gospel sent out Thomas McGhee as missionary to the parish in 1842, but after a year McGhee moved to assist the rector at St Andrews parish. Despite Owen's continuing efforts many islanders persisted in the New Light tradition [see Henry Alline*].

An exotic figure who became an admiral, Owen looms larger than life in the island's oral tradition. An authoritative, ageing man who was essentially benevolent in his intentions, he was not, like many of his peers, addicted to alcohol but rather to women. His ambition was to play the role of an English landed proprietor in a colonial island setting. As a justice of the peace from 1841, he exercised broad powers in criminal justice and local administration. His concurrent appointment as judge of the Inferior Court of Common Pleas, which handled civil cases, concerned him little. He held a commission to perform

Owen

marriages, there being no resident clergy, and it took him to the celebrations and parties at which he shone.

From at least August 1838 Owen had hoped to secure some professional appointment and in September 1842 he began the definitive survey of the Bay of Fundy for the Admiralty. In the winter of 1842–43 lines were measured on the ice of the Saint John River, and the survey of it and its harbour was completed in the next two years. A series of seven tide-gauges provided a statistical basis for understanding the action of the world's highest tides. The captain, who had served on local and provincial lighthouse commissions, was critical of the siting of lighthouses and pressed his views on the authorities in Saint John and Halifax, while various British and colonial authorities sought his advice, as a senior technical expert, about both the feasibility of a canal at the Nova Scotia–New Brunswick border and the best location for the ocean terminus of the proposed intercolonial railway. The old navy veteran longed for authority to act as an armed naval presence to overawe aggressive American fishermen but ships of the squadron at Halifax occasionally undertook to patrol instead.

Promoted rear-admiral on 21 Dec. 1847, Owen relinquished his surveying duties and was replaced by Peter Frederick Shortland*. Owen made one final voyage under his own pennant, returning his ship, the *Columbia*, to England for refit. At 73 he was content to let his son-in-law, Captain John James Robinson-Owen, assume more and more of his responsibilities at Campobello Island, with the St Andrew's and Quebec Railway, and in the Legislative Council. On the death of his first wife in 1852 he took up residence in Saint John in the home of Amy Nicholson, whom he married within a year. Promoted vice-admiral on 27 Oct. 1854, he was pensioned on the reserve list on 6 Feb. 1855. He died less than three years later and was buried in the churchyard on Campobello Island.

A man of enormous energy and single-mindedness of purpose in accomplishing the duty at hand, Captain Owen ploughed a deep and long furrow across the affairs of his age. Personal courage, religious faith, drive, and self-confidence explain his long record of achievement. His insistence on his rank and seniority, combative rivalry with his peers, and inability to appreciate the legitimate aspirations and goals of others, rendered him difficult. He received no mark of honour for his long service, no doubt because of his personality and the innumerable controversies that marked every stage of his career. Yet in his own circle of officers and acquaintances he made and maintained enduring friendships.

A legendary figure in the history of New Brunswick and of southern Africa, Owen inaugurated scientific hydrography in Canada and rightly achieved enduring fame for his service in Africa. As a master surveyor he began with the techniques pioneered by Captain James Cook* but developed his own system of procedure and notation and pressed the refinement of instruments and adaptations of their use. From 1810 he successfully experimented with the use of rockets, visible over considerable distances, to coordinate the recognition of a single moment in time. He attempted to refine the use of astronomical observations as aids to surveying and navigation, and his 1827 book of longitudes was a landmark in that field of endeavour.

For Charlotte County and New Brunswick he represented the half-pay officer, but writ in the largest characters. As holder of numerous civil commissions, landed proprietor, worldly senior naval officer, member of the legislature, and eccentric religious enthusiast, he left his imprint on the province's life.

PAUL G. CORNELL

William Fitz William Owen is the author of *Tables of latitudes and longitudes by chronometer of places in the Atlantic and Indian oceans, principally on the west and east coasts of Africa, the coasts of Arabia, Madagascar, etc. . . . to which is prefixed an essay on the management and use of chronometers, by Richard Owen, Commander R.N., an officer of the expedition* (London, 1827) and of *The Quoddy hermit; or conversations at Fairfield on religion and superstition*, published in 1841 in Boston under the signature William Fitzwilliam of Fairfield. Owen also prepared a translation of M. M. Franzini's *Roteiro das costas de Portugal, ou Instrucções nauticas . . .* ([Lisbon], 1812), entitled *Description of the coasts of Portugal and nautical instructions* ([London], 1814); the manuscript of the translation is preserved in G.B., Ministry of Defence, Hydrographic Dept. (Taunton, Eng.), Misc. papers, 105. The journals of his first African expedition were edited by H. B. Robinson and published as *Narrative of voyages to explore the shores of Africa, Arabia, and Madagascar; performed in H.M. ships "Leven" and "Barracouta," under the direction of Capt. W. F. W. Owen, R.N.* (2v., London, 1833).

An extensive collection of Owen's manuscript and printed charts is also available at the Hydrographic Dept., as are his remarks on the east coast of Africa and the Indian Ocean, 1813–34 (OD 26). Other collections of his papers are found in the National Maritime Museum (London), COO/3/A; N.B. Museum, which holds his estate papers; and the County of Grey–Owen Sound Museum (Owen Sound, Ont.), to which his journal of the east African survey of 1826–32 was donated in 1969 by the late Rear Admiral Sir Edward O. Cochrane, Owen's great-grandson. The Howell papers, a further collection of Owen letters and memorabilia assembled by Rear Admiral Cochrane, remain in the possession of his daughter, Mrs David Howell of London. Owen's correspondence with John and Amelia Harris between 1815 and 1850 can be found in the Harris papers; these belong to Dr Robin Harris of Toronto, but are temporarily deposited at the UCA.

G.B., Ministry of Defence, Hydrographic Dept., Letter-books, no.10 (1841–42); Minute-books, 3 (1837–42)–4 (1842–45); Misc. papers, 30–31, 58, 61, 64–65, 68, 86–91; OD 324, Lieut. Pullen, "Narrative of proceedings of a party from HMS *Columbia*, 1843, Captain W. F. W. Owen." National Maritime Museum, COO/1/A (William Owen papers); FL/1 (Matthew Flinders papers). N.B. Museum, W. F. Ganong coll., box 20, packet 1. PRO, ADM 1/ 2262–75; ADM 51/155, 51/221, 51/1914, 51/2162, 51/ 2229, 51/2355, 51/3254, 51/4094; ADM 52/3949; ADM 53/ 126, 53/364; CO 42/1, 42/172; CO 82/2–3, 82/10–11; CO 267/83, 267/94, 267/98; CO 324/81; FO 54/1. USPG, C/CAN/NB, 5: 91; Journal of SPG, 45.

Thomas Boteler, *Narrative of a voyage of discovery to Africa and Arabia, performed in his majesty's ships, "Leven" and "Barracouta," from 1821 to 1826, under the command of Capt. F. W. Owen, R.N.* (2v., London, 1835). William Owen, "The journal of Captain William Owen, R.N., during his residence on Campobello in 1770–71 . . . ," ed. W. F. Ganong, N.B. Hist. Soc., *Coll.* (Saint John), 1 (1894–97), no.2: 193–220; 2 (1899–1905), no.4: 8–29. *Report on the climate and principal diseases of the African station . . .*, comp. Alexander Bryson (London, 1847). SPG, [*Annual report*] (London), 1842–43. *An account of the Saint Andrews and Quebec Railway, being the original intercolonial railway, from its first inception in 1835 to the present time* (Saint John, N.B., 1869). R. T. Brown, "William Fitzwilliam Owen: hydrographer of the African coast, 1774–1857" (PHD thesis, Syracuse Univ., Syracuse, N.Y., 1972). E. H. Burrows, *Captain Owen of the African survey . . .* (Rotterdam, Netherlands, 1979). John Gray, *The British in Mombasa, 1824–1826: being a history of Captain Owen's protectorate* (London, 1957). M. V. Jackson, *European powers and south-east Africa; a study of international relations on the south-east coast of Africa, 1796–1856* (London, [1942]). J. G. Boulton, "[Paper on Admiral Bayfield]," Literary and Hist. Soc. of Quebec, *Trans.* (Quebec), new ser., 28 (1909–10): 27–95. P. G. Cornell, "William Fitzwilliam Owen, naval surveyor," N.S. Hist. Soc., *Coll.*, 32 (1959): 161–82. R. F. Fleming, "Charting the Great Lakes," *Canadian Geographic Journal* (Montreal), 12 (January–April 1936): 68–77. Robin Harris, "The beginnings of the hydrographic survey of the Great Lakes and the St. Lawrence River," *Historic Kingston*, no.14 (1966): 24–39. Olive [Mitchell] Magowan, "The Owens of Glensevern: part II, Admiral William Fitzwilliam Owen," *Saint Croix Courier* (St Stephen, N.B.), 12 Oct. 1977: 14.

P

PACK, ROBERT, merchant, politician, and justice of the peace; b. 1786 in Dorset, England, probably the son of Stephen Olive Pack and Olivia Horwood; m. 1809 Anna Ash in Carbonear, Nfld, and they had three daughters and two sons; d. there 1860.

The critical elements involved in understanding the career of Robert Pack lie in his ancestry, his occupation, and the era in which he lived in Newfoundland. The Pack family hailed from Christchurch in Hampshire and were old-established dissenters. Robert's father spent more than 40 years as a captain in the Newfoundland trade, much of the time as an employee of the large Poole–Carbonear concern of George and James Kemp. Robert came to Newfoundland in 1801 as an apprentice clerk in the Kemp establishment. Had he been of his father's generation he too would probably have been a ship's master, or at most a migratory agent for one of the large West Country firms. As it was, Pack was to become one of the early sedentary merchants who, after learning the trade with an older firm, established their own fisheries in Newfoundland. In the early years of his career Pack did travel back to England often, but after 1815 he seldom left the island.

In this respect, Pack merely reflected the change in Newfoundland from a largely migratory fishery to a settled colony. After 1800 the migratory fishery had decayed rapidly and the West Country fishermen and merchants had to choose between living in Newfoundland and thus keeping their occupations, or remaining in England and giving up the Newfoundland trade.

However, throughout his career, Pack relied heavily upon British merchants and bankers for his livelihood. In 1811 he ended his employment with the Kemps and went into business on his own account in Bay Roberts where he entered into a partnership with George Blackler of Dartmouth in Devon. Their trade was small and unlikely to get much bigger without an infusion of outside capital. In 1813 Pack terminated this partnership and entered into a new association with William Fryer of Wimborne, Dorset. Fryer was a partner in the important Wimborne bank of Fryer, Andrews and Company, which since the 1770s had played a large role in financing the Dorset merchants, shipowners, and planters involved with Newfoundland. Partnership with Fryer gave Pack a good source of capital, but he now faced another problem. Bay Roberts was at this time a prosperous community, but it was small and offered little opportunity for expanding a mercantile trade. In 1817 John Gosse of Ringwood, Hampshire, was taken into the partnership; he already had a growing trade in Carbonear, the second largest town in Newfoundland and, with its heavy involvement in the Labrador fishery and seal hunt, a far better place for expansion.

The new partner, who was older than Pack, had first come out to Newfoundland in 1789 as a clerk to the Kemps and later became their agent. Like Pack he was

Pack

a dissenter and like Pack he had quit the Kemps in 1803 to establish his own concern of Chancey, Gosse, and Ledguard. Gosse had established a flourishing trade at Carbonear but in 1816, at 49 years of age, he felt the need to establish a head office in Poole and to retire there. With Fryer and Pack, Gosse formed a new concern, Fryer, Gosse, and Pack in England and Pack, Gosse, and Fryer in Newfoundland. The new company was large from the start, having branches in Bay Roberts, Brigus, and Carbonear, and rapidly became heavily involved in the Labrador fishery and the seal hunt.

This arrangement allowed Gosse to run the firm's head office in Poole, with Fryer a sleeping partner and Pack managing the Newfoundland end. The company was able to expand even more after 1820 when the Kemps wound up their business in Carbonear. By 1825 Fryer, Gosse, and Pack employed 12 vessels in the trade between Europe and Newfoundland, and in the years 1820–58 they registered no fewer than 90 vessels for employment in the coasting and fishing trades of the island. They became, and remained until the 1850s, by far the largest firm in Carbonear, and were for a time among the largest shipowners in the west of England. Their success is all the more remarkable considering that it occurred in the 1820s, when most West Country–Newfoundland traders were retrenching. Apparently this success did not result in large fortunes for the partners – in part because the times were not propitious and in part because the fishery itself was not particularly profitable for outport merchants. Pack seems to have been the junior partner throughout. When his partners died, their sons inherited their full shares but Pack's two sons were unable to follow him in the firm. Pack did not (or could not) retire to England when his turn came around. He ran the Newfoundland business until the firm wound up in 1858, when he was 72, and then stayed in Carbonear until his death.

The fact that Pack, unlike many other merchants, did not retire to England in middle age had a profound effect upon his life. As a fully resident merchant, he took a far greater interest in the political, social, and economic development of Newfoundland than did many of his contemporaries. Thus he was an early supporter of the notion of representative government and took the lead in organizing support for it in Conception Bay. From 1832 almost all Protestant merchants joined the Conservative party, but in the elections of 1832 and 1836 Pack ran as a Liberal and set himself apart from the other merchants. Why did Pack differ politically from most merchants? The key to understanding him lies in the fact that he was a resident, a dissenter, and a merchant. In Dorset his relatives and friends, newly enfranchised by the repeal of the Test and Corporation acts in 1828, were bitterly fighting for local power against the old conservative oligarchies. They were often radical Whigs. Many of the Newfoundland merchants were also dissenters and until 1832 they supported the idea of representative government in Newfoundland as wholeheartedly as they did parliamentary reform in England. Thus neither Pack's support of representative government nor his running for election in 1832 is hard to understand. What was unusual was Pack's identification with the Liberal party. In both elections he was chosen by the largely Catholic interests in Conception Bay. The probable explanation is that in the first contest he was identified as the leading supporter of representative government in Conception Bay, and was asked to run, together with three Catholic colleagues, by Liberal party sympathizers. He came top of the poll – at the expense of all other Protestant Conservative candidates. In running on a Liberal slate, Pack ensured his own election, but alienated himself from his usually Protestant merchant colleagues and also, increasingly, from the Protestant electors of Conception Bay.

Between 1832 and 1836 Newfoundland politics polarized between a Protestant Conservative party and a Catholic Liberal party. Even in the elections of 1832 the Liberal party had committed several acts of intimidation and riot against would-be Conservative voters. Pack as a merchant was a consistent supporter of law and order, but elector intimidation worked in his favour and thus he did not protest. In the 1836 election intimidation was even more widespread – and indeed half a dozen men in Carbonear were charged. Much to his horror, Pack was one of them. He was acquitted but it marked the end of his active political life. When the election of 1836 was declared invalid and a new one called the following year, Pack was elbowed out by the Catholic Liberal party which ran and saw elected an entirely Catholic slate in Conception Bay. A radical liberal party, identified almost completely with the working class Irish and the Roman Catholic Church, was not the party for Pack: in 1837 the Liberal voters demonstrated that he was not the man for them either. From that time Pack played little or no part in political affairs – he did not, like so many of his associates, move into the Conservative party; he merely gave up politics altogether.

Robert Pack continued to play a leading role in the general life of Conception Bay and to be an advocate of "improvements." He spent a considerable amount of time and energy creating a model farm, and was a founding member of the Carbonear Commercial Society, a governor of the Newfoundland Savings Bank, and a justice of the peace for many years. He lived long and laboured hard.

KEITH MATTHEWS

Painchaud

Most of the information on which this biography is based was drawn from the Pack name file and other copies of records relating to the trade and fisheries of Newfoundland available at the MHGA.

Dorset Record Office (Dorchester, Eng.), D400/1–2; P34/OV9 (Apprenticeship indentures); P227/CW1–2, CW4 (Churchwardens, rates and accounts, 1751–1818), rates, vestry minutes; P227/OV15 (Apprenticeship indentures); P227/RE4 (Reg. of baptisms, marriages, and burials, 1740–90). Hunt, Roope & Co. (London), Robert Newman & Co., journals, 1801–6; Newfoundland letter-book, 1801 (mfm. at PANL). MHGA, Parish records of the county of Hampshire, Eng., reg. of baptisms, marriages, and burials for dissenting churches at Ringwood and Christchurch; Plantation books, Conception Bay, 1804–5 (copies). PANL, GN 2/1; GN 5/1/B/1, Harbour Grace, 1812–16; GN 5/4/B/1, Harbour Grace, 1790–91, 1793–1803; P1/5; P7/A/6, especially box 30 (Slade & Co., Catalina, letter-book, 1818–21). PRO, BT 107; CO 194/43–46, 194/49, 194/64, 194/70, 194/80; CO 199/18, Conception Bay plantation book, 1807, extracts (copies at MHGA); CUST 65/33. St Paul's Anglican Church (Harbour Grace, Nfld.), Conception Bay mission, reg. of baptisms, marriages, and burials (copies at PANL). Nfld., House of Assembly, Journal, 1832–36, 1857. Dorset County Chronicle (Dorchester), 1830–61. Lloyd's List (London), 1801–60. Newfoundlander, 1827–60. Newfoundland Express (St John's), 1851–60. Newfoundland Mercantile Journal, 1816–27. Public Ledger, 1827–60. Royal Gazette (Charlottetown), 1833. Royal Gazette and Newfoundland Advertiser, 1807–60. Times and General Commercial Gazette (St John's), 1832–60. Lloyd's register of shipping (London), 1801–60. Gunn, Political hist. of Nfld.

PAINCHAUD, ALEXIS, sea captain, shipowner, merchant, and justice of the peace; b. 22 Nov. 1792 at Quebec, son of Captain François Painchaud and Angélique Drouin; m. 19 Oct. 1815 Marguerite Arseneaux (Arsenault) in Carleton, Lower Canada, and they had ten children; d. 10 Feb. 1858 in Montreal.

Alexis Painchaud, a son and grandson of sailors, was the ninth of 12 children. His brother Joseph* became a doctor and his sister Marie-Louise, named de Saint-Augustin, the superior of the Hôtel-Dieu in Quebec. Alexis spent his childhood in the *faubourg* Saint-Roch at Quebec and was four years old when his father died of smallpox. His mother took a sailor, Pierre Laviolette, as her second husband.

Alexis's eldest brother, Abbé Charles-François Painchaud*, took him along when he was appointed missionary for the Baie des Chaleurs region. They set off from Quebec on 17 Sept. 1806 with their sister Victoire, the widow of François Normand, and her young son François. The journey by schooner to Carleton lasted six weeks because of storms and a stop at Halifax. Painchaud became the abbé's travelling companion on apostolic journeys undertaken by snow-shoe in winter and birchbark canoe in summer.

He was in good hands: his brother had been tutor to the children of Lieutenant Governor Sir Robert Shore Milnes* and would later found the Collège de Sainte-Anne-de-la-Pocatière.

The youth learned his trade with sailors from Carleton, among them his future brother-in-law, Captain Sébastien-Étienne Landry. At 18 he was skipper of the *Marie-Joseph*, a 40-ton schooner owned by Victoire's second husband, Gédéon Ahier. Soon he had schooners of his own and was known as a "trader in the Gaspé district." Painchaud carried cargoes of fish between Halifax, Newfoundland, and Quebec, where he decided to live shortly after his marriage in 1815. Around 1820 he settled his family in Montreal. He negotiated profitable deals in partnership with Montreal businessmen Félix Souligny and Hubert Paré*. His 122-ton brig, built at Caraquet, N.B., in 1825 and christened *Félix Souligny*, took him to Barbados and Trinidad on a number of occasions. He brought back rum and sugar for Jean-Olivier Brunet and Charles A. Holt, merchants at Quebec.

In 1828 Painchaud bought the *New Félix Souligny* (218 tons) and began trading with the British Isles. His brig took wheat to Liverpool, Cork, and Dublin, and returned with salt, coal, and iron for C. Noyes, G. Ross, and Félix Souligny. He also transported immigrants. The shipping news of 5 June 1833 announced details of the *New Félix Souligny*'s performance. Arriving from Dublin with iron, coal, and 54 passengers, the brig had covered the distance from Quebec to Montreal in 18 hours and 45 minutes. This was a record for a square-rigged vessel propelled by wind alone. The following autumn this magnificent ship was wrecked on its way back from Liverpool. The wreckage was sold for £250.

Using his schooners *Hubert Paré* (71 tons) and *Marie-Flora* (61 tons), Painchaud then developed a fish and oil trade with the Îles de la Madeleine. From 1838 he leased several pieces of land on the islands belonging to Isaac Coffin*, and to his successor, and when need arose acted as justice of the peace and conciliator there. His warehouses and fishing stations, which were on Havre Aubert Island and at L'Étang-du-Nord, were managed by his son Jean-Baptiste-Félix and employed about 50 people. In partnership with that son, who was a notary and merchant, and with another, Joseph-Alexis, a captain, he formed Painchaud and Sons on 23 March 1857.

For half a century Alexis Painchaud, with his score of ships, was a figure of note in the merchant navy. He gained recognition through his intelligence, boldness, enterprising spirit, and integrity. At his death in Montreal on 10 Feb. 1858 he left a flourishing business and a sizeable estate. The latter included a house in Montreal, several lots and beaches on the Îles de la Madeleine, a house, barn, large warehouse,

Painchaud

sheds, and three other buildings on the islands, and two schooners, one of which was outfitted for fishing. His sons continued the undertaking together until Joseph-Alexis was shipwrecked on the *Marie-Flora* in the autumn of 1860. Subsequently Jean-Baptiste-Félix bought back the share of his lost brother. He acted as a notary and served as a school inspector on the Îles de la Madeleine, and later owned coasting vessels that linked these islands to Halifax and Quebec.

CLOTILDE T. L. PAINCHAUD

ANQ-M, CE1-51, 13 févr. 1858; CN1-279, 23 mars, 4, 6 déc. 1857; 19 mars 1858. ANQ-Q, CE1-1, 22 nov. 1792. AP, Saint-Joseph (Carleton), Reg. des baptêmes, mariages et sépultures, 19 oct. 1815. PAC, RG 31, A1, 1825, 1861, Montreal; RG 42, ser.I. *Le Canadien*, 1834, 1838–40. *La Minerve*, 1832, 1852. *Le Pays*, 1857, 13 févr. 1858. *Quebec Gazette*, 1815, 1829. *Quebec Mercury*, 1811–15, 1823–24, 1831–34. *Le Spectateur* (Montréal), 1811–14. Bona Arsenault, *Histoire et généalogie des Acadiens* (éd. rév., 6v., [Montréal, 1978]). Antoine Bernard, *Histoire de la survivance acadienne, 1755–1935* (Montréal, 1935). N.-E. Dionne, *Vie de C.-F. Painchaud* (Québec, 1894). Rosa, *La construction des navires à Québec*.

PAINCHAUD, JOSEPH (baptized **Joseph-Louis**), doctor, surgeon, and philanthropist; b. 12 June 1819 at Quebec, son of Joseph Painchaud*, a doctor, and Marie-Geneviève Parant, and nephew of Alexis PAINCHAUD; d. probably 7 April 1855, in all likelihood near Tonila, Mexico.

Joseph Painchaud grew up in his father's spacious residence at the corner of Rue des Pauvres and Ruelle de l'Arsenal in Quebec. Third in a family of seven children, he suffered from delicate health and required attentive care from his mother, but he was brought up no less strictly than his brothers and sisters. His father was in comfortable circumstances, thanks to his medical practice, and had been able to protect his family from material worries. A fall down some school stairs had left the young Painchaud half-crippled and made it extremely difficult for him to walk. This handicap did not, however, deter him from beginning classical studies as a day-boy at the Petit Séminaire de Québec in 1835, and he completed them in 1840. During his fourth year (Versification) he felt himself called to be a missionary. At the end of his schooling he wanted to enter the priesthood but his infirmity prevented him from doing so. Accordingly, he studied medicine under his father and Dr James Douglas*, and then went to Paris to finish his training. On 28 Nov. 1846, having returned to Quebec, he received his licence as a doctor and surgeon. Shortly afterwards he entered the Marine and Emigrant Hospital, probably as an intern, under the direction of Dr Douglas. He received no remuneration at that time. In September 1847 he became a resident physician and

was granted an annual salary of £100. He remained at this hospital until the spring of 1848.

Unlike his father, Painchaud distinguished himself through neither medical practice nor public activity, but through the considerable though unobtrusive role he played in establishing the earliest conferences of the Society of St Vincent de Paul in Quebec. He had taken advantage of his stay in the French capital in 1845 to form numerous ties with that Catholic association. As well as joining various confraternities and visiting monasteries, he became a member of the society, which had been founded in 1833 by Antoine-Frédéric Ozanam and his friends. He had participated in the meetings and activities of the Saint-Séverin conference. Tradition has it that when he returned to his native city in 1846 he introduced the organization to Quebec, but in fact it had been established there two years before, although with aims and methods modelled only broadly on the Paris society. Apparently a circular letter of 16 June 1846 from the president general of the latter, Jules Gossin, prompted Archbishop Joseph Signay* to try to regularize the status of the Quebec conference. A meeting of 12 Nov. 1846, chaired by Charles-François Baillargeon*, who was then the parish priest of the cathedral, did not therefore constitute the beginning of the new society but rather a fresh start. At the next meeting, on 19 November, Jean CHABOT, a member of the House of Assembly who had previously presided over the conference, was elected president. It was not until the meeting of 26 November that the names of the two Painchauds, father and son, were mentioned for the first time in the society's minutes. The younger Painchaud worked to such good purpose that by 7 March 1847 Quebec had a total of nine conferences, all due to his indefatigable efforts. He even set one up at the Marine and Emigrant Hospital, dedicated to St Abysius Gonzaga. The Quebec conference formed in 1846 was granted affiliation with the Paris society in August 1847, as subsequently, in October, were the eight new conferences and the particular council of Quebec (a body encompassing the various conferences). Here, as would later be stressed, was indeed the "first link joining Old and New France since the separation of 1760."

Painchaud, who was quite familiar with the practices of the society in Paris, became both the guiding spirit and the driving force of the new organization at Quebec. None the less, following Ozanam's example, he did not hold any important office in it. Painchaud succeeded in bringing to Quebec the spirit of zeal and piety prevailing in Paris, but it cannot be said that he was imbued with the same social concerns as Ozanam. To Painchaud, material destitution was not an issue of social justice but an opportunity to do good and acquire spiritual merit.

The society's objective was to aid those in greatest need and to succour the unfortunate. Visits to the poor in their homes and the education of needy children were meant not only to provide material relief but to bring spiritual consolation and stir the recipients "to the depths of their souls."

These endeavours did not exhaust Painchaud's zeal. In 1845, when he was living in Paris, he had taken a vow to devote himself to missionary work should the day ever come when he could walk without difficulty. Four years later, as his condition had considerably improved, he offered his services as a doctor and catechist to Modeste Demers*, the bishop of Vancouver Island, making over to him his fortune and his estate. On 9 Sept. 1849 he set sail for Paris, where he stayed until the end of 1851, helping the bishop in his attempts to obtain assistance and introducing him into the society he had become acquainted with during his first stay in the city.

The rest of Painchaud's wanderings were marked by a series of misadventures. Having set out from Le Havre towards the end of 1851, he left New York for San Francisco the next spring aboard an immigrant ship on which he served as doctor. Following a mutiny, the vessel had to call at Rio de Janeiro, where the doctor and his companion, Abbé Laroche, decided to turn back and try to complete the journey by going through Nicaragua. Laroche died of exhaustion while crossing the isthmus. Painchaud embarked once more to go up the Pacific coast but was shipwrecked on the shores of Mexico. Unable to continue the voyage, he made his way to Colima, Mexico, where he erected a hospital and built up a highly lucrative practice. He wrote to Bishop Demers in 1852: "Divine Providence has probably put me here, in order to come more promptly to the assistance of the mission, for I am making money here, [and] I await your Excellency's orders." He then went to Tamazula, in the present state of Jalisco, to work a silver mine into which he sank all his new-found wealth. Shortly afterwards he fell ill and is believed to have died somewhere near Tonila and to have been buried there on 7 April 1855.

Joseph Painchaud has remained an unknown figure despite the role he played in establishing the Society of St Vincent de Paul in Quebec. Behind the clichés used by a pious press – "[a] heroic Christian, obedient child, model pupil, worthy and reserved student" – was hidden a tormented spirit inspired by an extraordinary, and at times excessive, religious zeal, but haunted above all by the thought of salvation. His devotion to Our Lady of La Salette, his participation in numerous confraternities, his activity within the Society of St Vincent de Paul, and his missionary vocation were all directed towards one end, to acquire as much merit as possible in this life in order to ensure his eternal salvation. In 1850 he had observed: "I am not much in favour of prayer and good works after one's death, [for] it is a bad system; it is better to deserve grace during life, for it is too late after one is dead. Doing good on earth means that much more merit in the eyes of God." His correspondence reflects a religious nature and reveals a personality which are symptomatic of the ideological evolution of French Canadian society around 1850. Father and son – the reform candidate in the elections of 1836 and the lay missionary, the founder of the Quebec Medical Society and the apostle of the Society of St Vincent de Paul – represent not only two generations, but two succeeding and sometimes conflicting visions of the world.

LOUIS PAINCHAUD

ANQ-Q, CE1-1, 5 juin 1815, 13 juin 1819; P-437. Private arch., Louis Painchaud (Quebec), Corr. of Joseph Painchaud, 1849–51. *Le Canadien*, 12 janv. 1859. P.-G. Roy, *Fils de Québec*, 4: 32–33. C.-J. Magnan, *Le docteur Joseph Painchaud, fondateur de la Société de Saint-Vincent de Paul au Canada, 1819–1919* (Montréal, 1919). Robert Rumilly, *La plus riche aumône: histoire de la Société de Saint-Vincent-de-Paul au Canada* (Montréal, 1946). [Henri Têtu], *Les noces d'or de la Société de Saint-Vincent de Paul à Québec, 1846–1896* (Québec, 1897). [Thomas Tremblay], *La Société de Saint-Vincent-de-Paul: son but, son esprit et ses avantages spirituels* (Québec, 1943). Sylvio Leblond, "Le Dr Jos. Painchaud et sa famille," SCHÉC *Rapport*, 23 (1955–56): 53–59. C.-J. Magnan, "La fondation de la première conférence de Saint-Vincent de Paul à Québec," *BRH*, 32 (1926): 699–702. Arthur Maheux, "L'Ozanam du Canada: Joseph Painchaud," *Rev. de l'univ. Laval*, 9 (1955): 735. "Petite galerie historique canadienne, le Dr. Jos. Painchaud," *L'Action catholique* (Québec), 19 sept. 1948: 2.

PANET, PHILIPPE, militia officer, lawyer, politician, judge, and justice of the peace; b. 28 Feb. 1791 at Quebec, son of Jean-Antoine Panet* and Louise-Philippe Badelard; m. 14 July 1819 Luce Casgrain in Rivière-Ouelle, Lower Canada, and they had 12 children, seven of whom died in infancy; d. 15 Jan. 1855 at Quebec.

After receiving a classical education at the Petit Séminaire de Québec from 1805 to 1810, Philippe Panet entered his father's office on 3 Dec. 1811 to study law. However, he broke off his studies at the time of the second American invasion and went through the whole campaign of 1812–13 as a captain in Quebec's 1st Militia Battalion. On 26 Oct. 1813 he served under Charles-Michel d'Irumberry* de Salaberry at the battle of Châteauguay. His mission was to hold the ford on the Rivière Châteauguay to prevent the enemy from crossing it and attacking the Voltigeurs from the rear. Panet was decorated for this action. He was to leave the militia on 1 Feb. 1833 with the rank of lieutenant-colonel.

Having managed to finish his legal training, Panet was called to the bar on 21 April 1817. The previous

Papineau

year he had been elected to the House of Assembly for Northumberland, which he represented from 25 April 1816 to 6 July 1824. Elections were held in 1824 but ill health prevented him from running. He was, however, a candidate in 1830, and won a seat in Montmorency. He served in the house from 26 Oct. 1830 to 3 July 1832. On 26 May 1831 the governor, Lord Aylmer [Whitworth-Aylmer*], appointed him to the Executive Council. As a councillor, Panet delivered the governor's messages to the assembly and became the executive's representative in the house.

On 29 June 1832 Lord Aylmer named Panet a judge of the Court of King's Bench for the district of Quebec, to replace Jean-Thomas Taschereau*, who had died. In 1833, from 1836 to 1838, and again in 1840 Panet also performed the duties of justice of the peace. After the reform of the Executive Council carried out by Lord Durham [Lambton*], he again served on that body from 28 June 1838. By this appointment he also became a member of the Court of Appeal.

It was as a judge that Panet became famous. During the disturbances of 1837–38, one John Teed, a tailor of American origin, was arrested for high treason on 11 Nov. 1838 and incarcerated in the Quebec jail. His lawyer, Thomas Cushing Aylwin*, sought a writ of habeas corpus for his client from Panet and his judicial colleague Elzéar Bédard*. The Special Council had suspended the law of habeas corpus by ordinances issued on 23 April and 8 November. Panet and Bédard declared these decrees unconstitutional and on 21 November issued their warrant for Teed to appear before them. In the mean time the accused had been transferred to the citadel under military authority. Thereupon the two judges sentenced to imprisonment the jailer of the Quebec prison, and held the commandant, Colonel George Bowles, to be in contempt of court. At the beginning of December, Panet and Bédard were suspended from their judicial duties by Sir John Colborne*, their judgements on the Teed case were quashed on appeal, and their related orders set aside by the Special Council.

Philippe Panet, whose stature in the eyes of his fellow citizens was enhanced by this ordeal, was reinstated as a judge of the Court of Queen's Bench on 8 Aug. 1840, and was reappointed to this court on 10 Feb. 1841. Following the reorganization of the courts of justice which was carried out in 1849, he sat on the Court of Appeal from 1 Jan. 1850 until his death at Quebec on 15 Jan. 1855. At the time of Panet's demise, the bar of Lower Canada expressed its highest "esteem for [his] independence of character and for [his] irreproachable integrity in the execution of the important duties of his office."

CLAUDE VACHON

ANQ-Q, CE1-1, 2 mars 1791, 18 janv. 1855; CE3-1, 14 juill. 1819. ASQ, Fichier des anciens. Le Canadien, 15, 19 janv. 1855. La Minerve, 19 janv. 1855. F.-J. Audet, "Les législateurs du Bas-Canada." P.-V. Charland, "Notre-Dame de Québec: le nécrologe de la crypte ou les inhumations dans cette église depuis 1652," BRH, 20 (1914): 313. Fauteux, Patriotes, 172, 379–80. Le Jeune, Dictionnaire, 2: 400–1. Officers of British forces in Canada (Irving), 119, 144. P.-G. Roy, Fils de Québec, 3: 50–52; Les juges de la prov. de Québec. Chapais, Cours d'hist. du Canada, 4: 224–25. P.-G. Roy, La famille Panet (Lévis, Qué., 1906), 91–121. Benjamin Sulte, Histoire de la milice canadienne-française, 1760–1897 (Montréal, 1897). Mason Wade, Les canadiens français, de 1760 à nos jours, Adrien Venne et Francis Dufau-Labeyrie, trad. (2v., Ottawa, 1963). "Les combattants de Châteauguay," BRH, 21 (1915): 28. Lucien Lemieux, "Juges de la province du Bas-Canada de 1791 à 1840," BRH, 23 (1917): 89.

PAPINEAU, DENIS-BENJAMIN, seigneurial agent, bookseller, seigneur, merchant, office holder, justice of the peace, and politician; b. 13 Nov. 1789 in Montreal, son of Joseph Papineau* and Rosalie Cherrier; m. there 14 Sept. 1813 Angélique-Louise Cornud, and they had nine children, including Denis-Emery*; d. 20 Jan. 1854 in Sainte-Angélique (Papineauville), Lower Canada.

Denis-Benjamin Papineau, the fifth in a family of ten, five of whom died in infancy, studied from 1801 to 1807 at the Petit Séminaire de Québec, where his elder brother Louis-Joseph* was also a student from 1802 to 1804. In his letters to his family he often expressed a desire to go to the seigneury of Petite-Nation, a property his father had bought from the Séminaire de Québec. From 1808 the young man lived at Petite-Nation, serving as seigneurial agent in the absence of his father, who from 1809 to 1814 represented Montreal East in the House of Assembly. Denis-Benjamin had a wide variety of occupations, which included settling the first censitaires, clearing land, and building a manor-house and a sawmill. To judge by the letters exchanged between father and son, Denis-Benjamin often committed blunders and made bad deals. When Louis-Joseph bought the seigneury from his father in 1817, he entrusted its management to Denis-Benjamin, who looked after it until his brother returned from exile in 1845. During that period Denis-Benjamin's particular concern was to increase the number of settlers and distribute lots. Lumbering was the chief economic activity. The sawmills were leased to local and regional lumberers, who were given cutting licences in return for paying rent. Papineau's task was to see that the privileges granted were respected. He also collected the rents, and on this score he regularly had to face the remonstrances of his brother, who was dissatisfied with the receipts and criticized him for not being firm enough.

Denis-Benjamin did not, however, confine himself to his role as seigneurial agent. In 1818 and 1819 he was the partner of bookseller Hector Bossange, who had been running a bookstore on Rue Notre-Dame in Montreal for several years. Around 1825 he was active in Petite-Nation as a merchant and also as postmaster. In addition, he held commissions as justice of the peace for the district of Montreal in 1826, 1828, 1830, 1833, and 1837, and was a commissioner of roads and bridges in 1829 and 1830. He had become seigneur of Plaisance fief, at the southwest extremity of the seigneury of Petite-Nation, in 1822, but seven years later was obliged to sell part of his land because of financial difficulties. Subsequently he tried, in vain, to breed horses, but he did succeed with sheep-farming and in 1844 owned a flock of 200.

Like his father and his brother Louis-Joseph, Papineau was interested in politics. He represented Ottawa in the assembly from 17 Aug. 1842 to 6 Dec. 1847. From September 1844 to June 1846, he was a member of the administration of William Henry Draper* and Denis-Benjamin Viger*. He helped form a government with Draper in June 1846, and then one with Henry SHERWOOD in May 1847. He discharged the duties of executive councillor and of commissioner of crown lands from September 1844 to December 1847, as well as those of commissioner of public works from October 1844 to June 1846.

The stands Papineau took made him a controversial figure. While the majority of French Canadians, under the leadership of Louis-Hippolyte La Fontaine*, took the path leading to ministerial responsibility, Papineau, whose family ties and principles associated him with the reform party, accepted office from Governor Sir Charles Theophilus Metcalfe*. According to historian Louis-Philippe Turcotte*, Metcalfe considered he must bestow ministerial appointments on persons he could fully trust. In appointing Papineau and his cousin Denis-Benjamin Viger, the governor sought to rally around him men whose very names would reassure French Canadians of the government's desire to serve their interests as best it could, especially since he felt sure that the people in general and a majority in the house were opposed to his views. In the opinion of historian Thomas Chapais*, Papineau, by accepting a post under Metcalfe, created dissension in the reform party; in Louis-Joseph Papineau's view, "One cannot accept a position as minister and remain an honourable man." For historian Jacques Monet, however, Denis-Benjamin's decision to accept a seat on the Executive Council was the best approach for him to have adopted in light of his personal principles: his behaviour implied a spirit devoted to the French Canadian cause.

Papineau's first act as a member of the assembly was to help choose a speaker for the house. According to Turcotte and Chapais, he committed a blunder in voting for Sir Allan Napier MacNab*, a unilingual anglophone, a decision that antagonized the Lower Canadian reform majority. In December 1844 he drew a positive response from the opposition when he moved approval of an address to the queen to annul the clause of the Act of Union which prohibited the use of the French language in legislative documents. For Turcotte, this step served to redeem to some extent his vote in favour of MacNab and to improve his image in the eyes of his compatriots. For Chapais, it was a political manœuvre: the Executive Council had anticipated that the reform party would make a resolution of this kind and decided to forestall it by taking the initiative itself through Papineau.

During his term as a minister Papineau again made his voice heard in ways that drew criticism from the opposition. He justified the government's action in 1845 in approving the grant of a substantial sum to compensate those in Upper Canada who had incurred losses during the rebellion of 1837–38, whereas nothing similar was granted in Lower Canada. The following year he also defended the government's intention to use for educational purposes the revenue from the Jesuit estates, as well as its proposal to make the expenses of administering criminal justice in Upper Canada a charge upon the consolidated revenue fund. These laws, which aroused violent opposition, were enough to make him thoroughly unpopular.

Papineau introduced in the assembly two important and highly controversial bills concerning schools and municipal administration in Lower Canada. The new school act passed in 1845 entrusted to school boards the management of public schools and the responsibility for collecting funds to operate them efficiently. For the Catholic clergy this legislation smacked of injustice. Fearful of losing control of education, the priests claimed their rights through a member of the opposition, Augustin-Norbert Morin*. Heated discussions led Papineau to accept in 1846 amendments favourable to the clergy, but not before he had held his ground and again incurred the censure of the opposition and the general public. As for the act dealing with municipalities in Lower Canada, passed during the same 1845 session, it replaced the old organization based on districts with an administration founded on parishes. It satisfied the opposition in principle, but the assessment rates, as in the case of the school act, were discussed for a long time and subsequently amended.

Papineau's short political career ended during the governorship of Lord Elgin [Bruce*]; influenced by Viger's resignation the previous year, Papineau gave up his duties in 1847. He retired to Plaisance fief, where he remained, embittered by illness, until his death. Historians generally agree that Denis-Benjamin Papineau played a minor role as a politician.

Paquet

Though he provoked controversy in this capacity, he seems more important as a seigneur and seigneurial agent.

CLAUDE BARIBEAU

ANQ-Q, P-417. ASQ, Fichier des anciens. PAC, MG 24, B2; RG 68, General index, 1651–1841: 200–1, 256, 358, 363, 368, 375, 383, 641, 697; 1841–67: 40, 73, 89, 91. Julie Bruneau, "Correspondance de Julie Bruneau (1823–1862)," Fernand Ouellet, édit., ANQ Rapport, 1957–59: 59–184. Debates of the Legislative Assembly of United Canada (Abbott Gibbs et al.), vol.4. L.-J. Papineau, "Correspondance de Louis-Joseph Papineau (1820–1839)," Fernand Ouellet, édit., ANQ Rapport, 1953–55: 191–442; 1955–57: 255–375. Joseph Papineau, "Correspondance de Joseph Papineau (1793–1840)," Fernand Ouellet, édit., ANQ Rapport, 1951–53: 169–299. F.-J. Audet, "Les législateurs du Bas-Canada." L.-O. David, Biographies et portraits (Montréal, 1876). Desjardins, Guide parl. Claude Baribeau, La seigneurie de la Petite-Nation, 1801–1854; le rôle économique et social du seigneur (Hull, Qué., 1983). Chapais, Cours d'hist. du Canada, vols.5–6. L.-O. David, L'union des deux Canada, 1841–1867 (Montréal, 1898). Monet, Last cannon shot. J.-L. Roy, Édouard-Raymond Fabre, 57. Rumilly, Papineau et son temps. L.-P. Turcotte, Le Canada sous l'Union, 1841–1867 (2v., Québec, 1871–72). [R.] C. Harris, "Of poverty and helplessness in Petite-Nation," CHR, 52 (1971): 23–50. É.-Z. Massicotte, "Les deux premiers avocats Bibaud," BRH, 44 (1938): 340–43. D.-B. Papineau, "Samuel Papineau," BRH, 39 (1933): 331–46.

PAQUET, *dit* **Lavallée, ANDRÉ,** carpenter and wood-carver; b. 2 Dec. 1799 in Saint-Charles, near Quebec, son of Jean-Baptiste Paquet, *dit* Lavallée, and Marie Baquette, *dit* Lamontagne; m. first 21 Nov. 1826 Sophie Lépine (Legris, *dit* Lépine) at Quebec; m. secondly 31 Jan. 1843 Marie-Hermine Turgeon in Saint-Charles; m. thirdly 21 June 1848 Joséphine (Josephte) Paquet at Quebec; d. 22 May 1860 in Charlesbourg, Lower Canada.

One of a family of five, André Paquet, *dit* Lavallée, served his apprenticeship with Thomas BAILLAIRGÉ, the Quebec architect, around 1820. He was on close personal terms with his master, for in 1826 on the occasion of his first marriage Baillairgé served as a witness. As well, Paquet's third wife was the architect's housekeeper. From 1830 to 1860 Paquet executed or saw to the execution of decorative ensembles designed by Baillairgé. The apprenticeship partly explains Paquet's artistic excellence and his pre-eminence among the creators of interior church architecture.

Paquet first became known as a master carpenter in 1829, when he obtained the contract to decorate the vault of the parish church at L'Ange-Gardien. From 1830 he was involved with a number of building sites, describing himself as wood-carver, contractor, and even architect. His principal achievements, in the order in which the work was begun, are the architectural decorations done in the churches of Saint-Pierre on the Île d'Orléans (1830, 1842), Saint-Charles (1830), Charlesbourg (1833, 1841), Saint-François on the Île d'Orléans (1834), Saint-Antoine-de-Tilly (1837), Deschambault (1840), Saint-Anselme (1845), Sainte-Luce (1845), Les Becquets (1849), Sainte-Croix (1850), and Notre-Dame-de-la-Victoire parish at Lévis (1850).

Through these works and complementary pieces made for existing interiors, such as the vaults of the churches at Saint-Jean on the Île d'Orléans (1831) and at Lotbinière (1840), Paquet ensured that Baillairgé's aesthetic concepts were being spread through the area influenced by the diocese of Quebec. Baillairgé himself was concerned solely with the design of volumes and spaces, which he rendered into drawings. These were first used jointly by a master mason and a master carpenter, who put up the fabric of the building. Then came – albeit sometimes years later – the phase of the interior décor, which in keeping with Baillairgé's aesthetics was to be a type of architectural decoration forming a logical unity with the edifice it adorned. Paquet usually began by installing both a false wooden vault embellished with carved motifs and the cornice separating it from the interior elevation. Then followed the retables (structures housing the altar) in the chancel and side chapels, which formed a continuous décor. In the final stages the pulpit, the churchwarden's pew, and the baptismal fonts received attention.

Although he could neither read nor write, Paquet prospered as a contractor. It is possible that at the beginning of his career he gave a hand on building sites, but later he confined himself to making models that his workmen followed. For instance, in 1841, when he was urging the churchwardens of Charlesbourg to give him the contract for the interior, he informed them that he would like "to have the time before leaving for the countryside to make a capital that will serve as a model for making the others." His decorative ensembles differed from those to which Baillairgé contributed in that they had no representational carving. The few figurative carvings of Moses that embellish the bodies of the pulpits at Saint-Charles, Charlesbourg, and Saint-Antoine-de-Tilly, and the busts of St Charles, at Saint-Charles and Charlesbourg, are the only exceptions to this rule, and the heavy-handed use of the chisel probably explains the absence of such ornamentation elsewhere. On the other hand, all the decorative schemes done by Paquet are embellished with trophies, garlands, and other stylized ornaments; this suggests that Baillairgé, aware of his disciple's inadequacies, had steered him in a direction more readily taken by a workshop with wood-carvers of uneven talent. It must also be noted that Paquet was confined to rural parishes; at Quebec,

Baillairgé could call upon specialized workmen to carry out his innovations. Hence while Paquet worked in wood, Baillairgé offered decorative ensembles made of plaster.

Unlike some of his colleagues, Paquet never seems to have been in financial difficulty. The inventory made after his death indicates that he owned several pieces of land, and that his estate included accounts receivable from a number of *fabriques* for work he had carried out. His success, of course, depended on the vogue enjoyed by Baillairgé's art, but it was also due to his particular abilities as a contractor. In creating interior décors for which he accepted payment over a period of years – up to 16 in the case of the church at Sainte-Luce – Paquet was in fact lending money to *fabriques* which otherwise would have postponed the work. It is to the business acumen Paquet showed that the extensive spread of Baillairgé's art should probably be attributed. The fact that similar if not identical ensembles were done in various places ensured that artistic schemes which by 1840 were obsolete at Quebec would persist in rural settings. The apparent success of these schemes helped perpetuate Baillairgé's style long after his death and that of Paquet.

Although André Paquet, *dit* Lavallée, had two sons from his first two marriages, it seems clear that neither of them carried on his work. On the other hand, his brother Jean learned the profession of wood-carver with him.

LUC NOPPEN

ANQ-Q, CE1-1, 21 nov. 1826, 21 juin 1848; CE1-7, 25 mai 1860; CE2-4, 31 janv. 1843; CN1-66, 7 janv., 20 juill. 1860; CN1-212, 19 nov. 1826, 8 mai 1841, 20 juin 1848. MAC-CD, Fonds Morisset, 2, P219.7/A555/2. Georges Côté, *La vieille église de Saint-Charles-Borromée, sur Rivière Boyer (comté de Bellechasse) en 1928* (Québec, 1928). Luc Noppen, *Les églises du Québec (1600–1850)* (Québec, 1977); "Le renouveau architectural proposé par Thomas Baillairgé au Québec de 1820 à 1850 (l'architecture néo-classique québécoise)" (thèse de PHD, univ. de Toulouse-Le Mirail, Toulouse, France, 1976). Luc Noppen et J. R. Porter, *Les églises de Charlesbourg et l'architecture religieuse du Québec* ([Québec], 1972).

PARANT (Parent), ANTOINE, Roman Catholic priest and seminary administrator; b. 27 Nov. 1785 at Quebec, son of Antoine Parant and Geneviève Bois; d. there 11 Feb. 1855.

Antoine Parant was a brilliant student at the Petit Séminaire de Québec from 1796 to 1804, and then for four years at the Grand Séminaire, where at the same time he taught the rudiments of Latin. He was ordained in the cathedral on 12 March 1808 by Joseph-Octave Plessis*, the bishop of Quebec, and was immediately sent to lend assistance at the new Séminaire de Nicolet. Writing to Jean Raimbault*, the

superior of this institution, on the day of Parant's ordination, the bishop assured him that he would find the abbé an "intelligent, pious, modest, studious young man" but "perhaps overly diffident." In a second letter dated 28 March, Plessis added, "I have deprived myself of an excellent ecclesiastic." Before leaving Quebec, Parant had nevertheless applied for membership in the community of the Séminaire de Québec. The directors, who knew how valuable he was, lost no time in granting his request and on 25 May 1809, soon after his return from Nicolet, invited him to join the seminary's council. Parant served first as a director of the Grand Séminaire and then became director-prefect (1810–12) and director (1810–17) of the Petit Séminaire. From 1817 until the end of his active life in 1849 he was alternately procurator and superior of the Petit Séminaire.

As Bishop Plessis had anticipated, Parant did not attract much comment and left few writings. He spent his entire life at the seminary and devoted all his talents to its administration. He seems to have left the seminary only once, in 1824. That year a committee of the House of Assembly, which included Louis Bourdages*, Andrew Stuart*, and Denis-Benjamin Viger*, was conducting an inquiry into the state of education in Lower Canada. Summoned to give testimony before the committee, Parant proposed that a system of primary schools be established under the direction and supervision of the *fabriques* and that the schools be financed directly by the funds each parish would be authorized to collect for their maintenance. This deposition was largely responsible for the assembly's passing a bill that year to establish and endow elementary schools in the parishes (commonly called the *fabrique* schools act).

Parant was lucky to find within the ranks of his colleagues two exceptionally valuable collaborators: Jérôme DEMERS, who alternated with him as procurator and superior from 1824 to 1848, and John HOLMES, a prefect of studies from 1830 to 1849. Under the impetus of these three educators, the Petit Séminaire reached a level of excellence which enabled it to found the Université Laval in 1852. Parant also shared with Demers in particular the supervision of construction work to enlarge the seminary. Undertaken to accommodate the growing number of pupils, this work was begun in 1823 and lasted for more than ten years. The wing and parlour of the Grand Séminaire were entirely rebuilt; the building of the Petit Séminaire looking onto the courtyard was enlarged, with a storey being added; and the wing of the procurator's office was extended on the garden side. The new building was intended to provide accommodation for students of the Grand Séminaire as well.

In intellectual matters Parant helped to improve the program of studies at the Petit Séminaire. When he accepted the office of director-prefect in 1810 the

Parant

curriculum was the same as in the previous century except for the addition of geography and history, which from 1808 had been taught as regular courses in all classes up to and including the fifth year (Belles-Lettres). In 1814, as prefect, Parant initiated the teaching of English for three hours a week starting in the fourth year (Versification). Later, as superior, he helped Holmes to introduce new subjects such as Greek in 1829, instrumental music in 1833, and drawing in 1835, and Demers to improve instruction in science. Étienne Parant* in Le Canadien never tired of praising the Petit Séminaire, and the memory of its educators, who made their mark on this period, remained alive for a long time. Joseph-Edmond Roy* wrote 50 years later: "The names Demers, Holmes, Parant, and Gingras [Louis Gingras*] mean nothing whatever to the new generations, but . . . we well know the extraordinary influence these men had on their contemporaries."

Before his retirement Parant became a member of the Catholic Board of Examiners of the City of Quebec. After 1849 he also continued to sit as first assistant on the council of the seminary, and he took part in deliberations leading to the approval of the plan Louis-Jacques Casault* put forward to establish the Université Laval. In 1850 he became a member of the bishop of Quebec's council, a post he retained until 1855, the year of his death.

NOËL BAILLARGEON

ANQ-Q, CE1-1, 27 nov. 1785, 14 févr. 1855. ASQ, MSS, 12–13; 431; 437: 363–64. Can., Prov. of, Statutes, 1846, c.27. L.C., Statutes, 1823–24, c.31. Le Séminaire de Québec: documents et biographies, Honorius Provost, édit. (Québec, 1964), 461. Allaire, Dictionnaire, 1: 415. P.-G. Roy, Fils de Québec, 3: 26. Tanguay, Répertoire, 171. L.-P. Audet, Le système scolaire, 3: 199–200, 215. André Labarrère-Paulé, Les laïques et la presse pédagogique au Canada français au XIX e siècle (Québec, 1963), 51, 147. Marc Lebel et al., Aspects de l'enseignement au petit séminaire de Québec (1765–1945) (Québec, 1968), 40–41. J.-E. Roy, Souvenirs d'une classe au séminaire de Québec, 1867–1877 (Lévis, Qué., 1905).

PARANT, JOSEPH, physician, surgeon, justice of the peace, and politician; b. 22 Aug. 1796 at Quebec, son of Antoine Parant, a wig-maker, and Geneviève Bois, and brother of ANTOINE; m. there 11 July 1822 Marie-Antoinette Doucet, and they had five children; d. there 28 Feb. 1856.

Joseph Parant received his classical education at the Petit Séminaire de Québec from 1806 to 1816. In 1818 he was in London studying medicine along with Jean BLANCHET and Augustin Mercier. After returning home, he was authorized on 29 Aug. 1820 to practise medicine in Lower Canada, and opened a surgery at Quebec. The next year he was listed for the first time in the Almanach de Québec as a physician and surgeon.

His considerable professional competence was quickly recognized. In 1824 the nuns of the Hôpital Général in Quebec were invited by Archbishop Joseph-Octave Plessis* to accept him as their acting doctor. On 16 April 1834, after the death of William Holmes*, who had been the physician there, Parant and his colleague Joseph Painchaud* offered themselves as replacements. Parant's work at the hospital came to an end in 1844, but in the preceding two years his activities there had been restricted because of illness.

Throughout his career Parant displayed a "zeal" and an "assiduity beyond all praise." The religious communities and the poor placed in their charge were the principal beneficiaries. As an instance, while working at the Hôpital Général Parant made his professional services available to the Ursulines of Quebec from 1828 to 1832, replacing Dr Thomas Fargues*. Then, for more than 20 years, from 1825 to 1847, he attended the sisters of the convent and the poor of the Hôtel-Dieu of Quebec without remuneration. Because of his ill health, he agreed to be replaced at the Hôtel-Dieu in 1847 by Charles-Jacques Frémont* and to take on the less onerous duties of visiting surgeon and consultant.

Along with his role as physician to religious communities, Parant gave his attention to medical publishing and education. In 1826 he was a member of the editorial committee of the Quebec Medical Journal, founded that year by François-Xavier Tessier*. His participation ended in 1827 when the journal ceased publication. Four years later Parant was nominated by his colleagues to the Medical Board of Examiners for the district of Quebec. In addition he was a member of the Quebec Education Society a number of times, notably in 1835 and 1841.

Parant's public-spiritedness was shown by his presence on the municipal scene. In 1837 he was one of the justices of the peace who administered the city of Quebec [see Hippolyte Dubord*], and in 1840 he became a town councillor. He participated at that time in the work of committees on public order, the watch and street lighting, and public health. The following year he was a member of the markets and stalls committee, and in 1842 he shared in the activities of the public schools committee. Parant gave up political involvement that year.

From 1835 to 1855 Parant served as medical inspector of the port of Quebec and was responsible for the quarantine station on Grosse Île [see George Mellis Douglas*]. These duties and the work he did at the Marine and Emigrant Hospital [see James Douglas*] "kept [him] so busy" that he complained in a letter to the mother superior of the Hôtel-Dieu. In the letter, dated 19 July 1847, Parant mentioned his poor health, and thanked the sister for her "kindnesses" towards him and for her "patience in putting up with [his] bad moods for more than twenty years." He asked one favour of her: he wanted to be given after his death "a little corner in [the] church where [his] body might be laid." This wish was to be granted.

Joseph Parant died at Quebec on 28 Feb. 1856. He was buried on 3 March at the Hôtel-Dieu convent in the nave of its church. In addition to the assets he left his family, Parant bequeathed a box of surgical instruments to the Hôtel-Dieu.

In collaboration with ÉDOUARD DESJARDINS

ANQ-Q, CE1-1, 23 août 1796, 11 juill. 1822, 15 juin 1823, 3 juin 1824, 12 nov. 1827, 11 janv. 1830; CE1-22, 23 oct. 1871. Arch. de l'Hôpital Général de Québec, Annales des Augustines du monastère, 1844–66: 13.14.2.4, 332. Arch. du monastère de l'Hôtel-Dieu de Québec, Actes capitulaires, I: f.132; Corr., Médecins, Joseph Parant, 1855; 29 févr., 1er, 13 mars 1856; Dispositifs et règlements, 1825–55, 22, 28 oct. 1825; Inventaires, 1791–1822, 21 oct. 1825; Médecine et chirurgie, 1818–1914, 10 oct. 1820; 7 avril 1825; 16, 19, 20 juill. 1847; Notes et mémoires des anciennes mères, tome 2, chap.94, no.6; Notes sur les médecins, no.31: 48–49; Rapports au sujet de l'administration et de la tenue de l'Hôtel-Dieu de Québec, avant 1724; Reg. des sépultures, 1847–57, V: f.85. Arch. du monastère des ursulines (Québec), Reg. des notes sur les médecins. ASQ, Fichier des anciens. AVQ, I, 1, mai 1836–août 1840; II, 1, b, août 1840–mai 1842. Morgan, *Sketches of celebrated Canadians. Quebec almanac*, 1821–41. *Quebec directory*, 1847–55. Abbott, *Hist. of medicine*. M.-J. et George Ahern, *Notes pour servir à l'histoire de la médecine dans le Bas-Canada depuis la fondation de Québec jusqu'au commencement du XIXe siècle* (Québec, 1923). J. J. Heagerty, *Four centuries of medical history in Canada and a sketch of the medical history of Newfoundland* (2v., Toronto, 1928), 2.

PARRY, Sir WILLIAM EDWARD, naval officer, Arctic explorer, and hydrographer; b. 19 Dec. 1790 in Bath, England, fourth son of eminent physician Caleb Hillier Parry and Sarah Rigby; m. first 23 Oct. 1826 Isabella Louisa Stanley (d. 13 May 1839), and they had eight children; m. secondly 29 June 1841 Catherine Edwards Hankinson, and they had three children; d. 8 or 9 July 1855 in Ems (Bad Ems, Federal Republic of Germany).

Educated at the Bath Grammar School, William Edward Parry entered the Royal Navy on 30 June 1803. In August of the same year he was rated midshipman and subsequently served aboard various vessels in the English Channel and the Baltic Sea during the Napoleonic Wars. He was promoted lieutenant on 6 Jan. 1810 and was assigned to the *Alexandria*, on duty protecting the Spitsbergen whale fishery and preparing marine charts in the Shetland Islands and along the coasts of Sweden and Denmark. With the outbreak of hostilities between Great Britain

and the United States, Parry was transferred to the North American station and, aboard the *Hogue*, participated in the destruction of 27 American vessels in the Connecticut River on 6 April 1814. That same year he prepared a short guide on nautical astronomy which was distributed to the officers stationed at Halifax and which was subsequently published. Returning to England early in 1817, Parry applied for and was granted an assignment with one of the Admiralty's two polar expeditions in search of a northwest passage, one under Commander John Ross and the other under Captain David Buchan*.

On the urging of John Barrow, second secretary of the Admiralty, Parry was given the command of the brig *Alexander*, which would accompany Ross aboard the sloop *Isabella*; Ross had instructions to seek a passage from the Atlantic to the Pacific through Davis Strait and Baffin Bay. Weighing anchor at London on 18 April 1818, the two vessels made a short stop in the Shetland Islands before heading west on 3 May. By the end of the month they had reached Davis Strait and, encountering ice floes, then followed the west coast of Greenland north. They continued as far as Smith Sound, where on 19 August Ross named the capes on either side of the sound after his two ships – Cape Isabella on Ellesmere Island and Cape Alexander on Greenland. Having erroneously concluded that the north end of Smith Sound was enclosed by land, Ross headed southwest towards Jones Sound and again mistakenly thought he observed land at the bottom of the inlet. Farther south the entrance to Lancaster Sound was found to be free of ice and on 31 August the two vessels proceeded west into it. As had often been the case during the voyage, the *Alexander* lagged a considerable distance behind the *Isabella*. With what appeared to be open water to the west, Parry remarked in his private journal that "the swell comes from the north-west, compass, (that is, south-southwest true,) and continues just as it does in the ocean. It is impossible to remark this circumstance without feeling a *hope* that it *may* be caused by this inlet being a passage into a sea to the westward of it." However, Ross was once again convinced that there was "land round the bottom of the bay," in the form of a chain of mountains blocking access to the west; he named them after the first secretary of the Admiralty, John Wilson Croker, and turned back to explore the east coast of Baffin Island. Parry, not having seen these mountains, was disappointed by his commander's decision and remained convinced of the possibility of a passage through Lancaster Sound. The expedition returned to England to avoid wintering in the Arctic, arriving at Deptford (London) on 21 November. Immediately the disagreement between Ross and Parry over the existence of Croker's Mountains became public, and Barrow was quick to criticize Ross's decision to turn back.

Parry

In order to resolve this confusion the Admiralty commissioned Parry on 16 Jan. 1819 to command a second expedition with specific instructions to investigate Lancaster Sound. Two vessels, the bomb *Hecla* and the gun-brig *Griper*, were specially fitted to meet Arctic conditions and sailed on 4 May. By 28 June they had reached Davis Strait. Parry then proceeded across Baffin Bay to Lancaster Sound and, heading into the inlet, discovered that his hopes of the previous year had been well founded and that Croker's Mountains did not exist. Having for the first time fully equipped an expedition to winter in the Arctic, the Admiralty had instructed Parry to continue westward as far as possible in the hope of reaching Bering Strait. Prince Regent Inlet was briefly explored and found to be closed off by ice, so the two ships pushed through Barrow Strait and along the south shore of the group of islands Parry named the North Georgian Islands (now Parry Islands). For the first time European vessels had penetrated the Arctic archipelago and, on 4 September, Parry crossed 110°W, off the south shore of Melville Island, earning for the expedition the prize of £5,000 offered by parliament for reaching this longitude.

Progress to the west was soon arrested by the ice, and the *Hecla* and *Griper* put into Winter Harbour on Melville Island, where they remained frozen in the ice until 1 Aug. 1820. Before leaving these moorings, Parry led a party of 12 men north across the island and explored the south shore of Hecla and Griper Bay. Unfortunately, westward progress during the second season was halted in the vicinity of Cape Dundas and, after new land (Banks Island) had been sighted to the south, the quest for the passage to the Pacific had to be forsaken and the ships turned back towards Britain. One of the most important naval expeditions to the Arctic, this voyage had not only determined that Lancaster Sound opened a passage towards the west but also laid the groundwork for the mapping of the maze of islands through which the much sought-after northwest passage would have to be traced. Parry had demonstrated the possibility of wintering in relative safety above the Arctic Circle and pioneered techniques for protection against the climate and illness. Landing at Peterhead, Scotland, on 30 October, he proceeded directly to London where he was welcomed by Lord Melville, first lord of the Admiralty, and given his promotion to commander. In England he was publicly honoured by a number of communities and institutions, and in February 1821 he was unanimously elected a fellow of the Royal Society.

Encouraged by the results of the 1819–20 voyage, the Admiralty commissioned Parry to the command of another expedition in search of a northwest passage. The *Hecla* and the bomb *Fury*, specially selected and fitted to duplicate the proven sailing characteristics of *Hecla*, left Deptford on 29 April 1821. Instead of pursuing the path already attempted through Lancaster Sound, Parry had been instructed to penetrate towards the west through Hudson Strait, between Baffin Island and the Ungava Peninsula. He reached the entrance to the strait by the end of June and continued westward to the north of Southampton Island into Repulse Bay, which was discovered to be closed to any further progress to the west. Parry then followed the coast of Melville Peninsula northward, being careful to investigate any possible passage to the west through its various bays and inlets. The expedition explored and charted the southern extremity of the peninsula and then proceeded to Lyon Inlet (which was named for the second officer of the expedition, Commander George Francis Lyon) before the season's navigation came to a halt. The vessels put into winter quarters off the south shore of Winter Island on 8 October and were quickly frozen into the positions they would keep for the next nine months.

The ships had their masts struck and their sails stowed. The heating system had been improved following the experience of the previous voyage so as to prevent the accumulation of moisture in the cabins and, to the same end, the traditional seamen's bunks had been replaced by hammocks to permit a freer circulation of air. The Royal Arctic Theatre, fully equipped with costumes and stage lights, was formed by crew members from both ships and presented a program each fortnight. To occupy the men further, a school was established aboard each vessel to teach reading and writing, and an observatory was installed on shore to take magnetic measurements and other scientific observations. The monotony of the long winter was further broken, on 1 February, by the arrival of a group of Inuit who had settled for the winter about two miles distant and kept in close communication with the expedition. From the Inuit, Parry learned that there was a strait north of Winter Island which provided access to open water to the west, and his hopes of finding the northwest passage were heightened.

The second season of navigation began on 2 July 1822 when *Hecla* and *Fury* were freed from the ice. With the help of the information provided by the Inuit, Parry made his way to the entrance of Fury and Hecla Strait, which he so named. Finding it barred by ice and being thus reduced to exploring it on foot, he none the less succeeded in sighting the body of water to the west. At the beginning of October winter quarters were prepared off Igloolik Island, Hooper Inlet, not far from the entrance to the strait, and the expedition passed a second winter in the company of Inuit who also used the island as a winter settlement. It had now become clear, however, that the expedition would not be able to reach its objective, Bering Strait, with the remaining provisions. When finally released from their winter moorings on 9 Aug. 1823, the vessels made one last attempt to explore Fury and Hecla Strait but found the ice still a solid barrier. Parry decided to turn back to England and the expedition arrived in the Thames at the end of October.

Having failed to discover a passage to the Pacific, Parry had none the less charted and explored a considerable area of the Arctic, previously unknown, stretching from Southampton Island north to Baffin Island. In addition, the almost continual contact with the Inuit of Melville Peninsula yielded a wealth of information on their culture, way of life, and language which was included in the published version of Parry's journal of this voyage.

On 8 Nov. 1821, during his absence, Parry had been promoted captain. On 1 Dec. 1823 he accepted the position of acting hydrographer of the Admiralty on the understanding that he would still be free to command another Arctic expedition. This commission was not long in coming. On 17 Jan. 1824 he was once again given the command of *Hecla* and *Fury* with instructions to search for a passage through Lancaster Sound, down Prince Regent Inlet, and then, if possible, along the north coast of North America. Leaving Deptford on 8 May, this expedition was to prove to be Parry's least successful. Heavy concentrations of ice were encountered in Baffin Bay which delayed its entering Lancaster Sound until 10 September, close to the end of practicable navigation. With considerable difficulty the expedition managed to reach Port Bowen, on the east coast of Prince Regent Inlet, where winter quarters were set up on 1 October. When the ice broke up the following July, Parry headed across to the other side of the inlet in the hope of finding an opening to the west. Fighting against the ice, the *Fury* was forced aground and severely damaged. There was no sufficiently secure harbour in which to effect the necessary repairs and Parry reluctantly decided to abandon the ship, to take both crews aboard the *Hecla*, and, because of the strain upon the resources of the one remaining vessel, to return immediately to England. Despite its limited contribution to the exploration of the Arctic this expedition collected significant information on the position of the magnetic pole, arctic wildlife, and other scientific questions.

On his return to England, Parry was formally appointed hydrographer. In spite of his duties he made one last voyage into Arctic waters. Following a plan originally proposed by Captain John Franklin*, he set out aboard *Hecla* on 4 April 1827 in an attempt to reach the North Pole by crossing the ice north of Spitsbergen. In two boats, *Enterprise* and *Endeavour*, fitted to act as sledges on the ice floes, Parry and Lieutenant James Clark Ross*, each commanding a crew of 12 men and one junior officer, took leave of the *Hecla* at Walden Island, to the north of Spitsbergen, on 21 June. Instead of the relatively

unbroken plain of ice he had expected, Parry found himself navigating through a pack of constantly moving small floes and against a southward current which moved the ice four miles south daily, drastically limiting the advance of the party. On 26 July they calculated that they had managed to advance their position only one mile northward in the previous five days, and Parry was forced to turn back to the ship. Not having reached his goal, Parry none the less set a new mark for the farthest north attained, 82°45′, which was not surpassed until 1876 when a sledge party from the expedition under George Strong Nares* managed to reach 83°20′26″. With the men back on the *Hecla* on 21 August, the expedition set sail for Great Britain, arriving in the Orkney Islands at the end of September 1827.

Parry resumed his duties at the Hydrographic Department until 13 May 1829, when for reasons of health, finances, and career opportunities he resigned. Accepting the offer of the Australian Agricultural Company to administer their operations in New South Wales, Parry agreed to a four-year appointment and was granted leave of absence from the navy. Before leaving England he shared in two public honours with John Franklin: on 29 April both were knighted and, in a joint ceremony at the University of Oxford on 1 July, they each received an honorary DCL degree. Parry served as commissioner of the Australian Agricultural Company, managing the company's monopoly over a large tract of land, for the four-year term. Upon his return to England in November 1834 no suitable employment with the Admiralty was to be found for him and on 31 Jan. 1835 he applied for the position of assistant poor-law commissioner for the county of Norfolk, a position he held until failing health forced him to resign in February 1836.

At the end of 1836 Parry was appointed by the Admiralty to reorganize the Home Packet Service, which had been transferred from the Post Office Department to the Admiralty, and in three months he succeeded in putting the delivery of mail on a sound footing. When the Steam Department of the Admiralty was created in April 1837, Parry was placed in charge as controller of steam machinery. During his service in this department he was instrumental in the rapid conversion of the Royal Navy to steam and oversaw the introduction of the screw propeller over other forms of steam propulsion. His health, however, was not robust and in November 1846 he requested permission to take his retirement. Instead of accepting his retirement, the Admiralty offered him the post of captain superintendent of the Royal Clarence Victualling Yard and Haslar Hospital, at Gosport near Portsmouth, where he began his duties on 2 December.

At Haslar, one of the largest naval hospitals of its day, Parry had as senior physician and inspector another naval officer renowned for his activity in the Arctic, Sir John Richardson*. Among the reforms effected during Parry's superintendency were the organization of care for the insane in place of the previous custodial incarceration, an improvement in the standard of nursing, and numerous changes in medical practice.

On 4 June 1852 Parry was promoted rear-admiral and retired to Northbrook House, Bishop's Waltham, Hampshire. In January 1854, however, he was appointed lieutenant governor of the Greenwich Hospital. His already deteriorating health worsened later that year when he suffered an attack of Asiatic cholera. Never fully recovering, he left in May 1855 for treatment at the baths at Ems, near Koblenz (Federal Republic of Germany), where he died on 8 or 9 July. He was interred in the mausoleum of the Greenwich Hospital on 19 July.

An active member of the Church of England, Parry had been a vigorous opponent of the Tractarian movement and had supported missionary work through such organizations as the Society for Promoting Christianity among the Jews, the Church Missionary Society, the Naval and Military Bible Society, and the British and Foreign Bible Society. In all of his posts, both at sea and ashore, he had gained recognition for his lectures on theology.

As an explorer and navigator in the Arctic, Sir William Edward Parry ranks in importance with Captain James Cook* and Sir James Clark Ross. He was the first explorer to penetrate the Arctic archipelago and open the passage through Lancaster Sound, Barrow Strait, and Viscount Melville Sound that subsequent expeditions would follow. Furthermore, he was the first to winter in the high Arctic deliberately and, through his experience, he developed techniques necessary for survival in these difficult conditions. Although his participation in Arctic exploration ended in 1827, he maintained a lively interest in the Admiralty's projects in this region and late in 1848 he was called upon to advise the Admiralty, as a member of the Arctic Council, on the measures to be taken in search of Sir John Franklin's expedition, lost in the Arctic since 1845. Parry's contribution to the exploration of the Arctic is recognized in the number of geographical features that bear his name.

ROBERT E. JOHNSON

Sir William Edward Parry wrote numerous works on exploration in the Arctic. His *Journal of a voyage for the discovery of a north-west passage from the Atlantic to the Pacific; performed in the years 1819–20* . . . (London, 1821; 2nd ed., 2v., 1821–24; new. ed., 1v., New York, 1968) was also published in Philadelphia in 1821 (with, as supplement, the *North Georgia Gazette, and Winter Chronicle*) and in French as *Voyage fait en 1819 et 1820, sur les vaisseaux de S.M.B., l'"Hecla" et le "Griper," pour découvrir un passage du nord-ouest de l'océan Atlantique à la mer Pacifique* . . . , [A.-J.-B. Defauconpret, trad.] (Paris, 1822). Following the 1821–23 expedition, he wrote *Journal of a second voyage for the discovery of a north-west passage from the Atlantic to the Pacific; performed in the years 1821–22–23* . . . (London, 1824; repr., New York, 1968; another ed., New York, 1824); a supplement containing scientific observations appeared in London in 1825. He then published *Journal of a third voyage for the discovery of a north-west passage from the Atlantic to the Pacific; performed in the years 1824–25* . . . (London, 1826; another ed., Philadelphia, 1826) and *Narrative of an attempt to reach the North Pole, in boats fitted for the purpose, and attached to his majesty's ship "Hecla," in the year MDCCCXXVII* . . . (London, 1828). These accounts were republished in three collections: *Journals of the first, second and third voyages for the discovery of a north-west passage from the Atlantic to the Pacific, in 1819–20–21–22–23–24–25* . . . (5v., London, 1828); *Voyages for the discovery of a north-west passage, 1819–25; and narrative of an attempt to reach the North Pole, 1827* (8v., London, 1821–28); *Three voyages for the discovery of a north-west passage from the Atlantic to the Pacific, and narrative of an attempt to reach the North Pole* (2v., New York, 1842). He also wrote *Nautical astronomy by night; comprehending practical directions for knowing . . . the principal stars . . . in the northern hemisphere* . . . (Bath, Eng., 1816); *Thoughts on the parental character of God* (London, 1841; 5th ed., 1855; new. ed., 1878), published in German as *Der vatersinn Gottes* . . . (Berne, Switzerland, 1844); *A lecture on the character, condition, and responsibilities of British seamen* (London, 1855).

Evangeliche Pfarramt II (Westbezirk) Bad Ems (Federal Republic of Germany), Evangeliche Kirchengemeinde Bad Ems, Sterberegister, 8 July 1855. *Gentleman's Magazine*, July–December 1855: 200–2. John Ross, *A voyage of discovery, made under the orders of the Admiralty, in his majesty's ships "Isabella" and "Alexander," for the purpose of exploring Baffin's Bay, and enquiring into the probability of a north-west passage* (2nd ed., 2v., London, 1819). Boase, *Modern English biog.*, 2: 367–68. Cooke and Holland, *Exploration of northern Canada*. L. S. Dawson, *Memoirs of hydrography including brief biographies of the principal officers who have served in H.M. Naval Surveying Service between the years 1750 and 1885* (2v., Eastbourne, Eng., 1885; repr. in 1v., London, 1969), 1: 97–103. O'Byrne, *Naval biog. dict.* (1849), 865–66. John Barrow, *Voyages of discovery and research within the Arctic regions, from the year 1818 to the present time* . . . (London, 1846). R. E. Johnson, *Sir John Richardson: Arctic explorer, natural historian, naval surgeon* (London, 1976). Ann Parry, *Parry of the Arctic; the life story of Admiral Sir Edward Parry, 1790–1855* (London, 1963). Edward Parry, *Memoirs of Rear-Admiral Sir W. Edward Parry, Kt., F.R.S., etc. late lieut.-governor of Greenwich Hospital* (2nd ed., London, 1857). F. W. Beechey, "Address to the Royal Geographical Society of London; delivered at the anniversary meeting on the 26th May, 1856," Royal Geographical Soc., *Journal* (London), 26 (1856): clxxxii–clxxxv.

PATERSON, JOHN, businessman and politician; b. 19 April 1805 at Blantyre Works (Blantyre), near Glasgow, son of Peter Paterson and Jean Frazer; m. 28

July 1831 in Dundas, Upper Canada, Grace Lesslie, sister of James Lesslie*, and they had no children; d. 1856, probably in Dundas.

In 1819 John Paterson settled with his family in York (Toronto), Upper Canada, where two years later his father established a hardware trade. John and a brother, Peter*, were apparently employed in the business as early as 1823, but were not admitted to partnership until 1833. John had been granted a lot on the waterfront at Coote's Paradise (Dundas) in 1823 and within six years had opened a store there, probably as a branch of the family business. One of the hamlet's earliest industrialists, he began building a brewery in 1830; a year later he sold his store to Thomas Stinson. Paterson also operated a glue factory and in 1845 established the Dundas Woolen Factory in partnership with Walter Gorham, whom he bought out in December 1846. The following year Paterson hired an experienced miller, William Slingsby, to manage this factory, which was renamed the Elgin Woolen Mills.

As a member of the Gore District Agricultural Association, Paterson diligently promoted the development of a vigorous frontier economy at the head of Lake Ontario. At the same time he attempted to advance his own interests through newspaper advertisements which urged potential customers to patronize "Home Manufactures," since a Canadian producer could best understand the needs of the domestic market. Although the woollens produced by Paterson and other Canadians drew praise in 1851 at the Great Exhibition in London, England, the home market was not well developed. Despite weaknesses in demand and distribution (indicated by the firm's reliance on custom work, its barter of finished products for wool, and its sale of retail products directly from the factory), Elgin Mills doubled its raw wool requirements in the first year of production.

Paterson's other major business interest was the Desjardins Canal Company, of which he was an original promoter in 1826. The canal was designed to link Dundas to Burlington Bay (Hamilton Harbour) and thus enhance the village's commercial position. The death in 1827 of Peter Desjardins*, the company's chief organizer, resulted in the suspension of construction. When work resumed in 1830 progress was too slow for Dundas's boosters. In 1833 Paterson headed a petition which resulted in a provincial investigation into the affairs of the company and the conduct of its president, Allan Napier MacNab*. At issue was a £5,000 government loan arranged in 1832 for the completion of the canal. Having mortgaged a large block of his own property as security, MacNab applied the loan instead to reducing the company's indebtedness. Although this action was not illegal and the inquiry exonerated MacNab, Paterson replaced him as president in 1834 and saw the canal through to completion in 1837.

Financial problems continued to plague both the company and Paterson. The canal's original capitalization was low and, rather than increase it, Paterson and the directors preferred to borrow more funds from the government in the vain hope that it would take over the project as it had done in 1843 with the Welland Canal [see William Hamilton Merritt*]. By 1846 £42,000 had been borrowed and within a few years Paterson's presidency would end, as it began, in controversy. In 1847 he was elected president of Dundas's first town council and, as head of the canal company, he authorized the loan of £1,500 to his municipal office for the construction of a town hall and market. During this transaction £500 disappeared. In February 1849 the company's shareholders initiated legal proceedings against the directors and Paterson, whom they charged with appropriating funds without properly consulting them. The personal property he was forced to convey to the company in trust was eventually signed back to him but, although the dénouement of the case is obscure, he was not re-elected president of either the canal company or the town council, being succeeded in the latter by James Bell EWART in 1849. The records of Paterson's land holdings suggest that, by the time of his death, his affairs were in disarray. In 1855 he had entrusted property to his brothers, David and Peter, a tactic occasionally employed in business to prevent dissatisfied creditors from forcing liquidation.

During his years as a prominent businessman, Paterson took an active part in the social and political life of Dundas. In 1829 he was a member of a committee formed to organize the Dundas Union Sabbath School, a cooperative effort of a number of local Protestant churches, and in 1831 he served as secretary of the Dundas Free Church. For several years prior to his election to town council, Paterson was a central figure in Dundas's municipal growth. With others, he had sought unsuccessfully to have it established as a police village in 1836 but the renewal of efforts in 1845 led to its incorporation as a town two years later. Paterson also maintained an interest in provincial politics at the local level. In 1836, during the tumultuous constitutional crisis within the Upper Canadian government, he had chaired a public meeting in Dundas which adopted a resolution proclaiming the loyalty of local citizens to Great Britain and to the British connection [see Sir Francis Bond Head*]. He eventually became a supporter of Robert BALDWIN and in the late 1840s helped to organize the Wentworth County Reform Association.

DAVID G. BURLEY

AO, RG 1, C-I-3, 43, warrant 2660. GRO (Edinburgh), Blantyre, reg. of births and baptisms, 19 April 1805. PAC, RG 1, L3, 404a: P13/37; RG 5, A1: 96972–74. Wentworth Regional Assessment Office (Hamilton, Ont.), Dundas town

Pattee

assessment and collectors' rolls, 1854–57 (mfm. at AO, GS 1437). Can., Prov. of, Legislative Assembly, *App. to the journals*, 1841, app.RR. *Debates of the Legislative Assembly of United Canada* (Abbott Gibbs *et al.*), 4: 902, 1051; 5: 344, 1218–19, 1450. U.C., House of Assembly, *Journal*, 1833–34, app., "Report of committee on Desjardins Canal affairs," 110; "Memorial of the inhabitants of Dundas," 215. *Colonial Advocate*, 11 Aug. 1831. *Dundas Warder* (Dundas, [Ont.]), 5 June, 13 Nov. 1846; 2 July 1847; 7 April 1848; 2, 9 Feb., 21 Aug. 1849. *Dundas Weekly Post*, 19 Jan., 5 April 1836. *Western Mercury* (Hamilton), 27 Jan. 1831. Great Exhibition of the Works of Industry of All Nations, *Official descriptive and illustrated catalogue* (3v., London, 1851), 3: 957–58, 966. *The history of the town of Dundas*, comp. T. R. Woodhouse (3v., [Dundas], 1965–68). C. M. Johnston, *Head of the Lake* (1967), 123, 127, 131. *Ontarian Genealogist and Family Historian* (Toronto), 1 (1898–1901): 8.

PATTEE, DAVID, farmer, businessman, justice of the peace, judge, and politician; b. 30 July 1778 in Goffstown, N.H., son of John Pattee and Mary Hadley; m. *c.* 1803 Clarissa Thomas, and they had three sons and five daughters; d. 5 Feb. 1851 near Hawkesbury, Upper Canada.

David Pattee received some medical training as a youth but the loss of an eye apparently prevented him from practising. In 1803, on the advice of his father, he left New Hampshire to escape both indebtedness and prosecution for forgery. He was drawn to Upper Canada by the presence of a cousin, Moses Pattee, and the large community of other New Englanders and New Yorkers who had settled on and about the lands of Nathaniel Hazard TREDWELL on the lower Ottawa River. Arriving on 3 June 1803, Pattee turned to the major economic opportunities offered by the district, farming and lumbering. An ambitious young man, he cleared land for a farm near the head of the Long Sault Rapids and in 1805 entered into partnership with Thomas Mears, a fellow American and an experienced mill proprietor, to exploit the water-power there for the purpose of milling lumber. In July of that year, with a Montreal merchant, John Shuter, Mears secured from the Algonkin and Nipissing Indians a long-term lease of two islands which could provide anchors for dams. He and Pattee soon acquired a 1,000-acre tract in the adjacent township, constructed wooden dams with flumes, and built the first sawmill on the Upper Canadian side of the Ottawa River to produce deals for the British export market. It was around this mill that the town of Hawkesbury developed.

By 1809 Mears and Pattee had contracted with the Quebec City firm of George* and William Hamilton to supply oak and elm timber, including deals, in exchange for mercantile goods, to be sold at Hawkesbury, and a series of mortgages and advances to finance their operation. Failure to fulfil the contract and financial strain eventually forced Mears and Pattee to sign over the mill to the Hamiltons, who

appear to have taken possession by October 1811. The take-over ended suspiciously, however, for the mill and its stock burned on 20 April 1812. The Hamiltons quickly rebuilt the mill.

Pattee returned successfully to full-time farming. His prominence, combined with his close connection with Mears and other leading members of the American community, the fact that he had some education, his membership in the Church of England, and an interest in public affairs, ensured his acceptance into the élite which dominated the area. Thus, when the Ottawa District was formed in 1816, he became a justice of the peace and a judge of the district's Surrogate Court, positions which he held until 1849. Mears, who had continued in lumbering, was appointed sheriff.

Pattee's position as a district official brought him once more into another, unhappy confrontation with the Hamiltons. The flash-point was the provincial election of 1820 in Prescott and Russell, but the problem stemmed from the long-festering friction over economic and political control in the two counties. Because rebuilding the Hawkesbury mill had left the Hamiltons in a precarious financial position, they were particularly aggressive in their attempts to establish their hegemony in the lower Ottawa valley. A rugged entrepreneur and an inveterate tory who was prepared to use innuendo and bullying to get his way, George Hamilton in particular viewed members of the American community such as Pattee and Mears as potential business rivals and as propagators of seditious democratic ideals who had access to political control. Hamilton also feared that Pattee and other officials might expose the fact that he and his brother, in common with most other lumberers, were illegally cutting timber on crown lands. To the American community, George Hamilton appeared a petty tyrant and, in the opinion of one settler, was "the greatest Blackguard in the said District."

When the election of 1820 was called, the Hamiltons were ready to reduce the political power of the American community. Pattee, fully supported by Mears, was opposed as a candidate by William Hamilton; Joseph Fortune, an associate of George Hamilton in the militia, was appointed returning officer. The campaign was a heated affair and the weeks-long poll tumultuous and violent, each side charging the other with intimidating voters. Pattee espoused the necessity of the people keeping power in their hands while the Hamiltons supported the "Executive Gover^t of the Country." George Hamilton attempted to ensure his brother's election by recalling the 1803 charge against Pattee of "forging & uttering conterfeit Bank Notes." Despite this disclosure, Pattee still polled a majority of votes and only when Fortune illegally annulled a number of them did Hamilton secure election.

George Hamilton, knowing the impropriety of the situation and aware that a petition from Pattee to the House of Assembly was inevitable, moved immediately to make charges against the various officials who supported Pattee in an effort to secure their dismissal and preserve the election of his brother. Throughout the late summer and fall of 1820 Hamilton attempted to compile full cases, most of a petty nature, against the officials. Attorney General John Beverley Robinson* reported in October that the charges, save that against Pattee, had little substance. Pattee, recognizing the seriousness of the charge against him, wrote early in the new year to the provincial civil secretary in his own defence. Maintaining that he had been falsely accused in 1803 by an admitted felon turned state's evidence, he claimed that officials in New Hampshire had refused him immunity to return to clear his name. In the intervening years he had sorted out his affairs and paid all his debts. Further, he offered to relinquish his offices if the lieutenant governor wished him to do so, but prayed that he not "gratify, the Spirit of Revenge and persecution" which, Pattee believed, lay behind the acts of George Hamilton.

Although Hamilton had dispatched an agent to New Hampshire to seek out the court records condemning Pattee, the assembly on 24 March overturned the election and gave the seat to Pattee. This victory was followed on 16 May by the Executive Council's decision that all the papers forwarded by Hamilton concerning Pattee's case did not contain "such Proof of Guilt of the Charge of forgery as to weigh against or outweigh eighteen years of irreproachable Conduct in this Province as certified by so many respectable Inhabitants." The council further recommended that Pattee retain his public offices since citizens of the district had indicated that he had more than satisfactorily filled them.

Politically, John Beverley Robinson loathed Pattee who, he stated in 1821, formed the "scum," along with Barnabas Bidwell* and Robert Randal*, which represented the "rascals of the Province." Pattee completed his term in parliament but did not seek re-election in 1824. His only other venture into provincial life took place in 1834 when, as a reformer, he sought election for Prescott but placed behind Charles Waters, another reformer, and Alexander Greenfield Macdonell*, a tory. Having reconciled his differences with the Hamiltons, Pattee remained a respected citizen of the Hawkesbury area, where he continued to farm until his death at his residence in 1851.

ROBERT PETER GILLIS

AO, MS 78, J. B. Robinson to John Macaulay, 18 Nov. 1821; MU 1129, Pattee family genealogy; RG 1, C-I-1, petition of David Pattee, 20 Feb. 1826; C-IV, West Hawkesbury Township, concession 2, lot 8, petition of David Pattee, 4 Jan. 1832. PAC, RG 1, E3, 61: 49–53; L3, 234: H17/53; 239: H20/30; 404a: P13/39; RG 5, A1: 23703–6, 23925–28, 24277–84, 24370–73, 24490–93, 25055–88, 25157–58c, 25163–65, 25177–79, 25182, 25373–85. Prescott Land Registry Office (L'Orignal, Ont.), Abstract index to deeds, West Hawkesbury Township (mfm. at AO, GS 5092–93). Armstrong, *Handbook of Upper Canadian chronology.* Lucien Brault, *Histoire des comtés unis de Prescott et Russell* (L'Orignal, 1965). S. J. Gillis, *The timber trade in the Ottawa valley, 1806–54* (Can., National Hist. Parks and Sites Branch, *Manuscript report,* no.153, Ottawa, 1975). M. A. Higginson and Mrs J. T. Brock, *The village of Hawkesbury, 1808–1888: the era of "Hamilton Brothers"* (Hawkesbury, Ont., 1961). Cyrus Thomas, *History of the counties of Argenteuil, Que., and Prescott, Ont., from the earliest settlement to the present* (Montreal, 1896; repr. Belleville, Ont., 1981).

PATTERSON, PETER, businessman, justice of the peace, and seigneur; b. 11 May 1768 in Bagdale (Whitby), England, son of Peter Patterson, labourer, and Mary ——; d. 12 June 1851 in his residence at Chute Montmorency, near Quebec.

Having grown up in or around Whitby on the Yorkshire coast, Peter Patterson conceivably found employment and acquired experience in the Baltic wood trade conducted at that port. In 1801 he arrived at Quebec, probably in the company of Henry Usborne*, a British merchant established in the Baltic trade, who came to initiate the timber business on a large scale between the St Lawrence River and Great Britain. By 1805 Patterson was employed in Usborne's Quebec branch.

Patterson is said to have had some experience in shipbuilding, and as part of his duties in 1805 he surveyed the construction of a ship at Quebec for Usborne. During its early years the Usborne firm carried on a business in masts, spars, bowsprits, pine and oak square timber, planks, and staves from the St Lawrence River and Lake Champlain areas. When Usborne returned to England in 1809 to direct the London end of affairs, Patterson took over the Quebec firm. Usborne remained in the Quebec partnership, and, with the addition of James Dyke of Quebec and Richard Collins of Montreal, the business was conducted at Wolfe's Cove (Anse au Foulon), at first under the name of Patterson, Dyke and Company, and by 1815 as Peter Patterson and Company. The firm served as agent and factor for the London partnership, managing the purchase, assemblage, and loading of cargoes.

For British North America and the port of Quebec these were years of rapid expansion in the timber trade to the mother country. A disruption in Baltic supplies, which Usborne had anticipated when he established the Quebec branch, came with the brief success of Napoleon's continental blockade in 1808–9; Baltic pine imports by Britain had plummeted from 213,637 loads in 1807 to 26,764 in 1808. The North American

Patterson

colonies picked up some of the slack in the supply of this commodity, crucial to the Royal Navy's war effort. In 1807–8 their exports more than doubled to 60,467 loads, and subsequent adjustments in British tariff policy, designed to encourage the colonial supply further, pushed exports to 171,796 loads by 1812. Following a disruption of transatlantic traffic during the War of 1812, colonial exports again increased, reaching 267,065 loads of pine alone by 1819. A trade virtually non-existent at the beginning of the century had taken root at Quebec and Saint John, N.B., as well as in the Miramichi region, and had grown to become the commercial mainstay of the colonial economy. Although at the outset the St Lawrence region was a secondary source of timber after New Brunswick, the growth of the trade conducted through the port of Quebec was rapid. In 1820 Usborne affirmed that since 1801 the number of ships engaged in the timber trade from Lower Canada had climbed from 80 to 800. The principal exports at the time were pine and oak square timber, pine and spruce deals (planks 12 feet in length, over 12 inches wide, and usually 3 inches thick), and staves, together with masts, spars, and other naval timbers.

Patterson and Usborne initially dealt in square timber, but they quickly turned to deals. In 1811 they acquired property around the Chute Montmorency, and by 1818 Peter Patterson and Company had completed construction there of one of the largest sawmill operations for the time in North America. To supply the mills, it purchased timber along the St Lawrence and in the Lake Champlain area, but apparently conducted some lumbering on its own in the Saint-Maurice valley as early as 1819. The firm also acquired undeveloped land about the province, presumably for timber.

Patterson's association with Usborne served him well. Not only did he become firmly established in the timber trade at Quebec, but he developed interests in shipbuilding, and efforts to rationalize round-trip charters drew him into the import trade and passenger service. In Quebec's commercial community, he became a well-known and respected figure. From 1813, with John Mure* and James Henderson, he served as attorney for a London firm of timber merchants, Linthorne and Jolliffe, and from 1815 he acted in the same capacity during the liquidation of the firm's holdings. In May 1819 he was nominated to the newly formed board of cullers along with William Bacheler Coltman* and five others. The board was established by the Lower Canadian House of Assembly to ensure the quality and fair measurement of timber and wood products at Quebec, and to examine and license cullers, who carried out measurements. Patterson appears also to have served briefly as justice of the peace from 1821.

In 1823 the partnership between Usborne and Patterson was dissolved. Patterson took over the firm's office at Quebec as well as the remainder of a nine-year lease on the "Domaine of Sillery" obtained from the colonial government in 1820 by George William Usborne, a relative of Henry. The property included a sizeable stretch of beach to the west of Quebec, of particular value for the reception, measuring, and loading of timber for export. From 1823 Patterson sublet coves along this beach to other merchants, among them George Longley* and John Richardson*. Patterson continued his specialization, developed during his partnership with Usborne, in the production and sale, either at Quebec or in Great Britain, of deals and boards. Among his accounts at Quebec were shipbuilders, timber merchants, and a cabinet-maker.

The centre of Patterson's business activity and his principal residence, even while he was in partnership with Usborne, were at Montmorency, where he operated the sawmills at the foot of the falls and occupied Haldimand House, the former residence of Governor Sir Frederick Haldimand*, above them. Equipped with a blacksmith's and a carpenter's shop, carts, scows, fire-engines, booms, and other equipment, the installation, together with the residence and land along the Rivière Montmorency upstream from the falls, would be valued at about £46,000 in 1852. Montmorency was not, however, the only site which Patterson exploited. Without reducing his operations there, in February 1842 he began leasing from the Dénéchaud family a sawmill on the Rivière Bécancour formerly operated by Claude Dénéchaud*. The lease was for five years at an annual rent of £120. From at least the early 1830s a large proportion of the saw logs for Patterson's operations had been coming from the area drained by the Bécancour; in renting the Dénéchaud mills, he felt he would benefit from manufacturing deals and boards closer to the source of the raw material, on a site where water power for the operation of a mill was readily available. The agreement was cancelled in November 1846 at the request of the Dénéchaud family. Three years later Patterson purchased from George William Usborne for £500 the lease (running until October 1852) on government-owned mills at the mouth of the Rivière Etchemin near Quebec. Built by Henry Caldwell* early in the century and later exploited by his son Sir John*, the Etchemin Mills were, with those operated by Patterson at Montmorency, among the largest in the colony and cost £585 a year in rent.

Patterson obtained the timber for his sawmills through various arrangements, including the acquisition of crown timber limits, the subleasing of limits held by others, the purchase of cutting rights on privately owned tracts, and the buying of extensive wooded lands. The acquisitions of land were probably also made as investments in their own right for speculative purposes. He made large purchases in Nelson, Somerset, and Stanfold townships during the 1830s, and in 1838 he was listed by Charles Buller*, secretary to Lord Durham [Lambton*], as one of the province's 105 principal owners of non-seigneurial lands; his holdings at that time totalled some 22,000 acres. During the 1830s and 1840s he acquired nearly 40,000 acres for his timber operations in the Eastern Townships and Bois-Francs and in Caxton and Somerset townships. He also greatly increased his holdings around Montmorency; on 27 May 1844 he purchased the seigneury of Beauport at auction for £8,300, and by 1851, through direct purchases, exchanges of property, and sheriff's sales, he also had acquired virtually all of the land along both banks of the Rivière Montmorency for a distance of about three miles upstream from the falls.

Most of Patterson's saw logs came from the Bois-Francs and Eastern Townships, particularly from shanties in Blandford, Bulstrode, Ireland, Maddington, Somerset, Stanfold, and Wolfestown townships, but he also contracted for logs from the Rivière de l'Achigan above L'Assomption, and by 1851 he was investing considerable capital in saw log production on the Ottawa River. That year he contracted with Ruggles Wright Jr and Joshua R. Wright for them to get out the timber on limits along the Rivière Gatineau, and he advanced them £4,679 on their production for 1852, slightly more than half the capital he advanced to all contractors for that year. Patterson's arrangement with the Wrights was typical of his and his competitors' business relationships with their suppliers. After having acquired a timber site or cutting rights, he contracted with a lumberer, usually a farmer residing near the site, to cut the desired quantity and category of timber. In this manner most of his raw material was ensured by contract in the fall for delivery at his mills the following summer. Throughout the winter Patterson provided specified periodical advances amounting to about two-thirds of the value of the contract, the balance to be settled after the last delivery. As a guarantee for the advances the terms of the contract gave Patterson ownership of the logs as soon as they arrived at the river nearest the site, but saddled the contractor with all risks encountered in the transport and classification of the timber until the logs arrived at the mills. In addition Patterson assumed costs involved in hauling and rafting, as well as boom and culling fees and other expenses for which the contractor was at least in part responsible. On occasion, at the closing of accounts, the producer found himself indebted to Patterson and obliged to mortgage his properties to him, be they residences or timber tracts.

Patterson sometimes would purchase logs on hand. In July 1837, for instance, he bought for £750 "all the saw logs on the Ottawa River near Hawkesbury [Ont.]

that may have gone adrift" from the booms at the mills operated by George Hamilton* and Charles Adamson Low. In the agreement of sale it was estimated that there were 18,000 logs strewn along the banks of the Ottawa, and, despite the cost involved in reclaiming and transporting them to Quebec, Patterson paid considerably less for this timber than if he had contracted to have it cut.

The real estate transactions completed by Patterson in 1843 and 1844 and his ability to make substantial advances to his suppliers indicate the measure of his success and a significant accumulation of capital. As a rule Patterson did not invest in private loans or mortgages, a form of investment generally favoured by the commercial class of the colony, but he appears to have made exceptions for close business acquaintances in need. In 1846 he lent £1,400 to William Price*, a Quebec timber merchant in financial difficulty. Patterson took a mortgage on the greater part of Price's ship the *Liverpool*. A much greater sum was advanced to Patterson's close friend George Pemberton, a well-established timber merchant at Quebec and a partner in the firm of Pemberton Brothers. In 1847 Pemberton Brothers were caught, as were other important Quebec commercial houses, by the excessively poor market for wood in Britain and were obliged to take a loan of £5,000 from Patterson on the Quebec-built ship the *Maple Leaf*. Despite business relations and a friendship with the Pembertons going back at least to the 1820s, Patterson became so alarmed by the firm's weakness that in December 1847 he gave power of attorney to Rankin, Gilmour and Company of Liverpool, England, to dispose of the vessel.

Successful in the timber trade and secure in his land investments, Patterson did not diversify his business activity much beyond these interests. Only towards the end of his life did he venture into other enterprises. With a group of investors that included Henry LeMesurier*, Patterson formed the Quebec and Lake Superior Mining Association in October 1846. He served as founding president of the company, and in 1848 held 6,100 of the 44,000 shares. He would also appear to have been the guiding spirit behind the formation of the Quebec and Richmond Railroad Company, sometimes called the Quebec and Melbourne Railway, in 1850. As its president, Patterson was joined on the board of directors by an impressive group of Quebec capitalists and political figures, including Louis-Joseph Massue*, Pierre-Joseph-Olivier Chauveau*, James Bell Forsyth*, and LeMesurier. To link Quebec with the St Lawrence and Atlantic Rail-road near Richmond, on the Rivière Saint-François, the railway was to pass through the townships in which Patterson held much of his property. However, construction did not get under way until January 1852, seven months after his death.

Peltier

As well, Patterson was a member of the Quebec Provident and Savings Bank in 1847. Interested in the affairs of the Church of England at Quebec, he was among a group of influential citizens who in 1843 had sought incorporation of the Church Society for the diocese of Quebec, an association formed, in part, to provide financial support for clergy and their families in the diocese.

Patterson seems never to have married, but he had a daughter, Mary Jane, who became the wife of George Benson Hall* in 1843. He took his son-in-law into the business at Montmorency, and they shared other business interests, such as the Quebec and Lake Superior Mining Association. The two appear to have had a disagreement, however, and in May 1851 Patterson excluded Hall from the firm. He granted Hall an annuity of £100 for the support of Mary Jane and the children on condition that Hall move to Upper Canada. These instructions were not acted upon before Patterson's death one month later, and Hall remained at Quebec where he took over the family business. Patterson's will, however, gave virtually all his property and wealth to his daughter, and after her death to her children. Although Hall operated the business, and the installation at Montmorency came to be called the Hall Mills, they were in fact owned by his wife.

The estate Patterson left was valued, after claims, at about £75,000. Nearly £65,000 before claims was in landed property, including Montmorency (valued at almost £45,000), Beauport, the banal mill, and wilderness lands, almost entirely in Lower Canada. A comparatively small amount was invested in stocks, including telegraph company shares in Montreal, Bytown (Ottawa), and Halifax, gas company shares, and the initial payment on stock in the Quebec and Richmond Rail-road. The balance of the estate was tied up directly in Patterson's timber business. The bills payable were almost exclusively related to the timber trade and included salaries and balances on accounts with timber merchants. The sum of £500 was credited to Judge Henry Black* by the terms of Patterson's will "in grateful recollection of the many friendly and professional services he has rendered me during our long intimacy."

Both the short obituary in the *Quebec Morning Chronicle* and the engraving on the impressive monument erected on the Patterson family plot in Mount Hermon Cemetery, Sillery, underline Peter Patterson's long and successful career in Quebec's business community, and although his will contained no provision for charitable bequests, he was remembered for his benevolence, especially towards "the poor in his immediate neighbourhood."

JOHN KEYES

ANQ-Q, 30076; CE1-61, 16 juin 1851; CN1-49, 25 juin 1814–7 mai 1852; CN1-67, 9 mai 1848–16 avril 1849; CN1-230, 15 août 1817; E21/35; T11-1, 4290, 4311, 4313, 4315. Arch. judiciaires, Québec, Testament olographe de Peter Patterson, 17 juin 1851 (*see* P.-G. Roy, *Inv. testaments*, 3: 110). Mount Hermon Cemetery (Sillery, Que.), Reg. of internments, F52, lot 144. North Yorkshire Record Office (Northallerton, Eng.), Whitby, Reg. of baptisms, 6 June 1768. PAC, RG 4, A1, 220, 5 May 1823; RG 68, General index, 1651–1841: 66; 1841–67: 353. L.C., *Statutes*, 1843, c.68; 1847, c.69; 1850, c.116. *Morning Chronicle* (Quebec), 27 May 1847: 13, 16, 18 June 1851. *Quebec Gazette*, 30 April 1812; 13, 20 May, 16 July 1813; 28 Sept., 5 Oct. 1815; 15 May, 18 Sept. 1817; 12 March, 21 Sept. 1818; 22 April 1819; 5, 30 July, 26 Nov. 1821; 12 May, 7 July 1823. *Quebec Mercury*, 13 June 1851. [J.-C. Langelier], *Liste des terrains concédés par la couronne dans la province de Québec de 1763 au 31 décembre 1890* (Québec, 1891), 14–16, 64, 82, 603, 609–11. *Quebec directory*, 1822, 1826, 1844–45, 1847–48, 1848–49, 1850. John Keyes, "La famille Dunn et le commerce du bois à Québec, 1850–1914" (thèse de PHD en cours, univ. Laval, Québec). D. T. Ruddel, "Quebec City, 1765–1831: the evolution of a colonial town" (D. ès L. thesis, univ. Laval, 1981). G. R. Stevens, *Canadian National Railways* (2v., Toronto and Vancouver, 1960–62), 1. *The storied province of Quebec; past and present*, ed. William Wood *et al.* (5v., Toronto, 1931–32), 4.

PELTIER (Pelletier), ORPHIR (baptized **Jean-Baptiste-Eustache-Orphire**), poet, composer, lawyer, and organist; b. 1 Sept. 1825 in Sainte-Geneviève (Sainte-Geneviève and Pierrefonds), Lower Canada, son of Jean-Baptiste-Généreux Peltier, a notary, and Marie-Scholastique Masson, sister of businessman Marc-Damase Masson*; d. 26 May 1854 in Montreal.

Orphir Peltier, the eldest of four surviving children in a family of 22, received his classical education at the Petit Séminaire de Montréal from 1834 to 1844. He then undertook legal training and was called to the Bar of Lower Canada on 6 May 1850. He practised in Montreal, but since he was in poor health and had been disabled as a result of an operation in early childhood, he turned particularly to literature and music. He had studied harmony and the organ; his nephew Romain Pelletier claimed that he was "the first Canadian to study harmony," but did not name his teachers. For an undetermined period Orphir held the post of organist at St Patrick's Church in Montreal. He is thought to have introduced the principles of harmony to his young brother Romain-Octave, who, preferring music to his profession of notary, was organist at the cathedral of Saint-Jacques for many years. Romain Pelletier further describes his uncle as "a kind of universal genius: a lawyer, physicist, poet, painter, and musician." He also states that he probably painted the picture *La mort de Saint Joseph*, which hangs above the right side-altar in St Patrick's Church. He makes no mention of his work as a physicist.

It is difficult even to speculate about the extent of Peltier's poetic work, for only a few of his poems have been published. "Sans son Dieu sur la terre, il n'est point de bonheur," written in 1842, appeared in the second volume of James HUSTON's *Répertoire national*, with a portrait of the poet. The poem is in nine quatrains. Another poem, "La vertu," signed O. P., was printed in the March 1846 issue of *L'Album littéraire et musical de la Revue canadienne*. A long allegorical poem, "Travail et paresse," was published in *La Ruche littéraire* of December 1853. Although Peltier handled the alexandrine with a certain dexterity, his poetry was somewhat ponderous and not very original in its inspiration.

As a composer, Peltier left only one piece, for four mixed voices with organ accompaniment, "O salutaris hostia!" This brief composition of 16 bars was published in *L'Album littéraire et musical de la Revue canadienne* in February 1846. Instead of naming his voices soprano, alto, tenor, and bass, Peltier used the old French designations of *dessus* (treble), *haute-contre* (counter-tenor), *taille* (tenor), and *basse-taille* (low tenor), rarely employed in Europe after the 17th century. A work of very conventional construction, it is rather like a music student's effort. Yet the summary in *L'Album* notes: "We thank M. Peltier of this city for his piece of sacred music. Such a composition is something new in the land. Honour to the young artist!"

Orphir Peltier died prematurely on 26 May 1854 in Montreal from the effects of his childhood operation. He was 28 years old. The foreword of *La littérature canadienne de 1850 à 1860*, the second volume of which came out in 1864 and included his poem "Travail et paresse," notes: "Another young poet, M. Orphir Peltier, has died, his classical studies but lately concluded. Although the sample verse of his that we give is far from perfect, it does however reveal a poetic talent that age and study would have developed."

GILLES POTVIN

Orphir Peltier is the author of a number of poems, some of which have been published in books and newspapers. They include "Sans son Dieu sur la terre, il n'est point de bonheur," written in 1842 and included in *Le répertoire national* (Huston; 1848–50), 2: 232–33, and (1893), 2: 260–61; "La vertu," published in *L'Album littéraire et musical de la Rev. canadienne* (Montréal), March 1846; and "Travail et paresse," published in *La Ruche littéraire* (Montréal), December 1853, and reprinted in *La littérature canadienne de 1850 à 1860* (2v., Québec, 1863–64), 2: 272–80. Peltier also composed a piece of sacred music, "O salutaris hostia!," published in *L'Album littéraire et musical*

de la Rev. canadienne, February 1846. His nephew Romain Pelletier attributes to him "La mort de saint Joseph," a painting hanging above the right side altar of St Patrick's Church, Montreal.

ANQ-M, CE1-28, 1er sept. 1825; CE1-51, 29 mai 1854. PAC, MG 30, D1, 24: 412–14. *Encyclopedia of music in Canada* (Kallmann *et al.*). Le Jeune, *Dictionnaire*, 1: 420. Morgan, *Bibliotheca Canadensis*, 305. Edmond Lareau, *Mélanges historiques et littéraires* (Montréal, 1877), 13–15. Maurault, *Le collège de Montréal* (Dansereau; 1967). Maréchal Nantel, "Les avocats admis au Barreau de 1849 à 1868," *BRH*, 42 (1936): 686. Romain Pelletier, "Octave Pelletier, organiste et pédagogue (1843–1927)," *Qui?* (Montréal), 4 (1952–53): 3–24.

PELTIER (Pelletier), TOUSSAINT, militia officer, lawyer, Patriote, and office holder; b. 7 Nov. 1792 in Montreal, son of Toussaint Peltier, a merchant, and Élisabeth Lacoste; m. there 11 July 1820 Émilie Hérigault (d. 1840), and they had several children of whom at least two attained adulthood; d. there 20 Aug. 1854.

Toussaint Peltier's forebear Guillaume Peltier immigrated to New France around the middle of the 17th century. A member of the seventh generation of the family, Toussaint was the eldest of three children whose father, a native of Kamouraska, had been married in Montreal in 1791. Toussaint studied at the Collège Saint-Raphaël from 1802 to 1806, and at the Petit Séminaire de Montréal from 1806 to 1811. He then began his legal training under a brother of Pierre-Stanislas Bédard*, Joseph, who was considered one of the foremost lawyers of his time. During the War of 1812 Peltier served as a lieutenant in Montreal's 2nd Militia Battalion, which was commanded by Lieutenant-Colonel Jacques Hervieux and had Louis-Joseph Papineau* as one of its captains.

Peltier was called to the bar on 23 Aug. 1816 and wasted no time in establishing his reputation. His extensive legal knowledge enabled him to acquire a large and varied practice which he kept all his life; his clients included the majority of Montreal's civil and religious institutions. Gradually he was entrusted with some of the most important contentious cases. In 1833 he took Joseph Bourret, who was ten years his junior and later became mayor of Montreal, into partnership. He had several students articling with him. One was Charles-Ovide Perrault*, who subsequently represented Vaudreuil in the House of Assembly and who was to die of wounds suffered at Saint-Denis on the Richelieu in November 1837. Another was Melchior-Alphonse de Salaberry*, son of Charles-Michel d'Irumberry* de Salaberry, hero of the battle of Châteauguay. By the time the rebellion broke out, Peltier had become one of the most prominent lawyers in Montreal.

Peltier took an active part in the events of 1837, but

Perry

adhered to constitutional means in endeavouring to ensure the success of the Patriote cause. He firmly supported the boycott of British products advocated by Papineau, and when he chaired several public meetings he wore rough, homespun clothes, as did Édouard-Étienne Rodier*, a lawyer who was the member for L'Assomption. With another lawyer, Côme-Séraphin Cherrier*, he attended the meeting in May at Saint-Laurent, on Montreal Island, and the one in August at Saint-Constant, near La Prairie. He was imprisoned for high treason on 1 December. William Walker* fought a hard legal battle to have him either brought to trial or released by habeas corpus. Peltier spent more than eight months in prison, almost died there, and was freed only on £1,000 bail, on 8 July 1838.

After the rebellion Peltier resumed practising law. On 2 Oct. 1844 he was appointed legal counsel to the city of Montreal, a post he retained until 1851. On 14 May of that year the municipal council, under pressure from its English-speaking members, named as his assistant Robert Abraham, a former militant journalist who had been called to the bar two years earlier. Deeply offended at having such a person associated with him, Peltier declared that he was humiliated by the council's action in making this move behind his back, and tendered his resignation to John Ponsonby Sexton*, the city clerk, on 4 June. Shortly after, the council, on the initiative of alderman Édouard-Raymond FABRE, appointed as his successor Joseph-Féréol Peltier, his nephew and son-in-law, who had been called to the bar in 1834. Toussaint Peltier pronounced himself satisfied.

Throughout his career as a lawyer, Peltier's exceptional qualities were recognized by the public, and the authorities several times bestowed on him the honours he deserved. He was offered a QC and a judgeship. He refused the first, and in 1849, with Cherrier, declined the second. On each occasion he displayed his independence of character, perhaps out of resentment for the incarceration he had suffered in 1837–38 at the hands of the government. When the Bar of Lower Canada was incorporated in 1849 Peltier had the honour of being chosen unanimously by his colleagues as the first bâtonnier (president) of the district of Montreal. He was re-elected to this office in 1850 and 1851, and sat on the bar council in 1852 and 1853; he had agreed in 1852 to sit on the board of the Montreal bar that examined candidates for the profession. In addition, from 1852 to 1854 he was a member of the Association Saint-Jean-Baptiste de Montréal.

During the night of 17–18 Aug. 1854, Peltier was paralysed by a stroke and died two days later at his home on Rue Craig (Saint-Antoine). He was deeply mourned by his sister Henriette (the wife of Alexis Bourret), his daughter Émilie (the wife of Joseph-Féréol Peltier), and his son Hector*. His colleagues attended the funeral as a group and, in accordance with the custom of the day, wore mourning for a month.

JEAN-JACQUES LEFEBVRE

A portrait of Toussaint Peltier hangs in the galerie des bâtonniers in the Montreal court-house. Restored in the 1930s, probably from a daguerreotype, this polished representation of him delineates very clear features and seems too idealized.

ANQ-M, CE1-51, 7 nov. 1792, 11 juill. 1820, 22 août 1854; CN1-194, 8 août 1811. ANQ-Q, E17/6, no.32; E17/7, no.85; E17/15, nos.902–20; E17/38, nos.3074–75. PAC, MG 30, D1, 24: 415–17; RG 4, B8, 19: 6873–946. Can., Prov. of, Statutes, 1849, c.46. La Minerve, 22 août 1854. L.-O. David, Biographies et portraits (Montréal, 1876), 215. Fauteux, Patriotes, 348. Montreal directory, 1842–54. Officers of British forces in Canada (Irving), 166–67. Tanguay, Dictionnaire, 1: 469. Pierre Beullac et Édouard Fabre Surveyer, Le centenaire du barreau de Montréal, 1849–1949 (Montréal, 1949), 21–28. Buchanan, Bench and bar of L.C., 88. David, Les gerbes canadiennes, 176–77. Maurault, Le collège de Montréal (Dansereau; 1967). F.-J. Audet, "1842," Cahiers des Dix, 7 (1942): 237; "Le Barreau et la révolte de 1837," RSC Trans., 3rd ser., 31 (1937), sect.I: 85–96. Guillaume Saint-Pierre, "Les avocats de la cité," La Rev. du Barreau, 4 (1944): 348–49.

PERRY, PETER, politician and businessman; b. 14 Nov. 1792 in Ernestown (Bath), Upper Canada, youngest child of Robert Perry and Jemima Gary Washburn; m. 19 June 1814 Mary Polly Ham, and they had seven daughters and two sons; d. 24 Aug. 1851 in Saratoga Springs, N.Y., and was buried near Oshawa, Upper Canada.

The Perry family's North American history was begun by Anthony Perry, who immigrated from England to Massachusetts in 1640. Peter Perry's father, a loyalist who had moved to Vermont in 1772, served during the American revolution in the Queen's Loyal Rangers and in Jessup's Rangers [see Edward Jessup*], and subsequently came to Township No.2 (Ernestown). Raised on his father's farm there, Peter married a daughter of another loyalist, John Ham, and settled near by in Fredericksburg (North and South Fredericksburg) Township.

Public involvement was not new to the Perry family; Peter's uncle Ebenezer Washburn* had been an outspoken member of the House of Assembly. Peter Perry first appeared in the public life of Upper Canada in January 1819. He was one of nearly 200 men of Ernestown Township who signed an address to Lieutenant Governor Sir Peregrine MAITLAND disavowing the activities of Robert Gourlay* and repudiating the criticism of government he had aroused, especially among recent American immigrants. That address was consistent with the loyalist political tradition which Perry had inherited and which he maintained throughout the most important years of his career. He accepted the land grants due to him as a reward for his father's decision to remain loyal and he often cited that decision as proof of his own adherence to the British constitution and the imperial connection.

But he had inherited more than loyalty. He was a North American whose family connection with the New World stretched back six generations. The appeal of the crown and the constitution were not, for him, based in any way upon the sentimental nostalgia of the newly arrived Briton. Nor was that appeal part of a tory political ideology. He was an egalitarian democrat for whom the rights and interests of the people of Upper Canada were the primary reality. He had no fear of American influence and, while he was prepared to defend the constitution against the "prejudices" of American-born settlers, he did not believe that they should be penalized for uttering them. Thus it was his interest in the alien question [see Sir Peregrine Maitland] that brought him into politics.

In 1823 Perry took the lead in protesting the exclusion of Marshall Spring Bidwell* from the ballot in a by-election in Lennox and Addington. On election day, it was later reported in the *Kingston Chronicle*, Perry spoke to a crowd "from an upper window," arguing ineffectively that the proceedings were illegal and that British subjects had been deprived of their rights. None the less, in the general election of the following year Perry, a reformer, joined Bidwell as a candidate for the county. The two men, each with American antecedents, led the polls and in January 1825 took their seats in the house. Their political partnership – an association of complementary qualities – lasted until they were both defeated 11 years later; their friendship persisted until Perry's death.

As a result of the election, the colonial assembly was divided between a small reform majority and a minority of conservatives led with consummate ability by Attorney General John Beverley Robinson*. The late 1820s were among the best years for the incipient reform party as its optimistic and enthusiastic members threw themselves into the task of reorganizing colonial society. In the attempt, they developed an *esprit de corps* that led them to affirm each legislative success in the house by discarding decorum, standing, waving their hats, and cheering tumultuously.

Perry fitted well into those parliamentary sessions. He was a man with little formal education, whose speeches contained no biblical quotations or classical allusions. Blunt, occasionally emotional, and often enlivened with imaginative, if homely, references to the common experiences of the inhabitants of Upper Canada, his speeches reveal him as an aggressive, sometimes overbearing man whose emphatic sincerity about the purity of his own motives reflects a certain self-righteousness. He conceived of himself as the spokesman of the common people and the defender of their rights. They were, he said, as talented and capable as any people anywhere and needed only "to have their paps brought out by education" in order to prove it.

When he spoke about Upper Canada, Perry had in mind primarily a society of small agricultural and, latterly, industrial producers. The people, with the farmers the most important group among them, were, he thought, the source of all political sovereignty. To express and protect their rights and interests, Upper Canadian society should, he believed, be democratic and egalitarian. He opposed, therefore, élites of all kinds and considered that the colonial government ought actively to discourage them. During the mid 1830s, for example, he spoke out against the "great power" enjoyed by the Bank of Upper Canada [see William ALLAN] and believed that bank directors in general should be required to guarantee deposits with their personal assets. When the first railways in Upper Canada were chartered in 1836 he tried to have their charters amended to allow the government to purchase them after 50 years. As well, he favoured local control over local affairs. He supported a decentralized political system with township officials elected by secret ballot. At a higher level he was willing to assert the economic and political interests of the colony over those of both Britain and the United States.

Perry's involvement in the business of the assembly after 1824 established him as an unimpeachable reformer. He moved or seconded the resolutions and voted for the bills – passed repeatedly by the house but rejected by the Legislative Council – that collectively defined the party's identity. On the alien question, he was consistently in favour of removing all restrictions on the civil status of American settlers and, indeed, wanted the colonial government to encourage additional immigration from the United States. He voted to abolish primogeniture in cases of persons dying intestate, for the abolition of imprisonment for debt, for the provision of counsel for accused felons, and for the repeal of the Sedition Act of 1804. Perry wanted to erase doubt about the independence of the judiciary by removing the colony's chief justice from the Executive Council. He was one of the minority in the house who, in the interest of taxpaying farmers, tried unsuccessfully to block government loans to the Welland Canal Company. He supported resolutions, again without success, by which control over colonial trade with the United States would be transferred from London to York (Toronto) and a protective duty on American livestock imports would be established.

Of all the issues that came before the assembly, the ones that most engaged Perry's attention were those complex questions involving the relationship of church and state. Although his family were Methodists and he had been married by a Presbyterian clergyman, Robert McDowall*, Perry had no denominational affiliation. He believed in what he called "pure and undefiled religion," simple and basic Christianity which, ideally, would be taught by enthusiastic clergy, financially dependent upon their congregations and intent only upon the salvation of souls. It was the ecclesiastical counterpart of the egalitarian community he favoured.

What he found in Upper Canada was quite different. The establishment there of the Church of England implied a society in which religious and social inequality was guaranteed by law. Anglicans constituted an élite and from his first days in the legislature Perry set about the work of levelling their pretensions. He voted consistently for the secularization of the clergy reserves, urging that they be sold and the proceeds be applied either to internal improvements or to popular education. He supported resolutions and formulated addresses to the imperial authorities requesting that all ecclesiastics be removed from the Legislative and Executive councils. He was convinced that King's College (University of Toronto), with its exclusive charter, was intended to produce an educated oligarchy that would oppress the common people of the colony and he was, therefore, determined that the charter's objectionable features be removed. Perry had minimal success in most of these attempts at ecclesiastical reform. But there was one exception. In each session of the legislature during the late 1820s Perry was either the mover or the seconder of a bill designed to permit clergymen of every legally recognized denomination to perform the marriage ceremony. His bills were turned back by the Legislative Council until the session of 1829. The measure he proposed that year was passed by both houses and, after being reserved by Lieutenant Governor Sir John Colborne*, it became law in 1831. It was the most important piece of legislation with which he was associated.

Perry was re-elected in 1828, 1830, and 1834. He was a member of the house, therefore, as the political constitution of the colony slowly began to break down. During those stormy years he was intent not on changing the constitution but on desperately striving to make it work. He accepted the result of the election of 1830, which reduced the reformers to a small group, and, unlike William Lyon Mackenzie*, was able to reconcile himself to the generally conservative consequences. Throughout the sessions of the 11th parliament (1831–34), the "glorious minority," though outvoted scores of times, persistently criticized the proposals of the conservative majority and brought forward its own resolutions and bills, with some success. In 1831 a resolution requesting the removal of Anglican privilege from the charter of King's College was approved by a large majority. The

assembly also voted to terminate the salary of its Church of England chaplain. The felon's counsel bill moved successfully through the house, and those amendments to the libel law of which reformers could approve were endorsed by the majority; neither measure, however, received royal assent at that time. In 1834, when confronted by possible imperial disallowance of recent banking legislation [see William Allan], the members voted almost unanimously for a resolution, moved by Bidwell and seconded by Perry, that unambiguously asserted colonial autonomy against imperial interference. There were other minor victories.

Put together with the reformers' triumph in the election of 1834, these successes allowed Perry at times to be mildly optimistic about the progress of reform. Nevertheless, it is quite clear that by 1835 the political constitution of Upper Canada was close to collapse. The balanced constitution of the colony could only operate properly in an atmosphere of moderation, in which divisive issues were avoided and cooperation among the three branches (elected assembly, appointed legislative council, and lieutenant governor) was made possible. What developed instead was political polarization that culminated in a crisis in the spring of 1836, precipitated when Robert BALDWIN and the rest of the Executive Council resigned in protest over actions by the new lieutenant governor, Sir Francis Bond Head*.

One source of that polarization was the conflict between William Lyon Mackenzie and the conservative majority in the assembly. Mackenzie posed serious problems for Perry. On the one hand, he and Mackenzie had similar ideas about the kind of society that ought to be established in Upper Canada. There was, therefore, a broad range of legislative matters on which they could cooperate. Moreover, from the time of Mackenzie's first expulsion in 1831 until parliament was dissolved in 1834, Perry and Bidwell defended Mackenzie in the house on numerous occasions and urged the angry members to moderate their treatment of him. In the session of 1835 not only did Perry vote to have the record of the expulsions expunged from the *Journal* of the house but he also declared that it ought to be publicly burned by the common hangman.

Nevertheless, Perry ultimately dissociated himself from Mackenzie. One reason was the latter's lack of moderation, his uncompromising intransigence. That was what Perry referred to when he remarked that he and Bidwell disapproved of Mackenzie's "occasional violence." There was another reason. Mackenzie was all too willing to depart from the British constitution. Perry was as dedicated to reform as Mackenzie but he was convinced that it could be achieved within the established constitutional framework. He could not, therefore, accept Mackenzie's suggestion that the

Legislative Council be made elective. To do so would be to modify seriously the constitution that his father had sacrificed "all but life" to defend. When he considered the question during the session of 1835, as chairman of a select committee on the Legislative and Executive councils, he carefully avoided recommending the extension of the elective principle to the upper chamber. To resolve the impasse between the two houses, he urged only that the imperial authorities change the composition of the Legislative Council.

By the time the session of 1836 had begun, Perry had ceased thinking about the upper house and had turned instead to a version of responsible government. In a proposed amendment to the reply to the speech from the throne, he took up the notion that the British constitution operated imperfectly in the colony. He drew a contrast between the convention in London, by which councillors were "only such men as enjoy the confidence of the people, expressed through their representatives," and the practice in Upper Canada, where positions of "trust, honor or emolument," from executive councillors to militia officers, were "bestowed on persons belonging to a particular party in politics." That, Perry said, directly contravened the constitution.

When the assembly rejected his amendment in favour of a more general statement, Perry did not pursue the matter. But when the Executive Council resigned on Saturday, 12 March, he seized upon the issue again. On Monday he immediately moved the preparation of an address to Head affirming approval in principle of a responsible Executive Council and requesting information on the resignations. The lieutenant governor's reply and related documents were laid before the assembly two days later and again Perry forced events. He moved the creation of a committee, of which he would be chairman, to report on the information the house had received. On the next day he also introduced a motion declaring an "entire want of confidence" in the four new councillors whom Head had appointed: William Allan, Augustus Warren Baldwin*, John Elmsley*, and Robert Baldwin Sullivan.

Perry presented his report on 15 April and after a long debate the house voted to accept it on the 18th. His solution to the crisis was, essentially, to extend the whole British constitution to Upper Canada. That would involve a system in which the lieutenant governor would be required to appoint executive councillors who had the confidence of the assembly, to consult with them on all important questions, and to follow their advice. In effect, as his critics immediately pointed out, Perry claimed colonial sovereignty over all local affairs. Given his loyalist background and his repeated insistence that he wished to maintain the imperial connection, the conclusion he reached in 1836 demands explanation.

What seems to lie at the bottom of it was that Perry did not see the crisis primarily as one involving an antithesis between colonial interest and imperial authority. He conceived of the crisis as an internal one precipitated by the aggressive behaviour of the executive branch of government. He cited two examples of the way in which the lieutenant governors had acted irrespective of popular wishes: patronage appointments and the creation of rectories as endowments for Anglican clergymen. Moreover, Head had informed the house that, in so far as the colony was concerned, he intended to retain total freedom of action in the future. Within the context of the balanced constitution, Perry saw those actions and that claim as despotism. He turned to the idea of responsibility as a means of restoring the balance and, like his 17th-century counterparts in the British parliament, recommended that the supplies be withheld.

Although Perry welcomed the election of 1836 – in fact he challenged Head to call it – he and Bidwell lost their seats to the conservatives John Solomon Cartwright* and George Hill Detlor. By that time Perry had accumulated an impressive list of political liabilities. Like Mackenzie, he had broken with Egerton Ryerson* and probably lost the support of some Methodists. He was accused in the Kingston press of using his political position to secure for himself and his friends appointments to government positions which the assembly intended to create. Perry was also an extensive speculator in loyalist land rights and had been a leader in the assembly in attempting to have the requirement of settlement duties removed from them. As well, despite his attempts to distance himself from Mackenzie – Perry voted against the adoption of the *Seventh report on grievances* in 1836 – the association between them remained too close for many. Similarly, the vigour of his denunciation of Head as a deliberate liar and a tyrant who would place "a yoke of despotism" on Upper Canada, was seen by the Kingston *Chronicle & Gazette* as an insult to the crown and a danger to the imperial connection.

There was another factor in the reaction against Perry which was of greater importance and was, moreover, largely beyond his control. When he and Bidwell had been first elected, the Bay of Quinte area was the most settled and prosperous region of the colony. By the mid 1830s, however, the rapid development of the western part of the province had made it appear a backwater. No politician could do much to improve those circumstances and the situation was made even more damaging politically when it was argued in the *Chronicle & Gazette* in 1834 that new settlers avoided the Quinte region because of its American reputation, the eradication of which demanded the defeat of Perry and Bidwell.

After the election Perry withdrew from public life.

Perry

There were rumours that he would return but in fact he had decided to leave Lennox and Addington to pursue another career. By the fall of 1836 he had moved to Whitby Township, on the north shore of Lake Ontario, and had begun business as a general merchant. The location was an excellent choice. Its most attractive feature was the harbour at Windsor Bay and Perry was fully aware of its potential; in 1831 it had been made a port of entry. Government engineers reported in 1835 that if improved, Windsor harbour would be the best facility between Toronto and Kingston. In the spring of 1836, a few days before he presented his final constitutional report, Perry personally guided legislation through the house that provided £9,000 to pay for improvements to the site. The bill died, however, when Head dissolved parliament and called an election. For a few months in the spring and summer of 1838 Perry may have seriously considered moving to the United States. At that time he was one of a group of reformers who organized the Mississippi Emigration Society; he was, in fact, chosen to act as its president. But a large-scale exodus from Upper Canada failed to materialize and in the end he decided to remain in Whitby Township.

Perry's business prospects were based on the capacity of the harbour to handle the commercial traffic of the extensive area to the north, at least as far as Lake Simcoe. By the 1840s, to exploit that traffic, Perry had constructed warehouses with access to the government wharf. The centre of his enterprise was the general store located slightly north of the port in the village of Windsor (Whitby), which became known as Perry's Corners. He also possessed a store at Port Perry, at the western end of Lake Scugog. In the mid 1840s Perry took the leadership in persuading the government to take over and improve the road from Windsor harbour to Lake Scugog. This Centre Line road was essential because it would direct the traffic of the northern area through Windsor rather than its rival, Oshawa.

Not only was the road built, but in 1850, acting on behalf of a company he had organized, Perry purchased the road from the government along with the harbour facilities at Windsor Bay at a price that was less than half of the original cost. With those components in place, he might well have been optimistic about his commercial future. During the late 1840s Windsor harbour handled a larger volume of traffic than any other Canadian port on Lake Ontario except Toronto and Kingston. But when Perry died in 1851, his personal financial situation seemed precarious. Although he had provided for his family, his will recorded debts of about £10,000 with virtually no assets with which to satisfy them. Perhaps the costs of establishing his enterprise, especially the purchase price of the road and harbour, were more than his resources could absorb.

Although Perry left public life in 1836, he did retain a connection with politics. Throughout the 1840s he worked in the reform interest in the riding to which he had moved, 3rd York. Consistent with his position in 1836, his immediate objective appeared to be the same as that of the reform party, a system of responsible government. To achieve it he was willing to accept the leadership of Robert Baldwin. Indeed, as the election of 1844 approached, he tried to persuade Baldwin to be the riding's candidate. When he declined, Perry threw his influence behind James Edward Small*, and four years later worked on behalf of William Hume Blake*. In fact, Blake, who did not appear in the riding during the campaign, seems to have owed his election largely to Perry's influence in Whitby Township.

Yet, by the fall of 1849, Perry was in the process of breaking with the reform majority. Although he left no testimony about his reason, his career surely reveals it. He was a North American for whom the interests of the people of Upper Canada were paramount. Those interests, he thought, would best be served by the establishment of a democratic and egalitarian society. But until the late 1840s Perry pursued that goal within the structure of the British constitution. His expectations of the new system of responsible government, however, were far more radical than those of the Baldwinite reformers. The performance of the ministry of Baldwin and Louis-Hippolyte La Fontaine* during the sessions of 1848 and 1849, therefore, must have been a bitter disappointment to him. When Blake resigned his seat in late 1849, Perry accepted the nomination in the ensuing by-election. He did so on a platform that could not be approved by the reform party leadership. By the fall of 1849 Perry had become a republican and he refused, despite pressure from Baldwin, Francis Hincks*, and George Brown*, to declare himself opposed in principle to annexation. Nevertheless, his election campaign was successful and at the convention in Markham in March 1850, he publicly abandoned the British constitution and emerged as one of the leading Clear Grits.

Perry, however, had little time left to work for radical reform. Severely ill in the spring of 1850, he was unable to take his seat in the legislature until early July and even after that his attendance was irregular. His voting record and the resolutions he introduced, notably on the Municipal Corporations Act, reveal his clear opposition to the reform leaders. When the session came to a close in early August, he had achieved little – even a bill he moved which would have created a new county, Ontario, with Whitby as its municipal centre, was refused second reading.

It was his last session. By the spring of 1851 he was again drastically ill. There was a brief recovery in early summer which allowed him to regain sufficient strength for a visit to Marshall Spring Bidwell in New

York City. But, before he could return, he died at Saratoga Springs on 24 August.

H. E. TURNER

AO, RG 1, C-I-3, 81: 170; 85: 55; 92: 14; 152: 121; C-I-4, 4: 43; C-III-3, 1: 88; 2: 12, 37, 74, 84, 148, 192; C-I-5, 1: 143, 310–11, 734; 14: 40; RG 22, ser.155, will of Peter Perry. MTL, Robert Baldwin papers, A43, Perry to Baldwin, 4 Dec. 1843; 1, 10 Oct., 13 Nov. 1845; 16 March, 3, 16 April, 9, 19 May, 25 July, 21 Dec. 1846; 21 Jan., 29 April, 15 June, 12 July, 12 Oct. 1847. PAC, RG 1, E1, 55; L3, 403: P11/62; 404: P12/28; 418: P misc., 1775–95/70. Whitby Hist. Soc. Arch. (Whitby, Ont.), Perry family genealogy. Can., Prov. of, Legislative Assembly, *Journals*, 1850. "The constitutional debate in the legislative assembly of 1836," ed. W. R. Riddell, Lennox and Addington Hist. Soc., *Papers and Records* (Napanee, Ont.), 7–8 (1916). R. H. Thornton, *A sermon preached at the interment of Peter Perry, esq., M.P.P., who died at Saratoga, 24 August, 1851, aged 51 years, 9 months, and 10 days* (Whitby, 1851; copy at Whitby Hist. Soc. Arch.). "United Empire Loyalists: enquiry into losses and services," AO *Report*, 1904: 1014–15. U.C., House of Assembly, *App. to the journal*, 1835, 2, nos.27, 53, 93; *Journal*, 1825–36. *British Colonist* (Toronto), 21 Jan. 1848. *British Whig*, 15, 18, 22 April, 30 Sept. 1834; 5 Feb., 16 March, 16 May, 22 Dec. 1835; 26 Jan., 27 Oct. 1836. *Chronicle & Gazette*, 11 Jan., 24 May, 26 July 1834; 11 Feb., 7, 25–26 March, 2, 8, 25 April, 13, 16, 25, 27 May, 22 Dec. 1835; 9, 16, 26 Jan., 24 Feb., 23, 26, 30 March, 18, 25 May, 4, 18, 22 June, 9 July 1836; 11 Sept. 1839; 12 Aug. 1840. *Colonial Advocate*, 24 Nov., 2 Dec. 1831. *Correspondent and Advocate* (Toronto), 21 March 1836. *Daily British Whig*, 27, 29 Aug. 1851. *Kingston Chronicle*, 29 Jan. 1819, 18 April 1823, 24 March 1832. *Kingston Gazette*, 22 June 1814. *Patriot* (Toronto), 19 Sept. 1837.

J. C. Dent, *The Canadian portrait gallery* (4v., Toronto, 1880–81), 3: 212–13. *Pioneer life on the Bay of Quinte, including genealogies of old families and biographical sketches of representative citizens* (Toronto, 1904; repr. Belleville, Ont., 1972), 940. William Canniff, *History of the settlement of Upper Canada (Ontario) with special reference to the Bay Quinte* (Toronto, 1869; repr. Belleville, 1971), 666. Cowdell, *Land policies of U.C.* Craig, *Upper Canada.* French, *Parsons & politics.* W. S. Herrington, *History of the county of Lennox and Addington* (Toronto, 1913; repr. Belleville, 1972), 369, 396. L. A. Johnson, *History of the county of Ontario, 1615–1875* (Whitby, 1973), 142–47. Patterson, "Studies in elections in U.C.," 405–6. G. M. Jones, "The Peter Perry election and the rise of the Clear Grit party," *OH*, 12 (1914): 164–75. R. S. Longley, "Emigration and the crisis of 1837 in Upper Canada," *CHR*, 17 (1936): 29–40. W. R. Riddell, "The law of marriage in Upper Canada," *CHR*, 2 (1921): 226–48.

PETERS, BENJAMIN LESTER, merchant, militia officer, politician, and justice of the peace; b. 29 June 1790 in Grimross (Gagetown), N.B., son of James Peters and Margaret Lester; m. 26 June 1823 Mary Ann Winnett in Annapolis Royal, N.S., and they had six daughters and four sons; d. 12 May 1852 in Saint John, N.B.

In 1783 James Peters, a prominent loyalist from Long Island, N.Y., arrived in the future province of New Brunswick as an agent for the Associated Loyalists and personally acquired grant P11 in Parrtown (Saint John). He gained virtual control over what was to become the community of Grimross when he obtained a grant of 360 acres in that location the following year. Peters planned and colonized the Grimross region, and he represented it in the House of Assembly until 1816, four years before his death. Benjamin Lester Peters, second last child in a family of ten, apparently received some formal education before leaving Grimross for Saint John. A freeman of that city in 1813, he was an established merchant on the lower end of South Market Wharf by the early 1820s, selling china, glass, paint, homespun, tallow, and whatever else trade demanded.

An Anglican, Peters served as both a vestryman and a churchwarden of Trinity Church in Saint John. He was also an active member of the masonic order, belonging to Saint John's Albion Lodge No.52. In 1826 he became the district grand master and deputy provincial grand master of the Grand Lodge of Free and Accepted Masons of New Brunswick. A son of the same name continued this connection into the 1890s. Peters was involved in the militia; a major of the 1st Battalion of Saint John militia in 1826, he was eventually appointed lieutenant-colonel commandant of the entire Saint John militia on 26 May 1845, the highest rank available to him.

Among Benjamin's siblings, Charles Jeffery* became solicitor general of New Brunswick in 1825 and three years later succeeded Thomas Wetmore*, a brother-in-law, as attorney general for life; Harry was a member of the Council; Valentine H. became a judge of the Inferior Court of Common Pleas for Queens County; and William Tyng* served as clerk of the Legislative Council. Through the marriages of his brothers and sisters, moreover, Benjamin was related not only to the Wetmores but also to such prominent families as the Ludlows and the Odells. These connections undoubtedly furthered his own political career. After serving for several years on the Saint John Common Council "with highly commendable zeal and activity," he was appointed mayor of the city in April 1834, an office in the gift of the Executive Council of the province. During his year as mayor, Peters strongly supported the building of the harbour bridge linking the east and the west sides of the city, and he was named first in the act incorporating the construction company in 1835. On 7 Aug. 1837, when the bridge was almost completed, it collapsed, killing seven workers.

Early in August 1849 Peters was made a stipendiary magistrate for Saint John, a position created earlier that year by the revision of the city's charter. According to the attorney general, Lemuel Allan

Peterson

Wilmot*, the office was "the most important one" proposed in the legislation, which consolidated several of the smaller municipal courts and was responsible for creating the city's first police force (30 constables under the authority of the magistrate). Peters received an annual salary of £300 and had the right to name a clerk who would be paid £150. Benjamin Lester Peters Jr filled that position. Over the next two and a half years Peters Sr established the force on a firm footing and upheld the law, receiving much credit in his obituary notice in May 1852 for the "present peaceable status of our city [compared] with its former disorderly condition." On 12 May 1852 he had died at home after a lingering illness.

CARL M. WALLACE

N.B. Museum, Jack Connell, geneal. notes, Peters family of Gagetown; Reg. of marriages for the city and county of Saint John, book A (1810–28), 1823. *Loyalist and Protestant Vindicator* (Saint John, N.B.), 15 May 1852. *Morning News* (Saint John), 1849, 14 May 1852. *New-Brunswick Courier*, 1834–35; 15 May 1852. *Star* (Saint John), 18 June 1822. *N.B. almanac*, 1851. W. F. Bunting, *History of St. John's Lodge, F. & A.M. of Saint John, New Brunswick, together with sketches of all masonic bodies in New Brunswick from A.D. 1784 to A.D. 1894* (Saint John, 1895), 81–83, 86. D. R. Jack, *Centennial prize essay on the history of the city and county of St. John* (Saint John, 1883). Lawrence, *Judges of N.B.* (Stockton and Raymond).

PETERSON, HEINRICH WILHELM (later **Henry William**), printer, publisher, editor, justice of the peace, and office holder; b. 27 May 1793 in Quakenbrück (Federal Republic of Germany), son of Johann Dietrich Peterson and Julianna Sophia Amelia von Borck; m. first 9 June 1825 Hannah Ann Hendrickson, and they had one daughter; m. secondly 12 Feb. 1831 Harriet Middleton Douglas, *née* Clayton, sister of John Middleton Clayton who later became American secretary of state (1848–50), and they had two children, one of whom died in infancy; d. 12 June 1859 in Guelph, Upper Canada.

Heinrich Wilhelm Peterson was two years old when, in August 1795, his family left Germany and immigrated to Baltimore, Md. In 1796 his father, a former printer and a Lutheran pastor, moved the family to Pennsylvania where Heinrich Wilhelm received his schooling. From August 1814 to March 1817 the younger Peterson published the *German Liberty Flag* at Carlisle, Pa. In February 1819 his father accepted a call to minister to Lutheran congregations in Markham and Vaughan townships, Upper Canada. Heinrich Wilhelm did not accompany his parents but he did visit them in 1823 or 1824.

Within a year of his marriage in 1825 Peterson had moved to Markham where, according to his son's later account, he printed a small news-sheet "more I think for his private amusement than anything else." By March 1827 he was working in Ancaster for George Gurnett* on the *Gore Gazette*. A short time thereafter he went to Dover, Del., where he opened a printing-shop and published the *Legislative Reporter* and then briefly the *Christian Magazine*. In 1830 both ventures failed for lack of support and in the same year Peterson's wife died, leaving an infant daughter. Peterson remarried the following year and returned to Upper Canada, staying temporarily at his parents' home in Markham before settling in Berlin (Kitchener) in 1832.

Although not an ordained clergyman, Peterson ministered to German settlers of the Lutheran and Anglican faiths in the Waterloo area during the 1830s. In December 1832 he was appointed catechist for the Church of England, assisting the itinerant Vincent Philip MAYERHOFFER. Peterson later joined the Methodist meeting at Berlin and he continued in the Methodist connection until his death, being a strong supporter of the Norfolk Street Methodist Church in Guelph during his later years.

By 1835 Peterson was in the printing business again. He himself lacked sufficient capital to open a publishing establishment, but local supporters interested in a German newspaper purchased stock at $20 a share so that he could procure the necessary equipment. Peterson's printing-press was transported by oxen from Pennsylvania to Berlin where it was installed in August 1835, and the first issue of the *Canada Museum, und Allgemeine Zeitung* appeared on 27 August. The *Museum* was printed on good quality paper, and its format revealed a skilled and experienced hand.

The weekly paper concentrated on international news, giving particular attention to events in Pennsylvania. Drawing from German newspapers printed in the United States, the *Museum* ran serialized stories and other contemporary German literature to keep up local interest in German language, literature, and social customs. In Canadian political affairs the *Museum* tried to pick a middle course, although Peterson made no secret of his support for government authority and was concerned that some Germans who opposed the government might become involved in the violence associated with the rebellions of 1837–38 [*see* William Lyon Mackenzie*]. In the aftermath of the uprising, Peterson urged the German community to accept the recommendations made by Lord Durham [Lambton*], hoping that such action would help restore civic peace in Upper Canada. The paper was also concerned with local affairs. It published news of town meetings, political rallies, and religious events in Wellington District. German poetry by Upper Canadian authors, including Peterson himself, was also published.

For four and a half years the *Museum*, which sold

for an annual subscription of two dollars, played a dominant role in introducing German immigrants to Canadian mores. According to a later report in the *Guelph Advertiser*, "the circulation of this journal extended beyond the Province, and exerted a considerable influence in promoting and encouraging German emigration to Canada. It was also the means of inducing many mechanics and others, to settle in Berlin, which was then composed of but a few houses."

In addition to the newspaper, Peterson published a number of secular and religious titles for the German community. One of the earliest German books printed in British North America was a hymn-book, *Die Gemeinschaftliche Liedersammlung*, compiled in 1836 by Benjamin EBY, the local Mennonite bishop. Between 1838 and 1841 Peterson published a series of German almanacs and in 1839 he printed a German primer prepared by Eby for use in schools. The *Museum* office further served as Berlin's first post office receiving bi-weekly mail deliveries from Toronto.

Peterson's interest in public affairs, his fluency in English and German, and his reputation as a friendly arbitrator in the community resulted in his appointment as a justice of the peace in August 1838. He was named registrar of Wellington District in 1840 and by December had decided to cease publication of the *Museum*. He sold his press to Heinrich Eby and Christian ENSLIN, his former assistants, who continued the paper as the *Deutsche Canadier und Neuigkeitsbote*.

In 1842 Peterson supported efforts to establish a tory newspaper, the *Guelph Herald and Wellington District Advertiser*, which lasted only nine months. The paper was reconstituted as the *Guelph Herald and Literary, Agricultural and Commercial Gazette* in 1847 and was funded for a short time by a joint-stock company formed by Peterson and several Guelph businessmen. In the mean time, Peterson had settled in Guelph. He continued to serve as registrar, for the district until 1849 and thereafter for the county until his death.

HERBERT K. KALBFLEISCH

Works published by Heinrich Wilhelm Peterson include *German Liberty Flag* (Carlisle, Pa.), 27 Aug. 1814–25 March 1817; *Christian Magazine* (Dover, Del.), 1 (1830); *Legislative Reporter* (Dover), 1830; *Canada Museum, und Allgemeine Zeitung* (Berlin [Kitchener, Ont.]), 27 Aug. 1835–18 Dec. 1840; *Die Gemeinschaftliche Liedersammlung . . .*, [comp. Benjamin Eby] (1st ed., Berlin, 1836; 2nd ed., 1838); and Benjamin Eby, *Neues Buchstabir- und Lesebuch . . .* (1st ed., Berlin, 1839).

As a lay minister in Berlin, Peterson kept a register of baptisms and burials presided over by himself and by visiting clergymen between 1833 and 1835, much of it written in German. This register has been translated by Paul Eydt *et al.* and published as "The records of H. W. Peterson of Kitchener, 1833–1835" in *Ontario Reg.* ([Madison, N.J.]), 1 (1968): 133–40.

AO, MU 2955, H. W. Peterson [Jr.] to Matthew Teefy, 13 July 1864. PAC, RG 5, A1: 92190–93. *Der Deutsche Canadier* (Berlin), 7 July 1859. *Gore Gazette, and Ancaster, Hamilton, Dundas and Flamborough Advertiser* (Ancaster, [Ont.]), 3 March 1827–8 June 1829. *Guelph Advertiser, and Elora and Fergus Examiner* (Guelph, [Ont.]), 23 June 1859. *Guelph Herald and Literary, Agricultural, and Commercial Gazette. Guelph Herald and Wellington District Advertiser*, 1842. C. A. Burrows, *The annals of the town of Guelph, 1827–1877* (Guelph, 1877). A. E. Byerly, *The beginning of things in Wellington and Waterloo counties . . .* (Guelph, 1935). C. R. Cronmiller, *A history of the Lutheran Church in Canada* (1v. to date, n.p., 1961–   ). Johnson, *Hist. of Guelph*. H. K. Kalbfleisch, *The history of the pioneer German language press of Ontario, Canada, 1835–1918* (London, Ont., and Münster, German Federal Republic, 1968). Millman, *Life of Charles James Stewart*. W. H. Breithaupt, "'The Canada Museum,'" Waterloo Hist. Soc., *Annual report*, 1939: 62–70; "Some German settlers of Waterloo County," 1913: 11–15; and "Waterloo County newspapers," 1921: 152–60. A. E. Byerly, "Henry William Peterson," Waterloo Hist. Soc., *Annual report*, 1931: 250–62. A. B. Sherk, "The Pennsylvania Germans of Waterloo County, Ontario," *OH*, 7 (1906): 98–109.

PETITCLAIR, PIERRE, notary's clerk, writer, and tutor; b. 12 Oct. 1813 in Saint-Augustin-de-Desmaures, Lower Canada, son of Pierre Petit-Clair, a farmer, and Cécile Moisan; d. unmarried, probably 15 Aug. 1860, at Pointe au Pot (Pointe à la Peau), Lower Canada.

Although he came from a farming family of modest means, Pierre Petitclair had the good fortune to receive an education and become broadly cultured. After four years of study at the Petit Séminaire de Québec from 1825 to 1829, he was employed as a clerk in the court record office in Quebec, and under the guidance of notary Joseph-François Perrault* he received his initial legal training. However, the bar held no attraction for him, and three years later he became a copyist for another notary, Archibald Campbell*. A patron of the arts, Campbell owned a well-stocked library, was interested in both arts and sciences, prizing the humanities in particular, and enjoyed encouraging young people of talent. He was a real benefactor to Petitclair and undoubtedly exercised a great influence on him. But then he was dealing with a gifted person, for Petitclair excelled in mathematics, geometry, and philosophy, played the clarinet, violin, and guitar, sang magnificently, tried his hand at musical composition, appreciated painting, was adept with a brush, and above all was passionately fond of literature. He not only read everything that came to hand, but he himself had begun to write, first poems and then two comedies entitled "Qui trop embrasse

Petit Pigeon

mal étreint" and *Griphon ou la vengeance d'un valet*. He remained with Campbell for about five years, until 1837.

It was probably during this period that Petitclair had a love affair, about which little is known but which appears to have marked him deeply. In three poems, "La somnambule," "À Flore," and "Sombre est mon âme comme vous," he dealt with the theme of infidelity, and in his plays he had a way of disparaging love which often went beyond mockery and satire to betray a good deal of bitterness. It appears, then, that a woman had disappointed his expectations and that the experience was a profound shock to him. It probably explains why he remained a bachelor and felt no regret at abandoning Quebec for the isolated north shore of the St Lawrence.

During the winter of 1837–38 Petitclair accepted a position as tutor in a family with 12 children. The father, Guillaume-Louis Labadie, spent his time fishing in summer and seal hunting in winter. Petitclair accompanied the family everywhere, and hence lived in a succession of places on the north shore and the Gaspé peninsula before finally settling with the Labadies at the Anse des Dunes near Blanc-Sablon. From then on he returned to Quebec only for short visits. He was there in the autumn of 1842; this was the period when he reached the peak of his literary career, publishing within a couple of weeks three poems, "Pauvre soldat! qu'il doit souffrir!," "À Flore," and "Le règne du juste," and also a comedy, "La donation," which was first performed on 16 November and was well received. Subsequently Petitclair produced only one more comedy, *Une partie de campagne*, performed at Quebec on 22 April 1857 and published in December 1865. This play, which had taken longer to shape than the others, is probably his best work. It portrays an anglomaniac who makes himself look ridiculous as much through naïvety as through pride. Consequently this comedy has lost none of its topicality.

Pierre Petitclair is now no more than a name in the history of Canadian literature, and with the exception of Louis-Michel Darveau*, who wrote a panegyric on him in *Nos hommes de lettres*, no one considers him highly talented. He is rightly criticized for failing in his poetry to free himself from the formalist stamp of the classical era, and for yielding too readily to pre-romantic sentimentality. As for his comedies, they contain a few good satirical scenes and might still amuse the young, but on the whole they reveal him to be a rather poor imitator of Molière, Jean-François Regnard, Eugène Scribe, and Shakespeare. Nevertheless, Petitclair's work is not without interest. Reading a poem such as "Le règne du juste" or a short story such as "Une aventure au Labrador," one discovers that Petitclair not only was aware of the problems of his time but also had the wisdom to laugh at them and the boldness to denounce those responsible. Hence one must be careful not to pass too hasty a judgement on his three comedies or to see them as no more than the experiments of an amateur bent merely on his own diversion. The conventional plot conceals the true purpose, which is satirical. And, even more surprising, Petitclair, instead of putting the blame solely on the despotic and all-powerful Englishman, took aim at his compatriots. Perhaps better than others, he was able to see that under the régime uniting the two Canadas the French Canadian was an innocent who allowed himself to be outwitted with an ease more incredible than disconcerting. Displaying an audacity rare in the 19th century, he even flung a few barbs at the church, which he held responsible for the ignorance and excessive simple-mindedness of the faithful in Lower Canada. Hence, although his work is disappointing as literature, Petitclair remains important as a keen observer of his century and his milieu. Cultured and perspicacious, he understood the forces pitted against each other and sensed who in French Canada were tipping the balance of ideas on the eve of confederation.

JEAN-CLAUDE NOËL

[Pierre Petitclair's poems, "La somnambule" (1835), "Sombre est mon âme comme vous" (1839), "À Flore" (1842), "Pauvre soldat! qu'il doit souffrir!" (1842), and "Le règne du juste" (1843), were published first in newspapers, and then brought together by James HUSTON in *Répertoire national* (1848–50), vols.1–2, which also contains a comedy, "La donation," previously published in *L'Artisan* (Québec), 15, 29 Dec. 1842. Two other comedies were also published at Quebec, *Griphon ou la vengeance d'un valet* in 1837 and *Une partie de campagne* in a posthumous edition in 1865; these two, along with "La donation," are analysed by Jean Du Berger in *DOLQ*, vol.1. The manuscripts of the plays "Qui trop embrasse mal étreint" and "Le brigand" have not been located and were apparently not published. Petitclair also wrote the short story, "Une aventure au Labrador," published in *Le Fantasque* (Québec), 2 and 9 Nov. 1840.

Except for biographical dictionaries, few works deal with Petitclair. There is a biography by Louis-Michel Darveau in *Nos hommes de lettres* (Montréal, 1873) and an article by Victor Morin, "Un pionnier de théâtre canadien: Pierre Petitclair," in *La Rev. moderne* (Montréal), 14 (1932), no.2: 6, but otherwise Petitclair is now mentioned only as the first French-Canadian playwright. J.-C.N.]

ANQ-Q, CE1-17, 12 oct. 1813. ASQ, Fichier des anciens.

PETIT PIGEON. See GUIBOCHE, LOUIS

PHELAN, PATRICK, Roman Catholic priest, Sulpician, and bishop; b. 1795, on or about 14 February, in Ballyragget (Republic of Ireland), son of Joseph Phelan and Catharine Brennan; d. 6 June 1857 in Kingston, Upper Canada.

After running out of funds to further his education,

Patrick Phelan became a teacher in a private school but soon decided to leave for America to continue his studies there. In the words of an anonymous biographer, "The impression that God had called him to America, and that there should be the field of his real usefulness, was deeply made and it remained." He embarked from Dublin in 1821 on the first ship sailing to America, which happened to be bound for Boston. On arrival he placed himself under the guardianship of its prelate who, three months later, sent him to Montreal to study for the priesthood. On 24 Sept. 1825, with Bishop Jean-Jacques Lartigue* presiding, Phelan became the first priest to be ordained in Montreal's newly consecrated church of Saint-Jacques. Following "the earnest solicitation" of the Séminaire de Saint-Sulpice, Phelan was allowed to remain in Montreal to serve in its parish, Notre-Dame. After being received as a member of the seminary on 21 Nov. 1825, he spent the next 17 years ministering to the city's Irish Catholics.

Given the nascent state of that community, his services had to embrace more than its spiritual needs. He was active in furthering the education of the young, providing medical care during the cholera epidemics of 1832 and 1834, seeing to the welfare of destitute widows and orphans, sometimes at his own expense, and, through the establishment of St Patrick's Total Abstinence Society in 1841, trying to curb the community's widespread abuse of alcohol. According to his biographer, Phelan's service during the epidemics "made such a great impression on the minds of his congregation, that they ever after had unlimited confidence in him." The timing was fortunate because Phelan soon needed to make demands on that trust. The first involved Maria Monk*, a former resident of the Montreal area who falsely claimed to have spent several years in a convent there and who, in the summer of 1835, began making slanderous allegations about members of the city's Catholic clergy. In one of many outrageous statements, she said that Phelan was the father of her illegitimate child and that conception had taken place in the convent. Phelan had little difficulty surviving the accusations and Maria Monk was soon revealed to be a liar and a prostitute. Another incident occurred during the political disturbances of 1837 when members of Montreal's Irish community spoke of holding an assembly under the Patriote orators Edmund Bailey O'Callaghan* and Thomas Storrow Brown*. Phelan's superior, Joseph-Vincent QUIBLIER, sent him to restore calm, which he did by preaching on the need to obey the government.

Perhaps as the result of favourable impressions Phelan made on missionary visits to the Ottawa valley in 1838 and 1841 (the latter in the company of Bishop Charles-Auguste-Marie-Joseph de Forbin-Janson*), Bishop Rémi GAULIN of Kingston, Upper Canada, requested in 1842 that Phelan be appointed parish priest of Bytown (Ottawa). Acceding to the request, church authorities created him vicar general of the dioceses of Montreal and Kingston. Prior to his departure, leading members of his parish, including John Ponsonby Sexton* and John Michael Tobin, presented him with a eulogistic farewell address, and the Irish soldiers of the Montreal garrison gave him an ornamental silver snuff-box in grateful memory of his services to them. Phelan took charge of the Bytown parish on 22 Nov. 1842, and was joined about a month later by an assistant, Hippolyte Moreau*.

It was at this time that Bishop Gaulin was suffering from the physical and mental debilities that forced the Canadian episcopate to replace him with a coadjutor bishop to administer a diocese then covering the entire eastern half of Upper Canada. Rome concurred in the choice of Phelan, but Gaulin, who only a short time earlier had spoken warmly of him, bitterly denounced him when he learned of the appointment in April 1843. Then began the most difficult years of Phelan's ministry.

On 20 Aug. 1843, in Montreal, bishops Ignace Bourget*, Pierre-Flavien Turgeon*, and Michael Power* consecrated Phelan bishop of Carrhae and coadjutor to the bishop of Kingston with right of succession. The new bishop had much to contend with. The diocese of Kingston, in common with others of the time, needed schools, hospitals, orphanages, and churches, as well as qualified clergy and religious to serve in them. Phelan had the additional problem of rarely being free of Gaulin's interference, even while the latter resided in Lower Canada (1843–49 and 1852–57). Gaulin initially refused to give up the idea of staying in the bishop's residence in Kingston, denied Phelan access to diocesan records, and allowed his housekeeper to maintain a spirited defence of his offices and effects. Only gradually, and then largely through the continuing encouragement and counsel of Bishop Bourget, did Phelan manage to assume the administration of the diocese.

Despite the opposition he encountered, Phelan achieved impressive results. The Oblates of Mary Immaculate established themselves in Bytown in 1844, as did the Grey Nuns a year later [see Élisabeth Bruyère*]. The Religious Hospitallers of St Joseph arrived in Kingston in 1845 to establish a hospital for the town. The diocese of Bytown was created in part from Kingston's territory two years later and its first bishop, Joseph-Bruno Guigues*, was consecrated in 1848. In the same year the first Jesuit began teaching at Kingston's Regiopolis College. Phelan, whose first official act in Kingston had been to lay the cornerstone of St Mary's Cathedral, participated in consecrating the church on 4 Oct. 1848 [see Patrick Dollard*]. Phelan's service and potential were recognized two years later when Turgeon appointed him vicar general of the archdiocese of Quebec. In 1853 the Christian Brothers established a school in Kingston, and in 1855

Picoté

a separate school system was organized there. Phelan consecrated John Farrell*, the first bishop of Hamilton, in 1856, and welcomed the Loretto sisters to Belleville a year later [see Ellen Dease*]. Educational institutions also appeared in St Andrews and Alexandria during his administration. But all progress was achieved only at the cost of severe and continuing personal rancour brought about by Gaulin's refusal to give up his power, increasingly incapable though he was of exercising it.

Most of Gaulin's resistance to Phelan was petty, with the exception of his attempt between 1849 and 1852 to resume control of the diocese. After moving back to Kingston, Gaulin made appointments to a number of diocesan offices and undertook far-reaching projects, only to have the Canadian episcopate promptly remind him that all power resided in Phelan. The pope's personal intervention warning Gaulin against further involvement in the government of the diocese was required to bring about his return to Lower Canada and to restore calm. Phelan managed to settle all these challenges to his authority, but never without a great deal of anguish as well as protracted negotiations and correspondence.

Gaulin's lengthy struggle with his illness ended when he died on 8 May 1857. Phelan, after 14 years of intense labour trying to handle the myriad problems of administering a diocese while coping with a sick man's interference at every step, at last succeeded to the bishopric free of personal encumbrances. His freedom, and the sense of relief that must have accompanied it, were to be short-lived. While attending Gaulin's funeral in Kingston on 13 May, Phelan contracted a cold. Several days later, feeling somewhat recovered, he went to Belleville, the scene of his first pastoral visit as coadjutor, to attend the consecration of the new cemetery. An account in the *Toronto Mirror*, perhaps written by its publisher, Charles DONLEVY, stated: "Here, from exposure to the open air a second time, he caught an inflammation of the lungs. . . . Upon his return to Kingston, the disease increased in virulence, and on the night of Saturday, the 6th of June, he breathed his last in the arms of his faithful and beloved clergy, and after the last sacraments had been administered by Bishop Bourget." Like his predecessor, Phelan was buried in St Mary's Cathedral. The fourth bishop of Kingston, Edward John Horan*, was consecrated the following May.

J. E. ROBERT CHOQUETTE

ACAM, 255.102, 842-16; 843-2, -8-9, -12-13; 844-3; 845-2, -6; 851-1; 255.104, 842-4; RC, I: ff.125-28v. AO, RG 22, ser.155, will of Patrick Phelan. Arch. of the Archdiocese of Kingston (Kingston, Ont.), BI (Remigius Gaulin, corr.), 2ED3-6-7; 2ER1-7-8; 2CL1-15; C (Patrick Phelan papers). *Life of Right Reverend Patrick Phelan, third bishop of Kingston, to which is added a synopsis of the lives of the two first bishops of Kingston; by the clergyman who served Bishop Phelan's last mass* (Kingston, 1862). Maria Monk, *Awful disclosures of Maria Monk . . .* (New York, 1836), 16, 228-29, and *Awful disclosures, by Maria Monk, of the Hotel Dieu nunnery of Montreal, revised, with an appendix . . .* (New York, 1836), 240, 307-21, 330, 337, 346-47; both repr. in *Awful disclosures of the Hotel Dieu nunnery*, intro. R. A. Billington (Hamden, Conn., 1962). *British Whig*, 7 Oct. 1848. *Chronicle & Gazette*, 15 July, 12, 23 Aug., 9 Sept. 1843. *Daily British Whig*, 8, 12 June 1857. *Toronto Mirror*, 6, 13 Oct. 1848; 15, 22 May, 12, 19 June 1857. Caron, "Inv. de la corr. de Mgr Plessis," ANQ *Rapport*, 1928-29. L.-A. Desrosiers, "Correspondance de Mgr Ignace Bourget . . .," ANQ *Rapport*, 1945-46, 1948-49; "Inv. de la corr. de Mgr Lartigue," 1941-42, 1945-46. Léon Pouliot et François Beaudin, "Correspondance de Mgr Ignace Bourget . . .," ANQ *Rapport*, 1955-57, 1961-64, 1969. Gaston Carrière, *Histoire documentaire de la Congrégation des missionnaires oblats de Marie-Immaculée dans l'Est du Canada* (12v., Ottawa, 1957-75), 1: 219, 223; 4: 123. L. J. Flynn, *Built on a rock; the story of the Roman Catholic Church in Kingston, 1826-1976* (Kingston, 1976) [reproduces a portrait of the subject]. Labarrère-Paulé, *Les instituteurs laïques*, 59-60, 75. Robert Rumilly, *Histoire de Montréal* (5v., Montréal, 1970-74), 2: 229, 282.

PICOTÉ, ALEXIS TREMBLAY, dit. *See* TREMBLAY

PIERRE. *See* BASQUET, PIERRE

PIERS, TEMPLE FOSTER, army officer and businessman; b. 9 Dec. 1783 in Halifax, second son of Temple Stanyan Piers and Mercy Foster; m. 15 Feb. 1807, in St John's, Elizabeth Thomas, daughter of prominent merchant William Bevil Thomas; d. 19 April 1860 in Halifax.

The paternal grandfather of Temple Foster Piers had been one of the original settlers of Halifax under Edward Cornwallis* in 1749, and his father, who died when Piers was two years old, was a moderately successful merchant of the town. Apprenticed to John Lawson, also a Halifax merchant and a relative by marriage, Piers later worked for Charles Hill*, his father's former partner. On 15 May 1806, through the influence of Hill and Richard John Uniacke*, he obtained an ensign's commission in the Nova Scotia Fencibles. He joined the regiment at St John's, Nfld, and, after being appointed its paymaster, was promoted lieutenant on 2 Aug. 1809. The following April, however, he resigned his commission and entered into business in Halifax with his younger brother Lewis Edward. They established themselves as general merchants and importers of British goods in premises between Bedford Row and Water Street, aiming mainly at the market provided by the fisheries.

In May 1810, for example, they advertised for sale cordage, sailcloth, nails, and spikes, all imported from England.

Although continuing as merchants, some time in 1826 the Pierses decided to take advantage of the opportunities offered by the expansion of shipping and the fisheries and established a rope factory on the Stanyan property, six five-acre lots in the north suburbs of Halifax left to Temple Foster by his father. Unlike their New England counterparts, the brothers did not turn to local sources for workers or capital but imported skilled Scottish spinners and their families and arranged to purchase all their hemp from the Scottish firm of William Kidston and Sons in exchange for long-term credit. In addition, stock and machinery "of the most approved and superior construction" were shipped from Britain at a total cost of £8,000.

By means of surviving documents it is possible to describe some details of the enterprise. Producing staple cordage, bolt-rope, prepared yarn, and 18-thread cod lines, the brothers generally employed a foreman and about 20 spinners, both skilled hands and apprentices, who worked from 5:30 in the morning to 6 at night in the summer and from 6 to 6 in the winter, with about two hours off for meals. A constant hourly production rate was demanded and in return the employees were granted a high degree of job security for the period. The original manufactory depended on horses to power the rope-making machinery but by 1837 the Pierses decided that the rope-works required water power, "for horses are too expensive & irregular in motion." In the spring of that year they obtained from the estate of Anthony Henry Holland* a five-year lease on the paper-mill at the foot of Paper Mill Lake at the north end of Bedford Basin and moved some machinery there.

When the Pierses began operations, there was minimal local competition, but the success of the Stanyan Rope Works, as the enterprise became known, depended on factors beyond the brothers' control. The hemp used for making rope was initially admitted duty-free but in 1829, under new imperial laws, a duty of seven and one-half per cent was imposed. Despite this additional cost, the Pierses' average price of 65 shillings per hundredweight of cordage was still 5 shillings lower than that of British-made rope but could not compete with Russian rope priced at 55 shillings. The brothers therefore petitioned the provincial legislature to request the British government to repeal the duty on hemp and, although they were unsuccessful, they were granted a subsidy of £300 to pay the duty on hemp they had imported in 1829. Since competition from foreign imports continued to harm the rope-works throughout the early 1830s, in 1836 the brothers petitioned the legislature for tariff protection, arguing that imports

duty-free or at very low rates lessened both provincial revenue and production. This attempt similarly failed.

The commercial difficulties of the early 1840s and the firm's continued inability to compete with foreign imports (caused in part by the brothers' refusal to lower prices) placed the Pierses in dire financial straits, and in 1844 they were forced to sell their waterfront buildings to William Machin Stairs*. The same year they mortgaged the Stanyan Rope Works to the Kidston firm, their largest creditors, for £5,195. Persistent problems over the next decade resulted in the brothers transferring the mortgaged property in 1855 to the Kidstons, who were anxious to dispose of it and turned over its supervision to Stairs. The following year he closed the rope-works and dismantled the machinery.

Despite the failure of the rope manufactory, the brothers remained in business, operating a grist-mill at Mill Cove on Bedford Basin which they had taken over in 1842 from Temple Foster's son William Bevil Thomas Piers. When the Halifax and Windsor Railway was being constructed in 1854, its contractors agreed to leave an opening in the planned embankment across Mill Cove to allow vessels access to the mill. This promise was not kept, however, and grain had therefore to be trucked across the railway to the mill. This operation required much extra labour and played havoc with the firm's costs. The brothers estimated in July 1857 that their losses had amounted to £2,350; the operation of the mill had been suspended for 15 months and a new wharf and storehouse had been constructed at a cost of £250. On 1 Aug. 1857 they were finally awarded £1,150 in damages by the Halifax County grand jury.

Temple Foster Piers continued to supervise the operation of the mill until he died of a heart attack in April 1860. In his will he left a cottage in Halifax to his wife and surviving daughter and equal shares in the mill to three sons, two of whom had aided him in the business. A Sandemanian by religion, Piers seems to have taken little part in community activities other than his involvement in the volunteer fire company. Although he was neither successful nor prosperous, Temple Foster Piers is representative of the new class of manufacturers which appeared on the provincial scene early in the 19th century.

PHYLLIS R. BLAKELEY

PANS, MG 1, 753, no.1, pts.v–vi; MG 100, 215, docs.17–17m; RG 1, 290, doc.49; 292, doc.147; 293, doc.20; RG 28, 18, no.11. "The Stanyan Ropeworks of Halifax, Nova Scotia: glimpses of a pre-industrial manufactory," ed. D. [A.] Sutherland, *Labour* ([Halifax]), 6 (1980): 149–58. *British Colonist* (Halifax), 26 April 1860. *Novascotian*, 4 Jan. 1827, 23 Oct. 1843. *Weekly Chronicle* (Halifax), 10 April 1807; 25 May, 15 June 1810. A. A. Lomas, "The

Pinhey

industrial development of Nova Scotia, 1830–1854" (MA thesis, Dalhousie Univ., Halifax, 1950), 310–15, 359–66.

PINHEY, HAMNETT KIRKES, landowner, businessman, office holder, politician, and author; b. 11 Dec. 1784 in Plymouth, England, son of William Pinhey and Mary Townley; m. 12 Dec. 1812 Mary Anne Tasker in London, and they had two sons and two daughters; d. 3 March 1857 in Ottawa and was buried in the graveyard of St Mary's Church, March Township, Upper Canada.

In many ways Hamnett Kirkes Pinhey exemplified the ideal Upper Canadian settler: well educated, vigorous, able, youthful, patriotic, and, most important, wealthy. These attributes virtually guaranteed that he would play a substantial role in the young colony and distinguish himself in a number of important capacities.

The name Pinhey is probably Portuguese and it is possible that Hamnett was a descendant of merchants engaged in the Anglo-Portuguese trade. Certainly his family was well established in England at the time of his birth and had acquired a considerable estate at Totnes. Pinhey was educated in London, to which his family had moved. He entered Christ's Hospital in 1792 and left in 1799. At an early age he went into trade and appears to have prospered. During the Napoleonic Wars he successfully ran the French blockade to carry dispatches to the king of Prussia, a task for which he was later publicly thanked and voted a sum of money. In 1814, two years after his marriage to the daughter of a London merchant and exporter, Pinhey entered into a partnership with Henry Crosley as ship and insurance brokers. For a number of years it seems that the business was enormously successful in its European trade, but Crosley, who was responsible for the continental end of the operation, appears to have been less than completely open in his dealings with Pinhey and by the end of 1817 the partnership had failed, with the resultant litigation lasting three years. The bitterness of this breakup, the problems attending business in the postwar recession, and doubtless a certain sense of adventure led Pinhey to turn his interests elsewhere. In 1819, at the age of 34, he officially retired from business.

In December of that year, by which time he was a citizen and liveryman of the Company of Grocers and a governor of Christ's Hospital, Pinhey petitioned Colonial Secretary Lord Bathurst for a land grant in Upper Canada. Noting that "I have recently retired with a small independent fortune," Pinhey announced his intention to "found a commercial establishment in the back-settlements of His Majesty's Possessions in Canada," provided he could obtain a grant of 1,500 to 2,000 acres "on the Banks of the Utawa." The grant was authorized but neither its size nor its precise location had been determined when Pinhey left for British North America in April 1820. He brought with him £300 in gold and silver. His ship, the *Lord Exmouth*, docked at Quebec on 22 May, 35 days out of Plymouth. Pinhey journeyed to Montreal and then up the Ottawa River to March Township north of Bytown (Ottawa) where, shortly thereafter, he formally took up his land. Eventually, his estate in March Township would amount to more than 2,000 acres.

His was only one of a number of large estates in the region, the others having been established after the War of 1812 by former naval and army officers. At an early date the whole area was reputed to have a settled and prosperous air. By the summer of 1821 Pinhey had brought out his wife and two children, along with personal possessions – more than 50 trunks containing his plate, china, jewellery, and furniture – amounting to a value of £800. Pinhey quickly established himself as a gentleman-farmer and as one of the luminaries of the district. Historian Michael Sean Cross has noted that after the War of 1812 a nascent aristocratic class sprang up among the half-pay officers and gentlemen in the village of Richmond and in March township, a tory élite that also composed the local compact. He suggests further that education, breeding, and background were the cement of this colonial gentry. Pinhey was well suited to the group, but he was far more active in commercial affairs and his opinions, at the outset at any rate, were rather less orthodoxly tory than Cross has suggested.

Pinhey set up the equivalent of a large English farm on his property along the Ottawa and christened the place Horaceville after his eldest son. Within a few years he had built a fine stone house (guests here were to include Governor Lord Dalhousie [Ramsay*] and John Strachan*), saw- and grist-mills, and the first stone church in the area, St Mary's, which was consecrated by Anglican bishop Charles James Stewart* in 1834. Pinhey's business acumen and experience set him in sharp contrast to the military settlers and he soon became the nascent community's financial adviser and banker. Meticulous in his financial records, Pinhey shows clearly in his files the minutiae of Upper Canadian estate management in an age when transportation was slow and seasonal. By 1827, with only 80 acres of his 1,000-acre grant under cultivation, he reported, in a remark that reveals much about the Upper Canadian economy, "I am not making a fortune but an estate. In truth I never see any money but my own." Pinhey and his family lived well, employed a large number of servants, travelled, and kept abreast of affairs in England.

Apart from acting as the local agent of the Canada Company, he himself dabbled in real estate. He also interested himself over the years in a number of ambitious development schemes and local philanthropies. Among the former were plans for agricultural societies, road companies, and of course – Pinhey, like others, caught the mania – railways. Some of his enthusiasms were quite successful, for example, the road companies. He appears to have considered education most significant and his philanthropy included sustaining Christ's Hospital (he used his governorship in the school to sponsor the education of young Canadians and Englishmen) and at least one attempt to create a local equivalent – a proposal for a Royal Union College which would be "most liberal" and attract "all denominations of Christians." The latter idea was simply not possible in capital-poor Upper Canada but was indicative of the mentality of Pinhey and those in his circle.

Inevitably, in such a small community, a man like Pinhey would become enmeshed in politics. He was temperamentally a tory if not a committed one upon his arrival in Upper Canada. Rather aloof from the whole political prospect in the 1820s, by 1832 he was ready to take the plunge for office. In a by-election that year he was returned for Carleton County in a race against another tory, George Lyon. The difficult fight proved to be more a display of tory factionalism than a manifestation of conservative political ideology. "I might have a rotten borough seat in the Imperial Parliament, for one half the sum this very enviable one has cost me," he wrote to James FitzGibbon*, and added, "It is a seat, I suspect that rather takes from than adds to the dignity of the gentleman who condescends to take it."

Pinhey had little time to find out. He was unseated in 1833 because of irregularities; it seemed not all the freeholders who supported him actually owned land. Pinhey moved his political enthusiasms now largely behind the scenes, and for the next two decades, under such pen-names as Vesper and Poor Correspondent, he composed piquant verse, essays, and letters for the *Bytown Gazette, and Ottawa and Rideau Advertiser*, edited by his friend Alexander James Christie*, and for the *Alymer Times*. He emerges in these pieces as a curmudgeon, not just ready to maul reformers, radicals, and potential or real rebels, but to criticize, wittily and often eloquently, all sides. He also shows himself to be as much a spokesman of the propertied middle classes as anything, although his toryism becomes more extreme on constitutional questions such as the granting of responsible government. Special venom is always reserved for the "refractory, turbulent, and insulting" William Lyon Mackenzie*, but his attack seems to be more on the man's deficient character than on his politics.

Much of the material relating to Pinhey's activities during the rebellions of 1837–38 appears to have been destroyed but one can assume that he was an active tory supporter. In the 1840s he turned his considerable wrath against the notion of responsible government. His concerns revolved not so much around the principle as around problems posed by the poverty –

both intellectual and pecuniary – of elected officials in the Canadas and his consequent fears of placing the public trust in their corruptible hands. At this time a chief villain seems to have been, for Pinhey, Francis Hincks*.

A certain amount of patronage was granted Pinhey. He served as local reeve, warden of Dalhousie District Council and later of Carleton County Council, deputy superintendent of schools for Carleton County, and eventually in 1847 as legislative councillor, a position he held until his death in March 1857. His estate, Horaceville, remained in the family until 1959 when it became the first property to pass under the control of the National Capital Commission. Like the reputation of its builder, it requires restoration.

Roger Hall

[Manuscript material relating to Hamnett Kirkes Pinhey includes his papers at the AO (MU 2322–25) and various items in volumes 9–11 of the PAC's Hill collection (MG 24, I9). The Pinhey family papers at the PAC (MG 24, I14) are a miscellaneous collection of original documents and photocopies from a number of sources; original material includes Pinhey's "notebooks" or diaries for 1821–29 and 1837. His diaries for 1829–40 are available in AO, MS 199.

Biographical material relating to Pinhey can be found in the F.-J. Audet papers (PAC, MG 30, D1), volume 24: 841–44, and in the H. T. Douglas collection at the AO (MU 934–44, especially in MU 937). The Douglas collection also contains a photograph of Pinhey taken around 1850, in MU 940. A room in the Historical Society of Ottawa's Bytown Museum is devoted to Pinhey memorabilia.

No full-scale biography of Pinhey exists. A reference of uncertain reliability is [M.] N. Slater Heydon, *Looking back . . . pioneers of Bytown and March: Nicholas Sparks and Hamnett Kirkes Pinhey; their antecedents and their descendants* (Ottawa, 1980). Some further information can be found in Lucien Brault, *Ottawa old & new* (Ottawa, 1946). An early work with references to Pinhey is M. H. Ahearn, "The settlers of March Township," *OH*, 3 (1901): 97–102. It should be supplemented by M. S. Cross, "The age of gentility: the formation of an aristocracy in the Ottawa valley," *CHA Hist. papers*, 1967: 105–17. R.H.]

AO, RG 1, C-I-3, 96: 133; C-I-5, 1: 475; 2: 294; 14: 55; C-III-3, 1: 136; 2: 313; C-III-4, 10: 55. State Library of New South Wales, Mitchell Library (Sydney, Australia), MS 338, geneal. information on the Pinhey family, copied from H. K. Pinhey's Bible (photocopies in PAC, MG 24, I14). *Bathurst Courier*, 26 Oct. 1834, 13 Feb. 1835, 1 July 1836. *Bytown Gazette, and Ottawa and Rideau Advertiser*, 1836–45. *Ottawa Citizen*, 14 March 1857. *Quebec Gazette*, 22 May 1820, 20 Aug. 1821. *Historical sketch of the county of Carleton*, ed. C. C. J. Bond (Belleville, Ont., 1971). Harry Walker and Olive [Moffatt] Walker, *Carleton saga* (Ottawa, 1968).

POWLIS (Powles), GEORGE, convicted murderer; b. 1812 in the Mohawk Village (Brantford), Upper Canada, son of Paul Powlis (Paulus Paulus) and

Powlis

Margaret Brant; m. Susannah Davis, and they had six children; d. in or after 1852 in Upper Canada.

The presence of Indians in Upper Canada posed special problems at times in the application of the law. Until 1825 the judiciary considered them to have – by virtue of their treaty rights and unceded lands – a legal immunity from prosecution for crimes committed by one of their number against another. Even when the law could be applied, there was an appreciable cultural problem and the case of Angelique Pilotte* in 1817 illustrated the intrinsic difficulties in judging the customs of one society by the laws of another. The judicial basis for the Indians' immunity was reinforced by the military threat they posed collectively and by the possibility of retaliation against sheriffs, constables, or magistrates acting against them.

After the War of 1812 white settlers increasingly deplored the behaviour of the Indians. In 1817 a Gore District grand jury condemned the Grand River settlement of the Six Nations as a "frequent scene of riot and tumult . . . out of the reach of the law." Its pressing concern was the effect of such activity on settlement and progress. A year later Peter Lossing* and others petitioned the Legislative Council about the "frequent depradations" of the Six Nations Indians against each other and neigbouring whites, and the "repeated instances of horrid murder . . . among themselves." The petitioners called "loudly" for "some further legislative interference . . . to establish civil authority," blaming "a laxity in [the Indians'] former modes of regulating and punishing offenders" on "the baneful effects of intoxication" and prolonged acquaintance with "white people." In 1822 Judge William Campbell* questioned the legal immunity of Indians in the case of Shawanakiskie*, who had killed an Indian woman in Amherstburg. Three years later it was finally determined that the criminal law could be fully extended to Indians.

George Powlis grew up on the Six Nations' lands. His lineage was distinguished: on his father's side he was a grandson of Sahonwagy*, a Mohawk sachem; on his mother's side, a grandson of Joseph Brant [Thayendanegea*]. Powlis, who was a member of the Church of England, was 5 feet 9¾ inches tall with black hair and hazel eyes. On 22 Feb. 1839 George, his brother Joseph, and their father were arrested for murdering Susannah Doxater, a Mohawk, and were incarcerated in the district jail at Hamilton. By this time there was no longer any judicial trepidation over prosecuting Indians.

The Powlises were tried on 6 June before Levius Peters Sherwood* and two local associate judges, John WILLSON and Richard Beasley*. The case was prosecuted by Hamilton's leading citizen, Sir Allan Napier MacNab*. The Powlises were defended by two local lawyers, Miles O'Reilly and George Sylvester Tiffany. Murder cases in Upper Canada were usually decided upon circumstantial evidence; this trial was no different. Some facts were beyond doubt. The victim had been seen walking home towards the Mohawk Village about sunset on the evening of 16 February. Two days later, her naked body was found on the side of Vinegar Hill, which was known locally as a "place of resort for dissolute people." The examining surgeon thought she might have died by strangulation. Evidence indicated that the murder had not occurred where the body was found but at one of two nearby sites littered with chestnut shells and food. The tracks of four men and one woman led from one site to the other. At one a ring was found. Sleigh tracks led to these locations. Witnesses established that Doxater, an old woman who "occasionally got drunk," had been sober and one witness thought she had been "ravished."

The Powlises were connected to the murder by slender evidence. They had been seen in Brantford on the day of the murder. They left for the Mohawk Village "about sunset"; George was dropped off at Vinegar Hill while Paul and Joseph went on to the village. Sleigh tracks were found leading from Joseph's log cabin to the murder site. His sleigh had distinctive tracks and he was not in the habit of lending it. George had bought chestnuts and had some with him on his way home; there were shells at the murder site and between it and Joseph's cabin. The ring was identified as one that had been sold to George in Brantford that day. Finally, he was not seen after being left at Vinegar Hill. That night someone called several times at Joseph's cabin. No one saw the visitor, but one witness, who had been sleeping there, thought he spoke Mohawk. These visits agitated Joseph and Paul (then living with his son), who left the cabin each time for prolonged periods.

In his charge to the petit jury Sherwood concluded that most of the evidence was circumstantial and that the "real difficulty" was establishing whether the Powlises had killed Doxater or were present as accomplices. The testimony concerning George's ring constituted "strong presumptive evidence against the owner" because no explanation for it was given. Sherwood instructed the jury that the whole testimony was not conclusive of the guilt of any of the prisoners and that they should be acquitted if there was any doubt. After little more than an hour, the jury acquitted Paul and Joseph. George, however, was found guilty and sentenced, two days later, to be executed on 18 June.

Powlis immediately petitioned for royal clemency, claiming his innocence and arguing that the evidence was so palpably insufficient that the jury's decision was unwarranted. His plea was supported by 14 chiefs and others of the Six Nations. On 11 June, Sherwood tendered his report of the trial for the consideration of Lieutenant Governor Sir George ARTHUR. The judge admitted his own doubt of Powlis's guilt but did not wish to intimate an error by the jury. The Executive Council, the provincial body which usually reviewed capital cases, met on 13 June. Sherwood appeared before it and reiterated his conclusion: there was sufficient evidence to find Powlis guilty but it was "wholly circumstantial." Moreover, several facts were wanting to make the case "so conclusive as would be satisfactory in a case of capital punishment." The council followed Sherwood's lead. Solicitor General William Henry Draper*, however, urged that a murder committed by an Indian "should be visited with a punishment calculated to produce a deep impression on the minds of those of his own race." He recommended that the sentence be commuted to transportation for 14 years, but the council, with Arthur's concurrence, decided upon 7 years of hard labour in Kingston Penitentiary. William ALLAN reasoned that "protracted imprisonment . . . would be more Salutary, and even felt to be more severe by the Indians."

Uncertainties about Powlis's conviction lingered. Andrew Drew*, who had known Powlis for seven years, sought clemency for him in February 1840. Aided by Miles O'Reilly and William Johnson Kerr*, a son-in-law of Joseph Brant, Drew had investigated the case and was convinced that Powlis had not "acted a principal part in the murder." O'Reilly felt there was "a possibility" of guilt but "the evidence did not show even a probability of it." Again, Arthur referred the case to the Executive Council and on 2 March 1840 Robert Baldwin SULLIVAN reported that no new facts had been disclosed to warrant a further commutation of punishment.

The case was reopened for the last time on the petition in May 1841 of Powlis's wife and his mother, supported by chiefs and warriors of the Six Nations. Emphasizing Powlis's "good character," his conviction upon "slight grounds," and his relationship to Brant, the women urged Governor Lord Sydenham [Thomson*] to pardon him. The matter was referred to Sherwood, who wrote on 6 July that although he still had some doubt of Powlis's guilt, he was not sure the verdict was wrong. Since the jury was better acquainted with the witnesses and the locale, he had reasoned that it was "more capable" of drawing a correct conclusion. Asked to comment on the judge's response, Samuel Peters JARVIS, chief superintendent of Indian Affairs, urged "favorable consideration" of the petition. Civil Secretary Thomas William Clinton Murdoch disagreed on the grounds that "it is with these people [Indians], more than others, that it is necessary to discourage the ideas that such crimes may be committed with impunity or atoned for by light punishment." Sherwood, however, had been troubled by the case. He reread his notes and discussed the case with Chief Justice John Beverley Robinson*. The

chief justice was a much more decisive and self-assured man than Sherwood and undoubtedly his influence can be seen in Sherwood's letter of 13 July declaring, "I now think there is sufficient doubt of his guilt to warrant his discharge." The following day Powlis was pardoned and released from penitentiary.

The decision was, undoubtedly, the correct one. Although Powlis had never explained his whereabouts on the night of the murder or why his ring had been found at the murder site, the evidence could not sustain the jury's verdict. From the outset Sherwood had legal grounds for recommending a pardon; it was his failings as a judge that had imprisoned Powlis. The convict, on the other hand, was not the paragon depicted by his family, friends, and Drew. Kerr had alluded to the "bad Company" he kept and the beneficial effect likely to result from his imprisonment. A Mohawk woman, Sarah Ruggles, complained in June 1841 that Powlis was a "wretch" who, with others, had cheated her of her lands. Subsequently, the only surviving mentions of Powlis are on an 1849 census list for the Six Nations and on the provincial census of 1852.

ROBERT LOCHIEL FRASER

AO, RG 22, ser.134, 6: 119. HPL, Gore District jail reg., 1839. PAC, RG 1, E3, 65: 105–41; L3, 402: P9/57; RG 5, A1: 14336–39; RG 10, A1, 6: 2702–11, 2724–25; A5, 153: 88360; B8, 999A, Six Nations census for presents, 1849; RG 31, A1, 1851. Wis., State Hist. Soc. (Madison), Draper MSS, ser.F (Joseph Brant papers), 13: 31. Can., Prov. of, Legislative Assembly, *App. to the journals*, 1842, app.H, schedule B, no.348; 1844–45, app.EEE. U.C., House of Assembly, *App. to the journal*, 1839–40, 1, pt.I: 236; 1840: 66, no.348. *British Colonist* (Toronto), 19 June 1839. G. J. Smith, "Capt. Joseph Brant's status as a chief, and some of his descendants," *OH*, 12 (1914): 89–101.

PRESCOTT, CHARLES RAMAGE, merchant, politician, justice of the peace, office holder, and horticulturist; b. 6 Jan. 1772 in Halifax, seventh child and fourth son of Jonathan Prescott and Anne Blagden; m. first 6 Feb. 1796 Hannah Whidden (d. 1813), and they had seven children; m. secondly 9 Feb. 1814 Mariah Hammill, and they had five children; d. 11 June 1859 in Cornwallis, N.S.

Charles Ramage Prescott was a Nova Scotian pre-loyalist of impeccable credentials. His father, a surgeon and engineer in the siege of Louisbourg, Île Royale (Cape Breton Island), in 1745, had settled in Halifax by 1752, where he established himself as a luckless entrepreneur under Joshua Mauger*'s influence. Charles's brothers were respectively a doctor, a yeoman farmer, and Halifax's first commercial brickmaker; a sister married the prominent merchant Rufus Fairbanks. Charles himself took up the profession of his brother-in-law, and by 1800 had

Prescott

established himself in partnership with another pre-loyalist, William Lawson*. During the next decade, Prescott and Lawson epitomized Halifax's prosperous waterfront in the Napoleonic era: trading to the Iberian Peninsula, the West Indies, and the Canadas; privateering on the south Atlantic; and trans-shipping British goods to the United States to thwart the embargo. In 1809 Joseph Allison, later the husband of Prescott's eldest daughter, joined the partnership to form Prescott, Lawson and Company. The following year Lawson, MLA for Halifax County since 1806, sold his interest in the firm to Prescott, who himself sold half their wharf a year later to entrepreneur Enos Collins*. On 31 Dec. 1811 Prescott, Lawson and Company was dissolved, Allison alone apparently remaining active in commerce. Throughout the life of the firm, Prescott had been its senior partner. As such, he played an active role in Haligonian commercial life, subscribing for the apprehension of naval deserters, buying government bills at discount, participating fully in the Halifax Committee of Trade, and favouring the formation of a local joint-stock bank.

The dissolution of the firm, however, brought an end to Prescott's mercantile career. By mid 1812 he had left Halifax, reportedly on account of his health, to settle in Cornwallis. Here, he built a handsome seat, the fine neoclassical "Acacia Grove," where he pursued the life of a country squire. A magistrate, warden of the parish church, and trustee of the grammar school, he invested in local mortgages and took part in regional improvement, serving as a commissioner for erecting a bridge and as president of the agricultural society. From 1818 to 1820 he was MLA for Cornwallis Township; he was not an active legislator and, upon dissolution of the assembly at the death of George III, he was replaced by John Wells.

Prescott fitted more comfortably into the Council, to which he was appointed in 1825. For over a decade the only councillor resident outside the capital, he attended his unremunerated duty with admirable regularity during legislative sessions, though not at other times. The brother-in-law of an Anglican clergyman, he maintained a conservative position on controversial religious and educational issues such as the Pictou Academy [see Thomas McCulloch*]. On commercial matters, his views were likewise conservative, befitting a successful, if retired, merchant and a substantial shareholder in the provincial debt. Host to successive lieutenant governors at his country estate, Prescott was "of the stuff councillors are made of." It was no doubt this quality which led to his retirement in 1838 when Lieutenant Governor Sir Colin Campbell* was instructed to broaden the representative character of his advisers. Prescott was succeeded by his former partner Lawson.

It was neither for his mercantile career nor for his political role that Prescott was renowned. Rather, it was for his horticultural exploits. Like many of his contemporaries, including John Young*, he was an enthusiastic promoter of scientific agriculture, testing, for example, different varieties of wheat as a cereal crop and Swedish turnips as feed for sheep. A subscriber to John Claudius Loudon's famed *Gardener's Magazine*, he also cultivated the ornamental shrubberies and colourful exotics characteristic of contemporary English landscape gardening. In a province where functional landscaping remained the norm, his property was a showpiece of the era's "taste for improvement."

Prescott's interests far exceeded those of a fashionable country gentleman. His principal horticultural contribution lay in pomology. Importing a wide variety of fruit-trees from England, the United States, and Lower Canada, he created extensive orchards and noted hot-houses where he cultivated apples, apricots, cherries, grapes, melons, nectarines, peaches, pears, plums, and strawberries. He reportedly grafted and tested more than 100 varieties of apples and nearly 50 varieties each of pears and plums, from which he willingly gave scions to other cultivators. Although his activity pre-dated commercial fruit-growing in the province, he is credited with having introduced six of the ten varieties of apples, including the Gravenstein, which led the market during Nova Scotia's heyday as an apple producer. President of the short-lived King's County Horticultural Society, vice president of the Nova Scotia Horticultural Society when founded in 1836, and a member of the Massachusetts Horticultural Society, Prescott was lauded for his "zeal in Horticulture . . . only equalled by his rare knowledge, and still rarer liberality."

SUSAN BUGGEY

Kings County Court of Probate (Kentville, N.S.), Loose wills and estate papers, no.36 (C. R. Prescott) (mfm. at PANS). N.S. Museum (Halifax), Prescott papers. PANS, MG 1, 793; MG 2, 728, nos.535a–b, 587; MG 100, 209, no.36; RG 1, 192: 196; 194–96; 218SS–218DDD; RG 8, 6, no.9 (especially 16 Oct. 1820; 10 March, 15 May 1823; 8 Jan. 1824); 15, no.25. PRO, CO 217/152: 201–4. Simeon Perkins, *The diary of Simeon Perkins, 1790–1796; 1797–1803; 1804–1812*, ed. C. B. Fergusson (Toronto, 1961; 1967; 1978). *Acadian Recorder*, 1 June 1816; 20 Feb., 6 March, 1 May 1819; 1 July 1820; 24 March 1821; 3 Sept. 1825; 18 June 1859. *Novascotian*, 24 Aug., 14, 21 Sept. 1836; 9 Oct. 1839; 17 July 1843; 29 Sept. 1845; 2 March 1846; 4 Sept. 1848; 20 Sept. 1852; 20 June 1859. *Nova-Scotia Royal Gazette*, 7 July, 1 Sept. 1807; 22 July, 30 Aug. 1808; 6, 27 June 1809; 27 Feb. 1810; 3, 20 Feb., 24 April 1811. *Times* (Halifax), 8 Sept. 1846. T. M. Punch, "Jonathan Prescott, M.D. – vincit qui partitur," *N.S. Hist. Quarterly* (Halifax), 9 (1979): 59–80. *The standard cyclopedia of horticulture . . .*, ed. L. H. Bailey (3v., New York, 1933), 2: 1590. Beck, *Government of N.S.* Susan

Buggey, "Some considerations regarding the Prescott House, Starr's Point, Nova Scotia" (paper prepared for Can., Parks Canada, National Hist. Parks and Sites Branch, Ottawa, 1973). Eaton, *Hist. of King's County.*

PRINCE, JEAN-CHARLES, Roman Catholic priest, teacher, seminary administrator, editor, and bishop; b. 13 Feb. 1804 in Saint-Grégoire (Bécancour), Lower Canada, son of Jean Prince, a farmer, and Rosalie Bourg; d. 5 May 1860 in Saint-Hyacinthe, Lower Canada.

Jean-Charles Prince received his classical education at the Séminaire de Nicolet from 1813 to 1822. He began to study for the priesthood in 1822. In 1823–24, while taking theology courses as a seminarist, he taught rhetoric and the humanities. In the following school year he was made responsible for the teaching of philosophy at the Collège de Saint-Hyacinthe, and then in 1825 he returned to the Séminaire de Nicolet as a teacher of rhetoric. After his ordination on 23 Sept. 1826, Prince was summoned by Jean-Jacques Lartigue*, the auxiliary bishop in Montreal to the archbishop of Quebec, to assume various duties, including those of secretary to the bishop. He was also appointed chaplain of Saint-Jacques church.

In 1831, after six years in active association with Lartigue, Prince was made principal of the Collège de Saint-Hyacinthe (incorporated as the Séminaire de Saint-Hyacinthe in 1833). There, in 1825, he had formed strong ties of friendship with some of his pupils, in particular with Joseph La Rocque*, Joseph-Sabin Raymond*, and Isaac-Stanislas Lesieur-Désaulniers*, who were later called upon in turn to become superior of the seminary. When he arrived at the college, the new principal therefore found himself on familiar ground. His correspondence with Raymond in 1830 reveals how far Prince had accepted the ideas of Hugues-Félicité-Robert de La Mennais, and how fervently he had championed them with his young disciple.

From 1831 until Prince ceased to be principal in 1840, his life was closely linked to the institution for which he was responsible. As well as his primary office, he took on the duties of prefect of studies (1832–39), teacher of theology (1831–40), and procurator. According to the seminary's principal historian, Canon Charles-Philippe Choquette*, during Prince's term of office the classical college experienced a period of considerable expansion. Construction to enlarge and renovate the building was underway by 1832.

The college functioned in a social and political context which, added to its geographical location, was unlikely to protect it from the unrest related to the events of 1837–38. Thus the administration and staff of the college more than once found themselves caught in conflicts in which their behaviour prompted diverse interpretations concerning their political leanings, or at least what the government and ecclesiastical authorities thought to be such. Moreover, the college had in its student population sons, nephews, or cousins of such well-known Patriote leaders as Louis-Joseph Papineau*, Wolfred Nelson*, and Jean Dessaulles*; some of these leaders also had friends on its teaching staff. It was therefore no surprise that Prince and the college were closely watched by the government and ecclesiastical authorities and were more than once suspected or accused of being well disposed towards the Patriotes.

Certain events lent further credence to such rumours. For example, in August 1833 Papineau, the speaker of the House of Assembly and leader of the Patriote party, received an enthusiastic welcome from the pupils when he visited the college to see his son Lactance, who was then a boarder. The pro-Patriote papers, such as *L'Écho du pays* of Saint-Charles-sur-Richelieu, or the pro-government ones, such as *L'Ami du peuple, de l'ordre et des lois* of Montreal, had no intention of letting such an event go unnoticed, and the college found itself at the centre of a brief but heated controversy. This intensified a few weeks later after a visit by Governor Lord Aylmer [Whitworth-Aylmer*]. Aylmer, who had decided to attend the final examinations and the prize-giving, got a reception that some thought too cold in comparison to the far warmer one that had greeted Papineau. From then on, Prince was seen by the authorities at Quebec as a man tainted with partisan spirit, and was held in suspicion.

But it was difficult, if not impossible, to preserve real neutrality on the issues then dominating politics in Lower Canada. Prince and his staff had to deal tactfully with both the susceptibilities of the government and the nationalistic pride of some of the prominent Patriotes. If the former represented legitimate power, the latter none the less held enough of it to be able to make use of various forms of patronage. It was Papineau who was behind the grants that the college received from the government beginning in 1828, and it was through the support of Patriote representatives such as Louis Bourdages*, Édouard-Étienne Rodier*, and John Neilson* that the college obtained its incorporation in 1833. Hence, looking beyond the political leanings of its staff, the seminary could not ignore the manifold interests that linked it to the politicians of the Patriote party. Prince accordingly resigned himself to the suspicions and reproaches emanating from the archbishop of Quebec, Joseph Signay*, or the somewhat more cordial warnings from the bishop of Montreal, Lartigue, and his coadjutor, Ignace Bourget*. In a letter to Prince dated October 1837 Bourget urged, "Keep a close eye on your associates so far as their patriotic conduct is concerned. In this respect the institution is in a difficult situation."

On 4 Nov. 1837 several priests from the parishes adjoining Saint-Hyacinthe met at the seminary and voiced their apprehension with regard to Lartigue's pastoral letter of 24 October, which severely denounced any form of opposition to authority. Prince undertook to forward to his bishop a resolution expressing a desire that the clergy send an address to the government in London seeking justice for French Canadians, while affirming their own loyalty to the British crown. Lartigue supported the plan as much to satisfy the moderate Patriotes as to show that the clergy were not Papineau's tool. Prince collected the necessary signatures and found himself heading a delegation to forward the petition to Archbishop Signay and Governor Lord Gosford [Acheson*]. Although the petition was abandoned at the beginning of December, Gosford having considered it untimely, it was replaced a few weeks later by another addressed this time to the queen, in which the loyalty of French Canadians after the insurrection was reaffirmed.

Immediately following the battles of Saint-Denis and Saint-Charles-sur-Richelieu, the Séminaire de Saint-Hyacinthe had to shelter for a few days 200 soldiers and six officers under the command of Colonel Charles Stephen Gore*. But at the same time the seminary was hiding within its walls two Patriote leaders on the run, Thomas Boutillier* and Pierre-Claude Boucher* de La Bruère. The soldiers were apparently treated with consideration by their hosts. "If that is what is needed to prove our loyalty," wrote Prince, "then we are the most royalist people alive." But this was not enough to protect the authorities of the seminary from suspicion and reproach. Prince was obliged to vindicate himself on many occasions, and to assert categorically that as far as the current political disputes were concerned his institution was entirely neutral. In February 1838 Prince, Raymond, and La Rocque even agreed to draft jointly a long "justificatory statement" to clear themselves from the suspicions weighing upon them concerning their political stance. The task was a difficult one and Bishop Bourget pointed out its magnitude in a letter to Prince, "You cannot imagine all the charges being levelled against your institution."

Towards the end of 1838, although Prince was worried about the plight of the residents of Saint-Hyacinthe after the "looting" perpetrated by Major-General Sir James MACDONELL's troops, the seminary and its director appeared to be no longer the centre of controversy as far as the rebellions were concerned. The last two years of Prince's term of office were, moreover, largely devoted to pedagogical changes and innovations. For example, he eliminated the long public examinations at year-end, encouraged the expansion of the seminary's library, and in the

same period equipped the physics laboratory with new apparatus.

In 1840 Bourget, who succeeded Lartigue as bishop of Montreal that year, decided to summon Prince to work with him. Among the numerous tasks the bishop proposed entrusting to him was the founding of a religious journal which would speak for the clergy and undertake to interpret contemporary ideas and events in the light of strict religious orthodoxy. This plan, which Lartigue had formulated in 1827, had of necessity been shelved after meeting stubborn resistance from the ecclesiastical authorities of Quebec. Bourget proposed in 1840 to give concrete form to a project that seemed as close to his heart as it had been to Lartigue's. Hence the *Mélanges religieux* was founded. A prospectus for the newspaper was published on 21 Nov. 1840, announcing its objectives: "We will make religion the basis of all our teaching; we will apply ourselves mainly to enlightening the people about their duties." Concerning secular matters of the day, particularly politics, the prospectus stated: "Despite their usefulness, it is felt that their place in a collection of this kind can be only a very secondary one."

What the priest in charge of the *Mélanges religieux* did not divulge in public were his apprehensions about a task he considered too heavy to shoulder. He often unburdened himself on this subject in his correspondence with his former colleagues of the Séminaire de Saint-Hyacinthe, whom he pressed to contribute regularly to the paper. On 14 Dec. 1840 Prince began publishing in an unpretentious octavo edition a volume entitled *Prémices des mélanges religieux*. This publication, put out in seven parts concluding on 20 Jan. 1841, gave particular attention to reporting the public retreat preached at Montreal in December 1840 by Charles-Auguste-Marie-Joseph de Forbin-Janson*. Finally, on 22 Jan. 1841, the first issue of the *Mélanges religieux* came out. The paper was printed by Jacques-Alexis Plinguet and published under Prince's direction, but it was learned later that the editorial team also included abbés Michael Power*, Antoine Manseau*, Hyacinthe Hudon*, and Jean-Baptiste Saint-Germain*. The publication of the newspaper was Prince's responsibility until 10 Nov. 1843, when it changed hands.

The articles in the *Mélanges religieux* seldom disclosed the identities of their authors, who for the most part observed the strictest anonymity – a practice fairly common in mid-19th-century journalism. It is therefore difficult to identify Prince's specific literary contribution in any precise way, although presumably it must have been considerable. It is even more certain that the ultramontane ideas the paper championed were entirely the responsibility of the person who directed it for almost three years. Through the medium of the *Mélanges religieux*, Prince was one of the advocates of that ideology in Lower Canada [*see* François-Xavier-Anselme Trudel*].

While in charge of the *Mélanges religieux*, Prince, who had become a canon of the cathedral chapter, also took on other duties entrusted to him by Bishop Bourget. For example, in 1841 he was appointed chaplain of the Montreal Asylum for Aged and Infirm Women, an establishment founded by a volunteer group of women, including Émilie TAVERNIER. Two years later he helped to train the novices who were to form the Daughters of Charity, Servants of the Poor. The bishop of Montreal had also in 1841 appointed him chief chaplain to the sisters of the Congregation of Notre-Dame and to the Religious Hospitallers of St Joseph of the Hôtel-Dieu in Montreal. He was given the added task of accompanying a contingent of the former community to Kingston, Upper Canada, at the request of the bishop there, Rémi GAULIN. Prince left for Kingston on 19 November and stayed a year. As well as helping the sisters to get settled and looking after preparations for the reception of a number of Religious Hospitallers of St Joseph, he ministered to the French Canadians of the region and studied English.

In 1842 Bourget, who seemed to value Prince's help and efficiency, wrote to Rome requesting that he be appointed his coadjutor. Despite the opposition shown by the Sulpicians of Montreal, Bourget's request was finally granted. On 5 July 1844 Prince was appointed bishop of Martyropolis and coadjutor to the bishop of Montreal. He was consecrated on 25 July 1845 by Bourget, assisted by Bishop Power and Bishop Pierre-Flavien Turgeon*.

As coadjutor, Prince was made responsible for managing the diocese of Montreal during Bourget's second journey to Rome in 1846–47. He was sent there himself in October 1851, having been deputed by the first provincial council of Quebec to seek Pope Pius IX's approval of the acts it had passed. The coadjutor of Montreal also conveyed the council's request that two new dioceses, Saint-Hyacinthe and Trois-Rivières, be set up and that he be appointed to head the former. The appointment was confirmed on 8 June 1852, while Prince was still in Rome.

Bishop Prince assumed office on 3 Nov. 1852 upon returning home. He was to draw on the resources of the Séminaire de Saint-Hyacinthe frequently. Before the year was out he decided to appoint its superior, Raymond, his vicar general. A year later he acquired, apparently at a reasonable price, the building that had been known as "the old college" ever since the completion of the seminary's second and larger building. Prince carefully transformed the old college into an episcopal palace and a cathedral chapel, but his purchase ended in tremendous disappointment on 17 May 1854 when the building was destroyed by a raging fire.

During his episcopacy Prince created a score of parishes and ordained 40 priests. Being concerned about the spiritual state of the Catholics who were dispersed among the Protestants of the Eastern Townships, he paid them frequent pastoral visits and opened several missions in the region. He also undertook to increase the number of teachers. While travelling in Europe he recruited members of the Sœurs de la Présentation de Marie to see to the education of girls. The sisters opened their first convent at Sainte-Marie-de-Monnoir (Marieville) in 1853, and at the time of Prince's death were also running four more. In addition, he took steps to ensure that a community of Dominicans and teaching brothers was founded at Saint-Hyacinthe.

On 5 May 1860 Jean-Charles Prince, first bishop of Saint-Hyacinthe, died at the age of 56 as a result of a disease from which he had been suffering for several years.

NADIA FAHMY-EID

ACAM, 295.101; 295.103; 901.078; RLB, I; RLL, IX. ANQ-MBF, CE1-30, 13 févr. 1804. Arch. de la chancellerie de l'évêché de Saint-Hyacinthe (Saint-Hyacinthe, Qué.), Reg. des lettres des évêques, sér.I, 1–3; VII.B.1; XIII.B.8, 1851–60. ASSH, A, B, Dossier 7; G; C, 1, Dossier 1.7; 2, Dossier 1.8; F, Fp-8. *Mandements, lettres pastorales et circulaires des évêques de Saint-Hyacinthe*, A.-X. Bernard, édit. (8v., Montréal, 1888–98), 1. *Le Courrier de Saint-Hyacinthe*, 11 mai 1860. *Mélanges religieux*, 21 nov. 1840 (prospectus); 14 déc. 1840–20 janv. 1841 (prémices); 22 janv., 19 nov., 3 déc. 1841; 14 janv. 1842. Allaire, *Dictionnaire*, 1: 450. Cécile Mondou, *Inventaire sommaire d'une collection de mandements, lettres pastorales et circulaires de Mgr Jean-Charles Prince (P72), 1846–1886* (Montréal, 1979). Choquette, *Hist. du séminaire de Saint-Hyacinthe*, vol.1. Douville, *Hist. du collège-séminaire de Nicolet*, vol.2. Jacques Grisé, *Les conciles provinciaux de Québec et l'Église canadienne (1851–1886)* (Montréal, 1979). Lemieux, *L'établissement de la première prov. eccl.* [D.-A. Lemire-Marsolais, dite Sainte-Henriette et] Thérèse Lambert, dite Sainte-Marie-Médiatrice, *Histoire de la Congrégation de Notre-Dame* (11v. en 13 parus, Montréal, 1941–). Pouliot, *Mgr Bourget et son temps*, vol.2. Henri D'Arles [M.-J.-H.-A. Beaudé], "Monseigneur Jean-Charles Prince," *BRH*, 31 (1925): 467–68.

PRITCHARD, JOHN, fur trader, politician, farmer, author, businessman, and teacher; b. 1777 in Shropshire, England; m. first, according to the custom of the country, a native woman, and they had at least one son, John; m. secondly 1816 Catherine McLean, and they had at least nine children; d. 1856 in the Red River settlement (Man.).

John Pritchard came to the Canadas in 1800 and on 20 Feb. 1801 signed up for a five-year term as clerk for Forsyth, Richardson and Company, a partner in the short-lived New North West Company (sometimes

Pritchard

called the XY Company). He was stationed on the Red River near Lake Winnipeg (Man.) until the union of the New North West Company and the North West Company in 1804. The following year he served as clerk for the NWC on the Souris River. That June he became lost on the prairies of what is now southwestern Manitoba and southeastern Saskatchewan, where he wandered for 40 days without gun, knife, provisions, or clothing. He was rescued by passing Indians and cared for by a friend, John McKay* of the rival Hudson's Bay Company. Probably late in 1805 Pritchard was sent to the Nipigon country where he remained for four years before being stationed once again in the Red River department.

In the spring of 1814 Pritchard offered little resistance to the group of men sent by Miles Macdonell*, governor of Assiniboia, which seized much of the supply of pemmican at Fort La Souris (Man.) on behalf of the Red River settlers. Pritchard was labelled a coward by his NWC superior, probably Duncan Cameron*, and left the company's service soon afterwards. He had decided to settle at Red River but went first to Montreal, and while there contemplated going to London to warn Lord Selkirk [Douglas*], founder of Red River, about the perilous state of the colony. He sought out Colin Robertson* of the HBC for assistance in either travelling to London or returning to Red River to warn the colonists of an imminent attack by the Indians and Métis spurred on by the NWC. Pritchard left Montreal for Red River with three American axe-men on 17 Oct. 1814, undertaking the difficult journey via Moose Factory (Ont.), York Factory, and Norway House (Man.), mainly on snow-shoes.

While Pritchard was en route, Selkirk appointed him to the Council of Assiniboia. Pritchard arrived at Red River in April 1815 with one remaining companion, just in time to witness the arrest of Governor Macdonell and the dispersal of many of the colonists by the NWC. Although he remained behind and attempted to farm his newly acquired lot, the depredations of the Métis under the command of Alexander Greenfield Macdonell* forced him and the remaining settlers to leave. Together with Robertson, he was later able to persuade some of the colonists who had fled to Jack River House (Man.) to return to the abandoned settlement. He himself farmed and hunted at Red River for a year before being taken prisoner by the Métis during the massacre at Seven Oaks (Winnipeg) in 1816 [see Cuthbert GRANT]. After the battle he was dispatched to Fort Douglas (Winnipeg) with a message from the Métis, asking for the surrender of the fort. The colonists were evacuated and the fort surrendered.

Pritchard was taken to Fort William (Thunder Bay, Ont.), the headquarters of the NWC, but was released after Selkirk's arrival there. He presented Selkirk with a petition from 13 Red River settlers regarding the plundering of the settlement and the inadequate protection against the NWC. On his way back to Red River he was stopped at Rainy Lake by NWC men who threatened that "if he proceeded, he would be assassinated." He went instead to Montreal where he testified at Robertson's trial in May 1818. He was also subpoenaed as a witness at the trial in York (Toronto) in October of two Nor'Westers charged with the murder of Robert Semple*. Returning to Montreal in December, he made arrangements to travel to London to lay the case of the Red River settlement before parliament.

Pritchard reached his destination by 8 May 1819 and the following month he presented his petition to parliament, requesting protection for the Red River settlement from further aggressions by the NWC. That year a work was published in London containing accounts by Pritchard, Pierre-Chrysologue Pambrun*, and Frederick Damien Heurter of the attacks by the NWC. While in London, Pritchard also conducted an unsuccessful search for a schoolmaster for Red River and laid the groundwork with the governor and London committee of the HBC for the Buffalo Wool Company. This business was to be established as a subsidiary of the HBC and financed by the sale of 100 shares at £20 each; Pritchard was appointed its general manager. He returned to Red River via the annual ship to York Factory in 1820. A year later he had erected buildings at Pembina (N.Dak.) – close to the buffalo ranges – for the "manufacture" of buffalo wool and the tanning of buffalo hides for domestic and foreign markets. Although George SIMPSON, governor of the HBC's Northern Department, was convinced of the feasibility of the plan, he had little confidence in Pritchard, writing to Andrew Colvile in 1821 that Pritchard was "a wild visionary speculative creature without a particle of solidity and but a moderate share of judgement." Pritchard's Buffalo Wool Company floundered for five years before the major flood of 1826 destroyed much of its inventory and persuaded its partners to quit. The HBC underwrote the company's debt of £4,500.

After Pritchard's return to Red River from England, he became a leading citizen in the young settlement. In the short history *Glimpses of the past in the Red River settlement . . . , 1805–1836*, a collection of Pritchard's letters published in 1892, he described his farm as being "nearly sufficient for maintenance and clothing" in 1825. He also taught Sunday school and was reputed to have established day-schools for children of both sexes at Middlechurch and East Kildonan, without regard for their parents' ability to pay. For these services the HBC paid him £25 per year. It is not known when he retired from teaching but he remained active as a councillor of Assiniboia until

1848, serving on the committees of economy and finance. He was also involved in the financially unsuccessful tallow company established at Red River in 1832.

John Pritchard was a small man who was not afraid to break new ground. The first half of his life was certainly more adventurous than the second but throughout he maintained a strong concern for the settlers of Red River and devoted himself to securing the welfare of its colonists.

CAROL M. JUDD

John Pritchard is one of the authors of *Narratives of John Pritchard, Pierre Chrysologue Pambrun, and Frederick Damien Heurter, respecting the aggressions of the North-West Company, against the Earl of Selkirk's settlement upon Red River* (London, 1819). His petition to the House of Commons appeared in *Substance of the speech of Sir James Montgomery, bart., in the House of Commons, on the 24th of June 1819, on bringing forward his motion relative to the petition of Mr. John Pritchard, of the Red River settlement* (London, 1819). Some of Pritchard's letters are included in *Glimpses of the past in the Red River settlement from letters of Mr John Pritchard, 1805–1836*, ed. George Bryce (Middlechurch, Man., 1892); one of these letters, entitled "Lost on the prairies," was published in the *Beaver*, outfit 273 (June 1942): 36–39.

PAC, MG 19, E1, ser.1, 3: 1255, 1257; 4: 1492, 1501; 8: 3260; 9: 3597; 14: 5518, 5578; 16: 6171; 18: 6967; 23: 8902; 24: 9178; 52: 20151. PAM, HBCA, A.1/52: f.74; D.5/1: ff.243, 263; E.10/1, 1; MG 7, B7; MG 9, A76, file 102. Andrew Amos, *Report of trials in the courts of Canada, relative to the destruction of the Earl of Selkirk's settlement on the Red River; with observations* (London, 1820). *Canadian North-West* (Oliver), vol.1. S. H. Wilcocke, *Report of the proceedings connected with the disputes between the Earl of Selkirk, and the North-West Company, at the assizes, held at York in Upper Canada, October 1818* (Montreal, 1819). H. V. Neufeld, "John Pritchard – unsung hero of the Red River settlement," *Winnipeg Free Press*, 18 Jan. 1964: 18. Ray Tulloch, "Manitoba – the terrible, turbulent years; 'a little toad' they called him," *Winnipeg Free Press*, 21 Sept. 1963: 28.

PROUDFOOT, WILLIAM, Presbyterian minister, editor, and educator; b. 23 May 1788 near Peebles, Scotland; m. 8 June 1814 Isobel Aitchison of Biggar, Scotland, and they had six sons and five daughters; d. 16 Jan. 1851 in London, Upper Canada.

William Proudfoot, after attending the Lanark grammar school, went on to the University of Edinburgh and then, in 1807, entered the Associate Synod of Scotland's divinity hall at Selkirk. Licensed by the Associate Presbytery of Edinburgh on 6 April 1812, he worked for a short time as a relief preacher before accepting a call from Pitroddie, where he was ordained on 11 Aug. 1813. A popular, energetic man, he built up a large congregation, constructed a new church, created a bible society, and opened both an elementary and a grammar school. However, the congregation, deep in debt from rebuilding the church and hurt by the general recession, could not meet his salary. He was forced to apply for one of the three missionary postings to the Canadas proposed by the United Associate Synod of the Secession Church. Successful, he resigned on 5 June 1832 and, a month later, set out across the Atlantic in search of a new congregation.

He and his two companions, Thomas Christie and William Robertson, were charged with spearheading the church's penetration of the North American mission field. After having made a rapid survey of the Canadas that took him as far west as Goderich, Upper Canada, Proudfoot concluded that his synod should concentrate on the western part of the province since the existing Presbyterian groups were well established east of Hamilton. He decided in late 1832, after some wavering, to settle in London.

Hoping soon to be self-sufficient, he bought a 200-acre farm just outside the town. He organized congregations in and around London and established a number of preaching stations in the surrounding region. However, he found his charges inconveniently far apart and, though he ministered conscientiously to them for the next seven years, he was happy when the Reverend James Skinner relieved him in 1840 of two of the remoter congregations, allowing him to concentrate on London and its immediate neighbourhood. The London congregation's first place of worship, a schoolhouse, was shared by Methodists led by James JACKSON and Anglicans under Benjamin Cronyn*; its church, First Presbyterian, was built in 1836.

A forceful man, Proudfoot had immediately assumed command of the Canadian mission and, during his first two years in the colony, he assessed the religious needs of western Upper Canada, channelled requests for missionaries to Scotland, and briefed the new men as they arrived. By the end of 1834 he and the eight others labouring in the Canadas needed a more formal organization. After a brief flirtation with the idea of cooperating with the independent United Synod of Upper Canada, in December 1834 Proudfoot and his colleagues, fearful of compromising their voluntarist principles, founded the Missionary Presbytery of the Canadas in connection with the United Associate Synod of the Secession Church in Scotland. He was at the heart of the new church. A lifelong clerk of the presbytery and, after its creation in 1843, of the synod, he cajoled, conciliated, and directed his colleagues. He was able to minimize the arcane religious disputes and fratricidal quarrels that at times threatened to dissipate the energies of the small group, which numbered 18 ministers in 1843. Determined that his church should become an influential force within the colony, he undertook preaching tours

Proulx

throughout western Upper Canada, helped create new missionary stations and congregations, and founded in January 1843 the *Presbyterian Magazine*, of which he was editor and chief contributor during its 12-month existence. Proudfoot's other writings, especially his diary and letters, in which he commented on both secular and religious matters, are interesting sources of information about the colony.

Despite his efforts, the growth of the church was painfully slow. Closely tied to the Scottish synod and imbued with a conservative, Calvinistic theology, it appealed mainly to recent lower class immigrants from the Scottish lowlands and, to a less degree, to those from northern Ireland. Yet it was hard pressed to serve even this limited group, for the home synod, its attention divided between the West Indies and the Canadas, sent out few missionaries. Desperate, Proudfoot argued from 1837 for a Canadian seminary that could fill the gap. He eventually overcame local indifference and hostility from Scotland and in 1844 was authorized to open a divinity school in London while retaining his pastoral charge. The students boarded with him and he received periodic teaching assistance from other ministers, but there were never more than four students at any one time and, although it was a step in the right direction, the college failed to resolve the church's difficulties.

The paramount influence Proudfoot initially exercised within his church began to wane in the 1840s as more ministers took their seats in the synod. His colleagues, mindful of the powerful appeal among the colonists of the newly formed Synod of the Presbyterian Church of Canada, popularly called the Free Church, pressed for a merger with that body. Proudfoot was fearful that his church's staunch voluntarist principles might be compromised but, despite his misgivings, he led the negotiating team that conferred with the Reverend John BAYNE and his committee. Proudfoot was relieved when, after three years of talks, negotiations broke down in 1846. The following year, as the result of mergers in Scotland, the synod formed in 1843 was renamed the Synod of the United Presbyterian Church in Canada in connection with the United Presbyterian Church in Scotland. In the summer of 1850 the church decided to transfer its seminary to Toronto so that students could take advantage of the courses offered at the University of Toronto. Proudfoot opposed this move but he was overruled and he taught there while retaining his congregation in London. That fall, in Toronto, he caught cold and the complications which followed led to his death. His successor as pastor in London was his son, the Reverend John James Aitchison Proudfoot*.

A sensitive, intelligent man, Proudfoot was conscious that he retained his Scottish ideas along with his Scottish brogue. In religious matters he had little sympathy for other denominations and in politics he was a convinced Whig in Scotland and a staunch reformer in the Canadas, championing with undiminished vigour constitutional reform, secular education, and the complete separation of church and state. Yet he was keenly aware of the nature of the society around him and, recognizing that the colony was not Scotland, pressed for Canadian ministers, who might preach with Canadian cadences to Canadian ears. Although he himself did not wish to change his ideas on theology and his assumptions about church, state, and society, he helped ensure that his church was able to evolve and merge into the mainstream of Canadian Presbyterianism.

H. J. BRIDGMAN

[Proudfoot's journals and papers held by the UWOL, Regional Coll., and the PCA, together with the minutes of the presbyteries and synods named in the text, provide the main insights into his life. Portions of his journals have been edited and published in several periodicals, including "The Proudfoot papers . . . ," edited by Harriet Priddis, which appeared in volume 6 (1915) and pp.20–33 of volume 8 (1917) of the London and Middlesex Hist. Soc., *Trans.* (London, Ont.); after her death a further selection, edited by Fred Landon, appeared in volume 11 (1922) of the same journal. Another series, edited by M. A. Garland, was likewise published under the name "The Proudfoot papers . . . ," in *OH*, 26 (1930): 498–572; 27 (1931): 435–96; 28 (1932): 71–113; 29 (1933): 141–59; 30 (1934): 121–42; 31 (1936): 91–113; and 32 (1937): 92–103. Garland also edited "From Upper Canada to New York in 1835: extracts from the diary of the Rev. William Proudfoot," which appeared in the *Mississippi Valley Hist. Rev.* ([Cedar Rapids, Ind.]), 18 (1931–32): 378–96.

For two differing interpretations of Proudfoot *see* J. A. Thomson, "Proudfoot and the United Presbyterians; research into the Proudfoot papers" (MTH thesis, Knox College, Toronto, 1967); and H. E. Parker, "Early Presbyterianism in Western Ontario," London and Middlesex Hist. Soc., *Trans.*, 14 (1930): 5–79.   H.J.B.]

GRO (Edinburgh), Errol, reg. of marriages, proclamation of banns, 5 June 1814. SRO, GD1/92/1–22. UCA, Biog. files. *Presbyterian Magazine* (London), 1 (1843). *Canadian Free Press* (London), 17 Jan. 1851. *Annals and statistics of the United Presbyterian Church*, comp. William MacKelvie et al. (Edinburgh, 1873), 672. Gregg, *Hist. of Presbyterian Church*. John McKerrow, *History of the foreign missions of the Secession and United Presbyterian Church* (Edinburgh, 1867), 115. Robert Small, *History of the congregations of the United Presbyterian Church from 1733 to 1900* (2v., Edinburgh, 1904), 2: 579.

PROULX, JEAN-BAPTISTE, farmer, militia officer, landowner, and politician; b. 13 July 1793 in Nicolet, Lower Canada, son of Joseph Proulx, a farmer, and Geneviève Crevier Descheneaux; d. there 17 July 1856.

Jean-Baptiste Proulx belonged to an old farming family which had come to Nicolet at the time of

French settlement. His personality, shaped in this milieu of farmers, was marked not only by rural values but also by social circumstances in which mutual help based on kin and marriage was of prime importance. Attached to rural society by his upbringing, revering the family values instilled in him, and eager to see his patrimony enlarged and improved, Proulx, like his close relations, became a farmer.

Before so doing, Proulx entered upon a classical education at the Séminaire de Nicolet in 1803. Little is known about the intellectual training he received there, or about the influence his teachers had upon him, since he made no comment on these matters. He finished his studies in 1811 and, unlike his classmates who chose the priesthood or the liberal professions, he decided to return to the family farm. During the War of 1812 he joined the militia and went to the border to fight the Americans.

When Proulx returned to Nicolet in 1814 his father granted him some 150 acres – a third of his land – along with livestock, seed grain, and a parcel of old clothes. Proulx settled in and soon proved a dynamic and efficient farmer. His strength and wealth depended less on the size of his property than on the area he brought under cultivation. From the beginning his land had one of the highest yields in the parish of Saint-Jean-Baptiste at Nicolet, and Proulx was one of the minority of farmers who had a surplus to sell in the adjoining region. Thus he became one of the leading citizens in Nicolet, playing a part in most areas of its collective life. The Saint-Jean-Baptiste registers show that he was often chosen as a godfather, and in the early 19th century such a position was still a sign of prestige within a community. He was prominent in the organizations of his village. Among other things, in 1817 he helped set up a market at Nicolet. He took an interest in the militia, and as a lieutenant in the 2nd Battalion of Buckingham militia exercised considerable influence in the Trois-Rivières region.

A fervent and well-known defender of French Canadian institutions, Proulx in 1820 got himself elected to the House of Assembly for Buckingham, along with his running mate Louis Bourdages*. He retained his seat until 1838. In the house he attracted no particular attention and was concerned mainly with the problems of his region and little interested in the great political debates or parliamentary struggles. This perspective did not prevent him from earning the respect of colleagues, who appreciated his industriousness and his unfailing attendance at committees to inquire into the development of agriculture and settlement. He had no difficulty in securing re-election in Buckingham in 1824 and was on his way to becoming the spokesman in the house for the farmers of the Trois-Rivières region. Returned again in 1827, he was dismissed from his post as a militia lieutenant because during the elections that year he had taken issue with the policy of the governor-in-chief, Lord Dalhousie [Ramsay*], and had made disrespectful remarks concerning Lieutenant-Colonel Kenelm Conor Chandler*, the commander of the 2nd Battalion of Buckingham militia, who was the seigneur of Nicolet.

In 1828 Proulx's father granted him a sub-fief of about 45 acres, exempt to all intents and purposes from seigneurial dues. His land holdings gave Proulx pre-eminence over the majority of the region's farmers. He enjoyed a manifest superiority also in various other aspects of his agricultural activity, the most significant undoubtedly being the extent of his livestock. At the end of the 1820s Proulx owned 40 cattle, 7 horses, 60 sheep, and 14 pigs. He was one of the largest suppliers of butcher's meat in Nicolet; he even sold hay at the market in Trois-Rivières. In such circumstances he was able to entertain the idea of taking a wife. On 5 July 1830 he married a young widow, Flore Lemire, of Baie-du-Febvre (Baieville), who came from a milieu of well-to-do merchants and farmers. Through this fine marriage – "arranged," as local tradition aptly puts it – he was able to consolidate his social and economic standing further, since his wife brought a dowry consisting of more than 500 *livres* and a rich stretch of grassland in the village of Baie-du-Febvre.

That year Proulx was elected to the assembly for the new riding of Nicolet. On his return to the house he was urged to take an increasingly firm stand against the British government; the Patriote party under Louis-Joseph Papineau*, being no longer content to demand administrative and legal reforms, was pressing for full control of the budget by the assembly and an elected legislative council. At the same time, the agricultural crisis, the scarcity of property on seigneurial territory, and land speculation in the townships by important British merchants heightened social tensions and made any reconciliation between the French Canadians and the English Canadians impossible. It was in this period that Proulx openly joined the Patriote party and adopted Papineau's ideas. During the election campaign in 1834 he warmly defended the 92 Resolutions, and as positions hardened he reached the point of demanding that Lower Canada become independent. In the elections that year he won a resounding victory as a result of the high level of participation of local farmers and day-labourers. His brother-in-law Jean-Baptiste Hébert, a farmer, was also elected without difficulty, becoming the second member for Nicolet. Around these two men, linked through family ties, there increasingly developed a real framework of local power. In 1835 Proulx acquired a quarter of Île Bougainville, near Nicolet, in the hopes of extending his grassland and his cattle raising. Despite heavy duties as a farmer, he continued to wage a bitter struggle in his region against the government.

Provencher

On the eve of the rebellion Proulx was one of the most active members of the revolutionary organization in his county. He set up local associations, arranged meetings on the steps of churches following Sunday mass, and openly asked his fellow-countrymen to support armed revolt. But he had little success. The repeated interventions of Jean Raimbault*, priest of the parish of Saint-Jean-Baptiste, against any form of rebellion proved persuasive and were much talked of throughout the county. Similarly, the rural populace, who were over-burdened by seigneurial dues, were in effect disarmed by the unconditional support given to the seigneurial class of the Trois-Rivières region by various members of the liberal professions and small merchants. Proulx was denounced by many of his friends, and was taken to jail in Montreal at the end of 1838. He was released the following year for want of evidence.

After the rebellion Proulx withdrew into private life as a result of the disappointments he had experienced, which left him with a deep sense of bitterness. He decided that he would devote himself solely to cultivating his land, and would endeavour to preserve the economic independence he had always cherished. He began by rounding out his lands, adding small parcels bit by bit. From 1844 to 1850 he bought at least 10 properties, acquiring in this way an estate of some 500 acres. His land holdings thus gave him control over a large part of the seigneury of Nicolet. Then, being aware of the developing urban market and of new prospects, he focused his efforts on cattle raising, as the conversion of several holdings into pasture indicates. The slaughterhouse and two dairies on the farm give further proof of the increasing importance of his livestock.

Towards the end of his life Proulx made plans to establish his six children. In 1854 he bought the eldest son a property in Durham Township, and made it over to him. In his last will he named his wife sole legatee, on condition that she bequeath the family inheritance to the children and that she make some kind of division between them. Until the day of his death Proulx acted like an all-powerful family head. He died on 17 July 1856 at Nicolet and was buried that day in the village church, an obvious sign of his pre-eminence. A few years later his wife, who had always been submissive to him, complied with his wishes to a large extent; the last two sons inherited their father's estate, while the three girls received generous dowries when they married.

No doubt Jean-Baptiste Proulx had led an ordinary life. It was none the less representative of the destinies of the minority of farmers who kept their eye on the market, strove to preserve their forebears' patrimony, and exercised considerable power in their communities in the first half of the 19th century in Lower Canada.

RICHARD CHABOT

ANQ-M, CE3-2, 5 juill. 1830; CN3-81, 1ᵉʳ juill. 1830. ANQ-MBF, CE1-13, 13 juill. 1793, 17 juill. 1856; CN1-23, 28 févr. 1860; CN1-35, 18 juill. 1814; CN1-47, 20 mars 1852, 28 déc. 1854; CN1-52, 30 mars 1835; CN1-56, 6 juill. 1828. ANQ-Q, E17/8, nos.232–51. ASN, AO, Polygraphie, IV, no.19; Séminaire, Cahier de cens et rentes de la seigneurie de Nicolet, 11: 15; 13: 15; Cahier de dîme du curé Jean Raimbault, 1809–40, paiement de la dîme de J.-B. Proulx écuyer; Censier de la seigneurie de Nicolet, 5, nos.28, 30–31, 35–38, 52; Lettres des directeurs et autres à l'évêque de Québec, 2, 23 juill. 1839; Terrier de la seigneurie de Nicolet, 2: 23. PAC, MG 30, D1, 25: 441–48; RG 31, A1, 1831, Nicolet. L.C., House of Assembly, *Journals*, 1823–24, app.R; 1828–29, app.II. *La Minerve*, 14 juill. 1856. F.-J. Audet, "Les législateurs du Bas-Canada." Desjardins, *Guide parl.* Fauteux, *Patriotes*, 358. J.-E. Bellemare, *Histoire de Nicolet, 1669–1924* (Arthabaska, Qué., 1924). Douville, *Hist. du collège-séminaire de Nicolet*. Maurice Grenier, "La chambre d'Assemblée du Bas-Canada, 1815–1837" (thèse de MA, univ. de Montréal, 1966). Laurin, *Girouard & les Patriotes*, 101. L.-O. David, "Les hommes de 37–38: Jean-Baptiste Proulx," *L'Opinion publique*, 13 sept. 1877: 433.

PROVENCHER, JOSEPH-NORBERT (baptized **Joseph**), Roman Catholic priest, bishop, and politician; b. 12 Feb. 1787 in Nicolet, Que., son of Jean-Baptiste Provencher, a farmer, and Élisabeth Proulx; d. 7 June 1853 in St Boniface (Man.).

Joseph-Norbert Provencher came from a large family of limited means, and had to wait to begin his studies until a free primary school opened at Nicolet in 1801. He attended the Collège Saint-Raphaël at Montreal in 1802–3, returned to Nicolet in 1803, and then enrolled in the classical program when the seminary opened there in January 1804. Provencher studied at this institution until 1808, along with Thomas Cooke*, who later became bishop of Trois-Rivières. He spent the school year 1808–9 at the Collège Saint-Raphaël as a regent, while starting theological studies. These studies were continued in 1809–11 at the Séminaire de Nicolet, where he also taught the third and fifth forms (Method and Belles-Lettres). After a few months at the Grand Séminaire de Québec, he was ordained priest on 21 Dec. 1811.

For the next seven years Provencher ministered in several parishes. At a time when there was a woeful lack of clergy, the availability of this young ecclesiastic made it easier for Joseph-Octave Plessis*, the bishop of Quebec, to fill vacant positions. Provencher was named curate at the cathedral of Quebec in 1811, and given the same post at Vaudreuil in 1812 and Deschambault in 1813. Plessis made him responsible for Saint-Joachim parish at Pointe-Claire in 1814, and for that of Kamouraska two years later.

Provencher's correspondence during these years brings out certain of his traits: humility, receptiveness, and apostolic zeal. Wherever he went he deplored his parishioners' lack of religious fervour. At

Vaudreuil there seemed to be too many dances, and some people, believing a spell had been cast on them, went to a faith-healer; at Pointe-Claire he found "the young people in an unwholesome state . . . and the old hardly fervent"; and at Kamouraska he regretted that "the sin of the flesh is the most prevalent." It appeared to him that there was "enough to occupy an evangelical worker more zealous and skilful" than himself.

Bishop Plessis had doubtless discerned the young priest's qualities, and in 1818 he suggested to Provencher that he should go to the Red River colony (Man.) and establish the Roman Catholic church there. The Earl of Selkirk [Douglas*], a Scotsman and a shareholder in the Hudson's Bay Company, had founded the settlement at the junction of the Assiniboine and Red rivers on a tract of land granted by the company in 1811, and the first settlers had arrived in 1812. This colonizing venture had not, however, been looked upon with favour by the North West Company, the HBC's rival in the fur trade, because the NWC considered it a threat to the free passage of supplies between its storehouse at Fort William (Thunder Bay, Ont.) and the fur-rich region of Lake Athabasca. Since 1812 there had been violent and at times bloody clashes between the two companies in the area around the Selkirk settlement [see Cuthbert GRANT]. In 1816 Selkirk and Miles Macdonell*, the HBC governor of Assiniboia, had asked Plessis to send a missionary to the Red River, in the hope that the presence of a mission would put the colony on a more solid footing. A Catholic himself, Macdonell was well aware that the majority of the new settlers were Irish and Scottish Catholics, and that the region's Métis and French Canadian population, consisting of former engagés of the NWC and their families, was also in large part Catholic. Plessis had responded in 1816 by sending Father Pierre-Antoine Tabeau* into the northwest to assess the prospects for a permanent mission at Red River and itinerant missions at Rainy Lake and Grand Portage (near Grand Portage, Minn.). Following the battle of Seven Oaks (Winnipeg) in June 1816, in which Robert Semple*, the governor of the HBC's territories, was killed, Tabeau decided not to venture farther west than Rainy Lake, and in his report to Plessis he recommended that no mission be set up at Red River so long as the conflict between the two companies persisted.

Plessis did not share Tabeau's opinion and, as a result of a petition signed in 1817 by 22 residents of the settlement requesting a permanent missionary, he decided to send Provencher, with Sévère DUMOULIN, a young priest, and William Edge, a seminarist. Provencher raised objections to the new appointment, citing his "lack of knowledge," his inability to speak English, a painful hernia, an outstanding debt of some £250, and the immense challenge facing the mission-aries. He was not, in his opinion, "the right man for the job." But when Plessis, convinced that Provencher had the necessary qualities, insisted, he accepted.

To raise money for the mission, Samuel Gale*, Selkirk's lawyer, launched a campaign throughout Lower Canada in January 1818. Sir John Coape Sherbrooke*, the governor-in-chief, and Plessis were among the contributors, but the directors of the NWC, Henry McKenzie*, William McGillivray*, Thomas Thain*, and others, refused to help. The subscription, which had the strong support of numerous Protestants, reached all the Catholics of Lower Canada.

Provencher, Dumoulin, and Edge left Montreal on 19 May 1818, and on 16 July reached Fort Douglas (Winnipeg), where the governor of Assiniboia, Alexander McDonell*, lived. They were warmly received by the Catholics in the settlement. Provencher was an impressive figure. He stood six feet four inches, and like his confrère Dumoulin had a noble bearing. The newcomers created a great stir, especially since the Métis and the children had never seen clerical garb. According to Plessis's instructions, the first two objectives of the mission were to convert the "Indian nations scattered over that vast country" and to care for the "delinquent Christians, who have adopted there the customs of the Indians." The missionaries had specific orders to learn the Indian languages, to instruct and baptize Indian women who had married French Canadians à la façon du pays, and then to bless these unions. They were to remain neutral in the conflict between the two companies and to teach "by word and deed the respect and allegiance owed to the sovereign."

Upon arriving, the missionaries set to work to provide for the sacramental needs of the Catholics and their offspring, performing 72 baptisms in less than two weeks. In addition, with the help of the voyageurs who had brought them from Montreal, they began building their house, but only a section 20 feet by 30 was finished before winter. This house, divided in two, served as both chapel and residence. Selkirk had made over some 25 acres to the missionaries for a church on the east bank of the Red River opposite the mouth of the Assiniboine, and a tract five miles by four to support the mission. The chapel was inaugurated on 1 November, with Boniface (who had brought the Gospel to the Germanic tribes in the Middle Ages) as its patron saint. Two months earlier Dumoulin had left with Edge to establish a mission farther south at Pembina (N.Dak.). A number of families from the Red River had gone to Pembina to seek their livelihood hunting buffalo after a plague of grasshoppers had destroyed their crops in August 1818. Provencher visited them during the winter of 1818–19, and in March went to the trading posts on the Souris and Qu'Appelle rivers; in the course of the 300-mile trip he met some 260 people attached to the two companies.

Provencher

Before Plessis sent Provencher to Red River, he knew he would have to appoint a bishop in the northwest, because the region was too far from his episcopal see of Quebec. When he visited Europe in 1819 he put this plan forward in London and Rome, along with the idea of appointing a bishop for Montreal; Provencher and Jean-Jacques Lartigue* were the candidates he proposed. Some of the Canadian clergy thought the appointment of a bishop for the northwest was premature, and the choice of Provencher inappropriate. Plessis stood firm and, having convinced the British government of the merits of his plan, he returned to Lower Canada in June 1820 with bulls that had been signed in Rome on 1 February nominating Provencher auxiliary bishop and suffragan to the archbishop of Quebec, as well as his vicar general.

Provencher set out for Lower Canada on 16 Aug. 1820, four days after Abbé Thomas-Ferruce Picard* Destroismaisons had arrived at Red River, and he reached Montreal on 17 October. When Plessis handed the papal bulls to him at Quebec, Provencher asked for time to think the matter over. Plessis appointed him provisionally to the parish of Sainte-Anne at Yamachiche. In January 1821 Provencher wrote to Plessis that he could not "accept a burden which is so obviously beyond my strength and my ability." Plessis was not, however, of this opinion, as he made clear to Jean Raimbault*, superior of the Séminaire de Nicolet: "The more I study him, the more equanimity, good sense, seriousness and wisdom I perceive in his character." That March, Provencher informed Plessis of his decision to accept the bulls. He spent 1821 in Lower Canada soliciting funds for his mission, and was consecrated bishop on 12 May 1822 at Trois-Rivières. Because there was as yet no diocese in the northwest, Rome made him titular bishop of Juliopolis, the former episcopal see of Galatia.

Provencher left again for Red River on 1 June, with a young priest, Jean Harper. He reached St Boniface on 7 August, shortly after the departure of John HALKETT, the executor of Lord Selkirk, who had died in 1820. Halkett, as a member of the HBC's London committee, had been anxious to strengthen the Red River colony. Thus he had ordered that the company's trading post at Pembina be abandoned, and had secured a promise from Plessis that the Catholic mission there would be closed so that the settlers would be encouraged to return to Red River. Provencher wrote to Halkett pointing out that the settlement at St Boniface would not be able to provide for all the residents of Pembina during the coming winter. He therefore delayed dismantling Dumoulin's mission until 1823. Rather disheartened, Dumoulin went back to Lower Canada. Bishop Provencher then took it upon himself to help newcomers settle at St

François Xavier, in the White Horse Plain on the Assiniboine River. Since the missionaries' arrival in the northwest, they had performed 800 baptisms, regularized or blessed 120 marriages, and given first communion to 150 people, more than half of these sacraments being administered at Pembina.

Those evangelizing in the northwest seem to have had in mind four important objectives: education of the young, assisted colonization, moral improvement of the whites, and conversion of the Indians. By 1819 Provencher had started instructing young children at St Boniface. He made no secret of his concern to find among the boys candidates for the priesthood, but he had no illusions about the prospects. The two students on whom he was counting when he returned in 1822 left him a few years later, and the other boys who might later become priests were still children. As it turned out, no young man in his territory would be made a priest during his episcopacy. The education of girls seemed no less important to Provencher. A small house was built for this purpose in 1823, but it burned down just after it was finished. He also lacked teachers. In 1824 Provencher sought the services of Angélique Nolin, the Métis daughter of Jean-Baptiste Nolin*, who had studied in Montreal and who spoke French, English, and some Indian languages fluently. Because of her father's opposition, it was not until January 1829 that the St Boniface school for girls opened, with Angélique and her sister Marguerite as teachers. Meanwhile, Provencher had adopted the practice of visiting children at the St Boniface school, where Harper taught boys and girls, and of giving catechism classes.

To assist settlers, Provencher encouraged cultivation of the land and cattle raising, and saw that seed and livestock were brought in from Lower Canada and the United States. He set up an "industrial school" for weaving in 1838 to use wool from the sheep brought into the colony, and from the buffalo.

Provencher, in his role as a missionary, had also to take action on moral grounds. Abuse of alcohol was common, particularly after some of the whites and Métis had managed to distil it locally. The priests urged the civil authorities to prevent the sale of spirits and even beer to natives, and during the 1840s the HBC began to restrict their use. The conjugal life of the settlers also posed problems. In 1819 Dumoulin had noted that the missionaries were having difficulty persuading Canadians to regularize their country marriages with Indian or Métis women, because they liked "this liberty of being able to get rid of their wives." That year Provencher in a letter to Lady Selkirk had noted that "concubinage" was "rife," especially in the distant posts. In his view, more regularity of conduct "would probably have diverted the plagues that have overwhelmed us," which were most often attributed to chance.

It took a long time to evangelize the Indians, and apart from Dumoulin's efforts in the Pembina region little progress was made before the 1830s. Neither Provencher nor any of the missionaries with him managed to familiarize themselves with the Indian languages, and they had to resort to interpreters. In 1830 Provencher returned to Lower Canada and the following year he brought back Abbé George-Antoine Bellecourt*, a young priest who had already studied Ojibwa. Bellecourt in 1832 began his mission among the Saulteaux to the west of St Boniface on the Assiniboine River, setting up the village of Baie-Saint-Paul (St Eustache, Man.). He endeavoured to settle the Indians into a sedentary way of life and encouraged them to become farmers; these efforts were a source of tension between him and Provencher, for the bishop wanted to see native customs respected.

The white and Métis population of the Red River colony in 1831 numbered 2,390, including 262 Catholic and 198 Protestant families. The first non–Roman Catholic missionary to work there was the Anglican minister John West*. He had arrived in August 1820, and while serving the Protestants, who for the most part were Scots Presbyterians brought in by Selkirk, he had opened a boarding-school for young Indian boys. Anti-Catholic, and not well received by the Scots who wanted a minister of their own church, West soon found himself in competition with Provencher, who had already sought the right to solemnize marriages for Protestants, in the hope of thereby "retarding the introduction of Protestant ministers" into the northwest. Relations between Provencher and later Anglican ministers, David Thomas Jones* and William Cockran*, seem, however, to have been more harmonious, although the bishop never ceased to regard their doctrine as dangerous.

During the first years of his ministry Provencher had run into some difficulties with the HBC directors, who seemed to him more interested in the fur trade than in the colony's progress. After Selkirk's death, the Catholic missionaries were less welcome in the company canoes journeying from Lower Canada to the Red River; Provencher concluded that "we must expect nothing of benefit to the mission from men to whom the word Catholic is odious." Although Provencher enjoyed good relations with Andrew H. Bulger, governor locum tenens of Assiniboia in 1822–23, he was not on similar terms with Halkett, of whom the bishop caustically observed, "He appears to be very devoted to the interests of the company . . . without apparently paying much attention to those of the colony." Provencher complained in 1823 that Halkett had forbidden Bulger and John Clarke, the HBC's chief factor at Red River, to supply the Catholic missionaries with wine, although it was required to celebrate the Eucharist. Moreover, he noted that the missionaries had not enjoyed the 20 per cent reduction in debts to the HBC that the company had granted to the settlers because it had overcharged on goods sold to them.

However, under the influence of George Simpson, the governor of the HBC's Northern Department, there was a distinct improvement. Simpson spent the winter of 1823–24 at Red River, and Provencher reported that he was on "good terms" with him. In 1825 the council of the department, under Simpson's chairmanship, gave the mission sugar, wine, tea, and other food valued at £20 to £25. The same year the council recommended that the London committee grant Provencher's mission £50 annually, to indicate their approval of his beneficent work. Simpson, Provencher reported, expressed astonishment at all the good the Catholic missionaries were doing with meagre resources "whereas their ministers with so much money do nothing." In the same year Simpson assured Provencher that he would raise no objection to granting ecclesiastics free passage in company canoes, and over the years he sponsored other gifts from the HBC, such as £100 in 1830 for a stone church to be built at St Boniface. The annual grant was raised to £100 in 1835, and when Provencher proposed to set up his weaving school in 1837 Simpson offered to pay the travel expenses and salaries for two weavers from Lower Canada to come and teach at it for three years. The governor recognized the value of Provencher's mission in the colony, where more than half the settlers were Catholics. The company's position was being increasingly challenged, and it was having difficulty preserving its exclusive right to the fur trade in the face of opposition from the independent Métis traders. The activities of Provencher and his priests tended to encourage among the Métis some respect for stability and the established order, a fact that Simpson was well able to appreciate.

In the 1830s the Roman Catholic Church became firmly established along the Red and Assiniboine rivers, among the whites and Métis of the colony and even of Pembina, which had not been completely deserted, as well as among the Indians. Young people were receiving a primary education and being introduced to trades they would find useful. Substantial financial aid had come from the fund-raising campaigns conducted in Lower Canada among priests and people in general. In February 1835 Provencher, by invitation, attended for the first time sittings of the Council of Assiniboia, the legislative body set up by the HBC to govern the colony. Two years later he was admitted as a councillor, and for the rest of his life he participated in the council's business. Provencher enjoyed a degree of influence in this body, and from 1845 was a member of its committee of economy; Governor Simpson also consulted him when choosing Métis councillors [see François-Jacques Bruneau*].

Provencher

In 1835 Bishop Provencher believed the time had come to visit Europe in order to provide a final impetus for the development of the church in the northwest. He also wanted to forward his plan to begin a mission in the Columbia country, beyond the Rocky Mountains. Some of the whites settled there had asked him for such a mission, and the HBC directors were ready to help him in this endeavour. Provencher left Red River in August 1835, went first to Lower Canada, and then embarked at New York. In London the bishop's expectations were fulfilled by the HBC directors, who in particular guaranteed him the priests' right to travel in the company canoes to Red River and even to the Columbia country. In Paris and Lyons he obtained an increase in the annual grant of the Society for the Propagation of the Faith. In Rome he informed the prefect of the Congregation of Propaganda about his work in the northwest and about his plans, to which he thought the principal obstacle was the lack of priests and money. Pope Gregory XVI received him graciously and affectionately, and presented him with a beautiful chalice; Propaganda gave him the equivalent of £225 and a case of valuable books. The pope accepted Provencher's plan for a mission on the Pacific coast and extended his episcopal jurisdiction to the Columbia.

Having returned to Lower Canada on 22 June 1836, Provencher undertook to organize committees of the Society for the Propagation of the Faith, and urged the bishops of Quebec and Montreal to introduce it into their dioceses. He spent the winter in Lower Canada, and before returning to Red River in the spring of 1837 he persuaded Modeste Demers*, the curate at Trois-Pistoles, and François-Norbert Blanchet, the parish priest at Les Cèdres, to venture on a mission beyond the Rockies. Demers was at Red River during 1837–38 before joining Blanchet for the journey to the west coast.

In March 1843 the Red River colony had 5,143 settlers; more than half (2,798) were Roman Catholics. Of the 870 families, 571 were Métis or Indian, 152 French Canadian, 110 Scottish, and 22 English. There were never enough missionaries, and worse still, they were always a changing group. By 1843, 13 missionaries had come to help Provencher, but only four – Bellecourt, Jean-Baptiste Thibault*, Joseph-Arsène Mayrand, and Jean-Édouard Darveau* – were still in the colony; in 1844 Darveau was killed by Indians at Baie-des-Canards (Duck Bay, Man.). The arrival of Louis-François Laflèche* that summer therefore served only to keep the personnel at the same strength. The bishop himself was afflicted with kidney stones and had to reduce his activities. For his part, Joseph Signay*, the archbishop of Quebec since 1833, considered that it would be difficult in the future for him or his successors to force any secular priest to go to the west. It was not that Provencher had ever

proved hard to please in the matter of colleagues. All the same, in a letter to Signay in 1839 he had set down some conditions: "They must have a liking for the work and be educated men, steadfast in character and not given to rancour, able to restrain themselves and refrain from losing their temper, men who are not at a loss for words and can also sing. English would be a real necessity." He knew, however, that the archbishops of Quebec had sent him young priests somewhat at random; they had generally been good and he made no complaints.

Provencher left for Lower Canada and Europe in May 1843, hoping to find the help essential to satisfy the needs of his mission. He went by way of the United States, with the object of persuading a number of nuns to take up residence at Red River and to teach and care for the sick there, but his efforts at Dubuque (Iowa), St Louis, Mo., Louisville, Ky, and Cincinnati, Ohio, were to no avail. In Montreal, thanks to Ignace Bourget*, who had been bishop there since Lartigue's death in 1840, he was able to persuade the Sisters of Charity of the Hôpital Général in Montreal, commonly called the Grey Nuns, to send some of their number to the colony [see Marie-Louise Valade*]. As for priests, he sought them first among the Jesuits, but they had only recently returned to Lower Canada and could not undertake such a responsibility. Provencher found himself increasingly in favour of priests who belonged to religious orders. In a letter to Charles-Félix Cazeau* in 1844 he set out his reasons: "Secular priests will make slow headway. There is no common accord in their thinking, except that they should only put their hand to the plough for a time, which they always find too long." In France he met Charles-Joseph-Eugène de Mazenod, the bishop of Marseilles, who had founded the Congregation of the Oblate Missionaries of Mary Immaculate. Mazenod responded to Provencher's appeal, and in the summer of 1845 two Oblates, Pierre Aubert* and Alexandre-Antonin Taché*, reached the colony; three others followed soon after. Provencher himself had returned to Red River in the summer of 1844.

On his trip through Lower Canada in 1843, Provencher had persuaded the archbishop of Quebec that it was an opportune time to erect an autonomous ecclesiastical division in the northwest. On 16 April 1844 Rome agreed to the proposal, and decided to establish the vicariate apostolic of Hudson Bay and James Bay. Meanwhile the Society for the Propagation of the Faith at Lyons guaranteed Provencher an annual payment of 30,000 francs, which eased his financial circumstances. On that score the presence at the mission of two communities of religious was reassuring to him, given their vows of poverty and their habitual generosity towards such undertakings. Personnel, whether priests or sisters, was thenceforth assured. There would no longer be a lack of money.

The church of the northwest, after 25 years of unremitting toil, was at last widely established and solidly organized.

Following the establishment of an ecclesiastical province on the Pacific coast with Blanchet as its archbishop in 1846, Rome considered taking a similar step in the northwest. But to Provencher the project appeared truly premature. Since he was not in agreement, on 4 June 1847, as a compromise, his vicariate apostolic was erected into the North-West diocese; as a diocesan church was normally an integral part of an ecclesiastical province, Provencher again became suffragan to the archbishop of Quebec. What he wanted first and foremost, however, was a coadjutor. He thought there would be serious disadvantages if he were to die without a successor to take his place quickly. Among the secular clergy who were with him or who had worked in the northwest, he saw only one as suitable for episcopal ministry – the young priest Laflèche. But Laflèche's state of health left much to be desired; he suffered so badly from rheumatism that he was unable to travel. Steps were accordingly taken to obtain the appointment of the young French Canadian Oblate Taché, and his consecration as bishop of Arath and coadjutor in the diocese of the northwest took place on 26 Nov. 1851. When Taché subsequently visited Rome, he obtained permission for the diocese to be renamed St Boniface.

Bishop Provencher died on 7 June 1853, having been struck down by "epilepsy" (more probably apoplexy) some three weeks earlier. He had accomplished the task entrusted to him 35 years before. The parish of St Boniface had more than 2,000 inhabitants, including 1,000 Catholics widely dispersed on farms along the banks of the Red and Assiniboine rivers; the village had a cathedral, a bishop's house, the sisters' residence, which doubled as a hospital, and a few small houses. The parish of St François Xavier had a church, a convent where the sisters ran a school, and 900 Catholics. St Charles, located between these two villages, formed a nucleus of 200 settlers, and was to become a new parish in 1854. St Norbert, which was also on the Red River and where there were 900 Catholics, would soon follow suit. As for the Indian missions, there were three: St Anne (Lac Ste Anne, Alta) to the east of Fort Edmonton (Edmonton), Saint-Jean-Baptiste at Île-à-la-Crosse (Sask.), and La Nativité on Lake Athabasca. Each had branches which the missionaries visited periodically. By 1 Jan. 1854 they had baptized 4,309 Indians in the northwest. A church had come to life.

Bishop Joseph-Norbert Provencher was a strict man who would accept no compromise in matters of duty. His devotion to people and interest in public affairs, his common sense, goodness, courage, and tenacity, his undoubted simplicity and spirit of self-denial (for a pillow he had a block of oak) were remarkable.

Laflèche, who assisted him in the last nine years of his life, gave this simple testimony: "How often have I admired in him the tender piety and the admirable trust in Providence that constitute the comfort and the joy of a true Christian." He must not be made larger than life. But it is important to recognize Provencher as a man who took with utter seriousness the mission to which he was called, and who strove to carry it out with realism and hope.

LUCIEN LEMIEUX

A good deal of the correspondence of Joseph-Norbert Provencher has been published in "Lettres de monseigneur Joseph-Norbert Provencher, premier évêque de Saint-Boniface," Soc. hist. de Saint-Boniface, *Bull.* (Saint-Boniface, Man.), 3 (1913). Many of these letters were translated in *Documents relating to northwest missions, 1815–1827,* ed. Grace Lee Nute (St Paul, Minn., 1942). The report drawn up by Provencher for his visit to Rome in 1836, *Mémoire ou notice sur l'établissement de la mission de la Rivière-Rouge, et ses progrès depuis 1818, présenté à la Propagande, le 12 mars 1836* ([Rome, 1836]), was also translated into English as "Memoir or account on the establishment of the Red River mission, and its progress since 1818; presented to the Propaganda, March 12, 1836 . . .," ed. J. E. Rea and trans. J. R. Turnbull, *Beaver,* outfit 303 (spring 1973): 16–23.

AAQ, 12 A, H; 210 A, IX–XIV, XVIII–XXII; 90 CM, Angleterre, II; 36 CN, 1; 330 CN, I–III; 331 CN. ACAM, 255.109, 831–33, 835; 295.101, 833–34; 355.110, 814; RC, I; RLL, II; VIII. ANQ-MBF, CE1-13, 12 févr. 1787. Arch. de la chancellerie de l'évêché de Valleyfield (Valleyfield, Qué.), Saint-Michel (Vaudreuil), I, 51. Arch. de l'évêché de Sainte-Anne-de-la-Pocatière (La Pocatière, Qué.), Kamouraska, I. Archivio della Propaganda Fide (Rome), Scritture riferite nei Congressi, America Settentrionale, 3 (1831–36); 4 (1836–42). A.-A. Taché, *Vingt années de missions dans le nord-ouest de l'Amérique* (nouv. éd., Montréal, 1888). Allaire, *Dictionnaire.* J.-É. Champagne, *Les missions catholiques dans l'Ouest canadien (1818–1875)* (Ottawa, 1949). J.-E. Cyr, *Monseigneur Joseph-Norbert Provencher: quelques considérations sur sa vie et son temps* (Saint-Boniface, 1919). Douville, *Hist. du collège-séminaire de Nicolet,* 1: 19–49, 2: 5*, 12*, 127*. Georges Dugas, *Monseigneur Provencher et les missions de la Rivière-Rouge* (Montréal, 1889). Donatien Frémont, *Mgr Provencher et son temps* (Winnipeg, 1935). B. J. Gainer, "The Catholic missionaries as agents of social change among the Métis and Indians of Red River: 1818–1845" (MA thesis, Carleton Univ., Ottawa, 1978). Lemieux, *L'établissement de la première prov. eccl.* A.-G. Morice, *Histoire de l'Église catholique dans l'Ouest canadien, du lac Supérieur au Pacifique (1659–1905)* (3v., Winnipeg et Montréal, 1912). Gaston Carrière, "Mgr Provencher à la recherche d'un coadjuteur," CCHA *Sessions d'études,* 37 (1970): 71–93. Gilles Chaussé, "Deux évêques missionnaires: Mgr Provencher et Mgr Lartigue," CCHA *Sessions d'études,* 37: 51–60. Raymond Douville, "Les trois abbés Harper," *Cahiers des Dix,* 13 (1948): 139–85. Lucien Lemieux, "Mgr Provencher et la pastorale missionnaire des évêques de Québec," CCHA *Sessions d'études,* 37: 31–49. David Roy, "Mgr Provencher

Pryor

et son clergé séculier," CCHA *Sessions d'études*, 37: 1–16. Albert Tessier, "Un curé missionnaire: l'abbé S.-N. Dumoulin (1793–1853)," *Cahiers des Dix*, 16 (1951): 117–31.

PRYOR, WILLIAM, ship's captain, businessman, and office holder; b. 1775 in New York City, son of Edward Pryor and Jane Vermilye; m. 19 March 1798 Mary Barbara Voss; d. 4 Sept. 1859 in Halifax.

The Pryors were a loyalist family that came to Halifax from New York in 1783. William's grandfather arrived in America as a master carpenter but quickly and with considerable success turned to trade, as did his son Edward. William, the youngest of Edward's three sons, followed his brothers into commerce, apprenticing during the 1790s as a ship's captain in the West Indies trade. According to tradition, William spent part of his early career as a prisoner of the French on Guadeloupe and served at least briefly as captain of a Nova Scotia privateer. About 1800 he established premises on Water Street, from which he carried on general trade. The scale of his business remained modest at first, and he operated very much in the shadow of his elder brother John. He did well enough during the Napoleonic Wars, however, to be able in 1816 to spend £587 for land on Halifax's Northwest Arm. Over succeeding years this property was developed into an estate of considerable elegance named Coburg.

Pryor's rise to prominence came mainly after the War of 1812 and was occasioned in part by the deaths of his brother John in 1820 and of his father in 1831. Through inheritance and purchase he became the owner of extensive waterfront property, later known as the Dominion Wharf complex. The scale of his business is indicated by the permits issued by the local custom-house to authorize the re-export of goods brought into Halifax. In 1833, for instance, William Pryor and Company dispatched 41 vessels, mostly to adjacent ports within British North America; included in their cargoes were 33,294 gallons of rum and 2,911 hundredweight of sugar. Pryor was not a major shipowner, but between 1821 and 1856 he had shares in 25 vessels totalling 3,510 tons. He favoured the brig, a ship particularly suited to the West Indies and British American carrying trades. The firm's vessels usually performed shuttle runs between Halifax and the ports of the other Maritime provinces but Pryor also participated in more speculative and far-flung ventures. For example, late in the 1820s his brig *Rival* proceeded from Halifax to Brazil, and thence to the Cape of Good Hope and St Helena before returning to Brazil. From there it sailed to Gibraltar, Leghorn (Italy), and Marseilles and then to Quebec and Cape Breton. Finally, two years after its departure, it returned to Halifax. Such employment, involving the purchase and resale of a wide range of cargo, earned Pryor profits as high as £2,000 per voyage. The risks of trade also involved the firm in losses but, on balance, Pryor derived a substantial income from shipping and general mercantile operations. In 1830 he further assured his fortunes by winning the contract to supply the Halifax garrison market with rum. As his activities expanded, Pryor brought his three sons and his son-in-law into the firm as partners.

Pryor's shrewdest business decision had come in 1825, when he invested £5,000 to become one of the eight founding partners of the Halifax Banking Company. This initiative brought annual dividends of up to 20 per cent as well as membership in the inner circle of Halifax commerce. Pryor's entrepreneurial prominence was also reflected in his membership on the executive of the Halifax Commercial Society through the period 1815–30. During the 1830s he was president of both the Halifax Fire Insurance Company and the Nova Scotia Marine Insurance Company. He also served as a director of the abortive Shubenacadie Canal Company and led the campaign to make Halifax a base for ocean whaling. In 1854, after long service as vice-president of the Halifax Banking Company, Pryor succeeded Henry Hezekiah COGSWELL as president.

Pryor's involvement in general community affairs, although relatively limited, was nevertheless tinged with controversy. For example, in 1826 he resigned as a churchwarden and member of St Paul's after he and other leading laymen had been defeated by Bishop John Inglis* in a quarrel over who should be the new rector of the church [*see* John Thomas TWINING]. Although never a magistrate, Pryor enjoyed the confidence of Lieutenant Governor Sir Peregrine MAITLAND and in 1831 was appointed to the newly created commission to supervise pilotage service at the port of Halifax. Office, property, and kinship ties made Pryor a member of the ruling oligarchy. Accordingly, he opposed the agitation for reform which emerged during the 1830s and 1840s. Although never a leading figure in the resistance to responsible government, he signed several petitions drawn up in protest against political change. A symbol of the old order, thanks mainly to his banking activities, he lost access to public office with the coming of reform [*see* Richard TREMAINE] but retained his central position within the Halifax commercial élite.

Pryor left an estate valued at £39,000, most of it consisting of local real estate. Never active in organized philanthropy, he limited his bequests to family members. His three daughters, all advantageously married, received small annuities, while most of the wealth went to his three sons. The eldest, William*, carried on the family business and eventually succeeded to the presidency of the Halifax Banking Company. Thus William Pryor Sr can be regarded as a case study in the emergence of indigenous family capitalism within early 19th-century Halifax.

DAVID A. SUTHERLAND

BLHU, R. G. Dun & Co. credit ledger, Canada, 11: 240; 12: 745. Halifax County Court of Probate (Halifax), Estate papers, no.867; Wills, 4: f.315; 6: f.420; P92 (William Pryor) (mfm. at PANS). Halifax County Registry of Deeds (Halifax), Deeds, 22: f.346; 32: f.452; 37: f.431; 42: f.443 (mfm. at PANS). MHGA, Atlantic Canada Shipping Project, "Halifax shareholders' file," comp. E. [W.] Sager. PANS, RG 1, 244, no.103; 290, no.1; 311, no.63; 314, no.26; RG 5, P, 121, 20 Feb. 1830; RG 31-104, 12–14, Customs House permits, 1831–33. *Acadian Recorder*, 9 Dec. 1820, 15 Feb. 1823, 3 Sept. 1825, 22 Nov. 1828, 10 Sept. 1859. *Journal* (Halifax), 14 Aug. 1834. *Morning Chronicle* (Halifax), 6–8 Sept. 1859. *Novascotian*, 16 March 1831, 25 Jan. 1832, 7 Jan. 1836, 30 Sept. 1850. *Belcher's farmer's almanack*, 1824–59. W. E. Boggs, *The genealogical record of the Boggs family, the descendants of Ezekiel Boggs* (Halifax, 1916), 81. [T. B. Akins], *History of Halifax City* (Halifax, 1895; repr. Belleville, Ont., 1973), 93. J. W. Regan, *Sketches and traditions of the Northwest Arm (illustrated) and with panoramic folder of the Arm* (2nd ed., Halifax, 1909), 14–16.

PURCELL, JAMES, architect; b. *c.* 1804; fl. 1841–58 in St John's.

Some time in or before 1841 the strong-willed Roman Catholic bishop of St John's, Michael Anthony Fleming*, had a serious disagreement with the architect he had hired to superintend the construction of the Cathedral of St John the Baptist and replaced him with James Purcell, a stone-cutter and masonry contractor from Cork (Republic of Ireland). What Purcell did before he assumed that position in 1841 or after his departure in 1858 is not as yet known, but it is clear that he must have had a more amenable personality than his predecessor and may have been more willing to accept – or to work around – Bishop Fleming's decisions.

It is likely that this amenability and Purcell's association with Patrick Kough*, superintendent of Newfoundland's public buildings, were the principal factors in making him the dominant architect in St John's during the 1840s and 1850s. His importance can be seen in the commissions he received as well as in the fact that, in sectarian St John's, he was patronized by the two major denominations. In 1842, while working on the cathedral, he designed and built an extension to the Orphan Asylum school run by the Benevolent Irish Society; two years later he added to it a combined portico and observatory. Also in 1842 the Anglicans asked him to produce designs for a small chapel in Quidi Vidi as well as for their proposed cathedral in St John's. Both were executed in the Gothic Revival style, newly fashionable in Newfoundland. Christ Church, Quidi Vidi, which opened

in 1843, was a small, cruciform frame structure with simplified Gothic detail in the form of windows and doors with pointed arches. The design is a considerably modified version of Purcell's original proposal which called for pinnacled buttresses at every corner and an inappropriate baroque bell-cote over the entrance. The cathedral design was accepted by Bishop Aubrey George Spencer*, but was decisively rejected by his successor, Edward Feild*, who described it in 1844 as a "wretched imitation" of a church by "an honest man [who] knows as much about ecclesiastical architecture as his drawings show." Feild, in contrast to Spencer, was a high churchman and, in matters of design, an ecclesiologist – a combination which allowed for only the most correct of Gothic design. Feild had his way and the cathedral was designed by George Gilbert Scott in the Old English style of Gothic architecture, with construction beginning in 1847. Purcell appears to have been responsible for the design of the Theological Lecture Room on Military Road which was built in approximately 1842. It was a small, gabled frame structure with detail similar to that found on Christ Church.

In 1846 Purcell designed his major work, the Colonial Building, which housed a bicameral legislature and government offices. This Classical Revival structure with an Ionic portico was officially opened on 28 Jan. 1850. It was originally meant to be situated in the lower town and to include a market-house but, as both Kough and Purcell pointed out, this first site – on a very steep hill – militated against the visual effect of the building. The assembly accepted this argument and the Colonial Building was erected on Military Road adjacent to Government House, while the market-house was combined with a court-house on the original Water Street site. The Colonial Building remained the seat of the House of Assembly until 1959 and now houses the provincial archives.

During the 1850s Purcell's patron appears to have been the Roman Catholic church. From 1850 to 1853 he worked, once again with Kough, on the construction of the Presentation Convent. His next design commission for the Roman Catholic authorities was St Bonaventure's College (1857–58), which is built of grey rough-cut granite – stone acquired cheaply when the government reduced the size of the proposed penitentiary. Certain features of the college, notably the treatment of the window surrounds and the coping at the roof gable, are also found in the bishop's palace constructed in 1854 and the Mercy Convent of 1858, such similarities suggesting that Purcell might also have been responsible for these buildings.

Purcell is not known to have carried out any private or commercial designs in Newfoundland and it may be that he was too much engaged in his public and ecclesiastical commissions to be otherwise involved. He purchased a number of properties in St John's

Pyke

between 1846 and 1849, presumably on speculation. However, the local economy fell in 1849, and by 1852 all of Purcell's land was mortgaged. His financial difficulties must have continued to increase because by 1857 he was in serious trouble. By August 1858 he had become insolvent and left Newfoundland.

The impression created by James Purcell's buildings is that he was a competent architect, although neither imaginative nor adventuresome. His association with Kough – who had a reputation for good and honest work – allowed him to pursue a fairly substantial career in a developing economy. This career was considerably assisted by the building boom that followed the fire of June 1846, but it could not survive his own speculations on that boom or the general economic decline that characterized the succeeding decade.

SHANE O'DEA

Nfld., Registry of Deeds, Companies & Securities (St John's), Deeds, Central District, 11: ff.219, 507; 12: ff.167, 197–98, 200; 13: ff.32, 436, 527; 16: f.46. USPG, C/CAN/Nfl., folders 276–94 (mfm. at PANL). *Newfoundlander*, 24 Feb. 1842. *Patriot* (St John's), 28 July 1841. *Public Ledger*, 1841–58. *Times and General Commercial Gazette* (St John's), 9 Nov. 1842, 28 June 1843. *Centenary volume, Benevolent Irish Society of St. John's, Newfoundland, 1806–1906* (Cork, [Republic of Ire., 1906?]), 68. Wallace Furlong, "The history of St. Bonaventure's College," *The Adelphian: 125th anniversary, 1857–1982, St. Bonaventure's School, St. John's, Newfoundland* ([St John's, 1982]), 14. Howley, *Ecclesiastical hist. of Nfld.* [M. P. Murphy], *The story of the Colonial Building, seat of parliament from 1850 to 1860, now the home of the Newfoundland and Labrador provincial archives* (St John's, 1972). O'Neill, *Story of St. John's*, vol.2.

PYKE, GEORGE, lawyer, office holder, politician, and judge; b. 19 Jan. 1775 in Halifax, son of John George Pyke* and Elizabeth D. Allan; m. 10 May 1809 Eliza Tremain, and they had three sons and three daughters; d. 3 Feb. 1851 in Pointe-à-Cavagnal (Hudson), Lower Canada.

Little is known about George Pyke's early years in Nova Scotia, except that from 1787 he prepared for a legal career by studying under Richard John Uniacke*. Probably some time after 1794 he left Nova Scotia for Quebec, where he was called to the bar on 6 Dec. 1796. He seems to have successfully integrated himself into society there and probably benefited from the support of James Monk*, chief justice of the Court of King's Bench at Montreal, and of Monk's family. He knew how to advance himself in government circles, for in 1799 he obtained the position of deputy surveyor general of land for Lower Canada.

From then on Pyke was, as it were, adopted by the government; he held a variety of offices in the public service without a break until 1820, including those of deputy clerk of the crown in 1800; protonotary, with Joseph-François Perrault*, of the Court of King's Bench at Quebec, and clerk of the Court of King's Bench from 1802 to 1812; advocate general of the province in 1812 in succession to Olivier Perrault*; law clerk of the Legislative Council from 1816 to 1819, and interim Vice-Admiralty judge in 1816; acting judge of the Court of King's Bench at Montreal from 1 June 1818 to 1820 in the absence of judge Isaac Ogden*, whom he replaced permanently on 1 May 1820. The various posts Pyke obtained at the outset of his career were not unrelated to the political patronage quite natural to the age, a favouritism accepted by those profiting from it and coveted by those excluded. His political ideas ensured that he would be a loyal subject of the crown in the House of Assembly, where he represented the constituency of Gaspé from 1804 to 1814.

Pyke's appointment to the bench did not remove him completely from politics. As a judge of the Court of King's Bench at Montreal from 1820 to 1842, he was called upon to hear several political cases directly connected with the rise of the Patriotes and the insurrections of 1837–38. Two of them have been of interest to historians. The first arose from an article by Ludger DUVERNAY published in *La Minerve* in 1836. Charged with libel for the third time since 1828, Duvernay was tried before Pyke, who denounced the newspaper's insinuations as likely to sully the reputations of jurors as well as the good name of justice itself. Proclaiming his own clemency, Pyke at the same time imposed upon Duvernay a fine and a month in prison, a sentence that only enhanced the convicted man's status with the Patriotes.

The other trial, more dramatic in its implications, took place from 3 to 10 Sept. 1839. François Jalbert, a militia captain from Saint-Denis on the Richelieu, had been in jail for two years on a charge of having murdered Lieutenant George Weir in 1837 when Weir was a prisoner of the Patriotes [see Charles-Elzéar Mondelet*]. The jury included eight French Canadians and four English Canadians, of whom only two were British in origin. Judges Pyke, Samuel Gale*, and Jean-Roch Rolland* heard the case in an emotion-charged court-room. After several days of waiting, the excited audience heard the verdict: by ten to two, the jurors found Jalbert not guilty. The crowd jumped up in fury; the judges and jurors barely managed to make their escape. The heroes in the room, the two British jurors who alone had favoured a conviction, were borne out on the shoulders of those loyal to the régime.

Immersed as he was in the events of his time, Pyke obviously did not lose his personal interest in politics. Although he said he was "not much of a politician," in the period 1839–50 he aired his views on the changing

726

political scene at length to various correspondents. His political creed does not seem to have changed: he professed an unswerving faith in the power of the British empire and considered it in the colonies' interest to remain dependent on Britain. That is why, in his opinion, the real danger came primarily from the reformers who were seeking responsible government, and from the weakness of the governor and his executive in following a policy of political appeasement.

The upheavals that shook the province did not leave the administration of justice unscathed. The courts were overwhelmed with work, and also suffered from various dismissals, deaths, and suspensions within the judiciary. Consequently, during the reorganization of the judicial system between 1839 and 1842, Pyke had to shoulder heavy responsibilities. To the detriment of his already failing health, he was obliged to carry out the duties of both puisne judge and chief justice, the latter without either the title or the salary of the office. His confrères, Gale and Rolland, complained as much as he did, but none of them dared press Governor Sir John Colborne* to fill the vacancies and appoint a chief justice.

Sir Charles Bagot*, who served as governor from January 1842, undertook to resolve the problem. Despite the judges' good will, there was increasingly insistent criticism, from which Pyke was not immune. Although the members of the bar at Montreal acknowledged that he had great qualities, in March they complained that "age, infirmities and poor health made it impossible for [Pyke] to attend to the duties of his office." In the spring, without consulting him, the governor asked him to resign. Embittered, Pyke ended his career on 1 July, believing that he would thereby enable Bagot to accomplish his plans for the peace and prosperity of the Canadas. He refrained from any action except to seek recognition for the work he had done as *de facto* chief justice, in order to obtain a more generous pension.

Pyke then went into retirement on his vast estate at Pointe-à-Cavagnal, where he was able to attend to his most troublesome concerns: his business affairs and his health. Pyke's children, about whom there is little information, seem to have done well and to have given him little cause for anxiety: one son became a lawyer, another a doctor, the third a pastor; his daughters, as he did, lived eminently respectable lives. His business activities, on the other hand, claimed more of his attention. The purchase of about 10,000 acres in the Eastern Townships around 1820, the acquisition of an immense estate at Pointe-à-Cavagnal, and other transactions, both for himself and his children, had entailed financial obligations that he could not always meet.

These worries notwithstanding, George Pyke enjoyed a tranquil retirement in the country, for despite frail health he lived to be 76. Shortly before he died, his intimate friend, Paul-Loup ARCHAMBAULT, parish priest of Vaudreuil, wrote urging him, albeit without success, to convert to Roman Catholicism. He exhorted him to rise above the combats, obstacles, and agitations besetting his "noble heart," for "in the sight of eternity all must fall, all must vanish, all must disappear." Pyke was interred in the Anglican parish of Vaudreuil.

JACQUES BOUCHER

George Pyke is the author of *Cases argued and determined in the Court of King's Bench for the district of Quebec in the province of Lower-Canada, in Hilary term, in the fiftieth year of the reign of George III* (Montreal, 1811), the first collection of judicial decisions published in Lower Canada, consisting of 16 civil and commercial cases heard in the Court of King's Bench at Quebec in February 1816. The cases were reported in the format being used in England, giving summaries of the pleadings of counsel and lengthy reports of the judgements of all the judges who drafted notes.

Letters from Judge Pyke to various people about his business affairs, career, and political opinions are at ASQ, Fonds Viger–Verreau, cartons 79, 80, 81, where there is also a collection of the cases on which he ruled from 1818 to 1841 (Fonds Viger–Verreau, Sér.O, 0189–96). The collection Baby (P 58, U) at the AUM contains some ten letters by Pyke written between 1815 and 1839, while the Antiquarian and Numismatic Society of Montreal is the principal repository for the Pyke papers, 1797–1850 (mfm. at PAC, MG 23, GIII, 25, D).

ANQ-M, CE1-67, 6 févr. 1851. PANS, MG 1, 926: 104; MG 100, 211: 41. St Paul's Anglican Church (Halifax), Reg. of baptisms, marriages, and burials, 5 March 1775. *Doc. relatifs à l'hist. constitutionnelle, 1791–1818* (Doughty et McArthur), 516–21, 525; *1819–1828* (Doughty et Story; 1935), 241–85. F.-J. Audet, "Les législateurs du Bas-Canada." P.-G. Roy, *Les juges de la prov. de Québec.* Buchanan, *Bench and bar of L.C.* David, *Patriotes.*

Q

QUIBLIER, JOSEPH-VINCENT (baptized **Josephe** and often referred to simply as **Joseph**), Roman Catholic priest, Sulpician, and educator; b. 26 June 1796 in Colombier, France, son of Jean Quiblier, a day-labourer, and Catherine Quiblier; d. 12 Sept. 1852 at Issy-les-Moulineaux, France.

Quiblier

Little is known about Joseph-Vincent Quiblier's early years. After a classical education, he studied theology from 1816 to 1819 at the Séminaire Saint-Irénée in Lyons, which was run by the Sulpicians. He was ordained priest at Grenoble on 7 March 1819; that year he ministered as curate in a parish at Montbrison, in the department of the Loire, and then for nearly six years held a similar charge at Notre-Dame in Saint-Étienne. In the summer of 1825 Quiblier broke off his pastoral career and left France in haste without having undergone the spiritual training usual with the Sulpicians; the reasons for this radical switch are unknown.

In September 1825 Quiblier arrived at Montreal with a young theology student named Joseph-Alexandre Baile*. It was probably to help Quiblier integrate himself into Sulpician and Montreal life, as well as to meet the urgent need of replacing Antoine-Jacques Houdet*, whose health had suddenly deteriorated, that he was immediately appointed professor of philosophy and natural sciences at the Petit Séminaire de Montréal. Although he was young, inexperienced, and largely untrained, he did have access to the detailed lecture notes of his predecessor. He was appointed director of the Petit Séminaire in August 1828 but continued to work until 1830 within the group of full-time professors; he later encouraged the publication of their lecture notes as textbooks. His appointment came at the time when the superior of the Séminaire de Saint-Sulpice in Montreal, Jean-Henry-Auguste Roux*, was returning from London after negotiating an agreement with the British authorities about the problem of the seigneurial rights of the institution. The agreement, which provided for the seminary to cede its rights of *lods et ventes* to the government of Lower Canada in return for an annuity, precipitated an acute internal conflict between the French Sulpicians, who supported it, and the French Canadian Sulpicians, who opposed it. In this context, Quiblier's rapid rise to the office of director testifies to the confidence he had inspired among the French members of the seminary, who were in the majority; he would quickly become the key person among them because of his dominant personality and his youth. He shared this group's royalist leanings as far as the state was concerned, and its gallican tendency as to the position of the church (and of the seminary); this fact closely linked the fate of the seminary to decisions of the British government and explains the endemic opposition of the institution to the rival episcopal power of Jean-Jacques Lartigue*, the auxiliary bishop in Montreal to the archbishop of Quebec.

Quiblier succeeded Jacques-Guillaume Roque* as vice-superior of the seminary in August 1830. Bernard-Claude Panet*, the archbishop of Quebec, recognized Quiblier as such, but refused to accord him the dignity of vicar general or to acknowledge that he had an automatic right to the cure of Notre-Dame in Montreal before the Holy See, to which the seminary had appealed, decided who the titular priest was. In 1831 Panet, Lartigue, and Quiblier had a unique opportunity to build a common front against the bill on *fabriques*, by which the Patriote party wanted to throw parish deliberations open to all landed proprietors [*see* Louis Bourdages*]. But the internal ecclesiastical quarrel evidently overrode the general interest of the clerical group. Quiblier's offer to publish an important work by Roux on the question of the right of the *fabriques* came to nothing in the end. He had wanted to assert the autonomy of the seminary by publishing the work on its own authority, whereas Panet and more particularly Lartigue insisted on approving and amending it in advance of publication.

Roux, having suffered increasing infirmity and the deterioration of his faculties, died in April 1831, and Quiblier thus became superior. The quarrel over his powers and those of the bishops then continued in various ways. It was brought out into the open with the furore over the appointment of the coadjutor to the archbishop of Quebec. The seminary promoted its own candidate, Jean-Baptiste Saint-Germain*, a priest dedicated to its interests, and not the archbishop of Quebec's candidate, Pierre-Flavien Turgeon*. After Panet died in February 1833, the choice of Turgeon by the new archbishop of Quebec, Joseph Signay*, and its immediate confirmation by London were interpreted as acts hostile to the seminary's interests. Consequently it resorted to secret manœuvres at the Holy See, using its agent, Jean-Baptiste Thavenet*, to get the nomination process reversed in Rome. Warned in April of Thavenet's intrigues and of the small likelihood that his cause would succeed, Signay waited until August before broaching the nub of the matter with Quiblier. He then asked Quiblier to allow him to silence the rumours that Saint-Sulpice – still seen as a group of foreigners – wanted to halt the normal process of episcopal appointment in Lower Canada. As far as the archbishop of Quebec was concerned, the seminary must disavow publicly every single step taken in Rome by Thavenet. From then on Quiblier resorted to mental reservations in his dealings with Signay, giving only vague answers to questions. But, finally backed against the wall by Signay's repeated demands, Quiblier got all the members of the seminary to sign a formal disavowal of having taken part directly or indirectly in the intrigues against the issuing of the papal bulls for Bishop Turgeon. This approach allowed him to plead the persistent reluctance of some members of the seminary to give their signature, a reluctance he justified by resorting to the ordinary rules of canon law, and of the constitutions of the Society of Saint-Sulpice, with which Signay was unfamiliar.

Beginning in October 1833 the Lower Canadian

newspapers had taken up the whole affair, interpreting it as a sign of hostility to French Canadians on the part of the seminary, whose refusal to repudiate the accusations being spread by the papers now constituted, even in Signay's eyes, an admission of guilt. But, in the light of the seminary's participation in the intrigue, Quiblier could only take refuge in the decision awaited from Rome and the respect owed to the supreme authority of the Holy See. Ultimately it was Signay who put an end to what was probably one of the worst cases of tension between the seminary and the archbishop. At the beginning of 1834 he described his attitude as that of a protector of the seminary against public opinion. He thought it regrettable that the seminary's refusal to comply with his request for a public statement had deprived him of an important means of counter-attack. He had to content himself with the rather ambiguous disavowal by the Conseil des Douze, the governing body of the seminary, and now regarded the matter as closed. In March, Rome granted Signay the victory when it issued the bulls for Bishop Turgeon. It was a major defeat for Quiblier's diplomacy in Rome. He now had to heal the wounds caused by the open dissension among the clergy.

The winter of 1834–35 marked a turning-point in Quiblier's relations with the episcopacy. Bishop Lartigue had conveyed to him that he was favourably disposed towards the seminary. He wanted to have a Sulpician succeed him as bishop of Telmesse so the two institutions could support each other. To link the seminary with the episcopate, he was even ready to accept Quiblier's proposal for a successor, Jean-Baptiste ROUPE, a less independent man than his own choice, Nicolas Dufresne*. Thus nearly 15 years after Lartigue had assumed episcopal office at Montreal, the superior of the Sulpicians and the bishop would reach an agreement. The celebration at Notre-Dame on 24 Sept. 1835 of Roque's jubilee as a priest was the occasion for publicly manifesting the reconciliation. A few days later Quiblier acknowledged that the erection of an episcopal see at Montreal depended on his intervention, and stated that Lartigue would be its first incumbent. With Lartigue's consent he drafted a petition to the Holy See and a letter to the archbishop of Quebec, which he signed and had all the members of the seminary and parish priests of the district of Montreal sign; he also informed Rome of the step taken by the Montreal clergy. In March 1836 Quiblier learned that Rome had reached favourable decisions: the district of Montreal was to be erected into a diocese; Bishop Lartigue would hold the see; subsequently a coadjutor acceptable to the bishop and the seminary would be appointed. After Lartigue's solemn enthronement in the cathedral on 8 September, the new bishop of Montreal lacked only the civil recognition that would incorporate the diocese and accord it the power to acquire and own landed

property. Here again it seems that Quiblier interceded effectively, this time with the governor-in-chief of British North America, Lord Gosford [Acheson*], and later with his successor, Sir John Colborne*, as well as with the attorney general of Lower Canada, Charles Richard Ogden*.

In 1836 the seminary still did not have any formal recognition clarifying the nature of its seigneurial property rights. The sharp reaction of the French Canadian Sulpicians and the episcopate, who saw in the agreement negotiated by Roux in October 1827 the veritable spoliation of a Canadian patrimony, had prevented both the British government and the seminary from implementing it. In the spring of 1832 Archbishop Panet remained afraid that Quiblier would give in to pressure from Britain, and the superior's evasive replies did not reassure him. Yet the archbishop of Quebec was being prevailed upon by Rome to facilitate the arrangements already sketched out, and to promote an agreement on the part of the Sulpicians to alienate their property rights in return for government provision of other landed property as compensation. At the beginning of 1834 some members of the Lower Canadian House of Assembly took the initiative of drawing up a bill authorizing the Séminaire de Saint-Sulpice at Montreal to come to terms with those of its *censitaires* in the city who wanted to convert the rights of *lods et ventes* into freehold tenure. Quiblier showed great interest in this solution, which might obtain unanimous support, satisfy the citizens of Montreal, and rule out any excuse for later settlements.

It took the social and political upheaval occasioned by the rebellion of 1837–38 to make the British government decide on this course of action. The loyal conduct of Quiblier and the seminary at this period certainly helped clear the way. As early as 1832 Quiblier, who was aware that it was in the seminary's interest to display the strictest loyalty, had encouraged Pierre-Édouard Leclère*, the chief of police in Montreal, and John Jones, the king's printer, to launch L'Ami du peuple, de l'ordre et des lois. Under Quiblier's unofficial guidance the newspaper was to defend "the true interests" of Lower Canada, advocating obedience to the law and the respect due to legitimate authority [see Alfred-Xavier RAMBAU]. This loyalty would inevitably arouse the Patriotes' anger. In the autumn of 1837 the seminary, knowing it was the object of the Patriotes' hatred and covetousness since its assets could finance the uprising, burned a number of compromising documents, lest they should fall into the hands of a crowd of rebel demonstrators. But Quiblier's principal endeavour was to prevent the Irish community from mobilizing in support of the Patriotes. First he used his great influence with the leaders Peter Dunn and Joseph Macnaughton, who withdrew their backing from the

Quiblier

Patriotes at the time of a meeting at which Irishman Edmund Bailey O'Callaghan* and Thomas Storrow Brown* were to speak. He also encouraged the Irish to shift from the neutrality he had at first recommended they adopt and begin enlisting in the British militia.

In February 1838 Quiblier agreed to undertake the ambivalent and dangerous mission of bringing back into Lower Canada the Patriotes who had sought refuge in the area of Lake Champlain. Few Patriotes accepted the safe conduct offered to them, but because of his actions Quiblier was treated as a patriotic hero by Charles Buller*, the secretary to the new governor-in chief, Lord Durham [Lambton*], and gained quite a reputation at the Colonial Office in London. That was how he also came to serve as an intermediary seeking clemency for some of the accused at a time when Bishop Lartigue, who was considered unreliable because of family ties with the Patriote leaders Denis-Benjamin Viger* and Louis-Joseph Papineau*, was thought by the principal Lower Canadian political figures to have swung towards those whom the authorities suspected of being disaffected.

Quiblier knew that his loyalty might count in his favour when the issue of the seminary's property was being settled; consequently he had reason to be pleased with the admission by the former governor, Lord Gosford, in January 1838 that without this "liberal conduct and public spirit" on Quiblier's part Lord Durham's commission would have had nothing positive to propose for the seminary. The settlement of the property would now move towards a happy solution. Quiblier agreed to hand over the seminary's statements of accounts for the preceding five years, lavished assiduous attention upon Lord Durham, secured changes in Colborne's draft legislation granting civil incorporation to the seminary in April 1839, and had the satisfaction of seeing his friends get the bill passed in London in the spring of 1840. By the terms of the new law, the seminary could draw from various sources an average annual income of £14,200 between 1840 and 1846 to meet expenses of £12,202, of which $12\frac{1}{2}$ per cent would go to social welfare and nearly 25 per cent to education.

At the outset of the 19th century the seminary had begun setting up free primary schools in Montreal. Quiblier pursued this organizational and financial endeavour, bending it to fit the clericalizing strategy of Lartigue, who sought to replace lay teachers by members of religious orders on whom the episcopate could rely. From the beginning of his administration, Quiblier took steps to bring in the Christian Brothers; his efforts culminated in the arrival in November 1837 of four brothers, who were quickly installed by the seminary in new buildings and fully subsidized [see Louis Roblot*]. The seminary thus found itself occupying an influential field that the bishop of Montreal himself would have liked to control.

Quiblier gave impetus to the expansion of education for girls, urging the sisters of the Congregation of Notre-Dame to open classes for non-resident pupils in the *faubourgs* (in 1846 there would be 1,359 in attendance). In the autumn of 1838 Quiblier continued to give support to the Petit Séminaire de Montréal, then being loudly decried in Patriote circles for its teachers' "despotic" ideology. He held out to Arthur William Buller*, the commissioner inquiring into education in Lower Canada, the attractive prospect of turning the seminary into a university. Whether this was an additional argument to justify the immense economic resources of the seminary, or a serious plan, cannot be determined. As for the original mission of Saint-Sulpice, which was to train candidates for the priesthood, the Montreal establishment had not discharged its essential duty for two centuries since it had never functioned as a *grand séminaire*. Calmer relations between the Sulpician seminary and the episcopate, and the growing number of vocations, prompted the new bishop of Montreal, Ignace Bourget*, to ask it to undertake the theological and spiritual education of future clergy. When the Conseil des Douze met on 24 Aug. 1840 it gave its assent, and an agreement spelling out the direct authority of the bishop over the candidates of his diocese was signed in November.

With regard to cultural matters, mention must be made of Quiblier's connection with the Paris publishing house of Gaume et Frères for the purchase of books, and of the fact that he stood surety for the solvency of bookseller Édouard-Raymond Fabre, a source of anxiety for the Gaume firm. In 1844 he took part in launching the first collectively owned francophone library in Montreal, the Œuvre des Bons Livres, whose books came from the holdings of the confraternities and the Sulpicians; it was intended to combat bad books, provide the means to while away winter evenings, and extend the work of the schools.

Paradoxically, the specifically pastoral role of the seminary's superior may be the one least remembered by historians. From the time of his appointment in April 1831, Quiblier had insisted on discharging his legal duty as titular priest of the parish of Notre-Dame in Montreal, despite the episcopal opposition – which lasted until May 1843 – to this type of permanent incumbency. He had not, however, deemed it advisable to replace Claude Fay, who had been appointed by Roux, even though his talents as *ex officio* parish priest were not impressive. Before the exceptional religious revival brought about in 1840 through the 40 days of preaching by Bishop Charles-Marie-Auguste-Joseph de Forbin-Janson*, the spiritual life of the parish remained at a low ebb. Between 35 and 45 per cent of the parishioners took Easter communion in 1831, but the rate declined progressively until 1841 when the figure increased by more than a half. This phenomenon, doubtless linked with the religious interpretation of the rebellion and of its failure, gave rise to a new period of pastoral initiatives under the leadership of Bourget, a period that found the Montreal Sulpicians inactive and wedded to routine. Their situation was marked by the increasing age of the priests, inability to cope with the visibly larger number of the faithful, and defensive, reactionary attitudes. For this state of affairs Quiblier was no doubt in good measure responsible.

In any case, Bourget apparently was of this opinion and, as Quiblier's third term as superior was drawing to an end, he made strong representations to him and to the other members of the seminary, even demanding an audience at a new meeting of the Conseil des Douze. The struggle for power between the seminary and the bishop now worked in favour of the latter, for on 21 April 1846 Quiblier, sensing the wish of the majority, resigned; he was replaced by Pierre-Louis Billaudèle*, the director of the Grand Séminaire. It may be supposed that this gesture was also a significant moment in his personal religious experience: he was obeying his bishop in renouncing his own wishes and judgement – no small thing, considering the Sulpician superiors' long tradition of independence. Quiblier set off quietly to spend some time outside Lower Canada; he attended the council at Baltimore at the beginning of May and then went to Kingston in Upper Canada, where he remained until the end of July. It had been his wish to stay at the seminary for the rest of his life, but the process which had led him to resign created such a climate of opinion within the house, and among the public, that Quiblier thought it wiser to leave in October for Europe.

Quiblier never saw Montreal again, but in 1847 and 1848 he spent some time, particularly in Ireland, giving talks on the work of the seminary in Lower Canada in order to recruit new associates. One of these was Patrick Dowd*, who was to become priest in charge of St Patrick's in Montreal, a church Quiblier had helped to build. But he gained the impression that the seminary was not backing his initiatives; thus, on the advice of the bishop of Westminster, Nicholas Patrick Stephen Wiseman, he undertook pastoral ministry to the Irish who were flocking into England. He established a mission for them at Norwood (London) which he installed in a spacious church. Hostile feeling towards the Catholics was apparently beginning to change. Quiblier devoted his attention to young nuns newly converted from Protestantism. Then in September 1848 he received a group of French nuns who had come to start an orphanage. The following year he set up a mission at Spitalfields (London), where there were 6,000 Irish living in poverty and an endemic problem of mixed marriages. On a trip to Lyons, in France, he managed to obtain the help of the Marist Fathers.

Joseph-Vincent Quiblier finished his career as he had begun it, ministering to a parish. He had never had

to worry about supporting himself, since the seminary provided for the needs of its former superior. Aware that his health was failing, he went to Paris in 1851 and again in the summer of 1852. He had to take to his bed then and he died at Issy-les-Moulineaux on 12 Sept. 1852. Quiblier was buried in France, in the little cemetery at Lorette where the superior generals of Saint-Sulpice traditionally are interred.

LOUIS ROUSSEAU

Joseph-Vincent Quiblier is the author of "Notice sur le séminaire de Montréal," a collection of notes about events during his 15-year administration. The manuscript is held at Arch. de la Compagnie de Saint-Sulpice (Paris), MSS 1208.

AAQ, 210 A, XV: 423. ACAM, 465.101, 840-5, 846-3, 850-1; 901.025, 834-1; RLL, V: 431, 442; VI: 114, 192; VII: 754. AD, Loire (Saint-Étienne), État civil, Colombier, 27 juin 1796. Arch. de la Compagnie de Saint-Sulpice (Paris), dossier 98. Arch. municipales, Issy-les-Moulineaux (France), État civil, Issy-les-Moulineaux, 17 sept. 1852. ASSM, 1 bis, tiroir 5, vol.2; 21, cartons 61, 61A; 27, tiroirs 96, 97. L.C., Special Council, Ordinances, February–April 1839, c.50. Beaulieu et Hamelin, La presse québécoise, 1: 74. Henri Gauthier, Sulpitiana ([2e éd.], Montréal, 1926), 185, 252, 267. Louis Bertrand, Bibliothèque sulpicienne, ou Histoire littéraire de la Compagnie de Saint-Sulpice (3v., Paris, 1900), 2: 202–4. Chaussé, Jean-Jacques Lartigue, 122–29, 177–78. Marcel Lajeunesse, Les sulpiciens et la vie culturelle à Montréal au XIXe siècle (Montréal, 1982). Yvan Lamonde, Les bibliothèques de collectivités à Montréal (17e–19e siècle) (Montréal, 1979), 51–53; La philosophie et son enseignement au Québec (1665–1920) (Montréal, 1980), 72. Lemieux, L'établissement de la première prov. eccl., 370–71. [D.-A. Lemire-Marsolais, dite Sainte-Henriette et] Thérèse Lambert, dite Sainte-Marie-Médiatrice, Histoire de la Congrégation de Notre-Dame (11v. en 13 parus, Montréal, 1941–), 8: 299–302. Maurault, Le collège de Montréal (Dansereau; 1967); Nos messieurs (Montréal, [1936]), 101–21. Meilleur, Mémorial de l'éducation (1876), 86, 101–2, 184–88. Pouliot, Mgr Bourget et son temps, 2: 26–30. Louis Rousseau, La prédication à Montréal de 1800 à 1830; approche religiologique (Montréal, 1976), 44, 70, 90–92. Olivier Maurault, "M. Vincent Quiblier, prêtre de Saint-Sulpice," RSC Trans., 3rd ser., 28 (1934), sect.I: 139–48.

QUIRK, JOHN, sailor and businessman; b. 12 Jan. 1783 near Peel, Isle of Man, son of John Quirk and Sarah Cowin; m. first 8 Feb. 1821 Eliza Chipman (d. 16 June 1833), and they had six children; m. secondly 1 Feb. 1834 Phebe Tupper, widow of Robert FitzRandolph, and they had four children; d. 17 Oct. 1853 in Bridgetown, N.S.

One of seven children, John Quirk grew up on his father's farm, attending school in nearby Peel. His copybooks show a fascination with the sea. Rude sketches of ships and nautical equipment are interspersed with exercises relative to ships' supplies and the West Indian trade. Little is known of his early life at sea but it would not have been an easy one for a

Radenhurst

young sailor. When the Napoleonic Wars depleted the reserves of the Royal Navy, mercantile ships were frequently harassed by press-gangs. In 1814, Quirk's ship, on a voyage to Jamaica, put in to Queenstown (Cobh, Republic of Ireland) and he was pressed into service. His enforced career lasted barely a year. In July 1815 he was on a naval vessel in Plymouth harbour where he saw the defeated Napoleon aboard the *Bellerophon*.

From November 1815, when Quirk immigrated to Saint John, N.B., British North America was his permanent home. He retained a great affection for his native island, however, and assisted fellow Manxmen in establishing themselves in his adopted land. The Quirk household became a place of refuge and a stopover for many of them. He was joined in Saint John by his younger brother Matthias, and together they engaged in building and sailing coastal trading vessels. Quirk began visiting settlements up the Annapolis River to the head of navigation at Hicks' Ferry, trading primarily in lumber and agricultural produce. Here his white vessel flying the Manx flag attracted crowds. Captain Quirk's name appears in the account-books of the local merchants beginning in 1820. The next year he married the youngest daughter of a Baptist clergyman, gave up the sea, and purchased a lot in the town at Hicks' Ferry, laid out that year by John Crosskill*. He built a house on his land in 1822 and settled down, becoming a leading figure in the community which was named Bridgetown two years later. Beamish Murdoch*, recalling only a house or two on the site in 1822, returned in 1824 to find that "quite a town had sprung up in the interim."

Quirk sold his river-front home in 1827 and the next year purchased a house at the town's main intersection where he "commenced keeping entertainment." He named his hostelry the "Golden Ball Inn," although it was familiarly known as "Quirk's Hotel." Acquiring the lot next to the inn, he put up a building in 1829 at a cost of £225. Housing two stores at street level and a "long room" upstairs, it became, along with the inn, the social centre of the new town. Coaches stopped there at the last stage between Halifax and Annapolis Royal after that run was inaugurated in 1828. The long room was the only public hall in Bridgetown for some years and was the scene of much activity. In 1840, at a dinner honouring Joseph Howe*, who was then at the beginning of his political career, 80 gentlemen are recorded as having sat at table.

Quirk's second marriage in 1834 had brought six stepchildren into the household. To supply the needs of both his growing family and the inn, he assembled 80 acres of farm land north of the town at a cost of £325. A devout Anglican, Quirk none the less purchased pews in the Baptist and Methodist meeting-houses, and his name appears as a leading contributor to every effort advancing the prosperity of his community. At a time when those Nova Scotian establishments professing to be inns were found by army officer William Scarth Moorsom* to have "little idea of acting up to their profession," Quirk's hostelry was noted for its high standards. A traveller described it in 1843 as "a very nice clean hotel in the pretty town of Bridgeton."

Quirk died in his Bridgetown home in 1853, leaving an estate valued at more than £1,600. He had contributed to the life and prosperity of the community since its founding. His widow survived until 1873.

FRANKLYN H. HICKS

Annapolis County Court of Probate (Bridgetown, N.S.), Q3 (estate papers of John Quirk). Annapolis Valley Regional Library, Bridgetown Branch, "Book of Bridgetown pictures," comp. E. R. Coward (MS photo. albums, 4v., plus scrapbook, 1958), 1. PANS, MG 1, 238; MG 3, 28; RG 14, 73. Private arch., F. H. Hicks (Ottawa), Memoranda written by John and James Quirk. [James Lumsden], *American memoranda, by a mercantile man, during a short tour in the summer of 1843* (Glasgow, 1844), 57. W. S. Moorsom, *Letters from Nova Scotia; comprising sketches of a young country* (London, 1830). E. R. Coward, *Bridgetown, Nova Scotia; its history to 1900* ([Kentville, N.S.], 1955). [When writing this book E. R. Coward had access to ships' logs and family papers that have since been lost. F.H.H.] Beamish Murdoch, *A history of Nova-Scotia, or Acadie* (3v., Halifax, 1865–67), 3: 516–17. John Irvin, "History of Bridgetown . . . ," N.S. Hist. Soc., *Coll.*, 19 (1918): 31–51.

R

RADENHURST, THOMAS MABON, lawyer, politician, and office holder; b. 6 April 1803 in Fort St Johns (Saint-Jean-sur-Richelieu), Lower Canada, son of Thomas Radenhurst and Ann Campbell; m. 9 Nov. 1834 his cousin Lucy Edith Ridout, daughter of Thomas Ridout*, in Toronto, and they had four sons and six daughters; d. 7 Aug. 1854 in Perth, Upper Canada.

Thomas Mabon Radenhurst's father came from Cheshire, England, to Lower Canada in February 1776 as storekeeper to the hospital at Trois-Rivières and ten years later married the daughter of a loyalist in

732

Montreal. His death in 1805 left Thomas and his seven brothers and sisters under the sole care of their strong-willed mother. She managed to get commissions in the army for two of her older sons and later to have Thomas accepted at John Strachan*'s Home District Grammar School at York (Toronto). From there he went on to study law in the office of his cousin George Ridout*. Called to the bar in the spring of 1824, Radenhurst left York for Kingston and then moved to the new community of Perth, which in 1823 had become the judicial seat of the Bathurst District. There he built a prosperous legal practice out of the usual material: trespasses, debts, petitions, and assaults. Typical were his cases on behalf of the settlers of McNab Township against Archibald McNab, his role as solicitor for William Morris's Tay Navigation Company, and his defence of the Reverend William Bell in a libel suit instituted by John Stewart of the *Bathurst Independent Examiner*. Also typical of his class and age were the land speculation and the various private commercial transactions with which he augmented his professional income.

Radenhurst moved in the upper ranks of Perth society among the half-pay officers, merchants, and lawyers who composed the town élite. In 1832 he bought the Reverend Michael Harris's magnificent stone residence (now known as the Inderwick House), a visible crown to his successful career. Radenhurst's hatred, however, of fellow lawyer James Boulton (brother of Attorney General Henry John Boulton*) climaxed in a duel they fought in 1830. Fortunately "the matter ended without injury to either party." More serious consequences attended the duel fought in 1833 by their law students John Wilson* and Robert Lyon. Robert, the brother of Radenhurst's old friend and brother-in-law George Lyon, was killed and was buried in the Radenhurst family plot.

The "Father and Champion of Reform" in Lanark County, Radenhurst dated his "adhesion . . . to Reform principles" to the general election of 1828 when he ran successfully for the Carleton seat in the House of Assembly, which he represented until 1830 when the house was dissolved after the death of George IV. Deeply affected by the dismissal of Judge John Walpole Willis*, he served in 1829 on the select parliamentary committee chaired by William Warren Baldwin* inquiring into the case. In February 1840 when Robert Baldwin was offered the position of solicitor general by Governor Charles Edward Poulett Thomson*, he wrote to Radenhurst for advice. Radenhurst warned Baldwin of the perils of compromising his principles and accepting office under "what [Sir Francis Bond Head*] would say is the *bread and butter* system." None the less the bread and butter system did not hurt Radenhurst. Treasurer of the Bathurst District since 1840, he was appointed judge

of the district court in December 1841, a position he declined on the grounds that it was not remunerative enough, and frequently served as crown prosecutor for the Eastern and Midland circuits. Criticized by Baldwin when a verdict went against him in 1851, Radenhurst could remind Baldwin of his impeccable handling of "all the public business you have entrusted to me since 1842." He could also ask Baldwin to "use your influence" to affect local appointments.

Radenhurst's local political influence, however, was overshadowed by that of Malcolm Cameron*, who in the election of 1836 emerged as the power of the reform party in the Bathurst District. When Cameron decided to run for the riding of Kent in 1847, Radenhurst, who had repeatedly withdrawn his candidacy in Lanark at the party's request, fully expected to win the reform nomination there. Instead, William Bell's son Robert was selected at a sparsely attended reform convention. Ignoring his promise to support the convention's candidate and his own earlier warnings against splitting the party, Radenhurst threw his hat into the ring, but despite the split Bell was able to carry Lanark for reform. In 1851 Radenhurst ran again and this time emerged as the sole reform candidate but, having "injured himself beyond recovery" because he "broke faith last election," he was defeated by tory James Shaw*.

Despite his lack of political success Radenhurst was admired by contemporaries "for his strict integrity in his professional pursuits." In 1847 an observer describing Radenhurst's courtroom manner commented that he "lounges in his chair with an easy familiarity." Yet despite his "seeming abstraction . . . nothing has escaped his notice. . . . The witness finds that he is in the hands of a master." Above all, Radenhurst could convince a jury that he believed "there is such a thing as truth" and that "whatever may be the merits of the suit the advocate is an honest man." He was made a queen's counsel in December 1850, but did not live long to enjoy the honour. Ill for several months, on 4 Aug. 1854 he suffered "a return of his disorder – (paralysis)" and died three days later. The mighty of Lanark County formed part of his funeral procession to the Perth Episcopal cemetery. At his death Radenhurst left behind a large family, an estate valued at more than £5,000, and a reputation as "a leading member of the Bar in Canada."

WILLIAM COX

AO, MS 35, unbound papers, 1805; MU 2367–68. MTL, Robert Baldwin papers. PAC, RG 8, I (C ser.), 278: 122, 175, 203; 547: 179; 548: 16; 634: 53; 720: 124; 1220: 289; RG 31, A1, 1851, Perth. Perth Museum (Perth, Ont.), Radenhurst papers. QUA, William Bell papers; William Morris papers. *Bathurst Courier*, 9 Nov. 1834; 24 June 1836; 23 March 1840; 4, 18 Jan. 1842; 9 Nov., 24, 31 Dec. 1847; 7 Jan. 1848; November–December 1851; 11 Aug.

Rae

1854. *Lambton Observer, and Western Advertiser*, 17 Aug. 1854. Edward Shortt, *The memorable duel at Perth* ([Perth, 1970]).

RAE, ANN CUTHBERT (Knight; Fleming), author and schoolteacher; b. 1788 near Aberdeen, Scotland, eldest child of John Rae and Margaret Cuthbert; m. first 3 July 1810 James Innes Knight; m. secondly 8 May 1820 James Fleming; d. 15 March 1860 in Abbotsford, Lower Canada.

The multiple names born by Ann Cuthbert Rae during her lifetime are more concealing than revealing. Eventually, only male connections reveal her whereabouts: her merchant father in Aberdeenshire; her political economist, schoolmaster, and adventurer brother John Rae* in Upper Canada; her first husband, James Innes Knight, a merchant in Portsoy, Scotland, and possibly in Montreal; and finally her second husband, James Fleming, also a merchant in Montreal, himself overshadowed by his brother John*, a prominent businessman and author. The relative wealth of Ann's male connections may also have saved her from historical oblivion.

Ann was educated privately, as befitted a daughter of the middle class, and well, as Scottish Presbyterians seem to have demanded. Her emotional and intellectual attachment to her governess lasted into her adult years and was publicly admitted in the dedication of her second book of poetry, *A year in Canada, and other poems*, published in Edinburgh in 1816. This work and its predecessor, *Home*, which appeared in 1815 (not to be confused with a poem of the same title attributed to John Blackwood Greenshields, published in 1806), had both been inspired by a year-long trip to the Canadas commencing in June 1811. Was her husband on business or had the young couple decided to emigrate? Was it a delayed honeymoon or was Ann anxious to be away from her squabbling parents? With her six-week-old son, Robert, and perhaps a nursemaid, Ann set out to enjoy, observe, and record the seasons and regions of the Canadas. Both books of poetry were polished while she was back in Scotland in 1813 and 1814. In June 1815, leaving a year-old daughter, Jessie, in Scotland, Ann, her husband, and Robert crossed the Atlantic again with every intention, it would seem, of settling in Montreal.

Within four months of her arrival Ann had opened a school, one of the few paying occupations available to educated women in the early 19th century. Was the family in financial difficulties or did Ann already know of the illness that would claim her husband in June 1816? Her poem *Home* speaks movingly of the death of a spouse as a prime cause of domestic unhappiness. Or perhaps housewifery did not command her full attention and Montreal's lack of schools

may have provided her with an opportunity. Not that she was an early advocate of women's rights: the few notes of scorn in *Home* are reserved for Mary Wollstonecraft, daring to rival "the rights of man."

As a young widow, Ann kept a boarding-school on Rue Saint-Vincent for at least four years, teaching "plain and fancy Needle Work, the English language, writing, arithmetic, geography and drawing" to some rather well-connected young ladies of Montreal. Jane Porteous received *Home* as a prize and the two Misses McDonald cost their fur-trading father, John*, £29 8s. 0d. in order to be housed, fed, educated, bonneted, shod, and laundered for three months. Perhaps the bonnets and shoes came from the dry-goods store of James Fleming near by on Rue Notre-Dame? Possibly Ann already knew Fleming; they were both from Aberdeenshire and the Scottish community in Montreal was quite small. That community, including schoolmaster Alexander Skakel*, who taught Ann's son, favoured her school with "flattering and liberal support" and in the spring of 1817 it moved to a larger house on the same street. There, more boarders were accommodated, an "Assistant from Britain" joined the existing staff, and history, music, and dancing were added to the program. But in 1820, when Ann married James Fleming in the Anglican garrison church at Chambly, the school seems to have disappeared, and Ann fades from view.

Ann's interest in teaching, however, appears to have been irrepressible. In the 1830s Mrs Fleming was again summoning students to class, this time at her seminary on Rue Saint-Jacques. There, presumably, she developed a series of school-books for young people and their teachers, with primers, readers, grammars, and teachers' guides to accompany them. She may even have tried the lessons out on her own children: a daughter may have been born in 1821; a boy, John Ramsay, later a lawyer in Aylmer and protonotary of the Superior Court of Lower Canada in Hull, was born in 1824; and an infant death may have occurred in 1832. Certainly the books – *First book for Canadian children*; *Views of Canadian scenery, for Canadian children*; *The prompter*; and *Progressive exercises on the English language, to correspond with "The prompter"* – were tested in theory and practice long before their publication in the 1840s. The teaching of grammar particularly intrigued Ann Fleming. In 1836 she had convinced a number of prominent people, including Anglican archdeacon John Strachan*, that her innovative method, concentrating on verbs, "will make it pleasant and agreeable to children, instead of being dull and irksome, as is at present too frequently the case." In 1843 she travelled to Hamilton and Kingston, Upper Canada, possibly at the instigation of her brother John, then headmaster of the Gore District Grammar School in Hamilton, to display her methods by teaching recalcitrant eight-year-old boys the delights of English grammar for a period of six weeks. She also spoke with educators, publicized her pedagogical innovations, and solicited favourable opinions of them. The *Literary Garland* (Montreal) assisted her by quoting the recommendations the *First book* had already received and by pointing out that the governor, Sir Charles Theophilus Metcalfe*, had subscribed for a number of copies of *The prompter*.

Whether Ann achieved the public acclaim she seems to have sought is unknown. With the exception of petitions presented to the Legislative Council and the Legislative Assembly in 1845 for financial aid to publish additional textbooks, and a brief tale published in the *Literary Garland* the same year, there is no further trace of her. Her adopted home inspired in her some of its earliest English-language poetry in the female voice and it provided her with an opportunity to earn her living, whether by necessity or by choice, in a manner additional to that of wife and mother. It coaxed out of her an early recognition that schoolbooks needed Canadian content. And perhaps it gave her the same type of life which she claimed for an old grandfather in one of her readings for young people, a life in "this country where he is now so much more comfortable than he would have been if he had remained in the land he was born in."

SUSAN MANN TROFIMENKOFF

[The author wishes to express her appreciation to R. W. James and Brian Whittle of Ottawa for their assistance. S.M.T.]

Ann Cuthbert Rae is the author of *Home: a poem* (Edinburgh, 1815); *A year in Canada, and other poems* (Edinburgh, 1816); *First book for Canadian children* (Montreal, 1843); *Views of Canadian scenery, for Canadian children* (Hamilton, Ont., 1843); *The prompter, containing the principles of the English language, and suggestions to teachers, with an appendix, in which are stated the opinions of different grammarians on disputed points* (Montreal, 1844); *Progressive exercises on the English language, to correspond with "The prompter"* (Montreal, 1845); and of "The first ewe," *Literary Garland* (Montreal), new ser., 3 (1845): 460–62. Reviews of her works also appeared in *Literary Garland*, new ser., 2 (1844): 144, 366.

ANQ-M, CE1-65, 8 mars 1820; CE2-23, 17 mars 1860. ASQ, Fonds Viger–Verreau, Sér.O, 01-C. GRO (Edinburgh), Aberdeen, reg. of births and baptisms, 4 Jan. 1789; reg. of marriages, 3 July 1810. McCord Museum, John McDonald of Garth, accounts. PAC, RG 31, A1, 1831, 1842, 1851, Montreal. Can., Prov. of, Legislative Assembly, *Journals*, 1844–45; Legislative Council, *Journals*, 1844–45. *Montreal Gazette*, 9 Oct. 1815, 5 Jan. 1836. *Montreal Herald*, 1 March 1817. *Montreal directory*, 1819, 1843–44. Morgan, *Bibliotheca Canadensis*, 125. R. W. James, *John Rae, political economist; an account of his life and a compilation of his main writings* (2v., Toronto, 1965).

Lit. hist. of Canada (Klinck *et al.*; 1965). V. B. Rhodenizer, *Canadian literature in English* ([Montreal, 1965]).

RAMBAU, ALFRED-XAVIER (he was baptized **Dominique-Flavien-Xavier Rombau**), journalist and lawyer; b. 23 Feb. 1810 in Chalain-d'Uzore, France, son of Claude-Joseph Rombau and Marie-Reine Métayer-Descombes; d. 30 Oct. 1856 in Montreal.

Alfred-Xavier Rambau was born in a village dating back to the Middle Ages, into a family with a Legitimist tradition. In his childhood, according to the author of the obituary published in Montreal's *La Patrie* the day after his death, he had been taught the motto *Dieu et le Roi*. The article added that the brilliant student at the Collège de Clermont-Ferrand "took top prizes in his classes. He was spoken of with pride, as a pupil of superior quality." Having finished his classical studies, Rambau stayed for some time in Italy to complete his education and sailed for the United States in 1832.

Rambau was made welcome in New York by a man named Peugnet who, observing his outstanding natural aptitudes, entrusted him with the management of his Franco-American newspaper. Soon after, Rambau received an invitation from Pierre-Dominique Debartzch*, a friend of Peugnet and the seigneur of Saint-Charles-sur-Richelieu, to come to work in Lower Canada as a correspondent for his new newspaper. In January 1833 Debartzch had founded *L'Écho du pays*, a weekly to be published in his village to champion the interests of the Canadian party, in which he was a leader. Rambau accepted the invitation and came to settle in Lower Canada. In no time at all he adjusted to his adopted country. His lively pen, prone to a caustic turn of phrase when occasion allowed, quickly drew attention to his ability as a journalist, just as the vivacity and wit of this man of the world and his handsome presence – he was nicknamed "le beau Rambau" – soon ingratiated him with the social élite of Montreal, where he had gone to live after a brief stay at Saint-Charles-sur-Richelieu.

Rambau began to contribute to *L'Ami du peuple, de l'ordre et des lois* in 1833 and that year was made its editor, a post he retained until 1840. This paper, which was first issued on 21 July 1832, had been started by printer-publisher Pierre-Édouard Leclère*, the chief of the Montreal police, and John Jones, the king's printer. Its title revealed its interests; the journal claimed to be moderate and, as a firm opponent of political ventures, was against the extreme measures advocated by Louis-Joseph Papineau* and his supporters. Leclère and Jones in truth were merely figureheads; the Séminaire de Saint-Sulpice in Montreal controlled the operation of the paper. Since the Sulpicians were negotiating with

Rankin

London to secure recognition of their property rights in Lower Canada, a display of the strictest loyalty towards the British crown was to their advantage [*see* Joseph-Vincent QUIBLIER]. Rambau, whose talent and fine mind they had been able to appreciate in *L'Écho du pays*, suited them admirably as editor for a paper wholly devoted to their interests. For his part, Rambau chose to have his marriage solemnized by Sulpician Claude Fay, the parish priest of Notre-Dame in Montreal and a compatriot from the Loire. In the ceremony on 16 June 1834 he took as his wife Marie-Antoinette Allard, the rich and beautiful young widow of Alexis Demers, a physician who had represented Vaudreuil in the House of Assembly from 1830 to 1833. The couple were to have a son and a daughter. The conspicuous loyalism of *L'Ami du peuple*, however, brought down on Rambau the wrath of the Patriotes, who found his volte-face unpardonable; as a result he became involved one way or another in a number of duels.

Continuing his work as a journalist, during the rebellion Rambau also studied law, but he must have interrupted his studies for he was not admitted to the bar until 31 March 1848. He was a member of the Institut Canadien in Montreal from March 1852; he considered it an honour to belong to this cultural organization, although he was grieved by the dissension among the members, which he attributed to the Rouges. On 10 July 1855 he wrote, "What has this institute, the hope of young Canadians, now become in their hands? By dint of intrigue, by bringing in all their associates, they have managed to obtain almost exclusive control of it, and they have transformed the rostrum of this national institution . . . into a pulpit for discord, rebellion, and irreligion."

These lines were published in *La Patrie*, a paper Rambau began publishing in Montreal in September 1854. As the organ for the liberal-conservative coalition of which George-Étienne Cartier* was a leader, *La Patrie* followed the conservative line unequivocally: it defended the seigneurs at the time of the abolition of the seigneurial system, and supported the "separate school" system in Upper Canada and the right of religious communities to own property. Together with *La Minerve*, it launched a steady stream of attacks on *Le Pays*, the organ of the liberals and of the Institut Canadien. The polemics reached a peak in 1855 when Joseph-Guillaume Barthe* published in Paris his noted work *Le Canada reconquis par la France*. Barthe's suggestion that the Institut Canadien affiliate with the Institut de France seemed ludicrous to Rambau, who thought this connection would over-enhance the prestige of the Canadian body. Rambau soundly trounced the author in the columns of his paper, with a score of articles that appeared between 13 July and 26 Oct. 1855. He intended to bring them out as a pamphlet but it was never published.

Rambau was defending his friends with all the verve at his command when his career as a journalist ended abruptly, only half completed. *La Patrie* noted on 22 Oct. 1856 that he had suddenly fallen ill five days previously, and on 31 October announced that he had died the day before, at the early age of 46. He was buried on 3 November at Saint-Charles-sur-Richelieu, near his benefactor Debartzch.

PHILIPPE SYLVAIN

[Alfred-Xavier Rambau wrote *Le bill seigneurial exposé sous son vrai jour par le journal "La Patrie" (réfutation victorieuse du rapport soumis à la convention anti-seigneuriale), et quelques avis d'un cultivateur aux censitaires du Bas-Canada* (Québec, 1855).

Édouard-Zotique Massicotte* gave a biographical sketch of Rambau in "Le journaliste-avocat Rambau," *BRH*, 46 (1940): 156–58, which was largely drawn from the obituary in *La Patrie*, 31 Oct. 1856. Ægidius Fauteux*, who was certainly not partial to Rambau, obligingly spelled out in his work, *Le duel au Canada* (Montréal, 1934), 126–53, the details of the duels in which Rambau was involved. His comments are unpleasant and seem to be occasionally unjust and inaccurate as well as to contain a hint of xenophobia. Filteau, *Hist. des Patriotes*, 2: 72–74, goes further than Fauteux, and makes particular use of the papers of Ludger DUVERNAY (ANQ-Q, AP-G-68), who at one point was an implacable political foe of Rambau. P.S.]

AD, Loire (Saint-Étienne), État civil, Chalain-d'Uzore, 23 févr. 1810. ANQ-M, CE1-51, 16 juin 1834; CE2-10, 3 nov. 1856. *Lettres à Pierre Margry, de 1844 à 1886 (Papineau, Lafontaine, Faillon, Leprohon et autres)*, L.-P. Cormier, édit. (Québec, 1968), 27–29. Beaulieu et Hamelin, *La presse québécoise*, 1: 73–74, 76, 190–91. *Institut-Canadien en 1852*, J.-B.-É. Dorion, édit. (Montréal, 1852). F.-J. Audet, "Pierre-Édouard Leclère (1798–1866)," *Cahiers des Dix*, 8 (1943): 109–40. J.-J. Lefebvre, "Pierre-Dominique Debartzch, 1782–1846," *Rev. trimestrielle canadienne* (Montréal), 27 (1941): 179–200.

RANKIN, ALEXANDER, timber merchant, justice of the peace, politician, and office holder; b. 31 Dec. 1788 in the parish of Mearns, Scotland, probably at Mains House, second son of James Rankin and Helen Ferguson; d. unmarried 3 April 1852 in Liverpool, England.

Alexander Rankin came from a family of prosperous farmers. He was educated at Mearns parish school and in 1806 was hired as a clerk by Pollok, Gilmour and Company, general merchants of Glasgow. The firm traded with the Baltic ports in tar, hemp, flax, and timber. The senior partners became interested in extending their business to British North America and in 1812 Alexander Rankin and James Gilmour were sent to the Miramichi area in New Brunswick to open the company's first branch. They founded Gilmour, Rankin and Company on the north side of the Miramichi River, about half-way between Chatham and Newcastle. Within a few years, they had constructed wharfs, stores, and a sawmill. A small community called Gretna Green (Douglastown) developed around their holdings: it quickly became in many ways a company town with the Rankin firm controlling the only stores. The company built homes for some of its employees and virtually every male in the community either worked for it or was in some way dependent upon it. The real leader of the firm was Alexander Rankin. Although a partner for 30 years, Gilmour was considered by many to be a "non-entity in the business." In 1842 he would sell his interest to Rankin and retire to Scotland.

Gilmour, Rankin became suppliers as well as employers. Using goods sent by Pollok, Gilmour in Scotland, the firm provisioned not only its own lumbermen but also independent operators, who were expected to do business solely with it. The parent company sent ships to pick up the timber, which was then sold by the Glasgow office. Gilmour, Rankin also supplied goods to shipbuilders such as William Abrams* and Joseph RUSSELL, from whom it purchased ships. These vessels were sent to Glasgow to be either sold by the parent firm or used in its own business. Only after Rankin's death did the company begin to build its own ships.

Few records of the firm have survived, and it is difficult to determine the extent of its business operations. In 1819, of 1,520 British vessels employed in the British North American timber trade, 297 loaded at Miramichi, the majority being ships of Gilmour, Rankin. Having obtained commercial and political support from the town of Newcastle, the company virtually controlled timber operations on the Miramichi River by the early 1820s. In 1824, largely owing to the growth of the firm, Miramichi surpassed Saint John as a timber-exporting port, shipping 141,384 tons of squared timber. Shortly thereafter, however, the company's superiority was challenged by Joseph Cunard* who, with his brother Henry, had established a firm at Chatham about 1820.

Rankin and William Abrams were the chief sufferers in the Miramichi fire of 1825, which took about 160 lives and destroyed property worth approximately £204,000. Rankin's firm lost stores and merchandise worth more than £15,000, only £4,400 of which was insured. In addition large quantities of timber were destroyed. Rankin's house was one of only six buildings in Douglastown to escape the fire and it became a refuge for hundreds of the destitute. Rankin did everything he could to aid the survivors, as did his rival Cunard. All animosities were forgotten for a time and both men served on the relief committee.

The firm suffered a severe set-back as a result of the fire. However, with the aid of the parent company, it was able to recover quickly. In the late 1820s a large

stone sawmill was built at nearby Millbank. The machinery was said to have been constructed "upon the most approved principles" and worked "twenty-eight perpendicular saws, and two circular ones, cutting each day, upon an average 18,000 to 20,000 feet, plank measure." This mill was built to counter Cunard's operations farther down the river at Bay du Vin. In 1831 it was valued at £15,000 and employed 170 men. At that time it was the largest mill operating in the province. The firm expanded its domination over timber operations as well and in 1828–29 it held twice as many timber licences as did Cunard. By 1830 the two companies controlled almost all the lumbering in the northern part of New Brunswick. Between 1830 and 1850 they shipped on average 70 cargoes of timber a year.

In 1832 Rankin was the senior partner in Ferguson, Rankin and Company, which was established that year at Bathurst with Francis Ferguson as a partner and manager. The firm was for many years really a branch of Gilmour, Rankin. Rankin expanded his business even farther north in 1832 when he became a partner in Arthur Ritchie and Company of Dalhousie and Campbellton. The partnership lasted until 1842, but its operations were not as extensive as those carried on in Bathurst.

The northern operations depended on the regular dispatch of ships and goods by Pollok, Gilmour. On occasion, Ferguson in Bathurst felt that his company was being neglected. In 1838 he claimed that Pollok, Gilmour had not sent ships for the past three years to pick up his timber, and suggested that the Miramichi firm was getting more attention that his own. He also objected to the parent company's demands for timber squared on four sides, which he felt was wasteful and costly.

In the early 1830s the rivalry between Rankin and Cunard centred on the control of reserves on the Nepisiguit and Northwest Miramichi rivers. Cunard held control of approximately 500 square miles. In spite of the fact that his firm had only recently surrendered a similar licence, Rankin launched a strong attack on government policy and the privileges granted to Cunard. Although he made it sound as if he were concerned about the fate of the independent lumbermen, Rankin was disturbed only that the reserves gave Cunard an advantage. At a public meeting in Chatham in October 1831, Rankin introduced a resolution stating the evils that would result from the grant of extensive reserves to individuals, and in March 1833 his partner Gilmour threatened that the firm would "invest no more capital in this province" unless it was "permitted fairly to participate in the natural resources of the country." The Rankin firm was supported by 374 county residents, including 13 magistrates, who on 15 Feb. 1833 had presented a lengthy petition to the House of

Rankin

Assembly attacking Cunard, the Crown Lands Office, and its commissioner, Thomas Baillie*. These complaints and others were discussed in the assembly, and a delegation consisting of Charles SIMONDS and Edward Barron Chandler* was sent to England later that year to complain about Baillie's policies and to present the legislature's offer to assume control of the crown lands.

Rankin also went to London to challenge Cunard's rights to the reserves and to threaten removal of his firm from the colony if the situation was not changed. He was successful. Lord Stanley, the colonial secretary, informed the government in August that Cunard would have to relinquish the reserves, which he did in October. The lands were later put up for auction and Rankin probably managed to acquire part of them.

Rankin gained control of large blocks of land through a licensing system which had evolved in the early 19th century. Timber operators could apply for annual licences to cut, for a fee, a certain amount of timber at a specific location. In 1835 the system was changed because Baillie wanted to force the larger operators to make long-term commitments to the province. He introduced five-year licences, sold at public auction, for large blocks of land. Those lumberers who took advantage of this opportunity had to pay tonnage on a certain amount of timber each year whether or not it was actually cut. However, the option of applying for one-year licences was also retained. In 1836–37 Gilmour, Rankin had 70 one-year licences enabling them to cut 12,570 tons of timber and 820,000 board feet of logs. They also had 6 five-year licences for 8 square miles in Gloucester County and more than 112 square miles in Northumberland County, which allowed them an additional 3,820 tons of timber and 505,000 board feet of logs. Their branches in the northern part of the province also held a number of licences. Rankin's younger brother Robert* estimated the profits at Miramichi for the season 1837–38 to be approximately £10,000.

These operations were even larger during the 1840s. In 1847 William Carman, one of the members of the assembly for Northumberland County, claimed that Rankin controlled 875 square miles of timber reserves and Cunard 1,100. Together they accounted for more than 30 per cent of the licensed area in the province, including most of the best timber land, and lumbermen therefore had the choice of working for the big firms, starving, or leaving the province. Carman may well have been exaggerating, but the system used by Rankin and Cunard to control their timber operations was resented by many people. It is true that both men provided employment and believed they were helping their workers and the semi-independent operators, but they did business only on their own terms. They controlled the mill reserves, thus keeping out competitors. As merchants, they forced lumbermen to buy their goods at prices a writer in 1846 claimed were inflated by 50 per cent. The same lumbermen had then to sell their timber to the Rankin firm at reduced prices; if they still had a credit when their accounts were settled they had to take it not in cash but in goods at inflated prices.

In 1847 Carman also pointed out that when the mill reserves were put up for auction in Northumberland and Gloucester counties, the small operators were inevitably outbid by the bigger firms who "upon these occasions . . . did not bid against each other." The large companies could always act together to protect their mutual interests; thus in 1835 and in 1841 they had joined forces to organize petitions protesting against any revision of the timber duties.

Although his business practices might have been questionable at times, Rankin was a leader in establishing and expanding the timber industry in New Brunswick. He had excellent business sense, and was called upon occasionally to visit Saint John to check on the operations of the branch in that city, which had been established by his brother Robert in 1822. The Rankin firms did not suffer the same ups and downs as Cunard's company did, partly because of Alexander Rankin's good management and partly because the firms had strong financial backing from the parent firm in Scotland.

In business, Rankin was a hard and ruthless opponent: rivals were shut down and debtors such as Thomas Boies, the founder of Boiestown, had their goods and property seized when they defaulted on their payments. He fought the Crown Lands Office any time restrictions were imposed which obstructed the activities of his firms. He was not above using bribery to lure away operators cutting timber for Cunard and for a time in the early 1840s he had a deputy surveyor, Michael Carruthers, completely under his thumb. The rivalry between Rankin and Cunard involved trespasses on each other's reserves which often implicated government officials and members of the Executive Council. At one point Carruthers illegally seized timber belonging to Cunard, which subsequently found its way into Rankin's possession. As a result of this and other actions, Carruthers was removed from Northumberland County and sent to Gloucester. Both in 1843 and in 1846 Rankin was forced to pay fines as well as double and then triple duty on timber cut illegally.

Rankin never married, but he shared his home with his clerks, most of whom had come from Scotland, and his office became a training-ground for the other branches of the firm. Working long hours himself, Rankin expected his employees to do the same. He was usually up at 5:00 A.M. for a walk around the wharfs and timber-yards before the office opened. One of his nephews, also named Alexander Rankin, who was later able to live off the interest from the money he had inherited from his uncle, described what it was like to work for the firm in the late 1840s: "I found it not an easy task – hours 5 a.m. till 7 p.m. Three-quarters of one hour allowed for breakfast, one hour for dinner. After tea, sometimes in the office till 10 o'clock or so making up the tally of the day's work. From December to May the hours were shorter, 6 till 9, but two or three times a week we had to get up at 4 a.m. to get twenty or thirty teams away laden with provisions for the lumber camps."

Rankin first entered politics in 1827 when he was elected to the House of Assembly as one of two members for Northumberland County. He was to hold the seat until his death. Regular in attendance, he seldom left the house until the day's work was finished. He rarely spoke, and when he did it was usually in so mild a voice that he was often inaudible to those in the gallery. His speeches were always short and to the point, and he possessed no great gifts of oratory. When he chose to use it, he had great influence on the members and his views on matters relating to trade and commerce were often sought and invariably given serious consideration. Occasionally, when annoyed, he would speak in a much more forceful manner and then he could be heard throughout the house. This forcefulness was most evident in 1846 when he made a strong speech supporting the continuation of the grant for the lazaret on Sheldrake Island at the mouth of the Miramichi River.

In the election of 1830 Rankin and Cunard were the only candidates for the two seats in Northumberland County. They were unopposed because in those days of open voting no one could hope to defeat them. Although Cunard was appointed to the Legislative Council in 1833, he continued to attempt to control at least one of the assembly seats in Northumberland. In the 1837 election there were three candidates, two from the north side of the river, Rankin and John Ambrose Sharman Street*, and one from the south side, William Carman. It had been hoped that only one candidate from each side of the river would run so that there would be no contest. Cunard was this time supporting Carman, while Street claimed he was neutral. Rankin and Street won, and Carman stated that the latter had won only because of the former's support; from the results of later elections, it is obvious that Rankin did use his influence to help Street on numerous occasions.

Rankin was offered a seat in the Legislative Council in 1839 but he declined. The constituents, he claimed, were happy with their incumbent members in the assembly, Street and himself, and he did not want a new election reviving old animosities "which have now happily subsided." "There is scarcely any Political Convulsion of a local nature in this county

which is more pernicious and dangerous in its character and consequences than a contested election." Rankin may also have feared that if he vacated his seat it might go to a Cunard supporter. If he believed that old animosities had subsided, he was badly mistaken.

During the "fighting elections" of 1843 Rankin was deeply involved. In the January election he was a successful candidate and in the July by-election he supported Street against Cunard's candidate, John Thomas Williston. In his nomination speech, in December 1842, Williston had declared that Rankin intended "if possible" to take Street into the house with him, which would "place the whole Legislative influence of this county into the hands of Messrs. Gilmour, Rankin and Co., whose power I feel persuaded many of you think sufficiently strong already." Williston later claimed that Rankin had threatened to leave the county if Street lost the by-election. The voting saw riots, bloodshed, the death of one man, and the arrival of troops; when it was over, Street had won and he and Rankin were the county's representatives.

In February 1847 Rankin was sworn in as a member of the Executive Council in the administration of John Richard Partelow*, and the following year, when Lieutenant Governor Sir Edmund Walker Head* introduced responsible government, Rankin was kept as a member because he had considerable influence in the assembly. Head's only reservation derived from the "violent party feud" which prevailed in Northumberland County. However, he felt he could keep this in check and, since Rankin was not controlled by either party in the assembly, Head felt he would be a valuable member of the government. Not everyone agreed. Earlier in 1847 Lemuel Allan Wilmot* had questioned Rankin's appointment because no one knew what his political principles were. It is doubtful whether Rankin himself knew; he served neither side. Nevertheless, he remained a member of the council until his death.

Rankin opposed Cunard and his Chatham supporters in almost everything they did. In 1826 he had helped defeat an attempt to have Chatham made the county seat instead of Newcastle; the following year he used his influence to have the custom-house built about a mile and a half above Chatham and directly across the river from Douglastown; and in 1830 he managed to have the new seamen's hospital built in Douglastown. Needless to say his success in these matters angered the people of Chatham, especially Cunard, who was able to persuade the customs officials that they should move to Chatham in 1838. However, before the move took place there were threats of violence from the north side of the river and in 1839 Lieutenant Governor Sir John HARVEY was able to prevent it. Harvey considered Cunard a

Rankin

conservative opposed to all reform, but he felt Rankin and his partners were liberals and "Staunch Supporters" of the government. He had intervened not because of the violence, but to please Rankin.

Rankin served the community in many ways as did Cunard, and in spite of their business rivalry they could work together on projects which either were mutually beneficial or in no way infringed on their commercial power. In 1829 both men had been appointed commissioners for lights in the Gulf of St Lawrence and the Miramichi River and in 1841, along with William Abrams, they supervised the construction of a lighthouse at Point Escuminac. They were appointed to the board of health for Northumberland and Gloucester counties in 1844 and they helped supervise the construction of the lazaret on Sheldrake Island. Rankin had been made a justice of the peace in 1819 and probably retained the position until his death. He was also a long-time member of the Northumberland Agricultural Society and the Miramichi Emigration Society; he belonged as well to the Chatham Mechanics' Institute. In 1841 he was one of the founders of the North British Society (in 1846 it was renamed the Highland Society of New Brunswick at Miramichi), serving as president in 1851 and 1852. In 1850 he was a member of the board of management for the branch of the Commercial Bank of New Brunswick at Miramichi.

Rankin had few close friends. He was a quiet man, not given to long conversations or small talk, and many people considered him cold. Others found he had a warm heart and he was always ready to help the distressed, especially widows and orphans and the sick. His sudden death in 1852, while he was on a visit to England, shocked the whole Miramichi area, especially Douglastown. From the newspaper obituaries it would appear that Rankin was the perfect Christian gentleman and his charitable works were certainly evident in Douglastown. He was a deeply religious man and a firm supporter of the Church of Scotland. He also assisted other churches in the region and in his will he left £25 to every Protestant church on the river. Occasionally his firm also aided Roman Catholics and in 1838 it received the grateful thanks of the people of Neguac for the gift of a chapel bell. However, his benevolence extended only to those who loyally supported him; few in Chatham saw him in quite the same light as did the people of Newcastle and Douglastown. Ruling Douglastown almost like a feudal baron, he was loved by many of his employees and hated and feared by his enemies and some of the semi-independent operators. Men like Rankin were needed in the early years of the timber trade and he was perhaps the most successful of the New Brunswick timber barons who operated during the first half of the 19th century.

WILLIAM A. SPRAY

BLHU, R. G. Dun & Co. credit ledger, Canada, 9: 59, 143, 222, 314, 343. N.B. Museum, Webster coll., Sir Howard Douglas, letter-book, Douglas to Sir James Kempt, 7 Feb. 1829 (typescript). PANB, MC 216/11, 216/46, notes on Alexander Rankin; "N.B. political biog." (J. C. and H. B. Graves), XI: 71–72; RG 1, RS345, A1: 6; RG 2, RS6, A3: 444, 447; RS7, 24–25, 65; RS8, Appointments and commissions, 2/1: 58; reg. of commissions, 1785–1840: 121–22; Surveyor General, files 233–35; RG 4, RS24, S36-P31; S37-P57–58; S54-P108; RG 18, RS153, G3/4. PRO, CO 188/46, Campbell to Goderich, 14 Oct. 1833; 188/64: 20–23, 30–31; 188/65: 212–14; 188/105: 179–202; 193/3: 124–34. UNBL, MG H33. [Beamish Murdoch], *A narrative of the late fires at Miramichi, New Brunswick . . .* (Halifax, 1825), 13, 25. N.B., House of Assembly, *Journal,* 1829: 118. *Gleaner* (Chatham, N.B.), 28 Sept. 1830; 27 Sept., 4 Oct. 1831; 7, 12, 14 May, 26 Sept. 1833; 4 April, 5 Sept., 3, 10 Oct. 1837; 23 June 1840; 19 Jan. 1841; 18 Oct., 20, 27 Dec. 1842; 3, 10, 17, 24, 31 Jan., 7, 14, 21, 28 Feb., 6, 13, 20, 27 March, 8, 20, 22 April, 22, 28 July, 25 Aug., 8, 29 Sept. 1843; 14 Dec. 1844; 7 Feb., 11 July 1846; 16 Feb. 1847. *Royal Gazette* (Fredericton), 8 Feb. 1843, 17 Feb. 1847, 5 May 1852.

Esther Clark Wright, *The Miramichi, a study of the New Brunswick river and of the people who settled along it* (Sackville, N.B., 1944), 41–51. Robert Cooney, *A compendious history of the northern part of the province of New Brunswick, and of the district of Gaspé, in Lower Canada* (Halifax, 1832; repub. Chatham, 1896), 86, 90–96, 105–6, 108, 142. G. E. Fenety, *Political notes and observations; or, a glance at the leading measures that have been introduced and discussed in the House of Assembly of New Brunswick . . .* (Fredericton, 1867), 242. J. A. Fraser, *By favourable winds: a history of Chatham, New Brunswick* ([Chatham], 1975), 34, 38, 44–51; *Gretna Green; a history of Douglastown, New Brunswick, Canada, 1783–1900* ([Chatham], 1969). A. R. M. Lower, *Great Britain's woodyard; British America and the timber trade, 1763–1867* (Montreal and London, Ont., 1973), 60, 146–47. MacNutt, *New Brunswick,* 119, 216, 230, 275. John Rankin, *A history of our firm, being some account of the firm of Pollok, Gilmour and Co. and its offshoots and connections, 1804–1920* (2nd ed., Liverpool, Eng., 1921), 49–61, 64, 124–25, 249–50. J. D. White, "Speed the plough: agricultural societies in pre-confederation New Brunswick" (MA thesis, Univ. of N.B., Fredericton, 1976), 25–26. Graeme Wynn, "The assault on the New Brunswick forest, 1780–1850" (PHD thesis, Univ. of Toronto, 1974), 287–99, 322–23, 331, 354; "Industrialism, entrepreneurship, and opportunity in the New Brunswick timber trade," *The enterprising Canadians: entrepreneurs and economic development in eastern Canada, 1820–1914,* ed. L. R. Fisher and E. W. Sager (St John's, 1979), 18–20; *Timber colony,* 125–29, 134. W. S. MacNutt, "The politics of the timber trade in colonial New Brunswick, 1825–40," *CHR,* 30 (1949): 47–65. Graeme Wynn, "Administration in adversity: the deputy surveyors and control of the New Brunswick crown forest before 1844," *Acadiensis* (Fredericton), 7 (1977–78), no.1: 49–65.

RANKIN, COUN DOULY (Condulli) (Conduiligh MacRaing), army and militia officer, politician, justice of the peace, and office holder; b. *c.* 1774 at Breachacha Castle, Isle of Coll, Scotland, third son of Neil Rankin and Catherine Maclean; m. first 4 Sept. 1804 Flora Morison on Coll, and they had five children; m. secondly 16 Feb. 1818 Margaret Maclaine on the Isle of Mull, Scotland, and they had seven children; d. 4 Feb. 1852 in Charlottetown.

For centuries the Rankins (Clann Duiligh) were hereditary pipers for the Macleans of Duart and conducted a college of piping on Mull. Neil Rankin, the last in this tradition, married a cousin of Alexander Maclean of Coll and became the resident piper at Breachacha Castle. Samuel Johnson and James Boswell, in separate accounts of their week-long visit there in 1773, comment enthusiastically on his piping. Condulli (later written as Coun Douly) Rankin was trained to succeed his father as piper but instead followed the six Maclean of Coll brothers into the army. In April 1802 Janet, daughter of Alexander Maclean of Coll, married George Vere Hobart, who shortly became lieutenant governor of Grenada. Rankin accompanied the couple's retinue to the West Indies. However, Hobart died of yellow fever at Grenada on 5 Nov. 1802, and Rankin was responsible for escorting home both the widow and the daughter born to her on the return voyage.

On 8 July 1804, shortly before his marriage, Rankin was appointed a temporary lieutenant in the New Brunswick Fencibles. One of four regiments raised in 1803 for the defence of British North America, the corps was authorized to recruit in Scotland, and Rankin under two superior but unilingual officers was engaged in this service in the Highlands. His effectiveness as a bilingual officer was clear in the fact that most of the 34 men and 65 family members who reached Fredericton in September 1805 were Gaelic-speaking. This contingent pushed the Fencibles over its qualifying complement and, with the subsequent inspection report being approved, the regiment was placed on the army establishment. The Fencibles continued to recruit aggressively and Rankin, after arriving on 14 July 1806 in Prince Edward Island, there enlisted an additional 72 men by 1808. At its own request, the corps was transformed in September 1810 into a regiment of the line, the 104th Foot, making it eligible for imperial service. Rankin was appointed ensign in the 104th on 21 June 1810 and on 2 Nov. 1811 was promoted lieutenant.

In the 1806 House of Assembly elections, Coun Douly Rankin was the most recent immigrant among the five newcomers endorsed as candidates by the Loyal Electors; the others were James Bardin Palmer*, Angus Macaulay*, James BAGNALL, and Alexander MacDonell. The Electors, determined to wrest power from the "old party" that dominated Island politics [see Charles Stewart*], were highly successful in the 1806 contest: all the candidates bearing their endorsement were victorious. Although Rankin was not a prominent figure in any of the four sessions of the eighth assembly, he was one of three

Highlanders in the house, the others being Macaulay and MacDonell, and clearly served the interests of both his ethnic and his military constituencies. As a justice of the peace, he lost a degree of public confidence in March 1811 when charges were made, and then dropped, regarding his marrying a young couple without authority. In January 1812 he served the interests of the Loyal Electors by taking evidence in Gaelic from a Highlander who had seen Chief Justice Cæsar Colclough* beating a servant and getting drunk in public.

After the onset of the War of 1812, Rankin for a time was an overseer with the Royal Engineers in New Brunswick but soon returned to Prince Edward Island. In February 1813, when all but the Charlottetown and Sydney, N.S., companies of the 104th Foot had departed for Lower Canada, another fencible corps was authorized for New Brunswick under Lieutenant-General John Coffin*. Recruiting for a captaincy in the new fencibles, Rankin encountered difficulty in obtaining men. As an officer in a regiment of the line, he was suspected of recruiting for active service and, to add to his problems, competition for new recruits had become intense since the 104th had already absorbed nearly all of the men available. A clash with John McGregor, also recruiting on the Island for a lieutenancy in Coffin's fencibles, led to McGregor's being cashiered, but the quarrel tarnished Rankin's reputation with his superiors. On 20 April 1814, five days after the death of his wife, Rankin had to leave his four small children in Charlottetown when he was compelled to take his incomplete complement of recruits to Fort Cumberland (near Sackville, N.B.). Failing to qualify for his captaincy, he turned over his recruits but later claimed that Coffin neglected to reimburse him for his expenses. Coffin maintained that Rankin refused him access to his accounts. As a result, on 13 July 1815 he was superseded in promotion in the 104th Foot. On 4 April 1816 he was exchanged to the 8th Foot and placed on half pay.

Returning to Scotland, Rankin remarried and lived in Kengharair (near Dervaig) on Mull until 1820 when he took a group of Coll emigrants to Prince Edward Island. Serving first as high sheriff of the Island, he then became deputy receiver general of quitrents. In January 1823, with Deputy Sheriff Cecil Wray Townshend, he was the agent in the countryside through whom Lieutenant Governor Charles Douglass SMITH attempted to enforce payment of quitrent arrears. The ensuing controversy led to Smith's recall. By 1829 Rankin had moved his family to a farm at Point Prim on the Selkirk estate [see Thomas Douglas*]. Succeeding Macaulay as major in the 4th (Highland) Battalion of Prince Edward Island Militia on 18 July 1829, he commanded 700 men, each "a downright Highlander by father and mother." In 1831 he went to Britain to petition the War Office to appoint sub-inspectors of militia for the Island. He and

Rankin

Ambrose LANE received commissions in this office but Lane, the senior officer, received the only salary. Rankin continued to petition both the Island and the British governments for a salary on the basis of the fact that many of his men did not understand English and were anxious that he should be remunerated as he was "the only Highland Officer of any Rank in this Province."

In the 1834 election Rankin stood among the land reform candidates of William Cooper*'s Escheat party. Losing narrowly to William Douse*, land agent for the 6th Earl of Selkirk, he contested the result. The assembly investigated irregularities at the polls, including violent clashes at Pinette between Rankin's and Douse's supporters, but found them irrelevant to the validity of the contest. On 14 April 1836 Rankin presided at a Belfast meeting that passed resolutions supporting a court of escheat and the exclusion of land agents from the assembly. Douse responded by advertising the sale of Rankin's lease and rent arrearages. In spite of the fact that Selkirk's tenants had better terms and conditions than they would have had under most other proprietors, discontent was rampant. It was expressly directed against the land agent. On 3 September Douse wrote in anger to the *Royal Gazette* about letters in the press that assailed his character. The Belfast district continued to send Rankin as a delegate to various meetings then being held in Kings and Queens counties.

In the fall of 1837, after Lieutenant Governor Sir Charles Augustus FITZROY published a circular letter advocating proprietorial leniency towards tenants, Rankin participated in a meeting at Belfast where the letter was purportedly translated into Gaelic. Douse contended that the letter was distorted by Rankin and before long not only claimed that rent collection was impossible but also expressed concern for his personal safety. Rushing to Government House on 10 November, he accused Rankin of sedition, arguing that "if it were not for him things would be quiet and orderly in the settlement." Scepticism on the part of officials about Douse's credibility and a letter from the Reverend John MACLENNAN of Belfast protected Rankin from efforts to have the War Office delete his name from the half-pay list. Later, in March 1838, Douse's attempt to evict rent-withholders was met with an assemblage of people armed with pitchforks and bludgeons. Douse requested an armed force but Colonial Secretary Lord Glenelg declared government intervention premature. By 1839, however, Selkirk's attorneys were successful in having Rankin removed from his Point Prim farm.

Living in Charlottetown in his later years, Rankin played a prominent part in the militia and in the Highland Society of Prince Edward Island, of which he was president in 1846 and again in 1851. But it was in the 1830s, as spokesman for an immigrant tenantry otherwise silenced by a language barrier, that he had

had his finest hours. His earlier life had involved struggle and contradiction. Heir to a rich Highland tradition, he was none the less part of the obsolete tacksman class and, like others of his class, became a typical promoter of emigration. The difficulties of his life in the army and during his early Island years were partly the result of his forceful personality. However, they educated him for the drastic antagonisms that he and his people and their Prince Edward Island compatriots encountered in the struggles for land reform in the 1830s.

KENNETH A. MACKINNON

GRO (Edinburgh), Coll, reg. of births and baptisms, 23 July 1776; reg. of marriages, 4 Sept. 1804; Kilninian and Kilmore, reg. of marriages, 16 Feb. 1818. PAC, MG 11, [CO 226] Prince Edward Island A, 21: 95, 103–5; 23: 59; MG 19, E1, ser.1, 73: 19226–27, 19252, 19272, 19276–77; 74: 19340–57 (transcripts); RG 8, I (C ser.), 719: 50–53, 64–68, 110–17, 123–24, 127–28, 130–31, 161–66, 170–72; 1024: 91–112; 1025: 17–18, 122; 1203½E: 55; 1226: 7, 9, 16, 42–43, 53. PAPEI, Acc. 2524/20; Acc. 2702; Acc. 2716/1–2; Acc. 2825/53–54. P.E.I., Dept. of Health, Division of Vital Statistics (Charlottetown), Records of births, marriages, and deaths for the Rankin family (transcripts at P.E.I. Museum). Private arch., Niel Morison (Tobermory, Scot.), Corr. and geneal. records. PRO, CO 101/39, Dent to Hobart, 10 Nov. 1802; 226/28: 240–47; 226/37: 132–33, 137–38, 156; 226/54: 293, 637–41, 648–51; 226/55: 168–80, 277–92; 226/56: 307; 226/57: 160; WO 1/548 (copy in PAPEI, Acc. 3002). SRO, CH2/70/1/29, 31, 35, 101. Samuel Johnson and James Boswell, *Johnson's journey to the western islands of Scotland, and Boswell's journal of a tour to the Hebrides with Samuel Johnson, LL.D.*, ed. R. W. Chapman (London, 1924). P.E.I., House of Assembly, *Journal*, 1831–34.

Acadian Recorder, 28 May 1814. *Colonial Herald, and Prince Edward Island Advertiser* (Charlottetown), 17 March 1838; 2 May, 12 Sept. 1840; 6 April 1844. *Islander*, 6 Feb. 1852. *Prince Edward Island Gazette*, 13 Sept. 1823, 21 July 1829. *Prince Edward Island Times* (Charlottetown), 23 April 1836. *Royal Gazette* (Charlottetown), 9, 23 Dec. 1834; 3, 10, 17, 24 Feb. 1835; 26 April, 3, 20 Sept. 1836; 10 Oct., 5 Dec. 1837; 23 Jan. 1838; 12 Feb. 1839; 9 Feb. 1852. *Weekly Recorder of Prince Edward Island* (Charlottetown), 9 Feb., 27 March, 31 Aug. 1811. G.B., WO, *Army list*, 1805–17. J. M. Bumsted, *The people's clearance: highland emigration to British North America, 1770–1815* (Edinburgh and Winnipeg, 1982). A. M. Sinclair, *The Clan Gillean* (Charlottetown, 1899). W. A. Squires, *The 104th Regiment of Foot (the New Brunswick Regiment), 1803–1817* (Fredericton, 1962). Henry Whyte, *The Rankins: pipers to the MacLeans of Duart, and later to the MacLeans of Coll* (Glasgow, 1907). J. M. Bumsted, "The Loyal Electors of Prince Edward Island," *Island Magazine* (Charlottetown), no.8 (1980): 8–14. N. R. Morrison, "Clann Duiligh: Piobairean Chloinn Ghill-Eathain," *Gaelic Soc. of Inverness, Trans.* (Inverness, Scot.), 37 (1934–36): 59–79. G. F. G. Stanley, "The New Brunswick Fencibles," *Canadian Defence Quarterly* (Ottawa), 16 (1938–39): 39–53.

READ, JOHN LANDON, farmer, militiaman, merchant, justice of the peace, and office holder; b. *c.* 1787 in Township No.7 (Augusta, Ont.), son of Obediah Read and Lydia Landon; m. first *c.* 1812 Jennet Breakenridge (d. 1832), and they had four sons, including David Breakenridge Read*, and four daughters; m. secondly 23 July 1835 Hannah Elizabeth Harper (d. 1836) of Ogdensburg, N.Y., and there were no children; m. thirdly 12 Sept. 1837 Ann Miller (d. 1845), with whom he had two children; d. 19 Feb. 1857 in Chatham, Upper Canada.

John Landon Read's father and his grandfather, Moses, came from Connecticut and arrived in Upper Canada as unincorporated loyalists, who had not done military service. Obediah settled on lot 37, concession 3, of Township No.7 (named Augusta in 1788), where he built a stone house, Readholme, which still stands. He was a deacon in the Baptist church and often held meetings in his home. John grew up in a large family of nine children. He served in the War of 1812 and reputedly was present at the taking of Ogdensburg in February 1813. From that year to 1829 he lived on lot 36, concession 2, in Augusta, where he placed 40 acres under cultivation and prospered enough to live in a frame-house. By 1819 he had become a Methodist and had established a mercantile business at Maitland.

In 1830 he moved north with his growing family to Merrickville, a milling centre founded about 1800 on the Rideau River in Wolford Township. With the construction of the Rideau Canal (1826–32), opportunities for secondary services such as stores increased. Read quickly established himself as a merchant, supplying settlers not only in Wolford and adjoining Montague Township but also as far away as Perth. In 1836 he joined three other merchants in petitioning the government, on behalf of the village, for land on which a joint-stock company could erect more mills. This petition, which was eventually placed before Captain Daniel Bolton, the royal engineer in charge of the canal, might be read as the rising élite challenging the old. In 1838 Read, now a member of the Church of England, headed a petition to Bishop George Jehoshaphat Mountain* asking him to consecrate Trinity Church in Merrickville.

Read became involved in municipal affairs at an early date. He received his first commission as a magistrate on 22 July 1833. During the troubled general election of 1836 he was returning officer for the riding of Grenville. The election was being held at Merrickville when, on the fourth day of voting, the poll was attacked by a mounted party from adjacent Leeds County, where a strong anti-reform coalition had been formed to support Lieutenant Governor Sir Francis Bond Head*. The horsemen seized the poll-books and proceeded to shred them over the village green. Read knew that the reform candidates, Hiram Norton and William Benjamin Wells*, were leading the poll at the time of the attack and confirmed their election, although he himself was a staunch tory. For a number of years Read also served as a road commissioner for Wolford Township and in 1850 was its first reeve.

By 1848 the operation of his store, which stood alongside the Rideau River where high waters occasionally caused problems, appears to have been taken over by William Case Read, his second son. In the 1851 census John Landon Read is still listed as a merchant in Merrickville, living with his youngest son. By 1853 he is no longer there and it seems probable that about this time he went to Chatham, where his eldest son, James, had lived. John Landon Read died there on 19 Feb. 1857 but was buried in Merrickville. Born into a prominent pioneer family, he had proved himself a man of integrity and substance.

SHIRLEY C. SPRAGGE

ACC-O, Merrickville parish records, J. L. Read *et al.*, petition to G. J. [Mountain], 4 Nov. 1838; reg. of baptisms, marriages, and burials. AO, RG 21, United counties of Leeds and Grenville, Augusta Township, list of inhabitants and assessment rolls; Wolford Township, assessment rolls, 1830, 1844–48; RG 22, ser.179, Moses Read. PAC, RG 1, L3, 423: R3/3; 427: R11/10; 435A: R20/58; RG 5, A1: 105277–79; RG 68, General index, 1651–1841: 479. QUA, United counties of Leeds and Grenville, land registry copy book, liber F, instrument 321. *A summary of the proceedings of the council of the District of Johnstown and the council of the united counties of Leeds and Grenville, 1842–1942*, comp. William Jelly (Brockville, Ont., 1943), 11, 58. *Chatham Planet* (Chatham, [Ont.]), 19 Feb., 6 March 1857. *Christian Guardian*, 7 March 1832. *Church*, 8 Aug. 1845. *Correspondent and Advocate* (Toronto), 20 Aug. 1835, 26 July 1844. Chadwick, *Ontarian families*. *Illustrated historical atlas of the counties of Leeds and Grenville* (Belleville, Ont., 1973). *Marriage notices of Ontario*, comp. W. D. Reid (Lambertville, N.J., 1980), 115. Ella Read Wright, *Reed–Read lineage; Captain John Reed of Providence, R.I., and Norwalk, Conn., and his descendants through his sons, John and Thomas, 1660–1909* (Waterbury, Conn., 1909). T. W. H. Leavitt, *History of Leeds and Grenville, Ontario, from 1749 to 1879 . . .* (Brockville, 1879; repr. Belleville, 1972). D. B. Read, *The Canadian rebellion of 1837* (Toronto, 1896).

REILLY. *See* O'REILLY

RICHARDSON, JOHN (he also on occasion used the middle name **Frederick**), army officer, author, newspaperman, and office holder; b. 4 Oct. 1796 probably at Fort George (Niagara-on-the-Lake), Upper Canada, son of Robert Richardson and Madelaine Askin; m. first 12 Aug. 1825 Jane Marsh; m. secondly 2 April 1832 Maria Caroline Drayson; he had no children; d. 12 May 1852 in New York City.

John Richardson was a grandson on his mother's side of the fur trader and merchant John Askin* and

Richardson

Manette (Monette), a native woman believed to have been an Ottawa. His father came to Upper Canada from the Annandale district of Scotland as a surgeon with the Queen's Rangers. He met and married Madelaine Askin in Queenston in 1793 and eventually settled in Amherstburg on the Detroit River. There John spent his adolescent years.

In July 1812, one month after war had broken out between the United States and Great Britain, Richardson, at the age of 15, joined the 41st Foot as a volunteer. He took part in several military engagements near Lake Erie. Fighting with Indian forces led by his hero Tecumseh*, Richardson had an opportunity to observe the character of Indian warriors. He relied upon this experience when he came to write the novels *Wacousta*, *Hardscrabble*, and *Wau-nan-gee*. On 5 Oct. 1813 he was captured at the battle of Moraviantown and imprisoned in Kentucky. He was later to describe his war service in an essay, "A Canadian campaign, by a British officer."

Released in July 1814, he joined the 8th Foot (in which he had been commissioned ensign on 4 Aug. 1813) in October and was sent to Europe with it in June 1815 to fight Napoleon's last army. Arriving too late to engage in the battle of Waterloo, he was promoted lieutenant in July and then went on half pay in London in February 1816 before joining the 2nd Foot as a second lieutenant in May. He served with this regiment for more than two years, primarily in Barbados and Grenada. As a result of a severe case of malaria and for personal reasons, he went on half pay again in the autumn of 1818 in the 92nd Foot. For at least three years Richardson lived in London and then moved to Paris, where in 1825 he married for the first time. His experiences in these cities were later to figure in the novels *Écarté* and *Frascati's*. By 1826 he was back in London, where he published the poem *Tecumseh; or, the warrior of the west* (1828). His personal narrative, "A Canadian campaign," was serialized in 1826–27 in the *New Monthly Magazine and Literary Journal* (London), and another, "Recollections of the West Indies," probably first appeared at this time (it was later serialized in the *New Era* in 1842). He also engaged in journalism, began writing novels, and pestered the War Office to be taken back on active duty.

Richardson's first novel, *Écarté; or, the salons of Paris*, was published by Henry Colburn in London in 1829. Although it became a reference for preachers who wished to warn their congregations against the evils of gambling, the novel was more sensitive and profound than a mere object lesson for preachers and was, as one reviewer remarked, full of "fine moral antithesis." In his novels Richardson aimed for a realistic depiction of life, a perspective he later commended in the writings of Charles Dickens, whom he considered "nature's purest and most faithful painter." *Écarté*'s sequel, *Frascati's; or, scenes in Paris* (1830), written with Justin Brenan, describes how Irish tourists were taken in by tricksters in Paris. It was his third work, the historical novel *Wacousta; or, the prophecy* (1832), which became popular and established Richardson's fame.

In *Wacousta*, Sir Reginald Morton, an English nobleman, comes to British North America to seek revenge for the loss of his fiancée to a fellow officer and friend, Charles de Haldimar. Disguised as an Indian and adopting the name Wacousta, he helps Pontiac* lead an armed uprising in 1763 against English forts in the northwest. Only Detroit is saved because an Indian woman in love with the elder son of the fort's commander, de Haldimar, gets word to him of the Indians' planned ruse: to play field hockey outside the fort, pretend to chase the ball into the fort, and then slay the inhabitants. Before the end of the novel Wacousta kills two of de Haldimar's children and a curse is uttered by Wacousta's niece which prophesies the end of the de Haldimar line.

In writing the novel, Richardson made use of accounts of the siege of Detroit in 1763 and of the attack on Fort Michilimackinac (Mackinaw City, Mich.) which he had heard as a boy [see Minweweh*]. Wacousta himself was loosely modelled after John Norton*, son of a Cherokee father and a Scottish mother, who was raised in Scotland and came to British North America in 1785 with the 65th Foot. Norton was later appointed a Mohawk chief (Teyoninhokarawen), and worked closely with Joseph Brant [Thayendanegea*] negotiating the controversial settlement of the Six Nations Indians near the Grand River. As a small boy Richardson had himself encountered Norton, who had been a trading agent for John Askin, and in 1816 he appealed to Norton for assistance when he was seeking to return to full pay in London. The name Sir Reginald Morton, however, Richardson derived from Sir Reginald Norton, who died at Faversham, England, in 1500. The Norton family was closely connected for centuries with the Drayson family; Sir Reginald himself married a Drayson, and members from both families filled the office of mayor of Faversham in the 16th century. At the time he was writing *Wacousta*, Richardson was courting Maria Caroline Drayson, whom he married in the year it was published, and he doubtless heard of the Norton connection from her father, William, who was interested in genealogy. There are also obvious literary progenitors for the mighty Wacousta, the outlaw wreaking revenge on society for an injustice done to him; Milton's Satan and Schiller's Karl Moor are among them, as are the heroes of Byron who seek redress for the betrayal of friendship. When the American edition of 1851 appeared, critic Evert Augustus Duyckinck wrote: "This is one of these curiously compounded works, criticism stops at, because, in the first place it is sure of the sympathies of a large circle of readers; shows talent throughout; and yet, at the same time, is scarcely amenable to the strict standards of judgement."

Richardson's use of historical events did not serve so well the sequel to *Wacousta*, entitled *The Canadian brothers; or, the prophecy fulfilled* (1840). He called this novel "a Canadian national novel" since he drew again upon his personal experiences to describe the border warfare in the War of 1812 from a Canadian viewpoint. *The Canadian brothers* lacked the intensity of *Wacousta* and was not as popular. It was published in Montreal in 1840, the only one of his novels to appear first in Canada. In 1851 it was issued in the United States in an altered version under the title *Matilda Montgomerie: or, the prophecy fulfilled*, but it was never published in England, owing no doubt to its Canadian character.

In 1835 Richardson's wish to return to active service had been realized after a fashion when, as a captain, he joined the British auxiliary legion raised for service in Spain during the First Carlist War. His *Journal of the movements of the British Legion*, published in 1836, and the next edition of the work, *Movements of the British Legion* (1837), were used by Tories to embarrass the Whig government of Lord Melbourne, whose representatives retaliated by making personal attacks on Richardson in parliament. But the troubles of the British Legion were internal as well, and Richardson, by describing his sufferings at the hands of its commander, Lieutenant-General George de Lacy Evans, exposed the petty intrigues of military adventurers and place-seekers. His *Personal memoirs* (1838) and a satirical novel, "Jack Brag in Spain" (serialized in the *New Era* in 1841–42), continued his exposé of the British Legion. While still serving in Spain he had been brought before a military court of inquiry for casting "discredit on the conduct of the Legion," a charge altered to "cowardice in battle." Richardson, who had been wounded in the campaign, was exonerated, and then promoted major in 1836. Henceforth, his books, which had been published anonymously, carried his name and rank.

Another product of the Spanish campaign was a knighthood in the military Order of St Ferdinand, which he had received for courage in battle. It was his most prized award aside from his majority. From boyhood Richardson had developed a passionate interest in chivalry, and while in Europe he became an adherent of Saint-Simon's belief that the individual is responsible for maintaining his personal dignity, a gift derived directly from the Creator. He was later to transform the role of knight into fiction in *The monk knight of St. John; a tale of the Crusades* (1850), in which a Crusader named Abdallah, the monk knight, is put to the test in that era of murder and rapine.

In the spring of 1838 the *Times* of London, a Tory

newspaper, hired Richardson on a year's contract as foreign correspondent to cover the rebellions of 1837–38 in Upper and Lower Canada, perhaps as compensation for his services to the Tories. After his arrival in Montreal, however, Richardson became a strong supporter of the governor-in-chief, Lord Durham [Lambton*], prompting the *Times* to dismiss him. Richardson was also left with political enemies in the Canadas when Durham was recalled.

Richardson, in *Eight years in Canada* (1847) and its sequel, *The guards in Canada; or, the point of honor* (1848), provides a valuable contemporary account of events under the administrations of Durham, Lord Sydenham [Thomson*], Sir Charles Bagot*, and Sir Charles Theophilus Metcalfe*, and describes his personal vicissitudes in the period from 1838 to 1848. In these years he threw himself into journalism and the political fray on behalf of the conservative opposition. Having sold his lieutenancy to buy a printing-press in June 1840, he settled in Brockville in July and published there from June 1841 to August 1842 the *New Era, or Canadian Chronicle*, in which he tried to bring "polite literature" to Canadians. Then, living in Kingston, he issued the *Canadian Loyalist, & Spirit of 1812* from January 1843 to July 1844. Once again Richardson made himself a controversial figure. He feuded with members of the British military and with French Canadian conservatives led by Clément-Charles Sabrevois* de Bleury who were opposed to Durham's plan for the union of the Canadas. In 1842 Richardson edited his earlier work, "A Canadian campaign," fleshed it out with excerpts from official war documents, and serialized it in the *New Era* as "Operations of the right division." The articles were well received and were republished in book form as *War of 1812*. Richardson hoped that the book would be used in schools, and applied to the Legislative Assembly for a grant to publish two more volumes. He received £250 but claimed that the grant did no more than cover his expenses in publishing the first volume. In fact, he placed the remaining copies of *War of 1812* on auction to pay creditors; only one was sold, and no further volumes were issued. Francis Hincks*, who had opposed the grant for fear that Richardson would use it to help his newspapers, became a relentless political enemy and attacked Richardson regularly in print. In 1843 Richardson stirred up yet more controversy when, on 17 October, he fought a duel with Stewart Derbishire* over the latter's ardent defence of those responsible for the death of a 16-year-old youth in an Orange Day confrontation.

Despite his frequent quarrels with senior political officials, Richardson repeatedly tried to win appointment to government office, but his enemies were too numerous. Early in 1842 he had petitioned Queen Victoria in vain for a pension, claiming to be "the only Author this Country has hitherto produced." After his newspapers failed he fell into debt. Finally in May 1845 Governor Metcalfe, whom Richardson had energetically supported in the *Canadian Loyalist*, appointed him superintendent of police on the Welland Canal, and Richardson and his wife moved to St Catharines.

With only a small band of men to help him, Richardson now faced the unenviable task of maintaining order on the Welland Canal, where rioting, often politically instigated to embarrass the government, had broken out among Irish canal workers, who also protested the starvation wages paid by private contractors. Despite the antagonism of his employer, the Board of Works, whose members were reformers opposed to Metcalfe, Richardson set out to fashion a disciplined force and end violence along the canal. He went through a series of humiliations, violent confrontations, and a farcical trial in his struggle to assert his authority before all real power was taken away from him. His troubles were compounded by the unexpected death on 16 Aug. 1845 of his wife from apoplexy provoked by the strain of her husband's difficulties. In December, when it appeared that relative peace had been restored, Samuel Power, the chief engineer and an employee in favour with the Board of Works, recommended that the police force be reduced and Richardson be dismissed since his presence was no longer required. Richardson was dismissed from office at the end of January 1846. His account of the Welland Canal episode was published that year as *Correspondence (submitted to parliament)*.

From August 1846 to January 1847 Richardson tried his hand at political muck-raking by publishing a weekly newspaper in Montreal, the *Weekly Expositor; or, Reformer of Public Abuses and Railway and Mining Intelligencer*. During this time he also did some writing for the Montreal *Courier*. The passage in April 1849 of the Rebellion Losses Bill, which granted the rebels of 1837–38 compensation equal to that received by the loyalists for losses suffered during the uprising, offended loyalists and led to rioting in Montreal. The troubles prompted Richardson to relocate in New York in the fall of 1849. Americans, after all, celebrated him as an author while Canadians showed little interest in his work.

Richardson's entry on the American literary scene was heralded by the serialization in *Sartain's Union Magazine of Literature and Art* (Philadelphia) from February to June 1850 of his new novel, *Hardscrabble; or, the fall of Chicago*, which centres around the Indian siege of Fort Dearborn (Chicago) in 1812. His writings resulted in an increased readership of *Sartain's*, just as the serialization of his next novel, *Wau-nan-gee; or, the massacre at Chicago*, did for the New York *Sunday Mercury* in 1851. Despite his apparent success, Richardson's financial situation does not seem to have improved. Although his novels *Écarté*, *Wacousta*, and *The Canadian brothers* (retitled *Matilda Montgomerie*) were republished with as much critical and popular success as his newer works, including *The monk knight*, he made little money from them because he was forced by his straitened circumstances to sell them to the publishers for reduced lump sums.

In New York he also wrote short stories for American periodicals and at least two songs. One of the latter, "All hail to the land," set to music by harpist Charles Nicholas Bochsa and published in October 1850, was a national song. A short story, "Westbrook; or, the renegade," was initially rejected in 1851 in a contest held by *Sartain's*, but Richardson subsequently extended it into a short novel, *Westbrook, the outlaw*, at the suggestion of the editor of the *Sunday Mercury*, where it was serialized in the fall of 1851. It was based on a real person, Andrew Westbrook*, a farmer living in Upper Canada in the vicinity of the village of Delaware on the Thames River. During the War of 1812 Westbrook led American marauding parties into the province and was branded an outlaw by the Upper Canadian courts in 1816. Richardson depicted him as a villain whose revenge for the loss of a district militia command to a young neighbour of the local gentry was to imprison the youth's sister in an isolated cabin and rape her every day until he was discovered. Richardson's inspiration may have come in part from the rebellion of New York farmers around Albany against landowners in the 1840s, and the portrayal of the farmers in New York City newspapers as bloodthirsty savages. Although published in book form in 1853, the novel to all intents and purposes was lost until 1973 when the newspaper serialization turned up at a book auction in New York.

Richardson's last publication, *Lola Montes: or, a reply to the "Private history and memoirs" of that celebrated lady* (1851), was written in defence of the dancer and actress who arrived in New York late that year. He published it anonymously at his own expense, but it was a commercial failure. His fortunes, which were at a "very low ebb," were hurt rather than revived. Richardson died in New York on 12 May 1852 of erysipelas brought on by undernourishment. His friends took up a collection to pay the expenses of his funeral but there is no record of where he is buried, other than that his body was removed from the city.

Throughout his life Richardson defended his individuality to a point where many considered him quarrelsome, unreasonable, and enigmatic. Sensitive to slights, he was ever ready to fight a duel, and took part in many. Although an excellent shot with pistols, he claimed that he did not provoke confrontations but rather became involved only when it was necessary to uphold his dignity. His sharp criticism of his contemporaries and their utilitarianism sprang from his belief in the overriding need to develop the individual personality. During the 1840s he became sympathetic to the fatalistic teachings of the American sect leader William Miller, with his prophecies of the end of the world. Later, when he lived in New York, Richardson followed the evangelical preacher William Augustus Muhlenberg, who proclaimed the universality of Christianity and emphasized the spiritual power of love.

Richardson's strengths included a dedication to Canada's national progress, particularly evident in his support of Lord Durham and responsible government, and his antagonism to what he regarded as corrupt and irresponsible bureaucracies. An over-zealous pursuit of his goals and ideals along with too great an expectation of reward and success brought him enemies unnecessarily. He was, moreover, of an impatient and egotistical temperament. Although a champion of integrity and considerate behaviour, which he saw as exemplified in the chivalric code, he was not above small lies and looking out for his own interests. Thus he too was human, like the fictional characters through whom he tried to bring reality into literature. Certainly he was quick to anger and he pursued his objectives with stubborn perseverance, but he was not without the foresight of a visionary, a subtle sense of humour, and literary talents that were recognized by some of his contemporaries.

Richardson described his "inventive genius" as a natural talent: "The power so to weave together the incidents of a tale that they may be made comprehensible and attractive to the reader, is a mere gift, which some persons possess in a greater or less degree than others; and can reflect no more credit upon him who is endowed with it, than can reasonably be claimed by any man or woman who has been, by nature, fortunately gifted with personal beauty and attraction superior to that enjoyed by the generality of their kind." He showed no patience for Canadians who, by neglecting their writers, demeaned themselves in the eyes of the civilized world. "True, I have elsewhere remarked that the Canadians are not a reading people. Neither are they: but yet there are many hundreds of educated men in the country, who ought to know better, . . . who possess a certain degree of public influence, and who should have been sensible that, in doing honor to those whom the polished circles of society, and even those of a more humble kind, have placed high in the conventional scale, they were adopting the best means of elevating themselves."

Unrecognized by Canadians, he was almost forgotten, and in one of his frequent moments of frustration in Canada wrote that "should a more refined and cultivated taste ever be introduced into the matter-of-fact country in which I have derived my being, its people will decline to do me the honor of placing my name in the list of their Authors." It was a long time before his life aroused interest and his novels began to receive attention as energetic and complex creations. A promoter of a Canadian national literature in his day, Richardson would have been pleased to find that his works are now recognized as a contribution to its development.

DAVID R. BEASLEY

Many of John Richardson's full-length works were published first in serial form; some, especially the novels and in particular *Wacousta*, were republished frequently and in different versions. The following lists his most important extant writings, and references to books give only the first date of known separate publication. Fuller bibliographies, which include references to works that have not survived in their entirety or at all, and more complete information on Richardson's literary production are given in the author's *The Canadian Don Quixote: the life and works of Major John Richardson, Canada's first novelist* (Erin, Ont., 1977), 198–202, which is also the first full-length biography of John Richardson, and in *A bibliographical study of Major John Richardson*, comp. W. F. E. Morley (Toronto, 1973), which includes a biographical introduction by Derek F. Crawley. The reader should also refer to *The Canadian Don Quixote* for additional sources on Richardson's career.

Richardson wrote the following novels: *The Canadian brothers; or, the prophecy fulfilled: a tale of the late American war* (2v., Montreal, 1840), republished as *Matilda Montgomerie: or, the prophecy fulfilled; a tale of the late American war, being the sequel to "Wacousta"* (New York, 1851); *Écarté; or, the salons of Paris* (3v., London, 1829); *Frascati's; or, scenes in Paris* (3v., London, 1830), written with Justin Brenan; *Hardscrabble; or, the fall of Chicago: a tale of Indian warfare* (New York, [1850 or 1851]); *The monk knight of St. John; a tale of the Crusades* (New York, 1850); *Wacousta; or, the prophecy: the tale of the Canadas* (3v., London and Edinburgh, 1832); *Wau-nan-gee; or, the massacre at Chicago: a romance of the American revolution* (New York, [1852]); and *Westbrook, the outlaw; or, the avenging wolf* (New York, 1853), which has been reprinted with a preface by D. R. Beasley (Montreal, 1973). His poetry includes *Kensington Gardens in 1830: a satirical trifle* (London, 1830); "Miller's prophecy fulfilled," *Canadian Loyalist, & Spirit of 1812* (Kingston, [Ont.]), 1 Feb. 1844 (a single copy is extant, at the PAC), which has been edited and republished by D. R. Beasley and W. F. E. Morley in the *Papers* of the Biblio. Soc. of Canada (Toronto), 10 (1971): 18–28; and *Tecumseh; or, the warrior of the west: a poem, in four cantos, with notes* (London, 1828).

Among Richardson's important works of non-fiction are "A Canadian campaign, by a British officer," *New Monthly Magazine and Literary Journal* (London), new ser., 17 (July–December 1826), pt.II: 541–48; 19 (January–June 1827), pt.I: 162–70, 248–54, 448–57, 538–51; *Correspondence (submitted to parliament) between Major Richardson, later superintendent of police on the Welland Canal, and the Honorable Dominick Daly, provincial secretary . . .* (Montreal, 1846); *Eight years in Canada; embracing a review of the administrations of Lords Durham and Sydenham, Sir Chas. Bagot, and Lord Metcalfe, and*

Ridout

including numerous interesting letters from Lord Durham, Mr. Chas. Buller and other well-known public characters (Montreal, 1847); The guards in Canada; or, the point of honor: being a sequel to ... "Eight years in Canada" (Montreal, 1848); Journal of the movements of the British Legion (London, 1836), published in a 2nd edition as Movements of the British Legion, with strictures on the course of conduct pursued by Lieutenant-General Evans (London, 1837); Lola Montes: or, a reply to the "Private history and memoirs" of that celebrated lady, recently published, by the Marquis Papon ... (New York, 1851); "Operations of the right division of the army of Upper Canada, during the American War of 1812," New Era, or Canadian Chronicle (Brockville, [Ont.]), 2 March–22 July 1842, republished as War of 1812, first series; containing a full and detailed narrative of the operations of the right division, of the Canadian army ([Brockville], 1842); Personal memoirs of Major Richardson ... as connected with the singular oppression of that officer while in Spain by Lieutenant General Sir De Lacy Evans (Montreal, 1838); and "Recollections of the West Indies," New Era, or Canadian Chronicle, 2 March–24 June 1842.

Reprints of Richardson's works which also contain useful biographical information include The Canadian brothers ..., intro. C. F. Klinck (Toronto and Buffalo, N.Y., 1974); Richardson's War of 1812, with notes and a life of the author, ed. A. C. Casselman (Toronto, 1902); and Tecumseh and Richardson: the story of a trip to Walpole Island and Port Sarnia, ed. A. H. U. Colquhoun (Toronto, 1924). See also Major Richardson's short stories, ed. D. R. Beasley (Penticton, B.C., 1985). In addition, the Centre for Editing Early Canadian Texts (Ottawa) has among its projects the republication of Wacousta.

New York Public Library, MSS and Arch. Division, Duyckinck family papers, E. A. Duyckinck diary, 13 Sept. 1851. PAC, RG 5, C1, 196, Richardson to Lord Elgin, 10 May 1847. PRO, WO 25/772: 130v. G.B., Parl., Hansard's parliamentary debates (London), 3rd ser., 38 (1837): 2–123. Literary World (New York), 1 March 1851. Mirror of Parliament (London), April 1837. New Monthly Magazine and Literary Journal (London), new ser., 27 (January–December 1829), pt.III: 189–90. Pick (New York), 22 May 1852. Sunday Mercury (New York), 16 May 1852. DNB. Major John Richardson; a selection of reviews and criticism, ed. Carl Ballstadt (Montreal, 1972). D. R. Cronk, "The editorial destruction of Canadian literature: a textual study of Major John Richardson's Wacousta; or the prophecy" (MA thesis, Simon Fraser Univ., Burnaby, B.C., 1977). Dennis Duffy, Gardens, covenants, exiles: loyalism in the literature of Upper Canada/Ontario (Toronto, 1982). Michael Hurley, "The borderline of nightmare: a study of the fiction of John Richardson" (PHD thesis, Queen's Univ., Kingston, Ont., 1984). Robert Lecker, "Patterns of deception in Wacousta," The Canadian novel, ed. John Moss (3v. to date, Toronto, 1978–), 2: 47–59. C. W. New, Lord Durham; a biography of John George Lambton, first Earl of Durham (Oxford, 1929). James Reaney, Wacousta! (Toronto, 1979). W. R. Riddell, John Richardson (Toronto, 1923). T. D. MacLulich, "The colonial major: Richardson and Wacousta," Essays on Canadian Writing (Downsview [Toronto]), no.29 (summer 1984): 66–84. Desmond Pacey, "A colonial romantic: Major John Richardson, soldier and novelist," Canadian Literature (Vancouver), no.2 (autumn 1959): 20–31; no.3 (winter 1960): 47–56.

RIDOUT, LIONEL AUGUSTUS CLARK, hardware merchant, land speculator, and militia officer; b. August 1817 in Bristol, England, son of George Charmbury Ridout and Mary Ann Wright; m. 17 Dec. 1846 Louisa Lawrason, eldest child of Lawrence Lawrason*, in London, Upper Canada, and they had one son and three daughters, one of whom died in infancy; d. there 10 Nov. 1859.

George Charmbury Ridout emigrated from Bristol to Philadelphia with his family in 1820, settling in York (Toronto), Upper Canada, the following year. When Upper Canada College opened its doors in 1830, Lionel Augustus Clark Ridout and his younger brother, Septimus Adolphus, were among the students admitted. Later, Lionel probably worked for his two eldest brothers, George Percival* and Joseph Davis*, of Ridout Brothers and Company, an iron and hardware firm formed in York in 1832, and for branches or agents in the United States of Joseph Tarratt and Sons, iron and hardware merchants of Wolverhampton, England. In November 1844 he was able to establish in London, near the court-house square, a hardware store as a branch of his brothers' business, most likely with backing as well from Tarratt's and with a $1,500 loan from another former employer, John Neilson of the Pioneer Iron Company, New York. Though Ridout would continue to buy in England through his brothers, he began operating on his own account about 1846. By early 1847 his business was well established on Dundas Street in a brick building in which he had a quarter interest.

As his business prospered, Ridout emulated his father-in-law, Lawrence Lawrason, by investing in real estate in London and in the counties of Middlesex, Elgin, Kent, and Oxford. Like Lawrason in London and Joseph Davis Ridout in Toronto, he played a leading role in local business organizations. He became one of the most substantial shareholders in the County of Middlesex Building Society, the City of London Building Society, the Proof Line Road Joint Stock Company, and the London and Port Stanley Railway Company. In 1856 he was a director of the road company and president of the Middlesex building society. In the same year he became a trustee of the London Savings' Bank. His desire to promote the commercial interests of his community led him to assume a founding role in the London Board of Trade. He chaired its organizational meeting in April 1857 and was elected first vice-president; the following year he succeeded Adam Hope* as president. Ridout was very active in the London Mercantile Library Association and served as its president in 1853. A further mark of his local status during the 1850s was his captaincy in the 2nd Battalion of London militia.

In 1856–58 Ridout spent nearly $20,000 on the construction of his residence in Rough Park, his 14-acre estate in the northwestern part of the city. Before the house was completed, however, his business had begun to suffer from the commercial depression of the late 1850s and he had developed cancer of the tongue. By early 1859 the cancer had become so advanced and painful that he was compelled to entrust the management of his business to Hiram Chisholm, Lawrason's partner, and to remove to Toronto in order to be under the care of Dr William Rawlins Beaumont*. Despite the hopelessness of recovery, Ridout was urged by his family to travel to Great Britain to consult the doctors of London and Edinburgh. This journey he and his wife undertook, along with a side trip to Paris, during the spring and summer of 1859. They returned to London, Upper Canada, several weeks prior to his death on 10 November. A conservative politically and a member of St Paul's Church (Anglican), he was highly esteemed within the community, and the *London Free Press* regarded him as "one of its ablest and most promising merchants."

Because of economic conditions and his state of health during the last two years of his life, however, Ridout had found it difficult to collect debts owed him and therefore to pay his creditors. These included the Tarratt company and the firm of Thomas Brown Anderson*, a Montreal hardware importer. Consequently, Ridout's properties had become heavily mortgaged and he borrowed several thousands of dollars, much of it from Lawrence Lawrason. Ridout died with debts approaching $100,000, and even his household effects were sold in 1860, by his executors, George Percival Ridout, Henry Corry Rowley Becher*, and Lawrason. The latter personally underwrote a substantial amount of Ridout's debt and took in his widow and children. Real-estate prices having fallen drastically during the depression, Rough Park sold in 1862 for a mere $12,130. It was to be another ten years before Ridout's estate was completely settled. Meanwhile Rough Park became the site for Huron College, established by Bishop Benjamin Cronyn* in 1863.

DANIEL J. BROCK

BLHU, R. G. Dun & Co. credit ledger, Canada, 19: 25. UWOL, Regional Coll., Laurason–Ridout–Pennington families, papers and scrapbooks; Lionel Ridout, estate papers. *London Free Press and Daily Western Advertiser* (London, [Ont.]), 11, 14 Nov. 1859. *Weekly Prototype and Farmers' Newspaper* (London), 12 Nov. 1859. *Hist. of Middlesex*, 222–23.

RIDOUT, SAMUEL SMITH, office holder, merchant, and militia officer; b. 7 Sept. 1778 in Annapolis, Md, eldest son of Thomas Ridout* and his first wife, Isabella ——; m. first 21 May 1805 Eliza Parsons (d. 1838), and they had four sons and five daughters; m. secondly 2 Oct. 1838 Mary Hardwick Unwin, widow of Francis Humphreys; d. 6 June 1855 in Toronto.

In the spring of 1788, when Samuel Smith Ridout was nine years old, his father was captured by Shawnees while on business in the Ohio country. Thomas Ridout was ransomed at Detroit that summer but did not return to Maryland, choosing instead to make his way to Montreal. He married for the second time and settled in Upper Canada, first at Newark (Niagara-on-the-Lake), where he entered government service, and then, in 1797, at York (Toronto). Samuel remained in Maryland where he was probably raised and educated under the care of his uncle John Donovan, postmaster of Hancock. Thomas, once settled himself, encouraged his eldest son to join him with the lure of a position in his own office of registrar of York County. By 1800 Samuel, aged 21, had arrived in the provincial capital of Upper Canada and was soon employed as deputy to David Burns, clerk of the crown and pleas, the administrative support for the Court of King's Bench.

Samuel was not satisfied for long with the low prestige, or the £80 per annum salary, of his first post. In 1801 he became a clerk in the Surveyor General's Office, where his father had served as first clerk since 1793. Though the annual salary of £125 was "a bare subsistence," he had hopes of rising in the department. Impatient for advancement, in the next few years he also contemplated the possibilities of a commercial or a military career, but his future seemed secure when he became a deputy provincial surveyor in 1806. Within a year, however, Samuel found himself caught up in the struggle between Lieutenant Governor Francis GORE and Surveyor General Charles Burton Wyatt*, who was "transmitting copies of official Papers, to England, clandestinely, and for the purposes of misrepresenting the acts of the late Government." Ridout was peremptorily dismissed on 6 Jan. 1807 because he, the only one with knowledge of the affair, had not informed on Wyatt. His apology was accepted, however, and he was reinstated ten days later. Ridout also turned briefly to a commercial career, joining with Andrew Mercer* to operate a general store at York in 1809–10 and at Markham in 1811. After his father had been appointed surveyor general in 1810, Samuel was soon hinting that he would resign as second clerk, complaining that, although he did the work of the first clerk in the department, William Chewett* enjoyed the rank and salary. Gore, however, had not forgotten the Wyatt affair and in Thomas Ridout's words was "not disposed to do any thing for him." Gore's leave of absence and the War of 1812 would combine to provide Samuel with a second chance.

Ridout had entered the militia as a lieutenant in 1807 and received a commission in the 1st York Militia in 1809. In April 1812, with war looming, he was promoted captain in the 3rd York Militia and assigned to garrison duty at York. The following April he was paroled with many of York's other inhabitants

Riely

after the Americans captured the town. Ridout continued to assist the war effort as a non-combatant, for instance in August 1814 when he supervised the transfer of 61 prisoners to Kingston. Before the war was over Ridout petitioned Sir Gordon DRUMMOND, administrator of Upper Canada, for the post of first clerk in the Surveyor General's Office, "the Duties whereof he has been actually executing for these four years past." Though not successful in this quest, he remained in the office until after his father's death in 1829, resigning in disappointment when Chewett was made acting surveyor general. In the mean time Samuel had received other civil appointments. In April 1815 he was commissioned sheriff of the Home District, a post he would hold for more than 12 years. The following year Gore named him agent for the collection of fees for land grants. When that position was abolished in 1834, Ridout obtained an annual pension of £200 which he retained for life.

In 1827 Ridout participated in one of the most blatant examples of office trading by the "family compact." Samuel resigned as sheriff to take the less-demanding post of registrar of York County from the retiring incumbent, Stephen Jarvis. The latter's son, William Botsford Jarvis*, replaced Ridout as sheriff and, by leaving his position in the office of the provincial secretary and registrar, opened a place there for Samuel Peters JARVIS, whose late father, William Jarvis*, had held the post of provincial secretary and registrar. The complex exchange of offices, overseen and acquiesced in by Lieutenant Governor Sir Peregrine MAITLAND, was a happy change of situations for all involved, but to the compact's opponents it seemed yet another example of the oligarchy's arrogance and power. Ridout held the post of county registrar until his death on 6 June 1855. He was succeeded by his son John, who had been deputy registrar since 1827. A younger son, George Samuel, also became deputy registrar and later city assessor for Toronto. A daughter, Caroline Amelia, married his stepson, Toronto singer and music teacher James Dodsley Humphreys*.

Though his half-brothers George* and Thomas Gibbs Ridout* would gain considerable prominence, Samuel Smith Ridout avoided political involvement and was not a major figure in Upper Canada's pre-rebellion oligarchy. His career, however, with its reverses and successes, illustrates the importance of kinship, ambition, proper attitudes, and wartime activities in the task of "getting on" in early Upper Canada.

ROBERT J. BURNS

AO, MS 537; RG 1, A-I-6: 3896, 7529–30. PAC, RG 5, B9, 13: 40. PRO, CO 42/493: 217–33. *Ten years of Upper Canada in peace and war, 1805–1815; being the Ridout letters*, ed. Matilda [Ridout] Edgar (Toronto, 1890). *Town of York, 1793–1815* (Firth). Armstrong, *Handbook of Upper Canadian chronology*. R. J. Burns, "The first elite of Toronto: an examination of the genesis, consolidation and duration of power in an emerging colonial society" (PHD thesis, Univ. of Western Ont., London, 1974).

RIELY. *See* O'REILLY

RINTOUL, WILLIAM, Presbyterian minister, missionary, teacher, and editor; b. 31 Oct. 1797 in Kincardine (Kincardine-on-Forth), Scotland, son of Robert Rintoul and Sophia Aitken; m. Christian MacGibbon in Maryport, England, and they had six sons and one daughter; d. 13 Sept. 1851 in Trois-Pistoles, Lower Canada.

William Rintoul, the second son of a merchant, was educated at the University of Glasgow. He was ordained by the Church of Scotland's Presbytery of Dunblane in 1821 after accepting a call from Maryport, England, and while holding that charge he received an MA degree from the University of Edinburgh in 1826. A pamphlet he wrote the same year, called *Remarks on the claims of Scotsmen abroad, on the Christian sympathy and exertions of their countrymen at home*, revealed his decided interest in missionary work and brought him to the attention of church authorities involved with missions. In 1830 the Glasgow Colonial Society received a letter from William MORRIS, a prominent Presbyterian in Upper Canada, stating that a Presbyterian congregation newly formed in York (Toronto) needed a Scottish minister "of superior acquirements," and was proposing an attractive bond of £200 currency per annum for three years. The society offered Rintoul the appointment in September 1830 and he accepted, but delayed sailing until the spring when his twin infant sons could safely travel.

The Rintoul family arrived at Quebec on 25 May 1831 and hurried on to Kingston where a convention of Canadian Church of Scotland clergymen was scheduled for 7–8 June. Rintoul attended the second day's session which saw the formation of the Synod of the Presbyterian Church of Canada in connection with the Church of Scotland, and his own appointment as clerk of its committee for missions. He then proceeded with his family to York.

His church, St Andrew's, was opened for worship on 19 June 1831 and Rintoul, introduced to his ministry by the Reverend Robert McGILL, was the first to preach in it. Accommodating 900, it was the home church of the 79th Foot and of many Scottish emigrants, including its designer, John EWART. Although Rintoul performed his duties faithfully, introducing Sunday schools, minister's classes, and pastoral visitations, a disagreement with members of his congregation who were irritated by his stiff manners and reading of sermons resulted in his contract not being renewed at the end of its three-year term. After his departure in the spring of 1834 he was temporarily replaced in the pulpit by the Reverend John BAYNE until the return from leave in Scotland of the new incumbent, the Reverend William Turnbull Leach*.

The developments at St Andrew's were probably for the best, because it was in missionary work that Rintoul excelled. As clerk of the synod's committee for missions he had travelled throughout Upper Canada searching out Presbyterian communities lacking Church of Scotland clergymen and alerting the Glasgow Colonial Society to their needs in long letters which "had great influence in leading to more active exertions on behalf of the Presbyterian colonists." He also wrote a lengthy report published in 1835. So successful had he been in such work that on the expiry of his contract at St Andrew's he was immediately appointed superintendent of missions by his synod. His salary remained at £200, the Glasgow Colonial Society adding £50 to the synod's offer of £150. In December 1834 Rintoul decided that, while maintaining his missionary post, he would accept a call in the new year to the small Presbyterian congregation at Streetsville (Mississauga), Upper Canada, which the Reverend Andrew BELL was prepared to resign in his favour. In 1836 he was appointed moderator of synod.

Rintoul's considerable experience with the difficulty of attracting qualified clergy to Canada was largely responsible for his long-standing interest in the establishment of a Canadian seminary. Years of effort culminated in his becoming a founder of Queen's College in Kingston and, in 1840, going to Scotland with the Reverend John Cook* of Quebec to raise funds for the college. Although a sum of about £2,000 was collected, the results were considered disappointing. Moreover, Rintoul's connection with Queen's College was to be short-lived. The disruption in the Church of Scotland in 1843 spilled over into Canada and divided the Canadian church the following year [see Robert Burns*]. Queen's College, which had held its first classes in theology in 1842, remained with the Church of Scotland whereas Rintoul and his Streetsville congregation joined what was popularly called the Free Church, with Rintoul appointed first clerk of synod. In 1847 he resigned from his charge and moved to Toronto where he taught biblical criticism and Hebrew at the Free Church seminary (after 1858 Knox College), until the chair was abolished a few sessions later. Rintoul's want of occupation and a vacancy at the Scotch Presbyterian Church in Montreal, later known as the St Gabriel Street Church, prompted its congregation to issue him a call; he accepted, and on 3 July 1850 entered into service there with vigour.

As always, however, missionary work remained one of his chief interests. While in Montreal he edited the *Ecclesiastical and Missionary Record* and undertook missionary travels. In September 1851 while on a trip to Métis (Métis-sur-Mer) on the lower St Lawrence River he contracted what was thought to be cholera and was forced to pause at Trois-Pistoles. Having caught cholera before, he was confident he would recover this time as well, but his condition worsened and he died. One of his sons as well as a physician, both of whom had travelled from Montreal to be with him, obeyed his wishes to be buried in the nearest Protestant cemetery and transferred his remains to Fraserville (Rivière-du-Loup). The obituary in the *Globe* noted that his wife and one child were believed to be on their way back to Canada from a visit to Scotland and would be greeted on landing with the news of his death.

ELIZABETH ANN KERR MCDOUGALL

[William Rintoul is the author of *Remarks on the claims of Scotsmen abroad, on the Christian sympathy and exertions of their countrymen at home* (Edinburgh, 1826), *A sermon on dancing* (Toronto, 1843), and the sermon in *Sermon and addresses, on the occasion of the admission, by the Presbytery of Toronto, of the Rev. John Barclay, A.M., to the pastoral charge of the congregation of St. Andrew's Church, Toronto, on the 6th December, 1842* (Toronto, 1843), 3–20, as well as several official statements on behalf of the church, including *Report of a committee of the Presbytery of Toronto, on the subject of a theological seminary* (Toronto, 1836), and *A pastoral address from the Synod of the Presbyterian Church of Canada, in connexion with the Church of Scotland* ([Niagara-on-the-Lake, Ont.]), 1837). As the synod's corresponding secretary he was also responsible for issuing its *Report of the missions of the Synod* (Toronto), 1833–34.   E.A.K.McD.]

GRO (Edinburgh), Tulliallan, Perth, reg. of births and baptisms, 5 Nov. 1797; reg. of proclamations of marriages, 23 May 1794. UCA, Biog. files; Glasgow Colonial Soc., corr., II (1829–30), nos.174, 206, 219, 223; III (1831–32), no.56; VI (1836–38), no.274; VII (1839–43), nos.5, 96; letter-books, II, Robert Burns to Rintoul, 8 June 1831; minute-books, I, 21 July, 20, 22 Sept., 8 Nov. 1830; 12 Jan. 1831. Croil, *Hist. and statistical report* (1868), 39–40. *Ecclesiastical and Missionary Record for the Presbyterian Church of Canada* (Toronto), 7 (1850–51): 182. Glasgow Colonial Soc., *Report* (Glasgow), 1831: 14–15; 1832: 12–13; 1835: 24. *Globe*, 20 Sept. 1851. Scott *et al.*, *Fasti ecclesiæ scoticanæ*, vol.7. Campbell, *Hist. of Scotch Presbyterian Church.* Gregg, *Hist. of Presbyterian Church.* S. C. Parker, *The book of St. Andrew's: a short history of St. Andrew's Presbyterian Church, Toronto* (Toronto, 1930), 10–20.

RITCHIE, THOMAS, lawyer, politician, judge, office holder, and militia officer; b. 21 Sept. 1777 in Annapolis Royal, N.S., son of John Ritchie* and Alicia Maria Le Cain (Le Quesne); m. first 30 June 1807 Elizabeth Wildman Johnston (d. 1819), daugh-

Ritchie

ter of Elizabeth Lichtenstein* (Johnston), and they had five sons, including John William*, and two daughters; m. secondly 20 May 1823 Elizabeth Best (d. 1825); m. thirdly 21 Sept. 1831 Anne Bond, daughter of Joseph Norman Bond*, and they had one son and one daughter; d. 13 Nov. 1852 in Annapolis Royal.

Little is known of Thomas Ritchie's early life. He studied law in Annapolis Royal under Thomas Henry Barclay* and, when Barclay became British consul general in New York in 1799, Ritchie inherited his lucrative practice. In 1815 alone he was involved directly in more than three-quarters of the 600 cases which went to law in Annapolis County. His ward, James William Johnston*, received his legal training in Ritchie's law office.

In 1806 Ritchie was elected by acclamation to the House of Assembly as member for Annapolis County. In subsequent elections until his resignation in 1824 he never faced an opponent, each time being re-elected "without a dissenting voice." A bill he proposed in 1808 to regulate black servitude by compensating from the public treasury slave owners who would release their slaves was of questionable wisdom and never became law. Though he had ambition to be chosen speaker, he never attained that position. Despite these early set-backs he was an active member of the assembly and, according to Beamish Murdoch*, Ritchie joined Simon Bradstreet ROBIE, William Hersey Otis Haliburton*, and Samuel George William Archibald* in guiding the major deliberations during the 1820s. On 30 July 1812 he presented the bill which created the first revenue-producing treasury notes in Nova Scotia; these notes became the bulwark of the colony's budget during the War of 1812. Seven years later he guided through the assembly a loan act for farmers in Annapolis and Kings counties. In 1819 he was also chairman of the assembly committee which prepared a report on the 1818 convention between Great Britain and the United States. The convention had readmitted Americans to the Nova Scotia fisheries and as a result met with vigorous opposition and criticism in the committee's report, which has been described by historian Daniel Cobb Harvey* as one of the important steps in the constitutional evolution of the British colonies. Ritchie later served as chairman of the committee which consolidated the revenue acts and in 1821 he was instrumental in bringing about long-needed changes in the militia act. The next year he chaired the committee on fisheries, agriculture, and commerce. This appointment by his fellow assemblymen was obviously in recognition of the expertise he had developed through his work on the 1818 convention and his successful efforts in creating a loan scheme for Annapolis valley farmers.

On 10 March 1824 he became first justice of the Inferior Court of Common Pleas for the western division, one of three such positions created by the assembly and described by Nathaniel Whitworth White as an "easy chair." The bill creating these positions had met vocal and sustained public opposition and passed by a single vote. Three of the assemblymen who supported the bill, Jared Ingersoll Chipman, W. H. O. Haliburton, and Ritchie, received the appointments. Ritchie held this post until the court was abolished in 1841 at which time he received lucrative compensation in the form of a £240 pension which by 1851 had increased to £300. In 1830 he had lobbied to be appointed attorney general but the vacancy went to S. G. W. Archibald. On 2 March 1831 Ritchie was named president of the Court of General Sessions for the western district of Nova Scotia. He performed with diligence and competence in these positions and submitted regular comprehensive reports to the lieutenant governor detailing the state of affairs in western Nova Scotia.

Ritchie had erected a mansion called the Grange in Annapolis Royal about 1810. The property befitted the stature, wealth, and landholdings of one of the old capital's most prominent citizens. It was a three-storey, eleven-bedroom edifice directly across from a three-tiered garden. Tragedy, however, entered these pleasant surroundings. Ritchie's first wife died in a bedroom fire just a few days after giving birth to a son and his second wife was thrown from a horse and killed.

Throughout his life Ritchie was a power in the community. He served in such positions as trustee of the local grammar school and Annapolis Academy; president of the board of health; lieutenant-colonel in the local militia; *custos rotulorum*; and vestryman, clerk, and treasurer of St Luke's Church (Anglican). A local saying opined, "Annapolis belongs to the Devil, the Church, and Judge Ritchie." He was of untiring industry, possessed keen powers of analysis, and was known for his sound ideas and logic. The "old judge" and his descendants played a distinguished role in the political, judicial, and diplomatic life of Nova Scotia and Canada.

ALLAN C. DUNLOP

PANS, RG 1, 236, no.90; RG 5, U, 4, 1808, "An Act for regulating Negro servitude within and throughout the province." Elizabeth Lichtenstein Johnston, *Recollections of a Georgia loyalist, written in 1836*, ed. A. W. H. Eaton (New York and London, 1901). W. A. Calnek, *History of the county of Annapolis, including old Port Royal and Acadia . . .*, ed. A. W. Savary (Toronto, 1897; repr. Belleville, Ont., 1972). B. [C. U.] Cuthbertson, *The old attorney general: a biography of Richard John Uniacke* (Halifax, [1980]). C. I. Perkins, *The romance of old Annapolis Royal, Nova Scotia . . .* (n.p., 1934). M. C. Ritchie, "The beginnings of a Canadian family," N.S. Hist.

Soc., *Coll.*, 24 (1938): 135–54. C. St C. Stayner, "John William Ritchie, one of the fathers of confederation," N.S. Hist. Soc., *Coll.*, 36 (1968): 183–277.

RITCHIE, WILLIAM, merchant; b. 24 Aug. 1804 in Langton (Strathclyde), Scotland, son of David Ritchie, a farmer, and Barbara Gilmour; m. 1 Sept. 1834 Mary Strang, the daughter of a New Brunswick merchant, and they had two sons and three daughters; d. 17 Jan. 1856 at Middleton House (Lothian), Scotland.

Following an education at Mearns parish school, William Ritchie was employed in the Glasgow offices of Pollok, Gilmour and Company where he worked with his cousin Allan Gilmour*. His mother's brother, Allan Gilmour Sr, was one of the founding partners in this firm of timber merchants. In 1821 Ritchie undertook a brief training in ship-draftsmanship at Grangemouth and in the following year, at 18, he travelled to British North America to work for Gilmour, Rankin and Company, a subsidiary partnership of Pollok, Gilmour at Miramichi, N.B. There, under the management of Alexander RANKIN, Ritchie again worked with his cousin Allan, and with him was responsible for provisioning teams of lumbermen working inland.

In 1828 Ritchie accompanied his cousin and uncle on an extensive tour of the Canadas to survey the potential of the region. As a result of the voyage, two new Pollok, Gilmour companies were formed. According to the draft of a partnership agreement dated 1829, Ritchie, his cousin Allan, Allan Gilmour Sr, and the brothers John and Arthur Pollok became partners in Allan Gilmour and Company at Quebec and William Ritchie and Company at Montreal, each of which had a capital of £2,000, contributed equally by the five partners. Ritchie was responsible for the management of the company which bore his name, at a salary of £50 per year. While the Quebec firm under his cousin's direction was involved directly in the timber trade and in the extensive shipbuilding business at Wolfe's Cove (Anse au Foulon), William Ritchie and Company dealt in provisions and general goods. Ritchie's firm was also responsible for managing the day-to-day trading capital of all the Pollok, Gilmour companies in British North America. The other partnerships drew their bills against William Ritchie and Company, who in turn drew accommodation bills on Pollok, Gilmour in London which were discounted with the banks in Montreal to meet the demands of the original bills. Ritchie's ability to negotiate such arrangements was no doubt aided by his involvement as a founding director of the City Bank (of Montreal), which had been established in 1831 to break the monopoly of the Bank of Montreal and increase the availability of credit.

Ritchie's trading enterprise at Montreal was successful, increasing from an annual profit of £3,383 in 1829 to approximately £16,000 in 1840, despite a general depression in trade in British North America at the end of the 1830s which saw other Pollok, Gilmour companies in difficulties. Ritchie's brothers Arthur and Robert, who managed the firm Arthur Ritchie and Company, established at Dalhousie and Campbellton, N.B., since at least 1832, were particularly badly hit. Ritchie complained that his brothers and other Pollok, Gilmour companies insisted on holding more stock than they could ever hope to dispose of, while his cousin Allan felt that these firms had been "too liberal in their credits to the lumbermen and others quite undeserving" and urged a general reduction of capital. Arthur Ritchie's firm separated from Pollok, Gilmour in 1842 and by the late 1850s he faced bankruptcy in both New Brunswick and Liverpool, England. Before these matters were resolved, however, William Ritchie had withdrawn from all business activities in British North America.

In 1837–38 an acrimonious dispute had arisen among the partners in Pollok, Gilmour which resulted in Gilmour Sr's withdrawal from the firm in 1838. The dispute cut across close family ties: John Pollok, Robert Rankin*, Gilmour Jr, and Ritchie had all married daughters of New Brunswick merchant John Strang. Gilmour Sr was deserted by his protégé, Allan Gilmour Jr, in favour of the Polloks, but he found an ally in his other nephew, William Ritchie. The basis of Ritchie's own dispute with the partners and his alliance with Gilmour Sr, despite the fact that, according to Gilmour Jr, "there never was two persons that disliked each other more than they did at one time," was the draft agreement drawn up on Gilmour's withdrawal in 1838 while Ritchie was still in Montreal. This agreement, Ritchie claimed, gave him an interest both in the British North American concerns and in the home company, Pollok, Gilmour and Company, and its subsidiary, Rankin, Gilmour and Company at Liverpool (established shortly after Robert Rankin assumed direction of Pollok, Gilmour). His claim was rejected by the partners of the reorganized firm but, urged on by the disaffected Gilmour, he threatened to prevent any business taking place in the Canadas, presumably by obstructing the credit facilities he had established at Montreal. He travelled to Glasgow in the winter of 1839 to meet the partners and also to obtain legal advice on his position. Following a number of meetings and some bitter correspondence, in which Ritchie's conduct was described by Allan Gilmour Jr as "monstrous and disgracefull," an agreement was reached. Ritchie renounced any claims against the company in return for a payment of £49,600, less £5,200 at his account with the businesses in the Canadas. The latter figure was the source of one final dispute between the former partners when it was alleged that Ritchie had

Robie

concealed personal expenditures in excess of £1,500 in the firm's accounts at Montreal. The resulting court case, centring on the interpretation of a number of draft agreements which had never been officially signed, dragged on for some ten years before being finally resolved in Ritchie's favour in 1851.

Ritchie returned to Scotland with his wife and children in 1841 and purchased the estate of Middleton, near Gorebridge. As in Lower Canada, he remained essentially a private person, playing little or no part in public life. He devoted his energies to agriculture and arboriculture, purchasing additional land at Lambhill (near Strathaven) and leasing from Allan Gilmour Sr the farm of West Walton in Eaglesham. When he died in 1856 he left a movable estate of £13,919, with the majority of his heritable property in entail to his eldest son, William. His comparatively short business career relied for its success, and ultimately its failure, on the influence and genius of Allan Gilmour Sr. Ritchie's major contribution to Pollok, Gilmour in British North America was the personal influence and skill he exerted in establishing the credit facilities which enabled the various companies to flourish. This contribution connected him with important developments in finance and credit introduced with the growth of commercial banking in British North America.

NICHOLAS J. MORGAN

BLHU, R. G. Dun & Co. credit ledger, Canada, 9: 222. SRO, SC70/1/90; SC70/4/44. Strathclyde Regional Arch. (Glasgow, Scot.), T-BK/66; T-HH/77; T-HH/78. Univ. of Glasgow Arch., UGD 36/6/2. L.C., *Statutes*, 1832–33, c.32. *Glasgow directory*, 1830–60. John Rankin, *A history of our firm, being some account of the firm of Pollok, Gilmour and Co. and its offshoots and connections, 1804–1920* (Liverpool, Eng., 1908). *Studies in Scottish business history*, ed. P. L. Payne (London, 1967). Wynn, *Timber colony*. C. R. Fay, "Mearns and the Miramichi: an episode in Canadian economic history," *CHR*, 4 (1923): 316–20.

ROBIE, SIMON BRADSTREET, lawyer, politician, and judge; b. 1770 in Marblehead, Mass., son of Thomas Robie and Mary Bradstreet; m. 6 Oct. 1806 Elizabeth Creighton in Halifax; d. there 3 Jan. 1858.

Simon Bradstreet Robie was directly descended from Simon Bradstreet, an early governor of Massachusetts, described by some as "the Nestor of New England." He arrived in Halifax with his loyalist parents early in the American Revolutionary War. A law student in the office of his brother-in-law Jonathan Sterns, he was admitted to the bar in the early 1790s. After first being elected to the House of Assembly in 1799, he remained a member of the Nova Scotia legislature until 1848. Yet, because the assembly debates were infrequently reported before the 1820s, and because, later, he had few opportunities for public

speech-making as speaker of the assembly, member of the Council, which met behind closed doors, and president of the Legislative Council, even fragments of his speeches are few and far between.

As the member for Truro Township until 1806, he grew to like the locality so much that he once expressed a desire to retire there; in turn, it named one of its streets after him. After 1806 he sat for Halifax County and, in response, the city of Halifax attached his name to one of its leading thoroughfares. While an assemblyman, he was sometimes described as a reformer, even a populist, and certainly was included in the "country party" of William Cottnam Tonge* – the first semblance of a political party in Nova Scotia. Above all, Robie was a zealous defender of the assembly's constitutional rights, and until the 1830s was at least a moderate liberal, although by no means a democrat.

Initially he appeared much more radical than he actually was because his first eight years in the assembly pitted him against Sir John Wentworth*, the most authoritarian of Nova Scotia's lieutenant governors. Although Wentworth described Tonge as a sower of "discord and hatred both in and out of the House," Robie generally supported him. Thus, in 1803, when the Council in its legislative capacity declared improper the assembly's request to examine its proceedings, Robie headed the assembly committee which, after studying British precedents, reported that the lower house was "guilty of no impropriety" and that it had an undoubted right to inspect the Council's *Journal*.

The most momentous confrontation with Wentworth occurred in 1804, when the lieutenant governor sought to eliminate a "mode of granting monies and [a] controul upon Expenditures" that had "gradually deviated into a manner totally opposite to the practice of Parliament." For some years the assembly had been permitted to perform functions normally regarded as the prerogative of the executive, including the initiation of the road estimates and the nomination and, for all practical purposes, appointment of road commissioners. "These Powers being Prerogative Rights," Wentworth argued, they might be "constitutionally resumed by His Majesty's Representative, whenever he thinks the general Interest requires it." The Council having also tried to turn the clock back, an assembly committee chaired by Robie asserted that road monies would continue to be granted, "expended and accounted for in the mode heretofore adopted." The outcome was that no appropriation act was passed in 1804 and, although the assembly was a little more cautious during the 1805–6 session, the following year it was back at its old tricks. Thereafter Wentworth and his successors acknowledged the futility of executive interference. The probability is that a reform movement developed slowly in Nova Scotia because the assembly had already secured a wide measure of control over the voting of funds for a service which its country members regarded almost as their *raison d'être*. In successfully upholding these assembly "prerogatives," Tonge and Robie played a major role.

Robie was not in the assembly when Wentworth rejected Tonge as speaker in 1806, but he again confronted the lieutenant governor in 1807–8 when the latter unwisely questioned the assembly's unseating of Thomas Walker of Annapolis Township. As a leading member of the committee of privileges, Robie forcefully defended the assembly's right, maintained successfully "since its first formation . . . of judging and deciding . . . on all questions relating to the elections," and eventually the law officers of the crown in England upheld its competency to "decide exclusively and without appeal on the validity of the Election of one of the Members." But Robie would not go along with Tonge in his more extreme measures, especially his attempt in 1808 to limit Wentworth's retiring allowance to a period of one year. In this case his action did him no harm in the eyes of the new lieutenant governor, Sir George Prevost*, who had recommended more generous treatment for Wentworth.

Robie expressed himself strongly in 1809 against the highly reactionary Alexander Croke*, senior councillor and the judge of the Vice-Admiralty Court, who administered the province in Prevost's absence. Croke had refused his assent to the appropriation bill without reason, and the committee of privileges, which included Robie, told him that he had weakened confidence in government at a time when relations with the United States were critical. Generally a supporter of economical government, Robie also protested in 1811 against the ills of Croke's court. Why, he asked, did custom-house officers always lay their prosecutions in the Vice-Admiralty Court where there was no jury and the fees were excessive instead of in the common law courts where neither disadvantage existed?

Robie's legal and legislative experience began to secure recognition in 1815 when he became solicitor general. Defeated for the speakership in 1812 by Lewis Morris Wilkins*, he secured it in 1817 and was re-elected by the new assembly a year later. As speaker, he incurred the displeasure of Lieutenant Governor Lord Dalhousie [Ramsay*], a person of great likes and dislikes, who described him as "an ill-tempered crab, deeply tinctured in Yankee principles," and a man who " 'neither fears God nor honours the King.' " Because of the assembly's failure to accept his proposals in 1820, an action which he blamed partly on the speaker, Dalhousie refused as a farewell gift, after initially accepting it, "a Star and a Sword" for which the lower house had voted £1,000. He complained bitterly of the assembly's "disposition to disregard the Prerogative rights, and the respect due

to [the] first branch of the Constitutional Legislature," singling out its failure to provide money for the inspection of the militia as he had requested and to answer his special messages. Robie sorrowfully accepted responsibility for the second failing and blamed it on special circumstances: the confusion resulting from King George III's death and the belief that the business of the assembly must come automatically to an end. After consulting other assemblymen, Robie felt better; one of them wondered what "evil *genie* has been at work" to produce Dalhousie's "inconsistent and absurd" action. The "evil genie" was the loss of dignity which Dalhousie believed he had suffered and which led him for the moment to abandon reason and accuracy for emotion and petulance. Later, while governor-in-chief, he would have a higher opinion of Robie; indeed, by 1826–27 he was even describing his old antagonist as one of his chief Nova Scotian allies.

Because "the Business of the House occupied so much of [his] time" and worries such as the Dalhousie contretemps were "so injurious" to his health, Robie decided not to contest the election of 1820 and, although his friends eventually persuaded him to run, his "opinion and wishes were unchanged." It was his last election, for in April 1824, during the lieutenant governorship of Sir James KEMPT, he was elevated to the Council; less than two years later he relinquished the solicitor generalship to become the province's first master of the rolls and as such presided over the Court of Chancery, a function hitherto performed reluctantly by the lieutenant governor. Normally a homogeneous body, the Council was divided on matters touching the relations between church and state. Although a zealous adherent of the established Church of England, Robie held that at least a moderate accommodation ought to be made with dissenters, who comprised a large proportion of the population. In 1818, in committee of the whole, he had supported their petition to have the power of issuing marriage licences granted to their own clergymen, calling it a grievance that dissenters were forced to apply for them to a church to which they did not belong. Two years earlier he had supported the establishment of the non-sectarian Pictou Academy and regretted the restrictions placed upon it by the extreme churchmen in the Council. When its trustees sought help to erect a building in 1818, Robie argued that a province which was "building a palace" like Province House [see John Merrick*] could easily provide for the propagation of knowledge. Ridiculing assemblyman John George Marshall*'s notion that an age of learning was generally not known for its virtue, he pointed to the great benefits that education had conferred upon Scotland and New England.

In assisting the academy, Robie developed a close friendship with its Presbyterian principal, Thomas McCulloch*, who wrote to him in 1822: "The

Robie

essential service which you have rendered to our Church gives you a claim upon the affection of the whole of us." But, though the assembly supported Robie in his efforts to provide the academy with the permanent grant that Anglican King's College had long enjoyed, the extreme church party in the Council led by Attorney General Richard John Uniacke* always defeated it. "Why do you not show [Uniacke] in his true character to the public?" McCulloch once asked Robie. But he was suggesting a course that was altogether contrary to the basic style of Robie's political life.

In 1826 Robie joined the three other moderate councillors in again pressing for a permanent grant, but they were outvoted by five to four. The minority then entered a long dissentient opinion on the Council's *Journal*, pointing out that the lieutenant governor's participation in the naming of trustees would prevent the employment of teachers whose "principles might be inimical to our political Institutions," that more than four-fifths of Nova Scotians were dissenters, and that the bill's defeat would increase hostility to the established church. The academy got its usual annual grant in 1826, but not in subsequent years: three of the four moderate councillors (James Stewart, Brenton HALLIBURTON, and Charles Morris*) deserted it after the Church of Scotland came out in opposition to the academy and to McCulloch, a Secessionist minister, and after the latter engaged in open wrangling with Bishop John Inglis* of the Church of England. Only Robie continued to give the academy his full support in 1827 and 1828, and by then it had become clear that the attempt to establish a non-sectarian college in Pictou had failed.

In the early 1830s, with political reform under way in England and the first glimmerings of a political awakening visible in Nova Scotia, Robie became much more conservative. For him, Britain and its colonies had all the maladies of sinking states. "I am glad there is such a fellow as Nicholas of Russia." Convinced that reform, once set in motion in England, could not be halted, he was particularly anxious about the future awaiting Nova Scotia. Demands to set up a separate legislative council would be followed by demands for an elective council, and the outcome would be to reduce the executive power to "a mere nothing" and "leave us a Pure Democracy if the word 'pure' can be applied with Truth to a Thing in its nature so the reverse of Purity."

In letter after letter, Robie bewailed "our paltry Politicks" and longed to be rid of them. Scornfully he watched the assemblymen discussing means to restore confidence in a seriously depreciated currency, a question "of which they know about as much as the Man in the Moon, perhaps less." He himself did not escape the political ferment that was brewing in Nova

Scotia. As master of the rolls, he had presided over the Court of Chancery without ever attempting to alter the rules which had developed haphazardly over many years. Joseph Howe* commenced the assault on him in 1832. If, said Howe, Robie had pointed out what could be discarded in chancery proceedings in the manner of Lord Brougham, he could not have been faulted. Instead, he had "year after year pocketed the public money, for keeping up a body of costly and dangerous absurdities, that he ought long ago to have denounced." Likewise the *Acadian Recorder* complained of "the abominable, heart-breaking, pocket-picking system" of the Court of Chancery, and in 1833 the assembly added its voice to the clamour for reform. Finally, in December 1833, 22 new rules initiated by Robie went into effect, but they did little to remove the major grievances. Later a retired chief justice, Sir Charles James Townshend*, would say that except for these changes, "nothing of special note" occurred during Robie's term on the Court of Chancery. Apparently he performed his duties competently within a framework he was reluctant to alter.

Outwardly, at least, Robie did not let the storm revolving about his head perturb him: "You know how they have been abusing the Court and me; fortunately the labours of many years have made me independent of Office." A lucrative law practice had, indeed, enabled him to accumulate about £60,000, far in excess of his needs. But, as a remarkable series of letters to retired judge Peleg Wiswall indicates, his malaise went far beyond the state of politics. He was tired, too, of the eternal broils of the bar: "The vices and follies of men have been too long the objects of my investigation." He had never liked the land of "my father's adoption for me," nor the climate and fashions of Halifax; even as he wrote, the fog was so thick "you could cut it, and this I do not think I am bound to endure, merely to add a few hundred pounds to what I may have," especially since he had no son to inherit it.

Most of all, Robie longed to be free to speculate about the only subject of any importance: "that distant and . . . more happy land where I hope we may . . . see more of each other than has been our lot in this." The more he thought about the world, the more mysterious it seemed; yet he yearned for the truth however difficult the search, and hoped to discern "the path by which it may be found." After the Black Death had desolated Asia and Europe, mothers began more often to bear twins and even triplets. "Now why did this desolation take place?" And "if by the appointment of Providence, why was the ruin repaired in the way that I have described?" Also, if Providence permitted poor people to exist in order to allow "a few others . . . an opportunity of shewing their benevolent Feelings," why should there be so many of them? In this manner

Robie explored in his correspondence with Wiswall a wide variety of subjects ranging from the meaning of comets to the possibility of humans communicating with disembodied spirits.

Robie did retire as master of the rolls in 1834, but did not leave Nova Scotia or the Council. Indeed, on the separation of the Council in early 1838, he became a member of the Executive Council and president of the Legislative Council. For the next ten years he remained the confidant of lieutenant governors in their less liberal stances. Thus, in 1840, he told Lieutenant Governor Sir Colin Campbell* that the Legislative Council could not possibly agree to the assembly's proposals for commuting the casual revenues without violating vested rights or its own sense of justice. For a similar reason Robie joined in a dissentient opinion in 1844 on a bill that removed Sir Rupert D. George as registrar of the province and transferred his duties to county registrars. When asked by Lieutenant Governor Lord Falkland [Cary*] for his views on a modified legislative council, he insisted that the crown retain an unfettered power of appointment, "for I do think that unless we are to have a Democracy unchastened by any Mixture of Monarchical Principles Concessions more than enough have already been made to the Advocates of such a Democracy."

Ever the reluctant politician, Robie had earlier been persuaded by Campbell and Falkland not to give up his offices, but the mood of the country was running against him. Following the reform victory of August 1847, he and his fellow tory executive councillors resigned on 28 Jan. 1848 to make way for the administration of James Boyle UNIACKE. As the session of 1848 progressed, Robie became increasingly uncomfortable as president of the Legislative Council. Although he did manage to dilute the government's bill permitting judges to be removed by an address of the legislature, the Legislative Council did not, in the end, adhere to the amendments. Equally obnoxious to him was the departmental bill, which eliminated the provincial treasurer and in his place introduced two political officers, a receiver general and a financial secretary with membership in the Executive Council; in Robie's view, this bill destroyed the public faith of the crown with its servants. Taking the dubious position that he could not support measures "violating those principles which I have endeavoured through life to preserve," and feeling that as president of the council he ought not to oppose the government's major legislative proposals, he resigned on 3 April 1848. Lieutenant Governor Sir John HARVEY wondered if his action was intended to embarrass the government, but actually it did little more than bring his political career to a close.

Competent in the law, possessed of a wide circle of friends, Robie was also widely known for his philanthropy; indeed, one account states that the poor would "lament his loss; for his charities were almost without limit." His career illustrates how, in altered circumstances, the liberal of one era may become a conservative in the next. Perhaps his speculations on the mysteries of life and the afterworld provided a welcome respite from his experiences in the real world which, after 1830, he had increasingly failed to relish or understand.

J. MURRAY BECK

A selection of Simon Bradstreet Robie's papers in PANS, MG 1, 793, has been printed in PANS, *Report of the Board of Trustees* (Halifax), 1961: 19–42.

PANS, MG 1, 550–58; 980; RG 1, 53; 113½; 120; 191, especially 1808; 218SS–218DDD. Univ. of King's College Library (Halifax), Israel Longworth, "A history of the county of Colchester" (2 pts., Truro, N.S., 1866–78; typescript at PANS), 1, especially 221–40. N.S., *Acts*, especially 1825, 1833, 1848; House of Assembly, *Journals and proc.*, 1800–24; Legislative Council, *Journal and proc.*, 1836–48. Ramsay, *Dalhousie journals* (Whitelaw). *Acadian Recorder*, especially 1818, 1832. *Novascotian, or Colonial Herald*, especially 1832. *Nova-Scotia Royal Gazette*, 14 Oct. 1806. *Directory of N.S. MLAs*. J. H. Stark, *The loyalists of Massachusetts and the other side of the American revolution* (Boston, [1907]), 457–59. Beck, *Government of N.S.*; *Joseph Howe*. W. B. Hamilton, "Education, politics and reform in Nova Scotia, 1800–1848" (PHD thesis, Univ. of Western Ont., London, 1970). Beamish Murdoch, *A history of Nova-Scotia, or Acadie* (3v., Halifax, 1865–67), 3. Israel Longworth, "Hon. Simon Bradstreet Robie: a biography," N.S. Hist. Soc., *Coll.*, 20 (1921): 1–15. Norah Story, "The church and state 'party' in Nova Scotia, 1749–1851," N.S. Hist. Soc., *Coll.*, 27 (1947): 33–57. C. J. Townshend, "History of the Court of Chancery in Nova Scotia," *Canadian Law Times* (Toronto), 20 (1901): 74–80, 105–17.

ROBINS, ANN. See VICKERY

ROBINSON, HEZEKIAH, businessman, justice of the peace, and office holder; b. 12 June 1791 in Newfane, Vt, son of Jonathan Robinson and Sarah Taylor; d. 7 Feb. 1851 in Waterloo, Lower Canada.

Hezekiah Robinson came from an American family of Congregational persuasion, and received his education at the college in Newfane. At the age of 18 he was working as a carder and manufacturer of "ready mades" in summer and as a schoolteacher in winter. On 30 June 1817 he married Selucia Knowlton, the elder daughter of Luke Knowlton, acting judge of Windham County, Vt, and they were to have nine children. In May 1821 he immigrated to Stukely Township in Lower Canada, following the path of his father-in-law, who had settled there with his family when the Eastern Townships were opened to the loyalists.

Roche

On arriving in Stukely, Robinson, who was now a merchant by trade, bought properties and opened a carding-mill. But in October 1821, realizing that the adjoining township of Shefford, which was supplied with water by the Rivière Yamaska and Lac Waterloo, would be a more advantageous location for his business, he bought from Lazard Létourneau lot 21 of the 4th concession, on which stood a frame-house, grist-mill, and sawmill. He built a carding-mill on the lot and repaired the other mills, which were operating again by 1 June 1823.

In succeeding years Robinson extended his business activity and became prosperous. He opened the Old Stone Store in 1829, where he did a flourishing trade in general merchandise. A year later he put up a house and a sawmill next to his store. However, Robinson did not have the money to carry out the further repairs he wished to make on his mills. In 1832 he went into partnership with Peasley and Copp, businessmen of Georgeville, who provided him with the capital to make the desired improvements. The old grist-mill was repaired and met the needs of the local inhabitants until 1835, when a new mill was erected. At this period Robinson also built a pearl-ash works.

Robinson's unswerving honesty won him the respect and confidence of the inhabitants of Shefford County, and as a result on several occasions he was given important positions. Thus in 1830 Sir James Kempt, the administrator of Lower Canada, appointed him justice of the peace for the district of Montreal; his commission was renewed in 1837 and 1838. In 1836 one of Kempt's successors, Lord Gosford [Acheson*], selected him as the first postmaster of Shefford County. During the rebellion of 1837–38 Robinson demonstrated his unquestioned loyalty to the government.

In 1841 Peasley, Copp, and Robinson was dissolved. The following year Robinson went into partnership with his son Jonathan and his son-in-law Roswell Albert Ellis to establish Robinson, Ellis and Company, transferring to his partners one-half of his productive assets, which were then valued at £902 15s. 0d. In 1847 he made over a third of his remaining assets in order to give each of his partners a share equal to his own. Three years later, just before his death, another son, Hezekiah Luke, bought Ellis's share, so that the Robinsons could form Robinson and Sons.

During the 1840s Robinson also engaged in land speculation. He bought properties in Shefford Township, on one of which the main part of Waterloo was later built. He sold several lots at high prices to *rentiers*, artisans, or people who had been farmers and wanted to settle in the new village. In addition he sold the land he owned in Stukely Township. These transactions seem to have made Robinson wealthy, as witness the 35 or so contracts he concluded between 1843 and 1850. However, his interests were not confined to speculation. For charity or the common good he gave 17 acres to the Church of England, which he had joined soon after coming to Lower Canada. It was on this ground that the Anglican church in Waterloo was erected in 1843, and Robinson was its largest regular contributor.

Hezekiah Robinson died on 7 Feb. 1851 at Waterloo. He was then a justice of the peace and the chief local magistrate. He was mourned by his wife and nine children. His sons Jonathan and Hezekiah Luke took over the firm and continued to do business in and about Shefford County. Robinson had become wealthy through speculation in land and at the same time had made an important contribution to the development of the southwestern part of the Eastern Townships.

ANDRÉE DÉSILETS

ANQ-E, CE2-42, 12 févr. 1851. BE, Shefford (Waterloo), reg. B, 1, -8, -10. Brome County Hist. Soc. Arch. (Knowlton, Que.), 1, Samuel Willard papers, corr.; 8, Miscellaneous family papers. PAC, RG 68, General index, 1651–1841: 369. Vt., Public Records Division (Montpelier), Newfane Congregational Church, reg. of marriages, 30 June 1817. Vt. Hist. Soc. (Montpelier), Newfane Congregational Church, reg. of baptisms, 12 juin 1791. *British Colonist and St. Francis Gazette* (Stanstead, [Que.]), 1821–31. *Le Canadien*, novembre–décembre 1834. *La Gazette de Québec*, 1764–1823; novembre–décembre 1834. *La Minerve*, novembre–décembre 1834. *Missiskoui Standard* (Frelighsburh, [Que.]), 1835–39. *Montreal Gazette*, 1823; December 1831–March 1833; November–December 1834; 1851. *Quebec Mercury*, November–December 1834. *St. Francis Telegraph* (Sherbrooke, Que.), 12 Nov. 1851. *Sherbrooke Gazette and Eastern Townships Advertiser*, 1832–51. *Stanstead Journal* (Rock Island, Que.), 1851–52. J. P. Noyes, *Sketches of some early Shefford pioneers* ([Montreal], 1905), 113–15, 125. *Centennial proceedings and other historical facts and incidents relating to Newfane, the county seat of Windham County, Vermont* (Brattleboro, Vt., 1877), 74, 77–79. Roberpierre Monnier, *Naissance et évolution architecturale et urbaine de Waterloo de 1650 à 1900 dans son contexte: l'Estrie* (Québec, 1979). Cyrus Thomas, *Histoire de Shefford*, Ovila Fournier, trad. (Île-Perrot, Qué., 1973), 31–35; *The history of Shefford, civil, ecclesiastical, biographical and statistical* (Montreal, 1877), 43–50. Fernand Bélanger, "'Old Stone Store': la bâtisse incendiée de Waterloo aurait eu 150 ans," *La Voix de l'Est* (Granby, Qué.), 5 mai 1978: 1, 5; "Un autre incendie majeur frappe la ville de Waterloo," 29 avril 1978: 1. Richard Danis, "Waterloo voudra-t-elle préserver l'historique Old Stone Store?" *La Voix de l'Est*, 7 août 1978: 2.

ROCHE, JOHN KNATCHBULL, land surveyor; b. 15 March 1817 in London, third son of Lieutenant John Roche, RN; m. Annie Elizabeth ——, and they had three sons and one daughter; d. 13 Sept. 1859 in Balsam Lake, Upper Canada.

John Knatchbull Roche was educated at Christ's Hospital in London before coming to Upper Canada about 1832 with his parents, who settled in Peterborough. He received his licence as a land surveyor on 1 Dec. 1841 and went on to conduct numerous government and private surveys in Upper Canada, especially in the counties of Northumberland, Durham, Peterborough, Victoria, and Haliburton, and in the district of Muskoka. His government assignments included surveys in the township of Hope (1845); park lots adjacent to the town plot of Lindsay (1846); surveys in the townships of Hamilton (1847), Murray (1848), Belmont (1852 and 1856), Draper (1857–58), Carden (1858), and Laxton (1859); and finally a road line from Bobcaygeon to Lake Nipissing (1859).

In 1849 the Province of Canada had set up a board to examine the qualifications of persons applying for licences as land surveyors. Two years later, owing mainly to the differences in regulations concerning landholdings in Upper and Lower Canada, the board was divided into two sections, one to meet in Quebec, the other in Toronto. The Board of Examiners of Surveyors for Upper Canada, established on 30 Aug. 1851, consisted of the commissioner of Crown Lands and eight competent persons appointed by the governor to examine candidates and decide on complaints against members of the profession. The board met four times a year and members were paid for their services. Roche was appointed to the Upper Canadian board on its establishment, was present at the first meeting in April 1852, and during the remainder of his life was influential in regulating and upgrading survey work in Upper Canada. He himself conducted a number of resurveys of areas which had been inadequately or only partially subdivided.

In the 1850s the government decided that the land lying between the Ottawa River and Georgian Bay should be opened for settlement and planned a system of east-west and north-south roads. One of these, the Bobcaygeon, was to extend north from Bobcaygeon to Lake Nipissing. Work began in 1856 and by 1858 it had been opened for traffic from Bobcaygeon to Burnt River and surveyed as far north as St Nora Lake, where it intersected the east-west line which had been laid out by Robert Bell* in 1847–48. On 19 May 1859 Roche was instructed to continue the survey to Lake Nipissing. He began work in July and by early September had reached the Magnetawan River. At that time he found it necessary to return south to report progress and obtain further supplies. While he was crossing Balsam Lake on 13 September, his bark canoe overturned in a storm and, although his canoemen escaped, Roche was drowned. Crosbie Brady, who was sent to replace Roche, was hampered by severe cold and snow as well as an outbreak of scurvy which claimed the life of Roche's brother David, who had served as picketman. The road, surveyed at the cost of two lives and much suffering, was not opened north of Dorset.

For several years before his death J. K. Roche had made his home in Port Hope. He died intestate and the

administration of the estate, valued at $5,612, was granted to his wife. He was survived by at least three brothers, one of whom, George Molyneux Roche, was Crown Lands agent for part of Victoria County.

FLORENCE B. MURRAY

AO, RG 1, A-I-6: 17509–10, 21214–17, 21486–90, 21805–7, 23732–34, 28208–9, 28228–29; A-VII, 49; B-IV, 1845–46, no.3; 1848, no.7; 1852, no.30; 1857, no.18; 1858, no.4; CB-1, J. K. Roche, Belmont diary and field notes; Hamilton Township field notes; Hope diary; Lindsay diary; RG 22, ser.187, administration of J. K. Roche estate. Ont., Ministry of Natural Resources, Surveys and Mapping Branch (Toronto), Instructions to land surveyors, V (mfm. at AO). Trent Univ. Arch. (Peterborough, Ont.), B77-1016 (G. M. Roche, corr. relating to the death of his brother John, October 1859; William Bell, diary extracts, July 1859–April 1860) (transcripts). Can., Prov. of, *Statutes*, 1849, c.35; 1851, c.4. *Canada Gazette*, 6 Sept. 1851: 11324. *Muskoka and Haliburton, 1615–1875; a collection of documents*, ed. F. B. Murray ([Toronto], 1963), lxviii, lxxii–lxxiii, 203–5. *Globe*, 17 Sept. 1859. *Weekly Guide* (Port Hope, [Ont.]), 17 Sept. 1859. "John Knatchbul Roche," Assoc. of Ont. Land Surveyors, *Annual report* (Toronto), 1916: 61–62.

ROGERS, THOMAS, architect, office holder, and land speculator; b. 1778 or 1782 in England; married and had two sons; d. 27 Feb. 1853 in Kingston, Upper Canada.

It is not known when Thomas Rogers and his family immigrated to the Canadas but his son Thomas was born in England in 1811. The elder Rogers may have begun his career as a craftsman since he left his carpenter's and joiner's tools to Thomas in his will. His surviving drawings, however, show that he must have had training in an architect's office at some stage. The family may have been connected to another Thomas Rogers, an English architect who died after 1808. The likelihood of this relationship is strengthened by an examination of the latter's best-known design, the Middlesex County Sessions House, Clerkenwell Green (London) (1779–82). Its decorative, Adamesque qualities and the use of the Greek Ionic order reflect the sort of architectural grounding which one might assume for the Canadian Thomas Rogers, on the basis of his known works. A letter which appeared in the *Kingston Chronicle* in 1831 suggests a familial tie to Whig poet and wit Samuel Rogers. Samuel's cousin Richard Payne Knight was a great amateur architect and aesthetician. These connections may help to explain the apparently immediate success of the architect in Kingston, and his attainment of a long professional career throughout the province.

Rogers's first known commission, in 1825, was for a large stone structure to replace the small, wooden Anglican church at Kingston, St George's. His plans

Rogers

called for a two-storey, galleried basilica, with a shallow apse at the altar end, an elaborate bell-tower at the entrance, and a grand Ionic portico. Only the main body and part of the tower were erected to Rogers's designs. His tower was later replaced by the present one and the body of the church was substantially enlarged, but his finely sculpted quoining, the upper parts of his massive side-window surrounds, and much of his side walls still survive.

At St George's, Rogers would have met John MACAULAY, a prominent Anglican and office holder. Over the next decade Macaulay's name is frequently found in connection with Rogers's works, suggesting that he may have become the architect's chief patron. For example, in 1829 the Cataraqui Bridge was erected at Kingston to Rogers's designs, the commission coming from the Cataraqui Bridge Company, of which Macaulay was a director. As commissioner of lighthouses for Upper Canada, Macaulay was responsible for commissioning three lighthouses from Rogers: False Ducks (1828) and Point Petre (1832, destroyed 1969), both in the Prince Edward District, and Nine Mile Point (1833) on Simcoe Island near Kingston. It also appears that Macaulay was behind Rogers's involvement in the new parliament buildings at York (Toronto) in 1828–29. Rogers provided some drawings, specifications, and criticisms of proposals made by others. In April 1829 William ALLAN, chairman of the commission for erecting the buildings, informed Rogers that he had already written to Macaulay, asking to know if Rogers, in the midst of his busy schedule, "would be likely to engage for the superintendence." Rogers did not accept the complete superintendence, which Allan offered him, suggesting that he had decided to make his primary base in Kingston. In the 1820s and 1830s Kingston appeared to many to be the place in Upper Canada with the greater future.

Yet Rogers continued to accept short-term commissions in York and places other than Kingston. In 1831 he provided designs for the second St James' Church, York. As Macaulay had been a pupil of its rector, John Strachan*, and was in close touch with him politically, it is likely that Rogers obtained this commission on Macaulay's recommendation. The plans for St James' show a colonnaded tower inspired by John Nash's Church of All Souls, Langham Place, London. But sadly, Rogers's design for the tower was not used and the whole structure was destroyed by fire in 1839. He may have been involved in superintending the erection of the second market in York in 1831.

In Kingston the early recognition of Rogers's professional ability had led to his securing at least one public office. From about 1827 he was employed by the Midland District Court of Quarter Sessions as street surveyor for Kingston and, later, as a police officer there. In May 1827 he paid the Reverend George Okill Stuart* £50 for part of a rural lot now situated at the intersection of King and Barrie streets. On this lot, with its splendid view of Wolfe and Simcoe islands and out to Lake Ontario, Rogers had built a house for himself and his family by 1832. He was evidently an active gardener. In September 1837 the *Chronicle & Gazette* noted that growing in his garden, "near Stuart's Point," was a "Radish measuring in circumference two feet eight inches and a half." His house has been almost completely engulfed by later additions, but some of the ground plan can still be discerned. Rogers's purchase of land for his own house was only the first of a series of property acquisitions from Stuart. They were wise investments for the land was annexed to the city in 1850. Rogers, however, was able to reap considerable rewards even earlier; in 1842, after Kingston had become capital of the united provinces, he disposed of several building lots. Nor was his land speculation confined to Kingston. In 1846, for example, he bought 100 acres in Loughborough Township from the Canada Company. As well, he lent out considerable sums for mortgages, some of which may have been attached to buildings which he designed and supervised. What emerges from all these transactions is the picture of a shrewd, successful businessman.

The domestic architecture of Rogers is the least documented, yet in some ways it is the most interesting part of his work. Knaresborough Cottage, which he designed in 1834 for John Macaulay's mother, is the only house which can be verified as his work. Although the house, on King Street near Earl, has been considerably altered, the original main entrance, on the side, survives. The tall door is surmounted by an elliptical arch, inscribed with semi-circular glazing bars. The outer stone surround consists of an arch of massive voussoirs, of alternating large and small stones, supported by imposing, monolithic piers. The striking effect of the entrance is the result of a combination of Adamesque elegance in the woodwork and primitive simplicity in the masonry which matches in mood the rough texture of the main walls and the quoins. The latter, like the masonry door surround, are ashlar, simply grooved or furrowed.

The distinctive characteristics of Knaresborough Cottage enable us to identify Rogers as the architect of a whole group of early Kingston buildings which might otherwise remain anonymous. Variations on the doorway are found in houses built for Henry GILDERSLEEVE (1825–26), James Nickalls (Charles Place, *c.* 1828–32), John Counter* (Plymouth Square, 1833, now destroyed), the Reverend Robert David Cartwright (1832–33), John Solomon Cartwright* (1833–34), and Charles William Grant (Alwington, 1834, now destroyed). The Commercial Bank of the Midland District at 44 Princess Street (1833) is related stylistically to these buildings; a letter which appeared in the *Kingston Chronicle* in 1831 suggests that Rogers may have had an interest in designing the bank. The central block of the Kingston General Hospital (1833–35) has been said to have been designed by Wells and Thompson of Montreal and only superintended by Rogers. But stylistic features such as the quoins, the monolithic window surrounds, and the umbrage or recessed porch (found also at Charles Place and Plymouth Square) seem to point to Rogers as the designer.

Most of these structures have quoins on either the back or the front. In several cases elongated quoins touch the long stone jambs projecting from adjacent windows. This distinctive feature is particularly prominent on the corner wings of Charles Place, on the back façade of the Gildersleeve house, and on the side of the Commercial Bank. The feature is also seen on two more Kingston buildings which may thus be attributed to Rogers, one at the corner of Ontario and William streets (1841–42) and the other at 65–67 Princess Street. Farther afield, the peculiarity is found in two stone buildings in Perth, the Matheson house (1840) and the triple house at Gore and Harvey streets. These structures may also be designs by Rogers.

Quoining belongs to the rustic, basic mode of architecture. Contrary to expectation, the peculiar linking of quoins and jamb blocks seems to appear only once in the works of Italian Renaissance theorists and not at all in the designs of the early 18th-century English architect James Gibbs. Indeed, it was evidently not used to any extent in England until the 1840s, or elsewhere in Upper Canada until its appearance on Frederic William Cumberland*'s and William George Storm*'s Hamilton Post Office (1854–56). The device is found, however, in French architecture, prior to, but most frequently in, the work of Claude-Nicolas Ledoux (1736–1806). Did Rogers go to France before coming to the Canadas, was he influenced by publications, or was the influence perhaps indirect? Conceivably it came through the architectural milieu of Lower Canada. However the idea of linking the quoins and jambs came to Rogers, it probably appealed to him because of its combination of the decorative and the structural, and its emphasis on the simple, primitive forms of architecture.

Rogers's architectural sophistication clearly reflected the social elegance so evident in Kingston during the boom days of the 1820s and early 1830s. In contrast, his office of street surveyor exposed him to the vagaries of local politics. On 30 Nov. 1835 James Sampson*, a prominent Kingston physician and magistrate, brought two charges against Rogers before the Court of Quarter Sessions. The first was one of "violent conduct" towards Sampson while Rogers was "under the influence of liquor"; the second that Rogers was "so much addicted to drinking as to render him an unfit person for the situations he holds as Police Officer and Street Surveyor." The first charge was accepted as "fully proved"; the second was dismissed. At this distance it is impossible to unravel the case. Edward John Barker*, the editor of the *British Whig*, wrote on the day after the trial that Rogers, "by his attention to his duty and general good conduct, had won golden opinions from every person in this town, with the exception of Dr. Sampson, and the consequent excitement of the public, when so serious a charge was alleged against so deserved a favourite, was great. . . . The whole affair reminds us of the sacred story of Haman and Mordecai the Jew." Barker thus implied that Sampson was deliberately, and unjustly, trying to vilify Rogers. And indeed it emerged during the trial that the physician and the architect had had an earlier disagreement about the cutting down of trees near Rogers's property.

The court decisions were a considerable rebuff for Sampson. He was unable to convince his fellow magistrates, who included John Macaulay as chairman, that Rogers was unfit for office. All that Rogers received on the first charge was a reprimand. Among the witnesses who spoke on his behalf were Edward Horsey, a fellow architect, and Antoine Boisseau, a French Canadian mason who had apparently known and worked with Rogers for several years.

There is no evidence that Rogers's professional career suffered from the Sampson affair. He continued to receive substantial commissions, both public and private, for many years afterwards. In 1837 he built the Victoria District Court-House at Belleville (destroyed 1960). A simple but imposing two-storey structure with a grand Ionic entrance portico, it had quoins and massive window surrounds of the kind used earlier on the J. S. Cartwright house and on Plymouth Square. Two years later Rogers was asked to make substantial changes and additions to the Midland District Court-House, originally designed by John Leigh Okill in 1824 (taken down in 1855). The Prince Edward District Court-House at Picton, apparently built between 1831 and 1840, has been attributed to Rogers but has none of his peculiar stylistic features.

In 1838, following Kingston's incorporation as a town, Rogers petitioned that he be retained as street surveyor. He was unsuccessful and was replaced by John Cullen. But 11 months later, after Cullen's death, Rogers petitioned again for his former office, this time successfully. In April 1841 town council asked William Coverdale* and Rogers each to prepare a plan for a new market house. At the same meeting, the latter was asked to prepare an estimate of the public work he had in hand. On 1 May he reported projects worth £584, an increase from the £497 reported in July 1839 and doubtless a result of new commissions ordered since the town had become the provincial capital in February 1841.

Rollin

On 17 May 1841 council met to discuss the office of street surveyor. It moved that because of Rogers's "infirmity" and the "circumstances of the Town requiring the Services of an active and efficient officer," the position be declared vacant. It has been stated by historians that Rogers's "infirmity" was alcoholism, but council's motion probably meant no more than it said. Rogers was then around 60, and the duties of street surveyor were heavy and had been expanding. An "active" officer was indeed required, not only to supervise the increasing amount of street flagging and sewer construction, but to check wharfs to see that they did not infringe on street rights of way and to inspect chimneys and stoves to see that they were not potential fire hazards. Ironically, an alderman who tried to prevent Rogers's dismissal had had his chimney condemned by Rogers two years before.

As late as 1852, one year before his death from dropsy, Rogers is listed as an architect in William Henry Smith*'s *Canada: past, present and future*. As yet, however, little is known of his last years. In 1844 a pair of elegant stone houses, at 53–55 Earl Street, were built for one Alexander Somerville. Four years later they were mortgaged to Rogers. This fact and some stylistic evidence (elliptical door transoms and a carriageway arch, all with stone voussoirs of alternating colours) suggest that they may have been designed by Rogers. Two fine brick houses, 195–97 Earl Street, listed in 1855 as unfinished and owned by the builder, James Renton, may be among Rogers's latest designs. The careful interlocking of finely cut elliptical arches and quoins suggests his hand. Though Rogers is claimed to have had a part in designing George Okill Stuart's great villa, Summerhill, none of the architect's personal stylistic characteristics appear there. Rogers's grandest late design may be the three-storey stone building erected at the corner of Princess and King streets in 1847 for the widow of Henry Cassady, a former Kingston mayor for whom Rogers had done work. The strip pilasters on the Princess Street elevation recall those employed at Plymouth Square, while the use of quoins superimposed on large ashlar plates is similar to the treatment of the corners of the J. S. Cartwright house.

Thomas Rogers occupies an important place in the architectural history of Upper Canada. He was perhaps the most competent and versatile practitioner of his profession in the province in the 1820s and early 1830s. The variety of his work and the widespread demand for his services attest to this. Although many of his buildings have been destroyed, or radically altered, enough survive to show that he was a designer of considerable individuality. In Kingston his consistent use of stylistic features of a rustic or primitive kind gave a distinctive character to the town's stone architecture. From this George Browne*, who arrived in 1841, was to develop more fully his architectural ideas of Kingston as a primitive, Tuscan town. Browne's Presbyterian manse (1841), with its monolithic door and window surrounds (albeit bevelled), is unthinkable without Rogers's J. S. Cartwright house. (Not surprisingly, the latter has been attributed to Browne.) And the basement rows of elliptical arches on Browne's Town Hall and Market Building (1841–44) are symbolic witnesses to the firm foundation Rogers had laid for Kingston's distinctive architectural style.

J. Douglas Stewart

ACC-O, St George's Cathedral (Kingston, Ont.), minutes of the building committee, 15, 20 April, 24 Dec. 1825. AO, MS 78, Stanton to Macaulay, 23 March, 15 April 1831; RG 21, Victoria District (later Hastings County), council minutes, 2 April, 8, 19 May, 1, 8 June, 2 Aug. 1837; 22 Oct. 1839; RG 22, ser.159, 1808–59, no.259. Cataraqui Cemetery Company (Kingston), Burial record. Frontenac Land Registry Office (Kingston), Loughborough Township, abstract index to deeds, concession 8, lot 24 (mfm. at AO, GS 3976). MTL, William Allan papers, letters received, 1820–52, Allan to Rogers, 6 April 1829. PAC, RG 5, A1: 36447–48, 48585, 49077–80, 128862–63. QUA, Arch. of the city of Kingston, assessment rolls, 53–55 Earl Street, 1844, 1848; city council minutes, 17 May 1838, 9 April 1839; J. S. Cartwright papers, Givins corr., 1835; John Macaulay papers, corr., May 1834; Thomas Rogers, signed plan for St George's Anglican Church, Kingston, 1822; unsigned plan for Cataraqui Bridge, Kingston, 1829. St James' Cathedral Arch. (Anglican) (Toronto), Thomas Rogers, drawings for St James' Church, 1831. *Town of York, 1815–34* (Firth). U.C., House of Assembly, *Journal*, app., 1832–33: 218; 1833–34: 184–86. *British Whig*, 1, 8 Dec. 1835. *Chronicle & Gazette*, 23 May, 9 Dec. 1835; 27 Sept. 1837; 22 June 1839; 26 March 1842. *Daily News* (Kingston), 1 March 1853. *Kingston Chronicle*, 22 June 1827; 6 Aug. 1829; 3, 24 Dec. 1831.

H. M. Colvin, *A biographical dictionary of English architects, 1660–1840* (London, 1954), 512–13. *Heritage Kingston*, ed. J. D. Stewart and I. E. Wilson (Kingston, 1973). W. H. Smith, *Canada: past, present and future. City of Kingston, Ontario: buildings of historical and architectural significance*, ed. Margaret [Sharp] Angus (5v., [Kingston], 1971–80), 2: 66; 4: 217–19; 5: 48, 207–8. MacRae and Adamson, *Cornerstones of order*, 31, 57–58. MacRae et al., *Hallowed walls*, 204–5, 207. Margaret [Sharp] Angus, *Kingston General Hospital, 1832–1972: a social and institutional history* (Montreal and London, Ont., 1973); *The old stones of Kingston: its buildings before 1867* ([Toronto], 1966). J. D. and Mary Stewart, "John Solomon Cartwright: Upper Canadian gentleman and regency 'man of taste,'" *Historic Kingston*, no.27 (1979): 61–77.

ROLLIN, PAUL, wood-carver, architect, landowner, and merchant; b. 25 Jan. 1789 in Longueuil, Que., son of Dominique Rollin and Magdeleine Bouthellier (Bouteiller); m. 3 April 1815 Zoé Pétrimoulx in Saint-Vincent-de-Paul (Laval), Lower Canada; d. 1 Dec. 1855 in Sainte-Thérèse-de-Blainville (Sainte-Thérèse), Lower Canada.

The son of a native of the Lorraine region in France who had settled at Longueuil, Paul Rollin was apprenticed to wood-carver Louis Quévillon* of Saint-Vincent-de-Paul. No apprenticeship contract has been found, but it is known that by 1812 Rollin was a master wood-carver. Quévillon considered him one of his most valuable helpers and set him up on a site adjoining his own. Rollin shared in the work done in Quévillon's workshop at Les Écorres, along with René Beauvais*, *dit* Saint-James, and Joseph Pépin*. He formed a partnership with these two to fulfil contracts for ornamental work in the churches around Montreal. Thus with Pépin he helped to decorate the first church of Notre-Dame at Montreal in 1808–9. He did the baldachin, vaulting, and cornices, and then the gilding of the carved pieces.

From 1815 until about 1822 Rollin trained his own apprentices, none of whom, however, became famous. He went into partnership with Quévillon, Pépin, and Saint-James in February 1815 "to carry out all the works of the said profession of wood-carving . . . for all comers." Their contract stipulated: "This company has the responsibility of seeing that the said parties, as they have mutually undertaken to do, shall each contribute equally to whatever is to be done and paid for. . . . And the moneys produced by the said works shall be received by any of the said parties without distinction, and they . . . shall share the profit equally." Their partnership ended in January 1817 after the carvers had worked together in the churches at Pointe-Claire and Varennes. Rollin, Quévillon, Pépin, and Saint-James made a contract with the churchwardens of Chambly in 1819 to undertake wood-carvings in connection with the church's vault, chancel, and jube. In the same period Rollin also collaborated with these craftsmen on the ornamentation of the churches at Longueuil and Lachenaie. Then around 1821 he joined with Saint-James to do wood-carving, including work finished in gold and silver leaf, at the church of Saint-Mathias. When Quévillon died in 1823 Rollin continued his activities as a carver, although hard times forced him to accept work as an architect and contractor. For example, he was commissioned to restore the church roof at Saint-Vincent-de-Paul in 1823, a responsibility he shared with Saint-James and master carpenter Simon Hogue.

Although Quévillon's workshop was less involved in statuary, Rollin was assigned to do a figure of the Virgin for the high altar in the first church of Notre-Dame in Montreal. This statue, which was carved around 1808, is believed to have been moved to the great second church of Notre-Dame built by James O'Donnell* from 1823 to 1829. Moreover, Rollin in 1828 helped decorate this second church by carving 243 bosses in the form of stars for the painted vault, and 213 acanthus leaves for the high altar. This work well illustrates the type of carving produced in the workshop at Les Écorres, repetitive pieces that were standardized rather than individualized. In an era when several churches had to be decorated at the same time, this approach to wood-carving offered nothing but advantages. But after 1830 the number of buildings to be decorated was dwindling because there was little new construction, and more refined work was consequently being demanded.

It is easy to reach a harsh judgement today about a carver content to make faithful reproductions of European models, especially when these were already outdated in France. But in an isolated region, such as Montreal at that period, to decorate the parish church with carved and gilded ornamentation seemed such an important achievement that few worried about how the work would be received by Europeans. The criticisms of the "Quévillon style" voiced in the Quebec region began, however, to cast doubt upon this kind of church ornamentation, and the severity of the strictures probably hastened the collapse of the workshop at Les Écorres and the consequent dispersal of the craftsmen into the surrounding regions. Wood-carving declined to some extent after 1830, but it returned to favour when Victor Bourgeau* attained prominence during the 1840s.

The prestige enjoyed by Rollin does not seem to have been affected by the disfavour into which the "Quévillon style" was falling. Admittedly this artist in wood-carving was able to broaden the field of his activities, and had become integrated into a cultured milieu of lawyers and other persons of importance, as the list of the witnesses to his marriage in 1815 demonstrates. He also proved a landowner to respect. The year he was married he bought some land in the Châteauguay seigneury, which he sold seven years later. In 1820 he acquired a property with a house in the village of Saint-Vincent-de-Paul, which he made over to Saint-James in 1830 for £2,400. A piece of land bought in the same region in 1823 was rented as a farm, and another at Saint-François-de-Sales (Laval) was sold in 1828. Rollin is also known to have bought some land at Sainte-Thérèse-de-Blainville before 1832, and to have established himself there as a merchant, but it is not known what the latter activity involved.

Paul Rollin's obituary in *La Minerve* termed him "the most senior Canadian wood-carver." It described him as "a good father, a good husband, and a good Christian. He always distinguished himself by his simplicity [and] his gentle and honest nature."

RAYMONDE GAUTHIER

ANQ-M, CE1-12, 25 janv. 1789; CE6-25, 4 déc. 1855; CN1-16, 19 sept. 1812; CN1-28, 24 mars 1824; CN1-68, 17 févr. 1825, 4 mai 1827; CN1-96, 28 févr. 1812; 13 avril 1815; 3 févr. 1816; 3, 24 févr., 6 juin 1817; 10, 19 févr. 1818; 27 juill. 1819; 20 janv. 1820; 10 sept. 1821; 22 févr., 9

Rolph

juill. 1822; 22 févr., 8 mars, 13 oct., 8 nov. 1823; 7 avril 1824; 11 juin 1825; 22 déc. 1828; 25 mai 1829; 11, 30 mars 1830; 20 nov. 1832; CN1-126, 11 févr. 1815; CN1-167, 8 juin 1815; CN1-334, 3 févr. 1815; CN1-375, 26 févr. 1821; CN6-29, 4 août 1823. AP, Saint-Vincent-de-Paul (Laval), reg. des baptêmes, mariages et sépultures, 3 avril 1815. MAC-CD, Fonds Morisset, 2, R754/P324. *La Minerve*, 7 déc. 1855. *L'église et l'enclos paroissial de Saint-Mathias-de-Rouville* (Québec, 1978). Olivier Maurault, *La paroisse: histoire de l'église Notre-Dame de Montréal* (2ᵉ éd., Montréal, 1957). Ramsay Traquair and G. A. Neilson, *The old church of St Charles de Lachenaie* (Montreal, 1934). Émile Vaillancourt, *Une maîtrise d'art en Canada (1800–1823)* (Montréal, 1920).

ROLPH, THOMAS, surgeon, author, and emigration agent; b. 1801 or 1802 in London; m. Frances ——; d. 17 Feb. 1858 in Portsmouth, England.

Thomas Rolph's family, social, and educational background is unknown. In 1823 he received an apothecary's licence from the Society of Apothecaries in London but there is no evidence that he took further medical qualifications. In 1832 he left England for a brief tour of the West Indies and the United States on his way to Upper Canada. He arrived there in the summer of 1833 and settled in Ancaster where he began to practise as a surgeon on 13 August. He also bought and sold small amounts of land in Brooke and Ancaster townships between 1834 and 1837. In July 1838 he was appointed surgeon to the 1st Regiment of Gore militia and in December to the 6th Provisional Battalion. In May 1840 the College of Physicians and Surgeons of Upper Canada refunded Rolph's membership fee on the grounds that he had "exhibited no qualifications for being elected a member." Thus, Rolph's status as a surgeon must be regarded sceptically.

Rolph became known as a proponent of assisted emigration from Britain to the Canadas along the lines being advocated by Sir Robert John Wilmot-Horton and Edward Gibbon Wakefield*. In 1836 he presented his views in *A brief account, together with observations, made during a visit in the West Indies, and a tour through the United States of America, in parts of the years 1832–3; together with a statistical account of Upper Canada*. This book and other evidence indicate that Rolph travelled widely in Upper Canada for he describes in detail many features of the province's towns, villages, and townships. He depicts Upper Canada as a desirable location for British emigrants with capital and farm labourers who would work hard and not expect an easy life.

Rolph began his career promoting emigration when he went to Britain with Roman Catholic Bishop Alexander McDonell* who had been interested in immigration for some years. They left in June 1839 and in September presented to Lord John Russell at the Colonial Office a scheme for large-scale systematic emigration with government assistance. The government rejected this scheme, as it did many others, on the grounds of expense.

Rolph remained in Britain until July 1840, travelling, speaking, and writing as an unofficial promoter of emigration to the Canadas. He assisted in the formation of societies which, along with landowners, were to provide the means for indigent emigrants to go to the Canadas. In December 1839 the Central Agricultural Society of Great Britain and Ireland made him an honorary member and corresponding secretary for British North America. In February 1840 the Highland and Agricultural Society of Scotland (an association of landowners) made him an honorary member of its emigration committee and the North American Colonial Committee appointed him its honorary secretary. He was a member of this committee's delegation to Russell seeking government aid for emigration, which Russell refused.

All these activities were fully reported in Canadian newspapers, thereby making Rolph a prominent figure upon his return in September 1840. He delivered speeches at dinners given in his honour and afterwards helped organize local emigration societies. In October a central coordinating body, the Canadian Emigration Association, was formed in Toronto to collect information on lands and jobs and send it to British emigration societies or make it available to arriving immigrants. The association delegated Rolph as its representative in the British Isles.

Rolph's prominence so impressed Governor Lord Sydenham [Thomson*] that he appointed him "Emigration Agent for the Canadas" in December 1840. Rolph was in the British Isles from January to August 1841, arriving back in Canada in September. In February 1842 Governor Sir Charles Bagot* reappointed him as official emigration agent. He returned to Britain but in July the colonial secretary, Lord Stanley, wrote to Bagot criticizing Rolph's activities and advising that his appointment be ended. The reason given was that Rolph had incautiously encouraged indigent emigrants with the expectation that they would receive government aid. Neither the British nor the Canadian government intended to assist penniless emigrants; indeed, Canada wanted them discouraged. Rolph left Britain in August and ceased to be Canada's emigration agent in December.

Another reason for official disfavour towards Rolph was his involvement, beginning in 1841, with the British American Association for Emigration and Colonization. This was a commercial association which intended to purchase lands in British North America and promote emigration of the poor on Wakefieldian principles. It collapsed early in 1843 because it did not get British or Canadian government approval and could not raise its projected capital.

Rolph was in Canada from September 1841 to

March 1842 and from August to November 1842. He delivered speeches about his work and defended his involvement with the association. In October 1842 the Legislative Assembly voted to pay him £500 for his services under Bagot's appointment. The next month he returned to England but by August 1843 was back in Canada.

Beginning in 1839 Rolph had also petitioned the Colonial Office on behalf of two other causes, but without success. He sought guarantees against deportation to the United States of fugitive slaves in Upper Canada as well as special government provision for their education. The other cause was the request of the Ursulines and Sulpicians in Lower Canada for the return of property which had been confiscated by the British. As well, from 1841 Rolph advocated the voluntary emigration of blacks from Canada to Trinidad where the sugar planters were seeking workers to replace their freed slaves. He even acted briefly in 1843 as an emigration agent in Upper Canada for the governor of Trinidad.

Rolph left Canada at the end of 1843 and probably never returned. In 1844 he published his best-known work, *Emigration and colonization; embodying the results of a mission to Great Britain and Ireland, during the years 1839, 1840, 1841, and 1842*. The book contains detailed descriptions of his travels in the British Isles and in Upper Canada, reports of speeches (by himself and by others), and accounts of the societies he formed or helped to form. Something of a trial of endurance, even for ardent admirers of Rolph, it also served as a justification of his activities and of himself. By January 1845 he was settled in Portsmouth where he practised as a surgeon until his sudden death on 17 Feb. 1858. The previous day he is supposed to have seen the tombstone of a young woman which carried the inscription "killed by Dr. Thomas Rolph." By ten that evening he had become "insensible" and the next morning he died of a "Serious apoplexy."

Opinions on Rolph vary. H. I. Cowan sees him as a minor figure in colonization, seeking to enrich himself from land sales, while W. S. Shepperson believes Rolph did much to promote Scottish emigration. The truth is difficult to discover because Rolph's claims cannot be taken at face value. Although emigration from the British Isles increased from 1839 to 1842, too many causes operated to give Rolph a major share of the credit. The most that can be definitely said for Rolph is that he expanded interest in Canada among prospective emigrants in England and Scotland.

WESLEY B. TURNER

Thomas Rolph is the author of *A brief account, together with observations, made during a visit in the West Indies, and a tour through the United States of America, in parts of the*
years 1832–3; together with a statistical account of Upper Canada (Dundas, [Ont.], 1836), a second edition of which was issued under the title *A descriptive and statistical account of Canada: shewing its great adaptation for British emigration; preceded by an account of a tour through portions of the West Indies and the United States* (London, 1841). Rolph's other works include *Canada v. Australia; their relative merits considered in an answer to a pamphlet, by Thornton Leigh Hunt, Esq., entitled "Canada and Australia"* (London, 1839); *Colonisation: a natural, safe and effectual mode of relief for national distress* (London, 1847); *Comparative advantages between the United States and Canada, for British settlers, considered in a letter, addressed to Captain Allardyce Barclay, of Ury* (London, 1842); *The emigrant's manual: particularly addressed to the industrious classes and others who intend settling abroad; together with "The memoranda of a settler in Canada"* . . . (London, n.d.); and *Emigration and colonization; embodying the results of a mission to Great Britain and Ireland, during the years 1839, 1840, 1841, and 1842* . . . (London, 1844). Additional works are listed in the *British Museum general catalogue*.

AO, RG 1, C-III-4, 10: 12; RG 53, ser.2-2, 3. GRO (London), Death certificate, Thomas Rolph, 17 Feb. 1858. PRO, CO 42/467, 42/468, 42/497; CO 43/98, 43/101, 43/102, 43/144–45 (copies at PAC). Wentworth Land Registry Office (Hamilton, Ont.), Alphabetical index to deeds, Ancaster Township (mfm. at AO, GS 1394). *Arthur papers* (Sanderson). *Debates of the Legislative Assembly of United Canada* (Abbott Gibbs *et al.*), vol.2. Morgan, *Bibliotheca Canadensis*. Canniff, *Medical profession in U.C.* H. I. Cowan, *British emigration to British North America; the first hundred years* (rev. ed., Toronto, 1961). W. S. Shepperson, *British emigration to North America; projects and opinions in the early Victorian period* (Minneapolis, Minn., 1957). J. K. A. Farrell [O'Farrell], "Schemes for the transplanting of refugee American negroes from Upper Canada in the 1840's," *OH*, 52 (1960): 245–49.

ROMBAU. *See* RAMBAU

ROSS, ALEXANDER, schoolmaster, fur trader, office holder, politician, justice of the peace, and author; b. 9 May 1783 in Morayshire, Scotland; d. 23 Oct. 1856 in the Red River settlement (Man.).

Alexander Ross was raised in Scotland on his father's farm, Layhill, in the parish of Dyke. Little is known of his life before his departure from Greenock aboard the *Countess of Darlington* in 1804. He would appear to have had some formal education because, soon after his arrival at Quebec in July, he found employment as a schoolmaster. The following year he left for Upper Canada and again secured a position as teacher, in Glengarry County. By 1809 he had saved enough to buy 300 acres of land. He had not immigrated to British North America, however, to become a yeoman or an underpaid schoolmaster; he had come to make his fortune, and in the Canadas it was the fur trade with its excitement and prospect of wealth that lured the young. In 1810, presumably in

Ross

Montreal, Ross met Wilson Price Hunt of the Pacific Fur Company, and soon afterwards signed up as a clerk. On 20 July he left Montreal for New York with two of the company's partners, Alexander MacKay* and Duncan McDougall*, and a group of clerks and voyageurs. In September the party sailed for the Pacific northwest coast aboard the *Tonquin*. The voyage was a stormy one, as much the result of the abrasive character of the captain, Jonathan Thorn*, as of the weather of the south Atlantic. The vessel made a short stop at the Falkland Islands to take on water, and Ross was among the group of eight or nine passengers left behind by the captain when the *Tonquin* lifted anchor on 11 December. Only after struggling for several hours against a rough sea in a boat designed for half their number did the party succeed in rejoining the vessel. According to Ross, the rescue had only been made possible by one of the PFC partners, Robert Stuart, who forced the captain at gunpoint to turn back for the boat.

The *Tonquin* arrived late in March 1811 at the mouth of the Columbia River, where the PFC party established Fort Astoria (Astoria, Oreg.). On 22 July, Ross went up the Columbia with a trading expedition under David Stuart. The PFC men were accompanied for a short distance by David THOMPSON, of the North West Company, who had arrived at the fort earlier in the month. At the junction of the Okanagan and Columbia rivers a small post, Fort Okanagan (Wash.), was built and, while the rest of the party continued north in search of furs, Ross was left behind to trade with the Indians around the fort. He remained at this post for the next few years and there took an Okanagan woman, Sally*, as his country wife.

When the NWC purchased the PFC establishment in the Columbia in 1813, Ross joined that company and took charge of the northern posts, working out of Fort Okanagan. In 1816, appointed second in command to James KEITH, who was charged with the trade on the Pacific coast, Ross spent a year at Fort Astoria, renamed Fort George by the NWC. He found the interior more to his liking, however, and in 1817 procured an assignment to Fort Thompson (Kamloops, B.C.). The following year he left with an expedition under Donald McKENZIE to establish Fort Nez Percés (Walla Walla, Wash.), which was to be the departure point for trapping and trading in the Snake River country to the south. When McKenzie left with the first expedition in September, Ross was instructed to complete the construction of the post and to man it during the winter. He remained there during McKenzie's subsequent expeditions in 1819–20 and 1820–21, and after the union of the NWC and the Hudson's Bay Company in 1821.

The first expedition into the Snake country under the HBC was conducted by Finan McDonald in 1823. Ross was given charge of the expedition in 1824 by the HBC's Northern Department council and set out from Flathead Post (Mont.) on 10 February with 54 men and 231 horses, equipped with 206 traps and 62 guns. After Ross's first expedition HBC governor George SIMPSON, who visited the Columbia district in 1824–25, was convinced that Ross did not have the talent to implement his policy of trapping out the Snake country and Peter Skene OGDEN was instructed to lead later expeditions.

Ross had been contemplating settling in the Red River colony since 1823 and, like so many who found themselves redundant after Simpson's careful pruning, he moved there with his wife and four children in 1825. He settled on a 100-acre grant of land near the junction of the Red and Assiniboine rivers, and in the next years he became a prominent member of the community. Upon his arrival Ross found the settlement in a state of starvation and took to the plains near Pembina (N.Dak.) with Andrew McDermot* to keep himself and his family supplied with fresh meat. Ross, whom Simpson always thought lacked loyalty to the HBC, traded meat and corn with the Americans, Indians, and settlers, and in the following spring he began to run York boats from Red River to Hudson Bay. Labelled a "petty trader" by the HBC officers, he shipped company goods out of the colony and brought in, both on his own account and for the HBC, trade goods and general merchandise. His brigades attracted the influential men of the settlement, and Louis GUIBOCHE, Cuthbert GRANT, and the sons of retired chief factors William Hemmings Cook* and James BIRD were among those who joined him. Ross does not seem to have continued his trading activity beyond the late 1820s; he may have capitulated to growing competition from other free traders or to pressures from Simpson who sought to discourage trade with the Americans at Pembina.

Ross was one of the few men in the colony capable of tackling its increasingly complicated administrative problems, and over the years, despite his unpopularity with Simpson, he assumed several positions of responsibility. In 1835 he was appointed sheriff of Assiniboia and on 12 February he attended the Council of Assiniboia as an invited observer. At this meeting he was named to the committee of public works with McDermot, Robert Logan*, John Bunn*, and Simpson, and was appointed commander of the Volunteer Corps of 60 men created by the council to maintain order in the colony. On 13 June 1836 he was sworn in as councillor himself. The internal workings of the council are not known since its minutes do not indicate the precise contributions of each member. It would seem, however, that Ross exerted a moderating influence. For example, the difficult and bigoted recorder, Adam Thom*, complained throughout the 1840s that Ross refused to enforce the HBC's monopoly over the trade in furs and the prohibition against free trade. In 1845 Ross argued with Thom and a few of the other magistrates. He claimed that they were excessively unreasonable and unjust in expecting the police to enforce the monopoly provision of the HBC charter to the letter, and as sheriff he refused to press the volunteer mixed-blood police to do so. It is probable that most of the officers and men were themselves involved in the free trade and prosecution would have led to revolt. Ross's own connection with the free traders has not been determined, but Thom believed he was involved. When James Green, an American free trader who was to marry Ross's daughter Isabella in 1845, was prosecuted late in 1844, Ross attempted an equivocal stance.

Ross accumulated several other positions in the civil administration of the colony. In 1837 he was named magistrate for the Red River middle district. With the modification of the judicial structure of the colony effected by the HBC in 1839 he was named sheriff, with Cuthbert Grant, and in that capacity acted as chief officer in the supreme court. In 1843 he was appointed governor of the new jail with an annual allowance of £30 and two years later he added to his charge that of collector of customs duty following Bird's resignation from that office. He was appointed by council to the committee of finance, with Bunn, Thom, and George Marcus CARY, in 1847. Ross's lenient position on free trading put him at odds with Thom and solidified his support among the Métis. The conflict between Ross and Thom came to a head in February 1850 when the case of *Matheson* v. *Thom* was heard in the General Quarterly Court. Ross refused to sit on the bench and Governor William Bletterman Caldwell* presided over the court. According to Ross, Thom conducted his own defence "stamping, ranting and lecturing some two hours, insulting the magistrates and turning the jury out of the box." When Thom apparently stormed out of the courtroom in contempt of court, Caldwell failed to bring him to order, but promptly called Ross to order when he stated that neither law nor justice existed in the colony. Ross and the other magistrates subsequently refused to sit on the bench with the governor and in July they drafted a petition, which was signed by all of the lay councillors and more than 500 others, addressed to Eden Colvile*, the recently appointed governor of Rupert's Land, calling upon him to assume Caldwell's responsibilities at Red River. Ross had in the mean time resigned both as sheriff and as councillor, and in October 1851 he resigned as governor of the jail.

Ross's greatest interest, and the concern of many of his contemporaries, was what was known in Red River as the "Presbyterian question." This issue, which consumed much of Ross's attention in his last years, had its roots in the migration of Scottish settlers to the area in 1812. Brought to North America by Lord Selkirk [Douglas*], they had been promised a clergyman of their own faith and language – Presbyterian and Gaelic. In the absence of their own minister, most of the Presbyterians submitted to the forms and practices of the Church of England.

After the departure of the first Church of England missionary, John West*, his successors, David Thomas Jones* and William Cockran*, eventually modified their liturgy to accommodate the Scottish settlers and were informally low church and without Catholic pretension. The Presbyterians nevertheless continued to petition the HBC for a clergyman and in June 1844 Ross, Logan, and James SINCLAIR presented their case to Governor Simpson. The company was asked to contribute to the support of a minister. Compensation both for the property originally set aside for a Presbyterian church – upon which the Anglican Upper Church (St John's) had been built – and for the contribution made by the Presbyterian settlers over the years to the Anglican parish was also demanded. In the fall of 1850, after the intervention of the reverends Robert Burns* and William RINTOUL of the Presbyterian Church of Canada (Free Church), Governor Colvile offered the Red River Presbyterians a glebe at Frog Plain and £150 for the construction of their own church. At the same time the Anglican bishop of Rupert's Land, David Anderson*, agreed to purchase 28 pews, at £2 each, from the seceding members of the Upper Church. In September 1851 the first Presbyterian minister, John Black*, arrived in the settlement. Although it is difficult to determine how many colonists left the Anglican Church after Black started his services, it is known that only 80 to 90 communicants were left at the Upper Church; 70 remained at the Middle Church (St Paul's), where before there had been approximately 200. Ross himself estimated at 300 the number of Presbyterians who rallied to their own church. When, in 1852, Anderson threatened to prevent burial by any but Anglican rite in the Upper Church graveyard, where the Scots had been burying their dead since their arrival in the colony, Ross successfully called upon the HBC to intervene in favour of an open churchyard. None the less, feelings between the Anglican and Presbyterian communities had become so vicious that relations were never to be the same as they had been before.

Ross and his wife, Sally, were married by Christian rite in the Upper Church on 24 Dec. 1828, and at their home, Colony Gardens, they raised a family of at least 13 children. There is every indication that their children were aware of their racial disadvantage. Ross himself regarded the mixed-bloods as genetically inferior, and felt that only with the greatest effort could they be a credit to their heritage. The children were all too aware that "Mama" was only an Indian and they had to remind themselves that she neverthe-

Ross

less deserved their love and respect. The Ross children, pressed by their father to preserve their station, did well. William was appointed assistant sheriff and governor of the jail in 1851, to succeed his father, and in 1853 was sworn in as councillor of Assiniboia. He also held the offices of petty judge, auditor of public accounts, and postmaster before his premature death in 1856. James* attended the University of Toronto and during the events of 1869–70 [see Louis Riel*] he was a principal spokesman for the English-speaking settlers. Henrietta Ross married John Black, and another daughter, Mary, married the Presbyterian minister George Flett. These marriages were exceptional for mixed-blood women, and in fact Black's marriage to Ross's daughter in 1853 created quite a stir in the colony. Jemima Ross married William Coldwell*, who with William Buckingham* founded the Nor'Wester, the first newspaper in the settlement, in 1859.

While at Colony Gardens, Ross also turned his talents to writing and, as the author of three books, he was the most prolific writer in the pre-1870 northwest. His first book, Adventures on the Columbia, published in 1849, carefully documented his voyage to the Columbia in 1810–11 and his years in the employ of the PFC. With the narratives of Gabriel Franchère* and Ross Cox, this volume is one of the three first-hand accounts of the enterprise of John Jacob Astor*. His second book, The fur hunters of the far west, was also largely written from his experiences in the fur trade. Published in 1855, this work covers his years with the NWC and the HBC up to 1825. The third volume, The Red River settlement, appeared in 1856, shortly before his death. In this last book, the best single piece of writing on the Red River, it is evident that Ross believed that the motley, quixotic settlement at the forks of the Red and Assiniboine rivers had a predestined purpose. To Ross it was a civilized nucleus in the wilderness, whose primary function was to bring civilization and Christ to the "heathen." Although Ross felt that his years in the Oregon country were spent in a smothering wilderness, he believed his years in Red River were filled with divine purpose. He never tried to escape his exile in the west as did so many fur traders who fled eagerly upon retirement to the Canadas or back to Great Britain. Red River was the catalyst that would convert the wilderness and Ross of course by extension felt he must function as "the example." This conviction might explain his tireless devotion to his community, his church, and the upbringing of his mixed-blood children.

FRITS PANNEKOEK

Alexander Ross is the author of Adventures on the Columbia; The fur hunters of the far west; a narrative of adventures in the Oregon and Rocky mountains (2v., London, 1855); The Red River settlement: its rise, progress and present state; with some account of the native races and its general history, to the present day (London, 1856; repr. Minneapolis, Minn., 1957; repr. Edmonton, 1972); "Journal of Alexander Ross – Snake country expedition, 1824," ed. T. C. Elliott, Oreg. Hist. Soc., Quarterly (Portland), 14 (1913): 366–88; and "Letters of a pioneer," ed. George Bryce, Man., Hist. and Scientific Soc., Trans. (Winnipeg), no.63 (1903). Some bibliographies also attribute the fictional Selma: a tale of the sixth Crusade (London, 1839) to him.

PAC, MG 25, 62. PAM, HBCA, A.34/1: f.107; B.202/a/1; B.235/a/7–12; D.5/1–29; E.16/2; MG 2, B2; B4-1; C3; C14; MG 7, B4-1, 21 Dec. 1853; B7-1, 8 Aug. 1830; C12. Canadian North-West (Oliver), vol.1. Cox, Adventures on the Columbia. Docs. relating to NWC (Wallace). HBRS, 3 (Fleming); 13 (Rich and Johnson); 19 (Rich and Johnson). Simpson, Fur trade and empire (Merk; 1968). Quebec Gazette, 19 July 1804. George Bryce, "Alexander Ross," Canadian Magazine, 49 (May–October 1917): 163–68; "Alexander Ross, fur trader, author and philanthropist," Queen's Quarterly (Kingston, Ont.), 11 (1903–4): 46–56. R. St G. Stubbs, "Law and authority in Red River," Beaver, outfit 299 (summer 1968): 17–21.

ROSS, GEORGE McLEOD, Church of England minister; b. 1804; m. 2 March 1829 Edith Hallowell in Montreal, and they had three children; d. 9 Aug. 1855 in Drummondville, Lower Canada.

George McLeod Ross seems to have immigrated to Lower Canada as an adult and established himself in Montreal as a tutor. In 1824 the Church of England ministers in that town recommended him as a candidate for holy orders; he was ordained deacon on 10 March 1827 and priest on 31 May 1828 by the bishop of Quebec, Charles James Stewart*. It is thought that he studied theology with the rector of Christ Church in Montreal, John Bethune*, who became his brother-in-law when he married Edith Hallowell, the sister of Bethune's wife, Elizabeth. Two days after being made a deacon, Ross had been appointed to St George's Church in Drummondville, a charge left vacant when the Reverend Samuel Simpson Wood* departed; on 29 Jan. 1829 he was granted the title of rector, which he retained until his death. This post, indeed, was one of three in the diocese which offered lifetime appointments, Quebec and Hatley being the others. The letters patent declared that he would be recognized as though he were rector of a parish in England, but the young minister faced a dismal situation: a fire had gutted virtually the whole village in 1826, scarcely ten years after it had been founded, and the destitute and heterogeneous population could look after only its own needs. Living in poor accommodation a long way from his unfinished church, Ross had to travel not only the wretched roads of Grantham and Wickham townships, his own parish territory, but also those of Durham, Melbourne, Shipton, Kingsey, Wendover, and Simpson townships, and even of the adjacent seigneuries of Courval, Rivière-David, and Baie-du-Febvre. The life of a missionary was hard; however, he was affiliated with the powerful Society for the Propagation of the Gospel, which paid most of his salary, some income being added in later years from the clergy reserves fund.

Despite these difficult conditions, Ross devoted himself whole-heartedly to his pastoral duties, visiting the faithful twice a year and celebrating church services at more than one place on Sundays and holy days. Bishop George Jehoshaphat Mountain*, to whom he submitted detailed reports on his ministry, noted his strict adherence to liturgical form. Ross gave constant attention to the education of his parishioners. An accredited visitor to the schools of the Royal Institution for the Advancement of Learning, he regularly corresponded with the authorities, relating mainly the set-backs he had encountered. He particularly dreaded the influence of the Roman Catholics, and deplored the apathy that had led to the discontinuation of a Sunday school which had had such promising beginnings in 1830. As a result of his efforts to bring instruction to the people of the region, Arthur William Buller*, who had been charged by Lord Durham [Lambton*] to inquire into education in Lower Canada, consulted him in 1838. Ross gave permission in 1845 for his presbytery to be used as a school since the village school was tumbling down. He also encouraged the circulation of books, particularly the Bible and the catechism, to such an extent that he ran into debt. He set up a library for his parishioners in 1851, offering them a hundred or so "carefully chosen" volumes, as well as some of his own books.

Ross was able to persuade influential people in Drummondville and the surrounding region to help consolidate and improve the parish's patrimony. On several occasions Frederick George Heriot*, Robert Nugent Watts, and William Sheppard* gave money, land, and material for the buildings and cemetery. In April 1839, having collected £230 through a subscription campaign in England, and gifts of land from local farmers, Ross undertook to erect a church at Kingsey. He wrote to Mountain, his bishop, in 1842 that despite a number of difficulties he had managed to assemble funds to build another one at Lower Durham (L'Avenir). Well aware of the fluctuations in the region's economy and sensitive to his parishioners' financial difficulties, he willingly let them contribute according to their means, often in the form of manual labour. Shortly before his death, work began at Drummondville on the fine stone building of St George's Church, which is still standing.

During his 28 years as minister at Drummondville, George McLeod Ross managed to avoid the religious controversies that might have arisen in this pluralistic

environment, contenting himself with the thought that the Catholics respected the Protestants even "if they do not exactly love us." As well, he seems to have maintained friendly relations with Abbé François-Onésime Belcourt of Drummondville, who visited him during his last illness. He lived quietly through the heroic pioneering era and left an enduring legacy. He was succeeded by a son, William Moray Ross, who served in the parish for a few years.

MARIE-PAULE R. LaBRÈQUE

ANQ-M, CE1-63, 2 mars 1829. Arch. de l'évêché de Nicolet (Nicolet, Qué.), Cartable Saint-Frédéric. BE, Drummond (Drummondville), reg. district Nicolet, I, no.1; reg. B, 2, no.1221. ÉÉC-Q, 28; 50; 99: 101. USPG, C/CAN/Que., IV, 36: f.404; E/Que./1845–46; 1854–55; Journal of SPG, 38: 146–50, 221–23. A. R. Kelley, "The Quebec Diocesan Archives: a description of the collection of historical records of the Church of England in the Diocese of Quebec," ANQ *Rapport*, 1946–47: 179–298. [J.-C. Langelier], *Liste des terrains concédés par la couronne dans la province de Québec de 1763 au 31 décembre 1890* (Québec, 1891). R.-G. Boulianne, "The Royal Institution for the Advancement of Learning: the correspondence, 1820–1829; a historical and analytical study" (PHD thesis, McGill Univ., Montreal, 1970). [Cuthbert Jones et al.], *A history of Saint Peter's parish, Sherbrooke, diocese of Quebec* . . . (Lennoxville, Que., 1947). Millman, *Life of Charles James Stewart*. A. W. Mountain, *A memoir of George Jehoshaphat Mountain, D.D., D.C.L., late bishop of Quebec* . . . (Montreal and London, 1866). J.-C. Saint-Amant, *Un coin des Cantons de l'Est* (2e éd., Drummondville, Qué., 1932). Côme Saint-Germain, *Regards sur les commencements de Drummondville* (Drummondville, 1978). J. H. Lambert, "The Reverend Samuel Simpson Wood, BA, MA: a forgotten notable, and the early Anglican Church in Canada," CCHS, *Journal* (Glen Williams, Ont.), 16 (1974): 2–22. N. D. Pilchard, "The parish of Drummondville," *Quebec Diocesan Gazette* (Quebec), 3 (1945), no.1: 15–17, 31; no.2: 35–37.

ROSS, HUGH, Presbyterian minister; b. *c.* 1797 in Rothiemurchus, parish of Kincardine, Scotland; m. 10 Oct. 1826 Flora McKay at the East River, Pictou County, N.S., and they had seven daughters and four sons; d. 1 Dec. 1858 in Tatamagouche, N.S.

Hugh Ross emigrated to Halifax with his family in 1813. After a brief business apprenticeship there, he followed his family to Pictou County where he was tutored by the Reverend James Drummond MacGregor*, taught a Sunday school class at New Glasgow, and became one of the first class of six ministers to graduate from Pictou Academy [*see* Thomas McCulloch*] and be licensed by the Pictou Presbytery of the Presbyterian Church in Nova Scotia in 1824.

From beginning to end, Ross's ministry was a series of unhappy conflicts. During a tour of Cape Breton with the Reverend Thomas TROTTER in July 1824, he

Ross

received a tentative call at Canso. While he was in other parts of the island, however, Donald Allan Fraser* and John MacLennan, Kirk ministers, visited Canso and in Ross's words, "without shame or delicacy . . . belied the venerable Dr. McGregor, calumniated our church, reproached our College, and stigmatized its Professors and Students." The call to Ross was withdrawn. By 1827 he was settled at Tatamagouche. A personal disappointment came in 1830 with his failure to be called to MacGregor's congregation after the latter's death, especially galling in that he had been selected to deliver the eulogy at MacGregor's funeral.

The sparsely settled New Annan–Tatamagouche charge was served by Ross with firmness and zeal. In 1840, however, his congregation split over the question of infant baptism. In essence, Ross's position was that parents who did not take communion could not expect their children to be accepted automatically for baptism when brought to the altar. He demanded adherence to "the Westminster Confession of Faith [and] the Catechism larger and shorter as a rule of faith and practice." The dissenting elders noted "a good many had never seen the Confession of Faith, and if they had, could not read it."

This storm might have passed had not Ross become embroiled in the controversy surrounding the 1841 election battle in Colchester County, won by Thomas Dickson who was supported by Alexander Campbell. The feelings were so virulent that a year after the election Ross was hung in effigy. Upheavals and divisions, especially in Presbyterian congregations in Nova Scotia, were quite common but the action that Ross and his supporters settled upon in November 1842 was unprecedented – they joined the Church of Scotland. That members of a congregation of the Presbyterian Church in Nova Scotia would turn Kirk was virtually inconceivable.

Almost immediately after these events, Ross accepted a call to Georgetown–Murray Harbour, P.E.I. This move improved his financial position and removed him from the political-religious controversy raging in Tatamagouche. In 1844, one year after the disruption of the Kirk in Scotland, Ross joined and became the first moderator of the free church Synod of Nova Scotia Adhering to the Westminster Standards. Ross resigned his Murray Harbour charge in 1847. Six years later his religious odyssey came full circle when he returned to Tatamagouche and on 26 July 1853 was readmitted to the ministry of the Presbyterian Church in Nova Scotia. He proceeded to serve in various places throughout the province. In November 1855 he was located at Baddeck and from March to May of the following year he was an itinerant missionary to Cape Sable Island. For the first two weeks of June 1856 he ministered to the railway workers at Grand Lake.

Ross was a powerful, logical reasoner and a clear, forceful preacher of the Gospel in English or in Gaelic. A quiet, retiring individual noted for useful talents, good disposition, and a kindly heart, he made diligent efforts to discharge his ministerial responsibilities. When aroused, as during the aftermath of the 1841 election, his passionate prose knew neither restraint nor retreat. A former elder suggested that Ross had been driven from Tatamagouche because "he was too faithful in reproving sin, and too zealous in the cause of truth." Ross, however, was very much a victim, partly of his own naïvety, certainly of the religious and political factions of his fellow Presbyterians. In a letter he wrote to the Pictou *Observer* in 1842 it is clear that in the face of adversity and criticism he was unwavering – "I have never sold my conscience: I have never compromised my principles: I have never veered with the wind, either to inhale the incense of popular applause or to grasp of the mammon of the world."

Allan C. Dunlop

MCA, A. B. Dickie papers, History of Presbyterian congregations. PANS, MG 1, 553, no.131. *An address to the members of the Presbyterian Church of Novascotia, on the impropriety and inconsistency of the conduct of parents, who solicit and claim baptism for their children, while they habitually neglect the observance of the Lord's Supper* (Pictou, N.S., 1847). *Christian Instructor, and Missionary Reg. of the Presbyterian Church of Nova Scotia* (Pictou), 4 (1859): 30–32. *Guardian* (Halifax), 1841–42; 14 June 1844. *Mechanic and Farmer* (Pictou), 17 Feb. 1841. *Observer* (Pictou), 1841–42, especially 22 March 1842. Alexander Maclean, *The story of the kirk in Nova Scotia* (Pictou, 1911). L. C. C. Stanley, *The well-watered garden: history of Presbyterians in Cape Breton, 1798–1860* (Sydney, N.S., 1983), 46–47.

ROSS, Sir JOHN, naval officer, explorer, and author; b. 24 June 1777 in Balsarroch, Scotland, fourth son of the Reverend Andrew Ross, minister at Inch, and Elizabeth Corsane; m. first 1816 Christian Adair (d. 1822), and they had one son; m. secondly 21 Oct. 1834 Mary Jones; d. 30 Aug. 1856 in London.

John Ross entered the Royal Navy as a first-class volunteer on 11 Nov. 1786 and served in the Mediterranean aboard the *Pearl* until December 1789. The following year he was transferred to the *Impregnable*, stationed at Portsmouth. During the next eight years he stayed on the ship's books but, on the advice of his captain, actually served in the merchant marine as an apprentice seaman in order to gain seagoing experience. Returning to the Royal Navy in September 1799, he was promoted midshipman and then served aboard various vessels in the North Sea and the Mediterranean until, with the outbreak of war in 1803, he was posted to the *Grampus*, under Admiral Sir James Saumarez. On 13

March 1805 he received his lieutenant's commission, and later that year was seriously wounded in a naval engagement under the batteries of Bilbao, Spain.

Some time during his merchant service, Ross had learned Swedish and in 1808, during a combined Swedish-English action against a Russian squadron, he was called upon to act as liaison officer and interpreter for Saumarez aboard the Swedish flagship. For this service he was nominated a knight commander of the Swedish Order of the Sword in August 1809. On 1 Feb. 1812 he was promoted commander and at the end of March placed in command of the *Briseis* on the Baltic station. He distinguished himself in several actions, most notably against French vessels, before being transferred to the sloop *Actæon* in June 1814 for service in the North and White seas and along the coast of Ireland. In August 1815 he was given command of the *Driver*.

By 1816 the Napoleonic Wars were over. Ross, at the age of 39, had been almost constantly at sea for 30 years and had apparently been wounded no fewer than 13 times. A vigorous, ambitious, competent officer, he prospered in his naval career through constantly increasing pensions and considerable prize money. While he was commanding the *Driver*, on duty along the Scottish coast, he and his first wife were happily planning and building their new home, North West Castle, at Stranraer near his place of birth on Loch Ryan. He was enjoying peace-time service and looking forward to retirement. In December 1817 he received orders that would, instead, open a new chapter in his naval career.

With the coming of peace the British Admiralty found itself at liberty to turn to preoccupations other than those of defence, and under the guidance of John Barrow, second secretary of the Admiralty, interest in the possible existence of a northwest passage was renewed. Barrow had been receiving reports from whaling vessels in the North Atlantic describing an unprecedented breaking up of the ice to the east of Greenland that had apparently sent exceptionally large packs of ice and an unusual number of icebergs as far south as 40°N. These observations led to speculation about a general reduction of the Arctic ice barrier and prompted Barrow, with the support of Sir Joseph Banks*, president of the Royal Society, to prepare plans for two simultaneous expeditions: one to proceed towards the North Pole in an attempt to find a passage through the ice to Bering Strait, and the other to search for a passage to the west through Davis Strait. Two series of graduated prizes were also drafted, and adopted by an act of parliament passed in 1818, to reward the first vessels to pass various longitudes westward from Davis Strait within the Arctic Circle and those reaching various latitudes in an effort to attain the North Pole. On 11 Dec. 1817 Ross received a letter from Sir George Hope, of the Admiralty, informing him that he had been selected to command the expedition through Davis Strait; Captain David Buchan* was commissioned to lead the polar expedition.

Ross arrived in London on 30 December and, after ascertaining from Lord Melville, first lord of the Admiralty, that his chances for promotion would be enhanced by accepting this service, he went to visit the ships being fitted out for the expeditions. He selected the 385-ton *Isabella* as his flagship and the somewhat smaller *Alexander* as its consort. Lieutenant William Edward PARRY was placed in command of the *Alexander* and among the junior officers attached to the expedition were Ross's nephew Midshipman James Clark Ross* and Lieutenant Henry Parkyns Hoppner*. Also, on the recommendation of the Royal Society, Captain Edward Sabine* of the Royal Artillery was assigned to the *Isabella* to conduct scientific observations. Ross's instructions, dated 31 March 1818, were to go northward in Davis Strait and Baffin Bay in an attempt to find an open passage round the northeast corner of North America and to proceed westward to the Pacific through Bering Strait. He was to make observations on currents, tides, ice conditions, and magnetism, and to collect natural history specimens.

Ross took his ships down the Thames in April and, after a brief stop in the Shetland Islands where he met with Buchan, he sailed for Greenland. During the first leg of the voyage the existence of the sunken land of Buss was disproved when the ships passed over the location where it had been laid down on the charts since 1578 and found no bottom at 180 fathoms. In Davis Strait by the end of May, the expedition encountered icebergs and, heading north, met a number of whaling vessels having difficulty with the pack-ice. At Waygatt Strait, between Disko Island and Greenland, Ross found 45 whalers detained by the ice and was himself held up for a few days. Finally leaving the last of the whalers behind him in Melville Bay, which he named, at the beginning of August, he entered waters that no other European had visited since William Baffin*'s voyage in 1616. With the help of John Sacheuse (a south Greenland Inuk who had gone to England with a whaler, learned English, and joined Ross's expedition as interpreter), contact was made with several groups of Inuit along the northwest coast of Greenland. Ross, who named these people "Arctic Highlanders," devoted a chapter in his journal of the voyage to his observations concerning them.

The expedition inched its way north past steep cliffs and through ice-tossed waters teeming with little auks, whales, and narwhals. Ross confirmed many of Baffin's observations and bestowed names of his own on various geographical features. He named the capes on either side of Smith Sound after the *Alexander*, to the east, and the *Isabella*, to the west, and erroneously

Ross

concluded that the sound was closed off by land to the north; it actually opens into Kane Basin [see Elisha Kent KANE] whence a channel leads to the Arctic Ocean. Turning to the south, Ross passed Jones Sound and again, claiming to have seen mountains across its western end, mistakenly declared it to be a bay. On 30 August he arrived off the inlet Baffin had named Lancaster Sound and in the early hours of 31 August sailed westward into the sound with the *Alexander* trailing behind. At about four in the morning Ross claimed he saw a ridge of high mountains across the bottom of the inlet and at three in the afternoon he once again observed what he believed to be mountains to the west. He named the range Croker's Mountains after John Wilson Croker, first secretary of the Admiralty, and against the wishes of his junior officers he decided to turn back. This was the critical moment of the whole voyage; Croker's Mountains were a mirage that would haunt Ross for the rest of his life. Heading south down the west coast of Davis Strait, on 1 October he passed Cumberland Strait (Sound), which he thought offered a better chance of a passage but which, because of the lateness of the season, he did not investigate. Turning back for England, he reached Grimsby on 14 November and two days later arrived in London with his logs and papers.

This voyage had confirmed many of Baffin's 17th-century discoveries and added the outline of Baffin Bay to the charts. Croker's Mountains, however, immediately became the centre of a controversy that pitted Barrow, Sabine, and Parry against Ross in a lively and at times acrimonious debate. Ross's *A voyage of discovery*, published in early 1819, was scathingly reviewed and ridiculed by Barrow in the *Quarterly Review*. Describing Ross as "an active and zealous officer in the ordinary duties of his profession," Barrow declared him singularly unqualified for the command of a voyage of discovery, which required "an inquisitive and perservering pursuit after details of fact not always interesting, a contempt of danger, and an enthusiasm not to be dampened by ordinary difficulties." Many points in Ross's narrative were questioned by Barrow, the most contentious being his decision to turn back in Lancaster Sound "at the very moment which afforded the brightest prospect of success." Citing passages from Parry's private journal, Barrow pointed out inconsistencies and weaknesses in Ross's account of the investigation of the sound and seriously questioned the existence of Croker's Mountains. Ross's presentation of scientific observations without giving credit to the officers responsible for them was also criticized. The polemic continued with the publication in 1819 of Sabine's *Remarks on the account of the late voyage of discovery to Baffin's Bay*, accusing Ross of plagiarism and misrepresentation of his opinions, and,

in the same year, of Ross's *An explanation of Captain Sabine's remarks*. This controversy did not interfere with Ross's promotion to captain, which he received on 7 Dec. 1818, although Barrow did prevent him from getting another ship.

Ross retired to North West Castle, which remained his home for the rest of his life, although he usually took a winter house in some agreeable part of London. He entertained old friends and carried on a voluminous correspondence on a wide assortment of subjects ranging from phrenology to nautical instruments. He was ahead of his time in recognizing the potential of steam in warships and in 1828 he published *A treatise on navigation by steam*. The natural conservatism of sailors, combined with the unreliability of early engines, had created a great prejudice against steam in the Royal Navy. At about this time Ross urged the Admiralty to send a steam vessel on an Arctic voyage. Barrow was still in office and, as could be expected, the proposal was rejected. Undeterred, Ross approached his wealthy friend Felix Booth, distiller of Booth's gin, seeking support for the project. The public-spirited Booth at first refused because of possible criticism that he was interested only in the parliamentary rewards offered for sailing through a northwest passage. However, when parliament abolished the Board of Longitude in 1828 it also eliminated the graduated rewards and Booth then agreed to sponsor the expedition.

A small Liverpool steamer, the *Victory*, was selected for the voyage and brought around to London for preparation. Its tonnage was increased from 85 to 150 and various improvements were made. Ross assembled an impressive battery of navigating and scientific instruments and laid in fuel and provisions to last a thousand days. The public announcement of the project was greeted by a flood of applications from volunteers, many of them, such as George Back* and Henry Parkyns Hoppner, veterans of other Arctic voyages. The officers, however, had already been chosen, and Ross's nephew James Clark Ross was to sail with the *Victory* as second-in-command. The expedition left London on 23 May 1829 and from the outset there were difficulties with the *Victory*'s machinery. After a short stop in Scotland, Ross crossed the Atlantic to Davis Strait and proceeded up the west coast of Greenland. He then crossed Baffin Bay and on 6 August entered Lancaster Sound. Commenting in his journal on his earlier adventure into these waters, Ross expressed bitterly his disappointment in the conduct of Parry and the other junior officers with him in 1818 who had so openly criticized his decision to turn back, claiming as justification for his action that they had not revealed their opinions to him at the time. He was nevertheless forced to concede the mistake, saying simply that "in reality, the whole history of navigation abounds with similar errors of false conclusions." Heading south in Prince Regent Inlet, the vessel stopped at Fury Beach, Somerset Island, and took on extra provisions from the wreck of the *Fury*, abandoned on this spot in 1825 [*see* Sir William Edward Parry]. The *Victory* then continued south and at the end of September 1829, after having gone about 250 miles farther south into the inlet than any previous expedition, it was stopped by ice and forced into winter quarters at what was named Felix Harbour, near Thom Bay.

The expedition spent the following four winters in the Arctic, unable to free the *Victory* from the ice-bound coast of Boothia Peninsula. During these years, with the help of Inuit who took up residence near the vessel, the area to the west and north was explored. Having failed to notice Bellot Strait in 1829 [*see* Joseph-René BELLOT], Ross concluded that there was no passage through the peninsula connecting the water to the west. To the east the Gulf of Boothia was discovered and explored. On 1 June 1831 James Clark Ross located the North Magnetic Pole on the west coast of Boothia Peninsula.

When it became apparent that the *Victory* would remain imprisoned for the winter of 1831–32, Ross decided he would have to abandon ship and in the spring of 1832 he led his men on foot north to Fury Beach where some supplies were still to be found. They constructed a shelter, Somerset House, and after repairing the *Fury*'s boats set off in late summer in an attempt to reach the whaling fleet in Baffin Bay. Unable, however, to make their way into Lancaster Sound because of the ice, they were forced to return to Fury Beach, where they passed their fourth Arctic winter. On 14 Aug. 1833 a lane of water opened up leading northward and the weary men set out once more in the boats. At the mouth of Prince Regent Inlet they proceeded easterly and on 26 August, a few miles west of Navy Board Inlet, a sail was sighted. Much to Ross's astonishment the vessel turned out to be his flagship of 1818, the whaler *Isabella*. The rescued men were landed at Stromness on 12 October and the Rosses arrived in London one week later, just as rescue expeditions were being organized to search for them. Three crew members had died and one had lost his sight during the long stay in the Arctic.

The expedition had established an impressive record for survival in the Arctic. Both Ross and his nephew were received by King William IV and John Ross became the social lion of London. Hostesses vied with each other to entice him to dinner parties. He received over 4,000 letters of congratulation, together with the occasional love-letter, and was given the freedom of the cities of London, Liverpool, Bristol, and others. He made a tour of the Continent and received a number of foreign awards and medals. Ross very much enjoyed all of the attention. The Admiralty generously assumed payment of the *Victory*'s crew at

double time up to the abandonment of the ship and then at regular navy pay to the date of their return. Parliament voted to reimburse Booth for his investment and awarded Ross £5,000. On 24 Dec. 1834 Ross was knighted and made a companion of the Order of the Bath.

Regardless of this hero's welcome, Ross once again found himself involved in controversy as a result of the voyage. A serious disagreement between him and his nephew arose over the presentation of the latter's discovery of the North Magnetic Pole in the narrative of the expedition, Ross wishing to take partial credit for an exploit his nephew considered exclusively his. The captain's comments on the unreliability of the *Victory*'s engines prompted the manufacturer, John Braithwaite, to publish in 1835 *Supplement to Captain Sir John Ross's narrative of a second voyage*, to which Ross replied in his *Explanation and answer to Mr. John Braithwaite's "Supplement."* Another interested party who was not pleased with Ross's narrative was the ship's steward, William Light, who provided the information for a highly critical 700-page account of the expedition compiled by Robert Huish. In 1846 the controversy arising from this voyage, as well as from the first one in 1818, was rekindled by Sir John Barrow's intemperate commentary in *Voyages of discovery and research within the Arctic regions*. Barrow unforgivingly repeated his assessment of the first voyage, articulated 25 years earlier, and then sarcastically dismissed the second as "a private speculation," happily saved from tragedy by the experience and leadership of James Clark Ross. John Ross responded that same year with another pamphlet, *Observations on a work, entitled, "Voyages of discovery and research within the Arctic regions."*

In March 1839 Ross had been appointed British consul at Stockholm, where he remained until 1846. Back in England, he was one of the first to express concern over the fate of the Arctic expedition of 1845 under Sir John Franklin*, and on 9 Feb. 1847 he offered his services to the Admiralty for the command of a search expedition. The Admiralty decided it was still too early to send out a rescue party and when one was finally organized in 1848 Ross was considered too old and the command was given to his nephew. Two years later Ross took command of a private search expedition, sponsored by the Hudson's Bay Company and various individuals, and at 72 years of age he made his third voyage into Arctic waters, aboard the 91-ton schooner *Felix*. Poorly equipped, the *Felix* was unable to be of much help and in fact was dependent upon supplies from other vessels involved in the search, under Captain Horatio Thomas Austin* and William Penny*, during the winter of 1850–51. Ross returned to England in September 1851 and was promoted rear-admiral on the retired list a short time afterwards. In poor health and possibly suffering from gradual senility, he divided his remaining years between Stranraer and London. In 1855 he published a short pamphlet on the Franklin search, bitterly criticizing almost everyone associated with it. He died during one of his visits to London and was buried in Kensal Green Cemetery.

The importance of Sir John Ross's career as an explorer of the Canadian Arctic rests less on any particular or comprehensive geographical discovery than on the fame and controversy that surrounded it. Following the 1818 voyage his reputation was indelibly tarnished by the unfortunate and erroneous conclusions that Lancaster, Jones, and Smith sounds were all closed in by land. The many geographical and scientific contributions made during the second expedition are generally attributed to the energetic efforts of his nephew. The survival of this expedition was none the less a considerable achievement and one which earned for Ross the recognition he felt he deserved and had been denied by his many detractors.

In collaboration with ERNEST S. DODGE

Sir John Ross is the author of numerous works on the exploration of the Arctic. After his first voyage in 1818, he published the journal *A voyage of discovery, made under the orders of the Admiralty, in his majesty's ships "Isabella" and "Alexander," for the purpose of exploring Baffin's Bay, and enquiring into the probability of a north-west passage* (London, 1819; 2nd ed., 2v., 1819), as well as *A description of the deep sea clamms, hydraphorous, and marine artificial horizon, invented by Captain J. Ross, R.N.* (London, 1819) and *An explanation of Captain Sabine's remarks on the late voyage of discovery to Baffin's Bay* (London, 1819). Following his second expedition he published *Narrative of the second voyage of Captain Ross to the Arctic regions in ... 1829–33; compiled principally from the evidence of Captain Ross ... before the committee of the House of Commons* (London, 1834) and *Narrative of a second voyage in search of a north-west passage, and of a residence in the Arctic regions during the years 1829, 1830, 1831, 1832, 1833 ...* (London, [1834]; re-ed., 2v., London, 1835; re-ed., 1v., Paris, 1835; re-ed., Philadelphia and Baltimore, Md., 1835); a French version appeared as *Relation du second voyage fait à la recherche d'un passage au nord-ouest, par sir John Ross ... et de sa résidence dans les régions arctiques ...*, A.-J.-B. Defauconpret, trad. (2v., Paris, 1835). In reply to John Braithwaite's charges about his ship's steam-engine on this trip he wrote *Explanation and answer to Mr. John Braithwaite's "Supplement to Captain Sir John Ross's narrative of a second voyage in the 'Victory,' in search of a north-west passage"* ([London, 1835]). Ross is believed to have twice released comments on his dispute with Sir John Barrow. The authorship of *A letter to John Barrow, Esq., F.R.S., on the late extraordinary and unexpected hyperborean discoveries* (London, 1826), which is signed Alman, has been attributed to him, and he published under his own name *Observations on a work, entitled, "Voyages of discovery and research within the Arctic regions," by Sir John Barrow ..., being a refutation of the numerous misrepresentations contained in that volume* (Edinburgh and London, 1846). He also wrote *A treatise on naval discipline; with an explanation of the important advantages which naval and military discipline might derive from the science of phrenology ...* (n.p., 1825); *A treatise on navigation by steam; comprising a history of the steam engine, and an essay towards a system of the naval tactics peculiar to steam navigation ...* (London, 1828; 2nd ed., 1837); *Memoirs and correspondence of Admiral Lord De Saumarez; from original papers in possession of the family* (2v., London, 1838); *On communication to India, in large steam-ships, by the Cape of Good-Hope; printed by order of the India steam-ship company, and addressed to the British public* (London, 1838); *A short treatise on the duration of the mariner's compass, with rules for its corrections, and diagrams* (London, 1849); and *On intemperance in the Royal Navy* (London, 1852).

John Braithwaite, *Supplement to Captain Sir John Ross's narrative of a second voyage in the "Victory," in search of a northwest passage ...* (London, 1835). [Alexander Fisher], *Journal of a voyage of discovery, to the Arctic regions, performed between the 4th of April and the 18th of November, 1818, in his majesty's ship "Alexander" ...* (London, [1820]). Robert Huish, *The last voyage of Capt. Sir John Ross, R.N. to the Arctic regions; for the discovery of a north west passage ..., compiled from authentic information and original documents, transmitted by William Light, purser's steward to the expedition ...* (London, 1835). Edward Sabine, *Remarks on the account of the late voyage of discovery to Baffin's Bay, published by Captain J. Ross, R.N.* (London, 1819). L. S. Dawson, *Memoirs of hydrography, including brief biographies of the principal officers who have served in H.M. Naval Surveying Service between the years 1750 and 1885* (2v., Eastbourne, Eng., 1885; repr. in 1v., London, 1969). *DNB*. O'Byrne, *Naval biog. dict.* (1849). John Barrow, *Voyages of discovery and research within the Arctic regions, from the year 1818 to the present time ...* (London, 1846). E. S. Dodge, *The polar Rosses: John and James Clark Ross and their explorations* (London, 1973). [John Barrow], "A voyage of discovery ..., by John Ross ...," *Quarterly Rev.* (London), 21 (1819): 213–62. R. I. Murchison, "Address to the Royal Geographical Society of London; delivered at the anniversary meeting on 24th May, 1858," Royal Geographical Soc., *Journal* (London), 28 (1858): cxxx–cxxxii.

ROSS, MARIE-HENRIETTE. *See* LEJEUNE

ROTTERMUND, ÉDOUARD-SYLVESTRE DE, Count de ROTTERMUND, chemist, miller, justice of the peace, inventor, and office holder; b. *c.* 1812 in the province of Volhynia (U.S.S.R.), son of François de Rottermund, Count de Rottermund, and Rosalie de Kaminska, Countess de Rottermund; m. 15 May 1845 Margueritte-Cordelia Debartzch, daughter of Pierre-Dominique Debartzch*; d. 2 Dec. 1859 in Montreux, Switzerland.

Édouard-Sylvestre de Rottermund was born in Russian Poland but little else is known of his early life. He arrived in Canada from Paris in June 1843 and the next day applied to William Edmond Logan*, the new director of the Geological Survey of Canada, for the post of chemist. Logan stated that Rottermund had excellent testimonials and had studied at the École polytechnique in Paris under Jean-Baptiste Dumas. Taken by Logan on an exploratory trip in 1844, Rottermund complained continuously about the insects, the hard work, the canoeing, and the camping, and had to be sent back to Montreal. Officially appointed on 20 Dec. 1844, he absented himself from his laboratory duties often, but the patient Logan explained, "He has been in love, and is to get married. . . . I fancy he will do, though, perhaps, he will require some management." After his marriage in May 1845, Rottermund spent much of his time at the Debartzch home in Saint-Césaire. He persisted in his refusal to comply with Logan's requests and, early in 1846, resigned pleading family business. Logan was not quit of him, however, for in April 1846 Rottermund demanded that Provincial Secretary Dominick Daly* name him director of an independent chemical survey separate from Logan's geological work. This controversy brought Governor Lord CATHCART into the matter and the Legislative Assembly requested all documentation in the case. Logan's correspondence with Rottermund shows great patience in the face of evasions, delays, and non-cooperation, from which Logan concluded, "Mr. de Rottermund's conduct in the whole of this appeared to me very extraordinary."

During his employment with the geological survey, Rottermund wrote a short report on Upper Canada's mineral springs which was published in 1846 without Logan's acquiescence. This report was attacked in Montreal's *British American Journal of Medical and Physical Science* in March 1847 by Henry Holmes Croft*, professor of chemistry at King's College (University of Toronto) and Canada's pre-eminent chemist. In Croft's view, the report, which shows little understanding of chemistry, was a work of pure imagination. Rottermund counter-attacked in the journal the following month with a virulent, mostly *ad hominem* response, but the controversy died out late that year.

By 1846 Rottermund was operating a grist-mill at Saint-Césaire and on 22 June he had become a naturalized citizen. He put his name forward for the magistracy in November and on 28 Jan. 1847 he qualified as a justice of the peace. That year he also patented new designs for a grist-mill and a flour sifter.

In 1849, when the geological survey's report for 1847–48 appeared, Rottermund wrote letters to *L'Avenir* and the *British American Journal* viciously attacking the chemical work of his successor, Thomas Sterry Hunt*. Hunt remained quiet until urged by friends to publish a rebuttal, which he did in January 1850 in the *British American Journal*, easily disposing of his opponent's erroneous chemical ideas.

Croft entered the fray with a letter to the *Globe* backing Hunt and dubbing Rottermund a charlatan. The controversy became so heated that the editor of the *British American Journal* refused to allow Rottermund further replies. His business affairs seemed to run into troubles about the same time and he was sued by Antoine-Aimé Dorion* in 1851.

Early 1854 found Rottermund in Paris, making the acquaintance of Napoleon III and the major figures of French chemistry and geology, who seem to have commented favourably on his "discoveries." At this time the provincial secretary, Pierre-Joseph-Olivier Chauveau*, prompted by Rottermund's brother-in-law, Lewis Thomas Drummond*, requested him to use his influence in Paris to obtain from the French government replacements for the books, maps, and government specimens lost in the burning of the Parliament Building in Montreal in 1849. Rottermund carried out this request. On his return to Canada late in 1854, he testified before the legislature's select committee on the geological survey, criticizing Logan. In 1855 controversy was kindled anew by Rottermund's report to the corporation of the city of Quebec stating his belief that an abundant, workable deposit of pure coal underlay the Upper Town. Although the survey had already shown such a deposit to be impossible, Rottermund raised doubts about Logan's competence in geology.

Now that he was claiming to be a geologist as well as a chemist, his personal charm (to which Logan attested) and connections garnered for him the position of inspector of mines for the Crown Lands Department. In this capacity he undertook an entirely unnecessary geological survey of the shores of lakes Superior and Huron and wrote two reports on this work in 1856 and 1857. Edward John Chapman*, professor of mineralogy at the University of Toronto and an outstanding geologist, reviewed the first report in the *Canadian Journal*, revealing geological inaccuracies and curious methods, and concluded, "We look in vain for a single new fact of any practical or scientific value." At this time Rottermund began signing himself as "former professor of analytical chemistry at l'École Normale de Bruxelles," which seems an improbable claim. According to his own statement he was "recognized by the leading chemists of l'Académie des sciences," but in Canada he was generally seen as a fraud. After a career swirling in controversy, he left Canada in 1857 or 1858 and died in 1859 in Switzerland at the age of 47.

RICHARD A. JARRELL

[Édouard-Sylvestre de Rottermund, Count de Rottermund, is the author of *Report of E. S. de Rottermund, Esquire, chemical assistant to the Geological Survey of the province* (Montreal, 1846), also published as *Rapport de E. S. de*

Roupe

Rottermund, écuyer, chimiste de l'exploration géologique de la province (Montréal, 1846). The report was also issued as part of Can., Prov. of, Legislative Assembly, *App. to the journals*, 1846, app.WW. The report is republished in *Report and critiques of E. S. de Rottermund, Esq., late chemical assistant to the Geological Survey of Canada, in 1846* (Montreal, 1850). The report section of this booklet reprints app.WW in its entirety, and the critique section reprints the correspondence arising out of the report, which was first published as the following articles in *British American Journal of Medical and Physical Science* (Montreal): H. [H.] Croft, "Critical remarks on the labours of E. S. de Rottermund, Esq., late chemist to the provincial geological survey," 2 (1846–47): 289–92; É.-[S.] de Rottermund, "To the editor of the British American Journal," 2 (1846–47): 318, and "Reply to Professor Croft's 'Critical remarks,'" 3 (1847–48): 10–14; H. [H.] Croft, "Reply to Mr. DeRottermund," 3 (1847–48): 36–39, and "Critical remarks on the labours of Mr. de Rottermund, late chemist to the Geological Survey, no.II," 3 (1847–48): 62–63; É.-S. de Rottermund, "Observations sur la partie chimique du rapport de progrès pour l'année 1847–8, de l'exploration géologique du Canada," 5 (1849–50): 201–6; and T. S. Hunt, "Réponse aux observations de É.-S. de Rottermund, Écr., sur la partie chimique du rapport de progrès pour l'année 1847–8, de l'exploration géologique du Canada," 5 (1849–50): 230–33. For a continuation of this debate see Rottermund's letter in *L'Avenir* of 5 Oct. 1850, and Croft's reply in the *Globe* of 14 Nov. 1850.

Rottermund's first account of his surveying expedition is found in his *Report on the exploration of lakes Superior & Huron, by Count de Rottermund* ([Toronto, 1856]), also published as *Rapport sur l'exploration des lacs Supérieur et Huron, par le comte de Rottermund* ([Toronto, 1856]) and as Can., Prov. of, Legislative Assembly, *App. to the journals*, 1856, app.37. A review of this account is found in E. J. Chapman, "Report on the exploration of lakes Superior and Huron, by the Count de Rottermund," *Canadian Journal* (Toronto), new ser., 1 (1856): 446–52. Rottermund's second report of his surveying expedition is found in *Second rapport sur l'exploration des lacs Supérieur et Huron par le comte de Rottermund* (Toronto, 1857), which was also published as Can., Prov. of, Legislative Assembly, *App. to the journals*, 1857, app.5. Rottermund's other writings include "Note sur les mines aurifères de Saint-Laurent situées dans le Bas-Canada (district de Québec)," *Annales des mines* (Paris), 5e sér., 4 (1853): 443–50; "Note de M. de Rottermund sur un instrument qu'il a établi pour mesurer les distances et les niveaux," Soc. géologique de France, *Bull.* (Paris), sér.2, 11 (1853–54): 230–32; and *Rapport géologique de M. de Rottermund à son honneur le maire de Québec* ([Québec, 1855]). R.A.J.]

AUM, P 58, U, Rottermund à Moreau, 18 déc. 1851. PAC, RG 4, C1, 157, file 629; 175, file 3524; 198, file 2334; 200, file 2598; 226, file 1619; 348, file 752; 369, file 1335. Morgan, *Bibliotheca Canadensis*; *Sketches of celebrated Canadians*. B. J. Harrington, *Life of Sir William E. Logan, Kt., LL.D., F.R.S., F.G.S., &c., first director of the Geological Survey of Canada . . .* (Montreal, 1883). Ludwik Kos-Rabcewics-Zubkowski, *The Poles in Canada* (Ottawa and Montreal, 1968). Morris Zaslow, *Reading the rocks: the story of the Geological Survey of Canada, 1842–1972* (Toronto and Ottawa, 1975).

ROUPE, JEAN-BAPTISTE, Roman Catholic priest, seminary administrator, missionary, and Sulpician; b. 9 Jan. 1782 in Montreal, son of Samuel Roupe and Marie-Joseph Clocher; d. there 4 Sept. 1854.

Jean-Baptiste Roupe was descended from a Protestant family whose native town was Linsbourg, Switzerland. His father came to New France in 1757 and was converted to the Roman Catholic faith at Quebec the following year. Jean-Baptiste was born in the family dwelling on Rue du Saint-Sacrement, Montreal, near the house of the Sulpicians, and attended the primary school they ran; he received his classical education from 1794 to 1802 at the Collège Saint-Raphaël (which in 1806 became the Petit Séminaire de Montréal). He was reasonably good in Latin, was noted especially for his diligence as a student, and at that time expressed a desire to join the Sulpicians, a desire not to be fulfilled until some years later. During his final years at the college he served as a regent, and on 23 Sept. 1800 he received the tonsure from Pierre Denaut*, bishop of Quebec. After a brief stay at the Grand Séminaire de Québec, where he undertook theological studies, he received the subdiaconate at Quebec on 30 Oct. 1803; his father had meanwhile settled on him an annuity of 150 *livres* secured by half the property on which he had been born.

Bishop Denaut wanted to found another seminary at Nicolet, and named Roupe, his protégé, as its first director of students. The institution opened in January 1804 under the leadership of Abbé Alexis-Basile Durocher, the local parish priest. Roupe's task was no sinecure. He had to serve concurrently as director, prefect of studies, bursar, professor, and regent, as well as assistant parish priest. On 27 Jan. 1805, when Roupe had completed his theological training, Denaut ordained him priest at Longueuil. After Denaut's death in 1806, Joseph-Octave Plessis*, the new bishop of Quebec, contributed from his own pocket to help Roupe meet the seminary's financial obligations. But observing that Roupe's health was deteriorating, Plessis sent him in August 1807 to serve as assistant priest in the parish of Sainte-Anne at Varennes.

A month later Plessis entrusted Roupe with the Indian mission of Saint-Régis, appointing him to replace Roderic MacDonell who had just died. When he arrived at the mission on 31 October, Roupe set about studying the Mohawk language and he mastered it in a short time. His parish covered a vast territory stretching from the village of Les Cèdres to Kingston in Upper Canada. His ministry among the Iroquois proved barren and difficult because their customs did not accord with his teachings. In addition, Bishop Plessis asked him to undertake the training of young clerics. Accordingly he prepared Joseph Marcoux for the priesthood in 1812 and 1813 and taught him the

Mohawk language; Marcoux subsequently took over the mission of Saint-Régis, in succession to Roupe. During the War of 1812 he exhorted his flock to obey the British authorities. The Americans took the mission by storm during the night of 23 Oct. 1812. Made prisoner, Roupe was soon released. He continued to serve in the mission until June 1813.

Through Bishop Plessis, Roupe then obtained permission from the governor of Lower Canada, Sir George Prevost*, to join the Séminaire de Saint-Sulpice, at Montreal, as a replacement for Michel Leclerc* (who had died the month before) at the mission of Lac-des-Deux-Montagnes (Oka) in the Petite-Nation seigneury. He worked there as a missionary until 1829. From the time of his arrival he devoted himself to spreading the gospel among the Iroquois; he also breathed new vigour into the Confrérie de la Sainte-Famille there. On 26 Oct. 1814 he was made a member of the community of the Grand Séminaire de Montréal. After September 1815 he made two pastoral visits a year to those of his flock scattered in missions along the Ottawa River. He founded the parish of Notre-Dame-de-Bon-Secours (at Montebello) in 1821 and established several other places of worship along the river, in the settlements that became Buckingham and Aylmer and on the Île des Allumettes. It was at this time that Roupe sparked a sharp public controversy with his views on "mixed" marriages between whites and Indians. He was strongly opposed to such marriages but his colleagues did not share his opinions. When a mixed marriage was sought in 1826, Governor Lord Dalhousie [Ramsay*] went to the mission to hear the reasons for Roupe's refusal to solemnize it.

Roupe was recalled to the Petit Séminaire de Montréal on 25 Sept. 1829, and began a new ministry during which he gave his attention to all kinds of charitable organizations. Among others, he reinvigorated the Congrégation des Hommes de Ville-Marie in the period up to 1833. From 1834 he was chaplain to the Confrérie de la Sainte-Famille in the parish of Notre-Dame in Montreal; he also held that office at the Hôtel-Dieu and at St Patrick's Hospital, serving both the Religious Hospitallers of St Joseph and their French-speaking patients. In 1834 as well the superior of the seminary, Joseph-Vincent QUIBLIER, put Roupe's name forward as a candidate to succeed Jean-Jacques Lartigue*, who was then ill, as bishop of Telmesse. That high office, however, went to Ignace Bourget* three years later, after Lartigue had become bishop of Montreal. Roupe continued to discharge the various offices he held until 1854. In addition, he acted as assistant priest of the parish of Montreal from 1851 until his death. There he was responsible for a considerable number of penitents, and his sermons were highly appreciated. He fell ill at the beginning of August 1854 and died on 4 September, apparently of some form of cholera. He was buried under the Cathedral of Notre-Dame in funeral rites presided over by Bishop Bourget.

Like many of his colleagues at the Grand Séminaire de Montréal, Jean-Baptiste Roupe was conspicuous for his willingness to accept every office his superiors gave him. He carried out humble but necessary tasks in sparsely populated missions. Yet he did not hesitate later to take on a host of responsibilities in the rapidly growing parish of Montreal.

J.-BRUNO HAREL

AAQ, 515 CD, I, nos.18–44. ANQ-M, CE1-51, 10 janv. 1782, 6 sept. 1854. Arch. des Religieuses hospitalières de Saint-Joseph (Montréal), Annales, 2. ASQ, C 38. ASSM, 8; 21; 24, Dossier 2; 36; 49. Allaire, *Dictionnaire*, 1: 480–81. Caron, "Inv. de la corr. de Mgr Denaut," ANQ *Rapport*, 1931–32: 173, 228; "Inv. de la corr. de Mgr Plessis," 1927–28: 257, 294; 1932–33: 17. Louise Dechêne, "Inventaire des documents relatifs à l'histoire du Canada conservés dans les archives de la Compagnie de Saint-Sulpice à Paris," ANQ *Rapport*, 1969: 206. Alexis De Barbezieux, *Histoire de la province ecclésiastique d'Ottawa et de la colonisation dans la vallée de l'Ottawa* (4v., Ottawa, 1897), 1: 140–44. Louis Bertrand, *Bibliothèque sulpicienne, ou Histoire littéraire de la Compagnie de Saint-Sulpice* (3v., Paris, 1900), 2: 284–85. Michel Chamberland, *Histoire de Montebello, 1815–1928* (Montréal, 1929), 106–28. Douville, *Hist. du collège-séminaire de Nicolet*, 2: 14, 21. Claude Lessard, *Le séminaire de Nicolet, 1803–1969* (Trois-Rivières, Qué., 1980), 38. Gérard Malchelosse, *La famille Roupe* (Montréal, 1918), 3–6. Maurault, *Le collège de Montréal* (Dansereau; 1967), 194. *Le nord de l'Outaouais* (Ottawa, 1938), 151, 153. Pouliot, *Mgr Bourget et son temps*, 1: 125–26. J.-A. Cuoq, "Anotc kekon," RSC *Trans.*, 1st ser., 11 (1893), sect.I: 137–79. [Antoine Mercier], "Notice sur Messire Jean-Baptiste Roupe," *L'Écho du cabinet de lecture paroissial* (Montréal), 9 (1867): 535–44.

ROUTH, Sir RANDOLPH ISHAM, commissary general and politician; b. 21 Dec. 1782 in Poole, Dorset, England, third son of Richard Routh*, later chief justice of Newfoundland, and his wife, Abigail Eppes; d. 29 Nov. 1858 in London.

Although Randolph Isham Routh may have descended from an old Yorkshire family of Routh, near Beverley, his father settled the family in Poole while he travelled to Newfoundland each year to fulfil the obligations of his post as collector of customs. Randolph Isham studied at Eton College from 1796 to 1803 and entered the commissariat in 1805. Stationed first at Jamaica, he then served in the Netherlands during the Walcheren campaign of 1809 and throughout the Peninsular War, becoming deputy commissary general in 1812 and senior commissariat officer at Waterloo in 1815. From 1816 to 1822 he served at Malta and for the next four years was senior officer in the West Indies. Promoted to the highest office in the

Routh

commissariat service in August 1826, Routh was sent to the Canadas where he remained for the next 17 years.

When Routh arrived at Quebec in 1826, he was in charge of all the financial transactions of the army in the Canadas and was guardian of a military chest with resources often equalling or exceeding those of Lower Canada's provincial treasury. One of his most persistent, though unsuccessful, endeavours was to try to influence the House of Assembly of Lower Canada to adopt British sterling as the official medium of exchange and thus eliminate the confusion resulting from the use of a variety of foreign currencies.

Routh was more effective in his vigorous protest against the proposal in the early 1830s to turn all the financial business of the military over to local banks. In a 17-page report submitted to the British Treasury, he pointed out that the Bank of Montreal was the only colonial bank stable enough to undertake such a commitment, but he argued against this move on the grounds that the directors of the bank would then become the "real capitalists of the country at little personal risk." He also believed that both the efficiency and the secrecy of troop movements would be jeopardized if the commissariat could not act independently of local banks. In 1838 Routh added his protest to that of the commander of the forces, Sir John Colborne*, against the recommendation by Sir George ARTHUR, lieutenant governor of Upper Canada, to have a separate commissariat establishment in that province. Routh's service in British North America included the years of the rebellions of 1837–38, when his department was suddenly faced with wartime conditions and criticized by regimental officers in the field. Lieutenant-Colonel George Cathcart commented that Routh had no notion of organizing a field commissariat and that nothing could have been more complicated or less efficient than his arrangements. Cathcart admitted that part of the confusion arose from Colborne's initial orders at the outbreak of the second rebellion in 1838 to have the troops live at free quarters, which led to plunder by them in the disturbed areas. None the less, Routh was appointed to the Executive Council by Lord Durham [Lambton*] and held office from 2 June 1838 to 10 Feb. 1841.

Routh married first, probably on 26 Dec. 1815, at Paris, Adélaïde-Marie-Joséphine Lamy (Laminière), granddaughter of the secretary general of the Gardes de Corps of Louis XVI. She died at Quebec in 1827. The couple had had five children, of whom Randolph, the eldest son, eventually became commissary general. By 1829 Routh was courting Marie-Louise Taschereau, daughter of Jean-Thomas Taschereau* and sister of the future cardinal Elzéar-Alexandre Taschereau*; he was approximately 30 years her

senior. Louis-Joseph Papineau*, after attending one of the numerous balls at Routh's residence, wrote to his wife: "I spoke at length with Madame [Marie] Taschereau about the widower's merits, his manners, his interest in uniting the two societies, English and French Canadian. The good mother spoke more favourably of his qualities than I and convinced me, inadvertently, that her opposition was designed to obtain better terms for her daughter." The couple were married on 16 Jan. 1830 in the church of the British garrison at Quebec. There were four sons and five daughters of this marriage and his expanding family probably explains Routh's eagerness to buy some 6,599 acres of land along the Rivière Etchemin in the townships of Ware, Cranbourne, and Standon, south of Quebec, a purchase completed some time before 1836.

Knighted in 1841, partly for his long service in the Canadas, Routh returned to England in January 1843 on half pay. At this time he wrote *Observations on the commissariat field service and home defences*, which remained the standard work on the commissariat for many years. From 1845 to 1848 he superintended the distribution of relief in Ireland during the famine, a situation in which he faced unparalleled emergency conditions as a result of successive potato crop failures. When first consulted about the secret purchase of some £100,000 of Indian corn in the United States for relief in Ireland, Routh suggested that one of his Taschereau relatives in Quebec could see to the business discreetly, but the Treasury preferred to let the firm of Baring Brothers undertake the purchase. Routh tried to limit the distribution of corn to the absolutely destitute and in 1847 he unsuccessfully urged that the export of higher-priced grains be prohibited when he became convinced that it was not resulting in an increase in the import of lower-priced food. For his work in Ireland he was created a KCB on 27 April 1848.

Routh's services, not only in the Canadas and Ireland but in the West Indies as well, drew acclaim for the efficiency with which he ran the commissariat operations, the skill with which he cleansed the department of jobbery by eliminating close associations between commissariat officers and contractors, and, above all, his emphasis on proper bookkeeping and auditing of accounts. None challenged his integrity in running the commissariat. Yet he had an eye for lucrative financial transactions outside the department, thus giving military colleagues an opportunity to observe privately and correctly that, "though a good servant to the treasury . . . [he] made his own fortune [in the Canadas] notwithstanding." It was Routh who restored to the commissariat officers their distinctive uniform with epaulettes. A contemporary observed that under the "calm, cautious and carefully reserved" Routh, the "Commissariat was subdued, sobered and raised in the most quiet manner."

ELINOR KYTE SENIOR

Sir Randolph Isham Routh is the author of *Observations on the commissariat field service and home defences*, originally issued in 1845; a second edition was published in London in 1852.

ANQ-Q, CE1-71, 16 janv. 1830. Arch. du monastère des ursulines (Québec), Annales, II: 65, 67; XI: 62–63. PAC, MG 30, D1, 26: 650; RG 8, I (C ser.), 79: 107–13, 121–38; 1274: 162–67. PRO, T 1/8274 (copy at PAC); WO 17/1547: 201. *Gentleman's Magazine*, January–June 1859: 92–93. *Minutes of evidence taken under the direction of a general commission of enquiry, for crown lands and emigration, appointed on the 21st June, 1838, by His Excellency the Right Honorable the Earl of Durham, high commissioner, and governor general of her majesty's colonies in North America* (Quebec, 1839). *Appleton's cyclopædia of American biography*, ed. J. G. Wilson *et al.* (10v., New York, 1887–1924), 5: 336–37. Boase, *Modern English biog.*, 3: 319–20. Borthwick, *Hist. and biog. gazetteer*. Desjardins, *Guide parl.* DNB. G.B., WO, *Army list*, 1838. Morgan, *Sketches of celebrated Canadians*. Prowse, *Hist. of Nfld.* (Thoms and Gill; 1971). P.-G. Roy, *Les cimetières de Québec* (Lévis, Qué., 1941); *La famille Taschereau* (Lévis, 1901). C. B. F. G. Woodham Smith, *The great hunger, Ireland, 1845–1849* (New York, 1922). J.-J. Lefebvre, "La vie sociale du grand Papineau," *RHAF*, 11 (1957–58): 463–516.

ROUVILLE, JEAN-BAPTISTE-RENÉ HERTEL DE. *See* HERTEL

ROWAND, JOHN, fur trader; b. *c.* 1787 in Montreal, son of Dr John Rowand; d. 30 May 1854 at Fort Pitt (Sask.).

John Rowand's boyhood was spent in Montreal. Although his father was a surgeon there, John had acquired only a rudimentary education when he became an apprentice clerk for McTavish, Frobisher and Company, partners in the North West Company, at age 16. His first posting in 1803 was to Fort Augustus (Edmonton, Alta) on the banks of the North Saskatchewan River and for the next decade he was to serve either at the fort or at one of the nearby outposts. Probably some time around 1810 Rowand broke his leg in a fall from his horse while out buffalo hunting. He was rescued by a mixed-blood woman named Lisette (Louise) Humphraville (Ompherville), probably the daughter of Edward Umfreville*, who became his wife *à la façon du pays*. Besides her knowledge of Indian custom, Lisette brought to the marriage a valuable herd of horses which added to her husband's prestige among the native people.

In the summer of 1815, as the conflict at the Red River colony (Man.) escalated because of Governor Miles Macdonell*'s ban on the export of pemmican, Rowand rode overland to the settlement to help defend his company's interests. He witnessed the first dispersal of the colony and the next summer was prepared to take on "those H Bay Scamps" but arrived too late, several days after the battle at Seven Oaks (Winnipeg) [*see* Cuthbert GRANT]. By 1820 Rowand's energetic and able service in the Saskatchewan department had earned him a partnership in the NWC. The next year, as a result of the coalition of the Hudson's Bay Company and NWC, he became a chief trader in the HBC. In 1822, in an attempt to counteract the American threat to the company's trade with the Plains tribes, he was appointed to assist Chief Factor Donald MCKENZIE in the command of the Bow River expedition. A base camp was established for the season up the South Saskatchewan River, but exploring parties along the Red Deer and the Bow rivers found the fur resources of this southern region so poor that the idea of establishing a permanent post was abandoned.

The following year Rowand succeeded to the command of the HBC's Saskatchewan district with headquarters at Fort Edmonton. He was to manage the many responsibilities of the difficult charge successfully for the next 30 years. In addition to its fur returns, Fort Edmonton was also an important centre for provisions. There native hunters traded buffalo meat, which provided hundreds of packs of pemmican each year, and Rowand developed a substantial farm, producing wheat, barley, hay, and potatoes. Fort Edmonton also became a vital link in the HBC's transcontinental transport system; it supplied not only York boats for the navigation of the Saskatchewan River, but also pack-horses for the trans-shipment of cargoes from the Columbia and Peace rivers to Fort Assiniboine (Alta) on the Athabasca River. Every summer Rowand supervised the passage of the large Saskatchewan brigade out to Norway House and York Factory (Man.). Regular in his attendance at the annual meetings of the Council of the Northern Department, where Governor George SIMPSON much valued his support and advice, Rowand was promoted chief factor in 1826 and was named a councillor of Rupert's Land in 1839.

At the time of the coalition of 1821, the Saskatchewan district was losing money, but within a few years, because of Rowand's superior management, it had become one of the most profitable in the Indian country. Much of his success lay in his ability to deal with the Plains Indians who frequented his post, no easy task since the prairies were constantly in a state of unrest due to the warfare between the Blackfoot confederacy and the Crees and the Assiniboins. The Indians, who referred to him as

Rowand

"Iron Shirt" or "Big Mountain," were impressed with his bravery. A little man and quite lame, Rowand was none the less powerful. He was described in Simpson's "Character book" as being "as bold as a Lion" and, in his relations with the Indians, "so daring that he beards their Chiefs in the open camp while surrounded by their Warriors." Wrongdoers, especially Stoney horse thieves, were severely punished, but fairness was the hallmark of Rowand's trade relations: "No one will say that I ever spoilt Indians. . . . I give them due but they must do their duty."

Although a stern disciplinarian, Rowand was, in fact, a warm-hearted man, and many contemporaries remarked on his friendliness, integrity, and sense of humour. Father Pierre-Jean De Smet*, in summing up his positive traits, remarked that Rowand "unites to all the amiable and polite qualities of a perfect gentleman, those of a sincere and hospitable friend; his goodness and paternal tenderness render him a true patriarch amidst his charming and numerous family." Between 1812 and 1832 Rowand and his wife had three boys and four girls. The father was proud of his two surviving sons, John Jr and Alexander, who became an officer in the HBC and a doctor at Quebec respectively. After his youngest son died at school in Red River in 1835, Rowand became increasingly protective of his daughters. He was afraid to send them away to be educated, providing them with a comfortable home in the Big House, an impressive three-storey structure built at Fort Edmonton after 1829. Only one daughter, Nancy, was married during her father's lifetime, to Chief Trader John Edward Harriott*, who was stationed in the district. Rowand was heart-broken when she died in 1850, a year after his wife, his "old friend" of 40 years.

In 1841 Rowand accompanied his close friend Governor Simpson on part of his trip around the world. At Rowand's instigation, they pioneered a shorter, more southerly route across the Rockies via the Bow River. Rowand then went north with Simpson as far as Fort Stikine (Alaska) in the steamship *Beaver*, sailed south to California, and ultimately spent several weeks in Hawaii.

Upon his return to the Saskatchewan district, Rowand became increasingly frustrated with the creeping changes and the general decline in the fur trade. Although a nominal Roman Catholic, he had little enthusiasm for the arrival of missionaries such as the Methodist Robert Terrill Rundle* in 1840 and the Roman Catholic Jean-Baptiste Thibault* in 1842, complaining that "the fort is not a place to keep ministers who are never pleased except when the Fort is full of Indians, doing nothing for the Company or themselves except learning to sing salms." The increased demand for supplies meant that the system of transport became overburdened while, at the same time, the quality of the boatmen declined. Rowand

came to be regarded as a tyrant by the men, who were subject to his frequent volleys of verbal abuse. "When they misbehave," he wrote to Simpson, "I will tell them of it without fearing to hurt their feelings – they must do their duty as I was *made* to do mine." To add to his problems, the late 1840s were lean years; the prairie fires that ravaged the plains and the poor buffalo hunts resulted in little pemmican and starving Indians. Rowand also denounced the free traders who were making serious inroads into the company's monopoly.

In 1847–48 Rowand went on furlough to Montreal, the first time he had been east since 1803. By then he was anxious to retire but could not make up his mind where. It was not until the spring of 1854, knowing he was to be replaced, that he decided to go to Montreal. En route he died suddenly at Fort Pitt in May, apparently of a stroke, while trying to break up a fight among the voyageurs. The chief factor died a wealthy man. He left £7,500 to each of his three daughters, whom he had finally sent to a convent at St Boniface (Man.) in 1853, and £3,000 to each of his sons. One of these daughters, Marguerite, later married James McKay*, an HBC employee who became a prominent Manitoba politician, and another, Sophia, married Chief Factor John H. McTavish. Simpson went to considerable trouble to carry out his friend's request to be buried in Montreal beside his father. Rowand's body was disinterred at Fort Pitt in 1856, was taken to Red River, and then, because Simpson feared that the superstitious voyageurs would throw it overboard, was shipped via York Factory and London to Montreal. An impressive tombstone marks his grave in the Mount Royal Cemetery.

At the time of his death John Rowand was the last of the HBC officers who had been commissioned by the deed poll of 1821. For well over 30 years he had been the most influential white man in the Saskatchewan district and, according to Simpson, "was not surpassed by any officer for unswerving devotion to the public interests."

Sylvia Van Kirk

ANQ-M, CN1-29, 20 avril 1803. PAC, MG 19, A21, ser.1, 16; E1, ser.1, 22 (copies). PAM, HBCA, D.4/18: f.11d; D.4/74: ff.409–10; D.4/75: ff.671a–72; D.5/6: ff.13–19; D.5/10: ff.43–44; D.5/22: ff.371–72. PRO, PROB 11/2199: 777. *Catholic Church records of Pacific northwest* (Munnick). P.-J. De Smet, *Life, letters and travels of Father Pierre-Jean De Smet, S.J., 1801–1873 . . .*, ed. H. M. Chittenden and A. T. Richardson (4v., New York, 1905). William Gladstone, "William Gladstone's diary," ed. Freda Graham, *Lethbridge Herald* (Lethbridge, Alta.), 15 April–25 Nov. 1958. [J.] H. Lefroy, "Sir Henry Lefroy's journey to the north-west in 1843–4," ed. W. S. Wallace, RSC *Trans.*, 3rd ser., 32 (1938), sect.II: 67–96. Simpson, "Character book," *HBRS*, 30 (Williams), 151–236. J. G.

MacGregor, *John Rowand, czar of the Prairies* (Saskatoon, Sask., 1978). Ross Mitchell, "John Rowand, chief factor," *Beaver*, outfit 266 (June 1935): 37–40. H. E. Rawlinson, "Chief Factor John Rowand," *Alberta Hist. Rev.* (Edmonton), 5 (1957), no.2: 9–14; "The portrait of Chief Factor John Rowand," *Beaver*, outfit 293 (summer 1962): 36–37.

ROY, JOSEPH (baptized **Joseph-Marie**), master wood-carver, merchant, militia officer, justice of the peace, politician, and office holder; baptized 8 Dec. 1771 in the parish of Saint-Henri-de-Mascouche (at Mascouche), Que., son of Charles Roy, a farmer, and Élizabeth Beauchamp; m. 23 Feb. 1819 Émilie L. Lusignany, daughter of Charles Lusignan* and Madeleine Laforce, in Montreal, and they had two sons and one daughter; d. there 31 July 1856.

Joseph Roy, who came from a rural family, showed a talent for wood-carving early in his life. He left his native parish around 1790 and went to Montreal, where he served an apprenticeship under a wood-carver named Pasteur. Little is known of his career as a craftsman, but it seems that at the beginning of the first decade of the 19th century he owned and operated a workshop in Montreal.

Having followed evening courses apparently to acquire some knowledge in the field of commerce, Roy decided to abandon wood-carving for a new career. The transition occurred between 1803 and 1805, at the time he opened a general store on Rue Saint-Paul near Bonsecours market. He built up a large clientele over the years, and was successful enough to be accounted one of the largest merchants in Montreal. In 1820 he was a director of the Montreal Fire Insurance Company, which had its head office on Rue Notre-Dame. There he came in contact with Augustin Cuvillier*, its president, and John Molson*, its vice-president.

In the course of his career as a merchant, Roy became involved in the political life of the colony. He stood as a candidate in a by-election for Montreal in 1811. Having been an ensign in Montreal's 3rd Militia Battalion from at least 1804, he benefited from the strong support of citizens who favoured the Canadian party. He was, however, defeated by James STUART, the former solicitor general. Promoted lieutenant in the same battalion in 1812 and captain two years later, Roy was also called upon to assume numerous public offices. He consistently proved an ardent Patriote and a defender of the interests of his fellow French Canadians. He was serving as a justice of the peace in 1832 when three French Canadians were killed by British soldiers during a by-election in Montreal West. He did not hesitate to issue warrants for the arrest of Lieutenant-Colonel Alexander Fisher MacIntosh and Captain Henry Temple, the two officers of the 15th Foot whom the supporters of Daniel Tracey*, the Patriote candidate, held responsible for the

incident. As a result, he lost his commission as justice of the peace and did not receive another until 1843.

Roy also took an interest in municipal politics, and at one period he had to carry out municipal and provincial responsibilities concurrently. He was among those chosen when the citizens of Montreal elected their first town councillors on 3 June 1833. The following year he became the member for Montreal East in the House of Assembly, where he sat from 22 Nov. 1834 to 27 March 1838. In addition he was re-elected a town councillor in 1835. He declined the office of mayor in 1842, but accepted that of alderman, which he held for the next two years.

Roy was a full-fledged member of the Patriote party, and an intimate friend of Louis-Joseph Papineau* and Édouard-Raymond FABRE. He supported the 92 Resolutions in 1834 and the following year helped found the Union Patriotique. This society, with Denis-Benjamin Viger* as president and Roy and Jacob DE WITT as vice-presidents, undertook to support the Patriote party's demands, particularly those connected with obtaining responsible government and the election of legislative councillors. Roy did not take a radical position as the rebellion of 1837–38 unfolded but continued to favour constitutional struggle without recourse to arms. He was not bothered by the authorities when they arrested numerous Patriotes. In 1842 he endorsed the campaign launched by *La Minerve* to raise the funds needed to finance the return of the exiled Patriotes [*see* Édouard-Raymond Fabre]. The following year he also signed a collective letter sent to John Arthur Roebuck*, a member of the British House of Commons, asking him to seek a pardon from the queen for these Patriotes. After Papineau returned from exile in 1845 Roy gave him his support, and in 1852 Roy and several other leading citizens signed a letter urging him to stand for election in the riding of Deux-Montagnes.

Roy's business had meanwhile changed in nature, and he now specialized in the sale of "church articles, silverware and vestments, brocaded damask, stoles, gold braid and fringes." His principal customers were, of course, the clergy, for whom he imported items from Europe. His reputation was excellent, his store flourishing, but in 1852 a fire at the end of the summer forced him to liquidate his business. In January 1853 Roy published an announcement in *Le Pays* informing his clientele that he had sold his business to J.-C. Robillard of New York. The sale marked the end of his business career, for he was then 81 years old.

Joseph Roy died in Montreal on 31 July 1856 "after a long illness." At the time of his death he was still serving as a justice of the peace, and since 1845 he had performed the duties of commissioner for the building and repair of churches. An obituary was published on 2 Aug. 1856 in *Le Pays*, the Rouge paper he had helped found in 1852. It paid tribute to "one of the most highly esteemed citizens of Montreal, [one of] the rare men who have always professed the same political principles, without once giving way to the temptations or threats [attached] to authority."

FRANCE GALARNEAU

ANQ-M, CE1-51, 23 févr. 1819, 2 août 1856; CN1-32, 15 janv. 1846, 10 mai 1852; CN1-194, 23 déc. 1801. AP, Saint-Henri (Mascouche), Reg. des baptêmes, mariages et sépultures, 8 déc. 1771. Arch. de la ville de Montréal, Documentation, Biog. des conseillers, Joseph Roy. ASQ, Fonds Viger–Verreau, Sér.O, 0140. AUM, P 58, U, Roy à Louis Guy, 29 oct. 1830; Roy à J.-B. Mason, 16 oct. 1840. PAC, MG 30, D1, 26: 721–38; RG 68, General index, 1651–1841; 1841–67. L'Ère nouvelle, 7 août 1856. Le Pays, 15, 22 janv., 16 déc. 1852; 17 janv. 1853; 2, 5 août 1856. Quebec Gazette, 27 March, 27 Nov. 1817; 6 April, 25 May, 7 Dec. 1820; 25 Jan., 2 Aug. 1821; 8 Dec. 1823. André Giroux et al., Inventaire des marchés de construction des Archives nationales du Québec à Montréal, 1800–1830 (2v., Ottawa, 1981). Montreal almanack, 1842, 1845–50, 1853–54. Montreal directory, 1819, 1842–45, 1848–50, 1852–55. T.-P. Bédard, Histoire de cinquante ans (1791–1841), annales parlementaires et politiques du Bas-Canada, depuis la Constitution jusqu'à l'Union (Québec, 1869). Camille Bertrand, Histoire de Montréal (2v., Paris et Montréal, 1935–42), 2. France Galarneau, "L'élection pour le Quartier-Ouest de Montréal en 1832: analyse politico-sociale" (thèse de MA, univ. de Montréal, 1978). Hist. de Montréal (Lamothe et al.). J.-L. Roy, Édouard-Raymond Fabre. L.-O. David, "M. Joseph Roy," L'Opinion publique, 21 nov. 1872: 553–54.

RUDOLF, WILLIAM, merchant, justice of the peace, office holder, militia officer, and politician; b. 6 June 1791 in Lunenburg, N.S., son of John Christopher Rudolf and Elizabeth Koch (Cook), and grandson of Leonard Christopher Rudolf, one of the "Foreign Protestants" who founded Lunenburg in 1753; m. first 23 Sept. 1824 Catherine Stevens of Halifax; m. secondly 7 Nov. 1833 Anna Matilda Oxner in Lower La Have, N.S., and they had six children; d. 1 Jan. 1859 in Lunenburg.

Supposedly descended from the von Rudolf family of Thuringia (German Democratic Republic), William Rudolf belonged to one of Lunenburg's élite families. For many years his establishment, William Rudolf and Company, engaged successfully in the West India trade from a store on Montague Street. From 1819 to his death he was a justice of the peace, and at various times he served as postmaster, registrar of deeds, and lieutenant-colonel of the 1st battalion of the county militia regiment.

A member of the House of Assembly for Lunenburg County from 1826 to 1838, Rudolf was appointed to the Legislative Council on its establishment in 1838 and remained a member until his death. Always zealous in supporting the interests of the Church of England, but otherwise only a moderate tory, he stands out for his actions in 1848 and 1849, which permitted the reformers to adapt the existing governmental system to the requirements of responsible government without creating a constitutional impasse.

When James Boyle UNIACKE's reform government came to power in 1848, it filled up the five vacancies in the Legislative Council with its own appointees. Even then, however, it had only 9 supporters to the tories' 12, although the tory majority was, in effect, reduced to one by the prolonged absence of the ailing Robert Molleson Cutler and the inability of president Simon Bradstreet ROBIE to vote except to break a tie. Arriving late for the session of 1848, Rudolf discovered that the council had already proposed amendments to the first of the reform government's principal measures, the judges bill, which in essence permitted a judge of the Supreme Court to be removed on the joint address of the legislature. When the assembly declined to accept the amendments, the council decided, by 10 to 9, not to adhere to them, Rudolf's vote making that outcome possible. Similarly, the civil list bill, which transferred the casual revenues of the crown to the provincial assembly in return for a guarantee of some of the principal officials' salaries, and the departmental bill, the very keystone of the new system, which required two responsible finance officers, a financial secretary and a receiver general, to sit in the Executive Council, passed the Legislative Council only because of Rudolf's vote.

Late again for the session of 1849, Rudolf missed the events of 14 February, the most exciting day in the history of Nova Scotia's Legislative Council. The legislature having been requested by Colonial Secretary Lord Grey to reconsider the departmental bill, the tories in the council took advantage of the absence of Rudolf and of new reform member William McKeen, who was delayed by a heavy snowstorm, to press for the adoption of an address withdrawing the council's assent to the bill. Only the action of the new reform president, Michael Tobin, who voted as an ordinary member, a practice of the lord chancellor in the House of Lords not hitherto adopted in Nova Scotia, created the tie vote that then caused the tory motion to be defeated. Later in the session Rudolf joined the reformers in confirming the council's support of the bill.

Although the Acadian Recorder suggested that Rudolf was likely to join the reformers, he made no move in that direction. Indeed, on matters unrelated to the effecting of responsible government, he behaved much as before; thus, in 1849 he joined his fellow tories in defeating a private member's bill that would have put all the denominational colleges on the same footing by repealing the permanent annual grant to

King's College. Amazingly, despite Rudolf's support of reform bills which the tories, including Anglican Bishop John Inglis* in his capacity as councillor, fought tooth and nail, he somehow escaped the criticism of tory newspapers and his fellow tory councillors. Since Rudolf did nothing else of great consequence in more than 30 years as assemblyman and councillor, and indeed seldom spoke, his sole claim to distinction as a legislator rests upon his common sense decision that "pressure of public opinion . . . could not long be pent up by so feeble a barrier" as a majority of one in the Legislative Council.

J. MURRAY BECK

PANS, Biog., Rudolf family, genealogy (mfm.); MG 3, 295–99. N.S., Legislative Council, *Journal and proc.*, 31 March, 4, 6 April 1848; 14 Feb., 5 March 1849. *Acadian Recorder*, 25 Sept. 1824; 9 Nov. 1833; 1848–49. *Morning Chronicle* (Halifax), 1848–49. *Novascotian*, 1848–49. *Directory of N.S. MLAs* [William Rudolf's biog. mistakenly appears under the name of his father, [John] Christopher Rudolf]. Beck, *Government of N.S.*, 103–4; *Joseph Howe*, vol.2. W. P. Bell, *The "foreign Protestants" and the settlement of Nova Scotia . . .* (Toronto, 1961), 411–12. M. B. DesBrisay, *History of the county of Lunenburg* (2nd ed., Toronto, 1895), 113.

RUSSELL, JOSEPH, businessman, shipbuilder, and office holder; b. 17 Aug. 1786 in Clackmannan, Scotland, son of Thomas Russell and Jannett ——; m. 20 Sept. 1819 in Chatham, N.B., Ann Agnes Hunter, also from Clackmannan, and they had four sons and five daughters; d. 10 March 1855 in Great Salt Lake City (Salt Lake City, Utah).

Joseph Russell met with success in life, from his service in the Royal Navy beginning at age 12 to his role as a major financier of the Church of Jesus Christ of the Latter-Day Saints (also known as the Mormon Church) in his sixties. Little is known of his early years, but New Brunswick legend claims that he was a midshipman on Horatio Nelson's *Vanguard* at the battle of the Nile in 1798. Russell's arrival in New Brunswick was unheralded and unrecorded; his first documented activity is his marriage in 1819. By 1826 he was the owner of several buildings in Chatham, one of which was the King's Arms, a hotel he also operated. As the focal point in the community, this inn was the site of a dance school, the sheriff's tax sales, and meetings of the fire company, the chamber of commerce, and the agricultural society.

Although shipbuilding is the activity for which Russell is best known in New Brunswick, he apparently did not become involved in the industry until 1827. That year he built and was one-third owner of a 387-ton schooner. Shipbuilding became his profession after fire destroyed his hotel and two other buildings on 19 Jan. 1831. The following year he purchased Francis Peabody*'s yard in Chatham and began constructing vessels as large as 732 tons at the rate of one a year. He sold this yard to Joseph Cunard* in 1839 and purchased John Fraser's shipbuilding establishment on Beaubears Island.

The new yard was ideal: there was room to expand, and ships of 1,000 tons could be launched there. As well, river and land traffic to the upper Miramichi and Fredericton passed near by, and the location was remote enough to support a general merchandising business. Between 1839 and 1850 Russell built 21 square-rigged vessels ranging in size from 354 to 850 tons; five were launched during his peak year of 1844. It was at the height of this activity that he hired John Harley* as his master builder and George Burchill as his business manager; these two men ran a successful operation for Russell. The firm's primary supplier and the purchaser of its ships was the British firm of Rankin, Gilmour and Company and its Miramichi branch, Gilmour, Rankin and Company [*see* Alexander RANKIN]. The relationship was a personal as well as a business one, with partners of the Liverpool firm spending the winter with Russell at Beaubears and not in Douglastown at their Miramichi branch.

Russell's success in shipbuilding was not reflected in his attempt in 1837, with six other businessmen, to establish the Bank of Miramichi. Although incorporated in January 1838, the bank was unable to sell shares beyond the initial subscription of £7,000, and did not open.

Russell did not neglect public responsibilities. He helped organize the Chatham Fire Company in 1824 and served as a fireman; 15 years later Captain Russell was still being praised for his efforts in containing fires. He was a member of the grand jury and overseer of the poor in Chatham in 1832. Although he never held elected office, he was involved in some minor political efforts and held appointed positions. In 1835 he was a member of the delegation which presented Lieutenant Governor Sir Archibald Campbell* with a petition from the citizens of Chatham asking that the increase in timber fees be rescinded. The petition was unsuccessful. Following the rebellions of 1837–38 in the Canadas, Russell's resolution "detesting the behaviour of the rebels in Lower Canada and offering praise to those restoring order and crushing rebellion" was passed at a Chatham businessmen's meeting. On 12 Feb. 1840 he was one of 17 men who successfully petitioned to have Richard Marshall Clarke, high sheriff of Northumberland County, removed for abuse of his office. After he established his business on Beaubears Island, he was overseer of the poor for Nelson Parish from 1840 to 1842 and was again a member of the grand jury in 1844 and in 1846. In the latter year he delivered a welcoming speech on behalf of the grand jury to Judge George Frederick STREET of

Russell

the Supreme Court on his arrival in the county to hold his circuit court sessions.

Russell was a founding member of the Anglican-oriented Miramichi Sunday School Society in 1832, and was a member of the first and several subsequent executive committees. The Russell family converted to Mormonism, probably as early as 1840 or 1841 when the missionary Alfred Dixon visited the Miramichi, but this conversion did not preclude involvement in other social and religious activities. In January 1841 the North British Society (after 11 April 1846 the Highland Society of New Brunswick at Miramichi) was established and Russell was not only an original member but also served as a director from 1841 until 1847. Russell's wife was elected an executive member of the Miramichi Ladies Bible Society on 29 Sept. 1843 and remained a member until 1847.

The family moved to Beaubears Island in 1846 or 1847, and the move meant a cessation of most of their civic and social involvement. Russell may have delayed changing his place of residence until his children were beyond school age. But the timing may also have been the result of religious persecution. He was a devout Mormon by this time, and in the winter of 1847–48, while trying to address an indoor meeting of Mormons in Chatham, he was harassed by a crowd. He attempted to reason with them but, despite his former association with the town, his civic involvement, and his age, he was physically beaten so that he had to stop preaching.

Russell's involvement with the Mormon Church continued to grow. In anticipation of its projected mission, a 627-ton barque launched in 1846 was named *Zion's Hope* and he sailed with it on its maiden voyage to Liverpool to offer it to the British church to carry emigrants to California on their way to Deseret (Utah). However, when the British church members were unwilling to operate the ship and to finance its voyage, the offer lapsed.

After meetings in Boston in 1848 with Wilford Woodruff, one of the 12 apostles of the Mormon Church, Russell made plans to sell his business and to move to Deseret. Woodruff maintained contact with Russell during that winter and went to Miramichi in July 1849. The two travelled to Bedeque (Central Bedeque), P.E.I., and re-established a church there, before parting company at Shediac, N.B., on 5 August. Russell continued his efforts to sell his business but an auction advertised for 12 September did not take place. Economic conditions were generally depressed and only the previous year the Cunard yard, the largest in the area, had gone bankrupt. Then, on 29 September, Harley and Burchill agreed to buy the business, tentatively valued at £750, although Russell claimed it was worth between £6,000 and £7,500. The final price of £1,000

for both business and inventory was set as Russell was about to set sail from the Miramichi for the last time.

The Russells probably left the Miramichi on the last ship that he had built, the *Omega*, when it sailed for Liverpool on 24 June 1850. There, he settled his accounts with his long-time mentors, Rankin, Gilmour and Company, and collected what was due to him, some £11–12,000. He also met with two of the Mormon apostles to discuss the creation of the Deseret Manufacturing Company. This firm was to manufacture beet sugar in Utah territory, thus eliminating the Mormons' dependence on imported sugar. When it was incorporated on 22 Aug. 1851, Russell's contribution of £4,500 made him the principal shareholder. He left Liverpool late in 1851 to set up the company, the machinery for which, sent from England, came overland from New Orleans. He was totally dissatisfied with the operations of the company, and it was dissolved on 5 March 1853. The enterprise was reorganized but was never successful; Russell died on 10 March 1855, without seeing it finally fail.

In neither New Brunswick nor Utah was Joseph Russell a dominant figure, but in both places he was respected and successful. In the Morman Church he had access to the leader, Brigham Young, and at his funeral in Utah one of the Mormon apostles delivered the eulogy. On the Miramichi he had been a successful shipbuilder and his community efforts were publicly praised. He had built 29 reputable ships, and had amassed $70,000 by the time he retired in 1850.

BURTON GLENDENNING

Church of Jesus Christ of Latter-Day Saints, Hist. Dept. (Salt Lake City, Utah), Journal hist. of the Church, Alfred Dixon, letter, 5 Oct. 1841; Patriarchal blessings, 12: 335; F. D. Richards, diary, 29 Aug. 1851; Wilford Woodruff, diaries, box 2, folder 3, 1848–49, especially 15 Feb. 1849; box 3, folder 1, 1855; Brigham Young coll., church related businesses, constitution of the Deseret Manufacturing Company, 22 Aug. 1851; miscellaneous minutes, box 47, folders 7–8. PANB, MBU, II/8/3/1; II/13/5/4; RG 18, RS153, A7–8; I7/1. *Highland Society of New Brunswick at Miramichi, A.D. 1847; incorporated 11th day of April 1846* (London, 1847). *Latter-Day Saints' Millennial Star* (Liverpool, Eng.), 17 (1855): 346. *Gleaner* (Chatham, N.B.), 1829–50. *Mercury* (Miramichi, N.B.), 1826–29. Burton Glendenning, "The Burchill lumbering firm, 1850–1906: an example of nineteenth century New Brunswick entrepreneurship" (MA thesis, Concordia Univ., Montreal, 1978). Louise Manny, *Ships of Miramichi: a history of shipbuilding on the Miramichi River, New Brunswick, Canada, 1773–1919* (Saint John, N.B., 1960). Grant Nielsen, *Joseph Russell, Miramichi shipbuilder and financier* (Brossard, Que., 1980). John Rankin, *A history of our firm, being some account of the firm of Pollok, Gilmour and Co. and its offshoots and connections, 1804–1920* (2nd ed., Liverpool, 1921).

RYKERT, GEORGE, militia officer, teacher, surveyor, merchant, politician, and office holder; b. 8 Aug. 1797 in Rhinebeck, N.Y., son of Zacherius and Catharine Reickert (Reichert, Rikert); m. 31 Oct. 1827 Ann Maria Mittleberger in Montreal, and they had three sons and a daughter; d. 1 Nov. 1857 in St Catharines, Upper Canada.

A member of a Lutheran family of Germanic origin, George Rykert came to the Niagara District of Upper Canada in about 1810. During the War of 1812 he served with the 1st Lincoln Militia, which saw action in the skirmishes near St Davids in July 1814. He subsequently settled at St Catharines, where he taught school and on 26 Nov. 1818 took the oath of allegiance to the crown. After training under Charles Kinsey Fell, a Pelham Township surveyor, he qualified on 9 Nov. 1821 as a deputy provincial land surveyor, an occupation which he practised until shortly before his death. He conducted surveys throughout the Niagara District, especially for the "German" settlers in the Jordan area, and participated with varying success in engineering projects throughout the province.

In 1826 Rykert laid out a village plot for St Catharines, which was beginning to grow as a result of the construction of the adjacent Welland Canal. With Samuel Clowes, an experienced civil engineer, he also completed in that year a survey and estimates for a canal system on the St Lawrence River. In 1827 Rykert, James Simpson, and Thomas Adams formed a company to build the Smiths Falls section of the Rideau Canal but their failure to complete the contract resulted in the firm's dissolution about 1829 and a prolonged legal dispute with the British military.

Rykert's association with the Mittlebergers, a Montreal family active in the supply and financing of Upper Canadian merchants, was probably the major factor in his decision to enter business after his attempt at canal construction. In 1829 he and his brother-in-law John Mittleberger opened a general store and wharf in St Catharines. With Mittleberger and Beacher Benham, he later expanded into distilling and grist-milling. The supply of goods from Montreal and the subsequent sale of produce there were normally handled by commission agents such as Charles Mittleberger. Rykert gradually became heavily indebted to Montreal businessmen, including Peter McGILL and Robert ARMOUR. The business periodically suffered losses in the grain trade but, shored up by the regional prosperity generated by the Welland Canal, Rykert experienced modest success until the mid 1830s and acquired various local positions. He was a founding subscriber, and later trustee, of Grantham Academy, established in St Catharines in 1829, and four years later he received his first commission of the peace for the Niagara District.

Supported by his long-time friend William Hamil-ton Merritt*, the influential St Catharines businessman and politican, Rykert contested the seat for 2nd Lincoln in the provincial election of 1834. Described by the *British American Journal* as "a Steadfast *Reformer*, (not a *Humite* revolutionist) – and an opponent of the 'church and state' doctrine of the Tories," he defeated radical reformer William Woodruff with a moderate reform platform. Though a member of the Church of England himself, through his entire political career Rykert advocated the sale of Upper Canada's clergy reserves and the application of the proceeds to public works, education, and the needs of all religious denominations, including the Tunkers and the Mennonites. Re-elected in 1836, he "generally acted together" with Merritt and they "voted uniformly in the direction of improvements." Rykert served as chairman of a parliamentary committee on banking, which proposed the formation of district banks; both he and Merritt supported a bill to establish a district bank at St Catharines, an institution they had sought since 1831 owing to the "largely increased business" stimulated by canal operations. In the growing climate of hostility from reformers towards the Welland Canal, Rykert, who had withdrawn his stock in 1825 for "various causes," denied in 1836 that he had profited from the venture and recommended public control of the canal, which he regarded as a "fine thing for St. Cath^s and the adjoining places."

Beginning in 1836, largely on issues relating to Lower Canada, he began moving from moderate reform politics to compact toryism, and a position of ruinous political divergence from Merritt. He firmly opposed the much-debated Upper Canadian annexation of Montreal, which Merritt supported. Union of the provinces and Upper Canada's economic and cultural subjugation, he argued, would follow and the rebellion of 1837 only served to strengthen this belief. In the turbulent weeks of December 1837 Rykert, citing a lack of efficient militia officers, lobbied without success to secure a captaincy in the 1st Regiment of Lincoln militia and reputedly rejected a subaltern's appointment. By early January 1838 he had, however, assumed command of a cavalry company although he saw no action. Rykert had reacted vehemently towards William Lyon Mackenzie*'s proclamation of a provisional government on Navy Island in the Niagara River, applauding the destruction in December 1837 of the steamer *Caroline* [see Sir Allan Napier MacNab*], which had served the rebel forces there. During the resulting border tensions, which were marked by sporadic rebel raids and rumours of American complicity, he deplored the encroachment of republicanism, the permissive response of the British government, and French Canadian insurgence on another frontier. "There is no doubt in my mind the next brush will be on the Niagara Frontier," he informed Christopher Alexander Hagerman*. "We *must* be prepared to meet them ['the Rabble of Buffalo'] – I trust we shall have some assistance from the other side of the Lake. . . . I have great fears that we shall be attacked in rear by the people in the Southern part of our District."

During the early months of 1838, as rebellion subsided in Upper Canada and debate in the assembly resumed, Rykert became increasingly fearful of renewed hostility and resentful towards the military and government authorities. He lamented his legislative presence in Toronto. "It is disgusting to see the train hanging about the Govt office," he confided to Charles Mittleberger. "Every little puppy connected in the remotest degree to the family Compact of this city is dubbed Col. or Major." The rebellion had convinced Rykert that only a greater number of political representatives from Upper Canada could counter the political, cultural, and economic evils which he foresaw in provincial union. "I have no desire to be connected with your french rebels," he bluntly told Mittleberger in January 1838. "We have enough to do to keep down our own vagabonds." In 1839, following the release of the famous report from Lord Durham [Lambton*], Rykert briefly recognized the principle of union but, overwhelmed by personal antagonisms towards Roman Catholicism, the French language, and imperial concessions since the conquest, he soon resumed his open opposition to union and responsible government.

Rykert's sense of crisis and extreme conservatism, which were particularly acute even given the hostility in the wake of the rebellion in Upper Canada, were intensified by business difficulties (possibly related to the depression of 1836–37) and perhaps by the death in 1838 of his young daughter. In 1836 he had sought unsuccessfully a commercial association with Merritt. Rykert was forced to discontinue credit transactions with store customers in January 1839 as a result of the "inconvenience and embarrassment" caused by losses in "flour matters" and by his over-extension of credit. In August his partnerships with Mittleberger and Benham were dissolved as part of a complicated business reorganization which was completed about 1841.

In spite of his withdrawal from business, Rykert entered the electoral campaign of 1840–41, the first of the union era, anticipating strong support in St Catharines and several key townships. He was unexpectedly opposed by Merritt, whose moderate reform platform of popular union politics and "commercial and industrial improvement" underscored the growing obsolescence of Rykert's political position. His opposition to union and responsible government, continued antagonism towards the United States, and desperate plea for the continuation of the direct "British connexion" in the Canadas (the hallmarks of tory groups bypassed by the mainstream

of politics) produced a bitter and "truly astonishing" rearguard campaign over which Merritt's supporters and such journalists as James H. Sears rode roughshod. Rykert's accusations that Merritt had resorted to "bribery and corruption" quickly drew counter-allegations that Rykert had used gangs of Orangemen to control polls but had "tumbled *flat* into the ditch of political degradation."

Confronting the realities of political defeat and commercial retreat, Rykert pursued a number of county and district offices between 1841 and 1844 without much success. He nevertheless retained some local prominence as a boundary line commissioner, rebellion losses commissioner, militia officer, Grantham Township councillor, and warden of St George's Church. In 1843 he secured the newly opened St Catharines agency of the Commercial Bank of the Midland District, an appointment which had been facilitated by his political alignment with its president, the staunch Kingston tory John Solomon Cartwright*.

Although direct political influence had been wrested from him, Rykert viewed with intense partisan rancour the progress of negotiations over that "fatal absurdity," responsible government, and the degree of control exercised by Louis-Hippolyte La Fontaine* in parliament in 1842–43. "Either through imbecility, or something worse," Governor Sir Charles Bagot* had "bartered away the Queens prerogative with a reckless french faction to the imminent danger of our connection." The resignation of the executive and the prorogation of the legislative assembly in late 1843 [see Robert BALDWIN] sparked Rykert's hopes for a tory resurgence. He revelled in such "stirring times" and urged Cartwright "to take office if asked even at some sacrifice, rather than allow the Govt. again to fall into the hands of the 'Philistines.'" In the 1844 election Rykert once more failed to oust Merritt. According to an obituary, however, he "was afterwards thoroughly convinced of the justice and wisdom of the decision of the majority" on the question of responsible government.

The incorporation of St Catharines in 1845 drew the former councillor back into municipal politics. A member of the town's police board (1845, 1848–49), Rykert promoted the formation of a fire brigade, the erection of a market and town hall, and the construction of the Great Western Rail-Road. Privately he participated in the new businesses and institutions fostered by the reconstruction of the Welland Canal (completed in 1845) and the province-wide boom of the 1850s. He held the presidency of the St Catharines Building Society in 1850 and by 1852 agencies for the British America Fire and Life Assurance Company, the Colonial Life Assurance Company, and the Church of England Life Assurance Company. A director in 1853, he was president from 1854 to 1857 of the Port Dalhousie and Thorold

Railway, which was to connect with the Great Western just south of St Catharines. He was elected to town council in 1855, and in 1856–57 served as reeve of St Catharines and warden of Lincoln County.

Following the Midland Bank's closure of his St Catharines agency in July 1856 because of diminishing financial resources, Rykert toured England, Ireland, and Europe in a futile bid to arrest the chest cancer that afflicted him. Upon returning he nevertheless resumed his banking interests in St Catharines, where "facilities are wholly inadequate to the business of the place" as he optimistically declared in December in an effort to raise capital from Merritt and others to establish a branch of the Union Bank of Canada. That same month his own financial situation, which had possibly worsened since his return, necessitated his mortgaging of property.

In September 1857 Rykert's debilitating illness forced his confinement to his residence, where "the friend of the farmer, merchant and mechanic" died. His funeral and procession attracted over 500 people, including the town's fire brigades, representatives of Grantham Academy, and a large masonic cortège led by a "rather unusual feature – an excellent Band."

DAVID ROBERTS

AO, MS 74, packages 34, 36; MS 393; RG 1, A-I-1, 10; A-I-6, 11–12, 16–18, 20–22, 25; RG 22, ser.235, will of George Rykert. AUM, P 58, U, Rykert to Mittleberger, 1, 10, 14 March 1832; 15, 18 Jan., 23, 28 Feb., 27 April, 11 June, 27 Dec. 1838 (transcripts at PAC). City of St Catharines Arch. (St Catharines, Ont.), Police Board and Council, minute-books, 1845–57 (mfm. at AO). MTL, "Reichert-Rikert-Rykert: a record of the descendants and ancestors of Zachariah Reichert . . . ," comp. S. H. Riker and Carroll Rikert (East Northfield, Mass., 1961) (typescript). Niagara North Land Registry Office (St Catharines), Abstract index to deeds, St Catharines, I (mfm. at AO, GS 2030); Deeds, St Catharines, 1847–76 (mfm. at AO). PAC, MG 24, E1, 11, 16, 18, 22, 26; I8, 28; I26, 15; RG 5, A1: 24816, 53656, 61204–6, 63672–79, 65330–36, 66389–91, 66700–1, 88931–33, 96368–76, 106975–76, 107901–6, 108545–46, 112872–78, 113122–25, 114487–94, 116164–65, 118185–88, 134135–243; C1, 3, 7–9, 11–12, 39, 75, 93, 101, 131, 190; RG 8, I (C ser.), 45, 52, 54–55, 58, 60, 435; RG 9, I, B7, 21. PRO, WO 55/865 (mfm. at PAC). QUA, J. S. Cartwright papers. *Arthur papers* (Sanderson). [Seymour Phelps], *St. Catharines A to Z, by Junius, 1856* ([St Catharines], 1967). *Select British docs. of War of 1812* (Wood), vol.3, pt.I. *British American Journal* (St Catharines), 17 June, 15, 22 July, 30 Sept., 10, 14, 28 Oct. 1834. *Christian Guardian*, 1836–40. *Constitutional* (St Catharines), 1855–57. *Daily Spectator, and Journal of Commerce*, 1857. *Royal Standard* (Toronto), 1836–37. *St. Catharines Journal* (St Catharines), 1826–57. *Semi-Weekly Post* (St Catharines), 1857. *Canada directory*, 1851. *Canadian biog. dict.*, vol.1. *Cyclopædia of Canadian biog.* (Rose and Charlesworth), vol.1. E. F. Bush, *The builders of the Rideau Canal, 1826–32* (Can., National Hist. Parks and Sites Branch, *Manuscript report*, no.185, Ottawa, 1976), 61–63. Careless, *Union of the Canadas*. Craig, *Upper Canada*. J. N. Jackson, *St. Catharines, Ontario; its early years* (Belleville, Ont., 1976). J. N. Jackson and John Burtniak, *Railways in the Niagara peninsula: their development, progress and community significance* (Belleville, 1978). J. P. Merritt, *Biography of the Hon. W. H. Merritt . . .* (St Catharines, 1875). S. F. Wise and R. C. Brown, *Canada views the United States: nineteenth-century political attitudes* (Seattle, Wash., and London, 1967). H. V. Nelles, "Loyalism and local power: the district of Niagara, 1792–1837," *OH*, 58 (1966): 99–114.

S

SANDOM, WILLIAMS, naval officer; b. *c.* 1785 in England; m. 12 March 1844 Jane Gabrielle Constables; d. 15 Aug. 1858 near Lowestoft, England.

In April 1798, "at an early age," Williams Sandom entered the Royal Navy as a midshipman, under the patronage of Captain Charles Elphinstone Fleeming. Sandom served on various stations and was present at Sir Robert Calder's action off Cape Finisterre, Spain, on 22 July 1805. For a long period he was in the Mediterranean, and he took part in the attack on Constantinople (Istanbul) in 1807. As a result of his endeavours during the assault on Copenhagen in 1808 he was promoted lieutenant, effective 30 May of that year. He distinguished himself in the capture by the *Bonne Citoyenne* in 1809 of the French frigate *Furieuse* and commanded the prize during an epic, 25-day tow to Halifax, N.S., with French prisoners below decks. During the War of 1812 Sandom served against the Americans in a small-boat action up the Penobscot River in Maine.

In peace-time he served on many overseas stations, mainly in small vessels of 50 guns or less. Promoted commander on 26 Dec. 1822, he acquired the reputation of being an expert at fitting out vessels in emergencies. This capacity was recognized by his promotion to captain on 23 March 1828. He went on half pay in 1829 and spent his time ashore, particularly at the shipbuilding yards of Liverpool and Glasgow, acquiring detailed knowledge of steam-engines. In three decades of service this thoroughly professional officer had been under fire 60 times and had participated in the capture or destruction of 26

Sandom

ships-of-the-line, 17 corvettes or brigs, and many a privateer or gunboat.

Sandom's career in Upper Canada began in the spring of 1838 when he arrived in Kingston as captain commanding on the lakes. The unrest caused by the rebellion of 1837–38 and the threatening posture of the many Hunters' Lodges in the northern United States, which advocated the liberation of Canada from British rule, had led to a desire for naval protection, despite the restrictive provisions of the Rush–Bagot agreement of 1817 regarding the employment of armed vessels on the lakes.

From a purely naval viewpoint Sandom's appointment was justified by his response to the invasion at the stone windmill near Prescott, between 11 and 16 Nov. 1838. The invading force, ultimately headed by Nils Gustaf von Schoultz*, a trained officer from Europe, consisted of 2 schooners (with intermittent support from the steamer *United States*), some 180 men, and 3 field pieces. Sandom, warned by a spy, had advance notice of these invasion plans, which he first attempted to frustrate by cooperation with the United States Army. From his headquarters in the *Niagara* at Kingston, Sandom had acquired or rented various steam vessels so that when the cross-river attack occurred he had posted at Brockville the small paddle-steamer *Experiment*. Under Lieutenant William Newton Fowell* it interdicted attempted landings there and at Prescott and then harrassed attempts by the invaders to enlarge the force at the windmill. On 13 November Sandom arrived on the scene with the small steamers *Queen Victoria* and *Cobourg*. A detachment of the 83rd Foot, serving as marines, and 30 Royal Marines were landed to head the two militia columns, all under Colonel Plomer Young*'s command, while Sandom positioned his steam vessels in front of the mill to create a diversion and batter it with artillery. The invaders' position at the windmill was a strong one defensively, and the attack failed. The naval force was immediately converted into a blockade, while other vessels brought up heavier guns and reinforcements from Kingston. The combination of regular and militia forces on shore, now under Lieutenant-Colonel Henry Dundas from Kingston, and the blockade on the St Lawrence, forced von Schoultz to surrender on 16 November. As Sandom landed to accept the surrender he was struck on the chest by a spent round but it did not draw blood. Since the success of this bizarre adventure presupposed general Canadian support, which was not forthcoming, the British military operation had been, in essence, a routine mopping-up exercise. Nevertheless Sandom had anticipated and decisively isolated this alien army, and his naval forces had transported the guns which effectively terminated the affair. Dundas was made a CB but an embittered Sandom strove for years for equal recognition, without success.

Having frustrated the would-be invaders, Sandom turned to the coordination of patrol work along the border, which included in 1839 a campaign against William Johnston*, a pirate in the Thousand Islands, and to the problem of the long-term defences of lakes Ontario, Erie, and Huron. In addition to vessels hired or purchased to meet naval needs on the lakes subsequent to 1838, by 1843 he had completed or begun building the steamers *Minos* (406 tons) for Erie, *Cherokee* (750 tons) for Ontario, and *Mohawk* (174 tons) for Huron. Sandom's placement of armed vessels on the lakes was done with Admiralty approval but seems to have been carried out without consultation at the political level in England, and very likely was in technical violation of the Rush–Bagot agreement.

Sandom's seafaring and fighting capabilities were not matched by corresponding talents in the areas of diplomatic and personal relations. In 1838, when he had first contacted the local American army commander in northern New York, Colonel William Jenkins Worth, he took that soldier's word, as of a gentlemen, in their attempt to solve the problem raised by the movement of Patriot enthusiasts across the border, which involved international rights of refuge and search. The two officers mutually agreed to do away with boundary lines when pursuing pirates such as William Johnston. Worth was soon obliged to disavow this agreement and Sandom, experiencing the difficulties of on-the-spot diplomacy, was left "much perplexed" as to whether his instructions on the matter should come from the Admiralty or from Lieutenant Governor Sir George ARTHUR in Toronto. The latter left him to find his own level, so that by the time Governor Charles Edward Poulett Thomson*, later Lord Sydenham, assumed office in 1839 Sandom had become accustomed to telling the colonial authorities one thing and his naval superiors another. Quite aside from his own inexperience in this field, there was a conflict of command responsibility that might have trapped even a sophisticated diplomat. The conflict was clearly demonstrated in 1839 when Sandom attempted to discipline Commander Andrew Drew*, an officer in the Royal Navy who also held a commission in the Provincial Marine. The colonial authorities, under Drew's prodding, forced the Admiralty to hold a court martial on the matter the following year. Sandom's sentence against Drew was reversed by that body and the formal charges on all but one count were dismissed. Sandom subsequently faced widespread criticism for his action and Sydenham bluntly demanded his recall.

Although Sandom sustained a considerable social presence in Kingston, his ungovernable temper prejudiced his relations with his officers and men. His public image was further damaged after the Drew incident when one of the non-commissioned officers of the *Niagara* successfully sued him in 1843 for unjust imprisonment. He left Kingston in July of that year and was succeeded by William Newton Fowell. When Sandom returned to England he was placed on half pay. He married in 1844 and resided in London. Promoted rear-admiral on 27 Oct. 1854, he died on 15 Aug. 1858 at Blundestone House near Lowestoft, Suffolk.

JOHN W. SPURR and DONALD M. SCHURMAN

PAC, MG 11, [CO 42] Q, 273, pt.III: 428–31; RG 5, A1: 115705, 116625–35, 117881–908, 122073–79, 134707–9. PRO, ADM 1/2565–66 (copies at PAC); PROB 11, will of Williams Sandom. *Arthur papers* (Sanderson). *Elgin–Grey papers* (Doughty), 1: 266; 4: 1604–5. *Gentleman's Magazine*, July–December 1858: 318. [C. E. P. Thomson, 1st Baron] Sydenham, *Letters from Lord Sydenham, governor-general of Canada, 1839–1841, to Lord John Russell*, ed. Paul Knaplund (London, 1931): 148–49. *Daily British Whig*, 21 June 1852. *Times* (London), 18 Aug. 1858. "Calendar of series Q . . . ," PAC *Report*, 1941: 224, 252–53, 259, 268–73. "The Durham papers," PAC *Report*, 1923: 130, 136. G.B., ADM, *Navy list*, 1855–58. John Marshall, *Royal naval biography* . . . (4v. in 6 and 2v. supp., London, 1822–35), 3, pt.II: 24–27. O'Byrne, *Naval biog. dict.* (1849), 1026. "State papers – U.C.," PAC *Report*, 1944: 29–31, 33, 73, 75–78, 118; 1945: 34–35, 41, 45–46, 72–74, 97–98, 130, 156–57. Kenneth Bourne, *Britain and the balance of power in North America, 1815–1908* (Berkeley, Calif., 1967), especially 75–90, 102–15. W. A. B. Douglas, "The blessings of the land: naval officers in Upper Canada, 1815–1841," *Swords and covenants*, ed. Adrian Preston and Peter Dennis (London, 1976), 60–66. David Lee, "The battle of the windmill: November 1838," *Hist. and Archaeology* (Ottawa), 8 (1976): 102–80. J. W. Spurr, "The Royal Navy's presence in Kingston, part II: 1837–1853," *Historic Kingston*, no.26 (1978): 81–94. G. F. G. Stanley, "Invasion: 1838," *OH*, 54 (1962): 237–52.

SCOBIE, HUGH, newspaperman, publisher, justice of the peace, and office holder; b. 29 April 1811 in Fort George, Scotland, third son of Captain James Scobie of the 93rd Foot; m. 27 April 1844 Justina McLeod, and they had one daughter; d. 4 Dec. 1853 in Toronto.

Hugh Scobie was raised in a military family and received a classical education in Scotland at the Tain academy. He articled in an Edinburgh law firm, and when his family decided to emigrate to Upper Canada he planned to pursue his legal career in the colony. However, on his arrival with his brothers and sisters in the late spring of 1833, he discovered that the legal system deprived him "of every advantage that my former course of study ought to have afforded me." Until 1838 he was occupied with helping to establish the family farm in West Gwillimbury Township near Bradford. An ambitious man, he quickly became a leading lay spokesman for the Church of Scotland,

acting as secretary of the Presbyterian conference held in 1837 at Cobourg to protest the creation of 44 Anglican rectories the previous year [*see* William MORRIS]. Also during this period he became the Upper Canadian agent for the New York *Albion*, a weekly journal for British emigrants.

Having already established himself in Toronto as a defender of Scottish interests in Upper Canada, Scobie was the logical choice to edit and publish a newspaper which prominent Scots hoped to establish. The new journal was to promote a moderate political alternative to reform, discredited by the 1837–38 rebellion, and to toryism, represented by a political oligarchy dominated by the Church of England. The first issue of the *Scotsman* appeared on 1 Feb. 1838. Two weeks later it became the *British Colonist*, an important change which may have reflected Scobie's assumption of personal control as well as his desire to remove distinctions based on "National Origins." His goal was to "make the paper as generally useful & instructive as possible." Moderate in tone, as a rule the *Colonist* resisted hyperbole, excessive partisanship, and attacks on personalities. Through its editorials and articles, Scobie sought to influence public opinion by advocating such causes as an open and liberal education system and by supporting Upper Canadian sectionalism while implacably opposing French Canadian nationalism. Many of his editorials, undoubtedly influenced by his early legal training, read like well-documented, closely argued, legal submissions.

Scobie was to remain financially dependent on his newspaper. When reformers led by Francis Hincks* became enraged by Scobie's support of Governor Sir Charles Theophilus Metcalfe* during the constitutional crisis of 1843–44, they nearly succeeded in bankrupting Scobie by a campaign to scuttle the *Colonist*. Yet it was during this same crisis, when his subscription list fell by 250 names, that the newspaper achieved new heights of influence, which it maintained following the victory of Metcalfe's candidates in the election of 1844. That year James Morris* wrote to Isaac Buchanan*, "Our friend Scobie is conducting his paper with much ability." Although rival newspaperman and reformer George Brown* described the *Colonist* at that time as the "literary common-sewer of Toronto," he nevertheless joined with Scobie in 1847 to obtain a shared telegraph information system to relay Atlantic shipping news. Scobie's success throughout this period was aided by his gathering about him a group of ambitious young journalists, some of whom, most notably Brown Chamberlin, would go on to achieve considerable recognition.

In November 1851 Scobie added the *Daily Colonist* to his now semi-weekly *British Colonist*, and the following August he introduced the *News of the Week, or Weekly Colonist*. These newspapers provided the forum in which Scobie developed his vision of government built upon the principle of the "common good." He believed that civil well-being, which would provide the foundation-stones of an emerging British Canadian identity, could only be guaranteed through education, material prosperity equitably distributed among all classes, the moral values of Christianity, and a political system that embodied the good of all members. Though a spokesman for the Church of Scotland, he resolutely opposed religious sectarianism, and he scorned parties and politicians who appeared to place their own passions before the best interests of the Upper Canadian community. He urged politicians to build roads, bridges, and schools instead of engaging in divisive and fruitless debates on political philosophy. Passionately biased in favour of the "productive classes" (domestic manufacturers, agriculturalists, and workers), Scobie railed against speculators who sought to manipulate the economy.

In the first issue of the *Scotsman*, Scobie had advertised his services as a "Bookseller, and stationer, printer, bookbinder, lithographer, copperplate and woodengraver," and during the 1840s and 1850s his job-printing firm had become an important adjunct to his other activities. The *Canadian Christian Examiner, and Presbyterian Magazine* was printed and published by him from October 1839 to December 1840; he also printed the *Minutes* of the Toronto Synod of the Presbyterian Church of Canada in connection with the Church of Scotland as well as other religious matter. His presses issued volumes of verse, agricultural lectures by Henry Youle Hind*, and political pamphlets by Egerton Ryerson* and Isaac Buchanan. In association with John Simpson* of Niagara (Niagara-on-the-Lake), he published *The Canadian mercantile almanack* from 1843 to 1848. From 1848 to 1850, in partnership with John Balfour, a fellow Scot, he published *Scobie & Balfour's Canadian almanac, and repository of useful knowledge*. The following year Scobie continued by himself and *Scobie's Canadian almanac* appeared until 1854. The association with Balfour also produced *Scobie & Balfour's municipal manual, for Upper Canada* in 1850, but it too was published with only Scobie's name in 1851 and 1852. The *Manual* contained thorough digests of important provincial laws and was sold cheaply in order to improve public welfare by enlightening citizens.

In an advertisement dated October 1843 Scobie had announced that he had obtained a lithographic press and was "prepared to execute orders in this department." According to historian Mary Allodi, this purchase was significant because "pictorial lithography, which had virtually ceased when [Samuel Oliver Tazewell*] left Toronto in 1835, flourished again under Scobie's patronage." From May 1846 to June 1850 Scobie again teamed with Balfour to produce the *Colonist* as well as a number of lithographed prints and maps.

During his years in Toronto, Scobie was involved in numerous social, economic, and political organizations. An active freemason, he was also a founding member of the Toronto Literary and Historical Society, which was formed in 1842, about the time he was appointed a magistrate of the city. His concern for educational reform was recognized in 1846 when Ryerson appointed him to the province's first board of education. An ardent protectionist, he played a prominent role in the British American League in 1849–50 [*see* George Moffatt*] and the *Colonist* became the league's voice in Toronto. He sat on the local board of trade, was a founding director of the Consumers' Gas Company, and was a vice-president of the Ontario, Simcoe, and Huron Rail-road Union Company. Following his death, his employees who belonged to the Toronto Typographical Society noted that he was, "as an employer, strictly honorable, and generous in overlooking faults, ever striving to place the profession in a high and exalted position before the world, and rendering to the employed that which was their just due."

His direct political involvement was limited, but Scobie campaigned incessantly in the *Colonist* for moderate "liberal conservatism." In 1839 he had accepted the nomination as an anti-tory candidate in Simcoe County for the next election but withdrew in favour of Elmes Yelverton Steele* who won the seat in the 1841 election. In 1844 Ryerson nominated him for the position of inspector general in the ministry of William Henry Draper*; Draper rejected him for political and personal reasons. Scobie did run in the 1847–48 election in the 4th riding of York against Robert BALDWIN but was soundly defeated. In an editorial which appeared in the *Colonist* on 21 Dec. 1847, he wrote, "Between a no-party candidate and a violent partisan, what choice is likely to be made by that class of electors who are more desirous to see the country opened up by emigration and settlement, and more concerned about internal improvements in agriculture and manufacture, than in the profitless pursuit of political shadows?" In 1851 Scobie was again soundly defeated, this time by Joseph HARTMAN.

After a painful illness which lasted about ten weeks, the result of an aneurysm, Hugh Scobie died at his Toronto residence on 4 Dec. 1853. Samuel Thompson*, in partnership with two others, bought the *Colonist* from Scobie's widow, and other parts of his business, including the *Canadian almanac*, were acquired by Thomas Maclear* with William Walter Copp*. Although only 42 at the time of his death, Scobie had contributed significantly to the publishing, political, and cultural realms of Upper Canadian life. Had he not died at such a young age, his talents might have led him to rival the success of his competitor George Brown.

DAVID OUELLETTE

Hugh Scobie's letters to Egerton Ryerson have been edited by Charles Bruce Sissons and published under the title "Letters of 1844 and 1846 from Scobie to Ryerson," *CHR*, 29 (1948): 393–411. The originals are among Ryerson's papers at the UCA.

Two facsimiles of a water-colour portrait of Scobie by Hoppner Francis Meyer are available. Meyer's engraving of it appears in *OH*, 37 (1945), facing page 28; and a water-colour reproduction is at the MTL.

AO, RG 1, C-I-3, 92: 6. PAC, MG 24, D16; RG 5, A1: 74364–66, 115995, 123063–64, 138463–65, 142498–99. QUA, William Morris papers. York County Surrogate Court (Toronto), no.5414, will of Justina Scobie (mfm. at AO). *British Colonist* (Toronto), 1838–53, especially obituary article of 6 Dec. 1853. *Christian Guardian*, 1 May 1844. *Globe*, 6 Oct. 1847. *North American* (Toronto), 8 Dec. 1853. *Scotsman* (Toronto), 1, 8 Feb. 1838. *Toronto Patriot*, 16 Oct. 1840, 28 July 1843. *Canada directory*, 1851: 429. *Dict. of Toronto printers* (Hulse). *Early Toronto newspapers* (Firth). "State papers – U.C.," PAC *Report*, 1943: 89, 114. *Toronto directory*, 1843–44, 1846–47, 1850–51. Mary Allodi, *Printmaking in Canada: the earliest views and portraits* (Toronto, 1980). J. M. S. Careless, *Brown of "The Globe"* (2v., Toronto, 1959–63; repr. 1972), 1. H. P. Gundy, *Book publishing and publishers in Canada before 1900* (Toronto, 1965). G. L. Parker, *The beginnings of the book trade in Canada* (Toronto, 1985). Paul Rutherford, *A Victorian authority: the daily press in late nineteenth-century Canada* (Toronto, 1982), 37–42, 116, 140–41, 253. Wilfred Campbell, "Four early Canadian journalists," *Canadian Magazine*, 43 (May–October 1914): 551–58.

SCOTT, WILLIAM HENRY, militia officer, merchant, politician, and Patriote; b. 13 Jan. 1799 in Scotland, son of William Scott and Catherine Ferguson; d. 18 Dec. 1851 in Saint-Eustache, Lower Canada.

William Henry Scott came from a thoroughly Presbyterian family which was vaguely related to Sir Walter Scott. His parents immigrated from Scotland to Lower Canada around 1800. He was still very young when they settled in Montreal; his father, who had set himself up as a merchant, died in 1804. Little is known about William Henry's education except that in the course of living in Montreal he learned French well.

It is not certain when Scott went to Saint-Eustache, but in June 1827 he was serving on a constitutional committee in York County formed to protest to London against the injustices done to the French Canadians. Although the committee had nothing radical about it, it had the misfortune to displease Nicolas-Eustache Lambert* Dumont, a co-seigneur of Mille-Îles, who as a supporter of the authorities lost no time in denouncing its members to the governor,

Lord Dalhousie [Ramsay*]. In July, Scott, Jacques Labrie*, Ignace Raizenne, and Jean-Baptiste Dumouchel*, among others, were dismissed as militia officers for having taken part in Patriote party meetings during the election campaign that year.

By 1829 Scott was established at Saint-Eustache as a general merchant. In a by-election in York that year he was elected to the House of Assembly to replace Jean-Baptiste Lefebvre, who had died as a result of an accident; Labrie held the county's other seat. In 1830 the riding was split into three – Deux-Montagnes, Vaudreuil, and Ottawa – and Scott and Labrie continued to sit for Deux-Montagnes.

Scott was imbued with liberal ideas and thus, although he was of Scottish origin, he attached himself to the predominantly French Canadian Patriote party in the house. In 1832 he plunged into the constitutional struggle, having formed friendships with Louis-Joseph Papineau* and Wolfred Nelson*. That year he signed a notice on the door of the church in Saint-Benoît (Mirabel), a village adjacent to Saint-Eustache, denouncing land speculation and other flagrant abuses, including the clergy reserves and the English schools, as injustices perpetrated by the British at the expense of the French Canadians.

In the general election of 1834 Scott, who had just voted for the 92 Resolutions outlining the main grievances and demands of the assembly, ran as a Patriote with Jean-Joseph GIROUARD in Deux-Montagnes against the tory candidates Frédéric-Eugène Globensky and his brother-in-law James Brown*. A group of Scots and Irish Orangemen from the neighbouring townships attempted to intimidate the French Canadian voters and turn them against Scott and Girouard at St Andrews (Saint-André-Est), where in the event the vote favoured the candidates loyal to the government. Scott immediately proposed to contest the results because of the irregularities at the polls, and he was set upon by a number of Scotsmen armed with staves. At Saint-Eustache the supporters of Globensky and Brown, led by Lambert Dumont, Maximilien Globensky*, and Eustache-Antoine Lefebvre* de Bellefeuille, who were also co-seigneurs of Mille-Îles, seized the opportunity to intimidate the French Canadians again, but their manœuvres almost touched off a riot in the village, and they had to retreat. Despite such tactics, Scott and Girouard managed to emerge victorious.

When the rebellion broke out in 1837 Scott, who by then was a rich merchant in Saint-Eustache and enjoyed the high regard of his constituents, became one of the natural leaders of his adopted village. Although during the events leading up to the rebellion he had uttered violent words in regard to the authorities, he remained firmly in favour of not resorting to force of arms. Seeing that things might take a disastrous turn at Saint-Eustache, he attempted with the support of the parish priest, Jacques Paquin*, to cool the pugnacious ardour of his friends Jean-Olivier Chénier* and "General" Amury Girod*, but to no avail.

From then on Scott was in an untenable position. Not only did the governor, Lord Gosford [Acheson*], put a price on his head on 1 Dec. 1837 but also the Patriotes were threatening him with proceedings of their own for treason, so Scott had no choice but to flee. Just before the middle of December he left Saint-Eustache in the greatest secrecy. He went first to his brother Neil's house in Sainte-Thérèse-de-Blainville (Sainte-Thérèse). Then, concealed in an empty barrel, he travelled to Montreal, where on 19 December he was captured and imprisoned. Meanwhile his house and store were sacked during the fighting at Saint-Eustache. He was charged with high treason against the government, and was released only on 10 July 1838 on bail of £5,000.

There is no further trace of Scott until 1844. In the general election of that year he was returned, again for Deux-Montagnes, to the Legislative Assembly of the Province of Canada. When the session opened he became a member of an assembly committee to study Paquin's claim for compensation to restore the church and presbytery of Saint-Eustache, which had been damaged by the battles of 1837.

This matter settled, Scott turned his attention to the need to regularize his relationship with Marie-Marguerite-Maurice Paquet of Saint-Eustache, with whom he had been living since 1829. As he was a Presbyterian and she a Catholic, Paquin had categorically refused to solemnize their union. They had four sons and a daughter, Caroline, who was to marry Wolfred Nelson's son Alfred in 1852, a year after her father's death. In 1845 Scott asked Félix Martin*, the superior of the Jesuits in Lower Canada, to put an end to a situation which could hardly have been pleasant for a man in public life. Unfortunately this first step proved unsuccessful because of the intransigence of both Martin and Scott. The matter did not end there, however, for Scott continued until his death to seek a solution to this vexing problem.

In 1845, along with other Lower Canadian reform members who had been Patriotes, among them Louis-Hippolyte La Fontaine*, Papineau, and Nelson, Scott participated in the assembly debate on the Rebellion Losses Bill. In the 1848 general election he was re-elected for his riding on the reform ticket. On 9 March 1849, by a vote of 47 to 18, the reformers of Upper and Lower Canada won the day: a grant of $400,000 was made to those in Lower Canada who had suffered material losses by the actions of troops during the rebellion [see James Bruce*]. Scott himself received a large sum for the loss of his house and furniture.

On 15 Dec. 1851, following a final campaign in which he spared no efforts to get re-elected while continuing to indulge his fondness for alcohol, Scott returned to his home in Saint-Eustache exhausted and ill. He died there three days later, at the age of 52, as a result of a fit of delirium tremens. He was buried the next day in the cemetery of the local Presbyterian church.

Shortly before his death, Scott had managed to persuade the bishop of Montreal, Ignace Bourget*, to relent about his domestic situation; on 16 December he was married and his five children were made legitimate. Prompted by the prospects of an inheritance or possibly by sectarian sentiment, one of his sisters, Ann, who lived in Montreal, challenged this eleventh-hour marriage. The case went before the Superior Court of Lower Canada in 1854, the Court of Queen's Bench of Lower Canada in 1857, and, lastly, the Privy Council in London in 1867; each in turn rejected the plaintiff's case. In Saint-Eustache a plaque on the door of a general store, once Scott's residence, commemorates his name and his political activity.

JACQUES GOUIN

ANQ-M, CE6-11, 16 déc. 1851; CE6-65, 18 déc. 1851; CN5-4, 16 déc. 1851. ANQ-Q, E17/13, nos.712–13; E17/14, nos.766–72, 775; E17/39, no.3149. PAC, MG 24, A27, 34. Can., Prov. of, Legislative Assembly, *App. to the journals*, 1852–53, app.VV; *Journals*, 1844–45. Amury Girod, "Journal tenu par feu Amury Girod et traduit de l'allemand et de l'italien," PAC *Rapport*, 1923: 408–19. [J.-J. Girouard], *Relation historique des événements de l'élection du comté du lac des Deux Montagnes en 1834; épisode propre à faire connaître l'esprit public dans le Bas-Canada* (Montréal, 1835; réimpr., Québec, 1968), 10, 13–15, 18–20. *Scott* v. *Paquet* [1867], 1L.R. 1P.C. 552. *Le Populaire* (Montréal), 13 déc. 1837. F.-J. Audet, "Les législateurs du Bas-Canada." Desjardins, *Guide parl.* Fauteux, *Patriotes*, 373–74. *The Lower Canada jurist* (35v., Montreal, 1857–91), 4: 149–208. L.-N. Carrier, *Les événements de 1837–1838* (Québec, 1877), 69–71, 76. Béatrice Chassé, "Le notaire Girouard, Patriote et rebelle" (thèse de D. ès L., univ. Laval, Québec, 1974). Cornell, *Alignment of political groups*, 15–16, 22, 24, 30, 32. David, *Les gerbes canadiennes*, 175; *Patriotes*, 45–47. Émile Dubois, *Le feu de la Rivière-du-Chêne; étude historique sur le mouvement insurrectionnel de 1837 au nord de Montréal* (Saint-Jérôme, Qué., 1937), 51–52, 119–20, 135, 145. Filteau, *Hist. des Patriotes* (1975), 358–59, 476–77. [C.-A.-M. Globensky], *La rébellion de 1837 à Saint-Eustache avec un exposé préliminaire de la situation politique du Bas-Canada depuis la cession* (Québec, 1883; réimpr., Montréal, 1974), 46–47, 66–67, 224–25. Jacques Gouin, *William-Henry Scott et sa descendance ou le destin romanesque et tragique d'une famille de rebelles (1799–1944)* (Hull, Qué., 1980), 1–22. Joseph Schull, *Rebellion: the rising in French Canada, 1837* (Toronto, 1971), 94–95, 105–6, 209. "Les causes célèbres," *La Patrie* (Montréal), 5 juin 1926: 9.

SEALGAIR, IAIN. *See* MacDhòmhnaill 'Ic Iain, Iain

SEROOSKERKEN, Baron van TUYLL VAN SEROOSKERKEN, VINCENT GILDEMEESTER VAN TUYLL VAN. *See* Tuyll

SHEAFFE, Sir ROGER HALE, army officer and colonial administrator; b. 15 July 1763 in Boston, third son of William Sheaffe, deputy collector of customs, and Susannah Child; m. 29 Jan. 1810 Margaret Coffin, daughter of John Coffin*, at Quebec, and they had two sons and four daughters, all of whom predeceased Sheaffe; d. 17 July 1851 in Edinburgh.

As a young boy Roger Hale Sheaffe became the protégé of the Duke of Northumberland, who during the American Revolutionary War had established his headquarters in Boston in the boarding-house run by the widowed Susannah Sheaffe. The duke initially sent the lad to sea, but then transferred him to Locke's military academy in Chelsea (London), England, where he was a class-mate of George Prevost*. Northumberland subsequently bought most of Sheaffe's commissions, beginning in May 1778 with that of ensign in the 5th Foot, of which the duke was colonel. After serving in Ireland for six years, Sheaffe arrived at Quebec in July 1787 with his regiment, which was transferred to Montreal the following year. The 5th was subsequently stationed at Detroit, from 1790 to 1792, and then at Fort Niagara (near Youngstown, N.Y.) until 1796, when it returned to Quebec. In August 1794, prior to the signing of Jay's Treaty, Sheaffe had acted as Lieutenant Governor John Graves Simcoe*'s emissary to Sodus, an Indian community on the south shore of Lake Ontario, where he protested seizures of Indian lands by a settlement agent, Charles Williamson. Described by Simcoe as a "Gentleman of great discretion, incapable of any intemperate or uncivil conduct," Sheaffe was promoted captain in May 1795.

As a result of his regiment's being drafted, he returned to England in September 1797 and three months later purchased a majority in the 81st Foot. The following March he became junior lieutenant-colonel of the 49th Foot. At this point his career became linked with that of Isaac Brock*, the senior lieutenant-colonel. They served in north Holland together in 1799. The next year, when Brock left Sheaffe in command of the regiment, then stationed on Jersey, Sheaffe became unpopular with the men. After serving in the Baltic campaign of 1801, the two officers were ordered to the Canadas in 1802, arriving with the 49th in Lower Canada late that summer and taking up commands in the spring of 1803 in the upper province: Brock at regimental headquarters in York

(Toronto) and Sheaffe, with a wing of the regiment, at Fort George (Niagara-on-the-Lake).

It was there that Sheaffe's abilities as a military commander were first subjected to serious question. In August 1803 he and other officers warned Brock of an incipient mutiny at Fort George, which Brock quickly suppressed. Brock believed that the fort's proximity to the American border had been the major cause for the attempted desertion. But, conscious of Sheaffe's past conduct when in command, he also censured him for being "indiscreet and injudicious," particularly by behaving like a martinet, working his men too hard, and disciplining them too harshly for small lapses. Brock identified his reduction of "too many non-commissioned officers" as another contributing factor. Writing about the incident to Lieutenant-Colonel James Green* in 1804, he mentioned that Sheaffe possessed "little knowledge of Mankind" and had many enemies, although he could not offer any reasons for this enmity other than the bitter feelings which existed between Sheaffe and the men he commanded. William Dummer Powell*, and possibly other friends of Sheaffe, claimed after the War of 1812 that some of the submerged hostility in 1803–4 was based on Sheaffe's American origin which raised doubts about his loyalty; Powell at least believed it to be faultless. Sheaffe's actions in wartime would provide both his critics and his friends with support for their opinions. In 1808 he attained the brevet rank of colonel; three years later, as a result of his promotion to major-general, he was obliged to give up his command in the 49th and with it at least half his income.

In July 1812, some time after Sheaffe had returned from a trip to England, without specific duties, Lieutenant-General Sir George Prevost, who had become governor-in-chief and commander of the forces, was anxiously looking for general officers to fill various wartime commands. Aware of Sheaffe's financial plight, he also believed him to be well qualified to serve in Upper Canada because he would be a "Valuable Officer to the service from his Ability to command and his extensive local information." In addition to his long service in the colony, he had useful connections within its social and political élites, principally through Powell, a pillar of the "family compact" and a long-time friend of the Sheaffe family. Without knowing if Sheaffe had been posted elsewhere by the military authorities in England, Prevost appointed him temporarily to the army staff in the upper province, thus putting him under Brock's command once again.

Sheaffe arrived at Fort George on 18 August to find himself, as a result of Brock's departure to repulse the American invasion on the Detroit frontier, in command of the forces on the Niagara frontier. Within days he learned of Prevost's truce with Major-General

Sheaffe

Henry Dearborn. Having received news of Brock's capture of Detroit before it reached Major-General Stephen Van Rensselaer, the opposing American commander on the Niagara River, Sheaffe slyly arranged with him a codicil to the armistice whereby no reinforcements or supplies could be forwarded to the upper Great Lakes, which meant that neither side could reinforce Detroit. Prevost, however, was incensed, for the truce had placed no restriction on troop and supply movements by either side. At the same time, he admitted to Brock, disavowal of Sheaffe's initiative would embarrass the British, so no action was taken.

Late in August Sheaffe relinquished command to Brock, who had returned to the Niagara peninsula. The general armistice was ended on 4 September and both Brock and Sheaffe worked determinedly to strengthen the frontier's defences. Early on 13 October the Americans attacked at Queenston. Brock hurried quickly from Fort George to take command on the battlefield, leaving Sheaffe to assemble and bring up the main body of defenders. When Brock was killed in a daring direct assault, Sheaffe took command, leading his force from the fort in a wide flanking movement to join with the Indians and a party from Chippawa under Captain Richard Bullock to attack the American flank on high ground. The invaders were routed and almost 1,000 prisoners were taken, with insignificant British losses. John Beverley Robinson*, a militia officer at the time, recalled Sheaffe's conduct in battle as "cool though determined and vigorous." His manœuvre had been brilliant and on 16 Jan. 1813 he would receive the deserved honour of a baronetcy for his achievement, though in the public's memory Brock was the victor.

Following the battle, a three-day armistice had been immediately arranged by Sheaffe to allow each side to attend to its wounded and dead and to exchange prisoners. After he agreed to the American request for an indefinite extension, however, Prevost criticized him for not seizing the chance to cross the river instead to take Fort Niagara and for not getting prior approval of the extension. Many commentators in both Upper and Lower Canada, including the *Quebec Gazette*, thought that his leniency betrayed weakness and benefited only the Americans by giving them time to reorganize.

On Brock's death, Sheaffe had succeeded him as military commander of Upper Canada, and also as president and civil administrator of the province's government. He transferred his headquarters to York and on 20 October took the oath of office. During his term the effects of the war became fully evident. The problems of the dependability and loyalty of civilians plagued Sheaffe as they had Brock. On 9 November Sheaffe appointed alien boards at Niagara (Niagara-on-the-Lake), York, and Kingston to examine all persons claiming to be American citizens and therefore exempt from military service [*see* Michael Smith*]. As military commander, Sheaffe had to deal with a weak militia force and with the inefficiencies of several army departments, particularly the barrack department and the commissariat. Despite his serious, sustained efforts to remedy organizational weaknesses and the attendant shortages of military supplies, such fellow officers as Thomas Evans* and Christopher Myers knew that Sheaffe would be blamed for problems inherited from Brock, who had been more interested in action than in bureaucratic efficiency. By January the first signs of food shortages had begun to appear, in the Western District, where Colonel Henry Procter* was empowered by Prevost through Sheaffe to impose a partial operation of martial law to force farmers to sell produce to the army.

During the winter of 1812–13, most of which Sheaffe spent on the Niagara frontier (probably at Fort George), he seldom dealt with civil matters because of poor health and preoccupation with military defence. The armistice negotiated after the battle of Queenston Heights ended on 20 November. After an unsuccessful American invasion near Fort Erie on the 28th, the commanding officer of the British forces there, Lieutenant-Colonel Cecil Bisshopp*, feared a second attempt and requested reinforcements. Sheaffe wisely responded that troops could not be sent to that distant position, where they could easily be isolated and defeated, and advised him to retreat to Chippawa if the Americans attacked. An indignant Bisshopp presented Sheaffe's proposal to a council of officers, who were outraged that their commander should countenance retreat. Although the suggestion was theoretically a valid military plan, Sheaffe was seen to be injudicious in recommending it before it became a necessity, and rumour quickly labelled him a traitor. He lost standing with many regular and militia officers, notably Captain Andrew Gray, the deputy quartermaster general, and with a significant portion of the civilian population, a shift in opinion that alarmed Prevost.

Throughout the winter months of 1812–13 Sheaffe continued his efforts to remedy defensive weaknesses in the province. One of his major concerns was the need to ensure naval supremacy on the lakes when the shipping season opened [*see* George Benson Hall*]. He was well aware that Commodore Isaac Chauncey of the United States Navy had virtually seized control of Lake Ontario just before the winter freeze-up. By mid December Sheaffe and others had devised a plan "for the improvement of our marine establishment" by fitting out and arming additional vessels at Kingston, York, and Amherstburg. During part of January and February, however, Sheaffe's illness so interfered with his work that Prevost ordered the next available senior officer in Upper Canada, Colonel John

Vincent*, to proceed to Fort George and to be ready to take over the command of the province. In spite of his sickness, Sheaffe was able to endorse the formation of new corps as another obvious means for bolstering the province's defences. He welcomed the suggestion initiated by Procter and promoted by Colonel William Caldwell* to form a corps of rangers similar to Butler's Rangers in the American Revolutionary War. In February, Sheaffe supported Caldwell's proposals before Prevost. The Western Rangers, also known as Caldwell's Rangers, was formed in March and part of the credit may belong to Sheaffe.

He opened the Upper Canadian legislature on 25 Feb. 1813 and prorogued it on 13 March. This was the only session that he presided over but it acceded to most of his requests. The principal measures passed were the recognition of army bills authorized by the Lower Canadian legislature as legal tender in Upper Canada, the authorization for the lieutenant governor to prohibit the export of grain or its distillation, and the provision of annuities for disabled militiamen and for the widows and children of those killed. Amendments to the militia laws formed perhaps the most significant legislation, for these were intended to improve the efficiency of Upper Canada's militia, an end Prevost had been urging on Sheaffe along with an expansion of the militia force. Under these amendments existing flank companies would be replaced by battalions of incorporated militia made up of volunteers who enlisted for the duration of the war. To attract volunteers a cash bounty was offered. Sheaffe claimed credit for this inducement but was disappointed that the amount authorized by the House of Assembly was only eight dollars. Drawing from the military chest, he raised the bounty to eighteen dollars and offered land grants to all ranks at the end of their service. Although it was expected that two or three battalions would be raised, only one was recruited in 1813, with its officers coming from regular regiments.

In his conduct of the war, Sheaffe consistently declined to take risks, a position which accorded with Prevost's policy of a defensive war based on holding Montreal and Quebec. In March 1813 he exhorted Sheaffe to conserve his resources "for future exertion" and to adopt "activity and perseverance in the measures of defence, for which your present force and recent preparations are so well calculated." A cautious and methodical commander, Sheaffe opposed John Vincent's proposal to attack Fort Niagara that spring because not enough boats or Indians were available at the time. He sought to strengthen the defences of York but efforts there were abruptly cut short.

On 26 April an American fleet appeared west of the capital and the next day the invading force began landing, quickly establishing a beach-head. Sheaffe had about 700 regulars and militia and between 50 and 100 Indians with which to oppose some 1,700 United States regulars, supported by the guns of 14 ships. All he could do was fight a delaying action; nothing would have been gained by getting himself killed or captured, or by exposing his forces to heavy losses. After a brief engagement, he decided to retreat eastward to Kingston, destroying first a partially built ship, the marine stores, and the grand magazine. The town's senior militia officers were left to make terms with the Americans. This was a sound military decision and perhaps the clearest evidence of its validity is contained in the reaction of the American secretary of war, John Armstrong: "We cannot doubt but that in all cases in which a British commander is constrained to act defensively, his policy will be that adopted by Sheaffe – to prefer the preservation of his troops to that of his post, and thus, carrying off the kernel leave us only the shell." Unfortunately for Sheaffe, the post he had abandoned was the provincial capital, the home of such influential citizens as John Strachan*, William ALLAN, and William Chewett*, whose bitter criticisms of Sheaffe's conduct and withdrawal helped to finish his career in the Canadas. Disagreement over his actions at York persists to the present day.

The problem of civilian loyalty increased following the American capture of York and during fighting on the Niagara peninsula in May and early June, at which time Sheaffe was still in Kingston. Prevost, who along with Commodore Sir James Lucas Yeo* had joined Sheaffe there, authorized him after his retreat to impose martial law if necessary in order to sustain his troops and control disaffected elements [see Elijah Bentley*]. Sheaffe saw no benefit in using martial law, however, and declined to employ this power, claiming that as president of the province he had no constitutional authority to do so.

After the American invaders had been forced back on the peninsula, Prevost removed Sheaffe from his civil and military commands, in which he was succeeded on 19 June 1813 by Major-General Francis de Rottenburg*. Four days earlier the members of the Executive Council then "resident" in Kingston, William Dummer Powell, Thomas Scott*, and John McGill*, had praised Sheaffe for his administration and for his part in the battle of York; apparently the general still had important friends in Upper Canada. Still, Prevost was so dissatisfied with him that he informed Lord Bathurst, the colonial secretary, that Sheaffe had "lost the confidence of the Province by the measures he had pursued for its defence." In the opinion of William Dummer Powell, probably Sheaffe's closest adviser on civil matters, he "was sacrificed to Ignorance & Jealousy of those who had not souls to comprehend his character in which truth & honor so much predominated as to give his Conduct the appearance of weakness."

Sheaffe was subsequently ordered to take command

Sherwood

of the troops in the Montreal District, a position which entailed little responsibility since there was no fighting taking place in that area. In July, Prevost nevertheless criticized him for "indifference" in the discharge of his duties and demanded his "active support." The charge mystified Sheaffe. Although their correspondence does not make clear precisely how he was failing in his duties, Prevost was completely disillusioned with him. Though Sheaffe had been more assiduous than Brock in conducting the defensive war envisaged by Prevost, he had failed to keep Prevost well informed of his plans and thoughts and was unable to convince him that he was following his instructions. Even when faced with removal from his Montreal command, he feebly protested that Prevost was misinformed but made no attempt to set the record straight. On 27 September he was superseded by Prevost, who had returned to Montreal from Upper Canada, and was placed in charge of the reserve forces. Prevost, however, had already written to London about Sheaffe's recall. Orders to that effect were sent in August 1813, but his departure was delayed until November.

On returning to England, Sheaffe and his family lived in Penzance and then Worcester, and in 1817 they moved to Edinburgh, where Sheaffe spent most of his remaining years. Although his appointment to the army staff on 25 March 1814 was later recalled and deferred, he was promoted lieutenant-general in 1821 and general in 1838. He had become colonel of the 36th Foot in 1829.

Sir Roger Hale Sheaffe was an experienced professional soldier who attempted to conduct the War of 1812 in Upper Canada in accordance with the defensive strategy of Sir George Prevost – an approach which undoubtedly suited Sheaffe's cautious personality. It is, therefore, ironic that Prevost lost confidence in him for carrying out this policy, and that Brock, not Sheaffe, is known for the one battle Sheaffe won by a brilliant, offensive manœuvre.

CAROL M. WHITFIELD and WESLEY B. TURNER

A letter-book kept by Sir Roger Hale Sheaffe during the War of 1812 has been edited by Frank H. Severance and published as "Documents relating to the War of 1812: the letter-book of Gen. Sir Roger Hale Sheaffe," Buffalo Hist. Soc., *Pub.* (Buffalo, N.Y.), 17 (1913): 271–381.

ANQ-Q, CN1-230, 29 janv. 1810. MTL, W. D. Powell papers. PAC, MG 23, HI, 4, vol.3: 1174; MG 30, D1, 27: 753; RG 8, I (C ser.), 230, 329, 677, 679, 922–23, 1170, 1218–21, 1694. *Annual Reg.* (London), 1851: 310–11. Boston, Registry Dept., *Records relating to the early history of Boston*, ed. W. H. Whitmore *et al.* (39v., Boston, 1876–1909), [24]: *Boston births, 1700–1800*, 197; [30]: *Boston marriages, 1752–1809*, 392. *The correspondence of Lieut. Governor John Graves Simcoe . . .*, ed. E. A. Cruikshank (5v., Toronto, 1923–31), 2: 364. *Doc. hist. of*

campaign upon Niagara frontier (Cruikshank), vols.3–8. *Gentleman's Magazine*, January–June 1855: 661. *The life and correspondence of Major-General Sir Isaac Brock . . .*, ed. F. B. Tupper (2nd ed., London, 1847), 18. *Select British docs. of War of 1812* (Wood). *The Talbot papers*, ed. J. H. Coyne (2v., Ottawa, 1908–9). Solomon Van Rensselaer, *A narrative of the affair of Queenstown: in the War of 1812; with a review of the strictures on that event, in a book entitled, "Notices of the War of 1812"* (New York, 1836).

Burke's peerage (1839), 938–39. *DNB*. G.B., WO, *Army list*, 1838–39. *Hart's army list*, 1851. Morgan, *Sketches of celebrated Canadians*, 185–86. *Officers of British forces in Canada* (Irving). D. B. Read, *The lieutenant-governors of Upper Canada and Ontario, 1792–1899* (Toronto, 1900). Lorenzo Sabine, *Biographical sketches of loyalists of the American revolution with an historical essay* (2v., Boston, 1864; repr. Port Washington, N.Y., 1966), 2: 280–93. "State papers – U.C.," PAC *Report*, 1893: 43–49. Richard Cannon, *Historical record of the Thirty-Sixth, or the Herefordshire Regiment of Foot . . .* (London, 1853), 118–19. J. M. Hitsman, *The incredible War of 1812: a military history* (Toronto, 1965). W. R. Riddell, *The life of William Dummer Powell, first judge at Detroit and fifth chief justice of Upper Canada* (Lansing, Mich., 1924), 112. C. P. Stacey, *The battle of Little York* (Toronto, 1963). W. B. Turner, "The career of Isaac Brock in Canada, 1807–1812" (MA thesis, Univ. of Toronto, 1961). H. M. Walker, *A history of the Northumberland Fusiliers, 1674–1902* (London, 1919). E. A. Cruikshank, "A study of disaffection in Upper Canada in 1812–15," RSC *Trans.*, 3rd ser., 6 (1912), sect.II: 11–65. W. M. Weekes, "The War of 1812: civil authority and martial law in Upper Canada," *OH*, 48 (1956): 147–61. Carol Whitfield, "The battle of Queenston Heights," *Canadian Hist. Sites: Occasional Papers in Archaeology and Hist.* (Ottawa), no.11 (1975): 10–59.

SHERWOOD, HENRY, office holder, militia officer, lawyer, businessman, politician, and judge; b. 1807 in Augusta Township, Upper Canada, eldest son of Levius Peters Sherwood* and Charlotte Jones, daughter of Ephraim Jones*; m. 22 July 1829 Mary Graham Smith, daughter of Peter Smith* of Kingston, Upper Canada, and they had 18 children; d. 7 July 1855 in Kissingen (Bad Kissingen, Federal Republic of Germany).

Henry Sherwood was of loyalist descent through both parents. Members of the Sherwood and Jones families formed a large part of the local élite which dominated affairs in the Johnstown District. Through Henry's father and his uncle Jonas Jones* in particular, they had close connections with the controlling élite at York (Toronto) and made a sustained, influential contribution to provincial politics and the judiciary. In consequence, Henry Sherwood grew up in close familiarity with the governing system, absorbing attitudes and experiences which were reinforced by his education at the Home District Grammar School under the Reverend John Strachan*.

After articling at York in the law office of his uncle,

Solicitor General Henry John Boulton*, Sherwood was admitted to the bar of Upper Canada in Michaelmas term 1828. He went into practice in Prescott and perhaps also in Brockville, his place of residence. He soon developed a broad range of economic interests. Like so many of his class, he speculated in wild lands, advertising for sale on a single occasion 3,274 acres scattered widely throughout eastern Upper Canada. In 1830 he was active in efforts to establish a branch of the Bank of Upper Canada in Brockville and, when that initiative appeared to have failed, he joined in the movement to establish an independent bank there. In 1832 this tilt at York achieved the object originally desired. Sherwood then became the Bank of Upper Canada's local solicitor, having failed to obtain the more lucrative post of cashier. He was also involved in attempts to develop the forwarding trade and to secure Brockville's place in it. Among other things, this activity led to his appointment as a director of the Saint Lawrence Inland Marine Assurance Company, a Prescott organization chartered in 1833. Sherwood also served as the first secretary of the district agricultural society. In short, he proved an enthusiastic promoter of the general prosperity of the Johnstown District as well as of his own welfare. The latter was assisted by his enjoyment of public office: while yet a law student, he had received appointment as clerk of assize on the western circuit, where his father, on occasion, presided, and in 1830 he was gazetted one of the three commissioners of customs for the Johnstown District. It was a short step from this sort of activity to involvement in local government. He was perhaps the foremost proponent of the establishment of a board of police in Brockville, contending forcefully against Andrew Norton Buell*, a reformer, for open voting and the division of the town into wards and against legislative stipulation of the market site. An enactment on these issues very much along the lines desired by Sherwood became law in 1832. That year he was elected one of the board's first members.

From his teens Sherwood had been involved in politics. Naturally, in view of his background, his opinions were tory. He took part in the infamous type riot of 8 June 1826 when the presses of the *Colonial Advocate* and other printing equipment of the radical York newspaperman William Lyon Mackenzie* were destroyed by a mob. In November 1827 he was among a group opposing Mackenzie at the nomination meeting for the constituency of York, and in 1828 he fell foul of the quarrelsome, dissident judge, John Walpole Willis*, who accused Sherwood of threatening his life and being drunk in the streets. Later his political conduct became more conventional. He stood for the riding of Leeds at the general election of 1830 but ended up at the bottom of the poll. In 1834 he was a candidate for Brockville, where traditional tory interests predominated. The contest developed into a factional struggle between the families of Ephraim and Solomon Jones*, Sherwood representing the former. He lost to David Jones by one vote.

Now Sherwood's attention began to shift to Toronto. On 29 July 1835 he and his eminent brother-in-law, John Elmsley*, were elected to the first board of the Farmers' Joint Stock Banking Company. The initial months of this private Toronto bank were marked by controversy, during which the reformers on the board and Captain George Truscott, head of the banking firm of Truscott, Green and Company, were forced out. In these manœuvres Sherwood appears to have played an active role but only hints of his course appear in the evidence. At about the same time attempts were being made to further plans for the projected railway between Toronto and Lake Simcoe. Sherwood also showed a significant interest in this concern. Finally, he took up residence in the city and in November 1835 established his law office in the south corner of the market buildings.

Sherwood maintained his interests in the Johnstown District; he retained his property there; his activity in local administration and politics continued; and in June 1836, claiming to have been forced to remove to Toronto by the hope of increasing his practice, he came out again as a candidate for Brockville. He received the nomination of the recently formed Brockville Constitutional Association, defeating his uncle Jonas Jones, another prominent tory James Morris*, and the sitting member David Jones. The latter threatened to divide the conservative vote but withdrew before the poll, leaving Sherwood an easy contest against another tory, lawyer John Bogert. Although the evidence is by no means conclusive, it appears that Sherwood's success was the product both of the eclipse of the Solomon Jones family, a process which had been gathering pace during the 1830s, and of the support given him by Ogle Robert Gowan*, the leader of the Orangemen who were settling in large numbers around and in the constituency.

Sherwood's first session in parliament, between November 1836 and March 1837, set much of the pattern of his later career. He rapidly learned the basics of procedure and debate; his exertions as a local member were constant; he spoke effectively and often on general issues. Many of the questions that concerned him then absorbed him throughout his career. For example, he showed great interest in improving the administration of justice and in raising the standards of his profession. Subsequently he would attempt to regulate the medical profession [*see* Christopher Widmer]. As chairman of a select committee, he drew up an able, if condescending, critique of the stand taken by the Lower Canadian House of Assembly in support of Louis-Joseph

Sherwood

Papineau*'s 92 Resolutions of 1834. This hostility to a program, a people, and a leader he considered inimical to the British connection drove Sherwood to a more extreme attitude than that of other tories on the port of entry question: when the Upper Canadian assembly voted by a huge majority in favour of annexing Montreal, Sherwood stood forth as the advocate of appending to the imperial address a strong statement against legislative union with Lower Canada, a reform which, in the last resort, many of his closest political associates were prepared to contemplate. He was strongly opposed to responsible government and an elective legislative council, yet he rejected imperial interference in the internal affairs of the province, justifying this stand by reference to the Constitutional Act of 1791. If dividing the clergy reserves among all the Christian sects would achieve religious harmony, he was prepared for the step. His bill to establish a chartered bank in Brockville, together with his support for the establishment of chartered and joint-stock banks elsewhere, demonstrated his continuing opposition to a centralized financial system whether in the form of the tory- and Toronto-dominated Bank of Upper Canada or of William Hamilton Merritt*'s proposed provincial bank. With Allan Napier MacNab* he unsuccessfully advocated the appointment of a provincial emigration agent. Sherwood thus combined a pragmatic concern for economic growth and social harmony with an unusual degree of ideological commitment.

Ensuing sessions of the legislature were somewhat overshadowed by outside events. When Mackenzie and his supporters rose in revolt early in December 1837, Sherwood, who had been commissioned lieutenant in the West York militia in 1827, was at once appointed as one of the provincial aides-de-camp to Lieutenant Governor Sir Francis Bond Head* together with Jonas Jones, James McGill Strachan*, and John Beverley Robinson*. On 7 December he marched in the force that attacked and dispersed the rebels at Gallows Hill just north of Toronto. Sherwood was appointed Queen's Counsel on 23 Jan. 1838 and in that capacity was employed in numerous trials arising from the rebellion and from the subsequent Patriot incursions into Upper Canada; he also acted as judge advocate in the court martial of 44 prisoners including Joshua Gwillen Doan* at London from 27 Dec. 1838 to 19 Jan. 1839. His conduct of these proceedings was praised not only by Lieutenant Governor Sir George ARTHUR and the members of the court but also by the prisoners.

Though he remained a figure of the second rank, Sherwood was increasingly prominent in parliament. In 1838, as chairman of the select committee on the political state of Upper and Lower Canada, he had brought down a report which ably and fully expressed tory indignation at the recent uprisings. When the question of legislative union of the Canadas arose in December 1839, Governor Charles Edward Poulett Thomson* (later Lord Sydenham) paid considerable attention to him. Sherwood was now prepared to consider such a union but only on the stringent conditions laid down by the assembly in March 1839. In particular, despite all the influence brought to bear upon him, he pressed hard but in vain for unequal representation of the provinces in the common legislature, in order to secure a pro-British majority. On the other hand, like other ultra-tories, he repeatedly declared that he was not an opponent of Thomson's new regime. Indeed, he voted for the governor's clergy reserves bill even though he believed the Church of England's claims to the whole of the reserves to be legally, if not politically, sound.

At the first general election for the united Legislative Assembly in 1841, Sherwood came forward for the prestigious seat of Toronto. The decision to abandon his safe Brockville constituency was perhaps rash. However, his prospects were encouraging. He ran in tandem with a well-established merchant and alderman, George Monro*, against two Sydenhamite candidates, John Henry DUNN and Isaac Buchanan*. Sherwood again claimed not to be an opponent of the governor-in-chief but increasingly spoke like one, particularly in relation to public expenditure. In the event, though the municipal corporation, Bishop Strachan of Toronto, and the Orange order were strong in their cause, he and his partner were defeated. Over-optimism, government influence, and poor support among merchants, professionals, and non-resident property owners were the principal causes.

Sherwood now faced the difficult task of resuscitating his political career and probably also his personal finances. As was common among people of his background, he was used to taking a leading role in society. He had been a founding member of the Upper Canada Club (Toronto Club) in 1837 and a member of its second committee of management in 1838–39, and he later served as steward of the Toronto Turf Club. He also gave generously to church organizations. This costly style of life and his large family placed demands on him which his income could barely support. In 1838 he had claimed to be very hard up. Three years later he appears to have had difficulty in paying his election expenses and in posting security for his appeal against the election result. To add to his problems, he was now deprived of legal business for the crown because of the political stand he had taken towards the government. However, he kept himself before the public with some well-publicized court appearances, notably a successful defence of one Thomas Kelly, who had been accused of committing murder during the Toronto election, and a prosecution of Francis Hincks*, the editor of the reform *Examiner*, for a libel on Archibald MCNAB. By 1843 he could claim to be in comfortable circumstances. Indeed 10 years later prominent lawyer Philip Michael Matthew Scott VanKoughnet* would state that Sherwood had had "the best professional practice of any lawyer in Toronto."

Desperate to return to politics, Sherwood set about strengthening his base of support in Toronto. Having made much of the issue during the election, he continued to agitate in favour of Toronto again becoming the seat of government, at least alternately with Quebec. In January 1842 he was elected alderman for St David's Ward and at the ensuing meeting of the city council he was chosen mayor of Toronto, defeating Captain John Simcoe MACAULAY. Sherwood was to remain mayor for three terms (1842–44) and an alderman until 1849. He promoted the rapid extension of sidewalks, sewerage drains, schools, and other services, kept taxes as low as possible, and adopted a vigorous, hard-headed approach to raising the loans necessary to fund the resulting deficits. His administration of the affairs of this conservative city appears to have been both energetic and popular.

Meanwhile, Sir Charles Bagot*, the new governor-in-chief, had been trying to strengthen his tottering Executive Council. In particular, he sought a conservative solicitor general to balance the appointment of the reformer Francis Hincks as inspector general of public accounts. After John Solomon Cartwright* had declined the post, Sherwood was offered it. Surprisingly, he accepted. In doing so, he explicitly put aside a personal repugnance towards Hincks, on which Cartwright had mainly grounded his refusal, and asserted the need for moderation in politics. At the same time he reaffirmed his adherence to conservative principles, which many of his former political associates thought a contradiction. There had previously been signs that a few conservatives were hostile towards Sherwood but this acceptance of office greatly augmented that feeling. Only in Toronto was there any party support for his action, and that did not come on the whole from the tory establishment. Nor were the costs of his action balanced by comparable benefits, for Sherwood's tenure of office was short. Sworn in on 23 July 1842, during the next ministerial reconstruction he was absent from the seat of government on public business and took no part in the negotiations which led to his loss of office on 15 Sept. 1842, and the formation of the first government to be headed by Robert BALDWIN and Louis-Hippolyte La Fontaine*.

Though now indelibly tainted by the charges of excessive ambition and betrayal of his party, Sherwood was more determined than ever to resume his career in provincial politics. In the by-election held for Toronto in March 1843 he stood again and was again opposed by Macaulay. Sherwood had the powerful Toronto corporation and Orange influence on his side, together with most officers of a neutral provincial government, three-quarters of the Catholics, and many of the reformers who voted. Macaulay, solidly supported by the old tory élite which included the Gamble, Boulton, and Jarvis families, attacked Sherwood for his acceptance of office in 1842 but, by injudicious professions of fervent toryism, alienated the reformers and adherents of the Church of Scotland who had been tempted to support him. Although the contest was bitter and expensive, Sherwood's victory was overwhelming. He returned to parliament with a vengeance, attacking the La Fontaine–Baldwin government on almost every conceivable issue and in terms of indignation often indistinguishable from those of ultra-tories. In particular, he made much, as time went by, of the allegedly sectional character of the government's legislation.

During the crisis of 1843–44 Sherwood was active in rousing public opinion in support of Governor Sir Charles Theophilus Metcalfe*. He also appears to have intrigued for his own advancement. On 7 Oct. 1844 he was gazetted solicitor general west, though without a seat in the Executive Council. Metcalfe wrote that, despite Sherwood's reputation, his principles were "liberal" and therefore befitting this moderate "no-party" administration. Indeed, after his victory in the general election of 1844 Sherwood himself declared publicly that he was "not for any ultra or proscriptive policy."

The first session of the new parliament which convened late in November 1844 was critical for this important ministry. Its majority was slim. Much depended on the tact and debating skills of the leaders. Here Sherwood was outstanding. Moreover, he was almost the only minister to wield substantial influence in the assembly. However, after the Christmas break difficulties surfaced between him and the executive. Full of prickly self-importance, Sherwood took offence at the cabinet's refusal to consult either him or its other supporters before introducing legislation which they were expected to support. The general breakdown of communication was highlighted by the university question. William Henry Draper*, the government leader, proposed to establish a single university in Upper Canada that would encompass the existing denominational colleges, though these would continue to function as centres of religious instruction and would be supported from the endowment formerly attached to the Anglican King's College (University of Toronto). Sherwood, who favoured this quasi-federal compromise, did in fact vote for the first and second readings of Draper's bill but he was under pressure from his constituents, particularly the Anglican bishop, John Strachan. In deference to their wishes, he urged and was instrumental in obtaining a

Sherwood

postponement. Draper, who had committed himself to the measure, was furious.

During the next session, in the spring of 1846, these difficulties multiplied. Sherwood objected to Draper's inordinate delay in reintroducing the university bill and to the presenting of it, when the measure was revived, as an open question. Consequently he voted with the ultra-tories, helping to defeat the scheme once again but at the same time raising further doubts as to his own sincerity. Sherwood was also incensed at the revelation of Draper's secret negotiations with René-Édouard Caron*, which had for their object the introduction of a substantial French Canadian element into the ministry. The precise grounds of his objection increased the suspicion with which he was now viewed: it was not the attempt to gain added French support but the apparent bartering of offices without the knowledge of the existing incumbents which he condemned. Lesser disputes occurred over the civil list and tariffs. In 1845 Sherwood had considered resigning his office because of his disagreements with the cabinet. However, his tory friends had urged him not to do so, as this would have weakened, perhaps destroyed, an already shaky régime. Now he stuck with that decision but increasingly absented himself from important divisions on which he could not conscientiously support the government. As soon as the session ended, Draper asked for his resignation. It was accepted on 30 June 1846.

Sherwood was soon back in office and, moreover, at the head of the administration. This sudden reversal occurred amid a welter of internal dissension. Sherwood's hatred of Draper was widely shared by Upper Canadian ministerialists. Draper fully reciprocated the feeling. Sir Allan Napier MacNab and Sherwood had been on poor terms since the latter's acceptance of office in 1842, and events of 1846, including Sherwood's opposition to MacNab's railway legislation, had greatly worsened that relationship. MacNab had also fallen out with Draper over the adjutant generalship of the militia. Many others were discontented and anxious for change. In the end, Draper retired to the bench. MacNab's image was too extreme to allow of his heading the administration at this stage; in any case, he may not have wanted such a dubious honour. Although Sherwood had politicked hard for the post, it was largely by default that on 29 May 1847 he acceded to the attorney generalship west and the leadership of the government.

Sherwood's cabinet was not strong. Although it was far from being entirely his creation, the Upper Canadian section contained a balanced representation of conservatives. William Cayley* and John Hillyard Cameron* were ultras, William MORRIS and John A. Macdonald* moderates. But in Lower Canada the cabinet was extremely weak, owing to the refusal of influential French Canadians to accept the offers which Draper, Sherwood, and even Governor Lord Elgin [Bruce*] had made to them. Apart from Denis-Benjamin PAPINEAU, who continued as commissioner of crown lands, the other Lower Canadian members were British: the stolid William Badgley* and Peter McGILL, president of the Bank of Montreal. Dominick Daly* continued as provincial secretary.

Short on ability, internal harmony, and popular respect, this cabinet also suffered the disadvantage of having a parliamentary majority of barely more than two. Nor could it be sure of controlling its supporters. Nevertheless, it carried a number of useful measures. The most significant was a reform of the provincial tariff, which eliminated imperial preference by placing an average duty of seven and a half per cent on both British and American manufactured goods. Bonding and warehousing privileges were extended, and conditional provision was made for reciprocity of tariffs with the United States. This enactment represented a first declaration of Canadian fiscal autonomy. Minor amendments were also made to mercantile law, to the criminal code, to municipal law in Lower Canada, and to the Upper Canadian Common Schools Act. The government's only attempt at controversial legislation was on the university question. Here another compromise was attempted, one more acceptable than Draper's to the high tories in that it abandoned the concept of a unified, non-sectarian provincial university in favour of four clerically organized and managed colleges, each to be supported from the original endowment of King's College but with that institution gaining a greater share of the funds than the others. This legislation, however, was defeated by the combined opposition of a unified reform party and two defecting conservatives, Walter Hamilton Dickson and John Wilson*. The defeat was a considerable blow. The government's handling of the problems presented by the large Irish emigration in 1847 also lacked vigour, while the onset of economic depression in the spring further tarnished its image. There were increasing signs of discontent within its own ranks. After only eight weeks the session was brought to a close.

This situation could not continue. Following some procrastination, the cabinet decided on an early election, simultaneously trying to strengthen its position by the appointment of François-Pierre BRUNEAU as receiver general and Joseph-Édouard Turcotte* as solicitor general east. The campaign spanned December 1847 and January 1848. Sherwood himself was returned for Toronto but his government was trounced in both sections of the province.

Although Sherwood was by no means entirely to blame, the result of this election discredited him. After it the leadership of Upper Canadian conservatives reverted to Sir Allan Napier MacNab, though Sherwood took a lively part in the enraged tory opposition to the Rebellion Losses Bill in 1849 and at last gained the house's support for having the seat of government alternate between Toronto and Quebec. The crisis of 1849 tended at first to obscure the divisions between moderate and extreme tories. However, the formation of the British American League [see George Moffatt*] in the summer of that year was essentially the work of the moderates, and Sherwood became one of its more prominent figures. He took up its program with vigour in 1850 and 1851, forcefully advocating in particular the federative union of British North America. In 1850 he explicitly accepted responsible government as then understood, announced his support for an elective legislative council but clashed acrimoniously with William Henry Boulton* over the latter's more extreme proposals for constitutional reform. While apparently working towards the formation of a liberal conservatism, Sherwood still opposed change in the clergy reserves settlement of 1840. Through the almost defunct City of Toronto and Lake Huron Rail Road Company, of which he had been a director from 1846 to 1848, he also had a small stake in the railway politics of the early 1850s.

Sherwood's career was now near its close. At the general election of 1851, over-confidence, division of the tory vote, and, in the last hours of polling, a sudden rush by reformers to support one of his conservative opponents, George Percival Ridout*, deprived him unexpectedly of his seat. Although he regained it late in April 1853, he was to serve only a further 15 months, during which parliament sat little. Moreover, his health was poor. He ran a weak campaign for re-election in July 1854 and was again defeated, a harsh blow to his spirits. To restore both health and humour, he undertook a European tour but died in Bavaria on 7 July 1855.

Henry Sherwood was a man of intense egotism and ambition. He had considerable abilities, particularly as a public speaker, but he lacked the skill necessary to disguise self-advancement and the changes of view inevitable during his career under a cloak of principle. In consequence, he was distrusted by conservatives and reformers alike, except in Toronto. Clever but without restraint, affable but unloved, he was soon forgotten even there. Yet his influence on events, even when negative, was by no means nugatory. As an exemplar of toryism's internal tensions, its progression from a predominantly ultra party to moderate conservatism, and its preoccupation with the professions, business, and the church, Sherwood's career has much significance.

DONALD ROBERT BEER

Henry Sherwood protested the allegations made against him by Justice J. W. Willis in a pamphlet *To the public*, probably printed at York (Toronto) around 1828. His other publications include *Federative union of the British North American provinces* (Toronto, 1850) and two committee reports issued under his signature as chairman: U.C., House of Assembly, Committee on the resolutions of the House of Assembly of Lower Canada, *Report* (Toronto, 1837), and the *Report* of the Select committee on the political state of the provinces of Upper and Lower Canada (Toronto, 1838); the latter also appears in the *App. to the journals*, 1837–38: 257–77.

AO, MS 35, unbound papers, alphabetical list of students, 26 Nov. 1827; letter-book 1844–49: 64, 67. BNQ, Dép. des mss, mss-101, Coll. La Fontaine, 2: 356–57; 5: 1289–99 (copies at PAC). MTL, Robert Baldwin papers, J. Elliott to Baldwin, 17 Oct. 1840; George Ridout to Baldwin, 6 March 1843; J. H. Cameron papers, Dominick Daly to Cameron, 27 June 1846; W. H. Draper to Cameron, 22 June, 8 July 1846. PAC, MG 24, A13; B30, 1: 390–91; B101 (transcript), D16, 58: 46369–83; 105: 69486, 69554–57; E1: 2855–56; I65. PRO, CO 42/430–594; CO 537/140–43. *Arthur papers* (Sanderson). *Debates of the Legislative Assembly of United Canada* (Abbott Gibbs et al.). *Elgin–Grey papers* (Doughty). *Town of York, 1815–34* (Firth). *British Colonist* (Toronto), 1838–54, especially 28 July 1846. *Brockville Gazette* (Brockville, [Ont.]), 1829–32. *Brockville Recorder*, 1836. *Daily Leader* (Toronto), 1854–55, especially 4 Sept. 1855. *Montreal Gazette*, 3 Aug. 1855. *Toronto Patriot*, 1832–47. Armstrong, *Handbook of Upper Canadian chronology*. *Toronto directory*, 1843–44, 1846–47. Wallace, *Macmillan dict.* D. R. Beer, "Transitional toryism in the 1840's as seen in the political career of Sir Allan MacNab" (MA thesis, Queen's Univ., Kingston, Ont., 1963). Careless, *Union of the Canadas*. D. [G.] Creighton, *John A. Macdonald, the young politician* (Toronto, 1952; repr. 1965). J. C. Dent, *The last forty years: Canada since the union of 1841* (2v., Toronto, [1881]). G. P. de T. Glazebrook, *Sir Charles Bagot in Canada: a study in British colonial government* (Oxford, 1929). F. J. K. Griezic, "An uncommon conservative; the political career of John Hillyard Cameron, 1846–1862" (MA thesis, Carleton Univ., Ottawa, 1965), 10–33. George Metcalf, "The political career of William Henry Draper" (MA thesis, Univ. of Toronto, 1959). Middleton, *Municipality of Toronto*. D. R. Beer, "Sir Allan MacNab and the adjutant generalship of militia, 1846–47," *OH*, 61 (1969): 19–32. George Metcalf, "Draper conservatism and responsible government in the Canadas, 1836–1847," *CHR*, 42 (1961): 300–24. E. M. Richards [McGaughey], "The Joneses of Brockville and the family compact," *OH*, 60 (1968): 169–84. Hereward Senior, "Ogle Gowan, Orangeism, and the immigrant question, 1830–1833," *OH*, 66 (1974): 193–210.

SHIWELEAN. *See* HWISTESMETXĒ′QEN

SHONONHSÉ:SE'. *See* MARTIN, GEORGE

SHORE, GEORGE, army officer, militia officer, office holder, politician, and landowner; b. c. 1787 in England; m. 8 Feb. 1815 Ariana Margaretta Jekyll Saunders in Fredericton, and they had two sons and three daughters; d. there 18 May 1851.

Appointed ensign in the New Brunswick Fencibles

Shore

on 9 July 1803, George Shore left England immediately to join the regiment, then stationed in Fredericton. He was promoted lieutenant on 25 March 1804 and in 1810 was made captain and put in command of the light company, succeeding Dugald Campbell*. That September the regiment became the 104th Foot and the following year Shore assumed command of one of its companies, which was stationed in Charlottetown. As senior officer of the garrison, he appears to have assumed that he was in complete charge of the military in the colony. This belief led to a dispute with Lieutenant Governor Joseph Frederick Wallet Des-Barres* and to Shore's being tried by court martial on a variety of charges, including those of making false reports to his commanding officer and of disseminating and nurturing the seeds of insubordination and mutiny. He was cleared on all counts at a trial in Halifax that lasted from 27 May to 8 June 1812. Under the command of Alexander Halkett, Shore led one of the six companies of the regiment on the famous winter march from Fredericton to Upper Canada in 1813; leaving on 21 February, they covered the 700-mile journey to Kingston in 52 days.

Slightly wounded at Sackets Harbor on 29 May 1813, Shore served on the Niagara frontier the following year. While in command of the 104th light company at Lundy's Lane in July, he used his knowledge of local geography, gained while stationed there that spring, to bring his troops quickly into position and was thus able to provide reinforcements at a critical point in the battle. In August he was in the vanguard of the unsuccessful attack on Fort Erie led by Gordon Drummond. When the 104th Foot disbanded on 24 May 1817 Shore was placed on half pay.

His wife, whom he married while on leave from service in Upper Canada, was a woman of intelligence and spirit, with an interest in politics. At the end of the war they returned to Fredericton where Shore became a confidant of the lieutenant governor, Major-General George Stracey Smyth*; beginning in 1819 he served as aide-de-camp, acting also as private secretary, and he was one of the executors of the estate when Smyth died in March 1823.

Smyth, who was old-fashioned and conservative in his politics, did his utmost to place Shore in a highly paid permanent position. He failed in efforts to make him surveyor general and receiver general, though Shore twice held both offices concurrently for several months on a temporary basis. In 1819 he became auditor general, in 1821 a member of the Council, and in 1822 clerk of the pleas of the Supreme Court, a position that provided about £600 annually. In order to make the last office available, Smyth dismissed Henry Bliss*, a member of the local "family compact" whose influence Smyth was attempting to counter. Bliss appealed successfully to the Colonial Office for reinstatement in 1824 but did not return to New Brunswick; Shore therefore continued in the position

and, on Bliss's resignation two years later, was confirmed in the appointment. In 1827 he resigned as auditor general.

Smyth had also named him adjutant general of the provincial militia with the rank of major. Shore's first orders, issued early in 1821, made it clear that he intended to make the force more effective. He promulgated the place and time of musters for each of the 14 units and proceeded to make an inspection of the force. His appointment was resented by some senior officers because of his lack of seniority and his political affiliation. One of them, Major John Allen, commanding officer of the 1st Battalion of the York County Militia, refused to drill his men for inspection. Shore put Allen on charge and ordered a court of inquiry, which arrived at a Solomonic verdict on 21 May 1822: Allen was found guilty of disobeying a lawful command but his appeal of seniority to Shore was upheld. Smyth then defined the status of adjutant general more clearly, stating that, in performing the duties of inspecting field officer, he need not be of a rank senior to that of the commander of the troops. Shore diligently carried out regulations, reprimanding commanding officers for not fining offenders, insisting on the prompt and regular submission of returns and reports, and bringing unit finances under his surveillance. When he was appointed clerk of the Supreme Court in 1822, he offered to resign his militia appointment as being inconsistent with his new duties, but there is no evidence that his resignation was accepted. In 1823, in a move designed to balance Shore's authority, John Allen was named inspecting field officer of militia. The two men were active in organizing the force in the following years, and during the régime of Lieutenant Governor Sir Howard Douglas* it achieved its greatest popularity, and probably its highest level of efficiency. The reduction of tension on the New Brunswick–Maine boundary in the early 1830s lowered interest in the militia; it revived again in the crisis period later in the decade, but then died out with the settling of the boundary question in 1842.

As a member of Douglas's Council, Shore was called upon to undertake many time-consuming tasks, such as acting as a commissioner for the rebuilding of Government House after it was destroyed by fire in 1825 and as a member of the central relief committee for the victims of the Miramichi fire which also occurred that year. He served on several *ad hoc* committees concerned with the administration of crown lands and the improvement of public roads. Shore was not, however, in the front rank of politicians and, when the Council was abolished at the end of 1832 during the term of Sir Archibald Campbell*, he was not named to the new Executive Council, though he did become a life member of the Legislative Council.

Next to the lieutenant governor, the central figure

on the provincial scene under the new arrangements was the commissioner of crown lands, Thomas Baillie*. When Baillie arrived in New Brunswick in 1824, the Shores had cultivated his acquaintance, hoping to benefit from his influence at the Colonial Office. However, for reasons that are not clear, Shore and Baillie parted ways and their names almost always appear on opposite sides in recorded votes in the Legislative Council. In 1837 the group in the assembly opposed to Baillie's policies succeeded in destroying his political power: the Colonial Office was persuaded to transfer control of public lands to the province. To carry out its new liberal program, in May of that year the Colonial Office appointed Sir John HARVEY as lieutenant governor, with instructions to make the Executive Council more responsive to local political opinion. He dismissed two councillors, one of whom was Baillie, and appointed three new members, Charles SIMONDS, Hugh Johnston*, and Shore. Shore thus became identified with the reform administration that governed the province during what historian William Stewart MacNutt* has named "the Age of Harmony." It seems likely that he owed his appointment mainly to the fact that he and Harvey had been comrades-in-arms. The contrast, both in political ideas and in style, between the Council to which he was appointed in 1821 and that of 1837 was remarkable. In 1821 he had been the protégé of the austere Smyth, the last lieutenant governor to be dedicated to ultra-tory principles; in 1837 he joined a government which reflected the ideas and manners of the new liberal era. Shore must have been extremely adaptable to move from the piety and narrowness of Smyth's time to the expansiveness of Harvey's, which was once described by journalist Thomas HILL as "an age of boisterous mirth and lavish expenditure," when amusements were "Balls, Billiards, and Brandy" and it was "fashionable to feast, revel, and swear."

Shore did not hold a portfolio but his duties as adjutant general of the militia saw him involved in events on the Maine border during the crisis that led up to the "Aroostook war" of 1839. In 1837 he played a confidential role in the release of the American agent Ebenezer Greeley. Later Harvey asked Shore and Charles Jeffery Peters*, the attorney general, to inquire into alleged partiality shown to Sir John Caldwell*; the lieutenant governor also consulted him in arranging for relief supplies to be sent to Acadians in the Madawaska settlement. Shore resigned from the Executive Council following the election of 1843, but was reappointed on 5 Feb. 1846 by Lieutenant Governor Sir William MacBean George Colebrooke* and served until May 1848, when the principles of responsible government were adopted.

Shore's father-in-law, John Saunders*, was one of the largest landowners in New Brunswick and Shore and his wife acquired a considerable amount of property by gift, inheritance, and purchase. Their homes were Rose Hall in Fredericton and Shore's Folly on an island in the Saint John River, nine miles above the city. Both Shores had some skill in drawing and painting, and he prepared a map of the province in 1822 which was considered "the most correct extant." In public life, he appears to have performed his duties competently, without either earning particular distinction or being subject to serious criticism. In private, he was known for his charity, for his kindness to friends, and as a family man who gave pleasant parties. On his passing, a friend noted that "as all his daughters had married the family suddenly disappeared like ice in July." His style of life represented the ideal to which the Fredericton bureaucracy came to aspire. He had grown to maturity in a section of society dominated by ideas of gentility and he continued to represent those values when he came to terms with the liberal and democratic age.

Shore did not exercise any extensive personal authority in his administrative positions but they were a source of influence, for through them he had regular access to the lieutenant governor and the chief justice, and could be of service to two influential groups, the lawyers and the notables who led the county militia units. As a devoted churchman and a large holder of landed property, he was a quiet and effective spokesman for those particular interests. His wife's family, the Saunders, had no marriage ties with members of the Hazen, Odell, and Simonds extended families which dominated the colony's politics, but this may not always have been a disadvantage, for it is likely that, at times, the community's recognition of his independent position helped his career.

It is for his military career and his connection with the militia that Shore is chiefly remembered. "Through his efforts, which were perhaps greater than any other man, the militia system had improved and survived. Only in his later years, did age deprive him of the energy to be of further service."

D. MURRAY YOUNG

N.B. Museum, Epitaphs, York County, N.B., CB DOC., Shore; Marriages, CB DOC., Shore–Saunders. PAC, MG 24, A3, 3: 58; A17, ser.I, 1: ff.116–18 (transcripts); ser.II, 3: ff.249–50; L6, 1. PANB, "N.B. political biog." (J. C. and H. B. Graves); RG 1, RS558, A1a, especially p.380; RG 2, RS6, A1–3, 1785–1825; RS8, Appointments and commissions, 1785–1825; RG 7, RS75A, 1851, George Shore; 1868, A. M. Jekyll Shore, W. H. Shore. PANS, MG 12, HQ, 9, 10 June 1812. PRO, CO 188/25; 188/29: 295–97, 299–300; 188/52: 12–51 (mfm. at PANB); CO 189/12, Bathurst to Smyth, 30 April 1823; Bathurst to Chipman, 10 Sept. 1823 (mfm. at PANB). Southampton City Record Office (Southampton, Eng.), List of J. G. Smyth papers in private possession (typescript, 1968; copy at National Reg. of Arch., London). UNBL, MG H1, "Old Fredericton and the college: town and gown as described in the letters of James and Ellen Robb," ed. A. G. Bailey (typescript, 1973); MG H11, Shore corr.

Simms

N.B., Legislative Council, *Journal* [1786–1830], vol.2, 1821–30; 1831–42. Robb and Coster, *Letters* (Bailey). *Carleton Sentinel* (Woodstock, N.B.), 1851, especially 27 May. *Head Quarters* (Fredericton), 21 May 1851. *Morning News* (Saint John, N.B.), 21 May 1851. *New-Brunswick Courier*, 24 May 1851. *New Brunswick Reporter and Fredericton Advertiser*, 23 May 1851. *Royal Gazette* (Fredericton), 1814–34. G.B., WO, *Army list*, 1805, 1817. D. R. Facey-Crowther, "The New Brunswick militia: 1784–1871" (MA thesis, Univ. of N.B., Fredericton, 1965), 87–171. I. L. Hill, *Fredericton, New Brunswick, British North America* ([Fredericton?, 1968?]). Lawrence, *Judges of N.B.* (Stockton and Raymond). MacNutt, *New Brunswick*. D. R. Moore, "John Saunders, 1754–1834: consummate loyalist" (MA thesis, Univ. of N.B., 1980), 108–9, 126–27. W. A. Squires, *The 104th Regiment of Foot (the New Brunswick Regiment), 1803–1817* (Fredericton, 1962).

SIMMS, SOPHIA (Dalton), newspaper publisher; b. 1785 or 1786, near Birmingham, England; m. *c.* 1805 Thomas Dalton*, and they had three sons and four daughters; d. 14 June 1859 in Toronto.

Sophia Simms was one of 15 children born to William and Mary Simms of Hall Green (Birmingham) and was a sister of James Simms*, the eminent Newfoundland jurist and statesman. Little is known of her early life. She married Thomas Dalton of Birmingham about 1805 and spent much of the next 12 years in Newfoundland. Her husband served in St John's as agent for mercantile houses in Birmingham and London and later had his own business. Bankrupted in the general economic decline that followed the end of the Napoleonic Wars, the family left Newfoundland in 1817 and settled in Kingston, Upper Canada, where Thomas set up a brewery and was made a director of the first Bank of Upper Canada.

The family prospered for a few years, but the failure in 1822 of the private Bank of Upper Canada, and the harsh sanctions subsequently imposed on the bank's directors, brought great hardship. A disastrous fire in the brewery late in 1828 completed their financial ruin. With the help of his family Thomas Dalton launched a new career in November 1829 as publisher of the *Patriot and Farmer's Monitor*, but he had to sacrifice the brewery property and their comfortable home to finance the project. Three years later, in October 1832, the family moved to York (Toronto) where the always staunchly pro-British and now strongly conservative *Patriot* became one of the most influential newspapers of its period. Life for the family was somewhat easier now, but Dalton, frustrated by the government's approach to the problems that beset the province, gave way to frequent intemperate editorial outbursts which Sophia tried her best to get him to moderate.

When Thomas died of apoplexy on 26 Oct. 1840, Sophia took over the management of the semi-weekly paper, becoming the first successful woman publisher in Toronto, but she did not undertake the editorial duties herself. J. P. Macklin, said to have worked at one time on the *Manchester Guardian* and already assistant editor of the *Patriot*, stepped into the gap. But Sophia made it clear that she had no intention of abandoning her husband's policy of uncompromising condemnation of perceived evils. In a confidential letter to Dominick Daly*, Macklin reported in November 1840 that he was "not unshackled, being obliged to bow to the dictum of my employers (his widow &c). I have however endeavoured to moderate the tone of the paper, and in doing so have drawn a nest of hornets about my ears." Other editors followed him, with Sophia keeping control of the paper until 9 Oct. 1848.

During Sophia Dalton's years as publisher, the *Patriot* lost none of its status as a leading conservative journal. In announcing her retirement, at age 63, she said that "although during [her] period the editorial department has been filled by gentlemen of ability, yet, from the peculiarity of her position, there must have been many deficiencies, chiefly on local matters, arising from a want of that energy and activity which are absolutely requisite in the publication of a newspaper. . . . [She] is happy in being able to say to the friends of *The Patriot*, that it is now in the hands of gentlemen, who will conduct it in the advocacy of those Conservative Principles hitherto maintained, and with vigour and ability beyond her power to accomplish." The *Patriot* was sold to Edward George O'Brien* and was edited for a short time by his brother, Lucius James O'Brien*, and later by Samuel Thompson*.

Sophia Dalton raised eight children, including one son from her husband's first marriage. Two sons, William Henry and Robert Gladstone, worked in the *Patriot* office as young men and went on to gain a degree of prominence as a physician and a lawyer respectively. Quiet and unassuming but apparently with great strength of character, Sophia was able to maintain domestic calm through the many storms that buffeted her family. Matthew Teefy, an apprentice at the *Patriot* at the time of Thomas's death, said of her later: "I shall remember with feelings of pleasure during my life . . . the civility of Mrs. Dalton. She was a kind, good person." She died possessed of a very modest estate, but she made special provisions for her daughters and daughter-in-law, setting up trusts "for their separate use free from the control of their husbands."

I. R. DALTON

The Daltons' *Patriot and Farmer's Monitor* appeared in Kingston, [Ont.], from 12 Oct. [actually 12 Nov.] 1829 to 23 Oct. 1832, and in York (Toronto) from 7 Dec. 1832 to 18 March 1834. It was called the *Patriot* from 21 March 1834, and became the *Toronto Patriot* on 3 Jan. 1840. Issues relevant to Sophia Dalton's life include 25 March, 1 April, 1 June 1830; 23 Oct., 7 Dec. 1832; 27 Oct., 20 Nov., 29 Dec. 1840; and 10 Oct. 1848.

ACC-O, St George's Cathedral (Kingston), reg. of baptisms, 7 May 1825. AO, MS 78; MU 2113, 1858, no.16; RG 22, ser.155, will of Thomas Dalton. Cathedral of St John the Baptist (Anglican) (St John's), Reg. of baptisms, 27 April 1807, 7 Sept. 1809, 9 March 1813. Frontenac Land Registry Office (Kingston), Deeds, vol.E, no.276 (mfm. at AO, GS 3928); vol.K, no.156 (mfm. at AO, GS 3932). PAC, RG 5, A1: 36415–25, 47740–43, 135347–50; RG 9, I, B1, 9, List of appointments, 16 Aug. 1821; 12, Markland to Coffin, 2 July 1824. PANL, P1/5, Thomas Dalton to Duckworth, 31 Aug. 1811 (mfm. at PAC). St James' Cemetery and Crematorium (Toronto), Record of burials, 16 June 1859 (Sophia Dalton), 24 July 1865 (Charles Simms). York County Surrogate Court (Toronto), no.1685, will of Sophia Dalton, proved 18 May 1874 (mfm. at AO). *Arthur papers* (Sanderson), 2: 436–37; 3: 165. [Thomas Dalton], *"By the words of thy own mouth will I condemn thee"; to Christopher Alexander Hagerman, esq.* ([Kingston?, 1824?]; copy at MTL). Murphy, *Winter studies and summer rambles*, 1: 272. U.C., House of Assembly, *Journal*, 1825, app.B. *Aris's Birmingham Gazette; or the General Correspondent* (Birmingham, Eng.), 9 April 1804. *Kingston Chronicle*, 16 July 1819, 29 Nov. 1828. *Royal Gazette and Newfoundland Advertiser*, 10 Jan. 1811, 3 Dec. 1816. *Upper Canada Herald* (Kingston), 1823. *Birmingham directory*, 1808. I. R. Dalton, "Thomas Dalton and the 'pretended bank'" (MS, Toronto, 1981, possession of the author). Raymond Card, "The Daltons and *The Patriot*," CHR, 16 (1935): 176–78. *Courier* (St John's), 9 Aug. 1865. I. R. Dalton, "The Kingston brewery of Thomas Dalton," *Historic Kingston*, no.26 (1978): 38–50. *Leader*, 22 July 1865. M. L. Magill, "James Morton of Kingston – brewer," *Historic Kingston*, no.21 (1973): 28–36.

SIMONDS, CHARLES, businessman, politician, office holder, and justice of the peace; b. 22 Aug. 1783 in Portland Point (Saint John, N.B.), son of James Simonds* and Hannah Peabody; m. first 27 May 1817 Catharine Mary Longmuir (d. 2 March 1820); m. secondly 31 July 1824 Lucy Anne Clopper, sister of Henry George Clopper*, and they had three sons and one daughter; d. 12 April 1859 in Saint John.

Charles Simonds was born into one of the most successful families in what was to become New Brunswick. His father, a modest trader from Haverhill, Mass., had responded to the invitation issued to the people of the Thirteen Colonies by Charles Lawrence*, governor of Nova Scotia, and by 1762 he had settled in the Saint John River valley. He formed a trading company with his cousin William Hazen* and several other Massachusetts merchants. The firm, later known as Simonds, Hazen, and White, acquired title to several large tracts of land, and was to direct the commercial growth of the valley for several decades. During the American revolution the partners maintained unwavering support for the royal cause, and

from 1781 became the principal beneficiaries of the British war effort in Nova Scotia, supplying masts for the fleet and provisions for loyalist refugees. As they owned most of the land north and east of Portland (Saint John), they also profited in a number of ways from the large influx of loyalist settlers. Within a single generation the Simonds, Hazen, and White families had become landed gentry.

After attending the parish school in Portland and receiving instruction from a private tutor, Charles Simonds entered his father's business while still a teenager. The partnership of Simonds, Hazen, and White was dissolved around the turn of the century (the final outstanding legal matter was resolved in 1810), and Simonds Sr concentrated on his interests in real estate transactions, the timber trade, milling, and the importation and wholesale merchandising of consumer goods from Britain. Charles eventually assumed his father's place in directing the family's business affairs at the Portland base; his younger brother Richard* would set up a branch establishment on the Miramichi River. For several years prior to 1820 Charles was also involved in a firm of auction and commission merchants with a brother-in-law, Henry Gilbert.

As a representative of one of Saint John's premier commercial enterprises, Simonds came to play a leading role in the business community; he was a promoter and one of the first directors of the Bank of New Brunswick, incorporated in 1820, and became its president in 1824. He also actively participated in the Saint John Chamber of Commerce. Following the death of his first wife in 1820, Simonds gradually abandoned direct involvement in all of his businesses except the timber trade and those centred on the bank. Later on he was to become associated with the Commercial Bank of New Brunswick as well as the Saint John Fire Insurance Company, established in 1834 and 1854 respectively. By the early 1830s he was independently wealthy. Apart from his own resources, after his father's death in February 1831 he and his brother Richard had become the principal beneficiaries of the estate, estimated to be worth more than one million dollars. Their inheritance was primarily several thousand acres of real estate comprising much of the parish and later the town of Portland. Around this time Charles decided to devote his energies to public service.

A formative force on young Simonds's development had been his father's ideology. Elected to the House of Assembly for Saint John in 1795, James Simonds had supported the popular opposition to Lieutenant Governor Thomas Carleton* and the Council and had participated in the movement to secure control of appropriations for the house. He remained in opposition throughout his political career. Another important element in the make-up of young

Simonds

Charles was his family's religious tradition. Although they accepted conformity, their Anglicanism was of the colonial American variety – low, independent in polity, and streaked with the influence of George Whitefield and New England revivalism. Simonds was an active member and officer of such non-sectarian evangelical associations as the British and Foreign Bible Society, the Portland Temperance Society, and the Religious Tract Society. Like most low churchmen in Saint John, he probably also attended services at the Methodist chapel on Sunday afternoons and in his middle age he even held office in some of their organizations although he remained an Anglican. Certainly he was to cultivate these ties after his entry into politics. And certainly his church background coloured Charles's responses to the great religious issues of the 1830s, 1840s, and 1850s.

Having neither the need for revenue from public service (and indeed some contempt for those who did) nor the personal influence to command the great offices, Simonds chose to begin his public career in the House of Assembly. In 1822 he successfully ran as one of the four representatives for the County and City of Saint John, joining in the assembly his brother Richard, a member for Northumberland County since 1816, and his brother-in-law Thomas Millidge*, who also sat for Saint John. His first few years were undistinguished. During the "succession crisis" occasioned by the death of Lieutenant Governor George Stracey Smyth* in 1823, he doubtless sympathized with Christopher Billopp, who represented the merchant community, in his conflict with the dominant official clique led by Ward Chipman* Sr. Simonds none the less maintained a low profile. He used his early years for building alliances: already the most prominent representative for Saint John, Simonds needed to forge relationships with the political élites from the other major communities in the province. It was no easy political task because the electorate in the interior viewed the Saint John commercial interests with considerable suspicion. Bills and causes could sometimes be lost simply because of their introduction by "city" members. The lead in political matters was generally taken by his younger, but more experienced, brother Richard who also had the advantage of representing the north shore. Like his brother, Charles began to acquire influence, chairing several important committees in the middle and late 1820s. When in 1828 Richard, who had been elected speaker the year before, resigned from the assembly to join the Council, Charles was unanimously elected to succeed him. By that date he and Edward Barron Chandler* of Westmorland County were clearly the two men who could control the house.

No government could hope to achieve its legislative objectives without the cooperation of the speaker. Antagonism between the assemblymen and the office holders who comprised the Council frequently ran so high that effective control of the government rested in the hands of the lieutenant governor, who personally negotiated the legislative program with the leading assemblymen. The most successful of these colonial administrators were Sir Howard Douglas* and Sir John HARVEY, both of whom assiduously cultivated friendships with Simonds. The importance of these relationships is perhaps best illustrated by the issue of a provincial college. An inveterate proponent of development, Douglas was the principal promoter of a New Brunswick university. Realizing the difficulties inherent in creating an institution resting solely on the support of the provincial legislature, on 15 Dec. 1828 Douglas procured a royal charter for King's College (University of New Brunswick) whereby roughly one-half the capital as well as all of the annual operating costs of the school would come from New Brunswick's casual revenues. He was successful in large part because he had been able to win Simonds's support for the undertaking. Bills to provide the requisite financing were forthcoming from the assembly although by 1829 payment on the overrun cost of the building (started in 1825) was made only when Simonds, as speaker, cast the deciding vote. Simonds became a member of the first college council.

Unfortunately for the infant institution, Douglas returned home in 1829 and the high churchmen who dominated the college council neglected to invite Simonds to attend their meetings. Moreover, the council's reluctance to submit its budgets for assembly approval and its failure to admit dissenters to its membership (an amendment made to the royal charter in England meant the council could not legally appoint non-churchmen) or to the faculty, quickly turned Simonds into the institution's most vehement critic. On one point Simonds had always been adamant: there must be no denominational restrictions at King's College. A consistent supporter of religious equality, as early as 1821 he had voted with the majority of the house in support of a bill to permit the clergy of dissenting traditions to perform marriage ceremonies, and in 1831 he would argue for equality in the distribution of public funds to all religious denominations for building purposes. Both of these measures, passed in the assembly, were effectively destroyed in the Council. By 1831 he was leading a substantial coalition of dissenters and of like-minded Anglicans in the assembly in an effort to reduce the college's annual grant from £1,100 to £600. He objected to both the sectarian bias of the school and the salaries paid to its faculty and officers. Fortunately for the future of the college, Simonds was unable to muster a majority in the assembly, but the constant attacks on the institution brought its very survival into doubt in the early 1830s.

Simonds's principal rival in the house was Chandler, who by 1830 spoke for the coastal communities of New Brunswick just as Simonds spoke for the Saint John River valley. At the opening of the session in 1831, Simonds and Chandler were both nominated as speaker. The assembly divided evenly and a speaker was found only when both men withdrew: William CRANE was elected by a majority of one. Simonds and Chandler remained powerful rivals in all the assemblies until 1836, and it was only on those infrequent occasions when they were in agreement that the house took a clear position on important questions.

Of all the issues which troubled Simonds in the first decade of his public life, he considered none as important as that of the salaries and fees received by public officials. He was opposed in principle to the payment of public monies to officials who could not be held accountable to the property-owners and taxpayers, and his opposition towards British-born office holders was exacerbated by xenophobia, an envy of those considered to be his social superiors, and a contempt for lawyers and others who lived off the body politic. In January 1829 he was almost successful in stopping the payment of fees to the solicitor general, and they were approved only after Douglas promised to investigate charges made against that official. Simonds's opposition to King's College had a good deal to do with the size of the salaries granted to the crown appointees such as the registrar, George Frederick STREET. His particular *bêtes noires* were imperial officials such as Henry Wright, the collector of customs at Saint John, who in a good year received in excess of £3,000 for a relatively simple and part-time function. Simonds would often draw comparisons between that office and the post of provincial treasurer, held by his brother Richard, which paid only £500 for a much more demanding job.

As the provincial tariff system was broadened in the early 19th century, the proportion of provincial revenues controlled by the assembly rose, and in 1825 the house obtained control of the net revenues raised from imperial duties collected in New Brunswick. Given the assembly's tradition of voting sums for specific purposes, the Council rapidly found itself a government in exile; decisions concerning appropriations rested in the hands of the powerful house committee on supply, which consisted of a representative from each of the province's constituencies. Thus the Council sought its financial salvation in the casual revenues remaining to the royal prerogative. These revenues, centred on the lands of the province, could be raised either through the imposition of an annual quitrent on freeholders or through the rental and disposal of the crown's timber lands which comprised approximately three-quarters of the province. The royal agent for these lands was the ambitious, arrogant, and well-connected young English-born Thomas Baillie*, whom the Colonial Office had appointed in 1824 over a native New Brunswicker. As commissioner of crown lands, he became a target of public anger not only because of his efforts to increase the revenue-producing capacities of the land and his rigorous enforcement of the land regulations, but also for his luxurious style of living and his arbitrary use of power against which there was no judicial appeal. Lieutenant Governor Douglas had kept the political situation stable but, with a constitutional crisis between the assembly and the Council looming, the new lieutenant governor, Sir Archibald Campbell*, came to depend more and more heavily on the controversial Baillie.

Simonds feared that Baillie would be able to secure the financial independence of the Council by milking the crown lands to produce a capital sum of sufficient size that the interest on it would support the executive body in perpetuity. These fears seemed realized in 1833 when the Council was divided into legislative and executive branches. Not only did Campbell name Baillie as one of the five members of the new Executive Council, but he gave him precedence, making him the second most powerful man in the colony after himself and bypassing several senior native New Brunswick politicians such as Street.

As an alien who had received his office through personal influence, who retained it in his own rather than the public interest, and who obtained from it one of the most substantial incomes in the province, Baillie offended a whole range of Simonds's prejudices. The acrimony was probably enhanced when Baillie prosecuted Simonds for trespass in Saint John in 1827. However, the reason for Simonds's leadership in the movement to oust Baillie went beyond personal biases. While Chandler and others deplored Baillie's attempts to maximize the revenues from the crown lands, at no point did they challenge his legal right as a servant of the crown to withhold from the house an accounting of the king's casual revenues. Simonds's unorthodox constitutional position was genuinely radical. He argued that the crown and its representatives did not have privileged rights, that they were dependent on the House of Assembly, and that the central issue was the question of arbitrary taxation without the consent of the governed. No lawyer, Simonds rejected with disdain the objections to his theories raised by Chandler, Crane, and William Boyd Kinnear*. Regardless of the constitutional correctness of his rhetoric, Simonds's stance became immensely popular as the crisis developed in 1833 and 1834.

During the 1833 session Simonds was chiefly responsible for the creation of a select committee on grievances. Chaired by him, the committee was given

Simonds

authority to investigate current grievances; it could call witnesses, compel testimony, and force submission of required documentation. After three weeks, Simonds presented its report from which the house prepared eight resolutions. Four of these condemned Baillie's activities and policies, another deplored the imposition of quitrents, and the last one proposed to send a two-man delegation to present the resolutions to the colonial secretary, Lord Stanley. Simonds and Chandler, the chosen representatives, left in May 1833, probably with high hopes of success. Simonds had recently won two rounds in his encounters with the local political establishment. In 1831 the assembly had protested to the Treasury the size of salaries paid to the customs officers and suggested large reductions. In February 1832 it had received word that its proposal had been accepted. Later that year the house had also rejected a bill permitting the enforcement of quitrents.

In England, Simonds and Chandler had considerable success with Stanley. He was prepared to suspend collection of quitrents and surrender control of the crown lands to the legislature under three conditions: a permanent annual civil list of £14,000 would be provided by the house, Baillie would be retained as commissioner, and the £70,000 from the proposed sale to the New Brunswick and Nova Scotia Land Company of the Stanley Tract in York County would be kept by the crown. These recommendations were debated during the 1834 session. Chandler and Simonds were bitterly divided, Chandler advocating their acceptance and Simonds arguing that they did not go nearly far enough. Simonds finally carried the day and the proposals were defeated largely because the assembly did not want to surrender the funds that would come from the sale of the Stanley Tract.

The next two years were a period of vicious sniping as relations between the assembly and the lieutenant governor collapsed completely. For the first time in the province's history the assembly's animosity was directed not only against the lieutenant governor's advisers, but against the lieutenant governor himself. Simonds led the attack: the annual training period of the militia, one of the lieutenant governor's priorities, was cut from three days to one. Campbell replied by dissolving the house on 22 March 1834, but in the election held later that year Simonds and his partisans were returned in undiminished strength. When Campbell attempted to collect the quitrents in 1835 the assembly refused to compromise, rejecting the Colonial Office's suggestion that the quitrents be commuted for a fixed sum. Furthermore, the assembly so reduced the militia funds that the inspector general had to be dismissed, and it declined to vote monies for the expenses of the legislative councillors. The latter replied in kind, whereupon the assemblymen attached their own expenses to a general appropriations bill. When the council turned it down, the legislature was prorogued without approving a supply bill.

The strategy of financial deadlock came from Simonds. Reiterating his theory that the assembly possessed the sole right to dispose of public monies, he once again, after quarrelling with the more moderate Chandler, carried the house. However, the victory was short-lived. The annual expenditures for public works had become so critical to the economic well-being of most New Brunswick communities that the legislature was recalled three months later, the supply bill passed, and the quitrents commuted for an annual payment of £1,000 to the casual revenues. During the 1836 session Simonds recommended that the assembly again send a delegation to the colonial secretary, the procedure they had employed in 1833. In the bitter debate which ensued, his proposals were sustained by a 20 to 9 majority over the combined opposition of Chandler and William End*. A second assembly delegation, of Lemuel Allan Wilmot* and William Crane, met with the new colonial secretary, Lord Glenelg, that summer. Faced with a steadily worsening situation in the Canadas, Glenelg readily acceded to the demands of the assembly. The crown lands and the revenues from the Stanley Tract were to be surrendered in return for an annual civil list of £14,000, the salaries of certain British appointees were to be gradually reduced, and the Executive Council was to be enlarged to reflect more clearly the popular will. Campbell resisted the changes and finally resigned.

His replacement, Sir John Harvey, sought out Simonds on his arrival in May 1837 and established a friendship that was to last throughout his administration. In compliance with his instructions, Harvey attempted to create an executive council which had the support of the assembly. Baillie and Street were removed and Simonds and his nephew Hugh Johnston* became the first assemblymen ever to sit on the council. During the next session of the house Simonds again was elected speaker, an office he was to hold for the next four years.

The years 1837 to 1841 were the zenith of Simonds's political influence. This period, which historian William Stewart MacNutt* has dubbed the "Age of Harmony," was the time when the New Brunswick system of assembly democracy came of age. In control of appropriations and every source of provincial revenue, and heir to the £70,000 that Baillie had built up from the casual revenues, the assemblymen embarked on a substantial program of public works. As principal councillor to the lieutenant governor and as speaker and government leader in the house, Simonds was the cornerstone on which the new order was built.

Harmony, however, was purchased at a considerable price. Although the Executive Council now contained two influential representatives from the assembly and no longer openly challenged the house on any important issue, the majority of its members were still appointed officials and it was still answerable to the lieutenant governor. The House of Assembly now controlled the revenues, but in Simonds's eyes it proved itself financially irresponsible. Individual members seemed to him to be more concerned with the interests of their friends and constituencies than with those of the province as a whole. In the period 1837–42 the legislature received revenues of £467,000 and disbursed more than £600,000. Arguing that the financial crisis enveloping the province was the fault of the "abominable system," in early 1842 Simonds supported a resolution in the house that no appropriation would thenceforth be made unless the Executive Council provided full budgets outlining the year's income and expenditures. The alternative, he felt, would be direct taxation. Despite his best efforts, the traditional mode of appropriation was upheld by a vote of 18 to 12.

Having failed in his first effort to secure fiscal responsibility, later in 1842 Simonds embraced the proposals of the new lieutenant governor, Sir William MacBean George Colebrooke*, to create municipal corporations that would relieve the legislature of a substantial part of the financial burdens of the province. Simonds successfully carried the bill through the assembly by virtue of his tie-breaking vote. Appropriately, the battle for the municipalities was lost in the Legislative Council [see Ward CHIPMAN]. In the face of this defeat, the lieutenant governor dissolved the house. During the ensuing election of 1842–43, Colebrooke was opposed by virtually every leading assemblyman except Simonds. Although Simonds was returned for Saint John, throughout the province the ranks of the traditionalists were strengthened.

Simonds's influence in the legislature was severely reduced in the days immediately following the election. In 1842 he had been charged with rape and common assault on his married housekeeper, Ellen Seely. Moses Henry Perley*, the commissioner of Indian Affairs, commented on the affair in a letter to his mother: "This matter of Simonds is a very awkward business to make the best of it. There seems to be no doubt that he has been following up the woman for no good purpose, and whether he used force or not, has proved himself an old goat. It seems he has pawed the woman three or four different times, and went on, till she would stand it no longer." On 13 Jan. 1843 the 59-year-old widower was found guilty by a *nisi prius* jury of five counts of rape and one of common assault. Later, in the Supreme Court, three of the original counts of rape were expunged, and he was finally convicted of two counts of assault with carnal intent and one of common assault. Even though the affair was apparently not taken up by the press, his conviction, and the repudiation of the lieutenant governor's program by the electorate, probably persuaded Simonds not to seek the speaker's chair

again. The decline of his influence in the assembly after 1843 is perhaps best illustrated by the fate of a resolution to limit the grant of supply in any session to the estimated revenues of the period. Simonds was able to secure only seven votes in its favour including those of Wilmot and Charles Fisher*, the more progressive liberals of the house.

In an effort to secure the support of the assembly, Colebrooke reorganized his Executive Council early in 1843 to encompass all talents and political views. Of the five assemblymen appointed, Johnston, Chandler, Wilmot, Simonds, and Robert Leonard Hazen*, only Simonds remained from the earlier administration. The new government functioned without serious incident until the death of the provincial secretary, William Franklin Odell*, on Christmas Day 1844. Colebrooke, without consultation, appointed his son-in-law Alfred Reade to the office. When the Executive Council divided equally on the issue, Wilmot resigned on the principle that the great offices must be given to the members of the legislature on the advice of the Executive Council, and Hazen, Johnston, and Chandler left because they felt the appointment should have been given to a New Brunswicker. Of the four councillors who supported Colebrooke – Joseph Cunard*, John Simcoe Saunders*, John Montgomery*, and Simonds – only Simonds could pretend to possess any kind of popular support.

In his defence of the lieutenant governor during the assembly debates, Simonds enunciated his concept of the possibilities and limitations of responsible government within a colonial setting. It was impossible, he argued, to demand a government identical to that of the United Kingdom because New Brunswick was not a sovereign state. To make the Executive Council a creature of the assembly would both destroy the authority of the royal prerogative, as exercised through the lieutenant governor, and turn the entire administration of the province into a battleground of partisan politics such as existed in Nova Scotia and the Province of Canada. He believed the assembly had gained in 1836 all of the authority it needed; the Executive Council should be left as the point where popular and imperial interests met and melded, and the administration of the province should be kept beyond the partisan interests of the house. For these reasons he rejected the claim that the provincial secretaryship should be a political appointment. Although he would have preferred that the office go to a New Brunswicker, he accepted and supported the lieutenant governor's judgement in the matter.

Simonds's spirited defence did not deter the assembly, by a vote of 19 to 13, from deploring the lieutenant governor's action in appointing Reade, or at the same time passing, by 23 to 10, a resolution of non-confidence in the Executive Council. The rump government continued to function for the remainder of

Simonds

the year but – despite approaches from the lieutenant governor – Chandler, Johnston, and Hazen refused to rejoin the council. Finally, just prior to the opening of the 1846 session, the remaining councillors submitted their resignations. At the same time, Simonds also resigned from the assembly. On 1 Feb. 1846 he was appointed to the Legislative Council.

In the late 1840s Simonds came to devote more and more of his time to local matters and his business concerns. He served as police commissioner in Portland, played an important role in the creation of a permanent police force for that town, and was involved in maintaining the peace between the two resident Irish factions.

On 28 June 1849, following the abrogation by the British parliament of the navigation acts, Simonds chaired a public meeting of the merchants and citizens of Saint John who were concerned about the future of the province. Out of this meeting came the New Brunswick Colonial Association; its purpose was "to devise a scheme for the general relief of British North America to be submitted to Her Majesty's Government." Throughout the summer of 1849 the views of the association rapidly moved towards the possibilities of a union of British North America, which its members saw as a federal union allowing considerable powers of local self-government and assuring the Maritime colonies of equal influence with the Province of Canada in a united legislature. In November, Simonds and John Robertson* met in Montreal with members of the British American League [see George Moffatt*] to discuss the issue, but nothing came of the meeting.

The association prepared a platform which became the basis of the reform group in Saint John. During the provincial election of 1850 the reformers entered a strong slate of candidates from the city – Simonds, Samuel Leonard Tilley*, William Hayden Needham*, William Johnstone Ritchie*, John Hamilton Gray*, and Robert Duncan Wilmot* – who succeeded in defeating all of the government's candidates. At the opening of the 1851 session, Simonds was elected once again as speaker. The honour was short-lived. That August, in an effort to strengthen his failing Executive Council, Sir Edmund Walker Head* persuaded two of the Saint John members, Gray and Wilmot, to abandon their commitments and join the council. Because Wilmot also accepted the office of surveyor general, he was forced to resign his assembly seat and seek a new mandate. Outraged by this betrayal, Simonds, Tilley, and Ritchie publicly condemned Gray and Wilmot and, when the latter won re-election, resigned from the house.

Most commentators of the period expressed their admiration for the political character demonstrated by the three Saint John reformers. Tilley and Ritchie created from it a myth of integrity that was to mark their whole careers. At 68, Simonds seemingly had deliberately chosen this path of glory as a means to a second retirement. It was no surprise that he did not contest the provincial election of 1854. In May 1856 John Henry Thomas Manners-Sutton*, who was now the lieutenant governor, dissolved the house and forced the dismissal of his reform government, led by Charles Fisher, over the issue of the Prohibition Act of 1855. In the general election which followed, Simonds offered himself once again to the electors of Saint John and was returned to the assembly for an eighth time. In July the aged veteran was elected speaker of the house and presided over the repeal of the controversial law.

The liquor issue had divided many of the quasi-party loyalties that had developed during the early 1850s. Although most reformers were sympathetic to the temperance movement, many had supported the law's repeal. They believed that the new government could not last a week once the issue had been removed from the political arena. Eager to test this hypothesis, Fisher introduced a motion of non-confidence after the opening of the 1857 session. Following a long debate, the house divided 20 to 20. From the chair, Simonds berated both parties for their lack of patriotism and their concern with the spoils of government. He ended by casting his vote in support of the government. The "speaker's government" lasted just five weeks before the defection of one of its supporters persuaded the Executive Council to ask for dissolution. Simonds returned to Saint John where he played no further part in the public life of the province. He died less than two years later.

Charles Simonds was probably the most important New Brunswick political figure in the first half of the 19th century. For 28 years he sat as a member of the House of Assembly for the County and City of Saint John. He held the critical office of speaker for 11 years and was a member of the Executive Council for 9. The first assemblyman to hold the latter office, he also sat briefly on the Legislative Council. But Simonds's importance goes beyond the offices he held. The decisions taken on most significant public issues between 1828 and 1843 conformed more closely to his views than to those of any other public figure in the province. The debate over the extent to which he formed public opinion or simply reflected the views of certain interests is of the essence of history. There can be no question that he was instrumental in ensuring that there be an orderly resolution of the principal public issues in New Brunswick during the 1830s, 1840s, and 1850s.

T. W. ACHESON

[There are numerous references to Charles Simonds and his activities in most of the standard political histories of colonial

New Brunswick including MacNutt, *New Brunswick*; James Hannay, *History of New Brunswick* (2v., Saint John, N.B., 1909); G. E. Fenety, *Political notes and observations: or, a glance at the leading measures that have been introduced and discussed in the House of Assembly of New Brunswick* . . . (Fredericton, 1867); and Lawrence, *Judges of N.B.* (Stockton and Raymond). The best source for the detail of Simonds's political views and activities are the summaries of the Legislative Assembly debates and proceedings which were published in the *New-Brunswick Courier*. Further information can be found in N.B., House of Assembly, *Journal*, for 1820–57, and Legislative Council, *Journal*, for 1846–50; in N.B. Museum, M. H. Perley, letters, 1813–54, Perley to [Mary Merritt Perley], 29 Oct. 1842 (transcripts); in PANB, RG 2, RS6, A, and RG 4, RS24; and in PRO, CO 188. Unfortunately there is no collection of private papers. The best study of the origins of the Simonds family in New Brunswick is R. C. Campbell, "Simonds, Hazen and White: a study of a New Brunswick firm in the commercial world of the eighteenth century" (MA thesis, Univ. of N.B., Saint John, 1970). T.W.A.]

SIMPSON, FRANCES RAMSAY (Simpson, Lady Simpson), diarist; b. c. 1812 in London, second child of Geddes Mackenzie Simpson and Frances Hume Hawkins; m. there 24 Feb. 1830 George SIMPSON; d. 21 March 1853 in Lachine, Lower Canada.

Frances Ramsay Simpson, the daughter of a successful London merchant, was brought up with all the accomplishments and graces expected of a Victorian lady. In 1830 her middle-aged cousin George Simpson, governor of the Hudson's Bay Company in North America, visited the Simpson household while on furlough and was so captivated by the sweet nature and genteel talents of the 18-year-old Frances that he quickly married her without much consideration as to whether one so young and delicate could successfully adapt to life in Rupert's Land. After a brief honeymoon the governor and his bride sailed from Liverpool on 8 March for North America.

During the voyage Mrs Simpson was grateful to have the company of Catherine Turner, the Scottish bride of HBC chief factor John George McTavish*, for the parting from her family in London had caused her "bitter sorrow." Although she was violently seasick during the ocean crossing, her health improved sufficiently after her arrival in Montreal for her to enjoy the canoe trip from Lachine to York Factory (Man.) in May and June. The two wives were the first British women ever to travel this route, and the diary that Mrs Simpson kept of their trip constitutes a unique record. She was awed by the magnificence of the scenery, admired the strength and skill of the voyageurs, two of whom were entrusted to carry the ladies over the portages, and was amused by the gallant attempts of the company's officers to welcome her along the way. After her visit to the post on Rainy Lake (Ont.), it was renamed Fort Frances in her honour.

Frances Simpson's arrival in Rupert's Land had serious repercussions on fur-trade society. Most of the HBC officers had married native women "after the custom of the country." But with the British marriage of Governor Simpson, who had himself cast aside a native wife and family, racial prejudice increased. Simpson determined that native women, regardless of the rank of their HBC husbands, should be excluded from respectable society, especially in the Red River settlement (Man.) where the Simpsons took up their winter residence.

The gracious manners of the governor's lady and her delightful playing on the newly imported pianoforte made Frances Simpson "the brightest star" in Red River; but personally she was homesick and lonely, her female acquaintances being restricted to the few white wives of company officers such as Chief Factor Donald MCKENZIE and the missionaries William Cockran* and David Thomas Jones*. In the early months of 1831 Mrs Simpson's health deteriorated rapidly as her first pregnancy advanced, and, despite the efforts of Dr William TODD, the lack of skilled medical attention compounded the difficult birth of her son, George Geddes, in September. The sudden death of this child the following spring was a grievous blow. Although his wife regained her strength somewhat during a trip to York Factory in the summer of 1832, Governor Simpson realized that he would have to take her back to her family in England if she were to recover fully. She was not strong enough to accompany him on his extensive travels throughout Rupert's Land and he could not leave her in the inhospitable seclusion of Red River society.

After her return to London in 1833, Mrs Simpson received the best medical attention available but she remained a semi-invalid for the rest of her life. Subsequent pregnancies continued to weaken her physically; three daughters were born in England, in 1833, 1841, and 1843. Psychologically, she suffered from her husband's habit of treating her like a child and from his long absences. In the summer of 1838 Simpson brought his wife temporarily to Lachine, and after leaving the family in England for several years while voyaging around the world, he decided to settle them permanently at Lachine in 1845. There, in Hudson's Bay Company House, they lived with Chief Factor Duncan Finlayson* and his wife, Frances's sister Isobel Graham Simpson*. Another child, John Henry Pelly, was born to the Simpsons in June 1850 and, never fully recovering from this confinement, Lady Simpson died at Lachine early in 1853.

To the fur-trade society of early 19th-century Rupert's Land, Frances Simpson embodied the civilizing attributes of a Victorian lady; in her personal and family life, however, this role exacted a considerable sacrifice. As one HBC officer said of her in the early 1840s, the governor's lady was a "pious

Simpson

creature who resigns herself patiently under all circumstances which will contribute to the Honor of her Gallant Knt."

SYLVIA VAN KIRK

The correspondence between Frances Ramsay Simpson and her husband, Governor George Simpson, is included in the latter's personal papers at PAM, HBCA, D.6/1. The journal she wrote during her canoe trip from Lachine to York Factory in 1830 is at PAM, HBCA, D.6/4. Historian Grace Lee Nute edited this account and wrote an introduction when she published it in the *Beaver*, outfit 284 (December 1953): 50–54; (March 1954): 12–17; and outfit 285 (summer 1954): 12–18.
ANQ-M, CE1-63, 24 mars 1853. PAM, HBCA, B.135/c/2; Edward Ermatinger corr., copy no.23. Mactavish, *Letters of Letitia Hargrave* (MacLeod). J. S. Galbraith, *The little emperor; Governor Simpson of the Hudson's Bay Company* (Toronto, 1976). C. W. Mackenzie, *Donald Mackenzie: "king of the northwest"* . . . (Los Angeles, 1937). Sylvia Van Kirk, "The impact of white women on fur trade society," *The neglected majority: essays in Canadian women's history*, ed. Susan Mann Trofimenkoff and Alison Prentice (Toronto, 1977), 27–48. Van Kirk, *"Many tender ties."*

SIMPSON, Sir GEORGE, governor of the HBC, author, and businessman; b. probably in 1786 or 1787 in the parish of Lochbroom (Highland), Scotland, son of George Simpson; m. 24 Feb. 1830 his cousin Frances Ramsay SIMPSON in the parish of Bromley St Leonard (London), and they had five children, four of whom survived infancy; d. 7 Sept. 1860 in Lachine, Lower Canada.

George Simpson was born out of wedlock, and the responsibility for his care as a child was assumed by members of his father's family. Young George's aunt, Mary Simpson, became in effect his foster mother and he was under her care during his years in the parish school. His formal education does not seem to have gone beyond the parochial level and probably around 1800 he went to London. His uncle Geddes Mackenzie Simpson was a partner in the London sugar brokerage firm of Graham and Simpson and he gave his nephew employment. The merger of Graham and Simpson with Wedderburn and Company in 1812 brought Andrew Wedderburn into the firm, and through his intervention the link, which was to last a lifetime, between George Simpson and the Hudson's Bay Company was forged. Wedderburn's sister Jean had married Lord Selkirk [Douglas*] in 1807 and through his brother-in-law Wedderburn had been drawn into the affairs of the HBC, becoming a shareholder in 1808 and a member of the governing board in 1810.

During the first 20 years of the 19th century the HBC was involved in a struggle for survival with the Canadian-based North West Company. At first the Canadian company seemed better equipped for the struggle; its officers in the field, who received a share of the profits, were able and energetic, and its agents were shrewd businessmen. But after 1810 the HBC became more aggressive. This new militancy led to clashes, first at the Red River settlement (Man.) and then in the Athabasca country, the most lucrative source of the NWC's revenue. In the battle for dominance both sides used any means to acquire furs and deny them to the opposition: high prices, lavish distribution of liquor, intimidation of Indians, and, on several occasions, the use of force to confiscate the furs and trade goods of the opposition. The leader of the HBC campaign in Athabasca, Colin Robertson*, was captured by the Nor'Westers in October 1818 and charged with attempted murder. Despite his escape in the summer of 1819, the HBC's London committee had lost confidence in him. In addition, the HBC's principal officer in North America, William Williams*, its governor-in-chief, was in danger of arrest. The uncertain future of these two men made it necessary for the London committee to select another manager for the North American trade, and upon the urging of Wedderburn, who in 1814 had changed his name to Andrew Colvile, George Simpson was appointed governor-in-chief locum tenens in 1820.

Colvile and others on the governing board of the HBC had concluded that the situation was ripe for an agreement between the two companies. Basic organizational weaknesses were threatening the unity of NWC and late in 1819 the London committee had learned that some of the NWC wintering partners had indicated their desire for a negotiated settlement. Also, the offer made by Edward Ellice*, London agent for the NWC, to buy out the HBC had been interpreted by the directors as a sign of weakness. Under these circumstances Simpson offered the clear-headed business outlook and bargaining ability that Colvile admired and considered essential in the changing conditions of the fur trade.

The appointment seems to have come as a surprise to Simpson. Colvile had apparently employed him in some HBC matters as early as 1818, but on the whole he knew little about the North American fur trade. Regardless of his lack of experience, he seized the opportunity with great enthusiasm and on 4 March 1820 sailed for New York, where he arrived one month later. He then proceeded to Montreal, the capital of the fur trade, where he learned what he could about the NWC and enjoyed the social status accorded by Montreal society to the representative of the HBC. Simpson then left Montreal by canoe, heading up the Ottawa River, across to Lake Nipissing, and down the French River to Lake Huron. Continuing westward through Lake Superior, he arrived at Fort William (Thunder Bay, Ont.), where the NWC partners were meeting, on 28 May. Here he delivered a message that

812

Lord Bathurst, secretary of state for war and the colonies, had entrusted to him, calling for an end to the violence between the two companies. He then moved on to Rock Depot (Man.) on the Hayes River, there to learn from Governor Williams that Robertson had been captured again, at the Grand Rapids (Man.), and that he would now have to take charge of the Athabasca campaign in Robertson's place. Robert Seaborn Miles, who had worked with Robertson, accompanied Simpson as clerk and kept the journal. He and other experienced employees were undoubtedly of great service to Simpson as advisers during his first season in the fur trade.

Simpson had to contend with problems much more suited to his business-oriented talents than would have been the case even a year earlier. His NWC opponents blustered but they were not disposed to initiate violence. Taking particular exception to the aggressive "bullying" tactics practised by HBC officer John CLARKE, he quickly grasped the changing requirements of the trade and noted that "the N. W. Co. are not to be put down by Prize fighting, but by persevering industry, Oeconomy in the business arrangements, and a firm maintenance of our rights not by the fist but by more deadly weapons." He devoted his energies to promoting economy and discipline which had been absent at the height of the fur war and his dedication to these principles earned him the admiration of his employers. He showed a remarkable ability to master quickly the problems of the trade and the art of managing men. This undoubtedly reflected his reliance on experienced officers whose ideas he appropriated.

The amalgamation of the HBC and the NWC, agreed upon in March 1821 [see Simon McGillivray*], created under the charter of the HBC a great monopoly which was to control the fur trade of British North America for over 40 years. The terms of agreement divided the trading territory into two regions, the Northern Department and the Southern Department, and gave to a governor the direction of each. Most of the profitable fur areas were in the former department which covered the region westward from Rainy Lake and Fort Albany (Ont.) to the Pacific coast. The London committee designated Williams as the senior governor, presumably for the Northern Department, and Simpson as the junior governor. However, in the arrangements made by HBC director Nicholas GARRY for the implementation of the agreement, Williams chose the governorship of the Southern Department, leaving to Simpson the more promising appointment. This decision was fortunate for Simpson; he was given far greater latitude for his talents than would have been the case had he been assigned to the overtrapped areas of the Southern Department.

During the early years of his governorship Simpson had to deal with contentious officers, many of whom had been bitter rivals in the years before 1821. He showed great ability in reconciling these strong personalities to the new era. On the surface he was affable but officers soon came to understand that he would brook no insubordination. Those who did not, found that advancement passed them by. Generally, however, promotion depended upon merit and Simpson devoted a great deal of thought to analysing the abilities of fur traders. Although his judgements, as reflected in his celebrated "Character book" of 1832, were sometimes erratic, they were generally shrewd and well informed. Beyond Simpson's qualities as a leader there was another reason behind the loyalty of the commissioned officers: the company was prosperous, and they received shares of the profits. The economy measures he introduced were predominantly at the expense of the men in the lowest ranks.

One of Simpson's first preoccupations as governor of the Northern Department was the trade on the Pacific coast. In August 1821 he ordered John Lee Lewes and John Dugald CAMERON to conduct an inspection of the old NWC posts west of the Rocky Mountains. They reported that many of the posts could be made profitable by the elimination of excess personnel. The Columbia River area was judged less promising economically but of considerable strategic importance as a buffer to keep American competitors out of the richer fur areas to the north. In 1824 the London board decided to compete more aggressively with the Americans in the Columbia district, if this could be done at little financial loss, and Simpson was instructed to visit the area and to institute measures for economy and efficiency. To carry out the mission Simpson had to postpone a planned visit to England, one purpose of which was to seek a wife.

Accompanied by James McMILLAN, Simpson left York Factory (Man.) on 15 Aug. 1824 in a north (or light) canoe manned by eight men and an Indian guide. This was the first, and in many respects the most remarkable, of his transcontinental journeys. The journal which he kept reflects the characteristics Simpson manifested throughout his life – exceptional observational powers, a compulsion to demonstrate courage and physical endurance in the face of adversity, and a passion for record-breaking speed. Six weeks after he left York Factory, Simpson overtook Chief Factor John McLOUGHLIN's party which had set out 20 days before him. McLoughlin, a veteran fur trader and former Nor'Wester, was on his way to the Columbia to take charge of the district. Simpson arrived at Fort George (Astoria, Oreg.) on 8 November, ending a journey of 84 days, 20 fewer than the previous record from Hudson Bay to the Pacific. During the next four months he and McLoughlin developed the plans that enabled the company to take the offensive against both the Russians, who were trading up the coast to the north, and the Americans, and eventually to dominate the fur trade from the Columbia to Alaska. As part of this strategy Peter Skene OGDEN was to conduct trading into the Snake River country to the south and McMillan was sent north in 1827 to establish Fort Langley (B.C.).

Simpson left Fort Vancouver (Vancouver, Wash.) for the return trip in March 1825 and, once again travelling at record-breaking speed, reached the Red River colony two and a half months later. He then made his way to York Factory from where he embarked, in the fall, for England to meet with the London committee. As governor of the Northern Department, he had been in a position to demonstrate to his employers his genius as a leader in contrast to the less dynamic Williams, and he had taken full advantage of the opportunity. Not only had he zealously promoted economy and efficiency but he had given an impetus to expansion on the Pacific coast. The result was predictable: in February 1826, before Simpson's return to North America, Williams was recalled by the London committee and Simpson was made governor of both departments, though the official unification of the two jurisdictions was not effected until 1839.

Despite his previously expressed desire to find a bride, Simpson returned to North America still unmarried. His responsibilities, as governor of both departments, were now increased and in recognition of his enlarged jurisdiction he transferred his headquarters to Lachine, Lower Canada. This village was a base for company canoes bound for the west, and nearby Montreal, in addition to its importance as a financial and commercial centre, was much more accessible to England than York Factory, his previous base.

Though his headquarters were at Montreal, Simpson's passion for arduous journeys continued unabated. He still drove himself at a frenetic pace. In 1826 he travelled to York Factory to meet with the Council of the Northern Department, and after spending the winter months in Montreal he set off in the spring of 1827 on a trip that took him to Michipicoten (Michipicoten River, Ont.), where he convened the Council of the Southern Department, and then again to York Factory. Heading back towards Montreal, he made a tour of the territory covered by the Southern Department, going up the English River (Ont.), through the rivers and lakes of the Lake Nipigon district to the Albany River, down to James Bay, on to Moose Factory, the departmental headquarters, and finally up the Abitibi and down the Ottawa rivers to the St Lawrence. During his visit to Moose Factory he had prepared a detailed report of the business of the department for the London committee.

In 1828 Simpson returned to the west coast, this time to inspect the territory of New Caledonia, west of the Rockies and north of the Columbia district, which was reputed to be potentially the most lucrative area for furs west of the mountains. He also inspected the Fraser River as a possible alternative route to the coast. New Caledonia was indeed profitable, but his hopes to increase profits still further by using the Fraser route were dashed, almost literally, in the rapids and whirlpools of the river. Simpson remained on the Pacific coast until the spring of 1829. His return trip took him to Norway House (Man.) and Moose Factory to meet with his councils and then to Lachine by the end of August 1829. He had written to Colvile from Red River in June expressing his desire to go to England to seek medical advice. Although he was not ill, his constant travelling seemed to be taking its toll: "Exertions which were formerly but exercise for me are now fatiguing, indeed my snow shoe walk across the Mountains and overland journey from Saskatchawaine have wrought me a good deal." There was, however, another and perhaps more pressing motive for this voyage – his desire for a suitable marriage. Sailing from New York on 24 September he was in London by 21 October and during the winter found his partner, the 18-year-old daughter of his uncle Geddes, Frances Simpson. He himself was now in his forties.

Before his marriage to Frances, Simpson, like many others engaged in the fur trade, had developed relations with mixed-blood women, formalized in a manner known as marriage *à la façon du pays*. The agreement to live together involved no legal obligation on the part of the man, though many of the unions were lifelong, and in cases where the man left his partner, he usually made some provision for her welfare and that of her children. Simpson did assign his rejected partners to new mates, but he treated his mixed-blood partners as little more than sexual objects, and his manner of disposing of them manifested little feeling of humanity. Even before his marriage to Frances he had taken a strong line opposing marriages between fur traders and Indian or mixed-blood women; afterwards he apparently had no more sexual contact with mixed-blood women. Non-white wives were not welcome in the Simpson household, and Frances fully supported her husband's decision to exclude them.

Simpson had fathered several illegitimate children. A daughter, name unknown, was born somewhere in Great Britain; Maria was born in Scotland of an unknown mother; another Maria, George Stewart, John McKenzie, and James Keith were born to mixed-blood women. Simpson made provision for all of these children, but they were kept at a distance from his life with Frances.

During the years 1830–33 the Simpsons took up residence at Red River, and for Frances the transition from life in London to that in Rupert's Land was traumatic. She had no friends and from the time of her arrival in 1830 she suffered from ill health. Simpson was a devoted husband but the difference in their ages and his autocratic ways produced a gulf between them. Both went to England in 1833 and it was decided that Frances would not return to North America with Simpson in 1834, but instead would stay in England to regain her strength. It was not until 1838 that she rejoined her husband.

With his headquarters and residence permanently established in Lachine from 1834, Simpson was drawn into Montreal society and became one of the leading figures of the Anglo-Scottish business community. On political questions, although he generally shared the views of this prominent group, he refrained from expressing his opinions publicly in deference to his position as governor of the HBC. His house in Lachine was the scene of sumptuous banquets attended by business and political leaders and Simpson used his contacts to benefit the HBC. His connections with politicians enabled him to prevent legislation detrimental to the interests of the company and to secure benefits from favourably disposed government leaders. Simpson's friend Francis Hincks* would make several decisions as a cabinet member and as premier that were advantageous to the company. For example, he assigned responsibility for making government payments to Indians in the Lake Huron area to the company's trading posts, thus keeping them attached to the company rather than having them travel to central distribution points where they would come in contact with influences which might seduce them from their roles as fur hunters.

Simpson's private business grew considerably during his years in Montreal and his associations with British and Montreal businessmen led him into a number of different ventures. In 1839 he joined the board of directors of the North American Colonial Association of Ireland, a joint-stock company founded to purchase the seigneury of Villechauve, generally known as Beauharnois, from Edward Ellice and to develop it for settlement. During the 1840s and 1850s he served as a director of the Bank of British North America, resigning but a few months before his death in 1860 to take up a directorship in the Bank of Montreal. He also had interests in mining concerns and is listed as a director of the Montreal Mining Company for 1848–49. This was a period of rapid growth in both rail and steamship transportation and Simpson concentrated much of his investment activity in these two sectors. With such prominent Montreal capitalists as James Ferrier* and William Molson*, he was a founding shareholder and director in the Montreal and Lachine Rail-road, chartered in 1846, and his influence over officers of the HBC was such that he persuaded several of them, including John BALLENDEN, John ROWAND, and John SIVERIGHT, to

subscribe. In 1850 this railway merged with the Lake St Louis and Province Line Railway to form the Montreal and New York Railroad, of which Simpson was also a director. Another road in which Simpson was interested, and on whose board he sat as a director, was the Champlain and St Lawrence Railroad. This line merged with the Montreal and New York in 1857 to establish the Montreal and Champlain Railroad, and Simpson served as a director of this company until his death. All of these lines were eventually absorbed into the Grand Trunk system. Furthermore, Simpson apparently had investments in the Atlantic and St Lawrence Railroad, an American line, and in the North Shore Railway Company, of which he was elected president in 1857. In 1852 Simpson was an associate of Hugh Allan* in the formation of the syndicate that was incorporated as the Montreal Ocean Steamship Company in December 1854 and he held 4 of the 64 original shares. In addition to his investment in this company, he is reported to have had interests in at least three steamships.

Some time during the 1840s Simpson engaged Stewart Derbishire*, queen's printer, to act as lobbyist both in official HBC matters and in his private ventures. Through the distribution of small gifts such as boxes of cigars and buffalo tongues, the good will of Canadian legislators was secured. Derbishire also arranged for more substantial gifts like the "10,000 golden reasons" offered to Hincks and his attorney general for Upper Canada, John Ross*, in March 1854 for their influence in obtaining government contracts for the steamship line.

Installed at Hudson's Bay Company House and well integrated into Montreal society, Simpson had by the mid 1830s become a man of substance in both Canadian and British circles. His superiors in London listened to his advice with respect, and frequently he virtually wrote the instructions that they sent to him. He was not the "Emperor of the Plains," as he was called by both admirers and detractors; there was never any question that the ultimate authority rested with the London committee. But Simpson exercised the plenary authority of a viceroy. A combination of good management and strong demand produced handsome profits; between 1835 and 1840 annual returns on capital ranged from 10 to 25 per cent. Under such favourable conditions there was little reason for the directors to entertain reservations about a governor whose zeal for efficiency and economy had helped to bring about this prosperity. In recognition of his assistance in the Arctic explorations of Thomas Simpson and Peter Warren Dease*, Simpson was knighted in 1841. This honour also acknowledged his position of importance in the business world and his contribution as an adviser on foreign affairs to the British government.

Simpson

The governor of a territory stretching over most of British North America, Simpson had to be more than an efficient businessman. He had to be a politician, and, since part of the HBC's domain was disputed by the United States and Russia, a diplomat as well. The conflict with the Russian American Company over trading territory on the northwest coast dated from the reorganization of the HBC at the time of the merger in 1821. Simpson and HBC governor John Henry Pelly travelled to St Petersburg (Leningrad, U.S.S.R.) in August 1838 to negotiate an agreement with Baron von Wrangel, the most influential director on the board of the Russian company. These talks became the basis for a contract between the two companies, signed in 1839 by Simpson and Wrangel, by which the Russians leased the Alaskan panhandle to the HBC. In return the British company undertook to provide the Russians, based at Sitka, with foodstuffs at favourable prices. The strength of this arrangement, which ceded *de facto* control over Russian territory to the HBC, was such that in 1854–55 during the Crimean War the terms were respected and, at the suggestion of Simpson, both the British and the Russian governments agreed to exclude the northwest coast from the theatre of war.

As for the disagreement with the United States over the Oregon country, Simpson had first been called upon for advice by the Foreign Office in 1825. At that time he had indicated to the British government that without control of the Columbia River the HBC would probably have to abandon the trade on the west coast. This position was adopted by Great Britain and remained a key element in British foreign policy after Simpson himself had abandoned it. For 13 years the Anglo-American dispute remained unresolved and the territory continued under joint occupation. During these years the HBC not only maintained but strengthened its position against American competition. By 1833 American maritime trade had been virtually crushed and the policy of vigorously trapping out the Snake country discouraged American inland traders. The company, however, was unable to meet the challenge of American agricultural settlement, particularly when it was supported by the United States government. In 1838 news of a Congressional bill aimed at establishing American authority in the disputed area prompted Simpson to take aggressive countermeasures. He instructed company officers to secure possession of all locations on the Columbia that would be suitable for American military establishments and ordered them to resist if the Americans attempted to oust them. His intention was to create an "incident" that would force the British government to back the company. American troops, however, did not come and in the 1840s American settlers began to arrive in such numbers that Simpson and the London committee recognized the company's pre-eminence in the Columbia valley was nearing an end.

With events in Oregon approaching a crisis, Simpson completed plans for a great adventure he had contemplated for many years. He would undertake a journey around the world and en route would make a first-hand inspection of the situation in Oregon and review with the Russian American Company the operation of the agreement he had negotiated in 1838. The journey would also allow him to visit exotic places and to indulge his penchant for record-breaking speed. Simpson left London on 3 March 1841 for North America, accompanied because of failing eyesight by a young secretary, Edward Martin Hopkins. He made his way across North America, by way of Halifax, Boston, Montreal, and the canoe route up the Ottawa, and on his arrival at Fort Colvile (near Colville, Wash.) he recorded that he had "performed a land journey of about 1,900 miles in 47 days out of which we had travelled but 41, having been detained 6 en route." To achieve this, he and his party had ridden 11 hours a day. Simpson reached Fort Vancouver at the end of August and on 1 September left, aboard the HBC's steamship *Beaver*, for a tour of the posts along the northwest coast, in company with Chief Factor James Douglas*. After meeting with Chief Factor John Work* at Fort Simpson (Port Simpson, B.C.) and with other HBC officers, Simpson decided upon a complete reorganization of the trade for the Pacific coast. The company had succeeded in eliminating the American coastal trade through direct competition and by monopolizing the trade in supplies with the Russians, and Simpson came to the conclusion that the expensive series of permanent posts which had guaranteed this success were no longer necessary. When he returned to Fort Vancouver he informed McLoughlin of his intention to close all of the posts except Fort Simpson and to conduct the trade in the *Beaver*. This decision sparked a bitter conflict between Simpson and McLoughlin, who had in many ways been the architect of the trade operated by these posts, and it resulted in their permanent alienation. At the end of 1841 Simpson made a short visit to California and then proceeded to the Sandwich (Hawaiian) Islands where, in February 1842, he met with McLoughlin for a final session of discussions on the Columbia district. In spite of McLoughlin's protests, Simpson gave him instructions to close forts Taku (Alaska) and McLoughlin (near Bella Bella, B.C.) and to begin the construction of new headquarters for the district on Vancouver Island to replace Fort Vancouver.

The HBC had established an agency in the Sandwich Islands in 1833 and traded timber, fish, and flour for Hawaiian products. Simpson's cousin, Alexander Simpson*, had come to the islands to serve as assistant to George Pelly in the direction of company business at Honolulu. Having left the HBC service, he had remained at Honolulu where, together with the British consul general, Richard Charlton, he was using his influence to try to induce the British government to claim the islands as a dependency. Governor Simpson was not in agreement with this position, feeling that the company's interests would best be served by an independent Hawaiian government, and during his visit he met with the king, Kamehameha III, and his advisers. In the face of French, American, and British manœuvres suggesting imperial designs upon the islands, Simpson provided a letter of credit, to be drawn on the HBC, for £10,000 sterling to cover the costs of a native diplomatic mission to seek international guarantees of Hawaiian independence. Later, after his return to London in 1842, he was instrumental in arranging conferences between Hawaiian representatives and the British Foreign Office which resulted in a British commitment to recognize the independence of the islands. In 1843 he accompanied the Hawaiian delegation to Brussels and Paris and contributed to securing similar declarations from France and Belgium.

Simpson left the Sandwich Islands in March 1842 and sailed to Sitka, intending to continue his trip round the world by way of Russia and Europe. Before doing so, however, he decided to make a last tour of the HBC posts on the northern coast. When he reached Fort Stikine (Alaska) on 25 April he discovered that John McLoughlin's son John, who was in charge of the post, had been murdered. Simpson concluded that young McLoughlin had been killed in a drunken fight. He was wrong and McLoughlin never forgave Simpson for blackening his son's reputation. The last phase of Simpson's journey took him across Siberia back to Europe and London, where he arrived on 21 October. The entire trip had taken only 19 months and 19 days. He did not set a record, which would have been impossible because his business responsibilities required considerable time, but his pace was nevertheless remarkable.

Simpson's travel fever did not subside after his journey round the world. Almost to the end of his life he continued his canoe voyages to various company posts. During his 40 years of service with the company, in fact, he made at least one major journey every year, with the exception of three years when he was in London. He explained this exhausting activity by the need to keep himself informed, but there was undoubtedly an element in his nature which required these repeated tests of his constitution. The travels also had a remarkable effect on him. He periodically suffered from eye trouble, but his vision seemed to improve when he stepped into a canoe. The depression which seized him several times during his life lifted when he went on his grand tours and he once noted, "It is strange that all my ailments vanish as soon as I seat myself in a canoe." In 1850, however, he wrote that "the journeys to the interior & the duties I have there discharged for upwards of thirty years are becoming increasingly irksome, & unless circumstances may

arise which appear to render my presence desirable I shall not in all probability recross the height of land." Though he returned to the interior on several occasions, in the 1850s his pace of life slowed somewhat, probably because of advancing age. He was also becoming more involved in the business community of Montreal and less inclined to visit Red River. During the few years that he and his wife had resided in the colony their first child died as an infant, in 1832, and Frances suffered the illness from which she never quite recovered. Red River was also the seat of a free-trade movement that threatened the company's fur monopoly in some of its richest preserves. The exclusive right to trade furs in Rupert's Land had been granted to the HBC by the terms of its charter. The release without punishment of a convicted free trader, Pierre-Guillaume Sayer*, on 17 May 1849 in response to pressure from Red River Métis brought this monopoly to an end [see Adam Thom*]. Simpson thereafter was happy to leave the affairs of Red River to others. Just before the trial, the London board, in response to Simpson's desire to be rid of direct involvement with Red River and to curtail his travels, had appointed Eden Colvile*, son of Andrew, governor of Rupert's Land and second in command to Simpson for HBC business in the west.

In 1858 Simpson journeyed to St Paul, Minn., with Edward Ellice, to investigate the possibility of shipping the company's trade goods west by rail rather than along the traditional route through Hudson's Bay. On the basis of their recommendations the London board decided to send a consignment from Montreal by Canadian and American railways to St Paul and thence by steamboat to Red River. The experiment was a success and after Simpson's death this became the principal route used by the company.

The expansion of rail communication ushered in a new era in the development of British North America and profoundly affected the HBC. By the late 1850s it became evident to Simpson and others that the company's unchallenged control over Rupert's Land would not long continue. Some Canadians, among them George Brown*, editor of the Toronto *Globe*, argued that Rupert's Land should be part of Canada. The British House of Commons appointed a select committee in 1857 to investigate all facets of HBC activity and Simpson testified before it. His remarks on the unsuitability of company territory for settlement were unconvincing and the committee recommended that parts of Rupert's Land, including the Red River and Saskatchewan districts, be annexed to the Province of Canada and opened for settlement. Canada, however, lacked the resources to purchase these territories or to open railway communications with them and they remained in the company's possession until after Simpson's death.

In the last years of his life Simpson retained his intellectual vigour but his physical condition deterio-

Simpson

rated. In March 1859 he notified the governor in London that he intended to retire soon thereafter; after almost forty years with the company, he felt that it was time for him to make way for a younger and more energetic person. In February 1860 he suffered a severe attack of apoplexy, but within a few weeks he was making plans for another trip to the interior, this time by rail and steamboat. He left Lachine on 14 May but by the time he reached St Paul he realized that he could not complete the journey and he returned to Montreal.

Simpson's life ended on a note befitting his character. During the visit of the Prince of Wales to Canada in the summer of 1860, the royal party was entertained by Simpson on 29 August at the governor's estate on Île Dorval, near Lachine. He arranged an exhibition featuring Iroquois bedecked with paint, feathers, and scarlet costumes. Nine days later Simpson was dead. He had appeared in good health during the celebrations, but on 1 September he suffered another attack of apoplexy and on the morning of 7 September he quietly lapsed into a coma and died. Alexander Grant Dallas*, who had been recommended by Simpson some months earlier, was named as his successor.

Simpson was buried in Mount Royal Cemetery, Montreal, beside his wife, who had died in 1853. He was a wealthy man and left an estate, including stocks, bonds, and real estate, of well over £100,000 sterling. Among the properties he had acquired was part of the estate of Sir Alexander Mackenzie* in Montreal as well as a beautiful 15-acre site on Mount Royal on which at one time he had contemplated building a home. The bulk of his estate was bequeathed to his son John Henry Pelly Simpson and each of his three legitimate daughters received £15,000, with the provision that if a daughter married without the consent of the executors she would lose the legacy. He also stipulated that if his son had no male heirs the estate would pass to his daughters' male heirs, provided they agreed to take the name of Simpson. Only one of his illegitimate children was named in his will: his Scottish daughter, Maria Mactavish, widow of Donald, was bequeathed an annuity of £100.

Simpson was one of the principal architects of the HBC monopoly which came to dominate the North American fur trade in the 19th century. At the time of his death the company's fortunes were still buoyant, but its future was increasingly threatened by the free-trade movement at Red River, demands for annexation of Rupert's Land to Canada, and the impetus to open up the territory to agricultural settlement by the extension of the railway system across British North America. Simpson foresaw the impact that these developments would have upon the fur trade but he died before it materialized. He was a controversial figure, sometimes ruthless, sometimes unscrupulous. As a husband he had been devoted to a wife whom he treated as a cherished possession, but his treatment of mixed-blood and Indian women was unfeeling. On one aspect of his character, however, there is unanimity: he served the HBC with great ability and with consummate devotion, and he stands as one of the great business leaders of his day.

JOHN S. GALBRAITH

Most of Sir George Simpson's business papers are at PAM, HBCA, in particular his correspondence with the London committee (D.4 and D.5). Two collections of this correspondence have been published in *HBRS*, 10 (Rich) and 29 (Williams). Simpson's account of his first season in the west can be found in *HBRS*, 1 (Rich). His "Character book," which contains notes he wrote in 1832 on the company's chief factors and chief traders and which shows the breadth of his knowledge of commercial matters and his involvement in the minute details of the company's management, is reprinted in *HBRS*, 30 (Williams). Although Simpson modified some of his judgements in later years [*see* Peter Skene Ogden], the "Character book" is an important biographical source in studying the HBC. Frederick Merk edited and published the journal which Simpson wrote during his voyage to the west coast as *Fur trade and empire* (1931; 1968). Simpson's *Narrative of a journey round the world, during the years 1841 and 1842* (2v., London, 1847) was the only one of his works brought out during his lifetime. Written with the help of his secretary, Edward Martin Hopkins, and of Alexander Rowand, and edited by Adam Thom* and the secretary of the HBC, Archibald Barclay, it was republished as *An overland journey round the world, during the years 1841 and 1842* (Philadelphia, 1847). His observations on California were published by John Taylor Hughes as *California: its history, population, climate, soil, productions, and harbors* . . . (Cincinnati, Ohio, 1848; 1849), and the full work was published again as *Narrative of a voyage to California ports in 1841–42, together with voyages to Sitka, the Sandwich islands & Okhotsk* . . . , ed. T. C. Russell (San Francisco, 1930). Other writings by Simpson were published by Joseph Shafer in *Letters of Sir George Simpson, 1841–1843* ([New York, 1908]), and by Grace Lee Nute in "Simpson as banker," *Beaver*, outfit 286 (spring 1956): 51–52.

Can., Prov. of, *Statutes*, 1846, c.82; 1854–55, c.44. *Colonization of the county of Beauharnois* . . . (London, 1840). *HBRS*, 19 (Rich and Johnson). *Montreal Gazette*, 8 Sept. 1860. *Montreal directory*, 1847–60. J. S. Galbraith, *The Hudson's Bay Company as an imperial factor, 1821–1869* ([Toronto], 1957); *The little emperor; Governor Simpson of the Hudson's Bay Company* (Toronto, 1976). A. S. Morton, *Sir George Simpson, overseas governor of the Hudson's Bay Company; a pen picture of a man of action* (Toronto, 1944). Tulchinsky, *River barons*; "Studies in the development of transportation and industry in Montreal, 1837 to 1853" (PHD thesis, Univ. of Toronto, 1971). Van Kirk, *"Many tender ties."* A. M. Johnson, "Simpson in Russia," *Beaver*, outfit 291 (autumn 1960): 4–12. G. L. Nute, "Jehu of the waterways," *Beaver*, outfit 291 (summer 1960): 15–19. Sylvia Van Kirk, "Women and the fur trade," *Beaver*, outfit 303 (winter 1972): 4–21. C. P. Wilson, "Sir George Simpson at Lachine," "The emperor at Lachine," and "The emperor's last days" in outfit 265 of *Beaver*, September

1934: 18–22, December, 1934: 49–51, and June 1934: 36–39 respectively.

SINCLAIR, JAMES, fur trader and merchant; b. 1811 in Rupert's Land, a younger son of HBC officer William Sinclair, an Orcadian, and his Cree or part-Cree wife, Nahovway; d. 26 March 1856 at the Cascades (Cascade Locks, Oreg.).

James Sinclair was sent to Scotland at the age of eight to be educated. He came back to Rupert's Land in 1826 and spent the winter working at the Hudson's Bay Company's Fort Albany (Ont.) and Chickney Goose Tent (Ont.). On 6 July 1827 he left Fort Albany for the Red River settlement (Man.) where he established himself as a private trader. Starting with a small bequest from his father, who had died in 1818, by 1849 Sinclair had property worth £4,500, including a river lot, house, stables, livestock, carts, and boats. At a date unknown, he became a partner of Andrew McDermot*, the colony's leading merchant and private fur trader. During the 1830s and 1840s the partners freighted goods for the HBC and for private shippers, and were engaged in the plains provision trade, the fur trade, and the retail trade, as well as a diversity of other activities, such as transactions in wood products, cattle, and hay, and furnishing accommodation for visitors to the settlement. In 1845 HBC governor Sir George SIMPSON wrote of the partners' "superior standing and comparative intelligence."

In 1824 the HBC had granted McDermot a licence to trade in furs and later he and Sinclair "trafficked largely" in them, selling the furs to the company, which hoped by this means to keep them from falling into the hands of its American competitors.

To counter the growing threat to the HBC monopoly posed by the illegal free trade in furs around Red River, the company initiated various schemes to reduce the excess population of the settlement. In 1841 it organized a party of 23 families to emigrate to the Columbia River, hoping that, as settlers, they would strengthen British claims to the Oregon, then in dispute with the United States. Sinclair led the party across the plains and through the little-known southern Rocky Mountains. With Sinclair's brother-in-law James Bird* and the Cree Maskepetoon* as guides, they crossed White Man Pass (Alta/B.C.) to Red Rock Gorge (Sinclair Canyon, B.C.), arriving at Fort Vancouver (Vancouver, Wash.) on 13 October.

Returning to Red River from this remarkable journey, Sinclair established contacts with American fur traders. He imported American goods and became involved with Peter Garrioch and others in establishing the "cart line" from the settlement to St Paul (Minn.). He rejected a contract to smuggle furs to Norman Wolfred Kittson* at Pembina (N.Dak.), but the HBC suspected both Sinclair and McDermot of

clandestine trade and encouraging Kittson's activities. In 1844 it terminated the partners' freighting contracts. The HBC's London committee had given Sinclair permission to ship tallow to Great Britain, but a consignment was left at York Factory (Man.). As well, the company introduced measures to check the import of American goods and the illicit export of furs. Sinclair, with the Garrioch group, resisted the collection of customs duties on their American imports. He struggled to get redress for broken freighting contracts and cancellation of long-standing fur-trading privileges. He joined Garrioch in smuggling to Kittson furs of an estimated value of over $2,000.

On 29 Aug. 1845 Sinclair and 22 other settlers addressed a letter containing a series of questions to the HBC's governor of Assiniboia, Alexander Christie*, concerning their rights as natives to trade. Christie replied that they did not have more rights than other British subjects and must respect the company's charter privileges. Sinclair carried to England a memorial in English and a petition in French which the disaffected settlers had drafted early in 1846. With the help of Alexander Kennedy Isbister*, a native of Rupert's Land resident in London, these were submitted to the government, which declined to take any action. Eventually, after Sinclair left London in 1847, they were laid before parliament in 1849.

Determined not to accept the limits imposed on economic opportunity by the HBC, Sinclair went to St Louis, Mo., in the spring of 1848, after taking his daughters Harriette and Maria to Knox College in Galesburg, Ill. He went on to California and there he was lucky, allegedly finding gold worth £1,300 in a single week. He returned early in the winter of 1848–49 to Red River where illicit trade in furs was again worrying the company. On 17 May 1849 Pierre-Guillaume Sayer* was brought to trial for trading furs illegally. A throng of armed Métis surrounded the court-house. Sinclair, as one of a delegation from the demonstrators, managed to stave off violence. He acted as counsel for Sayer, on whom no penalty was inflicted, though the verdict was "guilty." Charges against three other free traders were dropped, a result greeted by exultant cries of "Le commerce est libre!"

After transmitting one more petition, this time to Governor Simpson, Sinclair decided to migrate to the Oregon Territory. He sold his house and land at Red River, and in October 1849, at St Paul, he became a citizen of the United States. He spent the winter in St Louis, arranging for the shipment of his household goods round the Horn; all were lost in a shipwreck. Intending to lead another party of emigrants to the Oregon, he returned to Red River in the spring of 1850. Floods made any group migration impossible but, leaving his wife and family at Red River, he went west himself and spent some time exploring approach-

Siveright

es to the Rockies, no doubt in search of a new pass which he had mentioned to John Palliser* in 1848. With guides from Rocky Mountain House (Alta), where he bought supplies on 6 October, he again crossed the mountains. After some months in the Oregon and California, he returned via the Panama Isthmus, Havana, and New York to Red River, arriving on 6 June 1852.

Mysteriously reconciled with Simpson, and in 1853 in alliance with him against the free traders, Sinclair entered the HBC service at the rank of clerk but with the allowances of a chief trader to take charge of and restore to efficiency the post of Fort Walla Walla (Walla Walla, Wash.) and the Snake River country. He was promised 200 head of cattle for a personal cattle-raising enterprise. He undertook, as the company's secret agent, to conduct a second party of emigrants, including his own wife and family, to the Columbia. Leaving the settlement late in May 1854, the travellers crossed the plains and made their way up the Bow and Kananaskis rivers (Alta), over the Rockies, down another river, perhaps the Elk (B.C.), and on by a difficult route to Canal Flats (B.C.). Sinclair reached Walla Walla late in December. There, besides transacting company business, he established himself and his family as settlers.

In October 1855 trouble with the Indians flared up and the Indian agent ordered Sinclair to evacuate Walla Walla. He returned with 150 American volunteers to find, after several days' fighting, that the post had been looted and the livestock killed or dispersed. Travelling on HBC business, Sinclair was killed on 26 March 1856 in an Indian attack on the settlement at the Cascades.

James Sinclair had married Elizabeth Bird, daughter of retired Chief Factor James BIRD, on 3 Dec. 1829, and before her death in 1846 or 1847 they had had nine children, most of whom died young. The eldest surviving child, Harriette, remembered the world she grew up in as one of "comfort and happiness." Sinclair married on 20 April 1848 his second wife, Mary Campbell, daughter of Chief Trader Colin Campbell, and had three more daughters and a posthumous son.

Only 45 when he died, Sinclair had packed into his short life a many-sided career as the first to take large parties through the then unexplored southern Canadian Rockies; as a pioneer promoter of trade between the Red River settlement and American centres; as a shrewd and courageous leader of the natives of Rupert's Land in their struggle against the monopoly claims of the HBC. Paradoxically, his restless search for wider economic opportunities, which had brought him into conflict with the company, took him, before his life ended, into its service as a most valued officer.

IRENE M. SPRY

Minn. Hist. Soc. (St Paul), Ramsey County District Court, naturalization records; H. H. Sibley papers. PABC, A/ C/30Si6C; Add. mss 635, file 204; E/B/Si6. PAC, MG 19, E8. PAM, Copley, "The career of James Sinclair"; HBCA, A.6/25–26; A.12/1–3; B.3/a/130–31; B.123/a/25; B.184/ z/1; B.223/b/41; B.235/d/34, 38, 41, 56–57, 60, 67, 68b, 71–73, 77, 80, 82, 83, 88a, 90–92, 94–96, 100; C.1/187; 228–30; D.4/25, 34, 58, 59, 67, 74, 75; D.5/6, 8, 11–12, 14–15, 17, 26, 36–38, 41; D.5/24–25, 37–38, 41; E.4/1a, 1b, 2; E.5/6–11; E.6/1–6; E.7/34, 36; MG 2, C38. G.B., Parl., House of Commons paper, 1849, 35, no.227: 1–5, *Copies of any memorials presented to the Colonial Office by inhabitants of the Red River settlement. . . . HBRS,* 19 (Rich and Johnson). *The papers of the Palliser expedition, 1857–1860,* ed. I. M. Spry (Toronto, 1968). *The Prairie west to 1905: a Canadian sourcebook,* ed. L. G. Thomas (Toronto, 1975), 56–59. U.S., Senate report 528, Committee on Public Lands, 43rd Congress, 2nd session, 15 Jan. 1875. J. S. Galbraith, *The Hudson's Bay Company as an imperial factor, 1821–1869* ([Toronto], 1957). A. C. Gluek, *Minnesota and the manifest destiny of the Canadian northwest: a study in Canadian-American relations* (Toronto, 1965). W. J. Healy, *Women of Red River: being a book written from the recollections of women surviving from the Red River era* (Winnipeg, 1923). D. G. Lent, *West of the mountains: James Sinclair and the Hudson's Bay Company* (Seattle, Wash., 1963). A. D. Pambrun, *Sixty years on the frontier in the Pacific northwest* (Fairfield, Wash., 1978). W. J. Betts, "From Red River to the Columbia, the story of a migration," *Beaver,* outfit 301 (spring 1971): 50–55. J. V. Campbell, "The Sinclair party – an emigration overland along the old Hudson Bay Company route from Manitoba to the Spokane country in 1854," *Wash. Hist. Quarterly,* 7 (1916): 187–201. I. M. Spry, "Routes through the Rockies" and "West of the mountains – James Sinclair and the Hudson's Bay Company," *Beaver,* outfit 294 (autumn 1963): 26–39 and 56–57. "To Red River and beyond," *Harper's New Monthly Magazine* (New York), 22 (1861): 306–21.

SIVERIGHT, JOHN, fur trader; b. 2 Dec. 1779 in Drumdelgy, parish of Cairnie, Scotland, son of John Siveright, farmer, and Jannet Glass; d. 4 Sept. 1856 in Edinburgh.

John Siveright entered the fur trade in April 1799 as an apprentice clerk with the Montreal-based Forsyth, Richardson and Company, one of the firms in the New North West Company (sometimes called the XY Company), on a seven-year contract for service in the northwest. When the New North West Company merged into the North West Company in 1804 he stayed on. In 1806 he was posted as clerk to the Monontagué department, near Lake Nipigon (Ont.), under John HALDANE. In 1815, when he was at Portage la Prairie (Man.), the Hudson's Bay Company considered him party to the NWC conspiracy to destroy the Red River settlement (Man.). He was with Duncan Cameron* at the NWC's Fort Gibraltar (Winnipeg) on 17 March 1816 when the latter was taken prisoner by Colin Robertson* of the HBC, and he was still in the colony at the outbreak of violence in

June that culminated in the killing of Governor Robert Semple* and about 20 settlers at Seven Oaks (Winnipeg). As a result of these events Siveright was one of those, including Allan McDONELL, charged as an accessory in the murder of Semple, for which Cuthbert GRANT and other Métis were to be tried. His friendship with Grant, later eroded by time and distance, was regarded as suspicious in itself. But, in the trials at York (Toronto) in October 1818, it was apparent that his involvement was peripheral at most, and the charges against him were not upheld after the acquittal of the principals. Siveright had apparently killed a man early in his career. Although no details have been found concerning this incident, HBC governor George SIMPSON noted in 1832, "I believe he was more influenced by personal fear and want of Nerve than any worse feeling."

From 1816 to 1823 Siveright served at Sault Ste Marie, Upper Canada, employed as a clerk by the NWC until 1821 and then, after the coalition, by the HBC. James Hargrave* was stationed there during the 1820–21 season and a friendship that lasted the length of Siveright's career was quickly forged between the two men. In 1823 he was transferred, to his regret, from Sault Ste Marie to take charge of the Fort Coulonge district, at Fort Coulonge, Lower Canada, on the upper Ottawa River.

From the early 1820s the HBC monopoly in the Ottawa valley was being threatened by the activity of lumbermen and tavern-keepers who conducted a petty trade in furs. At first both Simpson and Chief Trader Angus Cameron* at Fort Timiskaming (near Ville-Marie, Que.) believed Siveright was not strict enough in his application of company rules. But within a few years it became evident that he was at least securing the furs which might well have been diverted to other hands and in 1828 he was promoted chief trader. By 1831 Simpson was able to report to the London committee of the HBC that Cameron and Siveright had driven out the opposition on the Ottawa. Simpson's conclusion, however, was premature. The lumbering operations of George McConnell and his sons from Hull had penetrated to Lake Timiskaming by 1836, and Cameron suggested that the HBC undertake lumbering of its own on the lake to discourage any further encroachment. When queried by Simpson about this possibility in 1839, both Siveright and Chief Factor James KEITH, in charge of the Montreal department at Lachine, were unenthusiastic about the prospects. Simpson none the less went ahead and from 1840 to 1843 Cameron combined lumbering with his fur-trade activities at Timiskaming. In the fall of 1843 Siveright was placed in charge of the Timiskaming district, and until Fort Coulonge was closed in 1844 he combined the direction of both districts. The collapse in the Canadian timber trade, anticipated following the reduction in 1842 of the

protective tariff granted colonial wood, did not materialize and, when in 1844 Siveright reported renewed activity on the part of the McConnells and the prospect that Allan Gilmour and Company [see Allan Gilmour*] would also begin operations in the Timiskaming area, Simpson once again thought of moving into the field. Losses from the earlier operations and the arrival of John EGAN and other lumbermen finally forced the abandonment of Simpson's project, and Siveright was directed to meet the competition for furs with superior trading.

He stayed in Timiskaming until 1847, having been promoted chief factor in 1846, and after two years' furlough he retired from the HBC in 1849. During his more than 20 years' tenure in the Ottawa valley, Siveright appears to have recognized far sooner than the aggressive Simpson that HBC control over the region would inevitably be weakened by the advance of Canadian business interests, and from Fort Coulonge and Timiskaming he successfully conducted a rearguard action against the competition.

In spite of Simpson's conclusion in 1832 that the "sickly Deaf & Worn out" Siveright should retire, he had remained in the service a further 17 years. Simpson had at times criticized him for "subterfuge" and "evasion" in the fulfilment of his duties, and, in Simpson's dismissal of clerks under Siveright's direction without his having been consulted, as in the case of Roderick McKenzie, son of Chief Factor Roderick McKENZIE, in 1845, there is a suggestion that he doubted Siveright's judgement. Others, such as Keith, had a higher opinion of his abilities, and he served temporarily in the Lachine office as Keith's replacement in 1835–37. Simpson himself seems to have modified his assessment, and in the 1840s he advised Siveright to defer his retirement in order to secure a chief factorship; indeed, by the time Siveright chose to retire Simpson would have preferred that he remain in the service a little longer. His honesty and attention to duty were thus recognized even by those whom his mannerisms never failed to irritate.

Siveright died of a disease of the kidneys and was buried in Warriston cemetery, Edinburgh. He was survived by several children, including a son and a daughter born of Indian mothers in the Timiskaming district, and a daughter, Josephte, born of a Métis mother at Sault Ste Marie. Josephte married Alexis Goulet of St Boniface (Man.) in 1833 and was the mother of Elzéar* and Maxime* Goulet.

ELIZABETH ARTHUR

PAM, HBCA, A.31/9; B.134/c/4: ff.107–8d, 189; B.134/c/28; B.134/c/35; B.134/c/44: ff.204–5; D.4/1: ff.26–30; D.5/1: f.20d; D.5/14: f.173. Private arch., E. A. Mitchell (Toronto), Æneas and Angus Cameron papers (mfm. at AO). Andrew Amos, *Report of trials in the courts of Canada,*

Smiley

relative to the destruction of the Earl of Selkirk's settlement on the Red River; with observations (London, 1820). Hargrave, Hargrave corr. (Glazebrook). HBRS, 3 (Fleming). John McLean, John McLean's notes of a twenty-five year's service in the Hudson's Bay territory, ed. W. S. Wallace (Toronto, 1932). Simpson, "Character book," HBRS, 30 (Williams), 151–236. [S. H. Wilcocke], A narrative of occurrences in the Indian countries of North America . . . (London, 1817; repr., East Ardsley, Eng., and New York, 1968). E. A. Mitchell, Fort Timiskaming and the fur trade (Toronto and Buffalo, N.Y., 1977). Rich, Hist. of HBC (1958–59), vol.2. C. C. J. Bond, "The Hudson's Bay Company in the Ottawa valley," Beaver, outfit 296 (spring 1966): 4–21.

SMILEY, ROBERT REID, printer, newspaperman, and businessman; b. 1817 in Ireland, son of Samuel and Agnes Smiley; m. 2 Nov. 1847 Margaret Switzer; d. 10 May 1855 in Hamilton, Upper Canada.

Robert Reid Smiley immigrated with his parents to Kingston, Upper Canada, at an early age. He was apprenticed as a printer with the *Kingston Herald*, rose to be foreman, and later worked, also as foreman, for the *British Whig*. In 1844 he moved with the seat of government to Montreal, where he was employed by the printers J. Starke and Company and wrote on political matters for various journals.

Hamilton at that time had a high tory newspaper, the *Hamilton Gazette, and General Advertiser*, run by George Perkins Bull*. Its style was mild mannered and its interests increasingly theological. A group of leading conservative businessmen, which may have included Sir Allan Napier MacNab*, wanted a newspaper to express their views with the same vigour and aggressiveness that Solomon Brega was showing in his reform paper, the *Journal and Express*. A member of the group, grocer and druggist Edwin Dalley, had discussions with Smiley in Montreal as a result of which Smiley agreed to set up a newspaper in Hamilton, Dalley having indicated that he would give any financial assistance required. Smiley brought his younger brothers, John Gibson and Hugh Creighton, with him to Hamilton.

On 15 July 1846 the first issue of the *Hamilton Spectator, and Journal of Commerce*, a four-page semi-weekly, appeared. In May 1850 a weekly edition was added "For Country Circulation" and two years later publication of a daily began. Each prospered. The circulation of the semi-weekly in 1850 rivalled that of Toronto's *Globe* and *British Colonist*. On the day of Smiley's death the *Spectator* appeared in a new enlarged format indicative of its continued influence throughout the large area west of Toronto. The key to this success lay in Smiley's great industry, his excellent business habits, and the scope and vigour of his writing.

The *Spectator*'s editorial policy was considered moderate conservative. It made attacks on reformers as violent and vituperative as any in the province, being especially uncompromising in its abuse of Louis-Hippolyte La Fontaine*, whom it denounced as a dictator. The moderation of its conservatism was confined to church-state issues. For example, in 1847 Smiley approved the unsuccessful compromise settlement of the university question proposed by the government of Henry SHERWOOD. In 1850 he condemned the revival of agitation over the clergy reserves question as a ministerial device intended to distract public attention from the Rebellion Losses Act, but later he came round to supporting secularization of the reserves. A Presbyterian of the Church of Scotland connection, he was critical of the privileges and claims of the Church of England, hostile to the Free Church, and proud of the unanimity with which his denomination voted tory.

But if contemporaries saw the *Spectator* as moderate conservative, they also regarded it as the mouthpiece of the ultra-tory leader, MacNab. The paradox was not as absolute as it appears. From the late 1840s MacNab's ultra-toryism was more a matter of past associations and the necessities forced upon him as party leader than of deeply held convictions. On the other hand, Smiley was more extreme than MacNab in his criticisms of Governor Lord Elgin [Bruce*], La Fontaine, and Francis Hincks*. In 1853 Smiley publicly denied that MacNab had influence over or a financial interest in the *Spectator*. Privately, he expressed distrust of the knight and was critical of his selfishness. Yet both locally and provincially the *Spectator* supported MacNab with remarkable consistency. It was, for example, bitterly hostile towards William Henry Draper*, a leader of moderate conservative governments from 1843 to 1847, towards his successor Henry Sherwood, and towards Ogle Robert Gowan*, all political enemies and rivals of the Hamilton tory. In 1854 Smiley, influenced in part by his friendship with John Sandfield Macdonald*, advocated a coalition between the conservatives and the independent or opposition reformers of Upper Canada, but when MacNab led the conservatives into government with not only the Lower Canadian moderates but also the Hincksites, whom Smiley had denounced, the editor executed an immediate about-face. The *Spectator* became the leading Upper Canadian press representative of the conservatives in the new combination of political groups.

Smiley was also interested in civic affairs. He was a keen advocate of local improvement, pressing for such developments as lighted streets. When the Hamilton Gas Light Company was formed in 1850, he was one of its first directors. Through all the vicissitudes of its early history, Smiley supported the Hamilton-based Great Western Rail-Road Company, faithfully reporting its progress, boosting its prospects, and defending it against rivals. When the Grand

Trunk Railway, Hincks's emerging colossus, threatened the Great Western's monopoly west of Toronto, the *Spectator* was outraged and subsequently Smiley resisted strenuously any suggestion of amalgamation of the two competing companies. From the complex and ferocious fighting which developed within the Great Western in 1853 and 1854 Smiley at first stood aloof. Ultimately he came out strongly against the prominent Hamilton merchant, Isaac Buchanan*, who, with Charles John Brydges*, dominated the board. The Buchanan–Brydges proposal to purchase the Erie and Ontario Railroad Company together with associated properties was one reason for his stand, since it meant the building up of Niagara (Niagara-on-the-Lake) at the expense of Hamilton. MacNab's opposition to Buchanan and Brydges was another.

Little is known of Smiley's private life. He was described as "a pale young man of short stature, slim build, and by no means robust health." There was one child of his marriage, a son who died in October 1850. That year Smiley purchased land in the eastern part of Hamilton on which he erected a large house in Tuscan villa style. Completed in 1854, the house was referred to as Smiley's Castle more often than by its real name, Rose Arden. Smiley enjoyed his castle for only six months before his death from consumption. The disease seemed to have been halted by a trip abroad in 1851. He was planning another, and had been appointed honorary commissioner to the universal exposition in Paris in 1855. But on 10 May 1855 he died, a few hours after leaving his work at the paper. His large funeral was attended by freemasons, Oddfellows, and members of the Hamilton Typographical Society. The tributes on his death were unusually warm and numerous.

Smiley left to his wife and his brothers a money-making newspaper which has lasted to this day, a first-class steam printing plant, a bindery, a lithographing and printing outfit, the Ancaster Woollen Mill, and one of the finest residences in the city, all acquired in less than ten years.

DONALD ROBERT BEER and
KATHARINE GREENFIELD

AO, RG 22, ser.155, will of R. R. Smiley. HPL, Arch. file, C. R. McCullough papers, pp.1–6 (photocopies); Clipping file, Newspapers – Canada, Canadian journalism ser., xvii–xix; Hamilton biog.; Hamilton – Newspaper, general, "A bit of local news history"; Scrapbooks, Richard Butler, "Saturday musings," 2: 9, 53, 63; 3: 40, 98, 126, 147, 201–2, 219; 4: 18–19; H. F. Gardiner, 216: 10; *Hamilton Spectator*, 1: 16; Historic houses in Hamilton, 1, pt.2. PAC, MG 19, A2, ser.2, 3, pt.2, Smiley to Ermatinger, 20 March 1850, 15 Feb. 1851. *British Colonist* (Toronto), 1850. *British Whig*, 1840. *Christian Guardian*, 19 June 1850. *Daily Spectator, and Journal of Commerce*, 5, 28 Aug., 15 Sept. 1854; 15, 17 May 1855. *Globe*, 1850. *Hamilton Gazette, and General Advertiser*, 1845. *Hamilton Spectator, and Journal of Commerce*, 15 July 1846–10 May 1855, especially 21 July 1847, 22 June 1850. *Journal and Express* (Hamilton), 1845. *Kingston Herald*, 1840. *Death notices of Ontario*, comp. W. D. Reid (Lambertville, N.J., 1980). *DHB*, 1: 24, 30, 37, 58, 135–44, 182–83. *Marriage notices of Ontario*, comp. W. D. Reid (Lambertville, 1980). *Montreal directory*, 1843. *Hamilton Spectator*, 15 July 1896, 16 July 1921, 15 July 1936. E. S. Vickers, "The Victorian buildings of Hamilton," *Wentworth Bygones* (Hamilton), 7 (1967): 50–51.

SMITH, CHARLES DOUGLASS, colonial administrator; b. *c.* 1761 in England, eldest son of John Smith and Mary Wilkinson; m. 1790 Frances Woodcock, and they had at least four sons and four daughters; d. 19 Feb. 1855 in Dawlish, England.

Charles Douglass Smith was born into a penurious and somewhat eccentric family. His father, a captain in the British army, had served as an aide-de-camp to Lord George Sackville, but when the latter was cashiered in 1759 for alleged disobedience of orders Smith resigned from the army in disgust and lived most of the rest of his life in virtual seclusion in a boat-house at Dover, "long known as Smith's folly." He married Mary Wilkinson, the daughter of a wealthy London merchant, in 1760, but she was disinherited for marrying without her father's consent and in later life they separated and fought over the custody of their three sons. None of the three received much of an education, although for a time they were placed under a private tutor at Tonbridge and then briefly in a boarding-school at Bath from which their father removed them against their mother's wishes. Since Captain Smith held a minor office in the royal household, as gentleman usher, he was able to secure military commissions for his sons. The youngest, John Spencer Smith, entered the army and later became a moderately successful diplomat. William Sidney Smith entered the Royal Navy in his early teens, achieved great fame for his defence of Acre against Napoleon in 1799, and rose to become a vice-admiral of the blue in 1810. He sat in the House of Commons from 1802 to 1806, had many friends among the aristocracy, may have had an affair with the Princess of Wales, Caroline Amelia Elizabeth, and was noted for "an eccentricity as engaging as it was original."

Charles Douglass Smith's career was less successful. He entered the 1st Horse as a cornet on 5 Oct. 1776 and transferred to the 22nd Light Dragoons as a lieutenant on 15 Dec. 1779. Apparently, as he later claimed, he served for a time in the Thirteen Colonies and became a captain on 20 Nov. 1782, but was placed on half pay when his regiment was disbanded the following year. On 1 Oct. 1795 he resumed active service in the 32nd Light Dragoons and on 20 April 1796 transferred to the 21st Light Dragoons, but he

Smith

was again placed on half pay in 1798. He had risen in the army to be a major on 1 March 1794 and a lieutenant-colonel on 1 Jan. 1798.

Smith was rescued from well-merited obscurity and probably from genteel poverty by the influence his brother William Sidney enjoyed with Lord Bathurst, the secretary of state for war and the colonies. In 1812 the recently appointed Bathurst was seeking "an Active and Efficient Officer" to replace Joseph Frederick Wallet DesBarres* as lieutenant governor of Prince Edward Island. By associating himself with James Bardin Palmer*, who had organized a political society known as the Loyal Electors, DesBarres had incurred the hostility of the chief justice, Cæsar Colclough*, and the powerful faction led by Charles Stewart* and Thomas Desbrisay*. He had also aroused the fears of the proprietorial lobby in Britain which saw the Loyal Electors as a dangerous radical movement. To alleviate these fears, and influenced by representations from the Island, Bathurst dismissed DesBarres and Palmer from office, transferred Colclough to Newfoundland, and commissioned Smith as the new lieutenant governor on 4 Aug. 1812.

After a "most tempestuous Passage" across the Atlantic that took from 9 November to 29 December, Smith wintered in Halifax and spent the spring waiting for the navy to provide him with suitable transportation to the Island. On 24 July 1813 he finally assumed control of the government from William Townshend*, who had administered the colony since DesBarres's departure on 5 Oct. 1812 and who predicted that Smith would find "a peaceable regular and . . . a well satisfied People." But because Smith, fearful of American intentions, was already convinced that he was to be "exposed to the efforts of a crafty, active and enterprising Enemy," he "hazarded the experiment of convening the General Assembly" in November 1813 with great reluctance.

When the assembly ignored his requests for legislation, particularly for a revised militia act, he prorogued it on 13 Jan. 1814, declaring that it was controlled by "a Confederacy of a very dangerous description known by the name of 'The Club' . . . of which Mr. Palmer was & I believe is, the main spring." Arguing that the local garrison, which he sought in vain to have placed under his command, was too small to maintain order, during 1814 and 1815 Smith attempted to reorganize the "most undisciplined" militia. When his authority to revise the militia regulations was challenged and a number of militia units refused to obey his orders during a parade on 2 Nov. 1815, he reacted angrily. He ordered George Wright*, a militia officer, to punish his men for insubordination; when Wright resigned his commission rather than do so, Smith tried to dismiss him from the Council. Smith also wished to dismiss the new chief justice, Thomas Tremlett*, for refusing

to "do his Duty" in quelling the disturbance, and when Captain Charles Barrington, whom Smith had instructed "to have his ammunition ready," would not use the regular troops against the militia, Smith placed him under arrest. Smith's efforts were counterproductive. In 1816 Barrington was released and Sir John Coape Sherbrooke*, commander of the forces in the Atlantic region, reduced the local garrison from a company to a mere 22 men because of Smith's tendency "to interfere unnecessarily with the Troops." This action served merely to increase Smith's fears. He compelled the militia to mount a permanent guard, winter and summer, outside the officers' barracks, which he had sequestered upon his arrival for an official residence, and he repeatedly appealed, without success, for a larger garrison to protect him against threats that appear to have existed only in his own mind.

Initially, Smith's paranoia was directed against Palmer, whom he held responsible for the opposition to his militia reforms, and the members of Palmer's "Diabolical Club," whom Smith suspected were acting in unison with the disturbers of the peace in Ireland. On 27 Feb. 1816 Smith appointed William Johnston*, the attorney general, to the Council and in November, with Johnston's assistance, he had Palmer removed from the roll of attorneys after a completely irregular trial in the Court of Chancery over which Smith, as chancellor, presided. Palmer departed for London to appeal for reinstatement, and during his absence, on 8 July 1817, Smith reconvened the assembly he had prorogued nearly four years earlier. On 14 August he again prorogued the assembly, claiming that "we have separated upon good terms." But his decision not to assent to the lower house's supply bill because it imposed a 2½ per cent duty on British imports was the subject of a critical address by the next assembly, which met in November 1818 following the general elections held in September. Smith refused to receive the address and, when the assembly demanded that the chief justice, Tremlett, and the sheriff be dismissed from office for prosecuting delinquents who had not paid their quitrents, on 15 December he hurriedly sent his son-in-law John Edward Carmichael* to compel the house to adjourn. Less than a week earlier, during the evening of 9 December, one of Smith's sons, Henry Bowyer Smith, had smashed a window of the assembly – whether by using his fists or by throwing snowballs is not clear – and two days after the house reassembled on 5 Jan. 1819 he was committed to jail under a warrant issued by the speaker, Angus Macaulay*. Smith prorogued the legislature the following afternoon, thereby freeing his son.

He further weakened his support at the beginning of 1819 when he dismissed William Johnston from Council. Smith had turned against him the previous

May after Palmer had come back to the colony with evidence that Johnston had misappropriated funds belonging to the proprietors for whom he had been acting as agent. At the same time, Smith also dismissed from Council the adjutant general of militia, John Frederick Holland*, one of the few members in whom he had previously expressed any confidence. These two men, Smith declared, were at the centre of a new conspiracy which used "Free Masonry . . . as a Cloak for secret political proceedings."

In June 1820 Smith called another general election, but when the assembly met on 25 July 1820 and prepared an address criticizing his arbitrary actions, he prorogued the house on 10 August and proclaimed that "there is now no necessity for calling a General Assembly for Years." In a limited sense he was correct. Because of the productivity of various permanent revenue acts placed at the government's disposal many years earlier, the provincial treasury had a steadily increasing surplus. Smith might have used these funds to undertake public works but he preferred to use statute labour. By allowing the surpluses to accumulate in the treasury he contributed to the shortage of currency on the Island. Moreover, by refusing to convene the assembly he ensured that essential legislation could not be passed. But Smith justified his refusal by arguing that the assembly could not be trusted since "a club of a secret & very improper nature under the title of 'The Loyal Electors' . . . has recently revived under the mask of Free-Masonry."

Although the conspiracy of freemasons was a figment of Smith's imagination, by his own actions he did drive into opposition virtually every important interest group on the Island. Inevitably, the agitation against Smith was led by those whose motives were less than pure. William Johnston allied himself with Smith's opponents out of simple self-interest, and John Stewart*, who was removed as receiver general of quitrents in 1816 for absenteeism, played a leading part in organizing the resistance to Smith upon his return to the Island. Stewart's hostility is understandable since Smith had vowed that he would "put an end" to the power of the Stewart and Desbrisay families who "have grasped at, & for a long continuance of Years have held at different times almost every Office under the Crown in this Colony."

Even though one may sympathize with Smith's desire to destroy the monopoly of office enjoyed by a handful of families who had benefited handsomely from their positions, in practice he dispensed his patronage to an equally select group. Distrusting the Irish, the Scots, and the American-born, all Catholics and most Protestants, he favoured recent emigrants from England, members of the Church of England, and retired army officers like himself. By the end of his tenure the Island Council had become, as his critics

alleged, a body lacking "weight and influence." Moreover, while condemning the nepotism of others, he practised it himself; "though he might have prayed against temptation for he professes much religion, he has not been delivered from evil," one of his critics declared. In 1816 he had tried unsuccessfully to appoint his son Henry Bowyer Smith collector of customs and in 1817 to secure for him the posts of naval officer and provost marshal. When Thomas Heath Haviland* received the latter appointments and applied for a leave of absence, Smith forced him to appoint Henry, who was not yet 19, as his deputy. Smith's son-in-law John Edward Carmichael would become acting receiver general of quitrents, colonial secretary, registrar, and clerk of the Council. Another son-in-law, Ambrose LANE, was appointed registrar and master of the Court of Chancery and was given a seat on the Council. John Spencer Smith became collector of impost and George Sidney Smith acted as his father's private secretary. Towards the end of his career on Prince Edward Island, Smith became a recluse, surrounded by his relatives and a handful of sycophants.

When he did venture into public view, he usually added to his list of enemies. He was arrogant, quick tempered, and vindictive. He possessed the typical prejudices of an English country gentlemen of the time but in an exaggerated form. Deploring "the despicable degeneracy of mind & manners that stigmatises the Yankey Tribes," he refused to make land grants to anyone who had experienced "the degenerating effect of residence in those Regions of Rum & Rascality." The Scottish Highlanders he dismissed as a people "whose want of Industry, Sobriety & Agricultural knowledge is so great that it is really wonderful how they have ever advanced towards Prosperity at all," and he lamented the influence of the Roman Catholics and "Sectarists" on the Island. When the Catholics petitioned for the same rights possessed by their co-religionists in Quebec, Smith refused to forward the petition to London, and he was determined to enforce the laws which prevented clergymen who were not members of the Church of England from officiating at marriages. He selected for distribution to the Church of England the best plots of land available even when they were in the midst of settlements of Catholics and Presbyterians. Smith does seem to have been motivated by a sincere desire to advance the interests of the Church of England but he managed to antagonize the resident minister in Charlottetown, Theophilus Desbrisay*, and he quarrelled with the missionary sent to Georgetown by the Society for the Propagation of the Gospel. Even among his natural allies Smith was little loved.

Smith's clumsy efforts to deal with the land question on Prince Edward Island set in motion the events that ultimately led to his recall. To some extent

Smith

Smith must be given credit for good intentions. He recognized that the colony's development had been retarded by the failure of the proprietors of the large blocks of land, into which the Island had been divided in 1767, to fulfil the original terms of settlement, and he was determined to compel them to do so. In the beginning of 1818 he instituted escheat proceedings against lots 55 and 15, both of which were sparsely settled, and he was preparing to institute similar proceedings against Lot 52 when Lord Bathurst ordered him to desist. Bathurst, under pressure from the proprietorial lobby in Britain, announced in May 1818 that the original terms of the grants which required the land to be settled by foreign Protestants were not to be enforced and that the proprietors would be given ten years to settle their estates with the requisite number of tenants. If Bathurst had adhered to this decision, the absentee landlord problem would have been much alleviated, although not resolved, and Smith deserves some credit for acting as a catalyst. Yet Smith should not be lionized as an early proponent of a system of land reform designed to benefit an oppressed tenantry. He believed in the proprietorial system and thought that tenants needed "the Stimulus of Rent, to compel them to exert Industry." "The Non payment of Rents in general, The low price of Spirits, & the High Price of Labour, are," he complained, "three very principal causes that retard the advancement of the Colony," and he suggested that a number of troops be established on the Island to work at fixed rates and thus lower the price of labour. Smith's original intention was to turn the tenants on Lot 55 into tenants of the crown, not to give them or their heirs freehold grants. Bathurst, however, decided that anyone who had occupied the land for 15 years should be given a grant subject only to the payment of quitrents, thereby establishing an important precedent that the land reformers of a later period would look back to [see William Cooper*]. By this decision Bathurst may also have earned for Smith more popularity among the tenantry than he deserved.

Whatever popularity Smith did win by his escheat program was dissipated by his determination to collect quitrents. In one respect the collection can be seen as a desirable policy since it was a method, as Smith maintained, of coercing the landlords into making their estates more productive of revenue and thus encouraging settlement. But the burden of paying quitrents also fell on the tenants, whose leases frequently included this obligation. In fact, it was the smaller proprietors with limited capital resources and the tenants with virtually none who were most easily coerced into payment. The widespread opposition to quitrents, common throughout British North America, also arose from the fact that these were crown revenues beyond the assembly's control. Although Smith argued that the revenues should be expended on

useful objects within the colonies, these useful objects included an increase in his salary and the construction of a proper residence for the lieutenant governor, for which he knew the assembly would never provide funds. Indeed, one reason for Smith's concern over the collection of quitrents was to increase the funds at the government's disposal so that he could show the members of the assembly "how easy it is to do without them."

Smith was hampered in his policy by the absence of the receiver general of quitrents, John Stewart, and by the lack of instructions from Bathurst. In 1816 he had appointed Carmichael acting receiver general and Bathurst had announced that quitrents were to be collected, although not the arrears due prior to 1816, and that a new schedule of fees was to be established. For nearly two years Smith waited for further instructions but none came and early in 1818 he ordered Carmichael to begin collections at the old rate. This decision created an outcry among the absentee proprietors and contributed to the discontent demonstrated by the assembly when it met in November. Upon learning of Smith's action Bathurst expressed "surprize and regret" but he also announced the new schedule of fees. No further effort was made to collect quitrents until June 1822 when Carmichael issued a notice asking that all arrears be paid in July. It was ignored and in December he issued another notice demanding payment by 14 Jan. 1823. When the demand was again ignored he suddenly instituted court proceedings against two of the resident proprietors, Donald McDonald and John Stewart. The tenants in the heavily populated eastern townships of Kings County, many of whom were Gaelic-speaking Highlanders, were then informed that unless they paid their quitrents promptly their property would be seized. A number of them trekked 50 to 70 miles across the Island to Charlottetown "with loads of wheat and such other produce" which they were forced to sell at low prices to Carmichael and his deputies. One man, it was claimed, "was compelled to part with his worsted mittens that he had worn on his journey" to raise money. If the affidavits later sworn are to be believed, Carmichael and his deputies treated the Highlanders with scant respect and even less sympathy. In February 1823 he obtained judgements in the Supreme Court against the small proprietors of some 40,000 acres in Kings County and, according to John Stewart, Smith's "Sons and Sons in law . . . were as usual the principal purchasers." This charge must be viewed with scepticism but there is little reason to doubt that Carmichael and his deputies profited handsomely for so diligently performing their duties.

These events spawned a series of public meetings in March 1823, and committees, one of which included John Stewart and Paul Mabey*, as well as John MacGregor, whom Smith had dismissed as high sheriff for calling the meetings, were selected to prepare petitions from the resolutions passed in each county asking for Smith's recall. These petitions were circulated across the Island and the resolutions and related material were published in the *Prince Edward Island Register* the following September and October by its editor, James Douglas Haszard*. Since the complaints contained the charge that Smith and Ambrose Lane had abused their positions in the Court of Chancery by charging exorbitant fees, Smith decided that it was time to move with "moderation & firmness" against the "Factious few" for contempt of court. Haszard was brought to trial on 14 October and named the seven men on the Queens County committee; Smith then issued warrants for their arrest. Stewart escaped to London carrying the petitions but the others surrendered and, defended by Charles Binns*, were brought to trial in the Court of Chancery at the end of the month. Smith presided and, not surprisingly, found the accused guilty. But the mood of the crowd which surrounded the court-house was so ugly that Smith suspended the proceedings on 30 October, until he could enforce his judgement, and released the prisoners. He retreated to the barracks and clandestinely sent one of his sons to Halifax to appeal, in vain, to Sir James Kempt, commander of the forces in the Atlantic region, for more troops; "he will naturally return," Smith wrote to Kempt, "to share the fate to which those he left behind him are exposed."

In fact, Smith's fate was to be decided in London, not in the colony. All of Lord Bathurst's instincts predisposed him to support Smith and for a time he continued to do so. When Smith announced that he was suspending William Johnston as attorney general for not supporting him during the trial, Bathurst approved of the decision, although Smith's subsequent appointment of Palmer, who had represented Lane at those proceedings and to whom Smith turned in desperation, was less enthusiastically endorsed. In March 1824 James Stephen, the legal adviser to the Colonial Office, presented a lengthy report, based upon an exhaustive examination of the documents in London, which established that there was sufficient evidence of misconduct to justify Smith's recall. It was this report, not Stewart's influence at the Colonial Office and certainly not the influence of the absentee proprietors, which persuaded Bathurst that he must act. Reluctantly he asked Smith to resign, promising that if he could disprove the charges brought against him he would be given a pension of £500 per annum. Smith's replacement, John Ready*, arrived to assume control of the administration on 21 Oct. 1824 and Smith departed on 12 November, reaching London in December.

During 1825 he sought to rehabilitate himself and in January 1826 Stephen prepared a curiously ambiguous report which declared "that the charges of corruption, oppression and insolence, are satisfactorily repelled, but that he was guilty in his Office of indolence and of an implicit and heedless confidence in the various family connections whom he placed in situations of trust. It is manifest also, that he was either very poor, or very penurious, or both; and consequently very unpopular." Smith was told that he would be given a pension out of the revenues derived from the collection of quitrents on Prince Edward Island, but since little was collected during the next two years he was reduced to dire straits and bombarded the Colonial Office with letters appealing for his pension. In 1829 Sir William Sidney Smith again came to his brother's aid and the government agreed to place Smith's pension on the annual estimates voted by the British parliament for the administration of Prince Edward Island. Fortunately for Smith, the Duke of Wellington's government was able to carry out this promise in 1830 before the Whigs came to power and until his death at his home in Devon in 1855 Smith continued to draw his pension of £500 from the British Treasury. Significantly, during the transition to responsible government on the Island in the early 1850s, when the colony was asked to assume responsibility for paying the various expenses previously defrayed by the British parliament [*see* George Coles*], the one item that Lord Grey, the colonial secretary, did not ask the colonial government to pay was Smith's pension.

In *The government of Prince Edward Island*, Frank MacKinnon describes Smith as "the worst Governor in the history of the province." There are so many examples of wilful wrongdoing by the early governors of Prince Edward Island that it is difficult to decide whether Smith merits this distinction. Certainly he was less overtly corrupt than some of his predecessors and in his efforts to resolve the land question and collect quitrents he appears to have been motivated, at least in part, by honourable intentions rather than by a desire to acquire land on the cheap. Much of the criticism directed against him was exaggerated and was motivated by self-interest. None the less, he was guilty of abusing his authority and of bringing the Island to the verge of an open rebellion in 1823 by the way in which he conducted proceedings in the Court of Chancery. The excessive zeal he showed in finding employment for his large family was perhaps excusable since it was typical of the age in which he lived. But the evidence is overwhelming that he exercised little control over his relatives and that they exercised little restraint in their efforts to exact as much profit from their positions as the law allowed. In May 1824 Judge Brenton Halliburton, who had been deputed to investigate the complaints made against the Court of Chancery, prepared a report condemning Ambrose Lane for breaking the spirit, if not the letter, of the law by exacting excessive fees.

Smith

Since Smith benefited from the same fee structure, he was as guilty as Lane of abusing his authority.

In fact, Smith treated the Island as if it were a large country estate and its people as if they were his tenants. His achievements were negligible. He tackled the land question but in such a clumsy way that he provided the proprietors with additional reasons to argue that they were justified in not living up to their commitments because of the misgovernment of the Island, and thus he may have delayed a more substantial reform of the landholding system. By treating the colonial assembly with scant respect he encouraged that body to demand the same control over public revenues possessed by the assemblies on the mainland, and during the crisis of 1823 he probably brought into the political arena popular forces that had previously been quiescent. But these were not his intentions and it is hard to avoid the conclusion that he was a man of limited intelligence and slight ability who ought never to have been appointed. Perhaps Prince Edward Islanders may take some consolation from the fact that for nearly 30 years the British Treasury was saddled with the responsibility of paying for that error in judgement.

PHILLIP BUCKNER

PAC, MG 40, B17: 76–77 (transcripts); RG 7, G7, 12: ff.9–42. PAPEI, RG 5, Minutes, 1812–24 (mfm. at PAC). PRO, CO 226/26: 13–17, 79, 81; 226/27: 5–5A, 10–11, 31–32, 35–37, 45–46, 117–18; 226/29: 3–5, 45–48, 57–60, 67–77, 80–85, 95–97, 109–10, 347–49; 226/30: 9–16, 18–21, 42–49, 54–63, 114–20, 128–49; 226/31: 5–6, 34–52, 60–61, 88–89, 109–11, 119–21, 126–29, 156–59; 226/32: 7–10, 17–18, 28, 52–57, 68–69, 74–75, 113–15, 135–36, 167–70, 194; 226/33: 19–22; 226/34: 13–19, 29–30, 57–60, 146, 160–61, 174; 226/35: 3–4, 15–17, 33–77, 158–59, 166–67, 255–56, 265–66, 304–42, 350–51, 408–9; 226/36: 52–54, 60–61; 226/37: 5–8, 11–13; 226/39: 11–13, 19–20, 26–28, 143–46, 153–61, 163–66, 184–85, 191–97, 232–45, 286–87; 226/40: 58, 130, 170, 184–85, 191–205, 232–34; 226/41: 5–34, 89–125, 168–73, 188–95, 233–50, 323–42, 421–54; 226/43: 10, 177–80; 226/44: 226/46: 151–54; 226/46: 200–1, 219–20, 223–35; 226/47: 243; CO 227/7: 55–56, 60, 63, 69–75, 77–78, 110–17. SRO, GD45/ 3/27A/229–35. USPG, C/CAN/NS, 4: 163i (mfm. at PAC).

Gentleman's Magazine, January–June 1855: 444. [Edward Howard], *Memoirs of Admiral Sir Sidney Smith, K.C.B., &c.* (2v., London, 1839), 1: 5–10, 17, 367–68; 2: 352. John MacGregor, *Historical and descriptive sketches of the Maritime colonies of British America* (London, 1828; repr. East Ardsley, Eng., and New York, 1968), 65–66, 92–95. *Petitions from Prince Edward Island . . .* (London, [1824]). P.E.I., House of Assembly, *Journal. Examiner* (Charlottetown), 2 April 1855. *Prince Edward Island Register*, 13 Sept., 4, 11, 25 Oct., 1, 8, 15 Nov. 1823; 3, 17, 24 Jan., 6 March, 24 July, 24 Oct. 1824. G.B., Parl., House of Commons, *Members of Parliament* (2v., London, 1878), 2: 218; WO, *Army list*, 1777–1807. John Barrow, *The life*

and correspondence of Admiral Sir William Sidney Smith, G.C.B. (2v., London, 1848), 1: 3–5; 2: 82–84. Duncan Campbell, *History of Prince Edward Island* (Charlottetown, 1875; repr. Belleville, Ont., 1972), 61–71. *Canada's smallest prov.* (Bolger), 84–94. Frank MacKinnon, *The government of Prince Edward Island* (Toronto, 1951). MacNutt, *Atlantic prov.* E. F. L. Russell, *Knight of the sword: the life and letters of Admiral Sir William Sidney Smith, G.C.B.* (London, 1964). D. C. Harvey, "The Loyal Electors," RSC *Trans.*, 3rd ser., 24 (1930), sect.II: 101–10.

SMITH, JOHN, Presbyterian minister; b. 19 Jan. 1801 in Cromarty, Scotland, son of the Reverend Robert Smith and Isabella Gair Rose; m. 30 Aug. 1838 Jane Morson, in Bytown (Ottawa), Upper Canada, and they had six children; d. 18 April 1851 in Beckwith Township, Upper Canada.

John Smith was the sixth of ten children, and, like his father before him, was educated at King's College (University of Aberdeen), from 1814 to 1819. A shy man, quiet and pious, he tutored while studying theology and later became assistant to the Reverend William Mackay, minister of Dunoon, one of the foremost Gaelic scholars of the time. Smith learned the language from Mackay, and in so doing acquired a skill that would later bring him to the attention of church authorities seeking a minister to serve in a remote bush settlement in Upper Canada.

Beckwith Township had been settled in 1818 by Scots from Laggan (Highland), Scotland. Early in the following year the Presbyterians among them wrote to the governor in Quebec, the Duke of Richmond and Lennox [Lennox*], for help in securing and supporting a minister able to preach in Gaelic. When no reply was received they turned to the Reverend William BELL, a nearby Presbyterian clergyman, and asked him to petition Scotland on their behalf. Bell, a secessionist, complied, and wrote to the Associate Synod of Scotland. In 1822, after the congregation had again given up hope, a secessionist minister, George Buchanan, was sent to be their pastor. Buchanan must have been a valuable member of this pioneer community: a minister who could preach in English and Gaelic, he had also received medical training. Initially pleased, the congregation welcomed him and his large family "and did all in their power to render them comfortable." However, differences, largely religious, gradually arose between Buchanan and his flock. The discontent came to a head in May 1832 when the barn Buchanan had used as a church was destroyed in an accidental fire. His parishioners decided to take the opportunity for a fresh start and planned to build a stone church where services would be held in connection with the Church of Scotland and not with the secessionist body to which Buchanan belonged. Although Buchanan, 70 and ailing (he died in 1835), was being considered for admission to the Church of Scotland connection, a call went out to the

Glasgow Colonial Society [*see* Robert Burns*] for a minister of the established church who was fluent in English and Gaelic.

The society requested the Reverend Thomas C. Wilson, minister at nearby Perth and himself only a recent arrival in Upper Canada, to comment on Beckwith's prospects. He reported that "the people are in general industrious and comfortable in worldly circumstances, and warmly attached to the Church of their fathers. And I know of few country places here, where, a faithful minister may be more agreeably situated." Satisfied, the society then sought a minister to serve in Beckwith. It was not easy to be chosen for that station since the society was adamant it should go to someone fluent in Gaelic. John Smith was well qualified and, on his decision to go to Canada, received the support of his colleagues. The Reverend William Mackay wrote a glowing letter to the society praising his character and abilities. Another clergyman wrote: "He is not a popular preacher but he is evangelical in his views and amiable in his disposition and conduct. His talents are respectable, his want of popularity is owing to a nervous diffidence that he cannot easily surmount." At a test sermon preached in Glasgow on 26 May 1833 Smith was well received and praised. One of the society's officials who assessed him wrote that "I could not have discovered that the Gaelic was an acquired language with him, had he not told me so." He did so well on the trial sermons that he was given the choice of two ministries, Lancaster Township, also in Upper Canada, or Beckwith; he chose the latter, perhaps feeling some kinship with the settlers from Laggan which he had recently visited. Smith received his appointment from the society on 27 May, and on 9 July was ordained by the Presbytery of Chanonry.

Travelling with two sisters, Smith arrived in Beckwith late in October 1833 and preached his first sermon in the nearly completed stone church, St Andrew's, on 3 November. Disappointed that a house had not been built, he lived for a time in a log building through the kindness of a member of the congregation, and in 1834 oversaw the building of a stone manse which subsequently housed four successive ministers. By autumn of that year work was completed on the church itself.

Smith's congregation soon came to consider him a kindly, understanding man, and particularly appreciated his fluency in Gaelic. His ministry flourished. In a letter dated 21 April 1834 Smith wrote: "As one called to minister in Holy things among them I have met with every mark of esteem and respect from my congregation; in every way also in which they can add to my personal comfort they have shown the utmost kindness – the most cheerful willingness to oblige. Upwards of 300 regularly attend my public ministrations. On some favourable days during the sleighing season the number attending could not have been less than 500. During the summer months when our roads are passable I hope the average number of hearers will be 400 or rather more. This in one of the back Townships is considered a very respectable audience."

Controversy seems not to have touched Smith's life, although William Bell, who described him as having "a great talent for silence," resented the appointment in Beckwith of a minister ordained by the Church of Scotland at a time when negotiations were underway to readmit the secessionists. Smith remained with the Church of Scotland connection during the disruption of 1844 which saw the formation, led by John BAYNE, of what was popularly called the Free Church. Smith's congregation supported him and responded generously to his fund-raising efforts on behalf of Queen's College, Kingston, which also retained its original affiliation. His congregation, whom Smith described as "working farmers," donated some £130 at a time when its account totalled only £34.

Although there is no evidence to support the belief, family tradition, citing Smith's "saintly and impractical character," has it that he died of pneumonia "as a result of giving his overcoat to a beggar." Three other ministers in turn succeeded him to the charge at Beckwith, but within 25 years of Smith's death the church closed its doors and was allowed to fall into ruin.

MABEL RINGEREIDE

PAC, MG 9, D7, 35, 30 Aug. 1838. QUA, Queen's Univ. letters, John Smith to F. A. Harper, 10 June 1840. UCA, Biog. files, John Smith, especially Mabel Ringereide, "The Rev. John Smith and his Rockcliffe kin" (typescript, 1976); Glasgow Colonial Soc., corr. Croil, *Hist. and statistical report* (1868), 89–90. *Bathurst Courier*, 2 May 1851. Scott et al., *Fasti ecclesiæ scoticanæ*, vol.7. Gregg, *Hist. of Presbyterian Church.* Mabel Ringereide, *The flourishing tree* (Ottawa, [1979]); "Beckwith Manse," *Presbyterian Record* (Don Mills [Toronto]), 99 (1975), no.11: 2–3.

SMYTH, JOHN (also known as **Sir John Smith**), farmer, land agent, and poet; b. *c.* 1792; d. 1 Sept. 1852 at the House of Industry in Toronto.

By his own account, John Smyth was "born and bred up in this Province of Canada" and worked as a farmer until he was 23 years old. About 1815 he left that occupation to become a land agent in York (Toronto). Smyth was a railway enthusiast and in 1837 he published a *Map of Upper Canada, shewing the proposed routes of rail roads, for the purpose of extending the trade of the province.* Copies of this map were sold by Toronto book-dealers Henry Rowsell*, Robert Stanton*, and James Lesslie*. Eight years later Smyth published a short essay entitled "Railroad

Solomon

communication" in which he made one of the first public proposals calling for the construction of an all-Canadian railway route, saying that, in the event of war between Great Britain and the United States, a branch of the railway should be built "to run in the rear of Lake Huron, and also in the rear of Lake Superior, twenty miles in the interior of the county of the lake aforesaid; to unite with the Railroad from Lake Superior to Winepeg at the north-west main trading post of the North West Company."

Smyth had started writing in 1837 or 1838 in response to an anonymous poem which he received in the mail. The discovery of his talent surprised him "as much so, as though I had seen a person fly to the moon." The British writer Frederick Marryat* included one of Smyth's early poems, "To the ladies of the city of Toronto," in his widely circulated *A diary in America* (1839). Smyth is best known, however, for his two books. The first, *Select poems*, was published in Toronto in 1841; a copy now in the Metropolitan Toronto Library bears the handwritten inscription "A Literary Curiosity." The volume contains a number of poems on topical subjects, for example, Toronto's celebration of the marriage of Queen Victoria and the vandalism of Sir Isaac Brock*'s monument at Queenston Heights. In a poem on the transfer of the seat of government from Toronto to Kingston, he predicted that Toronto would "flourish and blossom like a rose" despite the loss of government revenue.

Advertisements placed in some contemporary newspapers hailed Smyth's work with extravagant accolades. One in the *Toronto Patriot* on 14 May 1841 proclaimed: "He is alike beyond the reach of praise and censure. In some departments of literature Sir John MAY have been exceeded, but we hesitate not to say that for exquisitely musical versification, peculiar originality of conception, and the power of blending the keenest and most withering sarcasm with the purest breathings of Christian charity, he must be forever unsurpassed!"

Four years later Smyth published *A small specimen of the genius of Canada West, and the wonders of the world*. In its preface he claimed that his writing was spontaneous and effortless: "I am pretty astonished at myself that I can compose as well and elegant any subject that I attempt." He signed this volume of essays and poems with a self-created designation as "Sir John Smyth, Baronet, and Royal Engineer, Canadian Poet, L.L.D., P.L. [Poet Laureate], and Moral Philosopher."

In fact, Smyth was seen by many of his contemporaries as a laughing-stock. In an open letter to Governor Sir Charles Theophilus Metcalfe* published in *A small specimen*, he flatly denied rumours that he was mad, claiming that "such evil reports of me are all false, untrue, and most diabolical." A note attributed to Matthew Teefy of Richmond Hill reported that Smyth "never was an *active*, intelligent man; [but] was weak, and silly, − given to [*poetry* ?] and *love* making − and became a *butt* for the *young* men about town." Smyth's notoriety was further enhanced after he lost the use of his legs and got about by means of a carriage he could propel while sitting in it. He died in 1852, impoverished and dependent upon public charity.

Although his poetry was unspectacular, the eccentric Smyth was not soon forgotten. Twenty years after his death Henry Scadding* recalled, "Sir John Smythe found in the public papers a place for his productions which by their syntactical irregularities and freedom from marks of punctuation proved their author . . . to be a man *supra grammaticam* and one possessed of a genius above commas."

BEVERLY FINK CLINE

John Smyth is the author of the following publications, all of which are available at the MTL: *Map of Upper Canada, shewing the proposed routes of rail roads, for the purpose of extending the trade of the province* (New York, 1837); "To the ladies of the city of Toronto" in Frederick Marryat, *A diary in America, with remarks on its institutions* (3v., London, 1839), 1: 217; *Select poems* (Toronto, 1841); and *A small specimen of the genius of Canada West, and the wonders of the world* (Toronto, 1845), which includes his "Railway communication . . ." on pp.25–32. The MTL's copy of the *Select poems*, originally the property of Matthew Teefy, contains a handwritten note concerning Smyth. Its copy of *A small specimen* is the only one recorded and may be the only one extant; it is itself an incomplete copy, missing pp.13–24.

British Colonist (Toronto), 5, 12 May 1841. *Christian Guardian*, 8 Sept. 1852. *Toronto Patriot*, 14 May 1841. Scadding, *Toronto of old* (Armstrong; 1966), 118–19.

SOLOMON (Solomons), WILLIAM, clerk and Indian Department interpreter; b. 28 May 1777 in Montreal, son of Ezekiel Solomon and Elizabeth Dubois; d. in Penetanguishene, Upper Canada, and was buried 27 Jan. 1857.

William Solomon was the fourth child of a German Jewish merchant who had come to New France from Berlin during the Seven Years' War and acted as a supplier to the British army. Following the conquest, Ezekiel Solomon, one of the first non-French fur traders to penetrate as far as the upper Great Lakes, spent part of each year in the interior and the remainder at Montreal, where William apparently received some education. By the mid 1790s William was working in the interior as an employee of the North West Company, and he evidently lived for some time with his parents on Mackinac Island (Mich.). There he and an Ojibwa girl, Agibicocoua, had an illegitimate daughter, who was baptized on 28 July

1796. In 1797, 1799, and 1800 he fathered three other illegitimate children. Shortly thereafter he appears to have married Marguerite Johnston, who had been born on Mackinac Island. They were to have ten children.

Solomon supported his growing family by working at Michilimackinac, on Mackinac Island, as a clerk for the merchant Joseph Guy and occasionally by doing some interpreting, since he had learned several Indian languages. In 1809 his father died, leaving him land on Mackinac Island and on the mainland at Saint-Ignace (Mich.). Though Mackinac had been turned over by the British to the United States in 1796, in accordance with Jay's Treaty, Solomon felt no strong loyalty to the Stars and Stripes. After war broke out between the United States and Great Britain in 1812, a force assembled by Captain Charles Roberts* swiftly descended upon Mackinac Island and captured the fort and town for the British on 17 July, the first military action of the war and a source of some satisfaction to Solomon. By February 1814 he had secured a position with the Indian Department as an interpreter at 4s. 6d. per day.

Since the number of British soldiers at Mackinac Island was small, their Indian allies were vital for their survival. When the Americans attempted to recapture the island in 1814, it was the Indians who swung the battle in favour of the British. The Americans never took Mackinac, but under the Treaty of Ghent it was returned to the United States. In July 1815 the British, under Lieutenant-Colonel Robert McDouall*, withdrew their forces. The following month they settled on nearby Drummond Island and Solomon and his family accompanied them. Solomon was provided with a government lot on which he built a home for his family and established a small farm. His duties were to make out requisitions for provisions and to order the repair of the Indians' guns.

Along with Jean-Baptiste Assiginack* and a few others, Solomon was one of the interpreters kept on at Drummond Island as part of the peace-time garrison, which included the Indian Department establishment under the superintendence of William McKay*. Though characterized somewhat harshly by John Askin, an official in the department, in January 1816 as "a sober man" who could not interpret at Indian councils but who "may answer about a post to see an equal distribution of Provisions," Solomon did in fact interpret at various councils. As well, when the Indians of the Upper Lakes flocked to Drummond Island to receive the presents which the British doled out to ensure their loyalty, Solomon probably participated in distributing the goods. In 1816, when the Indian Department was reduced, he lost his job. He was reinstated, however, on 29 May 1821.

The British were not to remain long on Drummond Island, for when the border between Upper Canada and the United States was surveyed, it was found to be American territory. Once again the garrison, including Solomon, David Mitchell*, and other Indian Department officials, was forced to move, this time to Penetanguishene on Georgian Bay, where a British naval establishment had already been located. In late 1828 a brig was chartered to move the forces, but when it proved too small Solomon was instructed to charter a schooner as well. He did not accompany it, however, since he had been ordered to spend the winter at St Joseph Island, where he had lived briefly in 1825, in order to inform the Indians about the British move. In all, the families of between 75 and 100 soldiers, voyageurs, and small traders came from Drummond Island to Penetanguishene, which Lewis Solomon, a son, described as "then mostly a cedar swamp, with a few Indian wigwams and fishing shanties."

In 1829 Solomon and his family finally moved to Penetanguishene, although his livestock and implements were lost in a shipwreck on 12 July of that year. He built a home near by, on lot 105, and continued to work as an interpreter. In 1837 he attended, along with Thomas Gummersall Anderson*, Samuel Peters JARVIS, Jean-Baptiste Assiginack, and others, a major Indian conference on Manitoulin Island, which was graphically described by Anna Brownell Jameson [MURPHY] in her account of travels in Upper Canada. On a longer trip, made in the early 1840s for the distribution of presents, he served as interpreter for a party that included Lord Morpeth, Lord Lennox, Jarvis, and 56 voyageurs from Penetanguishene; they visited Manitoulin, Sault Ste Marie, and Detroit.

Solomon received his discharge on 30 June 1845 and retired on a pension of 75 cents a day, according to his son Lewis. William afterwards moved into town, where he died and was buried in the cemetery of St Anne's Church. Surviving him were a large family and his second wife, Josephine Légris, whom he had married late in life.

DAVID ARTHUR ARMOUR

ANQ-M, CE1-63, 23 juill. 1769, 18 juin 1777. Arch. paroissiales, Ste-Anne-de-Michilimackinac (Mackinac Island, Mich.), reg. de baptêmes, mariages et sépultures, 1695–1821. Bayliss Public Library, Steere Special Coll. Room (Sault Ste Marie, Mich.), Port Mackinac, records, 1, 20, 22 Oct. 1818; 29 Sept. 1827. Detroit Public Library, Burton Hist. Coll., American Fur Company, day book, 1804–5; ledger, 1803–6; James Henry, Mackinac Store journal, 1802–4; Robert McDouall, orderly book, Drummond Island, 1815–16. Mackinac County Court House (St Ignace, Mich.), Reg. of the post of Michilimackinac, begun 1 June 1785. PAC, RG 1, L3, 465: S16/45; RG 10, A2, 22, 28–32; A4, 49; 52; 509: 201; A5, 268. St Ann's Roman Catholic Church (Penetanguishene, Ont.), Reg. of burials, 26 Jan. 1857. Stuart House Museum of Astor Fur Post

Somerville

(Mackinac Island), American Fur Company, letter-book, 11 July 1820, 8 Sept. 1822, 22 Sept. 1824. Joseph Delafield, *The unfortified boundary: a diary of the first survey of the Canadian boundary line from St. Regis to the Lake of the Woods*, ed. Robert McElroy and Thomas Riggs (New York, 1943), 318–21, 461. *The John Askin papers*, ed. M. M. Quaife (2v., Detroit, 1928–31), 2: 525. *Mich. Pioneer Coll.* (Lansing), 16 (1890), 23 (1893). Murphy, *Winter studies and summer rambles* (Talman and McMurray; 1943), 249, 256, 267. U.S., Congress, *American state papers . . . in relation to the public lands . . .*, ed. Walter Lowrie (5v., Washington, 1834), 4: 810, 819–20, 826–27. Wis., State Hist. Soc., *Coll.*, 9 (1882): 202; 18 (1908): 501; 19 (1910): 104–5, 110, 120. "List of the Drummond Island *voyageurs*," *OH*, 3 (1901): 149–66. *Officers of British forces in Canada* (Irving), 211, 214. Leonard Bacon, *Sketch of the Rev. David Bacon* (Boston, 1876), 53. E. J. and E. L. Bayliss, *Historic St. Joseph Island* (Cedar Rapids, Iowa, 1938), 78, 144–45; *River of destiny, the Saint Marys* (Detroit, 1955), 135, 318. S. F. Cook, *Drummond Island; the story of the British occupation, 1815–1828* (Lansing, 1896). B. F. Emery, *Post cemetery, Drummond, Fort Collyer, 1815–1828* (Detroit, 1931), 5–6; *The story of Fort Drummond (Fort Collyer), the last British stronghold in Michigan, 1815–1828* (Detroit, n.d.), 16–17. I. I. Katz, "Ezekiel Solomon: the first Jew in Michigan," *Mich. Hist.* (Lansing), 32 (1948): 247–56. A. C. Osborne, "The migration of *voyageurs* from Drummond Island to Penetanguishene in 1828," *OH*, 3: 123–49.

SOMERVILLE, JAMES, educator and Church of England clergyman; probably b. *c.* 1775 near Forfar, Scotland; d. 1852 in Scotland, probably in Edinburgh.

Little is known about James Somerville's background or life before his emigration to New Brunswick in 1811. He had at least one sister, who remained in Scotland, and one brother, Alexander Carnegie, who was to serve as rector in Bathurst, N.B., in the late 1820s and 1830s. In 1795 James Somerville had graduated with an MA from King's College (University of Aberdeen). He arrived in Fredericton in 1811 to take up the post of preceptor at Fredericton Academy. With him came his wife, Pattison Brown, a sister of Colonel Andrew Brown of Londonderry (Northern Ireland); she was described as a "learned lady" who read "Latin, French, Italian and Greek and Hebrew with great fluency."

Fredericton Academy, which had opened its doors by 1793, was a collegiate school, intended as a feeder school for the proposed College of New Brunswick (later King's College and then the University of New Brunswick). For its first few years the college, which was chartered provincially in 1800, existed only on paper although it had a council to act as overseers. This same governing body also oversaw the academy, as a separate institution, and its early efforts were concentrated on running the junior school as a kind of preparatory institution. Finances were always a problem for the academy, and the council found it difficult to obtain the quality of teacher necessary both to run the school and, in anticipation of better times, to begin college-level courses. In 1809 the position of preceptor of the academy became vacant and the council, through Judge John Saunders* (one of its members) and Humphrey Henry Carmichael, conducted a search for a replacement. George Gleig, bishop of Brechin, Scotland, was asked for recommendations. When his first choice declined to fulfil his contract, he proposed James Somerville. The council took up Gleig's suggestion and concluded a "treaty" with Somerville.

Somerville immediately ran into difficulties with the council over the issue of money. His duties at the academy included teaching "correct Grammatical Knowledge of the English language, reading English with Grace and propriety, Writing and Arithmetic, with the elements of Geometry, Geography and Astronomy" plus some classics. The cost to each student for such an education was to be 25 shillings as an "entrance fee" and £5 per annum paid in tuition; Somerville was to receive £270 yearly plus living-quarters at the academy. Unfortunately the council seems rarely to have paid him.

In 1812, when Somerville put in a request for his salary as well as a share of the tuition money to which he believed he was entitled, the council refused it. The following year his suggestion that the differences between himself and the council be arbitrated by Bishop Gleig, who was familiar with the original agreement, was also turned down, and Somerville then approached the provincial administrator, George Stracey Smyth*, for help. In 1830, after the College of New Brunswick had become King's College, the council was still recording, as an outstanding debt, "about £2000 Due to Dr. Somerville from the old Establishment which the new one is answerable for."

Despite his lack of pay for the work he was already doing, Somerville in 1820 accepted the appointment as president of the College of New Brunswick, although he retained his position with the academy until May 1822. Along with his academic duties he had been conducting a ministry outside Fredericton; in May 1821 he was required to cease his missionary work under threat of losing the "Tuition money" from the academy. This order was rescinded in February 1822, and he was allowed to take church preferments provided he gave up his living-quarters at the college. That year he received permission to begin teaching college-level courses to those students "sufficiently advanced." In recognition of his work as "Principal of the Collegiate Establishment Fredericton," King's College, Aberdeen, awarded Somerville an LLD on 26 June 1827.

When the college received its royal charter as King's College, Fredericton, the council gave Somerville notice that his presidency would cease with the coming into operation of the charter on 1 Jan. 1829

Somerville did, however, continue to teach college-level courses as a professor of divinity and metaphysics at the reduced salary of £150.

In contrast to his dealings with the council, Somerville got along well in the community and with his students. He served as a member of several local and provincial organizations, such as the Fredericton district committee of the Society for Promoting Christian Knowledge and the Fredericton Emigrant Society, in addition to his clerical duties first as an Anglican missionary for the parish of Douglas and later as its rector. For a time he also served as an itinerant missionary to the parish of Queensbury. From 1816 until he left Fredericton, he was chaplain of the provincial House of Assembly and, in the 1820s at least, he was also chaplain to the garrison stationed in the city.

In 1838 American artist Albert Gallatin Hoit was commissioned by 17 of Somerville's former pupils to paint his portrait, which now hangs in the Old Arts Building on the University of New Brunswick campus in Fredericton. Somerville was deeply touched by this gesture and wrote, "Next to the approbation of my own mind, I value this token of their regard above all earthly rewards, and I want words to express the feelings which actuate me on this occasion."

Long years of struggle eventually took their toll on Somerville. Early in 1839, according to a petition of 1847 made on his behalf, an "Inquisition" found him "incapable of managing his affairs," and a committee of lunacy was established. In July his wife took him back to Scotland. That same month the *Royal Gazette* referred to him as "a Lunatic." At some point between the time of Somerville's illness and his departure from New Brunswick, he was appointed to the board of health for York County. His resignation from the college was officially accepted on 9 Sept. 1840 by the council. On his return to Scotland, Somerville was first committed to the Glasgow Lunatic Asylum although his wife hoped to have him moved to a private hospital located closer to her in Edinburgh. Evidently Somerville recovered, possibly by 1843 when he first brought suit against George Frederick STREET, the registrar of King's College, for back pay. Another attempt was made on his behalf in 1847. It is probable that he lived in Edinburgh until his death.

LINDA SQUIERS HANSEN

UNBL, MG H28, 9 May 1829; UA, College Council minutes, College of New Brunswick, 1810–28; King's College, 19 Oct. 1829, 9 Sept. 1840; UA, College of New Brunswick charter, 12 Feb. 1800; UA RG 42, 9 Oct. 1847; UA RG 109, I, 4 Jan. 1830. Univ. of Aberdeen Library, MS and Arch. Sect. (Aberdeen, Scot.), King's College matriculation records and biog. data (copy at UNBL). N.B., House of Assembly, *Journal*, 1816. Robb and Coster, *Letters* (Bailey). *New Brunswick Reporter and Fredericton Adver-tiser*, 15 Oct. 1852. *Royal Gazette* (Fredericton), 26 Dec. 1819, 13 April 1836, 28 Feb. 1838, 17 July 1839. *N.B. almanac*, 1829, 1836. G. H. Lee, *An historical sketch of the first fifty years of the Church of England in the province of New Brunswick (1783–1833)* (Saint John, N.B., 1880). J. D. Hazen, "The collegiate school," *Capital* (Fredericton), 24 Oct. 1882. [Linda Squiers Hansen], "Loyalists petitioned for 'Infant Establishment,'" Univ. of New Brunswick, *Alumni News* (Fredericton), March 1981.

SOMERVILLE (Sommerville), MARTIN, painter, art teacher, and illustrator; b. in 1796 or 1797; d. 31 May 1856 at Quebec.

Martin Somerville, an immigrant from England, was painting in the Canadas by 1839. He may also have exhibited miniatures and water-colours in New York City in 1841. From 1845 to 1855 he occupied a studio at 25 Rue Saint-Jacques, Montreal. Cornelius Krieghoff* rented a studio in the same building about 1846 and the two artists obviously influenced each other, particularly in their choice of subject-matter. Somerville's best-known oil paintings depict Indians, principally men on snow-shoes and young women selling moccasins. These, and other canvasses of gentlemen driving horses and tandem sleighs on the frozen St Lawrence River, are similar to works painted by Krieghoff. Several Somerville paintings have had forged "C. Krieghoff" signatures added to them; they differ from Krieghoff's works in their accent on linear draftsmanship and low-keyed colour harmonies.

In 1845 Somerville advertised in the *Montreal Gazette* as a "Professor of Painting" and he established classes in painting "Historical Subjects, Landscapes, Flowers &c. in Oil and Water Colours." He was an instructor in free-hand and perspective drawing at Miss Plimsoll's school for young ladies in Montreal, where Krieghoff became instructor in painting from 1847 to 1849. In January 1847 Somerville exhibited as a member of the Montreal Society of Artists, the city's first professional artists' association. His 21 contributions, including water-colours, sketches of Greek landscapes with ruins in the picturesque style, paintings of flowers, and copies of landscapes by the English artist James Duffield Harding, indicate that he was a prolific artist. Drawings of Indians and local Montreal views appeared in the *Illustrated London News* during 1849 and 1850. *Me-nifs-i-no-wen-in-ne, the great warrior*, a pencil drawing of an Indian chief, demonstrates his precise technical excellence.

Somerville may also have had a home or studio at Quebec; he was listed as a resident during 1854–55 and died there in 1856 at the age of 59. Because Somerville's work has not been thoroughly studied and few details are known of his personal life, he remains a shadowy figure in Canadian art.

J. RUSSELL HARPER

Soulard

The Royal Ontario Museum (Toronto), Canadiana Dept., Sigmund Samuel Coll., holds the drawing of *Me-nifs-i-no-wen-in-ne, the great warrior* by Martin Somerville. The work, which is described in Mary Allodi, *Canadian watercolours and drawings in the Royal Ontario Museum* (2v., Toronto, 1974), was published along with others by Somerville in *Illustrated London News*, 19 May, 15 Sept. 1849; 21 Dec. 1850.

ANQ-Q, CE1-61, 2 juin 1856. *Montreal Gazette*, 10 Oct. 1845, 15 Jan. 1847. *Pilot* (Montreal), 29 Jan. 1847. C. P. De Volpi and P. S. Winkworth, *Montreal; a pictorial record . . . 1535–1885* (2v., Montreal, 1963). G. C. Groce and D. H. Wallace, *The New York Historical Society's dictionary of artists in America, 1564–1860* (New Haven, Conn., and London, 1957; repr., 1964). Harper, *Early painters and engravers. Montreal directory*, 1845–55. *Quebec directory*, 1854–55. *Le peintre et le Nouveau Monde* (Montréal, 1967). Gérard Morisset, *La peinture traditionnelle au Canada français* (Ottawa, 1960). W. A. Craick, "Letters; Cornelius Kreighoff," *Atlantic Advocate* (Fredericton), 53 (1962–63), no.5: 11.

SOULARD, AUGUSTE (baptized **Augustin**), man of letters and lawyer; b. 13 March 1819 in Saint-Roch-des-Aulnaies, Lower Canada, son of François-Marie Soulard and Théotiste Voisine; d. there unmarried 27 June 1852.

Auguste Soulard's father, a militia captain known for his hospitality and his love of the poor, was one of the most highly regarded habitants of Saint-Roch-des-Aulnaies. From 1831 to 1836 Auguste was a brilliant student at the Collège de Sainte-Anne-de-la-Pocatière, and during these years he formed a strong friendship with François-Magloire Derome*. Soulard went to Quebec in 1837 and studied law successively under Joseph-Noël Bossé and George Okill Stuart*.

For a true estimate of Soulard, an understanding of the complexities of his period is required. At the time when he was beginning his studies, French Canadians for the first time since the conquest were experiencing normal conditions in the school system and the book trade. His generation was, then, a pioneering one. As a law student Soulard commanded the attention of his colleagues by his charm, cheerfulness, love of study, and above all his attachment to his native land, a sentiment he expressed in the poem "Mon pays," first published in *Le Canadien* in 1841. Hence he gathered around himself a small group of young people who were eager to restore that land to its original vitality through progress in the sciences and humanities. They contributed as amateurs to the newspapers of Quebec, thus giving a considerable stimulus to the first stirrings of French Canadian literature. In October 1840 Soulard and Derome made plans to publish the *Journal des familles*, which was to forgo political debate in order to open its columns to "the writings of lovers of literature, the essays of studious youth, and discussions." But not even the promise of collaboration by men such as Augustin-Norbert Morin*, Louis-David Roy*, François-Xavier Garneau*, and Pierre-Joseph-Olivier Chauveau* was enough to ensure the journal's success, and only the prospectus appeared.

Soulard was called to the bar on 27 June 1842 and settled permanently at Quebec. The young lawyer won friendships everywhere by his selflessness. According to Chauveau, magistrates soon listened to him with a marked attention rarely bestowed on men of talent when still young. His smooth and correct diction, the restraint and logic of his pleading, and the diligence and zeal with which he studied his cases earned him a position of honour. He had numerous and significant successes in criminal cases.

In 1842 Soulard assisted in organizing the Société Saint-Jean-Baptiste of Quebec. Then, in the autumn of 1843, he helped found the Société Canadienne d'Études Littéraires et Scientifiques, which in January 1844 inaugurated a series of public lectures. This initiative was imitated on 17 December by a number of Montrealers who founded the Institut Canadien. Soulard displayed his talents as a popular speaker at public meetings and in the patriotic addresses he delivered for three years at the banquets of the Société Saint-Jean-Baptiste. For the public lectures of the literary societies, Soulard gave a talk on the history of the Gauls, and another on trade in ancient times; these were carefully prepared pieces of work which he none the less declined to publish. A pleasant and even brilliant conversationalist, he was held in esteem by his close friends for his urbanity and the good humour tinged with melancholy that lent charm to his remarks.

Around 1846 Soulard's law office on Queen's Wharf became the meeting place for young people in the city who were eager for culture and progress. Some of them joined him as crew for the yacht *La Belle Françoise*. Among them was Charles-Vinceslas Dupont, a law student and poet, who fell off the ship and drowned. In October 1849 Soulard's name appeared, along with those of writers Napoléon Aubin*, Télesphore Fournier*, and Marc-Aurèle Plamondon*, at the head of a list of citizens supporting annexation to the United States in view of the "commercial, political, and social difficulties of Canada . . . and in particular the lack of interest that the mother country seems to have in it."

But Soulard was soon forced by tuberculosis to return to his father's house. On the eve of his death, buoyed up by an unshakeable Christian hope, he consoled and fortified his father, who was also stricken with tuberculosis and who preceded him to the grave by six days. Auguste Soulard, who had long been preparing for his death by pious meditation, died on 27 June 1852.

Soulard's literary output was slight: a few very witty articles published anonymously in *Le Canadien* and *Le Fantasque*, a Canadian legend, and a number of poems in a correct and elegant style. He left no work of major importance; on the other hand he displayed exquisite taste, sure judgement, and a fair but kindly critical spirit that enabled him to guide and stimulate others to thought.

Shortly after Soulard's death, his contemporary and friend Chauveau emphasized the factors that made his accomplishments so meritorious: the effort that young people just out of college had to make at that time to acquire a station in life; the countless obstacles besetting a professional career; the difficulties involved in the study of law in particular, as a result of the chaotic state of the legal system in Lower Canada, which incorporated the remnants of three or four legislative systems. Soulard had overcome these impediments and within a few years his talent would have matured. His friend Derome devoted a long poem to various facets of his personality. His colleagues at the bar undertook to wear mourning for a month.

Auguste Soulard's reputation as a brilliant lawyer and a skilful littérateur lasted until the end of the 19th century. Since then academic and specialized studies have occasionally mentioned his creative contribution. He deserves to be remembered as an unassuming, energetic, and determined architect of the cultural resurgence of the 1840s.

JEANNE D'ARC LORTIE

ANQ-Q, CE2-25, 20 oct. 1807; 13 mars 1819; 22, 27 juin 1852. Le Foyer canadien (Québec), 1 (1863); 4 (1866). Le Canadien, 26 oct. 1840; 31 oct. 1849; 23, 30 juin, 7 juill. 1852. Le Courrier du Canada, 21 mars 1866, 28 déc. 1870, 22 nov. 1889. P.-G. Roy, Les avocats de la région de Québec, 410–11. Jeanne d'Arc Lortie, La poésie nationaliste au Canada français (1606–1867) (Québec, 1975). Le Répertoire national (Huston; 1848–50), vol.2. BRH, 2 (1896): 128. D. M. Hayne, "Sur les traces du préromantisme canadien," Rev. de l'univ. d'Ottawa, 31 (1961): 141.

STAINES, ROBERT JOHN, Church of England clergyman, schoolmaster, and farmer; baptized 8 Nov. 1820 in the parish of Oundle, England, son of John Collins Staines, tailor, and his wife Mary; d. 1854, probably in March, off Cape Flattery (Wash.).

The eldest of nine children, Robert John Staines was educated at the Oundle Grammar School before entering St John's College, University of Cambridge, in 1840. Two years later he transferred to Trinity College where he progressed well, showing an aptitude for teaching, and in January 1845 he was awarded a Bachelor of Arts degree. In the fall of 1844 Staines had been appointed assistant classics and mathematics master at the Derby Grammar School, a post he held until October 1845 when he accepted employment as a private tutor in Gorey, County Wexford (Republic of Ireland). He returned to England some time after July 1846 and following his marriage to Emma Frances Tahourdin, a well-educated linguist and teacher, he and his wife established a school at Boulogne-sur-Mer, France.

Early in March 1848 Staines's former employer in Ireland recommended him to the Hudson's Bay Company for the projected school at Fort Vancouver (Vancouver, Wash.). The London committee of the HBC was impressed with the qualifications of both Staines and his wife. Furthermore, since the Columbia district had gone without a chaplain for close to ten years, the directors were pleased to learn that Staines had contemplated taking holy orders and offered him a double appointment as schoolmaster and chaplain, should he be ordained. Hastily wrapping up his affairs in France, he returned to England and upon the recommendation of the bishop of London was ordained deacon and priest in Norwich Cathedral in August 1848. On 12 September the now Reverend Robert John Staines, his wife, and her ten-year-old nephew, Horace Foster Tahourdin, sailed for Fort Vancouver aboard the HBC barque Columbia, commanded by James Cooper*. During the voyage, however, the company decided to transfer the Columbia district headquarters from Fort Vancouver to Fort Victoria (Victoria, B.C.) on Vancouver Island and as a consequence Staines's posting was changed to the new headquarters.

When the Staineses arrived at Fort Victoria on 17 March 1849 there was no residence, schoolhouse, or church ready for them and they took up temporary accommodation in the HBC Bachelors' Hall. Although disappointed in the conditions at the fort, they appeared at first to be settling well into their new life. Classes for the 20-odd students were initially conducted in Bachelors' Hall and Sunday services were held in the hall of the fort. Staines performed baptisms, marriages, and burial services at the fort, in the adjacent districts on Vancouver Island, and as far afield as forts Langley (B.C.) and Nisqually (near Tacoma, Wash.) on the mainland. Some time after his arrival he obtained a claim of 400 acres in the vicinity of Mount Tolmie; he subsequently added a second tract of 46½ acres, for which he paid £46 10s. He took a particular interest in livestock and soon developed a fine breed of pigs; furthermore, by 1854 his farms were yielding significant quantities of wheat and oats. The inadequacy of the facilities at Fort Victoria none the less persisted and the Staineses continued to board, with a certain number of their students, in the company hall; the church was not ready for religious services until August 1856, more than two years after Staines's death.

It had not been long before differences had arisen between Staines and the HBC chief factor in charge of the fort, James Douglas*. The chaplain became associated with Cooper, who had left the company

Stevenson

service, and other non-HBC settlers, such as Thomas BLINKHORN, dissatisfied with the company's management of the colony. In August 1851 Staines was among those who drafted a petition opposing, unsuccessfully, the nomination of Douglas to succeed Richard Blanshard* as governor. Late in 1852 the Colonial Office in London received an anonymous letter protesting against the company's administration, which, according to Douglas, was written by Staines. Unsigned letters appeared in various Oregon Territory newspapers voicing the same complaints and were attributed by the governor to "Captain Cooper, or some other member of a little clique consisting of that person, the Revd Mr. Staines, [James] Yates, a ship carpenter and Muir [probably John Muir*], a collier and publican; who do everything in their power to slander the Hudson's Bay Company, and to produce impressions unfavourable to their character and government." In the summer of 1853 a petition signed by Staines, Cooper, William Fraser Tolmie*, John Tod*, Roderick Finlayson*, and 85 others, calling for an independent governor, an elective legislative council, and other reforms, was forwarded to the House of Commons in London.

Staines's political activities inevitably interfered with his duties as schoolmaster and by May 1853 the parents of the schoolchildren, who were responsible for raising his salary of £340, were openly critical of his conduct. After consultation with the HBC London committee, Douglas and Chief Factor John Work*, as members of the board of management, informed Staines on 1 Feb. 1854 that his services as teacher would not be required after 1 June, although he would be free to continue in the office of chaplain. Three days later Staines was delegated by the dissatisfied colonists, united in a public meeting, to carry to England two petitions, each bearing 70 signatures, protesting against the nomination of the governor's brother-in-law David Cameron* as acting chief justice of the Supreme Court of Civil Justice. To cover the expenses of the voyage a subscription of $400 was taken up, and, without asking for a leave of absence from the company, Staines boarded the *Duchess of San Lorenzo*, bound for San Francisco, at Sooke on or about 1 March. The vessel, which was carrying a heavy deck load of timber, foundered in Juan de Fuca Strait and all aboard were lost. Some years later the HBC doctor John Sebastian Helmcken* remarked that when news of the disaster reached Victoria "there was a general pity – he was praised or blamed – a martyr or a fool as the case may be, but all nevertheless regretted his end." Emma Frances Staines sold off the farm stock and returned to England with her nephew in January 1855.

Recognized in the colony as an intelligent, well-informed, and gifted teacher, Robert John Staines, "priest, pedagogue, and political agitator," was none the less poorly adapted as a pioneer settler and he left his mark primarily as a fomenter of ill will. Both he and his wife are commemorated in minor place names on the southern coast of Vancouver Island.

In collaboration with MADGE WOLFENDEN

City of Vancouver Arch., Add. mss 145 (copy at PABC). Northamptonshire Record Office (Northampton, Eng.), Census for Oundle (Northants), 1851; Oundle parish reg. of baptisms, 8 Nov. 1820. PAM, HBCA, A.11/74: ff.240d–43. G.B., Parl., House of Commons paper, 1857–58, 41, no.524: 571–74, *A return of all lands in Vancouver's Island sold to any individual or company. . . .* Helmcken, *Reminiscences of Helmcken* (Blakey Smith and Lamb). W. G. Walker, *A history of the Oundle schools* (London, 1956). G. H. Slater, "Rev. Robert John Staines: pioneer priest, pedagogue, and political agitator," *BCHQ*, 14 (1950): 187–240.

STEVENSON, DAVID BARKER, businessman, justice of the peace, office holder, and politician; b. 17 Nov. 1801 in Clinton (Hyde Park), N.Y., son of Timothy Stevenson and Phoebe Barker; m. 14 Dec. 1830 Agnes Rebecca Dougall of Hallowell (Picton), Upper Canada, and they had one daughter; d. 3 March 1859 in Picton.

David Barker Stevenson's father died when he was ten, leaving a widow with three small children. David received a "limited education in . . . Poughkeepsie," N.Y., before moving in 1824 to Hallowell where he secured employment at the general store of his uncle, Abraham Barker. On the latter's death in 1828 Stevenson carried on the business with his widowed aunt until 1833. He then operated independently until 1848 when he went into partnership with Thomas W. Nichol.

By the late 1830s Stevenson's business operations were becoming increasingly diversified. Like most general merchants of the time, he maintained credit accounts with his customers and often received payment in produce. These arrangements were extended to his dealings with Montreal wholesalers and forwarders such as George Moffatt* and Samuel CRANE, who provided him with letters of credit to buy and forward grain or accepted shipments of pork and flour in partial payment for their dry goods. Stevenson also sent timber rafts to Quebec, dealt in real estate, and operated a distillery and an ashery in Picton. He was a shareholder in the Montreal-based Canada Inland Forwarding and Insurance Company and in 1836 became the first president of the Mutual Fire Insurance Company of the Prince Edward District. Despite the variety of his enterprises Stevenson suffered many business reverses, including the destruction twice by fire of his Picton store, and he eventually died in modest circumstances. The major source of his financial difficulties was the trade stagnation of 1847–49 which Stevenson experienced along with the Montreal merchants and forwarders and from which he never recovered.

Stevenson's involvement in politics began in 1834 when he was appointed a magistrate for the newly created Prince Edward District. He represented Hallowell Township on the district council between 1842 and 1849 and was district warden from 1847 to 1849. After the passage of the Municipal Corporations Act, he was reeve of Picton (1850–53), county warden (1851–53), and mayor of Picton (1854). A moderate tory, Stevenson was elected to the Legislative Assembly for Prince Edward in 1848 and again in 1851 and 1854 with the help and encouragement of the rising young politician John A. Macdonald*. Prior to the 1851 election Macdonald wrote to Stevenson that "the Rads are working like blazes," and exhorted him to "take the stump manfully." He promised in return to see all the Kingston residents eligible to vote in Picton and "send them on to you." True to his word, Macdonald and a group which included Alexander Campbell* and Henry Smith* crossed the treacherous ice over the Bay of Quinte on foot to vote for Stevenson. His win secured a sweep of the region for the conservatives.

Stevenson's parliamentary support for Macdonald was unswerving, particularly on issues unpopular in Upper Canada. He supported a separate school system for Upper Canada (he was himself a communicant of the Reverend William Macaulay*'s Anglican church). He also spoke and voted against representation by population and backed Kingston as the seat of government. In 1856 he reluctantly joined the committee appointed to investigate Macdonald's accusations that George Brown* had falsified evidence and suborned witnesses while secretary of the 1848–49 commission inquiring into abuses at the Kingston penitentiary. Stevenson prepared the committee's majority report which mildly rebuked Macdonald for laying the charges but did not clear Brown. The ensuing debate in the assembly witnessed a series of bitter exchanges between Stevenson and Brown, who described the former as one of "my bitterest enemies in this house." When Stevenson lost his seat the following year to Willet Casey Dorland, the Toronto *Globe* gleefully noted the defeat of "the most despicable Ministerial creature in [the] last Parliament."

Stevenson's career in parliament was undistinguished. His major speeches mirrored his business interests: trade and tariffs as they affected the commerce of the St Lawrence. He decried the reformers' "free trade notions" and "the tendency of our commercial legislation . . . to drive all trade from Montreal to New York and Toronto, or Hamilton." As late as 1856 he still believed that the St Lawrence "was destined soon to be a great medium of transport for western trade to the sea." Though not an important politician or businessman, David Barker Stevenson was one of a small group of moderate tories who provided Macdonald with the original nucleus of his support. His business career reflected in microcosm the decline of the commercial empire of the St Lawrence.

James A. Eadie

ACC-O, St Mary Magdalene Anglican Church (Picton, Ont.), reg. of marriages, 1830. AO, MU 479, Alexander Campbell to Parker Allen, 3 May 1892; Allen to Campbell, 6 May 1892; MU 2884–90; RG 21, Prince Edward District, minutes, 1842–56; RG 22, ser.83, 1. PAC, MG 26, A. QUA, D. B. Stevenson papers. Can., Prov. of, Legislative Assembly, Select Committee Appointed to Inquire into Certain Charges Against George Brown, *Proceedings and minutes of evidence . . .* (Toronto, 1856), 145–46. *Debates of the Legislative Assembly of United Canada* (Abbott Gibbs et al.), vol.8. "Parl. debates," 1854, 1856. *Globe*, 1 Jan. 1858. *Hallowell Free Press* (Hallowell [Picton]), 4 Jan. 1831; 24 July 1832; 23 July, 12 Aug. 1833; 31 March 1834. *Picton Gazette* (Picton), 15 July, 12 Aug. 1836; 9 July, 3 Sept. 1847; 14 July 1848; 18 March 1859 [the last issue cited was consulted in transcript in the Lennox and Addington County Museum (Napanee, Ont.), Lennox and Addington Hist. Soc. coll., T. W. Casey papers]. *Pioneer life on the Bay of Quinte, including genealogies of old families and biographical sketches of representative citizens* (Toronto, 1904; repr. Belleville, Ont., 1972). J. M. S. Careless, *Brown of "The Globe"* (2v., Toronto, 1959–63; repr. 1972), 1: 218–27. D. [G.] Creighton, *John A. Macdonald, the young politician* (Toronto, 1952; repr. 1965). Canniff Haight, *Country life in Canada fifty years ago . . .* (Toronto, 1885; repr. Belleville, 1971), 297–98. J. S. Barker, "A brief history of David Barker, a United Empire Loyalist," *OH*, 3 (1901): 168–70.

STEWART, JOHN, businessman, justice of the peace, office holder, and politician; b. 24 Nov. 1773 in Musselburgh, Scotland, son of John Stewart, a surgeon, and Sarah Jackson; m. 28 March 1814, at Quebec, Eliza Maria Green, daughter of Lieutenant-Colonel James Green*, and they had eight children, of whom five survived childhood; d. 5 June 1858 in Sillery, Lower Canada.

Nothing is known of John Stewart's youth in Scotland or of the factors that brought him to British North America. He was already 20 years old when he sailed from Greenock for Quebec in the spring of 1794. He was to remain a resident of the city for the next 64 years, during which time he rose to membership in the economic and political élite of Lower Canada.

In the late 1790s Stewart's career seems to have followed a fairly straightforward path. In both 1797 and 1798 he was employed by Monro and Bell, owned by Mathew Bell* and David Monro*; it is not at all clear in what capacity he served them. Gradually, over the next few years, he began to act on his own behalf in various commercial matters. Starting in 1807 he carried on an importing business. From stores and cellars located on Rue Saint-Pierre, he sold Madeira, port, and claret as well as rum, cognac, brandy, and London-bottled porter. Other imported goods were also found on the premises: muscovado, tea, coffee, spices, vinegar, English iron, hardware, and dry goods. Occasionally Stewart advertised that he had on hand such North American goods as wheat, flour, Newfoundland biscuit, and square timber. He does not appear to have been involved in the export of the North American produce.

Stewart continued on his own account until some time in the fall of 1816. On 26 October of that year, Monro, who had decided to withdraw from Monro and Bell, sold his interests in the firm to Bell for £14,350. Bell then chose Stewart as his former partner's successor. The two men carried on in Quebec under the name Bell and Stewart from 1816 until January 1822. Unfortunately, little is known of the internal organization of the firm: no information has been located to document what each man brought to the partnership, or to explain how responsibilities and revenues were shared. Bell had been a lessee of the Saint-Maurice ironworks since 1793 and Stewart seems to have become involved in this aspect of Bell's affairs, at least from 1817 to the early 1820s, but the extent of his affiliation with Bell is not known. During the same period Bell and Stewart also operated a foundry in Trois-Rivières and did business there as general merchants.

The formation of this partnership, linking Stewart with one of the most prominent businessmen of Lower Canada, coincided with Stewart's emergence as a recognized leader of Quebec's mercantile community and as one of its most visible spokesmen. He was appointed a justice of the peace in 1815. In February 1816 he and five other merchants from Quebec were chosen to testify before a committee of the House of Assembly formed to examine the incorporation of a bank in Lower Canada. The following year he was selected as a director of the Office of Discount and Deposit, which acted as the Bank of Montreal's branch at Quebec. He became the office's president in 1824. In May 1817 a meeting of the Quebec Exchange, established to facilitate the transaction of business by providing a central location for the gathering and dissemination of commercial information, offers graphic evidence of the prominent position Stewart occupied. He chaired the meeting flanked by four vice-presidents, James Irvine*, John Mure*, John William WOOLSEY, and Robert Melvin. In 1822 he was elected chairman of the Quebec Committee of Trade, a position he held for the next three years. In 1824 he began a lengthy term as master of Trinity

House of Quebec, the body that oversaw the activities of what was then the largest port in British North America. During these years he also played a central role in numerous organizations and committees through which the Quebec business community sought to express its concerns and to influence both the colonial and the British governments.

Stewart's success in business and his rise to prominence within the Quebec mercantile community seem to explain the decision of Governor Lord Dalhousie [Ramsay*] to appoint him first to the Legislative Council in May 1825 and next to the Executive Council in January 1826, thus opening up a new phase in Stewart's career. As Dalhousie himself wrote to him in December 1825, "You know it is no sinecure, and you know how important it is, that the respectable Members in this community of Quebec, should thus give their abilities to that Branch of Public Service."

On 26 June 1815 Stewart had been named a commissioner for the Jesuit estates. He became the sole commissioner in 1826 in a move by Dalhousie to cut expenses. During the 1830s the House of Assembly sought to exercise more control over the estates and, while Bell was negotiating to renew his lease on the Saint-Maurice ironworks, it became known that Stewart, as commissioner, had designated extensive lands in Cap-de-la-Madeleine as a reserve for the ironworks to ensure its supply of wood and ore. The assembly, especially the member for Trois-Rivières, René-Joseph Kimber*, resented the favouritism that Stewart had shown to a fellow legislative councillor and former business partner, and criticized the commissioner for failing to allow settlement on the estates, for permitting arrears to accumulate in the payment of dues to the estates, and for the negligence of his agents. No action was taken, however, because the brevity of the 1836 and 1837 sessions of the assembly prevented the committee on the Jesuit estates from presenting a report.

Little else is known of Stewart's political career. No documents have been located that shed light upon his particular contribution to the formulation of government policy during this period of growing political tension. He was president of the Executive Council when the rebellions broke out in the fall of 1837. He ceased to be a legislative councillor with the suspension of the constitution in March 1838 and his role as executive councillor came to an end with the act of union in 1841.

Thus, in 1842, at age 68, Stewart found himself at the end of another stage in his long career. His political life was seemingly at a close, while his business activities had gone into decline over the previous decade. As he embarked upon his retirement years, his major concern seems to have been to find ways to augment the apparently inadequate income that his appointments as master of Trinity House and commissioner for the Jesuit estates provided. Writing to Governor Sir Charles Bagot* in July 1842, he sought to obtain both an increase in salary for these positions and the reinstatement of his income as an executive councillor. He recalled that he had "at different times, within the last thirty three years filled many high and confidential offices . . . to the entire satisfaction of Your Excellency's Predecessors and the Government." He enclosed a list of the services he had rendered, from his work for Governor Sir James Henry Craig* in 1809, negotiating commissariat bills of exchange in New York, through his contribution as deputy paymaster general of the Lower Canadian militia during the War of 1812, to his numerous later appointments. His petitions proved unsuccessful. He appears to have lived quietly, and perhaps more modestly than in previous years, until his death 16 years later.

John Stewart has been remembered by historians for his role in the political life of Lower Canada in the years preceding the rebellions of 1837–38. This view of him is at best incomplete. Stewart, the politician and office holder, can be understood only if he is seen first as a merchant, as a man who devoted the greater part of his adult life to business pursuits. It is especially necessary to examine his relationship with the Quebec mercantile community, whose spokesman he became and whose interests he represented.

JOANNE BURGESS

Can., Parks Canada, Quebec region (Quebec), Centre de documentation, système infothèque. PAC, MG 24, B3: 1–3; D84: 220–21; L3: 8986, 8992–93; MG 30, D1, 28: 430–36; RG 1, L3, 4: 1355, 1446, 2021; 7: 2230; 8: 2462, 2566; 80: 558; 126: 62170; 187: 89812, 89817–19; RG 68, General index, 1651–1841. *Quebec Gazette*, 1794–1824. E. H. Dahl *et al.*, *La ville de Québec, 1800–1850: un inventaire de cartes et plans* (Ottawa, 1975). Morgan, *Sketches of celebrated Canadians. Quebec directory*, 1822. Turcotte, *Le Conseil législatif*. R. C. Dalton, *The Jesuits' estates question, 1760–1888: a study of the background for the agitation of 1889* (Toronto, 1968). Denison, *Canada's first bank*. Fernand Ouellet, *Histoire de la Chambre de commerce de Québec, 1809–1959* (Québec, 1959).

STEWART, WILLIAM, businessman, militia officer, politician, and farmer; baptized 24 July 1803 in Carbost, near Loch Harport, Isle of Skye, Scotland, son of Ranald Stewart and Isabella McLeod; m. 16 April 1838 Catherine Stewart of Cuidrach, Isle of Skye, and they had four sons and five daughters; d. 21 March 1856 in Toronto.

William Stewart was 13 when he arrived at Quebec in 1816 with his nine brothers and sisters, his widowed mother, his maternal grandmother, and his uncle. The family proceeded to Upper Canada and settled in

Lancaster Township, Glengarry County, where William's education was rounded out under the tutelage of army doctor Roderick Macleod. Stewart's first employment was with a Montreal merchant, whom he represented at the sale of timber rafts at Quebec in 1825. He spent the next two years at Longueuil before moving in March 1827 to Bytown (Ottawa), then a construction camp. There, in partnership with John G. McIntosh, Stewart acquired property adjoining the projected route of the Rideau Canal and opened a store carrying dry goods and supplies for timber shanties on the upper Ottawa River. Though a teetotaller, he added a taproom to the store, ownership of which he assumed in 1830 upon the death of his partner. Community-minded, Stewart was elected one of the original councillors for Bytown in 1828. During the cholera epidemics in 1832 and 1834 he made door-to-door surveys for the board of health and later was one of the founders of the County of Carleton General Protestant Hospital. He helped form the Bytown Association for the Preservation of the Peace during the Shiner riots [see Peter Aylen*] and was active in the local militia.

In the mid 1830s Stewart supervised, staffed, and equipped his own timber shanties on the upper Ottawa and its tributaries and sold rafts of red and white pine at Quebec. As a broker, he also financed small operators and sold timber on their behalf. Fluent in English and Gaelic and with a working knowledge of French, Stewart, a founding member of the Ottawa Lumber Association, quickly became a spokesman for lumberers operating above Bytown, especially on the need for appointing timber cullers independent of both buyers and sellers. While in London in 1835, he presented a memorial to the British government on behalf of Montreal merchants and Bytown residents seeking improvements to navigation on the Ottawa. In London again in 1838, he was examined by a committee of the House of Commons on the feasibility of Charles Shirreff*'s proposed water route to Lake Huron via the Ottawa, and later that year he had an interview with Lord Durham [Lambton*] at Quebec on the matter. In 1839, acting as agent for Louis-Théodore Besserer*, Stewart sold lots in what is now the Sandy Hill district of Ottawa.

Upon the union of Upper and Lower Canada in 1841, Stewart ran for election for Bytown against Stewart Derbishire*. Apparently at the suggestion of Governor Lord Sydenham [Thomson*], who was backing Derbishire, James Johnston*, Alexander James Christie*, and Robert Shirreff withdrew their candidacies, but Stewart refused to retire. Though defeated he harboured no grudge and assisted Derbishire in furthering local concerns. In 1843 Stewart was returned for nearby Russell in a colourful by-election campaign during which he was escorted from Bytown by a uniformed volunteer fire brigade.

Street

Intensely loyal to the crown, Stewart won the 1844 general election in Bytown on a pledge to support "the course pursued by the illustrious Individual at the head of the Government," Sir Charles Theophilus Metcalfe*.

During his years in the Legislative Assembly (1843–47), Stewart shepherded through legislation regulating the culling and measurement of timber and introduced a resolution calling for a start on a project to be known as the Georgian Bay ship canal, an undertaking which his son McLeod would urge at a future date but without success. In 1845 Stewart chaired the committee that secured the return from the Board of Ordnance of land belonging to Nicholas Sparks*, and the following year he drafted the bill to incorporate Bytown. The boundaries in the bill, which Stewart later claimed reflected those sanctioned by Lord Sydenham in 1841, left his farm outside the town limits and thus subject to a lower tax rate. Stewart was also accused of arranging the wards in Bytown so as to favour conservative ascendancy. In the general election of 1847–48, the conservatives of Bytown for unknown reasons abandoned "sweet William," as the reform Bytown *Packet* dubbed him, for John Bower Lewis*. But John A. Macdonald* had not lost confidence in Stewart and, in the spring of 1849, urged him to "organize at once for Bytown, Russell, Prescott, and Carleton," should Lord Elgin [Bruce*] call a snap election during the upheaval caused by the passage of the Rebellion Losses Bill. He became the candidate of the British American League [*see* George Moffatt*] for Bytown but there was to be no election until 1851, when he was defeated by reformer Daniel McLachlin*. He ran for the last time in 1854 for Russell, again unsuccessfully.

In the late 1840s Stewart had suffered financial set-backs. Reported to be worth £20,000 in 1846, he had invested heavily in lumber; losses sustained as a result of a glutted market and tight credit during 1847–48 forced him to sell his crown timber permits to John EGAN and give up his lumber business. By 1850 he had given up his store as well and thereafter devoted his time to his duties as superintendent of common schools for Bytown and to his farm. The latter ran west of the Rideau River for two miles and adjoined the Bytown parcel owned by the heirs of Lieutenant-Colonel John By*. Stewart won prizes for his saddle horses and field crops and used the hustings to lecture farmers on methods of fertilizing. In March 1856, while representing the city of Ottawa as a special agent in Toronto, then the seat of government, he suddenly took ill and died a few days later. With him at the end were Robert Bell* and John Sandfield Macdonald*. The latter prepared Stewart's bedside will.

Stewart is best remembered for the wide range of his community activities, including the following: he was a founding member of St Andrew's (Presbyterian) Church; vice-president of the Highland Society of Canada; director of the Bytown Emigration Society; president of the Agricultural Society of Carleton County; a member of the original Bytown board of trade; and a director of the Bank of British North America. An ambitious businessman, Stewart accumulated property in Bytown and in Carleton and Renfrew counties despite his chronic complaint of financial difficulties. His letter-books reveal the man: deeply religious, philanthropic, impatient with the shortcomings of others yet a person to whom friends turned for advice. For poet William Pittman Lett, Stewart was "a *man* among old Bytown's men."

R. FORBES HIRSCH

AO, MU 1729. BLHU, R. G. Dun & Co. credit ledger, Canada, 13: 247. Ottawa, Hist. Soc., Bytown Museum Arch. (Ottawa), AMIS, no.6. PAC, MG 11, [CO 42] Q, 224: 754; MG 24, D101; I9, 19, 22; MG 55/24, no.304. Can., Prov. of, Legislative Assembly, *Journals*, 1843–47; *Statutes*, 1843–47. *Bytown Gazette, and Ottawa and Rideau Advertiser* (Bytown [Ottawa]), 1836–54, especially 10 Oct. 1844. *Ottawa Citizen*, 1854. *Ottawa Tribune*, 1854. *Packet*, 1844–51, especially 27 Nov. 1847. M. S. Cross, "The dark druidical groves: the lumber community and the commercial frontier in British North America, to 1854" (PHD thesis, Univ. of Toronto, 1968). W. P. Lett, *Recollections of old Bytown*, ed. Edwin Welch (Ottawa, 1979). Michael Newton, *Lower Town, Ottawa* (2v., Can., National Capital Commission, *Manuscript report*, nos.104, 106, Ottawa, 1979–81).

STREET, GEORGE FREDERICK, lawyer, college administrator, public servant, politician, and judge; b. 21 July 1787 in Burton, N.B., fifth of 12 children of Samuel Denny Street* and Abigail Freeman; m. 26 March 1818 Frances Maria Stratton (Straton), and they had one son and one daughter who survived to maturity; d. 10 July 1855 in London.

Although George Frederick Street's father had served with the British forces in the Thirteen Colonies, received a large grant of land in Sunbury County (N.B.), and sat in the provincial House of Assembly, he was of English birth and was never a member of the inner circle of American-born loyalists who monopolized government patronage in early New Brunswick. Repeatedly he was passed over when vacancies occurred on the bench in favour of loyalists who were junior to him at the bar, much to his children's chagrin. Since he lacked access to patronage, he sought to provide his children with a superior education and sent two of his sons, John Ambrose Sharman* and George Frederick, to study law at the Inns of Court in London. George Frederick attended the Inner Temple in 1808 and practised as attorney at the Court of King's Bench until 1818 when he married the daughter of a major in the Royal

Engineers and returned to New Brunswick to join his father's practice in Fredericton. Because of his English experience, he was allowed to appear in the New Brunswick courts, even though he was not formally admitted to the provincial bar as a barrister until two years later.

Fredericton was little more than a village in the 1820s and the competition for business among its handful of lawyers was intense. The main rivals of the Streets were the attorney general, Thomas Wetmore*, and his son, George Ludlow*. Since the Wetmores were members of the loyalist élite, relations between the two families were not cordial. During a trial in 1821 the two sons carried their argument outside the courtroom and Wetmore challenged Street to a duel. On the morning of 2 Oct. 1821 Street shot and killed his opponent. Wetmore's friends persuaded the sheriff to issue a warrant for Street's arrest for murder. He had fled to the United States following the duel, but he returned to stand trial in Fredericton in February 1822 and was acquitted.

After 1819, when his father was appointed to the Council, Street's future was assured. On 24 June 1822 he was named treasurer and clerk for the College of New Brunswick and when it was incorporated as King's College in 1829 he became the registrar, a lucrative position which he held until 25 June 1846. On 12 April 1825 Street was appointed advocate general by Lieutenant Governor Sir Howard Douglas*, who much admired the elder Street. He also held a number of minor administrative posts and in February 1825 served with Ward CHIPMAN on the committee of management for the newly formed provincial barristers' association. However, when he ran for the House of Assembly in 1827 and again in 1830, he was unsuccessful. Part of the reason for his failure may have been his close association with the unpopular commissioner of crown lands, Thomas Baillie*. During the latter part of the 1820s a bitter feud erupted between the leading loyalist families and Baillie, an Englishman, who established a competing network of family alliances. Quite naturally, Street attached himself to Baillie, and Baillie began to direct much of the legal business of the Crown Lands Office to the Vice-Admiralty Court. Street, who acted as its prosecutor, started to earn substantial fees. Baillie also secured for Street an appointment as solicitor for the New Brunswick and Nova Scotia Land Company, formed in 1831, and the two were associated in the incorporation of a branch of the Bank of British North America in 1837. Although Douglas tried to arbitrate between the conflicting factions in the colony, his successor, Sir Archibald Campbell*, was less discreet. When Campbell divided the Council into two in 1833, he appointed Street, Baillie, and Baillie's father-in-law, William Franklin Odell*, to the Executive Council, which they dominated. The

following year Campbell chose Street as his solicitor general and promised to appoint him to the bench on the next vacancy. After 1833 the assembly sought to curb Baillie's authority over crown lands and to win control of the rapidly growing casual and territorial revenues, but Campbell, in part because of the legal advice given to him by Street, refused to negotiate. Street's brother, John Ambrose Sharman, was one of the few members of the assembly who defended the lieutenant governor's actions.

Unfortunately for the Streets, they had tied themselves to a losing cause. By 1836 the Colonial Office was determined to reach an agreement with the New Brunswick assembly and Campbell was instructed to surrender the revenues for a comparatively modest civil list. Prompted by Street, who raised a number of spurious legal objections to the arrangement, Campbell refused to consent to the civil list bill passed by the assembly and in February 1837 he sent Street to London to justify his decision. Street's mission was an abysmal failure. In May of that year Campbell was replaced by Sir John HARVEY who promptly assented to the bill. Harvey dismissed Baillie from the Executive Council, which he broadened to take in several of the leading members of the assembly, including the speaker, Charles SIMONDS. These actions won almost universal approval except from a rump of officials, among them Baillie, Odell, Charles Jeffery Peters*, and Street. When Baillie appealed against Harvey's decision to reduce his salary, Street acted as his legal adviser. In 1837 Harvey dismissed Street from the Executive Council, declaring that he had experienced "more opposition of opinion from Mr. Street, in Council, than from *any* other Member." Street also nearly lost his position as solicitor general when Harvey accused him, wrongly as it turned out, of writing an article in the Saint John *Chronicle* denying the legality of the civil list act.

The disadvantages of continuing to oppose Harvey were further brought home to Street when it became apparent that if a vacancy occurred on the bench it might go to Harvey's protégé, John Simcoe Saunders*. Making a virtue of necessity, Street dissociated himself from the ranks of the governor's critics and in October 1838 Harvey reported that he was "highly satisfied" with Street's behaviour and recommended his appointment to the Legislative Council. After taking his seat in 1839, Street voted for a motion to prosecute the *Chronicle* for libelling Harvey, and the following year he conducted the prosecution, unsuccessfully. During the next five years he avoided political activity, but on 22 Feb. 1845 Sir William MacBean George Colebrooke*, then lieutenant governor of the province, reappointed him to the Executive Council after the more prominent members of the existing council had resigned in protest against Colebrooke's decision to give his son-in-law, Alfred

Stuart

Reade, the position of provincial secretary. When a vacancy occurred on the bench later that year, Colebrooke submitted Street's name as a puisne judge and in January 1846 his appointment was confirmed by the colonial secretary, William Ewart Gladstone.

For the next decade Street regularly performed his judicial duties until he fell ill in 1855. While on a journey to London that year he died. Although the Fredericton *New Brunswick Reporter* described Street in his obituary as "a sound lawyer and an impartial judge," there is no evidence to indicate that he made any significant contribution to the colony's legal or judicial system. He trained several lawyers, such as Charles Fisher* and William Hayden Needham*, who became prominent New Brunswick citizens, and was effective at pleading a case, but his usefulness as a judge was impaired by partial deafness.

The historian William Stewart MacNutt* describes Street as "one of the few scions of the leading Loyalist families, who opposed reform" in the 1830s. In fact, in a strict sense the Streets were not a loyalist family, or at least they were not perceived as one by the loyalist élite, and their somewhat erratic political behaviour arose from this fact. Samuel Denny Street began his political career as a "tribune of the people," but after his appointment to the Council in 1819, he consistently supported the executive against the assembly; John Ambrose Sharman Street ended his political career in 1851 heading a government which he had recently been attacking. George Frederick Street was less erratic. None the less, it is difficult to believe that he was motivated primarily by ideological considerations. He was an outsider in loyalist New Brunswick and, unlike his father and his brother, he was unable to win a seat in the assembly. His only hope for advancement lay with the executive and so he supported George Stracey Smyth*, Douglas, Harvey, and Colebrooke in turn, and was rewarded with a series of positions culminating in his appointment to the bench. His insecurity manifested itself in the zeal with which he attached himself to Baillie and in his eagerness to engage in duels. Although he claimed to regret that he had killed Wetmore, in 1834 he outraged public opinion by challenging Henry George Clopper*. Street was undoubtedly an able man but his positive contribution to the history of New Brunswick was extremely limited.

PHILLIP BUCKNER

[There is a small collection of Street family papers in the N.B. Museum and a few letters in the Saunders papers in UNBL, MG H11, but the major source for this study were the Colonial Office records in the PRO, especially CO 188/21: 67–68; 188/43: 222–31, 272–74; 188/46: 9–11; 188/50: 13, 131, 370; 188/52: 93–98; 188/57: 50–51, 74–78, 114–23, 140–43, 176–77, 227–28, 258–66; 188/58: 348–62, 365–67, 373–75, 379–82; 188/59: 172–75, 178–85; 188/60: 2–5, 19–22, 202–7, 246–49, 278–80, 311–15; 188/64: 253–54; 188/65: 210–11; 188/69: 313–16, 328–30; 188/92: 70–75, 93–97, 381–82; and CO 323/165: 494–96. Also valuable were the New Brunswick Executive Council minutes in PANB, RG 2, RS6, A3–4, 1833–37; A5, 1845; and the Legislative Council *Journal*, 1839–45.

Useful biographical information is contained in PANB, RG 7, RS75, 1855, G. F. Street, and in N.B. Museum, Street family, CB DOC., C. F. Street, "Historical notes on the Street family of New Brunswick" (typescript, n.d.). There are many references to Street in the newspapers of the period, but of particular importance are the *Royal Gazette* (Fredericton), 2 Oct. 1821, 12 April 1825, 6 Oct. 1830; *New-Brunswick Courier*, 8 March 1834; and *New Brunswick Reporter and Fredericton Advertiser*, 3 Aug. 1855. The chapter on Street in Lawrence, *Judges of N.B.* (Stockton and Raymond) and MacNutt, *New Brunswick*, 250–52, 256, 262, were also useful. P.B.]

STUART, Sir JAMES, lawyer, office holder, politician, and judge; b. 2 March 1780 in Fort Hunter, N.Y., third son of the Reverend John Stuart* and Jane Okill; m. 14 March 1818 Elizabeth Robertson in Montreal, and they had three sons and a daughter; d. 14 July 1853 at Quebec.

A prominent member of the ruling élite of Lower Canada, James Stuart had pursued a career that was the logical outcome of his family background and his undoubted energy and talents. His father was not only a loyalist but also a respected Church of England clergyman, for many years the rector at Cataraqui (Kingston), Upper Canada. Despite some periods of financial difficulties, John Stuart took pains to ensure for his sons the best education available at the time to arm them against the possible influence of "the diabolical Principles of Equality" current south of the border.

James, a talented and precocious lad, completed his eminently conservative and Protestant schooling at King's College, Windsor, N.S., and at the early age of 14 began his apprenticeship in the law in Lower Canada. After four years with John Reid, clerk of the Court of King's Bench in Montreal, and two years at Quebec with Jonathan Sewell*, then attorney general, Stuart was called to the bar in the spring of 1801.

Favourably impressed with the young man, Sir Robert Shore Milnes*, the lieutenant governor, had already made Stuart his personal secretary. Although convinced that he could build a more flourishing practice in Montreal, Stuart filled this post in the hope of eventually obtaining a much better one from his patron – an expectation that was realized when he was made solicitor general on 1 Aug. 1805. Three years later he entered the House of Assembly as one of the two members for Montreal East. With his reputation in private practice growing apace at the same time, it is scarcely surprising that Stuart hoped to replace Sewell as attorney general when the latter was made chief justice of Lower Canada in September 1808. However, the new governor, Sir James Henry Craig*, named his own favourite, Edward Bowen*, to the post. As Bowen was less competent, Stuart, a man of arrogant and choleric temperament, confident of his own abilities and sensitive to slights, showed his resentment of Craig's action. Craig later wrote to the Colonial Office that Stuart had neglected the social obligation of paying his respects to the governor, and, more seriously, although both a law officer and a member of the house, had not only neglected to ask the governor if he wanted any business introduced into the house but had also frequently voted with the "obnoxious party" against government measures. Stuart was to pay dearly for these snubs: in May 1809 Craig dismissed him from his post as solicitor general and replaced him with Stephen Sewell*, brother of the chief justice. Stuart's bitterness over the dismissal was probably accentuated by his defeat in the elections of the following spring at the hands of Stephen Sewell.

Stuart harboured a fierce sense of grievance which appears, however, to have been focused primarily upon Jonathan Sewell. Elected for the riding of Montreal in a by-election in 1811, Stuart acquired the rather uncharacteristic role of leader of the Canadian party in the assembly, rallying it in a concerted attack on Sewell and his colleague James Monk*, chief justice of the Court of King's Bench at Montreal. Stuart seized upon the recently promulgated rules of practice for the courts of King's Bench at Montreal and Quebec and for the Court of Appeals, claiming that the judges had, by changing these rules, stepped outside the proper sphere of judicial activities, arbitrarily abrogating sections of the law and usurping the function of the legislature. On 27 Jan. 1813 he demanded an inquiry, with a view to impeaching the two chief justices. The assembly readily followed his lead and Stuart himself was the president of the special committee and author of the report it handed down in February 1814.

A close analysis of this report shows a mixture of ability and unscrupulousness characteristic of its author. A skilful lawyer, familiar with both the French and the English legal systems, Stuart pin-pointed a grave problem implicit in dispensing French civil law in British courts: judicial practice in a system of judge-made law was alien to the spirit underlying French civil law, and the judges were in fact usurping a function which, in the French legal system, belonged to the legislature. However, in a partisan spirit Stuart also threw in quite a few specious and tendentious arguments and couched the report in exaggerated and violent language that obscured the valid issues he raised and caused it to be dismissed by his contemporaries and later by historians such as Thomas Chapais* as a tissue of fabrications. Stuart's lack of interest in solving the real problem he had

raised is made clear by his refusal to acknowledge the judges' good intentions or to propose a workable alternative. As Chapais has pointed out, when Stuart, as chief justice, revised the rules of practice in 1850, he maintained intact several of the very ones he had earlier attacked.

The "Heads of impeachment" against Sewell finally adopted by the assembly included, in addition to the specifically legal charges, a variety of charges of a political nature, accusing Sewell of subverting the constitution and introducing arbitrary and tyrannical government through his influence as Craig's chief adviser. Stuart's personal motives are particularly clear in the 7th clause of impeachment, which accused Sewell of causing the governor to "remove and dismiss divers loyal and deserving Subjects" because they were his political opponents and "in one instance, to procure the advancement of his brother." Such disparate contemporary observers as Governor Sir George Prevost* and Pierre-Stanislas Bédard*, former leader of the Canadian party, agreed that in pressing such charges Stuart was motivated by "personal Animosity" and "works only for his own gratification." Nevertheless, Stuart became one of the foremost leaders of the Canadian party from 1813 to 1817, during which time he relentlessly strove to keep the issue of the impeachment of the two chief justices alive.

The assembly's charges, sent to England as an address to the Prince Regent, were submitted to the Privy Council. Sewell took a leave of absence to defend himself, and was spared a confrontation with Stuart in London by the Legislative Council's refusal to vote funds to send Stuart over as the assembly's agent. Not surprisingly, the Privy Council exonerated the two chief justices. When the assembly, led by Stuart, reacted early in 1816 to the news of the vindication of the judges with a series of resolutions complaining that it had been prevented from having its case fairly heard, the administrator of the colony, Sir Gordon DRUMMOND, acting on instructions from the colonial secretary, dissolved the assembly and called an election.

Although Stuart revived the issue in the new parliament in 1817, the recently appointed governor, Sir John Coape Sherbrooke*, handled the rather explosive situation more adroitly than his predecessor. On receiving a petition from the assembly for a salary for its speaker, Louis-Joseph Papineau*, Sherbrooke agreed, provided that a similar salary be approved for the speaker of the Legislative Council (none other than Sewell himself). Determined to secure a salary for their leader, Papineau's supporters voted as the governor had suggested. Stuart was absent at the time on business in Montreal. Subsequently, in spite of his most impressive and impassioned oratory, the assembly refused to support a motion reviving the impeachments. He never forgave his erstwhile followers for this betrayal and, in high dudgeon, he ceased to attend the assembly.

The 1820s were a decade of increasing conflict between the French Canadian majority in the assembly and the British merchants and bureaucrats in the councils. Stuart, now a strong supporter of British interests, played a notable role in these disputes. When the British party attempted to reunite the provinces of Upper and Lower Canada in 1822, he was a prominent speaker on behalf of union, and he was sent to London in February 1823 as the agent of the pro-unionists. He presented the officials of the Colonial Office with petitions in favour of union and also published a pamphlet entitled *Observations on the proposed union of the provinces of Upper and Lower Canada, under one legislature* that ably and forcefully presented the case for union, stressing not only the obvious economic and geographic arguments but also the necessity of union for British predominance and the assimilation of the French Canadians.

Stuart used his sojourn in London to impress the Colonial Office with his own abilities. In the process, he produced a severe critique of the plan for a general legislative union of British North America proposed by Jonathan Sewell and John Beverley Robinson* and an analysis of the defects of the clause in the Canada Trade Act of 1822 relating to the conversion from seigneurial to freehold tenure. He succeeded in making a favourable impression on the colonial secretary, Lord Bathurst, who offered him the post of attorney general of Lower Canada, to which he was named on 31 Jan. 1825. The governor, Lord Dalhousie [Ramsay*], called upon Stuart to run for election in order to represent the executive in the lower house. Stuart sat for the riding of William Henry from 1825 to 1827 and had the unenviable task of defending the Legislative Council's measures in the house, where the Patriotes did not hesitate to point out the contradiction between his current and former positions. Papineau's correspondence suggests that Stuart was frequently red with ill-suppressed rage and "overwhelmed with vexations and humiliations" by his former associates in the rough-and-tumble of assembly debates. In recognition of his valuable services, the governor named him to the Executive Council on 6 July 1827, a post he held until the union of the Canadas in 1841. Stuart contested his seat in the stormy election of 1827, but was narrowly defeated by Wolfred Nelson*.

Stuart continued to pursue the policies of the British party as attorney general. In 1828 he elaborated the government's case against the Séminaire de Saint-Sulpice, arguing that the seminary had no legal existence and hence no right to its property (most of Montreal Island), which, in his view, belonged to the crown. An opponent of seigneurial tenure and of the Lower Canadian laws applying to real estate, Stuart argued against a bill passed by the Legislative Council and the assembly in 1829 which attempted to eliminate the uncertainty caused by the Canada Tenures Act of 1825 as to the validity of titles in free and common socage that had been transferred or mortgaged by Lower Canadian law. Stuart deplored the "ill-defined inter-mixture" of English and French law that the bill allowed. In 1830 he also strongly advised the new governor, Lord Aylmer [Whitworth-Aylmer*], against granting a petition by Jean-Baptiste-René HERTEL de Rouville for a new seigneury, arguing that such a concession would be contrary to the policy of gradual extinction of seigneurial tenure implicit in the Canada Tenures Act.

Stuart's arrogance and his role as a pillar of the British party combined to make him the target of a series of accusations by the assembly culminating in a demand for his dismissal. In 1831 a committee on grievances collected evidence on four basic charges against the attorney general: encouraging the unnecessary issuing of new commissions to notaries upon the death of George IV in order to collect a fee for each one; prosecuting cases that should have been dealt with in inferior courts in superior ones, where fees were higher; abuses of his authority during the election of 1827; and conflict of interest in a case between William Lampson, lessee of part of the king's posts, and the Hudson's Bay Company, which had retained Stuart as a private attorney. Aylmer, though not necessarily agreeing with the assembly's charges, felt that the delicate political situation in the province left him no choice but to suspend Stuart and to refer the accusations and the final decision to London. In this assessment Aylmer was correct: Papineau maintained that failure to suspend Stuart would be a clear sign that the governor was a servile tool of the British party. Stuart was suspended on 9 Sept. 1831 and was temporarily replaced by Charles Richard Ogden*.

Stuart was not a man to take suspension lightly. He challenged Aylmer to a duel (which Aylmer declined, with London's approval), demanded compensation for the financial loss he was suffering, and prepared a voluminous defence against the assembly's charges. He passed the next three years in London defending himself and then trying to obtain redress. The assembly had its agent in England, Denis-Benjamin Viger*, present its case. The evidence and arguments on both sides leave one uncertain as to Stuart's guilt or innocence. Lord Goderich, the colonial secretary, eventually decided that, although some of the charges were absurd or unproven, others were not, and Stuart was dismissed in November 1832. This dismissal was not the result of a public trial and the counts on which Goderich considered Stuart guilty were not identical to the specific charges of the assembly. As a result, Stuart was able to appeal successfully to Goderich's successor, Edward George Geoffrey Smith Stanley, on the grounds that his case had been dealt with unfairly. Unwilling to reverse Goderich's decision, Stanley offered Stuart the chief justiceship of Newfoundland in recompense. Stuart refused and insisted on financial compensation, which neither Stanley nor his successor, Thomas Spring-Rice, was willing to concede. Angry and embittered, Stuart returned to his private practice in Lower Canada in 1834 without public exoneration or the satisfaction of his claim.

Stuart's talents and energy had enabled him to build up a substantial private practice which included such well-known clients as Edward Ellice*, Lord Selkirk [Douglas*], and the HBC. In a manner typical of his time, he viewed private and public practice as complementary, and indeed, as his demands for financial compensation suggest, his income from public office was important to him. Evidence indicates that he was above all a practical lawyer, interested in the broader historical and philosophical aspects of the law only to the extent that they might occasionally further his personal goals.

Four years after his return fortune favoured Stuart. Sir John Colborne* named him to the Special Council on 2 April 1838. Stuart held the post briefly, for two months later Lord Durham [Lambton*] dismissed the council's members and replaced them with his own appointees. However, Durham, finding in Stuart a man who shared his views, named him on 22 October as Jonathan Sewell's successor when the chief justice retired. Durham justified the nomination on the grounds that Stuart was universally held to be "the ablest lawyer in the Province" and that his previous dismissal had been a "signal injustice," the charges of the assembly having been the fruit of political animosity. After Durham's departure he was once again appointed to the Special Council, on 11 Nov. 1839, serving as its president until a few weeks before its dissolution in February 1841. He was created a baronet on 5 May 1841.

As a member of the Special Council, Stuart voted in favour of the union of the Canadas, and Lord Sydenham [Thomson*] is said to have asked him to draft the legislation. He was also the author of the ordinance passed by the Special Council that established registry offices throughout Lower Canada, and thus put an end to a controversy which had lasted for decades. Among the consequences of this law was the virtual abolition of customary dower; not surprisingly, it was much resented by legal traditionalists such as François-Maximilien Bibaud* who saw in it an assault on the basic social values embodied in Lower Canadian civil law.

During the 1840s and 1850s Stuart was no longer the centre of controversy and he ended his life in the enjoyment of his honours and in the fulfilment of his obligations as chief justice of Lower Canada. All three of his sons succeeded to the baronetcy, which was extinguished by the death of the youngest in 1915.

An able and ambitious man, James Stuart was inevitably drawn into the political and ethnic conflicts that dominated the period. As a politician, with the exception of the interlude of his attack on Sewell, he was a supporter of the British party. As a jurist, he recognized the potential of the law as a means of assimilation, and he was at one with many of his British colleagues in striving to introduce more English law into the province. Although he was respected for his legal knowledge and talent, his personality was unendearing. Preoccupied with personal advancement, Stuart lacked both the attractive character and the diversity of interests that distinguished his brother Andrew* and the literary ability and statesmanlike breadth of vision shown by his long-time rival Jonathan Sewell.

EVELYN KOLISH

James Stuart is the author of *Observations on the proposed union of the provinces of Upper and Lower Canada, under one legislature, respectfully submitted to his majesty's government, by the agent of the petitioners for that measure* (London, 1824) and of "Remarks on a plan, entitled 'A plan for a general legislative union of the British provinces in North America'" which appeared in *General union of all the British provinces of North America* (London, 1824).

ANQ-Q, CE1-61, 24 juill. 1835, 16 juill. 1853. AO, MU 2923. PAC, MG 11, [CO 42] Q, 109: 128–30; 188-2: 406–18; 195-2: 372; 198-1: 192; 210-1: 98–110; 212: 245; 220-2: 350, 356, 365, 377; 248-1: 159–62; MG 23, GII, 10, vol.5: 2457–60, 2580–83; MG 24, B1; B2; B12; C3; L3: 7622–23, 31098–108 (copies); MG 30, D1, 28: 531–34; RG 7, G1, 25: 156, 159. L.C., House of Assembly, *Journals*, 1814, app.E; 1831, app.AA; 1831–32, app.A; 1836, app.EE. *Docs. relating to constitutional hist., 1791–1818* (Doughty and McArthur); *1819–1828* (Doughty and Story). *Quebec Gazette*, 22 Oct. 1822, 21 Dec. 1836. *Quebec Mercury*, 15 March 1814. F.-M. Bibaud, *Le panthéon canadien* (A. et V. Bibaud; 1891). *DNB*. Morgan, *Bibliotheca Canadensis*; *Sketches of celebrated Canadians*, 324–27. F.-J. Audet, *Les juges en chef de la province de Québec, 1764–1924* (Québec, 1927), 59–66. A. H. Young, *The Revd. John Stuart, D.D., U.E.L., of Kingston, U.C. and his family: a genealogical study* (Kingston, Ont., [1920]). [F.-M. Bibaud], *Commentaires sur les lois du Bas-Canada, ou conférences de l'école de droit liée au collège des RR. PP. jésuites suivis d'une notice historique* (2v., Montréal, 1859–61). Buchanan, *Bench and bar of L.C.* Chapais, *Cours d'hist. du Canada*, vol.3. Evelyn Kolish, "Changement dans le droit privé au Québec et au Bas-Canada, entre 1760 et 1840: attitudes et réactions des contemporains" (thèse de PHD, univ. de Montréal, 1980). J.-E. Roy, *Hist. du notariat*, 2: 459–73. G.-É. Giguère, "Les biens de Saint-Sulpice et 'The Attorney General Stuart's opinion respecting the Seminary of Montreal,'" *RHAF*, 24 (1970–71): 45–77.

SULLIVAN, ROBERT BALDWIN, lawyer, office holder, politician, and judge; b. 24 May 1802 in Bandon (Republic of Ireland), son of Daniel Sullivan and Barbara Baldwin; m. first 20 Jan. 1829 Cecilia

Sullivan

Eliza Matthews, and they had a daughter; m. secondly 26 Dec. 1833 Emily Louisa Delatre, and they had four sons and seven daughters; d. 14 April 1853 in Toronto.

Robert Baldwin Sullivan's father was an Irish merchant, and his mother was a sister of William Warren Baldwin*. The first member of Robert's family to come to York (Toronto), Upper Canada, was Daniel, his eldest brother, who became a law student under Baldwin and lived with another uncle, John Spread Baldwin. The rest of the family immigrated in 1819 and the ambitious Daniel Sr established himself as a merchant in York, dealing in soap and tobacco. After a promising beginning, the Sullivans' aspirations were dashed. In 1821 Daniel Jr died; the following year his father's death left Robert as the head of the family. Once again the extended family lent its support; in 1823 William Warren Baldwin placed his nephew on the books of the Law Society of Upper Canada and secured for him a position as librarian to the House of Assembly. Having received a solid education in private schools in Ireland, Robert excelled in his law studies and was called to the bar in Michaelmas term 1828.

Sullivan first took an active role in politics during the exciting provincial election of 1828, as a campaigner for his uncle. Symptomatic of the increasing organization of the reform movement, John Rolph* had arranged W. W. Baldwin's candidacy in his home riding of Norfolk, though Baldwin remained in York to aid in the campaign of Thomas David MORRISON. Sullivan went to Vittoria to represent his uncle, who was elected, he noted, largely because of Rolph's influence. Sullivan subsequently returned to the capital and took part with Baldwin and his son ROBERT in Morrison's challenge to the return in York of their arch-foe, tory John Beverley Robinson*. He then gave counsel and support to Rolph in his legal defence of Francis Collins*, a supporter of his cousin Robert. Despite the fact that Morrison was defeated and Collins found guilty of libel, Sullivan's considerable legal talents did not go unnoticed.

His future looked bright indeed, but not in the provincial capital. He returned to Vittoria, apparently determined to settle there and take over the law practice vacated by Rolph as a result of his move to Dundas. Shortly afterwards, in early 1829, he married a daughter of John Matthews*, a reform colleague of Rolph's. But once again, after a promising beginning, successive tragedies unravelled Sullivan's personal life: on 20 Dec. 1830, six months after the birth of their daughter, Sullivan's wife died; three months later the baby died. Sullivan quit Vittoria and returned to York to seek the support of his family once more.

Upon his return, he again entered the law offices of W. W. Baldwin and Son, and later, in 1831, he established a partnership with Robert, who had married his sister. The firm, with such talented young lawyers, was soon prospering. On his birthday in 1833, the obviously bright and sensitive Sullivan reported to his brother Henry, then studying medicine in Ireland, that things were going well: "Augustus [another brother] . . . is now a Student of the Learned Society of Osgoode Hall – we have six clerks with plenty to do." The partners were preparing "to go into parliament with the honorable body of Colonial Whigs. next election." Sullivan and Baldwin had advanced their careers enough to consider themselves eligible to replace the recently dismissed attorney general, Henry John Boulton*, and solicitor general, Christopher Alexander Hagerman*. But, Sullivan said, because of their rumoured replacement by law officers from England, neither he nor Baldwin stood a good chance of getting "a silk gown." By the end of 1833 Sullivan was once again thriving and on Boxing Day, in Stamford (Niagara Falls), Upper Canada, he married Emily Louisa, daughter of Lieutenant-Colonel Philip Chesneau Delatre.

His contemplations aside, Sullivan did not seek a seat in the election of 1834. The following year, however, he stood successfully as an alderman for St David's Ward, Toronto, no doubt with the mayoralty in mind. A gentleman of Sullivan's social standing and proven ability would have had little interest in aldermanic duties on a council just one year old. The mayoralty was another matter, however, as John Rolph's actions the previous year had indicated. At the first meeting of council in 1835, Sullivan was confirmed mayor by tory and radical alike. As Toronto's second mayor, he proved himself a competent administrator, approaching the problems of council from a practical rather than partisan perspective. Contested ward elections were the first problem; under Sullivan's guidance, council adopted a set of regulations for hearing these grievances before proceeding with individual cases. Plagued with the same financial problems that had faced the first council [see William Lyon Mackenzie*], Sullivan turned his attention to amending the assessment laws. He was, as well, able to arrange financing for the city's first major works project, a trunk sewer.

Public interest in municipal affairs was, however, sporadic at best. During 1835 council frequently could not convene for want of a quorum and there was discussion about compelling aldermen to attend. Sullivan's last council meeting, lacking a quorum, was adjourned the following year and he declined to run again. There was, however, no lack of public interest in provincial politics, especially with the arrival of the new lieutenant governor, Sir Francis Bond Head*, in January 1836. And it was Sullivan, the erudite lawyer, who, as mayor of the provincial capital, delivered an address of welcome from the outgoing council.

The resignation on 12 March 1836 of Head's Executive Council, of which Robert Baldwin had been a member, plunged the colony into its greatest political and constitutional crisis up to that point. With a haste that was indecent if nothing else, Sullivan accepted appointment to council and on the 14th was sworn in along with Augustus Warren Baldwin* (another uncle), John Elmsley*, and William ALLAN. Upper Canadian history provides other possible examples of political turncoats: Henry John Boulton deserved the epithet, John WILLSON probably did not. But Sullivan's volte-face is without parallel. At the time of the reform brouhaha in 1828 over the dismissal of Judge John Walpole Willis*, Sullivan had declared, "It was against my principles to shew any respect to the present judges," and, like his cousin, refused to plead before the "Pretended" Court of King's Bench. A few years later he professed his eagerness to join the "Colonial Whigs" in the House of Assembly. Yet, without warning, he bedded down in 1836 with a group denounced by William Warren Baldwin as the "Tory junto."

Sullivan has, unfortunately, left no explanation, or even rationalization, of his flip-flop. Reward was not long in coming: on 13 July he accepted the commissionership of crown lands, a plum worth £1,000 per annum. The patriarch of the Baldwin–Sullivan family was scathing. "R.S.," W. W. Baldwin wrote to his son Robert, "is in the midst of enemies but he has thrown himself into their arms, & when they shake him over the precepice, he will not have a friend to console him." A pariah among acquaintances and an object of rebuke by the whig press, Sullivan was isolated, almost. Robert Baldwin reminded his irate father that "family love" was "heavens best gift ... let us not let political differences interfere with the cultivation of it – but on the contrary where such unhappily exist always forget the politician in the relation." Despite Baldwin's support for Sullivan, their legal partnership appears to have ended some time between 1836 and 1838.

Lord Durham [Lambton*] later derided Head's appointments as ciphers. Sullivan proved an administration man, but he was no one's tool. And what cannot be questioned is his ability. Head defended his choice, describing Sullivan as well-educated, a leading lawyer, and "a man of very superior talents ... and of irreproachable character." He quickly became the dominant figure in an increasingly active council. In a memorandum on the councillors prepared by Head, probably for his successor, Sir George ARTHUR, Sullivan was lauded as possessing "great legal talent [and] sound judgement particularly on financial questions," whereas Allan, although honest and honourable, had "not much talent or education" and Elmsley was a "wrong headed man but brave." Arthur relied heavily on forceful men with incisive analytical minds, such as Chief Justice John Beverley Robinson, John MACAULAY, and Sullivan. In June 1838 Sullivan assumed the additional office of surveyor general. During Robinson's long absence in England from 1838 to 1840, Arthur tended to ignore his law officers and other councillors in preference to Sullivan, who "takes a more enlarged view of the subjects, or, at all events, his sentiments fall more in with my motives of dealing with political questions in the present day; and, therefore, I have generally conferred with him in his office as presiding member of the Executive Council." In February 1839 Sullivan was appointed to the Legislative Council. So crucial was he to the business of council and to the lieutenant governor as a policy adviser, that Arthur appointed Kenneth Cameron to serve as surveyor general pro tem, between October 1840 and February 1841, so that more important business need not be neglected by Sullivan.

In 1838, in the aftermath of the rebellion, Arthur had relied on him increasingly. That year Sullivan prepared, for instance, a mammoth report on the state of the province. The degree to which his analysis fell in line with that of his old enemies can be measured by Robinson's enthusiastic approval. The report was "natural & forcible" and its tone "liberally conservative." Sullivan took for granted that without natural or cultural barriers separating Upper Canada from the United States, the colony "must be materially affected by the state of Politics and of the popular mind in the neighbouring republic." He uttered, albeit eloquently, the usual bromides that depicted American political culture in terms of "tyranny of a majority" and mob rule. He repeated, in short, current tory denunciations of responsible government and an elective legislative council as mere half-way houses to full-blown democratic institutions and chaos. In a manner worthy of Robinson at his best, he defended the Constitutional Act of 1791, the integrity of office holders, and the absolute need, if not the right, of an executive claim to revenues independent of control by the assembly.

Sullivan's foray, in the same report, into policies on immigration, finance, and land matters marked his point of departure from tory nostrums. To his mind, tranquillity was a corollary of prosperity, which could only be achieved through large-scale immigration, a rise in the value of land, and productive public works. These measures would make people much happier "than any abstract political measures" could, and would have the effect of restoring public confidence and the colony's trade. An enormous public debt sucked up available revenues and was responsible for leaving the province a largely inaccessible wilderness. The lack of superintendence of crown land produced a decline in revenue and immigration. Upper Canada, Sullivan maintained, must gain control of its major source of revenue, customs duties raised at Montreal

Sullivan

and Quebec. To this end he gave full voice to a favourite tory war cry – annex Montreal, Trois-Rivières, and the Eastern Townships to Upper Canada, thus leaving the French Canadians to enjoy their own "bad laws, bad roads bad sleighs, bad food . . . in peace and quietness injuring no others and not being interfered with themselves." The resurrection of union as a panacea for the Upper Canadian crisis would therefore be dangerous, since it would bring together and make supreme the democratic elements in Upper and Lower Canada. Over a year later, in 1839, Sullivan reiterated his hostility to union and his attachment to British institutions in a memorandum sent under Arthur's name to the Colonial Office. He was at pains to distinguish two elements among the "conservatives": those "who are so from principle, or attachment from sentiment to British institutions," and the "Commercial party" which supported "prosperity, public credit and public improvements" but was conservative out of self-interest and only in prosperous times.

Sullivan's lucid analysis of the province's problems was matched by his equally deft set of practical prescriptions. He favoured the centralization of power, having urged Arthur in April 1838 to retain the power of patronage over the militia and not relinquish it to local colonels. That same year he recommended suspending work on the St Lawrence canals, lest the work become a "perpetual monument of Legislative folly & extravagance," and he cautioned Arthur to rein in the commissioners responsible for the work. Although he supported the legitimacy of the constitutional privileges of the Church of England, the clergy reserves issue had to be settled in the interests of internal harmony. To this end he favoured dividing the reserves among the Anglicans, Presbyterians, and Wesleyan Methodists, with the proceeds from the reserves used "to secure religious instruction according to the protestant faith."

In 1839 Arthur directed the Executive Council to prepare a report on how best to adapt land policy to the anticipated increase in immigration. The council split. Minority reports were submitted in 1840 by Sullivan and Augustus Warren Baldwin on one side, and William Allan and Richard Alexander Tucker* on the other. In fact, the reports were the efforts of Sullivan and Allan. Sullivan's represents an eloquent and closely reasoned defence of an agrarian society, composed largely of independent farmers, as the basis for social and political stability and economic prosperity. Allan argued that the province's economic backwardness could only be overcome by capitalist undertakings. Possessed of a shrewd, intuitive grasp of Upper Canada's situation and its potential, Allan urged seizing the opportunity to establish "what we have been taught to consider a great desideratum, viz, a class of labourers, separate and distinct from Land

owners." Although Governor Charles Edward Poulett Thomson* (later Lord Sydenham) noted agreement with Allan's position "as applied to a country under ordinary circumstances," he saw the province's present situation as different and he dismissed Allan's opinion as biased and his arguments as "trashy in the extreme."

Thomson, the architect of union, soon realized how useful Sullivan could be. He abandoned his previous hostility to union, a position which, as Attorney General Hagerman found out, Thomson would not tolerate. Sullivan was prominent in shepherding the measure through the Legislative Council, and appeared a solid "Governor's man" at its inception. He was one of the four executive councillors, along with William Henry Draper*, Charles Richard Ogden*, and Charles Dewey Day*, in whom Robert Baldwin expressed want of confidence in February 1841. Sullivan retained the commissionership of crown lands until June of that year, in which month he was appointed to the new Legislative Council.

John Charles Dent*'s description of Sullivan, as a brilliant orator who charmed with his "Irish provincial accent" but who lacked conviction and steadiness of purpose, is accurate. He seems to have dozed through his duties as president of the Executive Council in 1841–42. He performed another wonderful turnaround in September 1842. When the new governor, Sir Charles Bagot*, was struggling to avoid a reform-dominated ministry, Sullivan supported him in the Legislative Council, asking, "Are we to carry on the government fairly and upon liberal principles or *by dint of miserable majorities*?" Yet he happily remained as president of council when the miserable majority prevailed, holding that position until November 1843.

Indeed, he rapidly became a partisan of the new order, presumably an indication of his love of intrigue, his respect for power, and his weakness for flamboyant oratory. In October 1842 he was involved in the obdurate politics of the newly formed ministry of Baldwin and Louis-Hippolyte La Fontaine*, chairing the committee of the Executive Council which recommended withdrawing government advertising from newspapers "found to join in active opposition to the Government." Sir Charles Theophilus Metcalfe*, Bagot's successor in March 1843, was relatively complimentary to Sullivan as a minister, given that Metcalfe thought most of the executive councillors were fanatics, villains, or incompetents. According to his biographer, John William Kaye, the governor saw Sullivan as talented but dismissed him as inconsistent and lacking the "weight of personal character." If a lightweight, Sullivan was prominent enough to be a target of the Orange order. After passage of the Party Processions and Secret Societies bills, there was a huge, furious Orange demonstration in Toronto on 8 Nov. 1843. Sullivan's name was joined with those of the "traitors Baldwin and [Francis Hincks*]" on the mob's banners.

During the ten-month crisis which followed the resignation of the Baldwin–La Fontaine ministry in November, Sullivan was in his element. His talents as an orator and pamphleteer gave him a prominent role in the reform campaign to justify the actions of the late ministry and win the election of 1844. His excessive zeal, however, at times injured the reform cause. He took part in the early meetings of the party's new provincial organization, the Reform Association of Canada. At its first public meeting, in Toronto on 25 March 1844, Sullivan – ironically, given his "miserable majorities" speech – moved the resolution insisting that provincial ministries required the support of parliamentary majorities. He campaigned in 4th York with Baldwin and advised him on tactics. In September Baldwin reported consulting with Sullivan, James Edward Small*, and John Henry DUNN about whether to resign his militia commission and relinquish his appointment as queen's counsel, in protest against Metcalfe's autocracy. On their advice Baldwin retained his militia commission.

Sullivan's most important role continued to be that of public controversialist. In May 1844 Egerton Ryerson* had begun a series of newspaper articles which supported the governor, and later published them as a pamphlet. He claimed to have been sympathetic to the councillors until their "real motives" were revealed by Sullivan and Francis Hincks, when he came to see Metcalfe as "a misrepresented and injured man." Under the transparent *nom de plume* of Legion, Sullivan answered in 13 letters in the *Examiner* and the *Globe*. The letters, which also appeared as a pamphlet, contained no new insights but were an effective summary of the Baldwinite arguments for responsible government and provided a puncturing lampoon of Ryerson's pomposity. They show, at places, Sullivan's tendency to get carried away with his rhetoric. Later in the year the tories made good use of his indiscretion at an election meeting in Sharon, where, in ridiculing the governor as "Charles the Simple," he seriously overstepped even the limits of that day. His excesses, however, were only one small factor in the reform defeat in the election of 1844. Sullivan ascribed it in large measure to the influence of the Orange order. "Ireland in its worst time," he told Baldwin in January 1845, "was not more completely under the feet of an orange ascendancy than is Canada at present."

With the party in opposition, Sullivan was not very active in the Legislative Council. He continued to be a close adviser to Baldwin on political matters, presumably more because of Baldwin's stout family loyalty than because of his chequered record as a political tactician. He had a good deal to say about the worst crisis facing the party between 1845 and 1847: the tories' wooing of French Canadians disenchanted with the reformers after the 1844 defeat. William Henry Draper came close to forging an alliance with René-Édouard Caron* and others in 1845–46. To Sullivan, writing to Baldwin in August 1846, Caron was "a false sneaking knave"; Hincks, who toadied to the French to maintain support, was nearly as bad. This outburst suggested that Sullivan had a conveniently short memory. La Fontaine did not. During the Draper–Caron flirtation, La Fontaine reminded Baldwin that Sullivan had made a similar attempt, in July 1842, to split the French from the reform party. He had approached both La Fontaine and Caron to enter the Bagot–Draper ministry and leave Baldwin behind.

There were issues on which the cousins differed. During the winter of 1844–45 Sullivan, who joined William Hume Blake* in a campaign to reform the Upper Canadian judicial system, expressed his deep disappointment that Baldwin would not give leadership on that effort in the assembly. More significant was their disagreement over tariff policy. After Britain's adoption of free trade, Baldwin urged Canada, in a speech in November 1846, to follow that lead. Sullivan, however, was an early advocate of a different approach. Speaking to the Hamilton Mechanics' Institute on 17 Nov. 1847, he championed the emerging capitalist interests of Canada, in sharp contrast to his position in 1840. Rapid industrial development was the solution to Canada's economic problems, and he suggested the adoption of protective duties as a means to foster the needed industry. Published the following year, Sullivan's Hamilton appeal was frequently cited when the protectionist movement began to gain strength after 1849.

Despite his political success in the 1840s Sullivan's heavy drinking and fecklessness in business matters nearly destroyed his career. In 1843 he lamented his difficulty in collecting accounts, suggesting that his hand was all too often limp. In this he stood in marked contrast to his cousin. Baldwin was especially fierce in pursuing payment from the wealthy, who, he believed, had a moral duty to meet their debts. In 1844, however, things looked up. Oliver Mowat*, then a gossipy young lawyer, reported that Sullivan had joined the "total abstinence society." It was a necessary step, in Mowat's view, for no one in Toronto's legal community had confidence in the drunken Sullivan. The reformation did not last. In the spring of 1848 Baldwin's property manager, Lawrence Heyden, told Baldwin that Sullivan was in serious difficulty: "It is very generally reported here that he is broken out again."

Dry or wet, Sullivan remained an intimate adviser to the party chief. His views were sought on delicate matters, such as the manœuvres in 1847 to find a seat for the recent convert from high toryism, Henry John

Sutherland

Boulton, who remained anathema to many local reformers. When the party swept the election of January 1848, Baldwin suggested to La Fontaine 24 names, including Sullivan's, as possibilities for the 11 cabinet positions. According to Baldwin, Sullivan preferred a judgeship, but his experience would be useful in cabinet. Presumably La Fontaine was not as generous about the missteps of Baldwin's errant cousin, for Sullivan's name did not appear on the cabinet list presented to Governor Lord Elgin [Bruce*] on 7 March 1848. La Fontaine and Baldwin told him they needed the seat to conciliate a faction in the party. On Elgin's urging, however, they reconsidered and the next day Sullivan was included as provincial secretary, becoming the most senior of the ministers in terms of service. The governor was delighted for he considered Sullivan both able and "more British" than any other Canadian politician. In July he described Sullivan to Colonial Secretary Lord Grey as the member of council "who has the strongest feeling in favor of settling the lands of the Province and has most influence with his colleagues on questions of this nature." Sullivan, for example, favoured free land grants and the construction of colonization roads – programs for these would be initiated in the 1850s.

Sullivan nevertheless played no major role in the "Great Ministry" and on 15 Sept. 1848, after resigning from council, he received his desired reward, a puisne justiceship on the Court of Queen's Bench. He did not, however, entirely give up a political interest. While in cabinet, in April 1848, he had dismissed the medical superintendent of the Provincial Lunatic Asylum, Walter TELFER, and replaced him with the apparently more politically sound George Hamilton Park. Park proceeded to feud with the staff and to fire employees without authorization. Sullivan followed the case closely and gave his assessment of it to Baldwin in January 1849; Park was dismissed that month and the radical newspaper, the *Examiner*, took his side against the "tyrannous" government. Sullivan guessed correctly that Park's brother-in-law, John Rolph, was behind the crisis and warned Baldwin that the case was being used by such dissident reformers to embarrass the ministry.

Sullivan held his seat on the Legislative Council until May 1851. In January 1850 he had moved from Queen's Bench to the newly formed Court of Common Pleas, where he sat until his death three years later. A superb orator and incisive analyst when sober, Sullivan nevertheless remained known as a flawed figure, devoid, in the opinion of Dent and others, of "genuine earnestness of purpose" and "strong political convictions."

VICTOR LORING RUSSELL, ROBERT LOCHIEL FRASER, and MICHAEL S. CROSS

Robert Baldwin Sullivan is the author of three pamphlets: *Address on emigration and colonization, delivered in the Mechanics' Institute Hall* (Toronto, 1847); *Lecture, delivered before the Mechanics' Institute, of Hamilton, on Wednesday evening, November 17, 1847, on the connection between the agriculture and manufactures of Canada* (Hamilton, [Ont.], 1848); and, under the pseudonym Legion, *Letters on responsible government* (Toronto, 1844).

AO, MS 78, John Macaulay to Helen Macaulay, 29 Nov. 1843; MU 2106, 1833, no.8; RG 22, ser.155, will of R. B. Sullivan. BNQ, Dép. des MSS, MSS-101, Coll. La Fontaine (copies in PAC, MG 24, B14). MTL, Robert Baldwin papers; W. W. Baldwin papers, B105, Robert Baldwin to W. W. Baldwin, 24 Sept. 1836; B136, Committee for the protection of the provincial press, 8 Nov. 1828; unbound misc., R. B. Sullivan to W. W. Baldwin, n.d.; Toronto papers. PAC, MG 24, B11, 9–10 (access restricted); B24, Robert Baldwin to G. H. Park, 31 March 1847; RG 1, E1, 45: 465–66; 52; 365. *Arthur papers* (Sanderson). Can., Prov. of, Legislative Assembly, *App. to the journals*, 1849, app.M, app.GGG. *Elgin–Grey papers* (Doughty). J. W. Kaye, *The life and correspondence of Charles, Lord Metcalfe* (new and rev. ed., 2v., London, 1858), 2: 339. Oliver Mowat, "'Neither radical nor tory nor whig': letters by Oliver Mowat to John Mowat, 1843–1846," ed. Peter Neary, *OH*, 71 (1979): 84–131. *Examiner* (Toronto), 27 March 1844. *Globe*, 18 June–16 July 1844. *Pilot* (Montreal), 14 June 1844. N. F. Davin, *The Irishman in Canada* (London and Toronto, 1877), 410. J. C. Dent, *The last forty years: Canada since the union of 1841* (2v., Toronto, [1881]). J. C. Hamilton, *Osgoode Hall, reminiscences of the bench and bar* (Toronto, 1904), 179. Edward Porritt, *Sixty years of protection in Canada, 1846–1907, where industry leans on the politician* (London, 1908). V. L. Russell, *Mayors of Toronto* (1v. to date, Erin, Ont., 1982–   ). C. B. Sissons, *Egerton Ryerson: his life and letters* (2v., Toronto, 1937–47).

SUTHERLAND, MURDOCH, Presbyterian minister and school administrator; b. c. 1826 in the parish of Kildonan, Scotland; m. 1853 Isabella Campbell, and they had one son and two daughters; d. 21 April 1858 in Rothesay, Scotland.

Murdoch Sutherland, the son of a shepherd in the Strath of Kildonan, entered the University of Edinburgh in 1845. His studies were soon subsidized by the Free Church of Scotland's Colonial Committee, a group responsible for the foreign missions of the new Presbyterian body. Sutherland's evangelical disposition and his fluency in Gaelic made him a valuable candidate for mission work in Nova Scotia, where dissatisfaction with the established Church of Scotland over its stance on relations between church and state had decimated ministerial ranks in 1844. The committee sent Sutherland to Halifax as a probationer in the summer of 1849, where he attended the fledgling Free Church College.

Shortly after his arrival, Sutherland assumed the superintendence of a growing Sabbath-school and regularly conducted spiritual visitations in the homes of his students' parents, work that was a carry-over from his days in Edinburgh. Attempts by Sutherland and other students at the college to form a visiting agency to bring religious tracts to the destitute of Halifax met with the decided opposition of Professor Andrew King, but ample opportunity for missionary work was provided at the preaching stations of Pictou, Rogers Hill, and Caribou River. These brief terms of labour during the summers of 1849 and 1850 developed a lasting bond between Sutherland and the people he served. Forced by ill health to return to Edinburgh, he completed his theological studies at New College between 1850 and 1853. Repeated calls from the Gaelic-speaking congregation at Pictou, however, induced the Colonial Committee to expedite Sutherland's ordination on 13 June 1853. He returned to Pictou in July and was inducted into Knox Church on 28 October.

Sutherland's efforts to create a secure foundation in the area for the Synod of the Free Church of Nova Scotia were indicative of the efforts of many in the growing denomination. His plain but earnest preaching style, combined with a rigorous scheme of visitations by himself and his elders, contributed to the steady increase in the number of adherents at the three preaching stations under his supervision. Although his manner was forthright and at times combative, it seemed to appeal to the desire of many Highland settlers for a minister with a controversial style. By 1857 the congregations at Pictou, Rogers Hill, and Caribou River were the fastest growing in the synod in spite of Sutherland's frequent absences. A chronic shortage of ministers made his early career resemble that of an itinerant missionary, and in 1854 he was instrumental in establishing many of the Free Church sessions on Prince Edward Island. Sutherland also played a major role in stabilizing the precarious financial position of the synod, and as a result of his constant exhortations Pictou's contributions to church schemes, such as the College Endowment Fund of the Free Church College, rose to major proportions.

Sutherland shared the spiritual and social concerns that dominated Presbyterian thought in the mid 19th century. He was an outspoken critic of Roman Catholicism, which caused him to chafe at Pictou's tendency towards a more expedient attitude of toleration. The defamation of the sabbath was an even greater source of worry, and Sutherland was chosen to investigate the problem by the synod and the recently formed Sabbath Alliance. His reports in 1856 and 1857 attacked a host of activities, ranging from the concerts of military bands to the movement of mail and commercial goods, but special attention was given to the transgressions of railway labourers. As a result of his efforts, missionaries from the synod, beginning with Sutherland himself in 1856, were assigned to the lines of the Nova Scotia Railway then

under construction in an attempt to mould a more acceptable life-style. His involvement in such problems as sabbath observance brought him into constant contact with other Presbyterian bodies, and like many of his peers Sutherland became an active participant in the movement for union between his own Free Church synod and that of the Presbyterian Church in Nova Scotia, which was finally accomplished in 1860.

By the summer of 1857 these diverse activities had taken their toll on Sutherland's frail constitution. Despite a gradual reduction in his duties in 1856 and a prolonged leave of absence from Pictou in the fall of the next year, his health failed to improve. Sutherland resigned from his duties on 11 Nov. 1857 and returned to Scotland in the hope of finding a charge in a more moderate climate, but he eventually succumbed to tuberculosis on 21 April 1858. He had been esteemed for his diligence, enthusiasm, and evangelical priorities, and it was generally agreed that these very qualities robbed the young church of a valuable cleric before his greatest contributions could be made.

MICHAEL B. MOIR

Edinburgh Univ., New College Library, New College enrolment book, 1843–95. First Presbyterian Church (Pictou, N.S.), "Record of the Kirk session of the United Congregation of Pictou, Roger's Hill and Carribo River in connection with the Free Church of Nova Scotia" (mfm. in PANS, Churches, Pictou: Pictou United Church). NLS, Dept. of MSS, Deposit no.298/260–62 (Free Church of Scotland, Colonial Committee, minutes, 1844–58) (mfm. at UCA). PANS, MG 20, 153. Univ. of Guelph Library, Archival Coll. (Guelph, Ont.), Urquhart–Campbell–Sutherland papers. Free Church of N.S., *Ecclesiastical and Missionary Record* (Halifax), 3 (1854–55)–6 (1858); *Minutes of the Synod* (Halifax), 1855–57. Free Church of Scotland, *Home and Foreign Missionary Record* (Edinburgh), 3 (1847–48)–4 (1849–50); *Home and Foreign Record* (Edinburgh), 1 (1850–51)–6 (1855–56); new ser., 1 (1856–57)–3 (1858–59). *Presbyterian Witness, and Evangelical Advocate* (Halifax), 1 (1848)–3 (1850); 6 (1853)–11 (1858). John Murray, *The Scotsburn congregation, Pictou County, Nova Scotia: its history, professional men, etc.* (Truro, N.S., 1925). E. Ross, "The history of Presbyterianism in the county of Pictou, from 1817 to the union of 1875," *Proceedings at the centennial celebration of James Church Congregation, New Glasgow, September 17th, 1886 . . .* (New Glasgow, N.S., 1886), 30–38.

SUTHERLAND, THOMAS JEFFERSON, Patriot filibuster and author; b. *c.* 1801 in Plymouth, N.Y.; m. Laura ——; d. 7 Sept. 1852 at Iowa and Sac Mission (near present-day Highland, Kans).

Thomas Jefferson Sutherland, who had been trained as a printer, enlisted in the United States Marines at Philadelphia on 5 Dec. 1821. Discharged with the rank of sergeant on 15 Feb. 1830, he returned to the newspaper trade. Over the next two years he

Sutherland

published or edited, in various towns in western New York, several short-lived newspapers, most of which espoused the anti-masonic movement then sweeping that region. His subsequent career is obscure: in 1832, while still engaged in journalism, he was "reading law" and, according to the *New-York Daily Tribune*, later emerged as "a lawyer of low standing" in Erie County, N.Y.

In late 1837, after news of the rebellion in Lower Canada had reached Buffalo, N.Y., sympathizers with the Canadian cause organized meetings to enlist volunteers for an "Independent Canadian Service." Sutherland spoke at one such meeting on 5 December, asking those assembled, "Shall we withhold our sympathies and as individuals our assistance?" Immediately afterwards he left for Toronto, probably with the letter which, according to James Latimer, a journeyman printer employed by William Lyon Mackenzie*, was read by Mackenzie on 6 December to the rebels assembled at Montgomery's Tavern. Written by the secretary of the Buffalo meeting of the 5th, this letter stated that 200 men were coming to their assistance. Although Sutherland later denied having had "any manner of intercourse" with Mackenzie before the latter reached Buffalo, he claimed to have left Toronto commissioned to raise a force to assist the rebellion and after returning to Buffalo he started to enlist volunteers. It was probably about this time that he began claiming that he had participated in South American wars of liberation under Simón Bolívar and had run a military school.

Sutherland next called on Rensselaer Van Rensselaer, who had already heard of the defeat of the rebels at Montgomery's Tavern. Sutherland presented him with a letter of introduction from John W. Taylor, a prominent New York politician, and informed him of what he and other supporters in Buffalo of the Canadian cause had already accomplished. Sutherland urged him to take over the command of the Patriot army since, as a son of a hero in the War of 1812, he could give their undertaking "the proper tone." On 12 December Sutherland, John Rolph*, and Mackenzie, who had arrived in Buffalo the previous day, went together and received Van Rensselaer's consent to take command of the Patriot force once it was assembled on Canadian soil. Sutherland claimed that it was he and "some others," rather than Mackenzie, who decided to take the Patriot force to Navy Island, on Canadian soil, where Van Rensselaer could take command. Before the force moved off on the 15th, Sutherland had annoyed his supporters in Buffalo, who were relieved to hear of the Navy Island plan, by his "lawless course," open recruiting, and theft of arms from city hall. Sutherland, however, did not accompany Van Rensselaer and Mackenzie to the island but arrived later.

Van Rensselaer subsequently sent Sutherland to Detroit to aid the Patriots along the western border and to organize a diversion there. On New Year's Day 1838, while en route, he spoke in Cleveland, Ohio, before a large "Canada meeting," which adopted resolutions of sympathy with the "interest of liberty in every country" and of alarm over the Upper Canadian government's use of "blood-thirsty savages" against "our unoffending brethren adjacent to the Canadian frontier." On the same day Sutherland issued a proclamation, which he signed as brigadier-general of the Patriot army and which offered volunteers 300 acres of land and $100 in silver before 1 May. As a result 100 men enlisted and left for Detroit under his command.

The officers of the Patriot Army of the North West, under the command of General Henry S. Handy, were not disposed to recognize the authority Sutherland had received from Van Rensselaer. In the end it was agreed that Sutherland should command an expedition to occupy Bois Blanc Island in the Detroit River and to capture Fort Malden, at Amherstburg, Upper Canada. From Bois Blanc, on 9–10 January, he issued proclamations asking the citizens of Upper Canada to join the Patriot forces and free the land "from Tyranny" and promising them "all the blessings of freedom." When the Patriots' schooner, commanded by Edward Alexander THELLER, ran aground off Amherstburg on the 9th and was captured by Canadian militiamen, Sutherland did not attempt a rescue but, despite the entreaties of his men, ordered them to retreat to American territory. As a result they voted to have Handy replace him as commander. He was accused of cowardice by Theller for his conduct on Bois Blanc Island. On the other hand, E. D. Bradley, a Patriot colonel, held both Sutherland and Theller responsible for the fiasco.

On 13 January Sutherland was arrested at Detroit for violating American neutrality laws but was found not guilty. He appeared before the court, according to historian Robert B. Ross, as a man "of large stature, weighing about 220 pounds, with dark hair and complexion, and was a very fine specimen of the genus homo. He was dressed in a blue blanket coat, under which he wore a Kentucky hunting shirt with two tawdry epaulettes on his shoulders." An articulate spokesman for the Patriot cause, he was nevertheless a vain and indecisive figure who, like many Patriot leaders, inspired only mistrust and jealousy.

After publicly resigning his commission in the Patriot army about 5 February, Sutherland left Detroit for Ohio but was captured on 4 March on the ice at the mouth of the Detroit River by Lieutenant-Colonel John Prince*. Taken to Toronto, Sutherland was interviewed by Lieutenant Governor Sir Francis Bond Head*, after which, convinced that he would be executed, he attempted suicide by slitting veins in his arms and feet. He was tried for treason at a court martial under Samuel Peters JARVIS and sentenced in April to be transported to one of the Australian colonies for life. It was questionable, however, whether, as law required, he had been taken within Canadian territory and in arms and whether his trial had been properly conducted (parts of his indictment were not proven and the court was not composed correctly). In Toronto it was believed that after his capture he had made some disclosures which revealed that the plans of the Upper Canadian rebels had rested wholly on American aid. Revelations were made, but not by Sutherland. His aide, a son of Chief Justice Ambrose Spencer of New York, had been captured with him and it was he who gave Lieutenant Governor Head information on the understanding that he would be pardoned.

While imprisoned at Quebec awaiting transportation, Sutherland appealed to Lord Durham [Lambton*] for pardons for himself and nine others, including Theller and William Wallin Dodge, on the ground that they were American citizens who had been misled. Sutherland's wife sent Durham a copy of his pamphlet, *The trial of General Th. J. Sutherland*, which he had managed to get published in Buffalo and which demonstrated his knowledge of international law. In August 1838 the imperial government, because of the irregularities in his trial, directed that he be set free upon giving security that he would not re-enter British territory. He was unable to find sureties. Finally he was sent to Cornwall, Upper Canada, in May 1839 and released.

Returning to New York State, Sutherland resumed his Patriot associations and that fall was reportedly involved at Detroit and at Lewiston, N.Y., with such filibusters as Donald M'Leod* and Benjamin LETT. Patriot activity subsequently declined on both sides of the border but, perhaps to keep interest in the cause alive, Sutherland produced a number of pamphlets relating to the rebellion. His *Canvass of the proceedings on the trial of William Lyon Mackenzie* (1840) minimizes Mackenzie's importance at Navy Island. *Loose leaves, from the port folio of a late Patriot prisoner in Canada* (1839–40) is a particularly flimsy account in which he devotes a good deal of space to his poetry and self-portrayal as a shrewd lawyer and a dignified prisoner respected by his jailers. In contrast, Theller later claimed that Sutherland's whining and whimpering while in prison, his "bad conduct and attempts to quarrel with every one in the room, his lying, his vanity, and assumption of importance, as well as his playing the spy upon us . . . made the men all despise him." Between 1840 and 1845 Sutherland, in other pamphlets, in several letters to editors, and at public meetings in western New York, argued strenuously for the release of the Patriots imprisoned in Van Diemen's Land (Tasmania, Australia) for their part in

the rebellion. As well, in 1841, he launched a newspaper in Buffalo in order to bring that cause before a larger audience.

In 1846, evidently with Whig support, he clashed publicly in New York City with Colonel Jonathan Drake Stevenson over the formation of a regiment to fight in California against Mexico. Sutherland's whereabouts for the next five years are unknown. In 1851 he appeared in the river towns of the American midwest, "a mysterious looking individual, who travelled with a carpet-sack slung across his shoulders," *Putnam's Monthly Magazine* later recorded, "and who paid his way wherever he went by 'phrenological' lectures and examinations." During these tours and in newspaper articles, he zealously boosted the exploration and settlement of the Nebraska territory. Although he could criticize the Mormons for their treatment of the Indians there, he "held that the Indians had no right to keep such fine lands," as *Putnam's* also noted, and he advocated reform of the laws on land grants and sales. An avid admirer of such revolutionary heroes as Lord Byron and Hungarian nationalist Lajos Kossuth, Sutherland proposed to establish in Nebraska a "Military agricultural school" to train officers for "a republican army in a revolutionary struggle in Europe."

On 7 Sept. 1852, while moving farther west to settle, he died of typhus fever at Iowa and Sac Mission. He was survived by a young girl, Viola, whom he had adopted during a lecture tour on the Mississippi River. "In his trunk," recalled Samuel M. Irvin, the Presbyterian minister in charge of the mission, "was found a large quantity of manuscript, made up of biography, history and poetry, much of it seemingly prepared for the press; but nothing was found to throw any light on his ancestry or personal history." Indeed, by the time of his death, Sutherland had achieved much success in shrouding or reshaping his career back as far as his days in the Patriot army. Thus, in his obituary in the *Sentinel* of Savannah, Mo., he was portrayed as a "somewhat noted" though eccentric and controversial figure, "a fine schollar, lawyer and politician," and "one of the leading spirits in the Canadian rebellion."

LILLIAN F. GATES

Thomas Jefferson Sutherland is the author of the following pamphlets: *The trial of General Th. J. Sutherland, late of the Patriot army, before a court martial convened at Toronto on the 13th day of March, A.D. 1838, by order of Sir Francis Bond Head, lieutenant governor of said province, K.C.B. &c. &c. &c., on a charge of having, as a citizen of the United States, levied war in the province of Upper Canada against Her Majesty the Queen of Great Britain, &c.; with his defence and other documents* (Buffalo, N.Y., 1838); *A canvass of the proceedings on the trial of William Lyon Mackenzie, for an alleged violation of the neutrality laws of*

Switzer

the United States; with a report of the testimony – the charge of the presiding judge to the jury – the arguments of the United States attorney – and a petition to the president for his release (New York, 1840); Loose leaves, from the port folio of a late Patriot prisoner in Canada (New York, 1840); Three political letters, addressed to Dr. Wolfred Nelson, late of Lower Canada, now of Plattsburgh, N.Y. (New York, 1840); A letter to Her Majesty the British Queen, with letters to Lord Durham, Lord Glenelg and Sir George Arthur: to which is added an appendix embracing a report of the testimony taken on the trial of the writer by a court martial, at Toronto in Upper Canada (Albany, N.Y., 1841); and A letter to Lord Brougham, in behalf of the captive Patriots; to which is annexed a list of their names (New York, 1841).

Kansas State Hist. Soc., MS Dept. (Topeka), S. M. Irvin coll., S. M. Irvin, "Reminiscences of T. J. Sutherland." National Arch. (Washington), RG 127, Enlisted men, Marine Corps. N.Y. Hist. Soc. (New York), J. W. Taylor papers, Sutherland to Taylor, 15 Feb., 19 April 1832. PAC, MG 24, A40, Foster to Colborne, 14, 20 March 1838; Arthur to Colborne, 5 April 1838; RG 1, E1, 57: 14; RG 5, A1: 103319–33, 105215–17, 106077–78, 106784–85, 108168–69, 108339–40, 108899–950, 109333–40, 109816–17, 111302–4, 111724–29, 112382–86, 112686–91, 113801–32, 115999–6006, 121300–6. Arthur papers (Sanderson). J. C. Dent, The story of the Upper Canadian rebellion; largely derived from original sources and documents (2v., Toronto, 1885), 2: 231. "Nebraska: a glimpse of it – a peep into its unwritten history – together with a few facts for the future historian," Putnam's Monthly Magazine (New York), 3 (January–June 1854): 457–60. E. A. Theller, Canada in 1837–38 . . . (2v., Philadelphia and New York, 1841). Buffalo Commercial Advertiser, 6 Dec. 1837. Chronicle & Gazette, 17 March 1838. Daily Nonpareil (Cincinnati, Ohio), 5 March 1852. Frontier Guardian (Kanesville [Council Bluffs], Iowa), 27 Jan. 1851. Mackenzie's Gazette (New York), 10 Nov. 1838. New-York Daily Tribune, 11, 19 Nov. 1844; 1 Jan. 1845; 7 Oct. 1852. Rochester Daily Advertiser (Rochester, N.Y.), 3 Feb. 1842. Sentinel (Savannah, Mo.), 25 Sept. 1852. Western Herald, and Farmers' Magazine (Sandwich [Windsor, Ont.]), 1, 13 Jan., 18 March, 12 June 1838.

"Calendar of state papers," PAC Report, 1936: 591. "The Durham papers," PAC Report, 1923: 259, 523. "State papers – U.C.," PAC Report, 1943: 178; 1944: 9, 11, 21, 26–27. A. B. Corey, The crisis of 1830–1842 in Canadian-American relations (New Haven, Conn., and Toronto, 1941). L. F. [Cowdell] Gates, William Lyon Mackenzie: the post-rebellion years in the United States and Canada (Ithaca, N.Y., 1978). Guillet, Lives and times of Patriots. O. A. Kinchen, The rise and fall of the Patriot Hunters (New York, 1956). Lindsey, Life and times of Mackenzie, 2: 176. C. V. [Van Rensselaer] Bonney, A legacy of historical gleanings (2v., 2nd ed., Albany, 1875), 1: 65–66, 74–81. J. C. Malin, "Thomas Jefferson Sutherland, Nebraska boomer, 1851–1852," Nebr. Hist. (Lincoln), 34 (1953): 181–214. W. R. Riddell, "A Patriot general," Canadian Magazine, 44 (November 1914–April 1915): 32–36. R. B. Ross, "The Patriot war," Mich. Pioneer Coll. (Lansing), 21 (1892): 517, 535, 540–41, 552, 580–82. Carl Wittke, "Ohioans and the Canadian-American crisis of 1837–38," Ohio Archaeological and Hist. Quarterly (Columbus), 58 (1949): 26–37.

SWITZER, MARTIN, farmer, blacksmith, and rebel; b. 9 Jan. 1778 on Newpark Farm, parish of Kilcooly, County Tipperary (Republic of Ireland), sixth child of John Switzer and his second wife, Anne Ryan; m. 22 Feb. 1803 Mary Maurice, and they had three daughters and four sons; d. 26 Feb. 1852 in St Charles, Ill.

Martin Switzer and his family sailed from Dublin for Boston on the *Atlantic* in July 1804; the passenger list described him as a 28-year-old labourer, five feet ten inches tall, and of fair complexion. The family first settled in Maine but in 1808 moved to New Jersey where Martin plied his trade as a blacksmith. Anti-British sentiment after the War of 1812 caused the family to decide to join a group of Irish immigrants, similarly disenchanted with the republic, in moving to Upper Canada. On 21 April 1819 the leaders petitioned Lieutenant Governor Sir Peregrine MAITLAND for land, and on 18 September Switzer was granted the western half of lot 11, concession 5 west, near Streetsville (Mississauga). As well as clearing his land and farming, Switzer operated a blacksmith shop. He also became a leader in agitating for local improvements; in 1832, and again in 1835, his name headed petitions to the House of Assembly requesting money for roads. When he complained to officials in York (Toronto) that settlers received virtually no services in return for tax money raised, he was told that such talk was seditious.

In politics Switzer supported the reformers. During the 1834 election, William Lyon Mackenzie*, running in the riding of 2nd York, which included Streetsville, was a guest in the Switzer home at the time of polling. Two years later Mackenzie again contested the riding. On nomination day a line of Orangemen blocked the reform leader's passage to prevent him from filing his nomination papers. Switzer, the muscular smith, shouldered a way through with the diminutive radical leader following in his wake. Switzer's friendship with Mackenzie and this incident earned him the enmity of his tory neighbours.

In 1837, as the news of the insurrection in Toronto spread, Switzer, fearing for his safety, left home at four in the morning of 7 December heading towards the Niagara border and American soil. A meeting at the inn of Caleb Hopkins* in Nelson (Burlington) with Charles Morrison Durand, who expressed the opinion that Mackenzie had more than 4,000 men and had probably captured Toronto, caused Switzer to change his direction and purpose. He decided to ride to an American Quaker community in Yarmouth Township (where in previous weeks men had demonstrated militancy at political rallies by carrying weapons) to foment an armed uprising in support of the Toronto rebels. He arrived in the village of Sparta on Saturday evening, 9 December, and found the climate suitable for rebellion. In the next few days he addressed two public meetings, urging the young men to join Charles Duncombe*'s patriots at Scotland. Claiming that Toronto might well be in Mackenzie's hands and that there would be little or no fighting, he added that local men must march to show solidarity and to secure the rebellion. He warned that the tories might turn the Indians loose on defenceless settlers, and invited his audience to "lay his head on a block and cut it off" if they thought he had deceived them.

At noon on 12 December the "Spartan Rangers," 56 strong, marched off under Captain David Anderson and Lieutenant Joshua Gwillen Doan*. The company included several Quakers, in addition to Doan, who thus chose to disregard the peaceful principles of their faith. That night the rangers stayed in Richmond (Bayham) and two Yarmouth men rode in to warn that a company of loyalist horse from St Thomas might be in pursuit. By an early departure they also narrowly missed interception on the Talbot Road by militiamen who had marched all night from Port Burwell. The company reached Dr Duncombe's encampment on 13 December, some time after Switzer and shortly before the doctor learned of Mackenzie's defeat six days earlier and ordered a retreat. Most of the Spartans were captured crossing the Big Otter Creek near Richmond and 23 were charged with high treason. One youthful prisoner declared that had it not been for "Old Switzer . . . no man would have started from Yarmouth."

In the mean time, Switzer returned home under cover of night to find that vigilantes had partially destroyed his house and had driven off livestock. He fled again, this time for three weeks, and then remained hidden at home until April, when the hangings of Samuel Lount* and Peter Matthews* in Toronto frightened him into fleeing to the United States. There he bought a farm in Illinois.

In mid August, when Switzer surfaced to sell his farm at Streetsville, Colonel William Chisholm ordered him arrested for treason. Taken to the Toronto jail, Switzer sought the advice of George Ridout* on how best to extricate himself from the treason charge. Disregarding Ridout's advice to stand trial, on 5 September Switzer addressed to Sir George ARTHUR a plea for clemency with an accompanying narrative intended to suggest a political refugee who, on reaching Yarmouth, had been more of an observer than a fomenter of rebellion. The attorney general, Christopher Alexander Hagerman*, recommended banishment. The Executive Council, although convinced that the prisoner had been guilty of treasonable actions, felt pressured by the inclination of Lord Durham [Lambton*] towards clemency in political cases. Switzer was pardoned on condition that he provide surety of $4,000 to keep the peace for three years, and was released from jail on 28 September.

Mary Switzer had already left on the long trek to Illinois with three wagons and a herd of dairy cattle. This herd provided the basis for what was to become a prosperous dairy and cheese business. In exile Switzer wrote on 7 Dec. 1838 to his friend Mackenzie: "We begun the Sport in Canada. We made a bad beginning but I look for a good ending and that before long."

BRUCE PEEL

AO, MS 516, Martin Switzer to W. L. Mackenzie, 7 Dec. 1838, 4 Nov. 1839, 19 Feb. 1840. PAC, RG 1, E3, 84: 206–12; RG 5, A1: 98959–106686, 113188–93; B36, 1–2. Guillet, *Lives and times of Patriots*. Read, *Rising in western U.C.*

T

TALBOT (Talbott), RICHARD, colonizer, office holder, and militia officer; b. 1772 in County Tipperary (Republic of Ireland), presumably a son of Edward Talbot and Esther Allen; m. 1795 Lydia Baird in Killaloe Diocese, Ireland, and they had five daughters and three sons, including Edward Allen* and John*; d. 29 Jan. 1853 in London Township, Upper Canada.

Richard Talbot, a member of the minor gentry in Ireland, is believed to have descended from the Talbots of Mount Talbot in County Roscommon, a cadet branch of the Talbots of Malahide Castle [see Thomas TALBOT]. A captaincy in the British army was purchased for him in 1783 and, from 1787 until 1790, he was a captain in the 5th Foot. He then served on half pay until 1795, when, prompted by his marriage, he retired from the army and settled in Garrane in King's (Offaly) County.

Over the next several years Talbot, generally in partnership with his brother-in-law Freeman Baird, purchased or rented a few parcels of land in both King's and Tipperary counties. By 1800 he had moved from Garrane to Cloughjordan, in Tipperary. There he became an officer in the Cloughjordan Yeomanry and was commissioned commissariat officer in charge of payments to the widows and

Talbot

orphans of British soldiers who died during the Napoleonic Wars.

As with many others of his class, Talbot suffered serious losses during these wars owing to the economic upheavals which beset not only Ireland but all of Europe, and, one suspects, because of his own mismanagement. These losses and the lack of opportunities for his two eldest sons, who had been educated for military careers, led Talbot to consider emigrating to Canada with his large family. Although by early 1816 he had been in correspondence with the colonial secretary, Lord Bathurst, on matters of emigration and government assistance, it was not until late 1817 that he was prepared to depart. Talbot, Francis Brockell Spilsbury*, John Robertson, and Thomas Milburn each led one of four groups to settle in Upper Canada under the £10 deposit plan of 1818. By the terms of this emigration plan, Talbot was to bring out and locate at least 10 settlers and would receive from the Colonial Office a grant in the proportion of 100 acres for each potential settler, after paying a refundable deposit of £10 per settler to ensure that the conditions would be fulfilled. While the expense of feeding the emigrants was to be borne by Talbot, the government undertook to have the lands granted free of expense and to provide the necessary means for the Atlantic crossing.

Many hardships were to plague Talbot and his settlers owing to the ambiguity surrounding many aspects of the plan, the lack of foresight on the part of the British government, and Talbot's own incompetence in carrying out the scheme. The 183 individuals who comprised his group, predominantly Anglicans from Tipperary, sailed from Cork in mid June 1818 on board the *Brunswick*. By the time the party had reached Prescott, Upper Canada, however, only about half that number were still under the leadership of Talbot and his eldest son, Edward Allen. Most of the disgruntled settlers who had left the group with their families were ultimately located by Deputy Quarter-master General Francis Cockburn* in the townships of Goulbourn, March, and Nepean in eastern Upper Canada.

Arriving at York (Toronto) on 9 September, Talbot met the new lieutenant governor, Sir Peregrine Maitland, and most probably his kinsman Colonel Thomas Talbot. From the former he received the promise of a personal grant of at least 1,000 acres of land, in place of the Colonial Office's proposal, if he agreed to allow his remaining settlers to be located by the provincial government under the normal terms for settlement. From the latter he learned of the choice lands available under the colonel's supervision near the forks of the Thames River, in newly opened London Township. About 70 settlers followed Richard Talbot to this township. In 1819 and in succeeding years they were joined by relatives, friends, and former neighbours to form a very successful settlement, which soon spilled over into the neighbouring townships to the north and east.

Although his settlement was a success, Talbot personally experienced both social and economic failure. At the first town meeting, held on 4 Jan. 1819, he was elected one of two assessors, not the most important office within township government, and his name is conspicuous by its absence from the minutes of subsequent meetings. Though appointed a captain in 1823 in the newly formed 4th Regiment of Middlesex militia, he was the last of the six captains listed. Finally, although satisfactory candidates for appointment as justices of the peace were scarce, Talbot, in spite of his background in the Anglican gentry and the military, was never made a magistrate, the mark of the squire he envisioned himself to be.

Within a few years of his selection in 1818 of 1,000 acres on some of the best land in London Township, he had built Mount Talbot, which was more pretentious than the original dwelling he had built there. He was nevertheless totally unsuited to the life of a country gentleman. The several servants he had brought with him from Ireland had left his employ, his two eldest sons had left the area (at least temporarily), and as early as 1823, according to Edward Allen Talbot, his health was "fast declining." Moreover, by 1825 he had sold off his entire 1,000-acre grant, partly to reduce the indebtedness resulting from his financial mismanagement, partly to support his eldest son's family and ventures, and partly to attempt, unsuccessfully, to promote another emigration scheme. Finally, in 1836 he sold to George Jervis Goodhue* and Lawrence Lawrason* the additional 200-acre lot which had been allowed him in 1822 in the northern part of London Township.

Talbot, his wife, and unmarried daughters continued to live at Mount Talbot, which had been sold to Edward Allen Talbot in 1823, until some time after 1842. He and his wife then lived with their youngest son, Freeman, in what is now the northern part of the city of London. It was there that Talbot died in 1853, a week before the death of Colonel Thomas Talbot.

Daniel J. Brock

PAC, RG 5, A1: 29967–69, 30292–94, 30355–58, 30375–77, 86779–82. Private arch., D. J. Brock (London, Ont.), Letter from Bruce Elliott, 9 Oct. 1979, and enclosures, containing geneal. information. UWOL, Regional Coll., F. B. Talbot papers. E. A. Talbot, *Five years' residence in the Canadas* . . . (2v., London, 1824; repr., 2v. in 1, East Ardsley, Eng., and New York, 1968). G.B., WO, *Army list*, 1788, 1791, 1795. "State papers – U.C.," PAC *Report*, 1896: 70, 77; 1898: 217. D. J. Brock, "Richard Talbot, the Tipperary Irish and the formative years of London Township, 1818–1826" (MA thesis, Univ. of Western Ont., London, 1969). H. I. Cowan, *British emigration to British*

North America; the first hundred years (rev. ed., Toronto, 1961). F. T. Rosser, *London Township pioneers, including a few families from adjoining areas* (Belleville, Ont., 1975).

TALBOT, THOMAS, army and militia officer, settlement promoter, office holder, and politician; b. 19 July 1771 in Malahide (Republic of Ireland), son of Richard Talbot and Margaret O'Reilly; d. 5 Feb. 1853 in London, Upper Canada.

An aristocrat by birth, Thomas Talbot was descended from a noble Anglo-Irish family which had ancestral lands in Ireland dating from the 12th century. He was the fourth son in a family of 12 children and enjoyed a secure childhood in Malahide Castle, the family seat, where he received his early education. On 24 May 1783, at the age of 11, he was commissioned ensign in the 66th Foot. With the American revolution drawing to a close, he was retired on half pay shortly after his promotion to lieutenant on 27 September. He then resumed his formal education, attending for several years Manchester Free Public School in England which had many paying pupils from well-to-do families. In 1787 he was selected, largely through family influence, as an aide-de-camp to a distant relative, the Marquess of Buckingham, lord lieutenant of Ireland. Talbot thereupon assumed the commission of lieutenant in the 24th Foot. During his two and a half years of service under Buckingham, he became fast friends with a fellow aide, Arthur Wellesley, later the Duke of Wellington. In Dublin, Talbot enjoyed the active social life of an aide-de-camp and emerged from it with a full complement of social graces combined with the confidence of a member of the Anglo-Irish aristocracy.

In 1790, the year after Buckingham's resignation, Talbot joined his regiment on garrison duty at Quebec and the following spring moved with it to Montreal. Partly on Buckingham's recommendation, the first lieutenant governor of Upper Canada, John Graves Simcoe*, named Talbot as his private secretary in February 1792. The young lieutenant was thus provided with unlimited opportunities to travel throughout the new province and to impress Simcoe with his abilities. The bond forged between the two men over the next four years seems crucial in explaining Talbot's subsequent actions.

In June and July 1792 he accompanied Simcoe and his wife, Elizabeth Posthuma Gwillim*, to Newark (Niagara-on-the-Lake), Upper Canada's first capital. Simcoe had planned to locate the capital at the head of navigation on the Thames River, the later site of London, and with Talbot and others undertook an overland expedition to that area and to Detroit in early 1793. Talbot was subsequently sent on several missions to the western end of Lake Erie to parlay on Simcoe's behalf with the Indians and to meet the Indian agent Alexander McKee*. He travelled as well to Philadelphia as Simcoe's courier to the British plenipotentiary, George Hammond. Travelling by land and water in considerable freedom undoubtedly gave him the chance to observe and make inquiries about the region north of Lake Erie, where he would eventually live.

In the early summer of 1794 Talbot, then 22, left Simcoe's staff. The previous fall he had been promoted captain in the 85th Foot and on 6 March 1794 received a further rapid promotion to major. Returning to England in September he subsequently served for two years on active duty: in Holland fighting the French, in Gibraltar on garrison duty, and in England. On 12 Jan. 1796 he purchased a lieutenant-colonelcy in the 5th Foot. He remained in England until September 1799 when war with France again took him to Holland. After the withdrawal of the British later that year he continued to live in England but on Christmas Day 1800 abruptly sold his commission. Almost immediately, at 29, he left to establish himself as a settler in Upper Canada – a sudden change in career that surprised most of his circle. The precise reason for Talbot's decision is unknown, although several theories have been proposed, including disappointment in love, thwarted political ambitions, failure to advance further in the military, and (as Talbot himself claimed) a desire to assist in the progress and development of Upper Canada.

Talbot began farming in 1801 at "Skitteewaabaa," believed to be near the mouth of Kettle Creek on the north shore of Lake Erie. He apparently hoped to assume a role that would fit in with Simcoe's attempt to institute in the 1790s a system by which entire townships were granted to prominent individuals who, as local gentry, would select settlers and allocate land. Disappointed that Simcoe had not reserved land for him, he soon contacted prominent individuals in England such as the Duke of Cumberland (the fifth son of George III) and Simcoe himself. Promoting his intention to bring in British rather than American settlers (and thereby, in the spirit of Simcoe, check "the growing tendency to insubordination and revolt" in Upper Canada), Talbot succeeded in obtaining a field officer's grant of 5,000 acres in May 1803. He selected his grant in the townships of Dunwich and Aldborough, in Middlesex County, and that same month settled at the mouth of Talbot Creek in Dunwich, the site of Port Talbot, his home for the next 50 years. To stimulate settlement in these townships, he acquired mill machinery in 1804 and two years later constructed a water-powered grist-mill which was of great value to the emerging settlement until its destruction by American troops in 1814.

Initially Talbot's plan differed little from those of other township developers in Upper Canada's early

Talbot

years. He was to give 50 of his original 5,000 acres to the head of each family he could attract and in return he would claim 200 acres for himself from reserved land adjoining Dunwich and Aldborough. Talbot could thus eventually accumulate for himself 20,000 acres, which would compare favourably with the holdings of landed magnates in Ireland and Britain. In topographical terms the scheme would create an area of concentrated population surrounded by Talbot's enlarged holdings. Such a settlement might be expected to prosper as population increased and geographical propinquity alleviated the burden of isolation in what Talbot later recalled as "impenetrable wilderness."

In 1807, however, he began ignoring the original terms of the scheme when he located settlers outside his 5,000 acres. Apparently, in the fashion of Anglo-Irish nobility, he wanted to create a demesne around his residence to insulate him from ordinary settlers. Although he had expressed to Simcoe in 1802 a desire for "the ultimate establishment of a comfortable and respectable tenantry around me," it was necessary to Talbot to maintain a suitable distance between Port Talbot and his settlers. In 1842 he was to explain to John Davidson, commissioner of crown lands, that "within my home Belt, . . . I do not like to have settlers, as I find too near Neighbours a great nuisance." The provincial government acquiesced in Talbot's departure and agreed in 1808 to grant him 200 acres as remuneration for each family settled, whether located within his original grant or not. He thus extended his own potential acreage. About this time the government also accepted his practice of claiming and privately allocating land without registering the transfers at the Surveyor General's Office in York (Toronto) – the sole record being in Talbot's possession. In these early years of the settlement the rate of growth was extremely slow (between 1803 and 1808 he had placed only 20 families) and settlers did not choose to take up 50-acre lots when they might obtain 200-acre lots elsewhere in the province.

Talbot seemed keenly aware that his isolated holdings required road links to other settlements. Earlier efforts to deal with that sort of problem, such as Simcoe's Yonge Street, were well known to him. In 1804 he secured his appointment as a London District road commissioner and was instrumental in planning a southerly and topographically superior alternative to both Dundas Street and the Commissioners Road, which linked the district's middle townships to the head of Lake Ontario. On 15 Feb. 1809 Talbot and Robert Nichol* received provincial commissions from Lieutenant Governor Francis GORE to determine the exact route of the proposed road, which would join Port Talbot and the Niagara District. The Talbot Road east, as it became known, was approved that month by the Surveyor General's Office and was surveyed by

Mahlon Burwell*. As a provincial commissioner Talbot was also responsible for supervising the allocation of lots adjacent to the road. He succeeded in having all provincially reserved lots moved back from the road, as had been done with Yonge Street, and by late 1810 there were numerous settlers with lots along the route. Talbot had to report on the settlers' progress in fulfilling provincial settlement duties, which comprised the erection of a dwelling and the clearance of land within two years of allocation. By these activities he extended his geographical area of influence far beyond Dunwich and Aldborough townships.

Talbot was assisted in extending his superintendence of land settlement by his close friendship with Gore. In 1811, instead of proceeding formally through a recorded order-in-council, Gore verbally authorized the construction of two other roads: the Talbot Road north, linking Port Talbot to the Westminster Township settlement in the upper Thames River valley, and the Talbot Road west, leading to Amherstburg on the Detroit River. At the same time Talbot gained his permission to superintend the allocation and settlement of vacant crown land in concessions remote from the Talbot Road east in Yarmouth, Malahide, and Bayham townships. Gore's authorization stimulated Talbot to immediate action and, informing Surveyor General Thomas Ridout* of his scheme, he quickly proceeded to have the new roads surveyed by Mahlon Burwell and to locate settlers on lots alongside the roads and in concessions farther back. The consequences of these actions were both profound and long lasting. A storm of protest, which embarrassed Gore and infuriated Talbot, came from provincial officials who had not been told of Gore's commitments and who had already allocated lands in Malahide and Bayham. The matter was not readily settled, partly because of the outbreak of the War of 1812. During the war Talbot carried out routine duties as commander of the 1st Middlesex Militia and supervisor of all the militia regiments in the London District.

The government continued to show close interest in the progress of settlement on the lands under Talbot's supervision. In 1815 and 1817, at the request of Gore, Talbot submitted to Ridout returns of the settlers he had located, revealing for the first time the size and rate of growth of his settlement. The 1815 return named 350 families and two years later the total was 804. A large proportion had not been issued fiats for land and thus were unknown to the provincial authorities. Furthermore, the payment of grant, survey, and patent fees to the government by numerous settlers, amounting to over £4,000 by 1818, was being arbitrarily blocked by Talbot, who wished to retain full control over the settlers until they had completed their settlement duties.

After 1817 the provincial government became

increasingly concerned about the collection of internal revenue and doubled its efforts to retrieve fees from settlers. New regulations emphasized fee payment rather than actual residence and were therefore anathema to Talbot. Faced with considerable opposition at York, he travelled to England early in 1818, partly on the advice of the Reverend John Strachan*, who thought he should "go home at once and get the matter settled, if he considered himself aggrieved." He obtained the support of Lord Bathurst, the colonial secretary, who recognized the value of his work, endorsed his system of personally selecting settlers and withholding their fees, and even permitted him to claim the vast area (over 65,000 acres) of Dunwich and Aldborough that had been reserved in 1803. Thus the extraordinary procedures which he had been using for more than a decade were given official sanction, much to the chagrin of hapless provincial officials. Eventually his authority was extended to include the placing of settlers on land grants and the sale of crown and school reserves.

The consequences of Bathurst's decision were manifold. For the government it meant a reduction in revenues because of the withholding of fees. As for the process of settlement, Talbot's set of large-scale township plans, on which he pencilled the name of each settler fortunate enough to be selected for a particular lot, remained the only record of land transactions under his supervision. Not only the allocation but also the forfeiture of land, without provincial involvement and by an easy rubbing out of the name, was thus theoretically possible but the number of settlers ousted by Talbot is not certain. His plans were not examined by the Surveyor General's Office until at least the mid 1830s and they remained in his possession until his demise. The system thus allowed the non-registration of property titles for many individuals and the absence of any provincial record of alienation for large areas of crown land. Yet most settlers appear to have been content with Talbot's method of land transfer. They performed the settlement duties, established farms, and did not press for formal evidence of land title, partly perhaps because of the trust they placed in Talbot. Examples exist where two or three decades passed between the initial settlement of lots and the issue of land patents.

By 1828 Talbot's personal land acquisitions had been terminated despite his vigorous appeals to imperial authorities. His settlement extended over 130 miles from east to west and involved portions of 29 townships in southwestern Upper Canada. He never controlled land allocation and settlement in an entire township, but some – Dunwich, Aldborough, Bayham, Malahide, and London – had large portions under his supervision. Official assessments of the extent of Talbot's work were provided in 1831 and 1836. The author of a report prepared for the British government in 1831 on land settlement in the British North American provinces commented favourably on the progress of the Talbot settlement but noted fee arrears in excess of £35,000, the payment of which Talbot had been blocking, and suggested that an account of his "landed concerns" be provided. Such a tabulation, made for the provincial assembly in 1836, revealed a total of 519,805 settled acres (excluding Talbot's personal holdings in Dunwich) on 3,008 lots in the 28 remaining townships. The statement did not describe the reserve land sold by Talbot. More important, it indicated that 63 per cent of the 3,008 lots had not been reported to the surveyor general as settled and that only a quarter of them were patented in spite of lengthy occupation in many instances.

Talbot's power of supervision was ended in 1838 when Lieutenant Governor Sir Francis Bond Head*, against the advice of his council but with the support of the colonial secretary, Lord Glenelg, asked Talbot to wind up his affairs and turn the settlement over to the province. It had become too large to be managed by an ageing man whose records were inaccessible. Head's decision was also prompted by the controversy surrounding Talbot's forfeiture in 1832 of lots he had allocated to four settlers. They appealed his decision and successive provincial administrations deliberated the question of abuse of power. He had clearly acted unjustly in the case of John Nixon, whose land he had forfeited owing to his strong distaste for Nixon's reform politics, and political antipathy may have played a significant part in two of the other cases. Talbot's removal appears to have encouraged large numbers of settlers to complete their settlement duties (or claim they had) in order to obtain full title to their land, but it did not detract from his significant record of achievement or his own singular image.

Talbot represented the aristocratic, 18th-century British landowner in the New World. The more than 65,000 acres he had acquired by 1821 in the townships of Dunwich and Aldborough were viewed by William Dummer Powell* as his "palatinate" and by John Strachan as his "Princely domain." Although Talbot's holdings in these townships undoubtedly retarded the progress of farming there, he appears to have allowed those who settled early outside his holdings a free choice of location. They chose good land close to kinsfolk and mill-sites. Despite his original intention to settle only British subjects, Talbot accepted from the outset large numbers of Americans, whose prowess as settlers he had quickly recognized. Further, Talbot was virtually excused by the imperial government from observing the province's post-war regulations which prohibited most Americans from taking the oath of allegiance and acquiring land in Upper Canada. Nevertheless, even if American-born settlers, many of loyalist background, predominated in the Talbot settlement in 1820, after 1815 increasing numbers of British immigrants started to arrive, altering its character. Certain areas became distinc-

Talbot

tively Scottish, English, or American as social propinquity and farming background influenced choice of land. Highland Scots, for example, initially accepted poor land in 1818 in small (50-acre) lots in Dunwich and Aldborough but later became indignant at the size of the grants, their isolation within Talbot's undeveloped holdings, and the delay in issuing patents, and this indignation resulted in profound antipathy to Talbot over several subsequent generations.

By the end of the War of 1812 he had acquired considerable political power, particularly in the Middlesex County area, and over the next decade he carefully consolidated this power within the "courtier compact," the tory oligarchy which had taken shape around him in the region north of Lake Erie. After 1825 his strength waned as political weight shifted towards London, the reform movement gained ground, and his authority in his own settlement began to erode. Associated with his early powers had been the right to allocate such local positions as land surveyor and collector of customs. Within the first six years of his settlement at Port Talbot he himself had acquired several public offices, including legislative councillor, county lieutenant, district magistrate, township constable, school trustee, and road commissioner. Talbot, however, paid remarkably little attention to his collective duties. He chose instead, from his position as father of the settlement, to exercise indirect influence, primarily through the election and control of such tory candidates for the House of Assembly as John Bostwick* and Mahlon Burwell, a neighbouring landholder and county registrar of lands from 1809 to 1843. On only two occasions, when his position appeared to be in jeopardy, did Talbot become directly involved in politics. In the provincial election of 1812, according to Asahel Bradley Lewis*, he blatantly helped Burwell defeat Benajah MALLORY. On St George's Day in 1832, in reaction to rampant political agitation instigated by American settlers in Yarmouth and Malahide townships, Talbot, then 61, spoke to a large meeting at St Thomas, which included hundreds from his settlement. He arrogantly attacked the reformers, whom he blamed for the agitation, but with no lasting impact. Both appearances drew unfavourable attention to Talbot and his reception justified his general reluctance to become openly involved in local politics. There were few who comprehended the complexity of Talbot's political thought. Deeply rooted in his own interests, it could on occasion differ from that of his associates. His earliest biographer, Lawrence Cunningham Kearney, whose reform newspaper, the *Canada Inquirer*, Talbot had supported, understood in 1857 that "the Colonel was not violent, if even decided, in politics."

With advancing years and his reduced role in the settlement Talbot became despondent. In February 1836 he had expressed to William ALLAN, his close friend and banking agent in Toronto, the wish to be "possessed of a sufficiency to enable me [to] remove to the *Moon* or some other more wholesome place of residence," and in 1837 Anna Brownell Jameson [MURPHY] observed the "slovenly" nature of much of his farm. Two years later, after the brief governorship of Lord Durham [Lambton*], Talbot commented, again to Allan, that he did not "expect to hear much relating to the plans for this miserable Country, . . . Lord Durham is a sad impostor."

Talbot was always concerned with property and wealth and their acquisition. In 1804 he had expressed to Simcoe his wish to be recommended for the Executive Council rather than the Legislative Council as he did "not like working for nothing, and . . . the £100 is as well to have as not." In 1822, finding his financial position weak, he appealed directly to Lord Bathurst for a pension, clerical assistance, and the remission of fees which he had paid on his own lands. Four years later only a pension was granted, £400 annually. In 1832, with cash from the sale of cattle, Talbot was able to build a new house. He never married but, in the hope of keeping the farm within his family, he brought a nephew, Julius Airey, to Port Talbot in 1833. The youth stayed for almost eight years but could not take to the isolated existence. His elder brother, Captain Richard Airey, who was stationed in Upper Canada, was a frequent visitor to Port Talbot in the 1830s. In 1843 Talbot first invited him to live there and four years later promised to pass on his estate to him. Airey and his large family arrived in late 1847, displacing Talbot from his house. In May 1848, accompanied by George Macbeth* (at once his servant, companion, and estate manager), Talbot left for an extended visit to England, his first in 19 years. After 10 months they returned and in October 1849 Talbot attended as guest-of-honour the ground-breaking of the Great Western Rail-Road at London.

In early 1850 Talbot quarrelled with Airey, perhaps over differences in their styles of living, and on 16 March he conveyed to him only half of his estate (almost 29,000 acres). The remainder, valued at about £50,000, was bequeathed to Macbeth with the exception of an annuity for the widow of a former servant, Jeffrey Hunter. After a period of sickness Talbot again went to England with Macbeth in July 1850. The Aireys left Port Talbot in April 1851 and that summer Talbot returned to his cherished preserve on Lake Erie. Although a new district had been separated from the London District in 1837 and named in his honour, he was disappointed in 1851 when the new county created from Middlesex was named Elgin, after the governor of Canada, rather than Talbot. Macbeth and his wife moved to London in 1852 and they took Talbot with them. He died at their home at the age of 81 and was buried in the Anglican cemetery at Tyrconnell, a few miles west of Port Talbot.

Thomas Talbot was, and is, an enigmatic character whose deeds are far better known than his personality. He left no autobiography or reminiscences and his bachelorhood dictated no legacy of family recollections. Certain eccentricities – alcoholism, snobbery, reclusiveness, and alleged misogyny – have featured prominently in various biographies and may have warped the public view of his character. But whether these traits were as important to his make-up as has been suggested is open to question, possibly with no satisfactory answer. Talbot was clearly the product of a privileged, aristocratic upbringing which may well have implanted in him strong feelings of superiority that prevailed throughout his life. These feelings may have been especially obvious in the pioneer society of Upper Canada, where few of his peers ventured let alone resided. His impeccable pedigree was probably a lifelong support. In spite of his geographical isolation he was recognized, visited, and entertained as an aristocrat, until his death, by eminent men and women in both Canada and Britain.

Talbot maintained geographical and social isolation at the local level in the manner of a British lord. To many visitors he was arrogant, impatient, and rude, without reverence for nationality or social status, but to others he was a gentleman, fully cognizant of the social graces. He appears to have been attracted to a number of ladies before emigrating and subsequently proved most gracious in certain female company, as testified by Anna Jameson after her visit to Port Talbot in 1837. Furthermore, at home, he seems to have developed extraordinary ties of affection for the members of his household closest to him, his servants, and their families. In any analysis Talbot's character is obscured by one overriding enigma – his voluntary exile to Upper Canada. This enigma persisted, for he clearly cherished his British background and sought out British company both in Canada and by returning to Britain on six occasions after 1803.

The achievements of Thomas Talbot are embodied in the settlement named for him. The vast region he supervised, particularly along the Talbot roads, was better developed in terms of agriculture and commerce than most of the rest of the province. The best features of his system of land supervision, such as the roads, were never implemented in settlements elsewhere in Upper Canada. He worked alone and placed himself above everyone, alienating most provincial officials by his apparent avarice for land and by his direct recourse to the imperial government. Nevertheless, for several decades, the benefit to the province which resulted from Talbot's solitary, honest supervision far outweighed the personal benefits he enjoyed.

ALAN G. BRUNGER

[Thomas Talbot's remarkable career has attracted the attention of several biographers from the 1850s to the present. The first biography, by Lawrence Cunningham Kearney, *The life of Colonel, the late Honorable Thomas Talbot, embracing the rise and progress of the counties of Norfolk, Elgin, Middlesex, Kent and Essex . . .* (Chatham, [Ont.], 1857), was a brief anecdotal tribute. Despite differences in political viewpoint between them, the reform-minded author credited Talbot with much of value. Of all the biographers, Kearney may have been the most perceptive in correctly identifying Talbot's unique political stance – neither tory nor reform in character.

Another contemporary description, *Life of Colonel Talbot, and the Talbot settlement . . .* (St Thomas, [Ont.], 1859; repr. Belleville, Ont., 1972), was by Edward Ermatinger*, an acquaintance and associate. This somewhat longer – and largely anecdotal – biography included a description of the Talbot settlement. Ermatinger shared many of Talbot's conservative views although he attributed the latter's flaws to lack of religious guidance.

Charles Oakes Zaccheus Ermatinger, a son of Edward, published a substantial biography, greatly expanding upon his father's work. *The Talbot regime; or the first half century of the Talbot settlement* (St Thomas, 1904) was a more scholarly account although not critical of its subject. It incorporated a reprinted collection of Talbot's correspondence.

Brief biographies appeared in the *Cyclopædia of Canadian biography* (Rose and Charlesworth), vol.2, in 1888, and in 1898 in the *DNB*.

A somewhat more critical view of Talbot was produced as part of an annotated collection of documents published as *The Talbot papers* (2v., Ottawa, 1908–9). The editor, James Henry Coyne*, was the grandson of an arch-foe of Talbot in the township of Dunwich, their mutual abode. Coyne achieved some objectivity in his biography. His principal criticism was the unjust treatment of the Scottish settlers of Dunwich and Aldborough townships who received only 50 acres and were effectively isolated behind Talbot's large undeveloped landholdings.

Another descendant from the Coyne family line, Fred Coyne Hamil, wrote a most scholarly biography of Talbot entitled *Lake Erie baron: the story of Colonel Thomas Talbot* (Toronto, 1955). A wide range of archival materials was tapped in Hamil's work. The result was a detailed chronological account of Talbot's career and a substantial sketch of the evolution of the Talbot settlement.

The interpretation of Talbot by G. H. Patterson in his 1969 thesis, "Studies in elections in U.C.," is most enlightening. The political structure of Upper Canada was based in part on local élite groups which Patterson terms "compacts." These controlled local affairs through key positions, such as members of the House of Assembly, and by the allocation of sinecures within the administrative districts. Talbot controlled a local system of privilege for several years in the London District and particularly in Middlesex County. His power diminished significantly only after 1820, when a well-organized local reform opposition emerged. A.G.B.]

Thomas Talbot's "Remarks on the province of Upper Canada; by the founder of the 'Talbot settlement'" were published as app.B of G.B., Parl., House of Commons paper, 1823, 6, no.561: 1–203, *Report from the select committee on the employment of the poor in Ireland*, 175–78.

PAC, RG 1, E3, 87; RG 68, General index, 1651–1841: 418, 542. PRO, CO 42/330: 203. [E. P. Gwillim] Mrs J. G.

Tanner

Simcoe, *The diary of Mrs. John Graves Simcoe . . .* , ed. J. R. Robertson (Toronto, 1911; repr. [1973]), 62. Murphy, *Winter studies and summer rambles*. John Strachan, *John Strachan: documents and opinions; a selection*, ed. J. L. H. Henderson (Toronto and Montreal, 1969), 66. *Weekly Dispatch, St. Thomas, Port Stanley, and County of Elgin Advertiser* (St Thomas), 15 Feb. 1853, 26 April 1855. *Burke's peerage* (1970), 2607. "Calendar of state papers," PAC *Report*, 1936: 525–26, 552. G.B., WO, *Army list*, 1784–1801. "State papers – U.C.," PAC *Report*, 1891: 32–33; 1892: 288, 298–99; 1893: 10–12; 1896: 21–24, 36; 1898: 211, 213; 1943: 106–7; 1944: 10. A. G. Brunger, "A spatial analysis of individual settlements in southern London District, Upper Canada, 1800–1836" (PHD thesis, Univ. of Western Ont., London, 1974). Cowdell, *Land policies of U.C.* Craig, *Upper Canada.* E. N. Lewis, *Sidelights on the Talbot settlement* (St Thomas, 1938). W. H. Murch, *Talbot settlement centennial celebration, May 21st to 25th, 1903, Saint Thomas, Ontario* (St Thomas, [1903]). Wayne Paddon, *The story of the Talbot settlement, 1803–1840: a frontier history of south western Ontario* (rev. ed., [St Thomas?], 1976). Read, *Rising in western U.C.* W. R. Riddell, *The life of John Graves Simcoe, first lieutenant-governor of the province of Upper Canada, 1792–96* (Toronto, [1926]), 143. Paul Baldwin, "The political power of Colonel Thomas Talbot," *OH*, 61 (1969): 9–18. J. H. Coyne, "An address at the unveiling of the Port Talbot memorial cairn," *OH*, 24 (1927): 5–9; "Colonel Talbot's relation to the early history of London," *OH*, 24: 10–16. F. C. Hamil, "Colonel Talbot and the early history of London," *OH*, 43 (1951): 159–75; "Colonel Talbot's principality," *OH*, 44 (1952): 183–93. Archibald McKellar, "Recollections of Col. Talbot and his times; sacrifice of the public domain," Wentworth Hist. Soc., *Papers and Records* (Hamilton, Ont.), 1 (1892): 115–19. Colin Read, "The London District oligarchy in the rebellion era," *OH*, 72 (1980): 195–209. F. T. Rosser, "Colonel Thomas Talbot *vs* John Nixon," *OH*, 38 (1946): 23–29.

TANNER, OLYMPE. *See* HOERNER

TASKER, PATRICK, merchant and office holder; b. 3 or 4 Dec. 1823 in Greenock, Scotland, third son of James Tasker, a merchant; d. 2 Nov. 1860 in St John's.

Patrick Tasker came out to Newfoundland in April 1842 to work as a clerk in the family-related business of Hunters and Company. A St John's branch of the Greenock-based James Hunter and Company, the firm had been active in the Newfoundland fish trade since the mid 18th century and, like all major St John's fish merchants, it exported fish to southern Europe and the West Indies, imported provisions and fishery supplies for the outports, and outfitted vessels for the spring seal-fishery. Although its stone premises were destroyed in the fire of 9 June 1846 that burnt much of the predominantly frame city, Hunters and Company survived this disaster and was able to resume business.

Throughout the 1840s the company at St John's had been operated for the Tasker family by a series of shareholder partners. With the withdrawal of George Logan in 1850, the Taskers became sole owners of Hunters and Company. Although young and inexperienced, Patrick Tasker became the new manager; for the first few years he sought the advice of Peter McBride, a Scots merchant of St John's with more than 25 years' experience in Newfoundland.

His new status allowed Tasker easy entry into the commercial leadership of the city. In 1850 he was elected to the board of directors of the St John's Hospital, a seamen's and fishermen's hospital which also served the poor and sick of the city. Since 1836 the selection of the 15 directors had been by a quadrennial vote of all the owners and masters of vessels registered at the port of St John's. Tasker's election thus shows that he had earned the respect of his older mercantile colleagues. In 1854 he was re-elected and selected as president of the hospital, a position he held for a year; after the introduction of responsible government the following year, the Liberal ministry of Philip Francis Little* assumed complete administrative and financial control of the institution. In the summer of 1854 Tasker was appointed chairman of the newly established group of health wardens, who imposed on a disbelieving populace stringent sanitary regulations to remove the sewage that was so prevalent, especially in the overcrowded streets and narrow lanes in the centre of the city. When a major cholera epidemic broke out later that year, killing more than 500 people, the cleanliness of St John's undoubtedly helped to keep the number of deaths from rising higher. By the time the epidemic had abated at the end of December, Tasker had won the respect and admiration of all classes in the community.

He was a member of the St John's Chamber of Commerce from 1852 until his death, and in 1854 served as president of the St John's Water Company, organized after the fire of 1846 to supply water to the commercial district. An active promoter, in 1854 he became both a member of the organizing committee which established the Union Bank of Newfoundland, the colony's first successful private banking institution, and a major shareholder in an oil, soap, and candle factory. A director of several local financial and insurance institutions, he was president of both the Newfoundland Marine Insurance Company and the Permanent Loan and Investment Society in 1860.

Like many other merchants, Tasker had not been opposed to the granting of responsible government in 1855. However, he did object to the consequent division of local politics along religious and sectarian lines and to the election of candidates to the legislature on that basis. The St John's merchants, who were predominantly Protestant (Tasker himself was a Presbyterian), were fearful that their interests would be underrepresented in any elective house. In this sense he typified the city's mercantile community which saw the encouragement and protection of its interests as crucial to the welfare of the colony, an attitude not surprising in a society where the fishery was the mainstay of the economy.

Tasker's popularity can be seen in his selection to the executive of several local societies. In October 1855 he was nominated president of the St Andrew's Society and four months later he was elected president of the non-sectarian Agricultural Society. Further, the growth of the masonic order in St John's in the 1850s owed much to Tasker's organizational ability as master in recruiting many of the city's young professionals and businessmen. By 1856 the freemasons were sufficiently strong financially to secure a long-term lease on one of the best ballrooms in the colony. Two years later they made Tasker the deputy provincial grand master of the order for Newfoundland. In January 1860 he also helped organize the St John's Volunteer Association, a rifle reserve intended to assist the Royal Newfoundland Companies stationed in the colony, and he was elected captain of the first company.

During the late 1850s Tasker's business began to decline. In 1857 the company suffered great losses at the fisheries and, despite considerable reductions in the volume of its operations, failed to recover. By May 1860 Tasker owed £2,000 within the St John's commercial community, and another £8,000 in Scotland, half to his father. What effect, if any, his business misfortunes had on his health is not known. However, while in the process of winding down the company's activities, he died of a "short but severe illness," just one month before his 37th birthday. After paying off its debts, Hunters and Company formally closed its doors in 1862 after a century of involvement in the Newfoundland trade.

Patrick Tasker was a leader of a younger generation of merchants and professionals as well as of the entire business community. His funeral procession on 5 November included many of the island's luminaries such as Thomas* and Charles James Fox* Bennett, Hugh William Hoyles*, Laurence O'Brien*, and the governor, Sir Alexander Bannerman*. In June 1861 the masonic order established a fund in his honour to provide for the education of children of deceased freemasons. The following year the order erected an impressive monument at his grave to commemorate his public service to the city. He was described by a contemporary as having a "gentlemanly deportment, kind and agreeable manner," while his "honourable nature, rectitude of character and amiable disposition marked him out for a distinctive place in the community."

MELVIN BAKER

AASJ, Edward Morris diary (mfm. copy at MHGA). BLHU, R. G. Dun & Co. credit ledger, Canada, 10: 27. MHGA, Tasker name file. Nfld., Dept. of Health (St John's), John Joy, "A sketchy survey of Newfoundland health services until the beginning of the 20th century" (typescript, 1971). PANL, GN 2/1, 1854; GN 9/1, 1856. *Courier* (St John's), 1862. *Newfoundlander*, 1842–60. *Newfoundland Express* (St John's), 1851–60. *Public Ledger*, 1842–60. *Royal Gazette and Newfoundland Advertiser*, 1842–60. *When was that?* (Mosdell). Gunn, *Political hist. of Nfld.* Keith Matthews, "A history of the west of England–Newfoundland fishery" (PHD thesis, Univ. of Oxford, Oxford, Eng., 1968). Prowse, *Hist. of Nfld.* (1895). Shannon Ryan, "The Newfoundland cod fishery in the nineteenth century" (MA thesis, Memorial Univ. of Nfld., St John's, 1971). David Alexander, "Newfoundland's traditional economy and development to 1934," *Acadiensis* (Fredericton), 5 (1975–76), no.2: 56–78.

TAVERNIER, ÉMILIE (baptized **Marie-Émilie-Eugène**; she signed **Amélie**) **(Gamelin)**, founder and first superior of the Daughters of Charity, Servants of the Poor; b. 19 Feb. 1800 in Montreal, daughter of Antoine Tavernier, a carrier, and Marie-Josephte Maurice; d. there 23 Sept. 1851.

Born of a father and mother, respectively of Picard and Norman ancestry, who were both Montrealers, Émilie Tavernier was the youngest of 15 children, only six of whom reached adulthood. Despite the precarious economic state of Lower Canada at the beginning of the 19th century, the Tavernier family was not impoverished. However, during her childhood and adolescence Émilie experienced a series of painful bereavements. She was not yet four when her mother died, and only 14 at the death of her father. In the intervening period she also suffered the loss of five more beloved relatives. Before her death Émilie's mother had entrusted the girl to the care of her sister-in-law Marie-Anne Tavernier, the wife of Joseph Perrault, who was quite well off. Mme Perrault had four children, the youngest of whom, Agathe and Joseph, were still at home. She loved her niece as if she were her own daughter and saw to Émilie's upbringing and education. Then for a couple of years she sent her to the boarding-school run by the Congregation of Notre-Dame, where she remained as a student probably until 1815. Émilie subsequently returned to her aunt's house. In 1818 she went to look after her brother François, who had just lost his wife. When she came back to her adopted home the following year her aunt, who was now old and infirm, committed her to the care of her daughter Agathe; 13 years her senior and now the widow of Maurice Nowlan, Agathe became Émilie's confidante and in effect her third mother.

By the age of 19, when she was taking care of her aunt, Émilie Tavernier was frequently to be seen at social gatherings. She rather enjoyed being in society and made many friends. Her company was sought after both in Montreal and in Quebec, where she stayed for two quite long periods between 1820 and 1822 to help one of her cousins, Julie Perrault, the

863

Tavernier

wife of Joseph Leblond. She kept up a correspondence at that time with Agathe, to whom she confided on 18 June 1822 that she felt "a strong vocation . . . for the convent." The letter went on, "I renounce for ever the young dandies and also the [vanities of this] world; I shall become a nun some time in the autumn." However, to the surprise of her circle, on 4 June 1823 she married Jean-Baptiste Gamelin, a respectable Montreal bachelor of 50 who resided in the elegant *faubourg* Saint-Antoine and who made his living dealing in apples. Despite the difference in their ages, the marriage was a happy one, but it lasted less than five years for Gamelin died on 1 Oct. 1827; two of the couple's three sons had died shortly after birth and the third survived his father by less than a year. Hence at the age of 27 Émilie Gamelin was again alone.

A widow with assets inherited from her husband, in the bloom of youth and in possession of all her charms, Mme Gamelin could easily have rebuilt her life. There was no dearth of suitors, but her feelings were changing. She was sorely tried by the death of her husband and children, and on the advice of her confessor, Jean-Baptiste Bréguier-Saint-Pierre, and of Bishop Jean-Jacques Lartigue*, auxiliary bishop in Montreal to the archbishop of Quebec, she began to take an interest in charitable works to assuage her grief. Towards the end of 1827 she joined two relief societies set up by the Sulpicians, the Confrérie du Bien Public, which sought work for a large number of unemployed, and the Association des Dames de la Charité, founded to help the victims of poverty and destitution then so numerous in Montreal. Home visits and the distribution of alms – charitable donations and money collected from those well off – constituted the main activities of the Dames de la Charité. The following year Mme Gamelin also joined the Confrérie de la Sainte-Famille, which aimed to foster the spiritual growth of its members and to encourage spreading the faith. Within these diverse bodies Mme Gamelin showed dedication and developed organizational skills. She also gave her assistance for a short period to the Charitable Institution for Female Penitents, which had been established in 1829 by Agathe-Henriette Huguet-Latour, the widow of Duncan Cameron McDonell. It was probably during this period that she began to divest herself of her properties, and to allocate the money from their sale to the relief of the poor under her care.

During her home visits Mme Gamelin was deeply touched by the physical and mental anguish suffered by frail or sick elderly women who had no one to support them and who faced a lonely death in unsanitary dwellings. To help them, on 4 March 1830 she opened a shelter at the corner of Rue Saint-Laurent and Rue Sainte-Catherine, in a building placed at her disposal by Claude Fay, the parish priest of Notre-Dame in Montreal. The dwelling soon proved too small, and the following year she rented a new one on Rue Saint-Philippe, which she managed and lived in with her first 15 boarders. The work of "providence" then began to take shape. In 1832 and 1834 cholera epidemics ravaged Lower Canada. Despite her fear of contracting the disease, Mme Gamelin regularly visited the cholera patients and succoured the sorrowing families of Montreal. By 1836 the home on Rue Saint-Philippe had in turn become too small. Mme Gamelin then appealed to Antoine-Olivier Berthelet*, a rich Montreal businessman and philanthropist. On 14 March Berthelet donated a house on the corner of Rue Sainte-Catherine and Rue Lacroix (Saint-Hubert), near the future episcopal palace. It was on 13 May, after several years of religious and political struggle, that the ecclesiastical district of Montreal was erected into a diocese, with Lartigue becoming its first bishop on 8 September. During the rebellion, Mme Gamelin obtained official permission to visit the imprisoned Patriotes who were under sentence of death; she put them in touch with their families and helped relieve their distress. Suffering from exhaustion, in March 1838 she fell seriously ill with typhoid fever, but she managed to recover and resumed her activity shortly afterwards.

On Lartigue's death in 1840 Ignace Bourget* was appointed bishop of Montreal. That year also marked the beginning of a religious revival in Lower Canada. Bourget planned to set up a charitable undertaking capable of meeting the needs of the city's poor. However, he had no intention of founding a religious community to handle it. He left for Europe on 3 May and went in particular to France, where he worked hard to persuade members of the Filles de la Charité de Saint-Vincent-de-Paul to come and put the planned endeavour on a permanent footing. During his absence the Legislative Assembly of the province of Canada on 18 Sept. 1841 incorporated Mme Gamelin's old people's shelter as the Montreal Asylum for Aged and Infirm Women. On 16 October, shortly after his return, Bishop Bourget affirmed his intention to entrust Mme Gamelin's charitable undertaking to the Filles de la Charité de Saint-Vincent-de Paul; that very day the ladies who formed the corporation of the Montreal Asylum for Aged and Infirm Women, among them Mme Gamelin, decided to buy land and build a house which they called the Asile de la Providence. They elected Mme Gamelin head of the corporation on 27 October, and on 6 November, doubtless at her prompting, they purchased a property bounded by Rue Sainte-Catherine, Rue Lacroix, and Rue Mignonne (Boulevard de Maisonneuve), near the bishop's palace. They decided on 20 December to begin construction at once. Thus the Asile de la Providence came into being. Mme Gamelin donated her last piece of property to its corporation on 16 Feb. 1842.

On 8 November Bourget learned that the Filles de la Charité de Saint-Vincent-de-Paul could not come to Montreal. He decided then and there to found a religious order and charge it with the responsibility of running the Asile de la Providence. On 25 March 1843 seven women responded to his call, and they started their noviciate under the direction of Jean-Charles PRINCE, a canon who in turn became coadjutor to the bishop of Montreal and first bishop of Saint-Hyacinthe. Mme Gamelin was not one of the novices, but Bourget was eager to associate her with his project and authorized her to serve as their superior. One of the novices withdrew on 8 July, and Mme Gamelin was free to take her place. However, before she entered upon her noviciate Bourget sent her to the United States to visit the Sisters of Charity, a community founded in 1809 by Elizabeth Ann Bayley Seton at Emmitsburg, Md, and gather information about the way they organized their good works and religious life. She brought back a handwritten copy of the rule of St Vincent de Paul which the bishop of Montreal wanted to give to his new Canadian community. On 8 October, shortly after returning, she took the novice's habit. In a ceremony on 29 March 1844 Bourget conferred canonical status on the Daughters of Charity, Servants of the Poor, known later as the Sisters of Charity of Providence (Sisters of Providence). Then with the six other novices Mme Gamelin took the vows of chastity, poverty, and obedience, as well as a vow to serve the poor, and she received the name of Mother Gamelin. The next day she was elected superior of the new order.

Under Mother Gamelin's leadership the young institute grew and soon launched several new charitable projects. The sisters took in orphan girls and elderly women boarders in 1844. In 1845 they opened the Hospice Saint-Joseph, to shelter elderly and infirm priests. That year they set up an employment office for those seeking and offering domestic work, and also began attending to the mentally ill. They opened two other homes in 1846, one at Longue-Pointe (Montreal) and the other at La Prairie. In 1847 Mother Gamelin aided victims of a typhus epidemic and assumed responsibility for the Hospice Saint-Jérôme-Émilien, a hospital for the children of Irish immigrants who had died of this illness; she also agreed to send some sisters to teach at the École Saint-Jacques, which was then short of staff. Two years later she opened a lazaret to assist those stricken by the cholera epidemic. At that time considerable progress was being made in the care of the insane, and she submitted to Louis-Hippolyte La Fontaine*, the attorney general of Lower Canada, a plan which led to the creation of an asylum at Longue-Pointe. The sisters established a convent at Sainte-Élisabeth, near L'Industrie (Joliette), also in 1849. The next year Mother Gamelin founded another

at Sorel and made a second trip to the United States, where she visited the establishments of the Sisters of Charity, in particular their lunatic asylums.

When she returned in 1851 she gave her attention to putting matters in order at the Asile de la Providence. But her extraordinary involvement in charitable works during the preceding years had undermined her health. That year cholera again raged in Montreal. Her strength depleted, Mother Gamelin succumbed to it and died on 23 September after an illness of less than 12 hours. She was buried the following day in the vault of the Asile de la Providence. At the time of her death the Institute of the Sisters of Charity of Providence had 51 professed sisters, 19 novices, 5 postulants, and 7 homes which sheltered 110 poor and elderly women (some mentally afflicted), 95 orphans, 6 infirm priests, 16 female boarders, and 700 young pupils.

Mother Gamelin was the first French Canadian founder of a religious community in Lower Canada after the conquest. By her devotion to the elderly, sick, and needy, and through the charitable works she founded and helped establish, Mother Gamelin in the first half of the 19th century ensured that the gates of charity were opened for future generations.

MARGUERITE JEAN

ANQ-M, CE1-51, 20 févr. 1800, 4 juin 1823, 4 oct. 1827, 24 sept. 1851; CN1-134, 4 juin 1823. Arch. des Sœurs de la charité de la Providence (Montréal), Fonds Émilie Gamelin, A3.1, A3.5, A3.7. Can., Prov. of, *Statutes*, 1841, c.67. *Mélanges religieux*, 30 sept. 1851. F.-M. Bibaud, *Le panthéon canadien* (A. et V. Bibaud; 1891), 102. [Thérèse Frigon, dite] sœur Paul-du-Sauveur, "Essai de bio-bibliographie de la révérende mère Gamelin, fondatrice des Filles de la charité servantes des pauvres dites Sœurs de la Providence" (thèse de bibliothéconomie, univ. de Montréal, 1958), 1–22. [L.-A. Huguet-Latour], *Annuaire de Ville-Marie, origine, utilité et progrès des institutions catholiques de Montréal . . .* (2v., Montréal, 1863–82), 1: 70–82. Le Jeune, *Dictionnaire*, 1: 685–86. [J.-P.] Archambault, *Sur les pas de Marthe et de Marie: congrégation de femmes au Canada français* (Montréal, 1929), 93–99. [M.-J.-L. Blanchard, dite mère Marie-Antoinette], *L'Institut de la Providence: histoire des Filles de la charité servantes des pauvres, dites Sœurs de la Providence* (6v., Montréal, 1925–40), 1–2; *Notes historiques, 1799–1893, Sœurs de la Providence* (Montréal, 1922), 61. Gustave Bourassa, *Madame Gamelin et les origines de la Providence* (Montréal, 1892), 15, 56–57. M.-C. Daveluy, *L'orphelinat catholique de Montréal (1832–1932)* (Montréal, 1933), 24–28, 314–16. N.-E. Dionne, *Serviteurs et servantes de Dieu en Canada: quarante biographies* (Québec, 1904), 212–19. [M.-L. Duchaîne, dite sœur Jean-Baptiste], *Biographies de la mère Gamelin et de ses six compagnes fondatrices de l'institut des Filles de charité servantes des pauvres, dites Sœurs de la Providence* (Montréal, 1918), 11–56. Henri Giroux, *Une héroïne du Canada: madame Gamelin et ses œuvres* (Montréal, 1885), 14–15, 17–18, 21–23. Maurice

Taylor

Hudon-Beaulieu, *Mère Gamelin* (Montréal, 1942), 6–27. Angelo Mitri, *Mère Gamelin et sa cause de béatification* ([Montréal], 1978), 3–7. Eugène Nadeau, *La femme au cœur attentif: mère Gamelin* (Montréal, 1969). Pouliot, *Mgr Bourget et son temps*, 2: 86–109. Irène Richer, *Un cœur qui bat: itinéraire spirituel de mère Gamelin* (Montréal, 1978), 30, 39, 69, 78. [Rose-de-Lima Tessier, dite sœur Rose-de-Marie], *Vie de mère Gamelin, fondatrice et première supérieure des Sœurs de la charité de la Providence* (Montréal, 1900), 7–10, 12–19, 24–25, 28, 30, 32, 91, 100, 102. Léon Trépanier, *On veut savoir* (4v., Montréal, 1960–62), 2: 179–80. É.-J.[-A.] Auclair, "Le centenaire des Sœurs de la Providence," *La Voix nationale* (Saint-Justin, Qué.), 17 (1943): 12–13. Madeleine Durand, "Mère Gamelin et le service social," CCHA *Rapport*, 28 (1961): 11–18. É.-Z. Massicotte, "Le refuge des filles repenties à Montréal," *BRH*, 46 (1940): 373–77.

TAYLOR, HENRY, businessman and author; fl. 1799–1859.

Identification of Henry Taylor is a problem since a number of minor authors bearing this name published in England and the colonies in the mid 19th century. This Henry Taylor may have been born around 1771, and was possibly the son of Dr Henry Taylor and his wife, Anne, of Quebec. He attended schools in England at Hoddesdon and Waltham Abbey. He later claimed to have been a class-mate of Sir Isaac Brock* and of James Hughes, who became a trader in the North West Company and an official in the Indian Department in Montreal, but it seems unlikely in the former's case. For a time in the 1790s Taylor was a chemist's apprentice in London and in his writings he professed an early admiration for pneumatic chemistry and the discoveries of Henry Cavendish, Joseph Priestly, and Antoine-Laurent de Lavoisier.

Taylor returned to British North America in 1799, establishing himself as an importer and distiller in Halifax. As a member of the Committee of Trade [*see* William Sabatier*], he presented a petition to the Nova Scotia House of Assembly in 1811 for a reduction of the import duties on rum and molasses from the West Indies. In 1819 he took up residence near Quebec where he wrote several articles, including "A representative union of the British North American provinces and the parent state" for the *Montreal Herald* in 1822 and others for the *Enquirer* (Quebec) in the same year on a policy of agricultural improvement; the latter he presented to Governor Sir James KEMPT around 1828. It was also in Quebec, some time between 1819 and 1825, that he drafted his first major treatise, "An attempt to form a system of the creation of our globe," the manuscript of which he presented to Anglican archdeacon George Jehoshaphat Mountain* in 1829. Mountain encouraged him to publish the work in England and in the fall of 1829 Taylor returned to London, where he stayed for five years. He failed to interest publishers in his lengthy manuscript, but he continued to write in support of various Canadian causes, addressing petitions to radical politician Joseph Hume in 1831 on colonial representation in the imperial parliament and to the East India Company on transportation through British North America to the Orient.

On his return from Britain in 1834, Taylor probably settled in or near Toronto, where he appears to have become a land agent. In 1836 at Toronto he published *An attempt to form a system of the creation of our globe*. The work purported to explain the origins of the solar system by biblical exegesis and the scientific method. Written in the same period as John Jeremiah Bigsby*'s scholarly paper of 1824 which took some account of debates about the geological origins of the earth, it appeared at a time when British scientists and theologians such as William Buckland and Edward Bouverie Pusey were publishing on similar subjects. Taylor's work was heavily derivative, relying upon extensive citations from William Paley's *Natural theology* (London, 1802), and his providential explanations of natural phenomena were simply popularizations of ideas accepted by Anglican divines a generation earlier. A larger edition of the work appeared in 1840 at Quebec, where Taylor, whose only source of livelihood appears to have been pamphleteering, moved to publish and advertise his works. This second edition added further scientific evidence from leading European astronomers and philosophers.

In 1840 Taylor also published a popular account of his journeys through the Eastern Townships of Lower Canada, *Journal of a tour from Montreal*. Obviously prejudiced against the primitive state of agriculture he saw practised in the seigneuries, Taylor gives many suggestions to improve productivity with the aim of making British North America a major exporter of grain; he displays considerable knowledge of the wheat-fly, then a menace in Lower Canada, and recommends the building of roads and a canal from the townships to the St Lawrence to improve the transportation of staples.

It was at this time that Taylor began to write political tracts on the unsettled state of affairs in the two provinces. Between 1839 and 1841, in two serialized works, *Considerations on the past, present & future condition of the Canadas* and *On the forthcoming union of the two Canadas*, he opposed a federal union of the British North American colonies. He preferred representation of the colonies in the British parliament in conjunction with a union of the Canadas in which there would be increased political power for the British parts of the province, and which would thus place the French Canadians in a small minority in the assembly, able only to vote on local improvements, education, and municipal services. Apparently unsuccessful in eliciting much public interest in his publications through advertisements in the *Montreal Gazette*, he also failed to persuade the city council of Montreal to purchase copies of the second one in 1841.

During the 1840s and 1850s Taylor seems to have followed the government as it moved between Quebec, Montreal, Kingston, and Toronto; he continued to seek official support for his writings. Yet another polemic, *On the present condition of United Canada*, strongly opposed responsible government as a republican remedy, comparing it by graphic analogy to "the dreadful effects of volcanic action." Unfavourable comparisons to the French revolution were amplified in a second edition of the work, substantially revised and expanded, which was published in 1849 by the reform newspaper the *Canadian Free Press* (London) and in 1850 by the Toronto *Patriot*. Taylor was contemptuous of the radical Parisian republicans of 1848, stressed the benefits of the British constitution, and pandered to fears of "Romanism and Infidelity" emanating from Lower Canada.

In Toronto in 1850 Taylor undertook the reprinting of this latest work at his own expense and two years later secured a small grant of £10 from the legislature to be applied towards its purchase for the parliamentary library. In 1853 he solicited financial aid from the governor, Lord Elgin [Bruce*], for "pursuit of his scientific research" and support of his publications, but was refused. A further request for assistance from the government at Quebec was made in 1854, this time for a ninth edition of his *A system of the creation of our globe*. Taylor did not obtain the grant because of the work's "unscientific nature," and he published this edition himself. Purporting to include new scientific discoveries, the work merely resurrected well-known works on magnetism by Michael Faraday and on astronomy by François Arago. In Toronto in 1856 Taylor unsuccessfully petitioned Governor Edmund Walker Head* for additional public assistance on account of his "various misfortunes" and "much advanced years." Ever hopeful, he took advantage of the Desjardins Canal disaster on the Great Western Railway in March 1857 [see Samuel ZIMMERMAN] to petition railway and public officials for the joint development of patents to prevent railway accidents. Then, in 1858, "in extreme poverty," he requested legislative support for a rambling pamphlet on federation and imperial representation for the colonies, then subjects of discussion in the province. With a final refusal in 1859, his prolific but undistinguished career as a publicist came to an end.

Taylor's conservative political views were natural extensions of his disquisitions on the earth's providential creation. Numerous theological digressions punctuate his political tracts, and he constantly refers to the divine nature of the social compact and to the similarities between the physical and the moral world,

to which politics belonged. His major work, *A system of the creation*, was clearly a popular exposition of the creationist views widely held before the publication of Charles Darwin's theories, and seems to have been the work most read in Canada on the subject at that time. In spite of its archaic and "unscientific" contents, it appears to have satisfied popular yearnings for a synthesis of biblical authority and emerging natural science.

ANTHONY W. RASPORICH

Henry Taylor is the author of *An attempt to form a system of the creation of our globe, of the planets, and the sun of our system; founded on the first chapter of Genesis, on the geology of the earth, and on the modern discoveries in that science and the known operations of the laws of nature, as evinced by the discoveries of Lavoisier and others in pneumatic chemistry* (Toronto, 1836; this work went through several later editions as *A system of the creation of our globe* . . .); *Considerations on the past, present & future condition of the Canadas* (Montreal, 1839); *Journal of a tour from Montreal, thro' Berthier and Sorel, to the Eastern Townships of Granby, Stanstead, Compton, Sherbrooke, Melbourne, &c., &c., to Port St. Francis* (Quebec, 1840); *On the forthcoming union of the two Canadas, addressed to the Canadian public and their representatives, in the honourable legislature of United Canada* (Montreal, 1841); *On the present condition of United Canada, containing plans for the advancement of its agriculture, commerce and future prosperity, with strictures on the eventful question of responsible government, and the present crisis of the province* (Montreal, [1843]; a second edition, substantially revised and enlarged, was published as *On the present condition of United Canada, as regards her agriculture, trade, & commerce: with plans for advancing the same, and for promoting the health, wealth, and prosperity of her inhabitants with reflections on the present state of the Protestant religion; with a view to harmonize its various sects and ultimately to bring them into one powerful united body, also a dissertation on the national debt of Great Britain, with a plan for its gradual payment* (London, [Ont.], 1849; repr., Toronto, 1850)); and *On the intention of the British government to unite the provinces of British North America, and a review of some events which took place during the last session of the provincial parliament* (Hamilton, [Ont.], 1857; 2nd ed., Toronto, 1858).

PAC, MG 24, D16, 56; RG 5, C1, 379, file 200; RG 7, G20, 62–67. PANS, RG 5, A, 17, 25 Feb. 1811. Can., Prov. of, Legislative Assembly, *Journals*, 1852–59; Legislative Council, *Journals*, 1852–53, 1858. *Enquirer* (Quebec), 1 Jan., 1 April 1822. *Montreal Gazette*, 5, 19 Nov., 26 Dec. 1840; 9, 28 Jan. 1841. *Nova Scotia Royal Gazette*, 1799–1816. *Quebec Gazette*, 18 Aug. 1766, 8 June 1769, 27 Jan. 1774. Morgan, *Bibliotheca Canadensis*, 368–69. *Lit. hist. of Canada* (Klinck *et al.*; 1965), 448–49.

TAYLOR, JAMES, businessman, politician, office holder, justice of the peace, and militia officer; b. *c.* 1794 in Fredericton, second son of James Taylor and Jane ——; m. 26 Aug. 1829 Nancy Hatfield, widow of

Taylor

William Fortune, a master mariner, and they had one daughter and two sons; d. 4 Feb. 1856 in Fredericton.

In 1783 James Taylor's father was among the first loyalists to settle at St Anne's Point (Fredericton), where he established "one of the largest and most respectable firms" in the colony. Initially involved in the mercantile trade, he later became active in the timber trade, shipbuilding, and general construction. His three sons, James, William*, and John F., formally entered into a partnership with him in August 1821, forming James Taylor Senior and Company. As a leading building firm in Fredericton, the company was selected in July 1826 as one of the contractors to construct what was to be King's College (University of New Brunswick). Following the deaths of their brother in March 1834 and their father that December, James and John continued in partnership until January 1838.

James Taylor was also a director of the Nashwaak Mill and Manufacturing Company, founded during the heady atmosphere of the 1836 boom. When the operating manager fled to the United States in 1840 after having allowed the firm to go bankrupt, Robert Rankin and Company, which had been responsible for providing its supplies and marketing its lumber, took the business over. By the early 1840s the firm was producing between seven and eight million feet annually. In October 1835 James and John had sold two mill reserves and some land on the Tobique River to Ephraim H. Lombard of Saint John. Backed by American capital, Lombard then organized the Tobique Mill Company. He leased some 100,000 acres of crown land and made plans for the erection of several sawmills. On 9 Jan. 1838 James became president of the milling operations. Unfortunately, with only one sawmill in production, this firm also collapsed in 1840.

Taylor nevertheless remained involved in the business community. A founder of the Central Bank of New Brunswick in 1834, he had served as a director the following year and was also a director of the Fredericton branch of the Bank of British North America, which was established in 1838. In 1836 he had been one of the incorporators of the Fredericton Hotel and Stage Coach Company. Eight years later he was a founding partner in Fredericton's first brass and iron foundry. It suffered during the recession of the 1840s, and in 1847 Taylor sold out to George Todd, who became the sole owner. Taylor was an early and enthusiastic advocate of reciprocity with the United States in 1848 following the repeal in Britain of the navigation acts. Whatever the economic climate, Taylor managed to carry on and he remained one of the most respected merchants in Fredericton until his death.

Taylor had run in 1830 for York County in the general election, but was defeated. Following his protest of the by-election results in September 1832, he was declared a winner and on 11 March 1833 he entered the House of Assembly. He continued to hold the seat for the rest of his life, frequently topping the polls for the constituency. Taylor had family connections in politics. His brother William had represented York since 1822 and his wife's sister's husband, Charles Fisher*, would join him in the house in 1838. A diligent parliamentarian, Taylor actively sought to advance the interests of York County. He presented innumerable petitions and served on the influential standing committee on public and private accounts. His career in the house coincided with those years in which the assemblymen achieved their greatest power; as private members they introduced and passed money bills for the benefit of their constituencies without any effective interference from the lieutenant governor or the executive. Taylor was a successful manipulator of this system, which was popularly known as log rolling. Reformers such as George Edward Fenety*, who viewed the executive's exclusive right to initiate money bills as a central principle of responsible government, regarded log rolling as wasteful, and Fenety described Taylor as an "anti-Reformer." During the 1830s Taylor consistently voted with the opposition against the government of Lieutenant Governor Sir Archibald Campbell*, but after 1837 he supported Campbell's successor, Sir John HARVEY. In fact, it was alleged that, as contractor for the extensive renovations made to Government House between the years 1837 and 1840, he gave Harvey £1,000 a year "under the head of repairs." Although the charge was never proven, Taylor clearly benefited from the association with Harvey. His relationship with Harvey's successors was less close and during the 1840s and 1850s his voting pattern showed no consistency except that he was usually found on the side which had a majority in the assembly.

As a politician, office holder, and prosperous merchant, Taylor naturally assumed a position of leadership in the community. He served, likely in 1839, as paymaster and a captain of the York County militia. In 1840 he became a justice of the peace for York County with the extensive authority that implied in the old system of county government. The same year he was one of the commissioners for the care and management of the lieutenant governor's official residence. In 1853 John G. Lorimer, publisher of the *Provincial Patriot and St. Stephen Banner*, would write that Taylor was in high favour with Lieutenant Governor Sir Edmund Walker Head* and his wife and that he catered to their every whim regarding the internal arrangements of Government House. In 1848 Taylor was named a member of the public buildings committee and two years later was made a controller of customs. A strong supporter of the Fredericton St

Andrew's Society, he was also a pillar of the Church of Scotland, regularly serving as a lay preacher. He attended St Paul's Church in Fredericton which had been built on land donated by his father; before St Paul's was constructed, he had been a member of the Congregational Church in Sheffield. As he possessed little sympathy for the pretensions of the Anglican members of the assembly, Taylor often acted as the voice of the dissenting congregations in the capital.

Apparently Taylor was a tiny man, weighing perhaps only 112 pounds. His features were "very sharp and very lean – eyes quite small, but beaming with kindness; hair dark and thin – the forehead is high and unusually large." "We think the whole head is a 'Bump of Benevolence,'" Lorimer remarked, a reference both to Taylor's personal charity and to his generosity with public money, which Lorimer deplored. Taylor died in February 1856 and his obituary in the *New-Brunswick Courier* confirmed his generosity. According to the newspaper, he had remained an enormously popular local figure, noted "for his many gratuitous acts of kindness, and his general benevolence to the poor."

PHILLIP BUCKNER and D. MURRAY YOUNG

PANB, MC 69; RG 2, RS8, Central Bank, 1836–59; RG 4, RS24, Central Bank, 1836–59; RG 7, RS75, 1835, James Taylor (Sr); RG 10, RS108, James Taylor (Sr), 30 Nov. 1825; James Taylor (Jr), 15 April 1841. PRO, CO 188/105: 401–4. St Paul's United Church (Fredericton), Records of St Paul's Presbyterian Church (mfm. at PANB). N.B., House of Assembly, *Journal*, 1833–56. *Head Quarters* (Fredericton), 31 July 1844, 6 Feb. 1856. *New-Brunswick Courier*, 29 Sept. 1832, 6 Aug. 1847, 9 Feb. 1856. *New Brunswick Reporter and Fredericton Advertiser*, 8 Feb. 1856. *Provincial Patriot and St. Stephen Banner* (St Stephen, N.B.), 5 Aug. 1853. *Royal Gazette* (Fredericton), 21 Dec. 1836, 23 May 1838, 2 Oct. 1839, 13 Feb. 1856. G. E. Fenety, *Political notes and observations: or, a glance at the leading measures that have been introduced and discussed in the House of Assembly of New Brunswick ...* (Fredericton, 1867). I. L. Hill, *The Old Burying Ground, Fredericton, N.B.* (2v., Fredericton, 1981), 2: 218–26. MacNutt, *New Brunswick*.

TELFER, WALTER, physician and surgeon; b. Sept. 1800 in Hawick, Scotland, second son of William Telfer; m. Euphemia Denham, and they had one daughter; d. 7 March 1857 in Toronto.

Walter Telfer was sent "early in life" to Edinburgh "to learn the silk mercery business." He later spent two years in Jamaica settling an uncle's estate before entering medicine. In 1824 Telfer was licensed by the Royal College of Surgeons of Edinburgh, and immigrated to Stamford (Niagara Falls), Upper Canada. The following year he settled at Niagara (Niagara-on-the-Lake) and built a large practice which included the garrison, the district jail, and the poor. From 1832 he served as a medical officer, executing the regulations of the town's board of health. Telfer joined others in 1832 in an unsuccessful attempt to secure the support of the Medical Board of Upper Canada for the formation of a professional medical society. He himself was licensed by the board in July 1833.

"Finding the field ... too limited" at Niagara, Telfer moved in 1835 to Toronto, where he resumed practice. A contentious and ambitious figure, he publicly questioned the competence of other surgeons and signed a petition for the enlargement of the medical board. Despite his expressed interest, Telfer was not appointed to the enlarged board in 1836. He subsequently protested that since he was "the oldest practitioner in Toronto with the exception of Dr Widmer [Christopher WIDMER] ... the public will naturally infer that some improper conduct of mine must have been the cause that younger practitioners are preferred." In 1838 Telfer was named to the board, where he acted as an examiner in surgery. Until his death he sat on successive bodies: the College of Physicians and Surgeons of Upper Canada and the reinstituted Medical Board. Telfer also served as an attending surgeon at the Toronto General Hospital, as physician to the St Andrew's Society, and on the executive of the Toronto Medico-Chirurgical Society, the province's first organized medical society.

Telfer wanted the prestige of office. From 1840, at each rumour that medicine was to be taught at King's College (University of Toronto), he applied for a teaching position in surgery or anatomy. When the temporary Provincial Lunatic Asylum opened in Toronto in 1841, he petitioned to become medical superintendent but was passed over in favour of Dr William Rees*. In 1844 Telfer, Dr William Rawlins Beaumont*, and Dr Joseph Hamilton were appointed to report separately on the asylum and make recommendations for a permanent institution. Telfer criticized Rees's administration and his frequent use of bleeding, blistering, and purgation – common medical practices which, in Telfer's opinion, "would rather confirm than remove the disease." In 1845, when Rees was dismissed, Telfer replaced him as superintendent.

Before taking up his position Telfer examined asylums in the United States and later joined the Association of Medical Superintendents of American Institutes for the Insane. This contact undoubtedly reinforced his belief in humane practice and current theories of moral treatment, which Rees had also adopted. Telfer reportedly accepted all sent to the asylum to save them from being "confined to Gaols where they are generally cruelly treated." He eased overcrowding by moving some patients from the asylum to quarters in the parliament building which looked "more like a Boarding House." Telfer

Tharoniakanere

continued Rees's practice of prescribing opiates and sleep. He introduced manual labour therapy and emphasized the importance to recovery of moral instruction through such activities as religious services, reading, dancing and "every proper . . . Amusement." During his tenure Telfer claimed a high rate of recovery.

Telfer's work at the asylum was hindered by problems of staff discipline and internal authority about which he complained to the asylum's board of commissioners. The asylum steward, Robert Cronyn, brought charges before the commissioners accusing Telfer of drunkenness and misappropriation of drugs and supplies. These charges led to Telfer's dismissal in 1848. Refused a hearing "of a judicial character," he answered the charges publicly in the newspapers. Telfer challenged several of the accounts, including that of Cronyn, who was later himself dismissed for drunkenness. Telfer accused the commissioners of ignoring his earlier complaints. He believed that some of them had conducted personal business with the steward while others wanted him replaced by their own candidate. Telfer's defence, and the possible political influence of Dr John Rolph* in the controversial appointment of Telfer's successor, Dr George Hamilton Park, sparked continued recriminations. The provincial assembly sent for the papers on Telfer's case but no action followed.

Telfer returned to private practice and remained active at the general hospital. He spent time daily in "devotion, religious reading and meditation," and remained a popular figure, respected for his charitable service and medical skill.

GEOFFREY BILSON

Academy of Medicine (Toronto), MS 137. AO, RG 22, ser.155, will of Walter Telfer; ser.305, Euphemia Denham [Telfer]. Niagara Hist. Soc. Museum (Niagara-on-the-Lake, Ont.), B.1, 1827–32 (mfm. at AO). PAC, RG 5, A1: 56425–27, 65996, 65998, 70569–70, 88245–47, 88253–55, 92151–52, 113393–95; B9, 62: 260, 262, 506; C1, 21, file 210; 56, file 3512; 99, file 4865; 133, files 8125–26, 8135; 139, file 5870; 167, file 11908; 178, file 13434; 201, file 16616; 223, file 20131; RG 7, G14, 10: 4611. Royal College of Surgeons of Edinburgh, Licenses, 1824. *American Journal of Insanity* (Utica, N.Y.), 3 (1846–47): 87–88. Can., Prov. of, Legislative Assembly, *App. to the journals*, 1849, app.GGG. *Daily Colonist* (Toronto), 10 March 1857. *Gleaner* (Niagara [Niagara-on-the-Lake]), 3 Oct. 1825; 21 April 1832; 20 May, 13 July 1833. *Globe*, 12, 16 Aug., 2, 20, 27, 30 Sept. 1848; 12 March 1857. *Niagara Herald*, 1 Sept. 1828. *Patriot* (Toronto), 11 July, 8, 15 Dec. 1835. *Upper Canada Gazette*, 11 June 1835. *Laws of the Toronto Medico-Chirurgical Society, together with a catalogue of books in its library; instituted 17th June, 1844* (Toronto, 1845). *Toronto directory*, 1846–47: 73; 1850–51: 126; 1856: 230. Canniff, *Medical profession in U.C.*, 63–65, 76–77, 85, 88–89, 107, 113, 164–65, 167, 213, 647–48. [G. H. Park], *Narrative of the recent difficulties in the Provincial Lunatic Asylum in Canada West; dedicated to the Christian community, and to the presiding officers of the lunatic asylums in Europe and America* (Toronto, 1849). *Robertson's landmarks of Toronto*, 1: 437–38.

THARONIAKANERE. *See* MARCOUX, JOSEPH

THELLER, EDWARD ALEXANDER, Patriot raider and author; b. 13 Jan. 1804 in Coleraine (Northern Ireland); m. *c.* 1827 Ann Wilson, *née* Platt, in Burlington, Vt, and they had five children; d. 7 Feb. 1859 in Hornitos, Calif.

As Edward Alexander Theller's family was a "highly respectable" one, he gained a good education in Ireland, eventually becoming a teacher at the Belfast Grammar School. When his father, an auctioneer, died in 1825 he left "a large family in comparative penury." An unverified report has it that about this time Edward became an assistant surgeon in the Royal Navy, serving in that capacity for some while, but this report seems unlikely, for in 1826 he set sail for Lower Canada. In Montreal he studied medicine briefly with Dr Daniel Tracey*, a fellow Irishman and later a radical editor, who, according to a distant relation of Theller, eventually formed "a very bad opinion of his character and spoke disparagingly of his abilities." By his own account Theller was "wild and reckless" in his youth. In 1827 he rushed off to Vermont with his intended wife; over the next few years, unable to obtain a medical licence and in frequent trouble with the law, he moved constantly, living for periods in Burlington, in Lower Canada, and in Washington, D.C. Finally, about 1836, he settled in Detroit, where he practised medicine and ran a grocer's store and an apothecary shop. His eloquence and easy charm won him influence among "the lower class of voters" and minor public office.

After the abortive rebellions of 1837 in Upper and Lower Canada, Canadian refugees and American sympathizers plotted to invade the two provinces. Theller felt that it was the duty of Americans "to assist" the cause. He was secretary in December at two Patriot meetings in Detroit, then he became a "general" in the "western division of the Patriot army." In early January 1838 he participated in an attempted attack on Fort Malden at Amherstburg, Upper Canada. On the 9th, while he was cruising the Detroit River in command of the schooner *Anne*, she ran aground near the fort. Canadian militiamen under Colonel Thomas Radcliff* opened fire, stormed the vessel, and took all 21 on board, including Theller, who was sporting "a kind of uniform" and a wound.

In April he was tried in Toronto for treason. He "conducted his defence principally himself," arguing that the charge against him was inapplicable since he was a naturalized American citizen. Chief Justice John Beverley Robinson*, who presided, disagreed, asserting "that the obligation of natural allegiance . . . was . . . perpetual and inalienable." Theller was found guilty and on 10 April sentenced to die. Though some, such as Attorney General Christopher Alexander Hagerman*, thought that "*Law* and *Justice* require that Theller should be executed," he was not, largely because Robinson now feared (rather oddly) that the doctrine of indefeasible allegiance had been carried too far. After being sent to the Citadel at Quebec in June, Theller learned that he was to be transported to New South Wales (Australia) for life.

At Quebec he shared a cell with other Patriots. Though they had enough guards "to prevent the least shadow of hope of escape," they did manage to file through the bars on their window. In the early hours of 16 October, aided by Charles Drolet* and John Heath*, Theller and four others fled; "a short stout man," Theller had difficulty getting through the window. Three were soon captured but Theller and William Wallin Dodge remained at large. Aided by sympathizers, they travelled south, crossing the American border on November 6. The escape created a sensation, and Theller made a triumphant tour of several major American centres. To his delight, he was "feasted and made a hero of." He deemed the tour "an *impudent*, but *a successful move*," which did "more for the cause of suffering Canada" than anything else.

Arriving back in Detroit in December, he was promptly arrested for violating American neutrality laws, but was freed, likely on bail. His trial during the summer of 1839 produced his acquittal and in no wise diminished his enthusiasm for the Patriot cause. He began, in August, a newspaper, the *Spirit of '76*, and was "in almost daily communication" with Patriots across the border. Writing to William Lyon Mackenzie*, with whom he often corresponded, in warm and friendly terms, he happily contemplated the prospect of all once again running "the risk of being shot or hung." Declining personal finances, however, prompted him in 1841 to take his family to upstate New York, where they eventually settled in Rochester. That year his Patriot convictions led to his involvement in an attempt to blow up a lock on the Welland Canal and to his planning the destruction of two Canadian vessels moored in the Niagara River. Another blow for the cause was struck in 1841 when his book *Canada in 1837–38* appeared. At the time anglophobia was reaching a crest in the United States. Grandiloquent but highly readable, the book did little to check the wave, as Theller vividly recounted the Patriots' struggles against the British tyrants and his part in them, which he was careful not to undervalue.

The next year he became involved with John Sheridan HOGAN and others in an unsuccessful attempt to inflame American opinion once more over the destruction in December 1837 of the Patriot supply ship *Caroline* and the death of Amos Durfee of Buffalo [*see* Andrew Drew*; John Elmsley*]. All in all Theller was a dedicated Patriot, a dangerous one in the eyes of Canadian authorities and one to be watched in case of any future incursions.

Why did Theller play such an active role within the Patriot movement and prove such an ardent foe of the British presence in North America? One reason is suggested by Lieutenant Governor Sir George AR-THUR's term for him, a "Supreme Vagabond": Theller was the sort who would seek out and revel in adventure. But another explanation lies in the fact that he also acted out of ideological conviction. In Montreal he had associated with political radicals and had come to regard their cause as the cause of the Canadas. Here his conclusions were reinforced by his Irish background as he saw parallels between English oppression in Ireland and the despotism that in his view existed in the Canadas. And he seems to have worked to link the two cases in the public mind. Significantly, in early 1838 it was to be his particular task as a Patriot leader to make a revolutionary appeal to the Irish and French Canadian residents of Upper Canada. At his trial in Toronto, according to his book, he denounced England for the wrongs it had inflicted on Ireland. During his triumphant tour of the United States he preached the Patriot cause in several cities with large Irish-American populations. Further, in *Canada in 1837–38*, he attempted to bring his Patriot and Irish ideologies into line with nationalist thinking in the United States, by means of references to the Greek struggle for independence, Russia's repression of Poland, and the creation of a republic in Texas. He never forsook Ireland. After settling in Rochester he became a leading figure in the Irish community there, appearing at public dinners and meetings and becoming a secretary of the local Repeal Association, which sought dissolution of the parliamentary union between Ireland and Britain.

Theller's Patriot activities were also influenced by the broad utopian streak in his make-up. Chosen in 1843 as a director of the Fourier Association of Rochester, he hailed those joining the first communitarian settlement in the area as the "pioneers of industrial combination; may their success be such that others may soon follow their glorious example and make the earth what God intended it." It was clear to Theller that men of good will must be active (else God's plan would be long in the realization), they must unite, and they must recognize the essential unity of their cause. Hence he enjoined the members of the Repeal Association to proclaim themselves "the enemies of slavery in every form and in every clime, and the friends of the oppressed of every creed and color." He was later described by the historian Robert B. Ross as an "earnest and self-sacrificing man, a warm friend and a bitter enemy."

Theller was certainly prepared to help those in other climes. In 1849 he moved to Panama to fight an epidemic of yellow fever; he eventually operated a hotel there and edited a newspaper. Characteristically, he reportedly became caught up in a rebellion to separate Panama from New Granada (Colombia). Like the Canadian rebellion, it failed and once more he was cast into jail.

In 1853 he settled with his family in San Francisco, where he edited two newspapers and, in 1856, was elected superintendent of public schools. About two years later he moved to Hornitos, in the California gold-fields, where he practised medicine. He died suddenly there in 1859, leaving, in the words of the *San Francisco Daily Herald*, a memory of himself as a "warm-hearted" and "talented" individual, one "generous to a fault." Closer to the scene of Theller's Patriot activities, the *Boston Weekly Courier* (which claimed that he had visited the Massachusetts capital in the late 1840s to collect money on behalf of annexationists in the Canadas [*see* Thomas D'Arcy McGee*]) had more precise recollections to offer. Theller, the paper opined, "was a clear and direct writer, but did not understand the business of conducting a newspaper much better than a revolution. In both kinds of enterprizes he made several spirited starts, but always stranded in the course of a few months. He was as courageous, honest, and true, as he was restless and visionary."

COLIN FREDERICK READ

Edward Alexander Theller is the author of *Canada in 1837–38, showing, by historical facts, the causes of the late attempted revolution, and of its failure; the present condition of the people, and their future prospects, together with the personal adventures of the author, and others who were connected with the revolution* (2v., Philadelphia and New York, 1841).

AO, MS 4; MS 74, package 10, item 11; MS 516. PAC, MG 24, B42; RG 5, A1: 103568–69, 103704–5, 106067–70, 106335–38, 106356–62, 106571–72, 109700–2, 109727–28, 110317–26, 125306–34, 126569–74, 136912–26, 139298–99; RG 7, G12, 62: 175. PRO, CO 42/446 (mfm. at PAC). *Arthur papers* (Sanderson). *Rochester Daily Advertiser* (Rochester, N.Y.), 21 March, 16 April, 8 July, 19 Aug., 8 Sept. 1843; 12 Nov. 1850. *Rochester Daily Democrat*, 25 March 1842; 18 April, 7 June, 8 July, 8 Sept., 15 Nov. 1843; 8 Jan., 8 Feb. 1844. *Rochester Union and Advertiser*, 11 March 1858, 11 March 1859. *Western Herald, and Farmers' Magazine* (Sandwich [Windsor, Ont.]), 5 June 1838. "Calendar of state papers," PAC *Report*, 1936: 588–89; "State papers – U.C.," PAC *Report*, 1944: 28–29. E. T. H. Bunje *et al.*, *Journals of the Golden Gate* (Berkeley, Calif., 1936), 14, 29, 46. A. B. Corey, *The crisis of 1830–1842 in Canadian-American relations* (New Haven, Conn., and Toronto, 1941). W. R. Cross, *The Burned-over District; the social and intellectual history of enthusiastic religion in western New York, 1800–1850* (Ithaca, N.Y., 1950). Guillet, *Lives and times of Patriots*. O. A. Kinchen, *The rise and fall of the Patriot Hunters* (New York, 1956). Hereward Senior, *The Fenians and Canada* (Toronto, 1978), 1, 19–20. R. B. Ross, "The Patriot War," *Mich. Pioneer Coll.* (Lansing), 21 (1892): 509–609.

THOMAS, WILLIAM, architect, water-colourist, and engineer; b. *c.* 1799 in Suffolk, England, son of William Thomas and Ann ——; m. 17 Sept. 1826 Martha Tutin in Birmingham, England, and they had four sons and six daughters; d. 26 Dec. 1860 in Toronto.

William Thomas's significance among his generation of architects in British North America lies not only in the outstanding nature of the work he executed but also in the unique opportunity his career affords of tracing the relationship between his extensive preparation in England and his work in Canada, the latter being more accomplished and much more important relatively. Other architects such as John George Howard*, George Browne*, Frederic William Cumberland*, and Thomas Fuller* arrived when they were much younger than Thomas, with the result that their early work is unknown. Thomas came in his maturity.

Shortly after William's birth, the family settled at Chalford, Gloucestershire, where his father was innkeeper of the Clothier's Arms. William and his three brothers all entered the building trades. John, the youngest, was apprenticed to a letter-carver or mason at first, studied briefly under William in the early 1830s, and achieved some success as an architect; he is, however, best remembered as one of the most prolific sculptors of the period. Between 1812 and 1819 William was apprenticed to John Gardiner, a local carpenter and joiner.

Some time after receiving his indenture papers, William moved to Birmingham, where he married Martha Tutin in 1826. He may have been the pupil of Richard Tutin, a builder-turned-architect who was apparently a relative of Martha. In 1829 Thomas entered into partnership with him, but it was probably dissolved the following year. In 1832 Thomas moved to nearby Leamington, a flourishing watering-place in Warwickshire. Here he had a varied career: initially serving as agent for a developer, he promoted and executed his own building speculation schemes and designed numerous buildings for clients. The failure of a local bank in 1837 may have obliged him to apply for the office of town surveyor – he was acting surveyor in 1838–39 – and undoubtedly precipitated his bankruptcy in 1840, along with those of most of the other building speculators in Leamington. Thomas had opened a branch-office in Birmingham, but there were few architectural commissions available because of widespread depression in the early 1840s.

Thomas's architectural work in England comprises designs for a remarkable range of structures, including houses, churches, shops, a conservatory, a public bath complex, and iron and stone bridges. The bulk of his work, however, consisted chiefly of speculative housing for the middle class in Leamington. He is known to have designed town houses on Beauchamp Terrace, beginning in 1831, and two chapels in 1834. Two impressive housing complexes followed the next year: Lansdowne Circus, a horseshoe-shaped grouping of plain Georgian-style semi-detached houses and villas (most with decorative cast-iron porches and balconies under tent-shaped roofs), and adjacent Lansdowne Crescent, a curving terrace of connected and landscaped town houses executed in a fully elaborated classical style. For Lansdowne Crescent, Thomas had acquired the property in partnership, furnished the designs, and developed some parcels with covenants requiring conformity in the design of façades. In a somewhat similar vein he was responsible for the development on Brandon Parade and Holly Walk (which adjoined both the crescent and the circus) of about ten villas, in a mixture of Grecian and Gothic Revival designs. Before his bankruptcy Thomas lived in one of these villas, Elizabethan Place, which is conspicuously dated 1836 and signed "WT." A combination of small volumes balanced in effective groupings with ornamental flourishes at the edges is characteristic of the mature Thomas. Victoria Terrace, Pump Room and Baths, a multipurpose building begun in Leamington in 1837, formed a major focus of the town and was his grandest work in England.

In Duddeston (Birmingham) he erected St Matthew's Church (Anglican) in 1839–40. This rectangular brick building, executed in a mixture of Early English and Decorated Gothic Revival styles with a projecting three-storey tower at the west end, would be used by Thomas as a basis in developing many of his Canadian churches. In the same years he was also responsible for a palatial draper's shop in Birmingham called Warwick House. A water-colour by Thomas of this highly ornamented block, which was bombed in World War II, shows a four-storey building of seven bays, with immense display windows set between graceful piers opening up the ground floor, while the second and third floors are set off by colossal columns and the fourth floor is richly treated as an attic. This was a successful formula for commercial structures and would be used for one of Thomas's best-known works in Canada. In essence, Thomas's career up to this point forms a modest and provincial parallel, in its range of activity, styles, and enterprise, to that of John Nash, the fashionable architect who had done so much to reshape London in the first quarter of the 19th century.

In December 1842 Thomas sent to press a slim book entitled *Designs for monuments and chimney pieces*, a discreet piece of self-advertisement which was published in London the following year. Consisting of 41 lithographed plates with 46 Grecian, Roman, Gothic and Elizabethan patterns, the book is indicative of the eclectic approach to architectural design prevalent during the late Georgian and early Victorian periods. Like most other designers, Thomas felt free to choose historical revival styles that were deemed fitting to the location and function of a work. His churches, for example, were generally designed in the Gothic style, which readily identified their religious function and association with the devout Christian beliefs of the Middle Ages.

In April 1843 Thomas left England for Toronto. Precisely what prompted him, in his early 40s, to emigrate with his wife and eight children or to choose Toronto for his new home is unknown. His forced bankruptcy three years earlier and the dearth of work must have been contributing causes, but the key factor was probably his ambition. Toronto, which was entering a boom period with a population of more than 15,000 but with only three practising architects, was an appealing location for an industrious architect. Thomas's journal of his transatlantic crossing in 1843 reveals an acute and well-informed observer. He emerges from the journal as a patient and loving father, a warm and sympathetic man. Possessed of a considerable sense of humour, he was very sociable as well and enjoyed chess, card-playing, conversation, singing, and dancing. Thomas settled with his family at 5 York Street and opened an office at 55 King Street East, in the city's main commercial district. His first major commission in Toronto seems to have been the Commercial Bank of the Midland District on Wellington Street. Designed in 1844 and built a year later, it was one of the earliest banks fashioned in the Greek Revival mode in British North America and its façade remains one of the best examples of that style in the city. The only other bank known to have been designed by Thomas, the Bank of British North America, Hamilton (1847–49), has been demolished.

It was, however, his churches that brought early acclaim. Reputedly there were eventually more than 30 of these, 12 in Toronto alone. The first, St Paul's Church (Anglican) in London, was erected in 1844–46 of red brick (with a white-brick front) in the Decorated Gothic style. Described by William Henry Smith* in the year of its completion as "the handsomest gothic church in Canada West," it was elevated to cathedral status in 1857 [*see* Benjamin Cronyn*] and extended in the 1890s by means of transepts.

Before St Paul's was completed, Thomas com-

Thomas

menced his most ambitious ecclesiastical work and the largest church in Toronto at the time, St Michael's Cathedral (Roman Catholic), which was constructed in 1845–48 of the then-fashionable white brick. Extending from Bond to Church streets on the north side of Shuter, its long flank commanded McGill Square before that area was built over. St Michael's too was designed in the Decorated Gothic style, but on a cruciform plan, and it was both more substantial and more ornamental in character than St Paul's. The congregation could not immediately afford Thomas's tower and spire; these and the dormers were later added by the firm of Thomas Gundry and Henry Langley*. A palace for Bishop Michael Power* was also designed by Thomas, in the Tudor Revival style, and was erected in 1845 on Church Street just north of the cathedral.

Thomas was especially favoured by Presbyterian congregations, particularly those created as a result of the disruption of 1844 [see Robert Burns*]. In Toronto alone he designed Knox's Church (Free Presbyterian), Queen Street (1847–48), a church for the United Presbyterian congregation of the Reverend John Jennings*, Bay Street (1848), and Cooke's Church (Free Presbyterian), Queen Street (1857–58). But he worked for many other denominations in the city, designing the Methodist New Connexion Church, Temperance Street (1846), the Unitarian Church, Jarvis Street (1854), Zion Church (Congregational), Bay and Adelaide streets (1855–56), and the German Evangelical Lutheran Church, Bond Street (1856–57). All have been torn down or replaced.

Although Thomas was unsuccessful in the 1849 competition for the Church of England cathedral in Toronto, he received commissions in 1851–52 from Anglican congregations in Guelph and Hamilton which resulted in churches of considerable significance. St George's Church in Guelph, begun in 1851, was not only one of the first churches executed in the Romanesque Revival style in British North America but was also one of the first based on an asymmetrical plan. Three bays, including a corner tower forming a porch on the axis of Wyndham Street, were added in stone to an existing wooden church. Designs drafted by Thomas in 1856 for the rest of the church and for an elegant interior were not implemented and the church was later demolished. In Hamilton, where he had opened an office by 1849, possibly in the care of his son William Tutin, Thomas began work on Christ's Church (now the Anglican cathedral) in 1852. This was his most adventurous work structurally, calling for a stone building on a basilican plan, with a tall nave carried on piers, a decoratively treated open wooden roof, clerestory lighting, flanking aisles, and a short but distinct chancel. These features suggest that the design was an early instance in this province of the ritualistic neo-medievalism advocated in architectural

design by the Ecclesiological Society in England, though Thomas was by no means doctrinaire in his designs for churches. Only the chancel and two bays of Christ's Church were built, as tall additions to Robert Charles Wetherell's neoclassical wooden church of 1842, and the disjointed effect gave rise to the name "the hump-backed church." In 1873–77 it was completed. Simpler churches were well within Thomas's capability and at least three still stand: St George's-on-the-Hill Church (Anglican) of 1847 in Etobicoke (Toronto), the Free Presbyterian Church (now Grace United) of 1852 in Niagara (Niagara-on-the-Lake), and MacNab Street Church (Presbyterian) of 1856 in Hamilton. Of these, the Niagara church is particularly appealing. Executed in a predominantly Romanesque mode, it features chunky corbel tables and pilaster strips which look less skimped than those in his conventional Gothic designs.

Thomas's design for another Presbyterian church in Hamilton, the well-preserved St Andrew's (renamed St Paul's in 1874), was his most successful composition. It was begun in 1854 on a large budget, which encouraged a rich treatment in stone and an elaborate interior. The tower is bold and massive, with deep angle buttresses and dense carving in areas such as the entrance and the gables. The octagonal spire is apparently the only stone spire erected in Ontario. The interior is equally striking in the richness of its sombre decoration, carved in dark wood. Although the cost proved ruinous for its congregation, the church has been consistently admired: in 1901 the *Canadian Architect and Builder* regarded it as still "well worth the study of architects" because "the construction is genuine" and "an essential part of the aim was honest work."

Thomas was busy almost continuously designing a succession of significant public buildings for centres throughout British North America. These include the Fireman's Hall and Mechanics' Institute building, Toronto (1845), the combined district court-house, town hall, and market, Niagara (1846–48), the Talbot District Jail, Simcoe (1847–48), the House of Industry, Toronto (1848), the Kent County Court-House, Chatham (1848–49), the St Lawrence Hall, Arcade, and Market building, Toronto (1849–51), the town hall and market-house, Peterborough (1851), the town hall and market, Guelph (1856–57), the custom-house, Quebec (1856–60), the town hall and market-house, Stratford (1857), the city jail (now known as the Don Jail), Toronto (1859–64), and the Halifax County Court-House, Halifax (1858–62). All survive except those in Peterborough and Stratford, and the Fireman's Hall and Mechanics' Institute building in Toronto. Most of these commissions were won in competition and follow a common formula in their design: a long symmetrical front, with a projecting frontispiece under a pediment, often with colossal orders, seated on a heavy base. Not all of Thomas's competition designs were successful. In 1859, for example, he was an unsuccessful entrant in the contest for the parliament buildings in Ottawa.

The best known of Thomas's public structures is undoubtedly St Lawrence Hall in Toronto which, with its original arcade and market, comprised the St Lawrence Buildings. An earlier town hall and market on the site, designed by Henry Bowyer Joseph LANE, were destroyed in the fire of 1849 and Thomas immediately received the commission for their replacements, his design closely following his successful (but unexecuted) competition design of 1845 for refronting the earlier buildings. The St Lawrence Buildings were I-shaped, with the hall fronting on King Street, the market on Front Street, and the 200-foot arcade between the two. The hall contained shops on the ground floor, committee rooms on the second, and an assembly room on the third, the latter offering a more dignified space for concerts, balls, lectures, and the like than those provided by local hotels or the earlier town hall and market. An enlarged and more controlled version of Thomas's Warwick House (executed in Birmingham nearly a decade earlier), St Lawrence Hall is his most graceful exercise in classical design. The market and arcade have been replaced, but the hall has been refurbished and remains an important civic focus.

Thomas's earlier public buildings at Niagara and Chatham are both Late Georgian in style and nearly as restrained as St Lawrence Hall, but most of his other public works were designed in a forceful Victorian version of the Renaissance Revival style. There is a deliberate crudity of scale and texture in these visually powerful buildings which reflects their association with the law, public administration, and commerce. They are characterized by blocky masses, rugged surfaces, and abrupt transitions. The Halifax County Court-House best displays these characteristics in Thomas's later public buildings. The dominant feature of this sandstone structure is its heavily textured frontispiece with bands of contrasting stone at every level up to the stout brackets that support the simple pediment. The three splendid keystones, which are carved in the form of sombre bearded heads and alternate with lion's-head medallions, are hallmarks of Thomas's last, and most vigorous, architectural phase.

His civic architecture also included public schools, which were just beginning to be designed in Canada as architecturally distinctive institutions. His Union School in London (1849), described two years later in a government report as "by far the finest school house in the Province," was followed by designs for two schools in Toronto. In 1851 the city's first elected school-board, under the chairmanship of Dr Joseph Workman*, launched a school-design competition.

Thomas's plan was used in 1852–53 for the Park and Louisa Street schools. These were designed in the Tudor style, which was popular for institutional buildings because it afforded ample lighting and ventilation as well as an interesting silhouette, all within a reasonable budget. All three schools have been demolished. In 1853 Thomas received the commission for the combined county grammar and common schools in Goderich.

The columnar monument to Sir Isaac Brock* on Queenston Heights (1853–56) is arguably Thomas's most florid composition. It is 185 feet tall, rising from a richly trophied base guarded by carved lions. A colossal statue of Brock stands on a lavish capital, designed by Thomas himself rather than drawn from the classical orders. Gates, a lodge, and steps, all completed in 1859, frame the monument in scenographic fashion. Thomas displayed a stone model of it at the universal exposition in Paris in 1855.

His English work had consisted largely of housing and numerous Canadian examples can be identified. In Toronto, a handsome row of houses called Wellington Terrace, built on Wellington Street in 1847, has been demolished, but three units of another group, built in 1848, survive on Church Street behind St Michael's Cathedral. In Hamilton, Thomas's firm was said by the *Halifax Reporter* in 1860 to be responsible for "the greater number of the very beautiful private residences that meet the eye in every direction." Surviving work there attributed to Thomas includes Undermount (on John Street), designed for John Young* in the Italianate style in 1847, and two Gothic villas: the Presbyterian manse (at Herkimer and Park streets), completed in 1854, and Inglewood (on Inglewood Drive), built for Archibald Kerr about the same date. Thomas's Wilderness House (1848–51), built for Aeneas Kennedy, was destroyed in 1853. Thomas also designed a villa in London for Lawrence Lawrason*. His own Toronto residence, Oakham House (1848), a Gothic composition on Church Street, stands but has been gutted and additions replace his office wing on Gould Street; his 1859 Italianate home on Mutual Street has been destroyed. He is also known to have built houses in Toronto for at least six prominent businessmen, including John McMurrich*. Among Thomas's last known residential works was the house, which still stands, built in St Catharines in 1859–60 for William Hamilton Merritt*.

Mixed commercial and residential buildings by Thomas were surely numerous too. The first of these was probably the Adelaide Buildings on Yonge Street (1844), which were altered in 1853 and subsequently torn down. In 1846 William Henry Smith described some stores designed by him and under construction on King Street, Toronto, as "the handsomest buildings of the kind in Canada, and equal to anything to be seen

Thomas

in England." Although some of the stores were damaged in the fire of 1849 and others were demolished later, several still survive, now generally altered. More stylish were two Italianate works, both large-scale dry-goods businesses: the 1847 store (named the Golden Lion in 1849) of Robert Walker and Thomas Hutchinson on King Street and the premises of Ross, Mitchell and Company, built at Yonge and Colborne streets about 1856. Both have been demolished. In a period of vigorous economic growth in Canada, at least three other Toronto firms, including Bryce, McMurrich and Company, commissioned buildings from Thomas, who also designed stores in Port Hope and Hamilton.

Thomas formally took two of his sons, William Tutin and Cyrus Pole, both of whom he had trained, into his flourishing business in January 1857 and the firm became William Thomas and Sons. It was shortly to expand again. Thomas's design for Knox's Church in Toronto had so impressed visiting members of St Matthew's Church (Presbyterian) in Halifax that, when it was destroyed by fire in 1857, his firm was asked to design its replacement, which was built on Barrington Street in 1858–59 and still stands. This project brought the Thomas firm to Halifax, where Cyrus opened an office in 1858. The firm's successful entry that year in the county court-house competition no doubt led to commissions after the fire of 1859 for rebuilding much of the commercial section at the north end of Granville Street [see George Lang*]. At least 12 four-storey buildings, more than half of the new construction, were designed by the firm and nearly all were completed by the end of 1860. The group is remarkable not only for the number and variety of the commissions (executed simultaneously for no less than eight different clients) but for the impact of the resulting streetscape, which survives. Contiguous properties called the Palace Buildings were handled uniformly as the largest single design. Unity of effect elsewhere in the group was achieved through the use of stone (from different Nova Scotian quarries), elevations of related height, and recurring rhythms. All but one building had decorative cast-iron shop-fronts, which are important as early examples of this type of construction in British North America. Cyrus Pole Thomas visited Daniel D. Badger's Architectural Iron Works in New York in 1860 to arrange for the shop-fronts and internal detailing, some of which were later reproduced in Badger's lavish publication, *Illustrations of iron architecture*.

Thomas had risen quickly in Canada and had made a number of connections in the Toronto community and elsewhere. Concerned for the public enjoyment of the arts, he was probably instrumental in establishing the Toronto Society of Arts in 1847; he was elected its first president and showed his architectural drawings at the society's exhibitions of 1847 and 1848. He maintained limited contact with English architecture through the publications that he bought and the visit he paid in 1851 to the Great Exhibition in London, where his brother John exhibited sculpture. When John George Howard made a trip to England in 1853, Thomas served as city engineer in his stead and was appointed to superintend the work on Toronto's Esplanade. He also trained architects of the next generation, including, in addition to his sons, William George Storm*, who became a leading architect in Toronto, first in partnership with Frederic William Cumberland and then on his own.

The role played latterly by the sons in Thomas's business is difficult to determine. The later work of William Tutin, who moved to Montreal about 1863, is both more assured and more flamboyant than that of his father; Cyrus, who worked in Montreal before settling in Chicago, claimed credit for the firm's Haligonian work. It is reasonable, however, to assume a division of labour in William Thomas's last years. He suffered "long and continued illness," necessitating a journey to England in 1858. The financial burden of illness and treatment is reflected in the firm's extra efforts to collect new commissions and overdue payments. There was ever-increasing competition for architectural work: by 1859 there were 16 architects in Toronto, many of them well trained in the latest developments in style and construction. Thomas's seniority was nevertheless recognized and he was elected president in 1860 of the Association of Architects, Civil Engineers and Provincial Land Surveyors of the Province of Canada, which had been established the previous year.

William Thomas died on 26 Dec. 1860 of diabetes, according to cemetery records. Survived by his wife and six of their ten children, he was buried in the family's plot at St James' Cemetery beneath the handsome Grecian tombstone which he no doubt had designed. Although his obituary in the *Globe* commented conventionally that he would be remembered for "his kindly social qualities which endeared him to a numerous circle of friends," the statement rings true. A portrait, a bust, and a photograph all show an engaging figure. Moreover, maintaining a successful practice required a diplomatic touch in an era when, increasingly, important commissions were for public buildings, which entailed intense professional competition and often difficult negotiations with building committees.

A combination of experience, ambition, and personality made him a leading architect, with the largest architectural practice in British North America. He apparently prided himself on his ability to design substantial structures which could be built at reasonable cost. When Upper Canada was experiencing a great wave of prosperity, Thomas and a handful of other architects, including William Hay* and Kivas

876

Tully*, were able to design major buildings for the fast-growing communities: churches to express their faith, civic structures to display their pride and their optimism about the future, and commercial buildings and residences to reveal their growing wealth.

Thomas was the versatile architect who, in the manner of his period, worked in various styles, some of which he rendered in a fashion that can be clearly identified as his. The prevailing aesthetic of the picturesque movement was especially important to him, with its emphasis on variety and richness of visual effect. But deeply rooted in his work too was the older Georgian tradition of compactness, balance, and regularity. Such conservatism of style is not surprising in one who immigrated to the colony in mid life and whose contact with professional developments in Britain was limited to rare return visits and the receipt of publications. What is all the more remarkable, in contrast to other designers of the same generation working in British North America, is Thomas's professional maturation and independence which was demonstrated, in the work he produced in his last decade, by his new-found confidence in large works, his use of cast-iron, and his own form of the Italianate style. But although he continued to develop, the financial constraints imposed by some clients, a limited range of materials, and a shortage of skilled workmen must have contributed to a certain severity that is also noticeable in his architecture.

It was no mean achievement to have made a major contribution to Leamington's residential street-scape; subsequently Thomas reshaped the skyline of Canadian cities from Halifax to London with a series of churches and public buildings. George P. Ure, in his *Hand-book of Toronto*, claimed that "his high professional talent and correct taste have tended greatly to the embellishment and improvement" of Toronto, above all. Thomas's obituary in the *Globe* concurred: "To him we owe some of the most tasteful buildings of which our city can boast." His contributions to the development of architecture as well as the scope and quality of his work substantiate Thomas Ritchie's claim that William Thomas was "one of the founders of the Canadian architectural profession."

NEIL EINARSON

The projects for which drawings and plans by Thomas survive include: proposed customs house, Toronto (PAC, RG 11, A1, 5, no.7353); Niagara court-house, town hall, and market building (AO, Picture coll., D 1572–75, and MS 542 (William Kirby coll.), E-35); waterfront and esplanade, Toronto, 1853 (AO, J. C. B. and E. O. Horwood coll. (uncatalogued)); Don Jail, Toronto, 1857 (CTA, CRC 606, 1888); house designs for Henry John Boulton*, 1856 (Univ. of Toronto, Thomas Fisher Rare Books Library, MS coll. 25 (William Tyrrell papers), architectural plans); alterations to Toronto city hall, 1851 (MTL, J. G.

Howard papers, sect.III, architectural plans, nos.416–17); St George's Church, Guelph, Ont. (MTL, Henry Langley papers, architectural plans, nos.191–96); and enlargement of Knox College, Toronto, 1856 (MTL, W. H. Pim papers). In England, the Warwickshire County Record Office (Warwick) and the Birmingham City Museums and Art Gallery hold drawings of some of Thomas's buildings there. Illustrations of other Canadian and English projects are mentioned in the catalogues of the Toronto Soc. of Arts, *Toronto Society of Arts: first exhibition, 1847 . . .* ([Toronto?, 1847?]), nos.140, 154, 170, 173, 294, 297, 305, and *second exhibition, 1848 . . .* ([Toronto?, 1848?]), nos.101, 120, 124–25, 127. Published examples of Thomas's work can be found in his *Designs for monuments and chimney pieces* (London, 1843).

An oil portrait of Thomas is held at the MTL.

AO, MS 74, Thomas to W. H. Merritt, 15 Sept. 1859; MU 296; RG 22, ser.302, William Thomas. CTA, RG 1, A, 1844, 1846, 1849–50, 1855; B, 1849. HPL, St Andrew's–St Paul's (Presbyterian) Church file. PAC, RG 11, A3, 129, no.22949. PANS, MG 4, St Matthew's Presbyterian Church (Halifax), minutes, 1857–60; MG 100, 104, nos.23, 230–36. St James' Cemetery and Crematorium (Toronto), Record of burials. St Michael's Cathedral Arch. (Toronto), William Thomas, receipt, 16 July 1845; Charbonnel to Thomas, 18 Feb. 1859. Toronto Board of Education Records and Arch. Centre, Public school board minutes, 1850–54: 146, 151–52, 158–59, 181, 183, 187, 189, 209, 220. *The battle of Queenston Heights: being a narrative of the opening of the War of 1812, with notices of the life of Major-General Sir Isaac Brock, K.B., and description of the monument erected in his memory*, ed. John Symons (Toronto, 1859). Can., Parl., *Sessional papers*, 1867–68, no.8: 259–60. Can., Prov. of, Executive Committee for the Paris Exhibition, 1855, *Canada at the Universal Exhibition of 1855* (Toronto, 1856), 35; Legislative Assembly, *App. to the journals*, 1851, app.KK, "Town of London." "Description of the new buildings on Granville Street," *Halifax Reporter*, 1 Nov. 1860. "Inauguration of Sir Isaac Brock's monument at Queenston," *Journal of Education for Upper Canada* (Toronto), 12 (1859): 162. [C. P. Mulvany], "County and town of Peterborough," *History of the county of Peterborough, Ontario . . .* (Toronto, 1884), 215–372. *Report of the past history, and present condition, of the common or public schools of the city of Toronto* (Toronto, 1859), 45. W. H. Smith, *Canada: past, present and future*, 1: 31. *Topographical plan of the city of Toronto, in the province of Canada*, comp. Sandford Fleming (Toronto, 1851).

Acadian Recorder, 26 Aug. 1858. *Banner* (Toronto), 7 Aug. 1846. *British Colonist* (Halifax), 1 Sept. 1857; 25 Oct., 29 Nov., 1, 10 Dec. 1859; 12 Jan. 1860. *British Colonist* (Toronto), 11 Feb., 29 Aug., 2 Sept. 1845; 29 Oct. 1847. *Canadian Free Press* (London, [Ont.]), 10 April 1849. *Chatham Gleaner* (Chatham, [Ont.]), 26 Dec. 1848. *Globe*, 27 Dec. 1860. *Gloucester Journal* (Gloucester, Eng.), 12 Jan. 1861. *Illustrated London News*, 27 June 1847, 30 Aug. 1862. *Novascotian*, 20 June 1859. *Royal Leamington Spa Courier* (Leamington, Eng.), 12 Jan. 1861. *Times and Commercial General Advertiser* (London, [Ont.]), 27 Feb. 1846. *Weekly Despatch* (Peterborough, [Ont.]), 2, 9 Jan. 1851. W. H. Smith, *Smith's Canadian gazetteer; comprising statistical and general information respecting all parts of the upper province, or Canada West . . .* (Toronto, 1846;

Thompson

repr. 1970), 100, 194. Alfred Sylvester, *Sketches of Toronto, comprising a complete and accurate description of the principal points of interest in the city, its public buildings* ... (Toronto, 1858), 70. *Toronto directory*, 1846–47, 1856, 1859–60. [G. P. Ure], *The hand-book of Toronto; containing its climate, geology, natural history, educational institutions, courts of law, municipal arrangements, &c. &c., by a member of the press* (Toronto, 1858), 238, 251–55.

Eric Arthur, *Toronto, no mean city* ([Toronto], 1964). D. D. Badger, *Illustrations of iron architecture, made by the Architectural Iron Works of the city of New York* (New York, 1865); repr. in *The origins of cast iron architecture in America*, ed. W. K. Sturges (New York, 1970). W. E. Barnett *et al.*, *St Lawrence Hall* (Toronto, 1969). Janet Carnochan, *History of Niagara* ... (Toronto, 1914; repr. Belleville, Ont., 1973), 212. *Concerning the Saint Paul's Presbyterian Church and congregation, Hamilton, Ontario, 1854–1904* (Hamilton, 1904). N. G. Einarson, "William Thomas (1799–1860), of Birmingham, Leamington Spa and Toronto" (M.PHIL. thesis, Univ. of Essex, Colchester, Eng., 1981). Katharine Greenfield, *The pilgrim's guide to Christ Church Cathedral* ([Hamilton, Ont., 1963?]; copy at HPL). Heritage Trust of N.S., *A sense of place: Granville Street, Halifax, Nova Scotia* (Halifax, 1970). Johnson, *Hist. of Guelph*. Marion MacRae and Anthony Adamson, *The ancestral roof: domestic architecture of Upper Canada* (Toronto and Vancouver, 1963); *Cornerstones of order*. MacRae *et al.*, *Hallowed walls. Robertson's landmarks of Toronto*, 4: 215, 311. *Toronto in the camera; a series of photographic views of the principal buildings in the city of Toronto* (Toronto, 1868), 4, 15, 22–24. "Association of Architects, Civil Engineers and P.L. Surveyors of the Province of Canada," Board of Arts and Manufactures for Upper Canada, *Journal* (Toronto), 1 (1861): 14, 130–31. Thomas Ritchie, "The architecture of William Thomas," *Architecture Canada* (Toronto), 44 (1967), no.5: 41–45. "St. Paul's Church, Hamilton, Ont.," *Canadian Architect and Builder* (Toronto), 14 (1901): 27–28. Kivas Tully, "Architectural history of Toronto," Toronto Architectural Eighteen Club, *Catalogue* (Toronto), 1 (1901): 10.

THOMPSON, DAVID, fur trader, explorer, surveyor, justice of the peace, businessman, and author; b. 30 April 1770 in the parish of St John the Evangelist, Westminster (London), son of David and Ann Thompson; d. 10 Feb. 1857 in Longueuil, Lower Canada.

David Thompson's origins were humble, his final years spent in poverty. Yet, as an explorer and surveyor, his work has earned him a reputation as one of the best pioneering geographers in North America. His parents had only recently migrated from Wales to London when he was born and less than two years later his father died, leaving David, his mother, and a younger brother, John, in financial difficulty. At age seven Thompson was admitted to the Grey Coat Hospital, a charity school established to provide a moral and practical education to the poor children of Westminster, and, once accepted, he appears to have maintained little direct contact with his family. He was subsequently enrolled in the Grey Coat mathematical school, where he received a rudimentary training in navigation, and on 20 May 1784 he was apprenticed to the Hudson's Bay Company for seven years.

Thompson's first year with the HBC was spent under Samuel Hearne* at Fort Churchill (Churchill, Man.), the company's most northerly post on the western shore of Hudson Bay. Thompson remembered the year as one spent in little productive activity, yet his experience copying parts of the manuscript of Hearne's *A journey from Prince of Wales's Fort* must have stirred his imagination and sense of adventure. In the fall of 1785 the London committee of the HBC ordered Thompson down to York Factory and he made the 150-mile trip south on foot with two Indians, living off the land. At York, despite orders from London that he be "kept from the common men and employed in the writings, accounts and warehouse duty," Thompson spent at least part of the winter at hunting camps with the labouring servants. This was a practical experience that offered a welcome break from his clerical duties assisting the irascible chief at York, Humphrey Marten*, or the newly appointed writer and accountant, Joseph Colen*.

Thompson was sent inland in the summer of 1786, and in September he left Cumberland House (Sask.) with Mitchell Oman, an able but illiterate Orkneyman, and 13 others to establish South Branch House (near Batoche) on the South Saskatchewan River. At Cumberland House the following summer he appears to have perfected a working knowledge of the Cree language, an essential skill for a prospective fur trader in that region. The chief at this post was George Hudson, a former Grey Coat Hospital boy and apprentice whose moral and physical deterioration served Thompson as a lasting object-lesson on the dangers of long isolation. During that summer Thompson also underwent a religious experience which he described as a game of draughts with the devil. The experience had a strong influence on his conduct for the rest of his life and confirmed him in his abstemious habits and pious beliefs.

Thompson remained inland in 1787 and 1788, serving under William Tomison* at Manchester House (near Standard Hill) and James Tate at Hudson House (near Brightholme). He passed the winter of 1787–88 with Peigan Indians in the Rocky Mountain foothills and learned their language. Back at Manchester House in the fall of 1788, he seriously fractured his right leg on 23 December in a sled accident. Severe swelling made it impossible for the leg to be set properly, so it healed slowly despite the best care that Tomison, who had taken a paternal interest in Thompson, could provide for his young protégé. In the spring he was carried down to Cumberland House where he was gradually nursed back to health. By the end of the summer of 1789 he had regained enough strength to move around with the help of crutches, although he was not ready to withstand the voyage back up the river and was left to spend the winter at Cumberland House.

This proved to be a major turning-point in Thompson's life. In early October, soon after the canoes had proceeded upriver, Malchom Ross*, master at Cumberland, and Thompson were joined by the surveying party under Philip Turnor*, who was being sent into the Athabasca country. Both Thompson and Peter Fidler* studied mathematics, surveying, and astronomy with Turnor during the winter of 1789–90. By the spring Thompson had not yet recovered his strength and, to make matters worse, he had lost the sight in his right eye. As a consequence he was not considered by Turnor for the expedition to Lake Athabasca. Instead, Fidler and Ross were chosen to complete the party. Thompson was sent down to York Factory to finish his apprenticeship under the direction of Colen, who had replaced Marten as resident chief there. Turnor's choice appears to have been a severe blow to Thompson's youthful pride and he never fully forgave Ross or Fidler for being selected in his place.

To his credit, Thompson was determined that his training under Turnor should not be wasted. His interest in surveying and astronomy had been thoroughly aroused. On 30 Aug. 1790, shortly after his arrival at Hudson Bay, he wrote to the secretary of the company in London offering to make observations along the coast and requesting a sextant, parallel glasses, and nautical almanacs in lieu of the suit of clothes normally presented to an apprentice on the completion of his indentured term of service. Over the next year, when not busy with his duties as clerk or writer, Thompson carefully worked up the survey observations he had made while travelling from Cumberland House to York Factory and he submitted them to the London committee with a further request to be sent on surveys. Thompson's letters were well received. Upon completion of his apprenticeship he was formally offered the usual first contract as a writer for three years at £15 a year, and in a series of private letters he was encouraged to pursue his interest in surveying. Furthermore, his request for surveying instruments was granted. He therefore had every reason to hope that he would soon be recognized as surveyor for the company and he probably contemplated replacing Turnor in that position. It was not a vain hope. In the fall of 1792 he was instructed by Colen to follow up on Turnor's work in the Athabasca with a survey of the waterways through the Muskrat country between the Nelson and Churchill rivers. This survey was to provide information about communications in the area, a new arena of competition between the HBC and the North West Company, and about the

rivers flowing through it, which were believed to provide a more direct route to Lake Athabasca by way of Reindeer Lake.

After wintering at a post he built on Sipiwesk Lake (Man.), Thompson surveyed a route to the Churchill by way of Burntwood River, noting the locations of wintering posts of both companies. Unable to proceed to Reindeer Lake without a proper guide, he returned to York Factory. The London committee had been convinced by Turnor of the importance of establishing posts in the Athabasca country to compete effectively with the Nor'westers and in May 1793 it sent instructions to Ross to conduct an expedition into that region. The route Thompson had partially explored was circuitous and still unproven so Colen decided that the planned expedition should use the NWC route from Cumberland House to Île-à-la-Crosse (Sask.) and the Methy Portage (Portage La Loche). Since it was too late to begin the expedition when the committee's instructions arrived, Ross passed the winter of 1793–94 at Cumberland House preparing for a start in the spring. Thompson was sent up the Saskatchewan. He arrived at Manchester House on 28 October, a few days after it had been sacked by a band of Fall (Gros Ventre) Indians, and he rode directly on to Buckingham House (near Lindbergh, Alta). Any plans for exploration that winter appear to have been abandoned because of the unsettled relations with the Indians. He spent the winter at Buckingham House and in the spring of 1794 returned to Cumberland House, surveying those portions of the North Saskatchewan River not already mapped.

Ross and Thompson, who was to accompany Ross as his assistant, were forced to abandon their plans to proceed from Cumberland House to Lake Athabasca when the canoemen refused to proceed on the expedition without new contracts at a higher rate of pay. Tomison, now inland chief, would not promise the higher rates, arguing that he did not have authorization from London to do so, but Colen and most of the other HBC officers believed that Tomison was opposed to the project out of fear that it would weaken his position. Convinced that Tomison would never willingly support an expedition from Cumberland House, Thompson and Ross decided to pursue the alternate route through Reindeer Lake. Accordingly, in June they headed off with the few servants specifically assigned to them over Cranberry Portage (Man.) and on to Reed Lake, where Ross settled down for the summer. Thompson continued northeastward to York Factory to obtain the additional men and supplies needed for the expedition. There he was delayed 21 days by the late arrival of the supply ship, and, by the time he arrived back at Reed Lake on 2 September, it was too late in the year to proceed any farther.

In the spring of 1795 Thompson, armed with the

Thompson

knowledge that he had been appointed HBC surveyor at the handsome salary of £60 a year in May 1794, returned with Ross to York for men and supplies. At last it seemed as if the long-delayed Athabasca expedition would get off the ground. Starting up the Nelson on 18 July, they were only able to reach the Churchill River before they had to set up quarters for the winter: Thompson at Duck Portage (Sask.) on Sisipuk Lake, and Ross at Fairford House near the mouth of the Reindeer River. Finally, in 1796, while Ross went down to the bay for a new outfit of supplies, Thompson dashed north from Fairford House with two young Chipewyan guides and reached the east end of Lake Athabasca. The six-week return trip was accomplished under difficult and sometimes hazardous conditions. The route surveyed, however, proved to be a major disappointment; barely passable in the early summer with a small canoe, it was impassable when Thompson and Ross attempted to reach Lake Athabasca in September with three large canoes loaded with trade goods. As a consequence, they were forced to spend an unproductive and uncomfortable winter at Bedford House, a post they built on the west side of Reindeer Lake.

By spring Thompson had arrived at his momentous decision to leave the HBC for the NWC, and on 23 May 1797 he set out from Bedford House to walk to Alexander Fraser*'s post on the Reindeer River. Both the morality of this action and the reasons for it have been the occasion for some controversy. Thompson has been justly criticized for leaving without giving the year's notice required both by his contract and by courtesy to his employers, who would have been left without anyone to replace him if Ross had not agreed to postpone his planned retirement. Thompson's later claim that he left because he was ordered to cease his work as a surveyor cannot be substantiated, but one can understand how he might have come to that conclusion. In the summer of 1796 he had been nominated to replace Ross as "Master to the Northward" and in that position his primary responsibility would have been the management of a successful fur trade. His motives for going to the NWC were probably not financial because his recent promotion within the HBC would have placed him in a position to earn substantial bonuses and would have facilitated further advancement. That he harboured personal grievances against his employers and superiors is clear from letters he wrote soon after arriving at Fraser's post, but in balance they appear insufficient in themselves to motivate such a decision. They may, however, have been necessary from a psychological perspective to give Thompson the moral sanction he needed for the break he was making from close and long-standing personal ties with the company that had been like a family to him.

Thompson now began 15 years of productive work

with the NWC. In 1797 the as yet unresolved question of the boundary between British and American territory west of Lake of the Woods, underlined by the terms of Jay's Treaty in 1794, was cause for concern among the NWC partners and, at the meeting of agents and winterers at Grand Portage (near Grand Portage, Minn.) that summer, Thompson was instructed to make a survey westward along the 49th parallel, considered the most likely boundary, and to chart the position of NWC posts. He worked at a hectic pace, completing in 10 months an exploratory survey of the major rivers and lakes from Lake Superior to Lake Winnipeg and on to the Swan River valley, then south along the Assiniboine and Souris rivers and overland to the Mandan villages on the Missouri River, back to the Assiniboine and up the Red River, across to the headwaters of the Mississippi, then over the divide to Lake Superior by way of Fond du Lac House, and finally along the south shore of Superior to Sault Ste Marie and back to Grand Portage. His conclusion that the Mississippi had its source in Turtle Lake (Minn.) was but a few miles off and his observations constituted by far the most accurate information on the headwaters of the river gathered to that date.

The amount of work Thompson had accomplished in one year was prodigious, and had been possible only because he had been relieved of other duties and given all the logistical support he required – a marked contrast to his experience in the HBC. The methods he employed were those he had learned with the HBC and his observations were taken with the instruments he had received while an employee of that company. The maps he later compiled were based on a series of fixed points, usually trading posts, located by means of astronomical observations for latitude and longitude. Waterways and other natural features between these key points were traced according to rough observations of the routes he followed. His calculations of latitude and longitude were usually fairly accurate, given his equipment and methods, and are a tribute to his care and diligence in taking multiple observations whenever possible. Direction of travel was established by compass and distances were usually estimated on the basis of elapsed time; these observations, especially his estimates of distance, show considerable inconsistency. His visual perception of distance was undoubtedly affected by his partial blindness.

In 1798 Thompson travelled through the English (upper Churchill) River department up the Beaver River (Sask.) to Red Deers Lake (Lac la Biche, Alta), where he established a trading post and spent the winter. In early spring he travelled overland to Fort Augustus (Fort Saskatchewan) and from there he investigated a new route from the North Saskatchewan River to the upper part of the Athabasca River by way of Lac la Nonne and the Pembina River. He then followed the Athabasca River to the Clearwater River (Sask.), from which point he took the usual route over Methy Portage down to Grand Portage. On the way he stopped at Île-à-la-Crosse where on 10 June 1799 he married, according to the custom of the country, Charlotte Small. Charlotte, the mixed-blood daughter of retired NWC partner Patrick Small, was only 13 years old, but she was to become Thompson's lifelong companion in a relationship that greatly exceeded the norm for country marriages in closeness and stability.

During the next few years Thompson's rate of travel slowed down considerably. He combined duties as a trader at Fort George (near Lindberg, Alta), Rocky Mountain House, and on the Peace River (Alta) with a number of short surveying trips, three of which took him into the Rocky Mountains in 1800 and 1801. The last of these three expeditions, prepared by Duncan McGillivray*, was an attempt to cross the mountains to establish a direct trade with the Kootenay Indians and, it was hoped, to find an economical route to the Pacific. Accompanied by James Hughes, Thompson travelled up the North Saskatchewan and Ram rivers before being forced back to Rocky Mountain House by the abnormally high waters in the latter river. At the annual meeting at Kaministiquia (Thunder Bay, Ont.) in July 1804, Thompson became a partner in the NWC. The following two years were spent in the Muskrat country, where as a wintering partner he assumed responsibility for managing the trade. He nevertheless found time to expand the surveys he had conducted in the area over a decade earlier. His career as a surveyor might have come to an end with his rotation on furlough in 1808, so dissatisfied was he by 1804–5 at not being able to pursue his interests in exploring and surveying. A change in company plans, however, led him to undertake the explorations for which he is best remembered.

After the annual meeting in 1806 Thompson set off for the Rocky Mountains to act upon the observations he had submitted to McGillivray after the failure of the Ram River expedition, observations on the ways in which the failure of a subsequent expedition to the Pacific coast could be avoided. The NWC was concerned about the implications of the successful American overland expedition to the Pacific coast, led by Meriwether Lewis and William Clark in 1806, and was anxious to determine whether the Columbia River could be used as a gateway to its trading territories. Thompson travelled up the North Saskatchewan River with Finan McDonald and eight other men, together with his wife and three children, and, after wintering at Rocky Mountain House, he crossed the height of land on 25 June 1807, through the pass that would later be named for the HBC trader Joseph HOWSE. The party descended the Blaeberry River (B.C.) to a river which Thompson at first named Kootana, unaware that he had reached the upper Columbia. There over

the next three years he extended his trade and surveys throughout the territory of the Kootenay Indians and south into the Flathead country, passing the first two winters at Kootenae House near Lake Windermere, and the third winter at Saleesh House (near Thompson, Mont.). Thompson successfully precluded the expansion by American traders into the area. But in doing so he had seriously undermined the position of the Peigan Indians as intermediaries in the trade across the mountains and created tensions that came to a head in 1810.

Thompson left Saleesh House for Montreal in the spring of 1810, intending to take his furlough which had been postponed since 1808. En route he left his wife and children at Fort Bas-de-la-Rivière (Fort Alexander, Man.) with her sister Nancy, country wife of John McDonald* of Garth. Upon his arrival at Rainy Lake (Ont.) on 22 July, however, he received new instructions, was hurriedly resupplied, and was sent back to the Columbia in response to the plans of John Jacob Astor* to trade through the Pacific Fur Company in the area west of the Rockies. The exact nature of these instructions is unknown and remains a matter of historical debate. On the one hand, it is possible that Thompson was ordered to reach the mouth of the Columbia before the PFC ship, which was to sail around Cape Horn from New York, in order to establish a prior presence and claim for the NWC. On the other hand, in view of the acceptance by the NWC wintering partners of Astor's offer of a one-third interest in the PFC venture, agreed to in July 1810 but never ratified, Thompson may simply have been instructed to survey a feasible route across the mountains to the mouth of the Columbia. Once there, he could represent the NWC, ensuring that the Astorians did not cut into the trade already established by the NWC in the interior. The few surviving documents tend to support the latter interpretation. Although Thompson undoubtedly hoped to arrive on the Pacific coast before the Astorians, he was more concerned to consolidate his influence in the interior.

Whatever his instructions, Thompson suffered a decisive delay before he even reached the mountains. The Peigan Indians, already restless over the NWC's trading activities, were in an ugly mood after suffering a stunning defeat earlier that summer at the hands of the Salish. The fact that Finan McDonald and two other NWC clerks left in the Columbia by Thompson had aided the Salish confirmed the Peigans in their resolve to block any further trading from the interior across the mountains. Separated from his canoes, Thompson learned in late September of a group of Peigans above Rocky Mountain House and decided to travel by land to the North Branch (Brazeau) River (Alta). His brigade found itself divided into three groups: some men and horses were waiting for him at the headwaters of the North Saskatchewan, on the

Thompson

Kootenay Plains; the men with the canoes had learned of the Peigan Indians and had turned back to Rocky Mountain House; and Thompson, with William Henry, was encamped 60 miles downstream from there. Thompson was slow in dealing with this situation and it was only with the help of Alexander Henry* the younger that the brigade was pieced together again. After over a month's delay, Thompson set off at the end of October to cross the mountains by way of the Athabasca River. His decision to make a detour north to the Athabasca was probably not inappropriate under the circumstances. However, in the face of the Peigan difficulties he appears to have been paralysed into inaction for a short time and was slow in making this decision.

After a difficult crossing through the previously unexplored Athabasca Pass in the months of December and January, many of his men who had not already left or been sent back deserted, and Thompson awaited the coming of spring with his three remaining men in a rudely constructed hut on the banks of the Columbia near the mouth of the Canoe River (B.C.). He and his men made a canoe out of cedar boards and in April he headed south to Saleesh House. From there, by canoe and on horseback, he made his way to Spokane House (near Spokane, Wash.) and then north to the Kettle Falls on the Columbia. There he built another canoe for the last leg of his journey to the sea. Setting off on 3 July, he proceeded down the river, pausing to treat with the Indians at every village as he passed and to lay claim to a new post at the mouth of the Snake River. On 15 July 1811 he arrived, flag flying, at the PFC's Fort Astoria (Astoria, Oreg.), where he found the former Nor'Wester Duncan McDougall* in charge.

During his short stay with the Astorians, Thompson appeared to be under the impression that the agreement between Astor and the NWC had been finalized. It is not clear if he learned from them that this was not the case, but at least one of the PFC men at the fort, Alexander Ross, perceived Thompson and his party as competitors. On 22 July Thompson set off back up the Columbia, accompanied by a PFC party under David Stuart. The two groups parted company at the Dalles and Thompson hurried on to the mouth of the Snake River, which he ascended as far as the Palouse River (Wash.) before obtaining horses to ride overland to Spokane House. From that point he returned to the Columbia at Kettle Falls and followed the river upstream back to the Canoe River, thus completing the survey, begun in 1807, of the river from its source to the sea. Thompson crossed the mountains to pick up supplies from William Henry's post on the Athabasca River and then returned to pass the winter of 1811–12 at Saleesh House. In the spring he retraced his steps and crossed the Rockies for the

last time, bound for Montreal and retirement from active participation in the fur trade.

The generosity of the NWC towards Thompson in the terms of his retirement suggests the high regard they had for the work he had accomplished. Thompson was granted an annual payment of £100 plus a full share of the profits of the company for three years, during which time he was to compile his observations and prepare maps for the NWC. After that, he was to retire officially from the company and to be granted the usual seven-year allowance of a one-hundredth share of the company's profits. Upon his arrival at Montreal, one of his first preoccupations was to see to the baptism of his wife and four of their five children, performed at the Scotch Presbyterian Church, Montreal, on 30 Sept. 1812, and to regularize his marriage with Charlotte on 30 October. Over the next 25 years he would go to considerable trouble to provide for the education of all his children. He moved with his family in October 1812 to Terrebonne, where he spent most of the next two years fulfilling his obligation to the NWC. In 1814 he completed a large map of the northwest from Lake Superior to the Pacific which was forwarded to the NWC and hung for many years in the great hall at Kaministiquia, renamed Fort William in 1807.

In the fall of 1815 Thompson purchased a farm at Williamstown, Upper Canada, from the estate of the Reverend John Bethune*. There he lived in close contact with a large number of former Nor'Westers including his close friend and brother-in-law John McDonald of Garth. Thompson accepted in January 1817 a position as astronomer and surveyor for the boundary commission created under the 6th and 7th articles of the Treaty of Ghent to determine the precise location of the border with the United States. For five years he was employed on surveys under the 6th article, from Saint-Régis, Lower Canada, on the St Lawrence River to Sault Ste Marie. His role with the commission expanded year by year and after the death in 1819 of John Ogilvy*, the first British commissioner, he was given increasing responsibilities in managing the field operations of the survey crews. Relations between the American and British commissioners and their parties were sometimes cool, but Thompson won the respect of fellow surveyors, scientific observers, and political appointees on both sides. In 1822 agreement was reached on the boundary surveyed under the 6th article, but Upper Canadian opinion widely regarded it as a sell-out of Canadian interests. Both Anthony Barclay, the second British commissioner, and Thompson were subjected to a good deal of personal criticism. For the next four years the commission, with Thompson as its only official astronomer, proceeded with surveys under the 7th article, west from Lake Superior to Lake of the

Woods. In 1827 Thompson remained in the employ of the commission, drawing maps and preparing position papers, but the claims of the two governments had become so divergent that no further agreement was possible.

As the work of the commission came to an end, Thompson turned his attentions to his family and to his responsibilities in Glengarry County as a landowner and as a justice of the peace, a commission he had held since 1820. The good fortune that had smiled on him through most of his life now deserted him. He would find no lasting satisfaction either in the accomplishments of his children, eventually numbering seven sons and six daughters, or in his life as a landed proprietor. Thompson's eldest son, Samuel, had assisted him in his surveys and map making since 1820, but now rebelled and turned to other pursuits; by 1831 they had quarrelled bitterly and were no longer on speaking terms. His financial fortunes began to decline in 1825 with the bankruptcy of the NWC agent McGillivrays, Thain and Company [see Thomas Thain*], in which he lost a considerable portion of his life savings. Most of his remaining wealth was invested in land, but attempts in the late 1820s to clear it and bring it into commercial production were costly and unsuccessful. He turned to other activities such as potash production and the operation of two general stores, one at Williamstown in 1830 and the other at Nutfield (near Maxville) in 1831, in order to supplement his income and provide his sons with a livelihood, but these efforts met with similar results. The most disastrous of all his ventures was the contract he accepted to supply the British army at Montreal with cordwood in 1829–30. The project was dogged by misfortune from the beginning: labour was expensive and scarce; cordwood obtained from jobbers was too short and therefore unsaleable; rafts ran aground and broke up in the rapids below Coteau-du-Lac, Lower Canada; and finally he was forced to fill the shortfall in his contract with wood purchased at Montreal for prices far higher than he was to receive for it. By 1831 his capital resources had been depleted; two years later he was so deeply in debt that he had to assign his lands to his creditors in order to avoid bankruptcy and, at the age of 63, he was forced to seek employment as a surveyor in order to maintain himself and his family.

With his third son, Henry, as assistant, Thompson found fairly steady employment for the next three years carrying out hydrographic surveys for proposed canal projects and exploratory land surveys in the Eastern Townships for the British American Land Company. In 1837 he was employed by the government on a survey of the waterways between Lake Huron and the Ottawa River but continuing resentment in Upper Canada over the boundary

decision 15 years earlier damaged his reputation and his findings were shelved. Over the next eight years employment became increasingly sporadic and, between such projects as the mapping of Lac Saint-Pierre and street surveys in Montreal, he was frequently in financial difficulty. He had already moved from Williamstown to a rented house in Montreal. There he was forced to move several times into progressively meaner quarters and on more than one occasion was reduced to pawning his instruments; once he even had to pawn his coat. His desperation was such that in August 1840, at age 70, he unsuccessfully applied for a position as clerk with the HBC. Pleas for pensions or positions in recognition of his past services fell on deaf ears and he found no ready publisher for his maps. He did receive £150 for a new version of his map of the northwest in 1843 from the British government, but the advice he tendered on the Oregon boundary question was largely ignored.

Reluctantly, he moved in with his daughter and son-in-law, in 1845 in Montreal and in 1850 in Longueuil. In the small whitewashed rooms he shared with his wife in Longueuil, Thompson wrote an account of his travels in North America. This work of his final years is in many ways his greatest achievement, but he never had the satisfaction of seeing it completed and published. Already in 1848 the sight in his remaining good eye had begun to fail; by 1851 he was completely blind and the manuscript remained unfinished. Through all these years of misfortune, Thompson retained his strong religious convictions and his belief in the ultimate goodness of Providence, and he found solace and support in the unfailing care of his wife.

His death in 1857 went almost unnoticed outside the circle of his own family, and his true stature as one of Canada's greatest explorers and geographers was completely unrecognized until Joseph Burr Tyrrell* began his campaign in the 1880s to give him his due. It was only when Tyrrell obtained the manuscript in the 1890s and edited it for publication by the Champlain Society in 1914 that *David Thompson's narrative*, covering Thompson's career up to his retirement in Montreal in 1812, became public. The *Narrative*, somewhat flawed because it was written so long after the events, remains a major work of autobiography and an invaluable source for historians. By 1927, the 70th anniversary of Thompson's death, when special ceremonies were held in Montreal to unveil a monument on his previously unmarked grave, David Thompson had become one of Canada's best-known and loved historical figures.

JOHN NICKS

David Thompson's manuscript was published as *David Thompson's narrative*, ed. J. B. Tyrrell (Toronto, 1916); a new edition, prepared by R. [G.] Glover (Toronto, 1962), was later abridged and published with some additional material as *Travels in western North America, 1784–1812*, ed. V. G. Hopwood (Toronto, 1971). A few of the journals he wrote in the course of his expeditions, which are at AO, MS 25 and MU 2982, have been published as "David Thompson and the Rocky Mountains," ed. J. B. Tyrrell, *CHR*, 15 (1934): 39–45; "David Thompson on the Peace River," ed. H. A. Dempsey, *Alberta Hist. Rev.* (Edmonton), 14 (1966): 1–10; "David Thompson's account of his first attempt to cross the Rockies," ed. F. W. Howay, *Queen's Quarterly* (Kingston, Ont.), 40 (1933): 333–56; *David Thompson's journals relating to Montana and adjacent regions, 1808–1812*, ed. M. C. White (Missoula, Mont., 1950); "David Thompson's journeys in Idaho," ed. T. C. Elliott, *Wash. Hist. Quarterly*, 11 (1920): 97–103, 163–73; "David Thompson's journeys in the Pend Oreille country," ed. T. C. Elliott, *Wash. Hist. Quarterly*, 23 (1932): 18–24, 88–93, 173–76; "David Thompson's journeys in the Spokane country," ed. T. C. Elliott, *Wash. Hist. Quarterly*, 8 (1917): 183–87, 261–64; 9 (1918): 11–16, 103–6, 169–73, 284–87; 10 (1919): 17–20; and "The discovery of the source of the Columbia River," ed. T. C. Elliott, *Oreg. Hist. Quarterly* (Eugene), 26 (1925): 23–49. Part of Thompson's work as surveyor on the boundary commission was published as "Remarks on the maps from St. Regis to Sault Ste. Marie," *OH*, 1 (1899): 117–21, and his comments on the Oregon boundary question appeared as "Letters and reports relating to the Oregon Territory," *PABC Report* (1913): 112–25. A few of his letters can be found in "Some letters of David Thompson," ed. L. J. Burpee, *CHR*, 4 (1923): 105–26.

ANQ-M, CE1-63, 14 févr. 1857, 7 mai 1857; CE1-126, 30 sept. 1812. PAC, MG 19, A17; MG 30, D49. PAM, HBCA, A.1/46–47; A.5/2–3; A.6/3: ff.128d–29; A.6/13–15; A.11/116–17; A.16/33–34; A.21/1; B.14/a/1; B.24/a/1–6; B.49/a/17–25; B.55/a/1; B.87/a/8–9; B.121/a/1–8; B.178/a/1; B.205/a/1–8; B.239/a/86–99; B.239/b/45–59; B.239/f/1. *Les bourgeois de la Compagnie du Nord-Ouest* (Masson), vol.2. Can., Prov. of, Legislative Assembly, *App. to the journals*, 1842, 2, app.Z. Cox, *Adventures on the Columbia*. [Joseph Delafield], *The unfortified boundary: a diary of the first survey of the Canadian boundary line from St. Regis to the Lake of the Woods*, ed. Robert McElroy and Thomas Riggs (New York, 1943). *Docs. relating to NWC* (Wallace). Gabriel Franchère, *Journal of a voyage on the north west coast of America during the years 1811, 1812, 1813, and 1814*, trans. W. T. Lamb, ed. and intro. W. K. Lamb (Toronto, 1969). *HBRS*, 26 (Johnson). "Journals of Legislative Assembly of U.C.," *AO Report*, 1914: 1–690. "The journals of the Legislative Council of Upper Canada . . . [1821–24]," *AO Report*, 1915: 1–286. *Muskoka and Haliburton, 1615–1875; a collection of documents*, ed. F. B. Murray ([Toronto], 1963). *New light on early hist. of greater northwest* (Coues). A. Ross, *Adventures on the Columbia. Illustrated historical atlas of the counties of Stormont, Dundas and Glengarry, Ont.*, comp. H. Belden (Toronto, 1879; repr., Owen Sound, Ont., 1972). M. W. Campbell, *The North West Company* (Toronto, 1973). H. G. Classen, *Thrust and counterthrust: the genesis of the Canada–United States boundary* (Don Mills [Toronto], 1965). C. N. Cochrane, *David Thompson, the explorer* (Toronto, 1924). *David Thompson sesquicen-tennial, 1809–1959, symposium, Sandpoint, Idaho, August 29, 1959*, ed. R. N. Cheetham (Sandpoint, [1959]). A. M. Josephy, "David Thompson," *The mountain men and the fur trade of the far west . . .* , ed. L. R. Hafen (10v., Glendale, Calif., 1965–72), 3: 309–37. D. [S.] Lavender, *Winner take all: the trans-Canada canoe trail* (New York and Toronto, 1977). A. S. Morton, *David Thompson* (Toronto, [1930]). J. S. Nicks, "The Pine Island posts, 1786–1794: a study of competition in the fur trade" (MA thesis, Univ. of Alberta, Edmonton, 1975). *Old trails and new directions; papers of the third North American Fur Trade Conference*, ed. C. M. Judd and A. J. Ray (Toronto, 1980). Rich, *Hist. of HBC*. J. K. Smith, *David Thompson: fur trader, explorer, geographer* (Toronto, 1971). D. W. Thomson, *Men and meridians: the history of surveying and mapping in Canada* (3v., Ottawa, 1966–69), 1. J. B. Tyrrell, *A brief narrative of the journeys of David Thompson, in north-western America . . .* (Toronto, 1888). Van Kirk, *"Many tender ties."* J. N. Wallace, *The wintering partners on Peace River from the earliest records to the union in 1821; with a summary of the Dunvegan journal, 1806* (Ottawa, 1929). John Warkentin, *The western interior on Canada, a record of geographical discovery, 1612–1917* (Toronto, 1964).

"David Thompson monument," *CHA Report*, 1927: 9–16. R. [G.] Glover, "The witness of David Thompson," *CHR*, 31 (1950): 25–38. Arthur Hawkes, "Montreal honors on Monday man she starved 90 years ago," *Montreal Daily Star*, 21 May 1927: 21. J. M. Hitsman, "David Thompson and defence research," *CHR*, 40 (1959): 315–18. [W. L. MacIlquham], "Memorial to David Thompson," *Journal of the Dominion Land Surveyors' Assoc.* (Ottawa), 1 (October 1922): 2–3. I. E. MacKay, "The David Thompson memorial," *Canadian Magazine* (Toronto), 60 (January 1923): 223–29. A. S. Morton, "Did Duncan M'Gillivray and David Thompson cross the Rockies in 1801?" *CHR*, 18 (1937): 156–62; "The North West Company's Columbian enterprise and David Thompson," *CHR*, 17 (1936): 266–88. Elizabeth Parker, "Early explorers of the west – David Thompson," *Canadian Alpine Journal* (Winnipeg), 29 (1946): 216–28. J. S. Plaskett, "The astronomy of the explorers," *BCHQ*, 4 (1940): 63–77. R. I. Ruggles, "Hospital boys of the bay," *Beaver*, outfit 308 (autumn 1977): 4–11. H. D. Smiley, "The dalliance of David Thompson," *Beaver*, outfit 303 (winter 1972): 40–47. W. M. Stewart, "David Thompson's surveys in the north-west," *CHR*, 17: 289–303. *Toronto Star Weekly*, 28 May 1927. J. B. Tyrrell, "David Thompson and the Columbia River," *CHR*, 18: 12–27; "The rediscovery of David Thompson," *RSC Trans.*, 3rd ser., 22 (1928), sect.II: 233–48.

THOMPSON, WILLIAM, militia officer, farmer, justice of the peace, miller, and politician; b. 17 June 1786 in New Brunswick, son of Cornelius Thompson and Rebecca ——; m. by 1813 Jane Garden, and they had six sons and three daughters; d. 18 Jan. 1860 in Toronto Township, Upper Canada.

William Thompson was the son of Cornelius Thompson, lieutenant and adjutant of the 2nd battalion of New Jersey Volunteers, who settled near St Anne's Point (Fredericton) in 1783. In 1808 Cornelius visited Upper Canada with Stephen Jarvis, whose cousin William* was the provincial secretary. Personally recommended for 1,200 acres of land by Lieutenant Governor Francis GORE, Cornelius returned with his family the following year, proceeding from York (Toronto) to Grantham Township on the Niagara peninsula.

All four of Cornelius Thompson's sons served in the militia during the War of 1812. William, the eldest, was appointed captain of the 2nd York Militia on 16 April 1812 and fought that October in the battle of Queenston Heights. On 22 July 1814, while a member of a party of scouts under the command of Captain James FitzGibbon*, he was involved in a skirmish with American troops led by Colonel Joseph Willcocks* and was taken prisoner. William Hamilton Merritt*, a Grantham neighbour held in captivity with Thompson in Cheshire, Mass., described him as "a man of most exemplary morals, a mild, good temper, and possessed of more fortitude than generally falls to the lot of mankind." That fortitude would be needed when Thompson was released after the end of the war and returned home. His father had died in August 1814, and the family had "sustained ... very severe losses." William received no compensation, however, and was forced to begin settlement a second time on "wild lands" in Toronto Township located by his father in 1812. In 1825 he himself was granted an additional 400 acres.

Despite the set-back in his fortunes as a result of the war and the responsibilities of a family, Thompson rapidly achieved a position of local prominence. In 1816 he became a justice of the peace and between then and 1838 received repeated commissions for the Gore and Home districts. In 1817 he and his brother Frederick erected a sawmill in nearby Trafalgar Township. William also served for many years as an officer of the West York militia. During the rebellion of 1837–38 he was on active service as colonel in command of his regiment in York County and at Chippawa. On 10 Nov. 1846, after the province-wide reorganization of the militia, he became lieutenant colonel of the 1st Battalion of York militia.

William Thompson also acted on occasion in a political role. In 1824 the inhabitants of the western part of the Home District unanimously nominated him to represent them in the assembly. He and Ely Playter were elected for the riding of York and Simcoe that July, replacing the incumbents William Warren Baldwin* and Peter Robinson*. Staunchly conservative, Thompson was a prominent member of the Church of England and a confidant of John Strachan* and other members of the "family compact." He frequently took part in the business of the house, particularly in matters affecting rural Upper Canada. Thompson's support of the government élite, especially on the contentious alien question [see Sir Peregrine MAITLAND], was to lose him the sympathy

of many of his American-born rural constituents. Rumours circulated, only to be denied in Robert Stanton*'s *U.E. Loyalist*, that Thompson had "been attacked on his way home, in consequence of his vote on the Naturalization bill" in February 1827. The following year William Lyon Mackenzie*, who was running in Thompson's riding, gave a prominent position to his opponent's voting record in the *Colonial Advocate*'s first "Black List." Thompson withdrew shortly before the opening of the polls in the general election of 1828 which brought Mackenzie into the assembly for the first time. Thereafter Thompson attempted to regain his seat several times, without success. He was recommended by Chief Justice John Beverley Robinson* for a place on an enlarged Legislative Council but was not appointed, and his political activity in later life was confined to local affairs. In 1844 he became a member of Toronto Township's first council, on which he served regularly in the 1840s and 1850s, becoming township reeve in 1851.

Members of the Thompson family continued to take a strong interest in political affairs. His sons Alfred Andrew and Henry Horace were mayors of Penetanguishene, and a grandson Alfred Burke Thompson served in the provincial legislature and the federal parliament.

J. K. JOHNSON

PAC, RG 1, L3, 499: T14/86; 510: T leases, 1801–36/28–29; RG 8, I (C ser.), 1855: 55, 68; RG 9, I, B5, 1, 3–4, 6; RG 68, General index, 1651–1841. PRO, WO 13/3716: 339. Stephen Jarvis, "Reminiscences of a loyalist," ed. Stinson Jarvis, *Canadian Magazine*, 26 (November 1905–April 1906): 373, 450–57. U.C., House of Assembly, *Journal*, 1825–28. *Colonial Advocate*, May–July 1828. *U.E. Loyalist* (York [Toronto]), 3 March 1827. *Upper Canada Gazette*, 12 Feb. 1824. Armstrong, *Handbook of Upper Canadian chronology*. *The Canadian album: men of Canada; or success by example . . .*, ed. William Cochrane and J. C. Hopkins (5v., Brantford, Ont., 1891–96), 5: 343–44. *The Canadian directory of parliament, 1867–1967*, ed. J. K. Johnson (Ottawa, 1968), 567. *Centennial edition of a history of the electoral districts, legislatures and ministries of the province of Ontario, 1867–1968*, comp. Roderick Lewis (Toronto, [1969]). Ernest Green, "A little study in loyalist genealogy: 'Tomsons of Perthshire,'" *OH*, 31 (1936): 114–34. *Officers of British forces in Canada* (Irving). W. H. Smith, *Canada: past, present and future*, 1: 81 (2nd group). W. P. Bull, *From Strachan to Owen: how the Church of England was planted and tended in British North America* (Toronto, 1937). A. C. Osborne, "Old Penetanguishene: sketches of its pioneer, naval and military days," *Simcoe County pioneer papers* (6 nos., Barrie, Ont., 1908–17; repr., 6 nos. in 1v., Belleville, Ont., 1974), no.6: 102–5.

THRESHER, GEORGE GODSELL, painter, art teacher, and office holder; b. 6 April 1780 in

Thresher

Salisbury, England, son of Thomas Thresher and Rachel ——; m. Eliza Wilson Brooks, and they had two sons and three daughters; d. 9 Dec. 1857 in Charlottetown.

Artists made a real contribution to the life of 19th-century North America in their own works and by teaching others to appreciate the fine arts. They also provided for succeeding generations a pictorial record of contemporary life. In spite of these services it was hard for an artist to make a reasonable living unless employed by a wealthy family. Early immigrant artists thus moved from city to city, often following the coastline.

George Godsell Thresher immigrated to New York City in 1806 and later worked in Philadelphia, Montreal, Halifax, and Charlottetown. He is said to have studied art under Ross Dodd in London, and to have served in the Royal Navy. He also stated in later advertisements that he had taught "in some of the most respectable Boarding Schools and private families in Europe." In New York Thresher obtained a teaching position with the family of Dr J. Wallis Brooks and married his daughter.

Thresher was primarily a marine artist and was said by a descendant to have done paintings during the War of 1812 for the city of New York depicting naval victories. These were to be given to American commanders. A work known to have survived from this period shows the engagement between the USS *Hornet* and HMS *Peacock*, a pictorial record done in 1813 of the American vessel's defeat of the British ship on 24 February of that year.

As well as working in New York until about 1813, Thresher is said to have taught art in Philadelphia before moving to Montreal with members of the Brooks family when Honoria Brooks, his sister-in-law, married a John Dillon of Montreal. In May 1816 Thresher announced the opening of an academy for drawing in crayon or chalk and painting in water-colours or oils. A receipt from 1818 states that he was paid £14 15s. 0d. for painting 59 street signs for the city.

By 1821 Thresher had moved to Halifax. He made it his headquarters for some years though he may have lived temporarily in other parts of Nova Scotia pursuing work in his profession. He was on board the schooner *Speculation* when it was wrecked off Cape Breton on 7 Nov. 1828, and he advertised in May 1829 for any effects from that wreck, identifying himself as "Drawing Master, Pictou."

By July 1829 he was in Charlottetown advertising that he would open a drawing and painting academy with instruction in penmanship and bookkeeping as soon as a sufficient number of pupils were obtained. His academy, "by Permission from his late Majesty, and under the Patronage of his Excellency the Lieut. Governor," John Ready*, opened in December.

Although Thresher remained in Charlottetown except for a brief period in the winter of 1829–30, teaching may not have provided a sufficiently remunerative living. He advertised that he would do ornamental drawing-room painting with landscape scenery; Scripture pieces for chapels and churches; masonic aprons and banners on velvet, silk, or muslin; coats of arms and crests on carriages; furniture painted in imitation of different kinds of woods and marbles; gilt work; and ornamental writing. His wife and daughter augmented the family income by operating a school for young ladies in the different branches of education, including drawing and painting. An oil painting by Mrs Thresher entitled *Man with pipe* (c. 1848) attests to her skill.

Beginning in September 1830 a large painting by Thresher was exhibited in Charlottetown. Its subject was the bombardment of Algiers (Algeria) by Lord Exmouth on 27 Aug. 1816, painted "from a correct sketch taken on the spot, by a gentleman who went for the entire purpose." The price of admission to see the painting was a costly one shilling for adults, and suggests that both artist and painting were held in high regard.

Apparently unable to support himself by art alone, Thresher accepted an appointment in 1838 as deputy registrar of deeds, relinquishing the position in 1851 to become deputy colonial secretary. When he was forced to retire in 1853 because of infirmity, the House of Assembly overwhelmingly voted to grant him £30 "in consideration of his services." He seems, however, to have continued to paint throughout his lifetime. His depiction of the great gale that swept the Island in 1851 was reputed to have been submitted to an industrial exhibition in New York City where it was awarded a prize. When Charlottetown was incorporated in April 1855, Thresher was asked to submit designs for a city seal. He was paid one shilling, and the by-law to establish the seal received sanction in December. He was also a member of the Charlottetown Mechanics' Institute and lectured several times on such subjects as aerial perspective and the first principles of drawing.

Prince Edward Island was fortunate in attracting artists. The main contribution of William Valentine*, Leon Rosse, and S. W. Martin was in the field of portraiture. George Thresher, Fanny Amelia Bayfield [Wright*], and George Hubbard, on the other hand, provided documentary accounts of life in 19th-century North America. As well, George Thresher is esteemed as a competent marine artist by collectors of naval paintings in both Canada and the United States.

IRENE L. ROGERS

[The most comprehensive list of the paintings done by Thresher in the United States is in the Inventory of American

886

paintings executed before 1914, a database compiled by the Smithsonian Institution's National Museum of American Art (Washington). Illustrations of some of those paintings, along with biographical information on Thresher, is found in Douglas Norris, "The Hornet and the Peacock," *Antiquarian* (New York), 11 (1929): 53, 80; "George Thresher, naval painter," *Antiques* (New York), 48 (July–December 1945): 230, 232; *Catalogue of a special exhibition of the Irving S. Olds collection of American naval prints and paintings . . .* (Salem, Mass., 1959), 34, 44; and D. B. Webster *et al.*, *Georgian Canada: conflict and culture, 1745–1820* (Toronto, 1984), 189, 218.

Among his paintings done in British America, *View of Charlottetown*, date unknown, and *Charlotte Town taken from J. S. McGill Esq. farm*, 1836, are held by the PAPEI. The former is reproduced in *Through Canadian eyes: trends and influences in Canadian art, 1815–1965*, comp. Moncrieff Williamson (Calgary, 1976), plate 10, where it carries a date that appears to be too early. In addition to owning his wife's painting *Man with pipe* (c. 1848), the Confederation Centre Art Gallery and Museum (Charlottetown) holds Thresher's *Harbour entrance, Halifax*, c. 1830 (illustrated in *Confederation Centre Gallery and Museum* (Charlottetown, 1969), under the name *Indian tepee and ship*, in J. R. Harper, *Painting in Canada, a history* ([Toronto], 1966), and in *The first decade, 1964–1974: a retrospective survey of works acquired by Confederation Centre Art Gallery*, selected by Ian Lumsden (Charlottetown, 1975)); *Battle of Trafalgar*, unsigned and undated; and *The Yankee gale*, signed and dated 1851 (reproduced in *Prince Edward Island Magazine and Educational Outlook* (Charlottetown), 6 (1904): 39, where it is called *The great gale of 1851*). Other paintings, including *Rolfe*, a self-portrait, and *The cottagers*, are held by descendants or private collectors. The Charlottetown city seal is illustrated in I. L. Rogers, *Charlottetown: the life in its buildings* (Charlottetown, 1983), v. I.L.R.]

PAPEI, Acc.3466; RG 1, Commission books, 13 Nov. 1838; 2 Dec. 1839; 28 April, 7 July 1851; RG 20, item 36, W. B. Wellner to Thresher, 6 Dec. 1855; Charles Desbrisay to Mayor, 8 Dec. 1855. *Acadian Recorder*, 10, 17 Feb., 8 Sept. 1821; 30 Aug. 1823. *Colonial Herald, and Prince Edward Island Advertiser* (Charlottetown), 11 Jan. 1840, 18 Feb. 1843. *Examiner* (Charlottetown), 8 Jan. 1848. *Islander*, 8 April 1853, 11 Dec. 1857. *Prince Edward Island Register*, 20 Jan., 26 May, 14, 21 July, 4 Aug., 29 Sept., 24 Nov., 8, 29 Dec. 1829; 18 May, 1 June 1830. *Royal Gazette* (Charlottetown), 28 Sept., 12 Oct. 1830; 4 Oct. 1831; 4 Feb. 1845. G. C. Groce and D. H. Wallace, *The New-York Historical Society's dictionary of artists in America, 1564–1860* (New Haven, Conn., and London, 1957; repr. 1964). Harper, *Early painters and engravers*. *Rolfe genealogical tree*, comp. W. J. Morrison (n.p., n.d.; copy at P.E.I. Museum). *Examiner* (Charlottetown), 2 April 1880. *Guardian* (Charlottetown), 21 Oct. 1944.

TIFFANY, GIDEON, printer, office holder, publisher, mill-owner, and militia officer; b. 28 Jan. 1774 in Keene, N.H., son of Gideon Tiffany and Sarah Farrar, *née* Dean; m. c. 1802 Ruth Tomlinson, and they had five children who reached adulthood; d. 29 Aug. 1854 in Delaware Township, Upper Canada.

The Tiffany family removed from Keene to Hanover, N.H., about 1782, and there young Gideon completed his secondary school education. He then became a printer, presumably by joining his eldest brother, Silvester*, who conducted a printing business in Lansingburgh (Troy), N.Y. It was probably through his brother-in-law, Davenport Phelps, who in 1794 was living in Newark (Niagara-on-the-Lake), that Gideon learned the office of king's printer for Upper Canada was available. In November he succeeded Louis Roy* in this appointment and on 3 December published his first issue of the *Upper Canada Gazette; or, American Oracle*. Tiffany also undertook job printing and in 1795 published a pamphlet by Richard Cockrell* entitled *Thoughts on the education of youth*; this is believed to be the earliest non-governmental publication in the province. By early 1796 he had been joined by his brother Silvester who became assistant to the king's printer.

Although the Tiffany brothers were experienced printers, they were viewed by provincial authorities as having pro-American leanings. This dissatisfaction led to Gideon's tendering his resignation as king's printer in May 1797 and the subsequent appointment of the loyalist Titus Geer Simons. As Simons was not a trained printer and as the government did not have a press, the Tiffanys continued to print the *Gazette* at their shop. Even after the appointment of William Waters as king's printer in July 1798, the government probably continued to use the Tiffanys' press until the publication of the *Gazette* was transferred to York (Toronto) that September.

On 20 July 1799 the Tiffanys began publication in Niagara of the first independent newspaper in Upper Canada, the *Canada Constellation* (later the *Canadian Constellation*). The issue of 18 Jan. 1800, however, announced that Gideon was to be the sole publisher of the weekly, and he appears to have carried on alone for several months thereafter. Although Silvester continued to publish newspapers until his death in 1811, Gideon abandoned publishing and printing by 1801.

In March of that year, with five-year promissory notes amounting to £3,050 New York currency, Gideon and another brother-in-law, Moses Brigham, purchased 2,200 acres in Delaware Township, Middlesex County, from Ebenezer Allan*. The property included two sawmills formerly owned by Allan, and by 1804 Tiffany and Brigham were annually producing 300,000 to 500,000 board feet of lumber for the Detroit market. They were apparently also engaged in fur trading with Indians in the area. In November 1806, possibly because of a dispute with Allan over the construction of a church on the lands originally granted to him and a lack of funds to make the final payment on them, Tiffany and Brigham, together with Allan, had the entire property conveyed to Dr Oliver Tiffany, a well-to-do older brother of Gideon then living in Ancaster Township. Gideon Tiffany and Brigham continued to reside in Delaware Township and operate the mills. As well as managing his brother's lands, Gideon purchased additional lands in both Delaware and Caradoc townships. In 1810 he rented out one of his farms in Delaware to a tenant for the purpose of cultivating hemp, while he himself was engaged in constructing a breaking-mill for its processing.

Although Lord Selkirk [Douglas*] thought that Tiffany and Brigham were "intellegent Yankees" who seemed "to have the manners of the world much beyond what would be expected in such a place," Tiffany was mainly content to confine his talents to Delaware, where for more than 30 years he served in various township offices, acting as assessor, pound-keeper, and overseer of roads and fences, as well as churchwarden. He was commissioned a lieutenant in the 1st Middlesex Militia in February 1812 but there is no record of his name on militia rolls beyond December of that year. He may have moved to Ancaster Township with his family during 1812–14.

One of the few incidents in which Gideon was involved that extended beyond the confines of Delaware was his successful effort in 1806 to enlist others in the London District to contribute to the hiring of an individual to "ride post." Thereafter newspapers, letters, and other mail were conveyed from Niagara every three weeks.

Another larger concern was his involvement in the reform movement. On 6 Oct. 1837 he was unanimously elected to chair a large, widely publicized meeting of reformers in adjacent Westminster Township. At the meeting of 2 December which led to the formation of the Delaware Reform Association or Branch Political Union, he was a signatory to its constitution and advocated civil disobedience by not paying provincial taxes. He also proposed a resolution declaring that the delegates, of which he was one, to the provincial convention in Toronto on 21 December "should be instructed to propose to the Convention to petition Her Majesty to effect a peaceful separation of the Province from the mother country in order to prevent a civil war." Consequently, on 15 December at the age of 63, he was jailed for his involvement in this "Delaware conspiracy" and, according to the records of his trial examination, the charges included "alleged attempts to spread disaffection among the Indians." On 7 May 1838 he was tried, acquitted, and freed.

Thereafter, he continued to live out his life quietly, engaged in farming in the township and well liked and highly respected by his neighbours who found him possessed of a great "fund of anecdotes and history" and "a very agreeable conversationalist, warm hearted, sympathetic and liberal in his sentiments."

Following his death at his residence, his remains were interred in the Tiffany Cemetery in the village of Delaware laid out by his brother Oliver in the mid 1820s in the anticipation of its becoming the administrative and judicial seat of the London District.

DANIEL J. BROCK

[This biography is based on the author's examination of diverse primary sources, including gravestone inscriptions in the Tiffany Cemetery (Delaware, Ont.), and corrects a number of factual errors found in the previous studies, N. O. Tiffany, *The Tiffanys of America: history and genealogy* ([Buffalo, N.Y., 1901]), W. S. Wallace, "The first journalists in Upper Canada," *CHR*, 26 (1945): 372–81, and "Historical plaque to commemorate Gideon Tiffany, 1774–1854" (press release issued by Ont., Dept. of Public Records and Arch., Hist. Branch, [Toronto], 27 May 1968), available at the AO. D.J.B.]

AO, RG 1, A-I-1, 63: 2728–29; RG 22, ser.321, nos.56, 131. Eva Brook Donly Museum (Simcoe, Ont.), Norfolk Hist. Soc. Coll., Thomas Welch papers, 1023–24. Middlesex West Land Registry Office (Glencoe, Ont.), Instruments 6–7, 68, 3168. PAC, RG 1, L3, 495: T2/54; 511: T misc., 1791–1819/4. UWOL, Regional Coll., Delaware Township, London District, minutes of annual town meeting, 1807. [Thomas Douglas, 5th Earl of] Selkirk, *Lord Selkirk's diary, 1803–1804 . . .* , ed. P. C. T. White (Toronto, 1958), 307. "Minutes of the Court of General Quarter Sessions of the Peace for the London District . . . ," AO *Report*, 1933: 135–36. *The Talbot papers*, ed. J. H. Coyne (2v., Ottawa, 1908–9), 1: 175. *Canada Constellation* (Niagara [Niagara-on-the-Lake, Ont.]), 20 July–7 Dec. 1799, called the *Canadian Constellation*, 14 Dec. 1799–1800. *Constitution* (Toronto), 18, 25 Oct. 1837. *Upper Canada Gazette; or, American Oracle*, 3 Dec. 1794–October 1798. Marie Tremaine, *A bibliography of Canadian imprints, 1751–1800* (Toronto, 1952), 649–53. *Hist. of Middlesex*, 478–79, 568. Read, *Rising in western U.C.* W. S. Wallace, "The periodical literature of Upper Canada," *CHR*, 12 (1931): 5–6, 11–12.

TODD, WILLIAM, fur trader and surgeon; b. between 1784 and 1787 in Ireland; m. first, according to the custom of the country, Marianne (d. between 1830 and 1835); m. secondly 20 Aug. 1839 Elizabeth Dennett in the Red River settlement (Man.); d. there 22 Dec. 1851.

William Todd joined the Hudson's Bay Company in 1816 and served during his first two years as clerk and surgeon at Cumberland House (Sask.). In the summer of 1819 he volunteered for service with Colin Robertson* in the Athabasca campaign against the North West Company and spent the winter at Fort Wedderburn (Alta). Robertson regretted the fact that Todd did not have much experience as a fur trader, but he concluded at the end of the season that Todd had been the only man under his direction who appeared fit for duty in the Athabasca and who had conducted himself with firmness. In particular, Robertson commented on the influence Todd had exerted over the Chipewyans in his capacity as surgeon; his successful treatment of an outbreak of whooping cough gained a certain advantage for the HBC over the NWC in its relations with the natives. After a year's furlough, Todd spent 1821–22 in the Lower Red River district, 1822–27 at York Factory (Man.), and 1827–29 at Fort Vancouver (Vancouver, Wash.) in the Columbia district. He returned in 1829 to the Red River, where he was stationed as clerk at Brandon House (Man.).

During these years, Todd acquired a reputation as a clever, attentive doctor who was extremely scrupulous on points of honour and etiquette. He was not, however, considered particularly useful as a trader. In 1830 HBC governor George SIMPSON abruptly changed his appraisal of Todd's abilities and, underlining his service in the Athabasca campaign, recommended that Todd be promoted chief trader. The next year he was placed in charge of the Upper Red River district, as chief trader at Fort Ellice. In 1833 he took over the responsibility for Red River from Chief Factor Donald McKENZIE. The following year he was given charge of the Swan River district, with his headquarters at Fort Pelly (Sask.), where, except for one year at Fort Severn (Ont.) and two years' furlough, he remained until his retirement.

Todd had a relatively uneventful career as a trader. As a doctor, however, he was probably the most famous surgeon in the west before 1850. In the early 1830s he served the needs of both Governor Simpson and his wife, Frances Ramsay SIMPSON, who took up residence in Red River in the summer of 1830. In December Frances began a difficult pregnancy and, although there were two doctors in the settlement, Richard Julian Hamlyn and John Bunn*, Simpson had no confidence in either of these men and sent for Todd at Brandon House. Todd arrived by 1 Jan. 1831 and kept a close vigil over Frances until he delivered her son in September. He also attended to Governor Simpson who, agitated by the condition of his wife, suffered from depression, anxiety, and fears of recurring attacks of apoplexy. Simpson was accustomed to being bled whenever he feared one of these attacks and asked Todd to administer this treatment. Todd refused; he believed that bleeding had already been done too often prior to his arrival and that, if continued, it would seriously weaken Simpson's health. Eventually, when the stress associated with his wife's illness had passed, the governor recovered and Todd believed his advice had probably saved Simpson's life.

In the summer of 1836 Simpson temporarily posted Todd to York Factory to deal with a mysterious disease that had broken out there. Since 1834 this affliction, known as the "York Factory complaint,"

had appeared each spring, affecting in particular the officers at the fort. Beginning with colic, vomiting, and restlessness, the symptoms progressed to convulsions, depression, loss of reason, and, in the most severe cases, death. By the summer of 1836 the men at the fort were in a state of alarm because of the recurrence and severity of the disease, and the sick officers, including the post surgeon, Elzeard H. Whiffen, were evacuated. The men who remained had great faith in Todd as a physician and applauded the governor's decision to send him to York. Unhappily for all concerned, Todd himself succumbed to the dreaded "complaint" within a week of his arrival at the post, and had four violent attacks in September which left him so weakened that everyone feared for his life. It was decided that he too would have to leave. Before he did so, however, he apparently took the precautions he judged necessary to bring the reign of terror to an end. Unfortunately, it is not known what he considered to be the cause of the illness, or what measures he took to combat it. He claimed to have been the last person to suffer from the malady. Although he did recover, his health was never fully restored and he was a sickly man for the rest of his life.

In the summer of 1837 Todd was back at Fort Pelly, in charge of the Swan River district, when he heard rumours of a malignant disease having broken out amongst the Indians who visited Fort Union (on the border between North Dakota and Montana) on the Missouri River. Although parts of these stories were conflicting, Todd concluded that, if there was any disease at all, it was probably smallpox; without waiting for confirmation of his suspicion, he launched an extensive program of inoculation with cowpox vaccine. This was the first time that the Jennerian type of vaccine was used in the west. Besides administering the vaccine himself, he taught chiefs and medicine men the procedure, supplied them with vaccine, and told them to inoculate anyone they met who had not been treated. He also dispatched vaccine to other HBC posts to the north. Todd's quick action saved the lives of countless numbers of Indians inhabiting the Swan River district and the woodlands north of the Saskatchewan River and greatly enhanced his already considerable reputation among the Indians as a man who possessed powerful medicine.

Todd stayed on as chief trader in charge of the Swan River district until the spring of 1851 when he asked to be retired with either three years' furlough or promotion to chief factor. The HBC Council of the Northern Department granted his retirement with a one-year leave, but did not accord him the rank of chief factor. In poor health and, according to HBC governor Eden Colvile*, addicted to opium, he settled at Red River where he died in December 1851, leaving his second wife, Elizabeth, three children from his first marriage, and seven from his second. During his

Tredwell

long career Todd had gained considerable renown as a physician, among both the employees of the company and the native people of the regions where he served. Although his critics accused him of having a high opinion of himself as a doctor, the record clearly indicates that his self-esteem in this regard was justified.

ARTHUR RAY

PAM, HBCA, A.11/51: ff.4–7; A.34/1: f.42d (mfm. at PAC); B.135/c/2: ff.54–57, 65 (mfm. at PAC); B.154/a/27: f.19; B.239/a/148: ff.41–48; B.239/z/26: ff.143–44; D.4/22: f.53d; D.5/25, ff.390–91. *HBRS*, 1 (Rich); 2 (Rich and Fleming); 3 (Fleming); 19 (Rich and Johnson). Simpson, "Character book," *HBRS*, 30 (Williams), 151–236. G. C. Ingram, "The Big House, Lower Fort Garry," *Canadian Hist. Sites: Occasional Papers in Archaeology and Hist.* (Ottawa), no.4 (1970): 94–99. A. J. Ray, "Smallpox: the epidemic of 1837–38," *Beaver*, outfit 306 (autumn 1975): 8–13.

TREDWELL (Treadwell), NATHANIEL HAZARD, seigneur, fur-trader, and miller; b. 17 Jan. 1768 in Smithtown, N.Y., eldest son of Thomas Tredwell and Ann Hazard; m. 1793 Margaret Platt, and they had two sons and four daughters; d. 22 Dec. 1855 in L'Orignal, Upper Canada.

The son of a prominent state politician and judge, Nathaniel Hazard Tredwell was educated at Clinton Academy in East Hampton, Long Island, and trained as a civil engineer and land surveyor. He carried out extensive surveys in northern New York and, when his father and family moved from Long Island, he reportedly set up a new home near Plattsburgh, on Lake Champlain. In the spring of 1794, accompanied by his wife and a retinue of black servants (all former slaves who had been manumitted by his father), he immigrated to Lower Canada, settling on the north bank of the Ottawa River near the mouth of the Rivière du Nord. One of several non-loyalist Americans drawn to that area in the 1790s, he occupied an abandoned trading post, known as "Red House," and engaged in fur trading with the Indians.

Tredwell soon became interested in the development of large tracts of land in the Montreal district. In 1796 he acquired 1,500 acres south of Lac Saint-François, the seigneury of Ramezay, and the seigneury of Pointe-à-l'Orignal (Pointe-à-l'Orignac) which he purchased for 1,000 guineas from Joseph-Dominique-Emmanuel Le Moyne* de Longueuil. Located in Upper Canada upriver from "Red House," Pointe-à-l'Orignal extended six miles back from the river and nine miles along its shore. It was one of only two seigneurial holdings to lie within the province following its creation in 1791. Despite the efforts of his attorney in York (Toronto), Christopher Robinson*, Tredwell had great difficulty in having his

seigneurial claim recognized by the province's Executive Council and administrator, Peter Russell*, a situation which resulted in part from uncertainty surrounding both the exact limits of the seigneury and the legality of Tredwell's title, and in part from distrust of American land speculators. Although Tredwell never tendered seigneurial fealty and homage to the governor at Quebec, as Russell had instructed in 1799, his seigneurial claim was recognized by the Executive Council in 1805 on the recommendation of Attorney General Thomas Scott*. Tredwell's difficulties over Pointe-à-l'Orignal may have been a factor in his unsuccessful attempts in 1798 to buy, in association with Ross Cuthbert*, Kildare Township from Pierre-Paul Margane* de Lavaltrie and open it for settlement.

Tredwell maintained his fur-trading business but gradually started to develop a settlement around a stream in his seigneury at what is now the village of L'Orignal. Roads were opened to Glengarry County, to Plantagenet Township, and to the sawmill of David PATTEE and Thomas Mears at Hawkesbury, and by 1810 Tredwell had erected a sawmill and a grist-mill at L'Orignal. He had settled there himself about 1800, possibly as a result of the sheriff's sale that year of both his land on the Rivière du Nord, at the suit of Pierre-Louis Panet*, and the seigneury of Ramezay, at the suit of the Montreal mercantile firm of John Bell and Company. Once established in L'Orignal, Tredwell encouraged other Americans to join him as settlers in what was then virgin bush. Most of his land sales in the seigneury seem to have followed the recognition of his claim in 1805. He was a commanding figure, 6 feet 2½ inches tall, and he became well known for his hospitality. Although, according to a daughter, he was unorthodox in his beliefs, reputedly preferring the revolutionary works of Thomas Paine to the Bible, he had a "religious mind and never omitted family prayers."

In 1812, at the outbreak of war with the United States, he was required, because of his prominence in public life before he came to Canada, to take the oath of allegiance to the crown. He refused, his seigneurial land was evidently sequestered (though none seems to have been sold), and he had to return to the United States. During his journey south he was imprisoned at Dorchester (Saint-Jean-sur-Richelieu), Lower Canada. When offered his liberty he accepted but insisted upon an escort to the border, which was provided. Re-establishing himself in Plattsburgh with his wife and children, he built a mill on the Saranac River. In 1830 a great flood swept it away, forcing him to start again.

After his return to New York, Tredwell had continued to transact the sale of lands in his seigneury, which lay within Longueuil Township. In 1823 his son Charles Platt Treadwell returned to Upper Canada and after prolonged negotiations with provincial authorities repossessed the seigneury. On 19 Jan. 1824 he purchased 1,500 acres of it from his father and on 17 November bought the remainder. He added several thousand acres to his holding and further developed the settlement at L'Orignal, becoming a prominent citizen in the process. In 1835 he was appointed sheriff of the Ottawa District. Five years later Nathaniel Tredwell joined him at L'Orignal, and there spent his remaining years. A notice of his death in the *Montreal Gazette* said of him that he had "united the culture of a gentleman with the stern endurance of a backwoodsman."

ROBERT FERGUSON LEGGET

ANQ-Q, CN1-92, 23 mai 1796. AO, RG 1, A-I-6: 970–75, 1346–49; A-II-1, 1: 167, 469; C-I-1, petition of C. P. Treadwell, 27 Jan. 1830. PAC, MG 24, L3: 7160–61, 7164–66, 7171 (copies); RG 1, L1, 22: 277, 597; 24: 285–89; 26: 217; L3, 495a: T3/54; T4/39, 49; 496: T7/15; 511: T misc., 1797–1824/26; L3ᴸ: 62360–63. Prescott Land Registry Office (L'Orignal, Ont.), Abstract index to grantors, Longueuil Township, 44–46 (mfm. at AO, GS 5105). QUA, C. P. Treadwell papers, N. H. Treadwell corr., 1829, 1832, 1840; Survey maps, plan of L'Orignal. "Upper Canada land book B, 19th August, 1796, to 7th April, 1797," AO *Report*, 1930: 98. "Upper Canada land book C, 29th June, 1796, to 4th July, 1796; 1st July, 1797, to 20th December, 1797," AO *Report*, 1931: 71. "Upper Canada land book D, 22nd December, 1797, to 13th July, 1798," AO *Report*, 1931: 180, 183, 185–86, 188–89. *Montreal Gazette*, 5 Jan. 1856. *Quebec Gazette*, 14 Aug. 1800 (supplement). *The national cyclopædia of American biography* (59v. to date, New York, [etc.], 1892–   ), 3: 158–59. *Princetonians, 1748–1768: a biographical dictionary*, comp. James McLachlan (Princeton, N.J., 1976), 460, 468–72. W. A. Robbins, "Descendants of Edward Tre(a)dwell through his son John," *New York Geneal. and Biog. Record* (New York), 43 (1912): 138–40. P.-G. Roy, *Inv. concessions*, 3: 145; 5: 33. Lucien Brault, *Histoire des comtés unis de Prescott et Russell* (L'Orignal, 1965), 20–25, 229–31. Cyrus Thomas, *History of the counties of Argenteuil, Que., and Prescott, Ont., from the earliest settlement to the present* (Montreal, 1896; repr. Belleville, Ont., 1981). B. N. Wales, *Memories of St. Andrews and historical sketches of the seigniory of Argenteuil* (Lachute, Que., 1934).

TREMAIN, RICHARD, merchant, miller, militia officer, justice of the peace, and office holder; b. 20 June 1774 in New York City, son of Jonathan Tremain* and Abigail Stout; m. 1801 Mary Boggs in Halifax, and they had seven daughters and five sons; d. there 30 July 1854.

Richard Tremain's father emigrated in 1760 from England to New York City, where he built up a successful mercantile business. Having fled to Quebec as a loyalist refugee in 1783, he moved on to Halifax in 1786. There he resumed trading, which he

complemented by investment in flour milling, fishing, land, and coal mining. The family, through its close association with Lieutenant Governor Sir John Wentworth* and other leading loyalist families, enjoyed a secure place within the local oligarchy.

Richard, the second son, probably served a commercial apprenticeship under his father. In 1801, immediately after his marriage to a daughter of another prominent loyalist family, he formed a partnership with his brother-in-law, Charles Boggs, to operate a general store and brewery. Finding trade more profitable than brewing, Tremain concentrated on the import-export operations connected with the store and in 1814 he landed £24,929 worth of European dry goods, along with 19,744 gallons of molasses and 919 hundredweight of brown sugar. Much of his business involved the purchase of prize goods for later sale in the United States, a lucrative enterprise at the height of the War of 1812. The partnership with Boggs had ended in 1813, having been replaced by one with Richard's younger brother, James, and a family friend, Robert Hartshorne. That association in turn ended in 1821, after which Tremain proceeded on his own. Through the 1820s he continued as a Halifax general merchant, but increasingly the focus of his business activity came to be a Dartmouth flour-mill and bakehouse originally owned by his father and Lawrence Hartshorne* and taken over by himself and his brother James in 1815. The success of this venture owed much to Tremain's having won an exclusive contract to supply flour to the local garrison market. Revisions to British tariff policy in 1826, which had the effect of throwing the Halifax market open to American flour, may have prompted Tremain's decision to sell the Dartmouth property to the Shubenacadie Canal Company in 1831 for £6,700. Thereafter Tremain withdrew from active business, his income apparently being that of a *rentier*.

Thus by the mid 1830s Tremain had the status of a gentleman able to live in considerable comfort at Oakland, his estate in Halifax's south suburbs. He enjoyed community recognition through his service as president of the chamber of commerce, churchwarden of St Paul's, chairman of the Halifax firewards, lieutenant-colonel in the local militia, and director of the Nova Scotia Bible Society. Moreover, he had served as a magistrate since 1810, was commissioner of the house of correction from 1825 to 1831, and was deputy chairman and treasurer of the poor-house commission from 1826 to 1830. The various offices to which Tremain had been appointed should have been a source of prestige and influence, but they became instead the means of his subjection to public vilification, in an incident which simultaneously launched Joseph Howe* on his campaign for responsible government.

Tremblay

The episode occurred during the mid 1830s, at a time of business recession and rising taxes. The board of magistrates which presided over Halifax's internal affairs aroused increasing ire among ratepayers by refusing to account for public expenditure and by ignoring calls from the grand jury for the reform of its financial administration. Public dissatisfaction led to the publication in January 1835 of a letter in Howe's newspaper the *Novascotian or Colonial Herald*, wherein the anonymous author accused the magistrates of being arrogant, incompetent, and corrupt. Singled out for particular criticism were those magistrates who also served as commissioners of the poor-house. They, it was alleged, employed the institutionalized poor as unpaid servants and fed them with inferior flour purchased at high prices from stores owned by the commissioners. This practice, which could be variously interpreted as either illegal or simply indiscreet, immediately became the focus of a major confrontation between Howe and the champions of oligarchy.

Tremain, who had already experienced a number of attacks on his role within the Halifax administration, assumed that he was the prime target of Howe's anonymous correspondent. In self-defence he maintained that although he had sold flour and meal to the poor-house while serving on the commission of that institution, all sales had proceeded through open bidding, with prices being controlled by competition. Moreover, other commissioners had done the same. To suggest that anything illegal or even immoral had been done, Tremain insisted, was to engage in a "malicious" attack on those who served as stewards of the community. Public criticism of this kind aroused Tremain's fighting spirit. He had a reputation for belligerency that went back to the War of 1812, when he had joined a press-gang riot to rescue local sailors from the Royal Navy. As recently as 1832 he had been indicted for assault after quarrelling with a fellow magistrate. Accordingly, it was in character for Tremain to initiate the magisterial demand that Howe be tried for criminal libel.

Tremain's zeal in defending his honour precipitated a major crisis in Halifax. Several members of the gentry, including Howe's father, had become convinced of the need for reform in order to conciliate the aroused mass of ratepayers. Taking advantage of these cross-currents within the élite and of public dissatisfaction, Howe turned his libel trial into a forum for renewed rhetorical attack on the deficiencies of magisterial rule. Acquitted by a sympathetic jury, Howe launched into a political career which climaxed some 13 years later with the achievement of responsible government in Nova Scotia. Tremain was left to plead his innocence in letters to Lieutenant Governor Sir Colin Campbell* and to the editor of the Halifax *Journal*. Admitting himself to be humiliated,

he warned that the incident had grave implications, stating that "if public men are to seek the approval of Editors of Newspapers, instead of the Government from whence their authority is derived, soon will they become the master power, and great & small must court their countenance."

Several of the magistrates responded to Howe's victory by resigning, but Tremain refused to capitulate. Although purged from the poor-house commission, he stayed on as a justice of the peace. The post lost most of its power in 1841, however, when the administration of Halifax was taken from the justices in the Court of Quarter Sessions and turned over to an elected city council. Tremain's final defeat came in 1849 when the newly victorious reform party cancelled his magisterial commission. Meanwhile his personal affairs appear to have suffered considerable decline. The bankruptcy of his brother John in the mid 1830s and the related loss of £800 had undermined his financial security. Then, in 1848, his house at Oakland burned. Tremain's death six years later drew no more response than a two-line obituary notice in the Halifax *Church Times*.

Richard Tremain is best seen as an embodiment of the old régime in Nova Scotia. He was not so much corrupt as conventional, discharging his offices of public trust by the norms of the pre-reform era. He achieved notoriety essentially because the standards by which he had been brought up had become obsolete. Rather than adapt, he resisted, and thereby assured the destruction of his public career.

DAVID A. SUTHERLAND

Halifax County Registry of Deeds (Halifax), Deeds, 35: f.681; 38: f.275; 42: f.422; 43: f.19; 50: f.342; 54: f.186; 59: f.43; 61: f.192 (mfm. at PANS). PANS, RG 1, 149, 23 March 1835; 150: f.19; 226: ff.90, 117; 248: f.79; 411, no.130; 412, nos.137–39; RG 5, P, 120, 21 Jan. 1824; RG 13, 25; RG 31-104, 9, 1814. PRO, CO 217/203: 323. *Acadian Recorder*, 17 March 1821, 18 Feb. 1826. *Church Times* (Halifax), 5 Aug. 1854. *Journal* (Halifax), 6, 20–27 April 1835. *Novascotian*, 12 Jan. 1832, 8 May 1834, 1 Jan. 1835, 19 June 1842. *Nova-Scotia Royal Gazette*, 4 June 1801, 7 Jan. 1802, 21 July 1813, 5 Oct. 1814, 15 Jan. 1820. *Belcher's farmer's almanack*, 1824–54. W. E. Boggs, *The genealogical record of the Boggs family, the descendants of Ezekiel Boggs* (Halifax, 1916), 17, 82. *Halifax almanack*, 1819. C. T. Harrington, *A general history of the Harrington, DeWolfe and Tremaine families, with a genealogical record of 1643 to 1938* (Newton, Mass., 1938), 79–80. J. M. and L. J. Payzant, *Like a weaver's shuttle: a history of the Halifax–Dartmouth ferries* (Halifax, 1979), 11–19.

TREMBLAY, *dit* **Picoté**, **ALEXIS**, farmer, merchant, and lumberman; b. 14 June 1787 in Saint-Louis-de-l'Isle-aux-Coudres, Quebec, son of François Tremblay and Magdeleine Beauché, *dit* Morency; m. first 4 Sept. 1810 Modeste Bouliane in La

Malbaie, Lower Canada, and they had 11 children; m. there secondly 7 Sept. 1842 Olive Gagné, widow of Louis Desgagnés; d. there 26 Jan. 1859.

The parents of Alexis Tremblay, *dit* Picoté, left Île aux Coudres to settle at La Malbaie in the Charlevoix region at the end of the 18th century. Tremblay married after obtaining a grant of land in the seigneury of Mount-Murray on 27 Aug. 1810. This property represented an essential economic base for him until 1830. Subsequently, taking advantage of the experience of some relatives in the business world at La Malbaie, he gradually turned from farming to commerce and lumbering.

Tremblay opened a number of lumber camps in the environs of La Malbaie at the beginning of the 1830s. To get his timber on the market he had to deal with merchants such as Thomas Simard, who later became his partner, and William Price*. From 1832 his name often turns up in the latter's account-books, and in subsequent years Tremblay and his brother François were regular associates of Price.

In 1833, with the support of Simard and several other influential residents at La Malbaie, Tremblay circulated a petition seeking the opening of the Saguenay region, an immense section of the king's domain which had thus far been closed to farming and lumbering. It was submitted to the government along with a plan for an agricultural settlement built on lumbering and free of the seigneurial system. The petition stressed the lack of land in the Charlevoix region. But the sequence of events shows clearly that the signatories' request stemmed primarily from the desire to have access to new forest resources for the sizeable lumber trade developing in their region in step with the expansion of Canadian lumbering that began in the early 19th century. Thus, without waiting for an official reply, Tremblay and Simard started to take pine logs on crown land, having obtained permission in January 1836 from Peter McLeod, then agent of the Hudson's Bay Company, which held the licence to exploit the king's posts. That month, in a by-election to fill the seat for Saguenay in the House of Assembly, Tremblay gave his support officially to Charles Drolet*, a Patriote who pledged to make the Saguenay region accessible to people in Charlevoix. Two months later Tremblay and Simard formed a partnership with three businessmen of La Malbaie to build a sawmill at the falls on Rivière Malbaie. In mid March the plan to settle the Saguenay region was rejected by Governor Lord Gosford [Acheson*] and his council. As a result, Tremblay and Simard sold their share to Price. Tremblay remained as manager of the sawmill and became the official agent of William Price and Company at La Malbaie.

In view of the deterioration of the social and political climate in Lower Canada, George Simpson, the HBC governor, had apparently judged it advisable by the beginning of 1837 to hand over the cutting licence in the territory of the king's posts, which the company had enjoyed since 1836, to French Canadian lumber merchants. On 23 September he offered the licence to Simard, who in order to acquire it joined with Tremblay and some well-to-do people in La Malbaie to form the Societé des Entrepreneurs des Pinières du Saguenay, a joint-stock company later known as the Société des Vingt et Un. The company was secretly financed by Price, who would thus secure control of the best sawmill sites in the Saguenay valley, having left the actual installation and operation of the mills to local lumbermen under the direction of Simard and Tremblay. Yet, despite the experience of several of its members and the support of Price, the company encountered one set-back after another. From 1840 to 1842 Price gradually bought up the shares of its members through Tremblay. Thus, even before the Saguenay was officially opened to settlement, Price managed to acquire practically all the mills in the area. Tremblay, who had become responsible for overseeing Price's establishments at La Malbaie, on the north shore of the St Lawrence, and in the Saguenay region, in subsequent years regularly negotiated on his employer's behalf the purchase of most of the sawmills built in these parts.

During this period of prosperity Tremblay was obliged to travel constantly between La Malbaie and the Saguenay and gave up farming. In 1840, in partnership with his sons Isaïe and Alexis, he built a storehouse and wharf at La Malbaie. As a business-man and Price's agent he was now part of an élite there.

In 1839 Tremblay had backed a new and successful petition for the granting of lands in the Saguenay region. His support was detrimental to his own interests in the long run since the settling of the area created a local élite that freed the new centres from the grip of the Charlevoix merchants. Furthermore, when Peter McLeod became Price's partner in November 1842 Tremblay found himself reduced to the role of manager of the establishment at Grande-Baie, McLeod becoming overseer of the Saguenay region.

From 1843 William Price and Company ran into a number of difficulties, and Tremblay concentrated more on attending to his own affairs. On 29 April 1844 he went into partnership with Pierre and André Harvey, brothers who were merchants in La Malbaie, to "do trading in the Saguenay." His storehouse and wharf were placed at the disposal of the Harveys, and he agreed to let them run the company during the periods that he spent at Grande-Baie. A few days later the three new partners, along with other members of the bourgeoisie and some 100 farmers of La Malbaie and Sainte-Agnès, set up the Société du Saint-Laurent to develop trade, agriculture, and lumbering in the section of Saguenay County running along the St

Lawrence. The partners undertook to respect the HBC rights in this territory, and chose Tremblay as their agent general. In little more than two months this new company was dissolved, on the ground that the exploration of the area had proved disappointing. But meanwhile Tremblay had been busy. First he mortgaged his land to obtain the funds to construct a new storehouse to keep supplies for the Saguenay. Then he dissolved his partnership with the Harvey brothers. In the autumn he was to open a lumber camp at Portneuf in the seigneury of Mille-Vaches, acting on behalf of James GIBB, a lumberman from Quebec who was a partner of Price.

Doubtless because he was too busy at Portneuf, Tremblay in 1846 made over his share of the storehouse to his son Alexis, who had become an active merchant at La Malbaie and a useful associate of Price. Furthermore, during the 1840s Tremblay was one of the largest money-lenders in La Malbaie. He continued to participate in some of Price's ventures until 1850, and even took an interest in 1847 in the formation at La Malbaie of the Société des Défricheurs de la Rivière-au-Sable, which was set up to exploit the territory that later became the township of Jonquière.

Widowed in the spring of 1842, Tremblay married again that year. A shrewd businessman, on his first wife's death he had refused to have an inventory and apportionment of his assets done, but eventually in December 1850 he relinquished most of his personal estate to some of his children. The others had already received their share of their mother's estate in cash. Tremblay did, however, retain ownership of the land that he farmed with his son Augustin. In 1852, shortly after leaving Portneuf for good, he was again running a successful farming operation. During his last years he busied himself in setting up his younger children and settled a number of old debts and some earlier financial claims. He called himself a "bourgeois" like Thomas Simard, from whom he bought a mill at Port-aux-Quilles in 1858. In December of that year, not two months before his death, he finally made over to his son Augustin his land in the Ruisseau-des-Frênes range of lots.

At the end of his life, Alexis Tremblay, dit Picoté, owned only the mill at Port-aux-Quilles. He had indeed managed to provide for his numerous children, but this was a meagre recompense for a man who had helped build the empire of William Price.

MARIO LALANCETTE

ANQ-Q, CE4-2, 14 juin 1787; CE4-3, 4 sept. 1810, 7 sept. 1842, 28 janv. 1859; CN1-197, 16 oct. 1837; CN1-232, 1837; CN4-8, 4 juill. 1839; 12 oct., 28 déc. 1840; 12 mars 1841; 12 oct. 1842; 29 avril, 1er mai, 13 juin, 24 sept. 1844; 26 juin 1846; 5 nov. 1852; CN4-9, 3 janv., 12 févr., 11, 28 mars, 8, 19 avril, 1er mai, 8 juin, 3, 12, 29 sept., 1er, 22, 24 oct. 1836; 8 janv., 9, 13 juin, 24 juill., 9, 16, 19 oct., 11, 27, 28 nov. 1837; 16 janv., 18, 19 févr., 21 avril, 24 juill., 26 sept., 4 oct. 1838; CN4-10, 30 juin, 5 oct. 1840; 15 févr., 30 août 1842; 13 sept. 1848; 14 août, 7–21 déc. 1850; 16 nov. 1858; 8 mars 1859; CN4-12, 22 juill. 1823; CN4-13, 1836–60; CN4-15, 24 nov. 1807; 23, 27 août 1810; CN4-16, 18 mai, 11 juin 1795; CN4-19, 25 juill., 27 août 1842; 19 août 1844; P-81. ANQ-SLSJ, P-2, Dossiers 335; 340; 1646, doc.79. ASQ, S, S-168. PAC, RG 31, A1, 1842, 1851, La Malbaie. L.C., House of Assembly, *Journals*, 1828–29, app.RRR; 1834, app.H; 1835–36, app.EEE. Can., Prov. of, Legislative Assembly, *Journals*, 1841; 1857, app.25; 1858, app.15. "Un document intéressant," Victor Tremblay, édit., *Saguenayensia* (Chicoutimi, Qué.), 11 (1969): 45–48. *Le Canadien*, 21 mars 1836, 18 déc. 1843. Arthur Buies, *Le Saguenay et le bassin du lac Saint-Jean; ouvrage historique et descriptif* (3rd ed., Québec, 1896). Louise Dechêne, "William Price, 1810–1850" (thèse de licence, univ. Laval, Québec, 1964). Victor Tremblay, *Histoire du Saguenay depuis les origines jusqu'à 1870* (Chicoutimi, 1968). "Mémoires d'un vieillard: Maxime Tremblay 'Picoté,'" Victor Tremblay, édit., *Saguenayensia*, 2 (1960): 10–11. Victor Tremblay, "Des types de chez nous," *Saguenayensia*, 13 (1971): 111–14.

TROTTER, THOMAS, Presbyterian minister, teacher, office holder, and author; b. 1781 in Berwickshire, Scotland; m. 1808 Elizabeth Eadie, and they had one son and one daughter; d. 20 April 1855 in Antigonish, N.S.

Little is known of the early years of Thomas Trotter except that he studied medicine for a period at the University of Edinburgh before changing to theology. After studying under George Lawson at Selkirk, he was ordained in the Presbyterian ministry, into the burgher branch of the Secession Church, on 13 April 1808. That year he married and was called to Johnshaven, where he served for the next ten years. He was described as having exercised his pastoral duties with diligence and fidelity; for some time he was also the clerk of the Aberdeen presbytery. Through his warm-hearted friendship and extensive scholarship he became well liked and widely respected. However, economic conditions were poor and a heavy work-load was beginning to affect his health so he decided to accept a call from the congregation in Antigonish, N.S. Upon his arrival on 20 June 1818, he was inducted as the successor to the Reverend James Munroe.

The parish at Antigonish covered an extensive area but its population was small. To augment his income Trotter farmed and, in 1819, opened a grammar school. His main purpose, however, was to remedy a serious weakness in the educational system and for some time the government, recognizing the need for the school, gave an annual grant of £100. Trotter taught Latin and Greek and lectured on a variety of scientific issues, particularly geology, in which he was keenly interested. The Antigonish congregation, along with those in surrounding districts, increased in numbers and influence during Trotter's pastorate. An intelligent man with a great capacity for work, Trotter involved himself in all facets of community life. In addition to his preaching, teaching, and writing on a variety of issues, he also served as a school trustee, devoted considerable time to agriculture in trying to promote better farming methods, and built a grist-mill and later a fulling-mill.

During his years in Antigonish the population of the district was heavily Roman Catholic but, nevertheless, the Presbyterian cleric was well received and respected and enjoyed a warm friendship with Bishop William Fraser, the Catholic prelate, who, like Trotter, had been born in Scotland. Trotter was not as deeply involved in the theological disputes of Presbyterianism as some of his colleagues but neither did he refrain from expressing his views. He remained an orthodox minister and, although he had some differences with colleagues, it was his strong wish that there be a general union of Presbyterians in Nova Scotia.

Trotter developed a reputation as a writer on theological and scientific topics. He contributed letters and articles to the provincial press and occasionally to British publications as well as maintained a regular correspondence with friends and colleagues in Scotland and Nova Scotia. Some of his letters concerned Pictou Academy [see Thomas McCulloch*], in which he took a lively interest. His articles covered a wide area of learning and reflected the great depth of his scholarly and religious pursuits. A paper he read before the Literary and Scientific Society of Pictou on 4 Jan. 1837 was published as *The principles of meteorology*, and in 1845 *A treatise on geology* represented his attempt to reconcile religion and geology. Three years later he published *Letters on the meaning of baptizo* in reply to the views of Baptist minister Charles Tupper* concerning baptism. It appears that he also wrote "on one or two occasions" political articles in support of the liberals in Nova Scotia.

Following a stroke in 1853 Trotter gradually relinquished his duties and was succeeded in 1854 by the Reverend David Honeyman*. Trotter died the following year and his passing ended a career of useful endeavour in the religious, educational, and agricultural spheres. Like so many educated clerics of his day, he contributed towards the evolution of a Nova Scotia society, one in which the colonial cocoon was being shed.

RAYMOND A. MacLEAN

Thomas Trotter is the author of *The principles of meteorology; read at the meeting of the Literary and Scientific Society of Pictou, 4th January, 1837* (Pictou, N.S., n.d.; copy at St James United Church, Antigonish, N.S.); *A treatise on geology; in which the discoveries of that science are reconciled with the Scriptures, and the ancient revolutions of the earth are shown to be sources of benefit to man* (Pictou, 1845); and *Letters on the meaning of baptizo, in the New Testament; in reply to the views of the Rev. Charles Tupper* (Pictou, 1848). A collection of unpublished sermons and essays is in the Thomas Trotter papers, PANS, MG 1, 914B, and a "Legendary history of Britain" in his hand is found in PANS, MG 100, 239, no.41.

PANS, Churches, Presbyterian: Presbyterian Church of N.S., minutes, 1817–60, pp.303–5 (mfm.); MG 1, 552; Places: Pictou, Pictou Academy papers, W. M. Hepburn papers, W. M. Hepburn, "The early newspapers of Pictou," 5 (mfm.); RG 1, 439; RG 5, P, 51, no.97; RG 14, 45; RG 32, 13, no.6. St James United Church (Antigonish), Presbyterian Church, Antigonish, minutes, 1818–53. *Casket* (Antigonish), 22 Jan. 1857. *Colonial Patriot* (Pictou), 18 Feb. 1832. Morgan, *Bibliotheca Canadensis. Lit. hist. of Canada* (Klinck et al.; 1976), vol.1. D. G. Whidden, *The history of the town of Antigonish* (Wolfville, N.S., 1934). *Casket*, 17 Dec. 1891.

TRUSCOTT, GEORGE, banker; baptized 7 June 1785 in the parish of West Teignmouth, Devon, England, ninth and youngest child of Rear-Admiral William Truscott and Mary Croucher; m. first 29 Nov. 1820 Mary Stritch (d. 1837) in Exeter, England; m. secondly Ann Norman of Black Rock (Buffalo), N.Y., and they had two sons and seven daughters; d. 2 July 1851 in Buffalo.

The Truscotts were Devonshire gentry. All six of Rear-Admiral Truscott's sons went into the services, with George entering the navy in March 1793 as a captain's servant on his father's ship in the West Indies. He served in the Mediterranean, the English Channel, and the West Indies, rising to the rank of commander by 21 March 1812. That year he worked at different arsenals before being placed on half pay. Returning to active duty in December 1813, he commanded the gun-brig *Havock* at stations in the Channel, the North Sea, and off North America. He was placed on half pay again in 1815 but remained in the navy for 30 years, being promoted captain on 1 Feb. 1845, the year he retired from the service.

Truscott lived at Exeter during the 1820s, becoming a justice of the peace and a deputy lieutenant of the county. In 1830 he was admitted to the freedom of the city. About 1831 he and John Cleveland Green, both apparently with considerable personal means and good connections, founded a private bank there. Green had had some experience of the Canadas for he had served there in the commissariat from 1811 to 1818. John Henry Dunn, the receiver general of Upper Canada and an open proponent of new banks and "abundant" supplies of money for commerce, may have suggested the transfer of their banking operation to that province. Truscott came to Upper

Truscott

Canada in 1833, when he applied for land, receiving 461 acres in Zorra (East and West Zorra) Township in Oxford County, where many naval officers had settled. Banking, however, was his primary interest and in March 1834 he deposited some "banknote moulds" with the London banking firm of Grote, Prescott, and Grote, which was to become his English representative. By early 1834 rumours were flying in Upper Canada that a major English banking-house would soon open a branch in Toronto. Truscott and Green arrived there in May and began operations in June just as a major economic boom was getting under way in North America. Their firm, Truscott, Green and Company, operating as the Agricultural Bank, was a private partnership: unlike a chartered bank, the partners were totally liable for losses. Such a partnership had been demanded by some reformers, particularly William Lyon Mackenzie*, but it was bound to irritate Toronto's tory establishment and its Bank of Upper Canada, which had been operating alone since the withdrawal of the Bank of Montreal's branch from the city in 1829. There were some reformers, however, who raised questions about the partnership's financial base. Under these circumstances it might be expected that the partners would proceed cautiously; instead, with Dunn's "every countenance," Truscott, always the dominating influence, conducted operations with tremendous competitive vigour.

Immediately after the Agricultural Bank opened, a series of incidents took place. The newly incorporated city of Toronto, of which Mackenzie was mayor, required a loan of £1,000 for public works. The province's leading financiers, including the Bank of Upper Canada and the Commercial Bank of the Midland District, refused funding but Truscott, Green and Company agreed to provide the loan. A more painful cause of friction between the banks quickly followed: although no bank in the province had ever paid interest, the Agricultural Bank gave $3\frac{1}{2}$ per cent on deposits, forcing the others to do the same. The real battle, however, was precipitated by Truscott's method of obtaining specie. There being no mint, the banks customarily imported their own metallic currency at a small charge. However, each bank issued its own paper money, which it had to exchange for specie upon demand. Using this lever, Truscott avoided the cost of importing specie by obtaining Bank of Upper Canada notes in the course of business – even buying them at a discount in the United States – and presenting them for payment in hard cash. William ALLAN, president of the Bank of Upper Canada, claimed these withdrawals exceeded £30,000. In 1835 Allan, followed by the Commercial Bank, struck back by refusing to accept Agricultural Bank notes. Truscott, professing that he was following the usual English practice of drawing specie from the Bank of England (although he must have known that it was not the practice in Upper Canada), claimed, correctly, that Allan was trying to put him out of business.

When his tactic did not have this effect, Allan began buying up all the Agricultural Bank notes he could obtain across the province and presenting them for specie. Truscott asserted that $145,000 was demanded in less than three months in the attempt to break him; that the Agricultural Bank survived is evidence of its extensive backing. Both banks were nevertheless put to great cost. Truscott may also have attempted a take-over of the Bank of Upper Canada, or at least election to its board of directors, by purchasing stock at a premium of $16\frac{1}{2}$ per cent. Nothing, however, came of this manœuvre.

Truscott's next sally was to appeal directly to Lieutenant Governor Sir John Colborne*, first in February 1835. After various exchanges with Allan, Truscott demanded an official investigation of the Agricultural Bank's affairs. This, he believed, could counter Allan's claim that the Bank of Upper Canada would not accept Agricultural Bank notes because its resources were not publicly known. He realized too that a House of Assembly dominated by reformers would probably produce a supportive report; that is exactly what a special committee, chaired by William Lyon Mackenzie, submitted in March 1835. The report lacked detail but it did not question the Agricultural Bank's balance of £9,688. The whole contest probably played a role in Allan's retirement at about this time.

In June 1835 Truscott helped to establish another partnership bank, the Farmers' Joint Stock Banking Company, the founders of which included John Elmsley*, Francis Hincks*, and William Ketchum. Why he involved himself in founding a rival reform bank is uncertain. However, he intended renting to it the Agricultural Bank's Front Street premises. Possibly he planned to involve wealthy reformers in his Canadian operations, and then to retire to take care of his American interests. Whatever the case, the election of the first board of directors in July led to internal dissension and by early September Truscott and the reform directors had been forced out. As well, by August Mackenzie had broken with both the Farmers' and the Agricultural banks, perhaps because of Truscott's resort to aggressive litigation in obtaining payments due to the former. Thenceforth Truscott found him attacking the Agricultural Bank just as he did the Bank of Upper Canada.

During the heat of the controversy with the Bank of Upper Canada, Truscott had made remarks in confidence about tory leader Allan Napier MacNab*, which Mackenzie heard and repeated in the assembly. The result, on 19 March 1835, was one of the last duels in Upper Canada, in which MacNab's pistol misfired and Truscott shot into the air. Later that year Truscott took Thomas Gibbs Ridout*, the cashier (general manager) of the Bank of Upper Canada, to court for verbal slander, winning judgement in October. In 1837 he applied for an injunction against the city of Toronto when it decided to issue paper money during the shortage of coinage that developed as part of the financial crisis of that year [see Sir Francis Bond Head*]. Thus, in law as in business, Truscott took forceful and immediate action, a point to remember given his later allegedly passive acceptance of the mismanagement of the Agricultural Bank's funds in the United States. Aside from his banking activities he played little role in the city, not a surprising fact in view of the number of enemies he must have made. He was, however, a member of the United Services Club, Toronto's first gentlemen's organization.

Although his Canadian operations may seem to have been complex enough to occupy his time, Truscott was simultaneously busy in the United States. The American operations arose through the development of the typical branch bank system of the period. In September 1834 the Agricultural Bank had opened its first branch, in St Thomas, Upper Canada; during the bank war others were added, principally at various centres in the southwest part of the province and at Montreal. These caused no problems; but in 1834 Truscott and Green had also established a branch in Buffalo, N.Y., managed by one of their Toronto employees, 19-year-old John Wellington Buckland, whose youth was balanced by his father's alleged position in the house of Rothschild. Then in April 1835, rather mysteriously but ostensibly at Buckland's urging, a partnership was formed in Buffalo between Truscott, Green and Company and Buckland and Russell Searle Brown of the drug firm of Starkweather and Brown. Under this agreement Buckland would receive 15 per cent of the profits and Brown 25 per cent, but it was Truscott, Green and Company which had put up the partnership's entire capital of $30,000.

Almost immediately Brown, presumably with the connivance of Buckland, violated the agreement by drawing advances from the Agricultural Bank of more than $30,000; by autumn advances to Buckland and Brown were up to $88,000. Later, Truscott and Green claimed that they had insisted on a reduction in these advances, yet, instead of demanding a return, they formed a revised partnership with Buckland and Brown in April 1836. By then transfers had reached $131,648. The new agreement established Brown, Buckland and Company in Buffalo, supposedly under the supervision of Truscott, and Green, Brown and Company in New York City, with Green as resident partner. Later, Truscott and Green were to claim that they had had only a very vague idea of the various transactions, stating that it had "never occurred to them . . . to enter upon any examination of the books at Buffalo for the purpose of verifying the statements of profit and loss" of the partnership.

Such assertions are hard to believe. Rather, Truscott and Green were in all likelihood hiding the fact that they had used, for American speculations, the money Upper Canadian and English investors had paid into Brown, Buckland and Company and Green, Brown and Company. Among the investors involved was Receiver General John Henry Dunn, who made special advances "for the collective benefit of the firms" totalling $74,281, much of this amount not being properly secured by the partners. It is uncertain whether this was the province's money, his own, or a mixture of both; in any case, under the lax administrative controls of the time he was allowed to keep any profits made from personal investments using the funds of the province. It seems obvious that all those participating were looking for windfall profits in the booming American economy.

Two factors checked the plans of Truscott and Green. The boom of the mid 1830s in both the United States and Canada was rapidly drawing to a close in 1837. Even had it continued they could not have made a profit, for Brown was secretly entering into assorted devious enterprises, including the transfer of assets amounting to $74,652 from his reorganized partnership to Starkweather and Brown. When confronted by Green, he hid evidence and gained control of securities by subterfuge. That Truscott and Green did not sue him may indicate that they were both trying to hide their own involvement and prevent a run on the Agricultural Bank. In the spring of 1837 Brown was expelled from the partnership, but making him provide assets to cover his defalcations proved difficult.

Faced with a shortage of funds, the New York office was closed on 9 Oct. 1837; at the same time the Agricultural Bank began issuing notes without Green's name on them. In November Truscott and Green were arrested in Toronto at the instigation of the City Bank of Buffalo; they put up as bail securities entrusted to them by English investors and fled to Buffalo. Simultaneously the Agricultural Bank collapsed and Mackenzie announced in the *Constitution*, with some glee, that "Truscott & Co. are Bankrupt in right earnest." In February 1838 the Upper Canadian House of Assembly estimated that the unpaid notes of the Agricultural Bank totalled $20,000; its depositors had nothing. In June, Truscott and Green issued an explanation from Buffalo along with a promise to make good their arrears. They never did. Upper Canada's most spectacular and speculative banking venture was at an end.

What part of their personal fortunes they saved, or even invested, is unknown. Truscott tried unsuccess-

Tubbee

fully to get a pension from the British government. In 1840 he appeared as an "exchange broker" in Buffalo and remained active in that occupation until his death in 1851, a development which provides some evidence that his wealth was not exhausted. Of even more significance, he owned property in Buffalo, including a residence on Delaware Avenue, long the élite residential thoroughfare of the city. In addition he still held property in England, protected by various trusts, and apparently he was able to leave a considerable competency to his family.

Exact details of what happened in Truscott's North American banking venture may never be known. It is difficult, however, to come to any other conclusion than that Truscott and Green were misusing investors' funds for speculation in New York State and that they were outfoxed by an unscrupulous partner, although not to the extent that they would have had others believe. That Truscott must have had an impressive appearance and used his captaincy to best advantage is obvious; that he may have found many of his chief victims among wealthy investors in Toronto, including John Henry Dunn, seems a distinct probability. Whatever else, the panic of 1837 and the default of the Agricultural Bank likely accelerated the institution of stricter banking controls in Upper Canada.

IN COLLABORATION

AO, MS 78, Stanton to Macaulay, 18 March 1835; Cozens to Macaulay, 18 March 1835; Macaulay to Ann Macaulay, 14 April 1837; RG 1, A-I-6, 14; A-II-2, 1: 287. Devon Record Office (Exeter, Eng.), St David parish, Exeter, reg. of marriages, 29 Nov. 1820. Erie County Surrogate's Court (Buffalo, N.Y.), will of George Truscott. PAC, MG 24, E1, 9: 1038–41; MG 30, D101, 2–4; RG 1, L3, 502: T18/16; RG 5, A1: 70797–800, 73499–503, 78719–20, 79494–96, 82370–72, 82674–84, 123472–74. PRO, ADM 107/31: 176. St James' Church (Church of England) (Teignmouth, Eng.), West Teignmouth, reg. of baptisms, 7 June 1785 (transcript at Devon Record Office). *Naval Chronicle* (London), 30 (July–December 1813): 177. Truscott, Green & Co., *Statement of the financial transactions of the banking firm of Truscott, Green & Co. of Toronto, in connection with Green, Brown and Co. of New York; and Brown, Buckland & Co. of Buffalo . . .* (Buffalo, 1838). U.C., *Statutes*, 1837, c.13; 1837, 2nd session, c.1, c.2; 1838, c.22, c.23. G.B., ADM, *Navy list*, 1851. John Marshall, *Royal naval biography . . .* (4v. in 6 and 2v. supp., London, 1823–35), 7: 68, 336. National Maritime Museum (London), *Catalogue of the library* (5v. in 7, London, 1968–76), 2. O'Byrne, *Naval biog. dict.* (1849). *Toronto directory*, 1837. *Visitation of England and Wales*, ed. J. J. Howard and F. A. Crisp (19v., [London], 1893–1917), 4: 99–103. Franklin Graham, *Histrionic Montreal; annals of the Montreal stage with biographical and critical notices of the plays and players of a century* (2nd ed., Montreal, 1902; repr. New York and London, 1969), 105. R. J. Graham, "Captain Truscott's Canadian banking adventures," *Canadian Paper Money Journal* (Toronto), 14 (1978): 71–82, 101–9. Adam Shortt,

"Founders of Canadian banking: Captain George Truscott, R.N., retired naval officer and adventurous banker," Canadian Bankers' Assoc., *Journal* (Toronto), 31 (1923–24): 38–49. E. L. Weekes, "History of Buckerell Bore," *Devon and Exeter Daily Gazette* (Exeter), 14 Nov. 1927.

TUBBEE, OKAH (William Chubbee, William McCarey), musician and doctor; fl. 1830–56.

All the details of the early life of Okah Tubbee must be taken from the various editions of his autobiography which appeared between 1848 and 1852. According to his claims, he was born a Choctaw Indian, kidnapped as a child by a white man, and raised by a black "mother" as William McCarey, a slave, in Natchez, Miss. Although always suspecting that he was an Indian, the boy knew nothing of his origins and endured a childhood filled with constant cruelty and racial abuse. His "violent temper" eventually led him to strike another youth on the head with a brick and landed him in prison briefly. Shortly thereafter he was apprenticed to a blacksmith in Natchez, but he left after receiving a brutal whipping. At about this point McCarey discovered that he was the son of the Choctaw chief Mosholeh Tubbee (William Chubbee). McCarey began styling himself Okah Tubbee or William Chubbee and became involved in a legal case, which apparently carried on for years, in which he attempted to have himself legally declared an Indian rather than a black slave.

As a child Tubbee had been a talented whistler and ventriloquist and throughout the 1830s he pursued the life of an itinerant musician, being at that time an accomplished flautist. Some time in the early 1840s he married Laah Ceil Manatoi Elaah, supposedly the daughter of a Mohawk chief, in Iowa City (Iowa), and they were to have at least one son and two daughters. During the 1840s the drama in Tubbee's life seems to have continued unabated: he was forced to leave a number of towns (because, he claimed, of false rumours about his former violent behaviour) and he acted as the self-proclaimed hero of a shipwreck. He also began to travel extensively among the Indian tribes throughout the United States as a musician and a temperance advocate.

By 1850 Tubbee was concentrating his various activities in the North and had begun advertising himself as a doctor. Making a good deal of the experience he had gained during a year spent in a "situation" with an army surgeon but mainly stressing Indian herbal remedies he had gleaned through his meetings with numerous medicine men, he had started making forays into Upper Canada by 1851. However, the many testimonials which accompany the 1852 Toronto edition of his autobiography suggest that, at least until the summer of 1852, it was his musical rather than his medicinal talents that the citizens of Upper Canada desired. Methodist missionaries Peter

JONES and William CASE attested to the success of a concert given by Tubbee at Cayuga on 8 Jan. 1852, and John Stoughton Dennis* commented on the excellence of one given at Weston (Toronto) two months later. Testimonials dated July and August from residents of Toronto thanked Tubbee for treating "Liver Complaint, Female Disability, Tumour of the Neck, Scrofula in the Leg, and Hereditary Consumption."

Unfortunately for Tubbee, his timing in relocation was bad. He had arrived in Upper Canada when the campaign against quacks and patent medicine vendors was taking shape. On 7 April 1854 a letter appeared in the daily Toronto *Globe* from A. B. McNab of Durham, Grey County, accusing Tubbee of accepting ten dollars for medicine from the family of a seriously ill young man, who had since died. Because no medicine had been forthcoming, McNab demanded that Tubbee repay the family. Two weeks later the *Globe* ran Tubbee's reply which asserted that McNab had pleaded with him to accept the money, that there had clearly been a misunderstanding, and that he would be happy to refund it. In the middle of this controversy, on 22 April, Robert Jackson Macgeorge* of the Streetsville *Weekly Review* entreated: "May the hospitalities of the Penitentiary be extended to all 'Herb Doctors,' 'Indian Physicians,' and 'German and Reform Practitioners of Medicine.'" On 3 May the *Globe* noted that it felt no need to publish McNab's rejoinder to the "Indian quack Doctor" since "every one understands the case perfectly, and nothing could be gained by it but adding to the notoriety of the charlatan." Tubbee then had a poetic advertisement printed in which he bemoaned the fact that "of late I've been shamefully (M')*Nab'd* at."

It seems that Tubbee's protestations fell upon deaf ears since by 1857 he appears to have left Toronto. He supposedly relocated in New York City, perhaps desiring the anonymity that only the largest city on the continent could provide.

CHARLES DOUGALL

[I should like to acknowledge the detective work of former *DCB* bibliographies editor Joan E. Mitchell, without which this biography would not have been written. C.D.]

Okah Tubbee's life story was told in at least three pamphlets. L. L. Allen produced *A thrilling sketch of the life of the distinguished chief Okah Tubbee, alias, Wm. Chubbee, son of the head chief, Mosholeh Tubbee, of the Choctaw nation of Indians* (New York, 1848). Tubbee's wife, Laah Ceil Manatoi Elaah Tubbee, published *A sketch of the life of Okah Tubbee, alias, William Chubbee, son of the head chief, Mosholeh Tubbee, of the Choctaw nation of Indians* (Springfield, Mass., 1848), and *A sketch of the life of Okah Tubbee, (called) William Chubbee, son of the head chief, Mosholeh Tubbee, of the Choctaw nation of Indians* (Toronto, 1852).

Globe, 7, 21 April, 3 May 1854 [this is the daily edition found in the Baldwin Room at the MTL, and not the one available on CLA microfilm]. *Weekly Review* (Streetsville, [Ont.]), 22 April 1854. *Toronto directory*, 1856. J. J. Talman, "Three Scottish-Canadian newspaper editor poets," *CHR*, 28 (1947): 166–77.

TUYLL VAN SEROOSKERKEN (de Tuyll de Serooskerken), VINCENT GILDEMEESTER VAN, Baron van TUYLL VAN SEROOSKERKEN, land speculator and developer; b. 13 March 1812 in Bath, England, son of Carel Lodewijk van Tuyll van Serooskerken and Marie Louise Gildemeester; m. 8 Aug. 1844 Charlotte Henrietta Mansfield in London, and they had three sons and four daughters; d. 17 March 1860 in The Hague, Netherlands.

The van Tuyll van Serooskerken family has had a long and distinguished history in the Netherlands. Its Upper Canadian connection began in the 1830s with the real estate speculations of Carel Lodewijk van Tuyll van Serooskerken on the western fringe of the Canada Company's vast Huron Tract. His son, Vincent Gildemeester van Tuyll van Serooskerken, inherited the lands after his father's death and with them a complex set of contractual responsibilities for their development. The colourful young baron attempted to open up and sell his large acreage but continuous financial problems, difficulties with transatlantic communications, the comparative remoteness of the property, and a mounting reluctance on the part of Canada Company officials to extend his credit forced him to reduce his ambitions and eventually to quit the speculation.

The family was well established in the Netherlands. With the Napoleonic occupation Carel Lodewijk escaped to England, where in 1811 he married the daughter of a former Dutch consul-general to Portugal. When Vincent Gildemeester was born at Bath the following year, his father enjoyed sufficient prestige to have him christened at Bath Abbey. After the restoration of the House of Orange the family returned to the Netherlands. In 1816 Carel Lodewijk became gentleman of the bedchamber to King Willem I, and a year later was appointed dike-reeve of the district of IJzendoorn. His title of baron was granted in 1822. Although much of his time thereafter seems to have been spent as a gentleman farmer at Hillegom, he had more than a passing interest in commerce, particularly in coal mining near Liège (Belgium). It is likely that through business connections made during his stay in England he heard of the Canada Company, which had been chartered in 1826, but nothing is known of the negotiations which preceded his association with the company and there is little evidence to suggest that he ever visited the Canadas.

The task of selecting or inspecting property in the Huron Tract fell to Carel Lodewijk's agent, Ed-

Tuyll

ward C. Taylor of Goderich, who began amassing land partly on the advice of Commander Henry Wolsey Bayfield*, a family connection. In 1832 Taylor arranged the baron's purchase of over 4,000 acres, including 1,800 in Goderich Township and a 388-acre town-plot, surveyed that year in Stanley Township at the mouth of the Bayfield River. The purchase price of £1,500 was to be paid with £300 down in 1832 and the balance in equal annual instalments between 1833 and 1837. Later, up to 700 acres were purchased in Colborne Township. The baron agreed to establish settlers, develop mill sites, and build a dam on the Bayfield River and erect a sawmill and a grist-mill there to serve the needs of the projected town of Bayfield – all before 1836. The scheme was potentially a good one for both the baron and the Canada Company. Thomas Mercer Jones*, one of its commissioners, initially showed a great deal of enthusiasm for the project. Van Tuyll's plans, however, largely fell victim to this ill-fated optimism for in the 1830s much excellent land closer to established centres was still available elsewhere in the province, frequently at prices lower than those offered by the company.

In the early 1830s Vincent Gildemeester inspected his father's estate and built an attractive Regency-style manor north of Goderich. He subsequently made several trips to Upper Canada, in the course of them travelling widely throughout the province and the United States. A mill was started at Bayfield in 1835; but the death that year of Carel Lodewijk meant delays and confusion while his Dutch affairs were settled. The resulting suspension of instalment payments greatly alarmed the Canada Company's directors in London. A threat of forfeiture was turned aside only by a special plea from Vincent Gildemeester, to whom company officials extended every courtesy at this juncture. In 1837 a new bargain was struck. Even so Vincent had trouble finding a guarantor and finally, in June of that year, the company agreed to accept £1,000 as security for the fulfilment of his debts and obligations. Baron Vincent deposited £500 with the company's bankers but, evidently pushed financially in the Netherlands (an international depression had begun in 1837), he had difficulty with the second half of the deposit. It was finally paid in August 1838.

It seems apparent that neither baron had any practical idea of the costs of the improvements which each contracted to make. Vincent had few problems in paying off the purchase price by August 1841, but it was minor compared to the improvements, which would nearly overwhelm his resources. Taylor was highly critical of the company's demands and informed Jones in 1838 that "the Russian Autocrat could not place his meanest vassals in a more helpless degrading position than the Canada Company have placed the Baron de Tuyll." The cost of forfeiture would be "about twenty times the original value of the purchase, and the purchase money to boot." Such, Taylor concluded, "is the contemplated reward for improving a Wilderness!!"

Certainly Jones now felt that the deal should never have been made. The Bayfield mill alone, he informed the company directors, would cost the baron £2,000 to complete, and he was further convinced that van Tuyll did not yet understand the continuing expenses that he would encounter, not simply in fulfilling his contract but in making his lands saleable. Jones's fears were soon realized. The Bayfield River dam cost £1,600 – fully £1,300 over the contract price Taylor had arranged. Moreover, land sales were sluggish in the aftermath of the rebellion of 1837–38 and the town of Bayfield was still largely a mass of uncleared lots and scattered wooden buildings. Although the baron made some efforts to meet his expenses, he borrowed increasingly from the company, either through its Canadian commissioners or by simply failing to meet the terms of the contract. The company's court of directors in London was furious with the commissioners for making advances to van Tuyll but still they were sympathetic to his difficulties and reluctant to become enmeshed in legal action against him. A court case could well be injurious not only to the company and to the baron, but also to immigration and settlement generally – not to mention the company's stock on the London exchange.

In 1841 the dam and bridge at Bayfield were swept away by floods, and the Canada Company was faced with the responsibility for their repair. Taylor's death the previous year had thrown the baron's affairs into confusion. By now desperate to meet the costs of improvements, in August 1841 van Tuyll coaxed the company into accepting a mortgage on his Bayfield properties for £1,130 payable in December 1842. A second mortgage of £800 was reluctantly granted in August 1844. Yet by February 1847 the indulgent company had not received a penny and, understandably, its patience was at an end. The Canadian commissioners were ordered to settle the affair and the baron was threatened with foreclosure and the seizure of his remaining Canadian property. Van Tuyll nevertheless had enough influence to have one final bargain negotiated. A new commissioner, Frederick Widder*, fully realized the costs and dangers of what could only be prolonged litigation, and the baron was granted more time to pay off a debt of almost £2,200. In 1849 he began making regular, substantial payments to the company through the Bank of Upper Canada, and by 1857 the company was able to report him as fully paid. The money had not, however, come from his Huron lands, which took many years to sell off.

In the late 1840s van Tuyll had evidently begun speculating in tin mining and pewter production on the island of Billiton (Belitong) in the Dutch East Indies (Indonesia). He was immediately successful (in 1850, to celebrate, he named a daughter Sophie Mathilde Henriette Bilitonia Wilhelmine). In 1852 van Tuyll and Prince Hendrik of the Netherlands were appointed government commissioners to develop the Dutch tin industry, an important sideline of which was the production of toy soldiers. The baron died in 1860, just before the establishment of the N.V. Billiton Maatschappij (the Billiton International Metals Company), of which both his son and his grandson became president-commissioners.

Throughout the years of his Canadian involvement, van Tuyll was prominent at the Dutch royal court. In 1838, he became a royal chamberlain and, as part of the Dutch delegation, attended Queen Victoria's coronation. In the Huron Tract he was viewed as a strange and picturesque character. Tall and bearded, athletic with a keen interest in fencing, sailing, and fishing, and known to be flirtatious, he affected the dress of the country and was frequently seen in a blanket coat and a close hat featuring a squirrel's tail. In 1844 he married Charlotte Henrietta Mansfield and appears to have settled down somewhat. During the 1850s he farmed the family estates at Hillegom, raised a large family, and travelled extensively, spending much time at the fashionable German spa of Baden-Baden and at Munich. He and the baroness took up residence for a short period in the Huron Tract and, although neither felt particularly at home there, the baron seems to have been a leader in Goderich's energetic society.

In a larger sense the barons' role in Upper Canada's development was a minor one. Yet, they are of interest in showing the variety of people who were interested in profiting from North American development projects, and Vincent's career adds another touch of colour to the already diverse social picture of the colony.

FREDERICK H. ARMSTRONG and ROGER HALL

Algemeen Rijksarchief (The Hague, Netherlands), Coll. Baud, inventory no.898; Royal Decrees, 17 Nov. 1816, no.44; 9 Dec. 1817, no.44; 21 May 1822, no.68; 7 Sept. 1830, no.84; 30 May 1838, no.69; 22 Nov. 1842, no.6; 3 June 1852, no.5; 19 June 1852, no.55. AO, Canada Company records, A-2, 3; A-3, 4–8; A-4-5, box 1a, vol.1; A-6-1, 2; A-6-2, 3–4; A-6-3, 1; B-3, 1, 3, 19, 49–50; C-1, 2–3. GRO (London), Reg. of marriages for the parish of St George Hanover Square (London), 8 Aug. 1844. Somerset Record Office (Taunton, Eng.), Reg. of baptisms, Bath Abbey, 17 April 1812. *Nederlands adelsboek* (The Hague), 45 (1952). R. D. Hall, "The Canada Company, 1826–1843" (PHD thesis, Cambridge Univ., Cambridge, Eng., 1973). Robina and K. M. Lizars, *In the days of the Canada Company: the story of the settlement of the Huron Tract and a view of the social life of the period* (Toronto and Montreal, 1896). F. H. Armstrong, "The elusive barons of Bayfield: an excursion into the byways of history," *Families* (Toronto), 18 (1979): 67–74.

TWINING, JOHN THOMAS, Church of England clergyman and teacher; b. 14 May 1793 in Cornwallis, N.S., second son of William Twining, rector of St John's Church, and Sarah Weeks, daughter of Joshua Wingate Weeks, another Anglican clergyman; m. 1814 Susan Mary Winnett (Winniett) of Annapolis Royal, N.S., and they had five sons; d. 8 Nov. 1860 in Halifax.

John Thomas Twining's father had emigrated from Britain in 1770 as an impecunious Welsh curate employed by the Society for the Propagation of the Gospel, first in the Bahamas and then in Nova Scotia and Cape Breton. He served at Cornwallis from 1789 to 1805; at Sydney, Cape Breton, until 1813; at Rawdon and Horton until 1819; and at Liverpool until his death in 1826. The frequent changes owed something to his Methodist leanings which were well suited to Americanized church-goers in the Annapolis valley and along the South Shore but tended to bring him into conflict with the Anglican conservative élite and the church authorities. William's sympathy for low church practices had its impact on John Thomas, who followed in his father's footsteps both as a clergyman and as an evangelical.

Educated on an SPG exhibition at King's College, Windsor (BA 1813, MA 1816, DD 1823), of which he was in later years a devoted alumnus, the younger Twining served between 1815 and 1817 as principal of King's College School in Windsor. He was ordained deacon in 1816 and priest in 1817, the year he began his career in the church as curate to John Inglis* at St Paul's, Halifax. That same year he became officiating chaplain to the British garrison at Halifax, a position he held until his death, and assistant to George Wright*, the headmaster of the Halifax Grammar School, whom Twining succeeded in 1819.

Influenced by the evangelical preaching of Isaac Temple, chaplain to Lord Dalhousie [Ramsay*], and by the zeal of the Church Missionary Society and the British and Foreign Bible Society, Twining accentuated the low church tendencies at St Paul's. In 1824–25 he became a focal point in the secession of dissidents who opposed the crown's interference in the appointment of a successor to Inglis on the latter's elevation to the bishopric of Nova Scotia. Although Twining's evangelicalism may have helped to inspire the disruption, the Paulines were mainly concerned with the refusal of the church and state authorities to recognize their right to choose their own clergyman. Twining was caught in the middle. He left St Paul's with the seceders but refused, perhaps for financial reasons, to become minister of the independent episcopal church they desired. He none the less continued to command the respect and affection of the parishioners of St Paul's who, through their representatives and friends in the legislature, secured him the lifelong sinecure of chaplain to the House of Assembly in 1825. Opposed in their choice of

Twining

chaplain by the Council, the MLAs stoutly refused to budge, and their successful endorsement of Twining can be interpreted as part of their mounting campaign against oligarchy. The St Paul's secession itself represented a demand for North American democratic over Old World autocratic procedures.

Unlike those seceders who eventually found their peace in the Baptist church, such as James William Johnston*, Twining tried to reach some accommodation with Anglican leaders. To satisfy the bishop and the SPG he admitted and repented several "grievous" doctrinal errors and ministerial practices as well as participation in, though not leadership of, the secession. In response, Inglis, ever vigilant about encouraging "dissenters within the church," blocked him from preferment in Halifax, and Twining's appeals to the SPG and Colonial Office for a church living elsewhere also ended in failure. For the next 20 years his activities on the fringes of Halifax Anglicanism included support for various religious and educational organizations disapproved of by the bishop and alliances with other evangelical clergy, including the sons of prominent Anglican families such as the Uniackes and the Cogswells. But he was expected not to interfere with the bishop's policies, and when, in 1847, he emerged with Robert Fitzgerald Uniacke* as a strong supporter of the Colonial Church Society, a low church educational society shunned by Inglis, the bishop accused Twining of "fomenting party" and leading Uniacke astray. Inglis unsuccessfully manœuvred to have Twining removed from Halifax by the chaplain general.

Frustrated in his ambition to rise in the hierarchy of his church, Twining devoted himself to his functions as teacher and chaplain. As headmaster of the Halifax Grammar School, he earned himself an unenviable reputation as a harsh disciplinarian. Undoubtedly his own rigidity and humourless approach to children were by-products of his evangelicalism. One of his pupils later recorded that he was a veritable tyrant and was especially severe on his own children. Frequent respites from the schoolroom routine were fortunately provided for the boys by Twining's responsibilities as chaplain. Military funerals meant both a holiday and entertainment for the budding grammarians.

Twining approached his military chaplaincy with considerable doubt about his tenure. His censure by the bishop in 1827 meant that he was prohibited from preaching in diocesan churches; his functions as Anglican chaplain had to be performed in the rented chapels of dissenters or in the commissariat store. While Twining was barred from entering the pulpits of the parish churches, the soldiers and their families were barred from the pews by lack of space. To meet the need, between 1817 and 1844 Twining held garrison services in 11 different buildings, and the uncertainty which constant uprooting induced was not alleviated by his apprehension that he might be replaced by a regularly commissioned army chaplain. Although he would have welcomed such an appointment for himself, he remained a civilian when the new garrison chapel opened in 1846. None the less, at that time he became full-time chaplain, with an augmented income of £400, and gave up the grammar school. The chapel finally provided him with a respectable fabric: the neat neoclassical building with seating for 1,200 drew not only Anglican soldiers but also what Inglis described as the "religious sentimentalists" of St Paul's Church.

Twining was chaplain during a period when something over half of the officers and men of the British army were Anglicans. It can probably be assumed that much of his attention was devoted to the officers. Even in the army's own chapel a nice sense of class was maintained by confining the NCOs and privates to the gallery, the same status they enjoyed as strangers in the civilian churches. But, since the evangelical movement had produced a following in the army, Twining was encouraged to go beyond the basic ceremonial functions of conducting services, administering the sacraments, and visiting the sick and imprisoned. He established a military Sunday school with the aid of evangelical officers such as Captain Maximilian Montague Hammond, supervised day-schools for the soldiers and their children, and initiated mid-week bible classes and prayer-meetings for the enlightenment of the rank and file. In the era of army reforms which marked the last decade or so of his chaplaincy, Twining proved to be a suitable overseer of the garrison's spiritual life.

JUDITH FINGARD

A lecture delivered by John Thomas Twining before the Young Men's Christian Association of Halifax, entitled "The age, and its demands on Christian young men," was printed in the *Presbyterian Witness, and Evangelical Advocate* (Halifax), 7 (1854): 201–2, 205.

PAC, RG 8, I (C ser.), 1340, 1353, 1355, 1357–61, 1721–25, 1727, 1747. PANS, MG 1, 804, no.1; RG 36, 31, no.680. PRO, CO 217/143: 133–35, 358–61; 217/144: 63–66; 217/146: 3–6, 59–61; 217/148: 338–39; 217/149: 367–68. USPG, C/CAN/NS, 5: 199–205, 209; 7: 282, 287, 292–93; 9: 26, 45; 11: 355, 357. [E. D. Hammond], *Memoir of Captain M. M. Hammond, rifle brigade* (8th ed., London, 1860). *Acadian Recorder*, 5 Oct., 9 Nov. 1816; 12, 19 July 1817; 20 Nov. 1824. *Halifax Morning Post & Parliamentary Reporter*, 28 Oct. 1844. *Morning News* (Saint John, N.B.), 14 Nov. 1860. *Novascotian*, 5 Nov. 1855. *Times* (Halifax), 29 Oct. 1844, 20 Jan. 1846. Eaton, *Hist. of King's County*. Judith Fingard, *The Anglican design in loyalist Nova Scotia, 1783–1816* (London, 1972); "The Church of England in British North America, 1787–1825" (PHD thesis, Univ. of London, 1970). R. V. Harris, *The Church of Saint Paul in Halifax, Nova Scotia: 1749–1949* (Toronto, 1949). *Halifax Herald*, 10 Oct. 1896. *Presbyterian Witness, and Evangelical Advocate* (Halifax), 14 (1861): 2, 56.

U

ULLEBUCK. *See* OOLIGBUCK

UNIACKE, JAMES BOYLE, lawyer, politician, office holder, and sportsman; b. probably 1799 and baptized 19 Jan. 1800 in Halifax, son of Attorney General Richard John Uniacke* and Martha Maria Delesdernier; m. there 18 Dec. 1832 Rosina Jane Black, and they had several children; d. there 26 March 1858.

By 1810 James Boyle Uniacke's father had established his position in the forefront of Halifax society. Although he was a stern man who expected from his sons accomplishments similar to his own, he used all of his influence to further their interests and no one could have been more helpful in their hours of need. James, after graduating from King's College, Windsor, in 1818, articled in his father's law office and was admitted attorney and barrister on 5 April 1823. Later that year he was off to London, by way of Boston and New York, to complete his legal studies at the Inner Temple. In London he was kept busy securing all sorts of things for a demanding father – livestock, spinning-wheels, engravings, books – but the senior Uniacke wanted most of all for his son to "return uncontaminated with the corruptions of a world new to you." Perhaps he had reason to fear since, in contrast with the industry of his father, James returned to Halifax to live a comfortable, somewhat carefree existence.

One contemporary said that he "looked the aristocrat . . . tall, graceful, and a 'prince among men' . . . always attired in the latest London fashion." Another account suggests that "in a heavy-eating, hard-drinking age, [he] made no bones about his intimate friendship with John Berleycorn as he raced his stable of fast horses on the Halifax Commons. He had a great thirst for companionship and conviviality." As a supporter of the turf, Uniacke maintained a racing stud, one of two in the province. Once, in the legislature, he sarcastically compared his horses with John Young*'s truck horses, but got better than he gave. Alluding to Rosina Jane Black, the unattractive daughter of wealthy merchant John Black* whom Uniacke had married in 1832, Young simply replied that Scotsmen like himself selected their horses "upon the same principle that *some* gentlemen select their wives – not for their beauty but for their *sterling worth*." It was the inheritances of both his wife and himself which permitted Uniacke the indulgent type of existence during the 1830s that some observers found objectionable. A poet of the day, Andrew Shiels*,

called him "a pompous piece of perishable clay!" Apparently Uniacke's outward conduct and traits hid from Shiels the talents of the ablest of Richard John Uniacke's sons.

Little is known of Uniacke's practice of law, although his foreclosure of a mortgage led, in 1848, to a celebrated case, *Uniacke* v. *Dickson*, in which his lawyers won a victory by successfully contending that none of the statute law of England was in force in Nova Scotia, "except such portions as are obviously applicable and necessary." In the 1830s and 1840s he participated in the establishment of some new business ventures in Halifax. In 1832 he became an incorporator and one of the first directors of the Bank of Nova Scotia. Seven or eight years later he helped to set up the Halifax Gas Light and Water Company and before long became its president.

Uniacke entered politics in 1830 by being elected to the House of Assembly for Cape Breton County, but was unseated because he lacked the necessary property qualification. Re-elected, he took his seat in January 1832 and remained in the assembly until 1854. Since the election of 1836 polarized assemblymen into tories and reformers, Uniacke had a chance to display his tory attitudes to the full in the session of 1837. Having taken a strong stand against Joseph Howe*'s 12 Resolutions, especially the tenth, which denounced the disposition of the councillors to "protect their own interests and emoluments at the expense of the public," he naturally gloated when, for tactical reasons, Howe withdrew the resolutions.

Before the assembly opened in 1838, Uniacke had become a member of the newly created Executive Council, although refusing to admit that it operated under any meaningful degree of responsibility. On a wide variety of matters the battle was again joined between him and Howe. Uniacke did not oppose the incorporation of Halifax in principle, but decried a bill which, unlike the London charter, "put the respectability of the town under the controul of others, who should not possess that power." Since the intent of the bill was to enfranchise only those freeholders who voted in provincial elections, Howe concluded that Uniacke and the Nova Scotia tories "believe, or affect to believe, that there is a danger in the very sound of British liberty." When Uniacke sought the assembly's approval of an address of the Constitutional Association of Montreal, Howe objected to any recognition of the ultra loyalists of the Canadas who, by seeking to continue a system rife with abuses, had helped to promote rebellion.

Uniacke

But the differences stemming from their backgrounds came out most strongly in the debate on the judiciary. In 1837 Howe had not protested against Uniacke's sallies, but in 1838 he let it be known that if "jest, and anecdote and raillery" were to take the place of argument, he would show he was blessed with "a little imagination" too. That time came when Uniacke suggested that Howe's proposals to cut costs meant that he was putting the judiciary up for sale to get the cheapest administration of justice: "What! £450 a year for a judge to travel the circuit? Why, *Tim O'Shaughnessy! Tim Shea! or Con Lahy!* would do the labour for half that sum." Tired of Uniacke's witticisms, Howe replied that he would like to have £450, the salary of a single judge, to distribute to the struggling residents of eastern Halifax County whom he had recently visited. Uniacke would always be an honoured guest in the homes of judges and leading officials where he would be dined at the public expense, "but give me a seat beneath the poor man's roof – a portion of his humble fare – let me . . . feel that I am welcomed as a friend, and I seek no higher distinction." The reformers, who had writhed under Uniacke's scorn and ridicule for two sessions, enjoyed every moment of it.

Again, in 1839, the real jousting took place between Howe and Uniacke, and their exchanges rank high among the oratorical spectaculars of the Nova Scotia House of Assembly. Uniacke compared Howe to the Babylonian king who set up a golden image and cast into a fiery furnace everyone who refused to worship it. "He may heat the furnace seven times hotter, and cast me in, and I trust to come out as unscathed as Shadrach, Mesheck, and Abendnego." When Howe labelled all his opponents as anti-reform, Uniacke replied, "I also am a reformer, we are all reformers," only to meet Howe's scornful comment that the tories were trying to cure Nova Scotia by using the new system of medicine known as homoeopathic: "They would administer the millionth part of a grain of *reform* every session, and that should satisfy all!" But however ferocious their exchanges, they always had a grudging admiration for each other; would that Uniacke were a reformer, said Howe, and "I would be proud to follow him." As a result, the reformer William Young* wrote disconsolately to his brother George Renny: "Uniacke & I had a set-to & are on terms of open hostility – Howe & [Laurence O'Connor Doyle*] cultivate his good graces rather than mine."

Essentially Uniacke and Howe differed on the very nature of colonial government. The latter had come to believe that, if Nova Scotians were to remain part of the British empire, they needed to be British subjects to "the fullest extent of British constitutional freedom," while Uniacke held that the reformers' proposals would reduce the governor to a cipher and lead to colonial separation: a colonial governor simply could not be responsible at the same time both to a colonial executive and to a colonial secretary pledged to sustain the unity of the empire.

Then almost like a bolt from the blue, Uniacke – always accepting without question what he thought were the intentions of the British government – changed his stance following a dispatch of 16 Oct. 1839, in which the colonial secretary, Lord John Russell, stated that colonial officers might have to retire "as often as any sufficient motives of public policy" required. Although the lieutenant governor of New Brunswick, Sir John Harvey, held that the dispatch conferred "a new . . . and improved constitution upon these Colonies," Sir Colin Campbell*, his Nova Scotian counterpart, denied it. It turned out that Campbell was right and Harvey and Uniacke wrong since Russell intended only the occasional displacement of a single leading public officer to meet an obvious need and not the removal of all the governor's advisers. Nevertheless, when Howe carried a vote of non-confidence in the Executive Council by a majority of three to one in February 1840, Uniacke resigned from it. He did so partly because he "owed it to the House" not to remain in a body "condemned by such an overwhelming majority." But mostly it was because he believed Russell's dispatch had granted new constitutions to the colonies and, as one whose first political principle was never to "withdraw [his] humble support from the Parent State," he could not oppose the colonial secretary's view. Although he still feared that the new system would transfer power from the government to a few popular leaders, he was "willing to try the experiment" because the British government had ordered it; in his view, however, it would have had a better chance of working in a united British North America, in which the executive council was converted into a genuine ministry. To the extent that Uniacke had become a reformer it was not because of personal conviction, but because of his interpretation of a dispatch, which was quite different from the colonial secretary's intention. Strangely, he escaped for the most part the angry criticism of his former associates, the usual experience of turncoats in those years.

In the coalition government instituted by the new lieutenant governor, Lord Falkland [Cary*], in October 1840 Uniacke was again an executive councillor, and solicitor general as well after April 1841; also in the government were Howe, James McNab, and the tory leader, James William Johnston*. In 1841 Uniacke contested the speakership of the new assembly with Howe, but lost by 26 to 22, even though supported by all the tories. In December 1843, after Falkland allegedly broke faith with the reformers by appointing the tory Mather Byles Almon* to the council, Uniacke, along with Howe and McNab, withdrew. Falkland invited Uniacke to return in July 1844, but he refused because he believed "the sense of the Assembly is that the Queen's Representative should be surrounded by Executive advisers sustained by a Representative majority."

Uniacke's position in the reform party was fully recognized when in February 1845 Falkland caused to be made public his dispatch of 2 Aug. 1844 in which he intimated a disposition by the reform party to exclude Howe from the council. Uniacke, with others, made an unequivocal denial. He, who had never before spoken with anything but veneration for the crown and its representative, heaped scorn on a governor who could "so far forget his high position as the Representative of Royalty" as to proscribe a single individual. If he could "proscribe one man, because he dislikes his politics, he may exclude another because he is not pleased with the contour of his features, or [because] he has not mixed in fashionable circles. . . . in a few years the country will teem with proscribed Councillors. . . . the cut of a coat, the curl of a whisker, scrofulous legs, or atheistical principles, may, at a whim of him in power, be sufficient grounds for proscription." Falkland's dispatch had also sought to denigrate the reformers generally by pointing out that they had "no acknowledged leader." Hardly had it been made public when Howe stated: "Let there be no mistake about that point hereafter, for the Opposition 'acknowledge' . . . [Uniacke] as their leader." Howe was, of course, accepting the fact that he had forfeited his own claims by his ridicule and otherwise harsh treatment of the lieutenant governor.

In the latter part of 1846 Falkland's successor, Sir John Harvey, who also disliked the idea of party government, sought to restore the coalition, but Howe and the leading reformers turned him down. Luckily for them, Uniacke was in England and learning of events in Nova Scotia only through Howe's letters. In a reply which throws a great deal of light upon a man who had been drawn almost unwillingly into the reform party, Uniacke wondered, since Harvey did not want a government of one party, if he "ought . . . to be pressed too closely on [a] point which will require a long time to work so as to be acceptable to the people." Would it not be enough to humiliate Johnston by requiring him to sit at the same board with Howe, the man he had forced out in 1843? Obviously Uniacke still had misgivings about the workability of party government in a small colony like Nova Scotia. Yet, almost in the same breath, he admitted he had no strong feelings on this point, promised to "keep these sentiments to himself," and wanted only a triumph over the party which had "planned and endeavored to work out the dirty intrigue of 1843." Clearly he

appreciated that he led the party largely in name and that the decision was not his to make.

More than once between 1845 and 1847 Howe expressed annoyance in private that he was getting little assistance in planning the party's strategy and in perfecting its organization for the next election. When the election came in August 1847, Howe campaigned in the key areas, while Uniacke did little more than get himself elected. Even with the reform victory, there were apparently some doubts about Uniacke. So, when the Halifax *Times* seemed to be inviting Uniacke to turn traitor and dismember the party he led, Howe thought the matter serious enough to have his friend William GRIGOR sound him out. Grigor reported that Uniacke was still loyal to the reform cause; he also noted Uniacke's insistence that "the first stroke of liberal policy" must be to "get hold of the government and then dictate terms . . . to stop at nothing but to clean out all."

Uniacke was almost up to his old oratorical form when, in January 1848, he moved non-confidence in Johnston's tory administration. On 2 February he was back in the Executive Council and leader (the title "premier" was, as yet, little used in Nova Scotia) of the first fully "responsible" government in Britain's overseas empire; a week later he became attorney general. Uniacke did not stand out during his six years as leader of the government. At this time, of course, collegiality was the operative principle of the Executive Council and the leader was, at most, no more than *primus inter pares*; also, Uniacke, who performed at the optimum only when the spirit moved him, could not have been fully comfortable in a ministry dominated by Howe's ideas and energy. Still, he participated actively in all the major political questions between 1848 and 1851, especially in the adaptation of the provincial institutions to the requirements of responsible government and the preparation of the province's first revised statutes. His last decisive actions occurred in 1851 when Howe was absent in England seeking a guarantee for the intercolonial railway. With the proponents of the European and North American Railway from Halifax to Portland, Maine, threatening action which might stymie Howe's efforts, Uniacke turned his old eloquence upon them: "Was it fair to stab him [Howe] in the back? You may try it . . . but if you do, the poinard will drop from your hand before you can strike." Later, when Howe secured the guarantee and Uniacke failed to have it approved because George Young called it "niggardly," he insisted that Young or himself must leave the cabinet.

Uniacke remained, but his activities in the legislature steadily diminished after 1851 because of failing health. According to his nephew, "the last 7 years of his life he was more or less paralyzed," and

Vanfelson

during the session of 1854 a reform member reported him as "fairly used up and wholly unfit for public business." He had lingered on only because of financial necessity, since he had apparently lost most of his own and his wife's capital in bad investments in British railways. Finally, in April 1854, his colleagues eased him out of the Executive Council and appointed him commissioner of crown lands in place of John Spry Morris, on leave of absence in Britain. Though incompetent to perform the duties of the office, he survived as long as the liberals retained office, but the conservatives were unwilling to show the same compassion after they took over the government in February 1857 and they terminated his services at the end of the year. Early in 1858 he petitioned the assembly for a pension or retiring allowance and a liberal member introduced a bill to that end, but Uniacke died before it passed beyond first reading.

Uniacke was a study in contrasts, if not contradictions. Aristocratic in traits and temperament, he formed firm and lasting friendships with Howe and Doyle, both of whom possessed the common touch. Almost unequalled in his oratorical talents, he only occasionally disturbed a comfortable existence to display them to full advantage. An equivocal reformer, he found himself thrust into the leadership of a party which wanted a thorough transformation of the province's political institutions. A free spender in earlier years, he ended up as a rather pitiful suppliant for government assistance. But whatever the contradictions he cannot be denied lasting recognition as leader of the first truly responsible government in the colonies.

J. MURRAY BECK

An oil portrait of James Boyle Uniacke hangs in Uniacke House (Mount Uniacke, N.S.).

Harvard College Library, Houghton Library, Harvard Univ. (Cambridge, Mass.), MS Can. 58 (Joseph Howe papers) (mfm. at PANS). PAC, MG 24, B29, 1, 10 (mfm. at PANS). PANS, MG 1, 926; 1490; 1769; MG 2, 732–33; MG 9, no.225; RG 1, 255; RG 5, P, 48. Joseph Howe, *The speeches and public letters of Joseph Howe . . .*, ed. J. A. Chisholm (2v., Halifax, 1909), 1. N.S., House of Assembly, *Journal and proc.*, 1841. *Uniacke* v. *Dickson* (1848), 2 N.S.R. 287. *Acadian Recorder*, 22 Dec. 1832; 1838. *Novascotian*, 1838–58. *Yarmouth Herald* (Yarmouth, N.S.), 1847. *Directory of N.S. MLAs.* Albyn [Andrew Shiels], *The preface; a poem of the period* (Halifax, 1876). Beck, *Government of N.S.*; *Joseph Howe.* Duncan Campbell, *Nova Scotia, in its historical, mercantile and industrial relations* (Montreal, 1873). B. [C. U.] Cuthbertson, *The old attorney general: a biography of Richard John Uniacke* (Halifax, [1980]). John Doull, *Sketches of attorney generals of Nova Scotia* (Halifax, 1964). E. M. Saunders, *Three premiers of Nova Scotia: the Hon. J. W. Johnstone, the Hon. Joseph Howe, the Hon. Charles Tupper, M.D., C.B.* (Toronto, 1909). George Mullane, "A sketch of Lawrence O'Connor Doyle, a member of the House of Assembly in the thirties and forties," N.S. Hist. Soc., *Coll.*, 17 (1913): 151–95. "The two Uniackes," *Journal of Education* (Halifax), 8 (1937): 614–17.

V

VANFELSON, GEORGE, lawyer, militia officer, politician, and judge; b. 23 April 1784 at Quebec, son of Antoine (Anthony) Vanfelson and Josephte Meunier; m. 4 Aug. 1806 Dorothée-Magleine Just, daughter of surgeon John Conrad Just, and they had at least two sons; d. 16 Feb. 1856 in Montreal.

George Vanfelson, whose father was of German extraction and had settled at Quebec after the conquest, began to study law in 1798 in the office of Jean-Antoine Panet*, and on 25 April 1805 he was called to the bar. Thus began a fruitful career which was to lead him to the offices of advocate general of the province and judge of the Superior Court.

During the War of 1812 Vanfelson held the rank of captain in Quebec's 1st Militia Battalion from 6 Aug. 1812 to 20 March 1813. He was then transferred to the 6th Select Embodied Militia Battalion and was garrisoned at Quebec until the corps was disbanded on 4 Sept. 1814. The following year he entered politics.

On 14 Feb. 1815 he was elected by acclamation to the House of Assembly as member for Quebec's Upper Town, to replace Jean-Antoine Panet, who had been called to the Legislative Council. In the general elections of March 1816 he was re-elected in the same riding, where he received a good portion of the English-speaking vote.

Vanfelson obtained two appointments as commissioner in 1817, the first, on 29 March, "for purchasing seed grain to assist parishes hard hit by the poor harvest," and the second, on 26 April, for opening roads in Quebec County. On 28 Jan. 1819, however, a more important public office was conferred on him when he succeeded George PYKE as the province's advocate general. As a result, he withdrew from the political scene in 1820, and did not return to it until 1827.

In the 1827 elections Vanfelson ran for Quebec's Upper Town as a Patriote candidate, alongside of

Amable Berthelot*, but the two were beaten by Joseph-Rémi Vallières* de Saint-Réal and Andrew Stuart*. Vanfelson stood again in 1829 in a by-election held for the seat left vacant by Vallières de Saint-Réal, but the latter's protégé, Jean-François-Joseph Duval, won. These successive defeats led Vanfelson to accept the advocate generalship for a second time on 11 Dec. 1830.

None the less, he did not abandon the idea of returning to politics. Accordingly, he ran in the 1832 by-election for Lower Town and was successful. At this time he was a supporter of Louis-Joseph Papineau*. Re-elected in 1834, he was one of the first to defend in the house the 92 Resolutions conveying the assembly's major grievances and demands. However, under the conciliatory rule of Governor Lord Gosford [Acheson*], the Patriotes became increasingly divided. The moderates, or Quebec party, led by Elzéar Bédard* and John Neilson*, attracted some of Papineau's former supporters, including Vanfelson, Berthelot, René-Édouard Caron*, and Augustin-Norbert Morin*.

When Bédard was appointed to the Court of King's Bench in February 1836, Vanfelson replaced him as head of the moderates. On 4 June 1837 a meeting to protest Lord John Russell's resolutions was held at the Marché Saint-Paul at Quebec. During this meeting the principal speakers, Morin, Charles Drolet*, Louis-Théodore Besserer*, and Jean BLANCHET, who were all members of the house, spoke very forcefully, although they did not openly advocate armed revolt. The next day Vanfelson, disapproving of the tenor of these remarks by his confrères and disturbed by the prospect of violence, gave up his seat and quit political life.

Vanfelson pursued his career as a lawyer, and on 27 March 1843 was made a QC. On the 28th he accepted the post of inspector of police for Montreal. Then, on 24 Dec. 1849, he went on the bench. Appointed to the Superior Court of Lower Canada, to sit at Montreal, he served until his death in that city on 16 Feb. 1856. A prominent figure at Quebec and Montreal, George Vanfelson was remembered as a judge with integrity who had displayed great qualities in performing the duties of his office.

CLAUDE VACHON

ANQ-Q, CE1-1, 6 nov. 1775, 23 avril 1784, 4 août 1806. *L'Avenir*, 22 févr. 1856. *Le Canadien*, 25 févr. 1856. *Quebec Gazette*, 2 May 1805, 10 April 1817. F.-J. Audet, "Les législateurs du Bas-Canada." P.-G. Roy, *Fils de Québec*, 3: 21–22; *Les juges de la prov. de Québec*. Chapais, *Cours d'hist. du Canada*, 4: 75, 85–87. Ouellet, *Bas-Canada*. Mason Wade, *Les canadiens-français, de 1760 à nos jours*, Adrien Venne et Francis Dufau-Labeyrie, trad. (2v., Ottawa, 1963). Philéas Gagnon, "Frédéric Rolette," *BRH*, 1 (1895): 25. Antoine Roy, "Les Patriotes de la région de Québec pendant la rébellion de 1837–1838," *Cahiers des Dix*, 24 (1959): 241–54.

VAN TUYLL VAN SEROOSKERKEN, Baron van TUYLL VAN SEROOSKERKEN, VINCENT GILDEMEESTER. *See* TUYLL

VAVASOUR, HENRY WILLIAM, army officer and military engineer; b. *c.* 1783 in County Dublin (Republic of Ireland), son of William Vavasour, LLD; m. Louisa Dunbar, daughter of Sir George Dunbar, and they had at least five children, including Mervin Vavasour*; d. 4 July 1851 in Montreal.

Henry William Vavasour received his early education from the Reverend Richard Carey and then entered Trinity College, Dublin, in 1799, graduating BA in the summer of 1804. He had received a commission as second lieutenant in the Royal Engineers on 1 Feb. 1804 and was one of the first of this corps to study surveying at the Trigonometrical Survey. Promoted lieutenant on 1 March 1805, he served in the Cape Colony from 7 Jan. 1806 to 11 Feb. 1809 when he became a second captain and was posted to Ireland. On 9 April 1811 he was sent to Gibraltar, and while based there he took part in the Peninsular War and the defence of Tarifa, Spain, receiving a promotion to the position of captain on 21 July 1813. After a brief tour of duty at Chatham, England, he was sent to British North America.

Arriving at Quebec on 1 Oct. 1815, Vavasour was initially stationed there. He then served as senior engineer at Fort George (Niagara-on-the-Lake), Upper Canada, where he was responsible for surveying military reserves and roads, as well as for building and maintaining forts on the Niagara frontier. Vavasour encountered some problems in carrying out his responsibilities, particularly in obtaining requisitions from the commissariat. The Royal Engineers came under the jurisdiction of the Board of Ordnance and Vavasour reported to the commanding engineer at York (Toronto) rather than to the army colonel at Fort George. The latter resented being bypassed and encouraged the commissariat to create difficulties for the engineer.

Vavasour, through his duties at Fort George, was brought into closer contact with the civilian population than were most regular army personnel. As a result, he was aware of the post-war unrest in the area and in 1818 recommended the establishment of a board of inquiry to investigate the claims of civilians who had suffered losses or had not been paid for services rendered. He had applied for land near Niagara (Niagara-on-the-Lake) in the previous year but was rejected under the terms of an order in council of 1797 that denied grants to soldiers on full pay. Lord Dalhousie [Ramsay*] visited the Niagara frontier in July 1819, and although he first commented that

Venant

Vavasour was "particularly intelligent & entertaining" he later noted in his journal that he found the officer to be "a Bombastic & discontented soldier, constantly speaking without any regard to truth." Vavasour returned to Quebec in September 1823 and served there until his departure for England on 27 June 1825.

Vavasour was stationed in Scotland from 1826 to 1829. In October of the following year he was promoted lieutenant-colonel and became commanding engineer in Ceylon (Sri Lanka), a post he occupied for almost six years. He held the same post in England, at Chatham from 1837 to 1839 and at Harwich from 1841 to 1845. Promoted colonel on 22 April 1845, he served in Dublin as senior engineer from 1847 to 1849; on 7 July he was again posted to British North America, this time as commanding engineer for the Province of Canada with headquarters in Montreal. In this capacity he was responsible for all military surveying, fortifications, and works, including the maintenance of the canals on the Ottawa and Rideau rivers. He was one of the few British officers to serve as a junior officer on the Canadian frontier and later to hold a commanding position in Canada. Referred to in an obituary as a "gallant and much respected officer," he died in office and was interred in the military burial ground in Montreal.

FRANCES M. WOODWARD

Institution of Royal Engineers, Corps Library (Chatham, Eng.), Connolly papers, "Notitia historica of the Corps of Royal Engineers," comp. T. W. J. Connolly (17v.), 10; "Skelton memoirs of officers," comp. T. W. J. Connolly. PAC, RG 1, L3, 515: V11/10; RG 8, I (C ser.), 93: 23–24; 401–7. PRO, PROB, 11/2144, 4 Nov. 1846; WO 54/ 250–59. *Montreal Gazette*, 9 July 1851. *Montreal Herald*, 9 July 1851. [George Ramsay, 9th Earl of] Dalhousie, *The Dalhousie journals*, ed. Marjory Whitelaw (3v., [Toronto], 1978–82), 134, 138. G.B., WO, *Army list*, 1800–50. *Roll of officers of the Corps of Royal Engineers from 1660 to 1898 . . .* , ed. R. F. Edwards (Chatham, 1898). E. A. Cruikshank, "Post-war discontent at Niagara in 1818," *OH*, 29 (1933): 14–46.

VENANT. *See* VIVANT

VICKERY, ANN (Robins), Bible Christian preacher; b. 1799 or 1800, probably in Luxulion (Luxulyan), Cornwall, England; m. 1831 Paul Robins, and they had two sons; d. 18 Sept. 1853 in Bowmanville, Upper Canada.

Ann Vickery experienced a religious conversion at Luxulion in 1819 during an evangelical revival in Devon and Cornwall brought about by the preaching of the Bible Christians, a Methodist sect founded in 1815. It was Bible Christian practice to involve young converts in witness and service, and Ann, after being encouraged to respond to a call to preach, "threw all the powers of her earnest nature into the service of her new Master." At the second Bible Christian conference, held in 1820, she was appointed an itinerant preacher and given several one-year assignments in the region. The church posted her to London in 1826 where she did evangelistic work for two years. She was afterwards in Portsea until 1831 when she married Paul Robins, a Bible Christian minister. The sect had long encouraged unions between its ministers and women itinerants and promised that such couples "shall be entituled to the first support from the connexion." Following her marriage she faithfully assisted her husband on all the preaching circuits he was appointed to serve.

Ann and Paul Robins and their colleagues in the Bible Christian ministry worked chiefly in the southwestern counties of England where the sect originated and where most of its adherents resided. In 1831, following the immigration of West Countrymen to British North America, the church began assigning clergymen to meet the needs of its followers living there. The efforts of missionaries such as Francis Metherall*, Philip JAMES*, John Hicks Eynon*, and his wife, Elizabeth [DART], were not sufficient, and in 1846 Ann and Paul Robins were appointed to serve on the Peterborough circuit in Upper Canada. She and her family set sail on 14 April, arriving in Cobourg in early June. She had always been zealous in the service of her church, and Canada was to provide additional scope for demonstrating her commitment.

Ann Robins never considered that marriage excused her from the obligation to continue her ministry as opportunity permitted, and she was quick to respond to the demands of her new setting. Except for a brief period after the birth of her second child, when she had some help in the house, she did almost all her own housework "by her own choice" while leading fellowship classes, assisting in prayer meetings, visiting the sick, and preaching the gospel. Often she walked with a child in her arms to a distant appointment, handed "the precious burden" to a member of the congregation, conducted the service, and then returned as she had come, on foot. Needless to say, she had little patience with preachers who neglected to carry out their duties because of inclement weather or some similar difficulty. She encouraged her husband to fulfil his responsibilities however painful or hazardous. As he described it, "a coward husband . . . would lead but a sorry life with such a partner." She also had a great concern for sabbath observance, regarding it as "a delight, holy of the Lord and honourable." She made a point of preparing food and getting changes of clothing ready the preceding day so that the family could quickly respond to Sunday's sacred duties, and was grieved when Christian believers disregarded the Lord's day by using it merely as a time for visiting. She also organized her family responsibilities so that in an emergency she could take the place of a regular itinerant preacher who was sick. Among the first to call on her for this service was her husband, who became so ill after arriving in the province that "his life was despaired of."

In 1849 the family left the Peterborough circuit for Cobourg, and in 1852 moved to the Darlington station in the Bowmanville area. There, on 5 Sept. 1853, she was "much struck" by the news of a brother's death. Eight days later, while her husband was travelling the circuit and her sons were in Toronto, she was taken seriously ill. After exhorting several members of her class meeting to seek holiness and counselling her husband and family on spiritual matters, she died on 18 September at the age of 53.

Ann Robins and other female preachers, although an early feature of the Bible Christian Church in England, were not widely accepted in pioneer Canada despite their zeal and commitment. As her husband had noted in 1848, "there appears to be a prejudice in the minds of the people against female preaching." Perhaps these women were ahead of their time, but in some fashion they helped to prepare the way for the emergence of professional women workers in the 20th-century church.

ALBERT BURNSIDE

Bible Christian Magazine (Shebbear, Eng.), 25 (1846): 357–63; 27 (1848): 123; 32 (1853): 474–76. Methodist Church (Canada, Newfoundland, Bermuda), Toronto Conference, *Minutes* (Toronto), 1890: 75–76. Cornish, *Cyclopædia of Methodism*, 2: 255. *United Methodist ministers and their circuits . . . 1797–1932*, comp. O. A. Beckerlegge (London, 1968), 199, 245. Albert Burnside, "The Bible Christians in Canada, 1832–1884 . . ." (THD thesis, Emmanuel College, Victoria Univ., Toronto, 1969), 375. Thomas Shaw, *The Bible Christians, 1815–1907* (London, 1965), 33.

VIGER, JACQUES, newspaperman, landowner, author, militia officer, office holder, politician, historian, and collector; b. 7 May 1787 in Montreal, son of Jacques Viger and Amaranthe Prévost; m. there 17 Nov. 1808 Marie-Marguerite La Corne, widow of Major John Lennox, and they had three children, all of whom died in infancy; d. there 12 Dec. 1858.

Jacques Viger was part of the powerful network of the Viger, Papineau, Lartigue, and Cherrier families. He was a cousin of Denis-Benjamin Viger*, Louis-Joseph Papineau*, Jean-Jacques Lartigue*, and Côme-Séraphin Cherrier* and kept in constant touch with them all his life, writing or visiting often. He served as a well-informed observer of the Montreal scene for them, and even compiled what in effect were dossiers. He also frequently acted as a courier for one or other of them.

In 1799, at the age of 12, Viger was enrolled in the Collège Saint-Raphaël, an institution run by the Sulpicians which provided a classical education for children of the Montreal bourgeoisie. After his studies he went to Quebec, where he worked as an editor of the newspaper *Le Canadien* from November 1808 to May 1809. In 1810, soon after his return to Montreal, he prepared a collection of the neologisms he had noted in use; it was to come out a century later as "Néologie canadienne ou dictionnaire des mots créés en Canada." In 1812 he brought out *Relation de la mort de Louis XVI, roi de France* by Henry Essex Edgeworth de Firmont, which subsequently appeared in an English version. During the War of 1812 he enlisted as a lieutenant in Montreal's 3rd Militia Battalion, and later was promoted captain in the Voltigeurs Canadiens. He was at the battle of Sackets Harbor, N.Y., in May 1813, and in August was granted leave to deal with family matters, including the death of his mother. Because of a misunderstanding, George Prevost*, the governor-in-chief of British North America, dismissed him in November for being absent without permission. In March 1814, after the mistake was acknowledged, he was reinstated in his rank.

All his life Viger remained fascinated by military matters, and particularly by what he had experienced while campaigning in the war. Louis-Joseph-Amédée Papineau*'s memoirs state that Viger had himself "painted in the uniform of a Voltigeur, with Shako, long sabre and Sabretache." Viger was also anxious to see the memory of the battle of Châteauguay kept alive. In 1816 he went with his friend Joseph-D. Mermet, a French royalist officer in the service of Great Britain, to the battleground, and he did a great deal to promote an engraving of the hero of Châteauguay, Charles-Michel d'Irumberry* de Salaberry.

However, Viger's own military career was unremarkable, apart from the incident of his dismissal. Following reinstatement, he served in the militia until the end of his life. For example, he held various posts including that of lieutenant-colonel in Montreal's 3rd Militia Battalion, an appointment he received in 1829. Historian Fernand Ouellet thinks that this interest partly stemmed from the desire of French Canadians at the beginning of the 19th century to express and demonstrate their loyalty to the authorities. According to him, Viger was motivated by a desire to show that the conduct of his compatriots in time of war was beyond suspicion. This interest later took a different turn when Viger sought to reconstruct the military tradition of New France. Hence Ouellet sees a direct link between the climate of the early 19th century and the scholarly works of Viger.

Meanwhile, in December 1813 Viger had replaced Louis Charland* as surveyor of highways, streets,

Viger

lanes, and bridges of Montreal. At that time local government was in an early stage of development. The justices of the peace who were charged with responsibility for the town's administration had at their disposal few powers and still fewer officials, chief of these being the surveyor of highways, streets, lanes, and bridges. In this capacity Viger prepared reports, saw to the grading of highways, the realignment of routes, and drainage, levelling, and paving operations. He bought stone, made arrangements for construction, and signed various supply contracts. He was also involved in enforcing police regulations.

Viger's activity led him to engage in rudimentary town planning. For example, when the mound where the Montreal citadel had stood (near the present Champ-de-Mars) was levelled, the question of how some of the cleared land should be used had to be resolved. To this end Viger drafted a plan which provided for the extension northwards of Rue Bonsecours. His endeavours did not please everyone but because he had been appointed by the governor of the colony he was not wholly under the jurisdiction of the justices of the peace. When one of them apparently remonstrated with him about the plan, Viger ignored his remarks and got a lawyer friend to present it to the governor.

As surveyor Viger also drafted a number of reports. For example, he appeared before the House of Assembly of Lower Canada in 1825 with a report, which came out first in the journal of the assembly that year and then was published as *Observations en amélioration des lois des chemins telles qu'en force dans le Bas-Canada en 1825* through his own efforts 15 years later. In 1841 he brought out his *Rapports sur les chemins, rues, ruelles et ponts de la cité et paroisse de Montréal, avril et mai 1840*. These two publications were probably pleas to the city council in support of his work. In addition, to help him carry out his duties, he had two Montreal street directories drawn up, in 1817 and 1837.

In 1825 Viger was also appointed, with Louis Guy*, census commissioner for Montreal County, which then covered Montreal Island. The document of exceptionally high quality which he produced was an indication of his desire to acquire detailed knowledge of his own society. For instance, he added to the questionnaire required by the census law a series of his own questions that make this document an excellent source of information for reconstructing the history of Montreal.

Viger unsuccessfully sought or aspired to some other public offices. For example, he solicited the position of inspector of police at Montreal in 1820. In 1825 he wanted to become a justice of the peace and commissioner of the House of Correction at Montreal. There was talk of his being made commissioner for Trinity House of Montreal in 1830, and in 1832 he

applied for the post of overseer of highways. On the other hand, in the period 1829–36 he held various appointments as commissioner, among them to improve the roads in and around Montreal.

Although he was involved in public affairs, Viger did not take much part in politics. He held only one important office, serving as the first mayor of Montreal, from 1833 to 1836. It was probably no coincidence that he was elected to the mayoralty. In 1828 he had advised his cousins Louis-Joseph Papineau and Denis-Benjamin Viger, who were both members of the assembly, not only on boundaries for the wards in the town, but also on the importance of keeping the property qualification low enough for the majority of small owners to vote. He thus deliberately ensured that French Canadians formed the majority of voters. Adam Thom* and William Kennedy, in their study on municipal government for the report of Lord Durham [Lambton*], indicated they understood the reasons for the criteria adopted and denounced them as weakening the power of the British merchants, who were paying a large share of municipal taxes. Occupying an important place on the municipal scene through his position as roads surveyor, Viger gave advice to his cousins at the time of the assembly debates on the bill to incorporate Montreal. The statute of incorporation passed in 1832 was the result of a compromise between the city's merchants and the supporters of Papineau's party there. The former wanted the Patriote party's backing to have Montreal declared a port of entry not subject to the supervision of the port of Quebec, while the latter sought municipal incorporation to remove Montreal from the control of the justices of the peace, who were responsible to the governor and who were unpopular in the town.

Things quickly took a turn for the worse. Soon after incorporation Montreal was shaken by two events that left deep scars and widespread distrust. The first was the intervention of British troops during a by-election for Montreal West in May 1832, which resulted in the death of three French Canadians [see Daniel Tracey*]. Then, at the beginning of June a cholera epidemic broke out, killing at least 2,000 Montrealers, with French Canadians being the worse stricken. Viger's election as mayor in 1833 failed to restore calm. Anxious to avoid a repetition of the troubles of 1832, Viger intervened in the 1834 election campaign by having the men of the watch maintain order, a step that earned him bitter criticisms from the conservative press. He was further reproached for holding the offices of both mayor and roads surveyor, and thus neglecting part of his duties. From 1833 to 1836 he had major drainage operations carried out in the *faubourgs* of the city. It was a period in which cholera raged and its virulence was being blamed partly on the marshy state of the area north of Rue Sainte-Catherine, at the foot of the slope rising to Rue

Sherbrooke. François-Maximilien Bibaud* later noted that Viger should be credited with the improved sanitation of these *faubourgs*. However, the city's revenue base was limited, both before and after its incorporation, and the work was done at the expense of the upkeep of other streets. When the law setting up the municipality expired in 1836, the previous system of government by justices of the peace was re-established, and thus Viger's office as mayor was eliminated. Four years later, when a new charter came into force, Viger was dismissed from his post as roads surveyor and replaced by John Ostell*, probably because the Montreal roads were still in poor repair and because he was regarded as suspect by reason of family ties. From then on his livelihood depended on income from a few properties he owned in Montreal as well as from the offices he held as commissioner for the erection of parishes and the building of churches and as member of the Rebellion Losses Commission.

Politically, Viger was in sympathy with Papineau's party – witness his roles as a source of information and messenger, as well as his correspondence. He presided at the first banquet of Saint-Jean-Baptiste Day in 1834. Although, like many Montrealers, he did not play an active part in the rebellion, this did not keep him from supporting Ludger DUVERNAY during his imprisonment in 1836. His quite moderate political stand, together with the obligations of his office as roads surveyor, presumably explains this attitude, for which he was severely criticized the next year by Papineau. Six years later he was a member of the organizing committee for the Association Saint-Jean-Baptiste de Montréal, and in 1856 he was elected its president.

Viger often helped run elections. According to his biographers he served as returning officer eight times. His love of detail makes some of his expense claims a good source of information on the whole electoral process. Even when playing no precise role, he took copious notes, which were the basis of valuable reports, for example during the 1832 election.

It was, however, by his work as scholar and collector that Viger made himself best known during his lifetime. He had a remarkable determination to discover and understand far exceeding the curiosity of a local expert. Indeed, when he interested himself in Montreal County, following his inquiry at the time of the 1825 census, the various calculations he produced and included in the "Tablettes statistiques du comté de Montréal en 1825" show his concern to understand how society functioned. He calls to mind the first amateur statisticians, who in concentrating on "social mathematics" and its explanatory potential foreshadowed the development of statistics and the social sciences in the late 19th and early 20th centuries. The value of his studies was recognized, particularly by John HOLMES, who reprinted extracts of the "Tablettes statistiques" in his own 1831 work, *Nouvel abrégé de*

géographie moderne suivi d'un petit abrégé de géographie ancienne à l'usage de la jeunesse. Some authors also claim that Viger collaborated with Joseph Bouchette*, either in developing the first map of Montreal or by contributing to his descriptive works. There appears to be some confusion about the help Viger provided and about how the map was created, as well as about whether Bouchette plagiarized William Berczy*'s work. Finally, Viger's reputation as a scholar brought him requests for information from all sides. Historians such as Étienne-Michel Faillon* and Francis Parkman* had recourse to his services, and his correspondence gives an indication of requests from other scholars, as the references in his letters to Pierre Margry illustrate.

Viger's more historical works deal with religious institutions. His *Archéologie religieuse du diocèse de Montréal*, published at Montreal in 1850, provides short accounts of the parishes in the diocese, with a list of officiating priests. In 1853, in honour of the visit of the papal nuncio, Mgr Cajetan Bedini, Viger prepared for him a series of water-colours depicting the apparel of the various religious orders for French Canadian women. As a result he was appointed commander of the papal order of St Gregory the Great in 1855. While preparing the collection Viger wrote accounts of each of the communities, which he transmitted to the French ultramontane Henry de Courcy. The latter, using the pseudonym C. de La Roche-Héron, produced a book of them, which was published in 1855 as *Les servantes de Dieu en Canada: histoire des communautés religieuses de femmes de la province*.

These various works made Viger an archivist as well as an historian. At this period in the development of French Canadian historiography, there was apparently as much preoccupation with writing history as with preparing "memoirs" on various subjects that would eventually make such writing possible. Viger clearly belonged to the second school, writing most often as a memorialist. He began with his recollections of the War of 1812 in "Mes tablettes de 1813," but it was particularly in his monumental 43-volume "Ma saberdache" that he recorded his observations. There were two series in this collection, which he began in 1808: the first, 30 volumes called "Saberdache rouge," included various materials that could be drawn on for a history of the Canadas; the second, 13 volumes called "Saberdache bleue," contained Viger's correspondence, notes, and various documents. These were not memoirs in the accepted sense, but rather diverse comments on events in which he had been involved. He contributed to *Le Spectateur canadien*, and then to his friend Michel BIBAUD's *Bibliothèque canadienne*, publishing numerous extracts of "Mes tablettes" and "Ma saberdache." Concerning the books brought out by contemporary historians, Viger was harsh in his criticism. As an ultramontane he had little respect for the works of

Viger

François-Xavier Garneau*, or of Charles-Étienne Brasseur* de Bourbourg, whom in his letters he nicknamed "Brasseur de Boue" (muckraker). However, apart from his ideological biases, he paid serious attention to accuracy and to the critical use of documents.

Viger's concerns as an archivist were matched by his tastes as a collector. For most of his life he gathered documents and material on the history of Canada, literature, and other subjects. His collections contain a bit of everything. In this respect his "Albums" are representative. Water-colours and original drawings are next to reproductions and decorative items, for example a design in lacy paper created by patient toil but significant only for its detail. Given Viger's keen interest in the preservation of old documents, it is not surprising that in 1858 along with several other scholars he helped found the Société Historique de Montréal, of which he was elected the first president. He was involved in preparing the first instalment of the society's transactions which came out in 1859, a year after his death. The collection included a study entitled "De l'esclavage en Canada," which Viger had prepared with Louis-Hippolyte La Fontaine*. The society was incorporated that year.

Viger was also interested in education. His 1825 census of Montreal contained specific notes on the staff of the schools he had located, along with information on the pupils and the curricula. In 1829 and 1835 he made a detailed list of the educational institutions in Montreal. In 1836 he was a member of the committee that administered the École Normale de Montréal. It is thus not surprising that Charles Buller* sought his help in preparing the inquiry into education he carried out for the Durham report. Subsequently Viger was recommended by Ignace Bourget*, the bishop of Montreal, for the post of superintendent of education for Lower Canada, but the governor, Sir Charles Bagot*, chose to appoint Jean-Baptiste Meilleur*.

Viger's relations with the church were always extremely cordial. From the time his cousin Jean-Jacques Lartigue was made auxiliary in Montreal to the bishop of Quebec in 1820, Viger backed him in his dispute with the Sulpicians concerning the cathedral and even got letters by Lartigue published under a pseudonym in the Montreal papers. Viger enjoyed Bourget's confidence during his episcopacy.

Viger apparently was not wealthy, but he had sufficient means to live in comfort. According to Fernand Ouellet, Viger improved his financial position at the beginning of his career when through his marriage he benefited from the Lennox estate. In succeeding years he seems to have maintained himself at the level he attained then. In addition to his salary as an office holder, he received income from a few properties. Notarial minute-books indicate that he engaged in various property transactions. In 1811 and 1812 he and his mother jointly sold some lots on Rue Saint-Paul in Montreal that were part of his father's estate. In 1816 he sold the Saint-Jean sub-fief in the seigneury of Boucherville, which he had also inherited upon the death of his father in 1798. In 1816 as well he disposed of some lots he had purchased from Joseph Papineau* on Rue Sanguinet in Montreal; at the same time he bought some land in the Faubourg des Récollets and jointly with his wife acquired a property on Rue Bonsecours, where he was to live for the greater part of his life. He sold his house on Rue Saint-Paul in 1832, and a lot in Saint-Antoine ward in 1840. The properties were sometimes rented out – for example one on Rue Saint-Paul and one on Rue Bonsecours which was eventually occupied by an innkeeper. The 1842 census gives a glimpse of his household: the Vigers lived with their three daughters-in-law, two maidservants and one manservant; they also had a horse and a cow, a not uncommon practice at that time, even in the city. In 1858 Viger still owned the lot on Rue Bonsecours. However, at the time of his death his debts exceeded his assets, and thus the heirs handed all his property over to the Misses Lennox, Viger's stepdaughters and the principal creditors of the estate.

It is not easy to grasp the many sides of Jacques Viger's life. His personality, the range of his activity, and the diversity of his interests marked him as unusual. As Ouellet says, he was an enigmatic and disconcerting person. All the details of his fellow-citizens' lives were known to him – his 1825 census enumerated all the houses and their occupants, including the least commendable. He was not very handsome, but his lively mind, caustic rejoinders, and proverbial joviality gave him his charm. Moderate in politics when the 1830s began, then firmly ultramontane after the rebellion, he exemplified the ambiguities and problems that beset one part of the petite bourgeoisie of French Canada in the first half of the 19th century. This group vacillated between liberalism and a form of nationalism, and finally chose the path of reform and moderation, and even of conservatism. By the end of his life Viger was a man of renown, as is evidenced by the title of commander which he bore proudly, his military rank, and his participation in a number of learned societies. His writings placed him among the intellectuals who sought to understand the workings of their society. His substantial collection of more than 1,200 books and his documents were purchased by friends, among them Hospice-Anthelme-Jean-Baptiste Verreau*.

JEAN-CLAUDE ROBERT

The Fonds Viger–Verreau at the ASQ is the chief source of information on Jacques Viger. It includes Viger's "Ma saberdache" (sér.O, 095–125, 0139–52) and his personal journal (sér.O, 0165–71). An inventory by Fernand Ouellet of the "Saberdache" was published in ANQ *Rapport*, 1955–57: 31–176. The Fonds Viger–Verreau also includes Viger's "Album"; another "Album" is at the BVM-G.

The collection of neologisms that Viger prepared in 1810 was published a century later as "Néologie canadienne ou dictionnaire des mots créés en Canada et maintenant en vogue; – des mots dont la prononciation et l'orthographe sont différentes de la prononciation et orthographe françaises, quoique employés dans une acception semblable ou contraire, et des mots étrangers qui se sont glissés dans notre langue" in *Bull. du parler français au Canada* (Québec), 8 (1909–10): 101–3, 141–44, 183–86, 234–36, 259–63, 295–98, 339–42. Viger's historical works include *Archéologie religieuse du diocèse de Montréal* (Montréal, 1850) and *Archéologie canadienne: souvenirs historiques sur la seigneurie de La Prairie* (Montréal, 1857). With Louis-Hippolyte La Fontaine he also wrote the essay "De l'esclavage en Canada," which came out in the first issue of Soc. hist. de Montréal, *Mémoires* (Montréal), 1 (1859): 12–65. In addition, Viger produced excellent works while discharging his official duties, in particular *Observations en amélioration des lois des chemins telles qu'en force dans le Bas-Canada en 1825* (Montréal, 1840); *Rapports sur les chemins, rues, ruelles et ponts de la cité et paroisse de Montréal, avril et mai 1840* (Montréal, 1841); and "Tablettes statistiques du comté de Montréal en 1825," held at ASQ, Fonds Viger–Verreau, sér.O, 018A. Further information on the last document can be found in P.-A. Linteau and J.-C. Robert, "Un recensement et son recenseur: le cas de Montréal en 1825," *Archives* (Québec), 8 (1976–77), no.2: 29–36.

ACAM, 901.023. ANQ-M, CE1-6, 15 déc. 1858; CE1-51, 7 mai 1787, 17 nov. 1808; CN1-7, 14 juin 1836; CN1-134, 19 mai 1840; CN1-243, 28 févr. 1816; CN1-270, 13 mars 1832; CN1-295, 19 mars 1816, 6 nov. 1825; CN1-312, 8 janv. 1859; CN1-313, 18 déc. 1819; CN1-334, 22 mars 1811; 5–6, 8, 13 mai, 13 juill. 1812; 30 juill. 1813; 3 juin 1814; 11 janv., 21, 26–27 nov. 1816; 17 janv., 31 juill. 1817; P-24; P1000-3-383; P1000-5-516; P1000-20-709; P1000-49-1097. Arch. de la ville de Montréal, Dossier surintendant, inspecteur, directeur des travaux publics depuis 1796; Dossiers Jacques Viger; Procès-verbaux des juges de paix. ASQ, Fonds Viger–Verreau, cartons 22, no.38; 24, no.196a; sér.O, 015A, 018A, 021. PAC, MG 24, B2; MG 24, L3; MG 30, D1, 30: 415; RG 31, A1, 1831, 1842, Montreal; RG 68, General index, 1651–1841, 1841–67. Marius Barbeau, "Vieux papiers," *Le Canada français* (Québec), 2e sér., 26 (1938–39): 286–96. Can., Prov. of, *Statutes*, 1859, c.119. "Documents inédits," *RHAF*, 6 (1952–53): 110–11. *Election of the West Ward of the city of Montreal 27 March 1810 from the poll books alphabetically arranged* (Montreal, n.d.). [J. G. Lambton], *Lord Durham's report on the affairs of British North America*, ed. C. P. Lucas (3v., Oxford, Eng., 1912; repr., New York, 1970). L.C., House of Assembly, *Journals*, 1825, app.X; *Statutes*, 1831, c.54. *Lettres à Pierre Margry de 1844 à 1886 (Papineau, Lafontaine, Faillon, Leprohon et autres)*, L.-P. Cormier, édit. (Québec, 1968). *Le Courrier du Canada*, 15 déc. 1858. *La Minerve*, 15 déc. 1858. *L'Ordre* (Montréal), 14 déc. 1858. *Le Pays*, 14 déc. 1858. Beaulieu et Hamelin, *La presse québécoise*, vol.1. F.-M.

Bibaud, *Le panthéon canadien* (1858; A. et V. Bibaud, 1891). *DOLQ*, vol.1. F.-X. Grondin, "Bio-bibliographie de Jacques Viger" (thèse de bibliothéconomie, univ. de Montréal, 1947). Reginald Hamel *et al.*, *Dictionnaire pratique des auteurs québécois* (Montréal, 1976). Le Jeune, *Dictionnaire*. *Montreal directory*, 1820, 1842–58. Wallace, *Macmillan dict.*

Chaussé, *Jean-Jacques Lartigue*. Serge Gagnon, *Le Québec et ses historiens de 1840 à 1920: la Nouvelle-France de Garneau à Groulx* (Québec, 1978). Pierre de Grandpré, *Histoire de la littérature française du Québec* (2e éd., 4v., Montréal, 1971–73), 1. F.-X. Grondin, *Jacques Viger* (Montréal, 1942). Labarrère-Paulé, *Les instituteurs laïques*. Robert Lahaise, *Les édifices conventuels du Vieux Montréal: aspects ethno-historiques* (Montréal, 1980). Monet, *La première révolution tranquille*. *Montréal: artisans, histoire, patrimoine*, Henri Béchard *et al.*, édit. (Montréal, 1979). Fernand Ouellet, *Histoire économique et sociale du Québec, 1760–1850: structures et conjoncture* (Montréal et Paris, [1966]). Gérard Parizeau, *La vie studieuse et obstinée de Denis-Benjamin Viger (1774–1861)* (Montréal, 1980). Meilleur, *Mémorial de l'éducation* (1860), 174. Pouliot, *Mgr Bourget et son temps*, vols.1–5. J.-C. Robert, "Montréal, 1821–1871; aspects de l'urbanisation" (thèse de PHD, univ. de Paris, 1977). Robert Rumilly, *Histoire de la Société Saint-Jean-Baptiste de Montréal: des patriotes au fleurdelisé, 1834–1948* (Montréal, 1975); *Histoire de Montréal* (5v., Montréal, 1970–74), 2–3. L. J. Ste Croix, "The first incorporation of the city of Montreal, 1826–1836" (MA thesis, McGill Univ., Montreal, 1971). Jules Bazin, "L'album de consolation de Jacques Viger," *Vie des arts* (Montréal), 17 (Noël 1959): 26–30. L.-O. David, "Viger," *La Patrie* (Montréal), 8 mai 1926: 31. France Galarneau, "L'élection partielle du Quartier-Ouest de Montréal en 1832: analyse politico-sociale," *RHAF*, 32 (1979): 565–84. J.-J. Lefebvre, "La famille Viger: le maire Jacques Viger (1858); ses parents – ses ascendants – ses alliés," SGCF *Mémoires*, 17 (1966): 203–38. É.-Z. Massicotte, "Jacques Viger et les Centenaires," *BRH*, 33 (1927): 100–2; "Jacques Viger et sa famille," 21 (1915): 148–49; "Jacques Viger et sa famille: autres notes," 24 (1918): 209. Olivier Maurault, "Souvenirs canadiens; album de Jacques Viger," *Cahiers des Dix*, 9 (1944): 83–99. Victor Morin, "Esquisse biographique de Jacques Viger," RSC *Trans.*, 3rd ser., 32 (1938), sect.I: 183–90. Gérard Morisset, "L'album de Jacques Viger," *Vie des arts*, 8 (automne 1957): 15–18. Camille Roy, "Jacques Viger," *Bull. du parler français au Canada*, 8 (1909–10): 42–55. Claude Tousignant, "Michel Bibaud: sa vie, son œuvre et son combat politique," *Recherches sociographiques* (Québec), 15 (1974): 21–30.

VIGER, LOUIS-MICHEL, lawyer, militia officer, landowner, politician, banker, Patriote, and seigneur; b. 28 Sept. 1785 in Montreal, son of Louis Viger and Marie-Agnès Papineau; d. 27 May 1855 in L'Assomption, Lower Canada, and was buried three days later in Repentigny.

The Vigers were an old family of craftsmen who soon after the conquest began a remarkable rise to prominence in French Canadian society. Louis Viger was living in Montreal and working as an blacksmith when the Treaty of Paris was signed in 1763. Four years later he married Marie-Agnès Papineau, sister of Joseph Papineau* and later the aunt of the great Louis-Joseph*. This marriage played a part in building the network formed by the important Papineau, Viger, Cherrier, and Lartigue families.

Louis-Michel Viger was the seventh of nine children. By the time of his birth his father had apparently become an ironmaster, the sign of an appreciable improvement in his status. Hence Louis-Michel was given a classical education at the Collège Saint-Raphaël from 1796 to 1803. He studied there with his cousin Louis-Joseph Papineau, and the two boys quickly formed a brotherly friendship that endured for the rest of their lives. Before his studies were completed Viger had decided to become a lawyer, and in 1802 had started legal training under his cousin Denis-Benjamin Viger*. Called to the bar on 5 July 1807, at the age of 21, Louis-Michel began to practise in Montreal.

A brilliant young lawyer of distinguished bearing, Viger had useful family connections and so was received into the homes of the new and increasingly important petite bourgeoisie in his native city. He was so popular that he was tagged "le beau Viger." Like many in the professions, Viger was exploring the ideas of liberty, equality, and sovereignty of the people, which were beginning to circulate in Lower Canada, and he was gaining a sense of his French Canadian nationality. Consequently, he soon became interested in politics. He may have joined the Canadian party in this period, probably at the same time as Louis-Joseph Papineau. Certainly, during the general election of 1810 precipitated by Governor Sir James Henry Craig* to deal with the political crisis in the colony, Viger declined to sign a congratulatory address to Craig endorsed by the senior officials and important British merchants; he also managed to dissuade a good many Montreal citizens from adding their signatures. In June of that year Thomas McCord* and Jean-Marie Mondelet*, justices of the peace in Montreal, accused Viger of being disloyal to the colonial authorities and trying to impede the English party's candidates, but nothing came of the matter.

Like others of the French Canadian petite bourgeoisie, Viger had heeded the official call to arms issued by administrator Thomas Dunn* during the summer of 1807 to meet a threatened American invasion. In 1808 he had enrolled as an ensign in Montreal's 2nd Militia Battalion. When the War of 1812 broke out he was made a lieutenant, and in 1814 a captain in the same battalion. During this period he also obtained a commission as lieutenant in the 5th Select Embodied Militia Battalion of Lower Canada. He served throughout the conflict, demonstrating his attachment to British institutions.

At the end of the war Viger resumed the practice of law. He soon became one of the best known lawyers of the Montreal bar and, through competence, diligence, and kindness, acquired a great many clients. In 1822 he took into partnership Côme-Séraphin Cherrier*, a cousin who had been called to the bar that year. On 19 July 1824, at Saint-Charles, near Quebec, Viger married Marie-Ermine Turgeon, a daughter of Legislative Councillor Louis Turgeon*, the seigneur of Beaumont, and niece of Pierre-Flavien Turgeon*, later archbishop of Quebec. The marriage was solemnized with great ceremony in the presence of numerous relatives and friends, including Viger's cousins, Denis-Benjamin and JACQUES Viger. Louis-Michel and his wife then went to live in the family residence on Rue Bonsecours in Montreal. Their four children were born in that house, which he apparently had inherited on the death of his father in 1812. In 1825 Viger also owned properties in the eastern part of the old town that earned him an annual income estimated at between £100 and £200.

While practising law, Viger had continued to involve himself in politics. He was one of a group of Montreal reformers who after 1815 steadily acquired influence within the Canadian party. During the 1820 election campaign he spoke at a meeting in support of Hugues Heney*, whom he helped to win a seat for Montreal East in the House of Assembly. Subsequently Viger began frequenting Édouard-Raymond FABRE's bookstore on Rue Saint-Vincent, where he regularly met the reform leaders of the Montreal region. In 1827 he was relieved of his captaincy in Montreal's 2nd Militia Battalion for having taken part in election meetings where resolutions were passed condemning the policy of Governor Lord Dalhousie [Ramsay*] concerning the civil list [see Denis-Benjamin Viger].

In 1830 Viger himself entered the political fray, probably at the urging of Papineau, who thought his cousin and best friend would be an excellent representative for his party. In the general election that year he was chosen with Frédéric-Auguste Quesnel* to represent Chambly. Once in harness at Quebec, Viger realized that public life was absorbing most of his time, and in 1832 he had to give up legal practice. In the house he proved a keen supporter of Papineau, and in particular voted for the 92 Resolutions. During the election campaign of 1834 he defended the Patriote party program with unflagging energy and had no difficulty winning in Chambly again, this time with Louis Lacoste*. Viger's political convictions led him to take part subsequently in several patriotic demonstrations. For instance, he participated in the Saint-Jean-Baptiste celebrations in 1835. The following year he was amongst the first to contribute to the fund organized to compensate Ludger DUVERNAY, the publisher of *La Minerve*, who was serving a third term in jail for contempt of court.

In 1835 Viger had also decided to go into business. He joined a group of merchants closely associated with the Patriote party who, considering themselves disadvantaged by the Bank of Montreal's stranglehold on credit in Lower Canada, proposed to set up a new bank which would provide the capital to foster small businesses and industries owned by French Canadians. Viger became the chief proponent of the plan, which to his credit he carried through successfully. In his colleague Jacob De Witt he found the man to help him organize and direct the new undertaking. The two formed Viger, De Witt et Cie, a limited partnership with an initial capital of £75,000 to which De Witt contributed heavily. This company, which was also known as the Banque du Peuple, had 12 principal partners, each of whom had to invest substantial capital and to assume responsibility for its operation. Papineau did not initially approve of the plan, and told Viger it would be "the tomb of your popularity and even your patriotism." He none the less realized that the bank might constitute a powerful weapon in the struggle against the important minority of major British merchants in the colony, and he soon urged his compatriots to support it. Viger and De Witt in any case forged ahead with their venture, and under their skilful guidance the company was assured of success from its earliest years. The bank's clients were chiefly farmers and artisans, who turned to it for loans.

When the British parliament in March 1837 adopted the resolutions of Lord John Russell, which proposed the removal of all assembly control over the executive, Viger strenuously opposed their application and committed himself to the Patriote movement. He was one of the members who supported the boycott of British products advocated by Papineau. Furthermore, along with such members as Édouard-Étienne Rodier* and De Witt, he appeared at the opening of the new session of the house in August dressed in homespun clothes. He took part in several of the gatherings held on the eve of the rebellion. On 4 June, with Lacoste and Timothée Kimber, he had attended a protest meeting in Chambly County. On 23 October at the Assemblée des Six Comtés at Saint-Charles-sur-Richelieu, he took his place on the platform as a member of Papineau's inner group and addressed the crowd immediately after his cousin.

In view of his part in various large pre-revolutionary meetings, Viger was recognized by the authorities as a leader of the Patriote movement. One of the 26 for whom a warrant of arrest was issued on 16 Nov. 1837, he was charged with high treason and thrown into prison two days later. As for the authorities' objective, Ægidius Fauteux* suggests: "It was not impossible that in arresting him they hoped especially to ruin his banking establishment. The claim was made that the real purpose behind this institution was to give cash advances to the rebels' army." It was an easy matter for members of the English party to spread this rumour when the rebellion broke out on 23 November.

There is some question about the nature of the links between the Banque du Peuple and the rebel movement, and, according to historian Fernand Ouellet, nothing can be said with certainty on the matter. The only explicit proof that there was a connection is the testimony of Étienne Chartier, who denounced those at the head of the bank because at the eleventh hour they had refused to finance the insurrection. In Ouellet's opinion there are various indications that the two were closely linked: the ties of kinship and friendship between Papineau and the bank's directors and shareholders, the steady contact Viger maintained with Papineau until the Patriote leader left Montreal, Viger's arrest, and the hasty visit that bank director Édouard-Raymond Fabre paid to Saint-Denis on the Richelieu where he met with Papineau and Edmund Bailey O'Callaghan* after Viger was jailed and just prior to the outbreak of fighting there.

Whatever the case, Viger's lawyer, William Walker*, had to engage in a real legal battle to secure the release of his client. Around the middle of December 1837 Walker made his first request for a writ of habeas corpus, which was rejected because martial law had just been declared. On 13 March 1838 he failed to obtain Viger's release because he had addressed his request to a sheriff who did not have the prisoner under his guard. On 21 April he again sought a writ of habeas corpus, this time from Lieutenant-Colonel George Augustus Wetherall*, but two days later the Special Council passed an ordinance suspending the use of habeas corpus in the colony until 24 August. Before it was reinstated, a general amnesty was decreed on 23 June 1838. Viger refused, however, to supply the security required and to give pledges of good conduct. Only in his fourth attempt, on 25 August, did Walker succeed in getting Viger set free, on bail of £2,000. Viger gave way then because most of the other prisoners had accepted the terms of the amnesty, and he had no desire to languish in prison. On 4 November, the day after the outbreak of the second rebellion, he was arrested again, but he was freed without trial on 13 December.

Viger had doubtless been exhausted by his two prolonged stays in prison, and was then severely tried by his wife's death on 9 June 1839. Thus for a period he concentrated exclusively on his own affairs. However, he was to involve himself in public affairs once more when in February 1840, along with a good many French Canadian politicians of the Montreal region, in particular Louis-Hippolyte La Fontaine* and Denis-Benjamin Viger, he signed a petition denouncing the resolutions passed by the Special Council in Lower Canada and the House of Assembly

Viger

in Upper Canada concerning the union of the two colonies. Their efforts proved vain. When the union was inaugurated in 1841, Viger was amongst those who called for its repeal. Standing in his old riding of Chambly in the general election that year, he was defeated by John Yule, the government candidate, after a campaign marred by irregularities and numerous acts of violence. In association with five other defeated reform candidates, among them La Fontaine, he presented a petition to have the election, which he termed fraudulent, declared null and void. The Legislative Assembly of the Province of Canada found technical reasons for turning down the request. In 1842, at a by-election for the seat vacated by Augustin-Norbert Morin*, Viger was elected member for Nicolet.

Viger married again on 10 Sept. 1843 at L'Assomption; he took as his second wife Aurélie – the daughter of Joseph-Édouard FARIBAULT, the widow of Charles Saint-Ours, and the seigneur of L'Assomption and of the Bayeul fief. They were to have no children. In this period the Banque du Peuple, which had survived the revolutionary upheaval, underwent considerable expansion, and Viger and De Witt were successful in seeking a charter by which it was incorporated in 1844 with a capital of £200,000. In 1845 Viger was appointed its president for life, and De Witt its vice-president. The following year Viger also agreed to join the honorary board of directors of the new Montreal City and District Savings Bank. By the time his term as member for Nicolet was up in 1844, he had decided not to stand at the next general election, and he retired for a few years with his wife to the manor-house of the seigneury of Saint-Ours in L'Assomption. He must already have amassed a sizeable fortune, for in 1848 he purchased the seigneury of Repentigny from Henry Ogden Andrews for £1,450.

Viger ran again, in the 1847–48 general election, and was elected member for Terrebonne. Papineau, whose interests during his exile had in part been looked after by Viger, also won a seat. When Robert BALDWIN* and La Fontaine were asked by Governor Lord Elgin [Bruce*] to form a new government, they approached Viger, who on 11 March accepted the office of receiver general with a seat on the Executive Council. But in so doing he incurred the censure of Papineau, who criticized him for approving of the régime he had sought to have repealed in 1841. As a former Patriote, Viger was one of the members who in March 1849 voted for the Rebellion Losses Bill. When the issue of annexation arose, along with the rest of the Executive Council he signed a declaration of loyalty published in *La Minerve* on 15 Oct. 1849 in reply to the Annexation Manifesto which had appeared four days earlier. After the Parliament

Building in Montreal had burned down, the Executive Council moved to Toronto, which in November became the new capital of the province. That month Viger protested against this decision and resigned as receiver general, insisting that he was unable to "share the views of [his] colleagues on the matter of the seat of government." He none the less continued to sit in the house as an ordinary member. In the general election of 1851 he was returned for Leinster, a seat he retained until 1854. He retired shortly afterwards to the manor-house of Saint-Ours in L'Assomption, where he died, apparently of a paralytic stroke, on 27 May 1855, at the age of 69.

The son of a skilled tradesman and entrepreneur, Louis-Michel Viger was a man who advanced to a markedly higher status, securing for himself an important place within the petite bourgeoisie of French Canada in the first half of the 19th century. He struggled ardently, first for the Patriote cause and then, after the rebellion and the union of the Canadas, for responsible government. A few days after his death, in a letter to Jean-Joseph GIROUARD dated 30 May 1855, Papineau expressed his grief at the loss of the man he considered his spiritual brother: "My friend and kinsman of the heart and of boyhood, with whom I grew up like a brother, Louis Viger, only one year older than I, is gone, and I learn this just as I write to you." According to the provisions detailed in the inventory of his estate, which was drawn up on 17 Oct. 1855, Viger left to his second wife a handsome fortune, the seigneury of Repentigny, and a few properties in Montreal.

MICHEL DE LORIMIER

ANQ-M, CE1-51, 19 janv. 1767, 28 sept. 1785; CE5-14, 10 sept. 1843; CE5-16, 30 mai 1855; CN1-194, 13 mai 1802; CN1-226, 7 déc. 1848; CN1-312, 17 oct., 28 nov. 1855; CN5-11, 10 sept. 1843; P1000-3-290. ANQ-Q, CE2-4, 19 juill. 1824; CN1-230, 19 juill. 1824; E17/6, no.44; E17/15, nos.921–25; E17/16, nos.926–61; E17/38, nos.3074–75; P-68; P-69. Arch. de l'Institut d'hist. de l'Amérique française (Montréal), Coll. Girouard, lettre de L.-J. Papineau à J.-J. Girouard, 30 mai 1855. ASQ, Fonds Viger–Verreau, Carton 46, no.9; Sér.O, 0139–40; 0144; 0147. BNQ, Dép. des MSS, MSS-101, Coll. La Fontaine (copies at PAC). BVM-G, Fonds Fauteux, notes compilées par Ægidius Fauteux sur les Patriotes de 1837–1838 dont les noms commencent par la lettre V, carton 10. PAC, MG 24, B2; B46; RG 4, B8, 18: 6501–4; RG 68, General index, 1651–1841; 1841–67. L.C., House of Assembly, *Journals*, 1830–37. Can., Prov. of, Legislative Assembly, *Journals*, 1842–44; 1848–54; *Statutes*, 1843, c.66. "État général des billets d'ordonnances . . . ," Pierre Panet, compil., ANQ *Rapport*, 1924–25: 229–359. "Un document important du curé Étienne Chartier sur les rébellions de 1837–38: lettre du curé Chartier adressée à Louis-Joseph Papineau en novembre 1839, à St Albans, Vermont," Richard Chabot, édit., *Écrits* de Canada français (Montréal), 39 (1974): 223–55. *La Minerve*, 17 déc. 1827; 12 juin, 26, 30 oct. 1837; 15 oct. 1849; 29 mai 1855; 28 juill. 1857. *La Patrie*, 5 juin 1855, 22 juill. 1857. *Le Pays*, 23 juill. 1857. *Quebec Gazette*, 13 March 1820. F.-M. Bibaud, *Le panthéon canadien* (A. et V. Bibaud; 1891). Borthwick, *Hist. and biog. gazetteer*, 295–96. Desjardins, *Guide parl.* Fauteux, *Patriotes*, 396–98. Lefebvre, *Le Canada, l'Amérique*, 350. Le Jeune, *Dictionnaire*, 2: 784. *Montreal directory*, 1842–55. *Officers of British forces in Canada* (Irving). *Quebec almanac*, 1807–41. Terrill, *Chronology of Montreal*. Wallace, *Macmillan dict.*

J.-G. Barthe, *Souvenirs d'un demi-siècle ou Mémoires pour servir à l'histoire contemporaine* (Montréal, 1885). Hector Berthelot, *Montréal, le bon vieux temps*, É.-Z. Massicotte, compil. (2v. in 1, 2nd ed., Montréal, 1924), 2: 28–29. Buchanan, *Bench and bar of L.C.* Campbell, *Hist. of Scotch Presbyterian Church*, 254–55. David, *Les gerbes canadiennes*, 175. Filteau, *Hist. des Patriotes* (1975). A.[-H.] Gosselin, *Un bon Patriote d'autrefois, le docteur Labrie* (3rd ed., Québec, 1907). R. S. Greenfield, "La Banque du peuple, 1835–1871, and its failure, 1895" (MA thesis, McGill Univ., Montreal, 1968). Clément Laurin, *J.-J. Girouard & les Patriotes de 1837–38: portraits* (Montréal, 1973), 112. Maurault, *Le collège de Montréal* (Dansereau; 1967). Monet, *La première révolution tranquille*. Ouellet, *Bas-Canada*; *Éléments d'histoire sociale du Bas-Canada* (Montréal, 1972); *Histoire économique et sociale du Québec, 1760–1850: structures et conjoncture* (Montréal et Paris, [1966]). C. Roy, *Hist. de L'Assomption*, 186, 206–7, 444. J.-L. Roy, *Édouard-Raymond Fabre*. P.-G. Roy, *Toutes petites choses du Régime anglais*, 1: 284–85; 2: 142–43. Robert Rumilly, *Artisans du miracle canadien: Régime anglais* (Montréal, 1936), 42–44; *Histoire de Longueuil* (Longueuil, Qué., 1974); *Histoire de Montréal* (5v., Montréal, 1970–74), 2; *Papineau et son temps*. T. T. Smyth, *The first hundred years: history of the Montreal City and District Savings Bank, 1846–1946* (Montreal, [1946]). Tulchinsky, *River barons*. L.-P. Turcotte, *Le Canada sous l'Union, 1841–1867* (2v., Québec, 1871–72). Mason Wade, *Les canadiens-français de 1760 à nos jours*, Adrien Venne et Francis Dufau-Labeyrie, trad. (2nd ed., 2v., Ottawa, 1966), 1: 189. J.-P. Wallot, *Un Québec qui bougeait: trame socio-politique du Québec au tournant du XIXe siècle* (Sillery, Qué., 1973). F.-J. Audet, "Le barreau et la révolte de 1837," RSC *Trans.*, 3rd ser., 31 (1937), sect.I: 85–96; "L'honorable Louis-Michel Viger," *BRH*, 33 (1927): 354–55. Édouard Fabre Surveyer, "Les trois Viger," *BRH*, 53 (1947): 29. Montarville de La Bruère, "Louis-Joseph Papineau, de Saint-Denis à Paris," *Cahiers des Dix*, 5 (1940): 79–106. J.-J. Lefebvre, "Les députés de Chambly, 1792–1967," *BRH*, 70 (1968): 3–19; "La famille Viger: le maire Jacques Viger (1858); ses parents – ses ascendants – ses alliés," SGCF *Mémoires*, 17 (1966): 203–38. Henri Masson, "Louis-Michel Viger, député de Terrebonne, procureur général – prisonnier politique," SGCF *Mémoires*, 18 (1967): 198–205. Louis Richard, "Jacob De Witt (1785–1859)," *RHAF*, 3 (1949–50): 537–55. "Une institution nationale: la Banque du peuple," *Rev. canadienne*, 31 (1895): 82–97.

VIGER, MARIE-AMABLE. *See* FORETIER

VINCENT DE PAUL, JACQUES MERLE, named **Father.** *See* MERLE

VIVANT, LAURENT (also called **Venant** or **Virant** and sometimes known as **Louis**), draftsman, painter, teacher, and photographer; b. *c.* 1806 in Saint-Aignan, France; d. 28 Nov. 1860 in Montreal.

According to the obituary in *Le Pays* of 1 Dec. 1860, Laurent Vivant is thought to have arrived in Lower Canada around 1848, but no trace of him has been found there before 1850. His coming may have had some connection with the presence in Montreal of a seaman named Pierre Gauthier, who is listed in the 1848 *Montreal directory* and who in the 1849 one is described as a "paper-hanger" and "map mounter." Gauthier becomes a "decorator" in the directory's pages as soon as Vivant moved in with him in 1851, and it is not beyond the realm of possibility that Vivant through this association collaborated in the appointing of private residences and even public buildings. Gauthier's name disappears from the Montreal directory after 1858, shortly before Vivant's death.

In May 1850 Vivant, who described himself as a "French artist," had placed an announcement in *La Minerve*. Eager to teach drawing, he offered lessons in "perspective, line drawing, likenesses, landscapes, etc.," and indicated he was prepared to give private lessons. This marks the beginning of his teaching activity in Montreal, which he carried on until at least 1855. His reputation as a "young man of irreproachable moral character" possessed of "quite an extensive knowledge of his art" was perfectly in keeping with the occupation of drawing master. The range of subjects offered by Vivant was gradually widened to include in 1851 "landscapes in colour, sketching in two colours, mechanical drawing, or drafting of plans." The following year he summed up his curriculum as "landscapes, flowers, and faces," and specified that his courses dealt with painting as well as drawing. That year he published an announcement illustrated with a floral vignette; this is the only extant illustration associated with his name but it is not known if it was his handiwork. Vivant also executed portraits, either in oil on canvas or in the form of daguerreotypes.

In January 1854 Vivant became the first to be taken on as a "teacher of drawing and painting" at the model school in Montreal. Calling him a "valuable acquisition," an advertisement in *La Minerve* went on to assert that the model school could "now be compared advantageously with any other institution of this type on the continent." The secure job he had just acquired may explain why subsequently he is seldom listed in the directories and no longer mentioned in announcements in Montreal newspapers, but, given that his name appears for the last time in the 1855 edition of

Voyer

the *Montreal directory* as a "teacher of drawing," he probably taught only a year at the model school and he may also have been unsuccessful. However, at the time of his death he was described as a "painter and language teacher."

Vivant is called a daguerreotypist in the *Montreal directory* of 1857, but his name is not on the lists of members of this growing profession that year or in subsequent years. Montreal photographers, following the experiments carried out by Charles Dion in 1853, were acquiring the art of printing and enlarging positive images on light-sensitive paper; the fact that Vivant did not use this technique may have contributed to his failure in the field.

It was as a view painter that Vivant enjoyed his greatest success in Montreal. In November 1853 he showed a "superb view" of the Grand Provincial Agricultural and Industrial Exhibition held there from 27 to 30 September, in hopes of making a profit of at least 18 "piastres" by a lottery. Sponsored by the government of the Province of Canada, this remarkable show had attracted large numbers of people, coming as it did in the wake of the Exhibition of the Industry of All Nations, opened at New York in July. Whatever the result of the lottery, his piece drew praise in the newspapers; the press emphasized the "extraordinary sharpness" of a view that "did honour" to him.

This was not the first opportunity the Montreal public had had of seeing Vivant's works, for he had exhibited a number of them in 1851, apparently at Pierre-Étienne Picault's pharmacy at the corner of Rue Notre-Dame and Rue Saint-Vincent. At the end of the summer of 1860 he also exhibited "a few pleasing canvases" at the industrial exhibition.

On 28 Nov. 1860 Laurent Vivant put an end to his life by taking prussic acid. His last words on a note found at the scene of the tragedy were: "The night is beautiful – the moon is shining – adieu, my friends."

DAVID KAREL

ANQ-M, CE1-51, 30 nov. 1860. MAC-CD, Fonds Morisset, 2, V855.5/L. *La Minerve*, 10 mai 1850; 13 sept.–14 oct. 1851; 7, 21 sept.–26 nov. 1852; 2 août, 17 nov. 1853; 14 janv. 1854. *Le Pays*, 1er déc. 1860. *Montreal directory*, 1848–50, 1855, 1857–58.

VOYER, ANTOINE, businessman, politician, and strong man; b. 23 May 1782 in Montreal, son of Jacques Voyer and Judith Taton, *dit* Brind'amour; m. there 26 Nov. 1804 Marie-Anne Sainte-Marie, and they had three children; d. there 27 Dec. 1858.

Like most of those renowned for performing great physical feats, Antoine Voyer is enshrined in a legend so that it is difficult to separate reality from folklore. The man nicknamed "le grand Voyer" lacked neither panache nor reputation. Twenty years older than Joseph Montferrand*, strong man extraordinary, Voyer apparently had such a commanding physical presence that Jos looked up to him as to a father. Voyer was also sufficiently active in civic affairs to acquire social status and even to hold office as a town councillor. Paradoxically, this phase of his life is the least known although it can be more readily traced in documents, whereas the mighty deeds that make up his legend seem to have been written down only after long years of being recounted by one generation to the next.

Voyer was the eldest of seven children. His father owned some land, including four properties in different locations in the *faubourg* Saint-Laurent and the Coteau-Saint-Louis, which constituted the estate inherited jointly by his mother and her children in 1803. Voyer's share may have given him the beginnings of financial independence, for he is not known to have had any recognized trade. According to legend he was an innkeeper, but no proof of this has been found. He is supposed to have been taller than average and slender, "six feet and a half" and weighing just over 200 pounds. His strength cannot be assessed because there is no known record of his involvement in any challenges or performances. Voyer reportedly took part in several of the election riots or social disturbances that marked the early years of the 19th century. During one election, he and Jos Montferrand are said to have used a 250-pound weight to clear a polling-station occupied by one of the political parties. He supposedly picked quarrels with members of the army: once, aided by another strong man, he beat up seven or eight soldiers who were harassing an old woman, and then himself successfully took on five soldiers who, because of that incident, attacked him not far from a sentry-box. Legend also has it that when he was an innkeeper on Rue Saint-Laurent in Montreal he once cleared the establishment by dumping a number of brawling seamen out of the window one by one.

Of all Voyer's exploits, however, there is documentary evidence for only one: his participation in the by-election in Montreal West in 1832, during which he laid out one of the most redoubtable bullies in Montreal. The election began on 25 April and pitted Stanley Bagg, who described himself as a businessman, against Dr Daniel Tracey*, publisher of the city's *Vindicator and Canadian Advertiser*, a reform newspaper. Bagg was supported by the tories and the *Montreal Gazette*; Tracey was backed by French Canadian reformers and *La Minerve*, and counted on the Irish vote. Voyer, who lived on Rue Saint-Laurent, was on the riding's electoral list. He gave his support to Tracey, and with Louis-Hippolyte La

Fontaine* signed a circular inviting other voters to do the same.

On the first day of the election, a group of toughs in Bagg's pay, some of whom had also been sworn in as special constables by local magistrates, attempted to gain control of the polling-station and prevent Tracey's supporters from getting near. On the second day Voyer was present and, when the trouble-makers again resorted to threats and violence, he knocked out their leader, a certain Bill Collins who had already been convicted of homicide, with one blow of his fist. Tradition has it that Collins died of Voyer's blow, but the outcome remains uncertain and no charges were brought against Voyer. However, Voyer's appearance served to rout the tory ruffians and to restore calm until the bloody incident of 21 May when the army fired on a crowd and killed three people.

Despite the bravado on which Voyer's legend is based, the label of ruffian did not stick to him; on the contrary, he was looked up to and respected by his contemporaries, including La Fontaine, and he was not given to picking fights over trifles. There is little if any doubt that Voyer did not depend on his physical prowess for a living. His reputation, unmarred by the incidents of 1832, was sufficiently solid for him to be on the city council of Montreal in 1834 and 1835. There, incidentally, he was among a number of well-known citizens who had been involved in the 1832 election: La Fontaine, Jacques VIGER, Charles-Séraphin Rodier*, and John Anthony Donegani*. The only evidence of Voyer's business activities dates from this period. Some 30 notarial instruments, concluded between 1834 and 1843, show him busy in real estate. Most of these are leases for houses, which suggests that Voyer was able to turn his paternal inheritance to good advantage and make a place for himself as a large property owner in Saint-Laurent ward. He died there in December 1858 at the age of 76.

Among strong men, Antoine Voyer is a special case. The legend surrounding him rests not so much on the number of his exploits as on their character; none the less it is sufficiently impressive for him to be regarded as a predecessor to Jos Montferrand. His civic life was that of a man in comfortable circumstances, one who was numbered among the prominent citizens of his district, who was only unintentionally involved in fights, and who lived on the income from his properties. Legend, however, has discarded the bourgeois side of this man, favouring instead the image of one who used his strength to protect his fellow citizens during the troubled period of the early 19th century in the Canadas that saw the introduction of the British parliamentary régime and the development of Anglo-Saxon social patterns.

PAUL BERNIER

[Three accounts of Antoine Voyer's feats, based on oral history and thus lacking in dates and places, are in Hector Berthelot, Montréal, le bon vieux temps, É.-Z. Massicotte, compil. (2v. in 1, Montréal, 1916), 1: 99–101; É.-Z. Massicotte, Athlètes canadiens-français; recueil des exploits de force, d'endurance, d'agilité, des athlètes et des sportsmen de notre race depuis le XVIIIᵉ siècle . . . biographies, portraits, anecdotes, records (2nd ed., Montréal, [1909]); and Sulte, Mélanges hist. (Malchelosse), vol.12. Massicotte*'s volume unquestionably provides the fullest treatment. P.B.]

ANQ-M, CE1-51, 23 mai 1782, 26 nov. 1804, 27 déc. 1858; CN1-32, 1834–35, 1837, 1839–43; CN1-194, 21 déc. 1803. L.C., House of Assembly, Journals, 1832–33, app.M; 1834, app.NN. La Minerve, avril–mai 1832. Montreal Gazette, April–May 1832. Vindicator (Montreal), April–May 1832. F.-M. Bibaud, Le panthéon canadien (A. et V. Bibaud; 1891). Montreal almanac, 1829, 1848. Montreal directory, 1820, 1850. Hist. de Montréal (Lamothe et al.). Robert Rumilly, Histoire de Montréal (5v., Montréal, 1970–74), 2.

W

WALSH, WILLIAM, Roman Catholic priest, archbishop, and author; b. 7 Nov. 1804 in Waterford (Republic of Ireland), eldest of 14 children of Joseph Walsh; d. 11 Aug. 1858 in Halifax.

William Walsh attended St John's College in Waterford and then went to the seminary in Maynooth. Ordained at Holy Trinity Church, Waterford, on 25 March 1828, he served as a curate near Dublin, at Clontarf and Kingstown (Dun Laoghaire), for the next 12 years and was also nominated for, but did not receive, the post of vicar apostolic of Calcutta.

His notebooks record a busy life during this period: hearing confessions, preaching, saying mass, and tending to the needs of the parishioners under his care.

In 1841 his name was again proposed for higher office; this time he was to be appointed to the position of coadjutor bishop of Nova Scotia. The decision to appoint a coadjutor to William FRASER, vicar apostolic of Nova Scotia, resulted from insistent lobbying by representatives of the Irish Catholic population of Halifax. They felt that their interests were being neglected by Bishop Fraser, who chose to live in Antigonish. On 1 May 1842, in Ireland, Walsh was consecrated titular bishop of Maximianopolis and coadjutor bishop of Nova Scotia with the right of succession.

Soon after his consecration Walsh received a petition from 13 Nova Scotian priests noting that his appointment had been made without consultation with either Bishop Fraser or the clergy of the diocese. They blamed the troubles in Halifax on "a contemptable faction of misbehaved Catholics in the Metropolis of this Vicariate." Walsh immediately wrote to Rome offering his resignation but the Sacred Congregation of Propaganda refused to accept it. Accompanied by Thomas Louis Connolly*, his secretary and eventual successor, Walsh arrived in Halifax on 16 Oct. 1842 and proceeded to Antigonish to meet with Fraser. Although he claimed to have been "most kindly received by the worthy Dr. Fraser," it soon became evident that his stay in Halifax would prove difficult. Besides not being consulted about the appointment of a coadjutor, Fraser had learned of the appointment not from Rome but from a newspaper article. Walsh's arrival only served to worsen matters.

Walsh found two opposing factions within the Catholic church in Halifax: one, led by Father John Loughnan, vicar general of the diocese, included those who supported the authority of Bishop Fraser; the other, led by Father Richard Baptist O'Brien, a recent arrival from Ireland, included prominent Irish merchants and professionals who had been in favour of the appointment of a coadjutor. Fraser gave Walsh control of the temporal powers of the church in Halifax but left Loughnan as vicar general with jurisdiction over ecclesiastical and spiritual matters.

For almost a year and a half Walsh attempted to work with Loughnan and tried to remain neutral in the dispute between the two factions. This was not easy since Walsh and not Loughnan, Fraser's appointed representative, was looked upon by his Irish compatriots as their spokesman in dealings with Fraser. Nevertheless, Walsh immediately took the initiative in a number of areas. As instructed, he took over control of the temporalities from the wardens and electors of St Mary's Cathedral, began the establishment of a new church in the city, supervised the construction of a new cemetery and chapel, and sought to reorganize the operation of St Mary's College. Throughout this period Walsh lived in a hotel since he had not been authorized by either Fraser or Loughnan to live in the glebe house. Walsh attempted to warn Fraser about the unrest which was being caused by Loughnan, calling him "your Lordships greatest enemy." Fraser, still smarting from the slight by Rome and confident that Walsh would be recalled, refused to intervene and remained in Antigonish. While trying to reach an accord with Loughnan and Fraser, Walsh was also urging Propaganda, the body that had placed him in this "cruel dilemma," to split

the diocese, giving Fraser and a coadjutor the eastern end of the province and him the rest. He noted that Fraser, while "guileless, good natured," and "honest hearted," was "unsuited to the present position, or the many wants of this vast Diocese."

On 3 March 1844 Walsh left for Rome to plead his case personally and to seek an early resolution to the situation. Both Fraser and Walsh agreed on the need to split the diocese but they were at odds on the conditions of such a division. Finally on 22 September the division was made "according to the limits proposed by Monsignor Fraser." On 20 July 1845 Fraser, without a coadjutor, became bishop of Arichat, which included all of Cape Breton and what are now the counties of Antigonish and Guysborough, and Walsh became bishop of Halifax, which included the rest of the province and the island of Bermuda. With his position assured, Walsh set about building new schools and providing more priests for the diocese. He established convents in Halifax of the Sisters of Charity [see Rosanna McCann*] and of the Religious of the Sacred Heart to teach in the Catholic schools.

On 4 May 1852, after Fraser's death, Walsh was appointed archbishop of Halifax, with jurisdiction over the newly formed ecclesiastical province of Nova Scotia, thus becoming the first archbishop in British North America outside Quebec. His presence in the capital and his enthusiasm offered Catholics a visible symbol of their growing status within the city and throughout the province. He travelled extensively in the archdiocese and encouraged the development of new parishes. He was also a prolific writer of letters, poems, and major works of pious and devotional literature which were published and widely distributed.

William Walsh died on 11 Aug. 1858 after a lengthy illness that had kept him out of public life for some time. An obituary noted: "He was an easy and fluent speaker, and a forcible writer; possessed a singularly ready and polished wit, and a graceful affability of manner, qualities which made him such a conversationlist as we have never seen, and do not soon expect to see, surpassed. We will only add, what we have every reason to believe strictly true, that on all great questions on which the opinions and feelings of men are much divided, Dr. Walsh had more enlarged views and evinced more liberality of sentiment than one usually finds among men whose professions and associations, like his, naturally incline them to regard such questions in a partizan light."

DAVID B. FLEMMING

AAH, T. L. Connolly papers; William Fraser papers; William Walsh papers. *Acadian Recorder*, 14 Aug. 1858. *Evening Express* (Halifax), 16 Aug. 1858. David Allison,

History of Nova Scotia (3v., Halifax, 1916), 2. A. A. Johnston, *Hist. of Catholic Church in eastern N.S.*, vol.2. T. M. Punch, *Irish Halifax: the immigrant generation, 1815–1859* ([Halifax], 1981); "The Irish in Halifax, 1836–1871: a study in ethnic assimilation" (MA thesis, Dalhousie Univ., Halifax, 1977); *Some sons of Erin in Nova Scotia* (Halifax, 1980). K. F. Trombley [Tremblay], *Thomas Louis Connolly (1815–1876): the man and his place in secular and ecclesiastical history* (Louvain, Belgium, 1983). J. E. Burns, "Archbishop William Walsh," *N.S. Hist. Soc., Coll.*, 25 (1942): 131–43. C. M. Kelly, "William Walsh, first archbishop of Halifax (1804–1858)," *Irish Ecclesiastical Record* (Dublin), 66 (1945): 11–18.

WARBURTON, GEORGE DROUGHT, army officer and writer; b. 2 June 1816 in Wicklow (Republic of Ireland), third son of George Warburton and Anna Acton; m. 30 June 1853 Elizabeth Augusta Bateman-Hanbury, and they had one daughter, who later married Lord Edward Spencer-Churchill; d. 23 Oct. 1857, by his own hand, in Frant (East Sussex), England.

George Drought Warburton was sent to the Royal Military Academy, Woolwich (London), by his father, who had been inspector general of the Irish constabulary. He entered the Royal Artillery as a 2nd lieutenant on 21 June 1833 and was promoted 1st lieutenant on St Patrick's Day 1836. Serving on the north coast of Spain from February 1837 to October 1838 during the Carlist War, Warburton was wounded on 15 March 1837 near Hernani and received the 1st class of the Order of St Ferdinand. Promoted 2nd captain in the late spring of 1844, he left Woolwich on 17 July for a posting in the Canadas. He was stationed at Montreal from 4 Sept. 1844 to 15 July 1845 and from 19 Dec. 1845 to 1 March 1847, when he was granted six months' leave on "Private affairs."

During his stay in Canada, Warburton wrote "an agreeable description of the dominion," *Hochelaga; or, England in the New World*, published anonymously in London in 1846. His older brother, Bartholomew Elliott George (usually Eliot), who edited the book, had himself established a reputation as a travel-book author two years earlier with *The crescent and the cross; or, romance and realities of eastern travel.* Eliot's friendship with Alexander William Kinglake, author of the travel classic *Eothen; or traces of travel brought home from the East*, and acquaintanceship with Alexis de Tocqueville suggest a family interest in sophisticated travel writing. *Hochelaga* reflects George's experiences in North America. While in Quebec City he witnessed two terrible fires, on 28 May and 28 June 1845. He describes Montreal, Kingston, and Toronto, diligently noting social and political features as well as geographical ones, and the book includes a lively history of the "rebellious movements" of 1837. His later tours included a sweep from Buffalo through Philadelphia to Washington and back via Boston to Montreal; his comparisons between Canada and the United States are perceptive and lively. He watched the progress of canal-building and was convinced of the need for a railway system in Canada to further British interests and to consolidate the colonies. *Hochelaga* went through several editions in England and the United States, and became staple reading for the next generation of travellers.

On 1 Nov. 1848 Warburton was promoted 1st captain and took command of the 4th Company of the 6th Battalion of Royal Artillery stationed at Corfu (Greece). His company returned to Woolwich in May 1849 and that year he published, again anonymously, his two-volume work *The conquest of Canada*. From a lively history of the military campaigns of the 18th century, including several vignettes of army figures, he broadens to a general history. He also sketches the geological and agricultural possibilities, even in the "dreary solitudes" north of Lake Superior, and adds a carefully researched account of Canadian Indians. His writing is as lively as that of John RICHARDSON in his history of the War of 1812: indeed, of early histories, only George Heriot*'s *The history of Canada* is comparable to Warburton's work in coverage and liveliness. *The conquest of Canada* enjoyed a second London edition as well as a New York edition in 1850, and was being reprinted as late as 1864.

In September 1850 the company under Warburton's command was stationed at Landguard Fort, near Harwich, and, during his frequent visits to London, George joined his brother as part of Lady Morgan's witty circle. A third literary production, *A memoir of Charles Mordaunt*, "by the author of *Hochelaga*," appeared in 1853. During that eventful year, Eliot died in a fire at sea, George married the daughter of Lord Bateman, his company was sent to Guernsey in September, and he retired from the army with full pay on 29 November. He moved to Henley House, Frant, and on 28 Nov. 1854 was promoted major of the Royal Artillery. On 28 March 1857 he was elected to parliament by a large majority as an Independent Liberal for Harwich. On 23 October, "in a fit of temporary insanity" induced by pains of indigestion to which he was subject, he shot himself through the head.

George Warburton's life was brief and his direct experience of Canada lasted less than two years. Yet his accounts of Canada remain as testimony to an agreeable, spirited personality. *The conquest of Canada* helped Britons understand Canadian history and aspirations and *Hochelaga* popularized the notions of Canadian landscape as attractive and Canadian society as engaging and entertaining.

ELIZABETH WATERSTON

George Drought Warburton is the author of *Hochelaga; or, England in the New World*, ed. [B.] E. [G.] Warburton (2v., London, 1846); *The conquest of Canada* (2v., London,

Ward

1849); and *A memoir of Charles Mordaunt, earl of Peterborough and Monmouth: with selections from his correspondence* (2v., London, 1853).

PRO, WO 17/1548–51 (mfm. at PAC). George Heriot, *The history of Canada, from its first discovery, comprehending an account of the original establishment of the colony of Louisiana* (London, 1804). [John] Richardson, *War of 1812 . . .* ([Brockville, Ont.], 1842). *Battery records of the Royal Artillery, 1716–1859*, comp. M. E. S. Laws (Woolwich, Eng., 1952). *DNB* (biogs. of George Drought Warburton, Bartholomew Elliott George Warburton, Sydney Morgan, Lady Morgan). G.B., WO, *Army list*, 1834–58. *Hart's army list*, 1840–57. Morgan, *Bibliotheca Canadensis*, 387. K. N. Windsor, "Historical writing in Canada to 1920," *Lit. hist. of Canada* (Klinck *et al.*; 1976), 1: 226, 228.

WARD, EDMUND, printer, newspaperman, author, office holder, and publisher's agent; b. 24 June 1787 in Halifax, son of Edmund Ward and Hannah Rogers; m. there 9 Nov. 1817 Eleanor Bowers Jackson, and they had five sons and two daughters; d. 31 Oct. 1853 in Hamilton, Bermuda.

Edmund Ward's father, a loyalist from Connecticut, met his wife while he was a prisoner in her father's home during the American Revolutionary War; Captain Ward later served as an official in the barracks department in Nova Scotia, where he received land grants after the war. Young Edmund was trained as a printer in the office of William Minns*. In 1809 the governor of Bermuda, Brigadier-General John Hodgson, invited him there to edit a newspaper, which became the *Royal Gazette*. In Bermuda, Ward also issued the *Gleaner*, a short-lived literary paper, and the *Weekly Gazette*; he held a clerkship in the Court of King's Bench and a post in the customs department; and he helped organize a Sunday school. Because he was an associate of the unpopular Hodgson, he became involved in local controversies; the House of Assembly sometimes withheld payment for printing, and in 1815 declined to give him its printing contract.

Ward's Bermuda career ended over the incident of the capture of the American warship *President* by the frigate *Endymion* and other ships of a blockading British squadron off Long Island on 14–15 Jan. 1815. When the *President* was brought to Bermuda, Ward reported that the *Endymion* alone had captured her (which was denied in the official American reports) and that 68 American seamen were discovered stowed away in an unsuccessful ruse to recapture the ship. Governor Sir James Cockburn ordered Ward to retract the latter statement, but Ward trusted the word of a British lieutenant and stuck to his story; he was beaten up by an American midshipman and lost his commission as king's printer on 12 April. He angrily issued a pamphlet on the whole affair, continued the *Weekly Gazette* for a short time, and then returned to Halifax.

In April 1816 Ward began the *Free Press*, a tory newspaper that reported the House of Assembly debates and took a lively interest in economic and cultural affairs. But his stubbornness and quick temper, as well as his need to increase circulation, soon gained the paper a reputation for political quarrelling and personal abuse. His chief antagonists were publisher Anthony Henry Holland* and the contributors to his liberal newspaper the *Acadian Recorder*. The enmity reached a climax in 1820, when Ward was horsewhipped by George Renny YOUNG, the son of *Recorder* contributor John Young*; the next year Ward was beaten up by Holland's brother Philip John. In court in the latter year Ward was fined £2 for libelling another *Recorder* contributor, James Irving, while Philip Holland was fined £9 0s. 3d. for his attack on Ward. In 1838 the Hollands' successors, John English and Hugh William Blackadar*, were to print a letter in the *Recorder* from one A. H. Duncan, who evidently had crossed swords with Ward in Fredericton, which stated that Ward was "celebrated for many a feat of thoroughbred swindling." Duncan then disappeared but English and Blackadar were fined £40 for libel in June 1840.

Ward's other publications included the *Nova-Scotia almanack*, *The farmer's almanack*, *Ward's almanack*, and one issue of the *British North American Magazine, and Colonial Journal*. Elected secretary of the Halifax Temperance Society in 1834, that May he began the *Temperance Recorder* to bring together the 10,000 persons in some 90 temperance societies around the province whom he hoped to attract with a low subscription rate. He always had trouble collecting subscriptions, and by 1837 was feeling the competition of the new Baptist paper, the *Christian Messenger*. His premises were offered for sale in May and auctioned in late October, by which time the *Temperance Recorder* had ceased to appear. For several years Ward had travelled extensively around the Maritime provinces lecturing on temperance, and after one such trip to New Brunswick in 1837 he began the *Sentinel and New Brunswick General Advertiser* on 16 December in Fredericton. Ward was appointed assistant emigrant agent for New Brunswick in 1840 through his friendship with the lieutenant governor, Sir John HARVEY, to whom he gratefully dedicated a pamphlet advocating the cultivation of the interior, *An account of the River St John, with its tributary rivers and lakes*. Ward is also reputed to have been the author of *Solitude and other poems; by an old resident of New Brunswick*, which was printed at his office.

When the *Sentinel* closed down some time early in 1844, Ward moved to Halifax to issue a short-lived tri-weekly, the *Evening Gazette*, but soon left for New York to work as a reprint publisher's agent, in which role he travelled extensively through the southern states. In June 1846 he was back in the Maritimes as the agent for the New York *Anglo-American* newspaper, and by late 1848 he was the agent for the New York firm of Leonard Scott and Company, which had just secured the American reprint rights for the major British magazines. Since Nova Scotia now allowed these reprints in legally, Ward pressed for reduced postal rates so that subscribers outside Halifax could get the periodicals at Halifax rates. Ward had lost the Scott agency by early 1850, at a time when he was burdened by the deaths of three sons. Forced to work as a manual labourer, he sought relief for his desperate condition from Harvey, now the lieutenant governor of Nova Scotia.

Little is known about the years Ward then spent in New York City before he went to Hamilton, Bermuda, in October 1853 to assist his son Robert, the editor of the *Bermuda Herald*, who had contracted yellow fever. Ward himself came down with the fever and died suddenly. He was buried in the parish of Pembroke. Although quarrelsome and vindictive in public, Ward was remembered with affection by his children. A good parliamentary reporter and an advocate of temperance and other social improvements, he was a journalist with a direct, simple style.

GEORGE L. PARKER

Edmund Ward is the author of *Report of a debate on the quit rent, which took place in the House of Assembly, in the province of Nova Scotia . . .* (Halifax, 1830) and *An account of the River St John, with its tributary rivers and lakes* (Fredericton, 1841). His account of his Bermuda career, apparently written in the 1840s, was published under the title "Seven years residence in Bermuda," in the *Bermuda Hist. Quarterly* (Hamilton), 5 (1948): 183–98; 6 (1949): 34–49. A typed note inserted opposite p.238 of a copy of Robert James Long's *Nova Scotia authors and their work, a bibliography of the province* (East Orange, N.J., 1918) held by the Acadia Univ. Library (Wolfville, N.S.) attributes the authorship of *Solitude and other poems; by an old resident of New Brunswick* (Fredericton, 1842) to Ward. The addendum is probably Long's own, but it may not be accurate and no other supporting evidence is available.

PAC, MG 23, D1, ser.1, 61, book 3, Robert Ward to J. W. Lawrence, 24 Sept. 1880; MG 24, B1, 3: 255a–c; 176: 6002–5. PANS, MG 100, 243, nos.35–36; RG 1, 120: 239; 227, no.113; 258, no.93; RG 5, GP, 9, petitions of Edmund Ward, 17 Nov. 1818, 19 Aug. 1820, 10 April 1821, 3 May 1822; RG 7, 19, Ward to Howe, 17 Oct. 1848; RG 20A, Ward, Edmund, 1804, 1805; RG 24, 2: 207. William James, *A full and correct account of the chief naval occurrences of the late war between Great Britain and the United States of America . . .* (London, 1817), 449–51; *An inquiry into the merits of the principal naval actions, between Great-Britain and the United States . . .* (Halifax, 1816), 90–91. N.S., House of Assembly, *Journal and proc.*, 1832, app.16.

Acadian Recorder, 27 Oct. 1821; 10 Nov. 1838; 2, 9 May 1840; 3 Feb. 1849. *Daily Sun* (Halifax), 31 [sic] Nov. 1853. *Free Press* (Halifax), 20 Oct. 1818; 19 June, 30 Oct. 1821. *New-Brunswick Courier*, 9 April 1831, 27 June 1846, 19 Nov. 1853. *New Brunswick Reporter and Fredericton Advertiser*, 18 Nov. 1853. *Novascotian*, 23 April 1834; 10 Sept. 1835; 1 Oct. 1840; 6 May, 23 June, 8 July 1844; 19 Feb., 5, 19 March, 24 Dec. 1849; 25 Feb. 1850; 14 Nov. 1853. *Times* (Halifax), 24 March 1846. J. R. Harper, *Historical directory of New Brunswick newspapers and periodicals* (Fredericton, 1961), no.96. *An historical directory of Nova Scotia newspapers and journals before confederation*, comp. T. B. Vincent (Kingston, Ont., 1977), nos.26, 46, 50, 126. W. G. MacFarlane, *New Brunswick bibliography: the books and writers of the province* (Saint John, N.B., 1895), 82. Morgan, *Bibliotheca Canadensis*, 387. G. E. N. Tratt, *A survey and listing of Nova Scotia newspapers, 1752–1957, with particular reference to the period before 1867* (Halifax, 1979), nos.144, 192, 200, 342, 344. Duncan Campbell, *Nova Scotia, in its historical, mercantile and industrial relations* (Montreal, 1873), 297. V. L. O. Chittick, *Thomas Chandler Haliburton: a study in provincial toryism* (New York, 1924), 69. W. H. Kesterton, *A history of journalism in Canada* (Toronto, 1967), 17. Beamish Murdoch, *A history of Nova-Scotia, or Acadie* (3v., Halifax, 1865–67), 3: 450. William Smith, *The history of the Post Office in British North America, 1639–1870* (Cambridge, Eng., 1920), 186–87. H. C. Wilkinson, *Bermuda from sail to steam; the history of the island from 1784 to 1901* (2v., London, 1973), 1: 233–34, 273, 350–53; 2: 680, 834–35. M. L. Chase, "Edmund Ward and the Temperance," *N.S. Hist. Quarterly* (Halifax), 5 (1975), special supp.: 19–36. D. C. Harvey, "The intellectual awakening of Nova Scotia," *Dalhousie Rev.* (Halifax), 13 (1932–33): 18; "Newspapers of Nova Scotia, 1840–1867," *CHR*, 26 (1945): 294. J. S. Martell, "The press of the Maritime provinces in the 1830's," *CHR*, 19 (1938): 35–36, 38–39.

WEBBER, GEORGE, poet and newspaperman; fl. 1851–57 in Newfoundland.

George Webber was probably born at Harbour Grace, Nfld, apparently in the second decade of the 19th century since he writes of himself in 1851 as being at "life's meridian," presumably half-way through the proverbial three score years and ten. He made a career in journalism, yet there is no obituary or death notice for him and little information about his personal life. From his own writings it seems that he was educated and travelled widely in Newfoundland, and he evidently spent some years elsewhere, probably in Canada. In 1851 he calls himself "a stranger in my native land" and laments that "all seems sadly alter'd here." In notes appended to his poem *The last of the aborigines: a poem founded in facts*, published in book form that year, he indicates that one section had been published over his initials "some years since in Harbour Grace" and refers to his having been in Quebec City.

By 1851 Webber's travels were over and he returned to Newfoundland where he was associated with the St John's *Morning Post, and Shipping Gazette*. The anonymity affected by most journalists of the time prevents use of its columns to obtain details of Webber's activities. On 1 March 1851 the *Morning*

Wedderburn

Post marked the beginning of the year's seal-fishery by publishing "Sealers' song," a poem "by G. W. for the Morning Post"; a later publication claims it was written in 1842 but may be in error. It is an exercise in the "come-all-ye" tradition, with the usual heartiness, forced rhymes, and verbal inversions.

> Come, sing the hardy sealer's song,
>   A wild and cheerful strain;
> Who coast each creek and shore along –
>   Or cross the billowy main:
> Not winter's storms, nor sea's alarms,
>   Can daunt the daring mind;
> Unknown to fear, away they steer,
>   Old Neptune's Fleece to find!

The "Fleece" is seal pelt; there is much more to the poem, of roughly equal quality.

In the same year, 1851, *The last of the aborigines* was published by the *Morning Post*. The work, headed with an apt quotation from William Cowper's "Charity," is in heroic style and consists of four cantos of rhyming couplets interspersed with occasional songs. Webber presents an imaginary account of the last days of the Beothuks, the Newfoundland Indians who were annihilated, apparently by tuberculosis and white hunting parties. Imitative of late-18th-century English verse at its most sentimental, it is nevertheless based on facts, primarily the well-known account of the killing of the husband of Mary March [Demasduwit*] and several interviews Webber had with old settlers. The incidents are carefully chosen to give the Beothuks the most admired of Victorian virtues: devotion, love and respect between the sexes, stoic courage, especially in defence of women and children, and greatness of spirit. The white hunters, on the other hand, appear as cowardly bullies, shooting Indians on sight simply because they are terrified of them, and Webber with deliberate and effective irony always uses the word "Christians" to refer to them. The tragedy of cowards with guns against almost defenceless people, whom Webber sees firmly within the "noble savage" tradition, is well developed. His interpretation of the Mary March incident is central: the authorities offered a reward for the capture of a Beothuk through whom they could then communicate with the Indians and in 1819 a white hunting party led by John Peyton* seized Mary March from a group which included her baby. Her husband, strikingly tall, accosted them with a long speech obviously demanding her release, but the hunters stabbed him in the back. Webber transmutes this incident into the killing of his Indian hero Bravora, supposedly the son of the victim, who at his own death sings of his father pleading "with pathos wild and high" that his own life might be taken to let the "mother join her child." The other episodes, gleaned from settlers whom Webber had questioned,

are similarly used to stress familial devotion and courage among Beothuks and cowardice and brutality among the whites.

Whether Webber was settled in St John's in 1851 cannot be ascertained from the texts, but in 1856 he began a new weekly newspaper in Harbour Grace, the *Conception-Bay Man*. The first issue came out on 3 September with a motto from Thomas Campbell celebrating "*Truth ever lovely since the world began, / The Foe of Tyrants and the friend of Man*," and a prospectus calling for responsible government, equality of political rights regardless of religious affiliation, and a non-partisan demand "for the greatest happiness for the greatest number." In the issue of 10 June 1857 Webber described himself as a "native of the Country, an advocate of liberal principles, and an experienced observer of the course of public events for the last twenty years."

The *Conception-Bay Man* continued until February 1859 but 1857 is the last year in which anything is known of Webber.

EDWARD JAMES DEVEREUX

George Webber's poem "Sealers' song" appeared on the front page of the *Morning Post, and Shipping Gazette* (St John's), 1 March 1851. *The last of the aborigines: a poem founded in facts*, originally published in St John's the same year, has been edited by E. J. Devereux and printed in *Canadian Poetry* (London, Ont.), no.2 (spring–summer 1978): 74–98, under the title "George Webber's 'The last of the aborigines.'"

Conception-Bay Man (Harbour Grace, Nfld.), 3 Sept. 1856–16 Feb. 1859. *Morning Post, and Shipping Gazette*, 1851. F. G. Speck, *Beothuk and Micmac* (New York, 1922). E. J. Devereux, "The Beothuk Indians of Newfoundland in fact and fiction," *Dalhousie Rev.* (Halifax), 50 (1970–71): 350–62. W. A. Munn, "Harbour Grace history, chapter twenty-three: concluded," *Newfoundland Quarterly* (St John's), 39 (1939–40), no.2: 10.

WEDDERBURN, JOHN. *See* HALKETT

WELD, ISAAC, traveller and author; b. 15 March 1774 in Dublin, son of Isaac Weld and Elizabeth Kerr; m. 1802 Alexandrina Home; they had no children; d. 4 Aug. 1856 near Bray (Republic of Ireland).

A descendant of learned and pious clergymen, Isaac Weld in 1795 found himself distressed by conditions in Ireland and in Europe generally, and set out on a voyage to North America to "ascertain whether in case of future emergency, any part of those territories might be looked forward to, as an eligible and agreeable place of abode." He reached Philadelphia in November 1795 and over the next 15 months travelled through Virginia, Pennsylvania, New York, and Lower and Upper Canada, returning to Ireland via New York City. In January 1799 he published an account of his voyage, *Travels through the states of*

North America, and the provinces of Upper and Lower Canada, during the years 1795, 1796, and 1797, which was an immediate success. It went through several editions and was translated into French, German, Dutch, and Italian.

In his account of the United States, Weld found more to criticize than to admire. He deplored slavery and the treatment of the Indians; Americans struck him as rude and covetous; farming methods were "slovenly." Although he praised aspects of Philadelphia and New York City, and declared himself to be "well pleased at having seen as much of [this continent] as I have done," nevertheless he concluded, "I shall leave it without a sigh, and without entertaining the slightest wish to revisit it." Nor did he.

Weld was more favourably impressed by the Canadian provinces. Between July and November 1796 he travelled from Lake Champlain to Montreal and Quebec, returning through Montreal and continuing his journey to Kingston, Newark (Niagara-on-the-Lake), Malden (Amherstburg), Detroit, Fort Erie, and into western New York. He declared the scenery from the Upper Town of Quebec to surpass "all that I have hitherto seen in America, or indeed in any other part of the globe," and travelling conditions between Quebec and Montreal to be the best in North America. He argued that "a man of moderate property could provide for his family with much more ease in Canada than in the United States" because the price of land was lower there. Like many other British travellers, then and later, Weld felt more at home in the provinces than in republican America.

Although some of his judgements were obviously rather subjective, Weld's book was a substantial piece of work. He spent more time in North America than did many other travel writers. He was fortunate in his timing: in the 1790s he was able to give an early, sometimes a first, account of many aspects of North American life. Finally, Weld had a special skill in describing the topographical and physical aspects of the country through which he travelled "on horseback, on foot, and by canoes." This aspect of the book was strengthened by good maps and by plates made from his own sketches.

During the remainder of his long life, Weld pursued various topographical and scientific interests, both at home and in Europe. For more than 50 years he was a member, and after 1849 vice-president, of the Royal Dublin Society, and he was also a member of the Royal Irish Academy. In 1855 Weld's much younger half-brother, Charles Richard Weld, published *A vacation tour in the United States and Canada*, dedicated to him, which contained various comparative references to conditions in North America nearly 60 years after Isaac's trip.

G. M. CRAIG

The popularity of Isaac Weld's *Travels through the states of North America, and the provinces of Upper and Lower Canada, during the years 1795, 1796, and 1797* is attested to by the number of editions and translations in which it has been issued. Originally published in London in 1799, it appeared first in a one-volume and then in a two-volume edition. The next year a two-volume edition was followed by another in one volume, and in 1807 a final two-volume edition appeared. The 1807 edition has twice been reprinted (New York, 1968 and 1970). An abridged version of Weld's account and one by François-Alexandre-Frédéric de La Rochefoucauld*, Duc de La Rochefoucauld-Liancourt (originally issued in Paris in 1799), were published together as *Travels through the United States of North America, and the province of Upper & Lower Canada . . .* (London, [1801]) and as *Travels in North America . . . and through the American states, country of the Iroquois, and Upper Canada . . .*, edited by William Mavor (London, 1807).

Several French editions appeared under various titles, the earliest of these being *Voyage au Canada, dans les années 1795, 1796, et 1797 . . .* (3v., Paris, [1799]) and the last *Voyage aux États-Unis d'Amérique, et au Canada . . .* (2v., Paris, 1807). Two German versions, *Isaac Weld's des jüngern Reisen durch die staaten von Nord-Amerika, und die provinzen Ober- und Nieder-Canada . . .* and *Reise durch die Nordamerikanischen Freistaaten und durch Ober- und Unter-Canada . . .*, were published in Berlin in 1800; two subsequent two-volume editions appeared there under different titles in 1800 and 1805. Other translations include a Dutch version, *Reizen door de staaten van Noord-Amerika, en de provintiën van Opper- en Neder-Canada . . .*, translated by Sander van Hoek (3v., The Hague, 1801–2), and an Italian one, *Viaggio nel Canada' . . .*, translated by Pietro Spada (3v., Milan, 1819).

Weld's later writings include *Illustrations of the scenery of Killarney and the surrounding country* (London, 1807), another edition of which appeared there in 1812; *Observations on the Royal Dublin Society, and its existing institutions, in the year 1831* (Dublin, 1831); and *Statistical survey of the county of Roscommon, drawn up under the directions of the Royal Dublin Society* (Dublin, 1832). These and additional titles are listed in the *British Museum general catalogue* and the *National union catalog*, both of which also contain entries for his father and half-brother.

Gentleman's Magazine, January–June 1855: 609–11. *Monthly Rev.* (London), ser.II, 30 (September–December 1799): 1–11, 200–7. C. R. Weld, *A vacation tour in the United States and Canada* (London, 1855). *Athenæum* (London), 3 Jan. 1857: 19. *DNB* (biogs. of C. R. Weld and Isaac Weld). J. L. Mesick, *The English traveller in America, 1785–1835* (New York, 1922). H. T. Tuckerman, *America and her commentators, with a critical sketch of travel in the United States* (New York, 1864; repr. 1961).

WELLS, JOSEPH, army officer, politician, and university official; b. 19 June 1773 in the parish of St Martin Ludgate, London, son of Joseph Wells, silk merchant, and Mary ——; m. 10 June 1813 Harriett King of St Botolph parish, Aldersgate, London, and they had eight sons and two daughters; d. 4 Feb. 1853 in Toronto.

Joseph Wells began his army career in 1798 after serving as a lieutenant with a locally raised unit, the

Wells

Sheffield Volunteers. In January he purchased an ensigncy and the following May he was promoted lieutenant in the 43rd Foot. Joining a portion of the regiment stationed in Martinique in 1799, he was appointed adjutant in 1800 and purchased a commission as captain in 1804. He was promoted to the rank of major seven years later and to lieutenant-colonel of the 2nd battalion in 1814. With his regiment he took part in some of the hardest fighting of the Napoleonic Wars. After having served in the expedition to Copenhagen in 1807, he was transferred to the Iberian Peninsula and fought under Sir John Moore during the latter's campaign and retreat of 1808–9. He was the senior surviving officer of the 1st battalion after the storming of Badajoz in April 1812, but was himself so severely wounded that he was unable to take command; he was awarded gold and silver medals for his bravery in this action and silver medals for service in two other battles.

With the return of peace in 1815, and an imminent and large reduction of forces, Wells, like other officers, was faced with the prospect of being placed on half pay. At first he appeared to avoid this fate when he secured an appointment as inspecting field officer of militia in Upper Canada in November 1815 and soon afterward he came out to North America with his wife of some two years and two infant children. "To his great mortification" the position was abolished shortly after his arrival. In 1817 he was placed on half pay, which he retained until 1827 when he sold his commission for £4,000.

The hope of pursuing his military career had brought Wells to Upper Canada and to its little capital, York (Toronto), but almost at once he appears to have been very much at home in his new surroundings. The province's closely knit governing group welcomed the handsome officer, with his relatively high military rank and honourable record of service to king and empire. Wells soon established himself as a significant figure in the community. He had been granted 1,200 acres of land in 1817 and could also buy land cheaply. In 1821 he purchased from the McGill family a 200-acre estate called Davenport about five miles north of York, where he and his descendants would live for the next half-century and more. He was on the first board of directors of the Bank of Upper Canada [see William ALLAN] in 1822 and was to become one of the original directors of the Welland Canal Company three years later. Wells had been named to the Legislative Council in 1820, a life appointment and strong proof of the high regard which he had quickly won from Lieutenant Governor Sir Peregrine MAITLAND and his circle. In the same year he was made a trustee of the Upper Canada Central School at York, a school run by Joseph Spragge* on Church of England principles and favoured by the governing group. Then in 1823 Maitland named him to the Board

for the General Superintendence of Education. Wells became treasurer of that board under the chairmanship of the Reverend John Strachan*, a post and an association which were later to lead him into much grief.

Further evidences of Wells's standing were forthcoming. After Strachan secured a charter, in 1827, for King's College (University of Toronto), Wells was appointed bursar, at an annual salary of £150, presumably because of his experience with the board of education. He had responsibility for administering the very considerable endowment, both in lands and in money, which had been assigned to the college. "Not, by profession, an accountant," Wells was quite unequipped to discharge these duties efficiently. Meanwhile, however, he continued to acquire new responsibilities. When the new lieutenant governor, Sir John Colborne*, determined that it would be premature to open King's College and that the province needed a good preparatory school instead, the way was open for the establishment in 1829–30 of Upper Canada College, to be funded in part from the King's College endowment. Fatefully, it seemed appropriate to name the bursar of the latter to be the treasurer of the former. It was clear that the lieutenant governor had high confidence in Wells: in 1830 Colborne appointed him to the Executive Council and three years later named him registrar of King's College. The regard in which he was held by his neighbours was indicated in the forming of the St George's Society; Wells's name stood first among those who proposed the society, and in 1836 he was elected its first president.

There is no evidence that Wells played a determining role in Upper Canada's political history, yet two events in 1836 gave him some prominence. First, Colborne, as the last notable act of his administration, signed patents for the endowment of some 44 Anglican rectories; clearly, Wells, as an executive councillor, endorsed this act, despite the uproar it caused in the province. Shortly afterward his conduct was somewhat more ambiguous. The new lieutenant governor, Sir Francis Bond Head*, enlarged the council by appointing two reformers, Robert BALDWIN and John Rolph*, as well as John Henry DUNN, a government official but not identified with the "family compact." After a few weeks, perhaps inevitably, the governor and the reformers fell out, and the council broke up. Somewhat unaccountably, Wells and the other conservative councillors, George Herchmer Markland* and Peter Robinson*, joined with the reformers and with Dunn in signing a protest against Head's manner of conducting the government, and on 12 March 1836 the entire Executive Council resigned. Wells may not have intended any flirtation with the reform cause, but the action allowed Head to write later in *A narrative* that by appearing to endorse the doctrine of responsible government the conservative councillors had "at once impeached the conduct and practice of their whole lives." Yet Head relented almost at once: in a footnote he wrote of Wells that "a more loyal man does not exist in Upper Canada."

Although secure in his reputation as a loyal and highly regarded officer, Wells was to suffer embarrassment and even humiliation in 1839. That March the House of Assembly requested information about the finances of King's College and Upper Canada College. The lieutenant governor, now Sir George ARTHUR, asked Wells for a report and in consequence discovered, as he later noted, that it was "impossible to conceive anything more neglected than the affairs of the University have been." Under Arthur's prodding, the council of King's College set up a special committee to investigate, and a sorry tale emerged. Although it appeared that Wells had been conscientious and personally honest, it was also clear that his business methods had been hopelessly sloppy, that clear records did not exist, and that he had not kept college finances separate from his own. The investigation further revealed that Wells had lent more than £5,000 to the president of King's College, John Strachan, without adequate security and had made unsecured loans to others as well. In consequence, on 8 July 1839 Wells sent a rather abject letter of apology to the college council, referring to his "self-acknowledged censurable conduct" and to his "unaccountable neglect" in keeping his accounts. He noted, however, that even if he had kept proper records, they would not have been available, for he had destroyed "a mass of papers" when his property and person were threatened during the rebellion of 1837–38. To make restitution for the more than £13,000 due the university, he assigned to the council mortgages and other securities worth more than half that amount and proposed to pay off the balance over the months and years to come. A few days later the council determined to dispense "with his further services as Bursar and Registrar," and on 27 July Henry Boys* was appointed to replace him.

There was little disposition, at least in official circles, to place heavy blame on Wells. Lieutenant Governor Arthur wrote, "Poor man he is much to be pitied, for had the College Council done their duty he never cd. so much have neglected his & have plunged himself into such difficulties." Chief Justice John Beverley Robinson* found it "hard to believe that he has done anything dishonestly." These estimates were a tribute to Wells's standing in the dissolving "family compact." A subsequent inquiry into university finances by Robert Easton Burns*, John Wetenhall, and Joseph Workman*, moreover, concluded in 1852 that "disbursements" in the decade 1829–39 had not been "extravagant"; indeed, they had been "moderate," compared with those of the years 1839–49.

Nevertheless, the incident was also proof of the need for the improved administrative procedures that were inaugurated by Arthur and by his successor Lord Sydenham [Thomson*].

During his last dozen or so years, Wells withdrew to the life of a gentleman farmer on his large estate north of the city. In the funeral sermon for Harriett Wells, who predeceased her husband by two years, the Reverend John George Delhoste MacKenzie* described Joseph Wells as "one of our christian patriarchs."

G. M. CRAIG

Guildhall Library (London), MS 3857/3 (St Botolph Aldersgate, London, Reg. of baptisms, marriages, and burials), 10 June 1813; MS 10214 (St Martin Ludgate, London, Reg. of baptisms, marriages, and burials), 16 July 1773. PAC, MG 25, 97. *Arthur papers* (Sanderson). J. C. Dent, *The story of the Upper Canadian rebellion; largely derived from original sources and documents* (2v., Toronto, 1885). *Gentleman's Magazine*, January–June 1853: 448. F. B. Head, *A narrative, with notes by William Lyon Mackenzie*, ed. and intro. S. F. Wise (Toronto and Montreal, 1969). J. G. D. McKenzie, *A sermon, on occasion of the death of Clarence Yonge Wells, preached October 20th, 1850, at St. Paul's Church, Toronto* (Weymouth, [Eng.?], 1852). Univ. of Toronto, Commission of Inquiry into the Affairs of King's College Univ. and Upper Canada College, *Final report* (Quebec, 1852). U.C., House of Assembly, *App. to the journal*, 1839, 2: 408–28. *Doc. hist. of education in U.C.* (Hodgins), vols.1–3. G.B., WO, *Army list*, 1799–1828. R. G. A. Levinge, *Historical records of the Forty-Third regiment, Monmouthshire Light Infantry, with a roll of the officers and their services from the period of embodiment to the close of 1867* (London, 1868). Morgan, *Sketches of celebrated Canadians*. Lucy Booth Martyn, *Toronto: 100 years of grandeur; the inside stories of Toronto's great homes and the people who lived there* (Toronto, 1978). *Robertson's landmarks of Toronto*, vol.3. A. S. Thompson, *Spadina: a story of old Toronto* (Toronto, 1975).

WELSFORD, AUGUSTUS FREDERICK, army officer; b. 7 March 1811 in Windsor, N.S., son of John Welsford and Mary Marchinton; d. 8 Sept. 1855 near Sevastopol (U.S.S.R.).

Augustus Frederick Welsford was named after, and was the godson of, the sixth son of George III, Augustus Frederick, under whom his father, an officer in the 101st Foot, had served. After his father's death on active service in 1813, his mother, the daughter of wealthy Halifax merchant Philip Marchinton*, took the child for a prolonged stay in England, where he may have gone to preparatory school. The two returned to Halifax to live in 1820 and Welsford probably attended the Halifax Grammar School before entering King's College, Windsor, in September 1828.

West

At King's, Welsford is usually portrayed as a lover of the classics wandering the halls reciting "the stirring lines of Greek and Latin Poets." One dimension of his life there, however, has hitherto gone unnoticed. In July 1829 he was one of five students who, though they were not proved guilty, refused to sign a pledge swearing their innocence of charges arising from a series of incidents at the college which included an explosion of gunpowder under the principal's porch. Welsford's punishment for this refusal was to be deprived of four terms (one school year), and to be expelled for four more. He probably returned to the college in September 1830 and stayed until the next July, thus completing one year.

After leaving King's, Welsford followed in his father's footsteps and entered the British army. His first commission, dated 24 Feb. 1832, was in the 97th Foot, in which regiment he remained, attaining the rank of major in June 1850. All his promotions were purchased, with at least some of the money coming from the sale of properties in Nova Scotia which had belonged to his grandfather, of whose estate Welsford, through his mother, was a legatee.

Welsford went through the usual round of postings in the United Kingdom and in the colonies, including a stint in Halifax from 1848 to 1853. While stationed there, he pursued his hobby as an amateur painter. In November 1854, after the Crimean War had broken out between Great Britain and Russia, he and his regiment were sent to join the forces besieging the city of Sevastopol. Welsford was mentioned in dispatches that December for resisting, with 200 men, a determined Russian sortie. On 8 Sept. 1855 he commanded a ladder party in the initial wave of an unsuccessful assault on the Great Redan, a large projecting fortification of the eastern defences of the city. He crossed a broad open space and a ditch in front of the work and proceeded to climb one of the ladders which had been placed against the counterscarp; but, as he rose above the lip of an embrasure at the top, a gun was fired from within which blew his head off. Judging from a number of accounts written then and later, Welsford was highly regarded in his regiment, and his death was much regretted. Another Nova Scotian officer, William Buck Carthew Augustus Parker, the great grandson of Benjamin Green*, successfully scaled the counterscarp, got inside the work, and made a vain attempt to stem the mounting British retreat before a hail of bullets swept him into the ditch.

On 17 July 1860 these two Nova Scotian officers, seen as imperial heroes, were commemorated by the unveiling of the Welsford Parker Monument in St Paul's Cemetery, Halifax. Built by George Lang* of free-stone in the form of a triumphal arch, surmounted by the British lion, this monument was financed partly through private subscription and partly by a grant from the Nova Scotia legislature.

Cameron W. Pulsifer

Halifax County Court of Probate (Halifax), Estate papers, nos.1–40 (mfm. at PANS). PANS, MG 100, 24, no.28. Univ. of King's College Arch. (Halifax), Minutes of the Board of Governors, 2 (1815–35): 126–48 (mfm. at PANS). *Gentleman's Magazine*, July–December 1855: 554. G. W. Hill, *[Oration at the] inauguration of the Welsford and Parker monument at Halifax, on Tuesday, 17th July, 1860* (Halifax, 1860). Catherine Marsh, *Memorials of Captain Hedley Vicars, Ninety-Seventh Regiment* (London, 1856). W. H. Russell, *The war* (2v., London, 1856), 2. *British Colonist* (Halifax), 19 July 1860. *Daily Sun* (Halifax), 22–23 Oct. 1855. *Illustrated London News*, 3 Nov. 1855. *Morning Chronicle* (Halifax), 3 Nov. 1855. *Novascotian*, 24 Dec. 1855. *Times* (London), 3, 30 Oct. 1855. Harper, *Early painters and engravers*. *Hart's army list*, 1855. E. P. Wainwright, "Augustus Frederick Welsford, 1811–1855" (typescript, [Halifax, 1968]; copy at PANS). "The 'Welsford–Parker' monument in Halifax, Nova Scotia," Soc. for Army Hist. Research, *Journal* (London), 8 (1929): 129–31.

WEST, JOHN CONRADE, sailmaker, merchant, politician, and office holder; b. 8 April 1786 in Halifax, son of John Wendel West, blacksmith, and Hannah Rachel Foseler; m. there 1807 Elizabeth Brechin, and they had 13 children; d. there 15 April 1858.

Little is known of John Conrade West until 1809, when he is listed in a deed transaction as a sailmaker in Halifax. He and his brother Jacob Bailey West formed a partnership in 1815 which lasted some four years; thereafter, West continued the business alone until at least 1835. By 1829 he was also a shipowner and the following year he is listed as a merchant with his own flag. Mainly by acquiring seasoned vessels rather than constructing his own, West built an integrated West Indies mercantile fleet, which included the schooner *Royal William*, the brigantine *Pearl*, and the brigs *Sophia* (his first ship), *Sir Peregrine Maitland*, and *Hypolite*.

In January 1837 he took his eldest son, Nathaniel Levy, into partnership and the firm became known as C. West and Son; five years later he retired in favour of his son James Thomas and the firm became N. L. and J. T. West. All indications are that he retired from active day-to-day involvement in the firm but it was his money that backed it, as well as the company of his son John Conrad West (J. C. West and Company). By 1847 C. West and Son was again in business, this time being made up of West and his son William Pryor. It appears that West insisted his sons learn the business from the bottom up; all of them who became involved in the mercantile business went to sea and eventually captained ships.

As he lessened his involvement in business, West became active in politics, serving at the municipal level on Halifax's first city council of 1841, and as a commissioner of streets and of public property. On the provincial level, his involvement was basically financial and, although he never ran for office, he became a liberal and a friend of Joseph Howe*. He also became a leader in forming the Universalist Church in Halifax in March 1843. Until his death he gave generously of his time and money to the growth and development of the church.

Of the last years of his life little is known. The "Shipping Intelligence" columns of local newspapers indicated that C. West and Son was actively involved in the West Indies trade from the same premises as N. L. and J. T. West. At the death of John Conrade West on 15 April 1858, the *British Colonist* aptly summed up his public life: "As a citizen he served in the city council and acquired by his unaffected courtesy the esteem of the board. As a merchant he was conspicuous for his integrity and enlarged views of commerce; few men passed through life more esteemed." His private life is best described by his friend Howe, who, on receiving a hair ring from the family, wrote: "Truer friend than your father no man ever had. He stuck to me 'closer than a brother' and never wavered in his confidence in the darkest hours of my public life."

GARRY DAVID SHUTLAK

Halifax County Registry of Deeds (Halifax), Deeds, 1810–58 (mfm. at PANS). PAC, MG 24, B29 (mfm. at PANS). PANS, MG 1, 942–46; MG 4, 191, 198–99, 215; RG 32, 140, 26 May 1807; RG 35A, 1–3. *Acadian Recorder*, 1815, 1820, 1837, 1841–42, 1845, 1858. *British Colonist* (Halifax), 17 April 1858. *Morning Chronicle* (Halifax), 19 March 1844. *Novascotian*, 1815–58. *Times* (Halifax), 10 Aug. 1847. *Belcher's farmer's almanack*, 1829–58. *Cunnabell's N.S. almanack*, 1842: 24–25. T. M. Punch, "The Wests of Halifax and Lunenburg," *N.S. Hist. Quarterly* (Halifax), 6 (1976): 69–86.

WHITE PETER. *See* KLINGENSMITH, PETER

WHITMAN, ABRAHAM, mariner, businessman, and justice of the peace; b. 10 Sept. 1761 in Stow, Mass., tenth child of John Whitman and Mary Foster; m. 1 March 1793 Hannah Webber in Chester, N.S., and they had five daughters and four sons; d. 24 March 1854 in Canso, N.S.

Abraham Whitman's family was among the New England planters attracted to Nova Scotia by the vacated Acadian lands which were offered in the proclamation of 1758 by Governor Charles Law-rence*. His father, Deacon John Whitman, arrived in Annapolis Royal on 25 June 1760, the family following some time later. In 1763 John died, leaving his wife with 11 children, all under 15 years of age. As a result, the family was broken up. Abraham was only two years old when his father died and it is not clear where he spent his youth. A family genealogy suggests that he "was of an active and energetic disposition, and at an early age started out to make his own living." A deed registered in 1793 refers to him as a "mariner," and later biographical accounts suggest that he lived in both Halifax and Liverpool, N.S., before settling in Chester by 1792. Here he married, farmed, ran a store and wharf, and here eight of his children were born. His business included building ships and shipping timber to England, apparently in association with the large importing firm of James FOREMAN and George Grassie in Halifax. By 1807 Whitman's business in Chester was not prospering and he looked seriously at prospects elsewhere. Local references maintain that he had visited Canso during business trips and "was favourably impressed with the advantages it possessed for the fishing trade." In the fall of 1809 he petitioned for land there and the following year received a grant of 500 acres, 300 of which were on Durell Island, a valuable location for one who wished to "carry on a Fishery."

Although Canso had been the most important fishing post in the province until the middle of the 18th century, by the first decade of the 19th century it was hardly a shadow of its former self: it contained only five households in 1810. Thrust into the North Atlantic, it was isolated and lonely for months of the year. Despite establishing a business in Canso, Whitman did not immediately move his family there, preferring to winter in Chester until the War of 1812, "with its attendant privateers, reduced communication extremely dangerous." When he moved his family to Canso in December 1812 or January 1813, his split with Chester was complete, since he left power of attorney to sell all his property there. His business in Canso consisted of "fitting out fishing vessels and selling the cargoes brought home from the Banks." He also purchased large quantities of land, had a store, and "built up a business of considerable volume, exchanging merchandise for fish and fur. He shipped his fish principally to the West Indies – some to the Mediterranean ports and the Azores – bringing back return cargoes." He also built and bought ships, which were sailed by his sons, two of whom were lost at sea.

As both Canso and his business grew, Whitman became "the leading man in the community," and for 40 years he was involved in every aspect of life there. A Congregationalist himself, he set aside a room in his house for public worship and cooperated with local Methodists. He helped organize a Sunday school; as

Whittemore

"Mr Whitman was versed in music scientifically, a singing school was also opened." In 1824 he completed the building of a Congregational church in which "all evangelical clergymen visiting Canso were invited to preach," and in 1846 he turned the building and land over to the congregation. He sold and gave land to the Baptists and the Methodists. Apparently Whitman was a man of conviction as well as of religion. Like most merchants of the period, he was a large importer of liquor until, impressed by the claims of the temperance society, he pledged total abstinence about 1830 and "never imported another gallon of spirits." He was also concerned with education. During his early years in Canso he had brought a teacher from Chester for his family. In 1846, when the community needed a public school, he supplied the land. His concern for civic affairs is also evident in his acceptance in 1840 of a commission as a justice of the peace for Guysborough County: in a community that seven years before had gone through religious riots, such a commission was not simply honorary.

The Whitman business, which flourished for many years after Abraham's death in 1854 at 92, played a central role in the life of the community, as did several generations of Whitmans. The family, the business, and Canso itself provide an interesting insight into the growth, development, and decline of a Nova Scotian outpost community in the 19th and early 20th centuries.

JOHN N. GRANT

Guysborough County Registry of Deeds (Guysborough, N.S.), Index to deeds, 1800–60; deeds, book D: 295; book H: 204, 540; book I: 279; book K: 137 (mfm. at PANS). Lunenburg County Registry of Deeds (Chester, N.S.), Deeds, book 3: 532; book 6: 20; book 7: 106 (mfm. at PANS). PANS, MG 4, 103: 1–12; MG 9, no.45: 276–77; MG 100, 42, no.57; 245, no.26; RG 1, 175: 138; RG 20A, Whitman, Abraham, 1809, 1810, 1820. C. H. Farnam, *History of the descendants of John Whitman of Weymouth, Mass.* (New Haven, Conn., 1889), 806. Harriet Cunningham Hart, *History of the county of Guysborough* (Belleville, Ont., 1975). *Canso News* (Canso, N.S.), May 1912. Harriet Cunningham Hart, "History of Canso, Guysborough County, N.S.," N.S. Hist. Soc., *Coll.*, 21 (1927): 1–34.

WHITTEMORE, EZEKIEL FRANCIS, businessman and politician; b. 2 July 1818 in Montreal, son of Thomas Whittemore, nail-maker, and Priscilla Belding, both from New England; m. 6 April 1843 Margaret Johnston, and they had six children (one of whom died in infancy); d. 19 Feb. 1859 in Toronto.

Ezekiel Francis Whittemore began his commercial career in Montreal in the 1830s but his first modest ventures ended in bankruptcy by 1840. Making a new start, he moved to Toronto to work as a clerk for the mercantile firm of Thomas Rigney and Company. By 1844 he had accepted a partnership and in 1848, following Rigney's move to New York as the firm's partner there, Whittemore and another partner, Edward Henderson Rutherford, reorganized the business in Toronto to form Whittemore, Rutherford and Company. A general wholesale and agency business dealing largely with New York, it sold dry goods, hardware, groceries, and "American" merchandise, dealt in produce and real estate, and represented several Hartford, Conn., insurance companies.

The business prospered greatly in the commercial boom of the 1850s in Toronto and Whittemore was said to have achieved financial independence. Apparently as a result the partnership with Rigney and Rutherford was dissolved in 1854. On 1 July 1855 Whittemore formed E. F. Whittemore and Company in partnership with two young but enterprising employees, Elswood Chaffey and Edmund Morris. The firm, which continued Whittemore's interests in the grain trade and insurance business, also entered private banking. It bought and sold banknotes and bills of exchange, and acted as agent for banks from Montreal, New York, Chicago, and other cities. This finance-oriented development, found also in the Toronto mercantile firm of Robert Henry Brett, indicated growing sophistication and specialization in the Toronto market, but Whittemore's initiative proved premature. Severe financial difficulties in the panic of 1857 forced him to sell land and other assets, and his firm failed. Whittemore nevertheless continued the banking and insurance business on a reduced scale with Chaffey and by 1859 had apparently begun to regain financial stability.

Widely respected for his integrity and business acumen, Whittemore was a leading participant in several of the financial and commercial institutions which had emerged in Toronto. A founding member in 1844 of the Toronto Board of Trade, he served as a member of its council, acted as vice-president (1856–58), and was elected its third president just a month before his death. On the board he consistently spoke for business strategies designed to solidify Toronto's commercial position and specifically to foster its role in the western grain trade and in the creation of transportation links to the northwest. In 1846 Whittemore participated in organizing Toronto's first telegraph company. He was a founder of the Toronto Building Society that year, a director by 1850, and vice-president of its successor, the Toronto Permanent Building Society. The society's directors were by 1850 among the city's most competent mercantile managers and included the merchants Thomas Dennie Harris* and Peter Paterson*. In 1855 the society became the Canada Permanent Building and Savings Society, of which Whittemore was a founding director. He was also a founder, treasurer, and director of the Toronto Exchange (organized in 1854–55 as a focus for the grain trade), a founder (1847) and president (1856–59) of the Consumers' Gas Company of Toronto, and a director and vice-president (1858–59) of the Provincial Mutual and General Insurance Company.

A keen proponent of Toronto's railway ambitions, Whittemore supported the Ontario, Simcoe, and Huron Rail-road Union Company in 1850 and a year later the Toronto and Guelph, of which, through his roles in business and civic politics, he became a founding director. As agent in the purchase of shares, he played a profitable part in this railway's take-over in 1853 by Gzowski and Company [see Sir Casimir Stanislaus Gzowski*] on behalf of the Grand Trunk Railway. Whittemore served as a director of the Grand Trunk until about 1857. He provided an important liaison with Toronto's business community but, as few Torontonians had even a nominal role in that company, it is unlikely that he was a powerful figure on its board.

Whittemore took an active interest in politics and public affairs. His defence of free trade, opposition to the clergy reserves, and support of Malcolm Cameron*, the outspoken reform politican, revealed Whittemore's strong reform orientation. At the municipal level he was elected a councilman in 1848 for St George's Ward, one of the few reformers to win election to the city's tightly tory council. With three others, however, he resigned in April 1849 to protest the council's refusal to condemn a Toronto riot sparked by the Rebellion Losses Bill controversy [see James Bruce*]. He resumed civic activity as a school-board trustee in 1850–51 and was re-elected to council in 1851 as an alderman for St James's Ward. Whittemore's defeat the following year ended his electoral career. He nevertheless took a continuing interest in the Toronto Mechanics' Institute and served as its vice-president (1854–55) and president (1856–57). A Congregationalist, he worked with strong conviction in a number of temperance, mission, and sabbath observance organizations.

Ezekiel Francis Whittemore was one of the outstanding figures in Toronto's dynamic business community of the 1840s and the 1850s. His comprehensive career, despite its brevity, reflects exceptionally well the city's business and political history in his time.

DOUGLAS MCCALLA

[A portrait and autograph of Whittemore are found in *Commemorative biographical record of the county of York, Ontario . . .* (Toronto, 1907), but the article on him contains a number of inaccuracies. D.McC.]

AO, RG 22, ser.302, administration of E. F. Whittemore estate. BLHU, R. G. Dun & Co. credit ledger, Canada, 26: 28, 128. CTA, RG 1, A, 1848–51. Metropolitan Toronto Board of Trade, Resource Centre (Toronto), Toronto Board of Trade, council minute book, 30 April 1850–24 Jan. 1871. PAC, RG 30, 485, 1000, 1597. PCA, St Gabriel Street Church (Montreal), reg. of baptisms, marriages, and burials, 30 Dec. 1818. Toronto Exchange, *Report, charter, and by-laws, of the Toronto Exchange . . .* (Toronto, 1855). *Globe*, 1849–59. *Leader*, 23 Feb. 1859. *Toronto directory*, 1843–56. B. D. Dyster, "Toronto, 1840–1860: making it in a British Protestant town" (1v. in 2, PHD thesis, Univ. of Toronto, 1970), 246–332. *Robertson's landmarks of Toronto*, 1: 81–82, 330; 2: 616; 3: 138, 143, 176, 206, 208–9, 246–47; 6: 53. Samuel Thompson, *Reminiscences of a Canadian pioneer for the last fifty years: an autobiography* (Toronto, 1884; repub. Toronto and Montreal, 1968), 192. J. F. Whiteside, "The Toronto Stock Exchange to 1900: its membership and the development of the share market" (MA thesis, Trent Univ., Peterborough, Ont., 1979). Douglas McCalla, "The commercial politics of the Toronto Board of Trade, 1850–1860," *CHR*, 50 (1969): 51–67.

WIDMER, CHRISTOPHER, physician, surgeon, army officer, medical educator and administrator, justice of the peace, office holder, and politician; b. 15 May 1780 in or near High Wycombe, England; m. first 27 Nov. 1802 Emily Sarah Bignell; they had no known children; m. secondly *c.* 1834 Hannah ——, and they had two sons, one of whom died in infancy, and two daughters; d. 3 May 1858 in Toronto.

Christopher Widmer's roots probably lay in the lesser gentry, his surname having been borne by a family of landowners near High Wycombe which can be traced back to the late 15th century. He is said to have moved as a child to Oxfordshire, although in the 1790s a surgeon and a grocer, both with the same name as he, lived in High Wycombe. Widmer seems to have trained as a surgeon by the normal method of several years' apprenticeship to a general practitioner followed by a short course at a teaching hospital: in his case the conjoint school of Guy's and St Thomas' hospitals, London, which he entered in October 1802. He became a member of the Royal College of Surgeons of London by examination the following March. In June 1804 he joined the British army as a surgeon's mate on the hospital staff. In August 1805 he became an assistant surgeon in the 14th Dragoons, with which he served in the Iberian Peninsula from 1808 to 1814. He had been promoted surgeon in October 1811 and staff surgeon in November 1812. Two years later he came to Canada, where at different times he was stationed near Montreal and at York (Toronto) and Niagara (Niagara-on-the-Lake).

Retiring on half-pay in February 1817, Widmer moved at once from Niagara to York. Here he developed a large and remunerative general practice and assumed a leading part in the advancement of medical services and the medical profession. In 1819 he became an original member of the Medical Board of Upper Canada, which examined and certified

Widmer

candidates for provincial medical licences. From 1822 he was its senior member and president, positions he retained on its successors: the College of Physicians and Surgeons of Upper Canada (from 1839 to 1841), and the reconstituted Medical Board (from 1841 until his death). In 1829 he set up the general hospital at York, acting as its senior medical officer (with an important teaching role) until 1853, when he became its first consulting physician and surgeon. He also served as a trustee of the hospital (1833–57) and as chairman of its board (1844–47, 1848–55). During the rebellion crisis of 1837–38 he was made general superintendent of the army medical department in Upper Canada, with the rank of assistant inspector of hospitals. In 1839 he was appointed a commissioner to supervise the erection of a provincial lunatic asylum and two years later was largely responsible for establishing a temporary asylum at Toronto [see William Rees*; Walter TELFER]. Upon the completion of the permanent asylum in 1850 he became chairman of its board of directors, serving until 1853.

No doubt helped by his marital connection with a wealthy legal and banking family, the Bignells of Oxfordshire, Widmer built up a large fortune, acquired property, and lent large sums for profit or friendship. His estate at death included much realty and more than £50,000 in mortgages, bonds, and debentures. Such wealth, along with his and his wife's social antecedents, made him welcome in the highest circles of provincial society and his abilities brought him several prestigious non-medical offices. He became a justice of the peace in June 1822 and for more than 20 years was one of the most assiduous members of the Home District bench. No doubt his command of the business of local government had much to do with his being offered the wardenship of the district (which he declined) in 1841. He was a director of the Bank of Upper Canada (1822–25, 1827–57) and served as its vice-president from 1843 to 1849. In 1829 he was appointed to both King's College Council and the provincial Board for the General Superintendence of Education, just when those bodies were becoming preoccupied with the building and organization of Upper Canada College, a preparatory school in which Lieutenant Governor Sir John Colborne* (a fellow veteran of the Peninsular War) took a special interest. These appointments may have reflected Colborne's desire to extend official responsibilities to appointees who were outside the small circle of people that had hitherto monopolized office, but the choice of Widmer must have stemmed as well from his wish to involve an able businessman in his favourite project. In 1834 Widmer was made a district school trustee.

Widmer was never primarily a politician, but it was impossible for a man so active in the public affairs of such a highly politicized community to remain wholly disengaged. His professional, public, and private lives, including his membership in a masonic lodge, all brought him into frequent contact with members of the Upper Canadian establishment, and his political début was made as an aldermanic candidate on the conservative ticket for Toronto's St David's Ward in 1834, when he lost to William Lyon Mackenzie* and James Lesslie*. Widmer's political preferences were consistently conservative up to and including the general election of 1836, when he voted in Toronto for William Henry Draper*, who soundly defeated the moderate reformer James Edward Small*. In January 1837, however, Widmer stood for alderman on a ticket of prestigious reformers that included Small, William Warren Baldwin*, George Ridout*, and Jesse Ketchum* and that was probably designed to encourage Toronto's reform sympathizers to declare themselves. Again he lost.

Widmer's open conversion to reform at this time of maximum political polarization leading up to the rebellion of 1837 may well have been unique among public figures in Upper Canada, and its cause can only be guessed at. His conservative vote in 1836 suggests that his conversion may not have been due to the constitutional principle at stake in the general election so much as to Lieutenant Governor Sir Francis Bond Head*'s dismissal of Small, Baldwin, and Ridout from public office later in the year for engaging in reform politics. Friendships may also have contributed to Widmer's conversion: he was close to both Baldwin, a long-time colleague on the Medical Board, and his son ROBERT, and was also a friend of John Rolph*, another member of the board and now the leading parliamentary critic of the provincial government. Widmer and Rolph stood godfather to each other's son and stayed on cordial terms even after the latter's treason and flight in 1837.

From 1838 Widmer was a consistent Baldwinite, and in 1840 Lieutenant Governor Sir George ARTHUR identified him, along with the Baldwins, Small, and Francis Hincks*, as one of the "respectables" of the reform "Party." In that year Widmer chaired Robert Baldwin's campaign committee during the latter's protracted, but ultimately abortive attempt to become a member of the House of Assembly for Toronto at the expected general election. Widmer also served on the campaign committees of John Henry DUNN and Isaac Buchanan*, who stood and triumphed as anti-tory candidates when the election took place, in March 1841. In August 1843, during the ministry of Baldwin and Louis-Hippolyte La Fontaine*, Widmer was appointed to the Legislative Council, having declined the honour a year earlier on the grounds that he could not attend sessions at Kingston. He sat regularly only when the legislature met at Toronto, but was willing to join council at Montreal or Quebec when his friends thought it necessary. The colour of his politics in these years is further indicated by his membership on the general committee of the Reform Association of Canada in 1844 and by his recommendation to Robert Baldwin in 1846 that the "Reform Party" should put all its funds for propaganda behind a single, "Whig-Radical" newspaper, which would advocate "the great principle of a stern opposition to Government influence thro' an Episcopal Establishment." Such a journal would be "supported by a liberal annual subscription for those who could afford it, and a comparative low charge for the masses." His opposition in 1856 to the creation of an elective legislative council, long a reform demand, suggests the limits of his liberalism.

As head of the medical profession in Upper Canada, Widmer was a central figure in the debates generated by three topics of particular importance to it: the establishment of a university medical school, professional self-regulation, and the administrative reforms of 1852–53. His views on these matters are not always easy to establish: he was at the centre of affairs but his voice is often buried in the collective utterances of the various bodies to which he belonged.

In 1830 Sir John Colborne, aware of public discontent over the religious exclusiveness of King's College, decided to open only its medical faculty. Upper Canadians desiring medical training would then be less tempted to seek it in the United States, where they might suffer political contamination. The college council objected that the demand for medical education in Upper Canada was limited and that York was too small to afford students the requisite practical experience. There is no evidence that Widmer dissented from this view but from 1834, after two cholera epidemics had underlined the province's shortage of medical expertise, he and others on the Medical Board pressed for the immediate establishment of a medical faculty. At different times Widmer, Rolph, and the board as a whole were consulted on the matter by Colborne, but to no practical effect.

In May 1837 Widmer resigned from the college council along with its other medical member, Grant Powell*, probably to protest against John Strachan*'s plan for commencing instruction at the college, recently adopted by the council, which established the medical faculty on an inferior footing, with only three part-time instructors. Between August and November 1837 the Medical Board engaged in an increasingly acrimonious dispute on the subject with Sir Francis Bond Head, the college's chancellor *ex officio*, but the outbreak of rebellion in December prevented Strachan's plan from being implemented. In 1839 the College of Physicians and Surgeons, led by Widmer, tried to induce the council to become its partner in setting up a large medical faculty, but nothing was achieved until plans were made to set up the college as a whole. In May 1842 Widmer was reappointed to the

council by Governor Sir Charles Bagot* to help institute medical instruction. In an era of struggle between allopathic (orthodox) practitioners and the various rival groups which they condemned as quacks, Widmer's advice reflected a wish to enhance the allopaths' social standing by making the school and its courses as prestigious as possible. He would have preferred to import the entire faculty from Britain but, acknowledging that "local interests must be yielded to," recommended Toronto doctors instead, including John King, William Charles Gwynne*, and William Rawlins Beaumont*. Widmer left the council late in 1842, once the medical appointments had been made, whereupon it modified his scheme in order to accommodate the objections of Strachan, who favoured a larger but less well paid faculty. Responsibility for the medical school was transferred in 1850 to the University of Toronto, formed that year from King's College.

The incorporation of the medical profession in Upper Canada was conceived partly as another means to eradicate unorthodox practice. Although proponents of the idea, who tended to be politically conservative, argued that professional self-government was the best way to suppress quackery, their politically radical opponents, even among the allopaths, denounced them as a clique intent on monopolizing medical services. Widmer seems to have vacillated on the issue. When incorporation was first proposed, in 1832, he and the Medical Board opposed it, claiming that existing licensing procedures, coupled with provincial statutes against unlicensed practice, provided sufficient regulation. Six years later, after the board had lost those members implicated in the rebellion (Rolph, Charles Duncombe*, and Thomas David MORRISON), the proposal was revived on the grounds that the licensing system no longer provided adequate regulation. Despite radical opposition in the House of Assembly to the board's initiative, the College of Physicians and Surgeons was chartered in 1839 but the statute was disallowed by the imperial government in 1840 after the Royal College of Surgeons of London complained that the charter infringed its privileges. Widmer opposed the next, tory-led attempt to achieve self-regulation in 1846 but in May 1852 took the lead in the incorporation movement by calling a meeting of doctors at Toronto. This attempt was no more successful than earlier ones in overcoming radical opposition and uniting the profession.

Widmer's initiative in 1852 was interpreted by Dr Joseph Workman* as "acting cat's paw for the tories," who wished to defeat the effects of a recent reform of the Medical Board by having it superseded as the regulating medical authority in Upper Canada. This reform was one of several exacted from the ministry of Francis Hincks and Augustin-Norbert Morin* in

Widmer

1852–53 by John Rolph, whose political support was essential to the ministry's survival. Rolph wanted above all to counteract the competitive edge of the University of Toronto's medical faculty over his own Toronto School of Medicine in attracting students. The faculty, which received financial support from the university endowment, dominated both the Medical Board and the staff of the Toronto General Hospital, whereas the Toronto School of Medicine, which depended entirely on students' fees, was unrepresented in either institution. Since the board certified candidates for provincial licences, while the hospital was a vital source of practical training, the university possessed a threefold advantage over Rolph's school. Soon after Rolph had joined the cabinet in December 1851 the board was packed with his supporters, who changed its by-laws to make its proceedings public and provide that no member should examine any of his own students for a certificate. In 1853 the hospital's charter was revised so that each medical school in Toronto, including the medical faculty of Trinity College, might be equally represented on its staff. At the same time Rolph was able to exploit widespread public hostility to the University of Toronto by securing the abolition that year of its medical faculty as part of the government's comprehensive reform of the institution.

Widmer's attitude towards these reforms varied from cordial approval to outright hostility. The hospital bill was as much his as Rolph's: it was Widmer who introduced it into the Legislative Council. He also admitted the fairness of the Medical Board reforms, while resenting the packing of his panel with radicals and the forceful conduct of their leader, Joseph Workman. The university reforms he opposed absolutely. After Robert Baldwin had publicly refused to be named chancellor in protest against them, Widmer accepted the office in January 1853 and strongly censured the government's proposed legislation at his installation. His chancellorship ended when the reform bill was enacted in April and the post became a government appointment. However, he served until his death in the university senate, to which he had belonged since 1850.

Widmer's differences with Rolph on these matters do not seem to have damaged their friendship. Nor did another controversial affair. Rolph wished to replace the unpopular medical superintendent of the Provincial Lunatic Asylum, John Scott*, with his own nominee, Joseph Workman. In February 1853 Widmer and five other members of the asylum's board of directors offered to resign in protest against the conduct of Rolph's supporters on the board, William McMaster* and Terence Joseph O'Neill*. However, after the introduction of a bill to reform the management of the asylum had prompted Scott to resign, Widmer did not quit his post as chairman,

though he was not reappointed to the board under the new act in September. Moreover, although he deprecated Rolph's attempt to slip Workman into Scott's post on the sly, he proved ready to help secure Workman's appointment even after his own formal connection with the asylum had ceased. He advised Rolph to advertise the position widely and then recommended Workman over better-qualified rivals when the government referred the resulting applications to him for appraisal. He also told Rolph in March 1854 how to diminish the outcry the appointment would evoke.

Although the friendship survived these trials, it did not prevent Widmer from voting in 1855 as a hospital trustee to dismiss the representatives of Rolph's medical school on the staff of the general hospital, William Thomas Aikins* and Henry Hover Wright, after they had given damaging evidence at a public investigation into the hospital's management. Though the accusations of mismanagement at the hospital were by no means all refuted, the trustees followed this dismissal with other actions which benefited the medical faculty of Trinity College at the expense of Rolph's school and probably strained his relationship with Widmer. Rolph tried to prevent Widmer's reappointment to the board of trustees in 1855, and the two quarrelled publicly on the Medical Board in October 1857 over its examination of a candidate.

Widmer was noted in the public mind for his professional talents, profanity of utterance (which the charitable ascribed to his military background), and generosity of spirit. His obituary in the *Daily Leader* recorded the "curious fact" that for most of his life he refused to take more than six per cent interest on loans. His kindness to the sick poor was noted by contemporaries, although, like most of his class, he lacked sympathy for the "undeserving poor." In old age, Henry Scadding* recalled, Widmer's "face in repose was somewhat abstracted and sad, but a quick smile appeared at the recognition of friends." Indeed, his friendship with Rolph suggests that he may have valued personal fidelity even above patriotism, and there is evidence that amity may have blinded him to the professional failings of such colleagues as William Rawlins Beaumont, John Scott, and Edward Clarke, the medical superintendent of the general hospital. The melancholy at which Scadding hinted may have stemmed partly from the world-view of one who, though formally an Anglican, was widely suspected of being an atheist, at least until his last years. His private life may also have played its part. According to William Canniff*, Widmer dressed smartly and was "an amazing favourite with the ladies"; his first wife, described in 1826 by Samuel Peters JARVIS as "a little, short, straight, tight built creature, with a damned ugly face," furiously resented his philandering. His second wife, though she made him very happy, was

934

far below him in social rank and may have been something of an embarrassment. Their son Christopher Rolph, who seems to have been conceived several months before the first wife's death in 1833, disappointed his devoted father by his idleness and dissipation and died a year before Widmer, who suffered a fatal seizure while visiting his son's grave. Widmer's elder daughter, Annie, exhibited a waywardness which seems to have stemmed from a sense of shame at her parentage.

The variety of Widmer's offices over four decades suggests that his contribution to Canadian life was greater than those of many whose careers are better documented. Although his reputation made him an ideal figure-head for the reform cause in the 1840s, there is no reason to suppose that he was a nonentity in any public capacity. Remembered by James Henry Richardson as a "small and wiry" man with "an active springy walk," he brought to his work a fierce energy, which was typified by his response when summoned in 1841 to attend the dying governor-in-chief, Lord Sydenham [Thomson*]. At the age of 61, Widmer, "an accomplished horseman," rode from Toronto to Kingston without pause.

His pre-eminence in the medical field, both as a practitioner and an administrator, was beyond doubt to his contemporaries. As a practitioner, he was reputed to be extremely skilful in diagnosis and prescription, and retained into his seventies, despite increasing infirmity, an aptitude in difficult operations which put younger men to shame. He remained in private practice at least until 1854, and his reading, as partially reflected in a catalogue of his medical books auctioned in 1866, shows that he kept up with advances in medicine. He reportedly "gave to the earlier practitioners of the province an enormous impulse towards scientific surgery." As an administrator, he did his best to prevent the era's endemic factionalism from harming the best interests of his profession, which he conceived to lie in suppressing quackery and enforcing the highest possible standards of general education and competence among provincial licensees. Any attempt to explain his shifts on the position of professional self-regulation can only be speculative. As the government's chief adviser on medical matters, he had little to gain from the ending of government regulation, and his support for incorporation in 1839 and 1852 was probably exceptional. The earlier occasion may reflect the hope that a more strongly organized profession would be able to press an obdurate university establishment to set up a suitable medical faculty. The later shift was almost certainly linked to Widmer's loss of pre-eminence to John Rolph.

Widmer's confrères showed their esteem for him in various ways. He was elected first president of the two professional organizations formed in Toronto during his lifetime: the Medico-Chirurgical Society of Upper Canada (1833) and the Toronto Medico-Chirurgical Society (1844). Wider recognition came in 1844, when he was elected a fellow of the Royal College of Surgeons of England, and three years later, when McGill College granted him the honorary degree of MD. In 1853 John Rolph wrote quite sincerely that Widmer was "still you know, as he ever has been, and well named *primus omnium.*" Rolph's estimate of Widmer may be taken as conclusive.

PAUL ROMNEY

Christopher Widmer is the author of at least one medical paper, "On purulent ophthalmia" in *Laws of the Toronto Medico-Chirurgical Society, together with a catalogue of books in its library; instituted 17th June, 1844* (Toronto, 1845). A copy of *Elements of the practice of physic, for the use of those students who attended the lectures read on this subject at Guy's Hospital* ([London], 1798) which belonged to Widmer and contains his notes on the lectures is held by the library of the Academy of Medicine (Toronto) in MS 3.

Academy of Medicine, W. T. Aikins papers; MS 137. AO, MU 1532; RG 1, C-I-3, 37: 17; 123: 1; RG 22, ser.94, 3–7; ser.155, will of Christopher Widmer. MTL, Robert Baldwin papers; J. R. Robertson MS coll., J. H. Richardson, "Reminiscences of Dr. James H. Richardson, 1829–1905" (typescript). PAC, RG 1, L3, 527: W11/32; RG 5, A1: 14495–97, 14577–78, 14867–68, 42422–25, 50327–28, 77580–88; C1, 77, file 2315; 133, file 8136; 373, file 1966; 1841, file 2786; 1855, file 959; 1862, file 1380; C2, 7: 559; 22: 28; 28: 46, 138–39, 269, 338; 30: 52–53, 118; 32: 424; 36: 115; RG 8, I (C ser.), 0: 278; 1203½P: 92; 1707: 109; RG 68, General index, 1651–1841: 214, 445, 472; 1841–67: 150. St James' Cemetery and Crematorium (Toronto), Record of burials. Univ. of Toronto Arch., A70-0005, 1850–58; A72-0024/001–2, King's College council minutes, 1829–43; A73-0015/001, 1829–33. Can., Prov. of, Legislative Council, *Journals,* 1843–58. *Catalogue of medical & miscellaneous books, the library of the late Dr. Widmer, surgical instruments, &c., to be sold . . . October 18, 1866* (Toronto, [1866]). *Gentleman's Magazine,* 1802: 1160. *Medical Chronicle* (Montreal), 6 (1858–59): 45. *Report of an investigation by the trustees of the Toronto General Hospital, into certain charges against the management of that institution* (Toronto, 1855). *Town of York, 1815–34* (Firth). *Upper Canada Journal of Medical, Surgical, and Physical Science* (Toronto), 1 (1851–52): 68; 2 (1852–53): 59, 107–12.

Constitution (Toronto), 24 May 1837. *Correspondent and Advocate* (Toronto), 4 Jan. 1837. *Daily Leader* (Toronto), 4 May 1858. *Globe,* 4 May 1858. *Sarnia Observer, and Lambton Advertiser,* 13 May 1858. *Dictionary of American medical biography: lives of eminent physicians of the United States and Canada, from the earliest times,* ed. H. A. Kelly and W. L. Burrage (New York, 1928), 1299–1300. William Johnston, *Roll of commissioned officers in the medical service of the British army . . .* (Aberdeen, Scot., 1917). *National encyclopedia of Canadian biography,* ed. J. E. Middleton and W. S. Downs (2v., Toronto, 1935–37), 1: 53–54. V. G. Plarr, *Plarr's lives of the fellows of the Royal College of Surgeons of England,* ed. D'Arcy Power *et al.*

Wilkie

(2v., Bristol, Eng., and London, 1930), 2: 520. Canniff, *Medical profession in U.C.* C. K. Clarke, *A history of the Toronto General Hospital* ... (Toronto, 1913). W. G. Cosbie, *The Toronto General Hospital, 1819–1965: a chronicle* (Toronto, 1975). B. D. Dyster, "Toronto, 1840–1860: making it in a British Protestant town" (1v. in 2, PHD thesis, Univ. of Toronto, 1970), chap.2. W. B. Geikie, "Reminiscences of two of Toronto's principal medical men in the early years of the city's history," *Canadian Journal of Medicine and Surgery* (Toronto), 25 (January–June 1909): 283–94. R. I. Harris, "Christopher Widmer, 1780–1858, and the Toronto General Hospital," *York Pioneer* (Toronto), 1965: 2–11. W. A. McFall, "The life and times of Dr. Christopher Widmer," *Annals of Medical Hist.* (New York), 3rd ser., 4 (1942): 324–34.

WILKIE, DANIEL, teacher, author, Presbyterian clergyman, and newspaperman; b. *c.* 1777 in Tollcross or Bothwell, Scotland, youngest son of James Wilkie, a farmer; m. 1 Nov. 1805 at Quebec Margaret Lawson, and they had five children; d. there 10 May 1851.

Apparently orphaned at an early age, Daniel Wilkie was enabled, by the pooling of his brothers' slim resources, to begin grammar school in Hamilton, Scotland, in 1789. Five years later he entered the University of Glasgow. He undertook divinity studies, possibly in 1797, and supported the moderate party of the Church of Scotland, which sought to reconcile Enlightenment rationalism and secularism with Christian belief [*see* Alexander Spark*]. A fellow divinity student called him a "Deist that does not abjure the bible" and observed that he was "of a temper curious and inquisitive, restless & turbulent, that would be free of all doubts, and understand the very nature of things." Wilkie rejoiced in intellectual confrontation and theological controversy. At the same time, his moderatism and Enlightenment tenets induced him to seek reconciliation and toleration in religious matters. His rationalism led him to defend Socinianism, and in 1803 he won a first prize, awarded by the university, for an essay on the Socinian controversy. He obtained his MA that year. Few careers except teaching and preaching were open to someone of his education. He refused connection with any church requiring subscription to articles of faith on the ground that it was an infringement on the right to private judgement. He had begun teaching by September 1800 but it paid poorly and, after a year in a Glasgow school and two more in the nearby parish school of Rutherglen, he decided in 1803 to try his fortune in British North America.

A schoolmate, James Somerville*, had left a teaching position in a Quebec academy to fill the Presbyterian pulpit in Montreal, and Wilkie may have gone out to replace him with the hope of eventually acceding to a pulpit himself. He was soon operating his own academy in a school formerly kept by John Fraser*. By the winter of 1807 Wilkie was offering evening courses in geography (which in 1809 included "a particular account of the British American provinces"), grammar, composition, algebra, geometry, plane trigonometry, and mensuration. In providing evening classes in practical subjects for young working adults, Wilkie was keeping pace with, and possibly introducing to Quebec, a new trend in Scottish education. By 1809, as a means of publicizing the effectiveness of his teaching, he had begun public examinations of his students.

Teaching directed Wilkie's taste for philosophical discussion to education. In June or July 1810 he published *A letter; most respectfully addressed to the Roman Catholic clergy and the seigniors of the province of Lower Canada: recommending the establishment of schools*. In it he expressed many Enlightenment views on the subject of popular education. Deploring the extent of illiteracy in the colony and the lack of effort on the part of parishes to avail themselves of the education act passed by the assembly in 1801 [*see* Joseph Langley Mills*], he undertook "to combat the prejudices which have prevailed in this age against the instruction of the lower orders, and particularly those . . . against the instruction of the Canadians." In the colony, as in Britain, many among the political and social élite feared that educating the masses would lead to revolution; Wilkie argued that education promoted stability because it eliminated the popular ignorance on which demagogues thrived and was the means by which the French Canadians and the British "may be blended into one people." He felt the lower classes should possess "that knowledge which gives a man resources within himself . . . which enables him to employ his talents, to the greatest advantage for himself, his family, and his country." The ignorance of the habitants, Wilkie asserted, also reinforced devotion to traditional farming technology and left them unaware of superior agricultural practices. Knowing that education of the masses required methods different from those employed for instructing the few children of the élite, Wilkie supported the Lancasterian system [*see* Joseph Lancaster*].

Although it did not sell well, *A letter* was a good advertisement for its author. Until 1810 Wilkie commanded £1 per quarter year for each student he taught, charged £25 a year for boarders, and sold to his students textbooks imported from Scotland; but the income provided by these revenues was modest and unstable. That year the school filled up, enabling Wilkie to double his teaching fees and increase his boarding rates to £32. About 1810 he also moved to a spacious house where he opened the Classical and Mathematical School. The following year he introduced the "representative system," possibly an adaptation of the Lancasterian system. By 1815 he was offering a balanced curriculum of practical and classical subjects, adding writing, orthography, bookkeeping, navigation, Latin, Greek, philosophy, and elocution, which drew a clientele increasingly composed of the scions of prominent British and French Canadian inhabitants such as Jonathan Sewell*, Thomas Dunn*, John Neilson*, François Baby*, François Huot*, and Pierre Brehaut*, as well as of officers of the garrison.

Yet, grave problems remained. Lack of financial support from the government, even though requested, obliged Wilkie to establish rates beyond the means of the mass of the population to whom he wished to extend education; by 1824 he was charging £3 a quarter for tuition in addition to the cost of texts, materials, and room and board. The social status of his "Quebec Bloods" created discipline problems. Many parents neglected to back up Wilkie's efforts so that by 1824, although he had taught 30 to 60 students a year for nearly 20 years (about one-quarter of them French Canadians), he had graduated only 100 to 120 into various professions. Finally, his numerous changes of location from 1816 to 1818 would seem to reflect a persisting financial instability that saw him buying "a fine house" and "making a great deal of money" in 1815 and his school in a "reduced state" in 1820.

Only Wilkie's reputation appears to have been solid. In 1823–24 a committee of the House of Assembly summoned the leading educators of the city, Joseph-François Perrault*, Jean-Baptiste Corbin, Antoine PARANT, Robert Raby Burrage*, Mills, and Wilkie, to dissect the educational situation in the colony. Like the others, Wilkie deplored the failure to broaden the dissemination of education. He continued to attribute the problem to the lack of parish schools, adding the insufficient training of teachers and the want of a university as other factors.

Although teaching had become Wilkie's profession, he continued to search for a position ensconced "snugly in a Country-manse." Probably before September 1804 he had been licensed by the Presbytery of Montreal, which undoubtedly included Somerville and Alexander Spark, Church of Scotland minister at Quebec, both of whom shared Wilkie's moderate views. But there were no more openings for a Church of Scotland minister in Lower Canada. In 1810 Wilkie's *Letter*, read in manuscript by Anglicans Richard Cartwright* and the Reverend John Stuart* in Upper Canada, so impressed them that Stuart urged the bishop of Quebec, Jacob Mountain*, to arrange for Wilkie's appointment as schoolteacher and Anglican clergyman in Augusta Township, Upper Canada. Mountain agreed, but Wilkie refused. In 1812 he was again invited to join the Church of England in order to accept Mountain's offer of the evening lectureship at the Cathedral of the Holy Trinity at Quebec. Wilkie felt that he could accept the

Thirty-Nine Articles of the Anglican faith, but he feared that his conversion would mark him as a time-server. He refused the post. Apparently he also preferred to remain at Quebec, since in 1818 he turned down a call from the Presbyterians of Kingston. He assisted Spark at St Andrew's Church, where he was chosen an elder in April 1818. He preached on occasion, with a moderate's emphasis on morality rather than spirituality or theology, prompting a friend to remark ironically on the "moral-mathematical" composition of his sermons. When Spark died suddenly in 1819, Wilkie may have hoped to succeed him, but the congregation chose to call a minister licensed in Scotland. Wilkie provided interim duty until his arrival, donating the salary to Spark's widow.

No doubt Wilkie wished to remain at Quebec in part for its intellectual and cultural life, in which he took an active interest. He was an organizer of the ephemeral Quebec Philosophical Society in early 1812 and a subscriber to the Agriculture Society. He took particular interest in immigration. With Chief Justice Sewell and Anglican clergymen George Jehoshaphat Mountain* and Mills, he formed a public committee in December 1818 to consider the means of affording relief to distressed immigrants. When, as a result, the Quebec Emigrants' Society was formed the following year, Wilkie was appointed to its governing committee. Emigrants were sent to his care by clerical acquaintances in Scotland, and in 1822 he returned from a trip to Scotland accompanied by 20 settlers.

Wilkie had long harboured a latent interest in politics. It burst into the open on 5 Dec. 1827 when the first number of the *Star and Commercial Advertiser/ L'Étoile et journal de commerce*, a bi-weekly, appeared; Wilkie was its proprietor and editor. Originally bilingual, it became an English newspaper after its first year of publication. Wilkie felt that the Lower Canadian press was so polarized between the Canadian and English parties that distortion and misrepresentation of facts made well-informed judgement by even the unbiased impossible, preventing the formation of an enlightened public opinion capable of restraining the excesses of both sides. He dedicated the *Star* to furnishing the facts and thus published full accounts of the debates in the House of Assembly and of decisions rendered by the courts. In addition he promised non-partisan analysis of public affairs within the framework of law, order, and the British connection and sought moderate approaches to controversial problems.

Wilkie also used the *Star* to promote exploration, immigration, settlement of the Eastern Townships, agriculture, and commerce, as well as technological advances, especially the railway. He printed minutes and accounts of religious, social, and scientific organizations. An admirer of Perrault, Wilkie also published, in French, long extracts from his educa-

Wilkie

tional works. He himself wrote a series of articles on education that demonstrate evolution in his thinking. He recognized as chief hindrances to progress the extinction after the conquest of educational institutions such as the Jesuit college, the control of secular education by religious denominations, and, again, the lack of proper teacher training. He denounced the Protestant perception of Catholicism as a promoter of ignorance and despotism, supported long-standing demands for the appropriation of the Jesuit estates to education, and urged the opening of schools and colleges to all without distinction of religion, which, he argued, ought to be taught by each denomination in Sunday schools. In 1822 he and James Thom had drafted the rules for the management of St Andrew's Church Sunday School, founded shortly before.

For reasons unknown, Wilkie sold the *Star* at the end of 1830; although the new proprietors had promised to continue it on his principles, they closed it down instead. He then became active in the Literary and Historical Society of Quebec, founded under the auspices of Governor Lord Dalhousie [Ramsay*] in 1824. Wilkie was chairman of the science section in 1830, librarian for several years, and, in 1836, president. Throughout the 1830s and into the 1840s he presented numerous papers on education, the fine arts, literature, historical criticism, the Greek, English, and French languages, astronomy, fluvial systems, morals, and superstitions. Appropriately, it was in this period of intense intellectual production that Wilkie received an honorary LLD from the University of Glasgow on 10 Nov. 1837. As well, he had been a founding member of the St Andrew's Society of Quebec in October 1835. He served on the committee that drafted its constitution, was president of a school apparently operated by the society, and was chaplain to the organization. At St Andrew's Church he was elected a trustee in 1835 and he served as chairman of several committees, including one in 1837 to establish a congregational library. For some time after 1828 he preached on alternate months at Valcartier; by then, however, the ministry was no longer a goal because Wilkie had found prosperity as a teacher. He had been residing at the same location on Rue des Jardins for 17 years when, in 1835, he bought three contiguous lots and two houses next to his own for £910; the following year he built a two-storey stone house on the vacant lot. These transactions left him £800 in debt to John Neilson, but Wilkie's income enabled him to pay it off within three years.

By the early 1840s Wilkie's health was failing. He may have become the first principal of the High School of Quebec in 1842 or 1843, but if so he soon resigned in favour of his nephew Daniel Wilkie. He died at Quebec following a "suffusion of the brain" on 10 May 1851, "after two years of wasting and unconsciousness." In his funeral sermon for Wilkie,

the Reverend John Cook* recalled the "form and figure of the old philosopher, moving slowly and sometimes incongruously enough, in the midst of our busy community, obviously abstracted from the common interests . . . and dwelling in a world of his own, a world of speculation, a world of theories, and fancies, and doubtings." While disapproving of the originality of Wilkie's religious ideas, Cook underlined his lifelong struggle to maintain "a high standard of education in a community but too much inclined to limit education to the more immediate wants of commercial business."

To what degree Daniel Wilkie influenced the extension of elementary education in Lower Canada will never be determined clearly. However, one must not neglect his influence on the thought of his friend John Neilson and on a whole generation of the Quebec élite, for, if Wilkie fought for the education of the masses, he ensured that of many of the colony's future leaders, French Canadian and British. A list of his students is the most eloquent measure of his contribution, for it includes Neilson's son Samuel*, Dr Joseph Morrin*, Alexander BUCHANAN, Charles HARPER, William Foster Coffin*, Henry Black*, Robert-Shore-Milnes Bouchette*, Thomas Cushing Aylwin*, George-Paschal Desbarats*, and Jean-Charles Chapais*. In Wilkie's honour a number of these men raised an impressive monument of imported Aberdeen granite in Mount Hermon Cemetery.

JAMES H. LAMBERT

Daniel Wilkie is the author of *A letter; most respectfully addressed to the Roman Catholic clergy and the seigniors of the province of Lower Canada: recommending the establishment of schools* (Quebec, 1810), which has been republished in large part in *Confrontations: choix de textes sur des problèmes politiques, économiques et sociaux du Bas-Canada (1806–1810)*, ed. J. [E.] Hare and J.-P. Wallot (Trois-Rivières, Qué., 1970), 187–200, and of a number of unsigned articles in his *Star and Commercial Advertiser/ L'Étoile et journal de commerce* (Quebec), 1827–30. He also published "On length and space," "The theory of parallel lines, being an attempt to demonstrate the twelfth axiom of Euclid," "A few observations, on the importance of aiming at the establishment of some general system of education, in Canada, at this time, 1841," and "An oration, delivered before the Literary and Historical Society of Quebec, at the anniversary prize meeting, May 3, adjourned from April 27th 1827," in the Literary and Hist. Soc. of Quebec, *Trans.* (Quebec), 2 (1830–31): 64–76; 3 (1832–37): 72–82; 4 (1843–60): 16–24; and 4 (1843–60): 387–98 respectively. The Daniel Wilkie papers at MTL, consisting of incoming correspondence, provides a great deal of information on Wilkie. A portrait of him hangs in the entrance to the Literary and Historical Society building at Quebec.

ANQ-Q, CN1-49, 6 août 1829; 12 juill. 1836; 28 févr., 2, 20 mars 1837; 2 mai, 3 déc. 1838; 3 févr. 1841; 29 juin, 3 déc. 1842; 2 févr., 1er avril, 17 août 1844; 7 févr. 1848;

CN1-116, 17 oct. 1835, sept. 1836, 21 sept. 1838, 12 avril 1844; CN1-178, 30 mai 1811; CN1-209, 22 mars 1831; CN1-285, 29 janv. 1805. St Andrew's Presbyterian Church (Quebec), Corr. on education, 9 Jan. 1829; Kirk session minute-book, 1822–37; Reg. of baptisms, marriages, and burials, 1 Nov. 1805, 10 Aug. 1806, 24 Aug. 1808, 3 March 1809, 17 Aug. 1810, 25 Dec. 1814, 15 Jan. 1820, 13 May 1851; Reg. of corr. and session minutes; St Andrew's Society minute-book. *Quebec Gazette*, 16 April, 2 July, 19 Nov. 1807; 15 Dec. 1808; 17 Aug. 1809; 12 July, 20 Dec. 1810; 21 May, 17 Dec. 1812; 15 April, 30 Dec. 1813; 25 May, 24 Aug., 28 Dec. 1815; 26 Sept. 1816; 30 Jan., 2 Oct. 1817; 29 Jan., 12 March, 7 Dec. 1818; 15 July, 2, 5 Aug. 1819; 20 Jan. 1820; 9 Aug. 1821; 14 Oct. 1822; 17 Nov., 22 Dec. 1823; 15 Jan., 1 March 1824. Beaulieu et Hamelin, *La presse québécoise*, 1: 62–63. J. [E.] Hare et J.-P. Wallot, *Les imprimés dans le Bas-Canada, 1801–1840, bibliographie analytique* (Montréal, 1967). *Index of the lectures, papers and historical documents published by the Literary and Historical Society of Quebec . . .*, comp. F. C. Wurtele and J. C. Strachan (Quebec, 1927). Morgan, *Sketches of celebrated Canadians*. Scott *et al.*, *Fasti ecclesiæ scoticanæ*, vol.2. L.-P. Audet, *Le système scolaire. The centenary volume of the Literary and Historical Society of Quebec, 1824–1924*, ed. Henry Ievers (Quebec, 1924). A. C. Chitnis, *The Scottish enlightenment: a social history* (London, 1976). Gregg, *Hist. of Presbyterian Church*. "The late Daniel Wilkie, L.L.D.," *Presbyterian*, 9 (1856): 20. "The late Rev. Daniel Wilkie, L.L.D.," *Presbyterian*, 4 (1851): 97–98. P.-G. Roy, "La famille Wilkie," *BRH*, 42 (1936): 58–60.

WILLIAMS, ELEAZER (Éléazar) (Onwaren-hiiaki, which means "his head has been split"; baptized **Razar Williams**), chief of the Caughnawaga (Kahnawake) reserve and Congregational and Episcopalian minister; b. May 1788 on the shores of Lake George, N.Y., son of Tehoragwanegen* (Thomas Williams), chief of the Caughnawaga reserve, and Konwatonteta (Mary Ann Rice); m. 4 March 1823 Madeleine (Magdelene) Jourdain (Jourdon) in Green Bay (Wis.), and they had two daughters who died in infancy and one son; d. 28 Aug. 1858 on the Saint-Régis reserve.

Eleazer Williams was the great-grandson of John Williams*, a Puritan minister who was taken prisoner during Major Jean-Baptiste Hertel* de Rouville's expedition against Deerfield, Mass., in February 1703/4. His father, Thomas Williams, had him baptized in the Roman Catholic faith the month he was born, and gave him the name Razar, a diminutive of Eleazer. Later, after injuring his head while diving into Lake George, he received the Indian name Onwarenhiiaki. But he was usually called Eleazer Williams. He grew up at Caughnawaga, Lower Canada. In 1800, when he had reached the age for formal education, his father (against the wishes of his mother, who was a devout Catholic) sent him with his brother John to the Congregational seminary at Longmeadow, Mass. At the suggestion of relatives

living in Massachusetts, the American Board of Commissioners for Foreign Missions undertook to meet the cost of the young man's education, providing he adhered to Congregationalism. Shortly afterwards he renounced the Catholic faith and became a Congregationalist.

His studies completed, Williams ministered among the Indians as an itinerant, impecunious preacher, staying principally in Caughnawaga, Oneida Castle, N.Y., Green Bay, and Saint-Régis. He used his spare time to study the history of the Iroquois country; he had already, over the course of time, become an authority on Indian history. An eloquent preacher, he exerted on those whom he called his "racial brothers" an influence that was both political and religious. At the request of the American Board of Commissioners for Foreign Missions, between 1809 and 1812 Williams made several trips to Caughnawaga to introduce Protestantism. In March of the latter year he spoke with such great eloquence that the Indians on the reserve named him their chief. At the beginning of the War of 1812 the American government appointed him superintendent general of the Northern Indian Department; during the conflict he endeavoured to persuade the Caughnawaga Indians to side with the United States [*see* Atiatoharongwen*], and tried to obtain information on British troop movements.

However, it was in the religious sphere that Williams brought all his resourcefulness into play. In May 1815, not hesitating to change his faith again, Williams joined the Episcopal Church, and then taught catechism at Oneida Castle. Ordained an Episcopalian minister in 1826, he proselytized for his denomination among the Indians of Green Bay, where he had gone to live three years earlier, and continued to work there until October 1834. He went to Saint-Régis in June 1835 and was officially appointed schoolmaster of this mission by the governor of Lower Canada, Lord Aylmer [Whitworth-Aylmer*]. Naturally enough he came into conflict with the Catholic missionaries Joseph MARCOUX and François-Xavier Marcoux, who were serving the Caughnawaga and Saint-Régis missions. Finally, as a result of steps taken by Bishop Jean-Jacques Lartigue*, the new governor of Lower Canada, Lord Gosford [Acheson*], intervened in 1836 on behalf of the two Catholic priests, and Williams had no choice but to resign as schoolmaster. Later, from 1846 to 1848 and from 1850 to 1853, he tried again to make converts among his "brothers" and "compatriots," but without success. On 19 Jan. 1854 Abbé Joseph Marcoux confided to Jacques VIGER that as missionary of Caughnawaga he had not "much to fear" from Williams.

In the same year Eleazer Williams suffered another set-back, this time a resounding one, for he found himself stripped of a claim he had cherished for some

Williams

years – nothing less than a pretension to royal blood: he was the real Louis XVII, who had been abducted from prison in 1795, and who, once in America, had been taken to Caughnawaga and placed by a man named Bellanger in the care of the mixed-blood Thomas Williams. Such was the strange story ("Have we a Bourbon among us?") given the readers of a newly launched journal, *Putnam's Monthly*, in its February 1853 issue. The author was an Episcopalian colleague of Williams, John Halloway Hanson. The French legitimist Henry de Courcy, the New York correspondent for *L'Univers* of Paris, hastened to demolish this literary extravagance from America in an article published in the 7 March 1853 issue of the Paris paper under the unambiguous title "Un roman d'imagination." Subsequently, with the help of his Montreal friend Jacques Viger, who provided him with decisive arguments buttressed principally by statements from Eleazer's mother, Courcy refuted point by point the 480-page volume entitled *The lost prince*, which Hanson published in 1854. For Courcy, the title of the book was perfectly correct: the prince was indeed lost, and he was not found again.

PHILIPPE SYLVAIN

Collections of Eleazer Williams papers can be found at the Newberry Library (Chicago), Detroit Public Library (Detroit, Mich.), Missouri Hist. Soc. (St Louis), Buffalo Hist. Soc. (Buffalo, N.Y.), and Wisconsin Hist. Soc. (Madison). The Fonda Department of Hist. and Arch. (Fonda, N.Y.) holds a two-volume manuscript biography of Williams. His writings and the works he translated are listed in *Bibliography of the Iroquoian languages*, comp. J. C. Pilling (Washington, 1888).

Wis., State Hist. Soc., Grignon, Lowe, Porlier papers, vol.55, 4 March 1823. *Handbook of American Indians* (Hodge), 2: 953–55. E. J. Devine, *Historic Caughnawaga* (Montreal, 1922), 316–22, 370–71. J. H. Hanson, *The lost prince: facts tending to prove the identity of Louis the seventeenth, of France, and the Rev. Eleazar Williams, missionary among the Indians of North America* (New York, 1854). Robert [Philippe] Sylvain, *La vie et l'œuvre de Henry de Courcy (1820–1861), premier historien de l'Église catholique aux États-Unis* (Québec, 1955), 224–61. W. W. Wight, *Eleazar Williams, not the dauphin of France* (Chicago, 1903). Guillaume de Bertier de Sauvigny, "Louis XVII, un métis indien," *Historia* (Paris), 112 (1956): 307–10. L. C. Draper, "Additional notes on Eleazer Williams," Wis., State Hist. Soc., *Coll.*, 8 (1879): 353–69. A. G. Ellis, "Fifty-four years' recollections of men and events in Wisconsin," Wis., State Hist. Soc., *Coll.*, 7 (1876): 207–68; "Recollections of Rev. Eleazer Williams," Wis., State Hist. Soc., *Coll.*, 8: 322–52. J. H. Hanson, "Have we a Bourbon among us?" *Putnam's Monthly Magazine* (New York), 1 (January–June 1853): 194–217. Moïse Mainville, "Louis XVII est-il venu au Canada?" *BRH*, 3 (1897): 66–71. Robert [Philippe] Sylvain, "Louis XVII vint-il en Amérique?" *Rev. de l'univ. Laval*, 3 (1948–49): 743–61, 857–82.

WILLIAMS, RICHARD, Wesleyan Methodist minister; b. *c.* 1790 in England; d. 1 Aug. 1856 in Bridgetown, N.S.; he was survived by his wife.

Richard Williams was raised in an Anglican home in England and in his youth was converted at a Methodist meeting. He served initially as a class leader and local preacher in the British Wesleyan Conference, and in 1813 became a probationer in the itinerancy. Two years later he volunteered to become a missionary and was appointed to Montreal.

The War of 1812 had temporarily disrupted the work in Upper and Lower Canada of the Methodist Episcopal Church, based in the United States, and caused a shortage of preachers. This disruption, in combination with the Wesleyan Methodist proclivities of some English immigrants, induced the missionary committee of the British Wesleyan Conference to send missionaries to the Canadas. Williams was one of the first missionaries to arrive in Lower Canada. The committee's action led to severe rivalry between the American and English branches of Methodism, which was eased temporarily by an agreement between them in 1820, leaving Lower Canada in Wesleyan hands. From 1815 to 1825 Williams served on the circuits of Quebec, Trois-Rivières, Melbourne Township, and Saint-Armand in Lower Canada, as well as in Kingston in Upper Canada, before moving to Saint John, N.B.

From the outset, Williams was an energetic itinerant, who doubtless assumed that Wesleyan Methodism was superior to the American variety. He found the Methodists in Kingston "very anxious to obtain an English missionary; and what a mercy it would be to grant them their request!" He located many erring Protestants in and around Montreal and described St John's (Saint-Jean-sur-Richelieu) as a large village whose "inhabitants are wicked to a proverb," a distinction shared by the people of Chambly.

On 18 Feb. 1819 at the district meeting in Kingston, Williams was elected chairman of the Canada District. The missionaries at that meeting prepared an address to the Duke of Richmond [Lennox*], governor-in-chief of British North America, assuring him that their object was to turn many from "darkness to light," and that they would not fail to give "strenuous exhortations to the people of our charge, that they may be taught, both by precept and example, while they fear God, to honor the King . . . and to adorn our holy religion by a uniformly peaceable demeanor, and cheerful subjection to lawful authority." By such means, Williams and his colleagues helped to build a loyal, British-oriented Methodist community in Lower Canada and thus kept alive the contest between British Wesleyan Methodists and Canadian Methodists, a dispute that would not be resolved until 1847.

Williams's arrival in New Brunswick coincided

with the decision of the missionary committee to divide the Nova Scotia District into two, an action that was unpopular among the missionaries and their adherents. In May 1826 he was appointed chairman of the newly created New Brunswick District, which also included the Annapolis valley in Nova Scotia. The committee's action was indicative of its determination to promote self-sufficiency and local initiative in its missions, a policy that was coupled unfortunately with an unwillingness to listen to its missionaries or to approve steps taken by them to strengthen the Methodist cause. Its attitude had grown out of the society's chronic shortage of funds and its insistence on replicating Wesleyan Methodism in the colonies.

From the time of his appointment to New Brunswick, Williams and his colleagues were in difficulty with the secretaries and the committee. The latter was tightening the system of allowances for missionaries, who in turn argued that the new arrangements would create personal inconvenience and hinder the development of new circuits. They urged the secretaries to pay some attention to their honest judgement. Williams himself put up a spirited defence of the costs he had incurred in his final year at Quebec. In 1832 the secretaries claimed that the New Brunswick District's financial statement was misleading and unbusinesslike and that Williams was "utterly unfit" to manage financial matters. He was replaced that year as chairman by the Reverend John Bass Strong, a former colleague in Lower Canada.

After 1832 Williams did not figure prominently in the district meetings or in correspondence with the secretaries in London. He served on several circuits in New Brunswick and Nova Scotia and in 1840, as a missionary who had entered the ministry in England, he was permitted to return to that country. He spent 1840–42 in Cornwall, before being sent back to New Brunswick. In 1844 he was appointed chairman of the Newfoundland District. He presided over the district meetings from 1844 to 1849, when he became a supernumerary because of illness. He moved to Bridgetown, N.S., in 1852 where, although retired, he continued to preach regularly. His last sermon was given at Tupperville five days before his death.

Richard Williams was a large man with a brusque temper and a strong devotion to the tenets and usages of Wesleyan Methodism. According to the Reverend George Oxley Huestis, "neither the face of clay, nor the presence of the devil, could divert him from his purpose or change his mind when he thought he was right." He helped to build some strong circuits on the unpromising soil of Lower Canada, strengthened the influential Saint John circuit in New Brunswick, and gave quiet leadership in the New Brunswick and Newfoundland districts. Assuredly, he was convinced that Wesleyan Methodism was the best, but he recognized also the necessity to adapt it to British North American conditions. His preaching, "always rich in evangelical truth, was characterized by . . . the prominence which he gave to those great scriptural doctrines, justification by faith, and entire holiness." Despite his commitment to preaching he believed funeral sermons to be evil; "in life and in death I am opposed to funeral sermons, and when I die let no funeral sermon be preached on my account." His wish was granted: an address was given instead at his funeral.

G. S. FRENCH

SOAS, Methodist Missionary Soc. Arch., Wesleyan Methodist Missionary Soc., corr., North America, New Brunswick District, minutes, May 1826, May 1828; letter to Strong, 13 July 1832 (mfm. at UCA). Wesleyan Methodist Church, *Minutes of the conferences* (London), 2 (1799–1807): 272–73; 4 (1814–18): 107; 6 (1825–30): 37, 142; 9 (1840–43): 24; 10 (1844–47): 50; 11 (1848–51): 220; 12 (1852–54): 62. Wesleyan Methodist Church of Eastern British America, *Minutes* (Halifax), 1857: 4–5. *Provincial Wesleyan* (Halifax), 14 Aug. 1856. Carroll, *Case and his cotemporaries*, 2: 23. French, *Parsons & politics*, 67–74. G. O. Huestis, *Memorials of Wesleyan missionaries & ministers, who have died within the bounds of the conference of Eastern British America, since the introduction of Methodism into these colonies* (Halifax, 1872), 128. J. G. Reid, *Mount Allison University: a history to 1963* (2v., Toronto, 1984), 1, chap.1.

WILLS, FRANK, architect and author; baptized 25 Dec. 1822 in Exeter, England, second son of Charles Wills and Elizabeth Bolt; m. first 8 May 1848 Emily Coster (d. 1850), fourth daughter of George COSTER and Eleanor Hansard of Fredericton, and they had one daughter; by a second marriage he had a son; d. 23 April 1857 in Montreal, and was survived by his second wife and both children.

It could be argued that Frank Wills was the most important Gothic Revival architect of his generation in North America, even though he is one of the least known figures today. His obscurity must be due partly to the widespread range of his work – from the Atlantic to the Pacific, from the Gulf of Mexico to the St Lawrence River – and partly to his early death. But there is no doubt that he was influential in British North America and in the United States.

The surname Wills is common in Devon, and records from the 15th century onward include various members of the building trades with that surname. Frank Wills's grandfather and father were plasterers and helliers (slaters or tilers). Though Charles Wills died in 1829 at age 36, he left a comparatively large estate, and his resourceful widow immediately advertised that she intended "carrying on the Business as before." It would seem that Frank was apprenticed to an architect during his teens.

Wills

Frank Wills's earliest executed design is likely the ambitious and accomplished canopied tomb in Gothic style beside the high altar in St Thomas's Church, Exeter. Unsigned, undated, and unidentified, it was erected by the Reverend John Medley* to honour his wife, Christiana Bacon, who had died in 1841. Although it has been said that the effigy was carved by her father, the noted sculptor John Bacon the Younger, Wills must have been responsible for the monument as a whole: his elevation of this handsome work survives today in the Public Archives of Canada.

In 1842 Wills exhibited in the architectural section of the Royal Academy of Arts, London, for the first time. He had very likely received training in the office of John Hayward, an Exeter specialist in Gothic architecture who directed Wills's work on illustrations of local antiquities published by the Exeter Diocesan Architectural Society in 1843 and 1847. Wills seems to have assisted with the architectural work on – possibly he was even responsible for the design of – the Chapel of St Andrew, Exwick, in St Thomas's Parish, which Hayward had carried out in 1841–42. Although slightly awkward in proportion, the chapel was an outstanding early example of Victorian neogothicism. In part it was the gift of Medley, who was also the secretary and founder of the diocesan architectural society. He was to become the first Anglican bishop of Fredericton in 1845, and Wills's patron.

Wills appears to have been exclusively a neo-medieval ecclesiastical architect to the Anglican communion. He was a younger contemporary of that remarkable generation of English Goths, including George Gilbert Scott and Augustus Welby Northmore Pugin, who turned antiquarian study of the Middle Ages into the "science of ecclesiology," which is to say church architecture and everything that could possibly pertain to it. It was his distinction that he showed himself an early follower of Pugin, and became one of the first transmitters of ecclesiological ideals to British North American and the United States.

The turning-point in Wills's career came during the winter of 1844–45 with his discovery that St Mary's in Snettisham, Norfolk, a 14th-century parish church which resembled a cathedral in a number of ways, might serve as a model for the new cathedral Medley would require in Fredericton. Wills had done restoration work on it and had made a record of the church as a whole at Medley's request. St Mary's was, as the recently consecrated bishop observed on his arrival in New Brunswick in June 1845, "in its architecture and proportions, betwixt an English Cathedral and a Parish Church and therefore better adapted to this Province, and to the means of the inhabitants." Evidently both bishop and architect held the ecclesiological view that "instead of new designs

. . . real ancient designs . . . should be selected for exact imitation."

Wills moved to New Brunswick to supervise the construction of Christ Church, the cornerstone of which was laid on 15 Oct. 1845. Only a handful of important Gothic Revival churches had been built in British North America – all in the bland, flat, thin Georgian manner. Christ Church was to be fully Victorian. For two years Wills watched over the construction of what was both the first colonial cathedral to be undertaken on ecclesiological principles and "the first pure cathedral in the Pointed styles that has ever been reared in a British colony." However, problems with materials, poor workmanship, high costs, adverse criticism, and lack of funds all bedevilled the project. They caused Medley to begin construction at the west end with the nave and aisles, which were built in 1845–49, until revised designs for the east end and more funds were available.

Medley turned the delays to advantage, giving Wills another commission in Fredericton, St Anne's Chapel. Built rapidly between May 1846 and March 1847, this small church of roughly dressed stone is aisleless, with a porch on one side and an open bell-cote instead of a tower. Executed for the most part in simple Early English style, the chapel and its furnishings formed a demonstration piece of ecclesiology. Drawing simultaneously on one of the Cambridge Camden (later the Ecclesiological) Society's favourite churches, St Michael's at Long Stanton, England, and on a design published by Pugin in 1843, St Anne's illustrated a more adaptive philosophy than the first project for Christ Church. In Wills's view, "The spirit which should actuate our imitation of ancient work . . . should not be a slavish literal copying of any particular building, but rather the adopting the spirit which actuated its builders: we should endeavour to get *that* by a comprehensive imitation, which realizes the deep and holy poetry of the structure rather than by a narrow-minded combination of its minute portions."

With St Anne's finished, but the western part of the cathedral still incomplete and its eastern end not yet begun, Wills moved to New York City and opened an office late in 1847 or early in 1848. He was involved in organizing the New-York Ecclesiological Society in the spring of 1848 before returning to Fredericton that May to be married. He may have worked for the Anglo-American architect Richard Upjohn in 1848, even though it is clear that Wills held Upjohn in some disdain. The New York society named Wills its architect in January 1849 and he reciprocated by contributing to its journal, the *New-York Ecclesiologist*, a design for a model church to be used as a guide by congregations unable to obtain or afford architectural advice. He also acted as co-editor of this

942

publication, "the first American journal devoted solely to Architecture."

Suddenly in 1849, and doubtless owing to the reputation he gained through the New-York Ecclesiological Society, Wills found himself with much work. There was another job in the Maritimes, projects in Upper Canada, commissions in the southern United States, on the east and west coasts, and in western New York. The plans for at least three (in Newark, N.J., Milford, Conn., and San Francisco) of the ten known projects were asymmetrical, a feature that was considered inappropriate to the dignity of a cathedral but otherwise progressive. The San Francisco design was not executed, nor was Wills successful that summer with his competition entry for St James', the new Anglican cathedral in Toronto, which was erected to the design of Frederic William Cumberland*. Of the commissions that were carried out, three were in stone while five, including St Andrew's in Newcastle, N.B., were wooden, a perennial architectural problem in many parts of North America but an unfamiliar challenge for an Englishman. Wills clad one church, in Albany, N.Y., in board-and-batten, an innovative, North American technique that complemented the verticality of Gothic design and was held by the American theorist Andrew Jackson Downing to be structurally expressive of the predominantly upright members in frame construction.

Early in 1850 Wills published a handsome and useful book of major importance in North America, *Ancient English ecclesiastical architecture and its principles, applied to the wants of the church at the present day*. There was nothing just like it on either side of the Atlantic – a blend of architectural history, principles of design, modern examplars (all by Wills), and a glossary. It was a sensible and concise book. All the plates for the illustrations were done by Wills, who was a skilful lithographic artist. The designs ranged from the small wooden chapel at Albany to a large stone church. A couple were markedly irregular in the placing of the tower. ("Only let circumstances, and not a morbid love of the picturesque, govern its position," wrote Wills.) All were more or less Puginian in architectural concept and consistent with English ecclesiological teaching. The text, however, was freer than Pugin's writing of controversial polemic and less rigid or inclined to excessive symbolism than Cantabrigian literature. Wills occasionally showed flashes of boldness in theory. His advice on colour anticipated High Victorian taste: "Let us dip our pencils in the hues of heaven, borrow the tints of a cloudless sky or a setting sun, transfer the bright star from its amethystine vault to our churches' ceilings. . . . and men will . . . confess the real loveliness and grandeur of colour."

Although the book was successful, in retrospect two things were missing: designs in brick (not then generally accepted for churches, but later used by Wills) and a discussion of the cathedrals that the author had designed. The problem of a church that combined parish functions with those of a cathedral and with the appearance of a cathedral was a topical one, but no doubt Wills had found his experience with Christ Church, Fredericton, and St James', Toronto, distressing and had decided to avoid controversy. The book was favourably received in the United Kingdom and the United States. In British North America, where architectural publication was non-existent, it enjoys a peculiar distinction: it seems to be the only book with architectural designs illustrating Canadian work that appeared before the last decade of the 19th century.

After the flurry of activity in 1849, Wills's production slowed, became routine, and showed little development beyond the stage recorded in his book. In any case a pall hung over its publication. His first wife, whose health had been poor almost since their marriage, died in 1850; that year as well he returned to his native Exeter for a visit. These events might explain the near absence of other work by Wills during 1850. From 1851 to 1853 he was in partnership with Henry Dudley, an older colleague from Hayward's office in Exeter, who joined him in New York. This arrangement enabled Wills to devote more attention to his work outside the city.

Since leaving Fredericton, Wills had kept in contact with Bishop Medley and had had some involvement in the completion of Christ Church. Responding to ecclesiological criticism from England that a cathedral ought to have at least two towers, Wills had offered a striking but costly suggestion in 1846: towers at the end of the transepts. This proposal would have avoided alteration of the work already undertaken, but it was impractical and reflected the young man's lack of experience. Surely for this reason and also to pacify critics, Medley consulted William Butterfield, then emerging as the paramount ecclesiological architect, about the cathedral's east end during a fund-raising trip to Britain in 1848. Butterfield's intervention was limited: he suggested a more economic profile with a short sanctuary, no transepts, and a simplified central tower. In the work completed from 1849 to 1853 a compromise was struck, presumably by the architecturally astute Medley, between the basic forms suggested by Butterfield and the exterior detailing from Wills's projects.

Despite his dissatisfaction with Christ Church, Wills obviously accepted the compromise design as his own, and it served as the basis of his other cathedral plans. The tactic was unsuccessful in Toronto, where the *Church* had flatly rejected his use of a "modern antique" from another colony, yet Wills in effect produced an enlarged version of the Fredericton cathedral for the new Christ Church

Wills

Cathedral in Montreal. Fire had destroyed the old one on 10 Dec. 1856 and Wills's design was accepted early in the new year. After his sudden death in that city on 23 April 1857, Thomas Seaton Scott* carried out the project.

Contemporary estimates of Wills as an architect vary considerably. Although some praised the excellence of his designs, others found them "rather common-place," "coldly correct," or ill suited to locality. In North America the very Englishness of Wills's ecclesiology was both its strength (in so far as it represented a high art form, one that only an Englishman was likely to appreciate fully) and its weakness (in that it was doctrinaire and insufficiently adapted to new contexts). The *Church* commented that his design for the cathedral in Toronto would "make a very good . . . country Parish Church situated close to some rugged shore of the mother country . . . but it certainly does not . . . idealize the great, in architecture, in a manner to make a *fit* model for the metropolitan Church of Western Canada."

Wills reportedly designed "upwards of fifty churches." This number would be remarkable for a man who was not 35 when he died and who had been in North America fewer than a dozen years; nevertheless the figure is undoubtedly on the conservative side. A list nearly that long can be drawn up still, a century and a quarter later. What is equally extraordinary is the territory covered by these churches and projects for churches. The plans are not wonderfully varied or adventurous: Wills was sometimes too busy, possibly moving about too much, and certainly working in isolation too long to maintain a developing and innovative edge.

His work was so scattered that it is difficult to assess from the viewpoint of his contemporaries. In the Maritimes his influence seems to have been fairly widely felt and to have endured for several decades. In Upper and Lower Canada he had less impact on leading architects. Wills was certainly more advanced – in theory and in practice – than men like Edward Staveley of Quebec or William THOMAS of Toronto; both of these men were more than 20 years older than Wills (although they immigrated to British North America only a year or two earlier than he) and their patterns of thought were already set whether or not they had any awareness of the work of Wills or like-minded writers and practitioners. Those who emigrated later from the United Kingdom, for example, F. W. Cumberland, Thomas Fuller*, and T. S. Scott, had imbited still more advanced ideas and showed a more flexible and eclectic approach to the problems of "modern gothic" (High Victorian) church design.

Though Frank Wills's architectural anglicism was more ardent than some could bear, it is impossible to deny his practical and theoretical contributions in four areas: the colonial cathedral as a distinct type, Canadian and American ecclesiology in general, the development of a distinctive North American idiom in wood, and architectural publishing on this continent. He is entitled to recognition for any one of these; for the breadth of his achievements he deserves to be better remembered.

DOUGLAS RICHARDSON

Several articles by Frank Wills and reviews of some of his designs for American churches are in the *New-York Ecclesiologist*, 1 (1848–49)–5 (1853). Much of the material covered in his articles subsequently appeared in his book, *Ancient English ecclesiastical architecture and its principles, applied to the wants of the church at the present day* (New York, 1850).

Surviving unpublished material includes a collection of drawings of ecclesiastical antiquities in the Exeter area and lithographed views (by Wills or from his drawings) of churches, mostly of his own design, preserved in the "Exeter Diocesan Architectural Society scrap book" at the Devon and Exeter Institution (Exeter, Eng.). His drawings for Christ Church Cathedral (Fredericton) are in the Anglican Church of Canada, Diocese of Fredericton Arch.

Anglican Church of Canada, Diocese of Fredericton Arch., Christ Church Cathedral, John Medley, "Annals of the See of New Brunswick," 15 Oct. 1845. ANQ-M, CE1-63, 28 avril 1857. St James' Cathedral Arch. (Anglican) (Toronto), Corr., Wills to T. D. Harris, 18 June 1849; Wills to Henry Grasset, 1 Aug. 1849. *Ecclesiologist* (Cambridge, Eng., and London; London), November 1841–December 1859. Exeter Diocesan Architectural Soc., *Trans.* (Exeter, Eng.), 1 (1843); 2 (1847). John Medley, *A charge delivered at his primary visitation held in Christ Church Cathedral, Fredericton, August 24, 1847* (Fredericton, 1847); *A statement respecting the condition and works of his diocese, by the bishop of Fredericton* (London, 1848). Robb and Coster, *Letters* (Bailey). *Church*, 13 Sept. 1849. *Illustrated London News*, 28 April 1849. *Montreal Gazette*, 25 April 1857. *Montreal Transcript*, 11 Dec. 1856, 25 April 1857. *New-Brunswick Courier*, 28 June 1845. *New Brunswick Reporter and Fredericton Advertiser*, 12 May 1848. *Pilot* (Montreal), 24 April 1857. D. S. Francis, *Architects in practice, New York City, 1840–1900* ([New York, 1980?]), 27, 83. W. Q. Ketchum, *The life and work of the Most Reverend John Medley, D.D., first bishop of Fredericton and metropolitan of Canada* (Saint John, N.B., 1893). H. E. MacDermot, *Christ Church Cathedral; a century in retrospect* ([Montreal, 1959]). S. G. Morriss, "The church architecture of Frederic William Cumberland" (2v., MA thesis, Univ. of Toronto, 1976), 26–29. D. S. Richardson, "Christ Church Cathedral, Fredericton, New Brunswick" (MA thesis, Yale Univ., New Haven, Conn., 1966). P. B. Stanton, *The gothic revival & American church architecture; an episode in taste, 1840–1856* (Baltimore, Md., 1968). James Patrick, "Ecclesiological gothic in the antebellum south," *Winterthur Portfolio; a Journal of American Material Culture* (Chicago), 15 (1980): 117–38. D. S. Richardson, "Hyperborean gothic; or, wilderness ecclesiology and the wood churches of Edward Medley," *Architectura* (Munich), 2 (1972): 48–74; letter to the editor,

Journal of Canadian Art Hist. (Montreal), 1 (1974), no.2: 43–45.

WILLSON, JOHN, politician, office holder, justice of the peace, and judge; b. 5 Aug. 1776 in New Jersey, son of Ann ——; m. 28 Feb. 1799 Elizabeth Bowlby (Boultby, Bowlsby), and they had nine children; d. 26 May 1860 in Saltfleet Township, Upper Canada.

In a land petition dated 16 June 1806, John Willson claimed to have been "upwards of thirteen years" in Upper Canada; other sources claim that he arrived in 1790. He settled first at Newark (Niagara-on-the-Lake) before moving to Saltfleet Township in 1797. Willson quickly established himself as a prosperous farmer and a leader in local Methodist circles. His chief claim to fame was a political career that began in 1809 when a local deputation encouraged him to contest a by-election for the West Riding of York. As Willson later explained, the "parties in politics known at that time, were the '*Government*' and the '*Opposition.*' I was called by the latter, – which was chiefly composed of dissenting religious people." It is also likely that Willson drew support from small farmers frustrated by the monopolistic practices of merchants such as Richard Hatt*. Willson's election was protested, unsuccessfully, by Hatt, Richard Beasley*, and others, who claimed that he was ineligible as a Methodist "Teacher and Preacher."

During the remaining sessions of the fifth parliament, Willson made an enduring reputation as a defender of civil and religious liberty. His voting record in 1810–11 indicates complete support for Joseph Willcocks*, the foremost opponent of the administration of Lieutenant Governor Francis GORE. Willson was elected in 1812 to the sixth parliament (1812–16). In the last years of the War of 1812 he became highly critical of the change in the climate of opinion, especially as reflected in the stern measures enacted by successive administrations, which he considered to be military despotism. On 26 Feb. 1814 he cast the sole vote against the bill suspending habeas corpus [*see* Sir Gordon DRUMMOND]. In 1816 he supported a more liberal marriage bill. More important, he introduced and, with James Durand*, drafted the Common Schools Bill, which provided for public support of elementary education.

There has been some historical confusion with respect to Willson's involvement in the seventh parliament (1817–20), but what happened is really straightforward. At the opening of parliament in February 1817, Gore asked that there be due representation for the recently established Gore District before any business was transacted. The legislature concurred, the requisite bill was passed, and parliament adjourned. Willson then opposed Durand for the new riding of Wentworth. In a handbill printed by Bartemas Ferguson* and published in the *Niagara Spectator* by Richard Cockrell*, Durand attacked Willson for duplicity, cowardice, and corruption, claiming that the erstwhile champion of liberty had become a tool of government in return for a magistracy in the new district. The election was held about 18 February; Willson attributed Durand's victory to the "spirit of Radicalism" which had begun "to diffuse itself more generally." If anything, that spirit manifested itself even more strongly in the widespread local support for Robert Gourlay*'s convention of 1818. The tide, however, was turning against Gourlay and his supporters at the Head of the Lake (the vicinity of present-day Hamilton Harbour). When Richard Hatt died in 1819, Willson won the by-election to replace him for the riding of Halton.

Local perception of Willson's politics had been changing since his defeat by Durand. Willson, he himself later recalled, was referred to as "a thorough-going tory." Elected along with George Hamilton* for Wentworth in 1820, he had the support of "the Conservative interest, both in and out of office." He was subsequently re-elected to the ninth (1825–28), tenth (1829–30), and eleventh (1830–34) parliaments, thus emerging as the first major politician from the Head of the Lake. "Honest John," as he was usually called, had made a local reputation from his continued advocacy of the interests of farmers, his espousal of universal education, and his unrelenting tirades against the inequity of the civil courts. From a strong regional base he moved to the front ranks of the House of Assembly. In 1824 the first issue of William Lyon Mackenzie*'s *Colonial Advocate* had lauded him: "Many members of our legislature get less *useful* the longer they are kept in parliament; but his talents appear to us the more eminent, and his knowledge the more solid and extensive, the longer he is there."

Willson was at the height of his political power and influence between 1825 and 1834, his prominence being reflected in his election to the speakership of the assembly for the ninth parliament. During his tenure the assembly handled some of the colony's most important and contentious issues: the alien bill, the partiality of the judicial system, and the large-scale provincial support needed for public works, such as the Welland Canal. Increasingly, Willson associated with such men as John Beverley Robinson* and John Strachan*, the closest advisers of Lieutenant Governor Sir Peregrine MAITLAND. Slowly but surely, the image of Willson as he had been in opposition changed until he had become the epitome of the political turncoat and double-dealer. In 1828 Mackenzie, who described Willson as "positively ministerial" and featured him prominently on his legislative "Black List," wrote, "The more I examined his past parliamentary conduct, the more I was satisfied that he was acting a double and deceitful part as a politician." In his resurrection of the province's political past,

Willson

Mackenzie, looking for patterns of parliamentary compliance with unpopular administrations, singled out for particular censure the session of 1816; an impression of Willson's role in this session stuck among the reform-minded of the 1820s and 1830s. In 1831 John Rolph* claimed the "Maitland Faction" rivalled "the ever memorable parliament of 1816: and John Willson appears to act over again the same character which at that time brought upon him the odium of the country."

Through the latter half of the 1820s and into the 1830s, politics in Hamilton became associated in the opposition press with the abuse of civil liberties: the tar and feathering and then the dismissal, from the position of clerk of the peace, of George Rolph, an ardent reformer and John's brother; the alleged violations of judicial principles by Judge Christopher Alexander Hagerman* during the murder trial of Michael Vincent; the failure of local magistrates to act against a tory mob in the so-called "Hamilton Outrage" in 1829 [see James Gordon Strobridge*]; and the beating of Mackenzie. In the town a distinctive local political culture was emerging, partly in response to attacks by reformers in York (Toronto) such as Mackenzie and Francis Collins*. The flashpoint was the decision by Mackenzie and Collins in 1825 to support Peter Desjardins*'s proposal to build a canal to connect Dundas and Burlington Bay (Hamilton Harbour). The scheme was derided by Willson who saw, in Hamilton's rival Burlington Bay Canal, "the life and soul of all prosperity to the Gore, the Wellington, and the Brock Districts." York reformers, especially Mackenzie, not only supported the Desjardins Canal, they sided with the pretensions of Dundas over those of Hamilton to become a commercial and administrative capital at the Head of the Lake. In Hamilton the cause of political reform withered as beleaguered residents, of disparate ethnic, religious, and political backgrounds, came together in common cause over local economic development. In defence of its economic ambitions, Hamilton began with John Willson to turn to political leaders who would represent its interests. Its first newspaper, the *Gore Balance*, begun in 1829 by Bartemas Ferguson, was hostile to radicalism (especially of the York variety), championed development, and ardently boosted John Willson.

For his part, Willson considered himself a conservative independent, a spokesman of the interests of small farmers. In 1819 he had offered himself for the office of district court judge as a means of obviating the "evil" that could result from the marriage of that office to a man of commerce. Eight years later, during his speakership and at a time when he was being vilified by reformers, he criticized an assembly "composed of government officers, placemen, and pentioners." His remedy was more farmers

and fewer lawyers in government – in other words, plain, ordinary folk who would attend to useful improvements rather than spending their time "in levees, balls, and dinners with a view to procure places and pensions." In 1832, for instance, while Marshall Spring Bidwell* was lashing him for being "opposed to popular measures," Willson supported Peter PERRY's bill for disposing of the clergy reserves. Willson, in fact, went further and argued that the entire proceeds be appropriated to education and, much to Bidwell's displeasure, that all denominations, including Roman Catholics, had a claim on the reserves. Willson had reservations about Perry's attempt to reform the jury laws but sympathized with its main thrust. "I am not fond of leaving the selection of juries to the Sheriff," Willson said in the assembly. Finally, he supported a bill to bar dower. Though wives "might not be actually employed in clearing the land," he reasoned, "they were often called upon to assist, and they were therefore as much entitled to a property in the land, and should have the right to dispose of that title."

Willson did not contest the election of 1834, a date that marks the ascendancy of Allan Napier MacNab* as chief advocate of Hamilton's interests. None the less, Willson continued to be a major force. On 11 Dec. 1839 he was appointed to the Legislative Council, just in time for the critical debate on the proposed union with Lower Canada. Willson, who had opposed the scheme when it first came up in 1822 because of the differences between the two colonies in law, language, and religion, voted with the minority against union. That vote cost him the chance of reappointment to the council after the declaration of union on 10 Feb. 1841. He had had enough of politics and decried the rise of party, "a grasping power exerted to confine . . . the whole patronage of the government." Thereafter, he retired from public life to his farm in Saltfleet.

Locally, Willson served for many years as a justice of the peace, surrogate court judge, road commissioner, inspector of licences and stills, trustee of the Gore District Grammar School, commissioner for the Burlington Bay Canal, and member of the district board of health. He also served as a commissioner for the Welland Canal but was removed in 1840 by Lieutenant Governor Sir George ARTHUR for urging completion of the work on "a scale of expence" which Arthur regarded as "quite improper." As well, Willson was active in the Gore District Emigrant Society and in the Agricultural Society of the Gore District.

John Willson died in 1860 at his farm and was buried in St Andrew's churchyard in Grimsby. He left a modest estate worth about $6,000; he had sold off most of his lands in the early 1850s to his sons. A Methodist and then a supporter of Henry Ryan*, he seems to have become an Anglican in later life. Contemporary political language serves no useful purpose in coming to terms with "Honest John." There was a measure of continuity to his politics and it was this continuity that best defines the man. To his mind, it was the times that had changed, not he himself. He was, as he put it, a "plain farmer," self-educated, and ever concerned "to reap the advantages of the country," by which he meant a due regard for the farmer, moderate constitutional reform, liberal marriage laws, cheap justice, universal and decentralized elementary education, and economic development. In the combination of moderate conservatism and unabashed support for development, one finds the defining characteristics of Hamilton's political culture to the present day. Willson was its first spokesman.

ROBERT LOCHIEL FRASER

John Willson is the author of *Address to the inhabitants of the district of Gore, and speeches upon the Trade Act, upon the bill for compensating the losses of sufferers by the late rebellion, upon the Bank Restriction Bill, and an extract from a speech upon the union of the provinces* (Hamilton, [Ont.], 1840).

AO, MS 74, package 12, Willson to Papineau, 17 Feb. 1827; RG 22, ser.94, 2: 81; ser.205, no.107. HPL, Arch. file, Willson papers. MTL, Robert Baldwin papers, unbound misc., Willson to Baldwin, 4 Sept. 1843; W. W. Baldwin papers, Rolph to Baldwin, 24 March 1831. PAC, RG 1, L3, 525: W8/9; 527: W11/10, 98; RG 5, A1: 3868–79, 9953, 21787–94, 21884–87; RG 68, General index, 1651–1841: 182, 403, 426, 432, 438, 446, 459, 463, 474, 510, 539, 671. Wentworth Land Registry Office (Hamilton), Abstract index to deeds, Saltfleet Township, 4–6, 41–42 (mfm. at AO, GS 1627). *Arthur papers* (Sanderson), 3: 32, 40, 390. "Journals of Legislative Assembly of U.C.," AO *Report*, 1911, 1912. *Canadian Freeman* (York [Toronto]), 18 Jan. 1827; 21 July, 8 Sept. 1831. *Colonial Advocate*, 18 May 1824; 29 May, 6, 12 June, 31 July 1828; 14 Oct. 1830; 13 Jan. 1831; 16 Oct. 1834. *Gore Balance* (Hamilton), 12 Dec. 1829, 3 June 1830. *Gore Gazette, and Ancaster, Hamilton, Dundas and Flamborough Advertiser* (Ancaster, [Ont.]), 13 March, 1 Sept. 1827. *Hamilton Spectator, and Journal of Commerce*, 31 May 1860. *Liberal* (St Thomas, [Ont.]), 22, 29 Nov. 1832. *Western Mercury* (Hamilton), 7, 28 June 1832. *DHB*. "Loyalist and pioneer families of West Lincoln, 1783–1833," comp. R. J. Powell, *Annals of the Forty* (Grimsby, Ont.), 9 (1958): 65–69. D. R. Beer, *Sir Allan Napier MacNab* (Hamilton, 1984). Charles Durand, *Reminiscences of Charles Durand of Toronto, barrister* (Toronto, 1897). R. L. Fraser, "Like Eden in her summer dress: gentry, economy, and society: Upper Canada, 1812–1840" (PHD thesis, Univ. of Toronto, 1979), 315–16.

WINTON, HENRY DAVID, printer and newspaperman; b. 10 June 1793 in the parish of Withecombe Raleigh, Exmouth, England, fifth son of the Reverend Robert Winton and Teresa Maria——; m. 3 Sept. 1816 Elizabeth Luttrell Nicholson, and they had four sons and two daughters; d. 6 Jan. 1855 in St John's.

Henry David Winton was apprenticed to a printer and bookbinder in Dartmouth, England, and at the end of his term proceeded to London where he worked in the same trades. On 28 Aug. 1818 he arrived in Newfoundland and the next month, designating himself as a "Stationer, Bookseller, & Book-binder," he announced that he had opened a wholesale and retail "Stationery Warehouse" in St John's. Throughout his career in Newfoundland he maintained a business as stationer, printer, bookseller, and publisher.

It is as a journalist, however, that Winton is best known. In 1820, with Alexander Haire, he founded the *Public Ledger and Newfoundland General Advertiser*, the fourth newspaper in St John's. Haire's connection with the *Ledger* ended in 1823 but Winton's continued until his death. Few issues survive from the years 1820–26, but from 1821 or 1822 Winton, by his own admission, "strenuously" advocated the creation of a "Local Legislative Assembly." Thus he was caught up in the reform movement in the colony, supported William Carson* and Patrick Morris* in their campaign for representative institutions, and allowed them access to his paper to publicize their accomplishments. From 1827 to 1832 he continued to press for a legislature. He also supported the movement for parliamentary reform in Britain, as well as Roman Catholic emancipation. In view of the later developments it may seem surprising that prior to 1832 Winton appeared at times to be not only pro-Catholic but also hostile to the Church of England. The first recorded action for libel against him was brought by an Anglican priest, Frederick Hamilton Carrington*, in 1827. By contrast, after the British parliament passed the Catholic Relief Bill in 1829, Winton received public thanks from Catholics in St John's for arguing that its provisions ought to be extended to Newfoundland. One observer in 1830 called him "a radical reformer and stickler for civil and religious liberty." But this impression was superficial. Mild criticism of the Church of England might have been expected from Winton, who was a Congregationalist. And as for his political views, even the early Winton was not a whig radical like Carson: there was a conservatism in his outlook well before 1832. This was revealed, for example, in his careful distancing of himself from the Irish Catholic favourite Daniel O'Connell, of whom he wrote in 1831, "we are no great admirer," and in the attitude he displayed towards the riots in Conception Bay during the years 1830–32. Winton called the rioters "a lawless mob," "ruffians," and "rabble." He was especially harsh on those who took part in the protest meetings on Saddle Hill, between Carbonear and Harbour Grace, in February 1832 over the truck system: the established

Winton

practice whereby the fishermen received "past payment in goods" rather than cash. Winton wanted civil and religious freedoms extended, but he also believed in defending the "established order of society" and the interests of "the respectable portion of the inhabitants" against those who would pander to the intellects of "the lower classes."

For several years prior to the granting of representative government in 1832 Winton was on friendly terms with Catholic bishop Michael Anthony Fleming*. In the campaign leading to the first general election under the new form of government, that friendship changed into an enmity so profound that it coloured Newfoundland politics for generations. On 7 Sept. 1832 the *Ledger* cautioned voters not to select as members of the new assembly "inflated schoolboys, or superannuated old men" – a clear allusion to John Kent*, a young Irish merchant patronized by Fleming, and (though Winton later seemed to deny this) to Carson. In a furious response printed in the St John's *Newfoundlander*, Kent stated that he detected "an odour of prejudice" in Winton, adding that there was "a party here" which "if I were an imbecile, would elect me." In this letter and in a circular issued a few days later he made it clear that he thought Winton's objections to him were based on "an uncompromising hatred to Irishmen and Catholics." On 18 September Winton responded in an editorial which changed the course of his life. After denying the charge of prejudice, he asked what party had sufficient influence "to command the return of an *idiot* to our local Parliament." Such an assertion, he said, was an insult not only to Protestants "but to every respectable Catholic in this district." To what influence was Kent referring? "Sure we are that the Right Rev. the Bishop as the head of the Church of which Mr. K. is a member will not tolerate such conduct, nor permit it to be tolerated by any of his respectable clergy." He then denied that Kent had any such influence at his command, and concluded that he was "a political *impostor*." This was not an editorial at which Fleming could readily take offence; yet he did. On 19 September he wrote a letter to the *Newfoundlander* to comment on "the unwarrantable and unjustifiable manner in which [Winton] brought my name before the public," and declared that he had the right "as a citizen" to recommend candidates to the electorate. He thereupon endorsed Kent, Carson, and William Thomas, a merchant of the city. The gauntlet was now thrown down, and Winton was just the man to pick it up. In his bold reply of 21 September he accused Fleming of "as gross and wilful a misrepresentation of our sentiments as the mind of a Jesuit could possibly conceive" and informed him that he had "justly forfeited" the respect not only of Protestants but of "the respectable portion of your own Catholic flock." In the heated atmosphere of the campaign, these and subsequent remarks by Winton stirred up deep animosities among long-frustrated Catholics. Meetings were called in St John's and Conception Bay to support Fleming and denounce Winton. Placards, Winton later recalled, "covered the walls of the town dooming me to destruction." For his part, Kent in his speeches asked supporters to "put down the PUBLIC LEDGER – put down the *Orange Press*." The seed of sectarian rivalry had been planted in what had hitherto been a comparatively peaceful colony. The following 50 years would show into what fertile ground it had fallen.

Even before the election had taken place, Winton became convinced that the extensive franchise granted in 1832 was "an egregious error" which would endanger the peace and prosperity of the colony. After several reformers, including Kent, were elected, this view settled into a deep conviction. His opinion was that only truly independent men should have the vote; those who could not think for themselves, such as the mass of the Catholics in St John's, who appeared to him to be mentally enslaved by their clergy, should be excluded [*see* Edward Troy*]. These voters were merely tools in a clerical conspiracy to gain control of the House of Assembly. Winton's high sense of responsibility as a journalist and his own bulldog courage would not allow him to desist from iteration of these themes as long as the Catholic clergy insisted on playing a role in politics. His opposition to "Priestcraft" was one factor which alienated him from reformers such as Kent and Carson, whom the priests invariably supported. But these men came to offend him anyway by their radicalism. As Winton grew older his conservative nature became more and more evident in his paper, and his hostility to those who claimed to represent popular interests grew stronger.

After the election of 1832 the reformers soon had in Winton an implacable enemy whose supremacy as a journalist in the narrow intellectual world of St John's gave him an influence that could not be ignored. In 1833 Carson, James DOUGLAS, and possibly others found it necessary to establish the *Newfoundland Patriot* as the new journal of reform in St John's. An early employee on this paper was Robert John Parsons*, the foreman in Winton's printing establishment for six years, whose connection with the *Ledger* had ended in 1833 in a savage fist fight with his employer. By 1840 Parsons had become the *Patriot*'s sole owner and editor, and bitter personal invective against Winton was a regular feature of his columns.

As sectarian tensions in the colony increased in the 1830s, Winton found himself a favoured target of Catholic hostility. In December 1833, following a by-election victory for Carson in St John's, it became apparent that Winton was in real danger. On Christmas night a crowd estimated at upwards of 1,000 gathered in the street near his home, and the magistrates had to call out the military to prevent a riot. Catholic feeling against the *Ledger* persisted through 1834. Winton continued his attacks on Fleming, and in February 1835 even directed an ironical paragraph at the Order of the Presentation of Our Blessed Lady [*see* Miss KIRWAN], for which he at once apologized. During the winter of 1834–35 Winton was attacked from the altar, and Fleming in effect prohibited his congregation from reading the *Ledger*. Catholics who were thought to be associated with the paper felt obliged to offer public apologies and Catholic merchants who took the *Ledger* were denounced and boycotted. On 14 May 1835 Governor Henry Prescott* expressed his concern about the antipathy to Winton in a dispatch to the Colonial Office, noting, however, that for "several weeks past" public denunciations of subscribers to the *Ledger* had been discontinued. In the late afternoon of 19 May, Winton was travelling on horseback from Carbonear to Harbour Grace in the company of William Churchward, who was on foot. While descending Saddle Hill, they were attacked by a group of about five people with painted faces. Winton was struck on the head by a stone – a blow that opened a large wound – and felled him from his horse. More blows on the head followed. His ears were then stuffed with mud and gravel. One of the attackers opened a clasp-knife, cut two pieces from his right ear, and cut off the left one. Winton survived the ordeal, but despite an immediate official inquiry and a reward of £1,500 offered by the government and merchants, the identity of his assailants remains a mystery. Thus proof is lacking that Catholic animosity had anything to do with the mutilation. It was widely believed, however, that Catholics were indeed responsible. According to Prescott, the event was "a matter of open triumph and rejoicing to the Catholics of low degree, even female servants and children expressing the greatest satisfaction." Proclamations announcing the reward were speedily torn from walls, and a joyful ballad about "Croppy Winton" was soon in circulation. The *Patriot*, in a distasteful editorial, commented that "if ever mercy was deservedly extended to crime – this case above all others deserves it."

The effects of this bizarre and cruel incident upon Winton are difficult to assess. However, because it was the merchants who offered him sympathy and support, undoubtedly he was drawn into a closer union with them. The *Ledger* now became the acknowledged proponent of "conservative principles" and the organ of the Protestant mercantile élite which controlled the Council and exerted the greatest influence over the governor. The newspaper was supported by advertisements both from prominent merchants and from the government. Yet Winton's success in the competitive field of local journalism was not altogether due to patronage, nor was he drawn

to defend the establishment merely for profit. He wrote from conviction. He was also a gifted and inventive journalist. His network of contacts included a Catholic who kept him informed of the content of sermons in the local chapel and, after 1841, a London correspondent. The *Ledger* appeared twice a week – a novelty in St John's – and its circulation was described by Governor Sir John HARVEY in 1842 as surpassing all but one of the six other papers in the city. It would be exaggerating to call Winton an impartial journalist but neither was he a bigot. Although he objected to clerical interference in politics, he rarely stated wider theological and historical objections to Catholicism. True, he had the normal Protestant suspicions of the Roman church, but in many respects, even occasionally in his attitude to Catholics, Winton was a broadminded and compassionate man. Yet it is also apparent that he failed to make an effort to understand the underlying causes of unrest among the Irish Catholic population in the colony.

The election of 1836 saw Winton's worst fears realized when the reformers won control of the House of Assembly, bringing the colony under the dominion of "the Priests and the dregs of our society." The following five years gave him ample opportunity to indulge his talent for opposition, and his criticism of the leading figures in the assembly was unrelenting and scathing. These were Winton's great years. Whatever may be said of his principles, it must be admitted that he showed tenacity, vigilance, and courage. Even when in December 1838 the assembly appeared to have won the right to commit a man to prison for contempt [*see* Edward KIELLEY], Winton did not waver in his assaults on the house. Nor was he silenced when the mutilation of 1835 was re-enacted in 1840 on his assistant Herman Lott. There was, too, the threat of libel suits. Winton, many times a juror, seemed to know exactly the boundary between fair comment and libel, and in any case was not inclined to follow the "un-English practice of assailing personal and private character." A suit brought against him in 1838 by John Valentine Nugent*, a leading Catholic member of the assembly, was unsuccessful; later cases also showed that he was a hard man to catch. Winton himself, though attacked mercilessly in the *Patriot* from its inception as a drunkard, lecher, "bedlamite," "lickspittal," and "maniac," did not bother to seek redress from the courts until the appearance of another pro-Catholic paper, the *Newfoundland Vindicator*, in 1841. When Kent expressed in its columns the view that Winton was "a hideous featured adulterer – a veteran drunkard – a father of a family imparting, by example, to [his] sons an education that makes them pests of society," he felt obliged to sue and was awarded £200 in damages. A similar punishment was administered to the printer of

Winton

the *Patriot* in 1842. Winton's sexual exploits, drinking habits, and harsh treatment of his children were often alluded to in the press, and in the absence of private papers it is hard to reach conclusions on these matters. According to friends who testified on his behalf in court, he was not an excessive drinker. His obituary, which was probably written by his son Henry*, said that in his relations with his family he was "deeply affectionate" but that "his ideas of the duty of a parent partook of rather a severe cast."

A revealing test of Winton's integrity as a journalist came after the arrival of Governor Harvey in 1841. It was Harvey who presided over the introduction of the constitution of 1842, under which the franchise was restricted somewhat and the upper and lower houses amalgamated into one chamber. By all appearances he was a vain, pompous man, anxious for popularity – not the sort of person who could keep the reformers in check. Winton had been alarmed even before Harvey's arrival by such concessions on the part of Governor Prescott as the removal of Chief Justice Henry John Boulton* in 1838 and his replacement by a "new whig Radical" John Gervase Hutchinson Bourne*. He had also called Prescott a "radical" for elevating Patrick Morris to the Council. But Harvey's hobnobbing with the radical and Catholic element was too much to bear. He was "*selling himself to the rabble,*" Winton declared in March 1842. Fears about the growing influence of the reformers under Harvey may have been a factor in leading Winton to run for election himself in December. He coveted the Burin seat to no avail, being defeated by a Catholic reformer, Clement Pitt Benning*. By 1844 Winton was calling for the abolition of the new system, and his criticism of Harvey was so outspoken that government advertising was withdrawn from his paper. Winton responded to this exhibition of official displeasure by defiantly asserting his right to comment freely on public affairs, but in fact he felt uncomfortable in the situation, and his criticism of the government became muted. In 1845 he admitted that he was "passively looking on" as events transpired. No "free commentary" on the government, he wrote, could be made "with advantage, or even with safety, to the journalist who would attempt it." It was the first and only time in Winton's career that he had been put down, although he still occasionally pointed to the "twaddle" in Harvey's comments on agriculture and ridiculed his "comical government." After the fire of June 1846, which devastated St John's, he was returned to official favour. He even accepted a position from Harvey as secretary to a committee administering relief to the sufferers.

The anti-Catholic note in the *Ledger* softened considerably during the period of the Amalgamated Legislature. When his old enemy Parsons was successful in an 1843 by-election, Winton had to

concede that the clergy had played no part. Nor were they active, he admitted, during the general election of 1848, when he again ran unsuccessfully in Burin. By the late 1840s we find an unexpected warmth in his comments on Kent and Morris, and when Fleming died in 1850 Winton printed a long obituary, which described the bishop as a "truly great man." (It should be noted, however, that he did not write the obituary.) This gentleness was not destined to last. As the by-election of November 1850 approached in St John's, Winton heard the rumour that the priests were again active in support of Philip Francis Little*, an advocate of responsible government. By this date Winton's antagonism towards the idea of responsible government was deeply entrenched. In fact he was fast coming to the view that the colony was unfit for even the old system of 1832, which had essentially been restored in 1848 after the experiment with amalgamation ended. When Little was returned, the *Ledger* thundered forth as of old that the "Priest's party" had called out "the sweepings of the gutters and sewers" to ensure his election. He was enraged even further in 1851 when it was revealed that Little was in league with Catholic bishop John Thomas Mullock*, who openly supported responsible government. The people of Newfoundland, Mullock wrote in a letter published in that year, "look with longing eyes to the day when they can manage their own affairs." Here, then, was another partisan bishop. Winton once again seized the gauntlet, and the last four years of his life were spent in a desperate, losing battle against responsible government, which to him meant control of the colony by the rabble. Before he died he came to regret deeply that he had helped bring representative institutions to the colony in 1832. He now called for a much simpler system, one consisting of "a Governor and Council, the Council partly elective, and partly nominated by the Crown." It was a view apparently shared by Governor John Gaspard Le Marchant*. But both men seemed like voices from the past, and the year Winton died saw the colony adopt a new constitution, with Little, a Catholic, as Newfoundland's first prime minister under responsible government.

On Winton's death, his son Henry became editor, printer, and publisher of the *Public Ledger* although his mother, as administrator of the estate, was the proprietor until 1860 when he took sole control. Two of his brothers, Robert and Francis, were also newspaper publishers in St John's during the 1860s, producing the *St. John's Daily News* and the *Day Book* respectively. His third brother, Ebenezer, had tried to establish a tri-weekly paper, the *Morning Advertiser*, in the city in 1844.

Henry David Winton was a journalist of uncommon ability. His paper represented Protestant and mercantile interests – the dominant elements in Newfound-

Wolhaupter

land at a time of bitter sectarian divisions. As a partisan he was feared and hated, but even his opponents conceded his sincerity and his courage, and he was capable of generosity of spirit to enemies. As an intellectual and a critic of Newfoundland society, he was perhaps equalled in his time only by Carson and Nugent.

PATRICK O'FLAHERTY

[The most revealing sources of information about Winton's Newfoundland career are the St John's newspapers, especially his own paper, the *Public Ledger and Newfoundland General Advertiser*, for the years 1827 to 1855, and Parsons's, the *Newfoundland Patriot* (later the *Patriot & Terra Nova Herald*), for 1834 to 1855. Issues of the *Public Ledger* for 1846 and 1848, unavailable elsewhere, can be found in the PRO (CO 199/7–8), as can the *Patriot* for 1838–39 (CO 199/1) and excerpts from certain numbers of the *Public Ledger* prior to 1827 (CO 194). The most trustworthy biography of Winton is his obituary, *Public Ledger*, 16 Jan. 1855.

For official documents relating to Winton's mutilation in 1835, see PRO, CO 194/90: 183–207, and PANL, GN 2/2, April–September 1835: 41–46, 57–60. *See also* NLS, Dept. of MSS, MS 2350: ff.147–54, 170, 175, and the *Public Ledger*, 2 June 1835. For Winton's own lengthy account of his relations with Fleming, *see* PRO, CO 194/99: 49–66. P.O'F.]

Devon Record Office (Exeter, Eng.), 2992 A/PR10 (St Saviour parish, Dartmouth, reg. of marriages, 1813–37), 3 Sept. 1816. NLS, Dept. of MSS, MS 2350. PANL, GN 2/2; GN 5/2/A/1-1832–35: 88–90. PRO, CO 194/61–146; RG 4/959; 4/1209: ff.9, 24v. Supreme Court of Nfld. (St John's), Registry, 3: f.235 (administration of H. D. Winton, 27 Jan. 1855). Nfld., House of Assembly, *Journal*, 1833–55. *Newfoundlander*, 1827–34, 1837–43. *Newfoundland Mercantile Journal*, 1816–27. *Newfoundland Vindicator* (St John's), 1841–42. *Royal Gazette and Newfoundland Advertiser*, 1810–18, 1828–31. Gunn, *Political hist. of Nfld.*

WOLHAUPTER, BENJAMIN, watchmaker, silversmith, justice of the peace, militia officer, and office holder; b. 10 July 1800 in Saint John, N.B., second son of John Wolhaupter* and Mary Payne Aycrigg; m. 1820 Catharine Phoebe Brannan of Fredericton, and they had six children; d. 27 Jan. 1857 in Fredericton.

Having spent his early years in Saint John and Sheffield, Benjamin Wolhaupter moved with his family to Fredericton in 1813. There, working under his father, he began his apprenticeship as a watchmaker and silversmith. He finished his term in 1820, bought a house, married, and commenced practising his craft, probably with his father. Shortly thereafter he opened his own watchmaking and jewellery shop which he continued to operate until 1825.

On 16 May 1821 Wolhaupter petitioned the lieutenant governor, George Stracey Smyth*, to grant him the small three-acre island, known as Rain Island, situated in the River Nash (Nashwaak River) just above its confluence with the Saint John River. Although he promised to cultivate and improve the land, the petition was denied by 22 May, perhaps because the island had been inundated by the spring runoff. Despite this unsuccessful petition, Wolhaupter soon secured a more valuable grant within the town limits of Fredericton at the site of the old jail. The 6 Dec. 1825 issue of the *New-Brunswick Royal Gazette* carried a notice to his customers in which he advised them of his change in locale. Wolhaupter had two apprentices: in 1824 he took on Benjamin Franklin Tibbits (Tibbets) who is credited by some with later inventing the compound steam-engine, and in 1832 Wolhaupter's eldest son, Charles John, joined him. Charles completed his training in 1839 and in August of that year opened his own business in Chatham.

In 1837 Wolhaupter had been appointed magistrate for York County, the first of a series of public offices he was to hold. He was called on for active service as captain and quartermaster of the York-Sunbury Regiment of militia during the 1839 confrontations which arose over the New Brunswick–Maine boundary dispute [*see* Sir John HARVEY]. On 15 February of that year, in a letter to his brother Charles, Wolhaupter explained that he was "no advocate of war . . . but if our country is threatened with invasion, it is the duty of every man and every Christian to turn out cheerfully and protect the Blessings and Privileges that we enjoy."

Once the threat of war was removed, he extended his business interests; he became a director of both the Commercial Bank of New Brunswick and the Quebec and St Andrew's Railroad, and in 1846 he was elected president of the Central Fire Insurance Company. A short time later Wolhaupter was appointed provincial commissioner for public buildings. In 1847 he became high sheriff of York County, a position he held until his death. His son Charles John, who had returned to Fredericton in the early 1840s and gradually assumed sole responsibility for his father's business, left in 1851 to join the adventurers going to the Australian gold-rush. It can be assumed that the Wolhaupter watchmaking and jewellery business was closed before he left. Wolhaupter Sr was a devout member of the Church of England, a vestryman of Christ Church, Fredericton, and a close friend of Bishop John Medley*.

Only a few pieces of Benjamin Wolhaupter's work as a watchmaker and silversmith are known to have survived: a grandfather clock and a silver teaspoon are part of the collection of the York-Sunbury Historical Society Museum, Fredericton; another clock, a few pieces of silver flatware, and a gold watch belong to his descendants. Letters to the Fredericton papers after his death extolled his virtues as a man and offered

Woolsey

tribute to his integrity and magnanimity in public office. The *Head Quarters* stated that "no man we know of had more of the milk of human kindness in his breast than Sheriff Wolhaupter. Always merry and jocose – always kind and humane – sympathizing warmly with the distressed – we do not believe that he left behind a single enemy."

DONALD C. MACKAY

PANB, MC 1, A. C. Wolhaupter, "Wolhaupter," 1960; MC 300, MS60; RG 10, RS107, C10: 143. *Gleaner* (Chatham, N.B.), 21 Aug. 1839, 6 Oct. 1842. *Head Quarters* (Fredericton), 27 Jan. 1857. *New-Brunswick Royal Gazette*, 6 Dec. 1825. *True Liberator* (Saint John, N.B.), 30 Aug. 1847. *The old grave-yard, Fredericton, New Brunswick: epitaphs copied by the York-Sunbury Historical Society Inc.*, comp. L. M. Beckwith Maxwell (Sackville, N.B., 1938). *Fredericton's 100 years; then and now*, ed. Frank Baird (Fredericton, [1948]). I. L. Hill, *Fredericton, New Brunswick, British North America* ([Fredericton?, 1968?]). D. C. Mackay, *Silversmiths and related craftsmen of the Atlantic provinces* (Halifax, 1973).

WOOLSEY, JOHN WILLIAM (baptized **Jean-Guillaume**), businessman and militia officer; b. 26 July 1767 at Quebec, son of John William Woolsey, merchant, and Marie-Joseph Trefflé, *dit* Rottot; m. 19 March 1797 Julie Lemoine in Montreal, and they had seven children; d. 9 May 1853 at Quebec and was buried on 12 May at Château-Richer, Lower Canada.

Shortly after the conquest of New France, the elder John William Woolsey and his brother Robert left Portadown in Ireland and came to settle in the new British colony. Following his marriage, he and his wife, a daughter of the Montreal merchant Pierre Trefflé, *dit* Rottot, settled at Quebec, where Woolsey launched into various business activities. During the siege of the city by the Americans in 1775–76, Woolsey, who held the rank of major in the local militia, was taken off to Philadelphia as a prisoner. John William, who was then eight years old, went with his uncle George Woolsey to live in Baltimore, Md. They returned to Quebec some years later and on 14 May 1781 John William was apprenticed to his uncle Robert Woolsey and George Gregory, merchants specializing in the imported dry goods trade. The contract, which bound him to them for a period of five years, was transferred on 22 May 1784 to Melvin, Wills, and Burns with John William's consent.

Six years later Woolsey became the partner of William Burns* in Burns and Woolsey. The two partners were auctioneers, commission merchants, and brokers. In 1797 the firm rented the Queen's Wharf at the foot of Rue Sous-le-Fort, a site which then belonged to William Grant*. Burns and Woolsey was dissolved in 1806. That year Woolsey bought the Queen's Wharf, which included three stone houses

three storeys high, four two-storey stone sheds, various other buildings, and a quay.

The following year Woolsey left the house he had lived in for 12 years on Rue du Sault-au-Matelot to take up residence on Rue des Pauvres (Côte du Palais). It was here in 1808–9 that the artist William Berczy* did a painting of the Woolsey family. Woolsey moved again in 1810, to be closer to his business, and for the next 16 years he was to occupy a house at Queen's Wharf, opposite Rue Saint-Pierre. Following his move Woolsey introduced various innovations, such as establishing uniform charges for warehousing and wharfage, and using a crane to unload goods. In 1819 he brought in a European fertilizer and had a steam-mill built in order to prepare it. It was at this juncture that he joined the Agricultural Society in the district of Quebec.

In the same period Woolsey played an important role in the city's business community. In December 1816, for example, he chaired a meeting called to plan the location for a stock exchange. Subsequently he served on a committee of five merchants to carry out the plan. Two years later he presided over the founding meeting of the Quebec Bank and he held office as the first president of its board of directors from 1818 to 1823. His reputation extended beyond business circles, and he was called upon to chair various public meetings, including one of the Quebec Constitutional Association held on the Esplanade on 31 July 1837, which attracted several thousand people.

In connection with his business operations, Woolsey set up various firms. John William Woolsey and Company was formed in 1810 with his brother-in-law Benjamin Lemoine. Then came Woolsey, Stewart and Company, from 1815 to 1820. On the dissolution of this partnership Woolsey ceased to act as an auctioneer, commission merchant, and broker, but he kept his fertilizer business and continued to use the port facilities of the Queen's Wharf, where he had a steam-mill built for grinding wheat. However, by 1822 he had returned to his first commercial interest, setting up Woolsey, LeMesurier and Company, in which his son William Darly and merchant Henry LeMesurier* participated. LeMesurier resigned within a month, and the firm took the name of Woolsey and Son. William Darly Woolsey soon chose the priesthood, but his brother John Bryan showed an interest in business and made a start in the fertilizer trade, buying a site at Saint-Roch where he had a steam-mill built. In 1838 Woolsey Sr turned this mill, which had been badly damaged by fire two years before, into a sawmill. It included at least three saws run by a six-horsepower motor.

At the time his wife died in 1840, Woolsey was living comfortably in a rented nine-room house on Rue Saint-Georges (Côte d'Abraham), in Upper

Town. The couple owned a library of some 60 volumes, with French and English books shelved side by side. A telescope was installed in the room at the top of the house. Subsequently Woolsey moved to various parts of Upper Town, and from 1847 to 1848 he even lived in a villa at Sainte-Foy. He had been residing for a short while on Rue Saint-François at Quebec when he died on 9 May 1853 after a brief illness, at the advanced age of 85 years and 10 months. Not long before, he had renounced Protestantism, to which he had been converted in 1787. On 21 Feb. 1851, in a letter to a niece in England, he complained that his greatest disappointment had been in the manufacture of fertilizer, which he had carried on for more than 30 years at a loss he estimated at over £8,000. In fact various debts had forced Woolsey to divest himself of his properties gradually during the final years of his life.

His obituary in the *Quebec Mercury* of 17 May 1853 described John William Woolsey as a man with an innovative, venturesome mind and exemplary public-spiritedness. It was doubtless this last quality that had earned him his commission as lieutenant-colonel of Quebec's 1st Militia Battalion in 1830.

MICHEL MONETTE

The papers of John William Woolsey and of his family are at PAC, MG 24, D1, 1–2.

ANQ-M, CE1-63, 19 mars 1797. ANQ-Q, CE1-6, 10 sept. 1840, 12 mai 1853; CE1-20, 28 juill. 1767; CN1-188, 4 mars 1841, 25 mai 1853; CN1-230, 31 oct. 1806. *Quebec Gazette*, 19 Jan. 1792; 23 Feb. 1797; 4 Dec. 1806; 22 May 1820; 17 June, 15 Aug. 1822. *Quebec Mercury*, 31 Dec. 1810; 17 Jan. 1815; 17 Dec. 1816; 10, 20 Feb., 7 Sept. 1818; 20 April 1819; 17 May 1853. Jean Trudel, *William Berczy; la famille Woolsey* (Ottawa, 1976).

WORRELL, CHARLES, lawyer, landowner, businessman, office holder, justice of the peace, militia officer, and politician; b. *c.* 1770, probably in Barbados, third son of Jonathan Worrell, perhaps by Catherine, his second wife; d. unmarried 6 Jan. 1858 in London.

Charles Worrell, born into a prosperous Barbadian landowning family which by 1800 had removed to Juniper Hall, Mickleham, in Surrey, England, was trained as a lawyer and practised briefly at Lincoln's Inn. This career was cut short when, in the first decade of the nineteenth century, Jonathan Worrell undertook to settle land on his sons in anticipation of his own death. Jonathan decided that the bulk of the family estates in Barbados was to go to the two eldest sons, William Bryant and Jonathan, and, in compensation, began in 1803 to purchase land on Prince Edward Island for Charles and the fifth son, Edward (the fourth son had taken up an army career). In the hope of imitating their father's success in Barbados, Edward

and, more especially, Charles were drawn into the Island's affairs.

Jonathan Worrell's acquisition of Lot 41 in 1803 began the formation of what was eventually a huge estate. Next year the father and his two sons purchased 17,000 acres on Lot 39 and one-third of Lot 40 (lots were approximately 20,000 acres each). Both Charles and Edward now moved to the Island and began construction of Morell House on Lot 40 as a base of operations. In 1804 Plowden Presland, an absentee proprietor, gave Charles control as his agent over Lot 42. Edward bought 10,000 acres of his own on lots 38 and 39 in 1813. When Jonathan died in 1814, the two brothers formed a firm, C. and E. Worrell, and transferred £3,286 to their father's estate in order to extinguish any claims by other family members to property on the Island. Charles also inherited a small portion of the Sedgepond plantation in Barbados, but apparently took no interest in it and sold it to Edward in 1841.

Charles had enrolled in 1810 as a barrister for the Supreme Court of Prince Edward Island, but used his profession only as a convenience for transacting land purchases and conducting commercial ventures. He was committed to, indeed almost obsessed with, the continued expansion of his land holdings. In 1824 he purchased 10,000 acres from Presland on Lot 42, and obtained the other half of this lot in 1839; he gained control of Lot 43 in 1834, and closed the mortgage on it in 1841. His final major purchase, in 1840, was the 10,000 acres of the undersized Lot 66. Edward had returned to England by 1830 and sold his portion of the partnership to Charles in 1836. The Worrell estate, at its peak in 1843, consisted of lots 39, 41, 42, 43, 66, and large sections of lots 38 and 40 – more than 100,000 acres.

Worrell's lands formed a solid block around St Peters Bay in Kings County. St Peters had been the centre of French settlement on the Island prior to the conquest and was attractive to British settlers at the turn of the century because over 2,000 acres were already cleared. To a proprietor this meant that, with little or no effort, he could attract settlers anxious to avoid the initial hardships of wilderness farming. As a result, much of the first settlement was secondary, involving Highlanders who had drifted eastward from the uncleared lands of lots 34–36 where they had originally been planted. Unfortunately, the long-term outlook for this north-shore community was not bright. The inescapable reality was that the lots Worrell collected were mostly poor agricultural land. As the century proceeded, and as the rest of the Island filled out, the population in his district and the number of acres under cultivation remained at a standstill. In 1803 the population on the lots Worrell would eventually control was just under 2,000, in 1833 just over 2,000; acres under cultivation went from 5,226 to

6,030. The importance of the community relative to the rest of the Island declined.

Worrell's determination to acquire lots persisted despite the agricultural deficiencies of the area and he made no sustained effort to attract new settlers, although in 1805 he did join William Townshend* and John Cambridge* in presenting Lieutenant Governor Joseph Frederick Wallet DesBarres* with a memorial claiming that he and other proprietors, including John MacDonald* of Glenaladale and Lord Selkirk [Douglas*], were making efforts to settle their lots and advance the Island's prosperity. His decision to set rents as high as two shillings sterling per acre on lots averaging only 50 acres, with leases of 40 years, when average rents on the Island were one shilling per acre on 100-acre lots with leases of much longer duration, merely reinforced geographic reality in discouraging settlement and gave him a reputation as an eccentric land manager. The only signs of improvement noted by travellers in the 1820s were Morell House and buildings on the adjacent farm. Nevertheless, Worrell did have some successes. As a resident, rather than an absentee proprietor, he took a passionate interest in the management of his estate. He reduced the impact of his high rents upon his tenants by his willingness to accept labour and/or produce (mostly potatoes) as payment. His constant supervision virtually eliminated squatters and free cutting of timber, problems which plagued other proprietors. With four shipyards, five sawmills, and a carding-mill on his land, he was able to exploit its non-agricultural resources and afford employment to many tenants. These ventures could not, however, compensate for the basic agricultural deficiencies of the land, and by the time Worrell left the Island he had dissipated his wealth, leaving himself, according to Edward Whelan*, "in a condition not superior to that of his poorest tenants."

Worrell occupied an anomalous social and political position on the Island: neither an absentee proprietor nor a member of the Charlottetown élite, he ruled over his own fiefdom on the north shore. Family ties and intermarriage were essential for social intercourse, and Worrell's unmarried state further isolated him from his neighbours and local peers. To visitors he appeared "rather shy and diffident." Given the size of his holdings, he could hardly avoid becoming a justice of the peace (1806), a high sheriff (for 1808), or a lieutenant-colonel in the local militia, but he did not enjoy such intrusions on his time and did not use the opportunities these offices provided to socialize with other Island worthies. And although he maintained a Kings County seat in the House of Assembly during the years 1812–13 and 1818–20 (by having his agents round up his tenants and escort them with banners and bagpipes to the polls), he was never permanently attached to any political faction. A member of the so-called "cabal" which unseated Lieutenant Governor DesBarres, and a conspirator in the movement which brought about the removal of Lieutenant Governor Charles Douglass SMITH, he was motivated in both cases by a personal concern to protect property from high taxes or escheat.

Worrell was appointed to the Council in 1825, acting as president that year, and retired in 1836 only to be reappointed to the Legislative Council three years later after Lieutenant Governor Sir Charles Augustus FITZROY restructured the councils. During this time Worrell was not an active or leading participant in the Council's affairs. His interest was aroused only by questions directly affecting proprietorial concerns, escheat being the most obvious but also such bread-and-butter issues as land tax assessment and road-building legislation. Worrell seems to have used his office primarily as a window on local political trends in order to transmit intelligence to fellow proprietors resident in London. It was London that Worrell saw as the centre of real political decision making on proprietorial questions, an understanding which, however correct, distanced him from a Charlottetown élite intent on expanding local power.

At the very time when his land acquisitions had reached their peak, Worrell began to consider retirement to England. He was now in his seventies and was, according to some, showing signs of senility. He resigned from the militia in 1840 and from the Legislative Council three years later. In 1844 he began to sell his land but, unfortunately, found less interest in it than he had hoped; two years later he advertised his property for sale as a block but no acceptable offers were forthcoming. Buyers hesitated, probably because of difficulties Worrell encountered in collecting rent from his 400 tenant families. Tired and frustrated, he turned over his Island affairs to a board of trustees headed by Theophilus DesBrisay and left for England in 1848. The board served him ill and he was to wait six more years before the estate was finally sold. In a transaction amounting to a swindle, William Henry Pope* purchased the land in 1854 for £14,000 and then sold it to the Island government later that year for £24,100. Worrell was thus provided with a belated taste of the problems absentee proprietors had often encountered by trusting local agents. The delay in the sale, the poor administration of the land in the interim, and the probable corruption of the trustees meant that Worrell's last years in London were property heavy and cash lean.

But his estate was to retain a symbolic significance, for the government's acquisition of it was a landmark in the evolution of the land question on the Island. It was the first in a series of government purchases intended to transfer land title from large proprietors to small tenant farmers [see Sir Samuel Cunard*]. Yet the importance of the estate as such should not overshadow the formidable character of Charles

Worrell himself, and the rare example he provides of a large resident proprietor.

M. BROOK TAYLOR

PAPEI, Acc. 2316/1–2; Acc. 2849/128–29; RG 1, Commission books, 13 Oct. 1806, 2 May 1808, 1 Feb. 1814; RG 5, Journals, 1825–26; RG 6, Supreme Court, barristers roll, 1 March 1810; RG 15, Crown lands, leases, nos.136, 180; RG 16, Land registry records, conveyance reg., especially liber 12: f.241; liber 23: f.447; liber 50: f.11. Private arch., J. C. Brandow (New York), [N. T. W. Carrington], "The journal of Nathaniel T. W. Carrington: a Barbados planter's visit to Nova Scotia, Prince Edward Island, Boston, New York, Long Island, Philadelphia and New Brunswick in 1837," ed. J. C. Brandow (typescript; photocopy at PAPEI). PRO, CO 226/25: 11–13; 226/26: 11, 152; 226/27: 82–88; 226/29: 70–71, 115; 226/37: 109–10; 226/39: 98–114, 129; 226/46: 108; 226/53: 13–14; 226/60: 552; 226/88: 248–69, 446–65. John MacGregor, *Historical and descriptive sketches of the Maritime colonies of British America* (London, 1828; repr. East Ardsley, Eng., and New York, 1968), 11. P.E.I., House of Assembly, *Journal*, 1812–13, 1818–20, 1841; Legislative Council, *Journal*, 1827–36, 1839–44. John Stewart, *An account of Prince Edward Island, in the Gulph of St. Lawrence, North America . . .* (London, 1806; repr. [East Ardsley and New York], 1967), 213–14, 217, 220–22. *Examiner* (Charlottetown), 31 July 1848, 15 May 1865. *Islander*, 5 Feb. 1858. *Prince Edward Island Gazette*, 14 Oct. 1818. *Prince Edward Island Register*, 20 Jan. 1825; 19 June 1827; 19 Aug., 2 Sept., 1828; 6, 27 April, 15 June, 3 Aug. 1830. *Royal Gazette* (Charlottetown), 3 April, 16 Oct. 1832; 9 April, 21 May, 13 Aug., 26 Nov. 1833; 18 March 1834; 3 Feb. 1835; 19 Jan., 28 June 1836; 12 March 1839; 8, 22 Sept. 1840; 8 June, 21 Dec. 1841; 26 April 1842; 7 Feb. 1843; 30 June 1846. *Weekly Recorder of Prince Edward Island* (Charlottetown), 31 Aug. 1811; 4 May 1812. *Canada's smallest prov.* (Bolger), 77. A. H. Clark, *Three centuries and the Island: a historical geography of settlement and agriculture in Prince Edward Island, Canada* (Toronto, 1959), 49, 58, 60–61, 70–71, 75, 84–86, 101. A. B. Warburton, *A history of Prince Edward Island from its discovery in 1534 until the departure of Lieutenant-Governor Ready in A.D. 1831* (Saint John, N.B., 1923), 310. [E. M. Shilstone], "The Worrell family in Barbados," Barbados Museum and Hist. Soc., *Journal* (Bridgetown), 29 (1961–62): 8–23.

Y

YORK, ERASMUS. *See* KALLIHIRUA

YOUNG, GEORGE RENNY, lawyer, newspaperman, author, and politician; b. 4 July 1802 in Falkirk, Scotland, son of John Young* and Agnes Renny; d. 30 June 1853 in Halifax.

Like his brother William*, George Renny Young was completely moulded in his formative years by his father, the well-known Agricola, who came to Halifax in April 1814 determined to accumulate "a fortune as quickly as possible, under any flag" and convinced he could be both a merchant and a literary man at the same time. Though only 12, George went to Castine, Maine, after British troops under Sir John Coape Sherbrooke* occupied it in September 1814, and for seven months helped his father conduct a thriving trade with a large stock of dry goods the Youngs had brought from Britain. Performing well, he won the plaudits of his father, who wrote that his faculties were "beginning to open & he will turn out a smarter fellow than I believed . . . should he persevere in his present very laudable conduct I shall give him a share of the profits." In time George, more than his brothers, would aspire, like his father, to combine a literary career with his vocation, and become his father's greatest champion, "lamenting the ingratitude of Nova Scotians who 'having slain a patriot refused to erect a monument to his memory.'"

For the next five or six years George continued working in his father's mercantile and agricultural concerns. In 1815 he took a small vessel to Fox Island in Chedabucto Bay and exchanged goods for fish. He found the islands the worst place he had ever seen for vice; when the fishermen were not at work, "they must be either fighting, frolicing, drinking or smoking." In 1821 he started his studies at Pictou Academy, despite the objections of his brother William, who thought it no place for him to attend. George enrolled in principal Thomas McCulloch*'s class in moral philosophy and found him despite "all his pecularities of character . . . a man of profound & accurate knowledge," who made his points so clearly and fully that no one could fail to understand them.

Late in 1824 Young started a weekly newspaper, the *Novascotian, or Colonial Herald*, eschewing at the outset anything that savoured of radicalism and declaring his attachment to the British constitution and the "enlightened character" of Britain's colonial policy. Rather than embroil the colony in political disputes, he did what he could to further material improvement. As a result, the *Novascotian* contained an amount of original material on provincial agriculture, industry, and commerce that made it unique among the province's newspapers. Young's few ventures into politics were to lecture the House of Assembly for its failure to promote provincial

Young

development. In 1826, when only 20 of the 41 former assemblymen were returned, he suggested that the rejected had paid the penalty for their negativism in this matter. As a newspaper publisher, he had many things going for him: his family saw that he had adequate capital, his father and brother William were frequent contributors, and his father's connections in eastern Nova Scotia and Britain assured him of correspondents outside Halifax. Not surprisingly, therefore, he quickly established the *Novascotian* as the best all-round paper in the province and Joseph Howe*, who lacked similar assistance, was somewhat fearful when he took it over in December 1827.

While publishing the *Novascotian*, Young had begun the study of law even though a Scottish acquaintance had warned him that, as a lawyer, he would be "constantly employed to confound right & wrong," that "the line of demarcation" between the two would become completely obscured, and that his sole objective in the end would be to win his cases no matter "what harm or injustice is done." At the end of 1827 he sold the *Novascotian* in order to pursue his legal studies full time, largely in Britain, and on 22 Jan. 1833 he was admitted as attorney, on 22 July 1834 as barrister. Thereafter he practised law in association with his brother William in Halifax. As a lawyer, he may have been outclassed, as a later biographer put it, in "the external graces of forensic eloquence," but easily held his own "in legal acumen, and profound research," especially in "ransacking legal authorities and precedents."

Just before entering upon his practice, Young had received publicity in two other matters, some of it wanted and some not. As part of a closely knit family, he worked vigorously to have William elected for Cape Breton County in 1832 and helped to make the campaign one of the best known of all provincial election contests when a committee of the assembly declared him to be a leader of the mob which, "armed with Sticks," expelled the friends of the opposing candidate from the hustings and inflicted physical injury "and the greatest insult and ill treatment" upon them. While in Britain in 1833, Young had been appalled by the ignorance of colonial resources and progress on the part of leaders of opinion. The outcome was the publication in 1834 of *The British North American colonies*, which, much as Howe would do later, showed the importance to Britain of the colonies and colonial trade, and emphasized particularly that the Royal Navy needed the support of a commercial marine plying between Britain and the colonies. In addition, he argued that the colonial fisheries were the best nursery of sailors for the navy, and that the colonies provided the most fitting station to maintain a navy against the United States.

Even more momentous was his lengthy trip to Britain in 1837–38 during which he received news of

his father's death – a traumatic shock for the entire family – and letters from his mother beseeching him to marry "some amiable woman at home" who might help her manage the farming operation at Willow Park. George, she emphasized, could never be happy with anyone who "was careless of your feelings . . . indifferent to your person . . . possessed of the love of fashion." But on 12 April 1838, even before she wrote, he had married a fashionable Londoner, Jane Brooking, daughter of Thomas Holdsworth Brooking*, a man of substance, élitist and authoritarian in outlook. The second personal object of his visit was to feather his own nest at a time when the separation of the Nova Scotia Council into executive and legislative branches was imminent. Unsuccessful in his first efforts to be appointed to the Legislative Council, George got his father-in-law to intervene on his behalf with Colonial Secretary Lord Glenelg only to be told that the matter rested between the lieutenant governor of Nova Scotia, Sir Colin Campbell*, and George Young himself. Not used to being spurned, Brooking was convinced that "foul play somewhere" would be discovered "when we come to sift the affair to the bottom." But for anyone to have expected that the young and inexperienced George would receive preferment of this kind seems nothing short of preposterous.

Professionally, Young acted during the trip for two absentee land proprietors in Prince Edward Island, David and Robert Bruce Stewart, who faced threats of non-payment of rents by their tenants and of hostile legislative action by the provincial legislature. He received assurances from the colonial secretary that he would take no action to escheat the lands of absentee proprietors, and in his turn proposed a plan, later elaborated in a pamphlet, which, it was hoped, would remove every ground of complaint and end the agitation upon escheats. Later in 1838, acting for his client-proprietors, Young worked with Samuel Cunard*, one of the Island's largest landowners, to draw up plans for the Prince Edward Island Land Company, in which the proprietors involved were to unite their holdings in a large-scale emigration scheme. George's mother was fearful because Cunard's power was "immense & . . . people fear him so much that they keep quite & submit. He never was friendly to our family & will give you a blow where he can." The scheme fell through when Cunard insisted on breaking some of the original arrangements, including the appointment of George's brother Charles as company solicitor. Brooking was so indignant at Cunard's treatment of his son-in-law that he hoped for "an opportunity of telling him so in person."

As a publicist and educator, Young could not be faulted for inactivity. His trip to England in 1837–38 produced a pamphlet on banking and currency in which he recommended sterling as the money of

956

account. He helped Abraham Gesner*, later to be the discoverer of kerosene, to establish a correspondence with natural historians in Britain. A past president and frequent lecturer of the Halifax Mechanics' Institute, he arranged communications between it and sister organizations in Britain, and in 1842 the Central Board of Agriculture thanked him for helping it make similar contacts. While mourning the loss of his wife, who died suddenly in December 1841, he devoted his time to carrying out an earlier idea of producing a volume of essays, in the manner of David Hume and Sir William Blackstone, on colonial education. The outcome was the publication in 1842 of *On colonial literature, science and education*, a collection of 12 lectures on general literature and science, national systems of education, colonial education, and eloquence, ancient and modern. The projected second and third volumes did not appear; the first evoked little interest and is today only a curio.

Young also turned his hand to writing a romantic tale, "The prince and his protégé," published anonymously in an eight-part serial in the *Halifax Morning Post & Parliamentary Reporter* early in 1844, and a little later under his own name in the New York *Albion*. Highly moralistic, it may perhaps be judged from its last two sentences: "Had Darnley not been a Christian, Edith Conway would never have been his. Religion was to him as it ever is here, the source of all our exquisite blessings." Young's papers indicate that he also tried to write poetry, apparently without much success.

Like his father and brother, George had attached himself to the reform cause, and like them he did not receive the recognition he hoped for because his political course seemed to be determined by self-interest. Certainly the Youngs' liberalism was strongly Whiggish and anti-democratic; from England, George's father-in-law warned them to have as little contact as possible with that windy demagogue Howe, a conclusion he could have reached only on information supplied by the Youngs themselves. Shortly after Howe addressed his celebrated letters on responsible government to Lord John Russell in 1839, George Young forwarded his own letters on the same subject. But though competent in substance, they were highly legalistic and lacking in the arresting analogies and the illustrative material that only a Howe could provide.

Young entered active politics in 1843 by being elected to the assembly for Pictou County and quickly became a potent spokesman for the reformers. In 1845 a reporter, hearing Young's speech condemning Lieutenant Governor Lord Falkland [Cary*] for making public certain dispatches unfavourable to Howe, wrote: "We have heard a good many speeches in our time, but one possessing more vigour and hard home thrusts we never heard." In 1846 the Halifax and

Quebec Railway became Young's chief concern and it was to have a major effect upon the rest of his life. When the project was first proposed to him in Britain in 1845, he had thought it "in advance of the age," but a subsequent visit to the Province of Canada and New Brunswick as well as an examination of the statistical information convinced him of its feasibility, and apparently he became the first prominent British North American to press for it energetically. In 1846 he got the assembly to promise its support as soon as the undertaking could be "entered upon . . . with prudence and propriety." During the same session Falkland, who had lost all sense of political objectivity, ordered tabled in the legislature a dispatch to Colonial Secretary Lord Grey in which he accused William and George Young of associating with English speculators of dubious reputation and of putting the names of respectable Nova Scotians on railway prospectuses without their consent. Outraged, Howe blurted out that such conduct would lead some colonist to "hire a black man, to horsewhip a Lieutenant Governor in the Streets." The Youngs, who had become colonial solicitors for the railway, showed that the prospectuses were tentative and intended to be kept secret, and it appears that any impropriety on their part was, at worst, grossly exaggerated. In 1847, as part of lengthy efforts by the Youngs, George got the assembly to adopt an address protesting the monopoly possessed by the General Mining Association over the mines and minerals of Nova Scotia.

Re-elected for Pictou County in the reform victory of 1847, on 2 Feb. 1848 Young became minister without office in the ministry of James Boyle UNIACKE, the first fully "responsible" government in the colonies. He was the government's most articulate spokesman while the ministers with office were seeking re-election. In 1849 he was one of three commissioners who supervised the efficient and economical construction of the electric telegraph between Halifax and the New Brunswick border. But the craving of the Youngs to be foremost in the public eye was already creating difficulties in the ministry. Even in 1848 Howe lectured George for wanting to transfer the responsibility for looking after the crossroads from the county members to the Executive Council, thus introducing the centralized control over roads that was in effect in the Province of Canada. As a penalty, he should be made to drive through the Canadas where, said Howe, he himself "once nearly had his neck broken by travelling by coach over rough roads." The next year the *British Colonist* was wondering whether the Youngs were intending to lead a party against Uniacke and Howe.

Again, in 1850, when Howe was pressing for the building of a railway from Halifax to Windsor – a project first proposed by William Scarth Moorsom* –

Young

the Youngs indicated lack of confidence in the survey and fears about its cost, perhaps because they did not want the line to supplant ones in which they were interested. Indignantly, Howe pointed out that they had attached their names to a much more speculative venture in 1845 and expressed his dislike of "this half friendship for a measure – which cuts its throat." When the assembly refused to proceed unless half the funds were privately subscribed, Richard NUGENT's *Sun* blamed its action on the "over-officious intermeddling of the Messrs. Youngs" and their "love and admiration of self." The break between George Young and the reform ministry came in 1851 after word arrived from England that Howe had secured an imperial guarantee for the intercolonial railway. When Uniacke sought the assembly's approval, Young called the British government's offer "niggardly" and argued that it should pay half the cost of the road to Quebec. He would later defend himself by saying that an opposition was developing to the Nova Scotia government's course and that he had attempted a *ruse de guerre* which, by occupying his opponents' position, would disarm them, but there was deep suspicion that he could not accept a project initiated by himself being taken over by someone else. In any case Howe returned from Britain to find suggestions in the press that "a foul disease" existed in the Executive Council that "nought but the surgeon's knife can cure." He also found that Uniacke had offered his resignation and refused to serve further with Young. While reluctant to interfere in a matter that had occurred in his absence, in his capacity as provincial secretary Howe secured Young's resignation at the request of Lieutenant Governor Sir John HARVEY. In his letter to Harvey, Young stated that truth was "the safest guide in the end" and that, although he had no differences with his other colleagues, he could no longer act usefully with Uniacke.

In July 1851 Young told his constituents that he would not offer himself in the general election to be held the following month. Partly, it was because he could not "give general satisfaction . . . among *so divided a constituency*" – his papers indicate great differences among Pictonians about such matters as the division of the county – but mostly it was because he was unwilling to pledge the provincial revenues for one-third the cost of the railway to Quebec and ill disposed to "get into any angry opposition with my former political friends" about it.

In a letter to Lord Grey, Howe attributed Young's aberrant conduct to a fall from his horse, "on his head on a very hard road, coming in from a Country dinner Party some years ago. I do not believe that he has been quite right since, he is now a confirmed monomaniac." Young was at his worst in a series of more than 20 letters, published in the *British North American* between July and October 1852, in which he fancied

he could discredit the press and leaders of both parties and "sit astride on a new world created out of chaos." Bearing the brunt of his attacks were Howe, William Annand*, and Nugent, who were told to "lay aside their blackguardism and masks . . . if we are to have the responsible system." In reply, Nugent told him that he was "notorious for companionship with characters which shall be nameless" and guilty of "bestialities, a knowledge of which broke the heart of a high-spirited lady, whose ample 'dowry' supported the means of his libertarian indulgences." Why, Nugent wondered, did not some friend of his bear the cost of "shipping him off where *madmen* are cared for and re-trained?" Whatever the accuracy of Nugent's comments, Young's mental condition in his last few years was such that no action on his part would have been surprising. Accompanying his "gloomy fits" were severe physical disabilities – failure of his digestive system, loss of strength, and intense pain – which made his last months a nightmare.

Talented in many ways, the most literary of the Youngs, more disposed to devote time to research and the collection of statistical information than any of his contemporaries, George Young died a tragic figure. Like his father and brother William, he pursued self-interest too obviously; unlike William, he lacked prudence, sagacity, and above all, the luck of being in the right place at the right time. His abilities made him deserving of a better fate.

J. MURRAY BECK

George Renny Young is the author of *The British North American colonies . . .* (London, 1834); *History, principles, and prospects of the Bank of British North America, and of the Colonial Bank, with an enquiry into colonial exchanges, and the expediency of introducing "British sterling and British coin" in preference to the "dollar"* (London, 1838); *A statement of the "Escheat question," in the island of Prince Edward; together with the causes of the late agitation, and the remedies proposed* (London, 1838); *Upon the history, principles, and prospects of the Bank of British North America, and of the Colonial Bank; with an enquiry into colonial exchanges, and the expediency of introducing "British sterling and British coin" in preference to the "dollar," as the money of account and currency, of the North American colonies* (London, 1838); *Letters on "Responsible government," and an union of the colonies of British North America to Lord John Russell* (Halifax, 1840); *Letters to the Right Hon. . . . Lord Stanley . . .* (Halifax, 1842); *On colonial literature, science and education . . .* (Halifax, 1842); and *Articles on the great colonial project of connecting Halifax and Quebec by a railroad: and ultimately the Atlantic and the waters of Lake Huron . . .* (Halifax, 1847). His romantic tale, "The prince and his protégé; or, 'tis fifty years since: a provincial tale, founded on fact," was published anonymously in eight instalments in the *Halifax Morning Post & Parliamentary Reporter*, 4–23 Jan. 1844; it was also issued as an anonymous pamphlet under the title *The prince and his protégé; a tale of the early history of*

958

Nova-Scotia (Halifax, 1844), and, under Young's name, as "The prince and his protégé: a tale of Nova Scotia," in the Albion (New York), 20, 27 April 1844.

PAC, MG 24, B29, especially vol.36 (mfm. at PANS). PANS, MG 1, 550–58, especially 554; MG 2, 719–25, 731–32. N.S., House of Assembly, Journal and proc., especially 1833, 1846–47. Acadian Recorder, especially 1821, 1851. British Colonist (Halifax), especially 1849, 1851. British North American (Halifax), 1852. Daily Sun (Halifax), especially 1852. Halifax Morning Post & Parliamentary Reporter, especially 1844. Halifax Sun, especially 1850. Morning Chronicle (Halifax), especially 1851. Novascotian, especially 1826–27, 1845–46. Times (Halifax), especially 1844, 1848. Belcher's farmer's almanack, 1836. Directory of N.S. MLAs. Beck, Government of N.S.; Joseph Howe. Robert Grant, Life and times of George R. Young (New Glasgow, N.S., 1886). D. C. Harvey, "Pre-Agricola John Young, or a compact family in search of fortune," N.S. Hist. Soc., Coll., 32 (1959): 125–59.

YOUNG, THOMAS, artist, teacher, architect, politician, civil engineer, and surveyor; b. c. 1805 in England, son of Thomas Young; he and his wife Mary Cordelia had two sons and four daughters; d. 3 Oct. 1860 in Toronto.

Thomas Young studied architecture in London with Charles Heathcote Tatham, a noteworthy exponent of the neoclassical style, and later acquired practical experience in that city with the engineering firm of Joseph Bramah and Sons. The reasons for Young's immigration to North America are not known, but by 1834 he had settled in Toronto, establishing himself as an art teacher and artist. From 1834 to 1839 he was a drawing master at Upper Canada College; in 1836 he conducted drawing classes at the Home District Grammar School. At the same time he sketched and painted the townscape, and in 1835–36 advertised for subscribers to his series of *Four views of the city of Toronto*, issued in New York City by the newly founded house of Nathaniel Currier. These accomplished lithographs, executed at an early stage in Toronto's development and the first generally available scenes of the city, provide valuable views of Upper Canada College, the recently erected provincial parliament buildings, King Street, and the city from the eastern shore-line. As was done in many of Currier's urban prints, Young's views were enhanced with architectural features then unrealized. To the parliament buildings, for example, Young added his own version of a porch that the government had been unable to build for lack of funds, and in the view of King Street he provided a steeple for the truncated tower of St James' Church.

Young remained active as an artist but, thoroughly acquainted with neoclassicism and other trends in British architecture, he soon gained greater prominence as an architect. At this time opportunities in that field were considerable in the rapidly expanding community. His first architectural work in Toronto seems to have been a house and outbuildings for Robert Baldwin SULLIVAN, completed in 1836. Later that year he prepared a plan for laying out the city's market block. Although considered by Charles Daly, the city clerk and an artist, to be "highly indicative of taste, talent, and perseverance," it was rejected in favour of the plan by John George Howard*, who had come to York (Toronto) in 1832 and was frequently to be Young's architectural rival. In 1837, following the rejection of a design submitted by Howard about 1835, Young obtained the attractive commission to design King's College. Retaining the monumental Greek Revival idiom of a plan drawn up a decade earlier by the English architect Charles Fowler, he reduced his scheme to one more suited to the Canadian climate but still magnificent both in effect and in its contemporary association with learning and refined culture. It consisted of a wide, porticoed central structure connected by a covered walkway to a pair of wings which would embrace a spacious forecourt, a traditional English layout clothed here in austere Neo-classical detail. The rebellion of 1837–38, financial constraints, and changes in government appointments delayed the start of construction until 1842; Young, however, modified the vacant parliament buildings to house temporarily the college classes which began in 1843 under the direction of the Reverend John McCaul*. Between 1843 and 1849 Young was retained by the college as its architect at an annual salary of £200. The southeast wing of the college, a three-storey structure of Kingston limestone with an imposing façade distinguished by a Greek Doric frieze and giant half-columns, was completed in 1845 in what would become Queen's Park. Now demolished, the building served as a residence and administrative centre until the passage of Robert BALDWIN's 1849 bill, which reorganized the college to form the University of Toronto, forced the abandonment of the remainder of Young's scheme. The university's attempt to proceed with renewed building in 1852, based on fresh plans from Young, was thwarted by Governor General Lord Elgin [Bruce*] for reasons which are not clear.

During the period of Young's concern with King's College, he secured major commissions from three new administrative districts: the Wellington District jail (1839–40) and court-house (1842–44) at Guelph, the Huron District jail (1839–42) at Goderich, and the Simcoe District jail (1840–41) at Barrie. The Guelph court-house, now much remodelled, was a symmetrical building with entrances into castellated corner towers and it had been conceived in the medieval mode then associated with administrative and legal authority, an early Canadian example being John EWART's London District court-house. The jails at Goderich and Barrie, which also survive, were

Young

distinctive forms based on the octagonal plan with radiating wings that was widely advocated in Britain in the first half of the 19th century.

Young's other known buildings were erected in the Toronto region. Of these, the only surviving structure is Trinity Church in Streetsville (Mississauga) (1842–43), now greatly altered. Following the destruction by fire of St James' Church in January 1839, he had designed a replacement and shortly after its designation later that year as cathedral church of the new diocese of Toronto [see John Strachan*] completed it with a handsome tower and steeple. The Anatomical School (named Moss Hall in 1879) was designed in 1850 for the University of Toronto's medical faculty. Located southwest of the former King's College, the school was a dignified Georgian form in classical style with colossal pilasters, complementary to the college but executed in white brick. As well, Young designed two market buildings, both in the Italianate style: St Andrew's Market, built of wood about 1849 with a surrounding piazza, and St Patrick's Market (1850–54), a compact, two-storey composition in brick, crisply detailed and set off with a tall bell-tower to announce its function.

Like all architects, Young produced a number of designs which were never executed. In Toronto neither his plan in 1839 to enlarge and complete Ewart's St Andrew's Church with a steeple nor his design a year later for the Church of St George the Martyr was implemented. In 1841 he designed a scheme for the city's Market Lane (Colborne Street) that was to have included a row of shops on either side of a masonic hall combined with a school or an exchange. Two years later his obelisk design won first premium in the competition for a new monument to Sir Isaac Brock* at Queenston Heights which would replace the one sabotaged in 1840 by Benjamin LETT. Rebuilding was deferred because of lack of funds and, when the competition was repeated in 1852, Young's composition of a gigantic Doric column was passed over in favour of the even larger and more flamboyant entry of William THOMAS. Young had also placed second to Thomas in 1847 in the competition for the design of Knox Church.

Young produced other architectural designs strictly for artistic purposes, and he continued to paint landscapes. As a committee member of the Toronto Society of Arts, which held exhibitions in 1847 and in 1848 to encourage a taste for the arts among local citizens, he submitted works that were largely architectural in character, such as his designs for Grecian and Anglo-Italian villas, his design for Brock's monument, and renderings of buildings in Hampshire, England. One of his water-colour landscapes won a first prize at the provincial exhibition of 1847 and his *View of Hamilton, from the mountain* was included in the Toronto Society of Arts exhibition

the next year. Of a specifically commercial nature were the sketches he made of Hamilton shop exteriors for advertising circulars. As in his prints of Toronto, Young effectively incorporated a lively portrayal of the daily activities of the townspeople. In the mechanics' institute exhibition of October 1848 four coloured engravings by Young and his model for Brock's Monument were displayed. The following year he lectured at the institute on the history of architecture, and was appointed drawing master for the Toronto Society of Arts. As well he was one of several local artists and architects to belong to the Canadian Institute, founded in 1849. For the 1851 topographical plan of Toronto, which was based on the surveys of two other institute members, John Stoughton Dennis* and Sandford Fleming*, Young drew the border illustrating the city's principal buildings.

For a brief period he involved himself in Toronto's municipal affairs, serving as a councilman for St Andrew's Ward in 1839–40. Between 1840 and 1842 he was employed part-time by the city as an architect, engineer, and surveyor. Late in 1842, however, he quarrelled with the city over matters of payment and threatened legal action. He was subsequently dismissed and replaced by John George Howard in May 1843. Young's professional life was further disrupted by marital difficulties. In 1841 he had left his wife, taking their youngest child with him, and, although a daughter was born a year later, the apparent reconciliation does not seem to have lasted.

Few details are known of Young's architectural office. For some months early in 1842 he worked in partnership with James Cane, another artist, surveyor, and civil engineer; during the early 1840s he employed William Robinson, who later became a surveyor, an architect, and London's city engineer. In 1847 Young worked with John Stoughton Dennis in laying out a parcel of land in the western area of Toronto. The professional climate in which Young practised was not always calm. During his work for St Andrew's Church he was taken to court and the project was taken over by Howard, who in competition with Young for other commissions was often incensed by his frequent pleas for extensions of time. In 1840 the intervention of the Goderich jail building committee in the execution of his plan led him to withdraw from the project; a prior letter from Howard to the committee outlining the proper duties of an architect cannot have smoothed the situation. During the construction of King's College a dispute arose between Young and the contractor, John Ritchey, over discrepancies in accounts and had to be adjudicated by a second architect, Henry Bowyer Joseph LANE. In 1844 Young, Lane, and William Thomas appear to have banded together to challenge Howard's appointment as architect of the proposed provincial lunatic asylum. About 1844 Young formed a partnership with the builder Daniel McDonald. They were awarded the contract for erecting the new market building on Front Street, designed by Lane and completed in 1845. Later that year Young was forced into personal bankruptcy, the reasons for which are not certain.

After the early 1850s Young's career clearly began to founder. His appointment in 1857 as clerk of the works for the construction of the city jail (now known as the Don Jail) displeased its architect, William Thomas, who evidently had not been consulted and furthermore would have preferred a more "practical man" such as a trades foreman. The municipal committee charged with investigating construction delays found Young's records of salaries and transactions lax and in 1859 he was replaced by James Price. Young's last known work was the arch erected by the Orange order in September 1860 for the Prince of Wales's visit to Toronto.

Young died suddenly of apoplexy a month later in a Toronto hotel and was buried, apparently by the benevolent St George's Society, in St James' Cemetery. According to an obituary in the Toronto *Daily Leader*, the "seductive but destroying influence of liquor" had undoubtedly contributed to the waning of his career as well as to the deterioration of his health. This and ever-increasing competition from other architects, often younger and better-trained, who had arrived in Upper Canada during the 1840s and 1850s, including William Thomas, Henry Bowyer Joseph Lane, Frederic William Cumberland*, and William Hay*, prevented him from fully realizing his potential.

His work demonstrates considerable range and ability. With choice of style carefully allied to function, his compositions, drawn from a variety of revival styles, reflect the eclecticism that prevailed in his period. That he was capable of richly conceived detail and design on a grand scale, with a sense of appropriate monumentality, is confirmed by his stately scheme for King's College.

SHIRLEY G. MORRISS

Surviving plans drawn by Thomas Young include those held by the MTL (J. G. Howard papers, sect.III, architectural plans, nos.220, 408–9, and plans of Toronto lots, no.726.5), the CTA (CRC 685.6, 1841), and the Univ. of Toronto Arch. (A65-0001). A drawing for King's College, unsigned but attributed to Young, is in the uncatalogued J. C. B. and E. O. Horwood coll. at the AO, as is a signed plan of the third St James' Church, Toronto. Other architectural drawings by Young and his sketch, *View of Hamilton, from the mountain*, are mentioned in the Toronto Soc. of Arts catalogues *Toronto Society of Arts: first exhibition, 1847* . . . ([Toronto?, 1847?] and . . . *second exhibition, 1848* . . . ([Toronto?, 1848?]). The *View of Hamilton* may be the same as Young's undated lithograph of *Hamilton, from the mountain road*, published in New York by the firm of Saxony & Major, and reproduced in C. P. De Volpi, *The Niagara Peninsula, a pictorial record* . . . (Montreal, 1966), plate 33. Coloured engravings by Young as well as his "model design" for Brock's Monument were exhibited in Toronto at the Mechanics Institute exhibition of 1848 (MTL, Toronto, Mechanics Institute papers, D25 (exhibitions, 1847–49: accounts and exhibits)). The Canadiana Dept. of the Royal Ont. Museum (Toronto) has in its Sigmund Samuel Coll. a set of Young's *Four views of the city of Toronto*, lithographed by Nathaniel Currier (New York, 1835). Young's commercial work also includes the pictorial border for the *Topographical plan of the city of Toronto, in the province of Canada*, compiled by Sandford Fleming and published in Toronto in 1851 by Hugh SCOBIE's firm.

ACC-T, St George the Martyr (Toronto), negotiations of the first building committee, 1840. AO, MU 296, sect.I, Thomas Young to Colonel Bullock, 31 Dec. 1842, 3 May 1843. CTA, RG 1, A, 1834–59; B, 1834–59; RG 4, D, 31 Aug. 1844, 19 Dec. 1845; E, 1858; F, 19 Jan. 1846. MTL, J. G. Howard papers, sect.II, diaries, 21 Jan.–4 Feb. 1837; 3, 22 July, 5 Aug. 1840; 28 Dec. 1841; 11 Dec. 1844. PAC, RG 5, C2, 26: 329, 359–60 (mfm. at AO). Royal Canadian Institute (Toronto), Canadian Institute, minutes, 7 Dec. 1850. St James' Cathedral Arch. (Anglican) (Toronto), Records of St James' Church, 1839–49; Reg. of baptisms, 1821–56; reg. of burials, 1835–50. St James' Cemetery and Crematorium (Toronto), Record of burials, 7 Oct. 1860. Univ. of Toronto Arch., A68-0010, I/A/3, 45: 2; A72-0024/001–2, King's College council minutes, 1828–42; A72-0050/002, especially Young to J. Joseph, December 1836; report of building committee, 2 Dec. 1843; Young to Boys, 20 Dec. 1843. UWOL, Regional Coll., Huron County, Ont., Clerk of the Peace, court-house building committee records, 1839–40. "The Brock Monument," *Canadian Journal* (Toronto), 1 (1852–53): 22. *Minutes of the Simcoe District Municipal Council, 1843–1847* (Barrie, Ont., 1895). "New plan of Toronto," *British Colonist* (Toronto), 29 Aug. 1851. Univ. of Toronto, Commission of Inquiry into the Affairs of King's College University and Upper Canada College, *Final report* (Quebec, 1852).

British Colonist (Toronto), 13 Sept. 1838; 29 May 1839; 2 Dec. 1845; 2, 27 July 1847; 27 March 1849. *Church*, 21 Oct. 1842. *Daily Leader* (Toronto), 4 Oct. 1860. *Examiner* (Toronto), 14 June, 13 Dec. 1848. *Globe*, 8 Sept., 4 Oct. 1860. *Hamilton Spectator, and Journal of Commerce*, 9 Oct. 1847. *Herald* (Toronto), 17 March, 16 May 1842; 15 June 1843; 9 Sept. 1844. *Independent* (Toronto), 1 Nov. 1849–17 April 1850. *Toronto Patriot*, 1 May 1835; 3, 27 May 1836; 19 Feb. 1841. *Weekly Mercury* (Guelph, [Ont.]), 8 March 1866. *Landmarks of Canada; what art has done for Canadian history* . . . (2v., Toronto, 1917–21; repr. in 1v., 1967). *Toronto directory*, 1837; 1843: 81; 1846–47: 82; 1850–51: lxxv–lxxvi, 141. William Dendy, *Lost Toronto* (Toronto, 1978). Ralph Greenhill *et al.*, *Ontario towns* ([Ottawa, 1974]), plate 21. MacRae and Adamson, *Cornerstones of order*. MacRae *et al.*, *Hallowed walls*.

YOUNG, THOMAS AINSLIE, office holder, militia officer, politician, and justice of the peace; b. 12 June 1797 at Quebec, son of John Young* and

Young

Christian (Christianna) Ainslie; m. there 27 Dec. 1823 Monique-Ursule Baby, daughter of the deceased François Baby*, and they had at least seven children; m. there secondly 31 May 1845 Ann Walsh; d. there 8 Feb. 1860.

Thomas Ainslie Young grew up in an environment oriented towards politics and trade. His father, a leading figure in the English party, was a member of the Executive and Legislative councils and also an important merchant at Quebec. His mother, a daughter of Thomas Ainslie*, Quebec's receiver of customs, proved an excellent business woman. Young received most of his schooling in Lower Canada, continuing his studies in London from 1814 to 1817.

Like other sons of influential people, Young quickly obtained posts in the administration. Before he was 21, he was appointed secretary to the committee of the Executive Council responsible for auditing public accounts. In 1820 he became controller of customs for the port of Quebec, an office his father had tried to obtain some ten years earlier without success. Moving up, he served as inspector general of the public accounts for Lower Canada from 1823 to June 1826, when Lord Dalhousie [Ramsay*] made him auditor general of the province. Young performed the duties of this office until 1834, but from 1829 there was virtually no provision for paying him a salary. In 1833 and 1834 he approached the governor and the House of Assembly to have this situation rectified. A committee recommended that he be paid the amount he was owed, but the assembly took no further steps. The reaction of the house may be attributed in part to the decline of Young's political influence after October 1834, and to its own struggle with political and economic problems of greater collective importance than individual administrative concerns.

Although he was an office holder, Young was elected to the assembly as member for Quebec's Lower Town in 1824, 1827, and 1830. In 1824 he maintained that he could reconcile his "public duties" with his "private interests." But it is possible that his first election tainted his political credibility, for he was accused of corrupt electoral practices. His opponent, James McCallum*, and a number of voters petitioned the House of Assembly, and the commission then set up heard the testimony of witnesses. Adjourned in 1825, the case was dropped by the petitioners two years later. It is not known whether Young was really out to take his father's place in the hearts of the Lower Town voters, as is suggested in a remark he made in 1834, "I counted on the well-known and long-tested character . . . of my late father." During the ten years he sat in the assembly, he was considered the spokesman for his riding's merchants. He took part in special and standing committees on economic questions, and particularly on finance and trade, matters in

which many people acknowledged his competence. Young voted against the 92 Resolutions drafted in 1834, for although he accepted the principle behind them, he objected to the methods proposed to carry them into effect. Before the elections of that year the merchants, "for reasons best known to themselves," chose to nominate another candidate, George Pemberton, and Young withdrew.

Young is chiefly remembered because he was inspector and superintendent (chief) of police for the city of Quebec from 1837 to 1840. Various factors doubtless account for this appointment: his role as sheriff of the district of Quebec (a responsibility he shared with William Smith Sewell from 1823 to 1827), his participation in parliamentary debates, his municipal experience (among other things as justice of the peace from 1828 to 1830), his "legal knowledge," his loyalty towards the colonial government, and the fact that he belonged to the predominant minority. *Le Canadien* considered the appointment "unfair," for Young had been reprimanded by the government for embezzling funds when he was sheriff. But the city of Quebec needed an administrator to ensure law and order. Even before the publication of the 1838 ordinance to establish an effective policing system in Montreal and Quebec, Young had brought the police in his own city under regulation, and he continued until 1840 to propose various measures to improve their efficiency.

By the autumn of 1837, in light of the real possibility of new disturbances, the government of Lower Canada needed a man who firmly respected the social and political order. Young hunted down the Patriotes and pseudo-Patriotes around Quebec, even as far as the American border. The 1838 ordinance gave him authority to act as a justice of the peace. Thus he obtained the right to issue warrants for search and arrest. The best known and most controversial of his raids was on the house of Mme Clouet, who was suspected of hiding Louis-Joseph Papineau* and a quantity of weapons. His most celebrated arrests were those of Étienne Parent* and Jean-Baptiste Fréchette, respectively the editor and the printer of *Le Canadien*, on 26 Dec. 1838, and Napoléon Aubin* and Adolphe JACQUIES, both of *Le Fastasque* of Quebec, on 2 Jan. 1839. Young accused these newspapers of publishing "articles of an inflammatory and very objectionable nature," creating discontent, and undermining confidence in the government. He used various methods of surveillance, such as scrutinizing the papers, visiting the post office and opening suspicious letters, receiving anonymous and sworn denunciations, and spying. For the sake of peace, he carried out preventive arrests of persons suspected of high treason or of "treasonable practices"; they were put in jail and released some time later.

Following this troubled period, the authorities

rewarded Young by appointing him police magistrate for the district of Quebec, a position he held from 1840 to 1842. After the post was abolished in 1843, he held no further public office of any importance. In 1845 he tried to get himself reappointed as inspector and superintendent of police of the city of Quebec, but without success. The following year he also failed to obtain the rank of major in the 1st Battalion of Quebec County militia. He may indeed have lost all political influence. Whatever the case, from 1846 to 1854 he addressed a new set of appeals to the government to recover his salary arrears from the period 1829–34, but again his requests fell on deaf ears.

Overshadowed by his father in the annals of Canadian history, Young had a career similar to that of numerous sons of the English-speaking élite in Lower Canada. His place in the public service was hand-picked, and he took advantage of the prevailing nepotism. Like many others, he enjoyed concurrently a number of lucrative offices and honours. For example, from 1826 to 1829 he was a member of the assembly, auditor general of the province, sheriff of the district of Quebec, a justice of the peace, a director of the Royal Institution for the Advancement of Learning, and a militia officer. His military career had begun when he joined the voluntary militia on 8 April 1814. He had been appointed an ensign in the 1st Select Embodied Militia Battalion of Lower Canada, stationed at Pointe-aux-Trembles (Montreal), and was then transferred to the Beauport battalion of militia on 24 Dec. 1817. On 1 May 1818 he was appointed "Capitaine Aide Major" (adjutant). He was promoted major in February 1825 and on 1 June became second major of this battalion.

Thomas Ainslie Young's loyalty to British institutions had led him to take an extremist attitude when he was made head of the Quebec police in 1837. The colonial government had found the ideal man for the job: respectful of authority, Young became a link in the administrative chain and carried out orders almost to perfection. He was an alarmist, and this trait served the interests of the authorities while provoking a good deal of anxiety in the Patriote population. His dogged persistence in hunting down rebels made him the "scourge of the Patriotes." From 1845, however, the wind of politics veered, and the last 15 years of Young's life were "uneventful."

MARCEL PLOUFFE

ANQ-Q, CE1-61, 26 sept. 1797, 27 déc. 1823, 10 févr. 1860; CE1-66, 31 mai 1845; E17/36, nos.2933–34, 2939; E17/42; E17/50, nos.4045, 4088. AVQ, I, 1, vol.3, 2 mai 1836–12 août 1840; II, 1, b, vol.4, août 1840–mai 1842; vol.5, mai 1842–septembre 1843; vol.6, septembre 1843–décembre 1845; Conseil et Comités, adresses de bienvenue; éloges funèbres, 1842–64; police, nos.1–2; policiers, no.1; prisonniers; V, B, 20 juill. 1814–10 mai 1833; IX, Administration, Dossiers administratifs, documents officiels, 1838–1920; émeutes, 1844–1919; estimations, 1842–69; finances, état général des dépenses, 1840–56; finances, liste de paie, 1841–42; habillement, 1841–54; mélange, 1844–1925; personnel, 1844–1921; prison, 1835–51; rapports du chef de police et des détectives, 1840–59; règlements, résolutions et ordonnances, 1833–1925; requêtes, 1840–52; requêtes des policiers, 1841–59. PAC, MG 24, B4. Can., Prov. of, Legislative Assembly, *Journals*, 1846, 1849, 1852–53, 1854–55. *Doc. relating to constitutional hist., 1819–1828* (Doughty and Story). L.C., House of Assembly, *Journals*, 1825–34. *Le Canadien*, 1814, 1817, 1820, 1823–28, 1830, 1832, 1834, 1837–40, 1860. *Le Courrier du Canada*, 1860. *Le Journal de Québec*, 1860. *Quebec Gazette*, 1797, 1814, 1817, 1823–34, 1837–40, 1860. *Quebec Mercury*, 1834. F.-J. Audet, "Les législateurs du Bas-Canada." P.-V. Charland, "Notre-Dame de Québec: le nécrologe de la crypte ou les inhumations dans cette église depuis 1652," *BRH*, 20 (1914): 301–13. Desjardins, *Guide parl. Officers of British forces in Canada* (Irving). *Quebec directory*, 1822, 1826, 1844–45, 1847–61. P.-G. Roy, *Fils de Québec*, vol.3. L.-P. Audet, *Le système scolaire*, vols.3–4. P.-B. Casgrain, *Memorial des familles Casgrain, Baby et Perrault du Canada* (Québec, 1898). Chapais, *Cours d'hist. du Canada*, vol.4. Chouinard *et al.*, *La ville de Québec*, vols.2–3. Ouellet, *Bas-Canada*. Rumilly, *Papineau et son temps*. Taft Manning, *Revolt of French Canada*. "Le choléra asiatique à Québec," *BRH*, 12 (1906): 88–92. Antoine Roy, "Les Patriotes de la région de Québec pendant la rébellion de 1837–1838," *Cahiers des Dix*, 24 (1959): 241–54. P.-G. Roy, "Le secret des lettres en 1829," *BRH*, 44 (1938): 123; "Les shérifs de Québec," *BRH*, 40 (1934): 433–46. "Shérifs de Québec," *BRH*, 7 (1901): 274.

Z

ZIMMERMAN, SAMUEL, businessman; b. 17 March 1815 in Huntington County, Pa; m. first 15 Aug. 1848 Margaret Ann Woodruff (d. 1851), and they had two sons; m. secondly 16 Dec. 1856 Emmeline Dunn, sister of Timothy Hibbard Dunn*; d. 12 March 1857 near Hamilton, Upper Canada.

Of German descent, Samuel Zimmerman was the fifth son in a family of seven sons and one daughter whose parents were "in humble circumstances." He received little formal education and began to work, originally as a labourer, at an early age. While employed on construction and public works projects in his native state he gained the basic experience which was to make him a rich man. In 1842 or 1843 he came to Thorold, Upper Canada, to become involved in the reconstruction of the Welland Canal being carried out by the Board of Works, in which the canal was widened and deepened and the original wooden locks were rebuilt in stone. By his own account he arrived "not with more capital than he knew what to do with" but he was ambitious and energetic. Between 1846 and 1849 he built, under contract to the board, four locks and an aqueduct. Though he required an extension of time to complete his contracts he gained a reputation, according to Francis Hincks*, as "one of the best and most successful contractors that had ever been employed by the Government at that time." This reputation was achieved at least in part by his refusal to allow work to be stopped on his projects during a series of strikes by canal workers. He afterwards claimed that he and other contractors had been close to bankruptcy during their work on the Welland but there is no doubt that he ultimately made a considerable profit, which became the basis of his later fortune. By 1848 at any rate he was able to travel widely and in comfort. In that year he married the daughter of a businessman and politician, Richard Woodruff of St Davids, and settled near Niagara Falls.

Zimmerman's success as a canal contractor brought him into contact with a number of influential businessmen and politicians, including Hincks, and into the field of railway construction and railway politics where Americans soon achieved a commanding presence. During the reconstruction of the Welland Canal, one of the "host of Yankees" employed by Zimmerman was an engineer from New York state, Roswell Gardinier BENEDICT, who had acquired extensive railway-building experience in the United States and who became assistant to the chief engineer of the Great Western Rail-Road in 1847 and chief engineer four years later. In 1849 he was influential in persuading its inexperienced board of directors to give a contract to Oswald, Zimmerman and Company, the firm organized by Zimmerman and James Oswald (another contractor on the Welland who was to be associated with Zimmerman in numerous business ventures). Construction did not begin until 1851, when the firm began building the eastern division of the Great Western, from Paris to Niagara Falls. Almost invariably Oswald and Zimmerman relied upon sub-contractors for actual construction. Zimmerman was also a promoter of and contractor for the Niagara Falls Suspension Bridge. Designed by the eminent American engineer John Augustus Roebling, it was completed in 1855 and connected the Great Western to the American railway network.

In his role of railway promoter and contractor,

embarking on the beginning of what many believed to be a golden age of progress and prosperity, Zimmerman quickly displayed a flair for publicity and showmanship. He organized free rides on the completed portion of the Great Western track out of Hamilton by day and lavish entertainments for prominent businessmen and politicians by night. Construction, however, was slow and in 1852 Oswald and Zimmerman were unable to complete the eastern division by the time specified in their contract. On the advice of Benedict the railway company nevertheless offered them a bonus of £17,500 if the work was finished by September 1853. Despite missing this extended deadline by two months, the firm was voted a bonus of £11,250 for "early completion," even though the line was in such an unfinished state on opening in November that the engine of the train carrying a group of dignitaries from Hamilton to Zimmerman's home at Niagara Falls fell off the track when loose rails gave way. Zimmerman's firm undoubtedly profited handsomely from the Great Western contract, which permitted extra charges above the agreed price per mile on the approval of the chief engineer, who, until his dismissal in November 1852 for grossly underestimating the cost of the work, was Zimmerman's friend Benedict.

Because the Great Western planned to build a number of branch lines during and after the construction of the main line from Niagara Falls to Windsor, Zimmerman attempted, with some success, to gain a degree of personal control over the company. His influence rested on a growing reputation for having the energy and resources to carry out large undertakings and on an equally useful reputation as a political lobbyist who operated on a grand scale. His lobbying on behalf of the Great Western had probably begun in the late 1840s when attempts were made in the provincial parliament to charter a rival ("southern") railway system, parallel to and south of the Great Western's route. The initial activities of the group advocating the southern railway, then led by Francis Hincks, culminated in a vote in the Legislative Assembly in 1850 in which a charter for the line was defeated by two votes. In 1852, when the Hamilton and Toronto Railway (built by a supposedly separate company but as part of the Great Western system) was seeking a provincial charter, Zimmerman "took an active interest in obtaining support from the members" of the assembly, according to Joseph Curran Morrison*, a member of the Legislative Assembly for Niagara and a director of the Hamilton and Toronto. Three years later, when the Great Western wanted its charter amended, its vice-president, William Longsdon, and its managing director, Charles John Brydges*, were told by Hincks, John Hillyard Cameron*, and Sir Allan Napier MacNab* that "the only sure way of getting our Bill" was with the help of Zimmerman – help which was provided on the condition that he receive a contract, on his own terms, to double the Great Western's track between Hamilton and London.

His system of lobbying, in the opinion of the engineer Thomas Coltrin Keefer*, included the maintenance of apartments at the provincial capital for the open-handed entertainment of "all the peoples' representatives, from the town councillor to the cabinet minister." As well he made full use of the favour of leading politicians with whom he was on friendly terms. He was known to be closely associated with Hincks while he was provincial inspector general and co-premier (1851 to 1854), despite their occasional support of rival railway interests. When Hincks left the country in 1855 to become governor of Barbados and the Windward Islands, Zimmerman publicly demonstrated his friendship and gratitude by entertaining 1,000 guests at his own expense at a testimonial dinner and ball. He also used the good offices of Sir Allan Napier MacNab, who was a past president (1845–49) and a director (1850–54) of the Great Western. In 1852 MacNab had tried to have the building contracts for both the Hamilton and Toronto Railway and the London to Sarnia extension of the Great Western given to Zimmerman, but a prior commitment to an English contractor, George Wythes, had been made by Peter BUCHANAN, London agent for the Great Western. Though an accommodation was reached by which Zimmerman received the contract for the Sarnia extension and compensation of £10,000 or £12,000 for his political services, MacNab, through the agency of Zimmerman and Isaac Buchanan* (a Hamilton merchant and Peter's brother), was replaced in 1853 as parliamentary agent for the Great Western by Joseph Curran Morrison, now the province's solicitor general and "a particular friend" of Zimmerman's.

Well before the completion of the Great Western, Zimmerman had begun to look for additional railway contracts. He belonged to a select group which grasped very quickly in the early 1850s how Canadian railway mania, American entrepreneurship, the province's new municipal system [see Robert BALDWIN], and public credit could be integrated for their personal and political benefits. He appears to have been extraordinarily adept in his use of the Municipal Loan Fund Act, introduced by Hincks in 1852. The act made rapid railway expansion feasible since it provided for a fund against which municipalities could borrow in order to invest in railways planned to run through them. This meant that if municipal officials, and the ratepayers through referenda, could be persuaded to contribute money to railway companies, lines could be built almost entirely at public expense.

Zimmerman took advantage of this new situation by using his growing reputation as a successful contractor and his powers of promotion and persuasion to become the contractor for a number of short railways.

In 1852, with A. P. Balch, he agreed to build the Cobourg and Peterborough Rail-way, of which Ira Spaulding, formerly engineer for the central division of the Great Western and an American friend of both Benedict and Zimmerman, was chief engineer. This railway, which depended for its operation on a bridge three miles long across Rice Lake, was badly engineered and built and was never successful, owing to the repeated collapse of the bridge as a result of ice. Despite the low quality of construction, Zimmerman refused to turn over the tracks or the engines and rolling-stock, which he also provided as contractor, until he had been paid in cash and bonds for alleged extra costs, greatly in excess of the original estimate. Meanwhile he had entered into a contract to build a parallel and rival railway, the Port Hope, Lindsay and Beaverton, which was constructed as far as Lindsay between 1854 and 1857. Though better built than the Cobourg and Peterborough, it also began operations in a near bankrupt state after paying Zimmerman's bills for the work. Zimmerman himself had contributed to the company's capital by buying $100,000 of first mortgage bonds, thereby effectively becoming a part owner.

As well as expanding his operations into new areas of the province, Zimmerman had soon changed his mind about the feasibility of a "southern" railway paralleling the Great Western. In the hope of building and running the proposed southern line, which could divert traffic (including the valuable American through-trade) from the Great Western, he became deeply involved in the affairs of two projected railways: the Woodstock and Lake Erie Rail-way and Harbour Company in 1853 and the Amherstburg and St Thomas Railway in 1856. The former, with the help of Zimmerman as lobbyist, was given parliamentary approval in 1853 and in 1855 to build extensions to St Thomas and to the Niagara Falls Suspension Bridge. With these extensions, the Woodstock and Lake Erie combined with the Amherstburg and St Thomas would constitute a southern route between the Niagara and the Detroit rivers. In November 1853 Zimmerman's company was hired to build the Woodstock and Lake Erie, of which Hincks was president and Benedict chief engineer. The contract had to be cancelled because of the railway company's lack of funds but in January 1854 Zimmerman's firm, which now included Luther Hamilton Holton* as a partner, regained it through the intervention of one of the railway company's directors, Henry de Blaquiere, who was paid $50,000 by Zimmerman for advising the rival contracting firm of Valentine, Hall and

Zimmerman

Company to submit a higher bid. Work began in the spring of 1854. When the railway company again ran out of money after paying Zimmerman $348,000, he lent it $50,000 to complete bridging and grading on part of the route. In October work was again suspended while negotiations were conducted among the directors, Zimmerman, and representatives of the municipalities through which the railway was to run and which had been asked to vote funds to support the line.

Zimmerman moved as well to gain effective control of the Amherstburg and St Thomas. In July 1856, as an initial step, he subscribed $1,000,000 of stock and deposited the 10 per cent required by law in his own bank. For negotiations with the railway company he enlisted the aid of Arthur Rankin*, MLA for Essex, by promising him a construction contract worth at least $100,000.

Zimmerman's organizational moves on both railways were blocked, however, by Isaac Buchanan, who, acting on his own but in the interests of Hamilton and the Great Western Railway, made an opposing bid to secure financial and directorial control over both halves of the proposed southern railway. This struggle reached a point in August 1856 at which two competing boards of directors for the Amherstburg and St Thomas were elected on the same day: one headed by Rankin, representing Zimmerman, and the other headed by Amherstburg businessman John McLeod, representing Buchanan. Buchanan's intervention, which involved an expenditure of $350,000 of his own and his firm's money to buy stock and influence, was repudiated by the British board of the Great Western. He eventually became convinced that only Zimmerman could bring the southern scheme to completion and worked for a reconciliation of the competing interests and for his own withdrawal from the affair. By early 1857 he and Zimmerman had completed arrangements which gave Zimmerman or his nominees control of the boards of both the Amherstburg and St Thomas and the Woodstock and Lake Erie. It was following a meeting held in Toronto to discuss the final details of the southern project (later built as the Canada Southern Railway) that Zimmerman "jauntily walked out of the hotel with his grip in his hand, and entered the omnibus for the Great Western Railway station," only to be "laid low in death" within 60 minutes. Just as his train reached the bridge over the Desjardins Canal, it left the tracks as a result of a broken axle on the engine, smashed through the side railings, and crashed into the frozen waters of the canal, killing Zimmerman in his attempt to escape. He was buried at Clifton but was later reinterred beside his first wife at St Davids.

Before his career was so suddenly cut short he had found time to become involved in a variety of ventures other than railways. In 1848 he bought the Clifton House, a large hotel at Niagara Falls, and began to renovate and upgrade it. At the same time he purchased several hundred acres of land on the Canadian side of the suspension bridge which he proceeded to develop by laying out streets, erecting commercial buildings, and selling building lots for a community named Elgin, which merged with Clifton in 1856 and eventually became Niagara Falls. A large part of his Niagara land holdings was sold in 1856 to R. G. Benedict and Ira Spaulding for $200,000. Zimmerman also built gasworks and waterworks for the growing town and in 1854, along with Luther Hamilton Holton, John Hillyard Cameron, and James Oswald, he founded there the Zimmerman Bank, of which he was president and Gilbert McMicken*, his lawyer, was cashier. It operated first as a private bank under the Freedom of Banking Act of 1850 and from 1856 as a chartered bank, and helped in the financing of Zimmerman's various undertakings. Almost the entire capital stock of the bank, $1,000,000, was held by Zimmerman, though only $453,000 was ever paid up. The bank, later described by a government commission as an "ephemeral" institution, was in fact badly underfinanced and was partially supported by public funds, loaned secretly and without government authorization in 1856 by Zimmerman's close friend, Joseph Curran Morrison, the province's receiver general. Zimmerman also owned the Niagara Harbour and Dock Company, which along with his own short railway, the Erie and Ontario, was sold to the Great Western Railway in 1854, an arrangement repudiated within months by the railway's British board. He owned one lake steamer, the 475-ton *Zimmerman*, commanded from 1854 by Duncan Milloy* and operated in connection with the Erie and Ontario, and had a part interest in a second, the *Peerless*. With James Oswald he took over the large flour-mills of Jacob Keefer* at Thorold in 1855 by foreclosing a mortgage which they held. In addition Zimmerman invested heavily in real estate in several areas of the province, especially at Hamilton and Toronto, his holdings amounting in 1857 to approximately 18,000 acres.

The precise extent of Zimmerman's wealth and power has been and must remain a matter of conjecture. It was widely believed by Zimmerman's contemporaries that he was one of the richest, if not the richest, man in the province. At the time of his death he was in the process of building a mansion to cost $175,000 on 52 acres of landscaped grounds overlooking Niagara Falls. Although he spent money lavishly, some of his ventures, particularly the bank and the Niagara Harbour and Dock Company, were decidedly unprofitable. His land holdings once said to be worth as much as $3,000,000, lost a great deal of their value in the depression which began in the fall of 1857. After his death the debt of the Zimmerman Bank to the Bank of Upper Canada was found to be nearly $248,000 and his personal debt to the same bank more than $348,000. Like many businessmen of the time he had operated largely on borrowed money.

His power as a political boss is more difficult to assess; it also, his contemporaries agreed, was far-reaching. The *Semi-Weekly Spectator* wrote in its obituary of Zimmerman that "his sway over other men was limited only by the boundaries within which he could possibly exercise it." Thomas Coltrin Keefer later maintained that he had "organized a system which virtually made him ruler of the province for several years." In a biography of Thomas TALBOT, written in the wake of the railway boom of the 1850s, Edward Ermatinger* went out of his way to articulate a more pointed reaction to Zimmerman: "His talismanic wand so operated on the minds of men, whether members of the Legislature, speculating engineers, or railway contractors, that they could only revel in golden dreams, or swim in champagne; and in this mesmerized state, Zimmerman did what he pleased with them." What can be said with certainty is that he was on intimate terms with many of the leading politicians of the time, and that he was highly successful in persuading members of parliament to support his schemes.

Zimmerman was characterized by Keefer as an unscrupulous "bold operator." Clearly he was no model of impeccable virtue. He offered and accepted bribes, and was ruthless in extracting maximum profits from the contracts he undertook. It must be said, of course, that his business ethics were no different from those of many of the businessmen and politicians with whom he dealt. As well he was an extraordinarily generous man whose public and private gifts to individuals, churches, municipalities, and the masonic order, of which he was a prominent member, were made on a large scale. He was also acknowledged, by Henry James Morgan*, to be a man of extraordinary energy who was prepared to work constantly to ensure the success of his many projects. He was a self-made man whose style was well suited to the circumstances in which he operated. He was very much a man of his time.

J. K. JOHNSON

AO, MU 2756, 85, Walter Shanly to Francis Shanly, 18 June 1847; RG 22, ser.155, will of Samuel Zimmerman. PAC, MG 24, D16; D80; RG 11, A2, 94: 321; RG 30, 2, 7 Sept. 1853, 4 Jan. 1854; RG 43, CVI, 2c, 2248: 344; 2249: 367. Can., Prov. of, Financial and Departmental Commission, *Report* (2v., Quebec, 1863–64), 1: 45–46; Legislative Assembly, *App. to the journals*, 1849, app.QQQ; *Journals*, 1857, app.6; Parl., *Sessional papers*, 1864, no.21; *Statutes*, 1853, c.234; 1855, c.179. Cobourg and Peterborough Railway Company, *Report of the directors . . .* (Cobourg, [Ont.], 1853). *Daylight through the mountain: letters and labours of civil engineers Walter and Francis Shanly*, ed. F. N. Walker ([Montreal], 1957). *Debates of the Legislative Assembly of United Canada* (Abbott Gibbs *et al.*), vols.5–9. Edward Ermatinger, *Life of Colonel Talbot, and the Talbot settlement . . .* (St Thomas, [Ont.], 1859; repr. Belleville, Ont., 1972), 227–30. *Full details of the railway disaster of the 12th of March, 1857, at the Desjardin Canal, on the line of the Great Western Railway* (Hamilton, [Ont.], 1857]). T. C. Keefer, *Philosophy of railroads and other essays*, ed. and intro. H. V. Nelles (Toronto, and Buffalo, N.Y., 1972), 159–60. "The late Samuel Zimmerman," *Canadian Merchants' Magazine and Commercial Rev.* (Toronto), 1 (April–September 1857): 177–81. *Daily Spectator, and Journal of Commerce*, 19 March 1857. *Examiner* (Toronto), 9 Nov. 1853. *Globe*, 14 March 1857. *Leader*, 7 Nov. 1855. *Mackenzie's Weekly Message*, 22 March, 12 June 1857. *Sarnia Observer, and Lambton Advertiser*, 19 March 1857. *Semi-Weekly Leader* (Toronto), 6 Nov. 1855. *Semi-Weekly Spectator*, 18 March 1857. *Weekly Dispatch, St. Thomas, Port Stanley, and County of Elgin Advertiser* (St Thomas), 10 July 1856.

DHB. Marriage notices of Ontario, comp. W. D. Reid (Lambertville, N.J., 1980). Morgan, *Sketches of celebrated Canadians*, 735–36. P. A. Baskerville, "The boardroom and beyond: aspects of the Upper Canadian railroad community" (PHD thesis, Queen's Univ., Kingston, Ont., 1973). D. R. Beer, *Sir Allan Napier MacNab* (Hamilton, 1984). M. F. Campbell, *Niagara: hinge of the golden arc* (Toronto, 1958). A. W. Currie, *The Grand Trunk Railway of Canada* (Toronto, 1957). *The history of the county of Welland, Ontario . . .* ([Welland], 1889; repr. with intro. by John Burtniak, Belleville, 1972), 342–43. Douglas McCalla, *The Upper Canada trade, 1834–1872: a study of the Buchanans' business* (Toronto, 1979). Walter Neutel, "From 'southern' concept to Canada Southern Railway, 1835–1873" (MA thesis, Univ. of Western Ont., London, 1968). F. J. Petrie, "Samuel Zimmerman, benefactor of Clifton (1815–1857)" (paper presented to the Lundy's Lane Hist. Soc., Niagara Falls, Ont., 1957). *Robertson's landmarks of Toronto*, 1: 50. J. M. and Edward Trout, *The railways of Canada for 1870–1: shewing the progress, mileage, cost of construction, the stocks, bonds, traffic, earnings, expenses, and organization of the railways of the dominion . . .* (Toronto, 1871), 117–18. P. [A.] Baskerville, "Americans in Britain's backyard: the railway era in Upper Canada, 1850–1880," *Business Hist. Rev.* (Cambridge, Mass.), 55 (1981): 314–36. J. A. Haxby and R. J. Graham, "The history and notes of the Zimmerman Bank," *Canadian Paper Money Journal* (Toronto), 13 (1977): 81–97. J. K. Johnson, "'One bold operator': Samuel Zimmerman, Niagara entrepreneur, 1843–1857," *OH*, 74 (1982): 26–44. B. A. Parker, "The Niagara Harbour and Dock Company," *OH*, 72 (1980): 93–121. R. D. Smith, "The early years of the Great Western Railway, 1833–1857," *OH*, 60 (1968): 205–27.

Appendix

PRESTON, RICHARD, Baptist minister and abolitionist; b. 1791 or 1792 in Virginia; m. 16 Aug. 1828 Mary ——, widow of "Cockney Bill" Maulibock; d. 16 July 1861.

The African Chapel in Halifax was filled to overflowing and its corridors formed packed spillways to the streets beyond. Hand in hand the mourners rocked and swayed together to the sounds of an old refrain. "The bishop is gone," said a forlorn voice. "He's crossed the flood to glory; protect him, Jesus!" said another. "A prince . . . a great man . . . has fallen in Israel," bellowed the Reverend Benson Smithers, stepping back as the choir renewed its refrain. He choked the words, "The founder of our churches, Father Richard Preston, is dead."

From a merchantman in Halifax harbour some 45 years earlier, young Richard had stolen his first glimpses of Halifax. A six foot one inch mulatto about 25 years old, Richard had been a slave in Virginia before purchasing his manumission. To Haligonians the literate former slave of manly bearing, who was a gifted orator with a disarming sense of humour, must have been an enigma. He had made his way north to Nova Scotia in search of his mother, one of about 2,000 refugee blacks who had left the United States during the War of 1812. Finding his mother must have seemed a hopeless quest to him; yet he persevered in faith, and, after many efforts, as he prepared to cease his search, he found her in the township of Preston. The rejoicing was longlasting and he remained with her there until her death. Finding his mother and having a home gave Richard a sense of greater purpose. He adopted the surname Preston, so as to celebrate the happiness and security which freedom had bestowed upon him. In Virginia he had been preacher to his people on the plantations and now, settled in Nova Scotia, he was to be an apprentice to John Burton*, a former Methodist missionary who at that time headed the Baptists in Halifax.

Since Burton's black worshippers were unwelcome in the other established churches, and since a black leader could not gain white approval, Burton's leadership of the black congregation was initially secure. In 1821 he was instrumental in having Preston act as the first black delegate to the Nova Scotia Baptist Association, and two years later he successfully moved that Preston be formally licensed to preach. However, as Burton's focus remained on the Baptist hierarchy, Preston had begun to realize the political potential of his black constituency, and the two men gradually embarked upon a collision course. By 1824 Preston was appealing to the bonding sentiments that were the cement of slave society in an attempt to coalesce the black congregations around his leadership. From rural area to rural area the news of Preston spread, followed by his authoritarian presence and his exhortations. Gradually, he strengthened his grip. He knew and understood the blacks' past, and his vision of their collective future was more to their liking. Put to this test, Burton lost his hold in the rural areas more and more. In the city, the upheaval in St Paul's Church (Anglican) in 1824–25 would mark the diminution of Burton's influence over his urban black congregation. When Bishop John Inglis* appointed the erudite Robert Willis* to the rectorship of St Paul's instead of the popular John Thomas TWINING, numerous dissenters, including Edmund Albern Crawley*, James William Johnston*, and James Walton Nutting*, left Bishop Inglis and descended upon Burton. Shortly thereafter, one of the leaders of the dissenters arose in Burton's meeting-house to declare his group's desire to be rid of the congregation's blacks. Despite Burton's disavowal of any intention of turning the blacks out, some black leaders began to make plans to secure their right of worship and, as Burton fell from acceptance, Preston's popularity grew.

If Preston was to preside at baptisms, marriages, and funerals, he would have to be ordained and he would need a chapel. Prince William Sport and John Hamilton, deacons of the congregation, collected money to send him to England to be ordained and to raise funds for the purchase of land and the erection of a chapel. Preston, carrying papers identifying him as a candidate for the Baptist ministry of a small church in Halifax, landed at Liverpool on 15 Feb. 1831.

At that time the battle for abolition was at its height in Britain and the abolitionists were making gains. In the midst of the eloquent arguments of such men as William Wilberforce and Thomas Fowell Buxton, Richard nurtured his own oratorical skills. He also found assistance and encouragement for his cause. A committee of the West London Baptist Association made churches and congregations available to him and Preston gave a good account of himself. There are records of some of his lectures on slavery and the sermons he preached. On 28 June 1832 the *Novascot-*

ian, reprinting an account from the *Brighton Herald* of a sermon in London, noted that "the Chapel was crowded to excess. . . . His manner of delivery is exceedingly pleasing, and in his dissertations he evinces much clearness and perspecuity." Preston had been ordained by the ministers of the association in May and that summer he returned to Nova Scotia with a little more than £600. Never forgetting the generosity of the British, he was also wiser in church polity, and the issue of emancipation burned stronger in his heart than ever before.

The official founding date of the African Chapel on Cornwallis Street was 14 April 1832, when Preston was in England. Construction began shortly after his return and by the spring of 1833 it was almost built. The congregation, however, required some additional financial assistance to complete the remaining work. On 6 April Preston presented a petition to the House of Assembly, which approved a grant of £25. The recommendation, however, was refused by the Council. Nevertheless, the chapel was completed, to the delight of the entire black community of Halifax.

The city's black citizens registered pride in this event for it was cogent evidence that former slaves could establish their own institutions in Nova Scotia, impediments imposed by the white population notwithstanding. As well as fulfilling its official functions, the chapel housed a school and served as a meeting-place. This humble little chapel was itself a symbol of freedom to its worshippers; yet freedom was denied American slaves. Hence, while acting as a prime mover in the expansion of his own congregation and assisting in the establishment of other black Baptist churches, Preston also turned his attention to the task of emancipation. To involve black Nova Scotians in pressuring for the release of American blacks from slavery, to inform all Nova Scotians of slavery's cruelties, and to campaign for the total abolition of slavery, Preston formed the African Abolition Society.

The earliest record of Preston's activities involving the abolition society comes from the year 1846. The *Novascotian* reported a meeting in August to decide upon a constitution and a further meeting in November during which Preston's views caused a disruption between blacks and whites present. None could refute the clarity of his argument, grounded as it was in the Christian doctrine that slavery was against the laws of God. It was through these meetings, and his able opposition to slavery in the United States, that Preston won support from the black and white citizens of Halifax and beyond. Such men as Charles Roan of Dartmouth, William Barrett of Halifax, and Septimus D. Clarke of Preston were counted among the executive members of the African Abolition Society. Nevertheless, although Preston's goals were genuine and his intentions were sincere, the society's success was limited. Although it managed to identify those

who were sympathetic to the blacks' cause and to improve racial relations, it had little if any effect upon the actual emancipation of American blacks.

On 1 Sept. 1854 at Granville Mountain, Preston launched his major contribution to Nova Scotian life, the African Baptist Association. This union of 12 Baptist churches, although a religious organization, was also formed to realize the socio-economic goals of its members and to safeguard their existing rights while working to establish further rights. However, the continuing spread of the Baptist faith and the creation of additional black churches were the main goals. The Halifax chapel was designated as the "Mother Church," and Preston was called its "Bishop." In fact, Preston was the association.

The success of Preston's ministry is beyond question. When he began the African Chapel in 1832 there were 29 baptized members. By the time the association was organized, its 12 churches contained 308 baptized members. In 1861, the year of Preston's death, there were 15 churches and 503 baptized members. One of the main reasons for this success was the combination of Preston's sharpness of mind and his delicate sense of humour. During one of his more successful "reformations" in the 1840s, he drew a large congregation within the Dartmouth Lake Church: without, however, a yet larger mob was determined to disperse the congregation and put the run to Preston. Said Father Preston: "We'll go outside, as the Grace of God gives me sufficient power over men and devils, I fear neither." The unruly mob thought they had succeeded in breaking up the meeting, but when Preston went to work praying for their souls "both saints and sinners were rejoicing. All was perfect peace." While exhorting in First Preston Church, Preston fell into prayer and, with the whole congregation quiet and absolutely still, the door of the church blew in. The giddy ones began to move around. Without changing the tone of his voice from that of prayer, Preston said: "Are you looking for Satan? Never mind looking for him, I'll tell you when he's coming in."

Richard Preston was one of those men whose great accomplishments were accompanied by obvious shortcomings. Through his efforts the African Chapel was established, the first meetings of the African Abolition Society were organized, and the African Baptist Association was born. Of these three major accomplishments, the first and the last have endured. But Preston had a major shortcoming in his failure to establish suitable democratic procedures for choosing his successor. On his death, the association went through a decade of succession struggles which nearly destroyed it. James Thomas, a white Welshman married to a black woman, succeeded Preston at the African Chapel and in the association. Almost immediately there was a movement to impeach Thomas and eventually a short-lived rival association

Preston

was formed by several of the churches. Preston could have prevented these struggles, but, having failed to do so, he left the institution in jeopardy. A second shortcoming was his apparent inability to link his organization's political potential with the need for improvement in his congregation's economic, political, and social standing within the province.

"Yes! . . . He was a great leader," said the Reverend Benson Smithers, "now it is time to bury him." "His ideals and thoughts will survive him," said the feeble Reverend Henry Jackson. "Can you remember him saying: 'Listen! Listen! At present we are a poor people. We have been so recently snatched from the cruel grasp of slavery and its concomitant degradations that . . . we have so little about which to be proud, compared to others to which my memories extend. Our change of life,' he would say, 'of soil – of climate – the substitution of a moral life for heretofore mere physical responsibilities, was so sudden and complete that it will take many years for us to readjust. But . . . readjust we must. The time will come when slavery will be just one of our many travails. Our children and their children's children will mature to become indifferent toward climate and indifferent toward race. Then we will desire . . . Nay!, we will demand and we will be able to obtain our fair share of wealth, status and prestige, including political power. Our time will have come, and we will be ready . . . we must be.'"

On 19 July 1861, at about 11 o'clock, a funeral procession passed through Halifax to the South Ferry, and then through Dartmouth on to Crane's Hill, where Richard Preston was brought to rest.

FRANK S. BOYD JR

ABHC, Menno [J. M. Cramp], "The Baptists of Nova Scotia (1760–1860)" (scrapbook of clippings of column by Cramp in the *Christian Messenger* (Halifax), 18 Jan. 1860–23 Sept. 1863), 241–44; "A sketch of the history (to 1897) of the Baptists in the city and county of Halifax" (typescript, [1897?]). PANS, RG 5, P, 42, 1833; 72, 1835; 80, 1824. African Baptist Assoc. of N.S., *Minutes* (Halifax), 1854–61. [John] Clarkson, *Clarkson's mission to America, 1791–1792*, ed. and intro. C. B. Fergusson (Halifax, 1971). N.S., House of Assembly, *Journal and proc.*, 1833. N.S. and N.B. Baptist Assoc., *Minutes* (Saint John), 1816–21. N.S. Baptist Assoc., *Minutes* (Halifax), 1822–50. David Nutter, "Reminiscences of the past," *Christian Visitor* (Saint John), 16 July 1856. *Acadian Recorder*, 30 Aug. 1828. *Christian Messenger*, 16 Feb. 1838. *Novascotian*, 28 June 1832; 24 Aug., 23, 30 Nov. 1846.

P. G. A. Allwood, "First Baptist Church, Halifax: its origins and early years" (M DIV thesis, Acadia Univ., Wolfville, N.S., 1978). A. P. [Borden] Oliver, *A brief history of the colored Baptists of Nova Scotia, 1782–1953; in commemoration of the African United Baptist Association of Nova Scotia, Inc.* ([Halifax, 1953]). F. S. Boyd, "Rebellion and peace in two plantation societies, Jamaica and Georgia, 1655–1802: a study in slave-planter social relations" (MA thesis, Dalhousie Univ., Halifax, 1975). S. E. Davidson, "Leaders of the black Baptists of Nova Scotia, 1782–1832" (BA thesis, Acadia Univ., 1975). C. B. Fergusson, *A documentary study of the establishment of the negroes in Nova Scotia between the War of 1812 and the winning of responsible government* (Halifax, 1948). C. V. Hamilton, *The black preacher in America* (New York, 1972). R. M. Hattie, *Old-time Halifax churches, some defunct, others absorbed, all either forgotten or on the way to be forgotten, but their memory and their name preserved herein: a compilation of their history* (mimeographed typescript, Halifax, 1943; copy at PANS), 31–35. [P. E.] McKerrow, *McKerrow: a brief history of the coloured Baptists of Nova Scotia, 1785–1895*, ed. F. S. Boyd, assisted by M. I. Allen Boyd (Halifax, 1976). H. H. Mitchell, *Black preaching* (Philadelphia, [1970]). *Repent and believe: the Baptist experience in Maritime Canada*, ed. B. M. Moody (Hantsport, N.S., 1980). R. W. Winks, *The blacks in Canada: a history* (Montreal, 1971). F. A. Cassell, "Slaves of the Chesapeake Bay area and the War of 1812," *Journal of Negro Hist.* (Washington), 57 (1972): 144–55.

GENERAL BIBLIOGRAPHY AND
LIST OF ABBREVIATIONS

List of Abbreviations

AAH	Archives of the Archdiocese of Halifax	GS	Genealogical Society of the Church of Jesus Christ of Latter-Day Saints
AAQ	Archives de l'archidiocèse de Québec		
AASJ	Archives of the Archdiocese of Saint John's	HBC	Hudson's Bay Company
		HBCA	Hudson's Bay Company Archives
AAT	Archives of the Archdiocese of Toronto	*HBRS*	Hudson's Bay Record Society, *Publications*
ABHC	Atlantic Baptist Historical Collection		
AC	Archives civiles	HPL	Hamilton Public Library
ACAM	Archives de la chancellerie de l'archevêché de Montréal	MAC-CD	Ministère des Affaires culturelles, Centre de documentation
ACC	Anglican Church of Canada	MCA	Maritime Conference Archives
AD	Archives départementales	MHGA	Maritime History Group Archives
ADB	*Australian dictionary of biography*	MTL	Metropolitan Toronto Library
ANQ	Archives nationales du Québec	NLS	National Library of Scotland
AO	Archives of Ontario	NWC	North West Company
AP	Archives paroissiales	*OH*	*Ontario History*
ASN	Archives du séminaire de Nicolet	PABC	Provincial Archives of British Columbia
ASQ	Archives du séminaire de Québec		
ASSH	Archives du séminaire de Saint-Hyacinthe	PAC	Public Archives of Canada
		PAM	Provincial Archives of Manitoba
ASSM	Archives du séminaire de Saint-Sulpice, Montréal	PANB	Provincial Archives of New Brunswick
ASTR	Archives du séminaire de Trois-Rivières	PANL	Provincial Archives of Newfoundland and Labrador
AUM	Archives de l'université de Montréal	PANS	Public Archives of Nova Scotia
AVQ	Archives de la ville de Québec	PAPEI	Public Archives of Prince Edward Island
BCHQ	*British Columbia Historical Quarterly*		
BE	Bureau d'enregistrement	PCA	Presbyterian Church in Canada Archives
BLHU	Baker Library, Harvard University		
BNQ	Bibliothèque nationale du Québec	PRO	Public Record Office
BRH	*Le Bulletin des recherches historiques*	QUA	Queen's University Archives
BVM-G	Bibliothèque de la ville de Montréal, Salle Gagnon	*RHAF*	*Revue d'histoire de l'Amérique française*
CCHA	Canadian Catholic Historical Association	RSC	Royal Society of Canada
		SCHÉC	Société canadienne d'histoire de l'Église catholique
CCHS	Canadian Church Historical Society		
CHA	Canadian Historical Association	SGCF	Société généalogique canadienne-française
CHR	*Canadian Historical Review*		
CLA	Canadian Library Association	SOAS	School of Oriental and African Studies
CTA	City of Toronto Archives	SPG	Society for the Propagation of the Gospel
DAB	*Dictionary of American biography*		
DCB	*Dictionary of Canadian biography*	SRO	Scottish Record Office
DHB	*Dictionary of Hamilton biography*	UCA	United Church Archives
DNB	*Dictionary of national biography*	UNBL	University of New Brunswick Library
DOLQ	*Dictionnaire des œuvres littéraires du Québec*	USPG	United Society for the Propagation of the Gospel
GRO	General Register Office	UWOL	University of Western Ontario Library

General Bibliography

The General Bibliography is based on the sources most frequently cited in the individual bibliographies of volume VIII. It should not be regarded as providing a complete list of background materials for the history of Canada in the 19th century.

Section I describes the principal archival sources and is arranged by country. Section II is divided into two parts: part A contains printed primary sources including documents published by the various colonial governments; part B provides a listing of the contemporary newspapers most frequently cited by contributors to the volume. Section III includes dictionaries, indexes, inventories, almanacs, and directories. Section IV contains secondary works of the 19th and 20th centuries, including a number of general histories and theses. Section V describes the principal journals and the publications of various societies consulted.

I. ARCHIVAL SOURCES

CANADA

ANGLICAN CHURCH OF CANADA, DIOCESE OF ONTARIO ARCHIVES, Kingston, Ont.
Records of various churches were consulted, in particular the following:
St George's Cathedral (Kingston)

ANGLICAN CHURCH OF CANADA, DIOCESE OF QUEBEC ARCHIVES, Lennoxville, Que. For a description of this archives, see: A. R. Kelley, "The Quebec diocesan archives; a description of the collection of historical records of the Church of England in the Diocese of Quebec," ANQ Rapport, 1946–47: 181–298; [A.] M. Awcock, "Catalogue of the Quebec diocesan archives" (typescript, Shawinigan, Que., 1973; copy available at the archives).
The following materials were cited in volume VIII:
  28: Letters patent setting apart burying ground in St John's suburbs, Quebec
47–71: Parish reports, correspondence, and other material relating to the parishes
    52: Gaspé, Granby, Grand River, Grimsby, Grosse-Île, Guelph
    71: Toronto, St Thomas, Valcartier, Waterloo, Waterville, Williamsburgh, Woodhouse, Yonge, Whitby
82–100: Copies of letters and papers referring to Diocese of Quebec
    99: 1844–45
  105: Stewart letters

ANGLICAN CHURCH OF CANADA, DIOCESE OF TORONTO ARCHIVES.
Records of various churches were consulted, in particular those of the following:
Church of St Peter (Cobourg, Ont.)
St George the Martyr (Toronto)

ARCHIVES CIVILES. See Québec, Ministère de la Justice

ARCHIVES DE LA CHANCELLERIE DE L'ARCHEVÊCHÉ DE MONTRÉAL. A detailed inventory of many of the registers and files of this depository can be found in RHAF, 19 (1965–66): 652–64; 20 (1966–67): 146–66, 324–41, 669–700; 24 (1970–1971): 111–42.
The following were used in the preparation of volume VIII:
Dossiers
  255: Diocèses du Canada
    .102: Kingston
    .104: Toronto
    .109: Saint-Boniface
  295: Diocèses du Québec
    .101: Québec
    .103: Saint-Hyacinthe
  355: Paroisses en particulier
    .110: Saint-Joachim (Pointe-Claire)
    .114: L'Assomption
  400: Clergé
    401.130: Conférences ecclésiastiques

420: Prêtres en particulier
.048: Chartier, Étienne
.101: Kelly, J.-B.
450: Prêtres étrangers au diocèse de Montréal
.904: "D"
465: Communautés d'hommes en particulier
.101: Compagnie de Saint-Sulpice
525: Communautés de femmes en particulier
.107: Filles de la Charité du Bon-Pasteur
576: Laïcs, "F"
901: Fonds Lartigue–Bourget
.017: Messieurs Maguire et Tabeau, prêtres; division de Québec et biens de Saint-Sulpice; missions à Rome; projet de journal ecclésiastique
.023: Mgr Lartigue; recensement; lettre de D.-B. et Jacques Viger; autres documents de Jacques Viger et Lennox
.025: Messieurs J.-G. Rocque et J.-V. Quiblier, p.s.s., à Mgr Lartigue et Mgr Bourget
.028: Mgr Lartigue; lettres de M. Montgolfier; lettres de prêtres et d'amis; règlements divers et documents
.078: Mgr Bourget; lettres de Mgr J.-C. Prince
.137: Notre-Dame et Saint-Sulpice
902: Fonds Fabre–Bruchési
.002: Mgr Fabre; lettres à sa famille et journal
RC: Registres de la chancellerie
RCD: Registres et cahiers divers
XXIX: É.-C. Fabre; cahier de notes; études à Paris
RL: Registres de lettres
RLB: Registres des lettres de Mgr Bourget. An analytical inventory of the correspondence of Mgr Ignace Bourget* from 1837 to 1850 was published in ANQ *Rapport*, 1945–46: 137–224; 1946–47: 81–175; 1948–49: 343–477; 1955–57: 177–221; 1961–64: 9–68; 1965: 87–132; 1966: 191–252; 1967: 123–70; 1969: 3–146.
RLL: Registres des lettres de Mgr Lartigue. The correspondence of Mgr Jean-Jacques Lartigue* from 1819 to 1840 is inventoried in ANQ *Rapport*, 1941–42: 345–496; 1942–43: 1–174; 1943–44: 207–334; 1944–45: 173–266; 1945–46: 39–134.

ARCHIVES DE L'ARCHIDIOCÈSE DE QUÉBEC. A guide to the collection is available in SCHÉC *Rapport*, 2 (1934–35): 65–73.
Series cited in volume VIII:
A: Évêques et archevêques de Québec
12 A: Registres des insinuations ecclésiastiques

20 A: Lettres manuscrites des évêques de Québec
210 A: Registres des lettres expédiées. Inventories of the correspondence of a number of the bishops of Quebec, compiled by Ivanhoë Caron, are available in ANQ *Rapport* [section III].
22 A: Copies de lettres expédiées
C: Secrétairerie et chancellerie
CB: Structures de direction
1 CB: Vicaires généraux
CD: Discipline diocésaine
515 CD: Séminaire de Nicolet
61 CD: Paroisses
69 CD: Visites pastorales
81 CD: Congrégations religieuses féminines
Diocèse de Québec (in process of reclassification)
CM: Église universelle
10 CM: Correspondance de Rome
7 CM: États-Unis
90 CM: Angleterre
CN: Église canadienne
30 CN: Terre-Neuve
301 CN: Îles-de-la-Madeleine
31 CN: Maritimes
310 CN: Île-du-Prince-Édouard
311 CN: Nouveau-Brunswick
312 CN: Nouvelle-Écosse
320 CN: Haut-Canada
330 CN: Rivière-Rouge
331 CN: Saint-Boniface
36 CN: Colombie-Britannique
60 CN: Gouvernement du Canada
CP: Église du Québec
26 CP: Diocèse de Montréal
E: Administration temporelle
J: Société ecclésiastique Saint-Joseph
T: Papiers privés
U: Archives des missions, paroisses et institutions

ARCHIVES DE LA VILLE DE QUÉBEC. A useful publication of this repository is *État sommaire des Archives de la ville de Québec* (Québec, 1977), edited by Murielle Doyle-Frenière.
Series cited in volume VIII:
I: Juges
1: Procès-verbaux des Sessions spéciales relatives aux chemins et ponts
II: Conseil de ville de la Corporation de la cité de Québec
1: Procès-verbaux
a: Journal des procédés du Conseil de ville de la cité de Québec
b: Procès-verbaux du Conseil de ville
Conseil et comités
V: Séries chemins
B: Juges de paix

VII: Série finances
  E: Bureau des cotiseurs
    1: Rôles d'évaluation et d'imposition
IX: Série police

ARCHIVES DE L'UNIVERSITÉ DE MONTRÉAL. The Service des archives of the Université de Montréal has prepared an important series of publications relating to its collections; a list of these can be found in *Bibliographie des publications du Service des archives* (3ᵉ éd., Montréal, 1980), compiled by Jacques Ducharme and Denis Plante.
  The following collections were cited in volume VIII:
P 58: Collection Baby. The researcher may usefully consult the *Catalogue de la collection François-Louis-Georges Baby*, compiled by Camille Bertrand, with preface by Paul Baby and introduction by Lucien Campeau (2v., Montréal, 1971). Transcripts of the bulk of this collection, which is being classified at present, are located at the PAC.
  A: Documents d'ordre familial
    A2: Notes généalogiques et biographiques
    A3: Contrats de mariage
    A5: Successions et tutelles
  C: Colonisation
    C2: Ventes et échanges
  G: Commerce et finance
    G1: Grandes compagnies – fourrures
    G2: Commerce, finance, affaires
  U: Correspondance générale
P 79: Fonds famille Lacoste

ARCHIVES DU SÉMINAIRE DE NICOLET, Nicolet, Qué. This repository, which is at present classifying its materials, has a catalogue index and both nominal and thematic card indexes.
  The following series were cited in volume VIII:
AO: Archives officielles
  Polygraphie
  Séminaire
AP: Archives privées
  G: Grandes collections
    L.-É. Bois
      D: Documents historiques
      G: Garde-notes

ARCHIVES DU SÉMINAIRE DE QUÉBEC. Analytical and chronological card indexes as well as numerous inventories are available in the archives.
  Series cited in volume VIII:
C: Livres de comptes du séminaire
  28: 1814–23
  31: 1823–36
  37: 1761–1809

  38: 1802–24
  39: 1810–21
  40: 1822–39
  41: 1825–43
  42: 1840–49
  43: 1844–49
  66: 1876–80
E: Cahiers et notes d'écoliers
Fichier des anciens
Fonds Plante
Fonds Viger–Verreau
  Cartons: Papiers de H.-A.-J.-B. Verreau; Jacques Viger
  Série O: Cahiers manuscrits
    01-C: Recensement des environs de Montréal
    015A: Pièce annexée par Jacques Viger au cahier intitulé "Chemins réparés à Montréal"
    018A: Tablettes statistiques du comté de Montréal
    021: Élection dans Montréal-Ouest, compilations et notes par Jacques Viger
    095–125: Ma saberdache de Jacques Viger
    0139–52: Ma saberdache de Jacques Viger
    0165–71: Journal personnel de Jacques Viger
    0189–96: Analyse des causes du juge George Pyke
    0521: Livre de comptes de la Compagnie du Nord-Ouest
Journal du séminaire
Lettres
  S: 1663–1871
  T: 1731–1875
  Y: 1742–1881
MSS: Cahiers manuscrits divers
    2: A.-J.-M. Jacrau, Annales du petit séminaire
    7: H.-F. Gravé, Application des fondations
    12: Grand livre du séminaire
    13: Plumitif du Conseil du séminaire commencé en 1678
    34: A.-E. Taschereau, Journal du séminaire commencé en 1849
    431–32: A.-E. Gosselin, Liste d'élèves, d'ordinations du grand séminaire
    433: A.-E. Gosselin, Officiers et professeurs du séminaire de Québec
    436–37: A.-E. Gosselin, Prêtres du séminaire
MSS-M: Cahiers de cours manuscrits
    15: Cours de physique par l'abbé Jérôme Demers
    16: Cours de physique par l'abbé Jérôme Demers
    16a: Charles Tardif, Cours de physique par l'abbé L.-J. Casault
    16b: Cours de physique par l'abbé L.-J. Casault

53: F.-G. Drolet, Cours abrégé d'histoire du Canada par l'abbé Jean Holmes
66: Edward Daveluy, Cours de philosophie par l'abbé P.-F. Turgeon
84: Hubert Hamel, Cours de physique et cours d'astronomie
86: Cours de botanique d'après M. Guyart par l'abbé Jérôme Demers
105: Cyrille Bochet et Octave Perron, Cours d'astronomie
109: Cours d'arithmétique par l'abbé Jérôme Demers
110: Cours de trigonométrie sphérique par l'abbé Jérôme Demers
115: Louis Gravel, Cours de physique par l'abbé Jérôme Demers
129: Cours d'architecture par l'abbé Jérôme Demers
131: Cours d'architecture par l'abbé Jérôme Demers
144: Cours de physique, cours de géométrie et cours d'architecture par l'abbé Jérôme Demers
155: Félix Gatien, Cours de philosophie par l'abbé J.-B. Castenet
159: Jean Holmes, Cours de philosophie par l'abbé Jérôme Demers et cours de théologie morale
160: É.-G. Plante, Cours de philosophie par l'abbé Jérôme Demers
161: Edward Daveluy, Cours de philosophie (2ᵉ partie) par l'abbé P.-F. Turgeon
162: Jean Holmes, Cours de philosophie et cours de grammaire par l'abbé Jérôme Demers
186: Cours de rhétorique et cours de philosophie par l'abbé Jérôme Demers
189: Cours de physique (vol.1) par l'abbé Jérôme Demers
190: Cours de physique (vol.2) par l'abbé Jérôme Demers
191: Cours de physique
192: Cours de physique
195: Cours de physique par l'abbé Ambroise Parent
197: Cours d'architecture, cours de géométrie et cours de physique par l'abbé Jérôme Demers
198: Cours de physique par l'abbé Jérôme Demers
214: Toussaint Papineau, Cours de philosophie et cours de grammaire par l'abbé Jérôme Demers
215: Joseph Petitclerc, Cours de philosophie par l'abbé G.-H. Besserer
219: François Morin, Cours de physique par l'abbé Jérôme Demers

232: Cours de physique et cours d'astronomie par l'abbé Jérôme Demers
266: Cours de physique (vol.2) par l'abbé Jérôme Demers
267: Cours d'arithmétique par l'abbé Jérôme Demers
433: Cahier de messe par l'abbé C.-E. Paradis
676: L.-N. Bégin, Cours de théologie morale
1014: Notes d'astronomie; définitions de la sphère, du soleil, des étoiles de l'abbé E. Montminy
1015: Traité élémentaire de physique; définitions de la physique de l'attraction, du mouvement et de ses lois; des causes qui changent la direction du vent; caloïque par l'abbé E. Montminy
1040–40a: Traité élémentaire de physique (4 vols.) par l'abbé Jérôme Demers
Polygraphie: Affaires surtout extérieures
Registre du grand séminaire
Registre du petit séminaire
S: Seigneuries du séminaire
S-168: Terrier censier, Petite-Rivière, Baie-Saint-Paul, Saint-Urbain, Île-aux-Coudres
Séminaire: Affaires diverses

ARCHIVES DU SÉMINAIRE DE SAINT-HYACINTHE, Saint-Hyacinthe, Qué.
The following series were cited in volume VIII:
Section A: Archives du séminaire
Série B: Relations avec les autorités ecclésiastiques, correspondance des évêques
Dossier 7: Prince, J.-C.
Série G: Personnel du séminaire
Dossier 1–13: Dossiers particuliers d'autres membres du personnel
Section C: Histoire religieuse, civile et politique
Série 1: Évêques et évêchés
Dossier 1: Histoire religieuse du diocèse: les autorités
1.7: Prince, J.-C.
Série 2: Paroisses, cathédrale, monographies paroissiales
Dossier 1: Paroisse de Saint-Hyacinthe-le-Confesseur
1.8: Requête de Mgr J.-C. Prince pour jugement de ratification, Cour supérieure de Montréal
Section F: Fonds particuliers
Fg-2: Chartier, Émile
Fg-41: Saint-Pierre, P.-A.
Dossier 5: Biographies
5.2: Blanchard, Meunier, Després
Fp-4: Chèvrefils, J.-O.
Fp-8: Prince, J.-C.

I. ARCHIVAL SOURCES

ARCHIVES DU SÉMINAIRE DE SAINT-SULPICE, Montréal.
Sections cited in volume VIII:
Section 1 bis: Démêlés relatifs aux biens
Section 8: Seigneuries, fiefs, arrière-fiefs et domaines
  C: Autres fiefs, arrière-fiefs et seigneuries
Section 21: Correspondance générale
Section 24: Histoire et géographie, biographie, divers
  Dossier 2: Biographies
Section 25: Séminaire de Saint-Sulpice
  Dossier 2: Emplois
Section 27: Le séminaire, les évêchés et les paroisses
Section 36: Missions
Section 49: Prédication

ARCHIVES DU SÉMINAIRE DE TROIS-RIVIÈRES, Trois-Rivières, Qué. A summary inventory for this repository was compiled by Yvon Thériault and published in ANQ *Rapport*, 1961–64: 67–134. A general inventory including the new classification system is in preparation.

The following were used in the preparation of volume VIII:
0009: Fonds Hart, famille
0032: Collection Montarville Boucher de la Bruère
0184: Fonds Dumoulin, famille
0296: Fonds J.-S.-N. Dumoulin
0368: Trifluviens du 19ᵉ et du 20ᵉ siècle

ARCHIVES NATIONALES DU QUÉBEC. In 1980 the archives undertook to establish a new uniform classification for its regional centres. Inventories, catalogues, guides, conversion tables, and useful finding aids on microfiche are available in all the regional centres of the ANQ.

CENTRE D'ARCHIVES DE QUÉBEC, Québec
The following materials were cited in volume VIII:
C: Pouvoir judiciaire, archives civiles
  CE: État civil
    1: Québec
      1: Notre-Dame de Québec
      2: Notre-Dame de l'Annonciation (L'Ancienne-Lorette)
      5: Notre-Dame de Miséricorde (Beauport)
      6: La Visitation de Notre-Dame (Château-Richer)
      7: Saint-Charles-Borromée (Charlesbourg)
      15: Saint-François-de-Sales (Neuville)
      17: Saint-Augustin-de-Desmaures
      20: Notre-Dame-de-Foy (Sainte-Foy)
      21: Saint-Nicolas
      22: Saint-Roch (Quebec)
      61: Holy Trinity Cathedral (Quebec)

      66: St Andrew's Presbyterian Church (Quebec)
      67: St John's Presbyterian Church (Quebec)
      71: Garrison of Quebec Anglican Church (Quebec)
      74: Anglican travelling missionaries, district of Quebec
      75: Aubigny Anglican Church (Lévis)
      91: Saint Sylvester's Presbyterian Church (Saint-Sylvestre)
    2: Montmagny
      3: Notre-Dame-de-Bon-Secours (L'Islet)
      4: Saint-Charles (Bellechasse)
      5: Saint-Michel (Bellechasse)
      6: Saint-Pierre-de-la-Rivière-du-Sud (Montmagny)
      25: Saint-Roch-des-Aulnaies
    3: Kamouraska
      1: Notre-Dame-de-Liesse (Rivière-Ouelle)
      12: Sainte-Anne-de-la-Pocatière (La Pocatière)
    4: Saguenay
      2: Saint-Louis (Île aux Coudres)
      3: Saint-Étienne (La Malbaie)
    5: Frontenac
      13: Leeds Anglican Church
  CN: Notaires
    1: Québec
      16: Bélanger, Jean
      17: Bélanger, J.-C.
      18: Belleau, R.-G.
      27: Besserer, L.-T.
      49: Campbell, Archibald
      60: Chavigny de La Chevrotière, Ambroise
      61: Chavigny de La Chevrotière, André
      62: Chavigny de La Chevrotière, J.-O.-M.
      64: Childs, John
      66: Cinq-Mars, Charles
      67: Clapham, J. G.
      80: DeFoy, C.-M.
      92: Dumas, Alexandre
      99: Faribault, Barthélemy
      102: Filteau, Joseph
      116: Glackmeyer, Edward
      138: Hunt, Joseph
      155: Larue, D.-E.
      157: Larue, F.-X.
      178: Lelièvre, Roger
      188: Lindsay, E. B.
      197: McPherson, L. T.
      198: Mercier, F.-X.
      208: Panet, Louis
      209: Panet, P.-L.
      212: Parent, A.-Archange
      213: Parent, A.-Ambroise
      219: Petitclerc, Joseph
      230: Planté, J.-B.

232: Prévost, Louis
253: Scott, W. F.
255: Sirois-Duplessis, A.-B.
256: Stewart, Charles
260: Tessier, Édouard
261: Tessier, Michel
262: Têtu, Félix
265: Trudelle, J.-B.
267: Vaillancourt, F.-X.
285: Voyer, Jacques
2: Montmagny
    30: Morin, Amable
4: Saguenay
    8: Gagné, Jean
    9: Gauvreau, C.-H.
    10: Hudon-Beaulieu, Heli
    12: Huot, C.-P.
    13: Kang, John
    15: Lévesque, Isidore
    16: Néron, Jean
    19: Tremblay, Édouard
E: Pouvoir exécutif
    17: Justice
        6–52: Événements de 1837–38
    21: Terres et forêts
P: Fonds et collections privées
    9: Bossange, Hector
    52: Couillard Després, Azarie
    68: Duvernay, Ludger
    69: Fabre, É.-R.
    75: Faribault, famille
    81: Fraser, famille
    92: Girouard, J.-J.
    174: Marchand, F.-G.
    193: Neilson, imprimerie
    240: Seigneuries
    316: Jobin, André
    417: Papineau, famille
    437: Société Saint-Vincent-de-Paul
P1000: Petits fonds
    11-203: Black, George
    22-399: Christie, Robert
    25-456: Crémazie, Jacques
    27-505: Deblois, J.-F.
    28-541: Desandrouins, J.-N.
    31-572: Dionne, Élézie
    37-694: Fabre, Hector
    65-1291: Lévesque, Guillaume
    76-1540: O'Callaghan, E. B.
T: Pouvoir judiciaire
    11-1: Cour supérieure
Z: Copies de documents conservés en dehors des ANQ
    Q: Québec (en dehors des ANQ)
        6-45: État civil, Catholiques, Sainte-Marie-
            de-la-Nouvelle-Beauce
    30076: Index des baptêmes, mariages et sépultures
        des protestants de la région de Québec,
        c. 1790–1815

CENTRE RÉGIONAL DE LA MAURICIE–BOIS-FRANCS,
Trois-Rivières
    Materials used in the preparation of volume VIII
include:
C: Pouvoir judiciaire, archives civiles
    CE: État civil
        1: Trois-Rivières
            2: Saint-François-Xavier (Batiscan)
            4: La Nativité-de-Notre-Dame (Bécancour)
            10: Saint-Joseph (Maskinongé)
            13: Saint-Jean-Baptiste (Nicolet)
            15: Saint-Antoine-de-la-Rivière-du-Loup
                (Louiseville)
            30: Saint-Grégoire-le-Grand (Nicolet)
            48: Immaculée-Conception (Trois-Rivières)
            52: Sainte-Anne (Yamachiche)
        2: Arthabasca
            72: Saint-Norbert (Norbertville)
    CN: Notaires
        1: Trois-Rivières
            6: Badeaux, Joseph
            7: Badeaux, J.-M.
            11: Rivard Bellefeuille, F.-A.
            19: Craig, L.-D.
            23: David, George
            25: Defoy, Augustin
            27: Deguise, Joseph
            32: Dumoulin, J.-E.
            35: Duvernay, J.-M. Crevier
            38: Gagnon, Antoine
            47: Guillet, Valère
            52: Labarre, D.-G.
            56: Leblanc, A.-Z.
            60: Leroy, Benoît
            62: Lemaître Lottinville, Flavien
        2: Arthabasca
            15: Côté, Théophile
            26: Pacaud, P.-N.

CENTRE RÉGIONAL DE L'ESTRIE, Sherbrooke
    The following sources were consulted in the
preparation of volume VIII:
C: Pouvoir judiciaire, archives civiles
    CE: État civil
        1: Sherbrooke
            41: Hatley Anglican Church
        2: Bedford
            38: Dunham Anglican Church (Dunham)
            42: Shefford Anglican Church (Waterloo)
    CM: Testaments
        1: Sherbrooke
    CN: Notaires
        1: Sherbrooke
            23: Richardson, C. A.
            24: Ritchie, William
T: Justice
    12: Cours des sessions de la paix
        501: Saint-François

Centre régional de Montréal
Sources cited in volume VIII include:
C: Pouvoir judiciaire, archives civiles
CA: Arpenteurs
1: Montréal
    17: Couillard-Després, Emmanuel
CC: Tutelles et curatelles
1: Montréal
CE: État civil
1: Montréal
    2: La-Nativité-de-la-Très-Sainte-Vierge
      (Laprairie)
    3: Saint-Antoine-de-Padoue (Saint-
      Antoine-sur-Richelieu)
    5: Saint-Enfant-Jésus (Pointe-aux-
      Trembles)
    6: Notre-Dame-de-Grâce (Montréal)
    8: Saints-Anges (Lachine)
    10: Sainte-Anne (Varennes)
    12: Saint-Antoine (Longueuil)
    16: Saint-Bruno (Saint-Bruno-de-
      Montarville)
    22: Sainte-Famille (Boucherville)
    26: Saint-François-Xavier (Verchères)
    28: Sainte-Geneviève (Montréal)
    37: Saint-Joachim (Pointe-Claire)
    39: Saint-Joseph (Chambly)
    48: Saint-Martin (Laval)
    51: Notre-Dame de Montréal
    57: Sainte-Rose (Laval)
    59: Saint-Vincent-de-Paul (Laval)
    63: Christ Church Anglican (Montreal)
    65: Garrison Anglican Church (Montreal)
    67: Hudson Heights Anglican Church
      (Vaudreuil)
    68: St George's Anglican Church (Montreal)
    81: St Stephen's Anglican Church
      (Montreal)
    92: Evangelical Congregational Church
      (Montreal)
    115: American Presbyterian Church
      (Montreal)
    125: St Andrew's Presbyterian Church
      (Montreal)
    126: St Gabriel's Presbyterian Church
      (Montreal)
2: Saint-Hyacinthe
    1: Saint-Hyacinthe-le-Confesseur (Saint-
      Hyacinthe)
    10: Saint-Charles (Saint-Charles-sur-
      Richelieu)
    12: Saint-Denis (Saint-Denis, sur le
      Richelieu)
    23: Saint-Paul (Abbotsford)
3: Sorel
    1: Christ Church (Sorel)
    2: Saint-Antoine (Baie-du-Febvre)
    12: Immaculée-Conception (Saint-Ours)

4: Saint-Jean
    10: Saint-Jean-l'Évangéliste (Saint-Jean-sur-
      Richelieu)
    28: Anglican Episcopal Congregation
      (Iberville)
5: Joliette
    1: Sainte-Geneviève-de-Berthier (Berthier-
      ville)
    4: Saint-Joseph (Lanoraie)
    8: Sainte-Mélanie
    12: Saint-Roch-de-l'Achigan
    14: Saint-Pierre-du-Portage (L'Assomption)
    16: Purification-de-la-Bienheureuse-Vierge-
      Marie (Repentigny)
6: Saint-Jérôme
    9: Saint-Benoît (Mirabel)
    11: Saint-Eustache
    25: Sainte-Thérèse de Blainville
    65: Presbyterian Church (Sainte-Thérèse
      de Blainville)
CL: Licitations, adjudications, ventes par shérifs
CM: Testaments
1: Montréal
CN: Notaires
1: Montréal
    7: Arnoldi, G.-D.
    12: Barbeau, Louis
    16: Barron, Thomas
    23: Beaudry, Édouard
    28: Bédouin, Thomas
    29: Beek, J. G.
    32: Belle, Joseph
    43: Boileau, René
    46: Boucher de la Broquerie, Joseph
    68: Cadieux, J.-M.
    69: Cadieux, G.-H.
    74: Chaboillez, Louis
    87: Chénier, Félix
    96: Constantin, J.-B.
    102: Crawford, W. N.
    110: Daveluy, P.-É.
    114: Decelles, A.-C. Duclos
    122: De Lorimier, F.-M.-C.
    125: Demuy, Charles Daneau
    126: Desautels, Joseph
    127: Desève, Charles
    128: Desève, J.-B.
    134: Doucet, N.-B.
    135: Doucet, Théodore
    143: Duplessis, A.-C. Le Noblet
    167: Gauthier, J.-P.
    175: Gibb, I. J.
    179: Girouard, J.-J.
    182: Grant, J. P.
    187: Griffin, Henry
    192: Guy, Étienne
    194: Guy, Louis
    208: Hunter, J. S.

213: Isaacson, J. H.
215: Jobin, André
216: Jobin, J.-H.
226: Lacoste, L.-R.
237: Laparre, Henry
243: Latour, Louis Huguet
269: Lukin, Peter (père)
270: Lukin, Peter (fils)
279: Mathieu, Pierre
295: Mondelet, J.-M.
304: Normandin, Louis
311: Papineau, C.-F.
312: Papineau, D.-É.
313: Papineau, Joseph
315: Paré, A.-P.
326: Pinet, Alexis
332: Prest, James
334: Prévost, Charles
353: Ross, William
372: Simonnet, François
375: Soupras, L.-J.
384: Trudeau, J.-F.
396: Weekes, George
2: Saint-Hyacinthe
  22: Dessureau, F.-L.
  29: Faribault, Barthélemy (père)
  73: Séguin, Michel
  80: Têtu, J.-F.
3: Sorel
  29: Crebassa, John George
  35: Desrosiers, Léopold
  81: Rousseau, Joseph
4: Saint-Jean
  15: Decoigne, L.-M.
  16: Démaray, P.-P.
  19: Faribault, J.-É.
  20: Gamelin, Pierre
5: Joliette
  3: Archambault, Eugène
  4: Archambault, J.-B.
  11: Brunelle, Joseph
  18: Faribault, J.-É.
  24: Joliette, Barthélemy
  30: Mercier, Pierre
  36: Raymond, Louis
  37: Raymond, J.-T.
  42: Therrien, J.-A.
6: Saint-Jérôme
  15: Lemaire, F.-H.
  29: Turgeon, Joseph
P: Fonds et collections privées
  24: Viger, famille
  76: Lacoste, famille
 155: Landry, famille
P1000: Petits fonds
  3-290: Viger, Louis
  3-309: McGill, Peter

3-383: Viger, Jacques
5-516: Viger, Jacques
10-596: Fils de la liberté
20-709: Viger, Jacques
34-805: Rébellion 1837–38
49-1097: Viger, Jacques

CENTRE RÉGIONAL DU BAS-SAINT-LAURENT–GASPÉSIE, Rimouski
  The following was used in volume VIII:
C: Pouvoir judiciaire, archives civiles
  CN: Notaires
    1: Rimouski
      5: Garon, Joseph

CENTRE RÉGIONAL SAGUENAY–LAC-SAINT-JEAN, Chicoutimi
  Materials used in volume VIII were the following:
C: Pouvoir judiciaire, archives civiles
  CE: État civil
    1: Chicoutimi
      2: Saint-François-Xavier (Chicoutimi)
  CN: Notaires
    1: Chicoutimi
      3: Chaperon, John
P: Fonds et collections privées
  2: Tremblay, Victor

ARCHIVES OF ONTARIO, Toronto. Unpublished inventories, calendars, catalogue entries, guides, and other finding aids are available in the archives, which is also producing finding aids on microfiche.
  Materials used in volume VIII include:
Canada Company records
  A: Administrative records
    2: Court of Directors reports
    3: Minutes of committees
    4: Reports
      5: Reports of the Court of Directors
        to the proprietors
    6: Correspondence
      1: Letter-books and general letters
      2: Correspondence with the commissioners
      3: Letters to the Court of Directors
  B: Land business records
    3: Registers and deed-books
  C: Accounting section records
    1: Ledgers
J. C. B. and E. O. Horwood collection
MS: Microfilm Series
    2: Records of the registrar general, Home District and Ingersoll
    4: Robinson (John Beverley) papers
    6: Crookshank–Lambert papers
    25: Thompson (David) journals
    35: Strachan (John) papers

I-6: Office of the registrar general
    A: District marriage registers
RG 20: Records of the Ministry of Correctional
    Services
RG 21: Municipal records
RG 22: Court records
Court of General Quarter Sessions of the Peace
    ser.7: Register of payment of land taxes
  Brockville
    ser.12: Minutes
    ser.14: Case files
    ser.14a: Crown Office fee-book by account
  Cornwall
    ser.47: Minutes
  Perth
    ser.75: Minutes
  Prince Edward District
    ser.83: Minutes
  Home District
    ser.94: Minutes
  Western District
    ser.103: Minutes
Court of King's Bench
    ser.125: Term-books
    ser.131: Judgement docket-books
    ser.134: Assize minute-books
    ser.143: High Treason (1814) records
    ser.144: Alien Act (1814) records
Court of Probate
    ser.155: estate files
Surrogate Court
    ser.159: Kingston (Frontenac), estate files
    ser.164: Perth (Lanark), registers
    ser.176: Brockville (Leeds and Grenville),
      registers
    ser.179: Brockville, estate files
    ser.187: Cobourg (Northumberland and
      Durham), registers
    ser.191: Cobourg, estate files
    ser.198: Cornwall (Stormont, Dundas, and
      Glengarry), estate files
    ser.204: Hamilton (Wentworth), registers
    ser.205: Hamilton, estate files
    ser.211: Kitchener (Waterloo), registers
    ser.214: Kitchener, estate files
    ser.224: Ottawa (Carleton), registers
    ser.235: St Catharines (Niagara North), estate
      files
    ser.256: Cayuga (Haldimand), registers
    ser.260: Cayuga, estate files
    ser.264: Whitby (Ontario), estate files
    ser.289: Welland (Niagara South), estate files
    ser.302: Toronto (York), registers
    ser.305: Toronto, estate files
    ser.310: Windsor (Essex), registers
    ser.321: London (Middlesex), estate files

RG 53: Records of the Department of the Provincial
    Secretary, recording office
    ser.2-2: Index to patents by name
RG 55: Companies Division
    ser.3: Toronto and York County, records of
      business partnership registration

ARCHIVES OF THE ARCHDIOCESE OF HALIFAX.
    Collections cited in volume VIII include:
Edmund Burke papers
Thomas Louis Connolly papers
William Fraser papers
William Walsh papers

ARCHIVES OF THE ARCHDIOCESE OF ST JOHN'S.
    Collections cited in volume VIII include:
Michael Anthony Fleming papers
John Thomas Mullock papers

ARCHIVES OF THE ARCHDIOCESE OF TORONTO.
    Material from the following series was cited in
the preparation of volume VIII:
Series 1: Documents and letters relating to the history
    of the Catholic Church in the western part of
    the diocese of Upper Canada prior to the
    establishment of the diocese of Toronto,
    December 17th, 1841. An inventory of the
    series has been compiled by the Reverend
    Gordon A. Bean (typescript, Toronto,
    1970).
  A: Administration of Bishop Alexander
    Macdonell
    AB: Letters and papers of others, clergy and
      lay, involved in the history of the church
    AC: Letters and other papers relating to
      various missions in the diocese
  C: Supplementary material
    CA: Letters, arranged by sender
    CB: Miscellaneous documents, arranged by
      place

ARCHIVES PAROISSIALES. The more noteworthy holdings of parish archives in Quebec are the registers of
baptisms, marriages, and burials; copies are deposited
with the Archives civiles of the judicial district in
which the parish is located [*see* Québec, Ministère de
la Justice]. Parish archives usually contain many other
documents, including parish account-books, records
of the *fabriques*, registers of parish confraternities,
notebooks of sermons, and sometimes correspondence.

ATLANTIC BAPTIST HISTORICAL COLLECTION, Acadia
University, Wolfville, N.S. Although outdated, *A
catalogue of the Maritime Baptist Historical Collection in the library of Acadia University* (Kentville,

N.S., 1955) provides useful information on the collection.

Collections cited in volume VIII include:
Edward Manning papers
Records of various churches

BIBLIOTHÈQUE DE LA VILLE DE MONTRÉAL, SALLE GAGNON.

The following were cited in volume VIII:
Collection Gagnon
Fonds Ægidius Fauteux
MSS

BIBLIOTHÈQUE NATIONALE DU QUÉBEC, DÉPARTE-MENT DES MANUSCRITS, Montréal. A description of the collections held in this department is found in *Catalogue des manuscrits* (Montréal), the latest edition of which was published in 1978.

Sections cited in volume VIII:
Manuscrits
MSS-101: Société historique de Montréal
Collection La Fontaine. For a complete inventory of this collection see: *Inventaire de la collection Lafontaine*, Elizabeth [Abbott] Nish, compil. (Montréal, 1967).

BUREAU D'ENREGISTREMENT. *See* Québec, Ministère de la Justice

CITY OF TORONTO ARCHIVES.

Materials used in the preparation of volume VIII include:
CRC: Architectural plans
RG 1: City Council
  A: Minutes
  B: Papers
RG 4: Finance Department
  D: Cash-books
  E: General journals
  F: General ledgers
RG 5: City Clerk's Department
  F: Assessment rolls

HAMILTON PUBLIC LIBRARY, Special Collections Department, Hamilton, Ont.

The following series were used:
Archives files
Clipping files
Hamilton – biography
Scrap-books
  H. F. Gardiner
  Historic houses in Hamilton

HUDSON'S BAY COMPANY ARCHIVES. *See* Provincial Archives of Manitoba

McCORD MUSEUM, Montreal.

The following were cited:
Jacob De Witt papers
Gerald Hart papers
McCord papers
John McDonald of Garth accounts
Molson family papers

MARITIME CONFERENCE ARCHIVES. *See* United Church of Canada

MARITIME HISTORY GROUP ARCHIVES, Memorial University of Newfoundland, St John's. For information on the collections held at the archives see *Preliminary inventory of records held at the Maritime History Group*, comp. Roberta Thomas under the direction of Keith Matthews ([St John's, 1978]); *Check list of research studies pertaining to the history of Newfoundland in the archives of the Maritime History Group* (7th ed., [St John's], 1984); and *An index to the name files . . .* , comp. Gert Crosbie under the direction of Keith Matthews ([St John's], 1981). Various other indexes to individual collections at the archives are also available.

Materials cited in volume VIII include:
Name file collection. This collection consists of some 20,000 files, arranged by surname, concerning anyone connected in any way with the Newfoundland trade or fisheries, 1640–1850. The files are compiled from a wide range of sources, and each entry includes a reference to the original source.

METROPOLITAN TORONTO LIBRARY. Canadian History Department, Baldwin Room. For information on the library's manuscript holdings, see *Guide to the manuscript collection in the Toronto Public Libraries* (Toronto, 1954).

Manuscripts consulted for volume VIII include:
William Allan papers
Robert Baldwin papers
William Warren Baldwin papers
John George Howard papers
Samuel Peters Jarvis papers
Henry Langley papers
William Dummer Powell papers
Toronto, Mechanics Institute papers

MINISTÈRE DES AFFAIRES CULTURELLES, CENTRE DE DOCUMENTATION. *See* Québec, Ministère des Affaires culturelles

NEW BRUNSWICK MUSEUM, Saint John, N.B. For a description of its holdings *see* New Brunswick Museum, *Inventory of manuscripts, 1967* ([Saint John, 1967]).

Materials cited in volume VIII include:

C: Clipping files; folders and scrap-books of newspaper clippings

CB DOC: Vertical files containing original and photocopied documents

F: Folders

F51: New Brunswick land grants, surveyed by Charles Morris, 1784

F64: Miscellaneous correspondence

W. F. Ganong collection

H. T. Hazen collection

    Ward Chipman papers

N.B. Hist. Soc. papers

Register of marriages for the city and county of Saint John, book A (1810–28)

SB 42: "Canadian history" scrap-book

PRESBYTERIAN CHURCH IN CANADA ARCHIVES, Toronto.

    Materials used in volume VIII include:

St Gabriel Street Church (Montreal), Register of baptisms, marriages, and burials

PRINCE EDWARD ISLAND MUSEUM AND HERITAGE FOUNDATION, Charlottetown. Various files were consulted in the preparation of volume VIII for biographical and genealogical data on Island residents.

PROVINCIAL ARCHIVES OF BRITISH COLUMBIA, Victoria. Manuscript collections are being listed in PABC, *Manuscript inventory*, ed. Frances Gundry (3v. to date, [Victoria], 1976–   ).

    The following were used in the preparation of volume VIII:

AB20: McDonald, Archibald

    C72M: Fort Colvile, correspondence

        .1: Archibald McDonald correspondence

    Ka3A: Fort Kamloops, correspondence

    L2: Fort Langley, journal

    L3A: Fort Langley, correspondence

AB40: McDonald, Archibald

    M142: Correspondence outward

A/C/20: Fort Victoria, correspondence outward to HBC

A/C/30Si6c: "James Sinclair: an early colonizer of Oregon" (n.d.)

Add. MSS 505: Helmcken, John Sebastian

    520: Victoria, Christ Church Cathedral

    635: Ross, Donald

C/AA/10: Vancouver Island, governor (Douglas)

    .1/2: Despatches to London

    .4/1: Correspondence outward

E/B/B62.3: Blinkhorn, Thomas, commission as justice of the peace and magistrate

E/B/Si6: James Sinclair, correspondence outward

PROVINCIAL ARCHIVES OF MANITOBA, Winnipeg. This repository puts at the disposal of researchers a central card index and unpublished preliminary inventories and finding aids.

    Materials used in the preparation of volume VIII:

MG 2: Red River settlement

    A: Selkirk period

        1: Selkirk, Thomas Douglas

        5: Pelly, Robert Parker

    B: Council of Assiniboia

        2: Papers and financial records of Council of Assiniboia

        3: Census

        4: Court records

        4-1: Minutes of General Quarterly Court

    C: Individuals and settlement

        3: Cary, George Marcus

        14: Ross, Alexander, family

        38: Garrioch, Peter

MG 3: Red River disturbance, Northwest rebellion, and related papers

    D: Louis Riel

MG 4: Canada

    D: Government departments and agencies

        13: Department of the Interior, Dominion Lands Branch

MG 7: Church records and religious figures

    B: Church of England

        4: St Andrew's Church

        7: St John's Cathedral

    C: Presbyterian

        12: Black, John

    D: Roman Catholic

        8: Saint-Boniface

MG 8: Immigration, settlement, and local histories

    C: Genealogies

        1: Lagimodière, Jean-Baptiste

MG 9: Literary manuscripts and theses

    A: Manuscripts and related papers

        76: MacLeod, M. A.

        78: Gunn, G. H.

Hudson's Bay Company Archives. The PRO and the PAC hold microfilm copies of the records for the years 1670 to 1870. For more information concerning the copies held at the PAC and the finding aids that are available, see *General inventory, manuscipts, 3*. The articles by R. H. G. Leveson Gower, "The archives of the Hudson's Bay Company," *Beaver*, outfit 264 (December 1933): 40–42, 64, and by Joan Craig, "Three hundred years of records," *Beaver*, outfit 301 (autumn 1970): 65–70, provide useful information to researchers. For series of HBCA documents published by the HBRS, *see* section II.

Section A: London office records

    A.1/: London minute-books

    A.5/: London correspondence books outward – general

A.6/: London correspondence books outward – HBC official

A.8/: London correspondence with the British government

A.9/: Memorial books

A.10/: London inward correspondence – general

A.11/: London inward correspondence from HBC posts

A.12/: London inward correspondence from governors of HBC territories

A.16/: Officers' and servants' ledgers and account-books

A.21/: Officers' and servants' bill-books

A.31/: Lists of commissioned officers

A.32/: Servants' contracts

A.33/: Commissioned officers' indentures and agreements

A.34/: Servants' characters and staff records

A.36/: Officers' and servants' wills

A.43/: Books of assignments of stock

A.44/: Register book of wills and administrations of proprietors, etc.

A.64/: Miscellaneous books

Section B: North America trading post records

B.3/a: Albany journals

B.3/b: Albany correspondence books

B.3/e: Albany reports on district

B.4/b: Fort Alexander outward correspondence

B.4/d: Fort Alexander account-books

B.14/a: Bedford House journals

B.24/a: Buckingham House journals

B.27/a: Carlton House (Saskatchewan) journals

B.34/a: Chesterfield House (Bow River) journals

B.42/a: Fort Churchill journals

B.49/a: Cumberland House journals

B.55/a: Duck Portage journals

B.60/a: Edmonton House journals

B.60/d: Edmonton House account-books

B.87/a: Hudson House journals

B.89/a: Île-à-la-Crosse journals

B.89/d: Île-à-la-Crosse account-books

B.97/a: Thompson's River journal and correspondence

B.107/a: Lac Seul journals

B.107/b: Lac Seul correspondence outward

B.107/d: Lac Seul account-books

B.107/e: Lac Seul reports on district

B.107/z: Lac Seul miscellaneous items

B.110/c: Lake of Two Mountains correspondence

B.118/a: Loon River post journals

B.121/a: Manchester House journals

B.123/a: Martin Fall journals

B.129/a: Michipicoten journals

B.129/b: Michipicoten correspondence books

B.129/e: Michipicoten reports on district

B.134/c: Montreal correspondence inward

B.134/g: Montreal abstracts and servants' accounts

B.135/c: Moose correspondence inward

B.135/k: Moose minutes of council, Southern department

B.148/a: Nipawi journals

B.149/a: Nipigon House journals

B.154/a: Norway House journals

B.157/a: Peel River journals

B.162/a: Pic journals

B.178/a: Reed Lake House journals

B.184/z: Rocky Mountain House miscellaneous

B.186/b: Rupert House correspondence books

B.194/a: Sault Ste Marie journals

B.194/b: Sault Ste Marie correspondence books

B.194/e: Sault Ste Marie reports on district

B.197/a: Setting River journals

B.198/e: Fort Severn reports on district

B.200/a: Fort Simpson (Mackenzie River) journals

B.200/b: Fort Simpson correspondence books

B.202/a: Snake Country journals

B.205/a: South Branch House journals

B.223/a: Fort Vancouver journals

B.223/b: Fort Vancouver outward correspondence books

B.231/a: Fort William journals

B.231/e: Fort William reports on district

B.235/a: Winnipeg journals

B.235/d: Winnipeg account-books

B.235/z: Winnipeg miscellaneous items

B.239/a: York Factory journals

B.239/b: York Factory outward correspondence books

B.239/c: York Factory correspondence inward

B.239/d: York Factory account-books

B.239/f: York Factory list of servants

B.239/z: York Factory miscellaneous items

Section C: Records of ships owned or chartered by the HBC

C.1/: Ships' logs

C.3/: Portledge books

Section D: Governors' papers

D.1/: William Williams outward correspondence books

D.2/: William Williams correspondence inward and miscellaneous items

D.4/: George Simpson outward correspondence books

D.5/: George Simpson correspondence inward

D.6/: George Simpson minutes and correspondence concerning will

Section E: Miscellaneous records

E.4/: Red River settlement church registers

E.5/: Red River settlement census returns

E.6/: Red River settlement land registers and records

E.7/: Red River settlement account-books

E.8/: Red River settlement deeds, agreements, Bathurst–Selkirk correspondence, and miscellaneous papers

E.10/: Colin Robertson papers

E.12/5: Isobel Finlayson journal
E.13/: John McLoughlin Jr papers
E.16/: Council of Assiniboia records
E.24/: John Stuart records
Section F: Records of allied and subsidiary companies
  F.1/: North West Company minute-book
  F.3/: North West Company correspondence
  F.4/: North West Company account-books
  F.8–F.26/: Puget's Sound Agricultural Company papers
Section G: Maps, plans, charts
  G.3/: Published maps

PROVINCIAL ARCHIVES OF NEW BRUNSWICK, Fredericton. The archives is in the process of reorganizing and reclassifying some material. As a result, individual references to PANB collections in volume VIII will not always correspond to those currently in use at the archives, although the old references are still usable for the purposes of location and retrieval. The following description is an attempt to indicate the latest changes as the volume goes to press. For information on the manuscript holdings, *A guide to the manuscript collections in the Provincial Archives of New Brunswick*, comp. A. C. Rigby (Fredericton, 1977) is useful.

Materials used in the preparation of volume VIII include:
MBU: George Burchill & Sons papers
MC 1: Family history collection
     7: William Brydone Jack papers
    58: Bishop Inglis letters
    69: Tobique Mill Company, minute-book
   211: Raymond Paddock Gorham collection
   216: Kathleen Williston collection
   218: Wood family papers
   288: New Brunswick Barristers' Society papers
   300: York-Sunbury Historical Society collection
MYY 262: Miramichi Fire Relief Committee records
"New Brunswick political biography." Compiled by J. C. and H. B. Graves. 11 vols., typescript.
RG 1: Records of the lieutenant governor
  RS2: Sir John Harvey
  RS345: Sir W. MacB. G. Colebrooke
  RS558: Lieut. Gov. George Stracy Smyth
RG 2: Records of the central executive
  RS6: Minutes and orders-in-council of the Executive Council
  RS7: Executive Council records, Ottawa series
  RS8: Executive Council records, New Brunswick series
    Appointments and commissions
    Banks and companies, including Central Bank of New Brunswick
    Education
    Estates
    Surveyor general

    Unarranged Executive Council documents
RG 3: Records of the provincial secretary
  RS13: Departmental correspondence
RG 4: Records of the New Brunswick General Assembly
  RS24: Legislative Assembly sessional records
RG 5: Records of the superior courts
  RS55: Court of Equity records, original jurisdiction
RG 7: Records of the probate courts
  RS64: Gloucester County
  RS68: Northumberland County
  RS69: Queen's County
  RS71: Saint John County
  RS74: Westmorland County
  RS75: York County
RG 10: Records of the Department of Natural Resources
  RS107: Crown Lands and Lands Branch records
  RS108: Land petitions
RG 18: Records of the Department of Municipal Affairs
  RS150: Kent County Council records
  RS153: Northumberland County Council records
  RS427: Records of the city of Saint John
  RS538: Records of warrants, appointments, and commissions

PROVINCIAL ARCHIVES OF NEWFOUNDLAND AND LABRADOR, St John's. For information on the collections see *Preliminary inventory of the holdings . . . and Supplement . . .* (2 nos., St John's, 1970–74).
The following materials were cited in volume VIII:
GB: Government records – Great Britain
GB 2: Board of Ordnance, Royal Engineers
  1: Newfoundland, general correspondence
GN: Government records – Newfoundland
  GN 2: Department of the Colonial Secretary
    1: Letter-books, outgoing correspondence
    2: Incoming correspondence
  GN 5: Court records
    1: Surrogate Court
     B: Northern District
      1: Minutes
    2: Supreme Court
     A: Central Circuit
      1: Minutes
      4: Sessions Court
     B: Northern District
      1: Minutes
  GN 9: Executive Council records
    1: Minutes
P: Private records
  P1: Governors' private papers
    5: Duckworth papers
  P4: Former designation for professionals
    17: P. T. Mcgrath collection re Labrador

P7: Businesses
A: Fishing related
6: Slade & Sons, Fogo, ledgers
P8: Benevolent organizations
A/11: Congregational Church

PUBLIC ARCHIVES OF CANADA, Ottawa. The PAC has published guides to its holdings in the various divisions, including *General guide series 1983, Federal Archives Division*, compiled by Terry Cook and Glenn T. Wright (1983), and *General guide series 1983, Manuscript Division*, compiled by Grace Hyam and Jean-Marie LeBlanc (1984).

The following inventories to materials in the Manuscript and the Federal Archives divisions which were used in the preparation of volume VIII have been published:

General inventory, manuscripts, volume 1, MG 1–MG 10 (1971)
General inventory, manuscripts, volume 2, MG 11–MG 16 (1976)
General inventory, manuscripts, volume 3, MG 17–MG 21 (1974)
General inventory, manuscripts, volume 4, MG 22–MG 25 (1972)
General inventory, manuscripts, volume 7, MG 29 (1975)
General inventory, manuscripts, volume 8, MG 30 (1977)
General inventory series, no.1: records relating to Indian affairs (RG 10) (1975)
General inventory series, no.6: records of Statistics Canada (RG 31) (1977)
General inventory series, no.8: records of the Department of Public Works (RG 11) (1977)

An older series of inventories has been largely superseded by unpublished inventories available at the PAC, but the following are still of some limited use:

Record group 1, Executive Council, Canada, 1764–1867 (1953)
Record group 4, Civil and Provincial secretaries' offices, Canada East, 1760–1867; Record Group 5, Civil and Provincial secretaries' offices, Canada West, 1788–1867 (1953)
Record group 7, Governor General's Office (1953)
Record group 8, British military and naval records (1954)
Record group 9, Department of Militia and Defence, 1776–1922 ([1957])
Record groups, no.14: Records of parliament, 1775–1915; no.15: Department of the Interior; no.16: Department of National Revenue (1957)

Also useful are *Census returns, 1666–1881, Public Archives of Canada* (1982) and *Checklist of parish registers* (3rd ed., 1981). The catalogue of the holdings of the National Map Collection has been printed in *Catalogue of the National Map Collection, Public Archives of Canada, Ottawa, Ontario* (16v., Boston, 1976).

The PAC publishes the *Union list of* MSS [*see* section III] which lists holdings of the Federal Archives and Manuscript divisions. It has also issued a *Guide to Canadian photographic archives*, ed. Christopher Seifried (1984). Addenda to published inventories, unpublished inventories of manuscript and record groups, and finding aids to individual collections are available at the PAC, which also makes available a large number of finding aids on microfiche.

Material from the following collections was cited in volume VIII:

MG 8: Documents relatifs à la Nouvelle-France et au Québec (XVIIe–XXe siècles)
F: Documents relatifs aux seigneuries et autres lieux
99: McGinnis papers
MG 9: Provincial, local, and territorial records
C: Prince Edward Island
8: Church records
5: Belfast, St John's (Presbyterian) Church
D: Ontario
7: Church records
4: Dundas, Presbyterian Church
25: L'Orignal, Presbyterian Church
27: Hamilton, Knox Church Young Men's Bible Class
35: Ottawa, St Andrew's Presbyterian Church
MG 11: Public Record Office, London, Colonial Office papers
[CO 42]. Q series. The Q transcripts were prepared by the PAC before the PRO reorganization of 1908–10 and include most of what is now in CO 42 up to the year 1841, plus material now found in CO 43, as well as items from other series. Documents for the period covered by volume VIII are calendared in PAC *Report*, 1893, 1899–1901, 1941–42.
[CO 217]. Nova Scotia A; Cape Breton A. From 1802 the transcripts in these series are from PRO, CO 217. Documents of Nova Scotia A for the period covered by volume VIII have been calendared in PAC *Report*, 1947.
[CO 226]. Prince Edward Island A. For the period prior to 1820 this is a composite series of transcripts derived primarily from sources now in PRO, CO 226, but also including material copied from the Dartmouth papers (PAC, MG 23, A1). Post-1820 documents are from CO 226

987

only. A calendar for vols. 1–16 (1763–1801) appears in PAC *Report*, 1895.

MG 19: Fur trade and Indians
  A: Fur trade, general
    2: Ermatinger estate
    7: Mackenzie, Sir Alexander
    17: Macdonald of Garth, John
    21: Hargrave family
    35: McGillivray, Simon
    41: Keith, James
    44: McKenzie, Charles
  B: Fur trade, companies and associations
    1: North West Company
    3: Beaver Club
  C: Fur trade, collections
    1: Masson collection
  E: Red River settlement
    1: Selkirk, Thomas Douglas, 5th Earl of
    2: Red River settlement
    5: Bulger, Andrew
    8: Cowan, William
  F: Indians
    1: Claus family
    24: Vardon, George
MG 23: Late eighteenth-century papers
  B: American revolution
    3: Continental Congress
  D: New Brunswick
    1: Chipman, Ward, Sr and Jr
    2: Winslow, Edward
    4: Botsford, Amos
    5: Crannell, Bartholomew
    8: Gray, Joseph
  GII: Quebec and Lower Canada: political figures
    10: Sewell, Jonathan, and family
    17: Prescott, Robert
  HI: Upper Canada: political figures
    4: Powell, William Dummer, and family
  HII: Upper Canada: merchants and settlers
    1: McDonald–Stone family
MG 24: Nineteenth-century pre-confederation papers
  A: British officials and political figures
    2: Ellice papers
    3: Douglas papers
    10: Grey of Howick papers
    13: Bagot, Sir Charles
    17: Harvey, Sir John
    20: Head, Sir Edmund Walker
    21: Campbell, Sir Archibald
    27: Durham, John George Lambton, 1st Earl of
    28: Russell, Lord John
    31: Colebrook, Sir William MacBean George
    40: Coleborne, Sir John, 1st Baron Seaton
    52: Vaughan, Sir Charles Richard
  B: North American political figures and events
    1: Neilson collection
    2: Papineau, famille
    3: Ryland papers
    4: Young, John, and family
    6: Viger, Denis-Benjamin
    11: Baldwin, William Warren and Robert
    12: Stuart papers
    13: Jarvis, Edward James
    16: Cochran, Andrew Wilson
    18: Mackenzie, William Lyon
    24: Rolph, John
    25: Bellingham, Sydney Robert
    29: Howe, Joseph
    30: Macdonald, John Sandfield
    37: Papiers Perrault
    42: Theller, Edward Alexander
    46: Cherrier, Côme-Séraphin
    50: O'Callaghan, Edmund Bailey
    101: Toronto election (1841)
    141: Hoyle, Robert
    147: Caldwell, William
  C: Correspondents of political figures
    3: Duvernay, Ludger
    10: Graham, Christopher H.
  D: Industry, commerce, and finance
    1: Woolsey family
    8: Wright family
    9: Carteret Priaulx and Company
    16: Buchanan papers
    24: Bethune, Donald
    66: Stevenson, James
    80: Young, John
    84: Bayley, H. C.
    101: Stewart, William
  E: Transportation
    1: Merritt papers
  F: Military and naval figures
    50: Antrobus, Edmund William Romer
  G: Militia
    3: Ryerse, Samuel
    39: Crooks, James
  H: Exploration, travel, and surveys
    10: Bell, William
  I: Immigration, land, and settlement
    3: McGillivray family of Glengarry
    8: Macdonell of Collachie family
    9: Hill collection
    14: Pinhey family
    26: Hamilton, Alexander
    31: Kerby, James
    33: Keefer family
    54: British American Land Company
    61: Joseph, Abraham
    65: Sherwood, Adiel
  J: Religious figures
    13: Macdonell, Alexander
  K: Education and cultural development
    2: Coventry, George
    36: Bois, Louis-Édouard

L: Miscellaneous
    3: Collection Baby
    6: Delancy–Robinson collection
MG 25: Genealogy
    14: Brouse family
    62: Kipling, Clarence
    97: De Pencier family
MG 26: Papers of the prime ministers
    A: Macdonald, Sir John Alexander
MG 27: Political figures, 1867–1950
    I: 1867–96
      E: Members of the House of Commons
        and the Senate
        30: Ferguson collection
    III: 1921–50
      C: Members of the House of Commons
        and Senate
        1: Good, William Charles
MG 28: Records of post-confederation corporate
    bodies
    II: Financial institutions
      2: Bank of Montreal
    III: Business establishments
      18: Robin, Jones and Whitman, Limited
      57: Molson's Brewery
MG 29: Nineteenth-century post-confederation
    manuscripts
    B: Scientific
      6: Smith, Marcus
    D: Cultural
      61: Morgan, Henry James
MG 30: Manuscripts of the first half of the twentieth
    century
    D: Cultural
      1: Audet, Francis-Joseph
      6: Morris, Edmund Montague
      49: Tyrrell, Joseph Burr
      101: Shortt, Adam
MG 32: Political figures, 1950–
    A: Governors general
      1: Massey family papers
MG 40: Records and manuscripts from British
    repositories
    B: Letters patent, commissions, instructions
      17: Warrants, colonial
MG 55: Miscellaneous documents
RG 1: Executive Council: Quebec, Lower Canada,
    Upper Canada, Canada, 1764–1867
    E: State records
      1: Minute-books (state matters)
      3: Upper Canada: submissions to the
        Executive Council on state matters
      14: Executive Council office: correspon-
        dence and records of the clerk
    L: Land records
      1: Minute-books (land matters)
      3: Upper Canada and Canada: petitions for
        land grants and leases

      3^L: Quebec and Lower Canada: land peti-
        tions and related records
      6: Departmental records
        B: Surveyor general's records, Lower
          Canada, Upper Canada, Canada
      7: Miscellaneous records
RG 4: Civil and Provincial secretaries' offices:
    Quebec, Lower Canada, and Canada East
    A: Secretaries' correspondence, 1764–1841
      1: S series
    B: Office records
      8: Notaries and advocates: applications for
        licences as
      15: Land records
      20: Pardons, petitions for
      28: Bonds, licences, and certificates
      30: School records
      36: Municipal records
      37: Rebellion records
      46: Miscellaneous records relating to Lord
        Selkirk's colony and the Red River
        disturbances
      58: Customs records
    C: Provincial secretary's correspondence,
      1841–67
      1: Numbered correspondence
RG 5: Civil and Provincial secretaries' offices:
    Upper Canada and Canada West
    A: Secretaries' correspondence
      1: Upper Canada sundries
    B: Miscellaneous records
      3: Petitions and addresses
      9: Bonds, licences, and certificates
      11: Education, records relating to
      25: Election returns, Upper Canada and
        Canada West
      26: Statistical returns
      36: Records of the London District magis-
        trates relating to the treason hearings
    C: Provincial secretary's correspondence
      1: Numbered correspondence files
      2: Letter-books
RG 7: Governor General's Office
    G1: Dispatches from the Colonial Office
    G7: Dispatches from the lieutenant governors to
      the governor general
    G8B: Records from the Office of the Lieutenant
      Governor of New Brunswick
    G12: Letter-books of dispatches to the Colonial
      Office
    G14: Miscellaneous records
    G20: Civil secretary's correspondence
RG 8: British military and naval records
    I: C series (British military records)
    IV: Vice-Admiralty Court records
RG 9: Department of Militia and Defence
    I: Pre-confederation records
    A: Adjutant General's Office, Lower Canada

5: Registers of officers
6: Officers' commissions
7: Nominal rolls and paylists
B: Adjutant General's Office, Upper Canada
  1: Correspondence
  2: Returns and nominal orders
  5: Registers of officers
  7: Nominal rolls and paylists
C: Adjutant-General's Office
  1: Correspondence
RG 10: Indian affairs
A: Administrative records of the imperial government
  1: Records of the governor general and the lieutenant governors
    1–7: Upper Canada, civil control
    486–87: Lower Canada, civil control
    712–13: Petitions
  2: Records of the Superintendent's Office
    8–21: Superintendent General's Office
    22–25: Chief Superintendant's Office correspondence
    26–46: Deputy Superintendent General's Office, correspondence
  3: Record of the military
    488–97: Military Secretary's Office, Montreal
  4: Records of the Chief Superintendent's Office, Upper Canada
    47–77: Correspondence
    124–39, 739, 748, 751: Jarvis correspondence
    498–509, 749: Letter-books
  5: Records of the Civil Secretary's Office
    142–262, 752–60: Correspondence
    263–72: General administration records
    510–20: Letter-books
  6: General office files
    718–19: Macaulay report
    720–21: Commissions of inquiry
    1011: Paudash papers
B: Ministerial administration records
  8: General headquarters administration records
    802: J. B. Clench
    999A: Census records
C: Field Office records
  I: Superintendency records
  2: Western (Sarnia) superintendency
    442–47A: General administration files
    569–71: Letter-books
    10017: Blue books
D: Indian land records
  10: Treaties and surrenders
    661, 769: Surrenders
RG 11: Department of Public Works
A: Board of Works records

1: Official correspondence
  1–39: Registered correspondence
  40–77, 148: Correspondence in subject files
2: Registers and indexes
  93–95: Subject registers
3: Minutes, letter-books, and reports
  116–31: Letter-books
RG 16: Department of National Revenue
A: Customs, excise, and inland revenue
  1: Correspondence and returns
RG 19: Department of Finance
RG 30: Canadian National Railways
  1–22: Great Western Railway
  361–63: Hamilton and Toronto Railway
  484–88: Toronto and Guelph Railway
  1000–55: Grand Trunk Railway, minutes
  1596–98, 2028–29: Ontario, Simcoe and Huron Union Railroad
RG 31: Statistics Canada
A: Census Division
  1: Census records
RG 42: Marine Branch
  I: Shipping registers
RG 43: Department of Railways and Canals
C: Canal Branch records
  V: St Lawrence canals
  1: Commission for Improving the Navigation on the River St Lawrence
  VI: Welland Canal
  2: Welland Canal
    C: General and departmental correspondence
RG 68: Registrar general

PUBLIC ARCHIVES OF NOVA SCOTIA, Halifax. For a description of the collections see *Inventory of manuscripts in the Public Archives of Nova Scotia* (Halifax, 1976).

Materials used in the preparation of volume VIII include:
MG 1: Papers of families and individuals
  226–27: Enos Collins papers
  238: Elizabeth [Ruggles] Coward documents
  334: Sir Brenton Halliburton papers
  544: T. H. Lodge collection, genealogies
  550–58: Thomas McCulloch papers
  753: Harry Piers papers
  793: Simon B. Robie documents
  797B: Sargent family documents
  799–805: Shannon family papers
  817–63: Thomas B. Smith, genealogy
  914B: Thomas Trotter papers
  926: Richard J. Uniacke papers
  979–80: Peleg Wiswall documents
  1490: James Boyle Uniacke papers

1595–1613: Bliss family papers
1729: McLelan papers
1769: Crofton James Uniacke papers
MG   2: Political papers
    719–25: George Renny Young papers
    726–30: John Young papers
    731–83: Sir William Young papers
    1250–55: John Howard Sinclair papers
MG   3: Business papers
    28: John Quirk, Bridgetown, register
    295–98: Joseph Rudolf, Rudolf's Cove, account-books, ledgers
    299: William Rudolf, Rudolf's Cove, day-book
    300: William Crane, Sackville, ledger
MG   4: Churches and communities
    James Presbyterian Church (New Glasgow), records (mfm.)
    94–105: Lunenburg County genealogies, comp. E. A. Harris
    190–215: Universalist Unitarian Church (Halifax), records
MG   5: Cemeteries
MG   9: Scrap-books
    no.45: Scrap-book on counties
    no.225: History of the Nova Scotia Light and Power Co. Ltd., no.1
MG 12: Great Britain, Army
    HQ: Headquarters papers, Nova Scotia
    1–94: General orders
MG 15: Ethnic collections
    3–7: Indians
MG 20: Societies and special collections
    153: Free Church College
MG 100: Documents, newspaper clippings, and miscellaneous items
RG   1: Bound volumes of Nova Scotia records for the period 1624–1867
    29–185: Documents relating to the government of Nova Scotia: dispatches, letter-books, and commission books
    186–214½H: Council, minutes
    215–218DDD: Legislative Council, journals
    219–85: Miscellaneous documents
    286–300: Legislative Council, selections from the files
    301–14: Legislative Assembly, selections from the files
    410–17: Papers of the settlement of Halifax
    430–32: Indians
    438–39: Schools and school lands
    440–42: Nova Scotia militia
    443–54: Census and poll tax
RG   5: Records of the Legislative Assembly of Nova Scotia
    A: Assembly papers

    E: Election writs
    GP: Governor's petitions
    P: Petitions
    U: Unpassed bills
RG   7: Records of the provincial secretary of Nova Scotia
    1–142: Letters received
RG   8: Records of the Central Board of Agriculture of Nova Scotia
RG 13: Customs
    22–28: Halifax port records
RG 14: Education
RG 20: Lands and Forests
    A: Land grants and petitions
    B: Cape Breton land papers
    C: Crown lands
        13–50, 85–93: Land grants, county papers
RG 22: Nova Scotia, military records
RG 24: Post Office records of Nova Scotia
RG 25: Public health
RG 28: Railways
RG 31: Treasury
    102–20: Impost, excise, and revenue
RG 32: Vital statistics
    6–86: Deaths
    132–69: Marriage bonds
RG 34: Court of General Sessions of the Peace
    312: Halifax County
RG 35A: Halifax city and county assessments
    1–4: Halifax city assessments
RG 36: Chancery Court
RG 39: Supreme Court
    J: Judgement books
    M: Miscellaneous

PUBLIC ARCHIVES OF PRINCE EDWARD ISLAND, Charlottetown.
    Materials used in the preparation of volume VIII include:
Acc. 2316: P.E.I. letter-books, Robert Bruce Stewart and David Stewart
    2353: John Mackieson, diaries
    2524: Miscellaneous documents
    2552: Miscellaneous documents
    2664: Copies of MacDonald family papers in possession of Jean and Colin MacDonald, St Peters, P.E.I.
    2685: Port Hill papers
    2702: Smith–Alley collection
    2716: Correspondence donated by Niel Morison, Tobermory, Scotland
    2810: Ira Brown papers
    2825: MacNutt family papers
    2849: Palmer family papers
    3466: P.E.I. Heritage Foundation collection
RG   1: Lieutenant Governor, commission books

RG 3: House of Assembly, journals
RG 5: Executive Council
Minutes
Petitions
RG 6: Courts
Court of Chancery
Supreme Court
RG 8: Warrant books
RG 15: Crown lands, leases
RG 16: Registry Office, land registry records
Conveyance registers
RG 18: Census records
RG 20: City of Charlottetown records

QUÉBEC, MINISTÈRE DE LA JUSTICE. The Archives civiles and the Archives judiciaires du Québec, which are under the joint jurisdiction of the courts and the Ministère de la Justice, are now separate repositories as a result of the reclassification of the former Archives judiciaires. They are deposited at the court-houses in the administrative centres of the 34 judicial districts of Quebec.

ARCHIVES CIVILES. These archives retain documents for the last 100 years, including registers of births, marriages, and deaths, notaries' *minutiers* (minute-books), and records of surveyors active in the district. Earlier documents are held by the ANQ.

BUREAU D'ENREGISTREMENT. The registry offices hold all property titles and contracts affecting real estate: sales, marriages, wills and estates, mortgages, conveyances, assignments, gifts, guardian- and trusteeships. At present there are 82 registry offices in Quebec.

A list of the judicial districts and registry offices can be found in *The Quebec legal telephone directory*, ed. Andrée Frenette-Lecoq (Montreal, 1980).

QUÉBEC, MINISTÈRE DES AFFAIRES CULTURELLES, CENTRE DE DOCUMENTATION, Québec. The Ministère des Affaires culturelles has consolidated into one documentation centre the collections of all its previously existing centres, including that of the Inventaire des biens culturels.

The following materials were used in the preparation of volume VIII:
Fonds Morisset
1: Architecture et œuvres d'art par localité
2695: Journal de François Baillairgé
2: Artistes et artisans
B157/T454: Baillairgé, Pierre-Florent
B853.5/P662.97: Brien, *dit* Desrochers, Urbain
F249/G537.5: Fassio, Gerome
H243/J27.5/2: Hanna, James
H243.1/J27.5/2: Hanna, James Godfrey
M829.2/P324: Morand, Paul
N845/F825: Normand, François

P219.7/A555/2: Paquet, *dit* Lavallée, André
R754/P324: Rollin, Paul
V855.5/L: Vivant, Laurent

QUEEN'S UNIVERSITY ARCHIVES, Kingston, Ont. For information on the collection see *A guide to the holdings of Queen's University Archives* (Kingston, 1978).
Materials used in volume VIII include:
William Bell papers
John Solomon Cartwright papers
John Macaulay papers
William Morris papers
Presbyterian Church of Canada in connection with the Church of Scotland, Synod papers
Queen's University records
Queen's University letters

UNITED CHURCH ARCHIVES. The present-day United Church Archives is a descendant of 19th- and 20th-century archival collections of various Canadian Methodist, Presbyterian, Congregational, and Evangelical/United Brethren in Christ bodies. The Central Archives of the United Church of Canada at Victoria University, Toronto, is national in scope. Material of local interest, including the official records of the conferences concerned, is housed in regional conference archives.

CENTRAL ARCHIVES, Toronto
Materials used in volume VIII include:
Bible Christian Church in Canada records
Biography files
James Croil papers, diary, 1866–67
Glasgow Colonial Society, correspondence

MARITIME CONFERENCE ARCHIVES, Halifax.
Official records, especially those of the following bodies, were used in volume VIII:
Presbyterian Church of Nova Scotia (United Secession), synod and presbytery minutes
Wesleyan Methodist Church, Eastern British America Conference, conference and district minutes

UNIVERSITY OF NEW BRUNSWICK LIBRARY, Archives and Special Collections Department, Fredericton.
Materials used in volume VIII include:
MG H: Historical
H 1: Bailey papers
H 2: Winslow family papers
H 11: Saunders papers
H 28: Fredericton Emigrant Society minute-book
H 33: W. I. Bedell letter-book
UA: University archives
RG 42: Petitions and memorials
RG 109: University manuscripts

992

UNIVERSITY OF WESTERN ONTARIO, the D. B. Weldon Library, London, Ont. Regional Collection. A description of the municipal record and personal manuscript collections is available on microfiche in *Regional Collection: the D. B. Weldon Library catalogue*, ed. S. L. Sykes (4 fiches, London, 1977).

Various municipal record and personal manuscript collections proved useful in the preparation of volume VIII.

FRANCE

ARCHIVES DÉPARTEMENTALES. For a list of analytical inventories *see*: France, Direction des archives, *État des inventaires des archives nationales, départementales, communales et hospitalières au 1er janvier 1937* (Paris, 1938); *Supplément, 1937–1954* [by R.-H. Bautier] (Paris, 1955); and *Catalogue des inventaires, répertoires, guides de recherche et autres instruments de travail des archives départementales, communales et hospitalières . . . à la date du 31 décembre 1961* (Paris, 1962). For copies of documents held by the PAC see *General inventory, manuscripts, 1*: 87–99. There is a uniform system of classification for all departmental archives. A list of the various series may be found in *DCB*, 2: 683–84.

GREAT BRITAIN

GENERAL REGISTER OFFICE, London. Death and marriage records for various individuals were consulted in the preparation of volume VIII.

GENERAL REGISTER OFFICE FOR SCOTLAND, Edinburgh. Information concerning the parish registers held by the GRO is available in the *Detailed list of old parochial registers of Scotland* (Edinburgh, 1872). Registers of baptisms, marriages, and burials for several Scottish parishes were used in the preparation of volume VIII.

NATIONAL LIBRARY OF SCOTLAND, Department of Manuscripts, Edinburgh. Information on the manuscript collections is available in *Catalogue of manuscripts acquired since 1925* (5v. to date [1–4, 6], Edinburgh, 1938–   ), and in *Summary catalogue of the Advocates' manuscripts* (Edinburgh, 1971). Descriptions of some materials concerning Canada appear in *A guide to manuscripts relating to America in Great Britain and Ireland*, ed. J. W. Raimo (Westport, Conn., 1979), and in *Britain and the Dominions: a guide to business and related records in the United Kingdom concerning Australia, Canada, New Zealand, and South Africa*, comp. C. A. Jones (Boston, 1978).

Materials used in the preparation of volume VIII include:

Advocates' manuscripts
    Adv. MSS 46.1.1–46.10.2: Murray papers
Deposits
    Deposit no. 298: Church of Scotland, Overseas
        Council records
Manuscripts
    MSS 2264–505, 2568–608, 3022: Cochrane papers
    MSS 3430–49: Lee papers
    MSS 4007–131: Blackwood's letter file
    MSS 15001–195: Ellice papers

PUBLIC RECORD OFFICE, London. For an introduction to the holdings and arrangement of this archives see *Guide to the contents of the Public Record Office* (3v., London, 1963–68). For copies of PRO documents available at the PAC see *General inventory, manuscripts, 2*.

The following series were used in the preparation of volume VIII:
Admiralty
    Accounting departments
        ADM 24: Officers, Full pay
        ADM 36: Ships' musters, ser.I
        ADM 37: Ships' musters, ser.II
    Admiralty and Secretariat
        ADM 1: Papers
        ADM 7: Miscellanea
        ADM 11: Indexes and compilations, ser.I
        ADM 51: Captains' logs
        ADM 52: Masters' logs
        ADM 53: Ships' logs
    Medical departments
        ADM 99: Minutes
    Navy Board
        ADM 106: Navy Board records
        ADM 107: Passing certificates
Board of Customs and Excise
    CUST 65: Outport records, Dartmouth, England
Board of Trade
    Registrar general of shipping and seamen
        BT 107: Ships' registers
Colonial Office. [*See* R. B. Pugh, *The records of the Colonial and Dominions offices* (London, 1964).]
    Canada
        CO 42: Original correspondence
        CO 43: Entry books
        CO 47: Miscellanea
    Dominica
        CO 71: Original correspondence
    Fernando Po
        CO 82: Original correspondence
    Grenada
        CO 101: Original correspondence
    Malta
        CO 158: Original correspondence
        CO 159: Entry books

New Brunswick
  CO 188: Original correspondence
  CO 189: Entry books
  CO 193: Miscellanea
Newfoundland
  CO 194: Original correspondence
  CO 195: Entry books
  CO 199: Miscellanea
Nova Scotia and Cape Breton
  CO 217: Original correspondence
  CO 218: Entry books
Prince Edward Island
  CO 226: Original correspondence
  CO 227: Entry books
  CO 229: Sessional papers
Sierra Leone
  CO 267: Original correspondence
Vancouver Island
  CO 305: Original correspondence
Colonies General
  CO 323: Original correspondence
  CO 324: Entry books, series I
Emigration
  CO 384: Original correspondence
Supplementary
  CO 537: Correspondence
Exchequer and Audit Department
  Claims, American loyalists
    AO 13: Series II
Foreign Office. [See *Records of the Foreign Office,*
  1782–1939 (London, 1969).]
  General correspondence
    FO 54: Muscat
Home Office.
  Channel Islands, Scotland, Ireland, etc.
    HO 100: Ireland, correspondence
Public Record Office
  Documents acquired by gift, deposit, or purchase
    PRO 30/22: Russell papers
Prerogative Court of Canterbury (formerly held at
  Somerset House)
    PROB 11: Registered copy wills
Registrar General
  RG 4/959: Authenticated register, Dartmouth
    Presbyterian Church
  RG 4/1209: Authenticated register, Glenorchy
    Chapel, Withycombe Raleigh
  RG 4/1718: Register of births, Bethesda Meeting
    House, Nottingham
Treasury
  In-letters and files
    T 1: Treasury Board papers
War Office
  Correspondence
    WO 1: In-letters
  Returns
    WO 13: Muster books and pay lists: militia and
      volunteers

WO 17: Monthly returns
WO 25: Registers, various
Ordnance office
  WO 54: Registers
  WO 55: Miscellanea

SCHOOL OF ORIENTAL AND AFRICAN STUDIES
LIBRARY, University of London. The archival collec-
tions of several missionary societies are deposited in
the library.
  The following collections were used in the
preparation of volume VIII:
Council for World Mission Archives. The library has
  published a general guide to the collection: C. S.
  Craig, *The archives of the Council for World
  Mission (incorporating the London Missionary
  Society): an outline guide* (London, 1973).
    London Missionary Society
      Correspondence, Canada
Methodist Missionary Society Archives. Canadian
  material was microfilmed by the PAC in 1955,
  when the originals were held by the Methodist
  Missionary Society; *see* PAC, *General inventory,
  manuscripts, 3*.
    Wesleyan Methodist Missionary Society
      Correspondence, North America

SCOTTISH RECORD OFFICE, Edinburgh. A comprehensive listing of materials relating to Canada is provided
by the SRO's "List of Canadian documents" (typescript, 1977, with updates to 1983). An appendix
records Canadian documents in private archives as
surveyed by the National Reg. of Arch. (Scotland).
This guide is based on an earlier compilation, *A source
list of manuscripts relating to the U.S.A. and Canada
in private archives preserved in the Scottish Record
Office* (Edinburgh, 1970), and is available at the PAC,
all provincial archives, and other selected Canadian
institutions. Some items are also described in *A guide
to manuscripts relating to America in Great Britain
and Ireland*, ed. J. W. Raimo (Westport, Conn.,
1979), and *Britain and the Dominions: a guide to
business and related records in the United Kingdom
concerning Australia, Canada, New Zealand, and
South Africa*, comp. C. A. Jones (Boston, 1978).
  The following were cited in volume VIII:
CH: Church of Scotland
  CH1: General Assembly papers
    2: Bound volumes of papers submitted to
      the General Assembly
  CH2: Records of lower courts (synods, presby-
    teries, and kirk sessions) prior to 1929
    70: Kirk session minutes, Coll
GD: Gifts and deposits
  GD1: Miscellaneous gifts and deposits
    92: James Aitchison, letters
  GD45: Dalhousie muniments

GD50: John MacGregor muniments
GD112: Breadalbane muniments
RD: Registers of Deeds of the Court of Session
   RD5: Deeds
RS: Registers of sasines
   RS14: Particular register of sasines for the shire
     of Ayr and bailieries of Kyle, Carrick and
     Cunninghame
SC: Scottish Sheriff Courts
   SC70: Sheriff Court of Lothians and Peebles
     (commissary business)

UNITED SOCIETY FOR THE PROPAGATION OF THE
GOSPEL, London. The archives is in the process of
reorganizing and reclassifying some material. Thus
classifications used by Canadian archives holding
USPG microfilm do not always correspond to those of
the archives itself. For information about materials
relating to Canada, *see* William Westfall and Ian
Pearson, "The archives of the United Society for the
Propagation of the Gospel and Canadian history,"
CCHS *Journal*, 25 (1983): 16–24. For copies of
USPG documents available at the PAC, see *General
inventory, manuscripts, 3*.
   The following were consulted:
C/CAN: Unbound letters from Canada, 1752–1860.
   Letters from New Brunswick, Newfoundland,
   Nova Scotia, and Quebec groupings were used. A
   nominal card index is available at USPG.
D: Original letters received from 1850, bound in
   volumes. A handlist of writers and places is avail-
   able at USPG.
E: Reports from SPG missionaries from 1856, bound
   in volumes. A handlist is available at USPG.

X: Miscellaneous volumes and papers, 18th–20th
   centuries
Journal of proceedings of the Society for the Propagation of the Gospel. Comprises bound and in-
dexed volumes of the proceedings of the general
meetings held in London from 1701, and four
appendices, A, B, C, D (1701–1860).

UNITED STATES

BAKER LIBRARY, Harvard University, Graduate
School of Business Administration, Boston.
   The following material was consulted in the
preparation of volume VIII:
R. G. Dun collection
   Manuscript credit ledgers, Canada

GENEALOGICAL SOCIETY OF THE CHURCH OF JESUS
CHRIST OF LATTER-DAY SAINTS, Salt Lake City,
Utah. As a result of the Mormons' international
microfilming program, over a million rolls of
microfilmed records of genealogical interest, including parish registers, land grants, deeds, probate
records, marriage bonds, and cemetery records, are
available in the church's central library and through its
branch libraries, as well as at various archives.
   GS microfilms cited in volume VIII consist
primarily of copies of Ontario land registry office
records available at the AO. These references are
entered under the name of the Land Registry Office
where the original documents are located; when the
location of the original record is not known, a
reference to the GS microfilm roll is entered under the
name of the repository in which it was consulted.

II. PRINTED PRIMARY SOURCES

A. OFFICIAL PUBLICATIONS AND CON-TEMPORARY WORKS

ARCHIVES NATIONALES DU QUÉBEC, Québec
   PUBLICATIONS [*see also* section III]
   Rapport. 54 vols. 1920/21–1976/77. There is an
   index to the contents of the first 42 volumes:
   *Table des matières des rapports des Archives du
   Québec, tomes 1 à 42 (1920–1964)* ([Québec],
   1965).
ARCHIVES OF ONTARIO, Toronto
   PUBLICATIONS
   Report. 22 vols. 1903–33.
*The Arthur papers; being the Canadian papers,
   mainly confidential, private, and demi-official of
   Sir George Arthur, K.C.H., last lieutenant-
   governor of Upper Canada, in the manuscript
   collection of the Toronto Public Libraries*. Edited

by Charles Rupert Sanderson. 3 vols. Toronto,
   1957–59.
BAS-CANADA. *See* LOWER CANADA
*Les bourgeois de la Compagnie du Nord-Ouest: récits
   de voyages, lettres et rapports inédits relatifs au
   Nord-Ouest canadien*. Louis-[François-]Rodrigue
   Masson, édit. 2 vols. Québec, 1889–90; réimpr.,
   New York, 1960.
CANADA, PROVINCE OF
   LEGISLATIVE ASSEMBLY/ASSEMBLÉE LÉGISLATIVE
   *Appendix to the . . . journals of the Legisla-
    tive Assembly of the Province of Canada/
    Appendice . . . des journaux de la province du
    Canada*, 1841–59. Continued by Canada,
    Province of, Parliament/Parlement, *Sessional
    papers/Documents de la session*. See also *The
    Legislative Assembly of the Province of
    Canada: an index to journal appendices and*

sessional papers, 1841–1866. Compiled by Patricia A. Damphouse. London, Ont, 1974.

Journals of the Legislative Assembly of the Province of Canada/Journaux de l'Assemblée législative de la province du Canada, 1841–59.

LEGISLATIVE COUNCIL/CONSEIL LÉGISLATIF

Journals of the Legislative Council of the Province of Canada/Journaux du Conseil législatif de la province du Canada, 1841–61.

PARLIAMENT/PARLEMENT

Sessional papers/Documents de la session, 1860–66.

Statutes of the Province of Canada . . . /Statuts de la province du Canada . . . , 1841–57. The statutes were published under the title *Provincial statutes of Canada/Les statuts provinciaux du Canada* from 1841 to 1851.

PUBLICATIONS

For a critical bibliography of the English-language publications of the Province of Canada, *see* Bishop, *Pubs. of government of Prov. of Canada* [section III].

Canada Gazette. Kingston; Montreal; Toronto; Quebec; Ottawa. Official publication of the government of the Province of Canada, published weekly from 2 Oct. 1841 to 26 June 1869. The journal moved to follow the seat of government.

The Canadian North-West, its early development and legislative records; minutes of the councils of the Red River colony and the Northern Department of Rupert's Land. Edited by Edmund Henry Oliver. (PAC publications, 9.) 2 vols. Ottawa, 1914–15.

Catholic Church records of the Pacific northwest: Vancouver, volumes I and II, and Stellamaris mission. Translated by Mikell de Lores Wormell Warner and annotated by Harriet Duncan Munnick. St Paul, Oreg., 1972.

CHAMPLAIN SOCIETY, Toronto

PUBLICATIONS

53 vols. to date, exclusive of the Hudson's Bay Company series [see *HBRS*], the Ontario series, and the unnumbered series. Issued only to elected members of the society who are limited in numbers.

13–15, 17: *Select British docs. of War of 1812* (Wood).

22: *Docs. relating to NWC* (Wallace).

24: Hargrave, *Hargrave corr.* (Glazebrook).

28: Mactavish, *Letters of Letitia Hargrave* (MacLeod).

ONTARIO SERIES

11 vols. to date. Available for sale to the general public.

1: *Valley of the Trent* (Guillet).

5: *Town of York, 1793–1815* (Firth).

8: *Town of York, 1815–34* (Firth).

COX, ROSS. *Adventures on the Columbia River, including the narrative of a residence of six years on the western side of the Rocky Mountains, among various tribes of Indians hitherto unknown: together with a journey across the American continent.* 2 vols. London, 1831. Another edition. 1 vol. New York, 1832.

[CROIL, JAMES.] *A historical and statistical report of the Presbyterian Church of Canada, in connection with the Church of Scotland, for the year 1866.* Montreal, 1867. 2nd edition. 1868.

Debates of the Legislative Assembly of United Canada, 1841–1867. General editor, Elizabeth Abbott [Nish] Gibbs. 12 vols. in 23 to date. Montreal, 1970– .

"Les dénombrements de Québec faits en 1792, 1795, 1798 et 1805." Joseph-Octave Plessis, compil. ANQ *Rapport*, 1948–49: 1–250.

Documentary history of education in Upper Canada from the passing of the Constitutional Act of 1791 to the close of Rev. Dr. Ryerson's administration of the Education Department in 1876. Edited by John George Hodgins. 28 vols. Toronto, 1894–1910.

The documentary history of the campaign upon the Niagara frontier. . . . Edited by Ernest [Alexander] Cruikshank. (Lundy's Lane Historical Society publication.) 9 vols. Welland, Ont., [1896]–1908.

Documents relating to the constitutional history of Canada. . . . Edited by Adam Shortt *et al.* (PAC publication.) 3 vols. Ottawa, 1907–35.

[1]: *1759–1791.* Edited by Adam Shortt and Arthur George Doughty. 2nd edition. (PAC, Board of Historical Publications.) 2 parts. 1918.

[2]: *1791–1818.* Edited by Arthur George Doughty and Duncan A. McArthur.

[3]: *1819–1828.* Edited by Arthur George Doughty and Norah Story.

Documents relating to the North West Company. Edited by William Stewart Wallace. (Champlain Society publications, 22.) Toronto, 1934.

The Elgin–Grey papers, 1846–1852. Edited with notes and appendices by Arthur George Doughty. (PAC publication.) 4 vols. Ottawa, 1937.

Gentleman's Magazine. London, 1731–1907. Monthly.

"Grants of crown lands, etc., in Upper Canada, 1792–1796." AO *Report*, 1929: 1–177.

HARGRAVE, [JAMES]. *The Hargrave correspondence, 1821–1843.* Edited with introduction and notes by George Parkin de Twenebrokes Glazebrook. (Champlain Society publications, 24.) Toronto, 1938.

HARMON, DANIEL WILLIAMS. *Sixteen years in the Indian country: the journal of Daniel Williams Harmon, 1800–1816.* Edited with an introduction by William Kaye Lamb. Toronto, 1957.

HELMCKEN, JOHN SEBASTIAN. *The reminiscences of*

Doctor John Sebastian Helmcken. Edited by Dorothy Blakey Smith with an introduction by William Kaye Lamb. [Vancouver], 1975.

HUDSON'S BAY RECORD SOCIETY, Winnipeg

PUBLICATIONS

33 vols. General editor for vols.1–22, Edwin Ernest Rich; vols.23–25, Kenneth Gordon Davies; vols.26–30, Glyndwr Williams; vols. 31–33, Hartwell Bowsfield. Vols.1–12 were issued in association with the Champlain Society [*q.v.*] and reprinted in 1968 in Nendeln, Liechtenstein; vol.13 was reprinted in Nendeln in 1979.

1: Simpson, George. *Journal of occurrences in the Athabasca Department by George Simpson, 1820 and 1821, and report.* Edited by Edwin Ernest Rich, with an introduction by Chester [Bailey] Martin. Toronto, 1938.

2: Robertson, Colin. *Colin Robertson's correspondence book, September 1817 to September 1822.* Edited with an introduction by Edwin Ernest Rich, assisted by Robert Harvey Fleming. Toronto, 1939.

3: *Minutes of Council, Northern Department of Rupert Land, 1821–31.* Edited by Robert Harvey Fleming, with an introduction by Harold Adams Innis. Toronto, 1940.

4: McLoughlin, John. *The letters of John McLoughlin from Fort Vancouver to the governor and committee, first series, 1825–38.* Edited by Edwin Ernest Rich, with an introduction by William Kaye Lamb. London, 1941.

6: McLoughlin, John. *The letters of John McLoughlin from Fort Vancouver to the governor and committee, second series, 1839–44.* Edited by Edwin Ernest Rich, with an introduction by William Kaye Lamb. London, 1943.

7: McLoughlin, John. *The letters of John McLoughlin from Fort Vancouver to the governor and committee, third series, 1844–46.* Edited by Edwin Ernest Rich, with an introduction by William Kaye Lamb. London, 1944.

10: Simpson, George. *Part of dispatch from George Simpson, esqr, governor of Ruperts Land, to the governor & committee of the Hudson's Bay Company, London, March 1, 1829; continued and completed March 24 and June 5, 1829.* Edited by Edwin Ernest Rich, with an introduction by William Stewart Wallace. Toronto, 1947.

13: Ogden, Peter Skene. *Peter Skene Ogden's Snake country journals, 1824–25 and 1825–26.* Edited by Edwin Ernest Rich, assisted by Alice Margaret Johnson, with an introduction by Burt Brown Barker. London, 1950.

18: [Black, Samuel]. *A journal of a voyage from Rocky Mountain Portage in Peace River to the sources of Finlays Branch and North West Ward in summer 1824.* Edited by Edwin Ernest Rich, assisted by Alice Margaret Johnson, with an introduction by R. M. Patterson. London, 1955.

19: Colvile, Eden. *London correspondence inward from Eden Colvile, 1849–1852.* Edited by Edwin Ernest Rich, assisted by Alice Margaret Johnson, with an introduction by William Lewis Morton. London, 1956.

21, 22: Rich, *Hist. of HBC* [*see* section IV].

23: Ogden, Peter Skene. *Peter Skene Ogden's Snake country journal, 1826–27.* Edited by Kenneth Gordon Davies, assisted by Alice Margaret Johnson, with an introduction by Dorothy O. Johansen. London, 1961.

26: *Saskatchewan journals and correspondence; Edmonton House, 1795–1800, Chesterfield House, 1800–1802.* Edited with an introduction by Alice Margaret Johnson. London, 1967.

28: Ogden, Peter Skene. *Peter Skene Ogden's Snake country journals, 1827–28 and 1828–29.* Edited by Glyndwr Williams, with an introduction and notes by David Eugene Miller and David H. Miller. London, 1971.

29: Simpson, George. *London correspondence inward from Sir George Simpson, 1841–42.* Edited by Glyndwr Williams, with an introduction by John S. Galbraith. London, 1973.

30: *Hudson's Bay miscellany, 1670–1870.* Edited with introductions by Glyndwr Williams. Winnipeg, 1975.

32: *Fort Victoria letters, 1846–1851.* Edited by Hartwell Bowsfield, with an introduction by Margaret Anchoretta Ormsby. Winnipeg, 1979.

"The journals of the Legislative Assembly of Upper Canada . . . [1792–1824]." AO *Report*, 1909, 1911–14. The journals for part of 1794 and for 1795–97, 1809, 1813, and 1815 are missing.

LOWER CANADA/BAS-CANADA

HOUSE OF ASSEMBLY/CHAMBRE D'ASSEMBLÉE

Journals/Journaux. Quebec, 1792/93–1837.

SPECIAL COUNCIL/CONSEIL SPÉCIAL

Journals/Journaux. Quebec, 1838–41.

Ordinances/Ordonnances. Quebec, 1838–41.

Provincial statutes/Les statuts provinciaux. Quebec, 1792/93–1837.

For further information *see* Thériault, *Les pub. parl.* [section III].

[MACTAVISH] HARGRAVE, LETITIA. *The letters of Letitia Hargrave.* Edited with an introduction and notes by Margaret Arnett MacLeod. (Champlain Society publications, 28.) Toronto, 1947.

[MURPHY] JAMESON, [ANNA BROWNELL]. *Winter studies and summer rambles in Canada.* 3 vols. London, 1838; reprinted Toronto, 1972. [New edition.] Edited by James John Talman and Elsie McLeod Murray. 1 vol. Toronto, 1943.

NEW BRUNSWICK

The Acts of the General Assembly of her majesty's province of New Brunswick, from the twenty sixth year of the reign of King George the Third to the sixth year of the reign of King William the Fourth [1786–1836]. Revised and corrected by George F. S. Berton. Fredericton, 1838.

HOUSE OF ASSEMBLY

Journal. Fredericton, 1816–53.

LEGISLATIVE COUNCIL

Journal. Fredericton, 1831–50. The pre-1831 journals were published as *Journal of the Legislative Council of the province of New Brunswick . . .* [1786–1830]. 2 vols. Fredericton, 1831.

NEWFOUNDLAND

Blue book, 1836.

HOUSE OF ASSEMBLY

Journal, 1832–57.

LEGISLATIVE COUNCIL

Journal, 1837–49.

New light on the early history of the greater northwest: the manuscript journals of Alexander Henry, fur trader of the Northwest Company, and of David Thompson, official geographer and explorer of the same company, 1799–1814. . . . Edited by Elliott Coues. 3 vols. New York, 1897; reprinted 3 vols. in 2, Minneapolis, Minn., [1965].

NOVA SCOTIA

Acts of the General Assembly. Halifax, 1829–48. Title varies; see Bishop, *Pubs. of governments of N.S., P.E.I., N.B.* [section III].

HOUSE OF ASSEMBLY

Journal and proceedings. Halifax, 1800–54.

LEGISLATIVE COUNCIL

Debates and proceedings. Halifax, 1858–60.
Journal and proceedings. Halifax, 1836–60.

"Parliamentary debates." Canadian Library Association project to microfilm the debates of the legislature of the Province of Canada and the parliament of Canada for the period 1846–74.

Presbyterian: a Missionary and Religious Record of the Presbyterian Church of Canada in Connection with the Church of Scotland. Montreal. 1 (1848)–28 (1875).

PRINCE EDWARD ISLAND

HOUSE OF ASSEMBLY

Journal. Charlottetown, 1812–61.

LEGISLATIVE COUNCIL

Journal. Charlottetown, 1827–60.

PUBLIC ARCHIVES OF CANADA, Ottawa

BOARD OF HISTORICAL PUBLICATIONS

Docs. relating to constitutional hist., 1759–91 (Shortt and Doughty; 1918).

NUMBERED PUBLICATIONS [*see also* section III]

9: *Canadian North-West* (Oliver).

OTHER PUBLICATIONS [*see also* section III]

Docs. relating to constitutional hist., 1791–1818 (Doughty and McArthur).
Docs. relating to constitutional hist., 1819–28 (Doughty and Story).
Elgin–Grey papers (Doughty).
Report/Rapport. 1881–19 . Annually, with some omissions, until 1952; irregularly thereafter. For indexes, *see* section III.

[RAMSAY, GEORGE, 9TH EARL OF] DALHOUSIE. *The Dalhousie journals.* Edited by Marjory Whitelaw. 3 vols. [Ottawa], 1978–82.

Le répertoire national, ou recueil de littérature canadienne. James Huston, compil. 4 vols. Montréal, 1848–50; réimpr., 1982. 2ᵉ éd. 1893.

ROBB, JAMES, AND ELLEN [COSTER] ROBB. *The letters of James and Ellen Robb; portrait of a Fredericton family in early Victorian times.* Edited by Alfred Goldsworthy Bailey. Fredericton, 1983.

ROSS, ALEXANDER. *Adventures of the first settlers on the Oregon or Columbia River: being a narrative of the expedition fitted out by John Jacob Astor, to establish the "Pacific Fur Company"; with an account of some Indian tribes on the coast of the Pacific.* London, 1849; reprinted Ann Arbor, Mich., [1966].

Select British documents of the Canadian War of 1812. Edited with an introduction by William [Charles Henry] Wood. (Champlain Society publications, 13–15, 17.) 3 vols. in 4. Toronto, 1920–28; reprinted New York, 1968.

SIMPSON, GEORGE. "The 'Character book' of Governor George Simpson, 1832." In *HBRS*, 30 (Williams), 151–236.

—— *Fur trade and empire: George Simpson's journal, "Remarks connected with the fur trade in the course of a voyage from York Factory to Fort George and back to York Factory, 1824–1825. . . ."* Edited with an introduction by Frederick Merk. (Harvard historical studies, 31.) Cambridge, Mass., and London, 1931. Revised edition. Edited with a new introduction by Frederick Merk. Cambridge, 1968.

Statistical account of Upper Canada, compiled with a view to a grand system of emigration. Compiled by Robert [Fleming] Gourlay. 2 vols. London, 1822; reprinted East Ardsley, Eng., and New York, 1966. Abridged and with an introduction by Stanley Robert Mealing. (Carleton library series, 75.) 1 vol. Toronto, 1974.

The town of York, 1793–1815: a collection of documents of early Toronto. Edited by Edith Grace Firth. (Champlain Society publications, Ontario series, 5.) Toronto, 1962.

The town of York, 1815–1834: a further collection of documents of early Toronto. Edited by Edith Grace Firth. (Champlain Society publications, Ontario series, 8.) Toronto, 1966.

"United Empire Loyalists: enquiry into the losses and services in consequence of their loyalty; evidence in the Canadian claims." AO *Report*, 1904.

UPPER CANADA
  HOUSE OF ASSEMBLY
    Appendix to the journal, 1835–1839/40.
    Journal, 1821, 1825–1839/40. For the period from 1792 to 1824, *see* "Journals of Legislative Assembly of U.C.," AO *Report*, 1909, 1911–14.
  LEGISLATIVE COUNCIL
    Journal, 1828–1839/40. The earlier journals are available in "The journals of the Legislative Assembly of Upper Canada . . . [1792–1824]," AO *Report*, 1910, 1915.
    Statutes, 1802–38.
The valley of the Trent. Edited with an introduction by Edwin Clarence Guillet. (Champlain Society publications, Ontario series, 1.) Toronto, 1957.
WISCONSIN, STATE HISTORICAL SOCIETY, Madison
  PUBLICATIONS
    Collections. 31 vols. 1854–1931.

B. NEWSPAPERS

The following newspapers were particularly useful in the preparation of volume VIII. Numerous sources have been used to determine their various titles and their dates of publication. The printed sources include, for all areas of the country: CLA, *Canadian newspapers on microfilm, catalogue* (2 pts. in 3, Ottawa, 1959–69), *Union list of Canadian newspapers held by Canadian libraries/Liste collective des journaux canadiens disponibles dans les bibliothèques canadiennes* (Ottawa, 1977), and, for pre-1800 newspapers, Marie Tremaine, *A bibliography of Canadian imprints, 1751–1800* (Toronto, 1952); for New Brunswick: J. R. Harper, *Historical directory of New Brunswick newspapers and periodicals* (Fredericton, 1961); for Newfoundland: "Chronological list of Newfoundland newspapers in the public collections at the Gosling Memorial Library and Provincial Archives," comp. Ian MacDonald (copy in the Provincial Reference Dept., Nfld. Public Library Services, St John's), and *Serials holdings in the libraries of Memorial University of Newfoundland and St. John's Public Library: alphabetical list*, comp. C. D. Evans (8th ed., 2v., St John's, 1973); for Nova Scotia: D. C. Harvey, "Newspapers of Nova Scotia, 1840–1867," *CHR*, 26 (1945): 279–301, G. E. N. Tratt, *A survey and listing of Nova Scotia newspapers, 1752–1957, with particular reference to the period before 1867* (Halifax, 1979), and *An historical directory of Nova Scotia newspapers and journals before confederation*, comp. T. B. Vincent (Kingston, Ont., 1977); for Ontario: *Catalogue of Canadian newspapers in the Douglas Library,*

Queen's University, [comp. L. C. Ellison *et al.*] (Kingston, 1969), *Early Toronto newspapers* (Firth) [*see* section III], and W. S. Wallace, "The periodical literature of Upper Canada," *CHR*, 12 (1931): 4–22; for Prince Edward Island: W. L. Cotton, "The press in Prince Edward Island," *Past and present of Prince Edward Island . . .* , ed. D. A. MacKinnon and A. B. Warburton (Charlottetown, [1906]), 112–21, and R. L. Cotton, "Early press," *Historic highlights of Prince Edward Island*, ed. M. C. Brehaut (Charlottetown, 1955), 40–45; and for Quebec: Beaulieu et Hamelin, *La presse québécoise*, vols. 1–2 [*see* section III]. Bishop, *Pubs. of governments of N.S., P.E.I., N.B.* [*see* section III], gives information on official gazettes in the Maritime provinces.

L'Abeille. Québec. Published from 27 July 1848 to 23 June 1881.

Acadian Recorder. Halifax. Published from 16 Jan. 1813 to 26 June 1869 as a weekly. A tri-weekly began on 5 Sept. 1864, and was joined by a daily on 1 Dec. 1868. Both editions ceased publication in May 1930.

L'Avenir. Montréal. Published from 24 June 1847 to 22 Dec. 1857.

Bathurst Courier. Perth, Ont. Published as a weekly under various titles from 8 Aug. 1834 to the present. Until 7 Aug. 1835 its full title was the *Bathurst Courier and Ottawa Gazette*; it continued as the *Bathurst Courier and Ottawa General Advertiser* until 30 June 1846, when the second half of the title was dropped. On 13 Nov. 1857 it became the *Perth Courier*.

British Colonist. Halifax. Its full title initially was *British Colonist: a Literary, Political and Commercial Journal*. Published from 25 July 1848 until 31 Dec. 1874 as a tri-weekly; a weekly was added in January 1849 and a daily on 13 Dec. 1869. From 11 Sept. 1851 until 20 Jan. 1855, the title was *British Colonist, and North American Railway Journal*.

British Colonist. Toronto. Began as a weekly on 1 Feb. 1838 and became a semi-weekly in August 1843. The *Daily Colonist* began in November 1851 and the *News of the Week, or Weekly Colonist* in August 1852. The daily and semi-weekly editions had ceased publication by September 1860, but the *News of the Week* continued until December 1861.

British Whig. Kingston, Ont. Began publication as a semi-weekly in February 1834. The paper became the *British Whig, and General Advertiser for the Midland District* on 25 Jan. 1835, and by the 1840s it was the *British Whig, and General Advertiser for Canada West*. A weekly from January 1849 (when a daily edition also began publication [*see Daily British Whig*]) until 1897, it assumed the title *Weekly British Whig* on 15 June 1849.

Brockville Recorder. Brockville, Ont. Published

weekly from 16 Jan. 1821 until 22 Feb. 1957, it was issued as the *Brockville Recorder, and the Eastern, Johnstown, and Bathurst Districts Advertiser* until 15 July 1847, as the *Brockville Recorder and Advertiser, for the Eastern, Johnstown, and Bathurst Districts* from 22 July 1847 to 26 Dec. 1850, and as the *Brockville Recorder and Advertiser* from 9 Jan. 1851 to 25 Aug. 1853; beginning with the issue of 1 Sept. 1853 it became simply the *Brockville Recorder*.

Bytown Gazette, and Ottawa and Rideau Advertiser. Ottawa. Published from 9 June 1836 until around 1861 under various titles.

Canadian Freeman. Toronto. Published weekly from 1825 until August 1834.

Le Canadien. Québec. Published from 22 Nov. 1806 to 11 Feb. 1893.

Christian Guardian. Toronto. Published as a weekly from 21 Nov. 1829 until 10 June 1925 when it was superseded by the *New Outlook*, which was in turn succeeded by the *United Church Observer* on 1 March 1939. A general index of the *Christian Guardian* for the years 1829–67 is available at the UCA.

Chronicle & Gazette. Kingston, Ont. Published as a weekly from 29 June 1833 to 1834, as a semi-weekly from 1835 to 1847, and again as a weekly to about 1899. Its full name was *Chronicle & Gazette and Kingston Commercial Advertiser* until 1840 when the last part of the title was dropped, and from 1847 it was the *Chronicle and News*. A daily edition was issued from 7 Oct. 1851 to 1908 as the *Daily News* and other titles. The paper's predecessors were the weekly *Kingston Gazette* (25 Sept. 1810–29 Dec. 1818) and the *Kingston Chronicle* (1 Jan. 1819–22 June 1833).

Chronicle and News. Kingston, Ont. See *Chronicle & Gazette*

Church. Cobourg, [Ont.]; Toronto; Hamilton, [Ont.]. Published as a weekly from 6 May 1837 to 25 July 1856, first at Cobourg, and then at Toronto from 11 July 1840 to 30 June 1843, at Cobourg again from 14 July 1843 to 3 July 1846, at Toronto from 17 July 1846, and finally at Hamilton from 3 Aug. 1855. Between 5 Aug. 1852 and 16 June 1853 the title was the *Canadian Churchman*.

Cobourg Star. Cobourg, Ont. Published weekly from 11 Jan. 1831, it became a daily on 15 Nov. 1856, and continued until 1879. Its full title was the *Cobourg Star and Newcastle District Gazette* until 22 Sept. 1841 when the subtitle was dropped.

Colonial Advocate. Queenston, [Ont.]; Toronto. A weekly founded on 18 May 1824, it moved to York [Toronto] in November 1824. Its full title was *Colonial Advocate and Journal of Agriculture, Manufactures and Commerce* until 7 Oct. 1824

when it became the *Colonial Advocate*; in December 1833 it became the *Advocate*, and on 4 Nov. 1834 it amalgamated with the *Canadian Correspondent* to form the *Correspondent and Advocate*.

Correspondent and Advocate. Toronto. See *Colonial Advocate*

Le Courrier du Canada. Québec. Published from 2 Feb. 1857 to 11 April 1901.

Daily British Whig. Kingston, Ont. Began publication on 1 Jan. 1849. On 1 Dec. 1926 it merged with the *Daily Standard* to form the *Whig-Standard*, which continues to the present. [See also its predecessor, the *British Whig* (1834–48).]

Daily Colonist. Toronto. See *British Colonist*

Daily Leader. Toronto. See *Leader*

Daily News. Kingston, Ont. See *Chronicle & Gazette*

Daily Spectator, and Journal of Commerce. Hamilton, Ont. See *Hamilton Spectator*

L'Ère nouvelle, journal du district des Trois-Rivières. Trois-Rivières, [Qué.]. Published from 9 Dec. 1852 to 1865.

Examiner. Charlottetown. Published under a variety of titles, it began on 7 Aug. 1847 as a weekly. For a brief period from 23 Feb. 1850 to 7 April 1851 it appeared as a semi-weekly, the *Examiner and Semi-Weekly Intelligencer*, and from 1877 both daily and weekly editions were published.

Examiner. Toronto. Published as a weekly from 3 July 1838 until 29 Aug. 1855 when it merged with the *Globe*.

La Gazette de Québec. See *Quebec Gazette*

Gleaner. Miramichi, N.B.; Chatham, N.B. Published from 28 July 1829 to 1880, it superseded the *Miramichi Mercury* (1826–29). Its title until 1 Sept. 1835 was *Gleaner: and Northumberland Schediasma*, and it continued under various other titles, including that of *Gleaner: and Northumberland, Kent, Gloucester and Restigouche Commercial and Agricultural Journal* in the 1840s and 1850s. The paper appeared weekly except for the period from 23 July to 31 Dec. 1853 when it was issued twice a week.

Globe. Toronto. Began as a weekly on 5 March 1844, became a semi-weekly on 11 Nov. 1846, a tri-weekly on 3 July 1849, and a daily on 3 Oct. 1853. A second weekly series began on 6 July 1849 and continued to 28 Jan. 1914. A second semi-weekly series was published from 19 Oct. 1853 to 2 July 1855 and became a tri-weekly which lasted until 1864. The *Western Globe*, published weekly in Toronto but issued from London, Upper Canada, lasted from 16 Oct. 1845 until at least 1851. The title became the *Globe and Mail* when the paper merged with the *Daily Mail and Empire* on 23 Nov. 1936 and publication continues under this title to the present.

Hamilton Spectator. Hamilton, Ont. Began on 15 July 1846 as the semi-weekly *Hamilton Spectator, and Journal of Commerce*, and then from July 1855 to December 1864 appeared as the *Semi-Weekly Spectator*. The *Weekly Spectator* was added on 23 May 1850, and continued under various titles until December 1894. A daily edition was launched on 10 May 1852 as the *Daily Spectator, and Journal of Commerce* and appeared under this title until 29 March 1865; after several title changes it became the *Hamilton Spectator* on 21 March 1890, which continues to the present.

Herald. Toronto. A semi-weekly, published from 28 June 1837 to 1841 as the *Commercial Herald* and then until 1846 as the *Toronto Herald*; the paper was issued as the *Herald* from 1846 until it ceased publication on 30 June 1848.

Islander. Charlottetown. Published as a weekly from 2 Dec. 1842 until June 1874. Its full title was the *Islander, or Prince Edward Island Intelligencer and Advertiser* until 21 Jan. 1853, when it became the *Islander, or Prince Edward Island Weekly Intelligencer and Advertiser*, and then in December 1872 the *Prince Edward Islander: a Weekly Newspaper of General Intelligence*. It was absorbed by the *Weekly Patriot* in July 1874.

Le Journal de Québec. Published from 1 December 1842 to 1 Oct. 1889.

Kingston Chronicle. Kingston, Ont. See *Chronicle & Gazette*

Kingston Gazette. Kingston, Ont. See *Chronicle & Gazette*

Lambton Observer, and Western Advertiser. Sarnia, Ont. See *Sarnia Observer, and Lambton Advertiser*

Leader. Toronto. Began publication as the *Weekly Leader* on 7 July 1852; the *Semi-Weekly Leader* followed on 13 July 1852, and the *Daily Leader* was added on 11 July 1853. All three editions adopted the title *Leader* in November 1855, although the weekly reverted to *Weekly Leader* in 1859. The semi-weekly ceased publication on 30 Sept. 1864, but the daily and weekly editions continued until 1878.

Mackenzie's Weekly Message. Toronto. Published from 27 Jan. 1853 until 15 Sept. 1860. On 15 Aug. 1856 it became the *Toronto Weekly Message*, and from July 1859 to 15 Sept. 1860 it appeared as *Mackenzie's Toronto Weekly Message*.

Mélanges réligieux. Montréal. Published from 14 Dec. 1840 to 6 July 1852.

La Minerve. Montréal. Published from 9 Nov. 1826 to 27 May 1899.

Montreal Gazette. First issued on 3 June 1778 as *La Gazette du commerce et littérature, pour la ville et district de Montréal*. A bilingual continuation of this paper, the *Montreal Gazette/La Gazette de Montréal*, began on 3 Aug. 1785. From August 1822 to the present it has appeared only in English, with several changes in title and frequency.

Montreal Herald. Published from 19 Oct. 1811 to 18 Oct. 1857.

Montreal Transcript. Published from 4 Oct. 1836 until around 1865.

Morning Chronicle. Halifax. Published under various titles from 24 Jan. 1844 to the present. It began as a tri-weekly which lasted until 1877; a daily was added on 3 Aug. 1864, and a weekly was also printed from 1844 until around 1926 [see *Novascotian*]. On 1 Jan. 1949 it merged with the *Halifax Herald* to become the *Chronicle-Herald*.

Morning Chronicle. Quebec. Began publication on 18 May 1847.

Morning News. Saint John, N.B. Began publication on 16 Sept. 1839 as the *Commercial News and General Advertiser*, becoming the *Morning News* on 3 April 1840. It continued on 8 April 1884 under a variety of titles, of which *Morning News* was the most common. The paper began as a tri-weekly, a weekly edition being added on 15 Dec. 1847, and a daily on 2 Jan. 1869.

New-Brunswick Courier. Saint John, N.B. A weekly, it was launched on 2 May 1811 and continued until 1865.

New Brunswick Reporter and Fredericton Advertiser. Began publication on 23 Nov. 1844 as the *New Brunswick Reporter*, with the subtitle being added in 1845. From 17 March to 29 Sept. 1888 it was published jointly with the *Temperance Journal* and appeared under various combined titles. On 6 Oct. 1888 it became the *Reporter and Fredericton Advertiser*. It was a weekly except for the period between 3 May 1882 and 10 March 1888 when it was issued semi-weekly.

New-Brunswick Royal Gazette. Saint John; Fredericton. See *Royal Gazette*

Newfoundlander. St John's. Published from 1827 until 1884. The paper was a weekly until 29 April 1852, then became a semi-weekly until it ceased publication.

Newfoundland Mercantile Journal. St John's. A weekly, published from 1816 to 1827.

Newfoundland Patriot. St John's. See *Patriot*

Novascotian. Halifax. Published weekly under various titles from 29 Dec. 1824 until some time in 1926, although no issues after 25 Dec. 1925 appear to have survived. Its full title was initially the *Novascotian, or Colonial Herald*, but on 2 Jan. 1840 it dropped the subtitle. After 1844 it was the weekly edition of the *Morning Chronicle*.

Nova-Scotia Royal Gazette. Halifax. Published under this title from 3 Jan. 1801 to 9 Feb. 1843. A weekly, it began as the *Halifax Gazette* on 23 March 1752. It was continued under various titles, including the *Royal Gazette and the Nova-Scotia Advertiser* (7 April 1789–30 Dec. 1800). On 16 Feb. 1843 the paper became the *Royal Gazette*, which continues to the present.

L'Opinion publique. Montréal. Published from 1 Jan. 1870 to 27 Dec. 1883.

Ottawa Citizen. Ottawa. Began publication on 17 April 1844 as the weekly Bytown *Packet*, becoming the *Ottawa Citizen* on 22 Feb. 1851. A semi-weekly edition also appeared from 4 Oct. 1859 and the daily *Ottawa Citizen* from 15 May 1865; the latter has continued, with a number of title changes, to the present.

Packet. Ottawa. See *Ottawa Citizen*

La Patrie. Montréal. Published from 24 Feb. 1879 to 9 Jan. 1978.

Patriot. Kingston, [Ont.]; Toronto. Began publication in Kingston on 12 Nov. 1829 as the weekly *Patriot and Farmer's Monitor*. The paper moved to York [Toronto] on 7 Dec. 1832, became a semi-weekly in November 1833, and was changed to the *Patriot* on 21 March 1834 and the *Toronto Patriot* on 3 Jan. 1840. A second weekly edition was begun around 1849 and continued under various titles until October 1878. The *Daily Patriot and Express* was published from 16 April 1850 to November 1855 when it was absorbed by the *Leader*, becoming its evening edition.

Patriot. St John's. Published from 1833 to June 1890 as a weekly; issues are available only from 1834. Its full title was the *Newfoundland Patriot* until 1842, when it became the *Patriot & Terra Nova Herald*.

Patriot and Farmer's Monitor. Kingston, [Ont.]; Toronto. See *Patriot*

Patriot & Terra Nova Herald. St John's. See *Patriot*

Le Pays. Montréal. Published from 15 Jan. 1852 to 26 Dec. 1871.

Perth Courier. Perth, Ont. See *Bathurst Courier*

Pilot. Montreal. Published from 5 March 1844 to 25 March 1862.

Prince Edward Island Gazette. Charlottetown. See *Royal Gazette*

Prince Edward Island Register. Charlottetown. See *Royal Gazette*

Public Ledger. St John's. Published from about 1820 to 1882 first as a semi-weekly, then as a tri-weekly, and finally, in 1859, as a daily. Its full title was originally the *Public Ledger and Newfoundland General Advertiser*; it later appeared under various other titles, including the *Daily Ledger*, *Public Ledger*, and *Public Ledger and Newfoundland Daily Advertiser*.

Quebec Gazette/La Gazette de Québec. Published from 21 June 1764, the paper remained bilingual from 2 May 1832 until 30 April 1842, but the French and English editions were published separately. From 29 Oct. 1842 to 30 Oct. 1874 only the English edition appeared.

Quebec Mercury. Published from 5 Jan. 1805 to 1 Oct. 1903.

Royal Gazette. Charlottetown. Published weekly from 24 Aug. 1830 to the present, becoming an official government gazette in 1851. Its predecessors include the *Weekly Recorder of Prince Edward Island*, published from 1810 to perhaps 1813, the *Prince Edward Island Gazette*, published on an irregular basis from 1814 to about 1821, and the *Prince Edward Island Register*, which appeared weekly from 23 July 1823 to 17 July 1830.

Royal Gazette. Saint John, N.B.; Fredericton. Published weekly from 11 Oct. 1785 to the present, first in Saint John until around February 1814, and then in Fredericton. It appeared originally as the *Royal Gazette, and the New-Brunswick Advertiser*; since 1 Dec. 1802 it has been called simply the *Royal Gazette*, except from 1808 to 1814 when it was the *Royal Gazette, and New-Brunswick Advertiser* and from April 1814 to 12 May 1828 when it was the *New-Brunswick Royal Gazette*.

Royal Gazette and Newfoundland Advertiser. St John's. Published from 27 Aug. 1807 as a weekly. In October 1924 the paper became the *Newfoundland Gazette*, the official government gazette which continues to the present.

Royal Gazette and the Nova-Scotia Advertiser. Halifax. See *Nova-Scotia Royal Gazette*

Sarnia Observer, and Lambton Advertiser. Sarnia, Ont. A weekly, it was published from 16 Nov. 1853 to 20 Nov. 1856 as the *Lambton Observer, and Western Advertiser*. On 10 Jan. 1879 the title was shortened to *Sarnia Observer*. A daily edition began publication in 1895 and has continued to the present under various titles, including *Canadian Observer* (1917–57).

Semi-Weekly Leader. Toronto. See *Leader*

Semi-Weekly Spectator. Hamilton, Ont. See *Hamilton Spectator*

Times. Halifax. Published weekly from 3 June 1834 to 27 June 1848.

Times. London. Published daily from 1785 to the present. Its title from 1785 to 1788 was the *Daily Universal Register*.

Times and General Commercial Gazette. St John's. Published from 15 Aug. 1832 until 23 March 1895. It was a weekly until 25 Dec. 1844, and thereafter a semi-weekly.

Toronto Herald. See *Herald*

Toronto Mirror. A weekly, it was published from 1 July 1837 to 1842 as the *Mirror* and continued to about 1866.

Toronto Patriot. See *Patriot*

Upper Canada Gazette. Newark, later Niagara

[Niagara-on-the-Lake, Ont.]; Toronto. Began 18 April 1793 and moved to York [Toronto] after the issue of 25 Aug. 1798. Irregular until 1800, when it became a weekly. Its full title to 28 March 1807 was the *Upper Canada Gazette; or American Oracle*, from 15 April 1807 to the end of 1816 the *York Gazette*, and after 1817 the *Upper Canada Gazette* once more. It is believed to have ceased publication in 1849.

Weekly British Whig. Kingston, Ont. See *British Whig*

Weekly Recorder of Prince Edward Island. Charlottetown. See *Royal Gazette*

Weekly Spectator. Hamilton, Ont. See *Hamilton Spectator*

Western Mercury. Hamilton, Ont. Published weekly and then semi-weekly from 20 Jan. 1831 until about 1835.

York Gazette. Newark [Niagara-on-the-Lake, Ont.]; Toronto. See *Upper Canada Gazette*

III. REFERENCE WORKS

ALLAIRE, JEAN-BAPTISTE-ARTHUR. *Dictionnaire biographique du clergé canadien-français*. 6 vols. Montréal et Saint-Hyacinthe, Qué., 1908–34.

[1]: *Les anciens*. Montréal, 1910.

[2]: *Les contemporains*. Saint-Hyacinthe, 1908.

[3]: [*Suppléments.*] 6 parts in 1 vol. Montréal, 1910–19.

[4]: *Le clergé canadien-français: revue mensuelle* ([Montréal]), 1 (1919–20). Only one volume of this journal was published.

[5]: *Compléments*. 6 parts in 1 vol. Montréal, 1928–32.

[6]: Untitled. Saint-Hyacinthe, 1934.

ALMANACS. The almanacs have been listed under this heading to facilitate their identification. Because titles within series vary and publishers or editors often change, the almanacs have in the main been listed under a general title, with the specifics found on title-pages following. The information in square brackets is given as a guide and may not be completely accurate.

Belcher's farmer's almanack. [Halifax, 1824–1930.] Edited by Clement Horton Belcher from 1824 to 1870 when its publication was taken over by the firm of McAlpine and Barnes, later the McAlpine Publishing Company. From 1824 to 1831 its title was *The farmer's almanack . . .* ; in 1832 it became *Belcher's farmer's almanack . . .* , a title it retained with minor variations until its disappearance.

Canadian almanac. Toronto, 1848– . Publishers: Scobie & Balfour, 1848–50; Hugh Scobie, 1851–54; Maclear & Co., 1855–61; W. C. Chewett & Co., 1862–69; Copp, Clark & Co., 1870 to the present. From 1848 to 1850 its title was *Scobie & Balfour's Canadian almanac, and repository of useful knowledge . . .* and from 1851 to 1854 *Scobie's Canadian almanac, and repository of useful knowledge . . .* ; it has continued under various other titles, adopting its present name, *The Canadian almanac and directory . . .* , in 1948.

Cunnabell's Nova-Scotia almanac. Halifax, 1834–68. Published by J. S. Cunnabell, 1834–36; William Cunnabell, 1837–68. From 1834 to 1841 its title was the *Nova-Scotia almanack . . .* , in 1842 it became *Cunnabell's Nova-Scotia almanac . . .* , and in 1851 *Cunnabell's Nova-Scotia almanac, and farmer's manual. . . .*

Halifax almanac. [Published in Halifax from 1790 to at least 1821.] Its actual title was *An almanack . . . calculated for the meridian of Halifax, in Nova-Scotia. . . .* Published by John Howe, 1790–1815; David Howe, 1816; John Munro, 1821.

Montreal almanack. [Montreal, 1829–72.] Publishers: Robert Armour, 1829–31; H. C. McLeod, 1839–42; Starke's, 1867–72. Its title varies: *Montreal almanack, or Lower Canada register . . .* , 1829–31; *Montreal almanack . . .* , 1833–72.

New-Brunswick almanac. [Published at Saint John from 1812 into the 20th century.] Compiled by Bernard Kieran from 1812 to 1824, by Uranophilus from 1825 to 1828, and prepared under the supervision of the Fredericton Athenæum from 1849 to 1851. Published by Henry Chubb, and later by his firm, from 1812 to 1864. From 1812 to 1830 its title was *An almanack . . .* ; in 1832 it became the *New-Brunswick almanack . . .* ; and in 1849, the *New-Brunswick almanac and register. . . .*

Newfoundland almanack. [St John's, 1844–1932.] Compilers: J. Templeman, 1844; Philip Tocque, 1849; Joseph Woods from around 1856 until 1878. The earlier title varied between *almanack* and *almanac*.

Prince Edward Island calendar. [Charlottetown, 1841–73]. Publishers include: James D. Haszard, 1836; George T. Haszard, 1855–60.

Quebec almanac/Almanach de Québec. Quebec, 1780–1841 (except for 1781, 1790, and 1793). Publishers: William Brown, 1780–89; Samuel Neilson, 1791–92; John Neilson, 1794–1823;

Neilson and Cowan, 1824–36; S. Neilson, 1837; W. Neilson, 1838–41. Title varies as to spelling and also as to language, but from 1813 to 1841 it was published in English only as *The Quebec almanack; and British American royal kalendar.* . . .

ARCHIVES NATIONALES DU QUÉBEC, Québec PUBLICATIONS [*see also* section II]
P.-G. Roy, *Inv. concessions.*
—— *Les juges de la prov. de Québec.*

ARMSTRONG, FREDERICK HENRY. *Handbook of Upper Canadian chronology and territorial legislation.* (University of Western Ontario, Lawson Memorial Library publication.) London, 1967.

AUDET, FRANCIS-JOSEPH. *Les députés de Trois-Rivières (1808–1838)* ("Pages trifluviennes," sér.A, 11.) Trois-Rivières, Qué., 1934.
—— "Les législateurs du Bas-Canada de 1760 à 1867." Manuscript held by the Morisset Library, University of Ottawa, 3 vols., 1940.

Australian dictionary of biography. Edited by Douglas Pike *et al.* 9 vols. to date. Melbourne, [1966]– . Arranged alphabetically, vols.1–2 cover the years 1788–1850; vols.3–6, 1851–90; and vols.7–9, "A to Las" for 1891–1939.

BEAULIEU, ANDRÉ, ET JEAN HAMELIN. *La presse québécoise des origines à nos jours.* [2ᵉ édition.] 6 vols. to date [1764–1934]. Québec, 1973– .

Belcher's farmer's almanack. See ALMANACS

BIBAUD, [FRANÇOIS-]MAXIMILIEN. *Le Panthéon canadien; choix de biographies.* Nouvelle édition, revue, augmentée et complétée par Adèle et Victoria Bibaud. Montréal, 1891.

A bibliography of Canadiana, being items in the Public Library of Toronto, Canada, relating to the early history and development of Canada. Edited by Frances Maria Staton and Marie Tremaine. Toronto, 1934; reprinted 1965.

A bibliography of Canadiana: first supplement. . . . Edited by Gertrude Mabel Boyle with Marjorie Colbeck. Toronto, 1959; reprinted 1969.

Birmingham directory. See DIRECTORIES

BISHOP, OLGA BERNICE. *Publications of the government of the Province of Canada, 1841–1867.* (National Library of Canada publication.) Ottawa, 1963.
—— *Publications of the governments of Nova Scotia, Prince Edward Island, New Brunswick, 1758–1952.* (National Library of Canada publication.) Ottawa, 1957.

BOASE, FREDERIC. *Modern English biography: containing many thousand concise memoirs of persons who have died between the years 1851–1900, with an index of the most interesting matter.* 3 vols. and 3 supplements. Privately printed in Truro, Eng., 1892–1921; reprinted [London], 1965.

BORTHWICK, JOHN DOUGLAS. *History and biographi-cal gazetteer of Montreal to the year 1892.* Montreal, 1892.

British Museum general catalogue of printed books. Photolithograhic edition to 1955. 263 vols. London, 1959–66. A new catalogue, *The British Library general catalogue of printed books to 1975,* began publication in 1979.

BURKE, JOHN. *A general and heraldic dictionary of the peerage and baronetage of the United Kingdom.* London, 1826. 105th edition. Edited by Peter Townend. 1970.

"Calendar of state papers addressed by the secretaries of state for the colonies to the lieutenant-governors or officers administering the government of the Province of Upper Canada, [1821–1841]." PAC *Report,* 1935: 171–398; 1936: 399–598; 1937: 599–802.

Canada directory. See DIRECTORIES
Canadian almanac. See ALMANACS
The Canadian biographical dictionary and portrait gallery of eminent and self-made men. 2 vols. Toronto, 1880–81.

CANADIAN PERMANENT COMMITTEE ON GEOGRAPHICAL NAMES
TOPONYMY STUDIES
1: Rayburn, *Geographical names of P.E.I.*
2: Rayburn, *Geographical names of N.B.*

CARON, IVANHOË. "Inventaire de la correspondance de Mᵍʳ Bernard-Claude Panet, archevêque de Québec." ANQ *Rapport,* 1933–34: 235–421; 1934–35: 341–420; 1935–36: 157–272.
—— "Inventaire de la correspondance de Mᵍʳ Jean-Olivier Briand, évêque de Québec." ANQ *Rapport,* 1929–30: 47–136.
—— "Inventaire de la correspondance de Mᵍʳ Joseph Signay, archevêque de Québec." ANQ *Rapport,* 1936–37: 125–330; 1937–38: 23–146; 1938–39: 182–357.
—— "Inventaire de la correspondance de Mᵍʳ Joseph-Octave Plessis, archevêque de Québec, 1797–1825." ANQ *Rapport,* 1927–28: 215–316; 1928–29: 89–208; 1932–33: 3–244.
—— "Inventaire de la correspondance de Mᵍʳ Pierre Denaut, évêque de Québec." ANQ *Rapport,* 1931–32: 129–242.

CHADWICK, EDWARD MARION. *Ontarian families: genealogies of United-Empire-Loyalist and other pioneer families of Upper Canada.* 2 vols. Toronto, 1894–98; reprinted, 2 vols. in 1, Lambertville, N.J., [1970]. Vol. 1 reprinted with an introduction by William Felix Edmund Morley, Belleville, Ont., 1972.

Chatham directory. See DIRECTORIES

COOKE, ALAN, AND CLIVE HOLLAND. *The exploration of northern Canada, 500 to 1920: a chronology.* Toronto, 1978.

CORNISH, GEORGE HENRY. *Cyclopædia of Methodism*

in Canada: containing historical, educational, and statistical information, dating from the beginning of the work in the several provinces of the Dominion of Canada, and extending to the annual conferences of 1880. 2 vols. Toronto and Halifax, 1881–1903.

Cunnabell's Nova Scotia almanac. See ALMANACS

A cyclopædia of Canadian biography. . . . Edited by George MacLean Rose and Hector [Willoughby] Charlesworth. (Rose's national biographical series, 1–3.) 3 vols. Toronto, 1886–1919. Vols. 1–2 were edited by Rose, vol. 3 by Charlesworth. Subtitles and series titles vary.

DESJARDINS, JOSEPH. *Guide parlementaire historique de la province de Québec, 1792 à 1902.* Québec, 1902.

DESROSIERS, LOUIS-ADÉLARD. "Inventaire de la correspondance de Mgr Jean-Jacques Lartigue." ANQ *Rapport,* 1941–42: 347–496; 1942–43: 3–174; 1943–44: 212–334; 1944–45: 175–226.

Dictionary of American biography. Edited by Allen Johnson *et al.* 20 vols., index, and 2 supplements [to 1940]. New York, 1928–[58]; reprinted, 22 vols. in 11 and index, [1946?–58]. 5 additional supplements to date [to 1965]. Edited by Edward Topping James *et al.* [1973]– . *Concise DAB.* [1964.] 2nd edition. [1977.] 3rd edition. [1980.]

Dictionary of Hamilton biography. Edited by Thomas Melville Bailey *et al.* 1 vol. to date [to 1875]. Hamilton, Ont., 1981– .

Dictionary of national biography. Edited by Leslie Stephen and Sidney Lee. 63 vols., 3 supplements, and index and epitome [to 1900]. London, 1885–1903; reissued without index, 22 vols., 1908–9. 7 additional supplements to date [to 1970]. Edited by Sidney Lee *et al.* 1912– . *Concise DNB.* 2 vols. [1953]–61. *Corrections and additions to the Dictionary of national biography.* Boston, 1966.

A dictionary of Toronto printers, publishers, booksellers, and the allied trades, 1798–1900. Compiled by Elizabeth Hulse. Toronto, 1982.

Dictionnaire des œuvres littéraires du Québec. Maurice Lemire *et al.,* éditeurs. 4 vols. to date [to 1969]. Montréal, [1978]– .

DIRECTORIES. Issued initially as single works, these frequently became regular, usually annual, publications in the 19th century. Because titles within series varied greatly and editors or compilers frequently changed, the directories used in the preparation of volume VIII have been listed below by region and under a general title, with the dates of the relevant years following. Details of various titles and publishers given on title pages, as well as of the places of publication of the Canadian directories cited, can be found in D. E. Ryder, *Checklist of Canadian directories, 1790–1950/*

Répertoire des annuaires canadiennes (Ottawa, 1979). For British directories, the following sources proved useful: *British Museum general catalogue* and J. E. Norton, *Guide to the national and provincial directories of England and Wales, excluding London, published before 1856* (London, 1950).

Birmingham directory. Cited in vol. VIII was *Chapman's annual directory of Birmingham & its vicinity.* Birmingham, Eng., 1808.

Canada directory. Issues used in vol. VIII include: *The Canada directory* . . . , ed. R. W. S. Mackay (Montreal, 1851); *The Canada directory for 1857–58* . . . (Montreal, [1857]); and *Mitchell's Canada gazetteer and business directory for 1864–65* (Toronto, 1864).

The Chatham directory and county gazetteer, for 1885–6. Compiled by James Soutar. Chatham, Ont., 1886.

City of Hamilton directory. . . . Hamilton, [Ont.], 1858.

Glasgow directory. Glasgow. Cited in vol. VIII were issues for 1826–60. The titles include *Glasgow Post-Office directory* . . . , *The Post Office annual directory* . . . , and *Post Office Glasgow directory.* . . .

London directory. Used in vol. VIII was *The Post-Office annual directory.* . . . London, 1815.

Montreal directory. Montreal. Issues cited in vol. VIII were *An alphabetical list of the merchants, traders, and housekeepers, residing in Montreal; to which is prefixed, a descriptive sketch of the town,* comp. Thomas Doige (1819; repr. 1899; 2nd ed., 1820); and the *Montreal directory,* 1842–60. Edited by Robert Walter Stuart Mackay, 1842–54; Mrs R. W. S. Mackay, 1855–63. Title varies: *The Montreal directory* . . . from 1842–43 to 1855; *Mackay's Montreal directory* . . . from 1856–57 to 1867–68.

Port Hope directory for 1856–57. Port Hope, [Ont.], 1856.

Quebec directory, used for 1822 to 1891. Issues cited were *The Quebec directory, for 1822, containing an alphabetical list of the merchants, traders, and housekeepers, &c., within the city* . . . , comp. T. H. Gleason (Quebec, 1822); *The Quebec directory, or strangers' guide to the city, for 1826; comprising an alphabetical list of the merchants, traders and house keepers within the city* . . . , comp. John Smith (Quebec, 1826); *The Quebec directory and strangers' guide to the city and environs, 1844–45,* comp. Alfred Hawkins (Quebec, 1844); *The Quebec directory, and city and commercial register, 1847–48,* comp. Alfred Hawkins (Montreal, 1847); *Mackay's Quebec directory* . . . (Quebec), for 1848–49 to

1852; *Quebec business directory, compiled in June and July, 1854* ..., comp. Samuel McLaughlin (Quebec, 1854); *McLaughlin's Quebec directory* ... (Quebec, 1855; 1857); *The Quebec directory for 1858–59* ..., ed. G.-H. Cherrier and P.-M. Hamelin (Quebec, 1858); *The Quebec directory* ... (Quebec), for 1860–61 to 1889–90, first published by Georges-Hippolyte Cherrier and then by A.-Benjamin Cherrier, with slightly varying titles; and *The Quebec and Levis directory* ... /*L'indicateur de Québec et Lévis* ..., ed. T.-L. Boulanger and Edward Marcotte (Quebec), 1889–90 to 1890–91.

Toronto directory. Toronto. Issues cited in volume VIII include: *York commercial directory, street guide, and register, for 1833–4* ..., comp. George Walton (York [Toronto], [1833]); *The city of Toronto and the Home District commercial directory and register with almanack and calendar for 1837* ..., comp. George Walton (1837); *The Toronto directory, and street guide, for 1843–4*, comp. Francis Lewis (1843); *Brown's Toronto City and Home District directory, 1846–7* ... (1846); *Rowsell's city of Toronto and county of York directory, for 1850–51* ..., ed. J. Armstrong (1850); *Brown's Toronto general directory* ... (1856; 1861); *Caverhill's Toronto City directory, for 1859–60* ..., comp. W. C. F. Caverhill ([1859]); *Hutchinson's Toronto directory, 1862–63* ..., comp. Thomas Hutchinson ([1862]); and *Mitchell & Co.'s general directory for the city of Toronto, and gazetteer of the counties of York and Peel, for 1866* (1866).

A directory of the members of the Legislative Assembly of Nova Scotia, 1758–1958. Introduction by Charles Bruce Fergusson. (PANS publications, Nova Scotia series, 2.) Halifax, 1958.

Early Toronto newspapers, 1793–1867: a catalogue of newspapers published in the town of York and the city of Toronto from the beginning to confederation. Edited by Edith Grace Firth, with an introduction by Henry Cummings Campbell. Toronto, 1961.

Encyclopædia Britannica. [14th edition.] Edited by Warren E. Preece *et al.* 23 vols. and index. Chicago and Toronto, [1966]. 15th edition. 30 vols. [1977].

Encyclopedia Canadiana. Edited by John Everett Robbins *et al.* 10 vols. Ottawa, [1957–58]. [Revised edition.] Edited by Kenneth H. Pearson *et al.* Toronto, [1975].

Encyclopedia of music in Canada. Edited by Helmut Kallmann *et al.* Toronto and Buffalo, N.Y., [1981].

FAUTEUX, ÆGIDIUS. *Patriotes de 1837–1838.* Montréal, 1950.

Glasgow directory. See DIRECTORIES

Grand Larousse encyclopédique. 10 vols. Paris, [1960]–64. Nouvelle édition. 1973. 2 supplements to date. 1969– .

GREAT BRITAIN, ADMIRALTY. *The navy list....* London, 1815– . Issues for 1815 to 1858 were used in vol. VIII.

——— WAR OFFICE. *A list of the general and field-officers, as they rank in the army....* [London, 1754–1868.] *See also* Hart, *The new annual army list.*

Guide to the reports of the Public Archives of Canada, 1872–1972. Compiled by Françoise Caron-Houle. (PAC publication.) Ottawa, 1975.

Halifax almanac. See ALMANACS

Hamilton directory. See DIRECTORIES

Handbook of American Indians north of Mexico. Edited by Frederick Webb Hodge. 2 parts. (Smithsonian Institution, Bureau of American Ethnology, *Bulletin*, 30.) Washington, 1907–10; reprinted New York, 1971. The Canadian material in this work has been revised and republished as an appendix to the tenth report of the Geographic Board of Canada, entitled *Handbook of Indians of Canada* (Ottawa, 1913; repr. New York, 1969).

Handbook of North American Indians. Edited by William C. Sturtevant *et al.* (Smithsonian Institution publication.) 6 vols. to date [5–6, 8–10, 15]. Washington, 1978– .

HARPER, JOHN RUSSELL. *Early painters and engravers in Canada.* [Toronto, 1970].

HART, HENRY GEORGE. *The new annual army list....* London, 1840–1916. The title on the cover is *Hart's army list.* Issues for 1840 to 1857 were used in vol. VIII.

Index to reports of Canadian archives from 1872 to 1908. (PAC publications, 1.) Ottawa, 1909.

LEBŒUF, JOSEPH-[AIMÉ-]ARTHUR. *Complément au dictionnaire généalogique Tanguay.* (Société généalogique canadienne-française publications, 2, 4, 6.) 3 séries. Montréal, 1957–64. *See also* Tanguay, *Dictionnaire.*

LE JEUNE, LOUIS[-MARIE]. *Dictionnaire général de biographie, histoire, littérature, agriculture, commerce, industrie et des arts, sciences, mœurs, coutumes, institutions politiques et religieuses du Canada.* 2 vols. Ottawa, [1931].

London directory. See DIRECTORIES

Montreal almanack. See ALMANACS

Montreal directory. See DIRECTORIES

MORGAN, HENRY JAMES. *Bibliotheca Canadensis: or, a manual of Canadian literature.* Ottawa, 1867; reprinted Detroit, 1968.

——— *Sketches of celebrated Canadians, and persons connected with Canada, from the earliest period in the history of the province down to the present time.*

Quebec and London, 1862; reprinted Montreal, 1865.

The national union catalog, pre-1956 imprints. . . . 754 vols. London and Chicago, 1968–81.

New-Brunswick almanac. See ALMANACS

Newfoundland almanack. See ALMANACS

O'BYRNE, WILLIAM RICHARD. *A naval biographical dictionary; comprising the life and services of every living officer in her majesty's navy, from the rank of the fleet to that of lieutenant, inclusive. . . .* London, 1849. New and enlarged edition, 1 volume published and 4 parts of a second. London, 1861, [1859–62].

Officers of the British forces in Canada during the War of 1812–15. Compiled by L. Homfray Irving. (Canadian Military Institute publication.) [Welland, Ont.], 1908.

Place-names and places of Nova Scotia. Introduction by Charles Bruce Fergusson. (PANS publications, Nova Scotia series, 3.) Halifax, 1967; reprinted Belleville, Ont., 1976.

Places in Ontario: their name origins and history. Compiled by Nick and Helma Mika. (*Encyclopedia of Ontario*, 2.) 3 parts. Belleville, Ont., 1977–83.

Political appointments and elections in the Province of Canada, 1841 to 1860. Compiled by Joseph-Olivier Coté. Quebec, 1860. *. . . from 1841 to 1865.* 2nd edition. Ottawa, 1866.

Port Hope directory. See DIRECTORIES

Prince Edward Island calendar. See ALMANACS

PUBLIC ARCHIVES OF CANADA, Ottawa
   NUMBERED PUBLICATIONS
   1: *Index to reports of PAC.*
   OTHER PUBLICATIONS [*see also* section II]
   Guide to reports of PAC (Caron-Houle).
   Inventories of holdings in the manuscript division [*see* section I].
   Union list of MSS (Gordon *et al.*; Maurice).
   Union list of MSS, suppl. (Maurice *et al.*).

PUBLIC ARCHIVES OF NOVA SCOTIA, Halifax
   NOVA SCOTIA SERIES
   2: *Directory of N.S. MLAs*
   3: *Place-names of N.S.*

Quebec almanac. See ALMANACS

Quebec directory. See DIRECTORIES

RAYBURN, ALAN. *Geographical names of New Brunswick.* (Canadian Permanent Committee on Geographical Names, Toponymy study, 2.) Ottawa, 1975.

—— *Geographical names of Prince Edward Island.* (Canadian Permanent Committee on Geographical Names, Toponymy study, 1.) Ottawa, 1973.

ROY, PIERRE-GEORGES. *Les avocats de la région de Québec.* Lévis, Qué., 1936.

—— *Fils de Québec.* 4 séries [4 vols.] Lévis, 1933.

—— *Inventaire des concessions en fief et seigneurie,* *fois et hommages et aveux et dénombrements, conservés aux Archives de la province de Québec.* (ANQ publication.) 6 vols. Beauceville, Qué., 1927–29.

—— *Les juges de la province de Québec.* (ANQ publication.) Québec, 1933.

SCOTT, HEW *et al.*, *Fasti ecclesiæ scoticanæ, the succession of ministers in the Church of Scotland from the Reformation.* 3 vols. in 6, Edinburgh, 1866–71. New edition. 9 vols. to date, 1915– .

SMITH, WILLIAM HENRY. *Canada: past, present and future; being a historical, geographical, geological and statistical account of Canada West.* 2 vols. Toronto, [1852]; reprinted Belleville, Ont., 1973–74. Also issued in a subscription edition, 10 parts, [1851–52].

SMITHSONIAN INSTITUTION, Washington
   PUBLICATIONS
   Handbook of American Indians (Hodge).
   Handbook of North American Indians (Sturtevant *et al.*).

"State papers – Upper Canada, [1791–1841]." PAC *Report*, 1891: 1–177; 1892: 286–399; 1893: 1–50; 1896: 1–79; 1897: 81–179; 1898: 181–329; 1899: 331–90; 1900: 391–540; 1901: 541–601; 1943: 1–186; 1944: 1–154; 1945: 1–200. From 1943 to 1945 the calendars appeared under the title "Calendar of series Q: a series of state papers composed of the official correspondence of the governors, lieutenant-governors, administrators and other officials of Quebec and Lower and Upper Canada for the years 1760–1841."

TANGUAY, CYPRIEN. *Dictionnaire généalogique des familles canadiennes depuis la fondation de la colonie jusqu'à nos jours.* 7 vols. [Montréal], 1871–90; réimpr., [New York, 1969]. *See also* Lebœuf, *Complément.*

—— *Répertoire général du clergé canadien par ordre chronologique depuis la fondation de la colonie jusqu'à nos jours.* Québec, 1868. [2ᵉ édition.] Montréal, 1893.

TERRILL, FREDERICK WILLIAM. *A chronology of Montreal and of Canada from A.D. 1752 to A.D. 1893, including commercial statistics, historic sketches of commercial corporations and firms and advertisements, arranged to show in what year the several houses and corporate bodies originated; together with calendars of every year from A.D. 1752 to A.D. 1925.* Montreal, 1893.

THÉRIAULT, YVON. *Les publications parlementaires du Québec d'hier et d'aujourd'hui.* (Vie parlementaire, 2.) Québec, 1978. 2ᵉ édition. 1982.

Toronto directory. See DIRECTORIES

TURCOTTE, GUSTAVE. *Le Conseil législatif de Québec, 1774–1933.* Beauceville, Qué., 1933.

Union list of manuscripts in Canadian repositories/

Catalogue collectif des manuscrits des archives canadiennes. Edited by Robert Stanyslaw Gordon *et al.* (PAC publication.) Ottawa, 1968. Revised edition. Edited by E. Grace Maurice. 2 vols. 1975. *Supplement/Supplément.* Edited by E. Grace Maurice *et al.* 3 vols. to date. 1976–   .

WALBRAN, JOHN THOMAS. *British Columbia coast names, 1592–1906, to which are added a few names in adjacent United States territory: their origin and history....* (Geographic Board of Canada publication.) Ottawa, 1909; reprinted with an introduction by G. P. V. Akrigg, Vancouver, 1971; reprinted Seattle, Wash., and London, 1972.

WALLACE, WILLIAM STEWART. *The Macmillan dictionary of Canadian biography.* Edited by William Angus McKay. 4th edition. Toronto, [1978]. First published as *The dictionary of Canadian biography* (1926).

WATTERS, REGINALD EYRE. *A check list of Canadian literature and background materials, 1628–1950.* ... 2nd edition. [... *1628–1960*]. Toronto [and Buffalo, N.Y., 1972].

When was that? A chronological dictionary of important events in Newfoundland down to and including the year 1922; together with an appendix, "St. John's over a century ago," by the late J. W. Withers. Compiled by Harris Munden Mosdell. St John's, 1923.

IV. STUDIES (BOOKS AND THESES)

ABBOTT, MAUDE ELIZABETH [SEYMOUR]. *History of medicine in the province of Quebec.* Toronto, 1931; Montreal, 1931.

ALLAIRE, JEAN-BAPTISTE-ARTHUR. *Histoire de la paroisse de Saint-Denis-sur-Richelieu (Canada).* Saint-Hyacinthe, Qué., 1905.

AUDET, LOUIS-PHILIPPE. *Le système scolaire de la province de Québec* [1635–1840]. 6 vols. Québec, 1950–56.

BECK, JAMES MURRAY. *The government of Nova Scotia.* (Canadian government series, 8.) Toronto, 1957.

—— *Joseph Howe,* 2 vols. Kingston, Ont., and Montreal, 1982–83.
1: *Conservative reformer, 1804–1848.*
2: *The Briton becomes Canadian, 1848–1873.*

BILL, INGRAHAM EBENEZER. *Fifty years with the Baptist ministers and churches of the Maritime provinces of Canada.* Saint John, N.B., 1880.

BUCHANAN, ARTHUR WILLIAM PATRICK. *The bench and bar of Lower Canada down to 1850.* Montreal, 1925.

CAMPBELL, ROBERT. *A history of the Scotch Presbyterian Church, St. Gabriel Street, Montreal.* Montreal, 1887.

Canada's smallest province: a history of P.E.I. Edited by Francis William Pius Bolger. [Charlottetown, 1973.]

CANNIFF, WILLIAM. *The medical profession in Upper Canada, 1783–1850: an historical narrative, with original documents relating to the profession, including some brief biographies.* Toronto, 1894; reprinted 1980.

CARELESS, JAMES MAURICE STOCKFORD. *The union of the Canadas: the growth of Canadian institutions, 1841–1857.* (Canadian centenary series, 10.) Toronto, 1967.

CARROLL, JOHN [SALTKILL]. *Case and his cotemporaries; or, the Canadian itinerants' memorial:* constituting a biographical history of Methodism in Canada, from its introduction into the province, till the death of the Rev. Wm. Case in 1855. 5 vols. Toronto, 1867–77.

CHABOT, RICHARD. *Le curé de campagne et la contestation locale au Québec (de 1791 aux troubles de 1837–38): la querelle des écoles, l'affaire des fabriques et le problème des insurrections de 1837–38.* Montréal, 1975.

CHAPAIS, [JOSEPH-AMABLE-]THOMAS. *Cours d'histoire du Canada* [1760–1867]. 8 vols. Québec, 1919–34. Another edition. 8 vols. Montréal, [1944–45]; réimpr., [Trois-Rivières, Qué., 1972].

CHAUSSÉ, GILLES. *Jean-Jacques Lartigue, premier évêque de Montréal.* Montréal, 1980.

CHOQUETTE, CHARLES-PHILIPPE. *Histoire du séminaire de Saint-Hyacinthe depuis sa fondation jusqu'à nos jours.* 2 vols. Montréal, 1911–12.

CHOUINARD, FRANÇOIS-XAVIER *et al. La ville de Québec, histoire municipale.* (Cahiers d'histoire, 15, 17, 19, 35.) 4 vols. Québec, 1963–83.

CHRISTIE, ROBERT. *A history of the late province of Lower Canada, parliamentary and political, from the commencement to the close of its existence as a separate province....* 6 vols. Quebec and Montreal, 1848–55. [2nd ed.]. Montreal, 1866.

CORNELL, PAUL GRANT. *The alignment of political groups in Canada, 1841–1867.* (Canadian studies in history and government, 3.) Toronto, 1962.

[COWDELL] GATES, LILLIAN FRANCES. *Land policies of Upper Canada.* (Canadian studies in history and government, 9.) Toronto, 1968.

CRAIG, GERALD MARQUIS. *Upper Canada: the formative years, 1784–1841.* (Canadian centenary series, 7.) [Toronto], 1963.

DAVID, LAURENT-OLIVIER. *Les gerbes canadiennes.* Montréal, 1921.

—— *Les Patriotes de 1837–1838.* Montréal, [1884]; réimpr., [1937].

IV. STUDIES

DENISON, MERRILL. *Canada's first bank: a history of the Bank of Montreal.* 2 vols. Toronto and Montreal, 1966–67. Translated into French by Paul A. Horguelin and Jean-Paul Vinay as *La première banque au Canada: histoire de la Banque de Montréal.* 2 vols. Toronto et Montréal, 1966–67.

DEVINE, PATRICK K. *Ye olde St. John's, 1750–1936.* [St John's, 1936]; republished as *Ye olde St. John's, 1750–1939,* [St John's, 1939.]

DOUVILLE, JOSEPH-ANTOINE-IRÉNÉE. *Histoire du collège-séminaire de Nicolet, 1803–1903, avec les listes complètes des directeurs, professeurs et élèves de l'institution.* 2 vols. Montréal, 1903.

EATON, ARTHUR WENTWORTH HAMILTON. *The history of Kings County, Nova Scotia, heart of the Acadian land; giving a sketch of the French and their expulsion; and a history of the New England planters who came in their stead; with many genealogies, 1604–1910.* Salem, Mass., 1910; reprinted as *The history of Kings County,* Belleville, Ont., 1972.

FILTEAU, GÉRARD. *Histoire des Patriotes.* Montréal, 3 vols. 1938–42. [Nouv. éd.]. 1975.

FRENCH, GOLDWIN [SYLVESTER]. *Parsons & politics: the rôle of the Wesleyan Methodists in Upper Canada and the Maritimes from 1780 to 1855.* Toronto, 1962.

GREGG, WILLIAM. *History of the Presbyterian Church in the Dominion of Canada, from the earliest times to 1834; with a chronological table of events to the present time, and map.* Toronto, 1885.

GUILLET, EDWIN CLARENCE. *The lives and times of the Patriots; an account of the rebellion in Upper Canada, 1837–1838, and the Patriot agitation in the United States, 1837–1842.* Toronto, 1938; reprinted 1963; reprinted 1968.

GUNN, GERTRUDE E. *The political history of Newfoundland, 1832–1864.* (Canadian studies in history and government, 7.) Toronto, 1966.

Histoire de la corporation de la cité de Montréal depuis son origine jusqu'à nos jours. . . . Jean-Claude Lamothe *et al.,* édit. Montréal, 1903.

History of the county of Middlesex, Canada, from the earliest time to the present; containing an authentic account of many important matters relating to the settlement, progress and general history of the county. . . . Toronto and London, Ont., 1889; reprinted with introduction and corrections by Daniel [James] Brock and index by Muriel Moon, Belleville, Ont., 1972.

HOWLEY, MICHAEL FRANCIS. *Ecclesiastical history of Newfoundland.* Boston, 1888; reprinted Belleville, Ont., 1979.

JOHNSON, LEO A. *History of Guelph, 1827–1927.* (Guelph Historical Society publication.) Guelph, Ont., 1977.

JOHNSTON, ANGUS ANTHONY. *A history of the Catholic Church in eastern Nova Scotia.* 2 vols.

Antigonish, N.S., 1960–71.
1: *1611–1827.*
2: *1827–1880; with a brief appendix surveying the years 1880–1969.*

JOHNSTON, CHARLES MURRAY. *The head of the Lake; a history of Wentworth County.* Hamilton, Ont., 1958. 2nd ed., 1967.

LABARRÈRE-PAULÉ, ANDRÉ. *Les instituteurs laïques au Canada français, 1836–1900.* Québec, 1965.

LAMBERT, JAMES HAROLD. "Monseigneur, the Catholic bishop: Joseph-Octave Plessis; church, state, and society in Lower Canada: historiography and analysis." D. ès L. thesis, Université Laval, Québec, [1981].

LAREAU, EDMOND. *Histoire de la littérature canadienne.* Montréal, 1874.

LAURIN, CLÉMENT. *J.-J. Girouard & les Patriotes de 1837–38: portraits.* Montréal, 1973.

LAWRENCE, JOSEPH WILSON. *The judges of New Brunswick and their times.* Edited and annotated by Alfred Augustus Stockton [and William Odber Raymond]. [Saint John, N.B., 1907.]

LEMIEUX, LUCIEN. *L'établissement de la première province ecclésiastique au Canada, 1783–1844.* (Histoire religieuse du Canada, 1.) Montréal et Paris, [1968].

LEVY, GEORGE EDWARD. *The Baptists of the Maritime provinces, 1753–1946.* Saint John, N.B., 1946.

LINDSEY, CHARLES. *The life and times of Wm. Lyon Mackenzie; with an account of the Canadian rebellion of 1837, and the subsequent frontier disturbances, chiefly from unpublished documents.* 2 vols. Toronto, 1862; reprinted 1971.

Literary history of Canada: Canadian literature in English. Edited by Carl Frederick Klinck *et al.* Toronto, 1965. New edition. 3 vols. 1976. Translated by Maurice Lebel as *Histoire littéraire du Canada: littérature canadienne de langue anglaise,* Québec, 1970.

MACNUTT, WILLIAM STEWART. *The Atlantic provinces: the emergence of colonial society, 1712–1857.* (Canadian centenary series, 9.) Toronto, 1965.

—— *New Brunswick, a history: 1784–1867.* Toronto, 1963.

MACRAE, MARION, AND ANTHONY ADAMSON. *Cornerstones of order: courthouses and town halls of Ontario, 1784–1914.* Toronto, 1983.

MACRAE, MARION, *et al. Hallowed walls: church architecture of Upper Canada.* Toronto and Vancouver, 1975.

MAURAULT, OLIVIER. *Le collège de Montréal, 1767–1967.* 2e édition. Antonio Dansereau, éditeur. Montréal, 1967. The first edition was published in Montreal in 1918 under the title *Le petit séminaire de Montréal.*

MEILLEUR, JEAN-BAPTISTE. *Mémorial de l'éducation*

du Bas-Canada. Montréal, 1860. 2ᵉ éd. Québec, 1876.

MIDDLETON, JESSE EDGAR. *The municipality of Toronto: a history.* 3 vols. Toronto and New York, 1923.

MILLMAN, THOMAS REAGH. *The life of the Right Reverend, the Honourable Charles James Stewart, D.D., Oxon., second Anglican bishop of Quebec.* London, Ont., 1953.

MONET, JACQUES. *The last cannon shot: a study of French-Canadian nationalism, 1837–1850.* Toronto, 1969; reprinted Toronto and Buffalo, N.Y., 1976. Translated by Richard Bastien as *La première révolution tranquille: le nationalisme canadien-français (1837–1850)*, Montréal, 1981.

MORGAN, ROBERT J. "Orphan outpost: Cape Breton colony, 1784–1820." PHD thesis, University of Ottawa, 1973.

MORISSET, GÉRARD. *Coup d'œil sur les arts en Nouvelle-France.* Québec, 1941; réimpr., 1942.

O'NEILL, PAUL. *The story of St. John's, Newfoundland.* 2 vols. Erin, Ont., 1975–76.
  [1]: *The oldest city.*
  [2]: *A seaport legacy.*

OUELLET, FERNAND. *Le Bas-Canada, 1791–1840: changements structuraux et crise.* (Université d'Ottawa, Cahiers d'histoire, 6.) Ottawa, 1976. Translated and adapted by Patricia Claxton as *Lower Canada, 1791–1840: social change and nationalism* (Canadian centenary series, 15), Toronto, 1980.

PATTERSON, GRAEME HAZLEWOOD. "Studies in elections and public opinion in Upper Canada." PHD thesis, University of Toronto, 1969.

POULIOT, LÉON. *Monseigneur Bourget et son temps.* 5 vols. Montréal, 1955–77.

PROWSE, DANIEL WOODLEY. *A history of Newfoundland from the English, colonial, and foreign records.* London and New York, 1895. 2nd edition. London, 1896. 3rd edition. With additions by James Raymond Thoms and Frank Burnham Gill. St John's, 1971. Reprint of 1895 edition, Belleville, Ont., 1972.

READ, COLIN [FREDERICK]. *The rising in western Upper Canada, 1837–8: the Duncombe revolt and after.* Toronto, 1982.

RICH, EDWIN ERNEST. *The history of the Hudson's Bay Company, 1670–1870.* (HBRS, 21–22.) 2 vols. London, 1958–59. [Trade edition.] 3 vols. Toronto, 1960. A copy of this work available at the PAC contains notes and bibliographical material omitted from the printed version.

Robertson's landmarks of Toronto; a collection of historical sketches of the old town of York from 1792 until 1833, and of Toronto from 1834 to [1914]. Edited by John Ross Robertson. 6 series. Toronto, 1894–1914; vols. 1 and 3 reprinted Belleville, Ont., 1976, 1974.

ROSA, NARCISSE. *La construction des navires à Québec et ses environs; grèves et naufrages.* Québec, 1897; réimpr., Montréal, 1973.

ROSS, VICTOR, AND ARTHUR ST L. TRIGGE. *A history of the Canadian Bank of Commerce, with an account of the other banks which now form part of its organization.* 3 vols. Toronto, 1920–34.

ROY, CHRISTIAN. *Histoire de L'Assomption.* L'Assomption, Qué., 1967.

ROY, JEAN-LOUIS. *Édouard-Raymond Fabre, libraire et Patriote canadien (1799–1854): contre l'isolement et la sujétion.* Montréal, 1974.

ROY, JOSEPH-EDMOND. *Histoire de la seigneurie de Lauzon* [1608–1840]. 5 vols. Lévis, Qué., 1897–1904; réimpr. 1984.

—— *Histoire du notariat au Canada depuis la fondation de la colonie jusqu'à nos jours.* 4 vols. Lévis, Qué., 1899–1902.

ROY, PIERRE-GEORGES. *Toutes petites choses du Régime anglais.* 2 sér. Québec, 1946.

RUMILLY, ROBERT. *Papineau et son temps.* 2 vols. Montréal, 1977.

SCADDING, HENRY. *Toronto of old: collections and recollections illustrative of the early settlement and social life of the capital of Ontario.* Toronto, 1873. Republished as *Toronto of old*, abridged and edited by Frederick Henry Armstrong. Toronto, 1966.

SMITH, THOMAS WATSON. *History of the Methodist Church within the territories embraced in the late conference of Eastern British America, including Nova Scotia, New Brunswick, Prince Edward Island and Bermuda.* 2 vols. Halifax, 1877–90.

SULTE, BENJAMIN. *Mélanges historiques.* . . . Gérard Malchelosse, édit. 21 vols. Montréal, 1918–34. The volumes in this series consist of articles and monographs.

TAFT MANNING, HELEN. *The revolt of French Canada, 1800–1835; a chapter in the history of the British Commonwealth.* Toronto, 1962.

TULCHINSKY, GERALD J. J. *The river barons: Montreal businessmen and the growth of industry and transportation, 1837–53.* Toronto and Buffalo, N.Y., 1977.

UPTON, LESLIE FRANCIS STOKES. *Micmacs and colonists; Indian-white relations in the Maritimes, 1713–1867.* Vancouver, 1979.

VAN KIRK, SYLVIA. *"Many tender ties": women in fur-trade society in western Canada, 1670–1870.* Winnipeg, [1980].

WYNN, GRAEME. *Timber colony: a historical geography of early nineteenth century New Brunswick.* Toronto and Buffalo, N.Y., 1981.

V. JOURNALS

Acadiensis: Journal of the History of the Atlantic Region/Revue de l'histoire de la région atlantique. Fredericton. Published by the Department of History of the University of New Brunswick. 1 (1971–72)– .

Beaver: Magazine of the North. Winnipeg. Published by the HBC. 1 (1920–21)– . *Index:* 1 (1920–21)–outfit 284 (June 1953–March 1954). Title varies.

British Columbia Historical Quarterly. Victoria. Published by the PABC in cooperation with the British Columbia Historical Association. 1 (1937)–21 (1957–58). Author/title and subject indexes are provided by *A two-part index to the "British Columbia Historical Quarterly," volumes I–XXI* . . . , published by Camosun College ([Victoria], 1977).

Le Bulletin des recherches historiques. Published usually in Lévis, Qué. Originally the organ of the Société des études historiques, it became in March 1923 the journal of the Bureau des archives de la province de Québec (now the ANQ). 1 (1895)–70 (1968). *Index:* 1 (1895)–31 (1925) (4v., Beauceville, Qué., 1925–26). For subsequent years there is an index on microfiche at the ANQ-Q.

Les Cahiers des Dix. Montréal et Québec. Published by "Les Dix." 1 (1936)– .

CANADIAN CATHOLIC HISTORICAL ASSOCIATION/ SOCIÉTÉ CANADIENNE D'HISTOIRE DE L'ÉGLISE CATHOLIQUE, Ottawa. Publishes simultaneously a *Report* in English and a *Rapport* in French, of which the contents are entirely different. 1 (1933–34)– . *Index:* 1 (1933–34)–25 (1958). Title varies: *Study sessions/Sessions d'étude* from 1966.

CANADIAN CHURCH HISTORICAL SOCIETY, Toronto. *Journal.* Place of publication varies. 1 (1950–52)– . *Index:* 1 (1950–52)–21 (1979) in 23 (April 1981).

CANADIAN HISTORICAL ASSOCIATION/SOCIÉTÉ HISTORIQUE DU CANADA, Ottawa. *Annual report.* 1922– . *Index:* 1922–51; 1952–68. Title varies: *Historical papers/Communications historiques* from 1966.

Canadian Historical Review. Toronto. 1 (1920)– . *Index:* 1 (1920)–10 (1929); 11 (1930)–20 (1939); 21 (1940)–30 (1949); 31 (1950)–51 (1970). Université Laval has also published an index: *Canadian Historical Review, 1950–1964: index des articles et des comptes rendus de volumes*, René Hardy, compil. (Québec, 1969). A continuation of the *Review of Historical Publications relating to Canada*: 1 (1895–96)–22 (1917–18); *Index:* 1 (1895–96)–10 (1905); 11 (1906)–20 (1915).

Canadian Magazine. Toronto. 1 (March–October 1893)–91 (January–April 1939). *Index:* 1 (March–October 1893)–25 (May–October 1905) in 25. Title varies: *Canadian Magazine of Politics, Science, Art and Literature* to 63 (May 1924–January 1925); *Canadian Magazine*, 64 (February–December 1925)–87 (January–June 1937); *Canadian*, 88 (July–December 1937)–91 (January–April 1939).

Historic Kingston. Kingston, Ont. Published by the Kingston Historical Society. No.1 (1952)– ; nos.1–10 reprinted in 1v., Belleville, Ont., 1972. *Index:* no.1 (1952)–no.20 (1972).

NOVA SCOTIA HISTORICAL SOCIETY, Halifax. *Collections.* 1 (1878)–40 (1980). Beginning with vol.41 (1982) the Society became the Royal Nova Scotia Historical Society. Vols.1–8 reprinted, 2v., Belleville, Ont., 1976–77. *Index:* 1 (1878)–32 (1959) in 33 (1961).

Ontario History. Toronto. Published by the Ontario Historical Society. 1 (1899)– ; vols.1–49 (1957) reprinted Millwood, N.Y., 1975. An index to volumes 1 (1899) to 64 (1972) appears in *Index to the publications of the Ontario Historical Society, 1899–1972* (1974). Title varies: *Papers and Records* to 1946.

Revue canadienne. Montréal. 1 (1864)–53 (1907); nouvelle série, 1 (1908)–27 (1922). Vols.17 (1881)–23 (1887) are also numbered nouvelle série, 1–7; vols.24 (1888)–28 (1892) are also called 3ᵉ série, 1–[5]. *Tables générales:* 1 (1864)–53 (1907).

Revue d'histoire de l'Amérique française. Montréal. Published by the Institut d'histoire de l'Amérique française. 1 (1947–48)– . *Index:* 1 (1947–48)–10 (1956–57); 11 (1957–58)–20 (1966–67); 21 (1967–68)–30 (1976–77).

La Revue du Barreau de la province de Québec. Montréal. 1 (1941)– . Title varies: *La Revue du Barreau du Québec* from 28 (1967).

ROYAL SOCIETY OF CANADA/SOCIÉTÉ ROYALE DU CANADA, Ottawa. *Proceedings and Transactions/ Mémoires et comptes rendus.* 1st ser., 1 (1882–83)–12 (1894); 2nd ser., 1 (1895)–12 (1906); 3rd ser., 1 (1907)–56 (1962); 4th ser., 1 (1963)– . *General index:* 1st ser.–2nd ser.; *Subject index:* 3rd ser., 1 (1907)–31 (1937); *Author index:* 3rd ser., 1 (1907)–35 (1941); *Index:* 1st series–3rd series, 37 (1943). The CLA has published *A subject index to the Royal Society of Canada Proceedings and Transactions: third series, vols. I–XXXI, 1907–1937*, comp. M. A. Martin (Reference publications, 1, Ottawa, 1947).

Société canadienne d'histoire de l'Église catholique. *See* Canadian Catholic Historical Association

Société généalogique canadienne-française, Montréal. *Mémoires*. 1 (1944–45)– . The society's numbered publications include 2, 4, 6: Lebœuf, *Complément* [*see* section III].

Washington Historical Quarterly. Seattle. 1 (1906–7)–26 (1935). Continued under the title *Pacific Northwest Quarterly*, 27 (1936)– . *Index*: 1 (1906–7)–10 (1919); 11 (1920)–20 (1929); 1 (1906–7)–29 (1938); 45 (1954)–47 (1956).

Waterloo Historical Society, Kitchener, Ont. *Annual report*. 1913– . Place of publication or printing varies: at Berlin [Kitchener], 1913–15, at Kitchener, 1916–24 and 1931– , at Toronto, 1925–26, and at Waterloo, Ont., 1927–30. Title varies: *Annual volume*, 1957–64; since 1965 the reports have been untitled, appearing simply under the Society's name.

CONTRIBUTORS

Contributors

ACHESON, T. W. Professor of history, University of New Brunswick, Fredericton, New Brunswick.
George Bond. Thomas Harding. John Haws. Charles Simonds.

ALLEN, ROBERT S. Deputy chief, Treaties and Historical Research Centre, Department of Indian and Northern Affairs, Ottawa, Ontario.
Andrew H. Bulger [in collaboration with C. M. Judd].

ANDREAE, CHRISTOPHER ALFRED. President, Historica Research Limited, London, Ontario.
Roswell Gardinier Benedict. Elijah Leonard.

ANDREW, SHEILA. Graduate student in history, University of New Brunswick, Fredericton, New Brunswick.
Jean-Marie Madran.

ANGUS, MARGARET SHARP. Kingston, Ontario.
John Mowat.

ARMOUR, DAVID ARTHUR. Assistant superintendent, Mackinac Island State Park Commission, Michigan, U.S.A.
William Solomon.

ARMSTRONG, FREDERICK H. Professor of history, University of Western Ontario, London, Ontario.
Thomas-René-Verchères Boucher de Boucherville. George Crookshank. Vincent Gildemeester van Tuyll van Serooskerken, Baron van Tuyll van Serooskerken [in collaboration with R. Hall].

ARTHUR, ELIZABETH. Professor of history, Lakehead University, Thunder Bay, Ontario.
Nicolas-Marie-Joseph Frémiot. John Haldane. Roderick McKenzie. James Sinclair. John Siveright.

BAILLARGEON, NOËL. Historien, Séminaire de Québec, Québec.
Antoine Parant.

BAKER, MELVIN. Researcher, Newfoundland House of Assembly, St John's, Newfoundland.
Patrick Tasker.

BALF, MARY. Formerly curator and archivist, Kamloops Museum, British Columbia.
Hwistesmetxē'qEn.

BARIBEAU, CLAUDE. Directeur, Centre universitaire Jock-Turcot, Université d'Ottawa, Ontario.
Denis-Benjamin Papineau.

BEASLEY, DAVID R. Librarian, New York Public Research Libraries, New York, U.S.A.
John Richardson.

BÉCHARD, HENRI, S.J. Centre Kateri, Kahnawake, Québec.
Joseph Marcoux.

BECK, J. MURRAY. Professor emeritus of political science, Dalhousie University, Halifax, Nova Scotia.
Richard Nugent. Simon Bradstreet Robie. William Rudolf. James Boyle Uniacke. George Renny Young.

BEER, DONALD ROBERT. Senior lecturer in history, University of New England, Armidale, New South Wales, Australia.

Henry Sherwood. Robert Reid Smiley [in collaboration with K. Greenfield].

BENSLEY, EDWARD HORTON. Honorary lecturer in the history of medicine and honorary Osler librarian, McGill University, Montreal, Quebec.
Andrew Fernando Holmes.

BERGERON, WILFRID. Prêtre à la retraite, Nicolet, Québec.
Charles Harper.

BERNATCHEZ, ANNE. Ethnologue, Lac-Saint-Augustin-Sud, Québec.
Édouard Gingras.

BERNIER, JACQUES. Professeur agrégé d'histoire, Université Laval, Québec, Québec.
Jean Blanchet.

BERNIER, PAUL. Conseiller, Ministère des Relations internationales du Québec, Québec.
Antoine Voyer.

BETTS, E. A. Retired archivist, Windsor, Nova Scotia.
William Bennett.

BILSON, GEOFFREY. Professor of history, University of Saskatchewan, Saskatoon, Saskatchewan.
Walter Telfer.

BISHOP, CHARLES A. Professor of anthropology, State University of New York, Oswego, New York, U.S.A.
Charles McKenzie.

BLACKWELL, JOHN D. Lecturer in history, Queen's University, Kingston, Ontario.
Robert Sympson Jameson.

BLAKELEY, PHYLLIS R. Formerly provincial archivist, Public Archives of Nova Scotia, Halifax, Nova Scotia.
Hugh Bell. Sir Brenton Halliburton. Richard McLearn. Temple Foster Piers.

†BLAKEY SMITH, DOROTHY. Formerly archivist, Provincial Archives of British Columbia, Victoria, British Columbia.
Thomas Blinkhorn.

BLISS, MICHAEL. Professor of history, University of Toronto, Ontario.
Daniel Massey.

BOIVIN, AURÉLIEN. Professeur de littérature québécoise, Université Laval, Québec, Québec.
François-Réal Angers. Guillaume Lévesque.

BOND, COURTNEY C. J. Formerly historian, National Capital Commission, Ottawa, Ontario.
Peter Fleming.

BORTHWICK, EDYTH B., S.P. Researcher and writer, Seattle, Washington, U.S.A.
Marie-Amable Foretier (Viger).

BOUCHER, JACQUES. Doyen des études supérieures, Université de Montréal, Québec.
Alexander Buchanan. Nicolas-Benjamin Doucet. George Pyke.

BOWN, M. PERPETUA, R.S.M. Formerly teacher; Mercy

Convent, St John's, Newfoundland.
Marianne Creedon, named Mother Mary Francis.

BOWSFIELD, HARTWELL. Associate professor of history, York University, Downsview, Ontario.
Sir Peregrine Maitland.

BOYD, FRANK S., JR. Free-lance writer and journalist, Halifax, Nova Scotia.
Septimus D. Clarke. Richard Preston (Appendix).

BRIDGMAN, HARRY.
Andrew Bell. William Bell. Alexander Gale. Robert McGill. John McKenzie. William Morris. William Proudfoot.

BROCHET, ALDO. Research and reporting consultant, Toronto, Ontario.
Peter Du Val.

BROCK, DANIEL J. Teacher, Catholic Central High School, London, Ontario.
Joseph Brant Clench. Lionel Augustus Clark Ridout. Richard Talbot. Gideon Tiffany.

BROWN, JENNIFER S. H. Associate professor of history, University of Winnipeg, Manitoba.
John Clarke. George Keith. George Nelson [in collaboration with S. Van Kirk].

BRUNGER, ALAN G. Associate professor of geography, Trent University, Peterborough, Ontario.
Richard Birdsall. Thomas Talbot.

BUCKNER, PHILLIP. Professor of history, University of New Brunswick, Fredericton, New Brunswick.
Introductory essay: *The Colonial Office and British North America, 1801–50. Sir George Arthur. Ward Chipman. Sir Charles Augustus FitzRoy. Sir John Harvey. Charles Douglass Smith. George Frederick Street. James Taylor* [in collaboration with D. M. Young].

BUGGEY, SUSAN. Chief, Historical research, Parks Canada, Winnipeg, Manitoba.
John Keir. Charles Ramage Prescott.

BUMSTED, J. M. Professor of history, University of Manitoba, Winnipeg, Manitoba.
Joseph Crandall. Harris Harding. Edward James Jarvis [in collaboration with H. T. Holman]. *John MacGregor.*

BURANT, JIM. Chief, Collections management, Picture Division, Public Archives of Canada, Ottawa, Ontario.
Frederick William Beechey. James Bucknall Bucknall Estcourt. George Frederick Mecham.

BURGESS, JOANNE. Professeure d'histoire, Université du Québec à Montréal, Québec.
John Stewart.

BURLEY, DAVID G. Assistant professor of history, University of Winnipeg, Manitoba.
Hugh Cossart Baker. James Bell Ewart. John Paterson.

BURNS, ROBERT J. Historian, Parks Canada, Ottawa, Ontario.
Samuel Peters Jarvis [in collaboration with D. Leighton]. *Samuel Smith Ridout.*

BURNSIDE, ALBERT. United Church minister, Kew Beach United Church, Toronto, Ontario.
James Jackson. Philip James. Ann Vickery (Robins).

BURROUGHS, PETER. Professor of history, Dalhousie University, Halifax, Nova Scotia.
Sir James Kempt.

BUSH, E. F. Historian, Parks Canada, Ottawa, Ontario.
Thomas McKay.

BUSSEY, DEREK. Library technician, Newfoundland Public

Library Service, St John's, Newfoundland.
Patrick Doyle.

CAMERON, ALAN. Keeper of manuscripts, University of Nottingham Library, England.
Archibald McNab, 17th Chief of Clan Macnab [in collaboration with J. Gwyn].

†CARRIÈRE, GASTON, O.M.I. Archiviste, Archives historiques oblates, Ottawa, Ontario.
Fleury Baudrand.

CHABOT, RICHARD, Professeur d'histoire, Université du Québec à Montréal, Québec.
Étienne Chartier. Jean-Baptiste Proulx.

CHAMPAGNE, GUY. Professionnel de recherche, *Corpus d'éditions critiques*, Département des littératures, Université Laval, Québec, Québec.
Charles-François Lévesque.

CHAMPAGNE, LYNNE. Historienne, Ministère de la Culture, du Patrimoine et des Loisirs du Manitoba, Winnipeg, Manitoba.
Jean-Baptiste Lagimonière.

CHASSÉ, BÉATRICE. Agente culturelle, Québec, Québec.
Jean-Joseph Girouard.

CHIASSON, PAULETTE M. Rédactrice-historienne, *Dictionnaire biographique du Canada/Dictionary of Canadian biography*, Les Presses de l'université Laval, Québec, Québec.
Jacques Merle, named Father Vincent de Paul.

CHOQUETTE, J. E. ROBERT. Professeur agrégé de sciences religieuses, Université d'Ottawa, Ontario.
Rémi Gaulin. Patrick Phelan.

CLARKE, JOHN. Professor of geography, Carleton University, Ottawa, Ontario.
François Baby.

CLOUTIER, NICOLE. Conservatrice de l'art canadien ancien, Musée des beaux-arts de Montréal, Québec.
Urbain Desrochers.

COLE, JEAN MURRAY. Writer and historian, Indian River, Ontario.
Archibald McDonald.

COLLARD, ELIZABETH. Writer and museum consultant, Ottawa, Ontario.
Edmond Baird.

COOKE, O. A. Historian, Directorate of History, Department of National Defence, Ottawa, Ontario.
Charles Murray Cathcart, 2nd Earl Cathcart [in collaboration with N. Hillmer].

CORNELL, PAUL G. Formerly professor of history, University of Waterloo, Ontario.
William Fitz William Owen.

COURVILLE, SERGE. Professeur agrégé de géographie, Université Laval, Québec, Québec.
François-Pierre Bruneau. Charles Caron. Jean-Baptiste-René Hertel de Rouville. Janvier-Domptail Lacroix. François-Xavier Malhiot.

COX, WILLIAM. Head, History Department, Carleton Place High School, Ontario.
Thomas Mabon Radenhurst.

CRAIG, G. M. Professor emeritus of history, University of Toronto, Ontario.
Peter Boyle de Blaquière. Isaac Weld. Joseph Wells.

CREIGHTON, PHILIP. Chartered accountant, Toronto, Ontario.
William Scott Burn.

CROSBIE, GERTRUDE. St John's, Newfoundland.
James Douglas.

CROSS, MICHAEL S. Dean of continuing education and professor of history, Dalhousie University, Halifax, Nova Scotia.
Robert Baldwin [in collaboration with R. L. Fraser].
Robert Baldwin Sullivan [in collaboration with R. L. Fraser and V. L. Russell].

CRUIKSHANK, KEN. Doctoral candidate in history, York University, Downsview, Ontario.
John Henry Dunn.

CYR, CÉLINE. Rédactrice-historienne, *Dictionnaire biographique du Canada/Dictionary of Canadian biography*, Les Presses de l'université Laval, Québec, Québec.
Michel Bibaud. Émile de Fenouillet. Narcisse-Charles Fortier.

D'AIGLE, JEANNE. Professeure, écrivaine et journaliste, Saint-Hyacinthe, Québec.
Emmanuel Couillard-Després.

DALTON, IAN R. Associate professor of electrical engineering, University of Toronto, Ontario.
Sophia Simms (Dalton).

DEMPSEY, HUGH A. Assistant director, Collections, Glenbow-Alberta Institute, Calgary, Alberta.
A-ca-oo-mah-ca-ye.

DENAULT, BERNARD. Professeur agrégé de sociologie, Université de Sherbrooke, Québec.
Charles-Joseph Ducharme.

DEROME, ROBERT. Professeur d'histoire de l'art, Université du Québec à Montréal, Québec.
Paul Morand [in collaboration with N. Morgan].

DÉSILETS, ANDRÉE. Professeure d'histoire, Université de Sherbrooke, Québec.
Hezekiah Robinson.

†DESJARDINS, ÉDOUARD. Ex-rédacteur émérite, *L'Union médicale du Canada*, Montréal, Québec.
Joseph Parant [in collaboration].

DESJARDINS, MARC. Chercheur, Institut québécois de recherche sur la culture, Québec, Québec.
Joseph-François Deblois.

DESLAURIERS, PETER. Doctoral candidate in history, Concordia University, Montreal, Quebec.
Samuel Gerrard.

DEVEREUX, EDWARD JAMES. Professor of English, University of Western Ontario, London, Ontario.
George Webber.

DODDS, GORDON. Chief, Government Records, Provincial Archives of Manitoba, Winnipeg, Manitoba.
Sir James Buchanan Macaulay.

†DODGE, ERNEST S. Formerly director, Peabody Museum, Salem, Massachusetts, U.S.A.
Sir John Ross [in collaboration].

DOUGALL, CHARLES. Supervisory editor, *Dictionary of Canadian biography/Dictionnaire biographique du Canada*, University of Toronto Press, Ontario.
William Henry King. Okah Tubbee.

DOUGLAS, W. A. B. Director, Directorate of History, Department of National Defence, Ottawa, Ontario.
Edward Boxer.

DUBÉ, MIREILLE. Chef, Service de l'information, Commission des normes du travail du Québec, Québec.
Thomas Marchildon.

DUBUC, ALFRED. Professeur d'histoire, Université du Québec à Montréal, Québec.
John Molson [in collaboration with R. Tremblay].

DUFOUR, PIERRE. Historien, Québec, Québec.
Laurent Leroux. James McKenzie [in collaboration with M. Ouellet].

DUMAIS, RAYMOND. Responsable, Division des services techniques, Archives nationales du Québec à Montréal, Québec.
Louis-René Lacoste.

DUNLOP, ALLAN C. Assistant provincial archivist, Public Archives of Nova Scotia, Halifax, Nova Scotia.
Thomas Dickson. Thomas Ritchie. Hugh Ross.

DYSTER, BARRIE. Lecturer in economic history, University of New South Wales, Kensington, New South Wales, Australia.
John Simcoe Macaulay.

EADIE, JAMES A. Head, History Department, Napanee District Secondary School, Ontario.
David Barker Stevenson.

EADIE, TOM. Head, Reference and Collection Development Department, Dana Porter Library, University of Waterloo, Ontario.
Christian Enslin.

EARLE, G. H. Formerly provost, Queen's College, Memorial University of Newfoundland, St John's, Newfoundland.
Jacob George Mountain.

EDWARDS, MARY JANE. Professor of English and principal investigator at the Centre for Editing Early Canadian Texts, Carleton University, Ottawa, Ontario.
Ebenezer Clemo.

EINARSON, NEIL. Chief, Architectural History, Historic Resources Branch, Manitoba Culture, Heritage and Recreation, Winnipeg, Manitoba.
William Thomas.

ENNALS, PETER. Associate professor of geography, Mount Allison University, Sackville, New Brunswick.
Zacheus Burnham. Robert Henry. Stuart Easton Mackechnie.

EPP, FRANK H. Professor of history, University of Waterloo, Ontario.
Benjamin Eby.

ERICKSON, VINCENT O. Professor of anthropology, University of New Brunswick, Fredericton, New Brunswick.
Noel Lola. Peter Lola.

EVANS, CALVIN D. Assistant librarian, University of Alberta, Edmonton, Alberta.
John Bell. Richard Knight.

FACEY-CROWTHER, DAVID R. Associate professor of history, Memorial University of Newfoundland, St John's, Newfoundland.
Thomas George William Eaststaff.

FAHEY, CURTIS. Manuscript editor, *Dictionary of Canadian biography/Dictionnaire biographique du Canada*, University of Toronto Press, Ontario.
Charles Donlevy.

FAHMY-EID, NADIA. Professeure d'histoire, Université du Québec à Montréal, Québec.
Jean-Charles Prince.

FARIBAULT-BEAUREGARD, MARTHE. Bibliothécaire-archiviste, Société généalogique canadienne-française, Montréal, Québec.

Joseph-Édouard Faribault.

FELLOWS, JO-ANN CARR. Economist, Province of New Brunswick, Fredericton, New Brunswick.
Mary Coy (Morris; Bradley).

FERRON, MADELEINE. Écrivaine, Québec, Québec.
Siméon Gautron, dit Larochelle.

FINGARD, JUDITH. Professor of history, Dalhousie University, Halifax, Nova Scotia.
John Thomas Twining.

FINK CLINE, BEVERLY. Writer, Willowdale, Ontario.
John Smyth.

FIRTH, EDITH G. Formerly head, Canadian History Department, Metropolitan Toronto Library, Ontario.
John Carey.

FLANDERS, DOUGLAS L. Statistician/administrator, Offices of the General Council, United Church of Canada, Toronto, Ontario.
Reuben Crandall.

FLEMMING, DAVID B. Curator, Maritime Museum of the Atlantic, Halifax, Nova Scotia.
William Fraser. William Walsh.

FLEURY, ALCIDE. Arthabaska, Québec.
Jean-Gaspard Dumoulin.

FORTIN, LIONEL. Notaire, Saint-André-Avellin, Québec.
Pierre-Paul Démaray. Pierre Gamelin. Gabriel Marchand.

FOSTER, JOHN E. Associate professor of history, University of Alberta, Edmonton, Alberta.
James Bird.

FRASER, ROBERT LOCHIEL. Hamilton, Ontario.
Robert Baldwin [in collaboration with M. S. Cross]. *John Macaulay. Benajah Mallory. George Powlis. Robert Baldwin Sullivan* [in collaboration with M. S. Cross and V. L. Russell]. *John Willson.*

FRENCH, GOLDWIN. President, Victoria University, Toronto, Ontario.
William Case. Albert Des Brisay. William Martin Harvard. Richard Williams.

FRENETTE, YVES. Assistant professor of history, University of Maine at Orono, U.S.A.
William Cuthbert.

GAGNON, GASTON. Historien, Centre d'interprétation de la pulperie de Chicoutimi, Québec.
Peter McLeod.

GAGNON, SERGE. Professeur d'histoire, Université du Québec à Trois-Rivières, Québec.
Amable Dionne.

GALARNEAU, CLAUDE. Professeur titulaire d'histoire, Université Laval, Québec, Québec.
Jérôme Demers. John Holmes. Augustin-René Langlois, dit Germain.

GALARNEAU, FRANCE. Rédactrice-historienne, *Dictionnaire biographique du Canada/Dictionary of Canadian biography,* Les Presses de l'université Laval, Québec, Québec.
Joseph Roy.

GALBRAITH, JOHN S. Professor of history, University of California, San Diego, California, U.S.A.
Sir George Simpson.

GALLACHER, DANIEL T. Curator of modern history, British Columbia Provincial Museum, Victoria, British Columbia.
Andrew Muir.

GATES, LILLIAN F. Ithaca, New York, U.S.A.
Thomas Jefferson Sutherland.

GAUTHIER, BENOÎT. Étudiant au doctorat en histoire, Université du Québec à Montréal, Québec.
Pierre-Benjamin Dumoulin.

GAUTHIER, RAYMONDE. Professeure d'histoire de l'art, Université du Québec à Montréal, Québec.
François Normand. Paul Rollin.

GIDNEY, R. D. Professor of education, University of Western Ontario, London, Ontario.
Robert Murray.

GILLIS, ROBERT PETER. Chief, Information Policy, Administrative Policy Branch, Treasury Board Secretariat, Ottawa, Ontario.
David Pattee.

GIRARD, CHARLOTTE S. M. Associate professor of history, University of Victoria, British Columbia.
John Nobili.

GLENDENNING, BURTON. Supervisor, Historical Division, Provincial Archives of New Brunswick, Fredericton, New Brunswick.
Joseph Russell.

GOLDRING, PHILIP. Historian, National Historic Parks and Sites Branch, Ottawa, Ontario.
James Keith.

GOUIN, JACQUES. Historien, journaliste et traducteur, Saint-Sauveur-des-Monts, Québec.
William Henry Scott.

GRANT, JOHN N. Associate professor of history, Nova Scotia Teachers' College, Halifax, Nova Scotia.
Abraham Whitman.

GREENFIELD, KATHARINE. Formerly head, Special Collections, Hamilton Public Library, Ontario.
James Gage. Robert Reid Smiley [in collaboration with D. R. Beer].

GREENHILL, BASIL. Chairman, SS *Great Britain* Project, Bristol, England.
William Ellis. John Lewellin Lewellin [in collaboration with H. T. Holman].

GREENWOOD, F. MURRAY. Associate professor of history, University of British Columbia, Vancouver, British Columbia.
John Henry. André Jobin.

GWYN, JULIAN. Professor of history, University of Ottawa, Ontario.
Archibald McNab, 17th Chief of Clan Macnab [in collaboration with A. Cameron].

HALL, ROGER. Assistant professor of history, University of Western Ontario, London, Ontario.
Hamnett Kirkes Pinhey. Vincent Gildemeester van Tuyll van Serooskerken, Baron van Tuyll van Serooskerken [in collaboration with F. H. Armstrong].

HANDCOCK, W. GORDON. Associate professor of geography, Memorial University of Newfoundland, St John's, Newfoundland.
Samuel Codner.

HANSEN, LINDA SQUIERS. Editorial assistant, *Conflict Quarterly,* Centre for Conflict Studies, University of New Brunswick, Fredericton, New Brunswick.
James Somerville.

HARDY, RENÉ. Professeur d'histoire, Université du Québec à Trois-Rivières, Québec.
Olympe Hoerner (Tanner).

HAREL, J.-BRUNO, P.S.S. Archiviste, Séminaire de Saint-Sulpice, Montréal, Québec.
John Larkin. Jean-Baptiste Roupe.

†HARPER, J. RUSSELL. South Lancaster, Ontario.
Martin Somerville.

HEADON, CHRISTOPHER FERGUS. Historian, West Wickham, Kent, England.
Vincent Philip Mayerhoffer.

HICKS, FRANKLYN H. Physician, Ottawa, Ontario.
John Quirk.

HILLMER, NORMAN. Senior historian, Directorate of History, Department of National Defence, Ottawa, Ontario.
Charles Murray Cathcart, 2nd Earl Cathcart [in collaboration with O. A. Cooke].

HIRSCH, R. FORBES. Graduate student in history, Carleton University, Ottawa, Ontario.
William Stewart.

HODGINS, BRUCE W. Professor of history, Trent University, Peterborough, Ontario.
Alexander Fraser.

HOLLAND, CLIVE. Archivist, Scott Polar Research Institute, Cambridge, England.
Joseph-René Bellot. Kallihirua.

HOLMAN, H. T. Lawyer and archivist, Ottawa, Ontario.
Edward James Jarvis [in collaboration with J. M. Bumsted]. *John Lewellin Lewellin* [in collaboration with B. Greenhill].

HOLMGREN, ERIC J. Historical consultant, Edmonton, Alberta.
Ross Cox.

HOSKINS, RONALD G. Associate professor of history, University of Windsor, Ontario.
Claude Cartier.

HOWELL, COLIN D. Associate professor of history, St Mary's University, Halifax, Nova Scotia.
William Grigor.

HUGHES, MALCOLM A. Canon residentiary, Christ Church Cathedral, and editor, *Montreal Churchman,* Montreal, Quebec.
William Arnold.

HUNTER, WILLIAM A. Formerly chief historian, Pennsylvania Historical and Museum Commission, Harrisburg, Pennsylvania, U.S.A.
Peter Klingensmith, known as *White Peter.*

HYATT, A. M. J. Professor of history, University of Western Ontario, London, Ontario.
James Kerby.

JANSON, GILLES. Responsable, Archives historiques, Service des archives, Université du Québec à Montréal, Québec.
Louis-Joseph-Charles Cazeneuve.

JANZEN, CAROL ANNE. Businesswoman, Kentville, Nova Scotia.
Eliza Ann Chipman (Chipman).

JARRELL, RICHARD A. Associate professor of natural science, York University, Downsview, Ontario.
Édouard-Sylvestre de Rottermund, Count de Rottermund.

JARVIS, ERIC. Associate professor of history, University of Western Ontario, London, Ontario.
Charles Albert Berczy. Joseph Hartman.

JEAN, MARGUERITE, S.C.I.M. Secrétaire générale, Congrégation des sœurs du Bon-Pasteur de Québec, Sainte-Foy, Québec.

Émilie Tavernier (Gamelin).

JOHNSON, J. K. Professor of history, Carleton University, Ottawa, Ontario.
George Brouse. John Joseph. George Lyon. William Thompson. Samuel Zimmerman.

JOHNSON, ROBERT E. President, Horn of the Moon Enterprises, Montpelier, Vermont, U.S.A.
Elisha Kent Kane. Sir William Edward Parry.

JOHNSTON, HOPE H. Formerly director of home economics, Halifax City Junior High Schools, Nova Scotia.
William Ayre.

JOLICŒUR, CATHERINE. Professeure de folklore et de littérature, Centre universitaire Saint-Louis-Maillet, Edmundston, Nouveau-Brunswick.
Louis Gamache.

JONES, ELWOOD H. Professor of history, Trent University, Peterborough, Ontario.
John Gilchrist.

JONES, FREDERICK. Senior lecturer in organizational behaviour, Dorset Institute of Higher Education, Bournemouth, England.
Charles Blackman. Thomas Finch Hobday Bridge.

JONES, ORLO LOUISE. Genealogist, Prince Edward Island Museum and Heritage Foundation, Charlottetown, Prince Edward Island.
Robert Jones.

JUDD, CAROL M. Manager, Participation Services, Canadian Amateur Swimming Association, Ottawa, Ontario.
Andrew H. Bulger [in collaboration with R. S. Allen]. *John Pritchard.*

KALBFLEISCH, HERBERT K. Professor emeritus of German, University of Western Ontario, London, Ontario.
Heinrich Wilhelm Peterson.

KALLMANN, HELMUT. Chief, Music Division, National Library of Canada, Ottawa, Ontario.
Ferdinand Griebel.

KAREL, DAVID. Professeur agrégé d'histoire, Université Laval, Québec, Québec.
Gerome Fassio. Laurent Vivant.

KERNAGHAN, LOIS KATHLEEN. Historical researcher and editor, Boutilier's Point, Nova Scotia.
Alexander Campbell. Marie-Henriette LeJeune (Comeau; Lejeune, dit Briard; Ross).

KESTEMAN, JEAN-PIERRE. Professeur d'histoire, Université de Sherbrooke, Québec.
Silas Horton Dickerson.

KEYES, JOHN. Historian, Quebec, Quebec.
Peter Patterson.

KLINCK, CARL F. Formerly professor of English, University of Western Ontario, London, Ontario.
William Fitz Hawley.

KOLISH, EVELYN. Historian, Laval, Quebec.
Sir James Stuart.

KULISEK, LARRY L. Associate professor and head, Department of History, University of Windsor, Ontario.
Francis Xavier Caldwell.

LABRÈQUE, MARIE-PAULE R. Directrice, Bibliothèque municipale, Acton-Vale, Québec.
William Arms. George McLeod Ross.

LAHEY, RAYMOND J. Vicar general, Archdiocese of St John's, Newfoundland.
Timothy Browne. Charles Dalton. James W. Duffy.

LALANCETTE, MARIO. Étudiant au doctorat en histoire,

McGill University, Montréal, Québec.
Alexis Tremblay, dit Picoté.

LAMB, W. KAYE. Formerly dominion archivist and national librarian; Vancouver, British Columbia.
John McLoughlin.

LAMBERT, JAMES H. Rédacteur-historien, *Dictionnaire biographique du Canada/Dictionary of Canadian biography*, Les Presses de l'université Laval, Québec, Québec.
Jean-Baptiste Kelly. Thomas Maguire. Daniel Wilkie.

†LANGDON, JOHN E. Toronto, Ontario.
James Godfrey Hanna.

LEBEL, JEAN-MARIE. Étudiant au doctorat en histoire, Université Laval, Québec, Québec.
Aimé Désilets. Ludger Duvernay.

LEEFE, JOHN G. Minister of Fisheries, Province of Nova Scotia, Halifax, Nova Scotia.
John Barss.

LEFEBVRE, JEAN-JACQUES. Ex-archiviste en chef, Cour supérieure, Montréal, Québec.
Toussaint Peltier.

LEGGET, ROBERT FERGUSON. Formerly director, Division of Building Research, National Research Council of Canada, Ottawa, Ontario.
Nathaniel Hazard Tredwell.

LEIGHTON, DOUGLAS. Associate professor of history, University of Western Ontario, London, Ontario.
Dominique Ducharme. Samuel Peters Jarvis [in collaboration with R. J. Burns].

LEMIEUX, LUCIEN. Vicaire épiscopal, Saint-Lambert, Québec.
Joseph-Marie Bellenger. Joseph-Norbert Provencher.

LEMIRE, MAURICE. Professeur titulaire de littérature québécoise, Université Laval; chercheur, Institut québécois de recherche sur la culture, Québec, Québec.
James Huston.

LEPAGE, ANDRÉ. Contractuel, Québec, Québec.
David Le Boutillier.

LITTLE, J. I. Associate professor of history, Simon Fraser University, Burnaby, British Columbia.
Marcus Child.

LORIMIER, MICHEL DE. Rédacteur-historien, *Dictionnaire biographique du Canada/Dictionary of Canadian biography*, Les Presses de l'université Laval, Québec, Québec.
Timothée Kimber. Siméon Marchesseault. André Ouimet. Louis-Michel Viger.

LORTIE, JEANNE D'ARC. Chercheuse en résidence, Centre·de recherche en civilisation canadienne-française, Université d'Ottawa, Ontario.
Pierre Laviolette. Auguste Soulard.

LORTIE, LÉON. Professeur à la retraite, Montréal, Québec.
Amable-Daniel Duchaîne.

LOWREY, CAROL. Librarian, E.P. Taylor Reference Library, Art Gallery of Ontario, Toronto, Ontario.
John Craig.

McCALLA, DOUGLAS. Professor of history, Trent University, Peterborough, Ontario.
Peter Buchanan. Ezekiel Francis Whittemore.

MacDONALD, ALLAN J. Supervisor, Private Manuscripts, Archives of Ontario, Toronto, Ontario.
Benjamin Lett. Alexander McMartin.

MacDONALD, G. EDWARD. Historical researcher and writer, Sherwood, Prince Edward Island.

Bernard Donald Macdonald.

McDOUGALL, ELIZABETH ANN KERR. Historian, Montreal, Quebec.
Henry Esson. William Rintoul.

McDOUGALL, JOHN LORN. Lawyer, Toronto, Ontario.
John Lorn McDougall.

McFARLAND, JOHN. Historic resources planner, Provincial Parks Branch, Winnipeg, Manitoba.
Nicholas Garry.

McGAHAN, ELIZABETH W. Assistant professor of history, University of New Brunswick, Fredericton, New Brunswick.
Noah Disbrow.

†MACKAY, DONALD C. Halifax, Nova Scotia.
Benjamin Wolhaupter.

MACKENZIE, A. A. Associate professor of history, St Francis Xavier University, Antigonish, Nova Scotia.
Herbert Huntington.

MacKENZIE, ANN. Instructor of history, University of Western Ontario, London, Ontario.
William Graham Edmundson.

McKENZIE, RUTH. Free-lance writer, editor, and researcher, Ottawa, Ontario.
Henry Gildersleeve. Samuel Proudfoot Hurd.

MACKINNON, KENNETH A. Professor of English, St Mary's University, Halifax, Nova Scotia.
Coun Douly Rankin.

MacKINNON, WILLIAM R. Archivist, Provincial Archives of New Brunswick, Fredericton, New Brunswick.
Robert Doak.

McLEAN, MARIANNE. Archivist, Public Archives of Canada, Ottawa, Ontario.
John McGillivray (Dalcrombie).

MacLEAN, RAYMOND A. Professor of history, St Francis Xavier University, Antigonish, Nova Scotia.
Henry McKeagney. Thomas Trotter.

MacLENNAN, JEAN M. Edinburgh, Scotland.
John MacLennan.

McNAB, DAVID T. Senior Indian land claims researcher, Ontario Ministry of Natural Resources, Toronto; adjunct associate professor of history, University of Waterloo, Ontario.
George Martin.

McNALLY, LARRY S. Archivist, Public Archives of Canada, Ottawa, Ontario.
Robert Hoyle.

McNALLY, PETER F. Associate professor of library science, McGill University, Montreal, Quebec.
Robert Walter Stuart Mackay.

MacRAE, MARION BELL. Lecturer in history of design, Ontario College of Art, Toronto, Ontario.
John Ewart. Henry Bowyer Joseph Lane [in collaboration with S. A. Otto].

MANNION, JOHN. Associate professor of geography, Memorial University of Newfoundland, St John's, Newfoundland.
John O'Brien.

MARCIL, EILEEN. Historian, Charlesbourg, Quebec.
John Munn.

†MATTHEWS, KEITH. Formerly professor of history and chairman of the Maritime History Group, Memorial University of Newfoundland, St John's, Newfoundland.
Robert Pack.

MEALING, STANLEY R. Professor of history, Carleton University, Ottawa, Ontario.
Francis Gore.

MICHAUD, GUY R. Bibliothécaire, Edmundston, Nouveau-Brunswick.
Antoine Langevin.

MILLAR, W. P. J. London, Ontario.
Thaddeus Osgood.

MILLER, CARMAN. Associate professor of history, McGill University, Montreal, Quebec.
Benjamin Hart.

MILOT, JOCELYNE. Chercheuse et auteure, Sainte-Foy, Québec.
Pierre Drouin.

MITCHELL, ELAINE ALLAN. Toronto, Ontario.
Allan McDonell.

MOIR, JOHN S. Professor of history, University of Toronto, Ontario.
John Bayne.

MOIR, MICHAEL B. Archivist, St Christopher House, Don Mills, Ontario.
Murdoch Sutherland.

MONETTE, MICHEL. Étudiant au doctorat en histoire, Université Laval, Québec, Québec.
William Hall. John William Woolsey.

MOODY, BARRY M. Associate professor of history, Acadia University, Wolfville, Nova Scotia.
Richard E. Burpee. Edward Manning.

MORGAN, NICHOLAS J. Lecturer in Scottish history, University of Glasgow, Scotland.
William Ritchie.

MORGAN, NORMA. Graduate student in art history, Concordia University, Montreal, Quebec.
Paul Morand [in collaboration with R. Derome].

MORIN, MICHEL. Professeur d'histoire, Collège Notre-Dame de l'Assomption, Nicolet, Québec.
Michel Carrier.

MORRISS, SHIRLEY G. Curator, Brampton Public Library and Art Gallery, Ontario.
Thomas Young.

MORROW, MARIANNE G. Writer and researcher, Charlottetown, Prince Edward Island.
James Bagnall.

MUIR, ELIZABETH. Doctoral candidate in history, McGill University, Montreal, Quebec.
Elizabeth Dart (Eynon).

MURRAY, FLORENCE B. Professor emeritus of library science, University of Toronto, Ontario.
John Knatchbull Roche.

NEARY, PETER. Professor of history, University of Western Ontario, London, Ontario.
Miss Kirwan, named *Sister Mary Bernard.*

NELLES, H. V. Professor of history, York University, Downsview, Ontario.
Bartholomew Crannell Beardsley. George Keefer.

NICKS, JOHN. Research coordinator, Reynolds-Alberta Museum, Wetaskiwin, Alberta.
David Thompson.

NOBLE, JOHN H. Doctoral candidate in history, University of Toronto, Ontario.
James Barnston [in collaboration with S. E. Zeller].

NOËL, JEAN-CLAUDE.
Pierre Petitclair.

NOPPEN, LUC. Professeur titulaire d'histoire de l'art,

Université Laval, Québec, Québec.
Thomas Baillairgé. André Paquet, dit Lavallée.

O'DEA, SHANE. Associate professor of English, Memorial University of Newfoundland, St John's, Newfoundland.
James Purcell.

O'FARRELL, JOHN K. A. Professor of history, University of Windsor, Ontario.
Henry Walton Bibb.

O'FLAHERTY, PATRICK. Professor of English, Memorial University of Newfoundland, St John's, Newfoundland.
Edward Kielley. Henry David Winton.

O'GALLAGHER, MARIANNA. Teacher of history, Quebec, Quebec.
Patrick McMahon.

OTTO, STEPHEN A. Private scholar, Toronto, Ontario.
Henry Bowyer Joseph Lane [in collaboration with M. B. MacRae].

OUELLET, MARC. Chercheur autonome, Sainte-Foy, Québec.
James McKenzie [in collaboration with P. Dufour].

OUELLETTE, DAVID. Conservator, W. B. Ready Division of Research Collections, Mills Library, McMaster University, Hamilton, Ontario.
James Crooks. Hugh Scobie.

PAINCHAUD, CLOTILDE T. L. Auteure, Sherbrooke, Québec.
Alexis Painchaud.

PAINCHAUD, LOUIS. Professeur, Collège d'enseignement général et professionnel de Sainte-Foy, Québec.
Joseph Painchaud.

PANNEKOEK, FRITS. Director, Historic Sites Service, Alberta Culture, Edmonton, Alberta.
Alexander Ross.

PARKER, GEORGE L. Professor of English, Royal Military College of Canada, Kingston, Ontario.
Robert Armour. Henry Chubb. John Henry Crosskill. Edmund Ward.

PAYMENT, DIANE PAULETTE. Historienne, Parcs Canada, Winnipeg, Manitoba.
Louis Guiboche.

PEEL, BRUCE. Formerly librarian, University of Alberta, Edmonton, Alberta.
Martin Switzer.

PIETERSMA, HARRY. Supervisor of agricultural interpretation, Upper Canada Village, Morrisburg, Ontario.
Samuel Crane.

PLOUFFE, MARCEL. Chef de division, Service de l'audiovisuel, Université Laval, Québec, Québec.
Thomas Ainslie Young.

POIRIER, LUCIEN. Professeur agrégé de musique, Université Laval, Québec, Québec.
Théodore-Frédéric Molt.

PORTER, JOHN R. Professeur agrégé d'histoire de l'art, Université Laval, Québec, Québec.
Joseph Légaré.

POTVIN, GILLES. Critique musical, *Le Devoir*, Montréal, Québec.
Orphir Peltier.

POULIN, PIERRE. Assistant de recherche, Institut québécois de recherche sur la culture, Québec, Québec.
David Burnet. John Saxton Campbell. Jean Chabot. James Gibb. François-Xavier Méthot.

PRINCE, SUZANNE. Professeure de littérature, Collège

Mérici, Québec, Québec.
Jean-Denis Daulé.

PRYKE, KENNETH GEORGE. Professor of history, University of Windsor, Ontario.
James Carmichael. Matthias Francis Hoffmann.

PULSIFER, CAMERON W. Historian, Parks Canada, Halifax, Nova Scotia.
Augustus Frederick Welsford.

PUNCH, TERRENCE M. Vice-president, Royal Nova Scotia Historical Society, and president, Genealogical Institute of the Maritimes, Halifax, Nova Scotia.
Hugh O'Reilly.

RASPORICH, ANTHONY W. Professor of history, University of Calgary, Alberta.
Henry Taylor.

RAY, ARTHUR. Professor of history, University of British Columbia, Vancouver, British Columbia.
William Todd.

READ, COLIN FREDERICK. Associate professor of history, Huron College, London, Ontario.
Francis Evans. Edward Alexander Theller.

REID, JOHN G. Associate professor of history and associate director, Centre for Canadian Studies, Mount Allison University, Sackville, New Brunswick.
Charles Frederick Allison.

REID, RICHARD M. Associate professor of history, University of Guelph, Ontario.
John Egan.

RICHARDSON, DOUGLAS. Associate professor of fine arts, University of Toronto, Ontario.
Frank Wills.

RINGEREIDE, MABEL. Free-lance writer, Carleton Place, Ontario.
John Smith.

ROBERT, JEAN-CLAUDE. Professeur d'histoire, Université du Québec à Montréal, Québec.
Louis-Marie-Raphaël Barbier. Jacob De Witt. William Evans. William King McCord. Jacques Viger.

ROBERTS, DAVID. Manuscript editor, *Dictionary of Canadian biography/Dictionnaire biographique du Canada*, University of Toronto Press, Ontario.
John DeCow. François-Xavier Larue. George Rykert.

ROBERTSON, IAN ROSS. Associate professor of history, University of Toronto, Ontario.
Donald McDonald. Duncan Maclean.

ROGERS, IRENE L. Architectural adviser, Prince Edward Island Museum and Heritage Foundation, Charlottetown, Prince Edward Island.
George Godsell Thresher.

ROLAND, CHARLES G. Jason A. Hannah professor of the history of medicine, McMaster University, Hamilton, Ontario.
Robert Douglas Hamilton. Walter Henry.

ROMNEY, PAUL. Historian, Baltimore, Maryland, U.S.A.
Christopher Widmer.

ROSENKRANTZ, OTTE A. Doctoral candidate in history, University of New Brunswick, Fredericton, New Brunswick.
Sir Richard Armstrong.

ROSS, ALEXANDER M. Formerly professor of English language and literature, University of Guelph, Ontario.
William Henry Bartlett.

ROUILLARD, JACQUES. Professeur agrégé d'histoire, Université de Montréal, Québec.
Adolphe Jacquies.

ROUSSEAU, LOUIS. Professeur de sciences religieuses, Université du Québec à Montréal, Québec.
Paul-Loup Archambault. Joseph-Vincent Quiblier.

ROY, JEAN-LOUIS. Directeur, *Le Devoir*, Montréal, Québec.
Édouard-Raymond Fabre.

RUGGLE, RICHARD E. Rector, St Paul's Anglican Church, Norval, Ontario.
Alfred Booker.

RUSSELL, HILARY. Historian, Parks Canada, Ottawa, Ontario.
Angus Bethune.

RUSSELL, VICTOR LORING. Manager, City of Toronto Archives, Ontario.
Thomas David Morrison. Robert Baldwin Sullivan [in collaboration with M. S. Cross and R. L. Fraser].

RYDER, DOROTHY E. Formerly reference collection development specialist, National Library, Ottawa, Ontario; Vancouver, British Columbia.
Alfred Hawkins.

SAINT-PIERRE, JOCELYN. Chef, Division de la reconstitution des débats, Bibliothèque de l'Assemblée nationale, Québec, Québec.
Ronald Macdonald.

SCHMIDT, GRACE. Formerly assistant chief librarian, Kitchener Public Library, Ontario.
Samuel D. Betzner.

SCHURMAN, DONALD M. Professor and head, Department of History, Royal Military College of Canada, Kingston, Ontario.
Williams Sandom [in collaboration with J. W. Spurr].

SCOLLARD, ROBERT JOSEPH. Archivist, University of St Michael's College, Toronto, Ontario.
Michel Moncoq.

SENIOR, ELINOR KYTE. Assistant professor of history, McGill University, Montreal, Quebec.
John Clitherow. Aaron Hogsett. Sir James Macdonell. Sir Randolph Isham Routh.

SHEPARD, C. J. Archivist, Archives of Ontario, Toronto, Ontario.
John Crysler. Richard Duncan Fraser. John McDonald.

SHUTLAK, GARRY DAVID. Map/architecture archivist, Public Archives of Nova Scotia, Halifax, Nova Scotia.
John Conrade West.

†SIMARD, JEAN-PAUL. Ex-professeur d'histoire, Université du Québec à Chicoutimi, Québec.
John Chaperon.

SMITH, DONALD B. Associate professor of history, University of Calgary, Alberta.
Peter Jones.

SMITH, SHIRLEE ANNE. Keeper, Hudson's Bay Company Archives, Provincial Archives of Manitoba, Winnipeg, Manitoba.
Charles Dodd. John Halkett (Wedderburn). Ooligbuck.

SPEISMAN, STEPHEN A. Director, Ontario Region Archives, Canadian Jewish Congress, Toronto, Ontario.
Judah George Joseph.

SPRAGGE, SHIRLEY C. Archivist, Queen's University Archives, Kingston, Ontario.

Robert Christie. John Landon Read.

SPRAY, WILLIAM A. Vice-president (academic), St Thomas University, Fredericton, New Brunswick.
John Baird. Pierre Basquet. Alexander Boyle. Robert Ferguson. Alexander Rankin.

SPRY, IRENE M. Professor emeritus of economics, University of Ottawa, Ontario.
James Sinclair.

†SPURR, JOHN W. Formerly chief librarian emeritus, Royal Military College of Canada, Kingston, Ontario.
Williams Sandom [in collaboration with D. M. Schurman].

STAGG, RONALD J. Professor of history, Ryerson Polytechnical Institute, Toronto, Ontario.
George Barclay. John McIntosh.

STANLEY, DELLA M. M. Part-time lecturer in history, St Mary's University, Halifax, Nova Scotia.
William Chandler.

STELTER, GILBERT A. Professor of history, University of Guelph, Ontario.
David Gilkison.

STEWART, J. DOUGLAS. Professor of art history, Queen's University, Kingston, Ontario.
Thomas Rogers.

STICKNEY, KENNETH. Staff writer, *Daily Commercial News*, Toronto, Ontario.
Sir Gordon Drummond.

SUTHERLAND, DAVID A. Associate professor of history, Dalhousie University, Halifax, Nova Scotia.
Henry Hezekiah Cogswell. James Foreman. William Pryor. Richard Tremain.

SWANICK, ERIC L. Librarian, Legislative Library, Fredericton, New Brunswick.
Thomas Hill.

SWEENY, ROBERT. Member, Montreal Business History Project, Montreal, Quebec.
Peter McGill (McCutcheon).

SYLVAIN, PHILIPPE. Professeur d'histoire à la retraite, Université Laval, Québec, Québec.
Robert Corrigan. Léon Gingras. Alfred-Xavier Rambau. Eleazer Williams.

TALMAN, JAMES JOHN. Professor of history, University of Western Ontario, London, Ontario.
John Howison [in collaboration with E. Waterston].

TAYLOR, M. BROOK. Graduate student in history, University of Toronto, Ontario.
George R. Dalrymple. Ambrose Lane. Charles Worrell.

THOMAS, CLARA. Professor emeritus of English, York University, Downsview, Ontario.
Anna Brownell Murphy (Jameson).

THOMAS, GREGORY. Interpretive planner, Parks Canada, Winnipeg, Manitoba.
George Marcus Cary. James McMillan.

THOMAS, PETER. Professor of English, University of New Brunswick, Fredericton, New Brunswick.
Anthony Lockwood.

THORNE, TANIS C. Graduate student in history, California State University, Fullerton, California, U.S.A.
Ramsay Crooks.

TONER, PETER M. Associate professor of history, University of New Brunswick, Fredericton, New Brunswick.
William Dollard.

TRAP, PAUL. Teacher, Grand Haven Public Schools, Michigan, U.S.A.
Jean-Baptiste Faribault. Laurent-Salomon Juneau.

TREMBLAY, ROBERT. Étudiant au doctorat en histoire, Université du Québec à Montréal, Québec.
John Molson [in collaboration with A. Dubuc].

TROFIMENKOFF, SUSAN MANN. Vice-rector (academic) and professor of history, University of Ottawa, Ontario.
Ann Cuthbert Rae (Knight; Fleming).

TUNIS, BARBARA R. Research historian, Ottawa, Ontario.
George Thomas Landmann.

TURNER, H. E. Associate professor of history, McMaster University, Hamilton, Ontario.
Dominick Edward Blake. Peter Perry.

TURNER, WESLEY B. Associate professor of history, Brock University, St Catharines, Ontario.
Thomas Rolph. Sir Roger Hale Sheaffe [in collaboration with C. M. Whitfield].

†UPTON, L. F. S. Formerly professor of history, University of British Columbia, Vancouver, British Columbia.
Peter Paul Toney Babey. Charles Glode. Gabriel Glode.

VACHON, CLAUDE. Chef de division, Gestion des documents, Régie des rentes du Québec, Québec.
Philippe Panet. George Vanfelson.

VAN KIRK, SYLVIA. Associate professor of history, University of Toronto, Ontario.
John Ballenden. John Dugald Cameron. Donald McKenzie. Nancy McKenzie (McTavish; Le Blanc). Sarah McLeod (Ballenden). Letitia Mactavish (Hargrave). George Nelson [in collaboration with J. S. H. Brown]. *John Rowand. Frances Ramsay Simpson (Simpson, Lady Simpson).*

VAUGEOIS, DENIS. Travailleur autonome, Sillery, Québec.
Aaron Ezekiel Hart. Moses Hart.

VOISINE, NIVE. Professeur titulaire d'histoire, Université Laval, Québec, Québec.
Sévère Dumoulin.

WAITE, P. B. Professor of history, Dalhousie University, Halifax, Nova Scotia.
Gloud Wilson McLelan.

WALLACE, CARL M. Associate professor and chairman, Department of History, Laurentian University, Sudbury, Ontario.
Benjamin Lester Peters.

WATERSTON, ELIZABETH. Professor of English, University of Guelph, Ontario.
John Sheridan Hogan. John Howison [in collaboration with J. J. Talman]. *George Drought Warburton.*

WEAVER, JOHN. Associate professor of history, McMaster University, Hamilton, Ontario.
Paola Brown. Colin Campbell Ferrie.

WHITELAW, VIRGINIA RYERSON. Writer, Vancouver, British Columbia.
Edmund William Romer Antrobus.

WHITFIELD, CAROL M. Chief of operations, Halifax Defence Complex, Parks Canada, Halifax, Nova Scotia.
Sir Roger Hale Sheaffe [in collaboration with W. B. Turner].

WILLIAMS, GLYNDWR. Professor of history, Queen Mary College, London, England.
Peter Skene Ogden.

WILLIAMS, MAUREEN LONERGAN. Librarian, Special Col-

lections, Angus L. Macdonald Library, and lecturer in Celtic studies, St Francis Xavier University, Antigonish, Nova Scotia.
Iain MacDhòmhnaill 'Ic Iain.

WILLIAMSON, MARY F. Fine arts bibliographer, Scott Library, York University, Downsview, Ontario.
John Allanson.

WILSON, J. DONALD. Professor of the history of education, University of British Columbia, Vancouver, British Columbia.
Alexander Davidson.

WOLFART, H. CHRISTOPH. Professor of general linguistics, University of Manitoba, Winnipeg, Manitoba.
Joseph Howse.

WOLFENDEN, MADGE. Formerly assistant provincial archivist, Provincial Archives of British Columbia; Vancouver, British Columbia.
Robert John Staines [in collaboration].

WOODCOCK, GEORGE. Writer and former editor, *Canadian Literature*, Vancouver, British Columbia.
Cuthbert Grant. Henry Jones.

WOODWARD, FRANCES M. Reference librarian, Special Collections Division, University of British Columbia Library, Vancouver, British Columbia.
Henry William Vavasour.

WUST, KLAUS. Editor, *Report; Journal of German-American History*, Edinburg, Virginia, U.S.A.
Friedrich Gaukel.

WYNN, GRAEME. Associate professor of geography, University of British Columbia, Vancouver, British Columbia.
William Crane. James Finlay Weir Johnston.

YOUNG, D. MURRAY. Professor of history, University of New Brunswick, Fredericton, New Brunswick.
George Coster. Benjamin Gerrish Gray. George Shore. James Taylor [in collaboration with P. Buckner].

YOUNG, MARY BERNITA. Archivist, Sisters of St Joseph of Toronto, Willowdale, Ontario.
Marie-Antoinette Fontbonne, named *Sister Delphine.*

ZELLER, SUZANNE E. Doctoral candidate in history, University of Toronto, Ontario.
James Barnston [in collaboration with J. H. Noble].

INDEX OF IDENTIFICATIONS

CATEGORIES

Accountants

Agriculture

Architects

Armed forces

Artisans

Arts

Authors

Blacks

Business

Education

Engineers

Explorers

Fur traders

Indigenous peoples

Inventors

Journalists

Labourers and labour
organizers

Legal professions

Mariners

Medicine

Office holders

Philanthropists and
social reformers

Politicians

Religious

Scientists

Sports

Surveyors

Women

Index of Identifications

Like the network of cross-references within biographies, this index is designed to assist readers in following their interests through the volume. Most of the groupings are by occupations carried on either by persons within Canada or by native-born Canadians in other countries, but some have been established to help readers who approach the past from other perspectives. Women appear in one grouping, as do blacks, a reflection of the interest in their history, but they may also be found under the occupations in which they engaged. Indigenous peoples include Indians, Inuit, and Métis. Readers interested in immigration or in the history of ethnic groups in Canada should consult the Geographical Index, where subjects are listed by their place of birth.

Some of the occupational categories require explanation so that users will be better able to find biographies of particular interest. Under "agriculture" is to be found a variety of people known to have been engaged in the development of land. "Seigneurs" form a readily identifiable sub-group; the sub-group "improvers" consists of those responsible for colonization; listed as "settlers" are individuals who pioneered in new territories; and "farmers" comprise only those for whom farming was the prime occupation. The people who speculated in seigneuries or other lands are to be found under "real estate" in the "business" grouping, along with land agents and major landowners. "Arts" includes both fine and performing arts. A distinction between fine arts and "artisans" was difficult to make in some instances; photographers, for example, appear under "arts" and silversmiths under "artisans."

Although some of the engineers and doctors in this volume are military officers and so appear under "armed forces," they also appear separately as "engineers" or under "medicine." Surveyors, hydrographers, and cartographers are found under "surveyors." Fur traders, although they might have appeared under "business," are given a separate listing for the benefit of readers interested in this aspect of the economy. "Mariners" includes civilian captains, pilots, and navigators; naval officers appear as a sub-group of "armed forces." Within "office holders," the sub-division "administrators" includes high-ranking officials: governors, lieutenant governors, and administrators.

The DCB/DBC attempts by its assignments to encourage research in new areas as well as familiar ones, but its selection of individuals to receive biographies reflects the survival of documentation and the areas historians have chosen to investigate. The index should not, therefore, be used for quantitative judgements; it is merely a guide to what is contained in volume VIII.

ACCOUNTANTS

Burn, William Scott

AGRICULTURE

Farmers

Barclay, George
Birdsall, Richard

Brouse, George
Burnham, Zacheus
Carey, John
Caron, Charles

Cary, George Marcus
Cazeneuve, Louis-Joseph-Charles
Clarke, Septimus D.
Corrigan, Robert

ARCHITECTS

ARMED FORCES

INDEX OF IDENTIFICATIONS

ARTISANS

INDEX OF IDENTIFICATIONS

ARTS

AUTHORS

BLACKS

BUSINESS

EDUCATION

INDEX OF IDENTIFICATIONS

ENGINEERS

EXPLORERS

FUR TRADERS

INDEX OF IDENTIFICATIONS

INDIGENOUS PEOPLES

INVENTORS

JOURNALISTS

LABOURERS AND LABOUR ORGANIZERS

LEGAL PROFESSIONS

INDEX OF IDENTIFICATIONS

MARINERS

MEDICINE

OFFICE HOLDERS

Administrators

Arthur, Sir George
Bulger, Andrew H.
Cathcart, Charles Murray,
    2nd Earl Cathcart
Clitherow, John
Drummond, Sir Gordon
FitzRoy, Sir Charles Augustus
Gore, Francis
Harvey, Sir John
Kempt, Sir James
McDonald, Archibald
McKenzie, Donald
Maitland, Sir Peregrine
Sheaffe, Sir Roger Hale
Smith, Charles Douglass

Officials

Allan, William
Angers, François-Réal
Antrobus, Edmund William Romer
Armour, Robert
Baby, François
Bagnall, James
Ballenden, John
Barbier, Louis-Marie-Raphaël
Barclay, George
Barss, John
Bell, Hugh
Berczy, Charles Albert
Betzner, Samuel D.
Bibaud, Michel
Bird, James
Birdsall, Richard
Boxer, Edward
Brouse, George
Bulger, Andrew H.
Burnham, Zacheus
Caldwell, Francis Xavier
Campbell, Alexander
Carmichael, James
Cartier, Claude
Chandler, William
Chaperon, John
Child, Marcus
Chipman, Ward
Christie, Robert
Clench, Joseph Brant
Cogswell, Henry Hezekiah
Crooks, James
Crookshank, George
Crosskill, John Henry
Crysler, John
Cuthbert, William
Davidson, Alexander
de Blaquière, Peter Boyle
DeCow, John

Démaray, Pierre-Paul
Désilets, Aimé
Dickerson, Silas Horton
Dickson, Thomas
Doak, Robert
Donlevy, Charles
Doucet, Nicolas-Benjamin
Douglas, James
Ducharme, Dominique
Duffy, James W.
Dumoulin, Jean-Gaspard
Dumoulin, Pierre-Benjamin
Dunn, John Henry
Duvernay, Ludger
Egan, John
Enslin, Christian
Ewart, James Bell
Faribault, Jean-Baptiste
Faribault, Joseph-Édouard
Ferguson, Robert
Ferrie, Colin Campbell
Fraser, Alexander
Fraser, Richard Duncan
Gamelin, Pierre
Gilchrist, John
Gilkison, David
Grant, Cuthbert
Grigor, William
Hart, Aaron Ezekiel
Hawkins, Alfred
Hawley, William Fitz
Haws, John
Henry, Robert
Hoffmann, Matthias Francis
Hogsett, Aaron
Hoyle, Robert
Huntington, Herbert
Hurd, Samuel Proudfoot
Huston, James
Jameson, Robert Sympson
Jarvis, Edward James
Jarvis, Samuel Peters
Jobin, André
Jones, Robert
Joseph, John
Juneau, Laurent-Salomon
Kerby, James
Kielley, Edward
Lane, Ambrose
Larue, François-Xavier
Leroux, Laurent
Lévesque, Guillaume
Lockwood, Anthony
Lyon, George
Macaulay, John
McCord, William King
McDonald, John
McDougall, John Lorn
McGillivray (Dalcrombie), John

MacGregor, John
McKay, Thomas
McMartin, Alexander
Marchand, Gabriel
Marchesseault, Siméon
Martin, George
Méthot, François-Xavier
Molson, John
Morris, William
Morrison, Thomas David
Mowat, John
Muir, Andrew
Murray, Robert
Papineau, Denis-Benjamin
Peltier, Toussaint
Peterson, Heinrich Wilhelm
Petitclair, Pierre
Pinhey, Hamnett Kirkes
Prescott, Charles Ramage
Pryor, William
Pyke, George
Radenhurst, Thomas Mabon
Rankin, Alexander
Rankin, Coun Douly
Read, John Landon
Richardson, John
Ridout, Samuel Smith
Ritchie, Thomas
Robinson, Hezekiah
Roche, John Knatchbull
Rogers, Thomas
Rolph, Thomas
Ross, Alexander
Rottermund, Édouard-Sylvestre de,
    Count de Rottermund
Routh, Sir Randolph Isham
Roy, Joseph
Rudolf, William
Russell, Joseph
Rykert, George
Scobie, Hugh
Sherwood, Henry
Shore, George
Simonds, Charles
Solomon, William
Stevenson, David Barker
Stewart, John
Street, George Frederick
Stuart, Sir James
Sullivan, Robert Baldwin
Talbot, Richard
Talbot, Thomas
Tasker, Patrick
Taylor, James
Thresher, George Godsell
Tiffany, Gideon
Tremain, Richard
Trotter, Thomas
Uniacke, James Boyle

RELIGIOUS

INDEX OF IDENTIFICATIONS

Mennonites

Eby, Benjamin

Methodists

Bell, John
Bennett, William
Case, William
Des Brisay, Albert
Harvard, William Martin
Jackson, James
Jones, Peter
Knight, Richard
Williams, Richard

Presbyterians

Bayne, John
Bell, Andrew
Bell, William
Esson, Henry
Gale, Alexander
Keir, John
McGill, Robert
McKenzie, John
MacLennan, John
Murray, Robert
Proudfoot, William
Rintoul, William
Ross, Hugh
Smith, John
Sutherland, Murdoch
Trotter, Thomas
Wilkie, Daniel

Protestant Episcopal Church

Williams, Eleazer

Roman Catholics

Augustinians

Browne, Timothy

Congregation of the Sisters of Mercy

Creedon, Marianne, named Mother
  Mary Francis

Franciscans

Dalton, Charles

Jesuits

Frémiot, Nicolas-Marie-Joseph
Nobili, John

Oblates of Mary Immaculate

Baudrand, Fleury

*Order of the Presentation of
  Our Blessed Lady*

Kirwan, Miss, named Sister
  Mary Bernard

Seculars

Archambault, Paul-Loup
Bellenger, Joseph-Marie
Carrier, Michel
Chartier, Étienne
Daulé, Jean-Denis
Demers, Jérôme
Dollard, William
Ducharme, Charles-Joseph
Duffy, James W.
Dumoulin, Sévère
Fortier, Narcisse-Charles
Fraser, William
Gaulin, Rémi
Gingras, Léon
Harper, Charles
Holmes, John
Kelly, Jean-Baptiste

Langevin, Antoine
Macdonald, Bernard Donald
McKeagney, Henry
McMahon, Patrick
Madran, Jean-Marie
Maguire, Thomas
Marcoux, Joseph
Moncoq, Michel
O'Reilly, Hugh
Parant, Antoine
Phelan, Patrick
Prince, Jean-Charles
Provencher, Joseph-Norbert
Roupe, Jean-Baptiste
Walsh, William

Sisters of St Joseph of Toronto

Fontbonne, Marie-Antoinette, named
  Sister Delphine

Sœurs de la Charité de la Providence

Tavernier, Émilie (Gamelin)

Sulpicians

Larkin, John
Phelan, Patrick
Quiblier, Joseph-Vincent
Roupe, Jean-Baptiste

Trappists

Merle, Jacques, named Father
  Vincent de Paul

Others

Enslin, Christian
Hoerner, Olympe (Tanner)

SCIENTISTS

Barnston, James
Duchaîne, Amable-Daniel
Evans, William

Holmes, Andrew Fernando
Johnston, James Finlay Weir
Prescott, Charles Ramage

Rottermund, Édouard-Sylvestre de,
  Count de Rottermund

SPORTS

Henry, Walter

Lola, Peter

Uniacke, James Boyle

SURVEYORS

WOMEN

GEOGRAPHICAL INDEX

CANADA

Alberta

British Columbia
  Mainland
  Vancouver Island

Manitoba

New Brunswick

Newfoundland and Labrador
  Labrador
  Newfoundland

Northwest Territories

Nova Scotia
  Cape Breton Island
  Mainland

Ontario
  Centre
  East
  Niagara
  North
  Southwest

Prince Edward Island

Quebec
  Bas-Saint-Laurent–Gaspésie/
    Côte-Nord
  Montréal/Outaouais
  Nord-Ouest/Saguenay–Lac-Saint-Jean/
    Nouveau-Québec
  Québec
  Trois-Rivières/Cantons-de-l'Est

Saskatchewan

OTHER COUNTRIES

PLACE OF BIRTH

Barbados
Bermuda
Federal Republic of Germany
France
Germany
Greece
Greenland
Hungary
Ireland
Isle of Man
Italy
Jersey
Republic of Ireland
Saint Helena
Spain
Switzerland
Union of Soviet Socialist Republics
United Kingdom
United States of America

CAREER

Barbados
Bermuda
Burma
Egypt
France
Grenada
Ireland
Italy
Jamaica
Malta
Mexico
Netherlands
Portugal
Spain
Union of Soviet Socialist Republics
United Kingdom
United States of America

ONTARIO

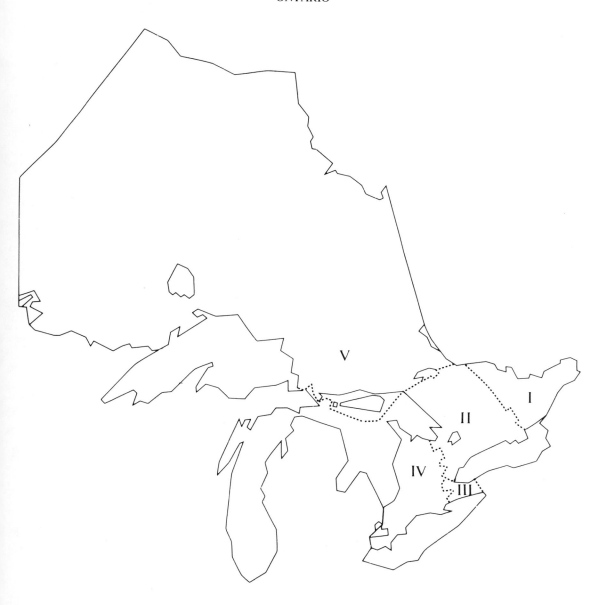

V North

I East
II Centre
III Niagara
IV Southwest
V North

QUEBEC

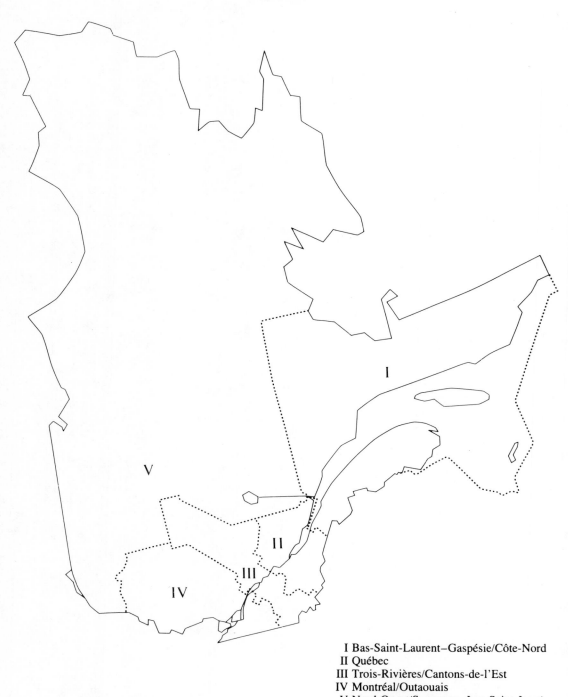

I Bas-Saint-Laurent–Gaspésie/Côte-Nord
II Québec
III Trois-Rivières/Cantons-de-l'Est
IV Montréal/Outaouais
V Nord-Ouest/Saguenay–Lac-Saint-Jean/
   Nouveau-Québec

Geographical Index

The Geographical Index, in two parts, provides a regional breakdown of subjects of biographies according to place of birth and according to career. Each part has two sub-sections: Canada and Other Countries.

For the purposes of this index, Canada is represented by the present provinces and territories, listed alphabetically. (The Yukon Territory does not appear here, however, since no one in volume VIII lived in or visited the region.) Five provinces are further subdivided. British Columbia, Newfoundland and Labrador, and Nova Scotia each have two subdivisions. Ontario and Quebec appear in five subdivisions as shown on the maps; those for Quebec are based on the administrative regions defined by the Direction général du domaine territorial. The section Other Countries is based for the most part on modern political divisions, but overseas territories of European countries are listed separately. Only the United Kingdom is subdivided.

Place of Birth. This part of the index lists subjects of biographies by their birthplace, whether in Canada or elsewhere. Where only a strong probability of birth in a particular region exists, the name of the subject is followed by a question mark; where no such probability exists, names have not been included. It should be noted that the use of modern political divisions produces some anachronisms; a person born in Würtemberg, for example, appears under "Federal Republic of Germany." To accommodate those individuals known only to have been born in Ireland, a separate listing under "Ireland" has been provided; readers interested in Irish personalities or in immigration from Ireland should consult also "Republic of Ireland" and "United Kingdom: Northern Ireland."

Career. Subjects appear here on the basis of their activity as adults. Places of education, retirement, and death have not been considered. Persons whose functions gave them jurisdiction over several regions, such as a bishop or governor, are listed according to their seat of office, but their activities as described in the biographies have also been taken into consideration. Merchants appear only in the area of the primary location of their business, unless the biographies indicate active personal involvement in other regions. Explorers are found in the areas they discovered or visited. Only individuals who were born in the territory of present-day Canada and whose lives took them elsewhere are listed in the section Other Countries; they are listed under the country or countries in which they had a career or were active.

PLACE OF BIRTH

Canada

ALBERTA

A-ca-oo-mah-ca-ye (?)

BRITISH COLUMBIA

Mainland

Hwistesmetxē′qɛn (?)

MANITOBA

Barnston, James

NEW BRUNSWICK

Basquet, Pierre (?)
Burpee, Richard E.
Chipman, Ward
Chubb, Henry
Coy, Mary (Morris; Bradley)

Harding, Thomas
Jarvis, Edward James
Lola, Noel (?)
Lola, Peter
Peters, Benjamin Lester

Simonds, Charles
Street, George Frederick
Taylor, James
Thompson, William
Wolhaupter, Benjamin

NEWFOUNDLAND AND LABRADOR

Newfoundland

Bulger, Andrew H.

Doyle, Patrick
Kielley, Edward

Webber, George (?)

NOVA SCOTIA

Mainland

Allison, Charles Frederick
Babey, Peter Paul Toney (?)
Bagnall, James
Barss, John
Campbell, Alexander (?)
Carmichael, James
Chandler, William
Chipman, Eliza Ann (Chipman)
Christie, Robert

Cogswell, Henry Hezekiah
Crane, William
Crosskill, John Henry
Dickson, Thomas
Glode, Charles (?)
Glode, Gabriel (?)
Harding, Harris
Huntington, Herbert
McLearn, Richard
McLelan, Gloud Wilson
Nugent, Richard

Piers, Temple Foster
Prescott, Charles Ramage
Pyke, George
Ritchie, Thomas
Rudolf, William
Twining, John Thomas
Uniacke, James Boyle
Ward, Edmund
Welsford, Augustus Frederick
West, John Conrade

ONTARIO

Centre

Baldwin, Robert
Hartman, Joseph
King, William Henry
Perry, Peter

East

Brouse, George

Macaulay, John
McMartin, Alexander
Read, John Landon
Sherwood, Henry

Niagara

Berczy, Charles Albert
Clench, Joseph Brant (?)
Jarvis, Samuel Peters

Jones, Peter
Macaulay, Sir James Buchanan
Richardson, John (?)

Southwest

Gilkison, David
Kerby, James
Powlis, George

PRINCE EDWARD ISLAND

Des Brisay, Albert
Macdonald, Bernard Donald

McDonald, Donald

Macdonald, Ronald

QUEBEC

Bas-Saint-Laurent–Gaspésie/Côte-Nord

Dionne, Amable
Gamache, Louis (?)
McLoughlin, John

Montréal/Outaouais

Antrobus, Edmund William Romer
Archambault, Paul-Loup
Barbier, Louis-Marie-Raphaël
Bibaud, Michel
Boucher de Boucherville, Thomas-René-Verchères
Bruneau, François-Pierre
Cameron, John Dugald (?)
Cartier, Claude
Cazeneuve, Louis-Joseph-Charles
Clarke, John
Desrochers, Urbain
Ducharme, Charles-Joseph
Ducharme, Dominique
Dumoulin, Sévère
Duvernay, Ludger
Fabre, Édouard-Raymond
Faribault, Jean-Baptiste
Faribault, Joseph-Édouard
Foretier, Marie-Amable (Viger)
Fraser, Richard Duncan (?)
Gamelin, Pierre
Hart, Benjamin
Hawley, William Fitz (?)
Hertel de Rouville, Jean-Baptiste-René
Jobin, André
Juneau, Laurent-Salomon
Lacoste, Louis-René
Lacroix, Janvier-Domptail
Lagimonière, Jean-Baptiste
Laviolette, Pierre
Leroux, Laurent
Lévesque, Charles-François
Lévesque, Guillaume
Madran, Jean-Marie
Malhiot, François-Xavier
Marchesseault, Siméon
Molson, John
Morand, Paul (?)
Nelson, George (?)

Ouimet, André
Papineau, Denis-Benjamin
Peltier, Orphir
Peltier, Toussaint
Radenhurst, Thomas Mabon
Rollin, Paul
Roupe, Jean-Baptiste
Rowand, John
Roy, Joseph
Solomon, William
Tavernier, Émilie (Gamelin)
Viger, Jacques
Viger, Louis-Michel
Voyer, Antoine
Whittemore, Ezekiel Francis

Nord-Ouest/Saguenay–Lac-Saint-Jean/Nouveau-Québec

McLeod, Peter (?)

Québec

Angers, François-Réal
Baillairgé, Thomas
Bellenger, Joseph-Marie
Blanchet, Jean
Caron, Charles
Carrier, Michel
Chabot, Jean
Chaperon, John
Chartier, Étienne
Couillard-Després, Emmanuel
Deblois, Joseph-François
Demers, Jérôme
Drouin, Pierre
Drummond, Sir Gordon
Fortier, Narcisse-Charles
Gaulin, Rémi
Gautron, dit Larochelle, Siméon
Gingras, Édouard
Gingras, Léon
Girouard, Jean-Joseph
Hanna, James Godfrey
Harper, Charles
Huston, James
Kelly, Jean-Baptiste
Kimber, Timothée
Langevin, Antoine

Langlois, dit Germain, Augustin-René
Larue, François-Xavier
Légaré, Joseph
Marchand, Gabriel
Marcoux, Joseph
Méthot, François-Xavier
Morrison, Thomas David
Normand, François
Ogden, Peter Skene
Painchaud, Alexis
Painchaud, Joseph
Panet, Philippe
Paquet, dit Lavallée, André
Parant, Antoine
Parant, Joseph
Petitclair, Pierre
Soulard, Auguste
Stewart, John
Tremblay, dit Picoté, Alexis
Vanfelson, George
Woolsey, John William
Young, Thomas Ainslie

Trois-Rivières/Cantons-de-l'Est

Démaray, Pierre-Paul
Désilets, Aimé
Doucet, Nicolas-Benjamin
Duchaîne, Amable-Daniel
Dumoulin, Jean-Gaspard
Dumoulin, Pierre-Benjamin
Hart, Aaron Ezekiel
Hart, Moses
Marchildon, Thomas
Prince, Jean-Charles
Proulx, Jean-Baptiste
Provencher, Joseph-Norbert

SASKATCHEWAN

Grant, Cuthbert

Other Countries

BARBADOS

Worrell, Charles (?)

BERMUDA

Hurd, Samuel Proudfoot

FEDERAL REPUBLIC OF GERMANY

Enslin, Christian

Gaukel, Friedrich

Peterson, Heinrich Wilhelm

FRANCE

Baudrand, Fleury
Bellot, Joseph-René
Daulé, Jean-Denis
Fenouillet, Émile de
Fontbonne, Marie-Antoinette,
  named Sister Delphine

Frémiot, Nicolas-Marie-Joseph
Jacquies, Adolphe
LeJeune, Marie-Henriette (Comeau;
  Lejeune, *dit* Briard; Ross)
Merle, Jacques, named Father
  Vincent de Paul

Moncoq, Michel
Quiblier, Joseph-Vincent
Rambau, Alfred-Xavier
Vivant, Laurent

GERMANY

Griebel, Ferdinand

Molt, Théodore-Frédéric

GREECE

Lane, Henry Bowyer Joseph

GREENLAND

Kallihirua

HUNGARY

Mayerhoffer, Vincent Philip

IRELAND

Ayre, William
Cary, George Marcus
Craig, John

Gerrard, Samuel
Manning, Edward
O'Brien, John (?)

Smiley, Robert Reid
Todd, William

ISLE OF MAN

Quirk, John

ITALY

Fassio, Gerome

Hoffmann, Matthias Francis

Nobili, John

JERSEY

Du Val, Peter

Le Boutillier, David

REPUBLIC OF IRELAND

Arnold, William
Baird, John
Blake, Dominick Edward
Browne, Timothy (?)
Carey, John
Cox, Ross

Creedon, Marianne, named Mother
   Mary Francis
Dalton, Charles
de Blaquière, Peter Boyle
Dollard, William
Donlevy, Charles

Duffy, James W.
Egan, John
Evans, Francis
Evans, William
Henry, John
Henry, Walter

UNITED STATES OF AMERICA

CAREER

Canada

ALBERTA

BRITISH COLUMBIA

MANITOBA

1055

NORTHWEST TERRITORIES

Beechey, Frederick William
Bellot, Joseph-René
Kallihirua

Kane, Elisha Kent
Leroux, Laurent
Mecham, George Frederick

Ooligbuck
Parry, Sir William Edward
Ross, Sir John

NOVA SCOTIA

Cape Breton Island

Ayre, William
Chartier, Étienne
Dollard, William
Duffy, James W.
Du Val, Peter
Fraser, William
Gaulin, Rémi
Halliburton, Sir Brenton
Kempt, Sir James
LeJeune, Marie-Henriette (Comeau;
  Lejeune, *dit* Briard; Ross)
MacDhòmhnaill 'Ic Iain, Iain
McKeagney, Henry
McLearn, Richard
MacLennan, John
Merle, Jacques, named Father
  Vincent de Paul
O'Reilly, Hugh
Ross, Hugh
Uniacke, James Boyle

Mainland

Allison, Charles Frederick
Ayre, William
Babey, Peter Paul Toney
Bagnall, James
Barss, John
Bartlett, William Henry
Bell, Hugh

Bennett, William
Bulger, Andrew H.
Campbell, Alexander
Carmichael, James
Chipman, Eliza Ann (Chipman)
Clarke, Septimus D.
Cogswell, Henry Hezekiah
Crandall, Joseph
Crosskill, John Henry
Des Brisay, Albert
Dickson, Thomas
Duffy, James W.
Du Val, Peter
Foreman, James
Fraser, William
Gaulin, Rémi
Glode, Charles
Glode, Gabriel
Gray, Benjamin Gerrish
Grigor, William
Halliburton, Sir Brenton
Harding, Harris
Harvey, Sir John
Haws, John
Henry, Walter
Hoffmann, Matthias Francis
Huntington, Herbert
Keir, John
Kempt, Sir James
Knight, Richard
Lockwood, Anthony
McLearn, Richard

McLelan, Gloud Wilson
MacLennan, John
Maitland, Sir Peregrine
Manning, Edward
Merle, Jacques, named Father
  Vincent de Paul
Nugent, Richard
O'Reilly, Hugh
Owen, William Fitz William
Piers, Temple Foster
Prescott, Charles Ramage
Preston, Richard (Appendix)
Pryor, William
Quirk, John
Ritchie, Thomas
Robie, Simon Bradstreet
Ross, Hugh
Rudolf, William
Sutherland, Murdoch
Taylor, Henry
Thresher, George Godsell
Tremain, Richard
Trotter, Thomas
Twining, John Thomas
Uniacke, James Boyle
Walsh, William
Ward, Edmund
Welsford, Augustus Frederick
West, John Conrade
Whitman, Abraham
Williams, Richard
Young, George Renny

ONTARIO

Centre

Allan, William
Allanson, John
Antrobus, Edmund William Romer
Arthur, Sir George
Baker, Hugh Cossart
Baldwin, Robert

Barclay, George
Bayne, John
Bell, Andrew
Berczy, Charles Albert
Bethune, Angus
Bibb, Henry Walton
Birdsall, Richard
Blake, Dominick Edward

Boucher de Boucherville, Thomas-
  René-Verchères
Buchanan, Peter
Burn, William Scott
Burnham, Zacheus
Carey, John
Cartier, Claude
Case, William

PRINCE EDWARD ISLAND

Keir, John
Lane, Ambrose
Lewellin, John Lewellin
Macdonald, Bernard Donald
McDonald, Donald

MacGregor, John
Maclean, Duncan
MacLennan, John
Rankin, Coun Douly
Ross, Hugh

Shore, George
Smith, Charles Douglass
Thresher, George Godsell
Worrell, Charles

QUEBEC

Bas-Saint-Laurent–Gaspésie/Côte-Nord

Arnold, William
Baillairgé, Thomas
Bellenger, Joseph-Marie
Chartier, Étienne
Christie, Robert
Clarke, John
Cuthbert, William
Deblois, Joseph-François
Dionne, Amable
Du Val, Peter
Estcourt, James Bucknall Bucknall
Gamache, Louis
Le Boutillier, David
McLeod, Peter
Madran, Jean-Marie
Painchaud, Alexis
Paquet, *dit* Lavallée, André
Petitclair, Pierre
Provencher, Joseph-Norbert
Pyke, George
Rintoul, William
Tremblay, *dit* Picoté, Alexis

Montréal/Outaouais

Antrobus, Edmund William Romer
Archambault, Paul-Loup
Armour, Robert
Arnold, William
Baillairgé, Thomas
Baird, Edmond
Baldwin, Robert
Barbier, Louis-Marie-Raphaël
Barnston, James
Bartlett, William Henry
Baudrand, Fleury
Bellenger, Joseph-Marie
Bennett, William
Berczy, Charles Albert
Bibaud, Michel
Booker, Alfred
Boucher de Boucherville, Thomas-René-Verchères
Bruneau, François-Pierre
Buchanan, Alexander
Bulger, Andrew H.
Carrier, Michel

Cathcart, Charles Murray, 2nd Earl Cathcart
Cazeneuve, Louis-Joseph-Charles
Chabot, Jean
Chartier, Étienne
Clarke, John
Clemo, Ebenezer
Clitherow, John
Couillard-Després, Emmanuel
Crane, Samuel
Crooks, Ramsay
Démaray, Pierre-Paul
Desrochers, Urbain
De Witt, Jacob
Dickerson, Silas Horton
Doucet, Nicolas-Benjamin
Duchaîne, Amable-Daniel
Ducharme, Charles-Joseph
Ducharme, Dominique
Duvernay, Ludger
Egan, John
Esson, Henry
Estcourt, James Bucknall Bucknall
Evans, William
Fabre, Édouard-Raymond
Faribault, Joseph-Édouard
Fassio, Gerome
Fleming, Peter
Foretier, Marie-Amable (Viger)
Fraser, Alexander
Gale, Alexander
Gamelin, Pierre
Gaulin, Rémi
Gerrard, Samuel
Girouard, Jean-Joseph
Hart, Benjamin
Hart, Moses
Harvard, William Martin
Harvey, Sir John
Hawley, William Fitz
Henry, John
Henry, Walter
Hertel de Rouville, Jean-Baptiste-René
Hoerner, Olympe (Tanner)
Holmes, Andrew Fernando
Hoyle, Robert
Huston, James
Jobin, André
Keith, James
Kelly, Jean-Baptiste

Kempt, Sir James
Kimber, Timothée
Lacoste, Louis-René
Lacroix, Janvier-Domptail
Lagimonière, Jean-Baptiste
Landmann, George Thomas
Larkin, John
Laviolette, Pierre
Leroux, Laurent
Lévesque, Charles-François
Lévesque, Guillaume
Lyon, George
McCord, William King
McDonald, Archibald
Macdonell, Sir James
McDougall, John Lorn
McGill (McCutcheon), Peter
McGill, Robert
Mackay, Robert Walter Stuart
McKay, Thomas
Maclean, Duncan
McMartin, Alexander
McMillan, James
Madran, Jean-Marie
Maguire, Thomas
Malhiot, François-Xavier
Marchand, Gabriel
Marchesseault, Siméon
Marcoux, Joseph
Molson, John
Molt, Théodore-Frédéric
Moncoq, Michel
Morand, Paul
Morris, William
Munn, John
Nelson, George
Normand, François
Ogden, Peter Skene
Osgood, Thaddeus
Ouimet, André
Painchaud, Alexis
Panet, Philippe
Papineau, Denis-Benjamin
Peltier, Orphir
Peltier, Toussaint
Phelan, Patrick
Prince, Jean-Charles
Provencher, Joseph-Norbert
Pyke, George
Quiblier, Joseph-Vincent

Rae, Ann Cuthbert (Knight; Fleming)
Rambau, Alfred-Xavier
Richardson, John
Rintoul, William
Ritchie, William
Robinson, Hezekiah
Rollin, Paul
Ross, George McLeod
Rottermund, Édouard-Sylvestre de,
    Count de Rottermund
Roupe, Jean-Baptiste
Roy, Joseph
Scott, William Henry
Sheaffe, Sir Roger Hale
Simpson, Frances Ramsay (Simpson,
    Lady Simpson)
Simpson, Sir George
Siveright, John
Smiley, Robert Reid
Somerville, Martin
Stewart, William
Stuart, Sir James
Talbot, Thomas
Tavernier, Émilie (Gamelin)
Taylor, Henry
Theller, Edward Alexander
Thompson, David
Thresher, George Godsell
Tredwell, Nathaniel Hazard
Vanfelson, George
Vavasour, Henry William
Viger, Jacques
Viger, Louis-Michel
Vivant, Laurent
Voyer, Antoine
Warburton, George Drought
Weld, Isaac
Whittemore, Ezekiel Francis
Widmer, Christopher
Williams, Eleazer
Williams, Richard
Wills, Frank
Young, Thomas Ainslie

Nord-Ouest/Saguenay–Lac-Saint-Jean/Nouveau-Québec

Chaperon, John
McDougall, John Lorn
McLeod, Peter
Ooligbuck
Tremblay, *dit* Picoté, Alexis

Québec

Angers, François-Réal
Antrobus, Edmund William Romer
Archambault, Paul-Loup
Arnold, William
Baillairgé, Thomas
Bartlett, William Henry
Black, George
Blanchet, Jean

Boxer, Edward
Bulger, Andrew H.
Burnet, David
Campbell, John Saxton
Carrier, Michel
Cartier, Claude
Chabot, Jean
Chartier, Étienne
Christie, Robert
Corrigan, Robert
Daulé, Jean-Denis
Deblois, Joseph-François
Demers, Jérôme
Désilets, Aimé
Desrochers, Urbain
Dollard, William
Drouin, Pierre
Drummond, Sir Gordon
Dumoulin, Sévère
Duvernay, Ludger
Eaststaff, Thomas George William
Egan, John
Estcourt, James Bucknall Bucknall
Faribault, Jean-Baptiste
Fassio, Gerome
Fenouillet, Émile de
Fortier, Narcisse-Charles
Gautron, *dit* Larochelle, Siméon
Gibb, James
Gingras, Édouard
Gingras, Léon
Hall, William
Hanna, James Godfrey
Harper, Charles
Hart, Aaron Ezekiel
Harvard, William Martin
Harvey, Sir John
Hawkins, Alfred
Henry, Walter
Hogan, John Sheridan
Holmes, John
Huston, James
Jacquies, Adolphe
Kempt, Sir James
Landmann, George Thomas
Langlois, *dit* Germain, Augustin-René
Larue, François-Xavier
Légaré, Joseph
Lévesque, Guillaume
McCord, William King
Macdonald, Ronald
Macdonell, Sir James
McKeagney, Henry
McKenzie, James
McMahon, Patrick
Madran, Jean-Marie
Maguire, Thomas
Marchand, Gabriel
Méthot, François-Xavier
Molson, John
Molt, Théodore-Frédéric
Munn, John
Normand, François

Osgood, Thaddeus
Painchaud, Joseph
Panet, Philippe
Paquet, *dit* Lavallée, André
Parant, Antoine
Parant, Joseph
Patterson, Peter
Petitclair, Pierre
Provencher, Joseph-Norbert
Pyke, George
Ross, Alexander
Rottermund, Édouard-Sylvestre de,
    Count de Rottermund
Routh, Sir Randolph Isham
Sheaffe, Sir Roger Hale
Somerville, Martin
Soulard, Auguste
Stewart, John
Stewart, William
Stuart, Sir James
Sutherland, Thomas Jefferson
Talbot, Thomas
Taylor, Henry
Theller, Edward Alexander
Thomas, William
Tremblay, *dit* Picoté, Alexis
Vanfelson, George
Vavasour, Henry William
Viger, Jacques
Warburton, George Drought
Weld, Isaac
Wilkie, Daniel
Williams, Richard
Woolsey, John William
Young, Thomas Ainslie

Trois-Rivières/Cantons-de-l'Est

Antrobus, Edmund William Romer
Archambault, Paul-Loup
Arms, William
Arnold, William
Baillairgé, Thomas
Bartlett, William Henry
Baudrand, Fleury
Bellenger, Joseph-Marie
Caron, Charles
Carrier, Michel
Chartier, Étienne
Child, Marcus
Désilets, Aimé
Desrochers, Urbain
Dickerson, Silas Horton
Doucet, Nicolas-Benjamin
Duchaîne, Amable-Daniel
Dumoulin, Jean-Gaspard
Dumoulin, Pierre-Benjamin
Dumoulin, Sévère
Duvernay, Ludger
Estcourt, James Bucknall Bucknall
Evans, Francis
Fassio, Gerome
Harper, Charles

SASKATCHEWAN

Other Countries

BARBADOS

BERMUDA

BURMA

EGYPT

FRANCE

Chartier, Étienne   Lévesque, Guillaume   Richardson, John

GRENADA

Richardson, John

IRELAND

Drummond, Sir Gordon

ITALY

Maguire, Thomas

JAMAICA

Drummond, Sir Gordon

MALTA

Jarvis, Edward James

MEXICO

Painchaud, Joseph

NETHERLANDS

Drummond, Sir Gordon

PORTUGAL

Antrobus, Edmund William Romer

SPAIN

Antrobus, Edmund William Romer   Richardson, John

UNION OF SOVIET SOCIALIST REPUBLICS

Welsford, Augustus Frederick

UNITED KINGDOM

England

Basquet, Pierre
Chipman, Ward
Drummond, Sir Gordon

Huntington, Herbert
Jones, Peter
McLoughlin, John
Richardson, John
Simonds, Charles

Scotland

Jones, Peter

UNITED STATES OF AMERICA

Bagnall, James
Bulger, Andrew H.
Cameron, John Dugald
Cartier, Claude
Chartier, Étienne
Clarke, John
Démaray, Pierre-Paul
Doucet, Nicolas-Benjamin
Drummond, Sir Gordon
Ducharme, Dominique
Dumoulin, Sévère

Duvernay, Ludger
Faribault, Jean-Baptiste
Fraser, Richard Duncan
Jarvis, Samuel Peters
Juneau, Laurent-Salomon
Lagimonière, Jean-Baptiste
Langevin, Antoine
Leroux, Laurent
McKenzie, Nancy (McTavish;
    Le Blanc)

McLearn, Richard
McLoughlin, John
Marchesseault, Siméon
Morrison, Thomas David
Nelson, George
Ogden, Peter Skene
Provencher, Joseph-Norbert
Richardson, John
Sinclair, James
Ward, Edmund

NOMINAL INDEX

As of 1985 the following volumes have been published, volumes I–V, VIII–XI, and an *Index, volumes I to IV*.

Nominal Index

Included in this index are the names of persons mentioned in volume VIII. They are listed by their family names, with titles and first names following. Wives are entered under their maiden names with their married names in parenthesis. Persons who appear in incomplete citations in the text are fully identified when possible. An asterisk indicates that the person has received a biography in a volume already published, or will probably receive one in a subsequent volume. A death date or last floruit date refers the reader to the volume in which the biography will be found. Numerals in bold face indicate the pages on which a biography appears. Titles, nicknames, variant spellings, married and religious names are fully cross-referenced.

ABBOTT, Frances (Baby), 33
Abell, Edward, 532
Abercromby, Sir Ralph, 458
Aberdeen, Earl of. *See* Hamilton-Gordon
Abernethy, George, 662
Abraham. *See also* Maskepetoon
Abraham, Robert, 22, 694
Abrams*, William (1785–1844), 737, 740
A-ca-oo-mah-ca-ye (Ac ko mok ki, Ak ko mock ki, A'kow-muk-ai, Old Swan), 3
A-ca-oo-mah-ca-ye (Ac ko mok ki, Ak ko mock ki, A'kow-muk-ai, Feathers, Old Swan) (uncle or father of A-CA-OO-MAH-CA-YE), 3
A-ca-oo-mah-ca-ye, **3–4**
Accolti, Michael, 654
Acheson*, Archibald, 2nd Earl of Gosford (1776–1849), xxiv, xxxii, 18, 22, 147, 207, 209, 210, 260, 261, 367, 407, 433, 434, 465, 586, 619, 712, 729, 730, 758, 792, 893, 907, 939
Ac ko mok ki. *See* A-ca-oo-mah-ca-ye
Acton, Anna (Warburton), 921
Adair, Christian (Ross), 770
Adams, Dorothea (Crysler), 194
Adams*, Mary Electa (1823–98), 15
Adams, Mary (Ferguson), 292
Adams, Thomas, 785
Adamson, Peter, 188
Addington, Baron. *See* Hubbard
Addison*, Robert (d. 1829), 276
Adonwentishon (Ahdohwahgeseon). *See* Ohtowaʔkéhson
Agibicocoua, 830
Ahier, Gédéon, 675
Ahier, Victoire. *See* Painchaud
Ahyonwaeghs (Ahyouwaeghs). *See* Tekarihogen (1794–1832)
Aidant, Brother. *See* Roblot
Aiken, Sarah (Gilchrist), 324
Aikins*, William Thomas (1827–97), 934
Ainslie, Christian (Christianna) (Young), 962
Ainslie*, George Robert (1776–1839), 459
Ainslie*, Thomas (1729–1806), 962
Airey, Julius, 860

Airey, Richard, Lord Airey, 275, 860
Airy, Sir George Biddell, 102
Aitchison, Isobel (Isabella) (Proudfoot), 715
Aitken, Sophia (Rintoul), 750
Ak ko mock ki (A'kow-muk-ai). *See* A-ca-oo-mah-ca-ye
Albert, George Dallas, 476
Albert, Thomas, 488
Alder*, Robert (1796–1873), 216, 361, 372, 373, 478
Alexander, Sir James Edward, 588
Alexandre, Victoire (Marchildon), 617
Allamand*, Jeanne-Charlotte (Berczy) (d. 1839), 83
Allan, Alexander, 4
Allan*, Ebenezer (1752–1813), 608, 887
Allan, Elizabeth (cousin of John MUNN), 649
Allan, Elizabeth (daughter of WILLIAM), 11
Allan, Elizabeth D. (Pyke), 726
Allan, Francis, 587
Allan*, George William (1822–1901), 11, 12, 486
Allan*, Sir Hugh (1810–82), 815
Allan, Leah Tyrer. *See* Gamble
Allan, Margaret. *See* Mowatt
Allan, William, **4–13**, 29, 191, 253, 255, 282, 338, 517, 519, 520, 521, 697, 709, 760, 795, 847, 848, 860, 896
Allanson, Elizabeth (wife of JOHN), 13
Allanson, John, **13–15**
Allard, Marie-Antoinette (Demers; Rambau), 736
Allcock*, Henry (d. 1808), 337
Allen. *See also* Allan
Allen, Anne (Coster), 171
Allen, Elizabeth. *See* Saul
Allen, Esther (Talbot), 855
Allen, John, 802
Allen, L. L., 899
Allin. *See* Allan
Alline*, Henry (1748–84), 177, 179, 610, 611, 612
Allison, Ann (Bell), 73
Allison, Charles Frederick, **15–16**, 183, 216
Allison, Elizabeth (Bennett), 82
Allison, James, 15
Allison, John C., 183
Allison, Joseph, 73, 710
Allison, Margaret. *See* Hutchinson

Campbell, Archibald (son of ALEXANDER), 123
Campbell*, Sir Archibald (1769–1843), xxiv, 183, 184, 377, 384, 495, 783, 802, 807, 808, 841, 868
Campbell*, Archibald (1790–1862), 123, 701, 702
Campbell, Charlotte. *See* Saxton
Campbell, Colin (architect), 39
Campbell, Colin (Hudson's Bay Company post chief), 820
Campbell*, Sir Colin (1776–1847), xxiv, 31, 74, 378, 379, 416, 603, 710, 757, 892, 904, 956
Campbell, David, 123
Campbell*, Sir Donald (1800–50), 485, 564
Campbell, Dugald, 324
Campbell*, Dugald (d. 1810), 802
Campbell, Duncan, 178
Campbell, Elizabeth (Esson), 272
Campbell, Isabella (Sutherland), 850
Campbell, J., 320
Campbell, James, 122
Campbell, Jane. *See* Hamilton
Campbell, John, 587
Campbell, John Duncan, 390
Campbell, John Saxton, 93, **123–24**
Campbell, Margaret. *See* Henderson
Campbell, Mary. *See* Archibald
Campbell, Mary (Sinclair), 820
Campbell, Mary Carne. *See* Vivian
Campbell, Rachel (Ferrie), 293
Campbell, Thomas, 386, 924
Campbell*, Thomas Edmund (d. 1872), 163, 394
Campbell, William (father), 122
Campbell, William, 122
Campbell*, Sir William (1758–1834), 5, 46, 69, 305, 511, 602, 708
Campion*, Étienne-Charles (d. 1795), 320
Canby, Amelia (Disbrow), 224
Cane, James, 960
Canniff*, William (1830–1910), 934
Cannon*, John (1783–1833), 581
Canterbury, Viscount. *See* Manners-Sutton
Cantin*, Augustin (1809–93), 559
Capreol*, Frederick Chase (1803–86), 10
Captain John. *See* Ogimauh-binaessih
Carcaud, Daniel, 494
Cardinal*, Joseph-Narcisse (1808–38), 364, 365
Carew. *See* Pole
Carey, Elizabeth. *See* Field
Carey, Eustace, 99
Carey, John, **124–26**
Carey, Margaret (wife of JOHN), 124
Carey, Richard, 907
Carleton*, Guy, 1st Baron Dorchester (1724–1808), 605
Carleton*, Thomas (d. 1817), xxiv, 805
Carlisle, Earl of. *See* Howard
Carlyle, Mary (McMartin), 582
Carman, Catherine (Brouse), 104
Carman, William, 738, 739
Carmichael, Ann (mother of JAMES), 126
Carmichael, Christian. *See* McKenzie
Carmichael, Humphrey Henry, 832
Carmichael, James (father of JAMES), 126
Carmichael, James (sergeant), 126
Carmichael, James, **126–28**
Carmichael, James William, 127

Carmichael*, John Edward (d. 1828), 444, 484, 531, 547, 824, 825, 826
Carmichael, John Robert, 127
Caroline Amelia Elizabeth of Brunswick (Caroline Amelia Elizabeth, Princess of Wales), 823
Caron, Barthélemy, 128
Caron, Charles, 18, **128–29**
Caron, Charles-François, 128
Caron, François, 128
Caron, Marie-Françoise. *See* Rivard
Caron, Marie-Françoise, *dite* de Saint-Charles, 128
Caron, Marie-Josephte. *See* Parent
Caron, Michel, 128
Caron*, Michel (1763–1831), 128
Caron*, René-Édouard (1800–76), 52, 138, 497, 800, 849, 907
Caron, Victoire (Gérin-Lajoie), 128
Carrier, Catherine. *See* Bleau
Carrier, Michel, 129
Carrier, Michel, **129–30**
Carrington*, Frederick Hamilton (d. 1839), 94, 103, 947
Carroll, John, 306, 307
Carroll*, John Saltkill (1809–84), 105, 310, 372, 422, 423
Carroll, Nancy (Manning), 610
Carruthers, John, 645
Carruthers, Michael, 738
Carson, Samuel, 468, 469
Carson*, William (1770–1843), 233, 234, 381, 403, 467, 468, 469, 470, 947, 948, 951
Carter*, Sir James (1805–78), 151, 174, 394
Carthew, Arthur, 486
Cartier, Anne (wife of CLAUDE), 130
Cartier, Claude, **130–31**
Cartier*, Sir George-Étienne (1814–73), 138, 231, 260, 262, 286, 402, 736
Cartier, Hortense. *See* Fabre
Cartier, William C., 131
Cartwright*, John Solomon (1804–45), 8, 520, 522, 697, 760, 786, 799
Cartwright*, Richard (1759–1815), 606, 607, 608, 937
Cartwright, Robert David, 760
Carver, William, 368
Cary, Anne Eliza (wife of GEORGE MARCUS), 131
Cary, George Marcus, **131–32**, 767
Cary, Joseph, 353
Cary*, Lucius Bentinck, 10th Viscount Falkland (1803–84), 74, 168, 193, 194, 334, 382, 417, 657, 757, 904, 905, 957
Cary, Mary Ann. *See* Shadd
Cary*, Thomas (1787–1869), 408
Casault*, Louis-Jacques (1808–62), 215, 406, 682
Casavant*, Joseph (1807–74), 243
Case, Eliza. *See* Barnes
Case, George, 132
Case, Hester Ann. *See* Hubbard
Case, William, **132–34**, 309, 422, 440, 441, 898
Casgrain, Luce (Panet), 677
Casgrain, Olivier-Eugène, 223
Casgrain*, Pierre (1771–1828), 223
Casirtan. *See* Bacelet
Casot*, Jean-Joseph (1728–1800), 201
Cassady, Henry, 762
Cassels*, Robert (1815–82), 9
Cassista. *See* Bacelet

Glegg, John Bachevoye, 161
Gleig, George, 832
Glenaladale. *See* MacDonald
Glenelg, Baron. *See* Grant
Gloade. *See* Glode
Globensky, Frédéric-Eugène, 331, 791
Globensky*, Maximilien (1793–1866), 791
Glode, Charles, **334–35**
Glode, Francis, 334
Glode, Gabriel, **335–36**
Glode, Jack, 335
Glode, John, 334
Glower. *See* Glode
Glyn, Thomas C., 427
Godefroy* de Tonnancour, Pierre-Joseph (1788–1828), 18
Goderich, Viscount. *See* Robinson
Godfrey, Philip, 257
Godin, Jean-Baptiste, 290
Godwin, Mary. *See* Wollstonecraft
Goethe, Johann Wolfgang von, 651
Goethe, Ottilie von. *See* Pogwisch
Goldie, Thomas Leigh, 394, 619
Goldschmidt, Johanna Maria. *See* Lind
Goldsmith, Elizabeth (Small), 336
Good, Mr (publisher), 266
Good, Allen, 44
Goodhue*, George Jervis (1799–1870), 856
Gordon. *See also* Hamilton-Gordon; Watson-Gordon
Gordon, Adam, xxxii
Gordon, Alexander, 4th Duke of Gordon, 295
Gordon, Lady Charlotte (Lennox, Duchess of Richmond and Lennox), 295
Gordon*, Edward John (1791–1870), 299
Gordon, Peter, 451, 452
Gore, Annabella. *See* Wentworth
Gore, Caroline. *See* Beresford
Gore*, Sir Charles Stephen (1793–1869), 18, 465, 712
Gore, Francis, 336
Gore, Francis, 4, 161, **336–41**, 387, 596, 597, 598, 607, 749, 750, 858, 885, 945
Gorham, Walter, 687
Gosford, Earl of. *See* Acheson
Gosse, John, 673, 674
Gosselin, Antoine, 302
Gosselin*, Léon (d. 1842), 260, 536
Gossin, Jules, 676
Gossip*, William (1809–89), 193
Goudge, Henry, 417
Goudie*, John (d. 1824), 558, 648
Goudreau, Monsieur (trapper), 313
Gouin, Josephte (Méthotte), 628
Goulburn, Henry, xxviii, xxix, 351
Gould, Ira, 220
Gould, Jason, 268
Gould, Nathaniel, 541, 542, 543
Goulet, Alexis, 821
Goulet*, Elzéar (1836–70), 821
Goulet, Josephte. *See* Siveright
Goulet*, Maxime (1855–1932), 821
Goupil, Joseph, 218
Gourlay*, Robert Fleming (1778–1863), 54, 69, 186, 305, 325, 337, 340, 409, 410, 450, 514, 515, 596, 597, 600, 604, 694, 945

Gove, Jonathan, 324
Gove, Lucretia (Gilchrist), 324
Gowan*, Ogle Robert (1803–76), 305, 426, 535, 797, 822
Gowan*, Robert (d. 1879), 157
Gowen, Hammond, 353
Gowen, Helenore (Hall), 353
Gower*, Sir Erasmus (1742–1814), 264
Grafton, Duke of. *See* FitzRoy
Graham, Margaret (Edmundson), 266
Graham, Thomas, 127
Grand Sauteux, Le. *See* Minweweh
Grannis, John, 147, 221
Grant. *See also* Ogilvie-Grant
Grant, Mrs. *See* Bennett
Grant*, Alexander (1734–1813), 4, 34, 336, 339
Grant, Ann (Gerrard), 320
Grant, Catharine (Fraser), 302
Grant, Charles, 1st Baron Glenelg, xxv, xxvii, xxxi, xxxiv, xxxvi, 29, 183, 207, 233, 251, 253, 254, 376, 377, 407, 419, 441, 523, 640, 641, 742, 808, 859, 956
Grant, Charles William, Baron de Longueuil, 760
Grant*, Cuthbert (d. 1799), 341, 500
Grant, Cuthbert, 5, **341–44**, 349, 482, 527, 537, 766, 767, 821
Grant, David, 121
Grant, Elizabeth. *See* MacKay
Grant, Isabella (Gilkison), 327
Grant, James, 341
Grant, John, 320
Grant, Sir Ludovic, 538
Grant, Madelaine. *See* Desmarais
Grant, Marie. *See* McGillis
Grant, Marie-Élisabeth (Montenach), 108
Grant, Marjory (Macdonell), 538
Grant, Peter, 121
Grant, Robert (businessman), 465, 466
Grant, Robert (fur trader), 341
Grant*, William (1744–1805), 952
Grant*, William (1743–1810), 320
Grassie, George, 300, 929
Gratton, Martin, 481
Gravé* de La Rive, Henri-François (1730–1802), 201
Gravel, Jean-Adolphe, 283
Gravel, Sophie. *See* Fabre
Gray, Andrew, 794
Gray, Benjamin Gerrish, 172, **344–47**
Gray*, Edward William (1742–1810), 389
Gray, Elizabeth (Ballenden), 59
Gray, Elizabeth (Jarvis), 428, 430
Gray*, John Hamilton (1811–87), 810
Gray*, John William Dering (1797–1868), 345
Gray, Joseph, 344
Gray, Mary. *See* Burns
Gray, Mary. *See* Gerrish
Gray, Mary. *See* Thomas
Gray*, Robert (d. 1828), 36, 428
Greeley, Aaron, 116
Greeley, Ebenezer, 378, 803
Greely, Adolphus Washington, 449
Green*, Anson (1801–79), 442
Green*, Benjamin (1713–72), 928
Green, Eliza Maria (Stewart), 837
Green, Ernest, 208, 209

McIntyre, Daniel Eugene, 53, 304
McIntyre, Margaret (McMartin), 582
MacIntyre*, Peter (1819–91), 247, 530
McKay, Alexander, 126
MacKay*, Alexander (d. 1811), 190, 557, 558, 580, 766
McKay, Ann. *See* Crichton
McKay, Annie (MacKinnon; Keefer), 552
Mackay, Christina (wife of ROBERT WALTER STUART), 551
McKay, Christina (mother of THOMAS), 552
Mackay, Donald, 551
MacKay, Elizabeth (Grant), 341
McKay, Flora (Ross), 769
McKay*, James (1828–79), 780
McKay, John, 552
McKay*, John (d. 1810), 714
McKay, Josette. *See* Latour
McKay, Marguerite. *See* Rowand
MacKay, Marguerite. *See* Waddens
MacKay, Mary (McKenzie; Sinclair), 556, 558
Mackay, Robert, 553
Mackay, Robert Walter Stuart, 385, **551**
Mackay, Stephen, 331
McKay, Thomas, 188, 269, **551–54**
Mackay, William, 828, 829
McKay*, William (1772–1832), 78, 112, 244, 287, 350, 831
McKeagney, Catherine. *See* McCarney
McKeagney, Henry, **554–55**
McKeagney, Patrick, 554
Mackechnie, Andrew, 555
Mackechnie, Anna Maria Barbara. *See* Poore
Mackechnie, Henry, 555
Mackechnie, Stuart Easton, **555–56**
McKee*, Alexander (d. 1799), 33, 857
McKeen, William, 782
Mackenzie, A. K., 229, 401
McKenzie, Adelgonde Humbert. *See* Droz
Mackenzie, Alexander, 557
Mackenzie*, Sir Alexander (1764–1820), 100, 321, 483, 500, 546, 818
Mackenzie, Catherine (mother of DONALD), 557
McKenzie, Charles, 559
McKenzie, Charles, 350, **556–57**
McKenzie, Christian (Carmichael), 126
McKenzie, Donald, 158, 190, **557–58**, 561, 766, 779, 811, 889
McKenzie, Elizabeth. *See* Cameron
McKenzie*, George Rogers (1798–1876), 126, 127
McKenzie, Hector Æneas, 556
McKenzie*, Henry (d. 1832), 557, 719
Mackenzie, Isabel. *See* Baxter
MacKenzie*, James (d. 1849), 350, 557
McKenzie, James, **558–60**
McKenzie, James (son of JAMES), 559
McKenzie, Janet. *See* Fraser
McKenzie, John, 126, 303
McKenzie, John, **560–61**, 640
MacKenzie*, John George Delhoste (1822–73), 927
McKenzie, Kenneth John, 222
MacKenzie, Lachlan, 569
McKenzie, Louisa (Bethune), 85
McKenzie, Mary. *See* MacKay
McKenzie, Nancy (McTavish; Le Blanc), 226, 558, **561**

McKenzie, Roderick, 821
McKenzie*, Roderick (d. 1844), 85, 453, 483, 556, 557, 561
McKenzie, Roderick, 350, **562–63**, 82
McKenzie, Samuel, 562
McKenzie, William, 560
Mackenzie*, William Lyon (1795–1861), xxiii, xxvii, 5, 6, 7, 8, 12, 46, 47, 48, 51, 54, 56, 57, 69, 105, 119, 120, 125, 178, 186, 187, 208, 229, 255, 256, 276, 305, 325, 340, 401, 431, 445, 466, 493, 501, 512, 523, 550, 598, 602, 603, 609, 622, 623, 642, 643, 696, 697, 707, 785, 797, 798, 852, 853, 854, 855, 871, 885, 896, 897, 932, 945, 946
Mackin, Denis, 475
MacKinlay*, Andrew (1800–67), 400
McKinlay, Archibald, 421
McKinley, Eleanor (McMillan), 584
MacKinnon, Annie. *See* McKay
MacKinnon*, Colin Francis (1810–79), 247, 308
MacKinnon, John, 552, 553
MacKinnon, Margaret (Macdonald), 535
Mackintosh, Sir James, 602
MacKintosh*, John (1790–1881), 376, 529, 530
Macklin, J. P., 804
McLachlin*, Daniel (1810–72), 268, 840
MacLaggan, Alexander, 224
Maclaine, Margaret (Rankin), 741
Maclaren*, James (1818–92), 553
Maclaren, John, 553
McLaren*, William Paterson (1810–66), 44
MacLean, Miss (McDougall), 539
MacLean*, Allan (1752–1847), 252
Maclean, Ann. *See* Smith
McLean*, Archibald (1791–1865), 195, 511, 514, 521, 608
McLean, Catherine (Pritchard), 713
Maclean, Catherine (Rankin), 741
Maclean, Duncan, **563–66**
McLean, Isabella (McGillivray), 546, 547
McLean, John, 479
McLean*, John (d. 1890), 309, 539
Maclean, John Bayne, 68
McLean*, Neil (1759–1832), 303, 546, 583
Maclean of Coll, Alexander, 741
Maclean of Coll, Janet (Hobart), 741
Maclear*, Thomas (1815–98), 14, 188, 189, 790
McLearn, Elizabeth. *See* Fenton
McLearn, Harriet. *See* Stout
McLearn, James, 566
McLearn, Richard, **566–68**
McLelan*, Archibald Woodbury (1824–90), 568, 569
McLelan, David, 568
McLelan, Gloud Wilson, 416, **568–69**
McLelan, Martha. *See* Spencer
McLelan, Mary. *See* Durling
McLelan, Peter, 568
McLellan. *See also* McClellan
McLellan, Archibald, 343
MacLennan, Catherine. *See* MacNab
MacLennan, John, 444, **569–70**, 742, 770
McLeod*, Alexander (1796–1871), 401
McLeod*, Alexander Roderick (d. 1840), 59, 573
McLeod*, Archibald Norman (fl. 1781–1839), 158, 453, 482, 546

Mary Catherine, Sister. *See* McAuley
Mary Francis, Mother. *See* Creedon
Mary John, Sister. *See* Power
Mary Joseph, Sister. *See* Nugent
Mary Magdalen, Sister. *See* O'Shaughnessy
Mary Martha, Sister. *See* Bunning
Mary of St John of God, Mother. *See* Nagle
Mary Vincent, Sister. *See* Nugent
Mary Xavier, Sister. *See* Lynch
Maseres*, Francis (1731–1824), xxv
Maskepetoon* (d. 1869), 819
Massey, Daniel, 621
Massey, Daniel, **621–22**
Massey*, Hart Almerrin (1823–96), 621
Massey, Lucina. *See* Bradley
Massey, Rebecca. *See* Kelley
Massicotte*, Édouard-Zotique (1867–1947), 736, 919
Masson, Damien, 332
Masson, Émilie (Jobin), 433, 434
Masson*, Joseph (1791–1847), 332, 479, 629
Masson*, Luc-Hyacinthe (1811–80), 331, 332
Masson*, Marc-Damase (1805–78), 433, 692
Masson, Marie-Scholastique (Peltier), 692
Massue, Aignan-Aimé, 605
Massue*, Louis-Joseph (1786–1869), 116, 323, 691
Massue, Pélagie (Morand), 637
Massy. *See also* Massey
Massy, Geoffrey, 621
Masta, Pierre-Paul. *See* Osunkhirhine
Mather, Henrietta (Cathcart, Countess Cathcart), 135
Mathew, Jane (Maitland), 596
Mathews. *See* Matthews
Mathieson*, Alexander (1795–1870), 560
Matlack, Lucius D., 90
Matooskie. *See* McKenzie, Nancy
Matthews, Cecilia Eliza (Sullivan), 846
Matthews, Ellen (Barnston), 61
Matthews*, John (b. 1797, d. *c.* 1832), 846
Matthews*, Peter (1786–1838), 27, 30, 61, 520, 643, 855
Mauger*, Joshua (d. 1788), xxv, 709
Maule, Anne (MacNab), 584
Maulibock, "Cockney Bill," 968
Maulibock, Mary. *See* Preston
Maurice, Marie-Josephte (Tavernier), 863
Maurice, Mary (Switzer), 854, 855
Mavor, William, 925
Mayerhoffer, Caroline. *See* Stahl
Mayerhoffer, Catharina. *See* Lublé
Mayerhoffer, Michael, 622
Mayerhoffer, Vincent Philip, **622–23**, 700
Maynard, Emma (wife of George), 427
Maynard, George, 427
Mayrand, Joseph-Arsène, 722
Mazenod, Charles-Joseph-Eugène de, 66, 722
Meagher, John, 196
Mearns, Duncan, 272, 640
Mears, Thomas, 688, 890
Measam, Dorothée (Méthot), 628
Measam, William, 628
Mecham, George Frederick, **623–25**
Medley, Christiana. *See* Bacon
Medley*, John (1804–92), 172, 173, 174, 228, 942, 943, 951

Megginch. *See* Drummond
Meilleur*, Jean-Baptiste (1796–1878), 87, 136, 137, 240, 241, 288, 426, 458, 912
Melbourne, Viscount. *See* Lamb
Melville, Viscount. *See* Dundas
Melvin, Robert, 353, 838
Ménard, *dit* La Fontaine. *See* La Fontaine
Menehwehna. *See* Minweweh
Mercer*, Andrew (d. 1871), 749
Mercier, Augustin, 682
Mercier, François-Xavier-Romuald, 487
Merivale, Herman, xxxiv, xxxv
Merle, Charles, 625
Merle, Jacques, named Father Vincent de Paul, 307, **625–28**
Merle, Louise. *See* Gagnon
Mermet, Joseph-D., 909
Merrick*, John (d. 1829), 755
Merritt*, William Hamilton (1793–1862), xxvi, 8, 9, 12, 52, 53, 56, 70, 208, 252, 253, 409, 450, 451, 523, 785, 786, 787, 798, 875, 885
Merton, Thomas, 628
Métayer-Descombes, Marie-Reine (Rombau), 735
Metcalf, Madeline Wharton (Hogan), 402
Metcalfe*, Charles Theophilus, 1st Baron Metcalfe (1785–1846), xxv, 18, 51, 52, 135, 137, 148, 205, 229, 256, 368, 379, 445, 571, 632, 641, 652, 679, 735, 745, 746, 789, 799, 830, 840, 848, 849
Metherall*, Francis (1791–1875), 424, 425, 908
Méthot. *See also* Méthotte
Méthot, Antoine-Prospère, 368, 628
Méthot, Dorothée. *See* Measam
Méthot, François-Xavier, 497, **628–30**
Méthot, Louis, 628
Méthot, Philéas, 629
Méthotte. *See also* Méthot
Méthotte, Joseph, 628
Méthotte, Josephte. *See* Gouin
Meunier, Josephte (Vanfelson), 906
Meyer, Hoppner Francis, 791
Meyers, Dorothy (Crysler), 194
Michaud, Magdelaine (Dionne), 222
Mignault*, Pierre-Marie (1784–1868), 626
Migneron, Marguerite (Kelly), 455
Milburn, Thomas, 856
Miles. *See* Henry, Walter
Miles*, Frederick W. (1805–43), 118
Miles, Mary Elizabeth (Bibb), 89
Miles, Robert Seaborn, 813
Miles*, Stephen (1789–1870), 514
Millar, John, 122
Mille, Claire-Sophie. *See* Bonnet
Mille, Hypolite, 291
Mille, Hypolite-Joseph. *See* Fenouillet, Émile de
Miller, Ann (Read), 743
Miller, Annie (Muir), 646
Miller, John, 369
Miller*, Linus Wilson (1817–80), 419
Miller, William, 106, 271, 747
Millidge*, Thomas (d. 1838), 224, 806
Milligan, Margaret Gordon (Hawkey; FitzRoy, Lady Fitzroy), 295, 297
Milloy*, Duncan (1825–71), 966
Mills*, Joseph Langley (d. 1832), 937

Morrison, Thomas David, 48, 358, **642–44**, 846, 933
Morrison, William, 642
Morrogh, Robert Lester, 502
Morse, Silas Livingston, 657
Morson, Jane (Smith), 828
Mortimer*, Edward (d. 1819), 122, 222, 355
Mortimer*, George (1784–1844), 95
Mortimer, William, 122
Mortin (Moreton), Catherine (Corrigan), 169
Morton, William, 449
Moscheles, Ignaz, 634
Mott*, Jacob S. (d. 1814), 156
Motz, James, 559
Mount*, Roswell (1797–1834), 438
Mountain, Frances Mingay. *See* Brooke
Mountain*, George Jehoshaphat (1789–1863), 25, 644, 743, 769, 866, 937
Mountain*, Jacob (1749–1825), 25, 94, 644, 665, 937
Mountain, Jacob George, **644**
Mountain, Jacob Henry Brooke, 644
Mountain, Sophia. *See* Bevan
Mowat, George, 645
Mowat, Helen. *See* Levack
Mowat, Jane. *See* Ewart
Mowat, Janet. *See* Bower
Mowat, John, **644–45**
Mowat, John Bower, 645
Mowat, Oliver, 644
Mowat*, Sir Oliver (1820–1903), 282, 402, 644, 645, 849
Mowatt, Margaret (Allan), 4
Mower, Nahum, 221
Muhlenberg, William Augustus, 747
Muir, Andrew, **646**
Muir, Annie. *See* Miller
Muir, Archibald, 646
Muir, Isabella. *See* Weir
Muir, Isabella Ellen, 646
Muir*, John (1799–1883), 646, 836
Muir, Michael, 646
Müller, Johannes von, 291
Mullock*, John Thomas (1807–69), 475, 950
Muncoq. *See* Moncoq
Mundy, Frances (FitzRoy), 295
Munn*, Alexander (1766–1812), 647
Munn, David, 647, 649
Munn, James, 647
Munn, John (brother of Alexander*), 647
Munn (McMunn), John (father of Alexander*), 647
Munn, John (father of JOHN), 646, 647, 648
Munn, John (nephew of John Munn, brother of Alexander*), 647, 649
Munn, John, 93, **646–49**
Munn*, John (1807–79), 199
Munro (Munroe). *See also* Monro
Munro, Henry, 575
Munro*, Hugh (d. 1846), 292
Munroe, James, 894
Murdoch*, Beamish (1800–76), 732, 752
Murdoch, Sir Thomas William Clinton, xxxii, xxxiii, 709
Mure*, John (d. 1823), 321, 690, 838
Murphy, Anna Brownell (Jameson), 177, 426, 427, 596, **649–51**, 831, 860, 861
Murphy, Denis Brownell, 649

Murphy, James, 475
Murray. *See also* Elliot-Murray-Kynynmound
Murray*, Anne (Powell) (1758–1849), 11
Murray, Daniel, 307, 665
Murray*, Sir George (1772–1846), xxvii, xxxi, xxxv, 462, 463, 583, 602
Murray, Jessie. *See* Dickson
Murray, John (father of ROBERT), 651
Murray, John (merchant), 642
Murray, Katharine (Haldane), 350
Murray, Robert, 426, **651–52**
Myers, Christopher, 161, 794

NAGLE, Honoria (Nano), known as Mother Mary of St John of God, 474
Nahnebahwequay* (Catherine Bunch Sonego) (Sutton) (1824–65), 440
Nahovway (Margaret) (mother of James SINCLAIR), 819
Napier*, Duncan Campbell (d. 1865), 245, 619
Napoleon I, Emperor of the French, 135, 214, 238, 391, 392, 418, 459, 596, 622, 625, 634, 689, 732, 744, 823
Napoleon III, Emperor of the French, 80, 619, 775
Nares*, Sir George Strong (1831–1915), 449, 624, 685
Nash, John, 760, 873
Nato'sapi (Old Sun), 3, 4
Nato'sapi* (d. 1897), 4
Nau*, Louis (fl. 1799–1850), 393
Nawahjegezhegwabe* (1786–1863), 440
Necker, Germaine, Baronne de Staël-Holstein, known as Madame de Staël, 650
Needham*, William Hayden (1810–74), 810, 842
Neilson, John, 748
Neilson*, John (1776–1848), xxvii, 154, 155, 156, 213, 214, 284, 433, 489, 536, 711, 907, 937, 938
Neilson*, Samuel (fl. 1790–1836), 408, 938
Nelson, Alfred, 792
Nelson, Caroline. *See* Scott
Nelson, George, **652–54**
Nelson, Horatio, 1st Viscount Nelson, 669, 783
Nelson, Jane. *See* Dies
Nelson, Jane, 653
Nelson*, Robert (1794–1873), 144, 145, 146, 285, 313, 471, 539, 653
Nelson*, William (1750–1834), 652
Nelson*, Wolfred (1791–1863), 49, 286, 392, 457, 471, 539, 616, 617, 653, 711, 791, 792, 844
Nemisses. *See* Guiboche, Louis
Nerbonne, Louis, 218
Nerval, Gérard de. *See* Labrunie, Gérard
Nesbitt, John James, 93, 559
Newechekeshequeby. *See* Nawahjegezhegwabe
Newton, Sir Isaac, 214, 240
Newton, Sir William John, 604
Nichol*, Robert (d. 1824), 340, 476, 515, 517, 518, 597, 608, 858
Nichol, Thomas W., 836
Nicholas I, Emperor of Russia, 756
Nicholson, Amy. *See* Vernon
Nicholson, Elizabeth Luttrell (Winton), 947
Nickalls, James, 760
Nicola. *See* Hwistesmetxē'qEn
Nimmo, Alexander, 541
Ninākon. *See* Minweweh

1111